June 26–July 1, 2016
San Francisco, California, USA

Association for Computing Machinery

Advancing Computing as a Science & Profession

SIGMOD'16

Proceedings of the 2016 International Conference on Management of Data

Sponsored by:

ACM SIGMOD

Supported by:

Microsoft, Oracle, Tableau, Alibaba, AT&T, Facebook, Google, IBM, Infosys, Platfora, Recruit, Salesforce, SAP, Snowflake, Amazon Web Services, Cloudera, Esgyn, Hewlett Packard, Intel, Linked In, LogicBlox, MemSQL, Splice Machine, VISA Research, Hewlett-Packard Enterprise, Morgan & Claypool, Elsevier, Springer, and National Science Foundation

Association for
Computing Machinery

Advancing Computing as a Science & Profession

The Association for Computing Machinery
2 Penn Plaza, Suite 701
New York, New York 10121-0701

ISBN: 978-1-4503-3531-7 (Digital)

ISBN: 978-1-4503-4604-7 (Print)

Additional copies may be ordered prepaid from:

ACM Order Department
PO Box 30777
New York, NY 10087-0777, USA

Phone: 1-800-342-6626 (USA and Canada)
+1-212-626-0500 (Global)
Fax: +1-212-944-1318
E-mail: acmhelp@acm.org
Hours of Operation: 8:30 am – 4:30 pm ET

Printed in the USA

Welcome Message from the SIGMOD Chairs

It is our great pleasure to welcome you to SIGMOD 2016, the 2016 edition of the ACM SIGMOD International Conference on Management of Data, at San Francisco, the heart of Silicon Valley. A unique bridge, cable cars, a sparkling bay, a famous prison, and steep streets with beautiful Victorian houses are just a few of the things that make San Francisco one of the world's greatest cities to visit. Located in the Bay Area along the Northern California coast, many attractions beyond those in the city can be easily reached: the world-famous wine country, including Napa and Sonoma Valley, beautiful beaches, the world's largest trees and wonderful hikes in nearby National Parks.

The conference itself is held in the Hyatt Regency Hotel, located in the financial district in downtown San Francisco. The hotel is very conveniently located nearby to many activities and landmarks, making this the ideal spot not only for an exciting conference but also for exploring the area. The banquet will be held in the California Academy of Sciences. The California Academy of Sciences is a Planetarium, Aquarium and Natural History Museum under a Living Roof in San Francisco, and it is among the largest museums of natural history in the world, housing over 26 million specimens.

This year's technical program features 137 papers in 22 sessions; 116 research papers, 17 industrial papers, and 4 invited papers. Research and industrial papers will be mixed together instead of separated into separate tracks as in past years. All papers will be presented at conference sessions, as well as at one of two plenary poster events. There are also 31 demos and 10 tutorials. Instead of running these concurrently with technical presentations, demos are now a separate plenary event in the conference and tutorials have been moved before and after the conference. There is just one panel, the Careers in Industry panel. Finally, this year's conference will feature one keynote, from the inimitable Jeff Dean (Google, USA), who will talk about how deep learning and software systems can support each other, with particular thoughts on the implications for data management. The net effect of these changes is that there are more plenary events, and at most three concurrent events ongoing (from 6 or more concurrent tracks in previous conferences). We hope this will make the SIGMOD experience more communal.

Other technical events of interest include the SIGMOD programming contest, featuring a $7,000 prize for the winning team plus a $3,000 dollar prize for the runner-up donated by Microsoft, with contest participants presenting their work during the poster session; the undergraduate poster competition, featuring 12 undergraduate posters from an outstanding group of young database researchers; the new research symposium on Tuesday night; and the business meeting, also on Tuesday evening.

We made a number of changes in the way we assembled this year's technical program with an eye towards improving review and paper quality. As in past years we had two submission deadlines, but we spread them out more (one in July and one in November). Each submission included one round of revisions, during which reviewers could request specific changes to papers. The vast majority of accepted papers underwent revision, which we believe significantly improved the quality of papers. All submissions were also discussed in a series of conference calls organized by our group leaders; this forced reviewers to defend their positions and helped achieve consensus. A post-review survey revealed 70% of reviewers felt this improved the review process, and 80% reported they worked harder in preparing and defending their reviews. We also asked reviewers and group leaders to request additional reviews when an additional opinion was needed; many papers received four reviews, and some papers received as many as six. Finally, we introduced an online conference organization tool, Confer, which we used to get the community's input about how papers should be grouped together, and which attendees can use throughout the conference to navigate the program.

SIGMOD 2016 is preceded and followed by 10 workshops, including the PhD symposium on Sunday, June 26. These workshops provide an opportunity for small groups of like-minded researchers to discuss areas of interest and new ideas, and we are pleased to see a diverse ecosystem of workshops with competitive submissions evolving at SIGMOD.

We are grateful to the many members of our community who made this technical program possible, especially the 247 reviewers whose hard work resulted in writing more than 2700 reviews for our research, industrial, and demo tracks. This work was coordinated by our fabulous program committee team, including our program track chairs, Alexandra Meliou (UMass Amherst, USA), and Tim Kraska (Brown University, USA), and our 14 group leaders, who coordinated conference calls and guided papers through the review process. The industrial program was created by Tyson Condie (UCLA, USA), and Carlo Curino (Microsoft, USA), and the demo program was organized by Jennie Duggan (Northwestern University, USA), and Aaron Elmore (University of Chicago, USA). Alexandros Labrinidis (University of Pittsburgh, USA), efficiently organized the tutorials program. The undergraduate poster competition was organized by Aditya Parameswaran (University of Illinois, Champaign Urbana, USA), and Anisoara Nice (SAP SE, Canada). Ken Salem organized this year's programming contest (finding shortest paths in a changing graph), and Peter Bailis (Stanford University, USA), and Andy Pavlo (Carnegie Mellon University, USA) organized the poster session. Anant Bhardwaj (MIT, USA), built the Confer online conference software. Finally, last but certainly not least Alekh Jindal helped organize the proceedings, tirelessly hounding authors to get their camera ready submissions uploaded!

SIGMOD is a volunteer effort and involved thousands of hours of work, thousands of emails, and thousands of hours in meetings during the last two years to put together. Please thank all these individuals involved if you see them around the conference. Also congratulate Alex Labrinidis, Alex Meliou, Melanie, Martin, Yunyao, and Stratos who became parents in the meantime.

We also acknowledge all members of the SIGMOD 2016 organizing committee, as well as the SIGMOD Executive Committee, for their invaluable help and guidance throughout the many months leading to the conference. The strong organizing team for SIGMOD 2016 includes finance chair Martin Theobald (University of Ulm, Germany), publicity chair Melanie Herschel (University of Stuttgart, Germany), social media chair Hakan Ferhatosmanoglu (Bilkent University, Turkey), sponsorship chairs Mohamed Mokbel (University of Minnesota, USA) and Stratos Idreos (Harvard University, USA), exhibit chair Huiping Cao (New Mexico State University, USA), local arrangements chairs Enela Pema (Facebook, USA) and Yunyao Li (IBM Research-Almaden, USA), registration chair Mohamed Sarwat (Arizona State University, USA) , workshop local arrangement chair Fei Chen (LinkedIn, USA), web chair Kostas Stefanidis (ICS-FORTH, Hellas), volunteer chair Maria Daltayanni (University of San Francisco, USA), and travel award committee chairs Eugene Wu (Columbia University, USA) and Peter Alvaro (University of California, Santa Cruz, USA. The success of this conference would be impossible without their hard work, persistent dedication, and hours of effort they committed to the conference. We also would like to thank K. Selçuk Candan for providing us with his advice and SIGMOD institutional memory, as well as for his help with logistics throughout the conference planning. We are also grateful to the Microsoft Research Conference Management Toolkit (CMT) team for their extremely prompt and helpful support throughout the complex conference reviewing process. We would also like to extend our appreciation to the student volunteers.

Finally, we would like to thank ACM, and particularly Fran Spinola and April Mosqus for helping with the conference logistics, Diana Brantuas for guidance and help with the budget, Stephanie Sabal for hotel site selection, Ann Lane for conference promotion, and Carolina Erazo for preparing the visa letters. Adrienne Griscti (ACM) and Lisa Tolles (Sheridan) have made the proceedings and the program booklet possible.

This year we are extremely grateful for all our corporate sponsors, whose contributions helped to keep the conference registration fees low, most significantly for student attendees. These include at the Platinum Level: Microsoft, Oracle, and Tableau; at the Gold Level: Alibaba.com, AT&T, Facebook, Google, IBM Research, Infosys, Platfora, Recruit, Salesforce, SAP, and Snowflake; and at the Silver Level: Amazon Web Services, Cloudera, esgyn, HP, Intel, LinkedIn, LogicBlox, memsql, Splice Machine, and Visa Research. Microsoft also supported the programming contest by providing the generous award to the winners. In addition, Microsoft, Google, the National Science Foundation and the SIGMOD Executive Committee have generously funded the SIGMOD 2016 student travel award program, Microsoft's donation provided 16 travel awards, Facebook's donation supported 4 travel awards, Snowflake's donation supported 1 travel award, and the NSF grant covered another 15 travel awards. Finally, the SIGMOD EC provided 27 awards, and covered all 63 free registrations for the student travel program awardees. Last but not least, we would like to thank Salesforce for organizing the reception at Exploratorium on Tuesday night for all SIGMOD attendees.

Welcome to San Francisco, and we hope you enjoy the conference!

Fatma Özcan	**Georgia Koutrika**	**Samuel Madden**	**Alekh Jindal**
General Chair	*General Chair*	*Program Chair*	*Proceedings Chair*

Table of Contents

Session 3 - Logical and Physical Database Design

Session 4 - New Storage and Network Architectures

Session 5 - Graphs 1: Infrastructure and Processing on Modern Hardware

Session 8 - Networks and the Web

Session 9 - Data Discovery and Extraction

Session 10 - Data Integration / Cleaning

Session 11 - Spatio / Temporal Databases

Session 12 - Distributed Data Processing

Session 13 - Graphs 2: Subgraph-based Optimization Techniques

Session 14 - Main Memory Analytics

Session 15 - Interactive Analytics ....

Session 16 - Streaming 2: Sketches

Session 17 - Transaction Processing

Session 18 - Transactions and Consistency

Session 19 - Query Optimization

Session 20 - Graphs 3: Potpourri

Session 21: Hardware Acceleration and Query Compilation

Session 22 - Nearest Neighbors and Similarity Search

Demonstrations

Tutorials

Undergraduate Student Abstracts

2016 SIGMOD Conference Organization

General Chairs:	Fatma Özcan (IBM Research, USA) Georgia Koutrika (HP Labs, USA)
Program Chair:	Sam Madden (Massachusetts Institute of Technology, USA)
PC Track Chairs:	Tim Kraska (Brown University, USA) Alexandra Meliou (University of Massachusetts, Amherst, USA)
Proceedings Chair:	Alekh Jindal (Microsoft, USA)
Tutorials Chair:	Alex Labrinidis (University of Pittsburgh, USA)
Industrial Program Chairs:	Carlo Curino (Microsoft, USA) Tyson Condie (University of California, Los Angeles, USA)
Demonstration Chairs:	Aaron Elmore (University of Chicago, USA) Jennie Duggan (Northwestern University, USA)
Workshops Chairs:	Anastasia Ailamaki (EPFL, Switzerland) Barzan Mozafari (University of Michigan, USA)
Poster Chairs:	Andy Pavlo (Carnegie Mellon University, USA) Peter Bailis (Stanford University, USA)
Undergraduate Poster Competition Chairs:	Anisoara Nica (SAP SE, Canada) Aditya Parameswaran (University of Illinois at Urbana Champaign, USA)
Local Organization Chairs:	Yunyao Li (IBM Research, USA) Enela Pema (Facebook, USA)
Finance Chair:	Martin Theobald (University of Ulm, Germany)
Sponsorship Chairs:	Mohamed Mokbel (University of Minnesota, USA) Stratos Idreos (Harvard University, USA)
Publicity Chair:	Melanie Herschel (University of Stuttgart, Germany)
Social Media Chair:	Hakan Ferhatosmanoglu (Bilkent University, Turkey)
Exhibits Chair:	Huiping Cao (New Mexico State University, USA)
Registration Chair:	Mohamed Sarwat (Arizona State University, USA)
Web/Information Chair:	Kostas Stefanidis (ICS-FORTH, Greece)

Travel Award Selection Committee Chairs: Eugene Wu (Columbia University, USA)
Peter Alvaro (University of California, Santa Cruz, USA)

Programming Contest Chair: Ken Salem (University of Waterloo, Canada)

New Researcher Symposium Chairs: Julia Stoyanovich (Drexel University, USA)
Fabian M. Suchanek (Telecom ParisTech University, France)

Volunteer Chair: Maria Daltayanni (University of San Francisco, USA)

Local Workshops Chair: Fei Chen (LinkedIn, Mountain View, USA)

Group Leaders: Sihem Amer-Yahia (CNRS, France)
Magdalena Balazinska (University of Washington, USA)
Carsten Binnig (DHBW Mannheim, Germany)
Mike Cafarella (University of Michigan, USA)
Philippe Cudre-Mauroux (University of Fribourg, Switzerland)
Amol Deshpande (University of Maryland, USA)
Ihab Ilyas (University of Waterloo, Canada)
Justin Levandoski (Microsoft Research, USA)
Amelie Marian (Rutgers University, USA)
Kyriakos Mouratidis(Singapore Management University, Singapore)
Paolo Papotti (QCRI, Qatar)
Daisy Zhe Wang (University of Florida, USA)

Program Committee: Daniel Abadi (Yale, USA)
Ashraf Aboulnaga (Qatar Computing Research Institute, Qatar)
Foto Afrati (NTU Athens, Greece)
Sameer Agarwal (Databricks, Inc, USA)
Yanif Ahmad (Johns Hopkins University, USA)
Reza Akbarinia (INRIA Sophia Antipolis, France)
Gustavo Alonso (ETH Zurich, Switzerland)
Peter Alvaro (UC Berkeley, USA)
Sihem Amer-Yahia (CNRS/LIG, France)
Aijun An (York University, Canada)
Arvind Arasu (Microsoft Research, USA)
Peter Bailis (UC Berkeley, USA)
Magda Balazinska (University of Washington, USA)
Zhuowei Bao (Facebook Inc., USA)
Denilson Barbosa (University of Alberta, Canada)
Srikanta Bedathur (IBM Research, India)
Philip Bernstein (Microsoft Research, USA)
Carsten Binnig (Brown University, USA)
Spyros Blanas (Ohio State, USA)
Michael Bohlen (University of Zurich, Switzerland)
Francesco Bonchi (Yahoo Labs, Barcelona, Spain)
Peter Boncz (CWI, Netherlands)

Program Committee (continued):

Angela Bonifati (Lille 1 University and INRIA, France)
Philippe Bonnet (IT University of Copenhagen, Denmark)
Stephane Bressan (NUS, Singapore)
Nico Bruno (Google, USA)
Michael Cafarella (University of Michigan, USA)
Mark Callaghan (Facebook, USA)
K. Selcuk Candan (Arizona State University, USA)
Kaushik Chakrabarti (Microsoft Research, USA)
Badrish Chandramouli (Microsoft Research, USA)
Kevin Chang (University of Illinois at Urbana-Champaign, USA)
Shimin Chen (ICT, Chinese Academy of Science, China)
Lei Chen (Hong Kong University of Science and Technology, Hong Kong)
James Cheng (CUHK, Hong Kong)
Alvin Cheung (University of Washington, USA)
Fei Chiang (McMaster University, Canada)
Sarah Cohen-Boulakia (LRI Universite Paris Sud, France)
Dario Colazzo (Universite Paris-Dauphine, France)
Tyson Condie (UCLA, USA)
Neil Conway (Typical Set LLC, USA)
Brian Cooper (Google, USA)
Philippe Cudre-Mauroux (University of Fribourg, Switzerland)
Bin Cui (Peking U., China)
Mahashweta Das (HP Labs, USA)
Sudipto Das (Microsoft Research, USA)
Antonios Deligiannakis (Technical University of Crete, Greece)
Amol Deshpande (University of Maryland, USA)
Stefan Dessloch (TU Kaiserslautern, Germany)
Jens Dittrich (Saarland University, Germany)
Luna Dong (Google, USA)
Chris Douglas (Microsoft, USA)
Eduard Dragut (Temple Univ., USA)
Jennie Duggan (Northwestern University, USA)
Curtis Dyreson (Utah State, USA)
Aaron Elmore (University of Chicago, USA)
Alan Fekete (U. Sydney, Australia)
Shel Finkelstein (UCSC, USA)
Peter Fischer (Universitat Freiburg, Germany)
Avrilia Floratou (IBM Almaden, USA)
Tim Furche (Oxford, United Kingdom)
Avigdor Gal (Technion, Israel)
Wolfgang Gatterbauer (CMU Tepper School of Business, USA)
Tingjian Ge (UMass Lowell, USA)
Floris Geerts (University of Antwerp, Belgium)
Rainer Gemulla (Max-Planck-Institut fur Informatik, Germany)
Boris Glavic (IIT Chicago, USA)
Lukasz Golab (University of Waterloo, Canada)

Program Committee (continued):

Todd Green (LogicBlox, USA)
Torsten Grust (U Tubingen, Germany)
Dimitrios Gunopulos (University of Athens, Greece)
Jiawei Han (UIUC, USA)
Wook-Shin Han (POSTECH, South Korea)
Carmem Hara (Universidade Federal do Parana, Brazil)
Oktie Hassanzadeh (IBM Research, USA)
Michael Hay (Colgate, USA)
Bingsheng He (Nanyang Technological University, Singapore)
Katja Hose (Aalborg University, Denmark)
Vagelis Hristidis (UC Riverside, USA)
Stratos Idreos (Harvard University, USA)
Ihab Ilyas (University of Waterloo, Canada)
Zachary Ives (University of Pennsylvania, USA)
Ruoming Jin (Kent State University, USA)
Alekh Jindal (MIT, USA)
Eser Kandogan (IBM Research, USA)
Panagiotis Karras (Skoltech, Russia)
Asterios Katsifodimos (TU Berlin, Germany)
Yannis Katsis (UC San Diego, USA)
Georgios Kellaris (Harvard, USA)
Anastasios Kementsietsidis (Google Inc., USA)
Alfons Kemper (University of Munich, Germany)
Oliver Kennedy (University at Buffalo, USA)
Eamonn Keogh (UC Riverside, USA)
Martin Kersten (CWI, Netherlands)
Daniel Kifer (Penn State, USA)
Christoph Koch (EPFL, Switzerland)
George Kollios (Boston University, USA)
Nick Koudas (University of Toronto, Canada)
Tim Kraska (Brown University, USA)
Hongrae Lee (Google, USA)
Wolfgang Lehner (TU Dresden, Germany)
Alberto Lerner (New York University, USA)
Justin Levandoski (Microsoft, USA)
Chengkai Li (UT Arlington, USA)
Feifei Li (University of Utah, USA)
Guoliang Li (Tsinghua University, China)
Yunyao Li (IBM Research, USA)
Erietta Liarou (EPFL, Switzerland)
Xuemin Lin (University of New South Wales, Australia)
Chengfei Liu (Swinburne University of Technology, Australia)
Eric Lo (Polytecnic University of Hong Kong, Hong Kong)
Guy Lohman (IBM Research, USA)
Jiaheng Lu (University of Helsinki, Finland)
Qiong Luo (Hong Kong University of Science & Technology, Hong Kong)

Program Committee (continued):

Shuai Ma (Beihang University, Beijing, China)
Ashwin Machanavajjhala (Duke U., USA)
Samuel Madden (MIT, USA)
Jayant Madhavan (Google, USA)
David Maier (Portland State University, USA)
Nikos Mamoulis (U. Hong Kong, Hong Kong)
Silviu Maniu (Universite Paris-Sud, France)
Essam Mansour (Qatar Computing Research Institute, Qatar)
Amelie Marian (Rutgers University, USA)
Davide Martinenghi (Politecnico di Milano, Italy)
Gianni Mecca (Universita della Basilicata, Italy)
Alexandra Meliou (UMass Amherst, USA)
Sergey Melnik (Google, USA)
Xiaofeng Meng (Renmin University of China, China)
Sebastian Michel (TU Kaiserslautern, Germany)
Umar Minhas (IBM Research, USA)
Zhou Minqi (East China Normal University, China)
Mohamed Mokbel (Northeastern University, USA)
Kyriakos Mouratidis (Singapore Management University, Singapore)
Barzan Mozafari (University of Michigan, USA)
Hannes Muhleisen (CWI, Netherlands)
Arnab Nandi (Ohio State University, USA)
Vivek Narasayya (Microsoft Research, USA)
Neha Narula (MIT, USA)
Felix Naumann (Hasso Plattner Institute, Germany)
Muhammad Naveed (University of Illinois at Urbana-Champaign, USA)
Rimma Nehme (Microsoft, USA)
Thomas Neumann (TU Munich, Germany)
Christopher Olston (Google, USA)
Dan Olteanu (Oxford University & LogicBlox, United Kingdom)
Beng Chin Ooi (National University of Singapore, Singapore)
Carlos Ordonez (University of Houston, USA)
M. Tamer Ozsu (University of Waterloo, Canada)
Ippokratis Pandis (Cloudera, USA)
Dimitris Papadopoulos (Boston University, USA)
Stavros Papadopoulos (Intel Labs and MIT, USA)
Olga Papaemmanouil (Brandeis University, USA)
Charalampos Papamanthou (UMD, USA)
Stelios Paparizos (Microsoft Research, USA)
Paolo Papotti (QCRI, Qatar)
Srinivasan Parthasarathy (Ohio State, USA)
Alex Passos (Google, USA)
Andy Pavlo (Carnegie Mellon University, USA)
Torben Bach Pedersen (Aalborg University, Denmark)
Jian Pei (Simon Fraser University, Canada)
Peter Pietzuch (Imperial College London, United Kingdom)

Program Committee (continued):

Holger Pirk (MIT, USA)
Evaggelia Pitoura (University of Ioannina, Greece)
Li Qian (Facebook, USA)
Jorge Quiane-Ruiz (Qatar Computing Research Institute, Qatar)
Karthik Ramachandra (Microsoft, USA)
Ravi Ramamurthy (Microsoft Research, USA)
Vijayshankar Raman (IBM Research, USA)
Christopher Re (Stanford University, USA)
Tore Risch (Uppsala Universitet, Sweden)
Florin Rusu (UC Merced, USA)
Russell Sears (PureStorage, USA)
Elaine Shi (Cornell University, USA)
Suvrit Sra (MIT, USA)
Ion Stoica (UC Berkeley, USA)
Kian-Lee Tan (National University of Singapore, Singapore)
Nesime Tatbul (Intel Labs and MIT, USA)
Anthony Tung (National University of Singapore, Singapore)
Daisy Zhe Wang (University of Florida, USA)
Jiannan Wang (UC Berkeley, USA)
Gerhard Weikum (Max-Planck-Institut fur Informatik, Germany)
Till Westmann (Oracle, USA)
Janet Wiener (Facebook, USA)
Xiaokui Xiao (Nanyang Technological University, Singapore)
Xiaochun Yang (Northeastern University, China)
Ken Yocum (Human Longevity, USA)
Cong Yu (Google Research, USA)
Matei Zaharia (MIT, USA)
Kai Zeng (UC Berkeley, USA)
Kevin Zheng (University of Queensland, Australia)
Jingren Zhou (Alibaba, USA)

Demo Program Committee:

Adam Silberstein (Trifacta, USA)
Alekh Jindal (MIT, USA)
Alexandros Labrinidis (University of Pittsburgh, USA)
Alvin Cheung (U. Washington, USA)
Arijit Khan (ETH Zurich, Switzerland)
Beng Chin Ooi (National University of Singapore, Singapore)
Danica Porobic (EPFL, Switzerland)
Darius Sidlauskas (EPFL, Switzerland)
Emad Soroush (Dato, USA)
Eugene Wu (Columbia University, USA)
Guy Lohman (IBM Almaden, USA)
Hannes Muhleisen (CWI, Netherlands)
Herodotos Herodotou (Cyprus University of Technology, Cyprus)
Holger Pirk (MIT, USA)
Isabel Cruz (Univ. of Illinois at Chicago, USA)

Demo Program Committee (continued):

Jagan Sankaranarayanan (NEC Labs, USA)
James Cheng (CUHK, Hong Kong)
Jens Teuber (TU Dortmund, Germany)
Jens Dittrich (Saarland, Germany)
Jeong-Hyon Hwang (SUNY Albany, USA)
Jiannan Wang (University of California, Berkeley, USA)
Jianyong Wang (Tsinghua, P.R. China)
Julia Stoyanovich (Drexel University, USA)
Junho Shim (Sookmyung Women's University, Rep. of Korea)
K. Selcuk Candan (Arizona State University, USA)
Kostis Kyzirakos (CWI, Netherlands)
Lei Chen (HKUST, Hong Kong)
Marco Serafini (QCRI, Qatar)
Martin Kersten (CWI, Netherlands)
Mike Carey (University of California - Irvine, USA)
Mohamed Mokbel (Univ of Minnesota, USA)
Mohamed Sarwat (Arizona State University, USA)
Paolo Papotti (QCRI, Qatar)
Pat Helland (Salesforce, USA)
Paul Brown (Paradigm4, USA)
Peter Bailis (University of California, Berkeley, USA)
Philippe Cudre-Mauroux (Univ. of Freiburg, Germany)
Pinar Tozun (IBM, USA)
Rachel Pottinger (University of British Columbia, Canada)
Ravi Ramamurthy (Microsoft Research, USA)
Reynold Cheng (Univ of Hong Kong, Hong Kong)
Ryan Stutsman (Microsoft Research, USA)
Shel Finkelstein (University of California, Santa Cruz, USA)
Spyros Blanas (Ohio State University, USA)
Sudeepa Roy (University of Washington, USA)
Sudipto Das (Microsoft Research, USA)
Christian Thomsen (Aalborg University, Denmark)
Tingjian Ge (U. Mass Lowell, USA)
Victor Alvarez (Saarland University, Germany)
Willis Lang (Microsoft Jim Gray Systems Lab, USA)
Yinghui Wu (Washington State University, USA)
Ziawasch Abedjan (MIT, USA)

Industrial Program Committee:

Philip Bernstein (Microsoft Research, USA)
Nico Bruno (Google, USA)
Michael Cafarella (University of Michigan, USA)
Mark Callaghan (Facebook, USA)
Neil Conway (Mesosphere, USA)
Brian Cooper (Google, USA)
Chris Douglas (Microsoft, USA)
Shel Finkelstein (UCSC, USA)
Konstantinos Karanasos (Microsoft, USA)
Guy Lohman (IBM Research, USA)
Ippokratis Pandis (Amazon Web Services, USA)
Karthik Ramachandra (Microsoft, USA)
Karthik Ramasamy (Twitter, USA)
Russell Sears (PureStorage, USA)
Till Westmann (Couchbase, USA)
Ken Yocum (Human Longevity, USA)
Jingren Zhou (Alibaba, USA)

Tutorials Program Committee:

Selçuk Candan (Arizona State University, USA)
Junghoo Cho (University of California, Los Angeles, USA)
Alex Delis (University of Athens, Greece)
AnHai Doan (University of Wisconsin, USA)
Luis Gravano (Columbia University, USA)
Guy Lohman (IBM Almaden, USA)
Qiong Luo (Hong Kong University of Science & Technology, Hong Kong)
Meral Ozsoyoglu (Case Western Reserve University, USA)
Alkis Polyzotis (Google, USA)
Mohamed Sharaf (University of Queensland, Australia)
Peter Triantafillou (University of Glasgow, UK)
Stratis Viglas (University of Edinburgh, UK)
Jun Yang (Duke University, USA)

Sponsors, Supporters, and Exhibitors

Sponsor:

Platinum Supporters:

Gold Supporters:

Silver Supporters:

Other Supporters:

Platinum Publisher:

Silver Publishers:

Student Travel Awards:

Building Machine Learning Systems that Understand

Jeff Dean
Google Research
jeff@google.com

ABSTRACT

Over the past five years, deep learning and large-scale neural networks have made significant advances in speech recognition, computer vision, language understanding and translation, robotics, and many other fields. Deep learning allows the use of very raw forms of data in order to build higher-level understanding of data automatically, and can also be used to learn to accomplish complex tasks. In the next decade, it is likely that a fruitful direction for research in data management will be in how to seamlessly integrate these kinds of machine learning models into systems that store and manage data. In this talk, I will highlight some of the advances that have been made in deep learning and suggest some interesting directions for future research.

CCS Concepts

• Theory of computation~Online algorithms • Theory of computation~Online learning theory

Short Bio

Jeff joined Google in 1999 and is currently a Google Senior Fellow in Google Research, where he leads the Google Brain team, Google's deep learning research team, working on machine learning systems and their use for speech recognition, computer vision, language understanding, and various predictive tasks. He has co-designed/implemented five generations of Google's crawling, indexing, and query serving systems, and co-designed/ implemented major pieces of Google's initial advertising and AdSense for Content systems. He is also a co-designer and co-implementor of Google's distributed computing and storage infrastructure, including the MapReduce, BigTable, Spanner and TensorFlow systems, protocol buffers, LevelDB, and a variety of internal and external libraries and developer tools.

He received a Ph.D. in Computer Science from the University of Washington in 1996, working with Craig Chambers on compiler techniques for object-oriented languages. He is a Fellow of the ACM, a member of the U.S. National Academy of Engineering and the American Academy of Arts and Sciences, and a recipient of the Mark Weiser Award and the ACM-Infosys Foundation Award in the Computing Sciences.

SIGMOD'16, June 26–July 1, 2016, San Francisco, California, USA.
ACM 978-1-4503-3531-7/16/06.
http://dx.doi.org/10.1145/2882903.2932259

Learning Linear Regression Models over Factorized Joins

Maximilian Schleich Dan Olteanu Radu Ciucanu

Department of Computer Science, University of Oxford
{max.schleich,dan.olteanu,radu.ciucanu}@cs.ox.ac.uk

Cultural Learnings of Factorized Joins for Make Benefit Glorious Family of Regression Tasks[1]

ABSTRACT

We investigate the problem of building least squares regression models over training datasets defined by arbitrary join queries on database tables. Our key observation is that joins entail a high degree of redundancy in both computation and data representation, which is not required for the end-to-end solution to learning over joins.

We propose a new paradigm for computing batch gradient descent that exploits the factorized computation and representation of the training datasets, a rewriting of the regression objective function that decouples the computation of cofactors of model parameters from their convergence, and the commutativity of cofactor computation with relational union and projection. We introduce three flavors of this approach: **F/FDB** computes the cofactors in one pass over the materialized factorized join; **F** avoids this materialization and intermixes cofactor and join computation; **F/SQL** expresses this mixture as one SQL query.

Our approach has the complexity of join factorization, which can be exponentially lower than of standard joins. Experiments with commercial, public, and synthetic datasets show that it outperforms MADlib, Python StatsModels, and R, by up to three orders of magnitude.

1. INTRODUCTION

There is increasing interest in academia and industry in building systems that integrate databases and machine learning [17, 34, 1, 18]. This is driven by web companies, e.g., Google Brain, Twitter, Facebook's DeepFace, or Microsoft's platform, though it is also prominent in other industry segments such as retail-planning and forecasting applications [2]. State-of-art commercial analytics systems support descriptive, or backward-looking analytics, predictive, or forward-looking analytics such as classification and regression, and prescriptive analytics, which are also forward-looking and usually take the output of a predictive model as input. The typical data sources of interest are weekly sales data, promotions, and product descriptions. In these settings, the input to analytics is a relation representing the natural join of those data sources stored in a database. A typical prediction a retailer would like to compute is the additional demand generated for a given product due to promotion.

In our exploration with such systems on a real dataset from a large US retailer and following discussions with industry experts [23], we realized three major shortcomings of these systems: (1) Poor integration of analytics and databases, which are traditionally confined to distinct specialized systems in the ever-growing technology stack [2]; (2) poor efficiency already for few data sources; and (3) insufficient accuracy due to omission of further relevant data sources.

The use of typical data sources already stretches the scalability of existing systems and the current processing regime is to manually partition the data, e.g., by market and category, and run analytics independently on each partition [23]. Domain-expertise focuses on how to best partition the data, to the point where it becomes black art. Data partitioning misses relevant correlations and prohibits common forecast patterns across different categories and markets. By processing separately by market/category, today's forecasting cannot leverage similar demand behavior across geography or time. For this reason, data partitioning is seen as a strong limitation of the state of the art and preference is given to running analytics on the entire dataset.

More data sources would enable forecasting with higher accuracy and at a more granular level, such as customer reviews, basket data transactions, competitive promotions and prices, flu trends, loyalty program history, customer transaction history, social media text related to the retailer products sold, store attributes such as demographics, weather, or nearby competition. Incorporating more data sources would allow customer-specific promotions and separate out the impact of actions taken by the retailer (e.g., changing discounts and prices) from weather and environment [23]. However, it can increase the load by several orders of magnitude as the size of the input to analytics explodes.

A feasible approach to address these shortcomings would at least need to support efficient joining of many relations and running in-database analytics on large join results.

The main contribution of this paper is a batch gradient descent approach that can build linear regression models on training datasets defined by arbitrary join queries on tables.

[1]With apologies to Sacha Baron Cohen and Borat

SIGMOD'16, June 26-July 01, 2016, San Francisco, CA, USA
© 2016 ACM. ISBN 978-1-4503-3531-7/16/06...$15.00
DOI: http://dx.doi.org/10.1145/2882903.2882939

Our key observation is that the intermediate join step represents the main bottleneck and it is unnecessarily expensive. It entails a high degree of redundancy in both computation and data representation, yet this is not required for the end-to-end solution, whose result is a list of real-valued parameters of the learned model. By computing a *factorized join* [5] instead of the standard flat join, we reduce data redundancy and improve performance for both the join and the learning steps. The theoretical and practical gains in both required memory space and time performance for factorized joins are well-understood and can be asymptotically exponential in the size of the join [28], which translates to orders of magnitude for various datasets reported in experiments [5, 4].

Our learning approach is based on several contributions:

- It uses an algebraic rewriting of the regression's objective function that decouples the computation of cofactors of model parameters from their convergence.
- Cofactor computation commutes with relational union and projection. The commutativity with union enables the computation of the parameter cofactors for the entire dataset as the sum of corresponding cofactors for disjoint partitions of the input dataset. This property is essential for efficiency in a centralized setting and also desirable for *concurrent learning*, where cofactors of partitions are computed on different cores or machines. The commutativity with projection allows us to compute all cofactors once and then explore the space of possible models by only running convergence for a subset of parameters. This property is desirable for *model selection*, whose goal is to find a subset of features that best predict a test dataset.
- We introduce three flavors of our approach: **F/FDB** uses FDB [5] to materialize the factorized join and computes the cofactors in one pass over it; our baseline **F** avoids this materialization and blends cofactor and join computation; and **F/SQL** expresses this mixture of joins and cofactors as one optimized SQL query.
- Given a database $\mathbf{D}$ and a join query Q, our approach needs $O(|\mathbf{D}|^{\mathit{fhtw}(Q)})$ time (modulo log factors), which is *worst-case optimal* for computing the factorized join whose nesting structure is defined by a hypertree decomposition of the query Q; in contrast, any relational engine can achieve at best $O(|\mathbf{D}|^{\rho^*(Q)})$ [3, 26, 41]. The gap between the fractional hypertree width $\mathit{fhtw}(Q)$ and the fractional edge cover number $\rho^*(Q)$ can be as large as the number of relations in Q. For instance, $\mathit{fhtw} = 1$ for acyclic queries and our approach takes linear time. Learning over traditional flat joins is thus bound to be suboptimal.
- We can also learn linear functions over arbitrary basis functions, which include feature interactions.
- We benchmarked **F** and its variants against R, which uses QR decomposition [15], Python StatsModels [40], which uses Moore-Penrose pseudoinverse to compute closed-form solutions (ols) [29], and MADlib [17], which also supports ols and Newton optimization for generalized linear models. In our experiments with public, commercial, and artificial datasets, **F** outperforms these competitors by up to three orders of magnitude while preserving the same accuracy.

2. FACTORIZED DATABASES: A PRIMER

In this paper, we rely on factorized databases to compute and represent join results that are input to learning regression models. We next introduce such databases by example and refer to the literature [5, 4, 28] for a rigorous treatment.

Factorized databases form a representation system for relational data that exploits laws of relational algebra, such as the distributivity of the Cartesian product over union, to reduce data and computation redundancy.

EXAMPLE 2.1. Figure 1(a) depicts a database consisting of three relations along with their natural join: The relation House records house prices and living areas (in squared meters) within locations given by zipcodes; TaxBand relates city/state tax bands with house living areas; Shops list shops with zipcode and opening hours (in our experiments, we consider an extended dataset from a large US retailer; the join condition may also use a user-defined distance function).

The join result exhibits a high degree of redundancy. The value z_1 occurs in 24 tuples, each value h_1 to h_3 occurs in eight tuples and they are paired with the same combinations of values for the other attributes. Since z_1 is paired in House with p_1 to p_3 and in Shops with h_1 to h_3, all combinations (indeed, the Cartesian product) of the former and the latter values occur in the join result. We can represent this local product symbolically instead of eagerly materializing it. If we systematically apply this observation, we obtain an equivalent *factorized representation* of the entire join result that is much more compact than the flat, tabular representation of the join result, cf. Figure 1(c) (the attribute names are clear from context). Each tuple in the result is represented once in the factorized join and can be constructed by following one branch of every union and all branches of a product. Whereas the flat join has 130 values (26 tuples of 5 values each), the factorized join only has 18 values.

The factorized join in Figure 1(c) has the nesting structure depicted in Figure 1(b): It is a union of Z-values occurring in the join of Shops and House on Z. For each Z-value z, we represent separately the union of H-values paired with z in Shops and the union of S-values paired with z in House and with T-values in TaxBand. That is, given z, the H-values are *(conditionally) independent* of the S-values and can be stored separately. This is where the factorization saves computation and space as it avoids an explicit enumeration of all combinations of H-values and S-values for a given Z-value. Also, under each S-value, there is a union of T-values and a union of P-values. The factorization can be compacted further by *caching* subexpressions [28]: The S-value s_2 occurs with its union of T-values $t_4 \cup t_5$ from TaxBand, regardless of which Z-values s_2 is paired with in House. This T-union can be stored once and reused for every occurrence of s_2. □

The nesting structures of factorized joins are called *d-trees* [28]. They are rooted forests representing partial orders of join variables. Each variable A in a d-tree Δ has a subset $\mathit{key}(A)$ of the set $\mathit{anc}(A)$ of its ancestor variables on which A and its descendant variables may depend. A d-tree satisfies the following constraints. (1) The variables of each relation symbol in Q lie along the same root-to-leaf path (since they depend on each other). (2) For any child B of a variable A, $\mathit{key}(B) \subseteq \mathit{key}(A) \cup \{A\}$. Caching of factorizations rooted at unions of A-values is useful when $\mathit{key}(A) \subset \mathit{anc}(A)$, since A and its descendant variables do not depend on variables in $\mathit{anc}(A) \setminus \mathit{key}(A)$ and thus factorizations rooted at A-values

Shops	
Z	H
z_1	h_1
z_1	h_2
z_1	h_3
z_2	h_4

House		
Z	S	P
z_1	s_1	p_1
z_1	s_1	p_2
z_1	s_2	p_3
z_2	s_2	p_4

TaxBand	
S	T
s_1	t_1
s_1	t_2
s_1	t_3
s_2	t_4
s_2	t_5

Shops ⋈ House ⋈ TaxBand				
Z	H	S	P	T
z_1	h_1	s_1	p_1	t_1
z_1	h_1	s_1	p_1	t_2
z_1	h_1	s_1	p_1	t_3
z_1	h_1	s_1	p_2	t_1
z_1	h_1	s_1	p_2	t_2
z_1	h_1	s_1	p_2	t_3
z_1	h_1	s_2	p_3	t_4
z_1	h_1	s_2	p_3	t_5
....				
the above for h_2 and h_3				
....				
z_2	h_4	s_2	p_4	t_4
z_2	h_4	s_2	p_4	t_5

(a) The three relations of database $\mathbf{D}$ and natural join $Q(\mathbf{D})$.

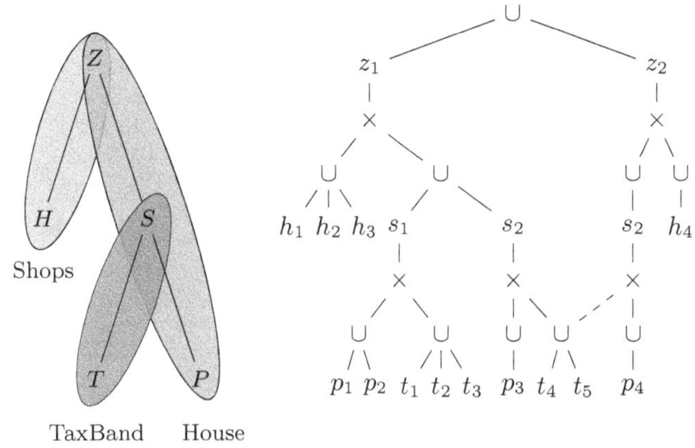

(b) D-tree Δ. (c) Factorization of $Q(\mathbf{D})$ over Δ.

Figure 1: (a) Database D with relations House(Zipcode, Sqm, Price), TaxBand(Sqm, Tax), Shops(Zipcode, Hours), where the attribute names are abbreviated and the values are not necessarily distinct; (b) Nesting structure (d-tree) Δ for the natural join of the relations; (c) Factorization $\Delta(\mathbf{D})$ of the natural join over Δ.

repeat for every tuple of values for these variables. For instance, $key(T) = \{S\} \subset anc(T) = \{S, Z\}$.

The construction of d-trees is guided by the joins, cardinalities, and join selectivities. They can lead to factorizations of greatly varying sizes, where the size of a representation (flat or factorized) is defined as the number of its values. Within the class of factorizations over d-trees, we can find the worst-case optimal ones and also compute them in worst-case optimal time:

PROPOSITION 2.2. *Given a join query Q, for every database $\mathbf{D}$, the join result $Q(\mathbf{D})$ admits*

- *a flat representation of size $\Theta(|\mathbf{D}|^{\rho^*(Q)})$* [3];
- *a factorization over d-trees of size $\Theta(|\mathbf{D}|^{fhtw(Q)})$* [28].

There are worst-case optimal join algorithms to compute the join result in these representations [26, 28].

The measures $\rho^*(Q)$ and $fhtw(Q)$ are the fractional edge cover number and the fractional hypertree width respectively. We know that $1 \leq fhtw(Q) \leq \rho^*(Q) \leq |Q|$, where $|Q|$ is the number of relations in query Q [28]. The gap between $fhtw(Q)$ and $\rho^*(Q)$ can be as large as $|Q|$. The fractional hypertree width is fundamental to problem tractability with applications spanning constraint satisfaction, databases, matrix operations, logic, and probabilistic graphical models [19].

A key observation is that aggregates defined by arithmetic expressions over data values with operations summation and multiplication, e.g., count and sum, can be computed in one pass over factorized joins [4]; we only need to change the union-Cartesian product semiring to the sum-multiplication semiring. For instance, to count the number of tuples of a relation represented by a subtree of the factorized join, we interpret each value as 1 and turn unions and Cartesian products into sums and multiplication respectively. The count at the topmost union node is then the number of tuples in the query result. To sum over all values of an attribute A, the only difference to the previous count algorithm is that we now preserve the A-values. The core computation underlying the construction of linear regression models concerns a family of such aggregates.

3. LEARNING REGRESSION MODELS OVER FACTORIZED JOINS

We are given a training dataset of size m that is computed as a join of database tables:

$$\{(y^{(1)}, x_1^{(1)}, \ldots, x_n^{(1)}), \ldots, (y^{(m)}, x_1^{(m)}, \ldots, x_n^{(m)})\}.$$

The values $y^{(i)}$ are called *labels* and the other values are called *features*. They are all real numbers. For our training dataset, a natural label would be P to predict the price given the other features. Our goal is to learn the parameters $\theta = (\theta_0, \ldots, \theta_n)$ of the linear function:

$$h_\theta(x) = \theta_0 + \theta_1 x_1 + \ldots + \theta_n x_n$$

that approximates the label y of unseen tuples $(x_1, \ldots, x_n)$. For uniformity, we add $x_0 = 1$ so that $h_\theta(x) = \sum_{k=0}^{n} \theta_k x_k$.

The error of our model is given by the so-called least squares regression objective function:

$$J(\theta) = \frac{1}{2}\sum_{i=1}^{m}(h_\theta(x^{(i)}) - y^{(i)})^2. \qquad (1)$$

This is a much studied objective function, since minimizing sum-of-squared errors is equivalent to finding a maximum likelihood solution under a Gaussian noise model [6].

We consider the *batch gradient descent* (BGD) [6], which repeatedly updates the parameters of h_θ in the direction of the gradient to decrease the error given by $J(\theta)$:

$$\begin{aligned}\forall 0 \leq j \leq n : \theta_j &:= \theta_j - \alpha \frac{\delta}{\delta\theta_j} J(\theta) \\ &:= \theta_j - \alpha \sum_{i=1}^{m} (\sum_{k=0}^{n} \theta_k x_k^{(i)} - y^{(i)}) x_j^{(i)}.\end{aligned}$$

The value α is the learning rate and can adapt with the iterations. A naïve implementation of the above expression would start with some initial values for parameters θ_k and perform one pass over the dataset to compute the value of the sum aggregate, followed by one approximation step for the parameters, and repeat this process until convergence.

This is not practical since it is inefficient to go over the entire dataset for each iteration. BGD can however become very competitive when adapted to work on factorized joins.

BGD has two logically independent tasks that are intertwined in the above expression: The computation of the sum aggregate and the convergence of the parameters. The sum aggregate can be rewritten so that the label y becomes part of the features and has a predefined parameter $\theta = -1$:

$$\forall 0 \leq j \leq n : S_j = \sum_{i=1}^{m} (\sum_{k=0}^{n} \theta_k x_k^{(i)}) x_j^{(i)} \tag{2}$$

Our approach is guided by two main insights.

Our **first insight** is that the sum aggregates can be rewritten so that we explicate the *cofactor* of each parameter θ_k in each sum aggregate S_j:

$$\forall 0 \leq j \leq n : S_j = \sum_{k=0}^{n} \theta_k \times \text{Cofactor}[k, j] \tag{3}$$

$$\text{where Cofactor}[k, j] = \sum_{i=1}^{m} x_k^{(i)} x_j^{(i)} \tag{4}$$

This reformulation allows to decouple cofactor computation from parameter convergence. This is crucial for performance as we do not require to scan the dataset for each approximation step. Our system **F** computes the cofactors once and performs parameter convergence directly on the matrix of cofactors, whose size is independent of the data size m. For convergence, **F** uses an adaptation of AdaGrad [13].

Furthermore, the cofactor matrix has desirable properties:

PROPOSITION 3.1. *Let $(Q, \mathbf{D})$ be a pair of join query Q and database $\mathbf{D}$ defining the training dataset $Q(\mathbf{D})$ with schema/features $\sigma = (A_0, \ldots, A_n)$. Let* Cofactor *be the cofactor matrix for learning the parameters $\theta_{A_0}, \ldots, \theta_{A_n}$ of the function $f_\theta = \sum_{k=0}^{n}(\theta_{A_k} x_{A_k})$ using batch gradient descent. The cofactor matrix has the following properties:*

1. Cofactor *is symmetric:*

$$\forall 0 \leq k, j \leq n : \text{Cofactor}[A_k, A_j] = \text{Cofactor}[A_j, A_k].$$

2. Cofactor *computation commutes with union: Given training datasets $Q(\mathbf{D}_1), \ldots, Q(\mathbf{D}_p)$ with cofactor matrices* $\text{Cofactor}_1, \ldots, \text{Cofactor}_p$ *where $\mathbf{D} = \bigcup_{l=1}^{p} \mathbf{D}_l$, then*

$$\forall 0 \leq k, j \leq n : \text{Cofactor}[A_k, A_j] = \sum_{l=1}^{p} \text{Cofactor}_l[A_k, A_j].$$

3. Cofactor *computation commutes with projection: Given a feature set $L \subseteq \sigma$ and the cofactor matrix* Cofactor_L *for the training dataset $\pi_L(Q(\mathbf{D}))$, then*

$$\forall 0 \leq k, j \leq n \text{ such that } A_k, A_j \in L : \quad \text{Cofactor}_L[A_k, A_j] = \text{Cofactor}[A_k, A_j].$$

The symmetry property implies that we only need to compute the upper half of the cofactor matrix.

The commutativity with union means that the cofactor matrix for the union of several training datasets is the entry-wise sum of the cofactor matrices of these training datasets. This property is key to the efficiency of our approach, since we can locally compute partial cofactors over different partitions of the training dataset and then add them up. It is also desirable for *concurrent computation*, where partial cofactors can be computed on different cores or machines.

The commutativity with projection allows us to use the cofactor matrix to compute any subset of the parameters: All it takes is to ignore from the matrix the columns and rows for the irrelevant parameters. This is beneficial if some features are necessary for constructing the dataset but irrelevant for learning, e.g., relation keys supporting the join such as zipcode in our training dataset in Figure 1(a). It is also beneficial for *model selection*, a key challenge in machine learning centered around finding the subset of features that best predict a test dataset. Model selection is a laborious and time-intensive process, since it requires to learn independently parameters corresponding to subsets of the available features. With our reformulation, we first compute the cofactor matrix for all features and then perform convergence on top of the cofactor matrix for the entire lattice of parameters independently of the data. Besides choosing the features after cofactor computation, we may also choose the label and fix its model parameter to -1.

The two commutativity properties in Proposition 3.1 hold under bag (SQL) semantics in the sense that the relational projection and union operators do not remove duplicates. This is important, since learning is sensitive to duplicates.

Our **second insight** is that we can compute the cofactors in one pass over *any factorized join* representing the training dataset, which has the flat join as a special case:

PROPOSITION 3.2. *Let $(Q, \mathbf{D}, \Delta)$ be a triple of a join query Q, a database $\mathbf{D}$, and a d-tree Δ of Q. Let the training dataset be the factorized join $\Delta(\mathbf{D})$ with features $(A_0, \ldots, A_n)$, and let* Cofactor *be the cofactor matrix for learning the parameters $\theta_{A_0}, \ldots, \theta_{A_n}$ of the function $\sum_{k=0}^{n}(\theta_{A_k} x_{A_k})$ using batch gradient descent. Then,* Cofactor *can be computed in one pass over the factorized join $\Delta(\mathbf{D})$.*

Section 4 gives an algorithm to compute the cofactor matrix over the materialized factorized join. Section 5 then shows how to avoid this materialization by intertwining cofactor and join computation. Finally, Section 6 shows how to encode the previous algorithm in one SQL query. An immediate implication is that the redundancy in the flat join result is not necessary for learning:

THEOREM 3.3. *The parameters of any linear function over features from a training dataset defined by a database $\mathbf{D}$ and a join query Q can be learned in time $O(|\mathbf{D}|^{fhtw(Q)})$.*

Theorem 3.3 is a direct corollary of Propositions 2.2 and 3.2. We recall our discussion in Section 2 that within the class of factorized representations over d-trees, this time complexity is essentially worst-case optimal in the sense that there is no join algorithm that can achieve a lower worst-case time complexity. To put this result into a broader context, any worst-case optimal join algorithm that would produce flat join results, such as NPRR [26] or LogicBlox's LeapFrog TrieJoin [41], would need time at least $O(|\mathbf{D}|^{\rho^*(Q)})$ to create the training dataset, yet the gap between $\rho^*(Q)$ and $fhtw(Q)$ can be as large as the number of relations in the join query.

Our approach extends to *linear functions* $\sum_{k=0}^{n} \theta_k \phi_k(\bar{x})$ *with arbitrary basis functions* ϕ_k over a tuple $\bar{x}$ of features. We previously discussed the identity basis functions $\phi_k(x_k) = x_k$. Further examples are polynomials and Gaussian Radial Basis Functions [6]. While basis functions over a single feature x_k are trivially supported, feature interactions are challenging as they may restrict the structure of the factorized join. For instance, the basis function $\phi_k(x_i, x_j) = x_i \cdot x_j$ can only be supported efficiently by d-trees where the attributes x_i and x_j are along the same root-to-leaf path as if they were attributes of a same relation, since we require to compute all possible combinations of values for x_i and x_j. We can enforce this path constraint by enriching the database with one (not materialized) relation over the schema $R_k(x_i, x_j)$ and the query Q with a natural join with R_k. The d-trees for the enriched query will necessarily satisfy the new path constraint and the factorization will have a new value for every combination of values for x_i and x_j along a same path. We can thus add to the factorization a value $\langle \phi_k : \phi_k(x_i, x_j)\rangle$ under each pair of values for x_i and x_j.

We can rephrase Theorem 3.3 for linear functions with basis functions as follows. We say that the basis functions $\phi_0, \ldots, \phi_b$ over the sets of features $S_0, \ldots, S_b$ *induce* a relational schema $\sigma = (R_0(S_0), \ldots, R_b(S_b))$. Given a join query Q and the above schema σ, an *extension of Q with respect to σ* is a join query $Q_\sigma = Q \bowtie R_0 \bowtie \cdots \bowtie R_b$.

THEOREM 3.4. *Let Q be a join query and $\mathbf{D}$ a database that define the training dataset $Q(\mathbf{D})$, and f_θ a linear function with basis functions that induce a relational schema σ. Let Q_σ be the extension of Q with respect to σ. Then, the parameters of f_θ can be learned in time $O(|\mathbf{D}|^{fhtw(Q_\sigma)})$.*

The **two insights** discussed above complement each other, in particular Proposition 3.1 still holds in the presence of factorized joins. The commutativity with projection is especially useful in conjunction with factorization since it does not restrict our choice of possible d-trees for the factorized join depending on the input features used for learning. We may choose the best possible factorization of the join result and at learning time skip over irrelevant attributes (e.g., join attributes). Explicitly removing join attributes from the factorized join may in fact lead to larger representations (this contrasts with the flat case). For instance, if we would eliminate from the factorized join in Figure 1(c) all Z and S-values, then the remaining attributes H, T, and P would become dependent on each other (they were independent conditioned on values for Z and S). The only permissible d-trees would be paths, and the factorized join may be asymptotically as large as the flat join.

For simplicity of exposition, we assume the following (not required in practice). Each relation has one extra attribute I with value 1 to accommodate the intercept θ_0. The d-trees for the join of the relations have the variable I as root. The fatorized join has the I-value 1 as root.

4. F/FDB: COFACTOR COMPUTATION ON MATERIALIZED FACTORIZED JOINS

The cofactors in Equation (4) can be rewritten to mirror the factorization in the factorized join. In this section, we introduce **F/FDB**, an approach that relies on FDB [5] to compute the factorized join and that computes the rewritten cofactors in one pass over the factorized join.

4.1 Cofactor Computation By Factorization

We explain cofactor factorization by examples.

EXAMPLE 4.1. For the training dataset TD in Figure 1(a), there is one sum aggregate in Equation (2) per feature (i.e., attribute) in the dataset. For feature Z, we obtain:

$$\begin{aligned}
S_Z =& (\theta_Z z_1 + \theta_H h_1 + \theta_S s_1 + \theta_P p_1 + \theta_T t_1) z_1 + \\
& (\theta_Z z_1 + \theta_H h_1 + \theta_S s_1 + \theta_P p_1 + \theta_T t_2) z_1 + \\
& (\theta_Z z_1 + \theta_H h_1 + \theta_S s_1 + \theta_P p_1 + \theta_T t_3) z_1 + \\
& \ldots \text{(the above block repeated for } p_2\text{)} \\
& (\theta_Z z_1 + \theta_H h_1 + \theta_S s_2 + \theta_P p_3 + \theta_T t_4) z_1 + \\
& (\theta_Z z_1 + \theta_H h_1 + \theta_S s_2 + \theta_P p_3 + \theta_T t_5) z_1 + \\
& \ldots \text{(all above repeated for } h_2 \text{ and } h_3\text{)} \\
& (\theta_Z z_2 + \theta_H h_4 + \theta_S s_2 + \theta_P p_4 + \theta_T t_4) z_2 + \\
& (\theta_Z z_2 + \theta_H h_4 + \theta_S s_2 + \theta_P p_4 + \theta_T t_5) z_2.
\end{aligned}$$

We can reformulate the aggregate S_Z using the rewritings

$$\sum_{i=1}^{n} x \to x \cdot n \text{ and } \sum_{i=1}^{n} x \cdot a_i \to x \cdot \sum_{i=1}^{n} a_i :$$

$$\begin{aligned}
S_Z =\ & \theta_Z[z_1 \underbrace{(z_1 + \cdots + z_1)}_{|\sigma_{Z=z_1}(TD)|} + z_2 \underbrace{(z_2 + \cdots + z_2)}_{|\sigma_{Z=z_2}(TD)|}] + \\
& \theta_H[z_1 (\sum_{i=1}^{3} \underbrace{h_i + \cdots + h_i}_{|\sigma_{Z=z_1, H=h_i}(TD)|}) + z_2 (\underbrace{h_4 + \cdots + h_4}_{|\sigma_{Z=z_2, H=h_4}(TD)|})] + \\
& \theta_S[z_1 (\sum_{i=1}^{2} \underbrace{s_i + \cdots + s_i}_{|\sigma_{Z=z_1, S=s_i}(TD)|}) + z_2 (\underbrace{s_2 + \cdots + s_2}_{|\sigma_{Z=z_2, S=s_2}(TD)|})] + \\
& \theta_P[z_1 (\sum_{i=1}^{3} \underbrace{p_i + \cdots + p_i}_{|\sigma_{Z=z_1, P=p_i}(TD)|}) + z_2 (\underbrace{p_4 + \cdots + p_4}_{|\sigma_{Z=z_2, P=p_4}(TD)|})] + \\
& \theta_T[z_1 (\sum_{i=1}^{5} \underbrace{t_i + \cdots + t_i}_{|\sigma_{Z=z_1, T=t_i}(TD)|}) + z_2 (\sum_{i=4}^{5} \underbrace{t_i + \cdots + t_i}_{|\sigma_{Z=z_2, T=t_i}(TD)|})].
\end{aligned}$$

We then obtain the following cofactors in the sum S_Z:

$$\begin{aligned}
& Q[Z, Z] = z_1 \cdot 24 z_1 + z_2 \cdot 2 z_2 \\
& Q[H, Z] = z_1 \cdot 8(h_1 + h_2 + h_3) + z_2 \cdot 2 h_4. \\
& Q[S, Z] = z_1 \cdot 3(6 s_1 + 2 s_2) + z_2 \cdot 2 s_2. \\
& Q[P, Z] = z_1 \cdot 3[3(p_1 + p_2) + 2 p_3] + z_2 \cdot 2 p_4. \\
& Q[T, Z] = z_1 \cdot 3[2(t_1 + t_2 + t_3) + t_4 + t_5] + z_2 \cdot (t_4 + t_5). \ \square
\end{aligned}$$

This arithmetic factorization is not arbitrary. It considers the arithmetic expressions grouped by the join Z-values, as done by the d-tree in Figure 1(b). Each cofactor in S_Z is expressed as a sum of terms with one term per each join Z-value z_1 and z_2. The numerical values occurring in the cofactors represent *occurrence counts*, e.g., 24 in $L[Z] = 24 z_1$ states that z_1 occurs in 24 tuples in the training dataset, while 8 in $L[H] = 8(h_1 + h_2 + h_3)$ states that each of h_1, h_2, and h_3 occurs in 8 tuples with z_1. The expressions $L[Z]$ and $L[H]$ represent *sums* of Z-values and respectively H-values that occur in the same tuples with z_1 and that are *weighted* by their occurrence counts.

The above rewritings do not capture the full spectrum of possible computational savings: They are sufficient for cofactors of features θ_X in Sum_Y, where X and Y are from the same input relation. Moreover, they do not bring asymptotic savings. In case X and Y are from different input relations, then we can potentially save more computation.

EXAMPLE 4.2. Consider now a rewriting of the cofactor of parameter θ_P in sum S_T:

$$Q[P, T] = 3[(p_1 + p_2) \cdot (t_1 + t_2 + t_3)] + 3[p_3 \cdot (t_4 + t_5)] + p_4 \cdot (t_4 + t_5).$$

The three terms in the outermost sum correspond to different pairs of join values for Z and S, namely (z_1, s_1), (z_1, s_2),

f-fdb (Factorization E)

if (*visited*) **return**;
switch E:

Case $\langle A : a\rangle \;\times\; (E_1 \cdots E_k)$:

$C_E = 1$;
foreach $j \in [k]$ **do** { **f-fdb**(E_j); $C_E = C_E \cdot C_{E_j}$; }
$L_E[A] = a \cdot C_E$; $Q_E[A, A] = a \cdot L_E[A]$;
foreach $j \in [k]$ **do** {
  foreach $B \in \mathsf{Schema}[E_j]$ **do** { $L_E[B] = L_{E_j}[B] \cdot C_E/C_{E_j}$; $Q_E[A, B] = a \cdot L_{E_j}[B] \cdot C_E/C_{E_j}$; }
  foreach $B, D \in \mathsf{Schema}[E_j]$ s.t. $B < D$ **do** $Q_E[B, D] = Q_{E_j}[B, D] \cdot C_E/C_{E_j}$;
  foreach $j < l \in [k], B \in \mathsf{Schema}[E_l], D \in \mathsf{Schema}[E_j]$ **do** $Q_E[B, D] = L_{E_l}[B] \cdot L_{E_j}[D] \cdot C_E/(C_{E_l} \cdot C_{E_j})$;
}

Case $\cup\; (E_1 \cdots E_k)$:

$C_E = 0$; **foreach** $j \in [k], B, D \in \mathsf{Schema}[E_j]$ **do** $\{L_E[B] = 0;\; Q_E[B, D] = 0;\}$
foreach $j \in [k]$ **do** { **f-fdb**(E_j); C_E += C_{E_j}; }
foreach $j \in [k], B \in \mathsf{Schema}[E_j]$ **do** {
  $L_E[B]$ += $L_{E_j}[B]$;
  foreach $D \in \mathsf{Schema}[E_j]$ **do** $Q_E[B, D]$ += $Q_{E_j}[B, D]$;
}

visited = *true*;

Figure 2: F/FDB: Algorithm for computing regression aggregates (constant C_E, linear L_E, quadratic Q_E) in one pass over a factorized join E.

and (z_2, s_2). This rewriting thus follows the same join order as the d-tree in Figure 1(b). These terms read as follows: Each of the P-values p_1 and p_2 occurs in three tuples with each of the T-values t_1 to t_3; the P-value p_3 occurs in three tuples with each of the T-values t_4 and t_5; the P-value p_4 occurs in one tuple with each of the T-values t_4 and t_5. □

The rewritten expression for $Q[P, T]$ factors out sums, e.g., $p_1 + p_2$, using a rewriting more powerful than those for the sum S_Z given in Example 4.1 that can transform expressions to exponentially smaller equivalent ones:

$$\sum_{i=1}^{r}\sum_{j=1}^{s}(x_i \cdot y_j) \rightarrow (\sum_{i=1}^{r} x_i) \cdot (\sum_{j=1}^{s} y_j).$$

The above rewritings are already implemented by the factorized join from Figure 1(c). For instance, the sums of values in the cofactors mentioned in Examples 4.1 and 4.2 can be recovered via unions of their corresponding values in the factorization. Since Z-values are above the values for the other attributes, the former are in one-to-many relationships with the latter. This explains the rewritings in Example 4.1 for the cofactors in sum S_Z: Each of z_1 and z_2 are paired with the weighted sums of all H-values underneath, namely $8(h_1 + h_2 + h_3)$ and respectively $2h_4$. Similar pairings are with the weighted sums of values for each of the other attribute. Since P and T are on different branches in the d-tree, a Cartesian product of a union of P-values and a union of T-values becomes a product of the sums of the corresponding P-values and T-values.

Examples 4.1 and 4.2 show that cofactor computation requires three types of aggregates: Constant aggregates that are occurrence counts; linear aggregates that are weighted sums, i.e., sums over features or products of linear and constant aggregates; and quadratic aggregates that are cofactors, i.e., products of features and/or linear aggregates, or of quadratic and constant aggregates. Constant aggregates are real numbers and denoted by C. Linear aggregates are arrays of reals, one per feature A and denoted by $L[A]$. Quadratic aggregates are matrices of reals, one per each pair of features (A, B) and denoted by $Q[A, B]$.

DEFINITION 4.3. A *regression aggregate* is a tuple (C, L, Q) of constant, linear, and quadratic aggregates. We use indices E and Δ to refer to the regression aggregates (C_E, L_E, Q_E) for a factorization E and $(C_\Delta, L_\Delta, Q_\Delta)$ for a d-tree Δ.

4.2 Computing Regression Aggregates

The algorithm **f-fdb** in Figure 2 computes the regression aggregates, and in particular the cofactors, at each node in the input factorization E in one pass over E.

Let us denote by $[\![E]\!]$ the relation represented by the factorization E. The schema $\mathsf{Schema}[E]$ of $[\![E]\!]$ is the set of features (or query variables) from the d-tree of E. The Cartesian product and union operators in the factorization translate to multiplication and summation for regression aggregates. Since they commute with union, we compute them for each child of a union and then add them entrywise.

The constant aggregate C_E is the number of tuples in $[\![E]\!]$. The constant aggregates are used to compute occurrence counts as follows. If E is the child of a product $E_\times$, its occurrence count in $E_\times$ (i.e., the occurrence count of each tuple in $[\![E]\!]$) is the product of the constant aggregates of its siblings. This is correct, since each of the tuples represented by E is extended in the relation $[\![E_\times]\!]$ by each tuple represented by each of E's siblings.

The linear aggregate $L_E[A]$ for a feature $A \in \mathsf{Schema}[E]$ is the sum of A-values in E, each weighted by their occurrence counts given by constant aggregates.

The quadratic aggregate $Q_E[B, D]$ for features $B, D \in \mathsf{Schema}[E]$ is the sum of quadratic aggregates $Q_{E_j}[B, D]$ for the child E_j of E if both B and D occur in E_j, or the product of linear aggregates for each of B and D weighted by their occurrence counts, if B and D are from different children of E. We use the symmetry of the cofactor matrix (cf. Proposition 3.1) to only compute the quadratic aggregates for B and D in case B occurs before D in the depth-first left-to-right preorder traversal of the d-tree (and factorization). The cofactor matrix is formed by the quadratic aggregates at the root of the factorization.

To support caching, we use a Boolean flag *visited* for each node in the factorization. Initially, this flag is false. After

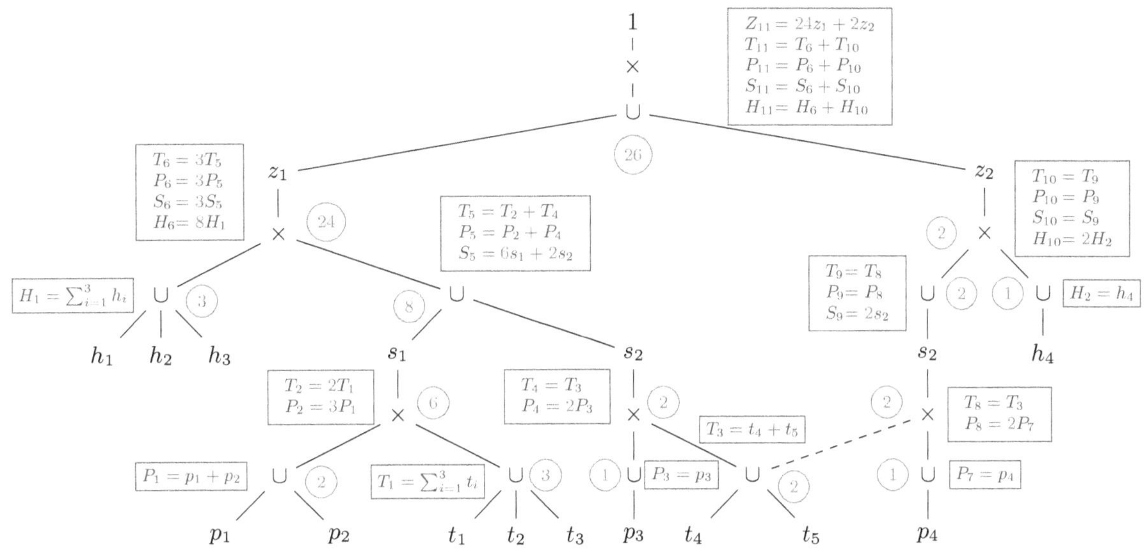

	θ_I	θ_Z	θ_S	θ_P	θ_T	θ_H
Σ_I	26	$24z_1 + 2z_2$	$3(6s_1 + 2s_2) + 2s_2$	$9(p_1 + p_2) + 6p_3 + 2p_4$	$6(t_1 + t_2 + t_3) + 3(t_4 + t_5)$	$8(h_1 + h_2 + h_3) + 2h_4$
Σ_Z	Σ_I/θ_Z	$24z_1^2 + 2z_2^2$	$z_1 S_6 + z_2 S_{10}$	$z_1 P_6 + z_2 P_{10}$	$z_1 T_6 + z_2 T_{10}$	$z_1 H_6 + z_2 H_{10}$
Σ_S	Σ_I/θ_S	Σ_Z/θ_S	$3(6s_1^2 + 2s_2^2) + 2s_2^2$	$3(s_1 P_2 + s_2 P_4) + s_2 P_8$	$3s_1 T_2 + 3s_2 T_4 + s_2 T_8$	$S_5 H_1 + S_9 H_2$
Σ_P	Σ_I/θ_P	Σ_Z/θ_P	Σ_S/θ_P	$9(p_1^2 + p_2^2) + 6p_3^2 + 2p_4^2$	$3P_1 T_1 + 3P_3 T_3 + P_7 T_3$	$P_5 H_1 + P_9 H_2$
Σ_T	Σ_I/θ_T	Σ_Z/θ_T	Σ_S/θ_T	Σ_P/θ_T	$6(t_1^2 + t_2^2 + t_3^2) + 3(t_4^2 + t_5^2)$	$T_5 H_1 + T_9 H_2$
Σ_H	Σ_I/θ_H	Σ_Z/θ_H	Σ_S/θ_H	Σ_P/θ_H	Σ_T/θ_H	$8(h_1^2 + h_2^2 + h_3^2) + 2h_4^2$

Figure 3: The factorized join in Figure 1(c) with extra root value 1 for intercept. Constant (encircled) and linear (boxed) aggregates are shown for product and union nodes. The cofactor matrix (bottom) is formed by the quadratic aggregates for the root node. We may first compute the matrix and then explore possible regression models by choosing different sets of features and label to predict.

the the node is visited, the flag is toggled so that we recognize visited nodes and skip them should we arrive again at them. The parent of an already visited node ν can just use the previously computed regression aggregates for ν.

EXAMPLE 4.4. Figure 3 shows the factorization in Figure 1(c) annotated with constant and linear aggregates as computed in one bottom-up pass. The cofactor matrix is computed in the same pass. The top left entry in the matrix is the cofactor of the intercept θ_I in the sum S_I and represents the number of tuples in the flat join result. Since the matrix is symmetric, we only compute the entries above and including the diagonal. □

Our algorithm inherits the data complexity of computing the factorized join as it is linear in its size. At each node ν, the algorithm **f-fdb** recurses once for each child of ν and we need time linear in its schema to compute the constant and linear aggregates, and quadratic in its schema to compute the quadratic aggregates. The time complexity is thus linear in the size of the input factorized data and quadratic in the size of the schema (number of features). We require space to store the factorized data. For each node in the factorization, we also require space quadratic in the schema size to store the regression aggregates. In the next section, we show how to avoid to store the factorized data and also to reduce the number of regression aggregates to only having one per variable in the d-tree.

5. F: MIXING COFACTOR AND FACTORIZED JOIN COMPUTATION

This section introduces two improvements to **F/FDB**. (1) We avoid the materialization of the factorized join. (2) We reduce the number of regression aggregates from one per node in the factorized join to one per node in its d-tree. This new algorithm is called **F**. It is an in-memory monolithic engine optimized for regression aggregates over joins.

Figure 4.2 gives **F**'s core procedure. It takes as input the database relations $R_1, \ldots, R_d$ and a d-tree Δ for the given join query. It computes a tuple $(C_\Delta, L_\Delta, Q_\Delta)$ of regression aggregates for the factorized join over Δ. Instead of materializing the factorized join, we iterate over its paths of values that are mapped to paths of variables in Δ. Such a mapping is kept in varMap. This join approach is reminiscent of LeapFrog TrieJoin [41] with the difference that instead of using a total variable (or join) order, we use a partial variable order defined by a d-tree. More branches in a d-tree mean a higher factorization degree and performance improvement.

The relations are assumed sorted on their attributes following a depth-first pre-order traversal of Δ. Each call takes a range defined by start and end indices in each relation. Initially, these ranges span the entire relations. Let us assume the variable at the root of Δ is A. Once A is mapped to a value a in the intersection of possible A-values from the relations with attribute A, then these ranges are narrowed down to those tuples with value a for A. We may further narrow down these ranges using mappings for variables below A in Δ at higher recursion depths. Each A-value a in this

f (d-tree Δ, varMap, ranges$[(start_1, end_1), \ldots, (start_d, end_d)]$)

$A = var(\Delta)$; keyMap $= \pi_{key(A)}$(varMap); reset$(C_\Delta, L_\Delta, Q_\Delta)$;

if $(key(A) \neq anc(A))$ { $(C_\Delta, L_\Delta, Q_\Delta) =$ cache[keyMap]; **if** $(C_\Delta \neq 0)$ **return**; }

foreach $a \in \bigcap_{i\in[d], A\in \mathsf{Schema}[R_i]} \pi_A(R_i[start_i, end_i])$ **do** {
  foreach $i \in [d]$ **do** find ranges $R_i[start'_i, end'_i] \subseteq R_i[start_i, end_i]$ such that $\pi_A(R_i[start'_i, end'_i]) = \{(A : a)\}$;
  switch(Δ) :
   leaf node $A : C_\Delta$ += 1; $L_\Delta[A]$ += a; $Q_\Delta[A, A]$ += $a \cdot a$;
   inner node $A(\Delta_1, \ldots, \Delta_k)$:
    foreach $j \in [k]$ **do** **f**$(\Delta_j$, varMap $\times \{(A : a)\}$, ranges$[(start'_1, end'_1), \ldots, (start'_d, end'_d)])$;
    $C = C_{\Delta_1} \cdot \ldots \cdot C_{\Delta_k}$;
    if$(C \neq 0)$ {
     C_Δ += C;
     foreach $j \in [k]$ **do** {
      foreach $B \in \mathsf{Schema}[\Delta_j]$ **do** { $L_\Delta[B]$ += $L_{\Delta_j}[B] \cdot C / C_{\Delta_j}$; $Q_\Delta[A, B]$ += $a \cdot L_{\Delta_j}[B] \cdot C/C_{\Delta_j}$; }
      foreach $B, D \in \mathsf{Schema}[\Delta_j]$ s.t. $B < D$ **do** $Q_\Delta[B, D]$ += $Q_{\Delta_j}[B, D] \cdot C/C_{\Delta_j}$;
      foreach $j < l \in [k], B \in \mathsf{Schema}[\Delta_l], D \in \mathsf{Schema}[\Delta_j]$ **do** $Q_\Delta[B, D]$ += $L_{\Delta_l}[B] \cdot L_{\Delta_j}[D] \cdot C/(C_{\Delta_l} \cdot C_{\Delta_j})$;
     }
    }
}
if $(key(A) \neq anc(A))$ cache[keyMap] $= (C_\Delta, L_\Delta, Q_\Delta)$;

Figure 4: F: Algorithm for computing regression aggregates (constant C_Δ, linear L_Δ, quadratic Q_Δ) for a given d-tree Δ of the join query and a database $(R_1, \ldots, R_d)$. The parameters of the initial call are the d-tree Δ, an empty variable map, and the full range of tuples for each relation.

intersection is the root of a factorization fragment over Δ. Instead of using one regression aggregate for each A-value, we may use one running regression aggregate for all of them since it commutes with their union. We thus only need as many regression aggregates as variables in the d-tree.

The regression aggregate for A is computed using the A-values and the aggregates for its children if any. We first reset it, since it might have been used for different factorization fragments with the same nesting structure Δ. We next check whether we previously computed this aggregate for the same factorization fragment and cached it. Whereas for **F/FDB** caching is done by FDB, **F** needs to manage the cache itself. As explained in Section 2, the *key* of each variable tells us when caching may be useful: This happens when $key(A)$ is strictly contained in $anc(A)$, since this means that the factorization fragments over the d-tree rooted at A are repeated for every distinct combination of values for variables in $anc(A) \setminus key(A)$. In this case, we probe the cache using as key the mappings from varMap of the variables in $key(A)$. If we have already visited that factorization fragment, then we can just use its previously computed regression aggregate and avoid recomputation. If this is the first visit, we insert the aggregate in the cache after we compute it. If the aggregate is not already in cache, we compute it precisely as for **F/FDB**. The case when Δ is an inner node is a combination of the two cases in Figure 2: We have a union of A-values, each on top of a product of subexpressions. The case when Δ is a leaf node corresponds to the first case in Figure 2 without subexpressions E_j.

F has the same time complexity as **F/FDB** (including FDB's computation of the factorized join). The key operation needed for joins is the intersection of the arrays of ordered values defined by the relation ranges. This is done efficiently using the unary leapfrog join [41]. Given d ordered arrays $L_1, \ldots, L_d$, where $N_{\min} = \min\{|L_1|, \ldots, |L_d|\}$ and $N_{\max} = \max\{|L_1|, \ldots, |L_d|\}$ are the sizes of the smallest and respectively largest array, their intersection takes time $O(N_{\min} \log(N_{\max}/N_{\min}))$, which is the size of the smallest array if we ignore log factors. The time to compute the regression aggregates is the same as for **F/FDB**. The amount of extra memory necessary for computing the join is however limited: For each relation, there is one index range that is a pair of numbers, varMap has at most one mapping per variable at any one time, and the number of regression aggregates is bounded by the number of variables in the d-tree.

6. F/SQL: F IN SQL

F's cofactor computation can be expressed using one SQL query whose result is a table with one row that contains all cofactors. This SQL encoding of **F**, called **F/SQL**, has desirable properties. (1) It can be computed by any relational database system and is thus readily deployable in practice with a small implementation overhead. (2) It works for datasets that do not fit in memory. (3) Like **F**, it pushes aggregates past joins for efficiency.

We generate the **F/SQL** query in two steps: We first rewrite the query so that cyclic joins are isolated and the rewritten query becomes (α-)acyclic. To retain the complexity of **F**, these isolated cyclic joins have to be computed using a worst-case optimal algorithm [41]. We then traverse bottom up an optimal d-tree Δ for the rewritten query and at each node with variable g we create a query that joins on g and then computes the regression aggregates for g. This evaluation strategy thus intertwines the joins and the aggregates like in **F**, which is prerequisite for its good complexity. In contrast to **F**, **F/SQL** requires as input an *extended*

rewrite(d-tree Δ)

$QS = \emptyset$; $\quad A = var(\Delta)$;
if $(\Delta = A(\Delta_1, \ldots, \Delta_k))$ $QS = \bigcup_{j \in [k]}$ **rewrite**(Δ_j);
Q_A = relations$(key(A) \cup \{A\})$;
if $(\nexists Q \in QS$ s.t. $Q_A \subseteq Q)$ **return** $QS \cup \{Q_A\}$
else **return** QS

Figure 5: F/SQL: Query rewriting procedure.

d-tree where each input table R becomes a leaf under the lowest variable that corresponds to an attribute of R.

6.1 Rewriting Arbitrary Joins to Acyclic Joins

The rewriting procedure is given in Figure 5 and works on a d-tree Δ of the input join query Q_{in}. The set QS is a disjoint partitioning of the set of relations in Q_{in} into sets of relations or partitions. Each partition Q_A corresponds to a join query that is materialized to a relation with the same name Q_A. The set $key(A) \cup \{A\}$ consists of those variables on which the variables in Δ depend. D-trees are a different syntax for hypertree decompositions and the set $key(A) \cup \{A\}$ represents the bag at a node in such a decomposition [28]. By materializing the joins defined by such bags, we simplify the hypertree decomposition or d-tree of Q_{in} to that of an acyclic query Q_{out} equivalent to Q_{in}. In case Q_{in} is already acyclic, then each partition has one relation and hence Q_{out} is syntactically equal to Q_{in}.

EXAMPLE 6.1. Consider the following bowtie join query Q over relations $R_1, \ldots, R_6$ together with a d-tree for it:

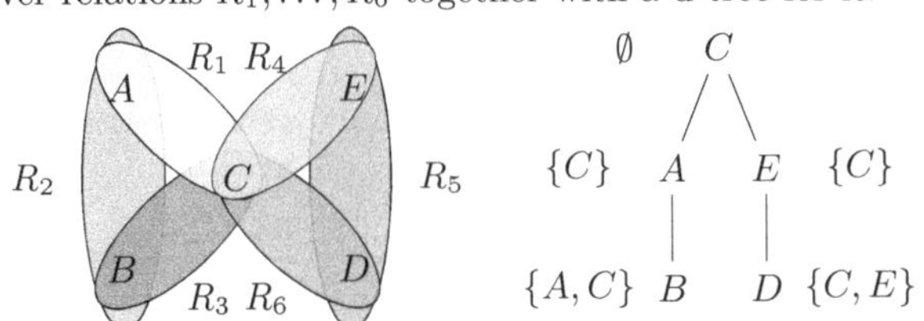

We state the keys next to each variable in the d-tree. We apply the rewriting algorithm. When we reach leaf B in the left branch, we create the join query Q_B over the relations $\{R_1, R_2, R_3\}$ and add it to QS. When we return from recursion to variable A, we create the query Q_A over the same relations, so we do not add it to QS. We proceed similarly in the right branch, create the join query Q_D over relations $\{R_4, R_5, R_6\}$, and add it to QS. The queries at E and C are not added to QS. Whereas the original query and the two subqueries Q_B and Q_D are cyclic, the rewritten query Q_{out} is the join of Q_B and Q_D on C and is acyclic. The triangle queries Q_B and Q_D cannot be computed worst-case optimally with traditional relational query plans [3], which calls for specialized engines to compute them [41].

The query in Figure 1(a) is acyclic. Using its d-tree from Figure 1(b), we obtain one identity query per relation. □

6.2 SQL for Learning over Acyclic Joins

The SQL construction algorithm is recursive on the structure of the extended d-tree. As we proceed bottom up, we aggregate over the input attributes $\mathcal{A}$ and create sets of constant $\mathcal{C}$, linear $\mathcal{L}$, and quadratic $\mathcal{Q}$ aggregates.

At a leaf for a table R, we create a trivial query $\mathbf{R}$:

$$\mathbf{R} = \textbf{SELECT } \mathcal{A}(R).*, \mathcal{C}(R).*, \mathcal{L}(R).*, \mathcal{Q}(R).* \textbf{ FROM } R;$$

where $\mathcal{A}$ is the schema of R, there is no linear and quadratic aggregate, and we add one constant aggregate with value 1.

At an inner node with variable g, where $\mathbf{G}_i$ is the query created at the i-th child, we create the aggregate query $\mathbf{G}$ over the natural join $\mathbf{G}_{\bowtie}$ of queries $\mathbf{G}_1, \ldots, \mathbf{G}_k$ on g.

$$\mathbf{G}_{\bowtie} = \textbf{SELECT } \mathcal{Q}(\mathbf{G}_{\bowtie}).*, \mathcal{L}(\mathbf{G}_{\bowtie}).*, \mathcal{C}(\mathbf{G}_{\bowtie}).*, \mathcal{A}(\mathbf{G}_{\bowtie}).* \textbf{ FROM } \mathbf{G}_1 \textbf{ NATURAL JOIN } \ldots \mathbf{G}_k;$$

$$\begin{aligned}\mathcal{Q}(\mathbf{G}_{\bowtie}) =& \{q \cdot \#_{-i} \mid q \in \mathcal{Q}(\mathbf{G}_i), i \in [k]\} \cup \{g \cdot 1 \cdot \#\} \cup \\ & \{l_i \cdot l_j \mid l_i \in \mathcal{L}(\mathbf{G}_i), l_j \in \mathcal{L}(\mathbf{G}_j), 1 \leq i < j \leq k\} \cup \\ & \{g \cdot l_i \cdot \#_{-i} \mid l_i \in \mathcal{L}(\mathbf{G}_i), i \in [k]\} \cup \{g^2 \cdot \#\} \\ \mathcal{L}(\mathbf{G}_{\bowtie}) =& \{l_i \cdot \#_{-i} \mid l_i \in \mathcal{L}(\mathbf{G}_i), i \in [k]\} \cup \{g \cdot \#\}\end{aligned}$$

$$\mathcal{C}(\mathbf{G}_{\bowtie}) = \{\#\} \qquad \mathcal{A}(\mathbf{G}_{\bowtie}) = \bigcup_{i=1}^{k} \mathcal{A}(\mathbf{G}_i) - \{g\}$$

$$\# = \Pi_{j=1}^{k}\{c \mid c \in \mathcal{C}(\mathbf{G}_j)\} \qquad \#_{-i} = \#/(\Pi_{c \in \mathcal{C}(\mathbf{G}_i)} c)$$

Two constant aggregates are used in several regression aggregates: $\#$ is the number of tuples in the result of $\mathbf{G}_{\bowtie}$ and $\#_{-i}$ is $\#$ where we ignore child i from the join. The regression aggregates are computed as for **F**. We next group by the remaining attributes $\mathcal{A}(\mathbf{G}_{\bowtie})$ and sum over each aggregate:

$$\mathbf{G} = \textbf{SELECT } \mathcal{A}(\mathbf{G}).*, \mathcal{C}(\mathbf{G}).*, \mathcal{L}(\mathbf{G}).*, \mathcal{Q}(\mathbf{G}).* \textbf{ FROM } \mathbf{G}_{\bowtie} \textbf{ GROUP BY } \mathcal{A}(\mathbf{G}).*;$$

$$\mathcal{Q}(\mathbf{G}) = \{\textstyle\sum q \mid q \in \mathcal{Q}(\mathbf{G}_{\bowtie})\} \quad \mathcal{L}(\mathbf{G}) = \{\textstyle\sum l \mid l \in \mathcal{L}(\mathbf{G}_{\bowtie})\}$$

$$\mathcal{C}(\mathbf{G}) = \{\textstyle\sum c \mid c \in \mathcal{C}(\mathbf{G}_{\bowtie})\} \quad \mathcal{A}(\mathbf{G}) = \mathcal{A}(\mathbf{G}_{\bowtie})$$

EXAMPLE 6.2. Consider the d-tree in Figure 1(b). We create the queries Q_P at node P and then Q_T at node T:

```
SELECT Z, S, sum(House_c) as P_c, sum(P) as P_l1,
       sum(P*P*House_c) as P_q1
FROM (SELECT Z, S, P, 1 as House_c FROM House)
GROUP BY Z, S;
SELECT S, sum(TaxBand_c) as T_c, sum(T) as T_l1,
       sum(T*T*TaxBand_c) as T_q1
FROM (SELECT S, T, 1 as TaxBand_c FROM TaxBand)
GROUP BY S;
```

At node S, we create the query Q_S using Q_P and Q_T:

```
SELECT Z, sum(S_c) as S_c, sum(S_l1) as S_l1,
       sum(S_l2) as S_l2, sum(S_l3) as S_l3,
       sum(S_q1) as S_q1, sum(S_q2) as S_q2,
       sum(S_q3) as S_q3, sum(S_q4) as S_q4,
       sum(S_q5) as S_q5, sum(S_q6) as S_q6
FROM (SELECT Z, P_c*T_c as S_c, P_l1*T_c as S_l1,
             T_l1*P_c as S_l2, S*S_c as S_l3,
             P_q1*T_c as S_q1, T_q1*P_c as S_q2,
             P_l1*T_l1 as S_q3, S*P_l1*T_c as S_q4,
             S*T_l1*P_c as S_q5, S*S_l3 as S_q6
      FROM Q_P NATURAL JOIN Q_T)
GROUP BY Z;
```

The nodes H and Z are treated similarly. The constructed query exploits caching: Indeed, for each distinct S-value s, Q_T computes once the aggregates over T in TaxBand. Without caching, we would repeat the computation of Q_T for every occurrence of the S-value s in House. □

F/SQL has the time complexity of **F** under the assumption that cyclic joins are computed using a worst-case optimal join algorithm like LFTJ. For (input and rewritten) acyclic queries, we may use standard query plans.

7. EXPERIMENTS

We report on the performance of an end-to-end solution for learning regression models over joins, which includes: (a) Constructing the training dataset via joins; (b) importing the dataset in the learning module; and (c) learning the parameters of regression functions. We show experimentally that the intermediate join step is unnecessarily expensive. It entails a high degree of redundancy in both computation and data representation, yet this is not required for the end-to-end solution, whose result is a list of real-valued parameters. By factorizing the join we reduce data redundancy while improving performance for both the join and the learning steps. A tight integration of learning and join processing also eliminates the need for the data import step.

We benchmark **F** and its flavors against three open-source systems: M (MADlib [17]), P (Python StatsModels [40]), and R [33]. We show that for the used datasets and learning tasks, **F** outperforms these systems by up to three orders of magnitude, while maintaining their accuracy; we verified that for all systems the learned parameters coincide with high precision. This performance boost is due to three orthogonal optimizations: Factorization and caching of data and computation; decoupling parameter convergence from cofactor computation; and shared cofactor computation.

Regression Learners. We implemented **F** and its flavors in C++. They all use AdaGrad to adapt the learning rate (α) based on history in the convergence component [13]. **F/FDB** uses FDB [5] to compute factorized joins via an in-memory multiway sort-merge join. **F/SQL** is **F**'s encoding in SQL. For R we used *lm* (linear model) based on QR-decomposition [15]. For P we used *ols* (ordinary least squares) based on the Moore-Penrose pseudoinverse [29]. For M we used *ols* to compute the closed-form solution and *glm* based on Newton optimization for generalized linear models. M (glm), P, and R use PostgreSQL 9.4.4 for join computation (done by query plans with sort-merge joins for the Housing dataset and with in-memory hash joins for the other datasets). We tuned PostgreSQL for in-memory processing by setting its working memory to 14GB and shared buffers to 128MB and by turning off parameters than affect performance (fsync, synchronous commit, full page writes, bgwriter LRU maxpages). We verified that it runs in memory by monitoring IO. From all the systems, M (ols), **F**, and **F/SQL** do not require the materialization of the join query. P and R need to export data from PostgreSQL and load it into their memory space, which requires one pass over the flat join and construction of its internal representation.

Experimental Setup. All experiments were performed on an Intel(R) Core(TM) i7-4770 3.40GHz/64bit/32GB with Linux 3.13.0/g++4.8.4 (no compiler optimization flags were used, `ulimit` was set to unlimited). We report wall-clock times by running each system once and then reporting the average of four subsequent runs with warm cache. For P, R, M (glm), and **F/FDB** we break down the times for: Computing the join in memory, importing the data, and learning the parameters; we do not report the times to load the database into memory as they can differ substantially between PostgreSQL and FDB and are orthogonal to this work. All tables are given sorted by their join attributes.

Datasets and Learning Tasks. We experimented with a real-world dataset, which is used by a large US retailer for forecasting user demands and sales, with two public datasets LastFM [10] and MovieLens [16], and a synthetic dataset modeling the textbook example on house price market [25]. We next briefly introduce the learning tasks for each dataset; a detailed description is given in Appendix.

US retailer: We considered three linear regression tasks that predict the amount of inventory units based on all other features: L considers all features; N_1 and N_2 also consider two interactions of features from the same tables (no factorization restructuring necessary), and respectively from different tables (factorization restructuring necessary).

LastFM: We consider two training datasets L_1 and L_2 to relate how often friends listen to the same artists.

MovieLens: The regression task is to predict the rating given by a user to a movie.

Housing: The regression task is to predict the housing price based on all the features in the dataset.

1. Flat vs. Factorized Joins. The compression ratio is a direct indicator of how well **F** fares against approaches that rely on flat representation of the training dataset. As shown in Table 1, the compression factor brought by factorizing the joins varies from 4.43 for MovieLens to 26.61 for US retailer and over 100 for LastFM. Caching can improve the compression factor even further: 3x for MovieLens and 8x for LastFM. The effect of caching for US retailer is minimal.

While the speedup of FDB over PostgreSQL is significant, it is less than the data compression ratio possibly due to the less optimized data structures to encode factorizations in FDB. As shown in Figure 6, for scale 10 the factorized join is computed in 1.25 seconds vs. 64 seconds for the flat join. All join queries used in the experiments are acyclic, which means that our **F** flavors can compute them in linear time (modulo log factors).

Table 1 reports the join time for the real-world datasets. For the US retailer, the flat join is too large to be handled by P and R. In practice, such large datasets are partitioned and learning happens independently for each partition. This entails a loss of accuracy as we miss correlations across features. We partitioned the largest table Inventory (84M tuples) into four (ten) disjoint partitions for R (respectively, P) of roughly equal sizes by hashing on the join values for location. By joining each partition with the other tables we obtain a partitioning of the join result. Table 1 reports the overall (starred) time to compute the join for all partitions.

2. Importing Datasets. P and R are the only systems that need one pass over the join result to load it into their internal data structures. This is typical for the existing solutions based on software enterprise stacks consisting of dozens of specialized systems (e.g., for OLAP, OLTP, and BI), where non-trivial integration effort is usually spent at the interface between these systems. Table 1 and Figure 6 report the times for importing the training datasets. For Housing, P and R failed to import the data starting with scale 10 and respectively 11. In contrast, **F** can even finish for scale 100.

3. Learning. Table 1 shows that the speedup factor of learning with **F/FDB** versus competitors is larger than the compression factor, which is partially due to sharing computation across cofactors and, when compared against the gradient descent approximation methods like M(glm), also due to our decoupling of cofactor computation from convergence. For R and P on US retailer, we partitioned the dataset as explained in Experiment 2. Table 1 reports the sum of learning times for all partitions. However, the learned parameters for each partition are arbitrarily far from true ones (although

		US retailer L	US retailer N_1	US retailer N_2	LastFM L_1	LastFM L_2	MovieLens L
# parameters		31	33	33	6	10	27
Join Size	Factorized	97,134,867	97,134,867	97,134,867	2,577,556	2,379,264	6,092,286
	cached	97,134,675	97,134,675	97,134,675	376,402	315,818	2,115,610
	Flat	2,585,046,352	2,585,046,352	2,585,046,352	369,986,292	590,793,800	27,005,643
	Compression	26.61×	26.61×	26.61×	143.54×	248.31×	4.43×
	cached	26.61×	26.61×	26.61×	982.86×	1870.68×	12.76×
Join Time	Fact. (FDB)	36.03	36.03	36.03	4.79	9.94	12.28
	Flat (PSQL)	249.41	249.41	249.41	54.25	61.33	1.30
Import Time	R	1189.12*	1189.12*	1189.12*	155.91	276.77	10.86
	P	1164.40*	1164.40*	1164.40*	179.16	328.97	11.33
Learn Time	**F/FDB**	9.69	9.82	9.79	0.53	0.89	3.87
	M (glm)	2671.88	2937.49	2910.23	572.88	746.50	31.91
	R	810.66*	873.14*	884.47*	268.04	466.52	6.96
	P	1199.50*	1277.10*	1275.08*	35.74	148.84	10.92
Total Time	**F**	16.29	16.56	16.50	0.11	0.25	2.12
	F/FDB	45.72	45.85	45.82	5.32	10.83	16.15
	F/SQL	108.81	109.02	109.07	0.58	2.00	14.26
	M (ols)	680.60	737.02	738.08	152.37	196.60	7.08
	M (glm)	2921.29	3186.90	3159.64	627.13	807.83	33.21
	R	2249.19*	2311.67*	2323.00*	478.20	804.62	19.12
	P	2613.31*	2690.91*	2688.89*	269.15	539.14	23.55
Speedup	**F** vs. M (ols)	41.78×	44.51×	44.73×	1385.18×	786.40×	3.34×
	F vs. M (glm)	179.33×	192.45×	191.49×	5701.18×	3231.32×	15.67×
	F vs. R	138.07×	139.59×	140.79×	4347.27×	3218.48×	9.02×
	F vs. P	160.42×	162.49×	162.96×	2446.82×	2156.56×	11.11×

Table 1: Performance comparison for learning over joins (size in number of values, time in seconds). F, F/SQL, and M(ols) intertwine the join and learning computation and we only show their total end-to-end times. P and R crashed for US retailer due to memory limitation, the starred numbers are for running them on disjoint partitions of the location values for the join (four for R and ten for P) and adding up the times.

not supported by P and R, they could have been made correct if the output parameters for a partition would serve as the initial parameter values for the next partition). Nevertheless, even under these simplifying assumptions for P and R, **F** learns the correct parameters at least two orders of magnitude faster than them.

The tasks N_1 and N_2 in Table 1 for US retailer consider feature interactions. The time to perform the regression task slightly increases, which is due to the fact that additional parameters are learned.

4. End-to-End Solution. Table 1 compares the performance of our end-to-end flavors of **F** and of our competitors, where we summed up their time components for the join, import, and learning. **F** performs the best for all datasets, which can be directly linked to the intermixing of the factorized join and cofactor computation. It is from 3x to 50x faster than **F/FDB** and from 5x to 8x faster than **F/FSQL**. For LastFM, **F** exceeds three-orders of magnitude improvement over its competitors. For US retailer, the performance speedup is around two orders of magnitude in comparison to R, P, and M(glm), and 40 times in comparison to the closest competitor M(ols). The performance gains for MovieLens are more limited, which is due to the comparatively smaller size of this dataset.

Figure 6 reports the performance of end-to-end solutions for Housing against M (ols), and R, which are the best competitors for this dataset. We stress-tested **F** for scale factors beyond 20 for Housing: The total time without data loading is 4.1 seconds for scale 50 (compression ratio 14K) and 5.9 seconds for scale 100 (compression ratio 69K).

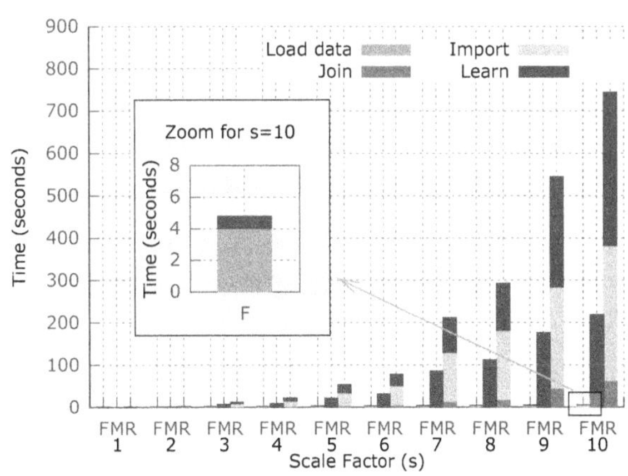

Figure 6: Total time for the end-to-end solution (loading data, join, import, learn) for F and the best competitors M(ols) and R on the Housing dataset. R runs out of memory starting with scale 11.

5. More features. We considered the Housing dataset with scale 15 and an increasing number of attributes per relation: 11, 18, 50, 100, and 168. This results in training datasets with around 60, 100, 300, 600 and 1000 features. Figure 7 shows the performance of **F** and M(ols) on these datasets (P and R already fail to load the original dataset with 27 features). M(ols) times out (i.e., it takes over four

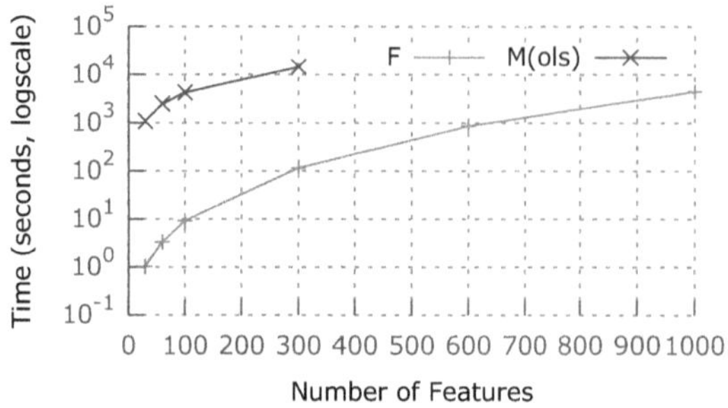

Figure 7: Total time for the end-to-end solution for F and M(ols) on the Housing dataset with scale factor scale 15 and increasingly many features. M(ols) times out after 300 features.

hours) for the dataset with 300 features. **F**'s performance is consistently two orders of magnitude better than of M(ols).
6. Model selection. In the previous experiments, we learned over all features of the training dataset. We further considered settings with fewer features, as used for model selection. The experiments validated that **F** only computes the parameter cofactors once and that the convergence time is consistently the smallest amongst all components of **F**. This contrasts with M, P, and R that need to independently learn over the entire dataset for each set of features.

8. RELATED WORK

Our contribution lies at the intersection of *databases* and *machine learning*, as we look at regression learning, which is a fundamental machine learning problem, through database glasses. The crossover between these two communities gained increasing interest during the past years, as also acknowledged in a SIGMOD 2015 panel [34].
Machine learning in databases. Our work follows a very recent line of research on marrying databases and machine learning [17, 14, 11, 36, 7, 20, 1, 24, 18, 9, 38, 34, 31, 32].

While **F**'s learning approach is novel in this landscape, two of these works are closest in spirit to it since they investigate the impact of data factorization for the purpose of boosting learning tasks. Rendle [36] considers a limited form of factorization of the design matrix for regression. His approach performs ad-hoc discovery of repeating patterns on the flat join to save up time in the subsequent regression task, though with two important limitations. This discovery does not seek to capture join dependencies, i.e., to recover the knowledge that the data has been produced via joins, since this is NP-hard. It also does not save time in join computation, but it instead needs additional time to perform the discovery on the flat join. Our approach is different since (i) we avoid the computation of the flat join as it is too expensive and entails redundancy; (ii) we exploit the join structure from the query to identify the repeating patterns due to join dependencies. Kumar et al. [20] propose a framework for learning generalized linear models over key-foreign key joins in a distributed environment and consider, amongst other techniques, factorized computation over the non-materialized join. **F** works for arbitrary join queries and factorizations with caching, linear regression with feature interactions, and has theoretical performance guarantees. We show that **F**'s cofactor computation commutes with union, and can thus be trivially distributed. Prior work on factorized databases discusses efficient support for joins [28] and simple aggregates [4]. **F** shows that factorization can benefit more complex user-defined aggregate functions, such as the cofactor matrix used in linear regression.

Most efforts in the database community are on designing systems to support large-scale scalable machine learning on top of possibly distributed architectures, with a goal on providing a unified architecture for machine learning and databases [14], e.g., MLLib [1] and DeepDist [24] on Spark [42], distributed gradient descent on GLADE [32], MADlib [17] on PostgreSQL, SystemML [18, 7], system benchmarking [9] and sample generator for cross-validate learning [38]. Our approach is more specialized as it proposes an efficient batch gradient descent variant for linear regression over joins. It achieves efficiency by factorizing data and computation, which enables more data to be kept in the memory of one machine and to be processed fast without the need for distribution. As pointed out recently [22], when benchmarked against one-machine systems, distributed systems can have a non-trivial upfront cost that can be offset by more expensive hardware or large problem settings.

The tight integration of the FDB query engine for factorized databases [5] with our regression learner **F** has been inspired by LogicBlox [2], which provides a unified runtime for the enterprise technology stack, and MADlib [17].
Gradient descent optimization. The gradient descent family of optimization algorithms is fundamental to machine learning [6] and very popular, cf. a ICML 2015 tutorial [37]. One of the applications of gradient descent is regression, which is the focus of this paper. A popular variant is the stochastic gradient descent [8] with several recent improvements such as faster convergence rate via adaptive learning rate [13] (which is also used by our system **F**) and parallel or distributed versions [43, 30, 35, 12, 27]. Some of these optimizations have made their way in systems such as DeepDive [39, 21] and DeepDist [24, 12]. Our contribution is orthogonal since it focuses on avoiding data and computation redundancy when learning over joins.

9. CONCLUSIONS AND FUTURE WORK

This paper puts forward **F**, a fast learner of least squares regression models over factorized joins that enjoys both theoretical and practical properties. The principles behind **F** are applicable beyond least squares regression models, as long as the derivatives of the objective function are expressible in a semiring with multiplication and summation operations (which is the case for gradient descent and Newton approximation methods), much in the spirit of the FAQ framework [19]. This is necessary since factorization relies on commutativity and distributivity laws. For this reason, least squares models are supported while logistic regression, which uses exponential functions, is not. A non-exhaustive list of analytics to benefit from our approach includes factorization machines, boosted trees, and k-nearest neighbors.

Acknowledgements

This work benefitted from interactions with Molham Aref (on **F/SQL**), Tim Furche (on experiments), Arun Kumar (on related work), Ron Menich (on problem setting and datasets), the MADlib team, and the anonymous reviewers. It was supported by a Google Research Faculty award, the ERC grant 682588, and the EPSRC platform grant DBOnto.

10. REFERENCES

[1] Apache. MLlib: Machine learning in Spark, https://spark.apache.org/mllib, 2015.

[2] M. Aref, B. ten Cate, T. J. Green, B. Kimelfeld, D. Olteanu, E. Pasalic, T. L. Veldhuizen, and G. Washburn. Design and implementation of the LogicBlox system. In *SIGMOD*, pages 1371–1382, 2015.

[3] A. Atserias, M. Grohe, and D. Marx. Size bounds and query plans for relational joins. In *FOCS*, pages 739–748, 2008.

[4] N. Bakibayev, T. Kociský, D. Olteanu, and J. Závodný. Aggregation and ordering in factorised databases. *PVLDB*, 6(14):1990–2001, 2013.

[5] N. Bakibayev, D. Olteanu, and J. Závodný. FDB: A query engine for factorised relational databases. *PVLDB*, 5(11):1232–1243, 2012.

[6] C. M. Bishop. *Pattern Recognition and Machine Learning (Information Science and Statistics)*, 2006.

[7] M. Boehm, S. Tatikonda, B. Reinwald, P. Sen, Y. Tian, D. Burdick, and S. Vaithyanathan. Hybrid parallelization strategies for large-scale machine learning in SystemML. *PVLDB*, 7(7):553–564, 2014.

[8] L. Bottou. Stochastic gradient descent tricks. In *Neural Networks: Tricks of the Trade (2nd ed)*, pages 421–436, 2012.

[9] Z. Cai, Z. J. Gao, S. Luo, L. L. Perez, Z. Vagena, and C. M. Jermaine. A comparison of platforms for implementing and running very large scale machine learning algorithms. In *SIGMOD*, pages 1371–1382, 2014.

[10] I. Cantador, P. Brusilovsky, and T. Kuflik. 2nd workshop on information heterogeneity and fusion in recommender systems. In *RecSys*, pages 387–388, 2011, http://grouplens.org/datasets/hetrec-2011.

[11] T. Condie, P. Mineiro, N. Polyzotis, and M. Weimer. Machine learning for big data. In *SIGMOD*, pages 939–942, 2013.

[12] J. Dean, G. Corrado, R. Monga, K. Chen, M. Devin, Q. V. Le, M. Z. Mao, M. Ranzato, A. W. Senior, P. A. Tucker, K. Yang, and A. Y. Ng. Large scale distributed deep networks. In *NIPS*, pages 1232–1240, 2012.

[13] J. Duchi, E. Hazan, and Y. Singer. Adaptive subgradient methods for online learning and stochastic optimization. *JMLR*, 12:2121–2159, 2011.

[14] X. Feng, A. Kumar, B. Recht, and C. Ré. Towards a unified architecture for in-rdbms analytics. In *SIGMOD*, pages 325–336, 2012.

[15] J. G. F. Francis. The QR transformation: A unitary analogue to the LR transformation–Part 1. *The Computer Journal*, 4(3):265–271, 1961.

[16] GroupLens Research. MovieLens, http://grouplens.org/datasets/movielens, 2003.

[17] J. M. Hellerstein, C. Ré, F. Schoppmann, D. Z. Wang, E. Fratkin, A. Gorajek, K. S. Ng, C. Welton, X. Feng, K. Li, and A. Kumar. The MADlib analytics library or MAD skills, the SQL. *PVLDB*, 5(12):1700–1711, 2012.

[18] B. Huang, M. Boehm, Y. Tian, B. Reinwald, S. Tatikonda, and F. R. Reiss. Resource elasticity for large-scale machine learning. In *SIGMOD*, pages 137–152, 2015.

[19] M. A. Khamis, H. Q. Ngo, and A. Rudra. FAQ: Questions Asked Frequently, CoRR:1504.04044, 2015.

[20] A. Kumar, J. F. Naughton, and J. M. Patel. Learning generalized linear models over normalized data. In *SIGMOD*, pages 1969–1984, 2015.

[21] J. Liu, S. Wright, C. Ré, V. Bittorf, and S. Sridhar. An asynchronous parallel stochastic coordinate descent algorithm. In *ICML*, pages 469–477, 2014.

[22] F. McSherry, M. Isard, and D. G. Murray. Scalability! but at what COST? In *HotOS*, 2015.

[23] R. Menich and N. Vasiloglou. The future of LogicBlox machine learning. LogicBlox User Days, 2013.

[24] D. Neumann. Lightning-fast deep learning on Spark via parallel stochastic gradient updates, www.deepdist.com, 2015.

[25] A. Ng. *CS229 Lecture Notes.* Stanford & Coursera, http://cs229.stanford.edu/, 2014.

[26] H. Q. Ngo, E. Porat, C. Ré, and A. Rudra. Worst-case optimal join algorithms. In *PODS*, pages 37–48, 2012.

[27] F. Niu, B. Recht, C. Ré, and S. J. Wright. Hogwild: A lock-free approach to parallelizing stochastic gradient descent. In *NIPS*, pages 693–701, 2011.

[28] D. Olteanu and J. Závodný. Size bounds for factorised representations of query results. *TODS*, 40(1):2, 2015.

[29] R. Penrose. A generalized inverse for matrices. *Math. Proc. Cambridge Phil. Soc.*, 51(03):406–413, 1955.

[30] F. Petroni and L. Querzoni. GASGD: stochastic gradient descent for distributed asynchronous matrix completion via graph partitioning. In *RecSys*, pages 241–248, 2014.

[31] C. Qin and F. Rusu. Scalable i/o-bound parallel incremental gradient descent for big data analytics in glade. In *DanaC*, pages 16–20, 2013.

[32] C. Qin and F. Rusu. Speculative approximations for terascale distributed gradient descent optimization. In *DanaC*, pages 1:1–1:10, 2015.

[33] R Core Team. *R: A Language and Environment for Statistical Computing.* R Foundation for Statistical Computing, www.r-project.org, 2013.

[34] C. Ré, D. Agrawal, M. Balazinska, M. I. Cafarella, M. I. Jordan, T. Kraska, and R. Ramakrishnan. Machine learning and databases: The sound of things to come or a cacophony of hype? In *SIGMOD*, pages 283–284, 2015.

[35] B. Recht and C. Ré. Parallel stochastic gradient algorithms for large-scale matrix completion. *Math. Program. Comput.*, 5(2):201–226, 2013.

[36] S. Rendle. Scaling factorization machines to relational data. *PVLDB*, 6(5):337–348, 2013.

[37] P. Richtárik and M. Schmidt. Modern convex optimization methods for large-scale empirical risk minimization. In *ICML*, 2015. Invited Tutorial.

[38] S. Schelter, J. Soto, V. Markl, D. Burdick, B. Reinwald, and A. V. Evfimievski. Efficient sample generation for scalable meta learning. In *ICDE*, pages 1191–1202, 2015.

[39] J. Shin, S. Wu, F. Wang, C. D. Sa, C. Zhang, and C. Ré. Incremental knowledge base construction using DeepDive. *PVLDB*, 8(11):1310–1321, 2015.

[40] The StatsModels development team. StatsModels: Statistics in Python, http://statsmodels.sourceforge.net, 2012.
[41] T. L. Veldhuizen. Triejoin: A simple, worst-case optimal join algorithm. In *ICDT*, pages 96–106, 2014.
[42] M. Zaharia, M. Chowdhury, T. Das, A. Dave, J. Ma, M. McCauly, M. J. Franklin, S. Shenker, and I. Stoica. Resilient distributed datasets: A fault-tolerant abstraction for in-memory cluster computing. In *NSDI*, pages 15–28, 2012.
[43] M. Zinkevich, M. Weimer, A. J. Smola, and L. Li. Parallelized stochastic gradient descent. In *NIPS*, pages 2595–2603, 2010.

APPENDIX

A. PROOFS

Proof of Proposition 3.1. 1. (*Symmetry*). Assume that $Q(\mathbf{D})$ has m tuples. We have:

$$S_k = \sum_{i=1}^{m}(\theta_0 x_0^{(i)} + \ldots + \theta_j x_j^{(i)} + \ldots + \theta_n x_n^{(i)})x_k^{(i)},$$

$$S_j = \sum_{i=1}^{m}(\theta_0 x_0^{(i)} + \ldots + \theta_k x_k^{(i)} + \ldots + \theta_n x_n^{(i)})x_j^{(i)}.$$

This implies that:

$$\text{Cofactor}[A_j, A_k] = \sum_{i=1}^{m} x_j^{(i)} x_k^{(i)} = \sum_{i=1}^{m} x_k^{(i)} x_j^{(i)} = \text{Cofactor}[A_k, A_j].$$

2. (*Commutativity with union*). For $1 \leq l \leq p$, assume that the training dataset $Q(\mathbf{D}_l)$ has m_l tuples, that we denote

$$Q(\mathbf{D}_l) = \{(x_{l,0}^{(1)}, \ldots, x_{l,n}^{(1)}), \ldots, (x_{l,0}^{(m_l)}, \ldots, x_{l,n}^{(m_l)})\}.$$

Then, $Q(\mathbf{D})$ has $\sum_{l=1}^{p} m_l$ tuples. Take $0 \leq k, j \leq n$. It holds that:

$$\sum_{l=1}^{p} \text{Cofactor}_l[A_k, A_j] = \sum_{l=1}^{p}(\sum_{i_l=1}^{m_l} x_{l,k}^{(i_l)} x_{l,j}^{(i_l)})$$
$$= \sum_{i=1}^{\Sigma_{l=1}^{p} m_l} x_k^{(i)} x_j^{(i)} = \text{Cofactor}[A_k, A_j].$$

3. (*Commutativity with projection*). Assume that $Q(\mathbf{D})$ has m tuples. Since we are under bag semantics, $\pi_L(Q(\mathbf{D}))$ also has m tuples. We assume that L has n_L features that we denote $x_{L,0}, \ldots, x_{L,n}$. Take $1 \leq k, j \leq n_L$. Then, $\text{Cofactor}_L[A_k, A_j] = \sum_{i=1}^{m} x_j^{(i)} x_k^{(i)}$, which moreover, is equal to $\text{Cofactor}[A_k, A_j]$.

Proof of Theorem 3.4. Take the basis functions $\phi_0, \ldots, \phi_b$ over the sets of features $S_0, \ldots, S_b$, the induced relational schema $\sigma = (R_0(S_0), \ldots, R_b(S_b))$, and $Q_\sigma = Q \bowtie R_0 \bowtie \cdots \bowtie R_b$ as the extension of Q w.r.t. σ.

First, we show that the extension $\mathbf{D}_\sigma$ of $\mathbf{D}$ with relations over the induced relational schema σ leads to a factorization of the join $Q_\sigma(\mathbf{D}_\sigma)$ of size $O(|\mathbf{D}|^{fhtw(Q_\sigma)})$. The extension $\mathbf{D}_\sigma$ has a relation instance R_i (for $1 \leq i \leq b$) for each schema $R_i(S_i)$ that is the projection of $Q(\mathbf{D})$ on S_i i.e., $\pi_{S_i}(Q(\mathbf{D}))$. It then holds that $Q(\mathbf{D}) = Q(\mathbf{D}_\sigma) = Q_\sigma(\mathbf{D}_\sigma)$. By Proposition 2.2, there exists a factorization of $\mathbf{D}_\sigma$ of size $O(|\mathbf{D}_\sigma|^{fhtw(Q_\sigma)})$. Under data complexity, the schema σ has constant size and thus $O(|\mathbf{D}_\sigma|^{fhtw(Q_\sigma)}) = O(|\mathbf{D}|^{fhtw(Q_\sigma)})$. Let us denote by E the factorization of $Q_\sigma(\mathbf{D}_\sigma)$ and let Δ be a d-tree under which we obtain the size of $O(|\mathbf{D}|^{fhtw(Q_\sigma)})$.

We next show that E can be augmented with values corresponding to the interaction terms ϕ_k while keeping the same asymptotic bound on its size. The query variables of any relation atom in the query, and in particular of relations over schemas $R_0(S_0), \ldots, R_b(S_b)$, are along the same root-to-leaf path in Δ. This means that E materializes all possible combinations of values for variables (corresponding to attributes) in each schema S_k. We can thus compute the result r_k of the basis function ϕ_k on the values for variables in S_k in one pass over E. For each tuple of values for variables in S_k, we add a product with the value r_k immediately under the lowest value in the tuple in E. We also add a variable ϕ_k in Δ immediately under the lowest variable in S_k. These additions do not modify the asymptotic size bounds of E since we add one value for each S_k-tuple of values in E. Let us denote by E_σ the factorization E extended with values for interaction terms. The factorization E_σ has size $O(|\mathbf{D}|^{fhtw(Q_\sigma)})$ and values for each basis function ϕ_k. Learning over E_σ has thus reduced to learning with identity basis functions and, by Proposition 3.2, this can be done in one pass over E_σ. The claim follows.

B. DESCRIPTION OF USED DATASETS

• **Housing** is a synthetic dataset emulating the textbook example for the house price market [25]. It consists of six tables: `House` (postcode, price, number of bedrooms/bathrooms/garages/parking lots, living room/kitchen area, etc.), `Shop` (postcode, opening hours, price range, brand, e.g., Costco, Tesco, Sainsbury's), `Institution` (postcode, type of educational institution, e.g., university or school, and number of students), `Restaurant` (postcode, opening hours, and price range), `Demographics` (postcode, average salary, rate of unemployment, criminality, and number of hospitals), and `Transport` (postcode, the number of bus lines, train stations, and distance to the city center for the postcode). The training dataset is the natural join of all relations (on postcode) and has 27 features. There are 25K postcodes, which appear in all relations. The scale factor s determines the number of generated distinct tuples per postcode in each relation: We generate s tuples in `House` and `Shop`, $\log_2 s$ tuples in `Institution`, $s/2$ in `Restaurant`, and one in each of `Demographics` and `Transport`. The numerical values for each attribute are randomly generated. The domains are intervals simulating the real-world semantics of attributes e.g., large intervals for attributes such as `price`, smaller intervals for attributes such as `nbtrainstations` and Boolean values for attributes such as `house`, `flat`, or `bungalow` indicating the type of housing.

We considered one linear regression tasks that predicts the price of a house based on all other features. Since all relations have a common attribute (`postcode`), the above query is acyclic and in particular hierarchical. An optimal d-tree that we would have each root-to-leaf path consisting of query variables for one relation. Caching in **F** is not useful here. The time complexity for **F** is linear (modulo log factors). We present a snapshot of it in Figure 8(a).

• **US retailer.** This dataset consists of three relations: `Inventory` (storing information about the inventory units for products in a location, at a given date), `Census` (storing demographics information per zipcode such as population, median age, repartition per ethnicities, house units and how

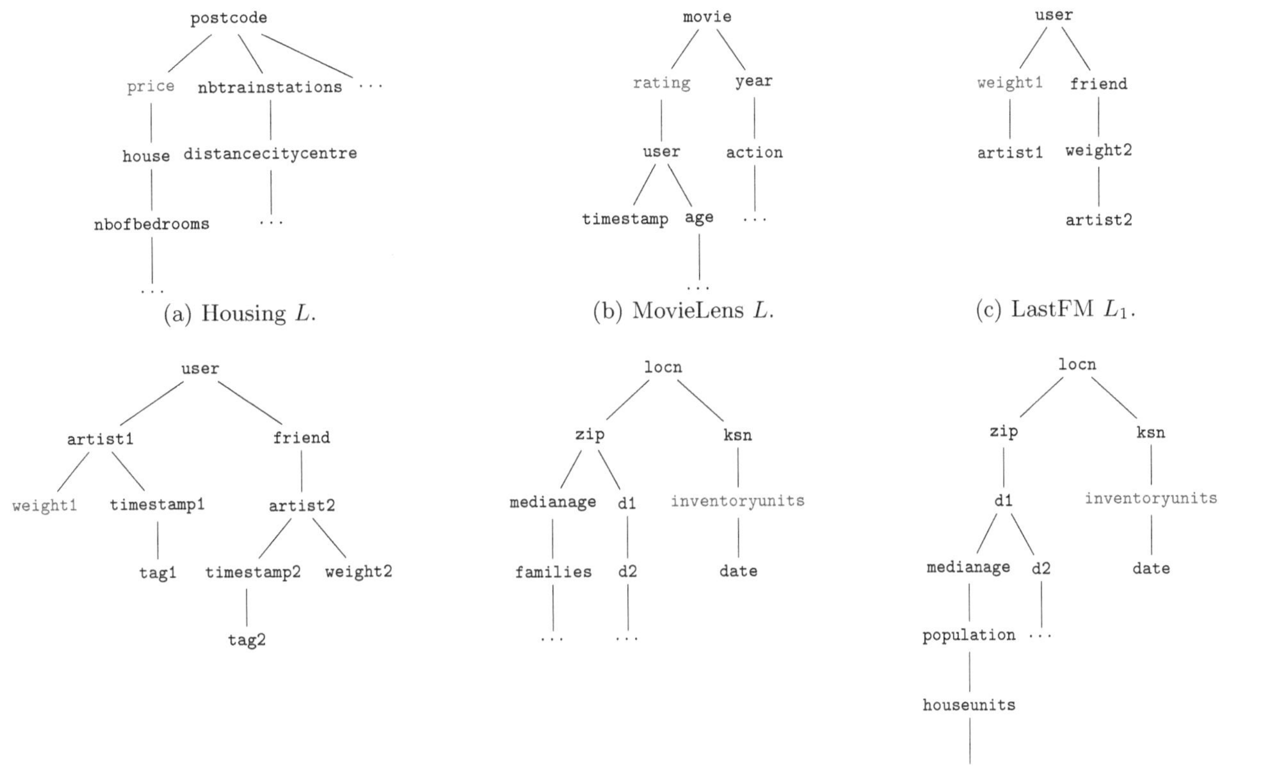

(a) Housing L. (b) MovieLens L. (c) LastFM L_1.

(d) LastFM L_2. (e) US retailer L and N_1. (f) US retailer N_2.

Figure 8: Snapshots of the d-trees considered in the experiments (root variable for intercept omitted).

many are occupied, number of children per household, number of males, females, and families), and `Location` (storing for each zipcode distances `d1` to `d10` to several other stores).

The training dataset is the natural join of the three relations and has 31 features. We considered three linear regression tasks that predict the amount of inventory units based on all other features. All join queries for these tasks are acyclic and under data-dependent functional dependencies (no store location can be in two zipcodes), they become hierarchical. Caching is not useful in their cases.

Task L considers the plain features. We consider an asymptotically optimal d-tree for the natural join query, a snapshot of which is presented in Figure 8(e). The relation `Inventory` is encoded along the path `locn/ksn/...`, the relation `Location` is encoded along the path `locn/zip/d1/...`, while `Census` is encoded along the path `zip/population/...`

Task N_1 considers two interactions of features from the same relation and for which no restructuring is necessary: (i) Between median age and number of families (both from `Census`) and (ii) between different distances to other stores (both from `Location`). The first interaction looks at the effect on inventory units while correlating the number of families and the median age, since the two features are strongly related. The second interaction looks at the effect of having competitors close to the store and how the interaction of the two competitors changes the effect on the inventory units in the given store. Since both features occurring in an interaction are from the same table, we can use the d-tree from the linear case, which is asymptotically optimal.

Task N_2 considers two interactions: (i) Between population and number of house units (both from `Census`), and (ii) between median age and distance to another store (features of `Census` and `Location`, respectively). The first interaction uses the insight that if we have a large population but few houses, then many people live in the same house. This can give an indication of what the general population is like, and therefore, can have a meaningful impact on our prediction. The second interaction looks at how the age of a person influences her tendency to look for satisfying stores at a further distance.

The d-tree used for N_2 needs to additionally satisfy the constraint that the features from its second interaction (population and house units) are on the same root-to-leaf path; a snapshot of it in Figure 8(f). For both tasks N_1 and N_2, each new interaction term can be seen as a newly-derived feature for learning in addition to the initial 31 features, hence for each task we have $31 + 2 = 33$ features.

• **LastFM [10]** has three relations: `Userfriends` (pairing friends in the social network from the LastFM online music system), `Userartists` (how often a user listens to a certain artist), and `Usertaggedartiststimestamps` (the user classification of artists and the time when a user rated artists). Our regression task is to predict how often a user would listen to an artist based on similar information for its friends. We consider two training datasets: L_1 joins two copies of `Userartists` with `Userfriends` to relate how often friends listen to the same artists; L_2 is L_1 where we also join in the

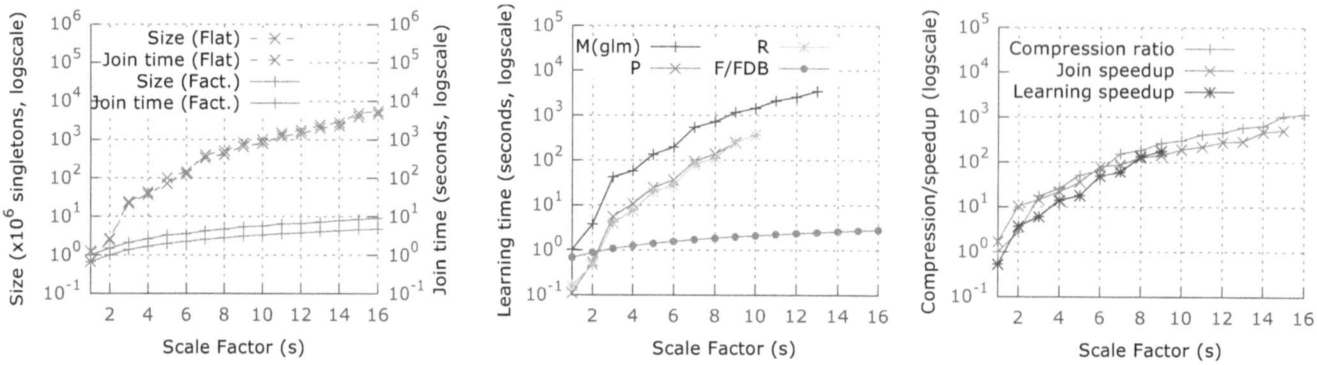

(a) Size and join time. (b) Learning time. (c) Compression ratio and speedup.

Figure 9: Housing dataset: (a) Size and join time for factorized vs. flat joins; (b) time for learning (excluding join time) with the four systems; (c) the learning speedup is for F/FDB relative to R, which is the fastest competitor in terms of learning time alone. P and R run out of memory starting at $s = 11$ for learning. M (glm) took longer than one hour after $s = 13$, and is not reported.

`Usertaggedartiststimestamps` copies of both friends:

$$L_1 : \texttt{UF} \ltimes_{\texttt{UF.user=UA1.user}} \texttt{UA1} \ltimes_{\texttt{UF.friend=UA2.user}} \texttt{UA2}$$

$$L_2 : \texttt{UF} \ltimes_{\texttt{UF.user=UA1.user}} \texttt{UA1} \ltimes_{\texttt{UF.friend=UA2.user}} \texttt{UA2} \ltimes \ltimes_{\texttt{UF.user=UTA1.user}} \texttt{UTA1} \ltimes_{\texttt{UF.friend=UTA2.user}} \texttt{UTA2}$$

Both queries are hierarchical since the `user` is common to all joined relations and use optimal d-trees for both of them. We illustrate them in Figures 8(c) and 8(d).

- **MovieLens [16]** has three relations: `Users` (age, gender, occupation, zipcode of users), `Movies` (movie year and its type, e.g., action, adventure, animation, children, and so on), and `Ratings` that users gave to movies on certain dates. The training dataset is the acyclic natural join of these tables and has 27 features. The regression task is to predict the rating given by a user to a movie. We depict a snapshot of the considered optimal d-tree in Figure 8(b). There are four versions of the MovieLens datasets and we only reported experimental findings for the largest available version (1M records) that has complete information for all three tables; there are two larger versions (10M and 20M) but without Users. We also experimented with the other versions (100K and the larger ones where we synthetically generated the Users relation) and found that they exhibit the same compression ratio and performance gain.

C. DATASET PREPARATION

The learning task requires to prepare the datasets. Firstly, we only kept features that represent quantities or Boolean flags over which we can learn and discarded string features (except if necessary for joins). Secondly, we normalized all number values of a feature A by mapping them to the $[0, 1]$ range of reals as follows. Let $\min_A$ and $\max_A$ be the minimum and respectively maximum value in the active domain of A. Then, a value v for A is normalized to $(v - \min_A)/\max_A$. Normalization is essential so that all features have the same relative weight, e.g., avoiding that large date values represented in seconds since Jan 1, 1970 are more important than, say, small integer values representing the number of house bedrooms. It also preserves the cardinality of the join results from the original datasets.

D. FURTHER EXPERIMENTS

Figure 9 outlines the relative performance of **F/FDB** over its competitors on the Housing dataset along three dimensions: Compression ratio, performance speedup, and learning speedup. For the first two dimensions we essentially compare FDB against PostgreSQL, since **F/FDB** uses the factorized join computed by FDB, while the competitors use the flat join computed by PostgreSQL.

Figure 9(c) shows that Housing can be compressed by a factor of over 10^3 for scale $s = 16$. For a scale factor s, the flat join of all tables on postcode has $25\text{K} \times s^3/2 \times \log_2 s$ tuples, each of 27 values, whereas the factorized join stay linear in the size of the input tables. The gap between the sizes of flat and factorized joins thus follows a quadratic function in s.

Figures 9(a) and 9(c) confirm the finding from the real datasets for join computation: There is a significant speedup for factorized over flat, which is upper bounded by the data compression ratio.

Figure 9(b) reports the performance of learning for up to scale 16 for **F/FDB**, up to 13 for M(glm), and up to 10 for P and R. At scale factor 10, the compression ratio is 240 and **F/FDB** takes 2.2 seconds for learning. M(glm) was stopped at scale factor 13, since it exceeded the timeout of one hour. Learning with R and P already fails for scale factor 11 due to memory limitation. We further tried with scale factors up to 20, where the compression ratio is 1.9K and **F/FDB** takes 3.4 seconds for learning.

To Join or Not to Join? Thinking Twice about Joins before Feature Selection

Arun Kumar Jeffrey Naughton Jignesh M. Patel Xiaojin Zhu
Department of Computer Sciences,
University of Wisconsin-Madison
{arun, naughton, jignesh, jerryzhu}@cs.wisc.edu

ABSTRACT

Closer integration of machine learning (ML) with data processing is a booming area in both the data management industry and academia. Almost all ML toolkits assume that the input is a single table, but many datasets are not stored as single tables due to normalization. Thus, analysts often perform key-foreign key joins to obtain features from all base tables and apply a feature selection method, either explicitly or implicitly, with the aim of improving accuracy. In this work, we show that the features brought in by such joins can often be ignored without affecting ML accuracy significantly, i.e., we can "avoid joins safely." We identify the core technical issue that could cause accuracy to decrease in some cases and analyze this issue theoretically. Using simulations, we validate our analysis and measure the effects of various properties of normalized data on accuracy. We apply our analysis to design easy-to-understand decision rules to predict when it is safe to avoid joins in order to help analysts exploit this runtime-accuracy trade-off. Experiments with multiple real normalized datasets show that our rules are able to accurately predict when joins can be avoided safely, and in some cases, this led to significant reductions in the runtime of some popular feature selection methods.

1. INTRODUCTION

The increasing use of machine learning (ML) in data-driven applications [2, 4] has led to a growing interest in more closely integrating ML and data processing [3, 16, 19, 23, 25, 47]. However, almost all ML toolkits assume that the input to an ML model is a single table even though many real-world datasets are stored as multiple tables connected by primary key-foreign key (KFK) dependencies. Thus, analysts typically perform KFK joins before ML to construct a single table that collects features from all base tables and then apply a feature selection method (either explicitly or implicitly [17]) over the entire set of features. Feature selection helps improve ML accuracy and is widely considered crucial for ML-based analytics [1, 17, 23, 46]. While this process certainly "works," it can be both painful and wasteful because the increase in the number of features might make it harder for analysts to explore the data and also increases the runtime of ML and feature selection methods. In some cases, the joins might also be expensive and introduce data redundancy, causing even more efficiency issues [29].

In this work, we help mitigate the above issues by studying a rather radical question: *Is a KFK join even needed for ML?* In other words, is it possible to ignore all "foreign" features (the features from the table referred to by the foreign key) in the first place without significantly reducing ML accuracy? We call this process "avoiding the join." At first, this seems preposterous: how can we be confident that ignoring some features is unlikely to reduce accuracy significantly without even running the feature selection method over the data (which requires the join)? The key turns out to be a rather simple observation: the KFK dependencies present in the *schema* enable us to avoid joins. Simply put, in an information theoretic sense [17], a foreign key encodes "all information" about all the foreign features brought in by a KFK join, which allows us to use it as a "representative" for the foreign features. Thus, this observation seems to make things stunningly simple: ignore all KFK joins and use foreign keys as representatives of foreign features!

Alas, the real world is not as simple as described above. Unfortunately, the information theoretic perspective is not sufficiently perspicacious to fully answer our core question of when it is safe to avoid a join. The finite nature of training datasets in the real world makes it necessary to analyze our problem using the standard ML notions of bias and variance [40]. This requires detailed, yet subtle, theoretical analysis (which we perform) of the effects of KFK joins on ML. It turns out that foreign features, which are safe to ignore from an information theoretic perspective, could be indispensable when both bias and variance are considered. This brings us back to square one with our conundrum: *given a KFK join, how to tell if it is safe to avoid or not?*

Answering the above core question could yield at least four benefits. First, it can help improve the performance of ML tasks without losing much accuracy. Second, in applications in which analysts explore features by being in the loop [27, 46], having fewer tables and features might make exploration easier. Third, it might help reduce the costs of data acquisition in applications where new tables (e.g., weather data) are purchased and joined with existing data. If we can show that such joins might not really help accuracy, analysts can reconsider such purchases. Fourth, in some applications, analysts have dozens of tables in the input and

SIGMOD'16, June 26-July 01, 2016, San Francisco, CA, USA
© 2016 ACM. ISBN 978-1-4503-3531-7/16/06...$15.00
DOI: http://dx.doi.org/10.1145/2882903.2882952

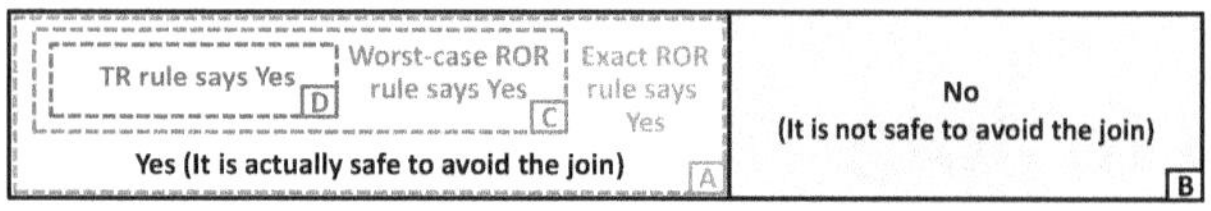

Figure 1: Illustrating the relationship between the decision rules to tell which joins are "safe to avoid."

prefer to join only a few "most helpful" tables (colloquially called *source selection*). Answering our question might help analysts assess which tables matter less for accuracy.

In this paper, we show that it is possible to answer our core question by designing practical heuristics that are motivated by our theoretical understanding. Thus, apart from establishing new connections between joins and ML, our work can help make feature selection over normalized data easier and faster. Indeed, the data management community is increasingly recognizing the need for more of such formal and systems support to make feature selection easier and faster [7, 27, 36, 46]. Ideally, we desire a *decision rule* that can help answer the question for analysts. Apart from being effective and concurring with our formal analysis, we desire that any such rule be *simple* (making it easy for analysts to understand and implement), *generic* (not tied too closely to a specific ML model), *flexible* (tunable based on what error is tolerable), and *fast*. These additional desiderata are motivated by practical real-world systems-oriented concerns.

Figure 1 illustrates our situation in a rough but intuitive manner. The whole box is the set of KFK joins that gather features. (Section 2.1 makes our assumptions precise.) Box A is the set of joins that are "safe to avoid," i.e., avoiding them is unlikely to blow up the test error (Section 4.2 makes this precise), while box B is the rest. Our goal is to characterize boxes A and B, and develop a decision rule to tell if a given join belongs to box A. We first perform a simulation study (using Naive Bayes as an example) to measure how different properties of the base tables affect the test error. We apply our theoretical and simulation results to devise an intuitive definition of box A and design a decision rule for it that exploits a powerful ML notion called the *VC dimension* [43]. Applying a standard theoretical result from ML, we define a heuristic quantity called the *Risk Of Representation* (ROR) that intuitively captures the increased risk of the test error being higher than the train error by avoiding the join. Using an appropriate threshold on the ROR yields a decision rule that can tell if a join is "safe to avoid" or not; this is how boxes A and B in Figure 1 are defined. Sadly, it is *impossible* in general to compute the ROR a priori, i.e., without performing the very feature selection computations we are trying to avoid. To resolve this quandary, we derive an upper bound on the ROR (we call it *worst-case* ROR) that is computable a priori. It yields a more *conservative* decision rule, i.e., it might wrongly predict that a join is not safe to avoid even though it actually is. Figure 1 illustrates this relationship: box C is contained in box A. The intersection of box A with the complement of box C is the set of missed opportunities for the worst-case ROR rule.

The worst-case ROR rule still requires us to inspect the foreign features (without having to do the join, of course). This motivates us to design an even simpler rule that does not even require us to look at the foreign features. We define a quantity we call the *tuple ratio* (TR) that only depends on the number of training examples and the size of the foreign key's domain. The TR is a conservative simplification of the worst-case ROR. Thus, the TR rule might miss even more opportunities for avoiding joins. Figure 1 illustrates this relationship: box D is contained in box C.

In the rest of this paper, we develop the precise theoretical machinery needed to explain our problem, characterize the effects of KFK joins on ML, and explain how we design our decision rules. Furthermore, since both of these rules are conservative, it is important to know how they perform on real data. Thus, we perform an empirical analysis with seven real-world datasets from diverse application domains: retail, hospitality, transportation, e-commerce, etc. We combine a few popular feature selection methods and popular ML classifiers. We find that there are indeed many cases on real datasets where joins are safe to avoid, and both of our rules work surprisingly well: out of 14 joins in total across all 7 datasets, both of our rules correctly classified 7 joins as safe to avoid and 3 joins as not safe to avoid but deemed 4 joins as not safe to avoid even though avoiding them did not blow up the test errors (note that our decision rules are conservative). Overall, our decision rules improved the performance of the feature selection methods significantly in many cases, including by over 10x in some cases.

In summary, our work makes the following contributions:

- To the best of our knowledge, this is the first paper to study the problem of formally characterizing the effects of KFK joins on ML classifiers and feature selection to help predict when joins can be avoided safely.
- We perform a simulation study using Naive Bayes as an example in order to measure how different properties of the normalized data affect ML error.
- We apply our theoretical and simulation results to design simple decision rules that can predict a priori if it is perhaps safe to avoid a given join.
- We perform an extensive empirical analysis using real-world datasets to validate that there are cases where avoiding joins does not increase ML error significantly and that our rules can accurately predict such cases.

Outline. Section 2 explains our problem setup and gives some background. Section 3 presents an in-depth theoretical analysis of the effects of joins on ML and feature selection. Readers more interested in the practical implications can skip to Section 4, which presents our simulation study and also explains how we design our decision rules. Section 5 presents our empirical validation with real data. Section 6 presents the related work. We conclude in Section 7.

2. PRELIMINARIES AND BACKGROUND

2.1 Setup, Example, and Assumptions

We focus on the same schema setting as [29] and adopt their terminology. The main table with the entities to model is called the *entity table*, denoted $\mathbf{S}$. There are k other tables called *attribute tables*, denoted $\mathbf{R}_i$, for $i = 1$ *to* k (if $k = 1$, we drop the subscript). The schema of $\mathbf{R}_i$ is $\mathbf{R}_i(\underline{RID_i}, \mathbf{X}_{R_i})$, where RID_i is its primary key and $\mathbf{X}_{R_i}$ is a vector (sequence) of features. We abuse the notation slightly to also treat $\mathbf{X}$ as a *set* since the order among features in $\mathbf{X}$ is immaterial in our setting. The schema of $\mathbf{S}$ is $\mathbf{S}(\underline{SID}, Y, \mathbf{X}_S, FK_1, \ldots, FK_k)$, where Y is the target for learning, $\mathbf{X}_S$ is a vector of features, and FK_i is a foreign key that refers to $\mathbf{R}_i$. Let $\mathbf{T}$ denote the output of the equi-join: $\mathbf{T} \leftarrow \pi(\mathbf{R} \bowtie_{RID=FK} \mathbf{S})$. In general, its schema is $\mathbf{T}(\underline{SID}, Y, \mathbf{X}_S, FK_1, \ldots, FK_k, \mathbf{X}_{R_1}, \ldots, \mathbf{X}_{R_k})$.

Example (based on [29]). Consider an insurance analyst predicting customer churn, i.e., will a customer leave the company (cancel their policy)? She decides to build a classifier using the table `Customers` (`CustomerID`, `Churn`, `Gender`, `Age`, `EmployerID`). The `EmployerID` feature is the ID of a customer's employer and is a foreign key referring to another table with data about companies and other organizations that potentially employ the customers: `Employers` (`EmployerID`, `Country`, `Revenue`). Thus, **S** is `Customers`, **R** is `Employers`, Y is `Churn`, FK is **S**.`EmployerID`, RID is **R**.`EmployerID`, $\mathbf{X}_S$ is {`Age`, `Gender`}, and $\mathbf{X}_R$ is {`Country`, `Revenue`}. She joins the tables to bring in $\mathbf{X}_R$ because she has a hunch that customers employed by rich corporations in rich countries are unlikely to churn.

We focus on the case in which all features (including Y) are *nominal*, i.e., each feature has a finite discrete domain.[1] Thus, we focus on *classification*. We assume that the foreign keys are not keys of **S** (e.g., `EmployerID` is clearly not a key of `Customers`). We also assume that the domains of all features in $\mathbf{X}_S$, $\mathbf{X}_R$, and all FK_i are "closed with respect to the prediction task" and the domain of FK_i is the same as the set of RID_i values in $\mathbf{R}_i$ (and there are no missing/NULL values)[2]. We explain the closed domain assumption. In ML, recommendation systems assume that the foreign keys of the ratings table, e.g., `MovieID` and `UserID` have closed domains, say, to enable matrix factorization models [24]. A movie might have several past ratings. So, `MovieID` can help predict future ratings. Note that closed domain does *not* mean new `MovieID` values can never occur! It means that analysts build models using only the movies seen so far but revise their feature domains and update ML models periodically (say, monthly) to absorb movies added recently. In between these revisions, the domain of `MovieID` is considered closed. `EmployerID` in our example plays exactly the same role: many customers (past and future) might have the same employer. Thus, it is reasonable to use `EmployerID` as a feature. Handling new movies (or employers) is a well-known problem called *cold-start* [39]. It is closely related to the *referential integrity constraint* for foreign keys in databases [35]. In practice, a common way to handle it is to have a special "Others" record in `Employers` as a placeholder for new employers seen in between revisions. Cold-start is orthogonal to our problem; we leave it to future work.

Overall, each feature in $\mathbf{X}_S$, $\mathbf{X}_{R_i}$, and FK_i is a discrete random variable with a known finite domain. We also assume that the foreign keys are not skewed (we relax this in a discussion in the appendix). We discuss the effects of KFK joins on ML classifiers and feature selection in general, but later we use Naive Bayes as an example.[3] Naive Bayes is a popular classifier with diverse applications ranging from spam detection to medical diagnosis [31,33]. It is also easy to understand and use; it does not require expensive iterative optimization or "black magic" for tuning hyper-parameters.

We emphasize that our goal is *not* to design new ML models or new feature selection methods, nor is to study which feature selection method or ML model yields the highest accuracy. Rather, our goal is to understand the theoretical and practical implications of ubiquitous database dependencies, viz., KFK dependencies (KFKDs) and functional dependencies (FDs) on ML. In this paper, we use the phrase "the join is safe to avoid" to mean that $\mathbf{X}_R$ can be dropped before feature selection without significantly affecting the test error of the subset obtained after feature selection. We make this notion more precise later (Section 4.2).

2.2 Background: Feature Selection

Feature selection methods are almost always used along with an ML classifier to help improve accuracy [17]. While our work is orthogonal to feature selection methods, we briefly discuss a few popular ones for concreteness sake. At a high level, there are three types of feature selection methods: *wrappers*, *filters*, and *embedded* methods [17,21].

A wrapper uses the classifier as a "black-box" and heuristically searches the space of feature subsets to obtain a more accurate subset. Sequential greedy search is a popular wrapper; it has two variants: *forward selection* and *backward selection*. Given a feature set **X**, forward (resp. backward) selection computes the *error* of an ML model for different subsets of **X** of increasing (resp. decreasing) size starting with the empty set (resp. full set **X**) by adding (resp. eliminating) one feature at a time. The error can be the holdout validation error or the k-fold cross-validation error. For our purposes, the simpler holdout method described in [18] suffices: the labeled data is split 50%:25%:25% with the first part used for training, the second part used for the validation error during greedy search, and the last part used for the holdout test error, which is the final indicator of the chosen subset's accuracy. Filters apply a specified scoring function to each feature $F \in \mathbf{X}$ using the labeled data but independent of any classifier. The top-k features are then chosen, with k picked either manually or tuned automatically using the validation error for a given classifier (we use the latter). Popular scoring functions include *mutual information* $I(F;Y)$ and *information gain ratio* $IGR(F;Y)$. Intuitively, $I(F;Y)$ tells us how much the knowledge of F reduces the *entropy* of Y, while $IGR(F;Y)$ normalizes it by the feature's entropy. Embedded methods are "wired" in to the classifier. A common example is L1 or L2 norm *regularization* for linear and logistic regression. These methods perform implicit feature selection by modifying the regression coefficients directly instead of searching for subsets, e.g., L1 norm makes some coefficients vanish, which is akin to dropping the corresponding features [18].

3. EFFECTS OF KFK JOINS ON ML

We start with a brief information theoretic analysis, and then dig deeper to establish the formal connections between KFKDs and the bias-variance trade-off in ML. For ease of exposition, we assume only one attribute table **R**. Readers more interested in the practical aspects can skip to the summary at the end of this section, or to Section 4.

3.1 The Information Theoretic Perspective

A standard theoretical approach to ascertain which features are "useful" is to use the information theoretic notions of feature redundancy and relevancy [17,22]. Thus, we now perform such an analysis to help explain why it might be safe to avoid the join with **R**, i.e., ignore $\mathbf{X}_R$.

[1] Numeric features are assumed to have been discretized to a finite set of categories, say, using binning [31].

[2] To handle RID_i values absent from FK_i in a given instance of **S**, we adopt the standard practice of *smoothing* [30].

[3] We present some empirical results and a discussion of some other popular ML models in Section 5 and the appendix.

3.1.1 Feature Redundancy

We start with some intuition. The foreign key FK is also a feature used to predict Y. In our example, it is reasonable to use `EmployerID` to help predict `Churn`. The equi-join condition $\mathbf{S}.FK = \mathbf{R}.RID$ that creates $\mathbf{T}$ causes FK to *functionally determine* all of $\mathbf{X}_R$ in $\mathbf{T}$. It is as if the FD $RID \rightarrow \mathbf{X}_R$ in $\mathbf{R}$ becomes the FD $FK \rightarrow \mathbf{X}_R$ in $\mathbf{T}$.[4] Thus, given FK, $\mathbf{X}_R$ is fixed, i.e., $\mathbf{X}_R$ does *not* provide any more "information" over FK. The notion of feature *redundancy* helps capture such behavior formally [22, 45]. Its rigorous definition is given in the appendix. This yields our first, albeit simple, result (let $\mathbf{X} \equiv \mathbf{X}_S \cup \{FK\} \cup \mathbf{X}_R$).

PROPOSITION 3.1. *In $\mathbf{T}$, all $F \in \mathbf{X}_R$ are redundant.*

The proof is in the appendix. This result extends trivially to multiple attribute tables. In fact, it extends to a more general set of FDs, as we show in the appendix. In the ML literature, the redundancy of a feature is often considered an indication that the feature should be dropped. In fact, many feature selection methods explicitly search for such redundancy in order to remove the redundant features [17,22,45]. However, they try to detect the presence of feature redundancy approximately based on the dataset *instance*. Our scenario is stronger because Proposition 3.1 *guarantees* the existence of redundant features. This motivates us to consider the seemingly "radical" step of avoiding these redundant features, i.e., avoiding the join with $\mathbf{R}$.

3.1.2 Feature Relevancy

A redundant feature might sometimes be more "useful" in predicting Y; this is captured using the formal notion of feature *relevancy*. This leads to the classical redundancy-relevancy trade-off in ML [17]. We provide some intuition. Suppose, in our example, that customers of rich corporations never churn and they are the only ones who do not churn; then `Revenue` is perhaps the most relevant feature, even though it is redundant. Thus, we would like to know if it is possible for some $F \in \mathbf{X}_R$ to be *more* relevant than FK. Feature relevancy is often formalized using scores such as the mutual information $I(F;Y)$ (a rigorous definition is given in the appendix) or the information gain ratio $IGR(F;Y)$. A feature with a higher score is considered to be more relevant [17, 45]. However, when we apply these two popular notions of feature relevancy to our setting, we realize that our information theoretic analysis hits a wall.

THEOREM 3.1. $\forall F \in \mathbf{X}_R, I(F;Y) \leq I(FK;Y)$

PROPOSITION 3.2. *It is possible for a feature $F \in \mathbf{X}_R$ to have higher $IGR(F;Y)$ than $IGR(FK;Y)$.*

The proofs are in the appendix. Basically, we get near-opposite conclusions depending on the score! If we use mutual information, features in $\mathbf{X}_R$ are no more relevant than FK. Coupled with the earlier fact that $\mathbf{X}_R$ is redundant, this suggests strongly that the join is not too useful and that we might as well stick with using FK as a "representative" of $\mathbf{X}_R$. However, if we use information gain ratio, a feature in $\mathbf{X}_R$ could be *more* relevant than FK. This suggests that we should bring in $\mathbf{X}_R$ by performing the join and let the feature selection method ascertain which features to use. We explain this strange behavior intuitively.

The domain of FK is likely to be much larger than any feature in $\mathbf{X}_R$. For example, there are fewer than two hundred countries in the world, but there are millions of employers. Thus, `EmployerID` might have a much larger domain than `Country` in `Employers`. Mutual information tends to prefer features with larger domains, but information gain ratio resolves this issue by penalizing features with larger domains [17, 31]. This brings us back to square one with our original conundrum! It seems the information theoretic analysis is insufficient to help us precisely answer our core question of when it is safe to avoid a join. Thus, we now dive deeper into our problem by analyzing the effects of KFK joins on ML and feature selection from the perspective of the bias-variance trade-off, which lies at the heart of ML.

3.2 The Join Strikes Back: KFK Joins and the Bias-Variance Trade-off

We now expose a "danger" in avoiding the join (using FK as a representative for $\mathbf{X}_R$). Our intuition is simple: information theoretic arguments are generally applicable to asymptotic cases, but in the real world training datasets are *finite*. Thus, we need to look to statistical learning theory to understand precisely how ML error is affected. We start with an intuitive explanation of some standard concepts.

The expected *test error* (i.e., error on an unseen labeled example) can be decomposed into three components: *bias* (a.k.a *approximation error*), *variance* (a.k.a. *estimation error*), and *noise* [18, 40]. The noise is an inevitable component that is independent of the ML model. The bias captures the lowest possible error by any model instance in the class of ML models considered. For example, using Naive Bayes introduces a bias compared to learning the expensive joint distribution since it assumes conditional independence [33]. The variance captures the error introduced by the fact that the training dataset is only a random finite sample from the underlying data distribution, i.e., it formalizes the "instability" of the model with respect to the training data. For example, if we train Naive Bayes on two different training samples, their test errors are likely to differ. And if we provide fewer training examples to the ML model, its test error is likely to increase due to higher variance. In colloquial terms, a scenario with high variance is called *overfitting* [18].

The crux of the argument is as follows: *using FK as a representative is likely to yield a model with higher variance than a model obtained by including $\mathbf{X}_R$ for consideration.* Thus, the chance of getting a higher test error might increase if we avoid the join. Perhaps surprisingly, this holds true irrespective of the number of features in $\mathbf{X}_R$! Before explaining why, we observe that there is no contradiction with Section 3.1; the information theoretic analysis deals primarily with bias, not variance. We explain more below.

Relationship between Hypothesis Spaces. To help formalize our argument, we first explain the relationship between the classes of models built using FK and $\mathbf{X}_R$. This is important to understand because a model with a larger hypothesis space might have higher variance.

As before, let $\mathbf{X} \equiv \mathbf{X}_S \cup \{FK\} \cup \mathbf{X}_R$. For simplicity of exposition, let $\mathcal{D}_Y = \{0, 1\}$. Also, since our primary goal is to understand the effects of the FD $FK \rightarrow \mathbf{X}_R$, we set $\mathbf{X}_S = \phi$ (empty) for ease of exposition. A learned ML

[4]KFKDs differ from FDs [5], but we can treat the dependencies in $\mathbf{T}$ as FDs since we had assumed that there are no `NULL` values and that all feature domains are *closed*.

Figure 2: Relationship between hypothesis spaces.

model instance is just a prediction function $f : \mathcal{D}_{\mathbf{X}} \to \{0,1\}$. The universe of all possible prediction functions based on $\mathbf{X}$ is denoted $\mathcal{H}_{\mathbf{X}} = \{f | f : \mathcal{D}_{\mathbf{X}} \to \{0,1\}\}$. A given class of ML models, e.g., Naive Bayes, can only learn a subset of $\mathcal{H}_{\mathbf{X}}$ owing to its bias. This subset of functions that it can learn is called the *hypothesis space* of the ML model. Let $\mathcal{H}^{NB}_{\mathbf{X}}$ denote the hypothesis space of Naive Bayes models on $\mathbf{X}$. Given $\mathbf{Z} \subseteq \mathbf{X}$, we define the *restriction* of $\mathcal{H}_{\mathbf{X}}$ to $\mathbf{Z}$ as follows: $\mathcal{H}_{\mathbf{Z}} = \{f | f \in \mathcal{H}_{\mathbf{X}} \wedge \forall \mathbf{u}, \mathbf{v} \in \mathcal{D}_{\mathbf{X}}, \mathbf{u}_{|\mathbf{Z}} = \mathbf{v}_{|\mathbf{Z}} \implies f(\mathbf{u}) = f(\mathbf{v})\}$. Here, $\mathbf{u}_{|\mathbf{Z}}$ denotes the projection of $\mathbf{u}$ to only the features in $\mathbf{Z}$. We now establish the relationship between the various hypothesis spaces. Figure 2 depicts it pictorially.

PROPOSITION 3.3. $\mathcal{H}_X = \mathcal{H}_{FK} \supseteq \mathcal{H}_{X_R}$

The proof is in the appendix. Note that the first part ($\mathcal{H}_{\mathbf{X}} = \mathcal{H}_{FK}$) is essentially the learning theory equivalent of Proposition 3.1. The second part might seem counter-intuitive because even if there are, say, a million features in $\mathbf{X}_R$ but only a hundred FK values, using FK instead of $\mathbf{X}_R$ is still more "powerful" than using $\mathbf{X}_R$ and dropping FK. But the intuition is simple: since $\mathbf{R}$ is fixed in our setting, we can only ever observe at most $|\mathcal{D}_{FK}|$ distinct values of $\mathbf{X}_R$, even if $\Pi_{F \in \mathbf{X}_R} |\mathcal{D}_F| \gg |\mathcal{D}_{FK}|$. Hence, using $\mathbf{X}_R$ instead of FK might increase the bias. For example, suppose that customers employed by Profit University and Charity Inc. churn and they are the only ones who churn. Then it is *impossible* in general to learn this concept correctly if `EmployerID` is excluded. Note that $\mathcal{H}^{NB}_{\mathbf{X}_R} \subseteq \mathcal{H}_{\mathbf{X}_R}$. Finally, $\forall X_r \in \mathbf{X}_R$, $\mathcal{H}^{NB}_{\mathbf{X}_R} \supseteq \mathcal{H}_{X_r} = \mathcal{H}^{NB}_{X_r}$ (and $\mathcal{H}^{NB}_{FK} = \mathcal{H}_{FK}$), since Naive Bayes has no bias if there is only one feature.

The relationship between the size of the hypothesis space and the variance is formalized in ML using the powerful notion of the *VC dimension* [40, 43]. We use this notion to complete the formalization of our argument.

VC Dimension. Due to space constraints, we only give an intuitive explanation and an example here. Intuitively, the VC dimension captures the ability of a classifier to assign the true class labels to a set of labeled data points of a given cardinality–a capability known as "shattering." For example, consider a linear classifier in 2-D. It is easy to see that it can shatter any set of 3 points (distinct and non-collinear). But it cannot shatter a set of 4 points due to the XOR problem [12]. Thus, the VC dimension of a 2-D linear classifier is 3. For finite hypothesis spaces (as in our case), the VC dimension is a direct indicator of the size of the hypothesis space [40]. A standard result from ML bounds the difference between the test and train errors (this difference is solely due to variance) as a function of the VC dimension (v) and the number of training examples (n):

THEOREM 3.2. (From [40], p. 51) *For every $\delta \in (0,1)$, with probability at least $1-\delta$ over the choice of the training dataset, and for $n > v$, we have:*

$$|Test\ error - Train\ error| \leq \frac{4+\sqrt{vlog(2en/v)}}{\delta\sqrt{2n}}$$

Thus, a higher VC dimension means a looser bound on the variance and, possibly, higher variance. The VC dimension usually increases with the number of features. For example, it is linear in the number of features for "linear" classifiers such as logistic regression and also Naive Bayes [43]. But note that we had assumed that all features are nominal in our setting. Thus, we recode the features to numeric space using the standard binary vector representation, i.e., a feature F is converted to a 0/1 vector with $|\mathcal{D}_F| - 1$ dimensions (the last category is represented as a zero vector). With this recoding, the VC dimension of Naive Bayes (or logistic regression) on a set $\mathbf{X}$ of nominal features is $1 + \sum_{F \in \mathbf{X}} (|\mathcal{D}_F| - 1)$. If we use FK alone, the maximum VC dimension for any classifier is $|\mathcal{D}_{FK}|$, which is matched by almost all popular classifiers such as Naive Bayes. However, as per the argument for Figure 2, the VC dimension of any classifier on $\mathbf{X}_R$ is at most the number of distinct values of $\mathbf{X}_R$ in the given table $\mathbf{R}$, say, r. Since RID is the primary key of $\mathbf{R}$, we have $|\mathcal{D}_{FK}| \geq r$. Thus, the VC dimension is likely to be higher if FK is used as a representative for $\mathbf{X}_R$.

In the Context of Feature Selection. The above variance-based argument gets stronger when we consider the fact that we might *not* retain all of $\mathbf{X}_R$ *after* feature selection. Consider an extreme scenario: suppose the "true" distribution can be succintly described using a lone feature $X_r \in \mathbf{X}_R$. In our churn example, this represents a case where all customers with employers based in "The Shire" churn and they are the only ones who churn (X_r is `Country`). Suppose an "oracle" told us to only use X_r. Clearly, $\mathcal{H}_{X_r}$ is likely to be much smaller than $\mathcal{H}_{FK}$, as illustrated in Figure 2. Thus, the variance for a model based on FK is likely to be higher than a model based on X_r, as per Theorem 3.2. For the opposite extreme, i.e., the true concept needs all of $\mathbf{X}_R$, the gap with $\mathcal{H}_{FK}$ might decrease, but it might still be large.

Alas, in the real world, we do not have oracles to tell us which features are part of the true distribution; it could be none, some, or all features in $\mathbf{X}_R$. What we do have instead of an oracle is a feature selection method, although it does the job approximately using a finite labeled sample. For example, in the above extreme scenario, if we input $\{FK, X_r\}$ to a feature selection method, it is likely to output $\{X_r\}$ precisely because a model based on $\{X_r\}$ is likely to have lower variance than one based on $\{FK\}$ or $\{FK, X_r\}$. By avoiding the join, we shut the door on such possibilities and force the model to work only with FK. Thus, overall, even though FK can act as a representative for $\mathbf{X}_R$, it is probably safer to give the entire set $\mathbf{X}$ to the feature selection method and let it figure out the subset to use. Finally, note that we had assumed $\mathbf{X}_S$ is empty for the above discussion because it is orthogonal to our core issue. If $\mathbf{X}_S$ is not empty, all the hypothesis spaces shown in Figure 2 will blow up, but their relative relationships, and hence the above arguments about the variance, will remain unaffected.

Summary. Our analysis reveals a dichotomy in the accuracy effects of avoiding a KFK join for ML and feature selection: avoiding the join and using FK as a representative of $\mathbf{X}_R$ might not increase the bias, but the variance (compared after feature selection) might increase significantly.

4. PREDICTING A PRIORI IF IT IS SAFE TO AVOID A KFK JOIN

Given our understanding of the dichotomy in the effects of joins, we now focus on answering our core question: how

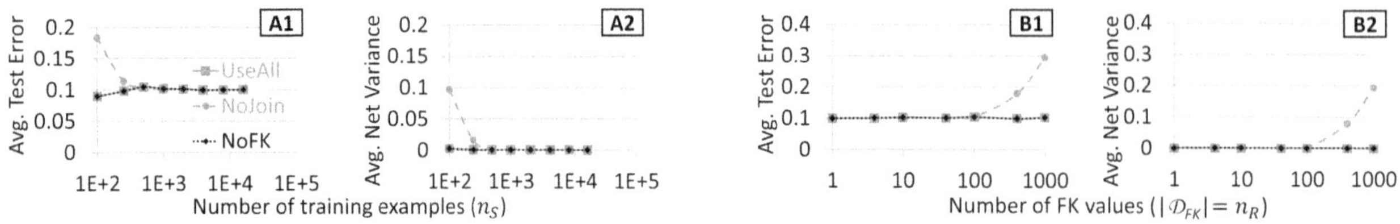

Figure 3: Simulation results for the scenario in which only a single $X_r \in \mathbf{X}_R$ is part of the true distribution, which has $P(Y = 0|X_r = 0) = P(Y = 1|X_r = 1) = p$. For these results, we set $p = 0.1$ (varying this probability did not change the overall trends). (A) Vary n_S while fixing $(d_S, d_R, |\mathcal{D}_{FK}|) = (2, 4, 40)$. (B) Vary $|\mathcal{D}_{FK}|$ $(= n_R)$ while fixing $(n_S, d_S, d_R) = (1000, 4, 4)$.

to predict a priori if a join with $\mathbf{R}$ is safe to avoid. We start with a simulation study using "controlled" datasets to validate our theoretical analysis and measure precisely how the error varies as we vary different properties of the normalized data. We then explain our decision rules and how we use our simulation measurements to tune the rules. All the plots in Section 4 are based on our synthetic datasets.

4.1 Simulation Study

We perform a Monte Carlo-style study. For the sake of tractability and depth of understanding, we use Naive Bayes as the classifier in this section. But note that our methodology is generic enough to be applicable to any classifier because we measure the accuracy only using standard notions of error, bias, and variance for a generic ML classifier.

Data Synthesis. We sample the labeled examples in an independently and identically distributed manner from a controlled true distribution $P(Y, \mathbf{X})$. Different scenarios are possible based on what features in $\mathbf{X}$ are used: it could be any or all features in $\mathbf{X}_S$, FK, and/or $\mathbf{X}_R$. Our primary goal is to understand the effects of the FD $FK \rightarrow \mathbf{X}_R$ and explain the danger in avoiding the join. Thus, we focus on a key scenario that intuitively represents the worst-case scenario for avoiding the join: the true distribution is succintly captured using a lone feature $X_r \in \mathbf{X}_R$. This corresponds to the example in Section 3.2 in which all customers with employers based in "The Shire" churn and they are the only ones who churn. In line with Proposition 3.3, we expect FK to play an indirect role in predicting Y in both scenarios. All other features are random noise. We also studied two other representative scenarios: one in which all of $\mathbf{X}_S$ and $\mathbf{X}_R$ are part of the true distribution, and one in which only $\mathbf{X}_S$ and FK are. Since these two did not yield any major additional insights, we present them in the appendix.

Simulation Setup. There is one attribute table $\mathbf{R}$ ($k = 1$), and all of $\mathbf{X}_S$, $\mathbf{X}_R$, and Y are boolean (i.e., domain size 2). The following parameters are varied one at a time: number of features in $\mathbf{X}_S$ (d_S), number of features in $\mathbf{X}_R$ (d_R), $|\mathcal{D}_{FK}|$ $(= n_R)$, and total number of training examples (n_S). We also sample $\frac{n_S}{4}$ examples for the test set. We generate 100 different training datasets and measure the test error and the variance based on the different models obtained from these 100 runs. This whole process was repeated 100 times with different seeds for the pseudo-random number generator [38]. Thus, we have 10,000 runs in total for one combination of the parameters studied. While the test error and variance were defined intuitively in Section 3.2, we now define them formally (based on [11]).

Definitions. We start with the formal definition of error (based on Domingos and Pazzani [13]).

DEFINITION 4.1. Zero-one loss. *Let t be the true class label of a given example with $\boldsymbol{X} = \boldsymbol{x}$, while $c_M(\boldsymbol{x})$ be the class predicted by a classifier M on $\boldsymbol{x}$. The* zero-one loss *(of M on $\boldsymbol{x}$), denoted $L(t, c_M(\boldsymbol{x}))$, is defined as $L(t, c_M(\boldsymbol{x})) = \mathbf{1}_{t=c_M(x)}$, where $\mathbf{1}$ is the indicator function.*

DEFINITION 4.2. *The* local error *(in short, the* error*) of M on $\boldsymbol{x}$, denoted $E_M(\boldsymbol{x})$, is defined as the expected value of the zero-one loss, where the expectation is over the values of Y, given $\boldsymbol{X} = \boldsymbol{x}$, i.e., $E_M(\boldsymbol{x}) = \sum_{y \in \mathcal{D}_Y} P(Y = y|\boldsymbol{X} = \boldsymbol{x}) L_M(y, c_M(\boldsymbol{x}))$.*

Since M depends on the training data, we compute the expectation of the error over different training datasets, say, by averaging over a given finite collection of training datasets $\mathcal{S}$ (typically, all of the same size). Note that $|\mathcal{S}| = 100$ for our Monte Carlo runs. The *expected error* of a classifier (across true distributions and $\mathcal{S}$) on $\mathbf{x}$ is decomposed as follows:

$$E[L(t, c_M(\mathbf{x}))] = B(\mathbf{x}) + (1 - 2B(\mathbf{x}))V(\mathbf{x}) + cN(\mathbf{x}) \quad (1)$$

Here, $B(\mathbf{x})$ is the bias, $V(\mathbf{x})$ is the variance, and $N(\mathbf{x})$ is the noise. The quantity $(1 - 2B(\mathbf{x}))V(\mathbf{x})$ is called the *net variance*, which is needed to capture the opposing effects of the variance on biased and unbiased predictions [11]. The *main prediction* on $\mathbf{x}$, given $\mathcal{S}$, is defined as the mode among the multi-set of predictions that result from learning M over each training dataset in $\mathcal{S}$. The main prediction is denoted y_m, while a single prediction based on some dataset in $\mathcal{S}$ is denoted y. The bias is defined as the zero-one loss of the main prediction, i.e., $B(\mathbf{x}) = L(t, y_m)$. The variance is defined as the average loss with respect to the main prediction, i.e., $V(\mathbf{x}) = E_D[L(y_m, y)]$. The *average bias* (resp. *average net variance* and *average test error*) is the average of the bias (resp. net variance and test error) over the entire set of test examples. Our goal is to understand how the average test error and the average net variance are affected by avoiding a join. Due to space constraints, we only discuss the key results here and present the others in the appendix.

Results. We compare three classes of models: *UseAll*, which uses all of $\mathbf{X}_S$, FK, and $\mathbf{X}_R$, *NoJoin*, which omits $\mathbf{X}_R$, and *NoFK*, which omits FK. Figure 3 plots the average test error and average net variance against n_S as well as $|\mathcal{D}_{FK}|$.

At a high level, Figure 3 validates our theoretical results on the dichotomy in the effects of avoiding the join. Both *UseAll* and *NoFK* use X_r, which enables them to achieve the lowest errors. When n_S is large, *NoJoin* matches their errors even though it does not use X_r. This confirms our arguments in Section 3.1 about FK acting as a representative of X_r. However, when n_S drops, the error of *NoJoin* increases, and as Figure 3(A2) shows, this is due to the increase in the net variance. Figure 3(B) drills into why that happens: for a fixed n_S, a higher $|\mathcal{D}_{FK}|$ yields a higher error for *NoJoin*, again because of higher net variance. This confirms our arguments in Section 3.2 about the danger of using FK as a representative due to the increase in the variance. Due to space constraints, we discuss other parameters and the other two simulation scenarios in the appendix.

4.2 Towards a Decision Rule

We now precisely define what we mean by "a join is safe to avoid" and devise intuitive decision rules to predict such cases. While our definition and decision rules are heuristic, they are based on our theoretical and simulation-based insights and they satisfy all the desiderata listed in Section 1. Our key guiding principle is *conservatism*: it is fine to not avoid a join that could have been avoided in hindsight (a missed opportunity), but we do not want to avoid a join that should not be avoided (i.e., the error blows up if it is avoided). This is reasonable since the feature selection method is there to figure out if features in $\mathbf{X}_R$ are not helpful, albeit with poorer performance. Designing a rule to avoid joins safely is challenging mainly because it needs to balance this subtle performance-accuracy trade-off correctly.

The Risk of Representation. We start be defining a heuristic quantity based on the *increase* in the error bound given by Theorem 3.2. Intuitively, it quantifies the "extra risk" caused by avoiding the join. We compare the bounds for a hypothetical "best" model that uses some subset of $\mathbf{X}_R$ instead of FK (join performed) against one that uses FK instead (join avoided). A subset of $\mathbf{X}_S$ might be used by both. We call this quantity the *Risk of Representation* (ROR):

$$ROR = \frac{\sqrt{v_{Yes} log(\frac{2en}{v_{Yes}})} - \sqrt{v_{No} log(\frac{2en}{v_{No}})}}{\delta\sqrt{2n}} + \Delta bias$$

In the above, v_{Yes} is the VC dimension of a classifier that uses FK as a representative and avoids the join, while v_{No} is for one that does not avoid the join (the appendix conveniently lists all the extra notation used in Section 4.2). We first define them and then explain the intuition behind their definition. For simplicity's sake, we restrict ourselves to models such as Naive Bayes and logistic regression that have VC dimension linear in the number of features, but discuss some other classifiers later.[5] We are given $\mathbf{X} = \mathbf{X}_S \cup \{FK\} \cup \mathbf{X}_R$. Suppose an "oracle" told us that $\mathbf{U}_S \subseteq \mathbf{X}_S$ and $\mathbf{U}_R \subseteq \mathbf{X}_R$ are the only features in the true distribution. We only consider the case where $\mathbf{U}_R$ is nonempty.[6] Thus, ideally, $v_{Yes} = \sum_{F \in \mathbf{U}_S}(|\mathcal{D}_F| - 1) + |\mathcal{D}_{FK}|$. Denote $\sum_{F \in \mathbf{U}_S}(|\mathcal{D}_F| - 1)$ by q_S; this is the sum of the number of unique values of all features in $\mathbf{U}_S$. Let q_R denote the number of unique values of $\mathbf{U}_R$ (taken jointly; not as individual features) in $\mathbf{R}$. In general, v_{No} does not have a closed form expression since it depends on $\mathbf{R}$, but we have $q_S < v_{No} \leq q_S + q_R$. Thus, $v_{No} \leq v_{Yes}$. Once again, since we do not have oracles in the real world, we will not know $\mathbf{U}_S$ and $\mathbf{U}_R$ a priori. Thus, it is *impossible* to compute the ROR exactly in general.[7] Furthermore, Theorem 3.2 only deals with the variance, not the bias. Thus, we denote the difference in bias using $\Delta bias$ in the ROR. Given this definition of the ROR, we now precisely state what we mean by the join with $\mathbf{R}$ is "safe to avoid."

DEFINITION 4.3. *Given a failure probability δ and a bound $\epsilon > 0$, we say the join with $\mathbf{R}$ is* (δ, ϵ)-safe to avoid *iff the ROR with the given δ is no larger than ϵ.*

The ROR Rule. While the ROR intuitively captures the risk of avoiding the join and provides us a threshold-based decision rule, we immediately hit another wall: it is *impossible* in general to compute $\Delta bias$ a priori without knowing $\mathbf{U}_S$ and $\mathbf{U}_R$. Thus, prima facie, using the ROR directly for a decision rule seems to be a hopeless idea to pursue! We resolve this quandary using a simple observation: we do not really need the exact ROR but only a "good enough" indicator of the risk of using FK as a representative. Thus, drawing upon our guiding principle of conservatism, we upper bound the ROR and create a more conservative decision rule. We explain the derivation step by step. Assume $n > v_{Yes}$. First, Proposition 3.3 showed that dropping $\mathbf{X}_R$ a priori does not increase the bias but dropping FK might, which means $\Delta bias \leq 0$. Hence, we ignore $\Delta bias$ entirely:

$$ROR \leq \frac{\sqrt{v_{Yes} log(\frac{2en}{v_{Yes}})} - \sqrt{v_{No} log(\frac{2en}{v_{No}})}}{\delta\sqrt{2n}}$$

Second, we substitute the values of some variables in the above inequality. Denote $q_{No} = v_{No} - q_S$ (the slack in the earlier inequality $q_S < v_{No}$). The inequality now becomes:

$$ROR \leq \frac{1}{\delta\sqrt{2n}}[\sqrt{(q_S + |\mathcal{D}_{FK}|) log(2en/(q_S + |\mathcal{D}_{FK}|))} \\ - \sqrt{(q_S + q_{No}) log(2en/(q_S + q_{No}))}]$$

Third, we observe that since $|\mathcal{D}_{FK}| \geq q_R \geq q_{No}$, the RHS above is a non-increasing function of q_S that is maximum when $q_S = 0$. This lets us eliminate $\mathbf{U}_S$ from the picture:

$$ROR \leq \frac{1}{\delta\sqrt{2n}}(\sqrt{|\mathcal{D}_{FK}| log(2en/|\mathcal{D}_{FK}|)} - \sqrt{q_{No} log(2en/q_{No})})$$

Fourth, let q_R^* denote the minimum possible number of unique values of $\mathbf{U}_R$ in $\mathbf{R}$, i.e., $q_R^* = min_{F \in \mathbf{X}_R}|\mathcal{D}_F|$. Now, we observe that since $q_{No} \leq |\mathcal{D}_{FK}| \leq n$, the RHS above is a non-increasing function of q_{No} that is maximum when $q_{No} = q_R^*$. Thus, finally, we get the following inequality:

$$ROR \leq \frac{1}{\delta\sqrt{2n}}(\sqrt{|\mathcal{D}_{FK}| log(2en/|\mathcal{D}_{FK}|)} - \sqrt{q_R^* log(2en/q_R^*)})$$

Intuitively, the above represents the worst-case scenario in which $\mathbf{U}_S$ is empty and $\mathbf{U}_R = \{argmin_{F \in \mathbf{X}_R}|\mathcal{D}_F|\}$. Thus, we call this bound the *worst-case* ROR, and its "gap" with the exact ROR could be large (Figure 1). Henceforth, we use the term "ROR" to refer to this worst-case upper bound. The ROR rule uses a threshold: given a parameter ρ, avoid the join if ROR $\leq \rho$.[8] This rule is conservative because given a join that is (δ, ρ)-safe to avoid, there might be some $\rho' < \rho$ such that the join is actually also (δ, ρ')-safe to avoid.

[5]The upper bound derivation is similar for classifiers with more complex VC dimensions, e.g., the joint distribution. We leave a deeper formal analysis to future work.

[6]If $\mathbf{U}_R$ is empty, $\mathbf{R}$ is trivially useless.

[7]A feature selection method can ascertain $\mathbf{U}_S$ and $\mathbf{U}_R$ approximately, but our goal is to avoid this computation.

[8]We set the failure probability δ to be always 0.1, but it can also be folded into ρ since $ROR \propto \frac{1}{\delta}$.

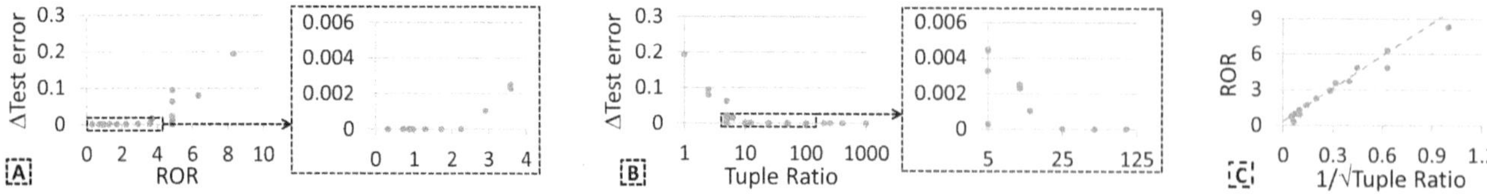

Figure 4: Scatter plots based on all the results of the simulation experiments referred to by Figure 3. (A) Increase in test error caused by avoiding the join (denoted "ΔTest error") against ROR. (B) ΔTest error against tuple ratio. (C) ROR against inverse square root of tuple ratio.

The TR Rule. The ROR rule still requires us to look at $\mathbf{X}_R$ to ascertain the features' domains and obtain q_R^*. This motivates us to consider an even simpler rule that depends only on n_S (number of training examples in $\mathbf{S}$) and $|\mathcal{D}_{FK}|$ ($= n_R$, by definition). We call $\frac{n_S}{n_R}$ the *tuple ratio* (TR). The key advantages of the TR over the ROR are that this is easier to understand and implement and that this does not even require us to look at $\mathbf{X}_R$, i.e., this enables us to ignore the join without even looking at $\mathbf{R}$. We now explain the relationship between the TR and the ROR.

When $|\mathcal{D}_{FK}| \gg q_R^*$, the ROR can be approximated as follows: $ROR \approx \frac{\sqrt{|\mathcal{D}_{FK}| log(2en/|\mathcal{D}_{FK}|)}}{\delta\sqrt{2n}}$. Since $n \equiv n_S$, we also have $ROR \approx (1/\sqrt{n_S/n_R})(\frac{\sqrt{log(2en_S/n_R)}}{\delta\sqrt{2}})$, which is approximately linear in $(1/\sqrt{TR})$ for a reasonably large TR. Thus, the TR is a conservative simplification of the ROR. The TR rule applies a threshold on the TR to predict if it is safe to avoid join: given a parameter τ, the join is avoided if TR $\geq \tau$. Note that since the TR rule is more conservative, it might lead to more missed opportunities than the ROR rule (Figure 1). We now explain why this "gap" arises. The key reason is that the TR cannot distinguish between scenarios where $|\mathcal{D}_{FK}| \gg q_R^*$ and where $|\mathcal{D}_{FK}|$ is comparable to q_R^*, as illustrated by Figure 5. When $|\mathcal{D}_{FK}| \gg q_R^*$, the ROR is high, which means the join may not be safe to avoid. But when $|\mathcal{D}_{FK}| \approx q_R^*$, the ROR is low, which means the join may be safe to avoid. The TR is oblivious to this finer distinction enabled by the ROR. But in practice, we expect that this extra capability of the ROR might not be too significant since it only matters if *all* features in $\mathbf{X}_R$ have domain sizes comparable to FK. Such an extreme situation is perhaps unlikely in the real world. In fact, as we explain later in Section 5.2.2, the ROR rule and the TR rule yielded identical results for join avoidance on all our real datasets.

Tuning the Thresholds. We now explain how to tune the thresholds of our decision rules (ρ for ROR and τ for TR). For our purposes, we define a "significant increase" in test error as an absolute increase of 0.001. This might be too strict (or lenient) based on the application. Our goal here is only to demonstrate the feasibility of tuning our rules. Applications willing to tolerate a higher (or lower) error can easily retune the rules based on our methodology.

Figure 4(A) shows a scatter plot of the (asymmetric) test error difference between *NoJoin* and *UseAll* based on our diverse set of simulation results (varying n_S, $|\mathcal{D}_{FK}|$, d_R, etc.) for the first scenario (a lone $X_r \in \mathbf{X}_R$ is part of the true distribution). We see that as the ROR increases, the test error difference increases, which confirms that the ROR is an indicator of the test error difference. In fact, for sufficiently small values of the ROR, the test error is practically unchanged. The zoomed-in portion of Figure 4(A)

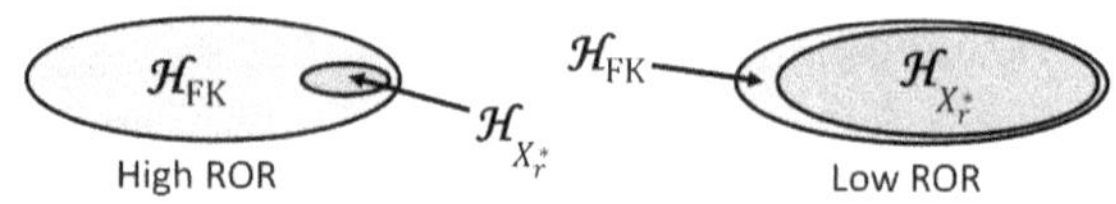

Figure 5: When $q_R^* = |\mathcal{D}_{X_r^*}| \ll |\mathcal{D}_{FK}|$, the ROR is high. When $q_R^* \approx |\mathcal{D}_{FK}|$, the ROR is low. The TR rule cannot distinguish between these two scenarios.

suggests that a threshold of $\rho = 2.5$ is reasonable. Figure 4(B) shows the same errors against the TR. We see that as the TR increases, the test error difference decreases. For sufficiently large values of the TR, the test error is practically unchanged. Thus, even the more conservative TR can be a surprisingly good indicator of the test error difference. The zoomed-in portion of Figure 4(B) suggests a threshold of $\tau = 20$ is reasonable. Finally, Figure 4(C) confirms the relationship between the ROR and the TR: the ROR is approximately linear in $1/\sqrt{TR}$ (Pearson correlation coefficient ≈ 0.97).

These thresholds need to be tuned only *once per ML model* (more precisely, *once per VC dimension expression*). Thus, they are qualitatively different from (hyper-)parameters in ML that need to be tuned *once per dataset instance* using cross-validation. The above threshold values can be directly used in practice for models such as Naive Bayes and logistic regression. In fact, they worked unmodified for *all* the real datasets in our experiments for both Naive Bayes and logistic regression! If the error tolerance is changed, one can use our simulation results to get new thresholds. For an ML model with a completely different VC dimension expression, our simulations have to be repeated with that ML model and new thresholds obtained in a manner similar to the above.

Multiple Attribute Tables. It is trivial to extend the TR rule to multiple $\mathbf{R}_i$: avoid the join with $\mathbf{R}_i$ if $\frac{n_S}{n_{R_i}} \geq \tau$. As for the ROR rule, since $\mathbf{U}_S$ was eliminated when deriving the worst-case ROR, we can ignore the other foreign keys in $\mathbf{S}$. Thus, we can avoid the join with $\mathbf{R}_i$ if the ROR computed using FK_i and $\min_{F \in \mathbf{X}_{R_i}} |\mathcal{D}_F|$ is $\leq \rho$. Making join avoidance decisions for multiple $\mathbf{R}_i$ jointly, rather than independently as we do, might yield less conservative (albeit more complex) decision rules. We leave this to future work.

Multi-Class Case. The VC dimension makes sense only when Y has two classes, which might limit the applicability of the ROR rule. In the ML literature, there are various generalizations of the VC dimension for multi-class classifiers, e.g., the Natarajan dimension or the graph dimension [40]. Intuitively, they generalize the notion of the power of the classifier by also considering the number of classes. However, it is known that these more general dimensions are bounded (for "linear" classifiers such as Naive Bayes or lo-

Dataset	#Y	(n_S, d_S)	k	k'	$(n_{R_i}, d_{R_i}), i = 1 \text{ to } k$
Walmart	7	(421570, 1)	2	2	(2340, 9), (45, 2)
Expedia	2	(942142, 6)	2	1	(11939, 8), (37021, 14)
Flights	2	(66548, 20)	3	3	(540, 5), (3182, 6), (3182, 6)
Yelp	5	(215879, 0)	2	2	(11537, 32), (43873, 6)
MovieLens1M	5	(1000209, 0)	2	2	(3706, 21), (6040, 4)
LastFM	5	(343747, 0)	2	2	(4999, 7), (50000, 4)
BookCrossing	5	(253120, 0)	2	2	(49972, 4), (27876, 2)

Figure 6: Dataset statistics. #Y is the number of target classes. k is the number of attribute tables. k' is the number of foreign keys with closed domains.

gistic regression) by a log-linear factor in the product of the total number of feature values (sum of the domain sizes for nominal features) and the number of classes [10]. Hence, intuitively, the ROR rule might be a stricter condition than needed for the multi-class case, which is in line with our guiding principle of conservatism for avoiding joins. We leave a deeper analysis of the multi-class case to future work.

5. EXPERIMENTS ON REAL DATA

Our goal here is three-fold: (1) verify that there are cases where avoiding joins does not increase error significantly, (2) verify that our rules can accurately predict those cases, and (3) analyze the robustness and sensitivity of our rules.

Datasets. Standard sources such as the UCI ML repository did not have datasets with known KFKDs/FDs. Thus, we obtained real datasets from other sources: Walmart, Expedia, and Yelp are from the data science contest portal Kaggle (www.kaggle.com); MovieLens1M and BookCrossing are from GroupLens (grouplens.org); Flights is from openflights.org; LastFM is from mtg.upf.edu/node/1671 and last.fm. Figure 6 provides the dataset statistics. We describe each dataset and the prediction task. We used a standard unsupervised binning technique (equal-length histograms) for numeric features. Links to the data and our scripts for data preparation will be made available on our project website. To the best of our knowledge, this is the first paper to gather and clean so many normalized real datasets for ML. We hope our efforts help further research on this topic.

Walmart. Predict department-wise sales levels by joining data about past sales with data about stores and weather/economic indicators. **S** is Sales (SalesLevel, IndicatorID, StoreID, Dept), while Y is SalesLevel. $\mathbf{R}_1$ is Indicators (<u>IndicatorID</u>, TempAvg, TempStdev, CPIAvg, CPIStdev, FuelPriceAvg, FuelPriceStdev, UnempRateAvg, UnempRateStdev, IsHoliday). $\mathbf{R}_2$ is Stores (<u>StoreID</u>, Type, Size). Both foreign keys (StoreID and IndicatorID) have closed domains with respect to the prediction task.

Expedia. Predict if a hotel will be ranked highly by joining data about past search listings with data about hotels and search events. **S** is Listings (Position, HotelID, SearchID, Score1, Score2, LogHistoricalPrice, PriceUSD, PromoFlag, OrigDestDistance). Y is Position. $\mathbf{R}_1$ is Hotels (<u>HotelID</u>, Country, Stars, ReviewScore, BookingUSDAvg, BookingUSDStdev, BookingCount, BrandBool, ClickCount). $\mathbf{R}_2$ is Searches (<u>SearchID</u>, Year, Month, WeekOfYear, TimeOfDay, VisitorCountry, SearchDest, LengthOfStay, ChildrenCount, AdultsCount, RoomCount, SiteID, BookingWindow, SatNightBool, RandomBool). HotelID has a closed domain with respect to the prediction task, while SearchID does not.

Flights. Predict if a route is codeshared by joining data about routes with data about airlines, source, and destination airports. **S** is Routes (CodeShare, AirlineID, SrcAirportID, DestAirportID, Equipment1, ..., Equipment20). Y is CodeShare. $\mathbf{R}_1$ is Airlines (<u>AirlineID</u>, AirCountry, Active, NameWords, NameHasAir, NameHasAirlines). $\mathbf{R}_2$ is SrcAirports (<u>SrcAirportID</u>, SrcCity, SrcCountry, SrcDST, SrcTimeZone, SrcLongitude, SrcLatitude). $\mathbf{R}_3$ is DestAirports (<u>DestAirportID</u>, DestCity, DestCountry, DestTimeZone, DestDST, DestLongitude, DestLatitude). All foreign keys have closed domains with respect to the prediction task.

Yelp. Predict business ratings by joining data about past ratings with data about users and businesses. **S** is Ratings (Stars, UserID, BusinessID). Y is Stars. $\mathbf{R}_1$ is Businesses (<u>BusinessID</u>, BusinessStars, BusinessReviewCount, Latitude, Longitude, City, State, WeekdayCheckins1, ..., WeekdayCheckins5, WeekendCheckins1, ..., WeekendCheckins5, Category1, ... Category15, IsOpen). $\mathbf{R}_2$ is Users (<u>UserID</u>, Gender, UserStars, UserReviewCount, VotesUseful, VotesFunny, VotesCool). Both foreign keys have closed domains with respect to the prediction task.

MovieLens1M. Predict movie ratings by joining data about past ratings with data about users and movies. **S** is Ratings (Stars, UserID, MovieID). Y is Stars. $\mathbf{R}_1$ is Movies (<u>MovieID</u>, NameWords, NameHasParentheses, Year, Genre1, ..., Genre18). $\mathbf{R}_2$ is Users (<u>UserID</u>, Gender, Age, Zipcode, Occupation). Both foreign keys have closed domains with respect to the prediction task.

LastFM. Predict music play levels by joining data about past play levels with data about users and artists. **S** is Plays (PlayLevel, UserID, ArtistID), Y is PlayLevel, $\mathbf{R}_1$ is Artists (<u>ArtistID</u>, Listens, Scrobbles, Genre1, ..., Genre5), and $\mathbf{R}_2$ is Users (<u>UserID</u>, Gender, Age, Country, JoinYear). Both foreign keys have closed domains with respect to the prediction task.

BookCrossing. Predict book ratings by joining data about past ratings with data about readers and books. **S** is Ratings (Stars, UserID, BookID). Y is Stars. $\mathbf{R}_1$ is Users (<u>UserID</u>, Age, Country). $\mathbf{R}_2$ is Books (<u>BookID</u>, Year, Publisher, NumTitleWords, NumAuthorWords). Both foreign keys have closed domains with respect to the prediction task.

Experimental Setup. All experiments were run on CloudLab, which offers free and exclusive access to physical compute nodes for research [37]. We use their default ARM64 OpenStack Juno profile with Ubuntu 14.10. It provides an HP Proliant server with 8 ARMv8 cores, 64 GB RAM, and 100 GB disk. Our code is written in R (version 3.1.1), and all datasets fit in memory as R data frames.

5.1 End-to-end Error and Runtime

We compare two approaches: *JoinAll*, which joins all base tables, and *JoinOpt*, which joins only those base tables predicted by the TR rule to be not safe to avoid (the ROR rule gave identical results). For each approach, we pair Naive Bayes with one of four popular feature selection methods: two wrappers (forward selection, and backward selection) and two filters (mutual information-based and information gain ratio-based). We compare only the runtimes of feature selection and exclude the time taken to join the tables. This can work against *JoinOpt*, but as such the joins took $< 1\%$ of the total runtime in almost all our results. As mentioned

A	Walmart		Expedia		Flights		Yelp		MovieLens1M		LastFM		BookCrossing	
Error Metric	RMSE		Zero-one		Zero-one		RMSE		RMSE		RMSE		RMSE	
Approach	JoinAll	**JoinOpt**	JoinAll	**JoinOpt**	JoinAll	**JoinOpt**	JoinAll	**JoinOpt**	JoinAll	**JoinOpt**	JoinAll	**JoinOpt**	JoinAll	**JoinOpt**
# Tables in i/p	3	1	3	2	4	3	3	3	3	1	3	2	3	3
# Features in i/p	14	3	29	21	40	35	40	40	27	2	13	6	8	8
Error with full set	0.9850	0.8927	0.2820	0.2417	0.2445	0.1699	1.3279	1.3279	1.1671	1.0671	1.2344	1.2145	1.4678	1.4678
Forward Selection														
Validation error	0.8927	0.8927	0.2338	0.2338	0.1390	0.1390	1.1361	1.1361	1.0670	1.0671	1.0247	1.0247	1.4313	1.4313
# Features in o/p	3	3	7	7	13	13	9	9	3	2	1	1	2	2
Holdout test error	0.8910	0.8910	0.2336	0.2336	0.1359	0.1359	1.1317	1.1317	1.0687	1.0685	1.0248	1.0248	1.4295	1.4295
Backward Selection														
Holdout test error	0.8961	0.8910	0.2337	0.2337	0.1390	0.1354	1.1330	1.1330	1.0693	1.0685	1.0475	1.0248	1.4422	1.4422
Mutual Information-based Filter														
Holdout test error	0.8910	0.8910	0.2339	0.2339	0.1610	0.1610	1.1676	1.1676	1.0685	1.0685	1.0248	1.0248	1.4327	1.4327
Information Gain Ratio-based Filter														
Holdout test error	0.9014	0.8910	0.2401	0.2352	0.1476	0.1476	1.1423	1.1423	1.0692	1.0685	1.0248	1.0248	1.4327	1.4327

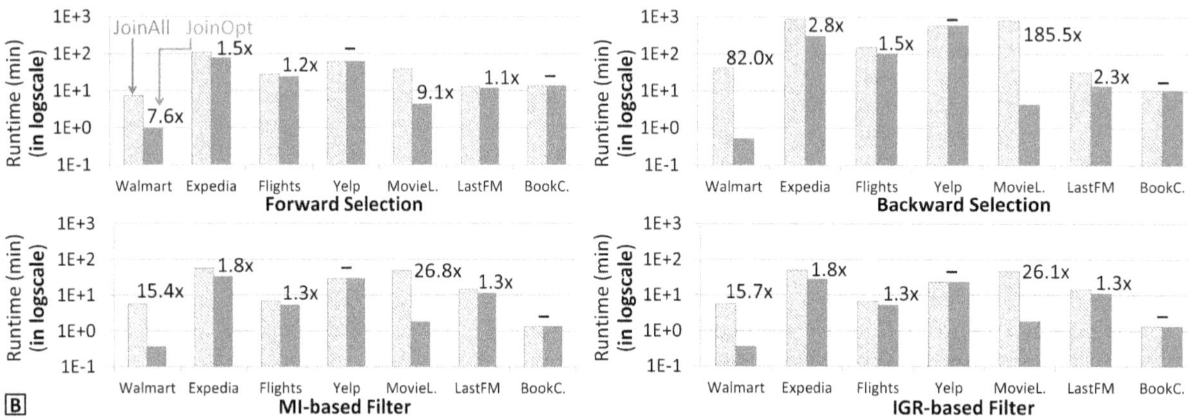

Figure 7: End-to-end results on real data. (A) Error after feature selection. (B) Runtime of feature selection.

before, we use the standard holdout validation method with the entity table (**S**) split randomly into 50%:25%:25% for training, validation, and final holdout testing. For the filter methods, the number of features filtered after ranking was actually tuned using holdout validation as a "wrapper."

In order to make the comparison more meaningful, the error metric used to report the error of the learned model depends on the type of the target and the number of classes. Specifically, the zero-one error is used for Expedia and Flights, which have binary targets, while the root mean squared error (RMSE) is used for the other datasets, which have multi-class ordinal targets. Note that our goal is to check if *JoinOpt* avoided any joins, and if so, whether its error is much higher than *JoinAll*. Figure 7 presents the results.

Errors and Output Features. The results in Figure 7(A) validate our key claim: *JoinOpt* did avoid some joins, and in all the cases where it did, the holdout test error did not increase significantly. For example, *JoinOpt* avoided both joins in both Walmart and MovieLens1M ("#Tables in input") without any increase in error. On Expedia, Flights, and LastFM, only one join each was avoided by *JoinOpt*, and the error did not increase much here either. Finally, on Yelp and BookCrossing, none of the joins were predicted to be safe to avoid. Furthermore, the trends are the same irrespective of the feature selection method used. In general, sequential greedy search had lower errors than the filter methods, which is consistent with the literature [17]. Surprisingly, in 12 of the 20 results (4 methods × 5 datasets; Yelp and BookCrossing excluded), *JoinOpt* and *JoinAll* had *identical* errors! This is because the output feature sets were identical even though the input for *JoinOpt* was smaller. For example, both *JoinAll* and *JoinOpt* had selected the same 3 features on Walmart for both forward selection and MI-based filter: {IndicatorID, StoreID, Dept}. Thus, none of the foreign features seem to matter for accuracy here. Similarly, on Expedia, the outputs were identical for forward selection: {HotelID, Score2, RandomBool, BookingWindow, Year, ChildrenCount, SatNightBool}, and backward selection but with 12 features. Thus, the HotelID sufficed and the hotel's features were not needed. On LastFM, for all methods except backward selection, both *JoinAll* and *JoinOpt* returned only {UserID}. It seems even ArtistID does not help (not just the artist's features), but our rules are not meant to detect this. Due to space constraints, we provide all other output features in the appendix.

In 3 of the 20 results, *JoinOpt* had almost the same error as *JoinAll* but with a different output feature set. For example, on MovieLens1M, for forward selection *JoinOpt* gave {UserID, MovieID}, while *JoinAll* also included a movie genre feature. More surprisingly, the error was actually significantly *lower* for *JoinOpt* in 5 of the 20 results (e.g., backward selection on Walmart and LastFM). This lower error is a serendipity caused by the variability introduced by the heuristic nature of the feature selection method. Since these feature selection methods are not globally optimal, *JoinAll*, which uses all the redundant features, seems to face a higher risk of being stuck at a poor local optimal. For example, for backward selection on Walmart, *JoinAll* dropped IndicatorID but retained many store and weather features even though it was less helpful for accuracy.

Runtime. The runtime speedup depends on the ratio of the number of features used by *JoinAll* against *JoinOpt*: the

A

Walmart

	JoinAll	No R1	No R2	*NoJoins*
FS	0.8910	0.8910	0.8910	0.8910
BS	0.8961	0.8910	0.8910	0.8910

MovieLens1M

	JoinAll	No R1	No R2	*NoJoins*
FS	1.0687	1.0685	1.0687	1.0685
BS	1.0693	1.0685	1.0699	1.0685

Yelp

	JoinAll	No R1	No R2	NoJoins
FS	1.1317	1.2350	1.2052	1.3322
BS	1.1330	1.2145	1.2446	1.3322

LastFM

	JoinAll	*No R1*	No R2	NoJoins
FS	1.0248	1.0248	1.0248	1.0248
BS	1.0475	1.0248	1.0456	1.0248

Flights

	JoinAll	*No R1*	No R2	No R3	No R1,R2	No R1,R3	No R2,R3	NoJoins
FS	0.1359	0.1359	0.1359	0.1359	0.1359	0.1359	0.1359	0.1359
BS	0.1390	0.1354	0.1363	0.1363	0.1354	0.1387	0.1363	0.1354

BookCrossing

	JoinAll	No R1	No R2	NoJoins
FS	1.4295	1.4295	1.4327	1.4327
BS	1.4422	1.4563	1.4422	1.4327

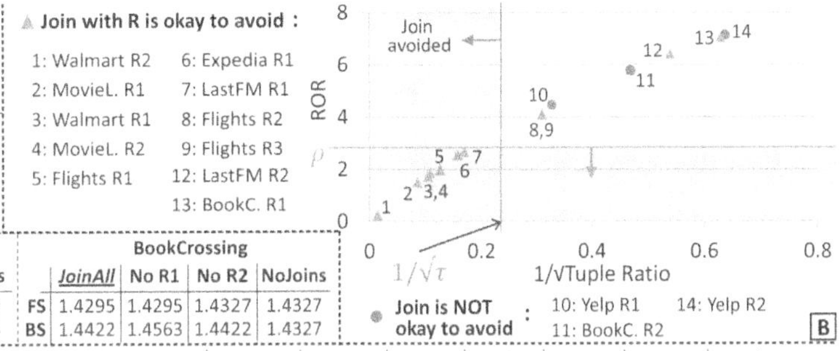

FS	Walmart	Expedia	Flights	Yelp	MovieL.	LastFM	BookC.
JoinOpt	0.8910	0.2336	0.1359	1.1317	1.0685	1.0248	1.4295
JoinAllNoFK	0.9477	0.2800	0.1688	1.1317	1.1940	1.5375	1.5347

BS	Walmart	Expedia	Flights	Yelp	MovieL.	LastFM	BookC.
JoinOpt	0.8910	0.2337	0.1354	1.1330	1.0685	1.0248	1.4422
JoinAllNoFK	0.9455	0.2760	0.1817	1.1381	1.1806	1.5863	1.5347

C

Figure 8: (A) Robustness. Holdout test errors after Forward Selection (FS) and Backward Selection (BS). The "plan" chosen by JoinOpt is highlighted, e.g., NoJoins on Walmart. (B) Sensitivity. We set $\rho = 2.5$ and $\tau = 20$. An attribute table is deemed "okay to avoid" if the increase in error was within 0.001 with either FS or BS. (C) Holdout test errors of JoinOpt and JoinAllNoFK, which drops all foreign keys a priori.

more features avoided, the higher the speedup. Hence, the speedup depends on the number of features in the base tables, as Figure 7(B) shows. Since *JoinOpt* avoided both joins on MovieLens1M and Walmart, the speedups were high: 186x and 82x resp. for backward selection; 26x and 15x resp. for the filter methods. But on Expedia, the ratio of the number of features used is lower (≈ 1.4), which yielded more modest speedups of between 1.5x to 2.8x. Similarly, the speedups are lower on Flights and LastFM. It is noteworthy that these datasets cover the entire spectrum in terms of how many joins can be avoided: Walmart and MovieLens1M on one end; Yelp and BookCrossing on the other.

Summary. In all 28 results, *JoinOpt* had either identical or almost the same error as *JoinAll* but was often significantly faster, thus validating our core claim.

5.2 Drill-down on Real Data

5.2.1 Robustness of Join Avoidance Decisions

JoinOpt avoids only the joins predicted by the TR rule as being safe to avoid. We would like to understand the robustness of its decisions, i.e., what if we had avoided a different subset of the joins? Due to space constraints, we focus only on sequential greedy search. Figure 8(A) presents the results. Expedia is absent because it has only one foreign key with a closed domain; so Figure 7 suffices for it.

On Walmart and MovieLens1M, it was safe to avoid both joins. Our rule predicted this correctly. At the opposite end, avoiding either join in Yelp and BookCrossing blows up the error. Our rule predicted this correctly as well. This shows the need for decision rules such as ours: the state-of-the-art *JoinAll* misses the speedup opportunities on Walmart and MovieLens1M, while its naive opposite *NoJoins* causes the error to blow up on Yelp and BookCrossing. On Flights, our rule predicted that Airlines is safe to avoid but not the other two attribute tables. Yet, it turned out that even the other two could have been avoided. This is an instance of the "missed opportunities" we had anticipated: recall that our rules are conservative (Figure 1). LastFM and BookCrossing also have an attribute table each that was deemed not safe to avoid, but it turned out that they could have been avoided. However, the results for *JoinAll* suggest that the features from those tables were not useful anyway; such opportunities are beyond the scope of this work.

5.2.2 Sensitivity to Thresholds

The TR rule uses $\tau = 20$ based on our simulation results. Similarly, we had picked $\rho = 2.5$ for the ROR rule. We now validate the sensitivity of the rules to the threshold settings by comparing them with the actual TR and ROR values on the real data. Figure 8(B) shows the results.

We see that the ROR is almost linear in the inverse square root of the TR even on the real data. Many attribute tables of Walmart, MovieLens1M, Flights, and Expedia lie below the thresholds chosen for either rule. They were all correctly predicted to be safe to avoid. Both attribute tables of Yelp and one of BookCrossing were correctly predicted to be not safe to avoid. The others fall in between and include some "missed opportunities." But note that there is no case in which avoiding an attribute table that was deemed safe to avoid by the TR rule caused the error to blow up.

Finally, we also tried a higher error tolerance of 0.01 instead of 0.001. This yielded new thresholds $\tau = 10$ and $\rho = 4.2$ based on Figure 4. This setting correctly predicted that two more joins could be avoided (both on Flights).

5.2.3 What if Foreign Keys Are Dropped?

Analysts sometimes judge foreign keys as being too "uninterpretable" and simply drop them. To assess the impact of this choice, we compare JoinOpt (whose accuracy is similar to JoinAll) with JoinAllNoFK, which is similar to JoinAll, but drops all foreign keys a priori. Figure 8(C) shows the results. In 6 of the 7 datasets, dropping foreign keys proved to be catastrophic for accuracy for both forward and backward selection. As we explained in our theoretical analysis in Section 3.2 (Figure 2), this is primarily because dropping foreign keys (JoinAllNoFK) might cause the bias to blow up drastically, while JoinOpt does not increase the bias.

5.3 Other ML Classifiers

It is natural to wonder if the trends observed on Naive Bayes would translate to other ML models. Note that the theoretical results and arguments in Section 3 apply to ML classifiers in general. Nevertheless, we now discuss another popular classifier: logistic regression. We also consider the popular Tree-Augmented Naive Bayes model (TAN) but, due to space constraints, we discuss TAN in the appendix.

Unlike Naive Bayes, the most popular feature selection method for logistic regression is the embedded method of

Dataset	Error Metric	L1 Regularization		L2 Regularization	
		JoinAll	JoinOpt	JoinAll	JoinOpt
Walmart	RMSE	0.8335	0.8335	1.1140	0.9370
Expedia	Zero-one	0.2130	0.2134	0.2559	0.2632
Flights	Zero-one	0.1167	0.1183	0.1494	0.1485
Yelp	RMSE	1.1426	1.1426	1.1744	1.1744
MovieLens1M	RMSE	1.0444	1.0459	1.1438	1.1940
LastFM	RMSE	1.0308	1.0300	1.5629	1.5605
BookCrossing	RMSE	1.3993	1.3993	1.6561	1.6561

Figure 9: Holdout test errors for logistic regression with regularization for the same setup as Figure 7.

regularization that constrains the L1 or L2 norm of the coefficient vector [17, 18]. We consider both and use the well-tuned implementation of logistic regression from the popular *glmnet* library in R [14]. Figure 9 presents the results. We see that the errors of *JoinOpt* are comparable to those of *JoinAll* with L1. Thus, the trends are the same as for Naive Bayes, which agrees with our theoretical results. Interestingly, L2 errors are significantly higher than L1 errors. This is an artefact of the data existing in a sparse feature space for which L1 is known to be usually better than L2 [18].

5.4 Discussion: Implications for Analysts

Our work presents at least three major practical implications. These are based on our conversations with analysts at multiple settings–a telecom company, a Web company, and an analytics vendor–about our results. First, analysts often join all tables almost by instinct. Our work shows that this might lead to much poorer performance without much accuracy gain. Avoiding joins that are safe to avoid can speed up the exploratory process of comparing feature sets and ML models. Our rules, especially the easy-to-understand TR rule, help with this task. Second, we found many cases where avoiding some joins led to a counter-intuitive *increase* in accuracy. Thus, at the least, it might help to try both *JoinOpt* and *JoinAll*. Third, analysts often *drop* all foreign key features (even if they have closed domains, e.g., `StoreID` in Walmart) since they subjectively deem such features as too "uninterpretable." Our work shows that this ad hoc step could seriously hurt accuracy. This finding helps analysts be better informed of the precise consequences of such a step.

Finally, most of the burden of feature engineering (designing and choosing features) for ML today falls on analysts [12, 20]. But the database community is increasingly recognizing the need to provide more systems support for feature engineering, e.g., Columbus [23, 46] provides declarative feature selection operations along with a performance "optimizer." We think it is possible for such systems to integrate our decision rules for avoiding joins either as new optimizations or as "suggestions" for analysts.

6. RELATED WORK

We now explain how our problem and ideas relate to prior work in both the database and ML literature.

Database Dependencies. Given a set of FDs, a relation can be decomposed into BCNF (in most cases) [5, 8]. Our work deals with the opposite scenario of joins resulting in a relation with FDs. This scenario was also studied in [29], but their goal was to avoid the materialization of the joins to improve ML performance. Our work focuses on the more fundamental question of whether such joins are even needed for ML in the first place from an accuracy perspective. There are database dependencies that are more general than FDs [5]. We think it is interesting future work to explore the implications of these more general database dependencies for ML and feature selection.

Graphical ML Models. The connection between embedded multi-valued dependencies (EMVDs) and probabilistic graphical models in ML was first shown by [34] and studied further by [44]. FDs are stronger constraints than EMVDs and cause feature redundancy. We perform a theoretical and empirical analysis of the effects of such redundancy in terms of its implications for avoiding joins.

Feature Selection. There is a large body of work in the ML and data mining literature whose focus is designing new feature selection methods to improve ML accuracy [17, 18]. Our focus is *not* on designing new feature selection methods but on understanding the effects of joins on feature selection. Our work is orthogonal to the feature selection method used. The redundancy-relevancy trade-off is also well-studied in the ML literature [17, 22, 45]. There is also some prior work on inferring approximate FDs from the data and using them as part of feature selection [42]. However, all these methods generally focus on approximately estimating redundancy and relevancy using the dataset *instance* [17]. In contrast, our results are based on the *schema*, which enables us to safely avoid features *without even looking at instances*, that is, using just the metadata. To the best of our knowledge, no feature selection method has this radical capability. A technique to "bias" the input and reduce the number of features was proposed by FOCUS [6]. At a high level, our rules are akin to a "bias" in the input. But FOCUS still requires expensive computations on the instance, unlike our rules.

Analytics Systems. There is growing interest in both industry and academia to more closely integrate ML with data processing [3, 9, 16, 19, 25, 26, 47]. In this context, there is a growing recognition that feature engineering is one of the most critical bottlenecks for ML [7, 27, 29, 36, 46]. Our work helps make it easier for analysts to apply feature selection over normalized data. We hope our work spurs more research in this important direction.

7. CONCLUSION AND FUTURE WORK

In this era of "big data," it is becoming almost "big dogma" that more features and data are somehow *always* better for ML. Our work makes a contrarian case that in some situations "less is more." Specifically, using theoretical, simulation, and empirical analyses, we show that in many cases, which can be predicted, features obtained using key-foreign key joins might not improve accuracy much, but degrade performance. Our work opens up new connections between data management, ML, and feature selection, and it raises new fundamental research questions at their intersection.

First, it is an open question as to how ML accuracy is affected by other database dependencies and how we can better exploit schema information to simplify feature engineering. Extending our results to numeric features and classifiers with infinite VC dimensions is another avenue. Finally, from conversations with analysts about our results, we learned that they were interested in our TR rule because it helps them quickly decide which tables to start with (often choosing from among over a dozen tables) for deeper analytics. This suggests the whole process of source selection and feature engineering might have more open questions.

8. REFERENCES

[1] Feature Selection and Dimension Reduction Techniques in SAS. nesug.org/Proceedings/nesug11/sa/sa08.pdf.

[2] Gartner Report on Analytics. gartner.com/it/page.jsp?id=1971516.

[3] Oracle R Enterprise.

[4] SAS Report on Analytics. sas.com/reg/wp/corp/23876.

[5] S. Abiteboul et al. *Foundations of Databases*. Addison-Wesley, 1995.

[6] H. Almuallim and T. G. Dietterich. Efficient Algorithms for Identifying Relevant Features. Technical report, 1992.

[7] M. Anderson et al. Brainwash: A Data System for Feature Engineering. In *CIDR*, 2013.

[8] C. Beeri and P. A. Bernstein. Computational Problems Related to the Design of Normal Form Relational Schemas. *TODS*, 4(1), Mar. 1979.

[9] Z. Cai et al. Simulation of Database-valued Markov Chains Using SimSQL. In *SIGMOD*, 2013.

[10] A. Daniely et al. Multiclass Learning Approaches: A Theoretical Comparison with Implications. In *NIPS*, 2012.

[11] P. Domingos. A Unified Bias-Variance Decomposition and its Applications. In *ICML*, 2000.

[12] P. Domingos. A Few Useful Things to Know About Machine Learning. *CACM*, 55(10), Oct. 2012.

[13] P. Domingos and M. Pazzani. On the Optimality of the Simple Bayesian Classifier under Zero-One Loss. *Machine Learning*, 29(2-3):103–130, 1997.

[14] J. H. Friedman et al. Regularization Paths for Generalized Linear Models via Coordinate Descent. *Journal of Statistical Software*, 33(1), 2010.

[15] N. Friedman, D. Geiger, and M. Goldszmidt. Bayesian Network Classifiers. *Machine Learning*, 29(2-3):131–163, Nov. 1997.

[16] A. Ghoting et al. SystemML: Declarative Machine Learning on MapReduce. In *ICDE*, 2011.

[17] I. Guyon, S. Gunn, M. Nikravesh, and L. A. Zadeh. *Feature Extraction: Foundations and Applications*. New York: Springer-Verlag, 2001.

[18] T. Hastie et al. *The Elements of Statistical Learning: Data mining, Inference, and Prediction*. Springer-Verlag, 2001.

[19] J. Hellerstein et al. The MADlib Analytics Library or MAD Skills, the SQL. In *VLDB*, 2012.

[20] S. Kandel et al. Enterprise Data Analysis and Visualization: An Interview Study. In *IEEE VAST*, 2012.

[21] R. Kohavi and G. H. John. Wrappers for Feature Subset Selection. *Artif. Intell.*, 97(1-2), Dec. 1997.

[22] D. Koller and M. Sahami. Toward Optimal Feature Selection. In *ICML*, 1995.

[23] P. Konda et al. Feature Selection in Enterprise Analytics: A Demonstration using an R-based Data Analytics System. In *VLDB*, 2013.

[24] Y. Koren et al. Matrix Factorization Techniques for Recommender Systems. *IEEE Computer*, 42(8), Aug. 2009.

[25] T. Kraska et al. MLbase: A Distributed Machine-learning System. In *CIDR*, 2013.

[26] A. Kumar et al. Hazy: Making it Easier to Build and Maintain Big-data Analytics. *CACM*, 56(3):40–49, March 2013.

[27] A. Kumar et al. Model Selection Management Systems: The Next Frontier of Advanced Analytics. *ACM SIGMOD Record*, Dec. 2015.

[28] A. Kumar et al. To Join or Not to Join? Thinking Twice about Joins before Feature Selection. *UW-Madison CS Tech. Rep. TR1828*, 2015.

[29] A. Kumar, J. Naughton, and J. Patel. Learning Generalized Linear Models Over Normalized Data. In *SIGMOD*, 2015.

[30] C. D. Manning, P. Raghavan, and H. Schütze. *Introduction to Information Retrieval*. Cambridge University Press, 2008.

[31] T. M. Mitchell. *Machine Learning*. McGraw Hill, 1997.

[32] A. Pavlo et al. Skew-aware Automatic Database Partitioning in Shared-nothing, Parallel OLTP Systems. In *SIGMOD*, 2012.

[33] J. Pearl. *Probabilistic Reasoning in Intelligent Systems: Networks of Plausible Inference*. Morgan Kaufmann Publishers Inc., 1988.

[34] J. Pearl and T. Verma. The Logic of Representing Dependencies by Directed Graphs. In *AAAI*, 1987.

[35] R. Ramakrishnan and J. Gehrke. *Database Management Systems*. McGraw-Hill, Inc., New York, NY, USA, 2003.

[36] C. Ré et al. Feature Engineering for Knowledge Base Construction. *Data Engineering Bulletin*, 2014.

[37] R. Ricci, E. Eide, and the CloudLab Team. Introducing CloudLab: Scientific Infrastructure for Advancing Cloud Architectures and Applications. *;login:*, 39(6), 2014.

[38] I. Rish et al. An Analysis of Data Characteristics that Affect Naive Bayes Performance. In *ICML*, 2001.

[39] A. I. Schein et al. Methods and Metrics for Cold-start Recommendations. In *SIGIR*, 2002.

[40] S. Shalev-Shwartz and S. Ben-David. *Understanding Machine Learning: From Theory to Algorithms*. Cambridge University Press, 2014.

[41] A. Silberschatz et al. *Database Systems Concepts*. McGraw-Hill, Inc., 2006.

[42] O. Uncu and I. Turksen. A Novel Feature Selection Approach: Combining Feature Wrappers and Filters. *Information Sciences*, 177(2), 2007.

[43] V. N. Vapnik. *The Nature of Statistical Learning Theory*. Springer-Verlag New York, Inc., 1995.

[44] S. K. M. Wong et al. A Method for Implementing a Probabilistic Model as a Relational Database. In *UAI*, 1995.

[45] L. Yu and H. Liu. Efficient Feature Selection via Analysis of Relevance and Redundancy. *JMLR*, 5, Dec. 2004.

[46] C. Zhang et al. Materialization Optimizations for Feature Selection Workloads. In *SIGMOD*, 2014.

[47] Y. Zhang et al. I/O-Efficient Statistical Computing with RIOT. In *ICDE*, 2010.

APPENDIX

A. ACKNOWLEDGMENTS

We thank David DeWitt, AnHai Doan, Robert McCann, and David Page for their feedback about this work. We thank Dan Olteanu for directing us to some of the datasets. We thank Pradap Konda and Wentao Wu for their feedback on an earlier version of this paper. This work is supported by a research grant from the Microsoft Jim Gray Systems Lab. All views expressed in this work are that of the authors and do not necessarily reflect any views of Microsoft.

B. EXTENDED BACKGROUND

DEFINITION B.1. Mutual information. *Given two random variables A and B with domains $\mathcal{D}_A$ and $\mathcal{D}_B$, their* mutual information *is $I(A;B) = H(B) - H(B|A)$, where $H(B)$ is the entropy of B. Thus, we have:*

$$I(A;B) = \sum_{a \in \mathcal{D}_A} \sum_{b \in \mathcal{D}_B} P(a,b) log \frac{P(a,b)}{P(a)P(b)}$$

DEFINITION B.2. Weak relevance. *A feature $F \in \boldsymbol{X}$ is* weakly relevant *iff $P(Y|\boldsymbol{X}) = P(Y|\boldsymbol{X} - \{F\})$ and $\exists \boldsymbol{Z} \subseteq \boldsymbol{X} - \{F\}$ s.t. $P(Y|\boldsymbol{Z}, F) \neq P(Y|\boldsymbol{Z})$.*

DEFINITION B.3. Markov blanket. *Given a feature $F \in \boldsymbol{X}$, let $\boldsymbol{M}_F \subseteq \boldsymbol{X} - \{F\}$; $\boldsymbol{M}_F$ is a* Markov Blanket *for F iff $P(Y, \boldsymbol{X} - \{F\} - \boldsymbol{M}_F | \boldsymbol{M}_F, F) = P(Y, \boldsymbol{X} - \{F\} - \boldsymbol{M}_F | \boldsymbol{M}_F)$.*

DEFINITION B.4. Redundant feature. *A feature $F \in \boldsymbol{X}$ is* redundant *iff it is* weakly relevant *and it has a* Markov blanket *in $\boldsymbol{X}$.*

C. PROOFS

PROPOSITION C.1. *In $\boldsymbol{T}$, all $F \in \boldsymbol{X}_R$ are redundant.*

PROOF. Consider an arbitrary feature $F \in \mathbf{X}_R$. We start by showing that F is weakly relevant. To show this, we need to prove that $P(Y|\mathbf{X}) = P(Y|\mathbf{X} - \{F\})$ and $\exists \mathbf{Z} \subseteq \mathbf{X} - \{F\}$ *s.t.* $P(Y|\mathbf{Z}, F) \neq P(Y|\mathbf{Z})$. For the first part, we observe that due to the FD $FK \rightarrow \mathbf{X}_R$, fixing FK automatically fixes $\mathbf{X}_R$ (and hence F). Thus, fixing $\mathbf{X}$ automatically fixes $\mathbf{X} - \{F\}$ and vice versa, which implies that $P(Y|\mathbf{X}) = P(Y|\mathbf{X} - \{F\})$. As for the second part, we only need to produce one instance. Choose $\mathbf{Z} = \phi$, which means we need to show that it is possible to have $P(Y|F) \neq P(Y)$. It is clearly trivial to produce an instance satisfying this inequality. Thus, F is weakly relevant. Next, we show that F has a Markov Blanket $\mathbf{M}_F \subseteq \mathbf{X} - \{F\}$. In fact, we have $\mathbf{M}_F = \{FK\}$. This is because the FD $FK \rightarrow \mathbf{X}_R$ causes F to be fixed when FK is fixed, which implies $\mathbf{M}_F \cup \{F\}$ is fixed when $\mathbf{M}_F$ is fixed and vice versa. Hence, $P(Y, \mathbf{X} - \{F\} - \mathbf{M}_F|\mathbf{M}_F, F) = P(Y, \mathbf{X} - \{F\} - \mathbf{M}_F|\mathbf{M}_F)$. Thus, overall, F is a redundant feature. Since F was arbitrary, all features in $\mathbf{X}_R$ are redundant. □

Next, we extend the previous result to a more general set of FDs. We start with a definition.

Definition C.1. *A set of FDs $\mathcal{Q}$ over $\boldsymbol{X}$ is* acyclic *iff the digraph on $\boldsymbol{X}$ created as follows is acyclic: include an edge from feature X_i to X_j if there is an FD in $\mathcal{Q}$ in which X_i is in the determinant set and X_j is in the dependent set.*

Corollary C.1. *Given a table $\boldsymbol{T}(\underline{ID}, Y, \boldsymbol{X})$ with a canonical acyclic set of FDs $\mathcal{Q}$ on the features $\boldsymbol{X}$, a feature that appears in the dependent set of an FD in $\mathcal{Q}$ is redundant.*

Proof. The proof is a direct extension of the proof for Theorem C.1, and we only present the line of reasoning here. We convert $\mathbf{T}$ into a relational schema in Boyce-Codd Normal Form (BCNF) using standard techniques that take $\mathcal{Q}$ as an input [41]. Since ID is the primary key of $\mathbf{T}$, both ID and Y will be present in the same table after the normalization (call it the "main table"). Now, features that occur on the right-hand side of an FD will occur in a separate table whose key will be the features on the left-hand side of that FD. And there will be a KFKD between a feature (or features) in the main table and the keys of the other tables in a manner similar to how FK refers to RID. Thus all features that occur on the right-hand side of an FD provide no more information than the features in the main table in the same way that $\mathbf{X}_R$ provides no more information than FK in Theorem C.1. Hence, any feature that occurs in the dependent set of an FD in $\mathcal{Q}$ is redundant. □

Theorem C.2. $\forall F \in \boldsymbol{X}_R, I(F;Y) \leq I(FK;Y)$

Proof. Let the FD $FK \rightarrow \mathbf{X}_R$ be represented by a collection of functions of the form $f_F : \mathcal{D}_{FK} \rightarrow \mathcal{D}_F$ for each $F \in \mathbf{X}_R$. Our goal is to show that $I(FK;Y) \geq I(F;Y), \forall F \in \mathbf{X}_R$.
Consider any $F \in \mathbf{X}_R$. We have the following:

$$I(F;Y) = \sum_{x,y} P(F = x, Y = y)\ log \frac{P(F = x, Y = y)}{P(F = x)P(Y = y)}$$

$$I(FK;Y) = \sum_{z,y} P(FK = z, Y = y)\ log \frac{P(FK = z, Y = y)}{P(FK = z)P(Y = y)}$$

Due to the FD $FK \rightarrow \mathbf{X}_R$, the following equalities hold:

$$P(F = x) = \sum_{z:f_F(z)=x} P(FK = z)$$

$$P(F = x, Y = y) = \sum_{z:f_F(z)=x} P(FK = z, Y = y)$$

Since, all the quantities involved are non-negative, we can apply the *log-sum inequality*, which is stated as follows.

Definition C.2. *Given non-negative numbers $a_1, \ldots, a_n$ and $b_1, \ldots, b_n$, with $a = \sum a_i$ and $b = \sum b_i$, the following inequality holds, and is known as the* log-sum inequality*:*

$$\sum_{i=1}^{n} a_i log(\frac{a_i}{b_i}) \geq alog(\frac{a}{b})$$

In our setting, fixing (x, y), we have $a = P(F = x, Y = y)$ and a_is are $P(FK = z, Y = y)$, for each $z : f_F(z) = x$. Similarly, $b = P(F = x)P(Y = y)$ and b_is are $P(FK = z)P(Y = y)$, for each $z : f_F(z) = x$. Thus, we have the following inequality:

$$\sum_{z:f_F(z)=x} P(FK = z, Y = y) log \frac{P(FK = z, Y = y)}{P(FK = z)P(Y = y)} \geq$$
$$P(F = x, Y = y) log \frac{P(F = x, Y = y)}{P(F = x)P(Y = y)}$$

Since this is true for all values of (x, y), summing all the inequalities gives us $I(FK;Y) \geq I(F;Y)$. □

Proposition C.2. *It is possible for a feature $F \in \boldsymbol{X}_R$ to have higher $IGR(F;Y)$ than $IGR(FK;Y)$.*

Proof. It is trivial to construct such an instance. Thus, we omit the proof here. □

Proposition C.3. $\mathcal{H}_{\mathbf{X}} = \mathcal{H}_{FK} \supseteq \mathcal{H}_{\mathbf{X}_R}$

Proof. Recall that we had assumed $\mathbf{X}_S = \phi$. Thus, $\mathbf{X} \equiv \{FK\} \cup \mathbf{X}_R$. We first prove the first part. By definition, given $\mathbf{Z} \subseteq \mathbf{X}$, we have: $\mathcal{H}_{\mathbf{Z}} = \{f | f \in \mathcal{H}_{\mathbf{X}} \wedge \forall \mathbf{u}, \mathbf{v} \in \mathcal{D}_{\mathbf{X}}, \mathbf{u}_{|\mathbf{Z}} = \mathbf{v}_{|\mathbf{Z}} \implies f(\mathbf{u}) = f(\mathbf{v})\}$. It is easy to see that the FD $FK \rightarrow \mathbf{X}_R$ automatically ensures that this condition is true for $\mathbf{Z} = \{FK\}$. This is because $\forall \mathbf{u}, \mathbf{v} \in \mathcal{D}_{\mathbf{X}}$ s.t. $\mathbf{u}_{|FK} = \mathbf{v}_{|FK}$, the FD implies $\mathbf{u}_{|\mathbf{X}_R} = \mathbf{v}_{|\mathbf{X}_R}$, which in turn implies $\mathbf{u} = \mathbf{v}$, and hence, $f(\mathbf{u}) = f(\mathbf{v})$. Thus, $\mathcal{H}_{\mathbf{X}} = \mathcal{H}_{FK}$.
As for the second part, we show that for any arbitrary $f \in \mathcal{H}_{\mathbf{X}_R}$, $\exists g_f \in \mathcal{H}_{FK}$ s.t. $f = g_f$. Note that an $f \in \mathcal{H}_{\mathbf{X}_R}$ satisfies the condition $\forall \mathbf{u}, \mathbf{v} \in \mathcal{D}_{\mathbf{X}}, \mathbf{u}_{|\mathbf{X}_R} = \mathbf{v}_{|\mathbf{X}_R} \implies f(\mathbf{u}) = f(\mathbf{v})$. Similarly, any $g \in \mathcal{H}_{FK}$ satisfies the condition $\forall \mathbf{u}, \mathbf{v} \in \mathcal{D}_{\mathbf{X}}, \mathbf{u}_{|FK} = \mathbf{v}_{|FK} \implies g(\mathbf{u}) = g(\mathbf{v})$. We now pick some $g_f \in \mathcal{H}_{FK}$ that also satisfies the following condition: $\forall \mathbf{u} \in \mathcal{D}_{\mathbf{X}}, g_f(\mathbf{u}) = f(\mathbf{u})$. Such a g_f necessarily exists because of three reasons: $\mathcal{H}_{\mathbf{X}_R}$ is defined based only on those values of $\mathbf{X}_R$ that are actually present in $\mathbf{R}$, the FD $FK \rightarrow \mathbf{X}_R$ ensures that there is at least one value of FK that maps to a given value of $\mathbf{X}_R$, and the same FD also ensures (by definition) that $\forall \mathbf{u}, \mathbf{v} \in \mathcal{D}_{\mathbf{X}}, \mathbf{u}_{|FK} = \mathbf{v}_{|FK} \implies \mathbf{u}_{|\mathbf{X}_R} = \mathbf{v}_{|\mathbf{X}_R}$. Thus, overall, $\mathcal{H}_{\mathbf{X}_R} \subseteq \mathcal{H}_{FK}$. Note that the equality arises when there is exactly one value of FK that maps to one value of $\mathbf{X}_R$ in $\mathbf{R}$, i.e., all tuples in $\mathbf{R}$ have distinct values of $\mathbf{X}_R$. □

D. MORE SIMULATION RESULTS

Figure 10 presents the remaining key plots for the simulation scenario in which the true distribution is succintly captured using a lone feature $X_r \in \mathbf{X}_R$. We also studied two other scenarios: one in which all of $\mathbf{X}_R$ and $\mathbf{X}_S$ are part of the true distribution, and another in which only $\mathbf{X}_S$ and

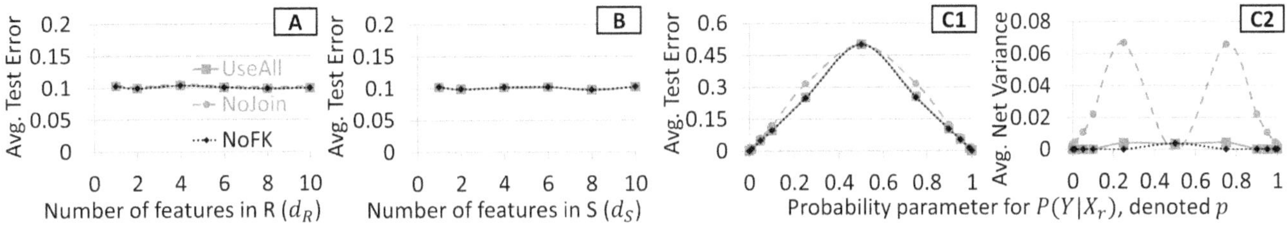

Figure 10: Remaining simulation results for the same scenario as Figure 3. (A) Vary d_R while fixing $(n_S, d_S, |\mathcal{D}_{FK}|, p) = (1000, 4, 100, 0.1)$. (B) Vary d_S while fixing $(n_S, d_R, |\mathcal{D}_{FK}|, p) = (1000, 4, 40, 0.1)$. (C) Vary p while fixing $(n_S, d_S, d_R, |\mathcal{D}_{FK}|) = (1000, 4, 4, 200)$.

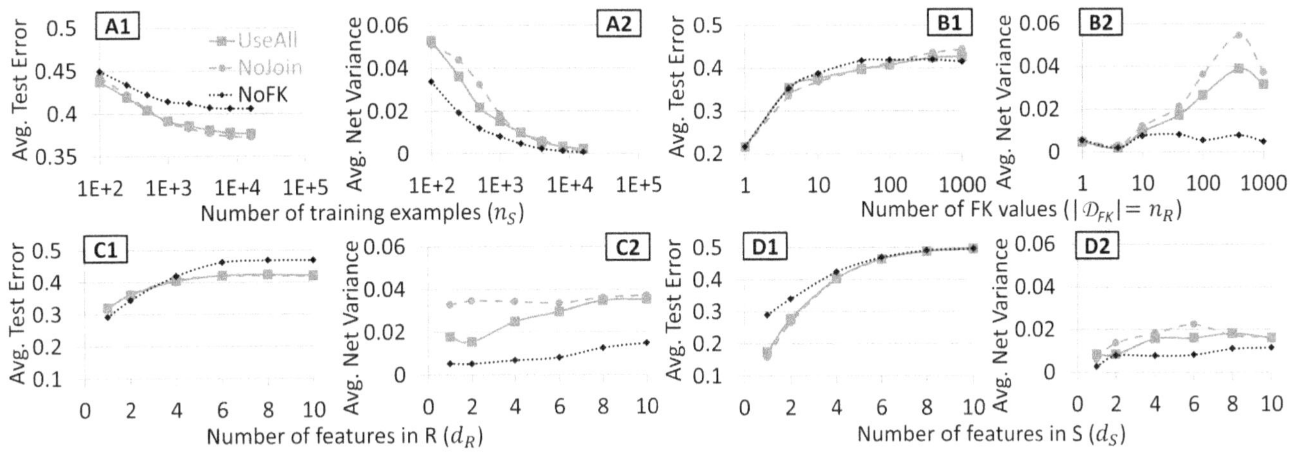

Figure 11: Simulation results for the scenario in which all of $\mathbf{X}_S$ and $\mathbf{X}_R$ are part of the true distribution. (A) Vary n_S while fixing $(d_S, d_R, |\mathcal{D}_{FK}|) = (4, 4, 40)$. (B) Vary $|\mathcal{D}_{FK}|$ while fixing $(n_S, d_S, d_R) = (1000, 4, 4)$. (C) Vary d_R while fixing $(n_S, d_S, |\mathcal{D}_{FK}|) = (1000, 4, 100)$. (D) Vary d_S while fixing $(n_S, d_R, |\mathcal{D}_{FK}|) = (1000, 4, 40)$.

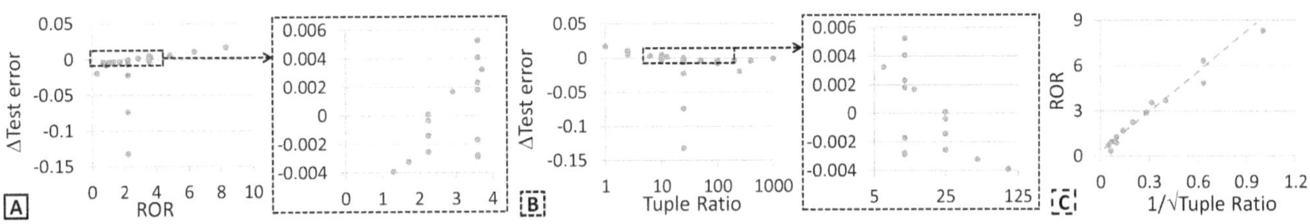

Figure 12: Scatter plots based on all the results of the simulation experiments referred to by Figure 11. (A) Increase in test error caused by avoiding the join (denoted "ΔTest error") against ROR. (B) ΔTest error against tuple ratio. (C) ROR against inverse square root of tuple ratio.

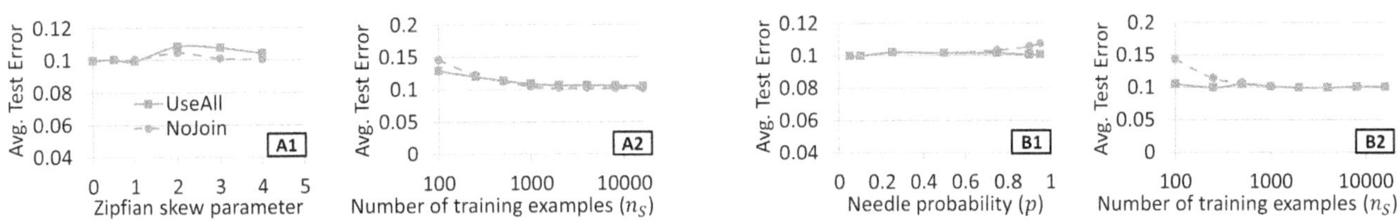

Figure 13: Effects of foreign key skew for the scenario referred to by Figure 3. (A) Benign skew: $P(FK)$ has a Zipfian distribution. We fix $(n_S, n_R, d_S, d_R) = (1000, 40, 4, 4)$, while for (A2), the Zipf skew parameter is set to 2. (B) Malign skew: $P(FK)$ has a needle-and-thread distribution. We fix $(n_S, n_R, d_S, d_R) = (1000, 40, 4, 4)$, while for (A2), the needle probability parameter is set to 0.5.

FK are. Figure 11 presents the plots for the former. Since the latter scenario in which $\mathbf{X}_R$ is useless did not reveal any interesting new insights, we skip it for brevity. We also plot the difference in test error between *NoJoin* and *JoinAll* for the scenario in which all of $\mathbf{X}_R$ and $\mathbf{X}_S$ are part of the true distribution in Figure 12. We see that the trends are largely similar to those in Figure 4 and that the same thresholds for ρ and τ work here as well.

Foreign Key Skew. So far, we had assumed that FK values are not skewed. Neither the ROR nor the TR account for skew in $P(FK)$. Foreign key skew is a classical problem in the database literature due to its effects on parallel joins [41] but its effects on ML have not been studied before. We now shed some light on the effects of skew in $P(FK)$ on ML.

We start by observing a key twist to the database-style understanding of skew: skew in $P(FK)$ *per se* is less important than its implications for learning the target. Thus, we classify skew in $P(FK)$ into two types: *benign* and *malign*. Loosely defined, benign skew in $P(FK)$ is that which does not make it much harder to learn the target, while malign skew is the opposite. We give some intuition using the scenario of a lone feature $X_r \in \mathbf{X}_R$ being part of the true distribution. Suppose $P(X_r)$ has no skew (the distribution is based on $\mathbf{T}$, not $\mathbf{R}$). Since multiple FK values might map to the same X_r value, there might still be high skew in $P(FK)$. But what really matters for accuracy is whether $P(Y)$ is skewed as well, and whether the skew in $P(Y)$ "colludes" with the skew in $P(FK)$.

There are three possible cases when there is skew in $P(FK)$: (1) $P(Y)$ is not skewed, (2) $P(Y)$ is skewed (some class label is dominant), and $P(FK)$ is skewed such that low-probability FK values co-occur mostly with high-probability Y values, and (3) $P(Y)$ is skewed, and $P(FK)$ is skewed such that low-probability FK values co-occur mostly with low-probability Y values. Cases (1) and (2) represent benign skew: even though some FK values have low probability, together they might still be able to learn the target concept reasonably well because there might be "enough" training examples for each class label. But case (3) is an instance of malign skew: essentially, FK "diffuses" the already low probability of some Y value(s) into a potentially large number of low-probability FK values. This issue might be less likely if X_r was used instead, i.e., the join was not avoided, since usually $|\mathcal{D}_{X_r}| \ll |\mathcal{D}_{FK}|$. Thus, malign skews in $P(FK)$ might make it less safe to avoid the join.

To verify the above, we performed two more simulation experiments. First, we embed a benign skew in FK using the standard Zipf distribution, which is often used in the database literature [32]. Second, we embed a malign skew in FK using what we call a "needle-and-thread" distribution: one FK value has a probability mass p ("needle" probability) and it is associated with one X_r value (and hence one Y value). The remaining $1-p$ probability mass is uniformly distributed over the remaining $(n_R - 1)$ FK values, all of which are associated with the other X_r value (and hence, the other Y value). Intuitively, this captures the extreme case (3) in which the skew in FK colludes with the skew in Y. Figure 13 presents the results for *UseAll* and *NoJoin*. As expected, the benign skew does not cause the test error of *NoJoin* to increase much, but the malign skew does. Figure 13(A) also suggests that benign skew might sometimes work in favor of *NoJoin* (this is primarily because the bias increased for *UseAll*). But as Figure 13(B1) shows, the test error of *NoJoin* increases when the skew in Y colludes with the skew in FK. However, as Figure 13(B2) shows, this gap closes as the number of training examples increases.

Overall, we need to account for malign skews in FK when using the ROR or TR rules for avoiding joins safely. While it is possible to detect malign skews using $H(FK|Y)$, we take a simpler, albeit more conservative, approach. We just check $H(Y)$, and if it is too low (say, below 0.5, which corresponds roughly to a 90%:10% split), we do not avoid the join. This is in line with our guiding principle of conservatism. It also captured all the cases of malign skews in our above simulations. We leave more complex approaches for handling skew to future work.

Symbol	Meaning
ϵ	Tolerance for safety with the ROR
δ	Failure probability for the VC-dim bound and the ROR
v_{Yes}	VC-dim of a (hypothetical) "best" classifier that avoids the join
v_{No}	VC-dim of a "best" classifier that does not avoid the join
q_S	$\sum_{F \in \mathbf{X}_S}(\lvert D_F \rvert - 1)$
q_R	Number of unique values of $\mathbf{X}_R$ in $\mathbf{R}$
q_{No}	$v_{No} - q_S$
q_R^*	$\min_{F \in \mathbf{X}_R} \lvert D_F \rvert$

Figure 14: Extra notation used in Section 4.2

E. OTHER ML MODELS: TAN

TAN strikes a balance between the efficiency of Naive Bayes and the expressive power of general Bayesian networks [15]. TAN searches for strong conditional dependencies among pairs of features in $\mathbf{X}$ given Y using mutual information to construct a tree of dependencies on $\mathbf{X}$. Surprisingly, TAN might actually be *less* accurate than Naive Bayes on datasets with the KFKDs we study because TAN might not even use $\mathbf{X}_R$. Intuitively, this is because the FD $FK \rightarrow \mathbf{X}_R$ causes all features in $\mathbf{X}_R$ to be dependent on FK in the tree computed by TAN. This leads to $\mathbf{X}_R$ participating only via unhelpful Kronecker delta distributions, viz., $P(\mathbf{X}_R|FK)$. Depending on how structure learning is done, general Bayesian networks could face this issue too. We leave techniques to solve this issue to future work.

F. OUTPUT FEATURE SETS

Due to space constraints, we only provide a summary here. We provide the detailed list of output feature sets in our technical report [28]. We omit Yelp and BookCrossing, since none of the joins were avoided by *JoinOpt* on those two datasets. On Walmart, the output of *JoinOpt* was identical to the respective output of *JoinAll* with forward selection and MI-based filter. On Expedia, the output of *JoinOpt* was identical to the respective output of *JoinAll* with forward selection, backward selection, and MI-based filter. On Flights, the output of *JoinOpt* was identical to the respective output of *JoinAll* with forward selection and MI-based filter. On MovieLens1M, the output of *JoinOpt* was identical to the output of *JoinAll* with MI-based filter. On LastFM, the output of *JoinOpt* was identical to the respective output of *JoinAll* with forward selection, MI-based filter, and IGR-based filter. In almost all the other cases, the outputs of *JoinOpt* and *JoinAll*, while different, differed only by a few features.

Real-time Video Recommendation Exploration

Yanxiang Huang[♯&§] Bin Cui[♯] Jie Jiang[§] Kunqian Hong[§] Wenyu Zhang[§] Yiran Xie[♯]
[♯]Key Lab of High Confidence Software Technologies (MOE), School of EECS, Peking University
[§]Tencent Inc.
[♯]{yx.huang, bin.cui, xie.yiran}@pku.edu.cn
[§]{zeus,kontenhong,gabyzhang}@tencent.com

ABSTRACT

Video recommendation has attracted growing attention in recent years. However, conventional techniques have limitations in real-time processing, accuracy or scalability for the large-scale video data. To address the deficiencies of current recommendation systems, we introduce some new techniques to provide real-time and accurate recommendations to users in the video recommendation system of Tencent Inc.. We develop a scalable online collaborative filtering algorithm based upon matrix factorization, with an adjustable updating strategy considering implicit feedback solution of different user actions. To select high-quality candidate videos for real-time top-N recommendation generation, we utilize additional factors like video type and time factor to compute similar videos. In addition, we propose the scalable implementation of our algorithm together with some optimizations to make the recommendations more efficient and accurate, including the demographic filtering and demographic training. To demonstrate the effectiveness and efficiency of our model, we conduct comprehensive experiments by collecting real data from Tencent Video. Furthermore, our video recommendation system is in production to provide recommendation services in Tencent Video, one of the largest video sites in China, and verifies its superiority in performance.

Keywords

Real-time; Video Recommendation; Big Data; Online Matrix Factorization; Real-time Collaborative Filtering

1. INTRODUCTION

The fast development of the Internet has changed everyone's daily life. People spend more and more time on the internet, such as shopping, ticket booking and other entertainment activities. Video sites provide large amounts of videos online, which attract many users with various purposes such as entertainment and news broadcasting. Millions of online videos are played over a billion times every day, by millions of users in YouTube [10], the world's most popular video site. In front of such a huge amount of data, navigating the information in an efficient and satisfying way becomes a hard task for normal users. Personalized recommendation systems are introduced to solve this problem by providing personalized service for every single user, and have been applied in many industrial fields in recent years [35, 34, 8]. As reported by Netflix [9], 75% of the content that people watch follows a recommendation. There is no doubt that video recommendation is of high demand in the era of information explosion. As one of the largest video sites in China, Tencent Video has more than 10 million daily active users and generates about one billion user actions every day. Some unique opportunities as well as challenges are presented for video recommendations in Tencent Video.

Generally, traditional video recommendation systems always produce relevant videos based on video content and user input profiles [33]. However, problems arise when it goes to unregistered users, since there are no profiles for them, while on the other hand unregistered users occupy a large proportion of the total video site users. People made a lot of attempts to improve the recommendation systems. For example, YouTube has introduced its video recommendation system in [10], which is based on user watch activities on the site. Although these works help a lot to improve the quality of recommendation services, they are far from perfect. First, most of the recommendation models are offline and the model training is carried out at regular time intervals. Second, most of the existing real-time recommendation models are too simple to generate satisfactory recommendations. Third, the lack of scalable models applicable to deal with the large amounts of noisy data seriously restrains the application of video recommendation service in the real world. Therefore, it still remains a challenging problem for a more practically efficient real-time video recommendation in the industrial community.

The real world conditions in the Tencent Video introduce multiple challenges for efficient real-time video recommendation. First of all, a large portion of the online users are not registered. It is also important to provide accurate recommendation services for these users. However, due to the lack of personal information of unregistered users, their profiles are unavailable. We need well-designed models and leverage multiple resources to improve the quality of recommendations. In the literature, collaborative filtering (CF) has achieved great success in recommendation systems [13]. One of CF's most successful techniques is matrix factorization (MF) [19], which assumes user preferences can be mod-

SIGMOD'16, June 26-July 01, 2016, San Francisco, CA, USA

DOI: http://dx.doi.org/10.1145/2882903.2903743

eled by only a small number of latent factors. MF based CF has become more popular since it's robust to the sparsity of the user-video collaborative matrix. However, due to the expensive cost to retrain the matrix factorization model, it is inapplicable to the fast changing trends in the presence of large scale data. Some online learning algorithms address this problem by keeping a representative sample of the data set in a reservoir to retrain the model [13], which however is not appropriate for large streaming data set. To avoid this problem, some other online algorithms propose to update the model based solely on the current observation [31], at the cost of reducing the quality of recommendations. What's more, the most convenient data for MF are high-quality explicit feedback. Unfortunately, the majority of the abundant data in the current online video systems, such as Tencent Video, are implicit feedback, which means that we can only guess users' preferences according to their behaviors. Implicit feedback raises additional challenges for efficient recommendation in Tencent Video. Last but not least, the high computational complexity of recommendation models as well as the massive data in Tencent Video lead to intensive calculations.

In this work, our goal for video recommendation is to provide real-time and accurate recommendation services for users in the condition of large data environment with large amounts of users and videos. Specifically, it demonstrates three requirements. First of all, the recommendation system needs to produce accurate recommendations for users. Second, the model should be updated in real-time to capture users' instant interests in very short delay (in seconds). Third, the processing need to be executed in parallel, i.e., scalable to handle large amounts of computations.

To fulfill the aforementioned goals, we propose a real-time top-N video recommendation system. We develop a real-time MF based CF algorithm, with an online updating strategy. Our online updating strategy takes the confidence levels of different implicit feedback data instances into consideration, where the learning rate in the training process is adjustable to each data instance. To produce top-N recommendations in real-time, we build similar video tables to select high-quality candidate videos for recommendation, which record the most relevant videos for each video. Besides the results of MF, we leverage other factors including video types and time factors to compute the similarity of videos. We present how to implement the model scalably on Storm [30], a distributed real-time computation system for processing streams of data. In addition, some optimization techniques in production are proposed, including demographic filtering and demographic training. We collect real data from Tencent Video to conduct experiments in order to discuss the effectiveness of our model, including the effectiveness of demographic training, and effectiveness of adjustable training. Our video recommendation system is in production at Tencent Video. By providing accurate real-time recommendation services for users, it demonstrates its superiority in performance.

In summary, this paper makes the following contributions:

- We develop a real-time MF based CF algorithm with an adjustable online updating strategy that takes the real-world implicit feedback into consideration.
- To generate top-N recommendations in real-time, we build similar video tables to select high-quality candidate recommended videos, where factors from different aspects are leveraged to compute relevant videos.
- We present some particular issues in production for our model, including scalable implementation, and two optimization techniques including demographic filtering and demographic training.
- We demonstrate the effectiveness of our model by conducting comprehensive experiments on real data and verify its superiority by deploying our recommendation system in production.

The rest of this paper is organized as follows. In Section 2, we review the related work. We present the real-time MF based CF algorithm in Section 3. Section 4 describes the procedure of real-time top-N recommendation generation where different factors are leveraged to compute relevant videos. Deployment issues along with some optimizations are discussed in Section 5. In Section 6, we investigate the effectiveness of our model and demonstrate its superiority in production. Finally, we conclude our work in Section 7.

2. RELATED WORK

There are two research fields closely related to our work, including video recommendation and online matrix factorization. Here we briefly review previous works on the corresponding literatures.

2.1 Video Recommendation

There exist many research works on video recommendation. In 2010, YouTube introduced its video recommendation system in [10], which recommends personalized sets of videos to users based on their activities on the site. In [37], the authors employed social and content information of videos, and proposed methods for video recommendation in sharing community, which fused the content relevance and social relevance to identify the relevant videos. To address the limitations of traditional Latent Factor Models and neighborhood-based collaborative filtering, Cui et al. [9] represented users with content attributes of videos, and represented videos with users' social attributes, so that both users and videos can be represented in a common space concatenated by social attributes and content attributes. In [11], the authors found candidate recommended videos by detecting the hot topics in Twitter, and generated final video recommendations by considering the user profile in YouTube, time factor, and quality factor. VecLp was proposed in [14], which recommends relevant Internet videos to the subscribers by collecting information from the live TV programs. In [23], the authors constructed user profiles as an aggregate of tag clouds and generated video recommendations according to similar view patterns. Mei at el. [33, 21] proposed video recommendation system based on multimodal fusion and relevance feedback. They combined features from three aspects including textual, visual, and aural to represent videos and expressed the relevance between two videos as the combination of relevance from three aspects. Chen et al. [5] provided personalized video suggestions for users on video search engines by exploring a tripartite graph over (user, video, query). They developed an iterative propagation scheme over the tripartite graph to compute the preference information of each user.

2.2 Real-time Collaborative Filtering

Recently, real-time collaborative filtering (CF) has attracted growing attention [27, 13, 36, 6]. Collaborative filtering can be divided into neighborhood-based CF and model-based CF. The neighborhood-based CF includes the user-based CF methods and the item-based CF methods, while the typical model-based CF is Latent Factor Models [19, 18] where matrix factorization (MF) techniques are usually used to solve the problem.

Real-time Neighborhood-based CF: StreamRec was proposed in [3] which implements a scalable item-based CF recommender model based on a stream processing system. In [15], the authors developed incremental and parallel versions of a co-clustering algorithm, and used it to build a real-time collaborative filtering framework, which predicts user-item ratings based on the average rating of co-clusters, users' bias and items' bias. To address the scalability problem of traditional user-based CF, Papagelis et al. [22] proposed a method to incrementally update user-to-user similarities by dividing the similarity computation into parts where each part could be computed incrementally. Similar strategies were used in [26], where the authors described a large scale implementation of a video recommendation system based on item-based CF, making use of a commercial cloud computing platform. A practical item-based CF was proposed in [17], with scalable incremental update mechanism considering several problems in real world production. However, it has been proven that model-based CF could achieve better performance than neighborhood-based CF in most cases [19]. Therefore, we focus on the matrix factorization method, one of CF's most successful techniques.

Real-time Model-based CF: Sarwar et al. [29] proposed an incremental singular value decomposition algorithm that could add new user or item vectors into the latent factor space utilizing the fold-in method. In [1], the authors proposed an online matrix factorization that could incorporate users' or items' properties. Ling et al. [20] developed an online learning framework consisting of probabilistic MF and ranking MF. In [27], an online regularized kernel MF model that can incrementally add new users or new items was proposed for large-scale recommender systems. Diaz et al. believed that recommendations based on pairwise ranking methodology could produce better results [13, 12]. In [12], to solve the short-term "memory" problem in online learning approaches, they proposed using the reservoir to sample the whole history data for training model. And in [13], they further developed a selective sampling strategy to perform online model updates based on active learning principles. Vinagre et al. [31] introduced a simple but fast incremental MF algorithm for positive-only feedback, which retrains the model at each new observation in a single step. In [32], the authors built a dynamic online MF model based on implicit user feedback stream, where whether a user was interested in an item or not was dependent on their adoption tendency.

3. ONLINE ADJUSTABLE MATRIX FACTORIZATION FOR IMPLICIT FEEDBACKS

In this section, we introduce our online adjustable matrix factorization for implicit feedbacks.

3.1 Basic Matrix Factorization

Collaborative filtering (CF) has achieved great success in recommendation systems. As one of CF's most successful techniques, matrix factorization (MF) [19] assumes user preferences can be modeled by only a small number of latent factors and tries to explain the observed user-item ratings by these factors inferred from the rating patterns. MF based CF has become popular because of its good scalability, good predictive accuracy, and robust to the sparsity of the user-video collaborative matrix. In addition, it offers much flexibility for modeling various real-life situations. So far, MF methods have proven to be generally superior to other alternatives.

Matrix Factorization models map both users and items to a joint latent factor space of dimensionality f, so that user-item interactions are modeled as inner products in that space. The goal of MF is to uncover the latent factors that can explain observed ratings. Specifically, each user u is associated with a vector $x_u \in \mathbb{R}^f$, and each item i is associated with a vector $y_i \in \mathbb{R}^f$. For a given item i, the elements of y_i measure the extent to which the item belongs to those factors. Similarly, for a given user u, the elements of x_u measure the extent of interest the user has in items that are high on the corresponding factors. We represent the user u's rating of item i as r_{ui}, which indicates the preference by user u of item i. Higher r_{ui} values mean stronger preference, and the goal of MF is to predict the unknown ratings. The prediction is done by taking an inner product, i.e., $\hat{r}_{ui} = x_u^T y_i$. The major challenge of MF is to compute the mapping of each user and item to factor vectors $x_u, y_i \in \mathbb{R}^f$. To learn the factor vectors (x_u and y_i), the training is performed by minimizing the regularized squared error on the set of known ratings:

$$\min_{x_*, y_*} \sum_{(u,i) \in D} (r_{ui} - x_u^T y_i)^2 + \lambda(\| x_u \|^2 + \| y_i \|^2) \quad (1)$$

where D is the set of user-item pairs for which r_{ui} is known, i.e., the training set, and λ is a parameter used to control the extent of regularization. The regularization term $\lambda(\| x_u \|^2 + \| y_i \|^2)$ is used to avoid overfitting, and the value of λ is data-dependent and usually determined by experiments.

Equation 1 tries to capture the interactions between users and items that produce the different rating values. However, much of the observed variation in rating values is independent of the interactions, yet is affected by the effects associated with either users or items, known as biases or intercepts. For example, some users tend to give higher ratings than others, and some items tend to receive higher ratings than others. Considering the biases effect, we extend the prediction of rating r_{ui} as follows:

$$\hat{r}_{ui} = \mu + b_u + b_i + x_u^T y_i \quad (2)$$

where μ denotes the overall average rating, and the parameters b_u and b_i indicate the observed deviations of user u and item i respectively, from the average. The observed rating is thus broken down into four components: global average, item bias, user bias, and user-item interaction. Then the objective function of the model for training, i.e., Equation 1 should be extended to:

$$\min_{x_*, y_*, b_*} \sum_{(u,i) \in D} (r_{ui} - \mu - b_u - b_i - x_u^T y_i)^2 + \lambda(\| x_u \|^2 + \| y_i \|^2 + b_u^2 + b_i^2) \quad (3)$$

The most successful methods to solve MF optimization

problem are Alternating Least Squares (ALS) [2] and Stochastic Gradient Descent (SGD) [1]. It has been shown [24] that SGD based optimization generally performs better than ALS when using sparse data, both in terms of model accuracy and running time efficiency. Given a training dataset consisting of tuples in the form <user, item, rating>, SGD performs several passes through the dataset until some stopping criteria is met, which is typically a convergence bound or a maximum number of iterations. At each iteration, SGD sweeps over all known ratings in the training set. For each rating, SGD updates the parameters by correcting them in the inverse direction of the gradient of error. The extent of correcting is determined by a factor of $\eta <= 1$, known as step size of the learning rate. Based on Equation 2, the associated prediction error of rating r_{ui} is computed as follows:

$$e_{ui} = r_{ui} - \mu - b_u - b_i - x_u^T y_i \tag{4}$$

The updating operations are performed as follows:

$$\begin{aligned} b_u &\leftarrow b_u + \eta(e_{ui} - \lambda b_u) \\ b_i &\leftarrow b_i + \eta(e_{ui} - \lambda b_i) \\ x_u &\leftarrow x_u + \eta(e_{ui} x_u - \lambda x_u) \\ y_i &\leftarrow y_i + \eta(e_{ui} y_i - \lambda y_i) \end{aligned} \tag{5}$$

3.2 Implicit Feedback Solution

We first introduce our solution to the implicit feedback problem, which to a large extent dictates our design of the online adjustable matrix factorization (MF) algorithm.

The most convenient data for matrix factorization are high-quality explicit feedback, i.e., explicit input by users regarding their interest in products, such as the star ratings, and thumbs-up or thumbs-down comments. However, explicit feedback is not always available in the practical situations. Actually, the majority of the abundant data are implicit feedback, i.e., user behaviors that indirectly reflect user opinions. Since we can only guess users' preferences according to the user behaviors, implicit feedback may reduce the recommender systems' performance if not appropriately handled [16].

There are various types of user behaviors in Tencent Video, including click, watch, comment, etc. The data that we have at our disposal is quite noisy since it measures a user's engagement and happiness indirectly. For example, the fact that a user watched a video in its entirety is not enough to conclude that he actually liked it, while a user may watch a favorite video for just a short period because of time limitation. Both the video length and the user engagement level influence the signal quality. Based on the intuition that different user actions represent different degrees of user's interests, we set proper weights to users' various action types. For example, a click behavior may correspond to a one star rating while a comment behavior equals a three star rating. The weights for various user actions are determined by experiences according to the real world condition in the application. Table 1 shows our settings in Tencent Video taking some action types as example. The *Impress* action represents video i is displayed to user u. And the *Play* action refers to that user u begins to watch a video i, while the *PlayTime* action reports the time period of video i viewed by user u.

[1]http://sifter.org/ simon/journal/20061211.html

Table 1: User Action Weight Settings

Actions	Impress	Click	Play	PlayTime
Weights	0	1	1.5	[1.5,2.5]

Specially, for users' *PlayTime* actions, we set their weights according to the percentile view time length, as follows:

$$w_{ui} = a + b\log(vrate_{ui}) \quad (a \geqslant b, 1 \geqslant vrate_{ui} \geqslant 0.1) \tag{6}$$

where $vrate_{ui} = t_{ui}/t_i$, t_{ui} is the user's viewing time and t_i denotes the full time length of the video.

We use view rate instead of user absolute viewing time to eliminate the variation on time length of videos of various types. To reduce the noise due to the various messy implicit feedback, we limit $rate_{ui} \geqslant 0.1$. In other words, we treat *PlayTime* actions with $vrate_{ui} < 0.1$ as inefficient ones that we set their weights the same as *Play* actions. Since we can hardly infer a user's real preference according to a stop watching action, it is unwise to generate a negative feedback, considering the diversity of recommendation. Actually, we have tested some alternatives such as $w_{ui} = a + b * vrate_{ui}$, and Equation 6 gave the best performance.

To train the MF model, we need r_{ui} values that indicate the preferences of user u for video i. For implicit feedback, a natural way is to treat the weights of user actions as the corresponding ratings, i.e., $r_{ui} = w_{ui}$, which is utilized in previous work [17]. However, although it works well in the item-based CF, there arise serious problems in the MF model, which we will illustrate in our experiments in Section 6.1.2. We attribute the poor performance to the noise raised by the inappropriate guess of implicit feedback, since MF is sensitive to the noisy data. Therefore, we turn to an alternative method. To be specific, we set r_{ui} to be binary variables, and denote the weight of user action w_{ui} as the confidence it measures, as inspired by the work in [16].

$$r_{ui} = \begin{cases} 1 & w_{ui} > 0 \\ 0 & w_{ui} = 0 \end{cases} \tag{7}$$

Simply speaking, a user u's interaction with video i ($w_{ui} > 0$) leads to an indication that u likes $i (r_{ui} = 1)$. On the other hand, if u never interacts with i, we believe no preference ($r_{ui} = 0$). Furthermore, our beliefs are associated with varying confidence levels, i.e., the user action weights w_{ui}, which will be utilized for the adjustable online updating strategy in the following section.

3.3 Adjustable Online Updating Strategy

As illustrated in Section 3.1, traditional matrix factorization (MF) is trained in a batch mode, which requires several passes or iterations through the dataset to train a model. As timeliness becomes more and more important in this rapidly changing world, traditional training method is not applicable for streaming data where ratings are continuously generated. Therefore, we propose a real-time MF algorithm with adjustable online updating strategy based on SGD.

First of all, our real-time video recommendation system requires a model that is able to capture users' recent activities and affect the recommendation results in real-time. To handle the huge amounts of streaming data where unbounded number of user actions increases, we need an incremental updating strategy that does not require iterations through the dataset. For the incremental updating strategy, each user action will be processed only once, and no iterations can ensure the model is converged. Actually, as the user actions are continuously generated at an unpredicted rate, the model will be updated all the time, thus is always not converged in terms of streaming data, which arises additional challenges for the real-time model training. Specially, the model in our streaming data condition should satisfy two requirements: able to produce satisfactory recommendations and always sensitive to new user actions. To be specific, first, the model needs to represent the attributes of users and videos to predict accurate preferences. Second, new user actions should have influence on the model in real-time, i.e., the model should quickly adapt to the new user actions, instead of staying the local optimal state of the historical data. These two requirements tend to conflict to some extent. To produce accurate recommendations at present, the model should adapt to current historical data, but this leads to its insensitivity to the new user actions, which may decrease its performance in the future. An efficient real-time MF model must take both aspects into consideration.

In this context, we propose an adjustable incremental SGD algorithm that can update the MF model in real-time to different extents for different user actions. We leverage the confidence levels of user actions in last section and reflect the difference of user actions in the updating strategy for incremental training. On one hand, for user actions with low confidence levels, which are more likely to be noise data, we decrease their influence on the model, to avoid overfitting the noise data or going to the wrong optimizing direction, thus sensitive to new user actions. On the other hand, the influence of user actions with high confidence levels is increased, which are more likely to represent users' true preferences, so that the model can represent attributes of users and videos, thus able to produce good performances. We employ the learning rate of the updating strategy to control the influence on the model, which is proportional to the confidence levels.

To be specific, we update the model at each new user action in a single step, no iterations required. For each user action, its influence on the model is dependent on both its rating and confidence level. We update the model only when the rating $r_{ui} = 1$, i.e., the impression records of users (video i is displayed to user u, $r_{ui} = 0$) do not have influence on the model. For user actions with $r_{ui} = 1$, the higher the confidence w_{ui}, the more influence on the model training procedure, i.e., a larger learning rate. Specifically, we update the model for different user actions according to their confidence levels, as follows:

$$\eta_{ui} = \eta_0 + \alpha w_{ui} \tag{8}$$

where η_0 is the basic learning rate of the training process, and α is a parameter to control the influence of confidence level on learning rate, which is determined by experiments.

The updating algorithm is shown in Algorithm 1. Since we use streaming data set in our scenario and user rating actions are generated at unpredicted rate, we just show the updating strategy for one user rating action for simplicity. For each user rating action, we first compute its preference and confidence, r_{ui} and w_{ui}. Providing the preference is positive ($r_{ui} = 1$), we will update the model according to the confidence level of the user rating action by Equation 8. Every user action will affect the model in real-time, and influence the recommendation results immediately. For new users or new items, we first initialize their vectors before the updating operation. We employ a distributed memory-based key-value storage to store the x_u and y_i vectors, as we will illustrate in Section 5.1. Thus new users and items can be easily added.

Algorithm 1: Real-time Matrix Factorization Model Update based on SGD

Input: user rating action tuple recording user u, video i and action information

Compute r_{ui} and w_{ui}
if $r_{ui} = 1$ **then**
  if u *is new* **then**
    Initialize x_u
  end
  if i *is new* **then**
    Initialize y_i
  end
  Compute η_{ui} by Equation 8
  Compute e_{ui} by Equation 4
  $b_u \leftarrow b_u + \eta_{ui}(e_{ui} - \lambda b_u)$
  $b_i \leftarrow b_i + \eta_{ui}(e_{ui} - \lambda b_i)$
  $x_u \leftarrow x_u + \eta_{ui}(e_{ui} x_u - \lambda x_u)$
  $y_i \leftarrow y_i + \eta_{ui}(e_{ui} y_i - \lambda y_i)$
end

4. REAL-TIME VIDEO RECOMMENDATION GENERATION

In this section, we introduce the procedure from receiving user recommendation request to generating real-time video recommendation in our recommendation system. Moreover, strategies to generate high-quality candidate videos are described.

4.1 Recommendation Request Processing

The goal of our recommendation system is to provide personalized recommendations that help users find high-quality videos consistent with their interests. In order to improve the degree of users' satisfaction, it is imperative that these recommendations are provided in real-time and reflect users' recent activities on the site. This requirement prevents us from generating recommendations by pre-computation that is adopted in many works, because pre-computed recommendations cannot reflect users' recent activities. Instead, we compute new recommendations for users in real-time for each user request.

The procedure from receiving user recommendation request to generating real-time video recommendation is shown in Figure 1, where real-time denotes that the delay is generally in mill-seconds. A typical situation where the recommendation happens is that when a user opens a video to watch, we need to produce similar videos as recommendations. After receiving the user recommendation request, we first get several seed videos and then expand the set of their relevant videos to select some candidates. Afterwards, we get the user & video vectors computed by MF model, and predict the preference of the user for these candidate videos according to Equation 2. Final recommendations are generated by ranking these candidate videos according to the predicted preferences. Specifically, example seed videos may be the video user currently watching in the aforementioned situation or historical videos a user interacted with (watched, liked) before in other scenarios where the user is not watching any videos. In addition, a distributed key-value storage is utilized to store the results of the MF model or user historical data, which we will illustrate in detail in Section 5.1.

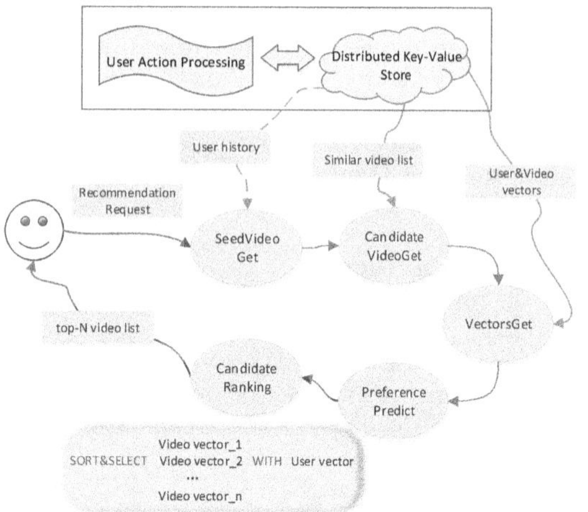

Figure 1: Procedure of Real-time Video Recommendation Generation

Note that we select some candidate videos to generate final recommendations by further ranking. The candidate videos selection is vital in real-time recommendation generation, since the computation through the whole video set is too expensive and time-costly to respond to users in real-time. Considering the dimension of user or video vector always ranges from 20 to 200, the preference prediction that takes the inner product of vectors is definitely a computing intensive task. In a large video site like Tencent Video, the whole video set contains millions of videos, and there are more than 1 billion user requests every day, with maximum 0.1 million requests in one second. The huge computation in real-time video recommendation generation will be a disaster without the candidate videos selection.

4.2 Candidate Video Preparation

From the discussion in above section, we can conclude the key of real-time video recommendation generation is the candidate videos selection. As illustrated previously, candidates are generated by expanding the set of relevant videos of seed videos. Therefore, to select candidate videos of high quality, we need an accurate mapping from a video i to a set of similar or relevant videos. In this context, we define similar videos as those that a user is likely to watch after having watched the given seed video i. To obtain the accurate similar videos, we combine the following three factors, collaborative filtering similarity, type similarity, and time factor.

4.2.1 Collaborative Filtering Similarity

Based on the matrix factorization model computed in Section 3, we can get a vector of latent factors $y_i \in \mathbb{R}^f$ for each video i. Considering the indication of these vectors, we can naturally compute the similarity between video i and j by taking an inner product, as follows:

$$s1_{ij} = y_i^T y_j \tag{9}$$

4.2.2 Type Similarity

In Tencent Video, every video has its type in a fine-grained category system. It is widely shared that same type videos are likely to be more similar than different types. Thus we take videos' types into consideration when computing similar videos. For video i and j, the type similarity is defined as follows:

$$s2_{ij} = \begin{cases} 1 & type(i)\ equals\ type(j) \\ 0 & type(i)\ not\ equals\ type(j) \end{cases} \tag{10}$$

4.2.3 Time Factor

To track the real-time changing trends in video recommendation, we add time factor into videos' similarity computation. We hold the view that the similarity between video pairs is time-sensitive and will descend as time goes on without new relevant user actions support. In other words, the past similar videos should be gradually forgotten. Therefore, we introduce time factor in the computation of similarity.

To be specific, the similarity of video pairs decreases as their update time goes far away from the current time. The update time refers to the time of the latest user action that touches off the similarity computation (similarity of video i and j will be updated only when new user action relating to i or j happens). Formally, we use a damping factor to measure this time factor, as follows:

$$d_{ij} = 2^{-\Delta t/\xi} \tag{11}$$

where Δt is the time difference between sim_{ij}'s(defined in the following section) update time and current time, and ξ is a parameter to control the rate of decay.

4.2.4 Fusion

In our context, each aforementioned similarity factor contributes to the final recommendation to different extent. We perform the relevance fusion by taking the advantage of each similarity factor. Given two videos i and j, the overall relevance between them is defined as:

$$sim_{ij} = d_{ij}((1-\beta) * s1_{ij} + \beta * s2_{ij}) \tag{12}$$

where β is a parameter adjusting the weight of different similarity factors in the final relevance function. The exact values of ξ and β are determined by the experiments.

5. DEPLOYMENT ISSUES

In this section, we present some deployment issues, including how to implement the model scalably to accomplish huge computations evolving large amounts of streaming data, and several optimization techniques in production, including demographic filtering and demographic training.

5.1 Scalable Implementation

We implemented the algorithm based on Storm [30, 7], a real-time stream data processing system. The primary concept in Storm is stream, which represents an unbounded sequence of data tuples. Storm provides "spouts" and "bolts" as the basic operations to conduct stream processing. A spout is responsible for producing the input streams, and passing the data to bolts. A bolt may consume any number of input streams and transform those streams in some way. Bolts can also emit new streams and pass them to some other bolts. Each spout or bolt can be executed in parallel, whose parallelism can be set by configuration. Complex stream processing may require a graph of multiple spouts or bolts where the edges indicate how the streams should be passed around. The graph is called a "topology", which is what we submit to Storm for real-time computation. A topology will process messages forever unless it is killed.

The topology framework of our real-time incremental matrix factorization based collaborative filtering is shown in Figure 2. The parallelism of different spout or bolts is determined by the data set. The grouping mode (denoted by "*value*" after colon in the figure) defines how to distribute the stream data to different workers of a spout or bolt. For example, in Figure 2, the spout emits data tuples in the form of $< user, video, action >$ and the $UserHistory$ bolt receives these data tuples that data tuples with the same user id will go to the same worker to be processed. In addition, we employ a distributed memory-based key-value storage (KVStore in the figure) to store the status data used in computations. We can access a vector x_u or y_i by its corresponding key (the user id or video id), without influencing other vectors. In this case, the KVStore helps distribute the computations among operators.

Specifically, the spout gets data from Tencent Video, parses the raw message, filters the unqualified data tuples, and transforms data tuples to the next bolts. The data tuples spout generated contains several fields, such as user id, video id, action type, action result, etc. For clear presentation, we just show the main fields of data tuples in the figure. The user action tuples are grouping by user id field, and flow to the next bolts. There are three main lines to process the user action tuples in parallel. First, the $ComputeMF$ bolt and $MFStorage$ bolt receive the user action tuples and update the vectors (x_us and y_is) in KVStore according to Algorithm 1. Second, the $UserHistory$ bolt receives the user action tuples and records users' behavior histories in KVStore. Third, the $GetItemPairs$ bolt, $ItemPairSim$ bolt and $ResultStorage$ bolt receive the user action tuples, do the video pair similarity computation utilizing user histories recorded by $UserHistory$ bolt, and finally store a top-N similar video list for each video in KVStore.

Note that the model updating is done by $ComputeMF$ and $MFStorage$ two bolts. First, the user action tuples are transferred to $ComputeMF$ bolt. $ComputeMF$ bolt reads user vectors and video vectors from KVStore and computes new vectors as in Algorithm 1. Then the new vectors will be sent to $MFStorage$ bolt, grouping by their corresponding keys used in KVStore storage. $MFStorage$ bolt receives the new vectors and writes them to KVStore. The key factor in this implementation design is the reassignment of new vectors from $ComputeMF$ bolt to $MFStorage$ bolt, grouping by their keys, which guarantees only a single worker node should operate over a specific video or user vector at some point. Using this method, the updating of vectors is atomic that no write conflict would happen. Thus the calculation can be safely scaled.

Video pair similarity computation is done by three bolts, including the $GetItemPairs$ bolt, $ItemPairSim$ bolt and $ResultStorage$ bolt. Different from model updating, the goal of this design is to reduce resource consumption and speed up computing. To be specific, by transferring the data streams with fields grouping, the queries of the same key for KVStore can be reduced to the same workers and thus we can employ optimizations for efficient processing. Some possible optimizations may be the *combiner* technique and the *cache* technique [17].

5.2 Some Optimizations

In this section, we introduce some useful optimizations in the production.

5.2.1 Demographic Filtering

One of the recommendation metrics is diversity and novelty. YouTube [10] expands the candidate video set by taking a limited transitive closure over the related videos graph to generate more diverse and novel recommendations. However, the number of candidate videos needed to be computed when generating recommendations is increased consequently. As a result, it will cost a longer time to produce recommendations, which may cause a recommendation delay to users, while long waiting time will decrease users' satisfaction. Therefore, in Tencent Video, we utilize another technique called the demographic based algorithm (DB) [25] to complement the recommendation results of matrix factorization (MF) based collaborative filtering (CF).

We first cluster users into different demographic groups according to their properties such as gender, age and education. Users in the same demographic group generally share similar interests or preferences. We compute the hot videos for each demographic group, i.e., the most popular videos. DB provides these hot videos as recommendations for a user based on his demographic group. By selectively merging the results of DB algorithm into the results of MF based CF algorithm, we broaden the span of recommendations and provide chances for users to discover new interests.

Demographic filtering has additional benefits. For new users or those users especially inactive who have little interaction with videos, the MF algorithm cannot produce enough efficient recommendations. In this case, we can rely on the demographic group information to better understand these users. Utilizing the results of DB algorithm, we can provide recommendation services for these users, so that the new user problem is partly solved. Specially, for new unregistered users, we generate the hot videos of global demographic group as recommendations, which was proven to work well in practice.

5.2.2 Demographic Training

Another optimization we utilized is demographic training, i.e., we run the recommendation algorithm within the aforementioned demographic user groups. To be specific, there will be a video vector y_i for each demographic group, and the similarity between video pairs is computed within the demographic group.

The demographic training gives two benefits. On one hand, the user-video matrix of a demographic group is obviously less sparse than the global user-video matrix, as illustrated in [17]. We will get a more accurate model by running the recommendation algorithm within the demographic user groups. On the other hand, a more fine-grained model will be generated by demographic training, which can capture the variation of rating patterns between different demographic groups.

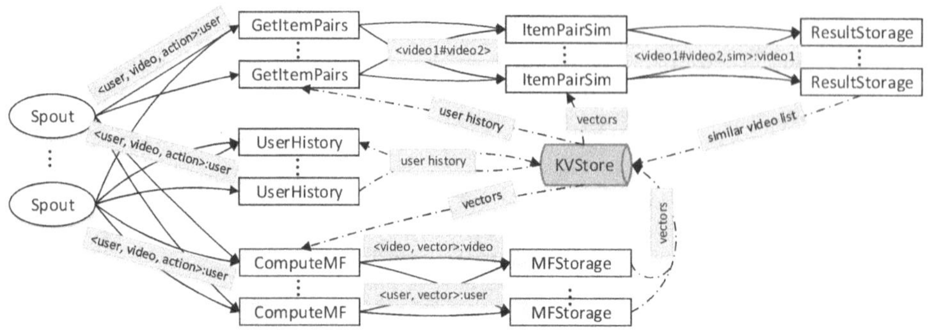

Figure 2: Topology Framework of the Recommendation System

6. EXPERIMENTAL STUDY

Our video recommendation system is now deployed to provide recommendation services for Tencent Video, one of the largest video sites in China. The Storm cluster used to deploy is composed of 100 computers equipped with a four-core processor and 32 GB memory. Every day, it deals with billions of user action tuples, with data size of more than 1 TB. Nevertheless, it can provide accurate real-time video recommendations steadily, handling millions of user requests every day, with latency of milliseconds.

In this section, we discuss the effectiveness of our model by conducting comprehensive experiments on real data collecting from Tencent Video, and demonstrate its superior performance in production.

Parameters Setting: Parameters used in our model are determined by using grid search to obtain the optimal values, as shown in Table 2.

Table 2: Parameter Settings

	f	λ	a	b	η_0	α	β	ξ
Values	70	0.02	2.5	1	0.00001	1	0.02	10

6.1 Offline Experiments

To discuss our model in detail, we collect data from Tencent Video, and conduct experiments to compare the effect of the factors in model, including the effectiveness of demographic training and the effectiveness of adjustable updating strategy. We first briefly introduce the experimental settings for the evaluation, including dataset, and evaluation criterion.

Data Sets: We collect data from Tencent Video in one week, and reserve users who have more than 50 actions and videos with more than 50 related actions. We take the data of first six days as training data set and the last day as test data set. Statistics of the dataset after cleaning are shown in Table 3.

Table 3: DataSet Statistics

	Users	Videos	Actions	Test Actions
Counts	846928	18198	74503804	13838594

Evaluation Criterion: We use two evaluation metrics to measure and compare the performance of various models.

Traditionally, collaborative filtering algorithms are evaluated by the accuracy of their predicted ratings. One commonly used performance metric for rating accuracy is the Mean Absolute Error (MAE). However, we are interested in measuring the top-N recommendation performance instead of rating prediction. Furthermore, the reliable feedback regarding how much users like the videos, i.e., the true ratings, is not available. Thus the MAE measure is not appropriate in our condition. Instead of MAE, we measure the quality of recommendation models by looking at the *recall* metric, also known as hit rate, which is widely used for evaluating top-N recommendation systems.

The *recall* metric is defined as follows:

$$recall = \frac{\sum_{u \in U_{test}} \sum_{i_u} \ell(i_u \in \text{top-N}_u)/N}{|U_{test}|} \tag{13}$$

where i_u indicates that video i is liked by user u in test data and $\ell(z)$ is an indicator function that returns 1 if condition z holds, and 0 otherwise. A larger recall value indicates that the system is able to recommend more satisfactory videos, leading to a better performance.

Another evaluation metric we used is average rank. We denote $rank_{ui}$ as the percentile-ranking of video i within the ordered list of all videos recommended for user u, and $rank^t_{ui}$ as the percentile-ranking of video i within the ordered interested video list of user u in test data. Here, the ordered interested video list of user u is ranked by the corresponding user actions' confidence levels in testing data. This way, $rank_{ui} = 0\%$ means that video i is predicted to be the most desirable for user u while $rank_{ui} = 100\%$ indicates that video i is not recommended to user u, as the same case for $rank^t_{ui}$s. We choose to use percentile-ranks rather than absolute ratings in order to make our comparison general and independent of the number of recommended videos, at the same time provide a more objective measure for implicit feedback. The average rank measure is then defined as the average percentile ranking of recommended videos, which is:

$$\overline{rank} = \frac{\sum_{u,i} rank^t_{ui}(1 - rank_{ui})}{\sum_{u,i}(1 - rank_{ui})} \tag{14}$$

where $1 - rank_{ui}$ measures the relative rating predicted by the model. For videos not recommended, $rank_{ui} = 1$, thus $1 - rank_{ui} = 0$. **Lower values** of $\overline{rank}$ is more desirable, indicating the recommended videos have an average lower rank in testing data, i.e., they lay closer to the top of actually watched video list.

6.1.1 *Effectiveness of Demographic Training*

In this section, we compare the models using demographic training and global training. Users in Tencent Video are clustered into dozens of groups, among which we select three largest demographic groups to do the comparison.

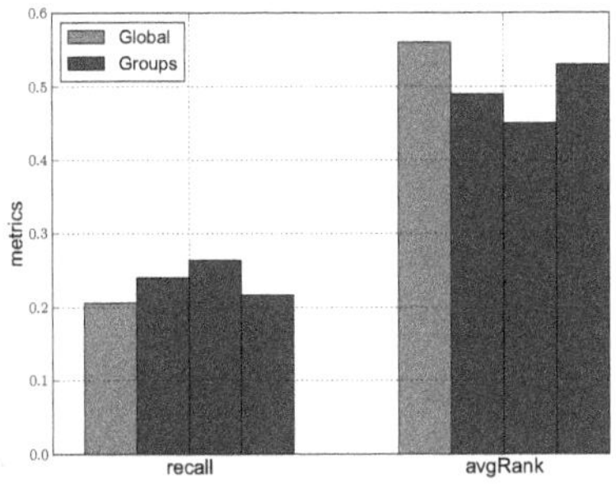

Figure 3: Comparison of Global vs Groups

The performance of global-model and group-models is shown in Figure 3, where the *recall* metric is shown by real numbers instead of percentage to make the values of $\overline{rank}$ (avgRank in the figure) and *recall* metric can be shown in the picture in an elegant way. From the figure, we can see that the *recalls* of group-models are higher than the global-model while the values of $\overline{rank}$ are lower than global-model, which suggests the performance of group-models is steadily superior to the global-model. The average improvement is more than 10%, while the maximum improvement is about 20%.

To explain the improvement of performance, we first show their statistics of training dataset in Table 4. The sparsity is defined by $\frac{\#Actions}{\#Users*\#Videos}$, which measures the quality of user-video matrix. Compared with the global dataset in Table 3 whose sparsity is 0.48%, the sparsity of dataset is greatly reduced within the demographic groups whose average sparsity is 1.45%. This is vital for the effectiveness of demographic training. Another reason why the group-models perform better should give the credit to the more fine-grained model generated by demographic training, which can capture the variation of rating patterns between different demographic groups.

Table 4: DataSet Statistics of Groups

	#Users	#Videos	#Actions	Sparsity(%)
Group1	166923	6594	14990035	1.36
Group2	152936	7161	13102179	1.20
Group3	95106	5010	8480328	1.78

6.1.2 *Effectiveness of Adjustable Updating Strategy*

In this section, we evaluate the effectiveness of our online adjustable updating strategy by comparing some alternative models.

First of all, we describe the alternative models as comparative methods.

- BinaryModel: This model uses the binary ratings but ignores the confidence levels of user actions, thus the learning rate is stable for all user action tuples.
- ConfModel: This model takes the confidence levels as ratings, and the learning rate is stable for all user action tuples.
- CombineModel: This model uses the binary ratings to train model and takes advantage of confidence levels of user actions to perform an adjustable updating, which is our ultimate recommendation model.

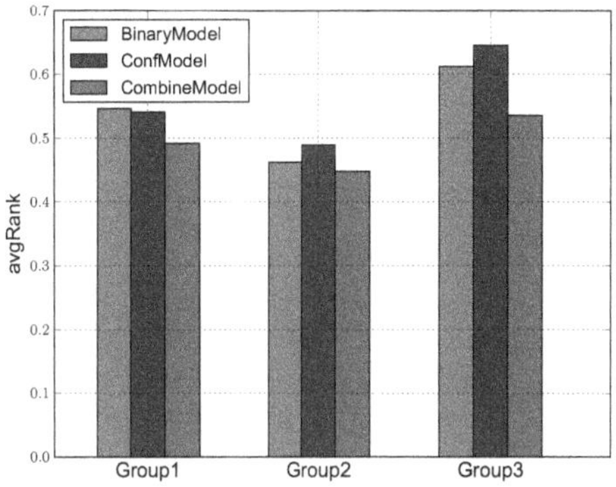

Figure 5: $\overline{rank}$ Comparison of Alternative Models

The performance of these models is shown in Figure 4 taking *recall@N* as metric, where N ranges from 1 to 10. We compare their performance in the three demographic groups. According to the figure, *CombineModel* steadily performs better than the other two models, with an average improvement about 10%. Specifically, we arrive at the following two observations. First, the *BinaryModel* performs slightly better than *ConfModel* in most cases but not all. The reason why *ConfModel* doesn't improve results is that it is sensitive to the settings in Table 1, which may raise noise due to inappropriate guess of implicit feedback. This verifies our statement in Section 3.2: if not appropriately handled, implicit feedback may reduce the performance of recommender systems, which is consistent with the results in [16]. Second, as we can see from the figure, *CombineModel* has a much desirable performance than *BinaryModel*. This demonstrates the benefits of our adjustable training strategy. What's more, because we take advantage of the information of different user actions to measure the confidence levels of binary ratings, *CombineModel* is more robust to the noisy data than *ConfModel*. As a result, *CombineModel*'s performance is much better than *ConfModel*.

Figure 5 compares alternative models' performances taking $\overline{rank}$ as metric. As expected, our *CombineModel* has a significant superior performance with $\overline{rank}$ metric as well, and the performance of *BinaryModel* is slightly better than *ConfModel*, as the same cases in Figure 4. As we can see, the values of $\overline{rank}$ metric of these models are around 0.5, indicating that the recommended videos rank in the middle of users' interested video list in average, which contributes to a considerable video recommendation list. Please note that the value of $\overline{rank}$ is not 0.5 for random model, since the total number of videos is much larger than the length of video recommendation list.

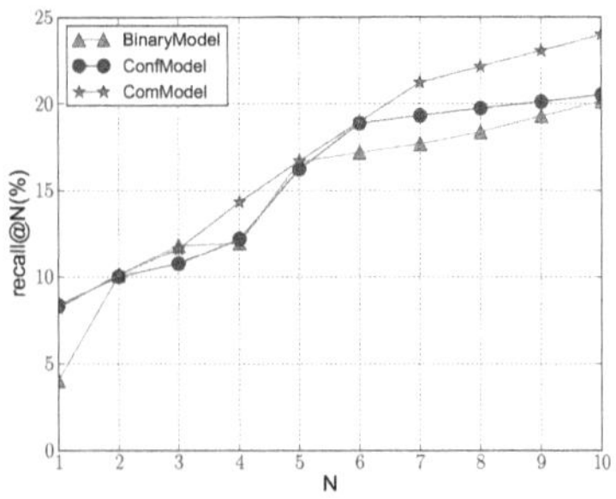

(a) *recall@N* of Group1

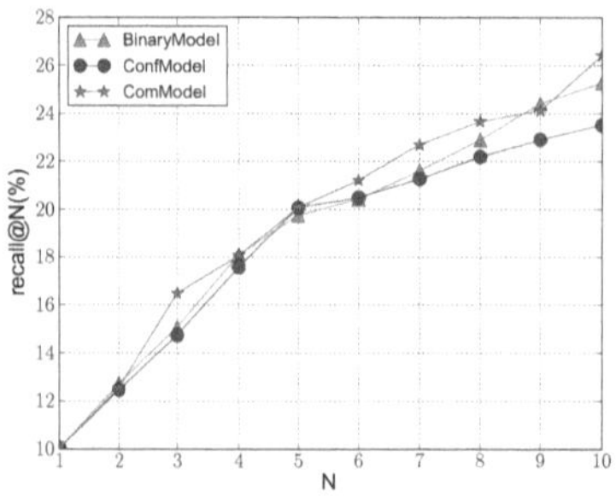

(b) *recall@N* of Group2

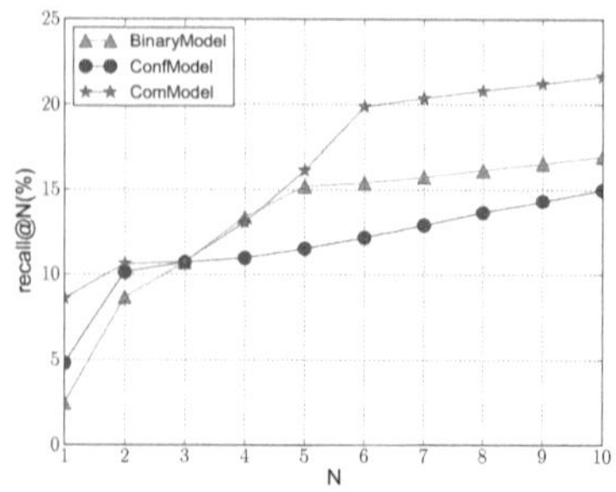

(c) *recall@N* of Group3

Figure 4: *recall@N* Comparison of Alternative Models

6.2 Online Testing

In this section, we show the practical performance of our recommendation system deployed in Tencent Video. The recommendation happens in two scenarios, as shown in Figure 6. The recommendations in Figure 6(b) are occurred when a user is watching a video, where we recommend similar videos of the current watching one. In the other scenario shown in Figure 6(a) where users open the site and have not watched any video yet, we first get the user history from KVStore, and then get the relevant videos of videos user liked before. Finally, video recommendations are generated by predicting user's preference for these videos utilizing the user vector and video vectors.

(a) Guess You Like Scenario

(b) Related Videos Scenario

Figure 6: Recommendation Scenarios

Comparative Methods: We compare our recommendation model with three competing methods that are used to produce video recommendations currently, as follows.

- *Hot* method recommends the most popular videos to users, a simple but powerful method, where the computation is in real-time.
- *AR* method represents the association rule based algorithm [28] whose model is trained in batch mode for every day.
- *SimHash* method denotes the user-based CF algorithm utilizing the SimHash technique [4], which is also offline that the model is trained at regular intervals.
- *rMF* method refers to our real-time MF recommendation algorithm.

Evaluation Metric: To evaluate the video recommendation quality, we use click through rate (CTR) as the metric for online testing since it is objective and can be quickly computed.

Experimental Setup: We use live evaluation via A/B testing [10] as the main method for evaluating the performance of the recommendation system. To be specific, live traffic is diverted into distinct groups among which one group acts as baseline and others are exposed to other comparative recommendation models. These groups then can be compared against one another. This approach allows that evaluation takes place in the context of the actual site UI. We do the A/B testing for the comparative methods over a period of ten days and recording their CTRs for comparison.

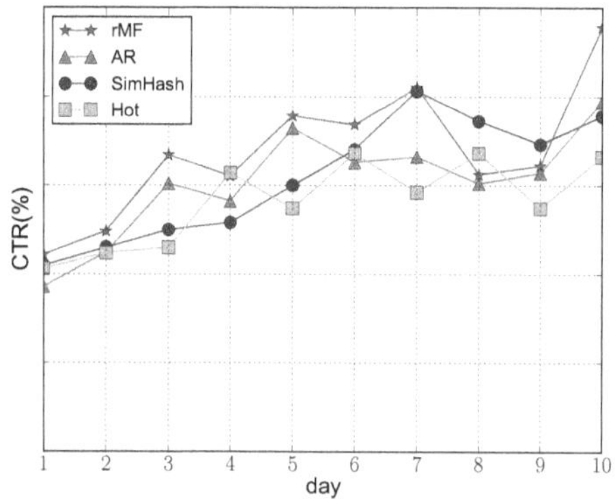

Figure 7: CTR Comparison in Online Testing

Figure 7 shows the performances of the alternative methods taking CTR as metric. We eliminate the specific values of CTR in the figure due to the proprietary concerns. Still, we can conclude according to the figure that *rMF* performs better than other competing methods in most cases. The

Table 5: Performance Improvement Comparison

Day	1	2	3	4	5	6	7	8	9	10	**Average**
rMF vs AR (%)	13.23	7.73	7.68	7.49	2.88	9.83	17.83	2.08	1.94	17.06	**8.82**
rMF vs SimHash (%)	3.81	5.29	23.89	14.80	19.36	6.12	0.68	-12.72	-5.52	20.69	**7.04**
rMF vs Hot (%)	5.24	7.46	31.19	-0.80	27.91	7.20	30.40	-5.78	12.87	33.41	**14.72**

performance of *Hot* method is worst among these methods, while the *AR* and *SimHash* have similar performances, and are better than *Hot* method. To better clarify the comparison, we show the performance improvement for different methods comparison in Table 5. From the table we can see that *rMF* has an average performance improvement of 8.82% and 7.04% comparing to *AR* and *SimHash* methods respectively. Compared to the *Hot* method, *rMF* performs more superior with an average improvement of 14.72%. Therefore, it is clearly verified that our recommendation system is effective in providing real-time accurate recommendation service. Note that, such improvement is already very valuable in real business applications. In addition, although *rMF* has a better performance in most cases, there exist some cases where it performs slightly poor. Actually, all the competing methods have both good cases and bad cases where their performances are excellent or poor, as the user behaviors may be affected by real-world events and are not fully predictable. For example, a user may have different preferences in different situations, depending upon his mood or with whom he's watching the video. The good and bad cases indicate that each method has its advantages and disadvantages, so that it may be better to combine results from different methods in an efficient way.

7. CONCLUSION AND FUTURE WORK

In this paper, we proposed a real-time top-N video recommendation system. First, we developed a real-time MF based CF algorithm, with an online updating strategy proposed. Our online updating strategy took the confidence levels of different implicit feedback data instances into consideration, and the learning rate of the training process is adjustable to each data instance. Second, we introduced the procedure of real-time video recommendation generation. To produce accurate video recommendations in real-time, we built similar video tables to select high-quality candidate videos for recommendation, recording the most relevant videos for each video. We leveraged factors from three aspects to compute the similarity of videos, including the matrix factorization similarity, the type similarity and the time factor. Third, we presented how to implement the model scalably on Storm, a distributed real-time computation system for processing streams of data. In addition, some optimization techniques in production were proposed, including demographic filtering and demographic training. At last, we conducted comprehensive experiments to evaluate our model, including offline experiments and online testing. In offline experiments, we collected real data from Tencent Video and conducted experiences to discuss the effect of factors in our model, including the effectiveness of demographic training, and effectiveness of adjustable training. Our video recommendation system was in production at Tencent Video and dealt with billions of user action tuples everyday, with data size of more than 1 TB. We show its superior performance in production in the online testing experiments.

There are a series of future works we can do for real-time video recommendations. First, we only utilized the videos' type information to measure the content features of videos in this work. There are still some other useful information can be employed, such as the videos' directors and actors. Second, there still remains much improving space for enhancing the diversity and novelty of video recommendations. A possible improvement may be a better methodology for combining results from different algorithms to leverage benefits of different methods.

8. ACKNOWLEDGMENTS

This work is supported by the National Natural Science Foundation of China under Grant No. 61272155 and 61572039, 973 program under No. 2014CB340405, Beijing Natural Science Foundation (4152023), Shenzhen Gov Research Project JCYJ20151014093505032, and Tecent Research Grant (PKU).

We thank all the Tencent Recommender Platform Team members for their contributions to this paper. Many thanks to Yu Xiang, Yong Wei, Qiaoxiong Lin, and Ruhai Luo for their kind suggestions and support.

9. REFERENCES

[1] J. Abernethy, K. Canini, J. Langford, and A. Simma. Online collaborative filtering. *University of California at Berkeley, Tech. Rep*, 2007.

[2] R. M. Bell and Y. Koren. Scalable collaborative filtering with jointly derived neighborhood interpolation weights. In *Proc of the 2007 7th IEEE ICDM Conference*, pages 43–52. IEEE, 2007.

[3] B. Chandramouli, J. J. Levandoski, A. Eldawy, and M. F. Mokbel. Streamrec: A real-time recommender system. In *Proc of the 2011 ACM SIGMOD Conference*, pages 1243–1246, 2011.

[4] M. S. Charikar. Similarity estimation techniques from rounding algorithms. In *Proc of the 34th ACM STOC Conference*, pages 380–388. ACM, 2002.

[5] B. Chen, J. Wang, Q. Huang, and T. Mei. Personalized video recommendation through tripartite graph propagation. In *Proc of the 20th ACM ICMM Conference*, pages 1133–1136. ACM, 2012.

[6] C. Chen, H. Yin, J. Yao, and B. Cui. Terec: A temporal recommender system over tweet stream. *Proc. VLDB Endow.*, 6(12):1254–1257, Aug. 2013.

[7] B. Cui, J. Jiang, Q. Huang, Y. Xu, Y. Gui, and W. Zhang. Pos: A high-level system to simplify real-time stream application development on storm. *Data Science and Engineering*, pages 1–10, 2015.

[8] B. Cui, H. Mei, and B. C. Ooi. Big data: the driver for innovation in databases. *National Science Review*, 1(1):27–30, 2014.

[9] P. Cui, Z. Wang, and Z. Su. What videos are similar with you?: Learning a common attributed

representation for video recommendation. In *Proc of the 2014 ACM ICMM*, pages 597–606. ACM, 2014.
[10] J. Davidson, B. Liebald, J. Liu, P. Nandy, T. Van Vleet, U. Gargi, S. Gupta, Y. He, M. Lambert, B. Livingston, et al. The youtube video recommendation system. In *Proc of the 4th ACM RecSys Conference*, pages 293–296. ACM, 2010.
[11] Z. Deng, M. Yan, J. Sang, and C. Xu. Twitter is faster: Personalized time-aware video recommendation from twitter to youtube. *ACM Transactions on Multimedia Computing, Communications, and Applications (TOMM)*, 11(2):31, 2015.
[12] E. Diaz-Aviles, L. Drumond, Z. Gantner, L. Schmidt-Thieme, and W. Nejdl. What is happening right now... that interests me?: online topic discovery and recommendation in twitter. In *Proc of the 21st ACM CIKM Conference*, pages 1592–1596. ACM, 2012.
[13] E. Diaz-Aviles, L. Drumond, L. Schmidt-Thieme, and W. Nejdl. Real-time top-n recommendation in social streams. In *Proc of the 6th ACM RecSys Conference*, pages 59–66, 2012.
[14] S. Gao, D. Zhang, H. Zhang, C. Huang, Y. Zhang, J. Liao, and J. Guo. Veclp: A realtime video recommendation system for live tv programs. In *Proc of the 29th AAAI Conference*, 2015.
[15] T. George and S. Merugu. A scalable collaborative filtering framework based on co-clustering. In *Proc of the 5th IEEE ICDM Conference*, pages 4–pp. IEEE, 2005.
[16] Y. Hu, Y. Koren, and C. Volinsky. Collaborative filtering for implicit feedback datasets. In *Proc of the 2008 8th IEEE ICDM Conference*, pages 263–272, 2008.
[17] Y. Huang, B. Cui, W. Zhang, J. Jiang, and Y. Xu. Tencentrec: Real-time stream recommendation in practice. In *Proc of the 2015 ACM SIGMOD Conference*, pages 227–238. ACM, 2015.
[18] Y. Koren. Factorization meets the neighborhood: a multifaceted collaborative filtering model. In *Proc of the 14th ACM SIGKDD Conference*, pages 426–434. ACM, 2008.
[19] Y. Koren, R. Bell, and C. Volinsky. Matrix factorization techniques for recommender systems. *Computer*, (8):30–37, 2009.
[20] G. Ling, H. Yang, I. King, and M. R. Lyu. Online learning for collaborative filtering. In *Proc of the 2012 IEEE IJCNN Conference*, pages 1–8. IEEE, 2012.
[21] T. Mei, B. Yang, X.-S. Hua, and S. Li. Contextual video recommendation by multimodal relevance and user feedback. *ACM Transactions on Information Systems (TOIS)*, 29(2):10, 2011.
[22] M. Papagelis, I. Rousidis, D. Plexousakis, and E. Theoharopoulos. Incremental collaborative filtering for highly-scalable recommendation algorithms. In *Foundations of Intelligent Systems*, pages 553–561. Springer, 2005.
[23] J. Park, S.-J. Lee, S.-J. Lee, K. Kim, B.-S. Chung, and Y.-K. Lee. Online video recommendation through tag-cloud aggregation. *IEEE MultiMedia*, 1(18):78–87, 2011.
[24] A. Paterek. Improving regularized singular value decomposition for collaborative filtering. In *Proc of 2007 KDD cup and workshop*, volume 2007, pages 5–8, 2007.
[25] M. J. Pazzani. A framework for collaborative, content-based and demographic filtering. *Artif. Intell. Rev.*, 13(5-6):393–408, Dec. 1999.
[26] R. Pereira, H. Lopes, K. Breitman, V. Mundim, and W. Peixoto. Cloud based real-time collaborative filtering for item–item recommendations. *Computers in Industry*, 65(2):279–290, 2014.
[27] S. Rendle and L. Schmidt-Thieme. Online-updating regularized kernel matrix factorization models for large-scale recommender systems. In *Proc of the 2008 ACM RecSys Conference*, pages 251–258, 2008.
[28] J. J. Sandvig, B. Mobasher, and R. Burke. Robustness of collaborative recommendation based on association rule mining. In *Proc of the 2007 ACM RecSys Conference*, pages 105–112, 2007.
[29] B. Sarwar, G. Karypis, J. Konstan, and J. Riedl. Incremental singular value decomposition algorithms for highly scalable recommender systems. In *Proc of the 5th IEEE ICIS Conference*, pages 27–28. IEEE, 2002.
[30] A. Toshniwal, S. Taneja, A. Shukla, K. Ramasamy, J. M. Patel, S. Kulkarni, J. Jackson, K. Gade, M. Fu, J. Donham, et al. Storm@ twitter. In *Proc of the 2014 ACM SIGMOD Conference*, pages 147–156. ACM, 2014.
[31] J. Vinagre, A. M. Jorge, and J. Gama. Fast incremental matrix factorization for recommendation with positive-only feedback. In *User Modeling, Adaptation, and Personalization*, pages 459–470. Springer, 2014.
[32] Z. Wang, Q. Li, Y. Liu, W. Liu, and J. Yin. Online personalized recommendation based on streaming implicit user feedback. In *Web Technologies and Applications*, pages 720–731. Springer, 2015.
[33] B. Yang, T. Mei, X.-S. Hua, L. Yang, S.-Q. Yang, and M. Li. Online video recommendation based on multimodal fusion and relevance feedback. In *Proc of the 6th ACM CIVR Conference*, pages 73–80. ACM, 2007.
[34] H. Yin, B. Cui, L. Chen, Z. Hu, and Z. Huang. A temporal context-aware model for user behavior modeling in social media systems. In *Proc of the 2014 ACM SIGMOD Conference*, pages 1543–1554, 2014.
[35] H. Yin, B. Cui, Y. Sun, Z. Hu, and L. Chen. Lcars: A spatial item recommender system. *ACM Trans. Inf. Syst.*, 32(3):11:1–11:37, July 2014.
[36] L. Yu, Y. Shao, and B. Cui. Exploiting matrix dependency for efficient distributed matrix computation. In *Proc of the 2015 ACM SIGMOD Conference*, pages 93–105. ACM, 2015.
[37] X. Zhou, L. Chen, Y. Zhang, L. Cao, G. Huang, and C. Wang. Online video recommendation in sharing community. In *Proc of the 2015 ACM SIGMOD Conference*, pages 1645–1656. ACM, 2015.

Towards Globally Optimal Crowdsourcing Quality Management: The Uniform Worker Setting

Akash Das Sarma
Stanford University
akashds@cs.stanford.edu

Aditya Parameswaran
University of Illinois (UIUC)
adityagp@illinois.edu

Jennifer Widom
Stanford University
widom@cs.stanford.edu

ABSTRACT

We study *crowdsourcing quality management*, that is, given worker responses to a set of tasks, our goal is to jointly estimate the true answers for the tasks, as well as the quality of the workers. Prior work on this problem relies primarily on applying Expectation-Maximization (EM) on the underlying maximum likelihood problem to estimate true answers as well as worker quality. Unfortunately, EM only provides a locally optimal solution rather than a globally optimal one. Other solutions to the problem (that do not leverage EM) fail to provide global optimality guarantees as well.

In this paper, we focus on filtering, where tasks require the evaluation of a yes/no predicate, and rating, where tasks elicit integer scores from a finite domain. We design algorithms for finding the global optimal estimates of correct task answers and worker quality for the underlying maximum likelihood problem, and characterize the complexity of these algorithms. Our algorithms conceptually consider all mappings from tasks to true answers (typically a very large number), leveraging two key ideas to reduce, by several orders of magnitude, the number of mappings under consideration, while preserving optimality. We also demonstrate that these algorithms often find more accurate estimates than EM-based algorithms. This paper makes an important contribution towards understanding the inherent complexity of globally optimal crowdsourcing quality management.

1. INTRODUCTION

Crowdsourcing enables data scientists to collect human-labeled data at scale for machine learning algorithms, including those involving image, video, or text analysis. However, since human workers often make mistakes while answering these tasks, *crowdsourcing quality management*, i.e., jointly estimating human worker quality as well as answer quality—the probability of different answers for the tasks—is essential. While knowing the answer quality helps us with the set of tasks at hand, knowing the quality of workers helps us estimate the true answers for future tasks.

We focus on *rating tasks*, i.e., tasks where the answer is one from a fixed set of ratings $\in \{1, 2, \ldots, R\}$. This includes, as a special case, *filtering tasks*, where the ratings are binary, i.e., $\{0, 1\}$. Consider the following example: say a data scientist intends to design a sentiment analysis algorithm for tweets. To train such an algorithm, she needs a training dataset of tweets, rated on sentiment. Each tweet needs to be rated on a scale of $\{1, 2, 3\}$, where 1 is negative, 2 is neutral, and 3 is positive. A natural way to do this is to display each tweet, or item, to human workers hired via a crowdsourcing marketplace like Amazon's Mechanical Turk, and have workers rate each item on sentiment from 1—3. Since workers may answer these rating tasks incorrectly, we may have multiple workers rate each item. Our goal is then to jointly estimate sentiment of each tweet and the accuracy of the workers.

Standard techniques for solving this estimation problem typically involve the use of the Expectation-Maximization (EM). Applications of EM, however, provide no theoretical guarantees. Furthermore, as we will show in this paper, EM-based algorithms are highly dependent on initialization parameters and can often get stuck in undesirable local optima. Other techniques for quality assurance, some specific to only filtering [5, 8, 12], are not provably optimal either, in that they only give bounds on the errors of their estimates, and do not provide globally optimal quality estimates. We cover this and other related work in detail in the next section.

In this paper, we present a technique for globally optimal quality management, that is, finding the maximum likelihood item (tweet) ratings, and worker quality estimates. A straightforward technique for globally optimal quality management is to simply consider all possible mappings from items to ratings, and for each mapping, infer its overall likelihood. (It can be shown that the best worker error rates are easy to determine once the mapping is fixed.) The mapping with the highest likelihood is then the global optimum.

However, even in this simple example, if we have 500 tweets and 3 possible ratings, the total number of mappings from tweets to ratings is 3^{500}, an exceedingly large number. Therefore, this straightforward technique is infeasible.

Key Insights. *To reduce this exponential complexity, we use two simple ideas to greatly prune the set of mappings that need to be considered, from* 3^{500}*, to a much more manageable number.*

Let us assume that workers are indistinguishable, and they all have the same quality (which is unknown). It is well-understood that at least on Mechanical Turk, the worker pool is constantly in flux, and it is often hard to find workers who have attempted enough tasks in order to get robust estimates of worker quality. (Our techniques also apply to a generalization of this case.)

Suppose we have 3 ratings for each tweet—a common strategy in crowdsourcing is to get a small, fixed number of answers for each question. First, we hash "similar" tweets that receive the same set of worker ratings into a common bucket. As shown in Figure 1, suppose that 300 items each receive three ratings of 3 *(positive), 100 items each receive one rating of 1, one rating of 2 and one*

SIGMOD'16, June 26-July 01, 2016, San Francisco, CA, USA

DOI: http://dx.doi.org/10.1145/2882903.2882953

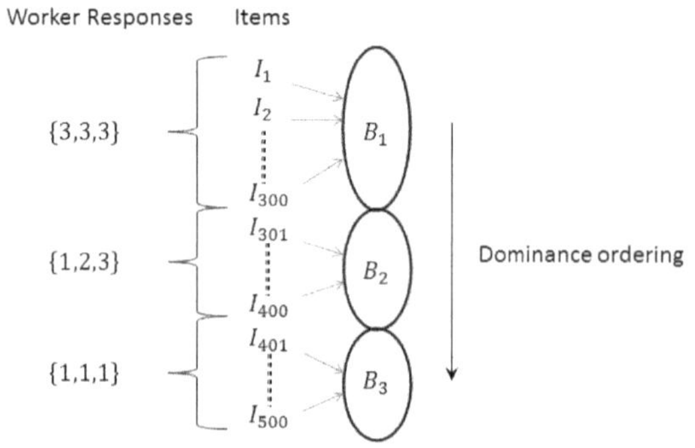

Figure 1: Mapping Example

rating of 3, and 100 items each receive three ratings of 1. *That is, we have three buckets of items, corresponding to the worker answer sets* $B_1 = \{3,3,3\}$, $B_2 = \{1,2,3\}$, *and* $B_3 = \{1,1,1\}$. *We now exploit the intuition that if two items receive the same set of worker responses they should be treated identically. We therefore only consider mappings that assign the same rating to all items (tweets) within a bucket. Now, since in our example, we only have 3 buckets each of which can be assigned a rating of 1,2, or 3, we are left with just* $3^3 = 27$ *mappings to consider.*

Next, we impose a partial ordering on the set of buckets based on our belief that items in certain buckets should receive a higher final rating than items in other buckets. Our intuition is simple: if an item received "higher" worker ratings than another item, then its final assigned rating should be higher as well. In this example, our partial ordering, or dominance ordering *on the buckets is* $B_1 \geq B_2 \geq B_3$, *that is, intuitively items which received all three worker ratings of* 3 *should not have a true rating smaller than items in the second or third buckets where items receive lower ratings. This means that we can further reduce our space of* 27 *remaining mappings by removing all those mappings that do not respect this partial ordering. The number of such remaining mappings is 10, corresponding to when all items in the buckets* (B_1, B_2, B_3) *are mapped respectively to ratings* $(3,3,3)$, $(3,3,2)$, $(3,3,1)$, $(3,2,2)$, $(3,2,1)$, $(3,1,1)$, $(2,2,2)$, $(2,2,1)$, $(2,1,1)$, *and* $(1,1,1)$.

In this paper, we formally show that restricting the mappings in this way does not take away from the optimality of the solution; i.e., there exists a mapping with the highest likelihood that obeys the property that all items with same scores are mapped to the same rating, and at the same time obeys the dominance ordering relationship described above.

We primarily focus on the setting where workers independently draw their responses from a common error distribution. That said, we do propose generalizations to the worker model in Appendix B, for instance, when workers are known to come from a small number of distinct classes with separate error distributions. In either case, one concern may be that these assumptions may be too restrictive, relative to the vast body of related work on the topic (Section 1.1). However, we still believe a thorough study of this setting is useful, for three reasons:

- To the best of our knowledge, no related papers provide global optimality guarantees (even for restricted settings), so it is of independent theoretical interest.
- It is common for practitioners to not track individual worker identities, but simply assume them to come from a generic pool, especially given the transient nature of crowdsourcing marketplaces, in which case our setting applies directly.
- Lastly, and most importantly, we find that even when the datasets violate our assumptions (that is, workers have distinct error rates), there are a variety of settings where our algorithms have higher accuracy than EM-based algorithms that take individual worker error rates into account. In fact, these settings correspond precisely to the real-world marketplace scenario where workers are fleeting and have limited attention spans.

Thus, our primary contributions are as follows:

- [Theoretical Insights] We develop an intuitive algorithm based on *simple, but key insights* that finds a provably optimal maximum likelihood solution to the problem of jointly estimating true item labels and worker error behavior for crowdsourced filtering and rating tasks. Our approach involves reducing the space of potential ground truth mappings while preserving optimality, *enabling an exhaustive search on an otherwise prohibitive domain.* Our work represents a significant *first step towards understanding the nature and complexity of exact globally optimal solutions* for the joint estimation problem.
- [Experimental Insights] We perform experiments to evaluate the performance of our algorithm on a variety of different metrics. Though we optimize for likelihood, we show that our algorithm also does well on other metrics such as the accuracy of predicted item labels and worker response distributions, and latency. We also test our algorithm in settings where certain worker model assumptions (uniformity of worker error rate) do not necessarily hold. We show that despite a competitive disadvantage in such settings, our algorithm still performs comparably to state-of-the-art EM-based algorithms, while having the advantage of simplicity and ease of implementation over them.

1.1 Related Literature

Crowdsourcing is gaining importance as a platform for a variety of different applications where automated machine learning techniques don't always perform well, *e.g.*, filtering [15] or labeling [17, 19, 26] of text, images, or video, and entity resolution [1, 24, 25, 27]. One crucial problem in crowdsourced applications is that of worker quality: since human workers often make mistakes, it is important to model and characterize their behavior in order to aggregate high-quality answers.

EM-based joint estimation techniques. We study the particular problem of jointly estimating hidden values (item ratings) and a related latent set of parameters (worker error rates) given a set of observed data (worker responses). A standard machine learning technique for estimating parameters with unobserved latent variables is Expectation Maximization [9]. There has been significant work in using EM-based techniques to estimate true item values and worker error rates, such as [7, 22, 28], and subsequent modifications using Bayesian techniques [3, 14]. In [18], the authors use a supervised learning approach to learn a classifier and the ground truth labels simultaneously. In general, these machine learning based techniques only provide probabilistic guarantees and cannot ensure optimality of the estimates. We solve the problem of finding a global, provably maximum likelihood solution for both the item values and the worker error rates. That said, our worker error model is simpler than the models considered in these papers—in particular, we do not consider worker identities or difficulties of individual items. However, we study this simpler model in more depth, providing optimality guarantees. Since our work represents the first providing optimality guarantees (even for a restricted setting), it represents an important step forward in our understanding of crowdsourcing quality management. Additionally, anecdotally, even the simpler model is commonly used for platforms like Mechanical Turk, where the workers are fleeting.

Furthermore, we experimentally test our algorithm on the general setting where worker identities are available. Although our algorithm is at a natural disadvantage due to its assumption of identical workers, we find that it compares well against EM-based heuristics that use the available worker-specific information.

Other techniques with no guarantees. There has been some work that adapts techniques different from EM to solve the problem of worker quality estimation. For instance, Chen et al. [4] adopts approximate Markov Decision Processes to perform simultaneous worker quality estimation and budget allocation. Liu et al. [13] uses variational inference for worker quality management on filtering tasks (in our case, our techniques apply to both filtering and rating). Venanzi et al. [23] uses a Bayesian Classifier Combination model and probabilistic inference to determine different classes of worker quality. Like EM-based techniques, these papers do not provide any theoretical guarantees.

Weaker guarantees. There has been a lot of recent work on providing partial probabilistic guarantees or asymptotic guarantees on accuracies of answers or worker estimates, for various problem settings and assumptions, and using various techniques. We first describe the problem settings adopted by these papers, then their solution techniques, and then describe their partial guarantees.

The most general problem setting adopted by these papers is identical to us (i.e., rating tasks with arbitrary bipartite graphs connecting workers and tasks) [29]; most papers focus only on filtering [5, 8, 12], or operate only when the graph is assumed to be randomly generated [11, 12]. Furthermore, most of these papers assume that the false positive and false negative rates are the same.

The papers draw from various techniques, including just spectral methods [5, 8], just message passing [12], a combination of spectral methods and message passing [11], or a combination of spectral methods and EM [29].

In terms of guarantees, most of the papers provide probabilistic bounds [5, 11, 12, 29], while some only provide asymptotic bounds [8]. For example, Dalvi et al. [5], which represents the most recent in a line of papers [8, 11, 12], show that under certain assumptions about the graph structure (depending on the eigenvalues) the error in their estimates of worker quality is lower than some quantity with probability greater than $1 - \delta$.

Thus, overall, all the work discussed so far provides probabilistic guarantees on their item value predictions, and error bound guarantees on their estimated worker qualities. In contrast, we consider the problem of finding a global maximum likelihood estimate for the correct answers to tasks and the worker error rates.

Other related papers. Joglekar et al. [10] consider the problem of finding confidence bounds on worker error rates. Our paper is complementary to theirs; while they solve the problem of obtaining confidence bounds on the worker error rates, we consider the problem of finding the maximum likelihood estimates to the item ground truth and worker error rates.

Zhou et al. [30, 31] use minimax entropy to perform worker quality estimation as well as inherent item difficulty estimation; here the inherent item difficulty is represented as a vector. Their technique only applies when the number of workers attempting each task is very large; here, overfitting (given the large number of hidden parameters) is no longer a concern. For cases where the number of workers attempting each task is in the order of 50 or 100 (highly unrealistic in practical applications), the authors demonstrate that the scheme outperforms vanilla EM.

Summary. In summary, at the highest level, our work differs from previous works in its focus on finding a globally optimal solution to the maximum likelihood problem. We focus on a simpler setting, but do so in more depth, representing significant progress in our understanding of global optimality. Our globally optimal solution uses simple and intuitive insights to reduce the search space of possible ground truths, enabling exhaustive evaluation. Our general framework leaves room for further study and has the potential for more sophisticated algorithms that build on our reduced space.

2. PRELIMINARIES

We start by introducing some notation, and then describe the general problem that we study in this paper; specific variants will be considered in subsequent sections.

Items and Rating Questions. We let $\mathbf{I}$ be a set of $|\mathbf{I}| = n$ items. Items could be, for example, images, videos, or pieces of text. Given an item $I \in \mathbf{I}$, we can ask a worker w to answer *a rating question* on that item. That is, we ask a worker: *What is your rating r for the item I?*. We assume that every item has a *true rating* in $[1, R]$ that is not known to us in advance, and allow workers to rate items with any value $\in \{1, 2, \ldots, R\}$.

Example 2.1. *Recall our example application from Section 1, where we have $R = 3$ and workers can rate tweets as being negative ($r = 1$), neutral ($r = 2$), or positive ($r = 3$). Suppose we have two items, $\mathbf{I} = \{I_1, I_2\}$ where I_1 is positive, or has a true rating of 3, and I_2 is neutral, or has a true rating of 2.*

Response Set. We assume that each item I is shown to m arbitrary workers, and therefore receives m ratings $\in [1, R]$. We denote the set of ratings given by workers for item I as $M(I)$ and write $M(I) = (v_R, v_{R-1}, \ldots, v_1)$ if item $I \in \mathbf{I}$ receives a rating of i, $1 \leq i \leq R$, from v_i workers. Thus, $\sum_{i=1}^{R} v_i = m$. We call $M(I)$ the *response set of* I, and M the *worker response set* in general.

Continuing with Example 2.1, suppose we have $m = 2$ workers rating each item on the scale of $\{1, 2, 3\}$. Let I_1 receive one worker response of 2 and one worker response of 3. Then, we write $M(I_1) = (1, 1, 0)$. Similarly, if I_2 receives one response of 3 and one response of 1, then we have $M(I_2) = (1, 0, 1)$.

Modeling Worker Errors. We assume every worker draws their responses from a common (discrete) *response probability matrix*, p, of size $R \times R$. Thus, $p(i, j)$ is the probability that a worker rates an item with true value j as having rating i. The matrix p is in general not known to us. We aim to estimate both, p and the true ratings of items in $\mathbf{I}$ as part of our computation.

Note that we assume that every response to a rating question returned by every worker is independently and identically drawn from this matrix: thus, each worker responds to each rating question independently of other questions they may have answered, and other ratings for the same question given by other workers; and furthermore, all the workers have the same response matrix. We recognize that assuming the same response matrix is somewhat stringent—to mitigate this, we evaluate our algorithm experimentally on settings where distinct workers have different error rates and show that making this assumption is appropriate (and leads to good performance) for certain settings that occur often in practice. We also consider generalizations of our algorithm to the case where we can categorize workers into different classes in Appendix B.

That said, while our (generalized) techniques can still indeed be applied when there are a large number of workers or worker classes with distinct response matrices, they may be impractical. Since our focus is on understanding the theoretical limits of global optimality for a simple case, we defer to future work fully generalizing our techniques to apply to workers with distinct response matrices, or when worker answers are not independent of each other.

Mapping and Likelihood. We call a function $f : \mathbf{I} \rightarrow \{1, 2, \ldots, R\}$ that assigns ratings to items a *mapping*. The set of actual ratings of

Symbol	Explanation
$\mathbf{I}$	Set of items
M	Items-workers response set
f	Items-values mapping
p	Worker response probability matrix
$\Pr(M\|f,p)$	Likelihood of (f,p)
m	Number of worker responses per item
T	Ground truth mapping

Table 1: Notation Table

items is also a mapping. We call that the *ground truth mapping*, T. For instance, for Example 2.1, $T(I_1) = 3, T(I_2) = 2$.

Let $\Pr(M|f,p)$ be the probability of workers providing the responses in M, had f been the ground truth mapping and p been the true worker error matrix. We call this value the *likelihood* of the pair, f, p. Thus, our goal is to solve the following problem:

Problem 2.1 (Maximum Likelihood Problem). *Given* $M, \mathbf{I}$, *find* $\underset{f,p}{\operatorname{argmax}} \Pr(M|f,p)$.

We illustrate this concept on our example. Consider the matrix:

$$p = \begin{bmatrix} 0.7 & 0.1 & 0.2 \\ 0.2 & 0.8 & 0.2 \\ 0.1 & 0.1 & 0.6 \end{bmatrix}$$

Let us compute the likelihood of the pair f,p when $f(I_1) = 2$, $f(I_2) = 2$. We have $\Pr(M|f,p) = \Pr(M(I_1)|f,p)\Pr(M(I_2)|f,p)$ assuming that rating questions on items are answered independently. The quantity $\Pr(M(I_1)|f,p)$ is the probability that workers drawing their responses from p respond with $M(I_1)$ to an item with true rating $f(I_1)$. Assuming independence of worker responses, this quantity can be written as the product of the probability of seeing each of the responses that I_1 receives. Therefore, the probability of seeing $M(1,1,0)$, that is, one response of 3 and one response of 2, is $p(3,2)p(2,2) = 0.1 \times 0.8 = 0.08$. Similarly, $\Pr(M(I_2)|f,p) = p(3,2) \times p(1,2) = 0.1 \times 0.1 = 0.01$. Combining, we have $\Pr(M|f,p) = 0.01 \times 0.08 = 8 \times 10^{-4}$. A naive solution would be to look at every possible mapping f', compute $p' = \underset{p}{\operatorname{argmax}} \Pr(M|f',p)$ and choose the f' maximizing the likelihood value $\Pr(M|f',p')$. The number of such mappings, $R^{|\mathbf{I}|}$, is however exponentially large, prompting the need for a more efficient algorithm. We list our notation in Table 1 for ready reference.

3. FILTERING PROBLEM

Filtering can be regarded as a special case of rating where $R = 2$. We discuss it separately, first, because its analysis is significantly simpler, and at the same time provides useful insights that we then build upon for the generalization to rating, that is, to the case where $R > 2$. For example, consider the filtering task of finding all images of Barack Obama from a given set of images. For each image, we ask workers the question "is this a picture of Barack Obama". We can represent an answer of "no" to the question above by a score 0, and an answer of "yes" by a score 1. Each item (image) $I \in \mathbf{I}$ now has an inherent true value in $\{0,1\}$ where 1 means that the item is one that satisfies the filter, in this case, the image is one of Barack Obama. Mappings here are functions $f : \mathbf{I} \to \{0,1\}$.

Next, we formalize the filtering problem in Section 3.1, describe our algorithm in Section 3.2, prove a maximum likelihood result in Section 3.3 and evaluate our algorithm in Section 3.5.

3.1 Formalization

Given the response set M, we wish to find the maximum likelihood mapping $f : \mathbf{I} \to \{0,1\}$ and 2×2 response probability matrix, p. For the filtering problem, each item has an inherent true value of either 0 or 1, and sees m responses of 0 or 1 from different workers. If item I receives $m - j$ responses of 1 and j responses of 0, we can represent its response set with the tuple $M(I) = (m - j, j)$.

Consider a worker response probability matrix of $p = \begin{bmatrix} 0.7 & 0.2 \\ 0.3 & 0.8 \end{bmatrix}$. The first column represents the probabilities of worker responses when an item's true rating is 0 and the second column represents probabilities when an item's true rating is 1. Given that all workers have the same response probabilities, we can characterize their response matrix by just the corresponding worker false positive (FP) and false negative (FN) rates, e_0 and e_1. Here, we can describe the entire matrix p with just the two values, $e_0 = 0.3$ and $e_1 = 0.2$.

Filtering Estimation Problem. Let M be the observed response set on item-set $\mathbf{I}$. Our goal is to find

$$f^*, e_0^*, e_1^* = \underset{f,e_0,e_1}{\operatorname{argmax}} \Pr(M|f,e_0,e_1)$$

Here, $\Pr(M|f,e_0,e_1)$ is the probability of getting the response set M, given that f is the ground truth mapping and the true worker response matrix is defined by e_0, e_1.

Dependance of Response Probability Matrices on Mappings. Due to the probabilistic nature of our workers, for a fixed ground truth mapping T, different worker error rates, e_0 and e_1 can produce the same response set M. These different worker error rates, however have varying likelihoods of occurrence. This leads us to observe that worker error rates (e_0, e_1) and mapping functions (f) are not independent and are related through any given M. In fact, we show that for the maximum likelihood estimation problem, fixing a mapping f enforces a maximum likelihood choice of e_0, e_1. We leverage this fact to simplify our problem from searching for the maximum likelihood tuple f, e_0, e_1 to just searching for the maximum likelihood mapping, f. Given a response set M and a mapping, f, we call this maximum likelihood choice of e_0, e_1 as the parameter set of f, M, and represent it as Params(f, M). The choice of Params(f, M) is very intuitive and simple. We show that we just can estimate e_0 as the fraction of times a worker disagreed with f on an item I in M when $f(I) = 0$, and correspondingly, e_1 as the fraction of times a worker responded 0 to an item I, when $f(I) = 1$. Under this constraint, we can prove that our original estimation problem, $\underset{f,e_0,e_1}{\operatorname{argmax}} \Pr(M|f,e_0,e_1)$ simplifies to that of finding $\underset{f}{\operatorname{argmax}} \Pr(M|f,e_0^*,e_1^*)$ where e_0^*, e_1^* are the constants given by Params(f, M).

Example 3.1. *Suppose we are given 4 items* $\mathbf{I} = \{I_1, I_2, I_3, I_4\}$ *with ground truth mapping* $T = (T(I_1), T(I_2), T(I_3), T(I_4)) = (1,0,1,1)$. *Suppose we ask* $m = 3$ *workers to evaluate each item and receive the following number of ("1", "0") responses for each respective item:* $M(I_1) = (3,0)$, $M(I_2) = (1,2)$, $M(I_3) = (2,1)$, $M(I_4) = (2,1)$. *Then, we can evaluate our worker false positive and false negative rates as described above:* $e_1 = \frac{0+1+1}{3+3+3} = \frac{2}{9}$ *(from items* I_1, I_3 *and* I_4*) and* $e_0 = \frac{1}{3}$ *(from* I_2*).*

We shall henceforth refer to $\Pr(M|f) = \Pr(M|f, \text{Params}(f, M))$ as the *likelihood of a mapping* f. For now, we focus on the problem of finding the maximum likelihood mapping with the understanding that finding the error rates is straightforward given the mapping is fixed. We formally show that the problem of jointly finding the maximum likelihood response matrix and mapping can be solved by just finding the most likely mapping f^* in Section 3.4 . The most likely triple f, e_0, e_1 is then given by f^*, Params(f^*, M).

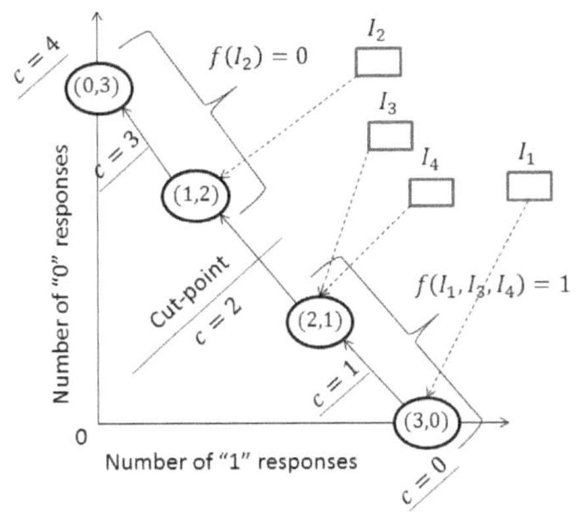

Figure 2: Filtering: Example 3.1 (cut-point = 2)

It is easy to calculate the likelihood of a given mapping. We have $\Pr(M|f) = \prod_{I \in \mathbf{I}} \Pr(M(I)|f, e_0, e_1)$, where $e_0, e_1 = \text{Params}(f, M)$ and $\Pr(M(I)|f, e_0, e_1)$ is the probability of seeing the response set $M(I)$ on an item $I \in \mathbf{I}$. Say $M(I) = (m - j, j)$. Then, we have

$$\Pr(M(I)|f) = \begin{cases} (1 - e_1)^{m-j} e_1^j & \text{for } f(I) = 1 \\ e_0^{m-j}(1 - e_0)^j & \text{for } f(I) = 0 \end{cases}$$

This can be evaluated in $O(m)$ for each $I \in \mathbf{I}$ by doing one pass over $M(I)$. Thus, $\Pr(M|f) = \prod_{I \in \mathbf{I}} \Pr(M(I)|f)$ can be evaluated in $O(m|\mathbf{I}|)$. We use this as a building block in our algorithm.

3.2 Globally Optimal Algorithm

In this section, we describe our algorithm for finding the maximum likelihood mapping, given a response set M on an item set $\mathbf{I}$. A naive algorithm could be to scan all possible mappings, f, calculating for each, $e_0^*, e_1^* = \text{Params}(f, M)$ and the likelihood $\Pr(M|f, e_0^*, e_1^*)$. The number of all possible mappings is, however, exponential in the number of items. Given $n = |\mathbf{I}|$ items, we can assign a value of 0 or 1 to any of them, resulting in 2^n different mappings. This makes the naive algorithm prohibitively expensive.

Our algorithm is essentially a pruning based method that uses two simple insights (described below) to narrow the search for the maximum likelihood mapping. Starting with the entire set of 2^n possible mappings, we eliminate all those that do not satisfy one of our two requirements, and reduce the space of mappings to be considered to $O(m)$, where m is the number of worker responses per item. We then show that just an exhaustive evaluation on this small set of remaining mappings is still sufficient to find a global maximum likelihood mapping.

We illustrate our ideas on the example from Section 3.1, represented graphically in Figure 2. We will explain this figure below.

Bucketizing. Since we assume (for now) that all workers draw their responses from the same probability matrix p (i.e., have the same e_0, e_1 values), we observe that items with the exact same set of worker responses can be treated identically. This allows us to bucket items based on their observed response sets. Given that there are m worker responses for each item, we have $m + 1$ buckets, starting from m "1" and zero "0" responses, down to zero "1" and m "0" responses. We represent these buckets in Figure 2. The x-axis represents the number of 1 responses an item receives and the y-axis represents the number of 0 responses an item receives. We hash items into the buckets corresponding to their observed response sets. Intuitively, since all items within a bucket receive the same set of responses and are for all purposes identical, two items within a bucket should receive the same value.

In our example (Figure 2), the set of possible responses to or bucket of any item is $\{(3,0), (2,1), (1,2), (0,3)\}$, where $(3-j, j)$ represents seeing $3 - j$ responses of "1" and j responses of "0". We only consider mappings, f, where items in the same bucket are assigned the same value, that is, $f(I_3) = f(I_4)$. This leaves 2^4 mappings corresponding to assigning a value of 0/1 to each bucket. In general, given m worker responses per item, we have $m + 1$ buckets and 2^{m+1} mappings that satisfy our bucketizing condition. Although for this example $m + 1 = n$, typically we have $m \ll n$.

Dominance Ordering. Second, we observe that buckets have an inherent ordering. If workers are better than random, we intuitively expect items with more "1" responses to be more likely to have true value 1 than items with fewer "1" responses. Ordering buckets by the number of "1" responses, we have $(m, 0) \to (m - 1, 1) \to \ldots \to (1, m - 1) \to (0, m)$. We eliminate all mappings that give a value of 0 to a bucket with a larger number of "1" responses while assigning a value of 1 to a bucket with fewer "1" responses. We formalize this intuition as a *dominance relation*, or ordering on buckets, $(m, 0) > (m - 1, 1) > \ldots > (1, m - 1) > (0, m)$, and only consider mappings where dominating buckets receive a value not lower than any of their dominated buckets.

Figure 2 shows the dominance relation in the form of directed edges, with the source node being the dominating bucket and the target node being the dominated one. Here, we discard all mappings which assign a value of "0" to a dominating bucket (say response set $(3, 0)$) while assigning a value of "1" to one of its dominated buckets (say response set $(2, 1)$).

Dominance-Consistent Mappings. We consider the space of mappings satisfying our above bucketizing and dominance constraints, and call them *dominance-consistent mappings*. We can prove that the maximum likelihood mapping from this small set of mappings is in fact a global maximum likelihood mapping across the space of all possible "reasonable" mappings: mappings corresponding to better than random worker behavior.

To construct a mapping satisfying our above two constraints, we choose a *cut-point* to cut the ordered set of response sets into two partitions. The corresponding *dominance-consistent mapping* then assigns value "1" to all (items in) buckets in the first (better) half, and value "0" to the rest. For instance, choosing the cut-point between response sets $(2, 1)$ and $(1, 2)$ in Figure 2 results in the corresponding dominance-consistent mapping, where $\{I_1, I_3, I_4\}$, are mapped to "1", while $\{I_2\}$, is mapped to "0". We have 5 different cut-points, $0, 1, 2, 3, 4$, each corresponding to one dominance-consistent mapping. Cut-point 0 corresponds to the mapping where all items are assigned a value of 0 and cut-point 4 corresponds to the mapping where all items are assigned a value of 1. In particular, the figure shows the dominance-consistent mapping corresponding to the cut-point $c = 2$. In general, if we have m responses to each item, we obtain $m + 2$ dominance-consistent mappings.

Definition 3.1 (Dominance-consistent mapping f^c). *For any cut-point $c \in 0, 1, \ldots, m+1$, we define the corresponding dominance-point mapping f^c as*

$$f^c(I) = \begin{cases} 1 & \text{if } M(I) \in \{(m, 0), \ldots, (m - c + 1, c - 1)\} \\ 0 & \text{if } M(I) \in \{(m - c, c), \ldots, (0, m)\} \end{cases}$$

Our algorithm enumerates all dominance-consistent mappings, computes their likelihoods, and returns the most likely one among them. The details of our algorithm can be found in our technical report. As there are $(m + 2)$ mappings, each of whose likelihoods can be evaluated in $O(m|\mathbf{I}|)$, (See Section 3.1) the running time of our algorithm is $O(m^2|\mathbf{I}|)$.

In the next section we prove that in spite of only searching the much smaller space of dominance-consistent mappings, our algorithm finds a global maximum likelihood solution.

3.3 Proof of Correctness

Reasonable Mappings. A reasonable mapping is one which corresponds to a better than random worker behavior. Consider a mapping f corresponding to a false positive rate of $e_0 > 0.5$ (as given by $\text{Params}(f, M)$). This mapping is *unreasonable* because workers perform worse than random for items with value "0". Given $\mathbf{I}, M$, let $f : \mathbf{I} \to \{0,1\}$, with $e_0, e_1 = \text{Params}(f, M)$ be a mapping such that $e_0 \leq 0.5$ and $e_1 \leq 0.5$. Then f is a *reasonable mapping*. It is easy to show that all dominance-consistent mappings are reasonable mappings.

Now, we present our main result on the optimality of our algorithm. We show that in spite of only considering the local space of dominance-consistent mappings, we are able to find a global maximum likelihood mapping.

Theorem 3.1 (Maximum Likelihood)**.** *We let M be the given response set on the input item-set $\mathbf{I}$. Let $\mathbf{F}$ be the set of all reasonable mappings and $\mathbf{F}^{dom}$ be the set of all dominance-consistent mappings. Then,* $\max_{f^* \in \mathbf{F^{dom}}} \Pr(M|f^*) = \max_{f \in \mathbf{F}} \Pr(M|f)$

Proof. We provide an outline of our proof below. Further details can be found in the Appendix A.1.

Step 1: Suppose f is not a dominance-consistent mapping. Then, either it does not satisfy the bucketizing constraint, or it does not satisfy the dominance-constraint. We claim that if f is reasonable, we can always construct a dominance-consistent mapping, f^* such that $\Pr(M|f^*) \geq \Pr(M|f)$. Then, it trivially follows that $\max_{f^* \in \mathbf{F^{dom}}} \Pr(M|f^*) = \max_{f \in \mathbf{F}} \Pr(M|f)$. We show the construction of such an f^* for every reasonable mapping f below.

Step 2: (Bucketizing Inconsistency). Suppose f does not satisfy the bucketizing constraint. Then, we have at least one pair of items I_1, I_2 such that $M(I_1) = M(I_2)$ and $f(I_1) \neq f(I_2)$. Consider the two mappings f_1 and f_2 defined as follows:

$$f_1(I) = \begin{cases} f(I_2) & \text{for } I = I_1 \\ f(I) & \forall I \in \mathbf{I} \setminus \{I_1\} \end{cases}$$

$$f_2(I) = \begin{cases} f(I_1) & \text{for } I = I_2 \\ f(I) & \forall I \in \mathbf{I} \setminus \{I_2\} \end{cases}$$

The mappings f_1 and f_2 are identical to f everywhere except for at I_1 and I_2, where $f_1(I_1) = f_1(I_2) = f(I_2)$ and $f_2(I_1) = f_2(I_2) = f(I_1)$. We show that $\max(\Pr(M|f_1), \Pr(M|f_2)) \geq \Pr(M|f)$. Let $f' = \text{argmax}_{f_1,f_2}(\Pr(M|f_1), \Pr(M|f_2))$.

Step 3: (Dominance Inconsistency). Suppose f does not satisfy the dominance constraint. Then, there exists at least one pair of items I_1, I_2 such that $M(I_1) > M(I_2)$ and $f(I_1) = 0, f(I_2) = 1$. Define mapping f' as follows:

$$f'(I) = \begin{cases} f(I_2) & \text{for } I = I_1 \\ f(I_1) & \text{for } I = I_2 \\ f(I) & \forall I \in \mathbf{I} \setminus \{I_1, I_2\} \end{cases}$$

Mapping f' is identical to f everywhere except at I_1 and I_2, where it swaps their values. We show that $\Pr(M|f') \geq \Pr(M|f)$.

Step 4: (Reducing Inconsistencies). Suppose f is not a dominance-consistent mapping. We have shown that by reducing either a bucketizing inconsistency (Step 2), or a dominance inconsistency (Step 3), we can construct a new mapping, f' with likelihood greater than or equal to that of f. Now, if f' is a dominance-consistent mapping, set $f^* = f'$ and we are done. If not, look at an inconsistency in f' and apply steps 2 or 3 to it. We can show that with each iteration, we are reducing at least one inconsistency while increasing likelihood. We repeat this process iteratively, and since there are only a finite number of inconsistencies in f to begin with, we are guaranteed to end up with a desired dominance-consistent mapping f^* satisfying $\Pr(M|f^*) \geq \Pr(M|f)$. This completes our proof sketch. □

3.4 Calculating error rates from mappings

In this section, we formalize the correspondence between mappings and worker error rates that we introduced in Section 3.1. Given a response set M and a mapping f, say we calculate the corresponding worker error rates $e_0(f, M), e_1(f, M) = \text{Params}(f, M)$ as follows:

1. Let $\mathbf{I_j} \subseteq \mathbf{I} \ni f(I) = 0, M(I) = (m-j, j) \forall I \in \mathbf{I_j}$. Then, $e_0 = \frac{\sum_{j=0}^{m}(m-j)|I_j|}{m\sum_{j=0}^{m}|I_j|}$
2. Let $\mathbf{I_j} \subseteq \mathbf{I} \ni f(I) = 1, M(I) = (m-j, j) \forall I \in \mathbf{I_j}$. Then, $e_1 = \frac{\sum_{j=0}^{m} j|I_j|}{m\sum_{j=0}^{m}|I_j|}$

Intuitively, $e_0(f, M)$ (respectively $e_1(f, M)$) is just the fraction of times a worker responds with a value of 1 (respectively 0) for an item whose true value is 0 (respectively 1), under response set M assuming that f is the ground truth mapping. We show that for each mapping f, this intuitive set of false positive and false negative error rates, (e_0, e_1) maximizes $\Pr(M|f, e_0, e_1)$. We express this idea formally below.

Lemma 3.1 ($\text{Params}(f, M)$)**.** *Given response set M, and mapping f, let $\Pr(e_0, e_1|f, M)$ be the probability that the underlying worker false positive and negative rates are e_0 and e_1 respectively, conditioned on f being the true mapping. Then,*

$$\forall f, \textit{Params}(f, M) = \underset{e_0, e_1}{\text{argmax}} \Pr(e_0, e_1|f, M)$$

Next, we show that instead of simultaneously trying to find the most likely mapping and false positive and false negative error rates, it is sufficient to just find the most likely mapping while assuming that the error rates corresponding to any chosen mapping, f, are always given by $\text{Params}(f, M)$. We formalize this intuition in Lemma 3.2 below. The details of its proof, which are simple and follow from Lemma 3.1, can also be found in the full technical report [6].

Lemma 3.2 (Likelihood of a Mapping)**.** *Let $f \in \mathbf{F}$ be any mapping and M be the given response set on $\mathbf{I}$. We have,*

$$\max_{f, e_0, e_1} \Pr(M|f, e_0, e_1) = \max_{f} \Pr(M|f, \textit{Params}(f, M))$$

3.5 Experiments

In this section, we evaluate the performance of our algorithm, OPT, on synthetic and real data, and compare it against baselines. We report our performance in terms of *(a) accuracy of label predictions*, *(b) accuracy of worker error rates*, and *(c) time taken.*

We discuss *four* experiments: our first experiment is on synthetic data, our second experiment is on data from [10] on image comparison, our third experiment is on data from [21] on classification, and our last experiment summarizes results on other datasets.

In all our experiments, our algorithm, OPT, assumes a single error rate across all workers, despite that not holding true, so is at a considerable disadvantage to other algorithms that do take individual worker identities and error rates into account.

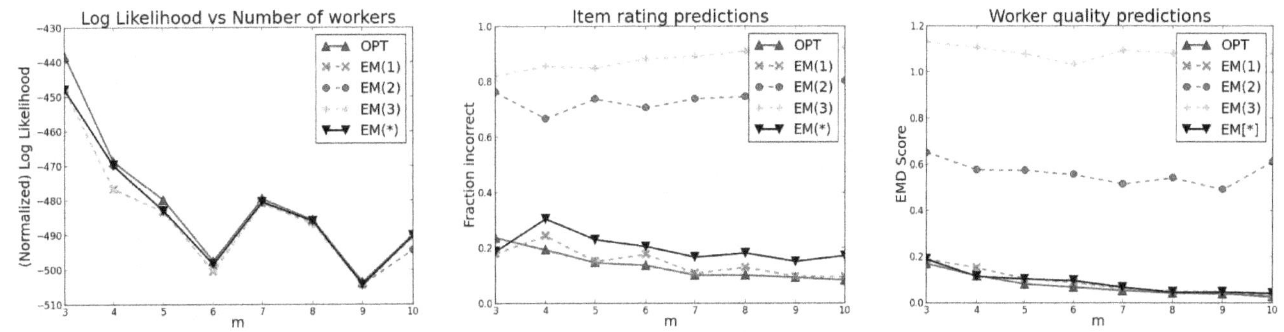

Figure 3: Filtering, Synthetic, Setting 1: (a)Likelihood, $s = 0.5$ (b) Fraction Incorrect, $s = 0.7$ (c) EMD Score, $s = 0.5$

We also note that while our gains for the filtering setting are small, as we will see in Section 4.3, the gains are *significantly higher* for the case of rating, where multiple error rate parameters are being simultaneously estimated. (For the filtering case, only false positive and false negative error rates are being estimated.)

Experiment 1: Synthetic Data Experiments

For the synthetic data, we perform experiments under two settings: In the first setting, data is generated using the assumption that workers draw their responses from a fixed common error distribution. This is the same assumption that is also made by our algorithm, denoted OPT. We compare OPT against an EM baseline that also makes the same assumption. Here, our goal is to explore the effects of optimizing on likelihood on other parameters of interest, e.g., the quality of the predicted item values, or the estimated error rates, on an equal footing with EM baselines.

In the second setting, data is generated using the assumption that different workers draw their responses from different error distributions, with worker identities known. While our algorithm continues to operate as before (with the single error rate assumption), for our EM baseline, we use a richer algorithm that can take worker identities and individual error rates into account. Here, our goal is to study the impact of OPT in settings where our assumptions do not hold, and when worker identities are indeed available.

Setting 1: Identical worker error distribution

Dataset generation. To generate ground truth values for items, given a fixed selectivity s, for each item, we assign a ground truth value of 1 with probability s, and 0 with probability $1 - s$. This gives a set of items $\mathbf{I}$, $|\mathbf{I}| = n$, and ground truth mapping T. Then, we generate an underlying worker response probability matrix, with the only constraint that workers are better than random (false positive and false negative rates are ≤ 0.5). We then simulate worker responses based on this matrix to generate a response set M. Different algorithms being compared now take $\mathbf{I}, M$ as input and return a mapping $f : \mathbf{I} \rightarrow \{0, 1\}$, and a worker response matrix p.

Algorithms. We compare our algorithm, OPT, against the basic EM algorithm that is also solving the same maximum likelihood problem. We discuss details of the EM algorithm in [6]. EM takes an initial estimate or guess for worker error rates as a parameter — we experiment with three different initializations here. EM(1) starts with an initialization of $e_0, e_1 = 0.25$ (workers are better than random), EM(2) with $e_0, e_1 = 0.5$ (workers are random), and EM(3) with $e_0, e_1 = 0.75$ (workers are worse than random). EM(*) is the consolidated algorithm which runs each of the three EM instances and best among them in terms of maximum likelihood.

Setup. We experiment with different choices over both input parameters and comparison metrics over the output. We observe that changing the number of items, n, does not significantly affect our accuracy results, so we set $n = 1000$. We vary the selectivity, s, and the number of worker responses per item, m; due to space limitations, we show a representative set of results below. Each experiment is repeated across 1000 random trials.

Likelihood. Figure 3(a) shows the likelihoods of mappings returned by OPT and different EM instances on varying the number of worker responses, for $s = 0.5$. The y-axis is on log scale, with a higher value being more desirable. We observe that OPT returns higher likelihood mappings with the marginal improvement going down as m increases. We believe that in practice it is unlikely that $m > 5$ (more than 5 answers per item).

Fraction incorrect. In addition to likelihood, we are also interested in other metrics that measure the quality of our predictions. In Figure 3(b) ($s = 0.7$), we plot the fraction of item values each of the algorithms predict *incorrectly* (a lower score is better). Here, again, OPT estimates true values of items with a higher accuracy than EM instances; with EM(2) and EM(3) being especially bad.

EMD score. Then, to evaluate the predicted worker error rates against actual ones, we plot the Earth Movers distance (EMD) between our predicted matrix and the actual one in Figure 3(c) ($s = 0.5$ – lower better). For a detailed description of distance metrics, see technical report [6]. We observe that OPT's predictions are closer to the actual probability matrix than all the EM instances. We observe that EM(2) and EM(3) get stuck in bad local minima.

Summary. For all metrics, OPT displays slightly higher accuracy, in addition to giving a global likelihood guarantee. (Our results for rating are even better since there are multiple parameters being estimated.) Our experiments also show that optimizing for likelihood does not adversely affect other metrics of interest. We experiment with additional parameter settings and comparison metrics, and present more extensive results in our technical report [6] .

Setting 2: Distinct worker error distributions

Next, we consider the setting where data is generated using distinct worker error rates, with worker identities available to the algorithms. Furthermore, different workers may respond to different items, giving a general *item-worker response matrix*. For this setting, we consider a generalized version of the previous EM, algorithm GEN_EM, that assumes and estimates a distinct error distribution for each worker. (The previous EM instances assumed a single common error distribution.) OPT, on the other hand, ignores worker identities, and uses a single common error distribution. The item-worker response matrix can be dense or sparse depending on how many items different workers respond to.

Our expectation is that if the matrix is dense, with a small number of workers, each answering many items, then GEN_EM will do well, since it will converge to high-confidence estimates for worker accuracies. If, on the other hand, the matrix is sparse, which is often the case when there is a large and fluid worker pool, with each worker answering a small number of items, then we expect OPT to do as well as GEN_EM, which may extrapolate worker accuracies without much evidence.

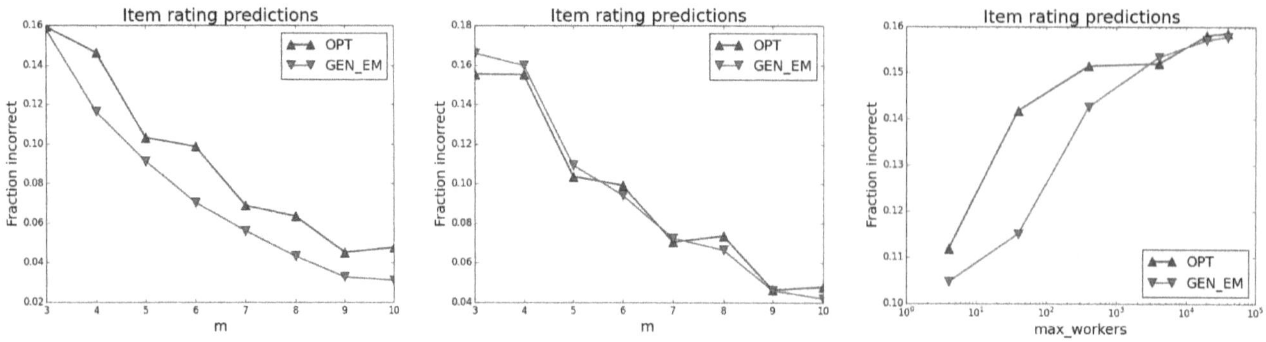

Figure 4: Filtering, Synthetic, Setting 2: (a) $m' = 50$, varying m (b) $m' = 1000$, varying m (c) ($m = 4$), varying m'

Dataset generation, Setup, and Algorithms. We use m' distinct workers each with a uniformly drawn, independent error rate that is better than random (≥ 0.5). Each of the n items receives responses from m workers randomly sampled from m', so workers answer an average of nm/m' items. We keep n constant at 1000, making m/m' a good measure of the density of the item-worker matrix.

The generalized version of EM for this setting, GEN_EM, starts with an initial error rate estimate for each worker, and then converges to distinct error rates for them. We use the same initialization as EM(1) from the experiments in Setting 1 for each worker, as that was observed to have the best performance.

Accuracy Results. Figure 4(a) depicts the performance as a function of m, when $m' = 50$. We observe that GEN_EM performs better throughout. This is not surprising given that with just 50 total workers, each worker would answer $1000 \times 10/50 = 200$ items for $m = 10$, giving GEN_EM very fine-grained information about each individual worker. Contrast this to Figure 4(b), where $m' = 1000$ — here, the item-worker response matrix is much sparser (average number of responses per worker is 10) and we consequently observe that OPT is comparable to (even marginally better than) GEN_EM in spite of working with a much coarser granularity of information! The latter case is often true in marketplaces where requesters have little control over which workers attempt their tasks, or if the workers are anonymous.

In Figure 4(c), we show the performance as a function of the maximum size of the worker pool, m' (log-scale), while keeping the number of responses per item, m, fixed. While GEN_EM outperforms OPT for smaller m' (dense response matrix), OPT catches up for $m' > 1000$.

Efficiency Results. In Figures 5(a), 5(b), 5(c), we compare the efficiency of OPT against GEN_EM in terms of actual execution time. As before, we explore the effects of both m and m'. In Figures 5(a), 5(b) we vary m from 3 to 10 along the x-axis, for a fixed value of $m' = 100, 1000$ in the two plots respectively. In Figure 5(c), we vary m' while keeping m fixed at 4. We observe that while the time taken by OPT is typically of the order of 0.001 seconds, GEN_EM (which scales linearly with number of iterations, set at 40 for these plots) takes several seconds to execute for higher values of m'. In fact, OPT is almost not visible in these plots. This further supports the case for OPT in settings with a large worker pool. Note that OPT is linear in m, but its low latency values hide this trend at this scale.

We also perform experiments where we inject a small fraction of "bad" (random) workers into the worker pool for both the settings above. We observe that for reasonable numbers, this injection does not significantly affect our previous results. More detailed experimental results on this can be found in our technical report.

Experiment 2: Real Data Experiment on [10]

We now describe our results on a real dataset. Since the dataset contains answers from a small worker pool, it is naturally dense, and is therefore unfavorable to OPT. We compare OPT versus GEN_EM here. Additional results can be found in the Appendix. For each of these experiments we "vary" the size of the dataset by hiding some of the worker responses and report results from the different, remaining, partial sets.

Dataset. Our dataset is an image comparison dataset [10], where 19 workers are asked to each evaluate 48 tasks. Each task requires a worker to identify if two images show the same sportsperson. We have ground-truth yes/no answers for each task, but do not know the worker error rates. To evaluate the performance of OPT with GEN_EM, we compare the estimates for the item values (the yes/no answers) against the given ground truth.

Results. While in our synthetic experiments, we had the luxury of generating datasets with arbitrary m', here, we have $m' \leq 19$. We fix m (number of responses per item) for a given plot and vary m' (number of total workers present) along the x-axis, and compare the fraction of item values predicted incorrectly along the y-axis. We show our results for $m = 5$ in Figure 6(a) and for $m = 2$ in Figure 6(b). Again, we observe that for the denser item-worker response matrix ($m = 5$), GEN_EM is more accurate than OPT, while for the sparser ($m = 2$) case, OPT is more accurate than GEN_EM. Thus, even on settings which violate our assumptions, such as this dataset with a finite, small worker pool, OPT is more accurate than GEN_EM for sparse item-worker response matrices.

Experiment 3: Real Data Experiment on [21]

We now present results on our second real dataset, from Tian et al. [21]. This is a dataset of images with simple classification (example, is this an image of the sky) or counting tasks. It contains a set of 64 images each responded to by 402 workers. From this, we selected the subset of 36 images corresponding to the filtering tasks, as opposed to the counting tasks. Below we show plots 6(c) and 7(a) where we keep m fixed for a plot and vary m' along the x-axis. We observe here that our algorithm OPT predicts item values more accurately than GEN_EM for nearly all parameter settings. Full details of our experimental setup can be found in [6].

Experiment 4: Comparison against other baselines

We also evaluated our approach on a few other datasets and against other baseline algorithms. We present our results on two datasets, *TEMP* and *RTE* from [16]—both these datasets are part of the SQUARE benchmark [20]. The *TEMP* dataset contains judgments for temporal ordering of events in text, while the *RTE* dataset contains judgments for textual entailment (both binary tasks).

OPT predicts the labels for *TEMP* with a 93.94% accuracy, similar to that of the best algorithm for this dataset, whose accuracy is 93.9% [20].

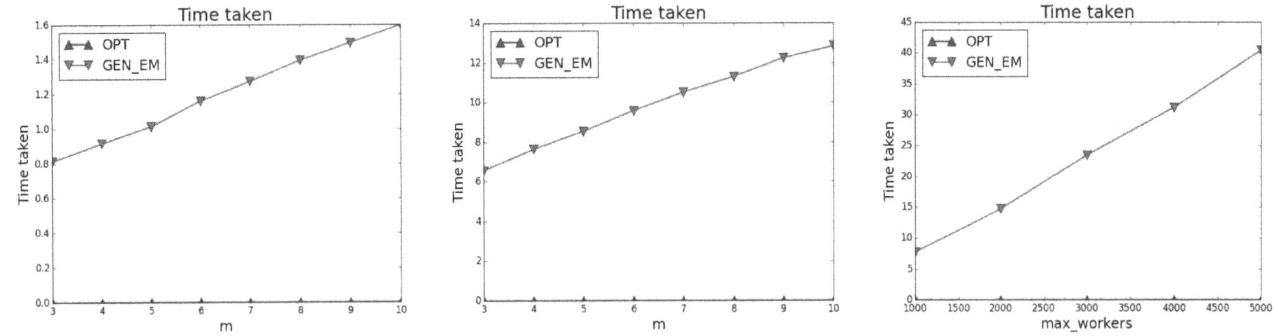

Figure 5: Filtering, Synthetic, Setting 2; Vary m: (a) $m' = 100$ (b) $m' = 1000$; Vary m': (c) $m = 4$

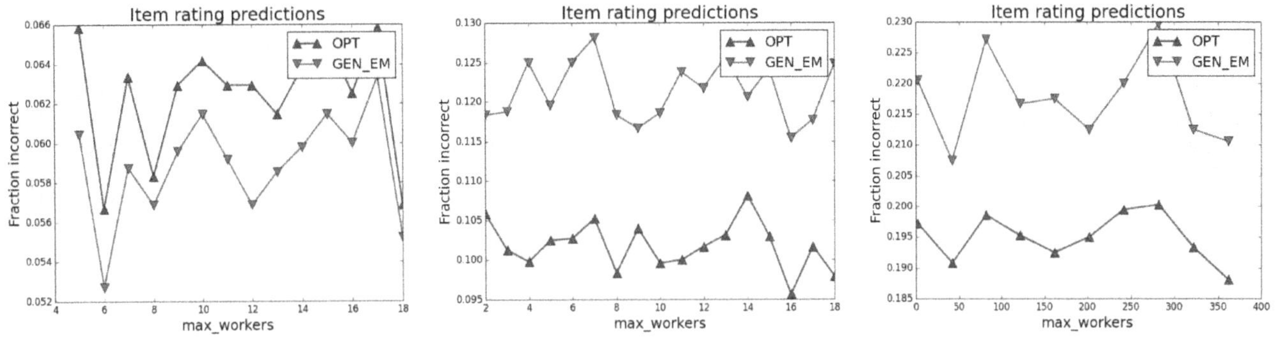

Figure 6: Filtering Real Dataset 1 (a) $m = 5$, (b) $m = 2$; Filtering Real Dataset 2 (c) $m = 2$

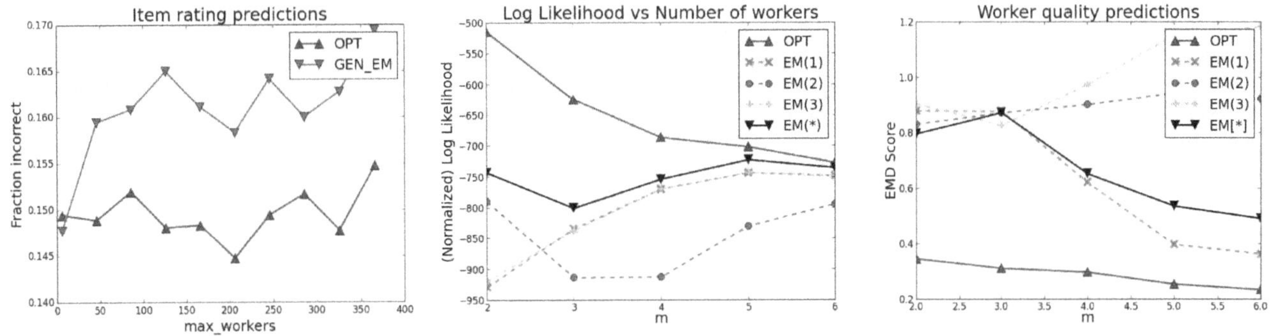

Figure 7: (a) Filtering, Real Dataset 2, $m = 6$; (b) Rating, Synthetic, Setting 1: Likelihood; (c) Rating, Setting 1: Worker Quality Predictions;

On the *RTE* dataset, OPT predicts labels with an error rate of 11.3% (accuracy of 88.7%). We compare this against the results from [29], where their sophisticated Opt-D&S algorithm has an error rate of 7.1% (while other methods have much poorer performance, for example, KOS — 39.7% [11] and Ghosh-SVD — 49.13% [8]). We argue that while OPT is not the most accurate (since it ignores worker identities), it is competitive in its accuracy while having the advantage of simplicity over some of the more sophisticated baselines such as Opt-D&S.

Indeed, all the datasets in the SQUARE benchmark are dense datasets; if the datasets were sparse (like in Experiment 3), we expect OPT to not just match the performance of these algorithms, but also beat them.

4. RATING PROBLEM

In this section, we extend our techniques from filtering to the problem of rating items. Even though the main change resides in the possible values of items ($\{0, 1\}$ for filtering and $\{1, \ldots, R\}$ for rating), this small change adds significant complexity to our dominance idea. We show how our notions of bucketizing and dominance generalize from the filtering case.

4.1 Formalization

Recall from Section 2 that, for the rating problem, workers are shown an item and asked to provide a score from 1 to R, with R being the best (highest) and 1 being the worst (lowest) score possible. Each item from the set $\mathbf{I}$ receives m worker responses and all the responses are recorded in M. We write $M(I) = (v_R, v_{R-1}, \ldots, v_1)$ if item $I \in \mathbf{I}$ receives v_i responses of "i", $1 \leq i \leq R$. Recall that $\sum_{i=1}^{R} v_i = m$. Mappings are functions $f : \mathbf{I} \to \{1, 2, \ldots, R\}$ and workers are described by the response probability matrix p, where $p(i, j)$ $(i, j \in \{1, 2, \ldots, R\})$ denotes the probability that a worker will give an item with true value j a score of i. Our problem is defined as that of finding $f^*, p^* = \underset{f,p}{\operatorname{argmax}} \Pr(M|f, p)$ given M.

As in the case of filtering, we use the relation between p and f through M to define the likelihood of a mapping. We observe that for maximum likelihood solutions given M, fixing a mapping f automatically fixes an optimal $p = \text{Params}(f, M)$. Thus, similar to Filtering, we can focus our attention on the mappings, implicitly finding the maximum likelihood p as well. Intuitively, Params$(f, M)(i, j)$ is just the fraction of times a worker responded i to an item that is mapped by f to a value of j. Let the ith dimension of the response set of any item I by $M_i(I)$. That is, if $M(I) = (v_R, \ldots, v_1)$, then $M_i(I) = v_i$. Let $\mathbf{I_i} \subseteq \mathbf{I} \ni f(I) = i \forall i, I \in \mathbf{I_i}$. Then, Params$(f, M)(i, j) = \frac{\sum_{I \in \mathbf{I_j}} M_i(I)}{m|I_j|} \forall i, j$.

Denoting the likelihood of a mapping, $\Pr(M|f, \text{Params}(f, M))$, as $\Pr(M|f)$, our maximum likelihood rating problem is now equivalent to that of finding the most likely mapping. Thus, we wish to solve for $\underset{f}{\text{argmax}} \Pr(M|f)$.

4.2 Algorithm

Now, we generalize our idea of bucketized, dominance-consistent mappings from Section 3.2 to find a maximum likelihood solution for the rating problem.

Bucketizing. For every item, we are given m worker responses, each in $1, 2, \ldots, R$. It can be shown that there are $\binom{R+m-1}{R-1}$ different possible worker response sets, or buckets. The bucketizing idea is the same as before: items with the same response sets can be treated identically and should be mapped to the same values. So we only consider mappings that give the same rating score to all items in a common response set bucket.

Dominance Ordering. Next we generalize our dominance constraint. Recall that for filtering with m responses per item, we had a total ordering on the dominance relation over response set buckets, $(m, 0) > (m-1, 1) > \ldots > (1, m-1) > (0, m)$ where no dominated bucket could have a higher score ("1") than a dominating bucket ("0"). Let us consider the simple example where $R = 3$ and we have $m = 3$ worker responses per item. Let (i, j, k) denote the response set where i workers give a score of "3", j workers give a score of "2" and k workers give a score of "1". Since we have 3 responses per item, $i + j + k = 3$. Intuitively, the response set $(3, 0, 0)$ dominates the response set $(2, 1, 0)$ because in the first, three workers gave items a score of "3", while in the second, only two workers give a score of "3" while one gives a score of "2". Assuming a "reasonable" worker behavior, we would expect the value assigned to the dominating bucket to be at least as high as the value assigned to the dominated bucket. Now consider the buckets $(2, 0, 1)$ and $(1, 2, 0)$. For items in the first bucket, two workers have given a score of "3", while one worker has given a score of "1". For items in the second bucket, one worker has given a score of "3", while two workers have given a score of "2". Based solely on these scores, we cannot claim that either of these buckets dominates the other. So, for the rating problem we only have a *partial* dominance ordering, which we can represent as a DAG. We show the *dominance-DAG* for the $R = 3, m = 3$ case in Figure 8. For arbitrary m, R, we can define the following dominance relation.

Definition 4.1 (Rating Dominance). *Bucket B_1 with response set $(v^1_R, v^1_{R-1}, \ldots, v^1_1)$ dominates bucket B_2 with response set $(v^2_R, v^2_{R-1}, \ldots, v^2_1)$ if and only if $\exists 1 < r' \leq R \ni (v^1_r = v^2_r \forall r \notin \{r', r'-1\})$ and $(v^1_{r'} = v^2_{r'} + 1) \wedge (v^1_{r'-1} = v^2_{r'-1} - 1)$.*

Intuitively, a bucket B_1 dominates B_2 if increasing the score given by a single worker to B_2 by 1 makes its response set equal to that of items in B_1. Note that a bucket can dominate multiple buckets, and a dominated bucket can have multiple dominating buckets, depending on which worker's response is increased by 1. For instance, in Figure 8, bucket $(2, 1, 0)$ dominates both $(2, 0, 1)$ (increase one score from "1" to "2") and $(1, 2, 0)$ (increase one score from "2" to "3"), both of which dominate $(1, 1, 1)$.

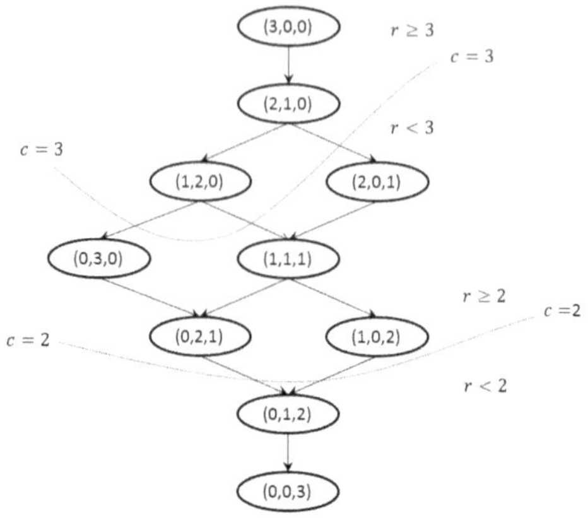

Figure 8: Dominance-DAG for 3 workers and scores in $\{1, 2, 3\}$

Dominance-Consistent Mappings. As with filtering, we consider the set of mappings satisfying both the bucketizing and dominance constraints, and call them *dominance-consistent mappings*.

Dominance-consistent mappings can be represented using *cuts* in the dominance-DAG. To construct a dominance-consistent mapping, we split the DAG into at most R partitions such that no parent node belongs to an intuitively "lower" partition than its children. Then we assign ratings to items in a top-down fashion such that all nodes within a partition get a common rating value lower than the value assigned to the partition just above it. Figure 8 shows one such dominance-consistent mapping corresponding to a set of cuts. A cut with label $c = i$ essentially partitions the DAG into two sets: the set of nodes above all receive ratings $\geq i$ while all nodes below receive ratings $< i$. To find the most likely mapping, we sort the items into buckets and look for mappings over buckets that are consistent with the dominance-DAG. We use an iterative top-down approach to enumerate all consistent mappings. First, we label our nodes in the DAG from $1 \ldots \binom{R+m-1}{R-1}$ according to their topological ordering, with the root node starting at 1. In the ith iteration, we assume we have the set of all possible consistent mappings assigning values to nodes $1 \ldots i-1$ and extend them to all consistent mappings over nodes $1 \ldots i$. When the last $\binom{R+m-1}{R-1}^{th}$ node has been added, we are left with the complete set of all dominance-consistent mappings. Details of our algorithm appear in [6].

Complexity. As with the filtering problem, an exhaustive search of only the dominance-consistent mappings under this dominance DAG constraint gives us a global maximum likelihood mapping across a much larger space of reasonable mappings. Suppose we have n items, R rating values, and m worker responses per item. The number of buckets of possible worker response sets (nodes in the DAG) is $\binom{R+m-1}{R-1}$. Then, the number of unconstrained mappings is R^n and number of mappings with just the bucketizing condition, i.e., where items with the same response sets get assigned the same value, is $R^{\binom{R+m-1}{R-1}}$. It is easy to see that this is an upper bound to the number of dominance-consistent mappings.

We can also derive a reasonable lower bound by observing that one way of generating (a subset of) dominance-consistent mappings is to assign ratings to the DAG such that all nodes at the same depth have identical ratings, and all nodes at any depth have a higher rating than all nodes at the subsequent lower depth. Note that all mappings generated this way are dominance-consistent, as no lower node can dominate a higher one. Furthermore, observe that this bound is achieved in the limiting case when the DAG has a width of 1, i.e., it is a chain. Suppose the DAG has a total depth of d. Then, using the standard combinatorial *stars and bars* technique, we can show that the number of such mappings is given

R	m	Unconstrained	Bucketized	Dom-Consistent
3	3	10^{47}	6×10^4	126
3	4	10^{47}	10^7	462
3	5	10^{47}	10^{10}	1716
4	3	10^{60}	10^{12}	2.8×10^4
4	4	10^{60}	10^{21}	2.7×10^6
5	2	10^{69}	10^{10}	2.8×10^4
5	3	10^{69}	10^{24}	1.1×10^8

Table 2: Number of Mappings for $n = 100$ items

by $\binom{d+R-1}{d}$. Now, by observing that the root node (depth 1) is given by $(m, 0, 0, \dots, 0)$, the bottom node (depth d) is given by $(0, 0, \dots, m)$, and that the ratings given to any node in depth d sum up to $Rm - d + 1$, we have $d = Rm - m + 1$. Substituting this value, we have $\binom{Rm-m+R}{Rm-m+1}$ as a lower bound for the number of dominance-consistent mappings for the rating problem.

We leave the (challenging) problem of finding a closed form expression for the actual number of dominance-consistent mappings as future work. Instead, we enumerate a sample set of values in Table 2 for $n = 100$ items. We see that the number of dominance-consistent mappings is significantly smaller than the number of unconstrained mappings. The fact that this greatly reduced set of intuitive mappings contains a global maximum likelihood solution displays the power of our approach. Furthermore, n is typically much larger, which would make the number of unconstrained mappings exponentially larger, while the number of dominance-consistent mappings remains unaffected.

4.3 Experiments

In this section, we evaluate the performance of our algorithm, OPT, on synthetic and real rating data. Similar to our analyses in Section 3.5, we report our performance in terms of (a) accuracy of label predictions, (b) accuracy of worker error rates, and (c) time taken. As before, in all our experiments, OPT assumes a single error rate across all workers. Here, we discuss *two* experiments: our first experiment is on synthetic data, and our second experiment is on data from [2], on website relevance judgment.

Experiment 1: Synthetic Data Experiments

We perform experiments on the identical, as well as distinct worker synthetic data settings using setups similar to those described in Section 3.5 . We present a sample of our experiments and results below, and refer interested readers to our technical report for a more extensive experimental analysis.

Setting 1: Identical worker error distribution

Similar to Section 3.5, we first perform experiments under the setting where data generation, OPT, as well as EM are all based on a single error rate matrix. Details of the setup can be found in [6].

Likelihood. Figure 7(b) plots the likelihoods (on log scale) of the mappings output by different algorithms along the y-axis. We observe that the likelihoods of the mappings returned by OPT, are *much higher* than those of any of the EM algorithms. For example, consider $m = 5$: we observe that our algorithm finds mappings that are on average 9 orders of magnitude more likely than those returned by EM(*) (here, the best EM instance). As with filtering, the gap between the performance of our algorithm and the EM instances decreases as the number of workers increases.

Quality of item rating predictions. In Figure 7(c) we compare the predicted ratings of items against actual values. We measure a weighted score based on how far the predicted value is from the true value. This score lies in the range $[0, 2]$ (details in [6]), with a lower score implying more accurate predictions. Again, we observe that in spite of optimizing for, and providing a global maximum likelihood guarantee, our algorithm predicts item ratings with a high degree of accuracy, with significantly better performance than all the EM instances. For example, at $m = 2$ we observe that OPT deviates from the true rating by less than 0.4 on average, while the EM instances are off by 0.8 or higher.

Setting 2: Distinct worker error distributions

Accuracy Results. Here, we compare the distance-weighted scores (plotted along the y-axis) of our algorithm, OPT, against GEN_EM while varying m (number of responses per item) along the x-axis (for a fixed m'). We observe that GEN_EM is more accurate than OPT for the case when $m' = 50$ (Figure 9(a)), but is significantly worse than OPT for the sparse item-worker response matrix setting (Figure 9(b)), where the size of the worker pool, $m' = 1000$ is large. For example, at $m = 5$, OPT deviates from the true ratings by less than 0.2 on average, while GEN_EM deviates by nearly 0.3. Comparing these results to those in Section 3.5, our gains in accuracy of item predictions for rating are significantly higher because the number of parameters being estimated is much higher, and the EM algorithm has more "ways" it can go wrong if the parameters are initialized incorrectly. That is, with a higher dimensionality we expect that EM converges more often to non-optimal local maxima.

Similar to Figure 4(c), in Figure 9(c), we also show the results obtained when we vary m' along the x-axis (log-scale), while keeping m fixed at 4. For $m' < 100$ (smaller worker pool, denser item-worker response matrix), GEM_EM outperforms our algorithm, while for higher values of m', OPT is significantly more accurate.

Efficiency Results. In Figures 10(a), 10(b), 10(c), we compare the efficiency of OPT against GEN_EM. Similar to our experiments for filtering, in Figures 10(a), 10(b) we vary m, for fixed values of $m' = 100, 1000$ respectively. In Figure 10(c), we vary m' while keeping m fixed at 4. We observe that OPT appears to scale exponentially in m, and is less efficient than GEN_EM for higher values of m and small values of m' ($m' \leq 100, m > 5$). However, for a large worker pool ($m' \geq 1000$), we see that OPT is much more efficient. Since typically m is fixed to be a small value by the task requester, we conclude that in practice OPT scales better than GEN_EM. Note again, that although these plots are drawn with GEN_EM performing 40 iterations, reducing the number of iterations (at the cost of accuracy) will only linearly scale down GEN_EM's latency; it will still be inefficient compared to OPT for higher values of m'.

Again, we conclude that even when distinct worker-level information is available to EM, OPT performs very well in spite of its simplifying assumptions, especially under the very realistic settings where worker pools are large and non-persistent.

Experiment 2: Real Data Experiment on [2]

We also performed experiments on a subset of the *HC* dataset from [2, 20]. This dataset contains judgements given by Mechanical Turk workers on the relevance of displayed webpages to given search queries. Relevance was judged on a ternary scale: highly relevant, relevant, and non-relevant. From this dataset, we chose the subset where every item (webpage-query pair) had gold truth available and at least 6 worker judgements. On this subset (spanning around 500 workers, 1000 items, 10000 judgements), we observed that both OPT and GEN_EM exactly matched the gold truth labels roughly 46% of the time, as compared to the Median strategy (always predict median of observed labels) which got roughly 35% correct. The distance weighted score (average absolute deviation from gold truth on a scale of 0 to 2) obtained by OPT was 0.65, while that by GEN_EM and Median were 0.74 and 0.85 respec-

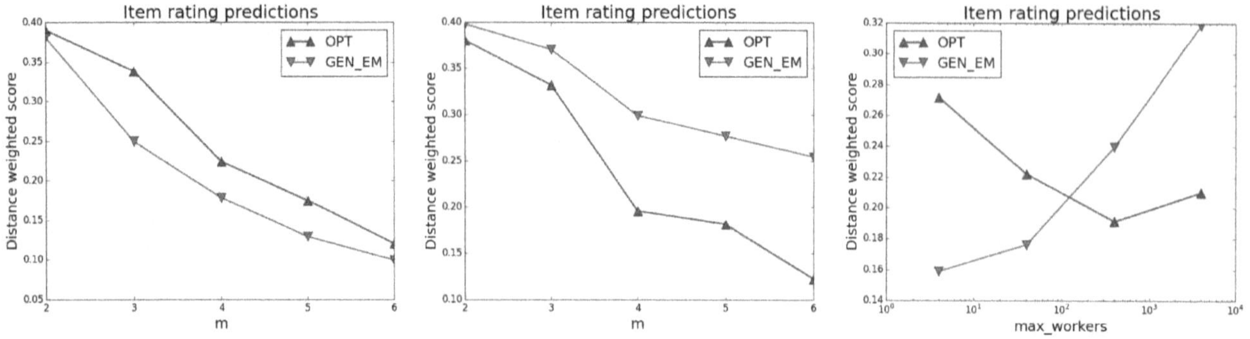

Figure 9: Rating, Synthetic: (a) Setting 2, item rating predictions: $m' = 50$, (b) $m' = 1000$ (c) Rating $(m = 4)$, Synthetic, Vary m'

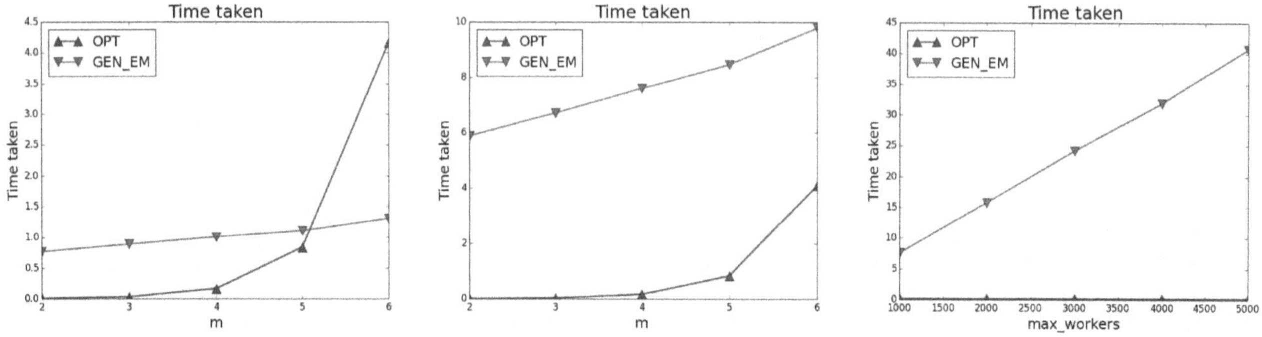

Figure 10: Rating, Synthetic, Setting 2; Vary m: (a) $m' = 100$ (b) $m' = 1000$; Vary m': (c) $m = 4$

tively, showing that OPT predicted values closer to the gold truth in more cases than simple vanilla-EM or Median based strategies.

5. CONCLUSIONS

We have taken a first step towards finding a global maximum likelihood solution to the problem of jointly estimating the item ground truth, and worker quality, in crowdsourced filtering and rating tasks. Given worker ratings on a set of items, we showed that the problem of jointly estimating the ratings of items and worker quality can be split into their two respective, independent estimation problems. We used a few key, intuitive ideas to first find a global maximum likelihood mapping from items to ratings, thereby finding the most likely ground truth. We then showed that the worker quality, modeled by a common response probability matrix, can be inferred automatically from the corresponding maximum likelihood mapping. We develop a novel pruning and search-based approach, in which we greatly reduce the space of (originally exponential) potential mappings to be considered, and prove that an exhaustive search in the reduced space is guaranteed to return a maximum likelihood solution.

Via our experiments, we demonstrated that our algorithm outperforms EM-based algorithms on datasets where worker errors are all alike, and in fact, even outperforms EM-based algorithms on datasets where the worker errors are distinct, as long the worker pools are large. The latter setting is common in practice in crowdsourcing marketplaces where workers are fleeting and easily distracted. It should be noted that even in the case of real datasets with a small set of distinct workers where our algorithm (due to its ignoring of worker identities) is at a disadvantage, its performance is still comparable to state-of-the-art algorithms while providing the significant benefit of being simple and intuitive. We also demonstrated that despite being optimized for the likelihood of mappings, our algorithm estimates ground truth of item ratings and worker error rates with high accuracy, and performs well on other metrics.

Our algorithms can be generalized to the setting where there is a small number of worker classes, each with their own error rates. Likewise, in this paper we assume a fixed number of responses for each item, but we can be generalized to the case where different items may receive different numbers of responses. We briefly discuss both these generalizations in our Appendix B.

It should be noted that although our framework extends to these generalizations, including the case where each worker has an independent, different quality, the algorithms can be inefficient in practice. We have not considered the problem of item difficulties in this paper, assuming that workers have the same quality of responses on all items. As future work, we hope that the ideas described in this paper can be built upon to design efficient algorithms that find a global maximum likelihood mapping under more general settings.

Acknowledgements:
We thank the anonymous reviewers for their valuable feedback. The authors acknowledge support from grant IIS-1513407 awarded by the National Science Foundation, grant 1U54GM114838 awarded by NIGMS through funds provided by the trans-NIH Big Data to Knowledge (BD2K) initiative (www.bd2k.nih.gov), and the Faculty Research Award provided by Google. The content is solely the responsibility of the authors and does not necessarily represent the official views of the funding agencies and organizations.

6. REFERENCES

[1] K. Bellare, S. Iyengar, A. Parameswaran, and V. Rastogi. Active sampling for entity matching. In *KDD*, 2012.

[2] C. Buckley, M. Lease, and M. D. Smucker. Overview of the TREC 2010 Relevance Feedback Track (Notebook). In *The Nineteenth Text Retrieval Conference (TREC) Notebook*, 2010.

[3] B. Carpenter. A hierarchical bayesian model of crowdsourced relevance coding. In *TREC*, 2011.

[4] X. Chen, Q. Lin, and D. Zhou. Optimistic knowledge gradient policy for optimal budget allocation in crowdsourcing. In *ICML*, pages 64–72, 2013.

[5] N. Dalvi, A. Dasgupta, R. Kumar, and V. Rastogi. Aggregating crowdsourced binary ratings. In *WWW*, pages 285–294. International World Wide Web Conferences Steering Committee, 2013.

[6] A. Das Sarma, A. Parameswaran, and J. Widom. Towards globally optimal crowdsourcing quality management: The uniform worker setting. Technical report, 2015.
[7] A. P. Dawid and A. M. Skene. Maximum likelihood estimation of observer error-rates using the em algorithm. *Applied Statistics*, 28(1):20–28, 1979.
[8] A. Ghosh, S. Kale, and P. McAfee. Who moderates the moderators? crowdsourcing abuse detection in user-generated content. In *EC*, pages 167–176, 2011.
[9] M. R. Gupta and Y. Chen. Theory and use of the em algorithm. *Found. Trends Signal Process.*, 4(3):223–296, Mar. 2011.
[10] M. Joglekar, H. Garcia-Molina, and A. Parameswaran. Evaluating the Crowd with Confidence . In *KDD*, 2013. Online: http://dl.acm.org/citation.cfm?id=2487575.2487595.
[11] D. Karger, S. Oh, and D. Shah. Effcient crowdsourcing for multi-class labeling. In *SIGMETRICS*, pages 81–92, 2013.
[12] D. R. Karger, S. Oh, and D. Shah. Iterative learning for reliable crowdsourcing systems. In *NIPS*, pages 1953–1961, 2011.
[13] Q. Liu, J. Peng, and A. Ihler. Variational inference for crowdsourcing. In *NIPS*, pages 701–709, 2012.
[14] P. Donmez et al. Efficiently learning the accuracy of labeling sources for selective sampling. In *KDD*, 2009.
[15] A. Parameswaran, H. Garcia-Molina, H. Park, N. Polyzotis, A. Ramesh, and J. Widom. Crowdscreen: Algorithms for filtering data with humans. In *SIGMOD*, 2012.
[16] R. Snow et al. Cheap and fast—but is it good?: evaluating non-expert annotations for natural language tasks. In *EMNLP*, 2008.
[17] V. C. Raykar and S. Yu. Eliminating spammers and ranking annotators for crowdsourced labeling tasks. *Journal of Machine Learning Research*, 13:491–518, 2012.
[18] V. C. Raykar, S. Yu, L. H. Zhao, G. H. Valadez, C. Florin, L. Bogoni, and L. Moy. Learning from crowds. *JMLR*, 11:1297–1322, 2010.
[19] V. S. Sheng, F. Provost, and P. Ipeirotis. Get another label? improving data quality and data mining using multiple, noisy labelers. In *SIGKDD*, pages 614–622, 2008.
[20] A. Sheshadri and M. Lease. Square: A benchmark for research on computing crowd consensus. In *HCOMP*, 2013.
[21] Y. Tian and J. Zhu. Learning from crowds in the presence of schools of thought. In *Proceedings of the 18th ACM SIGKDD international conference on Knowledge discovery and data mining*, pages 226–234. ACM, 2012.
[22] V. Raykar et al. Supervised learning from multiple experts: whom to trust when everyone lies a bit. In *ICML*, 2009.
[23] M. Venanzi, J. Guiver, G. Kazai, P. Kohli, and M. Shokouhi. Community-based bayesian aggregation models for crowdsourcing. In *Proceedings of the 23rd international conference on World wide web*, pages 155–164. ACM, 2014.
[24] N. Vesdapunt, K. Bellare, and N. N. Dalvi. Crowdsourcing algorithms for entity resolution. *PVLDB*, 7(12):1071–1082, 2014.
[25] J. Wang, T. Kraska, M. Franklin, and J. Feng. Crowder: Crowdsourcing entity resolution. In *VLDB*, 2012.
[26] P. Welinder, S. Branson, P. Perona, and S. J. Belongie. The multidimensional wisdom of crowds. In *NIPS*, pages 2424–2432, 2010.
[27] S. E. Whang, D. Menestrina, G. Koutrika, M. Theobald, and H. Garcia-Molina. Entity resolution with iterative blocking. In *SIGMOD '09*, pages 219–232, New York, NY, USA, 2009. ACM.
[28] J. Whitehill, T.-f. Wu, J. Bergsma, J. R. Movellan, and P. L. Ruvolo. Whose vote should count more: Optimal integration of labels from labelers of unknown expertise. In *NIPS*, pages 2035–2043, 2009.
[29] Y. Zhang, X. Chen, D. Zhou, and M. I. Jordan. Spectral methods meet em: A provably optimal algorithm for crowdsourcing. *arXiv preprint arXiv:1406.3824*, 2014.
[30] D. Zhou, S. Basu, Y. Mao, and J. C. Platt. Learning from the wisdom of crowds by minimax entropy. In *NIPS*, pages 2195–2203, 2012.
[31] D. Zhou, Q. Liu, J. Platt, and C. Meek. Aggregating ordinal labels from crowds by minimax conditional entropy. In *ICML*, pages 262–270, 2014.

APPENDIX

A. FILTERING

A.1 Proof of Correctness

In this section, we show that if a mapping, f, is not dominance-consistent for some given response matrix M, then we can construct an alternate, dominance-consistent mapping f', such that $\Pr(M|f') \geq \Pr(M|f)$. This is Step 3 in the proof for Theorem 3.3, and the proof for Step 2 follows in a similar fashion.

Suppose f does not satisfy the dominance constraint. Then, there exists at least one pair of items I_1, I_2 such that $M(I_1) > M(I_2)$ and $f(I_1) = 0, f(I_2) = 1$. Define mapping f' as follows:

$$f'(I) = \begin{cases} f(I_2) & \text{for } I = I_1 \\ f(I_1) & \text{for } I = I_2 \\ f(I) & \forall I \in \mathbf{I} \setminus \{I_1, I_2\} \end{cases}$$

Let I_1 have realization $(m-i, i)$, that is, it receives $m-i$ responses of 1 and i responses of 0 from workers. Similarly, let I_2 have realization $(m-j, j)$. Now, suppose $i < j$, that is, $M(I_1) > M(I_2)$ and $f(I_1) = 0, f(I_2) = 1, f'(I_1) = 1, f'(I_2) = 0$. Now, we need to show that $\Pr(M|f') \geq \Pr(M|f)$.

Let n_{k1}, n_{k0} denote the number of items mapped to 1 and 0 respectively under f (and f') in $\mathbf{I} \setminus \{I_1 \cup I_2\}$ with realization $(m-k, k)$. With this notation, we can compute each of $\Pr(M|f)$ and $\Pr(M|f')$.

<u>**Likelihood of $f' : I_1 \to 1, I_2 \to 0$.**</u>
Let

$$p'_{11} = \frac{\sum_k n_{k1}(m-k) + (m-i)}{\sum_k n_{k1} m + m}$$

and

$$p'_{00} = \frac{\sum_k n_{k0}(m-k) + j}{\sum_k n_{k0} m + m}$$

Here, p'_{11} (respectively p'_{00}) represents the underlying (maximum likelihood) probability of a worker responding 1 (respectively 0) for an item with true value 1 (respectively 0). Further, (for ease of exposition), let $a_1 = \sum_k n_{k1}(m-k)+(m-i)$, $a_0 = \sum_k n_{k0}(m-k) + j$, $c_1 = \sum_k n_{k1} m + m$, and $c_0 = \sum_k n_{k0} m + m$. Then, from the independence of items assumption, we have, $P(M|f') = (p'_{11})^{a_1}(1-p'_{11})^{c_1-a_1}(p'_{00})^{a_0}(1-p'_{00})^{c_0-a_0}$.

<u>**Likelihood of $f : I_1 \to 0, I_2 \to 1$.**</u>
Similarly, we let

$$p_{11} = \frac{\sum_k n_{k1}(m-k) + (m-j)}{\sum_k n_{k1} m + m}$$

and

$$p_{00} = \frac{\sum_k n_{k0}(m-k) + i}{\sum_k n_{k0} m + m}$$

Suppose $b_1 = \sum_k n_{k1}(m-k)+(m-j)$, and $b_0 = \sum_k n_{k0}(m-k)+i$, we can similarly show that $P(M|f) = (p_{11})^{b_1}(1-p_{11})^{c_1-b_1} \times (p_{00})^{b_0}(1-p_{00})^{c_0-b_0}$.

Therefore, we can write $\frac{P(M|f')}{P(M|f)}$ as $X_1 X_0$, where:
$X_1 = \frac{(p'_{11})^{a_1}(1-p'_{11})^{c_1-a_1}}{(p_{11})^{b_1}(1-p_{11})^{c_1-b_1}}$, and $X_0 = \frac{(p'_{00})^{a_0}(1-p'_{00})^{c_0-a_0}}{(p_{00})^{b_0}(1-p_{00})^{c_0-b_0}}$.
We claim, that for reasonable mappings, $X_1, X_0 \geq 1$, which implies that $P(M|f') \geq P(M|f)$, thereby completing our proof. We show below that $X_1 \geq 1$. The proof for X_0 follows in a similar fashion.

We can rewrite X_1 as $X_1 = \frac{(a_1)^{a_1}(c_1-a_1)^{c_1-a_1}}{(b_1)^{b_1}(c_1-b_1)^{c_1-b_1}}$. We drop the "1" subscript from this point for ease of notation. Here, we have $a < b$ (follows from $i < j$). It can be shown that when $a < b$, $a+b \geq c \Rightarrow X \geq 1$. It is easy to see that if f and f' are reasonable mappings, then we have $p'_{11}, p_{11} \geq 0.5$ (follows from the definition in Section 3.3). But $p'_{11} = \frac{a_1}{c_1}$, and $p_{11} = \frac{b_1}{c_1}$. Therefore, $a, b \geq \frac{c}{2} \Rightarrow a + b \geq c \Rightarrow X \geq 1$. This completes our proof.

A.2 Real Data Additional Experiments

Here, we report some additional experiments for our first real dataset [10]. In particular, we would like to estimate the performance of OPT versus vanilla EM instances. Under this setting,

OPT, as well as EM assume a single worker error distribution and infer item values based on this assumption and learned error distribution.

Setup. We vary the number of workers used from 1 to 19 and plot the performance of algorithms OPT, $EM(1)$, $EM(2)$, $EM(3)$, $EM(*)$ similar to Section 3.5. We plot the number of worker responses used along the x-axis. For instance, a value of $m = 4$ indicates that for each item, four *random* worker responses are chosen. The four workers answering one item may be different from those answering another item. This random sample of the response set is given as input to the different algorithms. Similar to our synthetic data experiments, we average our results across 100 different trials for each data point in our subsequent plots.

Likelihood. Figure 11(b) plots the likelihoods of the final solution for different algorithms. We observe that except for $EM(2)$, all algorithms have a high likelihood. This can be explained as follows: $EM(2)$ which starts with an initialization of e_0 and e_1 rates around 0.5 and converges to a final response probability matrix in that neighborhood. Final error rates of around 0.5 (random) will have naturally low likelihood when there is a high amount of agreement between workers. $EM(1)$ and $EM(3)$ on the other hand start with, and converge to near opposite extremes with $EM(1)$ predicting e_0/e_1 rates ≈ 0 and $EM(3)$ predicting error rates ≈ 1. Both of these, however, result in a high likelihood of observing the given response, with $EM(1)$ predicting that the worker is always correct, and $EM(3)$ predicting that the worker is always incorrect, i.e., adversarial. Even though $EM(1)$ and $EM(3)$ often converge to completely opposite predictions of item-values because of their initializations, their solutions still have similar likelihoods corresponding to the intuitive extremes of perfect and adversarial worker behavior. This behavior thus demonstrates the strong dependence of EM-based approaches on the initialization parameters.

Fraction Incorrect. Figure 11(a) plots the fraction of items predicted incorrectly along the y-axis for OPT and the EM algorithms. We observe that both $EM(1)$ and our algorithm OPT do fairly well on this dataset even when a very few number of worker responses are used. However, $EM(*)$, which one may expect would typically do better than the individual EM initializations, sometimes does poorly compared to OPT by picking solutions of high likelihood that are nevertheless not very good. Note that here we assume that worker identities are unknown and arbitrary workers could be answering different tasks — our goal is to characterize the behavior of the worker population as a whole. For larger datasets, we expect the effects of population smoothing to be greater and our assumptions on worker homogeneity to be closer to the truth. So, even though our algorithm provides theoretical global guarantees under somewhat strong assumptions, it also performs well for settings where not all our assumptions are true.

B. EXTENSIONS

In this section we discuss the generalization of our bucketizing and dominance-based approach to some extensions of the filtering and rating problems. Recall our two major assumptions: (1) every item receives the same number (m) of responses, and (2) all workers are randomly assigned and their responses are drawn from a common distribution, $p(i, j)$. We now relax each of these requirements and describe how our framework can be applied.

B.1 Variable number of responses

Suppose different items may receive different numbers of worker responses, *e.g.* because items are randomly chosen, or workers choose some questions preferentially over others. Note in this section we are still assuming that all workers have the same response probability matrix p.

For this discussion we restrict ourselves to the filtering problem; a similar analysis can be applied to rating. Suppose each item can receive a maximum of m worker responses, with different items receiving different numbers of responses. Again, we bucketize items by their response sets and try to impose a dominance-ordering on the buckets. Now, instead of only considering response sets of the form $(m-j, j)$, we consider arbitrary (i, j). Recall that a response set (i, j) denotes that an item received i "1" responses and j "0" responses. We show the imposed dominance ordering in Figure 13.

We expect an item that receives i "1" responses and j "0" responses to be more likely to have true value "1" than an item with $i - 1$ "1" responses and j "0" responses, or an item with i "1" responses and $j + 1$ "0" responses. So, we have the dominance relations $(i, j) > (i - 1, j)$ where $i \geq 1, j \geq 0, i + j \leq m$, and $(i, j) > (i, j + 1)$ with $i, j \geq 0, i + j + 1 \leq m$. Note that the dominance ordering imposed in Section 3, $(m, 0) > (m - 1, 1) > \ldots > (0, m)$, is implied transitively here. For instance, $(m, 0) > (m - 1, 0) \wedge (m - 1, 0) > (m - 1, 1) \Rightarrow (m, 0) > (m - 1, 1)$. Also note that this is a partial ordering as certain pairs of buckets, $(0, 0)$ and $(1, 1)$ for example, cannot intuitively be compared.

Again, we can reduce our search for the maximum likelihood mapping to the space of all bucketized mappings consistent with this dominance (partial) ordering. That is, given item set $\mathbf{I}$ and response set M, we consider mappings $f : \mathbf{I} \rightarrow \{0, 1\}$, where $M(I_1) = M(I_2) \Rightarrow f(I_1) = f(I_2)$ and $M(I_1) > M(I_2) \Rightarrow f(I_1) \geq f(I_2)$. We show two such dominance consistent mappings, f_i and f_j in Figure 13. Mapping f_i assigns all items with at least i "1" worker responses to a value of 1 and the rest to a value of 0. Similarly, mapping f_j assigns all items with at most j "0" responses a value of 1 and the rest a value of 0. We can construct a third dominance-consistent mapping f_{ij} from a conjunction of these two: $f_{ij}(I) = 1$ if and only if $f_i = 1 \wedge f_j = 1$, that is, f_{ij} assigns only gives those items that have at least i "1" worker responses and at most j "0" responses, a value of 1. We can now describe f_i and f_j as special instances of the dominance-consistent mapping f_{ij} when $j = m$ and $i = 0$ respectively.

We show below that all dominance-consistent mappings for this setting can be described as the union of different f_{ij}s for a set of $0 \leq i, j \leq m$, for a total of $O(2^m)$ dominance-consistent mappings. Note that although this expression is exponential in the maximum number of worker responses per item, m, for most practical applications this is a very small constant.

Let f be any dominance-consistent mapping under this setting. Let (i, j) be a response set with i responses of 1 and j responses of 0 such that $f(i, j) = 1$. Then, by our dominance constraint, we know that $f(i + \Delta i, j + \Delta j) = 1 \forall \Delta i \geq 0, \Delta j \geq 0$. We represent this figuratively in Figure 12(a). If $f(i, j) = 1$, then all response sets, or points, in the shaded area also get mapped to a value of 1.

Now, by applying the dominance constraint as shown in Figure 12(a) to every (i, j) such that $f(i, j) = 1$, we can show that f can now be described intuitively by its "boundary". We demonstrate this intuition in Figure 12(b). Every point, (i, j), on f's boundary satisfies $f(i, j) = 1$. Additionally, every point "within" the boundary, every point that is to the right of and below the boundary gets mapped to a value of 1 under f. Finally, every point that is not on or within the boundary gets mapped to a value of 0 under f.

It follows from the dominance constraint that every dominance-consistent mapping, f, can be represented by a unique such continuous boundary. Furthermore, it is easy to see that any such boundary satisfies three conditions:

- Its leftmost (corner) point lies on one of the axes.

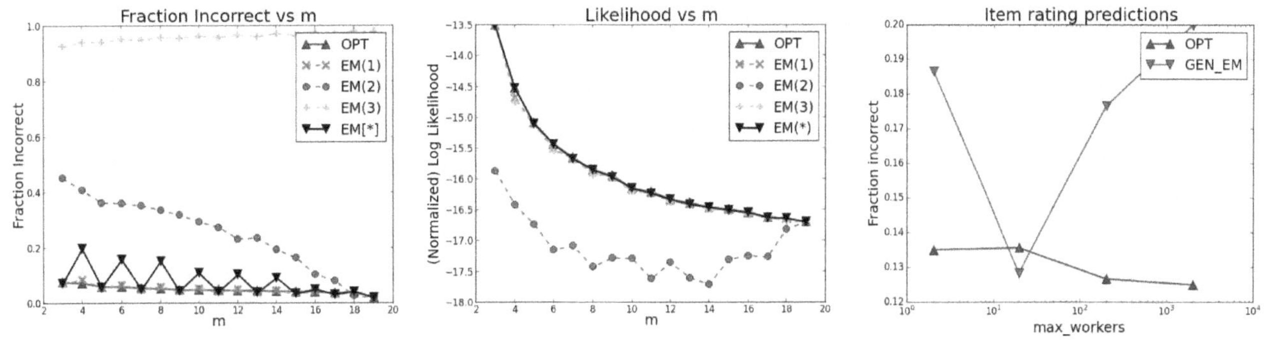

Figure 11: Filtering, Real, Setting 1: (a) Item predictions, (b) Likelihood; (c) 2 worker classes: Fraction incorrect

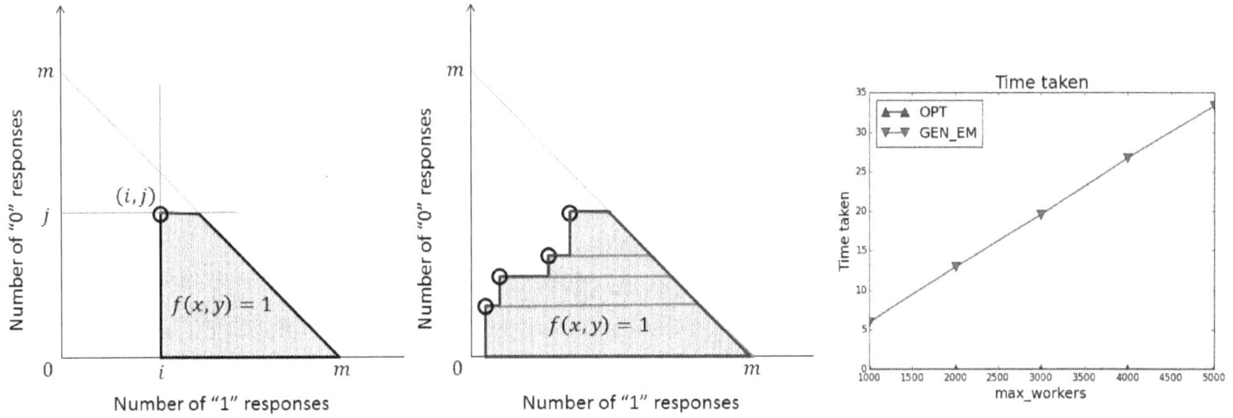

Figure 12: Variable number of responses: (a) Dominance constraint 1, (b) Dominance constraint 2; 2 worker classes: (c) Time taken

- Its topmost (corner) point lies on the line $x + y = m$.
- If (x_1, y_1) and (x_2, y_2) lie on the boundary, then $x_1 \leq x_2 \Leftrightarrow y_1 \leq y_2$.

Intuitively the above three conditions give us a constructive definition for any dominance-consistent mapping's boundary. Every dominance-consistent mapping can be constructed uniquely as follows: (1) Choose a left corner point lying on one of the axes. (2) Choose a topmost corner point (necessarily above and to the right of the first corner point) lying on the line $x + y = m$. (3) Finally, define the boundary as a unique grid traversal from the left corner to the top corner where you are allowed to extend the boundary only to the right or upwards. Each such boundary corresponds to a unique dominance-consistent mapping where every point on or under the boundary is mapped to 1 and every other point is mapped to 0. Furthermore, every dominance-consistent mapping has a unique such boundary.

Therefore our problem of counting the number of dominance-consistent mappings for this setting reduces to counting the number of such boundaries. We use our constructive definition for the boundary to compute this number. First, suppose the leftmost corner point, $L = (p, 0), 0 \leq p \leq m$, lies on the x-axis (we can calculate similarly for $(0, q)$). Now, the topmost corner point lies to the right of the first corner point, and on the line $x + y = m$. Therefore it is of the form $T = (p + i, m - (p + i))$ for some $0 \leq i \leq m - p$. The number of unique grid traversals (respectively boundaries) from L to T is given by $\binom{m-p}{i}$. Combining, we have the number of unique boundaries that have their left corner on the x-axis is $\sum_{p=0}^{m}\sum_{i=0}^{m-p}\binom{m-p}{i} = \sum_{p=0}^{m} 2^{m-p} = 2^{m+1} - 1$. Calculating similarly for boundaries that start with their leftmost corner on the y-axis ($(0, q), 1 \leq q \leq m$) and including the empty boundary (corresponding to the mapping where all items get assigned a value of 0), we get an additional 2^m boundaries. Therefore, we conclude that there are $O(2^m)$ such boundaries, corresponding to $O(2^m)$ dominance-consistent mappings. It should be noted that although this is exponential in the maximum number of worker responses to an item, typical values of m are small enough that all mappings can very easily be enumerated and evaluated.

B.2 Worker classes

So far we have assumed that all workers are identical, in that they draw their answers from the same response probability matrix, a strong assumption that does not hold in general. Although we could argue that different worker matrices could be aggregated into one average probability matrix that our previous approach discovers, if we have fine-grained knowledge about workers, we would like to exploit it. In this section we consider the setting where there are two of classes of workers, *expert* and *regular* workers to evaluate the same set of items. We discuss the generalization to larger numbers of worker classes below.

We now model worker behavior as two different response probability matrices, the first corresponding to expert workers who have low error rates, and the second corresponding to regular workers who have higher error rates. Our problem now becomes that of estimating the items' true values in addition to both of the response probability matrices. For this discussion, we consider the filtering problem; a similar analysis can be applied to the rating case.

Again, we extend our ideas of bucketizing and dominance to this setting. Let (y_e, n_e, y_r, n_r) be the bucket representing all items that receive y_e and n_e responses of "1" and "0" respectively from experts, and y_r and n_r responses of "1" and "0" respectively from regular workers. A dominance partial ordering can be defined using the following rules. An item (respectively bucket) with response set $B_1 = (y_e^1, n_e^1, y_r^1, n_r^1)$ dominates an item (respectively bucket)

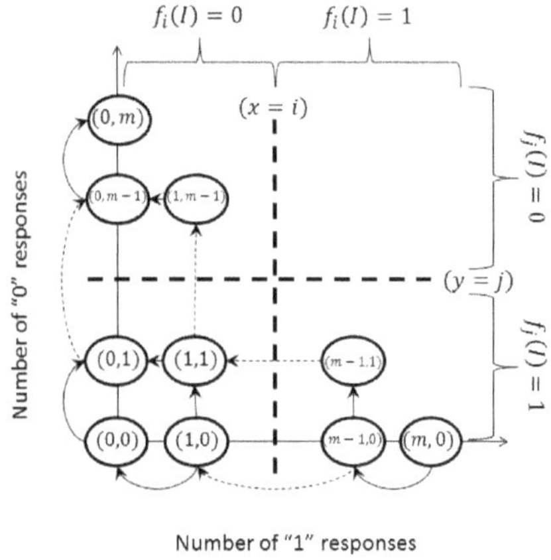

Figure 13: Variable number of responses

with response set $B_2 = (y_e^2, n_e^2, y_r^2, n_r^2)$ if and only if one of the following is satisfied:

- B_1 sees more responses of "1" and fewer responses of "0" than B_2. That is, $(y_e^1 \geq y_e^2) \wedge (y_r^1 \geq y_r^2) \wedge (n_e^1 \leq n_e^2) \wedge (n_e^1 \leq n_e^2)$ where at least one of the inequalities is strict.
- B_1 and B_2 see the same number of "1" and "0" responses in total, but more experts respond "1" to B_1 and "0" to B_2. That is, $(y_e^1 + y_r^1 = y_e^2 + y_r^2) \wedge (n_e^1 + n_r^1 = n_e^2 + n_r^2) \wedge (y_e^1 \geq y_e^2) \wedge (n_e^1 \leq n_e^2)$ where at least one of the inequalities is strict.

As before, we consider only the set of mappings that assign all items in a bucket the same value while preserving the dominance relationship, that is, dominating buckets get at least as high a value as dominated buckets.

Note that the second dominance condition above leverages the assumption that experts have smaller error probabilities than regular workers. If we were just given two classes of workers with no information about their response probability matrices, we could only use the first dominance condition. In general, having more information about the error probabilities of worker classes allows us to construct stronger dominance conditions, which in turn reduces the number of dominance-consistent mappings. This property allows our framework to be flexible and adaptable to different granularities of prior knowledge.

Example (2 worker classes, 2 responses per item). We demonstrate the OPT solution for a simple generalization to filtering, where we have two worker classes: "good", and "bad", and each item receives 2 responses. Suppose we denote the responses by a good worker as "Y" (yes, or 1) and "N" (no, or 0), and those by a bad worker as "y", and "n". Any item can receive one of the following 10 possible sets of responses: (YY), (Yy), (yy), (Yn), (yn), (YN), (yN), (nn), (Nn), (NN). If the only information about these worker classes is that the good class has lower (false positive and false negative) error rates, then the corresponding (least constrained) dominance-consistent DAG is shown in Figure 14. For this DAG, we have 18 dominance-consistent mappings.

We evaluated the performance of OPT against GEN_EM under this setting on a synthetic dataset. Workers were randomly chosen to belong to one of the two classes. Workers from the good class were uniformly randomly assigned an error rate between 0.9 and 1.0, while workers from the bad class were given an error rate between 0.6 and 0.7. In Figure 11(c) we vary the total size of the worker pool, m' along the x-axis, and show the fraction of items predicted incorrectly along the y-axis. We also plot the times taken by OPT and GEN_EM (20 iterations) to label all items in Figure 12(c). We observe that OPT is faster, as well as more accurate than GEN_EM under this setting.

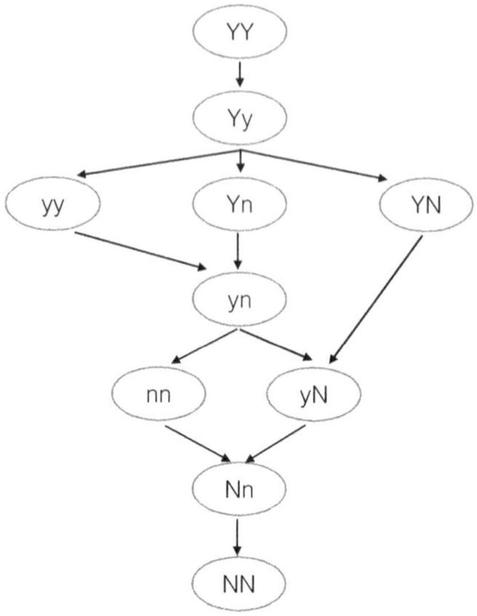

Figure 14: 2 worker classes: Dominance DAG

Complexity. The complexity introduced by worker classes can not be estimated for the general case, since it is governed not only by the number of worker classes, but also by the input constraints specified on the error rates of workers from different classes. Finer grained constraints imply fewer dominance-consistent mappings and hence, a lower complexity, while coarser grained (or fewer) constraints imply a higher complexity. For instance, in the limiting case where we have no prior information about the worker class error rates, we have no constraints, and the dominance-consistent DAG correspondingly has no edges. Therefore, the complexity of OPT, which scales linearly with the number of mappings, is $\mathcal{O}(R^k)$, where $R = 2$ for filtering, and k is the number of possible responses (or nodes in the DAG) seen by an item. At the other extreme, when the different error rates of the respective classes are highly constrained (for instance, if we know that one class is significantly better than another, and any responses from workers of the first class dominate all responses of workers from the second class), the dominance-consistent DAG can be reduced to a single chain: in this case, given any pair of sets of responses, it can be calculated exactly which set gives a higher likelihood of an item passing the filter. In this extreme, the resulting complexity of OPT is $\mathcal{O}(\binom{k+R-1}{k})$ (derivable in a similar fashion to the lower bound shown for rating in Section 4.2). Note that k itself is not easy to compute for arbitrary values of R, m and w (number of worker classes). For $m = 1$, we have $k = wR$ (each response can be given by any of the worker classes, and can be anything between $[1, R]$). For arbitrary values, k can scale exponentially with w.

While this extension is reasonable when the number of distinct worker classes is small, it is impractical to generalize it to a large number of classes. One heuristic approach to tackling the problem of a large number of worker classes, or independent workers, could be to divide items into a large number discrete groups and assign a small distinct set of workers to evaluate each group of items. We then treat and solve each of the groups independently as a problem instance with a small number worker classes. We leave the problems of formally computing the complexity, and finding more efficient algorithms for this general setting as a topic for future work.

Building the Enterprise Fabric for Big Data with Vertica and Spark Integration

Jeff LeFevre, Rui Liu, Cornelio Inigo, Lupita Paz
Edward Ma, Malu Castellanos, Meichun Hsu
HPE Vertica
Sunnyvale, CA
{first.last,r.liu}@hpe.com

ABSTRACT

Enterprise customers increasingly require greater flexibility in the way they access and process their Big Data while at the same time they continue to request advanced analytics and access to diverse data sources. Yet customers also still require the robustness of enterprise class analytics for their mission-critical data. In this paper, we present our initial efforts toward a solution that satisfies the above requirements by integrating the HPE Vertica enterprise database with Apache Spark's open source big data computation engine. In particular, it enables fast, reliable transferring of data between Vertica and Spark; and deploying Machine Learning models created by Spark into Vertica for predictive analytics on Vertica data. This integration provides a fabric on which our customers get the best of both worlds: it extends Vertica's extensive SQL analytics capabilities with Spark's machine learning library (MLlib), giving Vertica users access to a wide range of ML functions; it also enables customers to leverage Spark as an advanced ETL engine for all data that require the guarantees offered by Vertica.

1. INTRODUCTION

HPE Vertica is a massively parallel database system, ideal for read-intensive analytic database applications, with full support for SQL and robust data management based on columnar database technology. It is well-designed for managing critical data with atomicity, consistency, integrity, and durability. While our enterprise customers use Vertica for processing Big Data, new systems such as Apache Spark in the Hadoop ecosystem have been gaining momentum. Spark is a compute engine with a generalized multistage in-memory computation structure, instead of the two-stage disk-based MapReduce paradigm. It enables access to data in HDFS and supports batch, streaming, machine learning (MLlib), SQL, and graph processing (GraphX). However, its data management is weaker in enterprise readiness compared to a commercial database system. For example, Spark does not yet have adequate isolation semantics for data sharing, nor does it offer data integrity guarantees. Therefore, it is not the best choice for companies to store and manage their mission-critical business data.

SIGMOD'16, June 26-July 01, 2016, San Francisco, CA, USA

DOI: http://dx.doi.org/10.1145/2882903.2903744

Since Vertica is an enterprise class analytical database, it is a good target for storing data resulting from extract-transform-load (ETL) processes performed in Spark. We also leverage Spark for machine learning using data stored in Vertica. In this paper we present our solution to integrate Vertica and Spark into an enterprise fabric that supports robust data management, analytics and machine learning. We define the following two primary challenges to accomplish this integration:

1. Transferring data quickly, reliably, and robustly between Vertica and Spark in order to support:
    - A pipeline for Spark to use Vertica as a fast analytic data source.
    - Spark as an ETL engine for Vertica.
2. Creating and then deploying Spark ML models within Vertica for in-database scoring (i.e., prediction).

Our approach integrates Vertica and Spark with data flowing in either direction, Vertica to Spark (*V2S*) or Spark to Vertica (*S2V*) as shown in Figure 1. In the V2S direction for analytics, we provide a connector to efficiently read Vertica data into Spark and then leverage Spark's ML library (MLlib [9]) to train models in Spark. In the S2V direction for ETL workloads we provide a connector that efficiently loads the transformed data into Vertica. To support the full analytics pipeline, another essential component we provide is a mechanism to deploy the trained models (*MD*) to Vertica for in-database scoring. In addition, since Spark now supports export of some models in Predictive Model Markup Language (PMML) [7, 10], it makes sense to deploy PMML models from Spark to Vertica. Such capability can also serve other PMML producers such as SAS or Distributed R (DR) [14]. To make our Vertica and Spark integration easily accessible for Spark users, our architecture shown in Figure 1 allows each component (V2S, MD, S2V) to be initiated from within Spark. The approaches presented in this paper are available as a beta release on the HPE Marketplace [5].

Contributions

- Fast, reliable data transfer between Spark and Vertica with exactly once semantics.
    - Our parallelized method for V2S eliminates all data shuffling between Vertica nodes.

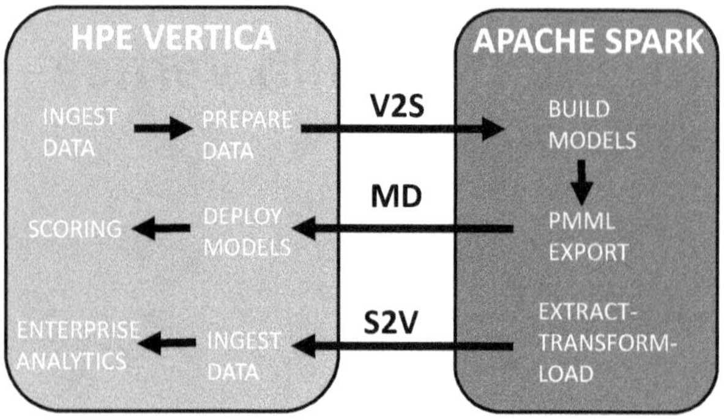

Figure 1: Overview of integration architecture and functionality.

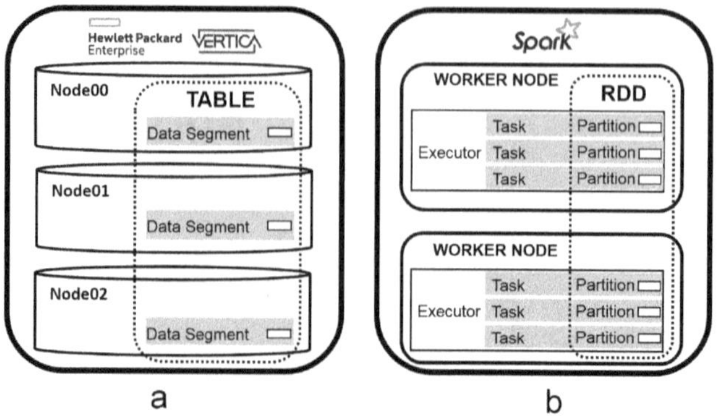

Figure 2: HPE Vertica (a) and Apache Spark (b).

- Our parallelized method for S2V prevents partial or duplicate loads.

- Our approach tolerates Spark job failures, task failures and restarts, as well as speculative execution; and it can be applied to the general class of MapReduce systems.
- We present experimental results evaluating our methods along different dimensions such as varying parallelism, data scaling, cluster scaling, and others. We also present a comparison with other approaches showing our methods have competitive performance.
- The capability to take machine learning models built in Spark to be deployed and executed within Vertica for in-database scoring.

In the following sections we describe each of these components and some of the challenges faced. We begin with an overview of the problem in Section 2, followed by the details of our approach in Section 3. The advanced analytics pipeline component V2S is described in Section 3.1 followed by the ETL pipeline component S2V in Section 3.2, while model deployment (MD) is described in Section 3.3. Experimental results that analyze many aspects of performance are provided in Section 4. Lastly, discussion, related work and brief conclusion are presented in Sections 5, 6, and 7.

2. PROBLEM OVERVIEW

Our goal is to integrate two distinct systems, HPE Vertica and Apache Spark for the following specific purposes. First we want to support the full analytics pipeline to extend Vertica's analytics capabilities with ML models created in Spark. Second we want to transfer data quickly and reliably between HPE Vertica and Apache Spark in support of the analytics pipeline (V2S component) and for using Spark as a fast ETL engine for Vertica (S2V component).

To achieve the first goal, we need to share and recreate ML models built in Spark with Vertica. Spark's MLlib includes a variety of machine learning algorithms such as classification, clustering, and regression, and models built with MLlib must be able to execute on Vertica. A common standard format helps to facilitate this task, and here we use PMML format to export the model and develop a mechanism to deploy the model on Vertica. To achieve the second goal, we need a reliable transfer mechanism that enables fast data transfer between HPE Vertica and Apache Spark in both directions, along with data semantics guarantees required for an Enterprise solution. Our focus in this paper is mainly on the data transfer mechanisms and their semantics.

Given these goals, our primary problem is to *reliably* transfer data between two distinct systems. From the user's perspective, ideally 'reliably' should indicate standard transactional semantics that a user expects in an enterprise database. Hence we desire *exactly-once semantics*, ensuring all of the data is transferred once and only once. Thus the data should move from one system to the other in its totality and current state at the time the move was requested. While there are database constructs to achieve transactional semantics within a single database, maintaining exactly-once semantics across systems is a challenge.

2.1 System Descriptions

In this section we briefly outline the characteristics of HPE Vertica and Apache Spark that are relevant in the discussion of our work. Figure 2 provides a high-level picture of each system and the details of each are described below.

2.1.1 HPE Vertica Database

Figure 2(a) provides an illustration of a Vertica database spanned over multiple nodes in a Vertica cluster. HPE Vertica is an MPP column-store [13, 15], distributed database with traditional transaction semantics (i.e., ACID). Tables in Vertica are segmented across nodes in the cluster as shown in the figure. *Segments* correspond to non-overlapping hash ranges, and each range is stored on a particular node. By default, tables are created using several columns in the segmentation (*hash*) expression, but segmentation columns may be explicitly provided, and it is possible to create unsegmented tables as well. For fault tolerance, Vertica provides replication of tables across nodes by setting its k-safety value where k is the number of failed nodes tolerated before data loss. When storing its data, Vertica uses a proprietary storage structure called *Read Optimized Storage*, or ROS, which is a highly optimized read-oriented disk storage that includes compression and indexing. Vertica also has a corresponding *Write Optimized Storage*, or WOS. The details of Vertica's ROS and WOS storage are beyond the scope of this paper but can be found in [13].

Vertica supports advanced SQL analytics, including the ability for users to write custom functions called User-Defined Extensions (UDx). In this way, Vertica's analytics functionality can be extended to support many algorithms.

2.1.2 *Apache Spark*

Figure 2(b) provides an illustration of Apache Spark, showing multiple nodes in a Spark cluster. Spark [17] is a compute engine and even though it provides SQL processing capabilities, it is not a database management system and does not provide shared data access nor ACID semantics. Spark's machine learning library, MLlib [9], provides parallelized versions of various ML algorithms. Spark's main abstraction is a Resilient Distributed Dataset (*RDD*), which is distributed throughout the cluster, and *worker nodes* manage local execution of tasks that operate on RDD data.

RDD. An RDD [16] is an immutable in-memory construct that is divided into *partitions* and distributed across a Spark cluster. RDDs themselves are not durable, but their data could be saved to an external storage location effectively creating a snapshot of the current RDD. However, since it is immutable any new manipulation performed on an RDD would produce a new RDD. In this way the in-memory RDD is simply a distinct copy of any data source from which it was created.

Spark Scheduler. Spark uses a batch-based task scheduler, where jobs are run asynchronously after they are submitted by the user. Jobs are composed of tasks, launched by *executors* and a job will create some number of tasks that execute independently of each other, with each operating on an associated partition of data as indicated in Figure 2(b). Tasks are coordinated by the Spark master (not shown), are stateless (ideally), and do not communicate or coordinate among themselves. Some of Spark's fault tolerance mechanisms include (a) maintaining the provenance (i.e., lineage) of an RDD such that an RDD partition's data can be recomputed any time and (b) the ability to restart failed or straggling tasks, i.e., speculative execution.

DataFrames. Recently Spark introduced DataFrames and its External Data Source API. A Spark DataFrame is effectively a wrapper around an RDD that provides a schema, where each of the RDD's rows is of Spark SQL Row type. A *DataFrame* in Spark is analogous to a database *table*, but since DataFrames are based on RDDs they are immutable. The External Data Source API was introduced in Spark to provide a standard API to save/load data to/from another data source. Developers may implement specific versions of the load/save functions for their data source. This is the interface we use in our work and have implemented load-/save functions specifically for Vertica. The API is based on enabling easy access for Spark users to external data but introduces several technical challenges, described below, due to Spark's compute architecture and especially its scheduler.

2.2 Possible Approaches and Challenges

Given the characteristics of each system, next we describe a first possible approach and the challenges that arise when introducing parallelism that results in competing design goals: performance versus consistency.

2.2.1 *Vertica-centric Approach*

A Vertica-centric approach would be one that enables Vertica to send the data to Spark (*push*-based) for the V2S direction, or let Vertica pull the data from Spark (*pull*-based) for the S2V direction. This Vertica-centric method can potentially have very high performance since it can rely on Vertica's query optimizer to plan and control the parallel data transfer in an efficient way because it is aware of the internal details of Vertica's data layout and cluster configuration. Although this would automatically provide parallelization and transactional semantics, this approach is not well-suited for Spark's batch-based scheduler as we describe next.

Since the Spark scheduler can only create a set of independent, stateless Spark tasks to perform the load or save actions, we do not have a direct way to coordinate the data push or pull actions with Vertica from Spark tasks. Spark tasks would need to start and then wait for some coordination to begin receiving or sending data to/from Vertica. Furthermore with a Vertica-centric approach, even if Vertica initiates the transfer by launching a Spark job, it is not clear when the tasks will be run or even *re-run* since tasks are scheduled by Spark and a submitted job can have an unbounded wait time depending upon how many other Spark jobs are currently executing in the system and on the scheduling algorithm (several are available). Alternatively, an independent third system with its own scheduler could be used to initiate and coordinate the actions. This approach to coordination is possible but adds extra complexity due to the need for a third system/process and scheduler, and in the end would still depend upon the Spark scheduler.

2.2.2 *Challenges with Parallelism*

To achieve performance we can potentially use many tasks, i.e., parallelism. By launching many tasks, a high degree of parallelism can be achieved but since they are independent and cannot coordinate with each other, there is no guarantee of reliable data transfer. For example, when saving data to Vertica, if a task fails or Spark itself crashes this could result in partial data transfer. If a task is restarted by Spark then it could repeat its own data transfer, potentially duplicating the data. Moreover, there is a subtlety in that even if a task only commits after it is completely done, it could still fail immediately *after* the commit and be restarted, again resulting in duplication. When loading data from Vertica, many independent tasks executing at different times or re-executing after failure can result in loading an inconsistent view of the Vertica data if a table is updated in-between tasks.

Compounding the problem further is that even if many parallel tasks connect to different Vertica nodes, it is not likely that a task will request data that is local to that node, hence in addition to the outbound network traffic sending the data out to Spark this will induce a lot of internal network traffic between Vertica nodes as they exchange data to answer each request. Hence, the technical challenges of our parallelized design include reducing internal data shuffling between Vertica nodes and how to provide a consistent view of the data while providing fast data transfer.

In this work we present and evaluate our approach that achieves parallelism and reliability with exactly-once semantics and with workload optimization. We describe this approach next in Section 3. Although this work is based upon Apache Spark, we believe that our methods can be applied to the general class of MapReduce [11] systems.

3. OUR APPROACH

Our approach for transferring data between Spark and Vertica utilizes the parallelism of the Vertica MPP DMBS as well as the parallelism inherent in Spark's computation model. Our key insights to solving the problem are that we

LOAD	SAVE
df.read .format(Def.Source) .options(opts) .load()	df.write .format(Def.Source) .options(opts) .mode(mode) .save()

Table 1: Spark's External Data Source API example

can rely on knowledge of the data layout in Vertica, and use Vertica itself and its ACID semantics as a way to guarantee reliable, fast data transfer with exactly once semantics. The connector is optimized to load large volumes of data from Spark to Vertica and designed to be robust to Spark failure scenarios such as total Spark failure, failed tasks, duplicated tasks, or speculative tasks and still provide exactly-once semantics. Next we discuss our approach that is implemented using DataFrames and Spark's External Data Source API. Our implementation using RDD (for Spark ML methods that operate on RDDs) provides a similar functionality. First in Section 3.1 we describe our approach for transferring data from Vertica to Spark, V2S. Then in Section 3.2 we describe our approach for transferring data from Spark to Vertica, S2V.

To help clarify the following discussions, Table 1 shows the current syntax for Spark's External Data Source API to load/save data from/to an external source assuming an existing Spark DataFrame `df`. The API includes a reference to the `DefaultSource` name, which is the implementation specific source code, in this case our Vertica-specific implementation, which is called "com.vertica.spark.datasource.DefaultSource". It also includes an arbitrary list of key=value options, `opts`; these typically include user names, passwords, table names, and host IP addresses among other parameters relevant for the source-specific implementation. Additional options available with our approach are described in the following V2S and S2V sections where relevant. When saving data, the API also requires a save mode, `mode`, which can include overwriting or appending to an existing table.

The benefit for users is that the API is standardized and simple. We note that this API only represents the current implementation while our below methodologies apply generally for load and save methods.

3.1 Transferring Data from Vertica to Spark (V2S)

In this this section we describe the design and semantics for the V2S component of the HPE Vertica Connector for Apache Spark. The connector is invoked with the `LOAD` API shown in Table 1, which also supports additional processing operations (e.g., `.filter()`, `.select()`, `.count()`) which can be applied to the DataFrame during load. The connector is optimized to pushdown these operations into Vertica in order to take advantage of the computational power of Vertica to both pre-process the data and minimize the amount of data transferred over the network. The transfer of a Vertica table to Spark is atomic and will load a consistent view of the table into Spark.

The key insight with our approach is that we can utilize Vertica's data layout and its ACID semantics to enable fast data transfer to load a consistent view of the data along with exactly-once semantics. To achieve the highest possible data transfer performance, our solution connects the computation pipelines of Vertica and Spark in an optimized way, which not only utilizes parallel channels for data movement, but also ensures:

1. Data flow optimization by pushing down computation into Vertica as appropriate.
2. Data request locality optimization on Vertica nodes.

Spark's computation is organized as a chain of RDDs (or DataFrames) which forms the execution pipeline and is evaluated *lazily*. Due to Spark's batch-style scheduler, the user can only request Vertica data by launching a Spark Job and then waiting for the Job to finish. For this reason, we require a *pull*-style approach whereby the user's Spark Job directly asks for the data that it wants, which is then pulled into Spark. For each Spark partition (i.e., task), our approach is to formulate a unique query requesting a non-overlapping subset of the desired Vertica data, as well as any pre-processing required (e.g., push-downs), and the union of the result of all queries represents the full table data. In Section 3.1.1 we describe the computation pipeline and pre-processing to achieve optimization (1) above, then in Section 3.1.2 we describe our query formulation to achieve optimization (2).

3.1.1 Reducing the Amount of Data in the Pipeline

Figure 3 shows the data flow in the computation pipeline of our V2S approach. The full computation job spans both Vertica and Spark: data from a Vertica table flows through multiple Vertica query execution plans in parallel on the different cluster nodes, and is then transferred into Spark's pipelines. Vertica can pre-process the data with project, filter, and count operators as supported by Spark's External Data Source API. By pushing these operators down into Vertica, only the pre-processed results are passed through the system boundary and into Spark's computation pipeline, potentially reducing the amount of data transferred.

Spark's External Data Source API currently does not support pushdowns for joins or aggregations, however, if the user pre-defines a view in Vertica that represents the join or aggregation our connector can load the view. V2S supports loading views (and similarly unsegmented tables) by producing *synthentic* hash ranges which allow us to also use parallelism during data transfer for views. In this way, views can enable pushdown of other operations such as joins and aggregations. All pushdowns are computed inside Vertica within our compute pipeline as shown by the connected arrows inside the Vertica nodes in Figure 3. In this way our notion of computation pushdown can extend beyond the simple pushdowns enabled by the Data Source API. This reduces data flow in the pipeline and helps us to achieve the data flow optimization (1) in Section 3.1.

3.1.2 Data Locality Aware Approach

As the number of parallel connections between the two systems increases, the network bandwidth between the Vertica nodes can become a bottleneck in the computation pipeline, potentially slowing it down. This is caused by the amount of data shuffling between Vertica nodes to retrieve all of the table data. This occurs because each Spark partition (task) connects via JDBC to a Vertica node and issues a query to pull a specific portion of the table data, which is typically scattered across all Vertica nodes.

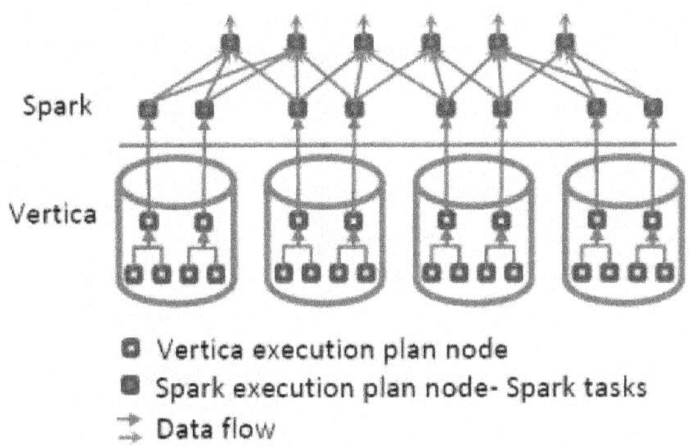

Figure 3: Connected computation pipeline.

Our novel solution to prevent unnecessary data shuffling between Vertica nodes is to have each Spark task formulate a query that only requests data that is local to the node to which it connects. Thus, each query to a Vertica node only targets the local *segment* of the data.

Vertica distributes its table data via hashing based on the SEGMENTED BY HASH(*columns*) clause or implicitly, storing segments with different contiguous hash ranges across the nodes based on hashing. This creates a hash-ring, whereby each node stores one segment of the ring. To formulate a pull query, we first look up the hash-ring segmentation boundaries, along with the node that contains each segment; this information is stored in the Vertica system catalog and can be queried. Then for each Spark task, we formulate a unique query that asks for a specific non-overlapping hash range within a segment boundary. This ensures that only one node will contain the requested data – the node which stores the segment range. The data locality aware approach has minimal data skew and respects the Vertica segment boundaries.

Figure 4 shows two examples of the Vertica table segments for a 4 node Vertica cluster and the corresponding Spark partition tasks. In both examples, the inner ring represents the Vertica hash ring, which indicates each of the four segments 0–3. The outer ring represents the Spark partitions (hence tasks), each of which will request one or more ranges of the hash ring. In Figure 4(a), there are only 2 Spark partitions, so each partition formulates a query requesting 2 segments (i.e., 2 hash ranges). In Figure 4(b), there are 8 Spark partitions, so each partition formulates a query requesting $\frac{1}{2}$ of a segment. The resulting data contained within each Spark partition is one or more contiguous hash ranges from Vertica segments. Since the desired number of Spark partitions is a user option in our implementation, the number of partitions is not restricted by the number of Vertica segments.

By ensuring the task only connects (via JDBC) to the Vertica node that stores the corresponding segment range, spurious network traffic between Vertica nodes is eliminated, effectively using the full network bandwidth between Vertica and Spark only for data transfer between the two systems, accelerating the entire computation pipeline. The data locality-aware partition queries help us to achieve the data locality optimization (2) in Section 3.1.

With many independent, parallel queries (one per task) that could access Vertica at different times, we need to ensure a consistent view of the table data. To do this, we can utilize Vertica's *epoch* feature which enables each query to request a specific version of the table data. In this way all tasks can formulate their queries to request data from the same epoch (e.g., last epoch). Although Spark tasks may fail and be restarted until they complete successfully, using epochs ensures that all tasks load a consistent view of the table. Together, our design for V2S is optimized for parallel data transfer, pushdown processing, takes advantage of data locality, is robust to Spark task failures, and preserves our desired exactly-once semantics.

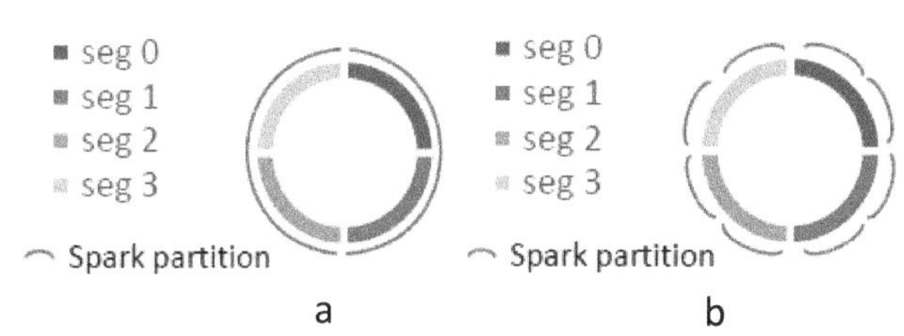

Figure 4: 4 Vertica data storage segments with (a) 2 Spark partitions and (b) 8 Spark partitions.

3.2 Transferring Data from Spark to Vertica (S2V)

In this this section we describe the design and semantics for the S2V component of the HPE Vertica Connector for Apache Spark. The connector is invoked with the `SAVE` API shown in Table 1, which supports saving to an existing table (append mode) or overwriting/creating a new table (overwrite mode). The transfer of a Spark DataFrame to Vertica is atomic and will never pollute the target table with partial loads or duplicate data, even though we optimize the performance by using many independent, parallel tasks.

The key insight with our approach is that we can use Vertica itself and its ACID properties to guarantee exactly-once semantics to save data, which is achieved within a single Spark job. In essence, since Spark tasks are stateless and do not communicate with each other as is typical in MapReduce [11] style batch processing systems, we use tables in Vertica to play the role of a durable log where we record the connector's progress and final status of success or failure. While the transfer is in progress, each task utilizes these tables to inquire the state of progress of all other tasks. Using these tables, the connector can ensure that tasks do not duplicate work, and that all tasks complete successfully. Since bulk loads may include rejected rows the connector API provides user control (optional parameter) to specify a tolerance for the number of rows rejected, and a sample of the rejected rows is provided. If the number of rejected rows falls within the user's tolerance level, the save is completed and considered successful; otherwise, it fails.

To launch S2V in Spark, the user specifies the save mode and target table along with a set of other options. (e.g., host, user, etc.). When an S2V job is launched, there is first a setup phase which includes creating the following 3 temporary tables, and 1 permanent table. A *Staging Table*, which has the same schema as the target table. A *Task Status Table*, which includes one row per task that includes task/-partition id, rows inserted/failed counts, and a task `done` status. A *Last Committer Table*, which includes the task id of the the last committer. A *Final Status Table*, which includes the unique job name, failed rows percentage, and final

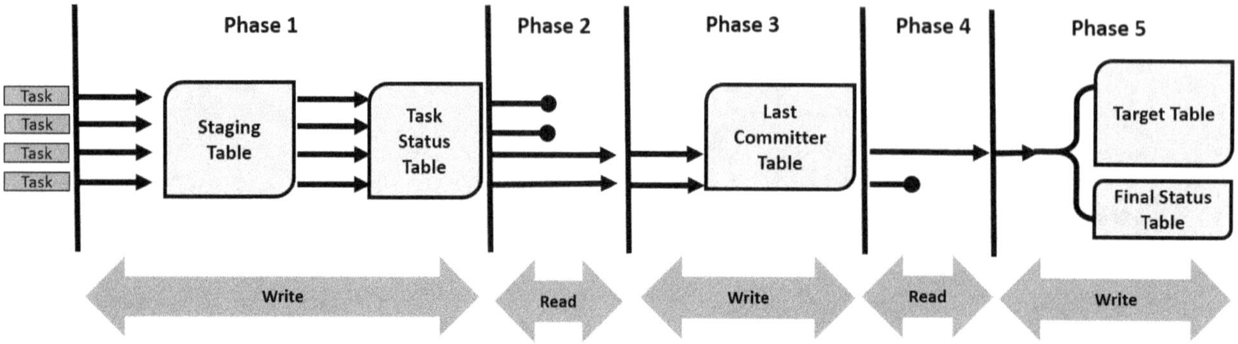

Figure 5: Phases of S2V tasks. Arrows and circles represent a single task's progression or completion.

status of each job. This table serves as a record of all S2V jobs and is not deleted upon termination. Because this table is always available, users can consult this table any time to verify the job's status, for instance in the case where there is a Spark error causing total Spark failure, which could leave the Spark user uncertain as to the job's final status.

Although the user provides only a single Vertica hostname to the API, all Vertica node IPs are looked up during setup so that tasks can connect to different Vertica nodes in order to balance the load across the Vertica cluster during data transfer. Also during this setup phase, we can repartition the DataFrame in order to obtain the desired parallelism, where the number of partitions is a user option. Typically with large data this is simply a coalesce of many partitions into fewer without any data shuffling.

Once the temporary tables have been created and the number of partitions and Vertica node IPs are known, the worker tasks can be started. We show later in Section 4.7.1 that the overhead for setup and teardown of these tables in S2V is on the order of a few seconds. Next, the challenge is to provide parallelism via independent tasks while guaranteeing that all independent tasks perform a single job of reliably saving the DataFrame to Vertica. This is achieved with the logic described in the next section.

3.2.1 Phases of tasks in S2V

Figure 5 shows the five phases of each task in a single S2V job that ensure each task completes saving its data only once, regardless of how many times an individual task is executed. In Phase 1, a task connects to one of the Vertica nodes and writes its data into the staging table and then updates its *done* status to true and commits, only if *done* is currently false otherwise it aborts the transaction. This check prevents the same task (i.e., a duplicate) from saving its data twice into the staging table. Writing to the staging table and updating the task status table are done under the same transaction in order to guarantee the record of the task saving its data is durable.

In Phase 2, the task reads the task status table to check if all tasks are done, including itself (since it could be duplicate). If any tasks are not done, then this particular task has no further work to do and it completes, as indicated by the terminal end point in phase 2 of the figure. However, if all tasks are done, then the task can advance to Phase 3. We note that several tasks can advance to Phase 3 at the same time, given they might finish in similar time frames.

In Phase 3, the task tries to update the last committer table with its task id, where the task id is empty, again committing if the id is still empty else it aborts. This is a race to update the table but ensures that *only one task* will be able to update the table with its id, which serves as a durable record of which task won the race (leader election).

In Phase 4, the task then reads back the last committer table to see if it had won the race. If it has not, it can terminate. Here we point out that each of the read phases of S2V are required since a task could have failed and been restarted at any point. By reading these tables at each phase before advancing to the next phase we prevent tasks from duplicating their previous work but ensure that they will complete all necessary work before terminating.

In Phase 5, the last committer task is the single remaining task, although due to speculative execution it could be duplicated. It verifies if the total number of failed rows is within the user's tolerance. If so, the task now commits the staging table into the target table and updates the final status table to finished, where finished is currently false; else it aborts. This check again prevents duplicate tasks from performing the same action, which ensures the final commit of the staging table data into the target table is only done once. In overwrite mode, this is simply an atomic rename of the staging table to the target table, and in append mode the task must copy the staging table data into the target table, which takes longer.

In summary, phases 1–2 ensure the reliable save of a Spark DataFrame to the staging table, which is the bulk of the work; phases 3–5 simply ensure the final atomic save of the staging table to the target table. The above process accounts for multiple task failures and restarts, speculative task execution, and also for complete Spark failure. Due to the use of a staging table, in the worst case of total Spark or Vertica failure the target table will not be affected.

3.2.2 Other Optimizations

During this entire process, S2V uses several optimizations. One is that we utilize the VerticaCopyStream Java API, which allows us to programmatically access Vertica's bulk load *COPY* utility, which is optimized for loading data quickly. Another is that we use the Avro [3] file format for each task to encode its data before sending to Vertica. The Avro format provides several benefits: it is a binary format, it does not require us to specify a delimiter (which can be difficult in the general case with unknown text data), and it also offers compression which can reduce the amount of data transferred over the network.

3.3 Model Deployment from Spark to Vertica (MD)

The goal of this component is to support in-database scoring of models generated by Spark MLlib and exported to Vertica. To this end, we have developed APIs for deploying and reading PMML models to/from Vertica. For storing PMML models in Vertica, one option is to store them into a table, but it is difficult to define a proper and generic schema for PMML models since there is a variety of model types (e.g., k-means, SVM, logistic regression, etc) and each model has a different number of features (i.e., fields). Instead, we store PMML models in an internal distributed file system (DFS) and hence are accessible to the database query engine and User-Defined Functions (UDF).

Our `DeployPMMLModel()` method stores the model itself into the DFS and also inserts its corresponding metadata (e.g., name, size, model type) into a Vertica table. Once the PMML models have been deployed, they can later be used for in-database model scoring. This requires to write a UDF that first reads the model from the DFS using our `GetPMML()` method and then uses JPMML [6] to build the corresponding model evaluator to perform scoring/prediction. To make it easier for the user, we have developed a generic model evaluator for models whose input is a numeric vector and the output is a number (e.g., logistic regression, k-means, etc).

Users can run predictions inside the database by using the scoring UDF in an SQL query. In the following example PMMLPredict() is the UDF which takes as arguments the column names corresponding to the features used by the model to do the predictions, along with the model name as a parameter.

```
SELECT PMMLPredict(
    sepal_length, sepal_width,
    petal_length, petal_width
USING PARAMETERS model_name='regression')
FROM IrisTable
```

In this way, prediction models can be trained in Spark using data from Vertica transferred with V2S, and then deployed into Vertica to do predictions on data stored in the database. This closes the loop on the full analytics pipeline with V2S and MD shown in Figure 1.

4. EXPERIMENTAL EVALUATION

In this section we evaluate our connector's functionality, performance, and scalability. We examine the connector's performance for both directions V2S and S2V. We evaluate the connector's sensitivity to parallelism, data size, data type, and data shape, as well as scalability with different cluster sizes for Vertica and Spark. Lastly, we compare V2S load (read) and S2V save (write) performance to other baselines including Spark's JDBC DefaultSource, HDFS, and Vertica's native bulk load utility.

4.1 Experimental Setup

Here we describe our software configuration, hardware configuration, datasets, and cluster configurations. For each experiment, the data originates in HDFS (co-located with Spark), and we use S2V in Overwrite mode to first save the data from Spark to Vertica then use V2S to load that same data back into Spark which ensures that the data used for S2V and V2S is exactly the same. All experimental results report the average execution time for 3 runs using a local cluster of machines.

Software Configuration. All of our experiments use HPE Vertica 7.2.1 and Apache Spark 1.5.2 configured for Hadoop 2.4+. Spark is configured with the Kryo serializer, and we assign roughly 75% of each machine's cores to Spark, leaving the remaining cores available for other background tasks including HDFS which is co-located with Spark. Spark Workers were allotted all local machine memory, and Spark executors were allotted 10GB each. We use HDFS from the Apache Hadoop 2.6 distribution, and HDFS is configured with the default block size (64MB) and replication (3×). Vertica is configured with the default settings except that replication (*k-safety*) is turned off simply for clarity of evaluation of data movement rather than database fault tolerance.

In Vertica we define a resource pool with default settings using $\frac{1}{2}$ of machine RAM (32GB in this case), and all Vertica connections use this pool. This simply helps to isolate and control the resources used by our data movement workloads from the normal database workloads. We also increased Vertica's `MAX-CLIENT-SESSIONS` parameter to 100, to allow for up to 100 connections per node during our experiments that vary the number of connections to Vertica (i.e., parallelism). The only other configuration settings explicitly modified for Vertica and Spark were temp directory paths. Other than as noted above, default settings were used; we performed no further optimizations.

Hardware Configuration. We use up to 24 machines running Red Hat Enterprise Linux Server release 6.7, each with 2 Intel Xeon 2.0GHz CPUs of 8 physical cores each with simultaneous multithreading (i.e.,hyper-threading) enabled resulting in 32 logical cores per machine. Each machine has 3 HDDs, one for the OS and applications, one for data storage, and one for temp space. Vertica table storage and HDFS block storage are located on the data storage disk. Vertica and Spark temp directories (used in part during shuffle/sort/spill) are located on the temp space disk. The machines have 64GB of RAM, and 2× 1GbE network interfaces. To separate the network traffic, we install Vertica onto one of the interfaces, and Spark onto the other. The keeps all Vertica internal traffic on one network and Spark traffic on the other, as would typically be done in a production environment with Enterprise Hardware.

Datasets. We use 2 datasets in our experiments. Dataset one (D_1) consists of 100 columns of randomly generated 8-byte float values in range [0–1), and in csv format consumes 140 GB on local disk. It contains 100 million rows (100M). Dataset two (D_2) consists of 2 columns of twitter data, the first column has a tweet_id (Long type) and the second column has tweet_text (String type), and in csv format consumes 140 GB on local disk. It contains 1.46 billion (1.46B) rows. In Vertica, string data types are represented as VARCHAR columns. In HDFS, all datasets are stored as delimited text files (CSV).

Cluster Configuration. Our primary cluster configuration uses 4 nodes for Vertica, and 8 nodes for Spark which is co-located with HDFS. We refer to this as our 4:8 cluster. This represents a 2× ratio of 2 nodes Spark/HDFS for 1 node Vertica. Empirically we observed the 2× ratio was able to sufficiently saturate network resources between the systems. All experiments use the 4:8 cluster except the cluster

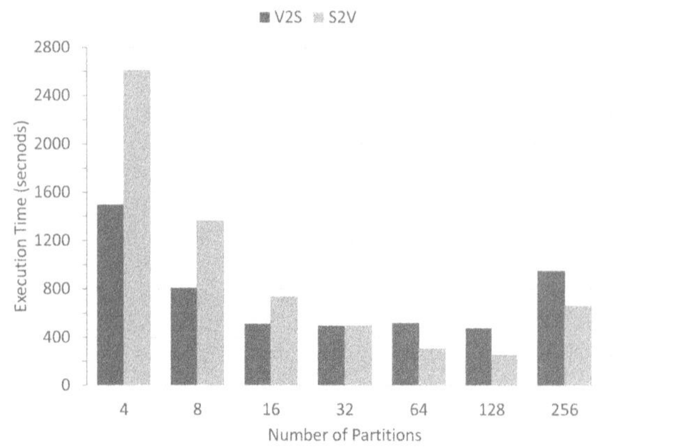

Figure 6: Varying the number of partitions.

scalability experiments. For cluster scalability experiments, we maintain the 2× ratio and vary the cluster sizes.

4.2 Performance While Varying Parallelism

In this experiment we evaluate how S2V and V2S perform as we vary the amount of parallelism. Here we use dataset D_1 with 100M rows. Figure 6 reports the execution time for V2S and S2V along the y-axis and the number of partitions along the x-axis. Given that our Vertica cluster has 4 nodes, on the far left we use 4 partitions resulting in 1 connection per Vertica node, and on the far right we use 256 partitions, resulting in 64 connections per Vertica node.

Figure 6 shows the best performance for V2S and S2V occurs somewhere in the middle ranges of partitions. For V2S, the fastest time is achieved with 128 partitions at 475 seconds. However, our experiences have shown that even though with 32 partitions performance is slightly slower at 497 seconds (<5%) using this lower value for the number of V2S partitions results in less resource usage on Vertica to achieve roughly the same performance, hence 32 is a better value in practice. For S2V, the fastest time is achieved with 128 partitions at 252 seconds.

Figure 6 clearly shows that both V2S and S2V are sensitive to the amount of parallelism. At a high level, 4 partitions is not enough parallelism (due to not enough work generated per connection) while 256 partitions is too much parallelism (due to the amount of overhead per connection). We drill down into this behavior in the following section.

4.2.1 *Resources Used with Varying Parallelism*

Next we examine the machine resources used during the experiments shown in Figure 6. That figure shows that both V2S and S2V performance degrades at the lower and higher ends of the parallelism spectrum tested. The Vertica resources are key, since Spark tasks are only formulating requests and sending those to Vertica for processing.

Table 2 shows the amount of CPU and network resources (outbound) used by a single Vertica node during the first 300 seconds of V2S with 4 partitions and 32 partitions during the experiments from Figure 6. In the plots shown in Table 2, max CPU usage possible is 100%, and max Network usage possible is about 125 MBps.

With 4 partitions, there is an initial burst of CPU, which then reaches steady-state at about 5% usage. Correspondingly, there is an initial saw-tooth behavior for network

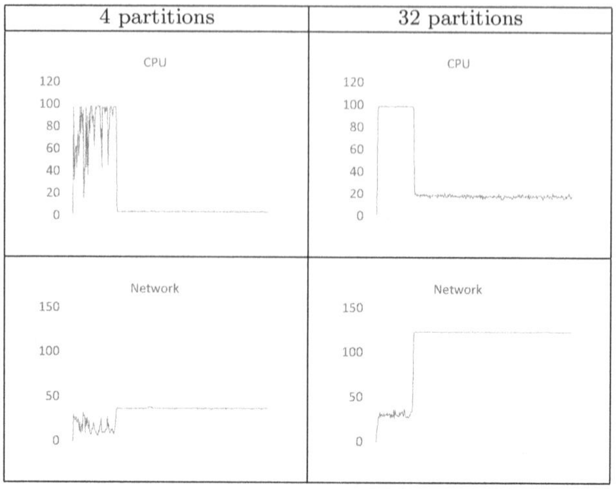

Table 2: Vertica node resource usage during V2S. The y-axis is percent CPU usage or Network MBps, the x-axis is the first 300 seconds of elapsed time.

MBps until it reaches steady-state at about 38 MBps. Because there are only a few requests, the network is not saturated and consequently it takes longer to complete the data transfer, as reflected in the execution time for V2S with 4 partitions in Figure 6. In contrast, with 32 partitions the CPU and network show the same initial behavior, after which the CPU reaches steady-state at about 20% usage and the network becomes fully saturated at about 120 MBps —thus the data transfer is faster as reflected in the lower execution time for V2S with 32 partitions in Figure 6. Because the network becomes saturated at this degree of parallelism, increasing the parallelism only increases the overhead without any data transfer benefit. This effect is reflected in the higher execution time for V2S with 256 partitions in Figure 6. A similar effect occurs with S2V (not shown here), although the best results are with 128 partitions instead of 32. This is because with S2V, each Spark task is alternately encoding its data into Avro format or transferring the data to Vertica so it benefits from more parallelism but S2V similarly becomes saturated with too much parallelism.

4.3 Data Scalability

Here we evaluate the performance of V2S and S2V as the data size is scaled up exponentially. We use dataset D_1 and vary the number of rows from 1 million (1M) to 1 billion (1000M). To set the parallelism for V2S and S2V, we choose the number of partitions with the best performance for each direction from Figure 6 which is 32 and 128 partitions respectively.

Figure 7 reports the total execution time in seconds (y-axis) as the number of rows is varied (x-axis), with both axes shown in log scale. The performance trend for both S2V and V2S is clearly linear, showing the connector scales well with the data size. With fewer rows, S2V is somewhat slower than V2S, most likely due to its additional overheads for batching and transactional consistency using the staging and commit tables. With more rows, the performance of each becomes similar and then S2V becomes somewhat faster than V2S. We performed additional experiments with 2 billion rows and greater, which showed these trends continued and thus are not presented here.

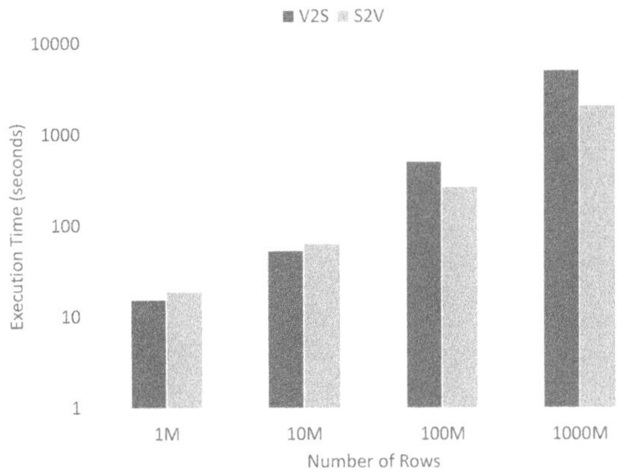

Figure 7: Varying the data size.

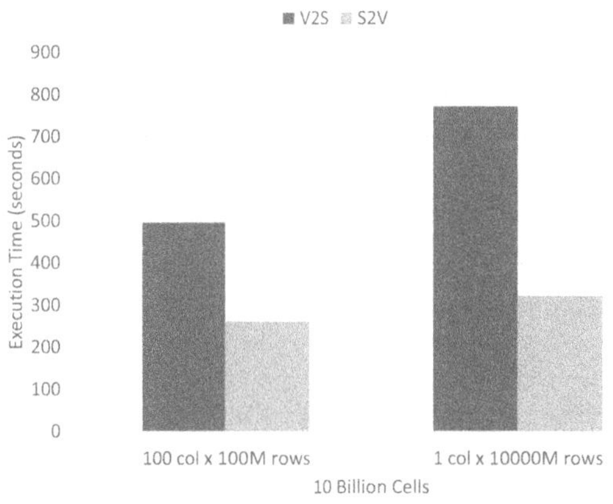

Figure 9: Varying the data dimensionality.

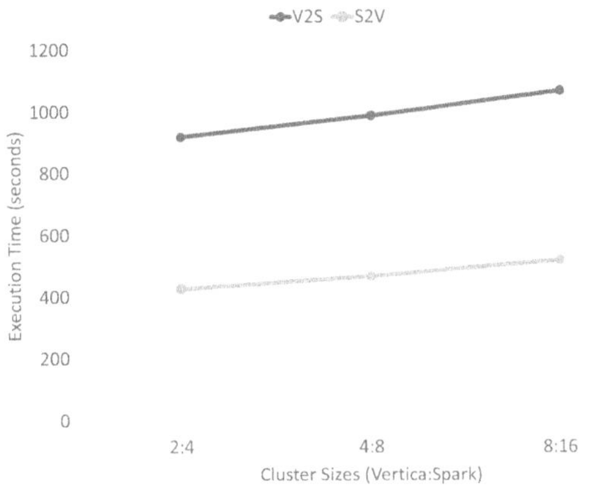

Figure 8: Varying the cluster sizes.

4.4 Cluster Scalability

In this experiment we vary the cluster sizes for our Vertica and Spark clusters while keeping the same 2× ratio. We start with 2 Vertica nodes and 4 Spark nodes denoted as 2:4, and then we double the cluster sizes to 4:8 and 8:16. We also double the data sizes with each cluster size, such that the amount of data per node is fixed. We use dataset D_1, with 100M rows for the 2:4 size, which is then doubled to 200M rows for the 4:8 cluster and then to 400M rows for the 8:16 cluster.

We base the number of partitions on the best values for V2S and S2V from Figure 6. Following these, we scale the number of partitions for V2S and S2V up and down respectively with the cluster size resulting in 16 and 64 respectively for the 2:4 cluster, 32 and 128 for the 4:8 cluster, and 64 and 256 for the 8:16 cluster.

Figure 8 reports the execution time of V2S and S2V as the cluster size and data size are scaled up in the corresponding 2× ratio. The results show that performance of V2S and S2V have a slight linear performance degradation (<10%) with each doubling of the cluster size. Overall, Figure 8 indicates that V2S and S2V scale reasonably well but we are considering optimizations as an area of future work.

	Execution Time (seconds)
V2S	378
S2V	386

Table 3: Performance with dataset D_2.

4.5 Varying the Data Dimensionality

In this experiment we examine what is the effect when the data size is the same, but the number of columns is varied. Here we use dataset D_1 which is 100 cols by 100M rows as our baseline, and this dataset has 10,000M cells. We then modify the dimensionality of this dataset to 1 col by 10,000M rows, which again has 10,000M cells. The goal is to show how performance can vary with the shape of the data.

Figure 9 reports the execution time for both variations of dataset D_1. The results show that execution time increases significantly when there is only 1 column but far more rows. This indicates there is some fixed amount of overhead per row, since even though the amount of data is the same, the results with 10,000M rows take longer to execute. For V2S, this includes the overhead for reading and encoding many more rows of data to send over JDBC, and for S2V this includes the fixed overhead to encode each row into Avro format in Spark and the overhead of parsing and unpacking each Avro row in Vertica.

4.6 Performance with Dataset D_2

In this experiment we evaluate performance with dataset D_2, which contains one column each of *Integer* and *String*. Although D_1 and D_2 are the same raw size on disk, 140 GB, D_1 has 100 million rows while D_2 has 1.46 billion rows. We again use V2S and S2V with 32 and 128 partitions, respectively. Table 3 reports the execution time in seconds for dataset D_2 using V2S and S2V. The results are interesting in that although the data sizes of D_1 and D_2 are the same, V2S is faster to load dataset D_2 (378 seconds here) than dataset D_1 (490 seconds from Figure 6). In contrast, S2V is slower to load dataset D_2 (386 seconds here) than dataset D_1 (252 seconds from Figure 6). This can be explained in part due to the performance variance of S2V and V2S seen in Figure 9, which shows the execution times change as the number of rows and columns is varied even though data size remains the same. There are also differences in the way Vertica stores and converts different data types to/from their native formats which can affect the reading and writing time.

4.7 Comparisons with Alternative Approaches

In this section we compare V2S and S2V with several alternative approaches to load and save Spark data using dataset D_1. We first compare V2S and S2V with Spark's JDBC DefaultSource, a basic implementation of Spark's External Data Source API. The JDBC default source implements both the load and save functions. Since load supports pushdown predicates, we also test with a selection predicate. We next compare V2S and S2V with reading and writing to/from HDFS. This is a less direct comparison than JDBC DefaultSource, but serves to show how our implementation performs to shuttle data between Spark and Vertica as compared to shuttling data between Spark and HDFS, which Spark supports natively. Last we compare S2V's performance with Vertica's native bulk load utility, the `COPY` statement.

4.7.1 Comparison with JDBC Default Source

Spark's JDBC Default Source provides both load and save methods and also supports parallelism, although with parallel approaches transaction control is not centralized and thus does not provide exactly once semantics.

For load, JDBC Default Source enables parallelism by issuing a unique query per Spark partition, where each query requests a range equally divided over a `min` and `max` value of the source table. Notably, in order to obtain parallelism the current implementation requires the source table to have an integer column, and the user to know its `min` and `max` values which are provided as arguments along with the column name to JDBC Default Source. If this is not done, it will default to a single partition which results in zero parallelism. To support this requirement, for our V2S experiments below we modify dataset D_1 to add an integer column with randomly assigned values from [0-100), allowing us to easily select any percentage of rows we wish.

Figure 10 reports the execution time to load data from Vertica to Spark with V2S and Spark's JDBC Default Source. Both approaches use Spark's External Data Source API, which supports predicate pushdown. In this experiment we use a select predicate with 5% selectivity, resulting in Vertica filtering out 95% of the data before sending the result back to Spark. The results show that by pushing down the filter, Vertica does most of the work and the output is significantly reduced (to just 5M rows) and thus both approaches have simlilar performance. However, although both approaches benefit from parallelism, the results without pushdown show a performance gain of nearly 4× for V2S over JDBC Default Source. This is due to the hash-ring based query approach used by V2S whereby each connection only requests node-local data from each Vertica node. Not only does this result in better performance, it also does not induce intra-node traffic within Vertica, leading to less Vertica resource usage overall than with the JDBC Default Source approach. JDBC Default Source also issues all queries throught a single Vertica node, it does not distribute the queries evenly across all nodes, although this is likely an easy change. Moreover, with V2S there is no requirement

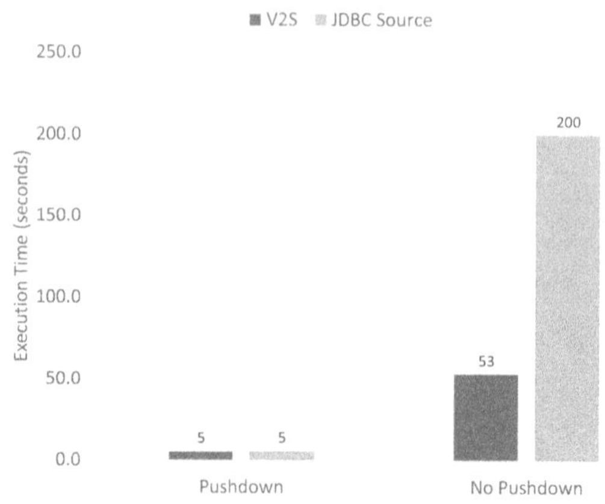

Figure 10: Load with V2S versus JDBC DefaultSource, with/without pushdown, 5% selectivity.

that the source table contains an integral column or that the user knows its `min` and `max` values. V2S's hash-ring query approach works with any existing Vertica table, and does not require the user to provide any special arguments other than the table name. For save, JDBC Default Source enables parallelism by each Spark partition issuing batches of insert statements to the target table. Notably, although each partition will commit its inserts at the end, these are independent queries thus they are not all under transaction control which can result in the target table being partially or duplicate loaded.

Figure 11 reports the execution time to save data from Spark to Vertica with S2V Spark's JDBC Default Source. In this experiment, we use dataset D_1 without any column modifications but we use only a subset of the rows. We report the execution times for 1 row, 1,000 rows (1K), 10,000 rows (10K).

The results for 1 row effectively show the overhead for both approaches; 5 seconds for S2V and 3 seconds for JDBC DefaultSource. For S2V, the overhead includes the one-time setup and teardown time of the temporary tables along with the logic to guarantee exactly-once semantics, which JDBC Default Source does not provide. Due to these overheads, S2V is slightly slower for the single row case. However, S2V's performance for larger numbers of rows is significantly better than JDBC Default Source. This is because S2V is designed for bulk loads as part of an ETL process, and it uses the `COPY` command along with batching, which is typically far faster than using a series of insert statements. We ran this experiment for larger data sizes but the trends shown in Figure 11 continued and hence results are not shown here. For example, for 1M rows S2V takes 19 seconds (as shown in Figure 7), while JDBC Default Source took longer than 3 hours, at which point we stopped the experiment.

4.7.2 Comparison with HDFS

In this section we compare our V2S and S2V approaches to load and save data between Spark and Vertica with that of reading and writing data between Spark and HDFS, for which Spark is natively integrated with HDFS source. We use our standard dataset D_1 with 100M rows. This experiment serves to show that reading and writing data between Spark and Vertica can be competitive with using HDFS. Here we use our standard 4:8 cluster (Vertica:Spark) for

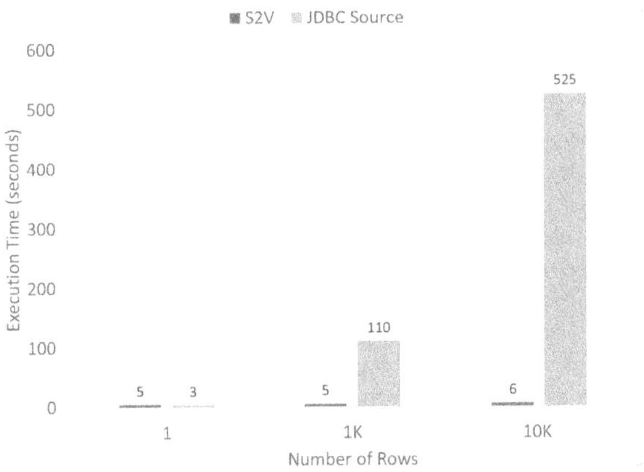

Figure 11: Save with S2V versus JDBC Default-Source.

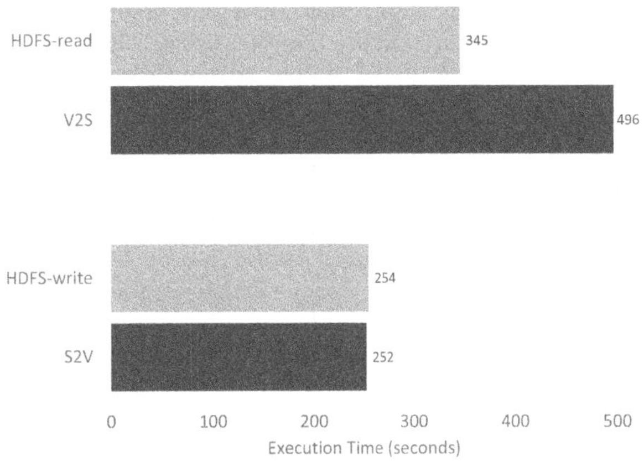

Figure 12: V2S and S2V versus HDFS read/write.

V2S and S2V, but in addition we create another 4:8 cluster (HDFS:Spark) for the HDFS experiment in order to perform a direct comparison with our approach. Note that just like our 4 Vertica nodes, the 4 HDFS nodes are not co-located with Spark. For HDFS read and write we use Spark's native read/write methods for parquet files using DataFrames. This dataset consists of 2240 HDFS blocks, which by default results in 2240 partitions in Spark. For V2S and S2V we use the values for 32 partitions and 128 partitions respectively from Figure 6. Figure 12 reports the time to load/save data from Vertica to Spark using V2S and S2V compared with reading and writing DataFrames using HDFS. Execution time is shown along the x-axis, and along the y-axis are our three comparative methods.

For reading, the results in Figure 12 show that reading from HDFS is about 30% faster than using V2S. This is not surprising given that Spark natively supports reading from HDFS. The primary reason is that the number of partitions with HDFS read is higher since it will default to one partition per HDFS block. This results in higher parallelism (2240 partitions) than with V2S (32 partitions). With HDFS, each partition is simply an HDFS block retrieval whereas with V2S each partition results in a separate query and together all queries result in loading a consistent view of Vertica data into Spark. Moreover, each V2S query executes a hash function on each data row which is the basis of our hash-ring approach. Since HDFS is not a database and HDFS files are not updated in place, there are no issues that can cause an inconsistent view of the data as there can be with a database. For writing, the results in Figure 12 show that writing to HDFS has about the same performance as S2V. Thus, considering the case when Spark is not co-located with Vertica or HDFS, these results show that data in Spark can be saved to a Vertica cluster about as fast as saving to an HDFS cluster.

4.7.3 Comparison with Vertica's bulk load utility

In this experiment we compare S2V with Vertica's native bulk load utility, i.e., the `COPY` command, which is the standard way to load large amounts of data into Vertica. Here we use `COPY` as a baseline to compare S2V and gauge its performance potential. To do a parallel `COPY`, a file is split into multiple parts, evenly distributed among the Vertica nodes, and a `COPY` is issued on all of the parts.

	Execution Time (seconds)
S2V	252
COPY	238

Table 4: Save with S2V versus native `COPY`.

In this experiment we use dataset D_1 to compare the loading time of S2V to parallel `COPY`. For S2V, we consider the execution times from Figure 6. For the parallel `COPY` approach, we split the original csv file into 4, 8, 16, 32, 64, and 128 parts and distribute them evenly across the 4 Vertica nodes onto their local disks We then record the total time to load the splits in parallel.

Table 4 reports the best time for S2V and the parallel `COPY` approach. The best time for `COPY` was 238 seconds, achieved with 8 file parts, 2 on each node. S2V's best time is about 6% slower than COPY; 252 seconds achieved with 128 partitions. This result shows that S2V's best time can be competitive with `COPY`, but it requires higher parallelism and consequently more Vertica resources to obtain similar performance.

5. DISCUSSION

The connector's sensitivity to the number of Spark partitions is a drawback, since it is not directly obvious what number will perform best given the user's machine configurations and cluster sizes. However, there is a clear bowl-shape to the performance as Figure 6 shows. While values at the outer ranges perform poorly, values in the middle ranges perform reasonably well. Best practices for tuning the parallelism are provided in the connector's user guide. Although memory can also be a constraint, the performance we report in this work was achieved with very modest memory sizes.

Another drawback is the connector's performance when using S2V in Append mode that requires to copy the entire staging table into the target table. While saving each task's data to the staging table is done in parallel under many independent transactions, saving the staging table into the target table must actually be a single atomic transaction which can have a higher execution time cost. We are currently exploring optimizations that can help to reduce the append time.

There are several other interesting areas of future work that we hope to investigate, in order to improve performance and scalability. One is to pre-hash the DataFrame in S2V to match the same partitioning (*segmented by* clause) as the target Vertica table similar to our approach for V2S in Section 3.1. Each pre-hashed partition can then connect to and load its data into the corresponding Vertica node that stores that particular segment, which eliminates the network traffic between nodes in the Vertica cluster.

Another is to consider a 2-Stage approach, that is, to first copy the data to an intermediate location that both systems can access, such as HDFS or S3 in the first stage then transfer the data to the other system in the second stage. This is the approach taken by the Spark-Redshift connector [8]. One drawback of using 2 stages is that it creates an extra dependency on an intermediate storage system, and it may be slower than our single-stage approach because it requires an intermediate write of a full copy of the data. As we showed in Section 4.7.2, our approach for reading/writing directly to Vertica can be competitive with reading/writing from Spark to HDFS. However, a 2-stage approach has the potential benefits of decoupling the systems and good performance given each system's native capabilities for reading/writing the intermediate storage.

6. RELATED WORK

In this section we describe some of the related work in the area of accessing external data sources with Spark.

Spark's JDBC Default Source. Spark provides a JDBC Default Source as an implementation of its External Data Source API. The implementation offers the ability to parallelize loads and saves, enabling load or save to any database that supports JDBC. Similar to our work, it also provides pushdown capabilities via the External DataSource API. However the current JDBC Default Source approach is only "best-effort" in that it does not guarantee a consistent view of the data due to task failures. In contrast, our approach for V2S and S2V includes several mechanisms to guarantee exactly once semantics resulting in a consistent view of the data. Moreover, in Section 4.7 we show that our connector can significantly outperform JDBC Default Source.

Additionally, as noted in Section 4.7.1, JDBC Default Source has some special requirements in that it can only parallelize the load of a source table if the table has an integer column, and the user provides the column name along with the column's `min` and `max` values. Furthermore, even when transfer is parallelized all connections go through a single database host, causing that host to do much of the work. In contrast, V2S requires no special table format nor any `min` and `max` values to be provided by the user. V2S parallelism is based on Vertica's data layout, and balances the load across Vertica nodes by enabling each Spark task to connect to a specific Vertica node and request only node-local data based upon a hash segment range.

When writing data to Vertica, JDBC Default Source parallelizes the writes but uses `INSERT` statements, whereas S2V utlizes Vertica's `COPY` command which is optimized for bulk loads. Additionally since each JDBC Default Source task performs its `INSERT`s independently and in parallel, a total Spark failure or failed/restarted tasks may leave the target table in an inconsistent state.

Datastax Cassandra Connector for Spark. Cassandra [12] is a key-value store that does not support a full relational model. There is available an open source package on GitHub [4], which provides both load and save functionality for Spark RDDs and DataFrames. The Cassandra connector provides partitioning by Cassandra ranges during load/save, similar to our hash segmentation approach. The consistency semantics (strong consistency via `LOCAL_QUORUM`) offered for writes are similar to our approach but specific to Cassandra, whereas our approach applies more generally to MapReduce-class systems and any database with ACID semantics.

Databricks Redshift Connector. Redshift [1] is a data warehouse available on Amazon AWS, and there is an open-source connector package available on GitHub [8]. The connector is similar in functionality to our connector, providing parellelized read and write between Spark and Redshift, and also supports transactional semantics and pushdowns. However, this connector uses a two-stage approach for both reads and writes. That is, it requires a common shared data landing zone (in this case Amazon S3 [2]) to write temporary files in the first stage to then be consumed by the other side in the second stage. For example, with writes Spark first saves all partition data in parallel to S3, and once that completes successfully a Redshift LOAD query(s) is issued. This load query is bookended by a `BEGIN` and `END` transaction statement, and between those is a sequence of individual load statements, one per each temporary file in S3. Like our S2V approach, this achieves exactly once semantics but has some extra overhead in that it requires an intermediate data landing zone large enough for the entire dataset.

MR as ETL Engine. MapReduce type systems may often be used for ETL, as they allow for massive parallelism as well as code-specific optimizations and transformations when loading data into the target system (e.g., Vertica). Such systems can be referred to generally as the class of batch-based task scheduler systems as noted previously. Our approach for reliably transferring data to/from an ACID compliant database is general in that it can be applied to any such class of system.

Read and Write using HDFS. HDFS is not a database and does not have transactional semantics like our approach that uses Vertica, but we do provide a comparison point for reference in Section 4.7.2 that shows our approach can be competitive with reading/writing HDFS from Spark. This is a key result in that it shows one could use Vertica as a durable storage for Spark DataFrames instead of HDFS.

7. CONCLUSION

In this work we have presented our design and implementation for fast, efficient, and reliable data transfer between HPE Vertica and Apache Spark with exactly once semantics. We have evaluated its performance across several dimensions and have compared with alternative approaches, and the current results show that our methods are competitive with the alternatives tested. The HPE Vertica Connector for Apache Spark is available as a beta release on HPE Marketplace [5] since November 2015.

8. REFERENCES

[1] Amazon Redshift. https://aws.amazon.com/redshift/.

[2] Amazon Simple Storage Service. https://aws.amazon.com/s3/.

[3] Apache Avro data serialization.

[4] DataStax Cassandra Connector. https://github.com/datastax/spark-cassandra-connector.

[5] HPE Vertica Connector for Apache Spark. https://saas.hpe.com/marketplace/big-data/hpe-vertica-connector-apache-spark.

[6] JavaPMML API. https://github.com/jpmml.

[7] PMML 4.1 general structure. http://dmg.org/pmml/v4-1/GeneralStructure.html.

[8] Redshift data source for Spark. https://github.com/databricks/spark-redshift.

[9] Spark MLlib. http://spark.apache.org/mllib/.

[10] Spark PMML model export. https://spark.apache.org/docs/latest/mllib-pmml-model-export.html.

[11] J. Dean and S. Ghemawat. MapReduce: Simplified data processing on large clusters. In *OSDI*, 2004.

[12] A. Lakshman and P. Malik. Cassandra: A decentralized structured storage system. *SIGOPS Oper. Syst. Rev.*, 44(2), Apr. 2010.

[13] A. Lamb, M. Fuller, R. Varadarajan, N. Tran, B. Vandiver, L. Doshi, and C. Bear. The Vertica analytic database: C-store 7 years later. In *VLDB*, volume 5, 2012.

[14] S. Prasad, A. Fard, V. Gupta, J. Martinez, J. LeFevre, V. Xu, M. Hsu, and I. Roy. Large-scale predictive analytics in Vertica: Fast data transfer, distributed model creation, and in-database prediction. In *SIGMOD*, 2015.

[15] M. Stonebraker, D. J. Abadi, A. Batkin, X. Chen, M. Cherniack, M. Ferreira, E. Lau, A. Lin, S. Madden, E. O'Neil, P. O'Neil, A. Rasin, N. Tran, and S. Zdonik. C-store: A Column-oriented DBMS. In *VLDB*, 2005.

[16] M. Zaharia, M. Chowdhury, T. Das, A. Dave, J. Ma, M. McCauley, M. J. Franklin, S. Shenker, and I. Stoica. Resilient Distributed Datasets: A fault-tolerant abstraction for in-memory cluster computing. In *NSDI*, 2012.

[17] M. Zaharia, M. Chowdhury, M. J. Franklin, S. Shenker, and I. Stoica. Spark: Cluster computing with working sets. In *Proceedings of the 2nd USENIX Workshop on Hot Topics in Cloud Computing*, 2010.

Truss Decomposition of Probabilistic Graphs: Semantics and Algorithms

Xin Huang Wei Lu Laks V.S. Lakshmanan
Department of Computer Science
University of British Columbia
Vancouver, B.C., Canada
xin0@cs.ubc.ca, welu@cs.ubc.ca, laks@cs.ubc.ca

ABSTRACT

A key operation in network analysis is the discovery of cohesive subgraphs. The notion of k-truss has gained considerable popularity in this regard, based on its rich structure and efficient computability. However, many complex networks such as social, biological and communication networks feature uncertainty, best modeled using probabilities. Unfortunately the problem of discovering k-trusses in probabilistic graphs has received little attention to date.

In this paper, given a probabilistic graph $\mathcal{G}$, number k and parameter $\gamma \in (0, 1]$, we define a (k, γ)*-truss* as a maximal connected subgraph $\mathcal{H} \subseteq \mathcal{G}$, in which for each edge, the probability that it is contained in at least $(k - 2)$ triangles is at least γ. We develop an efficient dynamic programming algorithm for decomposing a probabilistic graph into such maximal (k, γ)-trusses. The above definition is *local* in that the "witness" graphs that has the $(k - 2)$ triangles containing an edge in $\mathcal{H}$ may be quite different for distinct edges. Hence, we also propose *global* (k, γ)-truss, which in addition to being a local (k, γ)-truss, has to satisfy the condition that the probability that $\mathcal{H}$ contains a k-truss is at least γ. We show that unlike local (k, γ)-trusses, the global (k, γ)-truss decomposition on a probabilistic graph is intractable. We propose a novel sampling technique which enables approximate discovery of global (k, γ)-trusses with high probability. Our extensive experiments on real datasets demonstrate the efficacy of our proposed approach and the usefulness of local and global (k, γ)-truss.

1. INTRODUCTION

Network data analytics play a key role in many scientific fields such as biological, social and communication networks [18]. A large body of such real-world networks are associated with uncertainty, due to the data collection process, machine-learning methods employed at preprocessing, or privacy-preserving reasons. For instance, in Protein-Protein Interaction (PPI) networks, the edges represent interactions between proteins, which are derived through noisy and error-prone lab experiments and therefore entail uncertainty [19]; Moreover, many edges (interactions) in PPI networks are actually predicted by biologists using algorithms based on features of the proteins, instead of being actually observed in experiments [29]. Naturally, the predictions are associated with certain confidence levels, which are best modeled by probabilities [11, 12, 29]. As another example, in social networks, link prediction and peer influence motivate the need to model interactions between users with uncertainty, and in mobile ad-hoc networks, mobile nodes move and connect to each other, and a link between nodes can be unreliable and may fail with a certain probability. We model such uncertain networks as *probabilistic graphs*, also referred to as *uncertain graphs* in the literature. Each edge in a probabilistic graph is associated with a probability of existence [16, 27].

SIGMOD'16, June 26-July 01, 2016, San Francisco, CA, USA

DOI: http://dx.doi.org/10.1145/2882903.2882913

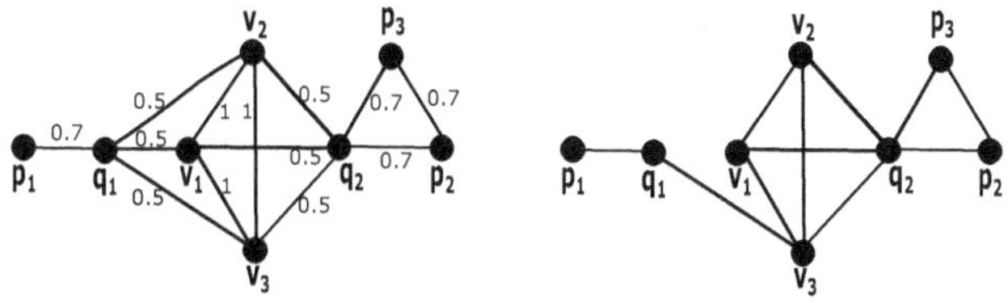

Figure 1: A running example

In many network analysis tasks, a fundamental problem is to identify various cohesive subgraphs [33]. Many notions of cohesive subgraphs have been proposed in the literature; these include cliques, quasi-cliques [24], n-clans [22], n-club [22], k-plexes [28]. The computation of all the above cohesive subgraphs is NP-hard.

A popular notion of cohesive subgraph that has found many recent applications is k-truss. A k*-truss* of a graph, is a subgraph in which each edge is contained in at least $(k - 2)$ triangles within that subgraph, i.e., its support is at least $(k - 2)$. A k-truss is maximal if it is not a proper subgraph of any other k-truss. For example, in Figure 1(a), ignoring probabilities, the entire graph G is a 2-truss but not a 3-truss. The subgraph induced by the nodes $\{q_1, q_2, v_1, v_2, v_3\}$ is a 4-truss, and the subgraph induced by all nodes but p_1 is a 3-truss. All of these are maximal k-trusses; the subgraph induced by $\{q_1, v_1, v_2, v_3\}$ is a non-maximal 4-truss. The set of all maximal k-trusses of a graph G, for various k, forms the truss decomposition of G. Recently, due to its efficient computability and cohesive structure, truss decomposition has attracted a lot of attention, and has been studied in various settings, including in-memory [9], external-memory [33], and dynamic graphs [15]. Unlike the aforementioned types of cohesive subgraphs, k-trusses [10] can be computed in polynomial time, similar to k-cores [2].

The closest work to us is the probabilistic extension to k-cores [4]. In addition to laying down the semantics, the authors provide efficient algorithms for finding subgraphs of probabilistic graphs that are k-cores with probability over a given threshold. A detailed comparison with this work appears in Section 2 but it's worth noting that k-trusses enjoy much more cohesiveness than k-cores.

(a) Local (4, 0.125)-truss $\mathcal{H}_1$ (b) Possible world of $\mathcal{H}_1$ as a connected 4-truss

Figure 2: A local (k, γ)-truss of $\mathcal{G}$ in Figure 1: $k = 4, \gamma = 0.125$.

The discovery of k-truss in uncertain graphs can be beneficial for a wide range of application domains. For instance, in network science domain, k-trusses as dense subgraphs can represent cohesive groups or communities. k-trusses have successfully become the basis of several community models [15,20]. Moreover, k-truss can be used to speed up the computation of finding maximum cliques as a k-clique must be in a k-truss, which can be significantly smaller than the original graph; Also, k-truss is a useful tool for visualization of complex networks [37]. All above applications can be naturally extended to uncertain graphs. In biology, a fundamental task is to detect and identify *functional modules*, which technically are cohesive subnetworks of proteins, from probabilistic PPI networks [1,11,12,25,29]. Modules capture subnetworks of proteins strongly expressed together by genes. Thus, detecting modules is highly important and valuable as it helps "assess the disease relevance of certain genes" [11], which further help critical clinical diagnosis of diseases such as cancer. Last but not the least, probabilistic k-truss can be directly applied to task-driven team formation in uncertain social networks, e.g., DBLP collaboration network, LinkedIn (with predicted links), etc. We conduct a case study on DBLP and report detailed results in Section 6.

In light of the above, mining k-trusses in probabilistic graphs is a pressing need. However, to the best of our knowledge, *truss decomposition over probabilistic graphs has not been studied yet.* In this paper, we present a principled extension of k-truss definitions in the presence of uncertainty, and propose efficient k-truss decomposition algorithms. Given a probabilistic graph $\mathcal{G}$, integer k and parameter $\gamma \in (0, 1]$, we define *local* (k, γ)*-truss* to be a connected subgraph $\mathcal{H} \subseteq \mathcal{G}$, in which for each edge, the probability that it is contained in at least $(k - 2)$ triangles is no less than γ. For example, consider the probabilistic graph $\mathcal{G}$ in Figure 1(a), the probability that the edge (q_1, v_1) is contained in two triangles is $0.5 \cdot (0.5 \cdot 1) \cdot (0.5 \cdot 1) = 0.125$. Figure 2(a) shows a local $(4, 0.125)$-truss $\mathcal{H}_1$ in $\mathcal{G}$. For each edge $e \in \mathcal{H}_1$, the probability that e is contained in at least 2 triangles is at least 0.125.

As with truss decompositions over deterministic graphs, we are interested in finding maximal local (k, γ)-trusses. However, efficient extraction of local (k, γ)-trusses raises challenges. In probabilistic graphs, to check if an edge belongs to a local (k, γ)-truss, the basic operation is to check if the edge has a large enough probability to be contained in at least $(k-2)$ triangles. A straightforward extension of the deterministic triangle counting operation leads to combinatorial blow-ups and is inefficient. Therefore, existing truss decomposition algorithms for deterministic graphs do not work for probabilistic graphs. Fortunately, local (k, γ)-truss has many desirable features. The key point is that the probability of edge support can be computed in polynomial time, relying only on the local structure. In other words, we can avoid its evaluation for every possible world of $\mathcal{G}$. Specifically, we are able to exploit this "locality" and develop an efficient dynamic programming algorithm for finding a decomposition of a probabilistic graph into maximal local (k, γ)-trusses, for various k, given a parameter $\gamma \in (0, 1]$.

The above definition of truss is *local* in that the "witness" graphs having the $(k - 2)$ triangles containing an edge in $\mathcal{H}$ may be quite different for different edges. To mitigate this, we explore another, "global" notion: in a *global* (k, γ)-truss $\mathcal{H} \subseteq \mathcal{G}$, for each edge in $\mathcal{H}$, the probability that it is contained in a k-truss must be at least γ. We show that unlike local (k, γ)-truss, the global (k, γ)-truss decomposition of a probabilistic graph is intractable: specifically, even computing the exact probability that a given subgraph contains a k-truss connecting its nodes is in general #P-hard. Given this, we tackle this issue with a novel sampling scheme that enables an efficient estimation of the said probability. We also show that there are instances where the number of maximal global (k, γ)-trusses can be exponential. Thus, we develop a heuristic approach combined with the sampling technique above for obtaining global (k, γ)-trusses. Each solution reported by our algorithm is guaranteed to be a maximal global (k, γ)-truss with high probability.

To summarize, we make the following contributions:

- We define local and global (k, γ)-truss over probabilistic graphs and motivate the problem of probabilistic truss decomposition associated with these notions (Section 3.1).
- We show that every global (k, γ)-truss is also a local (k, γ)-truss. We also show that computing the probability that a given probabilistic graph contains a k-truss connecting all its nodes is #P-hard and that there are instances where a given probabilistic graph has exponentially many maximal (k, γ)-trusses even when k and γ are fixed (Section 3.2).
- We show that the support probability of any edge, on which local (k, γ)-truss is based, is monotone w.r.t. k. Leveraging this and the structural locality, we develop an efficient dynamic programming algorithm for finding all maximal local (k, γ)-trusses of a probabilistic graph, given γ (Section 4).
- We develop a sampling scheme for approximating the probability of a graph containing a connected k-truss. We present an exact search algorithm and an efficient heuristic for finding approximate maximal global (k, γ)-trusses (Section 5).
- Using extensive experiments on eight real datasets, we test our proposed algorithms for finding maximal local and global (k, γ)-trusses. The results show that our algorithms significantly outperform natural baselines and alternative techniques based on probabilistic extensions to k-cores [4] (Section 6).

2. RELATED WORK

There are mainly two categories of previous work that are related to ours: querying and mining over probabilistic graphs and dense subgraph mining.

2.1 Probabilistic Graphs

The body of work on querying and mining probabilistic graphs is the closest to our work. In the literature, the studies on uncertain graphs have mainly focused on querying [17,27,30] and mining, specifically frequent subgraph mining [38,39], dense subgraph mining [4,23] and clustering [18,21]. Jin et al. [17] study the distance-constraint reachability problem, which is a generalization of the classic two terminal reliability problem: for a pair of nodes find the probability that their shortest path distance is under a threshold. This problem is #P-hard and they propose sampling schemes and experimentally show that they are efficient and produce accurate estimates. Potamias et al. [27] study the k-nearest neighbors problem over uncertain graphs and propose sampling strategies for answering k-nearest neighbor queries efficiently.

Zou et al. [38,39] consider the problem of discovering frequent pattern subgraphs in an input probabilistic graph. One of the key properties that helps efficient discovery of frequent pattern graphs is monotonicity: if a pattern graph is frequent then any subgraph of that pattern is also frequent. Jin et al. [16] investigate the problem of discovering highly reliable subgraphs of probabilistic graphs, in which the connectivity holds with a high probability. This problem is intractable and the authors develop an efficient approach using a combination of sampling and frequent cohesive set discovery. Bonchi et al. [4] extend the notion of k-core to probabilistic graphs. Since k-cores are a kind of dense subgraphs, a comparison with [4] appears in the next subsection. The problem of finding truss decomposition over probabilistic graphs has not been studied before, to our knowledge. Specifically, the notions of local and global (k,γ)-trusses proposed in this paper are novel. None of the techniques proposed in the aforementioned related work can be directly used to find maximal local/global (k,γ)-trusses. One unique challenge we face in case of global (k,γ)-trusses, unlike some of the related work, is the lack of any monotonicity properties (see Section 5): given two probabilistic graphs $\mathcal{H}_1 \subset \mathcal{H}_2$, if one of them is a global (k,γ)-truss, then the other may or may not be a (k,γ)-truss. This makes their discovery particularly challenging. Furthermore, unlike highly reliable subgraphs, our global (k,γ)-trusses needs to be not just connected, but also be densely connected with high probability.

2.2 Dense Subgraph Mining

In deterministic graphs, there are various definitions of dense subgraph patterns, including clique [5,7,34,35], quasi-clique [31], k-core [2,6] and k-truss [9,33]. Truss decomposition has been studied in various settings, including in-memory algorithms [9,36], external-memory algorithms [33], and MapReduce algorithm [10]. However, as far as we know, probabilistic truss decomposition has not been studied yet. Based on the k-truss definition [9], we propose two novel types of local and global (k,γ)-truss definitions appropriate for probabilistic graphs. Core decomposition has also been studied in both in-memory and external memory [6] settings. Recently, Bonchi et al. [4] extend the core decomposition from deterministic graphs to probabilistic graphs. They define a (k,η)-core as a subgraph of a probabilistic graph in which the degree of each node is at least k, with probability no less than η. Our local (k,γ)-truss is similar to (k,η)-core, since both are defined on the local structure. (k,γ)-Truss emphasizes the number of triangles supporting an edge, but (k,η)-core focuses on node degree. It is well-known that k-trusses enjoy a higher density (e.g., clustering coefficient) than k-cores and are more cohesive. This property carries over to probabilistic graphs and is also borne out by our experiments (see Section 6). On the other hand, in this paper, we also propose a global (k,γ)-truss, that is based on the probability of each edge belonging to a connected k-truss possible world. This is a graph-level, holistic constraint, which has no parallel in any of the previous work, to the best of our knowledge.

3. TRUSSES IN PROBABILISTIC GRAPHS

k-Truss in deterministic graphs. Let $G = (V, E)$ be an undirected, unweighted simple graph, with vertices V and edges $E \subseteq V \times V$. A cycle of length 3 is called a *triangle*; we let $\triangle_{uvw}$ denote a triangle with vertices $u, v, w \in V$. Let $H = (V_H, E_H)$ be an induced subgraph of G, i.e., $V_H \subseteq V$ and $E_H = \{(u,v) \in E \mid u, v \in V_H\}$. Henceforth, by subgraph we mean an induced subgraph. For any edge $e = (u,v) \in E_H$, we define the *support* of e in H as the number of triangles in H that contain e: $\mathsf{sup}_H(e) = |\{\triangle_{uvw} \mid (u,w),(v,w) \in E_H\}|$. A subgraph H of G is called a *k-truss* iff the support of every edge in this subgraph is at least $k-2$. Formally,

DEFINITION 1 (k-TRUSS). *Let $H = (V_H, E_H)$ be a subgraph of $G = (V, E)$ and $k \geq 2$ be any integer. Then, H is a k-truss if and only if for all $e \in E_H$, $\mathsf{sup}_H(e) \geq k-2$.*

A k-truss H is *maximal* if it is not a subgraph of any other k-truss. Given a deterministic graph G, the task of *truss decomposition* is to compute all maximal k-trusses of G for all $2 \leq k \leq k_{\max}$, where $k_{\max}$ is the largest support of any edge [33]; we do not need to know this value beforehand, since the decomposition process will automatically reveal it. A useful notion in truss decomposition is the *trussness* of an edge e in a graph G, defined as the maximum k for which e is contained in a k-truss subgraph of G.

Truss decomposition can be done in polynomial time using an iterative removal algorithm [9,33]. Observe that any connected graph is itself a 2-truss by definition, and thus we start from $k = 3$. The algorithm iteratively removes edges whose support is smaller than $k-2$ and updates the support of affected edges, until the remaining graph is a k-truss (or empty). The update is crucial for correctness, since when (u,v) is removed, all triangles $\triangle_{uvw}$ disappear and the support of (u,w) and (v,w) should be decreased by 1. As long as the remaining graph is not empty, we increment k by 1 and repeat the iterative edge removal process. We stop when the graph is empty, and the current k is thus $k_{\max}$. This algorithm is due to [9], which is then improved by [33] using hashing and sorting, achieving $O(m^{1.5})$ time and uses $O(m+n)$ space complexity.

Probabilistic graphs. Let $\mathcal{G} = (V, E, p)$ denote a *probabilistic* graph, where $p\colon E \to [0,1]$ is a function that maps each edge $e \in E$ to its existence probability $p(e)$. Each edge is typically assumed to exist independently [16]. A well-known approach to analyzing and reasoning about probabilistic graphs is to use *possible worlds*: each possible world is a deterministic graph instantiation of $\mathcal{G}$, where only a subset of edges exist for certain. Notice that by definition, *a possible world retains all nodes of $\mathcal{G}$*.

For a deterministic graph $G = (V, E_G)$ where $E_G \subseteq E$, the probability that G is observed as a possible world of $\mathcal{G}$ can be calculated as follows.

$$\Pr[G|\mathcal{G}] =_{\text{def}} \prod_{e \in E_G} p(e) \prod_{e \in E \setminus E_G} (1 - p(e)). \quad (1)$$

We use $G \sqsubseteq \mathcal{G}$ to indicate that G is a possible world of $\mathcal{G}$.

EXAMPLE 1. *Consider the probabilistic graph $\mathcal{G}$ in Figure 1(a) and the possible world $G_1 \sqsubseteq \mathcal{G}$ in Figure 1(b). By applying Eq. (1), we have* $\Pr[G_1|\mathcal{G}] = 0.7^4 \times 0.5^6 = 0.0037515625$.

3.1 Probabilistic Trusses

Local (k,γ)-truss. Next, we extend the concept of k-truss to probabilistic graphs. Let $\mathsf{sup}_{\mathcal{G}}(e)$ denote the support of $e = (u,v)$ in $\mathcal{G}$, and let $N(u) \subset V$ denote the set of *structural neighbors* of u in $\mathcal{G}$. Here, by a structural neighbor of u, we mean any node v that is adjacent to u according to the graph structure of $\mathcal{G}$, ignoring any probabilities. Thus, $N(u)$ is a deterministic set. Clearly, $\mathsf{sup}_{\mathcal{G}}(e)$ is a random variable which can take on any integer value from zero to $k_e =_{\text{def}} |N(u) \cap N(v)|$, the maximum possible support of e in any possible world of $\mathcal{G}$.

By definition of possible worlds, given any $t \in [0, k_e]$, the probability that $\mathsf{sup}_{\mathcal{G}}(e) \geq t$ is the sum of the probability mass of all possible worlds $G \sqsubseteq \mathcal{G}$ such that the (deterministic) support of e in G is no less than t. Mathematically,

$$\Pr[\mathsf{sup}_{\mathcal{G}}(e) \geq t] = \sum_{G \sqsubseteq \mathcal{G}} \Pr[G|\mathcal{G}] \cdot \mathbf{I}(\mathsf{sup}_G(e) \geq t), \quad (2)$$

where $\mathbf{I}(\mathsf{sup}_G(e) \geq t)$ is an indicator function which takes on 1 if $\mathsf{sup}_G(e) \geq t$, and 0 otherwise. If $e \notin E_G$, $\mathbf{I}(\mathsf{sup}_G(e) \geq t) =_{\text{def}} 0$.

Intuitively, a subgraph $\mathcal{H}$ of $\mathcal{G}$ [1] can be regarded as a cohesive subgraph of $\mathcal{G}$ if the support of every edge in $\mathcal{H}$ is no less than

[1]Note that $\mathcal{H}$ is still a probabilistic graph.

a threshold *with high probability*. Following this intuition, we define *local* (k,γ)*-truss* as follows, where by a connected subgraph $\mathcal{H} \subseteq \mathcal{G}$, we mean any subgraph $\mathcal{H}$ which is connected as a graph, ignoring probabilities.

DEFINITION 2 (LOCAL (k,γ)-TRUSS). *Let $\mathcal{G} = (V, E, p)$ be a probabilistic graph and $\mathcal{H} \subseteq \mathcal{G}$ any* connected *subgraph. Given a threshold $\gamma \in [0,1]$, and an integer $k \geq 2$, we say $\mathcal{H}$ is a* local (k,γ)-truss, *iff for every $e \in E_{\mathcal{H}}$, $\Pr[\mathsf{sup}_{\mathcal{H}}(e) \geq k-2] \geq \gamma$, i.e., for each edge, the probability that it has a support no less than $(k-2)$ in $\mathcal{H}$ is at least γ.*

The name "local" reflects that the support of each edge is evaluated individually, and there is no graph-wise global constraint that $\mathcal{H}$ must satisfy. The requirement that $\mathcal{H}$ is *connected* is natural, since it is possible to have two totally-separated connected components while still all edges have high support with high probability. For instance, as mentioned in Section 1, the subgraph $\mathcal{H}_1$ shown in Figure 2(a) is a local (k,γ)-truss where $k=4$ and $\gamma = 0.125$.

We are interested in finding all local (k,γ)-trusses that are *maximal*, i.e., those that are not proper subgraphs of any other local (k,γ)-truss. We formulate this problem as *Local Probabilistic Truss Decomposition*, dubbed LOCALDECOMP.

PROBLEM 1 (LOCALDECOMP). *Given a probabilistic graph $\mathcal{G} = (V, E, p)$ and a threshold $\gamma \in [0,1]$, find all* maximal local (k,γ)-trusses *of $\mathcal{G}$, for all $2 \leq k \leq k_{\max}$, where $k_{\max}$ is the maximum support of any edge in $\mathcal{G}$.*

Global (k,γ)-truss. As noted earlier, a local (k,γ)-truss does not have to satisfy any graph-wise global constraints: specifically, while Definition 2 ensures that for each edge, there are enough possible worlds where its support is $\geq (k-2)$, it does not ensure that the $(k-2)$ supporting triangles of different edges in $\mathcal{H}$ are present *together* in a fraction $\geq \gamma$ of the possible worlds. To mitigate this, we propose a stronger definition of a (k,γ)-truss which naturally incorporates a global constraint, thus strengthening the cohesiveness of a probabilistic truss. In the definition below, notice that all nodes of $\mathcal{H}$ are required to be connected in any connected possible world H of $\mathcal{H}$. Formally,

DEFINITION 3 (GLOBAL (k,γ)-TRUSS). *Let $\mathcal{G} = (V, E, p)$ be a probabilistic graph. Given a threshold $\gamma \in [0,1]$, and an integer $k \geq 2$, a connected subgraph $\mathcal{H} = (V_{\mathcal{H}}, E_{\mathcal{H}})$ of $\mathcal{G}$ is a* global (k,γ)-truss, *iff for each edge $e \in E_{\mathcal{H}}$,*

$$\alpha_k(\mathcal{H}, e) =_{\text{def}} \sum_{H \sqsubseteq \mathcal{H}} \Pr[H|\mathcal{H}] \cdot \mathbf{I}(H, k, e) \geq \gamma, \qquad (3)$$

where $\mathbf{I}(H,k,e)$ is an indicator function taking on 1 if the possible world H (thus $V_H = V_{\mathcal{H}}$) is a connected, deterministic k-truss containing e, and 0 otherwise.

Every global (k,γ)-truss is also a local (k,γ)-truss, as we show below. Hence, global (k,γ)-truss is a stronger and stricter notion, which intuitively corresponds to more cohesive (probabilistic) subgraphs.

LEMMA 1. *Let $\mathcal{G} = (V, E, p)$ be a probabilistic graph and $\mathcal{H} \subseteq \mathcal{G}$ be a global (k,γ)-truss. Then $\mathcal{H}$ is also a local (k,γ)-truss, for the same k and γ.*

PROOF. Every connected k-truss containing an edge e clearly has at least $(k-2)$ triangles containing that edge. The lemma follows from this and the fact that $\mathcal{H}$ is connected. □

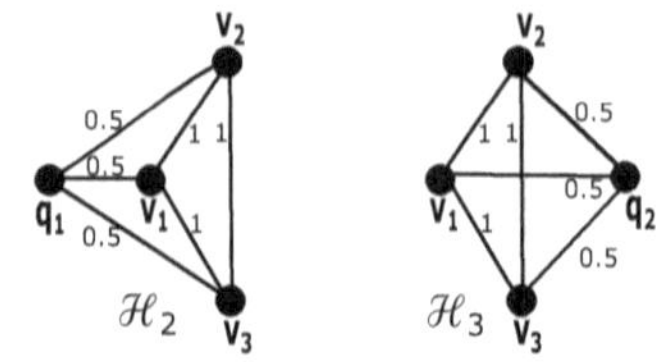

Figure 3: Two global (k,γ)-trusses of $\mathcal{G}$ in Figure 1. Here, $k=4$ and $\gamma = 0.125$.

EXAMPLE 2. Figure 3 depicts two global $(4, 0.125)$-trusses $\mathcal{H}_2, \mathcal{H}_3 \subseteq \mathcal{G}$, where $\mathcal{G}$ is shown in Figure 1. In both cases, the only supporting possible world is the one where all edges exist, whose existence probability is $(0.5)^3 \cdot 1^3 = 0.125$. Moreover, both $\mathcal{H}_2$ and $\mathcal{H}_3$ are maximal global $(4, 0.125)$-trusses and there exists no other global $(4, 0.125)$-truss in $\mathcal{G}$. To compare global and local (k,γ)-trusses, first, we note that $\mathcal{H}_2$ and $\mathcal{H}_3$ are also local $(4, 0.125)$-trusses, but the local $(4, 0.125)$-truss $\mathcal{H}_1$ in Figure 2(a) is not a global one. In fact, $\mathcal{H}_1$ is a global $(4, 0.5^6)$-truss, because the only possible world of $\mathcal{H}_1$ that is a connected k-truss containing all nodes in $\mathcal{H}_1$ is the one shown in Figure 2(b), and its existence probability is 0.5^6.

We are interested in the problem of finding all maximal global (k,γ)-trusses of a given probabilistic graph. Formally:

PROBLEM 2 (GLOBALDECOMP). *Given a probabilistic graph $\mathcal{G} = (V, E, p)$ and a threshold $\gamma \in [0,1]$, find all* maximal global (k,γ)-trusses *of $\mathcal{G}$, for all $2 \leq k \leq k_{\max}$, where $k_{\max}$ is the maximum support of any edge in $\mathcal{G}$.*

3.2 Hardness Results

As we shall see in Section 4, LOCALDECOMP can be solved in polynomial time. However, GLOBALDECOMP is generally intractable, since even computing $\alpha_k(\mathcal{H}, e)$ is #P-hard.

THEOREM 1. *Given a probabilistic graph $\mathcal{H}$ and an edge e in $\mathcal{H}$, computing $\alpha_k(\mathcal{H}, e)$ as in Eq. (3) is #P-hard.*

PROOF. The reduction is from the NETWORK RELIABILITY problem [16,32]. For a probabilistic graph $\mathcal{G}$, its network reliability, i.e., the probability that $\mathcal{G}$ is connected, is defined as

$$\mathsf{conn}(\mathcal{G}) = \sum\nolimits_{G \sqsubseteq \mathcal{G}} \Pr[G|\mathcal{G}] \cdot \mathbf{C}(G), \qquad (4)$$

where G is a possible world of $\mathcal{G}$, and $\mathbf{C}(G)$ is an indicator function taking on 1 if G is connected, and 0 otherwise. It is known that computing $\mathsf{conn}(\mathcal{G})$ is #P-hard [16].

Given an instance of NETWORK RELIABILITY with $\mathcal{G}$, we construct an instance of the problem of computing $\alpha_k(\cdot,\cdot)$ as follows. Let v be an arbitrary vertex in $\mathcal{G}$. We create a dummy node w and an edge (w,v) with $p(w,v) = 1$. Let the resulting graph be $\mathcal{H}$.

We show the following claim: a possible world $G = (V_G, E_G) \sqsubseteq \mathcal{G}$ is connected iff $H = (V_G \cup \{w\}, E_G \cup \{(w,v)\}) \sqsubseteq \mathcal{H}$ is a connected 2-truss that contains (w,v). The "if" direction is trivial. Now consider "only if". Since G is connected, then there exists a path between v and any other node in V_G. Also, since the edge (w,v) is in H, then there is also a path connecting w with any other node in V_G. Thus H is connected, contains (w,v) by construction, and is a 2-truss by definition.

Due to the one-to-one correspondence established between the possible worlds of $\mathcal{G}$ and $\mathcal{H}$ in the above claim, and the fact that $\Pr[G|\mathcal{G}] = \Pr[H|\mathcal{H}]$ as $p(w,v) = 1$, we can see that $\mathsf{conn}(\mathcal{G}) = \alpha_k(H, (w,v))$. The theorem follows. □

GLOBALDECOMP is as least as intractable as evaluating $\alpha_k(\mathcal{H}, k, e)$: since γ can be any real number in $[0, 1]$, checking if $\alpha_k(\mathcal{H}, e) \geq \gamma$ requires that $\alpha_k(\mathcal{H}, e)$ be computed to arbitrary accuracy. In addition, we show that the number of solutions to GLOBALDECOMP can in fact be exponential in graph size, adding another major computational challenge.

LEMMA 2. *There are probabilistic graphs $\mathcal{G}$ and parameter γ, such that the number of maximal global (k, γ)-trusses is exponential in $|V_\mathcal{G}|$. This is true even for fixed k.*

PROOF. Please refer to Appendix. □

Both Theorem 1 and Lemma 2 indicate the intrinsic hardness of GLOBALDECOMP. Although GLOBALDECOMP may have an exponential number of answers, it is still important to study for the following reasons. First, compared with the local (k, γ)-truss, global (k, γ)-truss is a more stringent and holistic definition, which ensures that the *entire* subgraph has a certain probability to exist as a k-truss. In critical applications such as identifying functional modules from protein-protein interaction networks, modules with a high probability of existence as a whole are more useful for making sure that any medical or clinical assessments are correct. In addition, as an analogy, consider the seminal Frequent Item-set (Pattern) Mining problem, where the number of satisfying item-sets is exponential in the number of items. However, this is still an extremely useful problem with wide applications. Besides, the number of frequent item-sets can be controlled by adjusting parameters such as support and confidence. In our global (k, γ)-truss decomposition problem, we can control the size of output by fine-tuning the value of k and γ. For a reasonably large k and γ, the number of satisfying subgraphs is unlikely to be enormous in real applications. This claim is experimentally verified on real datasets in Section 6.3. Finally, in Section 5.1, we make use of Hoeffding's inequality to develop a Monte Carlo sampling method, which lays the foundations of an approximation algorithm for finding maximal global (k, γ)-trusses.

4. LOCAL PROBABILISTIC TRUSS DECOMPOSITION

We now describe an algorithm for solving LOCALDECOMP. The general idea is based on the iterative edge removal process for truss decomposition in deterministic graphs [9, 33]. However, there are significant computational challenges brought about by probabilistic graphs. For example, we must combat the complications introduced by the *combinatorial nature* of the triangles in which an edge may participate. We will first give an outline of the algorithm and then describe two challenging tasks, namely computing and updating edge support probabilities, in detail.

4.1 Algorithmic Framework

For an edge $e = (u, v) \in E_\mathcal{G}$, let $\rho_\mathcal{G}(e, t)$ denote the probability that the support of edge e is at least t in $\mathcal{G}$, i.e., $\sigma_\mathcal{G}(e, t) =_{\text{def}} \Pr[\mathsf{sup}_\mathcal{G}(e) \geq t]$. Furthermore, let $\sigma_\mathcal{G}(e) =_{\text{def}} [\sigma_\mathcal{G}(e, 1), \sigma_\mathcal{G}(e, 2), \ldots, \sigma_\mathcal{G}(e, k_e)]$ be the vector of support probabilities of e for all possible t from 1 to k_e. We refer to $\sigma_\mathcal{G}(e)$ as the *edge support probability vector*. When it is clear from the context, we drop the subscript $\mathcal{G}$.

Note that the edge support probabilities in $\sigma(e)$ are well-defined only when e actually exists. Hence, in what follows, we assume that e does exist for the purpose of computing $\sigma(e)$. The "true" edge support probabilities can be easily derived by multiplying $\sigma(e)$ with $p(e)$ element-wise.

Algorithm 1 Local (k, γ)-truss decomposition

Require: $\mathcal{G} = (V, E, p)$; $\gamma \in [0, 1]$
Ensure: trussness score $\tau(e)$ of each edge $e \in E$
1: **for all** $e \in E$ **do**
2: compute $\sigma(e)$ using Algorithm 2
3: **for** $k \leftarrow 2$ **to** n **do**
4: **while** $\exists e = (u, v)$ such that $\sigma(e, k-1)p(e) < \gamma$ **and** $\sigma(e, k-2)p(e) \geq \gamma$ **do**
5: $\tau(e) \leftarrow k$
6: remove e from $\mathcal{G}$
7: **for** $w \in N(u) \cap N(v)$ **do**
8: update $\sigma_{(w,u)}$ and $\sigma_{(w,v)}$ {*cf.* Section 4.3}
9: **if** $\mathcal{G}$ is empty **then**
10: **break**

Monotonicity of $\sigma(e)$. In designing the decomposition algorithm, we make use of the fact that the edge support probabilities in $\sigma(e)$ are monotonically non-increasing. That is, for all $e \in E$, we have $\sigma(e, 1) \geq \sigma(e, 2) \geq \ldots \geq \sigma(e, k_e)$. This holds true by definition, because

$$\sigma(e, k) = \Pr[\mathsf{sup}_\mathcal{G}(e) = k] + \sigma(e, k+1) \geq \sigma(e, k+1).$$

Overview. Algorithm 1 presents the pseudo-code for our local (k, γ)-truss decomposition procedure. We begin by computing the edge support probability vector $\sigma(e)$ for all $e \in E$ (lines 1-2). Then, the algorithm iteratively finds all local (k, γ)-trusses starting from $k = 2$. For any particular k, if there exists an edge e such that $\sigma(e, k-1)p(e) < \gamma$ and $\sigma(e, k-2)p(e) \geq \gamma$, then e belongs to a local (k, γ)-truss, but does not belong to any local $(k+1, \gamma)$-truss. Then e will be assigned a trussness score of k, denoted by $\tau(e)$, and removed from the graph (lines 4-6). After the removal of e, all triangles in which this edge participates shall also be removed, and thus the support of the other two edges in each such triangle shall be updated (lines 7-8). This iterative process goes on until all edges are removed from the graph (lines 9-10). The value of k at which we stop is thus $k_{\max}$.

After obtaining the trussness score of all edges, we can easily construct all maximal local (k, γ)-trusses, for a particular k, by piecing together all edges e with $\tau(e) \geq k$. Note that by Definition 2, the output trusses for LOCALDECOMP must be connected subgraphs of $\mathcal{G}$. Thus, after Algorithm 1, we perform a post-processing step to extract all connected components. We have the following:

THEOREM 2. *Algorithm 1, with post-processing on connectivity, finds all and only maximal local (k, γ)-trusses of $\mathcal{G}$, for all $2 \leq k \leq k_{\max}$.*

PROOF. Please refer to Appendix. □

Although computing and updating edge support in deterministic graphs can be considered straightforward, it is far from trivial to compute and update edge support probabilities in probabilistic graphs. Next we give a dynamic programming algorithm for this task. We defer time complexity analysis of Algorithm 1 to the end of this section.

4.2 Computing Edge Support Probabilities

By definition, $\sigma(e, t) = \Pr[\mathsf{sup}_\mathcal{G}(e) \geq t]$, and thus

$$\sigma(e, t) = 1 - \sum_{i=0}^{t-1} \Pr[\mathsf{sup}_\mathcal{G}(e) = i]$$

Therefore, it is helpful for us to determine the formulas for computing $\Pr[\mathsf{sup}_{\mathcal{G}}(e) = i]$, given any i.

Zero triangles. Consider the special case of edge e having zero support, i.e., $\Pr[\mathsf{sup}_{\mathcal{G}}(e) = 0]$. Two cases arise: (i). e does not even exist, which happens with probability $1 - p(e)$; (ii). e exists but does not participate in any triangles, which happens with probability $p(e) \cdot \prod_{w \in N(u) \cap N(v)} (1 - p(w,u)p(w,v))$. Thus,

$$\Pr[\mathsf{sup}_{\mathcal{G}}(e) = 0] = (1 - p(e)) + p(e) \prod_{w \in N(u) \cap N(v)} (1 - p(w,u)p(w,v)). \quad (5)$$

The case of e not existing is not interesting, but for our dynamic programming algorithm in Section 4.2.1, we need to consider case (ii) above. Thus, the probability of zero support reduces to $\prod_{w \in (N(u) \cap N(v))} (1 - p(w,v)p(w,u))$ *under the assumption that e exists.*

Multiple triangles. Now, we consider the probability that edge e participates in one or more triangles. The most naive approach is to consider, for each $1 \le i \le k_e$, all sets of i triangles, and sum up all the probabilities as a final result.

$$\Pr[\mathsf{sup}_{\mathcal{G}}(e) = i] = \sum_{W \subseteq N(u) \cap N(v), |W| = i} \prod_{w \in W} p(w,u)p(w,v) \prod_{w \in N(u) \cap N(v) \setminus W} (1 - p(w,u)p(w,v)).$$

However, enumerating all subsets of $N(u) \cap N(v)$ of size i can be prohibitively expensive. The time complexity is $\binom{n}{i}$ where $|N(u) \cap N(v)| \in O(n)$, and thus is potentially exponential in n. To avoid this exponential blow-up, we devise a dynamic programming algorithm to compute $\Pr[\mathsf{sup}_{\mathcal{G}}(e) = i]$, $1 \le i \le k_e$, in polynomial time, as described next.

4.2.1 *Dynamic Programming for* $\Pr[\mathsf{sup}_{\mathcal{G}}(e) = i]$

Our purpose is to identify the structure of the problem so that we can derive a recursive formula for dynamic programming. Consider an edge $e = (u,v)$ and a fixed common neighbor $w \in N(u) \cap N(v)$. Note that if e participates in i triangles in $\mathcal{G}$, then either (i). $\triangle_{uvw}$ exists and e participates in $i-1$ other triangles in $\mathcal{G}$ excluding $\triangle_{uvw}$, or (ii). $\triangle_{uvw}$ does not exist and e participates in i other triangles. Thus, $\Pr[\mathsf{sup}_{\mathcal{G}}(e) = i]$ can be computed as a linear combination of the probabilities that e has $i-1$ or i triangles in $\mathcal{G}$ excluding $\triangle_{uvw}$. According to this rule, we can take advantage of the results of subproblems $\Pr[\mathsf{sup}_{\mathcal{G}}(e) = j]$, $0 \le j \le i-1$, to calculate $\Pr[\mathsf{sup}_{\mathcal{G}}(e) = i]$.

The recursion. Given a probabilistic graph $\mathcal{G} = (V, E, p)$ and an edge $e = (u,v) \in E$, we denote by $W =_{\text{def}} N(u) \cap N(v) = \{w_1, ..., w_{k_e}\}$, the set of all common neighbors of u and v in $\mathcal{G}$, ordered arbitrarily. Given a subset $W_\ell = \{w_1, ..., w_\ell\} \subseteq W$, where $1 \le \ell \le k_e$, we denote by $\Pr[\mathsf{sup}_{\mathcal{G}}(e) = i | W_\ell]$ the probability that e participates in i triangles with common neighbors from W_ℓ. For clarity of exposition, we use $f(i,\ell)$ as a shorthand for $\Pr[\mathsf{sup}_{\mathcal{G}}(e) = i | W_\ell]$. Now, for any two consecutive subsets $W_{\ell-1}$ and W_ℓ, the following recursive formula holds:

$$f(i,\ell) = p(w_\ell,u)p(w_\ell,v)f(i-1,\ell-1) + (1 - p(w_\ell,u)p(w_\ell,v))f(i,\ell-1), \quad (6)$$

where $-1 \le i \le k_e$ and $0 \le \ell \le k_e$. Note that $i = -1$ and $\ell = 0$ are "dummy" cases to set up the base cases:

Algorithm 2 Dynamic programming for computing $\sigma(e)$

Require: $\mathcal{G} = (V, E, p)$, an edge $e = (u,v) \in E$.
Ensure: $\sigma(e) = [\sigma(e,1), \sigma(e,2), \ldots, \sigma(e,k_e)]$
1: $f(0,0) \leftarrow 1$
2: $f(-1,\ell) \leftarrow 0$, for all $0 \le \ell \le k_e$
3: **for** $\ell \leftarrow 0$ **to** k_e **do**
4:     **for** $i \leftarrow \ell + 1$ **to** k_e **do**
5:         $f(i,\ell) \leftarrow 0$
6: **for** $i \leftarrow 0$ **to** k_e **do**
7:     **for** $\ell \leftarrow 1$ **to** k_e **do**
8:         $f(i,\ell) \leftarrow p(w_\ell,u)p(w_\ell,v)f(i-1,\ell-1) + (1 - p(w_\ell,u)p(w_\ell,v))f(i,\ell-1)$
9: $\sigma(e,0) \leftarrow 1$
10: **for** $t \leftarrow 1$ **to** k_e **do**
11:     $\sigma(e,t) \leftarrow \sigma(e,t-1) - f(t,k_e)$

- $f(0,0) = 1$;
- $f(-1,\ell) = 0$, for all $0 \le \ell \le k_e$;
- $f(i,\ell) = 0$, whenever $i > \ell$.

For any i, the value $f(i,k_e)$ is the desired edge support probability $\Pr[\mathsf{sup}_{\mathcal{G}}(e) = i]$.

Lines 1-8 of Algorithm 2 describe the dynamic programming procedure. After these steps, we can get the desired edge support vector $\sigma(e)$ via a single linear scan (lines 9-11), thanks to the following equations:

$$\begin{aligned}\sigma(e,t) &= \sigma(e,t-1) - \Pr[\mathsf{sup}_{\mathcal{G}}(e) = t-1] \\ &= \sigma(e,t-1) - f(t-1,k_e). \quad (7)\end{aligned}$$

Time complexity of Algorithm 2. For each edge $e = (u,v)$, Algorithm 2 runs in $O((\min\{d(u),d(v)\})^2)$ time, where $d(u)$ is the degree of u in $\mathcal{G}$. The entire dynamic programming procedure (lines 1-8) takes $O(k_e^2)$ time, where $k_e = |N(u) \cap N(v)| \in O(\min\{d(u),d(v)\})$. Calculating $\sigma(e)$ (lines 9-11) takes $O(k_e)$ time. As a result, the total time complexity is $O((\min\{d(u),d(v)\})^2)$.

4.3 Updating Edge Support Probabilities

We now describe how to update $\sigma(e)$ for edge $e = (u,v)$ if the triangle $\triangle_{uvw}$ is deleted from $\mathcal{G}$ where $w \in N(u) \cap N(v)$, owing to the removal of $e_1 = (u,w)$ or $e_2 = (v,w)$. Recall that the update step is fundamental and crucial in our (k,γ)-truss decomposition algorithm (line 8 of Algorithm 1). A naive approach is to compute $\sigma(e)$ from scratch by Algorithm 2 whenever the update is needed, but it will again incur $O((\min\{d(u),d(v)\})^2)$ overhead.

Assume, without loss of generality, that $e_1 = (u,w)$ was removed from $\mathcal{G}$ (the case of $e_2 = (v,w)$ being removed can be similarly analyzed). The following formula holds:

$$\begin{aligned}\Pr[\mathsf{sup}_{\mathcal{G}}(e) = i|W] = &(1 - p(e_1)p(e_2)) \Pr[\mathsf{sup}_{\mathcal{G}}(e) = i|W \setminus \{w\}] \\ &+ p(e_1)p(e_2) \Pr[\mathsf{sup}_{\mathcal{G}}(e) = i-1|W \setminus \{w\}]\end{aligned}$$

Re-arranging terms, we have:

$$\Pr[\mathsf{sup}_{\mathcal{G}}(e) = i|W \setminus \{w\}] = \frac{\Pr[\mathsf{sup}_{\mathcal{G}}(e) = i|W] - p(e_1)p(e_2) \Pr[\mathsf{sup}_{\mathcal{G}}(e) = i-1|W \setminus \{w\}]}{1 - p(e_1)p(e_2)}$$

Thus, to update $\sigma(e)$, we only need to update $f(t,k_e)$ using the following rule:

$$f^{new}(i,k_e) = \frac{f^{old}(i,k_e) - p(e_1)p(e_2)f^{new}(i-1,k_e)}{1 - p(e_1)p(e_2)}, \quad (8)$$

where the superscripts *old* and *new* correspond to before and after the edge e_1 is removed. Then, $\sigma(e)$ can be efficiently updated via a linear scan using f^{new} in $O(k_e)$ time as per Eq. 7. Furthermore, we can see that the update rule in Eq. 8 applies regardless of which edge, e_1 or e_2, is the one being removed.

Time complexity of Algorithm 1. The cost of computing $\sigma(e)$ for all $e \in E$ (lines 1-2) is $O(\sum_{(u,v)\in E}(\min\{d(u),\, d(v)\})^2) \subseteq O(d_{\max}\sum_{(u,v)\in E}\min\{d(u),\, d(v)\}) \subseteq O(d_{\max}\rho|E|)$, where $d_{\max}$ is the maximum degree and ρ is the arboricity of graph $\mathcal{G}$, i.e., the minimum number of spanning forests needed to cover all edges of $\mathcal{G}$. Notice that $\rho \leq \min\{d_{max}, \sqrt{|E|}\}$ [8]. The entire decomposition (lines 3-10) eventually will remove all edges from $\mathcal{G}$, and for each removal of an edge (u, v), we need to update $\sigma((v, w))$ and $\sigma((u, w))$ for all $w \in N(u) \cap N(v)$. For each removal, the number of updates is at most $2|N(u) \cap N(v)| \in O(\min\{d(u), d(v)\})$. Since a single update can be done in $O(k_e) \subseteq O(\min\{d(u), d(v)\})$ time as discussed, the total cost of doing updates pertaining to one edge removal is $O(\sum_{(u,v)\in E}(\min\{d(u), d(v)\})^2) \subseteq O(d_{\max}\rho|E|)$. In addition, edge selection (line 4) and edge removal (line 6) both can be done in $O(1)$ time by a variant of bin sort table [33]. Thus, the total time complexity of Algorithm 1 is $O(d_{\max}\rho|E|)$.

Space complexity of Algorithm 1. For each $e = (u, v) \in E$, we maintain a 2-dimensional table for dynamic programming in theory. In the implementation, for computing each $f(i, \ell)$, we only need to keep two arrays as $f(i-1, *)$ and $f(i, *)$, which consumes $O(\min\{d(v), d(u)\})$ space. Moreover, these two array can be released after obtaining $\sigma(e)$. In addition, the edge support vector $\sigma(e)$ only uses $O(\min\{d(v), d(u)\})$ space. The whole graph itself takes $O(|E|)$ space. Thus, the total space complexity is $O(|E| + \sum_{(u,v)\in E}\min\{d(v), d(u)\}) \subseteq O(\rho|E|)$.

5. GLOBAL PROBABILISTIC TRUSS DECOMPOSITION

5.1 Monte Carlo Sampling

First, we show how to use Monte Carlo sampling to estimate $\alpha_k(\mathcal{H}, e)$ (Eq. (3)) to circumvent the #P-hardness of its exact computation (Theorem 1). We apply a special case of the well-known Hoeffding's inequality [14], stated as follow. It specifies the minimum number of possible world samples required to get a bounded error for estimating $\alpha_k(\mathcal{H}, e)$.

PROPOSITION 1. *Let $X_1, X_2, \ldots, X_N$ be independent random variables such that $\Pr[0 \leq X_i \leq 1] = 1$. Let $\bar{X} = \frac{1}{N}\sum_{i=1}^{N} X_i$ and $\mu = \mathbb{E}[\bar{X}]$. Then,*

$$\Pr[|\bar{X} - \mu|] \geq \epsilon] \leq 2\exp\left(-2N\epsilon^2\right). \tag{9}$$

From Eq. (9), we have that for any $\delta \in (0, 1]$ and any $\epsilon \in (0, 1]$, $\Pr[|\bar{X} - \mu| \geq \epsilon] \leq \delta$, as long as $N \geq \frac{1}{2\epsilon^2}\ln(\frac{2}{\delta})$.

Given an error upper bound ϵ and a probability guarantee δ, a naive strategy would be to sample $N = \lceil \frac{1}{2\epsilon^2}\ln(\frac{2}{\delta})\rceil$ possible worlds of $\mathcal{H}$, for every subgraph $\mathcal{H} \subseteq \mathcal{G}$, and estimate $\alpha_k(\mathcal{H}, e)$ using the samples. This would be prohibitively expensive. Instead, our overall strategy is to sample $N = \lceil \frac{1}{2\epsilon^2}\ln(\frac{2}{\delta})\rceil$ possible worlds of $\mathcal{G}$, denoted $D_{\mathcal{G}} =_{\text{def}} \{G_i\}_{i=1}^{N}$. As the existence of each edge is independent, the resulting possible worlds are pairwise independent. Consider any subgraph $\mathcal{H} \subseteq \mathcal{G}$, we then obtain the N possible worlds of $\mathcal{H}$ by "projecting" each G_i to $\mathcal{H}$: $G_i \downarrow_{\mathcal{H}} =_{\text{def}} (V_{\mathcal{H}}, E_{G_i} \cap E_{\mathcal{H}})$. We also denote the projected world by H_i for simplicity. An estimation of $\alpha_k(\mathcal{H}, e)$ is then obtained via Monte Carlo sampling:

$$\widehat{\alpha}_k(\mathcal{H}, e) = \sum_{i=1}^{N} \mathbf{I}(H_i, e, k)/N, \tag{10}$$

where the indicator function $\mathbf{I}(H_i, e, k)$ is defined in Definition 3. Notice that by Proposition 1, an estimate of $\alpha_k(\mathcal{H}, e)$ obtained by sampling possible worlds of $\mathcal{H}$ is an unbiased estimate. Later, we shall show that the estimate $\widehat{\alpha}_k(\mathcal{H}, e)$ obtained by sampling (projected) possible worlds of $\mathcal{G}$ (as in Eq. (10)) gives the same result as the estimate obtained by sampling possible worlds of $\mathcal{H}$.

We say that $\mathcal{H}$ is an (ϵ, δ)*-approximate global* (k, γ)*-truss* if for any $e \in E_{\mathcal{H}}$, $\widehat{\alpha}_k(\mathcal{H}, e) \geq \gamma$. The following theorem establishes the theoretical foundation for our strategy that first samples N possible worlds of $\mathcal{G}$ and then projects them on to various subgraphs $\mathcal{H}$ throughout the decomposition process.

THEOREM 3. *Given a probabilistic graph $\mathcal{G}$ and parameters $\epsilon \in (0, 1]$ and $\delta \in (0, 1]$, let $D_{\mathcal{G}} = \{G_1, ..., G_N\}$ be N independently sampled possible worlds of $\mathcal{G}$, where $N \geq \frac{1}{2\epsilon^2}\ln(\frac{2}{\delta})$. Then, for any given $\mathcal{H} \subseteq \mathcal{G}$ and for any given $e \in E_{\mathcal{H}}$, we have*

$$\Pr[|\widehat{\alpha}_k(\mathcal{H}, e) - \alpha_k(\mathcal{H}, e)| \geq \varepsilon] \leq \delta,$$

where $\widehat{\alpha}_k(\mathcal{H}, e)$ is computed according to Eq. (10) using the projected possible worlds $D_{\mathcal{H}} =_{\text{def}} \{G_i \downarrow_{\mathcal{H}}\}_{i=1}^{N}$.

This is a non-trivial result, and to prove it, we first introduce a few notations and then give a useful lemma. Consider any subgraph $\mathcal{H} \subseteq \mathcal{G}$ and an arbitrary $H \sqsubseteq \mathcal{H}$. Let $X(H)$ denote the set of possible worlds of $\mathcal{G}$ whose projection to $\mathcal{H}$ results in H, i.e., $X(H) =_{\text{def}} \{G \sqsubseteq \mathcal{G} : G \downarrow_{\mathcal{H}} = H\}$.

LEMMA 3. *Given a probabilistic graph $\mathcal{G}$, a subgraph $\mathcal{H} \subseteq \mathcal{G}$, and any possible world $H \sqsubseteq \mathcal{H}$, we have*

$$\Pr[H|\mathcal{H}] = \sum_{G \in X(H)} \Pr[G|\mathcal{G}].$$

PROOF. Please refer to Appendix. □

COROLLARY 1. *Given any $\mathcal{H} \subseteq \mathcal{G}$, $\forall e \in E_{\mathcal{H}}$, we have*

$$\alpha_k(\mathcal{H}, e) = \sum_{G \sqsubseteq \mathcal{G}} \Pr[G|\mathcal{G}] \cdot \mathbf{I}(G \downarrow_{\mathcal{H}}, k, e).$$

PROOF. Please refer to Appendix. □

Note that Theorem 3 follows upon applying Proposition 1 to the result of Corollary 1. In particular, note that the probability of sampling a given possible world $H \sqsubseteq \mathcal{H}$ is the same as the probability of sampling some possible world $G \sqsubseteq \mathcal{G}$ such that G projects to H. Thus, we only need to sample N possible worlds of $\mathcal{G}$ which can be used to estimate $\alpha_k(\mathcal{H}, e)$ for any subgraph $\mathcal{H} \subseteq \mathcal{G}$ and edge $e \in E_{\mathcal{H}}$.

In what follows, we describe two algorithms for finding all *maximal* (ϵ, δ)-approximate global (k, γ)-trusses for a given γ and all possible k. For simplicity, we refer to such trusses as "satisfying trusses" in our algorithm descriptions.

5.2 Theoretical Analysis on Global (k, γ)-Truss

The search space for maximal global (k, γ)-trusses is huge. This is exacerbated by two challenging factors: (i) even computing the probability that a given subgraph $\mathcal{H} \subseteq \mathcal{G}$ contains a k-truss that connects all nodes of $\mathcal{H}$ is intractable (Theorem 1) and (ii) the number of maximal global (k, γ)-trusses can be exponential. In the previous section, we tackled the first factor using sampling. As for the second, a useful property that is often employed in efficient

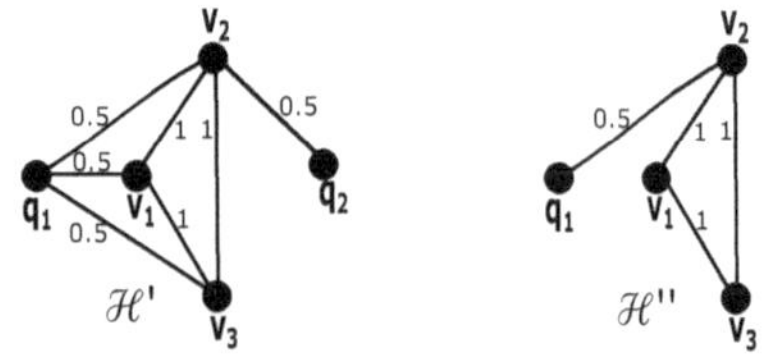

Figure 4: Two non-global (4, 0.125)-truss $\mathcal{G}'$ and $\mathcal{G}''$

discovery of frequent subgraphs is *monotonicity*. In our context, this reduces to asking, given graphs $\mathcal{H}_1 \subset \mathcal{H}_2$, whether one of them being a global (k, γ)-truss has any implications for the other graph. Unfortunately, this is not the case here.

EXAMPLE 3. In Figure 4, neither $\mathcal{H}'$ nor $\mathcal{H}''$ is a global (4, 0.125)-truss. For $\mathcal{H}'$, none of its possible worlds is a connected 4-truss containing node q_2 that is incident with just one edge. The same reasoning can be applied to $\mathcal{H}''$. Recall that as shown in Figure 3, $\mathcal{H}_2$ is a global (4, 0.125)-truss. Since $\mathcal{H}'' \subset \mathcal{H}_2 \subset \mathcal{H}'$, we can see that any monotonicity-driven pruning of search space does not work.

On the other hand, global (k, γ)-trusses do satisfy a monotonicity property w.r.t. k: every $(k+1, \gamma)$-truss is also a (k, γ)-truss. This follows from the fact that every $(k+1)$-truss is also a k-truss, although it is not guaranteed to be maximal. This observation can be exploited to develop a search framework and a bottom-up exploration strategy. The idea of the search framework is to start with a small k and find maximal global (k, γ)-trusses. Then we remove edges from them to find global trusses with larger k. In the bottom-up exploration strategy, we start with a single edge and then expand it by adding common neighbors of its endpoints and recursively following up until we obtain a maximal global (k, γ)-truss.

One of the challenges in case of maximal global trusses is that their number can be exponential (see Lemma 2 and the appendix). The reason for this is that different maximal global trusses can overlap. In case of maximal local trusses, the edge support probability is determined independently for each edge, so maximal local trusses (for any given k) are always disjoint. This is the reason they can be found efficiently.

5.3 Decomposition Algorithms

Overview. The decomposition process first samples N possible worlds from $\mathcal{G}$ (Theorem 3). Then, starting from $k = 2$, we apply local (k, γ)-truss decomposition (Algorithm 1) to construct a candidate graph, in which we search for maximal (ϵ, δ)-approximate global (k, γ)-trusses. The candidate graph varies with k, and higher k corresponds to smaller candidate graph (details to follow), thanks to the monotonicity property w.r.t. k discussed in the previous section. Since exhaustive search is prohibitive, we propose two more efficient search algorithms. The first one is a top-down, exact approach (Algorithm 4) that finds *all* satisfying trusses; The second one is a bottom-up heuristic (Algorithm 5) that is not guaranteed to find all satisfying trusses, but is significantly more efficient.

Backbone algorithm. Algorithm 3 is the backbone decomposition algorithm. It first samples $N = \lceil \frac{1}{2\epsilon^2} \ln(\frac{2}{\delta}) \rceil$ possible worlds from $\mathcal{G}$ to form $D_\mathcal{G} = \{G_i\}_{i=1}^N$ (lines 1–2), which will be used for estimating edge supports. Next, we apply Algorithm 1 to obtain all maximal local (k, γ)-trusses in $\mathcal{G}$ for all possible k (line 3).

The main decomposition procedure iterates over all possible k, starting from 2. In each iteration, we first generate the candidate set $\mathcal{C}_k$ that contains all edges that *may* be present in an (ϵ, δ)-approximate global (k, γ)-truss (line 5). In order to prune this set effectively, notice the following. An edge cannot belong to a global

Algorithm 3 Global (k, γ)-truss decomposition

Require: $\mathcal{G} = (V, E, p)$; γ, ϵ, δ
Ensure: All (ϵ, δ)-approximate global (k, γ)-truss $\mathcal{H}$
1: $N \leftarrow \lceil \frac{1}{2\epsilon^2} \ln(\frac{2}{\delta}) \rceil$
2: $D_\mathcal{G} \leftarrow \{G_1, \ldots, G_N\}$, sampled independently from $\mathcal{G}$
3: Apply Algorithm 1 on $\mathcal{G}$ for local (k, γ)-truss decomposition.
4: **for** $k \leftarrow 2$ **to** n **do**
5: $\quad \mathcal{C}_k \leftarrow$ Eq. ((11))
6: $\quad$ **if** $k > 2$ **then**
7: $\quad\quad$ Delete all edges with $< k - 2$ triangles in $\mathcal{C}_k$ (computed without considering edge probabilities)
8: $\quad$ **if** $\mathcal{C}_k = \emptyset$ **then**
9: $\quad\quad$ **break**
10: $\quad$ **for each** connected component $\mathcal{C}$ of $\mathcal{C}_k$ **do**
11: $\quad\quad \mathsf{S}_k \leftarrow$ all (ϵ, δ)-approximate (k, γ)-trusses in $\mathcal{C}$, found by Algorithm 4 or Algorithm 5
12: **return** all maximal (ϵ, δ)-approximate (k, γ)-trusses in $\mathsf{S}_k, \forall k$

Algorithm 4 Top-down exact search (TopDownSearch)

Require: $D_\mathcal{G} = \{G_1, ..., G_N\}, k, \mathcal{C} = (V_\mathcal{C}, E_\mathcal{C})$
Ensure: all (ϵ, δ)-approximate global (k, γ)-trusses in $\mathcal{C}$
Ans $\leftarrow \emptyset$.
if $\forall e \in E_\mathcal{C}$ such that $\widehat{\alpha}_k(\mathcal{C}, e) \geq \gamma$ **then**
$\quad$ **return** $\mathcal{C}$
else
$\quad$ **for** $e \in E_\mathcal{C}$ **do**
$\quad\quad \mathcal{C}' \leftarrow \mathcal{C} - \{e\}$ {remove e from $\mathcal{C}$}
$\quad\quad$ Delete edges in $\mathcal{C}'$ having $< k - 2$ triangles
$\quad\quad$ **for each** connected component $\mathcal{C}''$ of $\mathcal{C}'$ **do**
$\quad\quad\quad$ Ans $\leftarrow$ Ans $\cup$ TopDownSearch(D, k, $\mathcal{C}''$)
return Ans

(k, γ)-truss unless it also belongs to a local (k, γ)-truss. It also cannot belong to a maximal (k, γ)-truss unless it belongs to a maximal global $(k-1, \gamma)$-truss. Thus, edges outside this intersection can be safely pruned. Complications arise when dealing with approximate trusses, which are found by sampling. However, w.r.t. a given set of N possible worlds, it is easy to verify that every (ϵ, δ)-approximate maximal global (k, γ)-truss is also an (ϵ, δ)-approximate maximal global $(k-1, \gamma)$-truss. This observation allows us to prune the candidate set $\mathcal{C}_k$ significantly, as follows.

Let S_k denote the set of all (ϵ, δ)-approximate global (k, γ)-trusses produced by Algorithm 3 for any given $k \geq 2$. For convenience, we define $\mathsf{S}_1 = E_\mathcal{G}$, i.e., the set of all edges in the original graph $\mathcal{G}$ and we let $\bigcup \mathsf{S}_k$ denote the union of the edge sets associated with the satisfying trusses in S_k, for a given k. Hence, we have:

$$\mathcal{C}_k = \{e \in E_\mathcal{H} : \mathcal{H} \text{ is a maximal local } (k, \gamma)\text{-truss in } \mathcal{G}\} \cap (\bigcup \mathsf{S}_{k-1}). \tag{11}$$

For $k = 2$, $\mathcal{C}_2$ reduces to the set of edges present in some maximal local $(2, \gamma)$-truss. When $k > 2$, we perform an additional pruning step by removing from $\mathcal{C}_k$ all edges that are contained in less than $k - 2$ triangles (lines 6–7). The computation of triangles in this step does not take edge probabilities into account, which is equivalent to treating as if each edge had a probability of 1. Such removal clearly further prunes our search space, as those removed edges have no chance of being in any (ϵ, δ)-approximate global (k, γ)-trusses.

Algorithm 5 Bottom-up heuristic (BottomUpSearch)

Require: $D_{\mathcal{G}} = \{G_1, ..., G_N\}, k, \mathcal{C} = (V_{\mathcal{C}}, E_{\mathcal{C}})$
Ensure: all (ϵ, δ)-approximate global (k, γ)-trusses in $\mathcal{C}$

```
1: Ans ← ∅
2: for all e ∈ E_C do
3:     Q ← {e} {Q is an induced graph on e.}
4:     while ∃e ∈ Q such that sup_Q(e) < k − 2 do
5:         Add k − 2 triangles of C that have e to Q
6:     if ∀e ∈ E_Q, such that α̂_k(Q, e) ≥ γ then
7:         Extend Q to be maximal by adding edges.
8:         Ans ← Ans ∪{Q}
9: return Ans
```

After that, we search the subgraphs of each each connected component of $\mathcal{C}_k$ to identify all satisfying (ϵ, δ)-approximate global (k, γ)-trusses (lines 10–11). This is done by invoking a searching sub-procedure, Algorithm 4 or Algorithm 5, which we describe shortly. The whole process terminates as soon as the candidate set $\mathcal{C}_{k'}$ becomes empty, for a certain k'. By the monotonicity of global (k, γ)-trusses w.r.t. k mentioned above, for any $k'' > k'$, we know $\mathcal{C}_{k''}$ is also empty. Lastly, for each k such that $\mathcal{C}_k$ is non-empty, we return all maximal subgraphs in S_k as output, which are guaranteed to be the (ϵ, δ)-approximate global (k, γ)-trusses (line 12).

Top-down exact search. Algorithm 4 presents a DFS-based algorithm for finding all satisfying trusses, namely maximal (ϵ, δ)-approximate global (k, γ)-trusses, given as input k and a connected component $\mathcal{C}$ of candidate graph $\mathcal{C}_k$. The pseudo-code is mostly self-explanatory. It first checks if $\mathcal{C}$ is itself a satisfying truss. If so, then $\mathcal{C}$ is also maximal by construction, and thus is returned (lines 2–3). Otherwise, we remove an edge from $\mathcal{H}$, and recursively remove all edges whose support is less than $k - 2$ as a result (lines 6–7). Let the resulting graph be $\mathcal{C}'$. We then recursively run this search algorithm on each connected component of $\mathcal{C}'$ (lines 8–9). Finally, all satisfying trusses are gathered and returned to Algorithm 3.

Bottom-up heuristic search. The above top-down approach may suffer from inefficiency, as the search process that removes one edge at a time can be expensive. To combat this, we propose a bottom-up heuristic search method that provides significant speedup, in exchange for incompleteness. That is, it may not discover all satisfying trusses.

The pseudo-code is presented in Algorithm 5. This search method grows a potential satisfying truss from Q that is initialized to a single edge from the candidate component. For each edge $e \in Q$, we repeatedly add into Q the edges that can form triangles with e, until all edges in Q have a support of at least $k - 2$ (lines 3–5). We then check if Q satisfies the definition of (ϵ, δ)-approximate global (k, γ)-truss w.r.t. $D_{\mathcal{G}}$: if so, it will be included in a candidate solution. Since it may not be maximal, the algorithm will extend it by adding local edges to achieve maximality (lines 6–8).

The above bottom-up building process is repeated for all edges. As a heuristic, we rank edges in $\mathcal{C}$ in descending order of their edge probability. Also, when we grow Q, it is possible that an edge e may participate in more than $k - 2$ triangles, in which case we randomly select $k - 2$ of these. The reason for not adding all such triangles is that the more edges a subgraph includes, the more likely there is an edge that violates the constraint for a global (k, γ)-truss. There are other options such as choosing those triangles whose edges participate in the largest number of triangles. Such "look-ahead" strategies involve additional overhead and we do not explore them further in this paper. A careful study of the trade-off introduced by such additional heuristics is an interesting question for future work.

Network	$\lvert V_{\mathcal{G}}\rvert$	$\lvert E_{\mathcal{G}}\rvert$	d_{max}	$\lvert V_{\mathcal{C}}\rvert$	$\lvert E_{\mathcal{C}}\rvert$	#comp
FruitFly	3751	3692	27	2400	2771	435
WikiVote	7118	103689	1065	7066	103663	24
Flickr	24125	300836	546	21398	296202	840
DBLP	684911	2284991	611	581539	2169186	34132
BioMine	1008200	6742939	139624	961760	6688520	16242
LiveJournal	4847571	42851237	20333	4843953	42845684	914
Orkut	3072441	117185083	33313	3072441	117185083	1
Wise	58655849	261321033	278489	58655820	261321018	15

Table 1: Network statistics

6. EXPERIMENTS

We conduct extensive experiments to test the effectiveness and efficiency of our proposed algorithms for LocalDecomp and GlobalDecomp. All algorithms are implemented in C++, and all the experiments are conducted on a Linux Server with Intel Xeon CUP X5570 (2.93 GHz) and 100GB main memory.

6.1 Dataset and Experimental Setup

We use eight real-world probabilistic graphs, whose basic statistics are summarized in Table 1. For each network $\mathcal{G}$, besides the number of vertices $|V_{\mathcal{G}}|$, number of edges $|E_{\mathcal{G}}|$ and maximum degree d_{max}, we also report the size of the largest connected component $\mathcal{C}(V_{\mathcal{C}}, E_{\mathcal{C}})$ and the number of connected components (#comp).

Flickr (https://www.flickr.com/) is a popular online community for sharing photos. The network data contains 24.1K nodes (representing users) and 301K edges, where the probability of an edge between two users is calculated by the Jaccard coefficient of the interest groups of the two users [4,27].

DBLP (http://dblp.uni-trier.de/) is a computer science bibliography website. The probabilistic graph consists of 685K nodes and 2.3M edges. Here, each node corresponds to an author, and edges represent co-authorship relationships. Precisely, previous work [4, 27] measures the probability of each edge based on an exponential function of the number of collaborations.

BioMine is a snapshot of the database of the BioMine project [13] containing biological interactions (http://BioMine.cs.helsinki.fi/search/). The graph contains 1.01M nodes and 6.74M edges, where the probability of an edge corresponds to the confidence that the interaction actually exists [4,27].

FruitFly is a protein-protein interaction (PPI) network [23], obtained by integrating data from the BioGRID (http://thebiogrid.org/) database and data from the STRING database [27]. WikiVote, LiveJournal and Orkut are social networks downloaded from the Stanford Network Analysis Project (http://snap.stanford.edu/); Wise (http://www.wise2012.cs.ucy.ac.cy/challenge.html) is a micro-blogging network from WISE 2012 Challenge. For these four networks, the edge probabilities are assigned uniformly at random from the interval $[0, 1]$.

Comparison Methods. To evaluate the efficiency and effectiveness of local and global (k, γ)-truss decomposition methods, we test and compare three algorithms proposed in this paper, namely, Local, GTD, and GBU. Here, Local is the algorithm for LocalDecomp by combining Algorithm 1 and Algorithm 2 using dynamic programming strategies. GTD is the algorithm for GlobalDecomp by combining Algorithm 3 and Algorithm 4. GBU is also an algorithm for GlobalDecomp, which uses heuristic search strategies by combining Algorithm 3 and Algorithm 5.

Evaluation Metrics. For efficiency, we report running time in seconds. To evaluate the quality of an output truss, we use the following two metrics. We define the *density* (cohesiveness) of a proba-

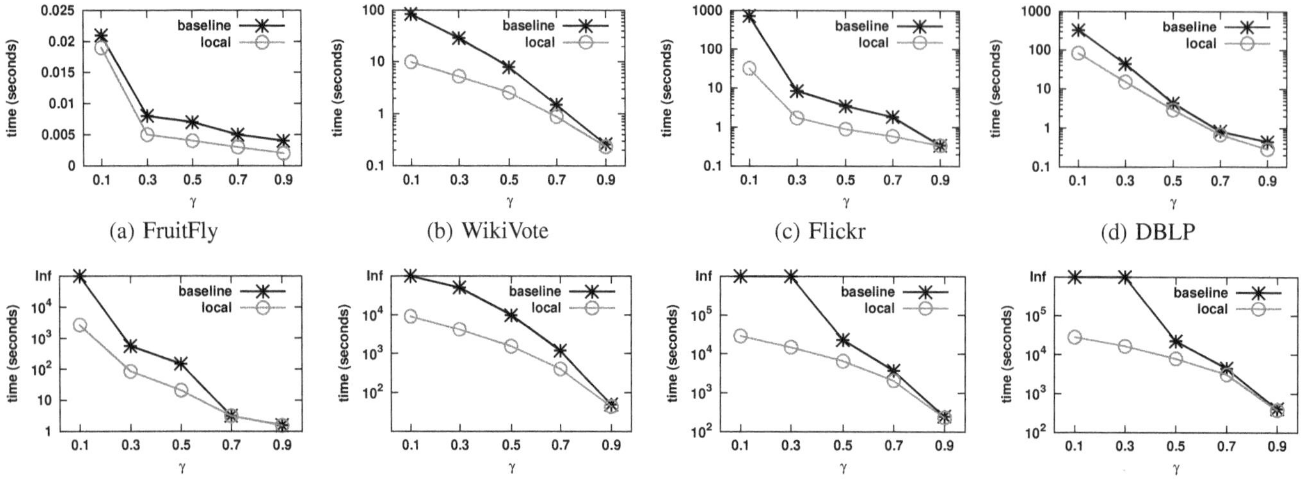

(a) FruitFly (b) WikiVote (c) Flickr (d) DBLP

(e) BioMine (f) LiveJournal (g) Orkut (h) Wise

Figure 5: Local (k,γ)-truss decomposition: dynamic programming vs. baseline (re-computing edge support probabilities from scratch after each edge removal) in terms of running time (in seconds)

bilistic graph $\mathcal{H}$ as

$$\mathsf{density}(\mathcal{H}) = \frac{\sum_{e \in E_{\mathcal{H}}} p(e)}{\frac{1}{2}|V_{\mathcal{H}}| \cdot (|V_{\mathcal{H}}| - 1)}, \tag{12}$$

where the numerator can be interpreted as the weighted sum of existing edges (where weights are existence probabilities) and the denominator is the maximum number of possible edges $\mathcal{H}$ can have. The second metric is the *probabilistic clustering coefficient* [26]:

$$\mathsf{PCC}(\mathcal{H}) = \frac{3\sum_{\triangle_{uvw} \in \mathcal{H}} p(u,v)p(v,w)p(w,u)}{\sum_{(u,v),(u,w) \in E(\mathcal{H}), v \neq w} p(u,v)p(u,w)}. \tag{13}$$

Note that, a graph $\mathcal{H}$ containing only a single edge is not considered for PCC in experiments. For GTD and GBU, we set the parameters $\epsilon = 0.1$ and $\delta = 0.1$, and randomly sample a total of $N = 150$ graphs where $N \geq \frac{1}{2\varepsilon^2}\ln(\frac{2}{\delta})$ by Theorem 3.

6.2 Efficiency Evaluation

Local (k,γ)-truss decomposition. For LOCALDECOMP, we test the proposed method Local, and compare its efficiency with a naive baseline, which still uses Algorithm 1 as its backbone, but whenever an update of edge support probabilities is needed (after an edge removal), it computes the entire vector $\sigma(\cdot)$ from scratch. The running time results are illustrated in Figure 5 by varying γ from 0.1 to 0.9. Note that the Y-axis for Figure 5(b) – 5(h) is in log-scale.

Overall, as γ increases, the requirement for a subgraph to be a local (k,γ)-truss becomes stricter, and the running time decreases. This is expected, as more edges can be pruned quickly and the algorithm enjoys working with a smaller graph. As can be seen, on all datasets, the version that uses dynamic programming for updating the probabilities is faster than the naive baseline. In particular, on large datasets (from WikiVote to Wise), the dynamic programming version is often more than one order of magnitude faster than the baseline, indicating its superior efficiency and scalability.

Global (k,γ)-truss decomposition. We next report the running time of our decomposition for (ϵ,δ)-approximate global (k,γ)-truss. As mentioned in Section 5, the top-down search algorithm GTD may suffer from inefficiency issues due to the inherent hardness of GLOBALDECOMP, and a bottom-up heuristic method GBU is proposed to alleviate the issue.

As can be seen from Figure 6, on a small probabilistic graph FruitFly, the GTD cannot finish in a reasonable amount of time for

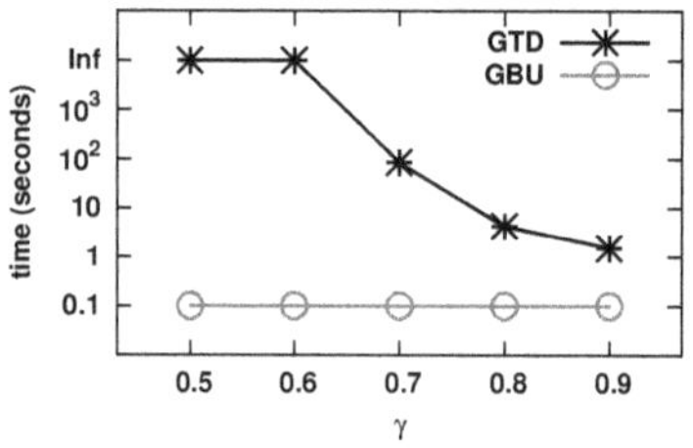

Figure 6: Running time (in secs) of GTD and GBU on FruitFly

Network	$\gamma = 0.1$	$\gamma = 0.3$	$\gamma = 0.5$	$\gamma = 0.7$	$\gamma = 0.9$
FruitFly	0.1	0.1	0.1	0.1	0.1
WikiVote	27.2	10.2	6.2	1.4	0.3
Flickr	40.9	11.7	11.4	11.1	11.0
DBLP	168	42.8	16.2	7.5	3.5
BioMine	2660	164	43.8	43.6	25.0
LiveJournal	24397	11828	4429	1173	146
Orkut	69870	33671	6178	2659	421
Wise	66085	49512	22861	8036	843

Table 2: Running time (in seconds) of GBU on all networks

$\gamma = 0.5$ and 0.6. GTD can accomplish the task in reasonable for $\gamma \geq 0.7$, but is often orders of magnitude slower than GBU. This indicates the scalability limitation of GTD. Thus, in subsequent experiments, we keep using the bottom-up heuristic for GLOBALDECOMP, whose running time on all datasets are shown in Table 2. As can be seen, similar to local (k,γ)-truss decomposition, the running time decreases as γ increases. The running time of GBU increases essentially linearly with graph size. Since all graphs tested have a single dominant connected component (see Table 1), these findings are reliable and attest to the scalability of GBU over graphs with millions of edges.

Memory Usage. In this experiment, we report the memory usage of proposed methods with $\gamma = 0.5$ in Figure 8. The black bar represents the space required for storing the graph on disk. As can be seen, the memory usage of GBU is the same memory as for Local. Both methods consume less than 20 times of graph size (see Figure 8). Local (k,γ)-truss decomposition takes $O(\rho|E_{\mathcal{G}}|)$ space complexity to store the edge support vectors, $|E_{\mathcal{G}}|$ being the number of edges. It can be inferred from Figure 8 that ρ tends to be small for real sparse networks. The memory consumption of GBU mainly consists of the edge support vectors and N sampled graphs. For an edge $e \in \mathcal{G}$, we use one bit '1' or '0' to record whether e exists in each sampled graph G_j, $1 \leq j \leq N$. It takes 192 bits

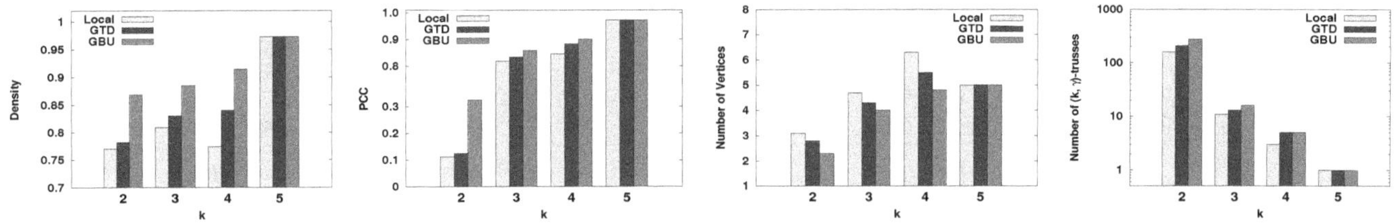

(a) Density (b) PCC (c) Number of Vertices (d) Number of (k, γ)-trusses

Figure 7: Quality Comparison on Fruit-Fly with $\gamma = 0.7$ varying k

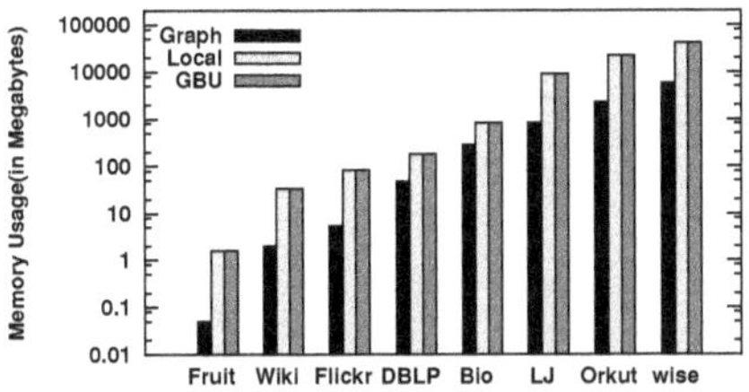

Figure 8: Memory Usage of proposed methods on all networks

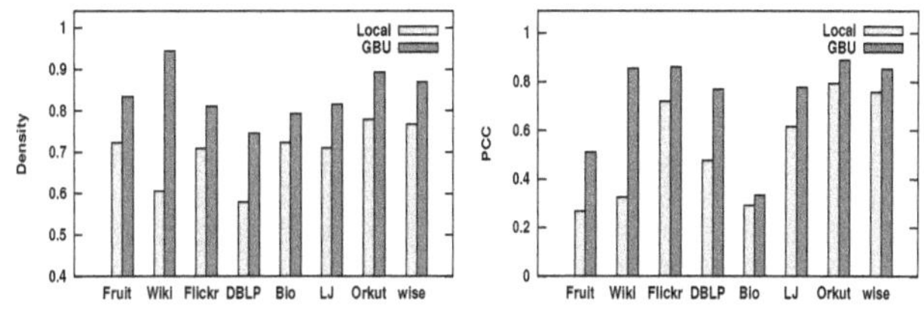

(a) Density (b) PCC

Figure 9: Quality Comparison between Local (k, γ)-truss and Global (k, γ)-truss with $\gamma = 0.5$ on all networks

(6 bytes) to record all sample results for one edge. Thus, the total memory cost of sampled graphs is significantly less than the cost of edge support vectors. Once we obtain the local truss-ness of all edges, we can release the memory used for storing edge support vectors, before creating sample graphs. As a result, GBU still costs the same memory as Local. Both methods show a good space scalability to large real networks.

6.3 Quality Evaluation

Recall that our motivation of proposing global (k, γ)-truss is to extract more cohesive subgraphs through more stringent definitions. To validate our proposal, in this experiment we directly compare the cohesiveness of these two types of probabilistic trusses using density and probabilistic clustering coefficient (PCC).

Figures 7(a)–(d) report the average density, the average PCC, the average vertex number of (k, γ)-truss and the number of (k, γ)-truss respectively found by all three methods on FriutFly[2], for varying k, with γ fixed at $\gamma = 0.7$. Figures 7(a)-(b) show that the output global (k, γ)-trusses consistently achieve higher density and PCC than the local ones, as expected. An exception is $k = 5$. For $k = 5$, all three methods find the same *one* (k, γ)-truss, which structurally is a 5-clique. The heuristic method GBU achieves higher density and PCC than GTD. The reason is two-fold. GBU always starts the exploration from edges with high probability to form (k, γ)-truss, which potentially leads to a higher density and PCC than GTD. Secondly, note that GBU cannot find all (k, γ)-trusses as GTD, and some of (k, γ)-trusses found by GBU may not be maximal, which may also increase density. Generally, for both local and global (k, γ)-truss, density and PCC become larger as k increases, as denser (k, γ)-trusses will be found by removing edges of low support and small probability. In Figure 7(c), GTD and GBU both found smaller (k, γ)-trusses than Local, reflecting that global (k, γ)-truss is a stricter definition than the local one. The (k, γ)-trusses of GBU are the smallest ones. In Figure 7(d), the number of output (k, γ)-trusses decreases as k goes up: indeed, increasing k leads to stricter a requirement by definition. For GBU, as a heuristic it may not discover some of the truly maximal satisfying trusses as found by GTD; instead it may find some other non-maximal ones. Thus, GBU sometimes outputs more trusses than GTD.

Next, we compare Local and GBU on larger networks. GTD is not compared here owing to its efficiency limitation. We report the results on average density and average PCC of all (k, γ)-trusses for all possible k with $\gamma = 0.5$ in Figure 9 (a)-(b). The results of the vertex size and the number of (k, γ)-trusses on these datasets are similar as FriutFly, and are thus omitted. As we can see, GBU achieves higher density and PCC than Local on all networks. Once again the superiority of global (k, γ)-truss is established.

[2]For all other datasets, under our parameter settings, GTD cannot finish. Thus Figure 7 demonstrates using FruitFly.

6.4 Comparisons with (k, η)-Cores

In this experiment, we show that local (k, γ)-truss is superior to (k, η)-core [4] as a type of cohesive probabilistic subgraphs when we take into account, not just graph structure, but also the *probability of existence* of that structure. For fairness of comparison, we use our local definition, since (k, η)-core is defined in a similar fashion to local (k, γ)-truss. For a given η, we use k_{cmax} to denote the maximum core number. Then, we set $\gamma = \eta$, and use k_{tmax} to denote the maximum truss number. For simplicity, we denote the (k_{cmax}, η)-core by C and the (k_{tmax}, γ)-truss by T. Table 3 reports the statistics of T and C on WikiVote, DBLP and Biomine. The results of other datasets are similar and are omitted. We vary the parameter $\eta = \gamma \in \{0.1, 0.5\}$. In terms of both the number of vertices and edges, we can see that the size of T is significantly smaller than that of C, which shows that the (k_{tmax}, γ)-truss and (k_{cmax}, η)-core are indeed quite different in terms of the kinds of cohesive subgraphs they extract. Note that k_{tmax} is always smaller than k_{cmax} for all $\gamma = \eta \in \{0.1, 0.5\}$.

First, ignore the edge probabilities and consider only the graph structure. The clustering coefficient of T is comparable to that of C on all datasets, and on Wikivote, T has a higher clustering coefficient. In addition, both C and T had nearly clique structure on DBLP and Biomine. However, this is not the true whole story as this ignores the probability of existence of the structure present in the found cores and trusses. As we can see, in terms of PCC and density, the (k_{tmax}, γ)-truss clearly outperforms (k_{cmax}, η)-core on all networks. This is because the (k, γ)-truss takes the probability of an edge contained in triangles into consideration, whereas (k, η)-core does not. As a result, (k, γ)-truss can prune edges with small probability as well as those having a small porbability of being contained in many triangles, and achieve a higher density and PCC. In conclusion, the results demonstrate that (k_{tmax}, γ)-truss is significantly more cohesive and tightly-knit than the (k_{cmax}, η)-

Network	$\eta = \gamma$	V_T/V_C	E_T/E_C	k_{tmax}/k_{cmax}	CC_T/CC_C	$\mathsf{PCC}_T/\mathsf{PCC}_C$	den_T/den_C
WikiVote	0.1	280/1080	7660/47873	8/21	0.386/0.200	**0.220/0.100**	**0.115/0.041**
WikiVote	0.5	82/985	891/44243	5/20	0.395/0.212	**0.305/0.105**	**0.210/0.046**
DBLP	0.1	34/112	261/6216	14/25	1.0/1.0	**0.619/0.316**	**0.611/0.263**
DBLP	0.5	10/114	45/6441	10/20	1.0/1.0	**0.992/0.319**	**0.992/0.265**
Biomine	0.1	102/199	5127/19701	33/58	0.996/1.0	**0.539/0.280**	**0.539/0.279**
Biomine	0.5	101/201	4996/20100	18/52	0.990/1.0	**0.536/0.280**	**0.536/0.279**

Table 3: Statistics of (k, γ)-truss, T, and (k, η)-core, C, on WikiVote, DBLP and Biomine. the number of vertices (V_T/V_C), the number of edges (E_T/E_C), the maximum truss/core number (k_{tmax}/k_{cmax}), the clustering coefficient (CC_T/CC_C), the probabilistic clustering coefficient ($\mathsf{PCC}_T/\mathsf{PCC}_C$) and the probabilistic density(den_T/den_C) respectively.

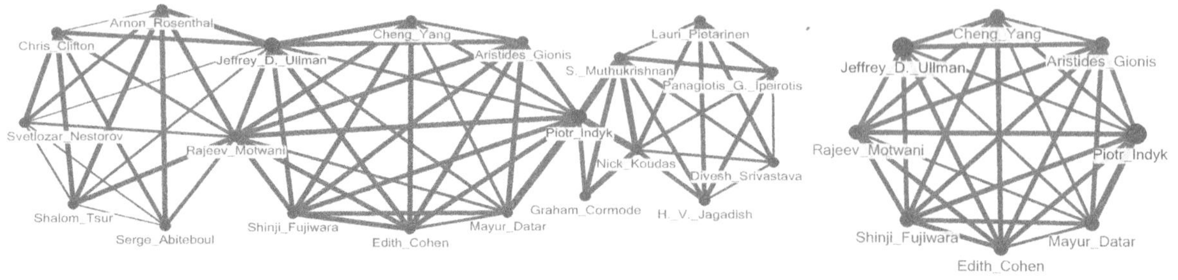

(a) Local (k, γ)-truss (b) Global (k, γ)-truss

Figure 10: An example of task-driven team formation with query nodes ={"Jeffrey D. Ullman", "Piotr Indyk"} and keywords ={"data", "algorithm"}. In the plots, a wider line indicates a higher probability on the edge.

core, for $\gamma = \eta$, when we take both structure and its existence probability into account.

6.5 Task-Driven Team Formation

We apply our local and global (k, γ)-truss decomposition algorithms to solve the task-driven team formation problem. The original problem definition [4] is w.r.t. (k, η)-core specifically. To be able to perform this experiment, we adapt the definition and make it specific w.r.t. (k, γ)-truss: Given a probabilistic graph $\mathcal{G} = (\mathcal{V}, \mathcal{E})$ derived specifically for a task T, a query (Q, T) with nodes $Q \subset \mathcal{V}$ and task T, as well as $\gamma \in (0, 1)$, find a local/global (k, γ)-truss from $\mathcal{G}$ that (i) contains all nodes in Q and (ii) has the highest truss-ness k that satisfies γ. The edge probabilities in $\mathcal{G}$ are defined w.r.t. task T, following the authors of [4].

We use a DBLP collaboration network with meta-data obtained from [4]. Each node represents an author, and an edge is drawn between two authors if they co-authored at least one paper. The resulting graph has 1.1M nodes and 4.1M edges. For each edge (u, v), the data contains the titles of all papers coauthored by u and v. Given a set W of keywords, the edge probability of (u, v) represents the collaboration strength of papers co-authored by u and v related to keywords W. For each edge, [4] takes the bag of words of the titles of all papers coauthored by the two authors, and applies the Latent Dirichlet Allocation (LDA) model [3] to infer its topics and calculates the edge probability. The probabilistic graph on keywords W is denoted $\mathcal{G}_W$.

We set $\eta = \gamma = 10^{-11}$ as suggested by authors of [4] due to the low edge probabilities in the data. The sample query is ({"Jeffrey D. Ullman", "Piotr Indyk"}, {"data", "algorithm"}). Figure 10(a) depicts a local $(4, 10^{-11})$-truss containing both authors. The local truss has 20 nodes, 67 edges, with density 0.002 and PCC 0.005. Furthermore, we use the local (k, γ)-truss shown in Figure 10(a) as the input of global (k, γ)-truss decomposition and obtain 17 global (k, γ)-trusses, one of which is shown in Figure 10 (b): It has 8 nodes, 28 edges, density 0.007, and PCC 0.007. Once again, the superiority of global (k, γ)-truss is shown.

In contrast, applying (k, η)-core decomposition [4] to this query results in a $(5, 10^{-11})$-core with 1153 nodes, 13355 edges, with density $6 \cdot 10^{-5}$ and PCC 0.002. As we can see, team formation by (k, γ)-truss produces a much more desirable team, i.e., it is much smaller and denser than (k, η)-core. Intuitively, this is arguably better for the task of writing a research paper related to "data" and "algorithm" as it is unrealistic for 1153 researchers to collaborate.

7. SUMMARY AND FUTURE WORK

Motivated by applications in biological, social, and communication networks, we propose, for the first time, extensions to the definition of a k-truss for probabilistic graphs. Our framework allows for a local as well as a global version of a probabilistic truss, a (k, γ)-truss, to be precise. (k, γ)-trusses correspond to probabilistic cohesive subgraphs and we motivate the truss decomposition problem for the world of probabilistic graphs as that of finding maximal (local or global) (k, γ)-trusses. We develop an elegant and efficient dynamic programming algorithm for finding all maximal local (k, γ)-trusses of a given probabilistic graph. For global (k, γ)-trusses, for a given probabilistic graph, the number of maximal global (k, γ)-trusses can be exponential; also even computing the probability of a given subgraph containing a k-truss that connects all its nodes, a task needed for finding global (k, γ)-trusses, is #P-hard. We thus propose an approach that combines sampling along with heuristic search, to find a subset of approximate (k, γ)-trusses efficiently. We conducted extensive experiments on 6 real datasets. Our results demonstrate that our algorithms significantly outperform natural baselines as well as alternative techniques based on probabilistic extensions to k-cores. The experiments show the efficiency and effectiveness of our proposed algorithms.

This work opens up several interesting questions. First developing further efficient and clever heuristics for finding maximal global (k, γ)-trusses is important. Second, given k, how to find maximal (local or global) (k, γ)-trusses for various possible γ? Notice that this problem is well defined even though γ is a real number, since there are only finitely many k-trusses in a (probabilistic) graph, each of which must be a (k, γ)-truss for some maximum possible γ. Finding efficient solution to this problem is wide open.

ACKNOWLEDGMENTS

This work was supported by a Discovery grant and a Discovery Accelerator Supplements grant from the Natural Sciences and Engineering Research Council of Canada (NSERC).

8. REFERENCES

[1] A.-L. Barabasi and Z. N. Oltvai. Network biology: understanding the cell's functional organization. *Nature Reviews Genetics*, 5(2):101–113, 2004.

[2] V. Batagelj and M. Zaversnik. An o (m) algorithm for cores decomposition of networks. *arXiv preprint cs/0310049*, 2003.

[3] D. M. Blei, A. Y. Ng, and M. I. Jordan. Latent dirichlet allocation. *Journal of Machine Learning Research*, 3:993–1022, 2003.

[4] F. Bonchi, F. Gullo, A. Kaltenbrunner, and Y. Volkovich. Core decomposition of uncertain graphs. In *KDD*, pages 1316–1325. ACM, 2014.

[5] C. Bron and J. Kerbosch. Finding all cliques of an undirected graph (algorithm 457). *Commun. ACM*, 16(9):575–576, 1973.

[6] J. Cheng, Y. Ke, S. Chu, and M. T. Özsu. Efficient core decomposition in massive networks. In *ICDE*, pages 51–62, 2011.

[7] J. Cheng, Y. Ke, A. W.-C. Fu, J. X. Yu, and L. Zhu. Finding maximal cliques in massive networks by h*-graph. In *SIGMOD*, pages 447–458, 2010.

[8] N. Chiba and T. Nishizeki. Arboricity and subgraph listing algorithms. *SIAM J. Comput.*, 14(1):210–223, 1985.

[9] J. Cohen. Trusses: Cohesive subgraphs for social network analysis. Technical report, National Security Agency, 2008.

[10] J. Cohen. Graph twiddling in a mapreduce world. *Computing in Science and Engineering*, 11(4):29–41, 2009.

[11] M. T. Dittrich, G. W. Klau, A. Rosenwald, T. Dandekar, and T. Müller. Identifying functional modules in protein–protein interaction networks: an integrated exact approach. *Bioinformatics*, 24(13):i223–i231, 2008.

[12] J. Dong and S. Horvath. Understanding network concepts in modules. *BMC Systems Biology*, 1(24), 2007.

[13] L. Eronen and H. Toivonen. Biomine: predicting links between biological entities using network models of heterogeneous databases. *BMC Bioinformatics*, 13, 2012.

[14] W. Hoeffding. Probability inequalities for sums of bounded random variables. *Journal of the American Statistical Association*, 58:13–30, 1963.

[15] X. Huang, H. Cheng, L. Qin, W. Tian, and J. X. Yu. Querying k-truss community in large and dynamic graphs. In *SIGMOD*, pages 1311–1322, 2014.

[16] R. Jin, L. Liu, and C. C. Aggarwal. Discovering highly reliable subgraphs in uncertain graphs. In *KDD*, pages 992–1000. ACM, 2011.

[17] R. Jin, L. Liu, B. Ding, and H. Wang. Distance-constraint reachability computation in uncertain graphs. *PVLDB*, 4(9):551–562, 2011.

[18] G. Kollios, M. Potamias, and E. Terzi. Clustering large probabilistic graphs. *TKDE*, 25(2):325–336, 2013.

[19] N. J. Krogan, G. Cagney, H. Yu, G. Zhong, X. Guo, A. Ignatchenko, J. Li, S. Pu, N. Datta, A. P. Tikuisis, et al. Global landscape of protein complexes in the yeast saccharomyces cerevisiae. *Nature*, 440(7084):637–643, 2006.

[20] Y. Li, T. Kuboyama, and H. Sakamoto. Truss decomposition for extracting communities in bipartite graph. In *Third International Conference on Advances in Information Mining and Management*, pages 76–80, 2013.

[21] L. Liu, R. Jin, C. Aggarwal, and Y. Shen. Reliable clustering on uncertain graphs. In *ICDM*, pages 459–468. IEEE, 2012.

[22] R. J. Mokken. Cliques, clubs and clans. *Quality & Quantity*, 13(2):161–173, 1979.

[23] A. P. Mukherjee, P. Xu, and S. Tirthapura. Mining maximal cliques from an uncertain graph. *arXiv preprint arXiv:1310.6780*, 2013.

[24] J. Pei, D. Jiang, and A. Zhang. Mining cross-graph quasi-cliques in gene expression and protein interaction data. In *ICDE*, pages 353–354, 2005.

[25] J. B. Pereira-Leal, A. J. Enright, and C. A. Ouzounis. Detection of functional modules from protein interaction networks. *PROTEINS: Structure, Function, and Bioinformatics*, 54(1):49–57, 2004.

[26] J. J. Pfeiffer and J. Neville. Methods to determine node centrality and clustering in graphs with uncertain structure. In *Fifth International AAAI Conference on Weblogs and Social Media*, 2011.

[27] M. Potamias, F. Bonchi, A. Gionis, and G. Kollios. K-nearest neighbors in uncertain graphs. *PVLDB*, 3(1-2):997–1008, 2010.

[28] S. B. Seidman and B. L. Foster. A graph-theoretic generalization of the clique concept*. *Journal of Mathematical sociology*, 6(1):139–154, 1978.

[29] R. Sharan, I. Ulitsky, and R. Shamir. Network-based prediction of protein function. *Molecular Systems Biology*, 3(1):88, 2007.

[30] Z. Sun, H. Wang, H. Wang, B. Shao, and J. Li. Efficient subgraph matching on billion node graphs. *PVLDB*, 5(9):788–799, 2012.

[31] C. E. Tsourakakis, F. Bonchi, A. Gionis, F. Gullo, and M. A. Tsiarli. Denser than the densest subgraph: Extracting optimal quasi-cliques with quality guarantees. In *KDD*, pages 104–112, 2013.

[32] L. G. Valiant. The complexity of enumeration and reliability problems. *SIAM Journal on Computing*, 8(3):410–421, 1979.

[33] J. Wang and J. Cheng. Truss decomposition in massive networks. *PVLDB*, 5(9):812–823, 2012.

[34] J. Wang, J. Cheng, and A. W.-C. Fu. Redundancy-aware maximal cliques. In *KDD*, pages 122–130, 2013.

[35] J. Xiang, C. Guo, and A. Aboulnaga. Scalable maximum clique computation using mapreduce. In *ICDE*, pages 74–85, 2013.

[36] Y. Zhang and S. Parthasarathy. Extracting analyzing and visualizing triangle k-core motifs within networks. In *ICDE*, pages 1049–1060, 2012.

[37] F. Zhao and A. K. Tung. Large scale cohesive subgraphs discovery for social network visual analysis. *Proceedings of the VLDB Endowment*, 6(2):85–96, 2012.

[38] Z. Zou, H. Gao, and J. Li. Discovering frequent subgraphs over uncertain graph databases under probabilistic semantics. In *KDD*, pages 633–642, 2010.

[39] Z. Zou, J. Li, H. Gao, and S. Zhang. Mining frequent subgraph patterns from uncertain graph data. *TKDE*, 22(9):1203–1218, 2010.

Appendix: Additional Proofs

Proof of Lemma 2. Consider an extension of the graph $\mathcal{G}$ shown in Figure 11, where there are n triangles attached to the central node, instead of 4. Consider $k = 3$ and $\gamma = (1/2)^{3\lceil n/2 \rceil}$. Then it can be easily verified that a maximal global (k,γ)-truss is a subgraph of $\mathcal{G}$ consisting of $\lceil n/2 \rceil$ triangles. There are $\binom{n}{\lceil n/2 \rceil}$ such choices, which is exponential in n.

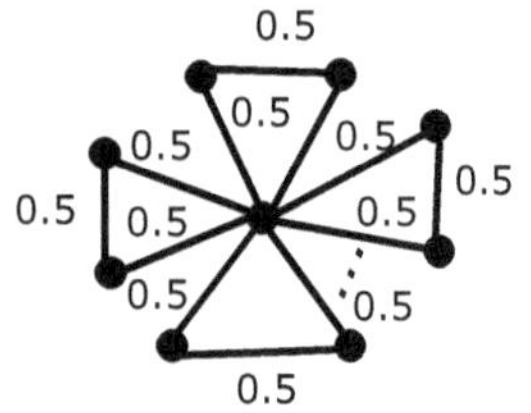

Figure 11: A "windmill" probabilistic graph

Proof of Theorem 2. We prove by contradiction. Suppose a maximal local (k,γ)-truss $\mathcal{H}$ is not in the answer set of Algorithm 1. First, for each edge $e \in \mathcal{H}$ has $\sigma(e, k-2)p(e) \geq \gamma$ by Definition 2, thus $\tau(e) \geq k$. Due to the fact that Algorithm 1 collects together all edges e with $\tau(e) \geq k$, no edges of $\mathcal{H}$ are missed by Algorithm 1. Moreover, all edges of $\mathcal{H}$ are connected, and will be assigned into the same component by the post-processing step. Thus, if $\mathcal{H}$ is not in the answer set of Algorithm 1, the only possibility is that there exists a larger local (k,γ)-truss containing $\mathcal{H}$. But this violates the maximal property of $\mathcal{H}$, a contradiction.

Proof of Lemma 3. First, the probability of a possible world H of $\mathcal{H}$ is

$$\Pr[H|\mathcal{H}] = \prod_{e\in E_H} p(e) \prod_{e\in E_{\mathcal{H}}\setminus E_H} (1-p(e)).$$

Next, for each possible world $G \sqsubseteq \mathcal{G}$ such that $G \in X(H)$, we have $E_G \cap E_{\mathcal{H}} = E_H$; we can divide the edge set E_G into two disjoint subsets E_1 and E_2, where $E_1 = E_H$ and $E_2 = E_G \setminus E_{\mathcal{H}}$. Since $E_G \cap E_{\mathcal{H}} = E_H$, we also have $E_2 = E_G \setminus E_{\mathcal{H}} = E_G \setminus E_H$ and $E_{\mathcal{H}} \setminus E_G = E_{\mathcal{H}} \setminus E_H$. Then, we obtain the probability

$$\begin{aligned}
&\Pr[G|\mathcal{G}] = \prod_{e\in E_G} p(e) \prod_{e\in E(\mathcal{G})\setminus E_G} (1-p(e)) \\
&= \prod_{e\in E_1\cup E_2} p(e) \prod_{e\in (E_{\mathcal{H}}\cup(E(\mathcal{G})\setminus E_{\mathcal{H}}))\setminus E_G} (1-p(e)) \qquad (14) \\
&= \prod_{e\in E_1} p(e) \prod_{e\in E_2} p(e) \prod_{e\in E_{\mathcal{H}}\setminus E_G} (1-p(e)) \\
&\quad \prod_{e\in (E(\mathcal{G})\setminus E_{\mathcal{H}})\setminus E_G} (1-p(e)) \qquad (15) \\
&= \prod_{e\in E_H} p(e) \prod_{e\in E_{\mathcal{H}}\setminus E_H} (1-p(e)) \prod_{e\in E_2} p(e) \\
&\quad \prod_{e\in (E(\mathcal{G})\setminus E_{\mathcal{H}})\setminus E_G} (1-p(e)) \\
&= \Pr[H|\mathcal{H}] \prod_{e\in E_2} p(e) \prod_{e\in (E(\mathcal{G})\setminus E_{\mathcal{H}})\setminus E_2} (1-p(e)) \\
&= \Pr[H|\mathcal{H}] \Pr[G'|\mathcal{G}'], \qquad (16)
\end{aligned}$$

where $\mathcal{G}' = (V(\mathcal{G}), E(\mathcal{G}) \setminus E_{\mathcal{H}})$ and $G' = (V(\mathcal{G}), E_2) = (V(\mathcal{G}), E_G \setminus E_{\mathcal{H}})$. Also notice that in going from Eq. (14) to Eq. (15), we have used the fact that $E_{\mathcal{H}} \setminus E_G$ and $(E_{\mathcal{G}} \setminus E_{\mathcal{H}}) \setminus E_G$ are disjoint. Now, clearly, G' has no edges in any possible world of $\mathcal{H}$, and $G' \sqsubseteq \mathcal{G}'$.

For a given possible world $H \sqsubseteq \mathcal{H}$, summing both sides of Eq. (16) over all possible worlds of $\mathcal{G}$ that project to H, we have

$$\sum_{G\in X(H)} \Pr[G|\mathcal{G}] = \sum_{G\in X(H)} \Pr[H|\mathcal{H}] \Pr[G'|\mathcal{G}'].$$

That is,

$$\begin{aligned}
\sum_{G\in X(H)} \Pr[G|\mathcal{G}] &= \sum_{G\in X(H)} \Pr[H|\mathcal{H}] \Pr[G'|\mathcal{G}'] \\
&= \Pr[H|\mathcal{H}] \sum_{G'\sqsubseteq \mathcal{G}'} \Pr[G'|\mathcal{G}'] \\
&= \Pr[H|\mathcal{H}].
\end{aligned}$$

This completes the proof.

Proof of Corollary 1. We define the indicator function $\mathbf{I}(G \in X_H)$ which takes on 1 if $G \in X_H$, and 0 otherwise. From Definition 3 and Lemma 3, we have:

$$\begin{aligned}
\alpha_k(\mathcal{H}, e) &= \sum_{H\sqsubseteq \mathcal{H}} \Pr[H|\mathcal{H}] \cdot \mathbf{I}(H,k,e) \\
&= \sum_{H\sqsubseteq \mathcal{H}} \sum_{G\in \mathbf{X}_H} \Pr[G|\mathcal{G}] \cdot \mathbf{I}(H,k,e) \\
&= \sum_{G\sqsubseteq \mathcal{G}} \sum_{H\sqsubseteq \mathcal{H}} \mathbf{I}(G \in X_H) \cdot \Pr[G|\mathcal{G}] \cdot \mathbf{I}(H,k,e) \\
&= \sum_{G\sqsubseteq \mathcal{G}} \Pr[G|\mathcal{G}] \sum_{H\sqsubseteq \mathcal{H}} \mathbf{I}(G \in X_H) \cdot \mathbf{I}(H,k,e), \qquad (17) \\
&= \sum_{G\sqsubseteq \mathcal{G}} \Pr[G|\mathcal{G}] \cdot \mathbf{I}(G\downarrow_{\mathcal{H}}, k, e). \qquad (18)
\end{aligned}$$

The last equality follows from the fact that although the second summation in (17) is over all $H \sqsubseteq \mathcal{H}$, the product $\mathbf{I}(G \in X_H) \cdot \mathbf{I}(H,k,e)$ is non-zero for at most one possible world of $\mathcal{H}$, namely $G\downarrow_{\mathcal{H}}$, and for this world, the product reduces to $\mathbf{I}(G\downarrow_{\mathcal{H}}, k, e)$.

Efficient and Progressive Group Steiner Tree Search

Rong-Hua Li
Shenzhen University
Shenzhen, China
rhli@szu.edu.cn

Lu Qin
University of Technology
Sydney, Australia
Lu.Qin@uts.edu.au

Jeffrey Xu Yu
CUHK
Hong Kong, China
yu@se.cuhk.edu.hk

Rui Mao
Shenzhen University
Shenzhen, China
mao@szu.edu.cn

ABSTRACT

The Group Steiner Tree (GST) problem is a fundamental problem in database area that has been successfully applied to keyword search in relational databases and team search in social networks. The state-of-the-art algorithm for the GST problem is a parameterized dynamic programming (DP) algorithm, which finds the optimal tree in $O(3^k n + 2^k(n \log n + m))$ time, where k is the number of given groups, m and n are the number of the edges and nodes of the graph respectively. The major limitations of the parameterized DP algorithm are twofold: (i) it is intractable even for very small values of k (e.g., $k = 8$) in large graphs due to its exponential complexity, and (ii) it cannot generate a solution until the algorithm has completed its entire execution. To overcome these limitations, we propose an efficient and progressive GST algorithm in this paper, called PrunedDP. It is based on newly-developed optimal-tree decomposition and conditional tree merging techniques. The proposed algorithm not only drastically reduces the search space of the parameterized DP algorithm, but it also produces progressively-refined feasible solutions during algorithm execution. To further speed up the PrunedDP algorithm, we propose a progressive A^*-search algorithm, based on several carefully-designed lower-bounding techniques. We conduct extensive experiments to evaluate our algorithms on several large scale real-world graphs. The results show that our best algorithm is not only able to generate progressively-refined feasible solutions, but it also finds the optimal solution with at least two orders of magnitude acceleration over the state-of-the-art algorithm, using much less memory.

CCS Concepts: Information systems→Graph-based database models

Keywords: Group Steiner Tree; DP; A^*-search Algorithm

1. INTRODUCTION

The Group Steiner Tree (GST) problem is a well-known combinatorial optimization problem that has been extensively studied in both research and industry communities [28, 18, 8, 22]. Given a weighted graph G and a set of labels P, where each node in G is associated with a set of labels. The GST problem seeks to find the minimum-weight connected tree (i.e., the top-1 connected tree with smallest weight) from G that covers all the given labels in P [28].

SIGMOD'16, June 26-July 01, 2016, San Francisco, CA, USA
© 2016 ACM. ISBN 978-1-4503-3531-7/16/06...$15.00
DOI: http://dx.doi.org/10.1145/2882903.2915217

The GST problem has a number of applications in the database and data mining communities. For example, the keyword search problem in relational databases has been formulated as a GST problem [8, 6]. Specifically, a relational database can be modeled as a graph, where each node denotes a tuple and each edge represents a foreign key reference between two tuples. Each edge is associated with a weight, representing the strength of the relationship between two tuples (nodes). The keyword search problem aims to find a set of connected nodes (tuples) that covers all the given keywords with minimum total weight of all induced edges. Clearly, the optimal solution for such a keyword search problem is a minimum-weight connected tree that covers the given keywords, and therefore it is an instance of the GST problem. Most existing keyword search systems such as BANKS-I [3], BANKS-II [19], BLINKS [17], STAR [20] and DPBF [8, 6] are based on approximate or exact GST search techniques. As indicated in [6], the GST based method (e.g., DPBF) is the most effective algorithm for keyword search in relational databases. Another notable application of the GST problem is to find a team of experts from a social network [22], also called the team formulation problem. Specifically, there is a set of experts that form a social network, and each expert is associated with a set of skills. Given a set of skills, the team formulation problem is to find a team of experts with all the skills at the minimum communication cost. In [22], the team is modeled as a connected tree covering all the given skills, and the goal is to find such a connected tree with minimum weight, where the weight measures the communication cost. Obviously, such a team formulation problem is an instance of the GST problem. Recently, the GST based method has been recognized as a standard technique to find a team of experts in social networks [30]. Many existing team search systems such as [22], [2] and [25] are based on the GST search technique.

Given its large number of applications, devising an efficient algorithm to solve the GST problem is crucial. Unfortunately, the GST problem is known to be NP-hard, and it even cannot admit a polynomial approximate algorithm with constant approximation ratio [18]. Thus, there is no hope to find the optimal GST (or constant approximate GST) from a graph within polynomial time unless P=NP.

Previous studies have adopted two main types of approach to solving the GST problem. First, many approximation solutions [5, 13, 3, 19, 17] have been proposed to solve the GST problem. In the theoretical computer science community, several LP (linear programming) based approximation algorithms [5, 13] have been developed, where the approximation ratio of these algorithms is polylogarithmic. Since these algorithms need to invoke the LP procedure, they are very hard to handle medium-sized graphs. In the database community, many practical approximation algorithms such as BANKS-I [3], BANKS-II [19], and BLINKS [17] have been devised for the keyword search application. The approximation ratio of these algorithms is $O(k)$, where k is the number of given labels. However, as shown in [6], all these approximation algorithms are still inefficient for large graphs due to the high time and space complexity. Second, faster parameterized dynamic programming (DP) algorithm has been devised [8] which takes $O(3^k n + 2^k(n \log n + m))$ time and $O(2^k n)$ space, where m and n are the number of the edges and nodes of the graph respectively. Unlike the approximate algorithms, the parameterized DP algorithm is able to find the optimal solution in reasonable time when k is very small. As indicated in [6], the parameterized DP algorithm significantly outperforms the above mentioned approximation algorithms for the keyword search application. The major limitations of the parameterized DP algorithm are twofold. First, due to the exponential time and space complexity, the parameterized DP algorithm quickly becomes impractical even for very small k (e.g., $k = 8$) in large graphs. Second, it cannot generate a solution until the algorithm has completed its entire execution, thus making the algorithm costly in practice.

Against this background, we propose an efficient and progressive GST algorithm, called PrunedDP. The PrunedDP algorithm quickly returns an initial solution, and then improves the quality of the solution that is found so far and achieves progressively better bounds, as the algorithm searches more of the search space, until an optimal solution is generated. The strength of the PrunedDP algorithm is founded on two main components. First, we propose a new approach to constructing a feasible solution for each state of the parameterized DP algorithm, and then keep refining those solutions during algorithm execution. Second, we develop two novel techniques, called optimal-tree decomposition and conditional tree merging, to reduce the search space of the parameterized DP algorithm. The general idea of these techniques is to obtain the optimal tree by merging several optimal subtrees with weights smaller than one half of the optimal solution. Moreover, we discover that there is no need to expand a state in the DP procedure by merging two optimal subtrees if their total weight is larger than two over three of the optimal solution. Armed with these techniques, the PrunedDP algorithm not only produces progressively-refined feasible solutions during algorithm execution, but it also drastically prunes the search space of the parameterized DP algorithm. Thus, the time and space overhead of the algorithm is significantly reduced.

To further speed up the PrunedDP algorithm, we propose a progressive A^*-search algorithm, called PrunedDP++, based on several carefully-designed lower-bounding techniques (more details can be found in Section 4). The PrunedDP++ algorithm is built on the PrunedDP algorithm. But unlike the PrunedDP algorithm, PrunedDP++ makes use of the A^*-search strategy to select the most promising state to expand, and thus many unpromising states can be pruned. We conduct extensive experiments on several large scale real-world graphs to evaluate the proposed algorithms. The results show that our algorithms are able to find progressively-refined feasible solutions during algorithm execution. Moreover, the reported feasible solutions can be quickly refined to a near-optimal solution in less than 10 seconds in large-scale graphs (≥ 10 million nodes) even for $k = 8$. In addition, when $k = 8$, our best algorithm finds the optimal solution in around 20 seconds in a large-scale graph, while the state-of-the-art algorithm cannot get the optimal solution within one hour. In general, the PrunedDP algorithm is around one order of magnitude faster than the state-of-the-art algorithm, and the PrunedDP++ algorithm can further achieves at least one order of magnitude acceleration over the PrunedDP algorithm, using much less memory.

The main contributions of this paper are summarized as follows.

- We propose an efficient and progressive GST algorithm, called PrunedDP, based on newly-developed optimal-tree decomposition and conditional tree merging techniques. The striking features of the PrunedDP algorithm are twofold: (i) the algorithm can generate progressively-refined feasible solutions during algorithm execution, and (ii) it finds the optimal solution one order of magnitude faster than the state-of-the-art algorithm.

Notation	Meaning
$G = (V, E)$	the graph
S	the set of labels
S_v	the set of labels associated with node v
P	the given label sets
$f^*(P)$	the optimal solution for the given label sets P
(v, X)	a state of the DP algorithm
$T(v, X)$	the minimum-weight tree rooted at v covering labels X
$f_T^*(v, X)$	the weight of $T(v, X)$
$\tilde{v}_p$	the virtual node corresponding to label p
V_P	the set of virtual nodes corresponding to labels P
$R(\tilde{v}_i, \tilde{v}_j, \bar{X})$	the minimum-weight route that starts from $\tilde{v}_i$, ends at $\tilde{v}_j$, and passes through all virtual nodes in $V_{\bar{X}}$
$W(\tilde{v}_i, \tilde{v}_j, \bar{X})$	the weight of the route $R(\tilde{v}_i, \tilde{v}_j, \bar{X})$
$R(\tilde{v}_i, \bar{X})$	the minimum-weight route that starts from $\tilde{v}_i$ and passes through all virtual nodes in $V_{\bar{X}}$
$W(\tilde{v}_i, \bar{X})$	the weight of the tour $R(\tilde{v}_i, \bar{X})$
$R(v, \bar{X})$	a tour starts from v and passes through all nodes in $V_{\bar{X}}$
$\tilde{R}(v, \bar{X})$	the minimum-weight tour over all $R(v, \bar{X})$
$f_{\tilde{R}}^*(v, \bar{X})$	the weight of the tour $\tilde{R}(v, \bar{X})$
$\pi_1(v, X)$	the one-label lower bound for a state (v, X)
$\pi_{t_1}(v, X)$	the first type of tour-based lower bound for a state (v, X)
$\pi_{t_2}(v, X)$	the second type of tour-based lower bound for a state (v, X)

Table 1: Summary of notations

- To further reduce the search space of the PrunedDP algorithm, we propose a progressive A^*-search algorithm, called PrunedDP++, based on several carefully-devised lower-bounding techniques. The PrunedDP++ algorithm also reports progressively-refined feasible solutions, and is at least one order of magnitude faster than the PrunedDP algorithm, using much less memory.
- We conduct comprehensive experiments on several large scale real-world graphs (≥ 10 million nodes) to evaluate our algorithms, and the results confirm our theoretical findings.

The rest of this paper is organized as follows. In Section 2, we formulate the problem and briefly review the parameterized DP algorithm. In Section 3, we propose the PrunedDP algorithm and develop the optimal-tree decomposition and conditional tree merging techniques. The PrunedDP++ algorithm and several nontrivial lower bounding techniques are proposed in Section 4. Finally, we review related work and conclude this paper in Section 6 and Section 7 respectively.

2. PRELIMINARIES

Let $G = (V, E)$ be a weighted graph, where V and E denote the set of nodes and edges respectively. Let $n = |V|$ and $m = |E|$ be the number of nodes and edges respectively. For each edge $e = (v_i, v_j) \in E$, $w(v_i, v_j)$ denotes the weight of e. For each node $v \in V$, there is a set of labels, denoted by S_v, associated with v. Let $S = \bigcup_{v \in V} S_v$ be the set of all labels. For each label $a \in S$, we let $V_a \subseteq V$ be the group (set) of nodes where each node in V_a contains the label a. Note that by this definition, each label corresponds to a group. Based on these notations, the Group Steiner Tree (GST) problem [28] is formulated as follows.

The GST problem. Given a weighted and labelled graph $G = (V, E)$ and a subset of labels P ($P \subseteq S$), the GST problem seeks to find the minimum-weight connected tree (i.e., the top-1 connected tree with smallest weight) from G that includes all the labels in P.

For convenience, in the rest of this paper, we assume without loss of generality that the graph $G = (V, E)$ is a connected graph. This is because if the graph is disconnected, we can solve the GST problem in each maximal connected component of the graph, and then pick the best connected tree as the answer.

It is well known that the GST problem is NP-hard [28], and is even inapproximable within a constant approximation factor by a polynomial algorithm [18]. Therefore, there is no hope to compute the GST (or find an approximate GST within constant preformation ratio) in polynomial time unless P=NP. In the literature, the state-of-the-art exact algorithm for the GST problem is a parameterized dynamic programming (DP) algorithm which runs in $O(3^k n + 2^k(n \log n + m))$ time [8], where $k = |P|$ denotes the number of given labels. Below, we briefly review such a parameterized DP algorithm, as it forms the basis for devising our progressive GST algorithms.

The parameterized DP algorithm. In the parameterized DP algorithm, a state, denoted by (v, X), corresponds to a connected tree rooted at v that covers all labels in X. Let $T(v, X)$ be the minimum-weight connected tree rooted at v that includes all labels in X, and $f_T^*(v, X)$ be the weight of $T(v, X)$ (i.e., the total weight of the edges in $T(v, X)$). Clearly, by these notations, the optimal weight of a state (v, X) is $f_T^*(v, X)$. Table 1 summarizes the important notations used in this paper.

Based on the definition of the state, the state-transition equation of the parameterized DP algorithm proposed in [8] is given by

$$f_T^*(v, X) = \min\{ \min_{(v,u)\in E} \{f_T^*(u, X) + w(v, u)\}, \min_{\substack{(X=X_1\cup X_2) \\ \wedge(X_1\cap X_2=\emptyset)}} \{f_T^*(v, X_1) + f_T^*(v, X_2)\}\}. \quad (1)$$

As shown in Eq. (1), the optimal weight of the state (v, X) could be obtained by either of the following two cases. The first case is that the optimal connected tree, denoted by $T(v, X)$, could be obtained by growing an edge (v, u) from the minimum-weight subtree of $T(v, X)$ rooted at u including all labels in X, where u is a child node of v (i.e., the first part of Eq. (1)). We refer to the state expansion operation in this case as the *edge growing* operation. The second case is that $T(v, X)$ could be obtained by merging two optimal subtrees rooted at v that includes all labels in X_1 and X_2 respectively, where $X_1 \cup X_2 = X$ and $X_1 \cap X_2 = \emptyset$ (i.e., the second part of Eq. (1)). Similarly, we refer to the state expansion operation in this case as the *tree merging* operation.

Initially, for each node v with labels S_v, we have $f_T^*(v, \{p\}) = 0$, for each label $p \in S_v$. By Eq. (1), Ding et al. [8] proposed a parameterized DP algorithm based on the best-first search strategy to compute the minimum $f_T^*(v, P)$ over all $v \in V$. Specifically, the parameterized DP algorithm uses a priority queue $\mathcal{Q}$ to maintain the states (e.g., (v, X)), in which the weight of a state is the priority of that state. Initially, the state $(v, \{p\})$ for each $p \in S_v$ is inserted into $\mathcal{Q}$. Then, the algorithm iteratively pops the smallest-weight state from $\mathcal{Q}$, and applies Eq. (1) to expand such a state. For each expanded state, if it is already in $\mathcal{Q}$, the algorithm updates its weight using the smaller weight. Otherwise, the algorithm inserts it into $\mathcal{Q}$. The algorithm terminates until the popped state covers all the labels in P. Clearly, by the best-first search strategy, the optimal state is always popped later than any intermediate state from the priority queue, and thus the weight of the popped intermediate state must be smaller than the optimal solution.

As shown in [8], the parameterized DP algorithm works well for keyword search applications when both the parameter k and the graph size are small. However, as discussed below, the parameterized DP algorithm becomes impractical when the parameter k and the graph size are large.

Limitations of the parameterized DP algorithm. First, the time complexity of the parameterized DP algorithm relies on the exponential factor 3^k. Thus, the algorithm only works well for very small values of k (e.g., $k = 4$ used in [8]) in large graphs. On the other hand, the space complexity of the parameterized DP algorithm is $O(2^k n)$. Clearly, when k is large, the algorithm will quickly run out of memory in large graphs. Indeed, as shown in our experiments, the parameterized DP algorithm does not work in large graphs with relatively large k values (e.g., $k = 8$). Second, the algorithm only generates a solution (i.e., the optimal solution) when it terminates. However, in many practical applications (e.g., keyword search), users may prefer a sub-optimal solution in less time, rather than wait for the algorithm to find the optimal solution.

The above discussions motivate us to answer the following question: can we develop an algorithm that is not only more efficient than the parameterized DP algorithm, but also reports sub-optimal solutions during execution (not only when the algorithm terminates)? In the following sections, we will propose several novel algorithms to achieve those goals.

3. THE PROGRESSIVE GST ALGORITHM

In this section, we first propose a basic progressive GST algorithm, called Basic, based on the parameterized DP algorithm in [8]. Then, we propose a novel algorithm, called PrunedDP, to reduce the search space of the Basic algorithm based on newly-developed optimal-tree decomposition and conditional tree merging techniques.

3.1 The Basic algorithm

We first introduce a progressive search framework, and then present the Basic algorithm following this framework.

The progressive search framework. Roughly speaking, a progressive search algorithm works in rounds, reporting a sub-optimal and feasible solution with smaller error guarantees in each round, until in the last round the optimal solution is obtained. More specifically, we refer to a search algorithm as a progressive algorithm when it satisfies the following two properties.

- **Progressive property.** The algorithm works in rounds. In each round, the algorithm returns a feasible solution, and reports the maximum error (with respect to the optimal solution) it may have.
- **Monotonic property.** The maximum error of a feasible solution does not increase after each round. In other words, the feasible solution reported in each round should be a refinement of the previous solution. Until in the last round, the optimal solution is obtained.

Clearly, the progressive property is desirable for many applications, because with the progressive property, we can always obtain a feasible solution and also know its bound to the optimal solution whenever we interrupt the algorithm. The monotonic property is also desirable, because the maximum error in each round is guaranteed to be non-increasing, and thus the algorithm can obtain a refined solution from one round to the next.

The basic progressive GST algorithm. Following the progressive search framework, we devise a progressive GST algorithm, called Basic, based on the parameterized DP algorithm in [8]. The general idea of Basic is that we first construct a feasible solution for an intermediate state (v, X) of the parameterized DP algorithm, then keep refining the feasible solution, and also compute the bound for that feasible solution.

Before proceeding further, we first introduce a preprocessing procedure for any query P and graph G, which will be used in all the proposed algorithms. Specifically, for a label $p \in P$, we create a virtual node $\tilde{v}_p$, and create an undirected edge $(\tilde{v}_p, v)$ with zero weight for each $v \in V$ that includes a label p. Then, we compute the single-source shortest path from $\tilde{v}_p$ to all the other nodes in the graph G. For each label $p \in P$, we independently perform this process. Let $dist(v, \tilde{v}_p)$ be the shortest-path distance between v and the virtual node $\tilde{v}_p$. For a query P, we can pre-compute all those shortest paths and $dist(v, \tilde{v}_p)$ by invoking the Dijkstra algorithm $k = |P|$ times, which takes $O(k(m + n \log n))$ time complexity.

After the above preprocessing, we can then construct a feasible solution as follows. First, for each state (v, X), let $\bar{X} = P \backslash X$

Algorithm 1 Basic(G, P, S)

Input: $G = (V, E)$, label set S, and the query label set P.
Output: the minimum weight of the tree that covers P.

```
1: Q ← ∅; D ← ∅;
2: best ← +∞; /* maintain the weight of the best feasible solution. */
3: for all v ∈ V do
4:     for all p ∈ S_v do
5:         Q.push((v, {p}), 0);
6: while Q ≠ ∅ do
7:     ((v, X), cost) ← Q.pop();
8:     if X = P then return cost;
9:     D ← D ∪ {(v, X)}; X̄ ← P\X;
10:    T'(v, X̄) ← ∅;
11:    for all p ∈ X̄ do
12:        T'(v, X̄) ← T'(v, X̄) ∪ Shortest-Path(v, ṽ_p);
13:    T̃(v, P) ← MST(T'(v, X̄) ∪ T(v, X));
14:    best ← min{best, f_T̃(v, P)};
15:    Report the approximation ratio for best;
16:    for all (v, u) ∈ E do
17:        update(Q, D, best, (u, X), cost + w(v, u));
18:    for all X' ⊆ X̄ and (v, X') ∈ D do
19:        update(Q, D, best, (v, X' ∪ X), cost + D.cost(v, X'));
20: return +∞;

21: Procedure update(Q, D, (v, X), cost)
22: if (v, X) ∈ D then return;
23: if cost >= best then return;
24: if X = P then best ← min{best, cost};
25: if (v, X) ∉ Q then Q.push((v, X), cost);
26: if cost < Q.cost((v, X)) then Q.update((v, X), cost);
```

(i.e., $\bar{X}$ be the complementary set of X with respect to the set P). For a node v and label set $\bar{X}$, there are $|\bar{X}|$ shortest paths from v to $\tilde{v}_p$ for all $p \in \bar{X}$. We merge all those $|\bar{X}|$ shortest paths, resulting in a tree denoted by $T'(v, \bar{X})$. Second, we unite the tree $T(v, X)$ (corresponding to the state (v, X)) and $T'(v, \bar{X})$, and then compute the minimum spanning tree (MST) of the united result, i.e., $\mathsf{MST}(T'(v, \bar{X}) \cup T(v, X))$). Let $\tilde{T}(v, P) \triangleq \mathsf{MST}(T'(v, \bar{X}) \cup T(v, X)))$. Clearly, $\tilde{T}(v, P)$ is a feasible solution, as it is a tree that covers all the labels in P.

Let $f_{\tilde{T}}(v, P)$ be the weight of the tree $\tilde{T}(v, P)$. Then, $f_{\tilde{T}}(v, P)$ is an upper bound of the optimal solution. On the other hand, we can always use $f_T^*(v, X)$ as a lower bound for the optimal solution. This is because by the best-first DP algorithm, the optimal solution is popped later from the priority queue than any computed intermediate state (v, X), and thus we have $f_T^*(v, X) \leq f^*(P)$, where $f^*(P)$ is the optimal solution for the GST query P. As a result, for any intermediate state (v, X), we can always report a feasible solution $\tilde{T}(v, P)$ and its approximation ratio $f_{\tilde{T}}(v, P)/f_T^*(v, X)$.

The algorithm is detailed in Algorithm 1. In Algorithm 1, we use a tuple $((v, X), cost)$ to denote the state (v, X), where $cost$ denotes the weight of the tree that corresponds to the state (v, X). Similar to the parameterized DP algorithm [8], Algorithm 1 follows the best-first search strategy. In each round, the algorithm pops the best state (v, X) from the priority queue $\mathcal{Q}$ (line 7), and uses a set $\mathcal{D}$ to maintain all the states that have been computed (i.e., the optimal weight of each state in $\mathcal{D}$ has been calculated). Based on (v, X), we construct a feasible solution $\tilde{T}(v, P)$ as described above (lines 10-13).

To make the algorithm progressive, we use a variable $best$ to record the best feasible solution found so far, and then keep refining $best$ in each round, and also report the approximation ratio for $best$ using the method described above (lines 14-15). In lines 16-19, the algorithm expands and updates the states based on the state-transition equation of the parameterized DP algorithm (i.e., Eq.(1)). Note that unlike the parameterized DP algorithm, in line 23, the Basic algorithm makes use of the current best solution for pruning the unpromising states. This pruning technique not only decreases the running time of the parameterized DP algorithm, but also reduces the space overhead as well (because the unpromising states will not be inserted into the priority queue $\mathcal{Q}$). Consequently, Basic is not just a progressive algorithm, it can also improve the efficiency of the parameterized DP algorithm. However, although the Basic algorithm is more efficient than the parameterized DP algorithm, it still needs to search a large number of states to find the optimal solution. Below, we propose a novel algorithm which drastically reduces the search space of the Basic algorithm.

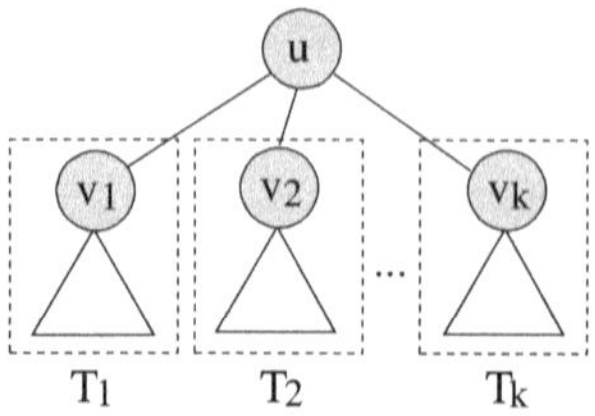

Figure 1: Illustration of the optimal-tree decomposition.

3.2 The PrunedDP algorithm

Recall that in the Basic algorithm, to obtain the optimal solution $f^*(P)$ for a query P, the algorithm must compute the optimal weights of all the intermediate states that are smaller than $f^*(P)$ in terms of the best-first search strategy. An immediate question is: can we avoid computing all such optimal weights to get $f^*(P)$? Below, we propose a new algorithm based on optimal-tree decomposition and conditional tree merging techniques to achieve this goal. Specifically, let $T^*(P)$ be the optimal tree with weight $f^*(P)$. For simplicity, we assume that $T^*(P)$ contains at least one edge. We then have the following optimal-tree decomposition theorem. Proofs of all the theorems and lemmas in this paper can be found in Appendix A.1.

THEOREM 1. ***Optimal-Tree Decomposition Theorem:*** *Assume that each edge in the graph G has a positive weight. Then, for the optimal tree $T^*(P)$, there always exists a node $u \in T^*(P)$ such that (i) the tree $T^*(P)$ rooted at u has k ($k \geq 1$) subtrees $T_1, T_2, \cdots, T_k$, and (ii) each subtree T_i (for $i \in \{1, 2, \cdots, k\}$) has a weight smaller than $f^*(P)/2$.*

Fig. 1 illustrates the idea of the optimal-tree decomposition, where every subtree rooted at v_i, for $i = 1, \cdots, k$, has a weight smaller than $f^*(P)/2$. According to Theorem 1, the optimal tree can always be decomposed into several optimal subtrees with weights smaller than $f^*(P)/2$. This result motivates us to devise a two-stage algorithm to compute the optimal tree. In the first stage, we compute all the optimal subtrees that have weights smaller than $f^*(P)/2$ by the best-first DP algorithm. Then, in the second stage, we merge the results obtained from the first stage to get the optimal tree. This is because, after the first stage, all the optimal subtrees with weights smaller than $f^*(P)/2$ have been generated, thus by Theorem 1, we can obtain the optimal tree via merging the optimal subtrees. To achieve this, we can apply the same method as used in the best-first DP algorithm to merge the optimal subtrees. Specifically, we can obtain the optimal tree by invoking two operations: (i) *edge growing*, and (ii) *tree merging*. For example, in Fig. 1, the optimal tree rooted at u can be obtained by growing an edge (v_i, u) from each optimal subtree rooted at v_i, and then merging all those edge-grown subtrees. Thus, without loss of optimality, for each optimal subtree generated in the first stage, we must perform an edge growing operation. Then, for every two subtrees, if they can be merged (i.e., share the same root), we need to perform a tree merging operation. Clearly, the optimal tree can always be obtained by invoking these two operations.

Since the second stage of our algorithm invokes the same operations that are used in the best-first DP algorithm, we can integrate

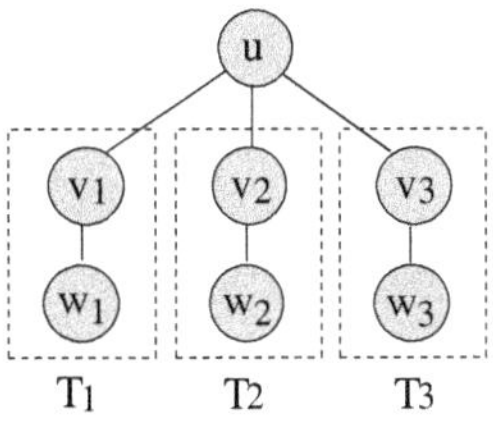

Figure 2: Illustration of the optimality of Theorem 2.

them into the first stage. In particular, when we pop a state from the priority queue in the best-first DP algorithm, we expand this state only when its weight is smaller than $f^*(P)/2$. Clearly, by adding this constraint to expand the states, all the optimal subtrees with weights smaller than $f^*(P)/2$ can be computed. Moreover, every subtree, which is obtained by invoking an edge growing operation on a computed subtree, is generated; and every subtree that is obtained by invoking a tree merging operation on two computed subtrees is also generated. After getting all these subtrees, we merge two subtrees if they can form a feasible solution (i.e., covers all labels in P), and then select the best one as the optimal tree.

Interestingly, we discover that there is no need to generate every subtree obtained by invoking the tree merging operation on two computed subtrees. Without loss of optimality, we can add an additional constraint in the tree merging operation to avoid generating unpromising subtrees in the best-first DP algorithm. Our technique is based on the following conditional tree merging theorem.

THEOREM 2. ***Conditional Tree Merging Theorem:*** *Without loss of optimality, to expand a state (v, X) by a tree merging operation in the best-first DP algorithm, we can merge two subtrees $T(v, X)$ and $T(v, X')$ for $X' \subset P\backslash X$ only when the total weight of these two subtrees is no larger than $2/3 \times f^*(P)$.*

By Theorem 2, we can further reduce a number of states generated in the best-first DP algorithm without loss of optimality, because any intermediate state (not a feasible solution) with a weight larger than $2f^*(P)/3$ does not need to be generated by the tree merging operation. It is important to note that this does not mean that all the states with weights larger than $2f^*(P)/3$ will not be generated by our algorithm, because a state with weight larger than $2f^*(P)/3$ may be generated by the edge growing operation, and also it may be generated by merging two *complementary* states (i.e., (v, X) and $(v, \bar{X})$ with $X = P\backslash X$) to form a feasible solution.

The optimality of Theorem 2. It should be noted that there is a factor of 2/3 in Theorem 2. Clearly, a small factor is better than a large one when pruning unpromising states. Thus, without loss of optimality, we strive to find the minimum factor to reduce the number of states generated by the best-first DP algorithm. However, interestingly, we find that the factor 2/3 is optimal. Below, we give an example in which the factor cannot be smaller than 2/3. Consider an optimal tree rooted at u as shown in Fig. 2. The optimal tree has three subtrees which are denoted by T_i for $i = \{1, 2, 3\}$ with roots v_i respectively. Suppose that the weight of each edge in this tree is 1. Note that by our algorithm, the optimal solution in this example must be obtained by merging two subtrees in which one of them must have a weight no smaller than $2f^*(P)/3$. Moreover, in this example, by our algorithm, we must invoke the tree merging operation to obtain a subtree that has a weight no smaller than $2f^*(P)/3$. This is because, we cannot obtain such a subtree by growing an edge from an optimal subtree with a weight smaller than $f^*(P)/2$. Therefore, in this example, we cannot set the factor to be a value smaller than $2/3$, otherwise we cannot generate such a subtree and thus cannot guarantee the correctness of the algorithm. As a result, the factor 2/3 given in Theorem 2 is optimal.

Based on the above theoretical results, we are now ready to present the PrunedDP algorithm. Note that to make the algorith-

Algorithm 2 PrunedDP(G, P, S)

Input: $G = (V, E)$, label set S, and the query label set P.
Output: the minimum weight of the tree that covers P.

1: $\mathcal{Q} \leftarrow \emptyset$; $\mathcal{D} \leftarrow \emptyset$;
2: $best \leftarrow +\infty$; /* maintain the weight of the best feasible solution. */
3: **for all** $v \in V$ **do**
4:   **for all** $p \in S_v$ **do**
5:     $\mathcal{Q}.push((v, \{p\}), 0)$;
6: **while** $\mathcal{Q} \neq \emptyset$ **do**
7:   $((v, X), cost) \leftarrow \mathcal{Q}.pop()$;
8:   **if** $X = P$ **then return** $cost$;
9:   $\mathcal{D} \leftarrow \mathcal{D} \cup \{(v, X)\}$; $\bar{X} \leftarrow P\backslash X$;
10:   $T'(v, \bar{X}) \leftarrow \emptyset$;
11:   **for all** $p \in \bar{X}$ **do**
12:     $T'(v, \bar{X}) \leftarrow T'(v, \bar{X}) \cup$ Shortest-Path$(v, \tilde{v}_p)$;
13:   $\tilde{T}(v, P) \leftarrow$ MST$(T'(v, \bar{X}) \cup T(v, X))$;
14:   $best \leftarrow \min\{best, f_{\tilde{T}}(v, P)\}$;
15:   Report the approximation ratio for $best$;
16:   **if** $(v, \bar{X}) \in \mathcal{D}$ **then**
17:     update$(\mathcal{Q}, \mathcal{D}, best, (v, P), cost + \mathcal{D}.cost(v, \bar{X}))$;
18:     **continue**;
19:   **if** $cost < best/2$ **then**
20:     **for all** $(v, u) \in E$ **do**
21:       update$(\mathcal{Q}, \mathcal{D}, best, (u, X), cost + w(v, u))$;
22:     **for all** $X' \subset \bar{X}$ **and** $(v, X') \in \mathcal{D}$ **do**
23:       $\overline{cost} \leftarrow \mathcal{D}.cost(v, X')$;
24:       **if** $cost + \overline{cost} \leq 2/3 \times best$ **then**
25:         update$(\mathcal{Q}, \mathcal{D}, best, (v, X' \cup X), cost + \overline{cost})$;
26: **return** $+\infty$;

m progressive, we can apply the same approach developed in the Basic algorithm to produce progressively-refined results. In addition, a final issue is that Theorem 1 and Theorem 2 rely on the optimal solution $f^*(P)$ of the GST problem which is unknown before the algorithm terminates. However, it is easy to verify that if we use an upper bound of $f^*(P)$ to replace $f^*(P)$ in Theorem 1 and Theorem 2, the results still hold. Therefore, in our algorithm, we can use the weight of the best feasible solution found so far as an upper bound of $f^*(P)$. Since the best feasible solution is progressively improved, the bound becomes tighter and tighter, as the algorithm searches more of the search space, and thus the pruning power of the algorithm is progressively enhanced.

The algorithm is detailed in Algorithm 2. Note that PrunedDP follows the same framework as the Basic algorithm to produce progressively-refined feasible solutions (see lines 10-15 of Algorithm 2). But drastically different from Basic, PrunedDP is based on the pruned DP-search strategy developed in Theorem 1 and Theorem 2. Specifically, in lines 16-18, the algorithm merges two *complementary* computed states once they can form a feasible state (a state that covers all query labels P), and then invokes the same update procedure as used in Algorithm 1 to update the feasible state. Then, in lines 19-25, the algorithm expands the state (v, X) only if its weight is smaller than $best/2$. This is because, according to the results in Theorem 1, the algorithm does not need to expand a state with weight no smaller than $f^*(P)/2$. In addition, in line 24, the algorithm merges two optimal subtrees only if their total weight is smaller than $2/3 \times best$ based on the *conditional tree merging* theorem. Clearly, the correctness of the algorithm can be guaranteed by Theorem 1 and Theorem 2.

Cost analysis of the PrunedDP algorithm. It is worth noting that the worst-case time and space complexity of the PrunedDP algorithm is the same as that of the Basic algorithm. However, compared to Basic, PrunedDP can prune a large number of unpromising states using *optimal-tree decomposition* and *conditional tree merging* techniques, and thus drastically reduces both the running time and memory overhead. In the experiments, we show that PrunedDP is one order of magnitude faster than the Basic algorithm, using much less memory.

4. THE PROGRESSIVE A^* ALGORITHM

Recall that the PrunedDP algorithm finds the optimal solution in a pruned search space based on the best-first DP search strategy. To further speed up the PrunedDP algorithm, we propose a novel progressive algorithm, called PrunedDP++, based on the A^*-search strategy over the pruned search space. Below, we first propose several lower bounding techniques, which are crucial to devise the PrunedDP++ algorithm.

4.1 Lower bounds construction

To devise an A^*-search algorithm for the GST problem, the key is to establish an effective lower bound for each state (v, X) in the search space [16, 7]. It is important to note that according to the A^*-search theory [16, 7], the lower bound in our problem denotes the bound from the current state (v, X) to its goal state (v, P). Thus, for a state (v, X), we need to design a lower bound for the weight of the optimal subtree $T(v, \bar{X})$ (i.e., $f_T^*(v, \bar{X})$), where $\bar{X} = P \backslash X$. In the following, we propose several effective lower bounds that are constructed via relaxing the constraints of the optimal subtree $T(v, \bar{X})$.

One-label lower bound. Note that the optimal subtree $T(v, \bar{X})$ must cover all the labels in $\bar{X}$. Here we develop a lower bound, called one-label lower bound, by relaxing such a *label covering* constraint. Our idea is that we consider the optimal connected tree rooted at v that covers only one label in $\bar{X}$, where $\bar{X} = P \backslash X$. Specifically, let $T(v, \{x\})$ be the optimal connected tree rooted at v that covers a label $x \in \bar{X}$, and $f_T^*(v, \{x\})$ be the weight of $T(v, \{x\})$. Further, we let $f_1^*(v, \bar{X})$ be the weight of the maximum-weight tree over all $T(v, \{x\})$ for $x \in \bar{X}$. Then, we define the one-label lower bound $\pi_1(v, X)$ as follows.

$$\pi_1(v, X) \triangleq f_1^*(v, \bar{X}) = \max_{x \in \bar{X}} \{f_T^*(v, \{x\})\}. \quad (2)$$

The following lemma shows that $\pi_1(v, X)$ is indeed a valid lower bound for a state (v, X).

LEMMA 1. *For any state* (v, X)*, we have* $\pi_1(v, X) \leq f_T^*(v, \bar{X})$.

Note that by definition, $f_T^*(v, \{x\})$ is equal to the shortest-path distance between the node v and the virtual node $\tilde{v}_x$ (i.e., $f_T^*(v, \{x\}) = dist(v, \tilde{v}_x)$), which can be obtained by invoking the same preprocessing procedure used in Algorithms 1 and 2. Therefore, for any state (v, X), the time complexity for computing $\pi_1(v, X)$ is $O(|\bar{X}|)$ after preprocessing.

Tour-based lower bounds. Recall that the optimal tree $T(v, \bar{X})$ must be a connected tree. By relaxing such a *connected tree* constraint, here we develop two novel tour-based lower bounds.

The first type of the tour-based lower bound is constructed as follows. First, for a given set of labels P with $k = |P|$, we create a virtual node $\tilde{v}_p$ for each label $p \in P$. Let V_P denotes the set of all virtual nodes. Then, we create an edge $(\tilde{v}_p, v)$ with zero weight for each $v \in V$ that includes a label p. After that, we can obtain a new graph, called the label-enhanced graph. Second, we compute the single-source shortest path from each virtual node $\tilde{v}_p$ to all the other nodes in the label-enhanced graph. It is worth mentioning that this procedure is different from the preprocessing procedure used for constructing the feasible solution in Algorithm 1 and Algorithm 2, and also for computing the one-label lower bound. Here we add all virtual edges simultaneously for all the virtual nodes, whereas in the previous preprocessing procedure, we independently process each virtual node. Third, for $\bar{X} \subseteq P$, we let $V_{\bar{X}}$ be the set of all virtual nodes that correspond to the labels in $\bar{X}$. For any $i, j \in \bar{X}$ and $\bar{X} \subseteq P$, we let $R(\tilde{v}_i, \tilde{v}_j, \bar{X})$ be the minimum-weight route that starts from $\tilde{v}_i$, ends at $\tilde{v}_j$, and passes through all the virtual nodes in $V_{\bar{X}}$. Further, we let $W(\tilde{v}_i, \tilde{v}_j, \bar{X})$ be the weight of the route $R(\tilde{v}_i, \tilde{v}_j, \bar{X})$.

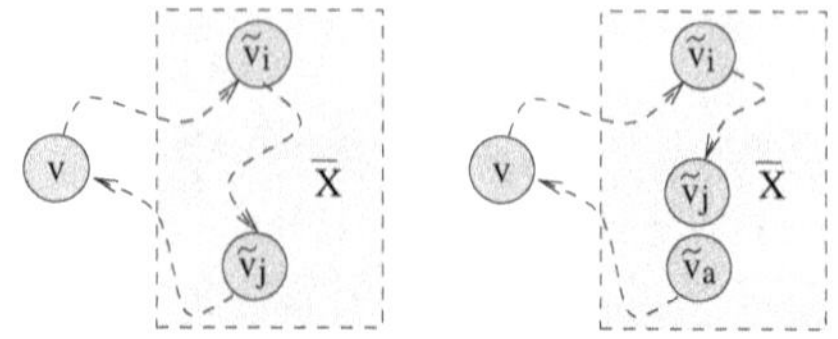

(a) (b)

Figure 3: Illustration of the tour-based lower bounds.

Based on these notations, for a state (v, X) of the GST problem, we can construct a tour $R(v, \bar{X}) \triangleq (v \sim R(\tilde{v}_i, \tilde{v}_j, \bar{X}) \sim v)$ that starts from v, ends at v, and covers all labels in $\bar{X}$. Fig. 3(a) illustrates such a tour. Note that for each virtual-node pair $(\tilde{v}_i, \tilde{v}_j)$, we have a tour $R(v, \bar{X})$. To construct the lower bound, we intend to find the minimum-weight tour. Specifically, we define $\tilde{R}(v, \bar{X})$ as the minimum-weight tour over all tours $R(v, \bar{X})$ for all $\tilde{v}_i, \tilde{v}_j \in V_{\bar{X}}$. Further, we let $f_{\tilde{R}}^*(v, \bar{X})$ be the weight of the optimal tour $\tilde{R}(v, \bar{X})$. Formally, we have

$$f_{\tilde{R}}^*(v, \bar{X}) = \min_{i,j \in \bar{X}} \{dist(v, \tilde{v}_i) + W(\tilde{v}_i, \tilde{v}_j, \bar{X}) + dist(\tilde{v}_j, v)\}, \quad (3)$$

where $dist(v, \tilde{v}_i)$ denotes the shortest-path distance between v and $\tilde{v}_i$. For a state (v, X), we define the first type of tour-based lower bound using the following formula:

$$\pi_{t_1}(v, X) \triangleq f_{\tilde{R}}^*(v, \bar{X})/2. \quad (4)$$

With this definition, we show that $\pi_{t_1}(v, X)$ is a valid lower bound.

LEMMA 2. *For any state* (v, X)*, we have* $\pi_{t_1}(v, X) \leq f_T^*(v, \bar{X})$.

With Lemma 2, we successfully construct a lower bound for any state (v, X) of the GST problem. The remaining question is how to compute such a lower bound efficiently. According to Eq. (3), the most challenging task is to compute $W(\tilde{v}_i, \tilde{v}_j, \bar{X})$ for all $i, j \in \bar{X}$. Below, we propose a DP algorithm to tackle this challenge.

For any $i, j \in \bar{X}$ and $\bar{X} \subseteq P$, we define $(\tilde{v}_i, \tilde{v}_j, \bar{X})$ as a state in our DP algorithm, denoting a route that starts from $\tilde{v}_i$, ends at $\tilde{v}_j$, and passes through all the virtual nodes in $V_{\bar{X}}$. Then, the recursive equation of the DP algorithm is given as follows.

$$W(\tilde{v}_i, \tilde{v}_j, \bar{X}) = \min_{p \in \bar{X} \backslash \{j\}} \{W(\tilde{v}_i, \tilde{v}_p, \bar{X} \backslash \{p\}) + dist(\tilde{v}_p, \tilde{v}_j)\}, \quad (5)$$

where $dist(\tilde{v}_p, \tilde{v}_j)$ denotes shortest path distance between two virtual nodes $\tilde{v}_p$ and $\tilde{v}_j$ in the label-enhanced graph. We explain Eq. (5) as follows. The optimal route w.r.t. the state $(\tilde{v}_i, \tilde{v}_j, \bar{X})$ can be obtained by expanding the optimal sub-route w.r.t. the state $(\tilde{v}_i, \tilde{v}_p, \bar{X} \backslash \{j\})$ with a path $\tilde{v}_p \sim \tilde{v}_j$. Initially, we have $W(\tilde{v}_i, \tilde{v}_i, \{\tilde{v}_i\}) = 0$, for all $\tilde{v}_i \in V_P$.

By Eq. (5), we can implement the DP algorithm using the best-first search strategy. Algorithm 3 details the DP algorithm. By invoking Algorithm 3, we can compute $W(\tilde{v}_i, \tilde{v}_j, \bar{X})$ for all $i, j \in \bar{X}$ and $\bar{X} \subseteq P$. Below, we analyze the complexity of Algorithm 3.

THEOREM 3. *The time and space complexity of Algorithm 3 is* $O(2^k k^3 + k(m + n \log n))$ *and* $O(2^k k^2 + n + m)$ *respectively, where* $k = |P|$ *is the number of given labels.*

PROOF. First, the shortest paths for all pairs $(\tilde{v}_j, \tilde{v}_p)$ can be pre-computed in $O(k(m + n \log n))$ time using the Dijkstra algorithm with a Fibonacci heap. Second, there are $2^k k^2$ states in total, thus the total cost for popping the top element from the priority queue is $O(2^k k^2 \log(2^k k^2)) = O(2^k k^3)$ using the Fibonacci heap (line 7). Also, for each state, the cost used in lines 10-15 is $O(k)$ using the Fibonacci heap and pre-computed shortest-path distances. Therefore, the total cost used in lines 10-15 is

Algorithm 3 AllPaths(G, P)

```
Q ← ∅; D ← ∅;
for all p ∈ P do
    Create a virtual node ṽ_p for p;
    Create an edge (ṽ_p, v) with zero weight for each v ∈ V including a label p;
    Q.push((ṽ_p, ṽ_p, {ṽ_p}), 0);
while Q ≠ ∅ do
    ((ṽ_i, ṽ_j, X̄), cost) ← Q.pop();
    W(ṽ_i, ṽ_j, X̄) ← cost;
    D ← D ∪ {(ṽ_i, ṽ_j, X̄)};
    for all p ∈ P and p ∉ X̄ do
        X̃ ← X̄ ∪ {p};
        cost~ ← cost + dist(ṽ_j, ṽ_p);
        if (ṽ_i, ṽ_p, X̃) ∈ D then continue;
        if (ṽ_i, ṽ_p, X̃) ∉ Q then Q.push((ṽ_i, ṽ_p, X̃), cost~);
        if cost~ < Q.cost(ṽ_i, ṽ_p, X̃) then Q.update((ṽ_i, ṽ_p, X̃), cost~);
```

$O(2^k k^3)$. Putting it all together, the time complexity of Algorithm 3 is $O(2^k k^3 + k(m + n \log n))$. For the space complexity, we need to maintain the priority queue $\mathcal{Q}$ and the set of all the computed states D which takes $O(2^k k^2)$. We also need to maintain the graph and the all-pair shortest-path distances between the virtual nodes which take $O(m + n + k^2)$ in total. As a result, the space complexity of Algorithm 3 is $O(2^k k^2 + n + m)$. □

It is worth mentioning that for a given query P, we can first invoke Algorithm 3 to pre-compute all the $W(\tilde{v}_i, \tilde{v}_j, \bar{X})$ for all $i, j \in \bar{X}$ and $\bar{X} \subseteq P$ in $O(2^k k^3 + k(m + n \log n))$ time. Moreover, the shortest-path distances $dist(v, \tilde{v}_i)$ and $dist(\tilde{v}_j, v)$ can also be pre-computed within $O(k(m + n \log n))$ time by invoking the Dijkstra algorithm. Consequently, for each state (v, X), we can compute $\pi_{t_1}(v, X)$ in $O(|\bar{X}|)$ time by Eq. (3) and Eq. (4).

Note that the first type of tour-based lower bound needs to find the minimum-weight tour over all virtual-node pairs $(\tilde{v}_i, \tilde{v}_j)$. Below, we propose the second type of tour-based lower bound, which does not take a minimum operation over all virtual-node pairs.

Let $R(\tilde{v}_i, \bar{X})$ be the minimum-weight route that starts from $\tilde{v}_i$ and passes through all virtual nodes in $V_{\bar{X}}$. Further, we let $W(\tilde{v}_i, \bar{X})$ be the weight of the route $R(\tilde{v}_i, \bar{X})$. Then, for a state (v, X), we construct the second type of the tour-based lower bound, denoted by $\pi_{t_2}(v, X)$, using the following formula.

$$\pi_{t_2}(v, X) \triangleq \max_{i \in \bar{X}} \{(dist(v, \tilde{v}_i) + W(\tilde{v}_i, \bar{X}) + \min_{j \in \bar{X}} \{dist(\tilde{v}_j, v)\})\}/2. \quad (6)$$

Eq. (6) includes three parts: (i) the shortest-path distance between the node v to a virtual node $\tilde{v}_i$, (ii) the route $R(\tilde{v}_i, \bar{X})$, and (iii) the minimum shortest-path distance between the virtual nodes in $V_{\bar{X}}$ to the node v. The second type of tour-based lower bound is constructed by taking the maximum weight of the sum over these three parts for all $\tilde{v}_i \in V_{\bar{X}}$. Fig. 3 illustrates the idea of this tour-based lower bound, where $dist(\tilde{v}_a, v) = \min_{j \in \bar{X}} \{dist(\tilde{v}_j, v)\}$. It should be noted that the end point of the route $R(\tilde{v}_i, \bar{X})$ could be any node in $V_{\bar{X}}$. The following lemma shows that $\pi_{t_2}(v, X)$ is indeed a valid lower bound.

LEMMA 3. *For any state* (v, X), *we have* $\pi_{t_2}(v, X) \leq f^*_T(v, \bar{X})$.

To compute $\pi_{t_2}(v, X)$, we can adopt a similar method as used for computing $\pi_{t_1}(v, X)$. Specifically, on the one hand, all the shortest-path distances in Eq. (6) can be pre-computed. On the other hand, we have $W(\tilde{v}_i, \bar{X}) = \min_{j \in \bar{X}} \{W(\tilde{v}_i, \tilde{v}_j, \bar{X})\}$ by definition. Thus, all $W(\tilde{v}_i, \bar{X})$ can also be pre-computed via invoking Algorithm 3. As a result, for each state (v, X), we are able to calculate $\pi_{t_2}(v, X)$ in $O(|\bar{X}|)$ time.

Compared to $\pi_{t_1}(v, X)$, the lower bound $\pi_{t_2}(v, X)$ does not take a minimum operation over all virtual-node pairs. Instead, it takes a maximum operation over all $\tilde{v}_i \in V_{\bar{X}}$. Theoretically, it is very hard to compare the performance of these two lower bounds. In practice, we can combine $\pi_{t_1}(v, X)$ and $\pi_{t_2}(v, X)$ by taking the maximum operation to obtain a better tour-based lower bound $\pi_t(v, X)$, i.e., $\pi_t(v, X) = \max\{\pi_{t_1}(v, X), \pi_{t_2}(v, X)\}$. In addition, we can further combine the one-label and tour-based lower bounds to achieve a better lower bound by taking the maximum operation. Let $\pi(v, X) = \max\{\pi_1(v, X), \pi_t(v, X)\}$, then we have the following lemma.

LEMMA 4. *For any state* (v, X), *we have* $\pi(v, X) \leq f^*_T(v, \bar{X})$.

4.2 The PrunedDP++ algorithm

Armed with the above lower bounds, we are ready to design the PrunedDP++ algorithm, which finds progressively-refined feasible solutions using A^*-search over the pruned search space. Specifically, PrunedDP++ is built on the PrunedDP algorithm. But unlike PrunedDP, PrunedDP++ makes use of $f^*_T(v, X) + \pi(v, X)$ as the priority for each state (v, X) to perform best-first search, where $\pi(v, X)$ is the combined lower bound developed in Section 4.1. Based on such an A^*-search strategy, PrunedDP++ can always select the most promising state to expand, and thus a large number of unpromising states can be pruned. In the experiments, we will show that PrunedDP++ is at least one order of magnitude faster than PrunedDP. The detailed implementation of PrunedDP++ is outlined in Algorithm 4.

The PrunedDP++ algorithm first invokes Algorithm 3 to compute $W(\tilde{v}_i, \tilde{v}_j, \bar{X})$ and $W(\tilde{v}_i, \bar{X})$ for all $\tilde{v}_i, \tilde{v}_j \in V_{\bar{X}}$ and $\bar{X} \subseteq P$ (line 1). Then, the algorithm initializes the priority queue $\mathcal{Q}$ and the set $\mathcal{D}$, and performs the best-first search using the A^*-search strategy (lines 3-26). Note that in Algorithm 4, each state (v, X) is represented by a tuple $((v, X), cost, lb)$, where $cost$ and lb denote the weight and the priority of the state (v, X) respectively. For each state (v, X), lb is obtained by the sum of the weight and the lower bound of that state (i.e., $cost + \pi(v, X)$) in terms of the A^*-search strategy. In Algorithm 4, the lower bound $\pi(v, X)$ and priority lb can be computed by invoking the lb procedure (lines 37-47).

The algorithm also applies the same method as used in Basic and PrunedDP to generate progressively-refined feasible solutions. Unlike Basic and PrunedDP, for any feasible solution constructed by the state (v, X) in PrunedDP++, we can report $f_{\tilde{T}}(v, P)/(f^*_T(v, X) + \pi(v, X))$ as the approximation ratio, because $f^*_T(v, X) + \pi(v, X)$ is a lower bound of the optimal solution by the best-first search strategy. The general framework of PrunedDP++ is very similar to that of PrunedDP, thus we omit the details.

The major differences between PrunedDP++ and PrunedDP are twofold. First, for each state (v, X), PrunedDP++ uses the sum of the weight and the lower bound as the priority, whereas PrunedDP only adopts the weight as the priority. Second, in the update procedure (lines 28-36), PrunedDP++ needs to invoke the lb procedure (lines 37-47) to compute the lower bound and the priority of the expanded state (line 30), and then determines whether the state can be pruned or not (line 32). If the state cannot be pruned, the algorithm needs to update the weight and the lower bound (or the priority) of the state (line 35-36). The PrunedDP algorithm, however, does not need to compute and update the lower bound. In addition, it is important to note that in line 31 of Algorithm 4, for each expanded state, the algorithm must take the maximum over the computed lb and the lb of its parent state, to ensure the *consistency* of the lower bound. After this process, the correctness of the algorithm can be guaranteed, which will be analyzed in the following.

Algorithm 4 PrunedDP++(G, P, S)

Input: $G = (V, E)$, label set S, and the query label set P.
Output: the minimum weight of the connected tree that covers P.

1: AllPaths(G, P);
2: $best \leftarrow +\infty$; /* maintain the weight of the current feasible solution. */
3: $\mathcal{Q} \leftarrow \emptyset$; $\mathcal{D} \leftarrow \emptyset$;
4: **for all** $v \in V$ **do**
5:   **for all** $p \in S_v$ **do**
6:     $\mathcal{Q}.push((v, \{p\}), 0, \mathsf{lb}((v, \{p\}), 0, P)$; /* lb is the priority in $\mathcal{Q}$. */
7: **while** $\mathcal{Q} \neq \emptyset$ **do**
8:   $((v, X), cost, lb) \leftarrow \mathcal{Q}.pop()$; /* pop the minimum lb element. */
9:   **if** $X = P$ **then return** $best \leftarrow cost$;
10:   $\mathcal{D} \leftarrow \mathcal{D} \cup \{((v, X), cost)\}$; $\bar{X} \leftarrow P \backslash X$;
11:   $T'(v, \bar{X}) \leftarrow \emptyset$;
12:   **for all** $p \in \bar{X}$ **do**
13:     $T'(v, \bar{X}) \leftarrow T'(v, \bar{X}) \cup$ Shortest-Path$(v, \tilde{v}_p)$;
14:   $\tilde{T}(v, P) \leftarrow$ MST$(T'(v, \bar{X}) \cup T(v, X))$;
15:   $best \leftarrow \min\{best, f_{\tilde{T}}(v, P)\}$;
16:   Report the approximation ratio for $best$;
17:   **if** $(v, \bar{X}) \in \mathcal{D}$ **then**
18:     update$(\mathcal{Q}, \mathcal{D}, P, best, (v, P), cost + \mathcal{D}.cost(v, \bar{X}), lb)$;
19:     **continue**;
20:   **if** $cost < best/2$ **then**
21:     **for all** $(v, u) \in E$ **do**
22:       update$(\mathcal{Q}, \mathcal{D}, P, best, (u, X), cost + w(v, u), lb)$;
23:     **for all** $X' \subset \bar{X}$ **and** $(v, X') \in \mathcal{D}$ **do**
24:       $\overline{cost} \leftarrow \mathcal{D}.cost(v, X')$;
25:       **if** $cost + \overline{cost} \leq 2/3 \times best$ **then**
26:         update$(\mathcal{Q}, \mathcal{D}, P, best, (v, X' \cup X), cost + \overline{cost}, lb)$;
27: **return** $+\infty$;

28: **Procedure** update$(\mathcal{Q}, \mathcal{D}, P, best, (v, X), cost, \tilde{lb})$
29: **if** $(v, X) \in \mathcal{D}$ **then return**;
30: $lb \leftarrow \mathsf{lb}((v, X), cost, P)$;
31: $lb \leftarrow \max\{lb, \tilde{lb}\}$;
32: **if** $lb >= best$ **then return**;
33: **if** $X = P$ **then** $best \leftarrow \min\{best, cost\}$;
34: **if** $(v, X) \notin \mathcal{Q}$ **then** $\mathcal{Q}.push((v, X), cost, lb)$;
35: **if** $lb < \mathcal{Q}.lb((v, X))$ **then**
36:   $\mathcal{Q}.update((v, X), cost, lb)$; /* update both $cost$ and lb */

37: **Procedure** lb$((v, X), cost, P)$
38: $\bar{X} \leftarrow P \backslash X$;
39: **if** $\bar{X} = \emptyset$ **then**
40:   $lb \leftarrow 0$;
41: **else**
42:   $lb_1 \leftarrow \min_{i,j \in \bar{X}}\{(dist(v, \tilde{v}_i) + W(\tilde{v}_i, \tilde{v}_j, \bar{X}) + dist(\tilde{v}_j, v))\}/2$;
43:   $lb_2 \leftarrow \max_{i \in \bar{X}}\{(dist(u, \tilde{v}_i) + W(\tilde{v}_i, \bar{X}) + \min_{j \in \bar{X}}\{dist(\tilde{v}_j, u)\})\}/2$;
44:   $lb \leftarrow \max\{lb_1, lb_2\}$;
45: **for all** $p \in \bar{X}$ **do**
46:   $lb \leftarrow \max\{lb, dist(v, \tilde{v}_p)\}$;
47: **return** $cost + lb$;

Correctness analysis. Recall that the PrunedDP++ algorithm relies on two types of operations to expand a state (v, X): edge growing and tree merging. For the edge growing operation, we can obtain a successor state (u, X) by expanding an edge (v, u), while for the tree merging operation, we can get a successor state $(v, X \cup X')$ through merging with a state (v, X'). To show the correctness of PrunedDP++, we need to prove that the developed lower bounds satisfy the *consistent* property defined in the A^*-search theory [16, 7, 14] for these two state-expansion operations. Below, we first prove that $\pi_1(v, X)$ and $\pi_{t_1}(v, X)$ are consistent, and then we introduce a technique to make $\pi_{t_2}(v, X)$ consistent. Finally, we show that the combination of all these lower bounds is also consistent.

Specifically, Lemma 5 and Lemma 6 show that $\pi_1(v, X)$ and $\pi_{t_1}(v, X)$ are consistent, respectively.

LEMMA 5. *For any state (v, X), we have (i) $\pi_1(u, X) + w(v, u) \geq \pi_1(v, X)$, and (ii) $\pi_1(v, X \cup X') + f^*_T(v, X') \geq \pi_1(v, X)$, where $X \cap X' = \emptyset$.*

LEMMA 6. *For any state (v, X), we have (i) $\pi_{t_1}(u, X) + w(v, u) \geq \pi_{t_1}(v, X)$, and (ii) $\pi_{t_1}(v, X \cup X') + f^*_T(v, X') \geq \pi_{t_1}(v, X)$, where $X \cap X' = \emptyset$.*

Unfortunately, we find in the experiments that $\pi_{t_2}(v, X)$ is not consistent. However, we can use the following technique to make it consistent. In particular, for a state (v, X), let (u, X) and $(v, X \cup X')$ be its successor states by the edge growing and tree merging operations, respectively. Then, for the successor state (u, X), we set $\pi_{t_2}(u, X) = \max\{\pi_{t_2}(u, X), \pi_{t_2}(v, X) - w(v, u)\}$ as the new second type of tour-based lower bound. Likewise, for the successor state $(v, X \cup X')$, we set $\pi_{t_2}(v, X \cup X') = \max\{\pi_{t_2}(v, X \cup X'), \pi_{t_2}(v, X) - f^*_T(v, X')\}$. After this process, it is easy to verify that such a new tour-based lower bound is consistent. According to A^*-search theory, the consistent property also implies that the new bound is a valid lower bound [14]. For convenience, in the rest of this paper, we refer to this new lower bound as the second type of tour-based lower bound, and also denote it by $\pi_{t_2}(u, X)$. We notice that in A^*-search theory, a similar process for inconsistent lower bounds was applied in [26]. In Algorithm 4, we implement this process in line 31.

Finally, we show that the consistent property can be preserved by taking the maximum operation over all the devised consistent lower bounds. In particular, we have the following result.

LEMMA 7. *Let $\pi(v, X) = \max\{\pi_1(v, X), \pi_{t_1}(v, X), \pi_{t_2}(v, X)\}$. Then, for a state (v, X), we have (i) $\pi(u, X) + w(v, u) \geq \pi(v, X)$, and (ii) $\pi(v, X \cup X') + f^*_T(v, X') \geq \pi(v, X)$, where $X \cap X' = \emptyset$.*

Armed with Lemmas 5, 6, and 7, we conclude that Algorithm 4 can find the optimal solution for the GST problem by the optimality of the A^*-search theory [16, 7].

Cost analysis. Note that the worst-case time and space complexity of PrunedDP++ are no higher than those of the PrunedDP algorithm. In the experiments, we show that the PrunedDP++ algorithm can achieve at least one order of magnitude acceleration over the PrunedDP algorithm, using much less memory. This is because in the PrunedDP++ algorithm, the lb in line 32 of Algorithm 4 can be much larger than the weight used in PrunedDP. Moreover, lb increases as the algorithm searches more of search space. On the other hand, the weight of the best feasible solution $best$ progressively decreases, thus the pruning power of our algorithm becomes increasingly strong. If both lb and $best$ are close to optimal, most of the unpromising states will be pruned by our algorithm (line 32). Therefore, compared to PrunedDP, PrunedDP++ will generate a much smaller number of states, and thus both the time and space overhead will be drastically reduced.

Remark. Note that some applications may require to find r connected trees with smallest weight (r is typically very small, e.g., $r \leq 50$). As discussed in [8], the parameterized DP algorithm can be adapted to find the top-r results. Specifically, the algorithm first finds the top-1 result, followed by top-2, top-3, and so on. Clearly, such an algorithm is rather costly, because it is expensive even for finding the top-1 result as analyzed in Section 2. Unlike the parameterized DP algorithm, all the proposed algorithms report progressively-refined results during execution, and the top-1 result is found until algorithms terminate. In the experiments, we find that our algorithms report many near-optimal solutions during execution, and thus we can select the best r results among them as the approximate top-r results. On the other hand, an efficient algorithm for finding the top-1 GST is sufficient for identifying the top-r GST with polynomial delay as shown in [21]. Thus, we can also apply the framework proposed in [21] to extend our algorithms to find the exact top-r results. As a consequence, we believe that our algorithms are also very useful for the applications that require to identify top-r results, albeit we mainly focus on finding the top-1 result (i.e., the minimum-weight connected tree) in this paper.

5. EXPERIMENTS

In this section, we conduct comprehensive experiments to evaluate the proposed algorithms. We implement four various progressive algorithms: Basic (Algorithm 1); PrunedDP (Algorithm 2); PrunedDP+, an A^*-search algorithm based on PrunedDP and the one-label lower bound; and PrunedDP++ (Algorithm 4). For a fair comparison, we use Basic as the baseline, because it produces progressively-refined results, and also is more efficient than the state-of-the-art parameterized DP algorithm, as discussed in Section 3.1. We evaluate the average query processing time, the average memory consumption, and the progressive performance of all algorithms. In all the experiments, the reported query processing time includes the time to pre-compute the shortest paths from each virtual node to the other nodes and the time to pre-compute $W(\tilde{v}_i, \tilde{v}_j, \bar{X})$ by invoking Algorithm 3. We only report the memory allocated for query processing as the memory overhead, without including the memory used to store the graph, because the graph size remains constant for all queries. In addition, we also implement BANKS-II [19], which is the widely-used approximation algorithm for GST search in the keyword search application, to compare the performance between our exact algorithms and existing approximation algorithms. All the experiments are conducted on a machine with two 3.46GHz Intel Xeon CPUs and 96GB main memory running Red Had Enterprise Linux 6.4 (64-bit), and all the algorithms are implemented in C++.

Datasets. We use two large scale real-world datasets, DBLP[1] and IMDB[2], which are two widely-used datasets for keyword search in graphs [8]. The DBLP dataset contains $15,825,211$ nodes and $19,609,604$ edges, while the IMDB datasets includes $30,407,193$ nodes and $46,971,820$ edges. Each node in these datasets consists of a set of labels (or keywords). Our main goal is to evaluate the performance of the GST search algorithms on these datasets. We also perform case studies on these datasets to evaluate the effectiveness of the proposed methods in the keyword search application.

Parameters and query generation. We vary two parameters in our experiments, namely, knum and kwf. knum is the number of labels in the query P (i.e., knum $= |P|$), and kwf is the average number of nodes containing each label in the query (i.e., the label frequency). knum is selected from 5, 6, 7, and 8 with a default value of 6, and kwf is selected from 200, 400, 800, and 1600 with a default value of 400. Unless otherwise specified, when varying a parameter, the values of the other parameters are set to their default values. Each query is generated by randomly selecting knum labels from the label set. In each test, we randomly generate 50 queries and report the average results over all of them.

We mainly perform six different experiments based on the above setting. In the first three experiments, we intend to test the query processing time and memory usage of various algorithms in a progressive manner. We vary the approximation ratio from 8 to 1 for each algorithm and report the average time/memory consumption with a decreasing approximation ratio during algorithm execution. In the fourth experiment, we aim to evaluate the progressive performance of various algorithms. In the last two experiments, we compare our best algorithm with the approximation algorithm BANKS-II, and conduct case studies to show the effectiveness of our approaches in the keyword search application. Additionally, we test the performance of our algorithms on graphs with different topologies, and also show the performance of our best algorithm for relatively large knum values. Due to space limit, these two additional experiments are reported in Appendix A.2.

Exp-1: Query processing time (vary knum). In this experiment, we vary knum from 5 to 8 and test the processing time of various algorithms with a decreasing approximation ratio. The results for the DBLP and IMDB datasets are shown in Fig. 4 and Fig. 5 respectively. Since the results on these two datasets are very similar, we focus on describing the results on the DBLP dataset. Specifically, from Fig. 4, we make the following observations.

First, all algorithms take a certain amount of initialization time to pre-compute the shortest paths from each virtual node to all the nodes in the graph, before reporting a feasible solution. PrunedDP++ also spends time pre-computing all $W(\tilde{v}_i, \tilde{v}_j, \bar{X})$ by invoking Algorithm 3. The initialization time increases when knum increases. The time to compute all $W(\tilde{v}_i, \tilde{v}_j, \bar{X})$ in PrunedDP++ can almost be omitted because such time cost is independent of the graph size as shown in Section 4.1.

Second, the approximation ratio for each algorithm becomes better when more time is spent, until it finally reaches 1, which indicates that the optimal solution has been found. The processing time of Basic and PrunedDP are very similar when the approximation ratio is larger than 2 because, in PrunedDP, the weight of most intermediate states cannot reach $f^*(P)/2$ and they apply the same process to compute the weights of those states. However, when the approximation ratio becomes smaller, the processing time of Basic increases sharply, while the processing time of PrunedDP becomes stable. PrunedDP+ shows significant improvement over PrunedDP using the A^*-search strategy, and PrunedDP++ makes further improvement over PrunedDP+ using the novel tour-based lower bounding techniques. For example, when knum $= 6$, Basic, PrunedDP, PrunedDP+, and PrunedDP++ take 732.4 seconds, 75.5 seconds, 22.2 seconds, and 7.1 seconds respectively to find the optimal solution as shown in Fig. 4 (b). In general, PrunedDP++ is more than one order of magnitude faster than PrunedDP and more than two orders of magnitude faster than Basic. These results are consistent with our theoretical analysis in Sections 3 and 4.

Finally, to achieve a certain approximation ratio, the processing time for each algorithm increases with increasing knum. Taking PrunedDP as an example, to achieve an approximation ratio of 1 for knum $= 5, 6, 7, 8$, the algorithm spends 34.1 seconds (Fig. 4 (a)), 75.5 seconds (Fig. 4 (b)), 404.7 seconds (Fig. 4 (c)) , and 750.9 seconds (Fig. 4 (d)) respectively. When knum increases, the gap between PrunedDP++ and PrunedDP+ increases and the gap between PrunedDP+ and PrunedDP decreases. This is because when knum increases, the lower bound used in PrunedDP+ tends to be more loose, which degrades the performance of the PrunedDP+ algorithm.

Exp-2: Query processing time (vary kwf). In this experiment, we vary kwf from 200 to 1600, and test the processing time with a decreasing approximation ratio. The results on the DBLP and IMDB datasets are reported in Fig. 6 and Fig. 7 respectively. Again, the results on these datasets are very similar, so we focus on describing the results on the DBLP dataset. From Fig. 6, we make the following observations: First, when kwf increases, the processing time of Basic, PrunedDP, and PrunedDP+ tend to decrease. The reason is that when kwf is small, the weight of the optimal tree tends to be large, which may result in longer processing time for Basic, PrunedDP, and PrunedDP+. For example, when kwf decreases from 1600 to 200, to achieve an approximation ratio of 1, the processing time of PrunedDP increases from 55.3 seconds to 141.5 seconds. However, the performance of PrunedDP++ is not largely influenced by kwf of the query due to the effective tour-based lower bounding techniques. Second, when kwf increases, the gap between PrunedDP+ and PrunedDP++ decreases. For example, for kwf $= 200, 400, 800$, and 1600, to achieve an approximation ratio of 1, the processing time of PrunedDP+ is 10 times (Fig. 6 (a)), 3 times (Fig. 6 (b)), 2.5 times (Fig. 6 (c)), and 1.4 times (Fig. 6 (d)) of that of PrunedDP++, respectively. The reason is that, when kwf increases, the lower bound computed by PrunedDP+ tends

[1] http://dblp.dagstuhl.de/xml/

[2] http://www.imdb.com/interfaces/

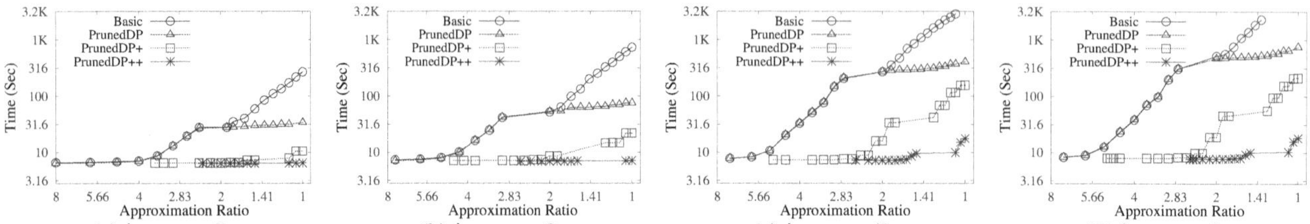

(a) knum = 5 (b) knum = 6 (c) knum = 7 (d) knum = 8

Figure 4: Query Processing Time vs. Approximation Ratio: Vary Number of Labels (knum) on DBLP

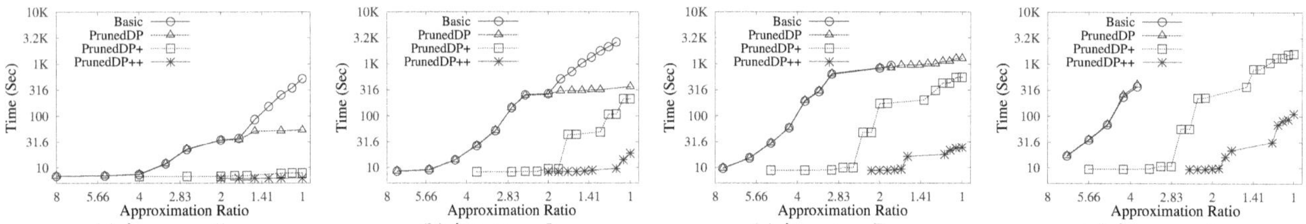

(a) knum = 5 (b) knum = 6 (c) knum = 7 (d) knum = 8

Figure 5: Query Processing Time vs. Approximation Ratio: Vary Number of Labels (knum) on IMDB

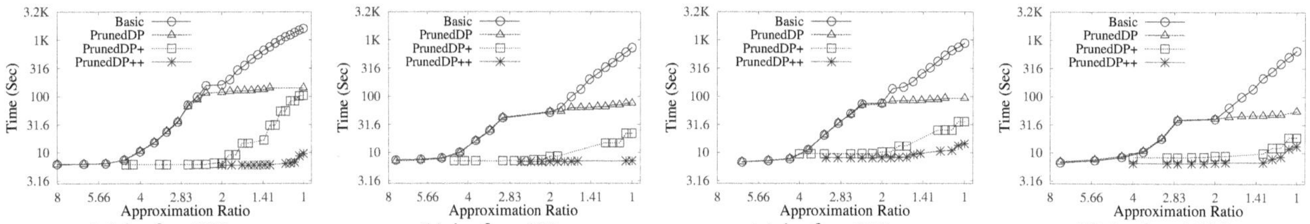

(a) kwf = 200 (b) kwf = 400 (c) kwf = 800 (d) kwf = 1600

Figure 6: Query Processing Time vs. Approximation Ratio: Vary Label Frequency (kwf) on DBLP

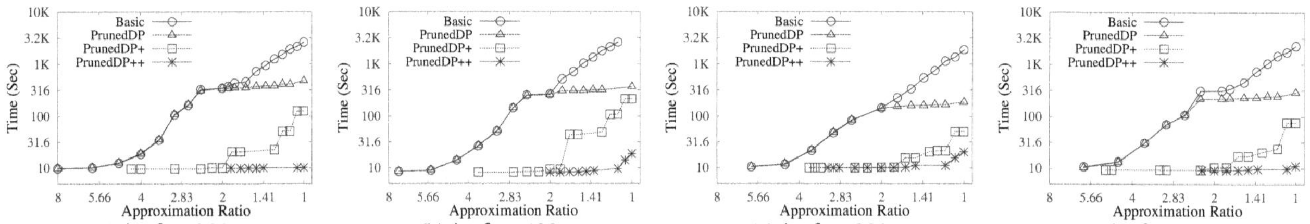

(a) kwf = 200 (b) kwf = 400 (c) kwf = 800 (d) kwf = 1600

Figure 7: Query Processing Time vs. Approximation Ratio: Vary Label Frequency (kwf) on IMDB

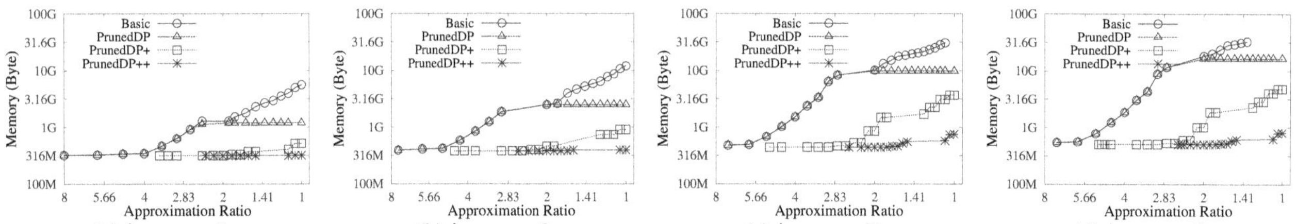

(a) knum = 5 (b) knum = 6 (c) knum = 7 (d) knum = 8

Figure 8: Memory Overhead vs. Approximation Ratio: Vary Number of Labels (knum) on DBLP

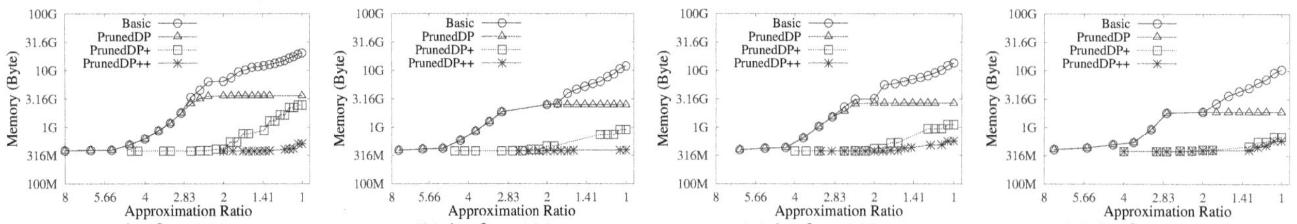

(a) kwf = 200 (b) kwf = 400 (c) kwf = 800 (d) kwf = 1600

Figure 9: Memory Overhead vs. Approximation Ratio: Vary Label Frequency (kwf) on DBLP

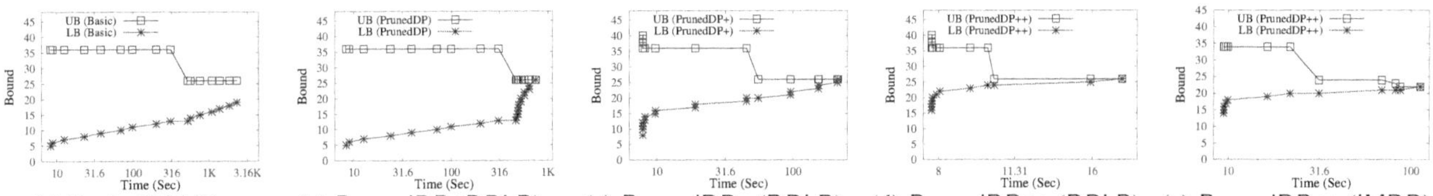

(a) Basic (DBLP) (b) PrunedDP (DBLP) (c) PrunedDP+ (DBLP) (d) PrunedDP++ (DBLP) (e) PrunedDP++ (IMDB)

Figure 10: Progressive Performance Testing (knum $= 8$, kwf $= 400$)

knum	kwf	Total Time BANKS-II	Appro Ratio BANKS-II	Total Time PrunedDP++	T_r PrunedDP++
5	400	88.0 secs	1.22	6.5 secs	6.4 secs
6	400	109.1 secs	1.40	7.1 secs	7.1 secs
7	400	131.2 secs	1.31	17.8 secs	9.9 secs
8	400	162.4 secs	1.38	18.4 secs	7.8 secs
6	200	110.8 secs	1.07	9.6 secs	6.4 secs
6	800	109.0 secs	1.20	14.4 secs	10.7 secs
6	1,600	109.1 secs	1.25	13.2 secs	6.8 secs

Table 2: Comparison with BANKS-II on DBLP

to be tighter and tighter, and thus the bounds of PrunedDP+ and PrunedDP++ tend to be similar.

Exp-3: Memory consumption. In this experiment, we evaluate the memory overhead of all the algorithms with a decreasing approximation ratio. To this end, we vary the parameters knum from 5 to 8 and kwf from 200 to 1600, respectively. We test all the algorithms on the DBLP dataset, and similar results can also be observed on the IMDB dataset. Fig. 8 and Fig. 9 depict the results with varying knum from 5 to 8 and varying kwf from 200 to 1600, respectively. Compared to Fig. 4 and Fig. 6, the curves for memory consumption for all the algorithms are very similar to those for query processing time under the same parameter settings. This is because both the memory and time overhead for each algorithm are roughly proportional to the number of states generated and, unsurprisingly, the curves are similar. In addition, PrunedDP++ uses less than 1GB memory to find the optimal solution even when knum =8. In the same setting, PrunedDP+ uses around 3.16GB memory and PrunedDP uses more than 10GB memory. The baseline algorithm (Basic) performs even worse, using more than 31.6GB memory to obtain a 1.41-approximation solution (see Fig. 8(e)). These results show that PrunedDP++ is indeed much more memory-efficient than the other algorithms.

Exp-4: Progressive Performance Testing. In this experiment, we test how well the reported feasible solutions are progressively improved during algorithm execution. To this end, we report the lower bounds denoted by LB and the weights of the feasible solutions denoted by UB (because it is an upper bound of the optimal solution) when a feasible solution is generated for all the algorithms. We set knum $=$ 8 and kwf $=$ 400, and similar results can also be obtained for the other values of knum and kwf. The results are shown in Fig. 10. As desired, for each algorithm, we can see that LB monotonically increases and UB monotonically decreases with increasing running time. In general, for each algorithm, the gap between the reported LB and UB becomes smaller with increasing running time. Clearly, if such a gap closes, the algorithm has found the optimal solution. However, the gap for the Basic algorithm (Fig. 10(a)) is relatively large compared to the other algorithms. Moreover, it dose not close within the one-hour time limit on the DBLP dataset. The gap between LB and UB for the PrunedDP algorithm (Fig. 10(b)) quickly closes on the DBLP dataset when the running time is larger than 316 seconds. The reason is as follows. After 316 seconds, the weight of most states in the PrunedDP algorithm may reach $f^*(P)/2$, thus such states will not be further expanded by the algorithm. As a consequence, the optimal solution can be quickly generated by merging these states. These results indicate that the PrunedDP algorithm exhibits much better progressive performance than the baseline algorithm. Furthermore, as can be seen from Fig. 10(c) and Fig. 10(d), PrunedDP+ shows much better progressive performance than PrunedDP, and PrunedDP++ can further achieve significant performance improvement over PrunedDP+ on the DBLP dataset. For example, the PrunedDP++ algorithm quickly narrows the gap between LB and UB in less than 10 seconds, and closes the gap within 20 seconds, whereas the PrunedDP+ algorithm does not close the gap in 100 seconds. We also show the result of PrunedDP++ on the IMDB dataset in Fig. 10(e). As can be seen, the PrunedDP++ algorithm results in a 2-approximation solution within 10 seconds, finds a near-optimal solution within 31.6 seconds, and obtains the optimal solution taking around 110 seconds. These results demonstrate that the PrunedDP++ algorithm exhibits excellent progressive performance in practice, which further confirm our theoretical findings.

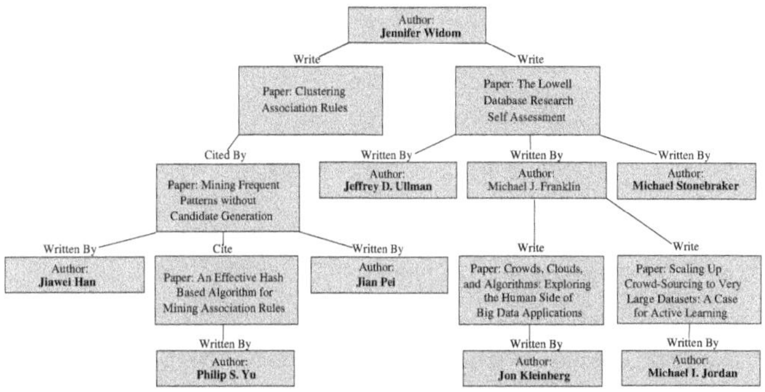

Figure 11: Case Study on DBLP using PrunedDP++ (knum $=$ 8, Processing Time $= 7.5$ Seconds)

Exp-5: Comparison with the Approximation Algorithm. In this experiment, we compare PrunedDP++ with the approximation algorithm BANKS-II [19]. We report the processing time of BANKS-II and PrunedDP++, as well as the approximation ratio of the best answer reported by BANKS-II. Since PrunedDP++ reports answers in a progressive manner, we also report the processing time of PrunedDP++ to generate an answer with at least the same quality as BANKS-II, and we denote such processing time as T_r. The results on the DBLP dataset are shown in Table 2, and similar results on IMDB dataset are shown in Appendix A.2. We test 7 different combinations of knum and kwf. As can be seen, PrunedDP++ is 7.4 to 15.4 times faster than BANKS-II, because BANKS-II typically needs to explore the whole graph to get an approximate answer while PrunedDP++ visits only a part of the graph to output the optimal answer. For example, with the default parameter setting (knum $=$ 6 and kwf $=$ 400), BANKS-II computes an 1.4-approximate answer in 109.1 seconds while PrunedDP++ outputs the optimal answer taking only 7.1 seconds. When knum $=$ 8, although PrunedDP++ requires 18.4 seconds to get the optimal answer, it only needs 7.8 seconds to obtain the answer with at least the same quality as the answer returned by BANKS-II. In this case, PrunedDP++ is 20.8 times faster than BANKS-II to generate the answer with the same quality.

Exp-6: Case Study. In this experiment, we conduct a case study on the DBLP dataset to compare the effectiveness of the exact GST computed by PrunedDP++ and the approximate GST calculated

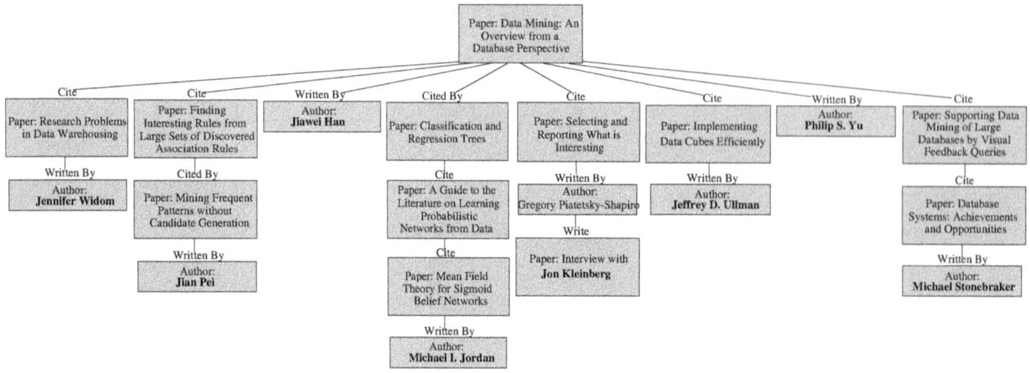

Figure 12: Case Study on DBLP using BANKS-II (knum $= 8$, Processing Time $= 151.6$ Seconds)

by the approximation algorithm BANKS-II [19]. An additional case study on the IMDB dataset can be found in Appendix A.2. We use the query $P = \{$"Jiawei Han", "Philip S. Yu", "Jeffrey D. Ullman", "Jian Pei", "Jennifer Widom", "Michael Stonebraker", "Jon Kleinberg", "Michael I. Jordan"$\}$, which includes 8 professor names. The answer reported by PrunedDP++ (taking 7.5 seconds) is shown in Fig. 11. As can be seen, the answer contains 14 edges, and the 8 professors are divided into two subgroups. The first subgroup contains "Jiawei Han", "Philip S. Yu", and "Jian Pei", in which "Jiawei Han" and "Jian Pei" collaboratively write a paper which cites a paper written by "Philip S. Yu". The second subgroup contains "Jeffrey D. Ullman", "Michael Stonebraker", 'Jon Kleinberg", "Michael I. Jordan", and "Jennifer Widom", in which "Jon Kleinberg" and "Michael I. Jordan" each collaborates with another professor "Michael J. Franklin" who further collaborates with "Jeffrey D. Ullman", "Michael Stonebraker", and "Jennifer Widom". The two subgroups are connected by "Jennifer Widom". The answer reported by BANKS-II (taking 151.6 seconds) is shown in Fig. 12. In this answer, a paper written by "Jiawei Han" and "Philip S. Yu" cites another five papers which is directly/indirectly related to five professor names in P, and there are 19 edges in total. Such a result does not exhibit any subgroup information. Obviously, the answer reported by PrunedDP++ is more compact and better captures the relationship among the 8 authors in P than the answer returned by BANKS-II. These results confirm the effectiveness of our approaches for the keyword search application.

6. RELATED WORK

The GST problem and its applications. The GST problem is a generalization of the traditional Steiner tree problem which was introduced by Reich and Widmayer in [28], motivated by an application in VLSI design. Recently, the GST problem has been widely used to keyword search in the database community [3, 19, 8], and it has also been applied to search for a team of experts in a social network [22]. From a computational point of view, the GST problem is known to be NP-hard [28]. In [18], Ihler showed that the GST problem cannot be approximated within a constant performance ratio by any polynomial algorithm unless P=NP. The lower bound of the approximation ratio is known to be $O(\ln k)$ [12], where k denotes the number of groups. The polylogarithmic approximation algorithms for the GST problem were obtained in [5, 13] based on the technique of linear programming relaxation. However, such approximation algorithms are very hard to handle large graphs, due to the high computational overhead of linear programming. To solve the GST problem optimally, Ding et al. [8] proposed a parameterized DP algorithm using the number of groups k as a parameter, which is a generalization of the well-known Dreyfus-Wagner algorithm for the traditional Steiner tree problem [9]. The parameterized DP algorithm was shown to be efficient for handling large graphs when the parameter k is very small (e.g., $k = 4$) [8]. However, the parameterized DP algorithm cannot provide progressively-refined solutions and it only works well for very small k values. Instead, in this paper, we propose several efficient and progressive algorithms to solve the GST problem. Our best algorithm is shown to be at least two orders of magnitude faster than the parameterized DP algorithm, using much less memory.

Anytime algorithms. Our work is also closely related to the anytime algorithms that have been studied in artificial intelligent and data mining communities [27, 32, 15, 29, 4]. For example, Mouaddib and Zilberstein [27] studied a knowledge-based anytime algorithm for real-time decision making applications. Hansen and Zhou [15] proposed an anytime heuristic search algorithm based on the technique of weighted heuristic search algorithm. Ueno et al. [29] proposed an anytime nearest neighbor classification algorithm for stream mining. Esmeir and Markovitch [10] studied an anytime decision tree induction algorithm for classification task. Mai et al. [4] proposed an anytime density-based clustering algorithm based on a lower-bounding technique for the similarity measure. Generally, all the above anytime algorithms are algorithms that can be terminated at any time to return an intermediate solution, and the quality of the intermediate solution can be improved progressively. However, unlike our progressive GST algorithm, all the above mentioned anytime algorithms do not focus on graph data. To the best of our knowledge, this is the first work to study progressive algorithms for the GST problem over large-scale graph data. It is worth mentioning that progressive algorithms were also studied in the computational geometry and database communities. For example, in [31], Zhang et al. proposed a progressive algorithm for computing the optimal location query problem in spatial databases. Alewijnes et al. [1] proposed several progressive algorithms for computational geometric problems. Once again, all of those algorithms do not focus on graph data. In addition, the term of progressive algorithms were also used in keyword search literature [23, 24]. However, substantially different from our progressive search algorithm, the algorithms proposed in [23, 24] are based on the classic threshold algorithm [11] to progressively identify the top-r answers.

7. CONCLUSION

In this paper, we first propose an efficient and progressive algorithm, called PrunedDP, based on two novel optimal-tree decomposition and conditional tree merging techniques. The PrunedDP algorithm is not only able to produce progressively-refined results during algorithm execution, but it is also one order of magnitude faster than the state-of-the-art algorithm. Second, to further speed up the PrunedDP algorithm, we propose a progressive A^*-search algorithm, named PrunedDP++, which can achieve at least one order of magnitude acceleration over the PrunedDP algorithm. Finally, we conduct extensive performance studies over several large-scale graphs (≥ 10 million nodes), and the results demonstrate the high efficiency and effectiveness, as well as excellent progressive performance of the proposed algorithms.

8. REFERENCES

[1] S. P. A. Alewijnse, T. M. Bagautdinov, M. de Berg, Q. W. Bouts, A. P. ten Brink, K. Buchin, and M. A. Westenberg. Progressive geometric algorithms. In *SOCG*, 2014.

[2] A. Anagnostopoulos, L. Becchetti, C. Castillo, A. Gionis, and S. Leonardi. Online team formation in social networks. In *WWW*, 2012.

[3] G. Bhalotia, A. Hulgeri, C. Nakhe, S. Chakrabarti, and S. Sudarshan. Keyword searching and browsing in databases using BANKS. In *ICDE*, 2002.

[4] C. Böhm, J. Feng, X. He, and S. T. Mai. Efficient anytime density-based clustering. In *SDM*, 2013.

[5] M. Charikar, C. Chekuri, A. Goel, and S. Guha. Rounding via trees: Deterministic approximation algorithms for group steiner trees and *k*-median. In *STOC*, 1998.

[6] J. Coffman and A. C. Weaver. An empirical performance evaluation of relational keyword search techniques. *IEEE Trans. Knowl. Data Eng.*, 26(1):30–42, 2014.

[7] R. Dechter and J. Pearl. Generalized best-first search strategies and the optimality of A*. *Journal of the ACM*, 32(3):505–536, 1985.

[8] B. Ding, J. X. Yu, S. Wang, L. Qin, X. Zhang, and X. Lin. Finding top-k min-cost connected trees in databases. In *ICDE*, 2007.

[9] S. E. Dreyfus and R. A. Wagner. The steiner problem in graphs. *Networks*, 1(3):195–207, 1971.

[10] S. Esmeir and S. Markovitch. Anytime induction of decision trees: An iterative improvement approach. In *AAAI*, 2006.

[11] R. Fagin, A. Lotem, and M. Naor. Optimal aggregation algorithms for middleware. *J. Comput. Syst. Sci.*, 66(4):614–656, 2003.

[12] U. Feige. A threshold of ln *n* for approximating set cover. *J. ACM*, 45(4):634–652, 1998.

[13] N. Garg, G. Konjevod, and R. Ravi. A polylogarithmic approximation algorithm for the group steiner tree problem. *J. Algorithms*, 37(1):66–84, 2000.

[14] A. V. Goldberg and C. Harrelson. Computing the shortest path: *A** search meets graph theory. In *SODA*, 2005.

[15] E. A. Hansen and R. Zhou. Anytime heuristic search. *J. Artif. Intell. Res. (JAIR)*, 28:267–297, 2007.

[16] P. E. Hart, N. J. Nilsson, and B. Raphael. A formal basis for the heuristic determination of minimum cost paths. *IEEE Trans. Systems Science and Cybernetics*, 4(2):100–107, 1968.

[17] H. He, H. Wang, J. Yang, and P. S. Yu. BLINKS: ranked keyword searches on graphs. In *SIGMOD*, 2007.

[18] E. Ihler. The complexity of approximating the class steiner tree problem. In *17th International Workshop, WG*, 1991.

[19] V. Kacholia, S. Pandit, S. Chakrabarti, S. Sudarshan, R. Desai, and H. Karambelkar. Bidirectional expansion for keyword search on graph databases. In *VLDB*, 2005.

[20] G. Kasneci, M. Ramanath, M. Sozio, F. M. Suchanek, and G. Weikum. STAR: steiner-tree approximation in relationship graphs. In *ICDE*, 2009.

[21] B. Kimelfeld and Y. Sagiv. Finding and approximating top-k answers in keyword proximity search. In *PODS*, 2006.

[22] T. Lappas, K. Liu, and E. Terzi. Finding a team of experts in social networks. In *KDD*, 2009.

[23] G. Li, C. Li, J. Feng, and L. Zhou. SAIL: structure-aware indexing for effective and progressive top-k keyword search over XML documents. *Inf. Sci.*, 179(21):3745–3762, 2009.

[24] G. Li, X. Zhou, J. Feng, and J. Wang. Progressive keyword search in relational databases. In *ICDE*, 2009.

[25] A. Majumder, S. Datta, and K. V. M. Naidu. Capacitated team formation problem on social networks. In *KDD*, 2012.

[26] L. Mero. A heuristic search algorithm with modifiable estimate. *Artificial Intelligence*, 23(1):13–27, 1984.

[27] A. Mouaddib and S. Zilberstein. Knowledge-based anytime computation. In *IJCAI*, 1995.

[28] G. Reich and P. Widmayer. Beyond steiner's problem: A VLSI oriented generalization. In *15th International Workshop, WG*, 1989.

[29] K. Ueno, X. Xi, E. J. Keogh, and D. Lee. Anytime classification using the nearest neighbor algorithm with applications to stream mining. In *ICDM*, 2006.

[30] X. Wang, Z. Zhao, and W. Ng. A comparative study of team formation in social networks. In *DASFAA*, 2015.

[31] D. Zhang, Y. Du, T. Xia, and Y. Tao. Progressive computation of the min-dist optimal-location query. In *VLDB*, 2006.

[32] S. Zilberstein. Using anytime algorithms in intelligent systems. *AI Magazine*, 17(3):73–83, 1996.

Acknowledgements. The work was supported in part by (i) NSFC Grants (61402292, U1301252, 61033009), NSF-Shenzhen Grants (JCYJ20150324140036826, JCYJ20140418095735561), and S-tartup Grant of Shenzhen Kongque Program (827/000065); (ii) AR-C DE140100999 and ARC DP160101513; (iii) Research Grants Council of the Hong Kong SAR, China, 14209314; (iv) Guangdong Key Laboratory Project (2012A061400024). Dr. Rui Mao is a corresponding author.

A. APPENDIX

A.1 Missing proofs

THEOREM 1. ***Optimal-Tree Decomposition Theorem:*** *Assume that each edge in the graph G has a positive weight. Then, for the optimal tree $T^*(P)$, there always exists a node $u \in T^*(P)$ such that (i) the tree $T^*(P)$ rooted at u has k ($k \geq 1$) subtrees $T_1, T_2, \cdots, T_k$, and (ii) each subtree T_i (for $i \in \{1, 2, \cdots, k\}$) has a weight smaller than $f^*(P)/2$.*

PROOF. We can construct the optimal-tree decomposition using the following procedure. First, we randomly select a node from $T^*(P)$ as the root u. If all the subtrees of the tree rooted at u have weights smaller than $f^*(P)/2$, we are done. Otherwise, there must be a subtree T_i that has a weight no smaller than $f^*(P)/2$. Let v_i be the root of such a subtree T_i. Then, we move the root from u to v_i, and recursively execute the same procedure. Fig. 13 illustrates this movement procedure. Note that the movement procedure is nonreversible (i.e., we cannot move the root from v_i to u), because the subtree rooted at v_i (i.e., T_i) has a weight no smaller than $f^*(P)/2$ whereas the remaining part of the tree rooted at u has a weight smaller than $f^*(P)/2$. More specifically, let us consider the tree shown in Fig. 13 (left panel). Since the tree rooted at v_i has a weight no smaller than $f^*(P)/2$ and the weight of the edge (u, v_i) is positive, thus the weight of the left-part subtree rooted at u must be smaller than $f^*(P)/2$. As a result, the procedure cannot move back from v_i to u, and thus in each movement, the procedure must replace the root with a new node. Since the number of nodes in $T^*(P)$ is bounded, the movement procedure must be terminated in finite number of steps. Once the procedure terminates, we obtain a tree rooted at u that satisfies the conditions as stated in the theorem. □

THEOREM 2. ***Conditional Tree Merging Theorem:*** *Without loss of optimality, to expand a state (v, X) by a tree merging operation in the best-first DP algorithm, we can merge two subtrees $T(v, X)$ and $T(v, X')$ for $X' \subset P \backslash X$ only when the total weight of these two subtrees is no larger than $2/3 \times f^*(P)$.*

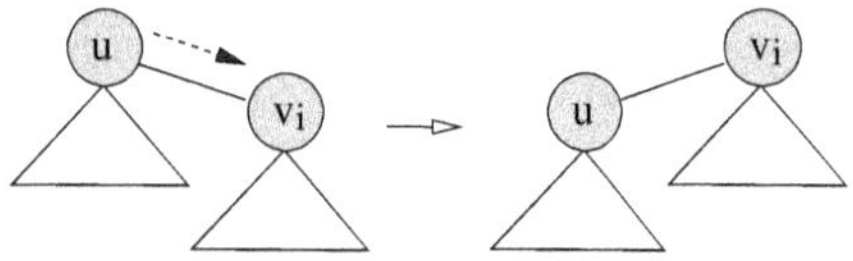

Figure 13: Illustration of the movement from a root u to v_i.

PROOF. To prove the theorem, we need to show that the optimal solution can still be obtained using the *conditional* tree merging strategy. By Theorem 1, we can assume, without loss of generality, that the optimal solution is a tree rooted at u with k subtrees, $T_1, \cdots, T_k$, whose roots are v_i respectively and weights are smaller than $f^*(P)/2$ (see Fig. 1). Let $\tilde{T}_i$ be the edge-grown subtree that is grown by T_i with an edge (v_i, u). Then, there are three different cases: (1) the weight of each $\tilde{T}_i$ is smaller than $f^*(P)/2$, (2) there is only one edge-grown subtree $\tilde{T}_i$ that has a weight no smaller than $f^*(P)/2$, and (3) there are two edge-grown subtrees and each one has a weight $f^*(P)/2$.

In case (1), we claim that the optimal tree can always be divided into two subtrees such that each of them has a weight no larger than $2f^*(P)/3$. In particular, we can obtain such a division using the following procedure. First, we pick the top-1 maximum-weight edge-grown subtree. If its weight is no smaller than $f^*(P)/3$, we are done. This is because, the union of the remaining edge-grown subtrees must have a weight no larger than $2f^*(P)/3$. Since the top-1 maximum-weight edge-grown subtree has a weight smaller than $f^*(P)/2$ (by the condition of case (1)), its weight is also smaller than $2f^*(P)/3$, and thus we obtain a feasible division. Otherwise, we pick the top-2 maximum-weight edge-grown subtree, and merge it with the top-1 maximum-weight edge-grown tree. If the merged edge-grown tree has a weight no smaller than $f^*(P)/3$, then we are done. Since the top-1 maximum-weight edge-grown subtree has a weight smaller than $f^*(P)/3$ in this case, the weight of the merged edge-grown tree must be smaller than $2f^*(P)/3$ (because the weight of the top-2 maximum-weight edge-grown subtree is also smaller than $f^*(P)/3$). On the other hand, the union of the remaining edge-grown subtrees must have a weight no larger than $2f^*(P)/3$. Thus, in this case, we obtain a feasible division. We can perform the same procedure recursively until we get a feasible division. Therefore, under the case (1), to expand a state (v, X) in the best-first DP algorithm, there is no need to merge two subtrees if the total weight of them is larger than $2f^*(P)/3$. This is because under the case (1), the optimal solution can always be obtained by merging two subtrees with weights no larger than $2f^*(P)/3$, and thus we do not need to generate a subtree that has a weight larger than $2f^*(P)/3$ via merging two subtrees.

In case (2), since there is an edge-grown subtree $\tilde{T}_i$ with weight no smaller than $f^*(P)/2$, thus by our best-first DP algorithm, the state corresponding to such a tree $\tilde{T}_i$ will not be expanded (see Theorem 1). On the other hand, the total weight of all the remaining edge-grown subtrees must be no larger than $f^*(P)/2$, and thus no larger than $2/3 \times f^*(P)$. In case (3), since both the two edge-grown subtrees have weights $f^*(P)/2$, there is no need to expand the states corresponding to these two subtrees by our algorithm. Putting it all together, the theorem is established. □

LEMMA 1. *For any state (v, X), we have $\pi_1(v, X) \leq f_T^*(v, \bar{X})$.*

PROOF. Since $\pi_1(v, X)$ denotes the weight of the optimal tree rooted at v that covers only one label in $\bar{X}$, $\pi_1(v, X)$ must be smaller than the weight of the optimal tree rooted at v that covers all labels in $\bar{X}$, which is exactly equal to $f_T^*(v, \bar{X})$. □

LEMMA 2. *For any state (v, X), we have $\pi_{t_1}(v, X) \leq f_T^*(v, \bar{X})$.*

PROOF. Recall that $f_T^*(v, \bar{X})$ denotes the optimal weight of a connected tree rooted at v that covers all the labels in $\bar{X}$. We can double every edge in this optimal tree $T(v, \bar{X})$, and thus obtain an Euler tour that starts from v and also ends at v. Clearly, the weight of such a tour should be no less than the weight of the optimal tour starting from v and ending at v, and covering all the labels in $\bar{X}$. As a result, we have $2f_T^*(v, \bar{X}) \geq f_{\tilde{R}}^*(v, \bar{X})$, and thereby the lemma is established. □

LEMMA 3. *For any state (v, X), we have $\pi_{t_2}(v, X) \leq f_T^*(v, \bar{X})$.*

PROOF. First, we can add the virtual nodes and virtual edges for the optimal tree $T(v, \bar{X})$, and thus result in a graph with weight $f_T^*(v, \bar{X})$. Then, we double the edges of such a graph, and obtain an Euler graph $\tilde{G}(v, \bar{X})$ with weight $2f_T^*(v, \bar{X})$. Clearly, in $\tilde{G}(v, \bar{X})$, we have an Euler tour that starts from v, ends at v, and passes through all edges in $\tilde{G}(v, \bar{X})$. For each virtual node $\tilde{v}_i \in V_{\bar{X}}$, we can always decompose such an Euler tour into three parts: (i) the path from v to $\tilde{v}_i$, (ii) the minimum-weight route $\tilde{R}$ that starts from $\tilde{v}_i$ and passes through all virtual nodes in $V_{\bar{X}}$, and (iii) the path from $\tilde{v}_j$ to v, where $\tilde{v}_j$ is the end node of the route $\tilde{R}$. By our definition, the total weight of these three parts must be no less than $dist(v, \tilde{v}_i) + W(\tilde{v}_i, \bar{X}) + \min_{j \in \bar{X}}\{dist(\tilde{v}_j, v)\}$. Since this result hold for every virtual node $\tilde{v}_i$, we can conclude that the weight of the Euler tour must be no less than $\max_{i \in \bar{X}}\{(dist(v, \tilde{v}_i) + W(\tilde{v}_i, \bar{X}) + \min_{j \in \bar{X}}\{dist(\tilde{v}_j, v)\})\}$, and therefore the lemma is established. □

LEMMA 4. *For any state (v, X), we have $\pi(v, X) \leq f_T^*(v, \bar{X})$.*

PROOF. Since $\pi(v, X) = \max\{\pi_1(v, X), \pi_{t_1}(v, X), \pi_{t_2}(v, X)\}$ and $\pi_1(v, X)$, $\pi_{t_1}(v, X)$, and $\pi_{t_2}(v, X)$ are the lower bounds of $f_T^*(v, \bar{X})$, thus the lemma holds. □

LEMMA 5. *For any state (v, X), we have (i) $\pi_1(u, X) + w(v, u) \geq \pi_1(v, X)$, and (ii) $\pi_1(v, X \cup X') + f_T^*(v, X') \geq \pi_1(v, X)$, where $X \cap X' = \emptyset$.*

PROOF. By definition, to prove the lemma, we need to prove that (i) $f_1^*(u, \bar{X}) + w(v, u) \geq f_1^*(v, \bar{X})$, and (ii) $f_1^*(v, \bar{X} \backslash X') + f_T^*(v, X') \geq f_1^*(v, \bar{X})$. First, we have $f_1^*(u, \bar{X}) + w(v, u) = \max_{x \in \bar{X}}\{f_T^*(u, \{x\}) + w(v, u)\}$. Clearly, $f_T^*(u, \{x\}) + w(v, u)$ is the weight of a tree that is rooted at v and covers a label x. Since $f_T^*(v, \{x\})$ is the optimal weight over all such type of trees, we have $f_T^*(u, \{x\}) + w(v, u) \geq f_T^*(v, \{x\})$, and thereby we have $\max_{x \in \bar{X}}\{f_T^*(u, \{x\}) + w(v, u)\} \geq \max_{x \in \bar{X}}\{f_T^*(v, \{x\})\} = f_1^*(v, \bar{X})$. Second, since $f_T^*(v, X') \geq f_1^*(v, X')$, it is sufficient to show $f_1^*(v, \bar{X} \backslash X') + f_1^*(v, X') \geq f_1^*(v, \bar{X})$. By the definition of the one-label lower bound, the above inequality clearly holds. □

LEMMA 6. *For any state (v, X), we have (i) $\pi_{t_1}(u, X) + w(v, u) \geq \pi_{t_1}(v, X)$, and (ii) $\pi_{t_1}(v, X \cup X') + f_T^*(v, X') \geq \pi_{t_1}(v, X)$, where $X \cap X' = \emptyset$.*

PROOF. First, we prove that the case (i) holds. Recall that $f_{\tilde{R}}^*(u, \bar{X})$ is the optimal weight of the tour (denoted by $(u \sim R(\tilde{v}_i, \tilde{v}_j, \bar{X}) \sim u)$) that starts from u, ends at u, and passes through all the virtual nodes in $V_{\bar{X}}$. Based on this optimal tour, we can construct a new tour $v \sim u \sim R(\tilde{v}_i, \tilde{v}_j, \bar{X}) \sim u \sim v$. Clearly, the weight of this new tour is $f_{\tilde{R}}^*(u, \bar{X}) + 2 \times w(v, u)$. Note that such a new tour is tour that starts from v, ends at v, and passes through all the virtual nodes in $V_{\bar{X}}$. Since $f_{\tilde{R}}^*(v, \bar{X})$ is the optimal weight of the tour that starts from v, ends at v, and passes through all virtual nodes in $V_{\bar{X}}$, we have $f_{\tilde{R}}^*(u, \bar{X}) + 2w(v, u) \geq f_{\tilde{R}}^*(v, \bar{X})$. Since $\pi_{t_1}(u, X) = f_{\tilde{R}}^*(u, \bar{X})/2$ by definition, we have $\pi_{t_1}(u, X) + w(v, u) \geq \pi_{t_1}(v, X)$.

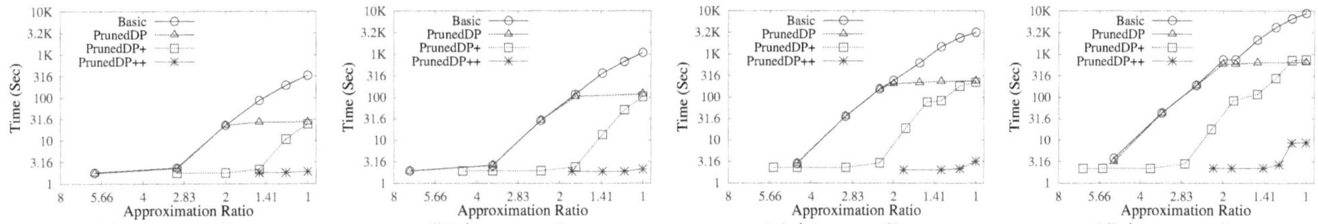

(a) knum = 5 (b) knum = 6 (c) knum = 7 (d) knum = 8

Figure 14: Query Processing Time vs. Approximation Ratio: Vary Number of Labels (knum) on LiveJournal

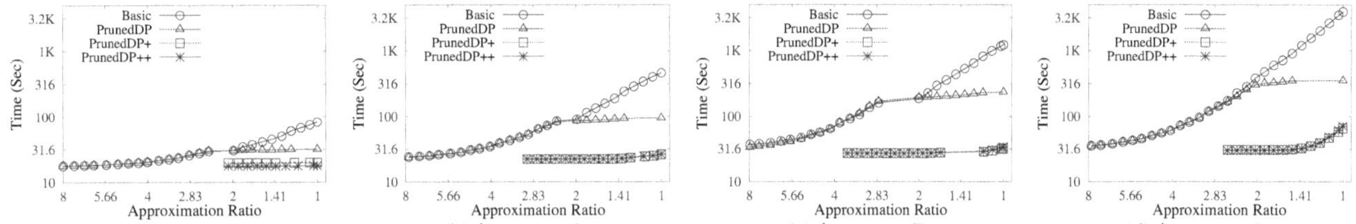

(a) knum = 5 (b) knum = 6 (c) knum = 7 (d) knum = 8

Figure 15: Query Processing Time vs. Approximation Ratio: Vary Number of Labels (knum) on RoadUSA

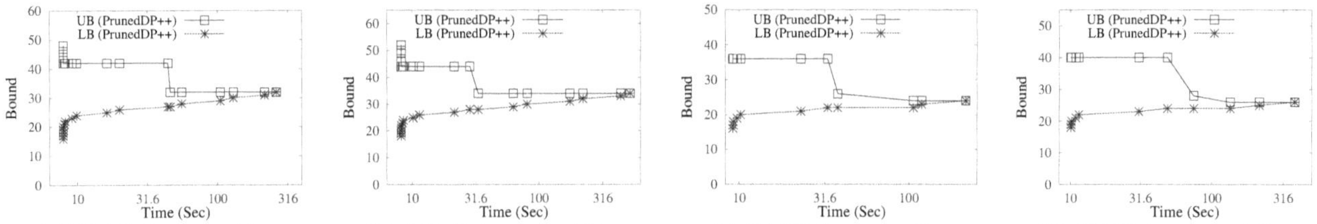

(a) DBLP (knum = 9) (b) DBLP (knum = 10) (c) IMDB (knum = 9) (d) IMDB (knum = 10)

Figure 16: Testing with Relatively Large knum for PrunedDP++ (kwf = 400)

Second, we show that the case (ii) also holds. Since $f_T^*(v, X') \geq f_{\tilde{R}}^*(v, X')/2$, it is sufficient to show $f_{\tilde{R}}^*(v, \bar{X}\backslash X') + f_{\tilde{R}}^*(v, X') \geq f_{\tilde{R}}^*(v, \bar{X})$. Let $v \sim R(\tilde{v}_i, \tilde{v}_j, \bar{X}\backslash X') \sim v$ and $v \sim R(\tilde{v}_i, \tilde{v}_j, X') \sim v$ be the optimal tours that starts from v, ends at v, and passes through all the virtual nodes in $V_{\bar{X}\backslash X'}$ and $V_{X'}$ respectively. We can merge these two tours and thus obtain a new tour that starts from v, ends at v, and passes through all the virtual nodes in $V_{\bar{X}}$. Since $f_{\tilde{R}}^*(v, \bar{X})$ is the optimal weight over all such type of tours, we have $f_{\tilde{R}}^*(v, \bar{X}\backslash X') + f_{\tilde{R}}^*(v, X') \geq f_{\tilde{R}}^*(v, \bar{X})$. Putting it all together, the lemma is established. □

LEMMA 7. *Let* $\pi(v, X) = \max\{\pi_1(v, X), \pi_{t_1}(v, X), \pi_{t_2}(v, X)\}$. *Then, for a state* (v, X), *we have (i)* $\pi(u, X) + w(v, u) \geq \pi(v, X)$, *and (ii)* $\pi(v, X \cup X') + f_T^*(v, X') \geq \pi(v, X)$, *where* $X \cap X' = \emptyset$.

PROOF. First, since all the developed lower bounds are consistent (for $\pi_{t_2}(v, X)$, we can use the technique proposed in Section 4.2 to make it consistent), we can easily prove that the inequality $\pi(u, X) + w(v, u) \geq \pi(v, X)$ holds.

Second, we prove that $\pi(v, X \cup X') + f_T^*(v, X') \geq \pi(v, X)$ also holds. Below, we consider nine different cases.

Case (1): if $\pi(v, X \cup X') = \pi_1(v, X \cup X')$ and $\pi(v, X) = \pi_1(v, X)$, then the result clearly holds by Lemma 5.

Case (2): if $\pi(v, X \cup X') = \pi_1(v, X \cup X')$ and $\pi(v, X) = \pi_{t_1}(v, X)$, then we have $\pi_1(v, X \cup X') + f_T^*(v, X') \geq \pi_{t_1}(v, X \cup X') + f_T^*(v, X')$. Since $\pi_{t_1}(v, X)$ is consistent by Lemma 6, we have $\pi_{t_1}(v, X \cup X') + f_T^*(v, X') \geq \pi_{t_1}(v, X) = \pi(v, X)$.

Case (3): if $\pi(v, X \cup X') = \pi_1(v, X \cup X')$ and $\pi(v, X) = \pi_{t_2}(v, X)$, then we have $\pi_1(v, X \cup X') + f_T^*(v, X') \geq \pi_{t_2}(v, X \cup X') + f_T^*(v, X')$. Since $\pi_{t_2}(v, X)$ is consistent, we have $\pi_{t_2}(v, X \cup X') + f_T^*(v, X') \geq \pi_{t_2}(v, X) = \pi(v, X)$.

Similarly, for the other six cases, we can also prove that $\pi(v, X \cup X') + f_T^*(v, X') \geq \pi(v, X)$ holds. Putting it all together, the lemma is established. □

A.2 Additional experiments

Results on Different Graph Topologies. In this experiment, we test the performance of the proposed algorithms on graphs with different topologies. To this end, we use two additional publicly available datasets LiveJournal[3] and RoadUSA[4] to evaluate our algorithms. LiveJournal is a social network with a power-law degree distribution. It contains 4,847,572 nodes and 42,851,237 edges with a diameter 20. The average degree is 17.7 and the maximum degree is 20,333. RoadUSA is the USA road network with a relatively uniform degree distribution. It contains 23,947,348 nodes and 28,854,312 edges with a diameter larger than 8,000. The average degree is 2.4 and the maximum degree is 9. For each dataset, we generate labels for nodes randomly with the default label frequency. We vary knum from 5 to 8 and test the performance of the four algorithms Basic, PrunedDP, PrunedDP+, and PrunedDP++.

The results on the LiveJournal dataset are shown in Fig. 14. As can be seen, when knum increases, the processing time for all algorithms increases. When knum = 8 (Fig. 14 (d)), to reach an approximation ratio of 1, PrunedDP++ is two orders of magnitude faster than PrunedDP+ and PrunedDP, and three orders of magnitude faster than Basic. For example, Basic computes the optimal solution within 8,871.9 seconds while PrunedDP++ only requires 8.7 seconds to calculate the optimal solution. As desired, PrunedDP+ is faster than PrunedDP. However, when the approximation ratio decreases to 1, the gap between PrunedDP+ and PrunedDP decreases. For example, for knum = 7 (Fig. 14 (c)), to achieve an approximation ratio of 2, PrunedDP+ only requires 16.2 seconds while PrunedDP needs 205.2 seconds. How-

[3] http://konect.uni-koblenz.de/networks/soc-LiveJournal1

[4] http://www.dis.uniroma1.it/challenge9/download.shtml

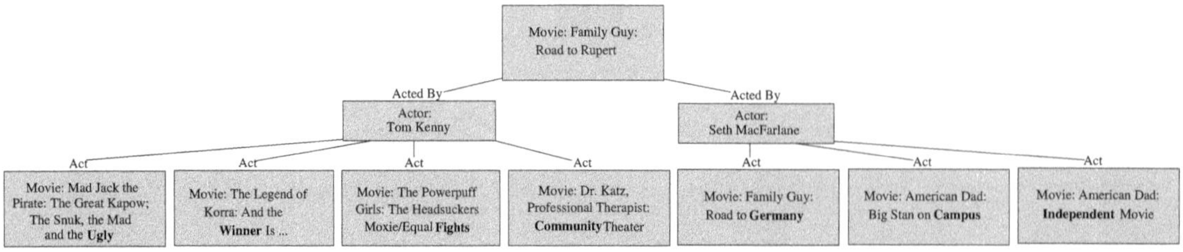

Figure 17: Case Study on IMDB using PrunedDP++ (knum $= 7$, Processing Time $= 40.9$ Seconds)

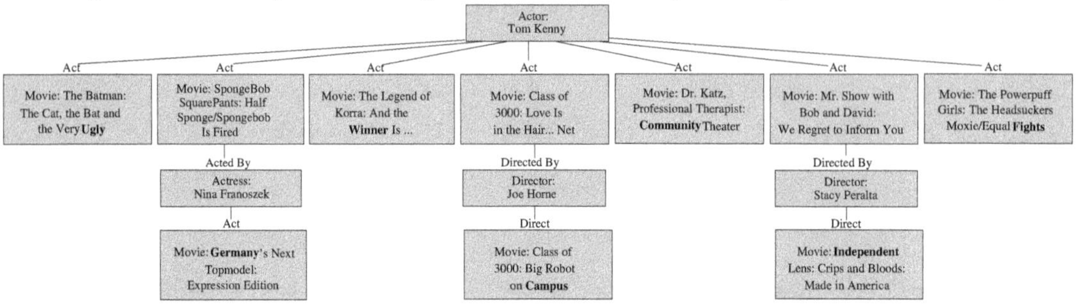

Figure 18: Case Study on IMDB using BANKS-II (knum $= 7$, Processing Time $= 252.7$ Seconds)

ever, to achieve an approximation ratio of 1, PrunedDP+ requires 169.7 seconds while PrunedDP needs 237.2 seconds.

The results on the RoadUSA dataset are shown in Fig. 15. Similar to the results on LiveJournal, PrunedDP++ is also the winner among all the algorithms on RoadUSA. However, different from the results on LiveJournal, the gap between PrunedDP++ and PrunedDP+ on RoadUSA is much smaller than that on LiveJournal. For example, when knum $= 6$, to reach an approximation of 1, PrunedDP++ is 48.8 times faster than PrunedDP+ in LiveJournal (Fig. 14 (b)), whereas PrunedDP++ is slightly faster than PrunedDP+ on RoadUSA (Fig. 15 (b)). This is because RoadUSA is a near planar graph, in which the difference between the one-label based lower bound and the tour-based lower bound is usually small. Instead, LiveJournal is a power-law graph, in which the one-label based lower bound is typically much smaller than the tour-based lower bound. These results indicate that the performance of PrunedDP++ is better on power-law graphs than that on near planar graphs.

Results on Relatively Large knum Values. In this experiment, we increase knum to 9 and 10 to test the scalability and progressive performance of the PrunedDP++ algorithm. Note that in many practical applications such as keyword search and team search problems, the number of given keywords is typically smaller than 10 [8, 6, 22, 30]. To the best of our knowledge, we are the first to handle knum > 6 to compute the exact GST on million-scale graphs. The experimental results on the DBLP dataset are shown in Fig. 16 (a) and Fig. 16 (b) for knum $= 9$ and knum $= 10$ respectively. As can be seen, when knum increases, the total processing time to compute the optimal answer increases. For example, PrunedDP++ requires 262.7 seconds and 520.6 seconds to compute the optimal answers for knum $= 9$ and knum $= 10$ respectively. Nevertheless, within 10 seconds, PrunedDP++ already generates answers with approximation ratios 1.31 and 1.29 for knum $= 9$ and knum $= 10$ respectively. The results on the IMDB dataset are similar to those on the DBLP dataset, which are shown in Fig. 16 (c) and Fig. 16 (d) for knum $= 9$ and knum $= 10$ respectively. As can be seen, when knum increases from 9 to 10, the processing time for PrunedDP++ increases from 214.7 seconds to 380.4 seconds. Likewise, within 37 seconds, PrunedDP++ generates an answer with approximation ratio1.083 for knum $= 9$, and within 72 seconds, PrunedDP++ generates an answer with approximation ratio 1.077 for knum $= 10$. These results indicate that the PrunedDP++ algorithm works well for relatively large knum values, and thus it is very useful for keyword search and team search related applications.

knum	kwf	Total Time BANKS-II	Appro Ratio BANKS-II	Total Time PrunedDP++	T_r PrunedDP++
5	400	211.3 secs	1.33	7.0 secs	6.9 secs
6	400	274.8 secs	1.22	18.7 secs	8.3 secs
7	400	332.1 secs	1.40	24.6 secs	18.0 secs
8	400	391.7 secs	1.45	112.4 secs	31.4 secs
6	200	275.4 secs	1.22	10.2 secs	10.1 secs
6	800	282.6 secs	1.14	20.3 secs	11.2 secs
6	1,600	266.0 secs	1.14	11.1 secs	9.8 secs

Table 3: Comparison with BANKS-II on IMDB

Additional Exp-5: Comparison with BANKS-II on IMDB. Here we compare PrunedDP++ and BANKS-II on the IMDB dataset. Table 3 reports the results on IMDB. Similar to the results on DBLP (Table 2), PrunedDP++ is 13.5 to 30.2 times faster than BANKS-II under all parameter settings on the IMDB dataset. For instance, under the default setting (knum $= 6$ and kwf $= 400$), BANKS-II computes an 1.22-approximate answer in 274.8 seconds while PrunedDP++ generates the optimal answer using only 18.7 seconds. When knum $= 8$, although PrunedDP++ takes 112.4 seconds to calculate the optimal answer, it only consumes 31.4 seconds to compute the answer with at least the same quality as the answer calculated by BANKS-II. These results further confirm the efficiency of the PrunedDP++ algorithm.

Additional Exp-6: Case Study. Here we report the case study on the IMDB dataset. In this case study, we use a seven keywords query $P = \{$ "Germany", "Campus", "winner", "independent", "fights", "ugly", "community" $\}$. With this query, the users may want to find some correlated actors/actresses who act movies with topics related to the keywords given in P. The answer reported by PrunedDP++ (taking 40.9 seconds) is shown in Fig. 17. This answer contains two actors who collaborate a movie and act movies with topics related to all the 7 keywords in P. Totally two actors and eight movies are included in this answer. The answer reported by BANKS-II (taking 252.7 seconds) is shown in Fig. 18. This answer contains an actor who acts seven movies directly/indirectly related to the seven keywords in P. Totally an actor, an actress, two directors, and ten movies are involved in this answer. Clearly, the answer reported by PrunedDP++ is more compact and may better meet the users' requirements than the answer reported by BANKS-II. These results further confirm the effectiveness of the proposed approach.

Publishing Attributed Social Graphs with Formal Privacy Guarantees

Zach Jorgensen
North Carolina State University, USA
zjorgen@ncsu.edu

Ting Yu
Qatar Computing Research Institute, Qatar
tyu@qf.org.qa

Graham Cormode
University of Warwick, UK
g.cormode@warwick.ac.uk

ABSTRACT

Many data analysis tasks rely on the abstraction of a graph to represent relations between entities, with attributes on the nodes and edges. Since the relationships encoded are often sensitive, we seek effective ways to release representative graphs which nevertheless protect the privacy of the data subjects. Prior work on this topic has focused primarily on the graph structure in isolation, and has not provided ways to handle richer graphs with correlated attributes.

We introduce an approach to release such graphs under the strong guarantee of differential privacy. We adapt existing graph models, and introduce a new one, and show how to augment them with meaningful privacy. This provides a complete workflow, where the input is a sensitive graph, and the output is a realistic synthetic graph. Our experimental study demonstrates that our process produces useful, accurate attributed graphs.

1. INTRODUCTION

Social network analysis (SNA) is an important tool with diverse applications, from marketing to counter-terrorism to the prediction of disease outbreaks. Recent years have seen massive growth in online social networking, which has created unique opportunities for SNA at unprecedented scales. Although the vast stores of social data hold great potential for research, they also present significant concerns for privacy. Social networks encode complex relationships among individuals (e.g., friendships, aquaintances, sexual relationships, disease transmission), which may be sensitive. Moreover, the nodes (e.g., users) in real-world social networks may be associated with various sensitive attributes, such as age, location or sexual preference. In order for the full benefit of SNA to be realized, effective privacy-preserving analysis techniques for this type of data are critical.

Much prior research on privacy for SNA has focused on graph anonymization techniques (e.g., [17, 38, 39]). Unfortunately, such approaches are now known to be vulnerable to deanonymization attacks (e.g., [1, 24]). Consequently, recent efforts have sought to provide the more rigorous guarantees of differential privacy for graph analysis. Two directions have emerged: (1) methods for privately computing specific statistics over sensitive graphs, such as degree distribution [11], subgraph counting [13, 2], clustering coefficient [35], and frequent subgraph mining [33]; and (2) private graph release, which typically involves (privately) fitting a generative graph model to input graphs in order to sample a synthetic graph, which can be used in analyses as a proxy for a real input graph (e.g., [23, 30, 34, 4, 36, 18, 29]). We follow this latter approach. Specifically, we address the important challenge of privately modeling social graphs in which the vertices have *sensitive attributes* that are correlated with the structure of the graph. Our goal is to generate synthetic graphs that mimic an input graph in terms of these important characteristics and that can be published without compromising the privacy of the individuals and relationships described in the input graph.

Three important motivations for producing a synthetic graph are highlighted by Hay [9]: (1) first, some analyses require running complex algorithms or simulations over actual network data, rather than via statistics. Using synthetic graphs in place of the true input allows an analyst to protect privacy without needing to analyze the privacy properties of each algorithmic approach; (2) synthetic graphs facilitate "exploratory, open-ended, and iterative" analyses, which can be very difficult to accommodate directly on an input graph with limited privacy budget under differential privacy; and (3) it eliminates the need to share the details of proprietary analyses with the data owner.

Existing work on differentially private graph learning and synthesis (cited above) has focused on modeling network structure alone, without taking into account *vertex attributes* and their correlations with graph structure. However, real-world graphs have vertex attributes and do exhibit such correlations. For example, in social graphs, user nodes often have many attributes such as age, gender, sexual preference, etc. and are well known to exhibit *homophily*, or the tendency for nodes with similar attributes to form connections [20]. Existing differentially private graph models do not capture such properties. However, there are many relevant analyses that rely on the presence of these correlations. In the field of relational machine learning, such correlations are exploited to predict missing or future attribute values; information diffusion in social networks has been shown to be influenced by both the graph structure as well as the attributes of the nodes.

In this work, we develop a differentially private framework for synthesizing attributed social graphs to mimic the structure and attribute correlations observed in an input graph. Our solution prevents disclosure of individual relationships (edges) and node attribute values associated with the individuals in the input graph. This is the first differentially private approach that targets both structural properties and attribute correlations.

To this end, we adapt the recent Attributed Graph Model (AGM) of Pfeiffer et al. [27] to add strong differential privacy guarantees

SIGMOD'16, June 26-July 01, 2016, San Francisco, CA, USA

ISBN 978-1-4503-3531-7/16/06...$15.00

DOI: http://dx.doi.org/10.1145/2882903.2915215

while preserving the utility of the synthesized graphs. AGM models a social network using three sets of parameters that describe (1) the distribution of attributes over the nodes, (2) the correlations between node attributes and edges, and (3) the modeling parameters for an underlying generative structural model. We show how to effectively compute each of these model parameters under differential privacy. While satisfying differential privacy for the attribute distribution is relatively straightforward, the other two sets of parameters present a significant challenge. Modeling the attribute correlations involves computing the fraction of edges that exist between nodes with every possible attribute configuration. Changing the attribute values associated with a single node can change many of these values, depending on the degree of the node. This translates to a high global sensitivity and standard techniques, such as the Laplace mechanism, will destroy utility. We propose a novel application of the the notion of edge truncation to avoid this problem, and show that it is superior to the more standard approaches of smooth sensitivity and sample-and-aggregate.

To capture the structural properties of the input graph, AGM incorporates an underlying generative structural model. Although several prior works have focused on extending existing structural models to satisfy differential privacy, none of these models sufficiently capture properties of typical networks, which are characterized by heavy tailed degree sequences and large amounts of clustering. Moreover, methods that do attempt to capture this structure appear less amenable to differential privacy. In response, we propose a *new* structural model, called TriCycLe, that captures the degree distribution and clustering coefficients of a social network, and is parameterized by statistics for which good differentially private estimators can be found. Specifically, TriCycLe extends the simple Chung-Lu random graph model with a triangle construction phase, in which existing edges in the Chung-Lu graph are iteratively rewired to create approximately the same number of triangles observed in the input graph. The model parameters are the triangle count and degree sequence of the input graph, both of which can be accurately estimated under differential privacy. We integrate this new model into AGM and outline the end-to-end workflow for generating differentially private synthetic graphs.

We evaluate the efficacy of the proposed framework on four real-world social network datasets and demonstrate that it is able to produce synthetic graphs that accurately mimic the structure and attribute correlations of an input graph, while also ensuring a strong level of privacy.

Outline. In the next section, we describe our problem and setting in more detail and introduce notation; we also provide an overview of AGM, the attributed graph model that we adapt to satisfy differential privacy. In Section 3 we present our approach for computing differentially private estimates of the three sets of modeling parameters used by AGM. In Section 4 we put the pieces together and outline the end-to-end workflow for synthesizing differentially private attributed graphs. Section 5 presents our experimental study on four real-world datasets. Related work and conclusions are in Sections 6 and 7 respectively.

2. PRELIMINARIES

2.1 Setting and Notation

We represent a social network (social graph) as an attributed simple graph (i.e., undirected, unweighted edges with no multiple or self-edges) denoted by the triple $G = (N, E, X)$. We use the terms network and graph interchangeably in the rest of the paper. $N = \{v_1, \ldots, v_n\}$ is a set of vertices (nodes), where each node typically represents a person or user. We assume that the number of nodes, n, is publicly known. $E = \{e_1, \ldots, e_m\}$ is a set of edges, where we write e_{ij} to refer to an undirected edge between nodes v_i and v_j (i.e., $e_{ij} \equiv e_{ji}$ and $e_{ij} \in E$ iff $e_{ji} \in E$). We write $\Gamma(v_i)$ to mean the set of v_i's neighbors, i.e., $\Gamma(v_i) = \{v_j \in N | e_{ij} \in E\}$, and we use $d_i = |\Gamma(v_i)|$ to denote the degree of v_i. $X = \{x_1, \ldots, x_n\}$ is a set of w-dimensional attribute vectors, where the vector $x_i = \langle x_{i1}, \ldots, x_{iw} \rangle$ contains the attributes associated with node v_i. In what follows, we assume that attributes are binary, i.e, $x_i \in \{0,1\}^w$; however, the ideas easily extend to attributes with larger domains.

Table 1: Summary of notation

N	Set of nodes, $\{v_i\}$
n	Number of nodes, i.e., $\|N\|$
$\Gamma(v_i)$	Set of nodes incident to node v_i
d_i	Degree of node v_i
d_{max}	Maximum degree among nodes in a graph
E	Set of edges, $\{e_{ij}\}$
e_{ij}	An (undirected) edge between v_i and v_j
E_{ij}	Binary random variable, $E_{ij} = 1$ if $e_{ij} \in E$
m	Number of edges, i.e., $\|E\|$
X	Set of attribute vectors, $\{x_i\}$
x_i	Attribute vector associated with node v_i
x_{ij}	The jth attribute in $x_i \in X$
w	Number of attributes
Y_w	Set of elements representing possible node attribute configurations
f_w	Function that maps an x_i to an element of Y_w
Y_w^F	Set of elements representing possible edge attribute configurations
F_w	Function that maps an e_{ij} to an element of Y_w^F
Θ_X	Set of attribute parameters used by AGM
Θ_F	Set of attribute correlation parameters used by AGM
M	Underlying structural model used by AGM
Θ_M	Set of structural model parameters
k	Truncation parameter
ε	Privacy parameter
n_Δ	Number of triangles in a graph
$\mathcal{S}$	Unordered degree sequence of a graph

Table 1 summarizes the notation introduced above, as well as other notation frequently used throughout this paper. We sometimes augment the notation with a superscript to explicitly connect the notation with a specific graph, e.g., $N^{(G_1)}$ refers to the set of nodes of graph G_1 and $d_i^{(G_1)}$ to the degree of node $v_i \in N^{(G_1)}$.

2.2 Attributed Graph Model (AGM)

In this work, we extend the recent Attributed Graph Model (AGM) of Pfeiffer et al. [27] to enable generation of synthetic graphs with formal differential privacy guarantees. AGM is capable of capturing both the structure and attribute correlations of a given input graph and efficiently sampling graphs from the learned model.

To simplify notation in the rest of the paper, we first define two functions to map a node attribute vector or an undirected edge to a unique integer. We use $f_w(x_i)$ to denote the function that maps maps a w-dimensional attribute vector x_i bijectively to an element of the set Y_w. We write $F_w(x_i, x_j)$ to mean the function that maps a pair of attribute vectors x_i, x_j associated with an edge to an element of Y_w^F, ignoring the direction of the edge.

AGM models graphs using parameters Θ_X, Θ_M, and Θ_F:

1. A set of attribute parameters Θ_X is used for modeling the distribution of attributes on the vertices, i.e., $\Pr[X|\Theta_X]$. Θ_X is computed from graph G as: $\Theta_X(y) = \frac{\sum_{v_i \in N}[f_w(x_i)=y]}{n}$, $\forall_{y \in Y_w}$, where $[\cdot] = 1$ if the statement within the brackets evaluates to

true, and 0 otherwise. In other words, $\Theta_X(y)$ is the fraction of total nodes whose attribute vectors are encoded as y.

2. A set of edge parameters Θ_M models the distribution of edges, $\Pr[E|\Theta_M]$. This uses an appropriate underlying generative structural model, M, parameterized by Θ_M. In general, M can be any generative model in which a graph can be generated by repeatedly sampling edges from the conditional distribution $\Pr[E_{ij}|\Theta_M, M]$, where $E_{ij} \in \{0,1\}$ denotes a binary random variable such that $E_{ij} = 1$ means $e_{ij} \in E$. Note that graphs generated by M are independent of X (i.e., the node attribute vectors).

3. Θ_F is the set of parameters for modeling the correlations between attributes and edges, $\Pr[F_w(x_i,x_j)|E_{ij} = 1, \Theta_M, \Theta_F]$. We can construct Θ_F from G as: $\Theta_F(y) = \frac{\sum_{e_{ij} \in E} [F_w(x_i,x_j)=y]}{m}$, $\forall_{y \in Y_w^F}$. In other words, $\Theta_F(y)$ is the fraction of all edges that connect two nodes whose associated pair of node attribute vectors is encoded as y.

Given the three sets of parameters, the procedure to generate a synthetic graph is relatively straightforward. We create a fresh set of nodes N' of the desired size, and sample a new set of attribute vectors X' for the nodes in N' independently from $\Pr[X|\Theta_X]$. Next, we sample a graph G' based on $\Pr[E_{ij} = 1|F_w(x'_i,x'_j), \Theta_M, \Theta_F]$. It is not convenient to sample from this distribution directly, so instead the approach of accept/reject sampling can be used. Essentially, the randomly produced attribute correlations observed in the generated graph are used to derive acceptance probabilities, which are in turn used to generate a new output graph [26].

2.3 Differential Privacy

The tools of differential privacy [7, 8] are by now well-known, so we give only a short summary of the main concepts. It provides a statistical notion of privacy, based on the concept of *neighboring data sets*, which differ in at most one element. We write $D \sim D'$to indicate that datasets D and D' are neighbors.

A randomized algorithm (mechanism) $\mathcal{M}$ is said to be *differentially private* (DP) if the probability distribution $\mathcal{M}(D)$ on any data set D is approximately the same as $\mathcal{M}(D')$, up to a factor of e^{ε}, for every $D \sim D'$. In other words, the algorithm's behavior should be (mostly) insensitive to the presence or absence of any one tuple in the input. Here, $\varepsilon > 0$ is a publicly known *privacy parameter* that controls the strength of the differential privacy guarantee: a larger ε yields weaker privacy, while a smaller ε leads to stronger privacy.

For real valued functions, i.e., $f : \mathcal{D} \to \mathbb{R}^d$, the most common way to satisfy differential privacy is to inject carefully chosen random noise into the output. The magnitude of the noise is adjusted according to the *global sensitivity* of the function, defined as $\Delta_f = \max_{D \sim D'} \|f(D) - f(D')\|_1$ ($\|\cdot\|_1$ is the L_1 norm). This measures the maximum extent to which any one tuple in the input can affect the output. A function f can be made ε-differentially private by adding random noise drawn from the Laplace distribution with mean zero and scale $\lambda = \frac{\Delta_f}{\varepsilon}$, denoted Lap($\lambda$), to its output.

Global sensitivity can be too blunt a tool when a few rare inputs can push up its value. *Smooth sensitivity* adapts the notion of sensitivity to the given data [25]. For $\beta > 0$, the β-smooth sensitivity of a function f at D is $S_{f,\beta} = \max_{D' \in \mathcal{D}} \left(LS_f(D') \cdot e^{\beta d(D,D')} \right)$ where $d(D,D')$ is the distance between D and D', i.e., the number of additions or deletions needed to turn D into D'. Adding noise from Lap$\left(\frac{2S_{f,\beta}(D)}{\varepsilon}\right)$ satisfies the slightly weaker model of (ε, δ)-differential privacy, where $\beta = \varepsilon / 2\ln(1/\delta)$ [25]. Smooth sensitivity has proven useful for certain tasks, such as the median and minimum spanning tree [25] and various graph analysis tasks [35]. But it is non-trivial to compute for arbitrary functions, in general; moreover, it can also be computationally hard to compute for some functions (e.g., [18]).

Properties of Differential Privacy. When multiple differentially private outputs are combined, there are simple rules for reasoning about the privacy level that results. The most basic is sequential composition [21]. If we run k mechanisms $\mathcal{M}_1, \ldots, \mathcal{M}_k$ on an input D in sequence and each independently satisfies ε_i-differential privacy, then the full output is ε'-differentially private, where $\varepsilon' = \sum_{i=1}^{k} \varepsilon_i$. That is, the privacy loss accumulates linearly. More strongly, if the mechanisms are applied to a set of *disjoint* inputs, the resulting sequence of computations is $(\max_i \varepsilon_i)$-differentially private. Lastly, any post-processing of the output of a DP algorithm does not impact the privacy guarantee [15]. Using these composition theorems, one can easily construct complex differentially private algorithms from individual differentially private components.

2.4 Differential Privacy for Attributed Graphs

Differential privacy was originally defined in the context of tabular data, where each row corresponds to an individual, so neighboring datasets differ in the presence of one individual [7, 8]. Translating differential privacy to the graph analysis domain requires defining what it means for two graphs to be neighboring. Most prior work in this area considers two graphs to be neighboring if they differ in the presence of a single edge; that is, given a graph G, the neighboring graph G' is formed by adding (or deleting) any one edge to (from) G. This *edge-differential privacy* [11] definition protects individual relationships from disclosure—an adversary will not be able to determine with high probability whether an edge exists between any pair of nodes (in the input graph).

Unlike most prior work (apart from [2]), we concentrate on graphs that have one or more attributes associated with each node. Edge-differential privacy is only concerned with edges; however, node attributes are typically highly sensitive as well, and should be protected. Thus, we adopt a notion for neighboring graphs from [2].

DEFINITION 1 (EDGE-ADJACENT ATTRIBUTED GRAPHS). *Two attributed graphs G, G' are said to be* edge-adjacent *(or neighboring) if they differ in the presence of a single edge or in the attribute vector associated with a single node.*

A core challenge is that the sensitivities of many graph-structural analyses are proportional to the number of nodes, n, since the impact of a node often depends on its degree, which is bounded by $n-1$. For example, in the subgraph counting task the goal is to count the number of subgraphs of a distinct shape (e.g., triangles) contained in a graph; in the worst case, it is possible to have a graph where the addition of a single edge could complete $n-2$ triangles.

3. COMPUTING MODEL PARAMETERS

In this section, we extend AGM to enforce differential privacy for the synthesized graphs. To do so, we develop procedures for learning differentially private approximations for each of the three model parameters, based on the sensitive input graph. Having approximated the model parameters in a differentially private way, we can then use them with the sampling algorithm (Section 2.2) to obtain a synthetic graph that closely approximates the input graph without loss of privacy. For clarity of exposition, formal descriptions of algorithms and their proofs are postponed to Appendix C.

3.1 Attribute-Edge Correlations

Recall that the attribute correlation parameters Θ_F describe the correlations observed between edges and node attributes in the input graph. Such correlations are a key characteristic of social graphs, which are well-known to exhibit phenomena such as homophily (the tendency for similar individuals to associate with one another). To compute Θ_F, we first find the connection probabilities $\Theta_F(y_j) = \frac{\sum_{e_{ij}\in E}[F_w(x_i,x_j)=y_j]}{m}$, for each $y_j \in Y_w^F$. Since we are assuming undirected graphs with w binary node attributes, we need to compute $y = \binom{2^w+1}{2}$ connection probabilities.

We can view the problem as computing a set of counting queries $Q_F = \{q_1,\ldots,q_y\}$ that count the edges between nodes with a particular attribute configuration y_i, i.e., $q_i = \sum_{e_{jk}\in E}[F_w(x_j,x_k) = y_i]$. Probabilities can be derived from private counts by normalizing. However, while adding or removing a single edge only increases or decreases one count by at most one, changing the attributes of a single node can have a significant impact on many counts (depending on the degree of the node). In the language of differential privacy, this entails a large global sensitivity. In fact, a naïve attempt to satisfy differential privacy through a direct application of the Laplace mechanism (Section 2.3), e.g. by computing Q_F and adding independent Laplace noise to each q_i will completely destroy the utility of the value. To understand why, consider an input graph containing a degree $n-1$ hub node; changing the attributes of this hub node will cause some subset of the counts to decrease by a total of $n-1$ and another subset to increase by the same amount, which means the global sensitivity is $2n-2$. Therefore, achieving differential privacy with good utility in this setting will require either finding a way to exploit the fact that such worst case nodes are extremely rare in real-world networks, or somehow limiting the worst-case impact of a single node by way of a transformation applied to the input graph.

We introduce a new approach to this problem, based on the idea of edge truncation. This generates a private approximation of the set of connection counts Q_F (i.e., noisy counts). These are then divided by their sum to get an approximation of the probability distribution Θ_F. In Appendix B, we describe two alternate approaches based on the DP techniques of smooth sensitivity and sample-and-aggregate, and show that edge truncation is preferable in practice.

Edge Truncation. Our approach enforces low global sensitivity by truncating high-degree nodes. The general idea of projecting an input graph of arbitrary degree onto the set of k-bounded graphs—that is, the set of graphs with degree at most k—was recently proposed in recent work [14, 2]. Specifically, [2] proposed a general edge truncation operation for transforming graphs in the edge adjacency model, which we extended to our task of computing Q_F.

DEFINITION 2 (EDGE TRUNCATION [2]). *Given a graph G and a truncation parameter $k > 0$, the truncation algorithm $\mu(G,k)$ starts by fixing a canonical ordering over all of the edges in E. Then, iterating through each edge $e_{ij} \in E$ in order, an edge is deleted if and only if $d_i > k$ or $d_j > k$.*

The notion of *restricted sensitivity* in [2] restricts the global sensitivity to consider just the set H_k of graphs with degree at most k. An important subtlety is that transformations applied to the input graph, such as μ from Definition 2, may amplify the restricted sensitivity of a function that is executed on the resulting truncated graph. For a function f with restricted sensitivity $RS_f(H_k)$, it is shown in [2] that the algorithm that applies this truncation operation to G and then runs f on the truncated graph, i.e., $A_f(G,k) = f(\mu(G,k))$, has a global sensitivity of $3 \cdot RS_f(H_k)$. The factor of 3 arises as adding or removing a single edge, prior to truncation, results in a difference of up to three edges in the truncated graph [2].

Our result improves over the general results in [2]. We show that for the special case of Q_F the truncation operation is "for free", resulting in the global sensitivity being equal to the restricted sensitivity, which is $2k$. The intuition is that, although the truncation routine can amplify the effects of an edge addition/deletion in the input graph, the global sensitivity is still dominated by the impact of changing an attribute vector, which is not affected by truncation.

PROPOSITION 1. *Let μ be the edge truncation algorithm of Definition 2 and let $k > 1$. The* global sensitivity *$GS(A_{\mu,Q_F}(G,k))$ of algorithm $A_{\mu,Q_F}(G,k) = f_{Q_F}(\mu(G,k))$, which truncates graph G then computes Q_F over the resulting k-bounded graph, is $2k$.*

PROOF. By Definition 1, neighboring graphs differ in the presence of a single edge *or* in the attributes associated with one node. Let v_i, v_j be two nodes in input graph G such that $d_i = d_j = k$ and no edge exists between v_i and v_j. Let G' be the neighboring graph formed by adding edge e_{ij} to G. Let $O = e_0, e_1, \ldots, e_m$ be the canonical ordering of the edges in G and let $O' = O + e_{ij}$ be the ordering for G'. Finally, assume that $e_0 = e_{rs}$ and $e_1 = e_{uv}$ such that $s \neq u$, $v \neq r$, $d_s \leq k$, $d_v \leq k$ and that $f_w(x_s) \neq f_w(x_v)$ (i.e., their attribute values are different). Observe that the graph resulting from truncating G, $\mu(G,k)$, contains edges e_0, e_1 since the nodes at both end points have degree $\leq k$, by our assumption. On the other hand, truncating G' results in both e_0 and e_1 being deleted, since at the time they are processed, both v_r and v_u have degree $k+1$ in G'. Moreover, by the time edge e_{ij} is considered, both u and v will have degree $\leq k$, so e_{ij} will not be deleted. Also observe that all other edges that are deleted from G are also deleted from G' and vice versa. Consequently, two of the connection counts will decrease by a total of two, while one count will increase by one. Therefore the outputs of $\mu(G,k)$ and $\mu(G',k)$ differ in exactly three edges.

Now consider the case in which G and G' are size n graphs and are identical except that the attribute vector associated with one node, say v_i, is changed from x_i to x_i', such that $f_w(x_i) \neq f_w(x_i')$, in G'. Assume that $d_i \geq k$. First observe that the difference in the attribute vectors has no impact on the edges that are deleted by μ, since μ only looks at the degrees, and after truncation, v_i will have degree k in both graphs. Since the attribute vector associated with v_i is changed in G', the k edges incident to v_i in $\mu(G',k)$ will now contribute to a different subset of the counts than the edges incident to u in $\mu(G,k)$; that is, one subset of the counts will increase by k and another disjoint subset will decrease by k, for a total difference of $2k$. Finally, since $2k > 3$ (for $k > 1$), the impact of changing the attributes of a single node dominates that of adding/removing an edge and we have $GS(A_{\mu,Q_F}) = 2k$. □

We provide pseudocode for this procedure (Alg. 4), and prove its privacy properties (Thm. 7) in Appendix C. Compared to using smooth sensitivity (Appendix B), we expect this approach to perform better when k is close to the true maximum degree, since smooth sensitivity with the Laplace mechanism requires using $\varepsilon/2$, whereas we can use the full ε with this approach. However, directly using the true maximum degree to set k does not satisfy differential privacy. Moreover, social networks tend to have a power law degree distribution, and the average degree is significantly smaller than the maximum degree. Therefore, setting $k \ll d_{\max}$, so that a few very high degree nodes are truncated while most nodes are untouched may give better performance due to the reduced sensitivity.

The best choice for k depends on ε and on the characteristics of the input graph; however, tuning k for the given input would consume privacy budget. Instead, we find that using the data-independent

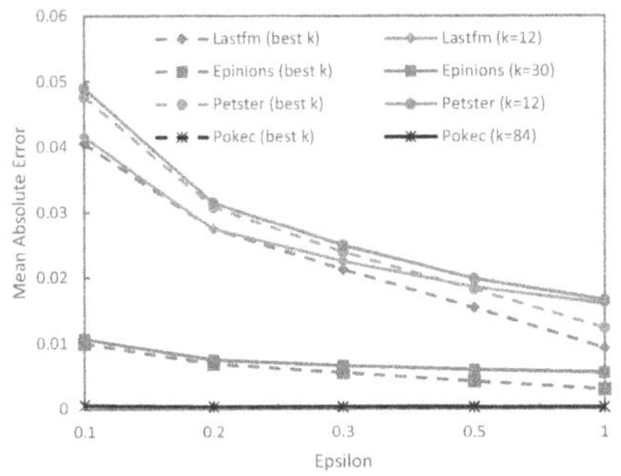

Figure 1: MAE of truncation approach when using the best truncation parameter k (dashed lines) vs. $k = n^{\frac{1}{3}}$ (solid lines).

heuristic $k = n^{\frac{1}{3}}$ works well in practice (a similar heuristic is given in [2]). A preliminary experiment to measure the Mean Absolute Error (MAE) between the input Θ_F and the noisy output over four datasets (described in Appendix A) is shown in Fig. 1. Since real-world social networks tend to have power-law degree distributions—meaning that only a small fraction of the nodes have very high degrees—this choice of k significantly lowers the sensitivity without deleting too many edges. For sufficiently large graphs (e.g., Pokec), the difference in error rates between the best k and the heuristically chosen k is negligible. Note that since n is assumed to be public in this work, setting k as a function of n does not affect the privacy guarantee of Thm. 7.

3.2 Node Attribute Distribution

The distribution of attributes on the nodes is modeled by Θ_X. Recall that Y_w is the set representing the 2^w possible attribute configurations that nodes can take, on a dataset with w binary attributes. We compute Θ_X as: $\Theta_X(y_i) = \frac{\sum_{v_i \in N}[f_w(x_i)=y_i]}{n}$, for $y_i \in Y_w$.

We can view the task of privately computing Θ_X as answering a set of $y = 2^w$ counting queries $Q_X = \{q_1, \ldots, q_y\}$ (where $q_i = \sum_{v_j \in N}[f_w(x_j) = y_i]$) under differential privacy. Here, we are counting disjoint sets of nodes, which has low global sensitivity. Observe that changing the attributes of a single node may, in the worst case, reduce at most one count $q_i \in Q_X$ by one and increase another count q_j by one, which means the global sensitivity is just 2. We are only counting *nodes*, so adding/removing edges has no impact on the counts. Therefore, we can obtain a private approximation of Θ_X, denoted by $\widetilde{\Theta}_X$, by computing counts on G, adding noise from $\text{Lap}(0, 2/\varepsilon)$, and finally dividing the noisy counts by their sum. As with Θ_F, we clamp the noisy counts to the range $(0, n)$ before dividing by the sum. For completeness, pseudocode of this procedure (Alg. 5) and a proof of its privacy properties (Thm. 8) are provided in Appendix C.2.

3.3 Structural Model: TriCycLe

AGM requires an underlying generative graph model, M, to capture the structural properties of the input graph. M is responsible for proposing new edges, which AGM then accepts or rejects to achieve the desired attribute correlations as it constructs a synthetic graph. An attractive feature of AGM is that it supports the use of any generative structural model in which a graph can be generated by repeatedly sampling edges. Therefore, our objective in this section is to (a) identify an appropriate structural model, and (b) to devise a way to compute its required model parameters, Θ_M, efficiently and accurately under differential privacy. For our purposes, the selected model should (1) capture structural features of social networks, including heavy-tailed degree distribution and high clustering; (2) be reasonably scalable (i.e., able to handle hundreds of thousands of nodes and millions of edges); and (3) be amenable to computation under differential privacy.

Recent work has extended popular structural models to support differential privacy, including exponential random graph models (ERGMs) [18] and the Kronecker graph model (KGM) [23]; however neither of these models meets our needs. ERGMs can reproduce the degree distribution and clustering coefficients of an input graph, but they do not scale well beyond a few thousand nodes. Conversely, KGMs are more scalable but fail to capture the high clustering characteristic of real-world social networks [32, 26].

From the broader graph analysis literature, two candidate models stand out: the Block Two-Phase Erdős-Rényi (BTER) model [31, 16], and the Transitive Chung-Lu (TCL) model [26]. Both allow efficient generation of synthetic graphs that mimic the degree distribution as well as the distribution of clustering coefficients in an input graph. The models both take as input the target degree sequence, and a measure of clustering. At a high level, BTER models a graph as a collection of dense Erdős-Rényi (ER) subgraphs that are sparsely interconnected to form the global graph structure and aims to reproduce the *degree-wise clustering coefficients*, i.e., $C_D = \{c_i\}$, where c_i is the ratio of the number of triangles involving nodes of degree i over the number of length-two paths centered at nodes of degree i. To do so, it requires C_D, along with the degree sequence $\mathcal{S}$, to be measured from the input graph and supplied as input to the algorithm. TCL, on the other hand, aims to reproduce the distribution of *local clustering coefficients* observed in the input graph. It extends the well-known Chung-Lu (CL) random graph model [6] by adding a transitive closure paramater, ρ, which controls the probability with which new edges create triangles (by connecting a node to a random two-hop neighbor), versus connecting two random nodes across the graph. The ρ parameter is a single value learned from the input graph via expectation-maximization.

From the privacy perspective, the degree sequence can be estimated from an input graph with reasonably high accuracy under differential privacy [11]. However, the clustering parameters used by these models are problematic. Under BTER, a single edge may be part of many triangles, and hence many coefficients can be affected. Moreover, adding or removing an edge e_{ij} will change the degrees of nodes v_i and v_j, which could cause a significant change in four different c_i's (i.e., those of the old degrees d_i, d_j and the new degrees $d_i \pm 1, d_j \pm 1$). This translates into a high global sensitivity, and it is unclear whether it is possible to circumvent this issue. Under TCL, the main difficulty comes from the fact that the ρ parameter is tuned through multiple iterations of an expectation maximization algorithm. The tools do not currently exist to bound the impact of such a change on the final value of ρ.

Proposed Approach. Motivated by the difficulty of incorporating differential privacy guarantees into existing generative social network models, we design a new model around a statistic for which accurate differentially private estimators are already known, namely the *triangle count*. Our model, which we call TriCycLe, is inspired by TCL. Rather than learning a transitive closure parameter, TriCycLe first estimates the number of triangles in the input graph and then rewires edges in a Chung-Lu seed graph until the desired number of triangles are present. In addition to being more amenable to differential privacy, we have found that TriCycLe often attains a better fit to the local clustering coefficient distribution than TCL.

In what follows, we give a brief overview of TCL and the CL model that it extends. We then describe how TriCycLe modifies TCL to replace the transitive closure parameter with the triangle count, and how that statistic is used to introduce the expected amounts of clustering into the output graph. The details of how the required model parameters—the degree distribution and number of triangles—can be estimated privately and efficiently are presented in Appendix C.3. Section 4 then explains how TriCycLe can be integrated into AGM as the underlying structural model.

A Review of CL and TCL. In the CL model, a graph is generated by (1) assigning a desired degree to every node based on the degree sequence of the input graph, and (2) sampling edges with a probability proportional to the desired degrees of the endpoint nodes; specifically, an edge e_{ij} is sampled with probability $\frac{d_i d_j}{2m}$. A graph matching a given degree sequence is generated in $O(m)$ steps by repeatedly sampling node pairs v_i, v_j independently from the distribution π, where $\pi(i) = \frac{d_i}{2m}$, and then adding edge e_{ij} to the sample graph. [28] gives an efficient implementation of the above idea, called Fast Chung-Lu (FCL). In FCL, nodes are sampled from π in constant time by constructing a vector of length $2m$ in which the ID of a node v_i is repeated d_i times, and then drawing nodes uniformly from this vector. Although CL therefore matches the desired degree distribution, it does not attempt to reproduce the amount of clustering in the input graph.

TCL extends CL to incorporate transitive edge formation, i.e., when a node connects to a friend of a friend. A transitive closure probability, ρ, controls the probability by which an edge is added between a randomly selected node and a two-hop neighbor (i.e., a friend of a friend), rather than to another randomly selected node, as in the CL model. Given a degree sequence $\mathcal{S}$ and ρ (learned from the input graph), TCL generates a synthetic graph in two phases. First, a *seed graph* of m edges is created using the CL procedure. Then TCL refines the seed graph by introducing triangles while preserving the expected degree sequence. Node v_i is first sampled from the π distribution; then with probability ρ, v_k is selected uniformly from v_i's neighbors and an edge is added between v_i and a uniformly selected neighbor of v_k, v_j (if it doesn't already exist), which results in at least one new triangle. With probability $1-\rho$, the endpoint v_j is sampled from π instead. After each new edge addition, the oldest edge in the graph is deleted to ensure that the expected degree sequence is maintained. The process of replacing edges continues until *all* old (seed) edges have been replaced.

TriCycLe Random Graph Model. Similarly to TCL, TriCycLe is based on the intuition that clustering in social graphs is attributable to triangles that form when a user is linked to a two-hop neighbor (i.e., a friend-of-a-friend). Therefore, TriCycLe attempts to reproduce the total number of triangles seen in the input graph by connecting nodes in this way. Like TCL, TriCycLe starts with a CL seed graph and iteratively replaces edges to create triangles. However, rather than using a transitive closure probability, we count the number of triangles in the input graph and then add transitive edges until the number of triangles in the resulting graph matches that of the input graph. The number of triangles in a graph can be accurately estimated under differential privacy using a recent technique [37] (Appendix C.3). Like TCL, for each transitive edge we add, we remove a seed edge to maintain the expected degree distribution; however, since the deleted edge may itself be part of one or more existing triangles, we reject proposed replacements that decrease the net triangle count. This check ensures that the algorithm terminates with the desired number of triangles.

Algorithm 1 gives the procedure for generating a graph with TriCycLe. The inputs to the algorithm are the degree sequence $\mathcal{S} = \{d_i | v_i \in G\}$ and the desired number of triangles n_Δ. For now, we assume that these two quantities have been directly measured from the input graph G (i.e., non-privately); in Appendix C.3, we explain how they can be accurately and efficiently estimated with

Algorithm 1 TriCycLe Graph Generation

Input: $N, \Theta_M = \{\mathcal{S}, n_\Delta\}$
Output: E_T

1: Compute π distribution from N and degree sequence $\mathcal{S}$
2: $E_T \leftarrow \text{CL}(\mathcal{S}, \pi)$
3: $\tau \leftarrow \text{COUNTTRIANGLES}(E_T)$
4: **while** $\tau < n_\Delta$ **do**
5:     $v_i \leftarrow \text{SAMPLE}(\pi)$
6:     $\gamma_i \leftarrow \Gamma(E_T, v_i) \setminus \{v_i\}$
7:     $v_k \leftarrow \text{SAMPLEUNIFORM}(\gamma_i)$
8:     $\gamma_k \leftarrow \Gamma(v_k)$
9:     $v_j \leftarrow \text{SAMPLEUNIFORM}(\gamma_k)$
10:     **if** $e_{ij} \notin E_T$ **then**
11:         $e_{qr} \leftarrow \text{OLDESTEDGE}(E_T)$ ▷ Get oldest edge to replace
12:         $CN_{qr} \leftarrow |\Gamma(v_q) \cap \Gamma(v_r)|$ ▷ Count common neighbors of v_q & v_r
13:         $E_T \leftarrow E_T \setminus e_{qr}$
14:         $CN_{ij} \leftarrow |\gamma_i \cap \Gamma(v_j)|$ ▷ Would proposed edge decrease τ?
15:         **if** $CN_{ij} \geq CN_{qr}$ **then**
16:             $E_T \leftarrow E_T \cup e_{ij}$ ▷ Update triangle count
17:             $\tau \leftarrow \tau + CN_{ij} - CN_{qr}$
18:         **else**
19:             $E_T \leftarrow E_T \cup e_{qr}$ ▷ Undo edge removal, making e_{qr} the *youngest* edge in E_T
20: **return** E_T

differential privacy. In line 2, a seed graph is sampled from the CL model[1], yielding edge set E_T. Recall that in CL, $m = \frac{1}{2}\sum_{d_i \in \mathcal{S}} d_i$ edges are sampled from the π distribution that is created from $\mathcal{S}$. In the main loop (line 4), we add transitive edges one at a time until E_T contains the desired number of triangles. A new edge is proposed by sampling a node v_i from the π distribution (i.e., with probability proportional to node degree) and then selecting a random "friend of a friend", v_j. Assuming the proposed edge e_{ij} does not already exist in E_T, we select the oldest edge e_{qr} (line 11) to be deleted in order to maintain the expected degree distribution. In lines 12–14 we calculate the number of triangles that would be created (destroyed) by adding (deleting) edge e_{ij} (e_{qr}). Note that we delete e_{qr} in line 13 before computing CN_{ij}, since its presence may affect the number of triangles created by connecting v_i and v_j. As long as the proposed edge addition/deletion does not decrease the number of triangles (line 15), we proceed with adding e_{ij} in line 16 and updating the triangle count in line 17. Otherwise, we undo the deletion of e_{qr} in line 19 before proceeding to the next iteration. Note that whenever the deletion of e_{qr} is reverted, its timestamp is reset so that it becomes the *youngest* edge in E_T; this is an important detail, since without it, the algorithm could get stuck, as there may not (at that moment) be any other edges in the graph that participate in more triangles than e_{qr}.

Extension to Handle Orphaned Nodes. A practical issue with the CL model, as well as TCL and TriCycLe, is that graphs generated by these models often contain many disconnected or *orphaned* nodes[2], compared to the input graph. Some fraction of nodes will not be assigned any edges, or will be connected only to nodes that are themselves disconnected from the rest of the graph. For large social graphs with many low-degree nodes, these models can generate many orphaned nodes. For example, on the large Pokec social network dataset (Appendix A), over 100K of its 720K nodes (many degree-one and degree-two nodes) are orphaned in the output.

We propose an extension to TriCycle to address this issue (it

[1] We use the FCL variant with bias correction (cFCL) in [26].

[2] A node is orphaned if it is not part of the main connected component of the graph. In this work, we assume the input graph is connected, and so the output graph should be too.

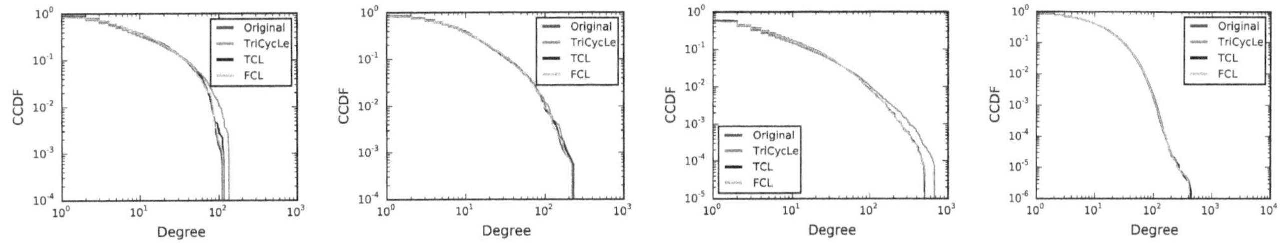

(a) Last.fm (b) Petster (c) Epinions (d) Pokec

Figure 2: Comparison of structural models in terms of their ability to reproduce the degree distribution

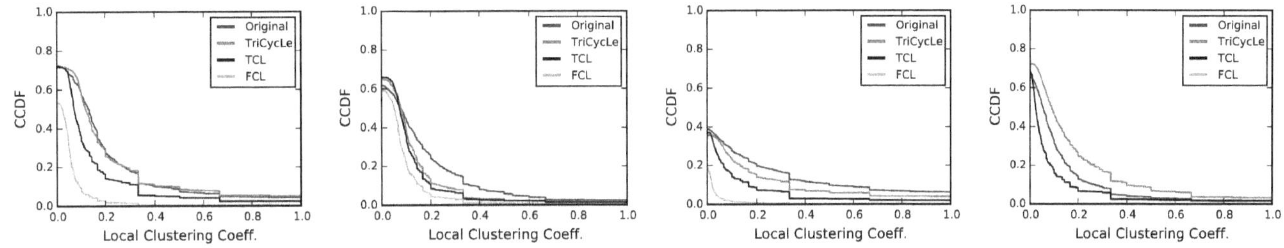

(a) Last.fm (b) Petster (c) Epinions (d) Pokec

Figure 3: Comparison of structural models in terms of their ability to reproduce the distribution of local clustering coefficients.

Algorithm 2 PostProcessGraph

Input: $N, E, \pi, \mathcal{S}$
Output: E'

1: $m \leftarrow \frac{1}{2}\sum_{v_i \in N} \mathcal{S}_{v_i}$
2: $E' \leftarrow E$
3: $m' \leftarrow |E'|$
4: **while** graph $G \leftarrow (N, E')$ is disconnected **do**
5: Select an orphaned node v_i
6: **if** $d_i^{(G)} > 0$ **then**
7: $m' \leftarrow m' - d_i^{(G)}$
8: Delete edges incident to v_i
9: **for** $j \leftarrow 1 \dots \mathcal{S}_{v_i}$ **do**
10: **repeat**
11: $v_k \leftarrow \text{SAMPLE}(\pi)$
12: **until** $d_k^{(G)} < \mathcal{S}_{v_k}$
13: $E' \leftarrow E' \cup e_{ik}$
14: **if** $m' = m$ **then**
15: Delete a random edge from E'
16: **else**
17: $m' \leftarrow m' + 1$
18: **return** E'

could also be applied to CL and TCL). We observe that (1) most nodes that end up orphaned are those with a degree of one in the input graph, and (2) since degree-one nodes cannot be part of any triangle, there is no reason to pick such nodes in line 5 of Algorithm 1. Let N_1 denote the set of degree-one nodes in the input graph. We make the following changes to Algorithm 1: (1) exclude degree-one nodes from the π distribution computed on line 1; (2) when generating the CL graph in line 2, generate $m - |N_1|$ edges, rather than m edges; (3) wire up the degree-one nodes, and any other orphaned nodes, in a separate post-processing step, given by Algorithm 2. Note that we apply post-processing to both the CL graph generated in line 2 (of Algorithm 1), and to the final output graph, before it is returned in line 20.

Post-processing takes as input nodes N and edges E, along with π and the degree sequence of the original input graph, which corresponds to the *desired* degrees for the nodes[3]. The main loop (lines 4–17) processes each orphaned node v_i by deleting any existing incident edges (which could only be connected to other orphaned nodes), then connecting v_i to the main connected component by adding edges to nodes in the main component (for which their desired degree has not yet been met) until v_i's desired degree is met. Upon adding a new edge, if we have more than the desired number of edges overall, we delete a randomly selected edge (line 15). Note that deleting existing edges (line 15) may result in additional orphaned nodes, therefore, we repeat this process as long as the graph is still disconnected. This process may destroy some triangles, but we found the impact to be minor in practice.

Empirical Evaluation. We validated the (non-private) graph models by generating synthetic versions of four real-world social graphs (see Appendix A) and comparing structural characteristics of the synthesized graphs to those of the original graphs. Figs. 2 (a)–(d) plot the degree distributions for the four datasets (on log-log scale), while Figs. 3 (a)–(d) plot the local clustering coefficient distributions. The y-axes give the complementary cumulative degree distribution (CCDF), i.e., the fraction of nodes with a greater degree or clustering coefficient than the x-value.

Figures 3(a)–(d) show that, as expected, the clustering coefficient distributions from TCL and TriCycLe were much closer to that of the input than for FCL (which does not model clustering). On the two largest graphs, the clustering coefficients for FCL were all very close to zero. Compared to TCL, TriCycLe more closely appoximated clustering coefficients of Last.fm and Epinions graphs, while its performance was comparable to that of TCL on the Pet-

[3] Degree-one nodes are included in $\mathcal{S}$, but excluded from π.

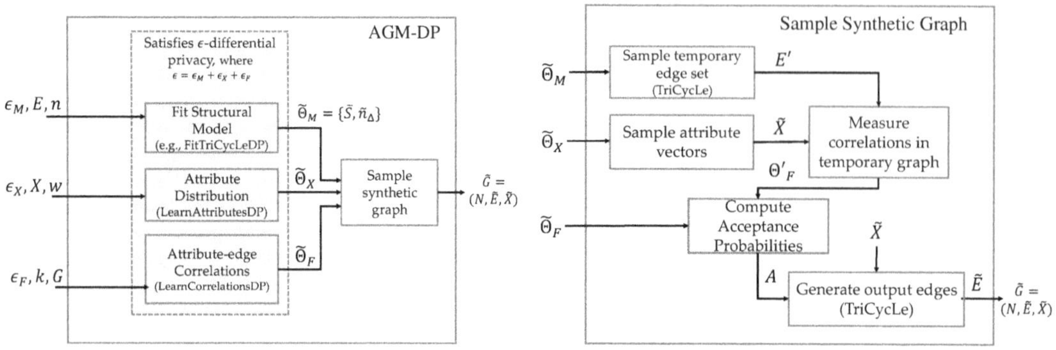

(a) Overview of AGM-DP

(b) Overview of Sampling Step

Figure 4: Fig. 4a gives an overview of our DP of AGM. Fig. 4b depicts the sampling step (corresponding to the right-most block in 4a).

ster graph. For Pokec, TriCycLe seems to over-estimate the clustering coefficients. All three models approximate the degree distributions reasonably well (Figs. 2(a)–(d)), though on two datasets, TriCycLe generated slightly more high degree nodes. The bias is a consequence of requiring edge replacements to increase the triangle count; removing edges from high degree nodes tends to remove more triangles, so fewer such edges are removed. There seems to be an inherent tension between the fidelity of the degree distribution and that of the clustering characteristics. Nevertheless, TriCycLe captures both properties sufficiently well for the purposes of this work, which focuses on the privacy aspect; therefore, we defer further analysis and improvement of TriCycLe to future work.

4. AGM-DP: PUTTING IT ALL TOGETHER

In the previous section we described how we model attributes on nodes and the graph structure, and learn the model parameters under DP. In this section, we put the pieces together and outline the end-to-end workflow for synthesizing differentially private graphs that mimic the attribute correlations and structural properties of a given social network. For concreteness, the presented algorithm uses TriCycLe as the structural model; however, other generative structural models (with DP) can be used in its stead.

The original AGM algorithm generates a synthetic graph based on G by repeatedly sampling edges from an underlying structural model M. Each sampled edge is either acceped or rejected to the output graph based on the acceptance probabilities A. This process ends when the desired number of edges (i.e., $m^{(G)}$) are generated. However, TriCycLe (Section 3.3) does not fit this pattern directly, as it continues to refine an initial seed graph by replacing edges to create new triangles until the desired number of triangles exists in the output graph. To accommodate models such as TriCycLe, we move the accept/reject step into the sampling algorithm for the structural model—that is, we still compute acceptance probabilities as in the original AGM algorithm (with the alterations required to satisfy differential privacy), but we then pass the probabilities A into M's specific sampling algorithm when generating the final output graph.[4] Since TriCycLe only replaces edges until the desired number of triangles exist, there may be many edges that are not replaced and thus are not subjected to the acceptance probabilities. Therefore, we also pass the acceptance probabilities into the CL seed graph generator on line 2 of Algorithm 1.

[4]Specifically, we change the condition in the *if* statement on line 10 of Algorithm 1 to "$e_{ij} \notin E_T \wedge \text{SampleUniform}(0,1) \leq A(F_w(\tilde{x}_i, \tilde{x}_j))$", where $\tilde{x}_i$ and $\tilde{x}_j$ are the attribute vectors generated for nodes v_i and v_j in Algorithm 5.

Algorithm 3 AGM-DP-TriCycLe

Input: $G = (N, E, X), w, \varepsilon, k$
Output: An ε-DP graph $\widetilde{G} = (\widetilde{N}, \widetilde{E}, \widetilde{X})$

1: $\widetilde{N} \leftarrow N$
2: $\varepsilon_X, \varepsilon_F, \varepsilon_M \leftarrow \text{SPLITBUDGET}(\varepsilon)$ ▷ Split privacy budget ε among the parameters to be learned
3: $\widetilde{\Theta}_X \leftarrow \text{LEARNATTRIBUTESDP}(\varepsilon_X, X, w)$ ▷ Learn DP approximations for each parameter from input graph G
4: $\widetilde{\Theta}_M \leftarrow \text{FITTRICYCLEDP}(\varepsilon_M, E)$
5: $\widetilde{\Theta}_F \leftarrow \text{LEARNCORRELATIONSDP}(\varepsilon_F, G, k)$
6: Sample new attribute vectors $\widetilde{X}$ using $\widetilde{\Theta}_X$
7: $\widetilde{E} \leftarrow \text{TRICYCLE}(\widetilde{N}, \widetilde{\Theta}_M)$
8: $A \leftarrow \emptyset$
9: **for** Iterations **do**
10: Compute Θ'_F from the graph $\widetilde{G} = \{\widetilde{N}, \widetilde{E}, \widetilde{X}\}$
11: **for** $y_i \in Y_F$ **do**
12: $R(y_i) \leftarrow \frac{\widetilde{\Theta}_F(y_i)}{\Theta'_F(y_i)}$
13: **if** $A_{old} \neq \emptyset$ **then**
14: $R(y_i) \leftarrow R(y_i) \times A_{old}(y_i)$
15: **for** $y_i \in Y_F$ **do**
16: $A(y_i) \leftarrow \frac{R(y_i)}{\text{SUP}(R)}$ ▷ Compute the acceptance probabilities
17: $\widetilde{E} \leftarrow \text{TRICYCLE}(\widetilde{N}, \widetilde{\Theta}_M, \widetilde{X}, A)$ ▷ Sample a new edge set using acceptance probabilities
18: $A_{old} \leftarrow A$
19: **return** $\widetilde{G} = (\widetilde{N}, \widetilde{E}, \widetilde{X})$

Our end-to-end differentially private workflow, AGM-DP, is given in Algorithm 3 and illustrated in Fig. 4. It takes input graph G with w attributes, a global privacy budget ε, and a truncation parameter k. We split the privacy budget ε evenly in our empirical analysis (Section 5), i.e, $\varepsilon_X = \varepsilon_F = \frac{1}{4}\varepsilon$, $\varepsilon_M = \varepsilon_S + \varepsilon_\Delta = \frac{1}{4}\varepsilon + \frac{1}{4}\varepsilon$, which seems to work well in practice; though other strategies could also be used. In lines 3–5, we learn the three sets of modeling parameters from the input graph using their respective differentially private learning procedures. Note that after line 5 we never look back at the raw input graph. Next we assign attribute vectors to nodes by sampling randomly from $\widetilde{\Theta}_X$. Temporary edge set E' is sampled independently of the node attributes. The loop beginning at line 9 computes edge acceptance probabilities by measuring the attribute correlations between Θ'_F in the current graph and $\widetilde{\Theta}_F$ derived from G Finally, new edges are sampled using the modified structural model discussed above (line 17). The process is iterated until the acceptance probabilities A converge (for simple models like FCL, only one iteration is required). In our experimental study, we found that A tended to converge after just a few iterations. The output graph $\widetilde{G}$ approximates a joint sampling of the structural model and the attribute correlations, and satisfies differential privacy.

THEOREM 2. *Algorithm 3 satisfies ε-differential privacy.*

PROOF. The privacy budget ε is split into three parts, $\varepsilon_X, \varepsilon_F, \varepsilon_M$, which are used in the learning procedures for the three sets of model parameters (lines 3–5). The fact that the learning procedures satisfy differential privacy with privacy parameters ε_F, ε_X, and ε_M, respectively, follows from Thm. 8, Thm. 7, and Thm. 9, respectively. After line 5, the algorithm never looks back at the raw input data again. Thus, by sequential composition and post-processing invariance, we have that the algorithm as a whole satisfies ε-DP. □

The time costs of our approach are discussed in Appendix C.4.

5. EMPIRICAL ANALYSIS

We present an experimental study of our DP adaptation of AGM on the four real-world social network datasets described in Appendix A. Our goal is to demonstrate that the synthetic graphs produced by AGM-DP reasonably preserve attribute correlations and structural properties of an input graph under privacy. We instantiate AGM-DP with the differentially private version of TriCycLe (referred to as AGMDP-TriCL henceforth), as well as a DP version of the simple FCL model (AGMDP-FCL henceforth) as the underlying structural models. For the latter, we modified the bias-corrected FCL algorithm (cFCL) described in [26] to take a noisy degree sequence as input, generated using the constrained inference approach of [11], just as was done for TriCycLe (Appendix C.3).

We experimented with four different privacy budgets, $\varepsilon \in \{0.2, 0.3, \ln(2), \ln(3)\}$; for the larger Pokec dataset, we used $\varepsilon \in \{0.01, 0.05, 0.1, 0.2\}$[5]. For AGM-DPTriCL, we divided the overall privacy budget ε evenly among the four model parameters: attribute distribution Θ_X, attribute correlations Θ_F, degree sequence $\mathcal{S}$ and number of triangles n_Δ. For AGMDP-FCL does not use n_Δ, so we allocated half of the budget to $\mathcal{S}$ and split the other half evenly between Θ_F and Θ_X. The truncation parameter, k, used in computing the private attribute correlations, was set to $n^{\frac{1}{3}}$ for all experiments. For both AGMDP-TriCL and AGMDP-FCL, on each setting of ε, we report average results over 1,000 synthetic graphs (100 for Epinions and Pokec). For comparison, we also report the results of AGM instantiated with the non-private versions of FCL and TriCycLe, denoted AGM-FCL and AGM-TriCL, respectively.

5.1 Statistics Evaluated

We compare synthetic and original graphs via several statistics.

Clustering Coefficients. We consider two measures of clustering. The *global clustering coefficient* (also called *transitivity*) of a graph G is defined as $C(G) = \frac{3 \times n_\Delta}{n_W}$ where n_Δ is the number of triangles in G and n_W is the number of wedges (i.e., length two paths) in G. Another measure is the average of the *local clustering coefficients*. The local clustering coefficient of a node $v_i \in N$ is given by $C_i = \frac{2|\{e_{jk} \in E | v_j, v_k \in \Gamma(v_i)\}|}{|\Gamma(v_i)| \times (|\Gamma(v_i)|-1)}$, and the average of the local clustering coefficients is denoted $\overline{C} = \frac{1}{n}\sum_{v_i \in N} C_i$. The reason for using both these measures is that the former tends to emphasize the low-degree nodes while the latter emphasizes high-degree nodes. We report the *mean relative error* (MRE) of C and $\overline{C}$ between the synthetic graphs and the original graphs (denoted C and $\overline{C}$ in the tables).

Degree Distribution. To evaluate how well a synthetic graph captures the degree distribution of the input graph, we use the *Kolmogorov-Smirnov* (KS) statistic, which quantifies the maximum distance between the two degree distributions. Let $F_{\mathcal{S}}$ and $F_{\widetilde{\mathcal{S}}}$ denote the cumulative distribution functions estimated from the sorted degree sequences of the original and synthetic graphs, respectively. Then $KS(\mathcal{S}, \widetilde{\mathcal{S}}) = \max_d |F_{\mathcal{S}}(d) - F_{\widetilde{\mathcal{S}}}(d)|$. Since the KS statistic is known to be less sensitive to differences in the tails of the distributions, we also report the *Hellinger distance* between the two degree distributions (denoted $D_{\mathcal{S}}, D_{\widetilde{\mathcal{S}}}$), defined as

$$H_{\mathcal{S}} = \frac{1}{\sqrt{2}}\sqrt{\sum_d \left(\sqrt{D_{\mathcal{S}}(d)} - \sqrt{D_{\widetilde{\mathcal{S}}}(d)}\right)^2}.$$

The smaller the values of both statistics, the closer (more similar) the degree distributions of the synthetic and original graphs.

Edge Count and Triangle Count. We report the mean relative error (MRE) for the number of edges (denoted simply as m in the tables) and the number of triangles (denoted as n_Δ in the tables) in the synthetic graphs relative to the original input graphs.

Attribute Correlations. To quantify the error in the attribute correlations in the synthetic graph, relative to the original graph, we report the MRE (denoted as simply Θ_F in the tables), as well as the Hellinger distance, defined as

$$H_{\Theta_F} = \frac{1}{\sqrt{2}}\sqrt{\sum_{y_i \in Y_w^F} \left(\sqrt{\Theta_F(y_i)} - \sqrt{\widetilde{\Theta}_F(y_i)}\right)^2},$$

where Θ_F and $\widetilde{\Theta}_F$ are the discrete probability distributions for the original and synthetic graphs, respectively. H_{Θ_F} lies in the range $[0,1]$, with a value near 0 meaning that the correlations in the synthetic graph closely approximate those in the input graph.

5.2 Results

Tables 2–5 summarize the experimental results on the four datasets. For each setting of the overall privacy budget (ε) we report the average error rates for the graphs synthesized by both AGMDP-TriCL and AGMDP-FCL. Recall that a smaller ε translates to a *stronger* privacy guarantee; so the level of privacy (and, in general, the amount of error) increases as we move down the tables. To make the impact of the privacy mechanism clear, we include, at the top of each table, the error rates for the non-private version of AGM instantiated with FCL and TriCycLe (denoted AGM-FCL and AGM-TriCL, respectively).

Clustering. Recall that the FCL structural model includes no mechanism for capturing and reproducing clustering in the input graph, so the error rates for the triangle count (n_Δ), average clustering coefficient ($\overline{C}$) and the global clustering coefficient (C) are larger for FCL-based models than for the TriCycLe-based models, as expected. For that reason, the error rates for AGMDP-FCL on those three statistics serve as a good reference point for interpreting the corresponding results of AGMDP-TriCL. For instance, looking at the results on the Last.fm and Epinions datasets (Tables 2 and 4, respectively) we see that even with a reasonably strong privacy budget of $\varepsilon = 0.2$, AGMDP-TriCL could reproduce the clustering observed in the input graph significantly better than AGMDP-FCL. For the large Pokec dataset, the error rates remained significantly below those of AGMDP-FCL, even with the extreme setting of $\varepsilon = 0.01$, typically the smallest ε seen in the DP literature. In

[5]The large size of this dataset makes it much more robust to injected noise, so we use smaller (stronger) values for ε.

Table 2: Results for AGMDP-FCL and AGMDP-TriCL structural models on the **Last.fm** dataset for different privacy settings, ε.

Last.fm	Model	Θ_F	H_{Θ_F}	KS_S	H_S	n_Δ	$\overline{C}$	C	m
non-private	**AGM-FCL**	0.00	0.01	0.05	0.15	0.59	0.75	0.61	0.0000
	AGM-TriCL	0.00	0.02	0.08	0.16	0.05	0.04	0.24	0.0001
$\varepsilon = \ln 3$	**AGMDP-FCL**	0.02	0.14	0.06	0.16	0.59	0.75	0.60	0.0076
	AGMDP-TriCL	0.02	0.14	0.09	0.17	0.05	0.07	0.23	0.0147
$\varepsilon = \ln 2$	**AGMDP-FCL**	0.03	0.18	0.07	0.17	0.56	0.74	0.58	0.0120
	AGMDP-TriCL	0.03	0.18	0.10	0.18	0.06	0.10	0.23	0.0222
$\varepsilon = 0.3$	**AGMDP-FCL**	0.05	0.27	0.09	0.19	0.42	0.68	0.48	0.0248
	AGMDP-TriCL	0.05	0.28	0.12	0.21	0.18	0.30	0.24	0.0499
$\varepsilon = 0.2$	**AGMDP-FCL**	0.06	0.32	0.11	0.20	0.39	0.65	0.43	0.0374
	AGMDP-TriCL	0.06	0.33	0.16	0.24	0.35	0.38	0.27	0.0769

Table 3: Results for AGMDP-FCL and AGMDP-TriCL on the **Petster** dataset for different privacy settings, ε.

Petster	Model	Θ_F	H_{Θ_F}	KS_S	H_S	n_Δ	$\overline{C}$	C	m
non-private	**AGM-FCL**	0.00	0.02	0.04	0.17	0.13	0.51	0.15	0.0001
	AGM-TriCL	0.00	0.01	0.05	0.17	0.00	0.35	0.07	0.0000
$\varepsilon = \ln 3$	**AGMDP-FCL**	0.03	0.16	0.05	0.17	0.18	0.51	0.19	0.0075
	AGMDP-TriCL	0.03	0.16	0.06	0.18	0.09	0.26	0.08	0.0136
$\varepsilon = \ln 2$	**AGMDP-FCL**	0.03	0.20	0.06	0.18	0.16	0.49	0.17	0.0117
	AGMDP-TriCL	0.04	0.20	0.07	0.19	0.13	0.29	0.10	0.0221
$\varepsilon = 0.3$	**AGMDP-FCL**	0.05	0.29	0.08	0.20	0.21	0.44	0.18	0.0268
	AGMDP-TriCL	0.06	0.30	0.12	0.22	0.39	0.32	0.24	0.0486
$\varepsilon = 0.2$	**AGMDP-FCL**	0.07	0.35	0.10	0.21	0.32	0.41	0.24	0.0388
	AGMDP-TriCL	0.07	0.36	0.14	0.24	0.72	0.32	0.40	0.0766

fact, the error rates for those statistics are nearly unchanged (compared to the non-private counterpart) until ε was set ≤ 0.05. This is because the amount of noise added to preserve privacy is independent of the size of the input graph, so larger graphs achieve a more favorable signal-to-noise ratio for the model parameters. On the other hand, we see that on the smaller Petster dataset, the clustering produced by AGMDP-TriCL was no better than that produced by AGMDP-FCL, when $\varepsilon < \ln(2)$ (≈ 0.69).

Attribute-Edge Correlations. A baseline for attribute-edge correlations is to set all correlation probabilities to be equal[6], independent of the data. This yields an average Hellinger distance of 0.37, 0.45, 0.55 and 0.5 and an MAE of 0.09, 0.11, 0.13 and 0.12 on Last.fm, Petster, Epinions and Pokec, respectively. Comparing against H_{Θ_F} and Θ_F in the tables, we see that the error rates for the synthetic graphs generated by AGMDP-FCL and AGMDP-TriCL were significantly lower than the baseline error rates on all datasets, even under the strongest privacy settings tested. The difference was most dramatic on the larger datasets (Epinions and Pokec).

Degree Statistics. The error in degree statistics (H_S and KS_S) grows more slowly for AGMDP-FCL than for AGMDP-TriCL (as ε decreases). This is because we allocated *half* of the privacy budget for computing the noisy degree sequence with AGMDP-FCL, while for AGMDP-TriCL we allocated only *a quarter* (the other quarter is used to estimate triangle counts, not needed by FCL). Thus, the degree sequence has more noise in AGMDP-TriCL for the same ε. To calibrate the error-rates, we note that the baseline model that assigns edges to nodes uniformly at random achieves KS error 0.51, 0.51, 0.61 and 0.43 and a Hellinger distance of 0.64, 0.63, 0.64 and 0.56 on Last.fm, Petster, Epinions and Pokec, respectively. The KS statistic was substantially below that of the baseline for both AGMDP-FCL and AGMDP-TriCL at $\varepsilon = 0.2$: the KS was ≤ 0.16 on Last.fm and Petster (Tables 2 and 3), and ≤ 0.09 on Epinions and Pokec (Tables 4 and 5). Similarly, the Hellinger distance for both models was less than half that of the baseline on all datasets: on Last.fm and Petster, we had $H_S \leq 0.24$, and on Epinions and Pokec we had $H_S \leq 0.12$. The number of edges in the synthetic graphs (m) is close to the input for small privacy budgets ($\varepsilon = 0.2$ for Last.fm, Petster and Epinions, and $\varepsilon = 0.01$ for Pokec) with the MRE below 0.08 on the small Last.fm and Petster datasets, below 0.04 on Epinions and below 0.085 on Pokec.

[6]So for $w = 2$ attributes, we set each of the ten probabilities to 0.1.

5.3 Discussion

Our experiments demonstrate that it is possible to generate synthetic attributed social graphs with reasonably high fidelity, without sacrificing privacy. An important takeaway from the results is that, while the proposed framework performs well even on very small graphs, its power really becomes evident when applied on moderate to large input graphs. In particular, we saw that on the reasonably large Pokec social network, we generated very accurate synthetic graphs even under the strongest privacy regime for DP used in the literature (i.e., $\varepsilon = 0.01$).

We focused our empirical analysis on graphs with $w = 2$ node attributes, however our framework is not limited to two-dimensional attribute vectors. Although the sensitivity of the approach is not affected by the number of attributes, we can expect the error rates to increase as w increases, since the number of counts that must be

Table 4: Results for AGMDP-FCL and AGMDP-TriCL on the **Epinions** dataset for different privacy settings, ε.

Epinions	Model	Θ_F	H_{Θ_F}	KS_S	H_S	n_Δ	$\overline{C}$	C	m
non-private	**AGM-FCL**	0.01	0.03	0.06	0.08	0.82	0.92	0.83	0.0008
	AGM-TriCL	0.00	0.01	0.04	0.08	0.27	0.06	0.53	0.0008
$\varepsilon = \ln 3$	**AGMDP-FCL**	0.01	0.06	0.06	0.08	0.83	0.92	0.84	0.0019
	AGMDP-TriCL	0.01	0.06	0.04	0.08	0.28	0.10	0.53	0.0057
$\varepsilon = \ln 2$	**AGMDP-FCL**	0.01	0.08	0.05	0.08	0.82	0.92	0.84	0.0042
	AGMDP-TriCL	0.01	0.09	0.04	0.09	0.28	0.11	0.52	0.0084
$\varepsilon = 0.3$	**AGMDP-FCL**	0.01	0.12	0.06	0.10	0.81	0.92	0.83	0.0128
	AGMDP-TriCL	0.02	0.14	0.07	0.11	0.23	0.14	0.48	0.0218
$\varepsilon = 0.2$	**AGMDP-FCL**	0.02	0.13	0.08	0.11	0.78	0.91	0.80	0.0157
	AGMDP-TriCL	0.02	0.17	0.09	0.12	0.20	0.19	0.46	0.0345

Table 5: Results for AGMDP-FCL AGMDP-TriCL on the **Pokec** dataset for different privacy settings, ε.

Pokec	Model	Θ_F	H_{Θ_F}	KS_S	H_S	n_Δ	$\overline{C}$	C	m
non-private	**AGM-FCL**	0.00	0.01	0.04	0.05	1.00	1.00	1.00	0.0000
	AGM-TriCL	0.00	0.02	0.03	0.04	0.24	0.37	0.30	0.0000
$\varepsilon = 0.2$	**AGMDP-FCL**	0.00	0.02	0.05	0.05	1.00	1.00	1.00	0.0020
	AGMDP-TriCL	0.00	0.03	0.03	0.05	0.24	0.39	0.30	0.0052
$\varepsilon = 0.1$	**AGMDP-FCL**	0.00	0.03	0.05	0.06	1.00	1.00	1.00	0.0057
	AGMDP-TriCL	0.00	0.04	0.05	0.07	0.24	0.37	0.30	0.0101
$\varepsilon = 0.05$	**AGMDP-FCL**	0.00	0.06	0.05	0.07	1.00	1.00	1.00	0.0108
	AGMDP-TriCL	0.01	0.09	0.07	0.10	0.25	0.35	0.33	0.0189
$\varepsilon = 0.01$	**AGMDP-FCL**	0.02	0.14	0.11	0.15	1.00	1.00	1.00	0.0510
	AGMDP-TriCL	0.03	0.20	0.15	0.19	0.46	0.37	0.50	0.0833

computed for Θ_X and Θ_F increase exponentially with w, leading to smaller counts and hence a higher noise-to-signal ratio. Likewise, we expect error rates to decrease when using $w = 1$.

6. RELATED WORK

Prior studies have shown that simple graph anonymization techniques are vulnerable to a number of attacks that can allow an attacker to reidentify individuals and determine the presence of specific edges [1, 10, 24]. Initial attempts to address these types of attacks (e.g., [17, 38, 39]) made strong assumptions about the attacker's background knowledge and lacked formal privacy guarantees. More recently, focus has shifted to extending the strong formal privacy guarantees of differential privacy to graph data. This work has generally pursued one of two directions: methods for privately computing specific statistics, and private graph release.

Private Graph Statistics. Hay et al. [11] considered releasing the degree distribution of a graph under edge-differential privacy using a constrained inference technique. The idea is to impose an ordering constraint on the pre-noise degree sequence, add Laplace noise to the sorted sequence then post-process the noisy sequence to restore the order constraint.

Subgraph counting queries ask how many "edge-induced isomorphic copies" of a query graph Q (e.g., triangle), are present in G. Although subgraph counting has high global sensitivity in general, Karwa et al. extend smooth sensitivity for specific queries such as triangles and k-stars. Wang et al. outlined a general, divide and conquer approach using smooth sensitivity for graph analysis tasks that have low *local* sensitivity, such as clustering coefficient [35]. Zhang et al. [37] defined the *Ladder* framework for producing accurate DP estimates of subgraph counting queries, including triangles and k-stars. The Ladder framework combines the concept of "local sensitivity at distance t" [25] with the exponential mechanism [22]. Shen and Yu [33] consider finding frequently occurring subgraphs under differential privacy.

Private Graph Release. Mir and Wright [23] focused on generating representative synthetic graphs via the *Kronecker graph model.* Their approach estimates the (single) model parameter from the input graph under edge-differential privacy. Sala et al.'s *Pygmalion* model uses the dK-series of the input graph, which records the distribution of the pairs of degrees observed on edges [30]. The proposed approach is based on local sensitivity, and so does not provide differential privacy. Subsequent work combined the dk-series model that constructs a synthetic graph via smooth sensitivity [34].

Xiao et al. encode the structure of a graph via private edge-counting queries, under the hierarchical random graph (HRG) model, and claim better results than the dK-series approach [36]. Chen et al. [4] use the exponential mechanism to sample an adjacency matrix after clustering the input graph. Proserpio et al. [29] suggest non-uniformly down-weighting the edges of a graph in order to reduce high global sensitivity due to the possibility of very high degree nodes. They demonstrate the approach, combined with MCMC-based sampling, to generate private synthetic graphs. Our work differs from all these prior works, in particular as we aim to (privately) model both structure and attribute correlations.

Node Differential Privacy. The prior work discussed above adopts edge-differential privacy. In the more challenging model of node-differential privacy, neighboring graphs differ in a single node and *all* of its incident edges. While smooth sensitivity has been useful for taming high global sensitivity under edge-differential privacy, it appears less effective for node differential privacy. This is because in node-differential privacy, even the local sensitivity of basic statistics can be very high. For example, the number of edges in a graph can increase by n (the number of nodes) if we add a new node connected to all others, so even the local sensitivity of edge counting is n. To disallow such cases, Chen and Zhou propose a *recursive mechanism* based on the notion of *local empirical sensitivity*, which considers only the effects of *deleting* of an existing node from the input graph [5]. Kasiviswanathan et al. [14] and Blocki et al. [2] independently proposed the idea of using low-sensitivity transforms to project an input graph onto the set of degree-bounded graphs. By bounding the maximum degree of the input graph, the sensitivity becomes bounded and can be significantly reduced. When the degree bound, D, is set so that most of the nodes in the graph have degree $\leq D$, very little error is introduced by the projection operation; however, choosing an appropriate bound can be difficult in practice.

7. CONCLUSIONS AND FUTURE WORK

This work proposed a differentially private adaptation of the Attributed Graph Model (AGM) of [27]. Our framework is capable of modeling and synthesizing attributed social networks that mimic the structural properties and attribute correlations of an input network, without disclosing individual relationships and attributes. We explored three different approaches for accurately modeling the attribute correlations under differential privacy, identifying edge truncation to be the most effective choice. We introduced a new structural model capable of reproducing the important structural properties of social networks, including the degree distribution and the distribution of local clustering coefficients, and showed that the parameters required by the model can be accurately estimated under differential privacy. Finally, we presented an end-to-end workflow for generating private, synthetic social graphs with our framework and demonstrated its efficacy through experiments on four real-world social network datasets.

We believe this work lays a good foundation for providing differential privacy guarantees for attributed graph analysis; however, there remain many avenues for future work. We limited our focus to achieving edge differential privacy for undirected social graphs with a relatively small number of binary node attributes. We conclude by briefly discussing what would be needed to remove each of these restrictions.

Other Graph Types. We chose to focus on attributed social networks in this work for concreteness; however the proposed framework could be extended to support other types of attributed graphs by plugging in an appropriate underlying structural model for M. As long as the structural model satisfies differential privacy, the framework as a whole will still satisfy differential privacy.

Non-Binary Attributes. Our framework can support non-binary categorical or continuous attributes by simply converting each attribute to a series of binary attributes, one per category or range[7]. Although increasing the number of attributes, w, has no impact on the sensitivity of our approach, it does increase the number of counts that need to be computed for Θ_X and Θ_F; thus we can expect the accuracy of the generated graphs to degrade as w increases, due to a higher noise-to-signal ratio for the counts. In general, the larger the graph, the more attributes that could be supported accurately, since the amount of noise is also independent of the size of the graph. It may also be of interest to support edge attributes (e.g., trust or friendship strength), which would need an additional correlation model.

Directed Edges. Modeling attribute-edge correlations under directed edges increases the number of counts computed for Θ_F from $\binom{2^w+1}{2}$ to 4^w. However, the sensitivity does not change. The structural model also needs to capture directionality. This is more challenging, since the current approaches (TriCycle and FCL) make use of the degree sequence. Switching to using the in-degree and out-degree sequence is not compatible with the constrained inference of [11], so this helpful post-processing step would be lost.

Node Differential Privacy. In this work we focused on satisfying edge-differential privacy, in which neighboring graphs differ in a single edge or the attributes of a single node. A stronger notion of adjacency which has been studied in a few recent works is node-differential privacy, in which neighboring graphs differ in a single node and all of its adjacent edges (and/or the attributes associated with one node). This is a more difficult definition to satisfy, as it translates to a much higher sensitivity for many tasks. A promising approach for computing Θ_F under node-privacy is to use the same edge truncation approach but then to add noise according to its smooth sensitivity in the node-adjacency model. In a preliminary experiment we found that using this approach, the Hellinger distance between the original and noisy correlation probabilities was still better than the baseline when $\varepsilon \geq \ln(2)$ on Last.fm, when $\varepsilon \geq 0.3$ on Petster, when $\varepsilon \geq 0.2$ on Epinions, and when $\varepsilon \geq 0.05$ on Pokec; δ was fixed at 0.01 for the experiment. The problem of developing a node-private approach for fitting a suitable structural model remains a challenging open problem.

8. ACKNOWLEDGMENTS

We thank the anonymous reviewers for their helpful feedback and suggestions. The work of Cormode is supported in part by European Commission Marie Curie Integration Grant PCIG13-GA-2013-618202 and a Royal Society Wolfson Research Merit Award.

9. REFERENCES

[1] L. Backstrom, C. Dwork, and J. Kleinberg. Wherefore art thou R3579X?: anonymized social networks, hidden patterns, and structural steganography. In *WWW*, 2007.

[2] J. Blocki, A. Blum, A. Datta, and O. Sheffet. Differentially private data analysis of social networks via restricted sensitivity. In *ITCS*, 2013.

[3] I. Cantador, P. Brusilovsky, and T. Kuflik. 2nd workshop on information heterogeneity and fusion in recommender systems (hetrec). In *RecSys*, 2011.

[4] R. Chen, B. C. Fung, S. Y. Philip, and B. C. Desai. Correlated network data publication via differential privacy. *VLDB Journal*, pages 1–24, 2013.

[5] S. Chen and S. Zhou. Recursive mechanism: towards node differential privacy and unrestricted joins. In *SIGMOD*, 2013.

[6] F. Chung and L. Lu. The average distances in random graphs with given expected degrees. volume 99, pages 15879–15882. National Acad Sciences, 2002.

[7] C. Dwork. Differential privacy. *ICALP*, 2006.

[8] C. Dwork, F. McSherry, K. Nissim, and A. Smith. Calibrating noise to sensitivity in private data analysis. In *Theory of Cryptography*, 2006.

[7]For example, marital status could be represented by the following three binary attributes: *isMarried*, *isDivorced*, *isSingleOrWidowed*.

[9] M. Hay. *Enabling accurate analysis of private network data.* PhD thesis, University of Massachusetts Amherst, 2010.
[10] M. Hay, G. Miklau, D. Jensen, D. Towsley, and P. Weis. Resisting structural re-identification in anonymized social networks. *VLDB*, 1(1):102–114, 2008.
[11] M. Hay, C. Li, G. Miklau, and D. Jensen. Accurate estimation of the degree distribution of private networks. In *ICDM*, 2009.
[12] Z. Jorgensen and T. Yu. A privacy-preserving framework for personalized, social recommendations. In *EDBT*, 2014.
[13] V. Karwa, S. Raskhodnikova, A. Smith, and G. Yaroslavtsev. Private analysis of graph structure. *PVLDB*, 2011.
[14] S. P. Kasiviswanathan, K. Nissim, S. Raskhodnikova, and A. Smith. Analyzing graphs with node differential privacy. In *Theory of Cryptography*, 2013.
[15] D. Kifer and B.-R. Lin. Towards an axiomatization of statistical privacy and utility. In *PODS*, 2010.
[16] T. G. Kolda, A. Pinar, T. Plantenga, and C. Seshadhri. A scalable generative graph model with community structure. SIAM J. Sci. Comput., 36(5), C424–C452, 2014.
[17] K. Liu and E. Terzi. Towards identity anonymization on graphs. In *SIGMOD*, 2008.
[18] W. Lu and G. Miklau. Exponential random graph estimation under differential privacy. In *KDD*, 2014.
[19] P. Massa and P. Avesani. Trust-aware bootstrapping of recommender systems. In *Workshop on recommender systems*, 2006.
[20] M. McPherson, L. Smith-Lovin, and J. M. Cook. Birds of a feather: Homophily in social networks. *Annual review of sociology*, pages 415–444, 2001.
[21] F. McSherry. Privacy integrated queries: an extensible platform for privacy-preserving data analysis. In *SIGMOD*, 2009.
[22] F. McSherry and K. Talwar. Mechanism design via differential privacy. In *FOCS*, 2007.
[23] D. J. Mir and R. N. Wright. A differentially private graph estimator. In *ICDMW*, 2009.
[24] A. Narayanan and V. Shmatikov. De-anonymizing social networks. In *Security and Privacy*, 2009.
[25] Nissim, Raskhodnikova, and Smith. Smooth sensitivity and sampling in private data analysis. In *STOC*, 2007.
[26] J. J. Pfeiffer, T. La Fond, S. Moreno, and J. Neville. Fast generation of large scale social networks while incorporating transitive closures. In *(PASSAT)*, 2012.
[27] J. J. Pfeiffer III, S. Moreno, T. La Fond, J. Neville, and B. Gallagher. Attributed graph models: modeling network structure with correlated attributes. In *WWW*, 2014.
[28] A. Pinar, C. Seshadhri, and T. G. Kolda. The similarity between stochastic kronecker and chung-lu graph models. *CoRR, abs/1110.4925*, 2011.
[29] D. Proserpio, S. Goldberg, and F. McSherry. Calibrating data to sensitivity in private data analysis. In *VLDB*, 2014.
[30] A. Sala, X. Zhao, C. Wilson, H. Zheng, and B. Y. Zhao. Sharing graphs using differentially private graph models. In *IMC*, 2011.
[31] C. Seshadhri, T. G. Kolda, and A. Pinar. Community structure and scale-free collections of erdős-rényi graphs. *Physical Review E*, 85(5):056109, 2012.
[32] C. Seshadhri, A. Pinar, and T. G. Kolda. An in-depth study of stochastic kronecker graphs. In *ICDM*, 2011.
[33] E. Shen and T. Yu. Mining frequent graph patterns with differential privacy. In *KDD*, 2013.
[34] Y. Wang and X. Wu. Preserving differential privacy in degree-correlation based graph generation. *Transactions on data privacy*, 6(2):127, 2013.
[35] Y. Wang, X. Wu, J. Zhu, and Y. Xiang. On learning cluster coefficient of private networks. Social Network Analysis and Mining (3), pages 925–938, 2013.
[36] Q. Xiao, R. Chen, and K.-L. Tan. Differentially private network data release via structural inference. In *KDD*, 2014.
[37] J. Zhang, G. Cormode, C. M. Procopiuc, D. Srivastava, and X. Xiao. Private release of graph statistics using ladder functions. In *SIGMOD*, 2015.
[38] B. Zhou and J. Pei. Preserving privacy in social networks against neighborhood attacks. In *ICDE*, 2008.
[39] L. Zou, L. Chen, and M. T. Özsu. K-automorphism: A general framework for privacy preserving network publication. PVLDB (2), 946–957, 2009.

APPENDIX

A. DATASETS

We make use of four real-world social network datasets:

Last.fm[8] is a social music platform where users listen to and rate music, as well as share their favorite music with friends. This publicly available dataset [3] contains undirected friendship edges between user nodes, as well as a set of "listened to" relations indicating which artists a user has listened to. Although the dataset does not contain node attributes, we created two attributes by selecting the two most popular artists and creating *listenedToArtistX* attributes, with a value of 1 if a user had listened to artist X at least once.

The Epinions dataset [19] was crawled from Epinions.com, a website where users review and rate products. The dataset contains directed edges between users that represent positive trust statements, e.g., that user A trusts the reviews/ratings produced by user B. We converted the directed edges to undirected edges by keeping only the *mutual* trust relationships, i.e., we keep edge e_{ij} only if both e_{ij} and e_{ji} were present. Similarly to the Last.fm dataset, we created binary node attributes by selecting the two most frequently-rated products in the dataset and creating attributes with a value of 1 if a user had rated the product.

Petster is a website where users create web pages for their pets and form friendships links with other pet owners[9]. The dataset[10] is a crawl of the undirected friendship network of pet hamster owners and includes node attributes such as the hamster's name, sex, age, etc. We used two binary attributes: *sex* and *is-living*, where is-

[8] http://www.last.fm

[9] www.petster.com.

[10] http://konect.uni-koblenz.de/networks/petster-friendships-hamster

Table 6: Dataset properties. The columns are number of nodes n, number of edges m, maximum degree $d_{\max}$, average degree d_{avg}, number of triangles n_Δ, and average local clustering coefficient $\overline{C}$.

Dataset	n	m	d_{max}	d_{avg}	n_Δ	$\overline{C}$
Last.fm	1,843	12,668	119	6.9	19,651	0.183
Petster	1,788	12,476	272	7.0	16,741	0.143
Epinions	26,427	104,075	625	3.9	231,645	0.138
Pokec	592,627	3,725,424	1,274	6.3	2,492,216	0.104

living was set to 0 if the value of the age attribute was "gone to hamster heaven", or 1 otherwise.

Pokec is a popular Slovakian online social network. This dataset is publicly available as part of the Stanford Large Network Dataset Collection[11] and contains directed friendship edges and node attributes such as gender, age, hobbies, etc. As with the Epinions dataset, we converted the edges to undirected by keeping mutual friendships. We used two attributes: *sex* and *age*. We converted age into a binary attribute by assigning a value of 1 for ages ≤ 30 and 0 for ages greater than 30. We ignored nodes with missing values for gender or age.

For all datasets, we considered only the main connected component (after converting to undirected edges, where applicable). Table 6 summarizes the four (pre-processed) datasets, with respect to various statistics.

B. ATTRIBUTE-EDGE CORRELATIONS

In this Appendix, we consider other approaches to generate the needed attribute edge correlation distribution Θ_F, and compare them to our proposed Edge Truncation method. The first generates connection counts which can be normalized to generate Θ_F, while the second directly produces a probability distribution.

B.1 Direct Approach with Smooth Sensitivity.

In real-world social graphs, most nodes share edges with only a small fraction of the other nodes in the graph. *Smooth sensitivity*, proposed by Nissim et al. [25], offers a general approach for getting around a high global sensitivity due to unlikely inputs. We add noise according to a smooth upper bound on the *local sensitivity*, which is based on the actual input rather than an improbable worst-case input. However, there is no automatic procedure for determining the smooth sensitivity of a computation, so we must derive it manually for our specific task. We begin by observing that the local sensitivity f_{Q_F} (that is, the function that computes the set Q_F) is twice the maximum node degree.

LEMMA 3. *The* local sensitivity *of f_{Q_F} is $LS_{Q_F}(G) = 2d_{\max}$, where $d_{\max} = \max_{v_i \in N(G)} d_{v_i}$.*

PROOF. The greatest impact to Q_F comes from changing the attribute vector associated with the highest degree node, which would have the effect of reducing some subset of the counts by an amount equal to $d_{\max}$, and increase another subset of the counts by the same amount. The impact of adding or removing an edge is just an increasing or decrease of one to a single count, which is negligible by comparison. □

Adding noise directly calibrated to the local sensitivity *does not* satisfy differential privacy, because the magnitude of the noise may itself leak information about the underlying data. Rather, smooth sensitivity can be expressed in terms of the local sensitivity at distance t from the input graph (Section 2.3).

PROPOSITION 4. *The β-smooth sensitivity of f_{Q_F} is*

$$\begin{aligned} S^*_{Q_F,\beta}(G) &= \max_{t\geq 0} e^{-t\beta} LS^t_{Q_F}(G) \\ &= \max_{t\geq 0} e^{-t\beta} \max_{G':d(G,G')\leq t} LS_{Q_F}(G') \\ &= \max_{t\geq 0} e^{-t\beta} \min(2d_{\max}+2t, 2n-2) \end{aligned}$$

where, $d(G,G')$ is fewest number of edges that would need to be added/removed or the fewest number of nodes whose attributes would need to be changed to transform G into G'.

For typical graphs and typical settings of $\varepsilon, \delta \approx 0$, this function is maximized when $t = 0$, yielding twice the maximum degree. Setting the derivative of the right hand side to zero and solving, we arrive at the following corollaries.

COROLLARY 5. *For a graph G with maximum degree $d_{\max}$,*

$$S^*_{Q_F,\beta}(G) = \begin{cases} 2d_{\max} & \text{if } \frac{1}{\beta} \leq 2d_{\max} \\ \frac{2e^{(\beta d_{\max}-1)}}{\beta} & \text{otherwise} \end{cases}$$

COROLLARY 6. *For a graph G with maximum degree $d_{\max}$, $\beta = \frac{\varepsilon}{2\ln(2/\delta)}$, and fixed ε, we have $S^*_{Q_F,\beta}(G) = 2d_{\max}$, for any $\delta \geq 2e^{-(\varepsilon d_{\max})/2}$.*

For many real-world social networks, we can expect the maximum degree to be a small fraction of the total number of nodes, and thus using smooth sensitivity should work reasonably well.

B.2 SA-Based Approach.

In the context of traditional databases, the *sample and aggregate framework (SA)* was originally proposed by Nissim et al. [25] as a general procedure for satisfying differential privacy in situations where determining the global (or smooth) sensitivity of a function is difficult or inefficient. The idea is as follows: to compute a differentially private estimate of a function f on dataset D, where $n = |D|$, first partition D into $t = n/k$ smaller datasets of k records each (for some k), denoted $D_1, \ldots, D_t$. Then, compute f on each of the t smaller datasets, yielding the set $Z = \{z_1, \ldots, z_t\}$, where $z_i = f(D_i)$. Finally, $f(D)$ is estimated by applying an aggregation function Agg (e.g., mean) to the set Z and adding noise according to the global (or smooth) sensitivity of Agg. For example, if the range of f is $[0,1]$ and A is the mean function, then we could add noise with sensitivity $1/t$ to the output of Agg(Z).

We extend this idea to the graph analysis domain to get around the high global sensitivity of Θ_F, as follows. For a given input graph G with n nodes, we first randomly partition the nodes into $t = n/k$ disjoint groups of k nodes each. Let $g_1, \ldots, g_m$ be the set of induced subgraphs, such that g_i is the subgraph induced by the nodes in group i. Note that (a) partitioning the nodes randomly does not impact the sensitivity, and (b) by working with the induced subgraphs, we ensure that a change to one node in the input graph G will only impact a single subgraph. Thus, we can apply a function f to each subgraph, aggregate the individual answers and add noise.

To compute Θ_F, we find the $\binom{2^w+1}{2}$ connection *probabilities* (not the *counts*) for each subgraph, average the corresponding probabilities across all subgraphs and add Laplace noise to each average. This approach has a global sensitivity of $\frac{2}{t}$, as illustrated by the following: let G, G' be a pair of neighboring graphs, where v_i is the node whose attributes were changed to get G' from G. Observe that, in the worst case, v_i is a member of a subgraph in which all of the internal edges are incident to v_i; if v_i's attribute values are different in G and G', then the L_1 difference of the corresponding sets of probabilities from G and G' will be 2. Since we are averaging over t subgraphs, the total impact on the set of average probabilities is $\frac{2}{t}$. Finally, after adding noise to the probabilities, we must divide them by their sum to ensure that they add up to one.

This approach introduces two types of error into the resulting probabilities: *estimation error*, due to averaging over outputs from the subgraphs, and *perturbation error* due to the Laplace noise.

[11] http://snap.stanford.edu/data/

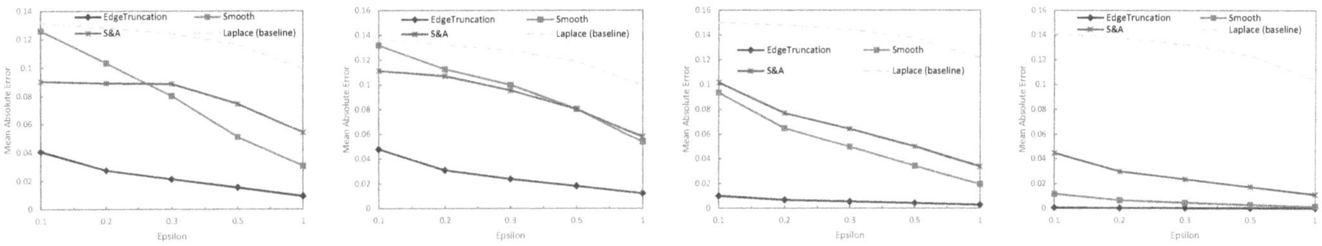

(a) Last.fm dataset (b) Petster dataset (c) Epinions dataset (d) Pokec dataset

Figure 5: Comparison of mean absolute error for different approaches for computing $\widetilde{\Theta}_F$ on four different datasets, under different privacy regimes. Note that privacy becomes weaker as we move rightward along the x-axis. The parameters for each approach were tuned empirically.

The accuracy will thus depend on balancing the two sources of error by selecting an appropriate size k for the subgraphs. A larger k gives fewer but bigger subgraphs, which reduces estimation error at the cost of increasing the perturbation error; conversely, a smaller k gives a greater number of small subgraphs, which reduces perturbation error at the cost of more estimation error.

B.3 Comparison of Approaches.

Figures 5(a)–5(d) compare the mean absolute errors[12] (MAE) of the three proposed approaches for different privacy settings, ε, on four datasets (Last.fm, Petster, Epinions and Pokec, described in Appendix A) with $w = 2$ attributes. The error-rates are taken over 10,000 trials (1,000 for the larger Epinions and Pokec datasets). In the plots, *Smooth* denotes the smooth sensitivity-based approach, *EdgeTrunc* is the edge truncation approach, and *S&A* is the sample and aggregate-based approach. The truncation parameter for EdgeTrunc and the group-size parameter for S&A were tuned empirically to minimize the MAE. Note that such tuning should be counted against the privacy budget for a real release; here, we discount this to see the relative performance. For the smooth sensitivity approach, we used negligible $\delta = 10^{-6}$.

As a baseline, we included results for the naïve approach (dashed line) in which noise from Lap $\left(\frac{2n-2}{\varepsilon}\right)$ is simply added to each connection count and then normalized by the sum to get Θ_F. A useful approach should have an MAE well below this line. The main takeaways from these results are that (1) all of the approaches work reasonably well at the weakest privacy setting tested ($\varepsilon = 1$), but edge truncation appears to be the best choice across all datasets and privacy settings tested; (2) in general, the larger the input graph, the lower the error. On the large Pokec dataset ($m = 3,725,424$) all of the approaches perform well, even with the strongest privacy setting tested. For EdgeTrunc, the MAE comes very close to zero, even for $\varepsilon = 0.1$. Given the superior performance of EdgeTrunc, we chose to limit our focus to that approach for privately computing Θ_F in the remainder of this work.

C. DP ALGORITHMS

For completeness, we summarize the procedure for computing a differentially private version of Θ_F, denoted $\widetilde{\Theta}_F$, with edge truncation, as described in Section 3.1. The pseudocode is in Algorithm 4 and we prove its privacy guarantee in Theorem 7.

C.1 Computing Correlations Privately

THEOREM 7. *Algorithm 4 satisfies ε-differential privacy.*

Algorithm 4 LearnCorrelationsDP

Input: ε, G, k, w
Output: $\widetilde{\Theta}_F$
1: $G' \leftarrow \mu(G,k)$ ▷ Truncate G using the truncation operator μ from Def. 2
2: $Q_F \leftarrow f_{Q_F}(G')$ ▷ Compute the set of counts on truncated graph G'
3: **for** $y_i \in Y_w^F$ **do**
4: $\widetilde{Q}_F(y_i) \leftarrow \min\left(n, \max\left(0, Q_F(y_i) + \text{LAP}(0, \frac{2k}{\varepsilon})\right)\right)$ ▷ Add Laplace noise to each count and clamp range
5: $q_{sum} \leftarrow \max_{y_i} \widetilde{Q}(y_i)$
6: **for** $y_i \in Y_w^F$ **do**
7: $\widetilde{\Theta}_F(y_i) \leftarrow \frac{\widetilde{Q}_F(y_i)}{q_{sum}}$
8: **return** $\widetilde{\Theta}_F$

PROOF. The global sensitivity of truncating G to get k-bounded graph G' followed by computing Q_F on G' (lines 1–2) was shown to be $2k$ by Proposition 1. In line 4, we add independent noise from $Lap\left(\frac{2k}{\varepsilon}\right)$, which gives ε-differential privacy (Laplace mechanism). The remainder of the algorithm, including clamping the noisy counts to the range $(0,n)$, operates only on the noisy counts, and therefore has no impact on the privacy guarantee. Thus, Algorithm 4 satisfies ε-differential privacy. □

C.2 Private Release of Attribute Distribution

Algorithm 5 outlines the procedure for computing the attribute distribution, $\widetilde{\Theta}_X$ that was described in Section 3.2. The formal statement of its privacy guarantee is then proved with Theorem 8.

THEOREM 8. *Algorithm 5 satisfies ε-differential privacy.*

PROOF. Let $G = (N,E,X)$ be an arbitrary input graph and let $G' = (N,E,X')$ be the neighboring graph created by changing the attributes of one node, say $v_i \in N$, from x_i to x_i', where $f_w(x_i) = y_i$ and $f_w(x_i') = y_j$ where $y_i, y_j \in Y_w, y_i \neq y_j$. Then we have that $q_i' = q_i - 1$ and $q_j' = q_j + 1$, and $q_k' = q_k, \forall_k k \neq i, k \neq j$. Thus, the global

Algorithm 5 LearnAttributesDP

Input: ε, X, w
Output: $\widetilde{\Theta}_X$
$Q_X \leftarrow f_{Q_X}(X)$ ▷ Compute the set of counts from X
for $y_i \in Y_w$ **do** ▷ Add Laplace noise to each count and clamp
$\widetilde{Q}_X(y_i) \leftarrow \min\left(n, \max\left(0, Q_X(y_i) + \text{LAP}(0, \frac{2}{\varepsilon})\right)\right)$
$q_{sum} \leftarrow \sum_{y_i} \widetilde{Q}_X(y_i)$
for $y_i \in Y_w$ **do**
$\widetilde{\Theta}_X(y_i) \leftarrow \frac{\widetilde{Q}_X(y_i)}{q_{sum}}$ ▷ Normalize
return $\widetilde{\Theta}_X$

[12]That is, the mean error between privately computed probabilities and true probabilities computed directly from the input graph.

sensitivity of $f_{Q_X}(X)$ (line 1) is 2. In line 3, we add independent Laplace noise with mean zero and scale equal to $\frac{2}{\varepsilon}$, which gives ε-differential privacy. (Laplace mechanism). The remainder of the algorithm, including clamping the noisy counts to the range $(0,n)$, operates on the noisy counts, and so does not impact privacy. □

C.3 Privately Fitting TriCycLe

The two inputs required by the algorithm are the degree sequence $\mathcal{S}$ and the number of triangles n_Δ, measured from the input graph G. Here we discuss how to compute differentially private estimates of these statistics using existing techniques, resulting in a DP graph generation process.

C.3.1 Degree Sequence

The degree sequence of input graph G is the multiset $\mathcal{S} = \{d_i | v_i \in N\}$. A straightforward way to satisfy DP for $\mathcal{S}$ is to apply the Laplace mechanism, adding independent noise from $\text{Lap}(2/\varepsilon)$ to each $d_i \in \mathcal{S}$; the global sensitivity is *two* because adding or removing an edge of G changes the degrees of exactly two nodes by one. However, this approach introduces a lot of noise, especially in low degree nodes, which are abundant in real social graphs. Instead, we can improve the estimate by observing that the mapping between a specific node and its degree is unimportant for how TriCycLe uses the degree sequence—we only need the sequence of degrees, the order is unimportant. [11] proposes an approach for accurately estimating the degree sequence of a graph based on constrained inference—recall that ε-differential privacy is invariant under post-processing, so this step does not affect the guarantee. The high-level idea is to sort the degree sequence prior to adding noise and then to post-process the noisy sequence to enforce the ordering condition, thereby canceling out much of the noise.

The algorithm in [11] starts by computing the actual degrees for each node, forming degree sequence S. It then sorts $\mathcal{S}$ in non-decreasing order and adds independent noise drawn from $\text{Lap}(2/\varepsilon)$ to each degree, yielding noisy degree sequence $\tilde{\mathcal{S}}$; the addition of noise may cause the ordering constraint to be violated. A constrained inference procedure is applied to $\tilde{\mathcal{S}}$ to find the $\overline{\mathcal{S}}$ that is "closest" to $\tilde{\mathcal{S}}$ (i.e., the minimum L_2 distance) that also satisfies the ordering constraint. A dynamic programming solution given in [11] performs the constrained inference operation in linear time.

C.3.2 Triangle Count

TriCycLe also needs the number of triangles in the input graph. The challenge here, from the privacy perspective, is that the global sensitivity of triangle counting is prohibitively high, since in the worst case there could be a single edge that is shared by every triangle in the graph—for a graph with n nodes, adding or removing a single edge could change the triangle count by up to $n-2$. Consequently, direct application of the Laplace mechanism yields a very inaccurate count. Fortunately, real-world graphs typically do not contain such pathological structures, and tend to have local sensitivities that are much lower. Triangle counting has been extensively studied in the context of differential privacy (e.g., [25, 37, 13, 5]). The most effective approaches take advantage of the above observation in some way to reduce the amount of noise required to satisfy differential privacy.

The state-of-the-art approach for differentially private triangle counting is based on the *Ladder* framework [37], which effectively combines the concept of "local sensitivity at distance t", from the smooth sensitivity framework [25], with the exponential mechanism [22]. In the context of triangle counting, it has been shown to provide better accuracy and has the added benefit that it provides pure differential privacy, rather than the weaker notion of (ε,δ)-

Algorithm 6 FitTriCycLeDP

Input: ε, E, n
Output: $\widetilde{\Theta}_M = \{\bar{\mathcal{S}}, \tilde{n}_\Delta\}$
1: $\varepsilon_\mathcal{S} \leftarrow \frac{\varepsilon}{2}$
2: $\varepsilon_\Delta \leftarrow \frac{\varepsilon}{2}$ ▷ Split the privacy budget (evenly) between the degree sequence and triangle count
3: $\mathcal{S} \leftarrow \langle d_1, \ldots, d_n \rangle$
4: $\mathcal{S} \leftarrow$ SORTASCENDING($\mathcal{S}$)
5: $\tilde{\mathcal{S}} \leftarrow \mathcal{S} + \text{LAP}(\frac{2}{\varepsilon_\mathcal{S}})^n$ ▷ Add independent Laplace noise to each coordinate of degree sequence $\mathcal{S}$
6: Apply constrained inference (Algorithm 1 from [11]) to $\tilde{\mathcal{S}}$ to get $\bar{\mathcal{S}}$
7: **for** $\bar{d}_i \in \bar{\mathcal{S}}$ **do**
8: Round $\bar{d}_i$ to the nearest integer in $\{0, \ldots, n-1\}$
9: $\tilde{n}_\Delta \leftarrow$ NOISESAMPLE($f_{n_\Delta}, E, \varepsilon_\Delta$) ▷ Get a differentially private estimate of the triangle count using Algorithm 1 from [37]
10: **return** $\widetilde{\Theta}_M = \{\bar{\mathcal{S}}, \tilde{n}_\Delta\}$

differential privacy provided by the smooth sensitivity framework. The local sensitivity of a function f at distance t (from the input graph) is denoted $LS_f^t(G)$, and quantifies the maximum local sensitivity among all graphs that can be formed from G by adding or deleting up to t edges. The resulting mechanism allows us to sample an approximate value for the triangle count, such that better approximations are exponentially more likely to be sampled.

C.3.3 Algorithm for Fitting TriCycLe-DP.

Algorithm 6 summarizes the procedure for fitting the parameters used by TriCycLe from an input graph G, while Thm. 9 shows that the algorithm satisfies ε-differential privacy.

THEOREM 9. *Algorithm 6 satisfies ε-differential privacy.*

PROOF. Let $G = (N, E, X)$ be an arbitrary input graph and, without loss of generality, suppose we form a neighboring graph G' by adding an arbitrary edge e_{ij}, such that the degrees of the two incident nodes in G are d, d' respectively. Let $\mathcal{S}$ and $\mathcal{S}'$ denote the degree sequence vectors for G and G' sorted in non-descending order, respectively. Thus, relative to $\mathcal{S}$, two values in $\mathcal{S}'$ are different: the right-most d has changed to $d+1$ and the right-most d' has become $d'+1$. Thus, the L_1 difference $|\mathcal{S}' - \mathcal{S}| = 2$, which gives a global sensitivity of 2. In line 5 we add Laplace noise to each coordinate of the sorted degree sequence vector. Since the global sensitivity is 2 and we add Laplace noise with a scale of $\frac{2}{\varepsilon_\mathcal{S}}$, giving $\varepsilon_\mathcal{S}$-differential privacy for the degree sequence. Performing the constrained inference procedure on the noisy degree sequence (line 6) has no effect on the privacy guarantee, since it does not look at the original degree sequence; likewise for the subsequent rounding of the post-processed degrees. Line 9 computes an ε_Δ-differentially private estimate of the number of triangles in G using the Ladder framework of [37]. By sequential composition, these two computations together satisfy ε-differential privacy, where $\varepsilon = \varepsilon_\mathcal{S} + \varepsilon_\Delta$. □

C.4 Running Time Analysis

Relative to the non-private version of AGM, the privacy mechanisms in AGM-DP add relatively little computational overhead. The truncation operation in LearnCorrelationsDP runs in $O(m)$ and sampling noise from the Laplace distribution takes constant time. The underlying structural model dominates the running time of our framework. Quantitatively, we note that on the largest graph in our experiments (Pokec), generating a synthetic graph with AGM-DP-TriCycLe took about 85 minutes on a Core i7 desktop with 12GB of RAM. Apart from sampling the edges, computing the private triangle count was the most expensive operation ($\approx$ 12 minutes using the Ladder framework of [37]). Our prototype was implemented in Python and was not optimized for speed; implementation in a faster language, such as C++, would likely result in significant speedups.

Publishing Graph Degree Distribution with Node Differential Privacy

Wei-Yen Day
Dept. of Computer Science
Purdue University
West Lafayette, IN USA
wday@purdue.edu

Ninghui Li
Dept. of Computer Science
Purdue University
West Lafayette, IN USA
ninghui@cs.purdue.edu

Min Lyu*
School of Computer Science and Technology
University of Science and Technology of China
Hefei, China
lvmin05@ustc.edu.cn

ABSTRACT

Graph data publishing under node-differential privacy (node-DP) is challenging due to the huge sensitivity of queries. However, since a node in graph data oftentimes represents a person, node-DP is necessary to achieve personal data protection. In this paper, we investigate the problem of publishing the degree distribution of a graph under node-DP by exploring the projection approach to reduce the sensitivity. We propose two approaches based on aggregation and cumulative histogram to publish the degree distribution. The experiments demonstrate that our approaches greatly reduce the error of approximating the true degree distribution and have significant improvement over existing works. We also present the introspective analysis for understanding the factors of publishing the degree distribution with node-DP.

Categories and Subject Descriptors

K.4.1 [**COMPUTERS AND SOCIETY**]: Privacy

Keywords

Differential privacy; Private graph publishing; Degree distribution

1. INTRODUCTION

Many kinds of interesting graph data exist, e.g., social networks, email networks. However, directly publishing graph data may reveal sensitive information of an individual even if the graph is anonymized [2, 27]. Starting from [12], researchers have been studying the problem of publishing information of a graph under *Differential Privacy* (DP) [7, 8]. An algorithm that satisfies DP guarantees that the output distribution does not change significantly from one dataset to a *neighboring* dataset. When applying DP to graph data, two variants of DP were introduced [12]: in edge-DP, two graphs are neighboring if they differ on a single edge; in node-DP, two graphs are neighboring if by removing one node and all edges incident to the node in one graph, one obtains the other graph. Obviously satisfying node-DP is much harder than satisfying edge-DP, since removing one node may cause, in the worst case, the removal of $|V| - 1$ edges, where V is the set of all nodes. Because of this reason, most existing approaches that apply DP to graphs consider edge-DP, under the rationale that doing so protects relationship between two entities from being disclosed. However, the privacy offered by edge-DP is much weaker than node-DP, and, as we argue in Section 2.3, is insufficient in most settings.

In this paper, we investigate the problem of publishing the degree distribution of a graph under node-DP. Given a graph $G = (V, E)$, the goal is to release a node degree distribution (or, equivalently, a node degree histogram) that approximates the true distribution of G as much as possible while satisfying node-DP. A key technique to satisfy node-DP is that of "graph projection", which transforms a graph to be θ-degree-bounded, i.e., the maximum degree in the graph is no more than θ. A key challenge is to preserve as much information as possible in the projection process, while bounding the sensitivity of the degree histogram constructed from a projected graph. In [18], a graph is truncated so that all nodes with degree above θ are removed; this approach, however, removes significantly more edges than necessary. In [31], projected histograms are constructed using an auxiliary flow graph, and it was shown that this has a sensitivity of 6θ.

We improve the current state of the art on publishing graph node degree distributions under node-DP by introducing two new approaches that have much higher accuracy. Both approaches use a new graph projection method that is based on an edge-addition process. We show that this method, unlike previous projection methods, ensures that the projected graph is *maximal* in the sense that adding any additional edge will make the graph no longer θ-degree-bounded. We also prove that publishing the degree histogram after projection has a sensitivity of $2\theta + 1$, lower than previous approaches. When projecting a graph, a larger θ causes noise with larger magnitude to be added; at the same time, a lower θ means more edges are pruned. The optimal choice of θ thus depends both on the dataset and on the value of ϵ. Further, when publishing noisy histograms, it is sometimes better to merge several adjacent bins based on a configuration Ω and publish the average of the noisy bins [1, 23, 34, 36], reducing the errors caused by noise. We observe that the optimal choices of θ and Ω are mutually dependent, and propose the (θ, Ω)-Histogram approach, which selects the pair (θ, Ω) in one step using the exponential mechanism, with a low-

*The work was done while the author was visiting Purdue University, West Lafayette, IN USA.

SIGMOD'16, June 26-July 01, 2016, San Francisco, CA, USA

© 2016 ACM. ISBN 978-1-4503-3531-7/16/06...$15.00

DOI: http://dx.doi.org/10.1145/2882903.2926745

sensitivity quality function that captures the resulting error due to the different factors, and then publishes a noisy histogram.

The second approach, which we call θ-CumulativeHistogram, is based on the observation that the edge-addition projection method will result in many nodes changing their degree by 1 between two neighboring datasets, and thus publishing a cumulative degree histogram after such a projection has sensitivity only $\theta + 1$. Furthermore, the monotonicity property of the cumulative degree histogram enables a calibrating step to further reduce the effect of noise. After obtaining a noisy cumulative histogram, one can then reconstruct the degree histogram. In both approaches, we also use an additional post-processing step to improve the accuracy of the histograms. We summarize the contributions of our paper in the following:

1. We have introduced an edge-addition based graph projection method, which preserves more information than previous approaches in the literature. We prove that publishing a degree histogram from the projected graph has sensitivity $2\theta + 1$, and publishing a cumulative degree histogram has sensitivity $\theta + 1$.

2. Based on the sensitivity bounds, we propose two approaches, (θ, Ω)-Histogram and θ-CumulativeHistogram, for publishing degree histograms under node-DP. We develop low-sensitivity quality functions that enable the selection of the parameters for these methods.

3. We have conducted extensive experiments using 8 real world datasets to compare our proposed methods with other existing methods. The experiments shown in Section 4 demonstrate that our proposed mechanisms have significant improvement over the state-of-the-art flow graph approach [31]. We also perform the introspective analysis to investigate the impacts of parameter selection, post-processing strategies for tail distribution, and edge ordering for projection. We demonstrate that our designed quality functions precisely evaluate the θ and Ω parameters with low sensitivities, which enable us to publish the degree distribution for a graph under node-DP.

The rest of this paper is organized as follows. We give the problem definition, discuss ϵ-DP and its application on graphs, and introduce existing approaches in Section 2. Section 3 introduces our proposed approaches. Experimental results are given in Section 4. We discuss related work in Section 5, and conclude in Section 6.

2. PRELIMINARIES

In this section, we introduce the problem definition, the notion of differential privacy and its application on graphs, and existing approaches.

2.1 Problem Definition

We consider undirected graphs with no additional labels on nodes and edges. Given an input graph $G = (V, E)$, we want to release a $|V|$-dimensional vector $\mathbf{d} \in \mathbb{R}^{|V|}$ that represents the probability distribution from degree 0 to $|V| - 1$, i.e., $\mathbf{d}_i$ is the probability that a uniformly randomly chosen node in the graph has degree i. Since the degree distribution can be obtained from normalizing the degree histogram, the problem can be equivalently stated as publishing the degree histogram of G, which we use $\mathsf{hist}(G)$ to denote.

Utility Metrics. Following previous works [18, 31], we use the L1 distance between the published distribution and the true distribution (or L1 error) to evaluate different approaches. More formally, the L1 distance between any two distributions $\mathbf{d}$ and $\mathbf{d}'$ with length $|V|$ can be computed by $||\mathbf{d} - \mathbf{d}'||_1 = \sum_{i=0}^{|V|-1} |\mathbf{d}_i - \mathbf{d}'_i|$. Some techniques may publish a distribution with size smaller than $|V|$. We follow the same procedure in [31] to pad $\mathbf{d}$ with 0 if its size is less than $|V|$ for comparison.

In addition to the L1 error, we also use the Kolmogorov-Smirnov distance (KS-distance) between two degree distribution, which was used in [12]. Given two degree distributions $\mathbf{d}$ and $\mathbf{d}'$, the KS-distance between $\mathbf{d}$ and $\mathbf{d}'$ is used to test the closeness between them and is defined as: $KS(\mathbf{d}, \mathbf{d}') = \max_i |CDF_{\mathbf{d}}(i) - CDF_{\mathbf{d}'}(i)|$, where $CDF_{\mathbf{d}}(i)$ is the value of cumulative distribution function on degree i from distribution $\mathbf{d}$.

2.2 ϵ-Differential Privacy

The notion of ϵ-differential privacy (ϵ-DP) [7] is defined based on the concept of *neighboring databases*.

DEFINITION 1. *A randomized algorithm $\mathcal{A}$ satisfies ϵ-differential privacy (ϵ-DP) when for any two neighboring databases, D and D', denoted by $D \simeq D'$,*

$$Pr[\mathcal{A}(D) \in S] \leq \exp(\epsilon) \times Pr[\mathcal{A}(D') \in S]$$

where $S \subseteq Range(\mathcal{A})$ and ϵ is a parameter for privacy level.

Laplace Mechanism. One way to satisfy DP is to add noise to the output of a query. In the Laplace mechanism [8], in order to publish $f(D)$ where $f : \mathbb{D} \to \mathbb{R}^d$ while satisfying ϵ-DP, one publishes

$$\mathcal{A}(D) = f(D) + \mathsf{Lap}\left(\frac{\Delta \mathsf{f}}{\epsilon}\right)^{\mathsf{d}},$$

$$\text{where} \qquad \Delta f = \max_{D \simeq D'} ||f(D) - f(D')||_1$$

$$\text{and} \quad \Pr\left[\mathsf{Lap}(\beta) = x\right] = \frac{1}{2\beta} e^{-|x|/\beta}$$

Exponential Mechanism. While the Laplace mechanism provides a solution to handle numeric queries, it cannot be applied to non-numeric valued queries. This motivates the development of the exponential mechanism [26], which can be applied whether a function's output is numerical or not. Given a dataset D, and a quality function $q : (\mathbb{D} \times T) \to \mathbb{R}$, which assigns a quality score $q(D, t)$ for outputting t on input D, the exponential mechanism outputs t with a probability proportional to $\exp\left(\frac{\epsilon q(D,t)}{2\Delta q}\right)$, where $\Delta q = \max_{\forall t, D, D'} |q(D, t) - q(D', t)|$ is the sensitivity of the quality function. This satisfies ϵ-DP.

Composition Properties. Differential privacy satisfies sequential composition and transformation invariance [25, 20]. In short, sequential composition guarantees that for any sequence of computations $\mathcal{A}_1, \mathcal{A}_2, \cdots, \mathcal{A}_k$, if each $\mathcal{A}_i$ satisfies ϵ_i-DP, then publishing the results of all of $\mathcal{A}_1, \mathcal{A}_2, \cdots, \mathcal{A}_k$ satisfies $\sum_i \epsilon_i$-DP. The transformation invariance property says that given $\mathcal{A}_1$ that satisfies ϵ-DP, and any algorithm $\mathcal{A}_2$, the new algorithm $\mathcal{A}(\cdot) = \mathcal{A}_2(\mathcal{A}_1(\cdot))$ satisfies ϵ-DP. In other words, performing post-processing on the output of an algorithm that satisfies DP does not affect the privacy guarantee.

2.3 Node-DP or Edge-DP

When applying DP to graph data, there are two variants of DP [12]: in edge-DP, two graphs are neighboring if they differ on a single edge; in node-DP, two graphs are neighboring if by removing one node and all edges incident to it in one graph, one obtains the other graph. They offer different kinds of privacy protection. As it has been extensively argued [7, 9, 21, 24], it is impossible to prevent an adversary with arbitrary background knowledge from learning sensitive information (e.g., by using correlation between data of different individuals) so long as one wants to preserve some utility of the data. What DP achieves is to approximate the effect of *opting out*. Suppose that one wants to publish $\mathcal{A}(D)$, where D consists of data of many individuals; and one individual, whose data is in D, complains that publishing $\mathcal{A}(D)$ violates her privacy. In this case, we can address the privacy concern by letting the individual "opting out", by removing the individual's data from D (or replacing her data with some arbitrary values) to obtain D' and publish $\mathcal{A}(D')$. Note that even after the removal of the individual's data, it may still be possible to learn information about the individual through correlation between this individual's data and others' data [7, 5, 10, 21]; however, such learning (while potentially harmful) is arguably not a privacy violation, since the learning can occur without accessing any personal data of the individual. For example, publishing study results that smoking increases one's chance of having lung cancer arguably leaks information about any smoker, even if the smoker does not participate in the study. However, one cannot say publishing the study results compromises the privacy of these people who are not even in the study. DP tries to approximate the effect of "opting out", by ensuring that any effect due to the inclusion of one's data is just a little more significant compared to the case in which her data is not included. We want to emphasize, however, that DP offers an approximation of "opting-out" **only when the difference of two neighboring datasets includes all the data one individual controls**.

We choose to use node-DP because we believe that edge-DP fails to provide adequate privacy protection. First, attacks on anonymized graph data are in the form of re-identifying nodes, illustrating that this is where the privacy concern lies [2, 27]. Second, edge-DP is often justified by the argument that one's goal is to protect the relationship between two entities encoded as an edge. Even if we accept that, edge-DP falls short of achieving that. DP offers effective protection only when the edges are independent from each other [21, 24]. However, it is hard to make the case that edges are independent. Conceivably, an edge between two high-degree nodes is much more likely than an edge between two low-degree nodes. Also, if two nodes share a lot of common neighboring nodes, then the probability that they are connected is higher too. Last but most importantly, while the above correlation argument can be applied to node-DP as well, node-DP can be justified because when using node-DP, one's goal is not to hide information of one node (which is unachievable), but only to approximate the effect of giving control of personal data to individuals. The same argument cannot be applied to justify edge-DP, since in most graph data, a node and its associated edges represent all personal data of an individual, and an edge does not represent all data controlled by one individual.

2.4 Existing Graph Projection Methods

The main challenge for satisfying node-DP is that the sensitivity is very high. Removing one node may cause, in the worst case, the removal of $|V|-1$ edges, where $|V|$ is the number of nodes in the graph. A natural approach is to apply the *projection* technique [3, 18, 31], which transforms the original graph G into a θ-bounded graph G^θ, such that the maximum degree in G^θ is less than or equal to θ; thus the sensitivity can be restricted. While the idea of projection is natural, how to use it most effectively turns out to be quite nontrivial. One challenge is that the projection operation may result in degree changes in a lot of nodes.

In [18], projection is done by truncation, i.e., removing all nodes with degrees larger than θ; and analyzing the sensitivity of publishing node-degree histograms after truncation is done in two steps. The first step is to compute S_T, the smooth bound on the number of nodes whose degrees may change because of the truncation. In order to keep S_T low, the cutoff threshold θ is randomized. The second step is to observe that changing one node in a θ-bounded graph can change the histogram by at most 2θ. The total sensitivity is the product of the two, i.e., $2\theta S_T$. Hence, it is suggested to add Cauchy noise with parameter $\frac{2\sqrt{2}\theta}{\epsilon}S_T$.

We observe two things. First, truncation removes more edges than necessary for the goal of ensuring a θ-bounded graph. One could keep up to θ edges for these nodes while ensuring θ-boundedness. Second, publishing a histogram after truncation has a global sensitivity of $2\theta+1$. Assume, wlog, that G_2 has one more node v^+ than G_1 such that removing v^+ and all its incident edges from G_2 results in G_1. If $deg(v^+) > \theta$, then G_1 and G_2 become the same after truncation. If $deg(v^+) \le \theta$, then at most θ nodes other than v^+ will have different degrees in G_1 and G_2 (both before and after truncation), resulting in an L1 distance of no more than $2\theta+1$ between two resulting degree histograms from G_1^θ and G_2^θ.

Another projection method is proposed in [3], in which one chooses an arbitrary order among the edges, traverses the edges in this order, and removes each encountered edge that is connected to a node that has degree $> \theta$. We refer to this method as "Edge-Removal". In [3], the sensitivities for queries such as subgraph counting after projection are shown to be $p(2\theta)^{p-1}$ for node-DP, where p is the number of nodes in the subgraph. However, publishing a degree histogram was not considered in [3]. It is unclear what is the sensitivity of publishing a degree histogram after Edge-Removal.

In a recent work for publishing degree distributions under node-DP [31], another projection method was introduced. Given a graph $G=(V,E)$ and a degree bound θ, the method first constructs a weighted graph as follows. Starting with a source node s and a sink node t, for each node $v \in V$, it creates two nodes, v_ℓ and v_r, and adds edges (s, v_ℓ) and (v_r, t) with capacity θ. For every edge $e=(u,v) \in E$, it then adds a new edge (u_ℓ, v_r) with capacity 1. With the weighted graph, the algorithm computes the maximum flow f from s to t, while minimizing $\sum_{v\in V}\left((\theta - f(s,v_\ell))^2 + (\theta - f(v_r,t))^2\right)$, where $f(u,v)$ is the flow from u to v. Finally, the algorithm removes s from the maximum flow graph, and, for each node $v \in V$, obtains the degrees of v_ℓ, and constructs the degree distribution from these degrees. The analysis given in [31] shows that the sensitivity of releasing the sorted degree list can be bounded by 3θ, and the sensitivity of publishing a histogram after projection is 6θ.

3. PROPOSED APPROACHES

We describe our proposed approaches, starting with our proposed projection approach in Section 3.1. Sections 3.2 and 3.3 describe two ways of this projection to publish degree histograms, and Section 3.4 describes some optimizations that are applicable to both approaches.

3.1 Our Proposed Projection Method

We propose a new projection method, π_θ, which is shown in Algorithm 1. Our algorithm requires a stable ordering of all edges in an input graph G, denoted by $\Lambda(G)$. We say that a graph edge ordering Λ is **stable** if and only if given two neighboring graphs

Algorithm 1 π_θ: projection by edge-addition.

Input: An input graph $G = (V, E)$, a degree bound θ, and a stable edge ordering $\Lambda = \langle e_1, \cdots e_n \rangle$.
Output: An output θ-bounded graph $\pi_\theta(G)$.
$E^\theta \leftarrow \emptyset$; $d(v) \leftarrow 0$ for each $v \in V$
for $e = (u, v) \in \Lambda$ **do**
  if $d(u) < \theta$ & $d(v) < \theta$ **then**
    $E^\theta \leftarrow E^\theta \cup \{e\}$; $d(u) \leftarrow d(u) + 1$; $d(v) \leftarrow d(v) + 1$
  end if
end for
return $G^\theta = (V, E^\theta)$

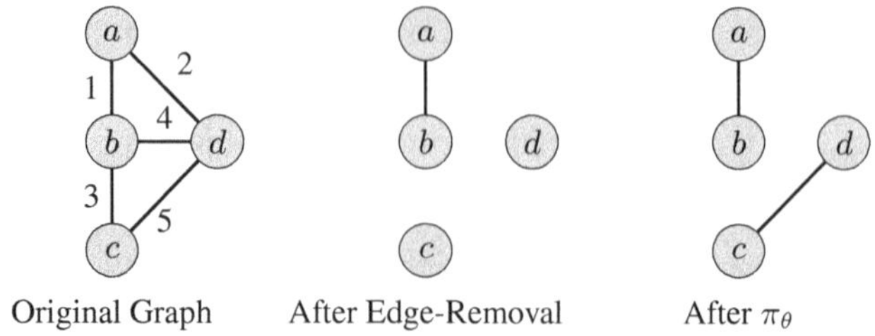

Figure 1: Comparison of Edge-Removal [3] and π_θ ($\theta = 1$). Edge order for removal in Edge-Removal: 5, 4, 3, 2, 1. Edge order for insertion in π_θ: 1, 2, 3, 4, 5.

$G = (V, E)$ and $G' = (V', E')$ that differ by only a node, $\Lambda(G)$ and $\Lambda(G')$ are consistent, in the sense that if two edges appear both in G and G', their relative ordering are the same in $\Lambda(G)$ and $\Lambda(G')$.

Such stabling edge ordering can be easily obtained in practice. For example, if G is abstracted from a data source where each node v has a unique id $id(v)$ (e.g., the account id in social network data), and these node ids can be totally ordered by an ordering $\prec$ (e.g., $\prec$ can be alphabetical ordering), then each edge (u, v) can be represented as a pair $(id(u), id(v))$ if $id(u) \prec id(v)$ and $(id(v), id(u))$ otherwise, and the lexicographical ordering of edges is stable.

The projection π_θ first forms a graph with all nodes in G but no edges, and then keeps inserting edges from Λ following the ordering whenever inserting an edge $e = (u, v)$ will not cause the degree of either u or v larger than θ. This is similar to Edge-Removal, except that π_θ inserts edges while Edge-Removal deletes edges. While this difference appears minor, π_θ can preserve more information. For example, in Figure 1, using π_θ results in two edges remaining; using Edge-Removal, in contrast, results in only one edge remaining.

In fact, **the projection result obtained from π_θ is maximal** in the sense that no additional edge from G can be added without making some node's degree be above θ. To see this, observe that any edge that could be added in the end can also be added when it is encountered while traversing Λ. Therefore, in the end, no additional edge can be added, making the result maximal. However, π_θ does not guarantee that the resulting graph keeps the largest possible number of edges, as the result depends on the insertion order and may be only locally optimal. The example in Figure 1 shows that the Edge-Removal process cannot guarantees maximality. In Section 4.2, we experimentally demonstrate π_θ's advantage over Edge-Removal and other projection methods.

Lemma 1 below shows that Δ_{hist}, the global sensitivity of releasing $\mathsf{hist}(\pi_\theta(G))$, i.e., one first projects G by π_θ and then releases the projected graph's degree histogram, is bounded by $2\theta + 1$.

LEMMA 1. *For any $G \simeq G'$ that differ in one node, we have*

$$||\mathsf{hist}(\pi_\theta(G)) - \mathsf{hist}(\pi_\theta(G'))||_1 \leq 2\theta + 1.$$

PROOF OF LEMMA 1. Assume, without loss of generality, that $G' = (V', E')$ has an additional node v^+ compared to $G = (V, E)$, i.e., $V' = V \cup \{v^+\}$, $E' = E \cup E^+$, and E^+ is the set of all edges incident to v^+ in G'. Let Λ' be the stable orderings for constructing $\pi_\theta(G')$, and t be the number of edges added to $\pi_\theta(G')$ that are incident to v^+. Clearly, $t \leq \theta$. Let $e'_{\ell_1}, \ldots, e'_{\ell_t}$ denote these t edges in their order in Λ'. Let Λ_0 be the sequence obtained by removing from Λ' all edges incident to v^+, and Λ_k, for $1 \leq k \leq t$, be the sequence obtained by removing from Λ' all edges that both are incident to v^+ and come after e'_{ℓ_k} in Λ'. Let $\pi_\theta^{\Lambda_k}(G')$, for $0 \leq k \leq t$, be the graph reconstructed by trying to add edges in Λ_k one by one on nodes in G', and λ_k be the sequence of edges from Λ_k that are actually added in the process. Thus λ_k uniquely determines $\pi_\theta^{\Lambda_k}(G')$; we abuse the notation and use λ_k to also denote $\pi_\theta^{\Lambda_k}(G')$. We have $\lambda_0 = \pi_\theta(G)$, and $\lambda_t = \pi_\theta(G')$.

We now show that $\forall k$ such that $1 \leq k \leq t$, at most 1 node (other than v^+) in λ_k will have a degree that is different from λ_{k-1}, and the difference is 1. This proves the lemma because there are at most t nodes that have a different degree in λ_t when compared with λ_0. Each such node induces a difference of at most 2 in the histograms, and v^+ contributes another difference of 1.

To prove this, consider how the sequence λ_k may differ from λ_{k-1}. The first difference must be that λ_k includes $e'_{\ell_k} = (u_j, v^+)$, and λ_{k-1} does not. (Recall that Λ_k contains e'_{ℓ_k} but Λ_{k-1} does not by construction.) The decisions for all edges coming before e'_{ℓ_k} in Λ' must be the same in both λ_k and λ_{k-1}. After e'_{ℓ_k}, the edges in Λ_k and Λ_{k-1} are exactly the same; thus we can consider each different decision regarding a future edge as one more difference. Assume that there are a total of $s \geq 1$ different decisions.

When $s = 1$, only u_j (other than v^+) has a degree in λ_k that is different from λ_{k-1}, and the difference is by adding 1. When $s > 1$, the second difference must be regarding an edge incident to u_j and is because θ edges incident to u_j are added in λ_{k-1}, and the last one of these, denoted by $(u_j, u_{i\theta})$, cannot be added in λ_k (because u_j's degree has reached θ in λ_k by then, due to the extra edge (u_j, v^+)). In this case, u_j has the same degree (i.e., θ) in both λ_k and λ_{k-1}. If $s = 2$, then only $u_{i\theta}$ (other than v^+) has a different degree, and its degree in λ_k is 1 less than that in λ_{k-1}. If $s > 2$, then the third difference must be about an edge incident to $u_{i\theta}$ and is because the edge is included in λ_k but not included in λ_{k-1}; this can only happen when $u_{i\theta}$ has degree θ in both λ_k and λ_{k-1}, and results in another node's degree change by 1. Since s is finite, this sequence of reasoning will stop, with only the last encountered node has a degree change from λ_{k-1} to λ_k (all nodes earlier must have degree θ in both λ_{k-1} and λ_k). □

3.2 Parameter Selection and Aggregation

In projection, the optimal choice of θ depends on both the distribution of the data and the privacy parameter ϵ. A larger θ means that more edges can be preserved in the projection process; however, larger noise needs to be added to the histogram. If most nodes in the graph have small degrees, then a smaller θ is preferred. At the same time, if ϵ is larger, then a larger θ is preferred. In previous work [3, 18], performing the projection step requires the prior knowledge of the projection level θ.

Furthermore, one way to improve the accuracy of publishing histograms after projection is to apply the idea of *aggregation* on histogram bins, which was investigated in the literature [1, 23, 34, 36]. The intuition is to find a structure Ω, in which some bins are grouped together, reducing the noise effect by averaging, with the cost of using an average to estimate each bin within a group. More specifically, $\Omega = \{\mathbf{g}_1, \mathbf{g}_2, \cdots \mathbf{g}_n\}$ is a set of disjoint groups of bins representing the aggregation strategy, where each $\mathbf{g}_k = (k_1, k_2, \cdots, k_{|\mathbf{g}_k|})$ corresponds to the bins of k_1'th, k_2'th, $\cdots$ $k_{|\mathbf{g}_k|}$'th degree in histogram. We use aggregation after the projection with a parameter θ, and thus have $\sum_{\mathbf{g}_k \in \Omega} |\mathbf{g}_k| = \theta$. The optimal aggregating structure Ω and projection level θ are related to each other.

We propose to estimate the optimal aggregation structure Ω and projection level θ simultaneously. To do so, we need to decide what is the candidate pool of (θ_i, Ω_j) pairs. The size of this pool should not be too large, as the running time is linear in the pool size and the quality of selection could deteriorate when the pool includes many poor choices. For the set of all choices for θ_i, we require as input Θ, and consider all integers from 1 to Θ as choices for θ_i. We use $\Theta = 200$ in the experiments. For $\boldsymbol{\Omega}$, the candidate pool of Ω, adopting a naive approach that considers all combinations results in a very large pool. Let K be the maximum number of groups after aggregation. The number of candidates is approximately on the order of Θ^K, even if we group only adjacent bins. To solve this problem, we exploit the long-tail property of the node degree distributions, and conjecture that a good candidate should group fewer bins on low degrees (usually with larger counts), and more bins on high degrees (long tail part). We then use geometric series, $r^0, r^1, r^2, \cdots$, to determine the size of each group in Ω, such that for each r, $\mathbf{g}_i = \{k : r^{i-1} \leq k < r^i\}$. That is, when $r = 1.5$, $\Omega = \{(1), (2), (3), (4, 5), (6, 7), (8, 9, 10, 11), \cdots\}$. We vary r such that $r \in [1, 2]$ to generate a good coverage of optimal Ω.

We also need to design a quality function to evaluate the desirability of any (θ_i, Ω_j) pair. Our quality function is similar to that used in [23], and has two components. The first component captures the errors introduced in the process of creating the noisy histogram, computed as follows:

$$\ell_{hist}(G, \theta_i, \Omega_j) = \sum_{\mathbf{g}_k \in \Omega_j} \sum_{d \in \mathbf{g}_k} \left(\left| c_d - \frac{\sum_{d \in \mathbf{g}_k} c_d}{|\mathbf{g}_k|} \right| + \frac{2\theta_i + 1}{\epsilon |\mathbf{g}_k|} \right),$$

where c_d denotes the number of nodes with degree d in $\mathsf{hist}(G^{\theta_i})$. The above sums over the error for all bins. For each bin, the first term captures the error due to the aggregation step and the second term captures the error due to added noises.

The second component captures the *projection loss*. Intuitively, we want to capture the number of nodes that have a degree above θ and will have degree changes after projection. However, directly using $|\{v | v \in V, deg(v) > \theta_i\}|$ has a high sensitivity; we thus choose to first project the graph G to a maximum degree of Θ, and then compute how many nodes have a degree above θ in the projected graph, i.e.,

$$\ell_{proj}(G, \theta_i) = 2 \cdot \left| \{v | v \in V, deg_{\pi_\Theta(G)}(v) > \theta_i\} \right|,$$

where $deg_{\pi_\Theta(G)}(v)$ gives v's degree in the graph $\pi_\Theta(G)$. This is two times the number of nodes with degree larger than θ_i in $\pi_\Theta(G)$. The intuition is that each of such nodes will have a degree change and result in a change of 2 in the degree histograms before and after projection.

Combining the two components, our proposed quality function is

$$q^h_\epsilon(G, \theta_i, \Omega_j) = -\ell_{hist}(G, \theta_i, \Omega_j) - \ell_{proj}(G, \theta_i). \quad (1)$$

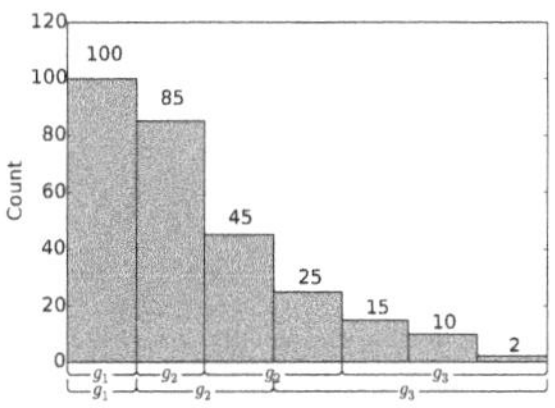

ϵ		Ω_1	Ω_2
$\epsilon = 0.2$	ℓ_{hist}	334	293
	ℓ_{proj}	4	4
	q^h_ϵ	-338	**-297**
$\epsilon = 1$	ℓ_{hist}	94	143
	ℓ_{proj}	4	4
	q^h_ϵ	**-98**	-147

Figure 2: An example of different structures. $\Omega_1 = \{(1), (2), (3, 4), (5, 6, 7)\}$, $\Omega_2 = \{(1), (2, 3), (4, 5, 6, 7)\}$.

A running example to demonstrate the advantage of this quality function is given in Figure 2. Consider two structures Ω_1, Ω_2, where Ω_1 has 4 groups and Ω_2 has 3 groups. Assuming that $\theta = 7$ and only 2 nodes have degree over θ, the projection loss is $\ell_{proj}(G, \theta) = 4$. When ϵ is small, i.e. $\epsilon = 0.2$, the quality function estimates that Ω_2, the coarser aggregation, has more advantage. When ϵ is 1, the quality function prefers Ω_1, the finer aggregation.

To apply the exponential mechanism to select a (θ, Ω) pair, we need to have a bound on the global sensitivity of q^h_ϵ given in Eq. (1); the following lemma establishes this to be $6\Theta + 4$.

LEMMA 2. *For any neighboring G and G', we have*

$$|q^h_\epsilon(G, \theta_i, \Omega_j) - q^h_\epsilon(G', \theta_i, \Omega_j))| \leq 6\Theta + 4$$

The proof is given in Appendix A.

Note that while our method avoids requiring θ as an input, it still requires Θ as an input. The difference is that the selection of Θ is much less sensitive and data-dependent than that of θ. In our experiments, we use $\Theta = 200$ for all datasets, and our method is then able to select different θ values that perform well for different datasets. We show that when using the same θ value for all datasets, invariably the method will perform poorly on some datasets. We also demonstrate that setting $\Theta = 400$ results in only slightly larger errors and is still able to significantly outperform existing methods.

We use (θ, Ω)-Histogram to denote the algorithm of releasing degree histogram from projection and aggregation, which is given in Algorithm 2. (θ, Ω)-Histogram first computes the quality of each candidate (θ_i, Ω_j) and performs the selection process through exponential mechanism. This step, for each θ_i, computes a projection of the graph from Algorithm 1, constructs a histogram, and then computes the quality for each Ω_j, resulting a $O(\Theta \cdot (|E| + |V| + \Theta \cdot |\boldsymbol{\Omega}|))$ running time. The second step is to perform projection using the selected (θ^*, Ω^*) and to publish the aggregated noisy histogram, which takes time $O(|E| + |V|)$. The final step for post-processing will be introduced in Section 3.4; it takes time at most $O(|V|)$. Thus the total time complexity is dominated by the step of computing quality functions, and is $O(\Theta \cdot |E|)$ for most practical cases.

Finally, we give the privacy guarantee of (θ, Ω)-Histogram as well as the proof in the following.

LEMMA 3. (θ, Ω)-Histogram *in Algorithm 2 satisfies* $(\epsilon_1 + \epsilon_2)$*-node-DP.*

PROOF OF LEMMA 3. In Algorithm 2, the steps of Lines 1-2 use exponential mechanism with privacy budget ϵ_1. The steps of projection (Line 3) and publishing histogram with aggregated counts (Line 4) use Laplace mechanism and satisfy node-DP for ϵ_2, and the post-processing step performs on the private output. By

Algorithm 2 (θ, Ω)-Histogram algorithm.

Input: A graph G, privacy budgets ϵ_1 and ϵ_2, candidates T and O
Output: A noisy degree distribution $\mathbf{d}$.

```
For each (θ_i, Ω_j) ∈ T × O, computes q_ε^h(G, θ_i, Ω_j, ε_2)
Select (θ*, Ω*) with prob. ∝ exp( ε_1 q_ε^h(G, θ_i, Ω_j, ε_2) / (2Δ_{q_ε^h}) )
G^{θ*} ← π_{θ*}(G) by Algorithm 1.
h ← Aggregate_{Ω*}( hist(G^{θ*}) ) + Lap(Δ_hist / ε_2)^{|Ω*|}
h' ← PostProcess(h) by Algorithm 5.
return d = h' / ||h'||_1
```

the composition theorem and transformation invariance properties, (θ, Ω)-Histogram satisfies $(\epsilon_1 + \epsilon_2)$-node-DP. □

3.3 Cumulative Degree Histogram

Releasing the degree histogram from projection and aggregation technique requires noise level of $\mathsf{Lap}\left(\frac{2\theta+1}{\epsilon}\right)$. One way to lower the noise magnitude is to publish a *cumulative degree histogram*, in which the k'th bin in the histogram is the answer of the query $\mathsf{cumhist}_k = |v : deg(v) \leq k|$, i.e., *"How many nodes in this graph have degree no higher than k?"*. Lemma 4 below shows that $\Delta_{\mathsf{cumhist}}$, the global sensitivity of releasing a cumulative degree histogram, i.e., the vector $\mathsf{cumhist}(\pi_\theta(G))$ where $1 \leq k \leq \theta$, is bounded by $\theta + 1$.

LEMMA 4. *Given $G \simeq G'$ that differ in one node, we have*

$$||\mathsf{cumhist}(\pi_\theta(G)) - \mathsf{cumhist}(\pi_\theta(G'))||_1 \leq \theta + 1$$

where π_θ is the projection function following Algorithm 1.

PROOF OF LEMMA 4. We follow the idea and notations in the proof of Lemma 1. Let t be the degree of v^+ in $\pi_\theta(G')$. Now consider the effect of v^+ in the cumulative histogram. Since v^+ appears in $\mathsf{cumhist}(\pi_\theta(G'))$ but not in $\mathsf{cumhist}(\pi_\theta(G))$, all $\theta - t + 1$ bins of $\mathsf{cumhist}(\pi_\theta(G'))$ from degree t to θ are increased by 1 compared to those in $\mathsf{cumhist}(\pi_\theta(G))$. Thus, there are at most $\theta - t + 1$ changes due to v^+.

Now consider other changes caused by adding edges incident to v^+. Recall that we use $\lambda_0, \lambda_1, \cdots, \lambda_t$ to denote the sequence of projected graphs resulted from keeping $0, 1, \cdots, t$ of such edges. We have shown that $\forall k$ such that $1 \leq k \leq t$, there is at most 1 node (other than v^+) in λ_k with the degree differs from λ_{k-1}, and the difference in the node's degree is 1. Thus, the cumulative histograms of λ_{k-1} and λ_k (ignoring v^+) have an L1 distance of at most 1. By the Triangular Inequality, the cumulative histograms of λ_0 and λ_t (ignoring v^+) have a distance of at most t. Combining this with the effect of v^+, the cumulative histograms of $\pi_\theta(G) = \lambda_0$ and $\pi_\theta(G') = \lambda_t$ have a distance of at most $\theta + 1$. □

Modeling the selection of the optimal θ requires a low-sensitivity quality function with the ability of estimating the error of cumulative histogram. Considering the property of a cumulative histogram, we point out, as θ is the cutoff point of the cumulative histogram in $\pi_\theta(G)$, the utility that $\mathsf{cumhist}(\pi_\theta(G))$ maintains is "how many nodes with degree equal to or under θ". We propose a quality function as follows:

$$q_\epsilon^c(G, \theta_i) = -2 \cdot \left|\{v : v \in V, deg_{\pi_\Theta(G)}(v) > \theta\}\right| - \sqrt{\theta} \cdot \frac{\theta + 1}{\epsilon}$$

The function q_ϵ^c captures the projection loss for computing histogram, and also considers the noise effect. The projection loss is the same as ℓ_{proj} for (θ, Ω)-Histogram. In the noise effect term, the coefficient $\sqrt{\theta}$ estimates the noise effect to the histogram extraction from the cumulative histogram, which includes the summation over bins. (Intuitively, the effect of summing θ independent noises have standard deviation $\sqrt{\theta}$ times that of the original noise.) $\Delta_{q_\epsilon^c}$, the sensitivity of q_ϵ^c, is $2\Theta + 2$, as analyzed in the proof of Lemma 2. With all these information on hand, one can perform projection π_θ on graph G and obtain $\mathsf{cumhist}(\pi_\theta(G))$.

Algorithm 3 ExtractHistogram algorithm.

Input: A noisy cumulative histogram hc with size θ.
Output: A degree histogram h with size θ.

```
1: hc_0 ← 0, i ← 1, hc_1 ← 0 if hc_1 < 0
2: while i ≤ θ do
3:     if hc_i < hc_{i+1} then
4:         h_i ← hc_i − hc_{i−1}
5:         i ← i + 1
6:     else
7:         For j from θ to i, find first j such that hc_{j−1} < hc_i
8:         Assign h_k ← (hc_j − hc_{i−1}) / (j − i + 1) for i ≤ k ≤ j
9:         i ← j + 1
10:    end if
11: end while
12: return h
```

In addition to the advantage of requiring less noise, the cumulative degree histogram also has the *monotonicity* property, i.e., the counts from degree 1 to degree θ are non-decreasing. This property provides a way of calibrating the noisy cumulative degree histogram while extracting the histogram from it. We give a histogram extraction algorithm ExtractHistogram based on the calibrating idea in Algorithm 3. Specifically, if the count of degree i is greater than the count of degree $i + 1$, either or both counts are undermined by too much noise injection. It then searches the first non-decreasing bin j from the last bin θ to bin i and assigns the counts uniformly between bin i to bin j (Lines 7-8). After that, it jumps to next non-decreasing bin and extracts the histogram continuously. An additional advantage of our extraction algorithm with calibrating the cumulative histogram is that it averages out the noise effect $\mathsf{Lap}\left(\frac{\theta+1}{\epsilon}\right)$, with the cost of viewing bin counts equally like aggregation in (θ, Ω)-Histogram approach.

Another calibration is based on constrained inference (monotonic regression) proposed in [13]. In Section 4.3, we also report the comparison between our calibration and constrained inference.

The overall algorithm of releasing the degree histogram from the cumulative histogram, named θ-CumulativeHistogram, is shown in Algorithm 4. Similar to Algorithm 2, θ-CumulativeHistogram first performs the computation of qualities and the exponential mechanism in Lines 1-2, and then projects the graph, computes the noisy cumulative histogram, calibrates and extracts, and finally publishes the post-processed histogram. The running time of θ-CumulativeHistogram is $O(|E| \cdot \Theta)$ for any given $G = (V, E)$ and Θ due to Lines 1 and 2, and it requires slightly less time than Algorithm 2 because it does not need to consider different Ω values. We report the experimental results for running time in Section 4.4. We also give the privacy guarantee for θ-CumulativeHistogram algorithm, as well as its proof.

LEMMA 5. *θ-CumulativeHistogram in Algorithm 4 satisfies $(\epsilon_1 + \epsilon_2)$-node-DP.*

PROOF OF LEMMA 5. In Algorithm 4, Lines 1-2 use exponential mechanism with privacy budget ϵ_1. Lines 3 and 4 uses Laplace mechanism with privacy budget ϵ_2. All other steps are indepen-

Algorithm 4 θ-CumulativeHistogram algorithm.

Input: A graph G, privacy budgets ϵ_1 and ϵ_2, candidates T.
Output: A noisy degree distribution $\mathbf{d}$.

For each $\theta_i \in T$, computes $q^c_\epsilon(G, \theta_i, \epsilon_2)$
Select θ^* from T with probability $\propto \exp\left(\frac{\epsilon_1 q^c_\epsilon(G,\theta_i,\epsilon_2)}{2\Delta_{q^c_\epsilon}}\right)$
$G^{\theta^*} \leftarrow \pi_{\theta^*}(G)$ by Algorithm 1.
$hc \leftarrow \mathsf{cumhist}\left(G^{\theta^*}\right) + \mathsf{Lap}\left(\frac{\Delta_{\mathsf{cumhist}}}{\epsilon_2}\right)^{\theta^*}$
$h \leftarrow \mathsf{ExtractHistogram}(hc)$ by Algorithm 3.
$h' \leftarrow \mathsf{PostProcess}(h)$ by Algorithm 5.
return $\mathbf{d} = h'/||h'||_1$

dent and performed on the noisy output. By the composition theorem and transformation invariance, θ-CumulativeHistogram satisfies $(\epsilon_1 + \epsilon_2)$-node-DP. □

3.4 Post-processing for Tail Distribution

After projection, most nodes that have original degree $> \theta$ will now have degree θ. This results in a high count for the last bin in the histogram. In other words, the count of last bin in histogram, which represents the number of nodes with degree θ in G^θ, actually contains the number of nodes with degree "at least" θ in G, i.e., $|v : deg(v) \geq \theta|$ in G. Releasing a histogram following either (θ, Ω)-Histogram or θ-CumulativeHistogram will preserve such information, given the assumption that the noise is not sufficiently large to destroy it. We can use this property to *reallocate* the counts of degrees larger than θ, making the published distribution be closer to the original distribution and more like a long-tailed distribution.

However, estimating the tail distribution using the noisy histogram is hard, given the perturbed histogram would unlikely to follow the original distribution. We design three simple approaches to allocate counts based on coefficients learned from linear regression, power law distribution, or uniform distribution. Specifically, the post-processing step either learns the slope m and the intercept b from $y = mx + b$ in linear regression, learns a and k from $y = ax^{-k}$ assuming it follows the power law distribution, or allocates the average count to each bin from degree θ to 2θ assuming the tail follows uniform distribution.

Algorithm 5 shows the detail steps of performing linear regression, assuming that from $\theta/2$th bin the counts drop linearly. In particular, Lines 1-2 first compute the average $\bar{c}$ from the second half of histogram H, and Line 3 learns the slope m and intercept b from H with linear regression. Ideally, m should be negative with a small quantity to approximate the long-tail, but m could be positive due to the effect of noise. If so, the algorithm simply assigns each bin with the average $\bar{c}$ (Line 8), otherwise it assigns the estimated count by m and b (Line 6) until the budget is out. For allocating tail distribution based on power law distribution or uniform distribution, we could modify steps in Lines 3 and 6 accordingly. We report the experimental result in Section 4.4 and show that the three approaches do not have significant difference on allocating tail distribution. We use linear regression in our other experiments.

4. EXPERIMENT

In this section, we report experimental results comparing our proposed approaches with approaches with the state of the art, and analyzing how different aspects of our proposed approaches affect the utility.

Algorithm 5 PostProcess algorithm.

Input: A degree histogram h, number of nodes n
Output: A post-processed degree histogram h'.

1: $budget \leftarrow h_\theta$, $H \leftarrow \{h_{\theta/2}, h_{\theta/2+1}, \cdots, h_{\theta-1}\}$
2: $\bar{c} \leftarrow \frac{2}{\theta}\sum_{k=\theta/2}^{\theta-1} h_k$
3: Learn the intercept b and slope m of linear regression on H.
4: **for** k from θ to n **do**
5:     **if** $m < 0$ **then**
6:         $h_k \leftarrow b + m \times k$
7:     **else**
8:         $h_k \leftarrow \bar{c}$
9:     **end if**
10:     $budget \leftarrow budget - h_k$; **break** if $budget < 0$
11: **end for**
12: **return** $h' = h$

4.1 Datasets and Settings

Our experiments use 8 real-world datasets downloaded from [22], as shown in Table 1. The datasets are from several different domains, including social networks, citation networks, and email networks. We pre-processed all graph datasets to be undirected. Table 1 also shows some additional information such as average degree, maximum degree, and the parameter α in α-decay [18] for the distribution (the larger α is, the long-tailed the graph is).

We compare our methods, (θ, Ω)-Histogram and θ-CumulativeHistogram, against two state-of-the-art methods for publishing node degree histograms while satisfying node-DP. The first algorithm is *Truncation* from [18]. The algorithm has two parameters: β and θ. We set $\beta = \epsilon \ln(|V|/\theta)$ as suggested in [18]. Since θ is manually specified in [18], we consider all θ values among $\{1, 2, 4, \cdots, 2^{\lfloor 2\log_2(|V|)\rfloor}\}$ and report the result with the smallest error. The second algorithm is *Flowgraph* [31], which uses the max-flow algorithm with minimizing L2 error of the remaining flows. Following [31], we select $\theta \in \{1, 2, 4, \cdots, 2^{\lfloor 2\log_2(|V|)\rfloor}\}$ by the generalized exponential mechanism.

We use L1 error and KS-distance to evaluate the approximation results on privacy budget $\epsilon \in [0.1, 2.0]$ in Section 4.3, where each privacy budget ϵ is divided into $\epsilon_1 = 0.1\epsilon$ and $\epsilon_2 = 0.9\epsilon$ in our proposed approaches. To evaluate the KS-distance on different approaches, we generate the degree sequence using the noisy degree distribution and then compare with the true degree sequence. All results on all approaches are the averages from 30 runs. We also show the complementary CDFs when $\epsilon = 1$ for all graph datasets.

4.2 Evaluating π_θ

We first directly compare our proposed graph projection method, π_θ, with three other existing graph projection methods mentioned in Section 2.4: **T** (Truncation), **FG** (FlowGraph), and **ER** (EdgeRemoval). Table 2 shows the results. We use two metrics: the L1 error of degree histogram after projection, and $\frac{|E'|}{|E|}$, where E' denotes the edges after projection. Since the histogram of $\pi_\theta(G)$ could have lots of counts with degree exactly θ (as all nodes with original degree over θ are *shaved* to θ), we compare π_θ after removing the bin of θ. We consider three θ values, $\theta = 16, 64, 128$.

The results show that Truncation and our π_θ have the lowest L1 error, meaning that these two approaches maintain the shape of distribution after projection. On the other hand, Flowgraph and π_θ preserve the most number of edges. In addition, because Flowgraph has a step to solve a max-flow problem with an objective

Graph	$\lvert V\rvert$	$\lvert E\rvert$	$d_{\max}$	d_{avg}	α
Facebook	4,039	88,234	1,045	43.69	2.39
Wiki-Vote	7,066	100,736	1065	28.32	1.94
Ca-HepPh	11,204	117,649	491	21.00	1.58
Email-Enron	33,696	180,811	1,383	10.73	1.76
Cit-HepPh	34,401	420,828	846	24.47	2.60
Loc-Brightkite	56,739	212,945	1,134	7.51	1.89
Twitter	81,306	1,342,310	3,383	33.02	2.15
DBLP	317,080	1,049,866	343	6.62	2.31

Table 1: Information about datasets. All graphs are connected (i.e. one connected component). $d_{\max}$ denotes maximum degree, and d_{avg} denotes average degree. α is the parameter for α-decay [18].

function, the running time of Flowgraph projection is roughly 10 to 20 times compared to other three approaches (we omit the result due to space limitation). Our proposed projection approach, π_θ, thus benefits from three sides: preserving well on the shape of distribution, the number of edges, and with better efficiency.

4.3 Evaluating (θ,Ω)-Histogram and θ-Cumulative

L1 and KS of Node Degree Distributions. Figure 3 compares the quality of the resulting node degree distributions of our two proposed method to those of *Truncation* [18] and *Flowgraph* [31]. We also report the result of a variant of our proposed θ-CumulativeHistogram. Instead of using our proposed method to exploit the monotonicity property to extract the resulting histogram from a noisy cumulative histogram, this variant uses the constrained inference (isotonic regression) technique in [13] for calibrating cumulative histogram (*θ-Constrained*). We also plot the standard deviation computed from 30 runs for each data point.

The experimental result shows that *Truncation* generally performs the worst, followed by *Flowgraph*, which has the largest variance. Looking at intermediate results, we note that *Flowgraph* tends to select very different θ values in different runs, and some of the values are very large. This combined with the high sensitivity of the resulting histogram (6θ) causes the high variance.

Our two proposed methods and the variant all perform significantly better than *Truncation* and *Flowgraph*, and result in quite accurate node degree histograms, especially when $\epsilon \geq 0.5$ and for the larger datasets. When looking at the L1 results, the *θ-Constrained* variant performs noticeably worse than the two proposed method. When looking at the KS results, we can see that *θ-Constrained* performs almost identically with θ-CumulativeHistogram, and they both perform noticeably better than (θ,Ω)-Histogram on the three datasets that are relatively small. The reason that *θ-Constrained* performs not as well as our proposed methods in terms of L1 distance is because when encountering an unversed pair in the noisy cumulative histogram, the isotonic regression method tends to result in stepwise cumulative histograms, which when converted to histograms results in many bins having 0 count. Overall, θ-CumulativeHistogram appears to be the best approach for publishing the degree distribution under node-DP.

Approximating the Node Degree Distributions. We now show the complementary cumulative distribution functions (CCDFs) from the distributions with median error out of 30 runs at $\epsilon = 1$ for each approach. As demonstrated in Figure 4, the distributions from (θ,Ω)-Histogram, θ-CumulativeHistogram, and θ-Constrained closely follow the true one, especially in the smaller degree part (less than 100); and θ-CumulativeHistogram performs the best. All approaches have a clear cutoff point, because they are all designed based on the idea of limiting sensitivity. Since these methods all underestimates the distribution for higher degree nodes, there may be ways to correct this systematic bias. This is an interesting future work. *Truncation* tends to perform the worst, often overestimating the number of low-degree nodes and underestimating the number of high-degree nodes. *Flowgraph*'s behavior appears more erratic, likely due to the high variance.

Running time analysis. Table 3 reports the average running time of our proposed approaches on an Intel i7-3770 3.40GHz machine with 12GB memory. As we have discussed in Section 3, the advantage that the time complexity of our algorithms is linear to number of edges ($O(|E|\cdot|\Theta|)$) enables both approaches handle the graphs with very large size. Besides, the computation of the quality on each candidate (which takes most of the time) can be easily parallelized, making our approaches scalable to very large graphs.

4.4 Introspective Analysis

In this section, we perform the introspective analysis, to try to understand how different aspects of our approaches affect the utility.

Analysis on tuning θ and Ω. In this analysis, we would like to know whether our quality functions for selecting the parameters θ,Ω are well-designed, to what extent the usage of aggregation affects the utility of (θ,Ω)-Histogram, and to what extent our proposed approaches are sensitive to the choice of $\Theta = 200$. Figure 5 shows the results.

The left half of Figure 5 shows different variants of (θ,Ω)-Histogram. The original method is dubbed (θ,Ω)-Hist; (θ,Ω)-Q-Best directly selects the value (θ,Ω) that has the best quality function (without using the exponential mechanism, and is thus non-private); (θ,Ω)-Oracle creates histograms using all (θ,Ω) values and select the one that results in noisy histograms with the least L1 error (also non-private); (θ,Ω)-Q-400 uses $\Theta = 400$ instead of $\Theta = 200$; (θ,Ω)-No-group does not use aggregation and is essentially θ-Histogram. From the results, we can see that not using grouping significantly impacts the accuracy. The curves for the original (θ,Ω)-Hist and for (θ,Ω)-Q-400 are very close, and in fact almost overlapping when $\epsilon \geq 0.5$. This suggests that our method is not very sensitive to the choice of $\Theta = 200$. We also see that the results for (θ,Ω)-Q-Best and (θ,Ω)-Oracle are almost overlapping, suggesting that our quality function is well-designed.

The right half of Figure 5 shows different variants of θ-CumulativeHistogram. Similarly, θ-Q-Best uses the θ value that has the best quality function (non-private), θ-Oracle uses the θ value that empirically has the lowest L1 error, and θ-Q-400 uses $\Theta = 400$ instead of $\Theta = 200$. In terms of L1 error, the curves for all methods are quite close. For the KS-error, the curves are also similar, although θ-Oracle sometimes deviates from the other curves slightly. Note that since θ-Oracle selects θ that optimizes L1 error, it may not produce the best KS result. The closeness of the 4 curves suggests the following: (1) the quality function for θ-CumulativeHistogram is well-designed; (2) we are able to select a θ that is quite close to optimal (because the low sensitivity of the quality function); and (3) the method is not sensitive to the choice of parameter Θ.

Analysis on choices of θ. To understand the effects from the choices of θs, we apply $\theta = 25, 50, 100, 200$ on θ-Histogram without aggregation and report the experimental result in Figure 6. The result shows that the utility of the published degree distribution is very sensitive to the choice of θ, i.e. if one chooses a "bad" θ, it easily leads to a noisy degree distribution with poor utility. Our proposed approaches solve the problem by applying the expo-

Graph	θ=16				θ=64				θ=128			
	T	**FG**	**ER**	π_θ	**T**	**FG**	**ER**	π_θ	**T**	**FG**	**ER**	π_θ
Face-	3828	5112	5122	**3228**	1923	2060	1880	**1313**	960	1092	976	**801**
book	0.03	0.30	0.20	0.27	0.27	0.70	0.62	0.66	0.57	0.90	0.86	0.88
Wiki-	5856	8232	4666	**4205**	**3546**	6018	4908	4991	**4622**	5404	5120	5054
Vote	0.00	0.25	0.12	0.19	0.11	0.57	0.45	0.51	0.36	0.76	0.70	0.73
Ca-	**4894**	8570	7198	5728	**4381**	5536	4868	4548	**4533**	4992	4712	**4533**
HepPh	0.11	0.36	0.28	0.33	0.23	0.51	0.43	0.48	0.55	0.81	0.76	0.78
Email-	14866	11200	9749	**8574**	**7361**	11216	10030	9848	**7223**	13602	12635	12577
Enron	0.13	0.37	0.27	0.34	0.33	0.62	0.56	0.60	0.50	0.75	0.72	0.74
Cit-	33657	33112	33373	**23724**	12297	7614	7906	**6401**	4888	4260	4329	**3825**
HepPh	0.05	0.45	0.30	0.39	0.49	0.82	0.77	0.80	0.80	0.93	0.93	0.93
Loc-Bri-	**31510**	43734	37554	36928	**35791**	39720	38629	38455	**37899**	39912	39616	39537
ghtkite	0.22	0.55	0.44	0.51	0.59	0.82	0.78	0.80	0.77	0.91	0.90	0.90
Twitter	78098	74286	75544	**53703**	39932	26358	23754	**20776**	18975	17116	17306	**15293**
	0.02	0.29	0.17	0.24	0.22	0.61	0.52	0.57	0.46	0.77	0.72	0.74
DBLP	**83630**	137112	119932	107484	**108997**	118798	117936	116764	**117225**	118464	118389	118273
	0.43	0.75	0.68	0.72	0.67	0.89	0.86	0.87	0.97	0.99	0.99	0.99

Table 2: L1 error (first row of each dataset) and the number of edges preserved $\frac{|E'|}{|E|}$ (second row of each dataset) of the degree histogram from different projection approaches on 8 datasets. **T** = Truncation, **FG** = Flowgraph, and **ER** = Edge-Removal.

Graph	(θ,Ω)-Histogram		θ-CumulativeHistogram	
	Quality	**Total**	**Quality**	**Total**
Facebook	78.86	79.43	74.38	74.98
Wiki-Vote	104.28	104.99	97.85	98.58
Ca-HepPh	130.84	131.70	119.50	120.39
Email-Enron	287.62	289.45	263.52	265.39
Cit-HepPh	574.06	578.13	548.25	552.41
Loc-Brightkite	407.69	410.29	367.38	370.08
Twitter	1867.66	1880.78	1833.84	1847.35
DBLP	2773.83	2791.14	2566.02	2582.96

Table 3: Running time (in seconds) for our proposed approaches.

nential mechanism with well-designed quality functions, making it only depending on Θ, which is not sensitive as discussed earlier.

Additional analysis. We also compared three different methods for allocating the tail distribution from counts of last bin (i.e., θ) to other bins: linear regression, power law distribution, and simple average. Experimental results are reported in Figure 7 in the appendix, and show that the three strategies produce similar results, suggesting that any of these can be used.

Finally, we analyze the influence from different edge orderings in the projection step. We pick up 10 random-ordered edge sequences, perform the projection and publish the degree distribution, and compare the highest and lowest error among these 10 results with our original approach. The result in Figure 8 in Appendix shows that edge orderings does not have significant impacts on our proposed projection approach and publishing the degree distribution.

5. RELATED WORK

DP on Graph Data. Applying differential privacy to the graph setting has been studied extensively; most use edge-DP [12, 15, 32, 16, 29, 17, 35], but some consider node-DP [18, 3, 4, 31]. We argue that using node-DP is more meaningful as node-DP gives the personal privacy control on graph data. The work in [12] studies the problem of publishing degree sequence from a graph under edge-DP, which has sensitivity of 2, as removing one edge will influence the degrees of two nodes. The approach in [12] applies the Laplace mechanism directly and performs a constrained inference to synthesize the degree sequence to be monotonic. Several following works have considered publishing the degree sequence or distribution and extended the technique to synthetic generation [32, 16, 29, 15, 16, 35]. These approaches are infeasible when the setting moves to node-DP, where the sensitivity of $\mathsf{hist}(G)$ becomes $2(|V|-1)$. The techniques of using "projection" to limit the sensitivity are studied to answer degree distribution under node-DP [18, 31]. The truncation approach is proposed in [18], and the Flowgraph approach is proposed in [31]. We have experimentally compared with these approaches. Researchers have proposed several approaches for answering a single-valued query, i.e., a certain statistics value about the graph. For example, subgraph counting queries (e.g., the number of triangles, the number of k-stars) have been studied under edge-DP [15, 35] and node-DP [18, 3, 4], and the computing cost of minimum spanning tree has been studied in [28] using smooth sensitivity.

Histogram publishing under DP. The problem of publishing histogram under differential privacy has been studied extensively [1, 6, 11, 13, 23, 30, 33, 34, 36]. The technique of using aggregation and averaging to reduce errors is studied in [1, 19, 23, 34, 36]. Publishing node degree histograms in graphs has the challenge that the sensitivity is much larger since removing one node may affect every other node; thus one has to consider histogram aggregation together with graph projection. We adopt the idea of aggregating bins for more accurate histogram from this line of work; however we exploit the power-law nature of graph node degree distributions to limit the candidates to those constructed using geometric series. An interesting approach to discover optimal aggregation configuration is proposed in [23], in which one adds the noise to the error estimation of each group of bins, and then uses dynamic programming to select a configuration that minimizes the sum of errors caused by grouping and errors caused by the noise. Fixing each θ value, one can use this method to select an aggregation structure Ω. It is an interesting future work to see whether this technique can be adapted to our problem of selecting (θ, Ω) together without divid-

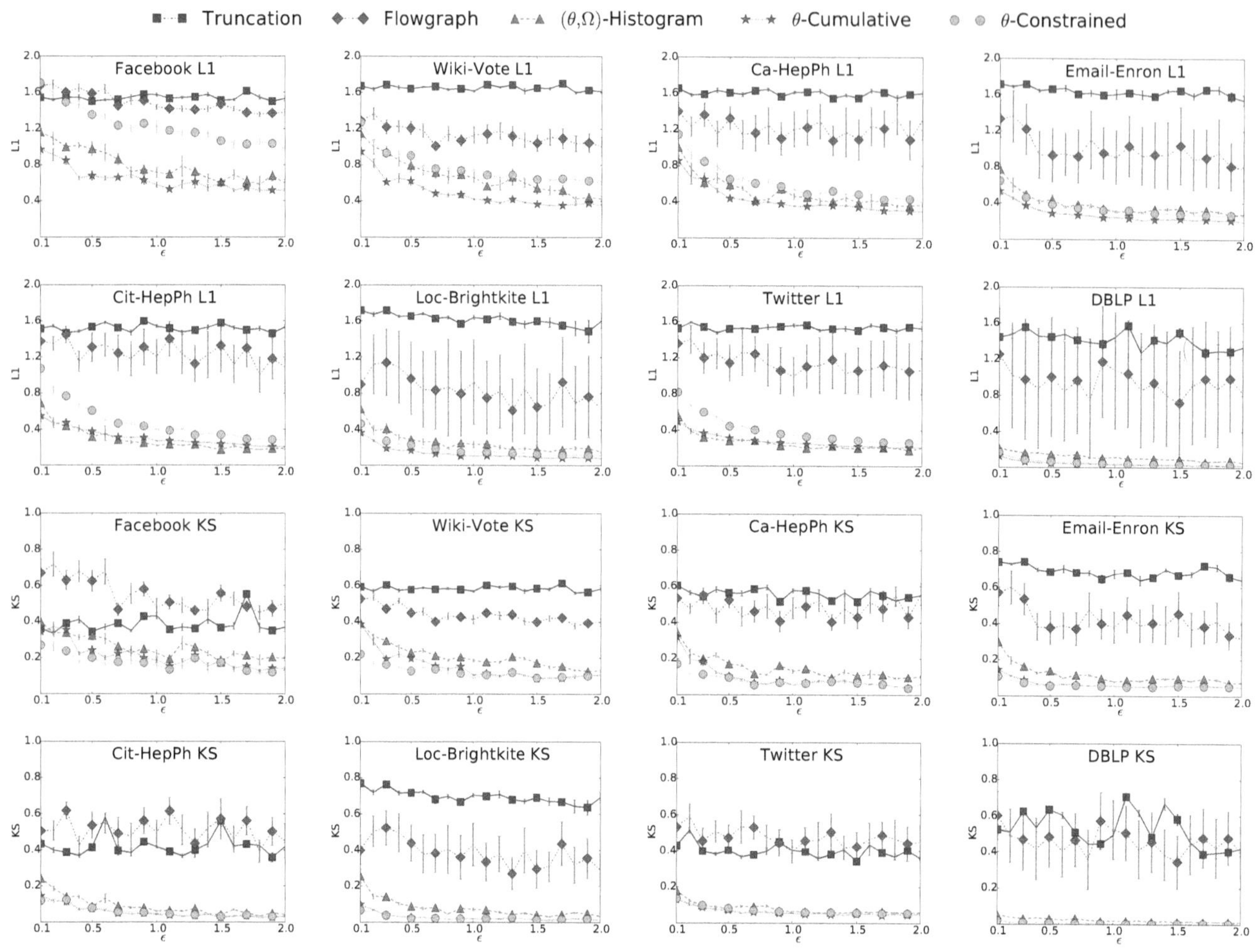

Figure 3: The L1 error (upper half) and KS distance (lower half) of approaches on different datasets.

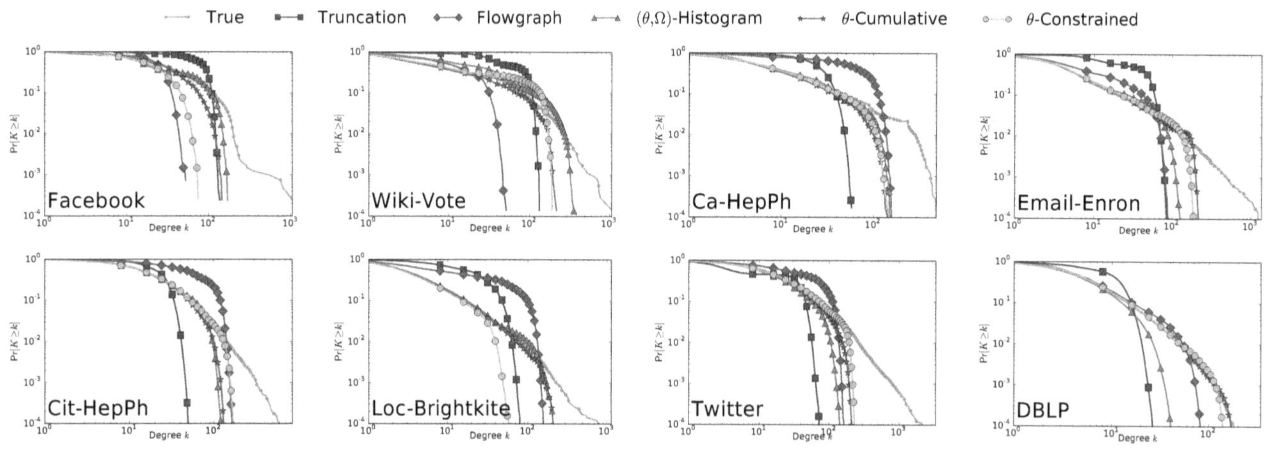

Figure 4: The complementary cumulative distribution function (CCDF) vs. degree of approaches on different datasets at $\epsilon = 1$. For any degree k in x-axis, the value in y-axis denotes the fraction of nodes with degree at least k ($\Pr[K \geq k]$).

ing the privacy budget, and if so, how this method compares with our approach of using geometric series.

It is suggested in [13] that when the number of bins to be published are relatively large, it is better to use hierarchical method to publish histograms under DP. In our work, the number of bins is usually small, and directly publishing the histogram without hierarchical method is preferred based on [30]. Releasing a cumulative histogram is also studied in [14]. While the global sensitivity of releasing a cumulative histogram is the number of bins in the cumulative histogram, the work proposes an ordered mechanism based

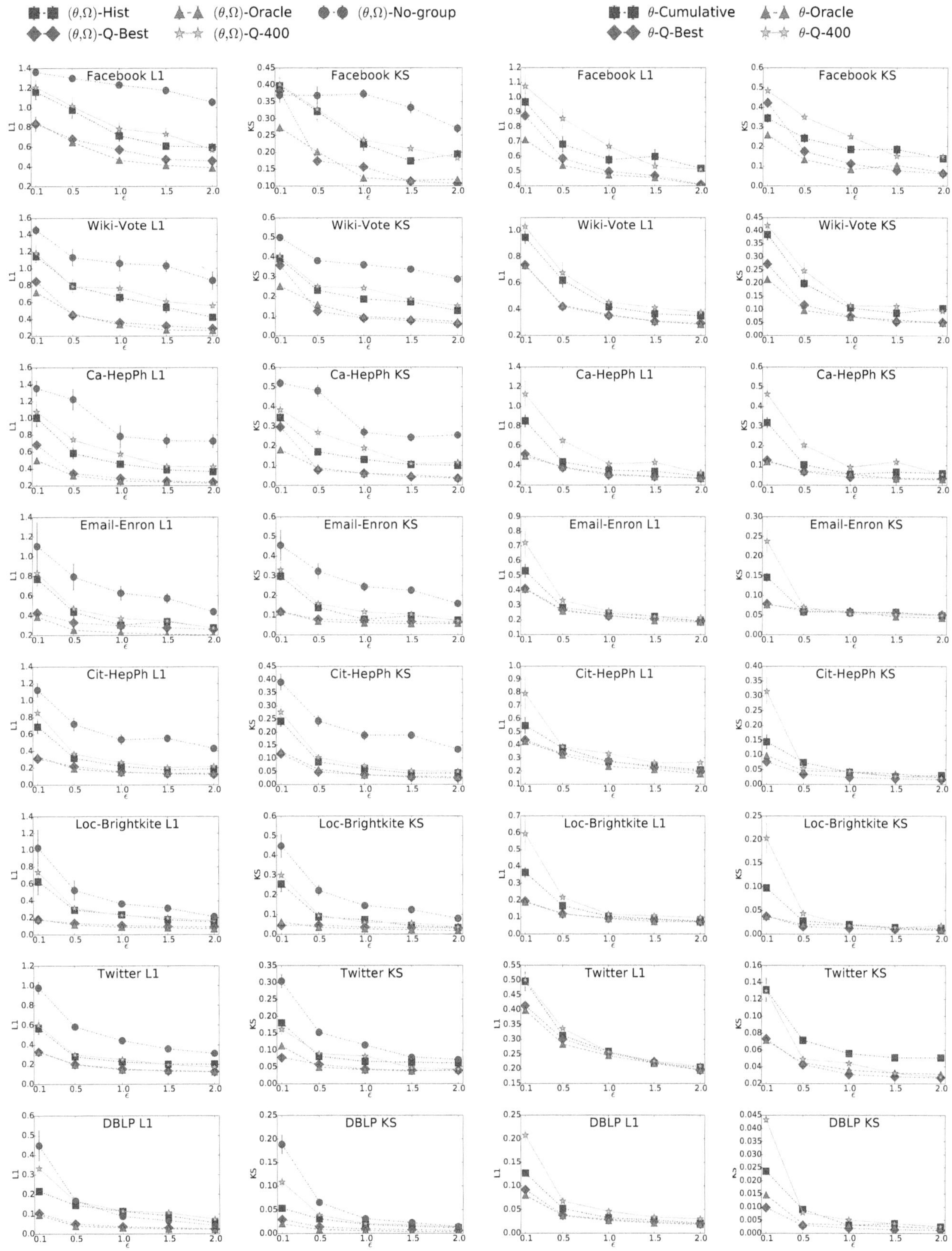

Figure 5: The experimental results on the effects of tuning the parameters θ and Ω for (θ,Ω)-Histogram (left half) and θ-CumulativeHistogram (right half).

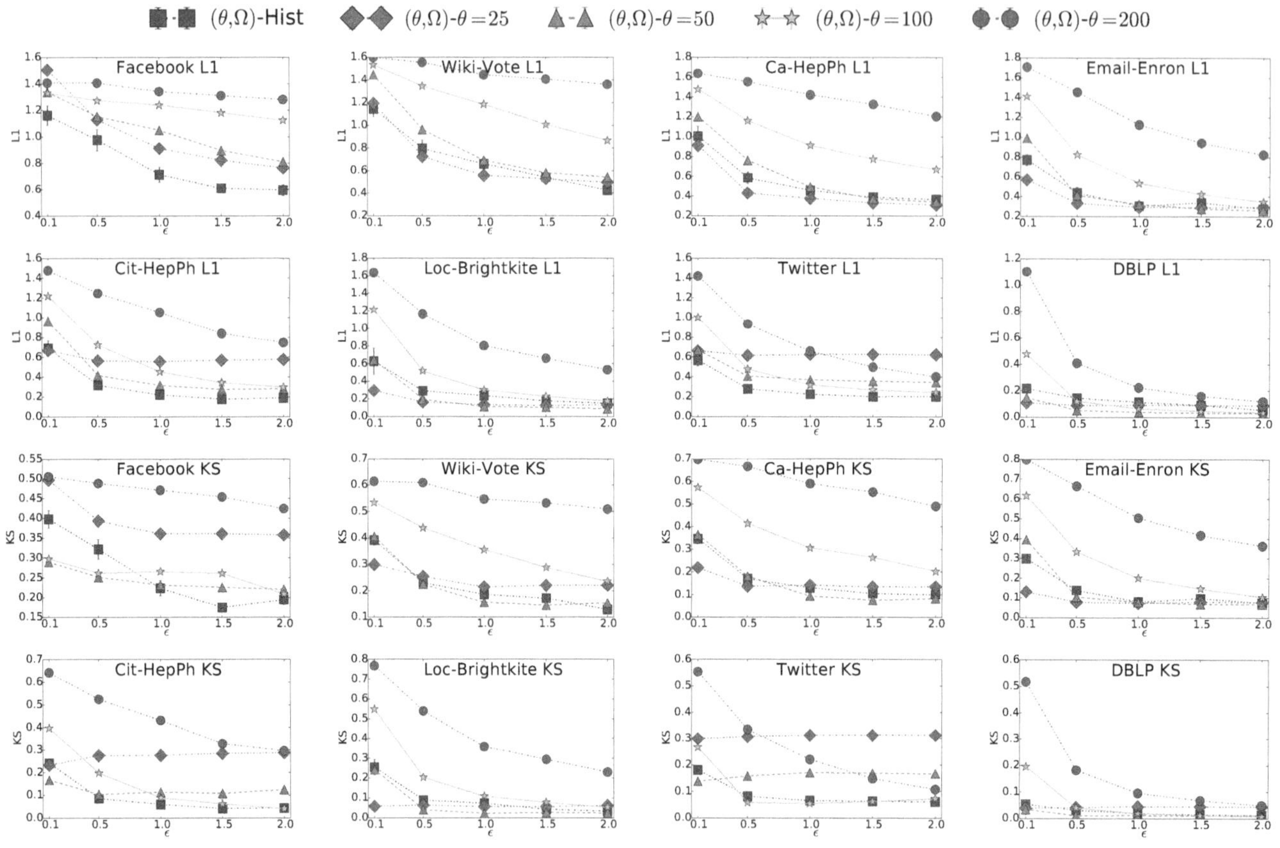

Figure 6: The L1 error (upper half) and KS distance (lower half) of (θ,Ω)-Histogram with manually setting $\theta \in \{25, 50, 100, 200\}$ on different datasets.

on a relaxed privacy notion named Blowfish privacy, in which the sensitivity becomes 1 for some predefined policy. In our work, we study the sensitivity of releasing a cumulative histogram after projection while satisfying node-DP.

6. CONCLUSION

In this paper, we discuss the necessity of using node-DP in private analysis of graph data, and study how to publish node degree histograms while satisfying node-DP. We propose a new projection method to preserve as much information of a graph as possible and limit the sensitivity of publishing the degree histograms on the projected graph. Based on the projection, we propose two approaches, (θ,Ω)-Histogram and θ-CumulativeHistogram, and experimentally compare with existing works for publishing degree distribution. The experimental results show that our proposed approaches have significant improvement over the state of the art. While these methods accurately capture the distribution of low degree nodes, future research is needed to better predict the distribution of higher-degree nodes using the preserved lower-degree information.

7. ACKNOWLEDGMENTS

This work reported in this paper is supported by National Science Foundation under grant CNS-1116991. We would like to thank Rui Chen and the reviewers for their useful comments.

8. REFERENCES

[1] G. Acs, C. Castelluccia, and R. Chen. Differentially private histogram publishing through lossy compression. In *ICDM*, pages 1–10, 2012.

[2] L. Backstrom, C. Dwork, and J. Kleinberg. Wherefore art thou r3579x?: anonymized social networks, hidden patterns, and structural steganography. In *WWW*, pages 181–190, 2007.

[3] J. Blocki, A. Blum, A. Datta, and O. Sheffet. Differentially private data analysis of social networks via restricted sensitivity. In *Proceedings of the 4th Conference on Innovations in Theoretical Computer Science*, ITCS '13, pages 87–96, New York, NY, USA, 2013. ACM.

[4] S. Chen and S. Zhou. Recursive mechanism: Towards node differential privacy and unrestricted joins. In *SIGMOD '13*, pages 653–664, 2013.

[5] G. Cormode. Personal privacy vs population privacy: Learning to attack anonymization. In *Proceedings of the 17th ACM SIGKDD International Conference on Knowledge Discovery and Data Mining*, KDD '11, pages 1253–1261, 2011.

[6] G. Cormode, C. Procopiuc, D. Srivastava, and T. T. L. Tran. Differentially private summaries for sparse data. In *ICDT '12*, pages 299–311, 2012.

[7] C. Dwork. Differential privacy. In *ICALP*, pages 1–12, 2006.

[8] C. Dwork, F. McSherry, K. Nissim, and A. Smith. Calibrating noise to sensitivity in private data analysis. In *TCC*, pages 265–284, 2006.

[9] C. Dwork and M. Naor. On the difficulties of disclosure prevention in statistical databases or the case for differential privacy. *Journal of Privacy and Confidentiality*, 2, 2008.

[10] M. Fredrikson, E. Lantz, S. Jha, S. Lin, D. Page, and T. Ristenpart. Privacy in pharmacogenetics: An end-to-end case study of personalized warfarin dosing. In *Proceedings of the 23rd USENIX Security Symposium, San Diego, CA, USA, August 20-22, 2014.*, pages 17–32, 2014.

[11] M. Hardt, K. Ligett, and F. Mcsherry. A simple and practical algorithm for differentially private data release. In *Advances in Neural Information Processing Systems (NIPS) 25*, pages 2339–2347, 2012.

[12] M. Hay, C. Li, G. Miklau, and D. Jensen. Accurate Estimation of the Degree Distribution of Private Networks. In *ICDM*, pages 169–178, 2009.

[13] M. Hay, V. Rastogi, G. Miklau, and D. Suciu. Boosting the accuracy of differentially private histograms through consistency. *PVLDB*, 3(1):1021–1032, 2010.

[14] X. He, A. Machanavajjhala, and B. Ding. Blowfish privacy: Tuning privacy-utility trade-offs using policies. In *SIGMOD*, pages 1447–1458, 2014.

[15] V. Karwa, S. Raskhodnikova, A. Smith, and G. Yaroslavtsev. Private analysis of graph structure. In *VLDB*, 2011.

[16] V. Karwa and A. B. Slavković. Differentially private graphical degree sequences and synthetic graphs. In *Proceedings of the 2012 International Conference on Privacy in Statistical Databases*, PSD'12, pages 273–285, Berlin, Heidelberg, 2012. Springer-Verlag.

[17] V. Karwa, A. B. Slavkovic, and P. N. Krivitsky. Differentially private exponential random graphs. In *Privacy in Statistical Databases - UNESCO Chair in Data Privacy, International Conference, PSD 2014, Ibiza, Spain, September 17-19, 2014. Proceedings*, pages 143–155, 2014.

[18] S. P. Kasiviswanathan, K. Nissim, S. Raskhodnikova, and A. Smith. Analyzing graphs with node differential privacy. In *Proceedings of the 10th Theory of Cryptography Conference on Theory of Cryptography*, TCC'13, pages 457–476, Berlin, Heidelberg, 2013. Springer-Verlag.

[19] G. Kellaris and S. Papadopoulos. Practical differential privacy via grouping and smoothing. *PVLDB*, 6(5):301–312, 2013.

[20] D. Kifer and B.-R. Lin. Towards an axiomatization of statistical privacy and utility. In *PODS*, pages 147–158, 2010.

[21] D. Kifer and A. Machanavajjhala. No free lunch in data privacy. In *SIGMOD*, pages 193–204, 2011.

[22] J. Leskovec. Stanford large network dataset collection. http://snap.stanford.edu/data/.

[23] C. Li, M. Hay, G. Miklau, and Y. Wang. A data-and workload-aware algorithm for range queries under differential privacy. *PVLDB*, 7(5), 2014.

[24] N. Li, W. H. Qardaji, D. Su, Y. Wu, and W. Yang. Membership privacy: a unifying framework for privacy definitions. In *2013 ACM SIGSAC Conference on Computer and Communications Security, CCS'13, Berlin, Germany, November 4-8, 2013*, pages 889–900, 2013.

[25] F. McSherry. Privacy integrated queries: an extensible platform for privacy-preserving data analysis. In *SIGMOD*, pages 19–30, 2009.

[26] F. McSherry and K. Talwar. Mechanism design via differential privacy. In *FOCS*, pages 94–103, 2007.

[27] A. Narayanan and V. Shmatikov. De-anonymizing social networks. In *IEEE Symposium on Security and Privacy*, pages 173–187. IEEE Computer Society, 2009.

[28] K. Nissim, S. Raskhodnikova, and A. Smith. Smooth sensitivity and sampling in private data analysis. In *STOC*, pages 75–84, 2007.

[29] D. Proserpio, S. Goldberg, and F. McSherry. A workflow for differentially-private graph synthesis. In *Proceedings of the 2012 ACM Workshop on Workshop on Online Social Networks*, WOSN '12, pages 13–18, New York, NY, USA, 2012. ACM.

[30] W. Qardaji, W. Yang, and N. Li. Understanding hierarchical methods for differentially private histograms. *PVLDB*, 6(14):1954–1965, 2013.

[31] S. Raskhodnikova and A. D. Smith. Efficient lipschitz extensions for high-dimensional graph statistics and node private degree distributions. *CoRR*, abs/1504.07912, 2015.

[32] A. Sala, X. Zhao, C. Wilson, H. Zheng, and B. Y. Zhao. Sharing graphs using differentially private graph models. In *Proceedings of the 2011 ACM SIGCOMM Conference on Internet Measurement Conference*, IMC '11, pages 81–98, New York, NY, USA, 2011. ACM.

[33] X. Xiao, G. Wang, and J. Gehrke. Differential privacy via wavelet transforms. *IEEE Trans. Knowl. Data Eng.*, 23(8):1200–1214, 2011.

[34] J. Xu, Z. Zhang, X. Xiao, Y. Yang, and G. Yu. Differentially private histogram publication. In *KDD*, 2012.

[35] J. Zhang, G. Cormode, C. M. Procopiuc, D. Srivastava, and X. Xiao. Private release of graph statistics using ladder functions. In *Proceedings of the 2015 ACM SIGMOD International Conference on Management of Data*, SIGMOD '15, pages 731–745, New York, NY, USA, 2015. ACM.

[36] X. Zhang, R. Chen, J. Xu, X. Meng, and Y. Xie. Towards accurate histogram publication under differential privacy. In *Proceedings of the 2014 SIAM International Conference on Data Mining, Philadelphia, Pennsylvania, USA, April 24-26, 2014*, pages 587–595, 2014.

APPENDIX

A. PROOF OF LEMMA 2

PROOF OF LEMMA 2. Lemma 2 says that for any neighboring G, G', we have $|q_\epsilon^h(G,\theta_i,\Omega_j) - q_\epsilon^h(G',\theta_i,\Omega_j))| \leq 6\Theta+4$. Since $q_\epsilon^h(G,\theta_i,\Omega_j) = -\ell_{hist}(G,\theta_i,\Omega_j) - \ell_{proj}(G,\theta_i)$, it suffices to show that (A) $\ell_{hist}(G,\theta_i,\Omega_j) - \ell_{hist}(G',\theta_i,\Omega_j) \leq 2(2\Theta+1)$ and that (B) $\ell_{proj}(G,\theta_i) - \ell_{proj}(G',\theta_i) \leq 2(\Theta+1)$.

The latter (B) holds because $\ell_{proj}(G,\theta_i) = 2 \cdot \left|\{v | v \in V, deg_{\pi_\Theta(G)}(v) > \theta_i\}\right|$, and from the proof of Lemma 1, at most $\Theta+1$ nodes will have different degrees in $\pi_\Theta(G)$ and $\pi_\Theta(G')$.

We now show that the former (A) holds. Note that $\ell_{hist}(G,\theta_i,\Omega_j) = \sum_{\mathbf{g}_k\in\Omega_j}\sum_{d\in\mathbf{g}_k}\left(\left|c_d - \frac{\sum_{d\in\mathbf{g}_k} c_d}{|\mathbf{g}_k|}\right| + \frac{2\theta_i+1}{\epsilon|\mathbf{g}_k|}\right)$,

The second term in ℓ_{hist}, i.e., $\frac{2\theta_i+1}{\epsilon|\mathbf{g}_k|}$ is independent of the input dataset and thus does not change between two neighboring graphs, so we only need to analyze the first term. We use $avg_{\mathbf{g}_k} = \frac{\sum_{d\in\mathbf{g}_k} c_d}{|\mathbf{g}_k|}$ to denote the average count within group $\mathbf{g}_k$ on $\pi_\theta(G)$, and similarly $avg'_{\mathbf{g}_k}$ on $\pi_\theta(G')$. We have

$$\begin{aligned}
&\sum_{\mathbf{g}_k \in \Omega_j} \sum_{d \in \mathbf{g}_k} \left|avg_{\mathbf{g}_k} - avg'_{\mathbf{g}_k}\right| \\
&= \sum_{\mathbf{g}_k \in \Omega_j} \sum_{d \in \mathbf{g}_k} \left| \frac{\sum_{d \in \mathbf{g}_k} c_d}{|\mathbf{g}_k|} - \frac{\sum_{d \in \mathbf{g}_k} c'_d}{|\mathbf{g}_k|} \right| \\
&= \sum_{\mathbf{g}_k \in \Omega_j} \left| \sum_{d \in \mathbf{g}_k} c_d - \sum_{d \in \mathbf{g}_k} c'_d \right| \\
&\leq \sum_{\mathbf{g}_k \in \Omega_j} \sum_{d \in \mathbf{g}_k} \left|c_d - c'_d\right| = 2\theta_i + 1
\end{aligned}$$

Thus, we have

$$\begin{aligned}
&\left| \sum_{\mathbf{g}_k \in \Omega_j} \sum_{d \in \mathbf{g}_k} |c_d - avg_{\mathbf{g}_k}| - \sum_{\mathbf{g}_k \in \Omega_j} \sum_{d \in \mathbf{g}_k} |c'_d - avg'_{\mathbf{g}_k}| \right| \\
&\leq \sum_{\mathbf{g}_k \in \Omega_j} \sum_{d \in \mathbf{g}_k} \left| \left(|c_d - avg_{\mathbf{g}_k}| - |c'_d - avg'_{\mathbf{g}_k}| \right) \right| \\
&\leq \sum_{\mathbf{g}_k \in \Omega_j} \sum_{d \in \mathbf{g}_k} \left| (c_d - avg_{\mathbf{g}_k}) - (c'_d - avg'_{\mathbf{g}_k}) \right| \\
&\leq \sum_{\mathbf{g}_k \in \Omega_j} \sum_{d \in \mathbf{g}_k} \left| (c_d - c'_d) - (avg_{\mathbf{g}_k} - avg'_{\mathbf{g}_k}) \right| \\
&\leq \sum_{\mathbf{g}_k \in \Omega_j} \sum_{d \in \mathbf{g}_k} \left| c_d - c'_d \right| + \sum_{\mathbf{g}_k \in \Omega_j} \sum_{d \in \mathbf{g}_k} \left| avg_{\mathbf{g}_k} - avg'_{\mathbf{g}_k} \right| \\
&\leq (2\theta_i + 1) + (2\theta_i + 1) \leq 2(2\Theta + 1).
\end{aligned}$$

□

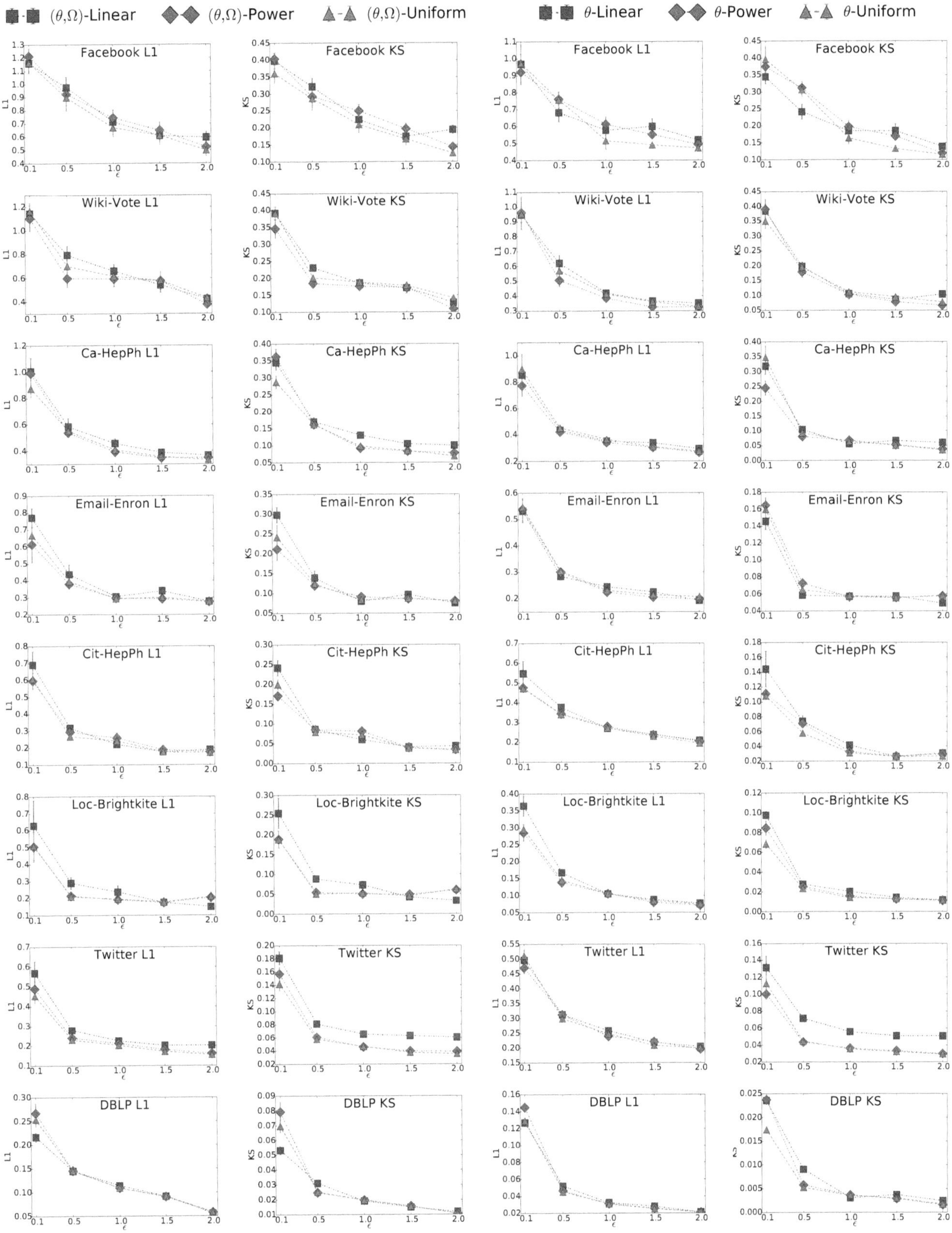

Figure 7: The experimental results on the effects of different allocation strategies for tail distribution for (θ, Ω)-Histogram (left half) and θ-CumulativeHistogram (right half).

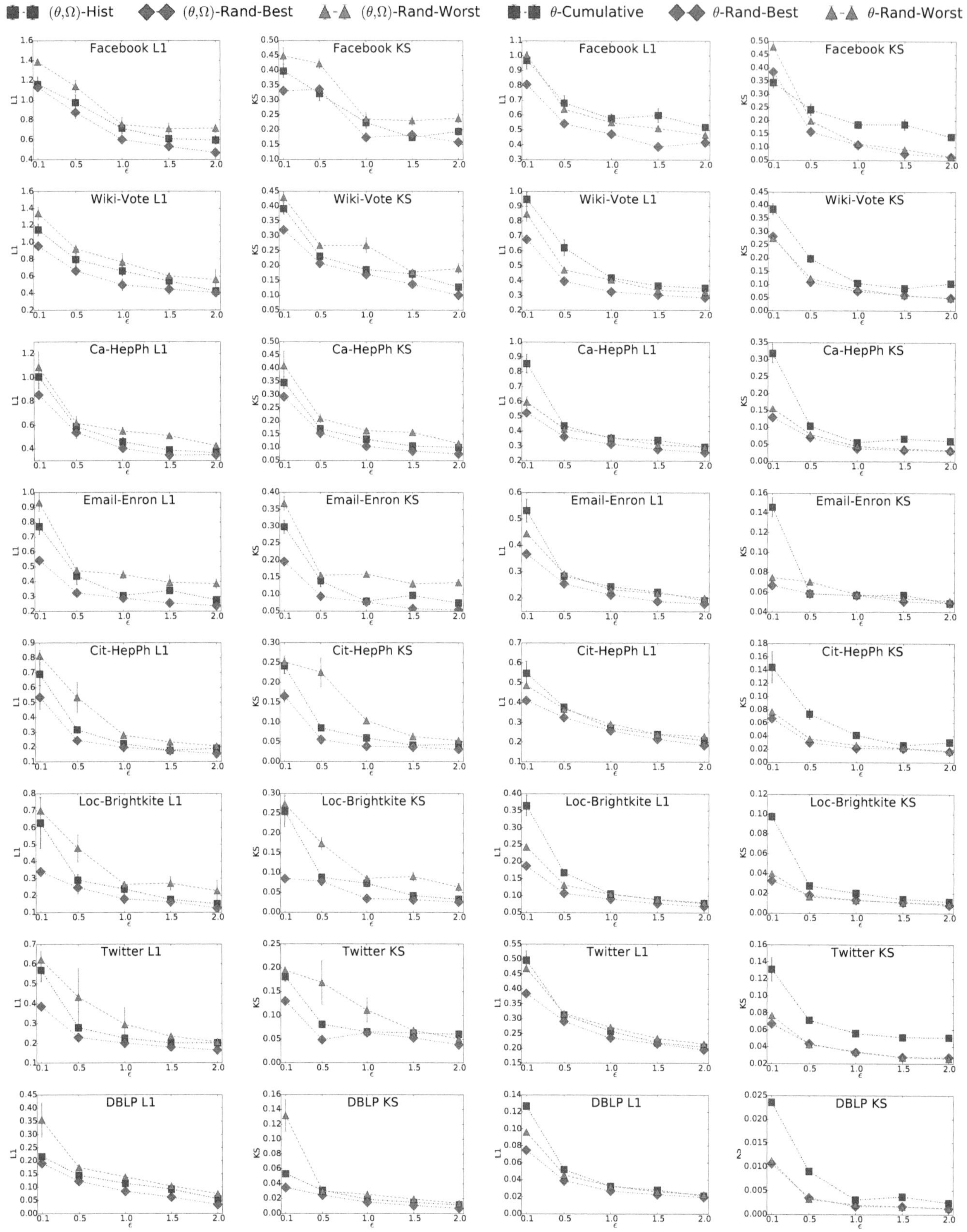

Figure 8: The experimental results on the effects of permutation on the edge orderings in projection for (θ, Ω)-Histogram (left half) and θ-CumulativeHistogram (right half).

Principled Evaluation of Differentially Private Algorithms using DPBench

Michael Hay*, Ashwin Machanavajjhala**, Gerome Miklau†, Yan Chen**, Dan Zhang†

* Colgate University
Department of Computer Science
mhay@colgate.edu

** Duke University
Department of Computer Science
{ashwin,yanchen}@cs.duke.edu

† University of Massachusetts Amherst
School of Computer Science
{miklau,dzhang}@cs.umass.edu

ABSTRACT

Differential privacy has become the dominant standard in the research community for strong privacy protection. There has been a flood of research into query answering algorithms that meet this standard. Algorithms are becoming increasingly complex, and in particular, the performance of many emerging algorithms is *data dependent*, meaning the distribution of the noise added to query answers may change depending on the input data. Theoretical analysis typically only considers the worst case, making empirical study of average case performance increasingly important.

In this paper we propose a set of evaluation principles which we argue are essential for sound evaluation. Based on these principles we propose DPBENCH, a novel evaluation framework for standardized evaluation of privacy algorithms. We then apply our benchmark to evaluate algorithms for answering 1- and 2-dimensional range queries. The result is a thorough empirical study of 15 published algorithms on a total of 27 datasets that offers new insights into algorithm behavior—in particular the influence of dataset scale and shape—and a more complete characterization of the state of the art. Our methodology is able to resolve inconsistencies in prior empirical studies and place algorithm performance in context through comparison to simple baselines. Finally, we pose open research questions which we hope will guide future algorithm design.

1. INTRODUCTION

Privacy is a major obstacle to deriving important insights from collections of sensitive records donated by individuals. Differential privacy [5–8] has emerged as an important standard for protection of individuals' sensitive information. Informally, differential privacy is a property of the analysis algorithm which guarantees that the output the analyst receives is statistically indistinguishable (governed by a privacy parameter ϵ) from the output the analyst would have received if any one individual had opted out of the collection. Its general acceptance by researchers has led to a flood of work across the database, data mining, theory, machine learning, programming languages, security, and statistics communities.

Most differentially private algorithms work by introducing noise into query answers. Finding algorithms that satisfy ϵ-differential privacy and introduce the least possible error for a given analysis task is a major ongoing challenge, in both research and practice. Standard techniques for satisfying differential privacy that are broadly-applicable (e.g. the Laplace and exponential mechanisms [8]) often offer sub-optimal error rates. Much recent work that deems differential privacy impractical for real world data (e.g., [13]) use only these standard techniques.

Many new differentially private algorithms have been proposed to address these limitations and reduce achievable error rates. Take the example task of privately answering 1- and 2-dimensional range queries on a dataset (the primary focus of this paper). Proposed techniques for this task include answering range queries using noisy hierarchies of equi-width histograms [4, 11, 16, 22], noisy counts on a coarsened domain [15, 21, 26, 27, 29], or by reconstructing perturbed wavelet [25] or Fourier [1] coefficients, or based on a synthetic dataset built using multiplicative weights updates [10]. These recent innovations reduce error at a fixed privacy level ϵ by many orders of magnitude for certain datasets, and can have a large impact on the success of practical differentially private applications.

However, the current state-of-the-art poses a new challenge of algorithm selection. Consider a data owner (say from the US Census Bureau) who would like to use differentially private algorithms to release a 1- or 2- dimensional histogram over their data. She sees a wide variety of algorithms in the published literature, each demonstrating settings or contexts in which they have advantageous theoretical and empirical properties. Unlike in other fields (e.g. data mining), the data owner can not run all the algorithms on her dataset and choose the algorithm that incurs the least error – this violates differential privacy, as the choice of the algorithm would leak information about the input dataset. Hence, the data owner must make this choice using prior theoretical and empirical analyses of these algorithms, and faces the following problems:

1. *Gaps in Empirical Evaluations:* As algorithms become progressively more complex, their error rates are harder to analyze theoretically, underscoring the importance of good empirical evaluations. For a number of reasons, including lack of benchmark datasets, space constraints in publications, and the chronology of proposed algorithms, existing empirical evaluations do not comprehensively evaluate all known algorithms leaving gaps (and even inconsistencies; see Section 3.2) in our knowledge about algorithm performance.

2. *Understanding Data-Dependence:* A number of recent algorithms are *data dependent*; i.e., their error is sensitive to properties of the input. Thus, a data dependent algorithm A may have lower error than another algorithm B on one dataset, but the reverse may be true on another dataset. While a few prior empirical evaluations evaluate algorithms on diverse datasets, there

SIGMOD'16, June 26-July 01, 2016, San Francisco, CA, USA

DOI: http://dx.doi.org/10.1145/2882903.2882931

is little guidance for the data owner on how the error would extrapolate to a new dataset (e.g., one with a greater number of tuples) or a new experimental setting (e.g., a smaller ϵ).

3. *Choosing Values for Free Parameters:* Algorithms are often associated with free parameters (other than the privacy parameter ϵ), but their effect on error is incompletely quantified. Published research provides little guidance to the data owner on how to set these parameters, and in many cases the default values are suboptimal.

4. *Unsound Utility Comparisons:* Even when empirical analyses are comprehensive, the results may not be useful to a practitioner. For instance, the error of a differentially private algorithm is a random variable. However, most empirical analyses only report the mean error and not the variability in error. Moreover, algorithm error is often not compared with that of simple baselines like the Laplace mechanism, which are the first algorithms a practitioner would attempt applying.

Given these problems, even as research progresses, the practitioner is lost and incapable of deploying the right algorithm. Moreover, researchers are likely to propose new algorithms that improve performance in narrow contexts. In this paper, we attempt to remedy the above problems with a rigorous framework for empirical evaluation, and we shed light on the algorithm selection problem for 1- and 2-dimensional range query answering. We make the following novel contributions:

1. We propose a set of principles that any differentially private evaluation must satisfy (Section 4). Based on these principles we develop DPBENCH, a novel methodology for evaluating differentially private algorithms (Section 5). Experiments designed using DPBENCH help tease out dependence of algorithm error on specific data characteristics like the size of the domain, the dataset's number of tuples (or scale) and its empirical distribution (or shape). DPBENCH provides an algorithm to automatically tune free parameters of algorithms, and ensures fair comparisons between algorithms. Finally, by reporting both the mean and variation of error as well as comparing algorithms to baselines the results of DPBENCH experiments help the practitioner get a better handle on the algorithm selection problem.

2. Using DPBENCH, we present a comprehensive empirical study of 15 published algorithms for releasing 1- or 2-dimensional range queries on a total of 27 datasets (Section 6). We evaluate algorithm error on 7,920 experimental settings. Our study presents the following novel insights into algorithm error (Section 7):

   (a) *Scale and Data Dependence:* The error incurred by recently proposed data dependent algorithms is heavily influenced by scale (number of tuples). At smaller scales, the best data-dependent algorithms can beat simpler data independent algorithms by an order of magnitude. However, at large scales, many data dependent algorithms start performing worse than data independent algorithms.

   (b) *Baselines:* A majority of the recent algorithms do not even consistently beat the Laplace mechanism, especially at medium and larger scales in both the 1- and 2-D cases.

   (c) *Understanding Inconsistencies:* Our results also help us resolve and explain inconsistencies from prior work. For instance, a technique that uses multiplicative weights [10] was shown to outperform a large class of data independent mechanisms (like [25]), but in a subsequent paper [15], the reverse was shown to be true. Our results explain this apparent inconsistency by identifying that the former conclusion was drawn using a dataset with small scale while the latter conclusions were made on datasets with larger scales.

3. While the DPBENCH algorithm for tuning free parameters is straightforward, we show a $13\times$ improvement in error for certain algorithms like the multiplicative weights method [10] over the original implementations with default parameters.

4. We formalize two important theoretical properties, *scale-epsilon exchangeability* and *consistency*, that can help extrapolate results from an empirical study to other experimental setting not considered by the study. For an algorithm that is *scale-espilon exchangeable*, increasing the scale of the input dataset and increasing epsilon have equivalent effects on the error. Thus, an algorithm's error is roughly the same for all scale and ϵ pairs with the same product. We prove that most algorithms we consider in this paper satisfy this property. An algorithm that is *consistent* has error that tends to 0 as the privacy parameter ϵ tends to ∞. That is, inconsistent algorithms return answers that are biased even in the absence of privacy constraints. While all the data independent algorithms considered in the paper are consistent, we show that some data dependent algorithms are not consistent, and hence a practitioner must be wary about using such algorithms.

While our analysis is restricted to 1- and 2-dimensional range queries, we believe our results will be useful beyond this context as the evaluation principles will extend to evaluation of differentially private algorithms for other tasks. We conclude the paper with comparisons to published results, lessons for practitioners, and a discussion of open questions in Section 8.

2. PRELIMINARIES

In this section we review basic privacy definitions and introduce notation for databases and queries.

2.1 Differential Privacy

In this paper we are concerned with algorithms that run on a private database and publish their output. To ensure the released data does not violate privacy, we require the algorithms to obey the standard of differential privacy.

Let I be a database instance consisting of a single relation. Let $nbrs(I)$ denote the set of databases differing from I in at most one record; i.e., if $I' \in nbrs(I)$, then $|(I - I') \cup (I' - I)| = 1$.

DEFINITION 1 (DIFFERENTIAL PRIVACY [7]). *A randomized algorithm $\mathcal{A}$ is ϵ-differentially private if for any instance I, any $I' \in nbrs(I)$, and any subset of outputs $S \subseteq Range(\mathcal{A})$,*

$$Pr[\mathcal{A}(I) \in S] \le \exp(\epsilon) \times Pr[\mathcal{A}(I') \in S]$$

For an individual whose data is represented by a record in I, differential privacy offers an appealing guarantee. It says that including this individual's record cannot significantly affect the output: it can only make some outputs slightly more (or less) likely – where "slightly" is defined as at most a factor of e^{ϵ}. If an adversary infers something about the individual based on the output, then the same inference would also be likely to occur *even if the individual's data had been removed from the database* prior to running the algorithm.

Many of the algorithms considered in this paper are composed of multiple subroutines, each taking the private data as input. Provided each subroutine achieves differential privacy, the whole algorithm is differentially private. More precisely, the sequential execution of k algorithms $\mathcal{A}_1, \dots, \mathcal{A}_k$, each satisfying ϵ_i-differential privacy, results in an algorithm that is ϵ-differentially private for $\epsilon = \sum_i \epsilon_i$ [19]. Hence, we think of ϵ as representing an algorithm's *privacy budget* which can be allocated across its subroutines.

A commonly used subroutine is the Laplace mechanism, a general purpose algorithm for computing numerical functions on the private data. It achieves privacy by adding noise to the function's output. We use Laplace(σ) to denote the Laplace probability distribution with mean 0 and scale σ.

DEFINITION 2 (LAPLACE MECHANISM [7]). *Let $f(I)$ denote a function on I that outputs a vector in $\mathbb{R}^d$. The Laplace mechanism $\mathcal{L}$ is defined as $\mathcal{L}(I) = f(I) + \mathbf{z}$, where $\mathbf{z}$ is a d-length vector of random variables such that $z_i \sim Laplace(\Delta f/\epsilon)$.*

The constant Δf is called the sensitivity of f *and is the maximum difference in f between any two databases that differ only by a single record, $\Delta f = \max_{I,I' \in nbrs(I)} \|f(I) - f(I')\|_1$.*

The Laplace mechanism can be used to provide noisy counts of records satisfying arbitrary predicates. For example, suppose I contains medical records and f reports two counts: the number of male patients with heart disease and the number of female patients with heart disease. The sensitivity of f is 1: given any database instance I, adding one record to it (to produce neighboring instance I'), could cause at most one of the two counts to increase by exactly 1. Thus, the Laplace mechanism would add random noise from Laplace($1/\epsilon$) to each count and release the noisy counts.

2.2 Data Model and Task

The database I is an instance of a single-relation schema $R(\mathbb{A})$, with attributes $\mathbb{A} = \{A_1, A_2, \ldots, A_\ell\}$. Each attribute is discrete, having an ordered domain (continuous attributes can be suitably discretized). We are interested in answering range queries over this data; range queries support a wide range of data analysis tasks including histograms, marginals, data cubes, etc.

We consider the following task. The analyst specifies a subset of target attributes, denoted $\mathbb{B} \subseteq \mathbb{A}$, and $\mathbf{W}$, a set of multi-dimensional range queries over $\mathbb{B}$. We call $\mathbf{W}$ the *workload*. For example, suppose the database I contains records from the US Census describing various demographic characteristics of US citizens. The analyst might specify $\mathbb{B} = \{age, salary\}$ and a set $\mathbf{W}$ where each query is of the form,

select count(*) from R
where $a_{low} \le$ age $\le a_{high}$ and $s_{low} \le$ salary $\le s_{high}$

with different values for $a_{low}, a_{high}, s_{low}, s_{high}$. We restrict our attention to the setting where the dimensionality, $k = |\mathbb{B}|$, is small (our experiments report on $k \in \{1, 2\}$). All the differentially private algorithms considered in this paper attempt to answer the range queries in $\mathbf{W}$ on the private database I while incurring as little error as possible.

In this paper, we will often represent the database as a multidimensional array $\mathbf{x}$ of counts. For $\mathbb{B} = \{B_1, \ldots, B_k\}$, let n_j denote the domain size of B_j for $j \in [1, k]$. Then $\mathbf{x}$ has $(n_1 \times n_2 \times \ldots \times n_k)$ cells and the count in the $(i_1, i_2, \ldots, i_k)^{th}$ cell is

select count(*) from R
where $B_1 = i_1$ and $B_2 = i_2$ and $\ldots B_k = i_k$

To compute the answer to a query in $\mathbf{W}$, one can simply sum the corresponding entries in $\mathbf{x}$. Because they are range queries, the corresponding entries form a (hyper-)rectangle in $\mathbf{x}$.

Example: Suppose $\mathbb{B}$ has the attributes age and salary (in tens of thousands) with domains $[1, 100]$ and $[1, 50]$ respectively. Then $\mathbf{x}$ is a 100×50 matrix. The $(25, 10)^{th}$ entry is the number of tuples with age 25 and salary \$100,000.

	Properties					*Analysis*	
Algorithm	H	P	Dimension	Parameters	Side info	Consistent	Scale-ϵ Exch.
Data-independent							
IDENTITY [7]			Multi-D	–		yes	yes
PRIVELET [25]	X		Multi-D	–		yes	yes
H [11]	X		1D	$b = 2$		yes	yes
H_b [22]	X		Multi-D	–		yes	yes
GREEDY H [15]	X		1D, 2D	$b = 2$		yes	yes
Data-dependent							
UNIFORM		~	Multi-D	–		no	yes
MWEM [10]			Multi-D	T	scale	no	yes
MWEM*			Multi-D	–		no	yes
AHP [29]		X	Multi-D	ρ, η		yes	yes
AHP*		X	Multi-D	–		yes	yes
DPCUBE [26]	~	X	Multi-D	$\rho = .5$, $n_p = 10$		yes	yes
DAWA [15]	X	X	1D, 2D	$\rho = .25$, $b = 2$		yes	yes
QUADTREE [4]	X	X	2D	c=10		no*	yes
UGRID [21]		X	2D	$c = 10$	scale	yes	yes
AGRID [21]	~	X	2D	$c = 10$, $c_2 = 5$, $\rho = .5$	scale	yes	yes
PHP [1]		X	1D	$\rho = .5$		no	yes
EFPA [1]			1D	–		yes	yes
SF [27]		X	1D	ρ, k, F	scale	yes*	no

Table 1: Algorithms evaluated in benchmark. Property column H indicates hierarchical algorithms and P indicates partitioning. Parameters without assignments are ones that remain free. Side information is discussed in Section 4.2. Analysis columns are discussed in Section 5.5 and Section 7.4. Algorithm variants MWEM* and AHP* are explained in Section 6.4.

We identify three key properties of $\mathbf{x}$, each of which significantly impacts the behavior of privacy algorithms. The first is the *domain size*, n, which is equivalently the number of cells in $\mathbf{x}$ (i.e., $n = n_1 \times \cdots \times n_k$). The second is the *scale* of the dataset, which is the total number of tuples, or the sum of the counts in $\mathbf{x}$, which we write as $\|\mathbf{x}\|_1$. Finally, the *shape* of a dataset is denoted as $\mathbf{p}$ where $\mathbf{p} = \mathbf{x}/\|\mathbf{x}\|_1 = [p_1, \ldots, p_n]$ is a non-negative vector that sums to 1. The shape captures how the data is distributed over the domain and is independent of scale.

3. ALGORITHMS & PRIOR RESULTS

3.1 Overview of Algorithm Strategies

The algorithms evaluated in this paper are listed in Table 1. For each algorithm, the table identifies the dataset dimensionality it supports as well as other key properties (discussed further below). In addition, it identifies algorithm-specific parameters and the possible use of "side information" (discussed in Section 4). The table also summarizes our theoretical analysis, which is described in detail later (Sections 5.5 and 7.4). Descriptions of individual algorithms are provided in Appendix B.

In this section, we categorize algorithms as either data-independent or data-dependent, and further highlight some key strategies employed, such as the use of hierarchical aggregations and partitioning. In addition, we also illustrate how algorithm behavior is affected by properties of the input including dataset shape, scale, and domain size.

First, we describe a simple baseline strategy: release $\mathbf{x}$ after adding independent random noise to each count in $\mathbf{x}$. To ensure differential privacy, the noise distribution is calibrated according to Definition 2, and each cell receives independent Laplace noise with a scale of $1/\epsilon$. The limitation with this simple strategy is that when answering range queries, the variance in the answer increases linearly with the number of cells that fall within the range. For large ranges, the error becomes intolerably high. Thus, the performance of this approach depends critically on the *domain size*.

Hierarchical aggregation: To mitigate the noise accumulation, several approaches not only obtain noisy counts for the individual cells in $\mathbf{x}$, but also obtain noisy estimates for the total count in hierarchically grouped subsets of cells. Because each record is now being counted multiple times, the noise must be proportionally increased. However, it has been shown in the 1D case that the increase is only logarithmic in the domain size and, further, any range query now requires summing only a logarithmic, rather than linear, number of noisy counts [11, 24]. For higher dimensions, the relative benefit of hierarchical aggregations diminishes [22]. Algorithms employing hierarchical aggregations include H [11], H_b [22], GREEDY H [15], DAWA [15], AGRID [21], DPCUBE [26], QUADTREE [4], HYBRIDTREE [4], PRIVELET [25].

For many of the algorithms mentioned above, the noise added does not depend on the data. Thus, the performance is the same on all datasets of a given domain size. Following [15], an algorithm whose error rate is the same for all possible datasets on a given domain is characterized as *data independent*. Table 1 indicates which algorithms are data-independent.

It can be shown that all of the data independent algorithms studied here are instances of the matrix mechanism [16, 18], a generic framework that computes linear combinations of cell counts, adds noise, and then reconstructs estimates for the individual cells by linear transformations. The algorithms differ in the choice of linear combination and thus experience different error rates on a given workload $\mathbf{W}$. (Computing the optimal linear combination is computationally infeasible.)

Thus, for data-independent algorithms, the only property of the input that affects performance is domain size. We next describe strategies of data-dependent algorithms, whose performance is affected by dataset shape and scale.

Partitioning: One class of data-dependent algorithm partitions the data, reducing the error due to noise by only computing noisy aggregations of cell groups. An example of such an approach is an equi-width histogram: the domain is partitioned into disjoint intervals (called "buckets") of equal size and a noisy count for each bucket is obtained. To approximate the count for a cell within a bucket, the standard *assumption of uniformity* is employed. The success of such a strategy depends critically on the *shape* of the dataset: If the distribution of cell counts within a bucket are nearly uniform, the noise is effectively reduced because each cell only receives a fraction of the noise; on the other hand, a non-uniform distribution implies high error due to approximating each cell by the bucket average. Algorithms that partition include AGRID, HYBRIDTREE, QUADTREE, DPCUBE, DAWA, as well as PHP [1], AHP [29], SF [27], UGRID [21].

Equi-width partitions are used by QUADTREE, UGRID, and AGRID whereas other algorithms select the partition adaptively based on the characteristics of the data. This is non-trivial because one must prove that the adaptive component of the algorithm satisfies differential privacy (and thus does not adapt too specifically to the input). Other algorithms, such as MWEM and EFPA [1], adapt to the data as well, but use a different strategy than partitioning.

While one might expect that the performance of data-dependent algorithms is affected by dataset shape, a novel contribution of this paper is to show that it is also affected by *scale*. The intuition for this can be seen by considering equi-width histograms. Holding shape fixed, as scale increases, any deviations from a uniform distribution become magnified. Thus, the relative benefit of partitioning cells into buckets diminishes. While data adaptive approaches could, in principle, adjust with increasing scale, our findings and theoretical analysis show that this is not always the case.

Baselines: IDENTITY is a data-independent algorithm described earlier: it adds noise to each cell count in $\mathbf{x}$, and is equivalent to applying the Laplace mechanism on the function that transforms I into $\mathbf{x}$. UNIFORM is the second baseline, which uses its privacy budget to estimate the number of tuples (scale) and then produces a data-dependent estimate of the dataset by assuming uniformity. It is equivalent to an equi-width histogram that contains a single bucket as wide as the entire domain.

With each baseline, the workload queries can be answered by summing the corresponding noisy cell counts.

3.2 Empirical Comparisons in Prior Work

We review prior studies with a focus on two things. First, we characterize what is known about the state of the art for both 1D and 2D settings and identify gaps and inconsistencies. Second, we look at the algorithmic strategies described in Section 3.1 and what is known about their effect on performance.

For the 1D setting, the study of Qardaji et al. [22] suggests that H_b generally is the best data-independent algorithm, achieving lower error than many competing techniques, including IDENTITY, H, PRIVELET, SF, and others [4, 17, 18, 28]. However, their study does not include any data-dependent algorithms other than SF. Thus, their study does not address whether H_b can outperform the data-dependent algorithms listed in Table 1, a gap in knowledge that has yet to be resolved.

The results of Hardt et al. [10] suggest that H_b and the other data-independent techniques studied in [22] would be outperformed by MWEM for both 1D and 2D range queries. In their study, MWEM almost always achieves an error rate that is less than a lower bound that applies to any instance of the matrix mechanism [16, 18], a generic class of differentially private algorithms that includes the top performers from the study of Qardaji et al. [22] and all of the data-independent techniques listed in Table 1.

Data-dependent and data-independent techniques are also compared in Li et al. [15] and their findings are inconsistent with the results of Hardt et al. Specifically, MWEM and other data-dependent techniques do not always outperform matrix mechanism techniques; for some "hard" datasets, the error of MWEM is 2-10× higher than PRIVELET, one of the matrix mechanism instances included in their study. The authors investigate the difficulty of datasets, but do not identify what properties of the input affect the performance of data-dependent algorithms. In this paper, by explicitly controlling for scale and shape, we are able to resolve this gap and offer a much richer characterization of when data-dependent algorithms do well and explain the apparent contradiction between [10] and [15].

For the 2D setting, we are not aware of any work that offers a comprehensive evaluation of all available techniques. The 2D study of Qardaji et al. [22] only compares H_b against IDENTITY. A second work by Qardaji et al. [21] compare their proposed algorithms with four techniques from the literature, and so is not as comprehensive as our study here. Li et al. [15] which appeared later did not compare to [21]. Thus, another gap in the literature is a clear picture of the state of the art for 2D.

Finally, we highlight key findings regarding the algorithmic strategies discussed in Section 3.1. For hierarchical aggregation, Qardaji et al. [22] carefully consider the effect of domain size and show that hierarchies can achieve significantly lower error than "flat" approaches like IDENTITY but only when the domain size is sufficiently large. Further, the minimum domain size increases exponentially with dimensionality. It must be at least 45 for 1D; at least 64^2 for 2D, and at least 121^3 for 3D. For the data-dependent strategy of partitioning, a number of works show that it leads to low error for some datasets [1,4,15,21,26,27,29]; however, we are not aware of any work that characterizes precisely when it improves upon data-independent techniques.

In summary, the existing literature has shown that data-dependent algorithms can sometimes do well and that domain size is an important factor in algorithm performance. However, it has not clarified whether the best data-dependent algorithms can consistently outperform data-independent algorithms, and also leaves open the question of what factors, beyond domain size, affect performance.

4. EVALUATION PRINCIPLES

In this section we present fundamental principles that our evaluation framework DPBENCH (see Section 5) is based on. These are principles that are often not followed in prior work, and when unheeded, can result in (a) gaps/incomplete understanding of the performance of differentially private algorithms, or (b) unfair comparison of algorithms. Our principles are categorized into three classes: *diversity of inputs*, *end-to-end private algorithms* and *sound evaluation of outputs*.

4.1 Diversity of Inputs

The first set of principles pertain to key inputs to the algorithm: the private data vector $\mathbf{x}$ and the differential privacy parameter ϵ. The intent of the principles is to ensure that algorithms are evaluated across a diverse set of inputs in order to provide a data owner with a comprehensive picture of algorithm performance. Almost all work adheres to Principle 1, but we state it for completeness.

PRINCIPLE 1 (ϵ DIVERSITY). *Evaluate algorithms under different ϵ values.*

In addition, most empirical work compares algorithms on several datasets. We identify three critical characteristics of the dataset – *domain size*, *scale*, and *shape*, as described in Section 2.2 – each of which significantly impacts the behavior of privacy algorithms. A novelty of our evaluation approach is to study the sensitivity of algorithm error to each of these properties (while holding the other two constant).

PRINCIPLE 2 (SCALE DIVERSITY). *Evaluate algorithms using datasets of varying scales.*

PRINCIPLE 3 (SHAPE DIVERSITY). *Evaluate algorithms using datasets of varying shapes.*

PRINCIPLE 4 (DOMAIN SIZE DIVERSITY). *Evaluate algorithms using datasets (and workloads) defined over varying domain sizes.*

We cannot anticipate in advance what dataset the algorithm might be run on, and what settings of ϵ a data owner may select. A sound evaluation should be able to predict algorithm performance on as many values of ϵ, scale, shape and domain size as possible. This is especially important for data-dependent algorithms as their performance changes not only quantitatively but also *qualitatively* when changing these settings.

Our empirical comparisons of differentially private algorithms for range queries (Section 7), in both the one- and two-dimensional cases, show that the algorithms offering least error vary depending on the values of ϵ, scale, shape, and domain size. Because current algorithms offer no clear winner, evaluation on diverse inputs remains very important.

Remarks on Prior Work. Empirical evaluations in prior work only compared algorithms on a single shape (e.g., [4, 26]), or a single domain size (e.g., [15]), or on multiple datasets without controlling for each of the input characteristics (e.g. [1,10,15,27,29]). These result in some of the gaps/inconsistencies in algorithm performance discussed in Section 3.2.

4.2 End-to-End Private Algorithms

The next three principles require that algorithms provide equivalent privacy guarantees to ensure fair comparisons. While all published algorithms include a proof of differential privacy, some actions taken during deployment or evaluation of the algorithm can undermine that guarantee in subtle ways.

PRINCIPLE 5 (PRIVATE PRE- AND POST-PROCESSING). *Any computation on the input dataset must be accounted for in the overall privacy guarantee of the algorithm being evaluated.*

Any computation that comes before or after the execution of the private algorithm must also be considered in the analysis of privacy. This includes pre-processing steps such as data cleaning as well as any post-processing (e.g., selecting the "best" output from among a set of outputs). If necessary, a portion of the user's ϵ privacy budget can be devoted to these tasks.

PRINCIPLE 6 (NO FREE PARAMETERS). *Include in every algorithm definition a data-independent or differentially private method for setting each required parameter.*

An important special case of preprocessing is parameter selection. Many published algorithms have additional parameters (beyond ϵ) whose setting can have a large impact on the algorithm's behavior. Borrowing a notion from physics, a parameter is considered *free* if it can be adjusted to fit the data – in other words, the value of the parameter that optimizes algorithm performance is data-dependent. Free parameters are problematic if they are later set by tuning them to the input data. In a production environment, it risks violating the differential privacy guarantee. In a research environment, it may impede a fair evaluation of algorithm performance, as some algorithms may be more sensitive to tuning than others. A principled methodology of parameter tuning is proposed in Section 5.2 and evaluated in Section 7.3.

PRINCIPLE 7 (KNOWLEDGE OF SIDE INFORMATION). *Use public knowledge of side information about the input dataset (e.g., scale) consistently across algorithms.*

Some algorithms assume that certain properties of the input dataset (e.g., scale) are considered public and use this during the execution of the algorithm. Other algorithms do not use this information, or allocate some privacy budget to estimate it, leading to inconsistent comparisons. In general, if the availability of "side information" is not accounted for properly, it can weaken the privacy guarantee.

Remarks on Prior Work. Some work on differentially private machine learning pre-processes the input dataset using non-private data transformation algorithms [3, 9]. In other work, parameters were tuned on the same datasets on which the algorithm's performance is later evaluated [4, 10, 24, 27, 29]. Moreover, a few algorithms [10, 21, 27] assume that the scale of the dataset is known.

4.3 Sound Evaluation of Outputs

The last four principles pertain to algorithm evaluation.

PRINCIPLE 8 (MEASUREMENT OF VARIABILITY). *Algorithm output should be evaluated by expected error as well as a measure of error variability.*

The error of a differentially private algorithm is a random variable. Most evaluations report its expectation or estimate it empirically. However, when the algorithm is deployed, a user will apply it to private data and receive a single output. Thus, it is also important to measure variability of error around its expectation. Note that this is different from reporting error bars representing standard error, which measures the uncertainty in the estimate of mean error and shrinks with increasing trials. Instead, we want to measure how much the error of any single output might deviate from the mean.

PRINCIPLE 9 (MEASUREMENT OF BIAS). *Algorithm output should be evaluated for bias in the answer.*

In addition to the expected error, a sound evaluation should also check whether the algorithm's output is biased. For instance, the Laplace mechanism is unbiased; i.e., the expected value of the output of the Laplace mechanism is equal to the original input. An attractive property of unbiased algorithms like the Laplace mechanism is that they are consistent – as ϵ tends to ∞, the error tends to 0. Recent data-dependent algorithms incur less error than the Laplace mechanism by introducing some bias in the output. Understanding the bias is important; we show in this paper (Section 7.4) that some algorithms incur a bias (and therefore incur error) even when ϵ tends to infinity.

PRINCIPLE 10 (REASONABLE PRIVACY AND UTILITY). *Evaluate algorithms for input settings that result in reasonable privacy and utility.*

Under extreme settings of the input parameters, one algorithm may outperform another, but both algorithms may produce useless results. Similarly, it is not meaningful to make relative comparisons of algorithm performance when a reasonable privacy guarantee is not offered.

Remarks on Prior Work. Almost all prior empirical work on differential privacy (with the exception of those that prove theoretical bounds on the error in terms of (α, δ)-usefulness [2]) focus on mean error and not its variability. Algorithm bias is seldom analyzed. While most algorithms are explicitly compared to a baseline like IDENTITY ([4] is an exception), none of algorithms have been compared with a data-dependent baseline like UNIFORM.

5. DPBENCH EVALUATION FRAMEWORK

In this section, we describe DPBENCH, a framework for evaluating the accuracy of differentially private algorithms. DPBENCH's goal is to formulate a set of standards for empirical evaluation that adhere to the principles from Section 4. The framework can be applied to a number of analysis tasks. Because different analysis tasks require the use of disparate algorithms, it is necessary to instantiate distinct benchmarks for each kind of task.[1] DPBENCH aims to provide a common framework for developing these benchmarks.

We define a benchmark as a 9-tuple $\{\mathcal{T}, \mathcal{W}, \mathcal{D}, \mathcal{M}, \mathcal{L}, \mathcal{G}, \mathcal{R}, \mathcal{E}_M, \mathcal{E}_I\}$. $\mathcal{T}$ denotes the task that the benchmark is associated with. $\mathcal{W}$ denotes the set of query workloads that are representative for the task $\mathcal{T}$. For instance, if $\mathcal{T}$ is the task of "answering one-dimensional range queries", $\mathcal{W}$ could contain a workload of random range queries. Note that one could use more than one workload to evaluate algorithms for a task. Evaluating differentially private algorithms is typically done on publicly available datasets, which we refer to as a *source* data instance I. $\mathcal{D}$ denotes a set of such source datasets. $\mathcal{M}$ lists the set of algorithms that are compared by the benchmark. $\mathcal{L}$ denotes *loss functions* that are used to measure the error (or distance) between $\mathbf{y} = \mathbf{W}\mathbf{x}$, the true answer to a workload, and $\hat{\mathbf{y}}$, the output of a differentially private algorithm in $\mathcal{M}$. An example of a loss function that we will consistently use in this paper is the L_2 norm of the difference between $\mathbf{y}$ and $\hat{\mathbf{y}}$; i.e. error is $\|\mathbf{W}\mathbf{x} - \hat{\mathbf{y}}\|_2$.

[1] This is akin to the various TPC benchmarks for evaluating database performance.

We call $\mathcal{W}, \mathcal{D}, \mathcal{M}$ and $\mathcal{L}$ *task specific components* of a DPBENCH benchmark, since they vary depending on the task under consideration. We discuss them in detail in Section 6. On the other hand the remaining components $\mathcal{G}, \mathcal{R}, \mathcal{E}_M, \mathcal{E}_I$ are task independent, and help benchmarks to adhere to the principles in Section 4. $\mathcal{G}$ is a *data generator* that ensures diversity of inputs (Principles 1 to 4). $\mathcal{R}$ defines a set of *algorithm repair functions* that ensure that the algorithms being evaluated satisfy end-to-end privacy (Principles 5 to 7). In particular, DPBENCH provides a technique to automatically train free parameters of an algorithm. $\mathcal{E}_M$ and $\mathcal{E}_I$ denote standards for measuring and interpreting empirical error. These help adhere to Principles 8 to 10 by explicitly defining standards for measuring variation and bias, declaring winners among algorithms, and defining baselines for interpreting error. Next, we describe these in detail, and on the way define two novel theoretical properties *scale-epsilon exchangeability* and *consistency*.

5.1 Data Generator G

Let $I \in \mathcal{D}$ be a source dataset with true domain $D_I = (A_1 \times \ldots A_k)$ and true scale s_I. The data generator $\mathcal{G}$ takes as input a scale m, and a new domain D, which may be constructed by (i) considering a subset of attributes $\mathbb{B}$, and (ii) coarsening the domain of attributes in $\mathbb{B}$. Note that m and D are possibly different from the true scale s_I and domain D_I. $\mathcal{G}$ outputs a new data vector $\mathbf{x}$ with the new scale m and new domain D as follows. First, $\mathcal{G}$ computes a histogram $\mathbf{x}'$ of counts on the new domain based on I. Then, $\mathcal{G}$ normalizes $\mathbf{x}'$ by its true scale to isolate the *shape* $\mathbf{p}$ of the source data on the new domain D. $\mathcal{G}$ generates $\mathbf{x}$ by sampling m times (with replacement) from $\mathbf{p}$. If we set the desired scale to the true scale s_I we will generate a data vector $\mathbf{x}$ that is approximately the same as the original (modulo sampling differences).

The output vector $\mathbf{x}$ of $\mathcal{G}$ is used as input to the privacy algorithms. Diversity of scale (Principle 2) is achieved by varying m. Diversity of domain size (Principle 4) is achieved by varying D. Shape is primarily determined by I but also impacted by the domain definition, D, so diversity of shape (Principle 3) requires a variety of source datasets and coordinated domain selection.

The data generator $\mathcal{G}$ outputs datasets that help evaluate algorithms on each of the data characteristics shape, scale and domain size while keeping the other two properties constant. Without such a data generator, the effects of shape and scale on algorithm error can't be distinguished, thus prior work was unable to correctly identify features of datasets that impacted error. For a fixed shape, increasing scale offers a stronger "signal" about the underlying properties of the data. In addition, this sampling strategy always results in datasets with integral counts (simply multiplying the distribution by some scale factor may not).

5.2 Algorithm Repair Functions $\mathcal{R}$

While automatically verifying whether an algorithm performs pre- or post-processing that violates differential privacy is out of the scope of this benchmark, we discuss two *repair functions* to help adhere to the free parameters and side information principles (Principles 6 and 7, respectively).

Learning Free Parameter Settings R_{param}. We present a first cut solution to handling free parameters. Let $\mathcal{K}_\theta$ denote a private algorithm $\mathcal{K}$ instantiated with a vector of free parameters θ.

We use a separate set of datasets to tune these parameters; these datasets will *not* be used in the evaluation. Given a set of training datasets $\mathcal{D}_{train}$, we apply data generator $\mathcal{G}$ and learn a function $R_{param} : (\epsilon, \|\mathbf{x}\|_1, n) \to \theta$ that given ϵ, scale, and the domain size, outputs parameters θ that result in the lowest error for the algorithm. Given this function, the benchmark extends the algorithm by adaptively selecting parameter settings based on scale and epsilon. If the parameter setting depends on scale, a part of the privacy budget is spent estimating scale, and this introduces a new free parameter, namely the budget spent for estimating scale. The best setting for this parameter can also be learned in a similar manner.

Side Information R_{side}. Algorithms which use non-private side information can typically be corrected by devoting a portion of the privacy budget to learning the required side information, then using the noisy value in place of the side information. This process is difficult to automate but may be possible with program analysis in some cases. This has the side-effect of introducing a new parameter which determines the fraction of the privacy budget to devote to this component of the algorithm, which in turn can be set using our learning algorithm (described above).

5.3 Standards for Measuring Error $\mathcal{E}_M$

Error. DPBENCH uses *scaled average per-query error* to quantify an algorithm's error on a workload.

DEFINITION 3 (SCALED AVERAGE PER-QUERY ERROR). *Let* $\mathbf{W}$ *be a workload of* q *queries,* $\mathbf{x}$ *a data vector and* $s = \|\mathbf{x}\|_1$ *its scale. Let* $\hat{\mathbf{y}} = \mathcal{K}(\mathbf{x}, \mathbf{W}, \epsilon)$ *denote the noisy output of algorithm* $\mathcal{K}$. *Given a loss function* L, *we define* scale average per-query error *as* $\frac{1}{s \cdot q} L(\hat{\mathbf{y}}, \mathbf{W}\mathbf{x})$.

By reporting scaled error, we avoid considering a fixed absolute error rate to be equivalent on a small scale dataset and a large scale dataset. For example, for a given workload query, an absolute error of 100 on a dataset of scale 1000 has very different implications than an absolute error of 100 for a dataset with scale 100,000. In our scaled terms, these absolute errors would be clearly distinguished as 0.1 and 0.001 scaled error. Accordingly, scaled error can be interpreted in terms of population percentages. Using scaled error also helps us define the scale-epsilon exchangeability property in Section 5.5.

Considering per-query error allows us to compare the error on different workloads of potentially different sizes. For instance, when examining the effect of domain size n on the accuracy of algorithms answering the identity workload, the number of queries q equals n and hence would vary as n varies.

Measuring Error. The error measure (Definition 3) is a random variable. We can estimate properties such as their mean and variance through repeated executions of the algorithm. In addition to comparing algorithms using mean error, DPBENCH also compares algorithms based on the 95 percentile of the error. This takes into account the variability in the error (adhering to Principle 8) and might be an appropriate measure for a "risk averse" analyst who prefers an algorithm with reliable performance over an algorithm that has lower mean performance but is more volatile. Means and 95 percentile error values are computed on multiple independent repetitions of the algorithm over multiple samples $\mathbf{x}$ drawn from the data generator to ensure high confidence estimates.

DPBENCH also identifies algorithms that are competitive for state-of-the-art performance for each setting of scale, shape and domain size. An algorithm is *competitive* if it either (i) achieves the lowest error, or (ii) the difference between its error and the lowest error is not statistically significant. Significance is assessed using a unpaired t-test with a Bonferroni corrected $\alpha = 0.05/(n_{algs} - 1)$, for running $(n_{algs} - 1)$ tests in parallel. n_{algs} denotes the number of algorithms being compared. Competitive algorithms can be chosen both based on mean error (a "risk neutral" analyst) and 95 percentile error (a "risk averse" analyst).

5.4 Standards for Interpreting Error $\mathcal{E}_I$

When drawing conclusions from experimental results, Principle 10 should be respected. One way to assess reasonable utility is by comparing with appropriate baselines.

We use IDENTITY and UNIFORM (described in Section 3.1) as upper-bound baselines. Since IDENTITY is a straightforward application of the Laplace mechanism, we expect a more sophisticated algorithm to provide a substantial benefit over the error achievable with IDENTITY. Similarly, UNIFORM learns very little about $\mathbf{x}$, only its scale. An algorithm that offers error rates comparable or worse than UNIFORM is unlikely to provide useful information in practical settings. Note that there might be a few settings where these baselines can't be beaten (e.g., when shape of $\mathbf{x}$ is indeed uniform). However, an algorithm should be able to beat these baselines in a majority of settings.

5.5 Scale Epsilon Exchangeability

We describe next a novel property of most algorithms due to which increasing ϵ and scale both have an equivalent effect on algorithm error. We say an algorithm is scale-epsilon *exchangeable* if increasing scale by a multiplicative factor c has a precisely equivalent effect, on the scaled error, as increasing epsilon by a factor of c. Exchangeability has an intuitive meaning: to get better accuracy from an exchangeable algorithm, a user can either acquire more data or, equivalently, find a way to increase their privacy budget. Moreover, for such algorithms, diversity of scale (Principle 2) implies diversity of ϵ (Principle 1).

DEFINITION 4 (SCALE-EPSILON EXCHANGEABILITY). *Let* $\mathbf{p}$ *be a shape and* $\mathbf{W}$ *a workload. If* $\mathbf{x}_1 = m_1\mathbf{p}$ *and* $\mathbf{x}_2 = m_2\mathbf{p}$, *then algorithm* $\mathcal{K}$ *is scale-epsilon exchangeable if* $error(\mathcal{K}(\mathbf{x}_1, \mathbf{W}, \epsilon_1)) = error(\mathcal{K}(\mathbf{x}_2, \mathbf{W}, \epsilon_2))$ *whenever* $\epsilon_1 m_1 = \epsilon_2 m_2$.

We prove in Appendix C that all but one of the algorithms we evaluate in this paper are scale-epsilon exchangeable. The exception is SF [27], which is not exchangeable but empirically behaves so. An important side-effect of this insight is that in empirical evaluations one can equivalently vary scale rather than ϵ if the algorithm is proven to satisfy scale-ϵ exchangeability.

5.6 Consistency

As ϵ increases, the privacy guarantee weakens. A desirable property of a differential privacy algorithm is that its error decreases with increasing ϵ and ultimately disappears as $\epsilon \to \infty$. We call this property consistency. Algorithms that are not consistent are inherently biased.

DEFINITION 5 (CONSISTENCY). *An algorithm satisfies consistency if the error for answering any workload tends to zero as* ϵ *tends to infinity.*

6. EXPERIMENTAL SETUP

In this section we use our benchmark framework to define concrete benchmarks for 1- and 2-D range queries. For each benchmark, we precisely describe the task-specific components of the benchmark $(\mathcal{D}, \mathcal{W}, \mathcal{M}, \mathcal{L})$, namely the datasets, workloads, algorithms and loss functions with the goal of providing a reproducible standard of evaluation. Experimental results appear in Section 7.

Dataset name	Original Scale	% Zero Counts	Previous works
1D datasets			
ADULT	32,558	97.80%	[10, 15]
HEPPH	347,414	21.17%	[15]
INCOME	20,787,122	44.97%	[15]
MEDCOST	9,415	74.80%	[15]
TRACE	25,714	96.61%	[1, 11, 27, 29]
PATENT	27,948,226	6.20%	[15]
SEARCH	335,889	51.03%	[1, 11, 27, 29]
BIDS-FJ	1,901,799	0%	new
BIDS-FM	2,126,344	0%	new
BIDS-ALL	7,655,502	0%	new
MD-SAL	135,727	83.12%	new
MD-SAL-FA	100,534	83.17%	new
LC-REQ-F1	3,737,472	61.57%	new
LC-REQ-F2	198,045	67.69%	new
LC-REQ-ALL	3,999,425	60.15%	new
LC-DTIR-F1	3,336,740	0%	new
LC-DTIR-F2	189,827	11.91%	new
LC-DTIR-ALL	3,589,119	0%	new
2D datasets			
BJ-CABS-S	4268780	78.17%	[12]
BJ-CABS-E	4268780	76.83%	[12]
GOWALLA	6442863	88.92%	[21]
ADULT-2D	32561	99.30%	[10]
SF-CABS-S	464040	95.04%	[20]
SF-CABS-E	464040	97.31%	[20]
MD-SAL-2D	70526	97.89%	new
LC-2D	550559	92.66%	new
STROKE	19435	79.02%	new

Table 2: Overview of datasets.

6.1 Datasets

Table 2 is an overview of the datasets we consider. 11 of the datasets have been used to evaluate private algorithms in prior work. We have introduced 14 new datasets to increase shape diversity. Datasets are described in Appendix A. The table reports the original scale of each dataset. We use the data generator $\mathcal{G}$ described before to generate datasets with scales of $\{10^3, 10^4, 10^5, 10^6, 10^7, 10^8\}$.

The maximum domain size is 4096 for 1D datasets and 256×256 for 2D datasets. The table also reports the fraction of cells in $\mathbf{x}$ that have a count of zero at this domain size. By grouping adjacent buckets, we derive versions of each dataset with smaller domain sizes. For 1D, the domain sizes are $\{256, 512, 1024, 2048\}$; for 2D, they are $\{32 \times 32, 64 \times 64, 128 \times 128, 256 \times 256\}$.

For each scale and domain size, we randomly sample 5 data vectors from our data generator and for each data vector, we run the algorithms 10 times.

6.2 Workloads & Loss Functions

We evaluate our algorithms on different workloads of range queries. For 1D, we primarily use the *Prefix* workload, which consists of n range queries $[1, i]$ for each $i \in [1, n]$. The *Prefix* workload has the desirable property that any range query can be derived by combining the answers to exactly two queries from *Prefix*. For 2D, we use 2000 random range queries as an approximation of the set of all range queries.

As mentioned in Section 5, we use L_2 as the loss function.

6.3 Algorithms

The algorithms compared are listed in Table 1. The dimension column indicates what dimensionalities the algorithm can support; algorithms labeled as Multi-D are included in both experiments. Complete descriptions of algorithms appear in Appendix B.

6.4 Resolving End-to-End Privacy Violations

Inconsistent side information: Recall that Principle 7 prevents the inappropriate use of private side information by an algorithm. SF, MWEM, UGRID, and AGRID assume the true scale of the dataset is known. To gauge any potential advantage gained from side information, we evaluated algorithm variants where a portion of the privacy budget, denoted ρ_{total}, is used to noisily estimate the scale. To set ρ_{total}, we evaluated the algorithms on synthetic data using varying values of ρ_{total}. In results not shown, we find that setting $\rho_{total} = 0.05$ achieves reasonable performance. For the most part, the effect is modestly increased error (presumably due to the reduced privacy budget available to the algorithm). However, the error rate of MWEM increases significantly at small scales (suggesting it is benefiting from side information). In Section 7, all results report performance of the original unmodified algorithms. While this gives a slight advantage to algorithms that use side information, it also faithfully represents the original algorithm design.

Illegal parameter setting Table 1 shows all the parameters used for each algorithm. Parameters with assignments have been set according to fixed values provided by the authors of the algorithm. Those without assignments are free parameters that were set in prior work in violation of Principle 6.

For MWEM, the number of rounds T is a free variable that has a major impact on MWEM's error. According to a pre-print version of [10], the best performing value of T is used for each task considered. For the one-dimensional range query task considered, T is set to 10. Similarly, for AHP, two parameters are left free: η and ρ which were tuned on the input data.

To adhere to Principle 6, we use the learning algorithm for setting free parameters (Section 5.2) to set free parameters for MWEM and AHP. In our experiments, the extended versions of the algorithms are denoted MWEM* and AHP*. In both cases, we train on shape distributions synthetically generated from power law and normal distributions.

For MWEM*, we determine experimentally the optimal $T \in [1, 200]$ for a range of ϵ-scale products. As a result, T varies from 2 to 100 over the range of scales we consider. This improves the performance of MWEM (versus a static setting of T) and does not violate our principles for private parameter setting. The success of this method is an example of data-independent parameter setting.

SF requires three parameters: ρ, k, F. Parameter F is free only in the sense that it is a function of scale, which is side information (as discussed above). For k, the authors propose a recommendation of $k = \lceil \frac{n}{10} \rceil$ after evaluating various k on input datasets. Their evaluation, therefore, did not adhere to Principle 6. However, because our evaluation uses different datasets, we can adopt their recommendation without violating Principle 6 – in effect, their experiment serves as a "training phase" for ours. Finally, ρ is a function of k and F, and thus is no longer free once those are fixed.

6.5 Implementation Details

We use implementations from the authors for DAWA, GREEDY H, H, PHP, EFPA, and SF. We implemented MWEM, H_b, PRIVELET, AHP, DPCUBE, AGRID, UGRID and QUADTREE ourselves in Python. All experiments are conducted on Linux machines running CentOS 2.6.32 (64-bit) with 16 Intel(R) Xeon(R) CPU E5-2643 0 @ 3.30GHz with 16G or 24G of RAM.

7. EXPERIMENTAL FINDINGS

We present our findings for the 1D and 2D settings. For the 1D case, we evaluated 14 algorithms on 18 different datasets, each at 6 different scales and 4 different domain sizes. For 2D, we evaluated 14 algorithms on 9 different datasets, each at 6 scales and 4 domain sizes. In total we evaluated 7,920 different experimental configurations. The total computational time was ≈ 22 days of single core computation. Given space constraints, we present a subset of the experiments that illustrate key findings.

In results not shown, we compare the error of data-independent algorithms (H_b, GREEDY H, H, PRIVELET, IDENTITY) on various range query workloads. The error of these algorithms is, of course, independent of the input data distribution, and the absolute error is independent of scale. (Or, in scaled-error terms, it diminishes predictably with increasing scale for all algorithms). The error for this class of techniques is well-understood because it is more amenable to analysis than data-dependent techniques. In order to simplify the presentation of subsequent results, we *restrict our attention to two data-independent algorithms:* IDENTITY, which is a useful baseline, and H_b, which is the best performing data-independent technique for 1D and 2D range query workloads with larger ranges.

7.1 Impact of Input Properties on Performance

As advocated in Principles 1 to 4, we now systematically examine the key properties of algorithm input that can affect performance: scale, domain size, shape, and ϵ. To aid in readability of figures, we report mean error without error bars but discuss variability over trials in detail in Section 7.4.

Scale: Figs. 1a and 1b compare algorithm performance at a fixed epsilon ($\epsilon = 0.1$) and increasing scales. Because of the scale-epsilon exchangeability property (Definition 4), which almost all algorithms satisfy,[2] the figures look identical if we fix scale and show increasing ϵ. For example, the first panel of Fig. 1a reports error for scale=1000 and $\epsilon = .1$ but the plotted error rates and relationships are identical to those for scale=10,000 and $\epsilon = .01$, scale=100,000 and $\epsilon = .001$, etc. Figs. 1a and 1b also capture variation across datasets (each black dot is the error of an algorithm on a particular dataset at the given scale; the white diamond is the algorithm's error averaged over all datasets).

FINDING 1 (BENEFITS OF DATA-DEPENDENCE). *Data-dependence can offer significant improvements in error, especially at smaller scales or lower epsilon values.*

The figures show that at small scales, almost all data-dependent algorithms outperform the best data-independent algorithm, H_b, on at least one dataset (black dot), sometimes by an order of magnitude. Further, the best data-dependent algorithms beat the best data-independent algorithms on average across all datasets (white diamonds), often by a significant margin. (For 1D, at the smallest scale, it is as much as a factor of 2.47; for 2D, it is up to a factor of 3.10.)

FINDING 2 (PENALTY OF DATA DEPENDENCE). *Some data-dependent algorithms break down at larger scales (or higher ϵ).*

Despite the good performance of data-dependent algorithms at small scales, at moderate or larger scales, many data-dependent algorithms have error significantly larger than IDENTITY, the data-independent baseline, which indicates quite disappointing performance. Even for the best data-dependent methods, the comparative advantage of data-dependence decreases and, for the most part, eventually disappears as scale increases. At the largest scales in both 1D and 2D, almost all data-dependent algorithms are beaten by H_b. At these scales, the only algorithms to beat H_b are DAWA and AHP*. In the 1D case, this only happens on a couple of datasets; in the 2D case, it happens on about half the datasets.

Shape: In Figs. 1a and 1b, the effect of shape is evident in the spread of black dots for a given algorithm.

[2] SF is not exchangeable, but it empirically behaves so.

FINDING 3 (VARIATION OF ERROR WITH DATA SHAPE). *Algorithm error varies significantly with dataset shape, even for a fixed scale, and algorithms differ on the dataset shapes on which they perform well.*

Even when we control for scale, each data-dependent algorithm displays significant variation of error across datasets. In the 1D case (Fig. 1a) at the smallest scale, EFPA's error varies by a factor of 24.88 from lowest error to highest. Across all scales, algorithms like MWEM, MWEM*, PHP, EFPA, and AHP* show significantly different error rates across shape. SF and DAWA offer the lowest variation across dataset shapes. In the 2D case (Fig. 1b), we also see significant variation at all scales. (Interestingly, DAWA exhibits high variation in 2D.)

While Figs. 1a and 1b show variation, one cannot compare algorithms across shapes. To do that, we use Figs. 2a and 2b, where scale is fixed and shape is varied. (For readability, we show only a subset of algorithms as explained in the caption for Fig. 2.) These figures show that the comparative performance of algorithms varies across shape. Fig. 2a shows that four different algorithms achieve the lowest error on some shape. In addition, a dataset that is "easy" for one algorithm appears "hard" for another: witness EFPA is able to exploit the shape of BIDS-ALL yet suffers on TRACE; the opposite is true for MWEM. In Fig. 2b, the shapes where DAWA performs poorly, AGRID does quite well. These results suggest that data-dependent algorithms are exploiting different properties of the dataset.

The unpredictable performance across data shape is a challenge in deployment scenarios because privacy algorithms cannot be selected by looking at the input data and because data-dependent algorithms rarely come with public error bounds. We discuss these issues further in Section 8.

Domain Size: Fig. 2c shows the effect of domain size for the 2D case. For two datasets (ADULT-2D and BJ-CABS-E) at two different scales (10^4 and 10^6), it reports error for domain sizes varying from 32 × 32 to 256 × 256.

FINDING 4 (DIFFERENT DOMAIN SIZE EFFECT). *Domain size affects data-dependent algorithms differently than data-independent algorithms.*

As discussed in [22], the error of data-independent algorithms IDENTITY and H_b is expected to increase with domain size, and at sufficiently large domains, H_b should achieve lower error than IDENTITY. Those effects are confirmed in Fig. 2c. However, the data-dependent algorithms exhibit different behavior. AGRID's error is nearly flat across domain size. This makes sense because the grid size is selected independent of domain size. DAWA's error is flat for some datasets but for others, it increases with domain size. DAWA selects a partition based on the data shape: for some shapes, the partition selected may grow increasingly fine-grained with domain size.

7.2 Assessment of State of the Art

Tables 3a and 3b show the number of datasets for which an algorithm is *competitive* for a given scale. We determine which algorithms are competitive by accounting for the variability in the mean error using t-tests (as discussed in Section 5.4).

FINDING 5 (COMPETITIVE ALGORITHMS). *No single algorithm offers uniformly low error. At small scales, data-dependent algorithms dominate; at large scales data-independent algorithms dominate.*

There is no algorithm that dominates all others by offering uniformly lower error. For 1D, 8 algorithms are competitive for at

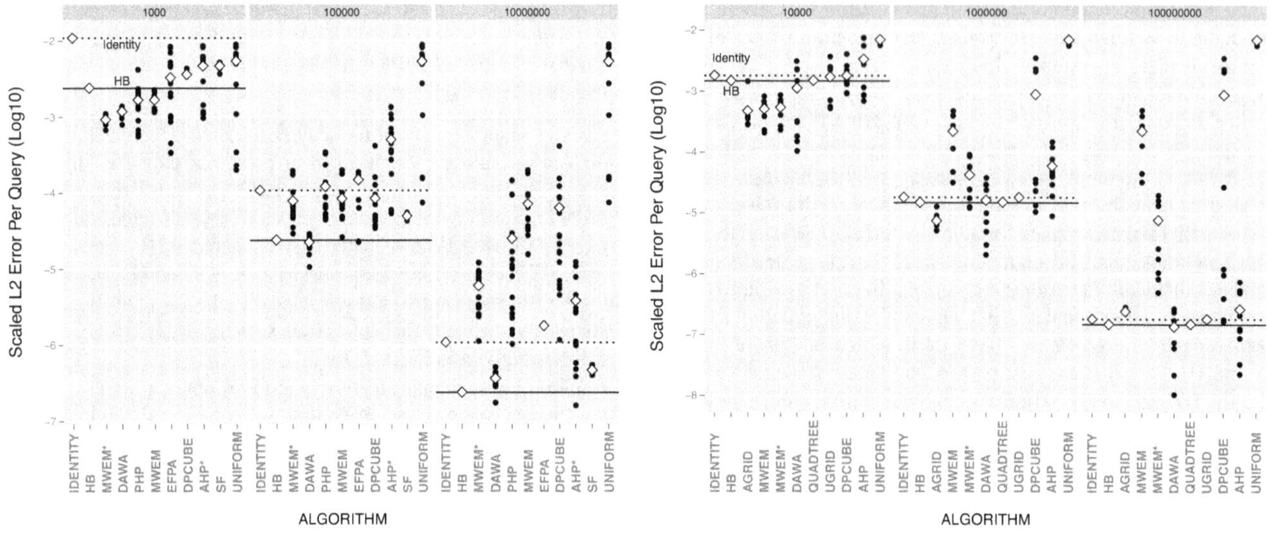

(a) 1D case: domain=4096, workload=Prefix

(b) 2D case: domain=128x128, workload=2000 random range queries

Figure 1: These figures show how average error rates of algorithms vary across the datasets described in Table 2, for both the 1D case (a) and 2D case (b). Each black dot (•) corresponds to average error for one dataset; white diamonds (◇) correspond to the mean error over all datasets. Horizontal lines are used to emphasize the error rates of the best and worst data-independent algorithms.

	Scale		
	10^3	10^5	10^7
DAWA	8	17	3
H_b		14	16
MWEM*	15		
EFPA	4	2	
PHP	2		
MWEM	3		
UNIFORM	3		
AHP*			1

(a) 1D case for domain size 4096

	Scale		
	10^4	10^6	10^8
DAWA	5	3	5
AGRID	5	6	
H_b			4
QUADTREE			4
AHP			1

(b) 2D case for domain size 128 × 128.

Table 3: Tables show the number of datasets on which algorithms are *competitive*, based on statistical significance of mean error.

least one combination of scale and shape; for 2D, 5 algorithms are competitive. At small scales for both 1D and 2D, the competitive algorithms are all data-dependent. At the largest scales, the only truly data-dependent algorithms are DAWA and AHP* (in the 2D case, QUADTREE is effectively data-independent at this domain size because the leaves of the tree are individual cells).

While no algorithm universally dominates across settings, DAWA offers the best overall performance in the following sense. We compare the error experienced by a user who selects a single algorithm to run on all datasets and scales to the error experienced by a user with access to an oracle allowing them to select the optimal algorithm (which would vary among the algorithms mentioned above on a case-by-case basis). We compute the ratio of errors per dataset/scale and then compute the average ratio, using a geometric mean. We call this measure "regret." DAWA has a regret of 1.32 on 1D and 1.73 on 2D. No single algorithm achieves lower regret (the next best on 1D is H_b with regret of 1.51 and on 2D it is AGRID with regret of 1.90).

7.3 Tuning Free Parameters

FINDING 6 (IMPROPER TUNING SKEWS EVALUATION). *For some algorithms tuning free parameters to fit the data can reduce error substantially, in some cases by a factor larger than 7.5.*

To demonstrate the sensitivity of performance to parameter settings, we ran AHP, DAWA, and MWEM under several different scenarios (i.e., 1D datasets of varying scale and shape) and found settings of their respective parameters that were optimal for some scenario (i.e., achieved lowest error on some 1D dataset at some scale). Then for a particular 1D dataset, MEDCOST, at a scale of 10^5, we measure the lowest error and the highest error achieved, considering *only those parameter settings that were optimal for some scenario.* All three algorithms are significantly impacted by the choice of parameters. Errors can be 2.5x (for DAWA) and around 7.5x (for MWEM and AHP) larger using sub-optimal parameters (even though those same parameters were in fact optimal for other reasonable inputs).

We proposed a method (Section 6.4) for setting free parameters in a manner consistent with Principle 6 and for removing dependence on side information (Principle 7). We applied this procedure to MWEM and AHP– violators of Principle 6 – to yield MWEM* and AHP* respectively. We report our results for the 1D case.

FINDING 7 (IMPROVED MWEM). *Training on synthetic data to decide free parameters (described in Section 6.4) leads to significant performance improvements for* MWEM, *especially at large scales.*

Ratio of error (MWEM/MWEM*), average all datasets						
Scale	10^3	10^4	10^5	10^6	10^7	10^8
Error ratio	1.799	.951	1.063	5.166	12.000	27.875

The reason for this improved performance is that a stronger signal (here higher scale; equivalently higher epsilon) allows MWEM to benefit from a higher number of rounds because a larger number measurements can be taken with reasonable accuracy. The training procedure, even with a single synthetic dataset, can help to find the right relationship between the scale-epsilon product and T. Since our method for setting T does not depend on the input data, this result shows that T can be set profitably in a data-independent way.

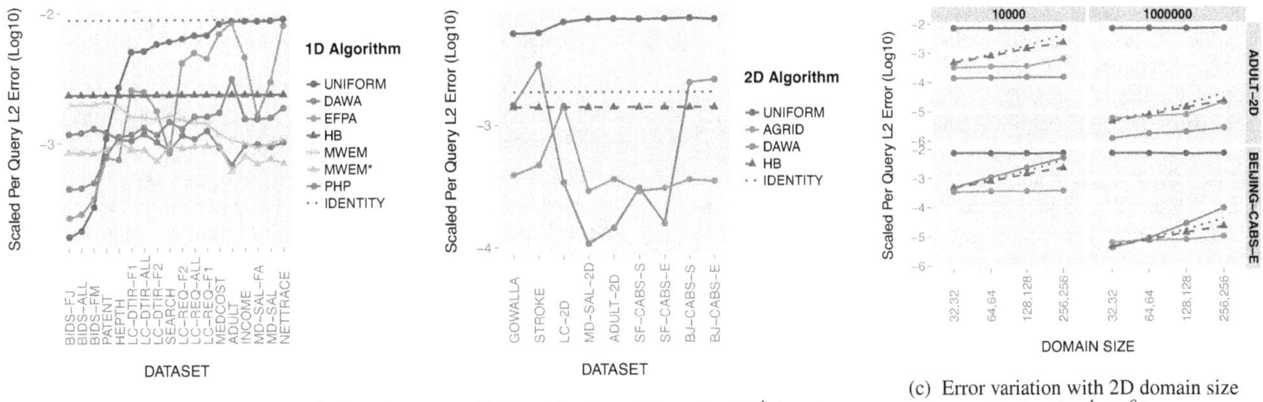

(a) Error by shape (1D, scale= 10^3, domain size= 4096)

(b) Error by shape (2D, scale= 10^4,domain size= 128×128)

(c) Error variation with 2D domain size (scale$\in \{10^4, 10^6\}$, shape$\in$ {ADULT-2D,BJ-CABS-E})

Figure 2: Error variation with data shape (1D and 2D cases) and domain size (2D case, for two shapes and two scales). The only algorithms shown are baselines, H_b, and those data-dependent algorithms that were competitive (on some dataset) for the scales shown.

This result also shows that we can cope with the removal of side information of scale without a significant impact on error.

For AHP, we applied our training method to determine parameters η and ρ. We compare the performance of AHP* against AHP using one of the several parameters settings used in [29]. At smaller scales, the error rates of both algorithms were similar. At larger scales, the results were mixed: one some datasets AHP* outperformed the fixed setting but on others vice versa. On average, over all datasets, AHP* was slightly better, with a ratio of improvement of 1.03 at scale 10^7. This shows that parameter tuning for AHP is more sensitive to shape and that it may be worth using a portion of the privacy budget to derive parameters.

7.4 Measurement of Variability and Bias

FINDING 8 (RISK AVERSE ALGORITHM EVALUATION). *Algorithms differ in the variation in error. The algorithm with lowest mean error may not be preferred by a risk averse user.*

In a real deployment scenario, a user will receive the output of a single run of the algorithm. Thus, she has no opportunity to reliably achieve mean error rates if error rates vary considerably around the mean. We are not aware of any prior work that has considered this issue in empirical algorithm evaluation.

While a risk-neutral user may evaluate algorithms with respect to mean error, a *risk averse* user should evaluate algorithms with respect to error rates she is very likely to achieve. Therefore, for the risk averse user, we consider the 95th percentile error rate (i.e. the error rate X for which 95% of trials have error less that X).

In most cases algorithms that are the best according to mean error are also the best according to 95th percentile error. In 1D, we see that DAWA has high variability in error and hence in ten scenarios (i.e., 10 scale-shape pairs at domain size 4096), we see DAWA being the best under mean error but not under 95% error. We see three scenarios (PATENT at scale 10^3, MD-SAL at scale 10^5 and TRACE at scale 10^7, all at domain size 4096) where an algorithm that was not competitive under mean error has the least 95% error. That algorithm was either UNIFORM or H_b, both of which have low variability in error. In 2D we see very few scenarios where an algorithm has the least mean error but not the least 95% error.

FINDING 9 (BIAS AND CONSISTENCY). *The high error of* MWEM, MWEM*, PHP, *and* UNIFORM *at large scales is due to bias. These algorithms are proven to be inconsistent.*

As scale increases, one expects error to decrease. However, Fig. 1 shows that the rate of decrease varies by algorithm. In fact, for some algorithms – PHP (1D only), MWEM, MWEM*, and UNIFORM– error remains quite high even at large scales. The cause is due to inherent bias introduced by these algorithms. In empirical results (not shown) we decompose error into bias and variance terms and find that at scale increases, the error of these algorithms becomes dominated by bias.

We complement our empirical findings with theoretical analysis. We show these algorithms are, in fact, inconsistent – implying that the bias does not vanish even as scale (or ϵ) goes to ∞. Table 1 reports a complete analysis of consistency for all algorithms; proofs appear in Appendix C.

7.5 Findings: Reasonable Utility

The previous section compared published techniques in a relative sense: it examined which algorithm performs the best in a given experimental setting. In this section, we evaluate the algorithms in an absolute sense: do the published algorithms offer reasonable utility? This is not an easy question to answer, as the notion of "reasonable" may be specific to the particular task that an analyst wishes to perform on the dataset. We address this by identifying situations when the error is unreasonably high for any application by comparing algorithms against a few simple baselines.

FINDING 10 (COMPARISON TO BASELINES). *For both 1D and 2D, many algorithms are beaten by the* IDENTITY *baseline at large scales. For 1D, the* UNIFORM *baseline beats all algorithms on some datasets at small scales.*

The experiments include two baseline methods (defined in Section 3.1) that can help us assess whether algorithms are providing meaningful improvements. The first baseline, UNIFORM learns virtually nothing about the input data (only its scale) and exploits a simplistic assumption of uniformity. Therefore, we argue that when sophisticated algorithms are delivering error rates comparable to UNIFORM, even on datasets that are decidedly non-uniform, they are not providing reasonable utility. Fig. 1 shows that most algorithms outperform UNIFORM at larger scales in 1D and at all scales in 2D. However, for the 1D case at scale 1000, UNIFORM achieves lowest error on some datasets. By examining Fig. 2a, one can see on which datasets UNIFORM beats competing algorithms. This figure shows that on some datasets, many algorithms do not offer much improvement over UNIFORM, suggesting that results for this scale (at least at this ϵ) are unlikely to be useful.

The second baseline is IDENTITY. A sophisticated algorithm that does not consistently and significantly improve over IDENTITY does not justify its complexity. This standard is highly dependent on scale, since, in terms of scaled error, IDENTITY improves with scale. For 1D, if we examine Fig. 1a and compare mean error across all datasets (the white diamonds), this standard rules out PHP, EFPA, AHP* at moderate scales (10^5) and EFPA, AHP*, MWEM, MWEM*, PHP, DPCUBE at large scales (10^7). For 2D (Fig. 1b), this standard rules out MWEM, MWEM*, DPCUBE, AHP at moderate scales (10^6) and AGRID, MWEM, MWEM*, DPCUBE, AHP at large scales (10^8).

8. DISCUSSION AND TAKEAWAYS

In this section, we synthesize our findings to (a) explain gaps or resolve inconsistencies from prior work, (b) present lessons for practitioners and (c) pose open research questions.

Explaining Results from Prior Work. We revisit the gaps and inconsistencies identified in Section 3.2 in light of our findings.

- We systematically compared data-dependent algorithms against the state of the art data-independent ones and learn there is no clear winner. Both scale and shape significantly affect algorithm error. Moreover, shape affects each data dependent algorithm differently.
- We can resolve the apparent inconsistency between [10] and [15] regarding the comparative performance of MWEM against data-independent matrix mechanism techniques by accounting for the effect of scale as well as the scale-epsilon exchangeability property. MWEM outperforms data-independent techniques (including instances of the matrix mechanism) either when the scale is small or when ϵ is small. Hardt et al. evaluate on small datasets and low ϵ whereas the datasets of Li et al. where MWEM struggled turn out to be datasets with large scale (over $335,000$). We demonstrated this by using the same datasets as [10,15] and controlling for scale.
- Our results are consistent with the findings of Qardaji et al. [22] regarding domain size and data-independent hierarchical algorithms. Interestingly, however, we show that data-dependent algorithms have a different relationship with domain size.
- We conduct a comprehensive evaluation of algorithms for answering 2D range queries, which is missing from the literature.

Lessons for practitioners. Our results identify guidelines for practitioners seeking the best utility for their task and facing the daunting task of selecting and configuring an appropriate algorithm.

The first consideration for a practitioner should be the overall strength of the "signal" available to them. This is determined by both the ϵ budget and the scale of the dataset. (We have shown that these two factors are exactly exchangeable in their impact on scaled error.) In a "high signal" regime (high scale, high ϵ), it is unlikely that any of the more complex, data-dependent algorithms will beat the simpler, easier-to-deploy, data independent methods such as IDENTITY and H_b. This greatly simplifies algorithm selection and deployment because error bounds are easy to derive, performance doesn't depend on the input dataset, and there are few parameters to set for these algorithms. In "low signal" regimes (low scale, low ϵ), deploying a data-dependent algorithm should be seriously considered, but with an awareness of the limitations: depending on the properties of the input data, error can vary considerably and error bounds are not provided by the data-dependent algorithms. For answering 1D range queries, DAWA is a competitive choice on most datasets in the low and medium signal regimes. For 2D range queries, AGRID consistently beats the data independent techniques, but DAWA can significantly outperform AGRID and the data independent techniques on very sparse datasets.

Open research Problems. Our experimental findings raise a number of research challenges we believe are important for advancing differentially private algorithms.

- *Understanding Data Dependence:* We have shown that data-dependent algorithms do not appear to be exploiting the same features of shape. The research community appears to know very little about the features of the input data that permit low error. Are there general algorithmic techniques that can be effective across diverse datasets, or should algorithm designers seek a set of specialized approaches that are effective for specific data properties?
- *Algorithm Selection:* While our evaluation of 1D and 2D algorithms identifies a class of state-of-the-art algorithms, it still does not fully solve the problem faced by the practitioner of selecting the algorithm that would result in the least error given a new dataset. We believe further research into analytical and empirical methods for algorithm selection would greatly aid the adoption of differential privacy algorithms in real world systems.
- *Error Bounds:* A related problem is that data-dependent algorithms typically do not provide public error bounds (unlike, e.g., the Laplace mechanism). Hence, users cannot predict the error they will witness without knowing the dataset, presenting a major challenge for algorithm deployment. Developing publishable error bounds is particularly important for this class of algorithms.
- *Parameter Tuning:* We showed that parameter tuning can result in significant gains in utility. Our training procedure is a first step towards setting parameters, but already distinguishes between a case where simple tuning can greatly improve performance over a fixed value (MWEM) and a case where parameter setting is more challenging because of data-dependence (AHP).
- *Expected Error versus Variability:* Existing empirical evaluations have focused on mean error while ignoring the variation of error over trials. We show that risk-averse users favoring low variability over low expected error may choose different algorithms than risk-seeking users. Current algorithms do not offer users the ability to trade off expected error and variability of achieved error, which could be an important feature in practice.

9. CONCLUSION

We have presented DPBENCH a novel and principled framework for evaluating differential privacy algorithms. We use DPBENCH to evaluate algorithms for answering 1- and 2-D range queries and as a result (a) resolved gaps/inconsistencies in prior work, (b) identified state-of-the-art algorithms that achieve the least error for their datasets, and (c) posed open research questions.

We are eager to extend our investigation in a number of ways. We have focused here primarily on evaluating the utility of algorithms, assuming that standard settings of ϵ offer sufficient privacy. We would like to provide meaningful guidelines for setting privacy parameters along with utility standards. We hope to expand our investigation to broader tasks (beyond 1- and 2-D range queries), and, as noted in Table 1, some of the algorithms considered support broader classes of workloads and may offer advantages not seen in our present experiments.

Acknowledgments We appreciate the comments of each of the anonymous reviewers. This material is based upon work supported by the National Science Foundation under Grant Nos. 1012748, 1253327, 1408982, 1443014, 1409125, and 1409143.

10. REFERENCES

[1] G. Ács, C. Castelluccia, and R. Chen. Differentially private histogram publishing through lossy compression. In *ICDM*, pages 1–10, 2012.

[2] A. Blum, K. Ligett, and A. Roth. A learning theory approach to noninteractive database privacy. *Journal of the ACM (JACM)*, 60(2):12, 2013.

[3] K. Chaudhuri and S. A. Vinterbo. A stability-based validation procedure for differentially private machine learning. In *Advances in Neural Information Processing Systems*, pages 2652–2660, 2013.

[4] G. Cormode, M. Procopiuc, E. Shen, D. Srivastava, and T. Yu. Differentially private spatial decompositions. In *ICDE*, pages 20–31, 2012.

[5] C. Dwork. Differential privacy: A survey of results. In *TAMC*, 2008.

[6] C. Dwork. A firm foundation for private data analysis. *Communications of the ACM*, 54(1):86–95, 2011.

[7] C. Dwork, F. M. K. Nissim, and A. Smith. Calibrating noise to sensitivity in private data analysis. In *TCC*, pages 265–284, 2006.

[8] C. Dwork and A. Roth. *The Algorithmic Foundations of Differential Privacy*. Found. and Trends in Theoretical Computer Science, 2014.

[9] M. Fredrikson, E. Lantz, S. Jha, S. Lin, D. Page, and T. Ristenpart. Privacy in pharmacogenetics: An end-to-end case study of personalized warfarin dosing. In *USENIX Security*, 2014.

[10] M. Hardt, K. Ligett, and F. McSherry. A simple and practical algorithm for differentially private data release. In *NIPS*, 2012.

[11] M. Hay, V. Rastogi, G. Miklau, and D. Suciu. Boosting the accuracy of differentially private histograms through consistency. *PVLDB*, 3(1-2):1021–1032, 2010.

[12] X. He, G. Cormode, A. Machanavajjhala, C. M. Procopiuc, and D. Srivastava. Dpt: differentially private trajectory synthesis using hierarchical reference systems. *Proceedings of the VLDB Endowment*, 8(11):1154–1165, 2015.

[13] X. Hu, M. Yuan, J. Yao, Y. Deng, L. Chen, Q. Yang, H. Guan, and J. Zeng. Differential privacy in telco big data platform. *Proc. VLDB Endow.*, 8(12):1692–1703, Aug. 2015.

[14] H. V. Jagadish, N. Koudas, S. Muthukrishnan, V. Poosala, K. C. Sevcik, and T. Suel. Optimal histograms with quality guarantees. In *VLDB*, pages 275–286, 1998.

[15] C. Li, M. Hay, and G. Miklau. A data- and workload-aware algorithm for range queries under differential privacy. *PVLDB*, 2014.

[16] C. Li, M. Hay, V. Rastogi, G. Miklau, and A. McGregor. Optimizing linear counting queries under differential privacy. In *PODS*, pages 123–134, 2010.

[17] C. Li and G. Miklau. An adaptive mechanism for accurate query answering under differential privacy. *PVLDB*, 5(6):514–525, 2012.

[18] C. Li, G. Miklau, M. Hay, A. McGregor, and V. Rastogi. The matrix mechanism: optimizing linear counting queries under differential privacy. *The VLDB Journal*, pages 1–25, 2015.

[19] F. D. McSherry. Privacy integrated queries: an extensible platform for privacy-preserving data analysis. In *SIGMOD*, pages 19–30, 2009.

[20] M. Piorkowski, N. Sarafijanovic-Djukic, and M. Grossglauser. CRAWDAD dataset epfl/mobility (v. 2009-02-24). Downloaded from http://crawdad.org/epfl/mobility/20090224, Feb. 2009.

[21] W. Qardaji, W. Yang, and N. Li. Differentially private grids for geospatial data. In *Data Engineering (ICDE), 2013 IEEE 29th International Conference on*, pages 757–768. IEEE, 2013.

[22] W. Qardaji, W. Yang, and N. Li. Understanding hierarchical methods for differentially private histograms. *PVLDB*, 6(14), 2013.

[23] P. A. Sandercock, M. Niewada, A. Członkowska, et al. The international stroke trial database. *Trials*, 12(1):1–7, 2011.

[24] X. Xiao, G. Bender, M. Hay, and J. Gehrke. ireduct: Differential privacy with reduced relative errors. In *SIGMOD*, 2011.

[25] X. Xiao, G. Wang, and J. Gehrke. Differential privacy via wavelet transforms. In *ICDE*, pages 225–236, 2010.

[26] Y. Xiao, L. Xiong, L. Fan, S. Goryczka, and H. Li. DPCube: Differentially private histogram release through multidimensional partitioning. *Transactions of Data Privacy*, 7(3), 2014.

[27] J. Xu, Z. Zhang, X. Xiao, Y. Yang, G. Yu, and M. Winslett. Differentially private histogram publication. *The VLDB Journal*, pages 1–26, 2013.

[28] G. Yuan, Z. Zhang, M. Winslett, X. Xiao, Y. Yang, and Z. Hao. Low-rank mechanism: Optimizing batch queries under differential privacy. *PVLDB*, 5(11):1136–1147, 2012.

[29] X. Zhang, R. Chen, J. Xu, X. Meng, and Y. Xie. Towards accurate histogram publication under differential privacy. In *ICDM*, 2014.

APPENDIX

A. DATASET DESCRIPTIONS

Table 2 provides an overview of all datasets, 1D and 2D, considered in the paper.

1D Datasets. The first seven were described in the papers in which they originally appeared [1,10,11,15,27,29]. The eleven new datasets were derived from three original data sources. A single primary attribute was selected for an initial shape distribution (denote by suffix -ALL). In addition, filters on a secondary attribute were applied to the data, resulting in alternative 1D shape distributions, still on the primary attribute.

The BIDS datasets are derived from a Kaggle competition whose goal is to identify online auctions that are placed by robots.[3] The histogram attribute is the IP address of each individual bid. BIDS-FJ and BIDS-FM result from applying distinct filtering conditions on attribute "merchandise": BIDS-FJ is a histogram on IP address but counting only individuals where "merchandise=jewelry", BIDS-FM is a histogram on IP address but counting only individuals where "merchandise=mobile".

The MD-SAL datasets are based on the Maryland salary database of state employees in 2012.[4] The histogram attribute is "YTD-gross-compensation". MD-SAL-FA is filtered on condition "pay-type=Annually".

The LC datasets are derived from data published by the "Lending Club" online credit market.[5] It describes loan applications that were rejected. The LC-REQ datasets are based on attribute "Amount Requested" while the LC-DTIR datasets are based on attribute "Debt-To-Income Ratio". In both cases, additional shapes are generated by applying filters on the "Employment" attribute. LC-REQ-F1 and LC-DTIR-F1 only count records with attribute "Employment" in range $[0,5]$, LC-REQ-F2 and LC-DTIR-F2 only count records with attribute "Employment" in range $(5,10]$.

2D Datasets. The BJ-CABS datasets and GOWALLA have been used and described in previous papers [12, 21]. The SF-CABS datasets are derived from well-known mobility traces data from San Francisco taxis [20].These location-based data are represented as latitude longitude pairs. To get more diverse data shape, we divide the two cab trace data into four by using only the start point and end point in a single dataset. BJ-CABS-S and SF-CABS-S contain only the start location of a cab trip, while BJ-CABS-E and SF-CABS-E record only the end locations.

ADULT-2D, MD-SAL-2D and LC-2D are derived from same sources as a subset of data we used in the 1D experiments. ADULT-2D is derived from source of ADULT. This source is also used in [10] with attributes "age" and "hours", but we use the attributes "capital-gain" and "capital-loss" in order to test on a larger domain. MD-SAL-2D is based on the Maryland salary database using the attributes "Annual Salary" and "Overtime earnings". LC-2D is derived from the accepted loan data from Lending Club with attributes "Funded Amount" and "Annual Income".

STROKE is a new dataset derived from the International Stroke Trial database [23], which is one of the largest randomized trial

[3] https://www.kaggle.com/c/facebook-recruiting-iv-human-or-bot/data

[4] http://data.baltimoresun.com/salaries/state/cy2012/

[5] https://www.lendingclub.com/info/download-data.action

conducted in acute stroke for public use. We used the attributes "Age" and "Systolic blood pressure".

B. ALGORITHM DESCRIPTIONS

Section 3.1 and Table 1 provide an overview of the algorithms studied; here we describe each algorithm individually. We begin with data-independent approaches, whose expected error rate is the same for all datasets, then describe data-dependent approaches. Baseline algorithms IDENTITY and UNIFORM are already described in Section 3.1.

Data-Independent Algorithms. Each of the data-independent approaches we consider can be described as an instance of the matrix mechanism [16, 18] (although a number were developed independently). The central idea is to select a set of linear queries (called the strategy), estimate them privately using the Laplace mechanism, and then use the noisy results to reconstruct answers to the workload queries. The strategy queries, which can be conveniently represented as a matrix, should have lower sensitivity than the workload and should allow for effective reconstruction of the workload.

If the discrete Haar wavelet matrix is selected as the strategy, the result is the PRIVELET method [25] which is based on the insight that any range query can be reconstructed by just a few of the wavelet queries and that the sensitivity of the Haar wavelet grows with $\prod_{i=1}^{k} \log_2 n_i$ where k is the dimensionality (number of attributes) and n_i is the domain size of the ith attribute.

Several approaches have been developed that use a strategy consisting of hierarchically structured range queries. Conceptually the queries can be arranged in a tree. The leaves of the tree consist of individual queries x_i (for $i = 1, \ldots, n$). Each internal node computes the sum of its children; at the root, the sum is therefore equal to the number of records in the database, $\|\mathbf{x}\|_1$. The approaches differ in terms of the branching factor and the privacy budget allocation. The H method [11] has a branching factor of b and uniform budget allocation. The H_b method [22] uses the domain size to determine the branching factor: specifically, it finds the b that minimizes the average variance of answering all range queries through summations of the noisy counts in the tree. It also uses a uniform budget allocation. GREEDY H is a subroutine of the DAWA [15] algorithm but can also be used as a stand-alone algorithm. It has a branching factor b and employs a greedy algorithm to tune the budget allocation to the workload. When used in DAWA, GREEDY H is applied to the partition that DAWA computes; by itself, it is applied directly to $\mathbf{x}$.

All of the above techniques reduce error by using a set of strategy queries which are a good match for the workload of interest. H, H_b, and PRIVELET were all initially designed to answer the set of *all* range queries, but the strategy each approach uses is static – it is not adapted to the particular queries in the workload. GREEDY H is the only technique that modifies the strategy (by choosing weights for hierarchical queries) in response to the input workload. In the table, it is marked as "workload-aware." While H and H_b naturally extend to the multi-dimensional setting (quadtrees, octrees, etc.), GREEDY H extends to 2D by applying a Hilbert transform to obtain a 1D representation.

Data-Dependent Partitioning Algorithms. Many of the data-dependent approaches use a partitioning step to approximate the input data vector and we discuss them as a group. These algorithms partition the domain into a collection of disjoint buckets whose union span the domain. The partition must be selected using a differentially private algorithm, since it is highly dependent on the input data, and this constitutes the first step for each algorithm in this group. Once a partition is selected, in a second step, they obtain noisy counts only for the buckets. A noisy data vector can be derived from the noisy bucket counts by assuming the data is uniform within each bucket, and this vector is then used to answer queries. Partitioning trades off between two sources of error: the error due to adding noise to the bucket count, which diminishes with increased bucket size, and the error from assuming uniformity within a bucket, which increases when non-uniform regions are lumped together. When the partition step can effectively find regions of the data that are close to uniform, these algorithms can perform well.

By the sequential composition property of differential privacy, any ϵ_1-differentially private algorithm for partition selection can be combined with any ϵ_2-differentially private algorithm for count estimation and achieve ϵ-differential privacy provided that $\epsilon_1 + \epsilon_2 \leq \epsilon$. All these algorithms therefore share a parameter that determines how to allocate the privacy budget across these two steps. We will use ρ to denote the proportion of ϵ used to identify the partition. Thus, $\epsilon_1 = \epsilon\rho$ and $\epsilon_2 = \epsilon(1 - \rho)$.

Unlike the first step, the approaches for estimating the bucket counts are typically data-*in*dependent. In fact, PHP, AHP, SF, and UGRID use the Laplace mechanism to obtain noisy counts.

The distinguishing features of each algorithm in this group are:

PHP [1] finds a partition by recursively bisecting the domain into subintervals. The midpoint is found using the exponential mechanism with a cost function based on the expected absolute error from the resulting partition. PHP is limited to 1D.

AHP [29] uses the Laplace mechanism to obtain a noisy count for each x_i for $i = 1, \ldots, n$ and sets noisy counts below a threshold to zero. The counts are then sorted and clustered to form a partition. As was done by [29], the greedy clustering algorithm is used in the experiments. The threshold is determined by parameter η. AHP extends to the multi-dimensional setting.

DAWA [17] uses dynamic programming to compute the least cost partition in a manner similar in spirit to V-optimal histograms [14]. The cost function is the same as the one used in the exponential mechanism of PHP [1]. To ensure differential privacy, noisy costs are used in place of actual costs. Once the partition is found, a hierarchical set of strategy queries are derived using GREEDY H. To operate on 2D data, DAWA applies a Hilbert transformation.

SF [27] aims to find a partition that minimizes the expected sum of squared error. While the aforementioned algorithms choose the size of the partition privately, in SF, the number of buckets is specified as a parameter k. Xu et al. [27] recommend setting k as a function of the domain size and we follow those guidelines in our experimental evaluation (see Section 6.5). Given the specified number of buckets, the bucket boundaries are selected privately using the exponential mechanism. Xu et al. [27] propose two variants of the algorithm, one based on the mean and another based on the median; our experiments evaluate the former. The parameters of SF include k, the number of buckets; ρ, the ratio for privacy budget allocation; and F, an upper bound on the count of a bucket (which is necessary for the cost function used in the exponential mechanism to select bucket boundaries). SF is limited to 1D.

DPCUBE [26], which is multi-dimensional, selects the partition by first applying the Laplace mechanism to obtain noisy counts for each cell in the domain, and then running a standard kd-tree on the noisy counts. Once the partition is selected it obtains fresh noisy counts for the partitions and uses inference to average the two sets of counts.

The remaining partitioning algorithms are designed specifically for 2D.

QUADTREE [4] generates a quadtree with fixed height and then noisily computes the counts of each node and does post-processing to maintain consistency. The height of the tree is a parameter. This algorithm becomes data-dependent if the tree is not high enough (i.e., the leaves contains aggregations of individual cells). Because the partition structure is fixed, this algorithm does not use any privacy budget to select it (i.e., $\rho = 0$).

HYBRIDTREE [4] is the combination of a kd-tree and the aforementioned quadtree. It uses a differentially private algorithm to build a kd-tree in a top down manner (DPCUBE goes bottom up). This tree extends a few levels and then a fixed quadtree structured is used for the remaining levels until a pre-specified height is reached.

UGRID [21] builds an equi-width partition where the width is chosen in a data-dependent way, based on the scale of the dataset. AGRID [21] builds a two-level hierarchy of partitions. The top level partition produces equi-width buckets, similar to UGRID. Then within each bucket of the top-level partition, a second partition is chosen in a data-adaptive way based on a noisy count of the number of records in the bucket.

Other Data-Dependent Algorithms. MWEM [10] is a workload aware algorithm that supports arbitrary workloads of linear queries (not just range queries). It starts with an estimate of the dataset that is completely uniform (based on assumed knowledge of the scale), and updates the estimate iteratively. Each iteration privately selects the workload query with highest error and then updates the estimate using a multiplicative weights update step. The number of iterations is an important parameter whose setting has a significant impact on performance. We propose a method for setting T, described in Section 6.4, that adheres to our evaluation principles.

EFPA [1] is based on applying the discrete Fourier transform (DFT) to a 1D data vector $\mathbf{x}$. It retains the top k Fourier coefficients, adds noise to them using the Laplace mechanism, and then inverts the transformation. By choosing $k < n$, the magnitude of the noise is lowered at the potential cost of introducing approximation error. The value of k is chosen in a data-dependent way using the exponential mechanism with a cost function that is based on expected squared error. The privacy budget is divided evenly selecting k and measuring the k coefficients.

C. THEORETICAL ANALYSIS

In this section, we theoretically analyze the properties of scale-epsilon exchangeability (Definition 4) and consistency (Definition 5) for the algorithms considered in the paper.

THEOREM 1. *Any instance of the Matrix Mechanism satisfies consistency and scale-epsilon exchangeability.*

PROOF. Given a $n \times k$ workload matrix $\mathbf{W}$, let $\mathbf{S}$ be a $p \times k$ *strategy* matrix, and $\mathbf{S}^+$ denote its Moore-Penrose pseudoinverse, such that $\mathbf{WSS}^+ = \mathbf{W}$. The matrix mechanism is given by the following:

$$\mathcal{M}_{\mathbf{S}}(\mathbf{W},\mathbf{x}) = \mathbf{Wx} + \mathbf{WS}^+ Lap(\Delta_{\mathbf{S}}/\epsilon)^p \quad (1)$$

where, $Lap(\lambda)^p$ denotes p independent random variables drawn from the Laplace distribution with scale λ, and $\Delta_{\mathbf{S}}$ is the sensitivity of the strategy workload.

The expected scaled per query error of this mechanism on a database $\mathbf{x}$ is given by:

$$\frac{E||\mathbf{WS}^+ Lap(\Delta_{\mathbf{S}}/\epsilon)^p||_2}{\|\mathbf{x}\|_1 \cdot k} = \frac{||\mathbf{WS}^+ \left(\frac{\Delta_{\mathbf{S}}}{\epsilon}\mathbf{1}_{p\times 1}\right)||_2}{\|\mathbf{x}\|_1 \cdot k} \propto \frac{1}{\epsilon \times \|\mathbf{x}\|_1} \quad (2)$$

where $\mathbf{1}_{p\times 1}$ is a column vector of p ones. This completes the proof. Matrix mechanism algorithms are consistent bacause the noise is additive and at high values of ϵ or high scales, the scaled error tends to 0. □

COROLLARY 1. IDENTITY, PRIVELET, H, H_b, GREEDY H *ensure both consistency and scale-epsilon exchangeability.*

PROOF. These techniques are instances of Matrix Mechanism and the proof follows from Theorem 1. □

LEMMA 1. *When ϵ goes to infinity, Exponential Mechanism picks one of the items with the highest score with probability 1.*

PROOF. Suppose T is the set of all items, T^* contains all the items with the highest score α. Since Exponential Mechanism picks any item t with the probability proportional to $e^{\epsilon score(t)}$, the probability of picking any item in T^* is

$$\begin{aligned} P(T^*) &= \frac{\sum_{t\in T^*} e^{\epsilon\alpha}}{\sum_{t\in T} e^{\epsilon score(t)}} = \frac{\sum_{t\in T^*} e^{\epsilon\alpha}}{\sum_{t\in T^*} e^{\epsilon\alpha} + \sum_{t\in T-T^*} e^{\epsilon score(t)}} \\ &= \frac{|T^*|}{|T^*| + \sum_{t\in T-T^*} e^{\epsilon(score(t)-\alpha)}} = 1(as \epsilon \to \infty) \end{aligned}$$

□

THEOREM 2. EFPA *ensures consistency.*

PROOF. EFPA works in two steps: (a) pick $k < n$ coefficients, and (b) add noise to the chosen coefficients. The number of coefficients k is chosen by Exponential Mechanism with the score function of expected noise added to the k chosen coefficients ($\frac{2k}{\epsilon}$) plus the error due to dropping $n - k$ Fourier coefficients. When ϵ goes to infinity, the noise term goes to zero. Thus $k = n$ (where all the coefficients are chosen) receives the highest score. By Lemma 1, this will be chosen as ϵ tends to infinity. Therefore, the scaled error from EFPA will tend to zero when ϵ tends to infinity, which satisfies consistency. □

THEOREM 3. AHP, DAWA *and* DPCUBE *are consistent.*

PROOF. All AHP, DAWA and DPCUBE noisily partition the domain and then estimate partition counts. When ϵ tends to infinity, these algorithms will use a partitioning with zero bias. Also, partition counts are estimated using Laplace Mechanism whose scaled error goes to zero as ϵ or scale tends to infinity. Thus AHP, DAWA and DPCUBE ensure consistency. □

THEOREM 4. AGRID *and* UGRID *ensure consistency.*

PROOF. When ϵ goes to infinity, both AGRID and UGRID are equal to IDENTITY having grids with size 1. Thus AGRID and UGRID are consistent. □

THEOREM 5. *On sufficiently large domains,* QUADTREE *and* HYBRIDTREE *do not ensure consistency.*

PROOF. Both QUADTREE and HYBRIDTREE set the maximum height of the tree. If the input dataset has large domain size, the leaf node in the tree contains more than one cell in the domain introducing bias. Therefore, QUADTREE and HYBRIDTREE are not consistent. □

THEOREM 6. *PHP does not ensure consistency.*

PROOF. PHP recursively bisects the domain but sets the maximum iterations to be $\log_2 n$ (n is the domain size). After $\log_2 n$ iterations, it is possible that there exist clusters with bias greater than zero. **Example**: Let the scale $m = 2^n - 1$ and $X = \{x_1, \ldots, x_n\}$ be the dataset with $x_i = 2^{n-i}$. In iteration j ($\epsilon = \infty$), PHP will divide the domain into $\{x_j\}$ and $\{x_{j+1}, \ldots, x_n\}$. After $\log_2 n$ iterations, the last partition will contain domain elements with different counts. Thus the bias of the partition does not go to zero even when ϵ tends to infinity. □

The consistency of SF depends on the implementation. Our experiments use the implementation provided by the authors that includes the modification described in Sec. 6.2 of [27].

THEOREM 7. *StructureFirst does not satisfy consistency. If the modification described in Sec. 6.2 of [27] is applied, then it does satisfy consistency.*

PROOF. StructureFirst fixes the number of clusters first (it sets the number k to be $\frac{n}{10}$ empirically, n is the domain size), which will introduce bias if the real number of clusters are greater than k. **Example**: Let $X = \{x_1, \ldots, x_n\}$ be the dataset with $x_i = i$. If we set the number of clusters $k < n$ (suppose $k = \frac{n}{10}$), there will be one cluster c containing more than one domain point. Since all the x_i are different, the bias of c does not go to zero even if ϵ tends to infinity. The modification proposed in [27] builds a hierarchical histogram (i.e., H) within each bin. This makes the algorithm consistent for the same reason that H is consistent. □

THEOREM 8. *MWEM does not ensure consistency.*

PROOF. MWEM fixes the number of iterations (it sets T = 10 empirically), which will introduce bias if T queries are not enough to update the estimate. **Example**: Let $X = \{x_1, \ldots, x_n\}$ be the dataset with $x_i = i$ and workload W contains all the single count queries. If the number of iterations T is less than n (suppose T = 10 < n), we can only pick T single count queries and correct T domain point when ϵ goes to infinity. The bias generated from other domain points will not go to zero even if ϵ tends to infinity. □

LEMMA 2. *Laplace Mechanism is scale-epsilon exchangeable. Exponential Mechanism is scale-epsilon exchangeable when the score is a linear function of scale.*

PROOF. Laplace Mechanism ensures scale-epsilon exchangeability since the scaled expected L_2 error for Laplace Mechanism is $\frac{\Delta}{\epsilon \|\mathbf{x}\|_1}$ (Δ is the fixed sensitivity given workloads).

Exponential Mechanism picks any item t with the probability proportional to $e^{\epsilon score(t)}$. When the score is a linear function of scale, Exponential Mechanism is scale-epsilon exchangeable. □

THEOREM 9. *PHP, MWEM, EFPA are scale-epsilon exchangeable.*

PROOF. All these three methods use Exponential Mechanism to choose clustering or parameter. Since their score functions are all linear functions of scale, based on Lemma 2, they will choose the same clustering or parameter with the same probability when ϵ * scale is fixed. Once they use the same clustering or parameter, the scaled error is the sum of the bias and the variance. The variance comes from Laplace Mechanism which is scale-epsilon exchangeable by Lemma 2. It is also easy to check those bias remain the same when fixing ϵ * scale. Thus PHP, MWEM, EFPA ensure scale-epsilon exchangeability. □

THEOREM 10. *StructureFirst does not satisfy scale-epsilon exchangeability.*

PROOF. The score function used in StructureFirst is a linear function of the square of scale. Based on Lemma 2, even if ϵ * scale is fixed, the probability of picking the same clustering will be different for different ϵ settings. Once the clustering is different, the bias will be different. **Example**: Suppose we use $\epsilon = 1$ on $D_1 = \{1, 2\}$ and $\epsilon = 0.5$ on $D_2 = \{2, 4\}$. For both D_1 and D_2, there are only two clusterings $C_1 = \{(x1, x2)\}, C_2 = \{(x1), (x2)\}$. For D_1, $P_1(C_1) = \frac{e^{\epsilon score(C_1)}}{e^{\epsilon score(C_1)} + e^{\epsilon score(C_2)}} = \frac{e^{1.5}}{e^{1.5}+e^2}$. For D_2, $P_2(C_1) = \frac{e^3}{e^3+e^4}$. We can see $P_1(C_1) \neq P_2(C_2)$. □

THEOREM 11. *DAWA ensures scale-epsilon exchangeability.*

PROOF. Let $D_1 = m_1 \cdot \mathbf{p}$ and $D_2 = m_2 \cdot \mathbf{p}$ be two datasets with the same shape $\mathbf{p}$, but different scales m_1 and m_2. Suppose we run DAWA on D_1 with privacy budget ϵ_1 and D_2 with privacy budget ϵ_2 such that $m_1\epsilon_1 = m_2\epsilon_2$. We show that the scaled expected error of the synthetic histogram output by DAWA ($\hat{\mathbf{x}}$) will be the same in both cases. The proof is in two steps:

1. In both cases, the probability that DAWA picks any paritioning $\mathcal{P}$ is identical.
2. Therefore, the scaled expected error of the noisy histogram $\hat{\mathbf{x}}$ is the same in both cases.

To prove the first statement, consider all partitionings considered by DAWA. Every partitioning $\mathcal{P}$ is associated with a score

$$\sum_{C \in \mathcal{P}} \left(\sum_{v \in C} |\mathbf{x}[v] - \frac{\mathbf{x}[C]}{|C|}| + \frac{1}{\epsilon} \right) \tag{3}$$

where $\mathbf{x}[v]$ is the count of domain value v, and $\mathbf{x}[C]$ is the total count of values in C. In fact, we can rewrite Eq 3 as

$$\|\mathbf{x}\|_1 \sum_{C \in \mathcal{P}} \left(\sum_{v \in C} |\mathbf{p}[v] - \frac{\mathbf{p}[C]}{|C|}| + \frac{1}{\|\mathbf{x}\|_1 \cdot \epsilon} \right) \tag{4}$$

DAWA uses the exponential mechanism to pick the best partitioning. Thus, $\mathcal{P}$ will be picked with a probability proportional to:

$$exp\left(\frac{\epsilon \cdot \|\mathbf{x}\|_1}{2\Delta} \sum_{C \in \mathcal{P}} \left(\sum_{v \in C} |\mathbf{p}[v] - \frac{\mathbf{p}[C]}{|C|}| + \frac{1}{\|\mathbf{x}\|_1 \cdot \epsilon} \right) \right) \tag{5}$$

Applying DAWA with budget ϵ_1 on $D_1 = m_1\mathbf{p}$ and with budget ϵ_2 on $D_2 = m_2\mathbf{p}$ will result in exactly the same probability distribution over partitionings.

Furthermore, the second step of DAWA adds noise to all the counts $\mathbf{x}[C]$, for $C \in \mathcal{P}$. If the partitioning in both datasets D_1 and D_2 is the same, then the resulting noisy histograms will have the same scaled expected error due to the scale epsilon exchangeability of the Laplace mechanism. The proof is complete since we showed that the partitionings have the same probability distribution in D_1 (with ϵ_1) and D_2 (with ϵ_2). □

THEOREM 12. *AHP ensures scale-epsilon exchangeability.*

PROOF. The proof is very similar to that of Theorem 11. □

THEOREM 13. AGRID, UGRID, QUADTREE *and* HYBRIDTREE *are scale-epsilon exchangeable.*

PROOF. The partitioning or the tree generation of these four algorithms are independent with $m \cdot \epsilon$, where m is the scale of the input dataset and ϵ is the privacy budget. After the partitioning or tree generation, each algorithm applies Laplace Mechanism to answer node queries. Laplace Mechanism is scale-epsilon exchangeable. Thus, AGRID, UGRID, QUADTREE and HYBRIDTREE ensure scale-epsilon exchangeability. □

PrivTree: A Differentially Private Algorithm for Hierarchical Decompositions

Jun Zhang[1] Xiaokui Xiao[1] Xing Xie[2]
[1]Nanyang Technological University
{jzhang027, xkxiao}@ntu.edu.sg
[2]Microsoft Research
xingx@microsoft.com

ABSTRACT

Given a set D of tuples defined on a domain Ω, we study differentially private algorithms for constructing a histogram over Ω to approximate the tuple distribution in D. Existing solutions for the problem mostly adopt a *hierarchical decomposition* approach, which recursively splits Ω into sub-domains and computes a noisy tuple count for each sub-domain, until all noisy counts are below a certain threshold. This approach, however, requires that we (i) impose a limit h on the recursion depth in the splitting of Ω and (ii) set the noise in each count to be proportional to h. The choice of h is a serious dilemma: a small h makes the resulting histogram too coarse-grained, while a large h leads to excessive noise in the tuple counts used in deciding whether sub-domains should be split. Furthermore, h cannot be directly tuned based on D; otherwise, the choice of h itself reveals private information and violates differential privacy.

To remedy the deficiency of existing solutions, we present *PrivTree*, a histogram construction algorithm that adopts hierarchical decomposition but completely eliminates the dependency on a pre-defined h. The core of PrivTree is a novel mechanism that (i) exploits a new analysis on the Laplace distribution and (ii) enables us to use only *a constant amount of noise* in deciding whether a sub-domain should be split, without worrying about the recursion depth of splitting. We demonstrate the application of PrivTree in modelling spatial data, and show that it can be extended to handle sequence data (where the decision in sub-domain splitting is not based on tuple counts but a more sophisticated measure). Our experiments on a variety of real datasets show that PrivTree considerably outperforms the states of the art in terms of data utility.

Keywords

Differential privacy; hierarchical decompositions

1. INTRODUCTION

Releasing sensitive data while preserving privacy is a problem that has attracted considerable attention in recent years. The state-of-the-art paradigm for addressing the problem is *differential privacy* [16], which requires that the data released reveals little information about whether any particular individual is present or absent from the data. To fulfill such a requirement, a typical approach adopted by the existing solutions is to publish a noisy version of the data in place of the original one.

SIGMOD'16, June 26-July 01, 2016, San Francisco, CA, USA
© 2016 ACM. ISBN 978-1-4503-3531-7/16/06...$15.00
DOI: http://dx.doi.org/10.1145/2882903.2882928

In this paper, we consider a fundamental problem that is frequently encountered in differentially private data publishing: Given a set D of tuples defined over a domain Ω, we aim to decompose Ω into a set S of sub-domains and publish a noisy count of the tuples contained in each sub-domain, such that S and the noisy counts approximate the tuple distribution in D as accurately as possible. Applications of the problem include:

- Private modelling of spatial data [12,41] often requires generating a multi-dimensional histogram of the input data.
- For differentially private data mining (e.g., k-means [48] and regression analysis [29]), one of the general approaches is to first coarsen the input data and inject noise into it, and then use the modified data to derive mining results.
- Existing algorithms for sequence data publishing [7] require identifying frequent patterns (e.g., prefixes) in a given set D of sequences. This is equivalent to asking for a decomposition of the sequence domain Ω into a set of disjoint sub-domains, such that (i) each sub-domain includes all sequences in D containing a particular pattern, and (ii) the number of sequences included in each sub-domain is larger than a given threshold.

To address the above decomposition problem, the prior art mostly adopts a *hierarchical* approach, which (i) recursively splits Ω into sub-domains and computes a noisy tuple count for each of them, and (ii) stops splitting a sub-domain when its noisy count is smaller than a threshold. This approach, albeit intuitive, requires a pre-defined limit h on the maximum depth of recursion when splitting Ω. The reason is that, to ensure differential privacy, the amount of noise injected in each tuple count has to be proportional to the maximum recursion depth, and hence, h must be fixed in advance so that the algorithm can decide the correct noise amount to use.

Nevertheless, the choice of h is a serious dilemma: for the algorithm to produce fine-grained sub-domains of Ω, h cannot be small; yet, increasing h would lead to noisier tuple counts, and thus more errors in deciding whether a sub-domain should be split. As a consequence, no choice of h could result in an accurate approximation of the input data. Furthermore, we cannot tune h directly on the input dataset; otherwise, the choice of h itself reveals private information and violates differential privacy. To mitigate these issues, existing work relies on heuristics to select an appropriate value of h, and to generate fine-grained decompositions even when h is small. As we show in our experiments, however, those heuristics are rather ineffective when the input data follows a skewed distribution (which is often the case in practice).

Contributions. Motivated by the limitations of existing solutions, we present *PrivTree*, an algorithm for the decomposition problem that adopts the hierarchical approach but completely eliminates the dependency on a pre-defined h. In particular, PrivTree requires only *a constant amount of noise* in deciding whether a sub-domain should be split, which enables it to generate fine-grained decompositions without worrying about the recursion depth. Such a surprising improvement is obtained with a novel mechanism for differential privacy that exploits a non-trivial analysis on the Laplace noise [17] to derive an extremely tight privacy bound. Its central insight is that, in the context of hierarchical decomposition, it is possible to publish a sequence S of $0/1$ values using $O(1)$ noise, regardless of the *sensitivity* of S [17]. In contrast, the standard Laplace mechanism [17] requires that noise amount must be proportional to S's sensitivity.

To demonstrate the applications of PrivTree, we apply it to the private modeling of spatial data, and present a non-trivial extension to tackle sequence data, for which we adopt an advanced Markov model and utilize a sophisticated measure (instead of tuple counts) to decide whether a sub-domain should be split. We experimentally evaluate our algorithms on a variety of real data, and show that they considerably outperform the states of the art in terms of data utility.

In addition, we present an in-depth analysis on the connection between PrivTree and the *support vector technique (SVT)* [18, 21, 28], a technique widely adopted for data publishing under differential privacy. We show that there exists a variant of SVT [28] that could have been used to implement PrivTree, if its privacy guarantees are as claimed in previous work [28]. Nevertheless, we prove that the SVT variant [28] does not satisfy differential privacy, which makes it inapplicable in our context.

In summary, we make the following contributions in this paper:

1. We propose PrivTree, a differentially private algorithm for hierarchical decomposition that eliminates the dependency on a pre-defined threshold of the recursion depth.
2. We present applications of PrivTree in modeling spatial and sequence data. (Sections 3 and 4)
3. We analyze the connection between PrivTree and the SVT, and point out a misclaim about the latter in [28]. (Section 5)
4. We conduct extensive experiments to demonstrate the superiority of PrivTree over the states of the art. (Section 6)

2. PRELIMINARIES

In this section, we introduce the concepts behind *differential privacy* [16], and define the problem of *spatial decomposition* [14, 46], which we will address with our PrivTree algorithm in Section 3.

2.1 Differential Privacy

Let D be a sensitive dataset with n tuples, and $\mathcal{A}$ be a data publishing algorithm that takes D as input and releases a set of information $\mathcal{A}(D)$. Differential privacy requires that $\mathcal{A}(D)$ should be insensitive to the presence or absence of any particular tuple in D, so that an adversary cannot infer much private information from $\mathcal{A}(D)$. More formally, differential privacy is defined based on the concept of *neighboring datasets*, as shown in the following.

DEFINITION 2.1 (NEIGHBORING DATASETS [16]). *Two datasets are neighboring if one of them can be obtained by inserting a tuple into the other.*

DEFINITION 2.2 (ε-DIFFERENTIAL PRIVACY [16]). *An algorithm $\mathcal{A}$ satisfies ε-differential privacy if, for any two neighboring datasets D and D' and for any possible output O of $\mathcal{A}$,*

$$\ln\left(\frac{\Pr\left[\mathcal{A}(D)=O\right]}{\Pr\left[\mathcal{A}(D')=O\right]}\right)\leq\varepsilon,$$

where $\Pr[\cdot]$ *denotes the probability of an event.*

There exist several mechanisms [17, 24, 38] for achieving differential privacy, among which the most fundamental one is the *Laplace mechanism*. Specifically, the Laplace mechanism considers a function f that takes D as input and outputs a vector of real numbers, and it aims to release $f(D)$ with differential privacy. To achieve this objective, it adds i.i.d. noise into each value in $f(D)$, such that the noise η follows a *Laplace distribution* with the following probability density function:

$$\Pr[\eta=x]=\frac{1}{2\lambda}e^{-|x|/\lambda}. \tag{1}$$

We denote the above distribution as *Lap*(λ), and refer to λ as the *scale* (since the standard deviation of *Lap*(λ) is proportional to λ). Dwork et al. [17] prove that the Laplace mechanism achieves $(S(f)/\lambda)$-differential privacy, where $S(f)$ is the *sensitivity* of f defined as follows:

DEFINITION 2.3 (SENSITIVITY [17]). *Let f be a function that maps a dataset D into a vector of real numbers. The global sensitivity of f is defined as*

$$S(f)=\max_{D,D'}\left\|f(D)-f(D')\right\|_1,$$

where D and D' are any two neighboring datasets, and $\|\cdot\|_1$ denotes the L_1 norm.

Intuitively, $S(f)$ measures the maximum possible change in f's output when we insert or remove one arbitrary tuple in f's input.

An important property of differential private algorithms is that their composition also ensures differential privacy:

LEMMA 2.1 (COMPOSITION RULE [37]). *Let $\mathcal{A}_1,\ldots,\mathcal{A}_k$ be k algorithms, such that $\mathcal{A}_i$ satisfies ε_i-differential privacy ($i\in[1,k]$). Then, the sequential composition $(\mathcal{A}_1,\ldots,\mathcal{A}_t)$ satisfies $(\sum_{i=1}^{k}\varepsilon_i)$-differential privacy.*

This lemma is particularly useful in proving that an algorithm ensures differential privacy: we can first decompose the algorithm into a few sequential components, and then analyze each component separately; after that, we can apply Lemma 2.1 to establish the overall privacy guarantee of the algorithm.

2.2 Spatial Decompositions

Let D be a set of data points in a multi-dimensional space Ω. A *spatial decomposition* [14, 46] of D consists of a tree-structured decomposition of Ω into its sub-domains, along with a partitioning of the data points among the leaves of the decomposition tree. For example, Figure 1 illustrates a spatial decomposition of a two-dimensional dataset D that contains 12 data points. The decomposition tree has 9 nodes, namely, $v_1, v_2, \ldots, v_9$, each of which is associated with a sub-domain of Ω (denoted as "*dom*" and visualized as a black rectangle in Figure 1). We refer to each sub-domain as a *region*. The root of the tree, v_1, corresponds to a region that covers the entire Ω; this region is recursively divided into four equal-size sub-regions in the lower levels of the tree, until each leaf node contains a sufficiently small number of data points.

The spatial decomposition in Figure 1 is referred to as a *quadtree* [14, 46], and is widely adopted in spatial databases for efficient

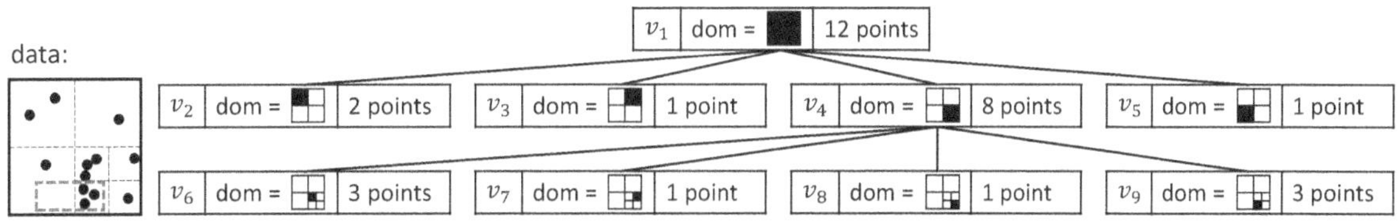

Figure 1: An illustration of a spatial decomposition tree.

query processing. In particular, suppose that we are to use the quadtree to answer *range count queries*, i.e., queries that ask for the number of data points contained in a rectangle q. In that case, we can pre-compute, for each node v in the quadtree, the number of data points contained in v's region. Then, we can answer any range count query q with a top-down traversal from the root node of the quadtree. Specifically, at the beginning of the traversal, we initialize the query answer as $ans = 0$. After that, for each node v that we traverse, we examine v's region $dom(v)$, and differentiate four cases:

1. If $dom(v)$ is disjoint from q, we ignore v;
2. If $dom(v)$ is fully contained in q, we increase ans by the point count pre-computed for v;
3. If $dom(v)$ partially intersects q and v is not a leaf node, then we visit every child of v with a region not disjoint from q;
4. If $dom(v)$ partially intersects q and v is a leaf node, then we inspect the data points in $dom(v)$, and add to ans the number of points contained in q.

After the traversal terminates, we return ans as the result. For instance, consider a range count query q that corresponds to the dashed-line rectangle in Figure 1. To answer q, we only need to examine four nodes, namely, v_1, v_4, v_5, v_9; the other nodes are all ignored since their regions are disjoint from q.

The efficiency of quadtrees results from its adaptiveness to the underlying distribution, i.e., it grows deep into the dense regions of Ω where there are a large number of data points (e.g., the region of v_4 in Figure 1), and it ignores those regions that are sparse (e.g., the regions of v_2, v_3, v_5). Such adaptiveness has motivated existing work [12] to utilize quadtrees for generating private synopses of spatial data. Specifically, the technique in [12] first applies a differentially private algorithm to generate a quadtree, and then employs the Laplace mechanism to inject noise into the point count of each node. The quadtree and the noisy counts can then be used to answer any range-count query q using the top-down traversal algorithm mentioned above, with two minor modifications. First, whenever we visit a node v whose region is fully contained in q, we add the noisy count associated with v (instead of the exact count) to the query answer ans. Second, if v is a leaf node whose region $dom(v)$ partially intersects q, then we multiply the noisy count of v by $\frac{|q \cap dom(v)|}{|dom(v)|}$ before adding it to ans, where $|\cdot|$ denotes the area of a region. That is, given only the noisy count of v, we estimate the number of data points in $dom(v)$ that are contained in q, by assuming that the points follow a uniform distribution. The rationale of this approach is that, given the adaptiveness of the quadtree, each leaf node v should cover a region where the data distribution is not highly skewed; otherwise, v should contain a dense sub-region, in which case the quadtree construction algorithm should have further split v (instead of making v a leaf node). This makes it relatively accurate to adopt a uniform assumption when estimating the contribution of v to the answer of q. In Section 3, we will present a more detailed analysis of the above quadtree approach, and then use it to motivate our PrivTree algorithm.

Table 1: Table of notations

Notation	Description
n, d	the cardinality and dimensionality of the input dataset D
$Lap(\lambda)$	a random variable following the Laplace distribution with 0 mean and λ scale
$dom(v)$	the sub-domain of a node v
$depth(v)$	the hop distance from a node v to the root of the tree
θ	the threshold used to decide if a node should be split
$c(v), \hat{c}(v)$	the point count of a node v, and its noisy version
$b(v), \hat{b}(v)$	the biased count of a node v, and its noisy version
$\rho(v)$	the privacy risk of a node v (see Equation (5))
$\rho^\top(v)$	an upper bound of ρ (see Equation (7))
β	the fanout of the spatial decomposition tree
δ	the decaying factor used by PrivTree
$\mathcal{I}$	the set of distinct items in a given set D of sequences

3. PRIVATE SPATIAL DECOMPOSITIONS

This section presents our solution for constructing private spatial decompositions. We first revisit the private quadtree approach (in Section 2.2) and discuss its limitations; after that, we elaborate our PrivTree algorithm, analyze its guarantees, and discuss its extensions. Table 1 shows the notations that we frequently use.

3.1 Private Quadtrees Revisited

Algorithm 1 presents a generic version of the private quadtree approach mentioned in Section 2.2. The algorithm takes as input four parameters: (i) a set D of spatial points defined over a multidimensional domain Ω, (ii) the scale λ of the Laplace noise to be used in the construction of the quadtree, (iii) the threshold θ used to decide whether a quadtree node should be split, and (iv) the threshold h on the maximum height of the decomposition tree. The output of the algorithm is a quadtree $\mathcal{T}$ where each node v comes with two pieces of information: the sub-domain of Ω corresponding to v (denoted as $dom(v)$), and a noisy version of the point count in $dom(v)$ (denoted as $\hat{c}(v)$). We define the *depth* of v as the hop distance between v and the root of $\mathcal{T}$, and denote it as $depth(v)$.

The algorithm starts by creating the root note v_1 of $\mathcal{T}$, after which it sets $dom(v_1) = \Omega$ and marks v_1 as *unvisited* (Lines 1-2). The subsequent part of the algorithm consists of a number of iterations (Lines 3-9). In each iteration, we examine if there is an unvisited node v in $\mathcal{T}$. If such v exists, we mark v as visited, and employ the Laplace mechanism to generate a noisy version $\hat{c}(v)$ of the number of points contained in $dom(v)$ (Lines 4-6). After that, we split v if the following two conditions simultaneously hold. First, $\hat{c}(v) > \theta$, i.e., $dom(v)$ is likely to contain a sufficiently large number of points. Second, the height of the tree is smaller than h, which, as we discuss shortly, ensures that the noisy counts generated by the algorithm would not violate differential privacy. If both of the above conditions are met, then we generate v's children and insert them into $\mathcal{T}$ as unvisited nodes (Lines 7-9); otherwise, v becomes a leaf node of $\mathcal{T}$. When all of the nodes in $\mathcal{T}$ become visited, the algorithm terminates and returns $\mathcal{T}$.

Algorithm 1: SimpleTree (D, λ, θ, h)

initialize a quadtree $\mathcal{T}$ with a root node v_1;
set $dom(v_1) = \Omega$, and mark v_1 as unvisited;
while *there exists an unvisited node* v **do**
  mark v as visited;
  compute the number $c(v)$ of points in D that are contained in $dom(v)$;
  compute a noisy version of $c(v)$: $\hat{c}(v) = c(v) + Lap(\lambda)$;
  if $\hat{c}(v) > \theta$ ***and*** $depth(v) < h - 1$ **then**
    split v, and add its children to $\mathcal{T}$;
    mark the children of v as unvisited;
return $\mathcal{T}$

Privacy and Utility Analysis. Algorithm 1 ensures ε-differential privacy if $\lambda \geq h/\varepsilon$. To understand this, suppose that we insert an arbitrary point t into D. Then, $\mathcal{T}$ has only h nodes whose exact point counts are affected by the insertion of t, i.e., the h nodes whose sub-domains contain t. In addition, the point count of those nodes should change by one after t's insertion. This indicates that the sensitivity (see Definition 2.3) of all point counts in $\mathcal{T}$ equals h, and hence, adding i.i.d. Laplace noise of scale $\lambda \geq h/\varepsilon$ into the counts would achieve ε-differential privacy.

As we mention in Section 1, however, requiring $\lambda \geq h/\varepsilon$ makes it rather difficult for Algorithm 1 to generate high-quality quadtrees. Specifically, if we set h to a small value, the resulting quadtree $\mathcal{T}$ would not adapt well to the data distribution in D, due to the restriction on the tree height; meanwhile, increasing h would also increase the amount of noise in each $\hat{c}(v)$, which makes Algorithm 1 more error-prone in deciding whether a node should be split, thus degrading the quality of $\mathcal{T}$. In other words, any choice of h inevitably leads to inferior data utility. Furthermore, we cannot directly tune h by (i) testing the performance of Algorithm 1 on D under different settings of h, and then (ii) selecting the one that yields the best result. The reason is that such a tuning process violates differential privacy: when we change the input data from D to a neighboring dataset D', the tuning process may select a different h, in which case Algorithm 1 would use different noise scales for D and D', invalidating its privacy guarantee.

To alleviate the above issue, existing work [12, 41, 42, 48] resorts to heuristics to choose h without violating differential privacy, and to enhance the performance of Algorithm 1, e.g., by avoiding the generation of noisy counts for certain levels of the decomposition tree (so that h can be reduced), and by exploiting correlations among the noisy counts to improve their accuracy [25]. However, none of those heuristics is able to thoroughly address the limitations of Algorithm 1. As we shown in our experiments in Section 6, existing approaches tend to provide inferior data utility, especially when the input data follows a skewed distribution.

3.2 Rationale Behind Our Solution

To remedy the deficiency of Algorithm 1, we aim to eliminate the requirement that $\lambda \geq h/\varepsilon$, and make λ a constant instead. This would not only resolve the dilemma in choosing h, but also unleash the potential of quadtrees as the tree height is no longer restricted. Towards this end, we first make a simple observation: after we finish constructing the quadtree $\mathcal{T}$ in Algorithm 1, we could remove all noisy counts associated with the intermediate nodes, and release only the noisy counts for the leaf nodes as well as the sub-domains of all nodes. The released tree, denoted as $\mathcal{T}'$, could still be used for query processing, since we can re-generate an alternative count for each intermediate node v in $\mathcal{T}'$ by summing up the published noisy counts of the leaf nodes under v. Intuitively, $\mathcal{T}'$ reveals less information than $\mathcal{T}$ does, and hence, we might use less noise in $\mathcal{T}'$ to achieve ε-differential privacy.

However, the above intuition does not hold in general, as $\mathcal{T}'$ and $\mathcal{T}$ require the same amount of noise to enforce the same privacy guarantee. To explain, consider two neighboring datasets D and D', such that D is obtained by inserting a point t into D'. Let $v_1, v_2, \ldots, v_h$ be the h nodes in $\mathcal{T}'$ whose sub-domains contain t. Then, these h nodes should form a path from the root of $\mathcal{T}$ to a leaf node. Furthermore, for any v_i, the point count of v_i is decreased by one when we change the input dataset from D to D'. We use $c(v_i)$ to denote v_i's exact point count on D.

Without loss of generality, assume that v_h is a leaf node (i.e., $v_1, \ldots, v_{h-1}$ are all intermediate nodes). Let $\Pr[D \rightarrow \mathcal{T}']$ (resp. $\Pr[D' \rightarrow \mathcal{T}']$) denote the probability that we obtain $\mathcal{T}'$ from D (resp. D') given fixed λ, θ, and h. Then,

$$\ln\left(\frac{\Pr[D \rightarrow \mathcal{T}']}{\Pr[D' \rightarrow \mathcal{T}']}\right) = \sum_{i=1}^{h-1} \ln\left(\frac{\Pr[c(v_i) + Lap(\lambda) > \theta]}{\Pr[c(v_i) - 1 + Lap(\lambda) > \theta]}\right) + \ln\left(\frac{\Pr[c(v_h) + Lap(\lambda) = \hat{c}(v_h)]}{\Pr[c(v_h) - 1 + Lap(\lambda) = \hat{c}(v_h)]}\right).$$

By Equation (1), for any $c(v_h) < \hat{c}(v_h)$,

$$\ln\left(\frac{\Pr[c(v_h) + Lap(\lambda) = \hat{c}(v_h)]}{\Pr[c(v_h) - 1 + Lap(\lambda) = \hat{c}(v_h)]}\right) = \frac{1}{\lambda}. \tag{2}$$

In addition, for any v_i ($i \in [1, h-1]$) with $c(v_i) \leq \theta$,

$$\ln\left(\frac{\Pr[c(v_i) + Lap(\lambda) > \theta]}{\Pr[c(v_i) - 1 + Lap(\lambda) > \theta]}\right) = \frac{1}{\lambda}. \tag{3}$$

Therefore, when $c(v_i) \leq \theta$ holds for every v_i ($i \in [1, h-1]$),

$$\ln\left(\frac{\Pr[D \rightarrow \mathcal{T}']}{\Pr[D' \rightarrow \mathcal{T}']}\right) = \frac{h}{\lambda}. \tag{4}$$

By Definition 2.2, this indicates that λ must be at least h/ε to ensure that $\mathcal{T}'$ achieves ε-differential privacy.

In summary, $\mathcal{T}'$ is no better than $\mathcal{T}$ in terms of the amount of noise required, because of the negative result in Equations (2) and (3). In other words, *in the worst case*, releasing the boolean result of $c(v_i) + Lap(\lambda) > \theta$ incurs the same privacy cost as releasing $c(v_i) + Lap(\lambda)$ directly. That said, if $c(v_i) > \theta$ for some v_i, then Equation (3) does not hold, in which case $\mathcal{T}'$ could entail a smaller privacy cost than $\mathcal{T}$ does. To illustrate this, we denote the l.h.s. of Equation (3) as a function ρ of $c(v_i)$, i.e.,

$$\rho(x) = \ln\left(\frac{\Pr[x + Lap(\lambda) > \theta]}{\Pr[x - 1 + Lap(\lambda) > \theta]}\right), \tag{5}$$

and we plot ρ in Figure 2. (Note that the y-axis of Figure 2 is in a logarithmic scale.) Observe that, when $x = c(v) \geq \theta + 1$, $\rho(x)$ decreases exponentially with the increase of x. This indicates that $\ln\left(\frac{\Pr[D \rightarrow \mathcal{T}']}{\Pr[D' \rightarrow \mathcal{T}']}\right)$ could be much smaller than h/λ, if $c(v_i) \geq \theta + 1$ holds for all $i \in [1, h-1]$. For example, if $c_{h-1} \geq \theta + 1$ and $c(v_i) - c(v_{i+1})$ is at least a constant for all $i \in [1, h-2]$, then

$$\sum_{i=1}^{h-1} \rho\big(c(v_i)\big) = \Theta\left(\frac{1}{\lambda}\right), \tag{6}$$

due to the exponential decrease of $\rho(v_i)$. In that case, we have $\ln\left(\frac{\Pr[D \rightarrow \mathcal{T}']}{\Pr[D' \rightarrow \mathcal{T}']}\right) = \Theta(1/\lambda)$ instead of $\ln\left(\frac{\Pr[D \rightarrow \mathcal{T}']}{\Pr[D' \rightarrow \mathcal{T}']}\right) = h/\lambda$, which would enable us to set λ as a constant independent of h.

The above analysis leads to an interesting question: can we ensure that Equation (6) holds for any input dataset? In Section 3.3, we will give an affirmative answer to this question. The basic idea of our method is to add a bias term to each $c(v_i)$, so that $c(v_i) - c(v_{i+1})$ ($i \in [1, h-2]$) is larger than a constant of choice. In addition, the bias term is independent of the input data, which

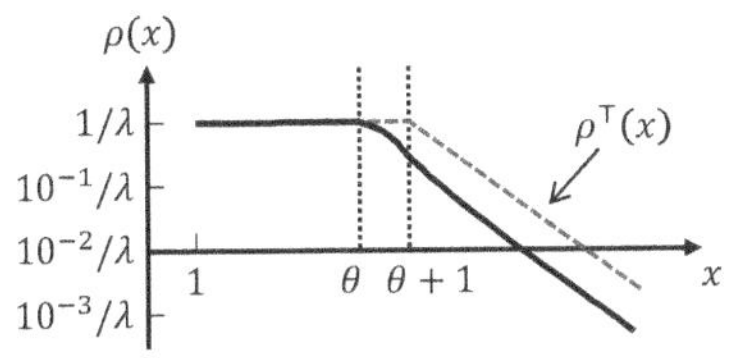

Figure 2: An illustration of $\rho(x)$ and $\rho^{\top}(x)$.

guarantees that its usage does not leak any private information. The derivation of the bias term requires a careful analysis of $\rho(x)$. To simplify our analysis, we devise a simple upper bound of $\rho(x)$:

LEMMA 3.1. *Let $\rho^{\top}$ be a function such that*

$$\rho^{\top}(x) = \begin{cases} 1/\lambda, & \text{if } x < \theta + 1 \\ \frac{1}{\lambda}\exp\left(\frac{\theta+1-x}{\lambda}\right), & \text{otherwise} \end{cases} \tag{7}$$

Then, $\rho(x) \le \rho^{\top}(x)$ for any x.

Figure 2 shows $\rho^{\top}$ with a dashed line. Observe that it closely captures the exponential decrease of ρ when $c(v) \ge \theta + 1$.

3.3 The PrivTree Algorithm

Algorithm 2 presents our PrivTree technique for private spatial decomposition. As with Algorithm 1, PrivTree asks for a spatial dataset D, the scale λ of Laplace noise to be used, and a threshold θ for deciding whether a node should be split. However, it does not request a threshold h on the maximum tree height; instead, it requires a positive number δ, the usage of which will be clarified shortly. The output of PrivTree is a quadtree $\mathcal{T}$, with the point count associated with each node removed. That is, $\mathcal{T}$ reveals the sub-domain of each node v, but conceals all information about $c(v)$. In Section 3.4, we will explain how we obtain the point count of each node, as well as our choices of θ and δ.

In a nutshell, PrivTree is similar to Algorithm 1 in that it also (i) generates $\mathcal{T}$ by recursively splitting a root node v_1 whose region $dom(v_1)$ covers the whole data space Ω, and (ii) decides whether a node v should be split based on a noisy point count of v. However, the method for obtaining noisy counts marks the crucial difference between the two algorithms. Specifically, given a node v, PrivTree does not generate its noisy count by directly adding Laplace noise to $c(v)$. Instead, PrivTree first computes a biased count $b(v) = c(v) - depth(v) \cdot \delta$, and checks if it is smaller than $\theta - \delta$; if it is, then PrivTree increases it to $\theta - \delta$. In other words,

$$b(v) = \max\left\{\theta - \delta,\ c(v) - depth(v) \cdot \delta\right\}. \tag{8}$$

After that, PrivTree produces a noisy count $\hat{b}(v) = b(v) + Lap(\lambda)$, and splits v if $\hat{b}(v)$ is larger than the given threshold θ. Notice that PrivTree does not restrict the height of $\mathcal{T}$, as the decision to split any node v solely depends on $\hat{b}(v)$.

Privacy Analysis. Consider any quadtree $\mathcal{T}$ output by PrivTree, and any two neighboring datasets D and D', such that D is obtained by inserting a point t into D'. In what follows, we show that setting $\lambda = \Theta(1/\varepsilon)$ is sufficient for ε-differential privacy, i.e.,

$$-\varepsilon \le \ln\left(\frac{\Pr[D \to \mathcal{T}]}{\Pr[D' \to \mathcal{T}]}\right) \le \varepsilon. \tag{9}$$

The proof for the first inequality in Equation (9) is relatively straightforward. For any node v in $\mathcal{T}$, let $c(v)$ be v's point count on D, and $b(v)$ be the biased version of $c(v)$ generated from Equation (8). Let $c'(v)$ and $b'(v)$ be the counterparts of $c(v)$ and $b(v)$, respectively, given D' as the input. Then, we have $c(v) = c'(v)$ for all nodes v in $\mathcal{T}$, except for the nodes whose sub-domains contain

Algorithm 2: PrivTree $(D, \lambda, \theta, \delta)$

```
initialize a quadtree T with a root node v1;
set dom(v1) = Ω, and mark v1 as unvisited;
while there exists an unvisited node v do
    mark v as visited;
    compute a biased point count for v with decaying factor δ:
    b(v) = c(v) − depth(v) · δ;
    adjust b(v) if it is excessively small: b(v) = max {b(v), θ − δ};
    compute a noisy version of b(v): b̂(v) = b(v) + Lap(λ);
    if b̂(v) > θ then
        split v, and add its children to T;
        mark the children of v as unvisited;
return T with all point counts removed
```

t. Note that those nodes should form a path from the root of $\mathcal{T}$ to a leaf. Let k be the length of the path, and v_i be i-th node in the path, with v_1 denoting the root of $\mathcal{T}$. We have $c(v_i) = c'(v_i) + 1$ and

$$b(v_i) = \begin{cases} b'(v_i) + 1, & \text{if } b(v_i) \ge \theta - \delta + 1 \\ b'(v_i), & \text{otherwise} \end{cases} \tag{10}$$

Then, by Equation (1),

$$\begin{aligned} \ln\left(\frac{\Pr[D \to \mathcal{T}]}{\Pr[D' \to \mathcal{T}]}\right) &= \sum_{i=1}^{k-1} \ln\left(\frac{\Pr[b(v_i) + Lap(\lambda) > \theta]}{\Pr[b'(v_i) + Lap(\lambda) > \theta]}\right) \\ &\quad + \ln\left(\frac{\Pr[b(v_k) + Lap(\lambda) \le \theta]}{\Pr[b'(v_k) + Lap(\lambda) \le \theta]}\right) \\ &\ge 0 - \frac{1}{\lambda} = -\frac{1}{\lambda}. \end{aligned}$$

This indicates that $\lambda \ge 1/\varepsilon$ ensures the first inequality in Equation (9).

Next, we prove the second inequality in Equation (9) by analyzing $\ln\left(\frac{\Pr[b(v_i)+Lap(\lambda)>\theta]}{\Pr[b'(v_i)+Lap(\lambda)>\theta]}\right)$, which we refer to as the *privacy cost* of v_i. The high-level idea of our proof is as follows. First, due to the way that we generate biased counts, each node v_i's bias count $b(v_i)$ is at least a constant δ smaller than that of its parent v_{i-1}, as long as $b(v_i) \ge \theta + 1$. Based on this observation and Lemma 3.1, we show that all nodes v_i with $b(v_i) \ge \theta + 1$ incur a total privacy cost of $\Theta(1/\varepsilon)$. After that, we prove that the total privacy cost of the remaining nodes is also $\Theta(1/\varepsilon)$.

By the definition of $v_1, \ldots, v_k$, we have $c(v_i) \ge c(v_{i+1})$ and $depth(v_i) = depth(v_{i+1}) - 1$ for any $i \in [1, k-1]$. This indicates that $b(v_i) \ge b(v_{i+1}) \ge \theta - \delta$, due to Equation (8). Without loss of generality, assume that there exists $m \in [1, k-1]$, such that $b(v_m) \ge \theta - \delta + 1$ and $b(v_{m+1}) = \theta - \delta$. Then,

$$\begin{cases} b(v_{i-1}) \ge b(v_i) + \delta \ge \theta + 1, & \text{if } i \in [2, m] \\ b(v_i) = \theta - \delta, & \text{otherwise} \end{cases} \tag{11}$$

Combining Equations (10) and (11), we have $b'(v_i) = b(v_i)$ when $i > m$, and $b'(v_i) = b(v_i) - 1$ otherwise. Therefore,

$$\begin{aligned} \ln\left(\frac{\Pr[D \to \mathcal{T}]}{\Pr[D' \to \mathcal{T}]}\right) &= \sum\nolimits_{i=1}^{k-1} \ln\left(\frac{\Pr[b(v_i) + Lap(\lambda) > \theta]}{\Pr[b'(v_i) + Lap(\lambda) > \theta]}\right) \\ &\quad + \ln\left(\frac{\Pr[b(v_k) + Lap(\lambda) \le \theta]}{\Pr[b'(v_k) + Lap(\lambda) \le \theta]}\right) \\ &\le \sum\nolimits_{i=1}^{k-1} \ln\left(\frac{\Pr[b(v_i) + Lap(\lambda) > \theta]}{\Pr[b'(v_i) + Lap(\lambda) > \theta]}\right) \\ &= \sum\nolimits_{i=1}^{m} \ln\left(\frac{\Pr[b(v_i) + Lap(\lambda) > \theta]}{\Pr[b(v_i) - 1 + Lap(\lambda) > \theta]}\right) \\ &= \sum\nolimits_{i=1}^{m} \rho\big(b(v_i)\big), \end{aligned}$$

where $\rho(\cdot)$ is as defined in Equation (5). By Lemma 3.1 and Equation (11),

$$\sum_{i=1}^{m} \rho\Big(b(v_i)\Big) \le \sum_{i=1}^{m} \rho^\top\Big(b(v_i)\Big)$$
$$= \rho^\top\Big(b(v_m)\Big) + \sum_{i=1}^{m-1} \frac{1}{\lambda} \exp\left(\frac{\theta + 1 - b(v_i)}{\lambda}\right)$$
$$\le \frac{1}{\lambda} + \frac{1}{\lambda} \cdot \frac{1}{1 - \exp(-\delta/\lambda)}$$
$$= \frac{1}{\lambda} \cdot \frac{2e^{\delta/\lambda} - 1}{e^{\delta/\lambda} - 1}.$$

Therefore, if we set $\delta = \gamma \cdot \lambda$, where γ is a constant, then

$$\ln\left(\frac{\Pr[D \to \mathcal{T}]}{\Pr[D' \to \mathcal{T}]}\right) = \sum_{i=1}^{m} \rho\Big(b(v_i)\Big) \le \frac{1}{\lambda} \cdot \frac{2e^{\gamma} - 1}{e^{\gamma} - 1} = \Theta\left(\frac{1}{\lambda}\right).$$

Summing up the above analysis, we have the following theorem:

THEOREM 3.1. *PrivTree satisfies ε-differential privacy if $\lambda \ge \frac{2e^{\gamma}-1}{e^{\gamma}-1} \cdot \frac{1}{\varepsilon}$ and $\delta = \gamma \cdot \lambda$ for some $\gamma > 0$.*

3.4 Noisy Counts and Parameterization

Generation of Noisy Counts. Recall that PrivTree outputs a quadtree with the point count for each node removed. However, if a quadtree with noisy counts is needed, we can easily obtain it by adding a postprocessing step to PrivTree. In particular, given a dataset D, we first invoke PrivTree to produce a $\frac{\varepsilon}{2}$-differentially private quadtree $\mathcal{T}$. After that, for each leaf node v of $\mathcal{T}$, we publish a noisy version of v's point count using Laplace noise of scale $2/\varepsilon$. It can be verified that this postprocessing step satisfies $\frac{\varepsilon}{2}$-differential privacy. Then, by Lemma 2.1, the generation of $\mathcal{T}$ and the noisy counts as a whole achieves ε-differential privacy. Finally, we compute a noisy count for each intermediate node v in $\mathcal{T}$, by taking the sum of the noisy counts of all leaf nodes under v.

Choice of δ. As shown in Theorem 3.1, when $\delta = \gamma \cdot \lambda$, PrivTree needs to use a noise scale $\lambda \ge \frac{2e^{\gamma}-1}{e^{\gamma}-1} \cdot \frac{1}{\varepsilon}$ to achieve ε-differential privacy. Intuitively, the choice of δ is a balancing act between the amount of bias and the amount of noise in each biased noisy count $\hat{b}(v)$ used by PrivTree. In particular, if δ is small with respect to λ, then the bias term in each $\hat{b}(v)$ is small, but the noise amount in $\hat{b}(v)$ would need to be large, since $\frac{2e^{\gamma}-1}{e^{\gamma}-1} \cdot \frac{1}{\varepsilon}$ increases when $\gamma = \delta/\lambda$ decreases. In contrast, if δ is large with respect to λ, then each $\hat{b}(v)$ would have small noise but a large bias.

That said, we observe that there is a more important factor in choosing δ. To explain, consider a node v with a biased count $b(v) = \theta - \delta$. Ideally, we would like PrivTree to avoid splitting such a node v, as its point count is likely to be small. Nevertheless, if $b(v) + Lap(\lambda) > \theta$, then PrivTree would split v and insert its children into the quadtree. In turn, each of v's children also has a certain probability to be split, and so on. If δ is excessively small, then each offspring of v has a relatively large splitting probability, in which case the splitting process may not *converge*, i.e., PrivTree may keep generating offsprings of v and does not terminate.

To address the above issue, we set δ in such a way to ensure that if $b(v) = \theta - \delta$, then in expectation, only 2 nodes would be generated from the subtree under v (including v itself). Specifically, we set $\delta = \lambda \cdot \ln \beta$, where β denote the *fanout* of $\mathcal{T}$, i.e., the number of children that each intermediate node in $\mathcal{T}$ has. (For example, $\beta = 4$ if $\mathcal{T}$ is a two-dimensional quadtree.) By Equation (1), this setting of δ guarantees that any node v with $b(v) = \theta - \delta$ has $\frac{1}{2\beta}$ probability to be split. Formally, we have the following lemma:

LEMMA 3.2. *Let $\mathcal{T}$ be the output of PrivTree given $\delta = \lambda \cdot \ln \beta$, and $\mathcal{T}^*$ be the output of PrivTree when it sets $\hat{b}(v) = c(v)$ for each node v (i.e., no noise or bias is introduced in the split decisions). Then, $\mathbb{E}[|\mathcal{T}|] \le 2 \cdot |\mathcal{T}^*|$ whenever $|\mathcal{T}^*| > 1$, where $|\cdot|$ denotes the number of nodes in a tree.*

The above setting of δ leads to the following corollary:

COROLLARY 1. *PrivTree satisfies ε-differential privacy if $\lambda \ge \frac{2\beta-1}{\beta-1} \cdot \frac{1}{\varepsilon}$ and $\delta = \lambda \cdot \ln \beta$, where β is the fanout of $\mathcal{T}$.*

Choice of θ. Intuitively, the threshold θ serves the purpose of ensuring that each leaf node v of $\mathcal{T}$ contains a sufficiently large point count $c(v)$, so that if we choose to output a noisy version of $c(v)$, it would not overwhelmed by the Laplace noise injected. The choice of θ, however, is complicated by the fact that PrivTree adds a negative bias to the point count of a node when it decides whether or not to split the node. In particular, due to the negative bias, even $\theta = 0$ could ensure that a node v with $b(v) > \theta$ has a sufficient large point count. Therefore, we use $\theta = 0$ in our implementation of PrivTree, and we observe that it leads to reasonably good results in our experiments.

3.5 Extensions

Although we have presented PrivTree in the context of spatial decomposition, we note that it could be extended in several different aspects for other applications. First, the decomposition tree used by PrivTree does not have to be a quadtree, but can be any other tree structure instead. For example, suppose that we are given a multi-dimensional dataset D containing both numeric and categorical attributes, and that each categorical attribute has a taxonomy. Then, we can still apply PrivTree on D to generate a private synopsis of D, by splitting each numeric dimension of D according to a binary tree and each categorical dimension based on its taxonomy.

Second, when PrivTree decides whether or not a node v should be split, the decision does not have to be based on the count of tuples contained in *dom*(v), but can also be based on any other score function $\mu(v)$ that is *monotonic*, i.e., $\mu(v) \le \mu(u)$ whenever v is a child node of another node u. The rationale is that, as long as μ is monotonic, we can add a bias to the score of each node v to ensure that it is at least a constant smaller that the score of v's parent. Then, we can apply Lemma 3.1 to show that PrivTree guarantees differential privacy, given that λ is properly set based on the sensitivity of the score function μ. In Section 4, we will apply this idea to extend PrivTree for private modeling of sequence data.

Finally, although the privacy analysis of PrivTree (in Section 3.3) assumes that the presence or absence of a tuple t only affects one leaf node and its ancestors, it can be extended to the case when multiples leaf nodes and their ancestors are impacted. In particular, if at most x leaf nodes can be affected, then we can apply PrivTree with the noise scale λ enlarged x times. The intuition is that each affected leaf node, along its ancestors, incurs one unit of privacy cost, which in turn requires one unit of noise to mitigate; as such, when there are x affected leaf nodes, we need x units of noise for sufficient privacy protection.

4. PRIVATE MARKOV MODELS

This section presents an extension of PrivTree for constructing Markov models on sequence data. We first introduce the basic concepts of sequences and Markov models in Section 4.1. After that, we elaborate our PrivTree extension in Section 4.2, and compare it with existing solutions in Section 4.3.

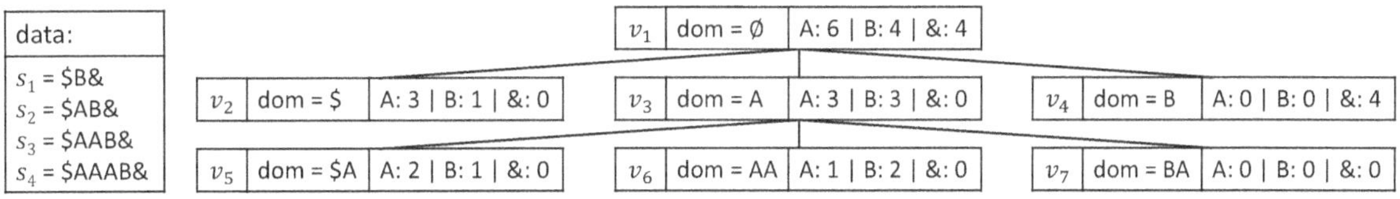

Figure 3: An illustration of a prediction suffix tree (PST).

4.1 Sequence Data and Markov Models

Given a finite alphabet $\mathcal{I}$, a *sequence* s of length l over $\mathcal{I}$ is an ordered list $x_1 x_2 \cdots x_l$, where each x_i ($i \in [1, l]$) is a symbol in $\mathcal{I}$. For convenience, we abuse notation and write $s = \$x_1 x_2 \cdots x_l \&$, where \$ and & are two special symbols that mark the beginning and the end of a sequence, respectively. Sequences are frequently used to represent user behavioral data, such as trajectories, web navigation traces, and product purchasing histories.

Markov models are a type of stochastic models commonly used to characterize sequence data. They assume the *Markov property* [44], i.e., a symbol x in a sequence s is decided by a few symbols that immediately proceeds x in s, but not any others. A Markov model over D is often represented as *prediction suffix tree (PST)* [3, 44], where each node v is associated with a *predictor string dom*(v), as well as a *prediction histogram hist*(v). In particular, *dom*(v) consists of symbols in $\mathcal{I} \cup \{\$\}$, while *hist*($v$) contains a count for each symbol x in $\mathcal{I} \cup \{\&\}$. The count, denoted as *hist*(v)[x], is computed as follows. We first inspect all occurrences of *dom*(v) in the sequences in D, and count the number y of occurrences when *dom*(v) is immediately followed by the symbol x; after that, we set *hist*(v)[x] $= y$. In other words, *hist*(v)[x] indicates how often an appearance of *dom*(v) would immediately lead to an appearance of x in a sequence.

For example, Figure 3 illustrates a PST constructed over a set D containing four sequences s_1, s_2, s_3, s_4, over an alphabet $\mathcal{I} = \{A, B\}$. The node v_6 has a predictor string *dom*(v_6) $= AA$, and prediction histogram *hist*(v_6) that contains a count for each element in $\{A, B, \&\}$. The counts in the histogram sum up to 3, since the string AA appears 3 times in D, i.e., once in s_3 and twice in s_4. In addition, *hist*(v_6)[A] $= 1$ because, among the 3 occurrences of AA, only one is immediately followed by A (i.e., the first occurrence of AA in s_4). The root node v_1 has an empty predictor string *dom*(v_1) $= \emptyset$, and its prediction histogram counts the occurrences of each individual symbol in $\mathcal{I} \cup \{\&\}$, e.g., *hist*(v_1)[A] $= 6$ since the symbol A appears 6 times in total in D.

The nodes in a PST are organized in such a way that each node v has $|\mathcal{I}| + 1$ children. Furthermore, for each child v' of v, *dom*(v') is obtained by adding a symbol in $\mathcal{I} \cup \{\$\}$ in the beginning of *dom*(v). That is, *dom*(v) is a suffix of *dom*(v'). For example, in the PST in Figure 3, v_3 is a parent of v_5; accordingly, *dom*(v_5) $= \$A$ is obtained by adding the symbol \$ to the beginning of *dom*(v_3) $= A$. The intuition here is that (i) each node v in a PST provides a way to predict the "next symbol" in a sequence based on a "predicate" *dom*(v), and (ii) when we split v, each child node would have a longer "predicate" that provides a more specific predication.

A PST $\mathcal{T}$ can be used to support a wide range of queries, such as estimating the number of times that a query string s_q appears in the sequences in D. Specifically, given $s_q = x_1 x_2 \dots x_l$, we first inspect the root node v_1's prediction histogram *hist*(v_1), and then initialize a temporary answer ans = *hist*(v_1)[x_1]. After that, we examine x_i ($i \in [2, l]$) in ascending order of i. For each x_i, we consider the length-($i - 1$) prefix of s_q, i.e., $s_i^* = x_1 x_2 \dots x_{i-1}$. We identify the node v in $\mathcal{T}$ whose predictor string is the longest suffix of s_i^*. Then, we compute the sum of the counts in v's prediction histogram *hist*(v), referred to as the *magnitude* of the histogram and denoted as $\|hist(v)\|_1$. After that, we set

$$ans = ans \cdot \frac{hist(v)[x_i]}{\|hist(v)\|_1}, \tag{12}$$

i.e., we multiple ans by the probability that the "next symbol" equals x_i, as predicted by *hist*(v). When all x_i ($i \in [1, l]$) are examined, we return ans as the query answer.

For example, consider a query sequence $s_q = AB$ on the PST in Figure 3. We first visit the root node v_1, and initialize ans = *hist*(v_1)[A] $= 6$. After that, we consider the length-1 prefix of s_q, i.e., $s_2^* = A$. We identify v_3 as the node whose predictor string is the longest suffix of s_2^*, and we set $ans = ans \cdot \frac{hist(v_3)[B]}{\|hist(v_3)\|_1} = 3$. Finally, we return $ans = 3$ as the answer.

In addition to the aforementioned query type, we can also utilize a PST $\mathcal{T}$ to generate a *synthetic sequence dataset*, by sampling sequences from $\mathcal{T}$ one by one. Specifically, to generate a sequence, we start from an initial sequence $s_0 = \$$ and insert symbols into s_0 iteratively. In the i-th iteration ($i \geq 1$), we inspect the sequence s_{i-1}, and identify the node v in $\mathcal{T}$ whose predictor string is the longest suffix of s_{i-1}. Then, we sample a symbol x_i from the symbol distribution represented by *hist*(v), i.e., $\Pr[x_i = x] = \frac{hist(v)[x]}{\|hist(v)\|_1}$. After that, we insert x_i to the end of s_{i-1}, and denote the resulting sequence as s_i. If x_i happens to be &, then we return s_i as the result.

4.2 Extension of PrivTree

To construct a PST $\mathcal{T}$ on a sequence dataset D, we can start from a root node v_1 with a predictor string *dom*(v_1) $= \emptyset$, and then recursively split v_1. This motivates us to adopt PrivTree for the generation of differentially private PSTs. However, we can no longer use a node v's noisy count $c(v)$ to decide whether v should be split, since $c(v)$ is undefined on a PST. Instead, as discussed in Section 3.5, we can redefine $c(v)$ as a score function that measures the suitability of v for splitting. In the non-private setting, existing work [44] typically avoids splitting a node v if any of the following conditions is satisfied:

C1. *dom*(v) *starts with* \$. In this case, no more symbol can be added to the beginning of *dom*(v); thus, v cannot be split.

C2. *The magnitude of hist*(v) *is small.* The rationale is that, when $\|hist(v)\|_1$ is small, further splitting v results in child nodes v' whose prediction histograms *hist*(v') have even smaller magnitudes. In that case, the symbol distribution captured by *hist*(v') is obtained from a tiny sample set of sequences, which leads to poor prediction accuracy.

C3. *The entropy*[1] *of hist*(v) *is small.* This is because when *hist*(v) has a small entropy, there is little uncertainty in the symbol prediction given by *hist*(v); as such, there is little benefit in splitting v. (See v_4 in Figure 3 for an example.)

Suppose that we are to adopt the above conditions into PrivTree.

[1]Here we treat *hist*(v) as a probability distribution.

Condition C1 can be straightforwardly applied, since it only depends on $dom(v)$ and does not rely on D, i.e., it does not leak private information. In contrast, conditions C2 and C3 cannot be directly adopted since the counts in $hist(v)$ depend on D. To address this issue, we aim to design a score function $c(\cdot)$ for PrivTree with the following two properties:

P1. $c(\cdot)$ is monotonic, i.e., $c(v) \leq c(u)$ for any node v and its parent u. This, as discussed in Section 3.5, is required to ensure that PrivTree satisfies differential privacy.

P2. If a node v's prediction histogram has a small magnitude or a small entropy, then $c(v)$ tends to be small. This is motivated by conditions C2 and C3 mentioned above.

Our construction of $c(\cdot)$ is based on the following observation: if a prediction histogram has a small entropy, it often has one symbol count that dominates the others, because a small entropy implies that the distribution of symbols in the histogram is skewed. (v_4 in Figure 3 shows an example.) Motivated by this, we define $c(v)$ as

$$c(v) = \|hist(v)\|_1 - \max_{x \in \mathcal{I} \cup \{\&\}} hist(v)[x], \tag{13}$$

i.e., $c(v)$ equals the magnitude of $hist(v)$ minus the largest count in $hist(v)$. The intuition is that if the magnitude of $hist(v)$ is small, then $c(v)$ must be small, regardless of the largest count in $hist(v)$; on the other hand, if the entropy of $hist(v)$ is small, then the largest count in $hist(v)$ tends to be close to the magnitude of $hist(v)$ (since the count often dominates all other counts in $hist(v)$), which results in a small $c(v)$ as well. Thus, $c(v)$ fulfills property P2. The following lemma show that $c(v)$ also satisfies property P1.

LEMMA 4.1. *$c(\cdot)$ is a monotonic function.*

In summary, we can construct a private PST on a sequence dataset D using PrivTree (i.e., Algorithm 2), with three minor changes. First, in Line 1 of Algorithm 2, $\mathcal{T}$ is a PST with a fanout $|\mathcal{I}|+1$ (instead of a quadtree), and v_1 is a PST node with a predictor string $dom(v_1) = \emptyset$ and a prediction histogram $hist(v_1)$. Second, in Line 5, $c(v)$ is as defined in Equation (13). Third, in Line 11, we return $\mathcal{T}$ after removing the biased score $\hat{b}(v)$ and the prediction histogram $hist(v)$ of each node v.

After we obtained the PST $\mathcal{T}$ (without prediction histograms) from the modified PrivTree, we can postprocess $\mathcal{T}$ to recover the prediction histograms. Specifically, for each leaf node v in $\mathcal{T}$, we derive the prediction histogram $hist(v)$ from D, and then compute a noisy version of $hist(v)$, denoted as $\widehat{hist}(v)$, by adding Laplace noise into each histogram count. After that, for any non-leaf node v', we construct a noisy prediction $\widehat{hist}(v')$, such that for any symbol $x \in \mathcal{I} \cup \{\&\}$,

$$\widehat{hist}(v')[x] = \sum_{v \text{ is a leaf node under } v'} \widehat{hist}(v)[x].$$

Finally, if any noisy histogram in $\mathcal{T}$ has a negative count, we reset the count to zero. This is to ensure that each histogram represents a distribution of symbols.

Privacy Analysis and Parameterization. To analyze the privacy guarantee of the modified PrivTree, we first introduce an assumption that is also adopted in prior work [6] on sequence data publication under differential privacy: we assume that the length of each sequence in D, when taking into account & but not \$, is at most $l^\top$, where $l^\top$ is a known constant. To explain why this assumption is needed, consider that we insert an *infinite* sequence s into D to obtain a neighboring dataset D'. In that case, the insertion of s incurs unbounded changes in the histogram counts of the PST, which makes it impossible to achieve differential privacy. In general, if $l^\top$ is unknown, we may choose an appropriate $l^\top$ and *truncate* any sequences s that is excessively long[2]. Specifically, if $s = \$x_1x_2 \ldots x_{l^\top}\&$, then we truncate it to $s = \$x_1x_2 \ldots x_{l^\top}$, i.e., s becomes an open-ended sequence. Note that the removal of & from s does not affect the construction of the PST.

Given the above assumption, we prove the privacy guarantee of the modified PrivTree as follows.

THEOREM 4.1. *Let $\beta = |\mathcal{I}|+1$. The modified PrivTree ensures ε-differential privacy when $\lambda \geq \frac{2\beta-1}{\beta-1} \cdot \frac{l^\top}{\varepsilon}$ and $\delta = \lambda \cdot \ln \beta$.*

In addition, we prove that the postprocessing of PrivTree's output (i.e., adding Laplace noise to the histogram counts of the leaf nodes) also achieves ε-differential privacy.

THEOREM 4.2. *Postprocessing PrivTree's output with Laplace noise of scale λ achieves ε-differential privacy, when $\lambda \geq \frac{l^\top}{\varepsilon}$.*

Finally, we clarify how we set θ and divide the privacy budget ε between PrivTree and its postprocessing step. First, we set $\theta = 0$, following our analysis in Section 3.4. Second, we set the noise scale in PrivTree and its postprocessing step, such that PrivTree achieves $\frac{\varepsilon}{\beta}$-differential privacy and the postprocessing procedure ensures $\frac{\varepsilon \cdot (\beta-1)}{\beta}$-differential privacy. To explain, recall that in PrivTree, we inject Laplace noise into each node v's score $c(v)$, which equals the sum of $\beta - 1$ counts in v's prediction histogram $hist(v)$ (i.e., all counts except the largest one). Meanwhile, in the postprocessing step, we add Laplace noise to each count y in the prediction histograms of $\mathcal{T}$'s leaf nodes. Intuitively, $c(v)$ is roughly $\beta - 1$ times more resilient to noise than y. Therefore, we set the privacy budget for the postprocessing step to be $\beta - 1$ times the budget for PrivTree, so as to balance the relative accuracy of $c(v)$ and y after noise injection.

4.3 Comparison with Previous Work

There exist two differentially private methods [6, 7] for modeling sequence data, and they both utilize hierarchical decompositions for model construction. However, they considerably differ from PrivTree in three aspects. First, they model sequences based on their prefixes [7] or n-grams [6], while PrivTree is based on a PST representation of the *variable length Markov chain model* [44]. Second, their algorithms for hierarchical decompositions are similar in spirit to Algorithm 1, due to which they also require a predefined threshold h on the maximum height of the decomposition tree. Consequently, they suffer from similar deficiencies to those of Algorithm 1, i.e., they cannot generate accurate models because of the dependency on h. Third, when constructing a decomposition tree, the methods in [6, 7] decide whether a node be split based only on a count associated with the node, whereas PrivTree adopts a more advanced strategy that takes into account three conditions commonly considered in the non-private setting. The above differences make PrivTree an effective approach for modeling sequence data, as we demonstrate in our experiments in Section 6.

5. CONNECTIONS TO SVT

In this section, we investigate the connection between PrivTree and the *sparse vector techniques (SVTs)* [18, 21, 28], which are a type of differentially private algorithms widely adopted in the literature. They take as input a sequence of queries and a threshold

[2] Such $l^\top$ can be chosen by first identifying the 90% or 95% quantile of the sequence lengths in D, and then computing a differentially private version of the quantile [54].

Algorithm 3: BinarySVT $(D, Q = \{q_1, q_2, \ldots\}, \theta, \lambda)$

```
1 compute a noisy version of θ:  θ̂ = θ + Lap(λ);
2 for i = 1, 2, ... do
3     compute a noisy version of q_i(D):  q̂_i(D) = q_i(D) + Lap(λ);
4     if q̂_i(D) > θ̂ then
5         output o_i = 1 and continue;
6     else
7         output o_i = 0 and continue;
8 return
```

θ, and output either a set of queries whose results are likely to be larger than θ [18, 28], or a noisy version of the answers for such a query set [21]. Intuitively, SVTs are similar in spirit to PrivTree since they both aim to identify some elements in a set (e.g., a node set or a query set) with "scores" above a given threshold. Motivated by this, in the following, we examine whether SVTs can be adopted for the hierarchical decomposition problem. Among the three existing variants of SVTs [18,21,28] that satisfy ε-differential privacy[3], we will focus on a variant dubbed *the binary SVT*, as it is most relevant to our problem. Interested readers are referred to the technical report of this paper for discussions on the other two variants.

Algorithm 3 presents a generic version of the binary SVT. Its input includes (i) a dataset D, (ii) a sequence $Q = \{q_1, q_2, \ldots\}$ of queries such that each q_i has sensitivity 1, (iii) a threshold θ, and (iv) a noise scale λ. Its output is a sequence of binary variables $\{o_1, o_2, \ldots\}$, such that $o_i = 1$ indicates that the result of q_i is larger than θ, and $o_i = 0$ indicates otherwise. The algorithm is fairly simple. It first computes a noisy threshold $\hat{\theta} = \theta + Lap(\lambda)$, and then, for each query q_i in the sequence, it generates a noisy query answer $\hat{q}_i(D)$ using Laplace noise of scale λ (Line 1-3). If $\hat{q}_i(D) > \theta$, then algorithm outputs $o_i = 1$; otherwise, the algorithm outputs $o_i = 0$ (Line 4-7). Previous work [28] makes the following claim about the privacy assurance of the algorithm:

CLAIM 1. *Algorithm 3 ensures ε-differential privacy if $\lambda \geq \frac{2}{\varepsilon}$.*

In other words, the noise scale required by the algorithm is $\Theta(\frac{1}{\varepsilon})$ and independent of the number of queries.

If Claim 1 holds, Algorithm 3 could yield highly competitive solutions for the problems that we consider. For example, consider the spatial decomposition problem studied in Section 3. Given a threshold θ and a set D of spatial points in a multi-dimensional space Ω, we first initialize (i) a quadtree $\mathcal{T}$ containing only a root node v_1 with $dom(v_1) = \Omega$, and (ii) a query sequence $Q = \{c(v_1)\}$, i.e., Q contains only one query that asks the number of points in $dom(v_1)$ (we will dynamically append queries to Q during the construction of the quadtree). After the initialization, we invoke the binary SVT to inspect each query in Q one by one; if the binary SVT outputs 1 for a query $c(v)$, then we split the node v in $\mathcal{T}$, and append a query $c(v')$ to the end of Q for each child node v' of v. When all queries in Q are inspected, we return the quadtree $\mathcal{T}$ obtained. By Claim 1, $\mathcal{T}$ ensures ε-differential privacy, as long as the binary SVT uses Laplace noise of scale $\lambda \geq \frac{2}{\varepsilon}$ when generating the noisy versions of $c(v_i)$. In contrast, PrivTree requires injecting Laplace noise of scale $\lambda \geq \frac{2\beta-1}{\beta-1} \cdot \frac{1}{\varepsilon} > \frac{2}{\varepsilon}$, which indicates that the solution based on the binary SVT is more favorable.

Unfortunately, we show that Claim 1 does not hold: in the worst case, Algorithm 3 requires $\lambda = \Omega(\frac{k}{\varepsilon})$ to achieve ε-differential privacy, where k denotes the number of queries.

[3]There exist other variants of SVT that satisfy a relaxed version of ε-differential privacy [23]. We do not consider those variants.

LEMMA 5.1. *There exists a sequence Q of k count queries for which Algorithm 3 violates ε-differential privacy if $\lambda \leq \frac{k}{4\varepsilon}$.*

Lemma 5.1 invalidates all solutions based on the binary SVT, including those in previous work [9,28,34]. In concurrent work [11], Chen and Machanavajjhala present a similar analysis on the binary SVT, and also come to the conclusion that it is not differentially private. In the full version of this paper[4], we discuss the other two variants of SVT [18,21], and show that one of them [21] also violates differential privacy, while the other [18] does not yield a competitive solution for our problem (even after we improve it with an optimization that leads to better data utility).

6. EXPERIMENTS

This section evaluates PrivTree against the states of the art on differentially private modelling of spatial and sequence data.

6.1 Experiments on Spatial Data

Datasets. We make use of four real spatial datasets shown in Table 2: road [12, 41], where each point represents the latitude and longitude of a road junction in the states of Washington and New Mexico; Gowalla [41,48], which contains check-in locations shared by users on a location-based social networking website; NYC[5] and Beijing[6], which are 4-dimensional datasets that record the pickup and drop-off locations of NYC and Beijing taxis, respectively. Figure 4 visualizes the points in road and gowalla, as well as the pickup locations in NYC and Beijing. Observe that the data distribution in road (resp. NYC) is more skewed than that in Gowalla (resp. Beijing).

Methods. We compare PrivTree against five state-of-the-art methods: UG [41, 42, 48], AG [41], Hierarchy [42], DAWA [30], and Privelet* [50]. UG partitions the data domain into m^d grid cells of equal size, and releases a noisy count for each cell, with $m = (n\varepsilon/10)^{2/(d+2)}$ [48]. AG is an improved version of UG that is specifically designed for two-dimensional data. It first employs a coarsened version of UG to produce a set of grid cells; after that, for each cell whose noisy count is above a threshold, AG further splits it into smaller cells and releases their noisy counts. Hierarchy utilizes a multi-level decomposition tree to generate spatial histograms, with the tree height and fanout heuristically chosen to minimize the mean squared error in answering range count queries. DAWA requires as input a workload of range count queries, and it employs the *matrix mechanism* [31] to generate a histogram that is optimized for the given workload. Privelet* publishes multi-dimensional datasets by utilizing the Haar wavelet transformation to reduce the errors of range count queries.

DAWA and Privelet* both require that the input data should have a discrete domain. Following [30], we discretize the domain of each dataset into a uniform grid with 2^{20} cells before feeding it to DAWA and Privelet*. The other parameters of each method (e.g., the height and fanout of the decomposition tree, and the grid granularity) are set as suggested in the original papers. For PrivTree, we set its fanout to 4 (resp. 16) for two-dimensional (resp. four-dimensional) datasets, which is standard for quadtrees.

We adopt the implementations of DAWA and Privelet* provided by their respective authors, and we implement all other methods in C++. All experiments are conducted on a windows/linux machine with a 2.4GHz CPU and 16GB main memory.

[4]http://arxiv.org/abs/1601.03229
[5]http://publish.illinois.edu/dbwork/open-data/
[6]http://research.microsoft.com/apps/pubs/?id=152883

Table 2: Characteristics of spatial datasets.

Name	Dimensionality d	Cardinality n	Description
road	2	$1,634,165$	Coordinates of road intersections in the states of Washington and New Mexico
Gowalla	2	$107,091$	Check-in locations shared by users of a location-based social networking website
NYC	4	$98,013$	Pickup and drop-off locations of NYC taxis
Beijing	4	$30,000$	Pickup and drop-off locations of Beijing taxis

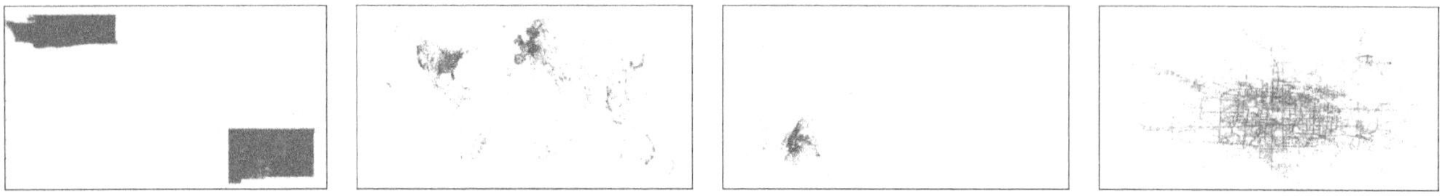

(a) road (b) Gowalla (c) NYC - pickup (d) Beijing - pickup

Figure 4: Visualization of datasets

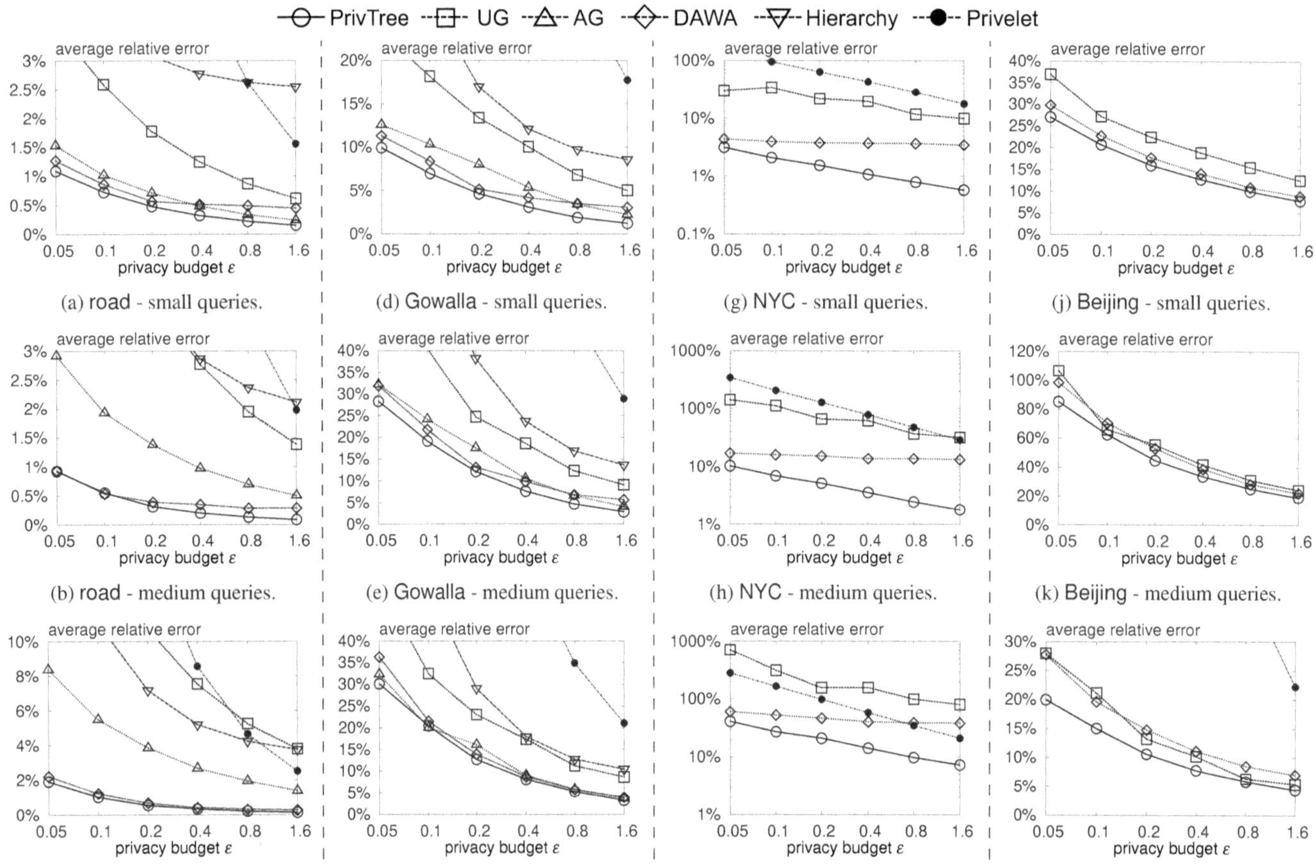

(a) road - small queries. (d) Gowalla - small queries. (g) NYC - small queries. (j) Beijing - small queries.

(b) road - medium queries. (e) Gowalla - medium queries. (h) NYC - medium queries. (k) Beijing - medium queries.

(c) road - large queries. (f) Gowalla - large queries. (i) NYC - large queries. (l) Beijing - large queries.

Figure 5: Results of range count queries on spatial datasets.

Tasks. We apply each method to create private synopses of every dataset, and we evaluate the quality of each decomposition by the accuracy of its answers to range count queries. In particular, we construct three query sets on each dataset: *small*, *medium*, and *large*, each of which contains $10,000$ randomly generated range count queries. Each query in the small, medium, and large set has a region that cover $[0.01\%, 0.1\%)$, $[0.1\%, 1\%)$, and $[1\%, 10\%)$ of the data domain, respectively. Following prior work [12, 41], we measure accuracy of an answer $\hat{q}(D)$ to a query q by its *relative error*, defined as

$$RE\left(\hat{q}(D)\right) = \frac{|\hat{q}(D) - q(D)|}{\max\left\{q(D), \Delta\right\}}.$$

where Δ is a smoothing factor set to 0.1% of the dataset cardinality n [41,50]. We repeat each experiment 100 times, and report the average relative error of each method for each query set. For DAWA (which is *query-dependent*), we allow it to generate a synopsis for each query set separately, based on a sample set of 500 queries.

Results. Figure 5 illustrates the average relative error of each method on each dataset as a function of the privacy budget ε. On road, PrivTree significantly outperforms UG, AG, Hierarchy, and

Table 3: Characteristics of sequence datasets.

Name	$\lvert\mathcal{I}\rvert$	Cardinality	Avg. sequence length	Description	$l^{\top}$	# of sequences with length $> l^{\top}$
mooc	7	80,362	13.46	Users' behavior sequences on a MOOC website	50	3,653
msnbc	17	989,818	4.75	Users' web navigation histories on a news portal	20	31,606

Privelet*, regardless of the query set used and the value of ε. In particular, on the large query set, the average relative error of PrivTree is at most $\frac{1}{4}$ (resp. $\frac{1}{10}$) of the error of AG (resp. UG and Hierarchy). This demonstrates the effectiveness of PrivTree in approximating the distribution of the input data. Meanwhile, AG is superior to UG and Hierarchy in all cases, which is consistent with the results in previous work [41]. DAWA is the only method that comes close to PrivTree, but its relative error is never smaller than that of PrivTree, and is 2 to 3 times higher than the latter for the small and medium query sets on road (resp. small query set on Gowalla) when $\varepsilon \geq 0.8$. Furthermore, we note that DAWA is given a sample query set in advance to optimize its query performance, whereas PrivTree is not given such an advantage.

On Gowalla, PrivTree still consistently achieves the best results, but the performance gaps between PrivTree and the other methods are reduced. The reason is that the data distribution in Gowalla is less skewed than that of road (see Figure 4), which makes Gowalla easier to dealt with for all methods. DAWA incurs relatively small errors in all cases, but is noticeably inferior to PrivTree on the small and medium query sets.

On NYC and Beijing, we omit AG and Hierarchy since (i) AG is only applicable on two-dimensional data, and (ii) when applied on a four-dimensional dataset, Hierarchy produces a decomposition tree with at least 2.18 billion leaf nodes [42], which cannot fit in the main memory of our machine. As shown in Figures 5g-5l, PrivTree consistently outperforms all other methods by a large margin on the highly skewed NYC, because its tree construction mechanism enables it to effectively adapt to the skewness of the data, by growing the tree tall (resp. short) in the dense (resp. sparse) regions of the data. On the other hand, on the less skewed Beijing, the accuracies of UG and DAWA are considerably improved. Nevertheless, PrivTree still incurs smaller query errors in all settings. One may notice that the error of DAWA on NYC only decreases around 2 times when ε increases from 0.05 to 1.6. We find that it is caused by a "private partitioning" step of DAWA [30], as well as the discretization of data domain Ω that it requires.

In summary, PrivTree provides better data utility than all baselines, especially when the input dataset follows a skewed distribution. This makes PrivTree a more favorable approach for releasing spatial data under differential privacy.

6.2 Experiments on Sequence Data

Datasets. We use two real sequence datasets: mooc[7] and msnbc [1, 6]. mooc contains 80,362 learners' behavior sequences on a MOOC platform, and the behaviors are divided into seven categories: working on assignments, watching videos, accessing other course objects, accessing the course wiki, accessing the course forum, navigating to other part of course, and closing the web page. msnbc consists of 989,818 sequences of URL categories, each of which corresponds to a user's browsing history during a 24-hour period on *msnbc.com*. Table 3 shows the key statistics of mooc and msnbc. Note that the total number $|\mathcal{I}|$ of symbols in mooc (resp. msnbc) is not excessively large. Otherwise (e.g., when $|\mathcal{I}| > 1000$), the domain of the sequence data would be extremely sparse, in which case it is enormously difficult to publish useful information under differential privacy.

[7] https://www.kddcup2015.com/

Tasks. We consider two analytical tasks on each sequence dataset D. The first task is to identify the top-k frequent strings in D, i.e., the k strings that appear the largest number of times in the sequences in D. This task is an important primitive in sequence data mining [20], and is also considered in existing work [6] on sequence data publishing. Following previous work [6], we measure the *precision* of the top-k strings returned by differentially private algorithm, i.e.,

$$\text{precision} = \frac{|K(D) \cap \mathcal{A}(D)|}{k},$$

where $K(D)$ is the exact set of top-k frequent strings in D, and $\mathcal{A}(D)$ is the set returned by algorithm $\mathcal{A}$.

The second task is to approximate the distribution of sequence lengths in D. In particular, we apply PrivTree and other existing methods to generate synthetic sequence data from D. Then, we compare the distribution of sequence lengths in the synthetic data with that in D, and we measure their *total variation distance* [13], i.e., half of the L_1 distance between the two probability distributions. For each task, we repeat each experiment 100 times and report the average measurements.

Methods. For the task of top-k frequent string mining, we compare PrivTree against two differentially private techniques: N-gram [6] and EM [38]. In particular, N-gram is the state-of-the-art solution for sequence data publishing, and it is based on a variable-length n-gram model. N-gram requires a pre-defined threshold n_{max} on the maximum length of n-grams; we set $n_{max} = 5$, as suggested in [6]. Meanwhile, EM is a standard application of the exponential mechanism [38] in our context. It first initializes a set R that contains $|\mathcal{I}|$ string of length 1, each of which consists of a unique symbol in $\mathcal{I}$. After that, it invokes the exponential mechanism k times. In each invocation, it selects the most frequent string r from R with differential privacy, and then replaces r in R with $|\mathcal{I}|$ strings, each of which is obtained by adding a symbol to the end of r. The k strings obtained are then returned as the result. For the task of approximating sequence length distributions, we omit EM since it is inapplicable.

Note that PrivTree, N-gram, and EM all require that the maximum sequence length in the input data is bounded by a constant $l^{\top}$ that is not excessively large (see Section 4.2 for a discussion on the necessity of $l^{\top}$). Following previous work [6], we set $l^{\top}$ to be roughly the 95% quantile of the sequence lengths in the input data, i.e., only around 5% sequences are truncated (see Table 3). To illustrate the effects of truncation, we also include in our experiments a baseline approach dubbed *Truncate*. This approach directly answers all queries on the truncated dataset, without any privacy assurance.

Results. Figure 6 shows the precision of each method (for top-k string mining) as a function of the privacy budget ε. The precision of Truncate remains unchanged for all ε, since it does not enforce differential privacy. Among the differentially private methods, PrivTree consistently outperforms N-gram and EM, in most cases by a large margin. Furthermore, in Figure 6d-6f, PrivTree has

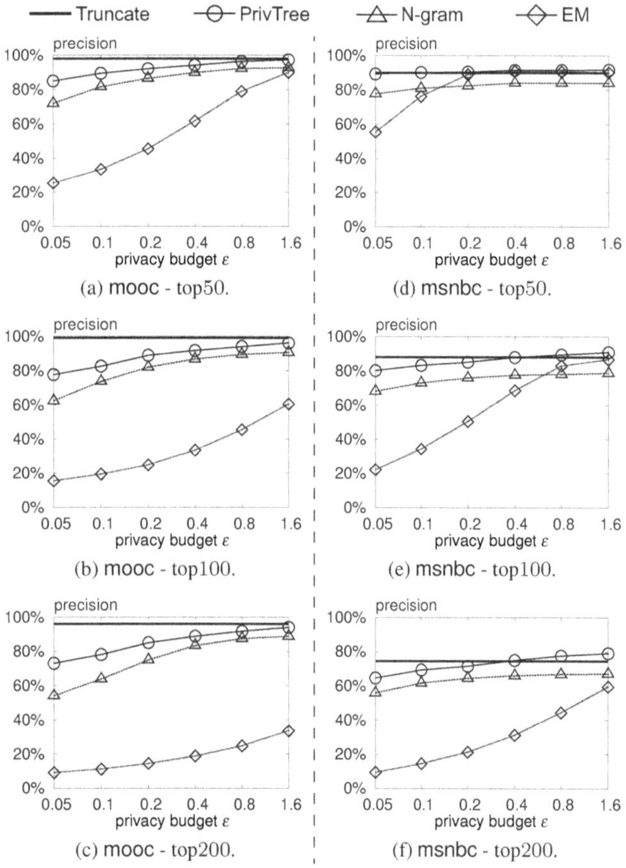

Figure 6: Results of top-k frequent string mining.

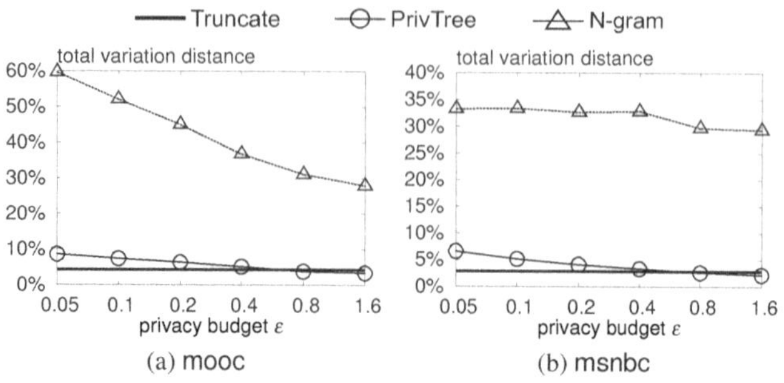

Figure 7: Errors of sequence length distributions.

an even higher precision than Truncate when $\varepsilon \geq 0.8$. The reason is that the Markov model adopted by PrivTree is able to *recover* some information that is lost due to the truncation of sequences. For example, suppose that the string aa appears in 5 sequences in a dataset D and, in each appearance, it is immediately followed by a symbol b. Assume that one of those 5 sequences (denoted as s) is truncated, and its suffix aab becomes aa after the truncation. In that case, the Markov model can be used able to accurately recover the truncated symbol of s, because, based on the truncated data, it would predict that the "next symbol" after aa is always b. Intuitively, such recovering of information is more effective when the amount of noise in the Markov model is small, which explains why PrivTree outperforms Truncate only when ε is large. In contrast, N-gram never outperforms Truncate, and its precision is lower than that of PrivTree by more than 10% in most settings. In addition, EM yields unattractive precision in almost all cases. Its accuracy degrades with the increases of k, since a larger k requires it to inject more noise into the selection procession of top-k frequent strings.

In the last set of experiments, we evaluate the accuracy of the sequence length distribution in the synthetic sequence data generated by each method. Figure 7 illustrates the total variation distance of each sequence length distribution. Observe that PrivTree incurs a small error comparable to that of Truncate, especially when $\varepsilon \geq 0.2$. In contrast, N-gram entails an enormous error in all cases. Based on the results in Figures 6 and 7, we conclude that PrivTree is a more preferable solution than N-gram to modeling sequential data under ε-differential privacy.

7. ADDITIONAL RELATED WORK

In Sections 3.1, 4.3, and 6, we have introduced the states-of-the-art solutions [6, 12, 30, 41, 42, 48, 50] for publishing spatial and sequence data under differential privacy. Besides those solutions, there are a few other methods for private modeling of spatial and sequence data. In particular, Xiao et al. [51] present a spatial decomposition algorithm based on the k-d tree [4]. It first imposes a uniform grid over the data domain, and then construct a private k-d tree over the cells in the grid. This method, however, is shown to be inferior to the UG and AG methods tested in our experiments, in terms of data utility [41]. Chen et al. [7] consider the publication of sequence data under differential privacy, and propose an algorithm that releases a prefix tree of sequences to support count queries and frequent string mining. Nevertheless, subsequent work by Chen et al. [6] shows that the prefix-based method is considerably outperformed by the N-gram approach in our experiment.

In addition, there is a long line of research on processing aggregate queries in a differentially private manner. Specifically, Barak et al. [2] investigate the publication of *marginals* (i.e., projections of a dataset on subsets of its dimensions), and propose a solution based on the Fourier transform. Ding et al. [15] publish multiple data cubes with both privacy and consistency guarantees. The *matrix mechanism* of Li and Miklau [32, 33] and follow-up approaches [22, 30, 52, 53] take into account a query workload, and aim to release a version of the data that maximizes the overall accuracy of the workload. DAWA [30] is the most advanced method among these approaches, but as shown in our experiments, it is outperformed by PrivTree in terms of the relative errors of range count queries on spatial data.

Moreover, there exists extensive work that addresses numerous other tasks under differential privacy, such as regressions [5, 27, 40, 47, 55, 57], clusterings [48], decision trees [19], recommendation systems [37], time-series data analysis [43], combinatorial optimizations [49], frequent itemset mining [35], and graph queries [10, 26, 36, 56]. Finally, recent research has also studied the adoption of differential privacy in various systems [8, 39, 45].

8. CONCLUDING REMARKS

In this paper, we study the problem of hierarchical decomposition under differential privacy, and address the central dilemma of choosing the maximum height h of the decomposition tree. We show that the constraint on h can be removed by introducing a carefully controlled bias in deciding when a node should be split. Based on this result, we propose PrivTree, a general approach for hierarchical decomposition on private data, and we showcase its applications on spatial and sequence data release. Our experimental results demonstrate that PrivTree significantly outperforms the states of the art in terms of data utility. For future work, we plan to extend the idea behind PrivTree to other problems that are based on a lattice-model instead of a tree-model, such as frequent itemset mining.

Acknowledgments

Xiaokui Xiao was supported by grant ARC19/14 from MOE, Singapore and gifts from MSRA and AT&T.

9. REFERENCES

[1] K. Bache and M. Lichman. UCI machine learning repository, 2013.

[2] B. Barak, K. Chaudhuri, C. Dwork, S. Kale, F. McSherry, and K. Talwar. Privacy, accuracy, and consistency too: a holistic solution to contingency table release. In *PODS*, pages 273–282, 2007.

[3] R. Begleiter, R. El-Yaniv, and G. Yona. On prediction using variable order markov models. *Journal of Artificial Intelligence Research*, pages 385–421, 2004.

[4] J. L. Bentley. Multidimensional binary search trees used for associative searching. *Commun. ACM*, 18(9):509–517, 1975.

[5] K. Chaudhuri, C. Monteleoni, and A. D. Sarwate. Differentially private empirical risk minimization. *Journal of Machine Learning Research*, 12:1069–1109, 2011.

[6] R. Chen, G. Acs, and C. Castelluccia. Differentially private sequential data publication via variable-length n-grams. In *CCS*, pages 638–649, 2012.

[7] R. Chen, B. Fung, B. C. Desai, and N. M. Sossou. Differentially private transit data publication: a case study on the montreal transportation system. In *SIGKDD*, pages 213–221. ACM, 2012.

[8] R. Chen, A. Reznichenko, P. Francis, and J. Gehrke. Towards statistical queries over distributed private user data. In *NSDI*, pages 169–182, 2012.

[9] R. Chen, Q. Xiao, Y. Zhang, and J. Xu. Differentially private high-dimensional data publication via sampling-based inference. In *SIGKDD*. ACM, 2015.

[10] S. Chen and S. Zhou. Recursive mechanism: Towards node differential privacy and unrestricted joins. In *SIGMOD*, pages 653–664, 2013.

[11] Y. Chen and A. Machanavajjhala. On the privacy properties of variants on the sparse vector technique. *CoRR*, abs/1508.07306, 2015.

[12] G. Cormode, C. M. Procopiuc, E. Shen, D. Srivastava, and T. Yu. Differentially private spatial decompositions. In *ICDE*, 2012.

[13] A. B. Cybakov. *Introduction to nonparametric estimation*. Springer, 2009.

[14] M. De Berg, M. Van Kreveld, M. Overmars, and O. C. Schwarzkopf. *Computational geometry*. Springer, 2000.

[15] B. Ding, M. Winslett, J. Han, and Z. Li. Differentially private data cubes: optimizing noise sources and consistency. In *SIGMOD*, pages 217–228, 2011.

[16] C. Dwork. Differential privacy. In *ICALP*, pages 1–12, 2006.

[17] C. Dwork, F. McSherry, K. Nissim, and A. Smith. Calibrating noise to sensitivity in private data analysis. In *TCC*, pages 265–284, 2006.

[18] C. Dwork and A. Roth. The algorithmic foundations of differential privacy. *Theoretical Computer Science*, 9(3-4):211–407, 2013.

[19] A. Friedman and A. Schuster. Data mining with differential privacy. In *KDD*, pages 493–502, 2010.

[20] J. Han, M. Kamber, and J. Pei. *Data mining: concepts and techniques: concepts and techniques*. Elsevier, 2011.

[21] M. Hardt. *A study of privacy and fairness in sensitive data analysis*. PhD thesis, Princeton University, 2011.

[22] M. Hardt, K. Ligett, and F. McSherry. A simple and practical algorithm for differentially private data release. In *NIPS*, pages 2348–2356, 2012.

[23] M. Hardt and G. N. Rothblum. A multiplicative weights mechanism for privacy-preserving data analysis. In *FOCS*, pages 61–70, 2010.

[24] M. Hardt and K. Talwar. On the geometry of differential privacy. In *STOC*, pages 705–714. ACM, 2010.

[25] M. Hay, V. Rastogi, G. Miklau, and D. Suciu. Boosting the accuracy of differentially private histograms through consistency. *PVLDB*, 3(1):1021–1032, 2010.

[26] V. Karwa, S. Raskhodnikova, A. Smith, and G. Yaroslavtsev. Private analysis of graph structure. *TODS*, 39(3):22, 2014.

[27] D. Kifer, A. D. Smith, and A. Thakurta. Private convex optimization for empirical risk minimization with applications to high-dimensional regression. *Journal of Machine Learning Research - Proceedings Track*, 23:25.1–25.40, 2012.

[28] J. Lee and C. W. Clifton. Top-k frequent itemsets via differentially private fp-trees. In *SIGKDD*, pages 931–940. ACM, 2014.

[29] J. Lei. Differentially private m-estimators. In *NIPS*, 2011.

[30] C. Li, M. Hay, G. Miklau, and Y. Wang. A data-and workload-aware algorithm for range queries under differential privacy. *PVLDB*, 7(5):341–352, 2014.

[31] C. Li, M. Hay, V. Rastogi, G. Miklau, and A. McGregor. Optimizing linear counting queries under differential privacy. In *PODS*, pages 123–134, 2010.

[32] C. Li and G. Miklau. An adaptive mechanism for accurate query answering under differential privacy. *PVLDB*, 5(6):514–525, 2012.

[33] C. Li and G. Miklau. Optimal error of query sets under the differentially-private matrix mechanism. In *ICDT*, pages 272–283, 2013.

[34] H. Li, L. Xiong, X. Jiang, and J. Liu. Differentially private histogram publication for dynamic datasets: an adaptive sampling approach. In *CIKM*, pages 1001–1010, 2015.

[35] N. Li, W. Qardaji, D. Su, and J. Cao. Privbasis: Frequent itemset mining with differential privacy. *PVLDB*, 5(11):1340–1351, 2012.

[36] W. Lu and G. Miklau. Exponential random graph estimation under differential privacy. In *KDD*, pages 921–930, 2014.

[37] F. McSherry and I. Mironov. Differentially private recommender systems: Building privacy into the netflix prize contenders. In *KDD*, pages 627–636, 2009.

[38] F. McSherry and K. Talwar. Mechanism design via differential privacy. In *FOCS*, pages 94–103, 2007.

[39] A. Narayan and A. Haeberlen. Djoin: Differentially private join queries over distributed databases. In *OSDI*, pages 149–162, 2012.

[40] K. Nissim, S. Raskhodnikova, and A. Smith. Smooth sensitivity and sampling in private data analysis. In *STOC*, pages 75–84, 2007.

[41] W. Qardaji, W. Yang, and N. Li. Differentially private grids for geospatial data. In *ICDE*, pages 757–768, 2013.

[42] W. Qardaji, W. Yang, and N. Li. Understanding hierarchical methods for differentially private histograms. *PVLDB*, 6(14):1954–1965, 2013.

[43] V. Rastogi and S. Nath. Differentially private aggregation of distributed time-series with transformation and encryption. In *SIGMOD*, pages 735–746, 2010.

[44] D. Ron, Y. Singer, and N. Tishby. The power of amnesia: Learning probabilistic automata with variable memory length. *Machine learning*, 25(2-3):117–149, 1996.

[45] I. Roy, S. T. V. Setty, A. Kilzer, V. Shmatikov, and E. Witchel. Airavat: Security and privacy for mapreduce. In *SIGMOD*, pages 297–312, 2010.

[46] H. Samet. *Foundations of multidimensional and metric data structures*. Morgan Kaufmann, 2006.

[47] A. Smith. Privacy-preserving statistical estimation with optimal convergence rate. In *STOC*, 2011.

[48] D. Su, J. Cao, N. Li, E. Bertino, and H. Jin. Differentially private k-means clustering. *arXiv preprint arXiv:1504.05998*, 2015.

[49] K. Talwar, A. Gupta, K. Ligett, F. McSherry, and A. Roth. Differentially private combinatorial optimization. *SODA*, 2010.

[50] X. Xiao, G. Wang, and J. Gehrke. Differential privacy via wavelet transforms. *TKDE*, 23(8):1200–1214, 2011.

[51] Y. Xiao, L. Xiong, and C. Yuan. Differentially private data release through multidimensional partitioning. In *Secure Data Management*, pages 150–168. Springer, 2010.

[52] G. Yaroslavtsev, G. Cormode, C. M. Procopiuc, and D. Srivastava. Accurate and efficient private release of datacubes and contingency tables. In *ICDE*, pages 745–756, 2013.

[53] G. Yuan, Z. Zhang, M. Winslett, X. Xiao, Y. Yang, and Z. Hao. Low-rank mechanism: Optimizing batch queries under differential privacy. *PVLDB*, 5(11):1352–1363, 2012.

[54] C. Zeng, J. F. Naughton, and J.-Y. Cai. On differentially private frequent itemset mining. *PVLDB*, 6(1):25–36, 2012.

[55] J. Zhang, G. Cormode, C. M. Procopiuc, D. Srivastava, and X. Xiao. Privbayes: Private data release via bayesian networks. pages 1423–1434, 2014.

[56] J. Zhang, G. Cormode, C. M. Procopiuc, D. Srivastava, and X. Xiao. Private release of graph statistics using ladder functions. In *SIGMOD*, pages 731–745, 2015.

[57] J. Zhang, X. Xiao, Y. Yang, Z. Zhang, and M. Winslett. PrivGene: differentially private model fitting using genetic algorithms. In *SIGMOD*, pages 665–676, 2013.

APPENDIX

A. PROOFS

Proof of Lemma 3.1. By Equations (1) and (5), for any x,

$$\rho(x) = \ln\left(\frac{\int_{\theta-x}^{+\infty}\frac{1}{2\lambda}\exp\left(-\frac{|y|}{\lambda}\right)dy}{\int_{\theta+1-x}^{+\infty}\frac{1}{2\lambda}\exp\left(-\frac{|y|}{\lambda}\right)dy}\right) \le \frac{1}{\lambda}.$$

Recall that $\rho^{\top}(x) = 1/\lambda$ when $c(v) < \theta + 1$. Therefore, $\rho(x) \le \rho^{\top}(x)$ holds if $x < \theta + 1$.

Now consider that $x \ge \theta + 1$. In that case,

$$\rho(x) = \ln\left(\frac{1-\frac{1}{2}\exp\left(\frac{\theta-x}{\lambda}\right)}{1-\frac{1}{2}\exp\left(\frac{\theta+1-x}{\lambda}\right)}\right).$$

For convenience, we let $\alpha = \frac{1}{2}\exp\left(\frac{\theta+1-x}{\lambda}\right)$, and define a function f of α as follows:

$$\begin{aligned} f(\alpha) &= \rho(x) - \frac{1}{\lambda}\exp\left(\frac{\theta+1-x}{\lambda}\right) \\ &= \ln\left(\frac{1-\alpha e^{-1/\lambda}}{1-\alpha}\right) - \frac{2\alpha}{\lambda}. \end{aligned}$$

Observe that $\alpha \in (0, 1/2]$ whenever $x \ge \theta + 1$. Therefore, we can prove the lemma by showing that $f(\alpha) \le 0$ for all $\alpha \in (0, 1/2]$. For this purpose, we first compute the second derivative of f with respect to α:

$$f''(\alpha) \;=\; (e^{1/\lambda} - 1)\cdot\frac{e^{1/\lambda} + 1 - 2\alpha}{(1-\alpha)^2\cdot(e^{1/\lambda}-\alpha)^2}.$$

Given that $e^{1/\lambda} - 1 > 0$ and $e^{1/\lambda} + 1 - 2\alpha \ge e^{1/\lambda} > 0$, we have $f''(\alpha) > 0$. This indicates that $\max_{\alpha\in(0,1/2]} f(\alpha) = \max\{f(0), f(1/2)\}$. Meanwhile, $f(0) = 0$, and

$$\begin{aligned} f(1/2) &= \ln(2 - e^{-1/\lambda}) - \frac{1}{\lambda} \\ &= \ln\left(e^{1/\lambda} - \left(e^{1/2\lambda} - e^{-1/2\lambda}\right)^2\right) - \frac{1}{\lambda} \\ &< \ln(e^{1/\lambda}) - \frac{1}{\lambda} = 0. \end{aligned}$$

Therefore, $\max_{\alpha\in(0,1/2]} f(\alpha) \le 0$, which proves the lemma. □

Proof of Theorem 3.1. The theorem directly follows from the privacy analysis in Section 3.3. □

Proof of Lemma 3.2. Let V be the set of all possible nodes in a quadtree built on D. We divide the nodes in V into three subsets: (i) the set V_1 of nodes that appear as non-leaf nodes in $\mathcal{T}^*$, (ii) the set V_2 of the nodes that appear as leaves in $\mathcal{T}^*$, and (iii) the set V_3 of the nodes that do not appear in $\mathcal{T}^*$. Let $g(S)$ be the expected number of nodes in a set S that appear in $\mathcal{T}$. Then, we have

$$\begin{aligned} \mathbb{E}[|\mathcal{T}|] &= g(V_1) + g(V_2) + g(V_3) \\ &\le |V_1| + |V_2| + g(V_3) \;=\; |\mathcal{T}^*| + g(V_3). \end{aligned}$$

Therefore, the lemma can be proved by showing $g(V_3) \le |\mathcal{T}^*|$.

Observe that each node in V_3 must be the descendant of a node in V_2, i.e., a node that appears as a leaf in $\mathcal{T}^*$. Therefore, we can divide the nodes in V_3 into $|V_2|$ subsets, such that all nodes in the same subset are descendants of the same node in V_2. Consider any such subset S that corresponds to a node $v \in V_2$. Given that v appears as a leaf in $\mathcal{T}^*$, we have $c(v) \le \theta$. In addition, since $|\mathcal{T}^*| > 1$, $depth(v) \ge 1$ holds. Therefore,

$$c(v) - depth(v)\cdot\delta \;\le\; c(v) - \delta \;\le\; \theta - \delta.$$

By Equation (8), we have $b(v) = \theta - \delta$. Furthermore, for any $v' \in S$, we have $c(v') \le c(v)$, which also leads to $b(v') = \theta - \delta$. Therefore, v and v' have the same probability p_s to be split. Given $\delta = \lambda \cdot \ln\beta$, we have

$$\begin{aligned} p_s &= \Pr[\theta - \delta + Lap(\lambda) > \theta] \;=\; \Pr[Lap(\lambda) > \delta] \\ &= \int_{\lambda\cdot\ln\beta}^{\infty}\frac{1}{2\lambda}\exp\left(-\frac{|y|}{\lambda}\right)dy \;=\; \frac{1}{2\beta}. \end{aligned}$$

Assume that v appears in $\mathcal{T}$. Then, given that v is split with $\frac{1}{2\beta}$ probability, each child of v has $\frac{1}{2\beta}$ probability to appear in $\mathcal{T}$. Therefore, in expectation, the number of v's children that appear in $\mathcal{T}$ should equal $\beta\cdot\frac{1}{2\beta} = \frac{1}{2}$. In general, for any $i \ge 1$, there exist β^i nodes $v' \in S$ with $depth(v') - depth(v) = i$, and each such v' has $(\frac{1}{2\beta})^i$ probability to appear in $\mathcal{T}$. Hence, the expected number of nodes in S that appear in $\mathcal{T}$ is

$$g(S) \;=\; \sum_{i=1}^{+\infty}\beta^i\cdot\left(\frac{1}{2\beta}\right)^i \;=\; \sum_{i=1}^{+\infty}\frac{1}{2^i} \;=\; 1.$$

Since each S uniquely corresponds to a node in V_2, we have

$$g(V_3) \;=\; |V_2|\cdot g(S) \;= |V_2| \;\le\; |\mathcal{T}^*|.$$

Therefore, the lemma is proved. □

Proof of Corollary 1. The corollary follows from Theorem 3.1 when $\gamma = \ln\beta$. □

Proof of Lemma 4.1. Let u and v be two nodes in $\mathcal{T}$, such that u is the parent of v. Then, $hist(v)[x] \le hist(u)[x]$ holds for every symbol $x \in \mathcal{I}\cup\{\&\}$. Let x_v (resp. x_u) be the symbol that has the largest count in $hist(v)$ (resp. $hist(u)$). We have

$$\begin{aligned} c(v) &= \|hist(v)\|_1 - hist(v)[x_v] \;\le\; \|hist(v)\|_1 - hist(v)[x_u] \\ &= \sum_{x\neq x_u} hist(v)[x] \;\le\; \sum_{x\neq x_u} hist(u)[x] \\ &= \|hist(u)\|_1 - hist(u)[x_u] \;=\; c(u). \end{aligned}$$

Therefore, $c(\cdot)$ is monotonic. □

Proof of Theorem 4.1. Let D and D' be two neighboring datasets, such that D is obtained by inserting a sequence s into D'. Assume that $s = \$x_1\ldots x_l$, where $x_i \in I\cup\{\&\}$ for $i \in [1, l]$. To facilitate our proof, we define l datasets $D_1, D_2, \ldots, D_l$, such that $D_i = D'\cup\{s_i\}$ and $s_i = \$x_1x_2\ldots x_i$ is the length-i prefix of s ended at symbol x_i. Observe that $D_l = D$. For convenience, we define $D_0 = D'$.

In the following, we will prove that for any $i \in [1, l]$ and any output $\mathcal{T}$ of the modified PrivTree,

$$-\frac{\varepsilon}{l^{\top}} \;\le\; \ln\left(\frac{\Pr[D_i \to \mathcal{T}]}{\Pr[D_{i-1}\to\mathcal{T}]}\right) \;\le\; \frac{\varepsilon}{l^{\top}}, \tag{14}$$

where $\Pr[D_i \to \mathcal{T}]$ denotes the probability that PrivTree outputs $\mathcal{T}$ given D_i. This would prove the theorem because, given that $l \le l^\top$,

$$\ln\left(\frac{\Pr[D \to \mathcal{T}]}{\Pr[D' \to \mathcal{T}]}\right) = \sum_{i=1}^{l} \ln\left(\frac{\Pr[D_i \to \mathcal{T}]}{\Pr[D_{i-1} \to \mathcal{T}]}\right) \in [-\varepsilon, \varepsilon].$$

Observe that D_i can be obtained by appending a symbol x_i to the end of the sequence s_{i-1} in D_{i-1}. Therefore, when we change the input data from D_{i-1} to D_i, the only changes in the PST are the histogram counts that x_i contributes to. Observe that if x_i contributes to the prediction histogram $hist(v)$ of a node v, then $dom(v)$ must be a suffix of s_{i-1}, and the only possible change in $hist(v)$ is that $hist(v)[x_i]$ would be increased by one. Then, by the definition of the PST, all of those nodes v should form a path from the root of the PST to a leaf. In addition, by Equation (13), the score $c(v)$ of each of those nodes v is changed by at most one. In that case, we can prove Equation (14) by reusing the analysis in the proof of Theorem 3.1.

To explain, recall that the correctness of Theorem 3.1 only replies on two conditions. First, the score $c(v)$ of each node v is monotonic. Second, when we change the input data, all of the nodes affected should form a path from the root of the decomposition tree to a leaf, and the score of each of those nodes should change by at most one. Notice that all three conditions are satisfied when we change the input of the modified PrivTree from D_{i-1} to D_i. Combining this with the fact that the modified PrivTree uses a noise scale that is $l^\top$ times that of Algorithm 2, it can be verified that Equation (14) holds. Therefore, the theorem is proved. □

Proof of Theorem 4.2. Let $\mathcal{T}$ be the output of the modified PrivTree. Let D and D' be two neighboring datasets, such that D is obtained by inserting a sequence s into D'. Assume that $s = \$x_1 \ldots x_l$, where $x_i \in I \cup \{\&\}$ for $i \in [1, l]$. Observe that each symbol x_i in s contributes to the prediction histograms of the nodes whose predictor strings $dom(\cdot)$ are suffixes of $\$x_1 \ldots x_{i-1}$. By the definition of PSTs, these nodes form a path from the root of $\mathcal{T}$ to a leaf. This indicates that each x_i gets counted in the histogram of *one* leaf node only. Taking into account $l \le l^\top$, it follows that the sensitivity of releasing the histogram counts of all leaf nodes in $\mathcal{T}$ is $l^\top$. By the property of the Laplace mechanism, the postprocessing step ensures ε-differential privacy if $\lambda \ge \frac{l^\top}{\varepsilon}$. □

Proof of Lemma 5.1. Consider three datasets $D_1 = \{a, b\}$, $D_2 = \{a, b, b\}$, and $D_3 = \{b, b\}$, where each tuple is either a or b. Observe that D_1 is a neighboring dataset of D_2, while D_2 is a neighboring dataset of D_3. Let q_a (resp. q_b) be a query that asks for the number of a (resp. b) in a dataset. Let Q be a sequence of k queries, such that first $k/2$ queries are all q_a, and the remaining $k/2$ queries are all q_b.

Suppose that we invoke Algorithm 3 on D_1, D_2, D_3, respectively, with Q, a noise scale λ, and a threshold $\theta = 1$. Let E be the event that Algorithm 3 outputs 1 for the first $k/2$ queries in Q, and 0 for the remaining $k/2$ queries. In addition, let $\Pr[D \to E]$ denote the probability that E occurs when the input dataset is D. If Algorithm 3 satisfies ε-differential privacy, then

$$\frac{\Pr[D_1 \to E]}{\Pr[D_2 \to E]} \le e^{\varepsilon}, \qquad \frac{\Pr[D_2 \to E]}{\Pr[D_3 \to E]} \le e^{\varepsilon}.$$

This indicates that

$$\frac{\Pr[D_1 \to E]}{\Pr[D_3 \to E]} = \frac{\Pr[D_1 \to E]}{\Pr[D_2 \to E]} \cdot \frac{\Pr[D_2 \to E]}{\Pr[D_3 \to E]} \le e^{2\varepsilon}. \quad (15)$$

In what follows, we prove the lemma by showing that Equation (15) does not hold when $\lambda \le k/4\varepsilon$.

Recall that Algorithm 3 generates a noisy threshold $\hat{\theta}$, and outputs 1 for a query q only when its noisy answer $\hat{q}(D)$ is larger than $\hat{\theta}$. Therefore,

$$\begin{aligned}
&\frac{\Pr[D_1 \to E]}{\Pr[D_3 \to E]} \\
&= \frac{\int_{-\infty}^{\infty} \Pr[\hat{\theta} = x] \cdot \left(\Pr[\hat{q_a}(D_1) > x] \cdot \Pr[\hat{q_b}(D_1) \le x]\right)^{\frac{k}{2}} dx}{\int_{-\infty}^{\infty} \Pr[\hat{\theta} = x] \cdot \left(\Pr[\hat{q_a}(D_3) > x] \cdot \Pr[\hat{q_b}(D_3) \le x]\right)^{\frac{k}{2}} dx} \\
&= \frac{\int_{-\infty}^{\infty} \Pr[\hat{\theta} = x] \cdot \left(\Pr[Lap(\lambda) > x - 1] \cdot \Pr[Lap(\lambda) \le x - 1]\right)^{\frac{k}{2}} dx}{\int_{-\infty}^{\infty} \Pr[\hat{\theta} = x] \cdot \left(\Pr[Lap(\lambda) > x] \cdot \Pr[Lap(\lambda) \le x - 2]\right)^{\frac{k}{2}} dx}
\end{aligned}$$

Consider any $x \in (-\infty, +\infty)$. If $x > 1$, then

$$\Pr[Lap(\lambda) > x - 1] = \frac{1}{2} e^{\frac{1-x}{\lambda}} = e^{\frac{1}{\lambda}} \cdot \Pr[Lap(\lambda) > x],$$

and $\Pr[Lap(\lambda) \le x - 1] > \Pr[Lap(\lambda) \le x - 2]$. This leads to

$$\begin{aligned}
&\Pr[Lap(\lambda) > x - 1] \cdot \Pr[Lap(\lambda) \le x - 1] \\
&\ge e^{\frac{1}{\lambda}} \cdot \Pr[Lap(\lambda) > x] \cdot \Pr[Lap(\lambda) \le x - 2] \qquad (16)
\end{aligned}$$

Meanwhile, if $x \le 1$, then

$$\Pr[Lap(\lambda) \le x - 1] = \frac{1}{2} e^{\frac{x-1}{\lambda}} = e^{\frac{1}{\lambda}} \cdot \Pr[Lap(\lambda) \le x - 2],$$

and $\Pr[Lap(\lambda) > x - 1] > \Pr[Lap(\lambda) > x]$. In that case, Equation (16) still holds.

Given that Equation (16) holds for all $x \in (-\infty, \infty)$, we have

$$\begin{aligned}
&\frac{\Pr[D_1 \to E]}{\Pr[D_3 \to E]} \\
&= \frac{\int_{-\infty}^{\infty} \Pr[\hat{\theta} = x] \cdot \left(\Pr[Lap(\lambda) > x - 1] \cdot \Pr[Lap(\lambda) \le x - 1]\right)^{\frac{k}{2}} dx}{\int_{-\infty}^{\infty} \Pr[\hat{\theta} = x] \cdot \left(\Pr[Lap(\lambda) > x] \cdot \Pr[Lap(\lambda) \le x - 2]\right)^{\frac{k}{2}} dx} \\
&> \left(e^{\frac{1}{\lambda}}\right)^{\frac{k}{2}} = e^{\frac{k}{2\lambda}}.
\end{aligned}$$

Therefore, $\frac{\Pr[D_1 \to E]}{\Pr[D_3 \to E]} > e^{2\varepsilon}$ when $\lambda \le k/4\varepsilon$, which proves the lemma. □

B. ADDITIONAL EXPERIMENTS

In this section, we evaluate the computation efficiency of PrivTree, and the impact of β (i.e., tree fanout) on the accuracy of PrivTree. Table B shows the processing time of PrivTree on each dataset (averaged over 100 runs), with ε varying from 0.05 to 1.6. The running time of PrivTree on road and msnbc are larger than that on the other datasets, since road and msnbc are larger in size than the others. In addition, the computation cost of PrivTree increases with ε. To understand this, recall that when PrivTree decides whether or not to split a node v, it first subtracts a bias term $depth(v) \cdot \delta$ from the score of v, and then injects noise into the biased score, after which it splits v if the noisy score is larger than the threshold θ. As δ is inversely proportional to ε (see Corollary 1), the bias term increases when ε decreases, in which case the noisy score of v is less likely to be larger than θ. Therefore, when ε is small, PrivTree has lower probabilities to split nodes, which leads to a small running time.

Previously, in Section 6.1, we evaluate the query accuracy of PrivTree on spatial data with its fanout β set to 2^d, where d is the dataset dimensionality. In that case, whenever PrivTree splits

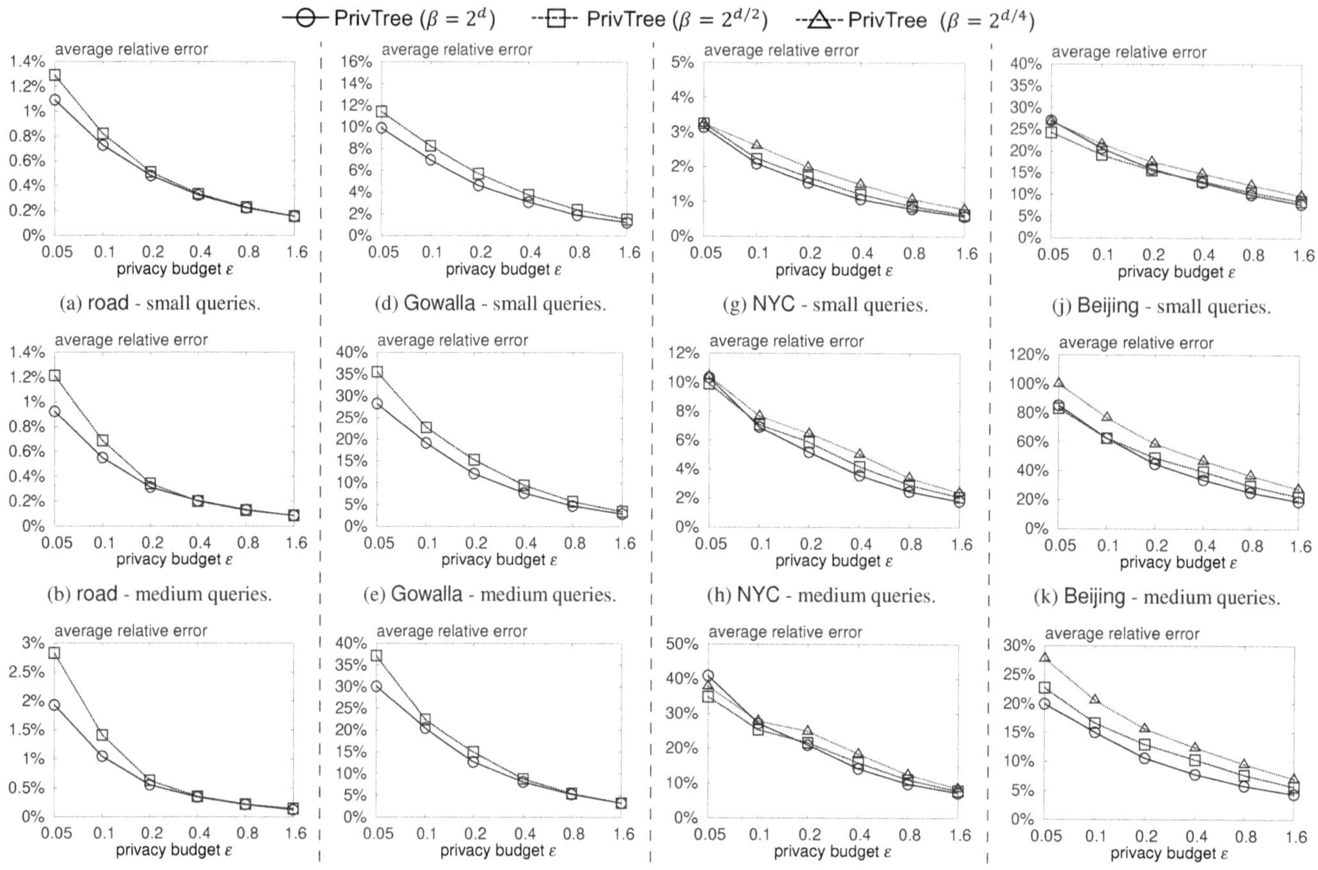

(a) road - small queries. (b) road - medium queries. (c) road - large queries. (d) Gowalla - small queries. (e) Gowalla - medium queries. (f) Gowalla - large queries. (g) NYC - small queries. (h) NYC - medium queries. (i) NYC - large queries. (j) Beijing - small queries. (k) Beijing - medium queries. (l) Beijing - large queries.

Figure 8: Impact of fanout on PrivTree.

Table 4: Running time of PrivTree (seconds).

Dataset	ε=0.05	ε=0.1	ε=0.2	ε=0.4	ε=0.8	ε=1.6
road	0.97	1.15	1.35	1.61	1.93	2.52
Gowalla	0.044	0.055	0.073	0.093	0.12	0.17
NYC	0.032	0.040	0.051	0.072	0.10	0.15
Beijing	0.0085	0.012	0.013	0.019	0.030	0.047
mooc	0.22	0.26	0.30	0.35	0.41	0.46
msnbc	1.73	2.03	2.21	2.50	2.72	3.05

a node v, the sub-domain $dom(v)$ of v is divided into 2^d parts by bisecting all dimensions of $dom(v)$. Figure 2 illustrates the results of the same experiments when β varies. In particular, when we set $\beta = 2^i$ with $i < d$, PrivTree would split the dimensions of each node in a round robin fashion, with i dimensions being bisected each time. Observe that, in general, the query error of PrivTree slightly increases when β decreases. This is mainly due to the bias term $depth(v) \cdot \delta$ that PrivTree subtracts from the score $c(v)$ of each node v, when it decides whether v should be split. Specifically, a decreased β increases the height of PrivTree's decomposition tree, in which case the nodes towards the leaf level of the tree would be given a larger bias term. In turn, the increased bias term renders it more difficult for PrivTree to correctly decide whether a node should be split, thus degrading the quality of PrivTree's output.

Nevertheless, on a few settings on NYC and Beijing, $\beta = 2^{d/2}$ entails smaller errors than $\beta = 2^d$. The reason is that, when β is large, any incorrect decisions made by PrivTree in node splitting would have a more pronounced negative effect, e.g., a quadtree node with a small count would be divided into a larger number of child nodes, each of which would have an even smaller count that is likely to be overwhelmed by the noise subsequently added. The increased number of noise-dominated nodes would then lead to less accurate query answers, which explains why $\beta = 2^{d/2}$ sometimes outperforms $\beta = 2^d$. That said, the overall result in Figure 8 indicates that $\beta = 2^d$ is still a preferable choice for PrivTree.

Adaptive Indexing over Encrypted Numeric Data

Panagiotis Karras[◇] Artyom Nikitin[◇] Muhammad Saad[◇]
Rudrika Bhatt[§] Denis Antyukhov[◇] Stratos Idreos[¶]
[◇]Skoltech [§]Rutgers University [¶]Harvard University

ABSTRACT

Today, outsourcing query processing tasks to remote cloud servers becomes a viable option; such outsourcing calls for encrypting data stored at the server so as to render it secure against eavesdropping adversaries and/or an honest-but-curious server itself. At the same time, to be efficiently managed, outsourced data should be indexed, and even adaptively so, as a side-effect of query processing. Computationally heavy encryption schemes render such outsourcing unattractive; an alternative, Order-Preserving Encryption Scheme (OPES), intentionally preserves and reveals the order in the data, hence is unattractive from the security viewpoint. In this paper, we propose and analyze a scheme for lightweight and indexable encryption, based on linear-algebra operations. Our scheme provides higher security than OPES and allows for range and point queries to be efficiently evaluated over encrypted numeric data, with decryption performed at the client side. We implement a prototype that performs incremental, query-triggered adaptive indexing over encrypted numeric data based on this scheme, without leaking order information in advance, and without prohibitive overhead, as our extensive experimental study demonstrates.

1. INTRODUCTION

We have entered the database-as-a-service era; data management capabilities need not be present at the data owner's locale, but can be provided *as a service* by a cloud-based service provider, to which the data is *outsourced*. This model provides users (i.e., the data owner and its trusted clients) power to create, store, modify, and retrieve data from anywhere in the world; the discussion about the applicability of this model has entered domains such as high-frequency trading, whereby a firm can use cloud providers' servers to test trading strategies, run time series analysis, assess risks, and even execute trades, while collecting financial data daily, or on a finer time scale [30, 2]. At the same time, such a model raises security and confidentiality concerns; to follow the same application area, a firm may deploy trading, analytics, and risk management modules to the cloud so as to filter out the most relevant financial data for in-house analysis. Thereby, sensitive data and query results may be leaked to malicious adversaries and/or an honest-but-curious service provider itself. Such concerns have motivated research on data encryption and query answering over encrypted data, starting with SQL query processing over encrypted data [19], and expanding to the design of tailor-made schemes that allow the processing of specialized queries over encrypted data, such as kNN [43] and skyline queries [10]. CryptDB has provided a coherent collection of efficient SQL-aware encryption schemes that allows for the execution of SQL queries over encrypted data [36].

SIGMOD '16, June 26–July 1, 2016, San Francisco, CA, USA.

ISBN 978-1-4503-3531-7/16/06. . . $15.00

DOI: http://dx.doi.org/10.1145/2882903.2882932

In all cases, the aim is to allow data to be managed by a server with minimal intervention by data owner and clients. The server should be able to process queries over the encrypted data, and deliver encrypted query results to the client, while the client should only have to decrypt the data and obtain the actual results thereby. Nevertheless, in order for a system to manage data and process queries efficiently, it should, first of all, be capable to *index* the data to the extent deemed necessary. In addition, modern applications, handling continuously arriving data, call for an inherent capacity to perform incremental indexing *on demand*, while processing user queries, and as a side-effect of such queries, requiring neither a priori idle time nor a priori workload knowledge; in other words, the system should not only be capable for indexing; it should be capable for *adaptive indexing* and *self-organization* [25, 20, 28].

These requirements for data management in the database-as-a-service era bring forth a contradiction. The requirement that data be kept confidential necessitates that it be *encrypted*; the requirement that data be efficiently managed necessitates that it be indexed. *Encryption* and *indexing* are in tension with each other; the former requires that the service provider knows nothing about the values of the data, while the latter necessitates that the same service provider knows, ideally, the exact values of the data under its purview. Given such conflicting aims, previous research has confronted these two challenges in isolation from each other and made no effort to face them in unison. Solutions for adaptive indexing and self-organization have not considered security and confidentiality, while secure database systems do not cater for adaptivity in dynamic environments. Unfortunately, by shying away from such an objective, such approaches offer fragmentary solutions to the problem of secure and efficient outsourced data management; in particular, extant encryption schemes suffer from one or more of the following drawbacks: (i) they are too computationally expensive; or (ii) leak too much information on the encrypted data, and/or (iii) require more data than the actual query results to be retrieved and then filtered in a post-processing step.

In this paper, we propose a model for breaking this isolation and achieving a seemingly contradictory target: allow for database systems that are both secure and adaptive. We examine the challenge of *adaptively indexing an encrypted database*. To bring about such a result, we investigate the extent to which encryption and indexing are in tension with each other: we study the bare-bones requirements for indexing, and the ways in which such requirements may be reconciled with encryption. We propose a lightweight and efficient encryption scheme that reveals less information than previous suggestions and allows for indexing encrypted numeric data adaptively. This indexing capacity does not aim to develop a complete index upfront, but to one built in an incremental, progressive manner, so that only those data which are queried get indexed. Such an *adaptive indexing* enables lightweight adaptation of the system to the workload at hand and also mitigates the tension between encryption and indexing. Our scheme relies on simple linear-algebra operations for encryption and decryption, while it can efficiently process range and point queries over ciphertexts without disclosing the order among attribute values, as an Order-Preserving Encryption Scheme [3], and without the computational and storage burdens of schemes like fully homomorphic encryption [14].

2. BACKGROUND AND STATE OF THE ART

We review prior work on data systems that support queries over encrypted data, as well as on adaptive indexing.

2.1 Processing Encrypted Data

Research on processing encrypted data can be classified in two broad classes. The former class of solutions propose processing the encrypted data **directly**. Hacıgümüş et al. [19] proposed a bucketization scheme that allows for approximate filtering of query results at the server, followed by the final processing at the client, after decryption. Hore et al. [22] expand on this scheme with an index that supports obfuscated range queries, extended to the multidimensional case [21]. However, such schemes reveal the data distribution and involve the client in query processing, while the only indexing capacity they offer is that afforded by bucketization.

An attempt for fine-grained indexing would necessitate *sorting* values at the server. Such an alternative is offered by Agrawal et al.'s *Order-Preserving Encryption Scheme* (OPES) [3], built on an encoding that preserves the order of numerical data. However, as previous research has noted [44, 6, 7, 37], OPES reveals the data order, hence cannot overcome attacks based on statistical analysis on encrypted data. Arguably, OPES provides an *overkill* solution: it delivers encrypted values in sortable form, hence allows such values to be compared to each other. We argue that a more conservative alternative would enable *selective indexing* without a priori leaking information about the order of values.

In the meantime, advances in cryptography have led to the capacity to perform arbitrary computations over encrypted data, so as to obtain a correct encrypted result, by fully homomorphic encryption (FHE) [14]. Such computations rely on an expensive public key cryptosystem, bringing forth prohibitive overheads of up to nine orders of magnitude [15]. Besides, FHE does not enable *indexing* encrypted data. With FHE, even while the server performs all computations correctly, it does so *only in the encrypted view of the world*. It has no access to any truth in the real world that would allow for building an index. Mani et al. [33] discuss the potential of FHE to enable the vision of secure database as a service, and conclude that practicality remains a very important concern. To process a simple select query by the two-step process proposed in [33], the server computes the query results first and sends to the client the encrypted number n of result tuples; the client decrypts n, and asks for $n' \geq n$ rows from the server. The server returns the top-n' rows in the result; thus, the client needs to be actively involved in simple query processing tasks.

Wang and Lakshmanan [42] propose a scheme for securely evaluating queries over encrypted XML data. They advocate an extension of OPES, order-preserving encryption with splitting and scaling (OPESS), whereby each plaintext is "split" into more ciphertexts and the split data are "scaled", so that the attacker cannot determine the identity of ciphertexts based on data frequency knowledge. However, this scheme cannot support updates; thus, it is unsuitable for a dynamic and adaptive database system.

Shi et al. [38] propose an encryption scheme for answering multidimensional range queries. Yet the problem they address is that of allowing an auditor to decrypt *those and only those* records (e.g., financial audit logs, medical anamneses, etc.) whose attributes fall within a specified range; privacy is not protected when an entry is matched by the query. Unfortunately, this *match-revealing* scheme does not allow for protecting attribute values while enabling a service provider to identify records matching queries over encrypted data in a way that can be exploited for indexing.

Boneh and Waters [9] process complex queries over encrypted data based on Hidden Vector Encryption (HVE). The notion of security in [9] is stronger than the one in [38]: query-matching records are identified, but their attribute values remain hidden. This *match-concealing* security notion fits the requirements for indexing while protecting the privacy of attribute values. However, the scheme in [9] is not practicable for vast volumes of dynamic data; it necessitates $O(DT)$ public key size, encryption time, and ciphertext size, for D attributes and T discrete values per attribute.

Tu et al. developed MONOMI [40], a system that can execute analytical queries over encrypted data. Building on CryptDB [36], MONOMI uses several techniques so as to improve performance, along with a designer that chooses efficient server-side physical designs and a planner that selects efficient query execution plans involving server and client. However, insofar as MONOMI allows for order-based indexing, it does so by relying on OPES. More recently, Li et al. [31] proposed a scheme for processing range queries over encrypted data in which inequality checks are conducted via exhaustive equality checks; no mechanism for pure inequality checks over encrypted data is suggested.

Overall, these approaches do not provide a good tradeoff between confidentiality and efficiency; lately, some research efforts have provided tailor-made encryption schemes that allow the processing of specialized queries over encrypted data, such as kNN queries [43], range search queries [45], and skyline queries [10].

An alternative to processing encrypted data directly is to maintain an **encrypted index** on the server, and rely on the client for traversing this index and locate the data of interest after a few iterations of retrieval and decryption. Damiani et al. [12] build a B-tree over plaintext values, but encrypt every tuple and the B-tree itself at node level; the tree's content is not visible to the server. Ge and Zdonik [13] propose *Fast Comparison Encryption* (FCE). An index traversal with FCE necessitates comparisons between plaintext and ciphertext key values by *partial decryption* on the client side. Wang et al. [41] provide a secure query processing framework that protects data both *in storage* and *at access*, based on Salted IDA (Information Dispersal Algorithm). By this scheme, a client maintains a secret *information dispersal matrix* and the keys for decoding a data matrix D; the client encodes and disperses D onto n servers, while using a pseudo-random number generator with a secret seed to add a random *salt* to each data entry; when retrieving data, salts are reconstructed and deducted from the decoded data, so as to recover D. Thus, query processing is directed by the client, while servers can only access data following the client's instructions. Overall, approaches based on an encrypted index do not allow the server to build, maintain, and traverse an index relying on its own devices.

A third direction involves processing encrypted data in **secure hardware**, most recently exemplified by Cipherbase [5]. Yet, for a range index Cipherbase reveals the full ordering information of index keys, even to a weak adversary; thus, range indexes in Cipherbase provide "similar confidentiality guarantees" [5], and have the same drawbacks as, order preserving encryption (OPE).

2.2 Adaptive Indexing

Apart from security requirements, data systems for modern applications need to be flexible and agile, easily adapting to rapidly changing requirements [11, 24]. *Adaptive indexing* is a recently introduced concept, by which index tuning need not be performed during system initialization [25, 26, 29, 20, 17, 18, 23, 34, 16, 35]; instead, it occurs during query processing: each query is interpreted not only as a request for a particular result set, but also as an advice on how to physically store the data, triggering small actions that refine the adaptive indexes. Those data portions that are queried become progressively and incrementally indexed. This capacity to index by continuously reacting to a changing query workload brings forth the property of *self-organization.*

In this section, we describe *database cracking* [23] in more detail. Database cracking introduced the notion of continuous, incremental, and on-demand adaptive indexing in the context of modern column-stores [1]. With cracking, the select operator of a database system performs index-building operations as a side-effect of processing a range (or equality) filtering action [25]; an index is built and refined collaterally to query execution: the more a data range is queried, the more its index is refined. The physical data store is changing with each incoming range query q, interpreting *q as a hint on how data should be stored.* That hint may explicitly use q's query bounds, or follow a more lax interpretation for the sake of robustness [20]. Without loss of generality, we discuss the strict interpretation. Assume a query requests $A<10$. A cracking DBMS responds to q by clustering all tuples of A with $A<10$ at the beginning of the respective column C, while pushing all other tuples to the column's end. A subsequent query requesting $A \geq v_1$, where $v_1 \geq 10$, will only need to look into the last piece of C, while a query that requests $A<v_2$, where $v_2 \leq 10$, searches its first part; each subsequent query cracks its respective piece further. Figure 1 shows how two queries crack a column by their selection predicates. Query Q1 cuts the column in three pieces, and Q2 enhances this partitioning by cutting the first and the last piece further. Each query collects its qualifying tuples in a contiguous area. Thereby, the original column A (including positions) is copied into a *cracker index* column, which is then continuously reorganized.

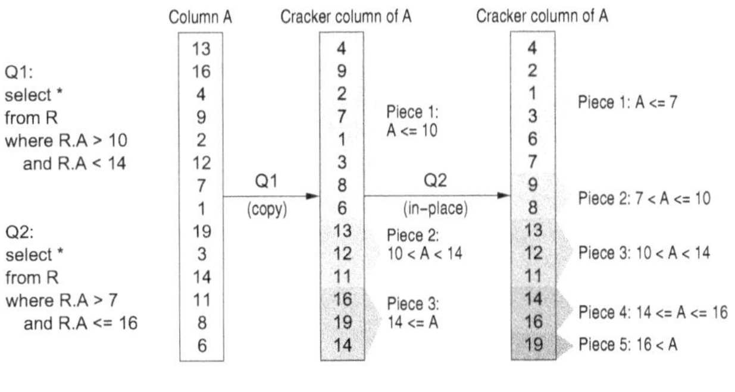

Figure 1: Cracking a column [25]

As queries are being processed, the adaptive index of a column is continuously split into more (and thus smaller) pieces. Therefore, we also need a data structure to localize a piece of interest. Past adaptive indexing literature has relied on an in-memory AVL-tree to keep track of all pieces created due to physical reorganization [25]. As a column becomes progressively indexed, queries requesting ranges that are exact matches of values known by the index are answered at the cost of searching only that tree-index; in all cases, even when there is no exact match, the index reduces the amount of data a query has to touch, as each range query reorganizes at most two pieces at the edge of the relevant range.

This on-the-fly physical reorganization is performed on individual pieces (or the whole column for the very first query) by in-place algorithms relying on sequential access patterns [25]. Algorithm 1 shows the most basic cracking algorithm that splits a piece into two, identifying tuples that need to be exchanged by *comparison* operations. Over the years, numerous algorithms have been proposed that split a piece of a column into three pieces [25], N pieces using radix clustering [29], partially sorting pieces in combination with partition/merge operations [29], fully sorting pieces when touched for the first time [18], and splitting pieces based on random pivots as opposed to query predicates [20, 34], yet the core idea remains the same. Figure 1 shows Query Q1, which partitions the whole column into three pieces, followed by Query Q2 that reorganizes Pieces 1 and 3 [25]. Other pieces of work accommodate updates [26], propagate the physical organization from one column to others on demand [27], and exploit multi-core CPUs [34, 35].

Algorithm 1 CrackInTwo(c,posL,posH,med,inc)
Physically reorganize the piece of column c between *posL* and *posH* such that all values lower than *med* are in a contiguous space. *inc* indicates whether *med* is inclusive or not, e.g., if *inc = false* then ϕ_1 is "<" and ϕ_2 is ">="

```
x1 = point at position posL
x2 = point at position posH
while position(x1) < position(x2) do
  if value(x1) φ1 med then
    x1 = point at next position
  else
    while value(x2) φ2 med &&
    position(x2) > position(x1) do
      x2 = point at previous position
    exchange(x1 ,x2 )
    x1 = point at next position
    x2 = point at previous position
```

In this work, without loss of generality, we consider the basic cracking design. We focus on the action of reorganizing a column into pieces with respect to a breakpoint as part of a query plan itself; thereby, a cracking select operator physically reorganizes the proper pieces of a column to bring all qualifying values in a contiguous area, which is leveraged to return the result, without additional result materialization [23]. Besides, with an AVL tree used for indexing, tree updates and rebalancing actions are also performed during query processing, in logarithmic time. This core operation is common and universally applicable to all adaptive indexing design. Our subsequent discussion shows how to apply this basic notion over encrypted data; we emphasize that our design extends the basic cracking design in a way that does not violate its assumptions about the underlying architecture: we assume that data is stored one column-at-a-time in *fixed-width* dense arrays as in modern column-stores [32, 39, 8], both on disk and in memory. Query processing may happen in bulk or vector-wise processing. These basic properties apply to all column-stores.

Crucially, adaptive indexing never necessitates fully sorting individual pieces [23, 29]; when a piece becomes small enough to fit in L1 cache, we scan the data at virtually no overhead. Thus, queries only cause reorganization for data pieces larger than a size threshold; that threshold can be bigger (e.g., L3 cache size) without a significant performance drop. In the context of our work, it follows that we *never* leak the *total data order* by a fully sorted index, as OPES does by default.

3. PROPOSED ENCRYPTION SCHEME

We aim to devise an encryption scheme that provides protection against attacks that aim to compromise data confidentiality, yet enables self-organizing indexing operations over encrypted numeric data, i.e. an *indexable encryption scheme*. However, unlike OPES [3], we do not wish our encryption to preserve the order of numerical data; we aim to enable efficient querying without leaking information about the order of tuples. An adversary can be either an external malicious entity or an honest-but-curious server. Insider attacks, such as those arising from malicious partners, are not considered. Client machines are assumed to be safe; confidential information such as secret keys on the client and client queries are not known to attackers. Attacker's computations are bounded by polynomial-size circuits. We first outline the requirements we would like our encryption scheme to satisfy.

1. It should provide the server with *some* capacity to **conduct inequality comparisons** between data values (plaintexts) employing their encrypted forms (ciphertexts).
2. This capacity to perform comparisons should **not directly reveal the order** among encrypted numeric data.
3. Comparison operations should not necessitate decryption at the server; attribute values should always **remain hidden** to the server.
4. The key sizes, encryption time, and ciphertext sizes should be **manageable** and not growing with the size of data, number of attributes, or number of discrete values.
5. The client should not be elaborately involved in processing simple queries; the server should deliver the encrypted results, and only those, to the client in a **single round** of communication.
6. The server should be capable to gracefully accommodate newly arriving data values and support **updates** in the encrypted data.

A prime challenge is to resolve the tension between requirements (1) and (2), i.e., enable inequality comparisons *without* revealing order. A way to achieve this result is to postulate that comparisons should *not* be possible *among* encrypted data residing at the server. If such data are not comparable to each other, then they cannot be straightforwardly brought to sorted order. We must then spell out under what circumstances a server should be able to perform an inequality check among ciphertexts. Such comparisons should be possible only *on demand*, between ciphertexts (e.g., a query bound and a tuple value) rendered comparable by their encryption; in effect, indexing actions would also be possible *only on client demand*. Such *on-demand indexing*, would be compatible with adaptive indexing: If we have to perform on-demand indexing for the sake of security, we also need to perform exactly such actions for the sake of adaptiveness, as the data has to be indexed in response to queries. Then, instead of being in tension with each other, the requirements for security and adaptivity reinforce each other.

We must then devise a method of creating *comparable ciphertexts*. Such a method could utilize two complementary encryption modes, A and B, *interfacing* with each other, so that a ciphertext encrypted in mode A can be compared to one encrypted in mode B. Then, encrypting attribute values in mode A and query bounds in mode B, we would offer the server a capacity to compare the former to the latter; as we saw, such comparisons form the backbone of adaptive indexing operations, and are performed with operators ϕ_1 and ϕ_2 in Algorithm 1. Assume a server needs to perform an inequality check between key value v in a column C and query bound value b, i.e., to check whether $v \geq b$. Equivalently, we need to check whether:

$$v - b \geq 0 \tag{1}$$

Using vector notation, we express Inequality (1) as

$$\begin{pmatrix} 1 \\ b \end{pmatrix} \cdot \begin{pmatrix} v \\ -1 \end{pmatrix} = v - b \geq 0 \tag{2}$$

Our objective is to devise an encryption scheme that allows the computation of such scalar vector products in obscured fashion. We employ three obscurement operations, to be be performed by the data vendor when uploading the data to the server and by a trusted client before issuing a query: (i) noise addition; (ii) scalar multiplication, and (iii) matrix multiplication. We elaborate on these in the following.

3.1 Noise Addition

Our noise addition operation builds two longer vectors $\mathbf{b}$, $\mathbf{v}$, by adding extra noisy elements to the length-2 vectors used in Inequality (2), such that the result of the vector product remains the same. We call $\mathbf{b}$ and $\mathbf{v}$ the encrypted *bound* and *value* vector, respectively. The specific length ℓ of vectors $\mathbf{b}$ and $\mathbf{v}$, and the positioning and distinction between the added *noisy contents* and original *value contents* therein constitute part of our *encryption key*, known to the data owner and trusted client, but not to the service provider. Without loss of generality, we present an example using vectors of length 5. We can rewrite Inequality (2) as follows:

$$\mathbf{b} \cdot \mathbf{v} = \begin{pmatrix} -4 \\ 1 \\ 8 \\ b \\ 4 \end{pmatrix} \cdot \begin{pmatrix} 3 \\ v \\ -2 \\ -1 \\ 7 \end{pmatrix} = v - b \geq 0 \tag{3}$$

In this example, the original contents of the vectors occupy positions 1 and 3 in them, whereas positions $\{0, 2, 4\}$ are reserved for noisy contents that cancel each other out in the scalar vector product, as they form two orthogonal length-3 embedded subvectors, $\mathbf{n}_b$ and $\mathbf{n}_v$, with inner product 0:

$$\mathbf{n}_b \cdot \mathbf{n}_v = \begin{pmatrix} -4 \\ 8 \\ 4 \end{pmatrix} \cdot \begin{pmatrix} 3 \\ -2 \\ 7 \end{pmatrix} = 0 \tag{4}$$

We call these orthogonal subvectors *noisy subvectors* of $\mathbf{b}$ and $\mathbf{v}$. We emphasize that we need not use the same exact noisy subvectors for each encrypted key value v or each encrypted bound value b, yet we do have to use the same *positions* for noisy contents across all encrypted values in the same column. We could use any pair of vectors orthogonal to each other, such that their inner product produces 0. Nevertheless, a vector $\mathbf{b}$ produced for a given bound value b should be orthogonal to *all* vectors $\mathbf{v}$ produced for attribute values. Therefore, we cannot choose our orthogonal vector pairs in an entirely arbitrary fashion. However, it suffices to select a unit vector $\mathbf{u}$, and make sure that each bound value b is obscured by embedding into the column vector $\left(\begin{smallmatrix} 1 \\ b \end{smallmatrix}\right)$ a randomly selected noise vector $\mathbf{n}_b$ collinear to $\mathbf{u}$, $\mathbf{n}_b = \lambda(b) \cdot \mathbf{u}$, with the values 1 and b occupying specific preselected positions, as shown above, to produce $\mathbf{b}$. Then, any data value v is obscured by similarly embedding a randomly selected vector $\mathbf{n}_v = \mathbf{u}^{\perp}(v)$, orthogonal to $\mathbf{u}$, into the column vector $\left(\begin{smallmatrix} v \\ -1 \end{smallmatrix}\right)$, to produce $\mathbf{v}$. We emphasize that the vectors $\mathbf{u}^{\perp}(v)$ do *not* need to be collinear to each other. Any vector orthogonal to $\mathbf{u}$ will suffice. Summing up, given a unit vector $\mathbf{u}$, the noisy subvectors embedded in $\mathbf{b}$ should be collinear to $\mathbf{u}$, while those embedded in $\mathbf{v}$ should be orthogonal to $\mathbf{u}$. Then an inequality check can be performed by means of a scalar vector product, as $v - b$ is calculated as $\mathbf{b} \cdot \mathbf{v}$.

In the above example, the unit vector used is $\mathbf{u} = \begin{pmatrix} \frac{-1}{\sqrt{6}} \\ \frac{2}{\sqrt{6}} \\ \frac{1}{\sqrt{6}} \end{pmatrix}$. Notably, $\|\mathbf{u}\| = 1$. A noisy subvector of $\mathbf{b}$ is produced by multiplying $\mathbf{u}$ by a randomly selected factor $\lambda(b)$. In above case, $\lambda(b) = 4\sqrt{6}$. On the other hand, a noisy subvector of $\mathbf{v}$ is produced by randomly selecting *any* vector of length $\ell - 2$, $\mathbf{u}^{\perp}(v)$, orthogonal to $\mathbf{u}$.

3.2 Scalar Multiplication

So far we have devised an encryption scheme that enables the calculation of the difference $v - b$ by the server, via the calculation of a scalar product of two vectors. Thus, we attain the objective of performing inequality checks, hence processing range queries, over the encrypted numeric data, while our encryption scheme does *not* preserve the order of the data in the way that OPES does. However, given an encrypted bound vector $\mathbf{b}$, an adversary can calculate any scalar product of the form $\mathbf{b} \cdot \mathbf{v}$, hence the difference $v - b$, for any encrypted value vector $\mathbf{v}$; then, by comparing the obtained $v - b$ values, one obtains not only the order, but also the exact differences among the encrypted data values.

To prevent this kind of leakage, we should not enable the calculation of exact differences of the form $v - b$. After all, we are not interested in obtaining the correct norms of those differences. Getting merely their *sign* would suffice. The norm of $|v - b|$ may be altered, as long as the sign is correctly obtained. We achieve this effect by adding a *scalar multiplication* in our obscurement operation. Then, for each data value v, the data vendor chooses a random positive multiplier $\xi(v) > 0$, and recalculates the encrypted value vector $\mathbf{v}$ as $\mathbf{v}' = \xi(v)\mathbf{v}$. Henceforward, we use $\mathbf{v}$ to refer to this recalculated value vector. In effect, the scalar product we calculate becomes $\mathbf{b} \cdot \mathbf{v} = \xi(v)(v - b)$. The server still obtains the correct *sign* of the difference $v - b$, *without* the exact norm of this difference being leaked. In effect, an adversary cannot reconstruct the order of data values using information obtained from scalar products.

3.3 Matrix Multiplication

Our noise addition and scalar multiplication operations produce a vector $\mathbf{v}$ representing each key value v and a vector $\mathbf{b}$ representing a query bound value b, so that *the sign*, but not the norm, of $v - b$ can be obtained from the scalar product $\mathbf{b} \cdot \mathbf{v}$. Still, the security these operations provide cannot withstand a simple breach: an adversary who learns the position within a vector $\mathbf{v}$ where the values $\xi(v)v$ and $-\xi(v)$ reside, can effectively acquire all original key values. We now provide an additional encryption layer that obstructs this breach.

Assume $\mathbf{v}$ and $\mathbf{b}$ are vectors of length ℓ, and let M be any invertible $\ell \times \ell$ matrix, and M^{-1} its inverse. M constitutes part of our encryption key; it is known to the data vendor and its trusted clients, but not to the service provider. We can then encrypt any key value v and any breakpoint b as follows.

$$\mathbf{E}_v(v) = M^{-1}\mathbf{v} \quad (5)$$

$$\mathbf{E}_b(b) = M^T\mathbf{b} \quad (6)$$

where $\mathbf{E}_v(\cdot)$, $\mathbf{E}_b(\cdot)$ are our encryption functions, $\mathbf{b}$ and $\mathbf{v}$ are represented as column vectors, and M^T is the transpose of matrix M. Then:

$$\begin{aligned} \mathbf{E}_b(b) \cdot \mathbf{E}_v(v) &= \mathbf{E}_b(b)^T \mathbf{E}_v(v) \\ &= (M^T\mathbf{b})^T(M^{-1}\mathbf{v}) \\ &= (\mathbf{b}^T M)(M^{-1}\mathbf{v}) \\ &= \mathbf{b}^T\mathbf{v} = \mathbf{b} \cdot \mathbf{v} = \xi(v)(v - b) \end{aligned}$$

where row vector $\mathbf{a}^T$ is the transpose of column vector $\mathbf{a}$.

In effect, any inequality check can be effectively conducted using the encrypted vectors $\mathbf{E}_v(v)$ and $\mathbf{E}_b(b)$. $\mathbf{E}_v(v)$ is generated by the data vendor and passed on to the server when the data (or an update) is generated. $\mathbf{E}_b(b)$ is produced by the trusted client, or again by the data vendor on behalf of the client, when issuing a query. These two encryption (and reverse decryption) steps are the only workload data vendor and client have to bear. Other computations and query processing are conducted by the server as with a non-encrypted database. At the same time, given those encrypted vectors, an adversary cannot determine the values of v or b without knowing the invertible matrix M.

3.4 The Encryption Key

In a nutshell, our total encryption key consists of:

1. The unit vector $\mathbf{u}$.
2. The arbitrary orientation of each vector $\mathbf{u}^{\perp}(v)$, orthogonal to $\mathbf{u}$, which is individually selected to construct $\mathbf{v}$ for a data value v.
3. Each factor $\lambda(b)$ used to produce a noisy vector collinear to $\mathbf{u}$, in order to construct $\mathbf{b}$ for a query bound b.
4. Each random positive multiplier $\xi(v)$ used to obscure the norm of $v - b$.
5. The positions occupied by the contents of $\begin{pmatrix} \xi(v)v \\ -\xi(v) \end{pmatrix}$ and $\begin{pmatrix} 1 \\ b \end{pmatrix}$ in $\mathbf{v}$ and $\mathbf{b}$, respectively.
6. The invertible matrix M.

3.5 Resistance to Attacks

We provide a sketch of the capacity of this lightweight encryption scheme to withstand attacks, assuming an honest but curious adversary, aware of the internal workings of our scheme, who aims to learn our key from known ciphertexts and potentially known plaintexts. As our scheme consists of three layers, we separate our discussion in two parts.

Noise and Scalar Multiplication Layers Leaving the matrix multiplication part aside, assume an adversary, Alice, who directly observes noisy vectors before they are multiplied by M. In such a known ciphertext attack, Alice would only be challenged to sort out the noisy contents from the value contents of those vectors. She can use the information that the noisy elements of an encrypted value vector $\mathbf{v}$ and an encrypted breakpoint vector $\mathbf{b}$ are orthogonal to each other, and make a hypothesis about the positions of the noisy contents vs. value contents in the observed vectors, i.e. arbitrarily select 2 positions out of ℓ in those vectors where the assumed value contents reside. To test this hypothesis, she can examine whether the assumed noisy subvectors produce consistently inner product 0 across many different observed $\{\mathbf{b}, \mathbf{v}\}$ pairs. If that is the case, then she can safely conclude that her hypothesis is verified. The question is how much Alice would have to try in order to reach a correct hypothesis by exhaustive search. Her hypothesis amounts to selecting 2 out of ℓ vector elements. As there are

$\binom{\ell}{2} = \frac{\ell(\ell-1)}{2} = O(\ell^2)$ ways of making such a selection, Alice can arrive at the correct hypothesis in polynomial time. We conclude that the noise layer of our scheme is easy to break. This is why we added the matrix multiplication layer, which we study next.

Matrix Multiplication Layer Once the noisy vectors Alice observes get multiplied by M, she cannot carry out the above attack. Now the multiplication matrix M enters the picture, consisting of ℓ^2 unknowns. The unit vector $\mathbf{u}$ brings $\ell - 2$ more unknowns into the picture; each encrypted vector $\mathbf{v}$ brings $\ell - 3$ more unknowns, as only one out of its $\ell - 2$ noisy elements can be derived using the $\ell - 3$ others and orthogonality to $\mathbf{u}$, and the $\xi(v)$ factor, which has multiplied $\{v, -1\}$ to produce its noisy contents; each encrypted vector $\mathbf{b}$ brings a $\lambda(b)$ factor, which multiplies $\mathbf{u}$ to produce its noisy contents. An attack that could still bear fruit is a known plaintext attack, in case Alice could gain access to pairs of an original value (either v or b) and its encrypted form ($\mathbf{E}_v(v)$ or $\mathbf{E}_b(b)$, respectively). For each such pair, she can construct ℓ scalar linear equations. Eventually, it can be shown that it suffices for Alice to know $N \geq \frac{\ell^2+\ell-2}{\ell-1} = O(\ell)$ plaintext-ciphertext pairs of values b; she can then solve the resulting system of equations for each of $\frac{\ell(\ell-1)}{2}$ ways of positioning noisy contents in $\mathbf{v}$ and $\mathbf{b}$, and, again, identify the one that leads to a solution consistently resulting in orthogonal noisy vector products. We conclude that the security of our encryption scheme against known plaintext attacks strongly depends on the chosen ciphertext size ℓ, while our scheme provides the data owner with the flexibility to choose the value of ℓ at will.

4. INDEXING ENCRYPTED DATA

We now discuss how our server can perform adaptive indexing over data encrypted by our encryption scheme. Notably, the choice of ℓ in our scheme determines the dimensions of matrix M, and incurs a ℓ-fold increase in our storage requirements. We contend that this storage overhead is an affordable price to pay for the sake for performing secure adaptive indexing operations.

4.1 The Problem of Leakage by Structure

We have so far emphasized that we eschew an order-preserving encryption scheme, so that the *order* of values does not leak to adversaries. Nevertheless, adaptive indexing operations do progressively bring the underlying data column in *sorted order*. After all, database cracking can be validly described as an *incremental quicksort*, while another alternative for adaptive indexing [18], adaptive merging, can be seen as an *incremental external merge sort*. An adaptive indexing mechanism, left to its own devices, will *tend* to bring the data in sorted order. Given a workload $\mathcal{W}$ such that, for any pair of values in the column v_1, v_2, there exists at least one query bound $b \in \{v_1, v_2\}$, adaptive indexing with $\mathcal{W}$ will eventually bring the data in an exact sorted order.

In effect, even though the encryption does not intrinsically betray the order of values, that order can eventually be observed in the order records are brought to after enough cracking operations have been applied. An adversary who can identify a target tuple can infer its position in the sorted order by observing the structure of the constructed index tree. The more refined the tree becomes, the more information it can leak about the order of underlying tuples.

4.2 Deliberately Allowing Errors

To mitigate the problem of leaking order by structure, we allow for erroneous interpretations of outsourced data, while the server cannot distinguish which interpretation is valid. Thus, even an adversary (or a server) knowing the internal workings of our scheme will not be able to make confident inferences about the relative positions of tuples.

We define *two* possible ways of interpreting each encrypted data value, without leaking which one of the two is correct for each tuple t. The server merely takes actions on both, by maintaining both possible interpretations of each record whenever needed. Only one of those versions corresponds to the true record, yet only the data owner and its trusted clients can make this distinction. From the point of view of the server, each interpretation is equally likely to be valid. In other words, the sever is concurrently managing multiple *possible worlds*. We configure such *multiple realities* by making each $\mathbf{E}_v(v)$ vector longer by a value θ, arbitrarily adding θ as a prefix *or* as a suffix to it, to obtain $\bar{\mathbf{E}}_v(v)$; we select θ so that both the ℓ-prefix and ℓ-suffix of $\bar{\mathbf{E}}_v(v)$ work consistently as valid $\mathbf{E}_v(v)$ vectors interfacing with $\mathbf{E}_b(b)$ vectors: in both, after multiplying by matrix M, the contents obtained in the positions reserved for noisy contents in a $\mathbf{v}$ vector are orthogonal to $\mathbf{u}$.

To facilitate the following discussion, we introduce a number of matrices useful so as to formally represent the creation of vectors and noise addition via linear-algebra operations. These matrices, and the purposes they serve, are gathered together in Table 1.

Matrix	Purpose
E_{nm}	*expansion matrix*: extends vector with $n - m$ zeros
P_{nm}	*permutation matrix*: shuffles extended value/bound vectors
P^c_{nm}	*complementary permutation matrix*: shuffles noise vector
S	*shift matrix*: cyclically shifts vector elements down
S^T	*symmetric shift matrix*: cyclically shifts vector elements up

Table 1: Employed matrices

We calculate the value of θ as follows. We are starting out from $(v; -1)^T$, the noisy subvector $\mathbf{n}_v \propto \mathbf{u}^\perp$, and $(1; b)^T$, the noisy subvector $\mathbf{n}_b = \lambda(b) \cdot \mathbf{u}$, where $\mathbf{u}$ is the secret unit vector and $\mathbf{u}^\perp$ a vector orthogonal to $\mathbf{u}$. Then, for the purposes of our encryption scheme, we first need to formally describe the *expanding* of these vectors into vectors of size ℓ. To that end, we employ two $n \times m$ *expansion matrices* that we denote as E_{nm}; such matrices multiply vectors from left and thereby extend those vectors with $n - m$ zeros. The structure of an E_{nm} matrix can be represented as $\begin{pmatrix} I \\ 0 \end{pmatrix}$, where I is the identity matrix. Then it holds that:

$$E_{\ell 2}\begin{pmatrix} v \\ -1 \end{pmatrix} = \begin{pmatrix} v \\ -1 \\ 0 \\ \dots \\ 0 \end{pmatrix}, E_{\ell(\ell-2)}\mathbf{n}_v = \begin{pmatrix} \mathbf{n}_v \\ \dots \\ 0 \end{pmatrix}$$

As a next step, we need to *shuffle* the contents of those expanded vectors so as to bring their contents in the positions predicted by our scheme. To that end, we employ two $n \times n$ *permutation matrices* that we denote as P_{nm} and P^c_{nm}; these matrices shuffle the extended value/bound and noise vectors, respectively, according to our noise addition scheme; only their first m rows have nonzero contents, hence it holds that $P_{nm}(P_{nm})^T = \begin{pmatrix} I_m & 0 \\ 0 & 0 \end{pmatrix}$; P^c_{nm} is chosen so that $P_{nm}(P^c_{nm})^T = 0$, i.e. P_{nm} and P^c_{nm} do not have permutation intersections: the one shuffles a vector's elements into positions complementary to those of the other. Last, let $\xi(v)$ and $\lambda(b)$ be the "scaling" functions we employ in our encryption scheme, as defined in Section 3.4. Thus, scaled noisy value and bound vectors can be represented as:

$$\mathbf{v} = \xi(v)\left(P_{\ell 2}E_{\ell 2}\begin{pmatrix} v \\ -1 \end{pmatrix} + P^c_{\ell(\ell-2)}E_{\ell(\ell-2)}\mathbf{n}_v\right)$$

$$\mathbf{b} = P_{\ell 2} E_{\ell 2} \begin{pmatrix} 1 \\ b \end{pmatrix} + P^c_{\ell(\ell-2)} E_{\ell(\ell-2)} \lambda(b) \mathbf{u}$$

We denote the final encrypted noisy value vector as $\mathbf{E}_v = M^{-1}\mathbf{v}$, where M is the encryption matrix. Our error-allowance scheme creates one of the following two vectors: $\begin{pmatrix} \mathbf{E}_v \\ \theta \end{pmatrix}$ or $\begin{pmatrix} \theta \\ \mathbf{E}_v \end{pmatrix}$. Without loss of generality, we consider only the first variant. In this first variant, we need to represent the *fake encrypted noisy value vector* $\mathbf{E}^f_v$, i.e., the ℓ-suffix of $\bar{\mathbf{E}}_v(v)$, which can be considered as true by an adversary. To this end, we employ an $\ell \times \ell$ *shift matrix* that we denote as S; multiplication by this matrix cyclically shifts vector components down. For example, for $n = 3$: $S = \begin{pmatrix} 0 & 0 & 1 \\ 1 & 0 & 0 \\ 0 & 1 & 0 \end{pmatrix}$. Symmetrically, its transpose, S^T, shifts vector components up. Thereby:

$$\mathbf{E}^f_v = S^T \mathbf{E}_v + (\theta - \mathbf{E}_v \cdot \mathbf{e}_1)\mathbf{e}_\ell$$

where $\mathbf{e}_k$ is a unit vector with all components zero except the kth; the above equation simply retains the $(\ell - 1)$-prefix of $\mathbf{E}_v$, shifted one position upwards, while it places θ at the ℓ-th position.

We want this $\mathbf{E}^f_v$ to have all properties of a real encrypted value vector. Then, the "noisy" $l - 2 \times 1$ subvector of the respective fake value vector $\mathbf{v}^f = M\mathbf{E}^f_v$ must be orthogonal to $\mathbf{n}_b$:

$$\mathbf{n}^f_v \cdot \mathbf{n}_b = E^T_{\ell(\ell-2)} (P^c_{\ell(\ell-2)})^T \mathbf{v}^f \cdot \mathbf{n}_b = 0 \Leftrightarrow$$

$$E^T_{\ell(\ell-2)} (P^c_{\ell(\ell-2)})^T M \left[S^T \mathbf{E}_v + (\theta - \mathbf{E}_v \cdot \mathbf{e}_1)\mathbf{e}_\ell \right] \cdot \mathbf{u} = 0 \Leftrightarrow$$

$$\left[\mathbf{E}^T_v S + (\theta - \mathbf{E}_v \cdot \mathbf{e}_1)\mathbf{e}^T_\ell \right] M^T P^c_{\ell(\ell-2)} E_{\ell(\ell-2)} \cdot \mathbf{u} = 0 \Leftrightarrow$$

$$\theta = \mathbf{E}_v \cdot \mathbf{e}_1 - \frac{\mathbf{E}^T_v S W \cdot \mathbf{u}}{\mathbf{e}^T_\ell W \cdot \mathbf{u}}$$

where $W = M^T P^c_{\ell(\ell-2)} E_{\ell(\ell-2)}$.

Figure 2 shows the form of an encrypted vector $\mathbf{E}_v$, while Figure 3 shows the encrypted vector $\bar{\mathbf{E}}_v(v)$, with ambiguity added. The size of the ambiguity-added vector is one more than original encrypted vector, hence each original value acquires two representations in the database: the one represented by the real encrypted vector, as the ℓ-prefix in the figure, and another represented by the fake vector, as the ℓ-suffix in the figure. Both are derived from the ambiguity-added vector as shown in Figure 3.

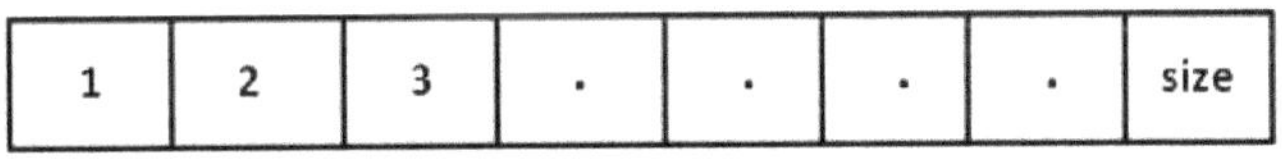

Figure 2: Encrypted Vector

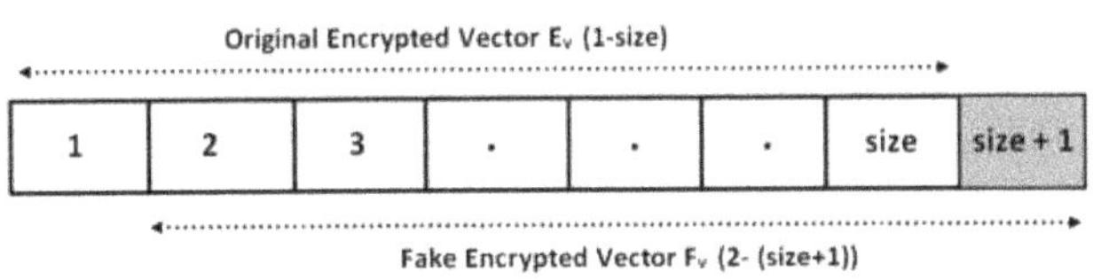

Figure 3: Encrypted Vector with Ambiguity

Having added this ambiguity about the identity of the real encrypted vector, we should render that identity identifiable by the trusted client. This can be achieved by selecting the (previously declared random) multiplier $\xi(v)$ in a particular way, e.g., postulating that it be an odd integer. The data owner and trusted client can then determine the real $\mathbf{E}_v(v)$ given $\bar{\mathbf{E}}_v(v)$ as follows: they decrypt both the ℓ-prefix and ℓ-suffix of $\bar{\mathbf{E}}_v(v)$, multiplying each by matrix M. The one that delivers an odd integer in the position of $\xi(v)$ is the real one. The fact that only one decryption attempt delivers an odd integer at that position is verified by the data owner during encryption.

However, what the client can determine so easily is inaccessible to the server. Under this arrangement, the server generates and manages each possible interpretation of $\bar{\mathbf{E}}_v(v)$ separately; this redundancy provides an obscurity that reduces the confidence of an adversary's inferences about the value order. Our end result is similar to adding counterfeit records in our database. However, the security provided by our scheme is higher than that provided by mere counterfeit insertion. In the case of adding counterfeits, an adversary with sufficient background knowledge may identify a *single* record of interest and infer information-leaking observations about its position in the index. On the other hand, with our scheme, the position of a record of interest in the index is uncertain *even when* that record of interest is identified, since each single record spawns two possible interpretations; this state of affairs confers additional security to our construction.

4.3 Managing an Encrypted AVL Tree

Our encryption scheme enables a server to manage a column of encrypted values, even with ambiguity inserted, and conduct comparisons between query bounds and data values. Yet, our system should also construct an AVL tree; in particular, query bounds, which correspond to the breakpoints b, are used as key values in tree nodes and utilized in subsequent tree traversals. During such a traversal, a new bound value b' has to be compared to a previous one, b, now used as key; then, at each node we need to compare two breakpoints values, b' and b, to each other.

In order to adapt this tree traversal mechanism to our encrypted data, the server needs to be able to compare two breakpoint values, b' and b, to each other. However, our encryption scheme uses two different encryption modes, one for breakpoints b, and one for values v, constructed so as to allow us to compare b to v only, but not different b and v values to each other. We solve this problem by having the query-issuing client encrypt a breakpoint b in both ways, i.e., in its native way, as $\mathbf{E}_b(b)$, and as an attribute value, $\mathbf{E}_v(b)$, and pass them on to the server. Subsequently, the former value is used for inequality checks with attribute values, while the latter is employed for storing it as a key in the constructed AVL tree index. When searching the encrypted AVL tree for a new breakpoint value b', the required comparison is conducted by calculating $\mathbf{E}_b(b') \cdot \mathbf{E}_v(b) = \xi(b) \cdot (b - b')$.

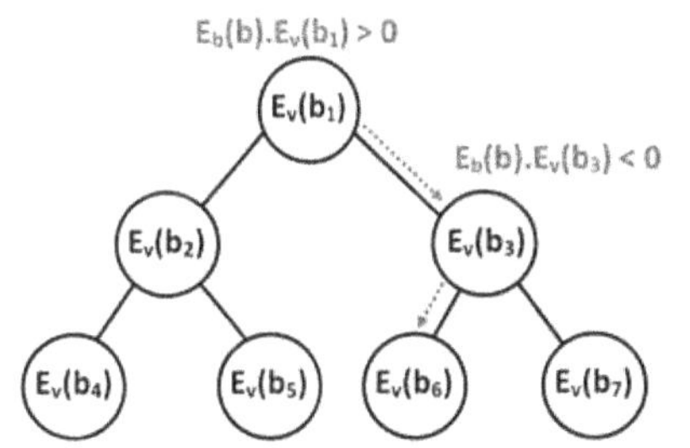

Figure 4: Finding a piece in an encrypted AVL Tree

Consider the example encrypted AVL tree in Figure 4. Finding a piece in this tree utilizes a query bound b encrypted as $\mathbf{E}_b(b)$, and key values in the tree itself encrypted as $\mathbf{E}_v(b)$; thus, the query bound and key values interface with each other and allow for conducting comparisons, resulting in the traversal shown in the figure.

Algorithm findpiece(objAVLTree,N,E_b,$posL$,$posH$)
Traverses AVL Tree and returns upper bound ($posH$) and lower bound ($posL$) values of the piece in which query bound vector $\mathbf{E}_b$ is located.

```
posL = 0
posH = N
isFound = true
rootNode = objAVLTree.getRoot()
if rootNode is not empty then
   minNode = objAVLTree.findMinNode(root)
   maxNode = objAVLTree.findMaxNode(root)
   fNode = objAVLTree.findNode(E_b)
   if ScalarProduct(E_b,maxNode.key) > 0 then
      isFound = false
   **Case 1**
   if isFound == false && fNode is not minNode then
      posL = maxNode.position
   **Case 2**
   else if fNode == minNode then
      if ScalarProduct(Eb,fNode.key) < 0 then
         posH = fNode.position
      else
         posL = fNode.position
         fNode = objAVLTree.findSuccessor(fNode)
         if ScalarProduct(fNode.key,maxNode.key) < 0 then
            posH = fNode.position
   **Case 3**
   else if ScalarProduct(Eb,fNode.key) < 0 then
      posH = fNode.position
      posL = objAVLTree.findPredecessor(fNode).position
   **Case 4**
   else
      posL = fNode.position
      fNode = objAVLTree.findSuccessor(fNode)
      if ScalarProduct(Eb,fNode.key) < 0 then
         posH = fNode.position
```

Algorithm `findpiece` illustrates the finding of the crack positions for a query bound b; it makes use of largest and smallest values in the AVL tree in order to determine whether the query bound is out of the tree's range; otherwise it obtains the leaf node $fNode$ by a search operation on the tree based on the given query bound $\mathbf{E}_b$; overall, it distinguishes the following cases:

- *Case 1* holds in case b is greater than the largest value in the tree; then the largest value in the tree is returned as the lower bound of the piece range.
- *Case 2* holds when the returned fNode is equal to the smallest value in the tree; then, if the query bound b is greater than that value, the range from that value to its successor is returned; if the query bound is smaller, then the smallest value is returned as the upper bound of the piece range.
- *Case 3* holds in case b is less than fNode; then the range between fNode and its predecessor is returned.
- *Case 4* holds when b is greater than fNode; then a range between fNode and its successor, if such exists, is returned.

In all cases, comparisons are performed via scalar vector products according to our scheme.

Having located a piece where a query bound b belongs, we need to complete the cracking operation by adding the bound b, represented by both $\mathbf{E}_v(b)$ and $\mathbf{E}_b(b)$, at a leaf node position in the AVL tree itself (and possibly rebalance the tree), so as to facilitate future searches. Figure 5 presents an AVL-tree traversal along with the addition of a leaf node for b_8 at the last step, after the piece in which b_8 belongs has been cracked in two. Algorithm `addCrack` illustrates how this operation is performed; its first three cases examine the situation where a node for b already exists in the tree; the fourth case adds a new node.

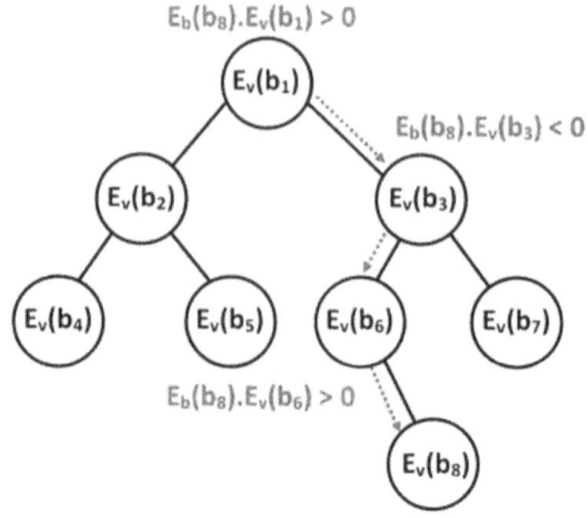

Figure 5: Adding a node in an encrypted AVL tree

Algorithm addCrack(objAVLTree,N,E_v,E_b,pos)
Adds a new node, for query bound b, to the AVL tree indexing N values, corresponding to position pos in the data array.

```
if pos == 0 or pos ≥ N then return
rootNode = objAVLTree.getRoot()
isFound = true
if rootNode is not empty then
   minNode = objAVLTree.findMinNode(root)
   maxNode = objAVLTree.findMaxNode(root)
   fNode = objAVLTree.findNode(E_b)
   if ScalarProduct(E_b,maxNode.key) > 0 then
      isFound = false
   **Case1**
   if isFound == true then
      if fNode.position == pos then return
      tmp = fNode
      if ScalarProduct(tmp.key,E_b) == 0 then
         tmp = objAVLTree.findSuccessor(tmp)
      if ScalarProduct(tmp.key,E_b) > 0 then
         if tmp.position == pos then return
   **Case2**
   if fNode is not minNode then
      if isFound == false then fNode = maxNode
      else fNode = objAVLTree.findPredecessor(fNode)
      if fNode.position == pos then return
   **Case3**
   if isFound == true && ScalarProduct(fNode.key,E_b) == 0 then
      fNode.setPosition(pos)
      return
   **Case4**
   objAVLTree.insert(E_v,pos,E_b)
   return
```

5. EXPERIMENTAL RESULTS

In this section we present an experimental analysis, demonstrating that secure adaptive indexing applying our schemes maintains all the adaptive properties and performance benefits of adaptive indexing while working over encrypted data. Our implementation is based on a stand-alone prototype in C++ that precisely implements the select operator of a modern column-store; it receives a column of values (fixed-width dense array) as input and returns a set of positions that mark qualifying values, represented again in a fixed-width dense array, as output. We keep this interface, common to all modern column-stores and all adaptive indexing approaches, intact. Our design affects only data manipulations that avoid data leakage. As our encryption scheme is based on precision-sensitive matrix operations, such as matrix inversion, matrix-vector multiplication, and vector-vector multiplication, we require high arithmetic precision; we employ the GNU Multi Precision Arithmetic

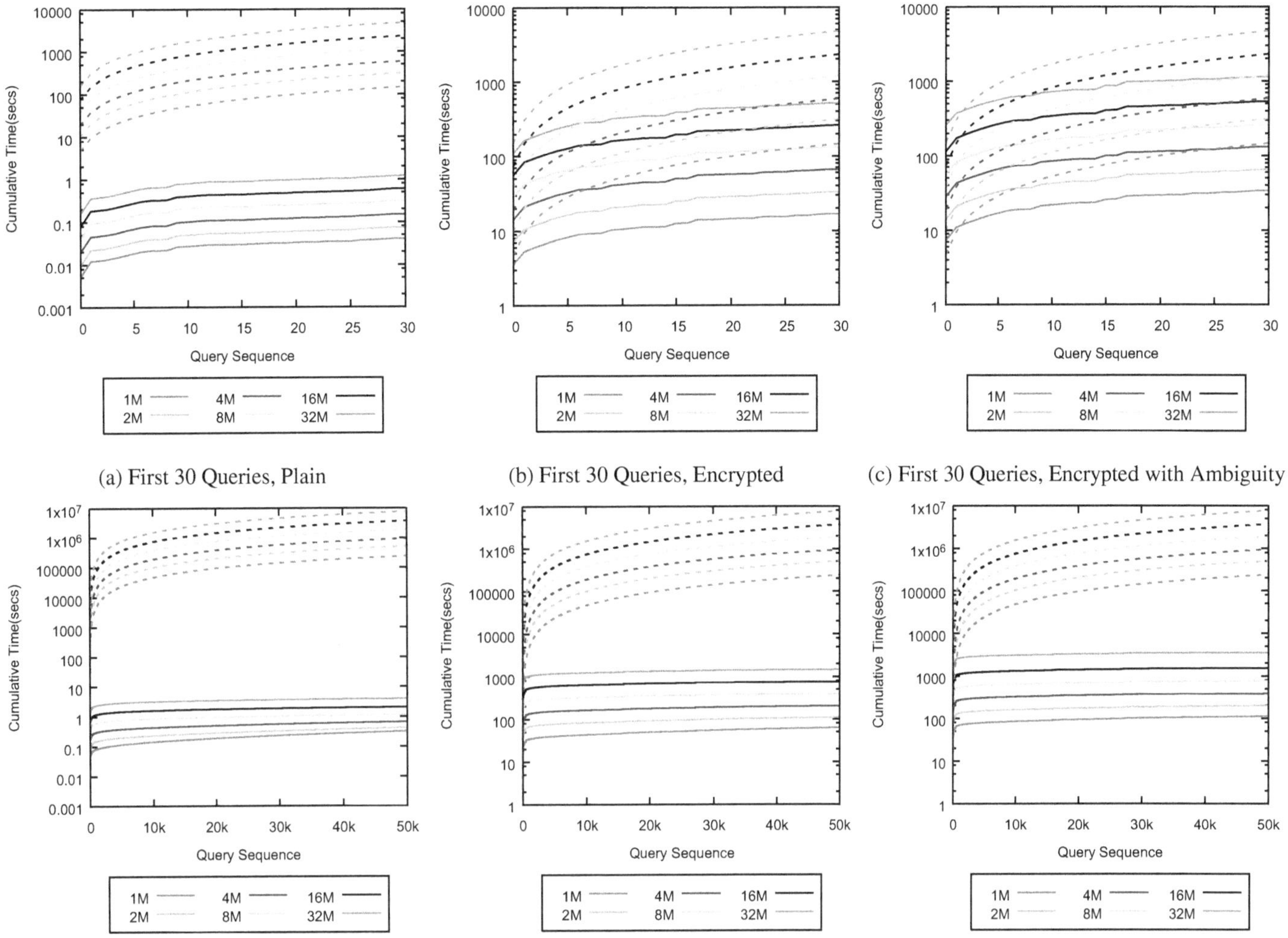

(a) First 30 Queries, Plain (b) First 30 Queries, Encrypted (c) First 30 Queries, Encrypted with Ambiguity

(d) 50k Queries, Plain (e) 50k Queries, Encrypted (f) 50k Queries, Encrypted with Ambiguity

Figure 6: Total Cumulative Time for different data sizes and types

Library (GMP)[1], a free library for arbitrary precision arithmetic, which operates on signed integers, rational numbers, and floating-point numbers, providing fast arithmetic operations for applications that need higher precision than is directly supported by the basic C types; GMP uses full *words* as the basic arithmetic type.

Our infrastructure consists of a 3.5 GHz Intel-Xeon machine with 12 CPU(s) and 32 GB of memory. In our core experiments, we run a query sequence that incrementally reorganizes a single column, and observe performance as the sequence evolves. In order to measure the effect of encryption, we perform such experiments on three types of data: (a) plain data without encryption, (b) data encrypted by the scheme introduced in Section 3, and (c) data encrypted along with the provision introducing added ambiguity, as described in Section 4.2. Moreover, we compare our cracking-based results against a plain scan of the encrypted numeric data, evaluating queries using comparisons via scalar products without any indexing or cracking; we call this approach **SecureScan**.

In all experiments, we encrypt data with default key size $\ell = 4$. The data are unique integers, drawn uniformly at random from $[0, 2^{31})$. The default workload is a sequence of 50K random selection queries with selectivity 1%; such workloads have been shown to be representatively challenging in terms of index adaptation [20].

[1]http://gmplib.org/

5.1 Cumulative Cost

We first present results based on the cumulative cost for processing a query workload. Figure 6 depicts our results for increasing data sizes ranging from 1M to 32M tuples, for Plain Data, Encrypted Data, and Encrypted Data with Ambiguity, along with the SecureScan method (based on simply scanning encrypted data with no ambiguity) in dashed lines; the x-axis in all graphs represents the query sequences, and the y-axis the cumulative response time up to query x. The top 3 graphs in Figure 6 focus on the first part of the workload, i.e., the first 30 queries, while the bottom 3 graphs show the complete query sequences. We focus separately on the beginning of a query sequence as this is where most of the heavy adaptive indexing actions take place, as the pieces being reorganized are much larger at this point [17].

The first row of figures shows that, in the first few queries, cumulative time grows significantly; this effect follows from the nature of cracking, as in the beginning more data is physically reorganized. On the other hand, in the second row of figures we notice that, as the workload evolves, for all data types, the cumulative time almost flattens, a result indicating that progressive physical reorganization renders query processing increasingly more efficient; moreover, this result applies irrespectively of data type, with encryption and with ambiguity as well as without. Furthermore, all figures show that, as the data size grows, the cumulative time increases in a scalable manner.

By comparing the plots across the three columns in Figure 6, we deduce that the trends observed for plain data are reproduced for encrypted data, as well as for encrypted data with ambiguity (which doubles data size). Remarkably, even the case of encryption with added ambiguity retains the fast convergence benefits of database cracking and vastly outperforms the SecureScan method in cumulative time on large query workloads. Besides, we note that the cumulative time for SecureScan keeps growing even after 50K queries have been processed, while the cumulative time for all cracking-based methods has flattened by that time.

Figure 7 puts together the cumulative times for the three tested types of data for different data sizes, as well as SecureScan for Encrypted Data. The figure shows that plain data require much less time than encrypted data to be processed; e.g., the cumulative time for the first 100 queries for the plain data of size 32M is 1.6 seconds, while the cost of the first query for the encrypted data of size 8M is 28.4 seconds. This is due to the fact that encrypted data necessitate costly vector-based comparisons and the high-precision arithmetic to retain correctness, whereas in the case of plain data we merely compare numbers in integer data type. However, scalability with encrypted data follows the trends for plain data, while the overall overhead for the sake of security remains manageable.

Besides, the figures shows that the cumulative time for encrypted data with ambiguity is double of that for encrypted data of the same size. This is due to the fact that, in the former case, the data size doubles, as each real value spawns a fake value in the database.

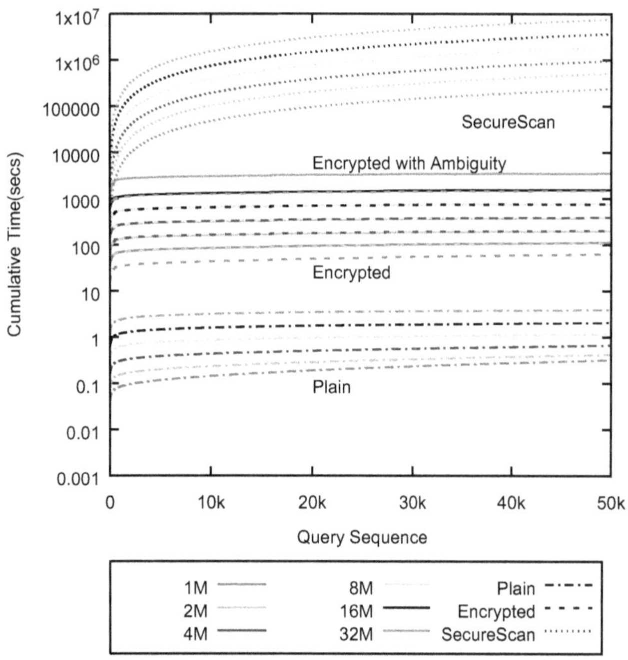

Figure 7: Total Cumulative Time Comparisons

5.2 Cost per Operation

As we have discussed, a cracking system invests its time in three main operations: (a) Cracking (b) Inserting query bounds in the AVL Tree (c) Searching for query bounds in the AVL Tree. We measure the time spent for each of these three purposes. Figure 8 shows the breakdown of the cost per operation for plain data. We observe that the core cracking operation is most expensive for the

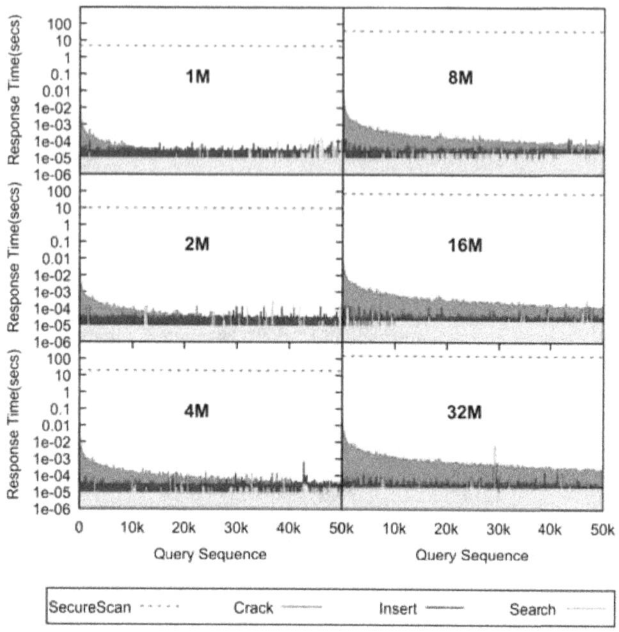

Figure 8: Cost per operation per query on Plain Data

initial queries, while it becomes progressively cheaper as the query workload evolves. In the case of smaller data sizes, as 1M and 2M, the Crack operation eventually becomes cheaper than the Insert and Search operations within the lifespan of the 50K workload, even while those other operations only take a few microseconds. Yet, overall, the Crack operation is more costly than the Insert and Search operations.

Figure 9 shows the cost per operation and per query for Encrypted Data. As in the case of plain data, the Crack operation be-

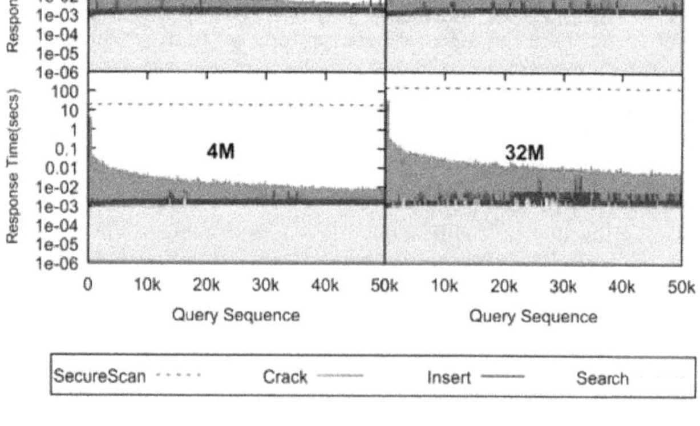

Figure 9: Cost per operation per query on Encrypted Data

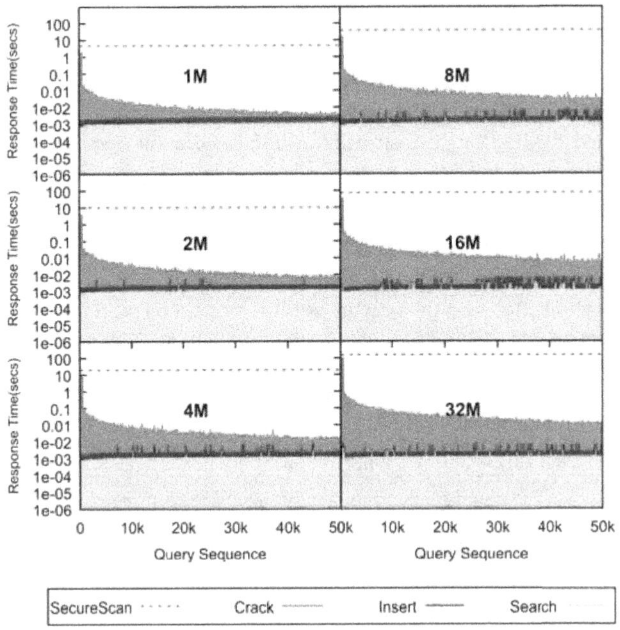

Figure 10: Cost per operation per query on Data with Ambiguity

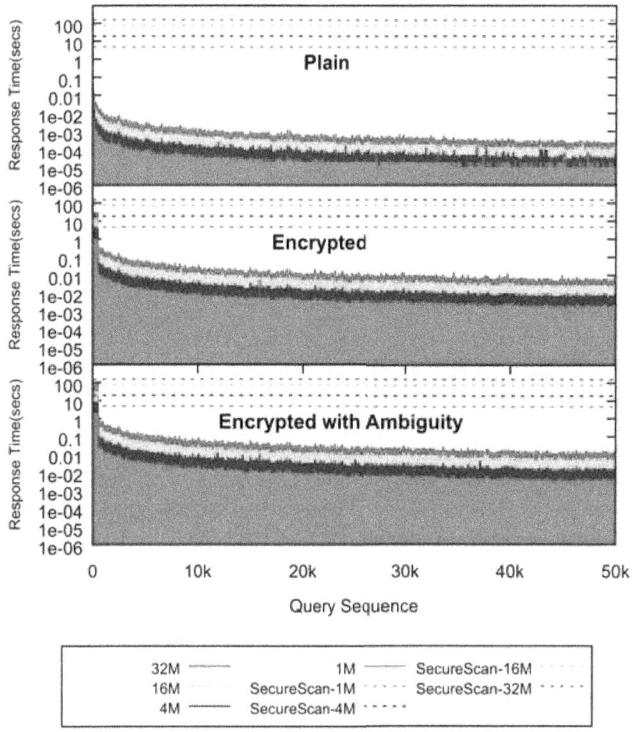

Figure 11: Cracking Time per query per data type

comes cheaper as the query workload evolves, with response time decreasing significantly. We also note that the Insert and Search operations become more costly from the initial query onwards, with their response times increasing from a few microseconds to a few milliseconds. Moreover, while cracking is more expensive at the early stages, after about 1000 queries for each data size the cost of cracking becomes less than 0.2 second.

Next, Figure 10 shows the cost per query for encrypted data with ambiguous values. All operations' trends remain the same as for encrypted data, with some higher peaks for cracking time, especially in the initial queries. This is due to the fact that physical reorganization is also done for ambiguous values along with real values. Thus, cracking becomes more expensive and burdens the initial queries of the workload. Even so, after about 2000 queries, response time again becomes approximately equal to 0.2 second. Besides, the time for cracking fluctuates a bit, as the cost of a cracking operation depends on the issued query's bounds; if the query falls on a previously unindexed piece, it requires more physical reorganization, hence higher response time.

We now focus on the time for cracking per query in particular. Figure 11 gathers together results for all data types, showing how cracking time grows as data sizes grow. Once gain, we observe that different data types present similar and comparable trends, while the overhead incurred for the sake of encryption and ambiguity, i.e., for the sake of security, remains manageable and reasonable.

5.3 Effect of Key Size

We now study the effect of our encryption key size on the system's performance. Figure 12 presents the total response time per query over encrypted data of size 10M, while varying encryption matrix key size from 4 to 64. This experiment is performed only for regular encrypted data, so as to examine the effect of key size in its native setting. The results we obtain show that a change in the key size bears a significant effect on performance across the query workload. This effect is felt most intensely with initial queries, which carry the heaviest burden anyway. However, in all cases, the response time increases proportionally to the key size change. For example, the initial response times shown in the figure are 2, 4, 8, 17, and 40 seconds for key sizes of 4, 8, 16, 32, and 64, respectively. The observed effect is due to the fact that vector comparisons become linearly more expensive with an increase of vector size. Nevertheless, as the cracking process progressively amortizes its cost while the query workload advances, the effect of encryption key size becomes negligible; for example, it makes a difference from a millisecond to 0.01 seconds between key size 4 and 64; we argue that this is an overhead that can be accepted for the sake of additional security.

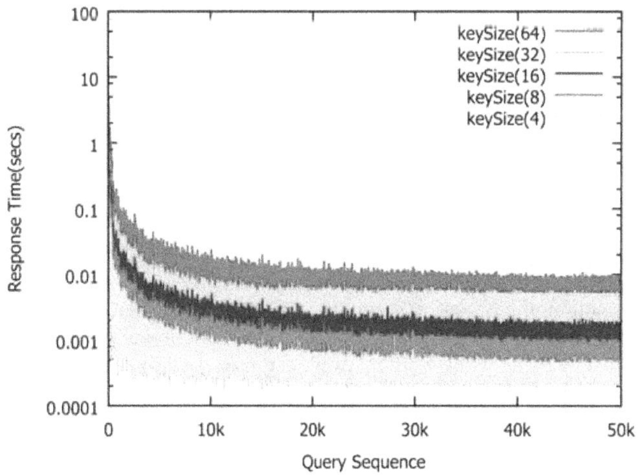

Figure 12: Cracking Time per query for different key sizes for Encrypted Data of size 10M

5.4 Client-Side Performance

All our experiments have hitherto studied the view from the server, as the server performs adaptive indexing actions. Yet a question arises about performance at the client, who receives query results, decrypts them, and, in the case of ambiguity, identifies and removes false positives. To address this question, we run a query workload of 1K random range queries of increasing selectivity from 0.1% upwards in geometric progress (0.1%, 0.3%, 0.9%, 2.7%, 8.1%) over data of size 10M; each group of 200 queries obtains a new selectivity value. Figure 13 shows our results. Figure 13a presents the *false positives rate* (FPR) at the client, i.e., the ratio of fake results over total results delivered to the client per query, while Figure 13b presents the runtime for decryption and filtering per query, comparing the case of Encrypted Data to that of Encrypted Data with Ambiguity, on a logarithmic time axis. We observe that the FPR fluctuates around 50%, as expected, and is unaffected by selectivity; besides, its fluctuation, with a variance of 7.1%, provides an additional security feature, as the exact number of returned results is not revealed and cannot be inferred by an adversary. Furthermore, we note that the decryption overhead is doubled due to ambiguity, presenting stability across different queries of the same selectivity, as well as scalability with increasing selectivity, with each new selectivity group coming one step upwards in the logarithmic time scale in the case with ambiguity just as in the case without ambiguity. Overall, the overhead remains manageable throughout the workload. We conclude that the client-side impact of our scheme is predictable and not detrimental to efficiency.

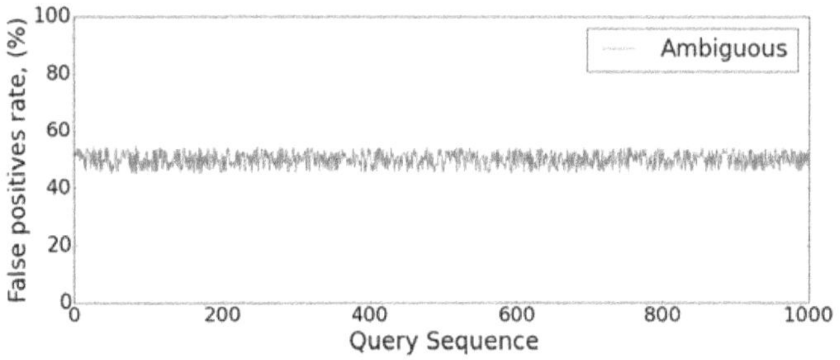

(a) False Positives Rate

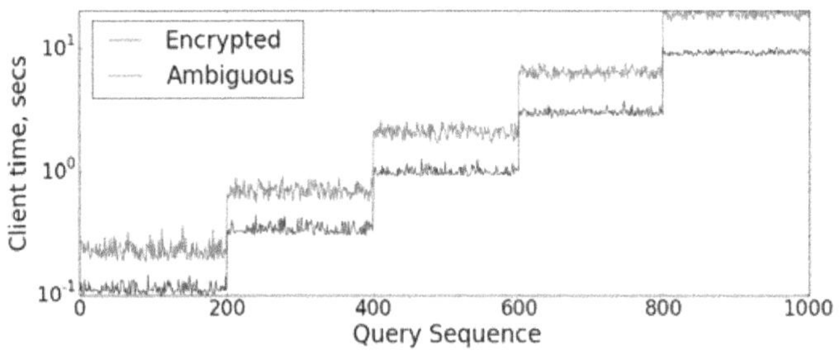

(b) Runtime for Decryption and Filtering

Figure 13: Client-Side Performance with increasing Selectivity

5.5 Discussion

In summary, our experimental analysis shows that our secure adaptive indexing schemes maintain the basic properties of adaptive indexing while working over encrypted data; by incrementally and adaptively focusing on hot data areas without requiring any initialization effort, they achieve significantly better performance compared to simply scanning encrypted data.

Naturally, working over encrypted data is more costly than working over plain data, for two reasons. First, we read and write more data due to auxiliary data for the sake of encryption and ambiguity. Second, we perform more computations, as comparisons are performed by vector operations. Even so, our schemes are several orders of magnitude faster than a secure scan.

An optimization that can be applied on top of our work is the utilization of modern hardware capabilities, such as multi-core CPUs and SIMD (Single Instruction Multiple Data) instructions. Past work has shown how to exploit multi-core CPUs for plain cracking, letting each core work on a single subpartition of a column in parallel and then merging these partitions to create new contiguous partitions [35]. A similar approach can be used in secure adaptive indexing out of the box. On the other hand, past work also attempted to reap the benefits of SIMD for plain cracking, with inconclusive results [35], as it is hard to map cracking comparison and swap actions to current SIMD instruction sets. On the other hand, the inner-product operations, on which our scheme relies (on top of plain cracking) to perform comparisons, are in principle amenable to SIMD-based vectorization: we multiply size-ℓ vectors; such vectorization should bring a significant performance boost, in the best case even *absorb* the computational cost of security at the server (assuming ℓ is not larger than modern SIMD vectors). Thus, secure cracking stands to gain from such optimizations. In our prototype implementation, we have opted for the arithmetic precision obtained by carrying out linear-algebra operations using the GMP arithmetic library, which does not inherently support vectorization, as it does not use primitive data types. In that sense, we have presented a *worst-case scenario* for our scheme in this paper. In our future work, we intend to examine the opportunity for SIMD utilization thoroughly by vectorizing GMP multiplication.

Past work has also speculated that sorting algorithms in highly-parallel environments could pose serious alternatives to plain cracking as modern CPUs evolve [4]. In that regard, we note that a highly-parallel sorting algorithm could not pose a legitimate algorithmic alternative to secure cracking, since our encryption scheme *does not allow* for sorting by cross-tuple comparisons; as we discussed, data encrypted by our scheme can be sorted *only* in a query-triggered manner, relying on encrypted pivot values provided by the client; thereby, our scheme *reinforces the rationale for cracking*.

6. CONCLUSION

This paper presents a novel, lightweight, linear-algebra-based encryption scheme that allows for (i) range query processing over encrypted numeric data outsourced in the cloud, and thereby for (ii) incremental, adaptive indexing whereby only data that are queried by trusted clients get indexed. Our scheme represents numerical values as short vectors, and relies on simple linear-algebra operations for encryption and decryption; it allows neither the actual data values nor their order to be disclosed. While the structure of the index may reveal order in the long-term, this only happens after crucial indexing operations have been performed; furthermore, we propose an additional obfuscation component in our scheme, which deliberately introduces ambiguity in our construction by allowing two variant interpretations of each encrypted value vector. We propose that our scheme assures the security needed in time-critical operations such as high-frequency trading and financial transaction processing over the cloud. We designed and implemented a prototype system that performs basic adaptive indexing operations, in the form of database cracking, over encrypted numeric data. Our experimental study demonstrates that our scheme preserves the graceful adaptation and hands-free self-reorganization advantages of cracking with a reasonable overhead incurred due to encryption.

In the future, we plan to (i) thoroughly analyze the properties of our encryption scheme, and (ii) utilize modern hardware capabilities for improved performance in cryptographic operations.

Acknowledgments

We thank Nickolai Zeldovich, Jaideep Vaidya, and David Cash for fruitful discussions on this topic.

7. REFERENCES

[1] D. Abadi, P. A. Boncz, S. Harizopoulos, S. Idreos, and S. Madden. The design and implementation of modern column-oriented database systems. *Foundations and Trends in Databases*, 5(3):197–280, 2013.

[2] A. Agopyan, E. Şener, and A. Beklen. Financial business cloud for high-frequency trading: A research on financial trading operations with cloud computing. *International Journal on Advances in Intelligent Systems*, 4(3):203–2017, 2011.

[3] R. Agrawal, J. Kiernan, R. Srikant, and Y. Xu. Order-preserving encryption for numeric data. In *SIGMOD*, 2004.

[4] V. Alvarez, F. M. Schuhknecht, J. Dittrich, and S. Richter. Main memory adaptive indexing for multi-core systems. In *DaMoN*, pages 3:1–3:10, 2014.

[5] A. Arasu, K. Eguro, M. Joglekar, R. Kaushik, D. Kossmann, and R. Ramamurthy. Transaction processing on confidential data using Cipherbase. In *ICDE*, pages 435–446, 2015.

[6] A. Boldyreva, N. Chenette, Y. Lee, and A. O'Neill. Order-preserving symmetric encryption. In *EUROCRYPT*, pages 224–241, 2009.

[7] A. Boldyreva, N. Chenette, and A. O'Neill. Order-preserving encryption revisited: Improved security analysis and alternative solutions. In *CRYPTO*, 2011.

[8] P. Boncz, M. Zukowski, and N. Nes. Monetdb/x100: Hyper-pipelining query execution. In *CIDR*, pages 225–237, 2005.

[9] D. Boneh and B. Waters. Conjunctive, subset, and range queries on encrypted data. In *TCC*, pages 535–554, 2007.

[10] S. Bothe, P. Karras, and A. Vlachou. eSkyline: Processing skyline queries over encrypted data. *PVLDB*, 6(12):1338–1341, 2013.

[11] S. Chaudhuri and G. Weikum. Rethinking database system architecture: Towards a self-tuning RISC-style database system. In *VLDB*, pages 1–10, 2000.

[12] E. Damiani, S. De Capitani di Vimercati, S. Jajodia, S. Paraboschi, and P. Samarati. Balancing confidentiality and efficiency in untrusted relational DBMSs. In *ACM CCS*, pages 93–102, 2003.

[13] T. Ge and S. B. Zdonik. Fast, secure encryption for indexing in a column-oriented DBMS. In *ICDE*, pages 676–685, 2007.

[14] C. Gentry. Fully homomorphic encryption using ideal lattices. In *STOC*, pages 169–178, 2009.

[15] C. Gentry, S. Halevi, and N. P. Smart. Homomorphic evaluation of the AES circuit. In *CRYPTO*, pages 850–867, 2012.

[16] G. Graefe, F. Halim, S. Idreos, H. A. Kuno, S. Manegold, and B. Seeger. Transactional support for adaptive indexing. *VLDB J.*, 23(2):303–328, 2014.

[17] G. Graefe, S. Idreos, H. Kuno, and S. Manegold. Benchmarking adaptive indexing. In *TPCTC*, pages 169–184, 2010.

[18] G. Graefe and H. Kuno. Self-selecting, self-tuning, incrementally optimized indexes. In *EDBT*, 2010.

[19] H. Hacigümüs, B. R. Iyer, C. Li, and S. Mehrotra. Executing SQL over encrypted data in the database-service-provider model. In *SIGMOD*, pages 216–227, 2002.

[20] F. Halim, S. Idreos, P. Karras, and R. H. C. Yap. Stochastic database cracking: Towards robust adaptive indexing in main-memory column-stores. *PVLDB*, 5(6):502–513, 2012.

[21] B. Hore, S. Mehrotra, M. Canim, and M. Kantarcioglu. Secure multidimensional range queries over outsourced data. *VLDB Journal*, 21(3):333–358, 2012.

[22] B. Hore, S. Mehrotra, and G. Tsudik. A privacy-preserving index for range queries. In *VLDB*, pages 720–731, 2004.

[23] S. Idreos. Database cracking: Towards auto-tuning database kernels. *CWI, PhD Thesis*, 2010.

[24] S. Idreos. Cracking big data. *ERCIM News*, 2012(89), 2012.

[25] S. Idreos, M. L. Kersten, and S. Manegold. Database cracking. In *CIDR*, pages 68–78, 2007.

[26] S. Idreos, M. L. Kersten, and S. Manegold. Updating a cracked database. In *SIGMOD*, pages 413–424, 2007.

[27] S. Idreos, M. L. Kersten, and S. Manegold. Self-organizing tuple reconstruction in column-stores. In *SIGMOD*, pages 297–308, 2009.

[28] S. Idreos, S. Manegold, and G. Graefe. Adaptive indexing in modern database kernels. In *EDBT*, pages 566–569, 2012.

[29] S. Idreos, S. Manegold, H. A. Kuno, and G. Graefe. Merging what's cracked, cracking what's merged: Adaptive indexing in main-memory column-stores. *PVLDB*, 4(9):585–597, 2011.

[30] E. Laursen. High-end trading strategists see cost savings in cloud computing. http://www.institutionalinvestor.com/Article/2750046/Search/High-End-Trading-Strategists-See-Cost-Savings-in-Cloud.html. [Online; posted on January 14, 2011].

[31] R. Li, A. X. Liu, A. L. Wang, and B. Bruhadeshwar. Fast range query processing with strong privacy protection for cloud computing. *PVLDB*, 7(14):1953–1964, 2014.

[32] S. Manegold, P. A. Boncz, and M. L. Kersten. Optimizing database architecture for the new bottleneck: memory access. *The VLDB Journal*, 9(3):231–246, 2000.

[33] M. Mani, K. Shah, and M. Gunda. Enabling secure database as a service using fully homomorphic encryption: Challenges and opportunities. *CoRR*, abs/1302.2654, 2013.

[34] E. Petraki, S. Idreos, and S. Manegold. Holistic indexing in main-memory column-stores. In *SIGMOD*, pages 1153–1166, 2015.

[35] H. Pirk, E. Petraki, S. Idreos, S. Manegold, and M. L. Kersten. Database cracking: fancy scan, not poor man's sort! In *DaMoN*, pages 4:1–4:8, 2014.

[36] R. A. Popa, C. M. S. Redfield, N. Zeldovich, and H. Balakrishnan. CryptDB: protecting confidentiality with encrypted query processing. In *SOSP*, pages 85–100, 2011.

[37] T. Sanamrad, L. Braun, D. Kossmann, and R. Venkatesan. Randomly partitioned encryption for cloud databases. In *DBSec*, pages 307–323, 2014.

[38] E. Shi, J. Bethencourt, H. T.-H. Chan, D. X. Song, and A. Perrig. Multi-dimensional range query over encrypted data. In *IEEE Symposium on Security and Privacy*, pages 350–364, 2007.

[39] M. Stonebraker et al. C-store: a column-oriented DBMS. In *VLDB*, pages 553–564, 2005.

[40] S. Tu, M. F. Kaashoek, S. Madden, and N. Zeldovich. Processing analytical queries over encrypted data. *PVLDB*, 6(5):289–300, 2013.

[41] S. Wang, D. Agrawal, and A. El Abbadi. A comprehensive framework for secure query processing on relational data in the cloud. In *Secure Data Management*, pages 52–69, 2011.

[42] W. H. Wang and L. V. S. Lakshmanan. Efficient secure query evaluation over encrypted XML databases. In *VLDB*, pages 127–138, 2006.

[43] W. K. Wong, D. W.-L. Cheung, B. Kao, and N. Mamoulis. Secure kNN computation on encrypted databases. In *SIGMOD*, pages 139–152, 2009.

[44] Z. Yang, S. Zhong, and R. N. Wright. Privacy-preserving queries on encrypted data. In *ESORICS*, pages 479–495, 2006.

[45] M. L. Yiu, G. Ghinita, C. S. Jensen, and P. Kalnis. Enabling search services on outsourced private spatial data. *The VLDB Journal*, 19(3):363–384, 2010.

Practical Private Range Search Revisited

Ioannis Demertzis *
University of Maryland
yannis@umd.edu

Stavros Papadopoulos
Intel Labs & MIT
stavrosp@csail.mit.edu

Odysseas Papapetrou *
EPFL, Lausanne, Switzerland
odysseas.papapetrou@epfl.ch

Antonios Deligiannakis
Technical University of Crete
adeli@softnet.tuc.gr

Minos Garofalakis
Technical University of Crete
minos@softnet.tuc.gr

ABSTRACT

We consider a data *owner* that outsources its dataset to an *untrusted server*. The owner wishes to enable the server to answer *range* queries on a single attribute, without compromising the privacy of the data and the queries. There are several schemes on *"practical"* private range search (mainly in Databases venues) that attempt to strike a trade-off between efficiency and security. Nevertheless, these methods either lack provable security guarantees, or permit unacceptable privacy leakages. In this paper, we take an *interdisciplinary* approach, which combines the rigor of Security formulations and proofs with efficient Data Management techniques. We construct a wide set of novel schemes with realistic security/performance trade-offs, adopting the notion of *Searchable Symmetric Encryption* (SSE) primarily proposed for keyword search. We reduce range search to *multi-keyword* search using *range covering* techniques with tree-like indexes. We demonstrate that, given *any* secure SSE scheme, the challenge boils down to (i) formulating leakages that arise from the index *structure*, and (ii) minimizing *false positives* incurred by some schemes under heavy data *skew*. We analytically detail the superiority of our proposals over prior work and experimentally confirm their practicality.

1. INTRODUCTION

We focus on a setting with two parties; a data *owner* and a *server*. The owner *outsources* its dataset to the server, and enforces the latter with answering *range* queries on a single attribute. The server is *untrusted*, and the goal is to protect the privacy of the dataset and the queries. The owner *encrypts* its data prior to sending them to the server. The challenge lies in enabling the server to process the owner's queries directly on the encrypted data, while achieving performance costs close to the non-private case. The benefits of data outsourcing and the importance of privacy have been stressed in numerous earlier works (e.g., [9, 31, 34, 38]).

*Work performed while the author was at the Technical University of Crete.

SIGMOD'16, June 26-July 01, 2016, San Francisco, CA, USA
© 2016 ACM. ISBN 978-1-4503-3531-7/16/06...$15.00
DOI: http://dx.doi.org/10.1145/2882903.2882911

Prior work. Privacy-preserving range queries can be solved with *optimal* security via powerful theoretical cryptographic tools, such as *Oblivious Random Access Memory* (ORAM) [17, 29] and *Fully Homomorphic Encryption* (FHE) [12, 13]. Nevertheless, despite their recent advances, both these tools are prohibitively costly for large database applications [37, 35, 36]. Motivated by this, there is a long line of work on private range search (especially in Databases venues) that attempts to strike a more desirable balance between security and practical efficiency [18, 19, 20, 31, 38].

All existing approaches either lack provable security guarantees, or permit unacceptable leakages. For instance, [18, 20, 19] employ *deterministic* encryption and bucketization techniques that map tuples with the same query attribute value to the same bucket. Deterministic encryption leaks the distribution of the data on the query attribute. Moreover, these schemes do not offer standard security definitions and proofs, which makes it hard to determine any other possible leakage. Another set of works utilizes *Order Preserving Encryption* (OPE), which has the property that the ciphertexts preserve the ordering of the plaintexts [2, 3, 23, 27, 30]. As such, traditional efficient indexes can be built directly on encrypted data, and queried in the same manner as for plaintexts. Nevertheless, OPE is also deterministic, inheriting the distribution leakage. In addition, it inevitably leaks the ordering of the data.

The work closest to ours is by Li et al. [26], which follows the notion of *Searchable Symmetric Encryption* (SSE) [5, 6, 8, 9, 22, 34]. SSE has been studied extensively for keyword queries. It relaxes the security of ORAM by leaking the *access patterns* of each query (i.e., which data it "touches"), as well as the *search patterns* (i.e., which queries are the same). However, nothing else is leaked (e.g., data distribution). The gain from allowing this leakage is efficiency, since SSE schemes typically build on fast inverted indexes and make use of lightweight cryptography, such as *Pseudorandom Function* (PRF) and hash evaluations. SSE also provides a rigorous framework for accurately defining *leakage* for any construction. Unfortunately, the scheme by Li et al. [26] relies on weak, obsolete SSE definitions (explained in detail in Section 2.1). Moreover, it unnecessarily introduces *false positives* and does not support updates. Most importantly, it does not define leakages that are introduced by the tree structure utilized in query execution. As we will show later, one of our baseline constructions is built on similar ideas to [26], but offers substantially better security and performance, accurately defining leakage, avoiding false positives, and supporting updates.

Scheme	Security	Query Size	Search Time	Storage	False Posit.
Li et al. [26]	0	$O(\log R)$	$\Omega(\log n \log R + r)$	$O(n \log n \log m)$	$O(r)$
Quadratic	6	$O(1)$	$O(r)$	$O(nm^2)$	–
Constant-BRC	1	$O(\log R)$	$O(R + r)$	$O(n)$	–
Constant-URC	2	$O(\log R)$	$O(R + r)$	$O(n)$	–
Logarithmic-BRC	3	$O(\log R)$	$O(\log R + r)$	$O(n \log m)$	–
Logarithmic-URC	4	$O(\log R)$	$O(\log R + r)$	$O(n \log m)$	–
Logarithmic-SRC	6	$O(1)$	$O(n)$	$O(n \log m)$	$O(n)$
Logarithmic-SRC-i	5	$O(1)$	$O(R + r)$	$O(n \log m)$	$O(R + r)$

n: dataset size, r: result size, m: domain size, R: query range size

Table 1: Summary of our RSSE schemes and analytical comparison to our closest competitor. Our schemes are named after the storage expansion factor and the range covering technique. A higher value in the Security column means better security guarantees.

Our contributions. In this paper, we revisit practical private range search, taking an *interdisciplinary* approach that combines the state-of-the-art definitional framework of SSE [9], with efficient data management methods. In particular, we reduce range search to *multi-keyword* search using *range covering* techniques with tree-like indexes, i.e., converting a range into sub-ranges, each representing an index node and receiving a keyword label. Contrary to off-the-shelf multi-keyword SSE schemes [6] that incur a prohibitive linear search time in the dataset size, we design efficient techniques based on single-keyword SSE protocols. We also show that we can use the (single-keyword) SSE security games to prove the security of a *Range SSE* (RSSE) scheme, by carefully defining the extra *structural leakage* stemming from the use of the tree index to convert a range into a set of keywords. This has the important benefit that *any* secure SSE scheme can be used as a black box to realize a RSSE scheme, which means that any future advances in the active area of SSE can be readily incorporated into a RSSE construction.

We emphasize that expressing a range with sub-ranges mapped to index nodes gives a lot of flexibility in designing RSSE schemes with variable efficiency and security guarantees. We also point out that the choice of the range covering method affects the security guarantees and could lead to false positives, especially under heavy data *skew*. To capture the above, we devise a wide set of solutions, which revolve around trading storage overhead and (potentially) false positives for security. Our constructions with their performance and security characteristics are summarized in Table 1 and discussed in detail throughout the paper. We also quantify the costs of Li et al. [26], which is clearly subsumed by our Logarithmic-BRC scheme.

Logarithmic-SRC-i offers the best trade-off between security and efficiency among all our solutions. It employs a novel directed-acyclic graph (DAG) structure that resembles a tree, and entails an extra round of communication between the owner and the server ("i" in its name stands for *interactive*). This index allows hiding even the order of the results, and minimizes the false positives. It is noteworthy that two of our schemes, namely Constant-BRC and Constant-URC, rely on the notion of *Delegatable PRFs* [24] and are motivated by a brief discussion included in [24]. Our contribution lies in formalizing the solutions and proving them secure.

Finally, contrary to existing *dynamic* SSE solutions (DSSE) [5, 21, 22, 34], we tackle updates in a manner closer to the one employed in large-scale database systems. In particular, the DSSE works attempt to devise dynamic indexes that handle updates with the minimum possible leakage. We stress that databases like Vertica [25] perform the updates in *batches*, such that (i) each batch is treated as an independent instance of the dataset, and (ii) multiple batches periodically get *consolidated* into a single dataset. This is to amortize the average update cost, and substitute numerous random disk accesses with a few linear scan operations. We formulate updates in our setting by effectively using multiple *static* RSSE instances that periodically get consolidated and re-encrypted.

Our contributions are summarized as follows:

- We are the first to formalize private range search in the context of state-of-the-art SSE, effectively introducing the first concrete *Range Searchable Symmetric Encryption* (RSSE) framework.
- We devise numerous RSSE schemes, identifying various trade-offs between efficiency and security.
- We tackle updates by adopting techniques from large-scale database systems, while formalizing the leakages.
- We analytically detail the superiority of our constructions over prior work and experimentally confirm their practicality.

Our paper is self-contained, in the sense that it does not require any particular knowledge on Security or Data Management. We provide both the rigorous definitions and the intuition behind all the formalism.

2. BACKGROUND

Section 2.1 surveys the related work, whereas Section 2.2 includes necessary preliminary information.

2.1 Related work

General privacy-preserving queries can be solved with optimal security guarantees using powerful cryptographic protocols, such as *Fully Homomorphic Encryption* (FHE) [12, 13] and *Oblivious RAM* (ORAM) [17, 29]. FHE enables the execution of *any* function directly on the ciphertexts, without revealing anything about the result. Unfortunately, despite the recent advances, FHE is still impractical due to the prohibitive ciphertext size and computational time. ORAM enables access to an encrypted memory space, without disclosing which memory location is accessed, thus hiding both the data and the *access patterns* of the queries. Currently, even the most efficient ORAM schemes [37, 35, 36] suffer from high bandwidth overhead and client storage cost, and require multiple rounds of communication. A wide set of techniques attempts to mitigate the above issues, trading security for efficiency. Below we focus mainly on those targeting range queries.

One class of techniques relies on *deterministic encryption* (DET) that maps two equal plaintexts to the same ciphertext [18, 19, 20] (its counterpart being *probabilistic encryption*), enabling *equality* queries on encrypted data. These schemes perform *bucketization* (accompanied by indexing) of data by encrypting based on the query attribute, and reduce range search to a set of equality queries that retrieve matching buckets. Although these schemes are quite efficient, they inherit the drawback of DET, which discloses the distribution of the data (since the bucketization essentially reveals a histogram of the data on the query attribute). Moreover, they do not offer rigorous security definitions and proofs. Another class of methods [2, 3, 23, 27, 30] utilizes *Order Preserving Encryption* (OPE). The latter has the property that the ciphertexts preserve the order of the plaintexts. Therefore, efficient traditional indexes can be built on the ciphertexts, in the same manner as on plaintexts. OPE is deterministic and, thus, inherits the data distribution leakage of DET. In addition, it also leaks the *order* of the data and, hence, offers even weaker security than DET.

Searchable Symmetric Encryption (SSE) [5, 6, 7, 8, 9, 14, 21, 22, 33, 34, 39, 28] has been initially proposed in the context of *keyword search*, having as main goals to (i) introduce rigorous security definitions, and (ii) enable the design of schemes that avoid the leakages of DET, while retaining high efficiency. There is currently no off-the-shelf SSE scheme that supports range queries. As we shall see, in our work (as well as in [26] described below) we effectively reduce range search into *multi-keyword* search. The only SSE scheme that seems applicable to multi-keyword search is that of Cash et al. [6] which targets *Boolean queries* and can express multi-keyword search as a *disjunction* of keywords. Unfortunately, disjunctions in [6] are answered in *linear* time in the number of documents, which conflicts with our performance desiderata.

The work closest to ours is the basic scheme of Li et al. [26][1]. Note that the authors also introduce another two schemes, which however share similarities with OPE and, hence, inherit its drawbacks explained above. In the sequel, any reference to [26] implies the *basic scheme*. This scheme assumes a binary tree over the query attribute domain, and computes for every tuple d in the dataset D the $\log m$ dyadic ranges covering its attribute value, where m is the domain size. Let the dyadic ranges of item d be denoted by $DR(d)$. Li et al. create a binary tree as follows. The root initially corresponds to all data items, and stores a *Bloom filter* [1] over $\{DR(d) : d \in D\}$. The algorithm works recursively, starting from the root and working *top-down*. At each node, it randomly *permutes* and splits the data items in two sets, each corresponding to one child. Then, it stores a Bloom filter over the DR values for the data items corresponding to each node. Eventually, each leaf contains a Bloom filter indexing only $DR(d)$ for a single d. A range query is answered by splitting the range into its $O(\log R)$ minimal dyadic ranges, where R is the range size over the domain, and traversing the tree by checking whether the Bloom filter in each node "contains" some minimum dyadic range.

[1] Faber et al. [11] also independently proposed schemes for range querying, after our work was submitted for publication. Two of their schemes are practically the same as our Logarithmic-BRC/URC, whereas their three-range cover solution is similar to our Logarithmic-SRC scheme (which is single-range cover). However, they did not consider false positives under data skew, which is efficiently captured by our most advanced method, Logarithmic-SRC-i.

The costs of [26] are included in Table 1. The scheme *fixes* the ratio of the *false positives* (inherent to Bloom filters) at each node. This results in $O(n \log n \log m)$ storage cost, and $O(r)$ false positives, where n is the dataset size and r the result size. Moreover, the query size is $O(\log R)$, whereas the search time is $\Omega(\log n \log R+r)$. Note that it is difficult (and out of our scope) to find a tight upper bound for the actual search time, due to the random perturbation of the items in the tree and the false positives, but [26] points out that this could be $O(r \log n)$. Performance aside, the most severe drawback of [26] is its security. First, it relies on the SSE definitions from Goh [14] which have been proven weak by [7, 9]; at a very high level, Goh [14] implies that the privacy of the encrypted queries (trapdoors) is not protected, whereas [9] protects both the data and the queries. Second, [26] focuses on *non-adaptive adversaries*; from a practical point of view, this means that [26] is secure only in applications that allow the users to ask all their queries *once in a batch*, and then they *shut down*. Contrary, it is not secure against adversaries that ask some queries first and, based on the responses they get, then *adapt* their attacks and ask more targeted queries later. This considerably limits the applicability of this solution in realistic settings. Finally, [26] does not support updates. We introduce Constant-BRC/URC (Section 5) and Logarithmic-BRC/URC (Section 6.1) that subsume [26] in all aspects.

There is a long line of work on creating *dynamic SSE* (DSSE) schemes to handle updates [5, 21, 22, 34]. The challenge in these works is to achieve a property called *forward privacy*; the server should not learn that a newly added item satisfies a query issued in the past. Most solutions focus on creating a dynamic secure index. In our work, we take an alternative approach that satisfies forward privacy, by utilizing only *static* SSE schemes and combining them with efficient bulk-loading techniques adopted from large-scale database systems (such as Vertica [25]).

Range queries have also been studied in a different setting where there are multiple parties contributing to the owner's dataset using her public key, and the owner issues its range queries on this collective dataset with her secret key [4, 32]. This setting is based on asymmetric cryptography and, hence, entails considerably higher computational costs than our schemes.

2.2 Preliminaries

We explain in turn two range covering techniques with binary trees, the PRF and DPRF cryptographic tools, and the required definitions we adopt from the SSE literature.

Range covering techniques. Consider a domain A. We construct a full binary tree over its values bottom-up. Given a range (i.e., a sequence of *contiguous* values) over A, a *range covering* technique selects a set of nodes whose subtrees collectively cover the given range entirely. We will describe two techniques, *best range cover* (BRC) and *uniform range cover* (URC). BRC essentially selects the *minimum* number of nodes that cover exactly the range (also called *minimum dyadic intervals*). For range size R, there are $O(\log R)$ such nodes. In Figure 1, for $A = \{0, \ldots, 7\}$, BRC covers range $[2, 7]$ with nodes $N_{2,3}$ and $N_{4,7}$ (shown in gray).

Consider now range $[1, 6]$ which has the same size as $[2, 7]$. BRC covers $[1, 6]$ with nodes $N_1, N_{2,3}, N_{4,5}$ and N_6, i.e., with a *different number* of nodes at *different levels*. We shall see later that this leads to extra leakage, since the number of nodes covering a range may *imply* where an encrypted range query may or may not be. Motivated by this fact, [24] introduces URC in the context of DPRFs (explained below). In particular, [24] points out that there is always a *worst-case decomposition* of *any* range of a given size R into a *certain number* of nodes at *certain levels*. Interestingly, this decomposition retains the $O(\log R)$ complexity, *regardless of where* this range is placed over the domain. Briefly stated, URC starts with the set of nodes output by BRC, and keeps on "breaking" certain nodes into their two children, until there is at least one node for each level $0, \ldots, max$, where max is the highest level of nodes in the result. In the example of Figure 1, for range $[2, 7]$, URC initially invokes BRC and retrieves $N_{2,3}$ and $N_{4,7}$. These nodes are at levels 1 and 2, respectively, but there is no node at level 0. Subsequently, it breaks $N_{4,7}$ into $N_{4,5}$ and $N_{6,7}$, as well as $N_{2,3}$ into N_2 and N_3. Now $[2, 7]$ is represented by nodes $N_2, N_3, N_{4,5}, N_{6,7}$ (enclosed in boxes in Figure 1), i.e., by two nodes at level 0 and two nodes at level 1. Observe that $[1, 6]$ is also represented by the same number of nodes at respective levels.

PRFs and DPRFs. A *Pseudorandom Function (PRF) family* $\mathcal{F}$ is a set of functions $\{f_k : A \to B \mid k \in \mathcal{K}\}$, where $A, B, \mathcal{F}, \mathcal{K}$ are indexed by a security parameter λ and such that $f_k(\cdot)$ is efficiently computable. The main property of a PRF is that an adversary that does not know the secret key k can distinguish $f_k \in \mathcal{F}$ from a truly random function only with negligible probability in λ, written as $\mathsf{negl}(\lambda)$.

A *Delegatable PRF (DPRF)* [24] is an enhancement of a PRF with an extra property: the party that knows the secret key k of f_k can allow another party that does not possess k to derive DPRF values for a *subset* of the domain A. The benefit is performance: the secret holder generates and outsources a small set of intermediate values, which can be used by an untrusted third party to produce an exponential number of DPRF values. Similar to a PRF, the intermediate and final DPRF values appear to be random.

In [24] the DPRF values are computed using the seminal GGM pseudorandom generator [16]. This is defined as $G : \{0,1\}^\lambda \to \{0,1\}^{2\lambda}$, i.e., on a λ-bit input x, $G(x)$ produces *two* λ-bit outputs $G_0(x)$ and $G_1(x)$ that appear to be random. Let $a_{\ell-1} \ldots a_0 = a \in A$ be some ℓ-bit domain value. Its DPRF value using secret key k is computed as $f_k(a_{\ell-1} \cdots a_0) = G_{a_0}(\ldots(G_{a_{\ell-1}}(k)))$, i.e., k serves as the *seed* to successive computations of G. For example, the binary representation of 6 is $(110)_2$. In Figure 1, observe that 6 is reached by a path starting from the root that chooses right, right and left. Assigning 0 to left and 1 to right, this path traversal uniquely identifies the binary expression of value 6. The DPRF of 6 is $f_k(6) = G_0(G_1(G_1(k)))$. The GGM values are practically organized into binary tree, hereafter called GGM tree.

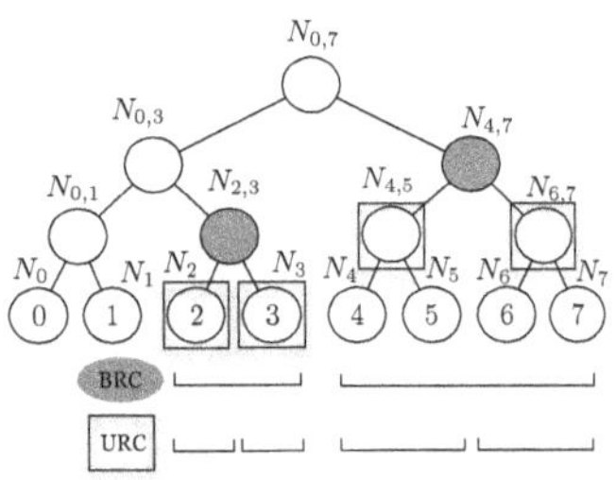

Figure 1: Covering range $[2, 7]$ with BRC and URC

The purpose of this particular construction is to permit delegation. Let us focus on range [4-7], completely covered by node $N_{4,7}$ in Figure 1. Observe that, given $G_1(k)$ and without possessing k, one can derive *all* DPRF values for 4-7; $G_1(k)$ is associated with node $N_{4,7}$, and all values corresponding to its descendants can be derived by applying G successively using $G_1(k)$ as the seed and choosing the G_0 (left) or G_1 (right) output based on the path.

When the input range is not covered completely with a single node, it is decomposed into a set of multiple nodes covering the range (following BRC or URC), and the appropriate GGM values corresponding to those nodes (paired with the node level) are provided. The receiver of these values can then easily derive all the DPRFs within the range. The GGM values are called *tokens* and produced by a function T that implements BRC or URC, whereas the derivation of the actual DPRF values (corresponding to the leaves) is performed by a function C. Both T and C are part of the specification of the DPRF function family.

SSE definitions. Let D be a collection of *documents*, where a document can be any data item, even a tuple. Each document $d \in D$ has a unique id, which could be the actual document id or an alias that allows easy mapping to d. Every d is also associated with a set of keywords from a dictionary Δ. We represent by $id(w)$ the ids of the documents that contain w. SSE schemes focus on building an *encrypted index* I on the document ids. For simplicity, we concentrate only on the ids, since the actual documents are encrypted independently and stored at the server separately from I; once some id is retrieved during search, the server can send the corresponding document to the owner, who decrypts in a final step that is *orthogonal* to the SSE instantiation.

An SSE *protocol* involves an *owner* and a *server* and consists of the following algorithms:

$k \leftarrow \mathsf{Setup}(1^\lambda)$: is a probabilistic algorithm run by the owner before commencing the system. It takes as input security parameter λ and outputs a secret key k.

$I \leftarrow \mathsf{BuildIndex}(k, D)$: is a probabilistic algorithm run by the owner prior to sending its data to the server. It takes as input the secret key k and the data collection D, and outputs an encrypted index I built on the document ids. Index I is sent to the server, along with the actual encrypted documents.

$t \leftarrow \mathsf{Trpdr}(k, w)$: is a deterministic algorithm executed by the owner when issuing a query. It takes as input key k and keyword w, and outputs a token t.

$X \leftarrow \mathsf{Search}(t, I)$: is a deterministic algorithm run by the server to retrieve the ids of the documents containing the query keyword. It takes as input a token t corresponding to the query keyword and the encrypted index I, and outputs a set X of document ids.

In state-of-the-art SSE constructions [9, 8, 22, 21, 34, 6, 5], I is essentially an encrypted *inverted index*, which allows

$\mathbf{Real}_{\mathsf{SSE},\mathcal{A}}(k)$	$\mathbf{Ideal}_{\mathsf{SSE},\mathcal{A},\mathcal{S}}(k)$
$k \leftarrow \mathsf{Setup}(1^\lambda)$	
$(D, st_\mathcal{A}) \leftarrow \mathcal{A}_0(1^\lambda)$	$(D, st_\mathcal{A}) \leftarrow \mathcal{A}_0(1^\lambda)$
$I \leftarrow \mathsf{BuildIndex}(k, D)$	$(I, st_\mathcal{S}) \leftarrow \mathcal{S}_0(\mathcal{L}_1(D))$
$(w_1, st_\mathcal{A}) \leftarrow \mathcal{A}_1(st_\mathcal{A}, I)$	$(w_1, st_\mathcal{A}) \leftarrow \mathcal{A}_1(st_\mathcal{A}, I)$
$t_1 \leftarrow \mathsf{Trpdr}(k, w_1)$	$(t_1, st_\mathcal{S}) \leftarrow \mathcal{S}_1(st_\mathcal{S}, \mathcal{L}_2(D, w_1))$
for $2 \leq i \leq q$	for $2 \leq i \leq q$
$(w_i, st_\mathcal{A}) \leftarrow \mathcal{A}_i(st_\mathcal{A}, I, t_1..t_{i-1})$	$(w_i, st_\mathcal{A}) \leftarrow \mathcal{A}_i(st_\mathcal{A}, I, t_1..t_{i-1})$
$t_i \leftarrow \mathsf{Trpdr}(k, w_i)$	$(t_i, st_\mathcal{S}) \leftarrow \mathcal{S}_i(st_\mathcal{S}, \mathcal{L}_2(D, w_1..w_i))$
let $\mathbf{t} = (t_1..t_q)$	let $\mathbf{t} = (t_1..t_q)$
output $v = (I, \mathbf{t})$ and $st_\mathcal{A}$	output $v = (I, \mathbf{t})$ and $st_\mathcal{A}$

Figure 2: SSE ideal-real security game

efficient retrieval of the document id list corresponding to the query keyword. The token t constitutes auxiliary information that allows the server to *partially decrypt* only the index components that lead to the retrieval of the result ids. However, once these index portions are decrypted, they become permanently known to the server. In other words, SSE inherently introduces certain information *leakage*.

An *ad-hoc* way of defining security would be to outline a set of adversarial attacks, and prove that the scheme is robust against these attacks. This is dangerous as we cannot anticipate the types of attacks an adversary is able to launch. A *rigorous* way to define security is to *formulate* the leakage, and *prove* that the adversary learns nothing more than this leakage. Curtmola et al. [9] introduced a framework for achieving this, following the seminal *ideal-real paradigm* by Goldreich [15]. In particular, after formulating leakage, we define two *games*. The *real* is essentially the execution of the actual SSE protocol. The *ideal* is a *simulation* of the real, i.e., an attempt to "fake" the real game, knowing only the formulated leakage. Finally, we prove that an adversary can *distinguish* the output of the first from that of the second with only *negligible* probability. Intuitively, this means that the adversary indeed does not learn anything more than the leakage, otherwise he would be able to distinguish the real from the ideal execution with non-negligible probability.

We focus on *semi-honest*, *adaptive* adversaries. "Semi-honest" means that the adversary is curious to infer information during the execution of the protocol, but does not deviate from the protocol. "Adaptive" means that the adversary attempts to learn information even in between query executions, and may adaptively select the next query based on the previous ones. A non-adaptive adversary submits all queries before starting to learn information. Clearly, adaptive adversaries are more realistic in database applications where the queries are not presented all at once to a system.

For completeness and to facilitate presentation in Section 3, in Figure 2 we present the SSE ideal-real games for (semi-honest) adaptive adversaries, as introduced in [10]. In $\mathbf{Real}_{\mathsf{SSE},\mathcal{A}}$, an adversary $\mathcal{A}$ interacts with the actual SSE protocol, *choosing* the initial document set and (adaptively) the keyword queries. The adversary gets access only to BuildIndex and Trpdr, since it does not know the secret key k. $st_\mathcal{A}$ is some *state* maintained by the adversary. The final *view* of $\mathcal{A}$ is the encrypted index I, and the set of generated tokens $\mathbf{t}$ and $st_\mathcal{A}$. Now observe the line correspondence between $\mathbf{Real}_{\mathsf{SSE},\mathcal{A}}$ and $\mathbf{Ideal}_{\mathsf{SSE},\mathcal{A},\mathcal{S}}$. In the latter, a *simulator* $\mathcal{S}$ (maintaining state $st_\mathcal{S}$) is enforced with "faking" BuildIndex and Trpdr for the same D and query keywords, *only using* leakage functions $\mathcal{L}_1$ and $\mathcal{L}_2$ (explained below). Security boils down to returning $(I, \mathbf{t}, st_\mathcal{A})$ that is distinguishable with negligible probability from the output by the real game. The challenge lies in properly using leakages $\mathcal{L}_1$ and $\mathcal{L}_2$ to create I and $\mathbf{t}$, such that (i) they "look" like those produced by real, and (ii) the Search algorithm in ideal is *consistent*, i.e., it functions similarly to that in real.

Although our schemes are independent of the underlying SSE construction, in order to provide context, we describe the leakage functions $\mathcal{L}_1, \mathcal{L}_2$ assuming the SSE scheme by [6]. $\mathcal{L}_1$ is associated with what is leaked from the index alone, whereas $\mathcal{L}_2$ accounts for the leakage from the queries.

- $\mathcal{L}_1(D) = \max_n$
  $\max_n$ is an upper bound on the size n of D.
- $\mathcal{L}_2(D, W) = \langle \alpha(W), \sigma(W) \rangle$
  W is a set of keywords, $\alpha(W) = (id(w))_{w \in W}$ is the *access patters*, i.e., the document ids returned by each keyword query, and $\sigma(W)$ is the *search patterns*, i.e., for every pair $w_i, w_j \in W$ such that $i \neq j$, it indicates whether $w_i = w_j$ or $w_i \neq w_j$.

In the next section, we explain that with minimal changes and by introducing extra leakage, we can use the described SSE security game to formalize the security of our RSSE framework as well.

3. PROBLEM DEFINITION

We define the problem of *Range Searchable Symmetric Encryption* (RSSE) in a very similar manner to SSE. In fact, the security game of RSSE is identical to that of SSE in Figure 2, where each w_i stands for a range query rather than a keyword. Moreover, similar to SSE, RSSE captures *index-based* schemes in its game; this is different from OPE that formulates a secure encryption scheme that allows ordered comparisons, without the need of an index. We employ this definitional framework to devise solutions that reduce range query search to *multi-keyword search.* This further allows us to build secure solutions on top of an existing secure SSE construction.

More specifically, we assume that data owner possesses a dataset D of tuples. We focus on range queries on a single attribute with domain A.[2]. We associate a pair (id, a) with each tuple $d \in D$, where id is a unique identifier for d and a is the value of d on A. We also write $d.id$ and $d.a$ to refer to the elements of this pair. We assume that the owner encrypts each $d \in D$ using a semantically secure encryption scheme, and sends the resulting ciphertext c along with $d.id$ to the server. The goal is to build a secure index I on the $d.id$ values, such that the server can perform range queries that retrieve the set of ids of the tuples satisfying the query. Note that, for each returned result $d.id$, the owner can retrieve from the server the corresponding ciphertext c of d and decrypt it in a subsequent step, orthogonal to the search process. In a nutshell, our RSSE framework can be summarized in the following main points:

- **Index creation:** Break A into a set of (potentially overlapping) ranges, and attribute a unique *keyword* to every range. Regard each $d \in D$ as a *document*, and associate it with the keywords of the ranges that include $d.a$. We hereafter use terms document and tuple interchangeably. Utilize a static SSE scheme to securely index D using as dictionary Δ the union of the range keywords of every $d \in D$.

[2]We assume that the values of A are *positive integers* Note that we can always convert any real domain to a discrete positive one by proper scaling and translation.

- **Query:** Break the query range into sub ranges, map them to keywords and generate tokens for searching the SSE index.
- **Security:** Augment the leakage functions $\mathcal{L}_1$ and $\mathcal{L}_2$ of the underlying SSE scheme, in order to capture the extra leakage stemming from the keyword mapping and index structure.
- **Updates:** Perform updates in batches. For every batch, create a separate index using new keys. Periodically, consolidate separate indexes into a single one (consolidation is performed hierarchically, similar to log-structured merge trees [25]). This requires the owner to download the involved indexes, and create a single (re-encrypted) index. The server must issue every range query on each "active" index, and return the separate result sets.

An *RSSE protocol* is specified by algorithms Setup, BuildIndex, Trpdr and Search, which are defined identically to those described in Section 2.2 for static single-keyword SSE, where w now stands for the query range. Their instantiation in each of our proposed schemes varies, but builds upon the constructions of traditional SSE. Our contribution revolves around the proper assignment of keywords to tuples in BuildIndex, the mapping of a range query to keywords/tokens in Trpdr, and potentially the adjustment of Search to function appropriately with the tokens of Trpdr.

Finally, we support updates using only static SSE schemes. Our goal is *forward privacy*, i.e., the server should not learn that a newly added item satisfies a query issued in the past. Our mechanism is generic capturing all schemes and, thus, is detailed separately in Section 7.

4. QUADRATIC SCHEME

Our Quadratic scheme is a naive baseline whose sole purpose is to help in conveying the basics of our RSSE framework. Let A be the query attribute domain, and m its total size. There are $O(m^2)$ possible range queries that can be applied in this domain. We enumerate all these possible sub ranges of A and assign a unique keyword to each range. Observe that a domain value belongs to $O(m^2)$ sub ranges. We associate each $d \in D$ with the keywords corresponding to the $O(m^2)$ ranges covering $d.a \in A$.

We start by replicating each $d \in D$ into $d'_1, \ldots d'_\nu$, where ν is the number of keywords d corresponds to, and include the replicated tuples in a new dataset D'. We then use any secure (single-keyword) SSE scheme *off-the-shelf* (i.e., without any changes), treating each $d' \in D'$ as a separate tuple. The Setup and BuildIndex algorithms are identical as in the SSE scheme, where the tuples in D' are now augmented with the keywords described above. Given a range query, Trpdr simply maps it to the *single* keyword associated with its range, and the rest of the algorithm is the same as in the SSE scheme. Finally, Search is also used as in SSE without changes, and returns exactly the tuples in D' containing the range keyword. By definition, the returned tuples are exactly those satisfying the range query (without replication).

Table 1 in Section 1 shows the costs of Quadratic. Each tuple is associated with at most $O(m^2)$ keywords and, hence, the index size is $O(nm^2)$, where n is the number of tuples in D. The search time is inherited from the SSE scheme, and assuming [6] this is $O(r)$, where r is the number of results. The query size is $O(1)$ as it involves a single keyword/token.

In terms of security, this technique does not introduce any additional leakage to what SSE reveals for D', namely its size. However, this may disclose information about the distribution of the values of D on A; two datasets with different distributions (e.g., one where all tuples have the same $d.a$ value, versus one where they all have a different one) will result in different D' sizes. This can be easily tackled by *padding* (e.g., as in [9, 5]); for any D', the mechanism takes as input the cardinality n of D and the domain size m, and always constructs a secure index corresponding to the maximum possible D' size. Hence, only n, m are leaked in Quadratic in $\mathcal{L}_1$ along with the $\mathcal{L}_2$ leakage of the underlying SSE scheme, which results in the highest security level for our setting. However, Quadratic clearly suffers from a prohibitive storage cost, which motivates our next solutions.

5. CONSTANT SCHEMES

In this section we present our Constant-BRC and Constant-URC schemes, which lie on the other side of the spectrum as far as the storage cost is concerned. Specifically, these techniques introduce a constant asymptotic overhead on the index size with respect to the dataset size n. Before embarking on their description, we first explain a naive variant.

We assign to each tuple $d \in D$ a *single* keyword, which corresponds to its actual value on A, namely $d.a$. In other words, the dictionary Δ is the values in A. No replication is involved. We then index D with an SSE scheme, yielding an index I of size $O(n)$. A query range of size R is simply mapped to R keywords, one for each value of A it covers. We trivially use these keywords as search tokens in the Trpdr and Search algorithms of the SSE scheme. The scheme will return the correct r results without false positives in $O(R + r)$ time. Disregarding security for now, the main drawback of this scheme is the potentially unacceptable query size $O(R)$ for very large ranges. This motivates our Constant-BRC and Constant-URC solutions, which take advantage of DPRFs (explained in Section 2.2) to reduce the query size to $O(\log R)$.

The instantiations of the RSSE algorithms for Constant-BRC and Constant-URC are the following (the two algorithms differ only in the range covering technique used for generating the trapdoor – BRC or URC):

$k \leftarrow$ Setup(1^λ): Output (k_1, k_2), where k_1 is a DPRF key and k_2 is the key of the underlying SSE scheme.

$I \leftarrow$ BuildIndex(k, D): Associate each $d \in D$ with keyword $d.a$. Invoke the BuildIndex algorithm of the SSE scheme on D and its keywords, but instead of using a PRF to encrypt the ids, use a DPRF instead. Each $d.id$ is decrypted only with token $f_k(d.a)$, where f_k is a DPRF function.

$t \leftarrow$ Trpdr(k, w): Invoke the token generation function (T) of the DPRF employing either BRC or URC, and retrieve the corresponding GGM values corresponding to range w from the GGM tree over A (see Section 2.2). Randomly permute these GGM values and output them as vector t. For each GGM value in t, provide the level of its respective node in the GGM tree as well.

$X \leftarrow$ Search(t, I): Derive the (leaf-level) DPRF values from the GGM values in t. Use these values as tokens in the Search algorithm of SSE and return the results.

We clarify the algorithm revisiting the example of Figure 1, where $A = \{0, \ldots, 7\}$. The owner first generates a DPRF key k_1 in Setup, and computes the DPRF values for the elements on A that appear in D, creating a GGM tree. Suppose that a $d \in D$ has $d.a = 6$. In BuildIndex, the owner assigns 6 as keyword to d. However, contrary to traditional SSE where this document can be decrypted by using as token a PRF value on keyword 6, Constant-BRC/URC use a DPRF value instead. Specifically, they invoke the same BuildIndex algorithm as SSE (using SSE key k_2 generated in Setup), but the token to decrypt d (or any other tuple d with $d.a = 6$) is $f_{k_1}(6) = G_0(G_1(G_1(k_1)))$. The algorithm proceeds similarly with every other $d \in D$.

Upon a query, Trpdr outputs as token t the GGM values corresponding to the nodes covering the range with BRC or URC. In our example in Figure 1, if BRC is used, then the output is $t = \langle (G_1(G_0(k_1)), 1), (G_1(k_1), 2) \rangle$, i.e., the GGM values of nodes $N_{2,3}$ and $N_{4,7}$ along with their levels, respectively. If URC is used, then t contains $(G_0(G_1(G_0(k_1))), 0)$ for node N_2, $(G_1(G_1(G_0(k_1))), 0)$ for N_3, $(G_0(G_1(k_1)), 1)$ for $N_{4,5}$, and $(G_1(G_1(k_1)), 1)$ for $N_{6,7}$. Note that the elements of t are *randomly permuted*.

In Search, the server first takes the GGM values of the non-leaf nodes and expands them to compute the DPRF values for the leaves. For instance, from $N_{2,3}$'s value $G_1(G_0(k_1))$, it generates DPRFs $G_0(G_1(G_0(k_1)))$ and $G_1(G_1(G_0(k_1)))$. It can do that because (i) G is public, and (ii) it knows the level of $G_1(G_0(k_1))$, i.e., 1. It finally uses as tokens the DPRFs to retrieve the results, invoking SSE's Search algorithm.

The cost complexities of Constant-BRC and Constant-URC are identical and provided in Table 1. Each tuple is associated with a single keyword and, hence, the storage cost is $O(n)$. Due to the BRC/URC techniques, the query size is $O(\log R)$ for a range size R. The search time at the server entails expanding the $O(\log R)$ GGM values into R DPRFs, and retrieving the r results from SSE, yielding a total $O(R + r)$ time. Both solutions do not introduce false positives.

We next turn to security. Our Constant constructions cannot be proven secure against adaptive adversaries that are allowed to issue *intersecting* range queries. This is an inherent limitation of our underlying DPRFs, as shown in [24]. Briefly stated, this is because the simulator must have *a priori* knowledge of the GGM sub-structure shared by the intersecting ranges, in order to produce consistent tokens. However, this is not possible in the adaptive case. In the example of Figure 1, suppose that some query generated a token that includes the GGM value for node $N_{2,3}$. Then, let another query involve producing as token a GGM value for node N_2. Without the a priori knowledge that the second range intersects the first at N_2, the simulator could not have generated the GGM value for $N_{2,3}$, in a way that it can produce the GGM value for N_2.

Consequently, the Constant schemes limit the functionality by *not allowing query intersections*. Note that this constraint can be enforced at the application level. For instance, the owner's program may maintain the history of queries and abort when an intersecting query is seen, or may try to answer the query from cached answers of previous queries that collectively encompass the new query range.

To prove security (under the constraint of non-intersecting queries), we define the two leakages as follows:

- $\mathcal{L}_1(D, A) = \langle m, n \rangle$
  D is the dataset, A is the query attribute domain, n is the cardinality of D, and m is the size of A.
- $\mathcal{L}_2(D, A, W) =$
  $\langle \alpha(W), \sigma(W), ((\mu(N_i), \ell(N_i), id_{map}(N_i))_{N_i \in RC(w)})_{w \in W} \rangle$
  $\alpha(W), \sigma(W)$ are the access and search patterns of the queries as defined for SSE. The extra leakage is as follows. For every query range $w \in W$, the leakage contains a tuple that consists of an alias $\mu(N_i)$ for every node N_i returned by the range covering $RC(w)$ – where the RC function is either BRC or URC – along with the level $\ell(N_i)$ of N_i, and the exact mapping $id_{map}(N_i)$ of the tuple ids to the leaves of $\mu(N_i)$'s sub tree.

Observe that, contrary to traditional SSE, the two leakage functions take as input also the query attribute domain A. This is because our constructions build an index considering the entire span of A. We further explain the extra leakage in $\mathcal{L}_2(D, A, W)$ incurred by our schemes with an example using Figure 1. Let the first query be $w_1 : [0, 3]$, with results d_1, d_2, such that $d_1.a = 0$ and $d_2.a = 3$. Then, $\mathcal{L}_2$ over $W = \{w_1\}$ is an alias for node $N_{0,3}$, its level (2), and the information that d_1 maps to its left-most leaf, and d_2 to its right-most leaf. Now suppose that the second query is $w_2 = [5, 7]$. Then, $\mathcal{L}_2$ over $W = \{w_1, w_2\}$ is what explained above, plus aliases for nodes $N_5, N_{6,7}$ (without disclosing their relative order) as well as the mappings of the qualifying tuples in these sub trees. Note that, neither the relative order of w_1, w_2 on A, nor the relative order of the sub trees of each query are revealed.

We will include the security theorems and proofs of all our schemes in the long version of our paper.

Qualitative comparison. The Constant schemes feature considerably better storage than Quadratic (at the expense of slightly increased query size and search time). However, they also introduce significantly higher leakage, since they disclose the exact mapping of the results in a sub tree, which further reveals relative order information. Comparing the BRC and URC variants, URC offers slightly better privacy; the BRC coverage may exclude mapping certain ranges to the query, whereas URC covers all ranges of the same size in an indistinguishable manner.

6. LOGARITHMIC SCHEMES

Motivated by the high structural leakage of the Constant schemes, in this section we design solutions that trade off storage for privacy. This is achieved by replicating tuples similar to Quadratic, but with a significantly lower expansion factor. Specifically, we present four constructions that increase the storage complexity only by a logarithmic factor, and differ in the other costs, the privacy level, and the false positives. Section 6.1 describes Logarithmic-BRC and Logarithmic-URC, Section 6.2 explains Logarithmic-SRC, and Section 6.3 presents Logarithmic-SRC-i.

6.1 Logarithmic-BRC/URC

The Logarithmic-BRC and Logarithmic-URC schemes mitigate the structural leakage of Constant-BRC/URC by avoiding the use of DPRFs and associating each tuple with a logarithmic, instead of constant, number of keywords. The RSSE protocol for Logarithmic-BRC and Logarithmic-URC is as follows (the two schemes again differ in the range covering technique used in Trpdr):

$k \leftarrow \mathsf{Setup}(1^\lambda)$: Same as in SSE.

$I \leftarrow \mathsf{BuildIndex}(k, D)$: Build a binary tree over domain A as described in Section 2.2, and assign a unique keyword at each node. For each tuple $d \in D$, find the nodes on the path from the tree root to $d.a$, and associate d with the node keywords. Replicate every d for each keyword it is associated with, and regard each replica as separate tuple as discussed in Quadratic. Let D' be the resulting dataset including all the replicas. Invoke the BuildIndex algorithm of the SSE scheme on D' and its keywords, after randomly permuting the documents that are associated with the same keyword.

$t \leftarrow \mathsf{Trpdr}(k, w)$: Let w represent the query range. Find the nodes that cover w using BRC or URC. Create a token for each node keyword invoking the Trpdr algorithm of the SSE scheme and include it in t. Randomly permute t prior to returning it.

$X \leftarrow \mathsf{Search}(t, I)$: Invoke the Search algorithm of SSE for every element in t, and output the union of the results.

The protocol associates each tuple with the *dyadic intervals* that cover its attribute value. For instance, if $d.a = 3$ in Figure 1, then d is associated with keywords $N_{0,7}$, $N_{0,3}$, $N_{2,3}$ and N_3 (where each N_i is the label of a node). We then replicate each d and index the augmented dataset D' with traditional SSE. Given a range query, we compute its cover with BRC or URC, and issue the output node labels of the range covering technique as keywords for traditional SSE search, i.e., we invoke the conventional Trpdr and Search algorithms of SSE for every node label and corresponding token, respectively. For example, for query $[2, 7]$ under BRC, Trpdr outputs an SSE token for $N_{2,3}$ and $N_{4,7}$ in random order, and the Search SSE algorithm is invoked for every such token separately.

The costs of Logarithmic-BRC and Logarithmic-URC are summarized in Table 1. The index size is $O(n \log m)$, where n is the number of tuples and m the domain size, since each tuple is associated with $O(\log m)$ keywords. The query size is $O(\log R)$, where R is the size of the query range, since this is the number of nodes covering the querying range in BRC and URC. The search time is $O(\log R + r)$, where r the result size, because there are $\log R$ tokens issued to the underlying SSE scheme, each incurring no additional cost to the retrieval of its results. Finally, the protocol returns correct answers without false positives, since BRC and URC cover the query exactly, and a tuple in the result is certainly associated with the keyword of a node in the cover.

The only extra information leaked is a *partitioning* of the result ids into groups. More formally:

- $\mathcal{L}_1(D, A) = \langle m, n\rangle$
  D is the dataset, A is the query attribute domain, n is the cardinality of D, and m is the size of A.

- $\mathcal{L}_2(D, A, W) =$
  $\langle \alpha(W), \sigma(W), ((\mu(N_i), id(N_i))_{N_i \in RC(w)})_{w \in W}\rangle$
  $\alpha(W), \sigma(W)$ are the access and search patterns of the queries as defined for SSE. For every query range $w \in W$, the leakage contains a tuple that consists of an alias $\mu(N_i)$ for every node N_i returned by the range covering $RC(w)$ – where the RC function is either BRC or URC – along with the list of tuple ids $id(N_i)$ associated with keyword N_i.

Qualitative comparison. Logarithmic-BRC/URC feature increased storage cost compared to Constant-BRC/URC, but slightly better search time (since the server does not need to generate DPRFs from the tokens). The main benefit of Logarithmic-BRC/URC is in the substantially reduced leakage, since they hide both the distribution and the total order of the tuples in each subtree of the query range cover. The difference between the BRC and URC variants of Logarithmic is similar to that in Constant; URC does not disclose information about the position of the range over the domain. Nevertheless, what is still leaked in both variants is the *partitioning* of the result tuples into distinct groups (each corresponding to a subtree), which may further disclose ordering information about the groups. This motivates our solution in the next section.

6.2 Logarithmic-SRC

The extra "result partitioning" leakage of the Logarithmic-BRC/URC schemes was due to the fact that Trpdr produces *multiple* tokens, one for each subtree with which BRC or URC cover the query range. Logarithmic-SRC, prevents this leakage by always covering the query range with a *single* range that is potentially a *superset* of the query range (SRC stands for *single range cover*). In addition to enhanced privacy, this also leads to *constant* query size, but may introduce *false positives*.

We can naively realize Logarithmic-SRC building upon the same binary tree over A as in Logarithmic-BRC/URC as follows. We assign once again to each $d \in D$ the keywords corresponding to the nodes whose subtrees cover $d.a$, and replicate tuples to create an augmented dataset D'. However, instead of invoking BRC or URC in Trpdr to find the cover of the query range with tree nodes, we could simply select the node of the smallest subtree fully covering the query, and use its keyword for searching. In our example of Figure 1, we would cover query $[2, 7]$ with the tree root $N_{0,7}$. Unfortunately, this solution features an unacceptable worst-case complexity for the number of leaves (i.e., domain values) contained in the single subtree, which is $O(m)$ where m is the domain size, regardless of the query range size R. This would further lead to an unacceptable number of false positives. For example, in Figure 1, query $[3, 4]$ is covered by the tree root that encompasses the entire domain and, hence, dataset D. Motivated by the above, in Logarithmic-SRC we produce keywords for the tuples in D based on a novel *tree-like Directed Acyclic Graph*, henceforth referred to as *TDAG*, which ensures that *any* query range of size R is covered by a single subtree with size $O(R)$.

We explain the TDAG structure using Figure 3. We start by building a binary tree over domain A, similar to the case of the previous schemes. We then inject one extra node between every two nodes at every level of the tree (depicted in gray), and connect it with the two nodes directly below it in the next level (i.e., the right child of the node in its left, and the left child of the node in its right).

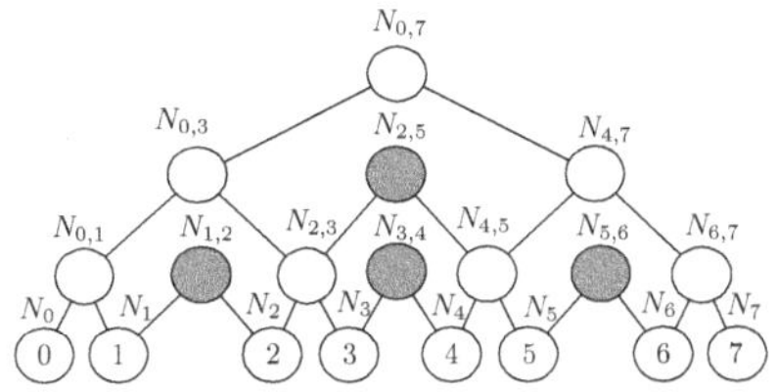

Figure 3: TDAG example

The following lemma is useful for our cost analysis of Logarithmic-SRC.

LEMMA 1. *Given a TDAG constructed over a domain A and any range in A of size R, there is always a subtree of size O(R) that can completely cover the range.*

PROOF. For any integer $R > 0$, there is an integer $j \geq 0$ such that $2^j \leq R \leq 2^{j+1}$. Any range of size R can be covered by at most 2 dyadic ranges (i.e., subtrees in the binary tree over A) of size 2^{j+1}; either the range is fully contained in such a subtree, or it is split between two *consecutive* subtrees of size 2^{j+1}. These two subtrees are either children of the same parent in the binary tree, or cousins. Recall that our TDAG structure essentially links every two cousins in each level with a new parent. Hence, there is always a node that covers the two subtrees each of size $2^{j+1} \leq 2R$. Thus, for any range of size R, there is always a subtree in TDAG with size at most $4R \in O(R)$. □

Given a range of size R, the SRC range covering algorithm simply finds the *lowest common ancestor* of the lower and upper bound of the range, which can be performed in $O(\log R)$ time. In the example of Figure 3, SRC covers range $[2, 7]$ by $N_{0,7}$, and range $[3, 5]$ by $N_{2,5}$.

The RSSE algorithms for Logarithmic-SRC are the same as in Logarithmic-BRC/URC with the following differences: (i) in BuildIndex, each $d \in D$ is associated with the keywords/labels of the nodes of TDAG that cover $d.a$ (instead of the nodes of the binary tree), and (ii) Trpdr generates a single token for the node label output by the SRC covering technique (instead of BRC/URC).

Table 1 summarizes the costs of Logarithmic-SRC. The query size is constant, since the query is represented by a single token. The index has size $O(n \log m)$; for each tuple $d \in D$, there are $O(\log m)$ nodes in the path from the root to $d.a$, and each such node is connected to at most one injected node in the TDAG; the subtrees of all these $O(\log m)$ nodes cover $d.a$ and, thus, each d is associated with $O(\log m)$ keywords. The false positives depend on the dataset *distribution* over A. If the distribution is *uniform*, then the false positives are $O(R)$ due to Lemma 1. However, if the dataset is *skewed*, then the false positives could be up to $O(n)$. For example, if $[3, 5]$ is the query in Figure 3 and there is a single tuple that satisfies the range, but the rest of the dataset has value 2 on A, then Logarithmic-SRC will return the entire dataset due to the used keyword $N_{2,5}$. The search time is linear in the result size plus the false positives and, thus, it is $O(n)$ in the worst case where there is heavy skew.

In Logarithmic-SRC, all range queries are reduced to single-keyword queries and, thus, the scheme degenerates to SSE, inheriting its security (assuming the padding technique discussed in Quadratic). However, for technical reasons in our proofs, we must define an extra subtle leakage, namely the fact that two different ranges may map to the same keyword. This can be modeled by extending the definition of search patterns. Nevertheless, from a practical point of view, this leakage is not observable by an adversary, since the mapping takes place at the owner. In particular, the adversary is unable to distinguish if the same token was produced twice for the same or for different range queries.

Qualitative comparison. Contrary to Logarithmic-BRC/URC, in Logarithmic-SRC the adversary is unable to infer ordering information about the results, since each range is mapped to a *single* keyword and the tuples associated with this keyword are *randomly permuted*. Logarithmic-SRC also features optimal query size and the highest achievable privacy in the our RSSE framework that builds upon single-keyword SSE. Similar to Logarithmic-BRC/URC, this comes at the cost of extra storage. Logarithmic-SRC is ideal for datasets with uniform distributions over the query attribute domain. However, it may feature an unacceptable number of false positives (and, thus, also search time) under heavy data skew. This is mitigated by our final solution described in the next section.

6.3 Logarithmic-SRC-i

The Logarithmic-SRC-i construction aims at reducing the false positives of Logarithmic-SRC from $O(n)$ to $O(R + r)$, where R is the query range size and r is the result size. It achieves this by building a *double* index $I = (I_1, I_2)$, where I_2 indexes the tuples in D similar to the previous schemes, and I_1 is an *auxiliary* index that guides the search to I_2. This construction is *interactive* (hence the "i" in the name), i.e., it involves an extra round of communication between the owner and the server during the query; the owner first queries I_1, it receives the result from the server, and based on the result it queries I_2.

We illustrate the construction of I_1 and I_2 with the example of Figure 4. Suppose that $D = \{d_0, \ldots, d_{15}\}$. Assume also for simplicity that $d_0, \ldots, d_{15}$ are sorted on A, so that the subscript i of each d_i implies its position in the total order of the tuples on A. Also consider that $d_0.a = \ldots d_9.a = 2$, $d_{10}.a = 4$, $d_{11}.a = d_{12}.a = 5$, $d_{13}.a = d_{14}.a = 6$, and $d_{15}.a = 7$. Consider TDAG$_1$ in the upper part of the figure, which is built on domain $A = \{0, \ldots, 7\}$, and let $[3, 5]$ be the query range. Recall that Logarithmic-SRC answers this query with TDAG$_1$ by using keyword $N_{2,5}$. This returns as false positives $d_0, \ldots, d_9$ corresponding to domain value 2, which comprise more than half of D.

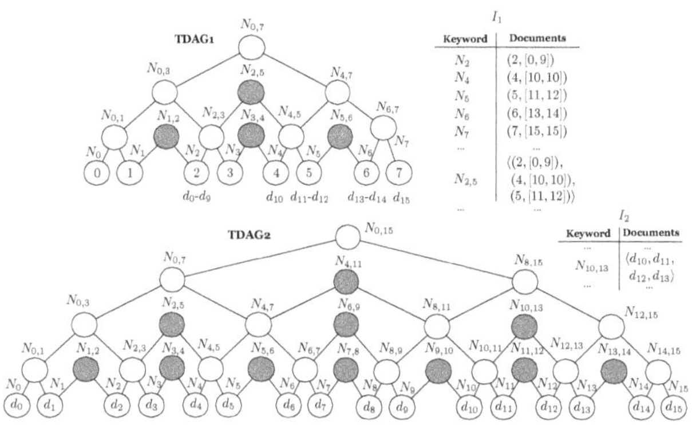

Figure 4: Building the index in Logarithmic-SRC-i

Instead of using $TDAG_1$ to index the tuples, Logarithmic-SRC-i uses it to index the *ranges* of tuples corresponding to the domain values, where a tuple range accounts for a range of tuple subscripts. Specifically, each leaf is associated with a pair (domain value, tuple range), e.g., N_2 is associated with $(2, [0, 9])$, since $d_0, \ldots, d_9$ all have domain value 2. The non-leaf nodes are associated with the lists of (domain value, tuple range) pairs of the leaves in their subtree, e.g., $N_{2,5}$ corresponds to $\langle(2, [0, 9]), (4, [10, 10]), (5, [11, 12])\rangle$. I_1 is constructed using the traditional SSE BuildIndex algorithm, where the documents are the pairs or lists of pairs described above, and the keywords are the $TDAG_1$ node labels.

The construction then builds a second TDAG, denoted by $TDAG_2$ in the lower part of the figure, which is built on the *tuples* sorted on A. Note that the order of the documents corresponding to the same keyword (i.e., to the same node in $TDAG_1$) does not affect the structure of $TDAG_2$. For instance, $TDAG_2$ would be equivalent if we swapped d_{11} with d_{12} in the leaf level (where d_{11} and d_{12} have the same keyword). Prior to constructing $TDAG_2$, we randomly shuffle the documents corresponding to the same keyword. Each node corresponds to the tuples covered by its subtree, e.g., $N_{10,13}$ is associated with d_{10}, d_{11}, d_{12} and d_{13}. I_2 is constructed using the traditional SSE BuildIndex algorithm, where the documents are $d_0, \ldots, d_{15}$, and the keywords are the $TDAG_2$ node labels.

The scheme performs the query in two stages. In the first, it issues the query range to I_1. For instance, for $[3, 5]$ it creates a token for $N_{2,5}$ (following always the SRC range covering technique on the TDAG), and receives $\langle(2, [0, 9]), (4, [10, 10]), (5, [11, 12])\rangle$. It then selects the pairs that satisfy the query, and creates a new, *single* query range on the document subscripts, by merging the qualifying ranges. In our example, it merges $[10, 10]$ and $[11, 12]$ to create new query $[10, 12]$ ($[0,9]$ does not satisfy the original query). In the second stage, it issues $[10, 12]$ to I_2, creating the token for node $N_{10,13}$ in $TDAG_2$, which fully covers the tuple range. The algorithm returns as result d_{10}, d_{11}, d_{12} and d_{13}. Observe that now there is only a single false positive, d_{13}, whereas Logarithmic-SRC returned 10 false positives for the same query. The RSSE protocol for Logarithmic-SRC-i is as follows:

$k \leftarrow$ Setup(1^λ): Generate and output two SSE keys (k_1, k_2).

$I \leftarrow$ BuildIndex(k, D): Build SSE index I_1 on the tuple ranges using $TDAG_1$ with key k_1, and index I_2 on the sorted tuples on A using $TDAG_2$ with key k_2. Output (I_1, I_2).

$t \leftarrow$ Trpdr(k, w): This is an interactive algorithm. Parse $k = (k_1, k_2)$. Generate SSE token t_1 with k_1 for the SRC node on $TDAG_1$ that covers range w, and send it to the server. Decrypt the answer to retrieve new range w'. Generate SSE token t_2 with k_2 for the SRC node on $TDAG_2$ that covers w', and output (t_1, t_2).

$X \leftarrow$ Search(t, I): This is an interactive algorithm. Parse $t = (t_1, t_2)$ and $I = (I_1, I_2)$. Retrieve t_1 from the owner, invoke the Search algorithm of SSE on I_1 and send the result to the owner. Retrieve t_2 from the owner, invoke the Search algorithm of SSE on I_2 and output the result X.

Table 1 illustrates the costs of Logarithmic-SRC-i. The number of documents indexed by I_1 is equal to the number of *distinct* domain values contained in the dataset, since we index the entire range of tuples on a specific domain value by a single (domain value, tuple range) document of constant size. Therefore, since I_1 is constructed using a TDAG similar to Logarithmic-SRC, its size is $O(n \log m)$. The number of documents indexed by I_2 is $O(n)$, i.e., the entire D. Contrary to I_1, the TDAG is built on n leaves and, thus, the size of I_2 is $O(n \log n)$. Assuming that m is typically larger than n, the total storage cost becomes $O(n \log m)$. The query size is $O(1)$, since there are only two tokens involved. The false positives are $O(R+r)$, considering also those of I_1. This is because the range size in I_1 is of size $O(R)$, whereas in I_2 is of size $O(r)$; due to Lemma 1, the number of false positives in each index is linear in the query range size and, thus, the total false positives are $O(R + r)$. The search time is dictated by the number of results plus the false positives and, thus, it is also $O(R + r)$.

Since I_1 and I_2 are built following the construction algorithm of the underlying SSE protocol and using two different keys, the leakage in each index is identical to that of the SSE scheme. Therefore, having the $\mathcal{L}_1$ and $\mathcal{L}_2$ leakages of SSE for *both* indexes, we can prove the security of Logarithmic-SRC-i.

Qualitative comparison. Logarithmic-SRC-i reduces the false positives as compared to Logarithmic-SRC, even in the case of heavy data skew, while retaining the optimal query size and linearithmic storage cost. As a downside, the usage of the auxiliary index leaks slightly more information than its counterpart. For instance, the size of I_1 (derived from $\mathcal{L}_1$ of I_1) leaks the number of distinct domain values covered by the dataset, whereas the size of a result from a query to I_1 (derived from $\mathcal{L}_2$ of I_1) reveals the number of distinct domain values covered by the result. Moreover, in *non-skewed datasets*, Logarithmic-SRC-i inflicts higher search cost than Logarithmic-SRC. This is because the benefits of using the extra I_1 index in Logarithmic-SRC-i to reduce the false positives diminish and, thus, the extra search overhead compared to Logarithmic-SRC becomes evident. In that sense, Logarithmic-SRC-i is better under data skew, whereas Logarithmic-SRC is preferable in non-skewed datasets.

7. UPDATES

Recall from Section 2.1 that most dynamic SSE (DSSE) schemes [22, 21, 34, 5] create a dynamic index that introduces the least possible leakage and provides *forward privacy*, i.e., it does not reveal that a new update satisfies a previous query. We follow an alternative methodology adopting a *bulk-loading* technique from commercial databases (e.g., Vertica [25]), which is simple from a Security point of view, but (i) builds upon static SSE schemes that are faster and easier to implement than their dynamic counterparts, (ii) enables easy formulation of leakage, and (iii) captures forward privacy. It is also *generic*; it applies to *all* our solutions and to *any* future static RSSE scheme.

We assume that updates come in batches, and each batch i is treated as a separate dataset D_i. The updates can be insertions of new tuples, or modifications/deletions of old tuples. Every update is treated as an insertion in the new dataset; deletions carry a small flag indicating that the tuple must be removed. For each new dataset D_i, the owner creates a new index I_i with a *fresh* key k_i following the BuildIndex of the utilized construction, and sends the encrypted data to the server. Suppose that the owner has uploaded b such indexes. Upon a query, the owner creates b separate tokens, one for each index with the corresponding key. The server processes them separately on the b indexes, and returns the results. The final refinement of the results occurs at the owner, who filters out the deleted tuples and appropriately performs the potential modifications.

Clearly, the number of keys, query size, storage cost, search time and result size increase linearly with b and, thus, the number of indexes should not increase indefinitely. Therefore, we adopt the approach of Vertica, which essentially organizes the datasets/batches into a *log-structured merge tree*. Specifically, the owner sets a parameter called *consolidation step*, denoted by s, which determines how frequently the indexes must be merged. After creating s new indexes, the owner downloads them, merges their tuples into a single index, re-encrypts the index and sends it to the server. This happens *hierarchically*; after consolidating s indexes s times, the s merged indexes are further consolidated into a new one. Conceptually, this is like organizing the indexes as leaves of a full s-ary tree created bottom-up, such that when s nodes are created in a level, they get consolidated creating a parent node at the next higher level. This leads to an *amortized logarithmic* merge cost in the number of batches [25]. Although this incurs extra periodic cost at the owner for the consolidation and re-encryption, it retains $O(s \log_s b)$ indexes at the server (and keys at the owner) at all times, instead of b. Finally, note that s should be tuned based on the application at hand. For instance, if the application expects frequent deletions, it is beneficial to set s to a small value, in order to perform merge operations more frequently, thus eliminating the extra cost for storing the deletions as insertions.

The leakage of this methodology is essentially the entire history of the $\mathcal{L}_1, \mathcal{L}_2$ leakages of every index that was once "active" at the server. For instance, from this leakage one could derive the number of deletions that occurred in one of the batches. Also observe that our technique satisfies forward privacy; every index is encrypted with a fresh key and, thus, a token created for one index in the past cannot be used to decrypt index components produced in the future.

8. EXPERIMENTAL EVALUATION

In this section we experimentally evaluate the performance of all our proposed schemes, excluding Quadratic that features a prohibitive storage cost. Based on our discussion in Section 2.1 about the three schemes of [26], we also include a comparison to the basic scheme of Li et al. [26], hereafter referred to as PB, recalling though that the latter offers unrealistically weaker security than our schemes. We also include additional experiments in the Appendix.

Setup. We implemented our solutions in Java, and conducted our experiments on a 64-bit machine with an Intel® Core™ i7-2720QM CPU at 2.2GHz and 16GB RAM, running Linux Ubuntu 14.10. We utilized the JavaX.crypto library for the entailed cryptographic operations. Specifically, we implemented PRF and GGM evaluations with HMAC-SHA-512, and hash computations with SHA-1. We also used AES128-CBC for encryption. We chose the construction by Cash et al. [6] as our underlying SSE scheme, setting its parameters to the values recommended in [6] for space-efficiency ($S = 6000$, $K = 1.1$).

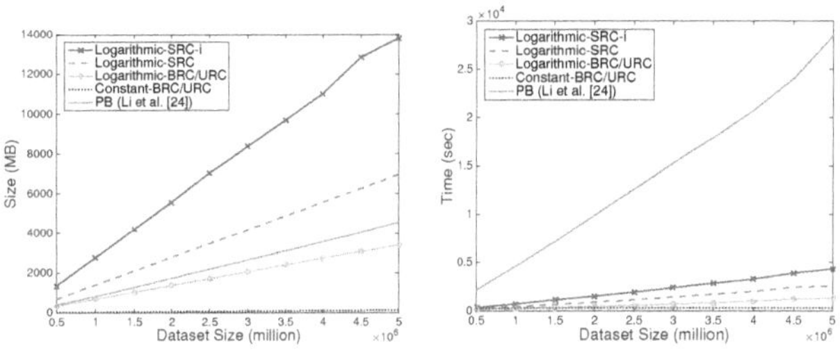

(a) Index size (b) Construction time

Figure 5: Index costs (Gowalla)

We experimented with two real datasets. The first is from the Gowalla geo-social network (`snap.stanford.edu/data/loc-gowalla.html`), hereafter called Gowalla. This dataset consists of 6,442,890 user location check-ins in a period between February 2009 and October 2010. We used as query attribute the date/time of the check-ins converted to 32-bit integers and translated such that the domain is $A = \{0, \ldots, 103017913\}$. The second dataset is from the US Postal Service (`www.app.com`), called USPS, and contains 389,032 employee records. We used as query attribute the annual salary field with domain $A = \{0, \ldots, 276840\}$. Note that Gowalla is relatively uniform on A (95% distinct values on A), whereas USPS is heavily skewed (5% distinct values on A). All datasets and respective indexes fit in memory.

Index costs. In the first set of our experiments we assess the index size and construction time in Gowalla when varying the dataset size n, and demonstrate the results in Figures 5(a) and 5(b), respectively. The construction time involves also the I/O cost for reading the dataset from the disk into main memory. As in [26], to retrieve the various datasets, we simply partition the initial dataset (sorted on A) into 10 sets of 500K tuples each, chosen uniformly at random from the entire data set, start with one partition, and gradually add the rest of the partitions. Note that the BRC and URC variants of the same scheme feature identical costs. The index size entails only the replicated tuple ids and their associated keywords. The curves in both figures have the same trends, since the index size dictates the construction time. Moreover, both the index size and construction time scale linearly with n, since even the logarithmic factors essentially add a constant factor to the overall size.

As expected, the Constant schemes achieve the smallest index size (12.63-131 MB), as well as the lowest construction time (288-332 s). The costs in Logarithmic-BRC/URC increase faster due to the logarithmic factor in the index size. Logarithmic-SRC incurs about twice the size and time compared to Logarithmic-BRC/URC, due to the nodes injected to form the TDAG. Logarithmic-SRC-i requires double the size and time compared to Logarithmic-SRC. Recall that Logarithmic-SRC-i entails building a second index on top of the one in Logarithmic-SRC, whose size depends on the distinct values on A covered by the dataset. In Gowalla, the tuples cover 95% of the query domain. Therefore, the size of the extra index is almost as large as the basic one, doubling the overall size. Finally, observe that Constant-BRC/URC and Logarithmic-BRC/URC outperform PB [26] in terms of index size, whereas the construction cost of all our schemes is significantly lower than PB.

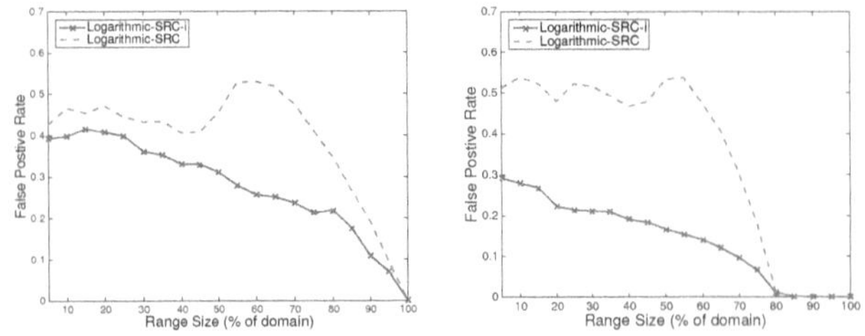

(a) Gowalla (b) USPS

Figure 6: False positives

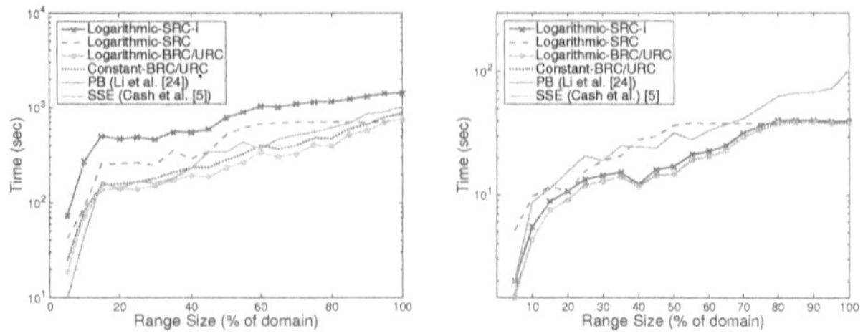

(a) Gowalla (b) USPS

Figure 7: Search time

Table 2 includes the index size and construction time for the USPS dataset. In this experiment we do not vary the dataset size because it is small. Similar to the case of Gowalla, the Constant schemes feature the smallest overheads, Logarithmic-BRC/URC add a constant factor to the costs of Constant, and Logarithmic-SRC incurs almost twice as high costs as Logarithmic-BRC/URC. However, the most interesting observation here is that, contrary to the case of Gowalla, Logarithmic-SRC-i adds minimal overheads to those of Logarithmic-SRC. This is because in USPS there are only 5% distinct values on A, which makes the extra index in Logarithmic-SRC-i very compact. Once again, Constant-BRC/URC and Logarithmic-BRC/URC feature a smaller index size than PB, whereas all our schemes have orders of magnitude faster construction time than PB.

Scheme	Index size (MB)	Constr. time (s)
Constant-BRC/URC	10.30	2.853
Logarithmic-BRC/URC	195.7	54.967
Logarithmic-SRC	391.4	106.970
Logarithmic-SRC-i	419.14	119.662
PB (Li et al. [26])	299.06	2374

Table 2: Index costs (USPS)

False positives. Figures 6(a) and 6(b) plot the average false positive rate (i.e., the average ratio of false positives over the total result size) as a function of the query range size, computed over the results of 200K random queries on each domain. We evaluate only Logarithmic-SRC-i versus Logarithmic-SRC, since these are the only schemes introducing false positives. The rate decreases almost linearly with the range size, since more tuples previously marked as false positives are contained in the range. In both datasets, Logarithmic-SRC-i incurs fewer false positives, outperforming Logarithmic-SRC by up to 27% in Gowalla and 38% in USPS. In USPS the rate drops more steeply in Logarithmic-SRC-i and the performance margin becomes wider, since USPS is more skewed than Gowalla, offering stronger opportunities to the auxiliary I_1 index in Logarithmic-SRC-i to eliminate false positives. Overall, the false positives in Logarithmic-SRC-i do not exceed 40% of the entire answer. Note that PB introduces a very small number of false positives for all range sizes. However, our Constant-BRC/URC and Logarithmic-BRC/URC schemes, whose performance has dominated that of PB in the investigated metrics so far, introduce no false positives at all.

Search cost. We evaluate the wall-clock time to execute Search at the server, as a function of the query range size. In Figures 7(a) and 7(b) We report the average CPU cost in Gowalla and USPS, respectively, for the same 200K queries of Figure 6. We compare all schemes, and provide also the inevitable cost of retrieving the actual results with the underlying SSE scheme of [6]. The search time is dominated by the PRF/DPRF evaluations entailed in [6] for each retrieved tuple. Consequently, Logarithmic-BRC (resp. Constant-BRC) and Logarithmic-URC (resp. Constant-URC) have negligible performance difference and we, thus, group them into a single curve.

Logarithmic-BRC/URC are the fastest and their performance coincides with that of pure SSE. This is expected since their search complexity is $O(\log R + r)$ and $\log R$ adds negligible overhead. The Constant schemes are slightly more expensive, due to the extra expansion of the GGM tokens into $O(R)$ DPRFs. Observe that this additional cost is more pronounced in Gowalla, due to its significantly larger domain (and, thus, query range sizes) than USPS. The SRC-based schemes are more costly, due to the false positives they introduce. In Gowalla, Logarithmic-SRC-i is more expensive than Logarithmic-SRC, due to the extra searches in its auxiliary index. Nevertheless, in USPS, Logarithmic-SRC-i outperforms Logarithmic-SRC, since its savings in false positives outweigh the extra index cost. PB features comparable search cost with that of Constant-BRC/ URC and Logarithmic-BRC/URC in the Gowalla dataset, but higher search cost in the case of USPS. In overall, the Constant-BRC/URC and Logarithmic-BRC/URC schemes subsume PB also in terms of performance.

9. CONCLUSION

In this paper we revisited the problem of range search over data outsourced to an untrusted server. Prior techniques are either secure but exhibit prohibitive performance cost, or efficient but with unacceptable privacy leakages. We presented the first concrete framework for practical private range search building upon the definitional framework of Searchable Symmetric Encryption (SSE). We introduced a variety of schemes with realistic security/efficiency tradeoffs. Our constructions utilize any secure (existing or future) SSE scheme as a black box, and appropriately convert range search to multi-keyword search. We formally defined the security of all proposed algorithms formulating the leakages, and experimentally demonstrated their practicality. In our future work, we plan to focus on the considerably harder setting of *multi-dimensional* (i.e., *multi-attribute*) range queries.

Acknowledgements

This work was partially supported by the European Commission under ICT-FP7-LEADS-318809 (Large-Scale Elastic Architecture for Data-as-a-Service) and ICT-FP7-QualiMaster-619525 (A Configurable Real-time Data Processing Infrastructure Mastering Autonomous Quality Adaptation).

10. REFERENCES

[1] B. H. Bloom. Space/Time Trade-offs in Hash Coding with Allowable Errors. *Commun. of the ACM*, 1970.

[2] A. Boldyreva, N. Chenette, Y. Lee, and A. O Neill. Order-Preserving Symmetric Encryption. In *EUROCRYPT*, 2009.

[3] A. Boldyreva, N. Chenette, and A. O'Neill. Order-Preserving Encryption Revisited: Improved Security Analysis and Alternative Solutions. In *CRYPTO*, 2011.

[4] D. Boneh and B. Waters. Conjunctive, Subset, and Range Queries on Encrypted Data. In *Theory of cryptography*, pages 535–554. Springer, 2007.

[5] D. Cash, J. Jaeger, S. Jarecki, C. Jutla, H. Krawczyk, M. Rosu, and M. Steiner. Dynamic Searchable Encryption in Very-Large Databases: Data Structures and Implementation. In *NDSS*, 2014.

[6] D. Cash, S. Jarecki, C. Jutla, H. Krawczyk, M.-C. Roşu, and M. Steiner. Highly-Scalable Searchable Symmetric Encryption with Support for Boolean Queries. In *CRYPTO*, 2013.

[7] Y.-C. Chang and M. Mitzenmacher. Privacy Preserving Keyword Searches on Remote Encrypted Data. In *ACNS*, 2005.

[8] M. Chase and S. Kamara. Structured Encryption and Controlled Disclosure. In *ASIACRYPT*, 2010.

[9] R. Curtmola, J. Garay, S. Kamara, and R. Ostrovsky. Searchable Symmetric Encryption: Improved Definitions and Efficient Constructions. In *CCS*, 2006.

[10] R. Curtmola, J. Garay, S. Kamara, and R. Ostrovsky. Searchable Symmetric Encryption: Improved Definitions and Efficient Constructions. *Journal of Computer Security*, 19(5):895–934, 2011.

[11] S. Faber, S. Jarecki, H. Krawczyk, Q. Nguyen, M. Rosu, and M. Steiner. Rich queries on encrypted data: Beyond exact matches. In *ESORICS*. 2015.

[12] C. Gentry. *A Fully Homomorphic Encryption Scheme*. PhD thesis, Stanford University, 2009.

[13] C. Gentry. Computing Arbitrary Functions of Encrypted Data. *Commun. of the ACM*, 2010.

[14] E.-J. Goh et al. Secure Indexes. *IACR Cryptology ePrint Archive*, 2003.

[15] O. Goldreich. *Foundations of Cryptography: Volume 1*. Cambridge University Press, 2006.

[16] O. Goldreich, S. Goldwasser, and S. Micali. How to Construct Random Functions. *J. ACM*, 33(4):792–807, 1986.

[17] O. Goldreich and R. Ostrovsky. Software Protection and Simulation on Oblivious RAMs. *J. ACM*, 43(3):431–473, 1996.

[18] H. Hacigümüş, B. Iyer, C. Li, and S. Mehrotra. Executing SQL over Encrypted Data in the Database-Service-Provider Model. In *SIGMOD*, 2002.

[19] B. Hore, S. Mehrotra, M. Canim, and M. Kantarcioglu. Secure Multidimensional Range Queries over Outsourced Data. *VLDB J.*, 21(3):333–358, 2012.

[20] B. Hore, S. Mehrotra, and G. Tsudik. A Privacy-Preserving Index for Range Queries. In *VLDB*, 2004.

[21] S. Kamara and C. Papamanthou. Parallel and Dynamic Searchable Symmetric Encryption. In *Financial Cryptography*, 2013.

[22] S. Kamara, C. Papamanthou, and T. Roeder. Dynamic Searchable Symmetric Encryption. In *CCS*, 2012.

[23] F. Kerschbaum and A. Schroepfer. Optimal Average-Complexity Ideal-Security Order-Preserving Encryption. In *CCS*, 2014.

[24] A. Kiayias, S. Papadopoulos, N. Triandopoulos, and T. Zacharias. Delegatable Pseudorandom Functions and Applications. In *CCS*, 2013.

[25] A. Lamb, M. Fuller, R. Varadarajan, N. Tran, B. Vandiver, L. Doshi, and C. Bear. The Vertica Analytic Database: C-store 7 Years Later. *PVLDB*, 2012.

[26] R. Li, A. X. Liu, A. L. Wang, and B. Bruhadeshwar. Fast Range Query Processing with Strong Privacy Protection for Cloud Computing. *PVLDB*, 2014.

[27] C. Mavroforakis, N. Chenette, A. O'Neill, G. Kollios, and R. Canetti. Modular Order-Preserving Encryption, Revisited. In *SIGMOD*, 2015.

[28] M. Naveed, M. Prabhakaran, and C. A. Gunter. Dynamic searchable encryption via blind storage. In *SP*, 2014.

[29] R. Ostrovsky. Efficient Computation on Oblivious RAMs. In *STOC*, 1990.

[30] R. A. Popa, F. H. Li, and N. Zeldovich. An Ideal-Security Protocol for Order-Preserving Encoding. *SP*, 2013.

[31] R. A. Popa, C. Redfield, N. Zeldovich, and H. Balakrishnan. CryptDB: Protecting Confidentiality with Encrypted Query Processing. In *SOSP*, 2011.

[32] E. Shi, J. Bethencourt, T.-H. Chan, D. Song, and A. Perrig. Multi-Dimensional Range Query over Encrypted Data. In *SP*, 2007.

[33] D. X. Song, D. Wagner, and A. Perrig. Practical Techniques for Searches on Encrypted Data. In *SP*, 2000.

[34] E. Stefanov, C. Papamanthou, and E. Shi. Practical Dynamic Searchable Encryption with Small Leakage. 2014.

[35] E. Stefanov and E. Shi. ObliviStore: High Performance Oblivious Cloud Storage. In *SP*, 2013.

[36] E. Stefanov, E. Shi, and D. Song. Towards Practical Oblivious RAM. *NDSS*, 2012.

[37] E. Stefanov, M. Van Dijk, E. Shi, C. Fletcher, L. Ren, X. Yu, and S. Devadas. Path ORAM: An Extremely Simple Oblivious RAM Protocol. In *CCS*, 2013.

[38] S. Tu, M. F. Kaashoek, S. Madden, and N. Zeldovich. Processing Analytical Queries over Encrypted Data. In *PVLDB*, 2013.

[39] P. Van Liesdonk, S. Sedghi, J. Doumen, P. Hartel, and W. Jonker. Computationally Efficient Searchable Symmetric Encryption. In *SDM*. 2010.

APPENDIX

A. ADDITIONAL EXPERIMENTS

Query costs at owner. To verify the practicality of the proposed approaches, we also evaluated experimentally the costs incurred at the owner during query execution. In particular, we generated random queries for ranges of size 1 to 100 over the domain $A = \{0, \ldots, 2^{20}\}$, and measured the size of each query (in bytes) and the time required for generating it. Figures 8(a) and 8(b) present the average results over 1000 executions for each query range size. For clarity, the curves corresponding to Constant and Logarithmic for the same range covering technique (i.e., BRC or URC) are grouped together in both figures, since (i) the same range covering technique leads to the same query size in both Constant and Logarithmic, and (ii) the difference in query generation time between Constant and Logarithmic is negligible, as token generation times of Constant are only slightly higher than those of Logarithmic (due to the GGM value expansion starting from the root).

As expected, Logarithmic-SRC and Logarithmic-SRC-i feature the smallest query sizes: the former always entails a single token per query, and the latter two tokens, where each token takes 24 bytes. On the other hand, the query size in both BRC- and URC-based schemes scales logarithmically with the range size. The saw-like trend of URC is due to the worst-case decomposition, whose size oscillates with the range size regardless of the randomly-selected query position. In contrast, in BRC, different query positions for the same range size lead to different numbers of tokens, which are smoothed by the averaging.

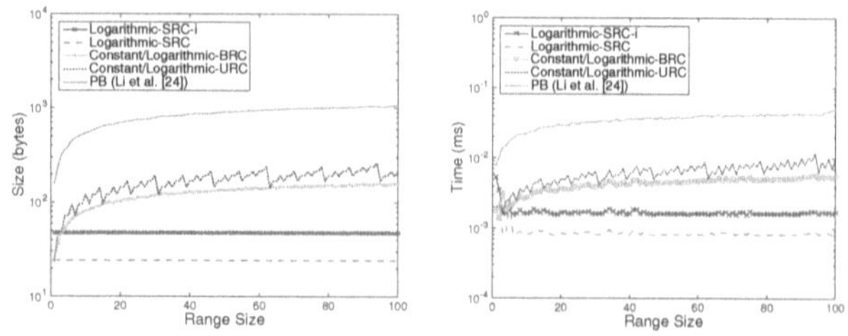

(a) Query size (b) Query generation time

Figure 8: Query costs at owner

Figure 8(b) depicts the wall-clock time required in Trpdr to compute the tokens for all nodes that are produced by the range covering technique. We see that the curves follow a similar trend to those of Figure 8(a), which is expected since the total time is dominated by the PRF evaluations (one for each covering node/keyword). Observe that these operations are lightweight, and are typically carried out in less than 0.01 milliseconds in all our schemes. PB, on the other hand, incurs larger query sizes and higher query generation times than all our schemes, mainly due to the excessive number of cryptographic hash functions involved in its Bloom filter approach.

It is important to note that the reported costs of our methods do not depend on the datasets, or on the domain; they only depend on the *position* of the range in the binary tree over the domain. As such, the presented results are representative of all possible domains and datasets.

Privacy Preserving Subgraph Matching on Large Graphs in Cloud

Zhao Chang[*,#], Lei Zou[*], Feifei Li[#]

[*]*Peking University, China;* [#]*University of Utah, USA;*

{changzhao,zoulei}@pku.edu.cn; {zchang,lifeifei}@cs.utah.edu

ABSTRACT

The wide presence of large graph data and the increasing popularity of storing data in the cloud drive the needs for graph query processing on a remote cloud. But a fundamental challenge is to process user queries without compromising sensitive information. This work focuses on privacy preserving subgraph matching in a cloud server. The goal is to minimize the overhead on both cloud and client sides for subgraph matching, without compromising users' sensitive information. To that end, we transform an original graph G into a privacy preserving graph G^k, which meets the requirement of an existing privacy model known as *k-automorphism*. By making use of the symmetry in a k-automorphic graph, a subgraph matching query can be efficiently answered using a graph G^o, a small subset of G^k. This approach saves both space and query cost in the cloud server. We also anonymize the query graphs to protect their label information using label generalization technique. To reduce the search space for a subgraph matching query, we propose a cost model to select the more effective label combinations. The effectiveness and efficiency of our method are demonstrated through extensive experimental results on real datasets.

1. INTRODUCTION

Owing to the rich semantic and structure information represented by a graph, structured graph data is used in numerous applications, such as social networks, web graphs, biological networks, transportation networks, knowledge base, and RDF graphs. Many emerging applications rely on large graphs to satisfy their query needs, such as Google's knowledge graph and Facebook's graph search. Thus, graph data management has attracted significant attention, and efficient graph query processing on large graph is an important subject of study. In this paper, we focus on subgraph matching query [25, 18, 12], which is a key component of numerous applications. For example, answering SPARQL query Q is equal to finding subgraph matches of Q on an RDF graph G [15]. Some graph databases also provide query language that is based on subgraph matching semantics, such as Cypher in Neo4j.

Meanwhile, increasingly, companies choose the "cloud" as their IT infrastructure platform. Using the cloud allows users to avoid expensive upfront infrastructure costs, and focus on projects that differentiate their businesses instead of on infrastructure [2]. Many public cloud services are available, such as Amazon cloud and Microsoft Azure. Some graph systems (such as GraphLab [14] and Neo4j [1]) offer SaaS (software-as-a-service)-style cloud services. In other words, they allow users to upload their graph data to their cloud platforms and provide cloud-based computing services over the outsourced graph data.

However, while utilizing cloud services for building graph applications is a cost-effective solution, the potential risk of compromising sensitive information is a serious problem.

One serious privacy leakage is the "identity disclosure" problem [20, 13]. Assume that an adversary can locate the target entity t as a vertex v of a social network graph G with a high probability. We say that the identity of t is disclosed. A naïve anonymization solution is to remove all identifiable personal information before publishing the network, such as names and social security numbers. However, even when a network is published without any identity information, it is still possible to locate the target with a high probability based on some structural information around the target [10].

For example, if an adversary knows the local graph structure (such as degree, 1-neighbor graph) around the target t, he/she may issue a subgraph query representing the local graph structure to find the matching position. If there are only few matches in graph G, the target will be identified with a high probability. Once it is determined that a vertex v corresponds to the target t, all sensitive attributes associated with v will be compromised. These are called *structural attacks*; see details in [13, 24, 10].

To address these threats, many privacy preserving graph data publishing techniques have been proposed [26, 6, 22]. A typical solution to protect graph privacy is based on the symmetry of the released graph data [26, 6, 22]. Specifically, given a graph G, we transform G into a k-automorphic graph G^k by introducing some noise edges, where each vertex has at least $(k-1)$ other symmetric vertices. It means there are no structural differences between v and each of its $(k-1)$ symmetric vertices. Thus it is impossible to distinguish v from the other $(k-1)$ symmetric vertices. In other words, the k-automorphism strategy [26] can defend against any structure-based attack.

These privacy preserving graph data publishing techniques seem like perfect solutions to our problem, but they *compromise the utility of query results*. In particular, they may return false positives regarding subgraph matching queries, due to the noise edges and vertices that were added. However, in a cloud setting, it is possible to offload most query processing costs to the cloud server and ask the clients to execute a simple and efficient filtering step to remove false positives and find the exact answers.

EXAMPLE 1. *Consider a professional social network in Figure 1 that is modeled as a graph G. Each vertex in G represents an*

SIGMOD'16, June 26-July 01, 2016, San Francisco, CA, USA

DOI: http://dx.doi.org/10.1145/2882903.2882956

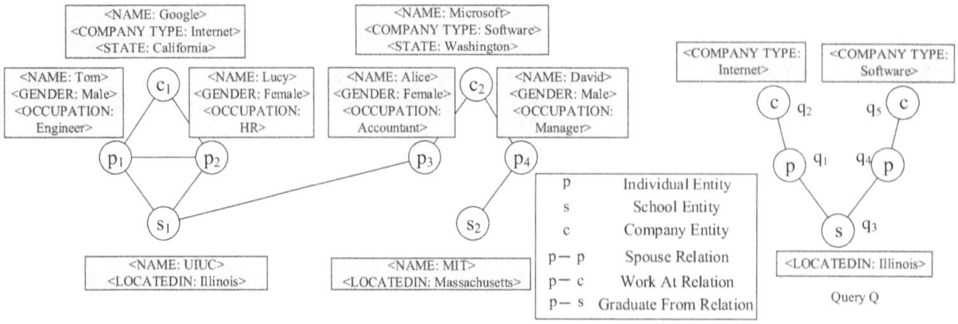

Graph G

Figure 1: An original data graph and a query graph on a professional social network graph.

entity, such as an individual (p_i), a company (c_j), or a school (s_ℓ). Each edge in G represents a relation between two entities, such as "spouse" relation, "work at" relation and "graduate from" relation. Each entity has some attributes. For example, the attributes associated with individuals are "gender", "occupation" and so on.

A user wants to find "two individuals satisfying (1) both of them graduated from the same university located in Illinois, and (2) one of them is working at a software company and the other one is working at an Internet company". The user issues a subgraph pattern matching query Q over G, as shown in Figure 1.

Sending the original graph G to the cloud will leak user privacy in G. Thus, we resort to the privacy preserving graph publishing techniques. For example, we can use the k-automorphism model [26]; the k-automorphic graph G^k for G and $k = 2$ is shown in Figure 2, where noise edges are shown by red dashed lines. Clearly, G^k protects the structure privacy of the graph G. To protect label privacy, we also use label anonymization where each vertex label in G^k is replaced by a label group (i.e., a generalized label). We use Label Correspondence Table (LCT) (in Figure 2) to represent the mapping between label groups and vertex labels. For example, vertex p_1 in G^k has label groups C and E in Figure 2.

A straightforward method is to upload G^k to the cloud and perform graph queries over G^k. Although the approach does not leak any sensitive information, the answers to query Q over graph G^k ($R(Q, G^k)$) are different from those over G ($R(Q, G)$). For example, there are only two subgraph matches of Q over the original graph G. However, due to the noise edges introduced into the k-automorphic graph G^k and the label anonymization, there are eight matches over G^k. Nevertheless, when the cloud returns $R(Q, G^k)$ with eight matches, the client can efficiently filter out false positives based on G to derive $R(Q, G)$.

Note that the filtering step at the client side is *much cheaper than asking the client to run the subgraph matching query Q over G* (which is known to be expensive especially over large graphs). In other words, the cloud server did most of the work in this process, making the cloud service worthwhile and attractive for the client. We do assume that the client is the data owner who has access to G for the filtering step. For the general case, a query client (who is trusted and authenticated by the data owner) can ask for the data owner to execute the (very lightweight) filtering step.

However, the example above shows some major limitations of directly applying the existing graph data publishing techniques [26, 6, 22]. Firstly, most of these techniques that focus on structural attacks do not protect label privacy at the same time. But more importantly, to achieve higher privacy, they need to add a lot of noise edges and/or vertices (e.g., a large k value in the case of the k-automorphism model) to the original graph G. This results in a much larger graph (than the original graph) on the cloud side, which leads to much more expensive storage cost, much larger communication overhead, and much higher query costs for both the cloud server and the query client.

This work focuses on *reducing these overheads without compromising either data and query graphs' privacy or the correctness of the final query results at the client side.*

Solution overview. In order to achieve that, we first propose a basic solution. We transform the data graph G into an outsourced graph G^k using existing privacy-preserving graph publication techniques, such as the k-automorphism model [26]; and then upload G^k to the cloud. At query time, we propose a *two-phase query evaluation strategy*. First, given a query graph Q, we transform Q into an outsourced query graph Q^o. In the cloud, we evaluate subgraph query Q^o over G^k to obtain query results $R(Q^o, G^k)$. Then, in the client side, we filter out false positives in $R(Q^o, G^k)$ based on G to find the final, correct results $R(Q, G)$, i.e., subgraph matches of Q over the original graph G. To improve the query performance, we propose a solution that only uploads a small part of G^k to the cloud by leveraging the symmetry of the k-automorphic graph G^k. This method saves both space cost and query processing time in the cloud significantly. Although only a (small) part of G^k is uploaded to the cloud, our method still guarantees the correctness of the query results. Furthermore, we also propose a cost model based label combination/generalization strategy to reduce the search space for subgraph matching queries in the cloud.

Contributions. To the best of our knowledge, this is the first work that supports privacy preserving subgraph matching queries over a large graph in the cloud while protecting privacy without undermining query results. In this paper, we consider the cloud server "honest-but-curious", which is consistent with most related works in the literature. In other words, the cloud server always offers correct computations without cheating. However, the cloud server is "curious" to learn the graph data, its index structure, and user queries so as to gain sensitive information if he can. Our main contributions are summarized as follows.

- We propose an effective strategy to provide exact subgraph matching query services in public cloud while preserving private information in the data graph and query graphs.
- To save both space cost and query processing cost, we only upload a small subset of the anonymized data graph to the cloud. We answer subgraph matching queries efficiently in the cloud by making use of the symmetry of the k-automorphic graph. These techniques contribute to saving cost while minimizing the overhead in the client side.
- In order to reduce the search space in answering subgraph matching queries, we design a novel cost model to select effective vertex label combinations for anonymizing labels in the data graph and query graphs.
- We study the effectiveness and efficiency of our method through extensive experiments over several large real graphs.

Label Group	Labels
A	{Internet, Software}
B	{California, Washington}
C	{Female, Male}
D	{HR, Accountant}
E	{Engineer, Manager}
F	{Illinois, Massachusetts}

Label Correspondence Table (LCT)

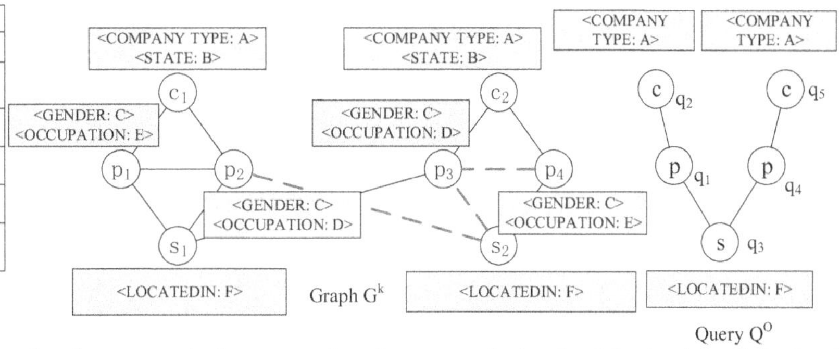

Figure 2: A k-automorphic graph and an anonymized query graph on the same professional social network graph for k = 2.

Table 1: Notations

G	The original data graph
G^k	The data graph released by k-automorphism algorithm
G^o	The outsourced data graph
Q	The original query graph
Q^o	The outsourced query graph
S_i	The i-th star of Q^o generated by query decomposition
R_{in}	The set of candidate matching results of Q^o generated in cloud
$R(Q,G)$	The set of subgraph matches of Q on G

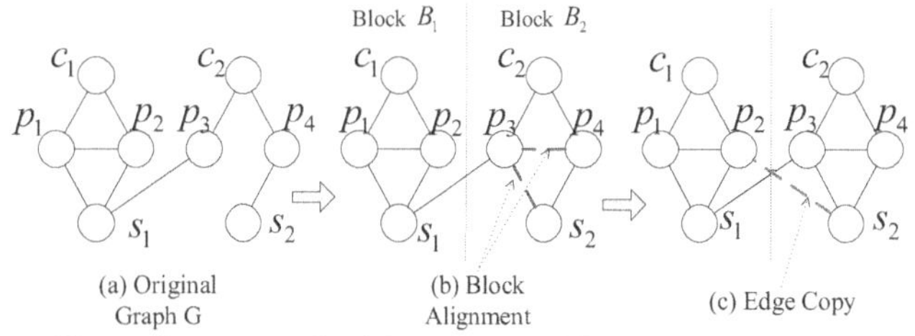

Figure 3: An example of the k-automorphism algorithm [26].

2. BACKGROUND

2.1 Preliminary

Traditional subgraph matching methods always adopt the vertex labeled graph model [23], where each vertex has a single label. But this model is not desirable to model complex graph data, such as social networks and RDF graphs. In this work, we adopt the *attributed graph model*, where each vertex has a rich data structure including vertex type, vertex attributes and vertex labels (i.e., attribute values). For simplicity, we only consider rich data structures on vertices and ignore those on edges, although handling the more general case is not more complicated. For example, we can introduce an imaginary vertex to represent an edge of interest and assign the rich data structure on the edge to the new vertex. Formally, our graph model is defined as follows. Table 1 lists some frequently-used notations in this paper.

Definition 1. ***Attributed Graph Model.*** *An attributed graph is defined as* $G = \{V(G), E(G), T, \Gamma, L\}$, *where (1)* $V(G)$ *is a set of vertices; (2)* $E(G) \subseteq V(G) \times V(G)$ *is a set of undirected edges; (3)* T *is a set of vertex types, where each vertex has and only has one vertex type; (4)* Γ *is a set of vertex attributes, where each vertex type has one or more vertex attributes and different vertex types have different vertex attributes; and (5)* L *is a set of vertex labels, where each vertex attribute has one or more vertex labels.*

The vertex type, vertex attributes and vertex labels of vertex v are denoted as $T(v)$, $\Gamma(v)$, $L(v)$, respectively. For any two different vertices v_1 and v_2, if and only if $T(v_1) = T(v_2)$, then $\Gamma(v_1) = \Gamma(v_2)$. For one vertex attribute $A \in \Gamma(v)$, $\langle A, \{a_1, \cdots, a_n\}\rangle$ represents the vertex attribute values on attribute A which are the vertex labels of A. Note that one vertex attribute may have multiple vertex labels (i.e., attribute values). For example, the "Company Type" of one company can be "Internet", "Software", and so on.

The data graph G and the query graphs Q in the running example follow the attributed graph model.

Definition 2. ***Subgraph Match.*** *Given a data graph* $G = \{V(G), E(G), T, \Gamma, L\}$ *and a query graph* $Q = \{V(Q), E(Q), T, \Gamma, L\}$, Q *is* subgraph isomorphic *to* G, *if and only if there exists at least one injective function* $g : V(Q) \rightarrow V(G)$ *such that*
1) $\forall q_i \in V(Q)$, $g(q_i) \in V(G) \Rightarrow L(q_i) \subseteq L(g(q_i))$*; and*
2) $\forall q_i, q_j \in V(Q)$, *edge* $\overline{q_i q_j} \in E(Q) \Rightarrow$ *edge* $\overline{g(q_i)g(q_j)} \in E(G)$.

If Q *is* subgraph isomorphic *to* G, *a* subgraph match M *of* Q *is a subgraph of* G, *represented as* $\langle g(q_1), \cdots, g(q_n)\rangle$.

The set of subgraph matches *of* Q *on* G *is denoted as* $R(Q, G)$.

Our problem can now be formalized as follows:

[Problem Definition] *Given a data graph* G *and a query graph* Q, *our problem is to find all subgraph matches of* Q *over* G, *denoted as* $R(Q, G)$, *through a cloud server, while preserving private information in data graph* G *and query graph* Q.

Note that the goal of our problem is to protect the privacy of data graph and query graph against the cloud, where clients who ask a subgraph query have the ability to de-anonymize, filter and verify the results returned from the cloud based on the original graph.

2.2 K-Automorphism

As explained in Section 1 (Example 1 and its discussion), it is possible to apply existing privacy preserving graph publication techniques in constructing a baseline solution. However, they suffer from major efficiency limitations. Furthermore, most of these techniques that focus on structural attacks do not protect label privacy at the same time. Nevertheless, we can use these techniques as a preprocessing step (e.g., k-automorphism [26]) towards constructing more effective and efficient solutions. That said, we will briefly review k-automorphism [26] next.

The basic idea of k-automorphism is as follows. Given a graph G to be published, we transform it into G^k by introducing more vertices and edges, where G^k satisfies the k-automorphic graph model (Definition 3). It means that any vertex v in graph G^k cannot distinguish itself from each of its symmetric $(k-1)$ vertices in G^k. Therefore, G^k is safe to publish. Here, it is assumed that the graph is unlabeled. Figure 3 shows an example of the algorithm in [26].

Definition 3. ***K-Automorphic Graph [26].*** *A* k*-automorphic graph* G^k *is defined as* $G^k = \{V(G^k), E(G^k)\}$, *where* $V(G^k)$ *can be divided into* k *blocks and each block has* $\left\lceil \frac{|V(G^k)|}{k} \right\rceil$ *vertices. Any vertex* v *has* $k-1$ symmetric vertices v' [1] *in the other* $k-1$ *blocks.*

The k-automorphic graph is generated with the help of the k-automorphic function defined as follows.

Definition 4. ***K-Automorphic Function [26].*** *Given a vertex* v *in a* k*-automorphic graph* G^k, v *and its corresponding* $k-1$ symmetric vertices *form an* alignment vertex instance *(AVI).*

[1] "symmetric" means swapping v and v' gives an isomorphic graph.

p_1	p_4
p_2	p_3
s_1	s_2
c_1	c_2

(a) Alignment Vertex Table

$F_1(p_1) = p_4; F_1(p_4) = p_1$
$F_1(p_2) = p_3; F_1(p_3) = p_2$
$F_1(s_1) = s_2; F_1(s_2) = s_1$
$F_1(c_1) = c_2; F_1(c_2) = p_1$

(b) Automorphic Function F_1

Figure 4: AVT and automorphic functions.

All AVIs are stored in an Alignment Vertex Table (AVT). Each AVI I in AVT is represented as a circularly-linked list. Specifically, $I.at(i)$ ($i = 0, \cdots, k-1$) denotes the i-th vertex in instance I. Suppose $v = I.at(i)$. If $i \leq k-2$, $v.next = I.at(i+1)$; else $v.next = I.at(0)$. For each vertex v in an AVI, we can define k automorphic functions F_i ($i = 0, \cdots, k-1$) in G^k based on the AVI, where

- $F_0(v) = v$;
- $F_i(v) = F_{i-1}(v).next$, *for* $1 \leq i \leq k-1$.

If M is a subgraph of G^k, each $F_i(M)$ ($i = 0, \cdots, k-1$) is defined as a mapping graph under function F_i, where:

- $V(F_i(M)) = \{u \mid \exists v \in V(M), u = F_i(v)\}$;
- $E(F_i(M)) = \{\overline{u_1u_2} \mid \exists\ \overline{v_1v_2} \in E(M), u_1 = F_i(v_1) \wedge u_2 = F_i(v_2)\}$.

A k-automorphic graph G^k (for $k = 2$) generated from G (in Figure 1) is given in Figure 2. The corresponding Alignment Vertex Table (AVT) is given in Figure 4(a). Each row of AVT shows k symmetric vertices. For example, the first row of AVT contains p_1 and p_4, meaning p_1 and p_4 are symmetric vertices. In other words, swapping vertices p_1 and p_4 will generate another isomorphic graph. Each column of AVT shows all vertices in one block of the k-automorphic graph. For example, there are two blocks $\{c_1, p_1, p_2, s_1\}$ and $\{c_2, p_4, p_3, s_2\}$ in the 2-automorphic graph in Figure 3. Based on AVT, we also show the automorphic function F_1 of the running example in Figure 4(b).

Given a graph G, we generate a k-automorphic graph G^k from G as follows. First, we adopt the METIS algorithm [11] to partition G into k blocks. For example, to generate the 2-automorphic graph for the graph G in Figure 1, we obtain two blocks $B_1\{c_1, p_1, p_2, s_1\}$ and $B_2\{c_2, p_4, p_3, s_2\}$ by partitioning G. If $|V(G)|$ cannot be divided by k, we will introduce some noise vertices to guarantee that every block has exactly $\left\lceil \frac{|V(G^k)|}{k} \right\rceil$ vertices. There is an efficient method to build the Alignment Vertex Table (AVT) (e.g., Figure 4) [26]. Based on the AVT, it is easy to define the k-automorphic functions. Finally, based on the k-automorphic functions, we build G^k by performing *graph alignment* and *edge copy*. For example, we perform graph alignment on B_1 and B_2 to obtain two alignment blocks B_1' and B_2' (adding edge (p_3, p_4) and edge (p_3, s_2) in Figure 3(b)), where B_1' and B_2' are isomorphic to each other. Lastly, the "edge copy" technique is used to deal with the crossing edges between different blocks (adding edge (p_2, s_2) that corresponds to edge (p_3, s_1) in Figure 3(c)). Readers can refer to [26] for further details. Furthermore, it is easy to show that any vertex in the k-automorphic graph G^k cannot distinguish itself from each of its $(k-1)$ symmetric vertices. It means that any adversary cannot identify any target vertex with a probability higher than $\frac{1}{k}$. [2]

2.3 Our Framework and Analysis Overview

In order to provide the correct cloud-based subgraph query services while preserving privacy in data graph and query graphs, our solution works as follows. We transform G into an outsourced graph G^o and upload G^o to the cloud. We guarantee that G^o does not leak any private information in the original graph G. Specifically, we require that any adversary, who sees G^o, cannot identify any target vertex in graph G with a probability higher than $\frac{1}{k}$. We adopt the *k-automorphism* model [26] to achieve this objective, by generating G^o based on G^k. At query time, given a query graph Q, we transform Q into an outsourced query graph Q^o. Leveraging the symmetry of the k-automorphic graph, the cloud server answers subgraph matching query Q^o based on G^o and returns R_{in} (a small subset of $R(Q^o, G^k)$, see Section 4.2.1) to the client. Based on R_{in}, the client can efficiently recover $R(Q^o, G^k)$ and finally find the final results $R(Q, G)$. We highlight several key requirements.

Firstly, we need to define what sensitive information is in data graph and query graphs. We do not consider the vertex types T and vertex attributes Γ as sensitive information, since they do not compromise users' privacy. For any vertex v in G or Q, we consider vertex labels $L(v)$ (i.e., attribute values) as private information. Thus, the "*label privacy*" considered in this paper refers to the privacy of the attribute values of each vertex in the graph. For example, given an "individual" vertex in graph G in Figure 1, the values of gender and occupation are users' privacy. Subgraph matching queries will reveal vertex labels in original data graph G, if we do not anonymize the vertex labels (i.e., attribute values) in query graphs. Thus, the vertex labels in query graph Q are also considered as sensitive information.

Secondly, we must reduce expenses for the cloud server; that is to say, we need to save query time and storage space in the cloud and reduce communication overhead between the client and the cloud. To protect data privacy, we have to introduce noise edges into the data graph and anonymize attribute values of vertices. Doing so will lead to larger search space in subgraph matching. Therefore, in Section 5, we propose a cost model to guide how to select a good graph anonymization strategy. We also study how to reduce the storage space and communication overhead by leveraging the symmetry of the anonymized graph in Section 4, which also helps reduce the cloud's query processing cost.

Thirdly, we should minimize the overhead in the client side. Subgraph matching is an expensive task in terms of both time and space complexity. In our framework, the client only needs to filter out false positives using a hash index in linear time complexity (in terms of the number of candidate results generated by the cloud).

3. A BASELINE SOLUTION

We first describe a simple scheme to help illustrate the basic principle of our approach. For a graph G, we first generate the k-automorphic graph G^k. A baseline solution is to upload G^k to the cloud directly. Note that k-automorphism [26] assumes that the graph is unlabeled. To protect the vertex labels in data graph and query graphs, we resort to the generalization technique, which is also used in k-anonymity [17, 19]. Specifically, each vertex label in data graph and query graphs is represented by a generalized label. We refer to a generalized vertex label as a "label group" in the following discussion. Here, we assume that each label group contains not less than θ distinct labels, where θ is a user-specified parameter. For example, a label group "A" in Figure 2 includes $\theta = 2$ labels {Internet, Software}.

The *Label Correspondence Table* (LCT) (in Figure 2) shows all label groups in the running example. Obviously, the label generalization strategy will affect the query performance. We assume that the label groups are given until Section 5, where we will propose a cost model to find a good label generalization strategy.

Using label generalization on a data graph G, we obtain a graph G' whose vertices hide vertex labels by label groups. Next, using the k-automorphism algorithm in [26], we obtain a k-automorphic data graph G^k and the corresponding AVT. Each vertex v in G^k has

[2] The proof was given in Theorem 4.4 of [26].

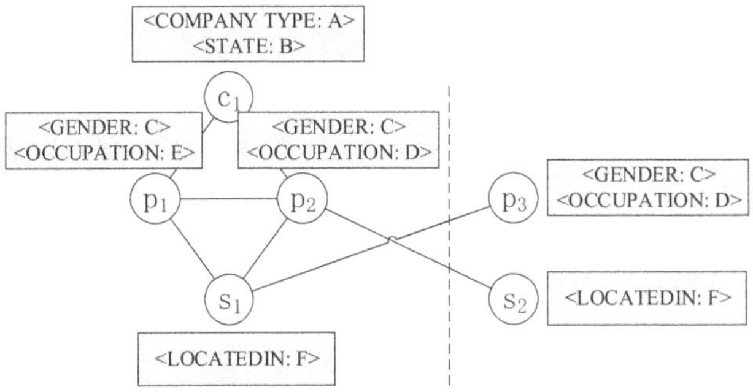

$\mathbf{G^o}$

Figure 5: The outsourced data graph G^o for G in Example 1.

$(k-1)$ symmetric vertices $F_i(v)$ under automorphic functions F_i for $i = 1, \cdots, k-1$. The k vertices, i.e., v together with $F_i(v)$ for $i = 1, \cdots, k-1$, form a symmetric vertex group, which corresponds to a row in AVT (an AVI). For each symmetric vertex group, we ensure that all vertices in it have the same label groups, i.e., a vertex v's label gropus are $L(v) \cup L(F_1(v)) \cup \cdots \cup L(F_{k-1}(v))$.

EXAMPLE 2. *Given the original data graph G in Figure 1, the k-automorphic graph G^k together with its label correspondence table (LCT) is given in Figure 2. A naïve solution is to upload G^k to the cloud directly.*

Given a query graph Q, we anonymize Q by representing each vertex label using its corresponding label group. The anonymized query graph is denoted as Q^o, which is submitted to the cloud. The cloud server answers subgraph query Q^o over the k-automorphic graph G^k. We know that $R(Q, G) \subseteq R(Q^o, G^k)$. Intuitively, we introduce more edges and vertices into G to form G^k, and Q^o and G^k's vertex labels are anonymized using the same LCT. Formally,

Theorem 1. *For graph G and query graph Q, $R(Q, G) \subseteq R(Q^o, G^k)$.*

Finally, $R(Q^o, G^k)$ are sent to the client and the client filters out false positives in $R(Q^o, G^k)$ based on G to obtain $R(Q, G)$.

The baseline solution suffers from the following limitations. First, we need to upload the k-automorphic graph G^k to the cloud. Since the size of G^k can be significantly larger than $|G|$, this introduces communication overhead and higher storage cost. Secondly, a larger graph G^k naturally leads to a larger search space for subgraph matching, which leads to higher query cost, especially as k increases.

Nevertheless, the baseline solution already saves the client from executing the very expensive subgraph matching query herself.

4. THE OPTIMIZED METHOD

4.1 Outsourced Graph

According to Definition 3, G^k is a k-automorphic graph consisting of k blocks. Each vertex v in G^k has $(k-1)$ symmetric vertices in the other $(k-1)$ blocks. Intuitively, we only need to upload a block of G^k together with k automorphic functions F_i $(i = 0, \cdots, k-1)$ to the cloud, since the cloud can recover the whole G^k based on G^o and the functions F_i. This is the motivation of defining the outsourced graph G^o (Definition 5), which is exactly the first block of G^k together with the 1-hop neighbors in G^k.

Definition 5. ***Outsourced Graph.*** *For a graph $G(V(G), E(G), T, \Gamma, L)$ and its k-automorphic graph $G^k(V(G^k), E(G^k), T, \Gamma, L)$, an outsourced graph of G is defined as $G^o = \{V(G^o), E(G^o), T, \Gamma, L\}$, where (1) G^o follows the* attributed graph model*; (2) $V(G^o)$ is the union of vertices in the first block of G^k, denoted as $V(B_1)$, together with their one-hop neighbors in G^k denoted as $V(N_1)$; and (3) $E(G^o)$ is the subset of undirected edges from $E(G^k)$ that connect vertices within $V(B_1)$ and vertics between $V(B_1)$ and $V(N_1)$.*

Given a k-automorphic graph G^k, according to Definition 5, we generate an outsourced graph G^o and upload it to the cloud. For example, given G and G^k in Figure 1 and Figure 2 from Example 1 respectively, an outsourced graph G^o is represented in Figure 5. G^o contains the vertices in the first block of G^k (i.e., the vertices in the first column of AVT) together with their 1-hop neighbors in G^k, and their corresponding edges in G^k. Note that the size of G^o is much smaller than the size of G^k (roughly an $1/k$ fraction of it).

Although G^o is a part of G^k, according to the k automorphic functions F_i (see Definition 4), each vertex/edge in G^k must have a counterpart in G^o. It means that we can easily recover G^k based on G^o and the k automorphic functions F_i $(i = 0, \cdots, k-1)$. This is the intuition that we only upload G^o to the cloud without compromising the accuracy of query results. More sophisticated technical details are discussed in the following subsection.

4.2 Privacy Preserving Subgraph Query

Given a query Q at the client side, we generalize its vertex labels to form Q^o. Specifically, for each vertex label in Q, we replace it with the corresponding label group according to the LCT (an example is shown in Figure 2). Q^o has the same size as Q, although each vertex of Q^o has a generalized label group. Q^o ensures the privacy of the vertex label information in Q. It is a trade-off between the query privacy and the query performance. Thus, label generalization is an interesting challenge in its own and we assume for now that this is done and present the details in Section 5.

The client then sends Q^o to the cloud. The cloud first finds subgraph matches of all *basic units* of Q^o over G^o, which will be defined shortly. Using the symmetry of the k-automorphic graph, the cloud can then obtain $R(Q^o, G^k)$, *but without G^k since it only has* G^o, by joining these intermediate results. Lastly, $R(Q^o, G^k)$ is sent back to the client, who can obtain $R(Q, G)$ by pruning the false positives in $R(Q^o, G^k)$. Theorem 1 guarantees the correctness of this framework.

4.2.1 Processing in the Cloud

A k-automorphic graph G^k consists of k symmetric blocks $(B_1, \cdots, B_k)$, while the outsourced graph G^o contains only one block together with the first-hop neighbors of its boundary vertices. *The challenge* is how to find subgraph matches *crossing* multiple blocks of G^k without accessing G^k, since only G^o resides in the cloud.

We adopt the query decomposition method. Given a query Q^o, the cloud server decompose Q^o into a set of stars $\{S_i\}$, $i = 1, ..., n$, where a star is a root vertex together with its adjacent edges and neighbors in Q^o. Then, it finds $R(S_i, G^o)$ for each star graph S_i for $i = 1, \cdots, n$. Leveraging the symmetry of G^k, we can then obtain $R(S_i, G^k)$ based on $R(S_i, G^o)$. Finally, we obtain $R(Q^o, G^k)$ by joining the matching results for these stars.

Query Decomposition. We first discuss how to decompose Q^o into a set of stars and how to find the optimal query decomposition.

Consider a query Q^o in Figure 2. The stars rooted at vertices with Type P are shown in Figure 6, where a shaded circle denotes the *center (aka root)* of a star.

Intuitively, a query decomposition is a set of stars that collectively cover the outsourced query graph Q^o. Figure 6 shows the query decomposition $\{S_1, S_2\}$ over query Q^o. The set of subgraph matches of a star graph S_i with respect to the outsourced graph G^o is $R(S_i, G^o)$, or simply $R(S_i)$ when the context is clear. To reduce the number of intermediate results, we design a *cost model* to estimate the number of matches, $|R(S_i)|$, for each star S_i. We will discuss the technical details of the cost model in Section 5. Here, we assume

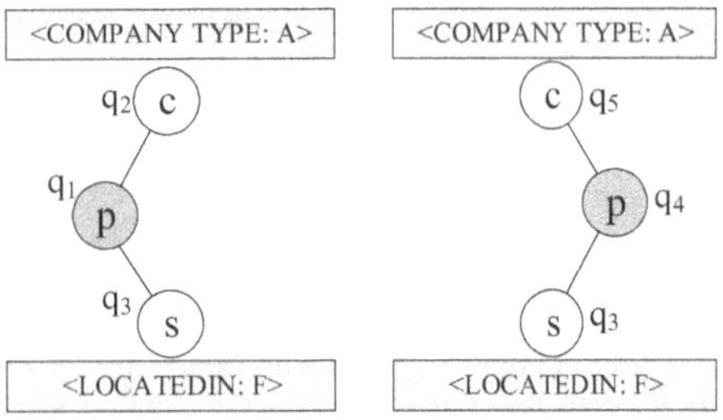

Star S_1 Star S_2

Figure 6: Star graphs after query decomposition.

Label Group	Vertex Type C <c_1>	P <p_1, p_2>	S <s_1>
A	<1>		
B	<1>		
C		<1, 1>	
D		<0, 1>	
E		<1, 0>	
F			<1>

Vertex Bit Vector Table (VBV)

Vertex	Label Groups of the Corresponding Neighbor Vertices <A, B, C, D, E, F>
c_1	<0, 0, 1, 1, 1, 0>
p_1	<1, 1, 1, 1, 0, 1>
p_2	<1, 1, 1, 0, 1, 1>
s_1	<0, 0, 1, 1, 1, 0>

Neighbor Label Bit Vector Table (LBV)

Figure 7: Index structure.

that each $|R(S_i)|$ $(i = 1, \cdots, n)$ is given. We define the cost of the query decomposition as follows.

Definition 6. ***The Cost of Query Decomposition.*** *Given a set of stars $\{S_1, \ldots, S_n\}$ that is a decomposition of an outsourced query graph Q^o, the cost of the query decomposition is:*

$$cost(Q^o) = \sum_{i=1}^{n} |R(S_i)|.$$

It is straightforward to reduce a minimum weighted vertex cover (a classical NP-hard problem) to the problem of finding the query decomposition with the minimum cost. Formally,

Theorem 2. *Given an outsourced query graph Q^o, finding the query decomposition with the minimum cost with respect to Definition 6 is an NP-hard problem.*

That said, we formulate finding the optimal query decomposition as the following ILP (integer linear programming) problem and use an available ILP tool, e.g, the Gurobi ILP solver, to solve this problem. Although ILP is still an NP-hard problem, Q^o is always a small-size graph. Thus in practice, it is actually very efficient to find the optimal query decomposition through this formulation. Solving this ILP also gives us the value n, the number of stars, in the query decomposition.

$$minimize \sum_{\text{all } v_i \in V(Q^o)} |R(S(v_i))| x_{v_i}$$

$$subject\ to \quad x_{v_i} + x_{v_j} \geq 1 \quad \text{for all } \overline{v_i v_j} \in E(Q^o)$$

*/*Each edge is contained in at least one star.*/*

$$x_{v_i} \in \{0, 1\} \text{ for all } v_i \in V(Q^o)$$

*/*A star rooted at each vertex v_i is either selected ($x_{v_i} = 1$) into the query decomposition or not ($x_{v_i} = 0$).*/*

Star Matching. Next, we present our star matching algorithm. The algorithm is designed to find the subgraph matches for each star S_i, in the query decomposition of Q^o, over G^o, i.e., $R(S_i, G^o)$. The cloud server builds a query index structure offline to improve the query efficiency.

The index can be considered as two parts: one is regarding the vertex label, and the other one is regarding the neighbourhood structure. Thus, there are two components in the index structure, as shown in Figure 7 which are constructed based on LCT (label correspondence table) and G^o (see Figure 2 and Figure 5 respectively). They are the *Vertex Bit Vector (VBV) Table* and the *Neighbor Label Bit Vector (LBV) Table*, respectively. For convenience, the first block of G^k is denoted as B_1. Obviously, B_1 is a subgraph of G^o.

Each VBV corresponds to a label group, where the corresponding bit in the VBV for a vertex $v \in B_1$ is set to 1 iff v contains that label group. For example, p_2 contains D but not E in B_1. Thus the two corresponding bits in VBV are 1 and 0, respectively.

In LBV, for each vertex v in B_1, the corresponding bit for a label group L is set to 1 if and only if L is contained in at least one label set for v's neighbor vertices. For example, D is contained in the label set of p_2 that is one of p_1's neighbors. However, E is not contained in the label set of any of p_1's neighbors. Thus the two corresponding bits for p_1 in LBV are 1 and 0, respectively.

Algorithm 1 Star Matching Algorithm

Require: Input: G^o (the outsourced data graph) and S^* (the set of stars that contains star S_i with center v_i, for $1 \leq i \leq n$).
Output: RS ($R(S_i, G^o)$ for $1 \leq i \leq n$).

1: Initialize $RS := \phi$.
2: **for** $i := 1$ to n **do**
3: Initialize $RS_i := \phi$.
4: Set $\alpha := VBV(L(v_i, 1)) \wedge VBV(L(v_i, 2)) \wedge \cdots \wedge VBV(L(v_i, |L(v_i)|))$.
5: **for** each vertex v_a that corresponds to a non-zero bit in α **do**
6: **if** $LBV(v_a) \wedge LBV(v_i) = LBV(v_i)$ **then**
7: Generate the set of matches of S_i with center v_a, denoted as RS_{temp}.
8: $RS_i := RS_i \cup RS_{temp}$.
9: $RS := RS \cup RS_i$.
10: Return RS.

The *Star Matching Algorithm* is presented in Algorithm 1. Without loss of generality, assume that the center of a star S_i is vertex v_i. For each star S_i for $1 \leq i \leq n$, we first find each *Vertex Bit Vector* that corresponds to every label group of v_i; e.g. VBV$(C) = (1, 1)$ in our example. Recall $L(v)$ is the set of label groups for vertex v. We use $L(v, j)$ to denote the j-th label group of v, for $1 \leq j \leq |L(v)|$.

Hence, the first step is to find $VBV(L(v_i, j))$ for $1 \leq j \leq |L(v_i)|$. We perform a *bitwise AND* operation on these $|L(v_i)|$ bit vectors to obtain the result vector α (Line 4). Each vertex v_a that corresponds to a non-zero bit in α is a candidate match of v_i. If each label group of v_i's neighbors can be found in the label sets of v_a's neighbors (Line 6), some of v_a's neighbors can be candidate matches of v_i's neighbors. By enumerating candidate vertex combinations of v_a and its neighbor vertices, we generate matches of S_i and add them to the result set (Line 7-Line 8).

Result Join. The next challenge is how to compute $R(Q^o, G^k)$ based on the star matching results $R(S_i, G^o)$, for $i = 1, ..., n$. A straightforward solution works as follows. First, using the k-automorphic function F_j $(j = 0, \cdots, k-1)$, we compute $R(S_i, G^k)$ based on $R(S_i, G^o)$. Then we compute $R(Q^o, G^k)$ by joining $R(S_i, G^k)$'s, i.e., $R(Q^o, G^k) = R(S_1, G^k) \bowtie R(S_2, G^k) \bowtie \cdots \bowtie R(S_n, G^k)$. Obviously, the cost of the join is $\prod_{i=1}^{n} |R(S_i, G^k)|$.

Figure 8 demonstrates the above process using the running example. In our example, Q^o is decomposed into two stars S_1 and S_2 (in Figure 6). Given the graph G^o (in Figure 5) on the cloud, we perform subgraph matching to obtain $R(S_1, G^o)$ and $R(S_2, G^o)$ (as shown in Figure 8), i.e., the subgraph matches of S_1 and S_2 over graph G^o, respectively. According to the automorphic function F_1 (defined in Figure 4), we can derive $R(S_1, G^2)$ and $R(S_2, G^2)$. Specifically, for each match M in $R(S_1, G^o)$, using the automorphic function F_1, $F_1(M)$ derives another match M' in $R(S_1, G^2)$. For example, (p_1, c_1, s_1) is a match of S_1 over G^o; thus, $(F_1(p_1), F_1(c_1), F_1(s_1))$ gives another match (p_4, c_2, s_2). Thus, we get $R(S_1, G^k) = R(S_1, G^o) \cup F_1(R(S_1, G^o)) \cup \cdots \cup F_{k-1}(R(S_1, G^o))$. We can obtain

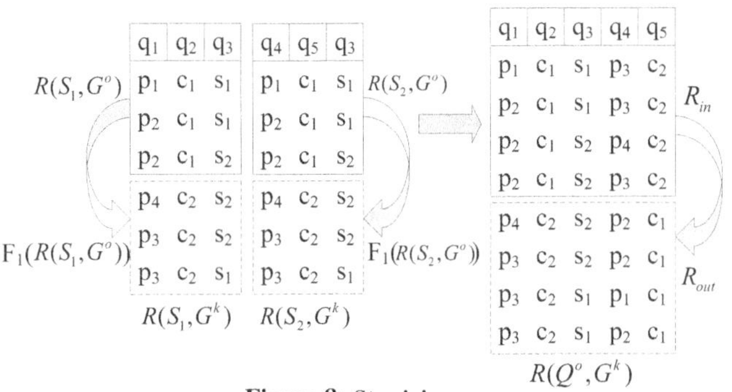

Figure 8: Star join.

$R(S_2, G^k)$ in a similar fashion. Figure 8 illustrates this process for our running example where $k = 2$.

Finally, we need to join $R(S_1, G^k)$ and $R(S_2, G^k)$ based on the topology relation between S_1 and S_2. Since S_1 and S_2 shares only one common vertex q_3 in this case, the join condition is that $R(S_1, G^k).q_3 = R(S_2, G^k).q_3$ but the other two columns of $R(S_1, G^k)$ and $R(S_2, G^k)$ do not match. The join results are $R(Q^o, G^k)$.

In this subsection, we propose an efficient technique to speed up the above process by leveraging the symmetry of the k-automorphic graph G^k. We conceptually divide $R(Q^o, G^k)$ into two parts: R_{in} and R_{out}. We only compute the subgraph matches in R_{in} through the above join process. The subgraph matches in R_{out} can be easily computed based on the automorphic functions (such as in Figure 8) without going through the expensive join process. For example, in Figure 8, we only expand $R(S_2, G^o)$ to $R(S_2, G^k)$ using the automorphic function. Then, we join $R(S_1, G^o)$ with $R(S_2, G^k)$ to obtain R_{in}. All other matches can be obtained by applying the automorphic function over matches in R_{in}. For n stars, we can apply this idea recursively over two star matches at a time, which can be done in parallel as well.

Consider a vertex q_1 in Q^o. For any match M' of Q^o over G^k, let v' denote the matching vertex of q_1 in this match. There are only two cases: v' is in B_1 (the first block of G^k) or not. If $v' \notin B_1$, there must exist another match M under automorphic function F_1 (i.e., $M' = F_1(M)$), where v is the matching vertex of q_1 in match M and v is in B_1. For example, in match $(p_1, c_1, s_1, p_3, c_2)$ in Figure 8, p_1 corresponds to q_1, where p_1 is in block B_1. In match $(p_4, c_2, s_2, p_2, c_1)$, p_4 corresponds to q_1 but p_4 is not in block B_1; but we know that $(p_4, c_2, s_2, p_2, c_1) = F_1(p_1, c_1, s_1, p_3, c_2)$, where F_1 is an automorphic function. In the latter match, p_1 matches q_1 and p_1 is in block B_1. Formally, we have the following theorem.

Theorem 3. *Given Q^o with m vertices q_a $(a = 1, \cdots, m)$, M' with m vertices v'_a $(a = 1, \cdots, m)$ is a subgraph match of Q^o over graph G^k, where v'_a matches q_a. Consider a vertex q_a in Q^o. If vertex v'_a matching q_a is not in B_1 (the first block of G^k), we can find another match M that contains a vertex v_a matching q_a, where $v_a \in B_1$ and $v'_a = F_j(v_a)$ under some automorphic function F_j. Furthermore, $M' = F_j(M)$, where $F_j(M)$ is a mapping graph of M under an automorphic function F_j, which is defined in Definition 4.*

Let us consider a vertex q_a in Q^o. Given q_a, the set of subgraph matches $R(Q^o, G^k)$ can be divided into the following two parts:

1. $R_{in}=\{M|M \in R(Q^o, G^k) \wedge (\exists v_a \in B_1, v_a \in M \wedge v_a \leftrightarrow q_a)\}$
2. $R_{out}=\{M|M \in R(Q^o, G^k) \wedge (\exists v_a \notin B_1, v_a \in M \wedge v_a \leftrightarrow q_a)\}$

where $v_a \leftrightarrow q_a$ means that vertex v_a matches q_a.

We only need to find subgraph matches in R_{in}. Then based on the automorphic functions, the client can obtain R_{out}. Note that the cloud server can do this step too if the goal is to minimize the processing cost at the client side, but with a higher communication overhead. Finally, $R(Q^o, G^k) = R_{in} \cup R_{out}$.

Algorithm 2 presents the join algorithm. Let us consider a query decomposition $\{S_1, \ldots, S_n\}$ over Q^o. Suppose that $|R(S_a)|$ $(1 \le a \le n)$ is the minimum over all stars, and without loss of generality star S_a roots at vertex q_a. Initially, we set answer set $R_{in} = R(S_a, G^o)$. We start with S_a and find another star S_i $(1 \le i \ne a \le n)$, where S_i overlaps with S_a and $|R(S_i)|$ is minimum over all such overlapping stars. Then, we compute $R(S_i, G^k)$ according to the automorphic functions F_j $(j = 0, \cdots, k-1)$ (Line 5-Line 8). We perform the natural join $R_{in} = R_{in} \bowtie R(S_i, G^k)$ (Line 9). Then we delete all the matches that contain duplicate vertices (Line 10-Line 12), since two query vertices cannot match the same vertex in the data graph, according to the definition of subgraph isomorphism. We iterate the above process until all stars in the query decomposition have been processed.

Algorithm 2 Result Join Algorithm

Require: Input: RS (the set of $R(S_i, G^o)$, $1 \le i \le n$) and Alignment Vertex Table (AVT).
Output: R_{in}.
1: Initialize $R_{in} := R(S_a, G^o)$, where $|R(S_a)|$ is minimum over all stars.
2: $RS := RS - R_{in}$.
3: **while** RS.size() > 0 **do**
4: Initialize a set $R_{next} := R(S_i, G^o)$ $(1 \le i \ne a \le n)$, where S_i overlaps with the part of query graph that corresponds to current matches in R_{in}, and $|R(S_i)|$ is minimum over all such overlapping stars.
5: Initialize a set $R^k_{next} := \phi$.
6: **for** $m := 0$ to $k-1$ **do**
7: $R^k_{next} := R^k_{next} \cup F_m(R_{next})$.
8: /* $F_m(R_{next}) = \{M|\exists M' \in R_{next}, M = F_m(M')\}$. */
9: $R_{in} := R_{in} \bowtie R^k_{next}$.
10: **for** each match $M \in R_{in}$ **do**
11: **if** M contains duplicate vertices **then**
12: $R_{in} := R_{in} - \{M\}$.
13: $RS := RS - R_{next}$.
14: Return R_{in}.

4.2.2 *Processing in the Client Side*

According to Algorithm 2, the cloud obtains the set R_{in} and transmits it to the client. There are two stages in the client side processing. The pseudocode is given in Algorithm 3.

First, we need to compute R_{out} according to the automorphic functions F_j $(j = 1, \cdots, k-1)$ (Line 1-Line 4 in Algorithm 3). For each match M in R_{in}, we compute $F_j(M)$ $(j = 1, \cdots, k-1)$ and put them into R_{out}. Obviously, $R(Q^o, G^k) = R_{in} \cup R_{out}$ (Line 5). Note that this step can also be done by the cloud.

Secondly, the client computes the final result set $R(Q, G)$ by filtering out the false positives in $R(Q^o, G^k)$ (Line 6-Line 23). The filtering process also has two steps. In the first step, we remove some matches in $R(Q^o, G^k)$ that contain vertices or edges that do not exist in the original graph G (Line 8-Line 20). Also note that we anonymize the vertex labels in the query graph by using vertex label groups. Thus in the second step, we need to filter out matches that contain vertices whose labels cannot match those of the corresponding vertices in the original query graph Q (Line 21-Line 22).

It is straightforward to see that the time complexity of the client processing is linear with the number of matches in $R(Q^o, G^k)$. Furthermore, it is easy to design some hashing techniques to speed up the filtering processing.

5. COST MODEL

In order to reduce the search space of subgraph matching, we need a cost model for both label generalization and query decomposition. Different label combinations lead to different search s-

Algorithm 3 Result Processing Algorithm

```
Require: Input: R_in (the set of candidate matching results generated in
    cloud), Alignment Vertex Table (AVT).
    Output: R (the set of final matching results).
Initialize R_out := φ.
for m := 1 to k − 1 do
    R_out := R_out ∪ F_m(R_in).
    /* F_m(R_in) = {M|∃M' ∈ R_in, M = F_m(M')}. */
Set R^k := R_in ∪ R_out.
Initialize R := φ.
for each match M ∈ R^k do
    find := true;
    for each vertex v ∈ V(M) do
        if v ∉ V(G) then
            find := false;
            break;
    if find = false then
        continue;
    for each edge e ∈ E(M) do
        if e ∉ E(G) then
            find := false;
            break;
    if find = false then
        continue;
    if M contains any vertices whose labels do not match those of the
    corresponding vertices on query Q then
        continue;
    R := R ∪ {M}.
Return R.
```

paces in subgraph matching. Since our subgraph matching algorithm is based on joining star matches, we require that the number of star matches ($|R(S)|$) should be as small as possible. Furthermore, the query decomposition method in Section 4.2.1 also relies on estimating $|R(S)|$. Thus, we propose a cost model for estimating $|R(S)|$.

5.1 Estimating $|R(S)|$

Given a star query S with center q, it matches a star with the center v in B_1 (i.e., the first block of G^k) if and only if the following two conditions hold. Therefore, we should consider the two factors while estimating $|R(S)|$.

- center q should match v;
- each neighbor of q should match one of v's neighbors.

First Factor. The first factor measures the number of candidate matching vertices of the center q of the star query S. Given an outsourced graph G^o, the vertices matching the center q of S only locate in the first block of G^k, i.e., block B_1. That is to say, we need to find the number of such candidate vertices v in B_1, where each v and q share the same vertex type and each such candidate v contains q's vertex label group. $\frac{|V(G^k)|}{k}$ is the number of vertices in B_1. Given a center q, we should estimate the probability that a vertex $v \in B_1$ has the same vertex type with q and v contains q's vertex label group.

Due to the symmetry in G^k, the first block B_1 has the same vertex label distribution with G^k. Thus, we use G^k to derive the probability. Let $V(G^k, j)$, $V_l(G^k, (j, i))$, and $V_g(G^k, (j, i))$ denote the set of vertices with the j-th vertex type, label $l_{j,i}$ (ith label of jth vertex type), and label group $L_{j,i}$ respectively. Then, we define:

$$F_{G^k}(j) = \frac{|V(G^k, j)|}{|V(G^k)|}, F^l_{G^k}(j, i) = \frac{|V_l(G^k, (j, i))|}{|V(G^k, j)|}, F^g_{G^k}(j, i) = \frac{|V_g(G^k, (j, i))|}{|V(G^k, j)|} \quad (1)$$

for the graph G^k.

Intuitively, $F_{G^k}(j)$ estimates the probability of a vertex being the jth vertex type; $F^l_{G^k}(j, i)$ estimates the probability of a vertex that's the jth vertex type having an ith label; lastly, $F^g_{G^k}(j, i)$ estimates the probability a vertex that's the jth vertex type having an ith label group *after the label generalization*.

Similarly, we can also define $F_S(j)$, $F^l_S(j, i)$ and $F^g_S(j, i)$ for a star query graph S, replacing G^k by star S in the equation.

Without loss of generality, assume that for the j-th ($1 \leq j \leq t$) vertex type, there are θh_j different labels ($l_{j,1}, l_{j,2}, \cdots, l_{j,\theta h_j}$). These labels can be combined into h_j label groups ($L_{j,1}, L_{j,2}, \cdots, L_{j,h_j}$). The i-th group $L_{j,i}$ contains θ different labels, which are $l_{j,p_{\theta(i-1)+1}}, l_{j,p_{\theta(i-1)+2}}, \cdots, l_{j,p_{\theta i}}$ for $1 \leq i \leq h_j$. Note that $\langle p_1, p_2, \cdots, p_{\theta h_j} \rangle$ forms a permutation of $\{1, 2, \cdots, \theta h_j\}$.

$F_{G^k}(j)F_S(j)$ is the probability that a vertex v in G^k has the same vertex type with the star center q. Consider each possible vertex type. For the j-th vertex type, $\sum_{i=1}^{h_j} F^g_{G^k}(j, i)F^g_S(j, i)$ denotes the probability that vertex v and the query center has the same label group. Therefore, the first factor estimating the number of vertices that can match the center of the star query is as follows.

$$\frac{|V(G^k)|}{k} \sum_{j=1}^{t} \left[F_{G^k}(j)F_S(j) \sum_{i=1}^{h_j} F^g_{G^k}(j, i)F^g_S(j, i) \right] \quad (2)$$

Second Factor. The second factor measures the search space of checking whether each of q's neighbors can find its matching vertex in v's neighbors. The estimation here is similar with that of the first factor. The difference is that the candidate matching vertex v of the center q of S has been given. Thus, to match the first vertex of q's neighbors, the number of candidate vertices that we should search is the degree of vertex v rather than $\frac{|V(G^k)|}{k}$. Since there are several candidate vertices v, we use the average degree of vertices in G^k to estimate the degree of vertex v. Here, we denote it as $D(G^k)$. Then, to match the second vertex of v's neighbors, the potential search space is $D(G^k) - 1$. The rest can be done in the same manner. Suppose the center of the star query S has $D^c(S)$ neighbors. Thus, this part of the search space can be estimated as $D(G^k) \cdot (D(G^k) - 1) \cdots (D(G^k) - D^c(S) + 1)$. For the sake of simplicity, we can estimate it as $D(G^k)^{D^c(S)}$. As with the estimation of the first factor, we should also consider the probability of sharing the same vertex type and containing the corresponding vertex label group.

Thus, we can define the second factor that estimates the search space of matching the star center q's neighbors as follows.

$$\left\{ D(G^k) \sum_{j=1}^{t} \left[F_{G^k}(j)F_S(j) \sum_{i=1}^{h_j} F^g_{G^k}(j, i)F^g_S(j, i) \right] \right\}^{D^c(S)} \quad (3)$$

The Cost Model. Our cost model is given by Expression 4, which is simply the product of factor 1 and factor 2 from (2) and (3).

It does assume independence among the label distributions for the neighbors of a vertex. This may not always hold in practice. But our experimental results show that our assumption is acceptable in three real large graphs and our cost model is very effective. We also note that $|V_g(G^k, (j, i))| \leq [1 + \delta(k)] \cdot \sum_{m=1}^{\theta} V_l(G^k, (j, p_{\theta(i-1)+m}))$ for some constant $0 \leq \delta(k) \leq k - 1$, i.e., the number of vertices from the jth vertex type having the ith label group is at most a constant factor of the total number of vertices with jth vertex type having a label that was generalized into this label group. Immediately, this implies that $F^g_{G^k}(j, i) \leq [1 + \delta(k)] \cdot \sum_{m=1}^{\theta} F^l_G(j, p_{\theta(i-1)+m})$. Intuitively, each vertex u in G^k has $(k - 1)$ symmetric vertices. To ensure that they have the same vertex groups, we require that u should have a union of all its symmetric vertices' label groups. In the worst case, $F^g_{G^k}(j, i)$ will increase by a factor of $(k-1)$. In fact, $\delta(k)$ can be much less than $(k - 1)$, and given G and the corresponding k-automorphic graph G^k, we can give a much tighter bound on the parameter $\delta(k)$. That is to say, if we do not introduce any unnecessary label groups during label generalization (just like the example in Figure 2), $\delta(k)$

will be 0. In practice, $\delta(k)$ is far less than 1 when k is small, as demonstrated in our experiments.

$$
\begin{aligned}
&|R(S)| \\
&= \frac{|V(G^k)|}{k} \sum_{j=1}^{t} \left[F_{G^k}(j) F_S(j) \sum_{i=1}^{h_j} F^g_{G^k}(j,i) F^g_S(j,i) \right] \\
&\quad \cdot \left\{ D(G^k) \sum_{j=1}^{t} \left[F_{G^k}(j) F_S(j) \sum_{i=1}^{h_j} F^g_{G^k}(j,i) F^g_S(j,i) \right] \right\}^{D^c(S)} \\
&= \left\{ \sum_{j=1}^{t} \left[F_{G^k}(j) F_S(j) \sum_{i=1}^{h_j} F^g_{G^k}(j,i) F^g_S(j,i) \right] \right\}^{D^c(S)+1} \cdot \frac{|V(G^k)| D(G^k)^{D^c(S)}}{k} \\
&\leq \left\{ \sum_{j=1}^{t} \left\{ F_{G^k}(j) F_S(j) \sum_{i=1}^{h_j} \left[\sum_{m=1}^{\theta} F^l_G(j, p_{\theta(i-1)+m}) \right] \left[\sum_{m=1}^{\theta} F^l_S(j, p_{\theta(i-1)+m}) \right] \right\} \right\}^{D^c(S)+1} \\
&\quad \cdot \frac{|V(G^k)| D(G^k)^{D^c(S)} [1+\delta(k)]^{D^c(S)+1}}{k}
\end{aligned} \tag{4}
$$

5.2 Label Combination

The cost model based query decomposition has been studied in Section 4.2.1. Hence, we only need to show how to do label generalization (label combination) based on the cost model above. Our solution works as follows. Let us consider the j-th vertex type and its θh_j different vertex labels $(l_{i,1}, l_{i,2}, \cdots, l_{i,\theta h_j})$. Assume that $P = \langle p_1, p_2, \cdots, p_{\theta h_j} \rangle$ is a permutation of $\{1, 2, \cdots, \theta h_j\}$. We divide P sequentially into h_j groups, where each group has θ vertex labels. Each permutation corresponds to one possible label combination. The goal is to find the optimal permutation, which leads to the minimum cost in star matching.

In the derivation of Expression 4, we only estimate the search space of a single star query S. However, to perform the label combination of the k-automorphic graph G^k, we need to estimate the search space of star queries in the average case. The average case can be estimated by exploring different query patterns. Suppose S_{set} is the set of all possible star queries. Similar to the definitions in Equation 1 in Section 5.1, we can define

$$
F_{S_{avg}}(j) = \frac{\sum\limits_{s \in S_{set}} \frac{|V(s,j)|}{|V(s)|}}{|S_{set}|},\ F^l_{S_{avg}}(j,i) = \frac{\sum\limits_{s \in S_{set}} \frac{|V_l(s,(j,i))|}{|V(s,j)|}}{|S_{set}|},\ F^g_{S_{avg}}(j,i) = \frac{\sum\limits_{s \in S_{set}} \frac{|V_g(s,(j,i))|}{|V(s,j)|}}{|S_{set}|}
$$

for star queries. These values rely on all possible star queries rather than any one single star query. Similarly, let $D^c(S_{avg}) = \frac{\sum_{s \in S_{set}} D^c(s)}{|S_{set}|}$.

Now similar to the derivation of Expression 4, we can estimate the search space of star queries in the average case, denoted as $|R(S_{avg})|$, in Expression 5 (the derivation follows the same steps as that in Expression 4). According to Expression 5, the component that concerns the label combination is given in Expression 6.

$$
\begin{aligned}
&|R(S_{avg})| \\
&\leq \left\{ \sum_{j=1}^{t} \left\{ F_{G^k}(j) F_{S_{avg}}(j) \sum_{i=1}^{h_j} \left[\sum_{m=1}^{\theta} F^l_G(j, p_{\theta(i-1)+m}) \right] \left[\sum_{m=1}^{\theta} F^l_{S_{avg}}(j, p_{\theta(i-1)+m}) \right] \right\} \right\}^{D^c(S_{avg})+1} \\
&\quad \cdot \frac{|V(G^k)| D(G^k)^{D^c(S_{avg})} [1+\delta(k)]^{D^c(S_{avg})+1}}{k}
\end{aligned} \tag{5}
$$

Therefore, we define the label combination cost as follows.

Definition 7. ***Label Combination Cost.*** *Given the j-th vertex type and its θh_j different vertex labels $(l_{j,1}, l_{j,2}, \cdots, l_{j,\theta h_j})$, we can form a list $\{(F^l_G(j,1), F^l_{S_{avg}}(j,1)), (F^l_G(j,2), F^l_{S_{avg}}(j,2)), \cdots, (F^l_G(j,\theta h_j), F^l_{S_{avg}}(j,\theta h_j))\}$, where $\sum_{i=1}^{\theta h_j} F^l_G(j,i) = 1$ and $\sum_{i=1}^{\theta h_j} F^l_{S_{avg}}(j,i) = 1$. Given $P = \langle p_1, p_2, \cdots, p_{\theta h_j} \rangle$ as a permutation of $\{1, 2, \cdots, \theta h_j\}$, the* label combination cost *of P for the j-th vertex type is defined as follows:*

$$
cost(P) = \sum_{i=1}^{h_j} \left[\sum_{m=1}^{\theta} F^l_G(j, p_{\theta(i-1)+m}) \right] \left[\sum_{m=1}^{\theta} F^l_{S_{avg}}(j, p_{\theta(i-1)+m}) \right] \tag{6}
$$

*/*G refers to the original data graph in this definition.*/*

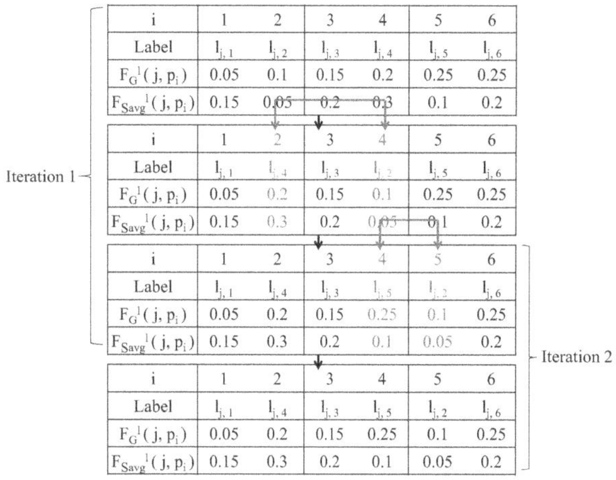

Figure 9: An example of label anonymization algorithm.

Thus we need to choose an effective permutation P to decrease $cost(P)$ as much as possible. To achieve that, we propose a heuristic solution. It works in an iterative manner. Initially, we generate a random label combination. Then, in each iteration, we try to swap two labels in two label groups, respectively. If the swap leads to smaller cost (see Expression 6), we keep the swap; otherwise, we ignore that. For example, we keep the swap between $l_{j,2}$ and $l_{j,4}$ (see Figure 9) in the first iteration. We consider all possible swaps sequentially. Once we cannot find a swap that leads to smaller cost, the algorithm stops. Our experimental results show that for each of the three datasets in Section 6 and each vertex type, we generally need no more than 10 such iterations before the results converge. An example of label anonymization algorithm for $\theta = 2$ (two lables in each label group) is represented in Figure 9, using our running example.

6. EXPERIMENTAL RESULTS

6.1 Datasets and Setup

We evaluated our method on three real datasets in our experiments. Statistics on these graphs are given in Table 2.

Table 2: Real graph datasets.

Dataset	$\|V\|$	$\|E\|$	# of Types	# of Attributes	# of Labels
Web-NotreDame	325,729	109,0108	1	1	200
DBpedia	3,243,606	8,588,047	86	101	6300
UK-2002	18,520,486	261,787,258	2500	2500	20,000

Web-NotreDame. Web-NotreDame is a web graph collected in 1999. Vertices represent pages from the University of Notre Dame and edges represent hyperlinks between them.

DBpedia. DBpedia is a crowd-sourced community effort to extract structured information from Wikipedia and generate a large semantic knowledge graph. Vertices correspond to entities in DBpedia and edges correspond to relationships among them. According to type information and property information from the dataset, we extract types, attributes and attribute values and add them for all the vertices.

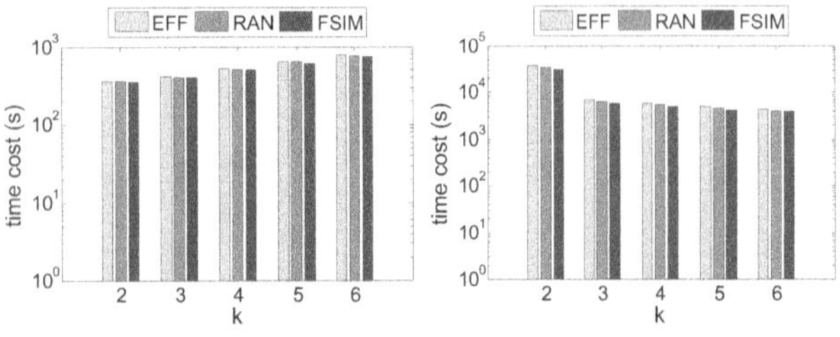

(a) Web-NotreDame (b) DBpedia

Figure 10: Time cost in generating G^k.

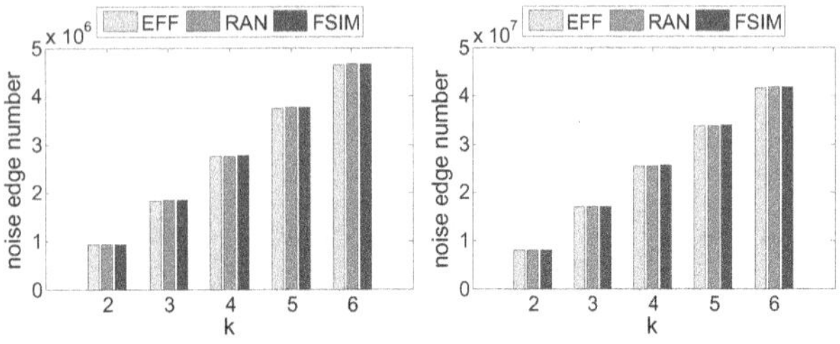

(a) Web-NotreDame (b) DBpedia

Figure 11: Number of noise edges in G^k.

Dataset		k = 2	k = 3	k = 4	k = 5	k = 6
Web-NotreDame	$\|E(G^o)\|$	1024152	1044054	1092048	1131386	1163919
	$\|E(G^k)\|$	2013828	2923686	3850740	4848650	5743884
DBpedia	$\|E(G^o)\|$	13000836	19106315	23923355	27285461	32653869
	$\|E(G^k)\|$	16582848	25561791	33971336	42268695	50278758
UK-2002	$\|E(G^o)\|$	351912573	502482658	618590274	737819332	848864429
	$\|E(G^k)\|$	487677404	713567550	952457696	1202931182	1460772185

Figure 12: Number of edges in G^o and G^k using EFF.

UK-2002. UK-2002 is obtained from a crawl of the .uk domain performed by UbiCrawler[3] in 2002.

We find that the frequencies of different vertex labels on these graphs all (roughly) obey Zipf's law of different skewness.

SETUP. We compare four methods EFF, BAS, FSIM and RAN, where EFF is our method with all optimizations discussed.

1. EFF applies both the "cost model based" label generalization and the graph size reduction (i.e., uploading G^o).

2. BAS applies the same cost model based label generalization approach with EFF; but BAS uploads the entire G^k directly.

3. FSIM and RAN adopt two different label generalization approaches. FSIM combines vertex labels with similar frequencies in the data graph into the same label groups, while RAN randomly combines vertex labels into label groups. However, *both FSIM and RAN adopt the graph size reduction approach proposed in this paper*, i.e., they upload G^o instead of G^k to the cloud.

We use a Windows 7 PC with 3.0 GHz Intel Core 2 Duo CPU and 8 GB main memory as the client side. The cloud server is on a virtualized Windows machine within Microsoft Azure cloud, providing 64 GB main memory and four CPU cores. All methods are implemented in C++. Some additional experimental results are presented in Appendix B.

6.2 Cost of Generating G^k and G^o

In this subsection, we evaluate the performance of generating G^k and G^o. The default value of θ (the number of labels contained in each label group) is 2 in all the experiments. The main results of these experiments are as follows.

[3]http://law.di.unimi.it/webdata/uk-2002

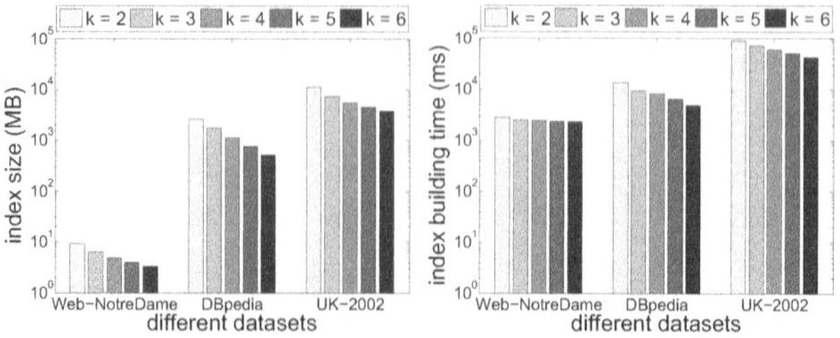

(a) Index size. (b) Index construction time.

Figure 13: Index cost of our algorithm.

The cost model based label anonymization approach EFF is as efficient as simple strategies like RAN and FSIM when generating G^k, as shown in Figure 10. The cost on Web-NotreDame slightly increases when k goes from 2 to 6, but the running time on DBpedia decreases as k becomes larger. The reason is that there are a few high-degree vertices on DBpedia. Since we use the BFS strategy in graph alignment for generating G^k, when k is small, such as 2, we have to do more explorations on these high-degree vertices. The experimental results on UK-2002 are similar with those on DBpedia; see Appendix B.

The number of noise edges ($|E(G^k)| - |E(G)|$) does not depend on the label anonymization approach. We find that the three approaches introduce nearly the same number of noise edges (as shown in Figure 11). The number of noise edges roughly grows linearly when k goes from 2 to 6. The experimental results on UK-2002 are also similar with those on the other two datasets; see Appendix B.

We also report the number of edges in G^o and G^k (i.e., space and communication cost) in Figure 12. Since the three approaches introduce nearly the same number of noise edges, we only report the results generated by EFF method. As shown in Figure 12, The edge number of G^o is much less than that of G^k. Especially, when k is small, $|E(G^o)|$ is close to $|E(G)|$. It shows that our method not only ensures the data privacy but also saves the online query cost, since online subgraph matching is performed on G^o rather than G^k.

Although the three label anonymization algorithms have similar efficiency in generating G^k, they do generate different G^k's. EFF produces G^k's that perform much better than the graphs produced by the other two methods in terms of the query performance. We will report these results shortly.

6.3 Performance in the Cloud

We first report the cost of index construction for our method. Figure 13 shows the space and time cost of constructing the index structure, which is discussed in Section 4.2.1. Both space and time costs of our index construction decrease while k increases from 2 to 6. The reason lies in the fact that the size of our index (see Figure 7) depends on the vertex number of G^o (i.e., $|V(G^o)|$). Obviously, $|V(G^o)|$ decreases with the increase of k, since G^o roughly contains only the first block of vertices in G^k and each block in G^k has about $\frac{|V(G^k)|}{k}$ vertices. Thus, larger k leads to less index size and less construction cost.

Then we pay attention to the cost of subgraph matching in the cloud. We generate query graphs by randomly extracting connected subgraphs from the data graph G, ensuring that $|E(Q)|$ meets a user-specified parameter value N. Specifically, we randomly locate the first edge e from the data graph G and set $E(Q) = \{e\}$. We then expand the current query graph Q through a random walk over G iteratively until it reaches N edges. We used 100 queries and report the average. We compared our method with the baseline BAS and the other two label generalization techniques. First, we report the query performance for different query graph sizes $|E(Q)|$. Figure

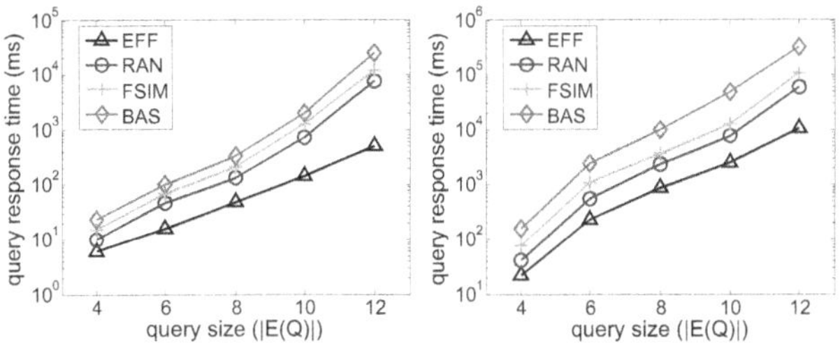

(a) $k = 3$ (b) $k = 5$

Figure 14: Query time vs. $|E(Q)|$ on Web-NotreDame.

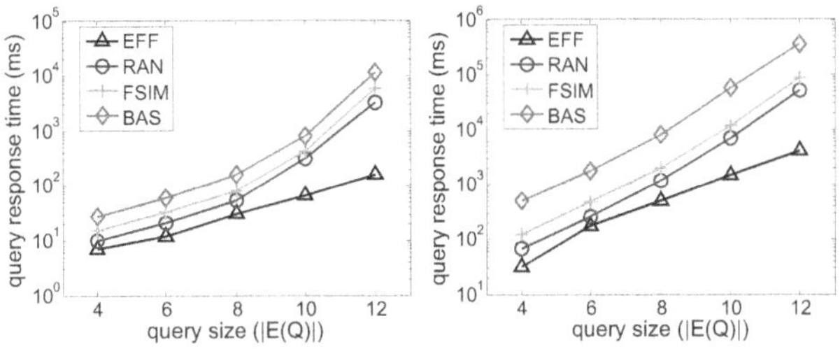

(a) $k = 3$ (b) $k = 5$

Figure 15: Query time vs. $|E(Q)|$ on DBpedia.

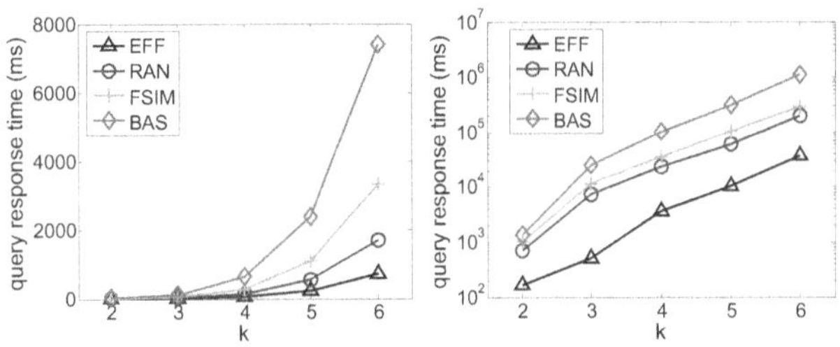

(a) $|E(Q)| = 6$ (b) $|E(Q)| = 12$

Figure 16: Query time vs. k on Web-NotreDame.

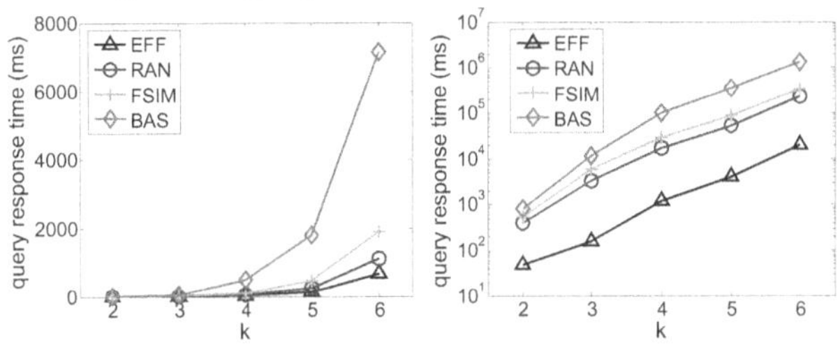

(a) $|E(Q)| = 6$ (b) $|E(Q)| = 12$

Figure 17: Query time vs. k on DBpedia.

14 shows that our method EFF performs much better than the other three approaches on Web-NotreDame. Note that RAN and FSIM use the same processing framework as EFF (i.e., they rely on G^o and our cloud processing algorithms as well); they only differ from EFF in how to generate the label combinations. Thus, the experimental results confirm the effectiveness of our cost model and the cost model based label combination.

We find similar results on DBpedia, as shown in Figure 15. The experimental results on UK-2002 are also similar with those on other datasets; see Appendix B. When the query size becomes larger, EFF outperforms the other three approaches by at least one order of magnitude. Furthermore, BAS always performs the worst, since the search space on G^k is much larger than that on G^o.

The running time of subgraph matching increases with k from 2 to 6, as shown in Figure 16 and Figure 17. This is because that $|E(G^o)|$ increases with k from 2 to 6, since we must insert more noise edges into G^o when k becomes larger. Nevertheless, EFF is always the best method. Furthermore, compared with other approaches, the advantage of EFF becomes even more significant for larger values of k.

Dataset		k = 3		k = 5	
		|E(Q)| = 6	|E(Q)| = 12	|E(Q)| = 6	|E(Q)| = 12
Web-NotreDame	EFF	9	31	42	137
	RAN	19	69	89	288
	FSIM	25	87	117	374
DBpedia	EFF	7	19	24	54
	RAN	11	36	41	110
	FSIM	14	50	50	149
UK-2002	EFF	7	24	34	125
	RAN	11	38	53	196
	FSIM	15	52	72	267

Star Matching Time (ms)

Figure 18: Star matching time.

Dataset		k = 3		k = 5	
		|E(Q)| = 6	|E(Q)| = 12	|E(Q)| = 6	|E(Q)| = 12
Web-NotreDame	EFF	96	188	487	696
	RAN	187	556	792	2089
	FSIM	252	729	1100	2858
DBpedia	EFF	64	126	296	431
	RAN	125	402	581	1920
	FSIM	163	478	759	2544
UK-2002	EFF	91	160	454	663
	RAN	127	431	638	1779
	FSIM	210	528	722	2668

|RS|

Figure 19: Result set size of the star matching algorithm ($|RS|$).

We also find that both the query decomposition algorithm and the star matching algorithm run very fast. Even when $|E(Q)|$ is as large as 12, the time cost of query decomposition algorithm is less than 1 ms. As for the time cost of star matching algorithm, Figure 18 shows the experimental results which are also very efficient. We also report the size of the set RS generated by our star matching algorithm in Figure 19. $|RS|$ has a large influence on the time cost of result join algorithm. These results show the importance of optimizing the result join algorithm.

6.4 Processing Cost in the Client Side

The last step of all methods involves processing in the client side. Figure 20 and Figure 21 illustrate this overhead on the first two real graphs. The goal of client side processing is to filter out all false positive matches due to the noise edges and labels in G^k.

First of all, note that for all methods, client processing cost is much less than cloud processing cost; it is orders of magnitude less. As Figure 20 and Figure 21 show, the overhead in the client side scales very well in terms of query size and k. EFF still outperforms both RAN and FSIM, but it is slightly worse than BAS in the client side. The reason is that EFF generates fewer intermediate results than RAN and FSIM, due to its effective label combination algorithm. However, following our processing framework, EFF, RAN, and FSIM produce R_{in} (i.e., a small subset of $R(Q^o, G^k)$, see Section 4.2.1) in the cloud, and the client needs to find $R(Q^o, G^k)$ based on R_{in} and our client side algorithm as shown in Section 4.2.2. In contrast, BAS obtains $R(Q^o, G^k)$ from the cloud directly (since the cloud has G^k instead of G^o as that in our method).

However, note that client processing time is a tiny fraction of the entire processing time. Furthermore, compared with our method like EFF, BAS has much more expensive communication cost, since $|R(Q^o, G^k)|$ is always much larger than $|R_{in}|$ (i.e., the size of a small subset of $R(Q^o, G^k)$, see Section 4.2.1). For example, the average size of matching results for $|E(Q)| = 6, k = 4$ on UK-2002 in BAS is 12,224 bytes, while EFF only transmits 3,056 bytes. Thus

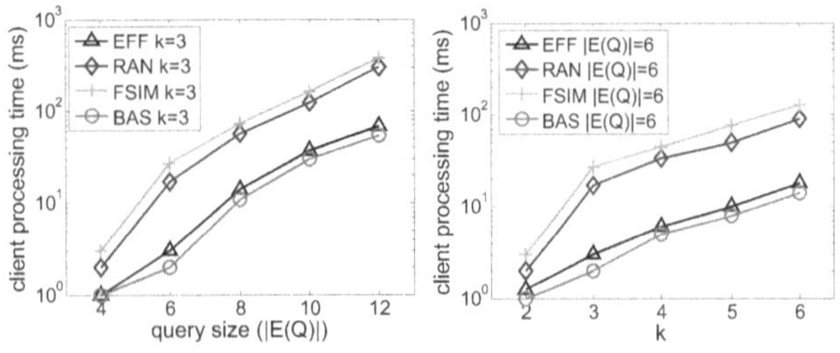

(a) vs. $|E(Q)|$, $k = 3$ (b) vs. k, $|E(Q)| = 6$

Figure 20: Client processing time on Web-NotreDame.

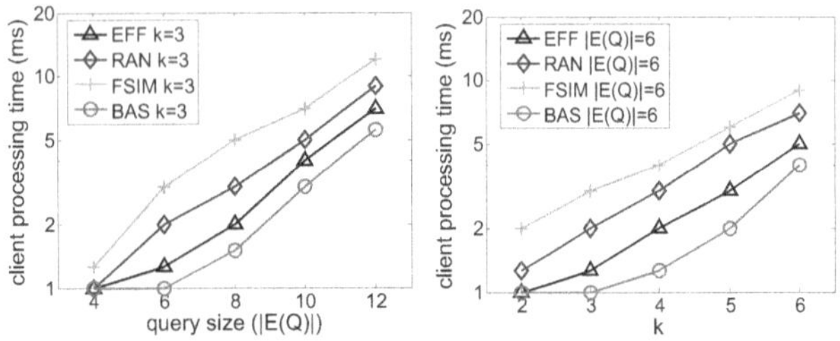

(a) vs. $|E(Q)|$, $k = 3$ (b) vs. k, $|E(Q)| = 6$

Figure 21: Client processing time on DBpedia.

Dataset		k = 3		k = 5	
		|E(Q)| = 6	|E(Q)| = 12	|E(Q)| = 6	|E(Q)| = 12
Web-NotreDame	EFF	21	608	249	10948
	RAN	73	7941	624	61306
	FSIM	110	12329	1197	108880
	BAS	109	25240	2423	318390
DBpedia	EFF	14	170	139	4144
	RAN	24	3263	265	52212
	FSIM	38	6048	492	86412
	BAS	64	11725	1805	350867
UK-2002	EFF	19	465	203	10076
	RAN	50	4721	400	50651
	FSIM	76	7956	550	96353
	BAS	112	17859	2381	277208

Overall Running Time (ms)

Figure 22: Overall running time.

the average communication time for transmitting results in BAS is 11 ms, but EFF only spends 3 ms. More importantly, as discussed in Section 4, the step of finding $R(Q^o, G^k)$ based on R_{in} in EFF can be easily moved to the cloud side if the priority is to lower the client processing cost and communication cost is a lesser consideration. As stated above, EFF runs much faster than other methods in terms of the overall running time, which is shown in the next subsection.

6.5 Overall Online Performance

Lastly, we report the end-to-end running time for privacy preserving subgraph matching queries in the cloud in Figure 22. The end-to-end time consists of three parts: the running time in the cloud, the network communication time, and the running time in the client side. Figure 22 shows that our method EFF, the cost model based label anonymization with graph size reducation approach, has the best overall running time. In particular, EFF outperforms other competing methods significantly.

7. RELATED WORK

Privacy preserving graph data publication. Lots of recent works pay attention to privacy protection for graph publication. The majority of these works [13, 24, 21, 26, 6] focus on protecting data privacy from structural attacks, they can be used as a baseline for our problem with significant overheads.

Some existing works [13, 24, 21] assume that the attacker only launches one type of structural attack. In fact, an attacker can launch multiple types of structural attacks to identify the target based on the strong background knowledge. The data graph produced from some privacy preserving techniques may lose a few edges because of edge delete operations [6]. The loss of structural information in original data graph will lead to the infeasibility of subgraph matching on published data graph. Thus, we utilize k-automorphism [26] to protect the data graph from compromising sensitive information. First, a k-automorphic graph can defend node re-identification based on any background information of any subgraph [26]. Second, a k-automorphic graph will not delete any vertices or edges from the original data graph. Third, the key point of utilizing k-automorphism is to enable us to leverage the symmetry of the k-automorphic graph, which allows our method to answer subgraph matching queries efficiently.

Differential privacy [8] is an effective model to protect against unknown attacks with guaranteed probabilistic accuracy. But due to the perturbation, these techniques [16, 4, 5] are useful in finding statistical information (e.g. aggregates) from a graph, but are not feasible in answering privacy preserving subgraph matching queries *exactly*.

Privacy preserving graph query processing in the cloud. For answering secure shortest path queries, Das *et al.* propose a linear programming method to anonymize edge weights of the original graph while preserving shortest paths [7]. However, any attacker with some topological knowledge can re-identify sensitive information easily. Gao *et al.* transform an original graph into a linked graph and a set of outsourced graphs to support privacy preserving shortest distance queries in the cloud [9]. However, it has much difficulty in answering subgraph matching queries, because of losing the connectivity in the original graph. Cao *et al.* propose a method to answer subgraph matching queries over encrypted graphs in the cloud [3], *for a database of graphs*. The method pre-builds a feature-based index for each data graph. After filtering in the cloud, each candidate supergraph is verified by checking subgraph isomorphism in the client. However, the method does not apply to our case where the goal is to find subgraph matches on a single large graph (instead of many small graphs).

8. CONCLUSION

In this paper, we present an efficient framework for privacy preserving subgraph matching on a large graph in the cloud. Our design protects both structural and label privacy in a graph, without losing data utility. By exploring a number of optimization techniques and leveraging an effective cost model, our method achieves superior query performance compared to the baseline method. Extensive experiments on large real graphs confirm the effectiveness and efficiency of our approach. Extending our framework to handling other important graph queries will lead to a number of interesting and important future works.

Acknowledgment. This work was supported by 863 project under Grant No. 2015AA015402, NSFC under Grant No. 61532010 and Beijing Higher Education Young Elite Teacher Project (YETP0016). This paper was also supported by "Special Program for Applied Research on Super Computation of the NSFC-Guangdong Joint Fund (the second phase)". Zhao Chang and Feifei Li were supported in part by NSF grant 1514520. Lei Zou is the corresponding author of this work.

9. REFERENCES

[1] http://neo4j.org/.

[2] What is cloud computing? *Amazon Web Services*, (3).

[3] N. Cao, Z. Yang, C. Wang, K. Ren, and W. Lou. Privacy-preserving query over encrypted graph-structured data in cloud computing. In *ICDCS*, pages 393–402, 2011.

[4] R. Chen, B. C. M. Fung, P. S. Yu, and B. C. Desai. Correlated network data publication via differential privacy. *VLDB J.*, pages 1–24, 2013.

[5] S. Chen and S. Zhou. Recursive mechanism: Towards node differential privacy and unrestricted joins. In *SIGMOD*, pages 653–664, 2013.

[6] J. Cheng, A. W. Fu, and J. Liu. K-isomorphism: Privacy preserving network publication against structural attacks. In *SIGMOD*, pages 459–470, 2010.

[7] S. Das, Ömer Eğecioğlu, and A. E. Abbadi. Anonymizing weighted social network graphs. In *ICDE*, pages 904–907, 2010.

[8] C. Dwork, F. Mcsherry, K. Nissim, and A. Smith. Calibrating noise to sensitivity in private data analysis. In *Theory of Cryptography Conference*, 2006.

[9] J. Gao, J. Y. Xu, R. Jin, J. Zhou, T. Wang, and D. Yang. Neighborhood-privacy protected shortest distance computing in cloud. In *SIGMOD*, 2011.

[10] M. Hay, G. Miklau, D. Jensen, D. F. Towsley, and P. Weis. Resisting structural re-identification in anonymized social networks. *PVLDB*, 1(1):102–114, 2008.

[11] G. Karypis and V. Kumar. Analysis of multilevel graph partitioning. In *SC*, 1995.

[12] J. Lee, W. Han, R. Kasperovics, and J. Lee. An in-depth comparison of subgraph isomorphism algorithms in graph databases. *PVLDB*, 6(2):133–144, 2012.

[13] K. Liu and E. Terzi. Towards identity anonymization on graphs. In *SIGMOD*, pages 93–106, 2008.

[14] Y. Low, J. Gonzalez, A. Kyrola, D. Bickson, C. Guestrin, and J. M. Hellerstein. Graphlab: A new framework for parallel machine learning. In *UAI*, 2010.

[15] J. Pérez, M. Arenas, and C. Gutierrez. Semantics and complexity of SPARQL. *ACM Trans. Database Syst.*, 34(3), 2009.

[16] A. Sala, X. Zhao, C. Wilson, H. Zheng, and B. Y. Zhao. Sharing graphs using differentially private graph models. In *IMC*, pages 679–688, 2011.

[17] P. Samarati and L. Sweeney. Protecting privacy when disclosing information: k-anonymity and its enforcement through generalization and suppression. *Technical report, SRI International*, 1998.

[18] Z. Sun, H. Wang, H. Wang, B. Shao, and J. Li. Efficient subgraph matching on billion node graphs. *PVLDB*, 5(9), 2012.

[19] L. Sweeney. k-anonymity: A model for protecting privacy. *International Journal of Uncertainty, Fuzziness and Knowledge-Based Systems*, 10(5):557–570, 2002.

[20] C. Tai, P. Tseng, P. S. Yu, and M. Chen. Identity protection in sequential releases of dynamic networks. *IEEE Trans. Knowl. Data Eng.*, 26(3):635–651, 2014.

[21] C.-H. Tai, P. S. Yu, D.-N. Yang, and M.-S. Chen. Privacy-preserving social network publication against friendship attacks. In *KDD*, pages 1262–1270, 2011.

[22] W. Wu, Y. Xiao, W. Wang, Z. He, and Z. Wang. K-symmetry model for identity anonymization in social networks. In *EDBT*, pages 111–122, 2010.

[23] X. Yan, P. S. Yu, and J. Han. Graph indexing based on discriminative frequent structure analysis. *TODS*, 30(4):960–993, 2005.

[24] B. Zhou and J. Pei. Preserving privacy in social networks against neighborhood attacks. In *ICDE*, pages 506–515, 2008.

[25] L. Zou, L. Chen, and M. T. Özsu. Distancejoin: Pattern match query in a large graph database. *PVLDB*, 2(1), 2009.

[26] L. Zou, L. Chen, and M. T. Özsu. K-automorphism: A general framework for privacy preserving network publication. In *VLDB*, 2009.

Appendix

A. Proof of Theorems.

Theorem 1. *Given a data graph G and a query graph Q, $R(Q,G) \subseteq R(Q^o, G^k)$.*

PROOF. For any match $M \in R(Q,G)$, we assume that $g : V(Q) \rightarrow V(G)$ is the injective function. We can let $g' : V(Q^o) \rightarrow V(G^k)$ have the same mapping relation with g, since G is a subgraph of G^k. Thus we have $\forall q_i \in V(Q^o) \Rightarrow g'(q_i) \in V(G^k)$ and $\forall q_i, q_j \in V(Q^o), \overline{q_i q_j} \in E(Q^o) \Rightarrow \overline{g'(q_i)g'(q_j)} \in E(G^k)$. Since we use the same label grouping strategy on G and Q, $\forall q_i \in V(Q^o) \Rightarrow L(q_i) \subseteq L(g'(q_i))$. According to Definition 2, $M \in R(Q^o, G^k)$, represented as $\langle g'(q_1), \cdots, g'(q_n)\rangle$. □

Theorem 2. *Given an outsourced query graph Q^o, finding the query decomposition with the minimum cost with respect to Definition 6 is an NP-hard problem.*

PROOF. Finding a minimum vertex cover is a classical NP-hard problem. When each $|R(S_i)| = 1$ $(i = 1, \cdots, n)$, finding the optimal query decomposition is equivalent to finding a minimum vertex cover. Thus finding a minimum vertex cover is a subproblem of finding the optimal query decomposition. □

Theorem 3. *Given Q^o with m vertices q_a $(a = 1, \cdots, m)$, M' with m vertices v'_a $(a = 1, \cdots, m)$ is a subgraph match of Q^o over graph G^k, where v'_a matches q_a. Consider a vertex q_a in Q^o. If vertex v'_a matching q_a is not in B_1 (the first block of G^k), we can find another match M that contains a vertex v_a matching q_a, where $v_a \in B_1$ and $v'_a = F_j(v_a)$ under some automorphic function F_j. Furthermore, $M' = F_j(M)$*[4].

PROOF. Since M' is a subgraph of G^k, we have $v'_a \in G^k$. Without loss of generality, assume that $v'_a \in P_i$ $(1 < i \leq k)$. We set $v_a = F_{k-(i-1)}(v'_a)$, i.e., $j = i - 1$ and $v'_a = F_j(v_a)$. Thus $v_a \in P_1$.

Here, we prove that $M = F_{k-(i-1)}(M')$ is another match of Q^o over G^k. Thus $M' = F_j(M)$.

For the match M', we assume that $g' : V(Q^o) \rightarrow V(G^k)$ is the injective function. Here, we prove that $g = F_{k-(i-1)}(g')$ is the injective function of M. Obviously, $\forall q_s \in V(Q^o) \Rightarrow g'(q_s) \in V(G^k) \Rightarrow F_{k-(i-1)}(g'(q_s)) \in V(G^k) \Rightarrow g(q_s) \in V(G^k)$. In a similar way, $\forall q_s, q_t \in V(Q^o), \overline{q_s q_t} \in E(Q^o) \Rightarrow \overline{g'(q_s)g'(q_t)} \in E(G^k) \Rightarrow \overline{F_{k-(i-1)}(g'(q_s))F_{k-(i-1)}(g'(q_t))} \in E(G^k) \Rightarrow \overline{g(q_s)g(q_t)} \in E(G^k)$. According to Definition 3, $\forall q_s \in V(Q^o) \Rightarrow L(q_s) \subseteq L(g'(q_s)) = L(F_{k-(i-1)}(g'(q_s))) = L(g(q_s))$. According to Definition 2, $M \in R(Q^o, G^k)$, represented as $\langle g(q_1), \cdots, g(q_n)\rangle$. □

B. Additional Experimental Results Figure 23 shows the time cost in generating G^k on UK-2002. Figure 24 shows the number of noise edges in G^k on UK-2002. Figure 25 and Figure 26 show the query time in the cloud on UK-2002. Figure 27 shows the filtering time in the client side on UK-2002. As these figures show, the experiment results on UK-2002 are similar with those on other datasets. Figure 28, Figure 29 and Figure 30 show the query time in the cloud on the three datasets, respectively. Figure 31 shows the time cost of our star matching algorithm on the three datasets. Figure 32 shows the size of the set RS generated by our star matching algorithm on the three datasets. Figure 33 shows the network overhead on the three datasets when transferring the candidate matching results from the cloud to the client side. Figure 34 shows the end-to-end running time on the three datasets. These results show similar trends as that in the experiment section and further confirm the superiority of our method.

[4] $F_j(M)$ is a mapping graph of M under an automorphic function F_j, which is defined in Definition 4.

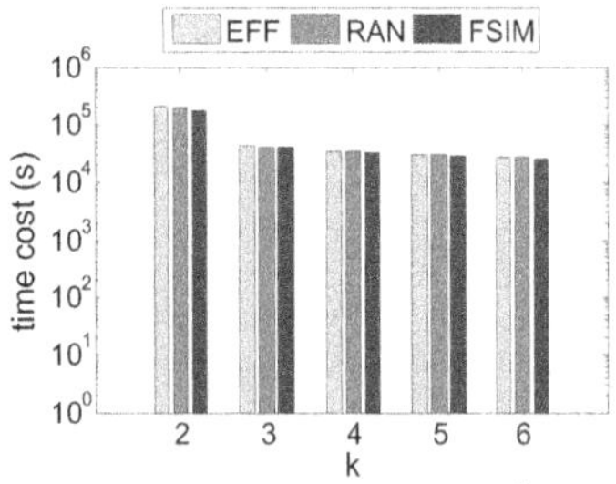

Figure 23: Time cost in generating G^k on UK-2002.

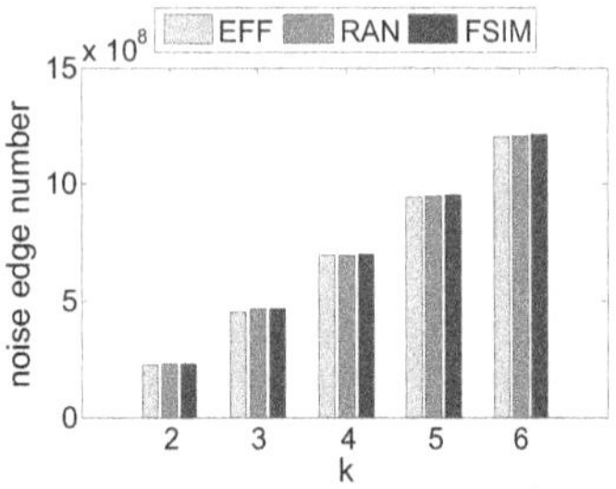

Figure 24: Number of noise edges in G^k on UK-2002.

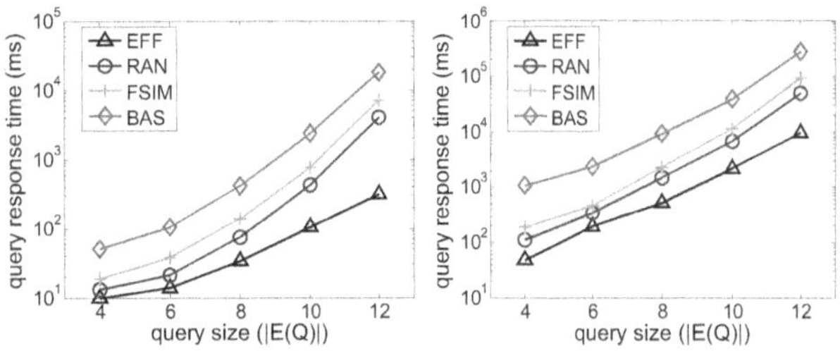

(a) $k = 3$ (b) $k = 5$

Figure 25: Query time vs. $|E(Q)|$ on UK-2002.

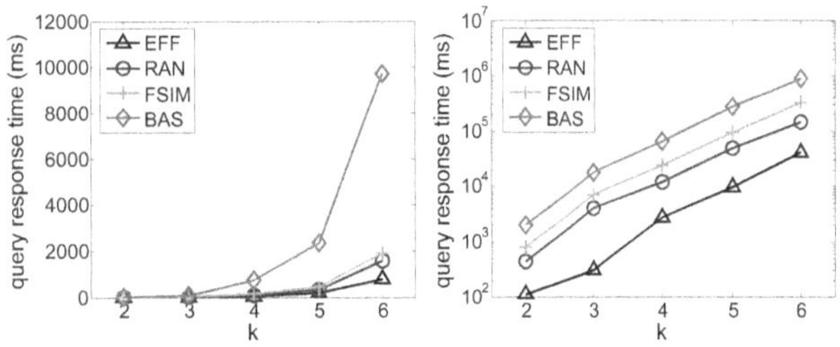

(a) $|E(Q)| = 6$ (b) $|E(Q)| = 12$

Figure 26: Query time vs. k on UK-2002.

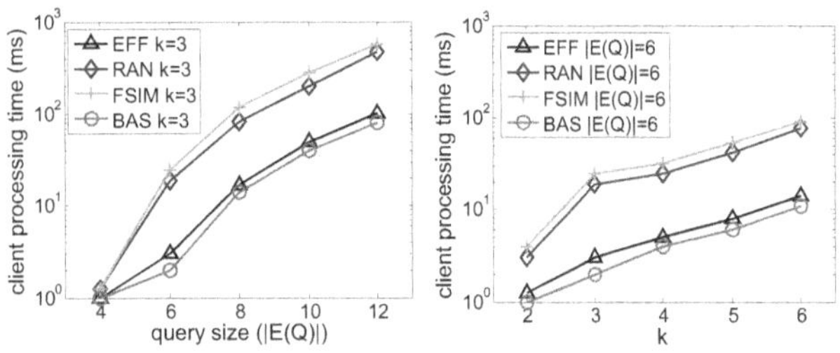

(a) vs. $|E(Q)|$, $k = 3$ (b) vs. k, $|E(Q)| = 6$

Figure 27: Client processing time on UK-2002.

Dataset		k = 2		k = 3		k = 4		k = 5		k = 6	
		|E(Q)| = 6	|E(Q)| = 12	|E(Q)| = 6	|E(Q)| = 12	|E(Q)| = 6	|E(Q)| = 12	|E(Q)| = 6	|E(Q)| = 12	|E(Q)| = 6	|E(Q)| = 12
Web-Notre Dame	EFF	3	10	9	31	22	70	42	137	77	254
	RAN	6	21	19	69	49	171	89	288	172	539
	FSIM	9	28	25	87	63	206	117	374	233	741
DBpedia	EFF	2	5	7	19	15	37	24	54	38	83
	RAN	3	10	11	36	23	66	41	110	60	168
	FSIM	4	14	14	50	32	101	50	149	89	264
UK-2002	EFF	2	6	7	24	19	68	34	125	57	192
	RAN	4	14	11	38	28	97	53	196	89	307
	FSIM	6	20	15	52	41	152	72	267	124	449

Star Matching Time (ms)

Figure 31: Star matching time.

Dataset		k = 2		k = 3		k = 4		k = 5		k = 6	
		|E(Q)| = 6	|E(Q)| = 12	|E(Q)| = 6	|E(Q)| = 12	|E(Q)| = 6	|E(Q)| = 12	|E(Q)| = 6	|E(Q)| = 12	|E(Q)| = 6	|E(Q)| = 12
Web-Notre Dame	EFF	53	131	96	188	210	416	487	696	955	1592
	RAN	98	225	187	556	344	1383	792	2089	1411	4286
	FSIM	119	262	252	729	727	1580	1100	2858	2007	4790
DBpedia	EFF	38	66	64	126	158	283	296	431	728	1215
	RAN	54	177	125	402	255	1032	581	1920	1246	4505
	FSIM	87	231	163	478	342	1427	759	2544	1633	4992
UK-2002	EFF	41	102	91	160	193	382	454	663	1007	1684
	RAN	63	186	127	431	331	787	638	1779	1390	3904
	FSIM	89	233	210	528	399	1391	722	2668	1634	4823

|RS|

Figure 32: The size of result set generated by star matching algorithm ($|RS|$).

Dataset		k = 2		k = 3		k = 4		k = 5		k = 6	
		|E(Q)| = 6	|E(Q)| = 12	|E(Q)| = 6	|E(Q)| = 12	|E(Q)| = 6	|E(Q)| = 12	|E(Q)| = 6	|E(Q)| = 12	|E(Q)| = 6	|E(Q)| = 12
Web-Notre Dame	EFF	1	14	2	34	3	61	5	108	9	184
	RAN	1	57	9	151	17	259	25	420	45	653
	FSIM	2	75	14	190	23	353	39	604	65	977
	BAS	1	27	6	100	12	242	23	522	50	1098
DBpedia	EFF	1	2	1	4	1	8	2	17	3	35
	RAN	1	2	1	5	2	11	3	26	4	69
	FSIM	1	3	2	6	2	14	3	33	5	81
	BAS	1	3	3	11	4	31	9	84	17	202
UK-2002	EFF	1	22	2	53	3	85	4	121	7	170
	RAN	2	100	10	235	13	342	21	501	39	759
	FSIM	2	123	13	286	16	447	27	688	46	1021
	BAS	1	44	7	155	11	336	19	598	39	1010

Network Transmission Time (ms)

Figure 33: Network overhead.

Dataset		k = 2		k = 3		k = 4		k = 5		k = 6	
		|E(Q)| = 6	|E(Q)| = 12	|E(Q)| = 6	|E(Q)| = 12	|E(Q)| = 6	|E(Q)| = 12	|E(Q)| = 6	|E(Q)| = 12	|E(Q)| = 6	|E(Q)| = 12
Web-Notre Dame	EFF	8	207	21	608	65	3871	249	10948	748	37561
	RAN	19	873	73	7941	192	24162	624	61306	1841	201831
	FSIM	27	1245	110	12329	347	36818	1197	108880	3519	300001
	BAS	38	1428	109	25240	664	101584	2423	318390	7472	1109777
DBpedia	EFF	5	54	14	170	45	1196	139	4144	671	19863
	RAN	7	402	24	3263	73	16823	265	52212	1115	232458
	FSIM	12	538	38	6048	118	29022	492	86412	1908	340659
	BAS	16	805	64	11725	516	97434	1805	350867	7158	1279688
UK-2002	EFF	5	177	19	465	68	3052	203	10076	800	41116
	RAN	12	749	50	4721	140	13055	400	50651	1704	149985
	FSIM	17	1176	76	7956	199	25316	550	96353	2065	324241
	BAS	22	2095	112	17859	764	64515	2381	277208	9763	909963

Overall Running Time (ms)

Figure 34: Overall running time.

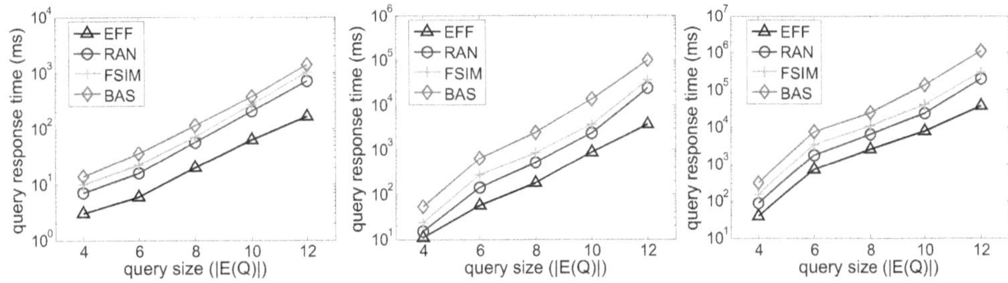

(a) $k = 2$ (b) $k = 4$ (c) $k = 6$

Figure 28: Query time vs. $|E(Q)|$ on Web-NotreDame.

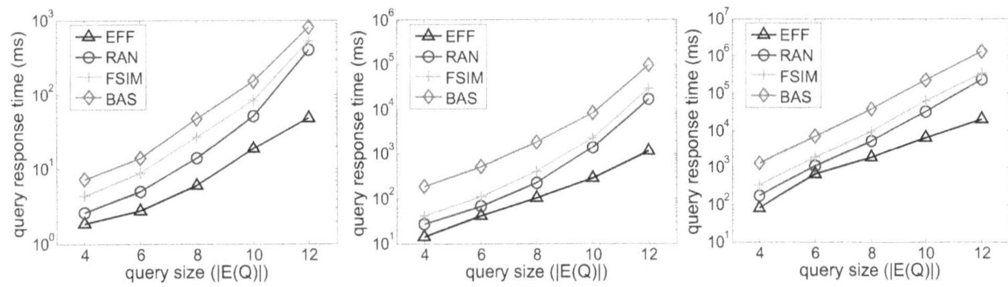

(a) $k = 2$ (b) $k = 4$ (c) $k = 6$

Figure 29: Query time vs. $|E(Q)|$ on DBpedia.

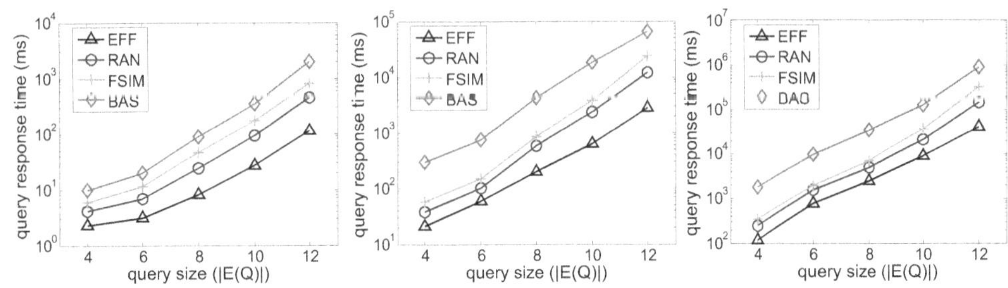

(a) $k = 2$ (b) $k = 4$ (c) $k = 6$

Figure 30: Query time vs. $|E(Q)|$ on UK-2002.

The Snowflake Elastic Data Warehouse

Benoit Dageville, Thierry Cruanes, Marcin Zukowski, Vadim Antonov, Artin Avanes, Jon Bock, Jonathan Claybaugh, Daniel Engovatov, Martin Hentschel, Jiansheng Huang, Allison W. Lee, Ashish Motivala, Abdul Q. Munir, Steven Pelley, Peter Povinec, Greg Rahn, Spyridon Triantafyllis, Philipp Unterbrunner

Snowflake Computing

ABSTRACT

We live in the golden age of distributed computing. Public cloud platforms now offer virtually unlimited compute and storage resources on demand. At the same time, the Software-as-a-Service (SaaS) model brings enterprise-class systems to users who previously could not afford such systems due to their cost and complexity. Alas, traditional data warehousing systems are struggling to fit into this new environment. For one thing, they have been designed for fixed resources and are thus unable to leverage the cloud's elasticity. For another thing, their dependence on complex ETL pipelines and physical tuning is at odds with the flexibility and freshness requirements of the cloud's new types of semi-structured data and rapidly evolving workloads.

We decided a fundamental redesign was in order. Our mission was to build an enterprise-ready data warehousing solution for the cloud. The result is the Snowflake Elastic Data Warehouse, or "Snowflake" for short. Snowflake is a multi-tenant, transactional, secure, highly scalable and elastic system with full SQL support and built-in extensions for semi-structured and schema-less data. The system is offered as a pay-as-you-go service in the Amazon cloud. Users upload their data to the cloud and can immediately manage and query it using familiar tools and interfaces. Implementation began in late 2012 and Snowflake has been generally available since June 2015. Today, Snowflake is used in production by a growing number of small and large organizations alike. The system runs several million queries per day over multiple petabytes of data.

In this paper, we describe the design of Snowflake and its novel multi-cluster, shared-data architecture. The paper highlights some of the key features of Snowflake: extreme elasticity and availability, semi-structured and schema-less data, time travel, and end-to-end security. It concludes with lessons learned and an outlook on ongoing work.

Categories and Subject Descriptors

Information systems [**Data management systems**]: Database management system engines

SIGMOD/PODS'16 June 26 - July 01, 2016, San Francisco, CA, USA

ACM ISBN 978-1-4503-3531-7/16/06.

DOI: http://dx.doi.org/10.1145/2882903.2903741

Keywords

Data warehousing, database as a service, multi-cluster shared data architecture

1. INTRODUCTION

The advent of the cloud marks a move away from software delivery and execution on local servers, and toward shared data centers and software-as-a-service solutions hosted by platform providers such as Amazon, Google, or Microsoft. The shared infrastructure of the cloud promises increased economies of scale, extreme scalability and availability, and a pay-as-you-go cost model that adapts to unpredictable usage demands. But these advantages can only be captured if the *software* itself is able to scale elastically over the pool of commodity resources that is the cloud. Traditional data warehousing solutions pre-date the cloud. They were designed to run on small, static clusters of well-behaved machines, making them a poor architectural fit.

But not only the platform has changed. Data has changed as well. It used to be the case that most of the data in a data warehouse came from sources within the organization: transactional systems, enterprise resource planning (ERP) applications, customer relationship management (CRM) applications, and the like. The structure, volume, and rate of the data were all fairly predictable and well known. But with the cloud, a significant and rapidly growing share of data comes from less controllable or external sources: application logs, web applications, mobile devices, social media, sensor data (Internet of Things). In addition to the growing volume, this data frequently arrives in schema-less, semi-structured formats [3]. Traditional data warehousing solutions are struggling with this new data. These solutions depend on deep ETL pipelines and physical tuning that fundamentally assume predictable, slow-moving, and easily categorized data from largely internal sources.

In response to these shortcomings, parts of the data warehousing community have turned to "Big Data" platforms such as Hadoop or Spark [8, 11]. While these are indispensable tools for data center-scale processing tasks, and the open source community continues to make big improvements such as the Stinger Initiative [48], they still lack much of the efficiency and feature set of established data warehousing technology. But most importantly, they require significant engineering effort to roll out and use [16].

We believe that there is a large class of use cases and workloads which can benefit from the economics, elasticity, and service aspects of the cloud, but which are not well served by either traditional data warehousing technology or by Big Data platforms. So we decided to build a completely new data warehousing system specifically for the cloud. The system is called the Snowflake Elastic Data Warehouse, or "Snowflake". In contrast to many other systems in the cloud data management space, Snowflake is not based on Hadoop, PostgreSQL or the like. The processing engine and most of the other parts have been developed from scratch.

The key features of Snowflake are as follows.

Pure Software-as-a-Service (SaaS) Experience Users need not buy machines, hire database administrators, or install software. Users either already have their data in the cloud, or they upload (or mail [14]) it. They can then immediately manipulate and query their data using Snowflake's graphical interface or standardized interfaces such as ODBC. In contrast to other Database-as-a-Service (DBaaS) offerings, Snowflake's service aspect extends to the whole user experience. There are no tuning knobs, no physical design, no storage grooming tasks on the part of users.

Relational Snowflake has comprehensive support for ANSI SQL and ACID transactions. Most users are able to migrate existing workloads with little to no changes.

Semi-Structured Snowflake offers built-in functions and SQL extensions for traversing, flattening, and nesting of semi-structured data, with support for popular formats such as JSON and Avro. Automatic schema discovery and columnar storage make operations on schema-less, semi-structured data nearly as fast as over plain relational data, without any user effort.

Elastic Storage and compute resources can be scaled independently and seamlessly, without impact on data availability or performance of concurrent queries.

Highly Available Snowflake tolerates node, cluster, and even full data center failures. There is no downtime during software or hardware upgrades.

Durable Snowflake is designed for extreme durability with extra safeguards against accidental data loss: cloning, undrop, and cross-region backups.

Cost-efficient Snowflake is highly compute-efficient and all table data is compressed. Users pay only for what storage and compute resources they actually use.

Secure All data including temporary files and network traffic is encrypted end-to-end. No user data is ever exposed to the cloud platform. Additionally, role-based access control gives users the ability to exercise fine-grained access control on the SQL level.

Snowflake currently runs on the Amazon cloud (Amazon Web Services, AWS), but we may port it to other cloud platforms in the future. At the time of writing, Snowflake executes millions of queries per day over multiple petabytes of data, serving a rapidly growing number of small and large organizations from various domains.

Outline.

The paper is structured as follows. Section 2 explains the key design choice behind Snowflake: separation of storage and compute. Section 3 presents the resulting multi-cluster, shared-data architecture. Section 4 highlights differentiating features: continuous availability, semi-structured and schema-less data, time travel and cloning, and end-to-end security. Section 5 discusses related work. Section 6 concludes the paper with lessons learned and an outlook on ongoing work.

2. STORAGE VERSUS COMPUTE

Shared-nothing architectures have become the dominant system architecture in high-performance data warehousing, for two main reasons: scalability and commodity hardware. In a shared-nothing architecture, every query processor node has its own local disks. Tables are horizontally partitioned across nodes and each node is only responsible for the rows on its local disks. This design scales well for star-schema queries, because very little bandwidth is required to join a small (broadcast) dimension table with a large (partitioned) fact table. And because there is little contention for shared data structures or hardware resources, there is no need for expensive, custom hardware [25].

In a pure shared-nothing architecture, every node has the same responsibilities and runs on the same hardware. This approach results in elegant software that is easy to reason about, with all the nice secondary effects. A pure shared-nothing architecture has an important drawback though: it tightly couples compute resources and storage resources, which leads to problems in certain scenarios.

Heterogeneous Workload While the hardware is homogeneous, the workload typically is not. A system configuration that is ideal for bulk loading (high I/O bandwidth, light compute) is a poor fit for complex queries (low I/O bandwidth, heavy compute) and vice versa. Consequently, the hardware configuration needs to be a trade-off with low average utilization.

Membership Changes If the set of nodes changes; either as a result of node failures, or because the user chooses to resize the system; large amounts of data need to be reshuffled. Since the very same nodes are responsible for both data shuffling and query processing, a significant performance impact can be observed, limiting elasticity and availability.

Online Upgrade While the effects of small membership changes can be mitigated to some degree using replication, software and hardware upgrades eventually affect *every* node in the system. Implementing online upgrades such that one node after another is upgraded without any system downtime is possible in principle, but is made very hard by the fact that everything is tightly coupled and expected to be homogeneous.

In an on-premise environment, these issues can usually be tolerated. The workload may be heterogeneous, but there is little one can do if there is only a small, fixed pool of nodes on which to run. Upgrades of nodes are rare, and so are node failures and system resizing.

The situation is very different in the cloud. Platforms such as Amazon EC2 feature many different node types [4]. Taking advantage of them is simply a matter of bringing the data to the right type of node. At the same time, node failures are more frequent and performance can vary dramatically, even among nodes of the same type [45]. Membership changes are thus not an exception, they are the norm. And finally, there are strong incentives to enable online upgrades and elastic scaling. Online upgrades dramatically shorten the software development cycle and increase availability. Elastic scaling further increases availability and allows users to match resource consumption to their momentary needs.

For these reasons and others, Snowflake separates storage and compute. The two aspects are handled by two loosely coupled, independently scalable services. Compute is provided through Snowflake's (proprietary) shared-nothing engine. Storage is provided through Amazon S3 [5], though in principle any type of blob store would suffice (Azure Blob Storage [18, 36], Google Cloud Storage [20]). To reduce network traffic between compute nodes and storage nodes, each compute node caches some table data on local disk.

An added benefit of this solution is that local disk space is not spent on replicating the whole base data, which may be very large and mostly cold (rarely accessed). Instead, local disk is used exclusively for temporary data and caches, both of which are hot (suggesting the use of high-performance storage devices such as SSDs). So, once the caches are warm, performance approaches or even exceeds that of a pure shared-nothing system. We call this novel architecture the *multi-cluster, shared-data architecture.*

3. ARCHITECTURE

Snowflake is designed to be an *enterprise-ready* service. Besides offering high degrees of usability and interoperability, enterprise-readiness means high availability. To this end, Snowflake is a service-oriented architecture composed of highly fault tolerant and independently scalable services. These services communicate through RESTful interfaces and fall into three architectural layers:

Data Storage This layer uses Amazon S3 to store table data and query results.

Virtual Warehouses The "muscle" of the system. This layer handles query execution within elastic clusters of virtual machines, called virtual warehouses.

Cloud Services The "brain" of the system. This layer is a collection of services that manage virtual warehouses, queries, transactions, and all the metadata that goes around that: database schemas, access control information, encryption keys, usage statistics and so forth.

Figure 1 illustrates the three architectural layers of Snowflake and their principal components.

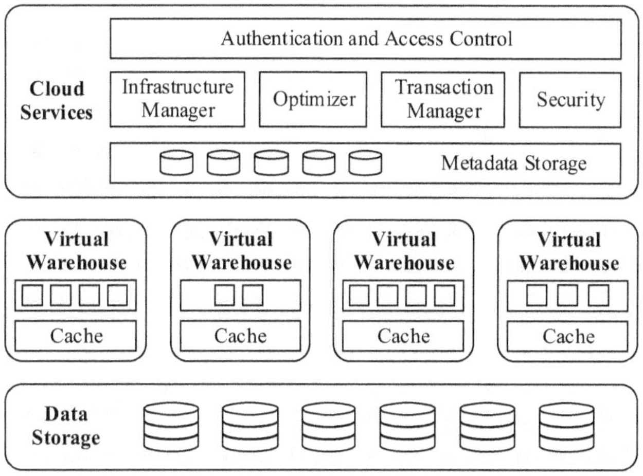

Figure 1: Multi-Cluster, Shared Data Architecture

3.1 Data Storage

Amazon Web Services (AWS) have been chosen as the initial platform for Snowflake for two main reasons. First, AWS is the most mature offering in the cloud platform market. Second (and related to the first point), AWS offers the largest pool of potential users.

The next choice was then between using S3 or developing our own storage service based on HDFS or similar [46]. We spent some time experimenting with S3 and found that while its performance could vary, its usability, high availability, and strong durability guarantees were hard to beat. So rather than developing our own storage service, we instead decided to invest our energy into local caching and skew resilience techniques in the Virtual Warehouses layer.

Compared to local storage, S3 naturally has a much higher access latency and there is a higher CPU overhead associated with every single I/O request, especially if HTTPS connections are used. But more importantly, S3 is a blob store with a relatively simple HTTP(S)-based PUT/GET/DELETE interface. Objects i.e. files can only be (over-)written in full. It is not even possible to append data to the end of a file. In fact, the exact size of a file needs to be announced up-front in the PUT request. S3 does, however, support GET requests for parts (ranges) of a file.

These properties had a strong influence on Snowflake's table file format and concurrency control scheme (cf. Section 3.3.2). Tables are horizontally partitioned into large, immutable files which are equivalent to blocks or pages in a traditional database system. Within each file, the values of each attribute or column are grouped together and heavily compressed, a well-known scheme called PAX or hybrid columnar in the literature [2]. Each table file has a header which, among other metadata, contains the offsets of each column within the file. Because S3 allows GET requests over parts of files, queries only need to download the file headers and those columns they are interested in.

Snowflake uses S3 not only for table data. It also uses S3 to store temp data generated by query operators (e.g. massive joins) once local disk space is exhausted, as well as for large query results. Spilling temp data to S3 allows the system to compute arbitrarily large queries without out-of-memory or out-of-disk errors. Storing query results in S3 enables new forms of client interactions and simplifies query processing, since it removes the need for server-side cursors found in traditional database systems.

Metadata such as catalog objects, which table consists of which S3 files, statistics, locks, transaction logs, etc. is stored in a scalable, transactional key-value store, which is part of the Cloud Services layer.

3.2 Virtual Warehouses

The Virtual Warehouses layer consists of clusters of EC2 instances. Each such cluster is presented to its single user through an abstraction called a virtual warehouse (VW). The individual EC2 instances that make up a VW are called worker nodes. Users never interact directly with worker nodes. In fact, users do not know or care which or how many worker nodes make up a VW. VWs instead come in abstract "T-Shirt sizes" ranging from X-Small to XX-Large. This abstraction allows us to evolve the service and pricing independent of the underlying cloud platform.

3.2.1 Elasticity and Isolation

VWs are pure compute resources. They can be created, destroyed, or resized at any point, on demand. Creating or destroying a VW has no effect on the state of the database. It is perfectly legal (and encouraged) that users shut down *all* their VWs when they have no queries. This elasticity allows users to dynamically match their compute resources to usage demands, independent of the data volume.

Each individual query runs on exactly one VW. Worker nodes are not shared across VWs, resulting in strong performance isolation for queries. (That being said, we recognize worker node sharing as an important area of future work, because it will enable higher utilization and lower cost for use cases where performance isolation is not big concern.)

When a new query is submitted, each worker node in the respective VW (or a subset of the nodes if the optimizer detects a small query) spawns a new worker process. Each worker process lives only for the duration of its query[1]. A worker process by itself—even if part of an update statement—never causes externally visible effects, because table files are immutable, cf. Section 3.3.2. Worker failures are thus easily contained and routinely resolved by retries. Snowflake does not currently perform partial retries though, so very large, long-running queries are an area of concern and future work.

Each user may have multiple VWs running at any given time, and each VW in turn may be running multiple concurrent queries. Every VW has access to the same shared tables, without the need to physically copy data.

Shared, infinite storage means users can *share and integrate* all their data, one of the core principles of data warehousing. Simultaneously, users benefit from *private compute* resources, avoiding interference of different workloads and organizational units—one of the reasons for data marts. This elasticity and isolation enables some novel use strategies. It is common for Snowflake users to have several VWs for queries from different organizational units, often running continuously, and periodically launch on-demand VWs, for instance for bulk loading.

Another important observation related to elasticity is that it is often possible to achieve much better performance for roughly the same price. For example, a data load which takes 15 hours on a system with 4 nodes might take only 2 hours with 32 nodes[2]. Since one pays for compute-hours, the overall cost is very similar—yet the user experience is dramatically different. We thus believe that VW elasticity is one of the biggest benefits and differentiators of the Snowflake architecture, and it shows that a novel design is needed to make use of unique capabilities of the cloud.

3.2.2 Local Caching and File Stealing

Each worker node maintains a cache of table data on local disk. The cache is a collection of table files i.e. S3 objects that have been accessed in the past by the node. To be precise, the cache holds file headers and individual columns of files, since queries download only the columns they need.

The cache lives for the duration of the worker node and is shared among concurrent and subsequent worker processes i.e. queries. It just sees a stream of file and column requests, and follows a simple least-recently-used (LRU) replacement policy, oblivious of individual queries. This simple scheme works surprisingly well, but we may refine it in the future to better match different workloads.

To improve the hit rate and avoid redundant caching of individual table files across worker nodes of a VW, the query optimizer assigns input file sets to worker nodes using consistent hashing over table file names [31]. Subsequent or concurrent queries accessing the same table file will therefore do this on the same worker node.

Consistent hashing in Snowflake is lazy. When the set of worker nodes changes—because of node failures or VW resizing—no data is shuffled immediately. Instead, Snowflake relies on the LRU replacement policy to eventually replace the cache contents. This solution amortizes the cost of replacing cache contents over multiple queries, resulting in much better availability than an eager cache or a pure shared-nothing system which would need to immediately shuffle large amounts of table data across nodes. It also simplifies the system since there is no "degraded" mode.

Besides caching, skew handling is particularly important in a cloud data warehouse. Some nodes may be executing much slower than others due to virtualization issues or network contention. Among other places, Snowflake deals with this problem at the scan level. Whenever a worker process completes scanning its set of input files, it requests additional files from its peers, a technique we call *file stealing.* If a peer finds that it has many files left in its input file set when such a request arrives, it answers the request by transferring ownership of one remaining file for the duration and scope of the current query. The requestor then downloads the file directly from S3, not from its peer. This design ensures that file stealing does not make things worse by putting additional load on straggler nodes.

3.2.3 Execution Engine

There is little value in being able to execute a query over 1,000 nodes if another system can do it in the same time using 10 such nodes. So while scalability is prime, per-node efficiency is just as important. We wanted to give users the best price/performance of any database-as-a-service offering on the market, so we decided to implement our own state-of-the-art SQL execution engine. The engine we have built is columnar, vectorized, and push-based.

Columnar storage and execution is generally considered superior to row-wise storage and execution for analytic workloads, due to more effective use of CPU caches and SIMD instructions, and more opportunities for (light-weight) compression [1, 33].

Vectorized execution means that, in contrast to MapReduce for example [42], Snowflake avoids materialization of intermediate results. Instead, data is processed in pipelined fashion, in batches of a few thousand rows in columnar format. This approach, pioneered by VectorWise (originally MonetDB/X100 [15]), saves I/O and greatly improves cache efficiency.

Push-based execution refers to the fact that relational operators *push* their results to their downstream operators, rather than waiting for these operators to *pull* data (classic Volcano-style model [27]). Push-based execution improves cache efficiency, because it removes

[1]Ephemeral processes are appropriate for analytic workloads but entail some query start-up cost. As an obvious optimization, we plan to recycle worker processes for small queries.

[2]Snowflake exposes T-shirt sizes rather than concrete node numbers, but the principle holds.

control flow logic from tight loops [41]. It also enables Snowflake to efficiently process DAG-shaped plans, as opposed to just trees, creating additional opportunities for sharing and pipelining of intermediate results.

At the same time, many sources of overhead in traditional query processing are not present in Snowflake. Notably, there is no need for transaction management during execution. As far as the engine is concerned, queries are executed against a fixed set of immutable files. Also, there is no buffer pool. Most queries scan large amounts of data. Using memory for table buffering versus operation is a bad trade-off here. Snowflake does, however, allow all major operators (join, group by, sort) to spill to disk and recurse when main memory is exhausted. We found that a pure main-memory engine, while leaner and perhaps faster, is too restrictive to handle all interesting workloads. Analytic workloads can feature extremely large joins or aggregations.

3.3 Cloud Services

Virtual warehouses are ephemeral, user-specific resources. In contrast, the Cloud Services layer is heavily multi-tenant. Each service of this layer—access control, query optimizer, transaction manager, and others—is long-lived and shared across many users. Multi-tenancy improves utilization and reduces administrative overhead, which allows for better economies of scale than in traditional architectures where every user has a completely private system incarnation.

Each service is replicated for high availability and scalability. Consequently, the failure of individual service nodes does not cause data loss or loss of availability, though some running queries may fail (and be transparently re-executed).

3.3.1 Query Management and Optimization

All queries issued by users pass through the Cloud Services layer. Here, all the early stages of the query life cycle are handled: parsing, object resolution, access control, and plan optimization.

Snowflake's query optimizer follows a typical Cascades-style approach [28], with top-down cost-based optimization. All statistics used for optimization are automatically maintained on data load and updates. Since Snowflake does not use indices (cf. Section 3.3.3), the plan search space is smaller than in some other systems. The plan space is further reduced by postponing many decisions until execution time, for example the type of data distribution for joins. This design reduces the number of bad decisions made by the optimizer, increasing robustness at the cost of a small loss in peak performance. It also makes the system easier to use (performance becomes more predictable), which is in line with Snowflake's overall focus on service experience.

Once the optimizer completes, the resulting execution plan is distributed to all the worker nodes that are part of the query. As the query executes, Cloud Services continuously tracks the state of the query to collect performance counters and detect node failures. All query information and statistics are stored for audits and performance analysis. Users are able to monitor and analyze past and ongoing queries through the Snowflake graphical user interface.

3.3.2 Concurrency Control

As mentioned previously, concurrency control is handled entirely by the Cloud Services layer. Snowflake is designed for analytic workloads, which tend to be dominated by large reads, bulk or trickle inserts, and bulk updates. Like most systems in this workload space, we decided to implement ACID transactions via Snapshot Isolation (SI) [17].

Under SI, all reads by a transaction see a consistent snapshot of the database as of the time the transaction started. As customary, SI is implemented on top of multi-version concurrency control (MVCC), which means a copy of every changed database object is preserved for some duration.

MVCC is a natural choice given the fact that table files are immutable, a direct consequence of using S3 for storage. Changes to a file can only be made by replacing it with a different file that includes the changes[3]. It follows that write operations (insert, update, delete, merge) on a table produce a newer version of the table by adding and removing whole files relative to the prior table version. File additions and removals are tracked in the metadata (in the global key-value store), in a form which allows the set of files that belong to a specific table version to be computed very efficiently.

Besides for SI, Snowflake also uses these snapshots to implement time travel and efficient cloning of database objects, see Section 4.4 for details.

3.3.3 Pruning

Limiting access only to data that is relevant to a given query is one of the most important aspects of query processing. Historically, data access in databases was limited through the use of indices, in the form of B^+-trees or similar data structures. While this approach proved highly effective for transaction processing, it raises multiple problems for systems like Snowflake. First, it relies heavily on random access, which is a problem both due to the storage medium (S3) and the data format (compressed files). Second, maintaining indices significantly increases the volume of data and data loading time. Finally, the user needs to explicitly create the indices—which would go very much against the pure service approach of Snowflake. Even with the aid of tuning advisors, maintaining indices can be a complex, expensive, and risky process.

An alternative technique has recently gained popularity for large-scale data processing: min-max based pruning, also known as small materialized aggregates [38], zone maps [29], and data skipping [49]. Here, the system maintains the data distribution information for a given chunk of data (set of records, file, block etc.), in particular minimum and maximum values within the chunk. Depending on the query predicates, these values can be used to determine that a given chunk of data might not be needed for a given query. For example, imagine files f_1 and f_2 contain values `3..5` and `4..6` respectively, in some column `x`. Then, if a query has a predicate `WHERE x >= 6`, we know that only f_2 needs to be accessed. Unlike traditional indices, this metadata is usually orders of magnitude smaller than the actual data, resulting in a small storage overhead and fast access.

Pruning nicely matches the design principles of Snowflake: it does not rely on user input; it scales well; and it is easy to maintain. What is more, it works well for sequential access of large chunks of data, and it adds little overhead to loading, query optimization, and query execution times.

Snowflake keeps pruning-related metadata for every indi-

[3]It would certainly be possible to defer changes to table files through the introduction of a redo-undo log, perhaps in combination with a delta store [32], but we are currently not pursuing this idea for reasons of complexity and scalability.

vidual table file. The metadata not only covers plain relational columns, but also a selection of auto-detected columns inside of semi-structured data, see Section 4.3.2. During optimization, the metadata is checked against the query predicates to reduce ("prune") the set of input files for query execution. The optimizer performs pruning not only for simple base-value predicates, but also for more complex expressions such as `WEEKDAY(orderdate) IN (6, 7)`.

Besides this *static* pruning, Snowflake also performs *dynamic* pruning during execution. For example, as part of hash join processing, Snowflake collects statistics on the distribution of join keys in the build-side records. This information is then pushed to the probe side and used to filter and possibly skip entire files on the probe side. This is in addition to other well-known techniques such as bloom joins [40].

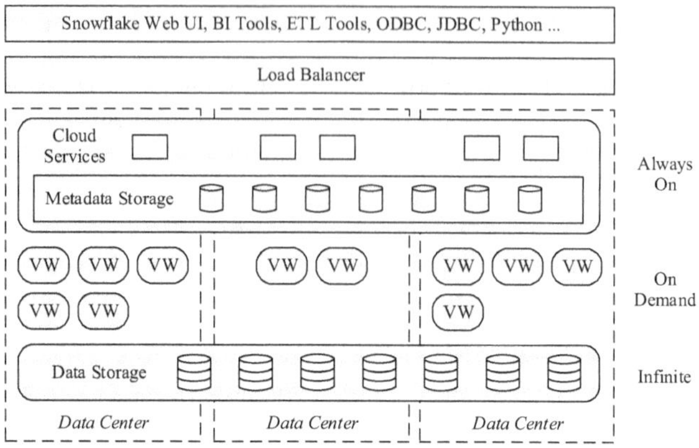

Figure 2: Multi-Data Center Instance of Snowflake

4. FEATURE HIGHLIGHTS

Snowflake offers many features expected from a relational data warehouse: comprehensive SQL support, ACID transactions, standard interfaces, stability and security, customer support, and—of course—strong performance and scalability. Additionally, it introduces a number of other valuable features rarely or never-before seen in related systems. This section presents a few of these features that we consider technical differentiators.

4.1 Pure Software-as-a-Service Experience

Snowflake supports standard database interfaces (JDBC, ODBC, Python PEP-0249) and works with various third-party tools and services such as Tableau, Informatica, or Looker. However, it also provides the possibility to interact with the system using nothing but a web browser. A web UI may seem like a trivial thing, but it quickly proved itself to be a critical differentiator. The web UI makes it very easy to access Snowflake from any location and environment, dramatically reducing the complexity of bootstrapping and using the system. With a lot of data already in the cloud, it allowed many users to just point Snowflake at their data and query away, without downloading any software.

As may be expected, the UI allows not only SQL operations, but also gives access to the database catalog, user and system management, monitoring, usage information, and so forth. We continuously expand the UI functionality, working on aspects such as online collaboration, user feedback and support, and others.

But our focus on ease-of-use and service experience does not stop at the user interface; it extends to every aspect of the system architecture. There are no failure modes, no tuning knobs, no physical design, no storage grooming tasks. It is all about the data and the queries.

4.2 Continuous Availability

In the past, data warehousing solutions were well-hidden back-end systems, isolated from most of the world. In such environments, downtimes—both planned (software upgrades or administrative tasks) and unplanned (failures)—usually did not have a large impact on operations. But as data analysis became critical to more and more business tasks, continuous availability became an important requirement for any data warehouse. This trend mirrors the expectations on modern SaaS systems, most of which are always-on, customer-facing applications with no (planned) downtime.

Snowflake offers continuous availability that meets these expectations. The two main technical features in this regard are fault resilience and online upgrades.

4.2.1 *Fault Resilience*

Snowflake tolerates individual and correlated node failures at all levels of the architecture, shown in Figure 2. The Data Storage layer of Snowflake today is S3, which is replicated across multiple data centers called "availability zones" or AZs in Amazon terminology. Replication across AZs allows S3 to handle full AZ failures, and to guarantee 99.99% data availability and 99.999999999% durability. Matching S3's architecture, Snowflake's metadata store is also distributed and replicated across multiple AZs. If a node fails, other nodes can pick up the activities without much impact on end users. The remaining services of the Cloud Services layer consist of stateless nodes in multiple AZs, with a load balancer distributing user requests between them. It follows that a single node failure or even a full AZ failure causes no system-wide impact, possibly some failed queries for users currently connected to a failed node. These users will be redirected to a different node for their next query.

In contrast, Virtual Warehouses (VWs) are not distributed across AZs. This choice is for performance reasons. High network throughput is critical for distributed query execution, and network throughput is significantly higher within the same AZ. If one of the worker nodes fails during query execution, the query fails but is transparently re-executed, either with the node immediately replaced, or with a temporarily reduced number of nodes. To accelerate node replacement, Snowflake maintains a small pool of standby nodes. (These nodes are also used for fast VW provisioning.)

If an *entire* AZ becomes unavailable though, all queries running on a given VW of that AZ will fail, and the user needs to actively re-provision the VW in a different AZ. With full-AZ failures being truly catastrophic and exceedingly rare events, we today accept this one scenario of partial system unavailability, but hope to address it in the future.

4.2.2 *Online Upgrade*

Snowflake provides continuous availability not only when failures occur, but also during software upgrades. The system is designed to allow multiple versions of the various services to be deployed side-by-side, both Cloud Services components and virtual warehouses. This is made possible by the fact that all services are effectively stateless. All hard state is kept in a transactional key-value store and is ac-

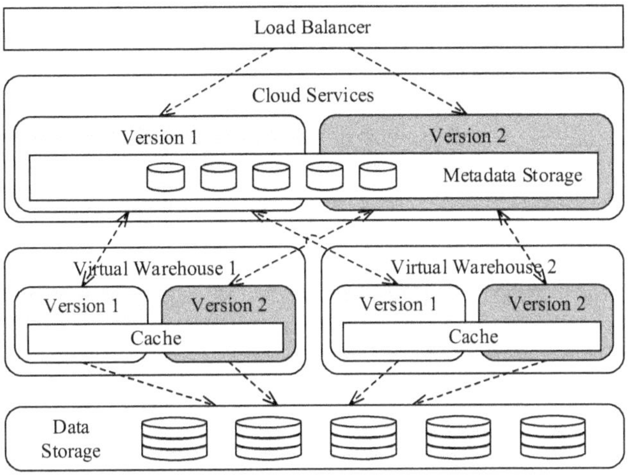

Figure 3: Online Upgrade

cessed through a mapping layer which takes care of metadata versioning and schema evolution. Whenever we change the metadata schema, we ensure backward compatibility with the previous version.

To perform a software upgrade, Snowflake first deploys the new version of the service alongside the previous version. User accounts are then progressively switched to the new version, at every which point all new queries issued by the respective user are directed to the new version. All queries that were executing against the previous version are allowed to run to completion. Once all queries and users have finished using the previous version, all services of that version are terminated and decommissioned.

Figure 3 shows a snapshot of an ongoing upgrade process. There are two versions of Snowflake running side-by-side, version 1 (light) and version 2 (dark). There are two versions of a single incarnation of Cloud Services, controlling two virtual warehouses (VWs), each having two versions. The load balancer directs incoming calls to the appropriate version of Cloud Services. The Cloud Services of one version only talk to VWs of a matching version.

As mentioned previously, both versions of Cloud Services share the same metadata store. What is more, VWs of different versions are able to share the same worker nodes and their respective caches. Consequently, there is no need to repopulate the caches after an upgrade. The entire process is transparent to the user with no downtime or performance degradation.

Online upgrade also has had a tremendous effect on our speed of development, and on how we handle critical bugs at Snowflake. At the time of writing, we upgrade all services once per week. That means we release features and improvements on a weekly basis. To ensure the upgrade process goes smoothly, both upgrade and downgrade are continuously tested in a special pre-production incarnation of Snowflake. In those rare cases where we find a critical bug in our production incarnation (not necessarily during an upgrade), we can very quickly downgrade to the previous version, or implement a fix and perform an out-of-schedule upgrade. This process is not as scary as it may sound, because we continuously test and exercise the upgrade/downgrade mechanism. It is highly automated and hardened at this point.

4.3 Semi-Structured and Schema-Less Data

Snowflake extends the standard SQL type system with three types for semi-structured data: `VARIANT`, `ARRAY`, and `OBJECT`. Values of type `VARIANT` can store any value of native SQL type (`DATE`, `VARCHAR` etc.), as well as variable-length `ARRAY`s of values, and JavaScript-like `OBJECT`s, maps from strings to `VARIANT` values. The latter are also called *documents* in the literature, giving rise to the notion of document stores (MongoDB [39], Couchbase [23]).

`ARRAY` and `OBJECT` are just restrictions of type `VARIANT`. The internal representation is the same: a self-describing, compact binary serialization which supports fast key-value lookup, as well as efficient type tests, comparison, and hashing. `VARIANT` columns can thus be used as join keys, grouping keys, and ordering keys, just like any other column.

The `VARIANT` type allows Snowflake to be used in an ELT (Extract-Load-Transform) manner rather than a traditional ETL (Extract-Transform-Load) manner. There is no need to specify document schemas or to perform transformations on the load. Users can load their input data from JSON, Avro, or XML format directly into a `VARIANT` column; Snowflake handles parsing and type inference (cf. Section 4.3.3). This approach, aptly called "schema later" in the literature, allows for schema evolution by decoupling information producers from information consumers and any intermediaries. In contrast, any change in data schemas in a conventional ETL pipeline requires coordination between multiple departments in an organization, which can take months to execute.

Another advantage of ELT and Snowflake is that later, if transformation is desired, it can be performed using the full power of a parallel SQL database, including operations such as joins, sorting, aggregation, complex predicates and so forth, which are typically missing or inefficient in conventional ETL toolchains. On that point, Snowflake also features procedural user-defined functions (UDFs) with full JavaScript syntax and integration with the `VARIANT` data type. Support for procedural UDFs further increases the number of ETL tasks that can be pushed into Snowflake.

4.3.1 Post-relational Operations

The most important operation on documents is extraction of data elements, either by field name (for `OBJECT`s), or by offset (for `ARRAY`s). Snowflake provides extraction operations in both functional SQL notation and JavaScript-like path syntax. The internal encoding makes extraction very efficient. A child element is just a pointer inside the parent element; no copying is required. Extraction is often followed by a cast of the resulting `VARIANT` value to a standard SQL type. Again, the encoding makes these casts very efficient.

The second common operation is flattening, i.e. pivoting a nested document into multiple rows. Snowflake uses SQL lateral views to represent flattening operations. This flattening can be recursive, allowing the complete conversion of the hierarchical structure of the document into a relational table amenable to SQL processing. The opposite operation to flattening is aggregation. Snowflake introduces a few new aggregate and analytic functions such as `ARRAY_AGG` and `OBJECT_AGG` for this purpose.

4.3.2 Columnar Storage and Processing

The use of a serialized (binary) representation for semi-structured data is a conventional design choice for integrating semi-structured data into relational databases. The row-

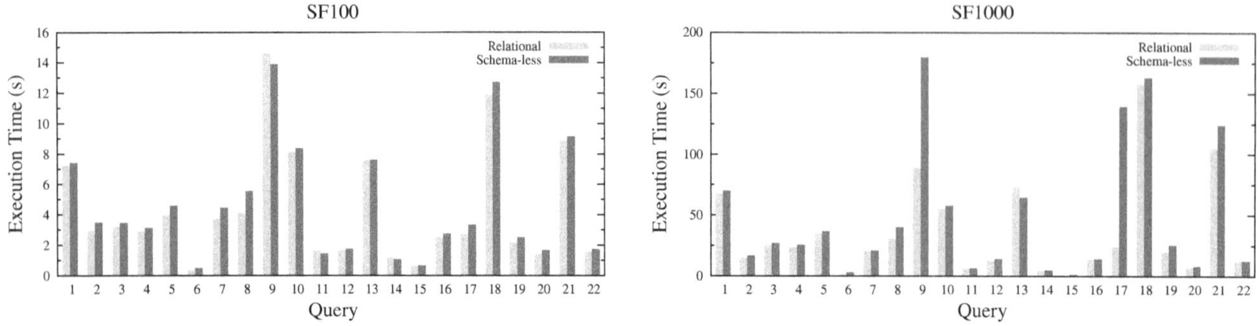

Figure 4: TPC-H SF100 and SF1000 Performance: Relational vs. Schema-less Row Format

wise representation, unfortunately, makes storage and processing of such data less efficient than that of columnar relational data—which is the usual reason for transforming semi-structured data into plain relational data.

Cloudera Impala [21] (using Parquet [10]) and Google Dremel [34] have demonstrated that columnar storage of semi-structured data is possible and beneficial. However, Impala and Dremel (and its externalization BigQuery [44]) require users to provide complete table schemas for columnar storage. To achieve *both* the flexibility of a schema-less serialized representation and the performance of a columnar relational database, Snowflake introduces a novel automated approach to type inference and columnar storage.

As mentioned in Section 3.1, Snowflake stores data in a hybrid columnar format. When storing semi-structured data, the system automatically performs statistical analysis of the collection of documents within a single table file, to perform automatic type inference and to determine which (typed) paths are frequently common. The corresponding columns are then removed from the documents and stored separately, using the same compressed columnar format as native relational data. For these columns, Snowflake even computes materialized aggregates for use by pruning (cf. Section 3.3.3), as with plain relational data.

During a scan, the various columns can be reassembled into a single column of type `VARIANT`. Most queries, however, are only interested in a subset of the columns of the original document. In those cases, Snowflake pushes projection and cast expressions down into the scan operator, so that only the necessary columns are accessed and cast directly into the target SQL type.

The optimizations described above are performed *independently* for every table file, which allows for efficient storage and extraction even under schema evolution. However, it does raise challenges with respect to query optimization, in particular pruning. Suppose a query has a predicate over a path expression, and we would like to use pruning to restrict the set of files to be scanned. The path and corresponding column may be present in most files, but only frequent enough to warrant metadata in some of the files. The conservative solution is to simply scan all files for which there is no suitable metadata. Snowflake improves over this solution by computing Bloom filters over all *paths* (not values!) present in the documents. These Bloom filters are saved along with the other file metadata, and probed by the query optimizer during pruning. Table files which do not contain paths required by a given query can safely be skipped.

4.3.3 *Optimistic Conversion*

Because some native SQL types, notably date/time values, are represented as strings in common external formats such as JSON or XML, these values need to be converted from strings to their actual type either at write time (during insert or update) or at read time (during queries). Without a typed schema or equivalent hints, these string conversions need to be performed at read time, which, in a read-dominated workload, is less efficient than doing the conversions once, during the write. Another problem with untyped data is the lack of suitable metadata for pruning, which is especially important in case of dates. (Analytical workloads frequently have range predicates on date columns.)

But applied at write time, automatic conversions may lose information. For example, a field containing numeric product identifiers may actually not be a number but a string with significant leading zeros. Similarly, what looks like a date could really be the content of a text message. Snowflake solves the problem by performing optimistic data conversion, and preserving both the result of the conversion and the original string (unless a fully reversible conversion exists), in separate columns. If a query later requires the original string, it is easily retrieved or reconstructed. Because unused columns are not loaded and accessed, the impact of any double storage on query performance is minimal.

4.3.4 *Performance*

To assess the combined effects of columnar storage, optimistic conversion, and pruning over semi-structured data on query performance, we conducted a set of experiments using TPC-H-like[4] data and queries.

We created two types of database schemas. First, a conventional, relational TPC-H schema. Second, a "schema-less" database schema, where every table consisted of a single column of type `VARIANT`. We then generated clustered (sorted) SF100 and SF1000 data sets (100 GB and 1 TB respectively), stored the data sets in plain JSON format (i.e., dates became strings), and loaded that data into Snowflake, using both the relational and schema-less database schemas. No hints of any kind regarding the fields, types, and clustering of the schema-less data were given to the system, and no other tuning was done. We then defined a few views on top of the schema-less databases, in order to be able to run the

[4]Experimental results were obtained using a faithful implementation of TPC-H data generation and queries. Nonetheless, the data, queries, and numbers have not been verified by the TPC and do not constitute official benchmark results.

exact same set of TPC-H queries against all four databases. (At the time of writing, Snowflake does not use views for type inference or other optimizations, so this was purely a syntactic convenience.)

Finally, we ran all 22 TPC-H queries against the four databases, using a *medium standard* warehouse[5]. Figure 4 shows the results. Numbers were obtained over three runs with warm caches. Standard errors were insignificant and thus omitted from the results.

As can be seen, the overhead of schema-less storage and query processing was around 10% for all but two queries (Q9 and Q17 over SF1000). For these two queries, we determined the reason for the slow-down to be a sub-optimal join order, caused by a known bug in distinct value estimation. We continue to make improvements to metadata collection and query optimization over semi-structured data.

In summary, the query performance over semi-structured data with relatively stable and simple schemas (i.e. the majority of machine-generated data found in practice), is nearly on par with the performance over conventional relational data, enjoying all the benefits of columnar storage, columnar execution, and pruning—without the user effort.

4.4 Time Travel and Cloning

In Section 3.3.2, we discussed how Snowflake implements Snapshot Isolation (SI) on top of multi-version concurrency control (MVCC). Write operations (insert, update, delete, merge) on a table produce a newer version of the table by adding and removing whole files.

When files are removed by a new version, they are retained for a configurable duration (currently up to 90 days). File retention allows Snowflake to read earlier versions of tables very efficiently; that is, to perform *time travel* on the database. Users can access this feature from SQL using the convenient `AT` or `BEFORE` syntax. Timestamps can be absolute, relative with respect to current time, or relative with respect to previous statements (referred to by ID).

```
SELECT * FROM my_table AT(TIMESTAMP =>
  'Mon, 01 May 2015 16:20:00 -0700'::timestamp);
SELECT * FROM my_table AT(OFFSET => -60*5); -- 5 min ago
SELECT * FROM my_table BEFORE(STATEMENT =>
  '8e5d0ca9-005e-44e6-b858-a8f5b37c5726');
```

One can even access different versions of the same table in a single query.

```
SELECT new.key, new.value, old.value FROM my_table new
JOIN my_table AT(OFFSET => -86400) old -- 1 day ago
ON new.key = old.key WHERE new.value <> old.value;
```

Based on the same underlying metadata, Snowflake introduces the `UNDROP` keyword to quickly restore tables, schemas, or whole databases that have been dropped accidentally.

```
DROP DATABASE important_db; -- whoops!
UNDROP DATABASE important_db;
```

Snowflake also implements a functionality we call *cloning*, expressed through the new keyword `CLONE`. Cloning a table creates a new table with the same definition and contents quickly and without making physical copies of table files. The clone operation simply copies the metadata of the source table. Right after cloning, both tables refer to the same set of files, but both tables can be modified independently thereafter. The clone feature also supports whole schemas or databases, which allows for very efficient snapshots. Snapshots are good practice before a large batch of updates, or when performing lengthy, exploratory data analysis. The `CLONE` keyword can even be combined with `AT` and `BEFORE`, allowing such snapshots to be made after the fact.

```
CREATE DATABASE recovered_db CLONE important_db BEFORE(
  STATEMENT => '8e5d0ca9-005e-44e6-b858-a8f5b37c5726');
```

[5]We currently do not disclose pricing and hardware details, but a medium standard warehouse consists of a very small number of inexpensive EC2 instances.

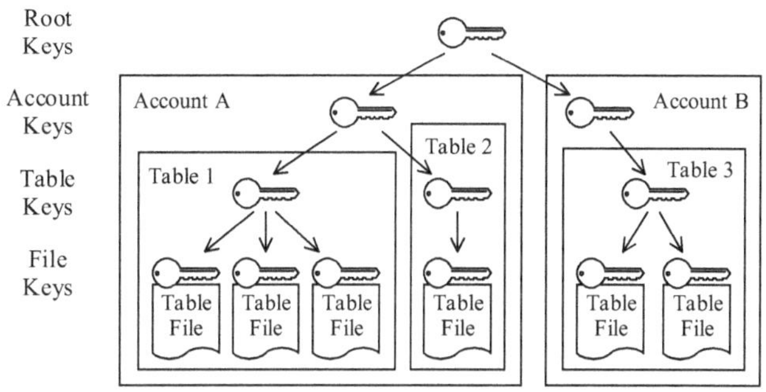

Figure 5: Encryption Key Hierarchy

4.5 Security

Snowflake is designed to protect user data against attacks on all levels of the architecture, including the cloud platform. To this end, Snowflake implements two-factor authentication, (client-side) encrypted data import and export, secure data transfer and storage, and role-based access control (RBAC [26]) for database objects. At all times, data is encrypted before being sent over the network, and before being written to local disk or shared storage (S3). Thus, Snowflake provides full end-to-end data encryption and security.

4.5.1 Key Hierarchy

Snowflake uses strong AES 256-bit encryption with a hierarchical key model rooted in AWS CloudHSM [12]. Encryption keys are automatically rotated and re-encrypted ("rekeyed") to ensure that keys complete the full NIST 800-57 cryptographic key-management life cycle [13]. Encryption and key management are entirely transparent to the user and require no configuration or management.

The Snowflake key hierarchy, shown in Figure 5, has four levels: root keys, account keys, table keys, and file keys. Each layer of (parent) keys encrypts i.e. *wraps* the layer of (child) keys below. Each account key corresponds to one user account, each table key corresponds to one database table, and each file key corresponds to one table file.

Hierarchical key models are good security practice because they constrain the amount of data each key protects. Each layer reduces the scope of keys below it, as indicated by the boxes in Figure 5. Snowflake's hierarchical key model ensures isolation of user data in its multi-tenant architecture, because each user account has a separate account key.

4.5.2 Key Life Cycle

Orthogonal to constraining the *amount* of data each key protects, Snowflake also constrains the *duration of time* during which a key is usable. Encryption keys go through four

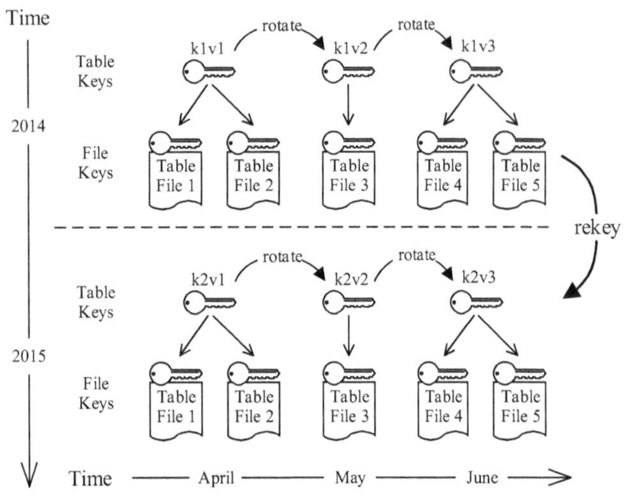

Figure 6: Table Key Life Cycle

phases: (1) a pre-operational creation phase, (2) an operational phase where keys are used to encrypt (originator-usage period) and decrypt (recipient-usage period), (3) a post-operational phase where keys are no longer in use, and (4) a destroyed phase. Phases 1, 3, and 4 are trivial to implement. Phase 2 requires one to limit the originator-usage and recipient-usage periods. Only when a key no longer encrypts any required data, it can be moved on to phases 3 and 4. Snowflake limits the originator-usage period using *key rotation* and the recipient-usage period using *rekeying*.

Key rotation creates new versions of keys at regular intervals (say, one month). After each such interval, a new version of a key is created and the previous version of the key is "retired". The retired version is still usable, but only to decrypt data. When wrapping new child keys in the key hierarchy, or when writing to tables, only the latest, active version of the key is used to encrypt the data.

Rekeying is the process of re-encrypting old data with new keys. After a specific time interval (say, one year), data that has been encrypted with a retired key is re-encrypted with an active key. This rekeying is orthogonal to key rotation. While key rotation ensures that a key is transferred from its active state (originator usage) to a retired state (recipient usage), rekeying ensures that a key can be transferred from its retired state to being destroyed.

Figure 6 shows the life cycle of a single table key. Assume keys are rotated once per month, and data is rekeyed once per year. Table files 1 and 2 are created in April 2014, using key 1 version 1 (k1v1). In May 2014, key 1 is rotated to version 2 (k1v2), and table file 3 is created using k1v2. In June 2014, key 1 is rotated to version 3 (k1v3), and two more table files are created. No more inserts or updates are made to the table after June 2014. In April 2015, k1v1 becomes one year old and needs to be destroyed. A new key, key 2 version 1 (k2v1), is created, and all files associated with k1v1 are rekeyed using k2v1. In May 2015, the same happens to k1v2 and table file 3 is rekeyed using k2v2. In June 2015, table files 4 and 5 are rekeyed using k2v3.

An analogous scheme is implemented between account keys and table keys, and between the root key and account keys. Each level of the key hierarchy undergoes key rotation and rekeying, including the root key. Key rotation and rekeying of account keys and the root key do not require re-encryption of files. Only the *keys* of the immediate lower level need to be re-encrypted.

The relationship between table keys and file keys is different though. File keys are not wrapped by table keys. Instead, file keys are cryptographically derived from the combination of table key and (unique) file name. It follows that whenever a table key changes, all of its related file keys change, so the affected table files need to be re-encrypted. The big benefit of key derivation, however, is that it removes the need to create, manage, and pass around individual file keys. A system like Snowflake that handles billions of files would have to handle many gigabytes of file keys otherwise.

We chose this design also because Snowflake's separation of storage and compute allows it to perform re-encryption without impacting user workloads. Rekeying works in the background, using different worker nodes than queries. After files are rekeyed, Snowflake atomically updates the metadata of database tables to point to the newly encrypted files. The old files are deleted once all ongoing queries are finished.

4.5.3 End-to-End Security

Snowflake uses AWS CloudHSM as a tamper-proof, highly secure way to generate, store, and use the root keys of the key hierarchy. AWS CloudHSM is a set of hardware security modules (HSMs) that are connected to a virtual private cluster within AWS. The root keys never leave the HSM devices. All cryptographic operations using root keys are performed within the HSMs themselves. Thus, lower-level keys cannot be unwrapped without authorized access to the HSM devices. The HSMs are also used to generate keys at the account and table levels, including during key rotation and rekeying. We configured AWS CloudHSM in its high-availability configuration to minimize the possibility of service outages.

In addition to data encryption, Snowflake protects user data in the following ways:

1. Isolation of storage through access policies on S3.
2. Role-based access control within user accounts for fine-grained access control to database objects.
3. Encrypted data import and export without the cloud provider (Amazon) ever seeing data in the clear.
4. Two-factor- and federated authentication for secure access control.

In summary, Snowflake provides a hierarchical key model rooted in AWS CloudHSM and uses key rotation and rekeying to ensure that encryption keys follow a standardized life cycle. Key management is entirely transparent to the user and requires no configuration, management, or downtime. It is part of a comprehensive security strategy that enables full end-to-end encryption and security.

5. RELATED WORK

Cloud-based Parallel Database Systems. Amazon has a number of DBaaS products with Amazon Redshift being the data warehousing product among these. Having evolved from the parallel database system ParAccel, Redshift was arguably the first real data warehouse system offered as a service [30]. Redshift uses a classic shared-nothing architecture. Thus, while being scalable, adding or removing compute resources requires data redistribution. In contrast, Snowflake's multi-cluster, shared data architecture allows users to instantly scale up, scale down, or even pause compute independently from storage without data movement—including the ability to integrate data across isolated compute resources. Also, following a pure service principle, Snowflake requires no physical tuning, data grooming, manual gathering of table statistics, or table vacuuming on the part of users. Although Redshift can ingest semi-structured data such as JSON as a `VARCHAR`, Snowflake has native support for semi-structured data, including important optimizations such as columnar storage.

Google's Cloud Platform offers a fully managed query service known as BigQuery [44], which is the public implementation of Dremel [34]. The BigQuery service lets users run queries on terabytes of data at impressive speeds, parallelized across thousands of nodes. One of the inspirations for Snowflake was BigQuery's support for JSON and nested data, which we find necessary for a modern analytics platform. But while BigQuery offers a SQL-like language, it has some fundamental deviations from the ANSI SQL syntax and semantics, making it tricky to use with SQL-based products. Also, BigQuery tables are append-only and require schemas. In comparison, Snowflake offers full DML (insert, update, delete, merge), ACID transactions, and does not require schema definitions for semi-structured data.

Microsoft SQL Data Warehouse (Azure SQL DW) is a recent addition to the Azure cloud platform and services based on SQL Server and its Analytics Platform System (APS) appliance [35, 37]. Similar to Snowflake, it separates storage from compute. Computational resources can be scaled through data warehouse units (DWUs). The degree of concurrency is capped though. For any data warehouse, the maximum number of concurrently executing queries is 32 [47]. Snowflake, in contrast, allows fully independent scaling of concurrent workloads via virtual warehouses. Snowflake users are also released from the burden of choosing appropriate distribution keys and other administrative tasks. And while Azure SQL DW does support queries over non-relational data via PolyBase [24], it does not have built-in support for semi-structured data comparable to Snowflake's `VARIANT` type and related optimizations.

Document Stores and Big Data. Document stores such as MongoDB [39], Couchbase Server [23], and Apache Cassandra [6], have become increasingly popular among application developers in recent years, because of the scalability, simplicity, and schema flexibility they offer. However, one challenge that has resulted from the simple key-value and CRUD (create, read, update, and delete) API of these systems is the difficulty to express more complex queries. In response, we have seen the emergence of several SQL-like query languages such as N1QL [22] for Couchbase or CQL [19] for Apache Cassandra. Additionally, many "Big Data" engines now support queries over nested data, for example Apache Hive [9], Apache Spark [11], Apache Drill [7], Cloudera Impala [21], and Facebook Presto [43]. We believe that this shows a real need for complex analytics over schema-less and semi-structured data, and our semi-structured data support is inspired by many of these systems. Using schema inference, optimistic conversions, and columnar storage, Snowflake combines the flexibility of these systems with the storage efficiency and execution speed of a relational, column-oriented database.

6. LESSONS LEARNED AND OUTLOOK

When Snowflake was founded in 2012, the database world was fully focused on *SQL on Hadoop*, with over a dozen systems appearing within a short time span. At that time, the decision to work in a completely different direction, to build a "classic" data warehouse system for the cloud, seemed a contrarian and risky move. After 3 years of development we are confident that it was the right one. Hadoop has not replaced RDBMSs; it has complemented them. People still want a relational database, but one that is more efficient, flexible, and better suited for the cloud.

Snowflake has met our hopes of what a system built for the cloud can provide to both its users and its authors. The elasticity of the multi-cluster, shared data architecture has changed how users approach their data processing tasks. The SaaS model not only has made it easy for users to try out and adopt the system, but has also dramatically helped our development and testing. With a single production version and online upgrades, we are able to release new features, provide improvements, and fix problems much faster than we would possibly be able to do under a traditional development model.

While we had hoped that the semi-structured extensions would prove useful, we were surprised by the speed of adoption. We discovered a very popular model, where organizations would use Hadoop for two things: for storing JSON, and for converting it to a format that can be loaded into an RDBMS. By providing a system that can efficiently store and process semi-structured data as-is—with a powerful SQL interface on top—we found Snowflake replacing not only traditional database systems, but also Hadoop clusters.

It was not a painless journey of course. While our team has over 100 years of database-development expertise combined, we did make avoidable mistakes along the way, including overly simplistic early implementations of some relational operators, not incorporating all datatypes early on in the engine, not early-enough focus on resource management, postponing work on comprehensive date and time functionality etc. Also, our continuous focus on avoiding tuning knobs raised a series of engineering challenges, ultimately bringing about many exciting technical solutions. As a result, today, Snowflake has only one tuning parameter: how much performance the user wants (and is willing to pay for).

While Snowflake's performance is already very competitive, especially considering the no-tuning aspect, we know of many optimizations that we have not had the time for yet. Somewhat unexpected though, core performance turned out to be almost never an issue for our users. The reason is that elastic compute via virtual warehouses can offer the performance boost occasionally needed. That made us focus our development efforts on other aspects of the system.

The biggest technical challenges we face are related to the SaaS and multi-tenancy aspects of the system. Building a metadata layer that can support hundreds of users concurrently was a very challenging and complex task. Handling various types of node failures, network failures, and supporting services is a never-ending fight. Security has been and will continue to be a big topic: protecting the system and the users' data from external attacks, the users themselves, and our internal users as well. Maintaining a live system of hundreds of nodes running millions of queries per day, while bringing a lot of satisfaction, requires a highly integrated approach to development, operations, and support.

Snowflake users continue to throw increasingly bigger and more complex problems at the system, influencing its evolution. We are currently working on improving the data access performance by providing additional metadata structures and data re-organization tasks—with a focus on minimal to no user interaction. We continue to improve and extend core query processing functionality, both for standard SQL and semi-relational extensions. We plan to further improve the skew handling and load balancing strategies, whose importance increases along with the scale of our users' workloads. We work on solutions simplifying workload management to the users, making the system even more elastic. And we work on integration with external systems, including issues such as high-frequency data loading.

The biggest future challenge for Snowflake is the transition to a full self-service model, where users can sign up and interact with the system without our involvement at any phase. It will bring a lot of security, performance, and support challenges. We are looking forward to them.

7. ACKNOWLEDGMENTS

Snowflake is the work of far too many people to list here. We would like to thank the entire Snowflake engineering team for their contributions to the product, and for all the hard work, effort, and pride they put into it. We also would like to thank all the other "Snowflakes" for their amazing work in bringing this product to the users and building a great company together. We are continuously impressed and humbled to work with such an excellent team.

8. REFERENCES

[1] D. J. Abadi, S. R. Madden, and N. Hachem. Column-stores vs. row-stores: How different are they really? In *Proc. SIGMOD*, 2008.

[2] A. Ailamaki, D. J. DeWitt, M. D. Hill, and M. Skounakis. Weaving relations for cache performance. In *Proc. VLDB*, 2001.

[3] S. Alsubaiee et al. AsterixDB: A scalable, open source DBMS. *PVLDB*, 7(14):1905–1916, 2014.

[4] Amazon Elastic Compute Cloud (EC2). aws.amazon.com/ec2/instance-types.

[5] Amazon Simple Storage Service (S3). aws.amazon.com/s3.

[6] Apache Cassandra. cassandra.apache.org.

[7] Apache Drill. drill.apache.org.

[8] Apache Hadoop. hadoop.apache.org.

[9] Apache Hive. hive.apache.org.

[10] Apache Parquet. parquet.apache.org.

[11] Apache Spark. spark.apache.org.

[12] AWS CloudHSM. aws.amazon.com/cloudhsm.

[13] E. Barker. *NIST SP 800-57 – Recommendation for Key Management – Part 1: General (Revision 4)*, chapter 7. 2016.

[14] J. Barr. AWS Import/Export Snowball – Transfer 1 petabyte per week using Amazon-owned storage appliances. aws.amazon.com/blogs/aws/aws-importexport-snowball-transfer-1-petabyte-per-week-using-amazon-owned-storage-appliances/, 2015.

[15] P. Boncz, M. Zukowski, and N. Nes. MonetDB/X100: Hyper-pipelining query execution. In *Proc. CIDR*, 2005.

[16] V. R. Borkar, M. J. Carey, and C. Li. Big data platforms: What's next? *ACM Crossroads*, 19(1):44–49, 2012.

[17] M. J. Cahill, U. Röhm, and A. D. Fekete. Serializable isolation for snapshot databases. In *Proc. SIGMOD*, 2008.

[18] B. Calder et al. Windows Azure Storage: A highly available storage service with strong consistency. In *Proc. SOSP*, 2011.

[19] Cassandra Query Language (CQL). cassandra.apache.org/doc/cql3/CQL.html.

[20] Cloud Storage – Google Cloud Platform. cloud.google.com/storage.

[21] Cloudera Impala. impala.io.

[22] Couchbase N1QL. couchbase.com/n1ql.

[23] Couchbase Server. couchbase.com.

[24] D. J. DeWitt, A. Halverson, R. Nehme, S. Shankar, J. Aguilar-Saborit, A. Avanes, M. Flasza, and J. Gramling. Split query processing in Polybase. In *Proc. SIGMOD*, 2013.

[25] D. J. DeWitt, S. Madden, and M. Stonebraker. How to build a high-performance data warehouse. db.csail.mit.edu/madden/high_perf.pdf, 2006.

[26] D. Ferraiolo, D. R. Kuhn, and R. Chandramouli. *Role-based access control*. Artech House Publishers, 2003.

[27] G. Graefe. Volcano: An extensible and parallel query evaluation system. *IEEE TKDE*, 6(1), 1994.

[28] G. Graefe. The cascades framework for query optimization. *Data Engineering Bulletin*, 18, 1995.

[29] G. Graefe. Fast loads and fast queries. In *Data Warehousing and Knowledge Discovery*, volume 5691 of *LNCS*. Springer, 2009.

[30] A. Gupta et al. Amazon Redshift and the case for simpler data warehouses. In *Proc. SIGMOD*, 2015.

[31] D. Karger, E. Lehman, T. Leighton, R. Panigrahy, M. Levine, and D. Lewin. Consistent hashing and random trees: Distributed caching protocols for relieving hot spots on the world wide web. In *Proc. STOC*, 1997.

[32] J. Krueger, M. Grund, C. Tinnefeld, H. Plattner, A. Zeier, and F. Faerber. Optimizing write performance for read optimized databases. In *Proc. DASFAA*, 2010.

[33] S. Manegold, M. L. Kersten, and P. Boncz. Database architecture evolution: Mammals flourished long before dinosaurs became extinct. *PVLDB*, 2(2):1648–1653, 2009.

[34] S. Melnik, A. Gubarev, J. J. Long, G. Romer, S. Shivakumar, M. Tolton, and T. Vassilakis. Dremel: Interactive analysis of web-scale datasets. *PVLDB*, 3(1-2):330–339, 2010.

[35] Microsoft Analytics Platform System. www.microsoft.com/en-us/server-cloud/products/analytics-platform-system.

[36] Microsoft Azure Blob Storage. azure.microsoft.com/en-us/services/storage/blobs.

[37] Microsoft Azure SQL DW. azure.microsoft.com/en-us/services/sql-data-warehouse.

[38] G. Moerkotte. Small materialized aggregates: A light weight index structure for data warehousing. In *Proc. VLDB*, 1998.

[39] MongoDB. mongodb.com.

[40] J. K. Mullin. Optimal semijoins for distributed database systems. *IEEE TSE*, 16(5):558–560, 1990.

[41] T. Neumann. Efficiently compiling efficient query plans for modern hardware. *PVLDB*, 4(9):539–550, 2011.

[42] A. Pavlo, E. Paulson, A. Rasin, D. J. Abadi, D. J. DeWitt, S. Madden, and M. Stonebraker. A comparison of approaches to large-scale data analysis. In *Proc. SIGMOD*, 2009.

[43] Presto. prestodb.io.

[44] K. Sato. An inside look at Google BigQuery. cloud.google.com/files/BigQueryTechnicalWP.pdf, 2012.

[45] J. Schad, J. Dittrich, and J.-A. Quiané-Ruiz. Runtime measurements in the cloud: Observing, analyzing, and reducing variance. *PVLDB*, 3(1):460–471, 2010.

[46] K. Shvachko, H. Kuang, S. Radia, and R. Chansler. The Hadoop distributed file system. In *Proc. MSST*, 2010.

[47] SQL DW Concurrency. azure.microsoft.com/en-us/documentation/articles/sql-data-warehouse-develop-concurrency.

[48] Stinger.next: Enterprise SQL at Hadoop scale. hortonworks.com/innovation/stinger.

[49] L. Sun, M. J. Franklin, S. Krishnan, and R. S. Xin. Fine-grained partitioning for aggressive data skipping. In *Proc. SIGMOD*, 2014.

Closing the functional and Performance Gap between SQL and NoSQL

Zhen Hua Liu, Beda Hammerschmidt, Doug McMahon, Ying Lu, Hui Joe Chang

Oracle Corporation

500 Oracle Parkway

Redwood Shores, CA 94065, USA

{zhen.liu, beda.hammerschmidt, doug.mcmahon, ying.lu, hui.x.zhang}@oracle.com

ABSTRACT

Oracle release 12cR1 supports JSON data management that enables users to store, index and query JSON data along with relational data. The integration of the JSON data model into the RDBMS allows a new paradigm of data management where data is storable, indexable and queryable without upfront schema definition. We call this new paradigm **Flexible Schema Data Management** (FSDM). In this paper, we present enhancements to Oracle's JSON data management in the upcoming 12cR2 release. We present **JSON DataGuide,** an auto-computed dynamic soft schema for JSON collections that closes the functional gap between the fixed-schema SQL world and the schema-less NoSQL world. We present a self-contained query friendly binary format for encoding JSON (**OSON**) to close the query performance gap between schema-encoded relational data and schema free JSON textual data. The addition of these new features makes the Oracle RDBMS well suited to both fixed-schema SQL and flexible-schema NoSQL use cases, and allows users to freely mix the two paradigms in a single data management system.

Categories and Subject Descriptors

H.2.4 [**Database Management**]: Systems – *Relational databases, transaction processing.*

General Terms

Algorithms, Management, Performance, Design, Standardization, Languages.

Keywords

JSON, SQL/JSON, Schema-less, Flexible Schema, NoSQL, XML, SQL/XML.

1. INTRODUCTION

Using a 'schema first, data later' approach, RDBMS platforms are very successful at managing well-structured relational data. NoSQL systems [4] are challenging this with a 'data first, schema later or never' paradigm. The fixed-schema paradigm of relational data management, which demands a schema before data can be stored and queried, is at odds with the NoSQL world where a variety of data in continually changing forms is available from diverse data sources. To address these challenges, the Oracle 12cR1 release supports JSON as a simple and practical example of FSDM to unleash the power of schema-less data management [21]. It is based on following three engineering principals originating from ORDBMS [11, 13]:

- Storing JSON objects as aggregated, self-described entities without shredding them into relational rows and columns. That is, embracing the document-object storage model. This resolves the "birth pain" usability problem of the schema-rigid classical RDBMS SQL world [8].
- Indexing JSON using a schema-agnostic strategy to support ad-hoc queries that search both schema and values together. That is, extending inverted index technology to index both data and schema together [18]. This resolves the problem of requiring knowledge of the query workload before an index can be defined in fixed-schema systems.
- Querying JSON using SQL as the inter-document query language and SQL/JSON path language as the intra-document query language [21]. This avoids the problem of creating a brand-new set-query language, such as JSONiq [12], to query JSON only.

These three principals have enabled FSDM [32] in RDBMS. However, we don't think that the relational model and SQL are out-dated [1] due to the demand for FSDM. The strength of the relational model [5] is that it avoids imposing a single hierarchy to manage data, and the strength of SQL is its ability to deliver powerful data analytics with its set-based declarative query language. These strengths motivate us to integrate FSDM capabilities with the relational model and with SQL. Our key insight is this: rather than integrate the two worlds by trying to impose a fixed relational schema into which FSD would be decomposed, we integrate them by dynamically projecting a relational schema **continuously derived** from collections of FSD instances. This **logical dynamic schema** allows users to view and query FSD relationally. *That is, a relational schema is not constructed as a physical frame to fit the data but rather as a logical lens to view the data.* We don't use schema to encode and store data, so FSD physical storage is free from the need for schema evolution.

To realize this vision, a relational view over JSON data can be defined using the SQL/JSON query construct JSON_TABLE() as a virtual function to derive relational rows from JSON data [21]. Once JSON relational views are defined, users can write queries on top of the relational views to achieve compile time schema check with the rich analytic power of SQL fully applied to JSON

SIGMOD'16, June 26–July 1, 2016, San Francisco, California, USA.

ACM 978-1-4503-3531-7/16/06…$15.00.
http://dx.doi.org/10.1145/2588555.2595628

data. To define such JSON_TABLE() views, users would need to figure out the implied schema within a collection of JSON instances so that they can write the SQL/JSON paths needed by the JSON_TABLE() operator. For relational data, the problem of deriving the relational schema from the data and then registering the relational schema with the RDBMS is traditionally accepted by the developers of the relational application. In FSDM, the schema derivation problem is the responsibility of the underlying DBMS. The "birth pain" [8] experienced by users in fixed-schema systems is resolved by having an FSD enabled RDBMS that *automatically computes and maintains the implied schema for an FSD collection and assists users in defining relational views to allow SQL access to the data.*

The computed schema must be *dynamic*: it must continually evolve as instances are added to or changed within FSD collections. For a JSON collection, the automatically computed schema should include a derivation of all the hierarchical structural paths that exist in that JSON collection, as well as the data types and statistics of leaf scalar values. We call this automatically-maintained schema the **JSON DataGuide**. We support two forms of the JSON DataGuide: persistent and transient. The persistent DataGuide is provided as a component of a schema agnostic JSON search index [21]. The transient schema is provided as a new SQL aggregate function over any JSON collections that can be computed from SQL declaratively. The concept of DataGuide has introduced a powerful new paradigm: "*write without schema, read with schema*". That is, users can store data without providing a schema definition, but they can still query the data as if a schema were defined and registered to the system ahead of storing the data. This is the key value proposition for the FSD enabled RDBMS.

The RDBMS uses relational schema information to encode data for storage and to decode data for query. The row format is optimized for fast query performance. To achieve query performance and minimize the storage size, row data is not self-describing; an external schema describing column meta-data is necessary to interpret the columns within the data. An FSD enabled RDBMS is **not** able to rely on column schema to encode data. Therefore, it needs an efficient binary format to encode data for fast query performance without relying on the existence of a central schema for column meta-data. For JSON, we have developed a binary format, called **OSON** (Oracle binary JSON encoding), to meet these requirements. OSON is a self-contained, compact representation of a tree of structures, arrays, and scalars. It's designed to provide rapid navigation to elements of the tree to resolve SQL/JSON path expressions. OSON bytes can be encoded from JSON text [10], BSON [16] or AVRO [15], and may either be stored persistently or loaded and used as structures in memory by Oracle's in-memory database option[19] for fast SQL/JSON query processing.

The main contributions of this paper are:

- To bridge the functional gap between the fixed-schema world of SQL and the schema-less NoSQL world, we introduce the concept of a DataGuide, a logical dynamic soft schema in RDBMS. We describe a practical SQL based solution to compute and maintain the DataGuide declaratively and automatically for both persistent and transient JSON collections so that they can be accessed relationally. The key idea here is that in an FSD enabled RDBMS, schema is no longer static meta-data but rather dynamically and continuously derivable via SQL over FSD collections.
- To bridge the performance gap between fixed-schema encoding of relational data and schema free JSON textual data, we describe a self-contained, compact binary encoding of JSON (OSON) which can be an order of magnitude faster than textual JSON for supporting SQL/JSON queries. The OSON format needs no central schema for column meta-data but still gives column data access performance that is close to a schema encoded row format.
- To bridge the conceptual gap between SQL and NoSQL world, we practically integrate the idea of '**Schema-less for Write**' from NoSQL [4] world and '**Schema-Rich for declarative Query**' from SQL world [5] through management of JSON data in a single RDBMS product without the need of polyglot persistence [7] . 'Schema-less for write' resolves the schema birth pain problem [8] and continuous schema evolution problem associated with classical RDBMS. 'Schema rich for declarative query' resolves the issue of developing code to discover data schema and to procedurally query data associated with pure NoSQL data stores. Figure 1 shows our architecture of connecting SQL and NoSQL world on top of a single RDBMS platform with SQL remains as declarative set query language.

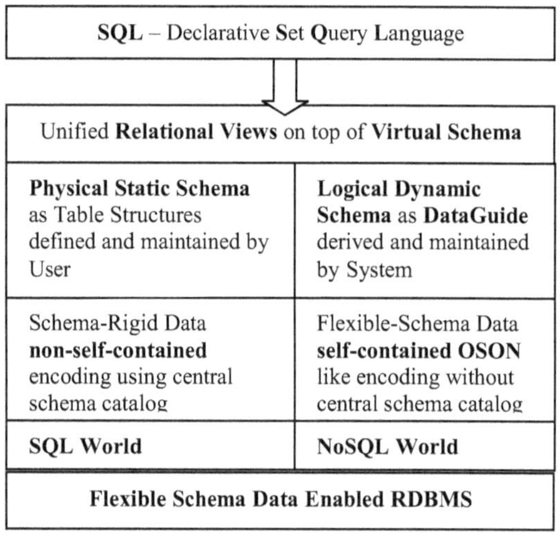

Figure 1 – Architecture connecting SQL and NoSQL World

Outline: Section 2 compares our work to related work. Section 3 describes the JSON DataGuide in detail. Section 4 describes the OSON design in detail. Section 5 describes SQL/JSON performance enhancements using OSON. Section 6 presents an evaluation of performance. Section 7 discusses future work. Section 8 concludes the paper with acknowledgements.

2. RELATED WORK

NoSQL vendors [4] have used JSON as a simple semi-structured data format for the document object model. RDBMS vendors are integrating support for JSON data with their SQL engines, including IBM DB2 [29], Microsoft SQL Server [25], TeraData [26], Vertica [27] and Oracle 12cR1 [21]. Another popular approach is to add a level of abstraction over polyglot persistence in middle-tier code. One example of this approach is Sinew [22]. However, Oracle 12cR2 takes this a step further. Recognizing that the lack of a schema presents a challenge in schema-less NoSQL world, Oracle offers the JSON DataGuide, allowing users to write queries over JSON collections with a de facto schema continuously derived from the instance documents. Concept of DataGuide was proposed by researchers in the LORE system [28]. Dynamic discovery and extraction of schema from a document store was presented in [20]. However, both these prior efforts dealt only with pure document store database, not in SQL based RDBMS. Our unique contribution is to deeply integrate DataGuide as a dynamic schema facility with existing SQL mechanisms: view, virtual column, index and aggregation. Our JSON DataGuide service provides automatic and customizable generation of SQL/JSON JSON_TABLE() based relational views for nested hierarchical documents, and virtual columns for singleton scalar values. While the flexible table approach of Vertica [40] is limited to singleton scalar fields from JSON collection, our approach handles JSON array expansion gracefully using the *NESTED PATH-* construct of JSON_TABLE(). That is, the contents of JSON arrays are un-nested automatically and become directly available to SQL queries as simple columns.

Unlike approach in Sinew [22], our JSON DataGuide is fully integrated with the Oracle RDBMS kernel and the SQL language. We provide support for both persistent and transient dynamic schemas. The *persistent JSON DataGuide* is integrated as a component of a schema agnostic JSON search index, ensuring that both discovery and search of JSON structures are completely in synch. Using a single index, users can discover JSON path structures within a collection, as well as what documents within the collection have particular path structures and values. The *transient JSON Dataguide* is provided as a SQL aggregation function. With this, computing an ad-hoc JSON DataGuide is simple, flexible, and declarative, and can be accomplished in one SQL statement!

There are number of popular binary encoding formats for hierarchical data objects, among them BSON [16], AVRO [15], and Protocol Buffers [14]. None of these is fast enough for all query situations, because the serialization formats lack efficient random field access, as discussed in Sinew[22]. Like Sinew [22], OSON encoding supports efficient random field access. Unlike Sinew [22], the OSON format is self-contained and doesn't rely on an external central catalog system to manage attribute ids. We have found that depending on such an external system is tantamount to maintaining a schema: exactly what users are trying to avoid with these NoSQL stores. The OSON format supports arbitrary SQL/JSON path navigation query efficiently. The self-contained format makes OSON as portable as JSON text or BSON binaries while still providing rapid random tree navigation; in contrast, BSON and textual JSON must be accessed in a serial fashion, with at best the ability to perform skip navigation. Although tree-encoding for XML is done in DB2 XML storage format [2], our OSON design is compact tree format: well-suited both as a persistent format and as the basis for an in-memory format. Our OSON and virtual column query access is tightly integrated with Oracle in-memory database architecture [19]. To the best of our knowledge, this is the first industrial paper that provides comprehensive SQL solution for providing dynamic schema support for JSON and in-memory query processing for JSON and thus towards the direction of closing schema and performance gap between SQL world and NoSQL world.

The comparison of OSON format and Dremel [24] representation is discussed in section 7.

3. JSON DataGuide

3.1 JSON DataGuide Conceptual Description

JSON is a language-neutral representation of data structures and scalar types common across different programming languages. The JSON data model is hierarchical and can be regarded as consisting of three types of nodes arranged in a node tree. The three node types are JSON objects, JSON arrays, and JSON scalars. JSON objects are structures consisting of key/value pairs with string keys and node values. JSON arrays are ordered lists of node values. JSON objects and JSON arrays are both considered container nodes. JSON scalars are always leaf values and may be strings, numbers, booleans, or null. A JSON document can be parsed and constructed as a JSON DOM tree using the JSON data model. SQL/JSON path language semantics [21] are based on the JSON DOM model.

A JSON DataGuide for a single JSON document instance is computed by extracting the container node *skeleton* of the JSON DOM tree. Leaf scalar values are replaced by data type and length. A JSON DataGuide for a collection of JSON documents is simply a merge of the instance DataGuides across all documents in the collection. The merge union process removes duplicate tree paths if they have the same tree node type for each step in the path. Paths having different tree node types at any step are considered different. Leaf scalar data information is merged by replacing conflicting data types with a more general type, and using the maximum length.

As an example of path merge, in one JSON document, path *'$.a.b'* with node *"b"* is a scalar tree node type, while in another JSON document, path *'$.a.b'* with node *"b"* is an object node type. The merged JSON DataGuide keeps both paths: *'$.a.b'* as a scalar node type and as an object node type, respectively. As an example of merging scalar nodes, in one JSON document, path *'$.a.b'* is a number, while in another JSON document, path *'$.a.b'* is a string. The resulting JSON DataGuide keeps one structural path *'$.a.b'* as scalar tree node type with *string* as leaf data type.

The JSON collection is stored in a column with an 'IS JSON' check constraint created. For such a persistent JSON column, we support a persistent JSON DataGuide that is incrementally maintained as new JSON documents are inserted into the collection.

3.2 Persistent JSON DataGuide Maintenance

3.2.1 DataGuide Evolution with DML

Consider a JSON column **JDOC** of a table **PO** storing the following purchaseOrder JSON documents. There is a nested detail hierarchy *"items"* under the master *"purchaseorder"* in each document.

DID	JDOC
1	*{"purchaseOrder":{"id" : 1, "podate" : "2014-09-08", "items" : [{"name":"phone" , "price" : 100, "quantity" : 2}, {"name":"ipad", "price" : 350.86, "quantity" : 3}]}}*
2	*{"purchaseOrder":{"id" : 2, "podate" : "2015-03-04", "items" : [{"name":"table" , "price" : 52.78, "quantity" : 2}, {"name":"chair", "price" : 35.24, "quantity" : 4}]}}*

Table 1 – JSON PurchaseOrder Collection

A persistent JSON DataGuide is maintained as a component of the JSON search index. The JSON search index is a general purpose schema agnostic index created on a JSON column by maintaining an inverted index for every JSON field name and every leaf scalar value (strings are tokenized into a set of keywords to support full-text searches). The index allows ad-hoc SQL/JSON path query predicates such as *JSON_EXISTS()*, *JSON_TEXTCONTAINS()*, and *JSON_VALUE()* to be evaluated efficiently [21] over the JSON collection. The JSON search index is the most natural place to support JSON DataGuide maintenance because this index is incrementally maintained when documents in the index JSON column are added, removed, or replaced. *To minimize the overhead, the DataGuide maintenance is incorporated directly into the processing of the IS JSON check constraint.* In the common case where a new JSON instance doesn't result in any new path structures or scalar node changes, the DataGuide processing terminates without the need to call any persistent DataGuide processing module.

The JSON search index internally stores the persistent JSON DataGuide in a relational table $DG. Using the data from Table 1 as an example, the contents of the $DG table are shown in Table 2. The $DG table captures all the distinct paths in the JSON document collection with its leaf type.

Path	Type
$.purchaseOrder	object
$.purchaseOrder.id	number
$.purchaseOrder.podate	string
$.purchaseOrder.items	array
$.purchaseOrder.items.name	array of string
$.purchaseOrder.items.price	array of number
$.purchaseOrder.items.quantity	array of number

Table 2 – JSON DataGuide Relational Format in $DG

To show how the DataGuide evolves in the face of new instances, consider what happens when the document shown in Table 3 is added to the collection. Note a new child object *"parts"* is added below the existing "*items*" array – this causes the DataGuide to grow **deeper**. A new top-level *"foreign_id"* field is also added.

DID	JDOC
3	{"purhcaseOrder":{"id" : 2, "podate" : "2015-06-03", **"foreign_id" : "CDEG35",** "items" : [{"name":"TV" , "price" : 345.55, "quantity" : 1, **"parts" : [** **{"partName" : "remoteCon", "partQuantity" : "1"},** **{"partName" : "antenna", "partQuantity" : "2"}** **]** }, {"name":"PC", "price" : 546.78, "quantity" : 10, **"parts" :** **[** **{"partName" : "mouse", "partQuantity" : "2"},** **{"partName" : "keyboard", "partQuantity" : "1"},** **]** }]}}

Table 3 – introducing a new child hierarchy

JSON search index maintenance inserts 4 new rows into $DG (see Table 4) to reflect the new path structures encountered for the document shown in Table 3.

Path	Type
$.purchaseOrder.items.parts	array of array
$.purchaseOrder.items.parts.partName	array of string
$.purchaseOrder.items.parts.partQuantity	array of string
$.purchaseOrder.foreign_id	string

Table 4 – four new rows added into $DG

Now consider what happens when the document show in Table 5 is added to the collection. A new hierarchy *"discount_items"* is added as a sibling of existing node "*items*" – this causes the DataGuide to grow **wider**.

DID	JDOC
4	{"purchaseOrder":{"id" : 98, "podate" : "2015-07-04", "items" : [{"name":"CD" , "price" : 5.55, "quantity" : 10, }, {"name":"DVD", "price" : 6.78, "quantity" : 20, }], **"discount_items":** **[** **{"dis_itemName" : "CPH", "dis_itemPrice" : 105.52, "dis_itemQuanitty":2,** **"dis_parts" :** **[** **{"dis_partName" : "phonejack", "dis_partQuantity" : 3},** **{"dis_partName" : "plug", "dis_partQuantity" : 2},** **]** **},** **{"dis_itemName" : "Printer", "dis_itemPrice" : 121.33,** **"dis_itemQuanitty":9,** **"dis_parts" :** **[** **{"dis_partName" : "toner", "dis_partQuantity" : 5},** **{"dis_partName" : "paper", "dis_partQuantity" : 20},** **]** **}** **]** }}

Table 5 - introducing a new sibling hierarchy

JSON search index maintenance inserts 7 new rows into $DG (see Table 6) to reflect the new path structures encountered for the document shown in Table 5.

Path	Type
$.purchaseOrder. discount_items	array of array
$.purchaseOrder. discount_items.dis_parts	array of array
$.purchaseorder. discount_items.dis_parts.dis_partName	array of string
$.purchaseOrder. discount_items.dis_parts.dis_partQuantity	array of number
$.purchaseOrder.discount_items.dis_itemName	array of string
$.purchaseOrder.discount_items.dis_itemPrice	array of number
$.purchaseOrder.discount_items.dis_itemQuanitty	array of number

Table 6 - seven new rows added into $DG

In addition to storing path and type information, the $DG table also has columns that store statistical information for a path such as frequency, minimum and maximum values, and number of null values. These statistical columns are populated when the JSON search index statistics are computed.

3.2.2 DataGuide Representation

The Persistent dataGuide can be presented in two forms: a *flatten form* as what is stored in $DG table and a *hierarchical form* with nested structures. Both forms are encoded as a JSON document that can be returned as a CLOB by invoking a PL/SQL function *getDataGuide()* from persistent indexing layer. In particular, this function can aggregate the information from the $DG table into a hierarchical format represented as a single JSON document. Users can annotate the computed DataGuide by picking fields, re-naming column names, changing the maximum length of data types, etc., and then call *CreateViewOnPath()* with the annotated DataGuide to generate customized relational views discussed in section 3.3.2.

3.3 Virtual Relational Schema for JSON

To realize the benefit of *'write without schema, read with schema'*, Oracle provides PL/SQL procedures to assist users in projecting relational views and virtual columns of the data, driven by information from the JSON DataGuide. The DataGuide is used as a dynamic schema to automatically compose SQL/JSON operators, making JSON data appear as if it were physically shredded and stored in master detail relational tables.

3.3.1 Adding Virtual Columns (VC) using JSON_VALUE()

With JSON DataGuide computed, user can run a PL/SQL procedure *AddVC()* to automatically add virtual columns to the base table. Each virtual column is defined using JSON_VALUE() to project a singleton scalar value out of the JSON document. Using the JSON DataGuide presented in section 3.2 as a starting point, Table 7 shows the definition of 3 virtual columns that are added to PO table via *AddVC()* calls. These virtual columns can be referenced in a query as if these fields in base JSON document were physically shredded and stored in them.

VC Name	VC
JCOL$id	*JSON_VALUE(JCOL, '$.purchaseOrder.id returning number)*
JCOL$podate	*JSON_VALUE(JCOL, '$.purchaseOrder.podate' returning varchar(16))*
JCOL$foreign_id	*JSON_VALUE(JCOL, '$.purchaseOrder.foreign_id returning varchar(8))*

Table 7 – JSON_VALUE() Virtual Columns

3.3.2 Creating De-normalized Master-Detail Views (DMDV) using JSON_TABLE()

Virtual columns can only project singleton scalar values; that is, values having a one-to-one relationship with document instances. Often, however, scalar values relevant to queries are nested within arrays and have a many-to-one relationship with document instances. If shredded into relational tables, the most natural way to view them is to form a left outer join of master record to detail records so that fields from a master record are repeated for each detail record. The outer join is used instead of an inner join to ensure that master records are captured in the view even if there are no matching detail records. In cases where there are more than one sibling detail arrays to be joined for the same master record, fields from the sibling records can be exposed using a union join. A union join is equivalent to a full outer join with an impossible condition, such as 0=1. By design, the default of the JSON_TABLE() *NESTED PATH* clause is to un-nest JSON arrays with left-outer join semantics for child hierarchies and do a union join for sibling hierarchies. With JSON DataGuide computed, user can run a PL/SQL procedure *CreateViewOnPath()* to automatically create a JSON_TABLE() view. We call such views as De-normalized Master Detail Views (DMDV) because the output is the same as the output of a view over physically decomposed master detail tables using the outer join and union constructs that we just described. DMDV is structurally similar to the wide table described in [30]. Table 8 shows the definition of a DMDV generated by calling *CreateViewOnPath('$')* . Users can also generate a DMDV view for a particular path. For example, users can generate a DMDV view for the items detail branch alone by executing *CreateViewOnPath('$.purchaseOrder.items')*. If JSON index statistics are collected, then frequency information can be passed to *CreateViewOnPath()* to project fields only if they occur more frequently than a given threshold value. In this way, sparse and outlier fields can be eliminated as columns of the DMDV.

```
CREATE VIEW PO_RV AS
SELECT PO.DID, JT.*
FROM PO, JSON_TABLE("JCOL" FORMAT JSON, '$'
COLUMNS
 "JCOL$id" number path '$.purchaseOrder.id',
 "JCOL$podate" varchar2(16) path '$.purchaseOrder.podate',
 "JCOL$foreign_id" varchar2(8) path '$.purchaseOrder.foreign_id',
NESTED PATH '$.purchaseOrder.items[*]' /*NP1*/
 COLUMNS (
  "JCOL$name" varchar2(8) path '$.name',
  "JCOL$price" number path '$.price',
  "JCOL$quantity" number path '$.quantity'),
 NESTED PATH '$.parts[*]' /*NP2*/
  COLUMNS ("JCOL$partName" varchar2(16) path '$.partName',
           "JCOL$part Quantity" varchar2(1) path '$.partQuantity'),
NESTED PATH '$.purhcaseorder.discount_items[*]' /*NP3*/
 COLUMNS (
  NESTED PATH '$.dis_parts[*]' /*NP4*/
   COLUMNS ("JCOL$dis_partName" varchar2(16) path '$.dis_partName',
            "JCOL$dis_partQuantity" number path '$.dis_partQuantity'),
            "JCOL$dis_itemName" varchar2(8) path '$.dis_itemName',
            "JCOL$dis_itemPrice" number path '$.dis_itemPrice',
            "JCOL$dis_itemQuanitty" number path '$.dis_itemQuanitty') ) JT
/* NP1 & NP2 are left outer join, so do NP3 & NP4; NP1 & NP3 are union join */
```

Table 8 – JSON_TABLE() DMDV View

3.4 Transient JSON DataGuide Computation

Note, persistent JSON DataGuide is additive, it does not remove paths for documents that are deleted. However, a JSON DataGuide can be computed dynamically by executing a SQL aggregation function *JSON_DataGuideAgg()* over the result of any SQL query returning a set of JSON documents. JSON_DATAGuideAgg() is implemented using user defined aggregation framework from ORDBMS [11,13]. It computes and returns JSON DataGuide as a single JSON document in either flatten form or hierarchical form as discussed in section 3.2.2. Table 9 shows SQL queries that compute transient JSON DataGuide. Q1 computes the DataGuide by sampling 50% of JSON documents in a JSON collection. Q2 computes the DataGuide group by their insertion date. Q3 computes the DataGuide for a filtered subset of JSON documents that have JSON path *'$.purchaseOrder.foreign_id'*. Integrating JSON DataGuide as a SQL aggregation function provides declarative way to compute DataGuide for JSON collection that may not be stored in Oracle. For example, Oracle external table can map file system data as virtual relational table on top of which JSON DataGuide can be computed and DMDV view can be created for query. Oracle SQL/JSON query support can transparently read from external virtual table and thus enables the In-Situ Query processing over JSON collection.

Q1	*Select json_dataguideagg(jcol) from po sample (50)*
Q2	*Select json_dataguideagg(jcol) from po group by insertion_date*
Q3	*Select json_dataguideagg(jcol) from po where json_exists(jcol, '$.purchaseOrder.foreign_id')*

Table 9 – Example queries computing JSON DataGuide Transiently

4. JSON Binary Format: OSON

4.1 OSON Design Criteria

In the classic relational approach to data management, schema information is separated from instance data, with the schema being defined in a central dictionary and then used to encode data instances for storage. In contrast, flexible storage models typically store metadata together with data instances, such that instances can be decoded and understood without the need to refer to a central dictionary. Self-contained JSON document instances can be more easily distributed, replicated, imported, exported, evolved, without the need for costly synchronization. *This property of self-containment is the first design criteria for our binary JSON format.*

BSON [16] is self-contained and is readable without costly textual parsing. The BSON format has a symmetric structure for nested child containers. Because of this, child containers can be extracted or inserted by simply copying byte ranges, a potentially big advantage when doing projections. Because containers have leading length words, a BSON decoder can skip unneeded child containers without decoding all of their descendants. The cost of nested symmetry is that the BSON format needs to store field names at each object level, and must repeat them for elements within arrays of objects. JSON path evaluations involving field name searches require relatively expensive string comparisons. A lesser problem is that field names are null terminated, necessitating a byte scan for the end of the field name string during searches. Finally, BSON, like JSON, is a stream format potentially requiring that an entire instance be read to resolve a JSON path, or, worse, to determine that it's not present in the instance. *Enabling readers to jump inexpensively to named fields and array locations is our second design criteria.*

JSON scalars can be numbers, strings, or Booleans. In binary formats this set is commonly extended to include date, timestamp, and raw data types. The SQL/JSON path language and SQL/JSON operators such as JSON_TABLE() support type-aware operations, such as type-based comparison semantics and arithmetic expressions. In a binary format, scalars can be stored in a format native to the database engine for maximum performance, especially when values pass between the JSON and SQL worlds. *Encoding scalar values in the same binary format as our SQL scalar columns is our third design criteria.*

4.2 OSON Format: Three-Segment Architecture

The OSON format separates a JSON document into 3 segments: a field-id-name dictionary segment, a tree node navigation segment and a leaf scalar value segment with navigation segment containing references to dictionary and value segment as shown in Figure 2. This division is done to reflect the different loading and access properties.

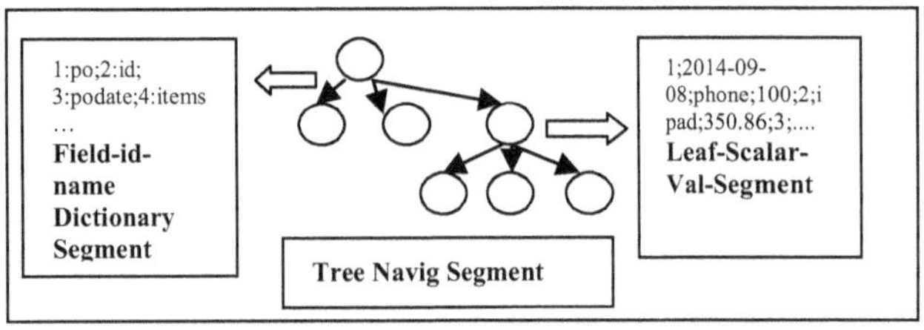

Figure 2 – OSON Format Architecture

4.2.1 Field-id-name-dictionary segment

Each unique field name within a JSON document is assigned an integer field name identifier and is stored only once so that multiple references to the same field name are replaced with its field name identifier. Because the identifiers take just a few bytes, the OSON encoding typically saves significant space when the original document has a nested array of sub-objects, or encodes a recursive hierarchical structure. *The biggest benefit of assigning identifiers is that they can facilitate rapid navigation to a child field given by performing a binary search using integer comparisons.* OSON stores the field name identifiers for each object in **sorted** order to support this type of access.

The field-id-name dictionary segment is responsible for providing a fast dictionary mapping between a field name and a field name identifier. The assignment of a field name identifier to a field name is done arbitrary using a hash function. The OSON encoder applies the hash function to each distinct field name referenced in a JSON document and builds a hash table containing all such mappings for the document. The hash table is compacted into a hash-id-array. Each array entry stores the field name and the hash id of the field name. The entire hash-id-array is **sorted** by the hash ids. *The ordinal position of an array entry containing a field name is used as the field name identifier for that field name.* To look up a field name identifier given a field name, we first apply the hash function to the field name to get its hash id. Then we perform a binary search on the hash-id-array using the hash id to locate the array entries having that hash id. Finally, we perform a field name string match to resolve any possible hash collisions.

To avoid repeatedly calling the hash function on field names and to avoid field name identifier lookup altogether, we have applied the following optimizations to the SQL/JSON query compilation and execution time.

- During the SQL query compilation phase, all SQL/JSON paths are compiled. The same hash function is called on all distinct field name references in all SQL/JSON paths so that their corresponding hash ids are stored in the SQL execution query plan.
- During SQL execution time, as the SQL/JSON path query is applied to each OSON instance, we use the pre-computed hash id and the field name that are stored in the execution plan to find the field name identifier using the field-id-name dictionary segment. This is done once for the OSON instance; afterwards, all field name searches are efficiently executed as binary searches using the instance-specific field name identifier.
- Finally, when the SQL/JSON path query is applied to the next OSON instance, the mapping determined on the previous OSON instance is checked to see if it matches the next instance. This single-row look-back is very effective on collections of structurally homogeneous JSON document instances, because the same field name identifiers are most likely used repeatedly, and therefore the cost of field-id resolution can often be skipped.

4.2.2 Tree-node Navigation Segment

The tree node navigation segment of OSON represents the JSON document as a tree-like skeleton of nodes that supports navigation from a parent node to its child nodes. There are 3 types of JSON tree nodes: JSON object nodes, JSON array nodes, and JSON scalar nodes. Each node is identified by its byte offset location from the beginning of the tree-node navigation segment. The byte offset is used as the tree node address and is stored in the child array of the parent tree node to jump to the child tree node. Each node has a common tree node header byte storing the type of the node (Object, Array, Scalar), and property flags that vary depending on the type of the node.

- For a JSON object node, the child array stores all of its children's field name identifiers and their corresponding tree node addresses. The array is sorted by the field name identifiers to support rapid navigation to the child node given its field name.
- For a JSON array node, the child array stores all of its children's node addresses. The child in Nth array position is accessed by taking the child node's offset from the Nth position in the array.
- For a JSON scalar node, this records the data type of the scalar value and an offset into the leaf-scalar-value segment where the data bytes are located. JSON boolean and null values are directly encoded as bit flags in the JSON scalar node and therefore have no offset. For fixed length scalar values, the length is inferred from the data type. For variable

length scalar values, bit flags are used to indicate if the length is encoded using one, two, or four bytes.

4.2.3 Leaf-scalar-value segment

The leaf-scalar-value segment is comprised of all leaf values in a JSON object instance. The bytes representing the values are concatenated together to form this segment. Each leaf scalar value is found by its byte offset from the beginning of the segment. The byte offset is used as the leaf value address and is stored in the JSON scalar node. For variable length data items, a length is stored before its value. For fixed length data, no length is stored. By default, OSON uses the Oracle binary number format to encode JSON numbers, minimizing the cost of using these values in SQL. JSON numbers can also be encoded using IEEE double-precision format, or encoded as strings in a canonical format.

No binary format is optimally efficient in its support for queries and updates. In designing OSON, we opted to maximize path query efficiency, so partial update support is limited to changes of existing leaf scalar values. However, we will work on enhancing OSON format to make intelligent trade-off to be more update friendly to handle future SQL/JSON partial object update language requirement.

5. SQL/JSON Query Performance Improvement

5.1 JSON DOM Path Engine using OSON based JSON DOM implementation

To evaluate SQL/JSON operators on textual JSON documents, we developed a JSON path engine that operates in a streaming fashion, using a series of *events* produced by the JSON text parser. These events allow evaluation of SQL/JSON operators without the need to materialize JSON objects in memory as document object model (DOM) instances. Generating the events requires costly text parsing. Worse still, evaluation of more complex operators requires the engine to memorize event sequences, in effect partially or completely negating the benefit of avoiding DOM construction. These operators include the JSON_TABLE() virtual table [21] as well as complex JSON_EXISTS predicates. In many cases it's simpler and more efficient to evaluate SQL/JSON operators on a DOM tree instance. The OSON format allows DOM read operations directly against the serialized instance, avoiding the need for a costly parse and DOM construction. Each JSON DOM tree node address is an offset within the tree-node-navigation segment of OSON, so DOM read operations can jump directly to desired nodes using the offsets in lieu of the machine pointer dereferences. This allowed us to extend the path engine so that it is capable of operating directly on DOM instances, without sacrificing efficiency, and without the need for memorizing events.

The DOM version of the JSON path engine calls the following interfaces to evaluate each step of a JSON path step and apply any predicate expression underneath it:

- *JsonDomGetNodeType(treeNodeAddress)*
- *JsonDomGetFieldValue(treeNodeAddress, fieldNameIdentifier)*
- *JsonDomGetArrayElement(treeNodeAddress, arrayIndexRange)*
- *JsonDomGetScalarInfo(treeNodeAddress)*

For path steps that require finding a child node given the name of a field, the path evaluator invokes *JsonDomGetFieldValue()*. The OSON DOM implements this by performing a binary search for the field name identifier over the child node array and then returning the corresponding child node address. For wildcard field steps, it simply returns the array containing all the child node addresses.

For array index path steps, the path evaluator invokes *JsonDomGetArrayElement()*. The OSON DOM implements this by directly accessing the desired position in the array and returning the child node.

In either case, the path engine then evaluates any predicate expression for the current step using each returned child node address as the context node. If the predicate evaluates to true, the path engine can recursively evaluate the next path step by again using the child node address as the context node.

The path engine invokes *JsonDomGetScalarInfo()* for each path predicate expression that reads a scalar value and applies built-in functions or range comparison operators as necessary. The OSON DOM implements this by returning a pointer within the leaf-scalar-value segment, computed using the offset from the node table.

The JSON_TABLE virtual function is designed as a built-in SQL iterator that supports the row source API [9], with implementations of start(), fetchNextBatch(), and close(). For each input document, a set of relational rows are computed by the JSON table driver and returned in response to fetchNextBatch() calls. The JSON table driver calls the DOM based path engine on the SQL/JSON path expression used for row generation to yield a set of tree node addresses. For each node, the path engine is called to evaluate the column path expressions to compute column value. If a NESTED PATH construct is used, the JSON table driver is called recursively on each nested row path expression.

5.2 SQL/JSON query evaluation leveraging Oracle Database in-memory Store Architecture

5.2.1 In-Memory Virtual column for JSON Scalar Value: Oracle 12cR1 supports IMC to improve OLAP query performance by loading rows in memory and organizing the information into an optimized columnar format suitable for SIMD processing [19]. In 12cR2, IMC has been extended to support virtual column expression as well. The JSON DataGuide can help users to discover and define virtual columns using JSON_VALUE() to extract singleton scalar values from JSON documents as discussed in section 3.3.1. Then just as normal SQL columns, JSON virtual columns can map directly to the in memory columnar format for fast SQL in-memory predicate, aggregation, group by and projection operations.

5.2.2 In-Memory OSON for any SQL/JSON query: For columns which have IS JSON check constraints, we automatically add a hidden virtual column defined using the OSON() constructor. Because it's a virtual column, the OSON bytes aren't stored on disk. However, when such a table is loaded in memory, the OSON() constructor is implicitly invoked to encode the textual JSON document column into OSON bytes which are then loaded in memory. During query compile time, SQL/JSON queries over the JSON textual column are transparently rewritten to access the OSON virtual column instead. During query execution, if an OSON binary is available in memory, it's used in lieu of the original textual JSON to evaluate the query more efficiently.

6. Performance Evaluation

We perform the performance evaluation with following criteria.

- For JSON textual documents, we remove all the non-significant white spaces so as to get the smallest possible JSON representation; this minimizes I/O and memory overhead and reduces the JSON text parsing overhead.
- We don't create any indexes over JSON document collections, and we configure enough memory so that the collections are cached entirely in memory. This ensures that any differences in SQL/JSON query processing efficiency among the different encoding methods are attributable solely to differences in their encoding formats.
- For all figures that show performance numbers, the y-axis shows the execution time in a time unit. Please keep in mind that the purpose of these experiments is not to demonstrate the absolute performance numbers that can be achieved, but rather comparing the **performance ratio** among different approaches to evaluate the relative performance characteristics of each approach.

Other than the NOBENCH[6] benchmark discussed in section 6.4, all other performance experiments are conducted on PC running Linux kernel 2.6.18 with a 2.53 GHz Intel Xeon CPU and 6GB of main memory.

6.1 JSON, BSON, OSON Size Statistics

We use various JSON collections including customer use cases and benchmark data from NOBENCH[6] and YCSB[31]. In our experience, customer data sets consist mostly of small to medium size JSON documents with a few large size JSON documents. The medium size JSON document (5MB) is a message archive for twitter postings. The large size JSON document (41.5MB) is from sensor data recording. Table 10 shows the average byte size per JSON document encoded using JSON, BSON and OSON formats respectively. JSON text is UTF-8 encoded with non-significant white space removed. All JSON documents are mainly ASCII characters with 1 byte per character encoding so that JSON text document is measured with its most optimal size. *For small documents, the JSON, BSON and OSON representations are of similar size. For medium and large size documents, the BSON and OSON representations are noticeably smaller than JSON. OSON is much smaller, especially for large documents.* This is because large documents typically have repetitive sub-structures in embedded arrays., The OSON encoding method has an advantage over the other formats because it stores repeated field names just once, in its field-id-name-dictionary segment.

Table 11 shows the average percentage of total space used by the three segments of the OSON format. For small documents, the field-id-name-dictionary segment typically occupies 40% of the total encoded output. For medium to large JSON documents with many structural repetitions, the relative size of field-id-name-dictionary segment is a small fraction of the total. We designed OSON to be self-contained in the same way as JSON text or BSON binary because this avoids many scalability and administrative problems that arise when a central mapping has to be maintained. In our experience, managing, synchronizing, merging, and evolving such a central dictionary is not scalable in an agile distributed computing environment.

JSON Document collection	**Average JSON Text Size per document in bytes**	**Average BSON binary Size per document in bytes**	**Average OSON binary Size per document in bytes**
workOrder	933	1000	952
salesOrder	670	710	732
eventMessage	1924	2117	2113
purchaseOrder	1117	1214	1080
bookOrder	2107	2283	1863
LoanNotes	5146	5353	5710
Twitter Msg	2974	2824	2951
AcquisionDoc	5904	6360	5462
NOBENCHDoc	533	551	654
YCSBDoc	1145	1160	1213
TwitterMsgArchive	5.05M	3.3M	2.5M
SensorData	41.5M	37.4M	18.9M

Table 10 – Avg Size with JSON, BSON, OSON encoding

JSON Document collection	**Average Field-id-name-dict Seg Ratio**	**Average Tree-Node Navigation Seg Ratio**	**Average Leaf-scalar-value Seg Ratio**
workOrder	34.55%	29.92%	35.52%
salesOrder	47.74%	25.94%	26.32%
eventMessage	41%	26.12%	32.65%
purchaseOrder	31.88%	26.89%	41.23%
bookOrder	43.09%	36.99%	19.91%
LoanNotes	62.68%	14.58%	12.29%
Twitter Msg	43.68%	17.61%	38.7%
AcquisionDoc	19.41%	23.51%	57.07%
NOBENCHDoc	40.56%	21.01%	38.44%
YCSBDoc	9.97%	5.6%	84.43%
TwitterMsgArchive	0.05%	42.71%	57.23%
SensorData	0.01%	80.77%	19.22%

Table 11 – OSON Three-Seg Size Statistics

6.2 JSON DataGuide Statistics

We compute a JSON DataGuide for various JSON collections, generate and query DMDV views starting from the root path '$'. Table 12 shows the JSON DataGuide statistics. Number of Distinct Paths is the row count of $DG table: it counts all the distinct JSON paths from the root to both intermediate and leaf nodes. Number of columns in DMDV counts all the distinct JSON paths from the root to leaf nodes only. It represents how "wide" the full master-detail expansion of the JSON hierarchy of the document collection is. DMDV-fan-out ratio, which is computed as the number of rows in DMDV divided by the number of documents in the JSON collection, represents how "tall" the full master-detail expansion of the JSON hierarchy of the document collection is. For medium to large JSON documents, the large DMDV-fan-out ratio occurs because the documents contain large arrays of repeated structures. Also note for NOBENCH [6] data, there are 1000 sparse fields with 11 common fields.

JSON Document collection	**Number of Distinct Paths**	**DMDV – number of columns**	**DMDV-fan-out ratio**
workOrder	29	24	5.5
salesOrder	20	19	3.0
eventMessage	79	55	10
purchaseOrder	29	21	5.0
bookOrder	86	62	11.7
LoanNote	153	122	3.0
TwitterMsg	362	316	1.8
AcquisionDoc	88	73	28
NOBENCHDoc	1011	1000	2
YCSBDoc	10	10	1
TwitterMsgArchive	316	267	5405
SensorData	68	63	32100

Table 12 – JSON DataGuide Statistics

6.3 Performance Comparison of OLAP query between JSON, BSON, OSON and relational storage methods

We used the purchaseOrder JSON collection. Table 1 shows a simplified sample of documents from this collection. We stored

100,000 documents using four storage methods. Figure 4 shows the storage size of each of these methods.

- JSON storage: storing JSON text in a varchar2(4000) JSON column with total storage of 136MB
- BSON storage: storing BSON binaries in a raw(4000) JSON column with total storage of 160MB
- OSON storage: storing OSON binaries in a raw(4000) JSON column with total storage of 136MB.
- REL storage: decomposing each purchaseOrder document relationally and storing the data in two relational tables: *purchase_master_tab* which stores all the top-level purchaseOrder scalar fields and *lineitem_detail_tab* which stores all the lineitems fields. The *lineitem_detail_tab* is linked with *purchase_master_tab* by a foreign key. Total storage of both tables plus primary key and foreign key indices is 112MB.

Table 13 shows the 9 OLAP queries for performance evaluation. These 9 queries are from customer OLAP application queries referencing two relational views *po_mv* and *po_item_dmdv* that serves as an abstraction to hide the underlying physical data storage models differences: schema-rigid relational storage (REL) and schema-less self-contained storage (JSON,BSON,OSON). *po_mv* view projects all the singleton scalar fields from the purchaseOrder whereas *po_item_dmdv* projects all fields from the purchaseOrder with master fields repeated for each detail field. For REL storage, *po_item_dmdv* is defined as a join of *purchase_master_tab* and *lineitem_detail_tab* representing de-normalized master-detail records. For JSON, BSON, and OSON storages, both *po_mv* and *po_item_dmdv* views are defined using JSON_TABLE() over the base JSON column. *Po_item_dmdv* requires one NESTED PATH to un-nest the item array in the same way as the DMDV view definition shown in Table 8. The views are dynamically computed during query processing time by invoking the JSON text parser, BSON decoder, or OSON decoder respectively. The WHERE predicates on the views are pushed down as JSON_EXISTS() with JSON path predicates to be filtered.

Q1, Q2 query only *po_mv*. Q3-Q9 queries query *po_item_dmdv*. Figure 3 Y-axis shows the query execution time for each query for each storage method. Query performance over OSON binary storage is faster than BSON storage which in turn is faster than JSON storage. BSON is marginally faster than JSON. For Q2, Q3, Q4, Q5, Q6, OSON storage is 5 to 10 times faster than JSON storage. Furthermore, OSON storage is on-par with REL storage for all queries. For querying *po_mv*, OSON storage is similar to REL storage to extract the top-level scalar fields. For querying *po_item_dmdv*, OSON storage avoids the need for a join because the master/detail information is de-normalized, whereas REL storage needs to use a hash join to join the master and detail table. Figure 4 shows the storage size comparison among JSON, BSON, OSON and REL. BSON is marginally bigger than JSON and OSON. JSON and OSON are of similar size, both of which are about 21% bigger than REL storage. This is expected because REL stores only data in the table rows, while storing schema in a central relational dictionary, while all other formats are obliged to store schema with each document. The 21% storage overhead is a reasonable trade-off for having self-contained schema flexibility store in exchange for centralized schema management system.

This performance experiment demonstrates that the OSON binary encoding format for JSON bridges the performance gap between schema-rigid relational row storage format and schema-less self-contained text storage format. OSON is self-contained but is more rapidly navigated than textual JSON. Its size is on par with JSON text for small JSON documents and is typically much smaller than JSON text for large JSON text documents because such documents commonly have repeated structures. *Therefore, OSON is an ideal JSON document binary instance format to bridge the performance gap between schema-based encoding and schema-free encoding.*

Q1	*select count(*) from po_mv p where p.reference = ?*
Q2	*select costcenter, count(*) from po_mv group by costcenter order by 1*
Q3	*select costcenter, count(*) from po_item_dmdv where PARTNO = '97361551647' group by costcenter*
Q4	*select REFERENCE, INSTRUCTIONS,ITEMNO, PARTNO, DESCRIPTION, QUANTITY,UNITPRICE from po_item_dmdv d where REQUESTOR = ? and d.QUANTITY > ? And D.Unitprice > ?*
Q5	*select l.Reference, L.Itemno, L.Partno, L.Description from DMDV l where l.PARTNO in (?, ?, ?)*
Q6	*select Partno, Reference, Quantity, QUANTITY - LAG(QUANTITY,1,QUANTITY) over (ORDER BY SUBSTR(REFERENCE,INSTR(REFERENCE,'-') + 1)) as DIFFERENCE from po_item_dmdv where Partno = ? order by SUBSTR(REFERENCE,INSTR(REFERENCE,'-') + 1) desc*
Q7	*select sum (quanTity * unitprice) from po_item_dmdv group by costcenter order by 1*
Q8	*select REFERENCE, INSTRUCTIONS,ITEMNO, PARTNO, DESCRIPTION, QUANTITY,UNITPRICE from po_item_dmdv where quantity > ? and unitprice > ?*
Q9	*select REFERENCE, INSTRUCTIONS,ITEMNO, PARTNO, DESCRIPTION, QUANTITY,UNITPRICE from po_item_dmdv*

Table 13 – OLAP queries

6.4 Performance Evaluation of integration of JSON with in-memory Store and Query Processing

We perform experiments to verify the orders of magnitude performance improvement by integrating JSON/OSON processing with Oracle 12.2 in-memory store. We show that it is feasible to store JSON text on disk but load its equivalent OSON binary into in-memory store so that all SQL/JSON queries can be evaluated using OSON transparently. Furthermore, singleton scalar fields of JSON document can be projected as columnar format and loaded into in-memory columnar store (IMC) for genuine columnar processing. We use NOBENCH benchmark [6] data and run all queries Q1 to Q11. NOBENCH represents a genuine semi-structured document collection with several common fields and many sparse fields. The collection has more than 1000 sparse fields so that it would exceed 1000 column limit imposed by Oracle relational storage if relational de-composition of NOBENCH data were attempted.

The experiment uses 64 million NOBENCH JSON text documents stored in varchar(4000) column and runs 11 NOBENCH SQL/JSON queries. The experiment is conducted on system using Intel Xeon with 16 CPU cores and 256GB DRAM running Linux and Oracle 12.2 Server. The experiment runs in 3 modes.

TEXT-MODE: All JSON text documents are fully cached in Oracle buffer cache and then run 11 queries over JSON text stashed in buffer cache.

OSON-IMC-MODE: OSON bytes for all JSON text documents are fully populated in IMC cache and then run 11 queries over OSON bytes stashed in Oracle IMEC.

VC-IMC-MODE: Following 3 virtual columns (VC) are added into the table:

JSON_VALUE(jobj,'$.str1')
JSON_VALUE(jobj, '$.num' RETURNING NUMBER)
JSON_VALUE(jobj, '$.dyn1' RETURNING NUMBER)

and load VC into IMC cache so that Q6,Q7,Q10,Q11 which use the above JSON_VALUE() functions can be processed using columnar format of scalar result from JSON_VALUE().

Figure 5 shows that OSON-IMEC-MODE has significantly improved performance compared with TEXT-MODE. This demonstrates that OSON can be used as an efficient in-memory JSON binary format to transparently improve ad-hoc SQL/JSON query performance despite the JSON is stored on disk in textual form. The advantage of using OSON as in memory format instead of being a persistent on disk format is that we can continuously improve binary encoding format for JSON without maintaining backward compatibility with on-disk format. Similar to Oracle IMC approach that avoids introducing new columnar storage, we've learned a key insight, that is, *decouple the storage format from in-memory query friendly format.* This insight is a principle to support trend of No-DB style In Situ query processing [23] where storage format is uncontrollable by database but any in-memory just-in-time data structure can be constructed and cached for query processing.

Figure 6 shows that VC-IMEC-MODE has significantly improved performance compared with OSON-IMEC-MODE for Q6, Q7, Q10, Q11 where the JSON_VALUE() on three singleton fields: '$.str1', '$.num', '$.dyn1' used in these queries have already been cached in IMC cache so that predicates and projections on JSON_VALUE() can leverage full performance power of Oracle IMC architecture [19].

6.5 Performance Evaluation of document insertion into JSON collection with enabled DataGuide maintenance

We use NOBENCH [6] data to measure the performance impact of maintaining the DataGuide over newly inserted JSON documents. As discussed in section 3.2, we have integrated the DataGuide maintenance with the *IS JSON* check constraint so that inserting JSON documents has minimal overhead in the common situation where no schema changes are discovered. We performed an experiment where we insert 10,000 NOBENCH JSON documents with identical structures. We repeated the experiment three times, each time in a different operating mode.

In "no-json-constraint" mode, we do insertion without the IS JSON check constraint; this measures the base cost of row insertion.

In "json-constraint" mode, we do the same insertion on the table with IS JSON check constraint enforced. This measures the base cost of insertion with the additional cost of reading and parsing the JSON data.

In "json-constraint-dataguide" mode, we turn on JSON DataGuide maintenance so that in addition to reading and parsing the JSON data, we also perform JSON path structural analysis to see if any schema changes need to be written to the $DG table of the JSON search index. Since the documents are identical, no writes to $DG are necessary after the first document is inserted, so this measures the cost of validating the dataguide.

Figure 7 shows insertion time for the 3 modes. With IS JSON check constraint enforced, we measured an overhead of 9.4% compared to not checking the constraint. With JSON DataGuide maintenance added, the overhead climbs to 17%. This means that for homogeneous JSON collections the overhead of the DataGuide is 7.6% versus simply enforcing the IS JSON constraint.

Our second experiment is to compare dataguide maintenance overhead for a heterogeneous JSON document collection with a homogeneous JSON document collection. In the experiment labelled homo, we inserted 10,000 JSON documents with identical structures. In the experiment labelled hetero, we inserted 10,000 JSON documents with every document adding a unique new field so that every insertion of a JSON document will cause a new JSON path to be inserted into the $DG table. Figure 8 shows that the heterogeneous collection incurred doubled the insertion cost of the homogeneous collection.

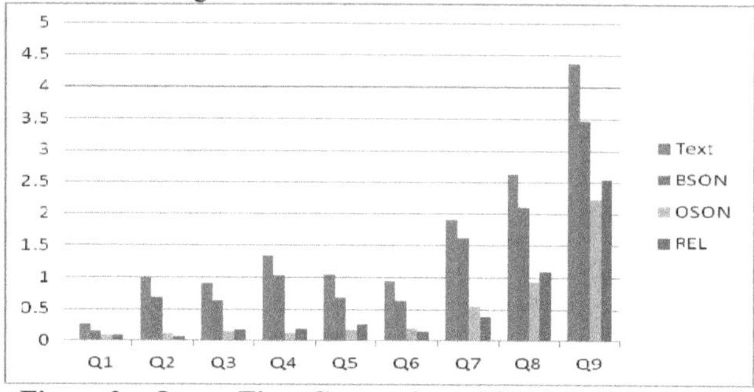

Figure 3 – Query Time Comparison: JSON, BSON, OSON, REL storages

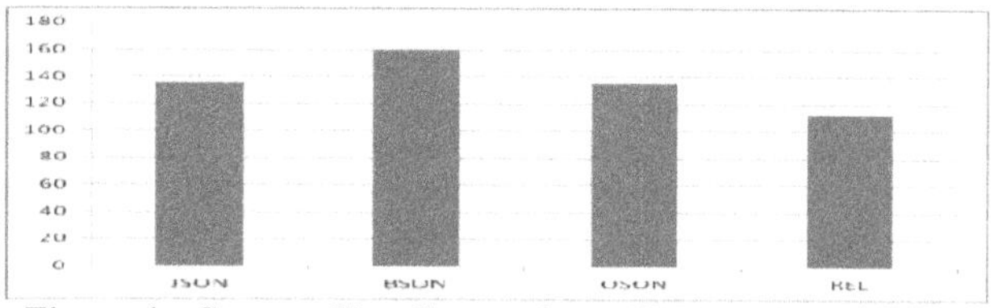

Figure 4 – Storage Size Comparison: JSON, BSON, OSON, REL

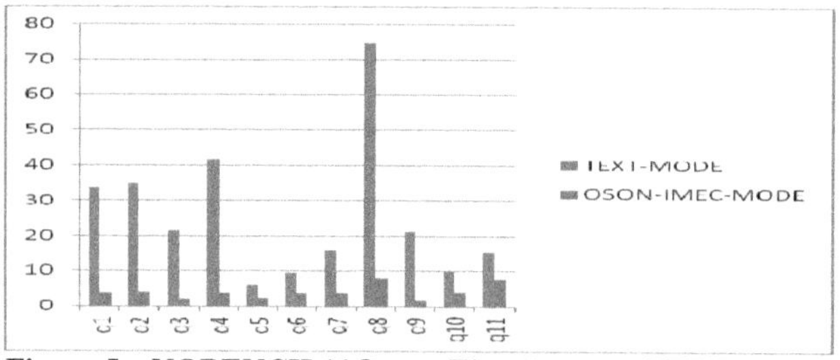

Figure 5 – NOBENCH 11Query Time between TEXT-MODE and OSON-IMC-MODE

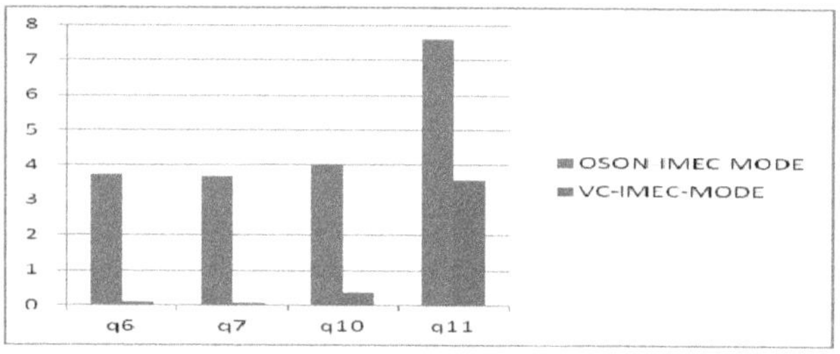

Figure 6 – Q6,Q7,Q10,Q11 11Query Time between OSON-IMEC-MODE and VC-IMC-MODE

6.6 Performance Evaluation of Transient DataGuide Aggregation

We loaded 2 million NOBENCH [6] JSON documents in a collection to measure the performance of transient dataguide computation and compare it with the cost of persistent dataguide creation. We ran a JSON_DataGuideAgg() SQL aggregation query with different sample percentage as Q1 in Table 9. Figure 9 shows the query execution time with sampling 25%, 50%, 75%, 99% of documents in the JSON collection. As expected, the execution time is linear with the number of samples used. We then compare the dataguide query execution time from the 99% sample with the creation time for the JSON search index, which computes a persistent dataguide over the collection. The persistent dataguide takes 27% more time than the transient dataguide. This is expected because both of them performed the same dataguide computation processing over almost the same number of samples, but the persistent dataguide did the additional work of persisting the information to the $DG table.

7. Future Work

Current OSON format is self-contained and instance based resembling a row format without relying on central schema registration and maintenance. We will work on OSON set encoding resembling a columnar format, however, *without reply on central schema definition and assuming homogenous instance collection*. This is different from the design of Dremel [24] which is a columnar encoding of hierarchically nested data conforming to a fixed homogenous hierarchical schema. Although Dremel [24] schema allows optional fields in the schema, it assumes an object field of all object instances within a collection having a fixed position and having the same datatype. For example, it cannot support the case that in one object instance, field 'name' is a string, in second object instance, field 'name' is an integer, in third object instance, field 'name' is a nested object, in fourth object instance, field 'name' is an array. However, such heterogeneous object instance collection is allowed in a JSON collection. Therefore, we want our OSON set format to be able to handle both homogeneous and heterogeneous JSON collections for the in-memory columnar store. Set OSON encoding may explore homogeneity for collection encoding if it can. For example, the common field-id-name dictionary segments can be extracted from each OSON instance and merged into a single dictionary in the in-memory store. This would reduce memory consumption and improve query performance because field name to id mapping can be done once for the entire in-memory store.

Furthermore, the DMDV generated by JSON DataGuide is structurally similar to the wide table [30]. Having many NULL columns and repeated master records per detail record, DMDV is ideal for in-memory columnar dictionary encoding and query processing. We will explore the design of encoding JSON collection as columnar DMDV format and loaded into in-memory columnar store.

In summary, our vision is: On-disk OSON is instance encoded and is self-contained and immune from schema birth and evolution problem to support 'Schema-less for write' No-SQL requirement. In-memory OSON is set encoded based on JSON Data-Guide and is non-self-contained to support 'Schema-Rich for declarative query' SQL requirement.

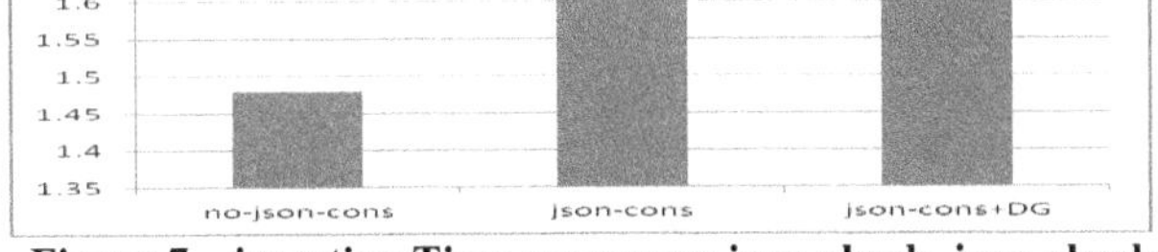

Figure 7 – insertion Time among no-json-check, json-check, json-check with dataguide on

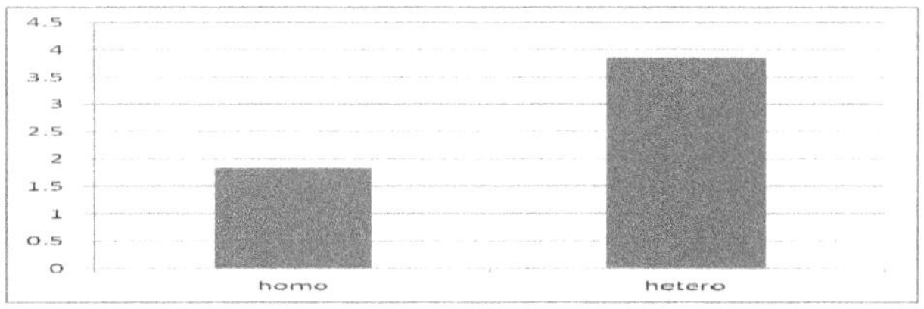

Figure 8 – Insertion Time of Homogenous Versus Heterogeneous Docs with enbled DataGuide

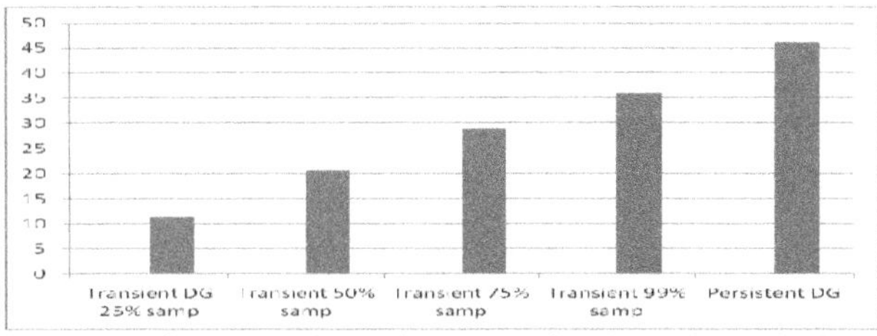

Figure 9 – Query Time for computing Transient JSON DataGuide Aggregation

8. Conclusion

Without JSON DataGuide support, users who adopt a polyglot persistence strategy [7] face two worlds: the relational world with a powerful query language (SQL) but with a requirement to carefully specify and manage schemas, and the NoSQL world with more agile application development and fast data ingestion, but with limited query capabilities. OLTP applications can use a NoSQL database to achieve fast document ingestion. However, afterwards, a relational schema needs to be developed to allow the data to be moved to an RDBMS for SQL analytics. Adding the JSON DataGuide and OSON binary format to the RDBMS shows us that the SQL and NoSQL worlds can be integrated, allowing users to manage both relational data and flexible schema data in a single database engine. The JSON DataGuide offers users a **schema-GPS** to write schema validated query: data schema goes from being hidden inside application data access code to being exposed via the familiar relational model well supported by many tools. OSON format allows JSON to be queried with efficiency that approaches that of schema-based relational tables. Loading OSON implicitly in memory as generic JSON query friendly format have transparently improved query performance.

9. Acknowledgements

We thank Vikas Arora, Asha Makur, Cetin Ozbutun, Mark Drake, George Lumpkin, for SQL/JSON product direction and development management support; Thank Prakashkumar Thiagarajan, Alfonso Colunga, and Rahul Kadwe for helping implementation; Thank Aurosish Mishra, Shasank Chavan, Allison Holloway, Jesse Kamp, Tirthankar Lahiri, Niloy Mukherjee, Vineet Marwah for supporting in-memory virtual column expressions; Thank Brian Chesebro, Srinivas Kareenhalli, Indira Patil, Manoj Sahoo for performance experiment; Thank Dieter Gawlick for evangelizing the concept of flexible schema data. Thank Oliver Kennedy, Boris Glavic for evangelizing future work on derivation of Dataguide from data with uncertainty and provenance tracking.

10. REFERENCES

[1] P. Atzeni, C.S. Jensen, G. Orsi, S. Ram, L. Tanca, R. Torlone: The relational model is dead, SQL is dead, and I don't feel so good myself. SIGMOD Record, 42(2):64-68, 2013

[2] K. Beyer, R. Cochrane, V. Josifovski, J. Kleewein, G. Lapis, G.M.Lohman, R.Lyle, F. Özcan, H. Pirahesh, N. Seemann, T. C. Truong, B.V. Linden, B. Vickery, C. Zhang: System RX: One Part Relational, One Part XML. SIGMOD Conference 2005: 347-358

[3] R. Murthy, Z. H. Liu, M. Krishnaprasad, S. Chandrasekar, A. Tran, E. Sedlar, D. Florescu, S. Kotsovolos, N. Agarwal, V. Arora, V. Krishnamurthy: Towards an enterprise XML architecture. SIGMOD Conference 2005: 953-957

[4] R. Cattell: Scalable SQL and NoSQL data stores. SIGMOD Record, 39(4):12-27, 2010.

[5] Chen P.: The Enity-Relationship Model: Toward a Unified View of Data. VLDB 1975: 173

[6] Chasseur, C; Li Y; Patel, J: *Enabling JSON Document Stores in Relational Systems* . WebDB 2013

[7] Fowler, M; Pramod Sadalage, P: *NoSQL databases and Polyglot Persistence:* http://martinfowler.com/articles/nosql-intro

[8] Jagadish, H: *Making Database Systems Usable*. SIGMOD 2007 Keynotes

[9] G. Grafe, Query Evaluation Techniques for Large Databases, in ACM Computing Surveys, 25(2):73–170, 1993.

[10] JSON: http://www.json.org/

[11] Z. H. Liu. "Object-Relational Features in Informix Internet Foundation."Informix technical notes. 9.4(Q4 1999):77-95.

[12] JSONiq: http://www.jsoniq.org/

[13] Stonebraker,M;, Brown,P; Moore, D. *Object-Relational DBMSs*, Second Edition Morgan Kaufmann 1998

[14] Protocol Buffers: http://code.google.com/p/protobuf/

[15] Avro http://avro.apache.org/docs/1.7.5/spec.html

[16] BSON http://bsonspec.org/

[17] Vertica Flex Table https://my.vertica.com/docs/7.0.x/PDF/HP_Vertica_7.0.x_Flex_Tables.pdf

[18] Z.H.Liu, Y. Lu, H.Chang: Efficient Support of XQuery Full Text in SQL/XML Enabled RDBMS. ICDE 2014: 1132-1143

[19] Lahiri, T. et al. Oracle Database In-Memory: A Dual Format In-Memory Database. Proceedings of the 2015 ICDE. Pp. 1253-1258, 2015

[20] L. Wang, O. Hassanzadeh, S. Zhang, J. Shi: Schema Management for Document Stores. PVLDB 8(9): 922-933 (2015)

[21] Z. H. Liu, B. Christoph Hammerschmidt, D. McMahon: JSON data management: supporting schema-less development in RDBMS. SIGMOD Conference 2014: 1247-1258

[22] D. Tahara, T. Diamond, D. J. Abadi: Sinew: a SQL system for multi-structured data. SIGMOD Conference 2014: 815-826

[23] Y. Tian, I. Alagiannis, E. Liarou, A. Ailamaki, P. Michiardi, M. Vukolic: DiNoDB: Efficient Large-Scale Raw Data Analytics. Data4U@VLDB 2014: 1

[24] Dremel: Interactive Analysis of WebScale Datasets S. Melnik, A. Gubarev, J. J. Long, G. Romer, S. Shivakumar, M. Tolton, T.Vassilakis VLDB 2010

[25] http://blogs.msdn.com/b/jocapc/archive/2015/05/16/json-support-in-sql-server-2016.aspx

[26] http://www.info.teradata.com/htmlpubs/DB_TTU_15_00/index.html#page/Teradata_JSON/B035_1150_015K/TeradataSupportJSON.html

[27] https://my.vertica.com/docs/7.0.x/PDF/HP_Vertica_7.0.x_Flex_Tables.pdf

[28] R. Goldman, J. Widom: DataGuides: Enabling Query Formulation and Optimization in Semistructured Databases. VLDB 1997: 436-445

[29] http://www.ibm.com/developerworks/data/library/techarticle/dm-1501sql-json-db2/index.html

[30] Y. Li, J. Patel:WideTable: An Accelerator for Analytical Data Processing. PVLDB 7(10): 907-918 (2014)

[31] YCSB:https://github.com/brianfrankcooper/YCSB/wiki/Running-a-Workload

[32] Z.H. Liu, D. Gawlick: Management of Flexible Schema Data in RDBMSs - Opportunities and Limitations for NoSQL -. CIDR 2015

Have Your Data and Query It Too: From Key-Value Caching to Big Data Management

Dipti Borkar
Couchbase Inc.
dipti@couchbase.com

Ravi Mayuram
Couchbase Inc.
ravi@couchbase.com

Gerald Sangudi
Couchbase Inc.
gerald@couchbase.com

Michael Carey
Couchbase Inc.
mike.carey@couchbase.com

ABSTRACT

Couchbase Server is a rethinking of the database given the current set of realities. Memory today is much cheaper than disks were when traditional databases were designed back in the 1970's, and networks are much faster and much more reliable than ever before. Application agility is also an extremely important requirement. Today's Couchbase Server is a memory- and network-centric, shared-nothing, auto-partitioned, and distributed NoSQL database system that offers both key-based and secondary index-based data access paths as well as API- and query-based data access capabilities. This is a major change from Couchbase's roots; in its early days, its focus was entirely on high performance and highly available key-value (memcache) based caching. Customer needs and competitive pressures in the evolving non-relational database market also accelerated this change.

This paper describes the architectural changes needed to address the requirements posed by next-generation database applications. In addition, it details the implementation of such an architecture using Couchbase Server and explains the evolution of Couchbase Server from its early roots to its present form. Particular attention is paid to how today's Couchbase Server cluster architecture is influenced by the memory-first, high-performance, and scalability demands of typical customer deployments. Key features include a layer-consolidated cache, a consistency-controllable interplay between updates, indexes, and queries, and a unique "multi-dimensional" approach to cluster scaling. The paper closes with a look at future plans for supporting semi-structured operational data analytics in addition to today's more OLTP-like, front-facing use cases

1. INTRODUCTION

Today's operational or OLTP applications have very different requirements than those of the past. Flexibility, scale, availability, and performance requirements have all seen dramatic changes. With population-scale user bases, the workload and throughput requirements have grown in many cases to hundreds of thousands of reads and/or writes per second. In addition, with the need to offer rich, on-line user experiences at high throughput, latency requirements are being pushed ever lower, with 1-3 milliseconds being a common latency expectation for applications like user profile stores. Applications such as catalog and SKU management systems need the ability to change and update information on the fly. All of these requirements come with the additional need to scale elastically with demand while being always available. These requirements call for a next-generation of database systems.

This paper begins by providing some general background on NoSQL systems followed by a brief history of Couchbase. We then describe the design choices that a database system needs to make to support OLTP workloads (vs. OLAP workloads) with a focus on the core principles underlying Couchbase Server. This is followed by an in-depth look at both its external interfaces and its under the hood architecture. We close with a look into the future.

NoSQL is a term applied to a class of DBMSs that are generally designed for use in high data volume, high throughput, and web-scale applications [3, 7]. NoSQL databases are sometimes also called non-relational databases because many of the systems in this category allow nesting and have no fixed schema, thus enabling the storage of complex entities as well as semi-structured data and allowing more flexible use by developers. Most have provided non-SQL-based APIs for accessing data since they were popularized primarily through grass roots developer adoption. However, over time, some have added query-based interfaces in addition to their APIs or MapReduce-style paradigms.

Common characteristics for NoSQL databases include horizontal scalability via a clustered approach and greater schema flexibility than relational databases. Beyond these characteristics, NoSQL databases are often classified into four categories, as indicated in Figure 1. Over time, these categories are starting to converge [10], and we believe that as NoSQL systems mature further, a single platform should be capable of supporting most of the features found in these categories today.

i. Key-Value Stores

Key-value stores provide fast access to a value when its key is known. They are the foundation of NoSQL databases and are typically implemented via a distributed hash table where each entry has a unique key plus an associated data value.

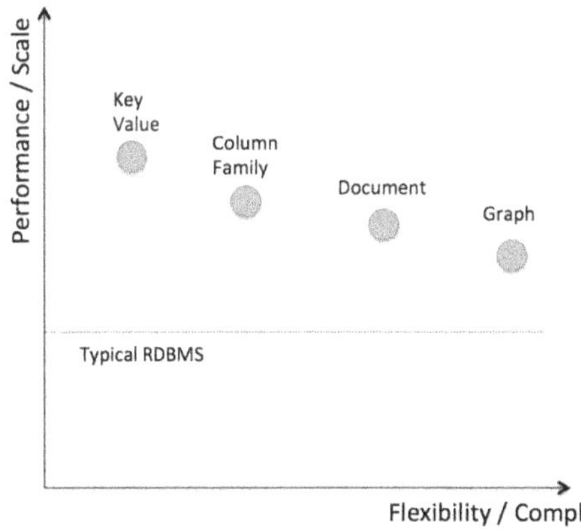

Figure 1. NoSQL database categories

SIGMOD'16, June 26-July 01, 2016, San Francisco, CA, USA

ISBN 978-1-4503-3531-7/16/06…$15.00
DOI: http://dx.doi.org/10.1145/2882903.2904443

The key-value model is the simplest and the easiest to implement. It also provides the highest raw performance; applications that need massive scale along with very low latency and/or high throughput are often implemented using this approach today. If the key for a given item (value) or set of items (values) is not knowable a priori, however, key-value systems are not a particularly good fit; most of the querying and management of relationships would then have to be handled in the application tier. Examples of key-value systems include Aerospike, Redis, and DynamoDB.

ii. Column Family Databases

Column family databases provide a bit more flexibility than key-value databases. A key is still needed to access the data, but the data value itself can consist of multiple columns. Schemas are flexible, and each keyed item can have its own set of columns (distinct from those of other items). Columns are organized as column families, and some such systems provide the ability to query by more than just the key. Examples of column family databases include BigTable, HBase, and Cassandra.

iii. Document Databases

Document databases provide still greater flexibility. The primary access path in a document database is still the key, but the value is typically based on a semi-structured data format like JSON (or XML). This allows complex objects and entities to be represented. These systems also typically provide more than just key-based access. Limited querying is usually supported as well, either through an API-based approach, MapReduce-based querying, or a (SQL-like) query language. Document database examples include Couchbase, MongoDB, and MarkLogic.

iv. Graph Databases

Graph databases build on document databases by adding a flexible graph model. Data is modeled as nodes, edges and properties. Typically these databases also use a semi-structured format like JSON to represent data. APIs are common to provide access to data, both for values and for following relationships, but support for full SQL-like query capabilities is rare since their focus is largely on querying graph structures. Examples of graph database systems include Neo4j and OrientDB.

1.1 Brief Couchbase History

Couchbase, Inc. was created through the merger of Membase, Inc. and CouchOne, Inc. in 2011. This combined two technologies, Membase Server and CouchDB. Membase Server was a key-value distributed database based on memcached, while CouchDB was a single-node document database supporting JSON. The goal of the merged company was to combine the strengths of Membase as well as CouchDB to create a highly scalable, high-performance, document-oriented database capable of addressing the needs of next-generation web, mobile and IoT applications.

1.2 Membase Server

When Couchbase began, Membase Server was a distributed key-value store built on top of memcached. Memcached itself is a widely used single-node caching technology in the Internet application space. It provides consistent, low-latency access to objects. Objects are binary in nature and similar to BLOBs in databases. Membase used memcached for its integrated caching layer and offered an API similar to the memcached API for user access to data.

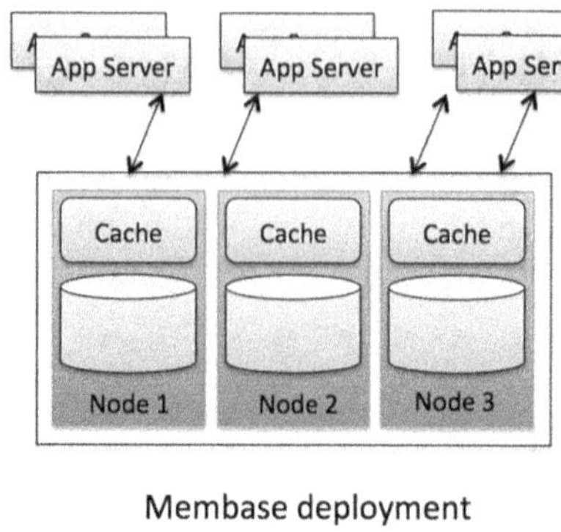

Figure 2. Membase deployment architecture

Membase added several major capabilities to the pure memcached system, including a distributed hash-partitioning scheme for scaling out, asynchronous persistence to disk to handle workload spikes at memory-first speeds, and asynchronous data replication within a cluster to achieve high availability.

Figure 2 illustrates a typical deployment of Membase for a web application. Since the caching layer is now consolidated with a persistent key-value data store, an additional external cache is no longer required for efficiently serving requests. Requests from the application servers are distributed across the collection of Membase nodes based on document hashing.

1.3 CouchDB

CouchDB was initially built as a single node database system with no partitioning capabilities and with several major differences from relational database systems. The first difference was schema flexibility. CouchDB chose JSON to serve as its data format, allowing agile application development without the need to conform to a strict schema. This difference also eliminated the need to perform complex multi-way joins just to reassemble normalized data.

The second difference from traditional relational database systems was tunable consistency between data and the associated indexes. Direct document access using a key was always consistent, but query access based on indexes was eventually consistent by default. A user could, however, specify a desired level of consistency at query submission time based on their type of data and their application's needs. CouchDB does support database-to-database replication (not partition level) to bring data closer to users. Figure 3 illustrates a CouchDB deployment with replication enabled.

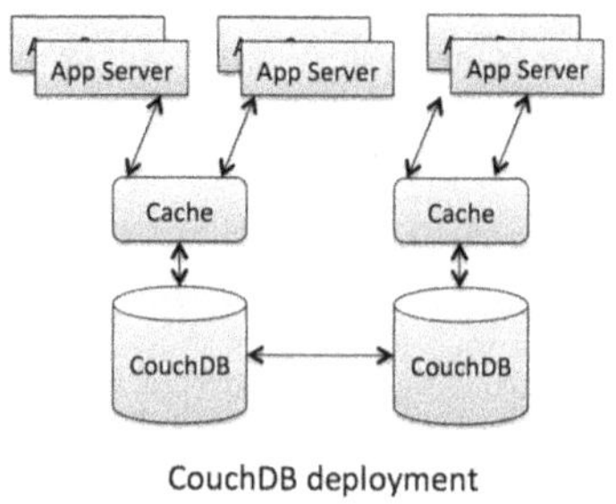

Figure 3. CouchDB deployment architecture

2. COUCHBASE SERVER OVERVIEW

2.1 Towards a Next-Generation DBMS

Couchbase set out to achieve specific technology goals, targeting new applications and their new requirements as explained earlier, through its merging of the Membase and CouchDB technologies. In general, many new applications (as well as some existing applications), including user profile services, custom content and metadata applications, and custom catalog or asset management applications, do not require a full relational database management system (RDBMS). Over time, their performance, scale, and flexibility needs outweigh their transactional requirements.

With Couchbase Server, it is not necessary to normalize natural application objects into multiple tables. As in CouchDB, objects can be stored in their unnormalized form as JSON documents. In addition, Couchbase Server allows users to access their data using either the key-value approach or a query-based approach. This means that applications that require high performance as well as the flexibility to access a sub-set of their data or parts of an object don't have to use two different systems; one database can support both of those access approaches.

RDBMs have dominated the IT industry for almost 40 years. However, NoSQL systems are now reaching a point where substantial functionality from the RDBMS world is available without the associated disadvantages of rigid schemas or lack of scaling. There are still areas, like transactionality, where further rethinking is needed regarding what is practical and needed by the next generation of applications, but the time seems right for next generation databases (such as Couchbase, of course) to transcend the relational model for many applications.

2.2 The OLTP vs. OLAP Design Tradeoff

Today, Couchbase Server is focused on handling OLTP-like workloads (i.e., OLTP workloads that do not need strong, multi-operation ACID transactionality). It offers a range of capabilities to manage and access data in real-time and allows users to isolate their workloads via a multi-dimensional scaling (MDS) approach. This will be explained in more detail in Sections 2.3.1 and 4.4. Couchbase Server can also handle limited OLAP-style workloads using pre-computed aggregates provided by a *view index*. N1QL, its query language, has many of the capabilities of SQL, but in general, its internal query processing architecture has very much been aimed at handling small, low-latency queries. This can be seen by comparing and contrasting the query execution pipeline described later in Section 4.5.3 with the data-parallel strategies found in parallel relational database systems that target large, warehouse-style use cases [5].

The longer-term goal and vision of Couchbase Server is to provide a single, unified platform that can be used for nearly all types of operational workloads – including operational analytics. Going forward, the support of such new analytic functionality cannot be added at the expense of the (sacred!) front-end OLTP workloads. To protect the front-end, there are some core principles that have been incorporated in the architecture and will be applied to future architectural changes as well.

2.3 Core Design Principles

2.3.1 Scaling workloads independently

This first core principle is applied to any service that manages data or data derived from the core key-value data set. Termed multi-dimensional scaling, this concept allows for services to be scaled up or out independent to one another from a hardware perspective. Each database workload has different needs, with some needing more I/O bandwidth and some needing more memory. Using this concept, hardware can be optimized based on the workload also making for more efficient use of hardware resources. This principle has been applied to Couchbase Server's data service, index service, and query service as well as to the services that will be introduced in the future like those for text search and analytics. Details of the implementation can be found in Section 4.4.

2.3.2 Asynchronous approach to everything

Relational databases mostly take a synchronous approach to data handling, which implies incurring a latency "hit" (penalty) at the time of a write (e.g., update, insert, or delete). However, given that the need for higher throughputs and lower latencies has only increased over time, Couchbase Server made a design choice to update all other components of the database asynchronously when a data update occurs. As a result, no immediate latency penalty is incurred at write time. This approach is used even for persisting updated data to disk.It is important to recognize that the rates at which new data can arrive and existing data can change may ultimately still be I/O limited, as, in the limit, the system must still be able to absorb the load offered by an application. However, asynchrony "buys time" for the system to handle spikes in the load; it also provides an opportunity for repeated updates to an object to be aggregated at the level of persistence.

Couchbase Server's asynchronous approach results in a world in which the data and its on-disk copy, the data and its replicas, and/or the data and its indices may become slightly out of sync. To make it easier for users to manage in such a world, Couchbase Server provides options for durability as well as consistency.

Durability guarantees

At write time, Couchbase provides client applications with the option to wait for replication and/or for persistence on a per mutation basis. This allows each application to make its own choice, based on its requirements, regarding taking (or not) the performance penalty associated with these options. Given that the latency expectations for modern large-scale OLTP applications are in sub-milliseconds, most users choose to receive a response immediately once the data hits memory or in some cases may choose to first replicate the data to one other node for safety. Since replication is memory-to-memory, the latency hit with the replication option is significantly less than waiting for persistence, especially when using spinning disks.

Configurable consistency for queries

Given that indexes in Couchbase are asynchronously updated, they can be out of sync with the data when a query makes a scan request. Couchbase supports two flavors of querying: N1QL and view queries. Both flavors allow users to specify the tolerable level of staleness on a per query basis. This means that users can choose between accessing an index as it is or waiting for the index to be updated up to the point in time when the query was initiated. The implementation of this concept for *view* queries is discussed in Section 3.1.2, and Section 3.2.3 discusses its implementation in the case of N1QL query processing.

2.3.3 Memory-first architecture

Couchbase follows a memory-first architecture when reading data as well as when distributing updates to the various components of the system. Almost all components are updated via DCP, which is the server's internal, in-memory database change protocol. This memory-first architecture makes it easier for all components to keep up with the system's high-throughput front-end loads.

3. COUCHBASE SERVER DATA BASICS

Couchbase Server is a distributed document database that supports various types of access paths and is built to scale in multiple ways [4]. It has a memory-first architecture that includes both an integrated caching layer and in-memory replication capabilities.

Couchbase Server stores data in JSON documents, where each document is a JSON object consisting of a number of fields. An application object can be stored using one or more documents, and the object's attributes become fields in the document(s). Documents are stored within a key space called a *Couchbase bucket,* and they can be directly accessed using a (user-provided) document ID much as one would use a primary key for lookups in an RDBMS.

The generally available version of Couchbase Server is currently version 4.1, with a preview of version 4.5 being available as of this writing. This paper's architectural description is thus based primarily based on version 4.1. The futures section will provide more insights into the system's upcoming capabilities and plans, including some of the highlights of version 4.5.

3.1 Client Access

Couchbase provides numerous client SDKs, including support for Java, .NET, php, Ruby, C, Python, node.JS and GoLang. Each of the client SDKs provides language-specific APIs or methods to access data via the various access paths available.

There are three main access paths by which a client application can talk to Couchbase Server:

1. Read / write JSON documents using key-value access via the primary key
2. Read / query JSON documents using the View API
3. Read / query JSON documents using N1QL queries

3.1.1 Key-value access using the primary key

Read access to DB

Couchbase provides a key-based lookup mechanism where the client is expected to provide the key, and only the cluster node hosting the data with that key will be contacted.

Write access to DB

Couchbase updates happen at the document level if the key-value API is used. A client SDK will retrieve a document that needs to be updated from the server, the user will modify certain fields, and the client SDK will then send the document back to the server for update.

To provide the required degree of isolation for concurrent access, Couchbase provides a CAS (compare and swap) mechanism for optimistic locking:

- When the client retrieves a document, a CAS ID (much like a revision number) is attached to it.
- While the client is manipulating the retrieved document locally, another client may modify this document. If this happens, the CAS ID of the document at the server will be incremented.
- Now, when the original client submits its modification to the server, it can choose to include the original CAS ID in its request. The server will then check this ID against the current ID in the server. If they differ, the document has been updated in between and the server will not apply the update.
- The original client can re-read the document (which now has a newer ID) and re-submit its modification.

Couchbase also offers its users a stricter locking mechanism; an application can opt to request a hard lock at the document level when performing its updates. (This lock will be released after a certain timeout to avoid deadlocks.)

Optimistic locking is what most large-scale online applications and production deployments use, as isolation is important to them, but not at the cost of a major performance penalty.

3.1.2 Read / query JSON using View API

Similar to the materialized view concept in the RDBMS world [11], Couchbase Server provides a MapReduce-style index called a *view.* A Couchbase *view* is essentially just a local (distributed) index that can be queried. A view is defined using a *Map function* that extracts data from the documents in a key space (bucket) and optionally a *Reduce* function that aggregates the data objects emitted by the map function. These are defined using JavaScript. A Couchbase view thereby provides a functional way to specify a materialized (and distributed) query result that client applications can directly utilize to improve their performance.

Queries that use views are static, meaning that a view needs to be defined and materialized before it can be used for querying data. An *emit( )* function that must be included in the *Map( )* function of a view is similar in its role to the query that would be specified in an RDBMS's CREATE MATERIALIZED VIEW statement. Every document that is a part of the key space upon which a view is defined will be processed by the view's *Map( )* and *Reduce( )* functions.

Once a view is materialized, it can then be queried for specific key(s) or a range of keys as follows:

- Return all values (as JSON) matching the supplied key, or
- Return all values (as JSON) matching any of the supplied keys, or
- Return all values (as JSON) starting with the provided key A and stopping on the last instance of a key B.

A given *view query* will be broadcast to all servers in the cluster and the results will be merged and sent back to the client SDK. To clarify all of these concepts, let us consider a simple example.

Sample document with key 'borkar123'

```
{
  ''name'': ''Dipti Borkar'',
  ''email'': ''Dipti@couchbase.com''
}
```

Example: Definition of View *Profile*

```
Function(doc){
if (doc.name){
      emit(doc.name, doc.email) }
```

This *map( )* function when executed will materialize a view and store the names and emails for all of the documents in the bucket that it is defined on. This *Profile View* can then be directly queried via the REST API or using a client SDK.

Example: REST query for View *Profile*

```
?key="Dipti"&stale=false
```

This REST call will return the value of the *doc.email* attribute from all documents where *doc.name* is "Dipti".

Views are eventually consistent [9] with respect to the underlying stored documents; they are kept up-to-date asynchronously, on demand, based on document writes/updates. As explained earlier, Couchbase provides users a choice to run a view query with configurable consistency. A *stale* parameter can be used as a part of the view query to specify the required level of consistency (i.e., the tolerable degree of staleness) for the query.

Supported values for the *stale* parameter are:

- *false*: Wait for the view indexer to finish processing changes that correspond to the current key-value document set and then return the latest entries from the view index.
- *ok*: Just return the current entries from the index file (including possibly stale entries).
- *update_after*: Return the current entries from the index, but then initiate a view index update. (This is the default.)

3.1.3 *Read / query JSON using N1QL*

Couchbase Server now prominently supports query-based access to data using its new SQL-inspired query language, N1QL, as described next. N1QL queries can enter the system via a REST call, an SDK call, or one of several interactive client tools.

3.2 The N1QL query language

3.2.1 *Overview and key capabilities*

Non-first Normal Form Query Language, or N1QL (pronounced "nickel"), is the first NoSQL query language to leverage the flexibility of JSON with nearly the full expressive power of SQL and an SQL-friendly syntax. Developed by Couchbase for use in Couchbase Server, N1QL provides a common query language and a JSON-based data model for distributed, document-oriented database management. (A nice comparison of various NoSQL query languages and associated systems can be found in [6,13].)

N1QL enables clients to access data from Couchbase Server using SQL-like language constructs, as N1QL's design was based on SQL. It includes a familiar data definition language (DDL), data manipulation language (DML), and query language statements, but can operate in the face of NoSQL database features such as key-value storage, multi-valued attributes, and nested objects.

3.2.2 *Features of N1QL*

N1QL provides a rich set of features that let users retrieve, manipulate, transform, and create JSON document data. Its key features include:

`SELECT` Statement: The `SELECT` statement in `N1QL` extends the functionality of the SQL `SELECT` statement to work with JSON documents. Of particular importance are the `USE KEYS`, `NEST`, and `UNNEST` sub-clauses of the `FROM` clause in N1QL.

At a high level, a `SELECT` statement supports the retrieval of data from specified keyspaces or Couchbase buckets. A simple query in N1QL has three parts to it:

`SELECT` - Portions of the document to return.

`FROM` - The keyspace or datastore with which to work.

`WHERE` – Conditions the retrieved data should satisfy.

Because data in Couchbase Server is stored in documents rather than in rigidly structured tables, N1QL queries can actually return a collection of different document structures or fragments.

Data Manipulation Language (DML): N1QL provides support for `INSERT`, `DELETE`, `UPDATE`, and `UPSERT` statements to create, delete, and modify data stored as JSON documents. These statements also support sub-document level lookups and updates.

3.2.3 *Salient clauses and parameters*

While N1QL supports an extensive set of clauses similar to SQL, there are certain clauses and parameters that differentiate it from other databases. Let us examine some of the key SQL clause additions that N1QL includes:

USE KEYS

This clause is the key (to so speak) to bridging the fundamental functionality gap between a key-value store and a document database. Its use provides the user with the flexibility to grab specific attributes or compose new values from existing objects while still getting key-value retrieval performance.

Specific primary keys within a key space (*Couchbase bucket*) can be specified in this clause. Only values having those primary keys will be included as inputs to the rest of the given N1QL query.

Example: To specify a single key:

```
SELECT * FROM profiles USE KEYS "acme-uuid-
1234-5678"
```

Example: To specify multiple keys:

```
SELECT * FROM profiles
USE KEYS ["acme-uuid-1234-5678", "roadster-
uuid-4321-8765"]
```

NEST and UNNEST Clauses

Supporting the JSON data format requires Couchbase to provide extensions to standard SQL to allow users to do more with JSON. Specifically, as JSON objects can be stored in the database as-is, without splitting or shredding them into multiple tables, users may need to flatten documents when reading them out, or if related documents are stored separately, to compose and combine them together into a single JSON document. Both of these goals can be achieved using the N1QL `UNNEST` and `NEST` clauses.

When the `NEST` clause is used, instead of producing a cross-product of the left and right hand inputs, it produces a single result for each left-hand input while its right-hand input is collected into an array and nested into a single array-valued field in the result.

Example: Consider a bucket that contains two types of documents, with *doc_type* 'user_profile' and 'order'. If we wish to assemble a list of products purchased by a user, we need to perform a `JOIN` across those two document types. However, a traditional relational join would yield a cross product instead of composing a result within which, for each user profile that matches the query criteria, its associated orders are embedded or nested within an array.

```
SELECT PO.personal_details, orders
FROM profiles_orders PO
USE KEYS 'borkar123'
NEST profiles_orders as orders
    ON KEYS ARRAY s.order_id FOR s
    IN PO.shipped_order_history END
```

The query above will return a JSON document with all the orders placed by the user whose key is 'borkar123' being nested into an array within the resulting user object.

In contrast, the UNNEST clause takes the contents of a nested array and joins them each with their parent object.

Example: Return a list of the existing (in-use) product categories in a world where products can fall into multiple categories

```
SELECT DISTINCT (categories)
FROM product
UNNEST product.categories AS categories
```

Query Scan Consistency

The consistency level for a given N1QL query can be configured using the staleness parameter for the query. The following consistency levels can be specified for the staleness parameter:

- `scan_consistency=not_bounded`

This level returns the query with the lowest latency, as it is the most relaxed consistency level. Selecting this option essentially means the query can return data that is currently indexed and accessible by the index or the view. The query output can be arbitrarily out-of-date if there are many pending mutations that have not been indexed by the index or the view. This consistency level is useful for queries that favor low latency and do not need the most up-to-date information.

- `scan_consistency=request_plus`

This level provides the strictest consistency level and thus executes with higher latencies than the other levels. This consistency level requires all mutations, up to the moment of the query request, to be processed before query execution can begin. This ensures that any writes that are done prior to issuing the query request, and possibly more recent mutations, have been indexed by the GSI or the view indexer and will be returned by the N1QL query if it qualifies for the result set. This guarantee is important to applications that require consistent reads or read-your-own-write semantics.

3.2.4 *Restrictions in N1QL*

While N1QL is very powerful (i.e., general), including its SQL extensions for dealing with nested objects in JSON, there are certain SQL language features supported by relational database management systems that – if permitted in Couchbase Server – could be very detrimental to runtime performance, given the larger data sets and the unnormalized approach to managing data in the NoSQL world. One example of this would be expensive (general, non-key) joins, as opposed to those joins needed to quickly traverse key-based relationships. A restricted Cartesian product across two secondary attributes of documents is not supported linguistically in N1QL. Instead, joins are only allowed when one of the two sides involves the primary key (document ID) within a bucket.

3.3 Indexing support

As would be expected of any database system, Couchbase Server provides indexing capabilities to speed up query performance. It provides two types of indexes.

3.3.1 *Local View Index*

As explained earlier, one type of index provided is the *view* index. Views are built asynchronously and are maintained for each mutation. Couchbase Server pre-computes and stores these view results before returning results to a client. Views are local indexes, i.e., they are co-located on each node where their associated indexed data lives, so they use the same hash-partitioning scheme discussed later for the data (see Figure 5).

Views can either be defined using Javascript (as in the earlier example) or via a SQL-like `CREATE INDEX` statement.

Example: Create an index using a local view on the email attribute of the profiles stored in the 'Profile' Couchbase Bucket

```
CREATE INDEX email on `Profile` (email)
USING VIEW;
```

3.3.2 *Global Secondary Index*

As their name suggests, a global secondary index (GSI) is a global index on all of the documents stored within a specified Couchbase bucket, and it is stored separately (hence "global") from the data itself. It can optionally use a range-partitioned scheme separate from the data's hash-partitioning scheme. GSI indexes reside on the nodes of the cluster where the index service is running. (Figure 9 in Section 4.3 shows a sample cluster topology.)

Example: Create an index using a GSI index on the email attribute of the profiles stored in the 'Profile' Couchbase Bucket

```
CREATE INDEX email on `Profile` (email)
USING GSI;
```

3.3.3 *Primary Index*

Typically, when describing the indexing capabilities of a database, one would expect to have the Primary Index described first. However, in the case of Couchbase Server, the "real" primary index in Couchbase is the hash table of keys that allows users to perform direct key value access. However, since this table doesn't provide a mechanism to perform range queries and other types of lookups on the attributes of JSON, Couchbase additionally allows users to define a PRIMARY INDEX similar to that of a RDBMS but based on the server's secondary indexing capabilities (either using a local view or a global secondary index) described above.

Example: Create a Primary Index on the Profile bucket

```
CREATE PRIMARY INDEX profile_pk_view ON
Profile USING VIEW;
```

or

```
CREATE PRIMARY INDEX profile_pk_gsi ON
Profile USING GSI WITH
{''defer_build'':true''};
```

3.3.4 *Selective or Partial Indexes*

Given that the data is stored in Couchbase is in a schema-free and unnormalized format, and that in many cases, documents (objects) of different types may be stored together in a given Couchbase bucket, N1QL allows users to create "selective indexes" (also sometimes called partial indexes [8]). Filtering the data to be indexed based on the anticipated query workload can significantly improve both indexing and query performance.

Example: Create an index using a global index on the age attribute of the profiles stored in the 'Profile' Couchbase bucket, but just for data where the age is > 21

```
CREATE INDEX over21 ON `Profile`(age)
WHERE age > 21
USING GSI;
```

4. A LOOK UNDER THE HOOD

4.1 Overview of clustered architecture

Couchbase Server has a shared-nothing architecture. It is typically set up as a cluster of multiple servers behind an application server. A cluster of Couchbase Servers consists of one or more nodes, with each containing a configurable set of services. This architecture allows the cluster to be scaled out horizontally, by adding more nodes, or scaled up vertically, by adding "beefier" hardware.

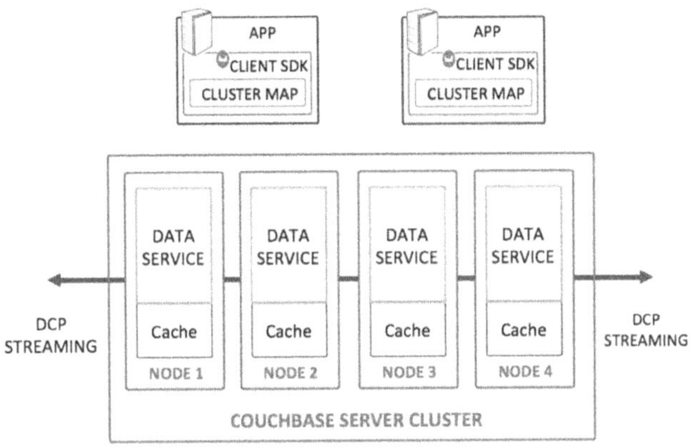

Figure 4. Couchbase Cluster Architecture

Figure 4 depicts a 4-node cluster. The figure's two application servers run the Couchbase client driver, and these clients can talk with any node in the cluster to read and/or write data. In this diagram, only the data service is running. There are additional services (described later) that can be added as the functionality required for an application becomes more complex.

A Couchbase bucket is the rough equivalent of a database and is better described as being a key space. Documents with different schemas can be stored in the same bucket. Each bucket is split into 1024 logical partitions called *vBuckets (vB)*. This is not a configurable number; any Couchbase server deployment has 1024 logical partitions. This number was selected to provide a good balance of cluster manageability from a size perspective and the amount of data that is managed per partition. The former is important for operational maintenance, and the latter is important for the performance of maintenance tasks that are carried out across the cluster. In general, cluster sizes as well as the amount of data managed by them have grown in production deployments; however, given the operational focus, in practice the number of nodes in our production clusters has yet to grow beyond about 150 nodes. A 150-node cluster can support many terabytes of data and has the capacity to handle millions of operations per second. Section 10.1.1 presents an overview of the Key Value performance.

vBuckets are mapped to physical servers across the cluster, and the mapping is stored in a lookup structure called the **cluster map**. Section 4.3.1 goes into more details about how this map is managed. Applications can use Couchbase's smart clients, which contain a copy of the cluster map, to interact with the server. Smart clients can hash the **document ID (key)**, which is specified by the application, for each document added to Couchbase. As shown in Figure 5, a client applies a hash function (CRC32) to every document that needs to be stored in Couchbase, and the document can then be sent directly from the client to the server where it should reside.

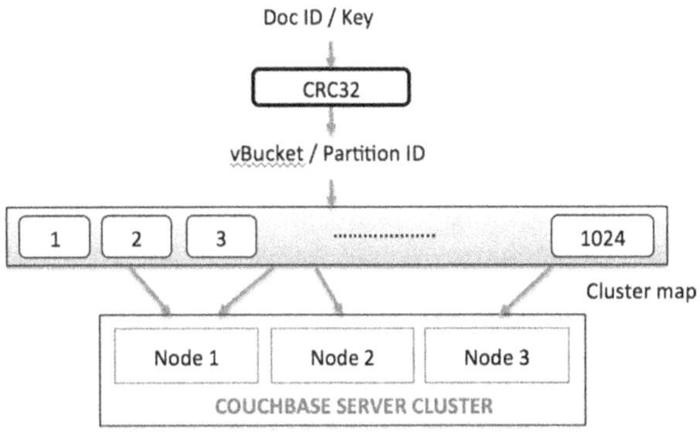

Figure 5. Mapping Keys to Partitions and Servers

4.1.1 Intra-cluster Replication

A bucket can be replicated up to 3 times, giving the user up to 4 copies of their data. An individual server manages only a subset of the active and replica partitions. At any point in time, for a given partition, only one copy of the partition will be active, with zero or more replica partitions on other servers. If the server hosting an active partition fails, the cluster will promote one of the replica partitions to active status, thereby ensuring that applications can continue to access the data without incurring downtime.

4.2 Asynchronous architecture

As explained earlier, in Couchbase Server all of the operations after a document is first written to memory will be performed *asynchronously*. This is a fundamental concept that extends to every facet of the server.

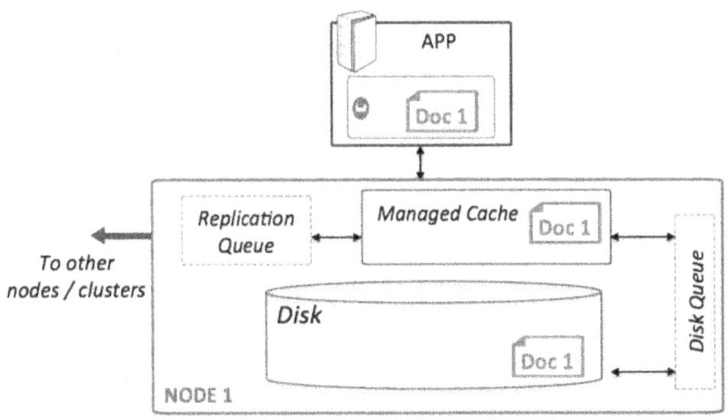

Figure 6. Couchbase Server Asynchronous Architecture

When data is written to Couchbase, it is first stored in the hash tables in the integrated (managed) cache. At this point, an initial acknowledgement of receipt of the mutation is sent back to the client SDK. This mutation is then asynchronously written to disk via the disk write queue, and at the same time it is also pushed into the in-memory replication queue to be replicated to other nodes within the cluster. This is summarized in Figure 6.

As explained in the earlier discussion of durability constraints, client applications are given a choice of whether or not to wait for replication and/or for persistence on a per mutation basis. This allows each application to make its own choice, based on its requirements and the nature of its data, regarding taking (or not) the performance penalty associated with these operations. When a document it written, a sequence number is generated and associated with the mutation. The maximum sequence number per vBucket is also tracked. This mechanism allows other parts of the system to provide an option for strong consistency.

Each mutation is also asynchronously fed to other parts of the system, such as cross-cluster replication, the view index engine, and the global secondary index (GSI) service. If a N1QL query chooses `request_plus` scan consistency, the query engine will wait until the index is updated up to the maximum sequence number for each vBucket.

4.3 Node-level architecture

The nodes in a Couchbase Server cluster can all look the same, or various subsets of the cluster nodes can be configured to run a particular (sub)set of services. This uniformity of architecture allows users to seamlessly scale a database linearly without a single point of failure. However, independent of what other services are running, there is some core functionality that runs on every node, *e.g.,* the cluster manager.

4.3.1 Cluster Manager

The Couchbase cluster manager supervises server configuration and interaction across all servers within a cluster. It is a critical component, as it manages the replication and data rebalancing operations in Couchbase. Although the cluster manager executes locally on each cluster node, the nodes also elect a cluster-wide *orchestrator node* to watch over the cluster conditions and carry out appropriate cluster management functions.

If a node in the cluster crashes or otherwise becomes unavailable, the orchestrator notifies all other machines in the cluster. It promotes to active status replica partitions associated with the server that went down. The cluster map will also be updated on all of the cluster nodes and the clients. The process of activating replica partitions is known as *failover*.

If the orchestrator node itself crashes, the existing nodes will detect the fact that it is no longer available and they will elect a new orchestrator immediately so that the cluster can continue to operate without disruption.

When the number of servers in a cluster changes due to scaling out or due to failures, data partitions must be redistributed. Doing this ensures that data will remain evenly distributed throughout the cluster and thus that application access to the data will be load-balanced evenly across all the servers. This process is called **rebalancing.**

When a rebalance begins, a new cluster map is calculated based on the current pending set of servers to be added and removed from the cluster. It is then streamed to all the servers in the cluster. During rebalance, the cluster moves the data directly between two server nodes (the source and destination) in the cluster. Once the cluster moves each partition from one location to another, an atomic and consistent switchover takes place between the two affected nodes, and the cluster updates each connected client library with the new cluster map. Throughout the migration and redistribution of partitions among servers, any given partition on a server will be in one of the following states:

Active: The server hosting the partition is servicing all types of requests for this partition.

Replica: The server hosting the partition cannot handle client requests, but it will receive replication commands. Rebalance marks the destination partitions as being replicas until they are ready to be switched to active.

Dead: This server is not in any way responsible for this partition.

4.3.2 Database Change Protocol

Any mutation that happens on an object in the data service must be propagated to all other parts on the system that need to know, including data replication, indexes, and so on. Couchbase has an internal Database Change Protocol (DCP) that is utilized to keep all of the different components in sync and to move data between the components at high speed. DCP lies at the heart of Couchbase Server and supports its memory-first architecture by decoupling potential I/O bottlenecks from many critical functions.

4.3.3 Data Service

As described above, Couchbase Server supports high speed, direct read/write operations based on a core Key-Value API (KV API). The Data Service provides the KV API that allows developers to create, retrieve, update and delete records by primary key. The Data Service forms the base data management layer of Couchbase and is leveraged by the Indexing and Query services. The data manager has a number of parts, including the object-managed cache, storage engine, view engine, and projector and router.

Object Managed Cache

Key-value pairs are stored in the object-managed cache. Hash tables for each virtual bucket reside in this cache and offer a quick way of detecting whether a given document currently exists in memory or not. Each document in a partition will have a corresponding entry in the hash table; each entry for a document stores the document's ID (i.e., its key), some document metadata, and the document's value.

By default the key and the metadata for every key in the bucket will be kept in memory, while the associated values can be evicted based on usage. Users also have the option to enable the eviction of the key and metadata based on usage.

Storage Engine

With Couchbase's append-only storage engine design, document mutations always go to the end of a file. When a new document is added in Couchbase, it is added at the end of a file. If an update is made to a document in Couchbase, it also is recorded at the end of the file. This improves disk write performance, as all updates are written sequentially. *Compaction* is periodically run, based on a fragmentation threshold, and while the system is online, to clean up stale data from the append-only storage.

View Engine

The view engine is responsible for building and querying ***view indexes.*** As explained earlier, views in Couchbase are defined using a map function, which extracts the data of interest from documents, and an optional reduce function, which aggregates the data that is emitted by the map function. Since the view index is a local index, the view engine runs within the data service. This component is a consumer of the DCP feed of the mutations needed to update the view indexes.

During initial view building or materialization of the view, Couchbase reads the partition's data files and applies the map function across every document. A key characteristic of a view index is that it stores the pre-computed aggregates defined in the Reduce function as a part of the index tree. This allows for very fast aggregation at query time.

As shown in Figure 8, applications can query views using one of the Couchbase SDKs. View query execution takes a scatter/gather approach: Queries are sent to a randomly selected server within the cluster. The server that receives a query sends the request to the other relevant servers in the cluster and then aggregates their results. The query's final result is then returned to the client.

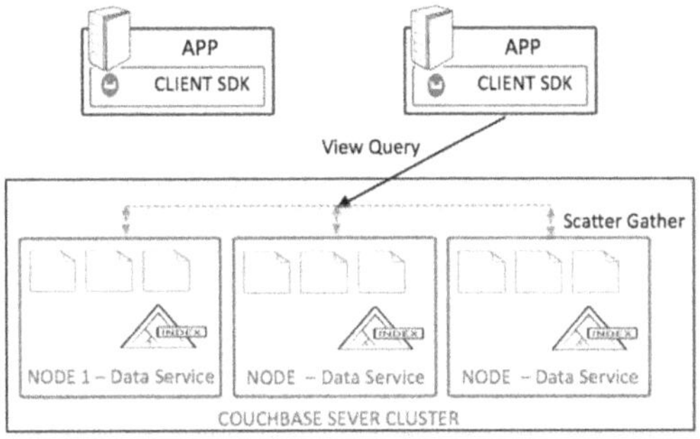

Figure 8. Distributed View indexing and querying

During a rebalance operation, partitions change state – the original partition transitions from *active* to *dead*, and the target partition transitions from *replica* to *active*. Since the view index on each node is synchronized with the partitions on the same server, when a partition has migrated to a different server, the documents that belong to the migrated partition should not be used in the view result anymore. To keep track of the relevant partitions that can be used in the view index, information about vBuckets is stored in the view B-tree itself. Using this information, parts of a B-tree can be deactivated as needed. This helps maintain consistency when querying a view index during rebalancing or failover operations.

Index Projector

The Projector is responsible for mapping incoming mutations to a set of Global Secondary Key Versions needed for secondary index maintenance. The Projector resides within the data service where the mutation originated, and it is a consumer of the DCP feed of mutations that sends its evaluated results to the Router.

Index Router

The Router is responsible for sending Key Versions to the index service. The router relies on the index distribution and partitioning topology to determine which indexer(s) should receive the key version. The router resides on the same node as the projector.

4.3.4 Index Service

The indexing service is responsible for managing all of the global secondary indexes. Various components work together to manage and maintain global secondary indexes. The projector and router live on the data service, while the index managers and indexers live on the index service. These together cooperate to manage the mutations coming from the Data Service via DCP. The projector extracts the secondary keys relevant to the indexes that have been defined and sends them to the router. The router then decides which indexer to send the message to. In case the index is partitioned, the partition key tells the router which indexer and which node to send the message to. An insert message may be sent to one indexer with a delete message being sent to another in the event that the value of the partition key itself has changed.

Index Manager

The *Index Manager* resides within the indexing service (see Figure 9) and is responsible for receiving requests for indexing operations (*e.g.,* creation, deletion, maintenance, scan, lookup).

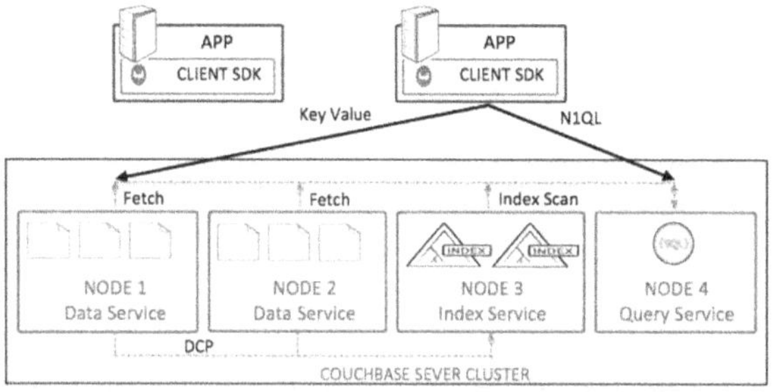

Figure 9. Index Service with Global Index

Indexer (Local Indexer)

The indexer component processes the changes received from the router and manages the on-disk index tree data structure. It also provides the interface for the query client to run index scans and it does scatter/gather for queries in case of a partitioned GSI index.

4.3.5 Query Service

At a high level, the Query Service takes an application query and performs the necessary functions to retrieve, filter, and/or project the data in order to resolve the application's request. Query execution is the job of the Query Service. To process a given user query, the query engine will issue requests to the index service, the data service, or both, depending on the chosen query plan.

Query Catalog

This Query Service component provides catalog support for the Query Service. This includes allowing it to perform Index DDL (*e.g.,* Create, Drop) and Index Scan/Stats operations. (Section 4.5 will discuss more of the details of query planning and execution.)

4.4 Multi-dimensional Scaling

As the earlier Sections described, an administrator can choose to run the Data, Index and Query Services on all or different nodes. This ability to have multiple "dimensions" in which to scale the cluster is called multi-dimensional scaling (MDS). This allows Couchbase users to scale workloads independently based on their needs – so a cluster can reflect and support the technical business requirements of an application.By separating its core data management functions into these three services, Couchbase Server enables users to control the scalability characteristics of their system based on workload characteristics. As those requirements change, Couchbase users can expand or shrink their cluster, adding data management resources to the function(s) where they are needed most in order to address the changing Data, Index, and Query Service requirements. A typical setup might have the Data Service running on nodes with more memory, the Query Service on nodes with more cores, and the Index Service on nodes with faster disks.

4.5 Deeper dive into indexing and querying

4.5.1 High-Level Query Service Interactions

Couchbase SDKs can route N1QL queries to any one of the nodes running the query service. The receiving node will analyze the query, use metadata on its referenced objects to choose the best execution plan, and execute the chosen plan. During execution, depending on the query and the available indexes, the query node works with the index and data nodes to retrieve keys and data, performing the required set of select-join-project operations.

The index service does not directly communicate with the data service. Instead, the query service issues all key-value access requests (unless a covering index can fully answer the query). An index simply returns the document ID for each attribute match found during index scans. This ID is then used by the query service to fetch the document itself in order to access and project out the additional fields that are needed.

4.5.2 Step-by-Step Query Execution Flow

Figure 10 enumerates the query processing steps for an example N1QL query. Once a query plan has been constructed, based on the operators and scans needed, the query service coordinates first with the index service and then with the data service. The query results are streamed to the client as they become available.

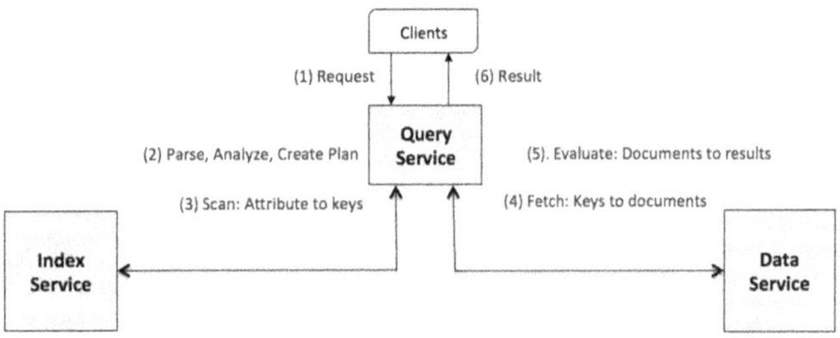

Figure 10. Data flow from query to index and data service

4.5.3 Query Execution Operators

Figure 11 shows the operators of query execution in more detail. Note that not all queries will have every operator in their plan, and some operators may appear and be executed multiple times. For example, the sort operator can be omitted if there is no ORDER BY clause in the query, while the scan, fetch, and join operators may be needed multiple times to perform multiple joins.

To see how a given N1QL query will be executed, an `EXPLAIN` statement can be used before any N1QL statement to request information about the execution plan for the statement.

Example:

```
EXPLAIN SELECT title, genre, runtime
FROM catalog.details
ORDER BY title
```

To optimize a query, the N1QL query planner analyzes the query and available access path options for each keyspace (bucket) in the query to pick an appropriate plan and execution infrastructure. The planner needs to first select the access path for each bucket, determine the join order, and then determine the type of the join operation. Once these big decisions have been made, the planner then creates the infrastructure needed to execute the plan. Some operations, like query parsing and planning, are done serially, while other operations, like fetch, join, and sort, are done in a local parallel (based on multicore) manner.

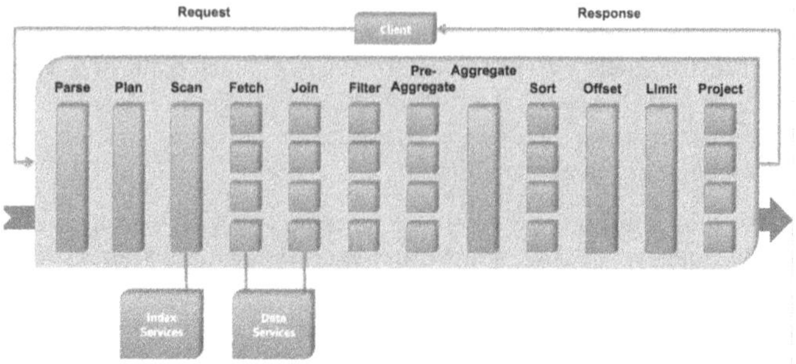

Figure 11. Operators in a N1QL query plan

In terms of the infrastructure available for query execution, some of the most important query plan operators are explained below:

Keyspace (bucket) scan – There are three types of scans:

- *Keyscan access:* When specific document IDs (primary keys) are available, the Keyscan access method retrieves the documents for those IDs. Any filters associated with that keyspace will be applied after retrieval. The Keyscan access method can be used either when a keyspace is being queried by itself or during join processing. A keyscan is commonly used to retrieve qualifying documents from the inner keyspace during join processing.

- *PrimaryScan access:* This is the equivalent of a full table scan in a relational database system. This is chosen when Documents IDs are not available and no qualifying secondary access methods are available for this keyspace. N1QL will again apply applicable filters on each document after retrieval. This access method is quite expensive, and the average time to return results increases linearly with number of documents in the bucket.

- *IndexScan access:* A qualifying secondary index scan is used to first filter the keyspace and determine the qualifying document IDs. The query executor then retrieves the qualifying documents from the data store by ID. In Couchbase, the chosen secondary index can be a (local) view index or a global secondary index.

Fetch – This operator reaches into the data service for the objects with a specific key. An index only contains document IDs, so the fetch operator is needed whenever a query includes additional projections that cannot be answered from the index alone. The execution of the fetch operator is parallelized.

Projection – There are two kinds of projection operators:
- *InitialProject*: This operator reduces the stream size to just the fields actually involved in query.
- *FinalProject*: This operator performs the final shaping of the result into the requested JSON schema.

Unnest – This is a join operation between a parent and a child object containing a nested array. In its result, the parent object is repeated for each child array item.

Nest: This inverse of **Unnest** is a grouping operation between a parent and a (desired) child with a nested array. In the result, the child array will be embedded in the parent object.

Join methods

N1QL supports a nested loop-based access method for all of the join types that it supports: `INNER JOIN` and `LEFT OUTER JOIN`. Consider the following `FROM` clause in a N1QL query:

```
FROM (ORDERS o INNER JOIN CUSTOMER c
ON KEYS o.O_C_ID)
```

For this join, ORDERS will serve as the outer keyspace and CUSTOMER will be the inner keyspace. The ORDERS keyspace will be scanned first (using one of the scan options described above). Then, for each of the qualifying documents from ORDERS, a KEYSCAN will occur on CUSTOMER based on the key O_C_ID in the ORDERS document.

4.6 Cross Cluster Replication

Cross datacenter replication (XDCR) provides a way to replicate active data to multiple, geographically diverse datacenters. This is done either for disaster recovery or to bring data closer to users.

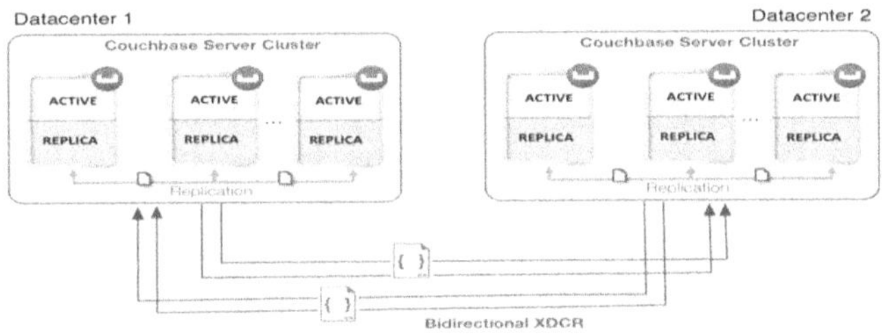

Figure 12. Cross datacenter replication architecture

Both intra-cluster replication and XDCR occur simultaneously, as Figure 12 illustrates. Intra-cluster replication takes place on both datacenters, and it happens within each cluster. At the same time, XDCR serves to replicate documents across datacenters. XDCR is also a consumer of the internal DCP stream, as it uses the DCP stream to push in-memory document mutations to the destination cluster. Some of the most notable attributes of XCDR are as follows:

XDCR can be setup on a per bucket basis. Depending upon application's requirements, only a subset of data may need to be replicated. This can be done either on a per bucket basis or even within a bucket by using filtered replication (based on a regular expression on the document ID, i.e., primary key, string).

XDCR is **cluster topology aware**. The source and destination clusters can have different numbers of servers and thus different data partitioning. If a server in the destination cluster goes down, XDCR is able to utilize the updated cluster topology information and can continue replicating data to the appropriate available servers in the destination cluster.

4.6.1 Consistency Across Clusters

Within a cluster, Couchbase Server provides strong consistency at the document level for the key-value API and controllable consistency when querying. Across clusters, XDCR provides **eventual consistency** [9]. This makes Couchbase a CP system within a cluster but an AP system across clusters with respect to the CAP theorem [12]. This choice was made to avoid taking a performance hit on writes, maintaining high performance while still providing 100% availability for reads / writes across clusters.

A built-in conflict resolution mechanism picks the same "winner" on both clusters if a document is mutated on both before being replicated. If such a conflict occurs, the document with the most updates is considered the "winner." If both clusters have the same number of updates for a document, additional metadata fields are used to pick the "winner." XDCR applies the same rule on both clusters to make sure that document consistency is maintained.

5. TUNING FOR OLTP PERFORMANCE

There are certain things commonly done in relational systems that would not work well with today's NoSQL data volumes and the scale of the systems needed to support them.

5.1.1 Avoid using a PRIMARY index

Couchbase allows users to create a PRIMARY index as a way to access all objects in a keyspace, but a best practice is to avoid queries requiring a PRIMARY index scan. The fastest data access will be via key-value look-ups or N1QL's USE KEYS clause.

5.1.2 Use of covering indexes

For the best performance, appropriate GSI indexes can be created to support a query without any document fetches. Such a covering index includes all of the information needed to satisfy the query and can thus avoid the need for an additional step to access the indexed data. Covered queries, that is, queries that get all their information from the index, deliver better performance. (This is actually a trick used in the relational world as well; it essentially uses an index as a "poor man's materialized view".)

6. A GLIMPSE INTO THE FUTURE

As described in the Introduction, Couchbase Server has evolved significantly since the early days, and its evolution is ongoing.

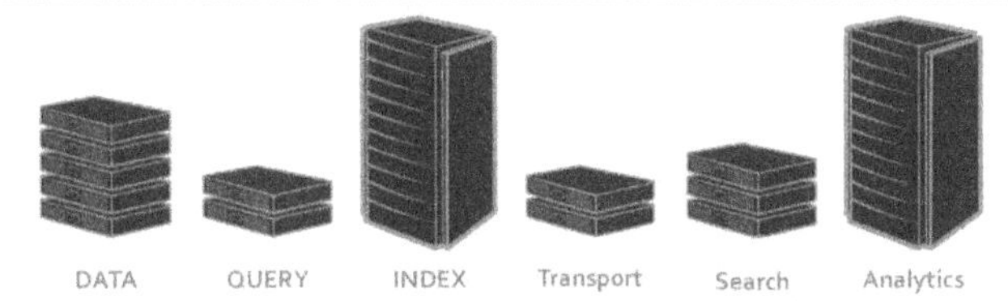

Figure 13. Services in a future Couchbase Server

With a vision to provide a single platform that can be used for all types of operational workloads, there are several key components that will be added to Couchbase in the near future. The resulting set of component services is sketched in Figure 13.

6.1 Near-term plans

6.1.1 Memory-optimized indexes

With a focus on its low-latency-driven memory-first architecture, a new feature in Couchbase version 4.5 is support for memory-optimized indexes.

These new indexes will reside completely in memory, dramatically reducing dependence on disk. Recoverability is provided via disk-backups. This functionality will allow users with very high write-heavy workloads to continue to utilize N1QL and indexing in addition to key-value access, as indexes can keep up with higher mutation rates. It will also allow very fast index scans to reduce query latencies. Section 10.1.2 presents an overview of query performance with memory-optimized indexes.

6.1.2 Array indexes

One of the key strengths of JSON is its ability to nest objects or items within arrays. Arrays are one very natural approach used to embed related data objects within a parent (e.g., think line items within orders). Nesting provides great flexibility from a data modeling perspective, but it is also important for those individual objects from within an array to be indexed and queried. N1QL today allows users to query items within an array, but without an index to support array predicates, the performance of such queries can be an issue. Version 4.5 will enable users to create indexes on array-valued fields, making those queries significantly faster.

6.1.3 Full-text search service

Another workload dimension that is required for some operational applications is full-text search. This is typically based on a reverse index, where all the *words* within the data are indexed to be able to do term-based, phrase-based, and/or prefix-based searches. Full-text search is another type of service currently being added that will receive data mutations via in-memory DCP and will be able to be scaled up or out independently as well.

6.2 Medium-term plans

One big area that Couchbase plans to add to the mix of services available to operational applications is operational analytics. By consolidating this into the core platform, rich applications can be built with a single platform that enables end-to-end management of operational data. Query-based insights from the latest updates can then be fed back into applications almost instantly without having to move data physically out of the cluster or being forced to restructure (*e.g.,* flatten) it via pre-analysis ETL.

The planned analytics service will be based on the open-source Apache AsterixDB Big Data Management System [1, 2]. The NSF-sponsored Asterix project set out to develop a next-generation system to ingest, manage, index, query, and analyze mass quantities of semi-structured data. The resulting platform, AsterixDB, has an extremely complementary data model to that of Couchbase. That commonality is one of the main reasons that the two teams decided to collaborate. The planned analytical service will be another new service that is fed via in-memory DCP and that can be scaled either out or up independently with respect to other services, especially the data service (to provide performance isolation for the all-important front-end OLTP workloads). The new analytics service will support a much wider range of queries and will include a parallel database inspired scalable runtime engine. Under the hood, AsterixDB includes partitioned, LSM-based data storage and indexing, support for both natively stored and external data, and a rich set of built-in types. A typical workload on the analytics engine, unlike the OLTP-like N1QL query engine, will include richer (and more expensive) queries such as large joins, aggregations, grouping, and so on.

7. CONCLUSION

We have described the history and evolution of Couchbase Server from its early roots as a key-value store to its current form, which is a full-featured and fully queryable document data manager. We pointed out a number of the unique features and requirements that arose from the need to support low-latency, OLTP-like workloads. We described the view from outside the system and the APIs available to users. These external interfaces were designed to be simple, but the internal architecture that supports them was built to support the OLTP requirements of next-generation applications, including flexible schemas, incremental scalability, and high performance. We explained how the components of Couchbase Server work together under the hood, including its data storage, indexing, and query services, and we closed with a glimpse into where things are expected to be going in the future.

8. ACKNOWLEDGEMENTS

The existence of Couchbase Server 4.1 (and 4.5) today is due to the combined efforts of many terrific Couchbase team members whose contributions we wish to acknowledge.

9. REFERENCES

[1] S. Alsubaiee *et al,* AsterixDB: A Scalable, Open Source BDMS, *Proc. VLDB Endowment* 7(14), October 2014.

[2] *Apache AsterixDB*, http://asterixdb.apache.org/.

[3] R. Cattell, Scalable SQL and NoSQL Data Stores, *ACM SIGMOD Record* 39(4), May 2011.

[4] *Couchbase NoSQL Database*, http://www.couchbase.com/.

[5] D. DeWitt and J. Gray, Parallel Database Systems: The Future of High Performance Database Systems, *CACM* 35(6), June 1992.

[6] Y. Papakonstantinou, Semistructured Models, Queries and Algebras in the Big Data Era, Tutorial in *Proc. ACM SIGMOD Conf.*, San Francisco, CA, June 2016.

[7] P. Sadalage and M. Fowler, *NoSQL Distilled: A Brief Guide to the Emerging World of Polyglot Persistence*, Addison-Wesley Professional, 2012.

[8] M. Stonebraker. The Case for Partial Indexes, *ACM SIGMOD Record* 18(4), December 1989.

[9] D. Terry, Replicated Data Consistency Explained Through Baseball, *CACM* 56(12), December 2013.

[10] *Magic Quadrant for Operational Database Management Systems,* Gartner, https://www.gartner.com/doc/3147919/magic-quadrant-operational-database-management.

[11] R. Bello *et al*, Materialized Views in Oracle, *Proc. 24th VLDB Conf.,* New York, NY, August 1998.

[12] S. Gilbert and N. Lynch, Perspectives on the CAP Theorem, *Computer* 45(2), February 2012

[13] K. Ong, Y. Papakonstantinou, and R. Vernoux, *The SQL++ Query Language: Configurable, Unifying and Semi-structured,* http://arxiv.org/abs/1405.3631.

[14] B. Cooper, A. Silberstein, E. Tam, R. Ramakrishnan, and R. Sears, Benchmarking Cloud Serving Systems with YCSB, *Proc. 1st ACM Symp. on Cloud Computing*, Indianapolis, Indiana, June 2010.

10. APPENDIX

10.1 Couchbase Server performance

In this section, we present some sample performance results, obtained using the Couchbase Server 4.5 Developer Preview, to provide a brief overview of the performance characteristics of Couchbase for both key-value and query workloads. The testing tool used was the Yahoo Cloud Serving Benchmark (YCSB) [14]. The Couchbase adapter for YCSB was built to operate against a Couchbase Server cluster using the official Couchbase Java SDK and provides a rich set of configuration options, including support for the N1QL query language.

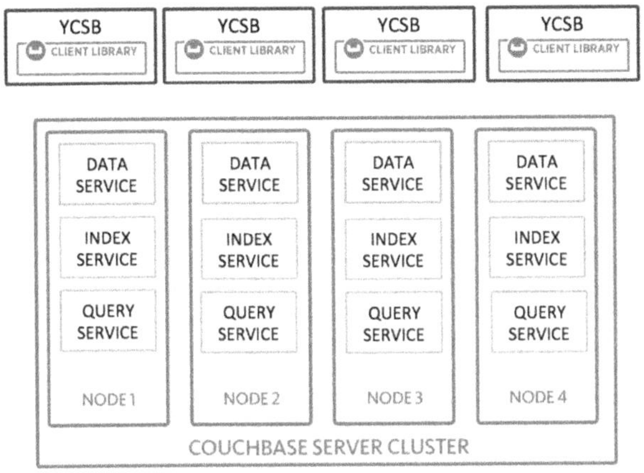

Figure 14. Performance test setup

The deployment topology used was simple, with the data, index and query services running on all nodes of a 4-node cluster. There are 4 YCSB clients that generate load. The number for threads for each client was scaled up from 12 threads to 32 threads and the maximum throughput was measured. There are two workloads presented here; each was run on the 4-node Couchbase cluster using an early version (Developer Preview) of the 4.5 release.

10.1.1 Key-value performance (YCSB workload A)

Workload A of YCSB is a mixed workload with 50% reads and 50% writes of keys. In this test, the thread counts for each of the four YCSB clients were varied from 12 to 32 threads. A data set of 10 million documents was used. The throughput in operations per second was measured and is plotted in Figure 15. As shown, a 4-node cluster with a total of 128 client threads driving load is capable of running approximately 178K operations per second.

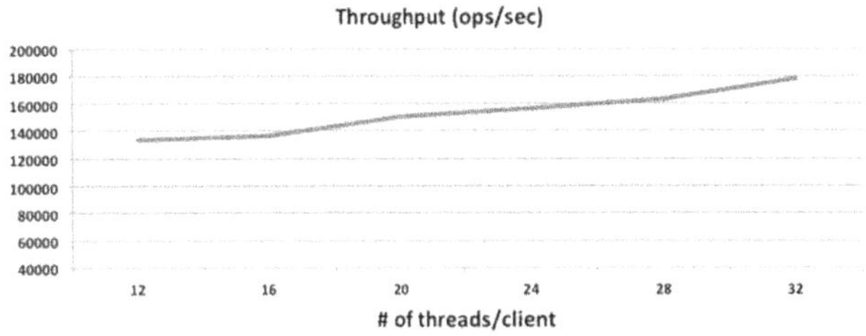

Figure 15. Simple operation throughput (ops/sec) *vs.* threads

10.1.2 Query performance (YCSB workload E)

Workload E of YCSB is a query workload consisting of small range queries. Short ranges of documents are queried via N1QL instead of performing individual document operations.

Sample query: `SELECT meta().id AS id FROM 'bucket' WHERE meta().id >= '$1' LIMIT $2;`

Similar to workload A, the thread counts for each of the four YCSB clients was varied from 12 to 32 threads. The throughput in queries per second was measured and is plotted in Figure 16 below. As shown, a 4-node cluster with a total of 128 client threads driving load is capable of running approximately 5400 small range queries per second.

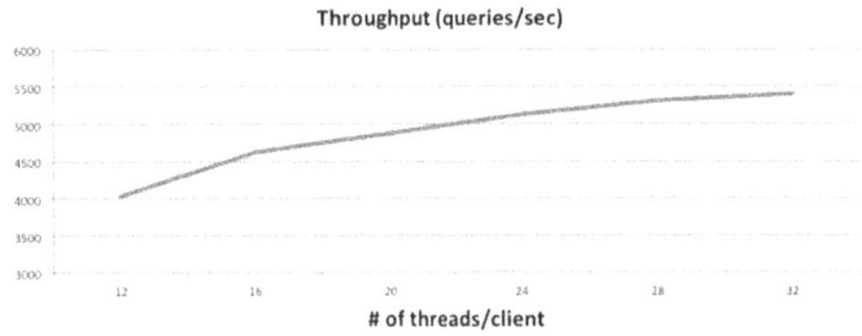

Figure 16. Range query throughput (queries/sec) *vs.* threads

Ambry: LinkedIn's Scalable Geo-Distributed Object Store

Shadi A. Noghabi[1], Sriram Subramanian[2], Priyesh Narayanan[2]
Sivabalan Narayanan[2], Gopalakrishna Holla[2], Mammad Zadeh[2], Tianwei Li[2]
Indranil Gupta[1], Roy H. Campbell[1]
[1]University of Illinois at Urbana-Champaign, [2]LinkedIn Corp.
{abdolla2, indy, rhc}@illinois.edu
{srsubramanian, pnarayanan, snarayanan, gholla, mzadeh, tili}@linkedin.com

ABSTRACT

The infrastructure beneath a worldwide social network has to continually serve billions of variable-sized media objects such as photos, videos, and audio clips. These objects must be stored and served with low latency and high throughput by a system that is geo-distributed, highly scalable, and load-balanced. Existing file systems and object stores face several challenges when serving such large objects. We present Ambry, a production-quality system for storing large immutable data (called blobs). Ambry is designed in a decentralized way and leverages techniques such as logical blob grouping, asynchronous replication, rebalancing mechanisms, zero-cost failure detection, and OS caching. Ambry has been running in LinkedIn's production environment for the past 2 years, serving up to 10K requests per second across more than 400 million users. Our experimental evaluation reveals that Ambry offers high efficiency (utilizing up to 88% of the network bandwidth), low latency (less than 50 ms latency for a 1 MB object), and load balancing (improving imbalance of request rate among disks by 8x-10x).

Keywords

Object Store, Geographically Distributed, Scalable, Load Balancing

1. INTRODUCTION

During the past decade, social networks have become popular communication channels worldwide. Hundreds of millions of users continually upload and view billions of diverse massive media objects, from photos and videos to documents. These large media objects, called *blobs*, are uploaded once, frequently accessed from all around the world, never modified, and rarely deleted. LinkedIn, as a global large-scale social network company, has faced the need for a geographically distributed system that stores and retrieves these read-heavy blobs in an efficient and scalable manner.

Handling blobs poses a number of unique challenges. First, due to diversity in media types, blob sizes vary significantly from tens of KBs (e.g., profile pictures) to a few GBs (e.g., videos). The system needs to store both massive blobs and a large number of small blobs efficiently. Second, there is an ever-growing number of blobs that need to be stored and served. Currently, LinkedIn serves more than 800 million put and get operations per day (over 120 TB in size). In the past 12 months, the request rate has almost doubled, from 5k requests/s to 9.5k requests/s. This rapid growth in requests magnifies the necessity for a linearly scalable system (with low overhead). Third, the variability in workload and cluster expansions can create unbalanced load, degrading the latency and throughput of the system. This creates a need for load-balancing. Finally, users expect the uploading process to be fast, durable, and highly available. When a user uploads a blob, all his/her friends from all around the globe should be able to see the blob with very low latency, even if parts of the internal infrastructure fail. To provide these properties, data has to be reliably replicated across the globe in multiple datacenters, while maintaining low latency for each request.

LinkedIn had its own home-grown solution called Media Server, built using network attached storage filers (for file storage), Oracle database (for metadata), and Solaris boxes. Media Server had multiple drawbacks. It faced CPU and IO spikes caused by numerous metadata operations for small objects, was not horizontally scalable, and was very expensive. Given that LinkedIn was scaling rapidly and the future web content will be largely dominated by media, we needed to find a replacement.

Several systems have been designed for handling a large amount of data, but none of them satisfactorily meet the requirements and scale LinkedIn needs. There has been extensive research into distributed file systems [10, 16, 22, 24, 28]. These systems have a number of limitations when used for storing blobs, as pointed out by [3, 11]. For instance, the hierarchical directory structure and rich metadata are an overkill for a blob store and impose unnecessary additional overhead.

Many key value stores [2, 5, 8, 14] have also been designed for storing a large number of objects. Although these systems can handle many small objects, they are not optimized for storing large objects (tens of MBs to GBs). Further, they impose extra overhead for providing consistency guarantees while these are typically not needed for immutable data. Some examples of these overheads include using vector clocks, conflict resolution mechanism, logging, and central coordinators.

A few systems have been designed specifically for large immutable objects including Facebook's Haystack [3] along with f4 [18] and Twitter's Blob Store [27]. However, these systems do not resolve load imbalance, especially when cluster expansions occur.

In this paper we present Ambry, a production-quality system designed specifically for diverse large and small im-

SIGMOD'16, June 26-July 01, 2016, San Francisco, CA, USA

ISBN 978-1-4503-3531-7/16/06...$15.00

DOI: http://dx.doi.org/10.1145/2882903.2903738

mutable data with read-heavy traffic, where data is written once, and read many times (>95% read traffic). Ambry is designed with four main goals in mind:

1) Low Latency and High Throughput: The system needs to serve a large number of requests per second in a timely fashion, while working on cheap commodity hardware (e.g., HDDs). In order to reach this goal, Ambry utilizes a number of techniques including exploiting the OS cache, using zero copy when reading data from disk to network, chunking data along with retrieving/storing chunks in parallel from multiple nodes, providing configurable polices for the number of replicas to write and read, and zero-cost failure detection mechanisms (Sections 2.3, 4.2, and 4.3).

2) Geo-Distributed Operation: Blobs have to be replicated in other geographically distributed datacenters for high durability and availability, even in the presence of failures. To achieve low latency and high throughput in this geo-distributed setting, Ambry is designed as a decentralized multi-master system where data can be written to or read from any of the replicas. Additionally, it uses asynchronous writes that write data to the closest datacenter and asynchronously replicate to other datacenter(s). Also, for higher availability, it uses proxy requests that forward requests to other datacenters when the data is not replicated in the current datacenter yet (Sections 2.3 and 4.2).

3) Scalability: With the ever-growing amount of data, the system has to scale out efficiently with low overhead. To achieve this goal, Ambry makes three main design choices. First, Ambry separates the logical placement of blobs from their physical placement, allowing it to change the physical placement transparently from the logical placement. Second, Ambry is designed as a completely decentralized system, with no manager/master. Third, Ambry uses on-disk segmented indexing along with Bloom filters and an in-memory cache of the latest segment, allowing for scalable and efficient indexing of blobs. (Section 4.3).

4) Load Balancing: The system has to stay balanced in spite of growth. Ambry uses chunking of large blobs along with a random selection approach to remain balanced in a static cluster, and a re-balancing mechanism to return to a balanced state whenever cluster expansion occurs (Section 3).

Ambry has successfully been in production for the last 24 months, across four datacenters, serving more than 400 million users. Our experimental results show that Ambry reaches high throughput (reaching up to 88% of the network bandwidth) and low latency (serving 1 MB blobs in less than 50 ms), works efficiently across multiple geo-distributed datacenters, and improves the imbalance among disks by a factor of 8x-10x while moving minimal data.

2. SYSTEM OVERVIEW

In this section we discuss the overall design of Ambry including the high-level architecture of the system (Section 2.1), the notion of partition (Section 2.2), and supported operations (Section 2.3).

2.1 Architecture

Ambry is designed as a completely decentralized multi-tenant system across geographically distributed data centers. The overall architecture of Ambry is shown in Figure 1. The system is composed of three main components: *Frontends* that receive and route requests, *Datanodes* that store the actual data, and *Cluster Managers* that maintain the state of the cluster. Each datacenter owns and runs its own set of these components in a decentralized fashion. The Frontends and Datanodes are completely independent of one another, and the Cluster Managers are synchronized using

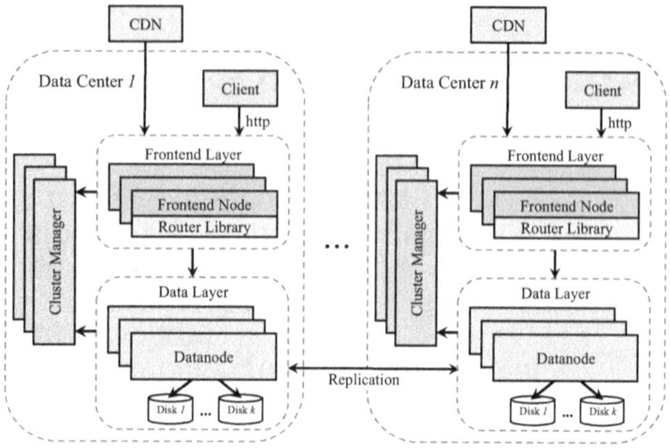

Figure 1: Architecture of Ambry.

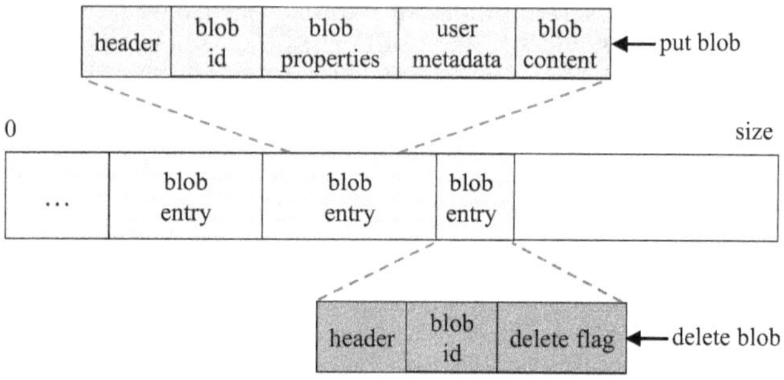

Figure 2: Partition and Blob layout.

Zookeeper [12]. We provide an overview of each component below (details in Section 4).

Cluster Manager: Ambry organizes its data in virtual units called *partitions* (Section 2.2). A partition is a logical grouping of a number of blobs, implemented as a large replicated file. On creation, partitions are read-write, i.e., immutable blobs are read and new blobs can be added. When a logical partition reaches its capacity, it turns read-only. The Cluster Manager keeps track of the state (read-write/read-only) and location of each partition replica, along with the physical layout of the cluster (nodes and disk placement).

Frontend: The Frontends are in charge of receiving and routing requests in a multi-tenant environment. The system serves three request types: put, get, and delete. Popular data is handled by a Content Delivery Network (CDN) layer above Ambry. Frontends receive requests directly from clients or through the CDN (if the data is cached). The Frontends forward a request to the corresponding Datanode(s) and return the response to the client/CDN originating the request.

Datanode: Datanodes store and retrieve the actual data. Each Datanode manages a number of disks. For better performance, Datanodes maintain a number of additional data structures including: indexing of blobs, journals and Bloom filters (Section 4.3).

2.2 Partition

Instead of directly mapping blobs to physical machines, e.g., Chord [26] and CRUSH [29], Ambry randomly groups blobs together into virtual units called *partitions*. The physical placement of partitions on machines is done in a separate procedure. This decoupling of the logical and physical placement enables transparent data movement (necessary for rebalancing) and avoids immediate rehashing of data during cluster expansion.

A partition is implemented as an append-only log in a pre-allocated large file. Currently, partitions are fixed-size during the life-time of the system [1]. The partition size should be large enough that the overhead of partitions, i.e., the additional data structures maintained per partition such as indexing, journals, and Bloom filters (Section 4.3), are negligible. On the other hand, the failure recovery and rebuild time should be small. We use 100 GB partitions in our clusters. Since rebuilding is done in parallel from multiple replicas, we found that even 100 GB partitions can be rebuilt in a few minutes.

Blobs are sequentially written to partitions as put and delete entries (Figure 2). Both entries contain a header (storing the offsets of fields in the entry) and a *blob id*. The blob id is a unique identifier, generated by the Frontend during a put operation, and used during get/delete operations for locating the blob. This id consists of the partition id in which the blob is placed (8 Bytes), followed by a 32 Byte universally unique id (UUID) for the blob. Collisions in blob ids are possible, but very unlikely (the probability is $< 2^{-320}$). For a collision to occur, two put operations have to generate equal UUIDs and chose similar partitions for the blob. Collisions are handled at the Datanodes by failing the late put request.

Put entries also include predefined properties including: blob size, time-to-live, creation time, and content type. Also, there is an optional map of user defined properties followed by the blob.

In order to offer high availability and fault-tolerance, each partition is replicated on multiple Datanodes. For replica placement, Ambry uses a greedy approach based on disk spaces. This algorithm chooses the disk with the most unallocated space while ensuring constraints such as: 1) not having more than one replica per Datanode and 2) having replicas in multiple data centers. Currently, the number of replicas per partition is configurable by the system administrator. As part of future work, we plan to adaptively change the number of replicas based on the popularity of the partition, and use erasure coding for cold data to even further reduce the replication factor.

On creation, partitions are read-write, serving all operations (put, get and delete). When the partition hits its upper threshold on size (capacity threshold) it becomes read-only, thereafter serving only get and delete operations.

The capacity threshold should be slightly less than the max capacity (80-90%) of the partition for two reasons. First, after becoming read-only, replicas might not be completely in-sync and need free space to catch-up later (because of asynchronous writes). Second, delete requests still append delete entries.

Deletes are similar to put operations, but on an existing blob. By default, deletes result in appending a delete entry (with the delete flag set) for the blob (soft delete). Deleted blobs are periodically cleaned up using an in-place compaction mechanism. After compaction, read-only partitions can become read-write if enough space is freed-up. In the rest of the paper we mainly focus on puts, due to the similarity of delete and put operations.

2.3 Operations

Ambry has a lightweight API supporting only 3 operations: put, get, and delete. The request handling procedure is shown in Figure 3. On receiving a request, the Frontend optionally conducts some security checks on the request. Then, using the Router Library (that contains the core logic of operation handling) it chooses a partition, communicates with the Datanode(s) in charge, and serves the request. In the put operation, the partition is chosen randomly (for data balancing purposes), and in the get/delete operation the partition is extracted from the blob id.

[1]As part of future work we plan to investigate potential improvements by using variable-size partitions.

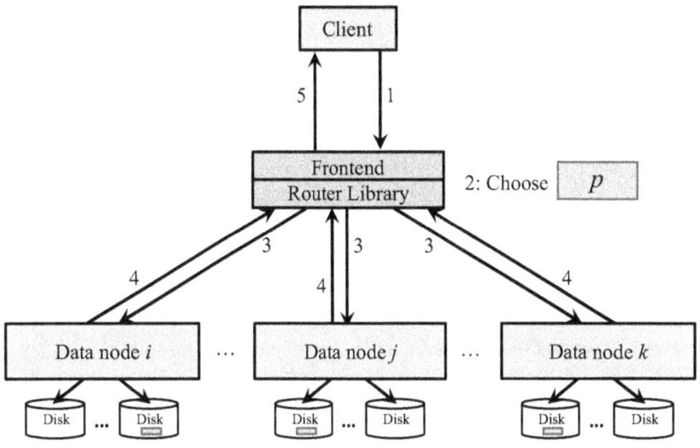

Figure 3: Steps in processing an operation.

Operations are handled in a multi-master design where operations can be served by any of the replicas. The decision of how many replicas to contact is based on user-defined policies. These policies are similar to consistency levels in Cassandra [14], where they control how many (one, k, majority, all) replicas to involve in an operation. For puts (or deletes), the request is forwarded to all replicas, and policies define the number of acknowledgments needed for a success (trade-off between durability and latency). For gets, policies determine how many randomly selected replicas to contact for the operation (trade-off between resources usage and latency). In practice, we found that for all operations the $k = 2$ replica policy gives us the balance we desire. Stricter polices (involving more replicas) can be used to provide stronger consistency guarantees.

Additionally, performing write operations to all replicas placed in multiple geo-distributed datacenters in a synchronous fashion can affect the latency and throughput. In order to alleviate this issue, Ambry uses asynchronous writes where puts are performed synchronously only in the local datacenter, i.e., the datacenter in which the Frontend receiving the request is located. The request is counted as successfully finished at this point. Later on, the blob is replicated to other datacenters using a lightweight replication algorithm (Section 5).

In order to provide read-after-write consistency in a datacenter which a blob has not been replicated yet (e.g., writing to one datacenter and reading from another), Ambry uses proxy requests. If the Frontend cannot retrieve a blob from its local datacenter, it proxies the request to another datacenter and returns the result from there. Although a proxy request is expensive, in practice we found that proxy requests happen infrequently (less than 0.001 % of the time).

3. LOAD BALANCING

Skewed workloads, massively large blobs, and cluster expansions create load imbalance and impact the throughput and latency of the system. Ambry achieves load balancing (in terms of disk usage and request rates) in both static and dynamic (scale-out) clusters.

Static Cluster: Splitting large blobs into multiple small chunks (Section 4.2.1) as well as routing put operations to random partitions, achieves balance in partition sizes. Additionally, using fairly large partition sizes along with relying on CDNs to handle very popular data significantly decrease the likelihood of hot partitions. Using these techniques the load imbalance of request rates and partition sizes in production gets to as low as 5% amongst Datanodes.

Dynamic Cluster: In practice, read-write partitions receive all the write traffic and also the majority of the read traffic (due to popularity). Since partitions grow in a semi-balanced manner, the number of read-write partitions becomes the main factor of load imbalance. After cluster expansion, new Datanodes contain only read-write partitions, while older Datanodes contain mostly read-only partitions. This skewed distribution of read-write partitions creates a large imbalance in the system. In our initial version, the average request rates of new Datanodes were up to 100x higher than old Datanodes and 10x higher than the average-aged ones.

To alleviate this issue, Ambry employs a rebalancing mechanism that returns the cluster to a semi-balanced state (in terms of disk usage and request rate) with minimal data movement. The rebalancing approach reduces request rate and disk usage imbalance by 6-10x and 9-10x respectively.

Ambry defines the ideal (load balanced) state as a triplet (idealRW, idealRO, idealUsed) representing the ideal number of read-write partitions, ideal number of read-only partitions and ideal disk usage each disk should have. This ideal state (idealRW, idealRO, idealUsed) is computed by dividing the total number of read-write/read-only partitions and total used disk space by the number of disks in the cluster, respectively. A disk is considered above (or below) ideal if it has more (or less) read-write/read-only partitions or disk usage than the ideal state.

The rebalancing algorithm attempts to reach this ideal state. This is done by moving partitions from disks above ideal to disks below ideal using a 2 phase approach, as shown in the pseudo-code below.

Algorithm 1 Rebalancing Algorithm

```
1: // Compute ideal state.
2: idealRW=totalNumRW / numDisks
3: idealRO=totalNumRO / numDisks
4: idealUsed=totalUsed / numDisks

5: // Phase1: move extra partitions into a partition pool.
6: partitionPool = {}
7: for each disk d do
8:     // Move extra read-write partitions.
9:     while d.NumRW > idealRW do
10:        partitionPool += chooseMinimumUsedRW(d)
11:    // Move extra read-only partitions.
12:    while d.NumRO > idealRO & d.used > idealUsed do
13:        partitionPool += chooseRandomRO(d)

14: // Phase2: Move partitions to disks needing partitions.
15: placePartitions(read-write)
16: placePartitions(read-only)

17: function PLACEPARTITIONS(Type t)
18:    while partitionPool contains partitions type t do
19:        D=shuffleDisksBelowIdeal()
20:        for disk d in D and partition p in pool do
21:            d.addPartition(p)
22:            partitionPool.remove(p)
```

Phase1 - Move to Partition Pool: In this phase, Ambry moves partitions from disks above ideal into a pool, called *partitionPool* (Lines 6-13). At the end of this phase no disk should remain above ideal, unless removing any partition would cause it to fall below ideal.

Ambry starts from read-write partitions (which are the main factor), and moves extra ones solely based on idealRW threshold. The same process is repeated for read-only partitions, but with considering both idealRO and idealUsed when moving partitions. The strategy of choosing which partition to move is based on minimizing data movement. For read-write partitions, the one with the minimum used capacity is chosen, while for read-only partitions, a random one is chosen since all such partitions are full.

Phase2 - Place Partitions on Disks: In this phase, Ambry places partitions from the partition pool on disks below ideal (Lines 14-16), starting from read-write partitions and then read-only ones. Partitions are placed using a random round-robin approach (Line 17-22). Ambry finds all disks below ideal, shuffles them, and assigns partitions to them in a round-robin fashion. This procedure is repeated until the pool becomes empty.

After finding the the new placement, replicas are seamlessly moved by: 1) creating a new replica in the destination, 2) syncing the new replica with old ones using the replication protocol while serving new writes in all replicas, and 3) deleting the old replica after syncing.

Datacenter	Datanode	Disk	Size	Status
DC 1	Datanode 1	disk 1 ... disk k	4 TB ... 4 TB	UP ... UP
DC 1	Datanode 2	disk 1 ... disk k'	4 TB ... 4 TB	DOWN ... UP
	...	...	...	...
DC n	Datanode j	disk 1 ... disk k''	1 TB ... 1 TB	DOWN ... UP

Table 1: Hardware layout in Cluster Manager.

4. COMPONENTS IN DETAIL

In this section we further discuss the main components of Ambry. We describe the detailed state stored by the Cluster Manager (Section 4.1), extra responsibilities of Frontends including chunking and failure detection (Section 4.2), and additional structures maintained by the Datanodes (Section 4.3).

4.1 Cluster Manager

The Cluster Manager is in charge of maintaining the state of the cluster. Each datacenter has its local Cluster Manager instance(s) kept in-sync with others using Zookeeper. The state stored by the Cluster Manager is very small (less than a few MBs in total), consisting of a hardware and logical layout.

4.1.1 Hardware Layout

The hardware layout includes information about the physical structure of the cluster, i.e., the arrangement of datacenters, Datanodes, and disks. It also maintains the raw capacity and status, i.e., healthy (UP) or failed (DOWN), for each disk. An example hardware layout is shown in Table 1. As shown, Ambry works in a heterogeneous environment with different hardware and configuration used inside and across different datacenters.

4.1.2 Logical Layout

The logical layout maintains the physical location of partition replicas, and the state (read-only/read-write) of each partition. In order to find the state of a partition, the Cluster Manager periodically contacts the Datanodes, and requests the state of their partitions. This layout is used for choosing a partition to write a new blob to (put operation), and locating the Datanode in charge of a given replica (all

Partition id	State	Placement
partition 1	read-write	DC 1: Datanode 1: disk 1 DC 1: Datanode 4: disk 5 ... DC 3: Datanode 7: disk 2
...	...	...
partition p	read-only	DC 1: Datanode 1: disk 1 ... DC 4: Datanode 5: disk 2

Table 2: Logical Layout in Cluster Manager.

operations). An example of this layout is shown in Table 2. As shown, replicas of a partition can be placed on multiple Datanodes in one datacenter, and/or in different datacenters. Additionally, one disk (e.g., DC 1: Datanode 1: disk 1) can contain replicas of distinct partitions, where some are read-only and some are read-write. Partitions are added by updating the logical layout stored in the Cluster Manager instances[2].

4.2 Frontend Layer

The Frontend is the entry point to Ambry for external requests. Each datacenter has its own set of Frontends. Frontends are decentralized involving no master or coordination, identically performing the same task, and stateless with all state stored in the Cluster Manager (which is periodically pulled). This design enhances scalability (new Frontends can be added without much performance penalty), fault-tolerance (requests can be forwarded to any Frontend), and failure recovery (failed Frontends can quickly be replaced) for Frontends. Frontends have three main responsibilities:

1. Request Handling: This involves receiving requests, routing them to the corresponding Datanode(s) using the Router Library (Section 4.2.1), and sending back the response.
2. Security Checks: Optionally performing security checks, such as virus scanning and authentication on requests.
3. Capturing Operations: Pushing events to a change capture system out of Ambry for further offline analysis, such as finding request patterns of the system. We use Kafka [13] as our change-capture system due to the high durability, high throughput, and low overhead it provides.

4.2.1 Router Library

The Router Library contains all the core logic of handling requests and communicating with Datanodes. Frontends simply embed and use this library. Clients can bypass Frontends by embedding this library and directly serving requests. This library includes four main procedures: 1) policy-based routing, 2) chunking large blobs, 3) failure detection, and 4) proxy requests.

Policy Based Routing: On receiving a request, the library decides which partition to involve (randomly chosen for puts and extracted from blob id for gets/deletes). Then, based on the policy used ({one, k, majority, all} discussed in Section 2.3), it communicates with the corresponding replica(s) until the request is served/failed.

Chunking: Extremely large blobs (e.g., videos) create load imbalance, block smaller blobs, and inherently have high latency. To mitigate these issues, Ambry splits large blobs into smaller equal-size units called chunks. A large chunk size does not fully resolve the large blob challenges and a small chunk size adds too much overhead. Based on our current large blob size distribution, we found the sweet spot for the chunk size to be in the range of 4 to 8 MB[3].

During a put operation, a blob b is split into k chunks $\{c_1, c_2, ..., c_k\}$, each treated as an independent blob. Each chunk goes through the same steps as a normal put blob operation (Section 2.3), most likely being placed on a different partition. It is also assigned a unique chunk id with the same format as a blob id. In order to be able to retrieve b Ambry creates a metadata blob $b_{metadata}$ for b. $b_{metadata}$ stores the number of chunks and chunk ids in order, as shown in Figure 4. This metadata blob is then put into Ambry as a normal blob and the blob id of $b_{metadata}$ is returned to the user as the blob id of b. If the put fails before writing all chunks, the system will issue deletes for written chunks and the operation has to be redone.

# Chunks	ChunkId*1*		...	ChunkId*k*	
	partitionId	UUID		partitionId	UUID

Figure 4: Content of the metadata blob used for chunked blobs.

During a get, the metadata blob is retrieved and chunk ids are extracted from it. Then, Ambry uses a sliding buffer of size s to retrieve the blob. Ambry queries the first s chunks of the blob independently and in parallel (since they are most likely written on unique partitions placed on separate Datanodes). When the first chunk in the buffer is retrieved, Ambry slides the buffer to the next chunk, and so on. The whole blob starts being returned to the user the moment the first chunk of the blob is retrieved.

Although an extra put/get is needed in this chunking mechanism (for the metadata blob), overall, our approach improves latency since multiple chunks are written and retrieved in parallel.

Zero-cost Failure Detection: Failures happen frequently in a large system. They range from unresponsiveness and connection timeouts, to disk I/O problems. Thus, Ambry needs a failure detection mechanism to discover unavailable Datanodes/disks and avoid forwarding requests to them.

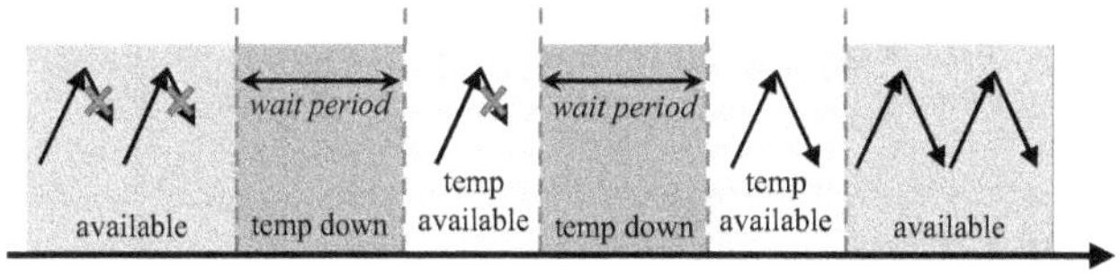

Figure 5: Failure detection algorithm with maximum tolerance of 2 consecutive failed responses.

Ambry employs a zero-cost failure detection mechanism involving no extra messages, such as heartbeats and pings, by leveraging request messages. In practice, we found our failure detection mechanism is effective, simple, and consumes very little bandwidth. This mechanism is shown in Figure 5. In this approach, Ambry keeps track of the number of consecutive failed requests for a particular Datanode (or disk) in the last *check_period* of time. If this number exceeds a MAX_FAIL threshold (in our example set to 2) the

[2]Currently, the system administrator manually adds partitions in order to prevent unwanted and rapid cluster growths. However, this can easily be automated.

[3]Chunk size is not fixed and can be adapted to follow the growth in blob sizes, improvements in network, etc.

Datanode is marked as *temporarily_down* for a *wait_period* of time. In this state all queued requests for this Datanode will eventually time out and need to be reattempted by the user. After the *wait_period* has passed, the Datanode becomes *temporarily_available*. When a Datanode is in the *temporarily_available* phase, if the next request sent to that Datanode fails, it will move to the *temporarily_down* phase again. Otherwise, it will be marked as *available*, working as normal again.

Proxy Requests: As described in Section 2.3, Ambry uses proxy requests to reach higher availability and read-after-write consistency in remote datacenters. When a blob has not been replicated in the local datacenter yet, requests for that blob are forwarded to other datacenters and served there (proxy requests). However, datacenter partitions can cause unavailability of unreplicated data until the partition is healed and replicas converge.

Proxy requests are handled by the Router Library, transparently from the user issuing the request. In practice, we found proxy requests occur less than 0.001% of the time, thus minimally affecting the user experience.

4.3 Datanode Layer

Datanodes are in charge of maintaining the actual data. Each Datanode manages a number of disks, and responds to requests for partition replicas placed on its disks. Puts are handled by writing to the end of the partition file. Gets can be more time-consuming, especially since the location of the blob in the partition is not known. To minimize both read and write latencies, Datanodes employ a few techniques:

- **Indexing blobs:** Ambry stores an index of blob offsets per partition replica to prevent sequential sweeps for finding blobs (Section 4.3.1).
- **Exploiting OS cache:** Ambry utilizes OS caching to serve most reads from the RAM, by limiting the RAM usage of other components (Section 4.3.2).
- **Batched writes, with a single disk seek:** Ambry batches writes for a particular partition together and periodically flushes the writes to disk. Thus, it incurs at most one disk seek for a batch of sequential writes. The flush period is configurable and trades off latency for durability. Although, batching can introduce overheads of flushing, dirty buffers, and tuning, the benefits outweigh these overheads.
- **Keeping all file handles open:** Since partitions are typically very large (100 GB in our setting), the number of partition replicas placed on a Datanode is small (a few hundred). Thus, Ambry keeps all file handles open at all times.
- **Zero copy gets:** When reading a blob, Ambry utilizes a zero copy [25] mechanism, i.e., the kernel directly copies data from disk to the network buffer without going through the application. This is feasible since the Datanodes do not perform any computation on the data at get operations.

4.3.1 Indexing

To find the location of a blob in a partition replica with low latency, the Datanode maintains a light-weight in-memory indexing per replica, as shown in Figure 6. The indexing is sorted by blob id, mapping the blob id to the start offset of the blob entry. The indexing is updated in an online fashion whenever blobs are put (e.g., blob 60) or deleted (e.g., blob 20).

Similar to SSTables [5], Ambry limits the size of the index by splitting it into segments, storing old segments on disk,

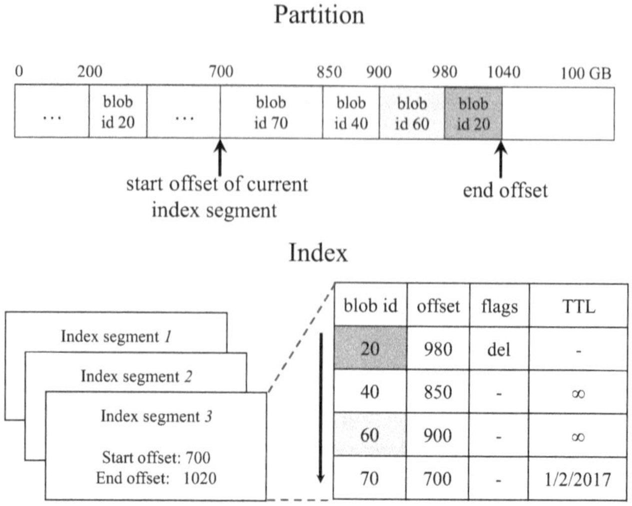

Figure 6: Indexing of blob offsets in a partition replica. When blobs are put (blob 60) or deleted (blob 20) the indexing stucture is updated.

and maintaining a Bloom filter for each on-disk segment (Section 4.3.2).

The indexing also stores a flag indicating if a blob has been deleted and optionally a time-to-live (TTL). During get operations, if the blob has expired or been deleted, an error will be returned before reading the actual data.

Note that the indexing does not contain any additional information affecting the correctness of the system, and just improves performance. If a Datanode fails, the whole indexing can be reconstructed from the partition.

4.3.2 Exploiting The OS Cache

Recently written data, which is the popular data as well, is automatically cached without any extra overhead (by the operating system). By exploiting this feature, many reads can be served from memory, which significantly improves performance. Thus, Ambry limits the memory usage of other data structures in the Datanode. Ambry bounds the indexing by splitting it into segments, with only the latest segment remaining in-memory (Figure 6). New entries are added to the in-memory segment of the indexing. When the in-memory segment exceeds a maximum size it is flushed to disk as a read-only segment. This design also helps toward failure recovery since only the in-memory segment needs to be reconstructed. Looking up blob offsets is done in reverse chronological order, starting with the latest segment (in-memory segment). Thus, a delete entry will be found before a put entry when reading a blob. This ensures deleted blobs are not retrievable.

Bloom Filters: To reduce lookup latency for on-disk segments, Ambry maintains an in-memory Bloom filter for each segment, containing the blob ids in that index segment. Using Bloom filters, Ambry quickly filters out which on-disk segment to load. Thus, with high probability, it incurs only one disk seek. However, due to our skewed workload a majority of reads just hit the in-memory segment, without any disk seeks.

5. REPLICATION

Replicas belonging to the same partition can become out of sync due to either failures, or asynchronous writes that write to only one datacenter. In order to fix inconsistent

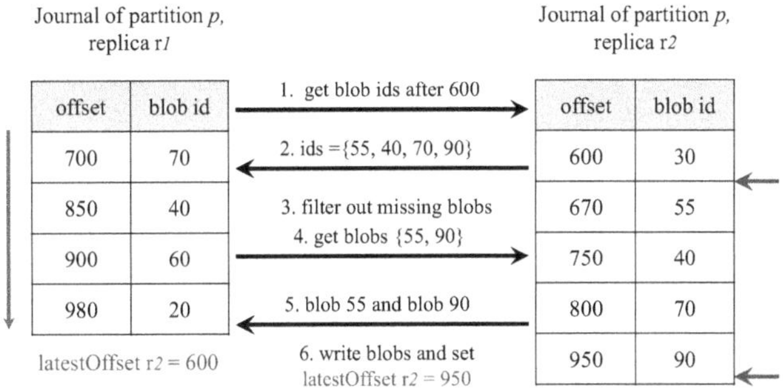

Figure 7: Journals for two replicas of the same partition and an example of the replication algorithm.

replicas, Ambry uses an asynchronous replication algorithm that periodically synchronizes replicas. This algorithm is completely decentralized. In this procedure each replica individually acts as a master and syncs-up with other replicas, in an all-to-all fashion. Synchronization is done using an asynchronous two-phase replication protocol as follows. This protocol is a pull-based approach where each replica independently requests for missing blobs from other replicas.

- **First Phase:** This phase finds missing blobs since the last synchronization point. This is done by requesting blob ids of all blobs written since the latest syncing offset and then filtering the ones missing locally.
- **Second Phase:** This phase replicates missing blobs. A request for only the missing blobs is sent. Then, the missing blobs are transferred and appended to the replica.

In order to find the recently written blobs quickly, the replication algorithm maintains an additional data structure per replica, called a *journal*. The journal is an in-memory cache of recent blobs ordered by their offset. Figure 7 shows example journals of two replicas (r_1 and r_2) and the two phase replication procedure for r_1 syncing with r_2 from latestOffset 600. In the first phase, r_1 requests all recently added blobs in r_2 after latestOffset; using the journal r_2 returns a list $B = \{55, 40, 70, 90\}$ of blob ids; and r_1 filters out the missing blobs (blob 55 and 90). In the second phase, r_1 receives the missing blobs, appends the blobs to the end of the replica, and updates the journal, indexing and latestOffset.

To provide improved efficiency and scalability of the system, the replication algorithm employs a number of further optimizations:

- Using separate thread pools for inter- and intra-datacenter replication with different periods.
- Batching requests between common partition replicas of two Datanodes, and batching blobs transferred across datacenters.
- Prioritizing lagging replicas to catch up at a faster rate (by using dedicated threads for lagging replicas).

6. EXPERIMENTAL RESULTS

We perform three kinds of experiments: small cluster (Section 6.1), production cluster (Section 6.2), and simulations (Section 6.3).

6.1 Throughput and Latency

In this section we measure the latency and throughput of the system using a micro-benchmark that stress-tests the system (Section 6.1.1), under read-only, write-only and read-write workloads.

6.1.1 Micro-Benchmark

We first measure the peak throughput. We designed a micro-benchmark that linearly adds load to the system (by adding more clients), until the saturation point where no more requests can be handled. Each client sends requests one at a time with the next request sent right after a response.

This benchmark has three modes: Write, Read, and Read-Write. In Write mode, random byte array blobs are put with varying number of clients. In Read mode, first blobs are written at saturation rate for a *write-period* of time. Then, randomly chosen blobs are read from the written blobs[4]. In most experiments we set the write-period long enough that most read requests (>80%) are served by disk, rather than RAM. Read-Write is a similar to Read, but serving 50% reads and 50% writes after the write-period.

Since latency and throughput are highly correlated with blob size, we use fixed-size blobs in each run, but vary the blob size.

6.1.2 Experimental Setup

We deployed Ambry with a single Datanode. The Datanode was running on a 24 core CPU with 64 GB of RAM, 14 1TB HDD disks, and a full-duplex 1 Gb/s Ethernet network. 4 GB of the RAM was set aside for the Datanode's internal use and the rest was left to be used as Linux Cache. We created 8 single-replica 100 GB partitions on each disk, with a total of 122 partitions. Using 14 disks with a 1 Gb/s network might look like an overkill. However, disk seeks are the dominant latency factor for small blobs. Since a large portion of blobs are small (< 50 KB), we need the parallelism created by using multiple disks (more detail in Section 6.1.4). Note that Ambry is designed as a cost-effective system using cheap HDD disks.

Clients send requests from a few machines located in the same datacenter as the Datanode. These clients, that are acting as Frontends, directly send requests to the Datanode. The micro-benchmark discussed above was used with varying blob sizes {25 KB, 50 KB, 100 KB, 250 KB, 500 KB, 1 MB, 5 MB}. We did not go above 5 MB since blobs are chunked beyond that point.

6.1.3 Effect of Number of Clients

We ran the micro-benchmark with varying blob sizes, while linearly increasing the number of clients. For Read mode, the write-period was set such that 6 times the RAM size, was first written. Figure 8a shows the throughput in terms of MB/s served by the system. Adding clients proportionally increases the throughput until the saturation point. Saturation occurs at 75%-88% of the network bandwidth. The only exception is reading small blobs due to frequent disk seeks (discussed in Section 6.1.4). Saturation is reached quickly (usually $\leq$ 6 clients) since clients send requests as fast as possible in the benchmark.

Figure 8b shows the latency normalized by blob size (i.e., average latency divided by blob size). Latency stays almost constant before reaching saturation point, and then increases linearly beyond the throughput saturation point. The linear increase in latency after saturation indicates the system does not add additional overhead beyond request serving.

[4]The random strategy gives a lower bound on the system's performance since real-world access patterns are skewed toward recent data.

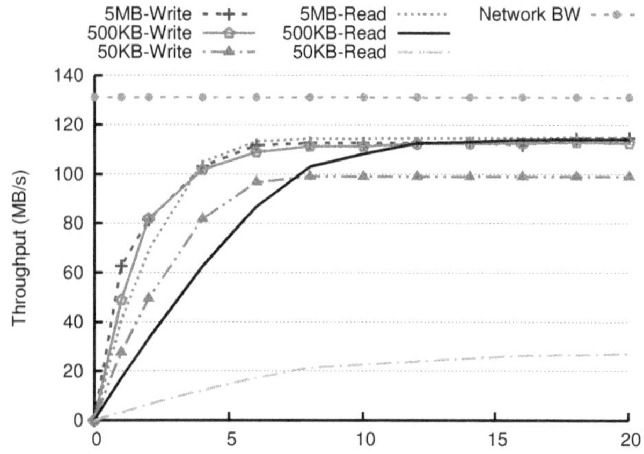

(a) Throughput

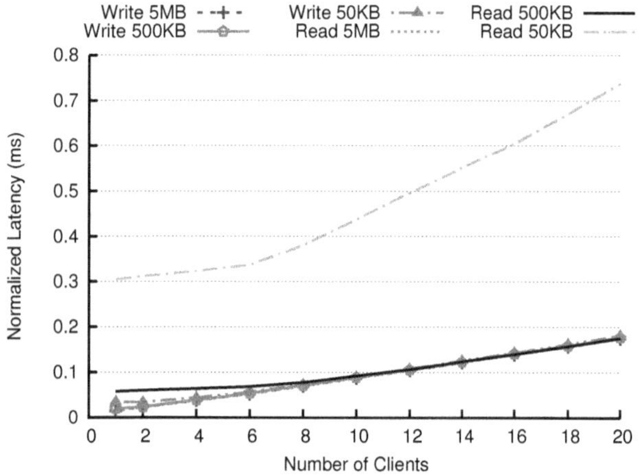

(b) Latency normalized by blob size

Figure 8: Throughput and latency of read and write requests with varying number of clients on different blob sizes. These results were gathered on a single Datanode deployment.

6.1.4 *Effect of Blob Size*

In Figures 9a and 9b we analyzed the maximum throughput (with 20 clients) under different blob sizes and workloads. For large objects (>200 KB), the maximum throughput (in MB/s) stays constant and close to maximum network bandwidth across all blob sizes. Similarly, throughput in terms of requests/s scales proportionally.

However, for Read and Read-Write, the read throughput in terms of MB/s drops linearly for smaller sizes. This drop is because our micro-benchmark reads blobs randomly, incurring frequent disk seeks. The effect of disk seeks is amplified for smaller blobs. By further profiling the disk using Bonnie++ [1] (an IO benchmark for measuring disk performance), we confirmed that disk seeks are the dominant source of latency for small blobs. For example, when reading a 50 KB blob, more than 94% of latency is due to disk seek (6.49 *ms* for disk seek, and 0.4 *ms* for reading the data).

Read and Write workload mostly utilize only the outbound and inbound link on the Datanode, respectively. However, Read-Write workload has a better mix and evenly utilizes both links reaching higher throughput. Therefore, in our full-duplex network infrastructure the Read-Write mode is able to saturate both links reaching almost double the network bandwidth ($\simeq$ 1.7 Gb/s in total out of the 2 Gb/s available). For smaller size objects it reaches twice the Read throughput, since Read-Write is a 50-50 workload with reads being the limiting factor.

Figure 9c demonstrates the trend in latency under various blob sizes. These results are before the saturation point with 2 clients. Similar to throughput, latency grows linearly except for reading small blobs. The higher latency in Read is because most read requests incur a disk seek, while write requests are batched and written together. The Read-Write latency falls halfway between Read and Write latency because of its mixed workload.

6.1.5 *Variance in Latency*

The tail and variance in request latencies are important. Figure 10 shows the CDFs of Write, Read, and Read-Write mode experiments with 2 clients. The CDF of Read and Write mode is very close to a vertical line, with a short tail and a majority of values close to the median. The jump around 0.15 in Read mode (for 50 KB blob size) is because a small fraction of requests are served using the Linux cache which is orders of magnitudes faster than disk (Section 6.1.6). The Read-Write mode is a mixture of the Read and Write CDF with a change around 0.5, following the 50% read - 50% write workload pattern.

6.1.6 *Effect of Linux Cache*

We ran the micro-benchmark on 50 KB blobs and 2 clients in two configurations: 1) writing 6 times more than the RAM size before reading, so that most requests (83 %) are served by disk (Disk Read), and 2) writing data equal to the RAM size to keep all data in RAM (Cached Read). Table 3 compares these two modes.

	Average	**Max**	**Min**	**StdDev**
Disk Reads	17 ms	67 ms	1.6 ms	9 ms
Cached Reads	3 ms	5 ms	1.6 ms	0.4 ms
Improvement	**5.5x**	13x	0	23x

Table 3: Comparision of get request latency when most of requests (83%) are served by disk (Disk Reads) and when all requests are served by linux cache (Cached Reads) for 50 KB blobs.

The Cached Read experiment performed more than 2100 requests/s (104 MB/s reaching 79% network bandwidth) matching the maximum write throughput (Section 6.1.3), compared to 540 requests/s for Disk Reads. We also measured the average, maximum, minimum, and standard deviation of latency, shown in Table 3. In both cases, the minimum is equal to reading from the Linux Cache. However, the Cached Read case improves the average and max latency by 5.5x and 13x, respectively. This shows the significance of exploiting the Linux Cache (Section 4.3.2).

6.2 Geo-distributed Optimizations

We analyzed our replication algorithm among 3 different datacenters at LinkedIn {DC1, DC2, DC3}, located all across the US. All experiments in this section are from production workloads.

6.2.1 *Replication Lag*

We define *replication lag* between a pair of replicas (r_1, r_2) as the difference of r_2's highest used offset and r_1's latest synced offset with r_2. Note that not all data in the replication lag needs to be transfered to r_1, since it could receive the missing blobs from other replicas as well.

We measured the replication lag among all replicas of a given Datanode and the rest of the cluster, and found that

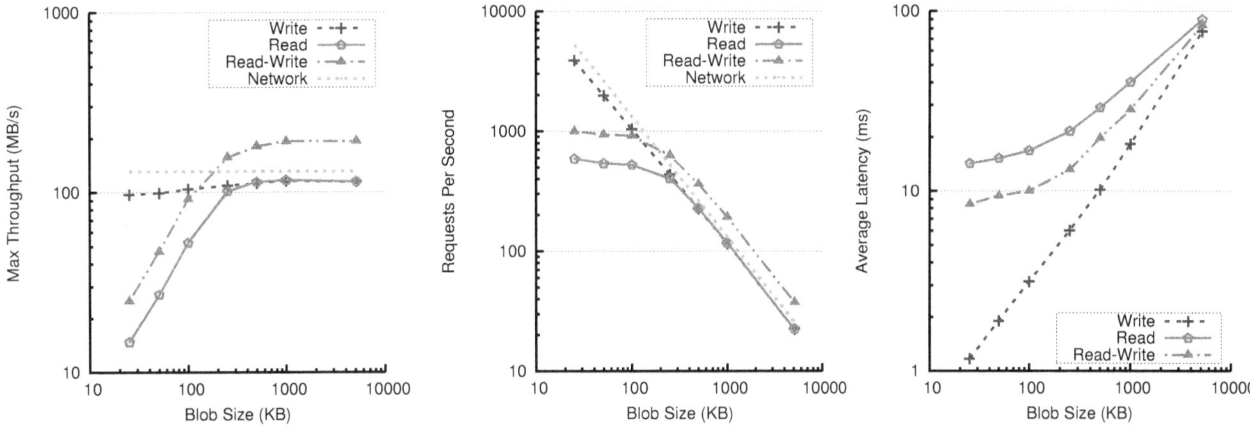

(a) Throughput (MB/s) (b) Throughput (requests/s) (c) Latency

Figure 9: Effect of blob size on maximum throughput, both in terms of MB/s and requests/s, and latency. Results were gathered on a write-only, read-only, and mixed (50%-50%) workload. Reads for small blob sizes (<200 KB) are slowed down by frequent disk seeks, while other requests saturate the network link.

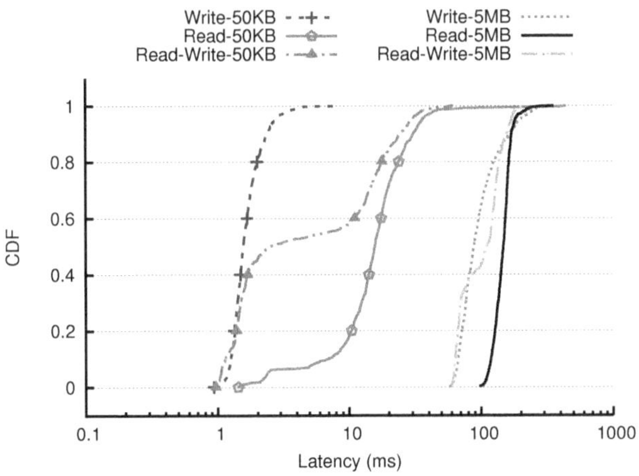

Figure 10: CDF of read and write latency with 2 clients for various blob sizes. Read-Write falls in the middle with change around 0.5 due to the 50-50 mixed workload.

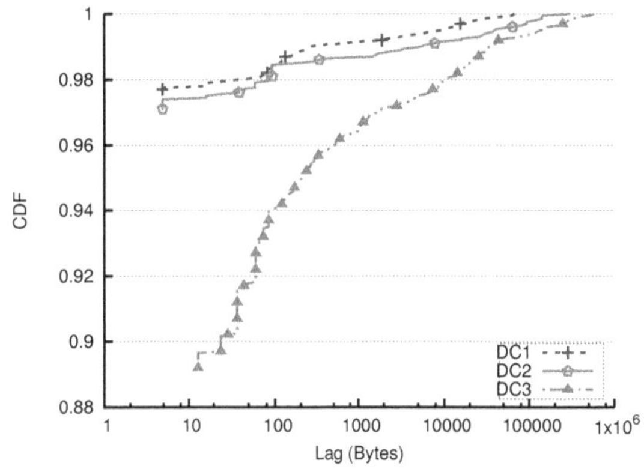

Figure 11: CDF of Replication Lag among replica pairs of a given Datanode and the rest of the cluster. Most values were zero, and are omitted from the graph.

more than 85% of the values were 0. Figure 11 shows the CDF of non-zero values grouped by datacenter. The 95th percentile is less than 1 KB for 100 GB partitions (in all datacenters), with slightly worse lag in datacenter 3 since it is placed farther apart from others.

6.2.2 Replication Bandwidth

Ambry relies on background replication to write data to other datacenters. We measured the aggregate network bandwidth used for inter-datacenter replication during a 24 hour period, shown in Figure 12. The aggregate bandwidth is small (< 10 MB/s), similar across all datacenters, and correlated to request rates with a diurnal pattern. This value is small because we batch replication between common replicas and due to the read-heavy nature of the workload.

Figure 13 demonstrates the CDF of average replication bandwidth per Datanode, for both intra- and inter-datacenter replication. Intra-datacenter bandwidth is minimal (< 200 B/s at 95th percentile), especially compared to inter-datacenter with 150-200 KB/s at 95th percentile (1000x larger). The higher value for inter-datacenter is because of asynchronous writes. However, the inter-datacenter bandwidth is still negligible ($\approx$ 0.2% of a 1 Gb/s link). The small difference among the 3 datacenters is due to the different request rates they receive.

Figure 14 shows a zoomed in graph of only inter-datacenter bandwidth. Inter-datacenter replication has a short tail with the 95th to 5th percentile ratio of about 3x. This short tail is because of the load-balanced design in Ambry. Intra-datacenter replication has a longer tail, as well as many zero values (omitted from the graph). Thus, replication either uses almost zero bandwidth (intra-datacenter) or almost balanced bandwidth (inter-datacenter).

6.2.3 Replication Latency

We define *replication latency* as the time spent in one iteration of the replication protocol, i.e., $T_{missing\_blobs\_received}$ minus $T_{replication\_initiated}$. Figure 15 demonstrates the CDF of average replication latency for intra- and inter-datacenter, in our production workload.

Inter-datacenter replication latency is low with a median of less than 150 ms, and a very short tail. Although this la-

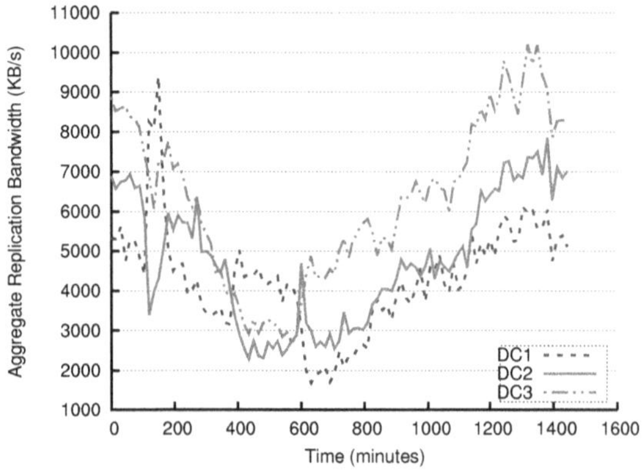

Figure 12: Aggregate network bandwidth used for inter-datacenter replication during a 24 hour period in production.

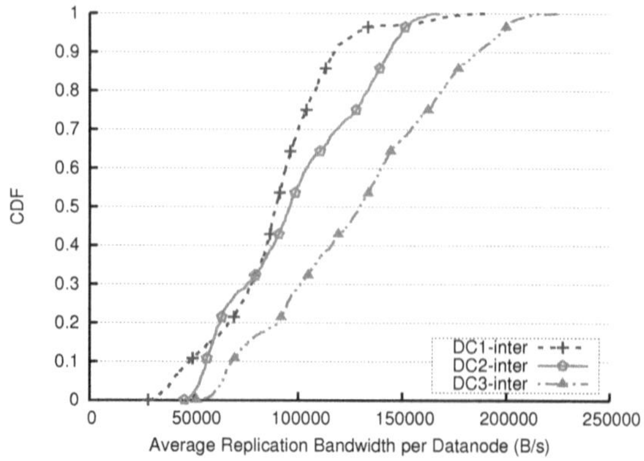

Figure 14: CDF of average inter-datacenter network bandwidth used per Datanode over a 24 hour period in production.

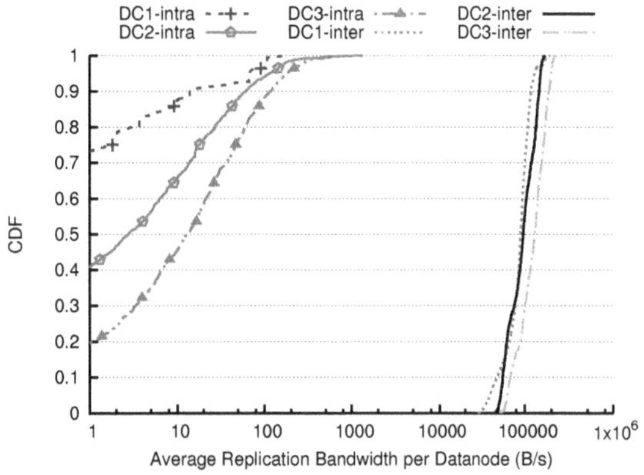

Figure 13: CDF of average network bandwidth used per Datanode for intra- and inter-datacenter replication over a 24 hour period in production.

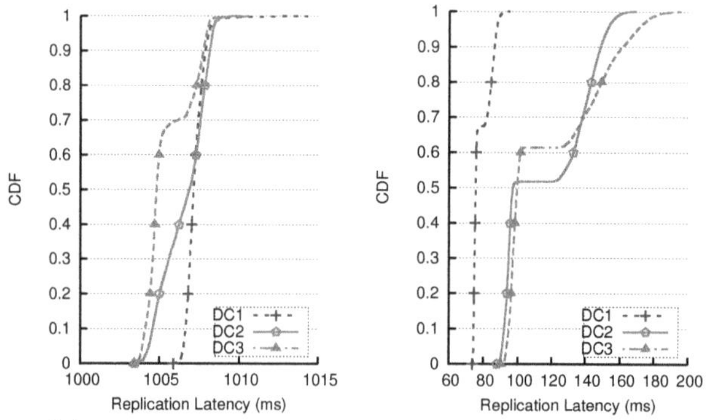

(a) Intra Datacenter (b) Inter Datacenter

Figure 15: CDF of average replication latency (i.e., time spent to recieve missing blobs) for intra- and inter-datacenter in production environment.

tency might appear to be high, the number of proxy requests remain near-zero ($< 0.001\%$). This is because users usually read data from the same local datacenter to which they have recently written. Therefore, replication has a minimal effect on user experience.

Surprisingly, intra-datacenter replication latency is relatively high (6x more than inter-datacenter) and with little variance. This pattern is because of a pre-existing and prefixed artificial added delay of 1 second, intended to prevent incorrect blob collision detections. If a blob is replicated in a datacenter faster than the Datanode receives the initial put request (which is possible with less strict policies), the Datanode might consider the put as a blob collision and fail the request. The artificial delay is used to prevent this issue in intra-datacenter replication. This relatively small delay does not have a significant impact on durability or availability of data since intra-replication is only used to fix failed/slow Datanodes, which rarely occurs.

6.3 Load Balancing

Since cluster growth occurs infrequently (every few months at most), we implemented a simulator to show the behavior of Ambry over a long period of time (several years), and at large scale (hundreds of Datanodes). We tried a workload that is based on production workloads. All results in this section are gathered using the simulator.

6.3.1 Simulator Design

The simulator's design resembles Ambry's architecture and requests are served using the same path. However, there are no real physical disks. For handling requests, only the metadata (blob id and size) is stored/retrieved, and the effect of requests are reflected (e.g., disk space increase).

Workload: We use a synthetic workload closely resembling the real-world traffic at LinkedIn. This workload preserves the rate of each type of request (read, write, and delete), the blob size distribution, and the access pattern of blobs (based on age).

Cluster Expansion: The simulator starts with an initial set of Datanodes, disks, and partitions in one datacenter. Over time, when partitions reach the capacity threshold, a new batch of partitions are added using the replica placement strategy from Section 2.2. If partitions cannot be added (e.g., if there is not enough unallocated space on disks), a batch of new Datanodes are added.

6.3.2 Experiment Setup

The simulation is run in a single datacenter, with 10 Frontend nodes. The experiment starts with 15 Datanodes, each with 10 4TB disks, and 1200 100GB partitions with 3 replicas. At each partition and Datanode addition point, a batch of 600 partitions and 15 Datanodes are added, respectively. The simulation is run over 400 weeks (almost 8 years) and

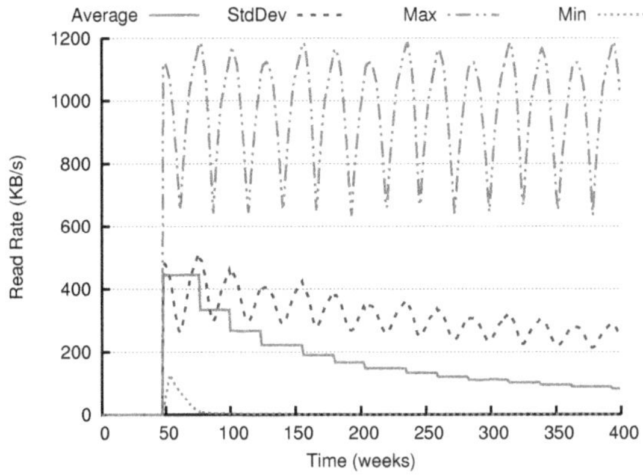

(a) Without rebalancing

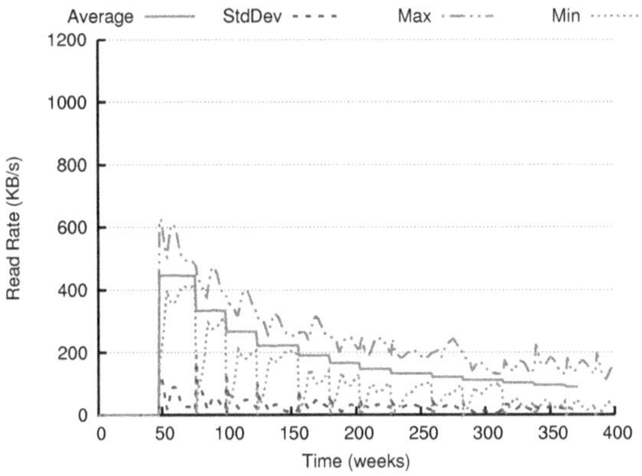

(b) With rebalancing

Figure 16: Average, standard deviation, maximum and minimum of average read rate (KB/s) among disks over a 400 week interval. The system is bootstrapping in the first few weeks, and the results are omitted.

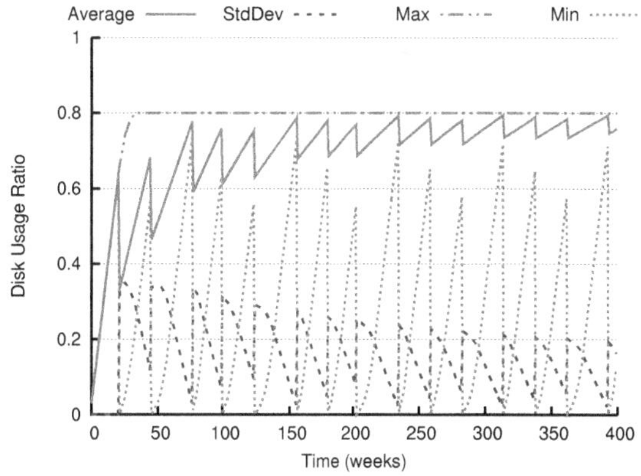

(a) Without rebalancing

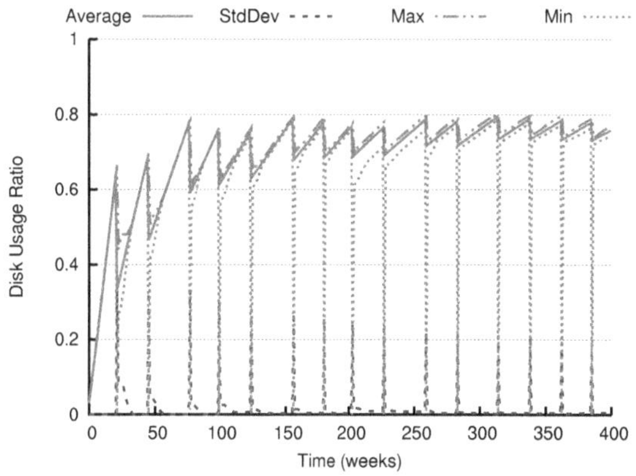

(b) With rebalancing

Figure 17: Average, standard deviation, maximum and minimum of disk usage ratio (i.e., used space divided by total space) over a 400 week interval.

up to 240 Datanodes. The simulation is run with and without rebalancing with the exact same configuration, while measuring request rates, disk usage, and data movement.

6.3.3 *Request Rate*

We measured the read rate (KB/s) for each disk at any point of time. Figure 16 demonstrates the average, standard deviation, maximum and minimum among these values, for the system with and without rebalancing. The results for write rates were similar and removed due to lack of space.

The average, which is also the ideal, is a dropping step function. The drops are points where new Datanodes were added to the cluster. In case of no rebalancing, a majority of the disks are old read-only disks with almost zero traffic, while a few disks receive most of the request. Thus, the minimum is close to zero. Also, the maximum and standard deviation are significant (3x-7x and 1x-2x larger than the average, respectively). When rebalancing is added, the minimum and maximum move close to the average, and the standard deviation drops close to zero. We conclude that Ambry's load balancing is effective.

6.3.4 *Disk Usage*

We analyzed the disk usage ratio, i.e., used space divided by total space among disks, with and without rebalancing. As seen in Figure 17, without rebalancing, the maximum stays at the capacity threshold since some disks become and remain full, while the minimum drops to zero whenever new Datanodes are added. With rebalancing, the maximum and minimum move closer to the average with temporary drops in the minimum until rebalancing is completed. Additionally, the standard deviation drops significantly, becoming almost zero with temporary spikes on Datanode addition points.

6.3.5 *Evaluation Over Time*

We evaluated the improvement over time by measuring the integral of range (max-min) and standard deviation for request rate and disk usage over the 400 week interval. As shown in Table 4, rebalancing has a prominent effect improving the range and standard deviation by 6x-9x and 8x-10x, respectively.

6.3.6 *Data Movement*

Whenever rebalancing is triggered, we measure the minimum data movement needed to reach an ideal state and the data movement caused by rebalancing. We calculate the minimum data movement by adding the difference between ideal and current disk usage among all disks above ideal disk usage. This value is a lower bound on the feasible minimum data movement since data is moved in granularity of partitions. As shown in Figure 18, the data movement of rebalancing is very close and always below the minimum. This is because the rebalancing algorithms trades off perfect balance (ideal state) for less data movement. Specifically, the rebalancing algorithm usually does not remove (or add)

Integral over 400 weeks	Write Avg	Read Avg	Disk Usage
Range w/o RB	63,000	340,000	200
Range w/ RB	8,500	52,000	22
Improvement	7.5x	6x	9x
StdDev w/o RB	21,00	112,000	67
StdDev w/ RB	2500	11,000	6.7
Improvement	8x	10x	10x

Table 4: Improvement of range (max-min) and standard deviation of request rates and disk usage over a 400 week interval. Results are from the system with rebalancing (w/ RB) and without rebalancing (w/o RB).

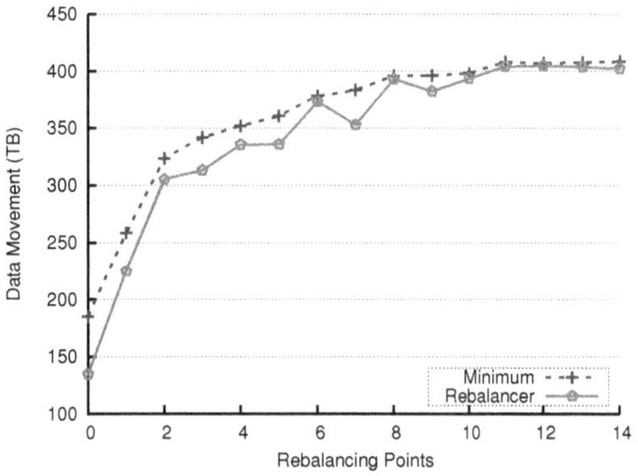

Figure 18: Data movement of the rebalancing algorithm at each rebalancing point (i.e., whenever new Datanodes are added) over a 400 week interval.

a partition from a disk if it would go below (or above) the ideal state, even if this were to cause slight imbalance.

7. RELATED WORK

File Systems: The design of Ambry is inspired by log-structure file systems (LFS) [21, 23]. These file systems are optimized for write throughput by sequentially writing in log-like data structures and relying on the OS cache for reads. Although these single machine file systems suffer from fragmentation issues and cleaning overhead, the core ideas are very relevant, especially since blobs are immutable. The main differences are the skewed data access pattern in our workload and additional optimization such as segmented indexing and Bloom filters used in Ambry.

There has been work on handling metadata and small files more efficiently. Some of these techniques include reducing disk seeks [9], using a combination of log-structured file systems (for metadata and small data) and fast file systems (for large data) [30], and storing the initial segment of data in the index block [17]. Our system resolves this issue by using in-memory segmented indexing plus Bloom filters and batching techniques.

Distributed File Systems: Due to the extremely large amount of data and data sharing needs, many distributed file systems such as NFS [22] and AFS [16], and even more reliable ones handling failures, such as GFS, HDFS, and Ceph [10, 24, 28] have emerged. However, all these systems suffer from the high metadata overhead and additional capabilities (e.g., nested directories, permissions, etc.) unnecessary for a simple blob store. In many of these systems (e.g., HDFS, GFS, and NFS) the metadata overhead is magnified by having a separate single metadata server. This server adds an extra hub in each request, becomes a single point of failure, and limits scalability beyond a point. Recent research has addressed this problem by either distributing the metadata [28] or caching it [20]. Although these systems alleviate accessing metadata, each small object still has a large metadata (usually stored on disk), decreasing the effective throughput of the system.

Distributed Data Stores: Many key-value stores, such as [2, 5, 8, 14], have been designed to handle a large number of requests per second. However, these systems cannot handle massively large objects (tens of MBs to GBs) efficiently, and add unnecessary overhead to provide consistency. Also, some systems [2, 8, 14] hash data to machines, creating large data movement whenever nodes are added/deleted.

PNUTS [6] and Spanner [7] are scalable geographically distributed systems, where PNUTS maintains load balance as well. However, both systems provide more features and stronger guarantees than needed in a simple immutable blob store.

Blob Stores: A similar concept to partitions in Ambry has been used in other systems. Haystack uses logical volumes [3], Twitter's blob store uses virtual buckets [27], and Petal file system introduces virtual disks [15]. Ambry is amenable to some optimizations in these systems such as the additional internal caching in Haystack. However, neither Haystack nor Twitter's blob store tackle the problem of load-imbalance. Additionally, Haystack uses synchronous writes across all replicas impacting efficiency in a geo-distributed setting.

Facebook has also designed f4 [18], a blob store using erasure coding to reduce replication factor of old data (that has become cold). Despite the novel ideas in this system, which potentially can be included in Ambry, our main focus is on both new and old data. Oracle's Database [19] and Windows Azure Storage (WAS) [4] also store mutable blobs, and WAS is even optimized for a geo-distributed environment. However, they both provide additional functionalities such as support for many data types other than blobs, strong consistency guarantees, and modification to blobs, that are not needed in our use case.

8. CONCLUSION

This paper described Ambry, a distributed storage system designed specifically for storing large immutable media objects, called blobs. We designed Ambry to serve requests in a geographically distributed environment of multiple datacenters while maintaining low latency and high throughput. Using a decentralized design, rebalancing mechanism, chunking, and logical blob grouping, we provide load balancing and horizontal scalability to meet the rapid growth at LinkedIn.

As part of future work we plan to adaptively change the replication factor of data based on the popularity, and use erasure coding mechanisms for cold data. We also plan to investigate using compression mechanisms and its costs and benefits. Additionally, we are working on improving the security of Ambry, especially for cross-datacenter traffic.

9. ACKNOWLEDGMENTS

We wish to thank the following people for their invaluable contributions towards the development and deployment of Ambry: our site reliability engineers, Tofig Suleymanov, Arjun Shenoy and Dmitry Nikiforov; our alumni Jay Wylie; our interns Tong Wei and Sarath Sreedharan; and our newest member Ming Xia for his valuable review comments.

10. REFERENCES

[1] Bonnie++. http://www.coker.com.au/bonnie++/, 2001 (accessed Mar, 2016).

[2] A. Auradkar, C. Botev, S. Das, D. De Maagd, A. Feinberg, P. Ganti, L. Gao, B. Ghosh, K. Gopalakrishna, et al. Data infrastructure at LinkedIn. In *Proceeding of the IEEE International Conference on Data Engineering (ICDE)*, 2012.

[3] D. Beaver, S. Kumar, H. C. Li, J. Sobel, and P. Vajgel. Finding a needle in Haystack: Facebook's photo storage. In *Proceeding of the USENIX Symposium on Operating Systems Design and Implementation (OSDI)*, 2010.

[4] B. Calder, J. Wang, A. Ogus, N. Nilakantan, A. Skjolsvold, S. McKelvie, Y. Xu, S. Srivastav, J. Wu, et al. Windows Azure storage: A highly available cloud storage service with strong consistency. In *Proceeding of the ACM Symposium on Operating Systems Principles (SOSP)*, 2011.

[5] F. Chang, J. Dean, S. Ghemawat, W. C. Hsieh, D. A. Wallach, M. Burrows, T. Chandra, A. Fikes, and R. E. Gruber. Bigtable: A distributed storage system for structured data. *ACM Transactions on Computer Systems (TOCS)*, 26(2), 2008.

[6] B. F. Cooper, R. Ramakrishnan, U. Srivastava, A. Silberstein, P. Bohannon, A. Jacobsen, N. Puz, D. Weaver, and R. Yerneni. Pnuts: Yahoo!'s hosted data serving platform. *In Proceeding of the Very Large Data Bases Endowment (VLDB)*, 1(2), 2008.

[7] J. C. Corbett, J. Dean, M. Epstein, A. Fikes, C. Frost, J. J. Furman, S. Ghemawat, A. Gubarev, C. Heiser, et al. Spanner: Google's globally-distributed database. In *Proceeding of the USENIX Symposium on Operating Systems Design and Implementation (OSDI)*, 2012.

[8] G. DeCandia, D. Hastorun, M. Jampani, G. Kakulapati, A. Lakshman, A. Pilchin, S. Sivasubramanian, P. Vosshall, and W. Vogels. Dynamo: Amazon's highly available key-value store. In *Proceeding of the ACM SIGOPS Operating Systems Review (OSR)*, 2007.

[9] G. R. Ganger and M. F. Kaashoek. Embedded inodes and explicit grouping: Exploiting disk bandwidth for small files. In *Proceeding of the USENIX Annual Technical Conference (ATC)*, 1997.

[10] S. Ghemawat, H. Gobioff, and S.-T. Leung. The Google File System. In *Proceeding of the ACM SIGOPS Operating Systems Review (OSR)*, 2003.

[11] Hortonworks. Ozone: An object store in HDFS. http://hortonworks.com/blog/ozone-object-store-hdfs/, 2014 (accessed Mar, 2016).

[12] P. Hunt, M. Konar, F. P. Junqueira, and B. Reed. Zookeeper: Wait-free coordination for internet-scale systems. In *Proceeding of the USENIX Annual Technical Conference (ATC)*, 2010.

[13] J. Kreps, N. Narkhede, J. Rao, et al. Kafka: A distributed messaging system for log processing. In *Proceeding of the USENIX Networking Meets Databases Workshop (NetDB)*, 2011.

[14] A. Lakshman and P. Malik. Cassandra: A decentralized structured storage system. In *Proceeding of the ACM SIGOPS Operating Systems Review (OSR)*, number 2, 2010.

[15] E. K. Lee and C. A. Thekkath. Petal: Distributed virtual disks. In *Proceeding of the ACM Architectural Support for Programming Languages and Operating Systems (ASPLOS)*, 1996.

[16] J. H. Morris, M. Satyanarayanan, M. H. Conner, J. H. Howard, D. S. Rosenthal, and F. D. Smith. Andrew: A distributed personal computing environment. *Communications of the ACM (CACM)*, 29(3), 1986.

[17] S. J. Mullender and A. S. Tanenbaum. Immediate files. *Software: Practice and Experience*, 14(4), 1984.

[18] S. Muralidhar, W. Lloyd, S. Roy, C. Hill, E. Lin, W. Liu, S. Pan, S. Shankar, V. Sivakumar, et al. F4: Facebook's warm blob storage system. In *Proceeding of the USENIX Symposium on Operating Systems Design and Implementation (OSDI)*, 2014.

[19] Oracle. Database securefiles and large objects developer's guide. https://docs.oracle.com/database/121/ADLOB/toc.htm, 2011(accessed Mar, 2016).

[20] K. Ren, Q. Zheng, S. Patil, and G. Gibson. Indexfs: Scaling file system metadata performance with stateless caching and bulk insertion. In *Proceeding of the IEEE High Performance Computing, Networking, Storage and Analysis (SC)*, 2014.

[21] M. Rosenblum and J. K. Ousterhout. The design and implementation of a log-structured file system. *ACM Transactions on Computer Systems (TOCS)*, 10(1), 1992.

[22] R. Sandberg, D. Goldberg, S. Kleiman, D. Walsh, and B. Lyon. Design and implementation of the Sun network file system. In *Proceeding of the USENIX Summer Technical Conference*, 1985.

[23] M. Seltzer, K. Bostic, M. K. Mckusick, and C. Staelin. An implementation of a log-structured file system for UNIX. In *Proceeding of the USENIX Winter Technical Conference*, 1993.

[24] K. Shvachko, H. Kuang, S. Radia, and R. Chansler. The Hadoop Distributed File System. In *Proceeding of the IEEE Mass Storage Systems and Technologies (MSST)*, 2010.

[25] D. Stancevic. Zero copy I: User-mode perspective. *Linux Journal*, 2003(105), 2003.

[26] I. Stoica, R. Morris, D. Karger, M. F. Kaashoek, and H. Balakrishnan. Chord: A scalable peer-to-peer lookup service for Internet applications. In *Proceeding of the ACM Special Interest Group on Data Communication (SIGCOMM)*, 2001.

[27] Twitter. Blobstore: Twitter's in-house photo storage system. https://blog.twitter.com/2012/blobstore-twitter-s-in-house-photo-storage-system, 2011 (accessed Mar, 2016).

[28] S. A. Weil, S. A. Brandt, E. L. Miller, D. D. Long, and C. Maltzahn. Ceph: A scalable, high-performance distributed file system. In *Proceeding of the USENIX Symposium on Operating Systems Design and Implementation (OSDI)*, 2006.

[29] S. A. Weil, S. A. Brandt, E. L. Miller, and C. Maltzahn. CRUSH: Controlled, scalable, decentralized placement of replicated data. In *Proceeding of the IEEE High Performance Computing, Networking, Storage and Analysis (SC)*, 2006.

[30] Z. Zhang and K. Ghose. hFS: A hybrid file system prototype for improving small file and metadata performance. In *Proceeding of the ACM European Conference on Computer Systems (EuroSys)*, 2007.

SQL Schema Design: Foundations, Normal Forms, and Normalization

Henning Köhler
Massey University
Palmerston North, New Zealand
h.koehler@massey.ac.nz

Sebastian Link
University of Auckland
Auckland, New Zealand
s.link@auckland.ac.nz

ABSTRACT

Normalization helps us find a database schema at design time that can process the most frequent updates efficiently at run time. Unfortunately, relational normalization only works for idealized database instances in which duplicates and null markers are not present. On one hand, these features occur frequently in real-world data compliant with the industry standard SQL, and especially in modern application domains. On the other hand, the features impose challenges that have made it impossible so far to extend the existing forty year old normalization framework to SQL. We introduce a new class of functional dependencies and show that they provide the right notion for SQL schema design. Axiomatic and linear-time algorithmic characterizations of the associated implication problem are established. These foundations enable us to propose a Boyce-Codd normal form for SQL. Indeed, we justify the normal form by showing that it permits precisely those SQL instances which are free from data redundancy. Unlike the relational case, there are SQL schemata that cannot be converted into Boyce-Codd normal form. Nevertheless, for an expressive sub-class of our functional dependencies we establish a normalization algorithm that always produces a schema in Value-Redundancy free normal form. This normal form permits precisely those instances which are free from any redundant data value occurrences other than the null marker. Experiments show that our functional dependencies occur frequently in real-world data and that they are effective in eliminating redundant values from these data sets without loss of information.

1. INTRODUCTION

Background of idealized instances. The relational normalization framework enables us to derive a database schema at design time that permits exactly those relations as instances that are free from any redundant data value occurrences at run time. This distinguished feature makes it possible to process updates efficiently. De-normalization refers to the process in which different relation schemata are

SIGMOD'16, June 26-July 01, 2016, San Francisco, CA, USA

ISBN 978-1-4503-3531-7/16/06...$15.00

DOI: http://dx.doi.org/10.1145/2882903.2915239

order_id	item	catalog	price
5299401	Fitbit Surge	Amazon	**240**
5299401	Fitbit Surge	Brookstone	240
7485113	Fitbit Surge	Amazon	**240**
7485113	Dora Doll	Kingtoys	25

Figure 1: The relation purchase

order_id	item	catalog
5299401	Fitbit Surge	Amazon
5299401	Fitbit Surge	Brookstone
7485113	Fitbit Surge	Amazon
7485113	Dora Doll	Kingtoys

item	catalog	price
Fitbit Surge	Amazon	240
Fitbit Surge	Brookston	240
Dora Doll	Kingtoys	25

Figure 2: Lossless decomposition of purchase

joined in order to process frequent queries more efficiently. The original techniques for this (de-)normalization framework are based on the fundamental notions of functional dependency, data redundancy, and Boyce-Codd normal form. As a simple running example consider the relation schema PURCHASE with four attributes *o(rder_id)*, *i(tem)*, *c(atalog)*, and *p(rice)*, which store information about items that have been ordered from a catalog for a price. Any reasonable instance is expected to satisfy the business rule that the same item from the same catalog cannot have different prices, which we can express as the functional dependency (FD) *item, catalog* $\rightarrow$ *price*. As an example, the relation `purchase` in Figure 1 satisfies this FD. The example also shows that {*item, catalog*} does not form a key over PURCHASE, because there are items from a catalog that occur in different orders.

This example illustrates the exact situation in which a schema permits instances in which redundant data values occur. Here, each bold occurrence of **240** in the *price* column is redundant in the sense that *any* change of one 240-value to a different value would result in a relation that violates the FD *item, catalog* $\rightarrow$ *price*. The Boyce-Codd normal form (BCNF) condition provides a syntactic characterization of those schemata which permit exactly those instances in which no redundant data values occur. In fact, a given relation schema T is in BCNF with respect to a given set Σ of FDs if and only if for every non-trivial FD $X \rightarrow Y$ in Σ it is the case that $X \rightarrow T$ is implied by Σ. Our PURCHASE example schema violates BCNF, and our relation `purchase` is an example of an instance in which redundant data values occur. Redundant data value occurrences can incur prohibitively expensive costs under updates, as all occurrences of a redundant data value must be modified consistently. In

item	catalog	price
Fitbit Surge	Amazon	240
Fitbit Surge	Amazon	240

Figure 3: Instance satisfying all FDs and no keys

order_id	item	catalog	price
5299401	Fitbit Surge	NULL	240
7485113	Fitbit Surge	NULL	200

order_id	item	catalog
5299401	Fitbit Surge	NULL
7485113	Fitbit Surge	NULL

item	catalog	price
Fitbit Surge	NULL	240
Fitbit Surge	NULL	200

Figure 4: Lossy decomposition based on the satisfied pFD *item*, *catalog* $_s\!\rightarrow$ *price*

relational databases it is always possible to obtain a lossless BCNF decomposition of a given schema. That is, if a given schema is not in BCNF, then we can always convert it into a schema that is. The foundation for this technique is the result that a T-relation I that satisfies a given FD $X \rightarrow Y$ is the lossless join of its projections on XY and $X(T-XY)$, that is, $I = I[XY] \bowtie I[X(T-XY)]$. In our example, we can decompose `purchase` into its two projections `purchase`[*oic*] and `purchase`[*icp*] as shown in Figure 2, without loss of information. The remarkable result of this decomposition is an exact representation of the original relation in which no redundant data values occur anymore. This magic is possible as the FD $X \rightarrow Y$ over T has become a key on the projected schema XY, which ensures that Y-values that occurred redundantly in I are now only stored once in the projected relation $I[XY]$. In our example, the projected relation `purchase`[*icp*] over {*item*, *catalog*, *price*} stores the two redundant occurrences of the price 240 from `purchase` only once. Note that the occurrence of 240 in the second tuple of `purchase`[*icp*] does not result from a redundant occurrence of 240 in the `purchase` relation. In addition, `purchase`[*icp*] satisfies the key {*item*, *catalog*} over {*item*, *catalog*, *price*}. These are the original fundamental ideas for the framework of relational normalization on which we will focus. Further developments of the relational normalization framework, such as other normal forms and classes of data dependencies, are outside the scope of this article. In particular, we defer the treatment of Third normal form and dependency-preservation to future work. We remark that dependency-preserving BCNF decompositions can always be obtained by attribute splitting [30].

Challenges of real-world instances. While Codd's relational model of data provides a sound foundation for relational database systems, the de-facto industry standard SQL exhibits features that have made an extension of the relational normalization theory to SQL-compliant data challenging. For example, SQL permits occurrences of a null marker in database instances, which makes it possible in practice to store and process incomplete information. In our example, catalog information may not exist for some ordered item or be unknown at the time of the order. Both interpretations of incomplete information are represented uniformly by the SQL null marker, here denoted by NULL or $\perp$, thereby consciously trading a loss of information for a gain in the efficiency of data management. The handling of null markers in query answering has been a long-standing problem in database research that has attracted continued interest since the beginnings, with remarkable insights and results produced over the years. While schema design has attracted some research, even the basics as mentioned above have not been adequately addressed so far. An additional challenge is caused by another distinguished feature of SQL. While the relational model is set-based and duplicates must not occur, SQL does permit duplicate tuples. The main reason is the importance of duplicates for aggregation queries, and another reason is that duplicate removal becomes prohibitively expensive in some situations. While duplicates offer opportunities for extending query languages, they incur additional challenges for schema design. We will now illustrate the challenges on our running example.

The first challenge is that the presence of duplicate tuples means that keys cannot be expressed by functional dependencies anymore. When duplicate tuples cannot be present, a relation I over relation schema T satisfies the key kX if and only if I satisfies the FD $X \rightarrow T$. When duplicate tuples may be present, I still satisfies the FD $X \rightarrow T$ whenever it satisfies the key kX, but not vice versa. That is, I may satisfy the FD $X \rightarrow T$ but violate the key kX. A simple and powerful illustration is the instance in Figure 3 which satisfies every FD but violates every key over {*item*, *catalog*, *price*}. The challenge means that FDs must be studied together with keys, because FDs can incur the presence of data redundancy while keys guarantee their absence. For example, the schema {*item*, *catalog*, *price*} with the FD *item*, *catalog* $\rightarrow$ *price* satisfies the traditional BCNF condition, but admits instances (with duplicate tuples) in which redundant data values occur, e.g., the instance above. As SQL permits the specification of attributes as `NOT NULL`, the actual challenge is to study the combined class of keys, FDs, and `NOT NULL` constraints.

The second challenge concerns the definition of the semantics of keys and functional dependencies in instances with duplicate and partial information. The challenge here is to define the semantics in such a way that i) many constraints that hold in an application domain can be expressed, ii) occurrences of null markers are handled appropriately by the dependencies, iii) the dependencies can be reasoned about efficiently, and iv) the dependencies are useful for designing SQL schemata. While the literature on functional dependencies in incomplete databases is rather rich, the only class of functional dependencies that has had a notable impact on schema design is that proposed by Lien [28]. We refer to these as possible FDs (p-FDs) and denote them by $X \,_s\!\rightarrow Y$. An instance I satisfies the p-FD $X \,_s\!\rightarrow Y$ if and only if all tuples $t, t' \in I$ have matching values on all the attributes in Y whenever they have strongly similar values on all the attributes in X, that is, when $t[X] \sim_s t'[X] \Rightarrow t[Y] = t'[Y]$. Here, $t[X] \sim_s t'[X]$ means that t and t' have the same matching non-null values on all the attributes in X, that is, $\perp \neq t(A) = t'(A) \neq \perp$ for all $A \in X$. The impact of this definition on schema design can be explained as follows. The X-total part of an instance I over schema T that satisfies the p-FD $X \,_s\!\rightarrow Y$ is the lossless join of the X-total projection $I_X[XY]$ and the X-total projection $I_X[X(T-XY)]$. The usefulness of p-FDs for schema design is therefore limited as a) their lossless join property does not extend to tuples in which null markers occur in X, as the example in

order_id	item	catalog	price
5299401	Fitbit Surge	Amazon	**240**
5299401	Fitbit Surge	NULL	**240**
7485113	Fitbit Surge	Amazon	**240**
7485113	Dora Doll	Kingtoys	25

order_id	item	catalog
5299401	Fitbit Surge	Amazon
5299401	Fitbit Surge	NULL
7485113	Fitbit Surge	Amazon
7485113	Dora Doll	Kingtoys

item	catalog	price
Fitbit Surge	Amazon	**240**
Fitbit Surge	NULL	**240**
Dora Doll	Kingtoys	25

Figure 5: Lossless decomposition and redundant values in bold based on the cFD *item, catalog* $_w\!\rightarrow$ *price*

Figure 4 illustrates. Indeed, while the given instance I satisfies the p-FD *item, catalog* $_s\!\rightarrow$ *price*, it is not the lossless join of $I[oic]$ and $I[icp]$. In fact, the usefulness of p-FDs for schema design is further limited as b) lossless decompositions do exist for instances with null marker occurrences, and c) p-FDs cannot capture many redundant data value occurrences. We illustrate these deficiencies on the example in Figure 5. Here, the given instance I satisfies a stronger notion of an FD, which we call a *certain FD* or c-FD for short. We say that two tuples t, t' are weakly similar on attribute A if $t(A) = \perp$ or $t(A) = t'(A)$ hold. Indeed, the first and second, as well as the second and third tuples in I are weakly similar on *item,catalog* and have matching values on *price*. That is, they satisfy the c-FD *item, catalog* $_w\!\rightarrow$ *price*. This also makes the occurrence of the value **240** in the second tuple redundant. Note the difference: The instance also satisfies the p-FD *item, catalog* $_s\!\rightarrow$ *price*, but the occurrence of the value **240** in the second tuple is not redundant with respect to this p-FD. This illustrates point c) above. To see point b), instance I in Figure 5 is indeed the lossless join of the two projections $I[oic]$ and $I[icp]$, where the join condition is based on matching values (and not weak similarity) on common attributes.

While the new notion of certain FDs is the right notion for SQL schema design, there are further challenges that must be dealt with. While the decomposition of the instance I in Figure 5 is lossless, it has not eliminated all data redundancy from the projected instance $I[icp]$. Indeed, each occurrence of the value **240** is redundant, as changing one of them to a different value will violate the c-FD *item, catalog* $_w\!\rightarrow$ *price*. The reason is that the projection of I onto *icp* did not imply that *item, catalog* is a key on $I[icp]$, in contrast to relations. This showcases again the necessity of studying keys and FDs together, but also the need to handle the semantics of keys in instances with null marker occurrences. As it turns out, the notions of possible and certain keys from [21] are very useful in our context. Indeed, a p-key $p\langle X\rangle$ (c-key $c\langle X\rangle$, respectively) holds on I if there are no two different tuples in I that are strongly (weakly, respectively) similar on all the attributes in X. In instance $I[cip]$ of Figure 5, for example, the first two tuples are weakly, but not strongly similar on *catalog*, which means that $I[cip]$ satisfies the p-key $p\langle item, catalog\rangle$ but not the c-key $c\langle item, catalog\rangle$. Indeed, the redundant data values **240** occur in $I[cip]$ because this instance does not satisfy the c-key $c\langle item, catalog\rangle$.

The major challenges are therefore to identify syntactic conditions that characterize SQL schemata that permit precisely those instances in which no redundant data values occur, and to identify when and how a given SQL schema can be transformed into one that satisfies these conditions.

Contributions. Main contributions of our research are:

1. We introduce the new class of c-FDs as a natural complement to Lien's class of p-FDs. C-FDs can express constraints not expressible by previously studied data dependencies. We show that c-FDs are the right notion for SQL schema design.

2. We establish axiomatic and linear-time algorithmic characterizations for the implication problem of the combined class of p-FDs, c-FDs, p-keys, c-keys, and `NOT NULL` constraints. This combination covers the main features of SQL instances in which duplicate and partial information readily occur. Duplicates make it necessary to include keys as these are no longer subsumed by FDs. Null markers make it necessary to investigate possible and certain variants of these constraints, and also to include `NOT NULL` constraints which largely determine the interaction of these constraints. Our results subsume and unify previous results by Lien on p-FDs [28], by Atzeni/Morfuni on p-FDs and `NOT NULL` constraints [4], and by Köhler/Link/Zhou on p- and c-keys [21], under our combined class of constraints, without time penalties to reason about them. These foundations enable us to propose a normal form for well-designed SQL schemata, and to justify it semantically by the absence of data redundancy.

3. Indeed, we propose a normal form in terms of our constraints and show that it syntactically characterizes SQL schemata that permit precisely those instances in which no data redundancy occurs. Our normal form reduces to the well-known Boyce-Codd normal form in the idealized special case where no duplicate tuples and null markers occur, that is, when all attributes are `NOT NULL` and some key holds on the schema. Our normal form condition is invariant under different representations of the given constraints, and can be verified in time quadratic in the input, thanks to our efficient algorithms to reason about the constraints.

4. In contrast to the idealized relational model, there are cases of SQL schemata that cannot be transformed into ones that satisfy our normal form condition. Nevertheless, we identify total FDs as an expressive sub-class of c-FDs, and combine them with c-keys, to establish a normal form condition that syntactically characterizes SQL schemata that permit precisely those instances in which no redundant data values occur except for redundant null markers. We further establish an algorithm that transforms any given SQL schema with total FDs and c-keys into one that satisfies this normal form condition. Our algorithm reduces to the classical BCNF decomposition algorithm in the idealized special case where all attributes are `NOT NULL` and some key holds on the schema. Thanks to our algorithms to reason about the constraints, our normalization algorithm is as efficient as the classical BCNF decomposition algorithm.

5. We have applied a data mining algorithm to discover c- and p-FDs in publicly available data sets. These experiments show that both c- and p-FDs frequently occur in practice, that c-FDs are often total, and that c-FDs are effective in eliminating data redundancy from real-world data sets, without loss of information.

Organization. Preliminaries are given in Section 2. Related work is discussed in Section 3. Schema design foundations are treated in Section 4. Normal forms are proposed and justified in Section 5. Section 6 introduces SQL schema normalization. Experimental results are presented in Section 7. We conclude in Section 8. Proofs are given in [20].

2. POSSIBLE AND CERTAIN FDS

Our data model and constraints are introduced in this section. Essentially, we will follow the *no information NULL* approach by [4, 16, 17, 21, 28], but extend it by introducing a new type of functional dependency which we call certain. The remainder of the article will establish the significance of certain functional dependencies for SQL schema design.

We begin with basic terminology. Let $\mathfrak{A} = \{A_1, A_2, \ldots\}$ be a (countably) infinite set of distinct symbols, called *attributes*. Attributes represent column names of tables. A *table schema* is a finite non-empty subset T of $\mathfrak{A}$. Each attribute A of a table schema T is associated with an infinite domain $dom(A)$ which represents the possible values that can occur in column A. In order to encompass incomplete information the domain of each attribute contains the null marker, denoted by $\perp$. The interpretation of $\perp$ is to mean "no information" [4, 16, 17, 21, 28]. We stress that the null marker is not a domain value. In fact, it is a purely syntactic convenience that we include the null marker in the domain of each attribute as a distinguished element.

For attribute sets X and Y we may write XY for their set union $X \cup Y$. If $X = \{A_1, \ldots, A_m\}$, then we may write $A_1 \cdots A_m$ for X. In particular, we may write A to represent the singleton $\{A\}$. A *tuple* over T is a function $t : T \rightarrow \bigcup_{A \in T} dom(A)$ with $t(A) \in dom(A)$ for all $A \in X$. For $X \subseteq T$ let $t[X]$ denote the restriction of the tuple t over T to X. We say that a tuple t is X-*total* if $t[A] \neq \perp$ for all $A \in X$. A tuple t over T is said to be a *total tuple* if it is T-total. A *table* I over T is a finite multiset of tuples over T. A table I over T is a *total table* if every tuple $t \in I$ is total. Let t, t' be tuples over T. We define *weak/strong similarity* of t, t' on $X \subseteq T$ as follows:

$$\begin{aligned} t[X] \sim_w t'[X] \quad &:\Leftrightarrow \quad \forall A \in X. \\ &\quad\; (t[A] = t'[A] \vee t[A] = \perp \vee t'[A] = \perp) \\ t[X] \sim_s t'[X] \quad &:\Leftrightarrow \quad \forall A \in X. \\ &\quad\; (t[A] = t'[A] \neq \perp) \end{aligned}$$

Hence, strong similarity of t, t' on X means for each attribute A of X that the two values $t[A]$ and $t'[A]$ are both total and identical, and weak similarity of t, t' on X means for each attribute A of X that the two values $t[A]$ and $t'[A]$ are identical or at least one of them is $\perp$. Weak and strong similarity coincide for tuples that are X-total. In such "classical" cases we denote similarity by $t[X] \sim t'[X]$. We will use the phrase t, t' *agree* interchangeably for t, t' *are similar*.

A *null-free subschema* (NFS) over table schema T is an expression T_S where $T_S \subseteq T$. The NFS T_S over T is satisfied by a table I over T iff I is T_S-total. In SQL, we can declare attributes to be `NOT NULL`, and the set of these attributes forms an NFS over the table schema. We sometimes refer to the pair (T, T_S) as table schema.

We say that $X \subseteq T$ is a *key* for the total table I over T, denoted by $I \vdash X$, if there are no two different tuples $t, t' \in I$ that agree on X. The following notions of possible and certain keys were introduced in [21]. Given a table I on T, we say that $X \subseteq T$ is a *possible/certain key* for I, denoted by $p\langle X\rangle$ and $c\langle X\rangle$ respectively, if no two tuples in I with distinct tuple identities are strongly (weakly) similar on X. In this paper, we introduce the following notions of possible and certain functional dependencies.

DEFINITION 1 (POSSIBLE/CERTAIN FD). *Let $X, Y \subseteq T$. We call an expression of the form $X \;_s\!\!\rightarrow Y$ a possible functional dependency (p-FD), and an expression of the form $X \;_w\!\!\rightarrow Y$ a certain functional dependency (c-FD) on T. A possible (certain) FD $X \;_s\!\!\rightarrow Y$ ($X \;_w\!\!\rightarrow Y$) holds for a table I over T, if for every pair of tuples $t, t' \in I$ strong (weak) agreement on X implies equality on Y.*

$$I \vdash X \;_s\!\!\rightarrow Y :\Leftrightarrow \forall t, t' \in I.\, t[X] \sim_s t'[X] \Rightarrow t[Y] = t'[Y]$$
$$I \vdash X \;_w\!\!\rightarrow Y :\Leftrightarrow \forall t, t' \in I.\, t[X] \sim_w t'[X] \Rightarrow t[Y] = t'[Y]$$

Intuitively, possible FDs hold if it is possible to satisfy the FD classically, that is, there is some replacement of $\perp$ occurrences in columns of the LHS by some domain values that will satisfy the FD classically; and certain FDs hold if it is certain to satisfy the FD classically, that is, every replacement of $\perp$ occurrences in columns of the LHS by some domain values will satisfy the FD classically. We do not impose weak or strong similarity for the RHS, in contrast to [24]. Intuitively, the LHS identifies a sub-entity (possibly or certainly), and the (possible or certain) FD expresses that matching sub-entities must have the same RHS value - this may be known or unknown (i.e., $\perp$), but if we know it in one case it should not be stored as unknown in the other. While p-FDs were introduced by Lien [28], and further investigated by Atzeni/Morfuni [4], and Hartmann/Link [17], c-FDs are new to the best of our knowledge.

For a set Σ of constraints over table schema T we say that a table I over T *satisfies* Σ if I satisfies every $\sigma \in \Sigma$. If for some $\sigma \in \Sigma$ the table I does not satisfy σ we say that I *violates* σ (and violates Σ). A table I over (T, T_S) is a table I over T that satisfies T_S. A table I over (T, T_S, Σ) is a table I over (T, T_S) that satisfies Σ.

One may wonder at this point whether our definition of c-FDs is practical, that is, whether it allows us to express "desirable" constraints that cannot be expressed with other notions of FDs. For this, consider Example 1.

EXAMPLE 1. *Consider the following relation where name and appointment are `NOT NULL`:*

n(ame)	*d(ob)*	*a(ppointment)*
John Smith	*19/05/1969*	*DB Admin*
John Smith	*01/04/1971*	*Finance Manager*
John Smith	$\perp$	*Programmer*
James Brown	$\perp$	*Programmer*

A reasonable constraint would be that every employee should be uniquely identifiable by their name and date of birth. This is violated in the table above: While rows 1, 2 and 4 clearly refer to distinct employees, it is not clear which of the two John Smiths the third row refers to, if either.

Our constraint can be expressed as the c-FD $nd \;_w\!\!\rightarrow d$. To satisfy it, we would have to (e.g.) assign a date of birth to the third row, identifying the employee as one of the two previous John Smiths (or as a distinct third John Smith). None of the previously studied notions of FD can express this constraint, as further explained in Section 3. While the c-key $c\langle nd\rangle$ comes close, it would prevent an employee from having two appointments, which may not be desirable.

The example shows that non-trivial c-FDs of the form $X \;_w\!\!\rightarrow X$ can be practical. Going further, we expect that one will be hard-pressed to find an example where a c-FD of the form $X \;_w\!\!\rightarrow Y$ is sensible, but $X \;_w\!\!\rightarrow XY$ is not. In Section 6 we will see that c-FDs, and particularly those of the form $X \;_w\!\!\rightarrow XY$, enable SQL schema decomposition.

3. RELATED WORK

Schema design is a core research topic for many data models: Relational [26, 31, 34], conceptual [37], nested [23, 34], object-oriented [8, 36], XML [2, 41], and RDF [19, 22]. Our main question asks how to generalize relational schema design to SQL, where duplicate and partial information readily occur, in particular in modern applications. The fact that only little research has been reported in over forty years is already witness to the challenges that this question poses.

As main enabling results we consider the lossless decomposition property of relations that satisfy FDs [35], the Boyce-Codd normal form (BCNF) [9, 18] and its semantic justification [6, 14, 40], the BCNF-decomposition [38], Armstrong's axioms [3] and linear-time algorithms to decide FD implication [5, 12] as tools that facilitate decompositions [7].

We review the most significant extensions of classical FDs in data models with partial information. The two most prolific interpretations of the null marker are "value unknown at present" [10] and "no information" [28, 42]. First we discuss the former interpretation, which has a possible world semantics as its foundation but cannot express non-existing data. In [39] a three-valued model of FD satisfaction is explored. Here, all possible worlds over an instance I are considered, and an FD either holds, does not hold, or may hold on I, iff it holds for all, none or some (but not all) possible worlds, respectively. In [24] the notions of weak and strong FDs are introduced. A weak FD holds on some possible world, while a strong FD holds on every possible world. The authors show that the combined class of weak and strong FDs does not enjoy any finite axiomatization. In [25] the same authors study several database design problems for partial relations. Here, a set of FDs is satisfied by such a partial relation, if there is some possible world in which all FDs of the given set are satisfied. Under such assumption, the issue of decomposing partial relations is avoided altogether. This, however, is the main focus in practice and of our current work. Secondly, we discuss proposals related to the "no information" approach, which encompasses unknown as well as non-existing data [28] and has therefore been adopted by SQL. Lien defined FDs in this context to hold if strong similarity on the LHS of an FD implies equality on its RHS [28]. Our p-FDs thus correspond to Lien's notion of an FD. P-FDs enjoy a partial decomposition theorem in the sense that the X-total projection of a partial relation I over schema T that satisfies the p-FD $X \rightarrow Y$ is the lossless join of the X-total projections of $I[XY]$ and $I[X(T-XY)]$. The work in [15] proposed an SQL normal form with respect to p-FDs, but lossless decompositions are only achievable with respect to p-FDs $X \;_s\!\!\rightarrow Y$ where all attributes in X are `NOT NULL`. What we show in our work is that c-FDs enjoy a full decomposition theorem. Atzeni/Morfuni characterized the implication problem for p-FDs together with `NOT NULL` constraints [4], and Hartmann/Link extended this work to include "possible" multivalued dependencies [16, 17]. Our notions of p-FDs and c-FDs are built on the notions of p-keys and c-keys recently introduced by Köhler/Link/Zhou [21]. Since duplicate information is present, p-FDs and c-FDs cannot express p-keys or c-keys. Hence it is necessary to consider all four notions together to accommodate partial and duplicate information that occur in SQL data.

Our main novelty are certain FDs (Definition 1) which have not been studied beforehand. Our results show that c-FDs are the right notion for SQL schema design. Previously studied notions of FDs are not suitable for decompositions. Indeed, c-FDs allow us to generalize the main enabling results from relational to SQL schema design. This is impossible to achieve with the other notions of FDs, as they cannot express many constraints that can be expressed by c-FDs. A brief comparison of the different notions is given by the following example.

EXAMPLE 2. *Consider the following relation:*

e(mployee)	*d(ept)*	*m(anager)*	*s(alary)*
Turing	*CS*	*von Neumann*	$\perp$
Turing	$\perp$	*Gödel*	$\perp$

Functional dependencies on this relation are satisfied (T) or violated (F) by the different definitions as follows:

	[39]	*[24] weak*	*[24] strong*	*[28] possible*	*here certain*
$e \rightarrow d$	*unk*	*T*	*F*	*F*	*F*
$e \rightarrow m$	*F*	*F*	*F*	*F*	*F*
$e \rightarrow s$	*unk*	*T*	*F*	*T*	*T*
$d \rightarrow d$	*T*	*T*	*T*	*T*	*F*
$d \rightarrow m$	*unk*	*T*	*F*	*T*	*F*
$m \rightarrow e$	*T*	*T*	*T*	*T*	*T*
$m \rightarrow d$	*unk*	*T*	*T*	*T*	*T*

Note that the c-FD $d \;_w\!\!\rightarrow d$ *does* not *hold.*

In summary, the novel notion of a certain functional dependency allows us to develop the first schema design approach to SQL that generalizes relational schema design. C-FDs ensure that the problems studied in this paper are substantially different from those in the research literature.

4. SCHEMA DESIGN FOUNDATIONS

The same way classical relation schema design is founded on the ability to efficiently reason about FDs, we will see that SQL schema design is founded on the ability to efficiently reason about the combined class of p-keys, c-keys, p-FDs, c-FDs and `NOT NULL` constraints. This chapter establishes these reasoning tools. Many other data management tasks, including data profiling, transaction processing, and query optimization, benefit from the ability to decide the implication problem of semantic constraints.

In our context, the implication problem can be defined as follows. Let (T, T_S) denote the schema under consideration. For a set $\Sigma \cup \{\varphi\}$ of constraints over (T, T_S) we say that Σ *implies* φ, denoted $\Sigma \models \varphi$, iff every table over (T, T_S) that satisfies Σ also satisfies φ. The *implication problem* for a class $\mathcal{C}$ of constraints is to decide, for arbitrary (T, T_S) and $\Sigma \cup \{\varphi\}$ in $\mathcal{C}$, whether Σ implies φ.

We will first establish axiomatic and algorithmic characterizations of the implication problem for the class of p- and c-FDs in the presence of `NOT NULL` constraints, and then show how to add p- and c-keys.

4.1 Possible and Certain FDs

Axioms facilitate our understanding and help us reason about constraints. In our case, the axioms enable us to establish a semantic justification for our normal form proposal of well-designed SQL schemata in Section 5. The definitions of *sound* and *complete* sets of axioms are standard [34]. Table 1 shows the set $\mathfrak{F}$ of inference rules which

Reflexivity (R):	$\dfrac{}{X \,{}_{s}{\to}\, X}$
L-Augmentation (A):	$\dfrac{X \to Y}{XZ \to Y}$
Strengthening (S):	$\dfrac{X \,{}_{s}{\to}\, Y}{X \,{}_{w}{\to}\, Y} \; X \subseteq T_S$
Union (U):	$\dfrac{X \to Y \quad X \to Z}{X \to YZ}$
Decomposition (D):	$\dfrac{X \to YZ}{X \to Y}$
Pseudo-Transitivity (T):	$\dfrac{X \to Y \quad XY \,{}_{w}{\to}\, Z}{X \to Z}$
Null-Transitivity (NT):	$\dfrac{X \,{}_{s}{\to}\, Y \quad XY \,{}_{s}{\to}\, Z}{X \,{}_{s}{\to}\, Z} \; Y \subseteq T_S$

Table 1: Axiomatization $\mathfrak{F}$ of p/c-FDs and `NOT NULL`s

forms a sound and complete axiomatization for p-FDs, c-FDs and `NOT NULL` constraints. Here, $X \to Y$ is to mean either $X \,{}_{s}{\to}\, Y$ or $X \,{}_{w}{\to}\, Y$, substituted uniformly for each rule. That is, either all unspecified FDs $X \to Y$ in a rule are certain, or all are possible.

THEOREM 1. *The set $\mathfrak{F}$ of inference rules from Table 1 are sound and complete for the implication of certain and possible functional dependencies and `NOT NULL` constraints.*

Given PURCHASE $= T = oicp$ with $T_S = ocp$, let Σ consist of the p-FD $oi \,{}_{s}{\to}\, c$ and the c-FD $ic \,{}_{w}{\to}\, p$. Applying L-augmentation to $ic \,{}_{w}{\to}\, p$ results in $oic \,{}_{w}{\to}\, p$, and applying pseudo-transitivity to $oi \,{}_{s}{\to}\, c$ and $oic \,{}_{w}{\to}\, p$ results in $oi \,{}_{s}{\to}\, p$. As $\mathfrak{F}$ is sound, we conclude that Σ implies $oi \,{}_{s}{\to}\, p$. For deciding if Σ implies the c-FD $oi \,{}_{w}{\to}\, p$, we could check if $oi \,{}_{w}{\to}\, p$ can be inferred from Σ using $\mathfrak{F}$. This is inefficient and does not make good use of the given input $oi \,{}_{w}{\to}\, p$.

The notion of an attribute closure was instrumental in deriving a linear-time decision algorithm for traditional FDs [5]. Here, we introduce the notions of p- and c-closures, and show that they serve the same purpose in the SQL context.

DEFINITION 2 (CLOSURE). *Let (T, T_S, Σ) be a schema with Σ containing c-FDs and p-FDs. The* p-closure (c-closure) *of $X \subseteq T$ is the set of all $A \in T$ such that $X \,{}_{s}{\to}\, A$ ($X \,{}_{w}{\to}\, A$) is implied by Σ:*

$$X^{*p}_{\Sigma,T_S} := \{A \in T \mid \Sigma \models X \,{}_{s}{\to}\, A\}$$
$$X^{*c}_{\Sigma,T_S} := \{A \in T \mid \Sigma \models X \,{}_{w}{\to}\, A\}$$

We simply write X^{*p}, X^{*c} when Σ, T_S is understood.

Classically, an FD $X \to Y$ is implied by an FD set Σ iff Y is a subset of the attribute closure of X. We establish corresponding properties for p- and c-closures. Hence, the implication problem reduces to their computations.

THEOREM 2. *Let (T, T_S, Σ) be a schema with Σ containing p-FDs and c-FDs. Then Σ implies $X \,{}_{s}{\to}\, Y$ if and only if $Y \subseteq X^{*p}$, and Σ implies $X \,{}_{w}{\to}\, Y$ if and only if $Y \subseteq X^{*c}$.*

In contrast to the relational model, neither $(\cdot)^{*c}$ nor $(\cdot)^{*p}$ is an actual closure operator: X^{*c} need not contain X, and

Algorithm 1 p-Closure

```
Input: Σ, T_S, X
Output: X^{*p}
C := X
repeat
    C_old := C
    for all Y w→ Z ∈ Σ with Y ⊆ C do
        C := C ∪ Z
    for all Y s→ Z ∈ Σ with Y ⊆ (C ∩ T_S) ∪ X do
        C := C ∪ Z
until C = C_old
return C
```

Algorithm 2 c-Closure

```
Input: Σ, T_S, X
Output: X^{*c}
C := X ∩ T_S
repeat
    C_old := C
    for all Y w→ Z ∈ Σ with Y ⊆ C ∪ X do
        C := C ∪ Z
    for all Y s→ Z ∈ Σ with Y ⊆ C ∩ T_S do
        C := C ∪ Z
until C = C_old
return C
```

$(X^{*p})^{*p} = X^{*p}$ does not hold in general. Nevertheless we will keep referring to them as closures for the sake of consistency with existing terminology. Indeed, the following properties are important in establishing the soundness of algorithms for the computation of p- and c-closures.

LEMMA 1. *The following statements holds: i) If $X \subseteq Y$ then $X^{*p} \subseteq Y^{*p}$ and $X^{*c} \subseteq Y^{*c}$, ii) $X, X^{*c} \subseteq X^{*p}$, and iii) $(X^{*c})^{*c} \subseteq X^{*c}$ and $(X^{*p})^{*c} \subseteq X^{*p}$.* □

Algorithms 1 and 2 compute the p- and c-closures of a given attribute set for a given set of p- and c-FDs. Both algorithms are provably correct and operate in quadratic time. In both cases, linear time complexity is achieved by applying the optimization techniques of [5].

THEOREM 3. *Algorithms 1 and 2 are correct, and the implication problem for the combined class of p-FDs, c-FDs, and `NOT NULL` constraints can be decided in linear time.* □

Recall our schema PURCHASE $= oicp$ with $T_S = ocp$ and where Σ consists of the p-FD $oi \,{}_{s}{\to}\, c$ and the c-FD $ic \,{}_{w}{\to}\, p$. We saw that $oi \,{}_{s}{\to}\, p$ is implied by Σ, which is confirmed by the p-closure $oi^{*p} = oicp$ of oi for Σ, and checking that $p \in oi^{*p}$. To see if $oi \,{}_{w}{\to}\, p$ is implied by Σ, we compute the c-closure $oi^{*c} = o$ of oi for Σ and realize that $p \notin oi^{*c}$. Hence, Σ does not imply $oi \,{}_{w}{\to}\, p$. This is confirmed by the following instance over (T, T_S, Σ) which violates $oi \,{}_{w}{\to}\, p$.

order_id	item	catalog	price
5299401	Fitbit Surge	Amazon	240
5299401	NULL	Kingstoy	25

4.2 Interaction with Keys

As FDs cannot express keys over instances with duplicate tuples, and keys are fundamental in schema design, we

key-Augmentation (kA):	$\dfrac{(p/c)\,\langle X\rangle}{(p/c)\,\langle XY\rangle}$
key-Strengthening (kS):	$\dfrac{p\,\langle X\rangle}{c\,\langle X\rangle}\; X \subseteq T_S$
key-Weakening (kW):	$\dfrac{c\,\langle X\rangle}{p\,\langle X\rangle}$

Table 2: The axiomatization $\mathfrak{K}$ for p/c-keys

key-FD-Weakening (kfW):	$\dfrac{(p/c)\,\langle X\rangle}{X \to Y}$
key-Transitivity (kT):	$\dfrac{X \to Y \quad c\,\langle XY\rangle}{(p/c)\,\langle X\rangle}$
key-Null-Trans. (kNT):	$\dfrac{X \;{}_s\!\!\to Y \quad p\,\langle XY\rangle}{p\,\langle X\rangle}\; Y \subseteq T_S$

Table 3: Set $\mathfrak{FK}$ of inference rules for the interaction of p/c-keys, p/c-FDs and NOT NULL constraints

extend our results to include p-keys and c-keys. For this purpose, we recall the axiomatization $\mathfrak{K}$ from [21] for p-keys, c-keys, and NOT NULL constraints, as shown in Table 2. Here, $(p/c)\,\langle X\rangle$ means either $p\,\langle X\rangle$ or $c\,\langle X\rangle$, substituted uniformly in the key-Augmentation rule.

We now target an axiomatization for p-keys, c-keys, p-FDs, c-FDs, and NOT NULL constraints together. We use the rules in $\mathfrak{F}$ for p-FDs and c-FDs, $\mathfrak{K}$ for p-keys and c-keys, and the rules in $\mathfrak{FK}$ from Table 3 that capture the interaction of p/c-keys and p/c-FDs. Here, $X \to Y$ is to mean either $X \;{}_s\!\!\to Y$ or $X \;{}_w\!\!\to Y$, while $(p/c)\,\langle X\rangle$ is to mean either $p\,\langle X\rangle$ or $c\,\langle X\rangle$, substituted uniformly for each rule. That is, either all unspecified keys and FDs are certain, or all are possible.

THEOREM 4. *The rules from sets $\mathfrak{F}$ in Table 1, $\mathfrak{K}$ from Table 2, and $\mathfrak{FK}$ from Table 3 together are sound and complete for the implication of p-keys, c-keys, p-FDs, c-FDs, and NOT NULL constraints.* □

Given PURCHASE $= oicp$ with $T_S = ocp$, let Σ consist of the p-FD $oi \;{}_s\!\!\to c$ and the p-key $p\,\langle oic\rangle$. An application of key-Null-transitivity to both elements of Σ is possible as $c \in T_S$, and results in $p\,\langle oi\rangle$, which is thus implied by Σ. The question remains how to decide implication efficiently, e.g., how to decide if Σ implies $oi \;{}_w\!\!\to p$.

Theorem 4 can be shown by reducing the implication problem to the class of p/c-keys and the class of p/c-FDs alone. The reduction is embodied in the following definition.

DEFINITION 3 (FD-PROJECTION/KEY-PROJECTION). *Let Σ be a set of p-keys, c-keys, p-FDs, and c-FDs over T. The* FD-projection *of Σ, denoted by $\Sigma|_{FD}$, is obtained by replacing each key X with an FD $X \to T$: $\Sigma|_{FD} := \{X \to Y \in \Sigma\} \cup \{X \;{}_s\!\!\to T \mid p\,\langle X\rangle \in \Sigma\} \cup \{X \;{}_w\!\!\to T \mid c\,\langle X\rangle \in \Sigma\}$. The* key-projection *$\Sigma|_{key}$ of Σ contains all keys in Σ: $\Sigma|_{key} := \{(p/c)\,\langle X\rangle \in \Sigma\}$.*

FD-projection reduces the implication of an FD by a set of keys and FDs to the implication of an FD by a set of FDs alone: For a p- or c-FD $X \to Y$ over (T, T_S) and a set Σ of p-keys, c-keys, p-FDs, and c-FDs over (T, T_S), Σ implies $X \to Y$ iff $\Sigma|_{\rm FD}$ implies $X \to Y$. Given PURCHASE $= oicp$ with $T_S = ocp$ and $\Sigma = \{oi \;{}_s\!\!\to c, p\,\langle oic\rangle\}$, we have $\Sigma|_{\rm FD} = \{oi \;{}_s\!\!\to c, oic \;{}_s\!\!\to p\}$. Now, Σ implies $oi \;{}_w\!\!\to p$ iff $\Sigma|_{\rm FD}$ implies $oi \;{}_w\!\!\to p$. However, the latter is true iff $p \in (oi)^{*c} = o$. Consequently, Σ does not imply $oi \;{}_w\!\!\to p$, as the following instance witnesses:

order_id	item	catalog	price
5299401	Fitbit Surge	Amazon	240
5299401	NULL	Kingstoy	25

Key-projection reduces the implication of a key by a set of keys and FDs to the implication of a key by a set of keys alone: (i) Σ implies $p\,\langle X\rangle$ iff $\Sigma|_{\rm key}$ implies $c\left\langle X^{*p}_{\Sigma|_{\rm FD}}\right\rangle$ or $p\left\langle X(X^{*p}_{\Sigma|_{\rm FD}} \cap T_S)\right\rangle$, and (ii) Σ implies $c\,\langle X\rangle$ iff $\Sigma|_{\rm key}$ implies $c\left\langle XX^{*c}_{\Sigma|_{\rm FD}}\right\rangle$. Given PURCHASE $= oicp$ with $T_S = ocp$ and $\Sigma = \{oi \;{}_s\!\!\to c, p\,\langle oic\rangle\}$, we have $\Sigma|_{\rm key} = \{p\,\langle oic\rangle\}$. By (i), Σ implies $p\,\langle oi\rangle$ if $\Sigma|_{\rm key}$ implies $p\left\langle oi(oi^{*p}_{\Sigma|_{\rm FD}} \cap ocp)\right\rangle = p\,\langle oic\rangle$. Consequently, Σ does imply $p\,\langle oi\rangle$. Our reduction and our closure algorithms entail the following result.

THEOREM 5. *The implication problem for the combined class of p-keys, c-keys, p-FDs, c-FDs, and NOT NULL constraints can be decided in linear time of the input.*

5. NORMAL FORMS

Generalizing from the relational model, we stipulate the absence of data redundancy from any database instance as a semantic criterion for an SQL schema to be well-designed. Using our axiomatization and linear-time decidability of the implication problem from Section 4 we establish an effective and efficient syntactic characterization for well-designed SQL schemata in the form of a Boyce-Codd normal form (BCNF) proposal, based on p-keys, c-keys, p-FDs, c-FDs, and NOT NULL constraints.

5.1 Normal Form Definitions

We first define the notion of data redundancy, and say that a schema is in Redundancy-free normal form if it only permits instances in which no data redundancy occurs. Our notion of data redundancy follows Vincent's seminal approach [40], which is independent from the type of constraint. Informally, an occurrence of a value in an instance is redundant if *every* change to a different value results in the violation of some given constraint.

DEFINITION 4 (REDUNDANCY). *Let (T, T_S, Σ) be a schema, I an instance over it, and p_0 a* position *(row and column) in I. A* p_0-value substitution *of I is an instance I' over (T, T_S, Σ) which differs from I precisely in the value at position p_0. We say that the value at position p_0 is* redundant *in I if I possesses no p_0-value substitution. We call I* redundancy-free *if it contains no redundant positions. We say that the schema (T, T_S, Σ) is in* Redundancy-free normal form *(RFNF) if and only if all instances over the schema are redundancy-free.*

Definition 4 stipulates what we want from a schema but does not allow us to identify schemata that meet the conditions of RFNF since there can be infinitely many instances over the schema. However, finding some instance with some redundant position tells us that the given schema is not in RFNF. For example, the schema PURCHASE $= oicp$ with $\text{PURCHASE}_S = oip$ and $\Sigma = \{ic \ _w\!\!\rightarrow p\}$ is not in RFNF: the top instance in Figure 5 contains redundant positions (marked bold). In the relational model, BCNF characterizes syntactically those schemata that are in RFNF [40]. The BCNF condition for schema (T, Σ) says that for every non-trivial FD $X \rightarrow Y$ that can be inferred from Σ by the Armstrong axioms, the FD $X \rightarrow T$ can also be inferred from Σ by the Armstrong axioms. Using our axiomatization for p-keys, c-keys, p-FDs, and c-FDs, we can extend the BCNF condition from relational to SQL databases. Naturally, it requires the left-hand sides of all inferable and non-trivial p- and c-FDs to be inferable p- and c-keys, respectively.

DEFINITION 5 (BCNF).
Let (T, T_S, Σ) be a schema, with Σ consisting of p-keys, c-keys, p-FDs, and c-FDs. We say that (T, T_S, Σ) is in Boyce-Codd Normal Form (BCNF) *if and only if (i) for all non-trivial p-FDs $X \ _s\!\!\rightarrow Y \in \Sigma^+$, $p\langle X\rangle \in \Sigma^+$, and (ii) for all non-trivial c-FDs $X \ _w\!\!\rightarrow Y \in \Sigma^+$, $c\langle X\rangle \in \Sigma^+$.*

Definition 5 is purely syntactic using our axiomatization for p-keys, c-keys, p-FDs, c-FDs, and `NOT NULL` constraints. Another important aspect of Definition 5 is its invariance under different representations of the given constraints. Indeed, two schemata are *equivalent* iff they have the same set of instances. For equivalent schemata (T, T_S, Σ_1) and (T, T_S, Σ_2), (T, T_S, Σ_1) is in BCNF iff (T, T_S, Σ_2) is in BCNF. In fact, (T, T_S, Σ_1) and (T, T_S, Σ_2) are equivalent iff the syntactic closures Σ_1^+ and Σ_2^+ are the same, i.e., the sets of constraints that can be inferred from Σ by a sound and complete axiomatization. So, Definition 5 ensures invariance under different constraint representations, but means we cannot directly decide if a given schema is in BCNF. Fortunately, we can show the following result.

THEOREM 6. *The schema (T, T_S, Σ) is in BCNF if and only if (i) for all non-trivial $X \ _s\!\!\rightarrow Y \in \Sigma$, $p\langle X\rangle \in \Sigma^+$, and (ii) for all non-trivial $X \ _w\!\!\rightarrow Y \in \Sigma$, $c\langle X\rangle \in \Sigma^+$.*

Theorem 6 shows that input p-FDs and c-FDs suffice to decide if a given schema is in BCNF. The linear-time decidability of the underlying implication problem gives us a quadratic upper time bound to decide the BCNF condition.

THEOREM 7. *The problem whether a given schema is in BCNF can be decided in time quadratic in the input.*

The schema PURCHASE $= oicp$ with $\text{PURCHASE}_S = oip$ and $\Sigma = \{ic \ _w\!\!\rightarrow p\}$ is not in BCNF as the c-FD $ic \ _w\!\!\rightarrow p$ is non-trivial, and the c-key $c\langle ic\rangle$ is not implied by Σ. Given $\text{PURCHASE}_S = \emptyset$ and $\Sigma = \{oic \ _w\!\!\rightarrow p, c\langle oicp\rangle\}$ instead the schema is indeed in BCNF: the c-key $c\langle oic\rangle$ is implied by Σ because $p \in (oic)^{*c}_{\Sigma|_{\text{FD}}}$.

Theorem 7 ensures that we can decide efficiently if a given schema is in BCNF. However, deciding if the projection of a given schema (T, T_S, Σ) onto a given attribute set $X \subseteq T$ is in BCNF is co-NP complete. Here, the projection of a given schema (T, T_S, Σ) onto a given attribute set $X \subseteq T$ is defined as the schema $(X, X \cap T_S, \Sigma[X])$ where $\Sigma[X] = \{Y \rightarrow Z \in \Sigma^+ \mid YZ \subseteq X\} \cup \{(p/c)\langle Y\rangle \in \Sigma^+ \mid Y \subseteq X\}$.

THEOREM 8. *The problem of deciding whether the projection of a given schema onto a given attribute set is in BCNF (RFNF) is co-NP complete.* □

5.2 Semantic Justification

We now pinpoint what our BCNF proposal achieves: It captures schemata that permit exactly those instances that are free from data redundancy.

THEOREM 9. *A schema (T, T_S, Σ) is in RFNF if and only if (T, T_S, Σ) is in BCNF.*

It is a corollary of Theorem 7 and Theorem 9 that we can decide efficiently whether a given schema is in RFNF.

THEOREM 10. *The problem whether a given schema is in RFNF can be decided in time quadratic in the input.*

PURCHASE $= oicp$ with $\text{PURCHASE}_S = oip$ and $\Sigma = \{ic \ _w\!\!\rightarrow p\}$ is not in RFNF, as it is not in BCNF. However, PURCHASE with $\text{PURCHASE}_S = \emptyset$ and $\Sigma = \{oic \ _w\!\!\rightarrow p, c\langle oicp\rangle\}$ is in RFNF, since it is in BCNF as observed earlier.

The proof of Theorem 9 requires us to construct instances with data redundancy whenever the BCNF condition is violated. This is achieved by the following lemma.

LEMMA 2 (CONSTRUCTION LEMMA). *Consider a schema (T, T_S, Σ) and table $I = \{t_0, t_1\}$ over (T, T_S).*

i) Let $\Sigma \nvDash p\langle X\rangle$ and t_0, t_1 constructed as

$$t_i[A] = \begin{cases} 0 & \text{if } A \in X^{*p} \text{ and } A \in X \cup T_S \\ \perp & \text{if } A \in X^{*p} \text{ and } A \notin X \cup T_S \\ i & \text{if } A \notin X^{*p} \end{cases}$$

Then Σ holds on I.

ii) Let $\Sigma \nvDash c\langle X\rangle$ and t_0, t_1 constructed as

$$t_i[A] = \begin{cases} 0 & \text{if } A \in XX^{*c} \text{ and } A \in T_S \\ \perp & \text{if } A \in XX^{*c} \text{ and } A \notin T_S \\ i & \text{if } A \notin XX^{*c} \end{cases}$$

Then Σ holds on I.

6. SQL SCHEMA NORMALIZATION

In practice we cannot expect that our first attempt at designing a suitable SQL schema meets the BCNF condition. Hoping to achieve BCNF with a new attempt is doomed for failure and a waste of resources. Instead, it is desirable to transform the current schema design into one that meets the normal form condition. This process is well-known as normalization, whose primary goal is the elimination of data redundancy. In relational databases, one can always transform a given schema into BCNF, without loss of information. The two enabling properties for this lossless BCNF decomposition process are that i) T-relations which exhibit an FD $X \rightarrow Y$ are the lossless join of their projections on XY and $X(T - XY)$, and ii) if X was not a key over T, then X will be a key over the schema XY. We now show that normalization of SQL schemata is more involved. First we show that c-FDs enable us to generalize the decomposition theorem from relations to SQL instances, using multiset/set-projections. Unlike the idealized special case of relations, decompositions do not always ensure that the resulting projected schema is in BCNF. For this purpose, we identify *total* FDs as an expressive sub-class of c-FDs that ensure the elimination of redundant data value occurrences different from the null marker. As the null marker is not a data value, we re-define RFNF to exclude null markers from redundant data value occurrences and term this normal form *Value redundancy-free normal form* (VRNF). We then propose *SQL-BCNF* as a normal form that characterizes VRNF syntactically. SQL-BCNF is invariant under different representations of constraint sets, and can be decided in quadratic time. Finally, we establish an algorithm that transforms a given schema into one in VRNF (SQL-BCNF).

6.1 Lossless Decompositions

In relational databases, FDs play a vital role in schema decomposition. The central decomposition theorem states that, given an FD $X \rightarrow Y$ over table schema T, we can decompose T into $X(T - XY)$ and XY without losing information, i.e., every instance I that satisfies $X \rightarrow Y$ also satisfies $I = I[X(T-XY)] \bowtie I[XY]$. Here, $I[X]$ denotes the set projection of I onto X. SQL instances can be multi-sets and we thus require different notions of projection.

Definition 6 (multi-set notations). *We denote multi-sets using the notation* $\{\{a, a, b\}\}$. *Let I be a table over T, and $X \subseteq T$. We denote the* multi-set projection *of I onto X by* $I[[X]] := \{\{t[X] \mid t \in I\}\}$. *As usual, set projection is denoted by $I[X]$.*

Accordingly, sub-schemata of a decomposition may contain set as well as multi-set projections.

Definition 7 (decomposition). *Let T be a schema and* $\mathcal{D} = \{[T_i], \ldots, [[T_j]], \ldots\}$ *consist of a set of sub-schemata with* $\bigcup \mathcal{D} = T$, *where the different notations indicate set and multi-set projection, respectively. Then $\mathcal{D}$ is a* decomposition *of T.*

Similar to the relational model, we can introduce lossless decompositions of instances and schemata. Intuitively here, a decomposition is lossless when it recovers the original instance by joining the projected components of its decomposition. We mean by join an *equality join*, that is we only require equality of data values on common attributes and not strong similarity.

Definition 8 (lossless). *We call a decomposition of an instance I* lossless *if a join of its components results in I. We call a schema decomposition lossless if it induces a lossless decomposition for all instances. We call a schema decomposition a BCNF decomposition if all its components are in BCNF.*

Lien studied only p-FDs and showed that lossless decomposition can only be done for p-FDs $X \,_{s}\!\!\rightarrow Y$ where $X \subseteq T_S$ [28]. Hence, we will focus on c-FDs. Theorem 11 shows that c-FDs $X \,_{w}\!\!\rightarrow Y$ over T enable lossless schema decompositions into $[[X(T - XY)]]$ and $[XY]$. It subsumes the classical decomposition theorem for relations.

Theorem 11. *Let (T, T_S, Σ) be a schema with $\Sigma \models X \,_{w}\!\!\rightarrow Y$, and I an instance over (T, T_S, Σ). Then the following holds:* $I = I[[X(T - XY)]] \bowtie I[XY]$.

For example, consider Purchase with c-FD $ic \,_{w}\!\!\rightarrow p$ and the top instance `purchase` from Figure 5. The decomposition of `purchase` into `purchase`[[oic]] and `purchase`[icp], as shown at the bottom of Figure 5, is lossless.

Theorem 11 shows the significance of c-FDs for achieving lossless SQL schema decompositions. However, the goal of schema design is to eliminate data redundancy. In our example, `purchase`[icp], shown at the bottom right of Figure 5, still contains redundant data value occurrences. The reason is that `purchase`[icp] does not satisfy the c-key $c\langle ic\rangle$. In fact, $c\langle ic\rangle$ does not hold on `purchase`[icp] because the c-FD $ic \,_{w}\!\!\rightarrow icp$ does not hold on `purchase`, even though $ic \,_{w}\!\!\rightarrow p$ does hold. Intuitively, the next result shows that c-FDs of the form $X \,_{w}\!\!\rightarrow XY$ eliminate data redundancy on the $[XY]$ component of a lossless decomposition.

Theorem 12. *Let (T, T_S, Σ) be a schema with $\Sigma \models X \,_{w}\!\!\rightarrow Y$, $X \cap Y = \emptyset$, and I an instance over (T, T_S, Σ). If $\Sigma \models X \,_{w}\!\!\rightarrow XY$, then $c\langle X\rangle$ holds on $I[XY]$.*

Theorem 12 establishes the significance of c-FDs $X \,_{w}\!\!\rightarrow XY$ for SQL schema design. Accordingly, we name them.

Definition 9 (total FD). *We call a certain FD of the form $X \,_{w}\!\!\rightarrow XY$* total.

We will focus on schema decompositions based on total FDs and c-keys. As this includes p-FDs $X \,_{s}\!\!\rightarrow Y$ where $X \subseteq T_S$, our decomposition approach generalizes that for p-FDs [28]. Still, our initial goal of obtaining lossless BCNF decomposition is elusive, even if we consider only total FDs.

Theorem 13. *There are schemata for which no lossless BCNF decomposition exists, even if only total FDs are given.*

The following example provides a proof for Theorem 13.

Example 3. *Consider the following variation of our running example:* $(oicp, oip, \{oic \,_{w}\!\!\rightarrow cp\})$. *Here, the same item may be ordered from different catalogues at different prices (e.g. promotions with purchase limits), as long as all catalogues are known. Applying Theorem 11, we get*

$$oicp \quad \{oic \,_{w}\!\!\rightarrow cp\}$$

$$[[oic]] \ \{oic \,_{w}\!\!\rightarrow c\} \qquad [oicp] \ \{c\langle oic\rangle\}$$

Here the sub-schema oic contains a non-trivial c-FD but no keys, and cannot be decomposed further.

6.2 Eliminating Value Redundancy

Theorem 13 showed that decomposing SQL schemata into BCNF without loss of information is elusive. While this makes it impossible to always eliminate all data redundancy, it is useful to investigate the type of data redundancy that resists elimination. For this purpose, consider the following instance over $[oic]$ from Example 3:

order_id	item	catalog
5299401	Fitbit Surge	**NULL**
5299401	Fitbit Surge	**NULL**
7485113	Dora Doll	Kingtoys
7485113	Dora Doll	Kingtoys

Here, the only redundant positions are those in which the null marker NULL ($\perp$) occurs. Substituting one occurrence of $\perp$ by any domain value will result in an instance that violates $oic \ {}_w\!\!\rightarrow c$. However, neither position of `Kingtoys` is redundant: After substituting one position by `Amazon` the given c-FD $oic \ {}_w\!\!\rightarrow c$ is still satisfied.

While it would be nice to also avoid redundant $\perp$-positions, it may not be appropriate to speak of redundant data occurrences in this case. In fact, $\perp$ is a marker not to be confused with a domain value. Furthermore, the amount of information duplicated by redundant $\perp$-positions is intuitively less than for any actual domain value. This insight provides a strong motivation to revise our original semantic normal form proposal of RFNF to the following.

DEFINITION 10 (VRNF). *We say that a position in an instance I is* value redundant *if it is not $\perp$ and redundant. We call I* free from value redundancy *if it contains no positions that are value redundant. We say that the schema (T, T_S, Σ) is in* Value redundancy-free normal form *(VRNF) if and only if all instances over the schema are free from value redundancy.*

We want to efficiently decide whether a given schema is in VRNF. Based on our findings on lossless decompositions we will focus on c-keys and c-FDs, and propose a syntactic normal form that we show to be equivalent to VRNF. For this purpose, we require one more definition that helps us distinguish between trivial FDs in the relational model (where an FD of the form $X \rightarrow Y$ with $Y \subseteq X$ is satisfied by all relations) from trivial c-FDs.

DEFINITION 11 (INTERNAL/EXTERNAL FD). *We call a functional dependency $X \rightarrow Y$* internal *if $Y \subseteq X$. Otherwise we call it* external.

Indeed, an internal c-FD $X \ {}_w\!\!\rightarrow Y$ is only trivial if $Y \subseteq T_S$. For example, on $(T = oicp, T_S = oip)$ the internal c-FD $oic \ {}_w\!\!\rightarrow c$ is not trivial since $c \notin T_S$. We now propose *SQL-BCNF* as another syntactic normal form, requiring the LHS of each inferable external c-FD to be an inferable c-key.

DEFINITION 12 (SQL-BCNF). *Let (T, T_S, Σ) be a schema, with Σ consisting of c-keys and c-FDs. We say that (T, T_S, Σ) is in* SQL-BCNF *if and only if for every* external *c-FD $X \ {}_w\!\!\rightarrow Y \in \Sigma^+$, $c\langle X\rangle \in \Sigma^+$.*

As for our BCNF, the SQL-BCNF condition is invariant under equivalent constraint representations, and using our linear-time decidability of the implication problem for c-keys and c-FDs, we can show that it is decidable in quadratic time in the input if a given schema is in SQL-BCNF.

THEOREM 14. *A schema (T, T_S, Σ) is in SQL-BCNF if and only if for every* external *c-FD $X \ {}_w\!\!\rightarrow Y \in \Sigma$, $c\langle X\rangle \in \Sigma^+$. It can therefore be decided in time quadratic in the input whether a given schema is in SQL-BCNF.*

The schema $(T = oicp, T_S = oip, \Sigma = \{oic \ {}_w\!\!\rightarrow cp\})$ of Example 3 is not in SQL-BCNF because the c-FD $oic \ {}_w\!\!\rightarrow cp$ is external but the c-key $c\langle oic\rangle$ is not implied by Σ. However, both schemata $(T_1 = oic, T_{1,S} = oi, \Sigma_1 = \{oic \ {}_w\!\!\rightarrow c\})$ and $(T_2 = oicp, T_{2,S} = oip, \Sigma_2 = \{c\langle oic\rangle\})$ are in SQL-BCNF.

Our semantic justification for proposing SQL-BCNF is its ability to permit exactly those instances that are free from redundant data value occurrences.

THEOREM 15. *A schema (T, T_S, Σ) is in VRNF if and only if it is in SQL-BCNF.*

For examples, the given schema $(T = oicp, T_S = oip, \Sigma = \{oic \ {}_w\!\!\rightarrow cp\})$ is not in VRNF, but both schemata $(T_1 = oic, T_{1,S} = oi, \Sigma_1 = \{oic \ {}_w\!\!\rightarrow c\})$ and $(T_2 = oicp, T_{2,S} = oip, \Sigma_2 = \{c\langle oic\rangle\})$ are in VRNF.

6.3 Lossless VRNF decompositions

We are now ready to compute lossless VRNF decompositions, based on any given set of total FDs and certain keys. Algorithm 3 generalizes the classical BCNF decomposition algorithm from relational databases, which is given by the special case where $T_S = T$ and Σ implies some p- or c-key. Already the classical algorithm runs in exponential time in the input, due to computing the set of constraints that hold on a sub-schema. Algorithms that produce lossless BCNF decompositions in polynomial time [38] decompose projected schemata that are already in BCNF, thereby making the denormalization effort more difficult.

Algorithm 3 VRNF decomposition

Input: Schema (T, T_S, Σ) where Σ consists of certain keys and total FDs.
Output: Lossless VRNF decomposition $\mathcal{D}$.

Initialize $\mathcal{D} := \{\ [[T]]\ \}$
while $\mathcal{D}$ is not in VRNF **do**
  pick $[[T_i]] \in \mathcal{D}$ or $[T_i] \in \mathcal{D}$ not in VRNF, remove from $\mathcal{D}$
  pick external $X \ {}_w\!\!\rightarrow XY$ on T_i implied by Σ where $\Sigma \not\models c\langle X\rangle$
  if $[[T_i]]$ picked **then**
    add $[[X(T_i - XY)]]$ and $[XY]$ to $\mathcal{D}$
  else
    add $[X(T_i - XY)]$ and $[XY]$ to $\mathcal{D}$
return $\mathcal{D}$

Algorithm 3 always returns a lossless VRNF decomposition of the given input in time exponential in the input.

THEOREM 16. *Algorithm 3 is correct and terminates in exponential time in the input.*

The correctness of Algorithm 3 is ensured as the totality of (LHS-minimal) FDs on sub-schemata is preserved during decomposition. That is, for every LHS-minimal FD $X \ {}_w\!\!\rightarrow Y$ implied by a set Σ of total FDs and certain keys, the total FD $X \ {}_w\!\!\rightarrow XY$ is also implied by Σ.

Continuing Example 3, on input $(T = oicp, T_S = oip, \Sigma = \{oic \ {}_w\!\!\rightarrow cp\})$, Algorithm 3 would return the lossless VRNF decomposition: $(T_1 = oic, T_{1,S} = oi, \Sigma_1 = \{oic \ {}_w\!\!\rightarrow c\})$ and $(T_2 = oicp, T_{2,S} = oip, \Sigma_2 = \{c\langle oic\rangle\})$.

Deciding if the projection of a given schema onto a given attribute set is in VRNF (SQL-BCNF) is co-NP complete.

THEOREM 17. *The problem of deciding whether the projection of a given schema onto a given attribute set is in SQL-BCNF (VRNF) is co-NP complete.* $\square$

7. EXPERIMENTS

We conducted experiments to get some indication of how frequent certain FDs are, and how often they can be used for schema decomposition. We also use a public data set to illustrate our techniques and their benefits, and comment on the overheads of discovering certain FDs from data sets.

Experiments were run in Ubuntu 14.04 LTS on an AMD FX(tm)-8350 Eight-Core Processor with 15.6 GB memory.

Quantitative Insights. We mined a total of 130 tables from the following publicly available data sets:

- GO-termdb (Gene Ontology) www.geneontology.org/
- IPI (International Protein Index) www.ebi.ac.uk/IPI
- LMRP (Local Medical Review Policy) www.cms.gov/medicare-coverage-database/
- PFAM (protein families) pfam.sanger.ac.uk/
- RFAM (RNA families) rfam.sanger.ac.uk/
- Naumann (benchmarks for FD mining) https://hpi.de/naumann/projects/repeatability/data-profiling/fd.html
- UCI (Machine Learning Repository) https://archive.ics.uci.edu/ml/datasets.html

We classify FDs into possible FDs (p-FDs), certain FDs (c-FDs) and not-null FDs (nn-FDs) containing no NULL columns in the LHS of the FD. Furthermore we record the number of certain FDs which are total (t-FDs), and the number of total FDs which (1) contain RHS attributes that do not occur on the LHS, and (2) are not certain keys. These criteria ensure that the FD can be utilized for VRNF decomposition, and we denote them as λ-*FDs*. Our results are given below. We record all non-trivial FDs with minimal LHSs, and only once per LHS (multiple FDs of the same type with identical LHS are combined and reported once).

nn-FDs	p-FDs	c-FDs	t-FDs	λ-FDs
847	557	419	205	83

Two factors are likely to have a significant impact on the figures above. First, constraints may only hold accidentally, especially when the tables examined are small. Second, constraints that should sensibly hold may well be violated due to lack of enforcement. We thus consider our results qualitative rather than quantitative. Still, they indicate that c-FDs do appear frequently in practice, and are helpful in decomposing schemas further to eliminate redundancy.

We report the relative size of tables projected onto λ-FDs, as this suggests the amount of data redundancy avoided by decomposing into VRNF. By eliminating data redundancy we minimize the overhead to maintain data consistency, which is the primary goal of normalization. Our results for the 83 λ-FDs (and the 620 nn-FDs whose LHSs are not keys) are visualized in Figure 6.

We observe a large gap in the distribution for λ-FDs, with no relative projection sizes between 52% and 78%. Closer manual examination of the FDs and tables involved reveals that for the majority of λ-FDs with projection size of 78% and over, the LHSs should really be certain keys, but are not due to dirty data (e.g. identical contact details being stored multiple times). This leaves 27 λ-FDs which could sensibly be used for decomposition to eliminate a significant number of redundant data values, plus an unknown number that *should* hold but are violated by dirty data. Similar observations hold for nn-FDs with no clear gap in their distribution but a large number of LHSs that should be keys.

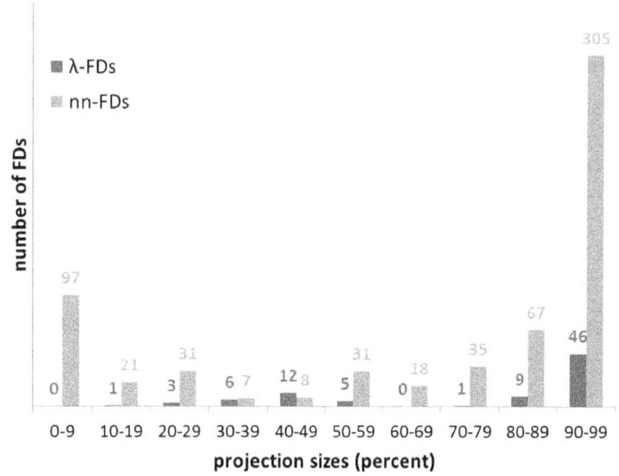

Figure 6: Relative sizes of projections on λ-FDs

contact_id	first_name	last_name	city	state_id
113	Michelle	Moscato	Carmel	20
110	Kathy	Sheehan	Columbia	48
51	Kathy	Sheehan	Columbia	48
64	Margaret	Cox	Columbia	48
120	Margaret	Cox	Columbia	48
60	Stacey	Brennan, M.D.	Columbia	48
6	Robert	Kamps, M.D.	Grove City	42
83	Michelle	Moscato	Indianapolis	20
19	Michelle	Moscato	Indianapolis	20
20	Nancy	Knudson	Indianapolis	20
18	Nancy	Knudson	Indianapolis	20
99	Stacey	Brennan, M.D.	Indianapolis	20
8	Carol	Richards	NULL	36
7	Pam	Baumker	NULL	36

Figure 7: Snippet I of `contact_draft_lookup`

Qualitative Insights. First, we illustrate the occurrence of a certain functional dependency in a real-world data set and its use for decomposing the data set without loss of information. For this purpose, we use the `contact_draft_lookup` table in the **LMRP** database. The actual table contains 14 columns and 124 rows. Figure 7 shows a snippet I consisting of only 5 columns and 14 rows.

The table `contact_draft_lookup` satisfies the λ-FD

$$\sigma : \mathit{first\_name}, \mathit{last\_name}, \mathit{city} \;{}_w\!\!\rightarrow \mathit{first\_name}, \mathit{last\_name}, \mathit{city}, \mathit{state\_id}\,.$$

In fact, the `contact_draft_lookup` even satisfies the λ-FDs

$$\mathit{first\_name}, \mathit{city} \;{}_w\!\!\rightarrow \mathit{first\_name}, \mathit{last\_name}, \mathit{city}, \mathit{state\_id}, \text{ and}$$
$$\mathit{last\_name}, \mathit{city} \;{}_w\!\!\rightarrow \mathit{first\_name}, \mathit{last\_name}, \mathit{city}, \mathit{state\_id},$$

but this is probably accidental. It can further be observed that a person alone does not functionally determine the state, because people can move. For example, Stacey Brennan, M.D. must have moved from Columbia to Indianapolis. In particular, the FD *first_name, last_name* $\rightarrow$ *state_id* does not hold on `contact_draft_lookup`. The possible and certain variants of this FD coincide because the columns

first_name	last_name	city	state_id
Michelle	Moscato	Carmel	20
Kathy	Sheehan	Columbia	48
Margaret	Cox	Columbia	48
Stacey	Brennan, M.D.	Columbia	48
Robert	Kamps, M.D.	Grove City	42
Michelle	Moscato	Indianapolis	20
Nancy	Knudson	Indianapolis	20
Stacey	Brennan, M.D.	Indianapolis	20
Carol	Richards	NULL	36
Pam	Baumker	NULL	36

contact_id	first_name	last_name	city
113	Michelle	Moscato	Carmel
110	Kathy	Sheehan	Columbia
51	Kathy	Sheehan	Columbia
64	Margaret	Cox	Columbia
120	Margaret	Cox	Columbia
60	Stacey	Brennan, M.D.	Columbia
6	Robert	Kamps, M.D.	Grove City
83	Michelle	Moscato	Indianapolis
19	Michelle	Moscato	Indianapolis
20	Nancy	Knudson	Indianapolis
18	Nancy	Knudson	Indianapolis
99	Stacey	Brennan, M.D.	Indianapolis
8	Carol	Richards	NULL
7	Pam	Baumker	NULL

Figure 8: VRNF-decomposition of *I* from Figure 7

first_name, last_name, state_id do not contain null marker occurrences in the whole table. A VRNF-decomposition of `contact_draft_lookup` using σ eliminates data redundancy: the set-projection on [*first_name, last_name, city, state_id*] contains 105 rows, i.e., 19 sources of potential inconsistency are eliminated. The c-key $c\langle first\_name, last\_name, city\rangle$ holds on this projection. For snippet I we obtain the decomposition shown in Figure 8. Finally, the c-FD *city* $\rightarrow$ *state_id* already fails to hold on our snippet I, so lossless decompositions according to this FD are not possible.

As a second example we apply Algorithm 3 to the `contractor` table of the **LMRP** database. This table has 22 columns and 173 rows. We decompose `contractor` into four tables with the following λ-FDs (without repeating LHS attributes on the RHSs)

1. *city,url* $_w\!\rightarrow$ *dmerc_rgn,status*
2. *cmd_name,phone,url* $_w\!\rightarrow$ *contractor_version,status_flag*
3. *address1,contractor_bus_name,contractor_type_id* $_w\!\rightarrow$ *url*.

Table 1 has 4 attributes and 38 rows, table 2 has 5 attributes and 67 rows, table 3 has 4 attributes and 73 rows, and the remaining table has 17 attributes and 173 rows (being the multi-set projection). In the process we eliminated 448 redundant data values, namely: 1 for *dmerc_rng*, 135 for *status*, 106 for *contractor_version*, 106 for *status_flag*, and 100 for *url*. The example shows that VRNF-decomposition can also eliminate null marker redundancies (but this is not guaranteed), in fact, we eliminated 134 of those in the *dmerc_rng* column. While storage saving is not the primary goal of normalization, we can compare the total number of cells over all tables (the sum of rows $\times$ columns). The original data set contains $173 \times 22 = 3806$ cells, while the decomposed tables contain $173 \times 17 + 38 \times 4 + 67 \times 5 + 73 \times 4 = 3720$ cells. Finally, we include a very simple comparison of the query and update performance between the normalized and non-normalized data set. Because of the small number of rows, we took the cross product of `contractor` with the new column $(1, \ldots, 1000)$, called *new*, in order to obtain a data set of a more typical size. The new column was then part of each FD and key, and each table in the decomposition. The time for validating the c-FD *new,city,url* $_w\!\rightarrow$ *dmerc_rgn,status* on the non-normalized data set took 122ms, while the time for validating the c-key *new,city,url* on the normalized table took 15ms. This shows a clear performance gain in validating consistency, the main purpose of normalization. In addition, the loss in efficiency when processing queries is rather small: Selecting all tuples from the non-normalized table took 2,957ms, while the selection of all tuples from the join of all normalized tables took 3,150ms.

Discovering c-FDs. The problem of computing a cover for the set of c-FDs from a given data set is not in the scope of this paper. Nevertheless, we provide some brief insight related to the performance of our discovery algorithm for c-FDs. Reference [33] contains a detailed performance analysis of the seven most popular algorithms that discover classical FDs (treating nulls as any other domain value). The following table shows for three of the Naumann data sets the number of classical FDs discovered, the time of the best performing algorithm to compute them according to [33], as well as the number of c-FDs we discovered and the time required by our algorithm.

data set	columns [#]	rows [#]	FDs [#]	time [s]	c-FDs [#]	time [s]
breast-cancer	11	699	46	0.5	54	0.1
adult	14	48,842	78	5.9	78	10.4
hepatitis	20	155	8,250	0.8	264	1.2

In general, c-FDs and classical FDs are incomparable which means that data sets may exhibit different numbers of them, and algorithms to discover them may perform quite differently. Nevertheless, we can say that the performance of our algorithm is rather competitive in comparison to that of the best breed discovery algorithms for classical FDs.

8. CONCLUSION AND FUTURE WORK

The impact of relational normalization theory on database practice has been limited. Well-known results that enable relational normalization do not apply to SQL-compliant data in which duplicate and partial information readily occur. We have developed the first SQL schema design framework based on the new notion of a certain functional dependency. Coupled with possible keys, certain keys, possible FDs, and `NOT NULL` constraints, certain FDs handle duplicate information and null marker occurrences in SQL data appropriately. These dependencies can express many desirable constraints in practice, form a rich source of SQL data redundancy, yet can still be reasoned about in linear time. We have proposed a normal form for well-designed SQL schemata, and semantically justified the proposal by showing that it permits exactly those instances that are free from data redundancy. In contrast to relational normalization, SQL schema normalization is not always achievable. Nevertheless, we identified total FDs for which we can transform any given SQL schema into one that permits exactly those instances that are free from redundant data values but not redundant null marker occurrences. Our experiments confirm that certain and total FDs occur frequently in real data sets, and our framework is effective in decomposing these data sets such that all data redundancy is eliminated and no information lost.

Future work will address the scalable discovery of certain FDs from large data sets, extending [1, 33] in which null markers are treated as any other domain value. Regarding SQL normalization, it is interesting to define notions of i) dependency-preservation and extensions of the Third normal form [7], ii) update anomalies and investigate what our normal forms achieve in terms of these [40], and iii) other dependencies and normal forms [11, 13, 27]. There are strong relationships with conditional independencies, paramount in statistics and machine learning [29, 32].

Acknowledgement. The research is supported by the Marsden Fund Council grant 3701176 from Government funding, administered by the Royal Society of New Zealand.

9. REFERENCES

[1] Z. Abedjan, L. Golab, and F. Naumann. Profiling relational data: a survey. *VLDB J.*, 24(4):557–581, 2015.

[2] M. Arenas. Normalization theory for XML. *SIGMOD Record*, 35(4):57–64, 2006.

[3] W. W. Armstrong. Dependency structures of data base relationships. In *IFIP Congress*, pages 580–583, 1974.

[4] P. Atzeni and N. M. Morfuni. Functional dependencies and constraints on null values in database relations. *Information and Control*, 70(1):1–31, 1986.

[5] C. Beeri and P. A. Bernstein. Computational problems related to the design of normal form relational schemas. *ACM Trans. Database Syst.*, 4(1):30–59, 1979.

[6] P. A. Bernstein and N. Goodman. What does boyce-codd normal form do? In *VLDB*, pages 245–259, 1980.

[7] J. Biskup, U. Dayal, and P. A. Bernstein. Synthesizing independent database schemas. In *SIGMOD*, pages 143–151, 1979.

[8] J. Biskup and T. Polle. Adding inclusion dependencies to an object-oriented data model with uniqueness constraints. *Acta Inf.*, 39(6-7):391–449, 2003.

[9] E. F. Codd. Recent investigations in relational data base systems. In *IFIP Congress*, pages 1017–1021, 1974.

[10] E. F. Codd. *The Relational Model for Database Management, Version 2.* Addison-Wesley, 1990.

[11] H. Darwen, C. Date, and R. Fagin. A normal form for preventing redundant tuples in relational databases. In *ICDT*, pages 114–126, 2012.

[12] J. Diederich and J. Milton. New methods and fast algorithms for database normalization. *ACM Trans. Database Syst.*, 13(3):339–365, 1988.

[13] R. Fagin. Multivalued dependencies and a new normal form for relational databases. *ACM Trans. Database Syst.*, 2(3):262–278, 1977.

[14] R. Fagin. A normal form for relational databases that is based on domains and keys. *ACM Trans. Database Syst.*, 6(3):387–415, 1981.

[15] F. Ferrarotti, S. Hartmann, H. Köhler, S. Link, and M. W. Vincent. The Boyce-Codd-Heath normal form for SQL. In *WoLLIC*, pages 110–122, 2011.

[16] S. Hartmann and S. Link. When data dependencies over SQL tables meet the logics of paradox and S-3. In *PODS*, pages 317–326, 2010.

[17] S. Hartmann and S. Link. The implication problem of data dependencies over SQL table definitions. *ACM Trans. Database Syst.*, 37(2):13, 2012.

[18] I. J. Heath. Unacceptable file operations in a relational data base. In *SIGFIDET Workshop*, pages 19–33, 1971.

[19] R. T. Herrera, J. Tekli, R. Chbeir, S. Laborie, I. Dongo, and R. Guzman. Toward RDF normalization. In *ER*, pages 261–275, 2015.

[20] H. Köhler and S. Link. SQL Schema Design. Technical Report TR-496, Centre for Discrete Mathematics and Theoretical Computer Science, The University of Auckland, 2016.

[21] H. Köhler, S. Link, and X. Zhou. Possible and certain SQL key. *PVLDB*, 8(11):1118–1129, 2015.

[22] G. Lausen. Relational databases in RDF: Keys and foreign keys. In *SWDB-ODBIS*, pages 43–56, 2007.

[23] M. Levene. *The Nested Universal Relation Database Model*, volume 595 of *LNCS*. Springer, 1992.

[24] M. Levene and G. Loizou. Axiomatisation of functional dependencies in incomplete relations. *Theor. Comput. Sci.*, 206(1-2):283–300, 1998.

[25] M. Levene and G. Loizou. Database design for incomplete relations. *ACM Trans. Database Syst.*, 24(1):80–125, 1999.

[26] M. Levene and G. Loizou. *A guided tour of relational databases and beyond.* Springer, 1999.

[27] M. Levene and M. W. Vincent. Justification for inclusion dependency normal form. *IEEE Trans. Knowl. Data Eng.*, 12(2):281–291, 2000.

[28] Y. E. Lien. On the equivalence of database models. *J. ACM*, 29(2):333–362, 1982.

[29] S. Link. Reasoning about saturated conditional independence under uncertainty. In *AAAI*, 2013.

[30] J. A. Makowsky and E. V. Ravve. Dependency preserving refinements and the fundamental problem of database design. *Data Knowl. Eng.*, 24(3):277–312, 1998.

[31] H. Mannila and K.-J. Räihä. *Design of Relational Databases.* Addison-Wesley, 1992.

[32] M. Niepert, M. Gyssens, B. Sayrafi, and D. V. Gucht. On the conditional independence implication problem: A lattice-theoretic approach. *Artif. Intell.*, 202:29–51, 2013.

[33] T. Papenbrock, J. Ehrlich, J. Marten, T. Neubert, J. Rudolph, M. Schönberg, J. Zwiener, and F. Naumann. Functional dependency discovery. *PVLDB*, 8(10):1082–1093, 2015.

[34] J. Paredaens, P. D. Bra, M. Gyssens, and D. V. Gucht. *The Structure of the Relational Database Model*, volume 17 of *EATCS Monographs on Theoretical Computer Science.* Springer, 1989.

[35] J. Rissanen. Independent components of relations. *ACM Trans. Database Syst.*, 2(4):317–325, 1977.

[36] Z. Tari, J. Stokes, and S. Spaccapietra. Object normal forms and dependency constraints for object-oriented schemata. *ACM Trans. Database Syst.*, 22(4):513–569, 1997.

[37] B. Thalheim. *Entity-relationship modeling - foundations of database technology.* Springer, 2000.

[38] D.-M. Tsou and P. C. Fischer. Decomposition of a relation scheme into Boyce-Codd normal form. *SIGACT News*, 14(3):23–29, 1982.

[39] Y. Vassiliou. Functional dependencies and incomplete information. In *VLDB*, pages 260–269, 1980.

[40] M. W. Vincent. Semantic foundations of 4NF in relational database design. *Acta Inf.*, 36(3):173–213, 1999.

[41] M. W. Vincent, J. Liu, and C. Liu. Strong functional dependencies and their application to normal forms in XML. *ACM Trans. Database Syst.*, 29(3):445–462, 2004.

[42] C. Zaniolo. Database relations with null values. *J. Comput. System Sci.*, 28(1):142–166, 1984.

SQLShare: Results from a Multi-Year SQL-as-a-Service Experiment

Shrainik Jain, Dominik Moritz, Daniel Halperin, Bill Howe, Ed Lazowska
Computer Science and Engineering Department, University of Washington, Seattle, WA, USA
{shrainik, domoritz, dhalperi, billhowe, lazowska}@cs.washington.edu

ABSTRACT

We analyze the workload from a multi-year deployment of a database-as-a-service platform targeting scientists and data scientists with minimal database experience. Our hypothesis was that relatively minor changes to the way databases are delivered can increase their use in ad hoc analysis environments. The web-based SQLShare system emphasizes easy dataset-at-a-time ingest, relaxed schemas and schema inference, easy view creation and sharing, and full SQL support. We find that these features have helped attract workloads typically associated with scripts and files rather than relational databases: complex analytics, routine processing pipelines, data publishing, and collaborative analysis. Quantitatively, these workloads are characterized by shorter dataset "lifetimes", higher query complexity, and higher data complexity. We report on usage scenarios that suggest SQL is being used in place of scripts for one-off data analysis and ad hoc data sharing. The workload suggests that a new class of relational systems emphasizing short-term, ad hoc analytics over engineered schemas may improve uptake of database technology in data science contexts. Our contributions include a system design for delivering databases into these contexts, a description of a public research query workload dataset released to advance research in analytic data systems, and an initial analysis of the workload that provides evidence of new use cases under-supported in existing systems.

1. INTRODUCTION

We recently completed a four-year exercise to study the use of database technology in science and data science, where scripts and files are the de facto standard for data manipulation and analytics. Database technology has had limited uptake in these environments, in part due to the overhead in designing a schema and setting up a permanent database infrastructure. Changing data and changing requirements make it difficult to amortize these upfront costs, and as a result analysts tend to retreat to manipulating files with scripts in R, Python and MATLAB. Simultaneously, there is no appropriate corpus available for researchers to use to study this problem effectively. Industry partners do not retain or do not share query workloads, and certainly do not provide public access to data. Query workloads that do exist are associate with conventional pre-engineered database applications rather than oriented toward ad hoc analysis of ad hoc datasets.

SIGMOD'16, June 26-July 01, 2016, San Francisco, CA, USA
© 2016 ACM. ISBN 978-1-4503-3531-7/16/06...$15.00
DOI: http://dx.doi.org/10.1145/2882903.2882957

Our hypothesis was that a relatively minor set of changes to how *existing* database technology is *packaged and delivered* would be sufficient to convince science and data science users to adopt SQL in their day-to-day data manipulation and analysis tasks, potentially displacing script-and-file based approaches. To test this hypothesis, we built SQLShare, a web-based system designed to make database technology easier to use for ad hoc tasks. We then deployed the system as a service and logged a multi-year query log as a research corpus for further analysis. This paper represents the release of the corpus to the database community, a description of the system that collected it, and an initial analysis of the data it contains. We also performed some informal ad-hoc interviews with our active user base, which is mostly comprised of *researchers and scientists*, and some of the results and conclusions drawn are influenced by our familiarity with these users..

Our ultimate goal is to design new systems to better support ad hoc data management and analytics. Although we target researchers in the physical, life, and social sciences, we find that the requirements in data-intensive science and data-intensive business have begun to converge. The data scientists that are in high demand share characteristics with academic researchers: a stronger math background and deep domain knowledge, traits that sometimes come at the expense of software and systems expertise. In response, we designed SQLShare [15, 14] to reduce the use of a database to a minimal workflow of just uploading data, writing queries, and sharing the results — we attempt to automate or eliminate steps for installation, deployment, schema design, physical tuning, and data dissemination. We deployed this system to determine its efficacy in attracting science users and understand their requirements. This experiment was not a controlled user study; rather, we deployed SQLShare as a production service — an "instrument" to collect measurements on the kind of datasets used in practice, the kinds of queries these scientists and data scientists would write, and how the specific SQLShare features would be used.

In this paper, we describe the corpus we collected during this experiment, describe the SQLShare system used to collect the corpus, and present findings from an initial analysis of the corpus. Our results show that the specific features of SQLShare are associated with specific usage patterns observed in the workload dataset, and that these patterns may motivate new kinds of data systems. We have made the query log dataset available to the research community to inform research on database interfaces, new languages, workload optimization, query recommendation, domain-specific data systems, and visualization. Our dataset is one of the only two known real-world SQL workloads publicly available to the database research community (the other being the Sloan Digital Sky Survey workloads [18]), and the only one containing primarily ad hoc, hand-written queries over user-uploaded datasets.

The workload suggests that some of our users are comfortable expressing complex tasks in SQL (binning, integration across many tens of datasets) and making use of advanced language features such as window functions. Further, there is evidence that by relaxing schema requirements and inferring structure automatically, we allow analysts to use SQL itself to incrementally impose structure by writing views: assigning types, renaming columns, cleaning bad values, reorganizing tables — tasks normally associated with offline preprocessing in a general purpose language.

Although SQL itself appears useful in this context, support for complex query authoring emerges as an important research topic: query recommendation, editors, debuggers, new languages supporting the common idioms found in this workload all appear well-motivated. SQL has enjoyed a resurgence as an important interface for analytics without necessarily relying on engineered schemas (e.g., HIVE [31], SparkSQL [4], and Schema-free SQL [22]). More recently Metanautix [2] has adopted SQL for image and video processing tasks. Our work provides further evidence of SQL's utility in non-traditional contexts, especially in science.

We find that conventional database views are remarkably useful for a variety of tasks in science and analytics environments: protected data sharing, workflow provenance, data publishing, abstraction for data processing pipelines. To encourage the use of views, we made view creation a side effect of query authoring and were careful to erase any distinction between physical tables and virtual views — both views and tables were considered a "dataset."

Sharing results with collaborators without emailing scripts and files emerged as an important use case. Collaborators reported browsing long chains of nested views to understand the provenance of a dataset. Snippets from one query were reused in other queries routinely. Shared datasets could be queried and manipulated without requiring data to be downloaded first. Altogether, these features led to workloads that involved very short data lifetimes: Data could be brought into the database easily, analyzed briefly with SQL, and shared with other partners with a click. The users report that these short-lifetime workloads were typically implemented as scripts in R or Python; SQLShare demonstrates that they can be supported in the database itself with minimal system changes.

We intend the database community to use this paper as a reference for understanding how non-experts use SQL "in the trenches," as a description of a workload dataset to drive further research, and as a baseline for comparison with new database systems targeting similar users. This paper makes the following contributions:

- A new publicly available ad hoc SQL workload dataset of 24275 hand-written queries over 3891 user-uploaded tables provided by scientists and data scientists in the life, physical, and social sciences.
- A description of the important features of the SQLShare, a system designed to increase uptake of database technology for ad hoc analysis and deployed as the instrument used to collect the workload.
- An initial analysis of the SQLShare workload linking the features of SQLShare to specific usage patterns typically associated with scripts-and-files, along with a general characterization of these usage patterns.
- A comparison of the SQLShare workload with that of a conventional schema-first science database to provide evidence that the characteristics we uncover are unique to the SQLShare experiment.

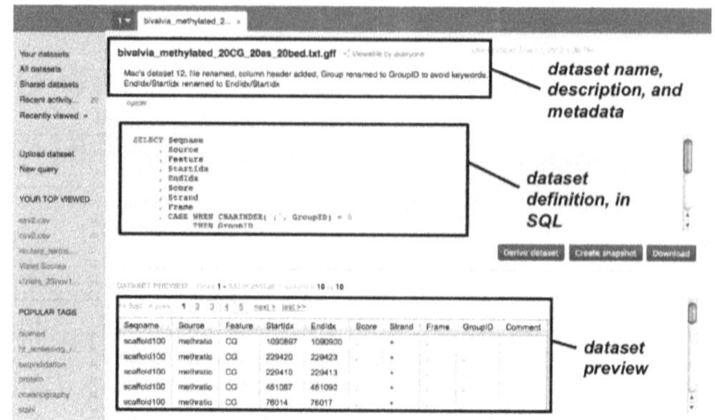

Figure 1: Screenshot of the SQLShare user interface. Each dataset is a view associated with some descriptive metadata and a preview. Creating and sharing views is the primary workflow in using the system.

2. PROBLEM CONTEXT

Relational databases remain underused in science (and data science) despite a natural fit between hypothesis testing and interactive query. Some ascribe this underuse to a mismatch between the requirements of scientific data analysis and the models and languages of relational database systems [29]. Our experience is that rows-and-columns datasets remain ubiquitous in science, and that standard relational models and languages remain a good conceptual fit. We find that the key barriers to adoption lie elsewhere:

- Although collections of records are generally appropriate, datasets in practice are *weakly structured*: they exhibit inconsistent types, missing and incorrect values, inconsistencies across column and table names, horizontal and vertical decomposition of logical datasets into sets of files. General purpose languages and collections of files are perceived to be the highest level of abstraction that can accommodate this heterogeneity.
- Daily activity results in long chains of *derived datasets*. Raw data are cleaned, restructured, integrated, processed, and analyzed — each step in the chain results in a derived dataset. The processing history of the dataset is important for provenance purposes. These derived datasets may be virtual or materialized, but in either case ease of recomputation is considered paramount. The natural inclination is to model the processing pipeline as a sequence of scripts, giving rise to workflow management systems designed to manage the execution and sharing of script-based processing [7, 9, 24, 30].
- As workloads become increasingly analytical, declarative languages are perceived to be increasingly limited. The emergence of impoverished SQL languages that lack support for standard features exacerbates the problem.[1]
- Inter-institution collaboration demands selective *sharing* of data, analysis steps, and results on-demand.
- Teams of researchers exhibit significant *diversity*, with varying backgrounds, varying experience levels, and varying tolerance for technical barriers. Data systems that require significant installation, configuration, and loading steps before

[1] For example, the popular HIVE SQL dialect only supports subqueries in the FROM clause and does not support window functions, complicating common analytical idioms that are naturally expressed in GPLs using loops.

Table 1: Summary of observed requirements in science and data science environments.

Requirement	Feature	Evidence
Weakly structured data	Relaxed schemas	Casting, cleaning, integration
Derived datasets	First-class views	Deep view chains, reuse, abstraction
Collaborative sharing	User-controlled permissions	Public datasets, fine-grained sharing
Complex manipulation	Full SQL	Use of complex idioms and features
Diverse users	SaaS	Broad use
Low data lifetime	Relaxed schemas	"One-pass" workloads

delivering value are perceived as "maybe good for database experts, but not right for me."

- Highly dynamic analysis environments result in *short data lifetimes*: datasets are presented to the system, analyzed, and then put aside. In contrast, conventional database applications tend to emphasize a permament, pre-engineered schema. The transient nature of data makes it difficult to amortize the cost of schema design and data loading in a conventional database and motivate a tighter interaction loop for incorporating new data sources.

Given these requirements, there is a temptation to design a new system from scratch targeting these requirements. Instead, we consider the null hypothesis: that existing database systems are largely equipped to support these new environments, provided we change their interfaces to support these new workflows. We consider how to change the "delivery vector" of relational databases by emphasizing certain features (full SQL, views) and de-emphasizing or automating the use of other features (fixed, pre-engineered schemas).

In this paper, we first formalize these requirement and show how we address them in SQLShare. Next we analyze SQLShare workload to show how we fared on fulfilling these requirements over the last 4 years. We then look at a comparison of SQLShare workload with the SDSS workload and show how SQLShare queries are more diverse and very complex. We conclude with a discussion about the non-traditional workflows generated over SQLShare. We show that by making use of databases simpler, SQLShare enabled novice database users to build data analytic skills and focus on science and domain expertise.

3. SQLSHARE PLATFORM FEATURES

The SQLShare [14] platform was designed, built and deployed to deliver database technology into science contexts, and, as a side effect, collect a workload dataset for use by the database research community. Table 1 summarizes the key features required to support science and data science use cases. Next we look at how each of these feature were built into SQLShare.

SQLShare is a cloud-hosted data management system for science emphasizing relaxed schemas and collaborative analysis. By "relaxed schemas," we mean that data can be uploaded as is, and column types are inferred automatically from the data upon ingest rather than prescribed by users. Moreover, the interfaces are designed to accommodate the management of hundreds or thousands of datasets per user instead of a single fixed schema linked by integrity constraints. SQLShare supports a "Sea of Tables" model rather than a pre-engineered schema. In this sense, it supports usage patterns like those of a filesystem rather than a database: Datasets can be freely created without regard to global constraints. Each dataset is a collection of typed records and has a name, but otherwise the system makes no assumptions.

SQLShare supports exploratory analysis by emphasizing the derivation and sharing of virtual datasets via relational views, and eschews destructive update at the tuple level in favor of dataset-level versioning. Tasks typically considered out of scope for relational databases, including preliminary data cleaning, timeseries analysis, and statistical analysis, are implemented by creating multiple layers of views. For example, nutrient information in an environmental sensing application may contain string-valued flags indicating missing numeric data, incorrect column names, and may comprise many separate files instead of one logical dataset. Instead of demanding that these issues be resolved prior to ingest into the system, SQLShare encourages data to be uploaded "as-is" and repaired using database features. Users may write one view to rename columns, another to replace missing values cast types, a third to integrate the files into one logical dataset, and a fourth to bin the data by time to compute an hourly average. Any of these views can be shared with collaborators as needed, and complete provenance of how the final result was constructed from raw data is available for inspection.

SQLShare was deployed and managed as a cloud-hosted service, which has been critical to the success of the experiment: The backend system was developed and supported by either zero or one developer at any time, thanks to the automatic failure handling and simplified deployment offered by the cloud providers.

The SQLShare experiment has been running in various forms since 2011, and we have attracted hundreds of science users who have run tens of thousands of queries over thousands of datasets.

3.1 Relaxed Schemas

Datasets are uploaded to SQLShare via the REST interface. Although we anticipated adding support for a number of different file formats, in practice we found that nearly all data was presented in some variant of row-delimited and field-delimited format, e.g. csv. Files are staged server-side and briefly analyzed to infer column types and assign default column names if necessary. Somewhat surprisingly, almost 50% of the datasets uploaded did not have column names supplied in the source file. Once a schema is derived, the appropriate table is created in the database and the file is ingested. By staging the file server-side we ensure robustness: if ingest fails, we can retry without forcing the user to re-upload the data. To infer

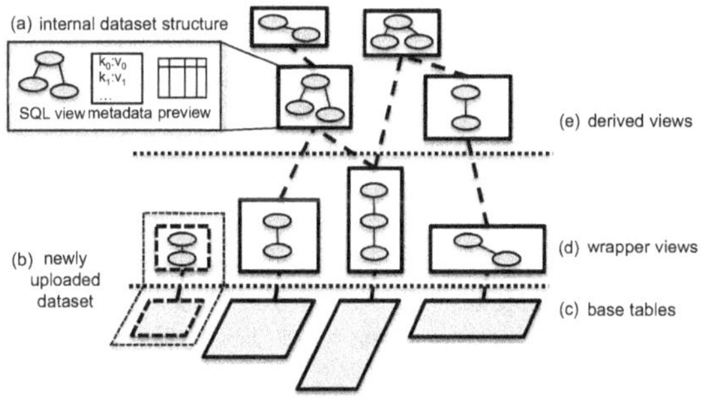

Figure 2: The SQLShare data model. (a) The internal structure of a dataset, consisting of a relational view, attached metadata, and a cached preview of the results. (b) A newly uploaded datasets creates both a physical base table and an initial (trivial) wrapper view. (c) The physical data are stored in base tables, but never modified directly. (d) Wrapper views are indistinguishable from other SQLShare datasets, except that they reference physical base tables. (e) Derived datasets can be created by any user. Permissions are managed in the underlying database.

the format, we consider various row and column delimiter values until the first N rows can be parsed with identical column counts. To infer column types, the first N records are inspected. For each column, the most-specific type is identified. For example, if every value can be successfully cast as an integer, the type is assumed to be an integer. This prefix inspection heuristic can fail, and non-integer types may be encountered further down in the dataset. In that case, the database raises an exception, we revert the type to a string via ALTER TABLE, and the ingest continues. Besides mixed-type columns, we also tolerate non-uniform row lengths. Additional columns are created as needed to accommodate the longest row, and these columns are padded with NULL for rows that do not supply appropriate values. A total of 9% of the datasets uploaded to SQLShare made use of this feature.

Our goal with this data ingest process is to tolerate (and ideally to flag and expose) many types of data problems, including problems with the structure, types, or values. We have designed the system to ensure that we do not reject such dirty data, because many of our target users (researchers in physical, life and social sciences) have no capacity to clean, reformat, or restructure the data offline. If we force them to use scripts (or even spreadsheets) to clean the data as a preprocessing step, we are essentially asserting that SQLShare is irrelevant for their day-to-day tasks. Instead, we want to tolerate malformed data and encourage the use of SQL itself to scale and automate cleaning and restructuring tasks.

3.2 Data Model: Unifying Views and Tables

We illustrate the data model of SQLShare in Figure 2.

Views are a first-class citizen in SQLShare. Views are created in the UI (or programmatically in the REST interface) by saving a query and giving it a name. Everything in SQLShare is accomplished by writing and sharing views: Users can clean data, assess quality, standardize units, integrate data from multiple sources, attach metadata, protect sensitive data, and publish results. We avoid forcing the user to use the CREATE VIEW syntax of the SQL standard, for two reasons: First, we want a view to be conceptually identical to a physical table — our design principle is "everything is a dataset." Second, the syntax proved awkward in initial tests with users.

All datasets are considered read-only; the only way to modify a dataset is by changing its view definition. Using UNION queries, a view definition can be extended with new data to simulate batch INSERTs. The advantage of this design is that provenance is maintained: an uploaded batch of data can be "uninserted" at a later date, and the substructure of the dataset as a sequence of batch inserts can be inspected and reasoned about. The disadvantage of this approach is that it prevents tuple-at-a-time updates and inserts. However, we find that a key characteristic of our target workloads is dataset-at-a-time processing, and we have not seen this design principle reported as a weakness. The REST interface provides some convenience features for appending batches of tuples: An `append` call accepts an existing dataset name E and a newly uploaded dataset name N as input, and, if the schemas are compatible, the query definition associated with E will be rewritten as $(E)UNION(N)$. Downstream views and queries will automatically see the new data with no changes required. For some applications, it is important that the data doesn't change without the consumers' knowledge. In these cases, the user can `materialize` the dataset to create a snapshot that is distinct from the original view definition. SQLShare does not automatically materialize views to improve performance; there is an application-specific tradeoff with freshness that we have not yet explored how to optimize. We are exploring certain "safe" scenarios where we can make materialization decisions unilaterally.

Each *dataset* in SQLShare is a 3-tuple $(sql, metadata, preview)$, where sql is a SQL query, $metadata$ consists of a short name, a long description, and a set of tags, and $preview$ is the first 100 rows of the dataset. When a user uploads a table to SQLShare, a *base table* `T` is created, along with a trivial *wrapper* query of the form `SELECT * FROM T`. This design helps unify the concept of tables and views and also provides an initial example query for novice SQL users to operate from. We find in practice that editing a simple query into an "adjacent" query is very easy for anyone in practice; only writing a complex query from scratch is difficult. The owner of the dataset is the user who created it; ownership cannot be transferred. Each dataset is associated with a set of keyword $tags$ to ease search and organization in the UI. The set of $permissions$ provides user-specific access. Users are not allowed to run DDL statements like `CREATE TABLE` etc. since that would make it difficult to automatically make a view on top of every table. Users can make a dataset public, share it with specific users, or keep it private. When sharing derived views, complex situations can arise. The semantics for determining access to a shared resource uses the concept of *ownership chains*, following the semantics of Microsoft SQL Server. If user A owns a table T, they can share a derived view $V_1(T)$ with user B even if the table T has not been shared, and user B will have access. But if user B then creates a derived $V_2(V_1(T))$ and shares it with user C, user C will encounter an error because the ownership chain $V2 \rightarrow V1 \rightarrow T$ is broken (i.e., it involves two different users, A and B.) We are exploring whether these semantics are too conservative for our requirements, given that sharing is a first-class concept.

3.3 Query Processing

Queries are submitted to SQLShare primarily via the WebUI or sometimes directly through the REST API. REST server receives the query request, and assigns an identifier to the request which is sent back to the requesting client. The WebUI uses this identifier to regularly get results or check for query status. This was an obvious choice over an atomic request for queries as long running queries would reduce the requests the REST server can handle. The REST server uses the MS SQL Azure's `C#` library to run queries internally. As of now, we do not create any automatic indices, however this is a feature we might build later. Since the dataset updates are allowed only via creation of newer datasets, we can assume that the result of query wouldn't change over time. This allows us to save the preview results for each dataset and serve them instead of running the query every time the dataset is accessed. However the query needs to be actually run if the user submits a 'download results' request.

3.4 Architecture

The architecture of SQLShare appears in Figure Figure 3. The core system consists of a REST interface in front of a database system that implements the data model, query log, ingest semantics, manages long-running queries, handles exceptions, and manages authentication. The SQLShare REST interface is compatible with any relational database, but it was originally deployed using the Microsoft Azure Database (originally SQL Azure). The Microsoft Azure Database is mostly interface compatible with Microsoft SQL Server, except that it requires all tables to be associated with clustered index. In SQLShare, we avoid exposing DDL to users and therefore create a clustered index by default on all columns in the database, in column order. The front-end UI is in no way a privileged application; it operates the REST interface like any other client. Indeed, other clients exist, in some cases built by the community. For example, the R client for SQLShare was written by a

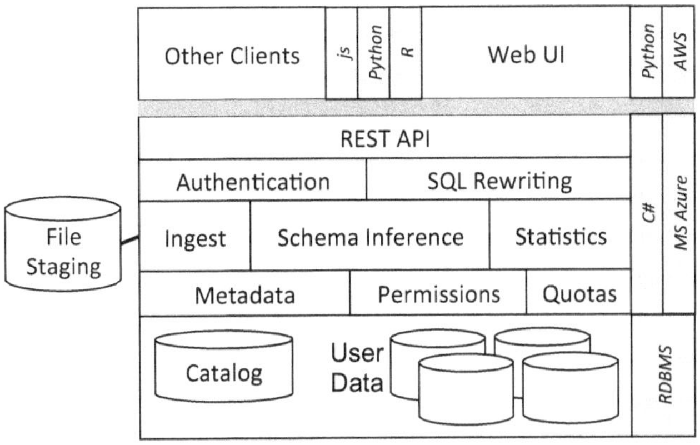

Figure 3: SQLShare architecture, primary user interface is the Web UI which communicates with the REST layer for dataset ingest, modification (via views) and querying. REST server interacts with the backend database which also keeps a catalog of user queries.

user based on their own requirements, and multiple javascript-based visualization interfaces have been developed.

3.5 Full SQL

We built SQLShare in part to faciliate access to the features of the full SQL standard, finding from our experience working with scientists that their use cases frequently required features that are not provided by simplified SQL dialects such as those found in HIVE [31] or Google Fusion Tables [12]. Specifically, window functions, unrestricted subqueries, rich support for dates and times, and set operations all appeared necessary in early requirements analysis. Since the interface is organized around a workflow of copying and pasting snippets of SQL from existing queries (a practice that in some cases may even be beneficial [26] [21]), we see evidence of users writing increasingly complex queries over time.

To support full SQL, we parse each query using a third-party standards-compliant SQL grammar in ANTLR, which we modified to accommodate details of the SQL Azure database and avoid common user pitfalls. For example, when creating a view, we automatically remove any ORDER BY clause to comply with the SQL standard.

Figure 1 shows a screenshot of the SQL editor. Users edit queries directly in the browser, but can access recently viewed queries to copy and paste snippets as needed. We analyze the usage of SQL features in Section 5.3.

4. OVERVIEW OF THE SQLSHARE WORKLOAD

SQLShare logs all executed queries; this log was collected to inform research on new database systems supporting ad hoc analytics over weakly structured data. With permission from the users, we are releasing this dataset publicly for use by the database research community. To our knowledge, no other workload in the literature provides user-written SQL queries over user-uploaded datasets.

The SQLShare workload has a total of 24275 queries on 7958 datasets (including 4535 derived datasets implemented as views), authored by 591 users over period of four years. Out of 591 users, 260 are from universities (indicated by a .edu address). In addition, we have interviewed a number of our top users and are familiar with their science and their requirements. There are a total of 3891 tables with an average of 12 queries per table. Figure 4 shows a histogram depicting the distribution of queries per table. Most tables are either accessed just once or they are queried >= 5 times.

The SQLShare system is not intended for large datasets; the total volume of data presently in the system is 143.02 GB. However, users delete datasets regularly so this number doesn't represent the size of all the datasets that have ever been present SQLShare. Indeed, based on our interactions with some users, they claimed to have developed a daily workflow of uploading data, processing it in SQL, downloading the results, and then deleting everything. Diversity rather than scale is the salient feature of the workload.

A short survey sent to all users to assess the effectiveness of SQLShare revealed that only 6 (out the 33 users who responded) felt that some other off-the-shelf database system could meet their data management needs. 18 of 33 reported that *no* other tool would work for their requirements. The remaining 9 users mentioned that non-database tools such as iPython notebooks might be appropriate for their tasks. 23 of 33 users mentioned that "*ease of data upload & cleaning*" and "*ability to share*" was the reason they found SQLShare most helpful.

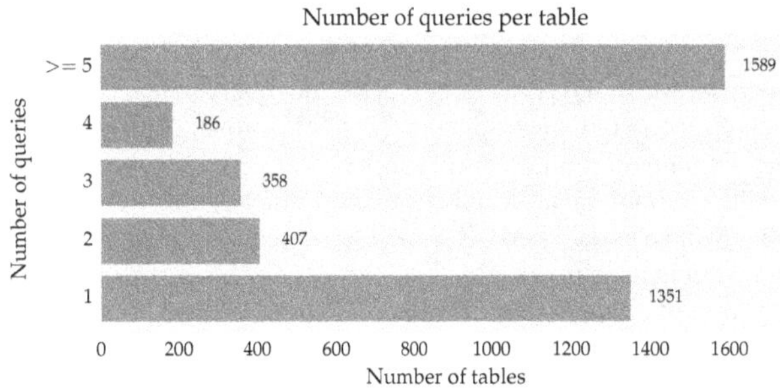

Figure 4: Distribution of queries per table. a) About a third of the tables accessed just once. b) Greater than a third of the tables are accessed many times, with the most common table being queried 766 times, suggesting two distinct use cases.

Extracting information from query logs.

To analyze the complexity and diversity of the SQLShare logs (Section 6), we developed a framework for extracting metrics from each query and its associated plan. The metrics of importance are query length, runtime, number & type of physical & logical operators, number & type of expression operators, tables & columns referenced and operator costs. We will use these metrics to drive the discussion the later sections.

The algorithm for extraction has 2 phases. In phase 1 each query in the SQLShare logs were sent to SQLServer, which returned the execution plan along with estimated result sizes and runtimes for each operator. The format of the execution plan is XML and is obtained by setting the SHOWPLAN_XML property[2]. The operator tree along with interesting properties needed for further analysis is extracted from the XML document with XPath [6]. These properties are estimated runtimes, estimated result sizes and predicates or other properties of an operator. Predicates for selections are split into clauses such that if one selection has a superset of predicates, it is more selective and filters out more tuples. Expressions are also extracted via XPath. Phase 1 extracts these properties and makes a simpler JSON plan for easier future consumption and saves it as an additional column in the query log. Figure 5a provides a conceptual visualization of Phase 1.

[2] http://msdn.microsoft.com/en-us/library/ms187757.aspx

Users	591
Tables	3891
Columns	73070
Views	7958
Non-trivial Views	4535
Queries	24275

(a) Workload Metadata

Feature	Mean Value
Length	217.32 char.
Runtime	3175.38 s.
# of Operators	18.12
# of Distinct Operators	2.71
# of Tables accessed	2.31
# of Columns accessed	16.22

(b) Query Metadata

Table 2: Aggregate summary of SQLShare metadata. SQLShare workload has an average 12 queries per table.

Phase 2 of the algorithm goes over each query and corresponding JSON plan and extracts other important query metadata like referenced tables, columns and views per query. This metadata is aggregated into separate tables in the query catalog for further analysis of the workload. Figure 5b shows a flowchart for this phase of the algorithm.

Listing 1 shows a sample query and the corresponding extracted properties. Most SQL providers support the 'query explain' feature, which returns a raw query plan in the XML format, so the methodology explained in this section can be applied to other workloads as well. We implemented and bundled all functionality as a python library whose source code is available online on demand [3]. As a sample implementation for other workloads, we have provided code to perform this analysis on SDSS and TPCH [8]. The python library also implements most of analysis that we make in the sections that follow.

Listing 1 Extracted structure and properties from a sample query.

```
query: "SELECT * FROM incomes
            WHERE income > 500000"
physicalOp: "Clustered Index Seek"
io: 0.003125
rowSize: 31
cpu: 0.0001603
numRows: 3
filters:
  - "income GT 500000"
operator: "Clustered Index Seek"
total: 0.0032853
children: []
columns:
  incomes:
    - "name"
    - "income"
    - "position"
```

The total size of the query logs along with this meta data (*e.g.* JSON query plans) is 398 MB. This will also be made available publicly. A summary of metadata extracted from SQLShare logs is shown in table Table 2a and Table 2b. As mentioned in §3.2 SQLShare creates trivial views over base tables to remove the distinction between a table and a view. Hence for analysis that follows in the later section, we will only look at the non-trivial views (*i.e.* the ones explicitly created by users) unless otherwise specified.

[3]https://github.com/uwescience/query-workload-analysis

5. EVALUATION OF SQLSHARE FEATURES

In this section, we consider the specific features of SQLShare and analyze their effect on the usage patterns we see in the workload. Each subsection represents a key finding associated with a specific feature of SQLShare. We have conducted interviews with our most active users, who are primarily researchers in the life, earth, and social sciences. Statements about our users' backgrounds and requirements are informed by these interviews.

5.1 Relaxed Schemas Afford Integration

The requirement for relaxed schemas is motivated by the ubiquity of *weakly structured* data. Further, the collaborative nature of data science results in a need to frequently share intermediate results before the data has been properly organized and described. As a result, we designed SQLShare to tolerate (and even embrace) upload of weakly structured data, encouraging users to write SQL queries to repair and reorganize their data. We build evidence to support this hypothesis by searching the corpus of 4535 derived datasets (views) for specific SQL idioms that correspond to "schematization" tasks: cleaning, typecasting, and integration.

NULL injection: About 220 of the derived datasets use a `CASE` expression to replace special values with NULL. ii) *Post hoc Column Types*: After removing bad tuples and replacing missing values with NULL, we find that about 200 of derived datasets used SQL `CAST` to introduce new types on existing columns.

Vertical Recomposition: Datasets presented to SQLShare are often decomposed into multiple files that reflect the manner in which the data was collected. Rather than requiring that these files be concatenated offline or requiring that a single table be designed to store all such data, we encourage users to "upload first, ask questions later." We found evidence of about 100 datasets that involved vertical recomposition using UNION in SQL.

Column Renaming: Datasets presented to SQLShare frequently had no column names in the source file; SQLShare automatically assigns default columns names in these cases and we encourage users to write SQL to assign semantic names. We see 1996 uploaded tables (about 50%) that had at least one default-assigned column name and 1691 uploaded tables for which *all* columns names were assigned a default value. Almost 16% of datasets involve some kind of column renaming step, suggesting that users have adopted SQL as a tool for adding semantics to their data. Rejecting datasets due to incomplete column names would have clearly limited uptake.

Overall, the data suggests that relaxed schemas played an important role in many use cases, and that tolerance for weakly structured data is an important part of any data system targeting science and data science environments.

5.2 Views Afford Controlled Data Sharing

The view-centric data model of SQLShare (Figure 2) allows users to think in terms of logical datasets rather than understanding a distinction between physical tables and virtual views. The hierarchy of derived views provides a simple form of provenance; the user can inspect (and with permission, edit) the specific steps applied to produce the final result. The view-centric data model also affords collaboration: users can share the derived dataset (and its provenance) without emailing files that get out of sync with the master data. Moreover, collaborators can directly derive their own datasets in the same system, and the provenance relationship is maintained. The view-centric data model was a very successful feature in SQLShare: About 56% of the datasets in the system are derived from other datasets using views. Among the top 100 most active users, multi-layer view hierarchies were quite common. Figure 6 shows

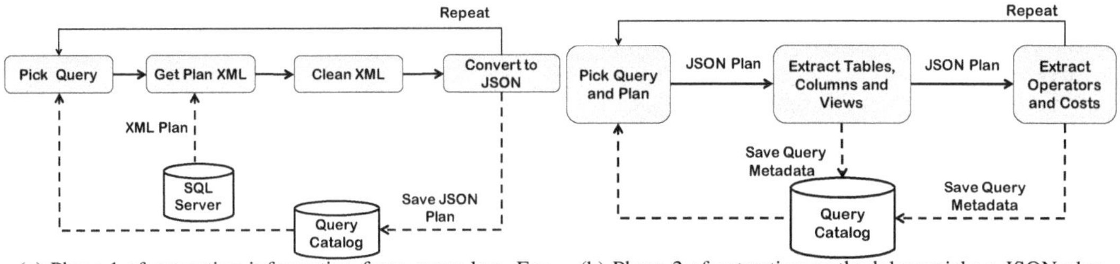

(a) Phase 1 of extracting information from query log. For each query, backend SQL Server is asked to explain it and return the corresponding XML plan. The XML is then cleaned for easier parsing and the extracted information is converted to a JSON plan for easier consumption by further steps. This JSON plan is saved back to query catalog as a new column.

(b) Phase 2 of extraction methodology picks a JSON plan from previous step. From the JSON plan, the referenced tables, columns and views are extracted and saved in separate tables in the query catalog. Next the operators, expressions and corresponding costs are extracted and saved into separate tables in the catalog as well.

Figure 5: Workload Analysis Methodology

the max depth of dataset hierarchies forthese 100 users. A view that references only base datasets is assigned a depth of 0. Other users would use views as query templates: They would use apply the same query to multiple source datasets, copying and pasting the view definition and only changing the name of a table in the FROM clause. Copy-and-paste seems inadequate here; motivated by this finding we intend to lift parameterized query macros into the interface as a convenience function[4].

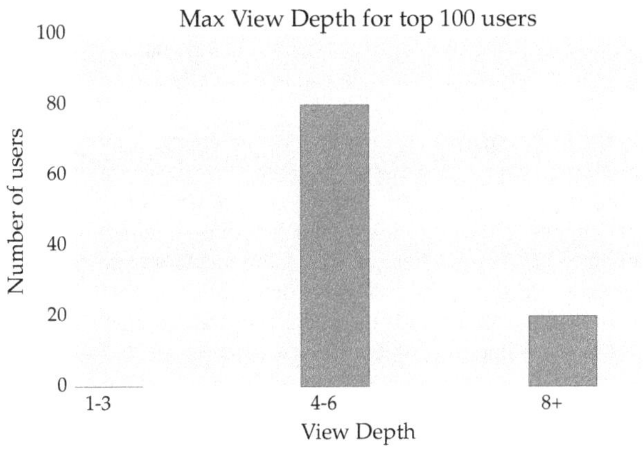

Figure 6: The maximum view depth for the 100 most active users of SQLShare. The data suggest that the ability to derive and save new datasets using views was an important features.

The view-centric data model also facilitates sharing: users can set daatset-level permissions, which are implemented in the database as view permissions. A dataset can either be private, public or shared with specific set of users. The permissions features were heavily used. About 37% of the datasets in SQLShare are publicly accessible, even though the default is to keep data private. About 9% of the datasets were shared with a specific other user. Moreover, about 2.5% of the views access other datasets that the author does not own, and over 10% of the queries logged in the system access datasets that the query author does not own. Beyond just collaborative analysis, the permissions feature allowed SQLShare to function as a data publishing platform. Several users cited SQLShare datasets in papers. One user minted DOIs for datasets in SQLShare; we are adding DOI minting into the interface as a feature in the next release.

5.3 Frequent SQL Idioms

SQLShare was designed to facilitate access to full, standards-compliant SQL as opposed to relying on the simplified SQL dialects often associated with analytics and sharing platforms (e.g., HIVE SQL [31], Google Fusion Tables [12]).

To evaluate whether full SQL was actually warranted, we counted the queries that use specific SQL language features that are sometimes omitted in simpler SQL dialects. As one might expect, queries involving sorting were comon (24%), and top k and outer join queries were frequent enough to justify support in any system (2% and 11% respectively). Perhaps more surprisingly, window functions (expressed using the SQL-standard OVER clause) appeared in about 4% of the workload. Virtually no systems outside of the major vendors support window functions; these newer systems will not be capable of handling the SQLShare workload!

In addition to specific SQL language features, we found evidence of recurring SQL "idioms" or "design patterns" that might motivate higher-level convenience functions to support query authoring. Aggregating timeseries and other data by computing a histogram was common enough (and awkward enough) that we are considering adding special support. Another common but tedious pattern was to rename a single column, and then be forced to explicitly list out every other column in the table. An expanded regular expression syntax raning over column names beyond just `*` is warranted: the ability to refer to all columns except a given column, or to replace a single column in its original order would be useful. More generally, the ability to refer to and transform a set of related columns in the same way would simplify query authoring: The expression `SELECT CAST(var* AS float) as $v FROM data` could indicate "replace each column with a prefix of `var` with an expression that casts it as a number and renames the expression appropriately."

6. WORKLOAD ANALYSIS

In contrast to the conventional relational use cases characterized by a pre-engineered schema and predictable query patterns generated by the constraints of a client application, we hypothesized that SQLShare users would write queries that are more complex individually and more diverse as a set, making the corpus more useful for designing new systems. A more complex workload, especially one derived from hand-written queries, provides a more realistic basis for experiments in optimization, query debugging, and language features than a workload from a conventional, sanitized environment.

[4]A query macro would be different than a conventional parameterized query, since it allows parameters in the `FROM` clause rather than only as expressions.

To test this hypothesis, we need to define metrics for query complexity and workload diversity. Since we are onboarding users with little or no database experience, query complexity needs to be measured in terms of the 'cognitive' effort it takes to express a task as a SQL query. Thus, the measures like query runtime or latency alone do not show the correct picture. In the discussion that follows, we have attempted to find proxy metrics to capture this 'cognitive' complexity. We develop simple metrics in this section and show that SQLShare queries on average tend to be more complex and more diverse than those of a conventional database workload generated from a comparable science domain: the Sloan Digital Sky Survey (SDSS) [18].

The SkyServer project of the SDSS is a redshift and infrared spectroscopy survey of galaxies, quasars, and stars. It led to the most detailed three-dimensional map of the universe ever created at the time. The survey consists of multiple data releases (10 to date), which represent different projects and different stages of processing refinement. Besides the survey data, the SDSS database contains one of the few publicly available query workloads from a live SQL database supporting both ad hoc hand-authored queries as well as queries generated from a point-and-click GUI. Singh *et al.*, in the Traffic Report for SDSS [28] describe how during the first five years itself the system generated $180GB$ of logs. These logs were then normalized and cleaned and auxiliary data structures were built for analysis. SDSS is a useful comparison: it is a conventional database application with a pre-engineered schema but the users and tasks are not dissimilar to those of SQLShare.

6.1 SQLShare Queries are Complex

We interpret query complexity primarily as a measure of the cognitive load on the user during query authoring as opposed to computational compelxity in optimizing or evaluating the query. Our goal is to design lightweight data systems that can be used as part of day-to-day analytics tasks, which means we are competing directly with general purpose scripting languages for users' attention. Any query corpus that purports to reflect the usage patterns of analysts cannot rely on vanilla query patterns typically assumed in the database literature. In this section, we consider ASCII character length as a simple proxy for query complexity and then argue why the number of distinct operators is an improvement.

ASCII Query Length. A naive estimate of query complexity from both the user and system perspective is the character length of the query as a string. The premise for character length as an indicator of complexity is is that the longer the query, the more a user has to write and read, and the more time and effort it takes to craft the query.

In both SQLShare and SDSS, most queries are short. But a significant number of queries in SQLShare, about 1500, are greater than 500 characters. This is not surprising given that users write queries over datasets which are often decomposed into multiple tables. Figure 7 shows the histogram of query length for both SQLShare and SDSS. SDSS has a high percentage of queries with similar length. We investigated this further and found that there are clear categories of SDSS queries corresponding to specific lengths. These categories correspond to particular query templates and example queries used many times, demonstrating that few of these queries should be considered hand-written. In addition, the shortest 20% of both workloads are less than 100 characters, which is quite short. But the longer queries in SQLShare range upto 11375 characters. However, query length does not necessarily capture cognitive complexity since long queries may involve repetitive patterns that are easy to write via copy-and-paste. We see examples of queries that are over 1000 characters long but involve just two operators (a filter applied to 50+ columns). The takeaway from the length comparison however is that SQLShare users write queries that the database community would consider unusual, which is precisely why this corpus is valuable. Such queries should be considered in any realistic workload targeting weakly structured data and non-expert users.

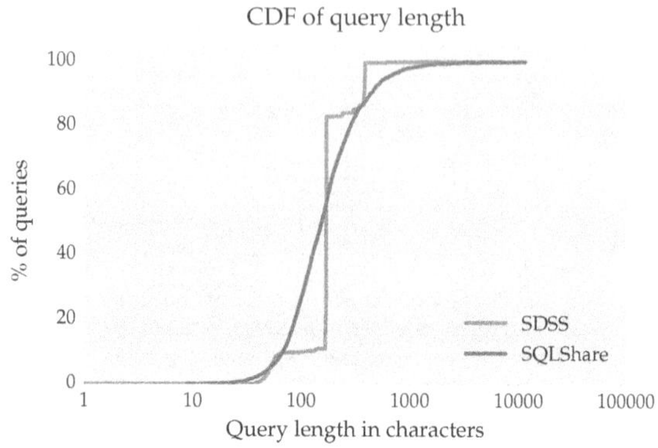

Figure 7: Hand-written SQLShare queries tend to vary more widely in length than SDSS queries. Short queries tend to be shorter, but long queries tend to be longer. SDSS queries show evidence of being "canned" rather than hand-written: only a few distinctive lengths are present and the majority of SDSS queries are about 200 characters. We explore these patterns in more detail in §6.2.

Distinct Operators in Query. To capture the complexity of a query more accurately, we look at the number of operations in the execution plan. More operations mean more steps of computation which increases the complexity of scheduling of data flow for the system. SQLShare queries use a lot more operators than SDSS on an average. Many operations alone does not necessarily lead to a complex query for a user if the query uses the same operator over and over *e.g.* a union of 10 relations. A better metric to capture this case is to look at the *diversity* of operators and count the number of unique operators per query. A combination of both the number of operations and the number of distinct operations intuitively captures complexity better than either of the two metric. Figure 8 shows the number of distinct operators for the three workloads.

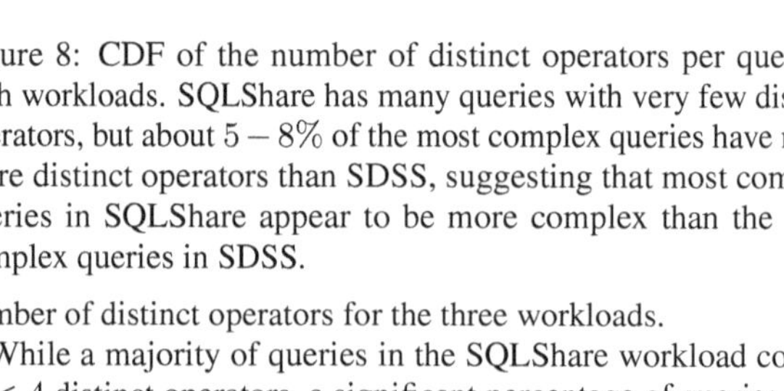

Figure 8: CDF of the number of distinct operators per query in both workloads. SQLShare has many queries with very few distinct operators, but about $5-8\%$ of the most complex queries have many more distinct operators than SDSS, suggesting that most complex queries in SQLShare appear to be more complex than the most complex queries in SDSS.

While a majority of queries in the SQLShare workload consist of < 4 distinct operators, a significant percentage of queries have significantly higher number of distinct operators, suggesting higher complexity. Among the top 10% of the queries with the highest number of distinct operators, the SQLShare queries tend to have almost double.

The next question one might ask is what type of the operators are present in the workload as a whole. This metric helps us understand workload complexity by providing the minimum requirement of SQL features for the workload to run, which is of interest to system designers.

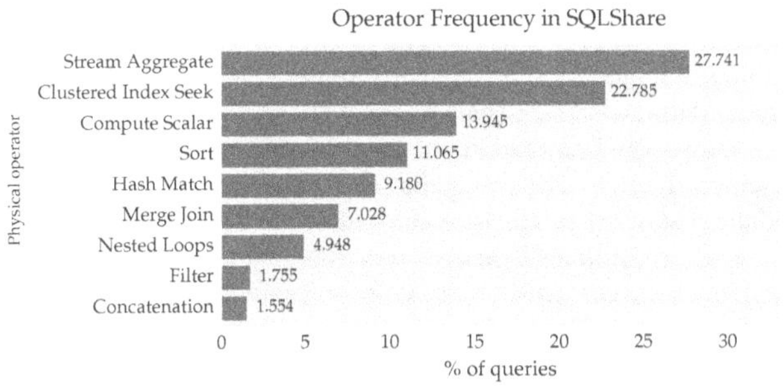

Figure 9: The most commonly used physical operators in SQLShare. We ignored Clustered Indexed Scan because SQLShare uses SQLAzure which requires them. Presence of a lot of aggregate and arithmetic operators in SQLShare suggests the presence of analytic workloads.

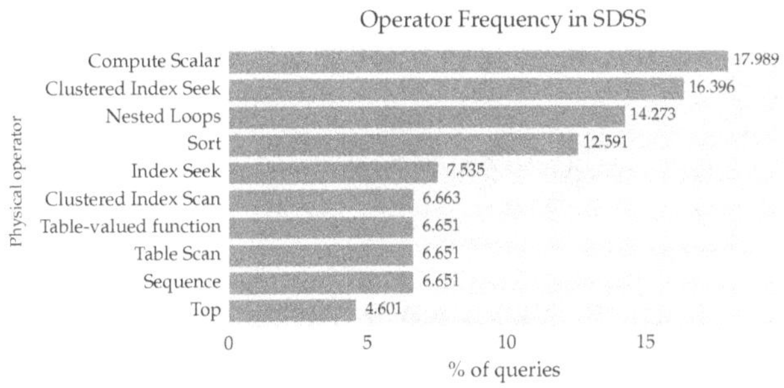

Figure 10: The most-used operator in SDSS is computation on scalars as a lot of queries use UDFs. Compared to SQLShare we see fewer arithmetic and aggregate operators.

Figure 9 and Figure 10 show the ten most common operators in SQLShare and SDSS. We ignored 'clustered index scan' for SQLShare workload because SQLShare uses SQLAzure as its backend and SQLAzure requires that every table be associated with a clustered index. SQLShare is dominated by aggregate queries, while SDSS has mostly computations on scalars most likely because it consists of a lot of user defined functions[5]. Overall, we find indications that users write more complex queries in SQLShare, suggesting that support for full SQL is useful for users.

6.2 SQLShare Queries are Diverse

If users are writing ad hoc queries rather than operating an application that generates queries on their behalf, we would expect that the *diversity* of the workload to increase. Rather than having the entire workload reduced to a few repeating templates, each query would be more likely to be unique. As the diversity of a query workload increases, system design and performance management becomes more challenging: up-front engineering and physical tuning becomes less efficacious. We consider high diversity a characteristic feature of the data science workloads and an important design goal of any system targeting this domain. This makes diversity an important feature to consider in database research. Current system overspecializes in simpler queries, since a corpus of hand-written real queries is unavailable. For example, research on query recommendation platform like SnipSuggest [20] can be further improved by taking real science queries into consideration to reflect the full complexity of the problem. Similarly, query optimizers should consider optimizations for arithmetic optimizations as well. New languages or user interfaces which make common science idioms simpler would greatly increase scientists' productivity.

We can consider the question of whether SQLShare workloads are measurably more diverse than the workloads of a conventional database application such as SDSS.

Workload Entropy. To quantify workload entropy, we must define query equivalence. A simple but naïve metric is exact ASCII string equivalence. ASCII string equivalence can only help eliminate very simple kinds of redundancies, such as identical queries generated by applications or repeated instances of copy-and-pasted sample queries. The SDSS workload contains both of these patterns, however, so we included this definition in our analysis.

A better measure of query equivalence was proposed by Mozafari *et al.* [23]: A query is represented by the set of all attributes (columns) referenced by the query. If two queries reference different sets of attributes, we say they are *column distinct*. A weakness of this metric in our context is that the set of attributes referenced does not capture the user's intended task, and can therefore fail to distinguish queries that differ widely in layers of nesting, use of complex expressions (e.g., theta joins or window functions), and grouping structures. The presence or absence of these features may be what determines whether a query is perceived as "difficult" to novice users, which is an important consideration in the design of a system.

ASCII string equivalence overlooks equivalences and the column-based metric proposed by Mozafari *et al.* appears to overlook differences. We therefore propose a simple third metric by extracting a query plan and normalizing it by removing all constants. We obtain an optimized query plan from the database, which also contains estimated result sizes and estimated runtimes for each operator. The query plan resolves any heterogeneity resulting from the syntax (order of conditions, JOIN vs. WHERE, nesting vs. joins, etc.) In addition, we remove all constants and literals from the plan to create the *query plan template* (QPT). The QPT seems to offer a better description of the user's intended task, as it unifies most semantically equivalent queries but still incorporates the operations.

The SDSS workload initially contained $7M$ queries. However, after resolving redundant queries using simple string equivalence, the SDSS workload contained only about $200K$; 3% of the total. Many queries in the SDSS are actually not handwritten; they were generated by applications such as the Google Earth plugin or the query composer from the SkyServer website . In contrast, the SQLShare workload from 2011 to 2015 contains about $25K$ queries, 24096 (96%) of which were unique.

If we group queries by the set of columns referenced following Mozafari *et al.*, we find that 45.35% of the queries are distinct in the SQLShare workload compared with only 0.2% of the 200K string distinct queries for SDSS.

Finally, SDSS only exhibits 686 unique query plan templates (0.3% of the $200K$ string distinct queries). The low entropy is not unexpected, given that many users manipulate a GUI and use

[5] http://skyserver.sdss.org/dr5/sp/help/browser/shortdescr.asp?n=Functions&t=F

Diversity Metric	SDSS	SQLShare
Total queries	$7M$	25052
String distinct queries	$200K$, 3% of $7M$	24096, 96% of 25052
Column distinct queries	467, 0.2% of $200K$	10928, 45.35% of 24096
Distinct query templates	686, 0.3% of $200K$	15199, 63.07% of 24096

Table 3: Workload Entropy: SQLShare queries are more diverse and have 63% distinct query templates. For SDSS, the number is very low (0.3%).

standard examples queries to study a fixed schema. The SQLShare workload contains significantly higher entropy: It has about 15199 (63.07% of the 24096 string distinct queries) unique query plan templates. We summarize these findings in Table 3. While none of these measures are perfect, a high value of ($\frac{\texttt{Unique Queries}}{\texttt{Total Queries}}$) and a high absolute number of unique queries indicate high diversity in a workload, suggesting that the SQLShare workload is an appropriate test case to drive requirements of new systems.

We see two distinct usage patterns here in the two database-as-a-service platforms, SQLShare and SDSS. Since SDSS relies on a fixed, engineered schema, the diversity of queries they can ask is obviously limited. SQLShare allows users to upload arbitrary tables; there is no expectation that queries will overlap in form or content.

Expression Distribution. Another measure of query diversity is the type and distribution of expression operators. We found the number of different expression operators to be 89 for SQLShare and 49 for SDSS. Moreover, we found that the workloads with intuitively higher variety not only use more diverse expressions but also more user defined functions (UDFs): SQLShare has 56 and SDSS 22. The most common intrinsic [6] and arithmetic expressions in SDSS are two scalar expressions followed by `BIT_AND`, `like` and `upper` (Table 4b). In SQLShare we found that six out of the ten most common expression operators (and again the vast majority) are operations on strings: `like`, `patindex`, `isnumeric`, `substring`, `charindex`, and `len` (Table 4a). Also, SQLShare has a higher expression diversity than other 2 workloads. This expression diversity backs our original hypothesis that use cases for SQLShare go beyond just data management and also include *data ingest, integration and cleaning* as suggested by the prevalence of string operations.

Operator	Count
like	61755
ADD	31570
DIV	17198
SUB	13707
patindex	8212
substring	7490
isnumeric	7206
charindex	6364
MULT	4162
square	2636
len	2608

(a) SQLShare

Operator	Count
GetRange ThroughConvert	25746
GetRangeWith MismatchedTypes	25746
BIT_AND	21850
like	2376
upper	2312

(b) SDSS

Table 4: Most common intrinsic & arithmetic expression operators. String operations are very common on SQLShare, suggesting a lot of data integration and munging tasks.

[6] https://technet.microsoft.com/en-us/library/ms191298(v=sql.105).aspx

Reuse: Compress Runtimes. The overall runtime of query is a measure of its complexity, but its misleading because runtime gets affected by the data size as well. However, runtime that can be saved by identifying re-occurring clauses in queries is a good measure of query diversity, *i.e.* lower reuse potential suggests higher diversity. Roy *et al.* show experiments in which 30% to 80% (depending on the workload) of the execution time can be saved by aggressively caching intermediate results [27]. Query optimization in the presence of cached results and materialized views is beyond the scope of this paper. Nonetheless, we implemented a simple algorithm to calculate reuse of query results that matches subtrees of query execution plans. While iterating over the queries, all subtrees are matched against all subtrees from previous queries. We allow a subtree that we match against to have less selective filters (filters are a subset) and more columns for the same tables (columns is a superset). If we find that we have seen the same subtree before, we add the cost of the subtree as estimated by the SQLServer optimizer to the saved runtime. Consequently, a precomputed intermediate result does not cost us anything when being reused.

Although this algorithm does not accurately model the actual execution time, we use it to estimate how diverse queries are. The algorithm can underestimate the potential for reuse since the matching misses cases when a rewriting would be needed. It could overestimate since we assume infinite memory as well as no cost for using a previously computed result. In this analysis we removed duplicate queries since a query that appears again will completely reuse previous results (recall that over 90% of SDSS queries are duplicates. But even for the distinct queries, 14% of the runtime could be saved. In SQLShare, we estimate saving to be around 37%. In all workloads, most of the saving per query was either very high (more than 90%) or very low (less than 10%). We conclude that most of the reuse could be achieved with a small cache if we have a good heuristic to determine which results will be reused. This also confirms our hypothesis that SQLShare queries are indeed more diverse.

6.3 Dataset Permanence Varies by User

In a conventional RDBMS, the schema is not expected to change much over time. We calculated the lifetime for the datasets in SQLShare, with lifetime defined as the difference in days between the first and the last time that dataset was accessed in a query and found that the SQLShare workload exhibits a variety of patterns. In particular, many users are operating in short-duration analysis loops, where they upload some data, write a few queries, and then move on to another task. This usage pattern is atypical for relational databases and seems to motivate new system features, including some of those already implemented in SQLShare.

Figure 11 shows the lifetime in days for the datasets for a user who both continuously updated new datasets and frequently accessed previous datasets. Each point represents one dataset for the given user. The y-axis is the number of days between the first and last query that accessed the dataset. While many datasets are used across periods of years, the majority are uploaded once, analyzed over a period of 5-7 days, and never accessed again. For this user, over half are only accessed once, on the same day they are uploaded. Some users operate exclusively in a "data processing" mode, where they upload data at a predictable rate, process it using the same queries, and move on. The shorter dataset lifetimes associated with science and data science workloads is significant because it suggests that the costs associated with creating schemas and loading data would be incurred so frequently as to make these workloads infeasible (or at least unattractive) for conventional database systems. This

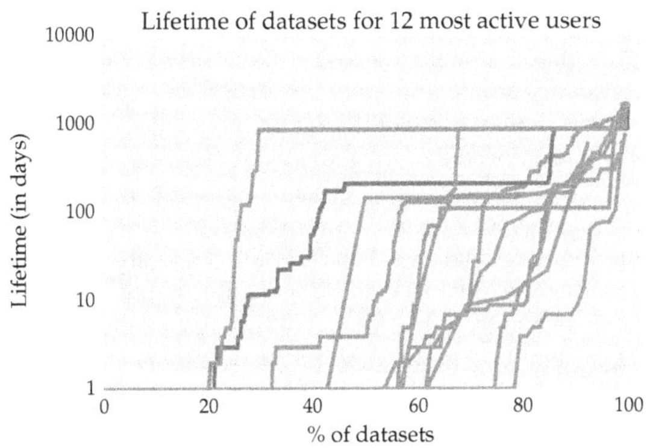

Figure 11: Dataset lifetimes for 12 most active users in SQLShare. Each curve is a user. The y-axis is the number of days between the first and last time the dataset was accessed. The x-axis is rank order. The great majority of datasets are accessed across a span of less 10 days, but some are accessed across periods of years. This type of a workload, where a user explores the data and never accesses it again, is a departure from a conventional RDBMS use case. The highlighted user is the most active user in SQLShare.

limitation does not exist in SQLShare due to the simple schema inference mechanisms and the web-hosted delivery vehicle.

SQLShare users in general are varied in their patterns of data upload and data analysis. Figure 12 shows table coverage for the most active users in SQLShare. Table coverage measures the cumulative count of tables referenced by queries upto a certain point in time. The figure shows how new datasets are being added all the time. This suggests that the use case is the following: user keeps adding datasets, and the queries are usually written on *all* of the datasets taken together, and that she may be uploading data to overwrite/replace old tables then re-running the same queries.

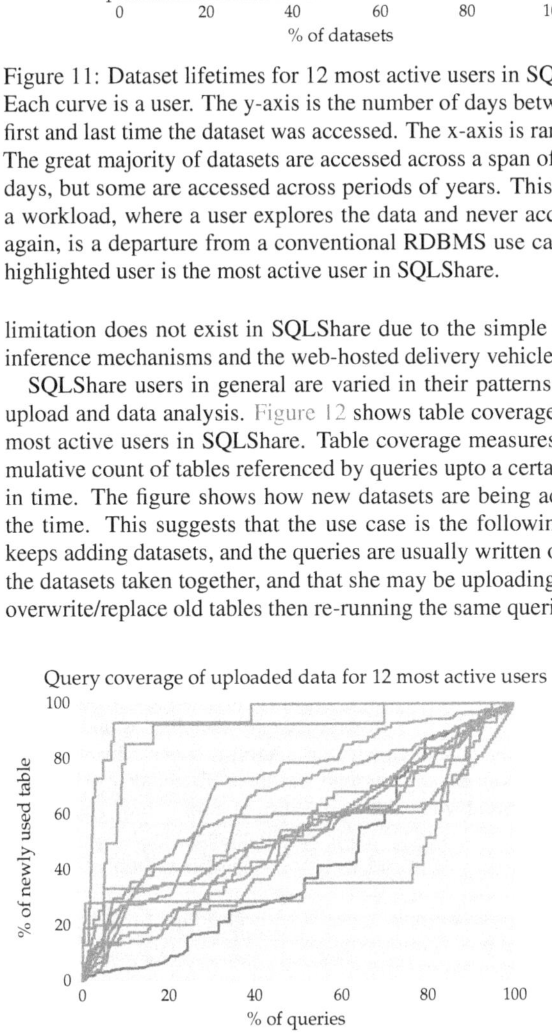

Figure 12: The rate of table coverage over time for the 12 most active users. Highlighted in red is the most active user for SQLShare. Each curve corresponds to a user and describes the percentage of tables accessed by the first N% of queries. A user who uploads one table at a time and queries it once would generate a line of slope one. Curves above slope one indicate a more conventional workload, where the user uploads many tables and then queries them repeatedly. Curves near to or below slope one indicate a more ad hoc workload, where queries are intermingled with new dataset uploads. We see both usage patterns in SQLShare, but the ad hoc pattern dominates.

6.4 SQLShare Attracts High-Churn Work

Based on interviews with users, SQLShare seemed to be used to support workloads that exhibited higher "churn" than conventional databases, where datasets would be uploaded, queried a few times, and then put aside. To attempt to quantify our anecdotal evidence, we considered the ratio of queries to datasets for each user, hypothesizing that this ratio would be very low for most SQLShare users.

Figure 13 shows the results. Each point is a single user. The x-axis is the number of distinct datasets owned by that user and the y-axis is the number of distinct queries submitted by that user. Both axes are on a log scale. The variety in workloads is also apparent: a few users upload relatively few tables (10-30) and query them repeatedly, which is reminiscent of a conventional database workload. These queries are labeled Analytical in the plot. But most users tend to upload approximately the same number of datasets as the number of queries they write, suggesting an ad hoc, exploratory workload. These users are labeled Exploratory. We also see that some users uploaded exactly one dataset, wrote 1-50 queries, and then never return. This group surely includes some users who were simply trying out the system and who either never had an intention to use it or did not find it useful. We label this group One-shot users.

To quantify the notion of workload diversity, we adapt the methodology of Mozafari et al [23]: break each user's workload into chronological blocks and measure the distance between the chunks. Each chunk is considered a separate workload and is represented by a row vector. Each position in this vector corresponds to a unique subset of attributes from the database. The value at that position represents the normalized frequency of queries that reference exactly this set of attributes. We then calculate the *euclidean* distance between these vectors, following Mozafari's algorithm [23]. The maximum distance found in the original paper was 0.003; this number was considered a high workload diversity. Among those users with sufficient queries to support this analysis, many exhibited *orders of magnitude* more diversity in their workload.

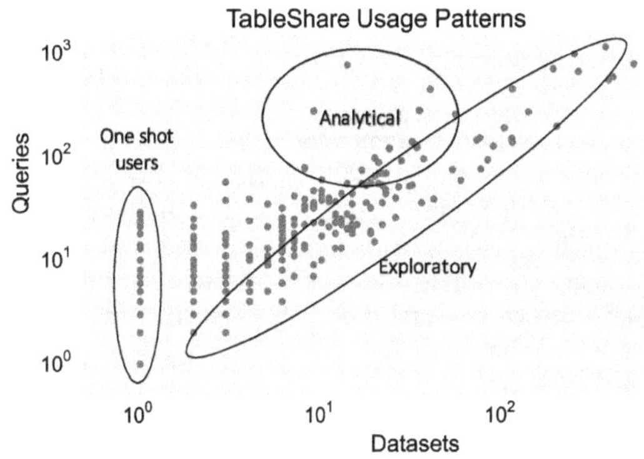

Figure 13: The ratio of datasets to queries suggests different usage patterns. The y-axis is the log of the number of queries, and the x-axis is the log of the number of datasets. Each point represents one user. Exploratory users only write a small number of queries over each dataset they upload. Some users exhibit a more conventional usage pattern, uploading a relatively small number of datasets and querying them repeatedly. A few non-active users upload one table and write very few queries.

7. RELATED WORK

Structure extraction tools cast the data variety problem as one of parsing complex formats to produce (weakly) structured data for further processing. OpenRefine [3] and Wrangler [16] are examples of this approach. These tools offer no support for working with multiple datasets or managing complexity once the parsing step has been completed, which has been shown to be a dominant cost [17]. In traditional data integration approaches the central goal is to derive a mediated schema from two or more source schemas, allowing all source data to be queried uniformly [10]. Tools and algorithms in this area induce relationships between database elements (tables, columns, rows) and use these relationships to rewrite queries or restructure data. Despite a long history of research (and a detour through XML in the early part of this century), these techniques do not seem to be widely used by analysts today, in part because of the assumptions that the input schemas are carefully engineered, information carrying structures on which the algorithms can gain purchase.

A welcome departure from the engineered schemas assumed by data integration techniques was *dataspaces* [11].The paper was prescient in its ability to capture important aspects of the high variety problem, but focused heavily on enterprise settings and managed environments rather than the ad hoc, one-off analysis that characterizes data science activities we see in practice. It is unusual to assume that we would know all kind of operations and all sources of data before hand. This approach misses the point that in Big Data, data sources and the operations required are usually not known beforehand. However, in case of SQLShare, the departure from the above mentioned approaches is that it enables scientific data analysis with a bare minimum set of changes to the original RDBMS. Infact, at its core, SQLShare uses pure relational models. It just hides these from the users. Our work shows that how even with these basic changes, we can cater to the entire data lifecycle, *i.e.* ingest, cleaning, synthesis, management, analytics, visualization and sharing.

Khoussainova *et al.* noted in [19] that the mode of interaction with databases is changing. Data analytics warrants the support for exploratory queries, query recommendations and collaborative query management. We believe SQLShare is a right step in this direction. Bhardwaj *et al.* presented DataHub [5], a system which provides the collaborative data management and versioning, but unlike SQLShare it lacks data querying capabilities and support for full SQL.

SnipSuggest [20] is an example of a system which can enable non-experts to write complex SQL queries and even teach them. This work is complementary to one aspect of SQLShare *i.e.* reducing 'friction' for query authoring. It would be interesting to see how user query complexity changes overtime using SnipSuggest with SQLShare. Ogasawara *et al.* [24] presented support for automatic optimization data science workflows, motivating research in database support for scientific workloads. Recently, Fei *et al.* presented Schema-Free SQL [22] which tries to enables faster analysis of data for which the schema is unknown. This approach is different from the automatic schema inference in SQLShare and builds language support for inaccurate/unknown schema.

Ren *et al.* performed a workload analysis over 3 different Hadoop [1] research clusters [25]. They noted underuse Hadoop features and significant diversity in workloads application styles motivating newer tools. Singh *et al.* published a 5 year usage study of SDSS [28] and reasoned about why it was so successful. Their work analyzed traffic and sessions by duration, usage pattern over time and found interesting factors like site's popularity and benefits of providing a framework for ad hoc SQL.

SQLShare takes this a step further by providing an SDSS like system for everyone. By enabling the user to upload datasets and enable sharing and dataset hierarchy, SQLShare unfolds a lot more avenues for easy scientific data management.

8. CONCLUSION

We presented a new public query workload corpus for use by the database research community and described the open source SQL-as-a-Service system SQLShare that was deployed to collect it. Further, we showed that the features of SQLShare were instrumental in attracting new kinds of ad hoc queries that are written to perform tasks usually reserved for scripts and files. Finally, we gave a preliminary analysis of the workload and argued that it is demonstrably more diverse than a comparable public workload in science, and that users are writing very complex queries by hand.

The SQLShare system was designed to be minimal adaptation of existing database technology to attract users in ad hoc, high-touch analytics environments. We relaxed assumptions about schemas, inferring structure automatically from the data and tolerating various structural problems (mismatched row lengths, non-homogeneous types, missing column names). We adopt a view-oriented data model to encourage reuse, track provenance, simplify editing, and facilitate data sharing. We support full SQL, finding that impoverised SQL-like languages are not sufficient to express the queries in our workload. We found these features of SQLShare to be demonstrably useful by analyzing patterns in the workload. More generally, we conclude that SQLShare is useful for short lifetime, one-shot analysis tasks that are typically ill-suited for databases, and that these tasks produced queries that are more complex and more diverse.

To define query complexity, we considered character length of the query as an ASCII string and the number of distinct operators. We showed that by these measures SQLShare had attracted hand-written queries that are more complex than the most complex queries in the comparable Sloan Digital Sky Survey workload, another public query workload associated with a conventional database application in a comparable domain.

To define workload diversity, we considered the entropy of the workload: the number of unique queries divided by the number of total queries. To define query uniqueness, we considered string uniqueness as a naive baseline, but recognizing that two queries that have an identical structure but differ in literal values should not be considered truly distinct. We therefore considered a templatization procedure that unified the structure of queries in the log and created equivalence classes based on query patterns. By both measures of entropy, the SQLShare workload was more diverse than the SDSS workload. We also considered the use of expressions and scalar functions. While expressions were more varied in the SQLShare dataset, the SDSS workload involved a significant number of user-defined functions.

In future work, we plan to use this workload to provide a formal definition for query complexity and design languages and editors that can provably reduce complexity. We can use this definition to build more effective query recommendation engines which recommends queries of comparable complexity to queries that user has written before. We also plan to use the complexity and diversity properties of the query workload to design a formal benchmark emphasizing high variety rather than hig volume or high velocity. Our analysis will also inform the development of new systems such as Myria [13] that are designed to address analytics workloads in science and data science.

9. ACKNOWLEDGEMENTS

This project was supported by NSF IIS award # 1247469, the Intel Science and Technology Center for Big Data and the University of Washington eScience Institute, which made this work possible.

10. REFERENCES

[1] Apache hadoop. https://hadoop.apache.org/. Accessed: 2014-10-14.

[2] Big data techniques applied to media and computer graphics applications. https://metanautix.com/tr/01_big_data_techniques_for_media_graphics.pdf.

[3] OpenRefine (formerly google refine). http://openrefine.org/. Accessed: 2014-10-14.

[4] M. Armbrust, R. S. Xin, C. Lian, Y. Huai, D. Liu, J. K. Bradley, X. Meng, T. Kaftan, M. J. Franklin, A. Ghodsi, et al. Spark sql: Relational data processing in spark. In *Proceedings of the 2015 ACM SIGMOD International Conference on Management of Data*, pages 1383–1394. ACM, 2015.

[5] A. Bhardwaj, S. Bhattacherjee, A. Chavan, A. Deshpande, A. J. Elmore, S. Madden, and A. G. Parameswaran. Datahub: Collaborative data science & dataset version management at scale. *arXiv preprint arXiv:1409.0798*, 2014.

[6] J. Clark, S. DeRose, et al. Xml path language (xpath). *W3C recommendation*, 16, 1999.

[7] S. Cohen-Boulakia and U. Leser. Search, adapt, and reuse: the future of scientific workflows. *ACM SIGMOD Record*, 40(2):6–16, 2011.

[8] T. P. P. Council. TPC-H benchmark specification. http://www.tpc.org/tpch/, 2008.

[9] E. Deelman, G. Singh, M.-H. Su, J. Blythe, Y. Gil, C. Kesselman, G. Mehta, K. Vahi, G. B. Berriman, J. Good, A. Laity, J. C. Jacob, and D. S. Katz. Pegasus: A framework for mapping complex scientific workflows onto distributed systems. *Sci. Program.*, 13(3):219–237, July 2005.

[10] A. Doan and A. Y. Halevy. Semantic integration research in the database community: A brief survey. *AI magazine*, 26(1):83, 2005.

[11] M. Franklin, A. Halevy, and D. Maier. From databases to dataspaces: a new abstraction for information management. *ACM Sigmod Record*, 34(4):27–33, 2005.

[12] H. Gonzalez, A. Y. Halevy, C. S. Jensen, A. Langen, J. Madhavan, R. Shapley, W. Shen, and J. Goldberg-Kidon. Google fusion tables: web-centered data management and collaboration. In *Proceedings of the 2010 ACM SIGMOD International Conference on Management of data*, pages 1061–1066. ACM, 2010.

[13] D. Halperin, V. Teixeira de Almeida, L. L. Choo, S. Chu, P. Koutris, D. Moritz, J. Ortiz, V. Ruamviboonsuk, J. Wang, A. Whitaker, et al. Demonstration of the myria big data management service. In *Proceedings of the 2014 ACM SIGMOD international conference on Management of data*, Sigmod '14, pages 881–884. ACM, 7 2014.

[14] B. Howe, G. Cole, E. Souroush, P. Koutris, A. Key, N. Khoussainova, and L. Battle. Database-as-a-service for long-tail science. In *Scientific and Statistical Database Management*, pages 480–489. Springer, 2011.

[15] B. Howe, F. Ribalet, D. Halperin, S. Chitnis, and E. V. Armbrust. Sqlshare: Scientific workflow via relational view sharing. *Computing in Science & Engineering, Special Issue on Science Data Management*, 15(2), 2013.

[16] S. Kandel, A. Paepcke, J. Hellerstein, and J. Heer. Wrangler: Interactive visual specification of data transformation scripts. In *Proceedings of the SIGCHI Conference on Human Factors in Computing Systems*, pages 3363–3372. ACM, 2011.

[17] S. Kandel, A. Paepcke, J. Hellerstein, and J. Heer. Enterprise data analysis and visualization: An interview study. In *IEEE Visual Analytics Science & Technology (VAST)*, 2012.

[18] S. M. Kent. Sloan digital sky survey. In *Science with Astronomical Near-Infrared Sky Surveys*, pages 27–30. Springer, 1994.

[19] N. Khoussainova, M. Balazinska, W. Gatterbauer, Y. Kwon, and D. Suciu. A case for a collaborative query management system. *arXiv preprint arXiv:0909.1778*, 2009.

[20] N. Khoussainova, Y. Kwon, M. Balazinska, and D. Suciu. Snipsuggest: Context-aware autocompletion for sql. *Proceedings of the VLDB Endowment*, 4(1):22–33, 2010.

[21] M. Kim, V. Sazawal, D. Notkin, and G. Murphy. An empirical study of code clone genealogies. In *ACM SIGSOFT Software Engineering Notes*, volume 30, pages 187–196. ACM, 2005.

[22] F. Li, T. Pan, and H. V. Jagadish. Schema-free sql. In *Proceedings of the 2014 ACM SIGMOD International Conference on Management of Data*, SIGMOD '14, pages 1051–1062, New York, NY, USA, 2014. ACM.

[23] B. Mozafari, E. Z. Y. Goh, and D. Y. Yoon. Cliffguard: A principled framework for finding robust database designs. In *Proceedings of the 2015 ACM SIGMOD International Conference on Management of Data*, pages 1167–1182. ACM, 2015.

[24] E. Ogasawara, J. Dias, F. Porto, P. Valduriez, and M. Mattoso. An algebraic approach for data-centric scientific workflows. *Proc. of VLDB Endowment*, 4(12):1328–1339, 2011.

[25] K. Ren, Y. Kwon, M. Balazinska, and B. Howe. Hadoop's adolescence: an analysis of hadoop usage in scientific workloads. *Proceedings of the VLDB Endowment*, 6(10):853–864, 2013.

[26] M. Rosson and J. Carroll. Active programming strategies in reuse. In O. Nierstrasz, editor, *ECOOPâĂŹ 93 âĂŤ Object-Oriented Programming*, volume 707 of *Lecture Notes in Computer Science*, pages 4–20. Springer Berlin Heidelberg, 1993.

[27] P. Roy, K. Ramamritham, S. Seshadri, P. Shenoy, and S. Sudarshan. Don't trash your intermediate results, cache'em. *arXiv preprint cs/0003005*, 2000.

[28] V. Singh, J. Gray, A. Thakar, A. S. Szalay, J. Raddick, B. Boroski, S. Lebedeva, and B. Yanny. Skyserver traffic report-the first five years. *arXiv preprint cs/0701173*, 2007.

[29] M. Stonebraker, J. Becla, D. J. DeWitt, K. Lim, D. Maier, O. Ratzesberger, and S. B. Zdonik. Requirements for science data bases and scidb. In *CIDR 2009, Fourth Biennial Conference on Innovative Data Systems Research, Asilomar, CA, USA, January 4-7, 2009, Online Proceedings*, 2009.

[30] I. J. Taylor, E. Deelman, D. B. Gannon, and M. Shields. *Workflows for e-Science: Scientific Workflows for Grids*. Springer Publishing Company, Incorporated, 2014.

[31] A. Thusoo, J. S. Sarma, N. Jain, Z. Shao, P. Chakka, S. Anthony, H. Liu, P. Wyckoff, and R. Murthy. Hive: a warehousing solution over a map-reduce framework. *Proceedings of the VLDB Endowment*, 2(2):1626–1629, 2009.

Automatic Generation of Normalized Relational Schemas from Nested Key-Value Data

Michael DiScala
Yale University
michael.discala@aya.yale.edu

Daniel J. Abadi
Yale University
dna@cs.yale.edu

ABSTRACT

Self-describing key-value data formats such as JSON are becoming increasingly popular as application developers choose to avoid the rigidity imposed by the relational model. Database systems designed for these self-describing formats, such as MongoDB, encourage users to use denormalized, heavily nested data models so that relationships across records and other schema information need not be predefined or standardized. Such data models contribute to long-term development complexity, as their lack of explicit entity and relationship tracking burdens new developers unfamiliar with the dataset. Furthermore, the large amount of data repetition present in such data layouts can introduce update anomalies and poor scan performance, which reduce both the quality and performance of analytics over the data.

In this paper we present an algorithm that automatically transforms the denormalized, nested data commonly found in NoSQL systems into traditional relational data that can be stored in a standard RDBMS. This process includes a schema generation algorithm that discovers relationships across the attributes of the denormalized datasets in order to organize those attributes into relational tables. It further includes a matching algorithm that discovers sets of attributes that represent overlapping entities and merges those sets together. These algorithms reduce data repetition, allow the use of data analysis tools targeted at relational data, accelerate scan-intensive algorithms over the data, and help users gain a semantic understanding of complex, nested datasets.

1. INTRODUCTION

Over the past two decades, self-describing semistructured data formats have become increasingly common solutions for storing and sharing information. As a recent example, NoSQL databases which implement key-value or document-based data models have gained traction among developers seeking to avoid rigid schemas. Human-readable key-value formats have emerged as the de facto message passing format used in modern APIs, allowing applications to interoperate with many services over standardized languages.

Although many semistructured formats exist, all typically support a set of common features. Notably, semistructured formats tend to inline attribute names within records instead of requiring clients to predefine their schemas. This allows records to contain arbitrary attributes with arbitrary types and allows records from within the same dataset to maintain different, potentially conflicting, attribute definitions.

Semistructured formats also tend to support deeply nested and hierarchical data structures. The popular JSON data format, for example, is recursively defined such that a key within a record may map to a nested record or even an array of nested records. Since most semistructured formats and their associated storage engines lack first-class support for modeling relationships across records (e.g. primary keys, foreign keys, joins, etc.), designers of semistructured data instead represent relationships with these nesting features and typically tend toward denormalized layouts.

The growing popularity of these formats has fueled interest in loading and processing semistructured data within relational database management systems (RDBMSes) so that more traditional business intelligence tools, query optimization techniques, and other tools from the relational world can be applied to these datasets [3, 4, 5, 6, 9, 21, 22, 23, 24, 27]. Efforts in this space typically propose mappings from semistructured formats to relational or mostly-relational structures that are compatible with standard SQL interfaces.

Once a mapping has been chosen, nearly any semistructured data can be represented within a relational framework. However, the schemas resulting from these mappings typically do not resemble anything a human designer would suggest. In some cases, this dissonance occurs because the mapping scheme is intended only to provide an efficient internal representation of semistructured data and does not attempt to provide a human-readable representation [3, 4, 9, 24, 21]. Even the mappings which attempt to generate human-readable schemas frequently fail to emulate human designers because they consider only the structure of input documents, rather than their values (e.g. for a key-value format, they consider the keys and their arrangement, but not their value distributions) [5, 23]. As a result, these mappings do not account for the denormalized data layouts that semistructured formats encourage. Even if an object is nested identically within two different records, these earlier strategies will doubly store the nested objects instead of creating a normalized, reference-based layout.

In this paper, we present a three-phase unsupervised machine learning algorithm that automatically designs a more traditional relational schema for an input dataset consisting of a set of related, denormalized, semistructured records. The first phase of the algorithm mines soft functional dependencies that exist within the semistructured dataset. It uses these dependencies to identify groups of attributes that are

SIGMOD'16, June 26-July 01, 2016, San Francisco, CA, USA

ISBN 978-1-4503-3531-7/16/06...$15.00

DOI: http://dx.doi.org/10.1145/2882903.2882924

likely to correspond to an independent semantic entity, and creates tables for these entities and associated foreign keys in parent tables. The second phase identifies entities found in the first phase with overlapping domains and merges them into a single entity structure. The final phase combines the intermediate results from the preceding two phases to produce a proposed schema that resembles a traditional normalized database schema (though not necessarily compliant with normalization schemes like BCNF, 3NF, or 4NF).

The advantages of this approach are two-fold. First, our algorithm simplifies the cognitively difficult task of exploring novel datasets by highlighting recurring structural and semantic patterns. Automated data exploration tools of this type are especially important while working with semistructured datasets, as these datasets are often semistructured precisely because their data sources are highly dynamic, and the set of attributes associated with any record is highly variable. Nonetheless, data exploration tools remain valuable even when the semistructured data originates from more ordered sources such as APIs, as these sources often lack extensive documentation and can be semantically inconsistent.

Second, our algorithm can significantly reduce the size of a dataset by eliminating redundancies. Whereas the denormalized data formats that we target store duplicate information whenever an instance of an entity is repeatedly referenced, normalized layouts avoid this repetition by storing instances of each entity a single time and replacing references to those instances with foreign keys. For semistructured formats that rely on inline attribute names, data size is further reduced by not repeatedly storing attributes names in the relational tables. The smaller size of our transformed datasets accelerates the scan-based queries that are especially common during an analyst's early interactions with a dataset.

Even as column-store technology reduces the need to normalize data in order to improve scan performance, scans of "dimension" tables corresponding to particular entities with a small number of rows can be performed much faster than scans of "fact" tables with a large number of rows. Hence, most column-stores continue to utilize separate tables for separate entities despite the overall reduced benefits of normalization. Furthermore, even when column-stores maintain physically denormalized data layouts, users still create logical views of the data in order to avoid losing the semantic connection to the actual entities within the dataset.

Therefore, the first two phases of our algorithm, which identify and match entities, are useful within both the column- and row- store contexts. The third phase of our algorithm, which analyzes the output of the preceding phases and decides which relations to normalize, is parameterized to target either a column- or row- store. If the final schema is destined for a row-store, phase 3 will normalize relations more aggressively. Conversely, if the schema is destined for a column-store, phase 3 will pre-join relations more frequently.

In Section 2, we summarize earlier works related to our algorithm. In Section 3, we explain each of our algorithm's three phases. In Section 4, we present our algorithm's performance on three semistructured datasets. In Section 5, we discuss our algorithm's limitations and areas for further investigation. In Section 6, we summarize our findings.

2. RELATED WORK

Functional dependencies: Largely due the close relationship between normalization and functional dependencies, functional dependency detection has been studied extensively [1, 2, 13, 14, 15, 18]. Mannila et al. prove that identifying the complete set of functional dependencies present within a relation is, in the worst case, exponential in the number of attributes [18]. Our work avoids this exponential search space by mining functional dependencies between pairs of attributes rather than arbitrary subsets of attributes. We note that this search space can be further reduced by applying the transitivity axioms that Bell presents [1].

Several of these dependency detection efforts attempt to identify "soft functional dependencies" or "approximate functional dependencies," which are similar to traditional functional dependencies, except that they are required to hold for most — but not all — data instances [13, 14, 15]. In particular, Ilyas et al. propose an approximate functional dependency detector which they use to improve query optimizer performance. We draw from their construction, applying it within the context of automated normalization and modifying it to function more robustly for skewed attributes.

Semistructured-to-relational mappings: Our work relates closely to previous mappings of semistructured data into relational data structures [4, 5, 6, 9, 21, 22, 23, 24, 27].

The most straightforward of these earlier efforts provide generic mapping rules that do not necessitate upfront analysis of the input dataset. One example, Chasseur et al.'s Argo, encodes JSON documents as ternary relations consisting of "object id," "attribute name," and "attribute value" columns [4]. Each attribute at the end of a nesting path through a record (i.e. a leaf attribute) is represented with a row in the ternary relation. Generic mappings of this sort achieve our goal of encoding semistructured documents in a relational system, but do not leverage the specific characteristics of the input dataset to achieve a more performant encoding or facilitate data exploration.

Other works are more similar to ours and generate schemas tailored to the input dataset. For example, Deutsch et al. present a language called STORED that maps semistructured data onto a combination of standard relational tables and an auxiliary data structure referred to as an "overflow graph"[1] [5]. They further present a data mining algorithm based on Wang and Liu's earlier work [25, 26], which identifies structures that appear frequently within the input dataset. They automatically translate these frequent structures into STORED mappings for the input data.

Shanmugasundaram et al. similarly present a mapping strategy based on structural analysis of the input dataset [23]. They design schemas for XML datasets by analyzing a graph of the DTD elements present in the input data; they apply a set of heuristics which dictate whether an element should be materialized as its own table or inlined within a parent element's table. Although their algorithm cannot operate directly on data that lacks a DTD specification, it can be applied within the schemaless context if the input dataset is first preprocessed by a schema discovery algorithm. One such discovery algorithm is Garofalakis et al.'s XTRACT system which produces a DTD from the arrangement of elements within a set of input XML documents [10].

Despite their overall differences, STORED's and Shanmugasundaram's approaches are similar in that they both extract their schemas from the original structures of the dataset and do not consider the distribution of data within

[1]This auxiliary structure limits STORED's ability to integrate with vanilla RDBMSes

those structures. In contrast, our approach ignores the original structure of the input and instead depends on patterns in the data (functional dependencies) to guide its schema generation. Our data-driven approach has three advantages over the prior structural approaches: 1) our analysis remains possible even when hierarchical structures are not present in the input dataset (e.g. flat CSV data files), 2) our algorithms can produce structures that were not present in the original encoding, and 3) our use of functional dependencies allows us to compress the input dataset through deduplication.

One previous approach to schema mapping that is sensitive to data distributions is Bohannon et al.'s LegoDB, which maps XML data to relational structures according to a search process that minimizes the cost of a user-specified workload [3]. LegoDB collects statistics about individual data attributes that it then feeds to a traditional query optimizer in order to estimate the cost of its workload for many candidate schemas. Since the system does not collect joint statistics about input attribute pairs, however, it cannot leverage functional dependencies as we do in our algorithm. Moreover, given that LegoDB requires users to define a query workload in advance of schema generation, it is less useful within the context of data exploration where queries are unlikely to be known in advance.

Another approach to schema mapping that is sensitive to data distributions is some very recent work by Pham et al. in the context of graph (RDF) data [19]. This work scans through a vertex-edge-vertex (SPO) dataset to find characteristic sets (CSs) consisting of edge-labels that co-occur as outgoing edges from multiple vertices. The CSs correspond to entities from which relations can be derived. Pham et al. use structural information in the graph (direct edges to non-literal vertices) to discover relationships between entities. In contrast, our algorithm does not rely on structural clues in the dataset to discover relationships.

A final approach related to our work is the xCurator system, which addresses our problems of schema generation, entity identification, and entity matching in the RDF context [12]. xCurator extracts entities by constructing and analyzing a structure graph from the dataset. Again, our algorithm differs in that it ignores structural information.

Schema matching: The second phase of our algorithm is closely related to earlier work on schema matchers, which identify mappings between independently designed schemas that model the same underlying domain. Rahm and Bernstein present an extensive survey of past approaches to this problem [20]. Despite the breadth of past work, earlier approaches are largely incompatible with our needs in phase 2: some require user-input (we intend our algorithm to be unsupervised), some rely on similarities in attribute names (we intend our algorithm to be entirely data driven), and some require rich schema information such as types or foreign-keys (we assume that this context will sometimes be unavailable). In this paper, we thus propose a matching scheme tailored to phase 2's restricted schema matching problem.

Our phase 2 algorithm borrows Li and Clifton's strategy of clustering attributes within a single schema into categories in order to reduce the number of potential matches the algorithm must consider [16].

3. ALGORITHM OVERVIEW

In this section, we provide a high-level overview of our algorithm, reserving more detailed discussion for later sections. We use a toy dataset of submissions to a journal in order to ground our description in concrete examples. Listing 1 shows a sample record from this dataset, which is encoded in the JSON format. The record includes the submission's title, author, and assigned reviewer, along with the author's and reviewer's associated institutions. A complete dataset would include many examples of this kind of submission record. While we expect that the structure of each record will vary, we assume that all of the records logically represent the same kind of object or entity.

```
{ 'submissionId': 1576,
  'title': 'Perils of DB',
  'author': {
    'email': 'js@e.pfl',
    'name': 'J. Snow',
    'institution': {
      'name': 'EPFL',
      'number': 1 } },
  'reviewer': {
    'email': 'dd@ca.uk',
    'name': 'D. Duck',
    'institution': {
      'name': 'Cambridge',
      'number': 14 }}}
```

Listing 1: Sample JSON

We begin constructing a relational schema for the data by temporarily transforming the raw data records from their semistructured format into a flat table akin to the "universal relation" model [7, 17]. In order to transform the JSON records from our journal submissions example, we create a table with a column for every attribute that originally contains an atomic value (e.g. a string or integer), where the column's name is the concatenated path through any nesting required to reach the atomic value. We then populate the table with a row for every record in the dataset by entering each record's values into their corresponding table column. Figure 1 illustrates this flattening process, as its first row contains the flattened form of the record shown in Listing 1 and its remaining rows represent additional submission records. Since our toy example does not rely on semistructured features more complex than nested attributes, this simple transformation procedure is sufficient for our needs here. We describe techniques for accommodating other semistructured features (e.g. creating relationship tables to model nested arrays of objects) in Appendix A.

This flat representation does not meet either of our primary goals: (1) offering users semantic insight into their datasets and (2) creating an approximately normalized schema for a dataset. This encoding nevertheless serves as a convenient starting point because it decouples our algorithm from a specific semistructured format and ensures that our results reflect the patterns implicit in the original data rather than the original data structure. We consciously ignore structural cues such as JSON's implicit object boundaries because these cues frequently derive from assumptions and needs that may not be borne out by the data itself (e.g. for development convenience, separate entities may be combined into a single JSON object). As our algorithm progresses, we refine this flat representation to expose more of the implicit structure of the data and thereby construct a more traditional relational schema.

In phase 1, we identify functional relationships between attributes in the dataset and leverage those relationships to decompose our initial table into a collection of smaller tables joined by primary-to-foreign key relationships. While the strict definition of a functional dependency from an attribute A to another attribute B requires that n-to-one relationships exist between *all* values of A and B, we adopt Ilyas et al.'s notion of a "soft" functional dependency which

subId	*title*	*authEmail*	*authName*	*authIName*	*authINum*	*revEmail*	*revName*	*revIName*	*revINum*
1576	Perils...	js@e.pfl	J. Snow	EPFL	1	dd@ca.uk	D. Duck	Cambridge	14
1680	Broken...	js@e.pfl	J. Snow	EPFL	1	nd@h.edu	N. Dame	Harvard	55
1559	Wins...	dd@ca.uk	D. Duck	Cambridge	14	js@e.pfl	J. Snow	EPFL	1

Figure 1: Collection of flattened records from the journal dataset (nested paths in column names shortened to save space)

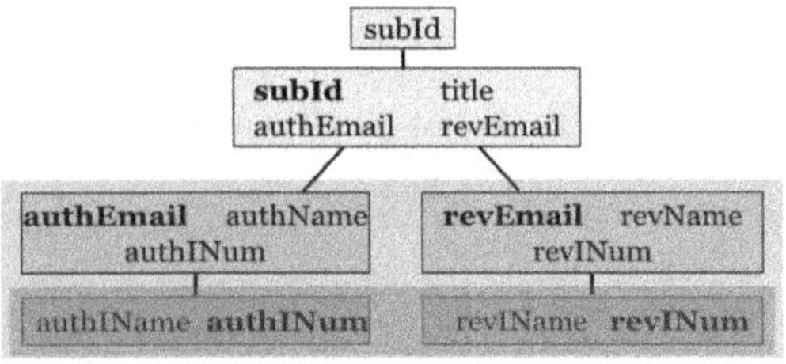

Figure 2: The ideal phase 1 attribute tree for the journal submission dataset, with parent attributes in bold and phase 2 entity matches highlighted in red and purple.

instead requires that the relationships exist for *most* values of A and B [14]. At the highest level, we identify these soft functional dependencies by considering pairs of attributes and observing how frequently the necessary n-to-one relationships exist between their values (described in Section 3.1.2). Even within the compact journal submission example, we would likely identify many functional relationships between pairs of attributes. Among others, we would identify that all attributes depend upon "subId" and that all attributes prefixed with "auth" depend upon "authEmail."

Based on an analysis of the identified dependencies, we group attributes that exhibit similar functional relationships and materialize these groups as new tables. In order to separate a group of attributes into their own table, every member of the group must depend upon some other attribute in the dataset. We refer to the attribute upon which all members depend as the *parent* of the group. For example, we might group the attributes prefixed with "auth" together because they share a common dependency on "authEmail." These attributes can be separated into their own table that is linked to the original through a primary-to-foreign key relationship on their parent attribute, "authEmail."

While this "auth" decomposition is valid, it is not the most expressive arrangement of the input: the dataset contains a chain of dependencies from "subId" to "authEmail" to "authINum" to "authIName," but the current decomposition reveals only functional relationships from "authEmail" to fields prefixed with "auth." We must further decompose our tables in order to expose the remaining functional relationships. To this end, we generate the attribute groups according to an algorithm that attempts to create the longest possible chains of groups from the identified functional dependencies.

The table structure resulting from this decomposition process can be modeled as a rooted tree in which every node represents a relation and every edge represents a primary-to-foreign key relationship. Figure 2 shows a potential attribute tree for the data contained in the journal submission example (ignore the purple and red boxes for now).

Phase 2 of the algorithm now begins. Unlike phase 1, which exclusively identifies relationships between attributes within a single record, phase 2 identifies relationships between *groups* of attributes *across* records. In particular, this phase searches for instances where the dataset contains multiple attribute groups that seem to represent similar entities in the dataset's domain model. As an example of this pattern, consider the group of journal submission attributes that contains "authIName" and "authINum" alongside the group that contains "revIName" and "revINum." Despite their distinct naming schemes, each group contains attributes describing a logical institution entity. When the fields are prefixed with "rev," the institution is associated with the reviewer, and when the fields are prefixed with "auth," the institution is associated with the author; regardless, the two groups always describe an institution. Moreover, the institutions that appear in the "revI" prefixed fields on some records will likely appear in the "authI" prefixed fields on others, as a single institution's professors may sometimes serve as reviewers and other times as authors.

We can therefore improve the relational design of our schema by merging these attribute groups together so that the resulting schema contains a single relation composed of all institutions, regardless of their author/reviewer classification. This merging operation eliminates redundant storage of records representing the same institutions in different tables, thereby reducing the overall size of the dataset. More importantly, it alerts users to the fact that some branches of the tree refer to an overlapping domain.

From a high level, phase 2 quantifies the overlap between the domains of subtrees within the attribute tree and declares that subtrees represent the same type of entities when their domains significantly overlap (described in Section 3.2). Phase 2 annotates the attribute tree with entity overlap information so that phase 3 can later merge the branches together. The purple and red boxes shown in Figure 2 represent the annotations we expect phase 2 to add to the journal submission attribute tree. The purple portion shows the earlier-described relationship between the "revI" prefixed fields and the "authI" prefixed fields. The red portion shows the overlapping relationship between the "rev" prefixed fields and the "auth" prefixed fields, which match because both groups contain attributes related to a person entity.

Phase 3 creates the final relational schema for the dataset by merging the subtrees identified by phase 2 and condensing long dependency chains (described in Section 3.3). Although these long chains reveal dependencies in the dataset, phase 3 condenses them because excessively normalized schemas are (1) less readable, (2) bloated by foreign keys, and (3) slow to query due to extensive JOIN operations.

Figure 3 shows one schema that the algorithm might create for the journal submission dataset. It contains three relations: one representing the root submission table, one representing people entities, and one representing institution entities. These relations are stitched together by primary-to-foreign key relationships that the algorithm introduces.

3.1 Phase 1 in-depth

In this section, we expand our earlier description of phase 1's mining of soft functional dependencies and its decomposition of the initial flat table into a tree of smaller tables.

subId	*title*	*revID*	*authID*	*ID*
1576	Perils...	3	1	1
1680	Broken...	5	1	3
1559	Wins...	1	3	4

email	*name*	*instID*	*ID*
js@e.pfl	J. Snow	1	1
dd@ca.uk	D. Duck	4	3
nd@h.edu	N. Dame	5	5

INum	*IName*	*ID*
1	EPFL	1
14	Cambridge	4
55	Harvard	5

Figure 3: The final relational schema generated for the data from the journal submission example.

3.1.1 Soft vs hard functional dependencies

We choose to mine soft functional dependencies instead of traditional functional relationships for two reasons. First, by mining soft relationships we allow our algorithm to operate on imperfectly curated datasets that contain a few erroneous records in violation of otherwise valid functional dependencies. Data inconsistencies of this type can arise in most any format, but are especially common within semistructured datasets because these formats often do not support schema level constraints (e.g. type or foreign key constraints).

Second, we favor soft functional dependencies because they philosophically align with our goal of helping users learn about their datasets. Even if they do not hold globally, soft functional relationships reflect the broad contours of the training dataset and can help users to understand the data structures prevailing within the majority of their data.

3.1.2 Identifying soft functional dependencies

We detect a soft functional relationship from a_1 to a_2 if the values of a_1 usually exhibit n-to-one relationships with values of a_2. Ilyas et al. [14] provide a light-weight formula to approximate the frequency of these n-to-one relationships:

FORMULA 3.1.1. *Let $strength(a_1,\ a_2)$ be:*

$$strength(a_1,\ a_2) = \frac{\#\ of\ unique\ values\ of\ a_1}{\#\ of\ unique\ (a_1,\ a_2)\ value\ pairs}$$

The strength measure ranges from 0 to 1, and is positively correlated with the degree to which a_1 predicts a_2. When individual values of a_1 pair with many values of a_2, the denominator grows and the strength measure approaches zero. Conversely, when a hard functional dependency exists and every value of a_1 pairs with a unique value of a_2, this measure equals one.

We found that Formula 3.1.1 works well most of the time. However, when a_2's distribution is significantly skewed toward a single value, it becomes possible that the strength value will be high as a result of coincidence rather than as a result of the dataset's semantics. The core problem is that a skewed value distribution of a_2 can produce patterns in the training data that resemble an n-to-one relationship where many values of a_1 map to the (skewed) modal value of a_2. We address this issue by modifying Formula 3.1.1 to discount the modal value of a_2:

FORMULA 3.1.2. *Let v_{2freq} be the modal value of a_2 in the dataset and let $m(a_1, a_2)$ be the number of unique $(a_1,\ a_2)$ value pairs where a_2 equals v_{2freq}.*

$$strength(a_1,\ a_2) = \frac{\#\ of\ unique\ values\ of\ a_1\ -\ m(a_1, a_2)}{\#\ of\ unique\ (a_1,\ a_2)\ pairs - m(a_1, a_2)}$$

Given a threshold, α, which corresponds to the allowable "softness" in the functional relationships, we use Formula 3.1.2 to discover soft functional dependencies in the dataset:

CONDITION 3.1.1. *Let $strength(a_1,\ a_2)$ be defined as in Formula 3.1.2, and $density(a)$ be the fraction of records where a is non-NULL. A soft functional dependency from a_1 to a_2 exists when:*
(1) $strength(a_1,\ a_2)$ has a non-zero denominator
(2) $strength(a_1,\ a_2) > \alpha$
(3) $density(a_1) \geq density(a_2)$

The threshold α should be set to a number close to 1 (0.99 in our experiments) in order to guarantee that a_1 reliably indicates a_2's value within the training set. This guarantee allows us to treat these relationships as approximate primary-to-foreign key links later in phase 1 and, consequently, is essential to our ability to decompose the initial flat table into many smaller relations.

3.1.3 Enumerating dependencies

For each pair of attributes, Condition 3.1.1 can be checked with algorithms that are either linear or linearithmic (n log n) in the size of the dataset. For simplicity, we identify dependencies by applying the conditions to every pair of attributes, in both directions ($O(N^2)$ comparisons where N is the number of attributes). This process enumerates all combinations of individual attributes that meet our conditions. However, this process cannot discover attributes that are functionally dependent on groups of attributes.

Our implementation can be optimized by leveraging the transitivity of functional relationships to avoid performing redundant dependency tests. Bell fully evaluates this strategy of optimizing dependency enumeration [1].

3.1.4 The longest path heuristic

After discovering dependencies, phase 1 forms groups of attributes. As described in Section 3, phase 1 forms these groups by identifying the longest chains of functional dependencies present in the dataset. Phase 1 employs this heuristic because it ensures that the attribute tree includes as many functional dependencies as possible and thus includes as much semantic information as possible. This strategy offers flexibility to the algorithm's later phases, allowing phase 2 to match entities within the tree's branches and phase 3 to selectively materialize the dependencies as relations.

Phase 1 begins its grouping process by constructing a dependency graph where nodes represent attributes and directed edges represent functional relationships (edges run from parent attributes to dependent attributes). The graph contains a node for every attribute in the training set and directed edges modeling each of the previously discovered dependencies. The graph also contains a special "ROOT" node that has outgoing edges to every other node. Figure 4(c) shows part of the journal submission example's graph.

For every attribute, a, phase 1 then computes $lp(a)$ which denotes the longest path through the dependency graph from "ROOT" to a. Ties are resolved according to the strength of the last functional dependency on the path, or are resolved randomly if the strengths are also tied.

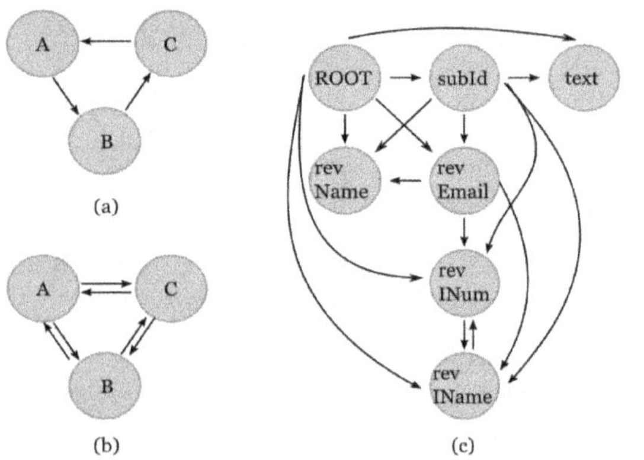

Figure 4: (a) An unlikely dependency graph cycle (b) A likely dependency graph cycle. (c) A subset of the dependency graph for the journal submission dataset.

Consider the value of $lp(revEmail)$ in Figure 4(c). There are two paths to "revEmail" in the dependency graph: "ROOT" $\rightarrow$ "revEmail" and "ROOT" $\rightarrow$ "subId" $\rightarrow$ "revEmail." Phase 1 chooses the latter path as $lp(revEmail)$ because it is longer.

In the general case, computing $lp(a)$ is an NP-hard problem and requires a brute-force examination of every possible path from "ROOT" to a. When the input is a directed acyclic graph (DAG), however, a linear time solution exists. Although we cannot assume that the phase 1 dependency graphs will be DAGs, the transitive nature of functional dependencies allows us to assume that the cycles in the graph will result from bidirectional dependencies between pairs of attributes as shown in Figure 4(b). Multi-node cycles similar to Figure 4(a) are only possible if a mistake was made in identifying functional dependencies, since multi-node cycles without bidirectional edges require that some functional dependencies do not exhibit the transitive property. We thus can usually transform our initial dependency graph into a DAG by removing bidirectional relationships. We remove a bidirectional relationship between attributes a_1 and a_2 according to the following rules:

1. If $descendants(a_1) - \{a_2\} = descendants(a_2) - \{a_1\}$, we merge the attributes together into a single node in the dependency graph. In this case, the attributes participate in the same functional dependencies so we treat them as a single unit. We would use this strategy to eliminate the cycle between "revIName" and "revINum" in Figure 4(c).
2. If the nodes cannot be merged, we break the cycle by removing the edge beginning at the node with fewer descendants in the graph.
3. If neither of the above conditions hold, we delete the edge with the lower strength, breaking ties randomly.

Once the longest paths have been identified, phase 1 forms attribute groups. For every attribute, it computes $parent(a)$ which denotes the attribute immediately preceding a on $lp(a)$. The algorithm then groups all attributes that share the same value of $parent(a)$. Throughout our remaining discussion, we refer to these groups by their shared parent attributes; we define A_{p1} to be the attribute group containing all attributes for which $parent(a)$ equals $p1$.

Finally, the algorithm splits the flat table into these attribute groups to form the tree structure that comprises the phase 1 output (as described above and shown in Figure 2).

3.2 Phase 2 in-depth

Phase 2 searches within the attribute tree to discover semantically equivalent entities that are embedded in multiple places within the dataset, as occurs in the algorithm overview's journal submission example with person entities (which exist as both authors and reviewers) and institution entities (which are nested underneath both authors and reviewers). In order to identify this behavior, phase 2 analyzes collections of attributes that — despite having different names (e.g "revIName" vs. "authIName") — have value distributions that suggest they represent the same entity.

We begin with Section 3.2.1 which explains why subtrees of the phase 1 attribute tree are a natural choice for searching for matching entities. We continue with Section 3.2.2 which presents our conditions for determining that two subtrees likely contain the same type of entities. For clarity, we first describe our algorithm in its most uncomplicated, but lowest performing variation. However, we describe four optimizations to this algorithm in Appendices B, C, D, E.

3.2.1 Entities and subtrees

We define entities as elements of the dataset's domain model that contain descriptive attributes and a unique identifier. For instance, the journal submission example includes person entities, which are uniquely identified by their emails and described by their names and institutional affiliations.

We classify attributes as "descriptive attributes" for a particular type of entity by examining the frequency with which the attributes change for a specific entity instance. On one hand, some attributes frequently hold different values throughout the dataset even when they are associated with the same entity. These frequently changing attributes typically model time-dependent information, where each record in the dataset contains a snapshot of the attribute's value. We are unconcerned with these kinds of attributes in phase 2, as they are not amenable to normalization and are not redundantly stored across repeated occurrences of an entity.

Instead, phase 2 searches for attributes that remain relatively fixed across all references to a specific entity; these attributes model concepts that are not time-dependent, such as a person's name. By virtue of their stability across references to single entity, a strong n-to-one relationship exists from an entity's unique identifier to its stable attributes. These stable attributes consequently tend to descend from their entity's unique identifier in the phase 1 attribute tree. Entities in a dataset thus correspond to subtrees of the phase 1 attribute tree:

DEFINTION 1. *If A_p is an attribute group in the tree with parent attribute p, then there exists a subtree beginning at A_p that contains all attribute groups A_{attr} such that the parent of A_{attr} equals p or one of p's descendants.*

For example, within the journal submission data, there is a perfect correspondence between the attribute tree's five subtrees and the domain model's 5 entities (1 submission entity, 2 person entities, and 2 institution entities)[2].

Since each semantic entity in the dataset usually corresponds to a subtree in the phase 1 attribute tree, entity matching reduces to a pairwise comparison of all subtrees ($O(N^2)$ in the number of subtrees). In many cases, this process identifies redundant matches because matching subtrees

[2]In general, not **every** subtree corresponds to an entity.

authEmail	*authName*	*authIName*	*authINum*	*revEmail*	*revName*	*revIName*	*revINum*
js@e.pfl	J. Snow	EPFL	1	js@e.pfl	J. Snow	EPFL	1
js@e.pfl	J. Snow	EPFL	1	js@e.pfl	J. Snow	EPFL	1
dd@ca.uk	D. Duck	Cambridge	14	dd@ca.uk	D. Duck	Cambridge	14

Figure 5: The result of joining the flat table on $authEmail = revEmail$.

often contain sub-subtrees that also match. Our algorithm exploits this redundancy to gain additional insight into the input data's semantics (discussed in Appendix C).

3.2.2 Detecting matching subtrees

Phase 2 uses a three step process to determine whether the subtrees S_1 and S_2 model the same underlying entity:

Step 1: This step identifies all pairs of training records where the subtrees seemingly describe the same entity. For example, when considering the person subtrees, $A_{authEmail}$ and $A_{revEmail}$, the algorithm must find all pairs of records where the author for the first record is the reviewer for the second. This process is essentially a join operation that returns records with matching values within their S_1 and S_2 subtrees. Given that the algorithm does not yet understand the relationships between S_1's and S_2's attributes, it cannot perform a direct subtree match. Instead, phase 2 approximates this join on the entire subtree by performing a join on the parent attributes of the two subtrees[3]. Due to the functional relationships from the parent attribute to the subtree's other attributes, this simpler join identifies all pairs of records that might contain the same entity. Figure 5 illustrates this process for the $A_{authEmail}$ and $A_{revEmail}$ subtrees. Appendix B outlines an optimization of this join.

When the result of this join is empty, we conclude that there is no possibility of S_1 and S_2 containing the same type of entity and skip the remaining two steps for this pair. This occurs whenever the subtrees' parent attributes have no common values, as in the example of $A_{authEmail}$ and $A_{authINum}$. When the result is non-empty, the joining records may reflect that 1) the two subtrees are related and the matches contain the same entities, or 2) the subtrees are unrelated and their parent attributes coincidentally overlap. The remaining two steps distinguish between these cases.

Step 2: This step analyzes the results from step 1 in order to identify correspondences between S_1's attributes and S_2's attributes. If the two subtrees truly represent the same underlying type of entity, we expect them to contain pairs of corresponding attributes. Consider, for example, the subtrees $A_{authEmail}$ and $A_{revEmail}$, which both model person entities. Their corresponding attributes can be mapped together as follows: "authEmail" maps to "revEmail," "authName" maps to "revName," "authINum" maps to "revINum," and "authIName" maps to "revIName." In this case, it is fairly trivial for a human observer to infer the appropriate mapping. In many other datasets, however, the mapping between subtrees will not be so obvious. For generality, we do not rely on information from attribute names.

Step 2 constructs attribute mappings by considering the frequency with which attributes from the two subtrees contain the same values on the same records in the step 1 join result. It tracks these frequencies in an attribute matrix that contains a cell for every pairing of S_1's and S_2's attributes.[4] We denote these pairs as (a_1, a_2). Every cell, $attrMatrix[a_1][a_2]$, is initialized to zero. The algorithm then iterates through every row, R, from the join result and increments $attrMatrix[a_1][a_2]$ by 1 if $R[a_1]$ equals $R[a_2]$.

For example, the matrix generated from the join in Figure 5 will have the value 3 in the cells for the pairs (revEmail, authEmail), (revName, authName), (revIName, authIName), and (revINum, authINum). All other cells contain zero.

From the attribute matrix we construct the mapping between S_1's and S_2's attributes. We attempt to map the S_1 attributes to the S_2 attributes that most frequently share their values across the join set. Formally, we define:

DEFINTION 2. *For every attribute a_1 in S_1, $match(a_1)$ equals the attribute a_2 in S_2 such that*

1. *$R[a_1] = R[a_2]$ for a threshold percentage of joined records:*
$$\frac{attrMatrix[a_1][a_2]}{\#\ records\ in\ join\ set} \geq \alpha^2$$
2. *$attrMatrix[a_1][a_2] \geq attrMatrix[a_1][a_2']$, for all other attributes a_2' in S_2*

Definition 2's first requirement excludes matches between attributes that coincidentally share the same value for some records in the join set. The threshold parameter α is the same α from Condition 3.1.1, which corresponds to the acceptable "softness" of the dataset. However, α^2 is used as the threshold here, since the errors multiply through a join. The *match* function is not guaranteed to be defined for all attributes; we refer to unmatched attributes as orphans. The definition's second requirement selects the best amongst multiple matches for an attribute that are above threshold. It allows *match* to map a single attribute from one tree to multiple attributes in the other when ties occur.

In Appendix E we describe an optimization to this process which clusters attributes based on their domain values. The algorithm leverages this clustering to improve accuracy and performance by excluding attribute matches across clusters.

Step 3: Finally, phase 2 analyzes the results from the previous two steps to determine whether the two subtrees likely model the same underlying entity. Phase 2 identifies an entity match only if the following three conditions hold:

1. *The subtrees' join result is at least (1-α)% the size of the original dataset.* This condition eliminates matches that result from extremely small, coincidental overlaps in the domains of the subtrees' parent attributes.
2. *The match function is defined for the majority of the attributes contained within the smaller subtree.* This condition allows us to identify subtree pairs that partially match, while also eliminating weak matches that may result from noise in the attribute matrix computations.

[3]When the parent attribute of a subtree is a merged attribute created during phase 1, we perform multiple joins and try all possible parent combinations. For example, if $parent(S_1)$ is the merged attribute "A, B" and $parent(S_2)$ is "C," we perform the join on both A = C and on B = C.

[4]In practice we do not compare every pair of attributes. See Appendix E for more details.

3. *The match function is defined for attributes other than the subtrees' parent attributes.* Parent attributes are guaranteed to match with each other since the subtrees are joined on these attributes. Thus, the *match* function provides no new information for parent attributes.

After identifying entity matches, phase 2 performs additional analysis to find partners for some orphaned attributes. The algorithm analyzes nested matches (e.g. the person and institution matches from the journal submission example) to find attribute matches that were overlooked during earlier phases. We outline this process further in Appendix D.

3.3 Phase 3 in-depth

Phase 3 produces a physical schema for the input data and a mapping of input attributes onto that physical schema. This phase begins by merging together the phase 2 entity matches. An entity's subtrees are merged in three steps:

1. Form groups of subtrees such that the members of each group are all phase 2 matches with one another. For example, if the phase 2 output contains the matches A-B, A-C, and B-C, then we form a group of all three trees.[5]
2. For each group of subtrees, designate the one with the most attributes as the canonical subtree for that group (resolve ties arbitrarily). Remove all non-canonical subtrees from the attribute tree.
3. Map each non-canonical subtree to its corresponding canonical subtree according to the pair's phase 2 *match* function. If the *match* function is undefined for any non-canonical attribute, add an attribute to the root of the canonical subtree and map the orphan to this new attribute. This ensures that every input attribute can be mapped to something in the physical schema.

Phase 3 then transforms the tree of canoncial subtrees into its final schema. The schema begins with a relation that corresponds to the root attribute group and contains all of the root attributes. The algorithm then performs a breadth-first traversal of the tree in order to build the complete schema. During each iteration of this traversal, the algorithm decides whether to create a new relation for the attribute group it's considering or to merge that group into an existing relation. As relations are created, the map of input attributes to physical attributes is updated accordingly.

The algorithm creates new relations if at least one of two conditions is satisfied. First, if the current attribute group corresponds to the root of a merged subtree, phase 3 always creates a new relation. This ensures that phase 3 can replace the original subtrees that were merged together with foreign key references into the newly created relation. Second, phase 3 creates a new relation if the cardinality of the current attribute group is at least $\epsilon\%$ less than the cardinality of the relation it would otherwise be condensed into (the group's nearest ancestor in the tree for which a relation has already been created). By default we set $\epsilon\%$ to 50%, but when a column-store is targeted, a larger ϵ is recommended. We choose to create relations for groups that correspond to significant cardinality shifts because the shifts usually signal the presence of a separate semantic entity. Even when they do not represent a new kind of entity, they represent a significant opportunity for normalization since they will reduce the size of the dataset if materialized as their own relation. This normalization and resulting data size reduction will generally improve row-store performance. However, column-stores usually perform better on denormalized data — this is why they benefit from a larger ϵ. Even though high ϵ values will reduce the number of entities that are revealed via the creation of separate tables, those entities that are hidden by a large value of ϵ can still be presented to the user separately from the final table schema.

If the attribute group under consideration does not meet either of these conditions, materializing the group as its own relation yields neither the benefits of entity identification nor significant redundancy elimination. The algorithm thus adds the attributes from the group to the relation corresponding to the group's nearest ancestor in the tree. This process concentrates the user's attention on the most important aspects of the dataset and may improve query performance by eliminating extra table joins.

Associations: The algorithm stitches together the created relations with primary-to-foreign key links. While the parent attributes would ideally be primary keys for their corresponding relations, this is often infeasible because parents are only required to be *approximately* unique within their relations. Instead, the algorithm adds an integer "id" attribute to each relation and designates "id" as the relation's primary key. Associations between relations are materialized as foreign keys from relations higher in phase 3's output tree to their children. By placing foreign keys in this way, phase 3 ensures that each relation can be deduplicated (if foreign keys were created in the opposite direction, every relation would have the same cardinality as the root relation).

Data loading: Each input record is loaded into the phase 3 schema by creating rows in phase 3's output relations according to the mapping of input attributes to physical attributes. Once all input records have been transformed, the phase 3 relations are deduplicated to reduce redundancy.

4. EXPERIMENTAL EVALUATION

We evaluate our algorithm with three real world datasets:

Dataset #1 — Flights: Our first dataset was collected by the US Bureau of Transportation Statistics and reports the timeliness of every non-stop flight within the United States. Each record corresponds to a single top-level flight entity and contains 64 attributes that collectively describe the flight's scheduled itinerary, any delays it experienced, and its affiliated airline. Within these flight objects, the dataset nests origin and destination airport entities.

Our training set includes 1.3 million flight records from the first months of 2014. The data is originally encoded in the CSV data format and, consequently, requires none of the preprocessing steps outlined in Appendix A.

Dataset #2 — Twitter: Our second dataset consists of 10 million records scraped from the JSON API of the social network Twitter, which allows its users to exchange messages called "tweets." Each record models a single top-level tweet entity and contains a short message along with more than 300 attributes of metadata. This metadata includes a user entity that identifies the author of the tweet and a place entity that specifies where the message was posted from.

10% of the experimental dataset models a special kind of tweet that users create by reposting a message that someone

[5]We simplify our implementation by assuming that subtree matches always behave transitively. While we expect this behavior to hold in most cases and observed no exceptions in our experiments, non-transitive matches are possible.

else previously authored. These special tweets, referred to as "retweets," are distinguishable because they embed the original tweet that they are derived from (this models the n-to-one relationship from retweets to original tweets).

This dataset contains arrays of nested objects. As described in Appendix A, our algorithm treats nested-object arrays as independent sub-instances of the original schema generation problem. In order to simplify our analysis of the Twitter results, we only focus on the first iteration of our algorithm, since this iteration contains the most important semantic entities (tweets, retweets, users, and places) and over 100 attributes on most records, while the subsequent sub-instances cover more fringe attributes and entities.

Dataset #3 — GitHub: Our third dataset was scraped from GitHub, which is a website allowing developers to collaborate on software projects managed by the Git version control system. At the top-level, records from this dataset contain a pull request entity which models a user's request to merge code across branches or different repositories. These pull request entities reference 7 embedded user entities, head and base commit entities (i.e. the new commit and the commit it's to be merged on top of), and head and base repository entities. Our training set contains 1M records scraped from GitHub's JSON API by the GHTorrent project [11].

Methodology: We have manually analyzed the raw data and documentation associated with each of the three datasets in order to gain insight into the semantics of their attributes and the relationships among their attributes. In Sections 4.1-4.3, we evaluate our algorithm's performance by comparing the output of each phase with the expectations developed during this analysis. In Section 4.4, we compare our algorithm with Argo [4] and an XML transformation algorithm from Shanmugasundaram et al. [23].

Due to the large number of attributes in all of these datasets, it is impossible to fit the full schema produced by our algorithm in the main part of this paper. However, Appendix F shows the final schema for the GitHub dataset.

Performance: Given that our algorithm is intended to be run once per dataset in an **offline** setting, we did not performance-optimize our implementation and do not present performance metrics in the body of the paper. In Appendix H, we provide details about our implementation, analyze its runtime, and describe the trade-offs of sampling.

4.1 Phase 1 results

Phase 1 produces attribute trees with many attribute groups for each of the datasets, with the Flights tree having the fewest at 22 and the GitHub tree having the most at 28.

Entities and stable attributes: As described in Section 3.2.1, each entity has a unique identifier and a set of descriptive attributes that are either stable or variable across repeated references to a specific instance of the entity. We expect entities to manifest in the phase 1 attribute tree as subtrees that begin with the entity's unique identifier and contain the entity's stable attributes. The phase 1 output for each of the experimental datasets generally shows this pattern. To illustrate, we consider the Flight dataset's origin airport entity which has the unique identifier "origin_airport_seq_id" and has descriptive attributes that specify the airport's short-code (e.g. "JFK") along with its location. These descriptive attributes are relatively stable across repeated references to the same airport and, consequently, form a subtree with the parent "origin_airport_seq_id." The subtree contains only attributes related to the origin airport.

In most cases, the entities contained within the experimental datasets behave similarly to this example and correspond to a single subtree in the phase 1 graph; the user entity from the Twitter dataset, however, is split across two subtrees. The first has "user_id" as its parent attribute and contains the user's basic information (e.g. screen name). The second has "user_profile_image_url" as its parent and contains attributes related to the visual design of the user's profile (e.g. text color and image URLs). This division occurs as a result of phase 1's strategy for assigning parent attributes: when choosing the parents for most of the user attributes, phase 1 finds that both the ID and URL are possible parents at a depth of one in the attribute tree; faced with a tie in the depth heuristic, phase 1 assigns each of the user attributes to the parent with which the attribute demonstrates the strongest functional relationship. The attributes for the user's basic information are most strongly dependent upon "user_id" and are correspondingly placed in that subtree; the visual attributes are most strongly dependent upon "user_profile_image_url" and are placed accordingly. This split suggests that the visual attributes associated with users behave as their own entity. Each *version* of a user's profile corresponds to an instance of this entity whose unique identifier is "user_profile_image_url" and whose descriptive attributes include the remaining visual attributes. Since these versions are neither unique to nor constant for a specific user, the algorithm produces two distinct subtrees that both attach to the attribute tree at the same depth.

The creation of this separate visual entity is another example of our phase 1 algorithm identifying semantic information missed during our manual analysis of the dataset. It is important to note that this semantic information is also absent in the original nesting of the JSON documents that comprise our training set, as those documents combine the user's basic information and visual attributes together in a single object. This example demonstrates the pitfalls of creating tables that exactly mimic the structures of the input data: even the designers of the input documents may be indifferent to or unaware of some important semantic details.

Entities and unstable attributes: Many entities from the experimental datasets contain unstable attributes that do not tend to retain their values across multiple references to the same instance of an entity. Due to the absence of functional relationships from an entity's unique identifier to its variable attributes, we expect unstable attributes to appear outside of their entity's subtree in the phase 1 output.

We observe this behavior in both the GitHub and Twitter datasets, which include several snapshot-in-time measurements. For example, GitHub's base repository entity includes "base_repo_forks_count" to track the number of times the base repository was forked, and Twitter's user entity includes "user_favourites_count" to track the number of tweets the user has saved to their favorites. These counting attributes vary over the lifetime of their associated entities and their values are only accurate as of the moment they were scraped from the GitHub and Twitter APIs. They consequently do not participate in functional dependencies and are placed in the root of their respective attribute trees.

There are, however, some exceptions, and in some cases these unstable attributes are placed in deeper attribute groups. For example, phase 1 places GitHub's unstable "head_user_

	Flights	*Twitter*	*GitHub*
# FDs from Formula 3.1.1	267	2497	3728
# FDs from Formula 3.1.2	112	1180	2603
Avg. skew of FD allowed by 3.1.1 but not by 3.1.2	97%	95%	91%

Table 1: Comparison of Formulas 3.1.1 and 3.1.2.

site_admin" attribute within the "head_repo_pushed_at" subtree. At first glance, there is no semantic justification for this placement. However, both attributes exhibit a hidden dependency on the record creation time, which creates a subtle, but strong, relationship between them. Since unstable attributes tend to be time dependent, phase 1 often places them within the subtrees of other time dependent attributes.

Skew performance: All three experimental datasets include attributes skewed toward a single value. As we described in Section 3.1.2, we expect these skewed attributes to frequently exhibit high values of Ilyas et al.'s strength formula (Formula 3.1.1) even when paired with semantically unrelated attributes in the dataset. We further expect that the modified strength formula we presented (Formula 3.1.2) will exclude these false pairings from the phase 1 output.

We observe this expected behavior across all three datasets. As shown in Table 1, Formula 3.1.2 excludes 30% to 60% of the column pairs that Formula 3.1.1 identifies as potential functional dependencies. These excluded column pairs tend to have dependent attributes that are highly skewed toward their modal value. On average, the dependent attributes from the excluded column pairs have the same value on 91% to 97% of all records in the dataset.

As a concrete example of the difference between the two strength formulas, consider the Flights dataset's "cancelled" and "cancellation_code" attributes. Both are NULL for the 95% of records that represent flights that were not canceled; for the remaining 5% of records, "canceled" contains the value 1.0 and "cancellation_code" contains one of the letters A though C. Both exhibit high values of Formula 3.1.1 with at least 10 other attributes in the dataset, the majority of which do not correspond to semantic relationships in the Flights domain model. However, these semantically unfounded relationships have near-zero values of our Formula 3.1.2 and the algorithm includes only the dependency from "cancellation_code" to "cancelled" in its output.

Attribute merging: As outlined in Section 3.1.4, we expect the algorithm to merge together attributes that contain the same information content in order to simplify its longest path computations. We observe correct attribute merges across all three datasets and observe no invalid merges.

A particularly interesting example of attribute merging occurs in the GitHub dataset where a pair of user entities are entirely merged together. The "base_user" and the "base_repo_owner" entities refer to the same user instance across every record in the dataset. As a result, their constituent fields always contain exactly the same value and are merged together. The two users are thus represented in the attribute tree by a single subtree of merged attributes.

4.2 Phase 2 results

Subtree matching: Our manual analysis of the experimental datasets identified several pairs of entities that had similar descriptive attributes and had good semantic basis to be matched and combined: Within the Flights dataset, the origin and destination airports should be matched. Within the Twitter dataset, the embedded retweet entity is really just a tweet, and should be matched with the top-level tweet entity. Similarly, the top-level user should match with the retweet's user, and the top-level place should match with the retweet's place. Within the GitHub dataset, there should be matches among all pairings of the 7 kinds of user entities, the 2 repository entities, and the 2 commit entities.

These expectations are summarized in Table 2's second column, which lists the number of matching entity pairs we manually identified in each dataset. The table's "Our algorithm" section compares phase 2's performance against those counts. It shows that phase 2 identifies all but one of the expected entity matches and also identifies semantically meaningful entity matches that we did not manually predict.

Phase 2 ignores the predicted entity match between the GitHub commit entities. We predicted this match because we noticed that the commits' unique identifiers — "head_sha" and "base_sha" — overlap and we assumed that they were each associated with a set of stable descriptive attributes describing associated user and repository entities. Our assumptions hold true for the head commit, which corresponds to a subtree that has "head_sha" as its parent and that embeds the head repository and head user entities. The base commits, however, are not stably associated with specific users or repositories. As a result, the base user and base repository attributes demonstrate weak functional relationships with "base_sha" and are not placed within the base commit's subtree. This leads the two commit entities to have dissimilar subtrees that do not match in phase 2. Given that the commits do not behave as we initially assumed, the phase 2 algorithm's output is a slightly more accurate reflection of the underlying data than our manual analysis. This is another example of our manual analysis being too sensitive to the attributes' original JSON nesting.

In addition to the 26 matches we anticipated during our analysis, seven matches were identified that we did not expect. For example, the algorithm reveals that Twitter's retweet entity contains an additional partial user to model whether the tweet is in reply to another member of the network. This partial user has only the fields "retweeted_status_in_reply_to_user_id," "retweeted_status_in_reply_to_user_id_str," and "retweeted_status_in_reply_to_user_name." Despite this sparsity of descriptive attributes, phase 1 allocates the partial entity its own subtree which matches with both the retweeted user and the top-level user during phase 2. These unexpected matches accurately reflect overlapping entities. Given that the in-reply-to user does not exist as its own object in the JSON input, this example represents another instance of our algorithm discovering semantic entities absent from the initial structure of the dataset.

There are no erroneous phase 2 matches found for any of the experimental data sets. All identified matches represent subtrees containing overlapping entities.

Attribute matching: Within each pair of matched entities, phase 2 highlights the pairs of semantically equivalent attributes that the two entities contain. In order to gauge phase 2's attribute matching performance, we consider three measures for each entity pair: 1) the number of attribute matches identified across the two entities, 2) the number of these attribute matches that accurately capture semantic equivalence, and 3) the number of these attribute matches do not accurately capture semantic equivalence and should

	# entity matches expected	Our algorithm				Shanmugasundaram et al.'s Algorithm			
		# expected found	# expected missing	# unexpected found	% unexpected meaningful	# expected found	# expected missing	# unexpected found	% unexpected meaningful
Flights	1	1	0	2	100%	0	1	0	N/A
GitHub	23	22	1	1	100%	5	18	0	N/A
Twitter	3	3	0	4	100%	2	1	0	N/A

Table 2: Summary of the entity matches found by both our algorithm and Shanmugasundaram et al.'s algorithm. Unexpected matches are considered "meaningful" if they have semantic underpinnings and correctly reflect overlapping domains.

	Flights	*Twitter*	*GitHub*
# attribute pairs	15	47	79
# correct attribute pairs	15	46	79
# incorrect attribute pairs	0	1	0
# missing attribute pairs	0	15	11

Table 3: Summary of attribute pairs found in each dataset.

not have been identified. The first three rows of Table 3 show the sum of these performance measures across all of the entity pairs found in each dataset. The numbers reflect that phase 2 correctly identifies equivalent attribute pairs in every dataset. Of the 141 attribute matches made across all three datasets, phase 2 only makes one incorrect match (it incorrectly matches two of Twitter's boolean fields).

While phase 2 rarely matches attributes incorrectly, it sometimes omits matches between semantically related attributes. We consider phase 2 to have missed a relevant attribute pair when an entity match contains an orphan attribute that has a semantically equivalent attribute elsewhere in the tree. The final row of Table 3 shows the number of these missing attribute pairs from each of the experimental datasets. In total there were 26 attributes across the datasets that could have been matched but were not. Of these 26, 24 were due to the fact that phase 2 only searches for matching attributes within matching subtrees of the attribute tree we construct in phase 1. In these 24 cases, the matching attribute was located outside of the relevant subtree being searched. This was usually due to the attribute being unstable, and phase 1 placing the attribute in the root instead of a particular subtree. The two remaining missed matches were a side-effect of the one incorrect match in the Twitter dataset — the two attributes that were incorrectly matched were not available for their correct partners.

4.3 Phase 3 results

Schema generation: For all three datasets, phase 3 creates a relational schema that contains a root relation that includes columns for (1) descriptive attributes of the top-level entity, (2) unstable attributes associated with embedded entities, and (3) foreign keys linking to the other relations in the final schema. As expected, the number of relations in the phase 3 schemas is significantly lower (50%-65%) than the number of phase 1 attribute groups. The Flights schema contains 10 relations, the Twitter schema contains 8, and the GitHub schema contains 8. For each of the three datasets, 4 of these relations result from phase 2 entity matches. The other relations result from large cardinality changes.

Phase 3's assumption that large drops in cardinality may signal the presence of an embedded entity frequently holds across all three datasets. For example, phase 3 detects GitHub's milestone entities due a large cardinality drop. In other cases, however, the relations due to cardinality are less semantically significant and instead represent opportunities for normalization. For example, the GitHub schema includes a relation off of the root that contains four semantically unrelated attributes that phase 3 creates because it has only 328K unique rows, while the root has 1M rows.

4.4 Comparison to Alternative Approaches

We compared our approach to two alternative approaches for mapping nested key-value data to relational schemas:

(1) Argo is significantly simpler than our algorithm because it does not perform entity identification and instead proposes a generic relational encoding of arbitrary JSON documents [4]. As described in Section 2, Argo stores documents in ternary relations that contain rows for every key in every document (each row stores the document ID, the key's name, and the key's value). Argo preserves type information by creating three ternary relations differentiated by the type of their "value" columns (boolean, text, and doubles).

(2) Shanmugasundaram et al. describe the shared inlining algorithm which generates a relational schema by analyzing a graph of the XML DTD associated with its input[6]. The DTD graph contains nodes for all elements in the input DTD and represents the nesting relationships between those elements with edges. The algorithm creates a relation for all nodes in the DTD graph with an in-degree of 0 (these are accessible only if made into relations) or with an in-degree greater than 1 (these are elements that are "shared" among multiple parent elements). Within our datasets, the algorithm inlines all other nodes into their nearest ancestors.

Note that the shared inlining approach requires XML DTDs, but none of our experimental datasets originally include this schema information. For the JSON-encoded GitHub and Twitter datasets, we generated DTDs with elements corresponding to the original nesting structure of the documents. For the CSV-encoded Flights dataset, we generated a DTD with a single element that contains all attributes.

Entity matching: Table 2 compares the number of entity matches identified by our algorithm and the number of matches identified by the shared inlining algorithm. We omit Argo from this part of the comparison, since it does not perform entity identification or matching.

While our algorithm identifies all three expected entity matches within the Twitter dataset, the shared inlining algorithm only matches the top-level user to the retweeted user and the top-level place to the retweeted place. The match between the top-level user and retweeted-user is identified because the two entities both appear beneath a "user" key in the original dataset ("user" and "retweeted_status.user" respectively). The generated DTD represents these keys

[6]We do not discuss their additional hybrid inlining algorithm because it produces a single relation for our datasets.

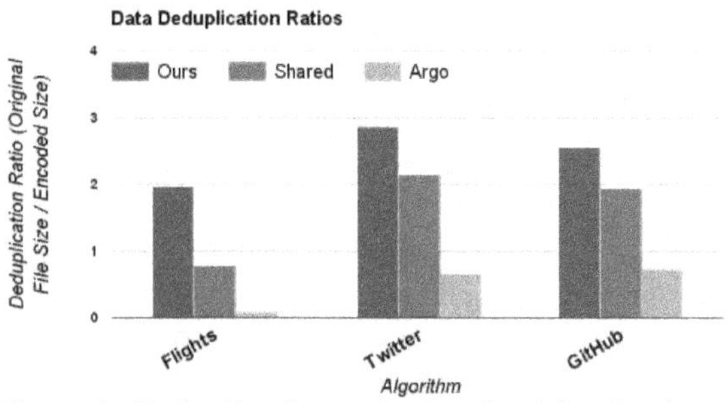

Figure 6: Deduplication ratios by algorithm by dataset.

with a single <user> element that may be nested within either a <root> element or a <retweeted_status> element. Since <user> may be nested within multiple elements, its in-degree in the DTD graph is greater than 1 and the shared inlining algorithm creates a separate relation to model the matched user entities. Similarly, the top-level place and retweeted place occur beneath a common key, enabling the shared inlining algorithm to merge them into one relation.

Since the top-level tweet and the retweeted-status do not appear beneath a common key in the input dataset, the shared inlining algorithm is not sensitive to their semantic relationship and cannot identify this expected entity match. Moreover, the shared inlining algorithm cannot detect any of the unexpected entity matches discovered by our algorithm because those matches involve groupings of input attributes that are not captured by the original JSON nesting.

The shared inlining algorithm similarly omits entities from GitHub dataset. The algorithm only successfully identifies 5 of the 23 expected entity matches — one match from the head repository to the base repository and four among pairings of the user entities. Only the user entities that are nested beneath the same key within the original JSON document are matched by the shared inlining algorithm. Since the seven user entities present in the dataset appear beneath four distinct keys ("milestone_creator," "user," "owner," and "assignee"), the shared inlining algorithm cannot identify the remaining 17 matches that occur among the dataset's users.

The shared inlining algorithm is unable to detect any entity matches from the flat Flights DTD.

Data deduplication: As described above, an advantage of converting nested data into relational data is the deduplication of records that are in multiple nested locations. Thus, we loaded each of the experimental datasets into the three proposed schemas and measured each schema's data size reduction ratio (the size of the input file divided by the size of the schema's relations). Figure 6 shows these results.

The Argo encoding carries significant storage overhead because it creates a large number of tuples (1 per key per document) that each require a 22-byte tuple header, an 8-byte document identifier ("objid"), and a variable length string to store key names. As a result of this storage overhead, the Argo encoding expands all of the input datasets.

The shared inlining algorithm exhibits better storage performance than Argo because it creates many fewer tuples (1 to 4 per document, depending on the dataset) and because it stores key names as column names. This latter optimization allows the algorithm to reduce the data size by roughly 2x for the Twitter and GitHub datasets. However, the Flights dataset does not reduce in size because its original CSV encoding already avoided redundant storage of key names. The shared inlining algorithm instead causes the Flights dataset to expand as a result of tuple headers and document ids.

Our algorithm achieves significantly more data size reduction for all three experimental datasets. Similar to the shared inlining algorithm, our algorithm stores key-names as column names which dramatically reduces the size of the Twitter and GitHub datasets. However, our algorithm achieves more data reduction for these datasets and for the Flights dataset because it uses foreign-key references to eliminate the duplication inherent in the entity matches it finds.

Query performance: In Appendix G, we analyze the runtimes of 5 queries to further compare and contrast these three approaches to schema generation.

5. FUTURE WORK

Our algorithm has two limitations which represent opportunities for future work. First, our algorithm does not support functional dependencies with multiple attributes on the left-hand side (e.g. functional dependencies in which one attribute depends on 2+ attributes). To support this class of dependency, our algorithm requires three extensions:

Dependency enumeration: Since it is computationally intractable to evaluate Condition 3.1.1 for all possible functional dependencies when multiple LHS attributes are allowed, a more intelligent exploration of the search space will be required. Flach et al. present a promising solution to this exploration problem which we could leverage [8].

Attribute tree construction: Our attribute tree construction algorithm creates a directed graph from the mined functional dependencies. If functional dependencies with multiple LHS attributes are allowed, we must either devise a strategy for modeling these attributes as merged nodes that are compatible with our existing algorithm or must extend the algorithm to handle the resulting hyper-graphs directly.

Entity matching: The entity matching algorithm identifies matches by joining subtrees on their parent attributes. Since subtrees will potentially have many parents when multiple LHS attributes are allowed, a new process for joining subtrees will be required. The naive approach simply joins subtrees on all combinations of their parent attributes; since this could greatly bloat the space of subtree matches, investigation of more efficient strategies will likely be needed.

The second limitation of our work is that we entirely ignore all structural information associated with our input datasets. While we contend that structural information is often misleading or otherwise unreliable, our approach of completely disregarding structural cues is heavy-handed. We expect that future research into a hybrid solution that integrates our data-driven approach with structural cues will yield higher quality schemas. We further expect that structural cues can also be leveraged to more intelligently explore the functional dependency search space.

6. CONCLUSION

We have presented an algorithm that identifies the structures implicit in semistructured datasets and materializes those structures as relational schemas. Our experiments show that our algorithm generates reasonable schemas for datasets from disparate domains, irrespective of their input format. While our algorithm's schemas often contradicted our expectations, the algorithm's schemas captured the patterns of the input data better than our manual analysis.

Acknowledgments This work was sponsored by the NSF under grant IIS-1527118. We thank Wenbo Tao, Lambros Flokas, and the anonymous SIGMOD 2016 reviewers for their insightful feedback on earlier versions of this manuscript.
Downloads Our experimental datasets are available at http://s3.amazonaws.com/discala-abadi-2016/index.html.

7. REFERENCES

[1] S. Bell. Dependency mining in relational databases. In *Qualitative and Quantitative Practical Reasoning*. 1997.

[2] D. Bitton, J. Millman, and S. Torgersen. A feasibility and performance study of dependency inference [database design]. In *Proc. of ICDE*, 1989.

[3] P. Bohannon, J. Freire, P. Roy, and J. Simeon. From xml schema to relations: a cost-based approach to xml storage. In *Proc. of ICDE*, 2002.

[4] C. Chasseur, Y. Li, and J. M. Patel. Enabling json document stores in relational systems. In *WebDB*, 2013.

[5] A. Deutsch, M. Fernandez, and D. Suciu. Storing semistructured data with stored. In *SIGMOD*, 1999.

[6] F. Du, S. Amer-Yahia, and J. Freire. Shrex: managing xml documents in relational databases. In *VLDB*, 2004.

[7] R. Fagin, A. O. Mendelzon, and J. D. Ullman. A simplied universal relation assumption and its properties. *ACM Trans. Database Syst.*, Sept. 1982.

[8] P. A. Flach and I. Savnik. Database dependency discovery: A machine learning approach. *AI Commun.*, 12(3), 1999.

[9] D. Florescu and D. Kossmann. A performance evaluation of alternative mapping schemes for storing xml data in a relational database. In *Inria Research Report*, 1999.

[10] M. Garofalakis, A. Gionis, R. Rastogi, S. Seshadri, and K. Shim. Xtract: A system for extracting document type descriptors from xml documents. In *SIGMOD*, 2000.

[11] G. Gousios. The ghtorrent dataset and tool suite. In *Conference on Mining Software Repositories*, 2013.

[12] O. Hassanzadeh, S. H. Yeganeh, and R. J. Miller. Linking semistructured data on the web. In *WebDB*, 2011.

[13] Y. Huhtala, J. Kärkkäinen, P. Porkka, and H. Toivonen. Tane: An efficient algorithm for discovering functional and approximate dependencies. *The computer journal*, 1999.

[14] I. F. Ilyas, V. Markl, P. Haas, P. Brown, and A. Aboulnaga. Cords: Automatic discovery of correlations and soft functional dependencies. In *SIGMOD*, 2004.

[15] J. Kivinen and H. Mannila. Approximate inference of functional dependencies from relations. *Theoretical Computer Science*, pages 129 – 149, 1995.

[16] W.-S. Li and C. Clifton. Semint: A tool for identifying attribute correspondences in heterogeneous databases using neural networks. *Data & Knowledge Engineering*, 2000.

[17] D. Maier, J. D. Ullman, and M. Y. Vardi. On the Foundations of the Universal Relation Model. *ACM Trans. Database Syst.*, 9(2):283–308, June 1984.

[18] H. Mannila and K.-J. Räihä. Algorithms for inferring functional dependencies from relations. *DKE*, 1994.

[19] P. Minh-Duc, P. Linnea, E. Orri, and P. Boncz. Deriving an emergent relational schema from rdf data. In *WWW*, 2015.

[20] E. Rahm and P. A. Bernstein. A survey of approaches to automatic schema matching. *VLDBJ*, 10(4):334–350, 2001.

[21] A. Schmidt, M. Kersten, M. Windhouwer, and F. Waas. Efficient relational storage and retrieval of xml documents. In *WebDB*, pages 47–52, 2000.

[22] J. Shanmugasundaram, E. Shekita, J. Kiernan, R. Krishnamurthy, E. Viglas, J. Naughton, and I. Tatarinov. A general technique for querying xml documents using a relational database system. *SIGMOD Rec.*, pages 20–26, 2001.

[23] J. Shanmugasundaram, K. Tufte, G. He, C. Zhang, D. DeWitt, and J. Naughton. Relational databases for querying xml documents: Limitations and opportunities. pages 302–314, 1999.

[24] D. Tahara, T. Diamond, and D. J. Abadi. Sinew: A sql system for multi-structured data. In *SIGMOD*, 2014.

[25] K. Wang and H. Liu. Schema discovery for semistructured data. In *KDD*, 1997.

[26] K. Wang and H. Liu. Discovering typical structures of documents: A road map approach. In *SIGIR*, 1998.

[27] H. Zhang and F. W. Tompa. Querying xml documents by dynamic shredding. In *DocEng*, 2004.

APPENDIX

A. FLATTENING INPUT DATA

As described above, input datasets must be flattened before phase 1. We accomplish this with three transformations:

Objects nested within objects: Objects nested inside of one another are flattened by creating a column for each of the leaf values contained in the objects. Each column is labeled with the concatenation of the attribute names that appear along the leaf's corresponding nesting path. Label collisions are resolved by appending the depth of the leaf within the original document to the concatenated name.

Arrays of scalar values: Scalar arrays (e.g. arrays of integers) are casted to strings for the algorithm's computations. When loaded into the final schema, the arrays are stored instead using the target database's preferred storage scheme (e.g. 1st-class array types or separate tables).

Arrays of nested objects: Objects containing arrays of other objects require the most involved transformations because they model either one-to-many or many-to-many associations, but our algorithm searches for one-to-one or many-to-one relationships. In order to overcome this incompatibility, each nested array can be treated as an independent sub-instance of the original schema generation problem. If the array models a one-to-many relationship, a foreign key is added from the sub-instance's root back to the schema for its parent instance. If the array models a many-to-many relationship, a linking object that joins the sub-instance to the schema for its parent instance must be introduced.

B. IMPROVING PHASE 2 PERFORMANCE

Although the join operation described in Section 3.2.2 effectively identifies record pairs with matching parent values, in many cases its computation will be expensive. In the worst case, when both subtrees' parent attributes contain a single shared value, the size of the join set is the square of the number of records in the training set. To reduce the size of the join and the cost of the subsequent operations, we preprocess each subtree before performing any join operations. For each subtree, we compute a deduplicated table that contains the unique permutations of the subtree's values, along with the frequency of each permutation in the training set. The result of this process for the $A_{authEmail}$ subtree is:

authEmail	*authName*	*authINum*	*authIName*	*freq*
js@e.pfl	J. Snow	1	EPFL	2
dd@ca.uk	D. Duck	14	Cambridge	1

Instead of performing subtree joins as self joins on the original flat table, we perform joins between the subtrees' deduplicated tables. Since all other attributes within the subtree exhibit soft functional dependencies on the parent attributes, the parents will be nearly unique within these deduplicated tables. Consequently, the upper bound on the size of the condensed join result is approximately the size of the training set and, in many cases, significantly smaller.

Every row in the condensed join set will contain a frequency column from each of the deduplicated tables. The product of these frequencies reflects the number of times that a row would repeat in the uncondensed join set. As a result, to compute the attribute matrices from the condensed join sets, we must modify phase 2 to increment cells by the product of the frequency columns, instead of by 1.

C. REDUNDANT PHASE 2 MATCHES

As described in Section 3.2.2, our matching algorithm attempts to match entire subtrees from the phase 1 attribute tree. In other words, it combines all attributes that descend from a particular node in the attribute tree into a single bucket, before attempting to match with a different bucket of attributes from a different subtree. As described in step 3 above, at least 50% of the attributes in the smaller bucket have to match with attributes in the larger bucket for the two subtrees to be considered a match. Therefore, once we discover that two subtrees are a match, additional matches will likely be found in subtrees of those subtrees.

On one hand, it is totally unnecessary to compare subtrees of matching subtrees. For example, as shown in Figure 2, once we have discovered that the subtree corresponding to "author" matches with the subtree corresponding to "reviewer" (shown in red), it is unsurprising that the nested institution information within the author and reviewer trees also matches (shown in purple). Checking the two institution subtrees therefore seems like a waste of effort.

We still check these sub-subtrees for a match because the inner match can reveal interesting insights into the relationship between the sub-subtrees and their parent subtrees. In particular, if the size of the join set between the two sub-subtrees is at least 50% larger than the join set between the two parent subtrees, we conclude that the entities represented by the sub-subtrees are semantically separate from the entities represented by their parent subtrees. We assume this because the join set's size can only increase significantly if either (1) some records from the training set do not join for the parent match but do join for the inner match or (2) the entity set represented by the inner match has significantly lower cardinality than the entity set represented by the parent match. Since both behaviors indicate the inner match behaves differently than the outer match, we show sub-subtree matches if the join set size increases sufficiently.

D. ATTRIBUTE TREE IMPROVEMENT

Due to the functional relationships entities typically exhibit, we expect phase 1 to isolate all of the stable attributes associated with an entity inside of a single subtree whose parent is the entity's unique identifier. Nevertheless, phase 1 sometimes produces suboptimal trees that place attributes outside of their entity's subtree. Although these erroneous placements do not reflect a correct semantic understanding of the data, they typically cannot be detected algorithmically because they do reflect the functional structures identified by phase 1. In the special case that these suboptimal placements occur within nested subtree matches, however, the phase 2 output provides a chance to correct these errors.

Matches between subtrees that begin at higher levels in the attribute tree cover more of the full tree and, consequently, are more likely to identify matching attribute pairs. Thus, if there is an orphaned attribute a_{orphan} in a subtree match, and the subtree match is nested within a match at a higher point in the tree, and the higher subtree match pairs a_{orphan} with another attribute, then there is likely an error within the original attribute tree. These errors are fixed by moving the attribute paired with a_{orphan} into the lower subtree.

E. ATTRIBUTE CLUSTERING

The algorithm above compares every pair of subtrees to see if there is a match, and during this comparison operation, compares every pair of attributes across these two subtrees. To reduce the space of both sets of comparisons, we analyze the domain of each attribute before we perform subtree matching, and cluster attributes into groups that contain similar values. The algorithm then only attempts to match subtrees whose parent attributes belong to the same cluster, as these are the only subtrees whose domains are likely to overlap. Similarly, when comparing two subtrees, phase 2 only considers pairs of attributes in same cluster.

We form these attribute groups according to a process inspired by Li and Clifton's clustering techniques [16]. For each text based attribute in the dataset we compute: 1) the maximum, minimum, variance, and average of the length of its values, 2) its proportion of numeric characters, 3) its proportion of punctuation characters, and 4) its proportion of whitespace characters. We use these statistics as the features for a bisecting k-means clustering instance. We choose K programmatically by computing clusterings with progressively increasing values of K and choosing the final clustering by analyzing the within-cluster-sum-of-squares:

$$\sum_{c \in clusters} \sum_{vector \in c} distance(vector, centroid(c))^2$$

We continue adding clusters until this function plateaus or increases from a previous value. Although lower K values limit the impact of this optimization, we favor lower values because they minimize the risk that matching attributes are erroneously separated into distinct clusters.

F. THE GITHUB SCHEMA

Interpreting the phase 3 diagrams: Figure 7 shows the phase 3 schema that our algorithm produces for the GitHub dataset. Each box in the diagram represents a relation in the final schema. For all relations:

- Attribute names that are written in upper-case letters are either primary or foreign keys inserted by phase 3.
- Foreign keys point to the relation whose header matches their name (e.g. the key "HR_ID" points to the relation with the header "HR").
- Relations joined by foreign key references are connected with lines (arrows point into the referenced relation).

For relations that do not participate in entity matches, a one-to-one relationship exists from input attributes to physical attributes in the phase 3 schema (these are the single-column boxes in the diagram). Each lower-cased cell in these relations represents an input attribute that phase 3 included directly in its physical schema. Consider the "MS1" relation in the diagram: "ms_title" is an input attribute mapped to a physical attribute of the same name.

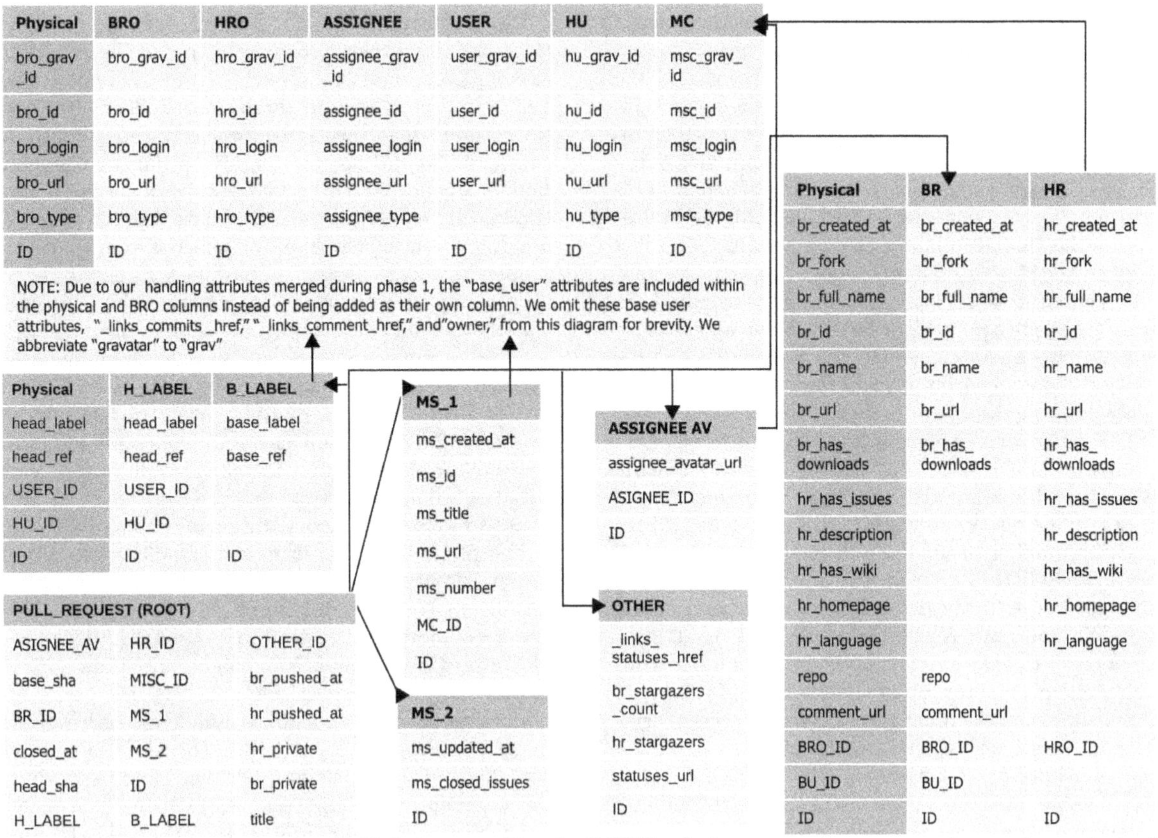

Figure 7: The phase 3 schema for the GitHub dataset. For the ROOT relation, we omit many attributes due to lack of space. We use the following abbreviations: "BR" is "base_repo," "BRO" is "base_repo_owner," "HR" is "head_repo," "HRO" is "head_repo_owner," "MS" is "milestone," "MC" is "milestone_creator," "BU" is "base_user" and "HU" is "head_user."

For relations that do participate in phase 2 entity matches, an n-to-one relationship exists from input attributes to physical attributes in the phase 3 schema (these are the multi-column boxes in the diagram). These relations include a dark gray column labeled "physical" that lists the names of the physical attributes in the phase 3 schema. Each additional column represents a distinct attribute group that was merged onto the relation. These columns show the mapping from that groups' input attributes to the physical schema: each attribute contained within the group appears on the same row as the physical attribute that it was mapped onto. Consider the relation containing "BR" (base_repo) and "HR" (head_repo) at the right of the figure: the first row indicates that input attributes "br_created_at" and "hr_created_at" both map onto the physical attribute "br_created_at."

Phase 1 attribute trees: Although we lack sufficient space to include the complete phase 1 attribute tree, the diagram shows nearly all of the original attribute groups because the phase 1 tree forms the basis of the phase 3 schema.

Phase 2 matches: The schema diagram shows all of GitHub's entity and attribute matches. Note that a single entity match may be represented by multiple relations if the matched entities contained several attribute groups.

G. QUERY PERFORMANCE COMPARISON

In Table 4, we present the runtimes of 5 queries over our algorithm's schema, the shared inlining schema, and Argo's schema. While the queries do not comprise a complete benchmark, they offer a view into the kinds of queries that may benefit from our algorithm's schema. All measurements represent cold-cache runtimes averaged over three runs. The queries were run on PostgreSQL on an Amazon EC2 instance with 8 vCPUs and 61 GiB of memory (this machine also was used for the performance evaluation in Appendix H).

Query #	*Our Algorithm*	*Shared-inlining*	*Argo*
1	0.7	28.7	559.1
2	32.7	95.1	1,635
3	1.9	5.6	6.7
4	25.2	37.1	36.9
5	23.9	16.3	35.5

Table 4: Runtimes in seconds for Appendix G's queries.

Query #1: This query projects a list of unique (user_id, user_login) pairs from the GitHub dataset, including pairs from all 7 kinds of user entities. This query requires only a sequential scan when expressed over our algorithm's schema because it merges all 7 users into a single relation. In contrast it must be expressed as the UNION of 4 queries in the shared inlining schema and as the UNION of 7 queries in Argo's schema. As a result, when run over our schema the query is 41x faster than it is over the shared inlining schema and 810x faster than it is over the Argo schema.

Query #2: This query identifies the average age of each Twitter user (current time - creation time). Argo's schema requires UNIONs and JOINs to express this query, which causes the query's runtime over Argo's schema to exceed the other schemas' runtimes by more than an order of magnitude. In contrast, both our algorithm's schema and the shared inlining schema store Twitter users as a single relation and implement this query as an aggregate over that single relation. Despite this similarity, on our schema this query runs 2.9x faster than on the shared inlining schema. This disparity exists because our schema contains only 5.9M user records while the shared inlining schema contains 20M user records. Since the shared inlining schema does not deduplicate its merged entities, its query performance usually benefits less from the entities it identifies than our algorithm.

Query #3: This query calculates the average flight time for all flights departing from "Anchorage, AK". Since the Flights dataset is significantly smaller when encoded in our schema than when encoded in either the Argo or shared inlining schemas, this query runs fastest over our schema (2.9x faster than shared inlining and 3.5x faster than Argo).

Query #4: This query calculates the number of pull requests and the number of unique pull requests authors per repository in the GitHub dataset. Since the query accesses many different entities in the dataset, all three schemas must perform JOINS and must read a large subset of the dataset from disk in order to answer this query. As a result, the runtime is relatively even across all of the schemas (our schema is only 1.4x faster than the other two schemas for this query).

Query #5: This query calculates the number of unique pull-request authors per repository in the GitHub dataset. This query demonstrates an advantage of the shared inlining schema over our algorithm's schema: since shared inlining includes the document ID on all records, repositories can be joined to authors without accessing the root pull-request data. In contrast, our algorithm must join the repository and user entities through the root relation. As a result, our schema is 1.4x slower than the shared inlining schema (although our schema still is 1.5x faster than Argo's).

H. IMPLEMENTATION & PERFORMANCE

Implementation: Given that performance is not a focus of this paper, we did not build a production-grade, highly optimized implementation of our algorithm. We instead implement the algorithm as a Ruby application which delegates as much computation as possible to a Postgres server. The Ruby application loads the input dataset into a single Postgres relation and then queries this relation for the values it requires (the attribute cardinalities required by phase 1 are performed via COUNT DISTINCT queries, and the subtree matching required by phase 2 is done via JOINS). These queries are performed in parallel to improve performance.

The decision to push this logic into Postgres simplifies our software, but couples our implementation to the peculiarities of the Postgres query optimizer. While the optimizer often chooses performant execution plans, on some inputs it selects plans that are significantly slower than equivalent alternatives. In particular, the optimizer struggles with queries involving strings with long common prefixes (e.g. URLs on the same domain or Twitter messages with identical content). When the optimizer chooses to sort the dataset to implement a COUNT DISTINCT or JOIN on these string attributes with common prefixes, the time required to compare the common prefixes becomes significant. In some cases we observe an order of magnitude slowdown compared to the same operation implemented with a hashing strategy.

Performance: For the Twitter dataset, which was the largest of the three we considered, phase 1 required 31 hours to complete, phase 2 required 3.7 hours, and phase 3 required 3.61 minutes. Although these times collectively seem high, we reiterate that they reflect only an upper bound on runtime since we did not thoroughly optimize our implementation. Many opportunities for optimization exist, including 1) eliminating comparisons of attribute pairs in phase 1 when functional relationships can be inferred from their transitive properties and 2) applying a hashing strategy to reduce time spent comparing frequently-occurring string prefixes.

Even without these implementation improvements, our algorithm's runtime can be reduced by sampling the input dataset. In order to explore sampling's feasibility, we ran phases 1 and 2 over a random subset of 1 million Twitter records (10% of the full dataset). Since phase 3's runtime was already short relative to the other phases, we continued with the full dataset in this stage. Over this random sample, phase 1 required 2.7 hours and phase 2 required 5.1 minutes.

The phase 1 output from the sampled data is generally similar to the phase 1 output from the entire dataset. Within specific subtrees, there is some shifting of parent attributes and some movement of attributes deeper into the same tree (downward movement is common because the sampled dataset includes less entity repetition and it is thus easier for functional dependencies to achieve a high strength value). Since these modifications occur within the same subtree, they do not affect phase 2 attribute matches and generally do not cause semantically important shifts in the final schema.

There are, however, 6 attributes that switch subtrees in the sampled attribute tree and no longer descend from their original parents. These movements negatively impact the semantic meaning of the attribute tree and interfere with subsequent matching in phase 2. Specifically, these changed attributes cause the sampled phase 2 output to exclude 3 of the 4 unexpected entity matches that were originally identified. These matches are between subtrees containing 2-3 attributes each. They are excluded because their constituent attributes do not form subtrees in the sampled attribute tree and are instead merged together. Despite the omission of these entity matches, we still believe that sampling is a viable strategy since phase 2 still identifies all 3 expected entity matches and 1 of the 4 unexpected matches.

The sampled phase 2 output additionally includes two matches that were not identified from the full dataset. The first match occurs between two small subtrees containing skewed boolean attributes. While some of the booleans are semantically related, the overall entity-match is not semantically meaningful and should not have been identified. The second match occurs between a subtree rooted at "retweeted_status_in_reply_to_status_id" and the root relation. Since both parent attributes contain Tweet IDs, their domains overlap frequently. However, this match also lacks semantic meaning because the attributes beneath the in-reply-to ID do not form a coherent entity and are instead introduced due to noise in the phase 1 tree. These erroneous matches introduce some noise into the phase 2 output, but only affect a few fringe attributes in the final schema.

While we recommend that users run our algorithm over their full datasets for the best results, we find that especially time-sensitive users can trade some output quality for time-savings by running our algorithm over a random sample of their data.

Data Blocks: Hybrid OLTP and OLAP on Compressed Storage using both Vectorization and Compilation

Harald Lang[1], Tobias Mühlbauer[1], Florian Funke[2,*],
Peter Boncz[3,*], Thomas Neumann[1], Alfons Kemper[1]

[1]Technical University Munich, [2]Snowflake Computing, [3]Centrum Wiskunde & Informatica
{harald.lang,muehlbau,neumann,kemper}@in.tum.de, florian.funke@snowflake.net, boncz@cwi.nl

ABSTRACT

This work aims at reducing the main-memory footprint in high performance hybrid OLTP & OLAP databases, while retaining high query performance and transactional throughput. For this purpose, an innovative compressed columnar storage format for cold data, called *Data Blocks* is introduced. Data Blocks further incorporate a new light-weight index structure called *Positional SMA* that narrows scan ranges within Data Blocks even if the entire block cannot be ruled out. To achieve highest OLTP performance, the compression schemes of Data Blocks are very light-weight, such that OLTP transactions can still quickly access individual tuples. This sets our storage scheme apart from those used in specialized analytical databases where data must usually be bit-unpacked. Up to now, high-performance analytical systems use either vectorized query execution or "just-in-time" (JIT) query compilation. The fine-grained adaptivity of Data Blocks necessitates the integration of the best features of each approach by an interpreted vectorized scan subsystem feeding into JIT-compiled query pipelines. Experimental evaluation of HyPer, our full-fledged hybrid OLTP & OLAP database system, shows that Data Blocks accelerate performance on a variety of query workloads while retaining high transaction throughput.

1. INTRODUCTION

In past years, a new database system architecture specialized for OLAP workloads has emerged. These OLAP systems store data in compressed columnar format and increase the CPU efficiency of query evaluation by more than an order of magnitude over traditional row-store database systems. The jump in query evaluation efficiency is typically achieved by using "vectorized" execution where, instead of interpreting query expressions tuple at a time, all operations are executed on blocks of values. The effect is reduced interpretation overhead because virtual functions implementing block-wise operations handle thousands of tuples

*Work done while at Technical University Munich.

SIGMOD'16, June 26-July 01, 2016, San Francisco, CA, USA

ISBN 978-1-4503-3531-7/16/06...$15.00

DOI: http://dx.doi.org/10.1145/2882903.2882925

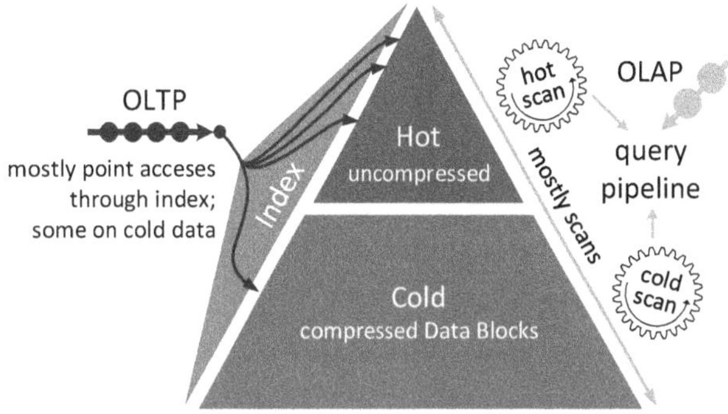

Figure 1: We propose the novel Data Block format that allows efficient scans and point accesses on compressed data and address the challenge of integrating multiple storage layout combinations in a compiling tuple-at-a-time query engine by using vectorization.

per function call, and the loop over the block inside these function implementations benefits from many loop-driven compiler optimizations including the automatic generation of SIMD instructions. Examples of such systems are IBM BLU [30], the Microsoft SQL Server Column Index subsystem [18], SAP HANA [12] and Vectorwise [39]. An alternative recently introduced way to accelerate query evaluation is "just-in-time" (JIT) compilation of SQL queries directly into executable code. This approach avoids query interpretation and its overheads altogether. Recent analytical systems using JIT are Drill, HyPer [16, 25] and Impala [34].

This paper describes the evolution of HyPer, our full-fledged main-memory database system, that was originally built with a JIT-compiling query engine to incorporate vectorization in the context of our novel compressed columnar storage format, "Data Blocks" (cf., Figure 1). HyPer differs from most of the aforementioned systems in that it aims to accomodate *both* high performance OLTP alongside OLAP running against the same database state and storage backend. Our primary goal is to reduce the main-memory footprint of HyPer by introducing compression while retaining the high OLTP and OLAP performance of the original system. To achieve this goal, we contribute (i) Data Blocks, a novel compressed columnar storage format for hybrid database systems, (ii) light-weight indexing on compressed data for improved scan performance, (iii) SIMD-optimized algorithms for predicate evaluation, and (iv) a blueprint for the integration of multiple storage layout combinations in a compiling tuple-at-a-time query engine by using vectorization.

Designing hybrid database systems is challenging because the technical demands of both types of workloads are very

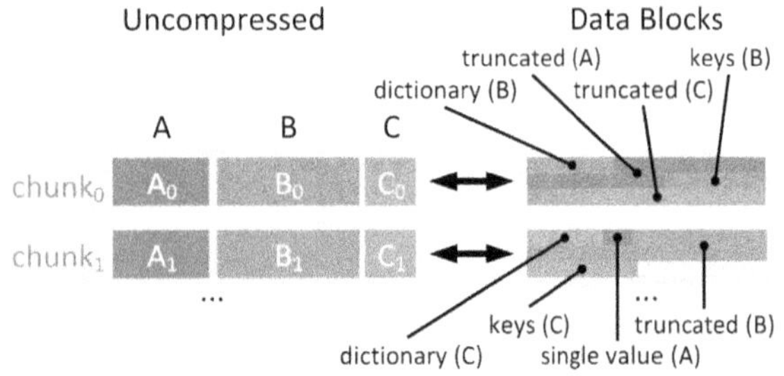

(a) Optimal compression techniques are chosen for each column in each block.

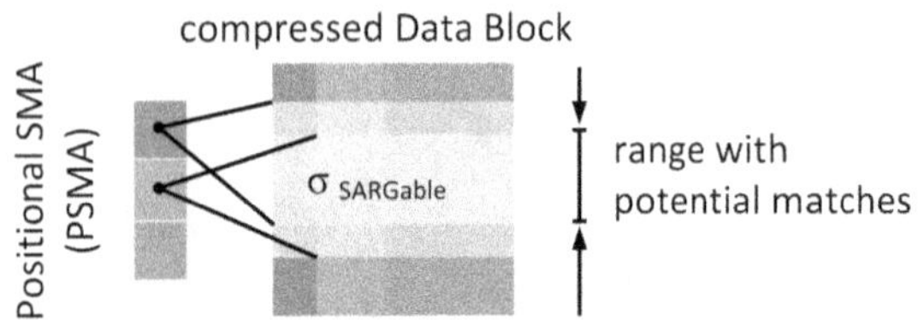

(b) Data Blocks store not only min and max values of attributes to skip blocks as a whole, but also light-weight indexes called Positional SMAs (PSMAs) that narrow the scan ranges on a per-attribute basis.

Figure 2: Overview of compressed Data Blocks

different and many fundamental physical optimizations are contradictory. Compression, for instance, reduces memory consumption and can improve analytical query performance due to reduced bandwidth usage. High performance transactional systems, on the other hand, refrain from using compression in order to keep individual tuple access fast. The fundamental difference to specialized analytical systems is that hybrids need to manage hot and cold data efficiently within a single database instance. One approach to address this problem is to divide relations into a read- and a write-optimized partition [17]. Updates are exclusively performed in the latter partition, which is then periodically merged into the read-optimized (compressed) partition. However, the merge process has $\mathcal{O}(n)$ time complexity (where n is the relation's cardinality) and requires re-compressing of the entire relation. This merge-process is a heavy-weight operation, which is why we propose an alternative strategy: Relations in our OLTP and OLAP system are divided into fixed-size chunks, which are individually compressed into read-optimized immutable Data Blocks when they are identified as cold using the compression scheme optimal for that chunk (Figure 2(a)). Once a chunk has been packed into a Data Block, the contained data is immutable (frozen). Updates are still possible by invalidating the cold record and moving it to the hot region. Thus, updates are internally transformed into a delete followed by an insert.

In order to allow for highly efficient access to individual records by tuple position, we only use light-weight compression schemes in Data Blocks. While many OLAP systems employ bit-packing techniques to achieve higher compression ratios, we refrain from doing so. Our experiments in Section 5.4 show that even with recent SIMD algorithms [27] for bit-packed data, scans only work very fast if their early filtering is either so selective that there are no qualifying tuples and entire blocks can be skipped, or all tuples in a block qualify. In case early filtering produces a sparse set of qualifying tuple positions, the cost of bit-unpacking the scan columns dwarfs the performance gains made by these recent techniques in early filtering. Our Data Blocks are designed to not only keep positional access on compressed data cheap, for OLTP workloads, but also to allow scan-based OLAP workloads to reap the benefit of early filtering while not losing this benefit in sparse tuple decompression.

To speed up scans on Data Blocks, we introduce a new "Positional" type of Small Materialized Aggregates [23] (PSMAs). PSMAs are light-weight indexes that narrow the scan range within a block even if the block cannot be skipped based on materialized min and max values (see Figure 2(b)).

The strength of tuple-at-a-time JIT compilation is its ability to generate code that is highly efficient for both OLAP and OLTP queries, in terms of needing few CPU instructions per processed tuple. Where vectorization passes data between operations through *memory*, tuple-at-a-time JIT passes data through CPU *registers*, saving performance-critical load/store instructions. Vectorization brings no CPU efficiency improvement at all for OLTP as its efficiency depends on executing expressions on many tuples at the same time while OLTP queries touch very few tuples and typically avoid scans. Choosing different compression schemes on a per-chunk basis, however, constitutes a challenge for JIT-compiling tuple-at-a-time query engines. As each compressed block can have a different memory layout, the number of code paths that have to be compiled for a scan grow exponentially. This leads to compilation times that are unacceptable for ad-hoc queries and transactions.

In this case, vectorized scans come to the rescue because their main strength is that they remain interpreted and can be pre-compiled. Further, vectorized scans are amenable to exploit SIMD and can express *adaptive* algorithms, opening a path to future further optimizations. As a final contribution we thus show how the strengths of both worlds, JIT compilation and vectorization, can be fused together using an interpreted vectorized scan subsystem that feeds into JIT-compiled tuple-at-a-time query pipelines. For vectorized predicate evaluation, we contribute new SSE/AVX2 SIMD algorithms. Overall, we show that this novel query engine together with our Data Blocks format yields a system that can save large amounts of main memory while still allowing for *both* highest performance OLTP and OLAP.

2. RELATED WORK

The work most closely related to Data Blocks is the storage format of IBM DB2 BLU [4, 30], which also consists of blocks representing all columns of a sequence of tuples stored in compressed columnar format inside the block (a concept introduced as PAX [3]) and provides mechanisms for early evaluation of range filters inside the scan. The main differences are that HyPer avoids bit-packing to keep positional access fast and introduces the PSMAs that further improve the evaluation of early selections.

We also note that recent work on advanced bit-packing schemes [22, 13] and their SIMD implementation [27] focus on the benefits of early filtering and either ignore the high per-tuple cost of bit-unpacking, or just position these bit-packed formats as a secondary storage structure. Our choice for byte-aligned storage mostly avoids this penalty and makes early filtering beneficial in a broader range of query workloads (see Section 5.4).

Vectorwise [39] proposed the idea to decompress chunks of the data into the CPU cache and process the decompressed data while it is cached. Vectorwise does not do any early filtering in scans and fully decompresses all scanned column ranges as it deems positional decompression too inefficient. In contrast, the efficient positional access of HyPer permits reaping the benefits of early evaluation of SARGable predicates inside the scan also in situations with moderate selectivities. Depending on the selectivity, early filtering can make scans in HyPer factors faster compared to Vectorwise (cf., Table 2); while on the other hand, byte-aligned compression on average increases space consumption $\leq \times 1.25$ (cf., Table 1).

Abadi et al. [1] thoroughly evaluated various compression schemes in column-oriented databases. They conclude that light-weight compression schemes should be preferred over heavy-weight schemes to operate directly on the compressed data. In contrast, we only consider filter operations and point-accesses on compressed data and do not pass compressed data to more complex operators like joins.

Oracle Database [28] uses block-wise compression but uses fewer compression schemes and is not built for efficient processing on modern CPUs. SAP HANA [12] is optimized for hybrid workloads, but as mentioned, follows a different approach where the entire relation is optimized for memory consumption and scan performance, whereas updates are performed in a separate partition, which is then periodically merged [17]. Thus, the distinction between hot and cold data is only implicit and depends on the size of the write-optimized partition. The Siberia framework [11], which is part of Microsoft's Hekaton engine [10], provides an interface for managing cold data. Unlike Data Blocks, it aims to reduce RAM usage primarily by evicting cold data to disk.

On the issue of integrating JIT-compiled query evaluation and vectorization, there has been work in Vectorwise on JIT-compiling projections and hash-joins [31]. This work showed only modest benefits of JIT integrated into vectorized operators, which subsequently remained an experimental feature only. The Impala [34] JIT approach is very different from our tuple-at-a-time JIT system which fuses all operators inside a query pipeline into a tight single loop. For each physical relational operator, Impala provides a C++ template class that is compiled with LLVM [19] into intermediate code in advance. During JIT query compilation, only the methods to handle tuples and expressions inside these operators are compiled directly into intermediate code and linked into this pre-compiled template class. The code of the different operators in a query pipeline are thus not fused. The Impala operators communicate with each other by using tuple buffers: in that sense they can be considered vectorized operators. The problem with this approach is that the main strength of JIT in minimizing the amount of needed instructions, passing data through registers and avoiding load/stores, is lost; the only real benefit is a more easy-to-understand and -test templated execution engine.

Vectorization enables the use of SIMD and facilitates algorithms that access data belonging to multiple tuples in parallel. In the database context, SIMD instructions have been used for example, to speed up selection scans [37, 35, 26], for bit unpacking [35, 27], bulk loading [24], sorting [6], and breadth-first search on graphs [32].

3. DATA BLOCKS

Data Blocks are self-contained containers that store one or more attribute chunks in a byte-addressable compressed format. The goal of Data Blocks is to conserve memory

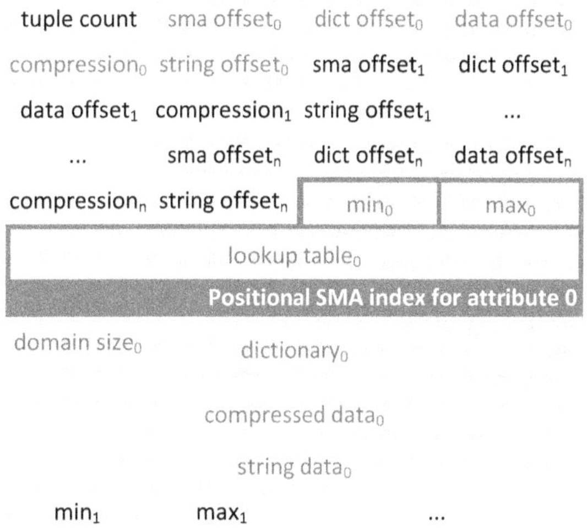

Figure 3: Layout of a Data Block for n attributes

while retaining the high OLTP and OLAP performance. By maintaining a flat structure without pointers, Data Blocks are also suitable for eviction to secondary storage. A Data Block contains all data required to reconstruct the stored attributes and our novel light-weight PSMA index structures, but no metadata, such as schema information, as replicating this in each block would waste space. Although orthogonal to this work, Data Blocks have further been designed with upcoming secondary storage solutions in mind, including non-volatile RAM (NVRAM) and byte-addressable flash storage. Data stored in Data Blocks on such storage devices can directly be addressed and read without bringing the whole Data Block into RAM. Several works have recently addressed the challenges of such storage devices [8, 33].

In HyPer, Data Blocks are used as a compressed in-memory storage format for cold data and for persistence. Identifying cold chunks of a relation is an orthogonal topic to the one addressed in this publication and has e.g., been addressed in [15, 9]. Once records have been packed into a Data Block, the contained data is immutable (frozen). Only delete operations are permitted where frozen records are marked with a flag. Updates are internally translated into a delete followed by an insert into a hot uncompressed chunk of the relation. In addition to immutability, Data Blocks have several convenient properties: (i) An optimal compression method is chosen based on the actual value distribution of an attribute within a chunk. This allows high compression ratios (cf., evaluation in Section 5). (ii) Only byte-addressable compression formats are used and the use of sub-byte encodings such as BitWeaving [22] is rejected in order to allow for efficient point accesses, which are required for OLTP and also for OLAP processing. (iii) SARGable scan restrictions, i.e., $=$, `is`, $<, \leq, >, \geq$, `between`, are evaluated on the compressed data representation using our aforementioned SIMD approach to find matches (cf., Section 4.2). As most compressed data in a Data Block is stored in either a 1-, 2-, or 4-byte integer, our SIMD algorithms provide even higher speedups than on uncompressed data. (iv) Data Blocks further contain Small Materialized Aggregates [23] (SMAs) that include a minimum and a maximum value for each attribute in the Data Block, which can be used to determine if a Data Block can be skipped during a scan. (v) Additionally, we include a novel light-weight index structure, PSMA, that maps a value to a range of positions on the Data Block where this value appears. Using the PSMAs, scan ranges can further be narrowed, even in cases where the value domain is large and entire blocks cannot be skipped.

SMAs and the PSMA indexes are not restricted to our Data Blocks format and could also be used for uncompressed chunks. However, in HyPer we refrain from using these for hot uncompressed data as maintaining the minimum and maximum information as well as updating the PSMA indexes would have a very high negative impact on transaction processing performance. The hot part of the database is usually rather small, such that the additional overhead is not justified.

3.1 Storage Layout

The first value in a Data Block is the number of records it contains. Typically, we store up to 2^{16} records in a Data Block. The tuple count is followed by information about each of the attributes. Per attribute we store the compression method that is used and offsets to the attribute's Small Materialized Aggregates (SMA) [23], dictionary, compressed data vector, and string data. The attribute information is followed by the actual data beginning with the SMA and PSMA for the first attribute. Figure 3 shows an example layout of a Data Block.

Since Data Blocks store data in a columnar layout, but can store all attributes of a tuple in the same block, they resemble the PAX [3] storage format.

3.2 Positional SMAs

Data Blocks store SMAs for each attribute in the block. The basic SMAs consist of the minimum (min) and maximum (max) value of each attribute stored in a Data Block. Similar to the Optimized Row Columnar (ORC) Hadoop file format [14], we use this domain knowledge to rule out entire Data Blocks if a SARGable (Search ARGument) predicate does not fall within the min and max values of a Data Block. Such min/max SMAs work particularly well on sorted attributes. In real data sets this is often the case for date or incrementing key attributes. If, for example, the `lineitem` relation of TPC-H is sorted on `l_shipdate`, Q_6, which has a highly selective predicate on `l_shipdate`, can be answered by only looking at a few Data Blocks as most blocks can already be ruled out by the basic SMAs. If, however, values are uniformly distributed over the relation, SMAs usually do not help. A single outlier can increase the min/max range to such an extent that the SMA cannot rule out the block anymore. In particular, this is also true for TPC-H data as generated by the *dbgen* tool. For our TPC-H evaluation of Data Blocks, we kept the insertion order of the generated CSV files, which are only sorted according to the primary keys. As all relevant attribute values are uniformly distributed over the blocks in this case, no blocks were skipped during query processing. Within a Data Block, however, usually only a fraction of the records will qualify.

To further narrow the scan range we thus extend an attribute's basic min/max information with a light-weight index structure, called Positional SMA (PSMA). Internally, PSMAs consist of a concise *lookup table* that is computed when a cold chunk is "frozen" into a Data Block. Each table entry contains a scan range $[b, e)$ that points to the compressed data inside a Data Block with potential matching tuples. For fixed size data types, the lookup table contains

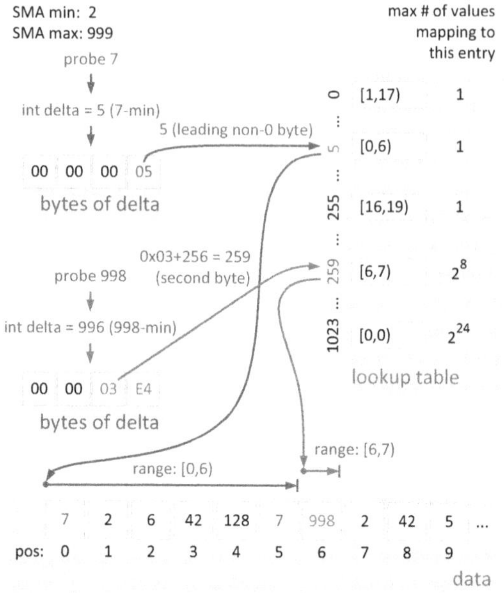

Figure 4: Examples of probing the lookup table of a Positional SMA index (PSMA)

2^8 entries for each byte of the data type, i.e., one entry for the values each byte can store. For example, for a 4-byte integer attribute, the lookup table contains $4 \times 2^8 = 1024$ entries. As such, multiple values map to the same lookup table entry stored in a single entry. If n values map to the same entry at index i and $[b_0, e_0), \ldots, [b_{n-1}, e_{n-1})$ are the ranges associated with these n values, then the range at entry i is widened to $[\min_{0 \leq j < n} b_j, \max_{0 \leq j < n} e_j)$. Thus, by design, the entries in the lookup table are more accurate for small values. Therefore, to improve the accuracy and the pruning power of the lookup table, we do not use the actual attribute value v itself, but its distance $\Delta(v)$ to the SMA's minimum value. The number of $\Delta(v)$ values whose range information is stored in the same lookup table entry increases with the size of the deltas. Delta values that fit into a single byte exclusively map to a single table entry (without collisions). For 2-byte delta values, 2^8 values map to the same table entry (2^{16} for 3-byte values, and 2^{24} for 4-byte values). Each entry points to a range on the compressed data where attribute values that map to this entry are stored. When looking for values equal to v, the associated scan range points to the position of first and one past the last element (right exclusive) where the most-significant non-zero byte equals the most-significant non-zero byte of v.

A lookup proceeds as follows: First, the delta between the probe value v and the SMA's min value is determined: $\Delta = v - \min$. Next, the highest non-0 byte of the delta, denoted as $\overline{\Delta}$, and the number of remaining bytes, denoted as r, are used to compute the index i into the lookup table: $i = \overline{\Delta} + r \times 256$. To determine the scan range for equality predicates, only a single lookup is required (Figure 4 illustrates example lookups and the implementation is sketched in Appendix B). For non-equality predicates like `between`, we perform multiple lookups and union the ranges of the entries. In the specific case of a `between a and b` predicate, we determine the lookup table indexes i_a of `a` and i_b of `b` and union the non-empty ranges for the indexes from i_a to i_b: range $= [\min_{i_a \leq i \leq i_b} b_b, \max_{i_a \leq i \leq i_b} e_i)$.

Building a lookup table is an $\mathcal{O}(n)$ operation. First, the table is initialized with empty ranges. Then, a scan over the column is performed. For each value v_i of the column $C = (v_0, \ldots, v_{n-1})$ the associated table entry is determined. If the entry contains an empty range, then the entry is set to $[i, i+1)$, otherwise the range end is updated to $i+1$.

As shown in Figure 3, an individual lookup table is stored for each attribute. In the presence of multiple SARGable predicates on different attributes, the individual lookup tables are queried and the returned scan ranges are then intersected to further narrow the scan range. Even though we store a lookup table for each attribute, the PSMAs consume only a fraction of the space of a Data Block. Each entry in the PSMA lookup table contains a range which is represented as two unsigned 4-byte integers. When n-byte values are indexed, the table consists of $n \times 2^8$ entries in total. Thus, typical memory footprints are 2 KB, 4 KB and 8 KB for values of type 1-, 2- or 4-byte integers, respectively. The PSMA lookup table is thus significantly smaller than a tree-based index structure on the 2^{16} values of a Data Block. Since the PSMA only limits the range that is scanned and generates the same access path as a full scan, the lookup table is also more robust than traditional index lookups and does not incur a performance penalty in cases when the range of potentially qualifying values is very large (or the entire vector qualifies). The precision of PSMAs depend on both the domain of the values as well as their order in the vector. Scan range narrowing works particularly well for values that have a small distance from the minimum value as fewer delta values share a lookup table entry.

PSMA range pruning is particularly efficient for data sets where similar values are physically clustered, such that values which share an entry have similar ranges. In the case of Data Blocks, such a clustering can be created when the data is re-ordered during freezing. If workload knowledge exists or was collected while processing queries on the uncompressed chunks, Data Blocks can be frozen based on a sort criterion to improve accuracy of PSMAs for similar queries.

3.3 Attribute Compression

The main requirement for our compression schemes is that compressed data needs to remain byte-addressable for efficient point accesses. As shown in our evaluation, sub-byte encodings (e.g., BitWeaving [22]) would indeed allow for greater compression ratios but increase the cost for point accesses and scans with low selectivities by orders of magnitude compared to our byte-addressable encodings (cf., Section 5.4). The following compression schemes have proven themselves useful and suitable in terms of compression ratio and overall scan and point access performance in the context of Data Blocks: (i) single value compression, (ii) ordered dictionary compression, and (iii) truncation. For each attribute, the compression scheme is chosen that is optimal with regard to resulting memory consumption and data is only stored uncompressed in the rare case that no compression scheme is beneficial. Note that the choice of the compression scheme depends largely on the value domain of the attribute in the specific block. Thus, different blocks that store different ranges of an attribute of a relation might be compressed using many different schemes.

Single value compression is a special case of run-length encoding and is used if all values of an attribute in a block are equal. This includes the case where all values are `NULL`.

As Data Blocks are immutable data structures, our *ordered dictionary compression* does not need to be capable of handling insertions of new values or other kinds of updates. Immutability allows us to use an order-preserving dictionary compression, a scheme that is too expensive to use if dictionaries can be updated or grow. In our ordered dictionary, if $k < k'$ holds for two uncompressed values, k and k', then the same holds for their dictionary-compressed values $d_k, d_{k'} : d_k < d_{k'}$. Immutability also frees us from the burden of reference counting and free space management. The byte-width of the dictionary keys is chosen depending on the number of distinct keys, i.e., 8-bit integers for up to 256 keys, 16-bit integers for up to 2^{16} distinct keys, and 32-bit for up to 2^{32} distinct keys. A major advantage of preserving the order and using byte-truncated keys is that we can use our SIMD-optimized algorithms to find matches (cf., Section 4.2) on the compressed data. In fact, finding the matches is likely faster on compressed data than on uncompressed data because only the truncated values need to be compared and thus more values will fit in a SIMD register.

The *truncation* compression scheme reduces the memory consumption by computing the delta between each value and the attribute's minimum value: Let $A = (a_0, \ldots, a_m)$ denote the uncompressed data and $\min(A)$ be the smallest element in A, then $\Delta(A) = (a_0 - \min(A), \ldots, a_m - \min(A))$ is the compressed data. For these delta values, our truncation scheme again uses byte-truncation to either 8-bit, 16-bit, or 32-bit integers. Truncation is not used for strings and `double` types. An exception is the string type `char(1)` which is always represented as a 32-bit integer (such that it can store any UTF-8 character). Our truncation scheme is a special case of Frame of Reference (FOR) encoding where in our case the minimum value is the reference and each Data Block contains exactly one frame.

Even though the Data Block compression schemes are light-weight, we measured compression ratios of up to 5× compared to uncompressed storage in HyPer. Compared to Vectorwise's compressed storage, Data Blocks consume around 25% more space (see Table 1).

As each Data Block is self contained, the attribute compression is as well limited to a single block. This blockwise approach has drawbacks in terms of compression ratio. For example, dictionary compressed string data causes redundancies when identical strings appear in multiple different chunks. In that case, these strings have to be stored in multiple dictionaries. However, blockwise compression offers the aforementioned opportunity to chose the best suitable compression scheme for each column in each individual block, which can amortize this overhead. Depending on the value distribution, the blockwise approach can result in better compression ratios, compared to when relations are compressed as a whole. Another opportunity is that in a chunked relation, the system can easily migrate chunks between their compressed and uncompressed representation based on OLTP access frequency.

3.4 Finding and Unpacking Matches

Finding and unpacking matches in Data Blocks proceeds as follows: First, a Data Block's SMAs and PSMAs are used to narrow the scan range based on the scan restrictions. If the resulting scan range is not empty, further checks are performed before the actual scan starts. E.g., in case of dictionary compression and an equality predicate, a block can be ruled out if a binary search on the dictionary does not find an entry. If the block cannot be ruled out, then the actual scan starts and all restrictions are evaluated on the compressed columns. The scan yields a vector which contains the *positions* (or offsets) of the matching tuples. These matches are unpacked by their positions before being pushed to the consuming operator. This vector-at-a-time processing is repeated until no more matches are found in the Data Block.

In contrast to a scan of an uncompressed chunk, restrictions are evaluated on compressed data. As we reject sub-byte compression techniques in Data Blocks, the search for matches is thus (in most cases) reduced to an efficient scan over small integers with a simple comparison. Note that also string types are always compressed to integers. The predicate evaluation on compressed data only adds a small overhead on a per-block-basis as restriction constants have to be converted into their compressed representation.

Point-accesses to tuples residing in Data Blocks do not require any of the previous steps. Instead, required attributes of a record are uncompressed from a single position.

4. VECTORIZED SCANS IN COMPILING QUERY ENGINES

Data Blocks individually determine the best suitable compression scheme on a per-block and per-column basis. The resulting variety of physical representations improves the compression ratio but constitutes a challenge for JIT-compiling tuple-at-a-time query engines: Different storage layout combinations and extraction routines require either the generation of multiple code paths or the acceptance of runtime overhead incurred by branches for each tuple.

Our goal, thus, is to efficiently integrate multiple storage layouts, most specifically for our novel compressed Data Blocks layouts, into our tuple-at-a-time JIT-compiling query engine, that is optimized for both OLTP and OLAP workloads. HyPer uses a data-centric compilation approach that compiles relational algebra trees to highly efficient native machine code using the LLVM compiler infrastructure. The compilation times from LLVM's intermediate representation (IR) which we use for code generation to optimized native machine code is usually in the order of milliseconds for common queries.

Compared to a traditional query execution model where for each tuple or vector of tuples the control flow passes from one operator to the other, our query engine generates code for entire query pipelines. These pipelines essentially fuse the logic of operators that do not need intermediate materialization together. A query is broken down into multiple pipelines where each pipeline loads a tuple out of a materialized state (e.g., a base relation or a hash table), then performs the logic of all operators that can work on it without materialization, and finally materializes the output into the next pipeline breaker (e.g., a hash table). Note that compared to traditional interpreted execution, tuples are not pulled from input operators but are rather *pushed* towards consuming operators. In this context, scans are leaf operators that *feed* the initial query pipelines. The generated scan code (shown in C++ instead of LLVM IR for better readability) of two attributes of a relation stored in uncompressed columnar format looks as follows:

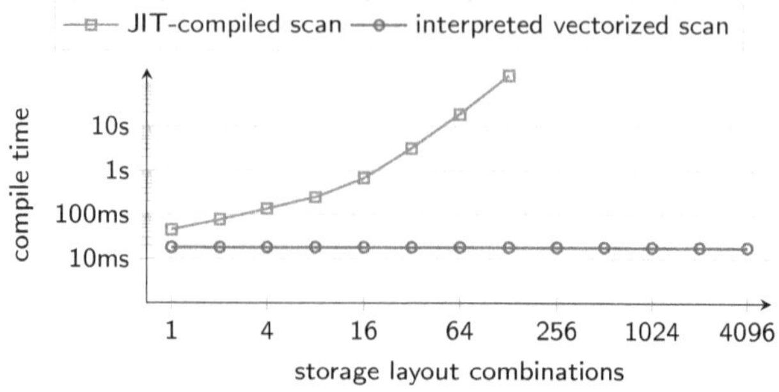

Figure 5: Compile times of a query plan with a scan of 8 attributes and a varying number of storage layout combinations of the base relation in HyPer.

```
for (const Chunk& c:relation.chunks) {
  for (unsigned row=0;row!=c.rows;++row) {
    auto a0=c.column[0].data[row];
    auto a3=c.column[3].data[row];
    // Check scan restrictions and push a0,a3
    // into consuming operator
    ...
} }
```

Note that for reasons of simplicity we omit multi-version concurrency control checks here. In order to perform the same scan over different storage layout combinations depending on the used compression techniques, the first possibility is to add a jump table for each extracted attribute that jumps to the right decompression method:

```
const Column& c0=c.column[0];
// Expensive jump table per attribute
switch (c0.compression) {
  case Uncompressed: ...
  case Dictionary: a0=c0.dict[key(c0.data[row])];
  ...
}
```

Since the outcome of the jump table's branch is the same within each chunk, there will not be a large number of branch misses due to correct prediction of the branches by the CPU. Yet, the introduced instructions add latency to the innermost hot loop of the scan code, and, in practice, this results in scan code that is almost 3× slower than scan code without these branches.

An alternative approach that does not add branches to the innermost loop is to "unroll" the storage layout combinations and generate code for each of the combinations. For each chunk, a computed goto can then be used to select the right scan code:

```
for (const Chunk& c:relation.chunks) {
  // Computed goto to specialized "unrolled"
  // code for the chunk's storage layout
  goto *scans[c.storageLayout];
  ...
  a0dicta3uncompressed:
  for (unsigned row=0;row!=c.rows;++row) {
    a0=c.column[0].dict[key(c0.data[row])];
    a3=c.column[3].data[row];
    ...
} }
```

Unrolling the combinations, however, requires the query engine to generate a code path for each storage layout that is used. The number of these layouts grows exponentially with the number of attributes n. If each attribute may be rep-

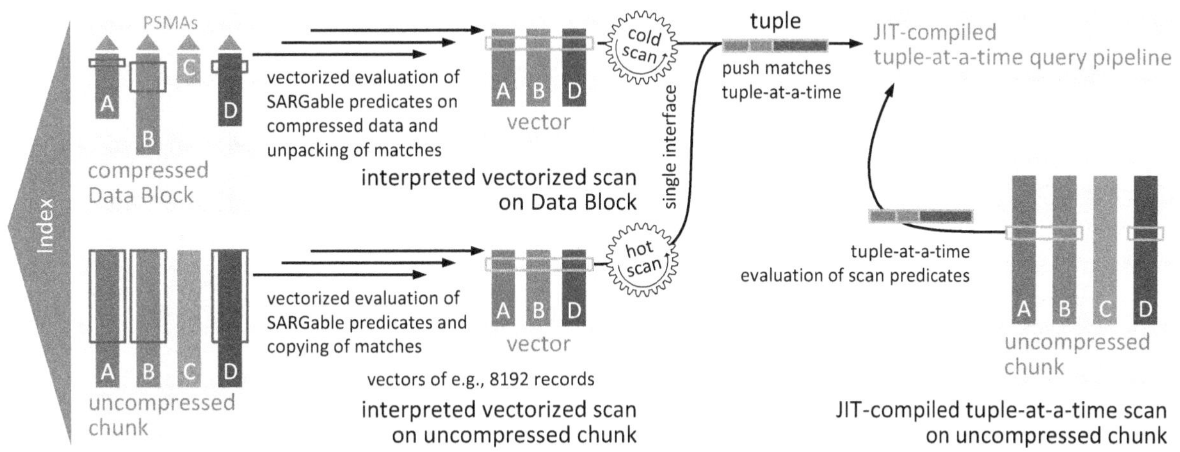

Figure 6: Integration of Data Blocks in our query engine: vectorized scans on Data Blocks and uncompressed chunks on the left share the same interface and evaluate SARGable predicates on vectors of records using SSE/AVX2 SIMD instructions (cf., Section 4.2). Matches are pushed to the query pipeline tuple at a time. The original JIT-compiled scan on the right evaluates predicates as part of the query pipeline.

resented in p different ways, the resulting number of code paths is p^n; e.g., for only two attributes and six different representations there are 36 generated code paths. While one can argue that not all of these combinations will actually occur in a relation[1], a small number of combinations will drastically increase code size and thus compilation time. This impact is shown in Figure 5, which plots the compilation time of a simple `select *` query on a relation with 8 attributes and a varying number of storage layout combinations.

Given the exploding compile time, we thus turned to calling pre-compiled interpreted vectorized scan code for vectors of say 8K tuples. The returned tuples are then *consumed* tuple-at-a-time by the generated code and pushed into the consuming operator:

```
while (!state.done()) {
  // Call to pre-compiled interpreted vectorized scan
  scan(result,state,requiredAttributes,restrictions);
  for (auto& tuple:result) {
    auto a0=tuple.attributes[0];
    auto a3=tuple.attributes[1];
    // Check non-SARGable restrictions and push a0,a3
    // into consuming operator
    ...
} }
```

Using the pre-compiled interpreted vectorized scan code, compile times can be kept low, no matter how many storage layout combinations are scanned (cf., Figure 5). Additionally, SARGable predicates can be pushed down into the scan operator where they can be evaluated on vectors of tuples.

4.1 Integration in HyPer

Our JIT-compiling query engine is integrated in our full-fledged main-memory database system HyPer that supports SQL-92+ query processing and ACID transactions. As illustrated in Figure 6, vectorized scans on hot uncompressed chunks and compressed Data Blocks share the same interface in HyPer and JIT-compiled query pipelines are oblivious to the underlying storage layout combinations.

[1]Our proposed compressed Data Blocks use over 50 different layouts for the lineitem relation of TPC-H scale factor 100.

In HyPer, vectorized scans are executed as follows: First, for each chunk of a relation a determination is made as to whether or not the block is frozen, i.e., compressed. If yes, then a Data Block scan is initiated, if not, a vectorized scan on uncompressed data is initiated. Next, the JIT-compiled scan glue code calls a function that generates a match vector containing the next n positions of records that qualify restrictions. n is the vector size and determines how many records are fetched before each of these records are pushed to the consuming pipeline one tuple at a time. The rationale for splitting the scan into multiple invocations is cache efficiency: As the same data is accessed multiple times when finding the matches, potentially unpacking these matches, if compressed, and passing them to the consumer, the vector-wise processing in cache-friendly pieces minimizes the number of cache misses (see Appendix A for an experiment with different vector sizes). In HyPer, the vector size is set to 8192 records. After finding the matching positions, scan glue code on a cold compressed Data Block calls a function that unpacks the matches into temporary storage, and a scan on an uncompressed chunk copies the matching required attributes into temporary storage. Finally, the tuples in the temporary storage are pushed to the consuming operator tuple at a time. Even though vectorized scans are indeed copying more data, our evaluation of vectorized scans in our JIT-compiling query engine shows that most of the time the costs for copying can be neglected and vectorized predicate evaluation can outperform tuple-at-a-time evaluation.

In this respect, Q_1 and Q_6 of TPC-H exemplify two extremes: for Q_1 most tuples qualify the scan restriction and vectorized scans copy almost all of the scanned data. As such, the runtime of Q_1 suffers by almost 50% (cf., Appendix). Note that without predicates, our vectorized scan uses an optimization whereby it does not copy data if all tuples of a vector match and performance is not degraded; due to the uniform value distribution of the restricted attributes, this optimization is not helpful if predicates are SARGd. For Q_6, on the other hand, only a small percent of tuples qualify the scan restriction. On uncompressed data, the vectorized evaluation of predicates improves runtime with vectorized scans over JIT-compiled scans up to 2.3× (cf., Appendix F).

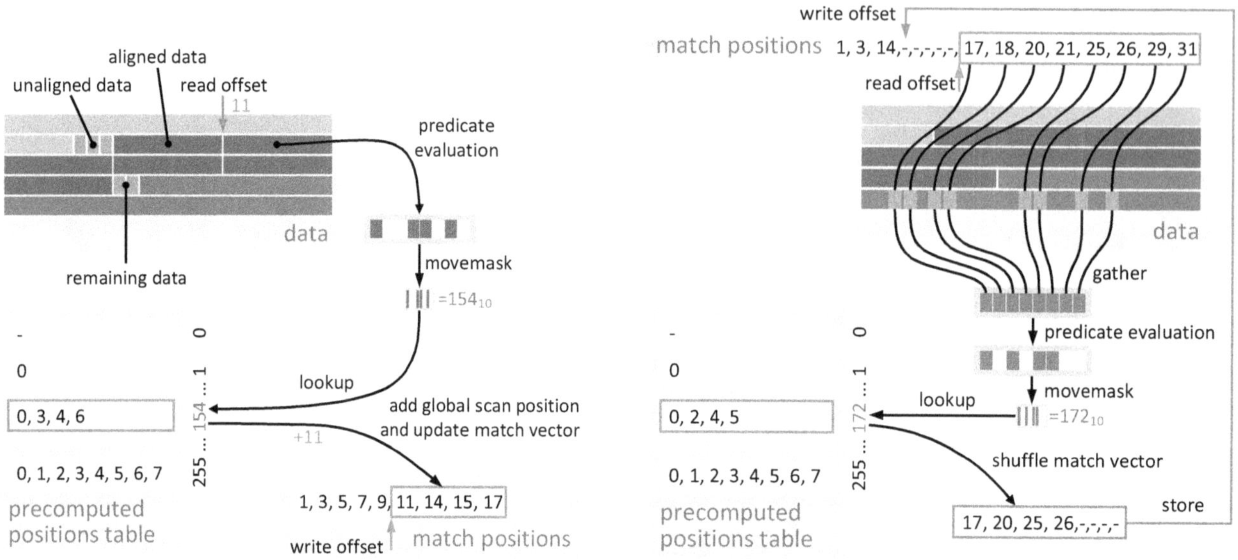

(a) The first applied restriction yields an initial vector of matching record positions. Positions for masks are stored in a lookup table to avoid costly computations.

(b) Additional restrictions reduce the initial match vector. Lookup table entries are used as shuffle control masks.

Figure 7: Evaluation of predicates on compressed and uncompressed data using SSE/AVX2 SIMD instructions

Using vectorized scans on our novel compressed Data Blocks, query runtimes on TPC-H improve by more than 2.3×: runtime of Q_6 improves by 6.7× and the geometric mean of the 22 query runtimes improves by 1.27×.

4.2 Finding Matches using SIMD Instructions

Vectorized processing enables us to employ SIMD instructions for evaluating SARGable predicates. As mentioned before, during the evaluation phase the *positions* (or offsets) of the qualifying elements are stored in a vector. We refer to the content of this vector as *match positions*[2]. For example, if the predicate $P(a) : 3 \leq a \leq 5$ is applied to the attribute vector $\vec{A}^T = (0, 1, 5, 2, 3, 1)$, then the resulting match positions are $\vec{M}^T = (2, 4)$. If additional conjunctive restrictions are present, then these restrictions need to be applied only to the tuples referred in M. At this low level, query engine only has to cope with conjunctive predicates, thus the match vector is shrunk with any additional predicate. Algorithmically, we distinguish between finding *initial* matches, which fill a match vector, and an optional *reduce* matches where an already existing match vector is shrunk.

In scalar (non-SIMD) code, restrictions are applied to a single attribute value at a time and evaluated to a single boolean value. When SIMD instructions are employed, the necessary comparisons are performed on multiple attributes in parallel. In contrast to the scalar code, a SIMD comparison yields a bit-mask which identifies the qualifying elements. When n elements are processed in parallel, then the resulting bit-mask is stored in a SIMD register where all bits of the n individual SIMD lanes are either set to 0 or 1. The challenging part is to compute the positions of matching records based on the given bit-mask. Possible solutions are (i) iterating over the bit-mask or (ii) performing a tree reduction where the complexity is $\mathcal{O}(n)$ or $\mathcal{O}(\log n)$, respectively.

[2]This concept is also known as *selection vector* [5].

We found that these conversions of the bit-mask into a match position vector is too expensive. Therefore, we make use of a pre-computed table to map the bit-masks to positions whereby a `movemask` instruction provides the necessary offset. With this approach, which is illustrated in Figure 7(a), the mapping can be done in constant time. Each table entry reflects a possible outcome of an n-way SIMD comparison. For example, in Figure 7(a) an 8-way comparison is performed where the 0 th, the 3 rd, the 4 th and the 6 th element (counted from left to right) satisfy the predicate. All bits of the 4 corresponding SIMD lanes are set to 1, whereas the others are all set to 0. The `movemask` instruction extracts the most significant bit of each SIMD lane and stores the result in an integer value. In the example, this value is $10011010_2 = 154_{10}$. This value is used as an offset to access the corresponding entry in the lookup table. The table entry reflects the outcome of the 8-way comparison. In the example, the result is an 32-bit integer vector where the positions of the matching elements are $(0, 3, 4, 6)$. The global scan position is added to the (local) match positions before the match vector is updated.

As each of the n attribute values stored in a SIMD register may or may not be a match, we have to store each possible outcome in the table which results in 2^n entries. Naturally, the table can become extremely large. E.g., for attributes of type 8-bit integer processed in 256-bit AVX2 registers (using a 32-way comparison), the table would contain 2^{32} entries (= 512 GB). Therefore, we limit the table size to 2^8 entries and perform multiple lookups if necessary. A single entry in the lookup table can therefore contain the positions of up to 8 matches. Each match position is represented as an unsigned 32-bit integer, thus the size of the entire lookup table ($2^8 \times 8 \times 4\,\text{B} = 8\,\text{KB}$) is sufficiently small to fit into L1 cache (which is 32 KB on recent Intel CPUs).

Along with the match positions, each table entry also contains the number of matching elements (not depicted). These values are stored in the low-order bits to keep the

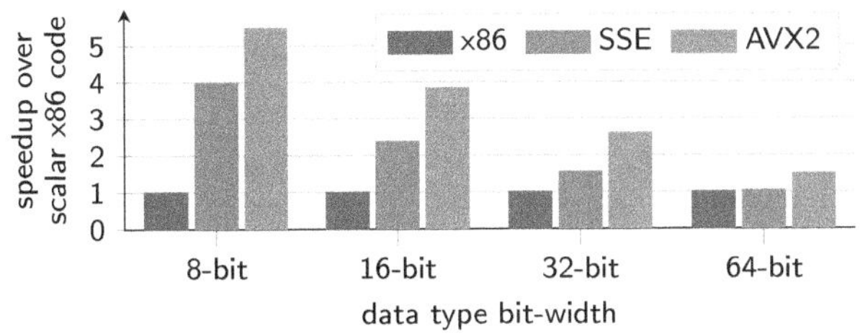

Figure 8: Speedup of SIMD predicate evaluation of type $l \leq A \leq r$ with selectivity 20%

memory footprint small and to avoid cache pollution. Thus, the extraction of the actual match positions requires an additional right-shift of the pre-computed position vectors. The number of matches per table entry are required to increment the write offset of the global match vector later on. We show the implementation details in Appendix C.

Applying additional restrictions is quite different to finding initial matches for two reasons: (i) The accessed elements are no longer contiguously stored in memory, as only elements are read that satisfy the first predicate, and (ii) a match vector already exists and needs to be shrunk. Nevertheless, our SIMD optimized implementation follows an approach similar to the one to find the initial matches. The most notable difference is that elements are directly *gathered* from their respective memory location into SIMD registers as sketched in Figure 7(b). Again, we make use of our lookup table consisting of pre-computed position vectors. In contrast to the find initial matches implementation, the table entries are now used as *shuffle control masks* to manipulate the match vector. In Figure 7(b), for example, the predicate is applied to the attributes at positions $(17, 18, 20, 21, 25, 26, 29, 31)$ where the elements in the SIMD lanes $(0, 2, 4, 5)$ qualify. The match positions are then shuffled according to the table entry: The zeroth element (value 17) remains in SIMD lane 0, the second element (value 20) is shuffled to the SIMD lane 1, and so on. Finally, the result $(17, 20, 25, 26, -, -, -, -)$ is written back to the match vector and the write offset is incremented by the number of matching elements. As only 4 of the 8 processed elements qualify the result contains *don't care* values (denoted as $-$) which are overwritten in the next iteration.

Unfortunately, the `gather` instruction is only available for 32- and 64-bit types. For 8- and 16-bit values we also draw on a 32-bit gather which reduces the degree of parallelism by a factor of 2 or 4, respectively. Thus, the performance improvements observed in our microbenchmarks are mostly independent from the underlying data types.

We observe speedups of almost $4\times$ with SSE and more than $5\times$ with AVX2 in microbenchmarks on a desktop Haswell CPU. Figure 8 shows the speedup of the evaluation of a *between* predicate where 20% of the tuples qualify. The degree of parallelism and therefore the performance gains highly depend on the bit-width of the underlying data type. For 64-bit integer attributes we observe speedups of $1.5\times$ with AVX2, whereas the degree of parallelism with SSE is too small to recognize performance benefits.

Our implementation for finding initial matches is insensible to varying selectivities due to the pre-computed positions table and varies only in the number of match positions written to the position vector. However, due to the fact that we process the input in a vectorized manner, the size of the match vector is limited to the number of tuples processed at a time (which is set to 16 K in this experiment). Thus, the number of matches written to the vector has no notable effects on performance.

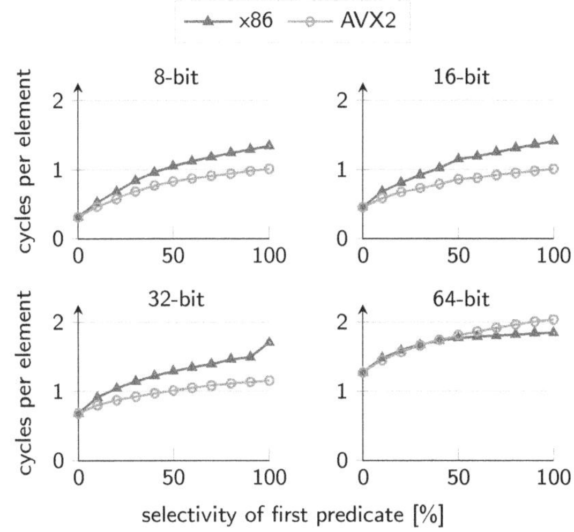

Figure 9: Applying an additional restriction with varying selectivities of the first predicate and the selectivity of the second predicate set to 40%

The implementation for reducing the match vector by applying additional restrictions is also insensible to varying selectivities of the applied restriction. However, scan performance highly depends on the selectivity of the preceding restrictions due to non-contiguous memory access pattern. When matching tuples are uniformly distributed, as they are in our experiment, the selectivity of the preceding predicates has the highest impact. Figure 9 shows these effects and compares the performance of our AVX2 implementation with a sequential version (branch-free scalar code). For integer attributes (up to 32-bit) we observe performance gains ranging from $1.0\times$ to $1.25\times$ with increasing selectivities. For 64-bit integer values, the reduction does not benefit from SIMD instructions. At higher selectivities, the SIMD implementation performs even worse than the scalar code.

Performance gains with other data types are almost identical, which is attributed to the missing `gather` instructions for 8- and 16-bit values. We would like to point out that the distribution of qualifying tuples is the crucial factor here, thus speedups of $1.25\times$ are also possible with highly selective predicates, e.g., when the data has a (natural) ordering.

The SIMD optimized algorithms presented here only work for integer data. For other data types and non-SARGable predicates we fall back to scalar implementations. However, our novel compressed Data Block format discussed in the previous Section compresses data into byte-addressable integer data, including string-like attributes. Thus, OLAP workloads highly benefit from the SIMD algorithms when large portions of the data are packed into Data Blocks.

5. EVALUATION

In this section we evaluate our implementation of interpreted vectorized scans, SIMD-optimized predicate evaluation, and the compressed Data Blocks format in our JIT-compiling query engine. The query engine we used for our experiments, is part of our full-fledged main-memory data-

	TPC-H SF100	IMDB cast info	Flights
	uncompressed		
CSV	107 GB	1.4 GB	12 GB
HyPer	126 GB	1.8 GB	21 GB
Vectorwise	105 GB	0.72 GB	11 GB
	compressed		
HyPer	66 GB	0.50 GB	4.2 GB
Vectorwise	54 GB	0.24 GB	3.2 GB

Table 1: Size of TPC-H, IMDB cast info, and a flight details database in HyPer and Vectorwise.

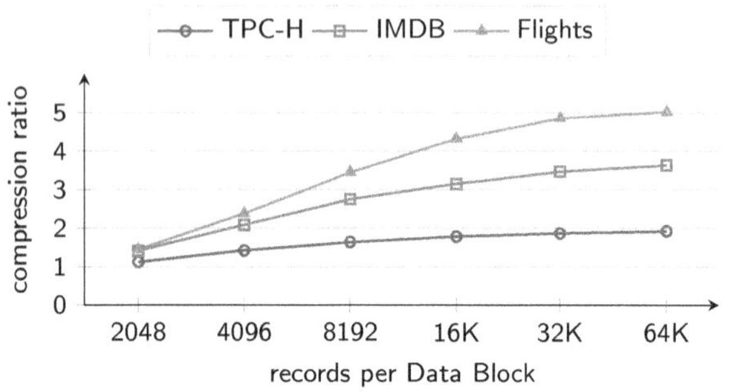

Figure 10: Compression ratio of TPC-H (scale factor 100), IMDB cast info, and a flight arrival and departure details data set for various Data Block sizes in HyPer (compared to uncompressed storage).

base system HyPer that supports SQL-92 queries and ACID transactions. We further show why we rejected sub-byte encodings of data by comparing our byte-addressable compression approach with SIMD-optimized *horizontal bit packing*.

Unless otherwise stated, the experiments were conducted on a 4-socket Intel Xeon X7560 2.27 GHz (2.67 .GHz maximum turbo) NUMA system with 1 TB DDR3 main memory (256 GB per CPU) running Linux 3.19. Each CPU has 8 cores (16 hardware contexts) and 24 MB of shared L3 cache. For experiments targeting the AVX2 ISA, we use an Intel Haswell i5-4670T CPU 2.3 GHz (3.3 GHz maximum turbo) with 16 GB DDR3 memory and 6 MB of shared L3 cache.

5.1 Compression

We evaluated the compression ratio of our compressed Data Blocks in an initial experiment. As input data sets we chose TPC-H scale factor 100, the largest relation of the Internet Movie Database (IMDB), which contains the casts of movies (cast info), and a data set consisting of flight arrival and departure details for all commercial flights within the USA, from October 1987 to April 2008[3]. Table 1 shows a comparison of uncompressed and compressed database sizes for these data sets in Vectorwise and HyPer.

Vectorwise is the commercial version of MonetDB/X100 [5] and uses a number of light-weight compression techniques that can handle non-compressible values (outliers) through a technique called "patching", which stands for the "P" in PFOR (Frame of Reference), PFOR-DELTA (delta encoding on PFOR), and PDICT (dictionary encoding) compression schemes [40, 38]. Run-length encoding is used where applicable. With these heavier compression schemes, Vectorwise

[3]http://stat-computing.org/dataexpo/2009/

scan type	geometric mean	sum
	HyPer	
JIT (uncomressed)	0.586s	21.7s
Vectorized (uncompressed)	0.583s (1.01×)	21.6s
+ SARG	0.577s (1.02×)	21.8s
Data Blocks (compressed)	0.555s (1.06×)	21.5s
+ SARG/SMA	0.466s (1.26×)	20.3s
+ PSMA	0.463s (1.27×)	20.2s
	Vectorwise	
uncompressed storage	2.336s	74.4s
compressed storage	2.527s (0.92×)	78.5s

Table 2: Runtimes of TPC-H queries (scale factor 100) using different scan types on uncompressed and compressed databases in HyPer and Vectorwise.

on average saves 25% more space than HyPer. However, this savings come at the cost of poorer query performance. Vectorwise's compression schemes were designed to work for situations where the database does not fit in memory and aims to accelerate disk load times. Processing compressed, memory-resident data is acceptably fast, but can be slower than processing uncompressed data [2]. In particular, we measured that TPC-H queries Q_1 and Q_6 were, respectively, 18% and 38% slower on compressed storage compared to uncompressed storage in Vectorwise (scale factor 10). Point accesses in Vectorwise are always performed as a scan; albeit on a scan range that is narrowed by indexes. Data Blocks, on the other hand, are designed around the assumption that most of the data fits into main memory. Performance-wise, our goal with Data Blocks is to be at least equally fast at query and transaction processing compared to uncompressed in-memory storage.

Figure 10 shows the compression ratio of the aforementioned data sets for various Data Block sizes from 2^{11} to our default of 2^{16} records per Data Block. As expected, if the number of compressed records in a block becomes too small, the overhead of block metadata worsens the compression ratio. In our experiments, 2^{16} records per Data Block proved to offer a good tradeoff between compression ratio and query processing speed as most values are still compressed into small integer types.

5.2 Query Performance

For our query performance evaluation, we first looked at TPC-H scale factor 100 and compared query runtimes in HyPer with JIT-compiled scans and vectorized scans on our uncompressed storage format, and vectorized scans on our compressed Data Block format. A summary of the results is shown in Table 2; full results are shown in Appendix F. 64 hardware threads were used and runtimes are the median of several measurements. Our results suggest that query performance does not change significantly with vectorized scans instead of JIT-compiled scans. This is also true if we push SARGable predicates (+SARG) into the vectorized scan. However, compilation times with vectorized scans is almost half of the time needed with JIT-compiled scan code (see numbers in parentheses in Appendix F). If we look at query performance on our Data Blocks format, we can see that if using only the compression aspect of Data Blocks, query performance also stays the same. If we push SARGable predicates (+SARG/SMA) into the scan on Data Blocks, we see a speedup of almost 26% in the geometric

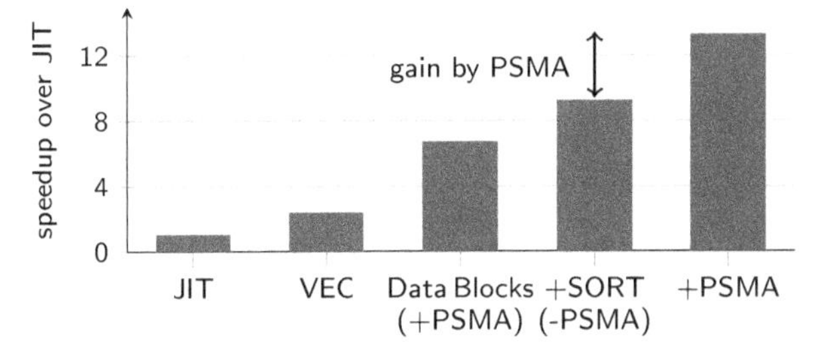

Figure 11: Speedup of TPC-H Q6 (scale factor 100) on block-wise sorted data (+SORT)

mean of query runtimes. We cannot measure the impact of SARGd predicates without SMA block skipping because our implementation of SARGing, by design, relies on block skipping. Nevertheless, no blocks were skipped in our experiment due to the uniform distribution of values in TPC-H and the performance improvement is only due to our efficient SIMD-optimized evaluation of predicates on vectors of the compressed data. As data is uniformly distributed, adding the PSMAs (+PSMA) does not provide a significant performance boost on TPC-H. We further compared HyPer to Vectorwise on its uncompressed and compressed storage formats. In Vectorwise, query processing on the uncompressed format is around 8% faster than on its compressed format when data is cached in memory. This suggests that even with light-weight compression techniques, such as those used in Vectorwise, it is actually very difficult to get a speedup from compression.

To further show the impact that PSMAs can have in more realistic scenarios than the default TPC-H, we conducted another TPC-H experiment for which we sorted each Data Block of the `lineitem` relation on `l_shipdate`. Due to the initial uniform distribution of dates, each block still contains data from every year of the data set, but inside the blocks the dates are sorted. Establishing this order can be done automatically when freezing a block (cf., Section 3.2). Figure 11 shows that a significant additional speedup can be gained by the PSMAs for TPC-H Q_6 in this scenario. Another query that profits even more from the SMAs and PSMAs is the following on the flights data set: select carriers and their average arrival delay in San Francisco for the years 1998 to 2008 (see Appendix D for the query text). As the relation is naturally ordered on date, most blocks are skipped due to the SMAs and on the remaining blocks the PSMAs narrow the scan range based on the restriction on the destination airport. Runtime of this query improves by more than 20×, compared to using a JIT-compiled scan on the uncompressed format.

5.3 OLTP Performance

To measure the overhead of accessing a record that is stored in a Data Block compared to uncompressed chunks, we performed a random point access experiment where we selected random records from a compressed TPC-H customer relation (scale factor 100, i.e., 15M records). Table 3 shows the measured lookup throughputs. With a primary key index (traditional global index structure), we measured an overhead of around 60% when accessing records in Data Blocks. Without the primary key index, all lookups are performed as scans. In this case the scans on Data Blocks can be faster than scanning uncompressed chunks because Data

		Ordered*	Shuffled°
uncompressed (JIT)	PK index	551,268	545,554
	no index	36	36
uncompressed (Vectorized)	PK index	550,661	566,893
	no index	26	26
Data Blocks	PK index	301,750	274,198
	no index	17,508	41
Data Blocks +PSMA	PK index	276,014	294,291
	no index	71,587	40

* customer is ordered on `c_custkey` as generated by *dbgen*
° shuffled customer relation (no longer ordered on `c_custkey`): SMAs/PSMAs can no longer narrow scan range

Table 3: Throughput (in lookups per second) of random point access queries `select * from customer where c_custkey = randomCustKey()` on TPC-H scale factor 100 with and without a primary key (PK) index on `c_custkey` and using JIT-compiled and vectorized scans on uncompressed storage and Data Block scans with and without PSMAs.

Blocks contain SMAs and PSMAs that can narrow the scan range. This is especially true if the customer relation is ordered on `c_custkey`, as is the case if the data is generated with the TPC-H *dbgen* tool. We also shuffled the data to show that without that order the SMAs and PSMAs cannot improve lookup performance. As such, for OLTP workloads, SMAs/PSMAs are not a general-purpose replacement for a traditional index structure. In Vectorwise, which uses no traditional index structure, we measured a random lookup throughput of 17 lookups per second.

We further ran TPC-C experiments with 5 warehouses. In a first experiment we only compressed old neworder records into Data Blocks, which reflects the intended use case as hot data should remain in uncompressed chunks. We measured a transaction throughput of 89,229 transactions per second on uncompressed storage and 88,699 transactions per second if the cold neworder records are stored in Data Blocks. The overhead stems from the additional switch on each access that determines if an uncompressed or a compressed chunk is accessed. In a second experiment, we executed only the read-only TPC-C transactions order status and stock level on an uncompressed TPC-C database and a TPC-C database that is completely stored in Data Blocks. On uncompressed storage we measured a transaction throughput of 119,889 transactions per second, on Data Blocks we measured 109,649 transactions per second; a difference of 9%. This shows that even if the individual record lookup throughput is decreased by 60%, in real transactional workloads this translates to a low percentage overhead if cold compressed data is accessed.

As Data Blocks primarily target OLAP workloads, we omit the mixed workload CH-benCHmark [7]. Our thorough evaluation with TPC-H and TPC-C covers the two extremes of the CH benchmark and we expect the results to be somewhere in between.

5.4 Advantages of Byte-Addressability

As previously mentioned, sub-byte encodings of values (e.g., BitWeaving [22]) can achieve higher compression ratios compared to byte-aligned truncation, which we use in

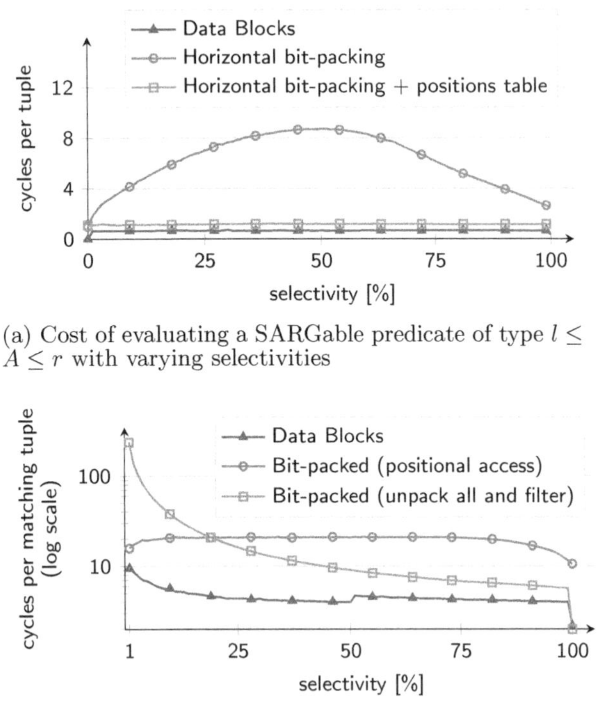

(a) Cost of evaluating a SARGable predicate of type $l \leq A \leq r$ with varying selectivities

(b) Cost of unpacking matching tuples (3 attributes)

Figure 12: Horizontal bit-packing compared to Data Blocks with byte-addressable compression schemes

Data Blocks. In this microexperiment, we show why we consciously decided against using sub-byte encodings in HyPer and how point accesses and scans with low selectivities suffer from these encodings.

For this experiment we use three columns A, B and C populated with 2^{16} integer values, whereas the domain of the values in column A and B is $[0, 2^{16}]$ and $dom(C) = [0, 2^8]$. Thus, the columns can be horizontally bit-packed into 9 bits or 17 bits, respectively. Intentionally, the domains exceed the 1-byte and 2-byte truncation by one bit which represents the worst case for Data Blocks as they are forced to use 2- and 4-byte codes. Therefore, the compression ratio of bit-packing is almost two times higher in this scenario. As workload, we evaluate a `between` predicate of the form $l \leq A \leq r$ and unpack the matching tuples into an output buffer. The benchmark is conducted on a Haswell i5-4670T CPU with the AVX2 instruction set. The codebase that we used for horizontal bit-packing is the highly SIMD-optimized implementation of [27]. The only bit-packing-related extension is a function that allows us to unpack a single tuple at a given position.

We first compare the costs for predicate evaluation without unpacking. The bit-packing implementation yields a bitmap where set bits identify matching positions. In contrast, our Data Blocks API returns a vector of 32-bit integers populated with the corresponding match positions. For our experiment we transform the bitmap in the case of bit-packing into a position vector to make the results comparable. Figure 12(a) shows that Data Blocks are robust with respect to varying selectivities. Horizontal bit-packing on the other hand is not. Bit-packing suffers from branch mispredictions in the aforementioned conversion of the bitmap. Therefore, we applied our *pre-computed position table* approach (cf., Section 4.2) to the bit-packing implementation, which makes bit-packing also robust to changing selectivities. Overall, predicate evaluation on Data Blocks is still 1.8× faster than predicate evaluation on the horizontal bit-packed format.

We compare Data Blocks to two bit-packing alternatives to evaluate unpacking performance: (i) *Positional access*, where all matching tuples are unpacked sequentially with scalar code, and (ii) *Unpack all and filter*, where all tuples are first unpacked using SIMD code and then sequentially filtered using the positions vector. Figure 12(b) shows the costs per extracted tuple for all three implementations with varying selectivities. Data Blocks outperform bit-packing in almost all cases, except when all tuples qualify where bit-packing is approximately 9% faster. The bit-packing implementation that extracts individual tuples based on the match vector performs well for selectivities less than 20%. If more than 20% of the tuples qualify, the *unpack all and filter* strategy performs better than positional accesses due to SIMD. The costs for unpacking are significantly higher for queries with moderate selectivities due to unpacking mostly non-qualifying tuples. Compared to the SARGing costs, unpacking clearly dominates in all cases. E.g., if 10% of the tuples qualify, then 10% of the cycles are spent in predicate evaluation with Data Blocks and only 5% for bit-packing, whereas 90% and 95% of the time is used for unpacking.

When a sparse set of tuples is selected by the SARGable predicate, we only benefit from this early selection iff individual tuples can be accessed and decompressed fast. On the other hand, if larger (dense) sets of tuples are selected, then early evaluation of predicates becomes increasingly pointless. In the above example (selecting 10% uniformly), extracting the selected tuples from a Data Block is more than 3× faster, while selection is 1.8× faster. As HyPer has to provide fast access to individual compressed records and also needs to deliver robust performance for scans with modest selectivities, we cannot use bit-packing in our Data Blocks.

We intentionally do not show results for *vertical bit-packing* as it trades faster SARGing for even higher decompression costs and is therefore even less suitable for our high performance OLTP and OLAP database system. Nevertheless, the recent work of Li et al. [21] shows how SARGing on vertical bit-packed data can be significantly improved, which might offer new applications of vertical bit-packed data, such as using it as secondary index.

6. CONCLUSION

The goal of this work was to reduce the main-memory footprint in high performance hybrid OLTP & OLAP database systems without compromising high query **and** transactional performance. To achieve this goal, we developed a novel compressed columnar storage format for hybrid database systems, termed *Data Blocks*. This compressed data format was further improved by light-weight intra-block indexing, called *Positional SMA*, for improved scan performance and SIMD-optimized predicate evaluation. The fine-grained adaptivity of Data Blocks necessitated the integration of JIT-compiled query execution with vectorized scans in order to achieve highest possible performance for compilation as well as query execution. This paper serves as a blueprint for integrating all these innovative techniques into a full-fledged hybrid OLTP & OLAP system. Further optimization potentials are outlined in Appendix E.

7. REFERENCES

[1] D. Abadi, S. Madden, and M. Ferreira. Integrating Compression and Execution in Column-oriented Database Systems. In *SIGMOD*, 2006.

[2] Actian Corporation. *Actian Analytics Database – Vector Edition 3.5*, 2014.

[3] A. Ailamaki, D. J. DeWitt, M. D. Hill, and M. Skounakis. Weaving Relations for Cache Performance. In *VLDB*, 2001.

[4] R. Barber, G. Lohman, V. Raman, R. Sidle, S. Lightstone, and B. Schiefer. In-memory BLU acceleration in IBM's DB2 and dashDB: Optimized for modern workloads and hardware architectures. In *ICDE*, 2015.

[5] P. A. Boncz, M. Zukowski, and N. Nes. MonetDB/X100: Hyper-Pipelining Query Execution. In *CIDR*, 2005.

[6] J. Chhugani, A. D. Nguyen, V. W. Lee, W. Macy, M. Hagog, Y.-K. Chen, et al. Efficient Implementation of Sorting on Multi-core SIMD CPU Architecture. *PVLDB*, 1(2), 2008.

[7] R. L. Cole, F. Funke, L. Giakoumakis, W. Guy, A. Kemper, S. Krompass, H. A. Kuno, R. O. Nambiar, T. Neumann, M. Poess, K. Sattler, M. Seibold, E. Simon, and F. Waas. The mixed workload CH-benCHmark. In *Proceedings of the Fourth International Workshop on Testing Database Systems, DBTest 2011, Athens, Greece, June 13, 2011*, page 8, 2011.

[8] J. DeBrabant, J. Arulraj, A. Pavlo, M. Stonebraker, S. Zdonik, et al. A Prolegomenon on OLTP Database Systems for Non-Volatile Memory. *PVLDB*, 7(14), 2014.

[9] J. DeBrabant, A. Pavlo, S. Tu, M. Stonebraker, and S. B. Zdonik. Anti-Caching: A New Approach to Database Management System Architecture. *PVLDB*, 6(14), 2013.

[10] C. Diaconu, C. Freedman, E. Ismert, P. Larson, P. Mittal, R. Stonecipher, et al. Hekaton: SQL Server's Memory-Optimized OLTP Engine. In *SIGMOD*, 2013.

[11] A. Eldawy, J. J. Levandoski, and P. Larson. Trekking Through Siberia: Managing Cold Data in a Memory-Optimized Database. *PVLDB*, 7(11), 2014.

[12] F. Färber, S. K. Cha, J. Primsch, C. Bornhövd, S. Sigg, and W. Lehner. SAP HANA Database: Data Management for Modern Business Applications. *SIGMOD Record*, 40(4), 2011.

[13] Z. Feng, E. Lo, B. Kao, and W. Xu. ByteSlice: Pushing the Envelop of Main Memory Data Processing with a New Storage Layout. In *SIGMOD*, 2015.

[14] A. Floratou, U. F. Minhas, and F. Özcan. SQL-on-Hadoop: Full Circle Back to Shared-nothing Database Architectures. *PVLDB*, 7(12), 2014.

[15] F. Funke, A. Kemper, and T. Neumann. Compacting Transactional Data in Hybrid OLTP&OLAP Databases. *PVLDB*, 5(11), 2012.

[16] A. Kemper and T. Neumann. HyPer: A Hybrid OLTP&OLAP Main Memory Database System based on Virtual Memory Snapshots. In *ICDE*, 2011.

[17] J. Krüger, C. Kim, M. Grund, N. Satish, D. Schwalb, J. Chhugani, et al. Fast Updates on Read-Optimized Databases Using Multi-Core CPUs. *PVLDB*, 5(1), 2011.

[18] P. Larson, C. Clinciu, E. N. Hanson, A. Oks, S. L. Price, S. Rangarajan, et al. SQL Server Column Store Indexes. In *SIGMOD*, 2011.

[19] C. Lattner and V. Adve. LLVM: A Compilation Framework for Lifelong Program Analysis & Transformation. In *CGO*, 2004.

[20] V. Leis, P. A. Boncz, A. Kemper, and T. Neumann. Morsel-driven Parallelism: A NUMA-aware Query Evaluation Framework for the Many-Core Age. In *SIGMOD*, 2014.

[21] Y. Li, C. Chasseur, and J. M. Patel. A Padded Encoding Scheme to Accelerate Scans by Leveraging Skew. In *SIGMOD*, 2015.

[22] Y. Li and J. M. Patel. BitWeaving: Fast Scans for Main Memory Data Processing. In *SIGMOD*, 2013.

[23] G. Moerkotte. Small Materialized Aggregates: A Light Weight Index Structure for Data Warehousing. In *VLDB*, 1998.

[24] T. Mühlbauer, W. Rödiger, R. Seilbeck, A. Reiser, A. Kemper, and T. Neumann. Instant Loading for Main Memory Databases. *PVLDB*, 6(14), 2013.

[25] T. Neumann. Efficiently Compiling Efficient Query Plans for Modern Hardware. *PVLDB*, 4(9), 2011.

[26] O. Polychroniou, A. Raghavan, and K. A. Ross. Rethinking SIMD Vectorization for In-Memory Databases. In *SIGMOD*, 2015.

[27] O. Polychroniou and K. A. Ross. Efficient Lightweight Compression Alongside Fast Scans. In *DaMoN*, 2015.

[28] M. Pöss and D. Potapov. Data Compression in Oracle. In *VLDB*, 2003.

[29] B. Raducanu, P. A. Boncz, and M. Zukowski. Micro Adaptivity in Vectorwise. In *SIGMOD*, 2013.

[30] V. Raman, G. Attaluri, R. Barber, N. Chainani, D. Kalmuk, V. KulandaiSamy, et al. DB2 with BLU Acceleration: So Much More Than Just a Column Store. *PVLDB*, 6(11), 2013.

[31] J. Sompolski, M. Zukowski, and P. A. Boncz. Vectorization vs. Compilation in Query Execution. In *DaMoN*, 2011.

[32] M. Then, M. Kaufmann, F. Chirigati, T.-A. Hoang-Vu, K. Pham, et al. The More the Merrier: Efficient Multi-source Graph Traversal. *PVLDB*, 8(4), 2014.

[33] S. D. Viglas. Data Management in Non-Volatile Memory. In *SIGMOD*, 2015.

[34] S. Wanderman-Milne and N. Li. Runtime Code Generation in Cloudera Impala. *DEBU*, 37(1), 2014.

[35] T. Willhalm, N. Popovici, Y. Boshmaf, H. Plattner, A. Zeier, et al. SIMD-scan: Ultra Fast In-memory Table Scan Using On-chip Vector Processing Units. *PVLDB*, 2(1), 2009.

[36] W. Yan and P.-A. Larson. Eager aggregation and lazy aggregation. In *VLDB*, 1995.

[37] J. Zhou and K. A. Ross. Implementing Database Operations Using SIMD Instructions. In *SIGMOD*, 2002.

[38] M. Zukowski and P. A. Boncz. Vectorwise: Beyond Column Stores. *DEBU*, 35(1), 2012.

[39] M. Zukowski, S. Héman, N. Nes, and P. A. Boncz. Super-Scalar RAM-CPU Cache Compression. In *ICDE*, 2006.

[40] M. Zukowski, M. van de Wiel, and P. A. Boncz. Vectorwise: A Vectorized Analytical DBMS. In *ICDE*, 2012.

APPENDIX

A. IMPACT OF VECTOR SIZE ON QUERY PERFORMANCE

Figure 13 shows the runtime of the TPC-H 100 benchmark with varying vector sizes. Query runtimes slightly increase for small vector sizes due to interpretation overheads (e.g., function calls). On the other hand, when the records stored in a vector exceed the cache size, query performance decreases as records are evicted to slower main memory before they are pushed into the JIT-compiled query pipeline.

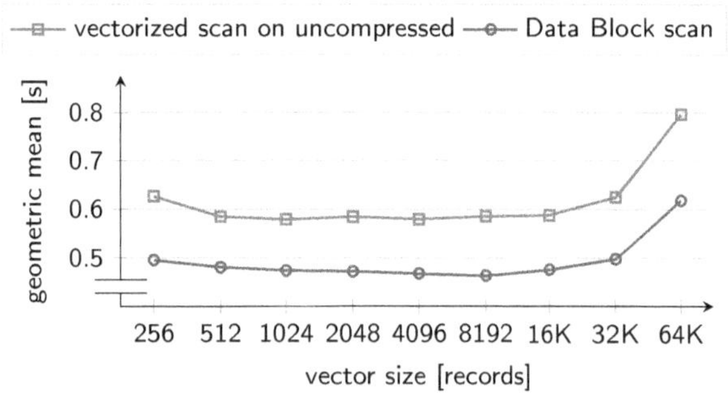

Figure 13: Geometric mean of TPC-H 100 query runtimes depending on vector size.

B. PSMA IMPLEMENTATION

The following listing sketches the code for constructing and probing the PSMAs. Before any PSMA access, the values are first converted into deltas relative to the smallest value in the current data block (*min*). The build scans the data block once and remembers the first and last occurrence of a value in the respective slot.

```
// Compute the PSMA slot for a given value
uint32_t getPSMASlot(T value,T min) {
  // d = delta
  uint64_t d=value-min;
  // r = remaining bytes (note: clz is undefined for 0)
  uint32_t r=d ? (7-(__builtin_clzll(d)>>3)) : 0;
  // m = most significant non-zero byte
  uint64_t m=(d>>(r<<3));
  // return the slot in PSMA array
  return m+(r<<8);
}

// Initialize all slots to empty ranges
for (auto& entry : psma)
  entry={0,0};

// Update ranges for all attribute values
for (uint32_t tid=0; tid!=values.size(); ++tid) {
  auto& entry=psma[getPSMASlot(values[tid],min)];
  if (entry.empty())
    entry={tid,tid+1};
  else
    entry.end=tid+1;
}
```

At query processing time, the potential range of tuples can now immediately be looked up in the PSMA:

```
// value = query constant of an equality predicate
auto scanRange=psma[getPSMASlot(value,min)];
```

C. SIMD IMPLEMENTATION OF FINDING INITIAL MATCHES

The following code listing shows the details of our find-matches implementation that makes use of the pre-computed table to map bit-masks to match positions. As the match table is limited to 256 entries, each entry can store 8 match positions. In most cases, we compare more elements in parallel which means multiple lookups are necessary. In the listing below, we evaluate a predicate on 32 8-bit integers at a time which results in 4 lookups.

Declarations:

```
// Vector of 8 32-bit integers.
typedef union {
 int32_t cell[8];
 __m256i reg256;
 __m128i reg128[2];
} vector8_int32;

using matchTableEntry = vector8_int32;

const matchTableEntry matchTable[256]{
 {{-256,-256,-256,-256,-256,-256,-256,-256}},
 {{1,-255,-255,-255,-255,-255,-255,-255}},
 {{257,-255,-255,-255,-255,-255,-255,-255}},
 // ...
 {{263,519,775,1031,1287,1543,1799,-249}},
 {{8,264,520,776,1032,1288,1544,1800}}
};
```

Find matches function:

```
if (reinterpret_cast<uintptr_t>(&column[from])%32) {
 // Process non-32-byte aligned elements sequentially
 ...
 // Recurse
} else {
 // Process 32-byte aligned elements (using SIMD/AVX2)
 const uint32_t simdWidth=32;
 const uint32_t numSimdIterations=(to-from)/simdWidth;
 const __m256i comparisonValueVec=set(comparisonValue);
 const __m256i vec16=_mm256_set1_epi32(16);
 uint32_t* writer=matches;
 for (uint32_t i=0;i!=numSimdIterations;i++) {
  uint32_t scanPos=from+(i*simdWidth);

  // Load and compare 32 values
  __m256i attributeVec=_mm256_load_si256(
      reinterpret_cast<__m256i*>(&column[scanPos]));
  __m256i selMask=cmp(attributeVec,comparisonValueVec);
  int bitMask=_mm256_movemask_epi8(selMask);

  // Lookup match positions and update positions vector
  auto& matchEntry0=matchTable[bitMask&0xFF];
  __m256i scanPosVec0=_mm256_set1_epi32(scanPos);
  _mm256_storeu_si256(
    reinterpret_cast<__m256i*>(writer),
    _mm256_add_epi32(scanPosVec0,
      _mm256_srai_epi32(matchEntry0.reg256,8)));
  writer+=static_cast<uint8_t>(matchEntry0.cell[0]);

  auto& matchEntry1=matchTable[(bitMask>>8)&0xFF];
  __m256i scanPosVec1=_mm256_set1_epi32(scanPos+8);
  _mm256_storeu_si256(
    reinterpret_cast<__m256i*>(writer),
    _mm256_add_epi32(scanPosVec1,
      _mm256_srai_epi32(matchEntry1.reg256,8)));
  writer+=static_cast<uint8_t>(matchEntry1.cell[0]);

  auto& matchEntry2=matchTable[(bitMask>>16)&0xFF];
  __m256i scanPosVec2=
      _mm256_add_epi32(scanPosVec0,vec16);
```

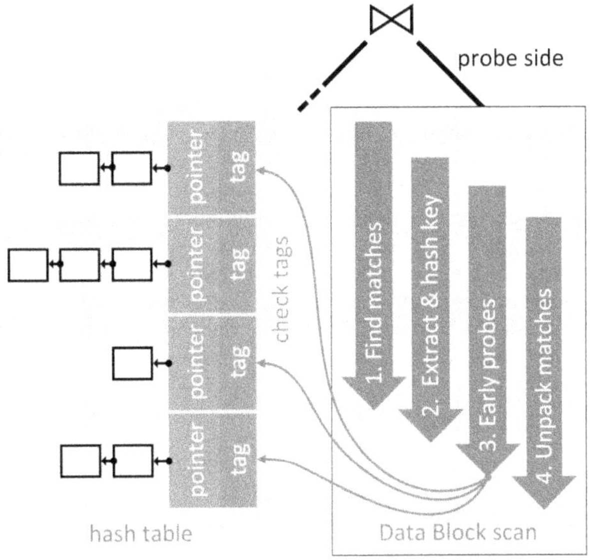

Figure 14: Early probing of vectors of matching keys from DataBlocks: pointer tags in the hash table are used to filter out keys that are not in one of the buckets (cf., tagged hash table pointers in [20]).

```
  _mm256_storeu_si256(
    reinterpret_cast<__m256i*>(writer),
    _mm256_add_epi32(scanPosVec2,
      _mm256_srai_epi32(matchEntry2.reg256,8)));
  writer+=static_cast<uint8_t>(matchEntry2.cell[0]);

  auto& matchEntry3=matchTable[(bitMask>>24)&0xFF];
  __m256i scanPosVec3=
      _mm256_add_epi32(scanPosVec1,vec16);
  _mm256_storeu_si256(
    reinterpret_cast<__m256i*>(writer),
    _mm256_add_epi32(scanPosVec3,
      _mm256_srai_epi32(matchEntry3.reg256,8)));
  writer+=static_cast<uint8_t>(matchEntry3.cell[0]);
 }
 // [...] Process remaining elements sequentially
 return writer-matches; // Number of matches
}
```

D. FLIGHT DATA SET QUERY

```
select
   uniquecarrier as carrier,
   avg(arrdelay) as avgdelay
from
   flights
where
   year between 1998 and 2008
   and dest = 'SFO'
group by
   uniquecarrier
order by
   avgdelay desc
```

E. FURTHER OPTIMIZATIONS

Vectorized scans that feed JIT-compiled query pipelines, as implemented in our hybrid OLTP and OLAP system, enable a large space of further optimization opportunities.

One research direction is to integrate more SIMD processing besides SARGable predicate evaluation in the vectorized scans. While SIMD processing is generally impossible in a tuple-at-a-time compiled loop produced by our JIT engine, vectorized scans will enable this possibility. One idea is to extend the vectorized scan with *eager aggregation* [36] functionality. This functionality would be able to calculate (arithmetic) expressions and evaluate aggregates only on the data inside one chunk. The resulting pre-aggregated data would then be re-aggregated by a true aggregation operator transforming the (non-holistic) aggregates in a way usually done for distributed, parallel, and indeed eager aggregation. This optimization mostly targets aggregates that just depend on a scan and are expected to have few groups, such as in TPC-H Q_1 and Q_6. In future work we intend to implement such early aggregation for vectorized scans on uncompressed chunks and compressed Data Blocks.

Another optimization opportunity is *early probing* of upstream hash-joins in the JIT-compiled query pipeline. When a vectorized scan of the probe side starts running in HyPer, the build side of the hash-joins in the JIT-compiled query pipeline has already been materialized. There are many situations in data warehousing workloads where such hash-joins can be very selective. For instance, this is the case when a fact table is used to probe a restricted dimension table. Scanning and decompressing all records of the fact table is a waste of CPU resources; hence, if the probe side is probed early inside the vectorized scan, touching attributes that would be eliminated later can be avoided. To enable such probing, systems like Vectorwise use bloom filters [29].

Probing a bloom filter is cheaper than performing a full hash lookup, for two reasons: First, a bloom filter is a much smaller memory object than a full hash table and thus typically fits in a lower-level CPU cache. Second, the JIT-compiled query pipeline contains the compiled hash lookup that performs the work in very few instructions; however, the loop in which it is placed also contains code for all subsequent operators in that query pipeline. The fact that this code is all part of the same code path means that this path potentially contains a large number of instructions and may thus be too complex to be executed efficiently. As such, even though modern out-of-order CPU cores can speculate deeply into a stretch of instructions if they hit stalls, it is improbable that the CPU is able to speculate through such a complex code path all the way up to the next loop iteration, i.e, up to the next input tuple. This means that in a JIT-compiled bloom filter, there is typically only one tuple at a time being looked up in the bloom filter and if this bloom filter is larger than the CPU cache, there will be only one outstanding memory load at any time. This is problematic because modern hardware is capable of handling multiple concurrent memory misses and limiting the number of outstanding loads available to the CPU core will make it impossible to use the available memory bandwidth. In contrast, vectorized bloom filter probing as part of a vectorized scan can be implemented as a simple loop that computes a boolean lookup result without any inter-tuple dependencies, and trivially generates the maximum number of parallel memory loads to saturate the memory bandwidth.

HyPer has a form of early probing, very similar to bloom filters, built into its hash table pointers (similar to tagged hash table pointers in [20]). This early probing is already used for tuple-at-a-time early probing in JIT-compiled pipelines. An implementation of this early probing for a vector of keys inside the vectorized scan (see Figure 14 for an example of vectorized early probing of matching keys from DataBlocks), directly after evaluating the SARGable predicates, allowed us to gain significant performance benefits on TPC-H Q_3–Q_5, Q_7–Q_8, Q_{10}–Q_{14}, and Q_{21}–Q_{22} in preliminary experiments. Overall, the geometric mean of query runtime improved by 1.2×. However, performing the early test for *all* joins inside the scan also slowed down a significant number of other queries. This provides a third optimization opportunity enabled by vectorization, namely to make query processing *adaptive*. Vectorwise has proposed *Micro Adaptivity* [29] where different implementations of particular vectorized functions ("flavors") are tried at runtime and performance is monitored. Given that inside a query a vectorized function might still be called millions of times, the micro-adaptive expression evaluator can experiment with the different flavors and stick most of the time with the flavor that performs best at that point in time. Micro-adaptivity captures the choice of flavors automatically and makes query performance more robust. Using such adaptive algorithms in a tuple-at-a-time JIT-compiled query pipeline is not possible, since every binary decision opportunity in the query pipeline duplicates the amount of possible code paths, which again leads to high compilation times (cf., Section 4). In vectorized scans, it is possible to employ such adaptive behavior and we experimented using micro-adaptivity to guide the decision whether or not to use the early join test inside the vectorized scan which allowed us to avoid performance penalties.

F. TPC-H RESULTS

	Uncompressed			Compressed			
	JIT scan	Vectorized scan	+SARG	Data Block scan	+SARG/SMA	+PSMA	over JIT
Q1	0.388s (45ms)	0.373s (29ms)	0.539s	0.431s	0.477s	0.478s	0.81×
Q2	0.085s (177ms)	0.097s (89ms)	0.086s	0.092s	0.086s	0.086s	1.00×
Q3	0.731s (64ms)	0.723s (34ms)	0.812s	0.711s	0.634s	0.627s	1.17×
Q4	0.491s (50ms)	0.508s (27ms)	0.497s	0.502s	0.457s	0.454s	1.08×
Q5	0.655s (120ms)	0.662s (57ms)	0.645s	0.691s	0.658s	0.655s	1.00×
Q6	0.267s (20ms)	0.180s (11ms)	0.114s	0.188s	0.040s	0.040s	6.70×
Q7	0.600s (124ms)	0.614s (62ms)	0.659s	0.632s	0.557s	0.548s	1.09×
Q8	0.409s (171ms)	0.420s (78ms)	0.401s	0.505s	0.458s	0.460s	0.89×
Q9	2.429s (121ms)	2.380s (59ms)	2.357s	2.423s	2.439s	2.453s	0.99×
Q10	0.638s (96ms)	0.633s (50ms)	0.691s	0.614s	0.521s	0.512s	1.25×
Q11	0.094s (114ms)	0.092s (56ms)	0.092s	0.087s	0.082s	0.081s	1.16×
Q12	0.413s (58ms)	0.447s (32ms)	0.430s	0.381s	0.305s	0.305s	1.35×
Q13	6.695s (45ms)	6.766s (27ms)	6.786s	7.260s	7.132s	7.098s	0.94×
Q14	0.466s (41ms)	0.410s (22ms)	0.438s	0.213s	0.145s	0.140s	3.33×
Q15	0.441s (48ms)	0.440s (37ms)	0.434s	0.359s	0.278s	0.275s	1.60×
Q16	0.831s (99ms)	0.836s (55ms)	0.842s	0.662s	0.669s	0.664s	1.25×
Q17	0.427s (74ms)	0.439s (41ms)	0.436s	0.504s	0.490s	0.487s	0.88×
Q18	2.496s (91ms)	2.418s (49ms)	2.401s	2.379s	2.366s	2.394s	1.04×
Q19	1.061s (70ms)	1.119s (34ms)	1.125s	0.682s	0.528s	0.521s	2.04×
Q20	0.602s (108ms)	0.596s (54ms)	0.610s	0.577s	0.529s	0.530s	1.14×
Q21	1.223s (129ms)	1.176s (65ms)	1.166s	1.212s	1.142s	1.136s	1.08×
Q22	0.265s (81ms)	0.321s (48ms)	0.261s	0.391s	0.278s	0.277s	0.96×
Sum	21.708s (1945ms)	21.649s (1016ms)	21.822s	21.497s	20.271s	20.179s	
Geometric mean	0.586s (78ms)	0.583s (42ms)	0.577s	0.555s	0.466s	0.463s	1.27×

Table 4: Query runtimes and compilation times (in parentheses) of TPC-H queries on scale factor 100 with (i) JIT-compiled tuple-at-a-time scans on uncompressed data, (ii) vectorized scans on uncompressed data, (iii) vectorized scans on uncompressed data with SARG-able predicate evaluation (+SARG), (iv) vectorized compressed Data Block scans, (v) vectorized compressed Data Block scans with SARG-able predicate evaluation and SMAs (+SARG/SMA), and (vi) (v) with Positional SMA indexes (+PSMA).

GeckoFTL: Scalable Flash Translation Techniques For Very Large Flash Devices

Niv Dayan
Harvard University
dayan@seas.harvard.edu

Philippe Bonnet
IT University of Copenhagen
phbo@itu.dk

Stratos Idreos
Harvard University
stratos@seas.harvard.edu

ABSTRACT

The volume of metadata needed by a flash translation layer (FTL) is proportional to the storage capacity of a flash device. Ideally, this metadata should reside in the device's integrated RAM to enable fast access. However, as flash devices scale to terabytes, the necessary volume of metadata is exceeding the available integrated RAM. Moreover, recovery time after power failure, which is proportional to the size of the metadata, is becoming impractical. The simplest solution is to persist more metadata in flash. The problem is that updating metadata in flash increases the amount of internal IOs thereby harming performance and device lifetime.

In this paper, we identify a key component of the metadata called the Page Validity Bitmap (PVB) as the bottleneck. PVB is used by the garbage-collectors of state-of-the-art FTLs to keep track of which physical pages in the device are invalid. PVB constitutes 95% of the FTL's RAM-resident metadata, and recovering PVB after power fails takes a significant proportion of the overall recovery time. To solve this problem, we propose a page-associative FTL called GeckoFTL, whose central innovation is replacing PVB with a new data structure called Logarithmic Gecko. Logarithmic Gecko is similar to an LSM-tree in that it first logs updates and later reorganizes them to ensure fast and scalable access time. Relative to the baseline of storing PVB in flash, Logarithmic Gecko enables cheaper updates at the cost of slightly more expensive garbage-collection queries. We show that this is a good trade-off because (1) updates are intrinsically more frequent than garbage-collection queries to page validity metadata, and (2) flash writes are more expensive than flash reads. We demonstrate analytically and empirically through simulation that GeckoFTL achieves a 95% reduction in space requirements and at least a 51% reduction in recovery time by storing page validity metadata in flash while keeping the contribution to internal IO overheads 98% lower than the baseline.

1. INTRODUCTION

In recent years, storage devices based on NAND flash memory such as eMMCs (embedded multimedia cards) and SSDs (solid state drives) have become widely used for various applications. Relative to hard disk drives, the benefits of NAND flash include superior read/write performance, shock-resistance, noiselessness, and lower power consumption.

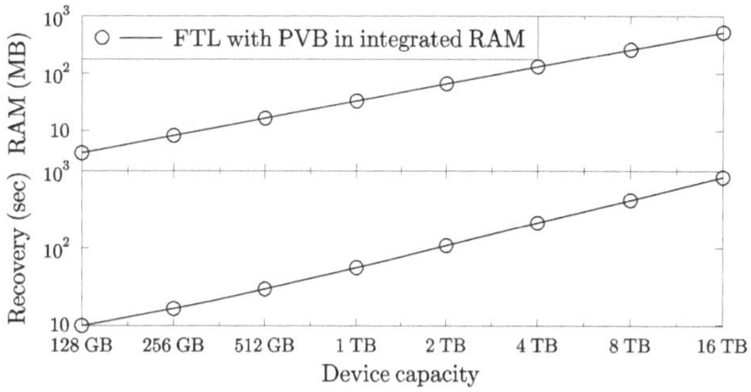

Figure 1: RAM-resident FTL metadata and recovery time are increasing unsustainably as device capacity grows.

The Need for a Flash Translation Layer. Flash memory is organized into thousands of flash blocks, each of which contains hundreds of atomic storage units called pages. A critical property of flash is that a page cannot be updated until the block that contains it is erased. This characteristic creates the requirement for a Flash Translation Layer (FTL). When a logical page is updated, its new version is written on a free flash page, and the original flash page is marked by the FTL as invalid. A lot of metadata is needed to support this task. At the very least, this metadata includes a translation table from logical to physical addresses (to keep track of the whereabouts of live logical pages), as well as a bookkeeping of which flash pages are invalid (to later reclaim them through garbage-collection).

Costly Integrated RAM. A small RAM module is integrated into flash devices to store FTL metadata. However, the amount of this integrated RAM is limited due to its costs. In lower-end devices like eMMCs, manufacturers use Static RAM (SRAM) due to its power-efficiency [27]. Today, the cost of SRAM is approximately \$5 per megabyte. This limits the amount of metadata that can be stored in integrated RAM to a few megabytes at most. Higher-end flash devices like SSDs typically embed an additional Dynamic RAM (DRAM) module comprising tens to hundreds of megabytes [13]. DRAM is 2 orders of magnitude cheaper than SRAM, but it also contributes to a device's cost by requiring a more sophisticated controller and circuitry. DRAM also increases runtime costs because it is more power-hungry than SRAM.

Scalability Problem. The amount of metadata needed by state-of-the-art FTLs is increasing in proportion to device capacity. This increases their minimum integrated RAM requirement. It also increases the time that it takes such FTLs to recover from power failure, because recovery time is proportional to the amount of metadata that has to be recovered.

SIGMOD'16, June 26-July 01, 2016, San Francisco, CA, USA

DOI: http://dx.doi.org/10.1145/2882903.2915219

A natural solution is to persist metadata in flash. This frees up integrated RAM and also reduces recovery time because flash is non-volatile and so metadata is not lost when power fails. Indeed, state-of-the-art FTLs already store the largest metadata structure, the logical to physical translation table, in flash [22, 26], while caching frequently accessed mapping entries in integrated RAM. This approach has kept the integrated RAM requirement and recovery time acceptable until now.

However, Figure 1 shows that the integrated RAM requirement and recovery time are increasing unsustainably as flash devices continue to grow in capacity. The results are based on an implementation of LazyFTL [22], which is a state-of-the-art FTL (we discuss the figure's derivation in detail in Section 5). In particular, the figure shows that integrated RAM reemerges as a dominant cost for low-end devices at capacities of $\approx$ 128 GB, at which point 4 MB of SRAM are needed. Similarly, recovery time becomes impractical at capacities of $\approx$ 2 TB, at which point recovery takes tens of seconds. Since there already exist 128 GB low-end[1] and 2 TB high-end[2] devices on the market, we are at the point in which these scalability challenges need to be addressed.

In this paper, we identify a key components of the metadata called the Page Validity Bitmap (PVB) as the bottleneck. PVB is used by state-of-the-art FTLs to keep track of which physical pages in the device are invalid. It is updated whenever a flash page becomes invalid, and it is queried by garbage-collection operations to determine which flash pages on a victim block are still valid. PVB accounts for 95% of all RAM-resident metadata and comprises a significant proportion of recovery time.

The simplest solution is storing PVB in flash. The problem is that PVB is frequently updated, so storing it in flash increases write-amplification, the phenomena whereby several internal flash reads and writes take place for every logical write issued by the application. Write-amplification harms throughput. It also wears out the device at a faster rate, since flash blocks have a limited lifetime with respect to the number of times they have each been overwritten.

Flash Devices and Databases. With more and more database systems and installations utilizing flash devices, it is increasingly important to scale flash devices to sustain the growth of very large database applications. At the same time, ensuring quick recovery in the presence of failures as devices grow is an essential property that very large databases require.

The Solution: GeckoFTL. To address these scalability challenges, we propose GeckoFTL. Its central innovation is storing page validity metadata in flash using a new write-optimized data structure called Logarithmic Gecko, where Gecko stands for **G**arbage-**C**ollector. Logarithmic Gecko is similar to an LSM-tree [32] in that it logs updates and later reorganizes them in flash to ensure fast and scalable access time. Relative to the baseline solution of storing PVB in flash, Logarithmic Gecko enables cheaper updates at the cost of slightly more expensive garbage-collection queries. We show that this is a good trade-off because (1) updates are much more frequent than garbage-collection queries to page validity metadata, and (2) flash writes are an order of magnitude more expensive than flash reads. Thus, Logarithmic Gecko reduces the write-amplification generated by a flash-resident PVB by 98% while still enabling a 95% reduction in the integrated RAM requirement. Even for devices that have enough integrated RAM to store PVB, we show that using Logarithmic Gecko reduces recovery time by at least 51% and improves performance as the freed integrated RAM is used to cache a larger proportion of the translation table.

[1]E.g. Samsung KLMDGAWEBD-B031

[2]E.g. Samsung MZ-7KE2T0BW

Since GeckoFTL involves storing more metatadata in flash, a natural question is how to garbage-collect flash-resident metadata. The GeckoFTL garbage-collector answers this by accounting for the different update frequencies of user data and metadata thereby further significantly decreasing the overall write-amplification.

Finally, GeckoFTL removes a significant contention between recovery time and write-amplification. In state-of-the-art FTLs, the flash-resident translation table is updated lazily and in bulk to amortize the cost of updates. Meanwhile, so-called dirty mapping entries for recently updated logical pages are cached in integrated RAM. When power fails, these dirty entries are lost, and the time to recover them is proportional to the number of dirty entries that were in the cache when power failed. To bound recovery time, existing FTLs limit the number of dirty entries in the cache. However, doing so also limits the amount by which updates to the flash-resident translation table can be amortized, so write-amplification increases. GeckoFTL presents a lazy recovery algorithm based on checkpoints that removes this contention between recovery time and write-amplification.

Contributions. Our contributions are as follows.

- We show that as flash devices scale, more metadata will need to be stored in flash to keep the integrated RAM requirement and recovery time practical. However, storing metadata naively in flash can significantly increase write-amplification thereby compromising throughput and device lifetime.
- We present GeckoFTL, a page-associative FTL that enables flash devices to scale while keeping the integrated RAM requirement, recovery time, and write-amplification low.
- GeckoFTL uses a novel data structure called Logarithmic Gecko to store page validity metadata in flash. Relative to the baseline solution of storing PVB in flash, Logarithmic Gecko generates 98% less write-amplification while still enabling a 95% reduction in the RAM requirement and at least a 51% reduction in recovery time.
- GeckoFTL keeps garbage-collection overheads low by differentiating between user data and flash-resident metadata.
- GeckoFTL includes a fast recovery algorithm for dirty cached mapping entries that neither requires a battery nor involves a contention between recovery time and write-amplification.

2. BACKGROUND

This section provides the necessary background on flash devices and flash translation layers.

Flash Devices. Flash devices consist of multiple NAND chips, each of which is organized into independent arrays of memory cells. An array is a flash block, and a row within the array is a flash page. A flash page typically stores 4-16 KB and a block typically contains 64-256 pages.

Idiosyncrasies. Flash memory is subject to several idiosyncrasies. (1) The minimum granularity of reads and writes is a flash page. (2) Before a flash page can be updated, the block that contains it must be erased. (3) Blocks become increasingly prone to random bit-shifts as a function of the number of erases and rewrites they have endured. Thus, they have a limited lifetime. (4) Writes must take place sequentially within a block to minimize bit-shifts due to electronic side-effects [1]. (5) Page reads and writes have asymmetric costs; they take tens and hundreds of microseconds to execute respectively [30], and this discrepancy is increasing as an industry trend [15]. Moreover, flash writes have an additional cost in that they wear out the device.

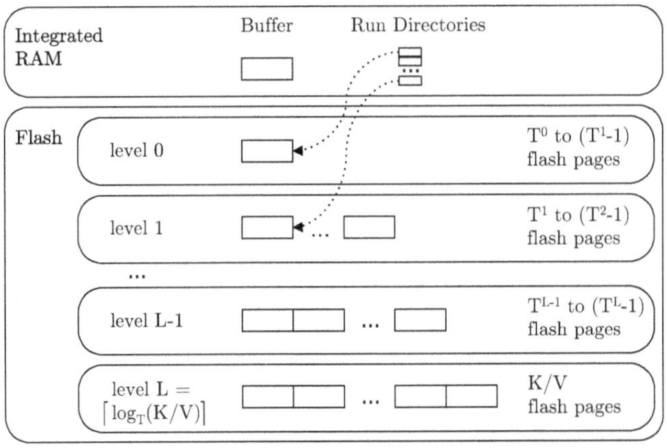

Term	Description	E.g.
K	Number of blocks in the flash device	2^{22}
B	Number of pages per block	2^7
P	Size of a flash page in bytes	2^{12}
R	Ratio of logical capacity to physical capacity	0.7
T	Size ratio between runs in Logarithmic Gecko	
L	Number of levels in Logarithmic Gecko	
V	Number of Gecko entries that fit into the buffer	
S	Entry partitioning factor in Logarithmic Gecko	
C	Capacity of LRU cache in GeckoFTL	
δ	Time to write flash page / time to read flash page	

Figure 2: Overview of Logarithmic Gecko, and terms used throughout the paper.

FTL Tasks. A layer of firmware called the Flash Translation Layer (FTL) manages these idiosyncrasies while exposing a simple block device interface to applications. Its principle tasks are performing out-of-place updates to avoid having to erase and rewrite an entire flash block for every page update, and performing wear-leveling to ensure that all blocks age at a similar rate.

Out-of-place updates have three important implications. (1) The physical capacity of the device must be larger than the logical capacity exposed to the application in order to accommodate free and invalid flash pages. This extra physical capacity is called over-provisioned space. (2) A translation table from logical to physical addresses is needed to keep track of the whereabouts of live logical pages. (3) A garbage-collector is needed to free space that is occupied by invalid pages.

FTL Metadata. The FTL relies on metadata to achieve these tasks. There is an integrated RAM module in flash devices whereon some of this metadata can be stored to enable fast access. However the amount of integrated RAM is limited by costs. Lower-end devices rely on power-efficient yet expensive SRAM, which limits capacity to few megabytes at most. Higher-end devices embed additional tens to hundreds of megabytes of DRAM, but this increases costs by requiring a more sophisticated controller and circuity as well as higher power-consumption during runtime.

In addition to integrated RAM, every flash page has an adjacent spare area whereon metadata about the page can be stored. The spare area is physically adjacent to its flash page and typically smaller by a factor of 32 [1]. Since a spare area cannot be updated before the underlying block is erased, it is used to store metadata that is relevant for a flash page during one of the page's life-cycles (e.g. current logical address, timestamp of when it was last written, error-correction code, etc).

Translation Table. The largest metadata structure in the FTL is the translation table from logical to physical addresses. The translation table is an associative array, and the value at offset i is the physical address of where logical page i currently resides in flash [16]. Using the terms in Figure 2, a device with physical flash capacity of $K \cdot B \cdot P$ bytes has a translation table of size $4 \cdot K \cdot B \cdot R$ bytes[3], which we denote as TT. For example, a 2 TB flash device described by the example values in Figure 2 has a 1.4 GB translation table. how to implement the translation table under integrated RAM constraints has been at the heart of FTL design for two decades [27].

Early FTL designs tackled this problem by increasing the mapping granularity from a page to a block [27, 14, 9, 10, 21, 23, 33]. This allows using one mapping entry per block rather than per page thereby reducing the size of the translation table by a factor of $\approx B$. The problem with these block-associative FTLs is that continuously reorganizing adjacent logical pages into the same flash block dramatically increases write-amplification, especially for update patterns that are random in the logical address space.

On the other hand, state-of-the-art FTLs [22, 26, 24, 18] store a page-associative translation table in flash while storing frequently accessed mapping entries in an LRU cache in integrated RAM. The flash pages that store the translation table are called translation pages, and each of them contains a contiguous range of mapping entries. Translation pages are also updated out-of-place, and so a Global Mapping Directory (GMD) is needed in integrated RAM to keep track of the most recent version of each translation page [22, 26]. The size of GMD is $(4 \cdot TT)/P$. Thus, for the 2 TB device described in Figure 2, GMD is 1.4 MB.

Recovering Dirty Entries. The flash-resident translation table is updated lazily and in bulk to amortize the cost of updates [16]. Meanwhile, dirty mapping entries for recently updated logical pages are stored in the LRU cache in integrated RAM. When power fails, these dirty mapping entries are lost and must be recovered to keep track of live user data. The brute-force recovery approach is to scan the spare areas of all flash pages in the device and create a dirty mapping entry for any page with user data that was updated after the last time its corresponding translation page was updated [23]. However, this approach is impractical for very large flash devices as it involves $K \cdot B$ spare area reads, which amount to $\approx$ 26 minutes[4] for the example values in Figure 2. An alternative is using a battery to synchronize all dirty mapping entries with the flash-resident translation table before power runs out [22]. However, a battery increases manufacturing costs.

The problem of how to efficiently recover dirty mapping entries without a battery is open, but the best known approach is to break it into two subproblems [26]: (1) identifying and recreating mapping entries for all recently updated logical pages (this should be done quickly while ensuring that we do not miss any unsynchronized logical pages), and (2) efficiently synchronizing these mapping entries with the flash-resident translation table. If step (2) is done before normal operation resumes, then it elongates recovery time by $\min(C, \frac{TT}{P})$ page reads and writes. When $C > \frac{TT}{P}$, this amounts

[3] Each physical address is 4 bytes.

[4] A spare area read takes $100/32 \approx 3$ μs since reading a page takes ≈ 100 μs [15] and a spare area is 32 times smaller than a page [1].

to ≈ 7 minutes[5] for the values in Figure 2. To bound recovery time, existing approaches restrict the number of dirty entries in the cache [26, 18]. The problem is that this also limits the amount by which updates to the flash-resident translation table can be amortized, and so write-amplification increases.

PVB. A page-associative FTL must maintain a Page Validity Bitmap (PVB) to keep track of which flash pages are invalid. PVB is structured such that bits that correspond to pages on the same block are adjacent. Whenever a flash page is invalidated, the FTL shifts the corresponding bit in PVB from 0 to 1. During a garbage-collection operation, the FTL queries PVB to determine which flash pages are still valid and need to be migrated before erasing the victim block. When the victim block is erased, all bits in PVB corresponding to pages on the erased block are set to 0.

Scalability of PVB. PVB contains one bit for each flash page in the device, and so its size is $\frac{B \cdot K}{8}$ bytes. For the example values in Figure 2, PVB comprises 64 MB. Thus, the RAM requirement for PVB is roughly 45 times larger than the RAM requirements for GMD. This makes PVB the primary bottleneck in terms of integrated RAM. Moreover, recovering PVB after failure takes a long time as it requires scanning all translation pages (to identify all valid flash pages). This takes $\frac{TT}{P}$ page reads, which amount to ≈ 36 seconds for the example values in Figure 2. To bound the integrated RAM requirement and recovery time for PVB, the simplest solution is to store it in flash [24]. The problem is that this requires updating one flash page of PVB for every application update. This significantly increases write-amplification.

3. LOGARITHMIC GECKO

Overview. Logarithmic Gecko is a novel write-optimized data structure that replaces PVB by indexing page validity metadata in flash. Figure 2 gives a high-level overview of Logarithmic Gecko as well as terms that we use throughout the paper.

The operations that Logarithmic Gecko supports at its interface are updates and garbage-collection queries (henceforth called GC queries). An update occurs when a flash page is invalidated. A GC query occurs during a garbage-collection operation to determine which flash pages are invalid in the victim block. The design goal of Logarithmic Gecko is to support both operations while minimizing the internal IO overhead.

Buffered Updates. Logarithmic Gecko handles an update by inserting the address of the invalidated flash page into a RAM-resident buffer. The buffer's size is one flash page, and we denote V as the number of entries that fit into it. When the buffer fills up, it is flushed to flash. Thus, V updates lead to one flash write. This is cheaper than PVB, for which V updates lead to V flash reads and writes.

Merge Operations. Logarithmic Gecko stores page validity metadata in substructures in flash called runs, which are organized into L levels. When the buffer is flushed, it is inserted as a run into level 0. Runs are merged in the background as an LSM-tree [32] to keep query time scalable. Whenever there are two runs in the same level, they are merged. The two original runs are then discarded, and the new run may be promoted to the next level based on its size. Thus, a merge operation may continue recursively. As shown in Figure 2, a run is placed in level i if it consists of between T^i and $T^{i+1} - 1$ flash pages, where T is a tuning parameter that controls a trade-off between the costs of updates and GC queries. The logical and physical details of merge operations are given in Section 3.1 and Appendix A respectively.

[5] A page read and write take $\approx 100\,\mu$s and ≈ 1 ms respectively [15].

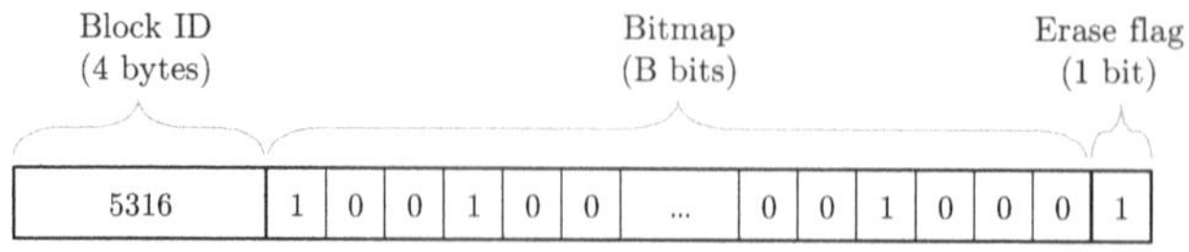

Figure 3: A Gecko entry

Gecko Entries. Logarithmic Gecko stores addresses of invalid flash pages in the buffer and in runs as key-value pairs called Gecko entries (Figure 3). The key of a Gecko entry is a block ID, and the Gecko entries in each run are sorted by this key. The value of a Gecko entry is a bitmap of size B, where the bit at offset i indicates if the physical page at offset i in the block is invalid.

A GC query for key X finds all Gecko entries with key X across all runs and merges their bitmaps using the bitwise OR operator. Similarly, when runs that contain two Gecko entries with the same key are merged, the two Gecko entries are merged in the resulting run by taking the OR product of their bitmaps. These operations are described in detail in Section 3.1.

Run Directories. The RAM-resident run directories in Figure 2 serve as indexes for the flash-resident runs. They contain the physical location of each flash page in each run and the key range of the Gecko entries that it contains. They speed up GC queries by enabling them to only read the flash page in each run that contains the relevant key range. A GC query always traverses the runs from most recently created to least recently created.

Erase Flag. When a block is erased, all of its pages become free. Thus, all Gecko entries for this block that were created before the erase become obsolete and must be ignored during subsequent GC queries. To accomplish this, a simple approach is to find every Gecko entry with the block's key and either erase it or mark it as invalid. However, this would be a costly operation involving $O(L)$ flash reads and writes. To avoid this cost, we add one bit to each Gecko entry called the erase flag (see Figure 3). When a block is erased, we insert a Gecko entry for the block to the buffer and set its erase flag to true. Moreover, we terminate a GC query when it encounters a Gecko entry for the target block with an erase flag set to true, because all Gecko entries on larger runs were created before the last time the block was erased and are therefore obsolete.

Logarithmic Gecko removes obsolete entries during merge operations so that they do not consume space. When two runs that contain Gecko entries with the same key are merged, the entry from the older run is discarded if the entry from the newer run has its erase flag set to true.

All in all, the erase flag allows handling a flash erase through one insertion to the buffer rather than through $O(L)$ flash reads and writes. This makes the performance of Logarithmic Gecko largely independent of the frequency of garbage-collection operations.

In Section 3.1, we describe the basic operations of Logarithmic Gecko in more detail and in Section 3.2 we analyze their costs. In Section 3.3, we introduce a technique called entry-partitioning that makes the performance of Logarithmic Gecko independent of the block size B. In Section 4, we describe how GeckoFTL and Logarithmic Gecko interact. We show how to recover Logarithmic Gecko's run directories and buffer after failure in Appendices C.1 and C.2 respectively.

3.1 Operations

Updates. Logarithmic Gecko's role is to keep track of invalid flash pages. Whenever the FTL identifies an invalid page (as explained later in Section 4.1) it reports it to Logarithmic Gecko via Algorithm 1. The algorithm checks if there is already a Gecko entry in the buffer corresponding to the invalid page's block and creates one if not. It then sets to 1 the bit in the Gecko entry's bitmap at

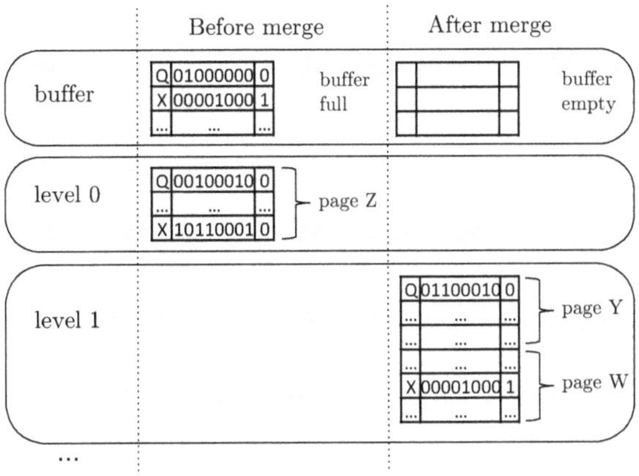

Figure 4: Example of a merge operation.

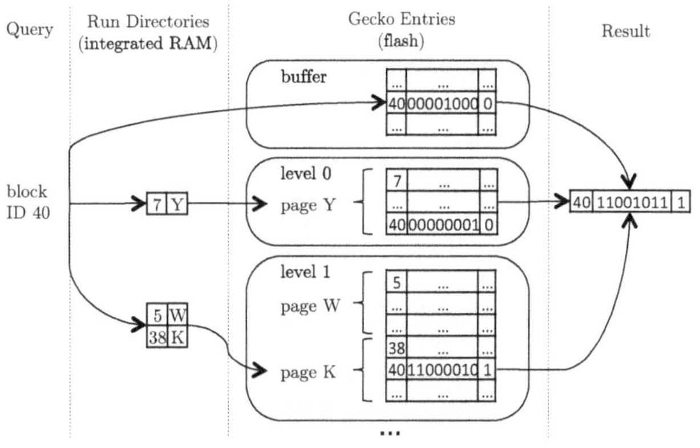

Figure 5: Example of a GC query for key 40.

the offset corresponding to the invalidated page in the block. If the buffer fills up, it is flushed to level 0 in flash.

Erases. When a flash block X is erased, all of its pages become free, and so we must ensure that all Gecko entries created before the block was erased are ignored in subsequent GC queries. This is done by invoking Algorithm 2, which takes as an input a block ID and inserts a Gecko entry with a corresponding key into the buffer with a blank bitmap and the erase flag set to 1.

Merging Runs. When we merge two runs, they may contain Gecko entries corresponding to the same flash block. We denote this as a collision. Collisions are easy to detect during a merge because the runs are sorted by key and we merge them through linear scans. Algorithm 3 is called to handle a collision. If the erase flag of the entry from the more recently created run is set to 1, it means that the other entry was created before the last time the corresponding block was erased, and so it is discarded. Otherwise, the bitmaps for the two entries are merged using the bitwise OR operator to save space.

Figure 4 shows an example of a merge operation. In the example, the buffer has filled up and is merged with the run at level 0. Two collisions occur during this merge for the entries with keys X and Q. For key X, the older entry is discarded since the newer entry's erase flag is set to 1. For key Q, the entries are merged using the bitwise OR operator. The resulting run consists of two flash pages. In this example, T is 2 so the new run is promoted to level 1.

```
Input: physical_address pa, logical_address la
block_id = pa.block_id;
page_offset = pa.page_offset;
if !buffer.contains(block_id) then
    buffer.insert(block_id);
    buffer[block_id].bitmap = blank bitmap;
    buffer[block_id].erase_flag = 0;
buffer[block_id].bitmap[page_offset] = 1;
if buffer is full then
    flush(buffer) ;
```

Algorithm 1: Insert an invalid page address into the buffer.

```
Input: block_id
if buffer.contains(block_id) = false then
    buffer.insert(block_id);
buffer[block_id].bitmap = blank bitmap;
buffer[block_id].erase_flag = 1;
if buffer is full then
    flush(buffer) ;
```

Algorithm 2: Insert the address of an erased block to the buffer.

GC Queries. A garbage-collection operation issues a GC query to determine which flash pages on the victim block are valid and must be migrated before erasing the victim. A GC query first searches the buffer and then the runs from smallest to largest for Gecko entries with keys matching the victim block's ID. It uses the run directories to only perform one flash read per run. Thus, its cost is $O(L)$ flash reads. It finishes once all runs have been searched or when it encounters an entry with an erase flag set to 1.

Figure 5 shows an example GC query for key 40. It first looks in the buffer and finds the first matching entry. It then probes the run directories for the location of the first run (at level 0), reads it from flash, and finds the second matching entry. It then probes the run directory for level 1, identifies flash page K as containing keys that overlap the target ID, reads it, and finds the third matching entry. Since this matching entry's erase flag is set to 1, the GC query terminates. Although there may be Gecko entries with key 40 in runs at higher levels, these entries must have been created before the last time that block 40 was erased, so they are ignored. The bitmaps of all found Gecko entries are finally merged using the bitwise OR operator.

```
Input: newEntry, oldEntry
if newEntry.erase_flag = 1 then
    return newEntry ;
else
    create resultEntry;
    resultEntry.bitmap = newEntry.bitmap OR oldEntry.bitmap;
    resultEntry.erase_flag = oldEntry.erase_flag;
    return resultEntry ;
```

Algorithm 3: Handling collisions during merge operations.

3.2 Analysis

The number of levels L in Logarithmic Gecko is $\lceil \log_T(\frac{K}{V})) \rceil$, where K is the number of flash blocks in the device and V is the number of Gecko entries that fit into one flash page. The reason is that the largest run consists of K/V pages, and subsequent runs have exponentially decreasing sizes, each by a factor of T. This gives way to a logarithmic number of levels.

Cost per Update. An update to Logarithmic Gecko involves inserting a Gecko entry to the buffer. This entry is later rewritten multiple times during merge operations. Although the overall IO cost of an update is indirect, we can capture it as follows. During a merge operation, each flash write copies V entries to the new run. The cost per entry per merge is thus $O(\frac{1}{V})$ of a flash read and write. Now, if an entry does not become obsolete earlier, then it participates on average in $O(T)$ merges per level and goes

Technique	Update		Garbage-Collection Operation		Integrated RAM
	flash reads	flash writes	flash reads	flash writes	
RAM-resident PVB	0	0	0	0	$O(B \cdot K)$
Flash-resident PVB	1	1	1	0	$O(\frac{B \cdot K}{P})$
Logarithmic Gecko	$O(\frac{T}{V} log_T(\frac{K}{V}))$	$O(\frac{T}{V} log_T(\frac{K}{V}))$	$O(log_T(\frac{K}{V}))$	$O(\frac{T}{V} log_T(\frac{K}{V}))$	$O(\frac{B \cdot K}{P})$

Table 1: Relative to a flash-resident PVB, Logarithmic Gecko offers cheaper updates and more expensive GC queries.

through $O(\log_T(\frac{K}{V}))$ levels before getting merged with the largest run. Thus, the amortized cost for an update is $O(\frac{T}{V} \cdot \log_T(\frac{K}{V}))$ flash reads and writes. Typically, V is much larger than $T \cdot \log_T(\frac{K}{V})$. Thus, the cost of an update is sub-constant (lower than 1); each update costs a small fraction of a flash read and a flash write.

Cost per Garbage-Collection Operation. A garbage-collection operation issues a GC query to Logarithmic gecko. A GC query traverses the levels from smallest to largest, issuing one flash read per level. The cost is $O(\log_T(\frac{K}{V}))$ flash reads.

A garbage-collection operation also inserts one entry to the buffer with the erase flag set to true. As we just saw, the cost of inserting a Gecko entry to the buffer is $O(\frac{T}{V} log_T(\frac{K}{V}))$ flash reads and writes.

Tuning. The parameter T controls a trade-off between the costs of updates and GC queries. The minimum value of T is 2. As T increases, there are less levels and so GC queries become cheaper. However, increasing T also increases the cost of updates, as each entry participates in $O(T)$ merge operations per level. In Section 5, we show how to tune T so as to minimize the overall IO overhead.

Comparison to PVB. Table 1 compares the IO costs and integrated RAM requirement of Logarithmic Gecko, a flash-resident PVB, and a RAM-resident PVB. The RAM-resident PVB has no IO overheads, but its integrated RAM requirement is high. The flash-resident PVB has a similar integrated RAM requirement to Logarithmic Gecko, but it is different in terms of IO costs. With a flash-resident PVB, the cost of an update is one flash read and one flash write while the cost of a GC query is one flash read. Compared to a flash-resident PVB, the cost of an update in Logarithmic Gecko is cheaper while the the cost of a GC query is more expensive. In Section 5, we show that this is a good trade-off because (1) flash reads are cheaper than flash writes, and (2) GC queries happen infrequently relative to updates to page validity metadata.

Space-Amplification. The existence of invalid entries leads to space-amplification in Logarithmic Gecko. However, because the largest run contains one of each entry, and since the runs at smaller levels are exponentially smaller, space-amplification is never beyond a factor of ≈ 2 for any value of T.

3.3 Entry-Partitioning

When a Gecko entry is inserted into the buffer, is contains a lot of space yet little information (i.e. most of the bits are set to 0). This waste of space limits V, the number of Gecko entries that fit into the buffer. As shown in Table 1, V is inversely proportional to the update cost in Logarithmic Gecko. We now show how to decrease the update cost by decreasing the amount of buffer space that is wasted.

Under the current design, $V \approx \frac{P \cdot 8}{key+B}$, where P is the size of a flash page in bytes, *key* is the size of a key of a Gecko entry in bits, and B is the number of page validity bits in a Gecko entry. Thus, the value of V depends on the value of B. In fact, since B tends to increase as flash devices grow in capacity, the dependency of V on B is a scalability problem. Our goal is to maximize V while eliminating its dependence on B.

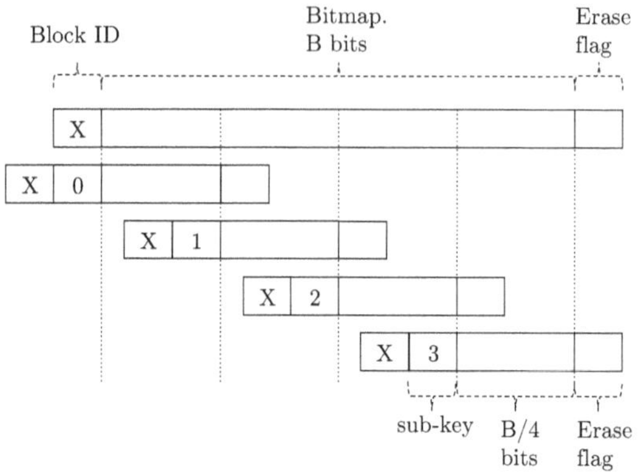

Figure 6: Entry-partitioning with a factor of 4.

To do so, we introduce entry-partitioning. The idea is to partition a Gecko entry into S equal sub-entries, where S is the partitioning factor. Figure 6 shows an example of entry-partitioning where $S = 4$. As shown, each of the partitioned sub-entries has an additional sub-key component to indicate which part of original bitmap it corresponds to. Thus, during an update to Logarithmic Gecko, we only need to insert one sub-entry for the part of the original bitmap that was updated.

An interesting question is how to tune S. To do so, it helps noting that the overall size of Logarithmic gecko in flash is $O(B \cdot K + S \cdot key \cdot K)$ bits, where $O(B \cdot K)$ is for the page validity bits and $O(S \cdot key \cdot K)$ is for the keys. One extreme is setting S to 1. This amounts to no entry-partitioning. In this case, $B \cdot K$ is typically larger than $key \cdot K$, and so the size of Logarithmic Gecko in flash simplifies to $O(B \cdot K)$ bits. The other extreme is setting S to B. In this case, the size of Logarithmic Gecko becomes dominated by the keys and simplifies to $O(B \cdot K \cdot key)$ bits. Thus, the space that Logarithmic Gecko takes up is amplified by a factor of $O(key)$. Space-amplification is harmful because it increases the number of levels in Logarithmic Gecko thereby increasing the costs of both updates and GC queries. It also increases the size of the run directories in integrated RAM. Thus, space-amplification should be bounded.

A good balance is setting $S = \frac{B}{key}$. This removes the dependence of V on B while restricting the size of Logarithmic Gecko to $O(B \cdot K)$ bits. For instance, if *key* is 32 bits and B is 128, than S is set to 4 so that each sub-entry contains a 32 bits key and a 32 bits chunk of the bitmap.

4. GECKO FTL

We now present GeckoFTL, a novel FTL whose design goal is to keep the integrated RAM requirement and recovery time practical for very large flash devices without paying a high price in terms of write-amplification. To do so, GeckoFTL makes three innovations. (1) It offloads page validity metadata to flash using Logarithmic Gecko. (2) It uses a garbage-collection scheme that prevents an increase in write-amplification as more metadata is offloaded to flash. (3) It uses a recovery approach for dirty mapping entries that does not exhibit a contention between recovery time and write-amplification.

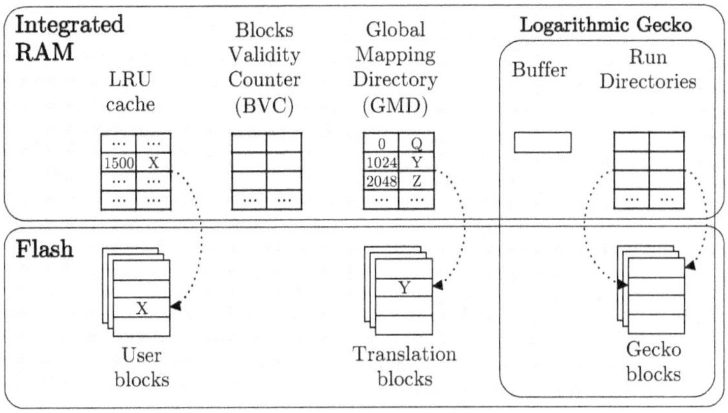

Figure 7: Overview of GeckoFTL.

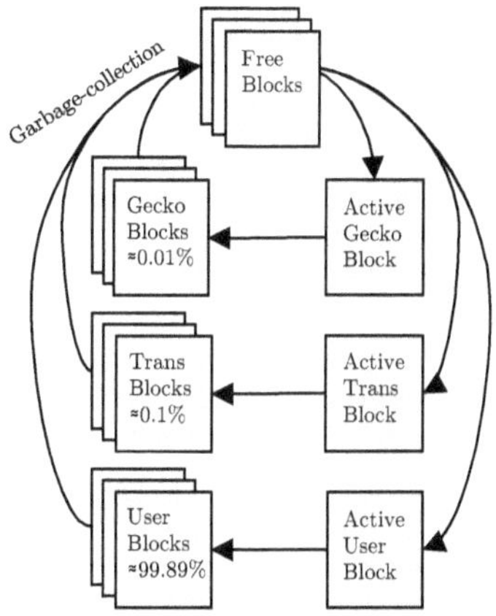

Figure 8: Lifecycle of a flash block.

The structure of the translation table in GeckoFTL is orthogonal to its core design. Thus, we use the simplest and original page-associative flash-resident translation table design first proposed in DFTL [22]: the translation table is stored in flash and a Global Mapping Directory (GMD) in integrated RAM keeps track of the physical location of every translation page. A RAM-resident LRU cache stores recently accessed mapping entries. The overall architecture of GeckoFTL is shown in Figure 7.

We now describe this translation scheme as well as how GeckoFTL lays out user data and metadata in flash. In Section 4.1, we describe how GeckoFTL and Logarithmic Gecko interact. In Sections 4.2 and 4.3, we describe the novel garbage-collection and recovery schemes respectively. We discuss wear-leveling in Appendix D.

Serving Application Reads. Figure 7 illustrates an example where the application issues a read to logical page 1500. To serve it, GeckoFTL first checks if the mapping entry is cached. If not, it finds the appropriate translation page in GMD, reads this translation page from flash, finds the mapping entry for logical page 1500 within the translation page, inserts this mapping entry into the LRU cache, and finally reads the user page.

Serving Application Writes. Now suppose the application updates logical page 1500. GeckoFTL immediately writes the new version of page 1500 on a free flash page Z. It then updates the cached physical address for the mapping entry to Z and marks the mapping entry as dirty using a bit flag.

Synchronization Operations. When the LRU cache fills up, the least-recently-used mapping entry is evicted. If this entry is dirty, a synchronization operation takes place. A synchronization operation identifies all dirty mapping entires in the LRU cache that belong to the same translation page as the evicted entry[6]. GeckoFTL then reads the translation page, updates the dirty cached mapping entries that it found on the translation page, and writes the updated translation page on a free page in flash. It then updates GMD to point to the updated translation page, and marks the cached dirty mapping entries that were included in the operation as clean.

Physical Layout. The flash pages in GeckoFTL have three types: (1) user pages, which contain user data, (2) translation pages, which store the translation table, and (3) Gecko pages, which store Logarithmic Gecko's runs. GeckoFTL separates these pages into different groups of flash blocks based on their types. This gives rise to 3 block groups, as illustrated in Figure 8. Each group has an active block to which updates are made in an append-only manner. When an active block runs out of free space, GeckoFTL allocates to the group a new active block from the pool of free blocks. The overall fraction of translation and Gecko blocks in a device is in the order of 0.1% and 0.01% respectively [7]. Thus, metadata consumes very little space in flash.

Garbage-Collection Operations. When the number of blocks with free space drops below a threshold, garbage-collection is triggered. The garbage-collection mechanism uses the Blocks Validity Counter (BVC) in Figure 7 to choose a victim. BVC keeps track of the number of valid pages in each flash block in the device. Once a victim is chosen, GeckoFTL issues a GC query to Logarithmic Gecko to identify which pages are still valid in the victim. These pages are migrated to a block with free space, and the victim block is erased. Note that garbage-collection migrations are treated like application writes; a dirty cached mapping entry is created for every page that is migrated.

4.1 Invalid Page Identification

We now show how Logarithmic Gecko efficiently identifies invalid pages during runtime. To do so, we denote a mapping entry as e = (logical_address, physical_address). As we just saw, when a logical page X is updated, a mapping entry $e_{cache} = (X,Z)$ is created for it and inserted into the cache. This entry is marked as dirty because the corresponding mapping entry $e_{flash} = (X,Y)$ in flash is now pointing to a before-image Y. Our goal is to guarantee that the invalid flash page Y is eventually identified and reported to Logarithmic Gecko. The greedy solution is to immediately read the translation page that contains e_{flash}. However, this would cost one extra flash read for every application write. We should avoid this extra cost. To do so, we augment synchronization operations to also lazily identify invalid pages.

UIP Flag and Synchronization Operations. We add one bit to each cached mapping entry called the Unidentified Invalid Page (UIP) flag. The UIP flag for entry $e_{cache} = (X,Z)$ is set to true if there is a flash page Y that contains a before-image of logical page X that has still not been identified and reported to Logarithmic Gecko as invalid. During a synchronization operation, before we replace $e_{flash} = (X,Y)$ by $e_{cache} = (X,Z)$, we report Y as invalid to Logarithmic Gecko if the UIP flag of e_{cache} is set to true.

Application Reads. When an application read fetches a mapping entry from the flash-resident translation table and inserts it

[6]The LRU cache is implemented as a tree to enable efficient range queries for mapping entries on a particular translation page.

[7] Assuming X mapping entries fit into each translation page, then the fraction of translation pages in the device is $\approx 1/X$. In practice, X is in the order of thousands, so the fraction of translation pages is in the order of 0.1%. Similarly, each Gecko page contains tens of thousands of page validity bits, and so the fraction of Gecko pages is in the order of 0.01%.

into the cache, we set both the dirty and the UIP flags for the new cached entry to false.

Application Writes. When a logical page X is updated by the application, we manage the cache as follows. If the mapping entry for page X is not already cached, we create a cached mapping entry for it and set both its dirty and UIP flags to true. On the other hand, if a mapping entry for page X is already cached, then we immediately report the old physical page as invalid to Logarithmic Gecko. We then set the entry's dirty flag to true (if it is not already) and leave the entry's UIP flag as it is (as there may be another before-image of logical page X that has still not been identified and reported to Logarithmic Gecko).

Garbage-Collection. Since invalid pages are identified lazily, it is possible that there are still unidentified invalid pages (UIPs) on a block when it is garbage-collected. These UIPs must be identified to avoid migrating invalid pages (doing so would overwrite valid pages). To identify such UIPs, we use the following policy. For every physical page Y in a victim block that Logarithmic Gecko reports as valid, we read the spare area of page Y and identify the logical page X last written on it. We then look up logical address X in the LRU cache. If there is a cached mapping entry for logical page X with the UIP flag set to true and with a different physical address than Y, then we know that the physical page Y is a UIP and do not migrate it as a part of the garbage-collection operation.

4.2 Garbage-Collection Victim-Selection

Since GeckoFTL stores metadata in flash, an interesting question is how metadata should be garbage-collected. Existing page-associative FTLs use a greedy victim-selection policy, which always targets the block with the least number of live pages in the device. The intuition is that this should minimize the number of garbage-collection migrations thereby minimizing their IO overhead. However, this intuition is wrong.

Flash-resident metadata is typically updated 2-3 orders of magnitude more frequently than user data. The key insight is that we should wait before garbage-collecting a block that contains frequently updated (hot) data because its valid physical pages will soon be invalidated anyways.

The question is by how much to defer garbage-collecting Gecko blocks and translation blocks. Our answer is to avoid garbage-collecting them altogether. Instead, GeckoFTL waits until all pages in a Gecko block or a translation block have become invalid and only then erases the block. In Section 5, we show that this policy significantly reduces garbage-collection overheads.

4.3 Recovery from Power Failure

When power fails, GeckoFTL must recover all RAM-resident data structures shown in Figure 7. The complete and detailed recovery algorithm is given in Appendix C. In this section, we focus on the bottleneck: recovering dirty cached mapping entries. We show how to quickly identify and recreate mapping entries for all non-synchronized pages. We also make the case for deferring synchronizing the recreated mapping entries with the translation table until after normal operation resumes.

Approach. The cache's capacity is C mapping entries. Thus, there are at most C dirty mapping entries when power fails. Our approach is therefore to recreate mapping entries for the C unique logical pages that were most recently updated. No mapping entry that was dirty before power failed can be outside of this set. To do this, we identify the most recently written user blocks based on timestamps in their spare areas. This takes K spare area reads, one per flash block. We then read the spare areas of these blocks' pages in reverse order starting from the most recently written block. For each new logical address that we encounter, we create a cached mapping entry.

Checkpoints. If the number of frequently updated logical pages before power fails is smaller than C, then some dirty entries can linger by the end of the LRU queue without ever getting evicted and synchronized. If so, the backwards scan must reach far back to find them. To bound the length of the backwards scan, we use runtime checkpoints. A checkpoint is taken every period of C inserts or updates to the LRU cache, and it synchronizes any mapping entry that has been in the LRU cache since the last checkpoint without getting updated itself. The checkpoints bound the backwards scan to $2 \cdot C$ spare area reads, as any logical page updated before the second last checkpoint must have been synchronized or updated again recently enough to be captured by the backwards scan.

In terms of implementation, a checkpoint inserts a dummy entry into the LRU cache called the checkpoint symbol. It then scans the cache's LRU queue from the end backwards until it finds and removes the symbol inserted by the last checkpoint. It synchronizes all dirty mapping entries encountered along the way.

Deferred Synchronization. Once GeckoFTL finishes recreating mapping entries for the most recently updated C unique logical pages, it still does not know which of these mapping entries are dirty. A natural approach is to access the flash-resident translation table to check. However, the cost would be at most $\frac{TT}{P}$ page reads, which amount to ≈ 36 seconds for the example values in Figure 2. Instead, GeckoFTL sets the dirty and UIP flags for all cached entries to true and corrects mistakes after normal operation resumes during regular synchronization operations. This is described in detail in Appendix C.3. Thus, synchronizing the recreated mapping entries does not elongate recovery time, and the penalty is amortized through synchronization operations that would be taking place anyways during normal operation.

5. EVALUATION

In this section, we present a detailed evaluation of GeckoFTL. We first evaluate Logarithmic Gecko in isolation to show how to optimally tune it and to demonstrate that its performance scales well with respect to different architectural parameters of a flash device. We then compare GeckoFTL to existing FTLs and show that it keeps the integrated RAM requirement and recovery time practical for very large flash devices while paying a lower price in terms of write-amplification.

Infrastructure: The FTL in commercial devices is an opaque black box because manufacturers complete with each other based on its design. Although it is possible to benchmark flash devices to determine the efficiency of different IO patterns [6, 7], it is impossible to disentangle the impact of different FTL components on performance let alone modify them. A part of the difficulty is that flash has no moving parts, so reverse-engineering a flash translation layer is impossible because there is nothing to observe (unlike for disks [2]). As a result, all work that we are aware of in this area relies on simulations [3, 22, 26, 24, 18]. Thus, we implemented GekoFTL and a few competitor FTLs within the flash simulation framework EagleTree [11]. This enables capturing the performance characteristics of different FTL components precisely.

Default Configuration: Unless otherwise stated, we simulate a 2 TB device with 4 KB flash pages and 128 pages per block. This is a standard architectural configuration [15, 3]. We set the ratio between the logical and the physical address spaces (a measure of over-provisioning) to 70%, which is common in practice [35]. We set the size of the LRU cache to 4 MB and assume that 8 bytes are needed per cached entry. Thus, the LRU cache accommodates $C = 2^{19}$ mapping entries. We denote the latency ratio between a

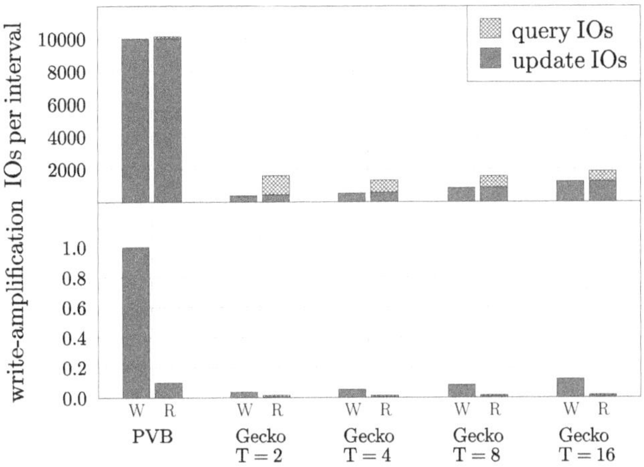

Figure 9: Logarithmic Gecko with a size ratio T of 2 minimizes write-amplification.

page write to a page read as δ and set it to 10, which is typical in practice [15]. We demonstrate throughout the evaluation how the performance of GeckoFTL scales with respect to all of these architectural parameters.

Metrics: We use three metrics to evaluate GeckoFTL: integrated RAM requirement, recovery time, and write-amplification. We measure write-amplification as $WA = (i\_writes + i\_reads/\delta)$ where i_writes and i_reads are the numbers of internal flash writes and flash reads that take place on average with respect to every logical page update issued by the application. Since write-amplification captures the impact on performance of garbage-collection and of updates to flash-resident metadata, it encompasses the entire impact of GeckoFTL's core design on performance. In terms of application reads, GeckoFTL performs the same as state-of-the-art FTLs [22, 26] because the structure of the translation table is the same. Thus, we do not consider application reads in the experimental workload. Nevertheless, our results are easily generalizable to a mixed workload. In particular, the slowdown factor for application reads throughput is the following expression, where RA is read-amplification caused by reading translation pages to fetch mapping entries, and RW is the ratio between application reads to application writes in the mixed workload.

$$\text{slowdown factor} = \frac{1}{RA \cdot RW + WA \cdot \delta}$$

5.1 Logarithmic Gecko vs. Flash-Based PVB

We first compare Logarithmic Gecko to a flash-resident PVB. Relative to this baseline, Logarithmic Gecko optimizes updates over GC queries because updates are at the critical path of performance. We now evaluate the impact of this design decision on write-amplification. We also show how Logarithmic Gecko performs under different tunings of the size ratio parameter T.

We evaluate Logarithmic Gecko under an adversarial application workload, which consists of uniformly randomly distributed page updates. Under this workload, Logarithmic Gecko's buffer absorbs as few updates as possible. This maximizes the overhead of merge operations. On the other hand, PVB is workload-insensitive; its IO overhead only depends on the number of page updates rather than the update pattern. Thus, evaluating PVB under this workload is fair.

The top part of Figure 9 shows the average number of internal flash reads and writes caused by updates and GC queries to PVB and Logarithmic Gecko over intervals of 10000 application writes. The bottom part of Figure 9 expresses these overheads in terms of write-amplification. Note that at this point, we do not capture the entire write-amplification in the device, which would also include garbage-collection and synchronization operations. We omit these overheads for now to enable an apples to apples comparison between Logarithmic Gecko and a flash-resident PVB.

As shown in Figure 9, PVB generates high write-amplification because each application update triggers one flash read and one flash write to PVB. Thus, PVB accumulates an overhead of 10000 flash reads and writes per interval. This results in a write-amplification of $\approx 1 + \frac{1}{\delta}$, which in this case is ≈ 1.1. Note that each garbage-collection operation also triggers one GC query to PVB, which involves one flash read. However, since garbage-collection operation are infrequent and since flash reads are inexpensive, the overhead of GC queries to PVB is negligible.

Logarithmic Gecko outperforms PVB under all tunings of the size ratio T. The reason is that the cost of updates is significantly reduced through buffering, and the time to execute GC queries remains fast and scalable because the number of runs is bounded and we only issue one IO per run during a GC query.

Finally, we observe that Logarithmic Gecko performs best when the size ratio T is set to 2. Recall that T controls a trade-off between the IO costs of updates and GC queries; as T increases there are less levels so GC queries become cheaper, but merge operations occur more frequently so updates become more expensive. Since 2 is the lowest value that T can take, the experiment shows that optimizing for updates as much as possible minimizes write-amplification. The reasons are that (1) updates are 1-2 orders of magnitude more frequent than GC queries, and (2) flash writes are an order of magnitude more expensive than flash reads. For all subsequent experiments, we set T to 2.

5.2 Logarithmic Gecko Scaling

We now show how Logarithmic Gecko's performance scales with respect to different architectural parameters of a flash device: the block size B, the number of blocks K, and the level of over-provisioning R.

Block Size and Entry-Partitioning. As the capacity of flash devices grows, the number of pages per flash block B tends to increase. In Section 3.3, we saw that this increases the size of a Gecko entry thereby reducing V, the number of entries that fit into the buffer, which in turn increases the cost of updates. To counter this trend, we proposed a technique called entry-partitioning to make the buffer size V independent of B (thereby also making the cost of updates independent of B). The idea is to partition a Gecko entry into S sub-entries, and to only insert to the buffer the sub-entry that corresponds to the part of the block that contains the page that was invalidated.

Figure 10 shows the impact of entry-partitioning on write-amplification as we vary the block size and the entry-partitioning factor. With no entry-partitioning (i.e. $S = 1$), write-amplification increases proportionally to the block size, whereas a moderate amount of entry-partitioning makes write-amplification independent of the block size. As the partitioning factor continues to increase, however, write-amplification begins to increase. The reason is that the keys of the partitioned entries lead to space-amplification. This increases the number of levels in Logarithmic Gecko thereby also increasing the cost of updates and GC queries. To choose the optimal value of S, the analytical technique at the end of Section 3.3 can be used. Overall, well-tuned entry-partitioning makes write-amplification independent of the block size.

Capacity. Logarithmic Gecko's goal is to enable flash devices to scale to multiple terabytes without incurring a significant performance degradation. However, as device capacity increases, the

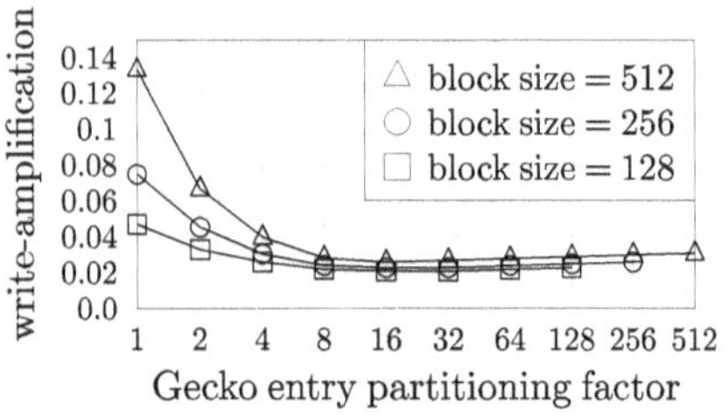

Figure 10: Entry-partitioning makes write-amplification independent of block size B.

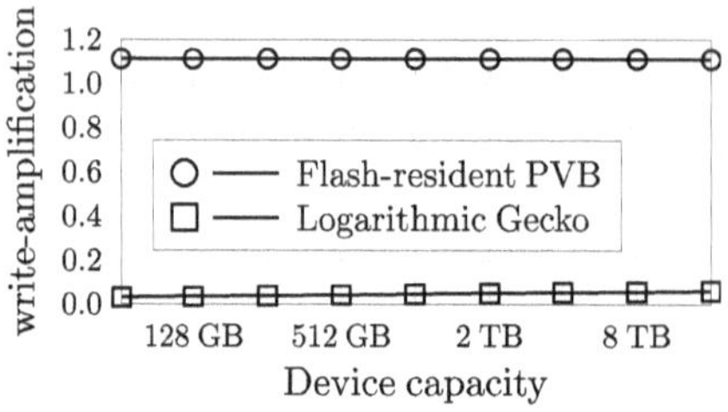

Figure 11: Logarithmic Gecko scales well for terabyte flash devices.

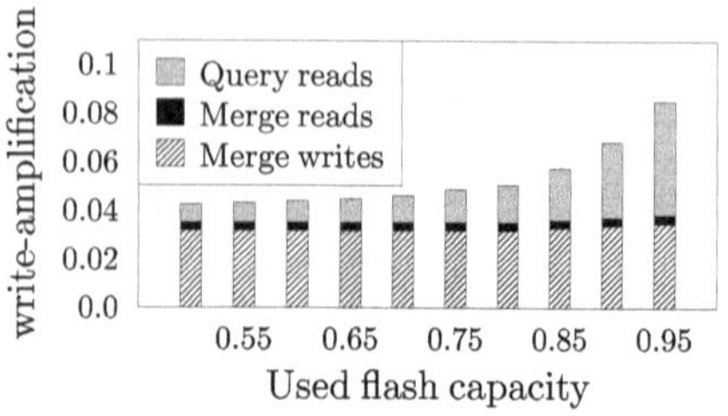

Figure 12: Over-provisioning level does not significantly affect write-amplification.

number of blocks K that are indexed in Logarithmic Gecko increases. This increases the number of levels, which, as we see in Table 1, increases the costs of updates and GC queries. It is therefore interesting to see the rate at which Logarithmic Gecko's performance deteriorates as device capacity increases.

In Figure 11, we compare write-amplification for Logarithmic Gecko and a flash-resident PVB as we increase the number of blocks K. For Logarithmic Gecko, write-amplification increases slowly with respect to device capacity because the costs of updates and GC queries are logarithmic with respect to the number of blocks K. On the other hand, for a flash-resident PVB, write-amplification is independent of device capacity since the cost of updates and GC queries each involve a fixed number of IOs. An interesting question is when the two curves cross. For this to happen, capacity has to increase by a large factor of $\approx 2^{100}$. Thus, Logarithmic Gecko outperforms PVB for any foreseeable device capacity.

Over-Provisioning. Since Logarithmic Gecko optimizes updates at the cost of more expensive GC queries, it is interesting to measure performance as the ratio between updates and GC queries changes. To do so, we vary over-provisioning, which affects the frequency of garbage-collection operations. As over-provisioning decreases, there are more live pages per flash block on average. Thus, garbage-collection victim blocks have more valid pages on average, so each garbage-collection operation reclaim less free space on average. As a result, garbage-collection operations take place more frequently relative to application writes.

In Figure 12, we vary the amount over-provisioning, expressed in terms of R, the ratio between the logical and the physical address spaces. As expected, the number of flash reads due to GC queries increases. Although more GC queries take place, the overall increase in write-amplification is low because flash reads are an order of magnitude cheaper than flash writes. Overall, Logarithmic Gecko works well for any reasonable level of over-provisioning.

5.3 GeckoFTL Vs. Existing FTLs

We now compare GeckoFTL to four state-of-the-art page-associative FTLs: DFTL [22], LazyFTL [26], μ-FTL [24] and Indexed-Based-FTL (IB-FTL) [18]. We compare these FTLs in terms of overall integrated RAM requirement, recovery time, and write-amplification. We show that GeckoFTL keeps the integrated RAM requirement and recovery time practical for very large flash devices without relying on a battery and while paying a lower price in terms of write-amplification than the other FTLs.

Competing FTLs. The FTLs we use differ in two critical ways from one another: (1) in how they store page validity metadata, and (2) in how they recover dirty cached mapping entries. In terms of page validity metadata, DFTL [22] and LazyFTL [26] both use a RAM-resident PVB, whereas μ-FTL uses a flash-resident PVB. IB-FTL logs the addresses of invalidated pages in flash in a page validity log (PVL) while maintaining a linked list of pointers between log entries of invalidated pages on the same block, where the first pointer for each chain is stored in integrated RAM [18]. We explain IB-FTL in detail in Appendix E.

In terms of recovery, DFTL and μ-FTL use a battery to recover dirty cached mapping entries. On the other hand, LazyFTL and IB-FTL restrict the number of dirty cached entries during runtime thereby navigating a trade-off between recovery time and write-amplification. In our experiments, we set the proportion of the cache that stores dirty mapping entries for LazyFTL and IB-FTL to 10% of C, the size of the cache.

(1) Integrated RAM Comparison. To compare the FTLs in terms of integrated RAM requirement, we modeled the sizes of their different data structures using the formulas in Section 2 and Appendix B. The top part of Figure 13 shows the amount of integrated RAM taken up by different data structures for each FTL. Note that the top part of Figure 1 in the introduction is simply the total integrated RAM requirement of LazyFTL under different device capacities.

DFTL and LazyFTL have the largest integrated RAM footprint because they both use a RAM-resident PVB. GeckoFTL, μ-FTL and IB-FTL avoid this overhead by storing page validity metadata in flash and instead only store BVC in integrated RAM to keep track of the number of valid pages in each block. IB-FTL stores additional metadata in integrated RAM to enable traversing and cleaning its page validity log.

GeckoFTL and μ-FTL achieve the lowest integrated RAM footprints. The bottleneck for both is BVC. This bottleneck can be alleviated by increasing the size of blocks, or by only storing a sample of BVC in integrated RAM. Note that μ-FTL achieves a slightly lower footprint than GeckoFTL since the translation table is a B-tree and so only the root has to be stored in integrated RAM rather than GMD. Indeed, in situations where integrated RAM is too scarce for storing GMD, structuring the translation table as a B-tree is a viable design decision.

(2) Recovery Time Comparison. To compare the FTLs in terms of recovery time, we modeled the number and types of flash IOs that are needed to recover each of their RAM-resident data structures. Appendix C shows the modeling in detail for GeckoFTL. In our models, reading a flash page takes 100 μs, reading a spare area takes 3 μs, and writing a flash page takes 1 ms [15]. The middle part of Figure 13 shows the results of our cost models. Note that the bottom part of Figure 1 in the introduction is based on the middle part of Figure 13 and captures the total recovery time for LazyFTL under different device capacities.

LazyFTL and IB-FTL exhibit significant bottlenecks to recovery time. Their shared bottleneck, denoted as "LRU cache", accounts for the time taken to recover and synchronize dirty mapping entries with the translation table. DFTL and μ-FTL avoid this bottleneck by relying on battery. In contrast, GeckoFTL eliminates this bottleneck by only identifying dirty entries during recovery and deferring their synchronization until after normal operation resumes.

LazyFTL's second bottleneck arises due to recreating the RAM-

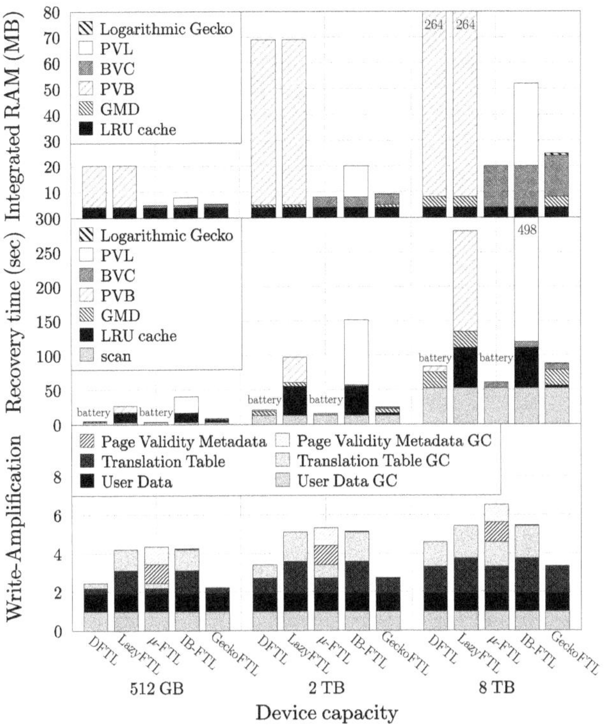

Figure 13: GeckoFTL achieves a better balance among integrated RAM, recovery time, and write-amplification than existing FTLs for large devices without relying on a battery.

resident PVB by scanning the translation table. DFTL avoids this bottleneck by using a battery to copy PVB to flash before power runs out. In contrast, μ-FTL and GeckoFTL avoid this overhead because they store page validity metadata in flash, and so it persists across failures.

IB-FTL's second bottleneck accounts for the time to recover metadata pertaining to its page validity log. Recovering this metadata entails scanning the whole log, whose size is proportional to device capacity.

Finally, Figure 13 shows that the time to initially scan the device to determine the types of blocks is emerging as a bottleneck for all FTLs. This bottleneck may be alleviated by using a larger block size or through parallelism, as a flash device typically consists of multiple logical units that can be accessed by the controller in parallel [3].

(3) Write-Amplification Comparison. To compare the FTLs in terms of write-amplification, we simulated each of them under uniformly randomly distributed writes and measured the number of IOs taking place for different purposes. The bottom part of Figure 13 shows write-amplification due to (1) application updates and garbage-collection of user data, (2) synchronization operations and garbage-collection of translation metadata, and (3) updates, GC queries and garbage-collection of page validity metadata.

The overhead of updating translation metadata is highest for LazyFTL and IB-FTL because they restrict the proportion of dirty mapping entries in the LRU cache. Thus, updates to the translation table are amortized to a lesser extent. For the other FTLs, the overhead of updating translation metadata is largely the same. Note that even though μ-FTL and IB-FTL structure the translation table as a B-tree, this does not increase the cost of updates to the translation table by much because the root and internal nodes of the B-tree are usually cached in integrated RAM.

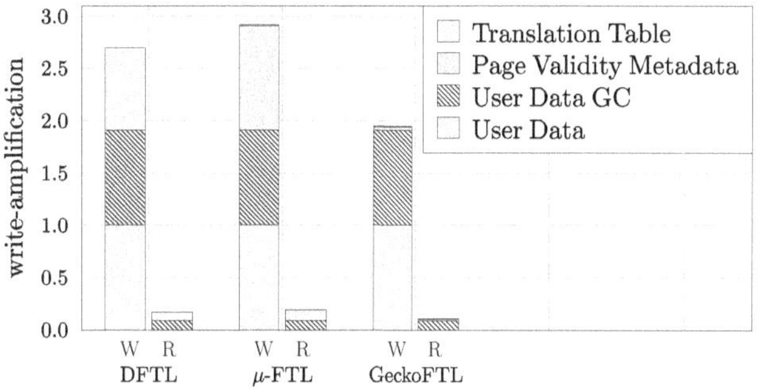

Figure 14: Even when integrated RAM is plentiful enough for storing PVB, GeckoFTL still improves performance by freeing integrated RAM to cache a larger proportion of the translation table.

Recall that GeckoFTL uses runtime checkpoints to bound recovery time by synchronizing dirty cached entries that have not been updated for a long time, as explained in Section 4.3. This leads to premature eviction and synchronization of dirty mapping entries and should result in an increase in the cost of updates to translation metadata in GeckoFTL. However, Figure 13 shows that the write-amplification induced by updating the translation table is largely the same in GeckoFTL as in DFTL and u-FTL, which rely on a battery. This demonstrates that the checkpoints in GeckoFTL increase write-amplification by a negligible amount.

In terms of page validity metadata, μ-FTL exhibits the highest write-amplification because it uses a flash-resident PVB. DFTL and LazyFTL avoid this overhead because they store PVB in integrated RAM. IB-FTL and GeckoFTL both achieve low write-amplification by virtue of buffering and later reorganizing page validity metadata in flash.

Finally, Figure 13 shows that garbage-collecting metadata blocks significantly increases write-amplification for DFTL, LazyFTL, μ-FTL and IB-FTL. GeckoFTL eliminates these overheads by not targeting blocks that contain metadata for garbage-collection, because such blocks contain frequently updated metadata that will soon be updated anyways.

Overall. Figure 13 shows that GeckoFTL achieves a better balance than existing FTLs among integrated RAM requirement, recovery time and write-amplification, and it does so without relying on a battery.

5.4 Better RAM utilization with GeckoFTL

Let us now suppose that integrated RAM is plentiful enough to store PVB, so storing page validity metadata in flash is not strictly necessary. We show that even in this case, using Logarithmic Gecko improves performance because the integrated RAM that it frees up is used to cache a larger proportion of the translation table.

In Figure 14, we compare three FTLs designs. All of these FTLs are given $\approx$ 70 MB of integrated RAM. The first is DFTL, which stores PVB in integrated RAM. It uses 64 MB of its integrated RAM for storing PVB, 4 MB for the LRU cache (as in the previous experiments), and $\approx$ 2 MB for the remaining RAM-resident data structures. The second FTL is μ-FTL, which stores PVB in flash. All of its remaining integrated RAM is allocated to the LRU cache, which has a size of 68 MB. The third is GeckoFTL. It also has a cache size of 68 MB, but it stores page validity metadata using Logarithmic Gecko rather than using a flash-resident PVB. To enable an apples to apples comparison, we give the implementations of DFTL and μ-FTL in this experiment the same garbage-collection scheme as GeckoFTL.

For DFTL, updating PVB involves no IO overheads since it is in integrated RAM, but the overhead due to updating translation metadata is significant. For μ-FTL, the overhead due to updating translation metadata drops to nearly 0 because the larger cache enables more amortization of synchronization operations, but the overhead due to updating PVB in flash is significant. In contrast, GeckoFTL achieves the best of both worlds. The cost of synchronization operations is nearly zero because of the larger cache, and the cost of updating page validity metadata in flash is low by virtue of using Logarithmic Gecko. Thus, GeckoFTL enables a more effective use of the available integrated RAM than existing FTLs even when integrated RAM is plentiful enough for storing PVB.

6. RELATED WORK

In this section, we describe how state-of-the-art page-associative FTLs maintain page validity metadata. We also discuss how they garbage-collect flash-resident metadata, as well as how they ensure quick recovery from power failure. We show how GeckoFTL advances the state-of-the-art in all of these respects.

Page Validity Metadata. DFTL and LazyFTL [22, 26] use one bit in the spare area of each flash page to indicate if the page is invalid. However, in modern flash devices the spare area of a flash page cannot be updated until the underlying block is erased [3, 24, 18]. Thus, an implementation of DFTL or LazyFTL would need to consolidate these bits into PVB and store it either in integrated RAM or in flash. On the other hand, μ-FTL [24] explicitly stores PVB in flash. The problem with these schemes is that storing PVB in integrated RAM is expensive and increases recovery time, whereas storing PVB in flash significantly increases write-amplification.

IB-FTL [18] logs the addresses of invalidated flash pages in flash while maintaining a linked list of pointers between log entries that correspond to invalid pages on the same blocks, and where the first link in each chain is stored in integrated RAM. Although it generates low write-amplification, the problem is that its RAM-resident metadata significantly increases the integrated RAM footprint and is slow to recover as the entire log must be scanned. Note that the log does not come with a cleaning mechanism, and so we extend it with one in Appendix E to enable an apples to apples comparison with other techniques in the evaluation.

In contrast, GeckoFTL uses Logarithmic Gecko, which generates low write-amplification while still enabling a great reduction in recovery time and integrated RAM.

Garbage-Collection. State-of-the-art page-associative FTLs [16, 26, 24] use a greedy garbage-collection policy that always chooses as a victim the block with the least number of valid pages in the device. In contrast, we propose a garbage-collection policy that never targets metadata. Instead, it waits for blocks containing metadata to become completely invalid and then erases them. This policy significantly reduces garbage-collection overheads.

Our policy in inspired by state-of-the-art garbage-collectors that separate logical pages into different groups of flash blocks based on update frequency [37, 8] and allocate relatively more over-provisioned space to hotter groups [35, 12]. However, state-of-the-art garbage-collectors rely on temperature detectors (e.g. [17, 34]) to determine the update frequency of a logical page. Temperature detectors exhibit a trade-off between accuracy and RAM-overheads, and in our environment integrated RAM is scarce. Moreover, temperature detectors fail when the workload changes or exhibits periodicity. In contrast, our approach leverages the type of data (i.e. user data vs. metadata) to infer its update frequency. This approach avoids the above-mentioned pitfalls of temperature detectors.

Recovery. State-of-the-art FTLs cache recently updated mapping entries in integrated RAM to amortize updates to the flash-resident translation table. When a failure occurs, the FTL need to recover these so-called dirty mapping entries.

The best known recovery algorithm for dirty mapping entries, proposed in LazyFTL, exhibits two shortcomings that GeckoFTL improves upon. In LazyFTL, whenever a dirty mapping entry is evicted from the cache, the cache is scanned and all other dirty entries that belong on the same physical block are also synchronized. This is done so that non-fully-synchronized blocks can be quickly identified during recovery. The problem is that scanning the cache for each eviction is computationally expensive. In contrast, GeckoFTL only scans the cache once per checkpoint thereby significantly reducing the computational overhead.

The second problem of LazyFTL's recovery approach is that it limits the number of dirty entries in the cache to bound the time it takes to synchronize all of them with the translation table. This decreases the amount by which updates to the translation table can be amortized, and so write-amplification during runtime increases. In contrast, GeckoFTL defers synchronizing the recreated mapping entries until after normal operation resumes. Thus, GeckoFTL does not need to bound the number of dirty entries in the cache. This removes the contention between recovery time and write-amplification.

Logarithmic Method. Various write-optimized key-value stores [32, 25, 4, 38] use the Logarithmic Method [5, 29], which involves logging updates and later reorganizing them through merge operations to guarantee logarithmic access time for queries. In this paper, we apply the logarithmic method outside of its traditional usage for key-value storage. We show how to use the logarithmic method to aggregate information about objects and report the aggregations through queries. Applying the logarithmic method for write-optimized aggregations in secondary storage is generalizable beyond Logarithmic Gecko.

7. CONCLUSION

In this work, we show that as flash devices scale in capacity to the order of terabytes, the metadata space requirement and the recovery time needed by state-of-the-art Flash Translation Layers are growing at an unsustainable rate. We identify the Page Validity Bitmap as the main bottleneck as it takes up 95% of all RAM-resident metadata and a large proportion of recovery time. We show that persisting PVB in flash is a poor solution because it increases write-amplification thereby harming performance and device longevity.

To solve this problem, we design a novel FTL called GeckoFTL. The central innovation of GeckoFTL is using an alternative data structure called Logarithmic Gecko, which logs updates about page validity in flash and later reorganizes them to ensure fast and scalable access time for queries. Logarithmic Gecko involves significantly cheaper updates yet costlier garbage-collection queries relative to the baseline. We show that this is a good trade-off since garbage-collection queries occur infrequently relative to updates to page validity metadata, and since flash reads are cheaper than flash writes. Logarithmic Gecko reduces write-amplification relative to the baseline by 98% while still enabling a 95% reduction in integrated RAM consumption and at least a 51% reduction in recovery time.

8. REFERENCES

[1] Small-block vs. large-block nand flash devices. *Technical Report, TN-29-07, Micron*, 2007.

[2] A. Aghayev, M. Shafaei, and P. Desnoyers. Skylight-a window on shingled disk operation. *ACM Transactions on Storage (TOS)*, 11(4):16, 2015.

[3] N. Agrawal et al. Design tradeoffs for SSD performance. In *USENIX*, pages 57–70, 2008.

[4] M. A. Bender, M. Farach-Colton, J. T. Fineman, Y. R. Fogel, B. C. Kuszmaul, and J. Nelson. Cache-oblivious streaming b-trees. In *Proceedings of the nineteenth annual ACM symposium on Parallel algorithms and architectures*, pages 81–92. ACM, 2007.

[5] J. L. Bentley and J. B. Saxe. Decomposable searching problems i. static-to-dynamic transformation. *Journal of Algorithms*, 1(4):301–358, 1980.

[6] L. Bouganim, B. Jonsson, and P. Bonnet. *uFlip: Understanding Flash IO Patterns*, pages 1–12. CIDR. 2009.

[7] F. Chen, D. A. Koufaty, and X. Zhang. Understanding intrinsic characteristics and system implications of flash memory based solid state drives. In *ACM SIGMETRICS Performance Evaluation Review*, volume 37, pages 181–192. ACM, 2009.

[8] M.-L. Chiang, P. C. Lee, and R.-C. Chang. Using data clustering to improve cleaning performance for flash memory. *SOFTWARE-PRACTICE & EXPERIENCE*, 29(3):267–290, 1999.

[9] T.-S. Chung, D.-J. Park, S. Park, D.-H. Lee, S.-W. Lee, and H.-J. Song. System software for flash memory: a survey. In *Embedded and Ubiquitous Computing*, pages 394–404. Springer, 2006.

[10] T.-S. Chung, D.-J. Park, S. Park, D.-H. Lee, S.-W. Lee, and H.-J. Song. A survey of flash translation layer. *Journal of Systems Architecture*, 55(5):332–343, 2009.

[11] N. Dayan, M. K. Svendsen, M. Bjørling, P. Bonnet, and L. Bouganim. Eagletree: Exploring the design space of SSD-based algorithms. *Proc. VLDB Endow.*, pages 1290–1293, Aug. 2013.

[12] P. Desnoyers. Analytic modeling of SSD write performance. In *SYSTOR*, pages 12:1–12:10, 2012.

[13] J. Do, Y.-S. Kee, J. M. Patel, C. Park, K. Park, and D. J. DeWitt. Query processing on smart ssds: Opportunities and challenges. In *Proceedings of the 2013 ACM SIGMOD International Conference on Management of Data*, SIGMOD '13, pages 1221–1230, New York, NY, USA, 2013. ACM.

[14] E. Gal and S. Toledo. Algorithms and data structures for flash memories. *ACM Comput. Surv.*, 37(2):138–163, June 2005.

[15] L. M. Grupp, J. D. Davis, and S. Swanson. The bleak future of NAND flash memory. In *Proceedings of the 10th USENIX Conference on File and Storage Technologies*, FAST'12, pages 2–2, Berkeley, CA, USA, 2012. USENIX Association.

[16] A. Gupta, Y. Kim, and B. Urgaonkar. DFTL: A flash translation layer employing demand-based selective caching of page-level address mappings. In *ASPLOS*, pages 229–240, 2009.

[17] J.-W. Hsieh, T.-W. Kuo, and L.-P. Chang. Efficient identification of hot data for flash memory storage systems. *ACM Transactions on Storage (TOS)*, 2(1):22–40, 2006.

[18] P.-C. Huang, Y.-H. Chang, and T.-W. Kuo. An index-based management scheme with adaptive caching for huge-scale low-cost embedded flash storages. *ACM Trans. Des. Autom. Electron. Syst.*, 18(4):56:1–56:26, Oct. 2013.

[19] A. Kawaguchi, S. Nishioka, and H. Motoda. A flash-memory based file system. In *USENIX*, pages 13–13, 1995.

[20] H.-J. Kim and S.-G. Lee. An effective flash memory manager for reliable flash memory space management. *IEICE Transactions on Information and Systems*, 85(6):950–964, 2002.

[21] J. Kim, J. M. Kim, S. H. Noh, S. L. Min, and Y. Cho. A space-efficient flash translation layer for compactflash systems. *IEEE Trans. on Consum. Electron.*, 48(2):366–375, May 2002.

[22] Y. Kim, A. Gupta, and B. Urgaonkar. A temporal locality-aware page-mapped flash translation layer. *Journal of Computer Science and Technology*, 28(6):1025–1044, 2013.

[23] S.-W. Lee, W.-K. Choi, and D.-J. Park. FAST: An efficient flash translation layer for flash memory. In *EUC Workshops*, pages 879–887, 2006.

[24] Y.-G. Lee, D. Jung, D. Kang, and J.-S. Kim. μ-ftl:: a memory-efficient flash translation layer supporting multiple mapping granularities. In *EMSOFT*, pages 21–30. ACM, 2008.

[25] Y. Li, B. He, R. J. Yang, Q. Luo, and K. Yi. Tree indexing on solid state drives. *Proceedings of the VLDB Endowment*, 3(1-2):1195–1206, 2010.

[26] D. Ma, J. Feng, and G. Li. Lazyftl: a page-level flash translation layer optimized for nand flash memory. In *SIGMOD*, pages 1–12. ACM, 2011.

[27] D. Ma, J. Feng, and G. Li. A survey of address translation technologies for flash memories. *ACM Comput. Surv.*, 46(3):36:1–36:39, Jan. 2014.

[28] J. M. Marshall and C. D. H. Manning. Flash file management system, Nov. 3 1998. US Patent 5,832,493.

[29] U. Meyer, P. Sanders, and J. Sibeyn, editors. *Algorithms for Memory Hierarchies: Advanced Lectures*. Springer-Verlag, Berlin, Heidelberg, 2003. pages 33-34.

[30] I. Micron Technology. Nand flash memory - mlc+. 2013.

[31] I. Micron Technology. Wear-leveling techniques in nand flash devices. 2013.

[32] P. O'Neil, E. Cheng, D. Gawlick, and E. O'Neil. The log-structured merge-tree (LSM-tree). *Acta Inf.*, 33(4):351–385, June 1996.

[33] C. Park, W. Cheon, J. Kang, K. Roh, W. Cho, and J.-S. Kim. A reconfigurable FTL (flash translation layer) architecture for NAND flash-based applications. *ACM Trans. Embed. Comput. Syst.*, 7(4):38:1–38:23, Aug. 2008.

[34] D. Park and D. H. Du. Hot data identification for flash-based storage systems using multiple bloom filters. In *Mass Storage Systems and Technologies (MSST), 2011 IEEE 27th Symposium on*, pages 1–11. IEEE, 2011.

[35] R. Stoica and A. Ailamaki. Improving flash write performance by using update frequency. *Proc. VLDB Endow.*, pages 733–744, July 2013.

[36] S. Wells. Method for wear leveling in a flash eeprom memory, Aug. 23 1994. US Patent 5,341,339.

[37] M. Wu and W. Zwaenepoel. envy: a non-volatile, main memory storage system. In *ACM SigPlan Notices*, volume 29, pages 86–97. ACM, 1994.

[38] X. Wu, Y. Xu, Z. Shao, and S. Jiang. Lsm-trie: An lsm-treebased ultra-large key-value store for small data. In *USENIX Annual Technical Conference*, 2015.

APPENDIX

A. MULTI-WAY MERGING

As mentioned in Section 3, a merge operation in Logarithmic Gecko may continue recursively. This is wasteful in terms of flash writes, as it involves rewriting Gecko entries from lower levels multiple times. We can reduce this overhead by foreseeing a recursive merge, and merging all the runs from the onset using a multi-way sort merge. This reduces the IO overhead of merge operations by a factor of $\approx 1/T$. To achieve this, we use the following policy. The run at level i participates in a commencing merge if (1) it is not already participating in another merge, and (2) there is at least one run at level $i-1$ participating in this merge. The downside of this policy is that it increases the number of input buffers needed in integrated RAM from 2 to L, the number of levels in the tree. Thus, this technique is only applicable for devices for which integrated RAM is larger than $P \cdot L$.

B. RAM BREAKDOWN

We now derive formulas for the amount of integrated RAM needed by the different data structures in GeckoFTL that are not already given in Section 2. The terms are given in Figure 2, and we denote I_X as an X byte integer.

Logarithmic Gecko's Run Directories

- *Number of entries:* The run directories contain one entry for every Gecko page in the device. Thus, we first derive the number of Gecko pages. Every Gecko entry takes up I_4 bytes for the key and $B/8$ for the page validity bitmap. Thus, the number of Gecko entries that fit into a flash page is $P/(I_4 + B/8)$. The largest run contains K entries, one for each block, and so its size in flash pages is $K/(P/(I_4 + B/8))$. The cumulative size of the rest of the runs is at most the size of the largest run. Thus, the total number of flash pages in Logarithmic Gecko is $(2 \cdot K)/(P/(I_4 + B/8))$.
- *Entry size:* Each entry in the run directories is a mapping from a block ID to the physical address of a flash page. This takes up $2 \cdot I_4$ bytes.
- *Total:* $2 \cdot I_4 \cdot (2 \cdot K)/(P/(I_4 + B/8))$ bytes.

Blocks Liveness Counter (BVC)

- *Number of entries:* There are K entries in BVC, one for each block.
- *Entry size:* I_2 bytes are needed to store the number of invalid pages in each block.
- *Total:* $I_2 \cdot K$ bytes.

Logarithmic Gecko's Buffers

- *Number of entries:* Logarithmic Gecko has one input buffer to which Gecko entries are inserted when physical pages become invalid. In addition, the multi-way merge strategy in Appendix A requires at most L input buffers, one for each level, and one output buffer.
- *Entry size:* The size of each buffer is P.
- *Total:* $P \cdot (2 + L)$ bytes.

C. RECOVERY

The recovery algorithm of GeckoFTL, which we call GeckoRec, comprises eight steps. In this section, we explain each of them and quantify their costs in terms of flash IOs.

Step 1. GeckoRec commences by creating a temporary data structure in integrated RAM called the Blocks Information Directory (BID). An entry in BID consists of 2 fields: the type of the block (Gecko, translation, user, or free), and a timestamp of when the first page in the block was written. To create BID, GeckoRec reads the spare area of the first flash page of each flash block, where the timestamp and the block's type are stored. Creating BID takes K spare area reads.

GeckoRec creates entries in BID for all translation, Gecko and free blocks. Since most flash blocks contain user data, creating a BID entry for every user block may cause BID to exceed the integrated RAM capacity. Thus, GeckoRec only creates BID entries for the most recently written $\max(\lceil \frac{2 \cdot C}{B} \rceil, V)$ user blocks. The reason this number must be at least $\lceil \frac{2 \cdot C}{B} \rceil$ is to enable scanning the last $2 \cdot C$ user pages to recover dirty mapping entries, as explained in Section 4.3. The reason it must also be at least as large as V, the size of Logarithmic Gecko's buffer, is to enable finding recently erased blocks that were lost from Logarithmic Gecko's buffer when power failed, as explained in Appendix C.2.

Step 2. Next, GeckoRec scans the spare areas of all translation pages, where the ID and last-update-timestamp for each of them are stored. It uses this to recover GMD by finding the most recent version of every translation page. This takes $O(\frac{K \cdot B}{P})$ spare area reads because the number of translation pages is $O(\frac{K \cdot B}{P})$.

Step 3. GeckoRec then recovers Logarithmic Gecko's run directories by scanning the spare areas of all flash pages in Gecko blocks. This takes $O(\frac{K \cdot B}{P})$ spare area reads because the number of Gecko pages is $O(\frac{K \cdot B}{P})$. Further technical details about recovering the run directories are given in Appendix C.1.

Step 4. Next, GeckoRec recovers Logarithmic Gecko's buffer, as explained in detail in Appendix C.2. This takes at most $2 \cdot V$ page reads.

Step 5. GeckoRec next recreates the Blocks Liveness Counter (BLC), which keeps track of the number of valid pages in each block in integrated RAM. It does this by scanning Logarithmic Gecko, reconstructing a page validity bitmap for every flash block, and computing its hamming weight to give the number of invalid pages in that block. This takes $O(\frac{K \cdot B}{P})$ flash reads, since Logarithmic Gecko consists of $O(\frac{K \cdot B}{P})$ flash pages.

Step 6. Next, GeckoRec recovers dirty mapping entries, as explained in Section 4.3. This step takes at most $2 \cdot C$ spare area reads.

Step 7. For all recreated mapping entries, GeckoRec sets the dirty and UIP flags to true. Mistakes will be fixed after normal operation resumes, as explained in Appendix C.3. The IO cost introduced by fixing mistakes is at most $O(\frac{K \cdot B}{P})$ flash reads as well as $O(C)$ spare area reads and redundant insertions into Logarithmic Gecko, but these overheads take place after recovery is complete and so they do not elongate recovery time.

Step 8. GeckoRec disposes of BID, and normal operation resumes.

C.1 Restoring the Run Directories

When power fails, we lose Logarithmic Gecko's run directories. We now show how to recover them. The challenge is that there may be multiple obsolete runs on Gecko blocks, but we must only recover the directories for the runs that were valid at the moment of power failure. Our approach relies on adding some metadata to each run to enable determining which run is the most recently created in each level.

We pad each run in flash with a preamble and a postamble. The preamble stores the run's level, a creation timestamp, and a unique ID. The postamble stores a copy of the run directory for this run. Every other page in the run begins with a header that contains the ID of the run that it belongs to.

During recovery, we examine the preamble and postamble of every run. We discard any run without a postamble as it is only partially written. We then use the creation timestamps to identify the most recently-created run in each level. For these runs, we recover the run directories from the postambles to integrated RAM.

C.2 Restoring the Buffer's Contents

When power fails, we lose the content of Logarithmic Gecko's buffer, which contains the addresses of recently erased blocks and recently invalidated flash pages. In this section, we show how to recover them.

C.2.1 Restoring Addresses of Erased Blocks

First, GeckoRec identifies and recreates Gecko entries for all blocks that were erased since the last time that Logarithmic Gecko's buffer flushed. To do this, it identifies the smallest run in Logarithmic Gecko and reads its preamble to find its creation timestamp. It then searches BID for all blocks that are free or whose first page was written after this timestamp. For each of these blocks, it invokes Algorithm 2, which inserts a Gecko entry into the buffer with the erase flag set to true. Since at most V blocks can be erased between two times that Logarithmic Gecko's buffer flushes, BID must contain entries for at least the most recently erased V user blocks to guarantee that GeckoRec does not miss any recently erased blocks.

C.2.2 Restoring Addresses of Invalidated Pages

Next, GeckoRec identifies and recreates Gecko entries for all flash pages that were invalidated since the last time that Logarithmic Gecko's buffer flushed. To do so, it exploits the property that an invalid flash page is only reported to Logarithmic Gecko during a synchronization operation, which updates a translation page. Thus, GeckoRec finds all translation pages that were updated since the last time that Logarithmic Gecko's buffer flushed. It compares each of these translation pages to the most recent previous version of the same translation page[8]. Every mapping entry in the previous translation page that mismatches the entry in the current translation page corresponds to a flash page that was invalidated since the last buffer flush. For each such mapping entry $e = (X, Z)$, we check if the physical address Z is still invalid by reading the spare area of flash page Z and checking if the logical address last written on it is still X. If so, GeckoRec inserts Z into Logarithmic Gecko's buffer via Algorithm 1.

For this approach to work, we must ensure that recently invalidated translation pages are not erased. To do so, we maintain a list of blocks in integrated RAM that cannot be erased. When a translation page is updated, we insert the ID of the block that contains the invalidated version of the translation page into the list. When Logarithmic Gecko's buffer is flushed, we clear the list.

The dominant cost of this phase is reading and comparing translation pages. Since the buffer contains up to V Gecko entries, then V flash pages are typically invalidated in-between two times the buffer flushes. In this case, as many as V translation pages could have been synchronized, so at most $2 \cdot V$ translation pages must be read and compared during this phase of recovery. Note that technically, if multiple logical pages that all correspond to different translation pages are stored on the same flash blocks and are updated at the same time, then the buffer can absorb as many as $V \cdot B$ inserts before flushing, in which case $2 \cdot V \cdot B$ translation pages must be read and compared during this phase of recovery. Although this scenario is unlikely, it is possible to restrict recovery time to $2 \cdot V$ by limiting the number of insertions that the buffer can absorb to V before it flushes.

[8] As long as $C > V$, the same translation page cannot be updated more than once in-between two times that Logarithmic Gecko's buffer flushes, so there is always at most one previous version for each updated translation page that we must examine.

C.3 Correcting Restored Cached Entries

GeckoRec defers synchronizing the recreated cached mapping entries with the flash-resident translation table until after normal operation resumes in order to shorten recovery time. Instead, it simply sets the dirty and UIP flags for each restored cached mapping entry to true. We now show how GeckoFTL corrects these flags after recovery during regular synchronization operations.

C.3.1 Dirty = false, UIP = false

We first consider a restored cached mapping entry for which the corresponding mapping entry before power failed had its dirty and UIP flags both set to false. When the restored mapping entry participates in a synchronization operation, GeckoFTL compares its physical address to the flash-resident mapping entry's physical address. If these addresses match, it means that the cached mapping entry was wrongly marked as dirty, and so GeckoFTL sets its dirty and UIP flags to false and omits it from the synchronization operation. If all cached entries participating in a synchronization operation are omitted, GeckoFTL aborts the synchronization operation thereby saving one flash write. The overhead introduced is $O(\frac{K \cdot B}{P})$ page reads because there are $O(\frac{K \cdot B}{P})$ translation pages and so the number of aborted synchronization operations is $O(\frac{K \cdot B}{P})$. However, this IO price is only paid after regular operation resumes, and so it does not lengthen recovery time.

C.3.2 Dirty = true, UIP = false

We now consider a restored cached entry for which the corresponding mapping entry before power failed had its dirty and UIP flags set to true and false respectively. In this case, only the UIP flag must be corrected after recovery. As before, when the cached entry participates in a regular synchronization operation after recovery, GeckoFTL compares the physical addresses of the cached entry and the flash-resident entry. Their addresses do not match (this is true by assumption that the cached entry before power failure was dirty), and so GeckoFTL replaces the flash-resident entry by the cached entry. After doing so, GeckoFTL would normally also report the physical address Z of the replaced entry as invalid to Logarithmic Gecko. However, address Z was already reported to Logarithmic Gecko before power failed (this is true by assumption that the cached entry's UIP flag was false before power failed). There is a danger in reporting page Z to Logarithmic Gecko a second time as invalid; page Z may have already been erased and rewritten before power failure, and so reporting it a second time as invalid can lead to losing live data currently written on it. To avoid this problem, GeckoFTL first checks in the spare area of page Z if the logical page written on it is the same as in the restored cached entry. It only reports Z as invalid to Logarithmic Gecko if these logical addresses match. Using this approach, GeckoFTL may still report a physical address to Logarithmic Gecko as invalid a second time after recovery, but the above check at least guarantees that GeckoFTL does not report a valid page as invalid.

Cost. This check introduces an overhead of one spare area read for every entry participating in a synchronization operation. This is not a large overhead since spare area reads are extremely cheap compared to flash writes. However, this overhead can also easily be restricted. The simplest method is to add an uncertainty flag to each cached mapping entry to signal that we are not sure if the UIP flag should be true or not. The uncertainty flag is set to true for any cached entry created during recovery. Otherwise, it is always set to false. Thus, we only perform the spare area check during a synchronization operation if the cached entry's uncertainty flag is set to true. After the check, we set the uncertainty flag of the entry to false. Since at most C entries can have their uncertainty flag set to true, then the overhead is $O(C)$ spare area reads and redundant insertions to Logarithmic Gecko.

We can also achieve the same effect without introducing an uncertainty flag. The dirty and UIP flags during normal operation can only ever be (false, false), (true, false) and (true, true). Thus, we can set the dirty and UIP flags for all restored cached mapping entries to (false, true), and use this combination to mean that the dirty flag and UIP flag are currently assumed to be true but that we are uncertain of this, so we should perform all the appropriate checks during a synchronization operation after power resumes.

D. WEAR-LEVELING

In this Appendix, we show how GeckoFTL performs wear-leveling. We show that the only necessary metadata in integrated RAM includes a few global statistics comprising $30-40$ bytes at most. The rest of the wear-leveling metadata can be stored in the spare areas of blocks.

Wear-Leveling Statistics. GeckoFTL relies on two statistics for each block to perform wear-leveling. The first statistic is erase-count, which is the number of times a block has been erased (used to identify blocks that are exceptionally unworn [36, 20, 3]). The second statistic is age, which is the number of erases that has taken place in the device as a whole since the last time that a given block was erased (used to identify blocks that contain static data [19]).

GeckoFTL maintains the erase-count for each block in one of its spare areas. An erase-count comprises 2 bytes per block because every block has a lifetime of at most a few thousands of erases [3]. The solution in [28] is used to maintain the erase-count in the presence of power failures.

To maintain the age of blocks, GeckoFTL uses a global erase counter (4 bytes) in integrated RAM. When any block is erased, the value of the global counter at that moment is saved as an erase-timestamp in one of the spare areas of the block, and the global counter is incremented. The age of any block can thus be calculated by subtracting its erase-timestamp from the global counter. The erase-timestamp comprises 4 bytes for each block.

Finding Wear-Leveling Victims. GeckoFTL only stores a few global statistics for the erase-counts and ages of blocks such as minimum, maximum and average (24 bytes). It periodically scans the device, issuing one spare area read per block, to update its global statistics and to identify wear-leveling targets based on how their erase-count and age compare to the global statistics. The scan takes place gradually with respect to flash writes. In particular, for every flash write that takes place, we read the spare area of the next block in the scan. When a scan is finished, we restart it. Since spare area reads are 3 orders of magnitude less expensive than flash writes, this ensures that scans do not introduce a significant performance overhead.

Scan Cost Analysis. Let us define a period as $K \cdot B$ flash writes, where K is the number of blocks in the device and B is the number of pages per block. By definition, B full scans take place during one period. Furthermore, let us assume that $1/X$ flash blocks contain non-static data. Thus, the blocks that contain non-static data each get erased X times on average during one period.

Clearly, as long as $X < B$ the policy does not fall behind. Under this condition, static blocks are inspected by the scan more frequently than the rate at which non-static blocks get erased. For example, suppose that X is 2, meaning that 50% of the blocks are non-static, and suppose that B is 128. During one period, the non-static blocks are each erased 2 times on average whereas the static block are inspected 128 times. It is therefore extremely easy to discover and address erase-count discrepancies as they arise.

This policy works well even when $X > B$. For example, suppose X is set to 1000, meaning that 0.1% of the blocks are non-static. In this case, the rate at which non-static blocks are erased is $1000/128 \approx 8$ times higher than the rate at which static blocks are scanned. Thus, each static block may be erased ≈ 8 times on average while we complete an entire scan to identify wear-leveling victims, and so the erase-count discrepancy will be no less than ≈ 8. This is acceptable seeing as the number of erases each block can undergo is in the hundreds or even thousands for modern flash devices [15]. In a stress case where $X >> B$, it is possible to increase the frequency of scans (i.e. read more than 1 spare area for each flash write) to ensure that the wear-leveling policy does not fall behind.

In summary, scans obviate the need for storing wear-leveling statistics for each block in integrated RAM in order to find wear-leveling victims. The frequency of scans is easy to tune such that they neither impact performance nor fall behind.

Dynamic Wear-Leveling. GeckoFTL uses a complementary dynamic wear-leveling technique to write frequently updated pages on unworn blocks (to accelerate their wearing rate) and seldom updated pages on worn blocks (to decelerate their wearing rate) [31]. To do this, GeckoFTL needs to know the update frequency of pages. It does this by keeping an update timestamp for each page in its spare area. When a page is updated or migrated, we can then tell based on the timestamp how long it has been since the last time it was updated relative to the average.

Overall, GeckoFTL uses a range of wear-leveling techniques, which only require storing a few bytes' worth of global statistics in integrated RAM.

E. PAGE VALIDITY LOG

IB-FTL [18] proposes to log the addresses of invalidated flash pages while maintaining a linked list of pointers between log entries that correspond to invalid pages on the same blocks, and where the first link in each chain is stored in integrated RAM. However, the original design in [18] does not include a cleaning mechanism, and so the page validity log (PVL) can grow indefinitely. To enable a fair comparison of Logarithmic Gecko and PVL in our experiments, we extended the design of PVL with a cleaning mechanism.

Our extension involves adding a timestamp to every log entry corresponding to when the page was invalidated. We also add a timestamp for every block in integrated RAM of the last time it was erased. We then bound the size of the log to X log entries. When the buffer is flushed and the log grows beyond X entries, we find the page that was inserted into the log the longest time ago. For every entry in this page, we compare its timestamp to the erase-timestamp of the corresponding block in integrated RAM. If the entry's timestamp is larger than the block's timestamp, it means the log entry was created after the last time the block was erased, and so we reinsert it into the log. On the other hand, if the log entry's timestamp is smaller, we discard it, because it was created before the last time the block was erased and is now obsolete.

A natural question is how to tune X, the size of the log. Our insight is that at any point, the number of invalid pages in the device is at most the difference between the sizes of the physical address space and the logical address space. We denote this difference as D. We propose to set X to double the size of D. Thus, when we reclaim the oldest page in the log, at least half of its log entries are discarded on average. Each log entry is reinserted into the log on average one time, and so the cost in terms of write-amplification is $O(\frac{1}{V})$, where V is the size of the buffer. In Section 5, we compare our version of PVL to Logarithmic Gecko.

SHARE Interface in Flash Storage for Relational and NoSQL Databases

Gihwan Oh
Sungkyunkwan University
Suwon, Korea
wurikiji@skku.edu

Chiyoung Seo
Couchbase, Inc.
Santa Clara, USA
chiyoung@couchbase.com

Ravi Mayuram
Couchbase, Inc.
Santa Clara, USA
ravi@couchbase.com

Yang-Suk Kee
Samsung Semiconductor, Inc.
San Jose, USA
yangseok.ki@samsung.com

Sang-Won Lee
Sungkyunkwan University
Suwon, Korea
swlee@skku.edu

ABSTRACT

Database consistency and recoverability require guaranteeing write atomicity for one or more pages. However, contemporary database systems consider write operations non-atomic. Thus, many database storage engines have traditionally relied on either journaling or copy-on-write approaches for atomic propagation of updated pages to the storage. This reliance achieves write atomicity at the cost of various *write amplifications* such as redundant writes, tree-wandering, and compaction. This write amplification results in reduced performance and, for flash storage, accelerates device wear-out. In this paper, we propose a flash storage interface, SHARE. Being able to explicitly remap the address mapping inside flash storage using *SHARE* interface enables host-side database storage engines to achieve write atomicity without causing write amplification. We have implemented *SHARE* on a real SSD board, OpenSSD, and modified MySQL/InnoDB and Couchbase NoSQL storage engines to make them compatible with the extended *SHARE* interface. Our experimental results show that this *SHARE*-based MySQL/InnoDB and Couchbase configurations can significantly boost database performance. In particular, the inevitable and costly Couchbase *compaction* process can complete without copying any data pages.

1. INTRODUCTION

In the era of *all-flash* cloud computing data centers, it is urgent to flash-optimize open source database engines, including traditional relational DBMSs (*e.g.*, MySQL/InnoDB) and emerging NoSQL storage engines (*e.g.*, Couchbase). Considering the intrinsically asymmetric performance between flash storage read and write operations, optimizing flash-based database write efficiency is a practical and critical problem that should be immediately addressed.

SIGMOD'16, June 26-July 01, 2016, San Francisco, CA, USA

DOI: http://dx.doi.org/10.1145/2882903.2882910

When considering that data consistency is a uncompromisable database requirement, optimizing reliable writes can be an intrinsic problem. With Hard Disk Drives (HDDs), a database update action may involve multiple pages, each in turn usually consisting of multiple disk sectors. A sector write requires a slow mechanical process and is susceptible to power failures. If a power failure occurs in the middle of a sector write, the sector might be only partially updated. So, a sector write operation is considered non-atomic by most contemporary database systems [3, 24].

To guarantee write atomicity, which is critical for database consistency, many database storage engines have assumed HDDs as their main storage media and resorted to either *copy-on-write* or *journaling*. With a journaling approach, each updated page's *before* or *after* image is redundantly stored in a dedicated journal area. Many database engines such as MySQL/InnoDB, PostgreSQL, SQLite, and Sybase SQL Anywhere rely on a journaling approach [3, 4, 6, 31]. In contrast, a copy-on-write approach, inspired by the shadow paging technique [21], does not update data pages in place, but instead writes all updated pages to other persistent storage locations, while the original pages remain immutable and become stale. Consequently, copy-on-write needs to reclaim stale pages periodically. It should be noted that these two techniques for guaranteeing atomic write are heavily used - not only in enterprise database applications but also in modern file systems [13, 22] and mobile databases [17].

These out-of-place write schemes for achieving atomicity, however, suffer from write amplification. The journaling approach requires writing one logical page *redundantly* to the storage. With the copy-on-write approach, the costly *compaction* process (a form of garbage collection) should be carried out [7]. The *wandering-tree* problem is additionally encountered in a tree-structured NoSQL storage engine and file system metadata [32]. This type of logical write amplification at the host layers is often cited as a primary cause of tardy performance and also aggravates flash storage wear-out [16, 17].

Meanwhile, because flash memory does not allow overwriting any page in place, a flash storage page update is commonly carried out by writing the new content into a clean flash page at another location, leaving the original page untouched [9, 20]. Due to this *out-of-place* strategy, flash storage devices are equipped with a firmware module called the FTL (flash translation layer), whose main role is to maintain the mapping between kernel block layer logical addresses and flash memory chip physical addresses. And, mainly for performance reasons, most contemporary flash storage devices have adopted fine-grained page unit mapping [23]. Fortunately, this indirection of *logical to physical* address mapping, which has been necessarily adopted to overcome flash memory's *no-overwrite* limitation provides an excellent opportunity in obviating the write amplification overhead data write reliability requires.

In this paper, we present the *SHARE* interface. This interface exposes an abstraction that allows host applications to explicitly change the *address mapping* inside flash storage. With *SHARE*, two different logical pages can share one physical page. This simple interface allows the host applications using either a journal or copy-on-write approach to achieve write atomicity without incurring write amplification. It also allows NoSQL storage engines, including Couchbase, to carry out a compaction process without copying data. The key contributions of this work are summarized as follows.

- *SHARE* provides an abstraction which allows host applications to change the address mapping table which has traditionally been managed internally only by FTL. Many database engines and file systems can easily exploit *SHARE* to achieve write atomicity without causing write amplification. In addition to atomic writes, *SHARE* can also make other numerous write-heavy cases almost cost free. This includes the NoSQL compaction process and file copy operations that can occur almost without copying data.

- We have implemented *SHARE* on an open SSD development hardware platform called *OpenSSD* by enhancing its FTL code with the *SHARE* features this paper presents. We have demonstrated both relational and NoSQL storage engines can easily exploit *SHARE* with only minimal code changes.

SHARE resembles the well-known *TRIM* command [30]. Both *SHARE* and TRIM allow upper-layer applications to provide useful information to flash storage devices, thus enabling them to achieve better performance. The TRIM command is successfully established as a new standard flash storage interface because it effectively improves the flash storage garbage collection process by informing flash storage devices which data blocks are no longer valid. We believe that the *SHARE* command could be incorporated into operating system kernel as easily as the TRIM command, and its performance benefit would be no less than the TRIM command's. Also, as is contrasted in Section 6, to our best knowledge, *SHARE* is the first work on ameliorating write amplifications for database engines utilizing the out-of-place update strategy.

The rest of the paper is organized as follows. Section 2 describes the I/O inefficiency for guaranteeing data write reliability in database engines and presents the motivation for our work. Section 3 presents the architecture of *SHARE* and its abstraction, and discusses its advantages for database storage engines. Section 4 gives the implementation details of *SHARE* architecture. In Section 5, we evaluate the performance impact of *SHARE* on MySQL/InnoDB and Couchbase storage engines using LinkBench benchmark and YCSB benchmark, respectively. Section 6 compares our work with the existing flash storage write optimization techniques. Lastly, Section 7 summarizes this paper's contributions and suggests future work.

2. MOTIVATION

A crucial assumption for database consistency and recovery is that each individual page is atomically written to storage. However, secondary storage devices such as spinning disks and flash memory SSDs do not generally guarantee page write atomicity. Hence, when a system crashes when a page write is in progress, the on-disk copy of the page may contain a mix of old and new data after system reboots. Such a *torn* page, however, cannot be completely restored - even with *Aries-style* write ahead logging (WAL) schemes [6, 24]. Therefore, for better recoverability, database systems should be armed with a mechanism to guarantee the atomic propagation of updated pages, which is orthogonal to the Aries-like recovery protocol. And, as solutions to achieve the write atomicity in databases and file systems, there have been two popular approaches: journaling and copy-on-write. However, the high write amplification these two approaches cause becomes a major obstacle to achieving scalable, consistent performance for normal read and write operations.

In this section, we explain how these two techniques are used in real database storage engines such as the MySQL/InnoDB server and the Couchbase storage engine. Then, we describe the definition of the problem this paper addresses and the opportunity flash storages provide.

2.1 Redundant Writes in MySQL/InnoDB

The MySQL/InnoDB storage engine takes a variant of journaling, called *double-write* [4], to deal with the partial page write problem. As shown in Figure 1(a), when a updated page is evicted from the buffer cache, prior to overwriting the old copy in its original database location, the InnoDB engine first appends its new copy (*i.e.*, *after-image*) to a separate journal area, *double-write-buffer*. And when the write to the journal area is forcefully completed (using `fsync` call), InnoDB writes the page to its original location. When the system recovers from a crash, InnoDB can always find a consistent page copy either in the database or in *DWB*.

The PostgreSQL server is also taking a redundant journaling approach to guarantee write atomicity. Specifically, when the server runs by default with the **`full_page_write`** option on, whenever a page is updated first after the last checkpoint, the *before-image* of the page is saved in the WAL log. It is also well known that SQLite, a popular embedded database system, provides two journaling modes, *rollback* and *write-ahead log*, to guarantee atomic page write, and the overhead of journaling either before-image or after-image of every updated page is very expensive [17].

This journaling-based redundant write paradigm has also been widely adopted in modern file systems such as `ext4` and `XFS` so as to guarantee the consistency of data and metadata despite the torn page problem [22]. However, because journaling both data and metadata pages (*i.e.*, `full` journaling mode) is too expensive, those file systems are by default configured to journal only metadata (*i.e.*, `ordered` journaling mode) so that the consistency of file system structure is at least preserved.

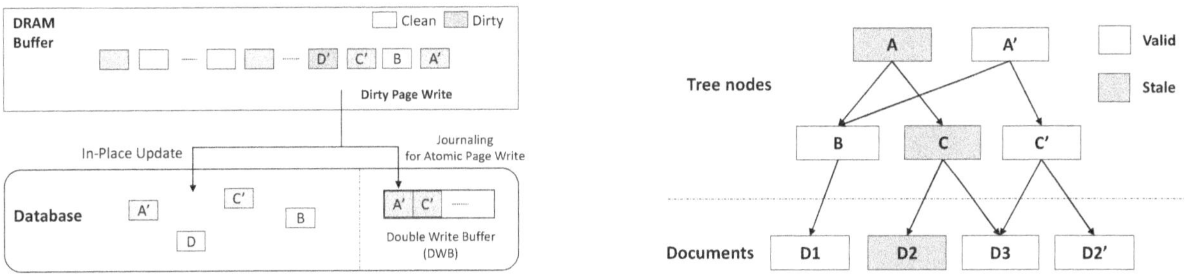

(a) Double Write Buffer in MySQL/InnoDB (b) Copy-On-Write in Couchbase

Figure 1: MySQL/InnoDB and Couchbase Journaling and Copy-on-Write

2.2 Copy-on-Write in Couchbase

Couchbase is a document-oriented NoSQL database system. Its storage engine is based on the append-only B^+-tree that takes a copy-on-write strategy for updating document(s) atomically: rather than overwriting the existing old document copy in place, it appends its new copy at the end of the database file. As is illustrated in Figure 1(b), when a document is updated, its new copy is written to the end of a database file while its old copy is left intact, but marked as *stale*. One undesirable consequence of this append-only update policy is that all tree nodes on a path from a leaf pointing to the document to the root should be updated and written in a cascaded way, where each node update also takes a copy-on-write strategy. The Couchbase storage engine relies on the so-called *wandering-tree* [32] scheme. A tree may be called a wandering tree if an tree node update requires updating its parent nodes up to the root due to inability to perform in-place updates. Consequently, the wandering-tree scheme amplifies the data to be written with N index node pages, where N is the height of B^+-tree.

Despite the high *write amplification*, Couchbase deliberately adopted this copy-on-write and wandering-tree combination mainly for two purposes: 1. as modern storage devices do not support an atomic write feature, the copy-on-write strategy has been adopted as an implementation method to support atomic writes [21]. 2. Couchbase has opted for the sequential write pattern of the copy-on-write strategy over the random write pattern of the update-in-place strategy. In particular, because spinning disk write latency is mainly dominated by the mechanical arm movement(*e.g.*, disk seek time), the write strategy Couchbase adopted can provide better write throughput than the traditional update-in-place policy.

As more documents are updated or newly-inserted under the copy-on-write and wandering-tree scheme, the percentage of stale database file pages increases. When the ratio of stale data reaches a configured database file threshold, the costly *compaction* operation is necessarily invoked to reclaim the unused space the stale data occupies. For this, the compaction task typically reads all non-stale documents and index nodes from the current database file and copies them to a new file. This incurs significant I/O overhead and write amplification. The current database file is later deleted when no longer accessed by any reader. Other NoSQL database systems, such as BigTable [11], Cassandra [19], and MongoDB [1] that adopt a Log-Structured Merge (LSM) tree [25] as their underlying storage engines have the similar issue.

2.3 Problem Statement

As aforementioned, journaling and copy-on-write commonly implement a two-phase write scheme to avoid the torn-write problem: perform a first write for recording updates (*e.g.*, *double-write-buffer* in the case of InnoDB and copy-on-write in the case of Couchbase) and perform a second write for applying the recorded writes to live data (*e.g.*, in-place update in the case of MySQL/InnoDB and compaction in the case of Couchbase). As a result, these systems double storage update write and thus the effective available user bandwidth is halved.

In particular, when database systems run on flash storage devices rather than on hard disks, the performance effect of this write amplification becomes more serious. A NAND flash page can be written only when it is in clean, empty state. Once it is written, it must be erased before it is rewritten. However, online erasure is impractical due to its several millisecond long erase time. Instead, SSD employs FTL that allows logical address to map to different physical locations, deferring page erasures. However, the stale pages eventually require a later clean up process. This garbage collection operation generates additional internal traffic (*i.e.*, read and write amplification) to relocate valid pages, causing a significant IO operations jitter. This paper refers to this activity as *copyback*. The more update data is written, the more garbage collection is required. That is, user writes are further amplified when the storage system uses SSD devices. Further, this undesirable write amplification shortens flash storage device lifespan.

Whether intended or not, the net effect of the copy-on-write operation inside flash storages remarkably resembles what database storage engine's out-of-place write schemes achieve. This provides an excellent opportunity to achieve the write atomicity almost at no cost of redundant writes, the tree wandering, and the compaction process. Based on this observation, we aim to develop a simple, but powerful abstraction at the flash storage level that allows database storage engines to avoid write amplification across storage systems and storage devices. Specifically, this interface allows host-side applications to explicitly change the address mapping inside flash storage.

3. SHARE INTERFACE

In this section, we present a new solution called *SHARE* that supports the atomic page writes at the flash storage layer, so that upper layers such as database and NoSQL engines can be freed from the burden of write amplifications.

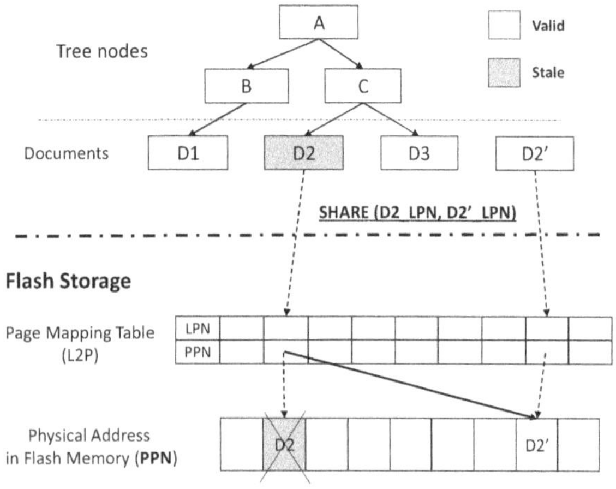

Figure 2: *SHARE* Architecture

The architecture, the interface, and the benefits of *SHARE* will be explained in turn.

3.1 SHARE Architecture

The solution discussed in this paper is based on the holistic understanding of problems across the layers of application, OS, and storage device. The FTL's *page-grained indirection* of logical-to-physical addressing mapping provides an excellent opportunity for solving the write amplification problem occurring in both the journaling and copy-on-write approaches. Let us first illustrate how we can, by exploiting the unique FTL page-level address mapping feature, avoid the Couchbase write amplification without compromising atomic write semantics. As is shown in Figure 2, when a new copy of document D2, denoted as D2', is written to flash storage media, each of two document copies, D2 and D2', has its own logical and physical address. Now, *what if the logical address of D2 in FTL can be remapped to point to the physical address of D2'?* The new D2' copy can be reached through D2's LPN. Hence, unlike the original Couchbase, all index nodes along the path from the corresponding leaf node to the root node need not to be copied-on-write. That is, the write amplification due to Couchbase's wandering-tree scheme can be totally avoided while still preserving the atomic write semantics required to update document D2. Similarly, with MySQL/InnoDB *double-write-buffer*, the redundant write of an updated page to the original location in the primary database can be avoided simply by FTL changing the logical address of its original location to point to the physical addresses of new copy written in the *double-write-buffer*, without losing the atomic write property.

From the examples described above, we know that write amplification can be completely avoided by providing upper-layer storage engines with an adequate abstraction (or API) which allows changing the logical-to-physical page mapping table flash storage devices internally manage.

3.2 SHARE Interface

The remaining issue is, then, how upper-layer applications can inform FTLs to enable two LPNs to share one physical address. For this purpose, we propose a new interface called `SHARE(LPN1, LPN2)` for flash storage. Upon receiving a *SHARE* command with a first LPN (LPN1) and a second LPN (LPN2) for an update, wherein the first LPN maps to a first PPN and the second LPN maps to a second PPN, FTL atomically remaps the first LPN so that the first LPN maps to the second PPN, trimming a mapping of the first LPN to the first PPN [30]. Since there is no matching command in current storage interface such as SATA, the `share` command has been added as a SATA vendor unique command as summarized below.

share(LPN1, LPN2, length) This is a new, added SATA command. When host issues a *SHARE* command, FTL changes the physical address mapped to `LPN1` to the physical address currently mapped to `LPN2` so both logical addresses share one physical data address. The third argument, `length`, is optionally used when the length of data to be shared is longer than the FTL mapping granularity. The length must be a multiple of mapping unit size. When the length is larger than 1, the range between LPN1 and LPN1+length cannot be overlapped with the range between LPN2 and LPN2+length.

Since the SATA command set is not always available to database storage engines and other applications that access files through a file system, we exploited the `ioctl` infrastructure so that the *SHARE* command can pass through the file system to the storage device, instead of invoking the SATA command directly from applications.

Even though our description so far assumes a SHARE command associated with a single pair of LPNs, this concept can be naturally extended to multiple LPN pairs in a batch. In this case, FTL should be able to support the atomic address remapping for the given set of LPN pairs upon a system crash or power-off failure. In this regard, the idea of *SHARE* resembles the shadow page technique [21], but it offloads the shadow paging overhead to the flash storage firmware, where the transactional atomicity can be implemented much more efficiently. Section 4 will describe one way to implement the *SHARE* command atomically. This batch SHARE operation can reduce the non-negligible round-trip overhead in the IO stack of issuing the command via ioctl [10]. In addition, this batch can reduce the number of potential flash writes to persist the updated mapping information.

3.3 SHARE Advantages

To the best of our knowledge, *SHARE* is the first work which exposes the existence of address mapping table inside flash storage to host applications, allowing them to explicitly change the mapping for their own purposes. The advantages of *SHARE* are threefold. First, *SHARE* exploits the address mapping mechanism every flash-based storage device uses [9], so that upper layer applications can complete the costly operations such as transactional atomicity and compaction at low cost with minimal writes. Second, since *SHARE* command semantics are simple and clear, it is easy to incorporate them into the existing storage interface frameworks (*e.g.*, using the vendor specific command) and does not require involving intermediate layers such as the kernel block layer. So standards such as SATA, SAS, NVMe, and FC (Fiber Channel) can incorporate the *SHARE* abstraction with minimal changes. Third, upper layer applications including MySQL/InnoDB and Couchbase storage engines can use the *SHARE* service with marginal code changes, and further those changes are limited to modules interacting flash storage via the *SHARE* command.

Our *SHARE* scheme is novel in that it attempts to convert a flash memory weakness (*i.e.*, being unable to update in place and thus maintaining another level of address mapping) into a strength (*i.e.*, atomic write without write amplification and zero-copy compaction). This enables applications with strict atomic write requirements to achieve low-cost transactional support as well as minimal write amplification. Moreover, reducing flash storage write prolongs a flash storage device's life span.

Compaction by SHARE

Let us explain how the *SHARE* interface can be effectively used in mitigating the costly compaction overhead in Couchbase. First, the compaction operation is less frequently triggered in Couchbase. Because the *SHARE* interface replaces the cascaded updates of index nodes with a simple host interface command, write amplification caused by the wandering tree in the original Couchbase can be avoided. Hence, the database file is filled with invalid pages at slower pace by the *SHARE*-assisted Couchbase than by the original Couchbase. Second, and more importantly, the *SHARE* interface can boost the compaction process itself. Given that all write transactions in most key-value stores slow down during database compaction, it is crucial to complete compaction as fast as possible.

When a compaction operation is triggered in the original Couchbase, it creates a new database file and copies all valid documents from the old database file to the new file. In contrast, with the *SHARE* interface, as depicted in Figure 3, compaction can proceed without copying any valid documents. That is, after creating a new file, it first allocates new address space for the new database file (*i.e.*, using `fallocate()` system call) and then invokes the *SHARE* command to make the valid document pages in the old file shared by the new LPN addresses in the new file. After the *SHARE* command is successfully completed, the only remaining thing is to build up tree index nodes for new database file.

Other Applications of SHARE

Though the benefit of *SHARE* will be, throughout this paper, demonstrated with two database systems, MySQL/InnoDB and Couchbase, we believe that the idea of *SHARE* is easily and generically applicable to other database systems such as PostgreSQL and SQLite. For example, if *SQLite* is minimally modified to run on *SHARE*, it can achieve the atomic propagation of updated pages in a transaction without using the costly journaling of either *rollback* or *write-ahead log* mode. Instead, it can simply turn them off, because *SHARE* supports transactional atomicity and durability at the storage level. Also, *SHARE* can be leveraged in journaling or copy-on-write file systems [13, 22] suffering from redundant write and tree-wandering problems.

4. IMPLEMENTATION

This section details the *SHARE* architecture and its prototype implementation. Most of the *SHARE* architecture is implemented as an OpenSSD development board firmware extension. New commands for the *SHARE* features are prototyped via vendor unique commands. A user-level library that implements a protocol for the new commands via the

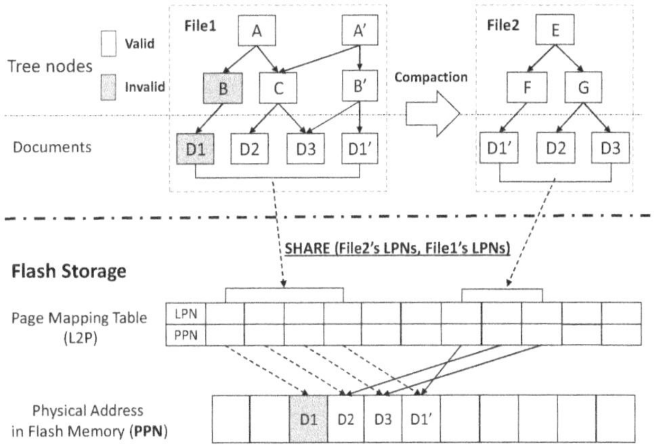

Figure 3: Couchbase Compaction with *SHARE*

ioctl system call supports applications and SSDs. This approach not only allows quickly prototyping the concept in development environments, i.e., Linux with ext4 file system, but also to make the prototype portable to most file systems. Please note that application changes to leverage the *SHARE* features are minimal - a few tens of lines of codes in Couchbase and MySQL/InnoDB total.

4.1 OpenSSD

OpenSSD is the first open development platform for SSD hardware/software. Its primary intent is to promote academia research [2, 17]. The first generation was introduced in 2011, and its third generation has been available since late 2014. This paper relies on the first generation, and the discussion in this section is limited to the first generation. Newer generation details are available at OpenSSD's project web site [2]. Since the WAF problem this paper discusses is independent of SSD performance, even though the actual performance observed by the end user can be influenced, this paper's claims are valid regardless of storage devices.

The first OpenSSD generation employs the *barefoot* controller and Samsung K9LCG08U1M NAND flash chips. The *barefoot* controller is a commercial product developed by Indilinx which was acquired by OCZ which was acquired by Toshiba Corporation. The controller is based on a 87.5MHz ARM processor and has a 96KB SRAM for the firmware and a 64MB Mobile SDRAM for metadata such as mapping tables. The type of NAND Flash is MLC (Multiple Level Cell) which contains two bits per cell. For flash memory management, a simple page mapping scheme is adopted, which is the most common management scheme used in contemporary SSD products and eMMC flash memory cards. We discuss more about FTL (Flash Translation Layer) and page mapping in the next section. The OpenSSD board is connected to the host system through a SATA interface.

4.2 Firmware Extension

4.2.1 SHARE *command*

A SSD FTL implements an indirection layer between a logical address space the host system sees and physical address space the FTL uses to store data on flash media. The most popular scheme is a page mapping which implements a mapping table that maps a logical NAND page (LPN) to a physical NAND page (PPN). When NAND Flash media page data is updated, the new content is written to a new physical NAND page and the mapping entry for the logical NAND page is updated to point to the new physical NAND page. We call this *forward mapping* or *L2P (logical page to physical page) mapping* in this paper.

The *SHARE* leverages this existing indirection. Instead of writing identical content twice for data consistency - as implemented in Couchbase compaction, InnoDB double write, and ext4 journaling - *SHARE* makes two logical NAND pages linked to the same physical NAND page, avoiding the second write.

This simple high-level description, however, imposes several technical challenges on firmware design and development. First, to preserve data consistency in the presence of failure, the sharing operation must be atomic. That is, the logical page must point to the old physical page if the operation fails, or to the new physical page if it succeeds. Second, a physical page can be accessed by two logical pages, complicating the SSD garbage collection process. A physical page can be recycled only when it is not referenced by any logical page. A simple solution to this problem is to maintain reverse mapping information for each physical page. If a physical page has a valid P2L (physical page to logical page) mapping and the logical page referenced by the mapping has a valid L2P mapping to the physical page, the physical page is valid. Therefore, each physical page needs to maintain multiple reverse mappings when using *SHARE*. Third, these extra data structures may compete with a normal mapping table for SSD memory space and this can have performance implications. The internal DRAM capacity of modern SSDs is proportional to the NAND capacity: roughly 1MB DRAM per 1GB NAND is available. Most of the DRAM space is used by the forward mapping table and the remaining space is used for I/O buffers and cache. To minimize the performance impact, we trade a portion of cache space for the reverse mapping and the size of reverse mapping table is empirically determined for the OpenSSD platform while the entire forward mapping table is kept in DRAM. The size of the P2L reverse mapping table is determined by several factors: the amount of available memory, the frequency of *SHARE* operations, and the lifespan of shared pages. The current implementation maintains only a small number of entries: 250 entries (4KB) or 500 entries (8KB).

4.2.2 *Atomicity*

As discussed in previous sections, double writes or journaling implement atomic data updates. Therefore, *SHARE* command must atomically update both the normal L2P mapping and the reverse P2L mapping. Furthermore, when such an update spans over multiple NAND pages, a *SHARE* operation for the update also applies to multiple pages. As such, a *SHARE* operation must be transactional and prevent any partial mapping updates in order to emulate the database semantics.

The FTL in modern SSDs maintains the consistency of the mapping table by logging mapping table state changes - called a Delta in this paper, since a reliably persistent version, i.e., a base mapping table, was created [18]. When a page is updated, the page is first written to a physical page and the mapping table entry in memory is updated. Then, a mapping table entry for the L2P is written to a log. Once a log entry is created, the update is deemed persisted. If an

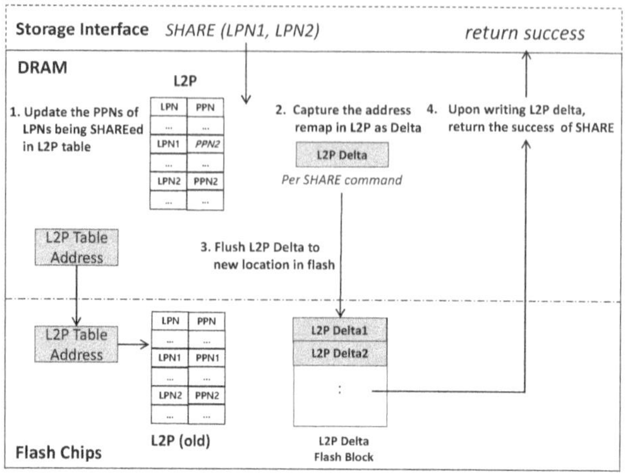

Figure 4: Atomicity in SHARE

SSD has an emergency power capacitor, the creation of an in-memory log entry guarantees persistency. Otherwise, the log entry must be flushed to flash. The modified portion of mapping table is flushed to flash and the log is truncated regularly to balance the update performance and the recovery overhead.

For *SHARE*, the first step of writing to the physical page is skipped. Instead, the delta that includes the changes of reverse mapping is written to the log in a form of (LPN, old PPN, new PPN). Figure 4 summarizes the procedure of *SHARE* operation. First, when a ***SHARE* (LPN1, LPN2)** command is received, the FTL updates the PPN entry for LPN2 in the L2P mapping table with the PPN1 for the LPN1. Then it generates a Delta, (LPN2, PPN2, PPN1), and writes it to a log. If a *SHARE* command is associated with multiple pages, a series of deltas are logged after updating all the mapping table entries. Thereafter, the **share** command is considered completed atomically and persistently. The maximum size of Deltas cannot exceed the mapping page size because only a page is written atomically to flash for most SSDs [16]. The *SHARE* command returns after logging finishes.

4.3 Application Extension

This section describes the changes we made in MySQL/InnoDB and Couchbase to enable them to run on the *SHARE* interface. As will be described below, the changes in both databases are minimal.

Changes made in MySQL/InnoDB

In the original MySQL/InnoDB, as explained in Section 2, when evicting a set of dirty victim pages from the buffer cache, each page is written to its original location after forcefully writing another copy in the *double-write-buffer* area.

In contrast, when MySQL/InnoDB runs on *SHARE*, it simply calls the **share** command with the LPN pair(s) (the database file LPN and the double write buffer LPN) after the victim page set is successfully written in the *double-write-buffer* area, instead of writing each page redundantly at its original location. When the **share** call terminates normally, it is guaranteed that each page is propagated to its original location in its entirety. On a system reboot after system crashes, because the address remapping between a dirty page in the *double-write-buffer* area and its original location is atomically guaranteed at the storage level, the modified MySQL/InnoDB server can find a consistent copy of the page in either the database or *the double-write buffer* area. The code changes made in InnoDB storage engine were minimal - less than 200 lines of new code were added to just two modules of `buffer` and `file`.

Changes made in Couchbase

Even though the Couchbase was designed to minimize unnecessary storage writes, write amplification caused by its tree wandering problem is inevitable. When a document is updated in the Couchbase storage engine, its new version is appended and a leaf node pointing to the old version is updated to point to the new version. This leaf node update triggers the cascading updates of parents nodes that incurs high write amplification. We have adapted the Couchbase storage's `commit` API to use *SHARE* interface to avoid a leaf node update for each document, which consequently prevents the cascading parent node updates.

For the database recovery, if Couchbase terminates abnormally without failing the entire system, its original recovery process is applicable since the Couchbase storage engine only appends a new document at the end of the database file. In case of the entire system failure (*e.g.*, by a power outage), the original recovery process can be still performed as the SSD page mapping changes are persisted in an atomic way (Section 4.2.2).

In addition, Couchbase performs the background compaction to reclaim stale pages by reading all active documents from the old file and writing them to the new file. To avoid this heavy read/write I/O overhead, we have adapted the Couchbase storage's `compact` API, so that the LPNs of the documents in the old file and the new LPNs of the documents in the new file can be passed to the SSD FTL layer via the *SHARE* interface. Upon crashing during this compaction, the partially compacted new file is deleted and the whole compaction process restarts at system reboot. Couchbase's *SHARE* integration required quite small code changes - less than 500 line of new codes were added to `commit` and `compact` APIs.

5. PERFORMANCE EVALUATION

In this section, we present performance evaluation results to analyze the impact of the *SHARE* interface on relational and NoSQL storage engines.

5.1 Experimental Setup

The experiments were performed on a Linux platform with the 3.13.0 kernel running on an Intel Core i3-3220 3.3GHz processor equipped with 8GB DRAM. The host machine had one 4GB OpenSSD drive and one Samsung PM853T 240GB SSD. The OpenSSD drive was used as the main storage device implementing the *SHARE* interface. In the case of MySQL/InnoDB benchmark, the Samsung PM853T SSD was used as a database log device. Both the OpenSSD drive and Samsung PM853T SSD connected to the host using SATA interfaces.

We used the *ext4* file system in the `ordered` mode for metadata journaling. The direct I/O option(O_DIRECT) was enabled to avoid the effect of file system page caching. The benchmarking clients were run along with the database processes on the same hardware to exclude network latency in evaluation results. For more realistic experimental environment, an aging operation of the OpenSSD drive was pre-run so that the overhead of garbage collections was reflected in the result.

5.2 Workloads

For relational database systems, we used LinkBench workload [8] to conduct the performance evaluations on MySQL/InnoDB under the two configurations (i.e., double write buffer enabled, *SHARE* with double write buffer disabled). We included a NoSQL benchmark (YCSB benchmark [14]) to evaluate the impact of *SHARE* on the performance of a Couchbase NoSQL system in normal writes as well as compaction operations. As benchmark workloads, transactions of LinkBench and YCSB are much smaller than a traditional TPC-C workload. On the other hand, they are quite similar to a TPC-C workload in that both benchmark tools generate a large number of small random reads and writes. Below are described the characteristics of two benchmarks, LinkBench and YCSB.

LinkBench LinkBench is a configurable open-source database benchmark for a large-scale social graph [8]. This benchmark tool reflects the characteristics of Facebook social graph data where the majority of read requests are served by a caching layer. This reduces the temporal and spatial locality of read requests reaching the underlying database servers [19]. However, the overall workload reaching the database servers is still read-intensive with approximately 30% writes. The force index option was turned on to avoid additional I/O operations required for query optimization. Also, the buffer flush neighbors option, which flushes any neighbor pages together for a dirty victim page, was turned off to reduce unnecessary write overhead.

YCSB Yahoo! Cloud Serving Benchmark (YCSB) is a benchmark framework created for evaluating cloud systems [14]. YCSB consists of six workload types and mimics web applications running a huge number of simple queries, each of which touches a single record. Since all the workloads except for workload-A and workload-F are read-intensive, workload-A and workload-F were used to evaluate the performance impact of *SHARE*.

5.3 Run-Time Performance

This section demonstrates the effectiveness of *SHARE* by comparing the performance of MySQL/InnoDB using LinkBench with and without *SHARE*. Similarly, the performance of Couchbase NoSQL system was tested using two YCSB workloads with and without *SHARE*. Each performance measurement in this section was an average of three runs.

5.3.1 MySQL/InnoDB for LinkBench

The version of MySQL/InnoDB used in the experiments was the most recent 5.7.5-m15 development release. We created three LinkBench databases of 1.5GB with page sizes of 4KB, 8KB, and 16KB to compare the effect of different page sizes. Throughout all the LinkBench experiments, 16 client threads were concurrently run. For steady performance measurement, the LinkBench was pre-run for a 300 second warm-up time to fill the InnoDB buffer cache. A total of 160,000 transactions (10,000 per client) were run in

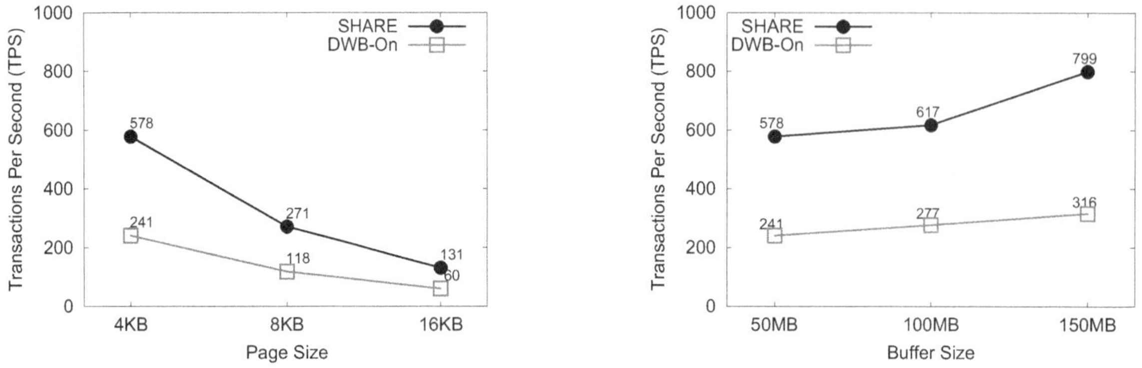

(a) Varying page size (b) Varying buffer size

Figure 5: LinkBench throughput on MySQL/InnoDB

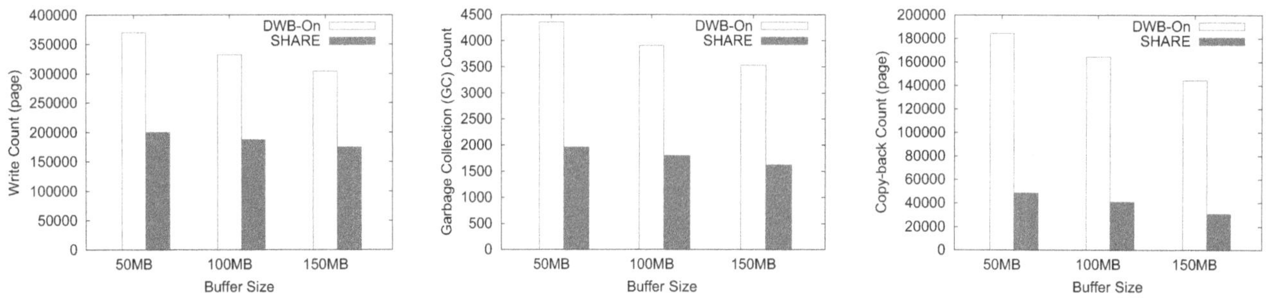

(a) OS page write count (b) Garbage collection count (c) Copyback page count

Figure 6: IO activities inside OpenSSD (50MB buffer cache, 4KB page)

each experiment. We use the `DWB-On` and `SHARE` symbol to denote MySQL/InnoDB execution in its default mode with the double-write-buffer on and in the *SHARE* mode with the double write buffer off, respectively.

The Effect of SHARE *on Throughput*

Two sets of experiments were conducted to evaluate the effect of *SHARE* on database throughput. In the first set, we ran the MySQL server with three LinkBench databases created with different page sizes when the buffer pool size was fixed to 50MB. For the second set, we ran the MySQL server by varying the buffer pool size from 50MB to 150MB when the LinkBench database page size was fixed to 4KB.

Figure 5 presents the results of measured transaction throughput. As clearly shown in Figure 5(a) and Figure 5(b), the *SHARE* consistently helped MySQL process LinkBench transactions much faster than the `DWB-On` mode by more than two times over all tested configurations regardless of buffer size and page size.

For all the experiments, we also measured the transaction throughput while running the MySQL server in the `DWB-Off` mode to compare the performance differences between three different modes. Interestingly, for all six configurations, although omitted from Figure 5 for clarity, the performance gaps between `DWB-Off` and `SHARE` modes were less than one percent. Recalling that the `DWB-Off` mode also avoids redundant writes, it is obvious that two modes generate the same IO traffic except the `share` commands issued in `SHARE` mode. This comparison derives two interesting points. One is that *SHARE* can achieve the write atomicity at almost no performance cost. The other is that the run-time overhead of our `share` implementation is very marginal.

The Effect of SHARE *on IO Activities*

This considerable performance gain of *SHARE*, which is shown in Figure 5, was a direct reflection of reducing the number of written pages. This is confirmed by the number of page writes requested by the host when running the same set of experiments for Figure 5(b). As is shown in Figure 6(a), the *SHARE*-based implementation reduced the number of requested page writes to the SSD by 45% compared to the original MySQL/InnoDB. The reduction ratio is less than 50% because the traffic includes file system metadata page write requests as well as MySQL data page write requests.

To understand how the input traffic reduction influences internal SSD behavior, we measured the number of garbage collection events and the number of valid pages copied-back due to garbage collection. As shown in Figure 6(b) and Figure 6(c), the `SHARE`-based implementation exacts much less SSD burden than the original MySQL/InnoDB. Regardless of buffer size, the garbage collection operations decreased by 55% while the number of copyback pages decreased by 75%.

It is interesting to observe the trend between the number of OS page writes, the number of SSD garbage collections, and the number of SSD copyback pages. *SHARE* contributed to 45% reduction of OS page writes, which led to 55% reduction of garbage collection events, and then ended up with 75% reduction of copybacks. By avoiding the redundant writes of pages, *SHARE* halves the number of page

Transactions		DWB-On						SHARE					
I/O Type	Name	Mean	P25	P50	P75	P99	Max	Mean	P25	P50	P75	P99	Max
Read	Get_Node	51.4	4	12	28	600	1363.3	23.9	5	10	23	300	901.1
	Count_Link	32.8	2	5	15	600	1244.4	14.4	2	5	17	200	747.4
	Multiget_Link	40.7	0.3	5	19	500	1573.5	15.2	0.8	6	17	200	313.3
	Get_Link_List	39.4	0.3	5	18	500	17467.4	17.2	0.3	5	17	200	6140.7
Write	ADD_Node	6.3	0.3	0.4	0.4	200	1521.0	1.5	0.3	0.3	0.4	24	554.6
	Update_Node	64.0	5	15	42	700	2071.4	28.3	5	14	27	300	823.8
	Delete_Node	62.6	5	13	40	600	1104.6	26.3	5	12	25	300	596.7
	Add_Link	119.3	17	40	200	1000	2248.2	49.7	14	27	57	400	730.4
	Delete_Link	70.5	4	16	55	800	1417.6	30.3	4	14	30	300	1132.8
	Update_Link	114.9	16	38	200	1000	2270.5	49.4	13	26	54	400	1102.5

Table 1: Distribution of LinkBench transaction latency (in millisec)

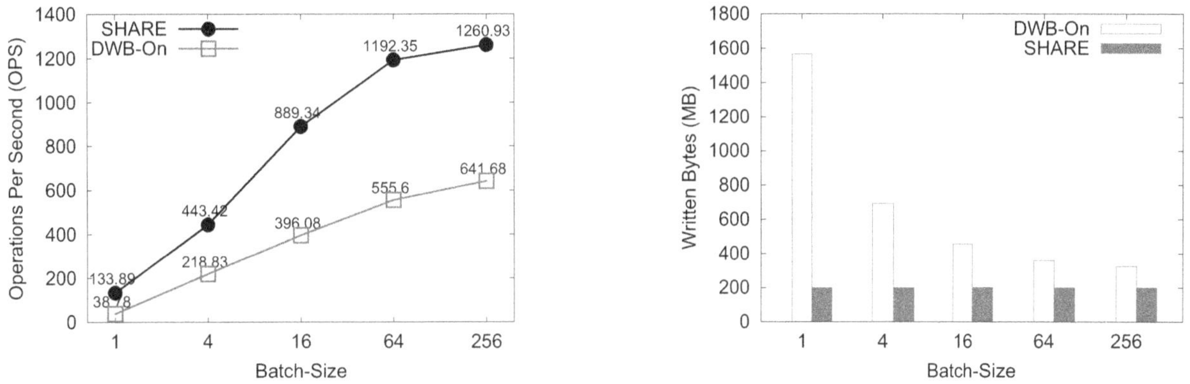

(a) Throughput (b) Total amount of written data

Figure 7: YCSB throughput on Couchbase: Workload-F

writes to the storage and thus triggers less garbage collections (*i.e.*, 10% less GCs). Further, this let a single block survive probabilistically 2x longer before it becomes a GC victim. As a result, data pages in each data block will have more chances to be invalidated before the data blocks are reclaimed for garbage collection. Therefore, in *SHARE*, a victim block likely has less valid data pages at GC time (*i.e.*, roughly a half copybacks per each victim block and quater copybacks in total). This implies that the *SHARE* interface can provide longer device lifespan while less garbage collection events provide more consistent IO performance with less performance jitter.

As is mentioned in Section 2, to guarantee write atomicity, PostgreSQL takes a similar approach to MySQL. In order to evaluate the performance impact of the `full_page_write` feature in the PostgreSQL server, we carried out a separate experiment using the `pgbench` benchmark [5]. In the experiment, when the `full_page_write` option was turned off, the transaction throughput approximately doubled and the amount of WAL log data reduction was roughly same as the total amount of data pages written to the database tables. This indicates that a PostgreSQL server also can expect significant performance gains by leveraging the *SHARE* interface as a mechanism to guarantee the atomicity of page writes.

The Effect of SHARE *on Tail Tolerance*

High tail latency poses serious challenges for online service providers since even small increase may result in reduced traffic and revenue [15]. In order to evaluate the impact of *SHARE* on read and write transactions latencies, we also measured the latencies while running LinkBench with a 50MB buffer cache and 4KB page size. The latency statistics were reported by the LinkBench script at the end of each benchmark run, and are summarized in Table 1.

Table 1 compares two modes of MySQL/InnoDB, **DWB ON** and **SHARE**, in terms of latencies at 25, 50, 75 and 99 percentiles as well as the average and maximum latencies for ten different types of read and write transactions. It is clear from this table that the *SHARE* interface significantly reduced the latency in all measurements. Specifically, the average latency was reduced by a factor of 2.1 to 4.2, while the maximum latency was reduced by a factor of 1.2 to 3.4. More importantly, the 99 percentile latency was also reduced by a factor of 2.0 to 8.3. Once again, this is clear evidence that *SHARE* reduces the tail latencies, contributing greatly to tail tolerance.

Another observation made from Table 1 is that *SHARE* could considerably lower the latency of read transactions as well as that of write transactions. One main reason is that faster write request completion by avoiding redundant writes can shorten the response time of read requests blocked by preceding writes on a page miss [16].

5.3.2 Couchbase for YCSB

To analyze the effect of *SHARE* on NoSQL workloads, we ran a Couchbase system against `workload-F` and `workload-A` of YCSB benchmark with a 1GB database consisting of 250,000 key-value records. The average size of key-value records in YCSB was 4KB. The workload-A consists of 50% read and 50% update operations by default. The workload-F consists of 100% read-modify-write operations by default.

The Couchbase throughput was measured in operations per second (OPS), where an operation is like a RDBMS system transaction. All the experiments were done in a single thread mode. The average index tree depth was three, and the size of each tree node was 4KB. Thus, the average amount of each update operation was about 16KB including the tree nodes and a document update. Couchbase can adjust the `fsync` frequency in order to trade durability for performance by changing the value of a `batch-size` parameter. If the `batch-size` is set to a positive integer, say k, a `fsync` call is executed every k updates.

Effect of SHARE *on Workload-F*

Figure 7 shows the experiment results in workload-F measured under different configurations created by changing the batch size from one to 256 and using *SHARE*. As Figure 7(a) clearly shows, the *SHARE* interface helped Couchbase process operations much faster than the original Couchbase by a factor of 1.96 (batch size 256) to 3.45 (batch size 1).

And Figure 7(b) demonstrates that the considerable performance gain reflected the reduction of the amount of the written pages. Recall that with *SHARE* interface, Couchbase does not update all tree nodes on a path from the root to a leaf pointing to an updated document. For this reason, the amount of written data with the *SHARE* interface is almost constant regardless of batch-size. On the other hand, the original Couchbase experiences less write amplification due to tree-wandering as the batch-size increases. Thus, the gap in the written data amount between the original and the *SHARE*-based Couchbase became much narrower from a factor of 7.86 to 1.64 by changing the batch-size from 1 to 256.

Reducing Couchbase's write amplification is crucial because NoSQL systems usually manage huge data volumes of mobile and web applications. In addition, less write amplification gives Couchbase various performance benefits, such as reduced compaction frequency, providing a consistent performance for normal operations, and prolonging the SSD lifespan.

Effect of SHARE *on Workload-A*

Similarly, in order to also evaluate the effect of *SHARE* on a mixed workload, we ran YCSB's workload-A. The experiments were conducted with the same configurations for the workload-F. Figure 8 shows that *SHARE*-based Couchbase outperformed its original version by a factor of 1.61 (batch-size 256) to 2.23 (batch-size 1).

Effect of SHARE *on Compaction*

In order to evaluate the effect of *SHARE* on compactions, we measured the elapsed times of compaction with the original and the *SHARE*-based Couchbase. As shown in Table 2, compared to the original Couchbase, the *SHARE*-based compaction completed faster by a factor of 3.1 and also reduced the amount of written data by a factor of 7.5. Though quite impressive, the improvement ratio in total elapsed time is less than the reduction ratio in total amount of written data. And the reason is that even with the *SHARE*-based compaction, the header page of each valid document in the old file should be read from the old database file so as to check the length of the document, which is required in the `share` command.

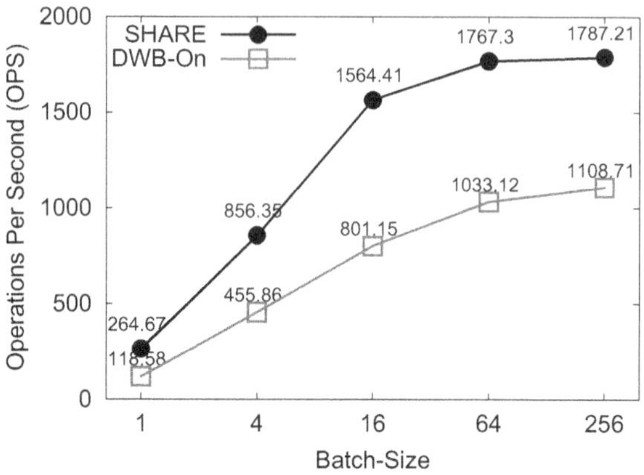

Figure 8: YCSB throughput on Couchbase: Workload-A

	Elapsed Time (sec)	Written Bytes (MB)
Original	277.52	1126.4
SHARE	88.38	150.6

Table 2: Effect of *SHARE* on compaction

6. RELATED WORK

Three types of existing work are closely related to *SHARE*: atomic write in flash storage [26, 27, 29], transactional FTL [17], and address remapping technique [12]. All these techniques exploit the copy-on-write approach used in FTL in order to provide host-side applications in place, page write atomicity. In contrast, with *SHARE*, host-side applications employ an out-of-place update approach and call the *SHARE* command to avoid the redundant write for the atomic writes. Now, let us briefly explain each work and compare it with *SHARE*.

6.1 Atomic Write in Flash Storage

Recently, several interesting suggestions have been made to efficiently support atomic updates on flash-based storage devices, mainly from the storage and file system communities [26, 27, 29]. These FTL approaches have focused more on ensuring the atomicity of a fixed set of pages, predetermined at write time.

To the best of our knowledge, the atomic write FTL by Park *et al.* [27] is the first study for supporting multiple flash storage page atomic writes by exploiting flash storage out-of-place update characteristics. This work only focuses on supporting multiple page atomic writes to be written in a single write request like `write(p1,..,pn)`. Upon receiving the write command, the FTL first writes all the pages into the flash chip media in a synchronous way, then leaves the commit record. If a crash occurs during the data page write or before writing the commit record, the FTL, upon rebooting, undoes all the page writes when the commit record is not found for the transaction. Recently, this approach was applied to FusionIO Atomic Write Extension, (the only device available in the market that supports page write atomicity at the storage level) [26]. And, Ouyan *et al.* [26] showed that it can be used to replace the double buffer area in MySQL/InnoDB, whose goal is to support the atomic data page writes. Similarly, Prabhakaran *et al.* [29] proposed an FTL called *txFlash*, which supports atomic writes semantics tailored for file system journaling.

While these existing approaches focus on supporting the atomic propagation of one or more pages written in an update-in-place manner inside flash storage, the *SHARE* scheme can efficiently support the atomic write of data pages in host applications without write amplification using the out-of-place update approach. And, unlike the existing approaches, our *SHARE* scheme does not require flushing the whole page set at once. Instead, with *SHARE*, applications can write any data page at any time and call the *SHARE* command against a set of pages at an appropriate time.

In this respect, *SHARE* more flexibly supports atomicity semantics. Moreover, *SHARE* can support the Couchbase compaction process, which is not possible with existing atomic write approaches.

6.2 Transactional FTLs

To support the transactional atomicity semantics database applications require, a transactional FTL called *X-FTL* [17] recently was proposed. It is more flexible than the FTLs described above in that *X-FTL* allows writing any data page at any time while still supporting atomicity of any group of pages belonging to a transaction. By also exploiting the flash storage *copy-on-write* mechanism, *X-FTL* can efficiently guarantee that, without resorting to amplified writes, all pages any transaction updates are successfully propagated or no pages are written upon a failure. In other words, it implements flash storage transactional atomicity, which is similar to the shadow paging technique [21]. With *X-FTL*, database applications such as SQLite are relieved from the burden of implementing their own proprietary transactional semantics and also benefit from better performance [17].

A common *X-FTL* and *SHARE* benefit is that they can guarantee transactional atomicity. However, *SHARE* is developed to support applications taking the out-of-place update approach for atomic write while *X-FTL* supports applications using update-in-place. Of course, *X-FTL*, like other related works, cannot be used to support the Couchbase compaction process either.

6.3 Address Remapping in JFTL

Regarding *SHARE*, other interesting flash storage work on and FTL community is JFTL [12]. Under the full journaling mode of a journaling file system [28], for higher file system consistency, the same data page in a file is redundantly written to both the journal area and the original file. To avoid redundant writes, JFTL (*i.e.*, FTL for journal mode) updates the mapping table instead of copying pages from the journal area to the original file. After writing a set of pages such as data pages and the file system's metadata (*e.g.*, inodes and superblocks) in the journal area, the journaling file system informs the flash storage of the list of the journaled data pages using a new interface. Upon receiving the list, the JFTL simply remaps the logical-to-physical mapping information of each data page in the list to the corresponding pre-written page in the journal area, thus avoiding writing the data pages redundantly. In this respect, JFTL is the closest approach to *SHARE*. However, unlike JFTL which is tailored to journaling file system and thus is based on a proprietary interface between OS kernel thread and FTL, *SHARE* is an explicit interface which any application can use. Also, *SHARE* is more flexible in that it supports the Couchbase compaction process.

7. CONCLUSION

Many database storage engines, as well as file systems, utilize a redundant write or copy-on-write approach for atomic writes. Consequent write amplification at the software level adversely impacts both performance and flash storage device lifespans. This paper proposes a novel interface for flash storage called *SHARE*, which allows the applications to explicitly change the FTL indirection address mapping, thus relieving costly write amplification from those applications without compromising atomic write properties.

We have implemented *SHARE* on an SSD development platform called OpenSSD by enhancing its FTL code with *SHARE* features. We have modified MySQL/InnoDB and Couchbase storage engine to exploit *SHARE* with only minimal code changes. Using a set of popular workloads for relational and NoSQL databases, we have demonstrated that *SHARE* achieves a significant performance improvement.

There are numerous applications that can benefit from the *SHARE* interface, including database systems such as PostgreSQL and SQLite and file systems such as Ext4 and BTRFS. As a future work,we will modify those systems to exploit the *SHARE* interface and evaluate its impact using various synthetic and real workloads.

Acknowledgments

This work was supported by Institute for Information & communications Technology Promotion(IITP) grant funded by the Korea government(MSIP). (R0126-15-1108, Flash-SQL: NVRam Based High Performance Open Source DBMS development and 1041244, SmartTV 2.0 Software Platform) And, the authors would like to express our sincere appreciation to Mark Callaghan of Facebook for his feedback on early draft of this paper.

8. REFERENCES

[1] mongoDB. https://www.mongodb.org/, 2007.

[2] OpenSSD Project. http://goo.gl/J0Ts5, 2011.

[3] Atomic Commit In SQLite. http://www.sqlite.org/atomiccommit.html, 2014.

[4] MySQL 5.7 Reference Manual. http://dev.mysql.com/doc/refman/5.7/en/, 2015.

[5] pgbench. http://www.postgresql.org/docs/devel/static/pgbench.html, 2015.

[6] PostgreSQL 9.4.4 Documentation. http://www.postgresql.org/docs/9.4/, 2015.

[7] Ahn, Jung-Sang and Seo, C. and Mayuram, R. and Yaseen, R. and Kim, Jin-Soo and Maeng, S. Forestdb: A fast key-value storage system for variable-length

string keys. *IEEE Transactions on Computers*, PP(99):1–14, May 2015.

[8] T. G. Armstrong, V. Ponnekanti, D. Borthakur, and M. Callaghan. LinkBench: a Database Benchmark based on the Facebook Social Graph. In *Proceedings of the 39th SIGMOD International Conference on Management of Data (SIGMOD '13)*, pages 1185–1196, 2013.

[9] A. Ban. Flash file system, Apr 1995. US Patent 5,404,485.

[10] A. M. Caulfield, A. De, J. Coburn, T. I. Mollow, R. K. Gupta, and S. Swanson. Moneta: A High-Performance Storage Array Architecture for Next-Generation, Non-volatile Memories. In *Proceedings of the 2010 43rd Annual IEEE/ACM International Symposium on Microarchitecture (MICRO '43)*, pages 385–395, 2010.

[11] F. Chang, J. Dean, S. Ghemawat, W. C. Hsieh, D. A. Wallach, M. Burrows, T. Chandra, A. Fikes, and R. E. Gruber. Bigtable: A distributed storage system for structured data. In *Proceedings of the 7th USENIX Symposium on Operating Systems Design and Implementation - Volume 7*, OSDI '06, pages 15–15, Berkeley, CA, USA, 2006. USENIX Association.

[12] H. J. Choi, S.-H. Lim, and K. H. Park. JFTL: A Flash Translation Layer Based on a Journal Remapping for Flash Memory. *ACM Transactions on Storage*, 4(4):14:1–14:22, Feb 2009.

[13] J. Condit, E. B. Nightingale, C. Frost, E. Ipek, B. Lee, D. Burger, and D. Coetzee. Better I/O Through Byte-addressable, Persistent Memory. In *Proceedings of the ACM SIGOPS 22Nd Symposium on Operating Systems Principles*, SOSP '09, pages 133–146, 2009.

[14] B. F. Cooper, A. Silberstein, E. Tam, R. Ramakrishnan, and R. Sears. Benchmarking Cloud Serving Systems with YCSB. In *Proceedings of the 1st ACM Symposium on Cloud Computing (SoCC '10)*, pages 143–154, 2010.

[15] J. Dean and L. A. Barroso. The Tail at Scale. *Communications of the ACM*, 56(2):74–80, Feb. 2013.

[16] W.-H. Kang, S.-W. Lee, B. Moon, Y.-S. Kee, and M. Oh. Durable Write Cache in Flash Memory SSD for Relational and NoSQL Databases. In *Proceedings of the 40th SIGMOD International Conference on Management of Data (SIGMOD '14)*, pages 529–540, 2014.

[17] W.-H. Kang, S.-W. Lee, B. Moon, G.-H. Oh, and C.-W. Min. X-FTL: Transactional FTL for SQLite Databases. In *Proceedings of the 39th SIGMOD international conference on Management of data (SIGMOD '13)*, pages 97–108, 2013.

[18] S.-Y. Kim and S.-I. Jung. A log-based flash translation layer for large nand flash memory. In *Advanced Communication Technology, 2006. ICACT 2006. The 8th International Conference*, volume 3, pages 1641–1644, Feb 2006.

[19] A. Lakshman and P. Malik. Cassandra: A decentralized structured storage system. *SIGOPS Oper. Syst. Rev.*, 44(2):35–40, Apr. 2010.

[20] S.-W. Lee, D.-J. Park, T.-S. Chung, D.-H. Lee, S. Park, and H.-J. Song. A Log Buffer-based Flash Translation Layer using Fully-associative Sector Translation. *ACM Transactions on Embedded Computing Systems*, 6(3):18, 2007.

[21] R. A. Lorie. Physical Integrity in a Large Segmented Database. *ACM Transactions on Database Systems*, 2(1):91–104, Mar 1977.

[22] L. Lu, A. C. Arpaci-Dusseau, R. H. Arpaci-Dusseau, and S. Lu. A Study of Linux File System Evolution. In *Proceedings of the 11th USENIX conference on File and Storage Technologies, FAST 2013, San Jose, CA, USA, February 12-15, 2013*, pages 31–44, 2013.

[23] D. Ma, J. Feng, and G. Li. A Survey of Address Translation Technologies for Flash Memories. *ACM Computing Survey*, 46(3):36:1–36:39, Jan. 2014.

[24] C. Mohan. Disk Read-Write Optimizations and Data Integrity in Transaction Systems Using Write-Ahead Logging. In *Proceedings of ICDE*, pages 324–331, 1995.

[25] P. O'Neil, E. Cheng, D. Gawlick, and E. O'Neil. The log-structured merge-tree (lsm-tree). *Acta Inf.*, 33(4):351–385, June 1996.

[26] X. Ouyang, D. W. Nellans, R. Wipfel, D. Flynn, and D. K. Panda. Beyond Block I/O: Rethinking Traditional Storage Primitives. In *Proceedings of International Conference on High-Performance Computer Architecture (HPCA '11)*, pages 301–311, 2011.

[27] S. Park, J. H. Yu, and S. Y. Ohm. Atomic Write FTL for Robust Flash File System. In *Proceedings of the Ninth International Symposium on Consumer Electronics (ISCE 2005)*, pages 155 – 160, Jun 2005.

[28] V. Prabhakaran, A. C. Arpaci-Dusseau, and R. H. Arpaci-Dusseau. Analysis and Evolution of Journaling File Systems. In *Proceedings of USENIX Annual Technical Conference*, 2005.

[29] V. Prabhakaran, T. L. Rodeheffer, and L. Zhou. Transactional Flash. In *Proceedings of Symposium on Operating Systems Design and Implementation (OSDI)*, 2008.

[30] F. Shu. Notification of Deleted Data Proposal for ATA-ACS2. http://t13.org, April 2007.

[31] Sybase. SQL Anywhere I/O Requirements for Windows and Linux. A Whitepaper from Sybase, an SAP Company, March 2011.

[32] D. Woodhouse. JFFS: The Journaling Flash File System. In *Proceedings of the Ottawa Linux Symposium*, 2001.

Accelerating Relational Databases by Leveraging Remote Memory and RDMA

Feng Li Sudipto Das Manoj Syamala Vivek R. Narasayya

Microsoft Research
Redmond, WA 98052, USA
{fenl, sudiptod, manojsy, viveknar}@microsoft.com

ABSTRACT

Memory is a crucial resource in relational databases (RDBMSs). When there is insufficient memory, RDBMSs are forced to use slower media such as SSDs or HDDs, which can significantly degrade workload performance. Cloud database services are deployed in data centers where network adapters supporting remote direct memory access (RDMA) at low latency and high bandwidth are becoming prevalent. We study the novel problem of how a Symmetric Multi-Processing (SMP) RDBMS, whose memory demands exceed locally-available memory, can leverage available remote memory in the cluster accessed via RDMA to improve query performance. We expose available memory on remote servers using a lightweight file API that allows an SMP RDBMS to leverage the benefits of remote memory with modest changes. We identify and implement several novel scenarios to demonstrate these benefits, and address design challenges that are crucial for efficient implementation. We implemented the scenarios in Microsoft SQL Server engine and present the first end-to-end study to demonstrate benefits of remote memory for a variety of micro-benchmarks and industry-standard benchmarks. Compared to using disks when memory is insufficient, we improve the throughput and latency of queries with short reads and writes by 3× to 10×, while improving the latency of multiple TPC-H and TPC-DS queries by 2× to 100×.

Keywords

Relational databases; RDMA; remote memory; opportunistic caching; buffer pool extension; semantic caching.

1. INTRODUCTION

Cloud database platforms, such as Amazon Relational Database Service, Microsoft Azure SQL Database, and Google Cloud SQL, are deployed in data centers comprising clusters of commodity servers with large memories and fast networks. Each server in the cluster runs an SMP relational database engine (RDBMS), such as MySQL or Microsoft SQL Server, and the service exposes a SQL API. Even parallel DBMSs, such as Actian Matrix MPP Analytics Database (formerly ParAccel) [31] Microsoft Analytics Platform System [26], and relational data warehouse services such as Amazon Redshift, run on similar clusters comprised of a collection of single server RDBMS. Memory is a crucial resource for RDBMS workloads. When memory is insufficient to meet the workload's demands, RDBMSs are forced to use disks (SSDs or HDDs) instead, which can result in significant performance degradation. In a database service, due to the variety and non-uniformity of workloads and resource demands, at any point in time, the memory usage of database servers can vary significantly from one server to another. One database server may experience *memory pressure*, i.e., demand exceeds available memory, while another server might have large amounts of *unutilized* memory which is not committed to any local process on the server.

An emerging infrastructure trend is the commoditization of network adapters that support remote direct memory access (RDMA). With the advent of technologies such as RDMA over Converged Ethernet (RoCE) [19] or iWARP [20], today RDMA is supported within data center environments at competitive prices. RDMA enables efficient, low latency ($\sim$10μsec), and high throughput ($\sim$56 Gbps) reads and writes of remote memory bypassing the operating system (OS) kernel at both the source and destination. Since the CPU is not involved in a transfer, RDMA avoids context switches and processor cache pollution, and incurs negligible performance impact on both the local and the remote servers.

The above trends open up an interesting opportunity for databases: can an SMP RDBMS with unmet memory demands efficiently leverage unused remote memory using RDMA to significantly improve performance of its workload? Databases have used RDMA primarily as a fast data transfer mechanism from storage to database servers or between database servers [17, 26, 29]. Rödiger et al. [34] present an approach where a parallel database can benefit from RDMA by redesigning the communication mechanism of the exchange operator. We consider an orthogonal problem of leveraging available remote memory to enable an SMP RDBMS to accelerate memory-intensive workloads without a major rewrite. We focus on scenarios where a mature database engine can leverage the benefits without a major rewrite.

Abstraction for remote memory in an RDBMS: The abstraction of distributed shared memory [1, 5] supported by the operating system is not suitable for RDBMSs that require control on which data is memory-resident. RDBMSs already explicitly manage the memory hierarchy and are adept in using disk-based file-oriented structures wherever memory is not adequate. Exposing remote memory via a lightweight file API gives the RDBMS explicit control over what data is placed in remote memory. This abstraction naturally aligns with our goal of integrating remote memory with modest changes to an existing RDBMS. We demonstrate the flexibility of this abstraction through a variety of scenarios that significantly improve the performance of memory-intensive workloads.

SIGMOD'16, June 26-July 01, 2016, San Francisco, CA, USA

ISBN 978-1-4503-3531-7/16/06...$15.00

DOI: http://dx.doi.org/10.1145/2882903.2882949

Scenarios for remote memory usage in RDBMS: We describe four novel scenarios where an SMP RDBMS can leverage remote memory to significantly improve performance of memory-intensive workloads. These scenarios are: (i) extending the RDBMS caches such as the buffer pool; (ii) spilling temporary data for memory intensive operators such as Sort and Hash; and (iii) supporting a semantic cache [10, 45]—which has traditionally been limited to application or middleware tiers—integrated into an RDBMS and pinned in available remote memory; and (iv) leveraging fast memory-to-memory transfer to prime and warm-up the buffer pool of a newly-elected primary in the event of a planned primary-secondary swap in an RDBMS cluster or a cloud database service. The first three scenarios leverage remote memory as a *a new level in the memory hierarchy of the RDBMS* whose performance lies between local memory and local SSDs or HDDs. While (i) and (ii) are handled by storage engine and lower layers, (iii) introduces interesting challenges of integrating this new form of cache within the RDBMS, query optimizer costing, plan selection, and identifying appropriate structures to cache. All four scenarios leverage the lightweight file API to access remote memory and can dramatically improve the performance of an SMP RDBMS, without affecting correctness and availability of the database server even if the remote server fails, rendering the memory unavailable.

Brokering of unutilized memory in the cluster: Unutilized memory on a subset of servers in a cluster of a cloud database service needs to be brokered to allow sharing among the different servers requesting additional memory. We use a design similar to many standard designs of resource negotiators, such as YARN [49]. Each server reports the unused memory to a memory broker. A server with unmet memory demand can request the broker for a lease to a remote memory region. This lease provides the database server exclusive access to the region. The database server *opportunistically* leverages this remote memory to improve the workload's performance without stealing memory committed to processes executing on the remote server.

Efficient implementation: There are several design decisions to consider to efficiently exploit remote memory. These include: (i) the suitable protocol to access remote memory via RDMA; (ii) whether to treat remote memory accesses as synchronous or asynchronous operations; and (iii) efficiently managing registration of memory regions to NICs which has non-trivial overheads [13]. We present a detailed implementation in Microsoft SQL Server (Section 4). While our implementation is specific to SQL Server, we expect our design to generalize to other RDBMSs particularly due to the choice of a lightweight file API to expose available remote memory in the cluster.

We conduct extensive experiments using a commodity RDMA-enabled cluster of ten servers, and using a variety of configurations, targeted micro-benchmarks and industry-standard TPC benchmarks (Section 5). We compare our implementation against several alternatives: (a) a baseline where the RDBMS uses locally-attached HDDs and SSDs when demand exceeds the memory available on the server; (b) two alternatives that leverage remote memory using off-the-shelf technologies but use different protocols to access remote memory; and (c) when the RDBMS server has sufficient local memory to serve the workload. In all our experiments, we use a high-performance enterprise-grade disk subsystem with a hardware RAID-0 controller and up to 20 disks. For queries with short reads and writes (similar to OLTP workloads), the throughput and latency improvements are $3\times$ to $10\times$. The latency of multiple TPC-H queries can be improved by $2\times$ to $10\times$, and the latency of many TPC-DS queries can be improved by $10\times$ to $100\times$ (Section 6 and Appendix B). For a variety of workloads, the throughput and latency is within 10% of that when the entire workload fits in the server's *local memory*. Moreover, there is no noticeable impact on the performance of workloads running on the server whose unused memory is being accessed remotely via RDMA. Further, by varying the number of remote memory servers a database server accesses, we demonstrate how our solution can scale by pooling memory available on multiple servers within the cluster. Ours is the first in-depth study to quantify the end-to-end benefits of remote memory and RDMA for complex RDBMS workloads. In Section 7, we also identify several potential directions of future work.

Contributions:

- We study the novel problem of how an SMP RDBMS can leverage RDMA and available remote memory in a cluster.
- We abstract remote memory, accessed via RDMA, as a lightweight file API. This abstraction enables easy integration of remote memory into existing RDBMSs and is flexible enough to support four novel scenarios that significantly improve performance of memory-intensive workloads.
- We articulate and address several crucial design challenges to efficiently support this abstraction in a mature RDBMS.
- We implement this abstraction and scenarios in Microsoft SQL Server and conduct extensive experiments to quantify the benefits using targeted micro-benchmarks as well as industry-standard benchmark workloads.

2. RELATED WORK

RDMA has been extensively used for fast data transfers in high performance computing systems using MPI implementations over Infiniband [24]. More closely related to our work are the applications of RDMA in storage and file systems, key-value stores, and relational database systems. We organize related work into the following categories: (a) using RDMA as a faster interconnection protocol; and (b) when multiple servers are accessing and sharing the same database, leveraging RDMA to efficiently exchange data between two servers. In contrast to existing approaches, our focus is on exploring remote memory as a new level in the memory hierarchy for an SMP RDBMS when the workload's memory demands cannot be met by local memory.

A common use of RDMA is in fast transfer of data from compute to storage servers in various application scenarios. For instance, many database appliances, such as Teradata Aster Big Analytics Appliance [43, 44] and Microsoft Analytics Platform System [26], use RDMA to transfer data in the storage servers to the database servers. Windows Server 2012 supports SMB Direct [37] which is a network file sharing protocol over RDMA. Applications, such as the Microsoft SQL Server database, can store data on a remote file server and efficiently transfer data using SMB Direct [39]. In addition, many projects have also explored leveraging RDMA to improve the performance of distributed file systems [21, 50].

The ability to efficiently transfer in-memory pages between two servers have been explored in various systems to improve performance. For instance, scale-out relational databases with a data-sharing architecture, such as IBM's DB2 Purescale [17] and Oracle Real Application Cluster (RAC) [29], uses RDMA to transfer database pages between the servers executing queries that access the shared database pages. The database nodes access the same database for both read and write operations through the global cache of pages through a centralized lock manager. Along similar lines, Barthels et al. [2] leverage RDMA as a fast data shuffling mechanism for distributed in-memory join processing. Rödiger et al. [34] present the architecture of a distributed query engine that re-architects the exchange operator for improved parallelism and proposes an RDMA-based communication multiplexer for fast intra-node data transfers. These approaches are orthogonal to our scenarios since we focus on scenarios where an SMP RDBMS can leverage RDMA and remote memory without a major architectural rewrite. The buffer pool priming scenario is similar to transferring data pages between servers, though only one server can execute transactions accessing the buffer pool.

Many distributed key-value stores have leveraged RDMA to improve performance of their respective systems. Jose et al. [22] extend Memcached, an in-memory caching infrastructure implementing a key-value API, to leverage RDMA for efficient inter-node communication. Along similar lines, Huang et al. [15] extend HBase, a key-value store implemented on top of a distributed file system, to leverage RDMA for efficient messaging. FaRM [12] exposes the memory of the machines in a cluster as a partitioned global address space and implements an efficient hashtable with lock free reads over RDMA. FaRM uses RDMA to efficiently and directly access data in a shared address space, and for fast messaging between the nodes. HERD [23] is also a distributed key-value store which uses RDMA for accessing the keys and values in the system. RamCloud, a distributed in-memory key-value store, uses Infiniband send/receive verbs to reduce the replication latencies leveraging kernel bypass [33].

3. NOVEL SCENARIOS

We now discuss four scenarios which provide a good trade-off between the potential performance benefits, complexity of implementing the remote memory abstraction, and ease of integration into an SMP RDBMS.

3.1 Extending the Caches

RDBMSs have several types of caches, such as procedure cache and buffer pool cache, which are critical to improve performance. When the size of a cache nears the available memory, an RDBMS must evict entries from the cache to accommodate newly-accessed entries. This eviction results in degraded performance if the evicted entry is accessed again. Instead of discarding the evicted entry, it can be cached in remote memory. When the evicted entry is accessed again, it can be fetched from remote memory, which is much faster for both sequential and random accesses compared to reading the entry from HDD or SSD. This extension of the cache can result in significant performance improvements when an application's working set does not fit in local memory. Such extension of the cache is similar to buffer pool extensions to SSDs supported in many commercial RDBMSs [3, 4, 28]. Similar to buffer pool, the procedure cache, which stores optimized query plans and partial execution results, can also be extended to remote memory.

3.2 Spilling Temporary Data

An RDBMS can generate a lot of temporary data during the execution of complex queries. Examples include user-generated temporary objects such as tables, table variables, or cursors, as well as system-generated temporary structures and data, such as intermediate results from data-intensive operators such as sorting and hashing. Depending on the workload, the size of such temporary data needed during query execution can be significant. If queries create a lot of temporary data and enough memory is not available, the RDBMS might need to spill the data to a temporary file. For instance, Microsoft SQL Server has a special database, called TempDB, for spilling such temporary data [42] and Oracle RDBMS uses Temporary Tablespaces [30]. Therefore, the I/O performance of the temporary file can significantly affect the performance of queries, specifically data analysis queries, as sort and hash are common operators used in many analysis queries. Storing this temporary data in remote memory and accessing it via RDMA can significantly improve query performance when compared to storing this temporary data in local HDDs or SSDs.

3.3 In-Memory Semantic Caching

Application-level semantic caches for RDBMSs, e.g., Oracle TimesTen Application Tier Database Cache [45], can speed up query execution significantly [10]. Such caches store the result of a SQL expression, support a standard SQL interface, and when possible, answer application queries by using results from the cache. If the query cannot be answered from the cache, the query is routed to the database engine for execution. Traditionally, such caching and opportunistic structures are used in the application-tier to avoid interfering with the memory requirements of the RDBMS. However, if remote memory is available, seamless semantic caching within the RDBMS can become attractive. The basic idea is to create specialized redundant structures, keep them pinned in remote memory, and access them via RDMA when executing queries that benefit from them. Examples include non-clustered indexes, partial indexes [35, 40], and materialized views, which can significantly speed up query execution and can be lazily built and maintained since they are redundant. Such structures are built opportunistically when remote memory is available, and is separate from the buffer pool memory local to the server. RDBMSs support a variety of memory brokers, such as buffer pool and procedure caches, and the semantic cache is yet another broker. In the presence of updates, these redundant structures are updated based on application-specified policies. They can be updated in-sync with transactions, updated asynchronously, maintained as a snapshot, or invalidated with an update. A key advantage of an integrated semantic cache is that it can leverage existing mechanisms within the RDBMS for view matching, and updating secondary indexes or materialized views [8, 14]. Since the semantic cache is entirely in remote memory, a remote node failure can be dealt in various ways. One approach is to invalidate the cache. Another alternative is to leverage the RDBMSs transaction log, which logs every update in the RDBMS, and REDO logic to recover the structures by replaying the log on another remote server with available memory.

Such in-memory semantic caching introduces many interesting challenges. First, the query optimizer's cost model, which is traditionally calibrated for on-disk structures, needs to be re-calibrated since seeks into remote memory is significantly faster compared to scanning HDDs or SSDs. Second, techniques to automate the selection of suitable structures is an interesting physical design problem along with policies to invalidate or update them. While an in-depth study of in-memory semantic caching in the RDBMS is beyond the scope of this paper, we empirically demonstrate the performance gains of integrating such a cache into the RDBMS.

3.4 Priming the Buffer Pool

Cloud database systems run multiple copies of a database for high availability. Typically, the primary copy processes update and read transactions and one or more secondary copies are kept up-to-date via logical or physical replication. If physical replication is used, the databases are kept identical at the page level. A *primary-secondary swap*, i.e., a secondary being promoted to a primary, is a common operation in such clusters due to failures and load balancing. While some failures are unplanned (e.g., machine crashes), there are a large number of swaps that are planned, for instance during load balancing, planned software or hardware upgrades etc. One major challenge with such swaps is that the application workload resumes on the newly-elected primary with a *cold* buffer pool, thus resulting in significant performance degradation until the buffer pool is warmed up. For physically-identical databases synchronized with physical replication, wire-speed RDMA transfers can be used to warm up the buffer pool of the newly-elected primary (S_2) using contents of the buffer pool of the old primary (S_1). This priming (or warming-up) of the buffer pool at S_2 can be proactive, where S_1 pushes the pages to S_2 or reactive, where S_2 fetches the pages from S_1 on-demand as the workload accesses them. The first scenario is similar to a push technique studied in the context of database and VM migration [9, 11]. The latter scenario is similar to the cache extension scenario described above. In either case, fast access to remote memory using RDMA can significantly reduce the impact of such planned primary-secondary swaps on application workloads.

4. DESIGN AND IMPLEMENTATION

Any RDBMS that aims to exploit remote memory must address several important design challenges. In this section, we first discuss these challenges and rationalize our choices with the goal of efficiency and ease of integration into a mature RDBMS. We then describe an implementation in Microsoft SQL Server, referred to as SQL Server for brevity, that embodies these choices.

4.1 Design Choices and Rationale

4.1.1 Abstraction for Remote Memory

The first design question is the abstraction to use for remote memory, i.e., how is remote memory exposed in the memory hierarchy on an RDBMS. We first discuss four alternatives and explain the abstraction we choose in our implementation.

Byte-addressable memory. Local memory is often accessed using byte-addressing and it is natural to expose remote memory also as byte-addressable memory, similar to that in distributed shared memory (DSM) [1, 5]. This allows existing applications to seamlessly extend their memory from local to remote, similar to the virtual memory abstraction exposed by the OS. However, it requires OS support to intercept memory accesses for address translation, which negates the kernel bypass benefits of RDMA. Moreover, it limits the RDBMS's ability to control which data is stored locally and which ones are moved to remote memory.

In-memory blocks. Many applications that manage their own memory, such as database systems, acquire memory from the OS in blocks. Therefore, remote memory can be exposed as blocks of fixed but configurable sizes. An application requests a block of remote memory which is identified uniquely. The application accesses a block using its unique identifier, an offset into the block, and the size of the data to be read or written. This abstraction allows the application to selectively read/write individual bytes within a block without having to read/write the entire block.

In-memory files. Database systems are designed to operate efficiently with files. Many in-memory structures in a database can be mapped to in-file representations, which makes a file abstraction suitable for databases. An in-memory file is a common abstraction supported by many operating systems [32], e.g., `ramfs` in Linux `Ramdisk` in Windows allow mounting a part of physical memory as a file system. Exposing a familiar file API, remote memory can be abstracted as in-memory files.

In-memory Key-value store. Caching variable-sized objects which are stored and retrieved as whole objects is a common requirement for many applications. A key-value store, where the keys and values are stored in remote memory, is another abstraction to expose remote memory. The key-value store hides the details of memory management and processing the remote reads and writes. The application only interacts through a get/put API which is common with key-value stores.

Our implementation builds on top of an in-memory block abstraction which provides flexible access to memory. To enable easy integration of remote memory into SQL Server, our implementation builds a lightweight file shim over fixed-size in-memory blocks, that exposes a subset of the standard file APIs but are sufficient for the scenarios we consider; the file API is specified in Table 2.

4.1.2 Protocols to Access Remote Memory

The protocol to access remote memory is also critical for performance. One class of protocols can be based on the standard TCP/IP stack in a client-server design using network sockets. TCP/IP uses the remote CPU, involves the OS at both the source and destination of the transfer, copies data from user space to the kernel, and incurs additional protocol overheads. However, the benefit is the standard implementations in both the Windows and the Linux platforms. Due to the common use of TCP-based protocols, we consider one such protocol as a baseline in our study. This baseline uses Server Message Block (SMB) [36], a network file sharing protocol (over TCP/IP or other network protocols), which has been supported in Windows since Windows 95. Though SMB is not directly associated with accessing memory, if remote memory is exposed as an in-memory file system, then SMB can be used to transfer data from remote to local memory over TCP/IP.

RDMA protocols bypass the OS and avoid TCP/IP overheads. However, the protocols for RDMA transfers are specific to the platform. For instance, the Windows ecosystem supports the Network Direct Service Provider Interface (NDSPI) where hardware vendors can implement advanced capabilities of their networking devices, such as RDMA over Infiniband. The Infiniband standard supports a variety of send/receive verbs as interface definitions, which has corresponding mappings to NDSPI. Another alternative is to use SMB 3.0 that supports RDMA transfers using SMB Direct. If the network adapter is RDMA-capable, SMB Direct uses RDMA. Our implementation uses RDMA reads and writes implemented over NDSPI which was the most efficient among the alternatives.

4.1.3 Synchronous vs. Asynchronous Operations

Database systems model I/O operations to the disk or over the network as *asynchronous* operations. This allows the system to hide I/O latencies by interleaving CPU activity on other threads. If a thread does not have any CPU activity after issuing an I/O, it yields the CPU, resulting in a context switch. The thread is switched back in after the OS processes the I/O completion. A remote memory access is an I/O and hence it is natural to treat such accesses as asynchronous. While such asynchronous accesses are efficient to hide disk I/O latencies, which is of the order of milliseconds, remote memory access latencies are in the order of tens of microseconds. A context switch itself consumes a few microseconds. In addition, pollution of the processor's cache lines and the delay between when the I/O is completed to when the thread is switched back in makes the overheads of a context switch comparable to remote memory access latencies. Therefore, even though remote memory access via RDMA is an I/O, we found treating it as *synchronous* accesses, similar to accesses to local memory, is important to enable the RDBMS leverage remote memory more effectively. This synchronous access model is efficient since it prevents unnecessary context switches and allows the database to process RDMA completions faster, thus resulting in significantly lower access latencies and higher throughput for remote memory accesses. While the synchronous model suits the small transfers in RDBMSs, an adaptive approach that switches to asynchronous when transfer

Table 1: **Summary of the design choices and alternatives.**

Design Choice	Alternative Chosen	Rationale
Remote memory abstraction	In-memory blocks with a file API shim	Ease of integration into existing DBMS engines
Protocol	NDSPI	Least overheads
Sync vs. async remote accesses	Synchronous	Avoid context switches, improve latency
Registering memory regions	Pre-register memory regions	Registration incurs fixed initialization cost
Fault tolerance	Best-effort	Correctness unaffected, simpler implementation

latencies are higher than typical context switches will be more general and is an interesting direction for future work.

4.1.4 *Registering Memory Regions*

RDMA transfers require that the source and the destination memory regions (MRs) be registered with the NIC. This registration of MRs can be done on-demand before every transfer, or large blocks of MRs can be pre-registered upfront at both the source and the destination. Both approaches have trade-offs, and present an important design choice. Considering a typical page in an RDBMS is $8K$, registering an $8K$ page has a latency of 50μsec on our hardware, which is of the same order as the cost to transfer the page itself. In addition, registering the page on-demand at the destination implies the destination server's CPU also needs to be involved to initiate the transfer, which partly defeats the benefits of RDMA transfers. Hence, efficient management of MR registration is critical to leverage the benefits of RDMA [13,34]. Our implementation preregisters in-memory blocks during initialization. Preregistration is straightforward if the memory region used for transfers is a contiguous block in physical memory. However, caches in an RDBMS, such as the buffer pool, are often not contiguous in physical memory, which introduces an implementation challenge for preregistration; we describe our solution in Section 4.2.

4.1.5 *Fault Tolerance and Availability*

In a cluster of commodity servers, failures and server restarts are common. When one server S_1 accesses memory of another server S_2, a failure of S_2 can impact S_1, depending on the fault-tolerance and availability guarantees provided by the remote memory abstraction. Exposing remote memory as *best-effort*, where failure of a server can make the memory unavailable, is the simplest abstraction to support, and is sufficient if an application uses remote memory only as a performance optimization. That is, if remote memory becomes unavailable, the RDBMS can continue to operate correctly, though likely with degraded performance. While it is possible to expose remote memory as a highly-available and durable abstraction, it increases the complexity of the implementation and also results in less performance gains due to the need to replicate data or write to non-volatile storage [27]. Since our scenarios can tolerate remote memory failures without affecting correctness, our implementation uses remote memory with best-effort fault tolerance and availability guarantees.

4.2 Implementation in SQL Server

We now present a detailed description of our implementation of the proposed remote memory abstraction in SQL Server deployed in a cluster environment. Our implementation embodies the design choices we discussed earlier which are also summarized in Table 1. Figure 1 presents a simplified illustration of the architecture we implement. The figure shows two sets of servers: the servers running the database process which are experiencing high memory

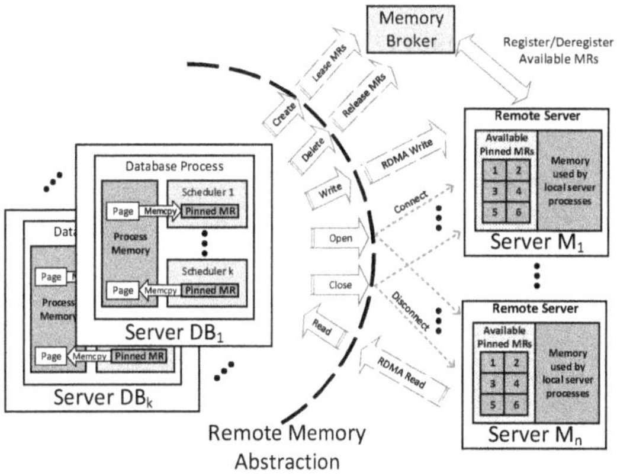

Figure 1: Integrating remote memory into an RDBMS.

pressure $(DB_1, \ldots, DB_k)$, and the servers with available memory which can be accessed via RDMA $(M_1, \ldots, M_n)$. For simplicity, the figure abstracts out the other processes running on the servers $(M_1, \ldots, M_n)$. These servers can also run a database process, which will typically be the case in a cloud database service. The only difference between $(M_1, \ldots, M_n)$ and $(DB_1, \ldots, DB_k)$ is there is available memory in the former set and unmet memory demand in the latter set.

Brokering available memory. Each server in the cluster reports the available and unused memory to a memory broker that tracks memory availability throughout the cluster. A server M_j with available memory divides its memory into configurable fixed-sized memory regions (MRs) depicted as numbered blocks in Figure 1. A memory brokering proxy process on M_j determines available memory not committed to any local process, pins the available MRs, registers them to the local NIC, marks them unavailable from the OS's perspective, and registers the MRs with the memory broker. Conceptually, the broker now controls the privilege to read and write to those MRs, which it can assign to any other server with unmet memory demands. Note that we do not steal memory committed to processes locally on a server, hence the memory on M_j registered with the broker cannot be committed to any local process on M_j. The memory brokering proxy at each M_j registers for OS memory pressure notifications such that if a local process on M_j requests additional memory from the OS, the proxy will detect such memory pressure. To prevent the OS from paging local applications, the proxy on M_j requests deregistration of one or more MRs from the memory broker. Once the memory broker frees the lease on the MR, they are freed to the OS at M_j which can allocate the pages to local processes. These memory notifications and adaptive memory brokering is a standard API supported by many OSs [25] and is transparent to applications running on M_j.

A database server with unmet memory demand (DB_i) can request the broker for a lease to a remote memory region. This lease provides DB_i exclusive access to the region. The memory broker's design is similar to many standard leasing mechanisms based on Zookeeper [16] which provides a fault-tolerant and highly-available mechanism to obtain timed leases. Many systems, such as the YARN scheduler [49] or the master in HBase which manages the mapping of regions to servers similar to that of Bigtable [6], have a similar use of Zookeeper. When DB_i requests a lease on an MR, the broker determines which server M_j has an unleased and available MR, registers this mapping in a lookup table, and creates the metadata for the lease. Zookeeper guarantees fault tolerance and high availability of this metadata for memory brokering. On obtaining the lease, DB_i directly communicates with M_j

Table 2: Simplified file API and RDMA operations.

File Operation	RDMA Implementation
Create (ServerEndpoint, Size)	Obtain lease on MRs
Open	Connect to server(s)
Read/Write (Offset, Size)	RDMA read/write
Close	Disconnect from server(s)
Delete	Relinquish lease on MRs

using the RDMA read/write commands. Since the memory broker is not in the data transfer path from M_j to DB_i, such a design can scale to thousands of servers [6,49]. In addition, since the broker's state is all stored in Zookeeper, a broker's failure is easy to tolerate by electing a new broker node orchestrated using Zookeeper. Before the lease for an MR expires, DB_i has to renew the lease. If the lease is successfully renewed, DB_i continues to use the MR. Otherwise, DB_i is forced to release the remote MR. DB_i can request a lease on another MR or continue with local disks. DB_i can also voluntarily release the lease on a remote MR if sufficient memory is available locally. There are many more details, such as how to deal with failures of both DB_i or M_j and the policies for lease management. These aspects are common of many distributed resource and lease negotiating systems, such as YARN, HBase, and Bigtable, and are omitted for brevity. Note that if a lease expiration is forced due to a failure or other policies, the correct operation of DB_i is not compromised and the DBMS can continue query execution, albeit with degraded performance.

Scenarios. SQL Server already has support to extend the buffer pool to an SSD to leverage the higher random I/Os available in SSDs. SQL Server implements the extension as a file by serializing the buffer pool contents. This logic to serialize buffer pool contents to a file is also leveraged to prime the buffer pool on the secondary. SQL Server spills temporary data into a file. Finally, structures in the semantic cache can also be stored and serialized as in-memory files. Therefore, exposing remote memory as a lightweight file API shim significantly reduces the changes needed in SQL Server to leverage benefits of remote memory. For all our scenarios, the database engine uses higher-level locks and latches to synchronize all I/Os. Hence, the in-memory files do not need many properties of files in a classic file system. A lightweight file API supporting reads/writes of a certain size from/to a specific offset is sufficient.

Implementing a lightweight file API. Table 2 summarizes the file API and the corresponding operations, which are also illustrated in Figure 1. To create a file of the specified size, a server DB_i requests a lease on MRs corresponding to the file's size. The broker provides the mapping of which MR is on which server M_j. On file open, DB_i initiates a connection and sets up an RDMA flow to all M_js that it will write to or read from. When a read or write operation is issued, we first translate the file offset into an MR backing the file and an offset within the MR. We then issue an RDMA read or write operation to the MR. A file close action terminates the connections. When a file is deleted, we free the lease on the corresponding MRs.

Our implementation of the RDMA read/write actions utilizes the C++ NDSPI API which is natively supported by the Mellanox NICs used in our implementation. The NDSPI library exposes RDMA accesses as an asynchronous operation which the database server can treat as asynchronous I/Os. However, as discussed in Section 4.1.3, treating RDMA requests as asynchronous I/Os is not efficient. Therefore, we use synchronous RDMA requests where if a thread does not have any additional CPU activity after issuing an RDMA request, it spins for a few microseconds until the RDMA request completes. If the request does not complete within a few tens of microseconds, we can switch to asynchronous mode

Table 3: System configurations

CPU	Intel(R) Xeon(R) CPU E5-2660 v2 @ 2.20 GHz (20 cores and 40 logical processors.)
Memory	384 GB DDR3, 1866 MHz
HDD	1 TB 7.2K RPM Near-line SAS 6 Gbps
SSD	400 GB SAS SLC 6 Gbps
RAID	Dell Perc H710P SCSI
Network Adapter	Mellanox ConnectX-3 VPI IPoIB (56 Gbps)
Operating System	Windows Server 2012 R2
Database System	SQL Server

to avoid spinning for long durations if the RDMA transfer latency increases. Such an adaptive strategy is left for future work.

Preregistration of MRs. As discussed in Section 4.1.4, another important consideration is preregistering the MRs with the NIC. Preregistration is straightforward when the memory region is a contiguous block of memory, which is the case with server (M_j) that has unused memory. We register large contiguous blocks of memory when the available MRs are registered with the broker. Preregistering MRs on the RDBMS server (DB_i) introduces a new challenge, especially for the buffer pool which in SQL Server is not a contiguous block of memory. First, the buffer pool might grow (or shrink) dynamically. Second, a single memory allocator services memory requests from the buffer pool as well as other consumers of memory within SQL Server. Hence, buffer pool pages can be interspersed with memory consumed by other engine components. Therefore, statically-registering the entire buffer pool could amount to registering the entire address space of the DBMS process, which comprises large chunks of memory which will never be used for RDMA transfers.

To avoid the cost of dynamic registration for every RDMA transfer, we use a preregistered staging buffer in database server's address space. The database server has multiple CPU schedulers and to maximize data parallelism each scheduler issues I/Os in parallel. We create a staging buffer for each scheduler, depicted as "Pinned MR" in Figure 1. When a scheduler evicts a buffer page and transfers the page to the extension on the remote server, it first copies the page into its local staging buffer using a `memcpy` operation. Registering an 8K page has a latency of 50μsec while `memcpy` has a latency of 2μsec. Therefore, introducing the additional `memcpy` actually results in a design that is far more efficient than dynamic registration of the buffer pool pages. The page in the buffer pool becomes available to hold another database page immediately after the `memcpy`. The scheduler initiates an RDMA write from the staging buffer to the appropriate location on the remote server. The staging area's buffer can be reused after the RDMA write completes. The pinned MR's size is a trade-off between memory overhead of the staging area and the number of pending RDMA transfers. We used 1MB for up to 128 pending RDMA transfers per scheduler which was tuned for our setup allowing us to sustain sufficient concurrent RDMA transfers to saturate the network. The "Pinned MR" is also used to fetch buffer pool pages from remote memory using RDMA reads.

5. EXPERIMENTAL SETTINGS

In this section, we present the system configurations, the benchmark workloads and the alternative designs evaluated in our experiments. For brevity, we use buffer pool extension as BPExt, and storage with spilled temporary data as TempDB.

5.1 System Specifications

We use a cluster of 10 servers each of whose hardware configuration is shown in Table 3; the servers are connected using a top-

Table 4: Summary of workloads

Work-loads	Data Size	Local Mem	BPExt Size	Tem-pDB Size	Concur-rency
RangeScan	110GB	32GB	128GB	8GB	80
Hash+Sort	227GB	256GB	N/A	320GB	1
TPC-H	840GB	64GB	256GB	64GB	5
TPC-DS	900GB	64GB	256GB	64GB	5
TPC-C	168GB	16GB	32GB	8GB	2000

of-rack Mellanox FDR MSX6036F-1BRR Infiniband Switch. We explore remote memory for scenarios where the DBMS is designed to use disks. Therefore, the performance of the I/O subsystem will have a significant impact on the benefits of using remote memory. We therefore use a few different configurations to control the bandwidth and access latencies of the I/O subsystem. We use a hardware RAID controller and a RAID 0 setup where data is striped across multiple drives. We vary the number of HDDs, or spindles, in a RAID 0 partition as 4, 8 and 20, respectively, and show how the performance of I/O subsystem affects the throughput/latency of the workloads. Unless otherwise specified, the default HDD set up has 20 spindles. For brevity, we refer to the RAID 0 I/O subsystem as HDD to differentiate from an SSD which is configured with its stand alone partition and used in some configurations.

5.2 Workloads

We use various micro benchmarks to test the scenarios in isolation, and then use standard benchmark workloads to quantify the overall benefits of using both optimization for more complex workloads. Table 4 summarizes the workloads that are evaluated in this paper. We measure native performance of the I/O subsystems and remote memory accesses using a standard benchmark SQLIO [38]. We use a ***RangeScan*** workload to micro benchmark buffer pool scenarios of extension and priming, and a ***Hash+Sort*** workload which is designed to stress TempDB by generating temporary data with Hash and Sort operators on large amounts of data. We also use a number of standard benchmark workloads: two decision support benchmarks (TPC-H [47] and TPC-DS [48]) and one on-line transaction processing benchmark (TPC-C [46]). Each benchmark has a scale-factor that determines the data sizes. The scale for TPC-H is 200, and the scale for TPC-DS is 300. For TPC-C, the number of warehouses is used to scale the database, which we set to 800. For the decision support workloads, we used SQL Server's Database Engine Tuning Advisor (DTA) to tune the physical design to avoid unnecessary I/Os and ensure we have a reasonably-tuned system. We use the query generator tools provided with TPC-H and TPC-DS benchmarks to generate the workload. DTA uses this workload to recommend index structures which we subsequently built. For TPC-C, we use the indexes as per the benchmark specification. The final database sizes after building the indexes is shown in Table 4. We now describe the two micro benchmarks in a bit more detail.

5.2.1 RangeScan

This benchmark is designed to stress the BPExt and priming scenarios. This workload generates queries that scan a range in a synthetically-generated `Customer` table that has the same schema as the `Customer` table of TPC-H. This table contains 500 million rows, and the average size of each row is 245 bytes. A clustered index is built on the `custkey`. The range scan query is of the form:

```
SELECT sum(acctbal) FROM customer
WHERE  custkey >= @start
AND    custkey <  @start + @range
```

We use two variants of this query: a read-only variant which calculates the average account balance for a range of rows starting from a start key, and an update variant which updates the account balance for the range selected. Since the table has an index on `custkey`, it results in seeks on that index. We fix `@range` to 100 to simulate short read-only queries which access three database pages on average. The `@start` parameter is randomly generated from a uniform distribution. With up to 80 concurrent threads issuing this query, the uniform access pattern creates a lot of churn in the buffer pool by accessing almost the entire database which does not fit in local memory. As a result, this query is suited to stress the BPExt by frequently moving pages to and from the extension. If the parameter is selected from a skewed or a hotspot distribution, it results in a small working set, which if in memory results in low tail latencies, but if not in memory, results in longer tail latencies. This setting is suited to test the priming scenario.

5.2.2 Hash+Sort

This query is designed to stress TempDB. It joins the `lineitem` and `order` tables from the TPC-H benchmark and returns the top 100,000 rows sorted by `extendedprice`.

```
SELECT    top 100000*
FROM      lineitem l JOIN orders o
ON        l.orderkey  = o.orderkey
ORDER BY  l.extendedprice
```

We built a clustered index on the `orderkey` of each table; Figure 2 shows the resulting execution plan for the query where the tables are joined with a hash join, which builds a hash table that will spill to TempDB if enough memory is not available, followed by a sort on the joined results, which will again use an external sort algorithm using TempDB if enough memory is not available. We assign 256 GB local memory to the database server which is enough to cache the data scanned by the query, thus making the reads and writes to TempDB during the Hash and Sort the bottleneck.

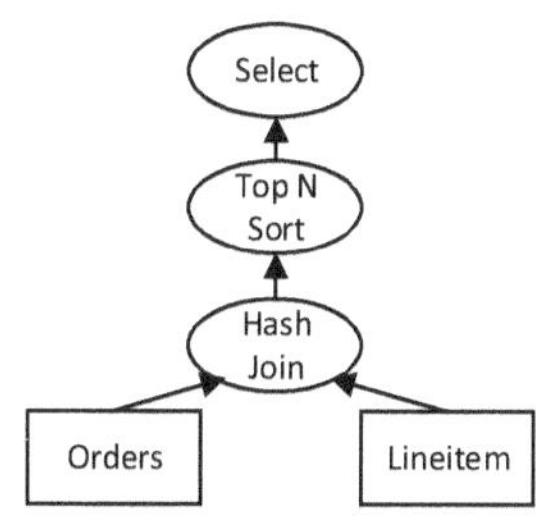

Figure 2: Execution Plan for Hash+Sort Query

5.3 Alternative Designs Evaluated

Table 5 summarizes the various design alternatives we consider for our empirical evaluation. The ***HDD*** and ***HDD+SSD*** are two baselines in which there is no remote memory available and the DBMS server uses local HDD or SSD for unmet memory demand. In the HDD setup, we disable BPExt since storing the BPExt on HDD which also has the data files degrades performance due to lower random read performance of HDD compared to SSD. For the data analysis workloads (such as *Hash+Sort*, TPC-H and TPC-DS), most of the I/Os are sequential. Considering that the HDD setup uses data striped across multiple disks (varied as $4, 8, 20$) in a RAID 0 configuration, the sequential throughput of the HDD setup can reach more than one GB/s, which is higher than the SSD's random access throughput. If the BPExt is enabled, sequential accesses are transformed to random accesses to the extension on the SSD. Therefore, for data analytics workloads, we disable BPExt for the *HDD+SSD* as well. For OLTP workloads (such as *RangeScan* and TPC-C), as most of the I/Os are random, and the SSD's random I/O throughput is higher than the HDD, we enable the BPExt for *HDD+SSD* and store it on SSD.

Table 5: Design alternatives evaluated.

Designs	Data Files	TempDB	BP Ext	Protocol
HDD	HDD	HDD	N/A	N/A
HDD+SSD	HDD	SSD	SSD	N/A
SMB+ RamDrive	HDD	Remote Memory	Remote Memory	SMB
SMBDirect +RamDrive	HDD	Remote Memory	Remote Memory	SMB Direct
Custom	HDD	Remote Memory	Remote Memory	NDSPI
Local Memory	HDD	SSD	N/A	N/A

Our abstraction of in-memory files can be implemented using various protocols to access remote memory and off-the-shelf components. We consider two such designs: ***SMB+RamDrive*** and ***SMBDirect+RamDrive***. We use a third party software that creates a fully-functional RamDrive on the remote server. SMB accesses RamDrive using TCP/IP (*SMB+RamDrive*). SMBDirect leverages RDMA for data transfer (*SMBDirect+RamDrive*). ***Custom*** is our implementation of the lightweight file API with data transfer using NDSPI (see Section 4.2).

Finally, to determine the best possible performance, we also consider a design where memory of equivalent size as remote memory is available locally at the server. We call this design ***Local Memory***. This alternative helps us to determine the overheads of using remote memory compared to when it is available locally.

6. EXPERIMENTAL RESULTS

We now present a thorough empirical analysis of our implementation to evaluate the effectiveness of remote memory in a cluster setting where a database service is deployed. Our experiments use a modified un-optimized build of SQL Server and hence our performance numbers should not be treated as official benchmark results. We first use a micro benchmark to evaluate the I/O throughput and latency for the different alternatives (Section 6.1), followed by micro benchmarks for BPExt (Section 6.2), TempDB (Section 6.3), semantic caching (Section 6.4), and buffer pool priming (Section 6.5). Appendix B presents additional experiments demonstrating the end-to-end benefits using industry-standard TPC benchmarks, impact of varying the amount of local memory, and varying the number of database servers accessing a memory server. Since the benefits of remote memory are significant only when local memory is insufficient to meet the workload's demands, our evaluation also focuses on configurations with memory pressure. Following are the key takeaways:

***Custom* significantly outperforms *HDD+SSD*.** In all experiments when the workload's memory demand exceeds the available local memory, *Custom* significantly outperforms *HDD+SSD* in both throughput and latency. For some TPC-DS queries, *Custom* achieves up to 100$\times$ improvement in terms of latency.

***Custom* outperforms *SMBDirect+RamDrive*.** Compared to *SMBDirect+RamDrive*, which requires no code changes, *Custom*'s results in around 3.4$\times$ improvement in random I/O throughput. For end-to-end SQL workloads, the improvements are in the range of $10 - 40\%$. This is mainly because for complex SQL workloads, CPU activity of query processing interleaves data accesses, which does not generate enough demand for remote memory to benefit from the lower overheads of *Custom*. That is, the workload are CPU-bound even with *SMBDirect+RamDrive*. Note that using CPU-efficient technologies such as column store and vectorized processing will further improve the benefits of remote memory, which is an interesting direction of future work.

***Custom* and *SMBDirect+RamDrive* outperform *SMB+RamDrive*.** The experimental results also show that both *Custom* and *SMBDirect+RamDrive* outperform *SMB +RamDrive*, which demonstrates the benefits of accessing remote memory via RDMA compared to TCP. This experiment highlights the importance of the choice of protocol for RDMA transfers.

RDMA has negligible performance impact on remote server. Accessing available memory via RDMA results in negligible impact on performance of workloads executing on the remote server providing the memory, compared to accessing memory over TCP which results in $\sim$ 10% overhead on both throughput and latency of workload on remote server.

***Custom* approaches performance of *Local Memory*.** For most of workloads, the performance of *Custom* is within $10 - 20\%$ of *Local Memory*. That is, even though accessing remote memory via RDMA (10μsec) is slower than accessing local memory (0.1μsec), for classic database systems, the difference of accessing data cached in local memory compared to remote memory is surprisingly small. The reason is that classic memory-optimized RDBMSs are not as optimized as purely in-memory databases and hence cannot effectively saturate the memory bandwidth. Analyzing RDMA's impact on in-memory technologies is beyond the scope of this paper.

Comparable improvements with multiple servers. In a cluster where a database server uses memory pooled aggregated from multiple servers or when multiple remote servers access memory available at one server, the overheads are negligible compared to when memory is obtained from one server.

6.1 I/O Micro benchmark Performance

We now present the read I/O throughput and latency using a micro benchmark. We first analyze the performance all alternatives with two servers, one database server (DB_i) and another memory server (M_j). We subsequently evaluate the performance of *Custom* with one DB_i accessing multiple M_js, and one M_j serving multiple DB_is. In a cluster with multiple servers, a database server might be accessing memory of multiple remote servers. Similarly, multiple database servers can concurrently access memory available at one server. Our multi-server experiments characterize performance for both scenarios.

For the two server setting, we evaluate the read performance for HDD, SSD, *SMB+RamDrive*, *SMBDirect+RamDrive* and *Custom*. For HDD, we evaluate the performance of our RAID 0 configuration with 4, 8, and 20 spindles, respectively. We evaluate both the random read and sequential read performance using SQLIO, a disk subsystem benchmark tool [38]. For random read, 20 threads issue the read requests of 8 KB pages concurrently. For sequential read, 5 threads issue read requests for blocks of size 512 KB.

Figure 3 plots the read throughput and Figure 4 plots the I/O latency for the different alternatives. As can be seen in this figure, the sequential read throughput of *Custom* is almost equal to that *SMBDirect+RamDrive*, but is higher than *SMB+RamDrive*. The sequential read throughput of both HDD and SSD is slower than the sequential read of the three remote memory designs, which shows the opportunity in exploiting remote memory for databases. In addition, since the HDDs on our server are configured as RAID 0, its sequential read throughput is much higher than the SSD. For random read, the throughput of our custom implementation is much higher than that of *SMBDirect+RamDrive*, which may be due to the overhead that is introduced by the RamDrive and the SMBDirect protocol. Access latencies for remote memory designs are also considerably lower than that of designs using locally-attached HDDs or SSDs. In addition, the low overheads of *Custom* is also evident in the lower latencies, especially for random page accesses.

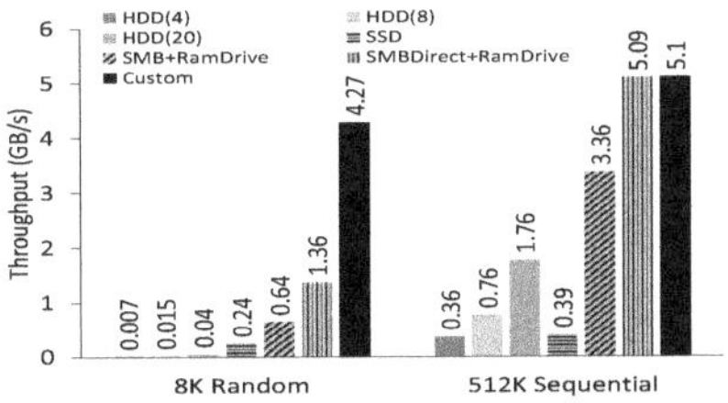

Figure 3: I/O micro benchmark throughput.

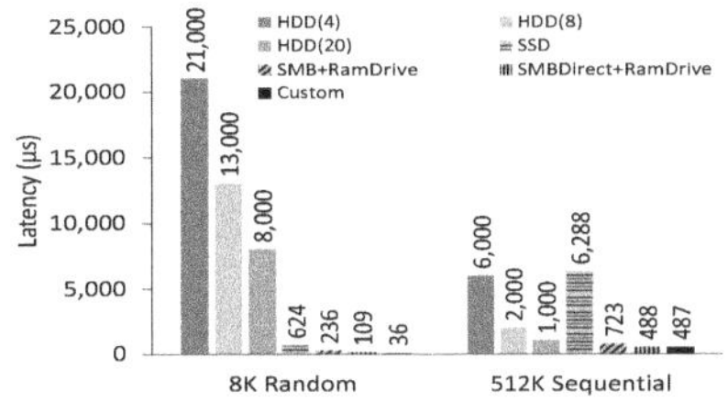

Figure 4: I/O micro benchmark latency.

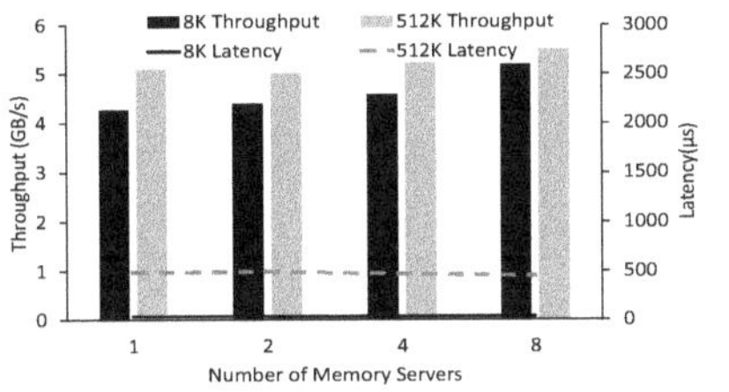

Figure 5: I/O performance with multiple memory servers.

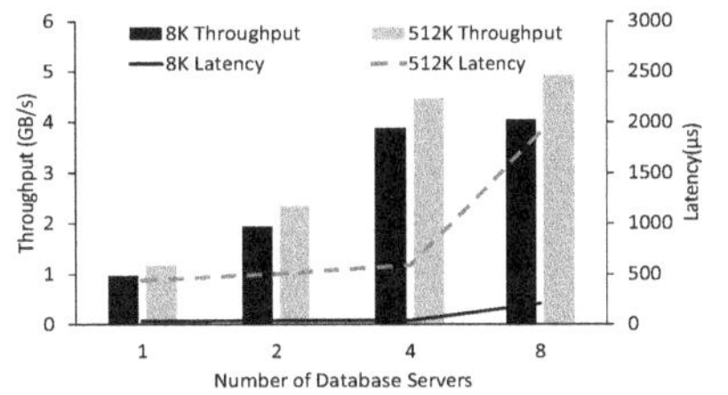

Figure 6: I/O performance with multiple database servers.

Figure 5 plots the I/O throughput and latency when one database server DB_i accesses remote memory from multiple memory servers M_j. The total amount of remote memory remains constant as we vary the number of memory servers from 1 to 8 which is plotted in the x-axis. The bars correspond to the throughput plotted on the left vertical axis and the lines correspond to latency plotted on the right vertical axis. As is evident from the figure, even when the network bandwidth of DB_i is saturated (which is the case even with one M_j), there is negligible impact on throughput and latency for accessing remote memory as we vary the number of M_js. In fact, with the higher parallelism available with 8 M_js, the latency of random I/Os is lower. This demonstrates our implementation can effectively leverage memory pooled across multiple servers.

Figure 6 plots the I/O throughput and latency when multiple DB_is access memory from on M_j. Each DB_i is accessing a fixed amount of memory and the number of accesses per second is tuned such that the NIC's bandwidth at M_j is saturated with four DB_is; we increase the number of DB_is from 1 to 8 which is plotted on the x-axis on Figure 6. The bars plot the aggregate throughput of all DB_is along the left vertical axis and the lines plot the average latency of all DB_is along the right vertical axis. There are two important observations. Before M_j's NIC was saturated, the aggregate throughput scales almost linearly with negligible change in latency as we increase number of DB_is. Once the NIC is saturated, increasing the number of DB_is results in higher latency, which is expected since contention for the resources increases. With four DB_is, the latency is comparable to that of Figure 4 where one DB_i was saturating the bandwidth of one M_j. When the link is saturated with 8 servers, the peak throughput for random I/Os in Figure 6 is comparable to that in Figure 3. Note that in this experiment, our goal was to saturate the NIC with a few servers to help us demonstrate linear scaling before saturation and the effect of contention after saturation. However, in a real cluster setting, it is unlikely that all remote database servers will continuously and concurrently overload the memory server, thus potentially allowing even more database servers to use memory available at an M_j.

6.2 Impact of Remote Memory on BPExt

6.2.1 Performance of RangeScan

We first measure the performance of *RangeScan* when 20% of the requests are updates; Figure 7 plots the throughput and Figure 8 plots the latency. Performance of the different alternative designs follow the trend observed with I/O performance discussed in Section 6.1: all the three scenarios that utilize remote memory have higher throughput compared to storing BPExt on local SSD. Furthermore, the throughput of *Custom* is only 10% lower compared to the ideal *Local Memory* scenario. It shows that with RDMA, caching pages in remote memory is a significantly better alternative when local memory is unavailable and the DBMS uses disks. Updates cause appends to the transaction log which is stored in the HDD. Therefore, as the number of spindles increases, the throughput increases and the latency decreases.

To eliminate this impact, we repeat the experiment without any updates; Figures 9 and 10 plots the throughput and latency for the corresponding experiment. Data is buffered into either SSD, remote memory or local memory depending on the alternative considered, and reading data from these structures is independent of the HDD performance. As a result, the throughput of *HDD* increases as the number of spindles increases, but the throughput of other methods remains the same in different spindle settings.

To better explain the observed behavior, we present a drill down on this experiment in terms of the I/O throughput, latency, and CPU utilization for *HDD+SSD*, *SMBDirect+RamDrive* and *Custom* for a 100 second period during the experiment (Figure 11). As seen in Figure 11(a), the I/O throughput is about 900 MB/s for *Custom*, which is much lower than the raw I/O throughput (~5 GB/s). The reason is that during the execution of this workload, as reading a data page from remote memory is so fast, I/O is no longer the bottleneck, instead it shifts to CPU. As shown in Figure 11(b), the CPU is almost entirely utilized for both *SMBDirect+RamDrive* and *Custom*, while the CPU utilization is only about 20% for *HDD+SSD*. Figure 11(c) shows the I/O latency of reading a page from BPExt during the executing of the workloads. The benefits of the *Custom* implementation is evident where the I/O latency of *Custom* is much lower (13μsec) compared to *SMBDirect+RamDrive* (272μsec). The higher latency can be attributed to how I/O is treated and overheads of a fully functional file system and the SMB Direct protocol for RDMA transfers. Without any code changes, SQL Server treats accesses to BPExt as an asynchronous I/O since BPExt is typically stored in a disk. For asynchronous I/Os, even though the I/O can be completed within 10μsec, the thread that issues this I/O must wait to be scheduled. By contrast, *Custom* treats remote memory accesses as synchronous operations.

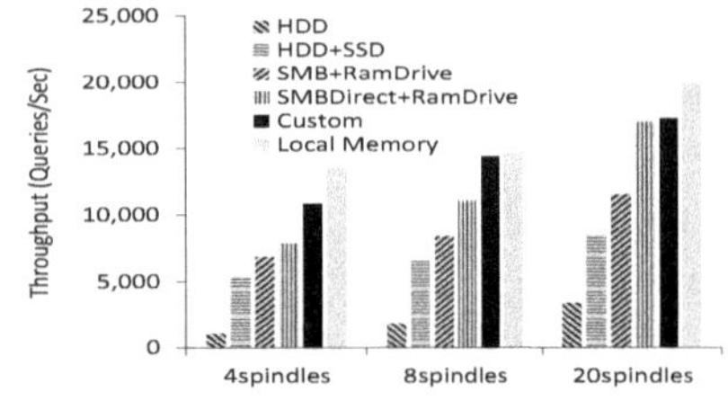

Figure 7: RangeScan throughput (20% updates).

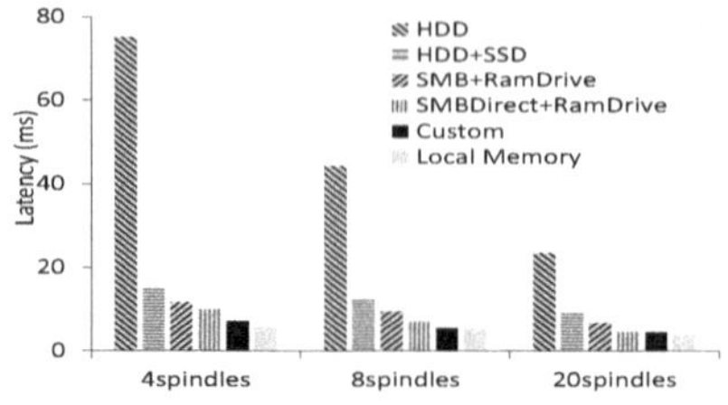

Figure 8: RangeScan latency (20% updates).

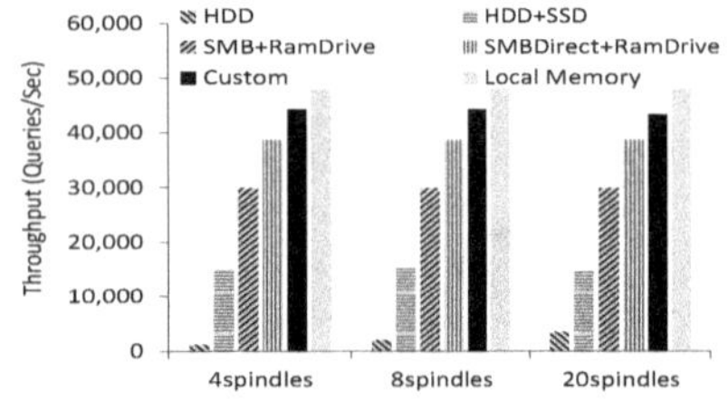

Figure 9: RangeScan throughput (no updates).

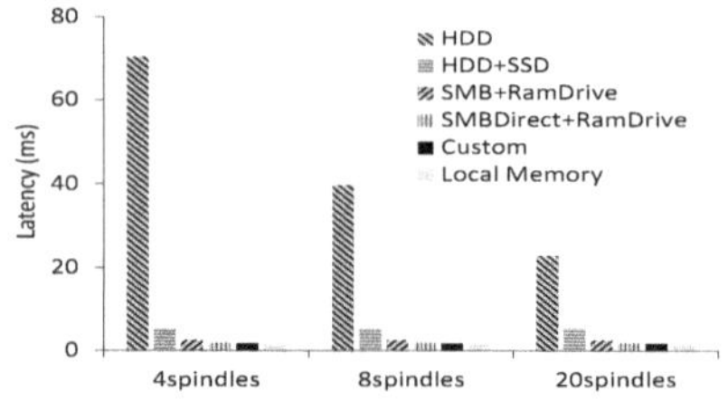

Figure 10: RangeScan latency (no updates).

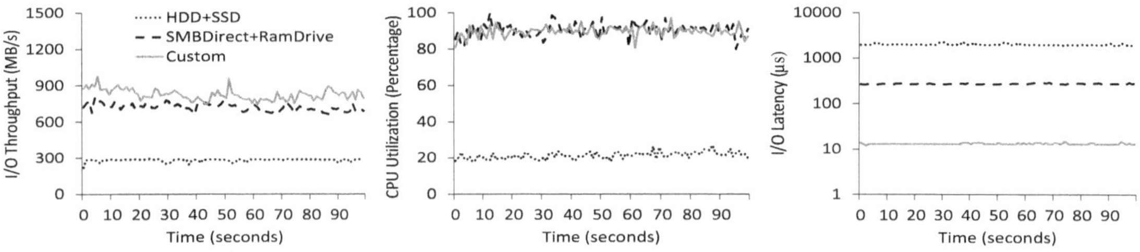

(a) I/O throughput (b) CPU utilization (c) I/O latency

Figure 11: Drill down of RangeScan.

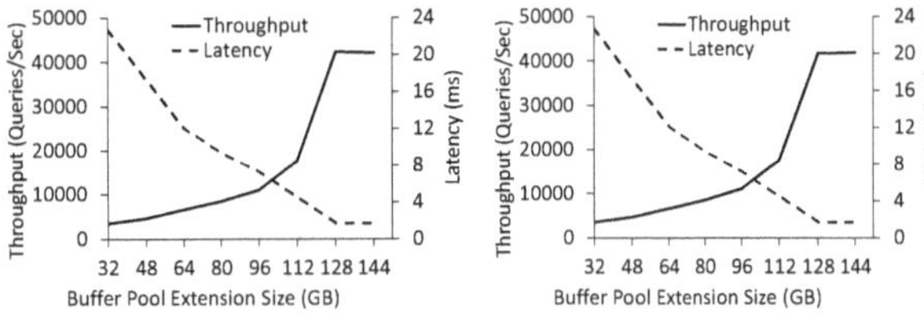

(a) One memory server. (b) Multiple memory servers.

Figure 12: Impact of varying BPExt size.

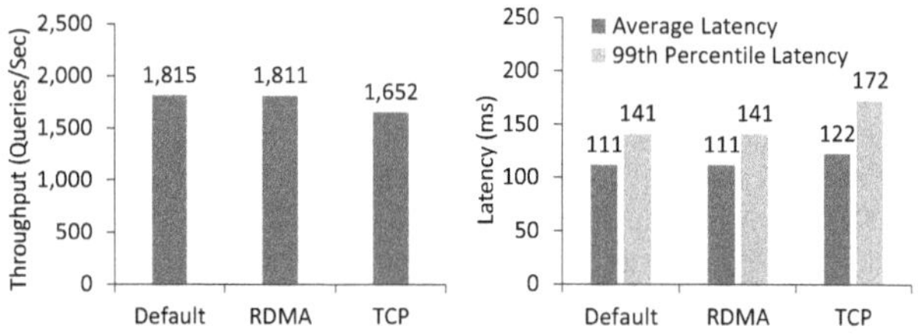

(a) Throughput. (b) Latency.

Figure 13: Impact on remote server.

6.2.2 *Impact of Memory Size*

The benefits of remote memory is dependent on the available local and remote memory. In this experiment, we keep the local memory at the server constant and vary the amount of remote memory allocated to the BPExt. Appendix B reports the experiment where we vary the amount of local memory available. When varying the remote memory, we report the results for two settings: when all the remote memory is on one server (Figure 12(a)) vs. the memory is spread evenly on multiple servers (Figure 12(b)) such that larger the size of the BPExt, higher is the number of M_js accessed. We vary the number of M_js from 2 to 9 where each server contributes 16GB of remote memory. The throughput and latency numbers depend on how much remote memory is available and independent of the number of servers contributing the memory, which is not surprising given the I/O performance reported in Figure 5. Each figure plots the throughput on the left vertical axis and latency on the right vertical axis, while the x-axis plots the increase in BPExt size. Both figures look identical, which demonstrates that remote memory continues to be equally beneficial even when it is pooled from multiple servers. In SQL Server, the size of BPExt is not allowed to be smaller than the local memory size. Thus, the size of BPExt starts from 32 GB. Because the range scan query selects the start of the range from a uniform distribution that spans the table, it accesses all data with equal probability. Therefore, until the point where the entire data is cached in (local or remote) memory, the workload can always benefit from more remote memory. That is, as we increase remote memory, the throughput increases and the latency decreases. The rate of improvement is lower for BPExt sizes below 96 GB when I/O is still the bottleneck. As the BPExt size reaches close to the data size, most of the data pages are cached, resulting in significant throughput and latency improvements.

6.2.3 *Impact on Remote Server*

One important benefit of RDMA, in contrast to TCP, is that memory accesses and transfers to do involve the CPU of the remote server, thus potentially having minimal impact on any workload executing on the remote server. In this experiment, we quantify how the performance of the server with available memory is affected when another server accesses the memory. In this experiment, we run workloads on two servers: S_A and S_B. S_B's unused memory is used to store S_A's BPExt, accessed through either RDMA or TCP. Both servers are executing the *RangeScan* workload without updates. We measure the performance of the workload on S_B. S_A's workload corresponds to the default configuration which generates high memory demand. Since we want to measure the impact of RDMA's ability to bypass the CPU, S_B's workload uses different parameters: (1) S_B uses 128 GB memory for the RangeScan workload, which is large enough to hold the entire data set in memory; and (2) the range size for *RangeScan* is set to $10,000$. These changes make S_B's workload to be CPU-intensive (with close to 100% CPU utilization). Figure 13(a) shows the throughput of the workload on S_B. *Default* corresponds to the scenario where S_A does not use S_B's available memory. As can be seen from the figure, the throughput is unaffected when remote memory is accessed via RDMA. In contrast, when S_B's available memory is accessed by TCP, its throughput degrades by about 10%. Figure 13(b) shows the average and the 99th percentile latency. The average latency with *TCP* is 10% higher than *Default* and *RDMA* and the impact is as high as 20% when considering the 99th percentile latency. That is, when S_B's memory is accessed using TCP, there is a noticeable performance degradation due to the CPU consumed to process the transfers, and secondary effects such as context switches and polluting the processor cache line. On the other hand, there is no noticeable impact when memory is accessed via RDMA.

6.3 Impact of Remote Memory on TempDB

The goal of this experiment is to quantify the benefits of remote memory on TempDB by using the *Hash+Sort* micro benchmark designed to stress TempDB. Since this is a long-running query, we only report the execution times (Figure 14(a)). As evident from the figure, the query running in the *HDD+SSD* configuration is about $5\times$ slower than *Custom*. Observe that HDD is faster than *HDD+SSD* because, as noted earlier, the sequential throughput of HDD is higher than that of the SSD and this workload results in large sequential reads and writes to TempDB. However, *HDD* is still significantly slower than leveraging remote memory with RDMA to store the TempDB. For *Hash+Sort*, the execution time of *SMBDirect+RamDrive* is roughly the same as *Custom* since, as shown in Figure 3, the sequential read throughput of *SMBDirect+RamDrive* is roughly the same as that of *Custom*.

Figure 14(b) shows the I/O throughput of TempDB reads and writes during query execution. The dashed line shows the throughput of TempDB reads and writes for *HDD+SSD* and the solid line plots that for *Custom*. The darker lines correspond to reads and the lighter lines correspond to writes. Recall that the execution of the *Hash+Sort* query consists of two phases (see Figure 2 for the execution plan). The first phase scans the data and builds the hash tables for the join. Since the hash table is too big to fit in memory, this build phase also writes data to TempDB. In the second phase where the join operator starts to generate the joined results, data is read from TempDB to compute the join and the sorted results are written to TempDB for the external sort.

In Figure 14(b), the first phase can be identified where only reads are happening, while the second phase has both reads and writes. As is evident, the phases are considerably shorter for when TempDB is stored in remote memory; the query ends at around 400 sec with *Custom* compared to 1800 sec for *HDD+SSD*. In phase 1, *Custom* achieves a throughput of around 400 MB/s mainly because this phase is CPU-intensive as the query scans the data pages cached in memory, builds the in-memory hashtable based on `orderkey`, and serializes the hash table to TempDB. Phase 2 is I/O-intensive dominated by TempDB reads and writes, where the aggregate throughput of reads and writes is close to 5 GB/s. The benefit of fast TempDB I/Os is evident from the CPU utilization

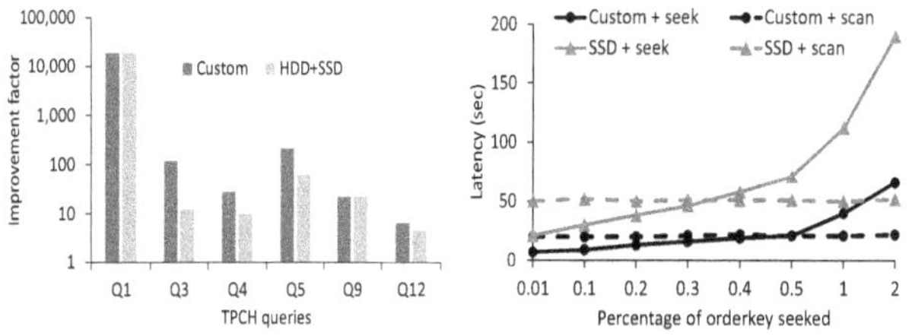

(a) Benefits of semantic cache (b) Seeking vs. scanning

Figure 15: Semantic caching.

during query execution which is shown in Figure 14(c). As the I/O throughput of *Custom* is much higher, the CPU utilization is much higher, especially in phase 2.

6.4 Remote Memory and Semantic Caching

The goal of this experiment is to evaluate the benefits of opportunistically building a semantic cache to improve query performance (Section 3.3). We use the TPC-H workload for this experiment. We consider materialized views (MV) which can often significantly improve performance for certain queries. We used SQL Server's DTA to generate MV recommendations for TPC-H queries; seven queries benefited from an MV. Since one of the goals of semantic caching is to not contend for buffer pool or other memory requirements of the RDBMS, these MVs are pinned in remote memory and the RDBMS accesses them through a semantic cache broker which is separate from the buffer pool. In the absence of remote memory, these MVs could still be created and stored in *HDD+SSD* to avoid contending for buffer pool memory, which is our baseline. Figure 15(a) plots the multiplicative factor improvement of the seven TPC-H queries compared to when they were executed without MVs using indexes tuned for the queries. As is evident from the figure, using MVs can result in one to four orders of magnitude improvement in query latency even when it is stored on *SSD+HDD*. Pinning the semantic cache in remote memory can result in another order of magnitude improvement. The relative improvement of the semantic cache being stored in *HDD+SSD* vs. remote memory depends on the size of the MV; pinning larger MVs to remote memory results in higher benefits.

Next we use a non-clustered index to demonstrate the fact that the query optimizers can benefit further with the knowledge that structures in the semantic cache are pinned in memory. We use an adapted version of TPC-H Q12 which joins `lineitem` with `orders`. We build a non-clustered index on `orders` which can either be seeked or scanned depending on whether an index nested-loop join (INLJ) or a hash join (HJ) plan is used. We vary the selectivity of the predicate on `lineitem` which determines the number of rows needed from `orders` for the join. Figure 15(b) plots the query latency as the percentage of `O_OrderKey` rows selected from `orders` changes. The dashed lines correspond to a HJ plan and the solid lines correspond to the INLJ plan. As expected, for high selectivity, the INLJ plan outperforms the HJ plan, and vice versa. However, the crossover points depend on whether the index is in remote memory or in SSD. Depending on whether the index is in the semantic cache or is accessed through the buffer pool (where it can be in memory or on disk), the optimal plan might vary. Thus, the optimizer's cost model must be tuned to select the optimal plan in the presence of such remote semantic cache.

6.5 Buffer pool priming

This experiment evaluates the costs and demonstrates the benefits of proactively priming the buffer pool of a newly-elected primary (S_2) using the warm buffer pool of the old primary (S_1) (Sec-

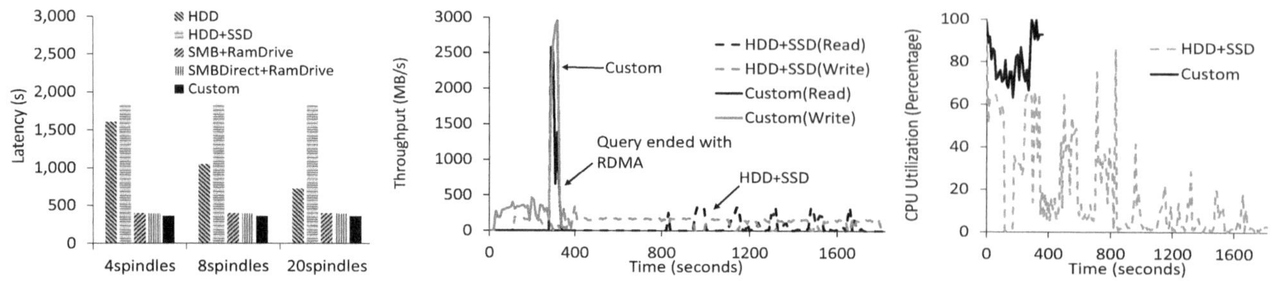

(a) Latency (b) I/O throughput drill down (c) CPU utilization drill down

Figure 14: Performance of Hash+Sort

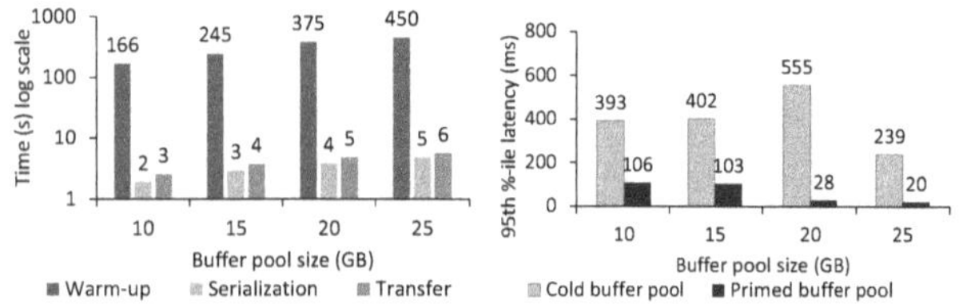

(a) Drill down of priming time. (b) Impact of priming on tail latencies.

Figure 16: Drill down of priming time vs. time to warm-up the buffer pool and its impact on tail latencies.

tion 3.4). We use the *RangeScan* workload with a database of about 100GB. The start key of the scan is selected from a hotspot distribution where 99% of the operation access about 20% of the data. Each query scans $5,000$ keys. Figure 16(a) plots the time in seconds (in log scale) to warm up the buffer pool at S_1 when executing the workload, scan through the buffer pool at S_1 and serialize the contents in an in-memory file to prepare for the priming transfer, and transfer the pages from the in-memory file into the buffer pool at S_2. We vary the size of the buffer pool from 10GB - 25GB. As is evident from Figure 16(a), the time to prime the buffer pool is about two orders of magnitude smaller than the time it takes to warm-up the buffer pool during the normal course of workload execution. Figure 16(b) plots the 95th percentile latency of the scan queries starting with a cold buffer pool during warm-up phase at S_2, and the latency of the same workload when the buffer pool was primed with pages from S_1. Unsurprisingly, a primed buffer pool results in $4\times - 10\times$ lower tail latencies, thus significantly reducing the impact of such planned primary-secondary swaps.

7. CONCLUDING REMARKS

We considered the setting of a cluster of RDBMS servers connected with RDMA-enabled NICs where some servers are experiencing memory pressure while other servers have available memory. We presented the abstraction of exposing unused memory on remote servers using a lightweight file API that allows a mature an SMP RDBMS to significantly improve performance of memory-intensive workloads with modest changes to the DBMS engine. We implemented this remote memory abstraction in Microsoft SQL Server and demonstrated the potential performance benefits using a variety of configurations and a combination of micro-benchmarks as well as the industry-standard TPC benchmarks. Compared to using disks when memory is insufficient, our abstraction improved the throughput and latency of queries with short reads and writes by $3\times$ to $10\times$, while improving the latency of multiple TPC-H and TPC-DS queries by $2\times$ to $100\times$.

While our work presents the first in-depth study of the end-to-end benefits of RDMA in an SMP RDBMS, we also highlight some potential areas of future research to further extend our abstraction and implementation. For instance, supporting flexible memory brokering policies, ensuring fairness across multiple workloads, and being more adaptive to the flux in memory requirements are important aspects for deploying this abstraction in a production service. The DBMS engine can also benefit from making remote memory as a first-class concept, and consider it similar to other sources and consumers of memory. For instance, remote memory can be exposed as a new type of memory broker, and techniques to detect a workload's memory requirements, such as Storm et al. [41], can be used to dynamically assign remote memory among the different consumers. In addition to the four novel scenarios of leveraging remote memory and fast RDMA transfers, in Appendix C, we highlight other potential scenarios where an SMP RDBMSs can leverage available resources on remote servers. Developing these techniques are interesting directions of future work. Furthermore, since today's data centers employ some form of virtualization. If the RDBMS is hosted within the guest OS, the performance implications of virtualization on the proposed abstraction needs to quantified. Finally, there are security implications since any remote process can DMA into a memory address once it is registered with the NIC. When processing an RDMA request, NICs have minimal support for authentication, checking privileges, or accounting for resources. Therefore, it is important to explore approaches for secure long-term memory registration or to efficiently encrypt data stored in remote memory.

Acknowledgements

We would like to thank Miguel Castro, Aleksandar Dragojević, and Dushyanth Narayanan for providing the code to implement RDMA transfers using NDSPI which we use in our custom implementation. We also thank Justin Levandoski, Ryan Stutsman, and Lidong Zhou for the useful feedback that helped improve this paper.

8. REFERENCES

[1] C. Amza, A. Cox, S. Dwarkadas, P. Keleher, H. Lu, R. Rajamony, W. Yu, and W. Zwaenepoel. TreadMarks: shared memory computing on networks of workstations. *Computer*, 29(2):18–28, Feb 1996.

[2] C. Barthels, S. Loesing, G. Alonso, and D. Kossmann. Rack-scale in-memory join processing using RDMA. In *SIGMOD*, pages 1463–1475, 2015.

[3] Microsoft SQL Server: Buffer Pool Extension. http://msdn.microsoft.com/en-us/library/dn133176.aspx.

[4] M. Canim, G. A. Mihaila, B. Bhattacharjee, K. A. Ross, and C. A. Lang. SSD Bufferpool Extensions for Database Systems. *Proc. VLDB Endow.*, 3(2):1435–1446, 2010.

[5] J. B. Carter, J. K. Bennett, and W. Zwaenepoel. Implementation and performance of munin. In *SOSP*, pages 152–164, 1991.

[6] F. Chang, J. Dean, S. Ghemawat, W. C. Hsieh, D. A. Wallach, M. Burrows, T. Chandra, A. Fikes, and R. Gruber. Bigtable: A distributed storage system for structured data. In *OSDI*, pages 205–218, 2006.

[7] S. Chaudhuri, U. Dayal, and V. R. Narasayya. An overview of business intelligence technology. *Commun. ACM*, 54(8):88–98, 2011.

[8] S. Chaudhuri, R. Krishnamurthy, S. Potamianos, and K. Shim. Optimizing queries with materialized views. In *ICDE*, pages 190–200, 1995.

[9] C. Clark, K. Fraser, S. Hand, J. G. Hansen, E. Jul, C. Limpach, I. Pratt, and A. Warfield. Live migration of virtual machines. In *2nd Symposium on Networked Systems Design and Implementation (NSDI 2005), May 2-4, 2005, Boston, Massachusetts, USA, Proceedings.*, 2005.

[10] S. Dar, M. J. Franklin, B. Þ. Jónsson, D. Srivastava, and M. Tan. Semantic data caching and replacement. In *VLDB*, pages 330–341, 1996.

[11] S. Das, S. Nishimura, D. Agrawal, and A. El Abbadi. Albatross: Lightweight elasticity in shared storage databases for the cloud using live data migration. *PVLDB*, 4(8):494–505, 2011.

[12] A. Dragojević, D. Narayanan, O. Hodson, and M. Castro. FaRM: Fast Remote Memory. In *NSDI*. USENIX, April 2014.

[13] P. Frey and G. Alonso. Minimizing the Hidden Cost of RDMA. In *ICDCS*, pages 553–560, June 2009.

[14] A. Gupta and I. Mumick. *Materialized Views:Techniques, Implementations, and Applications*. MIT Press, 1999.

[15] J. Huang, X. Ouyang, J. Jose, M. W. ur Rahman, H. Wang, M. Luo, H. Subramoni, C. Murthy, and D. K. Panda. High-performance design of hbase with rdma over infiniband. In *IPDPS*, pages 774–785, 2012.

[16] P. Hunt, M. Konar, F. P. Junqueira, and B. Reed. Zookeeper: Wait-free coordination for internet-scale systems. In *USENIX Annual Technical Conference*, 2010.

[17] IBM DB2 Pure Scale. http://www.ibm.com/developerworks/data/library/dmmag/DBMag_2010_Issue1/DBMag_Issue109_pureScale/.

[18] Mellanox Infiniband. http://www.mellanox.com/.

[19] Infiniband Trade Association. Supplement to InfiniBand Architecture Specification Volume 1 Release 1.2.2 Annex A16: RDMA over Converged Ethernet (RoCE), 2010.

[20] Internet Engineering Task Force. RFC 5040: A Remote Direct Memory Access Protocol Specification, 2007.

[21] N. S. Islam, M. W. Rahman, J. Jose, R. Rajachandrasekar, H. Wang, H. Subramoni, C. Murthy, and D. K. Panda. High Performance RDMA-based Design of HDFS over InfiniBand. In *SC*, pages 1–12, 2012.

[22] J. Jose, H. Subramoni, M. Luo, M. Zhang, J. Huang, M. W. ur Rahman, N. S. Islam, X. Ouyang, H. Wang, S. Sur, and D. K. Panda. Memcached Design on High Performance RDMA Capable Interconnects. In *ICPP*, pages 743–752. IEEE, 2011.

[23] A. Kalia, M. Kaminsky, and D. G. Andersen. Using RDMA Efficiently for Key-value Services. In *SIGCOMM*, pages 295–306, 2014.

[24] J. Liu, J. Wu, and D. Panda. High performance rdma-based mpi implementation over infiniband. *International Journal of Parallel Programming*, 32(3):167–198, 2004.

[25] Querymemoryresourcenotification function. https://msdn.microsoft.com/en-us/library/windows/desktop/aa366799(v=vs.85).aspx.

[26] Microsoft Analytics Platform System. http://www.microsoft.com/en-us/server-cloud/products/analytics-platform-system/.

[27] D. Ongaro, S. M. Rumble, R. Stutsman, J. K. Ousterhout, and M. Rosenblum. Fast crash recovery in ramcloud. In *SOSP*, pages 29–41, 2011.

[28] Oracle's Exadata Smart Flash Cache. http://www.oracle.com/technetwork/database/exadata/exadata-smart-flash-cache-366203.pdf.

[29] Oracle RAC over InfiniBand. http://www.cisco.com/c/en/us/products/collateral/cloud-systems-management/vframe-ib-software/prod_white_paper0900aecd8056d64c.html.

[30] Oracle Temporary Tablespaces. http://docs.oracle.com/cd/B28359_01/server.111/b28310/tspaces002.htm\#ADMIN11366.

[31] Actian Matrix MPP Analytics Database. http://www.actian.com/products/analytics-platform/matrix-mpp-analytics-database/.

[32] List of RAM drive software. http://en.wikipedia.org/wiki/List_of_RAM_drive_software.

[33] RDMA in RamCloud. https://ramcloud.atlassian.net/wiki/download/attachments/6848659/rdma_slides.pdf?version=1&modificationDate=1339212592571&api=v2.

[34] W. Rödiger, T. Mühlbauer, A. Kemper, and T. Neumann. High-speed query processing over high-speed networks. *PVLDB*, 9(4):228–239, 2015.

[35] P. Seshadri and A. Swami. Generalized partial indexes. In *Data Engineering, 1995. Proceedings of the Eleventh International Conference on*, pages 420–427, 1995.

[36] Server Message Block. https://en.wikipedia.org/wiki/Server_Message_Block.

[37] SMB Direct. http://technet.microsoft.com/en-us/library/jj134210.aspx.

[38] SQLIO Disk Subsystem Benchmark Tool. http://www.microsoft.com/en-us/download/details.aspx?id=20163.

[39] Install sql server with smb fileshare. http://msdn.microsoft.com/en-us/library/hh759341.aspx.

[40] M. Stonebraker. The case for partial indexes. *SIGMOD Rec.*, 18(4):4–11, Dec. 1989.

[41] A. J. Storm, C. Garcia-Arellano, S. S. Lightstone, Y. Diao, and M. Surendra. Adaptive self-tuning memory in db2. In *VLDB*, pages 1081–1092, 2006.

[42] Microsoft SQL Server: TempDB. http://msdn.microsoft.com/en-us/library/ms190768.aspx.

[43] Teradata selects MellanoxTechnologies's InfiniBand interconnect solution. http://cloud-computing.tmcnet.com/news/2012/12/19/6804961.htm.

[44] Big Data Analytics for Teradata Aster. http://www.teradata.com/Aster-Big-Analytics-Appliance/#tabbable=0&tab1=0&tab2=0.

[45] Timesten in-memory database and timesten application-tier database cache. http://www.oracle.com/technetwork/database/database-technologies/timesten/overview/index.html.

[46] TPC-C Benchmark. http://www.tpc.org/tpcc/.

[47] TPC-H Benchmark. http://www.tpc.org/tpch/.

[48] TPC-DS Benchmark. http://www.tpc.org/tpcds/.

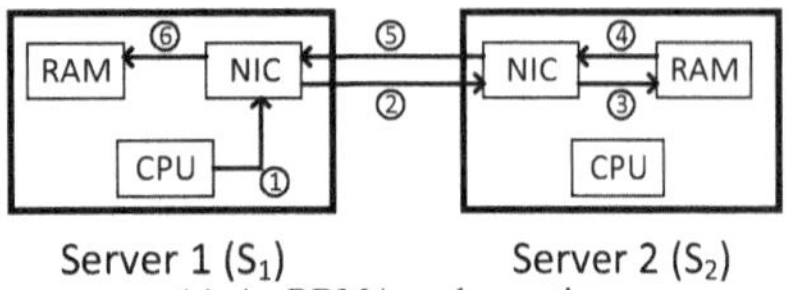

(a) An RDMA read operation.

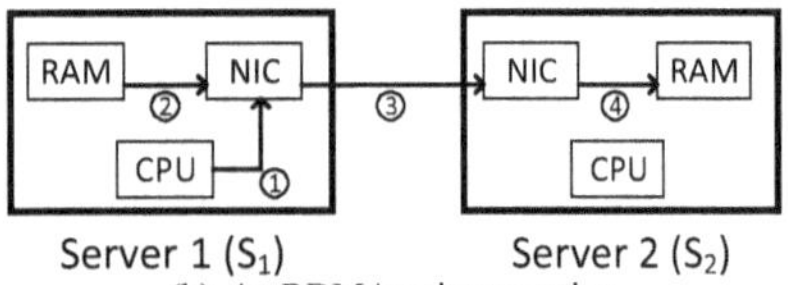

(b) An RDMA write operation.

Figure 17: Illustration of RDMA read and write operations.

[49] V. K. Vavilapalli, A. C. Murthy, C. Douglas, S. Agarwal, M. Konar, R. Evans, T. Graves, J. Lowe, H. Shah, S. Seth, B. Saha, C. Curino, O. O'Malley, S. Radia, B. Reed, and E. Baldeschwieler. Apache hadoop YARN: yet another resource negotiator. In *SOCC*, pages 5:1–5:16, 2013.

[50] J. Wu, P. Wyckoff, and D. Panda. PVFS over InfiniBand: design and performance evaluation. In *ICPP*, pages 125–132, 2003.

APPENDIX

A. RDMA BACKGROUND

RDMA allows computers in a network to exchange data from main memory of one server to the main memory of another server without involving the CPU on the remote server. RDMA bypasses the OS kernel, avoids the overhead of network protocol stacks, and performs DMA using only the NIC without copying data from the application's buffer to the OS buffers. Since the CPU is not involved in an RDMA transfer, it avoids context switches and cache line pollution. Figure 17 illustrates RDMA read/write operations between Server 2 (S_2, provider of remote memory) and Server 1 (S_1, accessor of remote memory).

The first step in initiating RDMA is setting up the network connection between the client (S_1) and the server (S_2). This setup also involves *registering* a part of the main memory, called a *memory region* (MR), with the respective NICs on both S_1 and S_2. During registration with the NIC, the device driver *pins* the registered memory pages to physical memory and stores the virtual to physical page mapping in a page table. Registering a memory region is a expensive operation (relative to RDMA transfers) since it involves the CPU and the OS kernel. There are also limits on the size of each MR (2 GB for our Mellanox NIC) and the number of registered MRs (around 130K for our NIC). The NICs also have limited memory for the page tables and uses the main memory to store this information. The NIC's memory is used as a cache and the NIC issues a DMA if there is a cache miss accessing the page table. Carefully managing registration of MRs and the available memory is crucial to leverage the performance benefits of RDMA [13].

RDMA communication is based on a set of queues. The send queue and receive queue, together called the *queue pairs*, process the RDMA transfer, and a completion queue notifies the application of the transfer's completion. RDMA requests are sent over a reliable channel and network failures are exposed as terminated connections. The NIC implements in hardware all the logic of the RDMA protocol, flow control, and reliability.

Figure 17(a) illustrates an RDMA read operation. When an application running on S_1 decides to read a memory location on S_2, S_1's CPU issues an RDMA request to the local NIC (Step ①) which in turn issues the request to the NIC on S_2 (Step ②). The request will specify the MR, the offset within the MR, the size of data read, and a memory location at S_1 where the remote memory contents will be transferred. S_2's NIC issues a DMA to access the pages in the memory (Steps ③ and ④) and transfers the contents to S_1's NIC (Step ⑤) which in turn performs another DMA to write the data to S_1's memory (Step ⑥). The steps for an RDMA write are also similar and are illustrated in Figure 17(b).

RDMA has many implementations such as in InfiniBand [18], RDMA over Converged Ethernet (RoCE) [19], and iWARP [20]. InfiniBand is a switched fabric link that provides RDMA capabilities. RoCE allows RDMA over Ethernet with data center bridging extensions where the connection state is managed in hardware providing a reliable communication channel without software protocols like TCP. iWARP implements RDMA on top of TCP/IP. It has fewer requirements on the network but the performance is worse compared to that on InfiniBand. RDMA protocols bypass the OS and avoid the overheads of TCP/IP. However, the protocols for RDMA transfers are specific to the platform. Section 4 discussed protocols in the Windows ecosystem. In the Linux ecosystem, alternative approaches include User Direct Access Programming Library (uDAPL) and the Sockets Direct Protocol (SDP). uDAPL defines a set of user-level APIs for all RDMA-capable transports. SDP is an Infiniband-specific upper-layer protocol that defines a standard wire protocol to support stream sockets networking over Infiniband allowing applications with minimal changes to leverage the benefits of the Infiniband protocols.

B. ADDITIONAL EXPERIMENTS

B.1 TPC Benchmarks

TPC-H. We now quantify the benefits of remote memory for both TempDB and BPExt using industry-standard benchmark workloads to analyze the holistic benefits for complex database workloads. Figure 18 shows the throughput of TPC-H with the different alternative designs. The experiment is repeated for three different configurations with 4, 8, and 20 HDD spindles. As can be seen in this figure, *Custom* outperforms both *HDD+SSD* and *SMBDirect+ RamDrive*. An interesting observation is that the throughput of *Custom* is even higher than *Local Memory* which has the 256 GB memory locally. This behavior is an artifact of SQL Server's query execution engine's admission control policy which does not assign all available memory to one long-running query, thus leaving memory available for subsequent queries and prevent runaway long-running queries from hogging the server's memory. Since memory provided to the operators are not enough for the data sizes, the execution resorts to using the TempDB to spill data. As a result, two of the TPC-H queries, $Q10$ and $Q18$, spill to TempDB. Since *Custom* stores the TempDB in remote memory, it is much faster than spilling to disk, thus resulting in *Custom* outperforming *Local Memory* for $Q10$ and $Q18$. For the other queries, most of the performance improvement comes from BPExt since their execution plans do not contain memory-intensive operators. Figure 19 plots a histogram of latency improvements of *Custom* compared to *HDD+SSD* for 20 spindles. As can be seen in this figure, the improvements are massive for TPC-H: 2× for 8 queries, 2× to 5× for 10 queries, and 5× to 10× for 3 queries.

TPC-DS. Similar improvements can be observed for the TPC-DS benchmark which has a more diverse set of queries. Figure 20 plots the throughput and Figure 21 plots the histogram of latency improvements of *Custom* compared to *HDD+SSD* for 20 spindles. The major difference from TPC-H results is that *Custom* has slightly lower throughput compared to *Local Memory* since queries do not

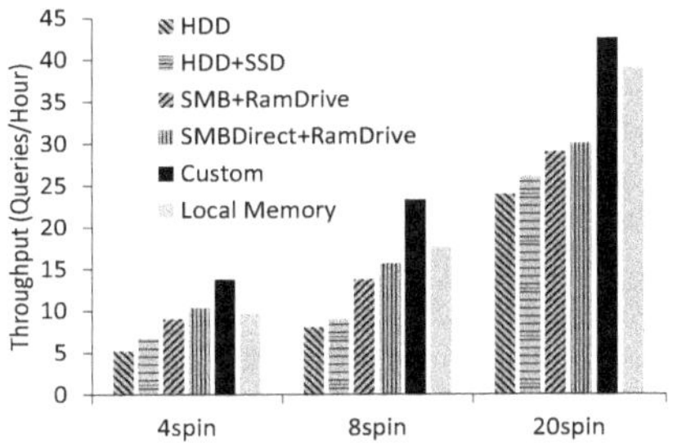

Figure 18: TPC-H throughput.

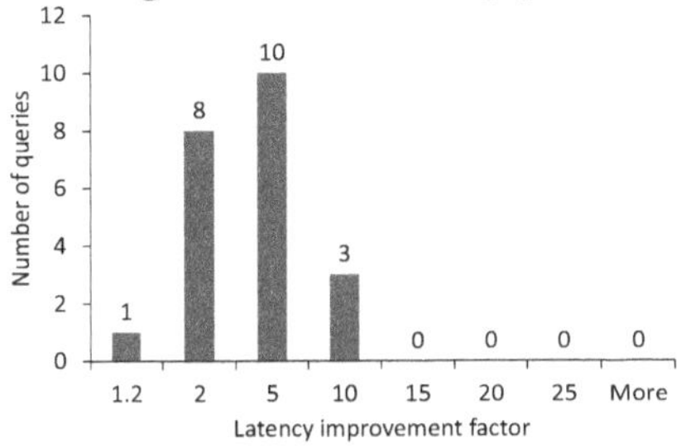

Figure 19: TPC-H latency improvement.

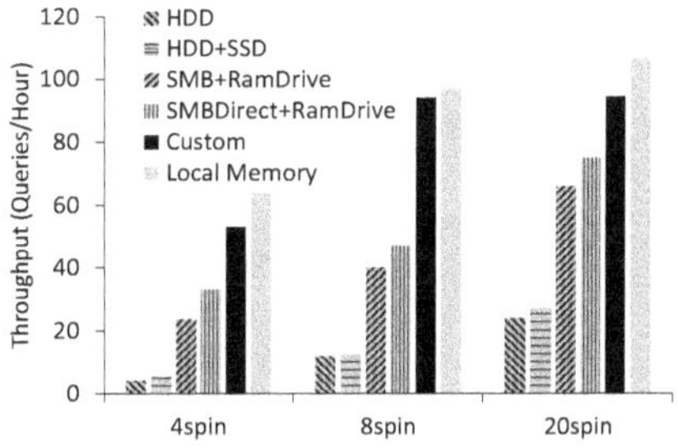

Figure 20: TPC-DS throughput.

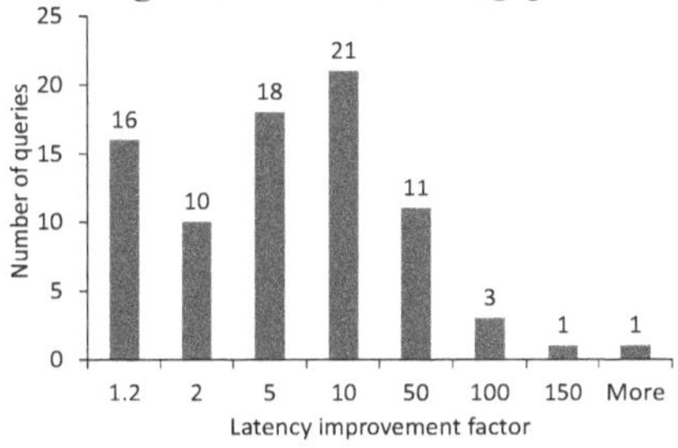

Figure 21: TPC-DS latency improvement.

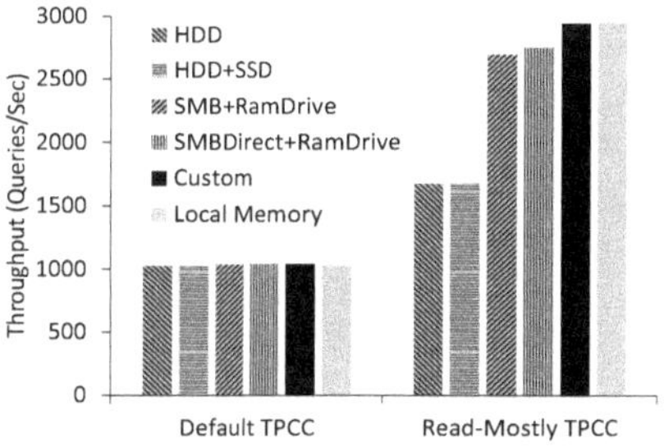

Figure 22: TPC-C throughput.

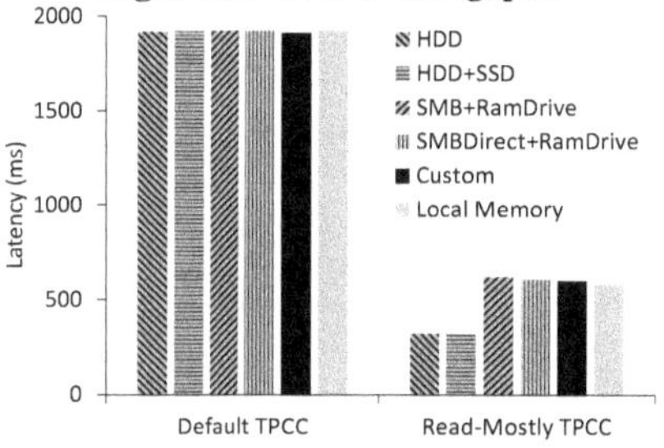

Figure 23: TPC-C latency.

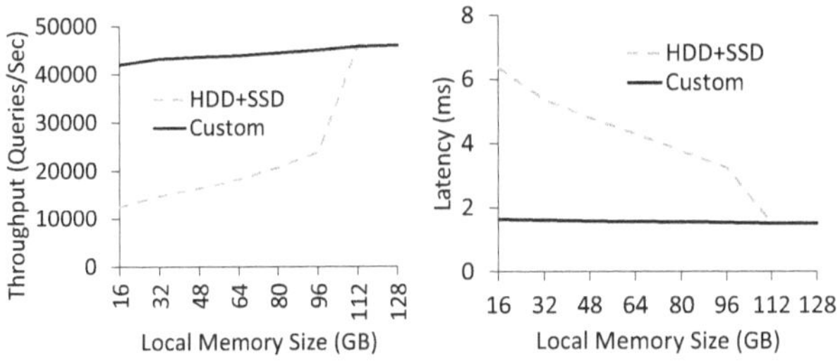

(a) Throughput. (b) Latency.

Figure 24: Performance impact of varying available local memory.

spill to TempDB for the *Local Memory* setting. In addition, we can see a much more significant improvement in terms of latency: 18 queries get 2× to 5× improvement, 21 queries get 5× to 10× improvement, and 11 queries get 10× to 50× improvement. Some TPC-DS queries can even get more than 100× improvement in latencies by leveraging remote memory.

TPC-C. OLTP workloads rarely have heavy demand for TempDB since more requests are short reads and writes. The RangeScan with update workload demonstrated some benefits of remote memory for OLTP workloads with short reads and writes. We now present results with the TPC-C workload. We report the throughput and latency of TPC-C workloads with two different parameter settings: (i) the default TPC-C transaction mix (Default TPCC); and (ii) where the read-only `StockLevel` transaction comprises 90% of the workload mix (Read-Mostly TPCC). We use an HDD setup with 20 spindles for both the experiments. As shown in Figure 22, the default TPC-C transaction mix does not benefit from remote memory even when the local memory does not cache the entire data. This is because in TPC-C, the `NewOrder` transactions create new orders which the `Payment`, `Delivery` and `OrderStatus` transactions access, which comprises 96% of the queries in the workload. Therefore, the working set for TPC-C workload is small and keeps changing as new orders are added to the database. Even with 32 GB local memory (the *Local Memory* setting), the throughput cannot be improved compared to *HDD+SSD* with 16 GB local memory. This experiment is an example where remote memory is not beneficial since there is not enough demand for memory. By contrast, with the read-mostly mix of TPC-C, most of the queries are `StockLevel` queries that also access the old data, accessing more database pages, resulting in a larger working set and more demand for memory. Hence, the alternatives with more available memory, whether local or remote, have higher throughput. Figure 23 shows the latency of different methods. For Read-Mostly TPCC, the latency of *HDD+SSD* is lower than the latency of the methods with remote memory. This is because with remote memory, the database is able to process more TPC-C queries (as seen from the throughput graph), which results in higher contention for resources, such as locks, resulting in higher latency. When the throughput of the different alternative design is set to the same target, the latency of *HDD+SSD* is higher compared to *Custom* with remote memory. Also, since this workload had lower demand for remote memory, even *SMB+RamDrive* has performance comparable to *SMBDirect+RamDrive*.

B.2 Varying available local memory

The benefits of remote memory is dependent on the available local memory and the workload's demand for additional memory. In this experiment, we vary the amount of local memory on the database server. We use the RangeScan workload used to stress the BPExt and store the BPExt on a fixed amount of remote memory sufficient to accommodate the working set. Figures 24(a) and 24(b) plot the throughput and latency of *Custom* and *HDD+SSD* as we vary the amount of local memory available from 16 GB to 128 GB. As is evident from the figures, as the amount of memory available locally increases, *Custom*'s benefits over *HDD+SSD* decreases. This decrease continues until the local memory is sufficiently large to cache the entire database. When the database is cached entirely in local memory, the throughput and latency of both alternatives are equal. In addition, as the amount of local memory increases, the throughput of *Custom* also increases slightly, since local memory is about two orders of magnitude faster than remote memory.

B.3 Multiple database servers

In the experiments presented in Section 6 we characterized the end-to-end workload performance in one multi-server setup where

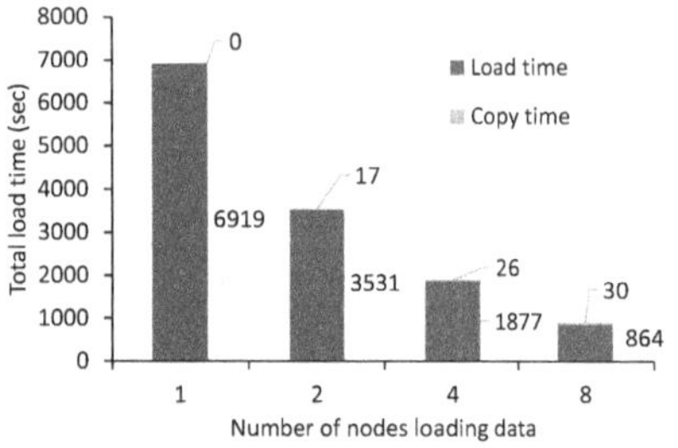

Figure 27: Parallel loading.

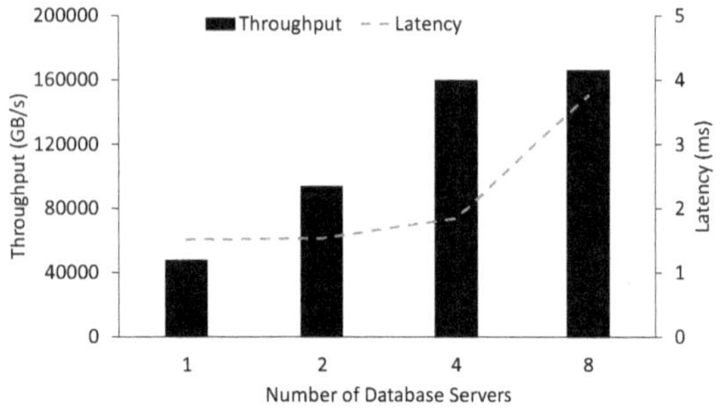

Figure 25: Performance of RangeScan when multiple database servers access remote memory at one server.

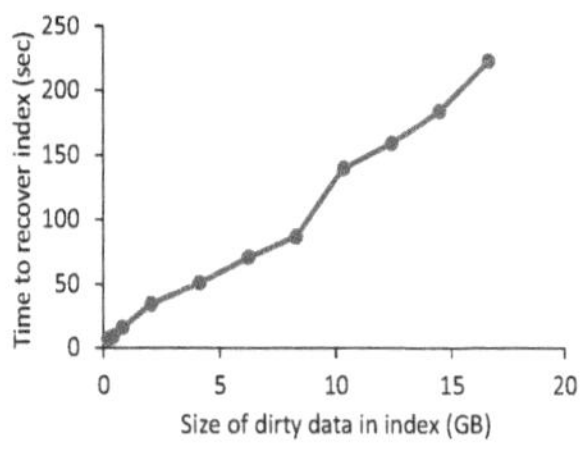

Figure 26: Recovering an index after remote node failure.

one database server accesses memory of multiple remote servers. In this section, we consider the complementary experiment where multiple database servers are accessing the memory on one remote server. We use the same RangeScan workload, though with a smaller database size (125 million rows) so that there is sufficient memory on one M_j to serve 8 DB_i servers. Each database server is configured with about 7GB local memory and 30GB remote memory. Figure 25 plots the throughput and latency as we increase the number of database servers which is plotted on the x-axis. The bars plot the aggregate throughput (queries per second) of all the database servers along the left vertical axis and the dashed line plots the average latency (ms) along the right vertical axis. Similar to the behavior we observed with the I/O micro benchmark, until the NIC at M_j saturates, the aggregate throughput increases almost linearly with the number of database servers, with negligible increase in latency. Once the NIC is saturated, increasing the concurrent load results in a noticeable increase in latency without much improvement in aggregate throughput.

B.4 Recovering the Semantic Cache

Since semantic cache is stored in remote memory and our remote memory abstraction is best effort, the remote server failure will completely wipe out the cache. Based on a user-specified policy, the queries can continue using the base indexes and ignore the cache. Alternatively, the cache can be rebuilt on another server. Even if we periodically checkpoint the cache, there might still be some trailing updates which might not be present in the checkpoint and need to be recovered from the transaction log. As a benefit of the cache being part of the RDBMS, we can use the REDO recovery logic to rebuild the index. Figure 26 plots the recovery time as a function of the amount of dirty pages in the non-clustered index since the last checkpoint. As is evident from the figure, the recovery time increases almost linearly with the size of dirty data. Less than a GB of dirty pages can be recovered in tens of seconds and about 16 GB of data can be recovered within four minutes. That is, if the data in the semantic cache is not being updated frequently, the cache can be recovered very fast. Therefore, even though we use remote memory with best-effort fault-tolerance guarantees, remote node failures only result in a small period of performance degradation since the cache can be reconstructed within minutes. Note that storing the semantic cache in HDD or SSD will not require recovery. Hence this experiment reports time to recover the cache into remote memory from the transaction log.

C. ACCELERATING DATA LOADING

In addition to the four scenarios discussed in Section 3, our lightweight file abstraction is also beneficial for other scenarios. For instance, efficiently loading new partitions of data into a data warehouse is crucial to enable querying newly-arriving data in a timely manner [7]. Parallel data loading into an RDBMS server is a CPU and I/O-intensive process which can be bottlenecked by the *single* server into which data is being loaded. Data often arrives as flat file which needs to be parsed, compressed, and converted into native database format. Each of these steps are CPU-intensive operations. If some remote database servers on the cluster have idle CPU along with unused memory, an additional scenario is to *offload* and parallelize the data load on multiple remote servers. Our key idea is to enable the remote database servers to load data for a set of partitions into local in-memory files. The CPU and memory-parallelism of multiple idle servers in the cluster can greatly speed up the data loading. Once the remote servers finish loading the partitions, the destination server *pulls* these loaded data partitions from the remote in-memory files using the API we support. Since the step of pulling data using RDMA is very fast relative to the actual data loading step, the overall data loading time can be dramatically reduced.

Figure 27 reports results from an experiment to demonstrate the benefits of such parallel loading. We consider the case where 160GB of raw data is being loaded into an existing TPC-H database. The data files are arriving from various sources and have 80 splits of approximately 2GB average size. The figure plots the time to load all the input files as we vary the number of servers loading the files. The bar with 1 server corresponds to data being loaded into the destination server using standard parallel loading tools. Since there is no copy needed, all the time is spent in loading. As we increase the number of servers, the data load is followed by a copy of the in-memory file to the destination server. As is evident from Figure 27, the data loading time reduces almost linearly, while the copy time continues to be negligible compared to the load time, thus allowing almost linear speedup in data loading. For instance, one server takes $6,919$ seconds to load the data while eight servers take 894 seconds, resulting in $\sim 7.7\times$ speedup. In addition to memory brokering which is implemented in our system, this scenario requires brokering of idle remote CPUs on database servers. A detailed design and implementation of such CPU brokering is an interesting area of future work, which can enable other interesting scenarios for CPU and memory offloading in a cluster of RDBMS servers.

FPTree: A Hybrid SCM-DRAM Persistent and Concurrent B-Tree for Storage Class Memory

Ismail Oukid[†‡] Johan Lasperas[‡] Anisoara Nica[‡]
Thomas Willhalm[*] Wolfgang Lehner[†]

[†]TU Dresden first.last@tu-dresden.de
[‡]SAP SE first.last@sap.com
[*]Intel Deutschland GmbH first.last@intel.com

ABSTRACT

The advent of Storage Class Memory (SCM) is driving a rethink of storage systems towards a single-level architecture where memory and storage are merged. In this context, several works have investigated how to design persistent trees in SCM as a fundamental building block for these novel systems. However, these trees are significantly slower than DRAM-based counterparts since trees are latency-sensitive and SCM exhibits higher latencies than DRAM. In this paper we propose a novel hybrid SCM-DRAM persistent and concurrent B$^+$-Tree, named *Fingerprinting Persistent Tree* (FPTree) that achieves similar performance to DRAM-based counterparts. In this novel design, leaf nodes are persisted in SCM while inner nodes are placed in DRAM and rebuilt upon recovery. The FPTree uses *Fingerprinting*, a technique that limits the expected number of in-leaf probed keys to one. In addition, we propose a hybrid concurrency scheme for the FPTree that is partially based on Hardware Transactional Memory. We conduct a thorough performance evaluation and show that the FPTree outperforms state-of-the-art persistent trees with different SCM latencies by up to a factor of 8.2. Moreover, we show that the FPTree scales very well on a machine with 88 logical cores. Finally, we integrate the evaluated trees in *memcached* and a prototype database. We show that the FPTree incurs an almost negligible performance overhead over using fully transient data structures, while significantly outperforming other persistent trees.

1. INTRODUCTION

The last few years have seen the rapid emergence of many novel types of memory technologies that have the additional characteristic of being non-volatile. These technologies are grouped under the umbrella term of *Storage Class Memory* (SCM) and include Phase Change Memory [6], Memristors [29], and Spin-Transfer Torque Magnetic Random Access Memory [4]. SCM combines the economic characteristics, capacity, and non-volatility property of traditional storage media with the low latency and byte-addressability of DRAM. Hence, SCM has a potential that goes beyond replacing DRAM: it can be used as universal memory, that is, as main memory and storage at the same time.

Given the characteristics of SCM, it is theoretically possible to persist data structures in SCM and at the same time obtain near-DRAM performance. This potential has been acknowledged by recent works and new systems that adopt this novel paradigm are emerging [5, 21, 18]. In this paper we investigate the design of index structures as one of the core database structures, motivated by the observation that traditional main memory B-Tree implementations do not fulfill the consistency requirements needed for such a use case. Furthermore, while expected in the range of DRAM, SCM latencies are slower and asymmetric with writes noticeably slower than reads. We argue that these performance differences between SCM and DRAM imply that the assumptions made for previous well-established main memory B-Tree implementations might not hold anymore. We therefore see the need to design a novel, persistent B-Tree that leverages the capabilities of SCM while exhibiting performance similar to that of traditional transient B-Tree.

Designing persistent data structures presents unprecedented challenges for data consistency since SCM is accessed via the volatile CPU cache over which software has only little control. Several works proposed SCM-optimized B-Trees such as the CDDS B-Tree [24], the wBTree [8], and the NV-Tree [28], but they fail to match the speed of an optimized DRAM-based B-Tree. Additionally, they do not address all SCM programming challenges we identify in Section 2, especially those of persistent memory leaks and data recovery.

To lift this shortcoming, we propose in this paper the *Fingerprinting Persistent Tree* (**FPTree**) that is based on four design principles to achieve near-DRAM-based data structure performance:

1. ***Fingerprinting***. Fingerprints are one-byte hashes of in-leaf keys, contiguously placed in the first cache-line-sized piece of the leaf. The FPTree uses unsorted leaves with in-leaf bitmaps –originally proposed in [8]–, such that a search would iterate linearly over all valid keys in a leaf. By scanning the fingerprints first, we are able to limit the number of in-leaf probed keys to **one** in the average case, which leads to a significant performance improvement.
2. ***Selective Persistence***. The idea is based on the well-known distinction between primary data, whose loss would infer an irreversible loss of information, and non-primary data that can be rebuilt from the former. Selective Persistence consists in storing primary data in SCM and non-primary data in DRAM. Applied to the FPTree, this corresponds to storing the leaf nodes in SCM and the inner nodes in DRAM. Hence, only leaf accesses are more expensive during a tree traversal compared to a fully transient counterpart.
3. ***Selective Concurrency***. This concept consists in using different concurrency schemes for the transient and persistent parts. Basically, the FPTree uses Hardware Transactional Memory (HTM) to handle the concurrency of inner nodes, and fine-grained locks to handle that of leaf nodes. Selective Concurrency elegantly solves the apparent incompatibility of HTM and persistence primitives required by SCM such as cache line flushing instructions. Con-

SIGMOD'16, June 26-July 01, 2016, San Francisco, CA, USA

ISBN 978-1-4503-3531-7/16/06...$15.00

DOI: http://dx.doi.org/10.1145/2882903.2915251

currency control techniques such as key-range locking [14] and orthogonal key-value locking [16] are orthogonal to our work as we focus on concurrency of physical operations.

4. ***Sound programming model***. We identify four SCM programming challenges: *data consistency*, *partial writes*, *data recovery*, and *memory leaks*, the last two of which are not fully addressed in related work. We solve all these challenges by relying on a sound programming model that encompasses the use of *Persistent Pointers*, an optimized, crash-safe, persistent allocator, and a memory leak prevention scheme. Contrary to existing work, this allows us to take into account the higher cost of persistent memory allocations in the performance evaluation.

We implemented the FPTree and two state-of-the art persistent trees, namely the NV-Tree and the wBTree. Using micro-benchmarks, we show that the FPTree outperforms the implemented competitors, with respectively fixed-size and variable-size keys, by up to 2.6x and 4.8x for an SCM latency of 90 ns, and by up to 5.5x and 8.2x for an SCM latency of 650 ns. The FPTree achieves these results while keeping less than 3% of its data in DRAM. In addition, we demonstrate how the FPTree scales on a machine with 88 logical cores, both with fixed-size and variable-size keys. Moreover, we show that the FPTree recovery time is 76.96x and 29.62x faster than a full rebuild for SCM latencies of 90 ns and 650 ns, respectively. Finally, we integrate the FPTree and the implemented competitors in *memcached* and a prototype database system. Compared with fully transient trees, results show that the FPTree incurs only 2% overhead in *memcached* using the *mc-benchmark* and that performance is network-bound. When using the TATP benchmark on the prototype database, the FPTree incurs a performance overhead of only 8.7% and 12.8% with an SCM latency of respectively 160 ns and 650 ns, while the overheads incurred by state-of-the-art trees are up to 39.6% and 51.7%, respectively.

The rest of the paper is organized as follows: Section 2 details our SCM programming model while Section 3 surveys related work. Section 4 presents our design goals and a description of our contributed design principles. Then, Section 5 explains the base operations of the FPTree. Thereafter, we discuss the results of our experimental evaluation in Section 6. Finally, Section 7 concludes the paper.

2. SCM PROGRAMMING MODEL

In the following we discuss SCM programming challenges and detail how we solve them with our programming model.

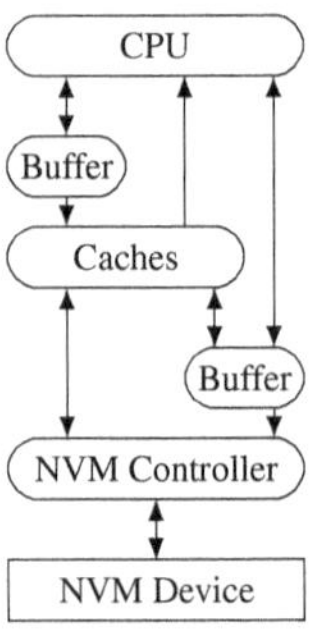

Figure 1: Volatility chain in x86-like processors.

Data consistency. SCM is accessed via a long volatility chain, illustrated in Figure 1, that includes store buffers, CPU caches, and the memory controller buffers, over all of which software has little control. The SNIA [3] recommends to manage SCM using an SCM-aware file system that grants the application layer direct access to SCM with *mmap*, enabling load/store semantics. Hence, ordering and durability of SCM writes cannot be guaranteed without software effort. To address this problem, we use, similarly to state-of-the art, persistence primitives, namely CLFLUSH, MFENCE, SFENCE, and non-temporal writes. CLFLUSH evicts a cache line from the cache and writes its content back to memory. When an MFENCE is issued, all pending load and store memory operations are completed before the program proceeds further. As for non-temporal writes, they bypass the cache and are buffered in a special buffer that is flushed when it is full or when an MFENCE is issued. Additionally, hardware vendors have announced new instructions to enhance SCM programming performance. For example, Intel has announced the CLFLUSHOPT (an optimized version of CLFLUSH), PCOMMIT, and cache line write back (CLWB) instructions [2]. When a PCOMMIT is issued, all pending writes that were evicted from the cache are made durable. Contrary to CLFLUSH, CLWB does not evict the cache line but simply writes it back, which can lead to significant performance gains when the cache line is re-used shortly after it was written back. In this work we assume the existence of a function *Persist* that implements the most efficient way of making data durable. In our evaluation systems, this function can correspond to either a CLFLUSH wrapped by two MFENCEs, since only MFENCE can order CLFLUSH [2], or a non-temporal write followed by an MFENCE.

Data recovery. When a program restarts, it does so with a new address space that renders all stored virtual pointers invalid. Therefore, there is a need for a mechanism that allows restoring data in SCM upon restart. We propose to use *Persistent Pointers* that encompass an 8-byte *File ID* and an 8-byte *Offset* inside that file. The file ID corresponds to a file that is created by the persistent allocator and used as an *Arena* to allocate memory. The persistent allocator provides bidirectional conversions between persistent and volatile pointers. Since persistent pointers stay valid across failures, they are used to refresh the volatile ones on restart.

Memory leaks. Since memory allocations are persistent in SCM, a memory leak would also be persistent. Hence, memory leaks have a deeper impact in SCM than in DRAM. For instance, let us consider a vector resize operation. The first step is to allocate a new, larger array. Then, the old array is copied into the new one. Finally, the old array is deallocated. If a crash occurs after the allocation of the new array but before the end of the copy phase, the persistent allocator will remember that it allocated the new array but the data structure will not, leading to a persistent memory leak. To solve this problem, we modify the interface of our persistent memory allocator so that it takes a reference to a persistent pointer that must belong to the persistent data structure that calls the allocator. In case of an allocation, the allocator persistently writes the address of the returned memory into that persistent pointer. In case of a deallocation, the allocator persistently resets (i.e., sets to null) that persistent pointer to convey that the deallocation has executed successfully. If a crash occurs during an allocation, upon recovery the allocator will either complete or roll-back the allocation, and the data structure will inspect the persistent pointer it used for the allocation. If the latter is not null, the data structure will know that it received memory. In brief, the task of discovering memory leaks is split between the allocator and the data structure.

Partial writes. Since writes to SCM have word granularity, partial writes may occur. Indeed, if a failure happens while writing data that is larger than the supported *p-atomic* write size, there is no guarantee on how much data was written. In contrast to *atomic* in the sense of concurrency, we mean by *p-atomic* a write that executes in one CPU cycle, i.e., a write that is immune to the partial write problem. To address this problem, we use flags that can be written p-atomically to indicate whether a larger write operation has completed. In this work we assume that only 8-byte writes are p-atomic.

3. RELATED WORK

Persistent trees. Data structures are traditionally persisted using undo-redo logging and shadowing techniques. The rise of flash memory lead to the emergence of new optimized data structures such as the Bw-Tree [19]. However, these remain intrinsically tied to the logging and paging mechanisms, which SCM can completely do without. Indeed, the advent of SCM enables novel and more fine-grained techniques in designing persistent data structures, but it presents unprecedented challenges as discussed in Section 2. Several works proposed global solutions to these challenges, such as NVHeap [10], Mnemosyne [26], and REWIND [7], which are based on garbage collection and software transactional memory. However, these solutions incur additional overhead due to systematic logging of changed data, which adds up to the overhead caused by the higher latency of SCM. Another line of work relies on the persistence primitives provided by the CPU, namely memory barriers, cache line flushing instructions, and non-temporal stores to design persistent data structures that are stored in and accessed directly from SCM.

In this context, Venkataraman et al. [24] proposed the CDDS B-Tree, a persistent and concurrent B-Tree that relies on versioning to achieve consistency. It recovers from failures by retrieving the version number of the latest consistent version and removing changes that were made past that version. Nevertheless, its scalability suffers from using a global version number, and it requires garbage collection to remove old versions. Chen et al. [8] proposed to use unsorted nodes with bitmaps to decrease the number of expensive writes to SCM. They extended their work by proposing the write-atomic B-Tree (wBTree) [9], a persistent tree that relies on the atomic update of the bitmap to achieve consistency, and on undo-redo logs for more complex operations such as splits. It employs sorted indirection slot arrays in nodes to avoid linear search and enable binary search. Following another approach, Yang et al. [28] proposed the NV-Tree, a persistent and concurrent B-Tree based on the CSB$^+$-Tree [23]. They proposed to enforce the consistency of leaf nodes while relaxing that of inner nodes, and rebuilding them in case of failure. This approach assumes an SCM-only configuration, while our proposed *Selective Persistence* assumes a hybrid SCM-DRAM configuration, stores only primary data in SCM, and keeps the rest in DRAM to enable better performance. The NV-Tree keeps inner nodes contiguous in memory and uses unsorted leaves with an append-only strategy. This design implies the need for costly rebuilds when a leaf parent node overflows, and leads to a high memory footprint.

While the wBTree and the NV-Tree perform better than existing persistent trees, including the CDDS B-Tree, their performance is still significantly slower than fully transient counterparts. Additionally, they are oblivious to the problem of persistent memory leaks. Indeed, both the wBTree and the NV-Tree do not log the memory reference of a newly allocated or deallocated leaf, which makes these allocations prone to *persistent* memory leaks. Moreover, while the NV-Tree can retrieve its data thanks to using offsets, the wBTree does not elaborate on how data is recovered: It uses volatile pointers which become invalid after a restart, making data recovery practically infeasible. Our proposed FPTree successfully solves these issues.

Other related work. Arulraj et al. [5] studied different SCM-based database architectures and recovery strategies. They concluded that using in-place updates is the optimal approach as there is no need to reload primary data or to apply a redo log upon recovery since transaction changes are made persistent at commit time. Oukid et al. [21] proposed a novel database architecture where data is stored in and directly accessed from SCM, eliminating the need for traditional logging mechanisms. Kimura [18] presented FOEDUS, a novel database architecture that aims at scaling with many cores and very large SCM capacity. The FPTree can be a building block for such systems since it is based on the same architectural assumptions.

To manage SCM, Condit et al. [11] presented BPFS, a high performance transactional file system that runs on top of SCM. Nayaranan et al. [20] proposed Whole System Persistence where data is flushed only on power failures using the residual energy of the system, but do not consider software failures. Zhao et al. [30] proposed Kiln, a persistent memory design that leverages SCM to offer persistent in-place updates without logging or copy-on-write. However, they assume a non-volatile last level cache. Several works used SCM to optimize OLTP durability management, mainly by optimizing the logging infrastructure [13, 22, 27]. Finally, other works focused on optimizing database algorithms on SCM such as sorts and joins, but without leveraging the non-volatility property of SCM [8, 25].

4. FPTree DESIGN PRINCIPLES

We put forward the following design goals for the FPTree:

1. *Persistence.* The FPTree must be able to self-recover to a consistent state from any software crash or power failure scenario. We do not cover hardware failures in this work.
2. *Near-DRAM performance.* The FPTree must exhibit similar performance to transient counterparts.
3. *Robust performance.* The performance of the FPTree must be resilient to higher SCM latencies.
4. *Fast recovery.* The recovery time of the FPTree must be significantly faster than a complete rebuild of a transient B$^+$-Tree.
5. *High scalability.* The FPTree should implement a robust concurrency scheme that scales well in highly concurrent situations.
6. *Variable-size keys support.* The FPTree should support variable-size keys (e.g. strings) which is a requirement for many systems.

Figure 2 depicts the inner node and leaf node layouts of the FPTree. Since inner nodes are kept in DRAM, they have a classical main memory structure with sorted keys. Leaf nodes however keep keys unsorted and use a bitmap to track valid entries in order to reduce the number of expensive SCM writes, as first proposed by Chen et al [8]. Additionally, leaf nodes contain fingerprints which are explained in detail in Section 4.2. The next pointers in the leaves are used to form a linked list whose main goals are: (1) enable range queries, and (2) allow the traversal of all the leaves during recovery to rebuild inner nodes. The next pointers need to be *Persistent Pointers* in order to remain valid across failures. Finally, a one-byte field is used as a lock in each leaf.

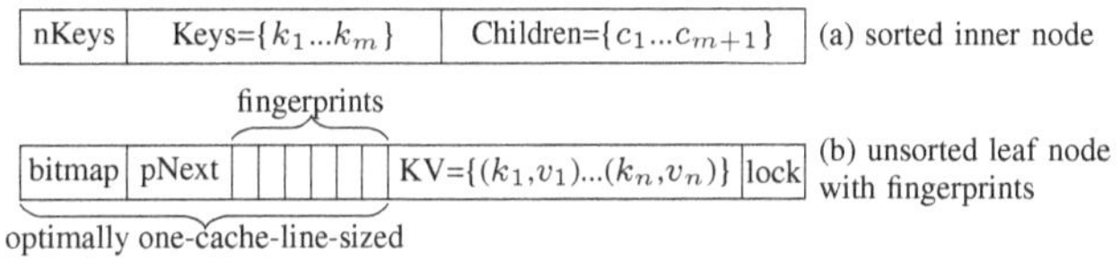

Figure 2: FPTree inner node and leaf node layouts.

In the following we present our proposed design principles that enable us to achieve the above design goals.

4.1 Selective persistence

Selective persistence can be described as keeping in SCM the minimal set of primary data on which all the implementation effort for consistency will be focused, and rebuilding all non-primary data that is placed in DRAM upon recovery. Applied to a B$^+$-Tree, as illustrated in Figure 3, the leaf nodes are placed in SCM using a persistent linked-list, while inner nodes are placed in DRAM and can be rebuilt as long as the leaves are in a consistent state. As a result only accessing the leaves is more expensive compared to a transient B$^+$-Tree. In addition, inner nodes represent only a small fraction of the total size of the B$^+$-Tree. Hence, selective persistence should enable our persistent tree to have similar performance to that of a transient B$^+$-Tree, while using only a minimal portion of DRAM. Our approach differs from that of the NV-Tree [28] in its underlying hardware assumptions: We assume a hybrid SCM-DRAM configuration while the NV-Tree assumes an SCM-only configuration.

In a nutshell, inner nodes will keep a classical structure and fully reside in DRAM without needing any special implementation effort, while leaf nodes will fully reside in SCM and require special care to

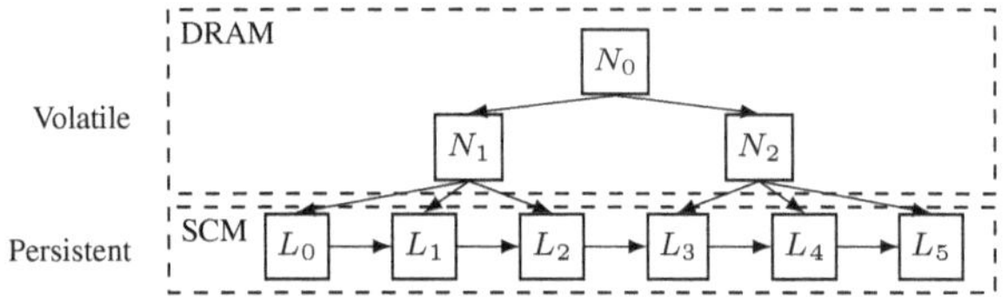

Figure 3: Selective persistence applied to a B+-Tree: inner nodes are kept in DRAM while leaf nodes are kept in SCM.

ensure their consistency. This interplay between SCM and DRAM is crucial for our concurrency mechanism we present in Section 4.4.

4.2 Fingerprints

Unsorted leaves require an expensive linear scan in SCM. To enable better performance, we propose a technique called *Fingerprinting*. Fingerprints are one-byte hashes of leaf keys, stored contiguously at the beginning of the leaf as illustrated in Figure 2. By scanning them first during a search, fingerprints act as a filter to avoid probing keys that have a fingerprint that does not match that of the search key. In the following we show that, theoretically, Fingerprinting enables a much better performance than the wBTree and the NV-Tree. We consider only the case of unique keys, which is often an acceptable assumption in practice [15]. We demonstrate that, using Fingerprinting, the expected number of in-leaf key probes during a successful search is equal to *one*. In the following we compute this expected number. We assume a hash function that generates uniformly distributed fingerprints. Let m be the number of entries in the leaf and n the number of possible hash values ($n = 256$ for one-byte fingerprints).

First, we compute the expected number of occurrences of a fingerprint in a leaf, denoted $E[K]$, which is equivalent to the number of hash collisions in the fingerprint array plus one (since we assume that the search key exists):

$$E[K] = \sum_{i=1}^{m} i \cdot P[K = i]$$

where $P[K = i]$ is the probability that the search fingerprint has exactly i occurrences knowing that it occurs at least once. Let A and B be the following two events:

- A: the search fingerprint occurs exactly i times;
- B: the search fingerprint occurs at least once.

Then, $P[K = i]$ can be expressed with the conditional probability:

$$P[K = i] = P[A|B] = \frac{P[A \cap B]}{P[B]} = \frac{\left(\frac{1}{n}\right)^i \left(1 - \frac{1}{n}\right)^{m-i} \binom{m}{i}}{1 - \left(1 - \frac{1}{n}\right)^m}$$

The nominator reflects the binomial distribution, while the denominator reflects the condition, i.e., the probability that at least one matching fingerprint exists, expressed as the complementary probability of that of no matching fingerprint exists.

Knowing the expected number of fingerprint hits, we can determine the expected number of in-leaf key probes, denoted $E_{FPTree}[T]$, which is the expected number of key probes in a *linear search* of length $E[K]$ on the keys indicated by the fingerprint hits:

$$E[T] = \frac{1}{2}\left(1 + E[K]\right) = \frac{1}{2}\left(1 + \sum_{i=1}^{m} i \frac{\left(\frac{1}{n}\right)^i \left(1 - \frac{1}{n}\right)^{m-i} \binom{m}{i}}{1 - \left(1 - \frac{1}{n}\right)^m}\right)$$

$$= \frac{1}{2}\left(1 + \frac{\left(\frac{n-1}{n}\right)^m}{1 - \left(\frac{n-1}{n}\right)^m} \sum_{i=1}^{m} \frac{i\binom{m}{i}}{(n-1)^i}\right)$$

$$= \frac{1}{2}\left(1 + \frac{\left(\frac{n-1}{n}\right)^m}{1 - \left(\frac{n-1}{n}\right)^m} \left(\frac{m}{n-1}\right) \sum_{i=0}^{m-1} \frac{\binom{m-1}{i}}{(n-1)^i}\right)$$

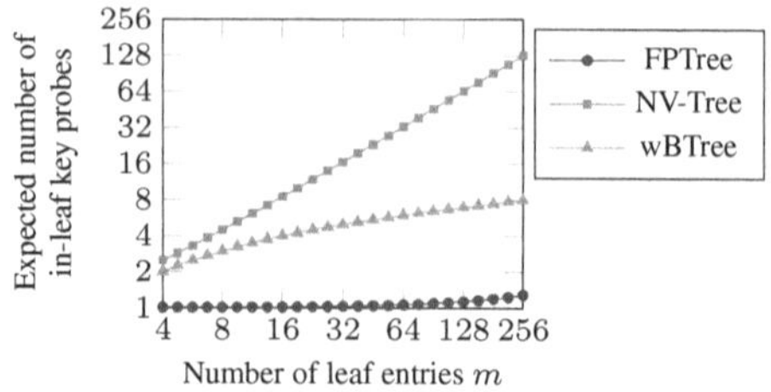

Figure 4: Expected number of in-leaf key probes during a successful search operation for the FPTree, NV-Tree, and wBTree.

By applying the binomial theorem on the sum we get:

$$E[T] = \frac{1}{2}\left(1 + \frac{\left(\frac{n-1}{n}\right)^m}{1 - \left(\frac{n-1}{n}\right)^m} \left(\frac{m}{n-1}\right)\left(\frac{n}{n-1}\right)^{m-1}\right)$$

$$= \frac{1}{2}\left(1 + \frac{m}{n\left(1 - \left(\frac{n-1}{n}\right)^m\right)}\right)$$

The wBTree is able to use binary search thanks to its sorted indirection slot arrays, hence, its expected number of in-leaf key probes is: $E_{\text{wBTree}}[T] = log_2(m)$. The NV-Tree scans a leaf by performing a reverse linear search, starting from the last entry of the leaf, so that if a matching key is found, it is guaranteed to be the most recent version. Then, the expected number of in-leaf key probes during a search operation for the NV-Tree is that of a linear search: $E_{\text{NV-Tree}}[T] = \frac{1}{2}(m + 1)$. Figure 4 shows the expected number of in-leaf key probes for the FPTree, the wBTree, and the NV-Tree. We observe that the FPTree theoretically enables a much better performance than the wBTree and NV-Tree. For instance, for $m = 32$, the FPTree needs a single in-leaf key probe, while the wBTree and NV-Tree need 5 and 16, respectively. Basically, fingerprinting requires less than two key probes in average up to $m \approx 400$. The wBTree outperforms the FPTree only starting from $m \approx 4096$. It is important to note that, in the case of variable-size keys, since only key references are kept in leaf nodes, every key probe results in a cache miss. Hence, every saved in-leaf key probe is a saved cache miss to SCM. This theoretical result is verified by our experimental evaluation as shown in Section 6.2.

4.3 Amortized persistent memory allocations

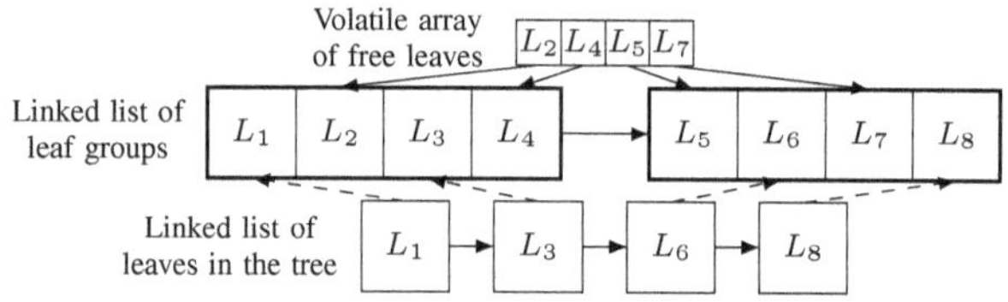

Figure 5: FPTree leaf groups management.

Since persistent allocations are expensive, allocating new leaves during splits is costly to the overall performance of the persistent tree. To remedy this issue, we propose to amortize the overhead of those allocations by allocating blocks of multiple leaves at once. As illustrated in Figure 5, leaves are managed through two structures:

- A linked-list of groups of leaves currently allocated;
- A volatile array of leaves currently free and not used in the tree.

Two methods are used to get and free leaves:

- *GetLeaf:* if the vector of free leaves is not empty, we pop the last element and return it. If it is empty, we allocate a new leaf group, append it to the linked list of groups, and add its leaves to the vector of free leaves, except the one that we return.
- *FreeLeaf:* when a leaf is freed, it is pushed into the vector of free leaves. If its corresponding leaf group is completely free, it is deallocated.

Using leaf groups allows to decrease the number of expensive persistent memory allocations which leads to better insertion performance, as shown in Section 6.2.

4.4 Selective concurrency

Transactional memory is a tool that simplifies concurrency by making a batch of writes atomically visible using transactions. HTM is hardware supported transactional memory. Several hardware vendors provide HTM, such as IBM on Blue Gene/Q and POWER8 processors, and Intel with Transactional Synchronization Extensions (TSX). Although we use Intel TSX in this work, our algorithms are valid for any currently available HTM implementation.

From a programmer's point of view, HTM is used as a coarse-grained lock around a critical section, but it behaves from the hardware point of view as a fine-grained lock: conflicts are detected between transactions at the granularity of a cache line. In the case of TSX, the critical code is put inside a transaction using the XBEGIN and XEND instructions. When a thread reaches the XBEGIN instruction, the corresponding lock is first read, and if it is available, a transaction is started without acquiring the lock. All changes made inside a transaction are made atomically visible to other threads by an atomic commit if the transaction is successful, that is, if it reaches the XEND instruction without detecting any conflicts. If the transaction aborts, all the buffered changes are discarded, and the operation is re-executed following a programmer-defined fall-back mechanism. In our implementation we use the Intel Threading Building Block[1] *speculative spin mutex* that uses a global lock as a fall-back mechanism.

To detect conflicts, each transaction keeps read and write sets in L1 cache. The read set comprises all the memory cache lines that the transaction reads, and the write set consists of all the memory cache lines that the transaction writes to. A conflict is detected by the hardware if a transaction reads from the write set of another transaction or writes to the read or write set of another transaction. When this happens, one of the two transactions is aborted. In this case, the aborted transaction falls back to a programmer-defined concurrency mechanism. To increase performance, a transaction is allowed to retry a few times before resorting to the fall-back mechanism. This is an optimistic concurrency scheme as it works under the assumption that only few conflicts will occur and the transactions will execute lock-free with high probability.

HTM is implemented in current architectures by monitoring changes using the L1 cache. Consequently, CPU instructions that affect the cache, such as CLFLUSH, are detected as conflicts which triggers the abortion of a transaction if they are executed within its read or write sets. A trivial implementation of HTM-based lock-elision for a standard B$^+$-Tree would be to execute its base operations within HTM transactions [17]. However, insert and delete operations would need to flush the modified records in the leaf, thus aborting the transaction and taking a global lock. This means that all insertion and deletion operations will in practice get serialized. Therefore, there is an apparent incompatibility between the use of HTM on the one hand and our need to flush the data to persistent memory to ensure consistency on the other hand. To solve this issue, we propose to use different concurrency schemes for the transient and the persistent parts of the data, in the same way we applied different consistency schemes for the data stored in DRAM and in SCM. We name our approach *Selective Concurrency*.

As illustrated in Figure 6, Selective Concurrency consists in performing the work that does not involve modifying persistent data inside an HTM transaction, and the work that requires persistence primitives outside HTM transactions. In the case of our FPTree, the

[1] https://www.threadingbuildingblocks.org/

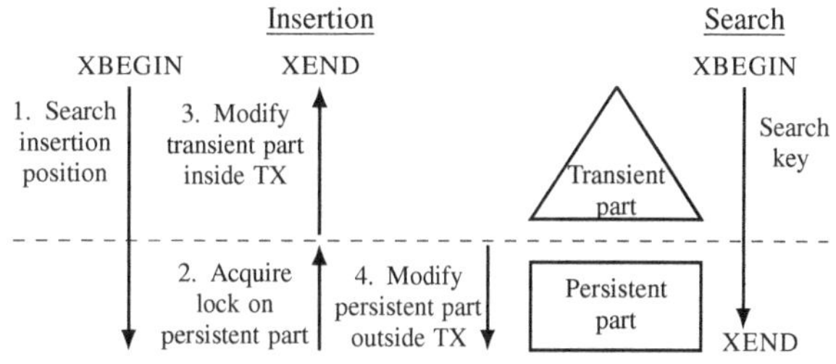

Figure 6: Selective Concurrency applied to a hybrid data structure.

traversal of the tree and changes to inner nodes only involve transient data. Therefore, these operations are executed within an HTM transaction and are thus protected against other operations done in concurrent HTM transactions. For other operations that cannot be executed inside the transaction, fine-grained locks are used. Basically, the leaf nodes to be modified are locked during the traversal of the tree inside the HTM transaction. After all modifications on the transient part are done, the transaction is committed. The remaining modifications on the persistent part are then processed outside of the transaction. Finally, the locks on the persistent part are released. The implementation of the base operations using TSX are detailed in Section 5.

5. BASE OPERATIONS

In this work, we implement three different persistent trees:

1. *FPTree.* It is the single-threaded version that implements selective persistence, fingerprinting, amortized allocations, and unsorted leaves.
2. *Concurrent FPTree.* This version implements selective persistence, selective concurrency, fingerprinting, and unsorted leaves. As for amortized allocations, since they constitute a central synchronization point, we found that they hinder scalability. Hence, they are not used in this version.
3. *PTree.* It reflects a light version of the FPTree that implements only selective persistence and unsorted leaves. Contrary to the FPTree and the wBTree, it keeps keys and values in separate arrays for better data locality when linearly scanning the keys.

In the following we discuss the base operations of the FPTree with fixed-size keys and explain how it can recover in a consistent state from any software crash or power failure scenario. A similar discussion is available for variable-size keys in Appendix C. Moreover, the algorithms for managing the leaf groups in the single-threaded version of the FPTree are explained in Appendix B. In the following, *speculative lock* denotes a TSX-enabled lock. Since leaf locks are only taken within TSX transactions, there is no need to modify them using atomics. Indeed, if many threads try to write the same lock –thus writing to the same cache line–, only one will succeed and the others will be aborted.

Find

Since search operations do not modify persistent data, they can be fully wrapped in a TSX transaction that protects them from conflicting with write operations of other threads. If another thread writes to a location read by the thread performing the lookup, the transaction will abort and retry, eventually taking a global lock if the retry threshold is exceeded. Search operations still need to check for any non-TSX lock (i.e., leaf locks) that might have been taken by another thread to perform changes outside a TSX transaction. Algorithm 1 shows the pseudo-code for the *Find* operation.

The *concurrent Find* is executed until it succeeds, making it retry as long as it aborts, which occurs either because the target leaf is locked or because a conflict has been detected. The speculative lock can execute in two ways: either a regular TSX transaction is started with the XBEGIN instruction as long as the TSX retry threshold is not reached, or a global lock is taken.

Algorithm 1 ConcurrentFind(Key K)

```
while TRUE do
    speculative_lock.acquire();
    Leaf = FindLeaf(K);
    if Leaf.lock == 1 then
        speculative_lock.abort();
        continue;
    for each slot in Leaf do
        set currentKey to key pointed to by Leaf.KV[slot].PKey
        if Leaf.Bitmap[slot] == 1 and Leaf.Fingerprints[slot] == hash(K)
        and currentKey == K then
            Val = Leaf.KV[slot].Val;
            Break;
    speculative_lock.release();
    return Val;
```

The way a transaction is aborted depends on the current situation: if a regular TSX transaction was started, the XABORT instruction will undo all changes (not relevant here since no changes were made), and rewind to the XBEGIN instruction. If the global lock was taken, the XABORT instruction has no effect. In this case, the ***while*** loop and the continue directive play the role of aborting and retrying. Upon reaching the leaf, and if its lock is not already taken, a lookup for the key is performed without taking the leaf lock. If another thread takes the leaf lock during the search for the key, a conflict is detected and one of the two transactions is aborted.

Insert

Algorithm 2 presents the pseudo-code of the *concurrent Insert* operation. It follows three steps: (1) Inside a TSX transaction, the tree is traversed to reach a leaf and lock it, and the information of whether a split is needed is propagated; (2) Outside a TSX transaction, changes to the insertion leaf are applied: a leaf split if needed, and the insertion of the key-value pair in the leaf. These operations use persistence primitives which would trigger an abort if used inside a TSX transaction; (3) If a leaf split occurred in step 2, the inner nodes are updated inside a second TSX transaction. This can be done in two ways: either by directly updating the leaf's parent node if it did not split while modifying the leaf, or by re-traversing the tree. The leaf lock is then released by setting it to 0. One can notice in Algorithm 2 that no **while** loop is used for the second transaction since inner nodes have no locks. Hence, there is no need to manually abort the transaction.

When no leaf split is needed, the key-value pair and the fingerprint are written to their respective slots and persisted. The order of these writes does not matter since they are not visible as long as the bitmap is not updated. Therefore, in case of a crash while writing the key and the value, no action is needed and the operation is considered as not completed. The bitmap is then p-atomically updated and persisted. In brief, if a failure occurs before the bitmap is persisted, the key-value pair was not inserted, otherwise, the operation successfully executed. In both cases, no action is required.

Algorithm 3 represents the pseudo-code for a leaf split. To ensure the consistency of the tree in case of failure during a split, we need to use a micro-log that consists of two persistent pointers: one pointing to the leaf to split, denoted *PCurrentLeaf*, and another pointing to the newly allocated leaf, denoted *PNewLeaf*. Basically, the concurrent FPTree contains split and delete micro-log arrays that are indexed by transient lock-free queues. A micro-log is provided by the lock-free queue and is returned at the end of the operation. The split recovery function is shown in Algorithm 4. The split operation starts by writing to *PCurrentLeaf* the persistent address of the leaf to split. If a failure occurs at this point, we only need to reset the micro-log, since *PNewLeaf* is still null. Then, we allocate a new leaf and provide a reference to *PNewLeaf* to the allocator, which persists the address of the allocated memory in *PNewLeaf* before returning. If a crash occurs at this point, the split recovery function checks whether *PNewLeaf* is null. If it is, it resets the micro-log and returns. Otherwise, it detects that the allocation did complete and thus continues the split operation. Thereafter, the content of the split leaf is persistently copied into the new leaf. The new key discriminator (split key) is then determined and the bitmap of the new leaf is updated accordingly. If a crash occurs during the latter two steps, the recovery function simply re-executes them when it detects that *PNewLeaf* is not null. Afterwards, the bitmap of the split leaf is updated and the next pointer of the split leaf is set to point to the new leaf. The latter write does not need to be p-atomic since in case of a failure at this point in time, the recovery function will redo the split starting from the copy phase. Finally, the micro-log is reset.

Algorithm 2 ConcurrentInsert(Key K, Value V)

```
Decision = Result::Abort;
while Decision == Result::Abort do
    speculative_lock.acquire();
    (Leaf, Parent) = FindLeaf(K);
    if Leaf.lock == 1 then
        Decision = Result::Abort; Continue;
    Leaf.lock = 1;            /* Writes to leaf locks are never persisted */
    Decision = Leaf.isFull() ? Result::Split : Result::Insert;
    speculative_lock.release();
if Decision == Result::Split then
    splitKey = SplitLeaf(Leaf);
slot = Leaf.Bitmap.FindFirstZero();
Leaf.KV[slot] = (K, V); Leaf.Fingerprints[slot] = hash(K);
Persist(Leaf.KV[slot]); Persist(Leaf.Fingerprints[slot]);
Leaf.Bitmap[slot] = 1; Persist(Leaf.Bitmap);
if Decision == Result::Split then
    speculative_lock.acquire();
    UpdateParents(splitKey, Parent, Leaf);
    speculative_lock.release();
Leaf.lock = 0;
```

Algorithm 3 SplitLeaf(LeafNode Leaf)

```
get µLog from SplitLogQueue;
set µLog.PCurrentLeaf to persistent address of Leaf;
Persist(µLog.PCurrentLeaf);
Allocate(µLog.PNewLeaf, sizeof(LeafNode))
set NewLeaf to leaf pointed to by µLog.PNewLeaf;
Copy the content of Leaf into NewLeaf;
Persist(NewLeaf);
(splitKey, bmp) = FindSplitKey(Leaf);
NewLeaf.Bitmap = bmp;
Persist(NewLeaf.Bitmap);
Leaf.Bitmap = inverse(NewLeaf.Bitmap);
Persist(Leaf.Bitmap);
set Leaf.Next to persistent address of NewLeaf;
Persist(Leaf.Next);
reset µLog;
```

Delete

The concurrency scheme of deletions, whose pseudo-code is shown in Algorithm 5, is very similar to that of insertions. The traversal of the tree is always done inside the TSX transaction which is aborted if the leaf is already locked by another thread. Upon reaching the leaf, three cases can arise: (1) The key to delete is not found in the leaf; (2) The leaf contains the key to delete and other keys; (3) The leaf contains only the key to delete.

Algorithm 4 RecoverSplit(SplitLog μLog)

```
1:  if μLog.PCurrentLeaf == NULL then
2:      return;
3:  if μLog.PNewLeaf == NULL then
4:      /* Crashed before SplitLeaf:4 */
5:      reset μLog;
6:  else
7:      if μLog.PCurrentLeaf.Bitmap.IsFull() then
8:          /* Crashed before SplitLeaf:11 */
9:          Continue leaf split from SplitLeaf:6;
10:     else
11:         /* Crashed after SplitLeaf:11 */
12:         Continue leaf split from SplitLeaf:11;
```

In the first case, we simply return that the key was not found (not indicated in Algorithm 5). In the second case that is similar to an insertion with no split, the leaf is locked and the TSX transaction is committed. Outside of the transaction, the bitmap position corresponding to the value to delete is set to 0 and persisted. Then, the leaf is unlocked. As discussed earlier this operation is crash-safe. In the third case, the leaf will be deleted. The inner nodes are modified inside the TSX transaction as no persistence primitives are needed. Basically, the key and pointer corresponding to the leaf are removed from its parent, possibly triggering further inner node modifications. We note that the leaf to be deleted does not need to be locked because it will become unreachable by other threads after the update of the inner nodes completes. The only node that needs to be updated outside of the TSX transaction is the left neighbor of the deleted leaf; its next pointer is updated to point to the next leaf of the deleted leaf. Before committing the transaction, this left neighbor is retrieved and locked. Finally, outside of the transaction, the next pointer of the left neighbor is updated, its lock released, and the deleted leaf is deallocated.

Algorithm 5 ConcurrentDelete(Key K)

```
1:  Decision = Result::Abort;
2:  while Decision == Result::Abort do
3:      speculative_lock.acquire();
4:      /* PrevLeaf is locked only if Decision == LeafEmpty */
5:      (Leaf, PPrevLeaf) = FindLeafAndPrevLeaf(K);
6:      if Leaf.lock == 1 then
7:          Decision = Result::Abort; Continue;
8:      if Leaf.Bitmap.count() == 1 then
9:          if PPrevLeaf->lock == 1 then
10:             Decision = Result::Abort; Continue;
11:         Leaf.lock = 1; PPrevLeaf->lock = 1;
12:         Decision = Result::LeafEmpty;
13:     else
14:         Leaf.lock = 1; Decision = Result::Delete;
15:     speculative_lock.release();
16: if Decision == Result::LeafEmpty then
17:     DeleteLeaf(Leaf, PPrevLeaf);
18:     PrevLeaf.lock = 0;
19: else
20:     slot = Leaf.FindInLeaf(K);
21:     Leaf.Bitmap[slot] = 0; Persist(Leaf.Bitmap[slot]);
22:     Leaf.lock = 0;
```

Algorithm 6 shows the pseudo-code for a leaf delete operation. Similarly to leaf splits, a leaf deletion requires a micro-log to ensure consistency. It consists of two persistent pointers, denoted *PCurrentLeaf* and *PPrevLeaf* that point respectively to the leaf to be deleted and to its previous leaf. The leaf delete function first updates *PCurrentLeaf* and persists it. If *PCurrentLeaf* is equal to the head of the linked list of leaves, its head pointer must be updated. If a crash occurs at this point, the delete recovery procedure (shown in Algorithm 7) detects that *PCurrentLeaf* is set and either itself or its next pointer is equal to the head of the linked list of leaves, and continues the operation accordingly. If the leaf to be deleted is not the head of the linked list of leaves, *PPrevLeaf* is updated and persisted. Then, the next pointer of the previous leaf of the leaf to be deleted is updated to point to the next pointer of the the latter. If a crash occurs at this point, the delete recovery procedure detects that the micro-log is fully set (i.e., both pointers are not null), and thus, it repeats the latter operation. Thereafter, in both cases, the deleted leaf is deallocated by passing *PCurrentLeaf* to the deallocate function of the allocator, which resets it to null. If a crash occurs at this point, the delete recovery function detects that *PCurrentLeaf* is null and resets the micro-log. Finally, the micro-log is reset.

Algorithm 6 DeleteLeaf(LeafNode Leaf, LeafNode PPrevLeaf)

```
1:  get the head of the linked list of leaves PHead
2:  get μLog from DeleteLogQueue;
3:  set μLog.PCurrentLeaf to persistent address of Leaf;
4:  Persist(μLog.PCurrentLeaf);
5:  if μLog.PCurrentLeaf == PHead then
6:      /* Leaf is the head of the linked list of leaves */
7:      PHead = Leaf.Next;
8:      Persist(PHead);
9:  else
10:     μLog.PPrevLeaf = PPrevLeaf;
11:     Persist(μLog.PPrevLeaf);
12:     PrevLeaf.Next = Leaf.Next;
13:     Persist(PrevLeaf.Next);
14: Deallocate(μLog.PCurrentLeaf);
15: reset μLog;
```

Algorithm 7 RecoverDelete(DeleteLog μLog)

```
1:  get head of linked list of leaves PHead;
2:  if μLog.PCurrentLeaf != NULL and μLog.PPrevLeaf != NULL then
3:      /* Crashed between lines DeleteLeaf:12-14 */
4:      Continue from DeleteLeaf:12;
5:  else
6:      if μLog.PCurrentLeaf != NULL and μLog.PCurrentLeaf == PHead
        then
7:          /* Crashed at line DeleteLeaf:7 */
8:          Continue from DeleteLeaf:7;
9:      else
10:         if μLog.PCurrentLeaf != NULL and μLog.PCurrentLeaf→Next
            == PHead then
11:             /* Crashed at line DeleteLeaf:14 */
12:             Continue from DeleteLeaf:14;
13:         else
14:             reset μLog;
```

Update

Algorithm 8 presents pseudo-code for the update operation. Although the update operation looks like an insert-after-delete operation, it is in fact much more optimized. Indeed, the update operation relies on the fact that the bitmap can be updated p-atomically to reflect both the insertion and the deletion at the same time. This has the advantage of maintaining the leaf size unchanged during an update, which makes leaf splits required only if the leaf that contains the record to update is already full. As for the recovery logic, it is exactly the same as for insertions, where a micro-log is needed to ensure consistency only in case of a leaf split.

Recovery

Algorithm 9 shows the pseudo-code for the concurrent FPTree recovery function. It starts by checking whether the tree crashed during initialization by testing a state bit. Then, for each micro-log in the micro-logs arrays, it executes either the leaf split or the leaf delete recovery function. Afterwards, it rebuilds inner nodes by traversing

Algorithm 8 ConcurrentUpdate(Key K, Value V)

```
Decision = Result::Abort;
while Decision == Result::Abort do
    speculative_lock.acquire();
    (Decision, prevPos, Leaf, Parent) = FindKeyAndLockLeaf(K);
    (Leaf, Parent) = FindLeaf(K);
    if Leaf.lock == 1 then
        Decision = Result::Abort; Continue;
    Leaf.lock = 1;
    prevPos = Leaf.FindKey(K);
    Decision = Leaf.isFull() ? Result::Split : Result::Update;
    speculative_lock.release();
if Decision == Result::Split then
    splitKey = SplitLeaf(Leaf);
slot = Leaf.Bitmap.FindFirstZero();
Leaf.KV[slot] = (K, V); Leaf.Fingerprints[slot] = hash(K);
Persist(Leaf.KV[slot]); Persist(Leaf.Fingerprints[slot]);
copy Leaf.Bitmap in tmpBitmap;
tmpBitmap[prevSlot] = 0; tmpBitmap[slot] = 1;
Leaf.Bitmap = tmpBitmap; Persist(Leaf.Bitmap);
if Decision == Result::Split then
    speculative_lock.acquire();
    UpdateParents(splitKey, Parent, Leaf);
    speculative_lock.release();
Leaf.lock = 0;
```

the leaves, resetting their locks, and retrieving the greatest key in each leaf to use it as a discriminator key. This step is similar to how inner nodes are built in a bulk-load operation. Finally, the queues of micro-logs are rebuilt.

Please note that micro-logs are cache-line-aligned. Thus, back-to-back writes to a micro-log that are not separated by other writes can be ordered with a memory barrier and then persisted together. Indeed, when two writes target the same cache line, the first write is guaranteed to become persistent no later than the second one.

Algorithm 9 Recover()

```
if Tree.Status == NotInitialized then
    Tree.init();
else
    for each SplitLog in Tree.SplitLogArray do
        RecoverSplit(SplitLog);
    for each DeleteLog in Tree.DeleteLogArray do
        RecoverDelete(DeleteLog);
RebuildInnerNodes();
RebuildLogQueues();
```

Variable-size keys

To support variable-sized keys (e.g., string keys), we replace the keys in inner nodes by virtual pointers to keys and those in leaf nodes by persistent pointers to keys. Ensuring consistency does not require any additional micro-logging compared to the case of fixed-size keys, although every insert or delete operation respectively involves a persistent allocation or deallocation of a key. Appendix C elaborates in detail on the FPTree base operations for variable-size keys and their corresponding recovery procedures.

6. EVALUATION

In this section we compare the performance of the FPTree with that of state-of-the-art persistent and transient trees.

6.1 Experimental setup

In addition to the PTree and the FPTree, we re-implemented the wBTree with indirection slot arrays and the NV-Tree as faithfully as possible with regard to their description in their respective original paper. To ensure the NV-Tree has the same level of optimization as the FPTree, we placed its inner nodes in DRAM. For the same purpose, we replace the wBTree undo-redo logs with the more lightweight FPTree micro-logs. As a reference transient implementation, we use the STXTree, an open-source optimized main memory B+-Tree[2]. The test programs were compiled using *GCC-4.7.2*. We use *jemalloc-4.0* as DRAM allocator, and our own persistent allocator for SCM.

Tree	Inner size	Leaf size	Key size	Memory
PTree	4096	32	8 bytes	SCM + DRAM
FPTree	4096	56	8 bytes	SCM + DRAM
NV-Tree	128	32	8 bytes	SCM + DRAM
wBTree	32	64	8 bytes	SCM
STXTree	16	16	8 bytes	DRAM
FPTreeC	128	64	8 bytes	SCM + DRAM
NV-TreeC	128	32	8 bytes	SCM + DRAM
PTreeVar	256	32	16 bytes	SCM + DRAM
FPTreeVar	2048	56	16 bytes	SCM + DRAM
NV-TreeVar	128	32	16 bytes	SCM + DRAM
wBTreeVar	32	64	16 bytes	SCM
STXTreeVar	8	8	16 bytes	DRAM
FPTreeCVar	64	64	16 bytes	SCM + DRAM
NV-TreeCVar	128	32	16 bytes	SCM + DRAM

Table 1: Chosen node sizes for the evaluated trees. Values are 8-byte integers for all trees. The suffixes *C* and *Var* indicate respectively the concurrent and variable-size keys versions of the trees.

To emulate different SCM latencies, we use a special system setup based on DRAM that provides two additional capabilities: (1) Part of the memory is separated out as a special memory region. We treat this memory region as *persistent memory*. It is managed by Persistent Memory File System (PMFS) [12], an open-source SCM-aware file system that like *tempfs*, gives direct access to the memory region with *mmap*; (2) Thanks to a special BIOS, the latency of this memory region can be configured to a specified value. A full description of this system can be found in [1].

This SCM evaluation platform is equipped with two Intel Xeon E5 processors. Each one has 8 cores, running at 2.6GHz and featuring each 32 KB L1 data and 32 KB L1 instruction cache as well as 256 KB L2 cache. The 8 cores of one processor share a 20 MB last level cache. The system has 64 GB of DRAM and 192 GB of emulated SCM. The same type of emulation system was used in [5, 12, 21]. In the experiments, we vary the latency of SCM between 160 ns (the lowest latency that can be emulated) and 650 ns. In addition, we use *ext4* with Direct Access[3] (DAX) support to emulate a DRAM-like latency of SCM (90 ns). DAX is a new feature in *ext4* that aims at supporting SCM-like devices. It is part of recent official Linux kernels releases. Similarly to PMFS, *ext4* DAX allows to do zero-copy memory mapping of files.

Unfortunately, the emulation system does not support TSX which prevents us from testing concurrency on this system. Hence, we use for concurrency tests a system equipped with two Intel Xeon E5-2699 v4 processors that support TSX. Each one has 22 cores (44 with HyperThreading) running at 2.1GHz. The system has 128 GB of DRAM. The local-socket and remote-socket DRAM latencies are respectively 85 ns and 145 ns. We mount *ext4 DAX* on a reserved DRAM region to emulate SCM.

We conducted a preliminary experiment to determine the best node sizes for every tree considered in the evaluation. Table 1 summarizes the results. We note that the best node sizes for the single-threaded and the concurrent versions of the FPTree differ. This is because larger inner nodes increase the probability of conflicts inside TSX transactions.

[2] https://panthema.net/2007/stx-btree/

[3] https://www.kernel.org/doc/Documentation/filesystems/dax.txt

6.2 Single-threaded micro-benchmarks

In this sub-section, we focus on the single-threaded performance of the base operations of the trees. In all our micro-benchmarks, we use uniformly distributed generated data. For fixed-size keys, keys and values are 8-byte integers, while for variable sized-keys, keys are 16-byte strings and values are 8-byte integers.

Base operations

To study the performance of the *Find*, *Insert*, *Update*, and *Delete* operations, we first warm up the trees with 50M key-values, then we execute back-to-back 50M *Finds*, *Inserts*, *Updates*, and *Deletes*. Figure 7 shows the performance results for different SCM latencies. For fixed-size keys, we observe that with an SCM latency of 90 ns (DRAM's latency), the FPTree outperforms the PTree, NV-Tree, and wBTree by 1.18x/1.48x/1.08x/1.08x, 1.47x/1.83x/2.63x/1.79x, and 1.97x/2.05x/1.81x/2.05x for *Find*/*Insert*/*Update*/*Delete*, respectively. The speedups increase up to 1.19x/1.63x/1.08x/1.02x, 1.92x/2.97x/3.65x/2.82x, and 3.93x/4.89x/4.09x/5.48x, respectively, with an SCM latency of 650 ns. We notice that compared with the STXTree, the FPTree and the PTree have better *Delete* performance with the lower SCM latencies because deletions consist in simply flipping a bit in the bitmap, while it consists in a sorted delete for the STXTree. Besides, the FPTree exhibits a slowdown of only 1.51x/1.67x/1.93x/1.21x and 2.56x/2.17x/2.76x/1.70x, for SCM latencies of 250 ns and 650 ns, respectively. The slowdowns for the PTree, NV-Tree, and wBTree are respectively 1.76x/2.46x/2.04x/1.21x, 2.47x/3.51x/5.78x/2.60x, and 4.32x/5.16x/5.25x/4.26x for an SCM latency of 250 ns, and 3.05x/3.55x/2.99x/1.73x, 4.92x/6.46x/10.09x/4.79x, and 10.07x/10.63x/11.30x/9.31x for an SCM latency of 650 ns. Moreover, we notice that the difference in performance between the FPTree and the PTree is greater for *Inserts* than for *Finds* and *Deletes*, showing the benefit of using leaf groups in addition to fingerprints.

At an SCM latency of 650 ns, the average time of an FPTree *Find* is 1.3 µs, which corresponds to the cost of two SCM cache misses: the first one to access the bitmap and fingerprints of the leaf node, and the second one to access the searched key-value. This is in line with our theoretical result of Section 4.2.

As for variable-size keys, the benefit of using fingerprints is more salient since any additional string key comparison involves a pointer dereferencing, and thus a cache miss. Indeed, for *Find*/*Insert*/*Update*/*Delete*, the FPTree outperforms the PTree, NV-Tree, and wBTree by 1.82x/1.65x/1.71x/1.24x, 1.72x/1.93x/4.80x/1.78x, and 2.20x/1.62x/2.15x/1.64x respectively for an SCM latency of 90 ns, and by increased speedups of 2.15x/2.16x/2.36x/1.35x, 2.50x/2.42x/8.19x/2.14x, and 2.93x/2.93x/5.43x/2.86x for an SCM latency of 650 ns. Another important observation is that the curves of the FPTree tend to be more flattened than those of the other trees, which denotes a decreased dependency with respect to the latency of SCM. Additionally, the FPTree outperforms the STXTree for *Find*/*Insert*/*Update*/*Delete* by 2.10x/ 1.13x/1.71x/1.22x at a latency of 90 ns, and thanks to fingerprinting, it is still 1.23x/1.02x faster for *Find*/*Update* at a latency of 650 ns, while the STXTree is 2.04x/1.99x faster for *Insert*/*Delete*.

Recovery

We evaluate the recovery performance of the trees, both for fixed-size and variable-size keys for different tree sizes and SCM latencies. Figure 7 depicts the experimental results. Since the wBTree resides fully in SCM, it exhibits constant recovery time, in the order of one millisecond, and thus it is not depicted in the figure. We observe that for a tree size of 100M entries, the FPTree recovers 1.52x/2.93x, and 5.97x/6.38x faster than the PTree and the NV-Tree for an SCM latency of 90 ns/650 ns, respectively. This difference between the FPTree and the PTree is explained by the leaf groups that provide more data locality when traversing the leaves. The slower recovery time of the NV-Tree is due to the inner nodes being rebuilt in a sparse way, requiring a large amount of DRAM to be allocated. The recovery of the FPTree is 76.96x and 29.62x faster than a full rebuild of the STXTree in DRAM, for an SCM latency of 90 ns and 650 ns, respectively.

Regarding variable-size keys, most of recovery time of the PTree, the FPTree and the NV-Tree is spent dereferencing the persistent pointers to the keys in the leaves to retrieve the greatest key in each leaf. The rebuild of the inner nodes itself represents only a minor part in the total rebuild time. This explains why all three implementations tend to perform the same for recovery. Nevertheless, for a tree size of 100M entries, the recovery of the FPTree is 24.68x and 5.68x faster than a full rebuild of the STXTree in DRAM, for an SCM latency of 90 ns and 650 ns, respectively.

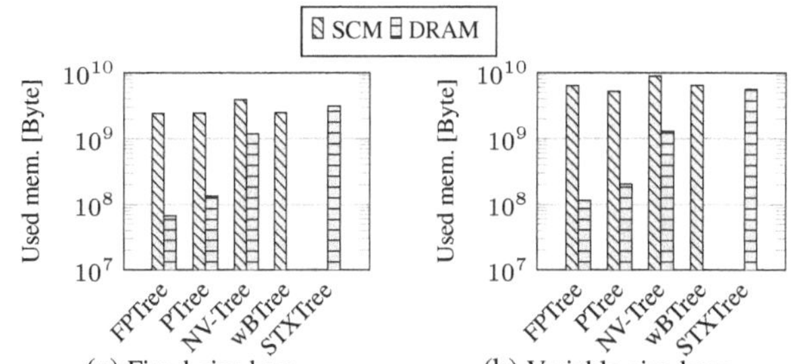

(a) Fixed-size keys (b) Variable-size keys

Figure 8: DRAM and SCM consumption of trees with 100M key-value: 8-byte and 16-byte keys for fixed-size and variable-size keys versions, respectively.

Memory consumption

Figure 8 shows DRAM and SCM consumption of the trees with 100M key-values and a node fill ratio of ~70%. Since the wBTree resides fully in SCM, it does not consume DRAM. We observe that for fixed-size keys, the FPTree needs 2.24 GB of SCM and only 64.12 MB of DRAM, i.e., only 2.71% of the total size of the tree. The PTree needs slightly more DRAM (5.19% of the size of the tree) because of its smaller leaves that lead to more inner nodes. The NV-Tree requires much more SCM and DRAM than the FPTree and the PTree: 3.62 GB of SCM and 1.09 GB of DRAM–which corresponds to 23.19% of the size of the tree. On the one side, the increase in SCM consumption is due to the additional flag that is added to every key-value and to the alignment of the leaf entries to be cache-line-aligned. On the other side, the increase in DRAM consumption is due to creating one leaf parent per leaf node when rebuilding the contiguous inner nodes. We observe similar results with variable-size keys, where consumed DRAM corresponds to 1.76% (108.73 MB), 3.78% (194.56 MB), and 12.67% (1.20 GB) of the total size of the tree for the FPTree, PTree, and NV-Tree, respectively. We note that the FPTree consumes slightly more SCM than the PTree due to the additional fingerprints in the leaves. The most salient observation is that the FPTree consumes one order of magnitude less DRAM than the NV-Tree.

6.3 Concurrent micro-benchmarks

For concurrency experiments, we use the HTM system that supports Intel TSX. We compare the fixed-size and variable-size concurrent versions of the FPTree and the NV-Tree. The experiments consist in warming up the trees with 50M key-values, then executing in order 50M concurrent *Finds*, *Inserts*, *Updates*, and *Deletes* with a fixed number of threads. We also consider a mixed workload made of 50% *Inserts* and 50% *Finds*. To eliminate result variations, we use the *numactl* utility to bind every thread to exactly one core. The resource allocation strategy is to first allocate all physical cores

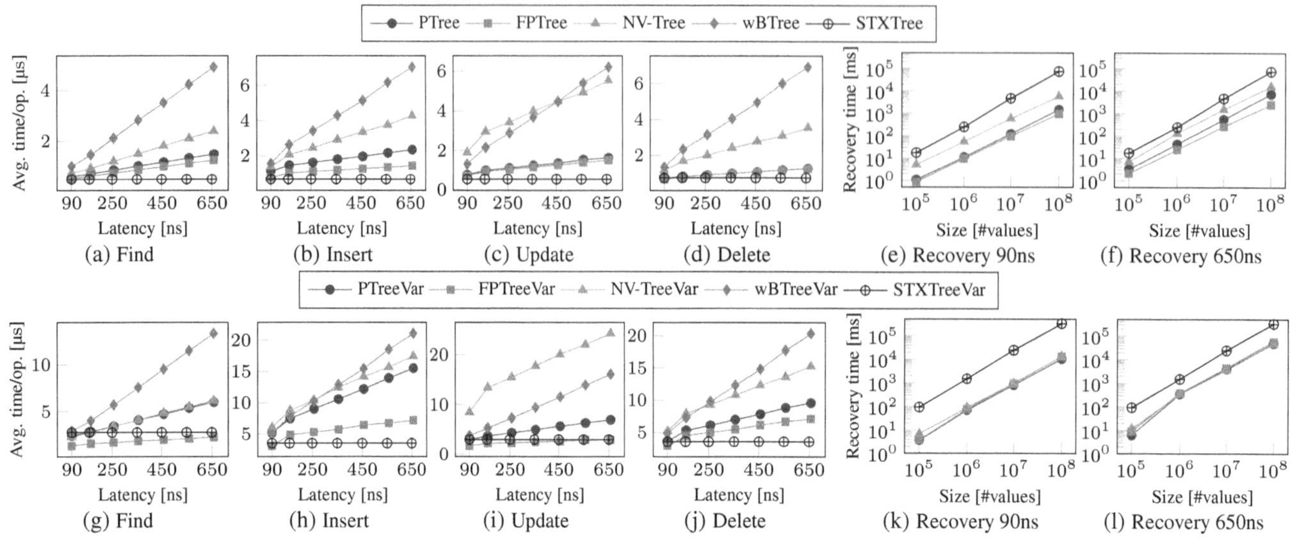

Figure 7: Effect of the latency of SCM on treess *Find*, *Insert*, *Update*, *Delete*, and *Recovery* operations performance.

before allocating the HyperThreads. When the two sockets are used, the cores are split equally between them.

We evaluate concurrency in three scenarios: on a single socket (up to 44 logical cores), on two sockets (up to 88 logical cores), and on one socket with a higher SCM latency. For each scenario we depict throughput figures alongside speedup figures over single-threaded execution. Ideal speedup is depicted with the mark-less line.

Single-socket experiments

Figure 9 depicts the results for scalability experiments on one socket. We observe that the FPTree scales well for both fixed-size and variable-size keys throughout the range of threads considered. In the case of fixed-size keys, performance is increased with 22 threads over single-threaded execution by a factor of 18.3/18.4/18.3/18.5/18.4 for the *Find/Insert/Update/Delete/Mixed* benchmarks, respectively. With 44 threads, and thus HyperThreading limiting the scaling, performance is increased over the execution with 22 threads by a factor of 1.57/1.55/1.56/1.63/1.56 for the *Find/Insert/Update/Delete/Mixed* benchmarks, respectively. Compared with the FPTree, the NV-Tree has lower base performances, and scales less. For fixed-size keys, its performance is increased with 22 threads over single-threaded execution by a factor of 16.4/11.5/14.1/11.2/15.1 for the *Find/Insert/Update/Delete/Mixed* benchmarks, respectively. With 44 threads, performance is increased over the execution with 22 threads by a factor of 1.49/1.73/1.07/1.74/1.61 for the *Find/Insert/Update/Delete/Mixed* benchmarks, respectively. We witness the same scalability patterns with variable-size keys. Between 45 and 88 threads, the performance of both the FPTree and the NV-Tree is stable and resists over-subscription.

Two-socket experiments

Results of the two-socket experiments are presented in Figure 10. We notice that the FPTree scales well for both fixed-size and variable-size keys. In the former case, the performance of the FPTree is increased using 44 threads compared with single-threaded execution by a factor of 36.8/36.3/37.5/37.6/36.7 for the *Find/Insert/Update/Delete/Mixed* benchmarks, respectively. Using HyperThreading, performance is increased with 88 threads over the execution with 44 threads by a factor of 1.50/1.30/1.34/1.53/1.37 for the *Find/Insert/Update/Delete/Mixed* benchmarks, respectively. As for the NV-Tree, it scales less than in the single socket scenario: performance is increased with 44 threads compared with single-threaded execution by a factor of 31.2/10.5/10.9/9.1/15.6 for the *Find/Insert/Update/Delete/Mixed* benchmarks, respectively. With 88 threads, performance is increased over the execution with 44 threads by a factor of 1.18/1.81/2.01/1.97/1.61 for the *Find/Insert/Update/Delete/Mixed* benchmarks, respectively.

Regarding variable-size keys, the FPTree's performance is increased with 44 threads compared with single-threaded execution by a factor of 37.2/35.0/38.4/38.5/34.9 for the *Find/Insert/Update/Delete/Mixed* benchmarks, respectively. Using HyperThreading, performance is increased with 88 threads over the execution with 44 threads by a factor of 1.54/1.63/1.63/1.62/1.67 for the *Find/Insert/Update/Delete/Mixed* benchmarks, respectively.

Single-socket experiments with a higher latency

To emulate a higher SCM latency, we bind the CPU and DRAM resources to one socket and use the memory of the second socket as emulated SCM. Hence, latency is increased from 85 ns (local socket latency) to 145 ns (remote socket latency). Figure 11 depicts the results for scalability experiments on one socket with an SCM latency of 145 ns. We observe that both the FPTree and the NV-Tree scale the same as with an SCM latency of 85 ns. The only difference is the decrease in throughput which is expected due to the higher emulated latency of SCM. Therefore, the scalability of our selective concurrency scheme is not affected by the latency of SCM.

Overall, the FPTree has better scaling and throughput performance than the NV-Tree, both for fixed-size and variable-size keys, for the three scenarios, namely using one socket, two sockets, and one socket with a higher SCM latency.

6.4 End-to-end evaluation

We integrated the evaluated trees in two systems: a single-level database prototype, and *memcached*, a popular key-value cache.

Database experiments

We replace the dictionary index of the dictionary-encoded, columnar storage engine of the database by the evaluated trees. Only the fixed-size keys versions of the trees are needed for the dictionary index. To measure the impact of the persistent trees on transaction performance, we run the read-only queries of the Telecom Application Transaction Processing Benchmark[4] (TATP) with 50M subscribers and 8 clients on the emulation system. The database size is ~45 GB.

During the warm-up phase where the database is created, *Subscriber Ids* are sequentially generated, thus creating a highly skewed

[4] http://tatpbenchmark.sourceforge.net/

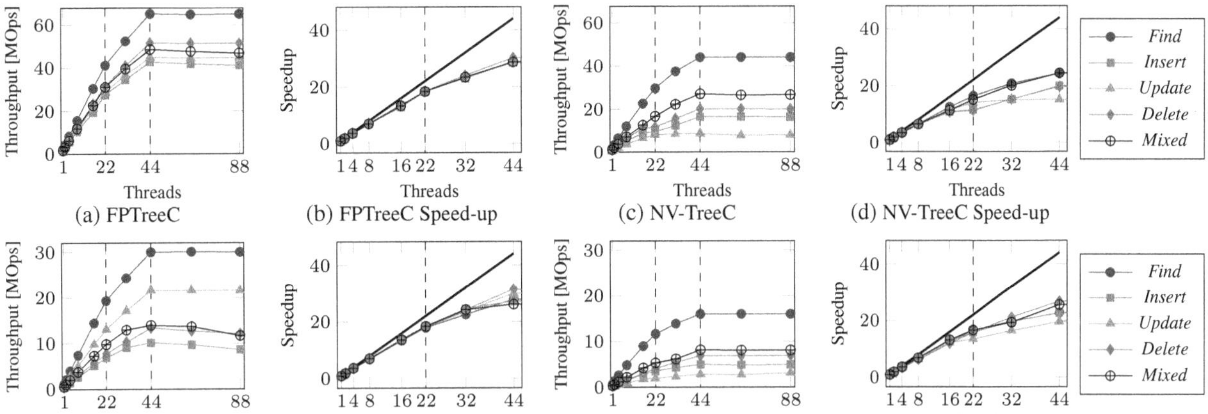

(a) FPTreeC (b) FPTreeC Speed-up (c) NV-TreeC (d) NV-TreeC Speed-up

(e) FPTreeCVar (f) FPTreeCVar Speed-up (g) NV-TreeCVar (h) NV-TreeCVar Speed-up

Figure 9: Concurrency performance on one socket – 50M key-values warmup followed by 50M operations.

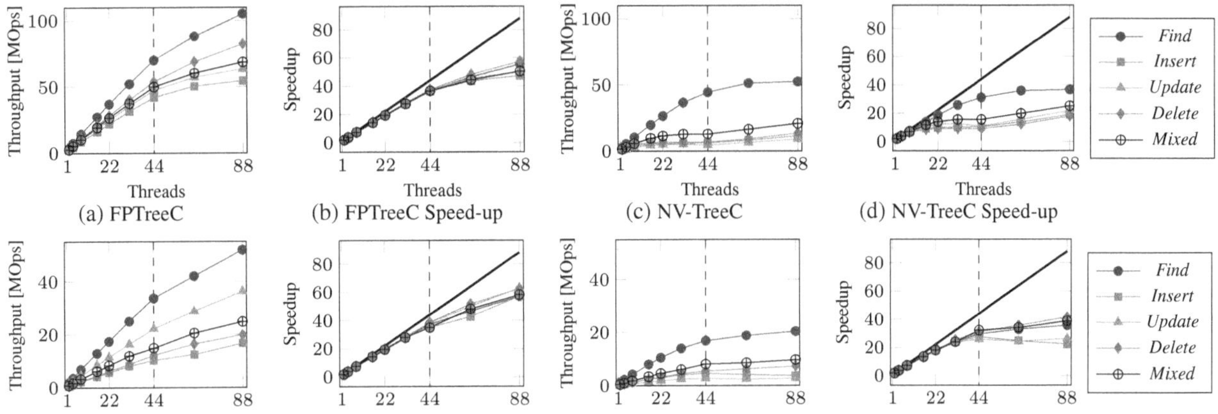

(a) FPTreeC (b) FPTreeC Speed-up (c) NV-TreeC (d) NV-TreeC Speed-up

(e) FPTreeCVar (f) FPTreeCVar Speed-up (g) NV-TreeCVar (h) NV-TreeCVar Speed-up

Figure 10: Concurrency performance on two sockets – 50M key-values followed by 50M operations.

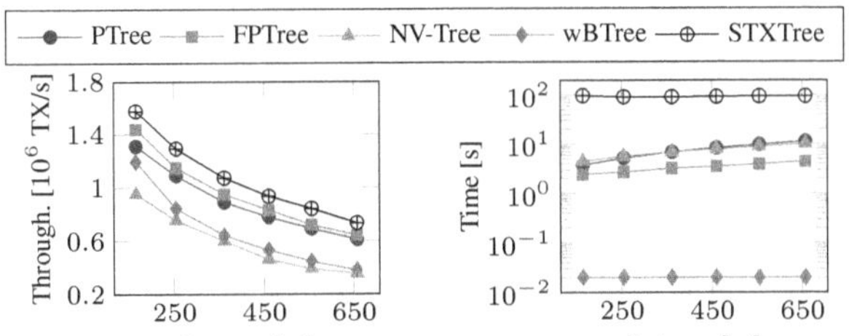

(a) DB throughput (b) DB restart time

Figure 12: Trees impact on database throughput and restart performance – TATP with 50M subscribers, DB size ~45GB.

insertion workload, a situation that the NV-Tree was unable to handle. Indeed, highly skewed insertions happen most often in the same leaf node. A last-level inner node will then quickly become full and trigger a costly rebuild of the inner nodes. The workload-adaptivity scheme of the NV-Tree tries to space the rebuild phases by dynamically increasing the size of write-intensive nodes at split time, which defers but does not solve the issue of frequent rebuilds in presence of sorted insertions. Eventually, the NV-Tree will have one parent node per leaf node which provokes a memory overflow in our system. To avoid this issue, we set the size of leaf nodes to 1024 and that of inner nodes to 8. The large leaf nodes aim at decreasing the number of inner node rebuilds, while the small size of inner nodes aims at keeping the memory footprint of inner nodes small, even in the case of having one parent node per leaf node.

The results are depicted in Figure 12a. We observe that compared with using the fully transient STXTree, the FPTree incurs an overhead of only 8.74%/12.80% for an SCM latency of 160 ns/650 ns, while the overheads incurred by the PTree, NV-Tree, and wBTree are 16.98%/16.89%, 39.61%/51.77%, and 24.27%/48.23%, respectively. On the one side, the limited slowdown caused by the FPTree and the PTree shows the significant benefit of selective persistence from which stems a decreased dependency with respect to the latency of SCM. On the other side, the FPTree outperforming the PTree shows the benefits of the fingerprints. The decrease in throughput with higher SCM latencies is due to other database data structures being placed in SCM. One can note that because of its larger leaf nodes, the NV-Tree performs worse than the wBTree.

To measure the impact on database recovery, we simulate a crash and monitor the restart time. We use the same benchmark settings as in the previous experiment. Recovery consists in checking the sanity of SCM-based data and rebuilding DRAM-based data. The recovery process is parallelized and uses 8 cores. Figure 12b shows restart time results. Since the wBTree resides fully in SCM, recovery is near-instantaneous –in the order of tens of milliseconds. However, using the wBTree incurs a severe overhead on query performance, as shown in Figure 12a. We observe that the FPTree, PTree, and NV-Tree allow respectively 40.17x/21.56x, 26.05x/8.32x, and 21.42x%/9.58% faster

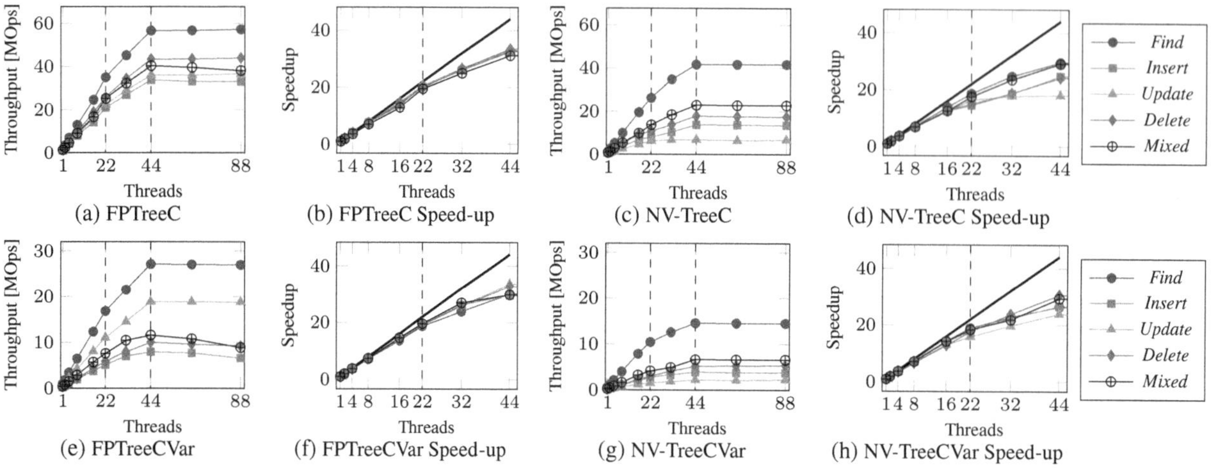

Figure 11: Concurrency performance on one socket with an SCM latency of 145 ns – 50M key-values warmup followed by 50M operations.

restart times for an SCM latency of 160 ns/650 ns than using the STXTree. One can note that the NV-Tree performs on par with the PTree thanks to its larger leaves which allow for more data locality while scanning the leaf nodes during recovery. Still, the FPTree outperforms the NV-Tree thanks to rebuilding compact inner nodes, and outperforms the PTree thanks to using leaf groups that provide better data locality when traversing the leaves during recovery.

Memcached experiments

Memcached[5] is a key-value cache that uses a main-memory hash table internally. It employs a locking mechanism on two levels: the first is global locks on the LRU lists of items, and the second is locks on the buckets of the hash table. We replace the hash table by the variable-size keys versions of the evaluated trees. Besides, we remove the bucket locking mechanism and replace it by global locks for non-concurrent trees and rely on the concurrency scheme of the concurrent ones. Another necessary change was to insert the full string key in the trees instead of its hash value to avoid collisions.

To measure the impact on performance, we run the *memcached* server on the HTM system, and the *mc-benchmark*[6] with 50 clients on the emulation system. The measured network bandwidth between the two machines is 940 Mbits/s. We found that using 2 workers in *memcached* yielded the best results for the single-threaded trees while 4 workers was the optimal for the concurrent ones. The *mc-benchmark* executes 50M SET requests followed by 50M GET requests. In addition, we use the same method as in the concurrency experiments to emulate a higher latency, that is, we bind *memcached* to one socket and use the memory of the other socket for SCM.

Figure 13 summarizes the experimental results. We observe that the NV-Tree and the concurrent version of the FPTree (denoted *FPTreeC* in the figure) perform nearly equally to vanilla *memcached* with the hash map table, for both latencies (85 ns and 145 ns) because their concurrent nature allows them to service requests in parallel and saturate the network. Indeed, the incurred overheads are less than 2% for the concurrent FPTree, and less than 3% for the NV-Tree. The single-threaded trees however incur significant overheads. Indeed, for SET/GET requests, the overheads incurred by the single-threaded FPTree, PTree, and wBTree are respectively 11.45%/0.29%, 40.37%/3.40%, and 45.57%/3.81% for an SCM latency of 85 ns. These overheads surge to respectively 37.28%/2.39%, 54.90%/24.06%, and 59.88%/32.40% with a higher SCM latency of

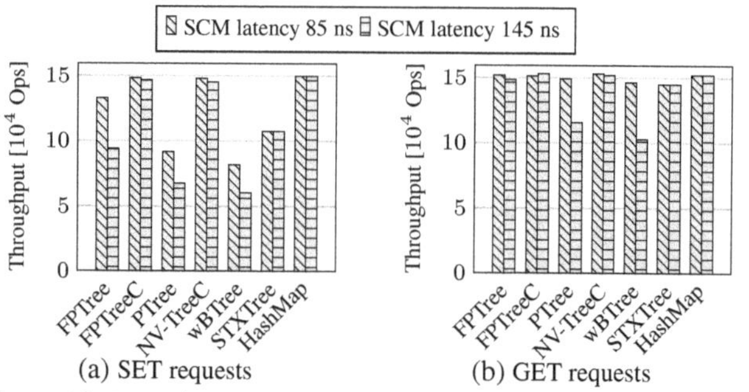

Figure 13: Trees impact on *memcached* performance for different latencies – *mc-benchkark* with 50M operations.

145 ns. As for the STXTree that resides fully in DRAM, it incurs an overhead of 28.29%/4.83% for SET/GET requests, respectively.

In conclusion, in both micro-benchmarks and end-to-end scenarios, the FPTree performs nearly equally to transient counterparts, significantly outperforms state-of-the-art persistent trees, and scales well in highly-concurrent situations.

7. CONCLUSION

In this paper, we proposed the *FPTree*, a novel hybrid SCM-DRAM persistent, concurrent B^+-Tree that supports both fixed-size and variable-size keys. Pivotal to the design of the FPTree are the following key principles: (1) fingerprinting; (2) selective persistence; (3) selective concurrency; and (4) state-of-the-art unsorted leaves.

These design principles make it possible to achieve the goals we put forward for our work: (1) the FPTree is persistent and guarantees any-point crash recovery to a consistent state without loss of information; (2) the FPTree exhibits fast recovery compared to a full rebuild; (3) the performance of the FPTree is similar to transient data structures, is resilient to high SCM latencies, and scales well in highly concurrent scenarios.

We perform an extensive experimental evaluation which shows that our FPTree exhibits significantly better base operation performance compared with state-of-the-art persistent trees, while using DRAM for less than 3% of its total size. Moreover, the FPTree recovery performance is almost one order of magnitude faster than a full rebuild. We conduct an end-to-end evaluation using *memcached* and a prototype database. We show that compared with a fully transient tree, the overhead of using the FPTree is limited to less than 2% and 13% for *memcached* and the prototype database, respectively, while using state-of-the-art persistent trees incur overheads of up to 60% and 52%, respectively.

[5] http://memcached.org/

[6] https://github.com/antirez/mc-benchmark

Acknowledgements

We thank the anonymous reviewers for their constructive comments that helped us improve the paper. We also thank Qingsong Wei for his help in figuring out the implementation details of the NV-Tree. Special thanks go to Ingo Müller for the fruitful discussions that helped refine the ideas of the paper, and to Roman Dementiev for his valuable help with TSX. This work is partially supported by the German Research Foundation (DFG) within the Collaborative Research Center "SFB 912/HAEC" as well as the Cluster of Excellence "Center for Advancing Electronics Dresden (cfaed)".

8. REFERENCES

[1] SR. Dulloor. *Systems and Applications for Persistent Memory.* PhD Thesis, 2016. https://smartech.gatech.edu/bitstream/handle/1853/54396/DULLOOR-DISSERTATION-2015.pdf.

[2] Intel®Architecture Instruction Set Extensions Programming Reference. Technical report, 2015. http://software.intel.com/en-us/intel-isa-extensions.

[3] SNIA NVM Programming Model V1.1. Technical report, 2015. http://www.snia.org/sites/default/files/NVMProgrammingModel_v1.1.pdf.

[4] D. Apalkov, A. Khvalkovskiy, S. Watts, V. Nikitin, X. Tang, D. Lottis, K. Moon, X. Luo, E. Chen, A. Ong, A. Driskill-Smith, and M. Krounbi. Spin-transfer torque magnetic random access memory (stt-mram). *ACM J. Emerg. Technol. Comput. Syst.*, 9(2), 2013.

[5] J. Arulraj, A. Pavlo, and S. R. Dulloor. Let's talk about storage & recovery methods for non-volatile memory database systems. In *ACM SIGMOD*, 2015.

[6] G. W. Burr, M. J. Breitwisch, M. Franceschini, D. Garetto, K. Gopalakrishnan, B. Jackson, B. Kurdi, C. Lam, L. A. Lastras, A. Padilla, et al. Phase change memory technology. *Journal of Vacuum Science & Technology B*, 28(2), 2010.

[7] A. Chatzistergiou, M. Cintra, and S. D. Viglas. Rewind: Recovery write-ahead system for in-memory non-volatile data-structures. *PVLDB*, 8(5), 2015.

[8] S. Chen, P. B. Gibbons, and S. Nath. Rethinking database algorithms for phase change memory. In *CIDR*, 2011.

[9] S. Chen and Q. Jin. Persistent b+-trees in non-volatile main memory. *PVLDB*, 8(7), 2015.

[10] J. Coburn, A. M. Caulfield, A. Akel, L. M. Grupp, R. K. Gupta, R. Jhala, and S. Swanson. Nv-heaps: Making persistent objects fast and safe with next-generation, non-volatile memories. *ACM SIGPLAN Not.*, 47(4), 2011.

[11] J. Condit, E. B. Nightingale, C. Frost, E. Ipek, B. Lee, D. Burger, and D. Coetzee. Better i/o through byte-addressable, persistent memory. In *ACM SOSP*, 2009.

[12] S. Dulloor, S. Kumar, A. Keshavamurthy, P. Lantz, R. Sankaran, J. Jackson, and D. Subbareddy. System software for persistent memory. In *EuroSys*, 2014.

[13] R. Fang, H.-I. Hsiao, B. He, C. Mohan, and Y. Wang. High performance database logging using storage class memory. In *IEEE ICDE*, 2011.

[14] G. Graefe. A survey of b-tree locking techniques. *ACM Transactions on Database Systems (TODS)*, 35(3):16, 2010.

[15] G. Graefe. Modern b-tree techniques. *Foundations and Trends in Databases*, 3(4):203–402, 2011.

[16] G. Graefe and H. Kimura. Orthogonal key-value locking. In *BTW*, 2015.

[17] T. Karnagel, R. Dementiev, R. Rajwar, K. Lai, T. Legler, B. Schlegel, and W. Lehner. Improving in-memory database index performance with intel® transactional synchronization extensions. In *IEEE HPCA*, 2014.

[18] H. Kimura. Foedus: Oltp engine for a thousand cores and nvram. In *ACM SIGMOD*, 2015.

[19] J. J. Levandoski, D. B. Lomet, and S. Sengupta. The Bw-Tree: A B-tree for new hardware platforms. In *IEEE ICDE*, 2013.

[20] D. Narayanan and O. Hodson. Whole-system persistence. In *ASPLOS XVII*, 2012.

[21] I. Oukid, W. Lehner, T. Kissinger, T. Willhalm, and P. Bumbulis. Instant recovery for main-memory databases. In *CIDR*, 2015.

[22] S. Pelley, T. F. Wenisch, B. T. Gold, and B. Bridge. Storage Management in the NVRAM Era. *PVLDB*, 7(2), 2013.

[23] J. Rao and K. A. Ross. Making B+- Trees cache conscious in main memory. In *ACM SIGMOD*.

[24] S. Venkataraman, N. Tolia, P. Ranganathan, and R. H. Campbell. Consistent and durable data structures for non-volatile byte-addressable memory. In *USENIX FAST*, 2011.

[25] S. Viglas. Write-limited sorts and joins for persistent memory. *PVLDB*, 7(5), 2014.

[26] H. Volos, A. J. Tack, and M. M. Swift. Mnemosyne: Lightweight persistent memory. *SIGPLAN Not., 47(4)*, 2011.

[27] T. Wang and R. Johnson. Scalable logging through emerging non-volatile memory. *PVLDB*, 7(10), 2014.

[28] J. Yang, Q. Wei, C. Wang, C. Chen, K. Yong, and B. He. Nv-tree: A consistent and workload-adaptive tree structure for non-volatile memory. *IEEE Transactions on Computers*, PP(99), 2015.

[29] J. J. Yang and R. S. Williams. Memristive devices in computing system: Promises and challenges. *ACM J. Emerg. Technol. Comput. Syst.*, 9(2), 2013.

[30] J. Zhao, S. Li, D. H. Yoon, Y. Xie, and N. P. Jouppi. Kiln: Closing the performance gap between systems with and without persistence support. In *IEEE/ACM MICRO-46*, 2013.

APPENDIX

A. PAYLOAD SIZE IMPACT

In this appendix we study the effect of the payload (value) size on the performance of the evaluated trees. We follow the same experimental setup as in Section 6 while varying the payload size from 8 bytes to 112 bytes. Figures 14b to 14d depict single-threaded performance results with an SCM latency set to 360 ns, while Figures 14e to 14f depict multi-threaded performance on a single socket with 44 threads. We observe two patterns: (1) The NV-Tree stands out as the tree that is most affected by larger payloads, which is explained by the fact that full linear scan of leaves needs to read larger amounts of data; (2) Insert operations tend to suffer more from larger payloads, which stems from the need for larger, more expensive SCM allocations. In general however, the performance of the FPTree and wBTree vary only slightly with larger payloads, thanks to them having respectively constant and logarithmic average leaf scan costs.

B. LEAF GROUPS MANAGEMENT

In this appendix we discuss how insert and delete operations make use of leaf groups in the single-threaded version of the FPTree.

Insert

The insert operation using leaf groups differs from the concurrent version of the FPTree in the split operation. Indeed the non-concurrent version of the FPTree employs leaf groups and does not allocate memory on every split. The same recovery logic as for insert operations without leaf groups applies and only the leaf allocation step is replaced by a call to the *GetLeaf* function (described in Algorithm 10). This function requires a micro-log that contains a single persistent pointer, denoted *PNewGroup*. Instead of directly allocating a new leaf, *GetLeaf* first checks whether there is a leaf that is available in the queue of free leaves, and if not, it will allocate a leaf group, add it to the linked list of leaf groups, and insert its members into the transient queue of free leaves, except the one that is returned. The corresponding recovery function is shown in Algorithm 11: if *PNewGroup* is not null, this means that the allocation took place and we can continue the operation as indicated in the pseudo-code. Otherwise, no action is required since the queue of free leaves is transient and rebuilt at recovery time.

Algorithm 10 GetLeaf(PLeafNode PLeaf)

```
1: μLog = Tree.GetLeafLog;
2: if Tree.FreeLeavesQueue.IsEmpty() then
3:     allocate(μLog.PNewGroup, sizeof(LeafNode)*GROUP_SIZE);
4:     Tree.PGroupsListTail.Next = μLog.PNewGroup;
5:     Persist(Tree.PGroupsListTail.Next);
6:     Tree.PGroupsListTail = μLog.PNewGroup;
7:     Persist(Tree.PGroupsListTail);
8:     μLog.Reset();
9:     insert Tree.PGroupsListTail in FreeLeavesQueue;
10: return Tree.FreeLeavesVector.Pop();
```

Algorithm 11 ReoverGetLeaf(GetLeafLog μLog)

```
1: if μLog.PNewGroup != NULL then
2:     if Tree.PGroupsListTail == μLog.PNewGroup then
3:         /* Everything was done except resetting the micro-log */
4:         μLog.Reset();
5:     else
6:         Continue from line GetLeaf:4;
```

Delete

The only difference between the Delete operation of the concurrent FPTree and the single-threaded FPTree is the leaf delete procedure. Indeed, the FPTree uses leaf groups and does not require a deallocation on every leaf deletion. Algorithm 12 shows the pseudo-code of the *FreeLeaf* function that replaces the deallocation function. This operation requires a micro-log that contains two persistent pointers, denoted *PCurrentGroup* and *PPrevGroup*. First, the procedure checks whether the leaf group to which the deleted leaf belongs is completely free. If it is, it will deallocate the leaf group and update the head of the linked list of groups if needed. Otherwise, it will push the deleted leaf into the transient queue of free leaves. The corresponding recovery function is depicted in Algorithm 13 and follows the same logic as the leaf delete recovery function that is detailed in Section 5: if *PCurrentGroup* is not null, this means that the micro-log was set but the deallocation did not take place. We can continue the operation starting by either updating the head of the linked list of groups, or by deallocating the group, as indicated in Algorithm 13. If *PCurrentGroup* is null, no action is needed since the queue of free leaves is transient and rebuilt at restart time.

Algorithm 12 FreeLeaf(LeafNode Leaf)

```
1: get head of the linked list of Groups PHead;
2: μLog = Tree.FreeLeafLog;
3: (Group,PPrevGroup) = getLeafGroup(Leaf);
4: if Group.IsFree() then
5:     delete Group from FreeLeavesQueue;
6:     set μLog.PCurrentGroup to persistent address of Group;
7:     Persist(μLog.PCurrentGroup);
8:     if μLog.PCurrentGroup == PHead then
9:         /* Group is the head of the linked list of Groups */
10:        PHead = Group.Next;
11:        Persist(PHead);
12:    else
13:        μLog.PPrevGroup = PPrevGroup;
14:        Persist(μLog.PPrevGroup);
15:        PrevGroup.Next = Group.Next;
16:        Persist(PrevGroup.Next);
17:    /* the deallocate function resets PCurrentGroup */
18:    deallocate(μLog.PCurrentGroup);
19:    reset μLog;
20: else
21:    push Leaf in FreeLeavesVector;
```

Algorithm 13 RecoverFreeLeaf(FreeLeafLog μLog)

```
1: get head of linked list of groups PHead;
2: if μLog.PCurrentGroup != NULL and μLog.PPrevGroup != NULL then
3:     /* Crashed between lines FreeLeaf:15-18 */
4:     Continue from FreeLeaf:15;
5: else
6:     if μLog.PCurrentGroup != NULL and μLog.PCurrentGroup ==
       PHead then
7:         /* Crashed at line FreeLeaf:10 */
8:         Continue from FreeLeaf:10;
9:     else
10:        if μLog.PCurrentGroup != NULL and
           μLog.PCurrentGroup→Next == PHead then
11:            /* Crashed at line FreeLeaf:14 */
12:            Continue from FreeLeaf:18;
13:        else
14:            reset μLog;
```

We note that to speed up *GetPrevGroup*, it can be implemented using a transient index on top of the linked list of free leaves.

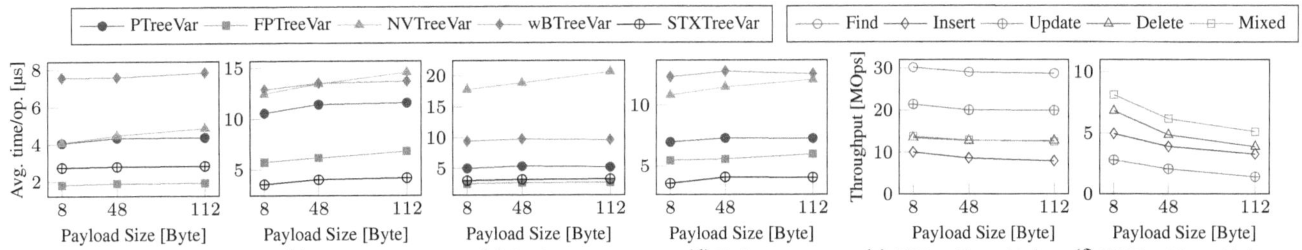

(a) Find (b) Insert (c) Update (d) Delete (e) FPTreeVar – 44 thr. (f) NVTreeVar – 44 thr.

Figure 14: Impact of payload size on the single-threaded and multi-threaded performance of the evaluated trees.

Algorithm 14 ConcurrentInsert_String(Key K, Value V)

```
Decision = Result::Abort;
while Decision == Result::Abort do
    speculative_lock.acquire();
    (Leaf, Parent) = FindLeaf(K);
    if Leaf.lock == 1 then
        Decision = Result::Abort; Continue;
    Leaf.lock = 1;
    Decision = Leaf.isFull() ? Result::Split : Result::Insert;
    speculative_lock.release();
if Decision == Result::Split then
    splitKey = SplitLeaf(Leaf);
slot = Leaf.Bitmap.FindFirstZero();
allocate(Leaf.KV[slot].PKey, strlen(K));
set NewKey to key pointed to by Leaf.KV[slot].PKey;
NewKey = K; Persist(NewKey);
Leaf.KV[slot].Val = V; Leaf.Fingerprints[slot] = hash(K);
Persist(Leaf.KV[slot].Val); Persist(Leaf.Fingerprints[slot]);
Leaf.Bitmap[slot] = 1; Persist(Leaf.Bitmap);
if Decision == Result::Split then
    speculative_lock.acquire();
    UpdateParents(splitKey, Parent, Leaf);
    speculative_lock.release();
Leaf.lock = 0;
```

Recovery

The recovery function of the non-concurrent FPTree is similar to that of its concurrent version, except that instead of iterating over the arrays of micro-logs, the non-concurrent version contains only one leaf split micro-log and one leaf delete micro-log. In addition, they differ in how the inner nodes are rebuilt. Indeed, the single-threaded FPTree traverses the linked list of leaf groups instead of traversing the linked list of leaves, which allows for more data locality. Besides, the keys that are retrieved from the leaves are unsorted and require to be sorted before proceeding to rebuilding inner nodes. Nevertheless, the benefits of increased data locality outperformed the cost of the additional sort, as shown in Section 6.2. We note that the transient vector of free leaves is rebuilt while traversing the list of leaf groups.

C. VARIABLE-SIZE KEY OPERATIONS

In this appendix we discuss the insert and delete operations of the concurrent FPTree with variable-size keys (string keys).

Insert

Algorithm 14 shows the pseudo code of the *concurrent Insert* operation. It is similar to its fixed-size keys counterpart. In particular, the leaf split operation is identical to that of fixed-size keys. The only difference is that for variable-size keys, we need to allocate persistent memory to store the insertion key. To ensure consistency, we do not need any additional micro-logging compared to fixed-size keys. When the insertion position is found, the new key is allocated by passing the key persistent pointer of the insertion position to the allocator that persistently writes the persistent address of the allocated memory to the provided persistent pointer. Then, the key to insert is persistently copied into the newly allocated key. Thereafter, the value and the fingerprint are persistently written in any order as they remain invisible until the bitmap is updated. Finally, the bitmap is persistently updated to make changes visible. If a crash occurs after the new key is allocated but before the bitmap is updated, the newly allocated key is a persistent memory leak. To detect this problem during recovery, it is sufficient to add the following additional check while traversing the leaves to rebuild inner nodes: for every unset bit in the bitmap of leaf, check whether its corresponding key persistent pointer is null (as it should be). If it is not, then we might have crashed during an insert operation, after having allocated the new key but before having updated the bitmap to reflect the insertion. Deallocating the key, as shown in the recovery procedure (Algorithm 17), is sufficient to set the tree back to a state of leak-free consistency.

Delete

Algorithm 15 shows the pseudo code of the *concurrent Delete* operation. It is similar to its fixed-size key counterpart. In particular, the leaf delete operation is identical to that of fixed-size keys. The only difference is that in this case, we need to deallocate the key that is deleted. Similarly to insert operations, there is no additional micro-log required to ensure crash-safety. Once the position of the key to be deleted is determined, the bitmap is updated and persisted to reflect the deletion. Finally, the deleted key is deallocated. A crash after updating the bitmap but before deallocating the key will lead to a persistent memory leak. Indeed, the key will be invisible since the bitmap has been updated and thus the key will never get deallocated. During recovery however, it is sufficient to conduct the same additional check as for insert operations: for every unset bit in the bitmap of leaf, check whether its corresponding key persistent pointer is null (as it should be). If it is not, then we might have crashed during a delete operation, after having updated the bitmap but before having deallocation the deleted key. All there is to do to recover to a consistent and leak-free state is to deallocate the keys pointed to by these non-null persistent pointers, as shown in Algorithm 17.

Update

Algorithm 16 shows the pseudo code of the *concurrent Update* operation. Similarly to the fixed-size key case, this operation is an optimized insert-after-delete operation where both the insertion and the deletion are made p-atomically visible by updating the bitmap. Compared to an insert operation, an update operation does not allocate memory, except when a split is needed. Indeed, instead of allocating a new key, the persistent pointer of the key is copied into a new location. After updating the bitmap, the persistent pointer of the old record location must be reset in order to ensure that a reference to a key exists only once. In the case of a crash after reflecting the update but before resetting the persistent pointer of the old record location, the recovery function might be mislead and

Algorithm 17 RebuildInnerNodes_String()

```
let MaxVector be a vector of keys;
for for Leaf_i in linked-list of leaves do
    let MaxKey be a key set to the smallest value of its domain;
    for each slot in Leaf_i.Bitmap do
        if Leaf_i.Bitmap[slot] == 1 then
            /* Find max key */
            set K to key pointed to by Leaf_i.KV[slot].PKey;
            MaxKey = MAX(K, MaxKey);
        else
            /* Test whether there is a memory leak */
            if Leaf_i.KV[slot].PKey != NULL then
                if KeyExists(Leaf_i, Leaf_i.KV[slot].PKey) then
                    Leaf_i.KV[slot].PKey.reset();
                else
                    deallocate(Leaf_i.KV[slot].PKey);
    MaxVector[i] = MaxKey;
rebuild inner nodes using MaxVector;
```

Algorithm 15 ConcurrentDelete_String(Key K)

```
Decision = Result::Abort;
while Decision == Result::Abort do
    speculative_lock.acquire();
    /* PrevLeaf is locked only if Decision == LeafEmpty */
    (Leaf, PPrevLeaf) = FindLeafAndPrevLeaf(K);
    if Leaf.lock == 1 then
        Decision = Result::Abort; Continue;
    if Leaf.Bitmap.count() == 1 then
        if PPrevLeaf->lock == 1 then
            Decision = Result::Abort; Continue;
        Leaf.lock = 1; PPrevLeaf->lock = 1;
        Decision = Result::LeafEmpty;
    else
        Leaf.lock = 1; Decision = Result::Delete;
    speculative_lock.release();
slot = Leaf.FindInLeaf(K);
Leaf.Bitmap[slot] = 0; Persist(Leaf.Bitmap);
deallocate(Leaf.KV[slot].PKey);
if Decision == Result::LeafEmpty then
    DeleteLeaf(Leaf, PPrevLeaf);
    PrevLeaf.lock = 0;
else
    Leaf.lock = 0;
```

might treat this as a crash during an insert or a delete operation, and deallocate the key, as described previously. To avoid this issue, whenever a deleted record with a non-null key persistent pointer is found, the recovery function checks whether there is a valid record in the same leaf that points to the same key. If there is one, the key persistent pointer simply needs to be reset. Otherwise, this means that the crash occurred during an insert or a delete operation and the key needs to be deallocated.

Algorithm 16 ConcurrentUpdate_String(Key K, Value V)

```
Decision = Result::Abort;
while Decision == Result::Abort do
    speculative_lock.acquire();
    (Decision, prevPos, Leaf, Parent) = FindKeyAndLockLeaf(K);
    speculative_lock.release();
if Decision == Result::Split then
    splitKey = SplitLeaf(Leaf);
slot = Leaf.Bitmap.FindFirstZero();
Leaf.KV[slot].PKey = Leaf.KV[prevSlot].PKey;
Leaf.KV[slot].Val = V;
Leaf.Fingerprints[slot] = Leaf.Fingerprints[prevSlot];
Persist(Leaf.KV[slot]); Persist(Leaf.Fingerprints[slot]);
copy Leaf.Bitmap in tmpBitmap;
tmpBitmap[prevSlot] = 0; tmpBitmap[slot] = 1;
Leaf.Bitmap = tmpBitmap; Persist(Leaf.Bitmap);
Leaf.KV[prevSlot].PKey.reset();
if Decision == Result::Split then
    speculative_lock.acquire();
    UpdateParents(splitKey, Parent, Leaf);
    speculative_lock.release();
Leaf.lock = 0;
```

Recovery

The recovery procedure of the FPTree with variable-size keys is identical to that with fixed-size keys, except for rebuilding inner nodes where the additional checks described above to catch memory leaks are added. Algorithm 17 shows the pseudo-code of the inner node rebuilding function.

Micro-architectural Analysis of In-memory OLTP

Utku Sirin* utku.sirin@epfl.ch
Pınar Tözün† ptozun@us.ibm.com
Danica Porobic* danica.porobic@epfl.ch
Anastasia Ailamaki* ‡ anastasia.ailamaki@epfl.ch

*École Polytechnique Fédérale de Lausanne
†IBM Almaden Research Center
‡RAW Labs SA

ABSTRACT

Micro-architectural behavior of traditional disk-based online transaction processing (OLTP) systems has been investigated extensively over the past couple of decades. Results show that traditional OLTP mostly under-utilize the available micro-architectural resources. In-memory OLTP systems, on the other hand, process all the data in main-memory, and therefore, can omit the buffer pool. In addition, they usually adopt more lightweight concurrency control mechanisms, cache-conscious data structures, and cleaner codebases since they are usually designed from scratch. Hence, we expect significant differences in micro-architectural behavior when running OLTP on platforms optimized for in-memory processing as opposed to disk-based database systems. In particular, we expect that in-memory systems exploit micro architectural features such as instruction and data caches significantly better than disk-based systems.

This paper sheds light on the micro-architectural behavior of in-memory database systems by analyzing and contrasting it to the behavior of disk-based systems when running OLTP workloads. The results show that despite all the design changes, in-memory OLTP exhibits very similar micro-architectural behavior to disk-based OLTP systems: more than half of the execution time goes to memory stalls where L1 instruction misses and the long-latency data misses from the last-level cache are the dominant factors in the overall stall time. Even though aggressive compilation optimizations can almost eliminate instruction misses, the reduction in instruction stalls amplifies the impact of last-level cache data misses. As a result, the number of instructions retired per cycle barely reaches one on machines that are able to retire up to four for both traditional disk-based and new generation in-memory OLTP.

Keywords

OLTP; Workload characterization; In-memory OLTP systems; Micro-architectural analysis

SIGMOD'16, June 26-July 01, 2016, San Francisco, CA, USA

DOI: http://dx.doi.org/10.1145/2882903.2882916

1. INTRODUCTION

Recent years have witnessed the rise of the in-memory or main-memory optimized OLTP systems [5, 19, 31]. Traditional OLTP engines are disk-based since they are designed in an era where the server hardware had a main-memory size in megabytes. Today, however, a server hardware with 1TB main-memory is a commodity. Therefore, the database management systems (DBMSs) are able to process the data working set of most OLTP applications in memory. This has led various vendors and researchers to design brand new OLTP engines optimized for the case where the hot dataset resides in memory [12, 14, 15, 27].

In-memory OLTP systems have several significant differences compared to disk-based systems. First, since the data working set resides mostly in memory, they omit the buffer pool component, which acts as the virtual memory of a DBMS and is, therefore, essential for the disk-based systems. Then, they tend to adopt more lightweight concurrency control mechanisms to avoid the scalability bottlenecks that arise due to traditional centralized locking. They also opt for cache-conscious indexes instead of the disk-optimized B-trees. Finally, since their codebases are written from scratch, they tend to have lighter storage engines in terms of the instruction footprint.

OLTP benchmarks are famous for their suboptimal micro-architectural behavior. There is a large body of work that characterizes OLTP benchmarks at the micro-architectural level [3, 6, 11, 23, 25, 28, 29]. They all conclude that OLTP exhibits high stall time ($>$ 50% of the execution cycles), and a low instructions-per-cycle (IPC) value ($<$ 1 IPC on machines that can retire up to 4 instructions in a cycle) [6]. The L1 instruction misses that mainly stem from the large instruction footprint of transactions are the main source of the stall time, while the next contributing factor is the long-latency data misses from the last-level cache (LLC) [28].

All the previous workload characterization studies, however, run the OLTP benchmarks on a disk-based OLTP engine. Considering the lighter components, cache-friendly data structures, and cleaner codebase of in-memory systems, one expects them to exhibit better cache locality (especially for the L1-I cache) and less memory stall time. Due to the distinctive design features of the in-memory systems from the disk-based ones, however, it is not straightforward to extrapolate how OLTP benchmarks behave at the micro-architectural level when run on an in-memory engine solely by looking at the results of previous studies.

In this paper, we perform a detailed analysis of the micro-architectural behavior of the in-memory OLTP systems. More specifically, we compare three in-memory OLTP systems (VoltDB [31], HyPer [9], and the in-memory OLTP engine of a closed-source commercial vendor) to two disk-based OLTP systems (Shore-MT [24] and a disk-based commercial DBMS) in terms of their IPC values, stall cycles, and cache misses while running simple micro-benchmarks as well as the more complex TPC benchmarks (TPC-B and TPC-C) [1]. Our analysis demonstrates the following:

- Despite all the design differences, in-memory OLTP behaves very similarly to the traditional disk-based OLTP at the micro-architectural level. More specifically, it spends more than half of the execution cycles in memory stalls, mostly due to L1-I misses, and exhibits low IPC.
- Even though the main-memory optimized DBMS components reduce the total instruction footprint at the storage manager side for the in-memory OLTP systems, the instruction footprint and code complexity of the rest of the components overshadow the benefits of these optimizations at the micro-architectural level.
- Transaction-specific compilation optimizations eliminate almost all the L1-I misses. However, the reduction in the instruction related stall time amplifies the impact of long-latency data misses when the data does not fit in LLC, and further reduces the IPC value.

The rest of the paper is organized as follows. Section 2 gives an overview of the in-memory OLTP systems and surveys related work on workload characterization and micro-architectural analysis studies. Section 3 describes the experimental methodology. Section 4 and Section 5 present the analysis results with a micro-benchmark and TPC benchmarks, respectively. Section 6 analyzes the effects of transaction compilation, index structures, and data types, whereas Section 7 investigates the impact of multithreading on the micro-architectural behavior. Finally, Section 8 discusses the results and Section 9 concludes.

2. BACKGROUND AND RELATED WORK

In-memory DBMSs have gained a lot of popularity in the last decade. In Section 2.1, we detail the underlying factors for this trend and the main design characteristics of in-memory OLTP systems. Then, in Section 2.2, we go over the recent workload characterization studies that focus on OLTP applications and highlight why they are not representative for in-memory OLTP systems.

2.1 In-memory OLTP

Commodity servers of the last decade follow two fundamental trends: (1) main-memory becoming cheaper and (2) number of cores increasing exponentially. Simply increasing the buffer pool size and the number of worker threads in the system to exploit the large main-memory and all the available cores, respectively, lead to marginal gains. Therefore, these two hardware trends have triggered alternative design opportunities for the new generation DBMSs.

As DRAM prices become cheap enough to buy 1TB main-memory for ~\$30K, today it is possible for most OLTP applications to keep all of their data working set in main-memory while running on a commodity server hardware. This has led to the development of various in-memory or main-memory optimized OLTP systems. These systems either manage all the data in main-memory or make sure that the hot data resides in main-memory. Since they manage to eliminate/minimize the disk I/O for the data page accesses, the overheads associated with managing the buffer pool overweigh its benefits [8]. Therefore, the in-memory OLTP systems omit the buffer pool component even though it is essential for the traditional disk-based DBMSs as it gives the illusion of an infinite main-memory to the system.

On the other hand, in step with Moore's law, the hardware vendors keep providing more and more opportunities for parallelism. Modern servers tend to have multiple multicore processors in the same machine and allow OLTP systems to handle increasing number of transactional requests in parallel. However, the traditional concurrency control mechanisms that ensure isolation among concurrent transactions using a centralized lock manager and two-phase locking are designed at an era where the server hardware were uniprocessors. Therefore, they do not scale on multicores preventing OLTP systems from exploiting the sheer number of cores available to them [22, 33].

In order to achieve better scalability on multicore architectures, in-memory OLTP systems adopt alternative concurrency control mechanisms. These mechanisms can be broadly grouped into two categories based on whether they partition the data or not. The ones that partition the data choose an extreme form of physical partitioning where there is a data partition for each core and a single worker thread for each partition. Systems like VoltDB [27] (or its ancestor H-Store [26]) and HyPer [12] deploy this approach. As a result, they can avoid any form of locking within a partition and need to coordinate worker threads only when a transaction requires data from multiple partitions (i.e., in the case of distributed transactions). On the other hand, the systems that prefer avoiding any kind of data partitioning, like Hekaton [14] or SAP HANA [15], rely on optimistic and multiversion concurrency control [4].

In addition to alternative concurrency control mechanisms, in-memory database systems also deploy cache-conscious index structures. They align the index page sizes to the size of a cache line as opposed to the size of a disk page and/or adopt lock-free index page access mechanisms rather than using traditional page latches [17, 30]. Moreover, the in-memory OLTP systems tend to depend on pre-determined stored procedures instead of ad-hoc queries [12, 14, 27] and apply efficient compilation optimization techniques that optimize the instruction stream for a particular transaction [14, 21]. Finally, the new-age in-memory OLTP systems have codebases that are implemented from scratch. Therefore, they are expected to have a cleaner codebase compared to the traditional disk-based systems where the codebase consists of many branch statements and patches due to different release versions spanning several decades of development.

Overall, in-memory OLTP engines deploy lighter storage manager components compared to the traditional disk-based systems aiming to utilize the resources of the modern server hardware in a more effective way.

2.2 OLTP at the Micro-architectural Level

There is a large body of related work analyzing the micro-architectural behavior of OLTP workloads. Barrosso et al. [3] investigate the memory system behavior of OLTP and DSS style workloads both on a real machine and with a full-system simulation. They argue that these two types of workloads would benefit from different architectural designs in terms of the memory system. Ranganathan et al. [23] perform a similar analysis. However, they only focus on the effectiveness of out-of-order execution on SMPs while running these workloads in a simulation environment. On the other hand, Keeton et al. [11] and Stets et al. [25] experiment only with OLTP benchmarks (TPC-B and TPC-C) on real hardware. All of these studies agree that OLTP workloads utilize the underlying micro-architectural resources very poorly, wasting most of the execution cycles on memory stalls and exhibiting a low IPC value.

Ailamaki et al. [2] examine where the time goes on four commercial DBMSs using a micro-benchmark to have a fine-grain understanding of the memory system behavior on multiprocessors, whereas Hardavellas et al. [7] analyze TPC-C and TPC-H on both in-order and out-of-order machines in a simulation environment. These studies focus on the implications for the DBMSs rather than the hardware to achieve better hardware utilization.

More recent workload characterization studies [6, 29] additionally analyze the TPC-E benchmark and show that micro-architecturally TPC-E behaves very similarly to the TPC-B and TPC-C benchmarks. These studies also corroborate the findings of the previous studies in terms of the inefficient use of the memory hierarchy when running OLTP. They highlight that the L1-I stalls are the dominant factor in the overall stall time followed by the long-latency data misses. Our experimental methodology while measuring various hardware events using counters on real hardware is very similar to the methodologies of these studies.

Harizopoulos et al. [8] demonstrate that traditional OLTP systems spend more than half of their execution time within the buffer pool, latching, locking, and logging components. On the other hand, Wenisch et al. [32] and Tozun et. al [28] tie the micro-architectural behavior of the disk-based OLTP into specific code modules by presenting the breakdown of the cache misses into specific code parts of the traditional OLTP software stack at different code granularities.

As Section 2.1 explains, the in-memory OLTP systems either remove or simplify most of the traditional disk-based OLTP components. Therefore, the micro-architectural behavior of OLTP workloads when run on disk-based systems cannot be representative for the in-memory systems. Even worse, the previous findings might mislead researchers and developers that aim to improve utilization at the micro-architectural level when running OLTP workloads using in-memory OLTP systems. Therefore, the focus of this paper is to perform a workload characterization study for OLTP benchmarks running on in-memory OLTP systems to understand the low-level differences between in-memory and disk-based OLTP; and based on these findings, provide valuable insights for OLTP systems' design.

3. SETUP AND METHODOLOGY

The experiments presented in this paper are executed on real hardware and performance is measured using event counters as opposed to hardware simulators since we are not investigating the impact of changing some of the hardware parameters on the micro-architectural behavior. The rest of this section details the setup and methodology for our study.

Hardware: We run experiments on a modern commodity server with Intel's Ivy Bridge processors. Table 1 shows the architectural details of this server. To collect numbers about various hardware events and break down the time spent in specific code modules, we use Intel VTune Amplifier XE 2015 [10], which provides an API for lightweight hardware counter sampling. We disable hyper-threading to obtain more precise hardware sampling values and increase predictability in measurements.

Table 1: Server Parameters

Processor	Intel(R) Xeon(R) CPU E5-2640 v2 (Ivy Bridge)
#Sockets	2
#Cores per Socket	8
#HW Contexts	16
Hyper-threading	Off
Clock Speed	2.00GHz
Memory	256GB
L1I / L1D (per core)	32KB / 32KB 8-cycle miss latency
L2 (per core)	256KB 19-cycle miss latency
LLC (shared)	20MB 167-cycle miss latency

OS: We run all the experiments using RHEL 6.5 with Linux kernel version 2.6.32.

Benchmarks: We run two types of benchmarks: micro-benchmarks and TPC benchmarks [1]. Our goal is to perform sensitivity analysis and have a more detailed understanding of the systems using the micro-benchmark, while the experiments using the TPC benchmarks serve to give an idea about the behavior of the systems when running well-known real-world applications.

The micro-benchmark uses a randomly generated table with two columns (`key` and `value`) of the type *Long*. It has two versions: read-only and read-write. The read-only version reads N random rows from the table, whereas the read-write version updates N random rows. Both versions use an index lookup operation on the randomly picked `key` value to reach the row to be read or updated. We also use a modified version of the micro-benchmark where we use the type *String* for both columns to quantify the impact of data type on micro-architectural utilization in Section 6.2.

As for the TPC benchmarks, we use TPC-B and TPC-C. We omit the more recent TPC-E benchmark since recent workload characterization studies demonstrate that TPC-E exhibits similar micro-architectural behavior to the TPC-B and TPC-C benchmarks [6, 29].

Analyzed Systems: We analyze three in-memory OLTP systems: *VoltDB* [31] (Community Edition Version 4.8), *HyPer* [9] (online demo-version), and the in-memory OLTP engine of a closed-source commercial vendor (*DBMS M*).

We pick these three systems as they are well-known in the community and their design characteristics represent a good variety among today's in-memory OLTP systems. While VoltDB and HyPer use physical data partitioning, DBMS M adopts optimistic multiversioned concurrency control. VoltDB uses traditional B-tree with node size tuned to the last-level cache line size [26]. HyPer implements adaptive radix tree with adaptive compact node sizes [16]. DBMS M implements both hash index and a variant of cache-conscious B-tree index similar to [17, 18]. For this system, we use the hash index for micro-benchmarks and TPC-B, and the B-tree index for TPC-C. Lastly, HyPer and DBMS M use transaction compilation techniques for the stored procedures [21], whereas VoltDB does not.

In order to gain better insights about the differences between the in-memory and disk-based OLTP systems, we also include two disk-based systems: the open-source *Shore-MT* [24] storage manager and a commercial system (*DBMS D*).

To implement benchmarks, we use VoltDB's Java-based developer front-end, HyPer's SQL-based programming language HyPerScript, Shore-MT's Shore-Kits suite that provides an environment to implement benchmarks for Shore-MT in C++, and the SQL frontend the closed-source commercial systems, DBMS M and DBMS D.

For all the systems, we use asynchronous logging. Therefore, there is no delay due to I/O in the critical path of the transaction execution.

Measurements: We populate the databases from scratch before each experiment and the data remains memory-resident throughout the experiment. In the following sections, we indicate the database sizes used in each experiment before discussing the results. In our experiments, both the database server process executing the transactions and the client processes generating the transactions run on the same machine. We first start the server process, populate the database, and then start the experiment by simultaneously launching all clients that generate and submit transactional requests to the database server.

We profile the database server process by attaching VTune to it during a 60-second benchmark run following a 60-second warm-up period. We report VTune counter results that correspond to the middle 30 seconds of the 60-second run in order to eliminate any peripheral effect that might happen during the initial or final part of the run. We repeat every experiment three times and report the average result.

In terms of micro-architectural efficiency, our goal is to observe how well each system exploits the resources of a single core regardless of the parallelism in the system. Therefore, all the experiments except for the ones in Section 7, use a single worker thread executing the transactions of the corresponding benchmark.

The choice of a single worker thread also eliminates contention due to several threads trying to access the shared data in the case of non-partitioned systems and distributed transactions in the case of partitioning-based systems. This way we avoid possible misleading micro-architectural conclusions. For example, high contention for a shared data page could lead to multiple threads spinning on a latch for that data page, thus artificially increasing the cache hit ratio.

We use one client to generate request in the single-threaded experiments. *Shore-MT*, *DBMS D*, *HyPer*, and *DBMS M* assign one worker thread per client. *VoltDB*, on the other hand, generates one worker thread per data partition, so we configure it to have only one partition. From VTune, we filter the hardware counter results particularly for the identified worker thread excluding the other threads that are responsible for background tasks, e.g., communication between the server and client, parsing transactions, etc.

In multi-threaded experiments (Section 7), we use multiple clients to generate requests for all systems except for *HyPer* whose online demo-version only supports single-client and single-threaded execution. For *VoltDB*, we also use multiple data partitions and ensure that all transactions access only a single partition. For each system, we gradually increase the number of clients, and profile the execution

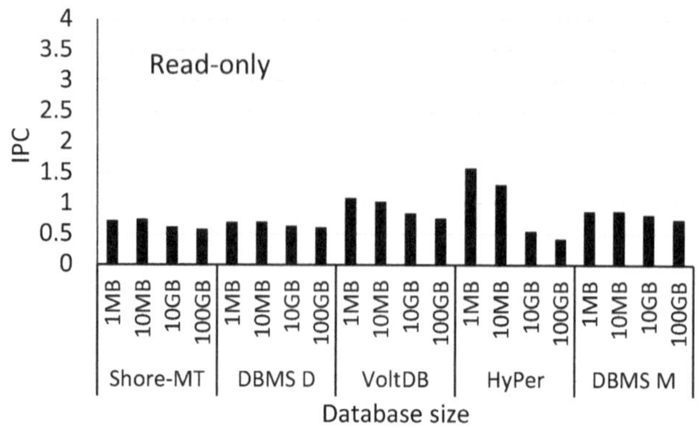

Figure 1: Effect of database size on the IPC value.

with the number of clients that give the highest aggregate throughput. From VTune, we filter hardware counter results for each worker thread separately and report their average.

Using the hardware performance counters, we measure the number instructions retired per cycle (IPC), and the instruction and data stall cycles from all the levels of the memory hierarchy. While reporting the stall cycles, we multiply the number of misses from each cache level with the expected penalty for that particular miss as specified in Table 1. For the last-level cache (LLC) misses, we average the penalty of going to local and remote memory. We note that one cannot be precise while showing the stall cycles breakdown on an out-of-order processor due to the overlapping of different execution components. Therefore, we draw the stall cycles due to different misses side-by-side rather than on top of each other.

4. MICRO-BENCHMARK

Before performing an analysis using the community standard TPC benchmarks, we devise a sensitivity study on the micro-architectural behavior of in-memory OLTP systems using the micro-benchmark. The goal of this study is to answer the following questions:

- How much instruction-level parallelism do OLTP benchmarks exhibit when run on an in-memory system? In other words, what is the number of instructions they can retire per cycle?
- Where do CPU cycles go when running in-memory OLTP? Are they wasted on memory stalls or used to retire instructions?
- Where do memory stalls come from within the memory hierarchy? Are they mainly due to instructions or data for in-memory OLTP?
- What is the impact of the database size on the above metrics?
- Does the amount of work done per transaction affect the results and, if yes, how?

To answer these questions, we break the analysis into two parts. The first part (Section 4.1) varies the database size by varying the number of rows in the table while keeping the amount of work done per transaction constant. On the other hand, the second part (Section 4.2) varies the amount

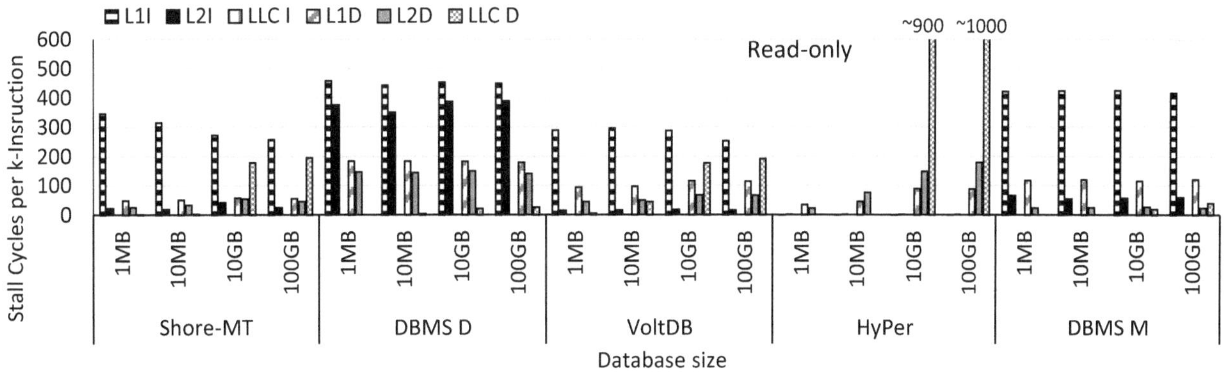

Figure 2: Stall cycles per 1000 instructions from the different levels of the memory hierarchy as we increase the database size.

of work done per transaction by increasing the number of rows read in a transaction while keeping the database size constant. Both parts measure the IPC value and stall cycles that arise due to different types of cache misses.

Since the trends are similar across the read-only and read-write versions of the micro-benchmark, we present the discussions about the read-only version of the micro-benchmark, and place the results and discussions about the read-write version in the Appendix, Section A.

4.1 Sensitivity to Data Size

To investigate the impact of database size on the micro-architectural behavior, we populate databases of size 1MB, 10MB, 10GB, and 100GB. Then, we collect hardware events as the systems run the micro-benchmark with a single transaction type that just reads/updates one random row after an index probe operation. While the results for the read-only version of the micro-benchmark are in the following sub-sections, the results for the read-write version of the micro-benchmark are in Section A.1 of the Appendix.

4.1.1 Instructions-per-Cycle

Figure 1 shows the number of instructions retired per cycle (IPC) on the y-axis for each system as the database size increases on the x-axis. The IPC values are similar for databases of sizes 1MB and 10MB since the data working set mainly fits in the last-level cache, which is 20MB (see Table 1). As we increase the database size to 10GB and 100GB, the IPC decreases since the data working set no longer fits in caches and the long-latency data misses become more significant (as shown in Section 4.1.2).

Where the two disk-based systems (*Shore-MT* and *DBMS D*) exhibit similar behavior in terms of their IPC values, the in-memory systems exhibit a slightly higher IPC value compared to the disk-based systems, except for *HyPer* with large database sizes.

Among the in-memory systems, *VoltDB* achieves a higher IPC value than *DBMS M*. On the other hand, *HyPer* achieves twice as high IPC value compared to the other systems when the data fits in the last-level cache. However, when the data does not fit in the last-level cache, *HyPer* suffers from long-latency data stalls, and hence, it has the lowest IPC value among all the systems.

Overall, even though the server used in our experiments is a 4-way issue one where each core has the ability to retire up to four instructions in a cycle, except for *HyPer* on datasets that fit in last-level cache, both the disk-based and in-memory OLTP systems barely achieve an IPC value of 1.

Since we investigate the impact of various memory-related stalls on the micro-architectural inefficiencies, we also conducted an experiment to measure IPC when there are no instruction or data misses in a program, which would be the ideal scenario in our study. For this experiment, we run a while loop accessing the same two integer variables repeatedly and assigning one's value to the other. The IPC value for this program after its cold start (after the compulsory data and instruction misses are over) is 3. Further investigation of this result is out of the scope of this paper.

4.1.2 Stall Cycles per 1000 instructions

Next, we analyze the causes of the low IPC values. Figure 2 plots the stall cycles per 1000 (k-)instructions coming from all the three levels of the cache hierarchy as we increase the data size on the x-axis. It also separates the instruction and data related stall cycles. For example, *L2D* represents the stall cycles due to data misses from the L2 cache.

From Figure 2, we observe that regardless of the database size, instruction stalls (mainly from *L1I* cache) are the most significant component in the overall stall cycles both for the disk-based and in-memory systems, except for *HyPer*. This shows that, despite all the optimizations described in Section 2.1, in-memory OLTP systems still dramatically suffer from instruction misses similar to the disk-based OLTP systems. On the other hand, these optimizations still help in reducing the instruction related stall time to some extent.

Among the traditional disk-based systems, *Shore-MT*'s instruction stalls are significantly lower than that of *DBMS D*. This is because *Shore-MT* is a storage manager and does not include the layers outside the storage manager component of an OLTP system such as query parser, query optimizer, and communication facilities. It hard-codes the query plan of the transaction in C++.

As the data size increases, *HyPer*'s data stalls increase dramatically, 5-10x more compared to the other systems. This mainly stems from *HyPer*'s high instruction locality. *HyPer* compiles transactions directly into machine code [20, 21]. Therefore, its transactions have an aggressively optimized instruction stream – small instruction footprint, few number of branches in the code, etc. As a result, *HyPer* is able to finish more transactions using the same number

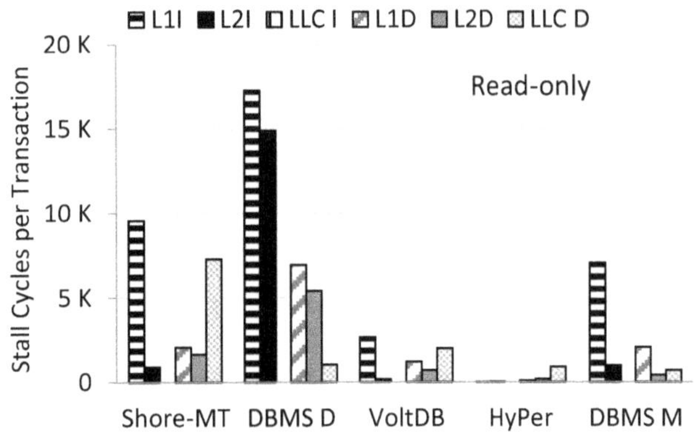

Figure 3: Stall cycles per transaction from the different levels of the memory hierarchy for a database of size 100GB.

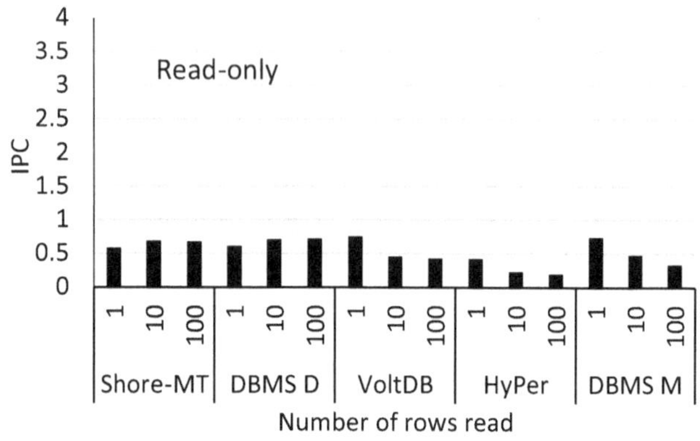

Figure 4: Effect of the amount of work per transaction on the IPC value with a database of size 100GB.

of instructions compared to the other systems. Hence, it touches more data randomly in a unit of time, which causes higher stall time due to long-latency data misses when the whole data set does not fit in *LLC*.

4.1.3 Stall Cycles per Transaction

The number of stall cycles per 1000 instructions provides an aggregated and normalized view of the stall cycles across different systems. In this section, we analyze the stall cycles per single transaction. Figure 3 shows the results for a database of size 100GB only since the results with different database sizes show similar trends.

The first observation is the dramatic decrease in *HyPer*'s LLC data stalls. While the *LLC* data stalls per 1000 instructions are 5-10x higher for *HyPer* than all the other systems, *HyPer*'s data stalls per transaction are among the lowest ones. This shows that *HyPer* executes large number of transactions in a period of time, and makes large number of random data accesses, hence, incurs many data stalls per 1000 instructions.

Except *Shore-MT*, all the other four systems have low *LLC* data stalls per transaction implying that they implement some variant of cache-conscious index structures. *VoltDB* implements a tree index where the node size is tuned to size of the last-level cache line [26]. While *HyPer* uses adaptive radix tree with adaptive compact node sizes [16], *DBMS M* implements hash index. *DBMS D* uses a traditional B-tree with page size of 8KB; however, we could not find any publicly available information about tuning the node size of *DBMS D* for being more cache-conscious. On the other hand, Shore-MT exhibits high *LLC* data stalls due to its non-cache-conscious index structure.

In terms of the instruction stalls, we observe that disk-based *DBMS D*'s instruction stalls are significantly higher than that of the in-memory systems. This highlights that the optimizations in-memory systems adopt help lower the instruction stalls. On the other hand, *DBMS M* has significantly higher *L1I* stalls than *VoltDB* and *HyPer*. This shows the relatively larger instruction footprint of *DBMS M* than that of the other in-memory systems. *DBMS M* is main-memory optimized OLTP engine of a traditional disk-based OLTP system similar to [5, 13, 18]. Therefore, it uses a lot of legacy code for the components outside the storage manager resulting in its relatively higher instruction footprint among the in-memory OLTP systems.

4.2 Sensitivity to Work per Transaction

To investigate the impact of the amount of work per transaction on the micro-architectural behavior, we increase the number of rows that a transaction accesses from 1 to 10 and then to 100. We perform these experiments with 100GB dataset. In the following sub-sections, we present the results for the read-only version of the micro-benchmark. The results for the read-write version of the micro-benchmark can be found in Section A.2 of the Appendix.

4.2.1 Instructions-per-Cycle

Figure 4 presents the IPC values as the number of rows read in a transaction increases on the x-axis. We observe that as the work done per transaction increases, the IPC values of the disk-based systems (*Shore-MT* and *DBMS D*) slightly increase, whereas the IPC values of the in-memory systems (*HyPer*, *VoltDB* and *DBMS M*) decrease. This stems from the changes in the instruction and the data stalls as more rows are read per transaction.

Instruction stalls decrease as the number of rows read increases. This is due to the repetitive work in a transaction which improves the instruction locality. On the other hand, increasing work per transaction in the micro-benchmark leads to more distinct data accesses in a period of time, which hinders data locality in caches and either limit the increase or cause a decrease in the IPC value.

4.2.2 Stall Cycles per 1000 instructions

To better understand the trends in the IPC values in Figure 4, we quantify the stall cycles per 1000 (k-)instructions coming from the different levels of the cache hierarchy similarly to Section 4.1.2. Figure 5 plots the results. The x-axis shows the number of rows read in a transaction.

As briefly explained in Section 4.2.1, the instruction stalls decrease as the number of rows read per transaction increase for all the systems. On the one hand, the repetitive behavior within a transaction leads to a better instruction cache locality. On the other hand, the code for the other layers of the system that surround a transaction's execution (e.g., the code outside the storage manager) is executed less frequently since the transactions get longer as we increase the amount of work done per transaction. For example, where

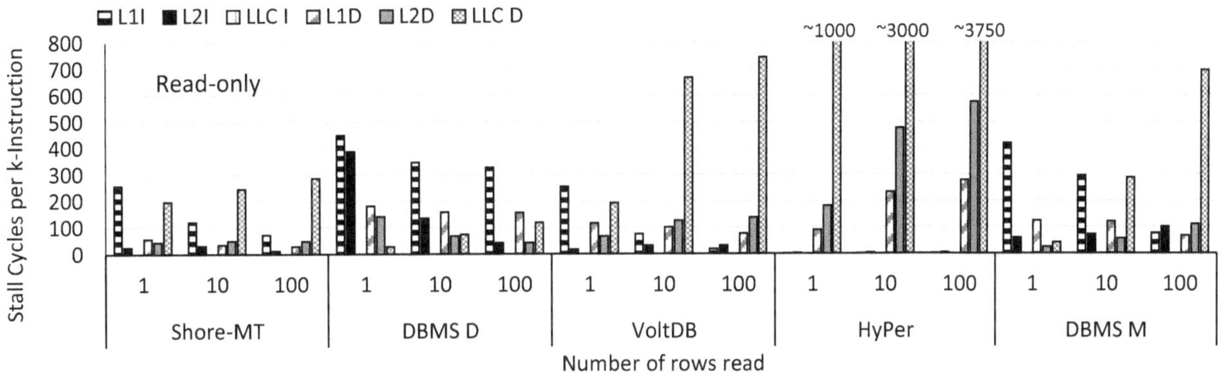

Figure 5: Stall cycles per 1000 instructions from the different levels of the memory hierarchy as we increase the amount of work done per transaction with a database of size 100GB.

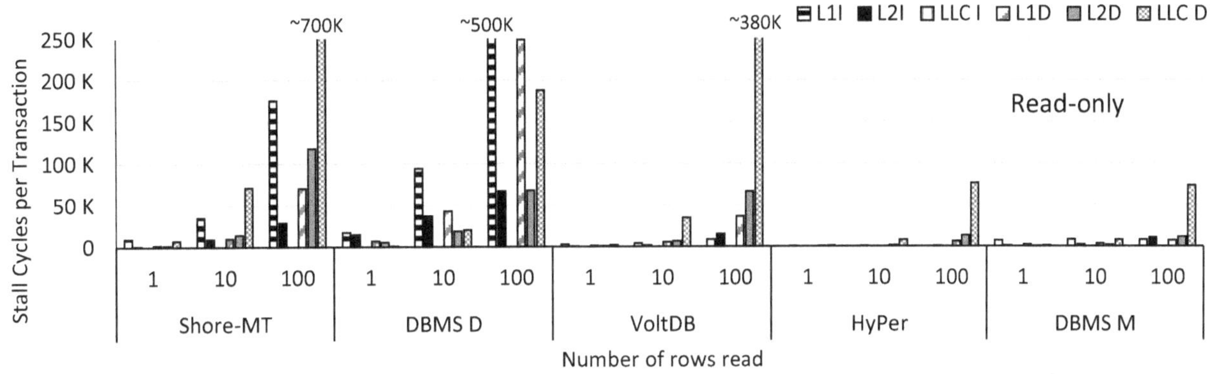

Figure 6: Stall cycles per transaction from the different levels of the memory hierarchy as we increase the amount of work done per transaction with a database of size 100GB.

probing 100 rows per transaction stresses purely the storage manager component of a system, probing 1 row also stresses the other layers such as query parsing, work done while starting/ending a transaction, etc.

While *DBMS M*'s instruction stalls are small for probing 100 rows, they are significantly higher for probing 1 and 10 rows compared to the other in-memory systems. This is because *DBMS M* inherits a lot of legacy code from the traditional disk-based OLTP system it belongs to. This brings a significant overhead on the total instruction footprint that can only be compensated by probing 100 rows per transaction. On the other hand, the low instruction stalls while probing 100 rows shows that the instruction footprint of the *DBMS M*'s storage manager (OLTP engine) is small. One reason for that is *DBMS M* compiles transactions into optimized machine code similar to, but less aggressively than, *HyPer*. Therefore, when stressed at the storage manager side, the compilation optimizations of *DBMS M* are also effective in reducing the instruction stalls. Section 6 quantifies the effect of compilation optimizations in *DBMS M* in more detail.

The data stalls increase as we increase the work done per transaction for all the systems. As we read more random rows per transaction, we access more distinct rows in a period of time. The more frequent random data accesses lead to a higher data miss rate for all the systems. *HyPer* has the highest data stalls for all the cases in Figure 5, since it executes more transactions, and hence, performs more frequent random data accesses compared to the other systems. For *Shore-MT*, *VoltDB*, and *DBMS M*, the *LLC* data stalls are also the dominant contributor to the stall time when accessing many rows per transaction. On the other hand, since *DBMS D* exhibits very high instruction stalls even when probing 100 rows per transaction, its throughput is lower and random data accesses are less frequent. Therefore, *DBMS D*'s LLC data stalls are the lowest.

4.2.3 Stall Cycles per Transaction

To better quantify the impact of accessing more data per unit of time, this section analyzes the stall cycles per transaction as the number of rows read increases from 1 to 100. Figure 6 plots the results. The x-axis shows the number of rows read in a transaction.

Unlike the results in the previous section, instruction stalls per transaction increase as the number of rows accessed in a transaction increases. When the instruction footprint of the loop that probes a random row in each iteration does not fit in the *L1I* and *L2I* caches, increasing the number of rows probed in a transaction increases the number of instruction stalls per transaction. We observe this effect for all the systems except for *HyPer*.

As we increase the number of rows read from 1 to 10, and then to 100, LLC data stalls increase almost linearly for all the systems. We observe that *Shore-MT* has the largest

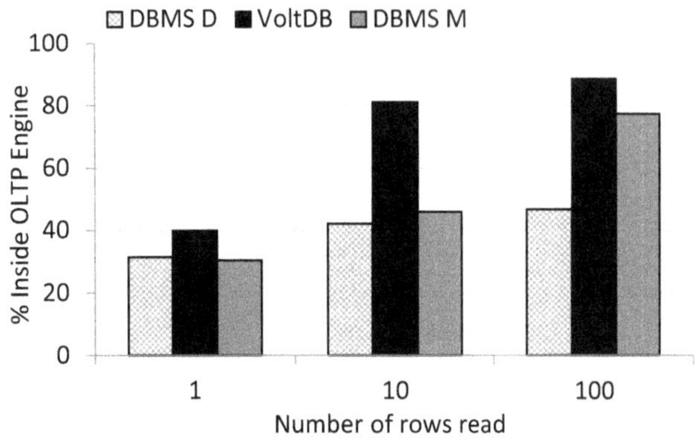

Figure 7: The percentage of the time spent inside the OLTP engine as we increase the amount of work done per transaction with a database of size 100GB.

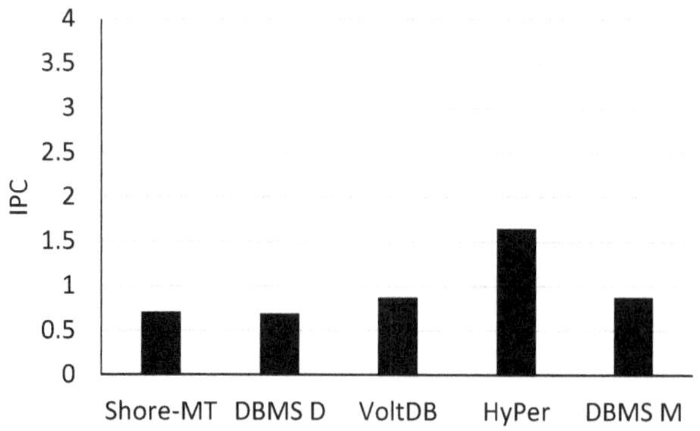

Figure 8: The IPC values while running TPC-B.

data stalls per transaction while probing 100 rows, followed by *VoltDB* and *DBMS D*. *DBMS M*'s hash-based index and *HyPer*'s adaptive radix tree lead to fewer random memory accesses during an index probe compared to the other system's B-tree-based index structures. Therefore, *DBMS M* and *HyPer* have the lowest LLC data stalls per transaction.

4.2.4 *Code Modules Breakdown*

To better understand the impact of legacy code, as well as components outside the storage manager, we quantify the percentage of the execution time spent in the OLTP engine as the amount of work per transaction increases for the disk-based system *DBMS D*, and the in-memory systems *VoltDB* and *DBMS M*. While performing this breakdown, we have done a best-effort categorization based on the code modules reported by VTune as part of the worker thread execution of each system. Figure 7 shows the results.

We observe that the amount of time spent inside the OLTP engine increases as the number of rows read increases for all three systems. This increase is modest for the disk-based system *DBMS D* showing the high overhead of the code outside the OLTP engine. For *DBMS M*, when we increase the number of rows from 1 to 10, the percentage inside the OLTP engine increases modestly showing the dominance of the legacy code overhead that *DBMS M* borrows from the traditional disk-based OLTP system it belongs to. However, when we increase the number of rows read from 10 to 100, we observe almost 2x increase in the percentage of time spent in the OLTP engine. For *VoltDB*, on the other hand, the amount of time spent inside the storage manager is small for probing 1 row showing the high overhead of the code outside the storage manager for light transactions. However, when we increase the number of probed rows to 10 or 100, the percentage increases more than 2x showing that *VoltDB* compensates this overhead for medium/large-sized transactions.

4.3 Summary

Overall, while the traditional disk-based systems, *Shore-MT* and *DBMS D*, have large instruction footprints and bad instruction locality; the in-memory-optimized systems, *HyPer*, *VoltDB*, and *DBMS M* (when stressed enough on the storage manager) have small, optimized instruction footprints and good instruction locality. The reduction in instruction footprint and the increase in instruction locality, however, lead to more random data accesses in a unit of time and, hence, increase long-latency data stalls when the data working set does not fit in the last-level cache. Therefore, all the systems suffer either from instruction or data stalls resulting in severe under-utilization of the micro-architectural resources having executed barely one instruction-per-cycle on a machine that has the ability of retiring up to four instruction-per-cycle.

5. TPC BENCHMARKS

Section 4 performs a sensitivity analysis using a simple micro-benchmark to gain a fine-grained understanding of the in-memory OLTP systems compared to the disk-based ones at the micro-architectural level. This section investigates the behavior of the same systems while running the more complex and community standard TPC-B (Section 5.1) and TPC-C (Section 5.2) benchmarks. All the experiments in this section use a database of size 100GB. Similar to Section 4, we analyze the IPC values, and the stall cycles per 1000 instructions and per transaction from different levels of the cache hierarchy. Our goal is to observe how the benchmark complexity affects the micro-architectural behavior of the in-memory OLTP systems.

5.1 TPC-B

TPC-B is an update-heavy benchmark that simulates a banking system. `AccountUpdate` is its only transaction type, which updates one row each in three tables, `Branch`, `Teller`, and `Account`, and appends a row to the `History` table.

5.1.1 *Instructions-per-Cycle*

Figure 8 shows the number of instructions retired per cycle (IPC) on the y-axis as each system runs TPC-B. *HyPer* exhibits the highest IPC value among all the systems, which is in contrast with its IPC being the lowest when running the micro-benchmark (Section 4.2.1). Moreover, we see that the IPC values are in general higher than the IPC values for the read-only micro-benchmark with 100GB data for probing 1 row (Figure 4). This is due to the higher data locality in TPC-B (see also Section 5.1.2). Since `Branch` and `Teller` tables have low cardinality, the probability of a randomly read row from one of these two tables being in *LLC* is high. In addition, `History` table accesses are only appends, which also increases the probability of the `History` table pages be-

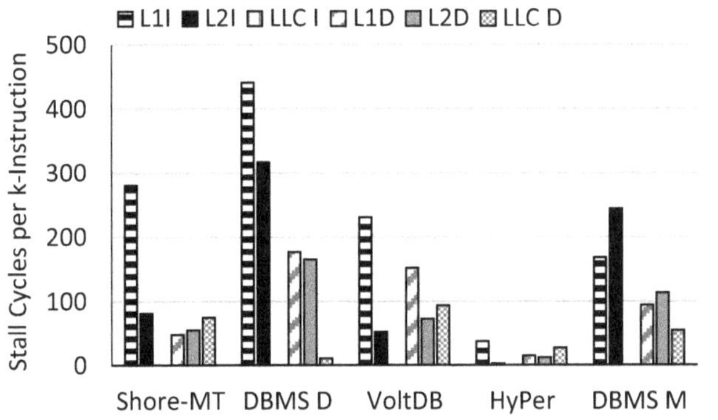

Figure 9: Stall cycles per 1000 instructions while running TPC-B.

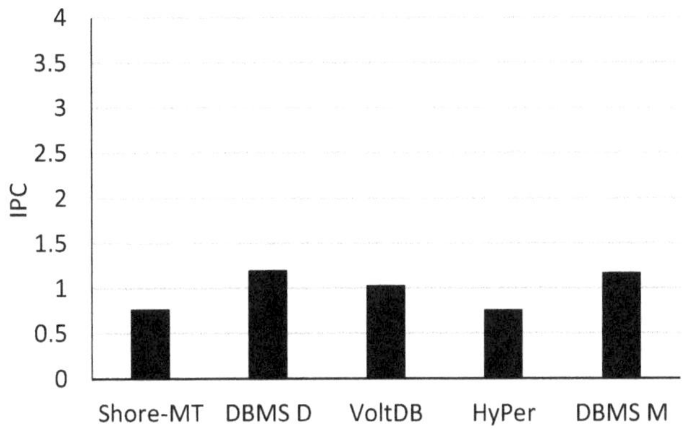

Figure 10: The IPC values while running TPC-C.

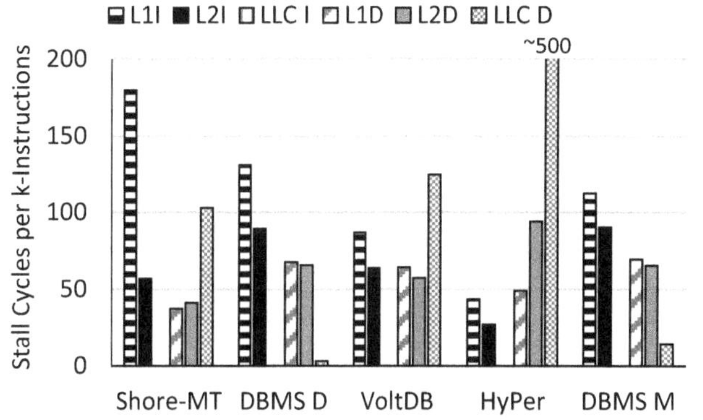

Figure 11: Stall cycles per 1000 instructions while running TPC-C.

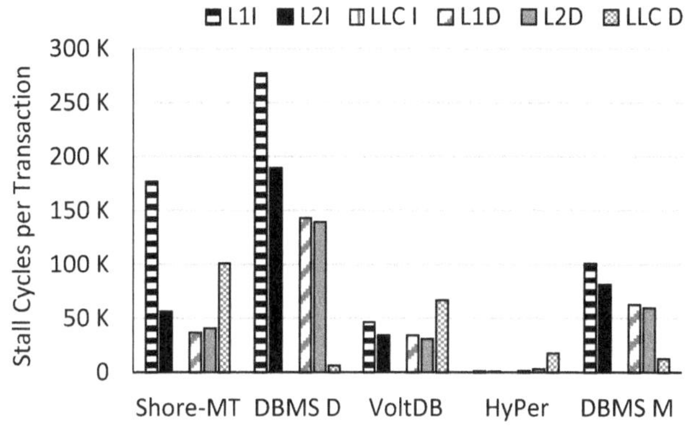

Figure 12: Stall cycles per transaction while running TPC-C.

ing accessed residing in the caches. Therefore, the only table that exhibits low data locality in TPC-B is the `Account` table.

5.1.2 *Stall Cycles*

Per 1000 instructions. To investigate the major causes of the stall cycles when running TPC-B, Figure 9 plots the instruction and data stalls per 1000 (k-)instructions for each level of the cache hierarchy for all the systems.

Figure 9 follows similar trends with Figure 5 for instruction stalls for probing 1 row. It demonstrates that the instruction stalls (from both *L1* and *L2* caches) are the dominant factor in the overall stall cycles for all the systems. *DBMS D* has the highest instruction stalls whereas *HyPer* exhibits very high instruction cache locality because of its aggressive query compilation techniques.

On the other hand, none of the systems suffer severely from the long-latency data misses even though we run TPC-B with 100GB data. This is mainly because TPC-B has better data locality compared to the micro-benchmark. When running the micro-benchmark, we randomly probe rows from a 100GB table, which includes more than one billion rows. On the other hand, TPC-B first probes one of the $\sim$ 20K `Branches` randomly. Then, it probes one of the $\sim$ 200K `Tellers` and one of the $\sim$ 2 billion `Accounts`. Finally, it inserts on row into the `History` table. Hence, the probability of re-accessing the same branch or teller as well as the same `History` table page is quite high compared to re-accessing a row from the micro-benchmark's single large table.

Per transaction. The stall cycles per transaction follows similar trends with the stall cycles per 1000 instructions. Therefore, we omit the discussion for stall cycles per transaction for TPC-B.

5.2 TPC-C

After investigating the micro-architectural behavior of the systems using TPC-B, this section focuses on the more complex TPC-C benchmark. TPC-C models a wholesale supplier with nine tables and five transaction types (2 of which are read-only and form 8% of the benchmark mix). In terms of the database operations, the TPC-C transactions contain probes, inserts, updates, and joins covering a richer set of operations than TPC-B. Therefore, we expect a different behavior for TPC-C than TPC-B.

5.2.1 *Instructions-per-Cycle*

Figure 10 reports the IPC values when the systems under analysis run TPC-C. Similar to the TPC-B results, the IPC values are in general higher than the IPC values observed with the micro-benchmark when probing 1 row (Figure 4). Unlike the TPC-B results, however, *DBMS D* and *DBMS M* exhibit the highest IPC among all the systems. In addition, except for *HyPer*, all the systems exhibit a higher IPC value for TPC-C than TPC-B. The differences between the TPC-B and TPC-C results stem from the lower data and higher instruction locality of TPC-C compared to TPC-B which also corroborates the results from [28, 29].

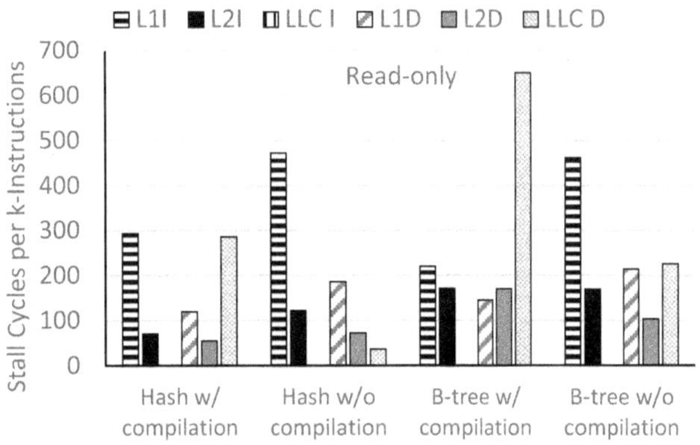

Figure 13: Stall cycles per 1000 instructions for different index structures with and without compilation optimizations while running the micro-benchmark.

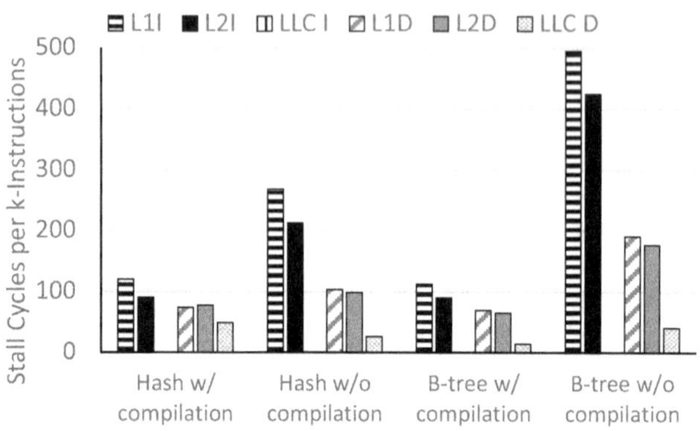

Figure 14: Stall cycles per 1000 instructions for different index structures with and without compilation while running TPC-C.

5.2.2 Stall Cycles

Per 1000 instructions. To better understand the IPC values in Figure 10, Figure 11 shows the instruction and data stalls per 1000 (k-)instructions for each level of the cache hierarchy.

The instruction stall cycles are considerably lower for TPC-C than TPC-B for all the systems. There are two main reasons for this outcome: the longer transactions of TPC-C compared to TPC-B and the number of scan-based accesses in TPC-C. TPC-C's longer transactions reduce the execution frequency of the components outside the storage manager increasing the instruction locality, which is similar to the difference between probing 100 rows vs probing 1 or 10 rows in Section 4.2. TPC-C also performs index-scans in several of its transactions, which increases instruction and data locality for this benchmark since a scan operation is a short loop that keeps fetching the next data item from a page or nearby pages.

With respect to the data stalls, unlike its TPC-B results, *HyPer* exhibits quite high *LLC* data stalls similar to the micro-benchmark experiments, which is due to the lower data locality of TPC-C compared to TPC-B. Even though the index-scans of TPC-C increase the locality of data accesses during the scan operation, in general, the TPC-C transactions access multiple tables with many rows and very little re-use.

Per transaction. Figure 12 shows instruction and data stall cycles per transaction for TPC-C. We observe the sharp decrease in *HyPer*'s *LLC* data stalls compared to per 1000 instructions results, similarly to the micro-benchmark case (Section 4.1.3). *DBMS D*'s instruction stalls are the highest among all the systems showing the large instruction footprint of the traditional disk-based *DBMS D*. *DBMS D* is followed by the disk-based system, *Shore-MT*, and the main-memory optimized OLTP engine *DBMS M*. While *DBMS M*'s instruction stalls are lower than the disk-based systems, they are still considerably large due to its legacy code components.

5.3 Summary

Overall, TPC experiments show similar trends to the micro-benchmark ones. The higher micro-architectural utilization (the higher IPC values) stems from the higher data (mainly TPC-B) and instruction (mainly TPC-C) locality in the TPC workloads compared to the micro-benchmark, which especially the in-memory systems can effectively exploit thanks to their optimized code and data structures.

6. INDEX AND COMPILATION OPTIMIZATIONS, AND DATA TYPES

This section analyzes the impact of index and compilation optimizations the in-memory systems adopt, as well as the impact of the data types, at the micro-architectural level. Among the systems used in this study, *DBMS M* is the only one that allows enabling/disabling the compilation optimizations and using two different index structures; hash index and a variant of cache-conscious B-tree index similar to [17, 18]. Therefore, while we use *DBMS M* for analyzing the impact of index and compilation optimizations, we experiment with all the three in-memory systems (*VoltDB*, *HyPer*, and *DBMS M*) to quantify the effect of different data types.

6.1 Impact of index type and compilation

To quantify the impact of the type of index and compilation on the micro-architectual utilization, we start with the read-only variant of the micro-benchmark and plot the stall cycles per 1000 instructions in Figure 13. The results for the read-write version of the micro-benchmark can be found in Section A.3 of the Appendix. We use the version of the micro-benchmark where we access 10 rows per transaction from the 100GB dataset. As expected, compilation optimizations have significant effect on the instruction stalls, resulting in $\sim$ 50% reduction regardless of the index type. On the other hand, while the choice of index does not change the instruction stalls behavior significantly, we observe that *LLC* data stalls are $2-4x$ larger for the B-tree index than the hash index. B-trees require traversing the entire index to probe a single row potentially touching many internal nodes of the B-tree. Hash index, on the other hand, directly goes to the hash bucket that corresponds to the probed keys. Therefore, hash index requires fewer random data requests incurring fewer data misses.

We repeat the experiment above using the TPC-C benchmark. Figure 14 shows the stall cycles per 1000 instructions from different levels of the cache hierarchy. Once again, compilation optimizations reduce instruction stalls significantly

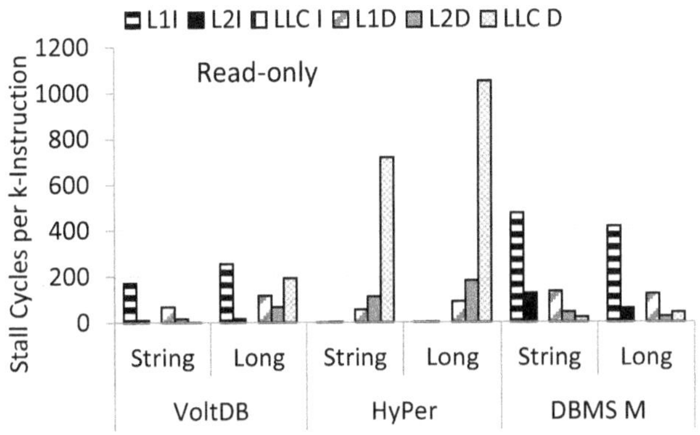

Figure 15: Stall cycles per 1000 instructions for String and Long data types while running the micro-benchmark.

for both index types. However, unlike the results with the micro-benchmark, instruction stalls are much higher for the B-tree index than the hash index without the presence of transaction compilation optimizations. This shows compilation is also effective in eliminating inefficiencies in the instruction stream when using a B-tree index. In the case of data stalls, since the TPC-C benchmark requires fewer random data reads compared to the micro-benchmark, we do not observe significant data stall time in Figure 14 for TPC-C regardless of the index types.

6.2 Impact of data type

To quantify the impact of different data types on micro-architectural utilization, we use the read-only version of the micro-benchmark where we probe 1 row per transaction over a 100GB database. The results for the read-write version of the micro-benchmark can be found in Section A.3 of the Appendix. We modify the micro-benchmark to use two 50 bytes *String* columns instead of two *Long* columns in the table and compare the two versions.

Figure 15 shows the results for *VoltDB*, *HyPer*, and *DBMS M*. We observe that the *LLC* data stalls are lower for *String* data type than for *Long* for *VoltDB* and *HyPer*. This is because larger data items such as 50 bytes *Strings*, provide better spatial locality than the smaller, 8 bytes *Longs*. While traversing a B-tree, comparing two 50 bytes of *Strings* would re-use the same cache line more frequently than comparing two 8 bytes of *Longs*. On the other hand, *DBMS M* does not have a significant difference in its data stalls while using *String* or *Long*. This is partly because of the larger instruction footprint of *DBMS M* and partly because of using a hash index structure rather than a B-tree.

6.3 Summary

Overall, we once again corroborate that the transaction compilation optimizations decrease the instruction related stall time fundamentally for OLTP systems by both reducing the instruction footprint and leading to a smoother instruction stream. The choice of index structures mainly affects the data locality especially for workloads that require frequent random data accesses. The data type, on the other hand, can affect the spatial locality of the workload, however, it does not affect the conclusions fundamentally.

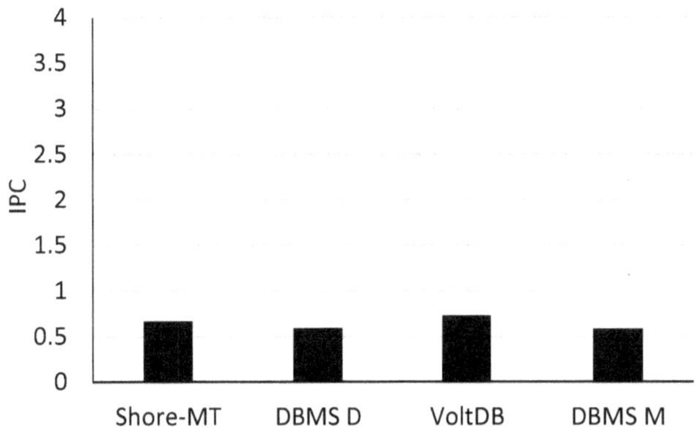

Figure 16: The IPC values for the multi-threaded experiments while running the micro-benchmark.

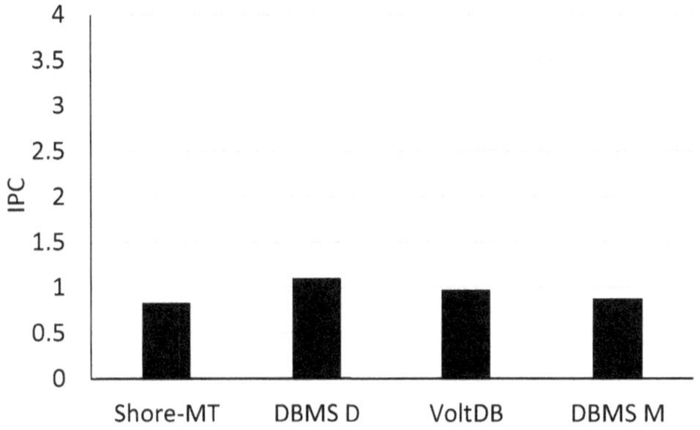

Figure 17: The IPC values for the multi-threaded experiments while running TPC-C.

7. IMPACT OF MULTI-THREADING

This section analyzes the effect of running multiple server side threads on the micro-architectural behavior. The single-threaded experiments aim to present an idealized case for all the systems since it avoids cache invalidations due to data sharing across different worker threads or misleading artificially high IPC values due to threads spinning under possible contention. On the other hand, multi-threaded experiments aim to investigate a more realistic scenario where systems are loaded with multiple threads executing transactions from multiple clients.

Figure 16 and Figure 17 show the IPC values while running the read-only version of the micro-benchmark when reading 1 row, and TPC-C benchmark, respectively. We use a database of size 100GB in both of the experiments. As can be seen from the figures, the IPC values are smaller than one for all the systems under both workloads (except for *DBMS D* running TPC-C) similar to the results from the single-threaded experiments (see Figure 1 and Figure 10).

Figure 18 and Figure 19 show the stall cycles per 1000 instructions while running the read-only version of the micro-benchmark and TPC-C benchmark, respectively. All the systems in Figure 18 and Figure 19 have similar stall cycles results for both the multi-threaded and single-threaded configurations.

As a side note, *VoltDB* adopts further optimizations in its concurrency control mechanism when it knows that there

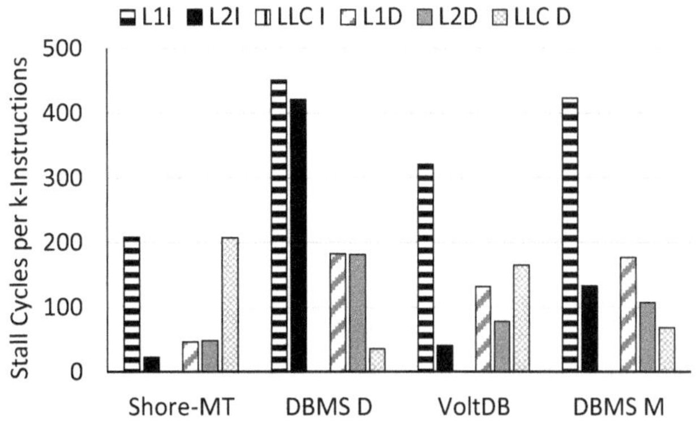

Figure 18: Stall cycles per 1000 instructions for the multi-threaded experiments while running the micro-benchmark.

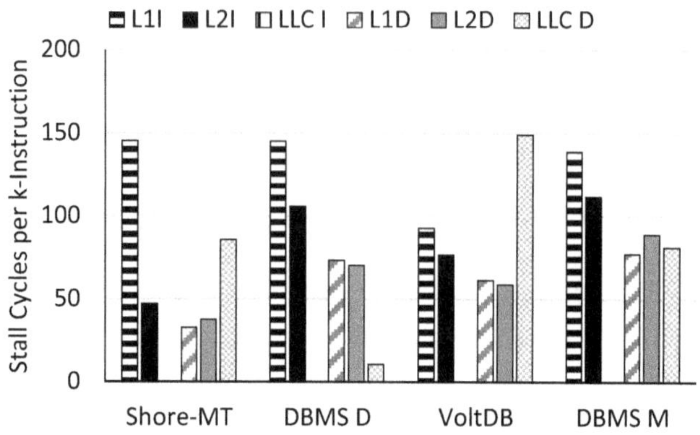

Figure 19: Stall cycles per 1000 instructions for the multi-threaded experiments while running TPC-C.

are no multi-partition transactions (as in the case for all the experiments with *VoltDB* in this paper). If we do not ensure single-site transactions, the instruction stalls of *VoltDB* increase significantly (by $\sim 60\%$).

Summary. Overall, the results in a multi-threaded configuration do not change the high-level conclusions from the results with a single-threaded configuration for the systems under analysis.

8. SUMMARY AND IMPLICATIONS

This section summarizes the highlights of our experimental study and discusses their implications.

In-memory OLTP systems implement a series of optimizations to reduce the instruction footprint and improve cache utilization. However, despite all of the optimizations, they severely under-utilize the micro-architectural features similarly to the traditional disk-based systems. The IPC values barely reach one on a machine that is capable of retiring four instructions per cycle.

Instruction stalls. *DBMS M* incurs the highest number of instruction stalls among the in-memory systems per transaction due to the large amount of legacy code it borrows from the traditional OLTP system it belongs to. On the other hand, *HyPer* is able to reduce the instruction stalls to almost zero thanks to its aggressive transaction compilation. However, high instruction locality amplifies the long latency data stalls resulting in low IPC values.

Data stalls. The data stalls when running OLTP workloads are affected by two factors: (1) whether the index is cache-conscious or not and (2) what the number of random data accesses per unit of time is. We observe that, except for *Shore-MT*, all the systems we analyze adopt some variant of cache-conscious index structures to improve data cache locality. On the other hand, systems that optimize instruction streams by transaction compilation, such as *HyPer* and *DBMS M*, perform more frequent random data accesses. Despite having cache-conscious index structures, they both suffer dramatically from long latency data stalls when requests do not exhibit data locality.

Implications. In this study, we conclude that software-level optimizations do not directly translate into more efficient utilization of micro-architectural resources, and might even hinder it, on modern processors. One needs to optimize the hardware and software together as the next step putting micro-architectural utilization as a high priority goal. This will, in turn, improve not only overall performance but also energy efficiency.

Exhibiting low instruction- and memory- level parallelisms, OLTP workloads are unable to utilize the wide-issue aggressive out-of-order cores that implement complex hardware mechanisms. Majority of the execution cycles go to the memory stalls for bringing either instructions from the *L1* cache or data items from the *LLC*. *L1* instruction cache sizes have been unchanged for the last decade due to the strict latency limitations and we cannot expect them to increase. On the other hand, whatever the size of the *LLC* is, megabytes of *LLC* will not be enough to keep the gigabytes of the data footprint of most standard OLTP benchmarks. Hence, instead of using beefy and complex out-of-order cores consuming large amount of energy, using simpler cores with caching mechanisms tailored toward the instruction and data accesses of typical OLTP applications would lead to higher energy-efficiency with better or similar performance.

9. CONCLUSION

In this paper, we perform a detailed micro-architectural analysis of the in-memory OLTP systems contrasting them to the disk-based OLTP systems. Our study demonstrates that in-memory OLTP system behave very similarly to the disk-based OLTP systems despite all the design differences and lighter storage manager components of the memory-optimized systems. The lighter storage manager components reduce the instruction footprint at the storage manager layer, but the overall instruction footprint of an in-memory OLTP system is still large, which leads to a poor *L1-I* locality and high number of *L1* instruction misses. Even though optimized compilation techniques help in minimizing the *L1* instruction misses, in the absence of the instruction misses the impact of long-latency data misses surfaces resulting in low IPC values.

Acknowledgements

We would like to thank the members of the DIAS laboratory for their constructive feedback and support throughout this work. The work in this paper has been partially funded by the Swiss National Science Foundation, project "200021-146407/1".

10. REFERENCES

[1] TPC transcation processing performance council. http://www.tpc.org/default.asp.

[2] A. Ailamaki, D. J. DeWitt, M. D. Hill, and D. A. Wood. DBMSs on a Modern Processor: Where Does Time Go? In *VLDB*, pages 266–277, 1999.

[3] L. A. Barroso, K. Gharachorloo, and E. Bugnion. Memory System Characterization of Commercial Workloads. In *ISCA*, pages 3–14, 1998.

[4] P. A. Bernstein and N. Goodman. Multiversion Concurrency Control—Theory and Algorithms. *ACM TODS*, 8(4):465–483, 1983.

[5] C. Diaconu, C. Freedman, E. Ismert, P.-A. Larson, P. Mittal, R. Stonecipher, N. Verma, and M. Zwilling. Hekaton: SQL Server's Memory-optimized OLTP Engine. In *SIGMOD*, pages 1243–1254, 2013.

[6] M. Ferdman, A. Adileh, O. Kocberber, S. Volos, M. Alisafaee, D. Jevdjic, C. Kaynak, A. D. Popescu, A. Ailamaki, and B. Falsafi. Clearing the Clouds: A Study of Emerging Scale-out Workloads on Modern Hardware. In *ASPLOS*, pages 37–48, 2012.

[7] N. Hardavellas, I. Pandis, R. Johnson, N. Mancheril, A. Ailamaki, and B. Falsafi. Database Servers on Chip Multiprocessors: Limitations and Opportunities. In *CIDR*, pages 79–87, 2007.

[8] S. Harizopoulos, D. J. Abadi, S. Madden, and M. Stonebraker. OLTP Through the Looking Glass, and What We Found There. In *SIGMOD*, pages 981–992, 2008.

[9] HyPer. http://hyper-db.de/.

[10] Intel. Intel VTune Amplifier XE Performance Profiler. http://software.intel.com/en-us/articles/intel-vtune-amplifier-xe/.

[11] K. Keeton, D. A. Patterson, Y. Q. He, R. C. Raphael, and W. E. Baker. Performance Characterization of a Quad Pentium Pro SMP Using OLTP Workloads. In *ISCA*, pages 15–26, 1998.

[12] A. Kemper, T. Neumann, J. Finis, F. Funke, V. Leis, H. Mühe, T. Mühlbauer, and W. Rödiger. Processing in the Hybrid OLTP & OLAP Main-Memory Database System Hyper. *IEEE DEBull*, 36(2):41–47, 2013.

[13] T. Lahiri, M. Neimat, and S. Folkman. Oracle TimesTen: An In-Memory Database for Enterprise Applications. *IEEE DEBull*, 36(2):6–13, 2013.

[14] P. Larson, M. Zwilling, and K. Farlee. The Hekaton Memory-Optimized OLTP Engine. *IEEE DEBull*, 36(2):34–40, 2013.

[15] J. Lee, M. Muehle, N. May, F. Faerber, V. Sikka, H. Plattner, J. Krüger, and M. Grund. High-Performance Transaction Processing in SAP HANA. *IEEE DEBull*, 36(2):28–33, 2013.

[16] V. Leis, A. Kemper, and T. Neumann. The Adaptive Radix Tree: ARTful Indexing for Main-memory Databases. In *ICDE*, pages 38–49, 2013.

[17] J. Levandoski, D. Lomet, and S. Sengupta. The Bw-Tree: A B-tree for New Hardware Platforms. In *ICDE*, pages 302–313, 2013.

[18] J. Lindstrom, V. Raatikka, J. Ruuth, P. Soini, and K. Vakkila. IBM solidDB: In-Memory Database Optimized for Extreme Speed and Availability. *IEEE DEBull*, 36(2):14–20, 2013.

[19] MemSQL. http://www.memsql.com/.

[20] T. Neumann. Efficiently Compiling Efficient Query Plans for Modern Hardware. *PVLDB*, 4(9):539–550, 2011.

[21] T. Neumann and V. Leis. Compiling Database Queries into Machine Code. *IEEE DEBull*, 37(1):3–11, 2014.

[22] I. Pandis, R. Johnson, N. Hardavellas, and A. Ailamaki. Data-oriented Transaction Execution. *PVLDB*, 3(1):928–939, 2010.

[23] P. Ranganathan, K. Gharachorloo, S. V. Adve, and L. A. Barroso. Performance of Database Workloads on Shared-memory Systems with Out-of-Order Processors. In *ASPLOS*, pages 307–318, 1998.

[24] Shore-MT. Shore-MT Official Website. http://diaswww.epfl.ch/shore-mt/.

[25] R. Stets, K. Gharachorloo, and L. Barroso. A Detailed Comparison of Two Transaction Processing Workloads. In *WWC*, pages 37–48, 2002.

[26] M. Stonebraker, S. Madden, D. J. Abadi, S. Harizopoulos, N. Hachem, and P. Helland. The End of An Architectural Era: (It's Time for a Complete Rewrite). In *VLDB*, pages 1150–1160, 2007.

[27] M. Stonebraker and A. Weisberg. The VoltDB Main Memory DBMS. *IEEE DEBull*, 36(2):21–27, 2013.

[28] P. Tözün, B. Gold, and A. Ailamaki. OLTP in Wonderland – Where Do Cache Misses Come From in Major OLTP Components? In *DaMoN*, pages 8:1–8:6, 2013.

[29] P. Tözün, I. Pandis, C. Kaynak, D. Jevdjic, and A. Ailamaki. From A to E: Analyzing TPC's OLTP Benchmarks – The Obsolete, The Ubiquitous, The Unexplored. In *EDBT*, pages 17–28, 2013.

[30] S. Tu, W. Zheng, E. Kohler, B. Liskov, and S. Madden. Speedy Transactions in Multicore In-memory Databases. In *SOSP*, pages 18–32, 2013.

[31] VoltDB. http://www.voltdb.com.

[32] T. F. Wenisch, M. Ferdman, A. Ailamaki, B. Falsafi, and A. Moshovos. Temporal Streams in Commercial Server Applications. In *IISWC*, pages 99–108, 2008.

[33] X. Yu, G. Bezerra, A. Pavlo, S. Devadas, and M. Stonebraker. Staring into the Abyss: An Evaluation of Concurrency Control with One Thousand Cores. *PVLDB*, 8(3):209–220, 2014.

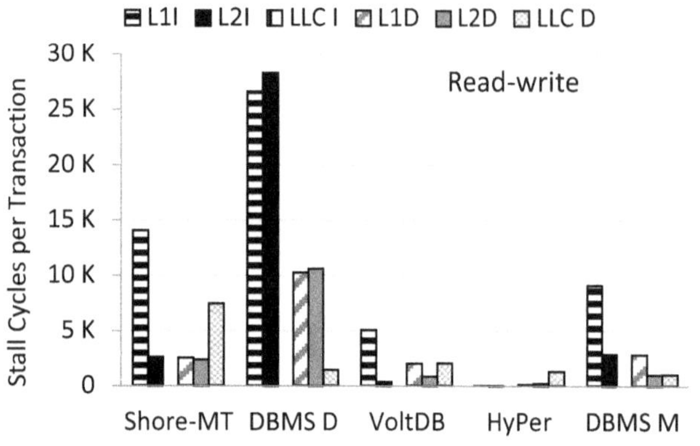

Figure 22: Stall cycles per transaction from the different levels of the memory hierarchy for a database of size 100GB.

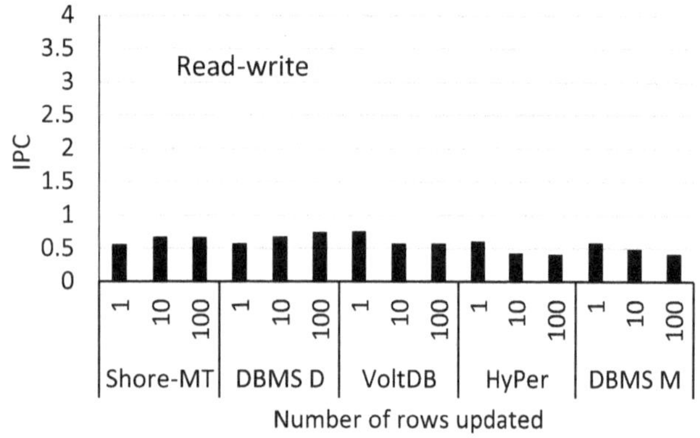

Figure 23: Effect of the amount of work per transaction on the IPC value with a database of size 100GB.

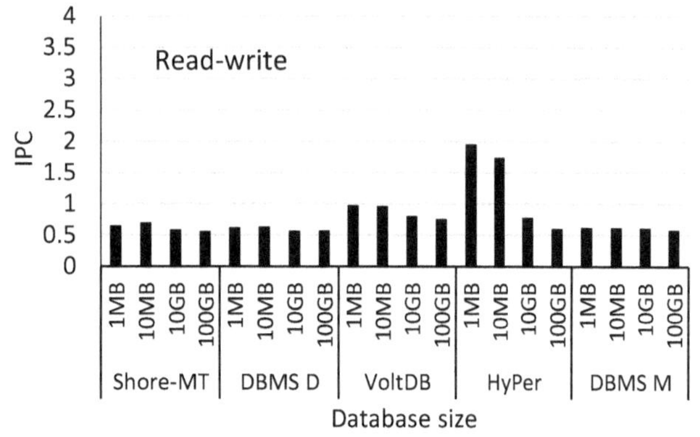

Figure 20: Effect of database size on the IPC value.

APPENDIX

In this appendix, we extend our sensitivity analysis with the results of experiments while running the read-write version of the micro-benchmark.

A. READ-WRITE MICRO-BENCHMARK

A.1 Sensitivity to Data Size

We start with the experiment where we increase the data size from 1MB, to 10MB, 10GB and 100GB. Figure 20 shows the IPC values when we run the read-write version of the micro-benchmark for 1 row.

The trends in IPC value do not differ much across read-only and read-write benchmarks, although, in general, the IPC values are higher for the read-only benchmark (see Section 4.1.1). The instruction footprint of the read-write micro-benchmark is larger than that of the read-only benchmark since, in the read-write benchmark, transactions both read and update the probed row as opposed to the read-only benchmark only reading the probed row. Therefore, all the systems, except for *HyPer*, have poorer instruction locality while running the read-write micro-benchmark (Section 4.1.2). This leads to the lower IPC value for this benchmark. *HyPer*, on the other hand, suffers less from the instruction stalls and more from the data stalls (Section 4.1.2), so it exhibits a higher IPC value for the read-write micro-benchmark compared to the read-only one.

As is for the read-only version of the micro-benchmark, IPC values are similar to each other when the data size is less than the capacity of the last-level cache (LLC), i.e., 20MB. As the data size increases to 10GB and 100GB exceeding the LLC capacity, IPC values decrease as the misses from *LLC* require accessing the main memory. This effect is dramatic for *HyPer* due to its sensitivity to the data stalls, and less observable for *DBMS D* and *DBMS M* due to their large instruction footprints. Even for small data sizes, e.g., 1MB and 10MB, the large instruction footprint of *DBMS D* and *DBMS M* causes high instruction stalls resulting in low IPC.

Figure 21 shows the stall cycles per 1000 (k-)instructions as we increase the dataset size for the read-write micro-benchmark. We observe that the instruction stalls are higher for the read-write micro-benchmark compared to the read-only micro-benchmark showing the larger instruction footprint of the read-write micro-benchmark. Similar to the read-only micro-benchmark, instruction stalls dominate the overall stall time.

Lastly, Figure 22 shows the stall cycles per transaction. Once again, we observe that the instruction stalls are higher for the read-write micro-benchmark compared to the read-only micro-benchmark.

A.2 Sensitivity to Work per Transaction

This section presents the results while running the read-write version of the micro-benchmark as we increase the amount of work per transaction by increasing the number of rows updated per transaction from 1, to 10 and 100.

Figure 23 plots the IPC values as the amount of work per transaction increases on the x-axis. We observe similar trends to the read-only micro-benchmark where IPC values increase for the disk-based systems (*Shore-MT* and *DBMS D*), and decrease for the in-memory systems (*VoltDB*, *HyPer*, and *DBMS M*). Moreover, IPC values are in general lower for the read-write micro-benchmark compared to the read-only micro-benchmark.

Figure 24 plots the stall cycles per 1000 (k-)instructions. We observe that the instruction stalls are higher and the data stalls are lower for the read-write micro-benchmark compared to the read-only micro-benchmark. Similarly to the read-only case, instruction stalls decrease as the number of rows updated per transaction increases due to higher locality within the instruction stream. *DBMS D*'s instruction stalls are high even when probing 100 rows implying the large instruction footprint of the commercial disk-based

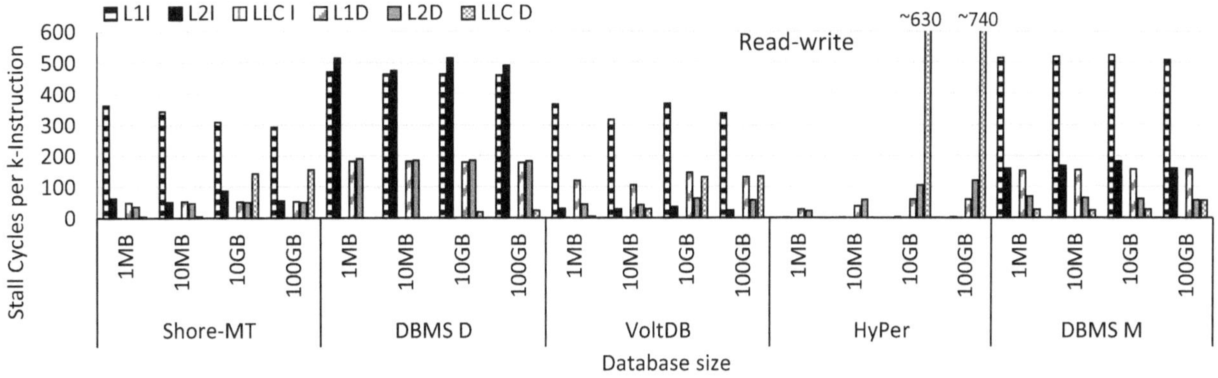

Figure 21: Stall cycles per 1000 instructions from the different levels of the memory hierarchy as we increase the database size.

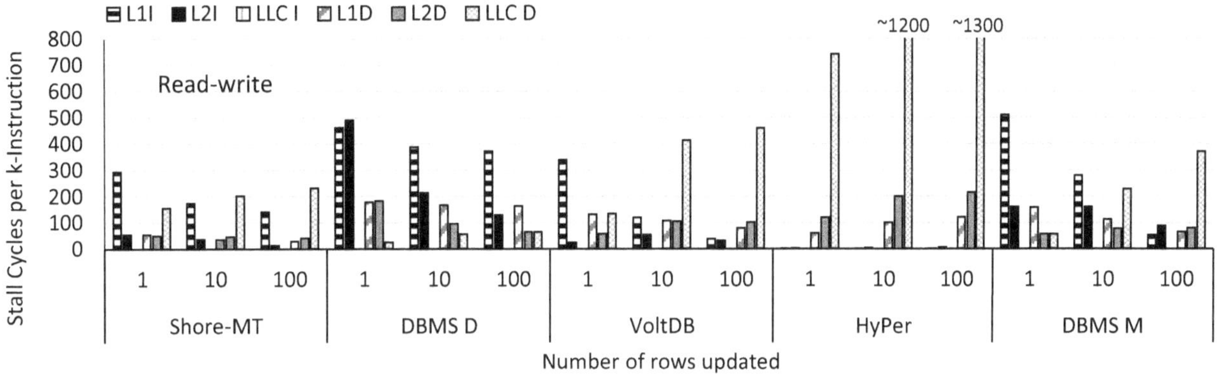

Figure 24: Stall cycles per 1000 instructions from the different levels of the memory hierarchy as we increase the amount of work done per transaction with a database of size 100GB.

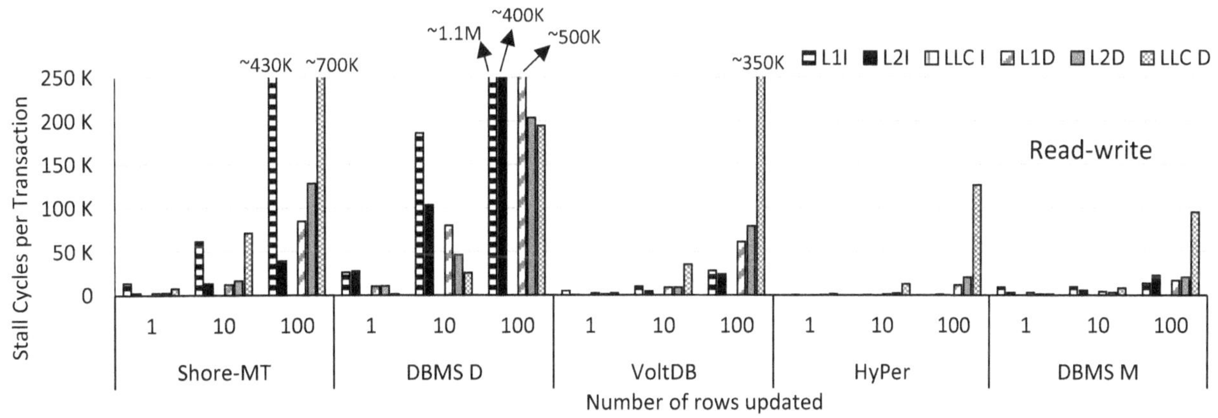

Figure 25: Stall cycles per transaction from the different levels of the memory hierarchy as we increase the amount of work done per transaction with a database of size 100GB.

OLTP system. *DBMS M*'s instruction stalls dominate for probing 1 and 10 rows showing the high overhead of the legacy code *DBMS M* uses from the traditional disk-based OLTP system it belongs to. For probing 100 rows, however, its instruction stalls become significantly smaller.

Lastly, Figure 25 shows the stall cycles per transaction as we increase the number of rows updated per transaction on the x-axis. Once again, we observe higher instruction stalls for the read-write micro-benchmark compared to the read-only micro-benchmark. Moreover, as the number of rows updated per transaction increases, the instruction stalls significantly increase for *Shore-MT* and *DBMS D*, and stay the same or slightly increase for *VoltDB*, *HyPer*, and *DBMS M*. The data stalls, on the other hand, increase almost linearly for all the systems as the number of rows updated increases. We observe that the data stalls of Shore-MT are 2-3.5x higher than the other systems suggesting that all the

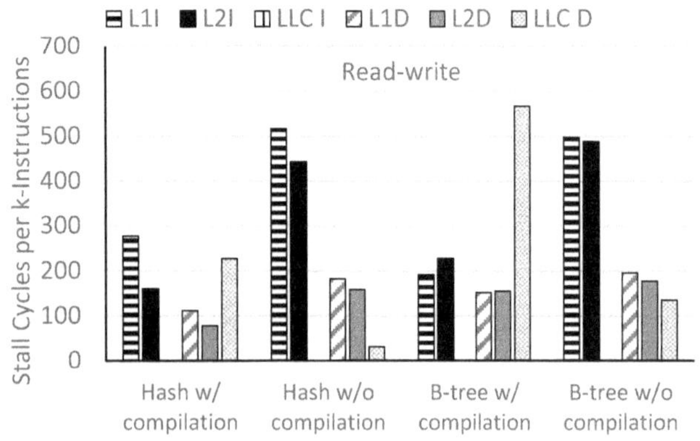

Figure 26: Stall cycles per 1000 instructions for different index structures with and without compilation optimizations when running the micro-benchmark.

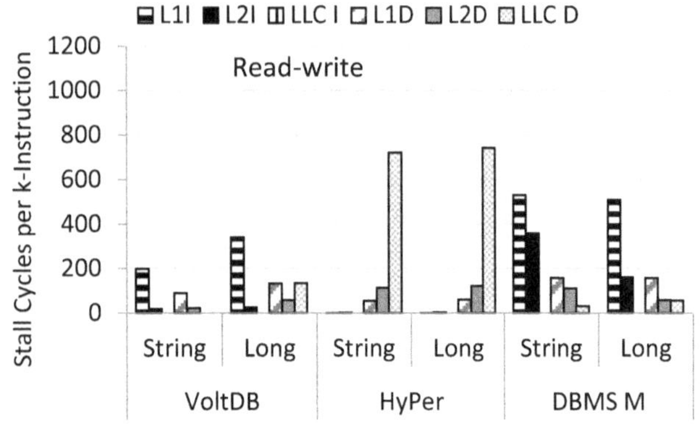

Figure 27: Stall cycles per 1000 instructions for String and Long data types when running the micro-benchmark.

other systems implement some variant of cache-conscious index structure.

A.3 Index, Compilation, and Data Type

Finally, this section presents the results while running the read-write version of the micro-benchmark as we use different index and compilation optimizations as well as different data types.

Figure 26 depicts the stall cycles per 1000 (k-)instructions for different index and compilation configurations for the read-write micro-benchmark. We observe similar trends to the read-only micro-benchmark. The instruction stalls decrease significantly when we use the compilation optimization for both hash and B-tree indexes, while different index structures do not affect the instruction stalls. On the other hand, B-tree index causes significantly higher data stalls than the hash index.

Figure 27 plots the stall cycles per 1000 (k-)instructions while running the read-write micro-benchmark with different data types, i.e, *String* and *Long*. We observe the slightly higher data stalls for *Long* than for *String* when using *VoltDB* and *HyPer*. Although this effect is similar to the one we observe while running the read-only micro-benchmark, the differences between the data stalls for *String* and *Long* are lower for the read-write micro-benchmark. This is because the read-write micro-benchmark has better spatial locality than the read-only micro-benchmark since the read-write micro-benchmark, after reading the cache line corresponding to the probed value, accesses the same cache line to write the updated value. *DBMS M*, on the other hand, exhibits similar data stalls for both of the data types, and has higher *L2* instruction stalls for the *String* data type.

iBFS: Concurrent Breadth-First Search on GPUs

Hang Liu H. Howie Huang Yang Hu
Department of Electrical and Computer Engineering
George Washington University
{asherliu, howie, huyang}@gwu.edu

ABSTRACT

Breadth-First Search (BFS) is a key graph algorithm with many important applications. In this work, we focus on a special class of graph traversal algorithm - concurrent BFS - where multiple breadth-first traversals are performed simultaneously on the same graph. We have designed and developed a new approach called *iBFS* that is able to run i concurrent BFSes from i distinct source vertices, very efficiently on Graphics Processing Units (GPUs). iBFS consists of three novel designs. First, iBFS develops a single GPU kernel for *joint traversal* of concurrent BFS to take advantage of shared frontiers across different instances. Second, *outdegree-based GroupBy rules* enables iBFS to selectively run a group of BFS instances which further maximizes the frontier sharing within such a group. Third, iBFS brings additional performance benefit by utilizing highly optimized *bitwise operations* on GPUs, which allows a single GPU thread to inspect a vertex for concurrent BFS instances. The evaluation on a wide spectrum of graph benchmarks shows that iBFS on one GPU runs up to 30× faster than executing BFS instances sequentially, and on 112 GPUs achieves near linear speedup with the maximum performance of 57,267 billion traversed edges per second (TEPS).

1. INTRODUCTION

Graph-based representations are ubiquitous in many applications such as social networks [1–3], metabolic networks [4], and computer networking [5]. As a result, graph algorithms have been an vital research topic in the era of big data, among which Breadth-First Search (BFS) draws a significant amount of interests due to its importance.

In this work, we focus on a special class of BFS algorithm - concurrent BFS - where multiple breadth-first traversals are performed simultaneously on the same graph. We refer to our solution to this problem as iBFS that is able to perform i multiple breadth-first traversals in parallel on GPUs, each from a distinct source vertex. Here i is between 1 and $|V|$, i.e., the total number of vertices in the graph.

SIGMOD'16, June 26-July 01, 2016, San Francisco, CA, USA

DOI: http://dx.doi.org/10.1145/2882903.2882959

Depending on the value of i, iBFS actually becomes a number of different problems. Formally, in a graph with $|V|$ vertices, iBFS is

- single source shortest path (SSSP) *if* $i = 1$ [6];
- multi-source shortest path (MSSP) *if* $i \in (1, |V|)$ [7,8];
- all-pairs shortest path (APSP) *if* $i = |V|$ [9,10].

Moreover, iBFS can be utilized in many other graph algorithms such as betweenness centrality [11,12] and closeness centrality [13]. For example, one can leverage iBFS to construct the index for answering graph reachability queries, that is, whether there exists a path from vertex s to t with the number of edges in-between less than k [14–16]. We will show in this paper this step can be an order of magnitude faster with iBFS. In all, a wide variety of applications, e.g., network routing [17–19], network attack detection [20], route planning [21–23], web crawling [24,25], etc., can benefit from high-performance iBFS.

This work proposes a new approach for running iBFS on GPUs that consists of three novel techniques: joint traversal, GroupBy, and bitwise optimization. Prior work has proposed to combine the execution of different BFS instances mostly on multi-core CPUs [26–28]. The performance improvement, however, is limited. For one, none of early projects has attempted to group the BFS instances to improve the frontier sharing during the traversal. Further, bottom-up BFS provides new additional challenges. For example, while MS-BFS [26] supports bottom-up, it does not provide early termination which iBFS leverages for faster traversal. In essence, BFS is a memory-intensive workload that matches well with thousands of lightweight threads provided by GPUs. Prior work such as [6,29–31] has shown great success of using GPUs for single-source BFS. To the best of our knowledge, this is the first work that supports concurrent BFS on GPUs.

The first technique of iBFS is motivated by the observation that a naive implementation that simply runs multiple BFS instances sequentially or in parallel would not be able to achieve high parallelism on GPUs. To address this challenge, iBFS proposes the technique of *joint traversal* to leverage the shared frontiers among different concurrent BFS instances, as they can account for as high as 48.6% of the vertices in some of the graphs we have evaluated. In particular, iBFS executes different traversals within a single GPU kernel. That is, all concurrent BFS instances share a joint frontier queue and a joint status array.

Second, to achieve the maximum benefit of joint traversal, iBFS shall execute all BFS instances together. However, this is impossible due to limited hardware resources, e.g., global memory size and thread count, on GPUs. Fortunately, we

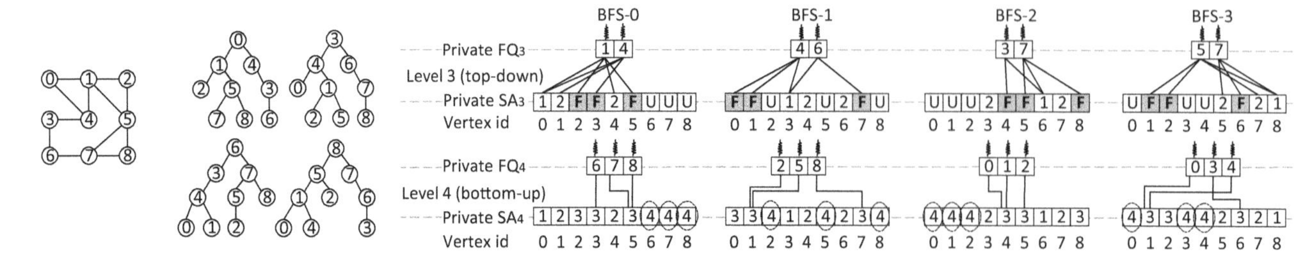

(a) An example graph (b) Four BFS traversal trees (c) Source vertex: 0 (d) Source vertex: 3 (e) Source vertex: 6 (f) Source vertex: 8

Figure 1: (a) An example graph used throughout this paper (b) Four valid BFS traversal trees from different source vertices, i.e., BFS-0, BFS-1, BFS-2, and BFS-3 starting from vertices 0, 3, 6, and 8, respectively. (c), (d), (e) and (f) are two levels traversal of the corresponding four valid trees, where the top half represents top-down traversal and the bottom half bottom-up. In all examples, FQ and SA stand for frontier queue and status array, respectively. The frontier queue stores frontiers while the status array indicates the status of each frontier in the current level where "F", "U" and numbers represent "Frontier", "Unvisited" and its depth (visited), respectively. The dotted circles indicate the updated depth for each frontier.

discover that grouping BFS instances can be optimized to ensure a high ratio of frontier sharing among different instances. Guided by a theorem on inter-group sharing ratio, iBFS develops the second technique of *GroupBy* that selectively combines BFS instances into optimized batches, which results in 2× speedup of the overall performance.

A typical BFS algorithm starts from the source vertex in a top-down fashion, inspects the frontiers at each level, and switches to bottom-up to avoid inspect too many edges unnecessarily. GroupBy improves iBFS performance in both top-down and bottom-up, although in different fashions. In top-down, higher sharing ratio directly reduces the number of memory access for inspection and expansion. In contrast, through sharing, GroupBy allows bottom-up traversals to complete in approximately the same amount of time, minimizing workload imbalance across multiple BFSes.

Third, iBFS would need to inspect a considerable amount of frontiers at multiple levels, in some case, upto 15× more than a single BFS. Although for each individual BFS not every vertex is a frontier at every level, concurrent BFS significantly increases the number of frontiers at each level. While GPUs offer thousands of hardware threads, traversing millions of the vertices of large graphs in parallel remains challenging. To this end, iBFS utilizes a *bitwise status array* that uses one bit to represent the status of the vertex for each BFS instance. This reduces the size of data fetched during inspection, and more importantly through bitwise operations reduces the number of threads needed for inspection, together accelerating the graph traversal by 11×.

In summary, the contributions of this paper are:

- iBFS combines joint traversal and GroupBy to allow both top-down and bottom-up BFS to run very efficiently within each group. This is achieved via utilizing a set of outdegree-based GroupBy rules to form good groups of concurrent BFS instances that are able to enjoy a high sharing ratio of frontiers among them. A theoretical study on frontier sharing and GroupBy is also presented.
- iBFS also develops bitwise-operations based inspection and frontier identification, which further simplifies the traversal on GPUs and delivers another key benefit of allowing early termination for bottom-up BFS. As a result, iBFS achieves up to 2.6× speedup compared to the state of the art [26].
- We have implemented and evaluated iBFS on a wide range of graphs, as well as on both a single GPU and a cluster. To the best of our knowledge, this is the first in both running GPU-based concurrent BFS on joint data structures, i.e., joint frontier queue and bitwise status array, and scaling to $\mathcal{O}(100)$ GPUs with unprecedented traversal rate, i.e., delivering 57,267 billion traversed edges per second (TEPS) on 112 GPUs.

The rest of the paper is organized as follows: Section 2 introduces the background on BFS, concurrent BFS, and the motivations. Section 4 presents the design of single-kernel and joint traversal. Section 5 discusses our GroupBy technique. Section 6 presents the bitwise optimization. Section 8 presents the evaluations on our iBFS system. Section 9 discusses the related work and Section 10 concludes.

2. BACKGROUND

BFS typically starts the traversal in top-down and switches to bottom-up in a later stage [32, 33]. Both directions perform three tasks at each level, namely, *expansion*, *inspection*, and *frontier queue generation*. To start, *frontier queue* (FQ) is initialized with the source vertex and will always contain the vertices (frontiers) to be expanded from at the next level. From the frontiers, *expansion* explores their edges to the adjacent vertices, and *inspection* updates the statuses of those neighbors in the *status array* (SA) which maintains a record (unvisited, frontier, or visited) for each vertex.

In top-down BFS, expansion and inspection aim to identify unvisited neighbors of each frontier. Figure 1 presents an example of breadth-first traversal. Given the graph in Figure 1(a), at level 3, a top-down BFS shown in the top half of Figure 1(c) (BFS-0 starting from vertex 0) will expand from the queue {1, 4} and mark their unvisited neighbors{2, 3, 5} as frontiers in the status array. Although vertices {0, 1, 4} have been visited before, they will still be inspected at this level, but their statuses will not be updated.

In contrast, bottom-up BFS tries to find a parent for unvisited vertices in expansion and inspection, and in this case, stores unvisited vertices in the frontier queue. In the bottom half of Figure 1(c), BFS-0 at level 4, {6, 7, 8} are unvisited vertices, i.e., treated as frontiers here. For vertex 6, since its first neighbor 3 is visited, bottom-up BFS will mark the depth of vertex 6 as 4, and there is no need to check additional neighbors. This is what we refer to as *early termination* in bottom-up BFS, which can potentially lead to significant performance gains. The newly proposed bitwise optimization in iBFS can further expedite this process for concurrent traversals and lead to even higher performance.

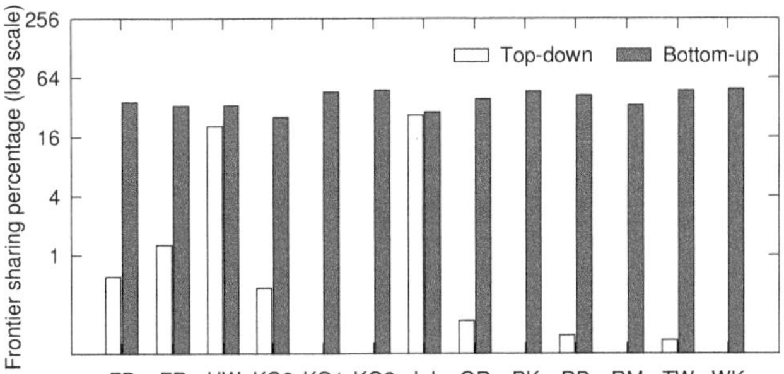

Figure 2: Average frontier sharing percentage between two different BFS instances.

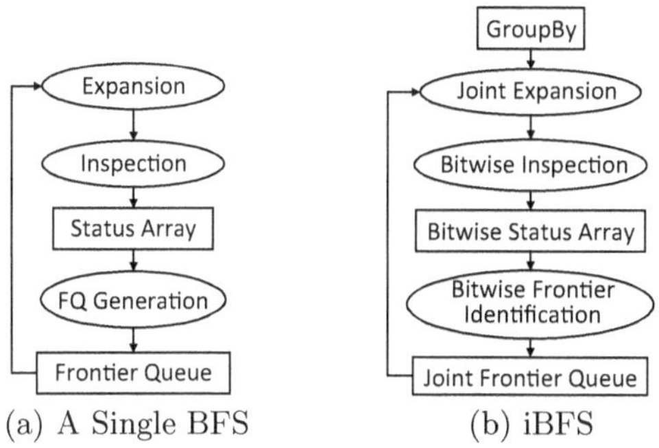

Figure 3: The flow charts of (a) BFS, (b) iBFS.

Among three tasks at each level, inspecting adjacent vertices of the frontiers involves a lot of random memory accesses (pointer-chasing), accounting for most of the runtime. This can be observed on four BFS traversals for both top-down and bottom-up in Figure 1.

Concurrent BFS executes multiple BFS instances from different source vertices. Using the example in Figure 1, four BFS instances start from vertex 0, 3, 6, and 8, respectively. A naive implementation of concurrent BFS will run all BFS instances separately and keep its own private frontier queue and status array. On a GPU device, each individual subroutine is defined as a *Kernel*. Therefore, in the aforementioned example, four kernels will run four BFS instances in parallel from four source vertices. NVIDIA Kepler provides *Hyper-Q* to support concurrent execution of multiple kernels, which dramatically increases the GPU utilization especially when a single kernel cannot fully utilize the GPU [34].

Unfortunately, this naive implementation of concurrent BFS takes approximately the same amount of time as running these BFS instances sequentially, as we will show later in Section 8. For example, for all the graphs evaluated in this paper, sequential and naive implementation of concurrent BFS take average 52 ms and 48 ms, respectively, with a difference in traversal rate of 500 million TEPS. The main reason for such a small benefit is because simply running multiple BFS instances in parallel would overwhelm the GPU, especially at the *direction-switching level* when a BFS goes from top-down to bottom-up. At that moment each individual BFS would require a large number of threads for their workloads. As a result, such a naive implementation may even underperform a sequential execution of all BFS instances.

Opportunity of Frontier Sharing: iBFS aims to address this problem by leveraging the existence of frontiers shared among different BFS instances. Figure 2 presents the average percentage of shared frontiers per level between two instances. The graphs used in this paper are presented in Section 8. Top-down levels have smaller number of shared frontiers (close to 4% on average) whereas bottom-up levels have much more as high as 48.6%. This is because bottom-up traversals often start from a large number of unvisited vertices (frontiers in this case) and search for their parents. The proposed GroupBy technique can improve the sharing for both directions to 10× and 1.7×, respectively.

Potentially, the shared frontiers can yield three benefits in concurrent BFS: (1). These frontiers need to be enqueued only once into the frontier queue. (2). The neighbors of shared frontiers need to be loaded in-core only once during expansion. (3). Memory accesses to the statuses of those neighbors for different BFSes can be coalesced. It is important to note that each BFS still has to inspect the statuses independently, because not all BFSes will have the same statuses for their neighbors. In other words, shared frontiers do not reduce the overall workload. Nevertheless, this work proposes that shared frontiers can be utilized to offer faster data access and saving in memory usage, both of which are critical on GPUs. This is achieved through a combination of bitwise, joint traversals and GroupBy rules that guide the selection of groups of BFSes for parallel execution.

3. iBFS OVERVIEW

In a nutshell, iBFS as shown in Figure 3, consists of three unique techniques, namely, joint traversal, GroupBy, and bitwise optimization, which will be discussed in Section 4, 5, and 6, respectively.

Ideally the best performance for iBFS would be achieved by running all i BFS instances together without GroupBy. Unfortunately, ever-growing graph sizes, combined with limited GPU hardware resources, puts a cap on the number of concurrent BFS instances. In particular, we have found that GPU global memory is the dominant factor, e.g., 12GB on K40 GPUs compared to many TB-scale graphs.

Let M be GPU memory size and N the maximum number of concurrent BFS instances in one group (i.e., the group size). If the whole graph requires S storage, a single BFS instance needs $|SA|$ to store its data structures (e.g., the status array for all the vertices), and for a joint traversal each group requires at least $|JFQ|$ for joint data structures (e.g., the joint frontier queue), then $N \leqslant \frac{M-S-|JFQ|}{|SA|}$. In most cases N satisfies $1 < N \ll i \leqslant |V|$. In this paper, we use a value of 128 for N by default.

Unfortunately, randomly grouping N different BFS instances is unlikely to produce the optimal performance. Care has to be taken to ensure a good grouping strategy. To illustrate this problem, for a group A with two BFS instances BFS-s and BFS-t, let $JFQ_A(k)$ be the joint frontier queue of group A at level k, $FQ_s(k)$ the individual frontier queue for BFS-s, and FQ_t for BFS-t. Thus, $|JFQ_A(k)| = |FQ_s(k)| \cup |FQ_t(k)| - |FQ_s(k)| \cap |FQ_t(k)|$, where $|FQ_s(k)| \cap |FQ_t(k)|$ represents the shared frontiers between two BFS instances. Clearly, the more shared frontiers each group has, the higher performance iBFS will be able to achieve. Before we describe the GroupBy technique in Section 5 that aims to maximize such sharing within each group, we will first introduce how iBFS achieves joint traversal in the next section which makes parallel execution possible.

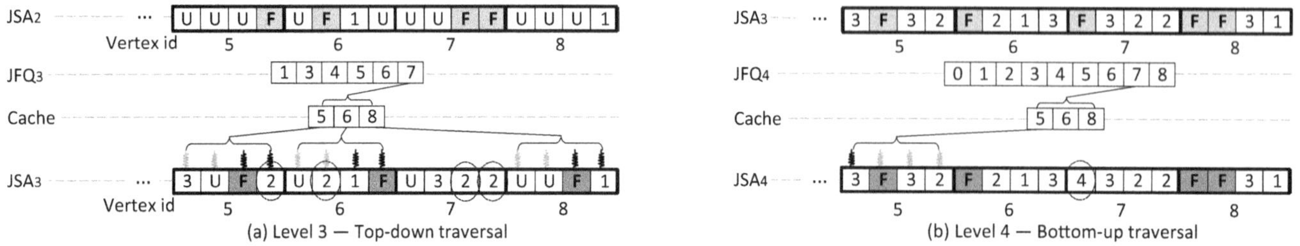

Figure 5: iBFS traversal on joint status array (a) Level 3 – top-down traversal and (b) Level 4 – bottom-up traversal using the example graph and four BFS instances from Figure 1, here i=4 and black threads are active while gray are not. While this figure only presents the inspection of one vertex 7, we keep JSA updated with the latest depth represented as dotted circles. Note that JSA_3 is different between (a) top-down and (b) bottom-up as frontiers are identified differently.

4. JOINT TRAVERSAL

In this work, we propose to implement iBFS in a single GPU kernel, different from prior GPU-based work [35]. This way, iBFS will be able to exploit the sharing across different BFS instances, e.g., if two threads of the same kernel are scheduled to work on a shared frontier, iBFS only needs to load adjacent vertices from global memory once. This benefit would be, otherwise, not possible on GPUs with a multi-kernel implementation which would be used for the aforementioned naive implementation.

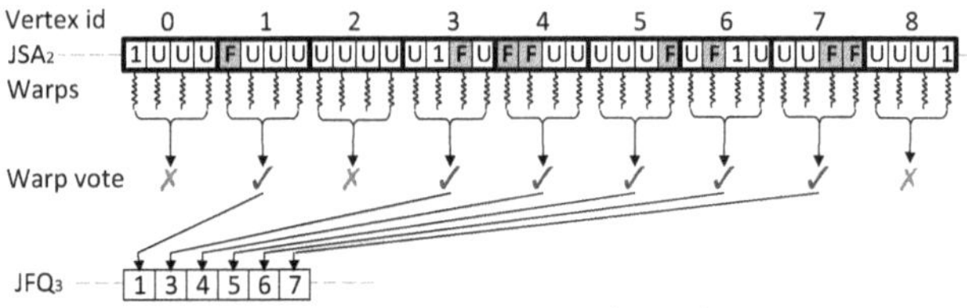

Figure 4: Generate joint frontier queue (JFQ_3) from joint status array (JSA_2). Assuming we are executing the four BFS traversals of Figure 1 in a single kernel.

The joint traversal of iBFS uses two joint data structures for all concurrent BFS instances: (1) **Joint Status Array (JSA)** is used to keep the status of each vertex for all instances. For each vertex, iBFS puts its statuses for different BFS instances sequentially. For example, in Figure 4, as we run four concurrent BFSes, four bytes are used for each vertex. For vertex 0, the first byte of 1 indicates that vertex 0 has been visited with the depth of 1 in BFS-0, and the next three bytes of U indicate that the same vertex 0 has yet been visited for all three other BFS instances. (2) **Joint Frontier Queue (JFQ)** is a set of all the frontiers from concurrent BFS instances, where any shared frontier appears only once. Thus, this queue requires the maximum size of $|V|$ to store the frontiers for all i BFS instances. In comparison, using a private frontier queue would require a much bigger queue with the size of $i \times |V|$.

A GPU uses single instruction multiple thread (SIMT) model and schedules threads in a *warp* that consists of 32 threads [36]. Several warps can form a thread block called *Cooperative Thread Array* (CTA). The threads within a block can communicate with each other quickly with *shared memory* and built-in primitives.

To generate the JFQ, iBFS assigns one warp to scan the status of each vertex as in Figure 4. If this vertex happens to be a frontier for any BFS instance, iBFS needs to store it in the joint frontier queue, e.g., vertex 1 is put in JFQ_3 because it is a frontier for BFS-0 at level 3. In contrast, vertex 0 is not considered a frontier for all four BFS instances.

It is worthy to note that iBFS uses a CUDA vote instruction, i.e., `__any()`, to communicate among different threads in the same warp and schedules one thread to enqueue the frontier. Furthermore, iBFS uses another CUDA feature `__ballot(parameter)` to generate a separate variable to indicate which BFS instances share this frontier. This is important for shared frontiers, e.g., while vertex 7 is a frontier in BFS-2 and BFS-3, it would appear once in the joint frontier queue. Removing such redundant frontiers from the queue substantially reduces the number of costly global memory updates, which contributes partly to performance gains obtained by iBFS.

iBFS's joint traversal introduces two unique memory optimizations to reduce the number of expensive global memory transactions: (1) during expansion, iBFS uses a new cache presented in Figure 5 to load the adjacent vertices of a frontier from GPU's global memory to its shared memory to feed all BFS instances. This way the neighbors from each frontier will only be loaded from global memory once, although numerous requests may come from multiple BFS instances. This benefit is not limited just to shared frontiers, rather every frontier in the queue. And (2) during inspection, iBFS schedules multiple threads with contiguous thread IDs to work on each frontier. Here the number of threads is the same as the that of concurrently executed BFS instances. This is because on GPUs one global memory transaction typically fetches 16 contiguous data entries from an array and only continuous threads can share the retrieved data. On the other hand, if continuous threads write to the same memory block, such writes are coalesced into one global memory transaction as well.

Now we will use an example to show how iBFS utilizes these new structures in both top-down and bottom-up traversal. Figure 5(a) exhibits the top-down traversal of vertex 7 which is a frontier in the proceeding level (i.e., level 2). During expansion, the neighbors {5, 6, 8} of vertex 7 are loaded in the cache. During inspection, BFS instances that do not have this frontier will not inspect the neighbors, specifically, the first and second threads in this figure. On the other hand, when the third and fourth threads access the statuses of three neighbors, it is performed in a single global memory transaction since these statuses are stored side by side and accessed by contiguous threads. At this level, vertex 7 will also have its status updated with the depth of 2.

The bottom-up traversal is performed in a different manner as shown in Figure 5(b). For the frontier vertex 7, iBFS will similarly load its adjacent vertices {5, 6, 8} into the cache. The difference here is that iBFS will check if {5, 6, 8} are already visited, if so, mark the depth of 7 as 4.

Note that a vertex can be a frontier at both top-down and bottom-up levels, for example, vertex 7 in Figure 5. In Figure 5(a), vertex 7 is a frontier for top-down traversal of the third and fourth BFSes, and in Figure 5(b) bottom-up of the first BFS. Clearly, as long as one BFS considers a vertex as a frontier at a particular level, this vertex shall be enqueued in iBFS.

5. GROUPBY

In this section, we will introduce the concept of sharing ratio, and propose several outdegree-based GroupBy rules. We will first use top-down traversal for the discussion of GroupBy and later present the impacts on bottom-up BFS.

5.1 Frontier Sharing Degree and Ratio

To a great extent, the performance of iBFS is determined by how many frontiers are shared at each level during the joint traversal of each group. This is because if multiple BFS instances have a common frontier in one level, all its edges will be checked only once, thus leading to overall performance improvement. In this work we define for any group, say group A with the size N, the Sharing Degree (SD_A) as the degree of sharing that exists in the joint frontier queue:

$$SD_A = \frac{\sum\limits_k \sum\limits_{j=1}^{N} |FQ_j(k)|}{\sum\limits_k |JFQ_A(k)|} \tag{1}$$

where $j \in$ [1, N] and represents the j-th BFS instance in the group A, and k represents the level (or depth) for the traversal. In essence, SD_A shows on average each joint frontier is shared by how many BFS instances in a group. Thus, the Sharing Ratio can be easily calculated as SD divided by the total number of instances in the group.

Traditionally, the time complexity of a BFS is calculated by the number of inspections performed, that is, the edge count $|E|$. Thus the time of a sequential execution of group A will be $\text{N} \cdot |E|$.

In this work, We use $T_A(k)$ to represent the time of the joint execution of group A at the level k, that is,

$$T_A(k) = \sum_{v \in JFQ_A(k)} outdegree(v)$$

where v stands for each frontier in the JFQ at the level k. And the total runtime T_A for group A can be calculated by summarizing the runtime of each level, which is:

$$T_A = \sum_k T_A(k) = \sum_k \sum_{v \in JFQ_A(k)} outdegree(v) \tag{2}$$

According to the Amdahl's Law, the speedup $Speedup_A$ of joint traversal for group A over sequential execution is:

$$Speedup_A = \frac{N \cdot |E|}{T_A} \tag{3}$$

Let $\bar{d}$ be the average outdegree, we can obtain the expected value of $Speedup_A$ using equations (2) and (3). Thus,

$$\begin{aligned}\mathbb{E}[Speedup_A] &= \mathbb{E}[\frac{N \cdot \bar{d} \cdot |V|}{\bar{d} \cdot \sum\limits_k |JFQ_A(k)|}] \\ &= \mathbb{E}[\frac{N \cdot |V|}{\sum\limits_k |JFQ_A(k)|}]\end{aligned} \tag{4}$$

LEMMA 1. *For any BFS group, say group A, its sharing ratio is equal to the expected value of $Speedup_A$, that is,*

$$SD_A = \mathbb{E}[Speedup_A] \tag{5}$$

PROOF. Because for the j-th BFS every vertex will become a frontier at one of the levels, the sum of $|FQ_j(k)|$ across all levels is equal to the total number of the vertices, that is, $\sum\limits_k |FQ_j(k)| = |V|$.

$$\begin{aligned}SD_A &= \frac{\sum\limits_k \sum\limits_{j=1}^{N} |FQ_j(k)|}{\sum\limits_k |JFQ_A(k)|} = \frac{\sum\limits_{j=1}^{N} |V|}{\sum\limits_k |JFQ_A(k)|} \\ &= \mathbb{E}[Speedup_A]\end{aligned} \tag{6}$$

□

Lemma 1 demonstrates that the sharing ratio reflects the performance of the joint execution when it is compared to the sequential execution of such a group. However, for any group, since the size of JFQ at each level is not known until runtime, we will not able to calculate a priori the sharing ratio as well as the expected performance. Fortunately, we discover that the sharing ratios at the first few levels can be used as a good metric, and there also exists an important correlation for sharing ratios at consecutive levels.

THEOREM 1. *Given any two BFS groups A and B with the same number of BFS instances, if at the level k their sharing ratios obeys $SD_A(k) > SD_B(k)$, at the level $k+1$ the following relationship, $\mathbb{E}[SD_A(k+1)] > \mathbb{E}[SD_B(k+1)]$, will hold.*

PROOF. Let us start with one group A. At the level k, the j-th BFS performs two main tasks for a frontier vertex v, i.e., expansion and inspection. In the first task, the j-th BFS fetches the neighbor list of frontier v, and in the second task, it checks all neighbors. The number of inspections is equal to the outdegree of v.

We define *null inspections* as those that do not lead to an increase in the size of the frontier queue at a particular level. Note that as vertices are shared, null inspections do not necessarily mean such inspections have not found a frontier at the next level. There are three cases that render a neighbor check as a null inspection. The first two cases are relevant to a single BFS, while all three are applicable to iBFS. For a neighbor w of the frontier v,

Case 1 : the neighbor w is visited.

Case 2 : the neighbor w has already been marked as a new frontier by other inspections at the level k. This check will be discarded, and will not increase the size of the frontier queue. This happens because w may have additional parents other than v.

Case 3 : the neighbor w has already been marked as a new frontier by other concurrent BFS instances. Similarly, in joint traversal, this check will be discarded, and will not increase the size of the frontier queue, because w may be shared by concurrent BFS instances.

We use three values to represent the occurring percentages of three cases: α accounts for case 1 and 2 for a single BFS, β for case 1 and 2 for iBFS, and γ for case 3 for iBFS alone. Thus, the probability of the complement of case 1 and 2 for a single BFS can be represented by $(1 - \alpha)$, and so on.

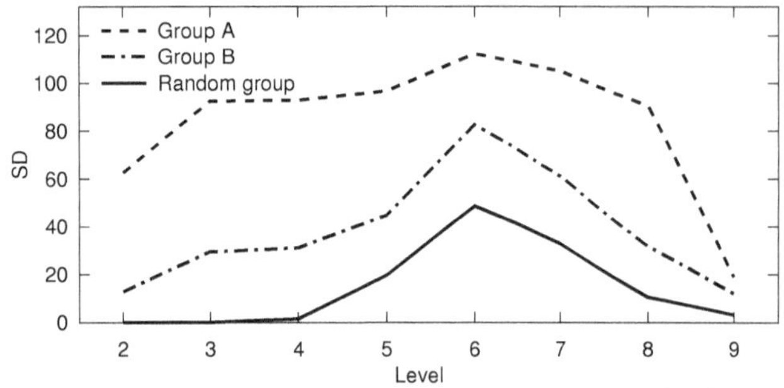

Figure 6: Sharing ratio trend of Facebook graph (FB).

Now for the level $k+1$, the size of JFQ is equal to the sum of the number of frontiers shared by different BFS instances within group A, from one to N instances. Thus, let $s_j(k)$ be the number of vertices that are shared by exactly j BFS instances, we have

$$SD_A(k+1) = \frac{\sum_{j=1}^{N} |FQ_j(k+1)|}{|JFQ_A(k+1)|} = \frac{\sum_{j=1}^{N} j \cdot s_j(k+1)}{\sum_{j=1}^{N} s_j(k+1)} = \frac{\sum_{j=1}^{N} j \cdot s_j(k) \cdot d_j \cdot (1-\alpha_j)}{\sum_{j=1}^{N} s_j(k) \cdot d_j \cdot (1-\beta_j-\gamma_j)} \tag{7}$$

where d_j denotes the average out-degree of these frontiers.

Since we do not know a priori the values for d_j, α_j, β_j, and γ_j, if replacing them with average values $\bar{d}$, $\bar{\alpha}(k)$, $\bar{\beta}(k)$, and $\bar{\gamma}(k)$, the expected value of $SD_A(k+1)$ is

$$\mathbb{E}[SD_A(k+1)] = \frac{\sum_{j=1}^{N} j \cdot s_j(k) \cdot \bar{d} \cdot (1-\bar{\alpha}(k))}{\sum_{j=1}^{N} s_j(k) \cdot \bar{d} \cdot (1-(\bar{\beta}(k)) - \bar{\gamma}(k))} \tag{8}$$

We assume that each single BFS has the same probability $\bar{\alpha}(k)$, so for iBFS, we have $\bar{\beta}(k) = \bar{\alpha}^j(k)$, and

$$\mathbb{E}[SD_A(k+1)] = \frac{\sum_{j=1}^{N} j \cdot s_j(k) \cdot \bar{d} \cdot (1-\bar{\alpha}(k))}{\sum_{j=1}^{N} s_j(k) \cdot \bar{d} \cdot (1-(\bar{\alpha}^j(k)) - \bar{\gamma}(k))} \approx SD_A(k) \cdot \frac{1-\bar{\alpha}(k)}{1-\bar{\gamma}(k)} \tag{9}$$

Now we consider two groups A and B. If $SD_A(k) > SD_B(k)$, as $\bar{\alpha}(k)$ and $\bar{\gamma}(k)$ are independent of groups, we get $\mathbb{E}[SD_A(k+1)] > \mathbb{E}[SD_B(k+1)]$ from equation (9). □

Figure 6 exhibits average sharing ratios for three different groups. We start from the second level as no BFS instances share the source vertices, and the maximum SD is equal to N, that is, 128. Since group A has a higher SD at the second level than group B, it always has higher ratios in the following levels. Similarly, group B has higher ratios than random. Clearly, as shown in Figure 6, sharing ratios would not increase monotonically for a group, which tend to peak at the first several bottom-up levels. Nevertheless, Theorem 1 implies that a higher sharing ratio of the initial levels can lead to a higher expected sharing ratio in later levels. Combining Lemma 1 and Theorem 1, we can see that a GroupBy strategy can achieve good speedup by focusing on the first several levels as described in Lemma 2.

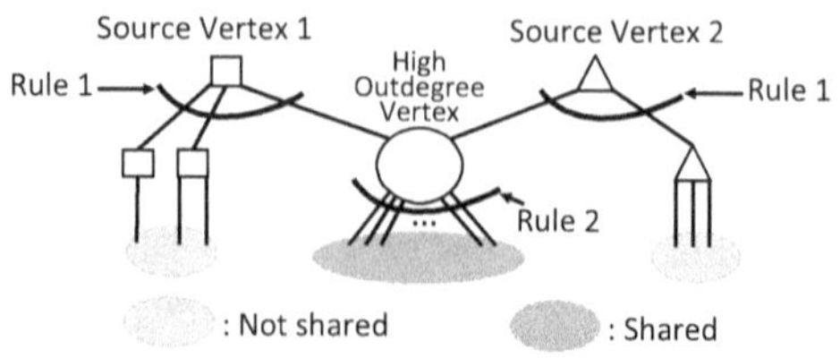

Figure 7: An illustration of a power-law graph.

LEMMA 2. *For two BFS groups A and B, for a small number k, if their initial sharing ratios obey $SD_A(k) > SD_B(k)$ at the level k, the expected values for the speedups will follow $\mathbb{E}[speedup_A] > \mathbb{E}[speedup_B]$.*

5.2 Outdegree-based GroupBy Rules

Lemma 2 states that a good GroupBy rule can be obtained by focusing on increasing the BFS sharing in the first several levels. Fortunately, an easy analysis on the outdegrees of the frontiers at these levels, coupled with a quick determination on the connectivity to *high-outdegree vertices*, can lead to two simple yet powerful **outdegree-based rules**:

Rule 1 The out-degrees of these two source vertices are less than p.

Rule 2 Two source vertices connect to at least one common vertex whose outdegree is greater than q.

Both rules are complementary to each other. Since the first rule ensures small outdegrees of the source vertices, other non-shared neighbors will not amortize the sharing ratio contributed by the shared vertex with high outdegrees from the second rule. With these two GroupBy rules, two BFS instances will likely get high sharing ratio.

Figure 7 shows an example of a power-law graph which is the focus of this work. In this example, many vertices are connected to a high-outdegree vertex, and the source vertices for different BFSes are not exception. When they share a common high-outdegree vertex, high sharing ratio across multiple BFSes can be easily achieved. It is not required that the source vertex directly connects to a high-outdegree vertex, as long as within the first several levels. Simply put, for two BFSes, it is beneficial to group them together if their source vertices have relatively small number of edges and also connect to high-outdegree vertices.

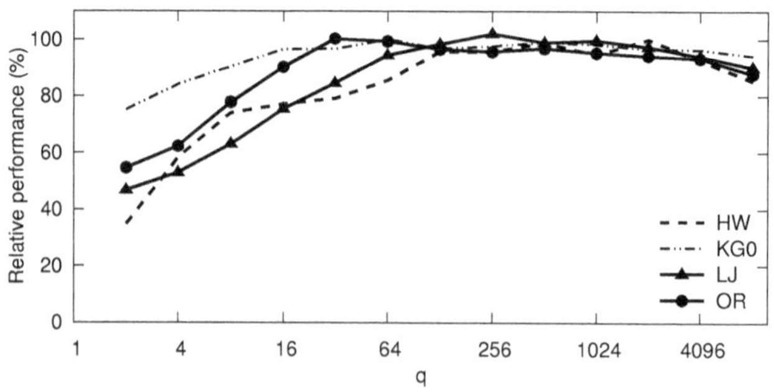

Figure 8: Performance of *GroupBy* for different q.

Selection of p and q. Figure 8 plots the GroupBy performance for different q values. One can see that the performance rises initially and reaches the peak, typically around the range of 128 – 1024. The lower performance is observed for both smaller and larger q. For smaller q, the groups would likely have small sharing ratios. On the other hand, for larger q, very few BFS instances would satisfy the GroupBy rules. In this paper q is 128 by default. Once q is decided, p is selected in the ascending order from a sequence of numbers that are the power of 2. Here we select p from a sequence of $4, 16, 64$, and 128.

The rules are applied as follows. First, iBFS selects all groups that satisfy both rule 1 and 2 with pre-determined p and q. iBFS will run such groups directly when their sizes are larger than N, the maximum group size described in Section 3. Otherwise, several small groups, likely using different values of p, will be combined and run together. Second, iBFS will try to combine the groups with different high-outdegree vertices. Last, when no BFS satisfies both rules, iBFS will group the remaining them in a random manner.

Sharing ratio improvement. Figure 9 plots the improvement on the sharing ratio using outdegree-based rules for both top-down and bottom-up. Specifically, for top-down, our GroupBy rules improves the sharing ratio by 10×, which increases from average 3.9% to 39.3% for 128 BFS instances. For bottom-up, although the relative improvement is smaller, the sharing ratio is greatly improved to average 66.1% which we will discuss shortly.

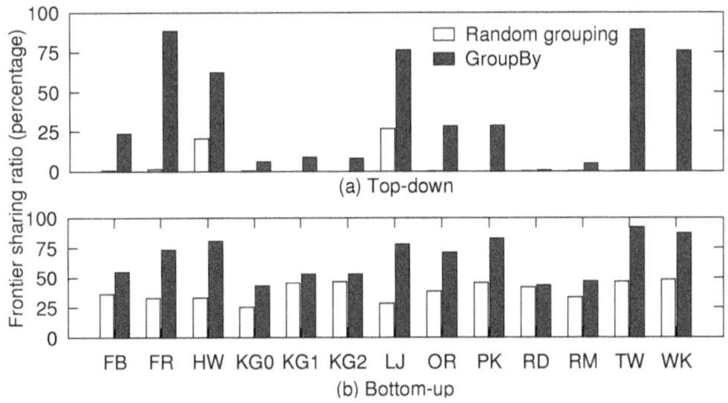

Figure 9: Frontier sharing ratio comparison between random and GroupBy.

For random graph that has a relatively uniform outdegree distribution, iBFS can adopt a slightly different rule. Since Theorem 1 and Lemma 2 still apply, iBFS can select a group of BFS instances if they share some common vertices from the sources. Our evaluation shows that such a rule may obtain 3.5× and 5% improvement in top-down and bottom-up respectively on a random graph, albeit much smaller compared to other graphs in our test suite.

5.3 GroupBy on Bottom-Up BFS

So far we have focused on GroupBy during the top-down stage of BFS. Surprisingly, good GroupBy rules for top-down will lend themselves to achieving great speedups during the bottom-up stage. Together, GroupBy further accelerates iBFS performance by increasing frontier sharing and more importantly balancing the workload across various BFS instances. These two effects can be best explained using an example of two BFS instances, say BFS-s and BFS-t, within a group. In Figure 10, Area I represents shared, visited vertices between two BFSes whereas Area III shared, unvisited vertices. When BFS-s and BFS-t share more frontiers at

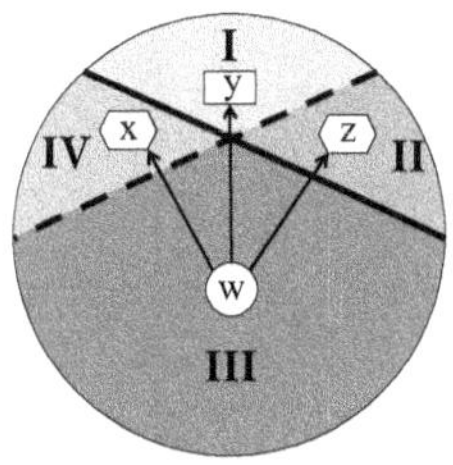

Figure 10: The circle represents all the vertices in a graph. There are two instances BFS-s and BFS-t. Area I and II represent the visited vertices for BFS-s (frontiers at top-down), and Area III and IV the unvisited vertices for BFS-s (frontiers at bottom-up). Similarly, Area I and IV represent the visited vertices for BFS-t, and Area II and III the unvisited vertices for BFS-t.

top-down, that is, bigger Area I, they share more frontiers at bottom-up, that is, bigger Area III. From Figure 9(b), one can see that for bottom-up, all the graphs still achieve 66.1% on average, close to 2 times improvement. This is significant because in bottom-up frontier sharing ratio is already high (38.7%) to begin with.

The most significant benefit of GroupBy when it comes to bottom up lies on the fact that it helps balance the workload. For a shared vertex w in Area III shown in Figure 10, depending on which BFS it belongs to and who is its parent, it may need to search all three other areas. Again, When BFS-s and BFS-t share more frontiers at top-down, that is, bigger Area I, this also increases the likelihood that both BFS instances discover the shared parent y in Area I. As bottom-up inspection terminates as soon as a parent is found, such sharing will further lead to similar runtimes across different BFSes, that is, reducing the variance in runtimes. To demonstrate this, Figure 11 shows the standard deviation for the number of inspections during bottom-up before and after GroupBy. Since GroupBy combines the BFS instances that would find their parent with a similar runtime, it lowers the standard deviation by 13×. Among all the graphs, it helps the TW graph the most – by 66×, reducing the number of inspections from 744 to 11.3. Clearly, GroupBy helps to transform a highly imbalanced workload to a much more balanced one.

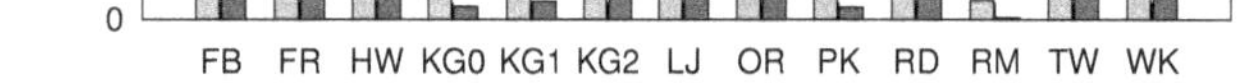

Figure 11: Standard deviation of the distribution for number of inspections during bottom-up before and after GroupBy.

6. GPU-BASED BITWISE OPERATIONS

Although joint status array removes random inspections on shared frontiers, assigning a warp of threads to work on each frontier is not feasible when a graph has millions of frontiers. While modern GPUs like NVIDIA K40 provide thousands of hardware threads, clearly we still need to find a smart way to utilize threads effectively when dealing with several millions of vertices in a graph. To this end, we propose a novel concept of **Bitwise Status Array (BSA)** in iBFS that uses a single bit to represent the status of each vertex for different BFS instances. And all bits of one vertex

Algorithm 1 Bitwise iBFS at Level $k+1$

```
BSA_{k+1} ← BSA_k
forall frontier f in parallel do
    foreach neighbor v of f do
        if Top-Down then
            BSA_{k+1}[v] = BSA_{k+1}[v] OR_atomic BSA_k[f]
        else // Bottom-up
            if BSA_{k+1}[f]==0xff...f then
                break; // Early termination
            end if
            BSA_{k+1}[f] = BSA_{k+1}[f] OR BSA_k[v]
        end if
    end for
end for
```

Algorithm 2 Frontier Identification at Level $k+1$

```
forall vertex v in parallel do
    if Top-down then
        if BSA_{k+1}[v] XOR BSA_k[v] then
            JFQ.enqueue(v)
        end if
    else // Bottom-up
        if NOT BSA_{k+1}[v] then
            JFQ.enqueue(v)
        end if
    end if
end for
```

are kept in a single variable. If this vertex is visited, we set it as 1, otherwise 0.

Figure 12 presents the mapping between joint and bitwise status array. Here for any vertex, while JSA uses the first four variables (3, U, 3, 2) to store the status for four BFS instances, BSA only needs a single variable (1011).

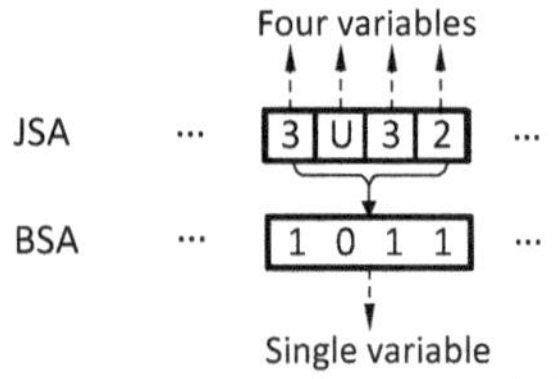

Figure 12: Mapping from joint status array (JSA) to bitwise status array (BSA) for one vertex.

With the bitwise status array, iBFS only needs one expansion thread to fetch the statuses of each vertex for all concurrent BFS. In addition, the inspection of concurrent BFS that will be described shortly can be executed by a single bitwise operation, which can be easily done with a single thread. In summary, this design frees up a substantial number of threads and further reduces the number of global memory access.

Bitwise Inspection. At level $k+1$, iBFS keeps a copy of bitwise status array – BSA_k. During traversal, the statuses for the most recently visited vertices are also marked as 1 in BSA_{k+1}. At the end of each level, the differences between BSA_k and BSA_{k+1} are used to identify the just visited vertices. Algorithm 1 shows the pseudo-code.

For top-down traversal, iBFS assigns a single thread to work on frontier f. This thread loads frontier's status (i.e., BSA_k[f]) from BSA_k and subsequently sets all neighbors' status in BSA_{k+1}[v] via a bitwise `OR` operation. For each neighbor, this `OR` operation only affects the bits for the corresponding BFS instances that share this frontier, because only these bits in $BSA_k[f]$ are recently updated as 1.

Using frontier 7 in Figure 13(a) as an example, vertex 7 is a frontier shared by the third and fourth BFS instances in Figure 1. During the inspection of vertex 7's neighbor – {5, 6, 8}, iBFS uses the bitwise `OR` operation between 7's status and each neighbor's status. Specifically, for vertex 5, it sets the third bit in BSA_3[5], and for vertex 6, the fourth bit in BSA_3[6]. One may also notice that, the `OR` operation does not affect the already set bits, like the fourth bit of vertex 5 in BSA_3[5]. The reason is that the fourth BFS instance has already visited vertex 5 in prior levels.

Because multiple BFS instances may want to set different bits of the same vertex in the bitwise status array concurrently, iBFS needs atomic operations to avoid overwrites of the updates to BSA_{k+1}, another difference from [26].

Bottom-up traversal, similarly assigns a single thread to work on each frontier. However, the frontier's status is updated by the neighbors' statuses, that is, iBFS uses `OR` between BSA_{k+1}[f] and BSA_k[v] and stores the result into BSA_{k+1}[f]. Using frontier 7 of Figure 13(b) as an example, its neighbors are {5, 6, 8}. iBFS executes `OR` between vertex 5's and 7's statuses and stores the result in BSA_4[7].

Early Termination. During bottom-up traversal for some frontiers, like frontier 7 in Figure 13(b), iBFS does not necessarily need to check all its neighbors because it is possible that some of its neighbors (e.g., vertex 5 for frontier 7) can set all bits of this frontier in the bitwise status array. When this happens, iBFS will terminate the inspection on this frontier, eliminating the need to further examine other neighbors (e.g., vertices 6 and 8), which we call early termination in this work. This newly freed-up thread will then be scheduled to work on other frontiers. This is not possible unless the bitwise operations already record all visited vertices as '1' in BSA, in this case before this level BSA_4[7] already has three bits set. In short, the early termination allows a great reduction in the traversal time compared to prior work such as [26].

Bitwise Frontier Identification. iBFS also needs a different approach for frontier identification that works efficiently with the bitwise status array. Algorithm 2 shows the pseudocode for bitwise frontier identification.

Top-down traversal executes the `XOR` operation between BSA_k[v] and BSA_{k+1}[v]. If *true* is returned, it means some BFS instances have just changed the corresponding bit of v and stored in BSA_{k+1}[v]. Since top-down treats most recently visited vertices as frontiers, iBFS hence stores the identified frontiers in the joint frontier queue. In contrast, bottom-up traversal, is much easier since it treats unvisited vertices as frontiers. Therefore, iBFS simply performs a `NOT` operation on BSA_{k+1}[v]. If it is evaluated as *true*, that is, some bits of BSA_{k+1}[v] are not set, then this vertex is a frontier and iBFS puts it in the joint frontier queue.

Vector data types on GPUs are also leveraged in iBFS. Clearly, the number of bits in each variable affects the number of concurrent BFS, e.g., if BSA is implemented with `int` type, one variable can represent the statuses for 32 BFS instances. In CUDA, the basic data are `char`, `int` and `long`, and on the other hand `vector` packs multiple basic types into one, e.g., `int4` contains four `ints`, similarly `char4`, `long4` etc. Using the vector data type in iBFS can further reduce the memory access time as it fetches four basic data elements together at one time.

Summary. Our bit-wise approach is novel in a number of ways, which leads to upto 2.6× speedup over [26]. First, [26]

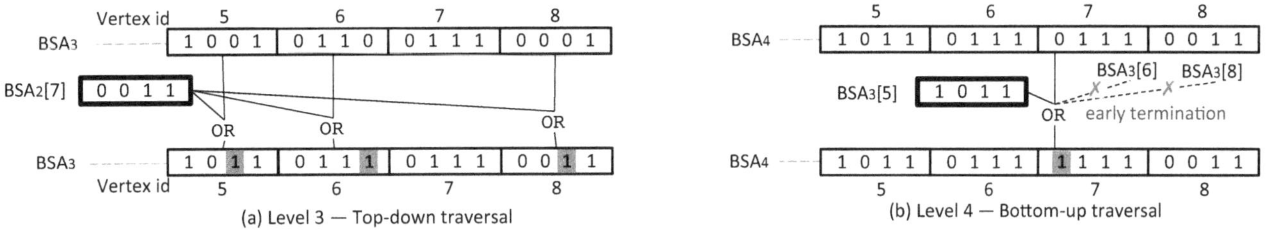

Figure 13: Traversing four BFS instances of the example graph from Figure 1 with bitwise status array: (a) Level 3 – Top-down traversal. (b) Level 4 – Bottom-up traversal. Shadow bits stand for updated status.

resets the bitwise status array at each level and only records the current level frontiers as 1. In comparison, iBFS records every visited vertex as 1 regardless of which level it is visited. This way our bitwise status array remembers all visited vertices, for which we also introduce a new frontier identification technique and early termination during bottom-up traversal as described earlier. Second, [26] is based on single thread BFS implementation, that is, each thread works on one BFS instance. In contrast, iBFS supports multi-threaded bitwise operation, that is, all available threads will work on a group of BFS instances. Inter-thread synchronization shall be carefully managed, because in iBFS multiple threads will need to update different bits of the same vertex simultaneously. In top-down, iBFS uses (manually controllable) shared memory on GPUs to cache and merge the updates in the same CTA (typically 256 threads), which avoids the overhead of atomic operations at this step. Next, iBFS has to rely on atomic operations to push the combined updates to the global memory. In bottom-up, iBFS performs multi-step tree-based merging of the updates within threads in a warp or CTA, again avoiding atomic operations.

7. iBFS ON CPUS

In principal iBFS can be implemented on CPUs. Specifically, *joint traversal* and *GroupBy* can follow the same design on GPUs. One notable difference is that iBFS would need atomic operation on CPUs for the multi-thread *bitwise operation.* Note that [26] does not need atomic operations because it is based on single-thread BFS. Generally speaking, concurrent BFS is an I/O intensive application, as it always has many frontiers to be processed. As modern CPUs provide tens of cores and thousands of registers [37,38], issuing a large number of CPU threads may improve memory throughput but inevitably would incur high overhead of context switches. On the other hand, GPUs not only provide a large quantity of small cores coupled with huge register files, e.g., 2,880 cores and 983,040 registers on NVIDIA Kepler K40 GPUs, but also support zero-overhead context switch [36]. As we will present shortly, compared to the CPU-based implementation, GPU-based iBFS runs 2× faster on average on various graphs.

8. EXPERIMENTS

iBFS is implemented in 4,000 lines of CUDA and C++ codes, extending a GPU-based high-performance BFS implementation – Enterprise [33]. Since it supports both top-down and bottom-up BFS, our iBFS can be easily configured to support conventional top-down BFS and traverse weighted graphs. iBFS is compiled using g++ 4.4.7, MPI (MVAPICH2) and NVIDIA CUDA 6.0 with the *-O3* flag. Our system is evaluated on NVIDIA Kepler K40 GPUs on our local cluster with Intel Xeon E5-2683 CPUs, and later on the Stampede supercomputer on NSF Extreme Science and Engineering Discovery Environment (XSEDE) program, where iBFS runs from 1 to 112 machines each of which is equipped with one NVIDIA Kepler K20 GPU.

We measure the execution time from when all the data are loaded in GPU memory to the traversal is completed and the results are stored in GPU memory. All the execution uses uint64 data type. We use the metric of *traversed edges per second* (TEPS) to measure the performance, which is calculated by the ratio of the number of directed edges traversed by the search, counting any multiple edges and self-loops, and the time elapsed during iBFS execution. In the tests, iBFS performs breadth-first search from all the vertices.

8.1 Graph Benchmarks

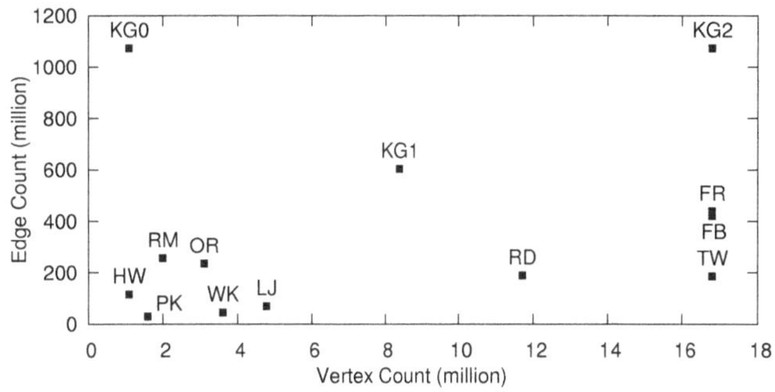

Figure 14: Graph benchmarks.

In this work we use total 13 graph benchmarks to evaluate iBFS, which as summarized in Figure 14 have upto 17 million vertices and 1 billion edges. In particular, there are seven real-world graphs of well-known online social networks. Facebook (FB) [39], a user to friend connection graph, contains 16,777,216 vertices and 420,914,604 edges. Twitter (TW) [40] is a follower connection graph, that is, if user v follows user u, (v, u) is considered as an edge. It also has 16,777,216 vertices and 196,427,854 different edges. Wikipedia (WK) [41] is a inter-website hyper-link graph, which consists of 3,566,908 vertices and 45,030,389 edges. We also obtain four popular online social network graphs, i.e., LiveJournal (LJ), Orkut (OR), Friendster (FR), and Pokec (PK), from Stanford Large Network Dataset Collection [42]. Specifically, LJ contains 4,847,571 vertices and 137,987,546 edges. OR has 3,072,627 vertices with an average outdegree of 75.27. FR contains 16,777,212 vertices and 439,147,122 edges. PK is the smallest graph with 1,632,804 vertices and 30,622,564 edges.

In addition, we generate three types of synthetic graphs with Graph 500 generator [43–45], namely, KG0, KG1 and

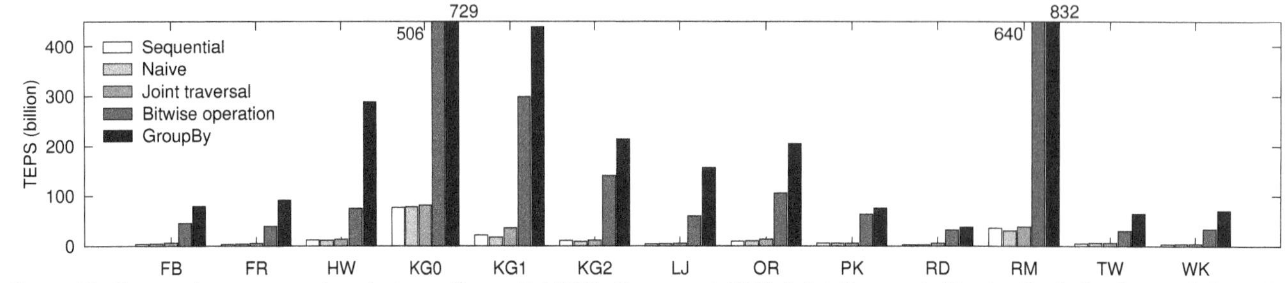

Figure 15: Traversal rate comparison between Sequential BFS, Concurrent BFS, Joint Traversal, Bitwise Optimization, and GroupBy.

KG2. The default value of (A, B, C) parameter is (0.57, 0.19, 0.19) per the requirement of Graph 500 [44]. Specifically, KG0 stands for the high average outdegree graphs, i.e., its average outdegree is 1024 and vertex count is 1,048,576. KG2 serves as the biggest graph in this paper, i.e., with both biggest vertex and edge count – 16,777,216 vertices and 1,073,741,824 edges. KG1 has 8,388,608 vertices and 603,979,776 edges. We also use the DIMACS graph generator [46] to generate the RM and RD graphs in this paper. RM follows the same theory from Graph 500 [43–45] but with a different (A, B, C) set of (0.45, 0.15, 0.15). RM has 2,097,152 vertices and 268,435,456 edges. RD [47] graph has uniform outdegree distribution, i.e., each vertex has roughly the same outdegree. RD contains 11,796,480 vertices and 188,743,680 edges.

All these graphs are stored in the *Compressed Sparse Row* (CSR) format. For graphs that are provided in the edge list format, we translate them into CSR while preserving the edge sequence. For undirected graphs, each edge is considered as two directed edges. For directed graphs, we also store the reversed edges to support the bottom-up traversal. The size of these graph ranges from 478 MB (PK) to 8.2 GB (KG2) when using *long integer* (8 bytes) to represent the vertex id.

8.2 iBFS Performance

We evaluate three techniques, *joint traversal*, *bitwise operation*, and *GroupBy*, and compare against running all BFS instances sequentially (*sequential*) or in parallel without any optimization (*naive*), both of which are based on state-of-the-art BFS implementation such as Enterprise [33]. In this test, we run APSP on all the graphs. As shown in Figure 15, sequential and naive implementation perform roughly the same. On average, the later traverses 1.05× faster, but a worse performance is observed in HW, KG1, KG2 and RM graphs, with only 78% of sequential performance on KG1.

In iBFS, joint traversal delivers 1.4× speedup compared to sequential implementation. The biggest performance gain of 2.6× speedup comes for RD, from 4.4 to 11.3 billion TEPS while the smallest is 1.03× speedup for PK . For other graphs, the performance improvement is more than 10%. On the other hand, bitwise iBFS, on average speedup the traversal by 11×. While the smallest improvement is 6.4× on HW from 11.7 to 75 billion TEPS, the biggest improvement is observed on RM – 18 × speedup from 36 to 640 billion TEPS. Astoundingly, **Groupby** improves iBFS by additional 2× on average beyond bitwise optimization, with the highest traversal rate of 832 billion TEPS on RM.

In this test, iBFS greatly reduces the run time of APSP on all graphs from average 123 hours of sequential traversal to 5.5 hours, where joint traversal helps to reduce to 87.8 hours, bitwise optimization 11.2 hours, and GroupBy the rest. GroupBy incurs a minimal processing time of less than 0.1 second on average.

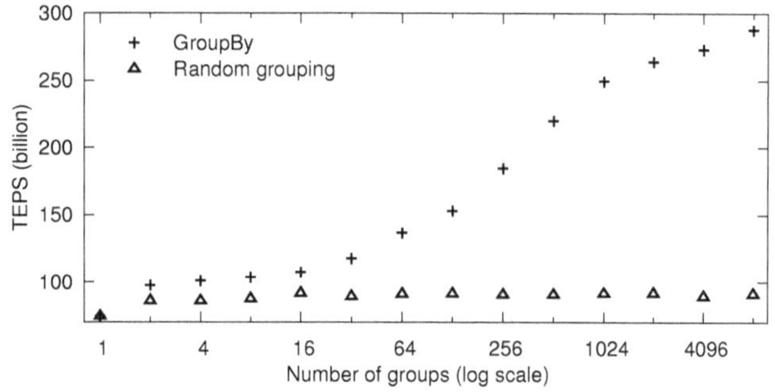

Figure 16: Traversal performance when running different number of BFS groups on HW.

We further evaluate the traversal performance of iBFS as the number of i varies, that is, running MSSP with varied number of source vertices. We observe similar performance on all the graph benchmarks. Figure 16 presents the TEPS when running different number of BFS groups on the HW graph, where the total number of BFS instances equals to the multiply of the number of groups and the group size. Clearly, as there are more BFS instances to run, the benefit of GroupBy – the gap between GroupBy and random grouping – increases because better groups can be formed. Specifically, with randomly formed groups, the traversal rate fluctuates in the range of 75 and 90 billion TEPS, which is raised to 288 billion TEPS with the help of GroupBy.

8.3 iBFS Scalability

In this test, we aim to evaluate the scalability of iBFS on a large number of distributed GPUs on the Stampede supercomputer at TACC. Clearly, as long as different GPUs work on independent BFSes, there is no need for inter-GPU communication. Therefore, the key challenge here is achieving workload balance on GPUs, especially when each individual BFS may inspect different number of edges during bottom-up. The longest time consumption of all the GPUs is reported in this test.

For the five graphs tested, iBFS achieves good speedup from 1 to 112 GPUs (the total number of GPUs on Stampede)[1]. As shown in Figure 17, from one to two GPUs, the biggest speedup, as expected, is from RD of 1.97× because RD graph has the most balanced workload. And even the

[1]As it took all the GPUs on Stampede, we were only given a small time window to conduct this test.

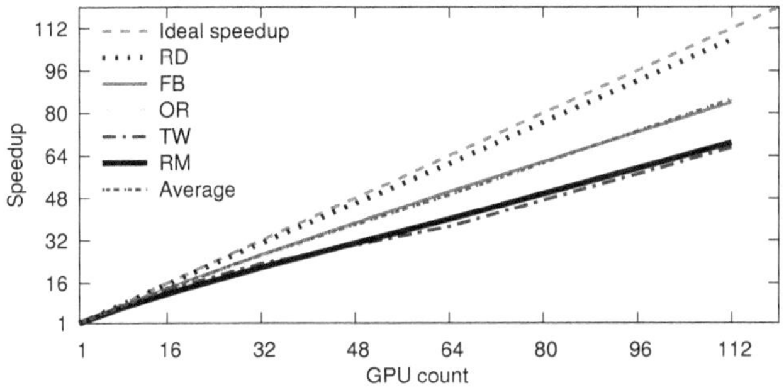

Figure 17: Scalability of bitwise iBFS from 1 to 112 GPUs.

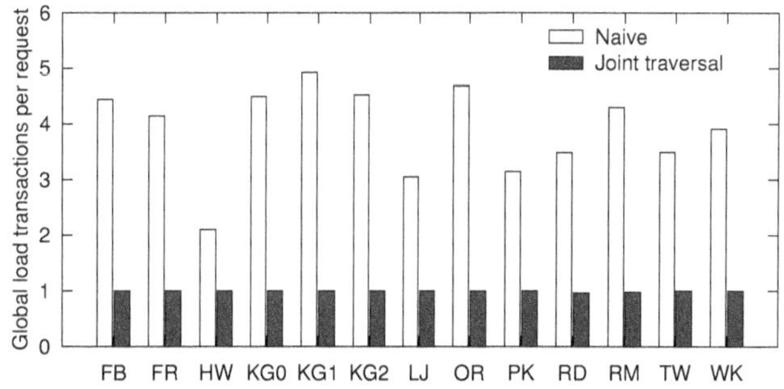

Figure 19: Load transaction count per request.

smallest speedup from OR is 1.9×. From one to four GPUs, the average speedup is 3.8× with the smallest speedup from OR of 3.6× while the biggest from RD graph – 3.9×. As the GPU count increases, workload imbalance slowly emerges and begins to negatively affect the performance. Specifically, iBFS achieves an average of 85× speedup for 112 GPUs. Again, RD gets the biggest speedup, i.e., 108×.

In all, iBFS achieves the average traversal rate of 16,509 billion TEPS across all the tested graphs with the maximum 57,267 billion TEPS on RM.

8.4 Joint Traversal and GroupBy

This section uses the NVIDIA profiler [48] to measure the impact of joint traversal and GroupBy on memory accesses. Having a joint frontier queue with only one copy of shared frontiers reduces the potentially large number of global memory writes, compared to having private frontier queues for each BFS instance. Figure 18 shows the number of global store transactions during the frontier queue generation of 1,024 BFS instances. Using private frontier queue, i.e., *private FQ*, executes 4 billion transactions on average across all the graphs, while joint frontier queue with random groups, i.e. *random FQ*, only needs one fourth transactions. The biggest reduction of over 11× is observed in the KG2 graph, from 8.3 billion to 700 million, the smallest saving is 1.2× on HW, i.e., 720 million to 580 million. With *GroupBy*, iBFS further saves the global stores by 2.6× with the largest from HW of 4×.

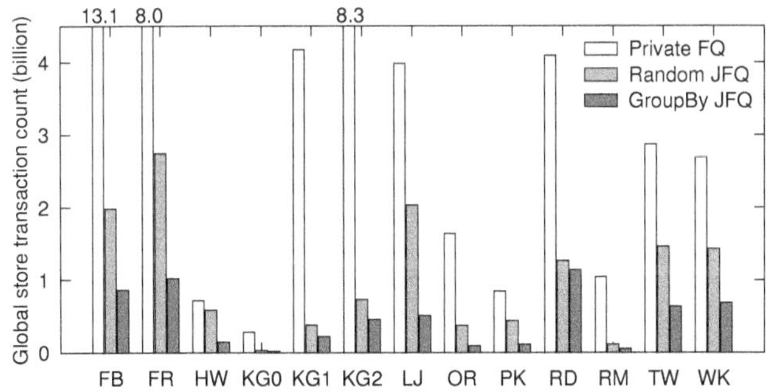

Figure 18: Global store transaction count during the generation of private frontier queue, random joint frontier queue and GroupBy joint frontier queue.

Combining joint status array with careful thread scheduling introduces significant performance benefits, as iBFS minimizes costly memory operations. Figure 19 exhibits global load transactions per request during traversal before and after this optimization. Note that global store transactions per request exhibits similar trend. Since joint status array of iBFS always coalesces the inspections and updates from contiguous threads into a single global memory transaction, our tests across 1,024 BFS instances show that we are able to reduce on average from four loads to a single load. The benefits add up quickly considering a large number of memory operations in concurrent BFS. On average each BFS instance executes 50 million of global load transactions.

8.5 Bitwise Operation

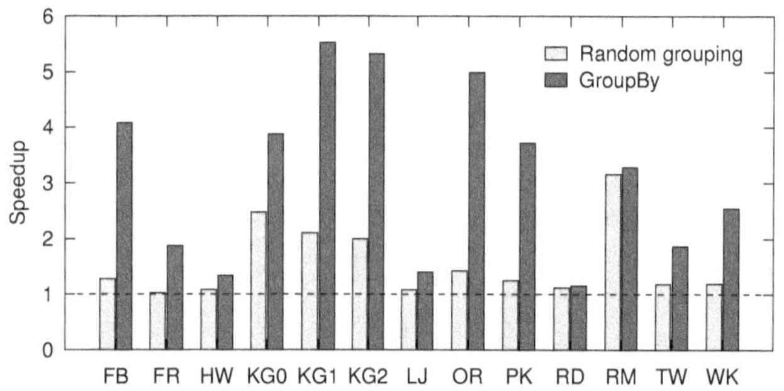

Figure 20: The speedup of our bitwise operation.

We implement the bitwise operation as in [26] and use it as baseline running all the benchmarks in our paper. Figure 20 plots the speedup of our bitwise operation. Even with random groups, we achieve 40% speedup, and our bitwise operation enjoys a better speedup with the outdegree-based GroupBy rules, i.e., 2.6×. Specifically, in random grouping, the maximum and minimum speedup is 2.5× of KG2 and 2% of FR. In comparison, the maximum and minimum speedup in GroupBy is 5.5× of KG1 and 15% of RD graph. Additional improvement from Groupby comes from the combined effect of high sharing ratio across grouped BFS instances and early termination enabled by bitwise traversal, which as a result allows concurrent instances to complete together and as early as possible.

In addition, we evaluate the impacts on the total number of global load transactions by bitwise traversal. Because bitwise status array consolidates the statuses of multiple (128 in our case) vertices into a single variable, we reduce the global load transactions of 1,024 BFS instances by 40%, i.e., from 53 to 38 million on average presented in Figure 21.

8.6 Comparison of State of the Art

We have implemented two CPU-based concurrent BFS, namely MS-BFS [26] and our own iBFS, both of which run 64 threads in total. In addition, we compare our GPU-based iBFS with B40C [29] and SpMM-BC [27]. B40C runs a single BFS instance on GPUs and has similar performance as the

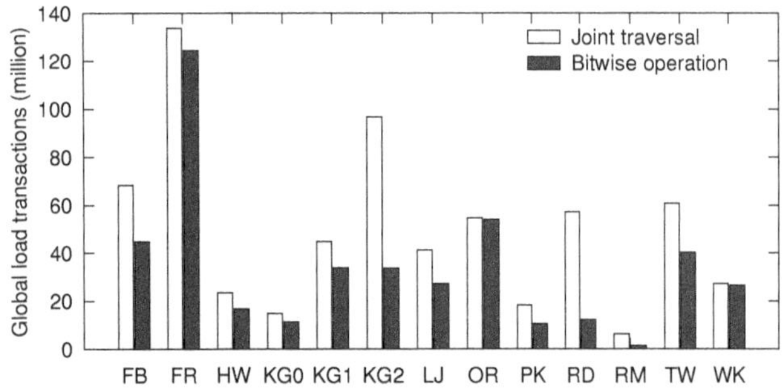

Figure 21: Total number of load transactions.

sequential or naive implementation presented in Figure 15, and SpMM-BC uses a simple GPU-based concurrent BFS to calculate betweenness centrality. Figure 22 presents the performance of all five implementations when running APSP on six different graphs.

CPU-based iBFS is significantly faster than MS-BFS thanks to the techniques such as GroupBy and early termination. The biggest speedup is achieved for the KG0 graph, where MS-BFS obtains 120 billion TEPS while our CPU-based iBFS reaches 397 billion TEPS. iBFS also achieves an average improvement of 45% on other five graphs. On GPUs, iBFS traverses on average 2× faster than SpMM-BC, and 19.3× than B40C. For graphs KG0 and HW, iBFS delivers about 700 and 300 TEPS respectively, greatly outperforming the other two implementations. Compared to the CPU-based implementation, GPU-based iBFS runs 2× faster on average across six different graphs.

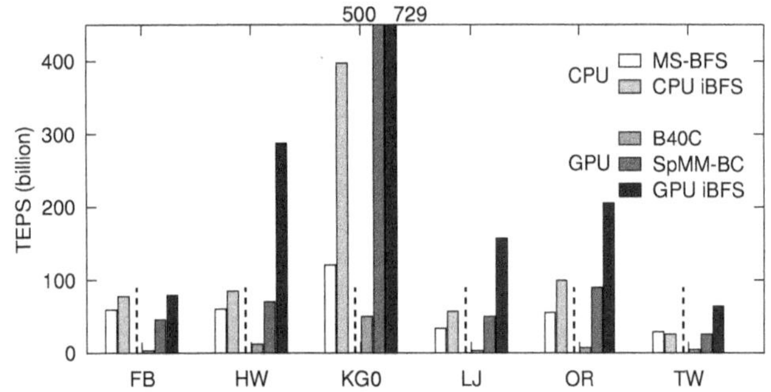

Figure 22: Comparison of CPU and GPU implementations.

8.7 Application: Reachability Index

To illustrate the broader application of iBFS on graph algorithms, in this paper we evaluate the benefits of using iBFS to construct the index for answering graph reachability queries, which computes the first k levels BFS for a large amount of selected vertices. Table 1 lists the runtimes of various implementations for constructing the index for 3-hop reachability. Clearly, GPU-based iBFS outperforms other concurrent BFS systems on four different graphs. Specifically, it is 21×, 3.3× and 2.2× faster than B40C, MS-BFS and CPU-based iBFS, respectively.

Dataset	CPU		GPU	
	MS-BFS	CPU-iBFS	B40C	GPU-iBFS
FB	19.2	16.5	302.8	14.3
KG0	1.85	0.56	2.9	0.31
OR	4.1	3.22	25.3	1.1
TW	2.1	2.7	27.8	0.9

Table 1: Runtime (hours) of 3-hop reachability index.

9. RELATED WORK

Our iBFS is closely related to CPU-based MS-BFS [26], which runs concurrent BFS by extending a single-threaded BFS, and compared to iBFS, underperforms on large graphs, e.g., it only achieves 10 billion TEPS on a graph with a billion of edges. In contrast, iBFS achieves more than 500 billion TEPS on a graph with billions of edges. Furthermore, the bitwise operation from MS-BFS cannot support early termination due to that it requires to reset the status array at each level, which leads to a much slower performance. Most notably, iBFS introduces a novel GroupBy strategy that improves the frontier sharing ratio dramatically and increases the benefit of concurrent traversal by another 2×.

Recent work has demonstrated that GPUs have great potentials in delivering high-performance breadth-first graph traversal [29,49]. One project SpMM-BC on regularized centrality [27] also extends the GPU-based BFS to concurrent BFS, but it does not support bottom-up BFS. On the other hand, the work [35] executes concurrent BFS to calculate the betweenness centrality [11] of a graph. However, each GPU in this work only executes a single BFS which is similar to the *naive* implementation in our work. In comparison, iBFS runs hundreds of BFS instances with one kernel and achieves on average 22× speedup compared to executing a single BFS on one GPU. Also, iBFS supports $\mathcal{O}(100)$ GPUs and achieves around 200 billion TEPS for graphs such as LJ and OR, significantly outperforming prior work [27, 35].

In addition, our work is related to three types of shortest path algorithms [50–56], namely, Dijkstra, Bellman-Ford and Floyd-Warshall. The first two algorithms focus on SSSP while the later APSP. Specifically, Dijkstra [57] applies to weighted graph where weight must be positive, with the complexity of $\mathcal{O}(|E| + |V|\log|V|)$. Bellman-Ford [58] extends Dijkstra by allowing negative weighted edges but non-negative cycles. Floyd-Warshall [59] works for APSP [60] with the same constraint as Bellman-Ford algorithm. In contrast, our iBFS applies to all types of shortest path problems on a unweighted graph with the time complexity of $\mathcal{O}(i|V|) \sim \mathcal{O}(i|E|)$.

PHAST [61] runs multiple SSSP on GPU concurrently. However, this work only applies to road network graphs and suffers from small-world graphs which do not have good separators as mentioned in [62]. Two MSSP algorithms [63,64] mainly focus on special graphs, i.e., planar and embedded graphs, respectively. In contrast, our iBFS applies to both small-world and random graphs, and leverages the opportunity of frontier sharing to accelerate concurrent BFS.

10. CONCLUSION

In this work, we present iBFS, a new GPU-based concurrent BFS system which leverages a novel GroupBy strategy, combined with joint frontier queue and bitwise operations, to achieve high-performance concurrent breadth-first traversals. iBFS achieves unprecedented performance of over 57,000 billion TEPS on over 100 GPUs. As part of future work, we plan to explore additional optimizations for iBFS and study its application on a wide range of domains.

ACKNOWLEDGMENTS

We would like to thank the anonymous reviewers for their comments and suggestions. This work was supported by NVIDIA and the National Science Foundation.

11. REFERENCES

[1] Stanley Milgram. The small world problem. *Psychology today*, 2(1):60–67, 1967.

[2] David Knoke and Song Yang. *Social network analysis*, volume 154. Sage, 2008.

[3] Juanzi Li, Jie Tang, Jing Zhang, Qiong Luo, Yunhao Liu, and Mingcai Hong. Eos: expertise oriented search using social networks. In *Proceedings of the 16th international conference on World Wide Web*, pages 1271–1272. ACM, 2007.

[4] Hawoong Jeong, Bálint Tombor, Réka Albert, Zoltan N Oltvai, and A-L Barabási. The large-scale organization of metabolic networks. *Nature*, 407(6804):651–654, 2000.

[5] David Easley and Jon Kleinberg. *Networks, crowds, and markets: Reasoning about a highly connected world*. Cambridge University Press, 2010.

[6] Pawan Harish and PJ Narayanan. Accelerating large graph algorithms on the gpu using cuda. In *High performance computing–HiPC*, pages 197–208. Springer, 2007.

[7] Hiroki Yanagisawa. A multi-source label-correcting algorithm for the all-pairs shortest paths problem. In *International Symposium on Parallel & Distributed Processing (IPDPS)*, pages 1–10. IEEE, 2010.

[8] I-Lin Wang, Ellis L Johnson, and Joel S Sokol. A multiple pairs shortest path algorithm. *Transportation science*, 39(4):465–476, 2005.

[9] Raimund Seidel. On the all-pairs-shortest-path problem in unweighted undirected graphs. *Journal of computer and system sciences*, 51(3):400–403, 1995.

[10] Abhinav Sarje and Srinivas Aluru. All-pairs computations on many-core graphics processors. *Parallel Computing*, 39(2):79–93, 2013.

[11] Ulrik Brandes. A faster algorithm for betweenness centrality*. *Journal of Mathematical Sociology*, 25(2):163–177, 2001.

[12] Kamesh Madduri, David Ediger, Karl Jiang, David A Bader, and Daniel Chavarria-Miranda. A faster parallel algorithm and efficient multithreaded implementations for evaluating betweenness centrality on massive datasets. In *International Symposium on Parallel & Distributed Processing (IPDPS)*, pages 1–8. IEEE, 2009.

[13] Paul W Olsen, Alan G Labouseur, and Jeong-Hyon Hwang. Efficient top-k closeness centrality search. In *International Conference on Data Engineering (ICDE)*, pages 196–207. IEEE, 2014.

[14] Hilmi Yildirim, Vineet Chaoji, and Mohammed J Zaki. Grail: Scalable reachability index for large graphs. *Proceedings of the VLDB Endowment*, 3(1-2):276–284, 2010.

[15] James Cheng, Zechao Shang, Hong Cheng, Haixun Wang, and Jeffrey Xu Yu. K-reach: who is in your small world. *Proceedings of the VLDB Endowment*, 5(11):1292–1303, 2012.

[16] Ruoming Jin, Yang Xiang, Ning Ruan, and David Fuhry. 3-hop: a high-compression indexing scheme for reachability query. In *Proceedings of the SIGMOD International Conference on Management of data*, pages 813–826. ACM, 2009.

[17] Shlomi Dolev, Yuval Elovici, and Rami Puzis. Routing betweenness centrality. *Journal of the ACM (JACM)*, 57(4):25, 2010.

[18] Shilpa Mahajan and Jyoteesh Malhotra. Energy efficient path determination in wireless sensor network using bfs approach. *Wireless Sensor Network*, 3(11):351, 2011.

[19] Vladimir Ufimtsev and Sanjukta Bhowmick. Application of group testing in identifying high betweenness centrality vertices in complex networks. In *11th Workshop on Machine Learning with Graphs, KDD*, 2013.

[20] Réka Albert, Hawoong Jeong, and Albert-László Barabási. Error and attack tolerance of complex networks. *nature*, 406(6794):378–382, 2000.

[21] Michael Bosse, Paul Newman, John Leonard, and Seth Teller. Simultaneous localization and map building in large-scale cyclic environments using the atlas framework. *The International Journal of Robotics Research*, 23(12):1113–1139, 2004.

[22] Shigeru Ichikawa. Navigation system and method for calculating a guide route, February 26 2002. US Patent 6,351,707.

[23] Angela Bonifati, Radu Ciucanu, and Aurélien Lemay. Learning path queries on graph databases. In *18th International Conference on Extending Database Technology (EDBT)*, 2014.

[24] Marc Najork and Janet L Wiener. Breadth-first crawling yields high-quality pages. In *Proceedings of the 10th international conference on World Wide Web*, pages 114–118. ACM, 2001.

[25] Xuesong Lu, Tuan Quang Phan, and Stéphane Bressan. Incremental algorithms for sampling dynamic graphs. In *Database and Expert Systems Applications*, pages 327–341. Springer, 2013.

[26] Manuel Then, Moritz Kaufmann, Fernando Chirigati, Tuan-Anh Hoang-Vu, Kien Pham, Alfons Kemper, Thomas Neumann, and Huy T Vo. The more the merrier: Efficient multi-source graph traversal. *Proceedings of the VLDB Endowment*, 8(4), 2014.

[27] Ahmet Erdem Sarıyüce, Erik Saule, Kamer Kaya, and Ümit V Çatalyürek. Regularizing graph centrality computations. *Journal of Parallel and Distributed Computing*, 2014.

[28] Ahmet Erdem Sariyuce, Erik Saule, Kamer Kaya, and Umit V Catalyurek. Hardware/software vectorization for closeness centrality on multi-/many-core architectures. In *International Parallel & Distributed Processing Symposium Workshops (IPDPSW)*, pages 1386–1395. IEEE, 2014.

[29] Duane Merrill, Michael Garland, and Andrew Grimshaw. Scalable gpu graph traversal. In *ACM PPoPP*, 2012.

[30] Rupesh Nasre, Martin Burtscher, and Keshav Pingali. Data-driven versus topology-driven irregular computations on gpus. In *27th International Symposium on Parallel & Distributed Processing (IPDPS)*, pages 463–474. IEEE, 2013.

[31] Sungpack Hong, Tayo Oguntebi, and Kunle Olukotun. Efficient parallel graph exploration on multi-core cpu and gpu. In *International Conference on Parallel*

Architectures and Compilation Techniques (PACT), pages 78–88. IEEE, 2011.

[32] S Beamer, K Asanovic, and D Patterson. Direction-optimizing breadth-first search. In *International Conference for High Performance Computing, Networking, Storage and Analysis (SC)*, pages 1–10. IEEE, 2012.

[33] Hang Liu and H. Howie Huang. Enterprise: Breadth-first graph traversal on gpu servers. In *International Conference for High Performance Computing, Networking, Storage and Analysis (SC)*, 2015.

[34] Nvidia. Nvidia kepler gk110 architecture whitepaper. 2013.

[35] Adam McLaughlin and David A Bader. Scalable and high performance betweenness centrality on the gpu. In *International Conference for High Performance Computing, Networking, Storage and Analysis (SC)*, pages 572–583. IEEE, 2014.

[36] Nvidia cuda c programming guide. *NVIDIA Corporation*, 2011.

[37] Intel Inc. Product brief intel xeon processor e7-8800/4800/2800 v2 product families. 2014.

[38] Intel Inc. Hpc code modernization workshop at lrz. 2015.

[39] Minas Gjoka, Maciej Kurant, Carter T. Butts, and Athina Markopoulou. Practical Recommendations on Crawling Online Social Networks. *JSAC*, 2011.

[40] Haewoon Kwak, Changhyun Lee, Hosung Park, and Sue Moon. What is twitter, a social network or a news media? In *WWW*, 2010.

[41] The University of Florida: Sparse Matrix Collection. http://www.cise.ufl.edu/research/sparse/matrices/.

[42] SNAP: Stanford Large Network Dataset Collection. http://snap.stanford.edu/data/.

[43] Deepayan Chakrabarti, Yiping Zhan, and Christos Faloutsos. R-mat: A recursive model for graph mining. In *SDM*, 2004.

[44] Graph500. http://www.graph500.org/.

[45] Green Graph500. http://green.graph500.org/.

[46] GTgraph: A suite of synthetic random graph generators. http://www.cse.psu.edu/~madduri/software/gtgraph/.

[47] Stéphane Bressan, Alfredo Cuzzocrea, Panagiotis Karras, Xuesong Lu, and Sadegh Heyrani Nobari. An effective and efficient parallel approach for random graph generation over gpus. *Journal of Parallel and Distributed Computing*, 73(3):303–316, 2013.

[48] Nvidia Profiler Tools. http://docs.nvidia.com/cuda/profiler-users-guide/.

[49] Sungpack Hong, Sang Kyun Kim, Tayo Oguntebi, and Kunle Olukotun. Accelerating cuda graph algorithms at maximum warp. In *PPoPP*, 2011.

[50] Philipp Klodt, Gerhard Weikum, Srikanta Bedathur, and Stephan Seufert. *Indexing Strategies for Constrained Shortest Paths over Large Social Networks*. PhD thesis, 2011.

[51] Huiping Cao, K Selçuk Candan, and Maria Luisa Sapino. Skynets: Searching for minimum trees in graphs with incomparable edge weights. In *Proceedings of the 20th ACM international conference on Information and knowledge management*, pages 1775–1784. ACM, 2011.

[52] Jun Gao, Jeffrey Xu Yu, Ruoming Jin, Jiashuai Zhou, Tengjiao Wang, and Dongqing Yang. Neighborhood-privacy protected shortest distance computing in cloud. In *Proceedings of the SIGMOD International Conference on Management of data*, pages 409–420. ACM, 2011.

[53] Weimin Yu, XINGQIN LIN, Wensheng Zhang, Julie McCann, et al. Fast all-pairs simrank assessment on large graphs and bipartite domains. 2014.

[54] Andy Diwen Zhu, Xiaokui Xiao, Sibo Wang, and Wenqing Lin. Efficient single-source shortest path and distance queries on large graphs. In *Proceedings of the 19th ACM SIGKDD international conference on Knowledge discovery and data mining*, pages 998–1006. ACM, 2013.

[55] Jianlong Zhong and Bingsheng He. Parallel graph processing on graphics processors made easy. *Proceedings of the VLDB Endowment*, 6(12):1270–1273, 2013.

[56] Jianlong Zhong and Bingsheng He. Medusa: A parallel graph processing system on graphics processors. *ACM SIGMOD Record*, 43(2):35–40, 2014.

[57] Roger Pearce, Maya Gokhale, and Nancy M Amato. Multithreaded asynchronous graph traversal for in-memory and semi-external memory. In *Proceedings of the International Conference for High Performance Computing, Networking, Storage and Analysis (SC)*, pages 1–11. IEEE Computer Society, 2010.

[58] Andrew Davidson, Sean Baxter, Michael Garland, and John D Owens. Work-efficient parallel gpu methods for single-source shortest paths. In *28th International Symposium on Parallel & Distributed Processing (IPDPS)*, pages 349–359. IEEE, 2014.

[59] Hristo Djidjev, Sunil Thulasidasan, Guillaume Chapuis, Rumen Andonov, and Dominique Lavenier. Efficient multi-gpu computation of all-pairs shortest paths. In *28th International Symposium on Parallel & Distributed Processing (IPDPS)*, pages 360–369. IEEE, 2014.

[60] Foto Afrati and Jeffrey Ullman. Matching bounds for the all-pairs mapreduce problem. In *Proceedings of the 17th International Database Engineering & Applications Symposium*, pages 3–4. ACM, 2013.

[61] Daniel Delling, Andrew V Goldberg, Andreas Nowatzyk, and Renato F Werneck. Phast: Hardware-accelerated shortest path trees. *Journal of Parallel and Distributed Computing*, 73(7):940–952, 2013.

[62] Edgar Solomonik, Aydin Buluc, and James Demmel. Minimizing communication in all-pairs shortest paths. In *27th International Symposium on Parallel & Distributed Processing (IPDPS)*, pages 548–559. IEEE, 2013.

[63] Philip N Klein. Multiple-source shortest paths in planar graphs. In *SODA*, volume 5, pages 146–155, 2005.

[64] Sergio Cabello, Erin W Chambers, and Jeff Erickson. Multiple-source shortest paths in embedded graphs. *SIAM Journal on Computing*, 42(4):1542–1571, 2013.

Tornado: A System For Real-Time Iterative Analysis Over Evolving Data

Xiaogang Shi Bin Cui Yingxia Shao Yunhai Tong
Key Lab of High Confidence Software Technologies (MOE), School of EECS, Peking University
{sxg, bin.cui, simon0227, yhtong}@pku.edu.cn

ABSTRACT

There is an increasing demand for real-time iterative analysis over evolving data. In this paper, we propose a novel execution model to obtain timely results at given instants. We notice that a loop starting from a good initial guess usually converges fast. Hence we organize the execution of iterative methods over evolving data into a main loop and several branch loops. The main loop is responsible for the gathering of inputs and maintains the approximation to the timely results. When the results are requested by a user, a branch loop is forked from the main loop and iterates until convergence to produce the results. Using the approximation of the main loop, the branch loops can start from a place near the fixed-point and converge quickly.

Since the inputs not reflected in the approximation is concerned with the approximation error, we develop a novel bounded asynchronous iteration model to enhance the timeliness. The bounded asynchronous iteration model can achieve fine-grained updates while ensuring correctness for general iterative methods.

Based on the proposed execution model, we design and implement a prototype system named Tornado on top of Storm. Tornado provides a graph-parallel programming model which eases the programming of most real-time iterative analysis tasks. The reliability is also enhanced by provisioning efficient fault tolerance mechanisms. Empirical evaluation conducted on Tornado validates that various real-time iterative analysis tasks can improve their performance and efficiently tolerate failures with our execution model.

1. INTRODUCTION

Real-time data analysis is very challenging as we must produce timely results at required instants while data continuously arrives and evolves over time. The ability of stream processing systems to achieve low latencies makes them attractive to real-time analysis. Recently, many stream processing systems have been proposed to facilitate real-time data analysis at scale [42, 35, 46]. But these systems are short of applicability as they provide little support for iterative methods which are often deployed in data analysis tasks.

Many machine learning and data mining problems are solved by starting with an initial guess and repeatedly refining the solution with iterations. These algorithms are traditionally performed on static datasets; but the requirement for timeliness now is leading to a shift to adaptive learning and stream mining [22, 49]. Given the wide adoption of iterative methods in data analysis and the increasing demand for timeliness, it's critical for us to develop a system that can perform real-time iterative analysis over evolving data.

A naive method to perform real-time computation over evolving data is collecting the inputs continuously and performing the computation when the results are required. It allows the deployment of existing systems designed for static data, e.g., Spark and GraphLab. Though these systems are efficient to process data with large volume, they usually experience high latencies because they have to load all collected data and perform computation from scratch.

Some attempts made on adaptive systems, e.g. Incoop [7] and Kineograph [13], provided methods to track the modification to the inputs so that they can reduce the cost of data collection. They also employed incremental methods to avoid redundant computation. But the incremental methods enforce a order on the execution of the requests. The enforced order disallows them to produce timely results at given instants because new inputs cannot be processed before the current computation completes. To reduce the dependencies between different epoches, Naiad [32, 33] decomposed difference traces into multiple dimensions and allowed them to be combined in different ways for different versions. The relaxation in dependencies allows an epoch to be processed without waiting for the completion of preceding epochs.

In all these systems, the latency is dominated by the amount of computation to perform at the required instant. Mini-batch methods are widely adopted to reduce the latency. In mini-batch methods, the inputs are organized into a series of epochs and the results are updated when an epoch ends. When the results at an instant is required, they can be incrementally computed from the results of the last epoch. Because the amount of updates to be processed at the required instant is limited by the epoch size, we can achieve a relatively low latency.

Though mini-batch methods are proved useful in non-iterative computation over data streams, they are not suited for real-time iterative computation. A mini-batch method works only when the cost to incrementally maintain the results scales sub-linearly or linearly with the number of updates. But the studies in adaptive computing suggest that the requirement is not satisfied in many iterative methods [16]. For example, when a graph is updated, the time needed to incrementally update PageRank results is proportional to the current graph size, but not the number of updated edges [5]. Therefore, shrinking epochs will not help reduce the latency.

In this paper, we propose a novel execution model that allows real-time iterative analysis over evolving data. We notice that *a loop starting with a good initial guess usually converges faster than*

SIGMOD'16, June 26-July 01, 2016, San Francisco, CA, USA

ISBN 978-1-4503-3531-7/16/06... $15.00

DOI: http://dx.doi.org/10.1145/2882903.2882950

those starting with poor guesses. If we can obtain a good approximation of a loop's results, then we can efficiently reduce the computation time of the loop. In mini-batch methods, the results of the last completed epoch are used as the initial guesses. But because the most recent inputs are not reflected in the initial guesses, the approximation error is relatively high. The observation motivates us to organize the computation into two separated parts: a main loop and several branch loops.

The main loop continuously gathers the incoming inputs and approximates the results at each instant. There already exist many studies in the approximation for iterative methods in the context of streaming mining [40, 14, 16]. Users can deploy them to approximate the initial guesses for specific iterative methods. For a wider range of iterative methods, users can approximate the initial guesses by performing the iterative methods on partial inputs. These approximation methods can provide better initial guesses than mini-batch methods because their computation complexity are much lower than the incremental counterparts. They can catch up with the evolving data, adapting the approximation to the changes.

Different branch loops correspond to different queries over the data. When a user issues a request to retrieve the results at a certain instant, a branch loop will be forked from the main loop and start its execution to return the precise results. The computation of different branch loops are independent of each other. They can benefit from the approximation of the main loop. Because the main loop can provide a good initial guess, they can start from a place near the fixed-point and converge quickly to return results.

In our execution model, the key to achieve low latency is reducing the approximation error. Because synchronous iteration models require global barriers to perform iterations, they are unable to gather inputs before all local computation completes. Many inputs are not reflected in the approximation. These inputs significantly increase the approximation error. On the other hand, asynchronous iteration models allow local computation to proceed to the next iteration individually. The ability to achieve low latencies and fine-grained updates allow them to efficiently adapt the approximation. But unfortunately, asynchronous iteration models cannot ensure correctness for many iterative methods when the degree of asynchronism is not bounded [12, 19, 37, 26].

To allow fine-grained updates while ensuring correctness for most iterative methods, we deploy a bounded asynchronous model to perform iterations. Though there exist some bounded asynchronous iteration models implemented in Parameter Servers [15, 26, 29, 45], they are designed for specific iterative methods. It's difficult for them to perform common graph analysis like PageRank and Shortest Single-Source Path. They are also unable to deal with retractable data streams. Different from these existing models, our iteration model utilizes data dependencies to manage iterations. With a three-phase update protocol, it can ensure correctness and consistency for general iterative methods over evolving data.

Based on the execution model of loops and iterations, we design and implement a prototype system named Tornado on top of Storm [42]. Tornado adopts a graph-parallel programming model which is similar to those in popular iterative computation systems [31, 30, 23]. Users can easily develop their applications to perform iterative analysis over data streams. Efficient fault tolerance and recovery mechanisms are provided so that user applications can achieve fault-tolerated execution at scale.

We implement many data analysis algorithms in Tornado and conduct a comprehensive analysis to study the benefits and costs of our designs. The evaluation demonstrates that Tornado can achieve significant performance gains from the main loop's approximation and can efficiently tolerate failures.

To summarize, the main contributions of our work include:

- We carefully analyze the challenges of real-time iterative data analysis over evolving data as well as the benefits and limitations of existing methods.
- We propose a novel execution model which can improve the timeliness without enforcing any partial orders.
- We propose a bounded asynchronous iteration model which provides correct and efficient execution.
- We design and implement a prototype system which allows easy programming and fault-tolerated execution at scale.
- We conduct extensive empirical studies on the prototype system. The experiments with various common iterative workloads validate that the execution can efficiently improve their performance while tolerating unexpected faults.

The rest of the paper is organized as follows. We first briefly review iterative computation in Section 2. Then we introduce the execution model for loops in Section 3. The details of the bounded asynchronous iteration model is given in the Section 4. The implementation and evaluation of Tornado are presented in Section 5 and 6 respectively. Finally we review the related work in Section 7 and conclude the work in Section 8.

2. ITERATIVE COMPUTATION

The researchers in the community of numerical analysis have put a lot of effort in implementing iterative methods under parallel and distributed settings. In this section, we briefly review the iteration models and their convergence properties. By extending these studies, we lay a sound theoretical foundation for our work, achieving guaranteed correctness for many real-time iterative methods.

2.1 Iterative Methods

Many iterative methods have similar programming structures. Suppose x_i is the i-th variable in the program and D_i is the domain of x_i. The state of a program with n variables then can be represented by $\sigma = (x_1, x_2, ..., x_n)$, $\sigma \in \Sigma$ and $\Sigma = \mathrm{D}_1 \times \mathrm{D}_2 \times ... \times \mathrm{D}_n$. x_i is also called a component of σ, $i = 1, 2, ..., n$.

Given a function $f : \Sigma \to \Sigma$, the problem is to find a fixed point of f which is an element $\sigma^\infty \in \Sigma$ and $f(\sigma^\infty) = \sigma^\infty$. It's usually solved by starting from an initial guess $\sigma^0 \in \Sigma$ and iteratively applying the function:

$$\sigma^{k+1} = f(\sigma^k) = f^k(\sigma^0), k \in \mathbb{N} \tag{1}$$

σ^k represents the value of σ in the k-th iteration and $f^k(\sigma^0)$ is the results if we start f from σ^0 and repeat the execution of f for k times. σ^∞ is approximated by $\sigma^{\hat{k}}$ where $|\sigma^{\hat{k}+1} - \sigma^{\hat{k}}| \leq \varepsilon$ and ε is the precision required in the computation.

2.2 Iteration Models

When performing iterative methods in parallel, the components of σ are distributed over a set of processing units. Different processing units communicate with each other through shared memory or message passing.

The execution of synchronous iteration models strictly obeys the definition of iterative methods. In each iteration, the processing units read the value of σ in the previous iteration and update the values of all components. The computation proceeds to the next iteration only when all components complete their updates.

The requirement for synchronization however is eliminated in asynchronous iteration models [12]. In asynchronous iteration models, a processing unit can update the components without the most recent value of σ and can delay the computation of some components for several iterations.

Let $\tau^k_{i\to j}$ be the iteration number of x_i that is read in the computation of x^k_j, S_i be the scheduling strategy of x_i which contains the iterations in which x_i is updated. Both synchronous and asynchronous iterations can be mathematically modeled as follows [6]:

Definition 1 (General Iteration Model) *Given an initial guess $\sigma^0 \in \Sigma$ and the scheduling strategies for all components $\{S_0, S_1, ...\}$, the iterative method:*

$$x^k_i = \begin{cases} x^{k-1}_i, & i \notin S_i \\ f_i(x_1^{\tau^k_{1\to i}}, x_2^{\tau^k_{2\to i}}, ..., x_n^{\tau^k_{n\to i}}), & i \in S_i \end{cases} \quad (2)$$

is said valid if the following assumptions hold:

1. ***Causality.*** *Only the values produced in previous iterations can be used in the computation, i.e.*

$$0 \le \tau^k_{i\to j} \le k-1, k \in \mathbb{N}$$

2. ***Eventual Scheduling.*** *Though the updates of some components may be delayed, these components will eventually be updates as time goes on, i.e.*

$$|S_i| = \infty, i = 1, 2, ..., n$$

3. ***Eventual Propagation.*** *A component will eventually receive new values of other components, i.e.*

$$\lim_{k\to\infty} \tau^k_{j\to i} = \infty, i, j = 1, 2, ..., n$$

$\{k - \tau^k_{j\to i}\}$ are the *delays* (or staleness in [26]) in the computation of x^k_i. When $S_i = \mathbb{N}$ and $k - \tau^k_{j\to i} = 1$, the iterations are synchronous; otherwise, the computation is asynchronous.

2.3 Bounded Asynchronous Iteration Models

As asynchronous iteration models eliminate the synchronization between different iterations, they can only ensure correctness for limited iterative methods. The convergence properties of asynchronous iterations are well understood in both linear and nonlinear cases [12, 19, 21]. These studies suggest that for most common iterative methods, including Stochastic Gradient Descent and Markov Chains, convergence is guaranteed only when the delays are bounded. Hence a bounded asynchronous iteration model is applicable for more iterative methods.

Definition 2 (Bounded Asynchronous Iterations) *A valid iterative method is said to be bounded asynchronous if there exists a delay bound $B \in \mathbb{N}$ s.t.*

1. *The delays of all components are less than B, i.e.*

$$k - B < \tau^k_{i\to j} < k, i, j = 1, 2, ..., n, k \ge 0$$

2. *All components are updated at least once in B iterations, i.e.*

$$\{k, k+1, ..., k+B-1\} \cap S^i \ne \emptyset, i = 1, 2, ..., n, k \ge 0$$

Obviously, a synchronous iteration model is also bounded asynchronous. Its delay bound B is 1.

3. REAL-TIME ITERATIVE COMPUTATION

In this section, we will introduce the problem of real-time iterative analysis over evolving data and describe the proposed execution model. We explicitly distinguish loops from iterations in this paper. We refer the procedure to obtain the value of f^∞ as a *loop* and each execution of f as an *iteration*. Obviously, the execution of a loop contains a number of iterations. A loop converges when its fixed-point is reached.

3.1 Problem Definition

In the real-time iterative analysis over evolving data, the inputs are continuously updated by external sources. The input data, $\mathcal{S}$ can be described as a unbounded sequence of stream tuples. Each stream tuple δ_t is associated with a timestamp t to identify the time when δ happens. In this paper, for simplicity and without loss of generality, we adopt the turnstile stream model [34] and assume that all stream tuples are updates to $\mathcal{S}$. The value of $\mathcal{S}$ at an instant $\bar{t}$ can be obtained by summing up all updates happening before $\bar{t}$:

$$\mathcal{S}_{[\bar{t}]} = \sum_{t\le\bar{t}} \delta_t$$

Definition 3 (Real-time Iterative Analysis over Evolving Data) *Given an instant t and a method f whose input data is $\mathcal{S}$, the problem of real-time iterative analysis over evolving data is to obtain the fixed-point of f at the instant t s.t.*

$$\sigma^\infty_{[t]} = \sigma = f(\mathcal{S}_{[t]}, \sigma)$$

A typical example of the problem is observed in search engines. In a simplified setting, the input of a search engine is a retractable edge stream which is produced by the crawlers. Iterative methods like PageRank are deployed to rank collected pages. When new pages are collected or old pages are updated, the search engine has to update its repository and adapt the ranking to the changes. To reflect the most recent updates, search engines usually updates its results at regular intervals, e.g. hourly or daily. In more general scenarios, a user may also commit ad-hoc queries to retrieve the results at specific instants. In all cases, the latencies of the queries should be as low as possible.

3.2 Design Consideration

Many existing systems organize the inputs into batches and deploy incremental methods to obtain timely results. They assume that the time complexity to incrementally update the results is proportional to the amount of new inputs. Under such assumption, the latency can be reduced by shrinking the batch as much as possible. But such assumption does not hold for most iterative methods. Consequently, the timeliness they achieve is limited.

The difficulty to develop efficient incremental methods to compute the results forces us to find alternative methods to satisfy the requirement of iterative analysis over evolving data. Our design is heavily encouraged by the following observations.

Observation One: Many iterative methods can converge to the same fixed-point with different initial guesses. The observation can be made in many iterative methods. For example, a Markov Chain starting from various initial distributions can converge to the same stationary distribution only if its transformation matrix is irreducible and aperiodic.

Definition 4 (Equivalence of Initial Guesses) *Given two different initial guesses σ^0_i and σ^0_j, we say they are equivalent in terms of input x if the loops starting from them can converge to the identical fixed-point, i.e.*

$$\sigma^0_i \sim \sigma^0_j \leftrightarrow f^\infty(x, \sigma^0_i) = f^\infty(x, \sigma^0_j)$$

Though loops from equivalent initial guesses will converge to the same fixed-point, the initial guesses have different effects on the convergence rate.

Observation Two: For many iterative methods, the execution time is closely relative to the approximation error. A loop starting from a good initial guess usually converges faster than those starting from bad initial guesses. If we can obtain a good initial guess, we can efficiently improve the performance of a loop.

Numerous methods have been proposed to approximate the results of iterative methods [40, 14]. These approximate methods all can provide a good approximation for the iterative computation over evolving data. Because their computation complexity is much less than the original iterative method, they can quickly adapt the approximation to the input changes.

Suppose at the time t, we have already obtained an approximation $\tilde{\sigma}_{[t]}$ with the approximation method g. We can produce the results of $\sigma_{[t]}^{\infty} = f^{\infty}(\mathcal{S}_{[t]}, \sigma^0)$ in two steps.

In the first step, we use an adaptive method $\mathcal{A}$ to obtain an valid initial guess from the approximation:

$$\sigma_{[t]}^{0} = \mathcal{A}(\tilde{\sigma}_{[t]}), \quad \text{where } \sigma_{[t]}^{0} \sim \sigma^0$$

In the second step, we iteratively perform the original method f to obtain the fixed point:

$$\sigma_{[t]}^{\infty} = f^{\infty}(\mathcal{S}_{[t]}, \sigma_{[t]}^{0})$$

As both the approximate method g and the original method f can be computed incrementally, we can avoid the difficult problem of incremental computation between different loops. Now the computation of $\sigma_{[t]}^{\infty}$ does not depend on previous results, $\sigma_{[t-\Delta t]}^{\infty}$. By not enforcing any order between the computation of different requests, we are able to produce timely results for ad-hoc queries. But to ensure correctness and benefit from the approximation, the following two conditions must be satisfied:

- **Correctness Condition.** $\tilde{\sigma}_{[t]}$ is equivalent to σ_0 in terms of the input $\mathcal{S}_{[t]}$.
- **Profitability Condition.** The execution time of f depends on the approximation error of the initial guesses and the approximate error made by g is kept small enough during the evolvement of $\mathcal{S}$.

Fortunately, the two conditions can be satisfied in most common iterative methods with minor changes. For example, Stochastic Gradient Descent (SGD) avoids the costly computation of gradients by approximating the gradient with an unbiased sampling of observation instances. The unbiased sampling is usually done by random sampling. But it's problematic because when the observation instances evolves over time, the old instances will be sampled more times than the new ones. The results produced by the approximate method hence are not valid initial guesses. In these cases, we should use reservoir sampling [44] instead to obtain the unbiased sampling of data streams. The correctness condition can be satisfied as reservoir sampling can ensure that all instances are sampled with identical possibility, regardless of the time when they come in.

3.3 Execution Model

Based on the ideas described above, we organize the iterative computation over evolving data into a main loop and several branch loops. The execution model of loops is illustrated in Figure 1.

The main difference made by the execution model of loops is that the collection of inputs and the computation of iterations are interleaved. In the main loop, we continuously gather incoming data and approximate the results at current instant. Let $\Delta \mathcal{S}_i$ be the inputs collected in the i-th iteration and $\tilde{\sigma}^i$ be the approximation in the i-th iteration, then we have $\tilde{\sigma}^i = g(\sum_{j=1}^{i} \Delta \mathcal{S}_j, \tilde{\sigma}^{i-1})$, where g is the approximation function.

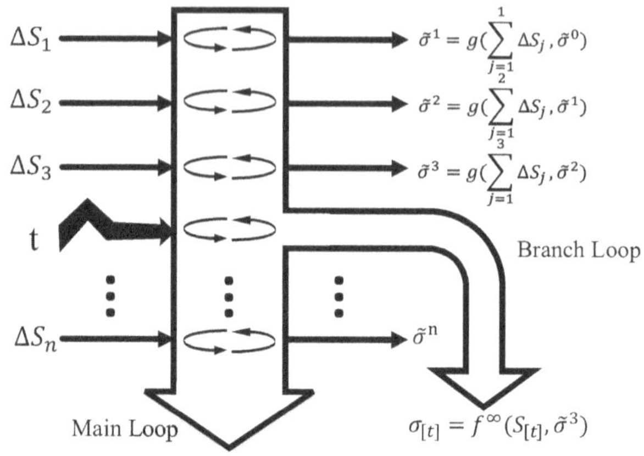

Figure 1: Illustration of the execution model of loops.

Users can issue their requests at regular intervals or send ad-hoc requests at specific instants. When the result at an instant t is required, we take a snapshot of $\mathcal{S}$ and fork a branch loop to perform iterations over the taken snapshot. Suppose by the time the user issues a request, the main loop has completed the execution of the i-th iteration. We can start the branch loop with the approximation obtained from the gathered input $\sum_{j=1}^{i} \Delta \mathcal{S}_j$. Though the inputs collected in the i-th iteration are not reflected in the approximation, the approximation error can be very small if $\|\mathcal{S}_{[t]} - \sum_{j=1}^{i} \Delta \mathcal{S}_j\|$ is small enough. The fixed-point at t, $\sigma_{[t]}^{\infty}$, is obtained when the branch loop converges.

Our execution model does not rely incremental methods to reduce the latency. Instead, the key to achieve low latency is reducing the approximation error. By starting from a place near the fixed-point, the performance of branch loops is improved. As the performance improvement is not gained from incremental methods, we avoid the partial orders between different loops. Besides, since the computation performed in the main loop can be shared by all branch loops, the overall amount of computation is also reduced.

4. ITERATION MODEL

To reduce the approximation error of initial guesses, the amount of the inputs that are not reflected in the approximation should be very small. To the satisfy the requirement, we propose a novel partially asynchronous iteration model which can guarantee correctness for most common iterative methods. We introduce the details of the iteration model in this section.

4.1 Determining Iterations

A key issue in the iteration management is to determine the iteration in which each update is performed. The iteration information then can be used to track progress and bound the iteration delays.

It's easy to determine iterations in synchronous models as all components must proceed to the next iteration with global synchronization barriers. Therefore, the iteration numbers of all components are the same. But as these global synchronization barriers don't allow fine-grained updates, we must develop a different method to determine the iteration of each update.

To support iterative computation over evolving data, we start from the general iteration model described in Section 2.2 and utilize the dependencies between different components to determine the iteration of each update.

Definition 5 (Dependency) *We say a component x_i depends on x_j if the value of x_j affects the value of x_i. If x_i depends on x_j, we call x_j is a* producer *of x_i. x_i in turn is a* consumer *of x_j.*

The dependencies can be easily obtained in many iterative methods where the dependencies are explicitly expressed as the edges of graphs. With the dependencies between different components, we can reason about the causality in the iterative computation. Suppose x and y are two components and y is a producer of x. We consider the cases when x receives the update of y to motivate our update rules. The iteration number of x and the update of y are τ_x and τ_y respectively:

- If $\tau_y \geq \tau_x$, it's indicated that y is updated in an iteration later than x. Hence according to Eq. 1, x should be updated in the next iteration. Therefore, we should set τ_x to $\tau_y + 1$. The iteration numbers of x may not be continuous as we allow delaying the update of a component. In this case, the update of x is not scheduled between the iterations from $\tau_x + 1$ to τ_y, i.e. $\{\tau_x + 1, ..., \tau_y\} \subseteq \mathbb{N} - S_x$.
- If $\tau_y < \tau_x$, y propagates to x an update which is produced in an iteration earlier than τ_x. Inconsistency arises in this case. Since x has proceeded to the iteration τ_x, it must have received an update from its producers in an iteration before τ_x. When x is updated, it doesn't observe the update of y in iteration τ_y. Now that y is updated, the fact is inconsistent with x's observation.

From the discussion above, we can see that to ensure consistency, the iteration in which a component is updated cannot be earlier than the iterations of its consumers. The following rules hence can be derived to ensure the validity of the iteration model:

1. When a component is updated in an iteration, the update should be observed by its consumers in the next iteration.
2. A component should be updated when it observes the update to its consumers, but the update can be delayed.
3. The iteration in which an update is performed cannot be later than the iterations of its consumers.

Rule 1 follows the definition of iterative methods, and Rule 3 is actually derived from the contraposition of Rule 1. By delaying the update of the component, we can achieve a valid and consistent iteration model with Rule 2. These update rules can ensure the validity and consistency of iteration models. An example which is executed using the update rules is illustrated in Figure 2.

Here we emphasize that the scheduling of updates is only *logical*. The concept of *scheduling strategy* helps us better understand the execution of our iteration model; but in practice, there does not exist a scheduler to update components according to the scheduling strategy. When a component receives an update, it can update itself and propagate its update immediately with the iteration information gained from its consumers.

4.2 The Three-Phase Update Protocol

The update rules imply that to determine the iteration number of a component, we should gather the iteration numbers of its consumers. Since all components are updated asynchronously and communicate with each other using message passing, it's possible that a component is updated after it replies to a producer with its iteration number. Inconsistency will arise in these cases.

To ensure that all updates are consistent with the observations, a component cannot update itself when it's still involved in the updates of its producers. Intuitively, the problem is a special case

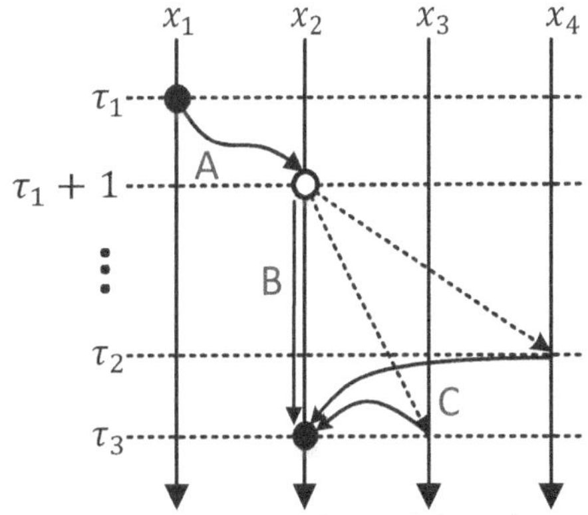

Figure 2: Illustration of the iteration model. x_2 is a consumer of x_1 and also a producer of x_3 and x_4. Suppose x_1 is updated in the iteration τ_1, then x_2 should update itself accordingly. The update of x_2 are performed in three steps: (A) When x_1 is updated, x_2 will observe the update in the next iteration and is prepared to update itself. (B) The update of x_2 however is *"delayed"* to make the scheduling strategy consistent with the observation of x_3 and x_4. (C) By the time x_2 is to update, x_3 and x_4 have proceeded to the iterations numbered with τ_2 and τ_3 respectively. In the progress towards the current iterations, they don't observe the update of x_2. Therefore, to make the scheduling strategy consistent with their observations, we update x_2 in an iteration whose number is no less than $\max(\tau_2, \tau_3)$.

of the well-known problem of *dining philosophers* [17]. When a component is to update itself, it must obtain the forks of its consumers and its consumer cannot update itself before the borrowed fork is returned. Generally, the dining philosophers problem can be solved by the Dijkstra [17] and Chandy-Misra [11] algorithms, but they both target at static dependency graphs and are not applicable in our cases where the dependency graph is continuously modified by the evolving inputs. Since the Dijkstra algorithm requires a component to acquire locks in sequence, it's inefficient when a component has a large number of neighbors or the list of neighbors is unknown at advance. The Chandy-Misra algorithm is also problematic as it avoids deadlocks by enforcing the resource priority graphs to be acyclic. When the algorithm starts, an initial acyclic priority graph is obtained by assigning forks to the nodes with lower IDs and no cycles are allowed to arise during the execution. But when new forks are created during the computation, it's difficult for us to assign these new forks. Cycles may arise if we continue assigning forks to the nodes with lower IDs.

To ensure the consistency of our iteration model, we adapt Chandy-Misra to our cases with a method based on Lamport Clocks [28]. Each component maintains a Lamport clock to record the time when it's updated. A component only replies to its producers when it's not updated or its update happens after that of its producers. Since an update is only blocked by the updates that *happen before* it, the implied partial orders make deadlocks and starvation impossible. As the partial orders in the execution are enforced by the logical clocks but not the acyclic priority graphs, we are flexible to deal with the evolvement of the dependency graph. The pseudo code of our iteration model is illustrated in Figure 3. The update of a component x is performed in three phases:

Update Phase. When x receives an input or an update, it first gathers the input/update and updates its iteration number. Suppose the iteration numbers of x and the update are $\tau(x)$ and $\tau(\delta)$ respectively. To preserve the causality, the new iteration number of

```
1  /* phase 1: gather updates from its producers */
2  OnReceiveUpdate(producer, iteration, data)
3    this.iteration = max(this.iteration, iteration+1);
4    /* gather the update with the user-defined function */
5    gather(id, iteration, data);
6    this.prepare_list.remove(producer);
7    /* prepare the update when it's not involved in any preparation */
8    if this.prepare_list is null and this.update_time is null
9      call OnPrepareUpdate();
10
11 /* phase 2: prepare to update itself */
12 OnPrepareUpdate()
13   this.update_time = LamportClock::get_time();
14   foreach consumer in this.consumer_list {
15     send (PREPARE, this.id, this.update_time) to the consumer
16     this.waiting_list.add(consumer);
17   }
18
19 OnReceivePrepare(producer, update_time)
20   this.prepare_list.add(producer);
21   /* only acknowledge those updates happening before */
22   if this.update_time is null or this.update_time > update_time
23     send (ACKNOWLEDGE, this.id, this.version) to the producer
24   else
25     this.pending_list.add(producer);
26
27 OnReceiveAcknowledge(consumer, iteration)
28   this.iteration = max(this.iteration, iteration);
29   this.waiting_list.remove(consumer);
30   /* commit the update when all its consumers have acknowledged */
31   if this.waiting_list is null
32     call OnCommitUpdate();
33
34 /* phase 3: commit the update to its consumers */
35 OnCommitUpdate()
36     this.update_time = null;
37     /* commit the update with the user-defined function */
38     scatter(UPDATE, this.id, this.iteration);
39     /* reply to all pending producers */
40     foreach producer in this.pending_list
41       send (ACKNOWLEDGE, this.id, this.iteration) to the producer
```

Figure 3: The pseudo code of the three-phase update protocol

x should be greater than $\tau(\delta)$. Therefore we update the iteration number of x as follows:

$$\tau'(x) = \max(\tau(x), \tau(\delta) + 1)$$

where $\tau'(x)$ is the new iteration number of x. If the update comes from one of the x's producers, x will also remove the producer from its `PrepareList`. When the `PrepareList` is empty, it can prepare its update. (`OnReceiveUpdate`, lines 1-9)

Prepare Phase. In the second phase, x first retrieves the Lamport clock to obtain the time it's updated. Then x should determine the iteration in which its update is scheduled. It sends `PREPARE` messages to its consumers to collect their iteration numbers. The timestamp obtained from the Lamport Clock is also attached in the message. (`OnPrepareUpdate`, lines 11-17)

Once a consumer y of x receives the `PREPARE` message from x, it replies to x with an `ACKNOWLEDGE` message which contains its iteration number. Then y will put x in its `PrepareList`. As a component can only start its update when its `PrepareList` is empty, to avoid the starvation of the update of itself, y will not acknowledge x if it's already updated and its update happens before that of x. Therefore y will not acknowledge a `PREPARE` message if it has updated itself and the update happens before the producer of the `PrepareMessage`. In these cases, y will put the `PREPARE` messages in a pending list. (`OnReceivePrepare`, lines 19-25)

When x receives the `ACKNOWLEDGE` message from its consumers, it will update its iteration number accordingly. During the preparation, x can continue gathering updates and acknowledging `PREPARE` messages. But it will not gather any input because new inputs may change the dependency graph. The results of the preparation will be incorrect if new consumers are added to x. (`OnReceiveAcknowledge`, lines 27-32)

Commit Phase. When x has received all the iteration numbers of its consumers and its `PrepareList` is empty, it can commit its update. The iteration in which x is updated, $\tau'(x)$, must be the maximum iteration number of all its consumers, i.e.

$$\tau'(x) = \max\Big(\tau(x), \tau(y_1), \tau(y_2), ..., \tau(y_n)\Big)$$

where y_i is a consumer of x. x will commit its new value and iteration number to all its consumers with `COMMIT` messages. It will also acknowledge all pended `PREPARE` messages (if any) with its new iteration number. (`OnCommitUpdate`, lines 35-41)

The timestamp obtained by x will be cleaned after the commitment. Now x can gather the inputs that come in during the preparation of the update. The update protocol will be executed again when x gathers any inputs or updates.

4.3 Terminating Iterations

In existing totally asynchronous iteration models, there is no method to detect the termination of an iteration. A loop converges when all components are updated and no updates are in transition. But in distributed settings, it's difficult to detect whether there are updates in transition. Some systems [30, 23] attempt to detect the convergence of loops using the Chandy-Lamport algorithm [10]. But their usage is problematic as the Chandy-Lamport algorithm only works for the detection of stable properties. The convergence of asynchronous loops however is not stable.

With the iteration numbers of each update, we can easily determine the termination of an iteration and step further to detect the convergence of a loop. According to the causality of iteration models, a component's update in an iteration will cause its consumers to update themselves a later iteration. Eventually all components will proceed to the succeeding iterations. The property implied by the causality allows us to terminate an iteration when all iterations preceding it have terminated and all vertices have proceeded to the iterations succeeding it.

The convergence of a loop is as same as the synchronous iteration models. When an iteration terminates, the loop can track the progress made in the iteration and evaluate the convergence condition with the progress. Generally a loop can converge when no updates are performed in an iteration.

A major difference made by our iteration model is that the iteration in which a vertex is updated is determined by the iterations of its consumers. In other systems, e.g., Naiad, the values of a vertex's versions form a continuous sequence. When a vertex completes its update in an iteration, its iteration number will be added by one. But in our iteration model, the iteration numbers of a vertex may not be continuous.

4.4 Bounding Delays

To ensure correctness for a wide variety of iterative methods, we must bound the iteration delays in the asynchronous execution. It can be done by blocking the propagation of all the updates that proceed too far.

Suppose the number of delays allowed in the execution is B and the first iteration that does not terminate is τ. We bound the delays by stopping the propagation of the updates in iteration $\tau + B - 1$. If a component is updated in iteration $\tau + B - 1$, then its update will not be gathered by its consumers. These updates are gathered only when iteration τ terminates. We can easily prove that the resulting iterations are valid bounded asynchronous iterations (see Appendix A for the proof).

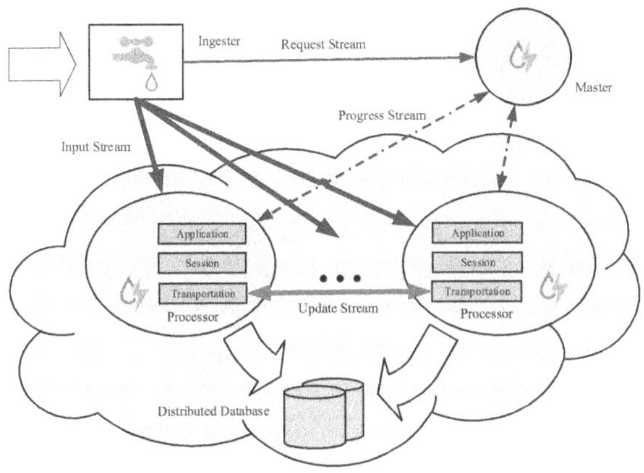

Figure 4: System architecture of Tornado.

The bounding of delays also allows the reduction in the number of PREPARE messages. If a component is updated in the iteration $\tau + B - 1$, we can commit its update without sending PREPARE messages. It's because the iteration numbers returned by its consumers cannot be larger than $\tau + B - 1$.

When B is set to 1, all updates will happen in the iteration $\tau + B - 1$ and they will not be gathered until all components have been updated in the iteration τ. In such cases, the execution of our partially asynchronous iteration model becomes exactly the same as the synchronous iteration models.

5. SYSTEM IMPLEMENTATION

Based on the execution model, we design and implement a prototype system named Tornado on top of Storm. All code is implemented in Java and the core library contains approximately 6000 lines of code. In this section, we will introduce the implementation details of Tornado, including the topology of Tornado, data storage and fault tolerance mechanisms.

Though this section focuses on the implementation on Storm, our techniques can be applied to any distributed systems that allow the components to communicate with each other by message passing.

5.1 Topology Setup

Storm is a popular system for distributed and fault-tolerated stream processing. An application in Storm can be developed by implementing two main components, *spout* and *bolt*, and connecting them to form a topology. A spout receives inputs from external sources and feeds them to the bolts. A bolt processes received messages and emits newly produced messages to other bolts. Both spouts and bolts are required to be stateless in Storm. Program states, if any, must be stored in external storage.

Tornado extends Storm with the ability to perform iterative computation over data streams. To ease the programming, Tornado adopts a graph-parallel programming model[1]. The execution of a user program is organized as a directed graph. Users can define the behavior of vertices and describe how the vertices are connected.

The topology of Tornado is illustrated in Figure 4. There are three different nodes in the topology, namely *ingester*, *processor* and *master*. Ingesters are implemented by spouts while the other ones are implemented by bolts. The ingesters collect inputs from external sources and send them to corresponding vertices. To utilize data parallelism, the vertices are partitioned and assigned to different nodes. The partitioning scheme of the vertices is stored in the shared data storage. Both the ingesters and processors retrieve the partitioning scheme to determine the location of a vertex.

Typically, a processor corresponds to a worker thread and is responsible for the management of vertices. The execution of the processors is organized into three layers. The transportation layer, the lowest layer, is concerned with the transmission and reception of messages. It packages the messages from higher layers and utilizes the interfaces provided by Storm to transfer them to other processors. It also ensures that messages are delivered without any error. When an input or an update is received, the transportation layer will unpack it and deliver it to the session layer. The session layer controls the updates of vertices, ensuring that the results are consistent and correct. The execution of the session layer strictly follows the iteration model described in Section 4. The three-phase update protocol is employed to update the vertex. The updates of vertices are coordinated so that the delays don't exceed the bound set by the users. The top most layer is the application layer which serves as the interface for users. By implementing the user-defined functions, users can describe how inputs and updates are processed and where outputs are sent.

The states of vertices are materialized in the external storage. When a vertex receives an input or an update, the processor first probes the vertex's state from the storage. After the vertex's update is committed in an iteration, the new version of the vertex will be deserialized and written to the storage.

When all vertices in an iteration have been updated, the processor will report the progress made in the iteration to the master. The master collects the progress from all processors and notifies the processors when an iteration terminates. The master also collects execution statistics, e.g. CPU usage and I/O utilization, to monitor the loads of processors. It will modify the partitioning when the load is heavily unbalanced. To ensure correctness, the master stops the computation before the modification to the partitioning scheme. After the partitioning scheme is modified, the computation will restart from the last terminated iteration.

5.2 Query Execution

Besides data collection, the ingesters are also responsible for the reception of users queries. When the results at an instant are required, the user can issue a request to the ingester. On receiving a request, the ingester will push it to the master. The master will start a branch loop to execute the query if there are sufficient idle processors. The branch loop will be forked at the place where the last iteration terminates. A message containing the iteration number will be sent to idle processors to fork the branch loop. When a processor receives the message, it will take a snapshot of the main loop and start the execution of the branch loop. If a branch loop is forked at iteration i, the most recent versions of vertices that are not greater than i will be selected in the snapshot.

The progress made in the branch loop will also be reported to the master. The master will detect the convergence of the branch loop with collected progress. Once the convergence condition holds, the processors will be notified to stop the execution of the branch loop. Users can retrieve the results from the storage with the number of the branch loop and the iteration at which the loop converges.

If there are no inputs are gathered during the computation of the branch loop, the results of the branch loop are also the precise results at the current instant. In these cases, the master will notify the processors to merge the results of the branch loop into the main loop to improve the approximation of the main loop. Though the computation of the main loop may be performed simultaneously during the merging, our execution model allows us to obtain a consistent snapshot of the main loop with little efforts.

[1]See Appendix B for the details of the programming model.

If the first iteration that does not terminate in the main loop is numbered τ, the results of the branch loop will be written with the iteration number $\tau + B$ into the main loop. During the merging of the results, the master will postpone the notification of the termination of iteration τ. The versions produced by the processors will not overwrite the results of the branch loop because the iteration numbers of the versions must be less than $\tau + B$. When the merging completes, the master can start the computation from iteration $\tau + B$. All the updates in transition will also be discarded because our iteration model requires that the iteration number of the a valid update must be no less than those of its consumers.

5.3 Fault Tolerance

Storm provides many mechanisms to tolerate faults and recover from failures. As Tornado is implemented on top of Storm, it can benefit from some of them. For example, as Storm can continuously monitor the status of the cluster, the failing workers can be detected and restarted efficiently.

Storm also provides some methods to achieve guaranteed message passing, but these methods do not work in our scenarios. For example, to ensure a tuple emitted by the spout is fully processed in the topology, Storm maintains a tree to track the propagation of the tuple and acknowledges the spout when all tuples produced by the tuple have been processed. But in Tornado, an update may lead to a large number of new updates. Besides, it's hard to track the propagation of the tuples because the topology is cyclic.

We deploy a mechanism based on checkpoints and message replaying to tolerate faults and recover from failures. We track all the passing of messages. When a sent message is not acknowledged in certain time, it will be resent to ensure at-least-once message passing. The causality of our iteration model ensures that our execution will not be affected by the duplicated messages. Any update whose iteration number is less than that of its receiver will be discarded.

When a processor has updated all its vertices in an iteration, it should report the progress to the master. But before doing that, it should flush all the versions produced in the iteration to disks. Hence when the master has received the progress of the iteration from all processors, we have already obtained a checkpoint of the computation. When some failures are detected, we can recover the computation with the results of the last terminated iteration.

Many efficient methods have been proposed to reduce the overheads of fault-tolerance and recovery. We now are investing them to help optimize our method. For example, the authors in [20] proposed an asynchronous parallel mechanism to minimize the processing interruption. Their techniques can also be applied in Tornado because currently Tornado deploys a synchronous method to perform checkpointing. Before terminating an iteration, the processor must flush all the updates made in the iteration onto disks. The computation hence is interrupted by the I/O operations. By deploying the asynchronous checkpointing method, we can proceed the computation without the waiting for the completion of the flushing. When the computation fails, we can recover from the last iteration whose results are all flushed onto disks.

6. EVALUATION

In this section, we present the experimental evaluation of the Tornado system. In the experiments, we will evaluate the effects of various factors on the execution of Tornado. We first introduce the experiment setup in Section 6.1. Then we will evaluate the effect of approximation and asynchronism in Section 6.2 and 6.3 respectively. Then we examine the scalability of Tornado in Section 6.4. Finally, we compare Tornado with other systems available for real-time data processing in Section 6.5.

6.1 Experiment Setup

The experiments are conducted on a cluster with 20 physical nodes. Each node has an AMD Opteron 4180 CPU clocked at 2.6GHz, 48GB memory and a 10TB hard disk. The version of Storm is 0.9.5. The maximum heap size of JVM is set to 16GB on each node. Unless otherwise stated, the number of threads is 200. Tornado allows the results to be stored in different external storage. In the following experiments, the intermediate results are materialized in Postgresql as default. Other different external storages will be described in the corresponding experiments.

Algorithm	Dataset	Description	Size
SSSP & PR	LiveJournal	4.84M nodes, 68.9M edges	1G
KMeans	20D-points	10M instances, 20 attributes	1.12G
SVM	HIGGS	11M instances, 28 attributes	7.48G
LR	PubMed	8.2M instances, 141K attributes	7.27G

Table 1: Data sets used in the iterative algorithms:

A range of analysis tasks and datasets, which are listed in Table 1, are used in our experiments. LiveJournal is downloaded from the SNAP project[2] while HIGGS and PubMed are from the UCI repository[3]. 20D-points dataset used in the experiments of KMeans is generated by choosing some initial points in the space and using a normal random generator to pick up points around them. PubMed is represented in the form of bag-of-words. In the experiments, we use LR to predict the relevance of each document to cancer.

6.2 Impact of Approximation

In this section, we evaluate the benefits of approximate methods and discuss the factors in the design of approximate methods.

6.2.1 *Comparison with Batch Methods*

We first validate that the approximation in the main loop can efficiently improve the performance of real-time iterative analysis. We read inputs from the datasets and fork a branch loop to compute the results when the number of required inputs is reached. We first do not perform any approximation in the main loop and use the results of the last batch as the initial guesses. Then we perform approximation in the main loop and probe the results at the same instants as in the batch methods. Three different workloads, namely SSSP, PageRank and KMeans are adopted in the experiments. The 99th percentile latencies of these workloads with different methods are plotted in Figure 5.

Figure 5a illustrates the latencies in the computation of SSSP under different methods. In the experiments of SSSP, we first obtain a fixed-point at the time when 4 million edges are read. Then we use incremental methods to calculate the results of each batch with the last fixed-point obtained. The cost to incrementally compute the results of SSSP is proportional to the number of updated edges. Therefore, the latency degrades linearly with the batch size when the batch size decreases from 20M to 1M. But when the batch size continues to decrease, the latency is not reduced as expected. It's likely that the performance is dominated by the communication cost when the batch size becomes small. Because the updated vertices randomly distribute over the clusters, the number of messages don't decrease with the reduction of inputs. Finally, the lowest latency achieved by batch methods is approximately 34.24s. Similar results are also observed in the experiments of PageRank. Figure 5b reports that the latencies of batch methods degrade quickly at first, but become stable afterwards.

[2]http://snap.stanford.edu

[3]http://archive.ics.uci.edu/ml/index.html

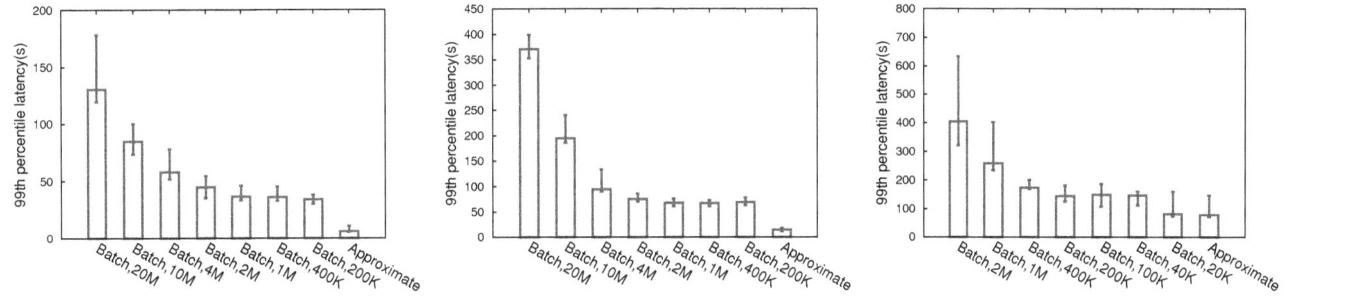

(a) SSSP (b) PageRank (c) KMean

Figure 5: Comparison between batch and approximate methods.

In both workloads, the approximate method achieves the lowest latency due to the smallest approximation error. As the incremental method of SSSP can catch up with the speed of data evolvement, we use it to approximate the results at each instant. In the main loop, each iteration takes approximately 4.13s to terminate and roughly 5K vertices are needed to be updated. When a branch loop is forked, the number of vertices to be updated in the approximate method is much less than the batch methods. Therefore, the branch loop can converge within only 6.10s on average.

Though the approximate method can also obtain good initial guesses for the KMeans workload, its latency roughly equals that of the batch method whose batch size is 20K (illustrated in Figure 5c. This is because the execution time of KMeans is not proportional to approximation error. KMeans has to rescan all the points even when only one centroid is updated. Hence, the initial guesses with less approximation error do not help reduce the latencies.

6.2.2 *Approximation Error vs. Adaption Rate*

We then exhibit the trade-off between the approximation error and adaption rate using SVM and LR workloads, both of which are solved by SGD. In the computation of SGD, the convergence rate is closely related to the descent rate. Typically the loop with a larger descent rate will converge faster. Therefore, if the main loop is configured with a large convergence rate, it will quickly adapt the approximation to the inputs. This assertion is ensured by Figure 6a. We plot the value of the objective function against the time in Figure 6a. We can see that the main loop with the descent rate whose value is 0.5 is reduced quickly. But the fast convergence rate does not help improve the performance of branch loops. As we see in Figure 6b, the branch loops forking from the main loop whose descent rate is 0.1 takes less time to converge. It's because the main loop can obtain better initial guesses when the descent rate is 0.1. We can see from Figure 6a that the approximation error in the main loop oscillates around 0.005 when the descent rate is 0.1. The achieved approximation error is much less than that in the main loop whose descent rate is 0.5.

But it's not always good to choose a small descent rate. Figure 7a exhibits another aspect of the problem. When the descent rate is 0.1, we observe the growth in the objective function. Then we decrease the descent rate to 0.05. The main loop now can efficiently adapt the approximation to the input changes. But if we continue decreasing the descent rate, the main loop fails to catch up with the input changes. Among all the three settings, the main loop whose descent rate is 0.05 achieves the best performance. The quick adaption of the approximation helps the branch loops to start from initial guesses with small approximation error.

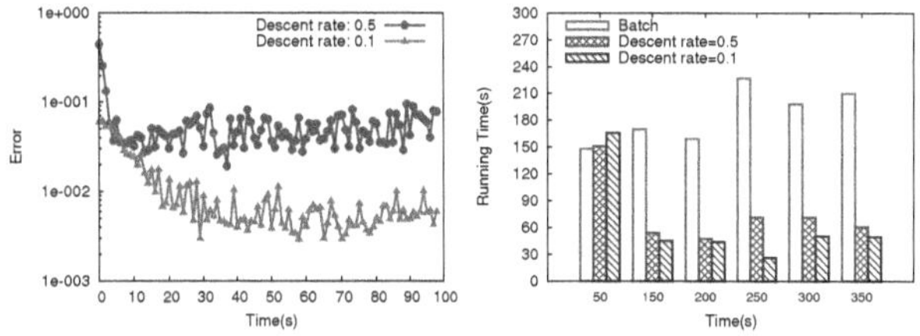

(a) SVM approximation error (b) SVM performance

Figure 6: Impact of approximation error on SVM.

The observation from Figure 6a and Figure 7a suggests that there exists trade-off between the approximation error and the adaption rate. A large descent rate allows the main loop to quickly adapt to the input changes, but it may achieve a relatively large approximation error. A small descent rate though can achieve small approximation error, but as they cannot adapt to the changes in time, the performance may still be degraded by the poor initial guesses.

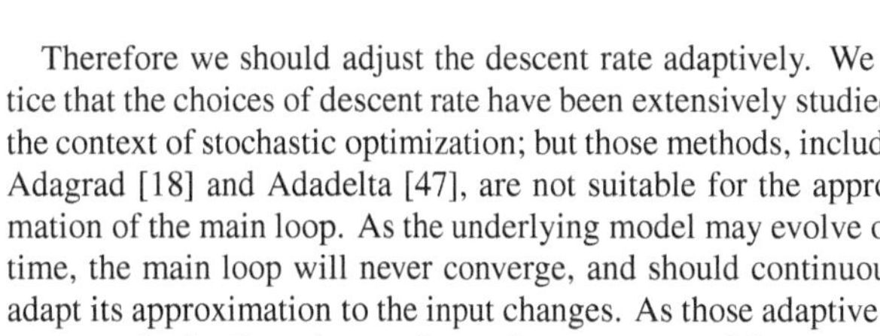

(a) LR with static descent rate (b) LR with dynamic descent rate

Figure 7: Approximation error vs. descent rate in LR.

Therefore we should adjust the descent rate adaptively. We notice that the choices of descent rate have been extensively studied in the context of stochastic optimization; but those methods, including Adagrad [18] and Adadelta [47], are not suitable for the approximation of the main loop. As the underlying model may evolve over time, the main loop will never converge, and should continuously adapt its approximation to the input changes. As those adaptive descent methods all produce a decreasing sequence of descent rates, they are unable to catch up with the input changes.

Currently, we deploy a heuristic method called *bold driver* [27, 38] to dynamically adjust the descent rate in the main loop. We decrease the descent rate by 10% when the value of the objective function increases and increase the descent rate by 10% when the value of the objective function decreases too slowly (less than 1%). The effect of the dynamic method on the LR workload is illustrat-

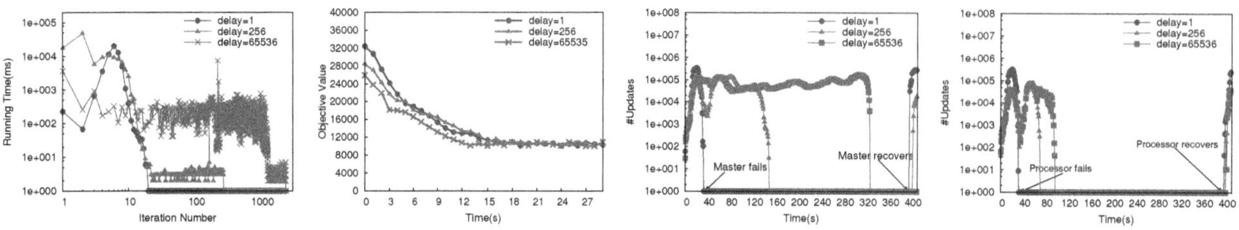

(a) SSSP branch loop (b) LR branch loop (c) Master failure (d) Single processor failure

Figure 8: Impact of asynchronism on performance and fault tolerance

ed in Figure 7b. When the main loop starts, the descent rate is set to an initial value and the approximation error drops sharply with the initial value. But when more inputs come in, the approximate error increases. Realizing the growth in the approximation error, the dynamic method increases the descent rate which helps the approximation to quickly adapt to the input changes. When the approximation error is small enough, the descent rate is decreased to achieve a better approximation. Compared with the static methods, the dynamic method can adjust the approximation to the inputs quickly and achieve relatively small approximation error.

6.3 Impact of Asynchronism

In this section, we verify that the degree of asynchronism has an impact on the performance and fault tolerance, and characterize the design trade-off. Three different delay bounds are chosen in the experiments, namely 1, 256 and 65536. In the loop whose delay bound is 1, the execution is equivalent to the one in synchronous iteration models, as described in Section 2.3. Hence we call this loop as the synchronous loop.

6.3.1 *Impact on Performance*

We first fork the branch loop of SSSP under three delay bounds. The branch loop starts from the default initial guess when the gathered inputs amount to half of the data sets. The computation time per iteration is plotted in Figure 8a and the summaries of the execution of these branch loops are listed in Table 2.

Bound	Time	#Iterations	#Updates	#Prepares
1	87.13s	22	104,668,914	0
256	227.811s	276	166,005,263	46,309,139
65536	335.521s	2370	119,634,766	119,634,766

Table 2: The summaries of the loops with different bounds.

We can see from Table 2 that the computation of the synchronous loop is performed without any prepare messages. That is because the computation progress completely replies on the notification of iteration termination, which performs as the synchronization barriers. All vertices are located at the same iteration, hence they do not need any PREPARE message to determine the iteration of each update. But as the delay bound increases, the loops become asynchronous and the number of prepare messages increases with the delay bound. When the delay bound is 65536, the numbers of prepare and update messages are the same. It indicates that the execution now does not depend on the information of iteration termination. The iteration in which each vertex is updated is completely determined by the vertex's consumers.

We also see that the synchronous loop can converge with the least number of iterations. Its computation completes in only 22 iterations while the other two loops need 276 and 2370 iterations respectively. Since the synchronous loop requires that the computation cannot proceed to the next iteration before all vertices have completed their updates, the computation can make sufficient progress in each iteration, which reduces the number of iterations. The reduction in the number of iterations has a measurable impact on the performance in our implementation. Figure 8a illustrates that the synchronous loop exhibits the best performance among the three loops. As explained in Section 5.3, to ensure data integrity, we require a processor to flush all the updates onto disks before it reports the progress to the master. Because asynchronous loops step more iterations to the fixed points, the performance of the asynchronous loops is degraded by the additional I/O cost. Besides, since more messages are needed in the computation, the performance is also hampered by the increasing communication cost.

But to make sufficient progress in each iteration, the synchronous loop takes a long time to terminate an iteration. An iteration in the synchronous loop takes 4.356s on average to terminate while in the loop whose delay bound is 65536, it takes only 0.141s on average. The growth in the computation time per iteration implies that we need a longer time to reflect the changes in the computation. In many workloads, it makes synchronous loops converge slower than their asynchronous counterparts.

In Figure 8b, we plot the objective value of the LR workloads versus time with different delay bounds. We increase the sample ratio to 10%. With the growth in the sample ratio, more computation is needed in each iteration and different workers will contend for computation resources. Consequently, the performance of the synchronous loop degrades significantly by the stragglers. On the other hand, the loop with the largest delay bound can quickly update the parameter model and is more tolerated to the unbalanced scheduling. Hence, it achieves a faster convergence rate than the synchronous one.

6.3.2 *Impact on Fault Tolerance*

Then we evaluate the impact of delay bound on the fault tolerance. We perform the branch loop of SSSP and kill the master node at a certain time. With the provisioned mechanism, the master node can recover from the failure and continue its execution. But during its recovery, the delay bound has different impact on the execution. In Figure 8c, we plot the number of updates performed per second against time under different delay bounds. To make the comparison fair, we ensure that all loops experience the same down time of the master node.

As the synchronous loop relies on the master node to detect the termination of iterations, its execution stops shortly after the failure of the master node. Different from the synchronous loop, the branch loop whose delay bound is 65536 is not affected by the failure of the master node. Because its execution can complete in 2370 iterations which is much smaller than the bound 65536, no updates will be blocked. The loop can continue its execution as nothing happens. The branch loop whose delay bound is 256 can continue its execution after the master node fails. But as it needs 276 iterations to complete its execution, eventually all updates are blocked by the delay bound. By that time, the execution completely stops.

Now we evaluate the impact of asynchronism on fault tolerance when a single processor fails. We randomly choose a processor node and kill it. Similar to the master node, the processor node can correctly recover from the failures but the branch loops with different delay bounds exhibit very different behaviors which is illustrated in Figure 8d.

As in the case of master failure, the synchronous loop stops shortly after the processor node fails. It's because an iteration cannot terminate when the vertices in the failing processors have not completed their updates. The asynchronous loops however can continue their execution as they don't require all vertices to be updated in each iteration. But as each vertex must prepare its updates before the commitment, the vertices cannot complete their updates if one of its consumers resides in the failing processor. The effect of the processor's failure then is propagated to the vertex's producers. Eventually all the vertices in the connected component will be unable to complete their updates.

The experiments with machine failures suggest that (1) When the master node fails, the computation stops when all updates are blocked by the delay bound. The computation of synchronous loop stops immediately after the master node is down. But if the execution of an asynchronous loop does not depend on the iteration termination, the loop can continue its computation as nothing happens. (2) When a vertex fails, the effect of the failure will propagate to its producers. The computation stops when the effect of the failure is propagated to all vertices.

6.4 Scalability

We now study the scalability characteristics of Tornado on various workloads. Ideally the performance should improve proportionally when the number of workers increases.

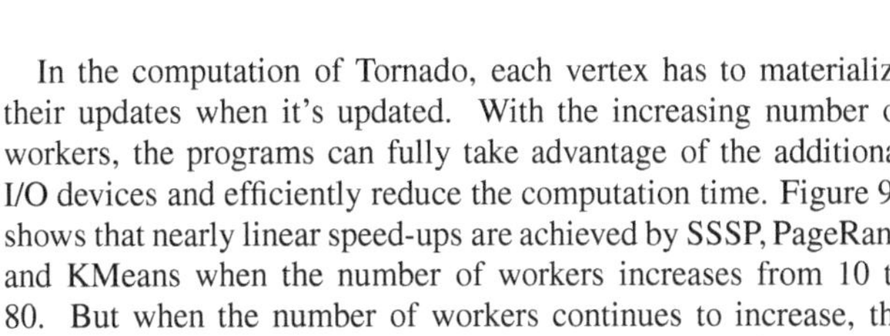

(a) Speedup (b) Message throughput

Figure 9: Scalability of Tornado

In the computation of Tornado, each vertex has to materialize their updates when it's updated. With the increasing number of workers, the programs can fully take advantage of the additional I/O devices and efficiently reduce the computation time. Figure 9a shows that nearly linear speed-ups are achieved by SSSP, PageRank and KMeans when the number of workers increases from 10 to 80. But when the number of workers continues to increase, the communication cost increases as well. We measure the network utilization by the number of messages sent per second. We can see in Figure 9b that with the growth in the number of workers, the throughput stops to increase when the number of sent message per second reaches 1.5M. At that time, more workers will not help SSSP and PageRank to improve the performance.

SVM exhibits very different scalability characteristics than SSSP and KMeans. The performance degrades when the number of workers increases. In SVM, the amount of computation is determined by the batch size and only the parameters are updated in each iteration. Hence its performance does not benefit from the increasing number of workers. On the contrary, more workers incur more communication cost, which degrades the performance.

6.5 Comparison with Existing Systems

In this section, we compare Tornado with other related systems. Three different systems are adopted in the comparison, namely Spark, GraphLab and Naiad. Spark is one of the most popular real-time systems in the industry. It also provides Spark Streaming which can process data streams with mini-batches. But as Spark Streaming does not allow iterative semantics, we does not adopt Spark Streaming in the experiments. Graphlab is a graph processing prototype which stands out with its excellent performance. Different from Spark, it adopts a graph-parallel model to execute programs at scale. Naiad is the system closest to Tornado. By tracking the dependencies between the inputs and the outputs, the results can be incrementally updated when the input changes.

Program	Spark	GraphLab	Naiad	Tornado
SSSP, 1%	364.16±23.13	43.12±5.67	26.41±4.12	5.76±2.13
SSSP, 5%	343.73±31.19	43.27±4.98	30.53±3.87	6.17±3.44
SSSP, 10%	352.98±29.92	45.11±4.63	32.48±4.84	6.71±2.03
SSSP, 20%	355.67±22.94	47.56±3.36	37.42±7.38	5.83±3.79
PR, 1%	461.25±25.21	95.85±2.39	100.46±12.08	13.72±2.02
PR, 5%	452.70±33.42	96.91±7.63	114.20±7.29	13.64±4.28
PR, 10%	449.13±35.61	99.75±5.27	135.19±10.07	12.53±4.12
PR, 20%	466.38±38.12	105.35±3.45	163.56±9.21	13.57±4.76
SVM, 1%	64.07±13.20	69.04±8.35	31.25±16.86	6.12±2.78
SVM, 5%	67.12±9.31	68.83±12.30	37.19±14.78	6.09±3.07
SVM, 10%	78.76±21.87	65.51±14.31	42.76±20.43	8.13±3.58
SVM, 20%	73.98±45.09	68.97±18.39	67.20±24.14	7.85±3.26
KM, 1%	644.08±43.10	154.07±2.47	-	64.23±18.23
KM, 5%	723.27±61.32	156.36±3.16	-	79.85±15.25
KM, 10%	686.21±67.12	156.96±7.03	-	89.64±19.49
KM, 20%	694.37±63.96	159.39±6.61	-	96.51±17.26

Table 3: Latency (seconds) in different systems

We evaluate the performance of these systems as well as Tornado with four different workloads, namely SSSP, PageRank, KMeans and SVM. Since other systems store results in memory, for fair comparison, Tornado stores the intermediate results in a distributed in-memory database backed by LMDB[4]. We continuously feed the inputs to these systems, and measure the latencies of these systems when the percentage of the accumulated inputs amount to 1%, 5%, 10% and 20% respectively. The results are illustrated in Table 3. In the experiments of KMeans, Naiad is unable to complete because it consumes too much memory.

Because both Spark and GraphLab target at batch-processing, we have to collect all produced inputs and run the iterative methods only when the results are required. Though Spark has been optimized for iterative algorithms by keeping intermediate results in memory and reusing them to reduce redundant results, it exhibits the worst performance in most workloads due to the I/O overheads in the data spilling.

Different from Spark and GraphLab, Naiad and Tornado are designed for real-time analysis. Similar to other adaptive systems, Naiad also utilizes incremental methods to reduce redundant computation. By decomposing the different traces, Naiad relaxes the dependencies among different epochs. But the decomposition also increases the time complexity of the incremental maintenance. When the inputs change, Naiad has to combine all previous difference traces to restore the current version. The performance hence degrades linearly with the number of epochs and iterations.

[4]http://symas.com/mdb

In the experiments, we set the epoch size of Naiad to be 1% of the size of the data set. In the computation of SSSP and SVM, Naiad achieves a much better performance than Spark and Graphlab. But in the computation of PageRank, it experiences longer execution time due to the growth in the number of iterations. The time needed to incrementally compute the results is even longer than the time needed by GraphLab to compute from scratch.

Tornado achieves the best performance on all the workloads against these adopted systems. The speedups vary from a fold of 1 to 50 with the accumulated changes ranging from 1% to 20%. Particularly, higher speedups are achieved when we can approximate the results well and the penalty of approximation error is small. In the experiments other than KMeans, the latency is independent from the amount of the changes and the size of historic data. The results show that Tornado can effectively reduce the latency with the proposed execution model.

7. RELATED WORK

The problem of iterative analysis over evolving data is closely related to many research areas. We briefly review the related work in this section.

Stream processing. Stream processing has been studied for many years in the context of both systems and algorithms. Early attempts made in stream processing systems [1, 9], have their roots in relational databases and allow users to perform relational queries on data streams. Recently, many distributed stream processing frameworks [42, 35, 2, 46] are proposed to facilitate fault-tolerant stream processing at scale. These stream processing systems, however, cannot efficiently handle cyclic data flows. Chandramouli et al. extended the punctuation semantics [43] and proposed Flying Fixed-Point [8] to support iterative queries over streams. But as their method targets at totally asynchronous iterations, its applicability is limited. Apache Flink[5] supports iterative computation over streams, but it does not provide an efficient method for users to retrieve the results at certain instants. A user has to collect all the results in the iterations and construct the results by himself.

Adaptive systems. Adaptive systems target at the applications whose inputs are incrementally updated. They avoid the need to compute from scratch by tracking the dependencies in the computation and employing incremental methods. Typical examples include Nectar [24] and Incoop [7]. But both of them do not support iterative computation. The iterative computation over dynamic data makes it hard to track the dependencies in the computation. Naiad [32, 33] proposed to decompose the different traces into multiple dimensions and combine them to allow incremental computation. By grouping inputs into small epochs, Naiad can produce timely results over data streams. But as we saw in the experiments, the decomposition degrades the performance as well. With the growth in the number of epochs, the latency of Naiad will become very high.

Iterative computation. In recent years, many graph processing systems have been proposed to allow general graph analysis, e.g., Pregel [31], GraphLab [30, 23] and Trinity [39]. By reducing materialization overheads and allowing incremental computation, these graph processing systems can achieve good performance for common iterative methods. But all these graph systems cannot deal with continuously changed inputs. Our iteration model allows iterative methods over dynamic graphs, hence can be deployed in these graph processing systems to enhance their applicability. For example, GraphLab deploys Chandy-Misra in its asynchronous engine to ensure consistency. Our extension to Chandy-Misra with Lamport Clock can be implemented in GraphLab to allow evolving inputs.

[5]http://flink.apache.org/

Kineograph [13] extends the functionality of these systems by allowing the collection of dynamic data. But newly-arrived updates cannot be processed immediately and must wait for the completion of the current epoch. Signal/Collect [41] and HAMA [3] adopt similar methods to Kineograph, but they allow the application of input changes when an iteration terminates.

Naiad provides different consistency levels across iterations. By default, the computation proceeds synchronously with the notify messages which indicates the termination of iterations. But users are free to proceed their computation, ignoring the notify messages. In such cases, the computation is totally asynchronous and can only ensure correctness for a limited number of iterative methods.

Besides these general-purpose iterative systems, there are many other systems targeting at specific workloads. For example, Hogwild! [37] is an efficient method to compute SGD on multi-core servers without locking. But it cannot be extended to distributing settings as the assumption that write latencies are limited will not hold. Parameter Servers [15, 26, 29, 45] are based on distributed shared memory and utilize weak consistency to implement bounded asynchronous iterations. But as they specialize the communication model, they can not support general iterative methods whose dependency graph are not bipartite.

Approximation methods. Many stream mining algorithms are developed for specific analysis tasks, such as clustering [40], link analysis [14] and frequent pattern mining [25]. These algorithms are usually assumed to be executed in a system with limited computation resources and the inputs will be discarded after they are processed [4]. Hence they usually approximate the results with constructed sketches and trade off space for passes [16]. These approximation methods can be adopted in Tornado to accelerate the convergence rate of branch loops.

Our method shares similar ideas with the practice of *warm starts* in gradient descent [36, 48]. But our work generalizes the idea and applies it to the iterative computation over evolving data. Such generalization is not trivial, since we have to deal with the complexity in distributed settings, e.g., the consistency and correctness of the computing results.

8. CONCLUSION

It's challenging to support real-time iterative analysis over evolving data. The observation that loops starting from good initial guesses usually converge fast encouraged us to develop an method to enhance the timeliness with better approximation but not incremental methods. To reduce the approximation error due the most recent inputs, we proposed a novel bounded asynchronous iteration model which can achieve fine-grained updates while ensuring correctness. The conducted experiments verified that many common iterative methods can benefit from our execution model.

There are several directions for the future development of Tornado. Currently, Tornado requires users to write their programs with procedural code. We are designing a high-level language to enhance the programmability. Ongoing research also involves the load shedding of branch loops so that given restricted resources, requests can be accomplished as many as possible.

9. ACKNOWLEDGEMENTS

This work is supported by the National Natural Science Foundation of China under Grant No. 61272155 and 61572039, 973 program under No. 2014CB340405, Beijing Natural Science Foundation (4152023), and Shenzhen Gov Research Project JCYJ2015101 4093505032.

10. REFERENCES

[1] D. Abadi, D. Carney, U. Çetintemel, M. Cherniack, C. Convey, S. Lee, M. Stonebraker, N. Tatbul, and S. Zdonik. Aurora: A new model and architecture for data stream management. *The VLDB Journal*, 12(2):120–139, 2003.

[2] T. Akidau, A. Balikov, K. Bekiroğlu, S. Chernyak, J. Haberman, R. Lax, S. McVeety, D. Mills, P. Nordstrom, and S. Whittle. Millwheel: Fault-tolerant stream processing at internet scale. *PVLDB*, 6(11):1033–1044, 2013.

[3] A. Andronidis. Hama wiki: Dynamic graphs. http://wiki.apache.org/hama/DynamicGraphs, 2013.

[4] B. Babcock, S. Babu, M. Datar, R. Motwani, and J. Widom. Models and issues in data stream systems. In *PODS*, pages 1–16, 2002.

[5] B. Bahmani, A. Chowdhury, and A. Goel. Fast incremental and personalized pagerank. *Proc. VLDB Endow.*, 4(3):173–184, 2010.

[6] D. Bertsekas and J. Tsitsiklis. *Parallel and Distributed Computation: Numerical Methods*. Prentice-Hall, Inc., 1989.

[7] P. Bhatotia, A. Wieder, R. Rodrigues, U. Acar, and R. Pasquin. Incoop: Mapreduce for incremental computations. In *SOCC*, pages 7:1–7:14, 2011.

[8] B. Chandramouli, J. Goldstein, and D. Maier. On-the-fly progress detection in iterative stream queries. *PVLDB*, 2(1):241–252, 2009.

[9] S. Chandrasekaran, O. Cooper, A. Deshpande, M. Franklin, J. Hellerstein, W. Hong, S. Krishnamurthy, S. Madden, F. Reiss, and M. Shah. Telegraphcq: Continuous dataflow processing. In *SIGMOD*, pages 668–668, 2003.

[10] K. Chandy and L. Lamport. Distributed snapshots: Determining global states of distributed systems. *TOCS*, 3(1):63–75, 1985.

[11] K. Chandy and J. Misra. The drinking philosophers problem. *TOPLAS*, 6(4):632–646, 1984.

[12] D. Chazan and W. Miranker. Chaotic relaxation. *LAA*, 2(2):199–222, 1969.

[13] R. Cheng, J. Hong, A. Kyrola, Y. Miao, X. Weng, M. Wu, F. Yang, L. Zhou, F. Zhao, and E. Chen. Kineograph: Taking the pulse of a fast-changing and connected world. In *EuroSys*, pages 85–98, 2012.

[14] A. Das Sarma, S. Gollapudi, and R. Panigrahy. Estimating pagerank on graph streams. In *PODS*, pages 69–78, 2008.

[15] J. Dean, G. Corrado, R. Monga, K. Chen, D. M., Q. Le, M. Mao, M. Ranzato, A. Senior, P. Tucker, K. Yang, and A. Ng. Large scale distributed deep networks. In *NIPS*, pages 1223–1231, 2012.

[16] C. Demetrescu, I. Finocchi, and A. Ribichini. Trading off space for passes in graph streaming problems. *TALG*, 6(1):6:1–6:17, 2009.

[17] E. Dijkstra. Hierarchical ordering of sequential processes. *Acta Informatica*, 1(2):115–138, 1971.

[18] J. Duchi, E. Hazan, and Y. Singer. Adaptive Subgradient Methods for Online Learning and Stochastic Optimization. *JMLR*, 12:2121–2159, 2011.

[19] M. El Tarazi. Some convergence results for asynchronous algorithms. *Numer. Math.*, 39(3):325–340, 1982.

[20] R. Fernandez, M. Migliavacca, E. Kalyvianaki, and P. Pietzuch. Making state explicit for imperative big data processing. In *USENIX ATC*, pages 49–60, 2014.

[21] A. Frommer and H. Schwandt. Asynchronous parallel methods for enclosing solutions of nonlinear equations. *IJCAM*, 60(1ĺC2):47 – 62, 1995.

[22] M. Gaber, A. Zaslavsky, and S. Krishnaswamy. Mining data streams: A review. *SIGMOD Rec.*, 34(2):18–26, 2005.

[23] J. Gonzalez, Y. Low, H. Gu, D. Bickson, and C. Guestrin. PowerGraph: Distributed graph-parallel computation on natural graphs. In *OSDI*, pages 17–30, 2012.

[24] P. Gunda, L. Ravindranath, C. Thekkath, Y. Yu, and L. Zhuang. Nectar: Automatic management of data and computation in data centers. Technical Report MSR-TR-2010-55, 2010.

[25] J. Han, H. Cheng, D. Xin, and X. Yan. Frequent pattern mining: Current status and future directions. *DMKD*, 15(1):55–86, 2007.

[26] Q. Ho, J. Cipar, H. Cui, S. Lee, J. Kim, P. Gibbons, G. Gibson, G. Ganger, and E. Xing. More effective distributed ml via a stale synchronous parallel parameter server. In *NIPS*, pages 1223–1231, 2013.

[27] H. Hsin, C. Li, S. M., and R. Sclabassi. An adaptive training algorithm for back-propagation neural networks. In *SMC*, volume 2, pages 1049–1052, 1992.

[28] L. Lamport. Time, clocks, and the ordering of events in a distributed system. *CACM*, 21(7):558–565, 1978.

[29] M. Li, D. Andersen, J. Park, A. Smola, A. Ahmed, V. Josifovski, J. Long, E. Shekita, and B. Su. Scaling distributed machine learning with the parameter server. In *OSDI*, pages 583–598, 2014.

[30] Y. Low, D. Bickson, J. Gonzalez, C. Guestrin, A. Kyrola, and J. Hellerstein. Distributed GraphLab: A framework for machine learning and data mining in the cloud. *PVLDB*, 5(8):716–727, 2012.

[31] G. Malewicz, M. Austern, A. Bik, J. Dehnert, I. Horn, N. Leiser, and G. Czajkowski. Pregel: A system for large-scale graph processing. In *SIGMOD*, pages 135–146, 2010.

[32] F. McSherry, D. Murray, R. Isaacs, and M. Isard. Differential dataflow. In *CIDR*, 2013.

[33] D. Murray, F. McSherry, R. Isaacs, M. Isard, P. Barham, and M. Abadi. Naiad: A timely dataflow system. In *SOSP*, pages 439–455, 2013.

[34] S. Muthukrishnan. Data streams: Algorithms and applications. *Found. Trends Theor. Comput. Sci.*, 1(2):117–236, 2005.

[35] L. Neumeyer, B. Robbins, A. Nair, and A. Kesari. S4: Distributed stream computing platform. In *ICDMW*, pages 170–177, 2010.

[36] B. O'donoghue and E. Candès. Adaptive restart for accelerated gradient schemes. *Found. Comput. Math.*, 15(3):715–732, 2015.

[37] B. Recht, R. Christopher, W. Stephen, and F. Niu. Hogwild: A lock-free approach to parallelizing stochastic gradient descent. In *NIPS*, pages 693–701, 2011.

[38] D. Sarkar. Methods to speed up error back-propagation learning algorithm. *CSUR*, 27(4):519–544, 1995.

[39] B. Shao, H. Wang, and Y. Li. Trinity: A distributed graph engine on a memory cloud. In *SIGMOD*, pages 505–516, 2013.

[40] J. Silva, E. Faria, R. Barros, E. Hruschka, A. Carvalho, and J. Gama. Data stream clustering: A survey. *CSUR*, 46(1):13:1–13:31, 2013.

[41] A. Stutz P.and Bernstein and W. Cohen. Signal/collect: Graph algorithms for the (semantic) web. In *ISWC*, pages 764–780, 2010.

[42] A. Toshniwal, S. Taneja, A. Shukla, K. Ramasamy, J. Patel, S. Kulkarni, J. Jackson, K. Gade, M. Fu, J. Donham, N. Bhagat, S. Mittal, and D. Ryaboy. Storm@twitter. In *SIGMOD*, pages 147–156, 2014.

[43] P. A. Tucker, D. Maier, T. Sheard, and L. Fegaras. Exploiting punctuation semantics in continuous data streams. *TKDE*, 15(3):555–568, 2003.

[44] J. Vitter. Random sampling with a reservoir. *TOMS*, 11(1):37–57, 1985.

[45] K. Vora, S. Koduru, and R. Gupta. Aspire: Exploiting asynchronous parallelism in iterative algorithms using a relaxed consistency based dsm. In *OOPSLA*, pages 861–878, 2014.

[46] M. Zaharia, T. Das, H. Li, T. Hunter, S. Shenker, and I. Stoica. Discretized streams: Fault-tolerant streaming computation at scale. In *SOSP*, 2013.

[47] M. D. Zeiler. ADADELTA: An Adaptive Learning Rate Method. *CoRR*, abs/1212.5701, 2012.

[48] M. Zinkevich. Theoretical analysis of a warm start technique. In *NIPS Workshop on Parallel and Large-Scale Machine Learning*, 2011.

[49] I. Zliobaite, A. Bifet, M. Gaber, B. Gabrys, J. Gama, L. Minku, and K. Musial. Next challenges for adaptive learning systems. *SIGKDD Explor. Newsl.*, 14(1):48–55, 2012.

APPENDIX

A. CORRECTNESS PROOF

In this section, we prove that the execution model described in Section 4 is a valid bounded asynchronous iteration model.

PROOF. (1) First, we prove that the iteration delay of each update is not greater than B. Since all components cannot gather the updates in iteration $\tau + B - 1$, the maximum iteration number of components must be less than $\tau + B$. As iteration $\tau - 1$ has terminated, the iteration numbers of all vertices must be in the range $[\tau, \tau + B - 1]$. As the iteration in which a component commits its update is determined by the iteration numbers of its consumers, the maximum delay of an update hence is less than B.

(2) Second, we prove that every component can be updated in the iterations from τ to $\tau + B - 1$. As all components will eventually be updated, we only to prove that all components in iteration τ can be updated. Because our iteration model don't allow the gathering of the updates in iteration $\tau + B - 1$, we have to prove that all components in iteration τ can receive an update whose iteration number is less than $\tau + B - 1$. Here we provide a proof sketch, without considering special cases.

Given any component x whose iteration number is τ. According to the causality, it must have a producer y who is updated in the iteration τ' and $\tau' < \tau$. As we have proved that the delay of each update cannot be greater than B, so we have $\tau - B < \tau' \leq \tau - 1$.

Since iteration τ is the first iteration that does not terminate, iteration τ' must have terminated. According to the requirement of iteration termination, y must have been updated before iteration τ' terminates. In combination with the delay bound, we can know that the new iteration number of y is less than $\tau' + B$ and also is less than $\tau + B - 1$.

Consequently, for each component x in iteration τ, it can receive an update from its producer whose iteration number is less than $\tau + B - 1$. The received update can be gathered by x and allow x to be updated in an iteration whose number is greater than τ. □

B. PROGRAMMING MODEL

The primary goal of Tornado is to provide efficient real-time iterative analysis over evolving data. To ease the programming, Tornado adopts a graph-parallel programming model similar to those in popular graph processing systems [23]. The programmer can define the behavior of a vertex by implementing the following interfaces:

```
vertex::init()
vertex::gather(iteration, source, delta)
vertex::scatter(iteration)
```

The `init` function defines how the vertex is initialized when it's created. When the vertex receives an update, it will use `gather` to receive the update. When the vertex can commit its update, it may call `scatter` to emit updates to its consumers. Both *gather* and *scatter* can modify the state of the vertex, but the updates of a vertex can only be propagated by *scatter*.

As the our iteration model utilizes the dependencies to ensure correctness, a vertex should invoke the system-provided methods to explicitly maintain the dependency graph:

```
vertex::addTarget(target)
vertex::removeTarget(target)
```

Besides the vertices, there are some other auxiliary classes in Tornado. For example, `ingesser` defines how the application receives the inputs from the external sources while `progress` is used to record the progress made in the computation.

```
vertex::init()
    length = (getID() == 0 ? 0 : INT_MAX);
    sourceLengths = new map();
vertex::gather(iteration, source, delta)
    delta.isType(ADD_TARGET) => addTarget(delta.value);
    delta.isType(REMOVE_TARGET) => removeTarget(delta.value);
    delta.isType(UPDATE) => sourceLengths[source] = delta.value;
vertex::scatter(iteration)
    length = min(min(sourceLengths.values()) + 1, length);
    if(!doBatchProcessing || getLoop() != MAIN_LOOP) {
        for(target : removedTargets)
            emit(UPDATE, INT_MAX);
        for(target : addedTargets + retainedTargets)
            emit(UPDATE, length);
    }
```

Figure 10: The pseudo code for Single-Source Shortest Path.

We use the pseudo code in Figure 10 as an example to illustrate the programming model. The example program performs the Single-Source Shortest Path algorithm on a stream which is composed of the insertion and deletion of edges.

The initial length of a vertex is initialized in the `init` function. The length of the source is initialized to 0 while the length of other vertices is set to `INT_MAX`.

There are three types of updates in the program: namely `ADD_TARGET`, `REMOVE_TARGET` and `UPDATE`. The first two types come from the input stream while the last one is sent by vertices. When a vertex receives an update, it calls function `gather` to update itself.

The `scatter` function will be called when the vertex completes the gathering in the iteration and is allowed to commit its update. In this program, each vertex reports its current length to its neighbors.

The computation of the vertex in the main loop and the branch loops are defined by the same functions. That is the code of the `gather` and `scatter` function is executed in both the main loop and the branch loops. The vertex can know the loop it's updated by calling the system-provided interface `getLoop()`. For example, if we want to perform batch processing, we should not emit any update in the main loop. In such cases, a branch loop will start from the place where all vertices are assigned with the initial value.

EmptyHeaded: A Relational Engine for Graph Processing

Christopher R. Aberger
Stanford University
caberger@stanford.edu

Susan Tu
Stanford University
sctu@stanford.edu

Kunle Olukotun
Stanford University
kunle@stanford.edu

Christopher Ré
Stanford University
chrismre@cs.stanford.edu

ABSTRACT

There are two types of high-performance graph processing engines: low- and high-level engines. Low-level engines (Galois, PowerGraph, Snap) provide optimized data structures and computation models but require users to write low-level imperative code, hence ensuring that efficiency is the burden of the user. In high-level engines, users write in query languages like datalog (SociaLite) or SQL (Grail). High-level engines are easier to use but are orders of magnitude slower than the low-level graph engines. We present EmptyHeaded, a high-level engine that supports a rich datalog-like query language and achieves performance comparable to that of low-level engines. At the core of EmptyHeaded's design is a new class of join algorithms that satisfy strong theoretical guarantees but have thus far not achieved performance comparable to that of specialized graph processing engines. To achieve high performance, EmptyHeaded introduces a new join engine architecture, including a novel query optimizer and data layouts that leverage single-instruction multiple data (SIMD) parallelism. With this architecture, EmptyHeaded outperforms high-level approaches by up to three orders of magnitude on graph pattern queries, PageRank, and Single-Source Shortest Paths (SSSP) and is an order of magnitude faster than many low-level baselines. We validate that EmptyHeaded competes with the best-of-breed low-level engine (Galois), achieving comparable performance on PageRank and at most 3x worse performance on SSSP.

Categories and Subject Descriptors

H.2 [**Information Systems**]: Database Management System Engines

Keywords

Worst-case optimal join; generalized hypertree decomposition; GHD; graph processing; single instruction multiple data; SIMD

SIGMOD'16, June 26-July 01, 2016, San Francisco, CA, USA

© 2016 ACM. ISBN 978-1-4503-3531-7/16/06...$15.00

DOI: http://dx.doi.org/10.1145/2882903.2915213

1. INTRODUCTION

The massive growth in the volume of graph data from social and biological networks has created a need for efficient graph processing engines. As a result, there has been a flurry of activity around designing specialized graph analytics engines [9, 22, 36, 43, 50]. These specialized engines offer new programming models that are either (1) low-level, requiring users to write code imperatively or (2) high-level, incurring large performance gaps relative to the low-level approaches. In this work, we explore whether we can meet the performance of low-level engines while supporting a high-level relational (SQL-like) programming interface.

Low-level graph engines outperform traditional relational data processing engines on common benchmarks due to (1) asymptotically faster algorithms [18, 49] and (2) optimized data layouts that provide large constant factor runtime improvements [36]. We describe each point in detail:

1. Low-level graph engines [9, 22, 36, 43, 50] provide iterators and domain-specific primitives, with which users can write asymptotically faster algorithms than what traditional databases or high-level approaches can provide. However, it is the burden of the user to write the query properly, which may require system-specific optimizations. Therefore, optimal algorithmic runtimes can only be achieved through the user in these low-level engines.
2. Low-level graph engines use optimized data layouts to efficiently manage the sparse relationships common in graph data. For example, optimized sparse matrix layouts are often used to represent the edgelist relation [36]. High-level graph engines also use sparse layouts like tail-nested tables [24] to cope with sparsity.

Extending the relational interface to match these guarantees is challenging. While some have argued that traditional engines can be modified in straightforward ways to accommodate graph workloads [21, 26], order of magnitude performance gaps remain between this approach and low-level engines [9, 24, 43]. Theoretically, traditional join engines face a losing battle, as all pairwise join engines are *provably suboptimal* on many common graph queries [18]. For example, low-level specialized engines execute the "triangle listing" query, which is common in graph workloads [31, 47], in time $O(N^{3/2})$ where N is the number of edges in the graph. Any pairwise relational algebra plan takes at least $\Omega(N^2)$, which is asymptotically worse than the specialized engines by a factor of $\sqrt{N}$. This asymptotic suboptimality

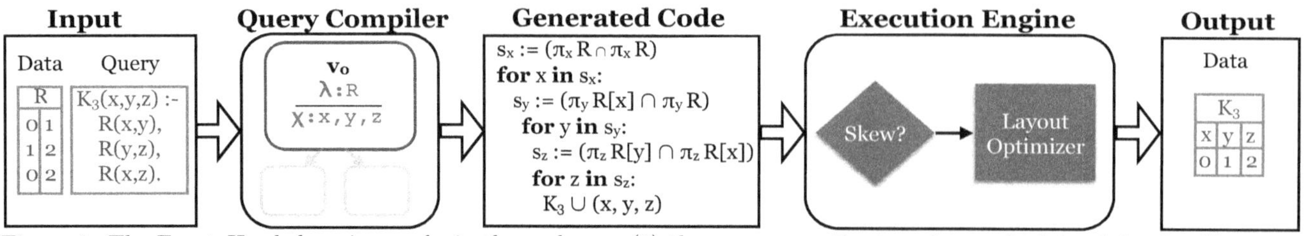

Figure 1: The EmptyHeaded engine works in three phases: (1) the query compiler translates a high-level datalog-like query into a logical query plan represented as a GHD (a hypertree with a single node here), replacing the traditional role of relational algebra; (2) code is generated for the execution engine by translating the GHD into a series of set intersections and loops; and (3) the execution engine performs automatic algorithmic and layout decisions based upon skew in the data.

is often inherited by high-level graph engines, as there has not been a general way to compile these queries that obtains the correct asymptotic bound [21, 24]. Recently, new multi-way join algorithms were discovered that obtain the correct asymptotic bound for any graph pattern or join [18].

These new multiway join algorithms are by themselves not enough to close the gap. LogicBlox [26] uses multiway join algorithms and has demonstrated that they can support a rich set of applications. However, LogicBlox's current engine can be orders of magnitude slower than the specialized engines on graph benchmarks (see Section 5). This leaves open the question of whether these multiway joins are destined to be slower than specialized approaches.

We argue that an engine based on multiway join algorithms can close this gap, but it requires a novel architecture (Figure 1), which forms our main contribution. Our architecture includes a novel query compiler based on *generalized hypertree decompositions* (GHDs) [2, 14] and an execution engine designed to exploit the low-level layouts necessary to increase single-instruction multiple data (SIMD) parallelism. We argue that these techniques demonstrate that multiway join engines can compete with low-level graph engines, as our prototype is faster than all tested engines on graph pattern queries (in some cases by orders of magnitude) and competitive on other common graph benchmarks.

We design EmptyHeaded around tight theoretical guarantees and data layouts optimized for SIMD parallelism.

GHDs as Query Plans. The classical approach to query planning uses relational algebra, which facilitates optimizations such as early aggregation, pushing down selections, and pushing down projections. In EmptyHeaded, we need a similar framework that supports multiway (instead of pairwise) joins. To accomplish this, based off of an initial prototype developed in our group [51], we use *generalized hypertree decompositions* (GHDs) [14] for logical query plans in EmptyHeaded. GHDs allow one to apply the above classical optimizations to multiway joins. GHDs also have additional bookkeeping information that allow us to bound the size of intermediate results (optimally in the worst case). These bounds allow us to provide asymptotically stronger runtime guarantees than previous worst-case optimal join algorithms that do not use GHDs (including LogicBlox).[1] As these bounds depend on the data and the query it is difficult to expect users to write these algorithms in a low-level framework. Our contribution is the design of a novel query optimizer and code generator based on GHDs that is able to achieve the above results via a high-level query language.

Exploiting SIMD: The Battle With Skew. Optimizing relational databases for the SIMD hardware trend has become an increasingly hot research topic [38, 44, 55], as the available SIMD parallelism has been doubling consistently in each processor generation.[2] Inspired by this, we exploit the link between SIMD parallelism and worst-case optimal joins for the first time in EmptyHeaded. Our initial prototype revealed that during query execution, unoptimized set intersections often account for 95% of the overall runtime in the generic worst-case optimal join algorithm. Thus, it is critically important to optimize set intersections and the associated data layout to be well-suited for SIMD parallelism. This is a challenging task as graph data is highly skewed, causing the runtime characteristics of set intersections to be highly varied. We explore several sophisticated (and not so sophisticated) layouts and algorithms to opportunistically increase the amount of available SIMD parallelism in the set intersection operation. Our contribution here is an automated optimizer that, all told, increases performance by up to three orders of magnitude by selecting amongst multiple data layouts and set intersection algorithms that use skew to increase the amount of available SIMD parallelism.

We choose to evaluate EmptyHeaded on graph pattern matching queries since pattern queries are naturally (and classically) expressed as join queries. We also evaluate EmptyHeaded on other common graph workloads including PageRank and Single-Source Shortest Paths (SSSP). We show that EmptyHeaded consistently outperforms the standard baselines [21] by 2-4x on PageRank and is at most 3x slower than the highly tuned implementation of Galois [9] on SSSP. However, in our high-level language these queries are expressed in 1-2 lines, while they are over 150 lines of code in Galois. For reference, a hand-coded C implementation with similar performance to Galois is 1000 lines.

Contribution Summary. This paper introduces the EmptyHeaded engine and demonstrates that a novel architecture can enable multi-way join engines to compete with specialized low-level graph processing engines. We demonstrate that EmptyHeaded outperforms specialized engines

[1] LogicBlox has described a (non-public) prototype with an optimizer similar but distinct from GHDs. With these modifications, LogicBlox's relative performance improves similarly to our own. It, however, remains at least an order of magnitude slower than EmptyHeaded.

[2] The Intel Ivy Bridge architecture, which we use in this paper, has a SIMD register width of 256 bits. The next generation, the Intel Skylake architecture, has 512-bit registers and a larger number of such registers.

on graph pattern queries while remaining competitive on other workloads. To validate our claims we provide comparisons on standard graph benchmark queries that the specialized engines are designed to process efficiently.

A summary of our contributions and an outline is as follows:

- We describe the first worst-case optimal join processing engine to use GHDs for logical query plans. We describe how GHDs enable us to provide a tighter theoretical guarantee than previous worst-case optimal join engines (Section 3). Next, we validate that the optimizations GHDs enable provide more than a three orders of magnitude performance advantage over previous worst-case optimal query plans (Section 5).
- We describe the architecture of the first worst-case optimal execution engine that optimizes for skew at several levels of granularity within the data. We present a series of automatic optimizers to select intersection algorithms and set layouts based on data characteristics at runtime (Section 4). We demonstrate that our automatic optimizers can result in up to a three orders of magnitude performance improvement on common graph pattern queries (Section 5).
- We validate that our general purpose engine can compete with specialized engines on standard benchmarks in the graph domain (Section 5). We demonstrate that on cyclic graph pattern queries our approach outperforms graph engines by 2-60x and LogicBlox by three orders of magnitude. We demonstrate on PageRank and Single-Source Shortest Paths that our approach remains competitive, at most 3x off the highly tuned Galois engine (Section 5).

2. PRELIMINARIES

We briefly review the worst-case optimal join algorithm, trie data structure, and query language at the core of the EmptyHeaded design. The worst-case optimal join algorithm, trie data structure, and query language presented here serve as building blocks for the remainder of the paper.

2.1 Worst-Case Optimal Join Algorithms

We briefly review worst-case optimal join algorithms, which are used in EmptyHeaded. We present these results informally and refer the reader to Ngo et al. [19] for a complete survey. The main idea is that one can place (tight) bounds on the maximum possible number of tuples returned by a query and then develop algorithms whose runtime guarantees match these worst-case bounds. For the moment, we consider only join queries (no projection or aggregation), returning to these richer queries in Section 3.

A ***hypergraph*** is a pair $H = (V, E)$, consisting of a nonempty set V of vertices, and a set E of subsets of V, the hyperedges of H. Natural join queries and graph pattern queries can be expressed as hypergraphs [14]. In particular, there is a direct correspondence between a query and its hypergraph: there is a vertex for each attribute of the query and a hyperedge for each relation. We will go freely back and forth between the query and the hypergraph that represents it.

A recent result of Atserias, Grohe, and Marx [3] (AGM) showed how to tightly bound the worst-case size of a join query using a notion called a fractional cover. Fix a hypergraph $H = (V, E)$. Let $x \in \mathbb{R}^{|E|}$ be a vector indexed by edges, i.e., with one component for each edge, such that $x \geq 0$; x is a *feasible cover* (or simply feasible) for H if

$$\text{for each } v \in V \text{ we have } \sum_{e \in E: e \ni v} x_e \geq 1$$

A feasible cover x is also called a *fractional hypergraph cover* in the literature. AGM showed that if x is feasible then it forms an upper bound of the query result size $|\text{OUT}|$ as follows:

$$|\text{OUT}| \leq \prod_{e \in E} |R_e|^{x_e} \quad (1)$$

For a query Q, we denote $\mathsf{AGM}(Q)$ as the smallest such right-hand side.[3]

EXAMPLE 2.1. *For simplicity, let $|R_e| = N$ for $e \in E$. Consider the triangle query, $R(x,y) \bowtie S(y,z) \bowtie T(x,z)$, a feasible cover is $x_R = x_S = 1$ and $x_T = 0$. Via Equation 1, we know that $|\text{OUT}| \leq N^2$. That is, with N tuples in each relation we cannot produce a set of output tuples that contains more than N^2. However, a tighter bound can be obtained using a different fractional cover $x = (\frac{1}{2}, \frac{1}{2}, \frac{1}{2})$. Equation 1 yields the upper bound $N^{3/2}$. Remarkably, this bound is tight if one considers the complete graph on $\sqrt{N}$ vertexes. For this graph, this query produces $\Omega(N^{3/2})$ tuples, which shows that the optimal solution can be tight up to constant factors.*

Algorithm 1 Generic Worst-Case Optimal Join Algorithm

```
//Input: Hypergraph H = (V,E), and a tuple t.
Generic-Join(V,E,t):
  if |V| = 1 then return ∩_{e∈E} R_e[t].
  Let I = {v_1} // the first attribute.
  Q ← ∅ // the return value
  // Intersect all relations that contain v_1
  // Only those tuples that agree with t.
  for every t_v ∈ ∩_{e∈E:e∋v_1} π_I(R_e[t]) do
    Q_t ← Generic-Join(V − I, E, t :: t_v )
    Q ← Q ∪ {t_v} × Q_t
  return Q
```

The first algorithm to have a running time matching these worst-case size bounds is the NPRR algorithm [18]. An important property for the set intersections in the NPRR algorithm is what we call the *min property*: the running time of the intersection algorithm is upper bounded by the length of the *smaller* of the two input sets. When the min property holds, a worst-case optimal running time for *any* join query is guaranteed. In fact, for *any* join query, its execution time can be upper bounded by $\mathsf{AGM}(Q)$. A simplified high-level description of the algorithm is presented in Algorithm 1. It was also shown that any pairwise join plan must be slower by asymptotic factors. However, we show in Section 3.1 that these optimality guarantees can be improved for non-worst-case data or more complex queries.

2.2 Input Data

EmptyHeaded stores all relations (input and output) in tries, which are multi-level data structures common in column stores and graph engines [29, 36].

[3] One can find the best bound, $\mathsf{AGM}(Q)$, in polynomial time: take the log of Eq. 1 and solve the linear program.

Name	Query Syntax
Triangle	`Triangle(x,y,z) :- R(x,y),S(y,z),T(x,z).`
4-Clique	`4Clique(x,y,z,w) :- R(x,y),S(y,z),T(x,z),U(x,w),V(y,w),Q(z,w).`
Lollipop	`Lollipop(x,y,z,w) :- R(x,y),S(y,z),T(x,z),U(x,w).`
Barbell	`Barbell(x,y,z,x',y',z') :- R(x,y),S(y,z),T(x,z),U(x,x'),R'(x',y'),S'(y',z'),T'(x',z').`
Count Triangle	`CountTriangle(;w:long) :- R(x,y),S(x,z),T(x,z); w=<<COUNT(*)>>.`

PageRank	`N(;w:int) :- Edge(x,y); w=<<COUNT(x)>>.`
	`PageRank(x;y:float) :- Edge(x,z); y= 1/N.`
	`PageRank(x;y:float)*[i=5] :- Edge(x,z),PageRank(z),InvDeg(z); y=0.15+0.85*<<SUM(z)>>.`

SSSP	`SSSP(x;y:int) :- Edge("start",x); y=1.` `SSSP(x;y:int)* :- Edge(w,x),SSSP(w); y=<<MIN(w)>>+1.`

Table 1: Example Queries in EmptyHeaded

Trie Annotations. The sets of values in the trie can optionally be associated with data values (1-1 mapping) that are used in aggregations. We call these associated values *annotations* [37]. For example, a two-level trie annotated with a float value represents a sparse matrix or graph with edge properties. We show in Section 5 that the trie data structure works well on a wide variety of graph workloads.

Dictionary Encoding. The tries in EmptyHeaded currently support sets containing 32-bit values. As is standard [22,38], we use the popular database technique of dictionary encoding to build a EmptyHeaded trie from input tables of arbitrary types. Dictionary encoding maps original data values to keys of another type—in our case 32-bit unsigned integers. The order of dictionary ID assignment affects the density of the sets in the trie, and as others have shown this can have a dramatic impact on overall performance on certain queries. Like others, we find that node ordering is powerful when coupled with pruning half the edges in an undirected graph [49]. This creates up to 3x performance difference on symmetric pattern queries like the triangle query. Unfortunately this optimization is brittle, as the necessary symmetrical properties break with even a simple selection. On more general queries we find that node ordering typically has less than a 10% overall performance impact. We explore the effect of various node orderings in Appendix A.1.1.

Column (Index) Order. After dictionary encoding, our 32-bit value relations are next grouped into sets of distinct values based on their parent attribute (or column). We are free to select which level corresponds to each attribute (or column) of an input relation. As with most graph engines, we simply store both orders for each edge relation. In general, we choose the order of the attributes for the trie based on a global attribute order, which is analogous to selecting a single index over the relation. The trie construction process produces tries where the sets of data values can be extremely dense, extremely sparse, or anywhere in between. Optimizing the layout of these sets based upon their data characteristics is the focus of Section 4. The complete transformation process from a standard relational table to the trie representation in EmptyHeaded is detailed in Figure 2.

2.3 Query Language

Our query language is inspired by datalog and supports conjunctive queries with aggregations and simple recursion (similar to LogicBlox and SociaLite). In this section, we describe the core syntax for our queries, which is sufficient to

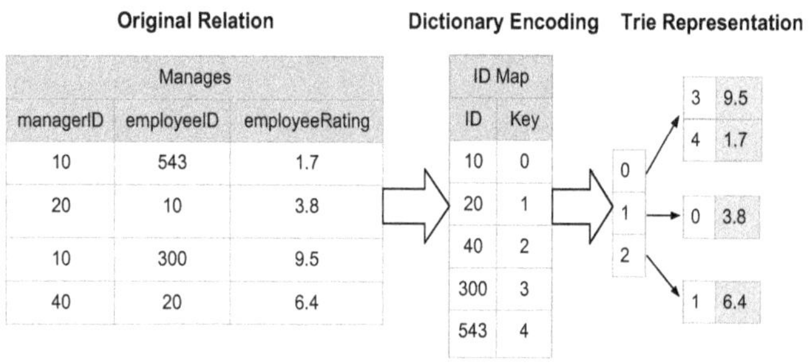

Figure 2: EmptyHeaded transformations from a table to trie representation using attribute order (*managerID,employerID*) and *employerID* attribute annotated with *employeeRating*.

express the standard benchmarks we run in Section 5. Table 1 shows the example queries used in this paper. Above the first horizontal line are conjunctive queries that express joins, projections, and selections in the standard way [52]. Our language has two non-standard extensions: aggregations and a limited form of recursion. We overview both extensions next and provide an example in Appendix A.2.

Aggregation. Following Green et al. [37], tuples can be annotated in EmptyHeaded, and these annotations support aggregations from any semiring (a generalization of natural numbers equipped with a notion of addition and multiplication). This enables EmptyHeaded to support classic aggregations such as `SUM`, `MIN`, or `COUNT`, but also more sophisticated operations such as matrix multiplication. To specify the annotation, one uses a semicolon in the head of the rule, e.g., `q(x,y;z:int)` specifies that each `x,y` pair will be associated with an integer value with alias `z` similar to a `GROUP BY` in SQL. In addition, the user expresses the aggregation operation in the body of the rule. The user can specify an initialization value as any expression over the tuples' values and constants, while common aggregates have default values. Directly below the first line in Table 1, a typical triangle counting query is shown.

Recursion. EmptyHeaded supports a simplified form of recursion similar to Kleene-star or transitive closure. Given an intensional or extensional relation R, one can write a

(a) Hypergraph (b) LogicBlox GHD (c) EmptyHeaded GHD

Figure 3: We show the Barbell query hypergraph and two possible GHDs for the query. A node v in a GHD captures which relations should be joined with $\lambda(v)$ and which attributes should be retained with projection with $\chi(v)$.

Kleene-star rule like:

$$\text{R*}(\bar{x}) \quad \text{:-} \quad q(\bar{x}, \bar{y})$$

The rule $R*$ iteratively applies q to the current instantiation of R to generate new tuples which are added to R. It performs this iteration until (a) the relation doesn't change (a fixpoint semantic) or (b) a user-defined convergence criterion is satisfied (e.g. a number of iterations, `i=5`). Examples that capture familiar PageRank and Single-Source Shortest Paths are below the second horizontal line in table 1.

3. QUERY COMPILER

We now present an overview of the query compiler in EmptyHeaded, which is the first worst-case optimal query compiler to enable early aggregation through its use of GHDs for logical query plans. We first discuss GHDs and their theoretical advantages. Next, we describe how we develop a simple optimizer to select a GHD (and therefore a query plan). Finally, we show how EmptyHeaded translates a GHD into a series of loops, aggregations, and set intersections using the generic worst-case optimal join algorithm [18]. Our contribution here is the design of a novel query compiler that provides tighter runtime guarantees than existing approaches.

3.1 Query Plans using GHDs

As in a classical database, EmptyHeaded needs an analog of relational algebra to represent logical query plans. In contrast to traditional relational algebra, EmptyHeaded has multiway join operators. A natural approach would be simply to extend relational algebra with a multiway join algorithm. Instead, we advocate replacing relational algebra with GHDs, which allow us to make non-trivial estimates on the cardinality of intermediate results. This enables optimizations, like early aggregation in EmptyHeaded, that can be asymptotically faster than existing worst-case optimal engines. We first describe the motivation for using GHDs while formally describing their advantages next.

3.1.1 Motivation

A GHD is a tree similar to the abstract syntax tree of a relational algebra expression: nodes represent a join and projection operation, and edges indicate data dependencies. A node v in a GHD captures which attributes should be retained (projection with $\chi(v)$) and which relations should be joined (with $\lambda(v)$). We consider all possible query plans (and therefore all valid GHDs), selecting the one where the sum of each node's runtime is the lowest. Given a query, there are many valid GHDs that capture the query. Finding the lowest-cost GHD is one goal of our optimizer.

Before giving the formal definition, we illustrate GHDs and their advantages by example:

EXAMPLE 3.1. *Figure 3a shows a hypergraph of the Barbell query introduced in Table 1. This query finds all pairs of triangles connected by a path of length one. Let* OUT *be the size of the output data. From our definition in Section 2.1, one can check that the Barbell query has a feasible cover of* $(\frac{1}{2}, \frac{1}{2}, \frac{1}{2}, 0, \frac{1}{2}, \frac{1}{2}, \frac{1}{2})$ *with cost* $6 \times \frac{1}{2} = 3$ *and so runs in time* $O(N^3)$. *In fact, this bound is worst-case optimal because there are instances that return* $\Omega(N^3)$ *tuples. However, the size of the output* OUT *could be much smaller.*

There are multiple GHDs for the Barbell query. The simplest GHD for this query (and in fact for all queries) is a GHD with a single node containing all relations; the single node GHD for the Barbell query is shown in Figure 3b. One can view all of LogicBlox's current query plans as a single node GHD. The single node GHD always represents a query plan which uses only the generic worst-case optimal join algorithm and no GHD optimizations. For the Barbell query, OUT *is* N^3 *in the worst-case for the single node GHD.*

Consider the alternative GHD shown in Figure 3c. This GHD corresponds to the following alternate strategy to the above plan: first list each triangle independently using the generic worst-case optimal algorithm, say on the vertices (x, y, z) *and then* (x', y', z'). *There are at most* $O(N^{3/2})$ *triangles in each of these sets and so it takes only this time. Now, for each* $(x, x') \in U$ *we output all the triangles that contain* x *or* x' *in the appropriate position. This approach is able to run in time* $O(N^{3/2} + \text{OUT})$ *and essentially performs early aggregation if possible. This approach can be substantially faster when* OUT *is smaller than* N^3. *For example, in an aggregation query* OUT *is just a single scalar, and so the difference in runtime between the two GHDs can be quadratic in the size of the database. We describe how we execute this query plan in Section 3.3. This type of optimization is currently not available in the LogicBlox engine.*

3.1.2 Formal Description

We describe GHDs and their advantages formally next.

Definition 1. Let H be a hypergraph. A ***generalized hypertree decomposition (GHD)*** of H is a triple $D = (T, \chi, \lambda)$, where:

- $T(V(T), E(T))$ is a tree;
- $\chi : V(T) \to 2^{V(H)}$ is a function associating a set of vertices $\chi(v) \subseteq V(H)$ to each node v of T;
- $\lambda : V(T) \to 2^{E(H)}$ is a function associating a set of hyperedges to each vertex v of T;

such that the following properties hold:

1. For each $e \in E(H)$, there is a node $v \in V(T)$ such that $e \subseteq \chi(v)$ and $e \in \lambda(v)$.

2. For each $t \in V(H)$, the set $\{v \in V(T) | t \in \chi(v)\}$ is connected in T.

3. For every $v \in V(T)$, $\chi(v) \subseteq \cup\lambda(v)$.

A GHD can be thought of as a labeled (hyper)tree, as illustrated in Figure 3. Each node of the tree v is labeled; $\chi(v)$ describes which attributes are "returned" by the node v–this exactly captures projection in traditional relational algebra. The label $\lambda(v)$ captures the set of relations that are present in a (multiway) join at this particular node. The first property says that every edge is mapped to some node, and the second property is the famous *"running intersection property"* [32] that says any attribute must form a connected subtree. The third property is redundant for us, as any GHD violating this condition is not considered (has infinite width which we describe next).

Using GHDs, we can define a non-trivial cardinality estimate based on the sizes of the relations. For a node v, define Q_v as the query formed by joining the relations in $\lambda(v)$. The ***(fractional) width*** of a GHD D is $\mathsf{AGM}(Q_v)$, which is an upper bound on the number of tuples returned by Q_v. The ***fractional hypertree width (fhw)*** of a hypergraph H is the minimum width of all GHDs of H. Given a GHD with width w, there is a simple algorithm to run in time $O(N^w + \text{OUT})$. First, run any worst-case optimal algorithm on Q_v for each node v of the GHD; each join takes time $O(N^w)$ and produces at most $O(N^w)$ tuples. Then, one is left with an acyclic query over the output of Q_v, namely the tree itself. We then perform Yannakakis' classical algorithm [54], which for acyclic queries enables us to compute the output in linear time in the input size ($O(N^w)$) plus the output size (OUT).

3.2 Choosing Logical Query Plans

We describe how EmptyHeaded chooses GHDs, explain how we leverage previous work to enable aggregations over GHDs, and describe how GHDs are used to select a global attribute ordering in EmptyHeaded. In Appendix B.1, we provide detail on how classic database optimizations, such as pushing down selections, can be captured using GHDs.

GHD Optimizer. The EmptyHeaded query compiler selects an optimal GHD to ensure tighter theoretical run time guarantees. It is key that the EmptyHeaded optimizer selects a GHD with the smallest width w to ensure an optimal GHD. Similar to how a traditional database pushes down projections to minimize the output size, EmptyHeaded minimizes the output size by finding the GHD with the smallest width. In contrast to pushing down projections, finding the minimum width GHD is NP-hard in the number of relations and attributes. As the number of relations and attributes is typically small (three for triangle counting), we simply brute force search GHDs of all possible widths.

Aggregations over GHDs. Previous work has investigated aggregations over hypertree decompositions [14,48]. EmptyHeaded adopts this previous work in a straightforward way.

	Operation	Description
Trie (R)	$R[t]$	Returns the set matching tuple $t \in R$.
	$R \leftarrow R \cup t \times xs$	Appends elements in set xs to tuple $t \in R$.
Set (xs)	for x in xs	Iterates through the elements x of a set xs.
	$xs \cap ys$	Returns the intersection of sets xs and ys.

Table 2: Execution Engine Operations

To do this, we add a single attribute with "semiring annotations" following Green et al. [37]. EmptyHeaded simply manipulates this value as it is projected away. This general notion of aggregations over annotations enables EmptyHeaded to support traditional notions of queries with aggregations as well as a wide range of workloads outside traditional data processing, like message passing in graphical models.

Global Attribute Ordering. Once a GHD is selected, EmptyHeaded selects a global attribute ordering. The global attribute ordering determines the order in which EmptyHeaded code generates the generic worst-case optimal algorithm (Algorithm 1) and the index structure of our tries (Section 2.2). Therefore, selecting a global attribute ordering is analogous to selecting a join and index order in a traditional pairwise relational engine. The attribute order depends on the query. For the purposes of this paper, we assume both trie orderings are present, and we are therefore free to select any attribute order. For graphs (two-attributes), most in-memory graph engines maintain both the matrix and its transpose in the compressed sparse row format [9,36]. We are the first to consider selecting an attribute ordering based on a GHD and as a result we explore simple heuristics based on structural properties of the GHD. To assign an attribute order for all queries in this paper, EmptyHeaded simply performs a pre-order traversal over the GHD, adding the attributes from each visited GHD node into a queue.

3.3 Code Generation

EmptyHeaded's code generator converts the selected GHD for each query into optimized C++ code that uses the operators in Table 2. We choose to implement code generation in EmptyHeaded as it is has been shown to be an efficient technique to translate high-level query plans into code optimized for modern hardware [46].

3.3.1 Code Generation API

We first describe the storage-engine operations which serve as the basic high-level API for our generated code. Our trie data structure offers a standard, simple API for traversals and set intersections that is sufficient to express the worst-case optimal join algorithm detailed in Algorithm 1. The key operation over the trie is to return a set of values that match a specified tuple predicate (see Table 2). This operation is typically performed while traversing the trie, so EmptyHeaded provides an optimized iterator interface. The set of values retrieved from the trie can be intersected with other sets or iterated over using the operations in Table 2.

3.3.2 GHD Translation

The goal of code generation is to translate a GHD to the operations in Table 2. Each GHD node $v \in V(T)$ is associated with a trie described by the attribute ordering in $\chi(v)$. Unlike previous worst-case optimal join engines, there are two phases to our algorithm: (1) within nodes of $V(T)$ and (2) between nodes $V(T)$.

Within a Node. For each $v \in V(T)$, we run the generic worst-case optimal algorithm shown in Algorithm 1. Suppose Q_v is the triangle query.

EXAMPLE 3.2. *Consider the triangle query. The hypergraph is $V = \{X, Y, Z\}$ and $E = \{R, S, T\}$. In the first call, the loop body generates a loop with body Generic-Join($\{Y, Z\}, E, t_X$). In turn, with two more calls this generates:*

for $t_X \in \pi_X R \cap \pi_X T$ *do*
    for $t_Y \in \pi_Y R[t_X] \cap \pi_Y S$ *do*
        $Q \leftarrow Q \cup (t_x, t_y) \times (\pi_Z S[t_Y] \cap \pi_Z T[t_X])$.

Across Nodes. Recall Yannakakis' seminal algorithm [54]: we first perform a "bottom-up" pass, which is a reverse level-order traversal of T. For each $v \in V(T)$, the algorithm computes Q_v and passes its results to the parent node. Between nodes (v_0, v_1) we pass the relations projected onto the shared attributes $\chi(v_0) \cap \chi(v_1)$. Then, the result is constructed by walking the tree "top-down" and collecting each result.

Recursion. EmptyHeaded supports both naive and seminaive evaluation to handle recursion. For naive recursion, EmptyHeaded's optimizer produces a (potentially infinite) linear chain GHD with the output of one GHD node serving as the input to its parent GHD node. We run naive recursion for PageRank in Table 1. This boils to down to a simple unrolling of the join algorithm. Naive recursion is not an acceptable solution in applications such as SSSP where work is continually being eliminated. To detect when EmptyHeaded should run seminaive recursion, we check if the aggregation is monotonically increasing or decreasing with a `MIN` or `MAX` operator. We use seminaive recursion for SSSP.

EXAMPLE 3.3. *For the Barbell query (see Figure 3c), we first run Algorithm 1 on nodes v_1 and v_2; then we project their results on x and x' and pass them to node v_0. This is part of the "bottom-up" pass. We then execute Algorithm 1 on node v_0 which now contains the results (triangles) of its children. Algorithm 1 executes here by simply checking for pairs of (x, x') from its children that are in U. To perform the "top-down" pass, for each matching pair, we append (y, z) from v_1 and (y', z') from v_2.*

4. EXECUTION ENGINE OPTIMIZER

The EmptyHeaded execution engine runs code generated from the query compiler. The goal of the EmptyHeaded execution engine is to fully utilize SIMD parallelism, but extracting SIMD parallelism is challenging as graph data is often skewed in several distinct ways. The density of data values is almost never constant: some parts of the relation are dense while others are sparse. We call this *density skew*.[4]

[4]We measure density skew using the Pearson's first coefficient of skew defined as $3\sigma^{-1}(mean - mode)$ where σ is the standard deviation.

n	o_1	...	o_n	b_1	...	b_n

Figure 4: Example of the `bitset` layout that contains n blocks and a sequence of offsets (o_1-o_n) and blocks (b_1-b_n). The offsets store the start offset for values in the bitvector.

A novel aspect of EmptyHeaded is that it automatically copes with density skew through an optimizer that selects among different data layouts. We implemented and tested five different set layouts previously proposed in the literature [6,8,16,40]. We found that the simple `uint` and `bitset` layouts yield the highest performance in our experiments [7]. Thus, we focus on selecting between (1) a 32-bit unsigned integer (`uint`) layout for sparse data and (2) a `bitset` layout for dense data. For dense data, the `bitset` layout makes it trivial to take advantage of SIMD parallelism. But for sparse data, the `bitset` layout causes a quadratic blowup in memory usage while `uint` sets make extracting SIMD parallelism challenging.

Making these layout choices is challenging, as the optimal choice depends both on the characteristics of the data, such as density, and the characteristics of the query. We first describe layouts and intersection algorithms in Sections 4.1 and 4.2. This serves as background for the tradeoff study we perform in Section 4.3, where we explore the proper granularity at which to make layout decisions. Finally, we present our automatic optimizer and show that it is close to an unachievable lower-bound optimal in Section 4.4. This study serves as the basis for our automatic layout optimizer that we use inside of the EmptyHeaded storage engine.

4.1 Layouts

In the following, we describe the `bitset` layout in EmptyHeaded. We omit a description of the `uint` layout as it is just an array of 32-bit unsigned integers. We also detail how both layouts support associated data values.

BITSET. The `bitset` layout stores a set of pairs (offset, bitvector), as shown in Figure 4. The offset is the index of the smallest value in the bitvector. Thus, the layout is a compromise between sparse and dense layouts. We refer to the number of bits in the bitvector as the *block size*. EmptyHeaded supports block sizes that are powers of two with a default of 256.[5] As shown, we pack the offsets contiguously, which allows us to regard the offsets as a `uint` layout; in turn, this allows EmptyHeaded to use the same algorithm to intersect the offsets as it does for the `uint` layout.

Associated Values. Our sets need to be able to store associated values such as pointers to the next level of the trie or annotations of arbitrary types. In EmptyHeaded, the associated values for each set also use different underlying data layouts based on the type of the underlying set. For the `bitset` layout we store the associated values as a dense vector (where associated values are accessed based upon the data value in the set). For the `uint` layout we store the associated values as a sparse vector (where the associated values are accessed based upon the index of the value in the set).

4.2 Intersections

We briefly present an overview of the intersection algorithms EmptyHeaded uses for each layout. This serves as

[5] The width of an AVX register.

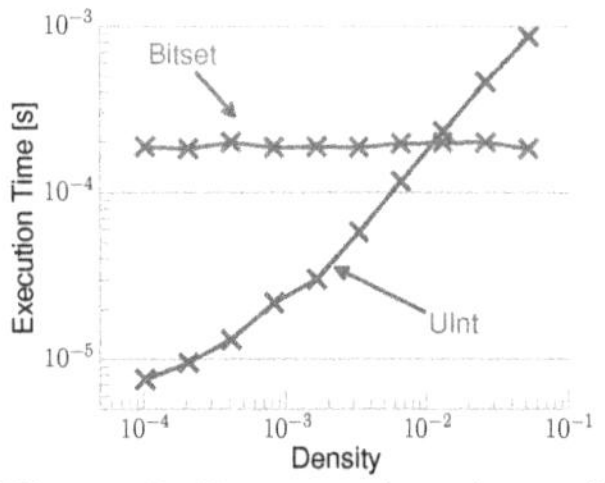

Figure 5: Intersection time of uint and bitset layouts for different densities.

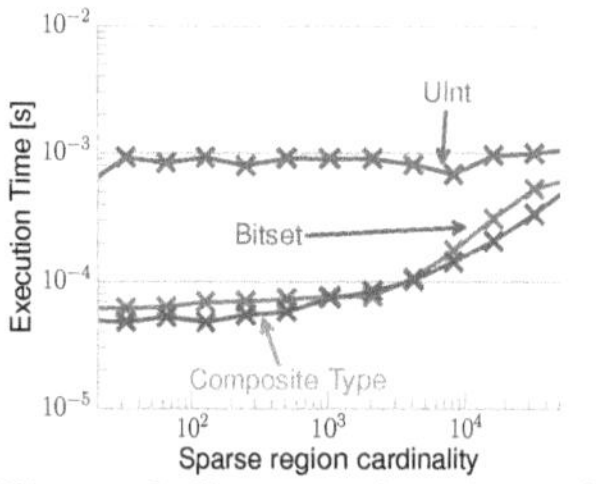

Figure 6: Intersection time of layouts for sets with different sizes of dense regions.

the background for our tradeoff study in Section 4.3. We remind the reader that the *min property* presented in Section 2.1 must hold for set intersections so that a worst-case optimal runtime can be guaranteed in EmptyHeaded.

UINT ∩ UINT. For the `uint` layout, we implemented and tested five state-of-the-art SIMD set intersections [6, 8, 16, 40]. For `uint` intersections we found that the size of two sets being intersected may be drastically different. This is another type of skew, which we call *cardinality skew*. So-called *galloping* algorithms [53] allow one to run in time proportional to the size of the smaller set, which copes with cardinality skew. However, for sets that are of similar size, galloping algorithms may have additional overhead. Therefore, like others [8, 16], EmptyHeaded uses a simple hybrid algorithm that selects a SIMD galloping algorithm when the ratio of cardinalities is greater than 32:1, and a SIMD shuffling algorithm otherwise.

BITSET ∩ BITSET. Our `bitset` is conceptually a two-layer structure of offsets and blocks. Offsets are stored using `uint` sets. Each offset determines the start of the corresponding block. To compute the intersection, we first find the common blocks between the `bitsets` by intersecting the offsets using a `uint` intersection followed by SIMD `AND` instructions to intersect matching blocks. In the best case, i.e., when all bits in the register are 1, a single hardware instruction computes the intersection of 256 values.

UINT ∩ BITSET. To compute the intersection between a `uint` and a `bitset`, we first intersect the `uint` values with the offsets in the `bitset`. We do this to check if it is possible that some value in a `bitset` block matches a `uint` value. As `bitset` block sizes are powers of two in EmptyHeaded, this can be accomplished by masking out the lower bits of each `uint` value in the comparison. This check may result in false positives, so, for each matching `uint` and `bitset` block we check whether the corresponding `bitset` blocks contain the `uint` value by probing the block. We store the result as a `uint` as the intersection of two sets can be at most as dense as the sparser set.[6] Notice that this algorithm satisfies the min property with a constant determined by the block size.

[6] Estimating data characteristics like output cardinality a priori is a hard problem [34] and we found it is too costly to reinspect the data after each operation.

Dataset	Nodes [M]	Dir. Edges [M]	Undir. Edges [M]	Density Skew	Description
Google+ [42]	0.11	13.7	12.2	1.17	User network
Higgs [42]	0.4	14.9	12.5	0.23	Tweets about Higgs Boson
LiveJournal [23]	4.8	68.5	43.4	0.09	User network
Orkut [4]	3.1	117.2	117.2	0.08	User network
Patents [1]	3.8	16.5	16.5	0.09	Citation network
Twitter [17]	41.7	1,468.4	757.8	0.12	Follower network

Table 3: Graph datasets presented in Section 5.1.1 that are used in the experiments.

4.3 Tradeoffs

We explore three different levels of granularity to decide between `uint` and `bitset` layouts in our trie data structure: the relation level, the set level, and the block level.

Relation Level. Set layout decisions at the relation level force the data in all relations to be stored using the same layout and therefore do not address density skew. The simplest layout in memory is to store all sets in every trie using the `uint` layout. Unfortunately, it is difficult to fully exploit SIMD parallelism using this layout, as only four elements fit in a single SIMD register.[7] In contrast, bitvectors can store 256 elements in a single SIMD register. However, bitvectors are inefficient on sparse data and can result in a quadratic blowup of memory usage. Therefore, one would expect unsigned integer arrays to be well suited for sparse sets and bitvectors for dense sets. Figure 5 illustrates this trend. Because of the sparsity in real-world data, we found that `uint` provides the best performance at the relation level.

Set Level. Real-world data often has a large amount of density skew, so both the `uint` and `bitset` layouts are useful. At the set level we simply decide on a per-set level if the entire set should be represented using a `uint` or a `bitset` layout. Furthermore, we found that our `uint` and `bitset` intersection can provide up to a 6x performance increase over the best homogeneous `uint` intersection and a 132x increase over a homogeneous `bitset` intersection. We show in Sections 4.4 and 5.3 that the impact of mixing layouts at the set level on real data can increase overall query performance by over an order of magnitude.

Block Level. Selecting a layout at the set level might be too coarse if there is internal skew. For example, set level layout decisions are too coarse-grained to optimally exploit a set with a large sparse region followed by a dense region. Ideally, we would like to treat dense regions separately from sparse ones. To deal with skew at a finer granularity, we propose a *composite set* layout that regards the domain as a series of fixed-sized blocks; we represent sparse blocks using the `uint` layout and dense blocks using the `bitset` layout. We show in Figure 6 that on synthetic data the composite layout can outperform the `uint` and `bitset` layouts by 2x.

[7] In the Intel Ivy Bridge architecture only SSE instructions contain integer comparison mechanisms; therefore we are forced to restrict ourselves to a 128 bit register width.

Dataset	Relation level	Set level	Block level
Google+	7.3x	1.1x	3.2x
Higgs	1.6x	1.4x	2.4x
LiveJournal	1.3x	1.4x	2.0x
Orkut	1.4x	1.4x	2.0x
Patents	1.2x	1.6x	1.9x

Table 4: Relative time of the level optimizers on triangle counting compared to the oracle.

4.4 Layout Optimizer

Our synthetic experiments in Section 4.3 show there is no clear winner, as the right granularity at which to make a layout decision depends on the data characteristics and the query. To determine if our system should make layout decisions at a relation, set, or block level on real data, we compare each approach to the time of a lower-bound oracle optimizer. We found that while running on the real graph datasets shown in Table 3, choosing layouts at the set level provided the best overall performance (see Table 4).

Oracle Comparison. The oracle optimizer we compare to provides a lower bound as it is able to freely select amongst all layouts per set operation. Thus, it is allowed to choose any layout and intersection combination while assuming perfect knowledge of the cost of each intersection. We implement the oracle optimizer by brute-force, running all possible layout and algorithm combinations for every set intersection in a given query. The oracle optimizer then counts only the cost of the best-performing combination (from all possible combinations), therefore providing a lower bound for the EmptyHeaded optimizer. On the triangle counting query, the set level optimizer was at most 1.6x off the optimal oracle performance, while choosing at the relation and block levels can be up to 7.3x and 3.2x slower respectively than the oracle. Although more sophisticated optimizers exist, and were tested in the EmptyHeaded engine, we found that this simple set level optimizer performed within 10%-40% of the oracle optimizer on real graph data. Because of this we use the set optimizer by default inside of EmptyHeaded (and for the remainder of this paper).

Set Optimizer. The set optimizer in EmptyHeaded selects the layout for a set in isolation based on its cardinality and range. It selects the `bitset` layout when each value in the set consumes at most as much space as a SIMD (AVX) register and the `uint` layout otherwise. The optimizer uses the `bitset` layout with a block size equal to the range of the data in the set. We find this to be more effective than a fixed block size since it lacks the overhead of storing multiple offsets.

5. EXPERIMENTS

We compare EmptyHeaded against state-of-the-art high- and low-level specialized graph engines on standard graph benchmarks. We show that by using our optimizations from Section 3 and Section 4, EmptyHeaded is able to compete with specialized graph engines.

5.1 Experiment Setup

We describe the datasets, comparison engines, metrics, and experiment setting used to validate that EmptyHeaded competes with specialized engines in Sections 5.2 and 5.3.

5.1.1 Datasets

Table 3 provides a list of the 6 popular datasets that we use in our comparison to other graph analytics engines. LiveJournal, Orkut, and Patents are graphs with a low amount of density skew, and Patents is much smaller graph in comparison to the others. Twitter is one of the largest publicly available datasets and is a standard benchmarking dataset that contains a modest amount of density skew. Higgs is a medium-sized graph with a modest amount of density skew. Google+ is a graph with a large amount of density skew.

5.1.2 Comparison Engines

We compare EmptyHeaded against popular high- and low-level engines in the graph domain. We also compare to the high-level LogicBlox engine, as it is the first commercial database with a worst-case optimal join optimizer.

Low-Level Engines. We benchmark several graph analytic engines and compare their performance. The engines that we compare to are PowerGraph v2.2 [22], the latest release of commercial graph tool (CGT-X), and Snap-R [43]. Each system provides highly optimized shared memory implementations of the triangle counting query. Other shared memory graph engines such as Ligra [50] and Galois [9] do not provide optimized implementations of the triangle query and requires one to write queries by hand. We do provide a comparison to Galois v2.2.1 on PageRank and SSSP. Galois has been shown to achieve performance similar to that of Intel's hand-coded implementations [30] on these queries.

High-Level Engines. We compare to LogicBlox v4.3.4 on all queries since LogicBlox is the first general purpose commercial engine to provide similar worst-case optimal join guarantees. LogicBlox also provides a relational model that makes complex queries easy and succinct to express. It is important to note that LogicBlox is full-featured commercial system (supports transactions, updates, etc.) and therefore incurs inefficiencies that EmptyHeaded does not. Regardless, we demonstrate that using GHDs as the intermediate representation in EmptyHeaded's query compiler not only provides tighter theoretical guarantees, but provides more than a three orders of magnitude performance improvement over LogicBlox. We further demonstrate that our set layouts account for over an order of magnitude performance advantage over the LogicBlox design. We also compare to SociaLite [24] on each query as it also provides high-level language optimizers, making the queries as succinct and easy to express as in EmptyHeaded. Unlike LogicBlox, SociaLite does not use a worst-case optimal join optimizer and therefore suffers large performance gaps on graph pattern queries. Our experimental setup of the LogicBlox and SociaLite engines was verified by an engineer from each system and our results are in-line with previous findings [10, 24, 30].

Omitted Comparisons. We compared EmptyHeaded to GraphX [20] which is a graph engine designed for scale-out performance. GraphX was consistently several orders of magnitude slower than EmptyHeaded's performance in a shared-memory setting. We also compared to a commercial database and PostgreSQL but they were consistently over three orders of magnitude off of EmptyHeaded's performance. We exclude a comparison to Grail [21] as its performance has been shown to be comparable to or substantially worse than PowerGraph [22], to which we provide a comparison.

5.1.3 Metrics

We measure the performance of EmptyHeaded and other engines. For end-to-end performance, we measure the wall-clock time for each system to complete each query. This measurement excludes the time used for data loading, outputting the result, data statistics collection, and index creation for all engines. We repeat each measurement seven times, eliminate the lowest and the highest value, and report the average. Between each measurement of the *low-level* engines we wipe the caches and re-load the data to avoid intermediate results that each engine might store. For the *high-level* engines we perform runs back-to-back, eliminating the first run which can be an order of magnitude worse than the remaining runs. We do not include compilation times in our measurements. Low-level graph engines run as a stand-alone program (no compilation time) and we discard the compilation time for high-level engines (by excluding their first run, which includes compilation time). Nevertheless, our unoptimized compilation process (under two seconds for all queries in this paper) is often faster than other high-level engines' (Socialite or LogicBlox).

5.1.4 Experiment Setting

EmptyHeaded is an in-memory engine that runs and is evaluated on a single node server. As such, we ran all experiments on a single machine with a total of 48 cores on four Intel Xeon E5-4657L v2 CPUs and 1 TB of RAM. We compiled the C++ engines (EmptyHeaded, Snap-R, PowerGraph, TripleBit) with g++ 4.9.3 (-O3) and ran the Java-based engines (CGT-X, LogicBlox, SociaLite) on OpenJDK 7u65 on Ubuntu 12.04 LTS. For all engines, we chose buffer and heap sizes that were at least an order of magnitude larger than the dataset itself to avoid garbage collection.

5.2 Experimental Results

We provide a comparison to specialized graph analytics engines on several standard workloads. We demonstrate that EmptyHeaded outperforms the graph analytics engines by 2-60x on graph pattern queries while remaining competitive on PageRank and SSSP.

5.2.1 Graph Pattern Queries

We first focus on the triangle counting query as it is a standard graph pattern benchmark with hand-tuned implementations provided in both high- and low-level engines. Furthermore, the triangle counting query is widely used in graph processing applications and is a common subgraph query pattern [31, 47]. To be fair to the low-level frameworks, we compare the triangle query only to frameworks that provide a hand-tuned implementation. Although we have a high-level optimizer, we outperform the graph analytics engines by 2-60x on the triangle counting query.

As is the standard, we run each engine on pruned versions of these datasets, where each undirected edge is pruned such that $src_{id} > dst_{id}$ and *id*'s are assigned based upon the degree of the node. This process is standard as it limits the size of the intersected sets and has been shown to empirically work well [49]. Nearly every graph engine implements pruning in this fashion for the triangle query.

		Low-Level			High-Level	
Dataset	EH	PG	CGT-X	SR	SL	LB
Google+	**0.31**	8.40x	62.19x	4.18x	1390.75x	83.74x
Higgs	**0.15**	3.25x	57.96x	5.84x	387.41x	29.13x
LiveJournal	**0.48**	5.17x	3.85x	10.72x	225.97x	23.53x
Orkut	**2.36**	2.94x	-	4.09x	191.84x	19.24x
Patents	**0.14**	10.20x	7.45x	22.14x	49.12x	27.82x
Twitter	**56.81**	4.40x	-	2.22x	t/o	30.60x

Table 5: Triangle counting runtime (in seconds) for EmptyHeaded (EH) and relative slowdown for other engines including PowerGraph (PG), a commercial graph tool (CGT-X), Snap-Ringo (SR), SociaLite (SL) and LogicBlox (LB). 48 threads used for all engines. "-" indicates the engine does not process over 70 million edges. "t/o" indicates the engine ran for over 30 minutes.

Takeaways. The results from this experiment are in Table 5. On very sparse datasets with low density skew (such as the Patents dataset) our performance gains are modest as it is best to represent all sets in the graph using the `uint` layout, which is what many competitor engines already do. As expected, on datasets with a larger degree of density skew, our performance gains become much more pronounced. For example, on the Google+ dataset, with a high density skew, our set level optimizer selects 41% of the neighborhood sets to be `bitsets` and achieves over an order of magnitude performance gain over representing all sets as `uints`. LogicBlox performs well in comparison to CGT-X on the Higgs dataset, which has a large amount of cardinality skew, as they use a Leapfrog Triejoin algorithm [53] that optimizes for cardinality skew by obeying the min property of set intersection. EmptyHeaded similarly obeys the min property by selecting amongst set intersection algorithms based on cardinality skew. In Section 5.3 we demonstrate that over a two orders of magnitude performance gain comes from our set layout and intersection algorithm choices.

Omitted Comparison. We do not compare to Galois on the triangle counting query, as Galois does not provide an implementation and implementing it ourselves would require us to write a custom set intersection in Galois (where >95% of the runtime goes). We describe how to implement high-performance set intersections in-depth in Section 4 and EmptyHeaded's triangle counting numbers are comparable to Intel's hand-coded numbers which are slightly (10-20%) faster than the Galois implementation [30]. We provide a comparison to Galois on SSSP and PageRank in Section 5.2.2.

5.2.2 Graph Analytics Queries

Although EmptyHeaded is capable of expressing a variety of different workloads, we benchmark PageRank and SSSP as they are common graph benchmarks. In addition, these benchmarks illustrate the capability of EmptyHeaded to process broader workloads that relational engines typically do not process efficiently: (1) linear algebra operations (in PageRank) and (2) transitive closure (in SSSP). We run each query on undirected versions of the graph datasets and demonstrate competitive performance compared to specialized graph engines. Our results suggest that our approach is competitive outside of classic join workloads.

		Low-Level				High-Level	
Dataset	EH	G	PG	CGT-X	SR	SL	LB
Google+	0.10	**0.021**	0.24	1.65	0.24	1.25	7.03
Higgs	0.08	**0.049**	0.5	2.24	0.32	1.78	7.72
LiveJournal	0.58	**0.51**	4.32	-	1.37	5.09	25.03
Orkut	0.65	**0.59**	4.48	-	1.15	17.52	75.11
Patents	**0.41**	0.78	3.12	4.45	1.06	10.42	17.86
Twitter	**15.41**	17.98	57.00	-	27.92	367.32	442.85

Table 6: Runtime for 5 iterations of PageRank (in seconds) using 48 threads for all engines. "-" indicates the engine does not process over 70 million edges. EH denotes EmptyHeaded and the other engines include Galois (G), PowerGraph (PG), a commercial graph tool (CGT-X), Snap-Ringo (SR), SociaLite (SL), and LogicBlox (LB).

		Low-Level			High-Level	
Dataset	EH	G	PG	CGT-X	SL	LB
Google+	0.024	**0.008**	0.22	0.51	0.27	41.81
Higgs	0.035	**0.017**	0.34	0.91	0.85	58.68
LiveJournal	0.19	**0.062**	1.80	-	3.40	102.83
Orkut	0.24	**0.079**	2.30	-	7.33	215.25
Patents	0.15	**0.054**	1.40	4.70	3.97	159.12
Twitter	7.87	**2.52**	36.90	-	x	379.16

Table 7: SSSP runtime (in seconds) using 48 threads for all engines. "-" indicates the engine does not process over 70 million edges. EH denotes EmptyHeaded and the other engines include Galois (G), PowerGraph (PG), a commercial graph tool (CGT-X), and SociaLite (SL). "x" indicates the engine did not compute the query properly.

PageRank. As shown in Table 6, we are consistently 2-4x faster than standard low-level baselines and more than an order of magnitude faster than the high-level baselines on the PageRank query. We observe competitive performance with Galois (271 lines of code), a highly tuned shared memory graph engine, as seen in Table 6, while expressing the query in three lines of code (Table 1). There is room for improvement on this query in EmptyHeaded since double buffering and the elimination of redundant joins would enable EmptyHeaded to achieve performance closer to the bare metal performance, which is necessary to outperform Galois.

Single-Source Shortest Paths. We compare EmptyHeaded's performance to LogicBlox and specialized engines in Table 7 for SSSP while omitting a comparison to Snap-R. Snap-R does not implement a parallel version of the algorithm and is over three orders of magnitude slower than EmptyHeaded on this query. For our comparison we selected the highest degree node in the undirected version of the graph as the start node. EmptyHeaded consistently outperforms PowerGraph (low-level) and SociaLite (high-level) by an order of magnitude and LogicBlox by three orders of magnitude on this query. More sophisticated implementations of SSSP than what EmptyHeaded generates exist [33]. For example, Galois, which implements such an algorithm, observes a 2-30x performance improvement over EmptyHeaded on this application (Table 7). Still, EmptyHeaded is competitive with Galois (172 lines of code) compared to the other approaches while expressing the query in two lines of code (Table 1).

Dataset	Query	EH	-R	-RA	-GHD	SL	LB
Google+	K_4	4.12	10.01x	10.01x	-	t/o	t/o
	$L_{3,1}$	3.11	1.05x	1.10x	8.93x	t/o	t/o
	$B_{3,1}$	3.17	1.05x	1.14x	t/o	t/o	t/o
Higgs	K_4	0.66	3.10x	10.69x	-	666x	50.88x
	$L_{3,1}$	0.93	1.97x	7.78x	1.28x	t/o	t/o
	$B_{3,1}$	0.95	2.53	11.79x	t/o	t/o	t/o
LiveJournal	K_4	2.40	36.94x	183.15x	-	t/o	141.13x
	$L_{3,1}$	1.64	45.30x	176.14x	1.26x	t/o	t/o
	$B_{3,1}$	1.67	88.03x	344.90x	t/o	t/o	t/o
Orkut	K_4	7.65	8.09x	162.13x	-	t/o	49.76x
	$L_{3,1}$	8.79	2.52x	24.67x	1.09x	t/o	t/o
	$B_{3,1}$	8.87	3.99x	47.81x	t/o	t/o	t/o
Patents	K_4	0.25	328.77x	1021.77x	-	20.05x	21.77x
	$L_{3,1}$	0.46	104.42x	575.83x	0.99x	318x	62.23x
	$B_{3,1}$	0.48	200.72x	1105.73x	t/o	t/o	t/o

Table 8: 4-Clique (K_4), Lollipop ($L_{3,1}$), and Barbell ($B_{3,1}$) runtime in seconds for EmptyHeaded (EH) and relative runtime for SociaLite (SL), LogicBlox (LB) and EmptyHeaded while disabling features. "t/o" indicates the engine ran for over 30 minutes. "-R" is EH without layout optimizations. "-RA" is EH without both layout (density skew) and intersection algorithm (cardinality skew) optimizations. "-GHD" is EH without GHD optimizations (single-node GHD).

5.3 Micro-Benchmarking Results

We detail the effect of our contributions on query performance. We introduce two new queries and revisit the Barbell query (introduced in Section 3) in this section: (1) K_4 is a 4-clique query representing a more complex graph pattern, (2) $L_{3,1}$ is the Lollipop query that finds all 3-cliques (triangles) with a path of length one off of one vertex, and (3) $B_{3,1}$ the Barbell query that finds all 3-cliques (triangles) connected by a path of length one. We demonstrate how using GHDs in the query compiler and the set layouts in the execution engine can have a three orders of magnitude performance impact on the K_4, $L_{3,1}$, and $B_{3,1}$ queries.

Experimental Setup. These queries represents pattern queries that would require significant effort to implement in low-level graph analytics engines. For example, the simpler triangle counting implementation is 138 lines of code in Snap-R and 402 lines of code in PowerGraph. In contrast, each query is one line of code in EmptyHeaded. As such, we do not benchmark the low-level engines on these complex pattern queries. We run `COUNT(*)` aggregate queries in this section to test the full effect of GHDs on queries with the potential for early aggregation. The K_4 query is symmetric and therefore runs on the same pruned datasets as those used in the triangle counting query in Section 5.2.1. The $B_{3,1}$ and $L_{3,1}$ queries run on the undirected versions of these datasets.

5.3.1 Query Compiler Optimizations

GHDs enable complex queries to run efficiently in EmptyHeaded. Table 8 demonstrates that when the GHD optimizations are disabled ("-GHD"), meaning a single node GHD query plan is run, we observe up to an 8x slowdown on the $L_{3,1}$ query and over a three orders of magnitude performance improvement on the $B_{3,1}$ query. Interestingly, density skew matters again here, and for the dataset with the largest amount of density skew, Google+, EmptyHeaded observes the largest performance gain. GHDs enable early aggregation here and thus eliminate a large amount of computation on the datasets with large output cardinalities (high density skew). LogicBlox, which currently uses only the generic worst-case optimal join algorithm (no GHD optimizations) in their query compiler, is unable to complete the Lollipop or Barbell queries across the datasets that we tested. GHD optimizations do not matter on the K_4 query as the optimal query plan is a single node GHD.

5.3.2 *Execution Engine Optimizations*

Table 8 shows the relative time to complete graph queries with features of our engine disabled. The "-R" column represents EmptyHeaded without SIMD set layout optimizations and therefore density skew optimizations. This most closely resembles the implementation of the low-level engines in Table 5, who do not consider mixing SIMD friendly layouts. Table 8 shows that our set layout optimizations consistently have a two orders of magnitude performance impact on advanced graph queries. The "-RA" column shows EmptyHeaded without density skew (SIMD layout choices) and cardinality skew (SIMD set intersection algorithm choices). Our layout and algorithm optimizations provide the largest performance advantage (>20x) on extremely dense (`bitset`) and extremely sparse (`uint`) set intersections [7] , which is what happens on the datasets with low density skew here. Like others [41], we found that explicitly disabling SIMD vectorization, in addition to our layout and algorithm choices, decreases our performance by another 2x (see Appendix A.1.2). Our contribution here is the mixing of data representations ("-R") and set intersection algorithms ("-RA"), both of which are deeply intertwined with SIMD parallelism. In total, Table 8 and our discussion validate that the set layout and algorithmic features have merit and enable EmptyHeaded to compete with graph engines.

6. RELATED WORK

Our work extends previous work in four main areas: join processing, graph processing, SIMD processing, and set intersection processing.

Join Processing. The first worst-case optimal join algorithm was recently derived [19]. The LogicBlox (LB) engine [53] is the first commercial database engine to use a worst-case optimal algorithm. Researchers have also investigated worst-case optimal joins in distributed settings [35] and have looked at minimizing communication costs [11] or processing on compressed representations [48]. Recent theoretical advances [25, 27] have suggested worst-case optimal join processing is applicable beyond standard join pattern queries. We continue in this line of work. The algorithm in EmptyHeaded is a derived from the worst-case optimal join algorithm [19] and uses set intersection operations optimized for SIMD parallelism, an approach we exploit for the first time. Additionally, our algorithm satisfies a stronger optimality property that we describe in Section 3.

Graph Processing. Due to the increase in main memory sizes, there is a trend toward developing shared memory graph analytics engines. Researchers have released high performance shared memory graph processing engines, most notably SociaLite [24], Green-Marl [36], Ligra [50], and Galois [9]. With the exception of SociaLite, each of these engines proposes a new domain-specific language for graph analytics. SociaLite, based on datalog, presents a engine that more closely resembles a relational model. Other engines such as PowerGraph [22], Graph-X [20], and Pregel [15] are aimed at scale-out performance. The merit of these specialized approaches against traditional online analytical processing (OLAP) engines is a source of much debate [5], as some researchers believe general approaches can compete with and outperform these specialized designs [13, 20]. Recent products, such as SAP HANA, integrate graph accelerators as part of a OLAP engine [28]. Others [21] have shown that relational engines can compete with distributed engines [15,22] in the graph domain, but have not targeted shared-memory baselines. We hope our work contributes to the debate about which portions of the workload can be accelerated.

SIMD Processing. Recent research has focused on taking advantage of the hardware trend toward increasing SIMD parallelism. DB2 Blu integrated an accelerator supporting specialized heterogeneous layouts designed for SIMD parallelism on predicate filters and aggregates [38]. Our approach is similar in spirit to DB2 Blu, but applied specifically to join processing. Other approaches such as WideTable [45] and BitWeaving [44] investigated and proposed several novel ways to leverage SIMD parallelism to speed up scans in OLAP engines. Furthermore, researchers have looked at optimizing popular database structures, such as the trie [39], and classic database operations [55] to leverage SIMD parallelism. Our work is the first to consider heterogeneous layouts to leverage SIMD parallelism as a means to improve worst-case optimal join processing.

Set Intersection Processing. In recent years there has been interest in SIMD sorted set intersection techniques [6, 8, 16, 40]. Techniques such as the SIMDShuffling algorithm [40] break the min property of set intersection but often work well on graph data, while techniques such as SIMDGalloping [8] that preserve the min property rarely work well on graph data. We experiment with these techniques and slightly modify our use of them to ensure min property of the set intersection operation in our engine. We use this as a means to speed up set intersection, which is the core operation in our approach to join processing.

7. CONCLUSION

We demonstrate the first general-purpose worst-case optimal join processing engine that competes with low-level specialized engines on standard graph workloads. Our approach provides strong worst-case running times and can lead to over a three orders of magnitude performance gain over standard approaches due to our use of GHDs. We perform a detailed study of set layouts to exploit SIMD parallelism on modern hardware and show that over a three orders of magnitude performance gain can be achieved through selecting among algorithmic choices for set intersection and set layouts at different granularities of the data. Finally, we show that on popular graph queries our prototype engine can outperform specialized graph analytics engines by 4-60x and LogicBlox by over three orders of magnitude. Our study suggests that this type of engine is a first step toward unifying standard SQL and graph processing engines.

Acknowledgments We thank LogicBlox and SociaLite for helpful conversations and verification of our comparisons. Andres Nötzli for his valuable feedback on the paper and extensive discussions on the implementation of the engine. Rohan Puttagunta and Manas Joglekar for their theoretical underpinnings. Peter Bailis for his helpful feedback on this work. We gratefully acknowledge the support of the Defense Advanced Research Projects Agency (DARPA) XDATA Program under No. FA8750-12-2-0335 and DEFT Program under No. FA8750-13-2-0039, DARPA's MEMEX program and SIMPLEX program, the National Science Foundation (NSF) CAREER Award under No. IIS-1353606, the Office of Naval Research (ONR) under awards No. N000141210041 and No. N000141310129, the National Institutes of Health Grant U54EB020405 awarded by the National Institute of Biomedical Imaging and Bioengineering (NIBIB) through funds provided by the trans-NIH Big Data to Knowledge (BD2K, http://www.bd2k.nih.gov) initiative, the Sloan Research Fellowship, the Moore Foundation, American Family Insurance, Google, and Toshiba. Any opinions, findings, and conclusions or recommendations expressed in this material are those of the authors and do not necessarily reflect the views of DARPA, AFRL, NSF, ONR, NIH, or the U.S. government.

8. REFERENCES

[1] U.S. patents network dataset – KONECT, 2014.
[2] C. Chekuri and A. Rajaraman. Conjunctive query containment revisited. In *ICDT '97*, pages 56–70. Springer.
[3] A. Atserias et al. Size bounds and query plans for relational joins. *SIAM Journal on Computing*, 42(4):1737–1767, 2013.
[4] A. Mislove et al. Measurement and analysis of online social networks. In *Proc. Internet Measurement Conf.*, 2007.
[5] A. Welc et al. Graph analysis: Do we have to reinvent the wheel? GRADES '13, pages 7:1–7:6.
[6] B. Schlegel et al. Fast sorted-set intersection using simd instructions. In *ADMS Workshop*, 2011.
[7] C. Aberger et al. Emptyheaded: A relational engine for graph processing. *Technical Report*, abs/1503.02368, 2016.
[8] D. Lemire et al. SIMD compression and the intersection of sorted integers. Software: Practice and Experience, 2015.
[9] D. Nguyen et al. A lightweight infrastructure for graph analytics. SOSP '13, pages 456–471.
[10] D. Nguyen et al. Join processing for graph patterns: An old dog with new tricks. *arXiv preprint arXiv:1503.04169*, 2015.
[11] F. Afrati et al. Gym: A multiround join algorithm in mapreduce. Technical report, Stanford University.
[12] F. Chierichetti et al. On compressing social networks. KDD '09, pages 219–228.
[13] F. McSherry et al. Scalability! but at what cost? HOTOS '15, pages 14–14, Berkeley, CA, USA, 2015. USENIX Association.
[14] G. Gottlob et al. Hypertree decompositions: Structure, algorithms, and applications. In *Graph-theoretic concepts in computer science*, pages 1–15. Springer, 2005.
[15] G. Malewicz et al. Pregel: A system for large-scale graph processing. SIGMOD '10, pages 135–146.
[16] H. Inoue et al. Faster set intersection with simd instructions by reducing branch mispredictions. *VLDB '14*, 8(3).
[17] H. Kwak et al. What is Twitter, a social network or a news media? In *WWW*, 2010.
[18] H. Q. Ngo et al. Worst-case optimal join algorithms: [extended abstract]. In *PODS '12*, pages 37–48. ACM.
[19] H. Q. Ngo et al. Skew strikes back: New developments in the theory of join algorithms. *CoRR*, abs/1310.3314, 2013.
[20] J. E. Gonzalez et al. Graphx: Graph processing in a distributed dataflow framework. In *OSDI '14*, pages 599–613. USENIX Association, October 2014.
[21] J. Fan et al. The case against specialized graph analytics engines. In *CIDR '15*.
[22] J. Gonzalez et al. Powergraph: Distributed graph-parallel computation on natural graphs. OSDI '12, pages 17–30.
[23] J. Leskovec et al. Statistical properties of community structure in large social and information networks. In *Proc. Int. World Wide Web Conf.*, pages 695–704, 2008.
[24] J. Seo et al. Socialite: Datalog extensions for efficient social network analysis. In *ICDE '13*, pages 278–289. IEEE, 2013.
[25] M. A. Khamis et al. FAQ: Questions asked frequently. *arXiv preprint arXiv:1504.04044*, 2015.
[26] M. Aref et al. Design and implementation of the logicblox system. In *SIGMOD '15*, pages 1371–1382. ACM, 2015.
[27] M. Joglekar et al. Aggregations over generalized hypertree decompositions. *arXiv preprint arXiv:1508.07532*, 2015.
[28] M. Rudolf et al. The graph story of the SAP HANA database. In *BTW*, volume 13, pages 403–420. Citeseer, 2013.
[29] M. Stonebraker et al. C-store: a column-oriented dbms. In *VLDB '05*, pages 553–564.
[30] N. Satish et al. Navigating the maze of graph analytics frameworks using massive graph datasets. SIGMOD '14, pages 979–990.
[31] R. Milo et al. Network motifs: simple building blocks of complex networks. *Science*, 298(5594):824–827, 2002.
[32] S. Abiteboul et al. *Foundations of databases*, volume 8. Addison-Wesley Reading, 1995.
[33] S. Beamer et al. Direction-optimizing breadth-first search. SC '12, pages 12:1–12:10.
[34] S. Chaudhuri et al. On random sampling over joins. volume 28 of *SIGMOD '99*, pages 263–274.
[35] S. Chu et al. From theory to practice: Efficient join query evaluation in a parallel database system. In *SIGMOD '15*, pages 63–78. ACM, 2015.
[36] S. Hong et al. Green-marl: A dsl for easy and efficient graph analysis. ASPLOS XVII, pages 349–362, 2012.
[37] T. J. Green et al. Provenance semirings. In *SIGMOD '07*, pages 31–40. ACM.
[38] V. Raman et al. DB2 with BLU acceleration: So much more than just a column store. *VLDB.*, 6(11):1080–1091, 2013.
[39] S. Z. F. Huber and J. Freytag. Adapting tree structures for processing with simd instructions.
[40] I. Katsov. Fast intersection of sorted lists using sse instructions. https://highlyscalable.wordpress.com/2012/06/05/fast-intersection-sorted-lists-sse/, 2012.
[41] Christian Lemke, Kai-Uwe Sattler, Franz Faerber, and Alexander Zeier. Speeding up queries in column stores: A case for compression. DaWaK '10, pages 117–129.
[42] J. Leskovec and A. Krevl. SNAP Datasets: Stanford large network dataset collection. http://snap.stanford.edu/data, June 2014.
[43] J. Leskovec and R. Sosič. SNAP: A general purpose network analysis and graph mining library in C++. http://snap.stanford.edu/snap, 2014.
[44] Y. Li and J. M. Patel. Bitweaving: Fast scans for main memory data processing. SIGMOD '13, pages 289–300.
[45] Y. Li and J. M. Patel. Widetable: An accelerator for analytical data processing. *VLDB*, 7(10), 2014.
[46] T. Neumann. Efficiently compiling efficient query plans for modern hardware. *VLDB '11*, 4(9):539–550.
[47] M. E. J. Newman. The structure and function of complex networks. *SIAM review*, 45(2):167–256, 2003.
[48] D. Olteanu and J. Závodný. Size bounds for factorised representations of query results. *TODS '15*, 40(1):2.
[49] T. Schank and D. Wagner. Finding, counting and listing all triangles in large graphs, an experimental study. WEA '05.
[50] J. Shun and G. E. Blelloch. Ligra: A lightweight graph processing framework for shared memory. *SIGPLAN Not.*, 48(8):135–146, 2013.
[51] S. Tu and C. Ré. Duncecap: Query plans using generalized hypertree decompositions. In *Proceedings of the 2015 ACM SIGMOD International Conference on Management of Data*, pages 2077–2078. ACM, 2015.
[52] J. Ullman. Conjunctive queries. http://infolab.stanford.edu/~ullman/cs345notes/slides01-6.pdf.
[53] T. L. Veldhuizen. Leapfrog triejoin: a worst-case optimal join algorithm. *arXiv preprint arXiv:1210.0481*, 2012.
[54] M. Yannakakis. Algorithms for acyclic database schemes. In *VLDB*, pages 82–94, 1981.
[55] J. Zhou and K. A. Ross. Implementing database operations using simd instructions. In *SIGMOD '02*.

APPENDIX

A. APPENDIX FOR SECTION 2

A.1 Dictionary Encoding and Node Ordering

A.1.1 Node Ordering

Because EmptyHeaded maps each node to an integer value, it is natural to consider the performance implications of these mappings. Node ordering can affect the performance

Ordering	Higgs	LiveJournal
Shingles	1.67	9.14
hybrid	3.77	24.41
BFS	2.42	15.80
Degree	1.43	9.93
Reverse Degree	1.40	8.47
Strong Run	2.69	21.67

Table 9: Node ordering times in seconds on two popular graph datasets.

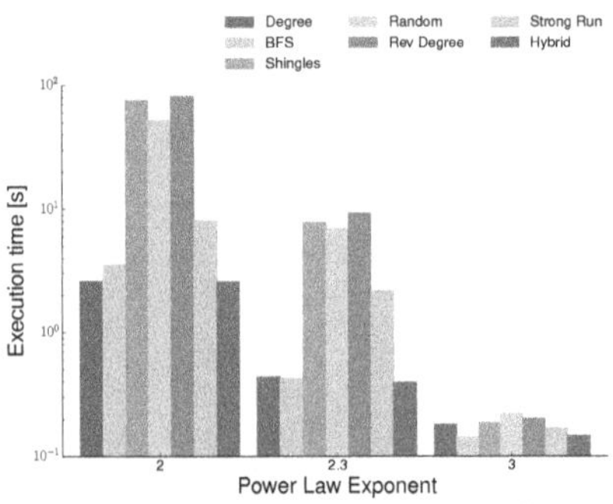

Figure 7: Effect of data ordering on triangle counting with synthetic data.

in two ways: It changes the ranges of the neighborhoods and, for queries that use symmetry breaking, it affects the number of comparisons needed to answer the query. In the following, we discuss the impact of node ordering on triangle counting with and without symmetry breaking.

We explore the impact of node ordering on query performance using triangle counting query on synthetically generated power law graphs with different power law exponents. We generate the data using the Snap Random Power-Law graph generator and vary the Power-Law degree exponents from 1 to 3. The best ordering can achieve over an order of magnitude better performance than the worst ordering on symmetrical queries such as triangle counting.

We consider the following orderings:

Random random ordering of vertices. We use this as a baseline to measure the impact of the different orderings.

BFS labels the nodes in breadth-first order.

Strong-Runs first sorts the node by degree and then starting from the highest degree node, the algorithm assigns continuous numbers to the neighbors of each node. This ordering can be seen as an approximation of BFS.

Degree this ordering is a simple ordering by descending degree which is widely used in existing graph systems.

Rev-Degree labels the nodes by ascending degree.

Shingle an ordering scheme based on the similarity of neighborhoods [12].

In addition to these orderings, we propose a hybrid ordering algorithm `hybrid` that first labels nodes using BFS followed by sorting by descending degree. Nodes with equal degree retain their BFS ordering with respect to each other. The `hybrid` ordering is inspired by our findings that ordering by degree and BFS provided the highest performance on symmetrical queries. Figure 7 shows that graphs with a low power law coefficient achieve the best performance through

	Default		Symmetrically Filtered	
Dataset	`uint`	EmptyHeaded	`uint`	EmptyHeaded
Google+	1.0x	1.4x	1.8x	4.7x
Higgs	0.9x	1.2x	3.0x	1.9x
LiveJournal	1.2x	1.1x	1.7x	1.6x
Orkut	1.1x	1.1x	1.4x	1.5x
Patents	1.2x	1.1x	1.9x	1.3x

Table 10: Relative time of random ordering compared to ordering by degree.

	Default			Symmetrically Filtered		
Dataset	-S	-R	-SR	-S	-R	-SR
Google+	1.0x	3.0x	7.5x	1.0x	4.9x	13.4x
Higgs	1.5x	3.9x	4.8x	1.2x	0.9x	1.7x
LiveJournal	1.6x	1.0x	1.6x	1.2x	0.9x	1.2x
Orkut	1.8x	1.1x	2.0x	1.4x	1.0x	1.6x
Patents	1.3x	0.9x	1.1x	1.0x	0.7x	0.8x

Table 11: Relative time when disabling features on the triangle counting query. Symmetrically filtered refers to the data preprocessing step which is specific to symmetric queries. "-S" is EmptyHeaded without SIMD. "-R" is EmptyHeaded using `uint` at the graph level.

ordering by degree and that a BFS ordering works best on graphs with a high power law coefficient. Figure 7 shows the performance of hybrid ordering and how it tracks the performance of BFS or degree where each is optimal.

Each ordering incurs the cost of performing the actual ordering of the data. Table 9 shows examples of node ordering times in EmptyHeaded. The execution time of the BFS ordering grows linearly with the number of edges, while sorting by degree or reverse degree depends on the number of nodes. The cost of the `hybrid` ordering is the sum of the costs of the BFS ordering and ordering by degree.

A.1.2 Pruning Symmetric Queries

We explore the effect of node ordering on query performance with and without the data pruning that symmetrical queries enable. Symmetric queries such as the triangle query or the 4-clique query on undirected graphs produce equivalent results for graphs where each src, dst pair occurs only once and datasets where each src, dst has a corresponding dst, src pair (the latter producing a result that is a multiple of the former). Specialized engines take advantage of restricted optimization that only holds for symmetric patterns. For this experiment, we measure the effect of the node orderings introduced in Appendix A.1.1 on five datasets with different set layouts. We show that node ordering only has a substantial impact on queries that enable symmetry breaking and that our layout optimizations typically have a larger impact on the queries which do not enable symmetry breaking, which is the more general case.

We use the relative triangle counting performance on 5 datasets with a random ordering and ordering by degree as a proxy for the impact of node ordering. For each dataset, we measure the triangle counting performance with random ordering and ordering by degree (the default standard), with and without pruning, and with the EmptyHeaded set level optimizer and with a homogeneous `uint` layout. We call pruned data on symmetrical queries *symmetrically filtered.* We report the relative performance of the random ordering compared to ordering by degree. Table 10 shows that ordering does not have a large impact on queries that do not enable symmetry breaking. In addition, Table 10 shows that our optimizer is more robust to various orderings in the special cases where symmetry filtering is allowed. Table 11 shows that our optimizations typically have a larger impact on data which is not symmetrically filtered. This is important as symmetrical queries are infrequent and their symmetrical property breaks with even a simple selection.

A.2 Extended Query Language Discussion

Conjunctive Queries: Joins, Projections, Selections. Equality joins are expressed in EmptyHeaded as simple conjunctive queries. We show EmptyHeaded's' syntax for two cyclic join queries in Table 1: the 3-clique query (also known as triangle or K_3), and the Barbell query (two 3-cliques connected by a path of length 1). EmptyHeaded easily enables selections and projections in its query language as well. We enable projections through the user directly annotating which attributes appear in the head. We enable selections by directly annotating predicates on attribute values in the body (e.g. b = 'Chris').

We illustrate how our query language works by example for the PageRank query:

EXAMPLE A.1. *Table 1 shows an example of the syntax used to express the PageRank query in EmptyHeaded. The first line specifies that we aggregate over all the edges in the graph and count the number of source nodes assuming our Edge relation is two-attribute relation filled with (src, dst) pairs. For an undirected graph this simply counts the number of nodes in the graph and assigns it to the relation N which is really just a scalar integer. By definition the $COUNT$ aggregation and by default the SUM use an initialization value of 1 if the relation is not annotated. The second line of the query defines the base case for recursion. Here we simply project away the z attributes and assign an annotation value of $1/N$ (where N is our scalar relation holding the number of nodes). Finally, the third line defines the recursive rule which joins the Edge and $InvDegree$ relations inside the database with the new $PageRank$ relation. We SUM over the z attribute in all of these relations. When aggregated attributes are joined with each other their annotation values are multiplied by default [27]. Therefore we are performing a matrix-vector multiplication. After the aggregation the corresponding expression for the annotation y is applied to each aggregated value. This is run for a fixed number (5) iterations as specified in the head.*

B. APPENDIX FOR SECTION 3

B.1 Selections

Implementing high performance selections in EmptyHeaded requires three additional optimizations that significantly effect performance: (1) pushing down selections within the worst-case optimal join algorithm, (2) index layout tradeoffs, and (3) pushing down selections across GHD nodes. The first two points are trivial so we briefly overview them next while providing a detailed description and experiment for pushing down selections across GHDs in Appendix B.1.1. We narrow our scope in this section to only equality selections, but our techniques are general and can be applied to general selection constraints.

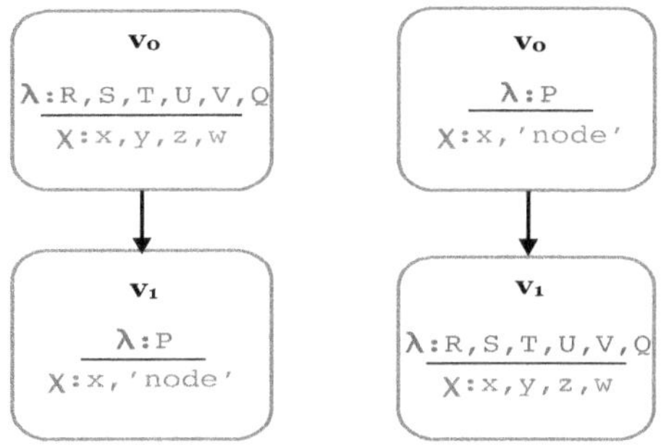

(a) GHD without pushing down (b) GHD with pushing down

Figure 8: We show two possible GHDs for the 4-clique selection query.

Within a Node. Pushing down selections within a GHD node is akin to rearranging the attribute ordering for the generic worst-case optimal algorithm. Simply put, the attributes with selections should come first in the attribute ordering forcing the attributes with selections to be processed first in Algorithm 1.

Index Layouts. The data layouts matter again here as placing the selected attributes first in Algorithm 1, causes these attributes to appear in the first levels of the trie which are often dense and therefore best represented as a bitset. For equality selections this is enables us to perform the actual selection in constant time versus a binary search in an unsigned integer array.

B.1.1 Across Nodes

Pushing down selections across nodes in EmptyHeaded's query plans corresponds to changing the criteria for choosing a GHD described in Section 3.2. Our goal is to have high-selectivity or low-cardinality nodes be pushed down as far as possible in the GHD so that they are executed earlier in our bottom-up pass. We accomplish this by adding three additional steps to our GHD optimizer:

1. Find optimal GHDs $\mathcal{T}$ with respect to fhw, changing V in the AGM constraint to be only the attributes without selections.
2. Let R_s be some relations with selections and let R_t be the relations that we plan to place in a subtree. If for each $e \in R_s$, there exists $e' \in R_t$ such that e' covers e's unselected attributes, include R_s in the subtree for R_t. This means that we may duplicate some members of R_s to include them in multiple subtrees.
3. Of the GHDs $\mathcal{T}$, choose a $T \in \mathcal{T}$ with maximal selection depth, where selection depth is the sum of the distances from selections to the root of the GHD.

B.1.2 Queries

To test our implementation of selections in EmptyHeaded we ran two graph pattern queries that contained selections. The first is a 4-clique selection query where we find all 4-cliques connected to a specified node. The second is a barbell selection query where we find all pairs of 3-cliques connected to a specified node. The syntax for each query in EmptyHeaded is shown in Table 12.

Consider the 4-clique selection query:

Name	Query Syntax
4-Clique-Selection	`S4Clique(x,y,z,w) :- R(x,y),S(y,z),T(x,z),U(x,w),V(y,w),Q(z,w),P(x,'node').`
Barbell-Selection	`SBarbell(x,y,z,x',y',z') :- R(x,y),S(y,z),T(x,z),U(x,'node'), V('node',x'),R'(x',y'),S'(y',z'),T'(x',z').`

Table 12: Selection Queries in EmptyHeaded

EXAMPLE B.1. *Figure 8 shows two possible GHDs for this query. The GHD on the left is the one produced without using the three steps above to push down selections across GHD nodes. This GHD does not filter out any intermediate results across the potentially high selectivity node containing the selection when results are first passed up the GHD. The GHD on the right uses the three steps above. Here the node with the selection is below all other nodes in the GHD, ensuring that high selectivities are processed early in the query plan.*

B.1.3 Discussion

We run `COUNT(*)` versions of the queries here again as materializing the output for these queries is prohibitively expensive. We did materialize the output for these queries on a couple datasets and noticed our performance gap with the competitors was still the same. We varied the selectivity for each query by changing the degree of the node we selected. We tested this on both high and low degree nodes.

The results of our experiments are in Table 13. Pushing down selections across GHDs can enable over a four order of magnitude performance improvement on these queries and is essential to enable peak performance. As shown in Table 13 the competitors are closer to EmptyHeaded when the output cardinality is low but EmptyHeaded still outperforms the competitors. For example, on the 4-clique selection query on the patents dataset the query contains no output but we still outperform LogicBlox by 3.66x and SociaLite by 5754x.

Dataset	Query	|Out|	EH	-GHD	SL	LB
Google+	SK_4	1.5E+11	154.24	6.09x	t/o	t/o
		5.5E+7	1.08	865.95x	t/o	50.91
	$SB_{3,1}$	4.0E+17	0.92	3.22x	t/o	t/o
		2.5E+3	0.008	351.72x	t/o	t/o
Higgs	SK_4	2.2E+7	1.92	14.48x	t/o	58.10x
		2.7E+7	2.91	9.50x	t/o	52.44x
	$SB_{3,1}$	1.7E+12	0.060	17.36x	t/o	t/o
		2.4E+12	0.070	14.88x	t/o	t/o
LiveJournal	SK_4	1.7E+7	6.73	18.05x	t/o	14.83x
		5.1E+2	0.0095	13E3x	t/o	10.46x
	$SB_{3,1}$	1.6E+12	0.27	6.47x	t/o	t/o
		9.9E+4	0.0062	278.16x	t/o	70.23x
Orkut	SK_4	9.8E+8	208.20	1.26x	t/o	t/o
		2.8E+5	0.020	13E+3x	t/o	18.79x
	$SB_{3,1}$	1.1E+15	3.24	3.20x	t/o	t/o
		2.2E+8	0.0072	1314x	21E+3X	23E+3x
Patents	SK_4	0	0.011	121.70x	5754x	3.66x
		9.2E+3	0.011	117.56x	5572x	10.72x
	$SB_{3,1}$	1.6E+1	0.0060	77.82x	223.29x	15.17x
		1.1E+7	0.0066	71.22x	1073x	3296x

Table 13: 4-Clique Selection (SK_4) and Barbell Selection ($SB_{3,1}$) runtime in seconds for EmptyHeaded (EH) and relative runtime for SociaLite (SL), LogicBlox (LB) and EmptyHeaded while disabling optimizations. "|Out|" indicates the output cardinality. "t/o" indicates the engine ran for over 30 minutes. "-GHD" is EmptyHeaded without pushing down selections across GHD nodes.

B.2 Eliminating Redundant Work

Our compiler is the first worst-case optimal join optimizer to eliminate redundant work across GHD nodes and across phases of code generation. Our query compiler performs a simple analysis to determine if two GHD nodes are identical. For each GHD node in the "bottom-up" pass of Yannakakis' algorithm, we scan a list of the previously computed GHD nodes to determine if the result of the current node has already been computed. We use the conditions below to determine if two GHD nodes are equivalent in the Barbell query. Recognizing this provides a 2x performance increase on the Barbell query.

We say that two GHD nodes produce equivalent results in the "bottom-up pass" if:

1. The two nodes contain identical join patterns on the same input relations.
2. The two nodes contain identical aggregations, selections, and projections.
3. The results from each of their subtrees are identical.

We can also eliminate the "top-down" pass of Yannakakis' algorithm if all the attributes appearing in the result also appear in the root node. This determines if the final query result is present after the "bottom-up" phase of Yannakakis' algorithm. For example, if we perform a `COUNT` query on all attributes, the "top-down" pass in general is unnecessary. We found eliminating the top down pass provided a 10% performance improvement on the Barbell query.

C. APPENDIX FOR SECTION 5

C.1 Extended Triangle Counting Discussion

PowerGraph represents each neighborhood using a hash set (with a cuckoo hash) if the degree is larger than 64 and otherwise represents the neighborhood as a vector of sorted node ID's. PowerGraph incurs additional overhead due to its programming model and parallelization infrastructure in a shared memory setting. CGT-X uses a CSR layout and runs Java code for queries which might not be as efficient as native code. Snap-R prunes each neighborhood on the fly using a simple merge sort algorithm and then intersects each neighborhood using a custom scalar intersection over the sets. We note that the runtimes in Table 5 do not reflect the cost of pruning the graph in our system, PowerGraph, SociaLite, or LogicBlox, while CGT-X and Snap-R include this time in their overall runtime. In Snap-R we found, depending on the skew in the graph, the pruning time accounts for 2%-46% of the runtime on the triangle counting.

C.2 Memory Usage

We utilize a small amount of the available memory (1TB RAM) for the datasets run in this paper. For example, when running the PageRank query on the LiveJournal dataset our engine uses at most 8362MB of memory. For comparison, Galois uses 7915MB and PowerGraph uses 8620MB.

GTS: A Fast and Scalable Graph Processing Method based on Streaming Topology to GPUs

Min-Soo Kim, Kyuhyeon An, Himchan Park, Hyunseok Seo, and Jinwook Kim
Department of Information and Communication Engineering
DGIST
Republic of Korea
{mskim,khan,chan150,hsseo,bm010515}@dgist.ac.kr

ABSTRACT

A fast and scalable graph processing method becomes increasingly important as graphs become popular in a wide range of applications and their sizes are growing rapidly. Most of distributed graph processing methods require a lot of machines equipped with a total of thousands of CPU cores and a few terabyte main memory for handling billion-scale graphs. Meanwhile, GPUs could be a promising direction toward fast processing of large-scale graphs by exploiting thousands of GPU cores. All of the existing methods using GPUs, however, fail to process large-scale graphs that do not fi in main memory of a single machine. Here, we propose a fast and scalable graph processing method GTS that handles even RMAT32 (64 billion edges) very efficientl only by using a single machine. The proposed method stores graphs in PCI-E SSDs and executes a graph algorithm using thousands of GPU cores while streaming topology data of graphs to GPUs via PCI-E interface. GTS is fast due to no communication overhead and scalable due to no data duplication from graph partitioning among machines. Through extensive experiments, we show that GTS consistently and significantl outperforms the major distributed graph processing methods, GraphX, Giraph, and PowerGraph, and the state-of-the-art GPU-based method TOTEM.

Keywords

Graph processing; GPUs; SSDs; Stream

1. INTRODUCTION

Graphs are widely used to model real-world objects in many disciplines such as social networks, web, business intelligence, biology, and neuroscience, due to their generality of modeling. As the sizes of real graphs are growing rapidly, fast and scalable graph processing methods have become more important than ever before.

In order to handle large-scale graphs efficientl , there have been proposed a number of distributed graph processing methods. Apache Giraph [1, 11] is an alternative implementation of Google's Pregel [22]. It follows the Bulk-Synchronous Parallel (BSP) message passing model where all vertex kernels run simultaneously in a sequence of supersteps. Within a superstep, each kernel receives all messages from the previous superstep and sends them to its neighbors in the next superstep. Apache Spark GraphX [10, 33, 35] is a graph-parallel framework built on top of Apache Spark. PowerGraph [9, 20, 21] is a graph processing framework considering the power-law distribution of real graphs. It follows the Gather-Apply-Scatter (GAS) model, where Gather collects the information about adjacent vertices/edges, Apply updates the new value of the central vertex using the information, and Scatter updates the data on adjacent edges using the new value. Although they follow their own architectures and models, they all require a lot of machines equipped with a total of thousands of CPU cores and a few terabyte main memory for handling billion-scale graphs.

Meanwhile, the continuous advancement of GPU technology makes the theoretical computing power of modern computers ever-increasing. Due to the much higher theoretical computing performance of GPUs than CPUs, it becomes more and more important to exploit GPUs in a wide range of problems requiring high performance computing such as graph processing. Exploiting GPUs could be a promising direction toward fast processing of large-scale graphs mainly due to their implementation of the characteristics of the Parallel Random Access Machine (PRAM) abstraction. The PRAM abstraction has been widely used to investigate theoretical performance of parallel graph algorithms. It assumes an infinit number of processors and uniform memory latency. GPUs implement these characteristics with a very large number of hardware threads and uniform memory latency. In addition, GPUs have massive memory bandwidth. Conventional CPUs are far from those characteristics and only can traverse or calculate on a few vertices at a time. On the contrary, GPUs can do on a much large number of vertices at a time, without a severe memory bottleneck to shared memory and without excessive concern about different memory latency. Since many real graphs have millions or billions vertices, GPUs are potentially well suited to fast processing of such graphs.

Nevertheless, there is a major challenge associated with exploiting GPUs for processing large-scale graphs. Many real graphs do not fi in the GPU device memory with this tendency becoming more marked as the sizes of graphs are growing [7, 8]. Lack of support for large-scale graphs beyond the capacity of device memory is pointed out as one of the most critical problems of the existing graph processing methods using GPUs [7, 8, 15]. There is almost no study on solving this problem yet, in spite of its importance. To the best of our knowledge, TOTEM [7, 8] is the only work to systematically process a graph that does not fi in the GPU device memory. To solve the problem, it partitions a graph into two parts, one part in main memory and the other part in GPU device memory. GPUs process the part in GPU device memory, while CPUs process the part in main memory. Though it can handle large-scale graphs, it has many fundamental drawbacks such as underutilization of the

SIGMOD '16, June 26–July 1, 2016, San Francisco, CA, USA.

DOI: http://dx.doi.org/10.1145/2882903.2915204

computational power of GPUs, lack of scalability in terms of the number of GPUs, and the difficult of optimizing performance due to a lot of options. Furthermore, it still cannot process larger-scale graphs beyond the capacity of main memory.

We propose a fast and scalable GPU-based graph processing method called GTS that can process even RMAT32 (64 billion edges) graphs very efficientl . GTS fully exploits the computational power of GPUs by processing the entire graph only using GPUs. It does not rely on the graph partitioning scheme and not require a bunch of options for optimization. To overcome the limit of GPU memory capacity and moreover the limit of main memory capacity, we propose a concept of *storing only updatable attribute data and moving topology data*. Here, the attribute data means the information about vertices and edges that are required and updated during execution of vertex kernels. The proposed method stores graphs in PCI-E SSDs and executes a graph algorithm using thousands of GPU cores while streaming topology data of graphs to GPUs via PCI-E interface. More specificall , GTS firs copies attribute data to GPU device memory, and then, processes a graph algorithm by applying a user-define GPU kernel function on each piece of topology data being copied in a streaming fashion from main memory to device memory. In GPUs, asynchronous data transfer can be achieved by using the asynchronous GPU streams (e.g., CUDA Streams), which could hide memory access latency from GPUs to main memory and so utilize GPU's computing power more. For efficien streaming, GTS adopts the slotted page format [12] that divides a graph into fi ed-size units. In terms of exploiting multiple GPUs and SSDs, we also propose two strategies, (1) the strategy for performance (shortly, Strategy-P) for high performance with a limit on scalability and (2) the strategy for scalability (shortly, Strategy-S) for high scalability with a limit on performance. GTS can achieve higher performance compared with the existing methods, due to no communication overhead among machines and due to exploiting massive parallelism of GPU cores. In addition, it could achieve higher scalability compared with the existing methods, due to no data duplication from graph partitioning among machines and due to storing graphs on secondary storage, i.e., SSDs. For example, it can easily store and process an RMAT33 graph (8 billion vertices and 128 billion edges) only using 1 TB PCI-E SSDs, theoretically. GTS is also fairly scalable in terms of the number of GPUs and SSDs, and so, shows a stable speedup when adding a GPU or an SSD to the machine. It is because GTS almost uniformly distributes the units of graph data to GPUs, which again perform graph processing almost independently of each other.

The main contributions of this paper are as follows:

- We propose a novel concept of *storing only updatable attribute data and moving topology data* that is counter-intuitive in terms of the conventional models (e.g., GAS) of storing topology data and moving attribute data.
- We propose a parallel graph processing method GTS on GPUs that can perform graph algorithms very efficientl for large-scale graphs (e.g., billions vertices) by fully exploiting the asynchronous GPU streams.
- We present two strategies that can improve the performance or the scalability further by exploiting multiple GPUs and multiple SSDs: Strategy-P and Strategy-S.
- Through extensive experiments, we demonstrate that GTS consistently and significantl outperforms the major distributed graph processing methods, GraphX, Giraph, and PowerGraph, and the state-of-the-art GPU-based method TOTEM, across wide range of benchmarks.
- Especially, we show that GTS can process an RMAT32 graph within a reasonable time in a single machine that the existing distributed methods fail to process by using 30 machines of a total of about 2 TB memory.

The rest of this paper is organized follows. Section 2 reviews the data format adopted by GTS. In Section 3, we propose the GTS method. In Section 4, we present two strategies for exploiting multiple GPUs and SSDs. In Section 5, we present the cost models of GTS, and in Section 6, we address several implementation issues. Section 7 presents the results of experimental evaluation, and Section 8 discusses related work. Finally, Section 9 summarizes and concludes this paper.

2. PRELIMINARIES

In this section, we explain the data formats proposed for storing graph data, especially with focusing on the format for storing a graph on secondary storage (e.g., SSD). Most of real graphs are known as to be sparse, and various kinds of in-memory formats for a sparse graph have been proposed. They include Diagonal (DIA) [13], ELLPACK (ELL) [2], Compressed Sparse Row (CSR), Compressed Sparse Column (CSC), and Coordinate list (COO) [3]. They might have a limit on the size of graphs to process since they usually require a very long contiguous edge array in main memory for large-scale graphs.

Besides, there is an external memory (i.e., out-of-core) graph format called the *slotted page format* [12]. It represents a graph in a set of fi ed-size slotted pages. A slotted page consists of two parts, *records* and *slots*, where records grow forward from the start of the page, but slots grow backward from the end of the page. A slot consists of a vertex ID (*logical ID*), denoted as VID, and the start offset of the corresponding record, denoted as OFF. A record consists of the size of the adjacency list, denoted as ADJLIST_SZ, and the adjacency list itself, denoted as ADJLIST. Here, the adjacency list again consists of a list of *record IDs* of neighbor vertices. A record ID is a *physical ID* consisting of a pair of the page ID (of 2-byte), denoted as ADJ_PID, and the slot number (of 2-byte) where the corresponding vertex is located, denoted as ADJ_OFF. By using physical IDs, graph algorithms can access to the physical locations of neighbor vertices easily during traversal. This concept of physical ID is commonly used for performance in database area [14]. The vertex IDs and record IDs are consecutive and ordered within a page.

Figure 1 shows an example graph G and the slotted pages of G. In Figure 1(a), the vertices v_0, v_1, and v_2 have a relatively small number of neighbor vertices, while v_3 has a relatively large number of neighbor ones. Such skewness of the node degree distribution is common in real graphs. The low-degree vertices like $\{v_0, v_1, v_2\}$ can be stored in a single page SP_0 as in Figure 1(b), which is called a *Small Page* (SP). In contrast, a high-degree vertex like v_3 might not be stored in a f xed-size slotted page, but can be stored in multiple pages $\{LP_1, LP_2\}$ instead as in Figure 1(c), which are called *Large Pages* (LPs).

3. STREAMING GRAPH TOPOLOGY

In this section, we present the proposed method GTS. Section 3.1 explains the concept of streaming topology, and Section 3.2 describes the streaming scheme of GTS in detail. Section 3.3 presents the scheme to process various types of graph algorithms, and Section 3.4 shows the algorithm of the GTS framework.

3.1 Concept

In general, graph algorithms require both graph topology data (shortly, topology data) and attribute data for vertices and/or edges.

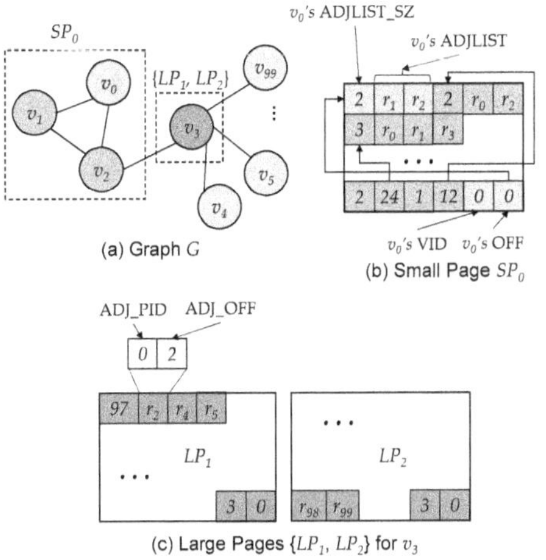

Figure 1: Example graph G and the slotted pages of G.

For example, in addition to topology data, PageRank requires two attribute vectors for vertices: a vector of the previous PageRank values (shortly, prevPR) and a vector of the next PageRank values (shortly, nextPR). As another example, BFS requires one attribute vector for keeping traversal levels for vertices (shortly, LV). The attribute vectors again can be divided into read-only ones and read/write ones. For example, for PageRank, prevPR is a read-only attribute vector, while nextPR is a read/write attribute vector, in a specifi iteration. For BFS, LV is a read/write attribute vector.

Most of the existing graph processing systems [9,20,22] follows the concept that topology data is stored on main memory in a cluster of machines, and attribute data is moved among machines (e.g., the Gather-Apply-Scatter (GAS) model). Without loss of generality, the amount of attribute data to be moved is smaller than that of topology data, and so, it is beneficia to follow that concept for a distributed shared-memory system where each local memory can be accessed via a relatively slow interconnection network. However, it might not be true for a machine equipped with GPUs that have limited device memory and are connected with main memory via a much faster interconnection, i.e., PCI-E interface.

Here, we propose a concept of *storing only updatable attribute data and moving topology data*, where a relatively small amount of attribute data is stored in GPU's limited device memory, and topology data is moved via a high-speed interconnection. Moving topology data from main memory or SSDs to GPUs takes some amount of time even using PCI-E interconnection. However, we can hide that time by processing a given graph algorithm simultaneously with moving attribute data. A graph algorithm θ is executed through a corresponding user-define GPU *kernel* function, denoted as K_θ. In our method, K_θ is executed using thousands of GPU cores for both a part of topology data and attribute data within GPU device memory.

Intuitively, GTS firs copies read/write attribute data to device memory, and then, processes graph algorithms by copying read-only attribute data and topology data in a streaming fashion to device memory. GTS considers that each attribute vector is conceptually partitioned into multiple subvectors, and topology data consists of multiple fi ed-size units, especially, in the slotted page format described in Section 2. For example, prevPR for PageRank can be conceptually decomposed into a lot of subvectors, where a subvector corresponds to a slotted page in terms of the range of vertex IDs. That is possible since the vertex IDs are consecutive in each slotted page. Let attribute data be X and topology data be $Y = \{y_1, \cdots, y_n\}$. Then, the amount of device memory required for processing the graph algorithm θ completely becomes $|X| + |y_i|$. It is obviously important to reduce $|X|$ or $|y_i|$ in order to process a large-scale graph with the limited size of device memory. In general, since $|X| >> |y_i|$, we focus on reducing $|X|$. Between read-only attribute vector (shortly, RA) and read/write attribute vector (shortly, WA), GTS keeps only WA in device memory for reducing the amount of device memory used. Since WA is frequently and randomly updated during graph algorithm in general, it is important to keep WA in device memory for performance. However, RA is not updated during processing, and so can be fed into device memory together with the corresponding topology data. For example, for PageRank, we keep the entire nextPR in device memory, but feed each subvector of prevPR together with the corresponding topology page to device memory.

Figure 2 shows the data fl w of GTS. We suppose WA is divided into W chunks ($W = 1$ in default), and RA is divided into R subvectors. We also suppose the numbers of small pages and large pages are S and L, respectively. The number of units of RA, i.e., R is usually equal to S since most of the topology pages are SP, which will be shown in Section 7.5. RA_j represents the subvector of RA corresponding to SP_j. For WA, GTS performs the following three steps: (1) copying WA to GPU device memory; (2) processing graph algorithms while copying the topology pages $\{SP_j\}$ (or $\{LP_j\}$) together with the read-only attribute vectors $\{RA_j\}$ to GPU device memory in a streaming fashion; and (3) copying WA, which has been updated during graph processing, back to main memory for (data) synchronization.

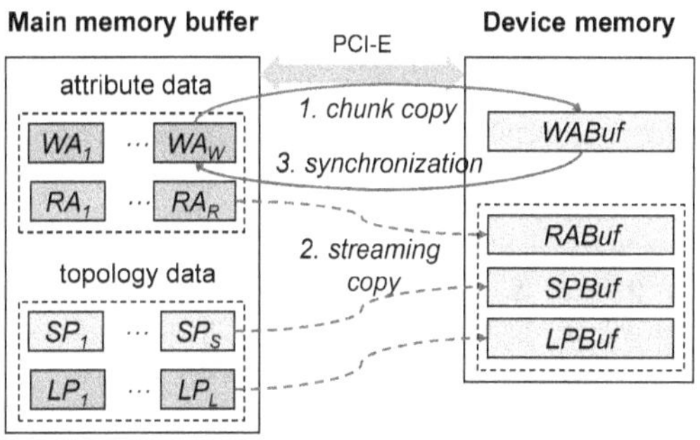

Figure 2: Basic data fl w of GTS.

3.2 Asynchronous multiple streaming

GTS copies topology data from main memory to GPU device memory via the PCI-E bus asynchronously in a streaming way. For streaming topology data, GTS adopts the slotted page format, but it is not a necessary condition that GTS uses the slotted page format. GTS may adopt any format that can divide topology data into fi ed-size units for streaming. GTS rather adopts the slotted page format since it considers workload balancing and coalesced memory access to some degree, which will be discussed in Section 6.2. For streaming RA, SP, and LP to device memory, GTS allocates three kinds of streaming buffers in device memory, called RABuf, SPBuf, and LPBuf, respectively, as in Figure 2. In addition, for WA, GTS also allocates a chunk buffer called WABuf.

GTS exploits multiple GPU streams for streaming. Figure 3 shows the timeline of copy operations of attribute and topology data to device memory. A CPU thread firs transfers WA to WABuf. Then, it starts multiple GPU streams, each of which performs a series of operations, (1) copying SP_j (or LP_j) to SPBuf, (2) copying RA_j to RABuf, and (3) executing the kernel function, repeatedly. In general, transfer operations for WA, RA_j, and SP_j to device memory cannot overlap with each other, at least in the current GPU architecture [5]. Instead, they can overlap with kernel execution [5,27]. Theoretically, the suitable number of streams k can be determined by using the ratio of the transfer time of SP_j and RA_j to the kernel execution time. For example, in Figure 3, if the kernel execution time is k times longer than transfer time, then the transfer operation for SP_{k+1} would start right after the transfer operation for RA_k at time t. Table 1 shows the ratios of the transfer time to the kernel execution time for BFS and PageRank on three real data sets used in experimental evaluation. BFS has relatively high ratios since it is not computationally intensive, while PageRank has relatively low ratios since it is computationally intensive. Thus, the optimal k seems to be dependent on graph algorithms.

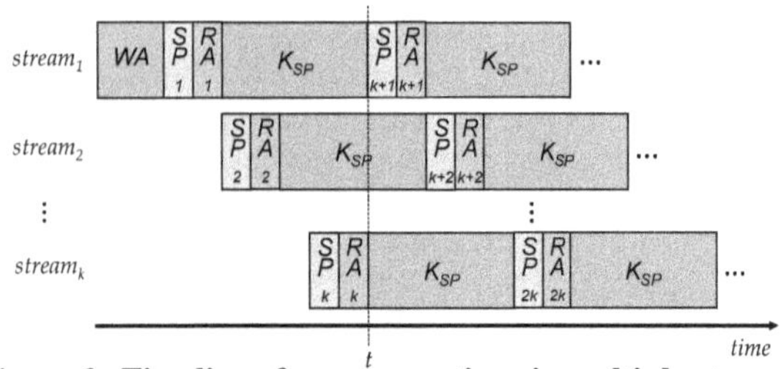

Figure 3: Timeline of copy operations in multiple streams.

Table 1: The ratios of transfer time to kernel execution time for BFS and PageRank on real data sets.

Algorithm	Twitter [18]	UK2007 [32]	YahooWeb [34]
BFS	1:3	1:1	2:1
PageRank	1:20	1:6	1:4

However, in practice, the performance continuously increases until using 32 streams, which will be shown in Section 5.4. This is because the kernel execution becomes faster when SP_j and RA_j are prepared in the queues of GPU in advance. The maximum number of streams that can execute a kernel function concurrently is 32 in the current CUDA technology [5]. After streaming and processing all $\{SP_j\}$ for WA, GTS performs streaming and processing all $\{LP_j\}$ for WA. The reason separating processing SPs from processing LPs is reducing the kernel switching overhead among SPs and LPs. After processing all data streamed to GPU is done, the updated WA is copied back to main memory for bulk synchronization, which is omitted in Figure 3. Figure 4 shows the actual timelines of copy operations for BFS and PageRank when using 16 streams on a synthetic data, which is obtained by profiling In Figure 4, the very short red colored bars indicate copying SP_j and RA_j to device memory, while the long green colored bars indicate executing a kernel function. The timeline for PageRank in Figure 4(b) is denser than that for BFS in Figure 4(a) since PageRank is computationally intensive, whereas BFS is not.

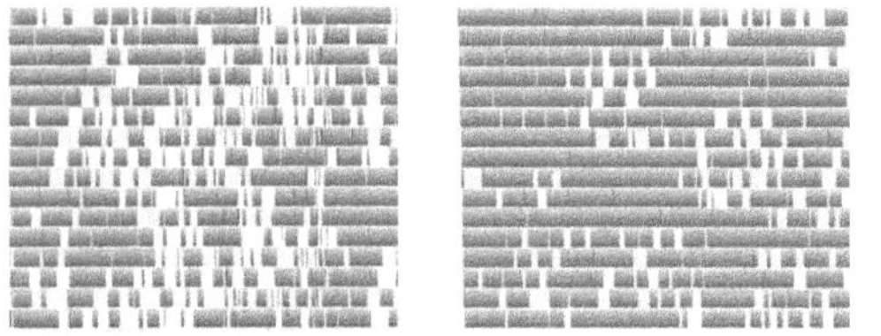

(a) Streaming for BFS (b) Streaming for PageRank

Figure 4: Actual timeline of copy operations for BFS and PageRank when using 16 streams.

3.3 Handling BFS-like algorithms

We consider two major types of graph algorithms: (1) accessing a part of a graph via graph traversal and (2) accessing a whole graph by linear scanning vertices and edges [12]. The former algorithms are usually less computationally intensive, but causes non-coalesced memory accesses due to the irregular structure of graphs. They include Breadth-First Search (BFS), Single-Source-Shortest-Path (SSSP), neighborhood, induced subgraph, egonet, K-core, and cross-edges. BFS is the typical one [7, 8, 12], and hereafter, we denote them as BFS-like algorithms. The latter algorithms are usually computationally intensive, and the scan order of vertices and edges is not important in many cases. They include PageRank, degree distribution, Random Walk with Restart (RWR), radius estimations, and connected components. PageRank is the typical one [7, 8, 12], and hereafter, we denote them as PageRank-like algorithms.

The processing scheme described in Sections 3.1 and 3.2 is typically suitable for processing a single iteration of PageRank-like graph algorithms that access the entire topology data once. However, BFS-like algorithms requires level-by-level traversal, where a single level traversal accesses a very small portion of topology data and does not require streaming the entire topology data. Each traversal just requires streaming a set of topology pages containing the vertices to be visited. For that purpose, GTS keeps the data structure called nextPIDSet that contains the IDs of pages to be accessed at the next level. The local version of nextPIDSet is updated in each GPU during a single level traversal and copied back to main memory, and then, a CPU thread merges the local versions into a single global version. At the next level, the CPU thread copies the set of topology pages in the global nextPIDSet to GPU. As a result, GTS can integrate two types of algorithms having quite different access patterns into a single framework, which will be explained in Section 3.4.

After GTS allocates four buffers WABuf, RABuf, SPBuf, and LPBuf in the GPU device memory, there might be free memory available in GPU device memory. Especially, for BFS, since GTS allocates a small amount of WABuf due to small WA data, where WA is just a LV attribute vector for vertices, there might be a lot of free memory left in GPU device memory. In that case, GTS tries to maximize the performance of graph processing by caching topology data, i.e., SPs and LPs. The BFS-like algorithms could access the same topology pages repeatedly during traversal, and thus the caching scheme could avoid unnecessary copying from main memory to device memory. In general, the cache hit rate increases as the size of cache memory increases. When the total number of topology pages of a graph is $S + L$, a naive approximation of the cache hit rate using B pages would be $B/(S + L)$ for random graphs, though it also depends on a caching algorithm used. GTS basically adopts the LRU algorithm for the caching algorithm, but other algorithms can be used as well.

3.4 Algorithm of the framework

In this section, we present the algorithm of the GTS framework. Algorithm 1 presents the pseudo code of the framework. It performs a user-define kernel function K_{SP} and K_{LP} for a specifi graph algorithm on a graph G, where K_{SP} is a kernel for SPs and K_{LP} is a kernel for LPs. GTS requires such two kinds of kernels since SPs and LPs have a little different structure. As an initialization step, GTS loads G into main memory (MM), creates the streams for small pages and large pages for each GPU, and allocates the buffers WABuf, RABuf, SPBuf, and LPBuf in the device memory (DM) of each GPU. Then, it sets nextPIDSet, a set of page IDs to process next, depending on the type of the graph algorithm. If the graph algorithm is of BFS-like, the page ID containing the start vertex is assigned to nextPIDSet. Otherwise, the constant ALL_PAGES is assigned to it. The map data structure cachedPIDMap$_i$ is initialized, which is used for storing the IDs of cached pages within GPU$_i$ (Line 8). We note that cachedPIDMap$_i$ is updated within GPU$_i$ during streaming topology data (Lines 14-27) and copied back to main memory (Line 29). Here, MMBuf indicates main memory buffer used for fetching the slotted pages from SSDs to main memory.

Algorithm 1 Framework of GTS

```
Input: Graph G, /* input graph */
       K_SP, /* GPU kernel of Q for small pages */
       K_LP, /* GPU kernel of Q for large pages */

Variable: nextPIDSet, /* set of page IDs to process next */
          cachedPIDMap_{1:N}; /* cached page IDs in GPU_{1:N} */
          bufferPIDMap; /* buffered page IDs in MMBuf */
 1: /* Initialization */
 2: Create SPStream and LPStream for GPU_{1:N};
 3: Allocate WABuf, RABuf, SPBuf, LPBuf for GPU_{1:N};
 4: if Q is BFS-like then
 5:    nextPIDSet ← page ID containing start vertex;
 6: else
 7:    nextPIDSet ← ALL_PAGES;
 8: cachedPIDMap_{1:N} ← ∅;
 9: if |G| < MMBuf then
10:    Load G into MMBuf;
11: Copy WA to WABuf of GPU_{1:N};
12: /* Processing GPU kernel */
13: repeat
14:    /* repeat Lines 15-31 for LPs */
15:    for j ∈ nextPIDSet.SP do
16:       if j ∈ cachedPIDMap_{h(j)} then
17:          Call K_SP for SP_j in GPU_{h(j)};
18:       else if j ∈ bufferPIDMap then
19:          Async-copy SP_j in MMBuf to SPBuf in GPU_{h(j)};
20:          Async-copy RA_j to RABuf in GPU_{h(j)};
21:          Call K_SP for SP_j in GPU_{h(j)};
22:       else
23:          Fetch SP_j from SSD_{g(j)} to MMBuf;
24:          Async-copy SP_j in MMBuf to SPBuf in GPU_{h(j)};
25:          Async-copy RA_j to RABuf in GPU_{h(j)};
26:          Call K_SP for SP_j in GPU_{h(j)};
27:    Thread synchronization in GPU;
28:    Copy WA of GPU_{1:N} to MMBuf;
29:    Copy nextPIDSet_{1:N} and cachedPIDMap_{1:N} to MMBuf;
30:    nextPIDSet ← ∪_{1≤i≤N} nextPIDSet_i;
31: until nextPIDSet = ALL_PAGES ∨ nextPIDSet = ∅
```

The *repeat-until* loop (Lines 10-34) takes charge of level-by-level traversal. For a PageRank-like algorithm, this loop is performed only once. Lines 15-27 are performed for processing small pages and performed similarly for processing large pages. We note that Lines 19-20 and 24-25 asynchronously transfer a topology page SP$_j$ (or LP$_j$) in nextPIDSet to a specifi GPU$_{h(j)}$ according to the return value of $h(j)$, which will be explained in Section 4. Here, before transferring the page, GTS firs checks if the page already exists in the cache of GPU$_{h(j)}$ by looking up cachedPIDMaph(j) (Line 16). We note that RA$_j$ for LP is a subvector of a single attribute value since LP$_j$ deals with only a single vertex. While executing a kernel, a new set of page IDs to process at the next level is assigned to local $nextPIDSet_i$ in device memory of each GPU$_i$, which is copied back to MMBuf (Line 29), and then merged into the global nextPIDSet (Line 30). The updated set of cachedPIDMap$_{1:N}$ are also copied back to MMBuf and used in the next level traversal. In the case of PageRank-like algorithms, both nextPIDSet and cachedPIDMap$_{1:N}$ are actually not used. The detailed kernel functions for BFS and PageRank are explained in Appendix B. In the case of PageRank, since the pseudo code in Algorithm 1 is for a single iteration of PageRank, users might need to perform Lines 13-31 as many times as necessary in their applications. Here, at the end of every iteration, nextPR should be initialized after being copied to prevPR.

4. EXPLOITING MULTIPLE GPUS

In this section, we present two strategies for exploiting multiple GPUs. GTS can be easily extended to exploit multiple GPUs. We let the number of GPUs be N. Section 4.1 presents the strategy for high performance with a limit on scalability, whereas Section 4.2 presents the strategy for high scalability with a limit on performance.

4.1 Strategy for performance

The firs strategy of GTS for multiple GPUs is copying the same attribute data, especially WA, to all GPUs and copying a different topology data to each GPU. Figure 5(a) shows the data fl w scheme of that strategy, which consists in four different steps. In Step 1, GTS copies the same WA to all $\{\text{GPU}_1, \cdots, \text{GPU}_N\}$, which are denoted as solid arrows. In Step 2, it executes a given GPU kernel K_{SP} while streaming a different $\langle$ SP$_k$, RA$_k$ $\rangle$ to each GPU$_k$ for $1 \leq k \leq N$, which are denoted as dotted arrows. More specificall , it copies $\langle$ SP$_{i*N+j}$, RA$_{i*N+j}$ $\rangle$ to GPU$_j$ for $0 \leq i \leq \lceil \frac{S}{N} \rceil - 1$ and $1 \leq j \leq N$. LPs are processed in the same way. Here, each GPU can execute the same GPU kernel function independently for a different part of topology data. Steps 3 and 4 perform the data synchronization of WA that has been updated during Step 2, which are denoted as double-lined arrows. GTS exploits the peer-to-peer memory copying feature of modern GPUs. When using multiple GPUs, a naive synchronization method is performing N times synchronization from GPUs to main memory directly, one time per each GPU. This approach might suffer from synchronization overhead as N increases. GTS largely reduces such synchronization overhead by exploiting peer-to-peer memory copying among GPUs, which speed is much faster than that of between GPU and main memory. In Step 3, the WA data of each GPU is copied and merged to the device memory of a master GPU (e.g., GPU$_1$), and then, in Step 4, the updated WA data in GPU$_1$ is copied to main memory.

In terms of the framework of GTS (i.e., Algorithm 1), Step 1 corresponds to Line 11, Step 2 to Lines 16-26, and Steps 3-4 to Line 28. In Step 2, for load balancing, the function $h(x)$ returns a hash value for a page ID j of SP$_j$ (or LP$_j$) such that the page SP$_j$ (or LP$_j$) is streamed to GPU$_{h(i)}$. Typically, GTS uses the *mod* function for the default hash function.

This strategy of GTS potentially can achieve fairly linear parallel speedup with respect to the number of GPUs for graph processing, as long as the capability of data streaming is sufficient Moreover, since the different topology data distributed over GPUs have almost equal sizes, i.e., almost the same amount of workload under this strategy, the speedup ratio can be fairly stable regardless of the characteristics of a graph (e.g., its size and its density). The capability of data streaming largely depends on (1) the speed of PCI-E interface and (2) the I/O performance of SSDs. Under the current computer architecture, the I/O speed of SSDs (e.g., about up to 2 GB/sec) is much slower than that of PCI-E interface (e.g., 16 GB/sec). Thus, the overall performance of this strategy is limited to the I/O performance of SSDs. To alleviate this performance problem, GTS exploits multiple SSDs. In detail, GTS stores each slotted page SP$_j$ of $G (1 \leq j \leq S)$ in a specifi SSD$_{g(j)}$, where

$g(j)$ returns a hash value for a page ID j, and fetches the corresponding page from $SSD_{g(j)}$ according to the I/O request at Line 23 in Algorithm 1. If the size of G is smaller than main memory buffer (MMBuf), fully loading G into MMBuf might be a better method (Lines 9-10), especially for BFS-like algorithms. In that case, the speed of PCI-E interface would become a performance bottleneck.

Although this strategy shows high and stable performance of fairly linear speedup with multiple GPUs, it could suffer from GPU's limited device memory. It could not process a graph algorithm requiring WA larger than the size of a single GPU's device memory. For example, this strategy can process the PageRank algorithm only up to RMAT30 using a GPU having 6 GB device memory.

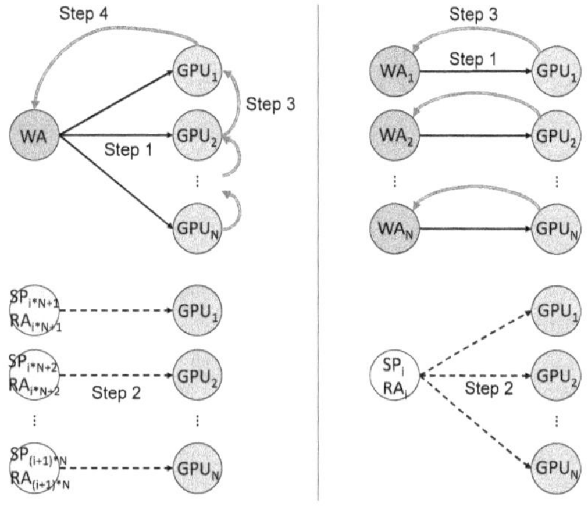

(a) Strategy for performance (b) Strategy for scalability

Figure 5: Two strategies of GTS exploiting multiple GPUs.

4.2 Strategy for scalability

The second strategy of GTS for multiple GPUs is copying a different attribute data, especially a different WA_i chunk to each GPU and copying the same topology data to all GPUs. Figure 5(b) shows the data fl w scheme of that strategy, which consists three steps. In Step 1, GTS copies a different WA_i to each GPU_i for $1 \leq i \leq N$, which are denoted as solid arrows. In Step 2, it executes a given GPU kernel K_{SP} while streaming the same $\langle$ SP_j, RA_j $\rangle$ to all GPUs, which are denoted as dotted arrows. LPs are processed in the same way. Here, each GPU can execute the same GPU kernel function independently for a different part of attribute data. Step 3 performs the data synchronization of all $\{$ WA_i $\}$ that has been updated during Step 2, which are denoted as double-lined arrows. Since all WA_i chunks are disjoint with each other, GTS cannot use the peer-to-peer memory copying feature of GPUs. This strategy just uses a naive synchronization method of performing N times synchronization from GPUs to main memory directly, one time per each GPU.

In terms of the framework of GTS, as in Section 4.1, Step 1 corresponds to Line 11, Step 2 to Lines 16-26, and Steps 3-4 to Line 28. However, in Step 2, the function $h(x)$ returns a set $\{1, \cdots, N\}$ instead of a single hash value for a page ID j such that the page SP_j (or LP_j) is streamed to all GPUs.

This strategy of GTS tries to maximize the size of a graph to process. Especially, it can achieve linear increase of the size of a graph to process, with respect to the number of GPUs, as long as the capacity of main memory or SSDs is sufficient Since the different attribute data distributed over GPUs have almost equal sizes, and at the same time, the same topology data is fed into those GPUs, each GPU has almost the same amount of workload under this strategy. That is, the workload of graph processing is well balanced among GPUs regardless of the characteristics of a graph. This strategy is logically analogous to using a single GPU of large device memory. Thus, although increasing the number of GPUs, the performance of graph processing itself does not change, and the capability of data streaming to GPU also does not change. If we have a large amount of main memory, and so, perform this strategy without accessing to SSDs, the speed of PCI-E interface would be a performance bottleneck. Otherwise, the I/O performance of SSDs would be a bottleneck. However, when we exploit multiple SSDs as described in Section 4.1, the gap between the I/O performance of SSDs and the logical speed of PCI-E interface is not so much due to the fi ed capability of data streaming to the logical single GPU. That means the overall performance of this strategy would not increase much even though processing an entire graph in main memory.

Consequently, the strategy for scalability of GTS is suitable to process a relatively large-scale graph where its WA cannot fi in a single GPU's device memory by storing the graph on SSDs (e.g., an RMAT32 graph in a machine of 6 GB GPUs and 500 GB SSDs). On the contrary, the strategy for performance of GTS (in Section 4.1) is suitable to process a relatively small-scale graph where its WA can fi in a single GPU's device memory by storing the graph in main memory (e.g., an RMAT30 graph in a machine of 6 GB GPUs and 128 GB main memory).

5. COST MODELS

In this section, we present the cost models of GTS, which allow us to understand the performance tendency and further improve the performance later through the cost-based optimization. We only consider major factors that could affect the performance of GTS. Since PageRank-like algorithms and BFS-like algorithms show a quite different tendency, we present two cost models. For simplicity, we present the cost models for Strategy-P without I/O.

5.1 Cost model for PageRank-like algorithms

The cost model for PageRank-like algorithms is given by

$$\frac{2|WA|}{c1} + \frac{|RA|+|SP|+|LP|}{c2 \times N} + t_{call}\Big(\frac{S+L}{N}\Big) + t_{kernel}(SP_{|1|} + LP_{|1|}) + t_{sync}(N). \quad (1)$$

where N is the number of GPUs, $c1$ is the communication rate (e.g., in MB/s) between main memory and device memory in a chunk copy mode, $c2$ is the communication rate in a streaming copy mode, $t_{call}(x)$ is the time overhead of calling a kernel function x times, $t_{kernel}(y)$ is the kernel execution time to process y pages, and $t_{sync}(z)$ is the time overhead of synchronization among z GPUs. Here, $c1$ is usually higher than $c2$ for GPUs. For example, in PCI-E 3.0 x16 interface, $c1$ is about 16 GB/s, while $c2$ is about 6 GB/s. In Eq. 1, $\frac{2|WA|}{c1}$ indicates the total amount of time for copying all WA to device memory and copying the updated ones back to main memory. That time does not decrease while using multiple GPUs. The transfer time of $\frac{|RA|+|SP|+|LP|}{c2}$ is divided by N since the data is transferred concurrently to N GPUs. The time overhead of calling the kernel function $t_{call}(S+L)$ is also divided by N. The term $t_{kernel}(SP_{|1|}+LP_{|1|})$ indicates the last kernel execution time for the last single SP and the last single LP that are not hidden by data streaming. They are not negligible since PageRank-like algorithms are usually computationally intensive. They also cannot be divided by N since every GPU does the same thing. We note that the time overhead $t_{sync}(N)$ increases as N increases in order to synchronize WAs among more GPUs.

5.2 Cost model for BFS-like algorithms

The cost model is for BFS-like algorithms is given by

$$\frac{2|WA|}{c1}+\sum_{l=0}^{depth}\Bigg(\frac{|RA_{\{l\}}|+|SP_{\{l\}}|+|LP_{\{l\}}|}{c2\times N\times d_{skew}}\times(1-r_{hit})+t_{call}\Big(\frac{S_{\{l\}}+L_{\{l\}}}{N\times d_{skew}}\Big)\Bigg). \quad (2)$$

where depth is the number of traversal levels, $SP_{\{l\}}$ is a set of small pages visited at an l-th level of traversal, d_{skew} is the degree of workload skewness (i.e., imbalance) among GPUs, and r_{hit} is the cache hit rate $\frac{B}{S+L}$ discussed in Section 3.3. The operations in the braces at different levels of traversal cannot overlap with each other due to synchronization barrier, and thus the total amount of time is just a sum of the times from level 0 to level depth. The transfer time of data $\frac{|RA_{\{l\}}|+|SP_{\{l\}}|+|LP_{\{l\}}|}{c2}$ is divided by N due to using N GPUs, and moreover divided by d_{skew}, which is between $\frac{1}{N}$ (most imbalanced) and 1 (most balanced). We need to consider this factor since page access patterns of BFS-like algorithms might not be quite balanced different from PageRank-like algorithms. In the most imbalanced case, the transfer time of data is the same with that of using only one GPU. The term (1-r_{hit}) represents the caching effect, where r_{hit} is between 0 (no cache hit) and 1 (all cache hits). There is no term $t_{kernel}(y)$ in this cost model since the kernel execution time of BFS-like algorithms is not a major factor. There is also no term $t_{sync}(z)$ since the size of WA to be synchronized (e.g., LV) is usually negligible. In the term $t_{call}(\frac{S_{\{l\}}+L_{\{l\}}}{N\times d_{skew}}$, $S_{\{l\}}$) indicates the number of small pages visited at an l-th level of traversal.

6. IMPLEMENTATION

6.1 Data format for trillion-scale graphs

In terms of the slotted page format, although the one proposed in [12] is useful for representing a graph topology data for secondary storage, there is a clear limit to the maximum size of a graph to represent. The physical ID of 4-byte (2 bytes for page ID and 2 bytes for slot number) can theoretically represent a graph of up to $2^32 = 4$ billion vertices. In practice, however, it fails to represent an RMAT30 graph of 1 billion vertices and 16 billion edges due to the two-level addressing scheme (of page ID and slot number) and the skewness of the node degree distribution. Thus, in order to handle even a trillion-scale graph, we slightly generalize the existing format such that p-byte page ID (ADJ_PID) and q-byte slot number (ADJ_OFF) are used for addressing. For example, when considering the physical ID of 6-byte, there are three possible configuration as in Table 2, where $(p = 2, q = 4)$ means a small number of large-sized pages, $(p = 3, q = 3)$ a medium number of midium-sized pages, and $(p = 4, q = 2)$ a large number of small-sized pages. In the table, the maximum page size is calculated under the assumption that ADJLIST_SZ is of 4-byte, VID of 6-byte, and OFF of 4-byte. Among configurations we choose $(p = 3, q = 3)$ and implement our method using 64 MB page size, since both p and q are well-balanced, and the page size of 64 MB is compatible with the default block size widely used in many big data framework such as Hadoop [31] and Spark.

6.2 Micro-level parallel processing

GTS mainly focuses on coarse-granular or macro-level parallel graph processing for handling large-scale graphs that do not fi in GPU device memory. However, when GTS calls a given GPU kernel on topology data page-by-page, the GPU kernel can apply various kinds of fine-granula or micro-level parallel graph processing techniques to each page. The kernel can apply a better/different technique to each page depending on the characteristics of the page (e.g., density, i.e., the ratio of the number of vertices to the number of edges within a page).

Table 2: Three possible configuration of physical ID of 6-byte.

p	q	max. page ID	max. slot number	max. page size
2	4	64 K	4 B	80 GB
3	3	16 M	16 M	320 MB
4	2	4 B	64 K	1.25 MB

For example, we exploit the VWC technique [15] as a default technique for processing each slotted page, where the threads in each warp process the outgoing edges of each vertex simultaneously. We presents the GPU kernels for BFS and PageRank exploiting the VWC technique in Appendix B. We denote the VWC technique as edge-centric in this paper. On the contrary to edge-centric, we can use another micro-level technique that makes each GPU thread process each vertex and its entire outgoing edges. We denote that technique as vertex-centric. Then, we can consider a hybrid micro-level technique combining both edge-centric and vertex-centric. In general, the vertex-centric technique might be suitable for very sparse graphs where each vertex has only few outgoing edges, while the edge-centric one might be suitable for less-sparse graphs. The hybrid technique can handle both types of graphs by applying a different micro-level technique to each page depending on the density of the page. We will show the effectiveness of each technique in Appendix E.

7. PERFORMANCE EVALUATION

In this section, we present experimental results in four categories. First, we evaluate the performance of GTS compared with the state-of-the-art distributed graph processing methods, Apache Giraph [1,11], Apache Spark GraphX [10,33,35], PowerGraph (GraphLab v2.2) [9, 20, 21], and Naiad [23, 25] to show the superiority of our method. Second, we evaluate the performance of GTS compared with the state-of-the-art CPU-based graph processing methods, Ligra [29], Ligra+ [30], and Galois [26], to show the superiority of our method. For reference, we also evaluate the performance of the parallel graph processing method using CPUs called MTGL [2], which is widely used for comparison [36]. Third, we evaluate the performance of GTS compared with the state-of-the-art GPU-based graph processing method, TOTEM [7,8], to show the superiority of our method. To the best of our knowledge, TOTEM is the only method to process large-scale graphs that do not fi in GPU device memory and also to exploit multiple GPUs. For reference, we also evaluate the performance of Cusha [16] and MapGraph [6], which can process only the graph data that can fi in GPU memory. Fourth, we evaluate the performance of GTS while varying strategies (of Section 4), storage types (i.e., SSD and HDD), the number of streams, and the densities of graphs to show the characteristics of GTS.

7.1 Experimental setup

For experiments, we use both synthetic and real datasets. For synthetic datasets, we generate scale-free graphs following a power law degree distribution by using RMAT [4]. We generate from RMAT27 to RMAT32, where the ratio of the number of vertices to the number of edges is set to 16. For real datasets, we use three well-known graphs of Twitter [18], UK2007 [32], and YahooWeb [34], which all have different sizes and characteristics. Table 3 shows the basic statistics of those data sets. For GTS, we use ($p = 2, q = 2$) in Section 6.1 for storing RMAT27-29 graphs and real graphs since their sizes are relatively small. In the table, #SP and #LP mean the number of small pages and that of large pages, respectively, under the corresponding configuratio ($p = 2, q = 2$). Most of topology pages are small pages in both synthetic and real graphs. We use ($p = 3, q = 3$) for storing RMAT30-32, where there is no LP due to the large page size of 64 MB.

Table 3: Statistics of graph datasets used in the experiments.

data	#vertices	#edges	statistics for GTS		
			(p,q)	#SP	#LP
RMAT27	128 M	2,048 M	(2,2)	9,724	58
RMAT28	256 M	4,096 M	(2,2)	19,533	62
RMAT29	512 M	8,192 M	(2,2)	38,747	937
RMAT30	1 B	16 B	(3,3)	1,786	0
RMAT31	2 B	32 B	(3,3)	3,584	0
RMAT32	4 B	64 B	(3,3)	7,175	0
Twitter	42 M	1,468 M	(2,2)	5,418	1,029
UK2007	106 M	3,739 M	(2,2)	15,484	0
YahooWeb	1,414 M	6,636 M	(2,2)	32,807	0

We summarize the statistics of the size of WA data versus the size of topology data in the slotted page format in Table 4. We can see the ratio of the WA data to the topology data is very small, which is between 1.7% and 10%. The WA data for up to RMAT32 can fi in two NVIDIA TITAN X GPUs' memory (i.e., 24 GB), except RMAT32 for CC.

Table 4: Statistics of the sizes of WA data versus topology data in the slotted page format (GByte).

data	topology	WA			
		BFS	PageRank	SSSP	CC
RMAT28	20	0.5	1	1	2
RMAT29	40	1	2	2	4
RMAT30	114	2	4	4	8
RMAT31	229	4	8	8	16
RMAT32	459	8	16	16	32

We conduct all the experiments of four distributed graph processing methods on the same cluster of one master node and 30 slave nodes connected via Infiniban QDR (40 Gbps), each node of which is equipped with two Intel Xeon 8-core 2.60 GHz CPUs, 64 GB memory, and two 3 TB HDDs (RAID 0). The cluster has a total of 480 CPU cores and 1,920 GB memory. We also conduct all the experiments of four CPU-based methods and four GPU-based methods on the same workstation equipped with two Intel Xeon E5-2687W 3.1GHz CPUs of eight cores, 128 GB main memory, two NVIDIA GTX TITAN X GPUs of 12 GB device memory, and two Fusion-io's PCI-E SSD. The CPUs and GPUs are connected with PCI-E 3.0 x16 interface. For graph processing, GTS uses only GPUs, while TOTEM uses both two CPUs and GPUs. All CPU-based methods use 16 threads after turning off the Hyper-Threading (HT) option for performance.

In terms of software versions and configurations we use Scala 2.11.7 and Spark 1.5.1 for GraphX, MPI ICC 14.0.0 for PowerGraph, and Hadoop 1.2.1 for all three distributed methods. For Giraph, we set the size of mapper memory to 60 GB. For Spark, we set the size of executor memory to 60 GB. Naiad requires the.NET framework, and so, we use Mono (JIT compiler version 3.2.8) for running Naiad on Linux. For MTGL, Galois, Ligra, Ligra+, TOTEM, CuSha, and MapGraph, we download their latest source codes. We compile all single-machine methods with the same optimized option of -O3 with gcc 4.9 and CUDA 7.5. If a method requires its own data format, we convert graph data to its own format (e.g., Galois, Ligra, Ligra+, CuSha, and MapGraph). Different from GTS, TOTEM requires a different set of options for each graph algorithm and each data set in order to achieve the best performance [8]. We use the sets of options recommended by the authors of TOTEM for most of experiments. We also have found Naiad often failed to process graph queries due to lack of memory, and so, adjusted its configuratio to achieve its best scalability and performance (e.g., sizes of heaps and arrays).

7.2 Comparison with Distributed Methods

Figure 6 shows the comparison results among GraphX, Giraph, PowerGraph, Naiad, and GTS, for BFS and PageRank. Y-axis represents the elapsed times in seconds (in log-scale), and O.O.M means out of memory error. In the case of PageRank, we measure the total elapsed times of ten iterations. For four distributed methods, we measure the elapsed time, excluding loading and finaliza tion times. For GTS, we measure the elapsed times between starting reading the firs page from main memory (for real graphs and RMAT28-30) or SSDs (for RMAT31-32) and showing the query results. Here, for real graphs and RMAT28-30, since they can fi in main memory, we exclude loading time (Lines 1-10 in Algorithm 1) for a fair comparison. We set the buffer size of GTS to 20% of a graph size for RMAT31 and RMAT32 (e.g., 45 GB for RMAT31).

For all datasets used, GTS significantl outperforms the distributed graph processing methods using 30 machines, for both BFS and PageRank. Moreover, GTS shows the best scalability among the methods compared. Only GTS can process all graphs of up to RMAT32 for both BFS and PageRank. Among four distributed methods, Naiad shows the worst scalability, Giraph shows the worst performance, and PowerGraph the best scalability and performance, in general. The reason that the processing time of GTS rapidly increases between RMAT30 and RMAT31 is due to including I/O time of SSDs and changing the strategy from performance (of Section 4.1) to scalability (of Section 4.2). Theoretically, the processing time of GTS should increase linearly between RMAT31 and RMAT32 since GTS uses the secondary storage and the same strategy for both datasets, but it actually does not. This is because there are higher-degree vertices in RMAT32, and the performance of GPUs tends to be degraded (e.g, down-clocking) due to overheat when processing for a long time.

7.3 Comparison with CPU-based Methods

Figure 7 shows the comparison results among MTGL, Galois, Ligra, and Ligra+, and GTS, for BFS and PageRank. In the fig ure, except GTS, there is no results for relatively large-scale graphs such as RMAT29-30 and YahooWeb, since the CPU-based methods cannot load data into main memory or process graph algorithms due to lack of main memory. Among the CPU-based methods, Galois, Ligra, and Ligra+ have significantl outperformed the multi-threaded graph library (MTGL) in terms of both the elapsed time and the size of a graph to process, except the case of Twitter for PageRank. Among three CPU-based methotds, Ligra and Ligra+ show a better performance than Galois, except the case of UK2007 for BFS. Ligra shows a similar performance with Ligra+. However, we could not execute Ligra+ for UK2007, RMAT27, and RMAT28, due to segmentation fault errors, which were executed successfully in Ligra. We guess the Ligra+ source code is not stable yet. Compared with GTS, either Galois or Ligra slightly outperforms GTSfor relatively small graphs for BFS. This is because the CPU-based methods perform edge-level random access for traversal algorithms, while GTS performs page-level random access with data transfer overhead between main memory and GPUs. For relatively

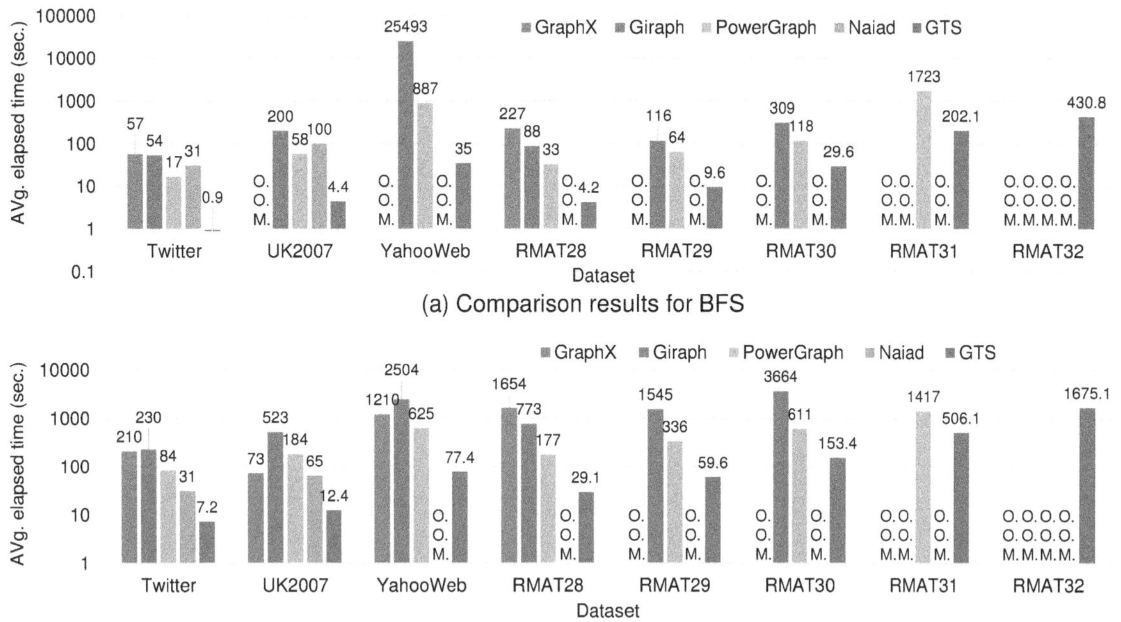

(a) Comparison results for BFS

(b) Comparison results for PageRank (#iterations = 10)

Figure 6: Comparison with GraphX, Giraph, PowerGraph, and Naiad for BFS and PageRank (Y-axis is log-scale).

large graphs (e.g., YahooWeb, RMAT29-30), only GTS could process BFS. For PageRank, GTS significantl outperforms all CPU-based methods in terms of both the elapsed time and the size of a graph to process.

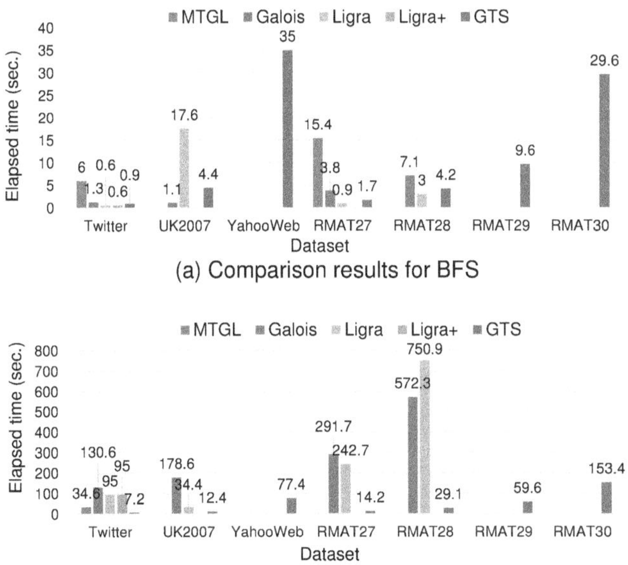

(a) Comparison results for BFS

(b) Comparison results for PageRank (#iterations = 10)

Figure 7: Comparison with MTGL, Galois, Ligra, and Ligra+ for BFS and PageRank.

7.4 Comparison with GPU-baesd Methods

Figure 8 shows the comparison results among MapGraph, CuSha, TOTEM, and GTS, for BFS and PageRank. Both CuSha and MapGraph can process only the graph data that can fi in GPU memory, and so, the size of a graph to process is very small. CuSha can process BFS only up to Twitter data. It cannot process other data (e.g., RMAT27) due to lack of GPU memory. We expected CuSha would be faster than GTS as long as a graph could fi in GPU memory. However, CuSha was slower than GTS, and even than TOTEM for Twitter. It cannot process PageRank for all graphs tested, since PageRank requires more memory than BFS due to prevPR and nextPR. MapGraph is worse than CuSha in terms of scalability. It cannot process even BFS for Twitter. It can just process a tiny graph like LiveJournal. It is because the Market Matrix format of MapGraph is less space-efficien than the G-Shard format of CuSha.

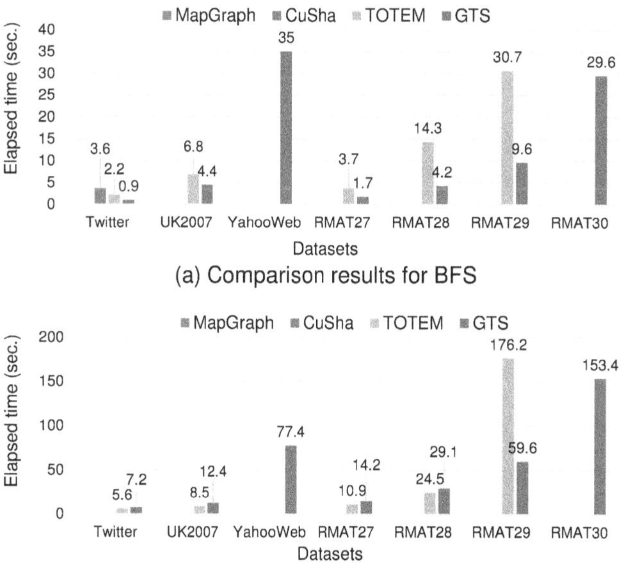

(a) Comparison results for BFS

(b) Comparison results for PageRank (#iterations = 10)

Figure 8: Comparison with TOTEM, MapGraph, and CuSha for BFS and PageRank.

We compare the performance of GTS with the best performance of TOTEM using the set of options carefully selected. In the case of TOTEM, we can minimize the amount of graph data processed by slower processors, i.e., CPUs, by fittin as much graph data as possible in device memory, and thus, maximize its performance. Appendix C shows the set of options including the ratios of graph data processed by GPUs to that by CPUs in TOTEM (GPU%:CPU%), most of which are the ones recommended by the authors. For PageRank, TOTEM slightly outperforms GTS for relatively small-scale graphs such as RMAT27, Twitter, and UK2007. GTS, however, significantl outperforms TOTEM for large-scale graphs such as RMAT29. For BFS, GTS consistently outperforms TOTEM. Here, TOTEM cannot process YahooWeb due to some bugs, and so, there is no corresponding result. In addition, TOTEM cannot process RMAT30-32 since it relies on in-memory data format requiring a contiguous array in main memory. We note that GTS processes PageRank for RMAT29 only in about 59 seconds, which indicates the graph processing speed of GTS is about 7 GB/s, since the size of RMAT29 is about 40 GB in the slotted page format, and the number of PageRank iterations is ten in the experiments. We also note that GTS shows the performance of up to 1,500 MTEPS (millions traversed edges per second) for Twitter.

7.5 Characteristics of GTS

Figure 9 shows the performance of GTS while changing the strategy explained in Section 4 for RMAT30. Strategy-P indicates the strategy for performance in Section 4.1, and Strategy-S the strategy for scalability in Section 4.2. Both strategies show similar performance with each other when using 1 SSD or 2 HDDs since the I/O performance is a bottleneck. However, Strategy-P shows a slightly better performance than Strategy-S when using main memory or 2 SSDs due to no or less I/O bottleneck.

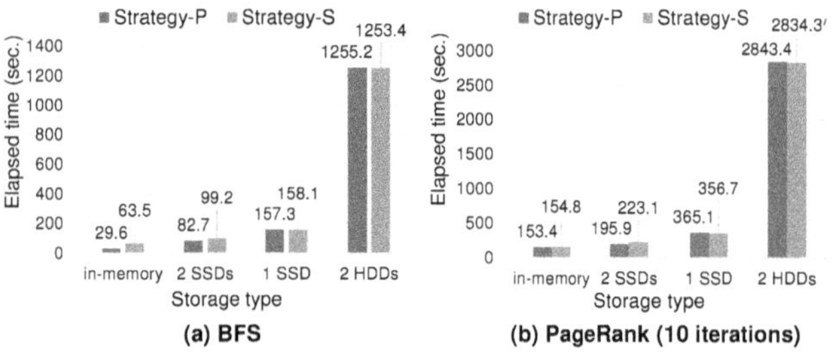

Figure 9: Comparison between two strategies for BFS and PageRank (RMAT30).

In terms of the overall performance, we note that the speed of PCI-E bus becomes a bottleneck in memory setting, and the I/O performance of PCI-E SSDs becomes a bottleneck in SSD setting. For example, for ten iterations of PageRank using RMAT30, GTS in memory setting takes about 153 seconds, which is approximately equal to $114 \times 10 \div 6 = 190$ seconds, where 6 means the communication rate in a streaming copy mode $c2$ in Section 5.1. Here, actual elapsed time of 153 seconds is smaller than the calculated time of 190 seconds due to caching mechanism described in Algorithm 1. For another example, GTS using two SSDs takes about 196 seconds, which is approximately equal to $114 \times 10 \div 5 = 228$ seconds, where 5 (GB/s) means the sequential read performance of two PCI-E SSDs. Here, actual elapsed time of 196 seconds is smaller than the calculated time of 228 seconds due to the page buffering mechanism in Algorithm 1. The performance of GTS using two HDDs is completely bound by the I/O performance of HDDs. When using two HDDs in the Strategy-P mode, its sequential read I/O bandwidth is about 330 GB. The elapsed time of PageRank for RMAT30 is about 2,843 seconds, where the calculated time is $114 \times 10 \div 0.33 = 3,454$ seconds. Here, actual elapsed time of 2,843 seconds is smaller than the calculated time of 3,454 seconds due to the page buffering mechanism.

Figure 10 shows the performance of GTS while varying the number of streams for RMAT26-29. The performance increases steadily as the number of streams increases for all data sets. Even for BFS where the ratios of transfer time to kernel execution time are much smaller than 32, it does due to the reason explained in Section 3.2.

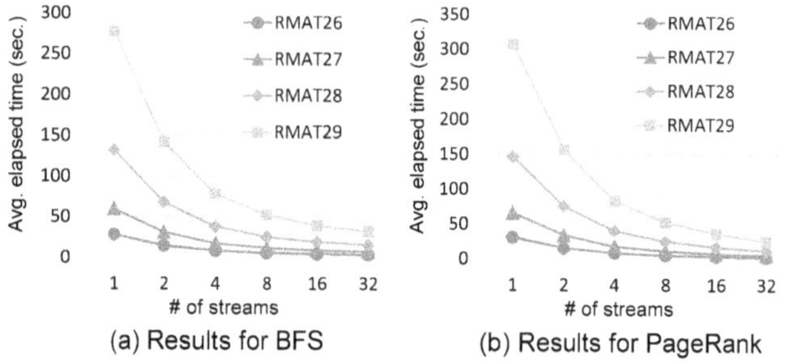

Figure 10: Performance when varying the number of streams.

Figure 11(a) shows the performance of GTS for BFS while varying the cache size from 32 MB to 5,120 MB, and Figure 11(b) shows the corresponding cache hit rates. For RMAT29, there is no result at the cache size 5,120 MB due to a large size of WABuf. We can easily adjust the size of cache since it is allocated by a CPU thread (i.e., the framework thread of GTS). For example, for the cache of 1,024 MB, GTS allocates the array of 16 slotted pages of 64 MB within GPU_i and make $cachedPIDMap_i$ maintain up to 16 page IDs. In Figure 11(b), the cache hit rates increase linearly as the cache sizes increase, but decrease linearly as the sizes of topology data increase, as discussed in Section 3.3.

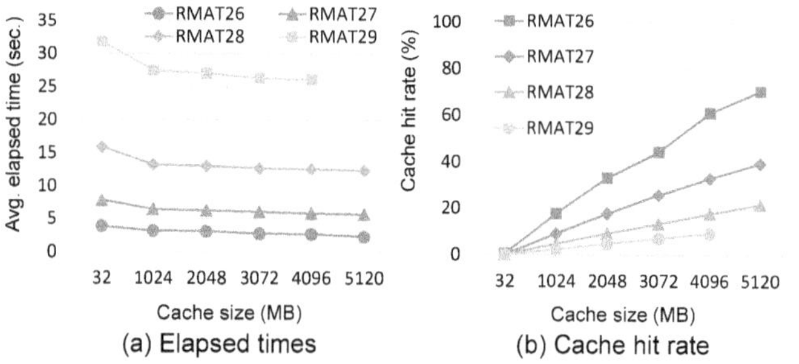

Figure 11: Effectiveness of caching for BFS.

8. RELATED WORK AND DISCUSSION

Most of the existing graph systems (e.g., Apache Giraph, PowerGraph) follow the *vertex-centric* scatter-gather model involving random access to topology data (i.e., vertices and edges), and so, require topology data to be in main memory for performance. In contrast, X-Stream [28] has proposed the *edge-centric* scatter-gather model that can exploit sequential access to edge data, and so, only requires both vertex data and update data to be in main memory. These two approaches are two extremes in terms of edge access: the former relies on only fine-graine (i.e., edge level) random access, and the latter relies on only fine-graine sequential access (i.e., streaming edges). As a result, the latter approach has a significan performance penalty for traversal algorithms (e.g., BFS, SSSP) which the former approach does not have. For a large-scale graph (e.g., YahooWeb) having a high diameter, X-Stream executes a very large number of scatter-gather iterations, each of which requires streaming the entire edge list but doing little work. Accordingly, for traversal algorithms for such a graph, X-Stream did not finis in a reasonable amount of time [28]. GraphChi [19] has the similar problem, but shows a worse performance than X-Stream, due to requiring fully loading (not streaming) a shard fil and no overlapping between disk I/O and computation. GTS is quite different from the above two extremes, since it exploits coarse-grained (i.e., page level) sequential access, and at the same time, coarse-grained (i.e., page level) random access. We have presented this *hybrid* mechanism supporting both sequential and random accesses in detail in Section 4.3, Algorithm 1, and Appendix A. Due to exploiting both, GTS requires streaming only the relevant pages for traversal algorithms.

We discuss how GTS is differ from the streaming mechanism used in X-Stream and other existing work in more detail. Like other methods following the scatter-gather model, X-Stream needs to update the data fiel of each vertex after each scatter-gather iteration. In order to do that, it tries to maintain the whole vertex data including both read-only attributes and updatable attributes in main memory. However, since the size of the whole vertex data might not fi in main memory, X-Stream partitions the vertex and edge data into multiple partitions, where each partition can fi in main memory, and performs the three phases of scatter, shuffle and gather for each partition (not two phases of scatter and gather). In order to update the vertex data of other partitions, the shuffl phase is essential. In the shuffl phase, X-Stream builds the *update* data structure, which is used for updating the vertex data structure later. In this scheme, both vertex data and update data take a substantial amount of main memory, and the computational overhead of the shuffl phase is also considerable. In contrast, GTS separates the data field of vertices into read-only (i.e., RA) and updatable (i.e., WA), and maintains the only and entire WA data in GPU memory. By minimizing the amount of data to be kept in memory, it can keep the entire WA data in GPU memory even for billion-scale graphs, and moreover, do not need to build the update data structure and perform the shuffl phase. If the WA data is larger than the single GPU memory, we can spread it to multiple GPUs' memory in Strategy-S. As long as the WA data can fi in GPUs' memory, GTS can perform high-performance streaming in the hybrid mechanism described above. Unlike X-Stream, it has no shuffl phase and no write operations to secondary storage. It performs read-only streaming from beginning to end, while X-Stream performs a mixture of read and write streaming. It fully exploits sequential streaming bandwidth, while X-Stream only partially exploits the bandwidth.

There are a number of graph processing methods using GPUs on a single computer [7, 8, 13, 15, 16, 24, 36]. The VWC method [15] proposes the virtual warp scheme that enables trading off between workload imbalance and ALU underutilization with a single parameter, the number of threads per virtual warp. It usually partitions a physical warp of 32 threads into multiple virtual warps of 4, 8, or 16 threads. Too large virtual warp could cause unused ALUs within a warp, which could limit the parallel performance of kernel executions. CuSha [16] adopts the shards format [19] for solving the non-coalesced memory access problem and presents two graph representations: G-Shards and Concatenated Windows (CW). It focuses on fully utilizing the GPU computing power by processing multiple shards in parallel on GPU's streaming multiprocessors. Medusa [36] proposes a programming framework that can simplify implementation of GPU programs for graph processing. [24] presents a BFS parallelization method that focuses on fine-graine task management constructed from efficien pre-fi sum, which achieves an asymptotically optimal $O(|V| + |E|)$ complexity. All the work mentioned above lack support for large-scale graphs that do not fi in the GPU's limited device memory. However, many techniques addressed in the above work belong to micro-level parallel processing techniques and are orthogonal to our method GTS, and so they can be applied to processing each topology page.

TOTEM [7, 8] is the only work to process large-scale graphs and exploit multiple GPUs, to the best of our knowledge. It partitions a graph into two parts: (1) the main memory part processed by CPUs and (2) the device memory part processed by GPUs. Although it can handle large-scale graphs that other methods cannot, it still has three major drawbacks. First, it completely underutilizes the computational power of GPUs. It processes only a small fraction of a graph by using GPUs. The remaining part of the graph is processing by relatively slow CPUs. This underutilization becomes more and more marked as the graph size increases, since the size of the part processed by GPUs is fi ed. Second, it it is not very scalable in terms of the number of GPUs used. TOTEM demonstrates the graph processing power of GPU is higher than that of CPUs, and so it concludes that using more GPUs instead of more CPUs are required for faster graph processing. However, under the partitioning scheme like edge-cut, the number of cut edges among main memory and multiple GPUs increases as the number of GPUs increases, which means the amount of data to be communicated among main memory and GPUs also increases [9]. As a result, the speedup tends to decrease as well. Third, it is difficul for users to optimize the performance due to a lot of configuratio options. Different from GTS, TOTEM requires a different set of options for each graph algorithm and for each data set in order to achieve good performance. If users do not carefully tune a bunch of options, its performance could be significantl degraded. Although TOTEM does not outperform GTS, we consider that hybrid computation using both CPUs and GPUs is potentially will be superior to our method GTS using only GPUs.

9. CONCLUSIONS

In this paper, we proposed a fast and scalable GPU-based graph processing method called GTS that can process even RMAT32 (64 billion edges) graphs very efficientl . GTS fully exploits the computational power of GPUs by processing the entire graph only using GPUs. To overcome the limit of GPU memory capacity and moreover the limit of main memory capacity, we proposed a concept of storing only updatable attribute data and moving topology data. The proposed method stores graphs in PCI-E SSDs and executes a graph algorithm using thousands of GPU cores while streaming topology data of graphs to GPUs via PCI-E interface. For streaming topology data, GTS exploits the asynchronous GPU streams (e.g., CUDA Streams), which could hide memory access latency from GPUs to main memory and so utilize GPU's computing power more. For efficien streaming, GTS adopted and generalized the slotted page format that divides a graph into fi ed-size units. In terms of exploiting multiple GPUs and SSDs, we also proposed two strategies, the strategy for performance and the strategy for scalability. GTS is fairly scalable in terms of the number of GPUs and SSDs, and so, shows a stable speedup when adding a GPU or an SSD to the machine. Through extensive experiments, we demonstrated that GTS consistently and significantl outperforms the major distributed graph processing methods, GraphX, Giraph, and PowerGraph, and the state-of-the-art GPU-based method TOTEM, across wide range of benchmarks. Especially, we demonstrated that GTS can process an RMAT32 graph within a reasonable time in a single machine that the existing distributed methods fail to process by using 30 machines of a total of about 2 TB memory.

10. ACKNOWLEDGMENTS

This work was partly supported by Institute for Information & communications Technology Promotion(IITP) grant funded by the Korea government(MSIP) (No. R0190-15-2012, High Performance Big Data Analytics Platform Performance Acceleration Technologies Development), Basic Science Research Program through the National Research Foundation of Korea(NRF) funded by the Ministry of Science, ICT & Future Planning (2014R1A1A1008227), and Samsung Research Funding Center of Samsung Electronics under Project Number SRFC-IT1401-04.

11. REFERENCES

[1] Apache Giraph. http://giraph.apache.org/, 2015.

[2] B. W. Barrett, J. W. Berry, R. C. Murphy, and K. B. Wheeler. Implementing a portable multi-threaded graph library: The mtgl on qthreads. In *IPDPS*, pages 1–8, 2009.

[3] G. E. Blelloch, M. A. Heroux, and M. Zagha. Segmented operations for sparse matrix computation on vector multiprocessors. *Technical Report CMU-CS-93-173*, 1993.

[4] D. Chakrabarti, Y. Zhan, and C. Faloutsos. R-mat: A recursive model for graph mining. In *SDM*, volume 4, pages 442–446, 2004.

[5] CUDA Stream. http://on-demand.gputechconf.com/gtc-express/2011/presentations/StreamsAndConcurrencyWebinar.pdf, 2011.

[6] Z. Fu, M. Personick, and B. Thompson. Mapgraph: A high level api for fast development of high performance graph analytics on gpus. In *GRADES*, pages 1–6, 2014.

[7] A. Gharaibeh, L. B. Costa, E. Santos-Neto, and M. Ripeanu. A yoke of oxen and a thousand chickens for heavy lifting graph processing. In *PACT*, pages 345–354, 2012.

[8] A. Gharaibeh, T. Reza, E. Santos-Neto, L. B. Costa, S. Sal-linen, and M. Ripeanu. Efficien large-scale graph processing on hybrid cpu and gpu systems. *Technical Report arXiv:1312.3018*, 2014.

[9] J. E. Gonzalez, Y. Low, H. Gu, D. Bickson, and C. Guestrin. Powergraph: distributed graph-parallel computation on natu-ral graphs. In *OSDI*, volume 12, pages 17–30, 2012.

[10] J. E. Gonzalez, R. S. Xin, A. Dave, D. Crankshaw, M. J. Franklin, and I. Stoica. Graphx: Graph processing in a distributed datafl w framework. In *OSDI*, 2014.

[11] M. Han and K. Daudjee. Giraph unchained: barrierless asynchronous parallel execution in pregel-like graph processing systems. In *PVLDB*, pages 950–961, 2015.

[12] W.-S. Han, S. Lee, K. Park, J.-H. Lee, M.-S. Kim, J. Kim, and H. Yu. Turbograph: A fast parallel graph engine handling billion-scale graphs in a single pc. In *KDD*, pages 77–85, 2013.

[13] P. Harish and P. J. Narayanan. Accelerating large graph algorithms on the gpu using cuda. In *HiPC*, pages 197–208, 2007.

[14] G. M. Hector, J. D. Ullman, and J. Widom. *Database Systems: The Complete Book*. Prentice Hall, 2008.

[15] S. Hong, S. Kim, T. Oguntebi, and K. Olukotun. Accelerating cuda graph algorithms at maximum warp. In *PPoPP*, pages 267–276, 2011.

[16] F. Khorasani, K. Vora, R. Gupta, and L. N. Bhuyan. Cusha: vertex-centric graph processing on gpus. In *HPDC*, volume 23, pages 239–252, 2014.

[17] M. Kim. Towards exploiting gpus for fast pagerank computation of large-scale networks. In *EDB*, 2013.

[18] H. Kwak, C. Lee, H. Park, and S. B. Moon. What is twitter, a social network or a news media? In *WWW*, pages 591–600, 2010.

[19] A. Kyrola, G. Blelloch, and C. Guestrin. Graphchi: large-scale graph computation on just a pc. In *OSDI*, volume 12, pages 31–46, 2012.

[20] Y. Low, J. Gonzalez, A. Kyrola, D. Bickson, C. Guestrin, and J. M. Hellerstein. Distributed graphlab: A framework for machine learning and data mining in the cloud. In *PVLDB*, pages 716–727, 2012.

[21] Y. Low, J. E. Gonzalez, A. Kyrola, D. Bickson, C. E. Guestrin, and J. Hellerstein. Graphlab: A new framework for parallel machine learning. In *arXiv:1408.2041*, 2014.

[22] G. Malewicz, M. H. Austern, A. J. Bik, J. C. Dehnert, I. Horn, N. Leiser, and G. Czajkowski. Pregel: a system for large-scale graph processing. In *SIGMOD*, pages 135–146, 2010.

[23] F. McSherry, M. Isard, and D. G. Murray. Scalability! but at what cost? In *HotOS*, pages 1–6, 2015.

[24] D. Merrill, G. Michael, and A. Grimshaw. Scalable gpu graph traversal. In *PPoPP*, pages 117–128, 2012.

[25] D. G. Murray, F. McSherry, R. Isaacs, M. Isard, P. Barham, and M. Abadi. Naiad: a timely datafl w system. In *SOSP*, pages 439–455, 2013.

[26] D. Nguyen, A. Lenharth, and K. Pingali. A lightweight infrastructure for graph analytics. In *SOSP*, pages 456–471, 2013.

[27] S. Pai, M. Thazhuthaveetil, and R. Govindarajan. Improving gpgpu concurrency with elastic kernels. In *ASPLOS*, pages 407–418, 2013.

[28] A. Roy, I. Mihailovic, and W. Zwaenepoel. X-stream: edge-centric graph processing using streaming partitions. In *SOSP*, pages 472–488, 2013.

[29] J. Shun and G. E. Blelloch. Ligra: a lightweight graph processing framework for shared memory. In *PPoPP*, pages 135–146, 2013.

[30] J. Shun, L. Dhulipala, and G. Blelloch. Smaller and faster: Parallel processing of compressed graphs with ligra+. In *DCC*, pages 403–412, 2015.

[31] A. Thusoo, J. Sarma, N. Jain, Z. Shao, P. Chakka, S. Anthony, H. Liu, P. Wyckoff, and R. Murthy. Hive: a warehousing solution over a map-reduce framework. In *PVLDB*, pages 1626–1629, 2009.

[32] Webspam-uk2007. http: //barcelona.research.yahoo.net/webspam/datasets/uk2007, 2007.

[33] R. S. Xin, J. E. Gonzalez, M. J. Franklin, and I. Stoica. Graphx: A resilient distributed graph system on spark. In *GRADES*, 2013.

[34] Yahoo webscope. ahoo! altavista web page hyperlink connectivity graph. http://webscope.sandbox.yahoo.com, 2009.

[35] M. Zaharia, M. Chowdhury, M. J. Franklin, S. Shenker, and I. Stoica. Spark: cluster computing with working sets. In *USENIX Conference on Hot Topics in Cloud Computing*, volume 10, 2010.

[36] J. Zhong and B. He. Medusa: Simplifie graph processing on gpus. In *TPDS*, 2013.

APPENDIX

In this appendix, we present the details on GPU kernel functions of GTS for two typical graph algorithms, BFS and PageRank, used in the experiments. GTS requires two different kinds of GPU kernels for processing SPs and LPs, as explained in Section 3.4, since SPs and LPs have a little different structure. Thus, we present a total of four kernels: two kernels K_{BFS_SP} and K_{BFS_LP} for BFS and two kernels K_{PR_SP} and K_{PR_LP} for PageRank. Appendix A presents the mapping table of the slotted page format required for understanding the four GPU kernels.

A. MAPPING TABLE FROM RID TO VID

Each record ID (i.e. physical ID) in ADJLIST consists of a pair of the page ID (ADJ_PID) and the slot number (ADJ_OFF) where the corresponding vertex is located. For example, in Fig. 1, ADJLIST of v_3 in LP_1 contains r_2, which points to v_2 in SP_0, and thus consists of a pair of 0 (ADJ_PID) and 2 (ADJ_OFF). Since the graph algorithms usually require vertex IDs for traversal instead of record ID, they need a method to translate a record ID to the corresponding vertex ID. For that purpose, The slotted page format maintains a kind of mapping table from RID to VID, called RVT in main memory. Fig. 12 shows RVT for G in Fig. 1. In RVT, there exists a tuple for each slotted page, and a tuple consists of a pair of START_VID and LP_RANGE, where START_VID means the firs VID in the corresponding page, and LP_RANGE means the range of large page IDs. We can easily and quickly translate RID to VID by calculating RVT[ADJ_PID].START_VID + ADJ_OFF for a given RID, i.e. (ADJ_PID, ADJ_OFF). For example, r_2 is $(0, 2)$ as explained above, and so its VID is calculated by RVT[0].START_VID + 2 = 2. That is, r_2's VID is 2. In Appendix B, we denote the VID calculated using (ADJ_PID, ADJ_OFF) as ADJ_VID.

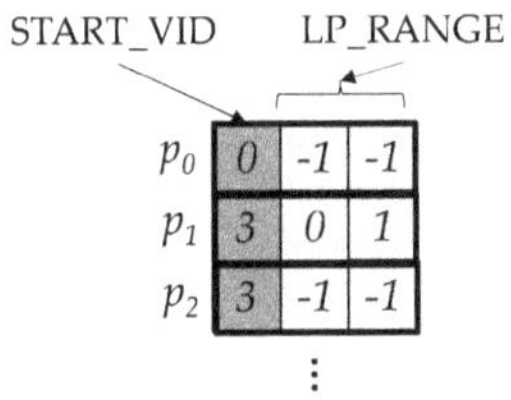

Figure 12: The RVT table for mapping RID to VID.

B. GPU KERNELS IN GTS

B.1 Kernel for BFS

We exploit the virtual warp-centric (VWC) technique [15] as a default technique for the BFS graph algorithm, where the threads in a warp process the outgoing edges of a vertex simultaneously. Algorithm 2 shows the GPU kernel K_{BFS_SP} for processing SPs. Since it is a kind of θ-join operator between topology data and attribute vector, it takes SP and LV as inputs, where LV is WA for traversal levels of vertices. It also takes a fla finishe and a current traversal level curLevel, as in [15]. As the last input, it takes the local nextPIDSet maintained in each GPU, denoted as nextPIDSet_{GPU}. It is a bit vector where the number of bits is equal to the number of pages, and a bit 1 means that the corresponding page should be visited next. The overall structure of the kernel is similar with that of the kernel in [15], since both follow the same VWC technique. It firs calculates the warp ID (W_ID) and the offset in the

Algorithm 2 BFS Kernel for SP

```
Input: SP; /* a small page */
       LV; /* WA for level */
       finished /* fla for finishin traversal */
       curLevel; /* current traversal level */
       nextPIDSet_GPU; /* local nextPIDSet in GPU */

__kernel__ K_BFS_SP(SP, LV, finished curLevel, nextPIDSet_GPU) {
ID ← THREAD_ID;
W_ID ← ID / W_SZ;
W_OFF ← ID % W_SZ;
while W_ID < SP.NUM_NODES do
    VID ← SP[W_ID].VID;
    ADJLIST_SZ ← SP[W_ID].ADJLIST_SZ;
    ADJLIST ← SP[W_ID].ADJLIST;
    if LV[VID] = curLevel then
        expand_warp(W_OFF, ADJLIST_SZ, ADJLIST, LV, finished
        curLevel, nextPIDSet_GPU);
}
__device__ expand_warp(W_OFF, ADJLIST_SZ, ADJLIST, LV, fin
ished, curLevel, nextPIDSet_GPU) {
for i ← W_OFF; i < ADJLIST_SZ; i ← W_SZ+i do
    ADJ_PID ← ADJLIST[i].PID;
    ADJ_OFF ← ADJLIST[i].OFF;
    ADJ_VID ← RVT[ADJ_PID].START_VID+ADJ_OFF;
    if LV[ADJ_VID] = NULL then
        LV[ADJ_VID] ← curLevel + 1;
        nextPIDSet_GPU[ADJ_PID] ← true;
        finishe ← false;
__threadfence_block();
}
```

Algorithm 3 BFS Kernel for LP

```
Input: LP; /* a large page */
       LV; /* WA for level */
       finished /* fla for finishin traversal */
       curLevel; /* current traversal level */
       nextPIDSet_GPU; /* local nextPIDSet in GPU */

__kernel__ K_BFS_LP(LP, LV, finished curLevel, nextPIDSet_GPU) {
ID ← THREAD_ID;
VID ← LP.VID;
while ID < LP.ADJLIST_SZ do
    if LV[VID] = curLevel then
        ADJ_PID ← LP.ADJLIST[ID].PID;
        ADJ_OFF ← LP.ADJLIST[ID].OFF;
        ADJ_VID ← RVT[ADJ_PID].START_VID+ADJ_OFF;
        if LV[ADJ_VID] = NULL then
            LV[ADJ_VID] ← curLevel + 1;
            nextPIDSet_GPU[ADJ_PID] ← true;
            finishe ← false;
}
```

warp (W_OFF) for each thread (Lines 2-4). Then, each warp processes a single vertex in SP (Lines 5-12). A warp checks the corresponding VID, ADJLIST_SZ, and ADJLIST (Lines 6-8) and then calls the expand_warp routine if the corresponding vertex should be traversed, i.e. LV[VID] is equal to curLevel (Lines 9-11).

The expand_warp routine processes all neighbor vertices in ADJLIST in a warp centric manner. That is, it processes the firs W_SZ neighbor vertices, and then processes the next W_SZ neighbor vertices, and so on (Line 15). Each thread in a warp checks ADJ_PID and ADJ_OFF of the corresponding neighbor vertex (Lines 16-17) and calculates ADJ_VID (Line 18). If the corresponding neighbor vertex ADJ_VID is not visited yet (Line 19), the thread sets LV[ADJ_VID] to curLevel + 1 (Line 20) and sets the fla finishe to false (Line 22). The thread also sets the bit nextPIDSet$_{GPU}$[ADJ_PID] to true (Line 21) such that the GTS framework could asynchronously copy the page ADJ_PID from main memory to GPU at the next level traversal. Finally, the routine calls CUDA's __threadfence_block() function to synchronize all of the threads within the warp (Line 29).

Algorithm 3 shows the GPU kernel K_{BFS_LP} for processing LPs. It is basically similar to K_{BFS_SP}, except that multiple warps for a large page processes ADJLIST of the page together. Since a single warp does not need to process an entire ADJLIST of a vertex, there is no loop like Line 15 in the K_{BFS_SP} kernel. Instead, each thread performs the body of the expand_warp routine of K_{BFS_SP} directly (Lines 6-13) if the current vertex should be traversed, i.e. LV[VID] is equal to curLevel (Line 5). In K_{BFS_LP}, since there is no calling of the warp-level routine like expand_warp in the kernel, there is no warp-level synchronization like __threadfence_block().

B.2 Kernel for PageRank

We exploit the edge-based method proposed in [17] in addition to the VWC technique for the PageRank graph algorithm. In the edge-based method, a GPU thread takes responsibility for partial updating the PageRank value of the source (or destination) node of an edge. Algorithm 4 shows the GPU kernel K_{PR_SP} for processing SPs. Since it is also a kind of θ-join operator between topology data and attribute vector, it takes SP and two required attribute vectors nextPR and prevPR as inputs. Since nextPR is WA, the kernel requires the entire nextPR. In contrast, prevPR is RA, and so the kernel only requires the partial prevPR corresponding to the given SP as explained in Section 3.1. We denote such a subvector of prevPR as prevPR[$v{:}w$]. Before calling the kernel K_{PR_SP}, each element of nextPR is initialized to $\frac{1-df}{|V|}$ in main memory, where df means the damping factor. Thus, the kernel only needs to add the value of the remaining part of the PageRank equation to nextPR. The outline of K_{PR_SP} is similar to that of K_{BFS_SP} (Lines 2-8). A warp calls the expand_warp routine in order to update the PageRank values for the outgoing edges from VID (Line 9). The expand_warp routine processes all neighbor vertices in ADJLIST in a warp centric manner, as in K_{BFS_SP}. Each thread in a warp calculates ADJ_VID of the corresponding neighbor vertex as in A.2 (Line 16) and calculates the partial PageRank value for ADJ_VID with considering the edge between VID and ADJ_VID (Line 17). The calculated value is added to nextPR[ADJ_VID]. Here, since multiple GPU threads could update nextPR[ADJ_VID] simultaneously, we should use the atomicAdd operator to avoid a race condition. CUDA supports several atomic operators including atomicAdd. At the end of the routine, the synchronization function is called as in K_{BFS_SP} (Line 19).

Algorithm 5 shows the GPU kernel K_{PR_LP} for processing LPs. It is basically similar to K_{PR_SP}, except that multiple warps for a large page processes ADJLIST of the page together. As in K_{BFS_LP}, each thread performs the body of the expand_warp routine of K_{PR_SP} directly (Lines 4-7).

Algorithm 4 PageRank Kernel for SP

```
Input: SP; /* a small page (for vertices [v:w]) */
       nextPR; /* WA */
       prevPR[v:w]; /* subvector of RA */

1:  __kernel__ K_PR_SP(SP, nexPR, prevPR[v:w]) {
2:  ID ← THREAD_ID;
3:  W_ID ← ID / W_SZ;
4:  W_OFF ← ID % W_SZ;
5:  while W_ID < SP.NUM_NODES do
6:      VID ← SP[W_ID].VID;
7:      ADJLIST_SZ ← SP[W_ID].ADJLIST_SZ;
8:      ADJLIST ← SP[W_ID].ADJLIST;
9:      expand_warp(W_OFF, ADJLIST_SZ, ADJLIST, VID, nextPR, prevPR[v:w]);
10: }
11: __device__ expand_warp(W_OFF, ADJLIST_SZ, ADJLIST, VID, nextPR, prevPR[v:w]) {
12: for i ← W_OFF; i < ADJLIST_SZ; i ← W_SZ+i do
13:     ADJ_PID ← ADJLIST[i].PID;
14:     ADJ_OFF ← ADJLIST[i].OFF;
15:     ADJ_VID ← RVT[ADJ_PID].START_VID+ADJ_OFF;
16:     atomicAdd(nextPR[ADJ_VID], df * prevPR[VID] / ADJLIST_SZ);
17: __threadfence_block();
18: }
```

Algorithm 5 PageRank Kernel for LP

```
Input: LP; /* a large page (for vertex v) */
       nextPR; /* WA */
       prevPR[v]; /* subvector of v */

1: __kernel__ K_PR_LP(LP, nexPR, prevPR[v]) {
2: ID ← THREAD_ID;
3: while ID < LP.ADJLIST_SZ do
4:     ADJ_PID ← LP.ADJLIST[ID].PID;
5:     ADJ_OFF ← LP.ADJLIST[ID].OFF;
6:     ADJ_VID ← RVT[ADJ_PID].START_VID+ADJ_OFF;
7:     atomicAdd(nextPR[ADJ_VID], df * prevPR[v] / v.ADJLIST_S);
8: }
```

C. OPTIONS OF TOTEM

Table 5 shows the ratios of graph data processed by GPUs to that by CPUs in TOTEM (GPU%:CPU%) when following the options recommended by the authors. In general, as the size of a graph increases, the size of the GPU partition decreases. However, it is not for RMAT29 since the mapped memory options of TOTEM allocates a part of the GPU partition as mapped memory [8].

D. ADDITIONAL GRAPH ALGORITHMS

In addition to BFS and PageRank, for a wider range of benchmarks, we implement the following three additional graph algorithms using GTS: Single-Source Shortest Path (SSSP), Connected Components (CC), and Betweenness Centrality (BC). It demonstrates the adaptability of GTS. We select those three graph algorithms since Giraph, GraphX, PowerGraph, and TOTEM commonly support them. Figure 13 shows the comparison results among f ve methods (BC between two methods). GTS significantl outperforms other four methods for SSSP and CC, and also largely outperforms TOTEM for CC. Here, we perform the experiments of BC using the default mode, i.e., the single node mode for both methods.

Table 5: Ratios of partition sizes in TOTEM (GPU%:CPU%).

data	one GPU		two GPUs	
	BFS	PageRank	BFS	PageRank
RMAT27	65:35	60:40	80:20	80:20
RMAT28	15:85	60:40	40:60	80:20
RMAT29	50:50	15:85	75:25	30:70
Twitter	50:50	80:20	75:25	85:15
UK2007	35:65	30:70	70:30	60:40
YahooWeb	10:90	15:85	N/A	N/A

E. MICRO-LEVEL PARALLEL PROCESSING

Figure 14 shows the performance of GTS for BFS and PageRank while changing the density (i.e., #vertices : #edges) of RMAT28 from 1:4 to 1:32 and changing a micro-level parallel processing technique for each slotted page. The three techniques discussed in Section 6.2 show similar performance for very sparse graph of 1:4. However, for denser graphs, the edge-centric strategy outperforms the vertex-centric strategy largely. The hybrid strategy improves the performance slightly (up to 6% for BFS and up to 24% for PageRank) compared with the edge-centric one.

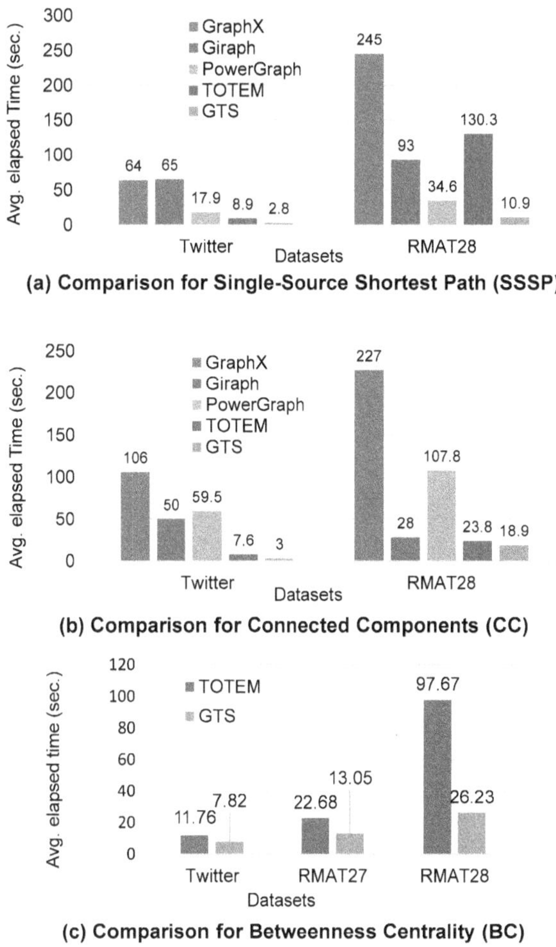

Figure 13: Comparison for additional graph algorithms: SSSP, CC, and BC.

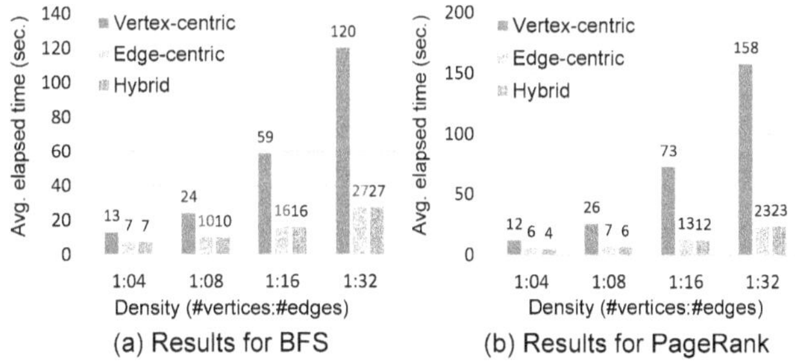

Figure 14: Performance when changing micro-level parallel processing techniques and graph density.

Graph Analytics Through Fine-Grained Parallelism

Zechao Shang†, Feifei Li‡, Jeffrey Xu Yu†, Zhiwei Zhang§, Hong Cheng†

†The Chinese University of Hong Kong, ‡University of Utah, §Hong Kong Baptist University

{zcshang,yu,hcheng}@se.cuhk.edu.hk, lifeifei@cs.utah.edu, cszwzhang@comp.hkbu.edu.hk

ABSTRACT

Large graphs are getting increasingly popular and even indispensable in many applications, for example, in social media data, large networks, and knowledge bases. Efficient graph analytics thus becomes an important subject of study. To increase efficiency and scalability, in-memory computation and parallelism have been explored extensively to speed up various graph analytical workloads. In many graph analytical engines (e.g., Pregel, Neo4j, GraphLab), parallelism is achieved via one of the three concurrency control models, namely, bulk synchronization processing (BSP), asynchronous processing, and synchronous processing. Among them, synchronous processing has the potential to achieve the best performance due to fine-grained parallelism, *while ensuring the correctness and the convergence of the computation, if* an effective concurrency control scheme is used. This paper explores the topological properties of the underlying graph to design and implement a highly effective concurrency control scheme for efficient synchronous processing in an in-memory graph analytical engine. Our design uses a novel hybrid approach that combines 2PL (two-phase locking) with OCC (optimistic concurrency control), for high degree and low degree vertices in a graph respectively. Our results show that the proposed hybrid synchronous scheduler has significantly outperformed other synchronous schedulers in existing graph analytical engines, as well as BSP and asynchronous schedulers.

1. INTRODUCTION

Graph is a perfect model to represent complex relationships among objects, in particular, data interconnectivity and topology information. As a result, the graph data model has been used extensively to store, query, and analyze data from a number of important application domains ranging from social media data to large computer or transportation networks to knowledge bases (semantic web) and to biological structures [1, 17]. Large amounts of graph data and many applications running on top drive the needs for efficient and scalable graph analytics.

To increase both efficiency and scalability, *in-memory computation* and *parallelism* have been explored extensively as two very useful techniques to speed up analytics over large graphs. Inspired by the design and success of early systems like Pregel [35], most graph systems support the *vertex-centric* data model and programming paradigm, in which a graph is represented by a set of vertices and their edge lists. An edge list for a vertex v simply stores all neighboring vertices of v in the graph. A typical analytical workload over a vertex-centric graph model can often be represented as follows (suppose the graph has N vertices and UDF is some user defined function):

```
for iteration i = 1...n      // in iteration
   for j = 1...N             // all vertices
         UDF(v_j, edgeList_j)
```

For example, the classic PageRank algorithm is an instantiation of the above computation framework. We often speed up this computation through parallelism, and existing graph systems have used different consistency models for such parallelism. The most popular choices are the following three consistency models, namely, *the bulk synchronous parallel* (BSP), *asynchronous, and synchronous parallel processing*. A major difference among these models is their message passing mechanism and the staleness of messages.

BSP proceeds in iterations (or super-steps), and message passing takes place at the end of an iteration, therefore the message staleness is exactly one iteration. AP may introduce a delay (of uncertain length) in delivering messages. In contrast, in SP processing, a worker (thread) receives messages without any degree of staleness. In other words, the implication is that workers in the BSP model reach synchronized states at the end of an iteration, but they will proceed with asynchronized states in the asynchronous model, and they have to wait for synchronization and only proceed when a synchronized state is obtained in the synchronous model. In the context of vertex-centric analytics, data consistency model decides whether vertices are able to access up-to-date and consistent data values from other vertices during the computation.

BSP is the most popular model in practice due to its simplicity; it is adopted by the general parallel computing frameworks such as MapReduce [8], Spark [66], and graph analytical systems such as GraphX [64] that is based on Spark. Systems and programming frameworks using the asynchronous model, including PowerGraph, Galois, Grace [15, 45, 59], were also proposed. The synchronous model was explored by a few existing systems (e.g., in GraphLab [33]), however, the overhead in ensuring synchronization needs to be carefully addressed to avoid introducing significant negative impacts to system efficiency.

Ideally, no message staleness is the most desirable design since it leads to synchronized states for all workers in a parallel computation framework. However, ensuring this in a synchronous model is not trivial and waiting for synchronization may introduce significant overheads in a system. In practice, the BSP and asynchronous models address this issue by exploring the trade-off between mes-

SIGMOD'16, June 26-July 01, 2016, San Francisco, CA, USA

© 2016 ACM. ISBN 978-1-4503-3531-7/16/06... $15.00

DOI: http://dx.doi.org/10.1145/2882903.2915238

sage staleness and efficiency. In particular, the BSP model limits the massage staleness by introducing a barrier in its computation, i.e., workers need to wait for the completion of the last thread from the current iteration, which ensures that the states of different workers are synchronized by the end of each iteration. However, it suffers from the infamous *straggler problem.*

The asynchronous model, on the other hand, removes the restriction of synchronization altogether, hence, can be very efficient. However, since asynchronous message might be significantly delayed in reaching its target, which could lead to incorrect or unstable computations. For many graph analytical workloads, the algorithms can recover the correct, synchronized states in next iteration. However, this is not the case for all analytics, and there are algorithms that do not have an implementation that will eventually converge using the asynchronous model. Even algorithms on convex problems which always leads to the correct answer may fall into local minimum caused by the chaos of asynchrony, e.g., SGD (stochastic gradient descent) may fail to converge [69, 42].

Our contributions. In light of these limitations, we focus on improving the efficiency and scalability of parallel graph analytics using *synchronous parallel processing*. We assume an in-memory computing engine, to focus on the effects of the concurrency control model and eliminate the impacts of disk I/Os. We encapsulate the computations initiated by each vertex in a given round as a transaction. Using this view, the synchronous computation is made of transactions. Each transaction is an atomic unit of operations. By ensuring conflict serializability among these transactions, the results of the concurrent execution of these transactions are equivalent to the results from a sequential execution of these transactions. The synchronous model eliminates unbounded latency in communication and relieves developers from reasoning and debugging a non-deterministic system as that in the asynchronous model.

That said, we can use a standard concurrency control scheme, such as strict 2PL (two phase locking) or OCC (optimistic concurrency control) to ensure the concurrent execution of these transactions. We define the degree of a vertex v as the number of edges connected to v. An important observation is that the distribution for degrees of vertices in a graph has a strong influence on the likelihood of having a transaction conflict. This observation explains why traditional schedulers such as 2PL or OCC lead to bad performance for graph analytics using the synchronous model. In particular, degrees of vertices in a graph often follow a very skewed distribution. This means that the locking-based approaches such as 2PL will often lead to high locking overhead, while the non-locking based scheduler such as OCC will suffer from high abort rates at the time of transaction commit.

Inspired by this observation, we propose *HSync*, a *hybrid scheduler* that combines both locking-based and non-locking based schedulers, to achieve high performance graph analytics through synchronous parallel processing. HSync adapts to a scale-free graph where the degrees of vertices may vary: it uses *a locking-based scheduler for high degree vertices*, and *a non-locking-based scheduler for low degree vertices*. This design ensures that transactions for high degree vertices will never need to abort due to low degree ones (which is important since it is expensive to abort these transactions). But transactions for low degree vertices may need to abort, however, they are not expensive, and doing so ensures that almost no deadlocks will ever occur as transactions for low degree vertices will never block the execution and commit of a high degree vertex's transaction. Extensive experimental results confirmed the superior performance of our hybrid scheduler over existing schedulers for the synchronous model. They also show that by using our hybrid scheduler, the synchronous model will outperform the asynchronous and BSP models for in-memory parallel graph analytics.

Organization: In Section 2, we formalize the *vertex-centric parallel programming and computing* framework, and compare different task schedulers and data consistency models in this framework. In Section 3, we formalize and describe synchronous parallel processing for fine-grained parallelism in graph analytics. In Section 4, we discuss the impact of large scale-free graphs on synchronous parallel processing for graph analytics. In particular, we identify that the skew distribution for degrees of vertices in a graph is the root cause for the poor performance of existing schedulers. In Section 5, we propose our hybrid scheduler HSync that uses the locking-based approach and the non-locking based scheme for high-degree and low-degree graph vertices respectively. We show our experimental results in Section 6 and discuss the related work in Section 7. The paper is concluded in Section 8.

2. BACKGROUND AND FORMULATION

As introduced in Section 1, we focus on *in-memory graph analytics*. We assume that the graph data is owned and used by *a single user* for each analytical workload, which is fairly common in in-memory analytical systems, e.g, in Spark [66], GraphX [64], GraphLab [33], and many other graph analytical systems. A simple way to generalize to multiple users is to make a copy of the underlying graph for the execution of each analytical workload. We also assume that the graph data is static during the execution of an analytical workload, i.e., there are no updates to the graph during the execution of a graph analytics job. A user submits an analytical job and expects the exact results at the end of task completion. Reducing the wall-clock processing time is the main objective.

We also assume that the data resides in memory during the entire execution. We make this assumption for two reasons. First, in-memory computing is increasingly common [67], and many graph data does fit in memory. For example, as reported in [52], the median size of data used in Yahoo's and Microsoft's analytics jobs is 14GB. On the other hand, memory capacity increases quickly and it is not uncommon for many desktop machines nowadays to have memory in tens of GB, and commercial multi-core servers can support up to 6TB of memory.[1] Moreover, high speed network and RDMA (remote direct memory access) significantly reduce the latency of remote memory accessing and the speed of accessing memory in a remote node is close to the speed of accessing local memory. Therefore, with the help of middleware like FARM and RAMCloud [11, 46], even really large data can still reside entirely in memory over a cluster. Secondly, the focus of our work is to analyze the impacts of concurrency control schedulers for synchronous parallel processing in graph analytics. Thus, we would like to eliminate the impacts by other factors such as disk I/Os and highlight the bottlenecks introduced by the concurrency model.

2.1 Vertex-Centric Parallel Computing

Most graph analytical systems, like Pregel [35], GraphLab [33], and GraphX [64], are built based on the vertex centric (VC) model. In this model, user implements a user-defined function (UDF), which is executed on each vertex iteratively as shown in Section 1.

The vertex-centric computing model can be made to run in parallel, which leads to vertex centric parallel programming and computing. We illustrate a simplified framework of vertex centric parallel programming and computing in Fig. 1. The system consists of multiple workers (computer nodes and/or cores). Each worker executes the UDF on a vertex through the coordination of the task scheduler.

[1]For example, Dell R920 by November 2015

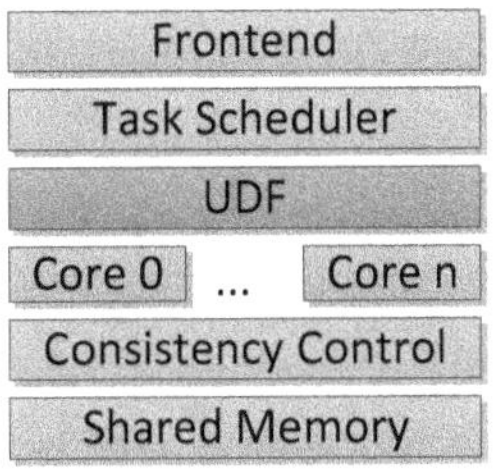

Figure 1: Vertex-centric parallel programming and computing.

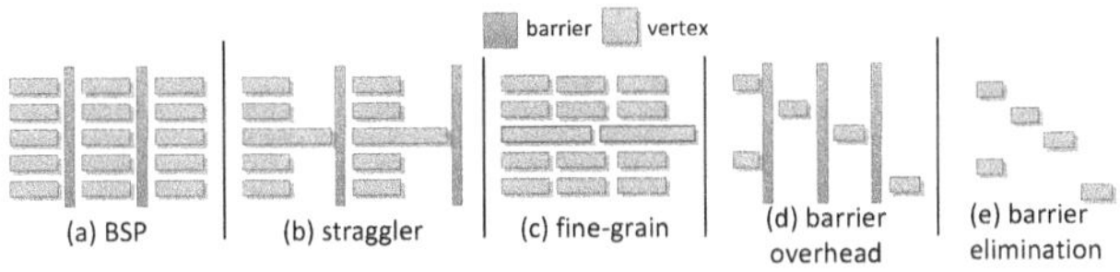

Figure 2: Coarse-grained vs. fine-grained scheduling

The UDF may be executed multiple times on the same vertex until a convergence condition is met. The concurrency control model dictates the consistency states among different vertices.

Although this simple framework is being used on literally all graph analytics systems, differences in two key components often lead to very different instantiation and performance in practice. The first design choice is *how to pick the next vertex v in task scheduler*. Jobs associated with different vertices may execute simultaneously, or in a random order, or by a user-defined priority assignment. The other design choice is *the data consistency model*: when more than one workers are executing the UDF over multiple vertices concurrently, it is entirely possible that they will interfere with each other, for example, UDF (v_1) updates the states of some vertices that are also used by UDF (v_2) when UDF (v_1) and UDF (v_2) are running concurrently. Systems may choose a strong data consistency model (e.g., synchronous parallel processing), a weak consistency model (e.g., BSP processing), or no consistency control at all (e.g., asynchronous parallel processing).

2.1.1 Task Scheduler

In VC graph analytics, the task scheduler is in charge of the strategy used to select the next vertex to run the UDF on. A popular choice is the BSP processing introduced by Pregel [35]. BSP works in iterations. All vertices run the same UDF *in parallel* in each iteration, and each vertex executes the UDF exactly once in one iteration. A barrier is enforced after each iteration to ensure that all workers complete their jobs before entering the next iteration, and synchronization messages are exchanged as well so that vertices reach synchronized states at the beginning of the next iteration. BSP is a coarse-grained scheduling method as illustrated by Fig. 2(a).

In contrast, a fine-grained scheduling method eliminates all barriers. Each execution of the UDF on a vertex becomes a computing task. A (centralized) global scheduler, usually a work queue, is responsible for scheduling. We illustrate its execution in Fig. 2(c).

The main advantage of coarse-grained scheduling like BSP is its simplicity and low overhead in concurrency control, since vertices run in parallel and isolation in one iteration and they only coordinate and send update messages to each other at the end of one iteration. If all tasks in one iteration have similar costs, *and* all iterations have similar number of tasks, as shown in Fig. 2(a), BSP will be highly effective. However, in practice this assumption usually does not hold and the coarse granularity in parallelism may suffer from several drawbacks.

The first limitation is *task straggler*: some tasks may run (much) longer than others. Therefore, as illustrated as Fig. 2(b), the completion time of each iteration is determined by the slowest task.

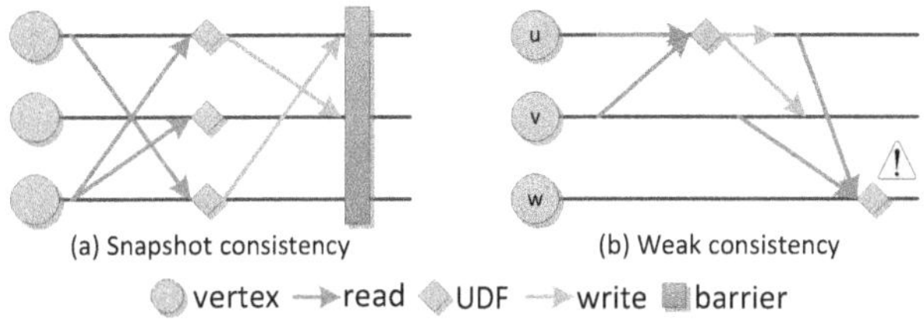

Figure 3: Snapshot and weak data consistency models.

Secondly, the overhead of enforcing the barriers becomes significant especially if not all tasks are active in an iteration. As illustrated in Fig. 2(d), if only a small number of tasks are being executed in each iteration, the workers (e.g., CPU cores) are underutilized and the time spent on barrier synchronization becomes a major bottleneck. Fine-grained scheduling is able to remove this overhead as shown in Fig. 2(e). *Third*, the coarse-grained scheduling prohibits application-specific intra-iteration optimizations. For example, for some problems assigning different (scheduling) priorities to tasks helps speed up the convergence rate [68]. Such prioritized scheduling is only feasible under a fine-grained scheduling methods. *Lastly*, in BSP a new iteration cannot start until all workers finish their communications in the last iteration. In other words cores are idling while waiting for network communication and synchronization. In contrast, finer-grained scheduling is able to reduce CPU idling significantly.

2.1.2 Data Consistency Model

If UDFs on different vertices are allowed to execute concurrently without control, they may interfere with each other and lead to inconsistent states. BSP overcomes this data consistency problem by working on a *snapshot*. In particular, each vertex reads data from last iteration and emits messages (to update other vertices) that will only be visible in next iteration. In other words, each vertex is not aware of other vertices' work (that run concurrently in parallel) until next iteration. This data consistency model is shown in Fig. 3(a). Clearly, this approach eliminates a lot of synchronization overheads, but limits the rate of state synchronization which in turn leads to slow convergence and longer job completion time.

Using the asynchronous model for fine-grained parallelism relaxes the data consistency requirement: there is little or no control on the data consistency at all. Each worker is allowed to *write to shared data anytime in any order*. As illustrated in Fig. 3(b), this approach suffers from the *weak data consistency* problem: the transaction w reads an inconsistent snapshot of the vertex u and v, which one have been update by transaction u and the other not. In order to compute exact and correct results, developers have to maintain data consistency somehow by themselves. This dramatically increases the complexity for programming and code maintenance. Nevertheless, this approach is very useful when an approximate result is acceptable or even desirable for better efficiency, which is usually satisfied by machine learning and data mining applications. However the exact trade-off between efficiency and accuracy is unclear and hard to model and reason about.

Lastly, strong data consistency model in fine-grained parallelism can be achieved by using synchronous parallel processing. In particular, for all workers that are being executed concurrently in parallel, the strong data consistency model requires that they satisfy *conflict serializability*. In other words, the concurrent execution of these workers leads to a state that is the same as the state from one of the serial executions of these workers. We will detail and formalize this framework in next section.

3. SYNCHRONOUS PARALLEL PROCESSING FOR FINE-GRAINED PARALLELISM

In this section we propose the fine-grained parallelism for graph analytics with strong data consistency by using synchronous parallel processing. Following the general VC framework, user will submit an UDF and it is executed over vertices in a graph. UDF (v_j) may read other vertices' attribute values and write values back. The *task scheduler* consists of the following modules:

1) The class `vertex` models the actions related to a vertex. It asks for an implementation of the UDF for this vertex, that may be called multiple times and may have different actions in each execution depending on the current states of the vertices in a graph. It also provides the interfaces for reading and writing values from and to other vertices. `vertex` can access its edge lists. For simplicity we do not distinguish the direction of edges. Instead we model them as undirected ones with tags. In other words, a `vertex` object represents a task related to a specific vertex.

2) `addTask` adds a task into the scheduler's queue, possibly with a priority assignment. Each task is removed from the scheduler's queue before its execution.

3) `barrier` introduces a global barrier; all workers enter this barrier after completing its currently assigned task. And they will execute a user-specified function f before leaving the barrier. The barrier can be used for synchronization. The function f may use `addTask` to add more tasks back to the queue. For example, to implement BSP-style scheduling, user adds each vertex using `addTask` and imposes the barrier based on a global value for iteration that is only updated when all workers in the current round have completed. Tasks in the next iteration are added back to the queue using f. `barrier` is also used for progress monitoring, checking for termination condition, debugging and profiling, etc.

```
// global functions and class
class vertex {
    abstract UDF(vertex v);
    value_t readVertex(vertex v);
    writeVertex(vertex v, value_t val);}

addTask(vertex v, priority = 1.0);
barrier(function f);
```

Figure 4: The API of fine-grained parallelism.

```
in parallel for each worker (executed by a
    thread)
    if at barrier
        wait until all workers reach barrier
        execute the function f
        continue
    if no more tasks in the scheduler queue
        exit
    retrieve (and remove) task vertex v
    begin transaction
        execute UDF(v) as a transaction t(v)
    end transaction
```

Figure 5: The workflow of fine-grained parallelism.

The workflow of fine-grained parallelism is shown as Fig. 5. Once a worker becomes available, it retrieves a task from the scheduler and executes the task *concurrently in parallel* with other active workers while *ensuring strong data consistency*. The UDF is treated as an *atomic unit*. Atomic units run concurrently, but each of them behaves like *running by its own in isolation*. Although users can define such atomic unit with arbitrary logic, the most common form in graph analytics involves computations over a single vertex and its neighbors and the edges between them if applicable (i.e., its edge list). These computations form an atomic unit and are encapsulated by the UDF. Each such UDF proceeds as long as it does not interfere (i.e., conflict with) other concurrently running UDFs. For example, a conflict is identified if UDF (v_1) tries to update the attribute values

```
void UDF(vertex v) {
    // calculate the page rank value
    double sum = 0, previous = readVertex(v);
    for (all neighbors u)
        sum += readVertex(u);
    sum = sum * (1 - d) + d;
    writeVertex(v, sum);

    // schedule v with priority
    double gap = abs(sum - previous);
    if (gap > 1e-6)
        addTask(v, gap);

    // report vertices with top-k page rank
        values periodically
    if (time elapsed 1 sec since last report)
        barrier({
    // find current top-k vertices and print
        });
}
```

Figure 6: PageRank in fine-grained parallelism framework.

of v_3 that is being used by UDF (v_2) running concurrently (suppose v_3 is a neighbor of both v_1 and v_2).

This computation model bears great similarity to *transaction processing* in relational databases. In particular, each UDF as described above forms an atomic unit that satisfies the *atomicity* and *isolation* properties that are exactly the same as *'A' and 'I'* requirements in the ACID definition for transactions in RDBMS. Henceforth, we can enforce fine-grained parallelism for active workers in Fig. 5 through *transactions*.

UDF (v) is represented by a *transaction on vertex class* v. Unless specified we will denote fine-grained parallelism as transaction handling in following. Active workers lead to the set of actively running transactions. Using a *transaction scheduler* for concurrency control among these transactions, the system keeps the transactions from interfering each other while running concurrently. Formally speaking, the end effect of running them in parallel is equivalent to the results of a sequential execution of these transactions.

An example. We use the classic PageRank algorithm (PR) (Fig. 6) to illustrate the realization of fine-grained parallelism through this API. This UDF calculates the PageRank value of vertex v by reading neighboring vertices' PageRank values and writing back the updated PageRank value to the vertex v itself. After which, it adds the vertex back to the scheduler's queue, using `addTask`, if and only if the PageRank value for v has changed for more than a threshold. It reports the vertices with top-k PageRank values periodically by using the `barrier` function.

Remarks. The fine-grained parallelism through synchronous parallel processing has several advantages compared to other approaches (namely, BSP and asynchronous processing).

First, it is more flexible compared to BSP and asynchronous models. In fact, we can use the above fine-grained parallelism framework to realize BSP and asynchronous processing, simply by using different `barrier` functions and different concurrency control schemes for the *transactions*. BSP and asynchronous processing also suffer from the snapshot and weak data consistencies as discussed in Section 2.1.2. In particular, asynchronous computing introduces uncertainty to the computations, which brings extra troubles for users to reason the correctness of analytics.

Second, by modeling synchronous processing of active workers as transaction processing, fine-grained parallelism greatly reduce the system complexity. This frees other system modules from considering the concurrency control and synchronization issues. For example, dynamic workload balancing which aims at re-balancing the workloads during the parallel processing is critical to the performance. However such re-balancing is a sophisticated process in BSP: a typical workflow is by exchanging the workload information several times before each worker agrees with the workloads to be migrated. Additional communications are needed to perform the migration and notification [54, 23, 65]. Such complexity are due to the staleness introduced by the coarse grain parallelism. For fine-grained parallelism re-balancing is much simpler: underloaded workers can steal the work from overloaded ones on the fly.

Lastly, dissemination of states among vertices is faster and synchronization reaches other vertices much quicker than using BSP, and ensures correctness that might not be possible in asynchronous model. For algorithms on convex problems like stochastic gradient descent (SGD), the flexibility of fine-grained parallelism makes it possible to support arbitrary update orders. Some gradients may get updated more frequently than others, and these updates are instantly visible to others once the transactions commit. Therefore the algorithm may converge faster. Non-convex and/or discrete problems may have problem-specific constrains or dependencies on the update orders. Consider graph coloring as an example: each vertex shall find a color distinct from its neighboring colors. It is important to ensure a vertex can access up-to-date and consistent color values of its neighbors during the computation. Fine-grained parallelism helps enforce such constraints: user program does not have to worry about a vertex u's neighbors concurrently alter their colors and lead to incorrect coloring assignment. Instead, the system itself will take over the concurrent executions while ensuring isolation. In contrast, the BSP model will incur significant overhead, and the asynchronous model may not even be able to implement this correctly because each vertex cannot be sure to read its neighbors' correct and consistent status.

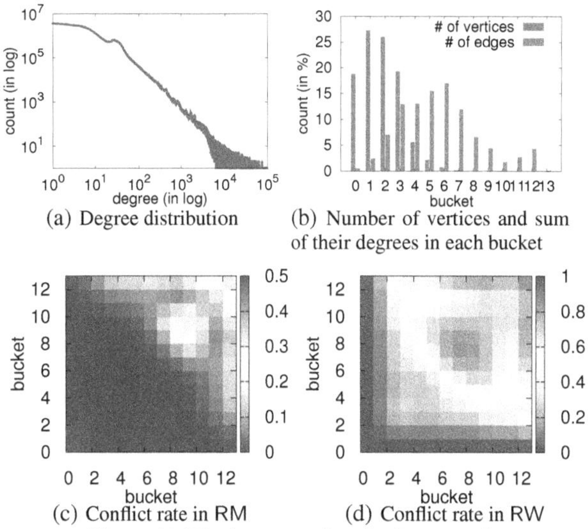

(a) Degree distribution (b) Number of vertices and sum of their degrees in each bucket

(c) Conflict rate in RM (d) Conflict rate in RW

Figure 7: The impacts of scale-free graphs.

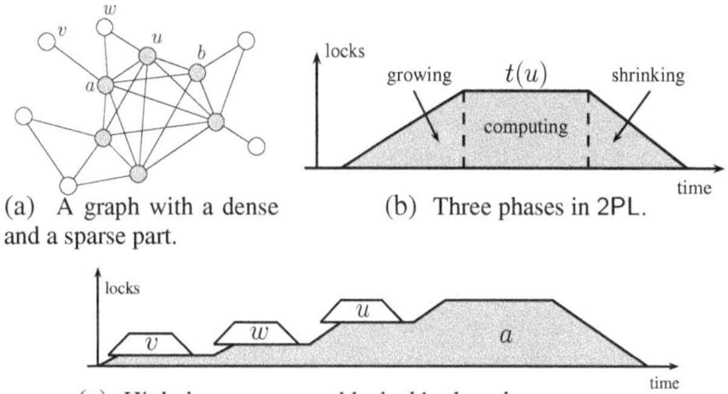

(a) A graph with a dense and a sparse part. (b) Three phases in 2PL.

(c) High degree vertex a blocked by low degree ones u, v, w

Figure 8: Inefficiency of 2PL.

4. THE SCALE-FREE GRAPH CHALLENGE

Although fine-grained parallelism has several significant advantages against other consistency models including BSP and asynchronous processing, it can lead to considerable overheads in order to maintain strong data consistency. In particular, its *transaction scheduler* may perform poorly on large graph analytical processing due to the overhead in doing concurrency control over many vertex transactions. Many large graphs in real applications are *scale-free graphs, i.e., whose degree distribution (for vertices) follows a power law* [6]. In this section, we discuss the properties of scale-free graphs and investigate the impacts of pow law graphs have for the transaction scheduler in fine-grained parallelism.

4.1 Large Scale-Free Graphs

Consider the `twitter-mpi` graph which is a follower network in Twitter, crawled by MPI in 2010, and represents friendships among twitter users. It has more than 52 million vertices (twitter users) and around 2 billion edges (follower-followee). Its degree distribution is shown in Fig. 7(a), where the *x-axis* is the vertex degree, and *y-axis* is the number of vertices with a particular degree value. Both axises are in *log scale*. This is clearly a *power law* distribution. We divide vertices into buckets. In Fig. 7(b), we show the percentage of vertices, and the percentage of edges *(reflects the sum of the number of vertex neighbors, i.e., total degrees of vertices)*, that fall in a bucket in the graph, where a vertex with degree d is assigned to the $\lfloor 2\log_{10}(d)\rfloor$-th bucket. Note that the number of neighbors for a vertex v is a good indicator for the amount of updates and the workload (assuming that the time complexity of UDF is linear) of transaction $t(v)$ in one execution. Clearly, most vertices fall into buckets with small degrees yet the total number of neighbors for these buckets is small compared to those buckets with larger degree vertices (even though very few vertices are in those buckets).

Next, we investigate the likelihood of conflicts by showing the probability of conflicts of two vertex transactions, one from each of every two buckets, for Read Mostly (RM) and Read Write (RW) workloads in Fig. 7(c) and Fig. 7(d) respectively. In Fig. 7(c), the RM workload asks every transaction $t(v)$ writes vertex v and reads its neighbors. In Fig. 7(d), the RW workload asks every transaction $t(v)$ writes vertex v as well as its neighbors. Details of these workloads can be found in Section 6. As can be seen in Fig. 7(c), if two transactions in RM are from buckets 0 to 7, their conflict rates are under 1%. For transactions on vertices with larger degrees, their conflict rates could be as large as 20% even for RM workloads. Conflict rates are higher for RW workloads as shown in Fig. 7(d). Consider two transactions in bucket 3, where transactions are over vertices with a degree about 30. The conflict rate is around 30%. For large degree vertices, the conflict rate could be as high as 100%.

Clearly, the higher the degree of the two vertices, the more likely their transactions are going to conflict, and the conflict rates of RW are much higher than that of RM.

4.2 Limitations of Existing Schedulers

Several existing designs are available to serve as the *transaction scheduler* in the fine-grained parallelism framework as presented in Section 3. Unfortunately, when being applied over large scale-free graphs, they suffer from various limitations as we will investigate next. We use a toy example (Fig. 8(a)) to represent a large scale-free graph. This graph G has a large fully connected component consisting of blue vertices. Based on our analysis from last subsection, the conflict rates among vertex transactions for blue vertices are going to be very high, whereas the conflict rates among white vertices will be fairly small. Note that recent research [34] confirms

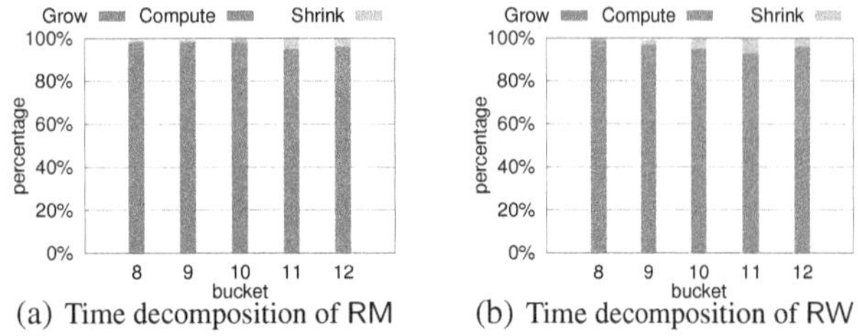

(a) Time decomposition of RM

(b) Time decomposition of RW

Figure 9: 2PL **on** `twitter-mpi`**:** RM **and** RW.

that large scale graphs have both a dense part and a sparse part that are similar to this graph G.

Locking based schedulers. We use two phase lock (2PL) as the representative for locking-based schedulers. 2PL is used in one of the GraphLab's engines [33]. 2PL requires locks to be obtained for all vertices that the transaction needs to access. If all lock requests are successful, the transaction proceeds. Otherwise the transaction must wait till it can acquire these locks.

As illustrated in Fig. 8(b), there are three phases in a transaction following 2PL. The transaction requests all locks in the *growing phase*, and releases all locks in the *shrinking phase*. The computation is performed between the growing and shrinking phases.

In multi-core in-memory graph analytics, the locking overhead becomes a significant overhead. A vertex v with a high degree may require as many as millions of locks in a large graph. There is a very high probability that transaction $t(v)$ will be blocked by the locks held by some of its neighbors and their neighbors. In Fig. 8(c), it shows that the growing phase of $t(a)$ can be very expensive. In particular, a has many white vertices as its neighbors and the lock requests by $t(a)$ on these vertices are likely to be blocked by transactions running concurrently over these white vertices (which have low degrees).

Using both the RM and RW workloads on the `twitter-mpi` graph, we measured the total clock time (over all vertex transactions) of the three phases in Fig. 9 for buckets 8 to 12 (refer to Fig. 7(b)). The growing phase for requesting locks accounts for 60% to 90% of the overall processing time, which is too high.

Optimistic schedulers. In an optimistic scheduler like OCC [28], a transaction $t(v)$ does not lock vertices it needs to access, and is allowed to execute while all its reads and writes are being logged. When $t(v)$ is ready to commit, the scheduler will replay the log to ensure all its operations are still valid in order to commit: for all read operations the current values for objects read by $t(v)$ should be same as the values in the log for those reads; for all write operations the values written by $t(v)$ should not have been overwritten. If this validation succeeds, $t(v)$ commits; otherwise, the scheduler aborts $t(v)$ (even with only one violation) and $t(v)$ will be queued again for execution.

Compared to locking based schedulers, the optimistic scheduler does not block transactions. Thus, the overheads on locking are eliminated. On the other hand, if two transactions conflict with each other, at least one of them will be forced to abort and redo all the work. This is bad news when we apply OCC for the fine-grained parallelism framework on large scale-free graphs, as shown in Figures 7(c) and 7(d), the conflict rates can be very high especially for the dense part of a graph like the graph G.

TO schedulers. Timestamp ordering (TO) schedulers assign a timestamp for each transaction (as ts_v) and each data item (as TS_v). Usually the transaction's timestamp is assigned as the time it starts. During the execution of the $t(v)$, each read/write operation is allowed to operate on an item only if the timestamp of $t(v)$ satisfies a condition determined by the data item's timestamp.

TO scheduler suffers from the following issues over vertex transactions in large scale free graphs. Suppose $t(v)$ reads u. It can perform the read *if and only if* $ts_v \geq TS_u$, where $TS_u = max\{ts_w \mid t(w)$ writes u, $t(w)$ has committed$\}$. Otherwise $t(v)$ will have to abort. In large scale free graphs the degree of v could be millions. It is very likely that one of its neighbors has been overwritten by another $t(w)$ which starts later than $t(v)$ but finishes earlier than $t(v)$. Thus $t(v)$ on vertices with large degree is very likely to abort.

MVCC and SI schedulers. Multi-version concurrency control (MVCC) [63, 30, 31, 9, 44, 27, 13, 53, 32] increases transaction throughput, especially for read-only transactions, by keeping multiple versions of the same object (each update creates a new version). With extra storage cost, the strength of MVCC is to not block any read-only transactions. Snapshot isolation (SI) works on the snapshot of data instead of up-to-date values. Grace [50] is a graph database that supports snapshot isolation, but it does not provide serializable schedule. Serializable snapshot isolation (SSI) [14] builds on top of SI, with an extra component for correcting the errors/anomalies (w.r.t. serializability) brought by SI.

These schedulers work better than other single-versioned schedulers when there are *many read-only transactions*: they handle non-read-only transactions via other schedulers like 2PL and read-only transactions with snapshots. If there are no read-only transactions, these schedulers degenerate to 2PL. However for most analytical graph processing workloads using fine-grained parallelism, most if not all vertex transactions are NOT read-only. A graph analytics job often needs to update values associated with vertices throughout its computation, e.g., PageRank in Figure 6. Thus, MVCC, SI and their variants are not likely to help in this situation.

Chromatic scheduler. First proposed in [33], chromatic scheduler ensures data consistency in graph analytics by *assigning colors to vertices*. Assume that UDF(v) reads/writes vertex v and (only) reads its neighbors (RM), chromatic scheduler colors vertices so that adjacent vertices have different colors. The execution of UDFs consists of the following recursive phases: in each phase, only vertices in one particular color are active (note that UDF(v) may add one or more vertex UDFs back to the queue). Coloring ensures that active workers for computing vertex UDFs will not interfere with each other. This idea is further developed in [22, 21].

Compared to the *transaction scheduler* in fine-grained parallelism, all transaction scheduling overheads are eliminated in this approach. However its performance often suffers from the large number of colors that are needed in real large graphs. It is observed that the large scale graphs or networks usually have one or more dense subgraphs. Say the graph G has a k-clique where any two vertices in this clique are connected. Using the chromatic scheduler, each vertex in the k-clique shall have a unique color. Therefore we have at least k colors for graph G. Chromatic scheduler will have to schedule UDFs for vertices in the clique to run *sequentially*. But a typical value of k could range from several hundreds to tens of thousands in a large graph. Sequential execution on this large sub-graph drastically degrades the performance of chromatic scheduling. Furthermore, for RW workloads, where each vertex reads and writes itself and its neighbors, the graph shall be colored *such that each vertex's color is different from the colors of its 2-hop neighbors*. This is a hard problem to solve, since for each vertex we shall inspect its 2-hop neighbors and the total number of 2-hop neighbors over all vertices is a large search space. The cost of maintaining a valid coloring in case of incorporating changes to the underlying graph is significant too. Hence, it was once employed in GraphLab [33], but has been replaced by a locking-based scheduler like 2PL.

Remarks. Our analyses reveal that existing schedulers are not

Algorithm 1 *TX-START* (v)

```
Require: vertices values in D[]                      ▷ Graph data
Require: vertices version in ver[]                   ▷ Meta-data for scheduling
Require: vertices locks in L[]                       ▷ Fine-grained locks

if d(v) ≥ threshold τ then
    BIG ← true; TX-START-B (v);
else
    BIG ← false; TX-START-S (v);
set version = concatenation of ThreadID and counter;
counter++;
```

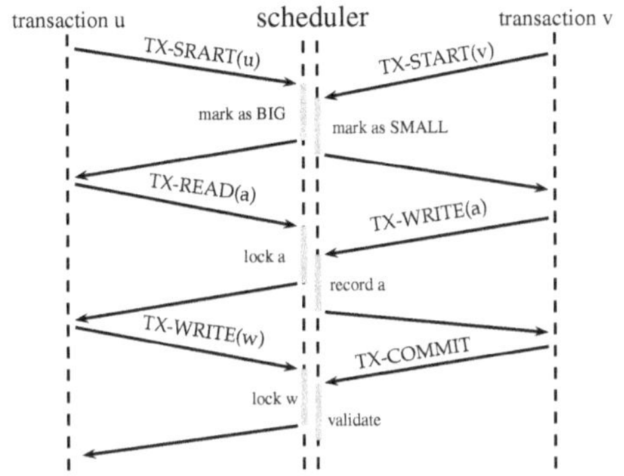

Figure 10: Illustration of transaction-scheduler interaction

likely to perform well for vertex transactions in a large scale-free graph. A better design is to be able to adapt to high conflict rates on high degree vertices and low conflict rates on low degree vertices.

5. HSync: A HYBRID SCHEDULER

The above discussion shows none of the existing schedulers will perform well for graph analytics over large scale-free graphs. This inspires us to design a hybrid scheduler, HSync, which combines the advantages of 2PL and OCC by routing vertex transactions to an appropriate scheduler based on the degrees of the vertices. Intuitively, there are a few high degree vertices in a large scale-free graph and the UDFs on these vertices are more costly to compute, thus we want to ensure that they do not abort using 2PL. On the other hand, there are many low degree vertices and we want to ensure that they don't create too many conflicts that will block the execution of UDFs for high degree vertices, and aborting these vertex transactions is not expensive since low degree vertices have small computation workload. Thus, we use OCC for these vertices.

A hybrid approach. We take a hybrid approach HSync, which uses 2PL for the transactions over *big* vertices and OCC for the transactions over *small* vertices. A vertex v is a big vertex if its degree $d(v)$ is greater than or equal to a threshold τ; otherwise, it is a small vertex. Using HSync in our fine-grained parallelism framework, a UDF on the vertex v initiates a vertex transaction $t(v)$ by *TX-START*, and ends the transaction $t(v)$ by either *TX-COMMIT* or *TX-ABORT*.

We show *TX-START* in Algorithm 1. It checks the degree of the vertex v, if $d(v) \geq \tau$, it will call *TX-START-B*; otherwise it will call *TX-START-S*. A transaction is assigned a unique identifier by concatenating the `ThreadID` of a thread (which is unique) and a local `counter` variable. Note that with the help of the `BIG` variable, all subsequent transaction procedures, e.g. *TX-COMMIT*, will call a procedure with *-B* suffix for big vertices, and a procedure with *-S* suffix for small vertices. That said, procedures for big vertices are shown in Algorithm 2, and procedures for small vertices are shown in Algorithm 3. In all these procedures, the variables `D[]`, `ver[]`, and `L[]` refer to the same data structures in

Algorithm 2 Transaction Processing for Big Vertices

```
procedure TX-START-B(v)
    locks ← ∅;                                       ▷ Reset locks

procedure TX-READ-B(v)
    request lock L[v] for read mode;                 ▷ Request lock first
    locks ← locks ∪ {v};
    return value of vertex v;

procedure TX-WRITE-B(v, value)
    request lock L[v] for exclusive mode;            ▷ Request lock first
    locks ← locks ∪ {v};
    D[v] ← value;
    ver[v] ← version;                                ▷ Update the version

procedure TX-COMMIT-B()
    for v in locks do                                ▷ Release locks
        release the lock L[v];

procedure TX-ABORT-B()
    for v in locks do                                ▷ Recover and release locks
        recover the value of v in D[] and ver[] from the log;
        release the locks L[v] if held;
```

Algorithm 3 Transaction Processing for Small Vertices

```
procedure TX-START-S(v)
    reads ← ∅;
    writes ← ∅;

procedure TX-READ-S(v)
    if v found in writes then                        ▷ Find the vertex in written log
        return writes[v];
    if v not in reads then                           ▷ Add the read access to log
        reads ← reads ∪ {(v, ver[v])};
    return D[v];

procedure TX-WRITE-S(v, value)
    writes ← writes ∪ {(v, value)}                   ▷ Append to log

procedure TX-COMMIT-S()                              ▷ Validation phase
    for v in writes do                               ▷ Request locks for modification
        try-request lock L[v] for exclusive mode;
        if fails then
            TX-ABORT-S();
    for v in reads do                                ▷ Verify read access
        if ver[v] ≠ reads[v] or
           v locked by another thread exclusively then
            TX-ABORT-S()
    for v in writes do                               ▷ Update data and version
        D[v] ← writes[v];
        ver[v] ← version;
    for v in writes do
        release the locks L[v] held;

procedure TX-ABORT-S()
    for v in writes do
        release the locks L[v] if held;
```

Algorithm 1. Basically, the procedures for big vertices follow the 2PL protocol, and the procedures for small vertices follow the OCC protocol. But they share data values, data versions, and data locks. Note that a data version here *does not* represent a multi-version data, rather it simply *shows which transaction has the latest update to the data value in concern.*

User is unaware of such a hybrid approach, nor her involvement is needed. The system decides automatically if a vertex transaction is big or small based on the threshold τ. In other words, the fine-grained parallelism API always calls, for example, *TX-READ*, but not *TX-READ-B* or *TX-READ-S* (and similarly for other API calls to any transaction procedure). A workflow chart that illustrates the interaction between two transactions and the HSync scheduler is shown as Fig. 10. In this example, when transaction u enters the system, the scheduler marks it as BIG, so for following operations issued from transaction u, HSync will request locks on the corresponding vertices. On the other hand, for transaction v, the scheduler marks it as SMALL, and simply records its write operations `TX-WRITE(a)` on its private write log without requesting any locks and verify if they are still valid at the time of commit.

The details of HSync. We first discuss the procedures for big vertices (Algorithm 2). In *TX-START-B*, it initializes the `locks` to empty. In the growing phase of 2PL, a transaction needs to lock all vertices it tends to access, using shared locks for read access and exclusive locks for write access. In *TX-COMMIT-B*, it releases all locks it has held. All operations are recorded in a log for recovery during transaction abort. In *TX-ABORT-B*, it recovers and restores the value and the version of v back into `D[]` and `ver[]` using the old values kept in the log before releasing the locks held.

Note that in our implementation of 2PL in Algorithm 2, we did not use the traditional data structures used in the lock manager for disk-based RDBMS [63, Chapter 10]. Traditional scheduler registers the transaction $t(v)$ on the waiting list of the lock, suspends the $t(v)$ and switches to another transaction (when $t(v)$ can not acquire a lock). The cost of doing so is relatively small since a dominant cost in disk-based RDBMS is disk I/Os. However, for in-memory graph analytics, the cost of context switching and the cost associated with cache misses hurt the performance significantly [18, 47, 43]. Hence, we use the spinlock instead, i.e., each vertex has a light-weight spinlock to indicate if it is currently locked by a transaction or not. The transaction simply waits for the lock release, when a lock can not be acquired. We resolve deadlocks using deadlock prevention: since the lock set for a vertex transaction for vertex u in a graph analytical workload is known before the execution of the transaction, which is a subset of u's neighbors (may include u itself), we request locks following a global ordering of locks. In our implementation we used the vertex ids as this global ordering for locks. Note that similar approaches have also been adopted in other systems [51, 43, 58].

We next discuss the procedures for small vertices (Algorithm 3). Recall that in OCC, a transaction keeps a local set `reads` to maintain all reads executed, and a local set `writes` to maintain all writes executed. OCC allows all reads/writes to be executed without locking. It will check their validity at the validation phase when the transaction is about to commit. In *TX-START-S*, it initializes both `reads` and `writes` to empty. In *TX-READ-S*, it first checks if v had been updated by the current transaction. If so, it returns the updated value of v from `writes[`v`]`. If v is not in `writes`, it further checks if it is already recorded in `reads`, returns the value kept in `D[`v`]` if not and records it in `reads`. In *TX-WRITE-S*, it keeps the newly updated value in `writes`, and *does not update* the value in `D[`v`]`.

The validation phase is done in *TX-COMMIT-S*. *TX-COMMIT-S* will abort the transaction by calling *TX-ABORT-S*, if one of the following conditions is met: 1) the transaction cannot get exclusive locks for all objects in `writes`. Here the lock requests are non-blocking, i.e., if a lock cannot be acquired, the transaction thread will not wait for its availability, and will return fail and abort the transaction immediately. If all locks are successfully obtained, it will update `D[`v`]` for every vertex v in `writes` before releasing any locks; 2) the transaction finds a mismatch between the version of a vertex v in its `reads` and the version of the vertex from `D[`v`]`. This implies that another transaction has updated v since v was read by the current transaction. Lastly, *TX-ABORT-S* simply releases all locks held by the current transactions.

In traditional implementation, the validation of a transaction in OCC is a non-interruptible critical section, and all other transactions will be declined to enter validation if there is an actively running critical session of a transaction. This is not efficient nor scalable for in-memory graph analytics over large graphs. We adopt an optimization that is similar to Silo [58]. In the validation phase, the transaction requests locks on vertices. If the transactions are less likely to conflict, which is the case for transactions over small vertices, the locks will be in the cache of the workers of these transactions during the whole validation phase. There are two ways to validate a transaction in OCC [63]. One is BOCC (backward-oriented optimistic concurrency control), and the other is FOCC (forward-oriented optimistic concurrency control). In our system, we use FOCC which validates a transaction against all the transactions that run in concurrent but have not committed yet.

To reduce overhead while integrating OCC with 2PL, we let small transactions access vertices' values where possible and then request all locks before their validation phases. Due to the low conflict rates for the small transactions as they do not have a large number of neighbors (see Figures 7(c) and 7(d)), it is likely that most small transactions will successfully commit without being aborted. The main advantage of using OCC for small transactions rather than using 2PL is that a small transaction has a chance to commit much early. This is because that the time taken from requesting locks to releasing locks in OCC is very small (especially for small transactions) which means they will not interfere with the execution of big transactions under 2PL too much. In addition, in the worst case, if a small transaction gets aborted, it is very inexpensive to re-execute it and let it try to commit again.

Note that in HSync, 2PL and OCC share the same locks. 2PL uses locks for transaction scheduling, and OCC utilizes locks to replace the usage of critical section as discussed above and prevents other transactions to write concurrently. By sharing the same set of locks, small transactions under OCC acquire locks to prevent potential data racing from both OCC and big transactions under 2PL. Although small transactions under OCC may request locks that may conflict with big transactions, they hold these locks for very minimum time. Compared to the 2PL-only scheduler, our hybrid scheduler essentially ensures that big transactions have higher priorities against small transactions.

Correctness. We briefly discuss the proof sketch of our theorem showing that the hybrid scheduler HSync ensures serializable. Full details can be found in appendix.

Theorem 1 *HSync permits only conflict serializable schedules.*

We define the *commit time* as the time when a transaction decides to commit. Transactions satisfy **commit order-preserving** (CO) if for any two transactions $t(i)$ and $t(j)$ that are in conflict, $t(i)$'s conflicting operation is earlier than $t(j)$'s, and $t(i)$'s commit time is also earlier than $t(j)$'s. Our proof goes by case analysis; we show that under the hybrid scheduler HSync, any two transactions that are in direct conflict with each other will guarantee to satisfy CO. We enumerate four cases that both $t(i)$ and $t(j)$ could be scheduled by 2PL or OCC. Based on this, we show that all transactions' conflict relationships are ordered by their commit time which has a total order. Therefore there must be no cycles of conflicts in HSync, which is a sufficient condition for conflict serializability. ■

We take one step forward and proved that under some reasonable assumptions, our approach *achieves the optimal concurrency for any two schedulers to form a hybrid scheduler*, where the degree of concurrency is measured by the possible transaction execution

(a) 2PL	$t(u)$				u	……	✓
	$t(v)$	v	a	✓			
	$t(w)$	u	w	a	✓		
(b) OCC	$t(u)$	u	w	a	b	…	✗
	$t(v)$	v	a	✓			
	$t(w)$	u	w	a	✓		
(c) HSync	$t(u)$	u	w	a	b	…	✓
	$t(v)$	v	a	✓			
	$t(w)$	u	w	a	✗		

time →

Figure 11: An example using three different schedulers.

traces allowed by the scheduler [63]. The details of this discussion and its proof could be found in appendix.

An example. We show the advantages of our hybrid scheduler by illustrating the execution of three transactions from the graph in Fig. 8(a). Assume three transactions, namely $t(u)$, $t(v)$ and $t(w)$, where u is a big vertex , and v and w are small vertices. We assume all operations are `write`, and their operations follow the order as shown in Figure 11.

In 2PL, a transaction can easily be blocked by other transactions. In this case, transaction $t(w)$ competes for lock on vertex u with transaction $t(u)$. Assume $t(w)$ acquires the lock successfully, then $t(u)$ has to wait for $t(w)$'s completion. In the toy example u has only six neighbors, but in a real large graph, a big vertex like u may have millions of neighbors. Thus, during the execution of a transaction on a big vertex like u, it may be blocked numerous times. To make the situation even worse, it is possible that $t(u)$ has to wait for a lock near the end of its growing phase, while it already holds millions of locks. Many other transactions cannot proceed if they require any one of these locks. In short, a small transaction may block a big transaction, which further blocks millions of small transactions. This exacerbates the congestion among transactions and may even stall the whole system. The failure of 2PL is caused by the fact that big transactions are blocked by small transactions.

For OCC, two small transactions are able to commit but the big transaction $t(u)$ has to abort in its validation phase. The committed transaction $t(v)$ "contaminates" the value read by $t(u)$ and so does $t(w)$. This is a great waste considering such big vertex u may have millions of neighbors in a large graph.

For our HSync approach, $t(u)$ is never blocked nor interrupted by $t(v)$ and $t(w)$. For data racing between $t(u)$ and $t(w)$, $t(u)$ wins due to the hybrid policy: $t(w)$ is scheduled by an optimistic scheduler and it does not acquire any lock; therefore it will not block $t(u)$, nor will it contaminate the value read by $t(u)$ because all modifications it made are recorded in its local private log. During $t(w)$'s validation phase, it will find out that the vertex a's lock is held by another transaction ($t(u)$) so it aborts. This will not affect the execution of $t(u)$ at all. But aborting and re-executing a small transaction is not costly. On the other hand, $t(v)$ is still able to finish and commit before $t(u)$ produces conflicts with it.

Optimization and extension. When a small transaction fails to commit, by default it will be rescheduled for another execution. Most existing optimistic schedulers adopt this policy because they assume that the chance of having conflicts during validation is small and re-trying several times is sufficient for the transactions to eventually progress. However in our problem, although the conflicts among small transactions are indeed infrequent, the rate for a small transaction to be in conflict with a big transaction that is concurrently running is not negligible, and a big transaction could be long standing as well due to its heavier workload. Thus, simply retrying the small transaction is not necessarily a good solution. To address this issue, we adopt a new policy that when a small transaction has failed to commit too many times, we will execute it as a big transaction (using 2PL).

Dataset	$\|V\|$	$\|E\|$	$\|E\|/\|V\|$	Size
sk-2005	50,636,154	1,949,412,601	38.50	17G
twitter-mpi	52,579,682	1,963,263,821	37.33	18G
wdc-sd	89,2472739	2,043,203,933	22.89	20G
uk-2007-05	105,896,555	3,738,733,648	35.31	33G

Table 1: Four real graph datasets

Our discussion so far assumes that the graph edges have no values and they are not involved in the analytics. If they do, we propose two extensions to handle them. Taking big transactions as example (small transactions are handled similarly), the first method is to treat edges as vertices as well. Each edge e has a fine-grained lock `L[e]`. When a big transaction tries to access e, it requests its lock. The second method does not assign a lock to an edge e. Instead, if a big transaction tries to access $e = (u, v)$, it must own both locks for u and v. The first method has a finer locking granularity, and hence, potentially better concurrency, while the second method saves space and reduces the number of locks to manage.

In contrast to classic OLTP environments like online banking, graph analytics, like other OLAP workloads, does not require durability: in case of a system crash, it is safe to restart the computation from the beginning. Thus, HSync eliminates write-ahead-logging at per-operation level (which is only needed for durability). Rather, it periodically records a snapshot of states as a checkpoint for more efficient fault recovery [63]. Users may adjust how frequent the checkpointing process is in HSync. Such fault tolerance avoids re-execution from the beginning in case of a crash.

As shown in our experiments, HSync is not very sensitive to the choice of τ (i.e., there is a relatively wide safe region to choose the value of τ from to define BIG and SMALL). That said, to facilitate choosing a good τ value, HSync uses a sampling approach. It executes the UDF on a small sample graph, sampled from the input graph using weighted sampling over vertices where the sampling weight for a vertex u is proportional to its degree, to estimate the vertex transaction conflict rates and a heat map similar to Fig. 7(c) and 7(d). The value of τ is then chosen to separate the intense conflict and occasionally conflict regions.

6. EXPERIMENTS

Experiment Setting: We have conducted extensive experiments on Amazon EC2 `c4.8xlarge` instance which has 36 cores and 60GB memory. All experiments were repeated 10 times with the average value being reported. We implemented all methods in C++.

Real large graphs: We used 4 real large graph data sets in the experiments. The dataset **twitter-mpi** is a follower network from Twitter, crawled by MPI in 2010.[2] The dataset **wdc-sd** is a hyperlink graph crawled in 2012.[3] All other data sets are large social networks and web page graphs used in different domains which can be downloaded from WebGraph.[4] Table 1 summarizes these datasets. The number of vertices of these graphs are in the range from 50 million to 106 million, the numbers of edges are in the range from 1.9 billion to 3.7 billion, where the average degrees are in the range of 22.89 and 38.50. The sizes of these graphs are from 17 gigabytes to 33 gigabytes, assuming that a graph is represented using the adjacency lists. We also conducted experiments on synthetic graphs at Appendix D.

[2] http://twitter.mpi-sws.org/

[3] http://webdatacommons.org/hyperlinkgraph/

[4] http://law.di.unimi.it/datasets.php

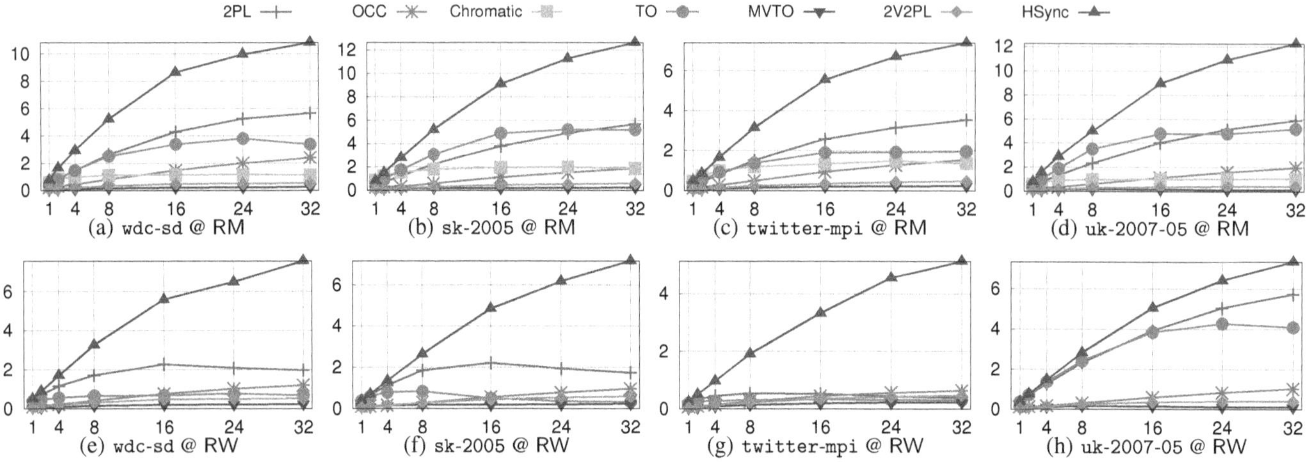

Figure 12: Throughput on RM and RW ***(x-axis for number of cores, y-axis for throughput*** **($\times 10^6$ *tps*))**

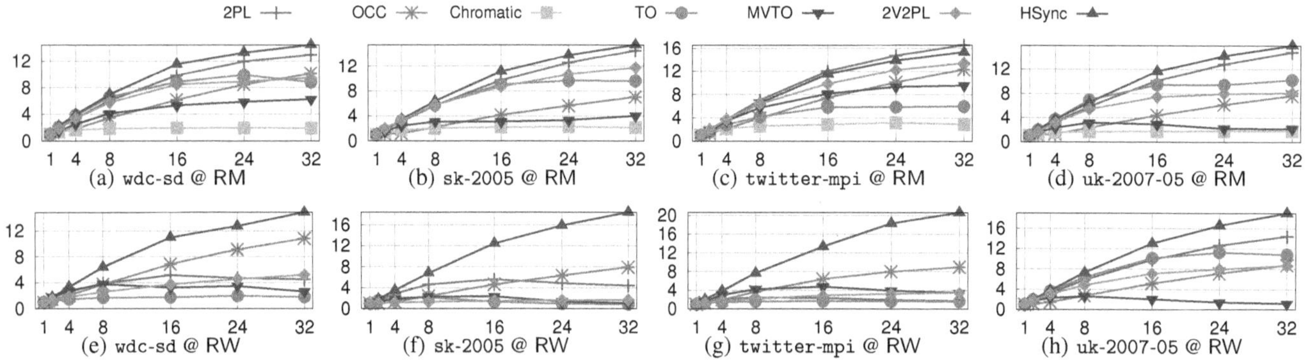

Figure 13: The scalability on RM and RW (normalized as the ratios to the throughput using 1 core)

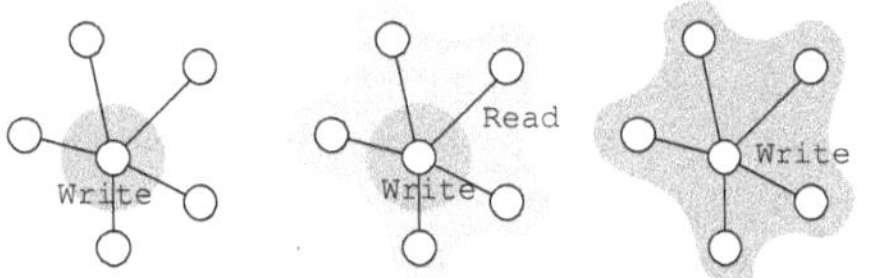

Figure 14: Different workload behavior: WO, RM, RW

Various Workload Behavior: In practice, for a vertex transaction in $t(v)$, v itself and its neighbors usually play different roles: for example, in some cases we only need to read v's neighbors but write to v. Depending on the amount of different operations, there are three possible modes of vertextransactions, shown in Fig. 14, namely *(i)* write to v; *(ii)* write to v and read from neighbors; *(iii)* write to v and neighbors. A similar consistency model has been proposed by GraphLab in [33], with data item on edges. We name these different workloads WO (Write Once), RM (Read Mostly), RW (Read Write). Among these three, WO is not interesting as it degrades to a key-value database.

6.1 Schedulers Performance

We first study the performance of different schedulers by measuring the throughputs of vertex transactions. The throughput of a scheduler is defined as the number of *t*ransactions successful committed in every *s*econd (*tps*). We define the performance gain as the ration between the throughput of the HSync scheduler vs. *the best throughput of all other schedulers*. Another important metric is the scalability. It measures the improvements on throughput when we increase the computing resources, i.e., the number of cores. To make a fair comparison, each scheduler is assigned to schedule the same set of workloads, and the throughput is measured by the wall clock time taken for each scheduler from start to the completion of last worker. For the RM workload, the sequential greedy coloring algorithm for the chromatic scheduler takes several hours for each graph. For the RW workload, chromatic scheduler is not even available because computing the appropriate graph coloring didn't finish after running for more than 100 hours for each dataset (it needs to explore 2-hop neighbors in this case).

Throughput. The throughput of transaction schedulers are shown in Fig. 12, for workload RM and RW. For RM, with 32 cores, HSync's performance gain ranges from 1.91 to 2.23 for different data sets (note that this is against the best performance from all other schedulers), with an average performance gain of 2.07. For workload RW, HSync's performance gain is from 1.28 to 8.2, with a an average gain of 3.57. In short HSync is on average 2 to 4 times more efficient than the best state-of-the-art graph vertex transaction schedulers. We note although our scheduler performs well on all data sets, the throughput gains on uk-2007-05 are less ideal. For this dataset, the throughput of 2PL is much better than OCC for both workloads. It indicates that this graph is much denser than other graphs. In a denser graph, the transactions are more likely to conflict and the throughputs of all schedulers are limited by the severe degree of conflicting operations.

Scalability. We consider the scalability of different transactions up to 32 cores. The results are shown in Fig. 13. Recall that this is defined as the throughput value of a transaction at 32 core divided by the throughput value for the same transaction at 1 core. For RM, the scalability of HSync ranges from 14.44 to 15.92, with an average 15.28, for the four data sets tested. The second best scheduler on RM, which is 2PL, only has an average scalability of 14.64. For workload RW, the scalability of HSync ranges from 14.88 to 20.65, with an average 18.1 for the same four data

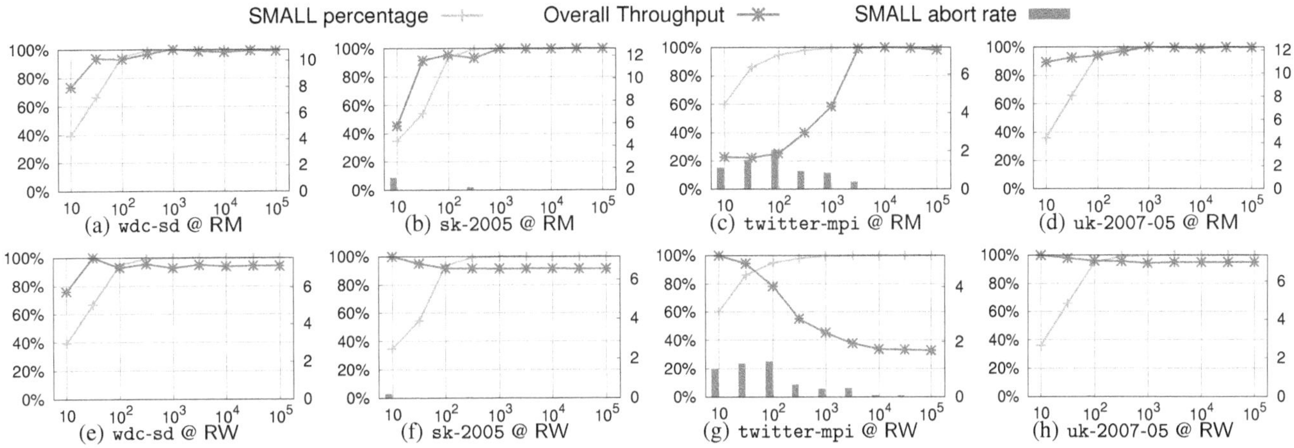

Figure 15: The effect of degree threshold τ *(x-axis for degree threshold τ, right y-axis for throughput ($\times 10^6$ tps))*

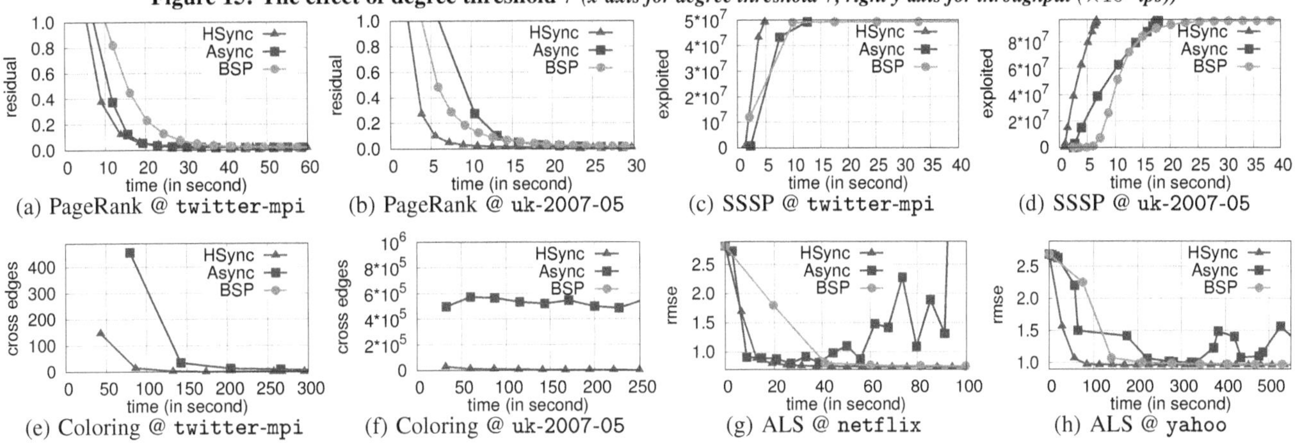

Figure 16: Four graph analytics workloads: PageRank, SSSP, graph coloring and ALS.

sets. The second best scheduler on RW, which is OCC, only has an average scalability of `9.05`.

Threshold τ in HSync. Our hybrid scheduler is almost parameter-free. The only parameter that may affect its performance is the threshold of degree τ, which determines whether a transaction is BIG or SMALL. We vary the value of τ from `10` to `100,000`, and measure the overall throughput, the percentage of transactions that are processed by the SMALL transaction scheduler (OCC), the abort rate of SMALL and the lock conflict rate for BIG transactions respectively. The results are shown in Fig. 15.

These results show that HSync is relatively insensitive to the value of τ. The workload RM has lower conflict rates (see Fig. 7(c)), therefore it performs better when τ is large, i.e., most of the transactions are processed by OCC. Similarly the workload RW performs better for a lower threshold. Among these figures, the throughput is stable for the most part, when τ changes from 10^2 to 10^4. Compared to the web graphs, social network `twitter-mpi` is more sensitive to the choice of the parameter. It is due to its higher degree of skewness. In general, we can just use a large τ value for RM workloads and a small τ value for RW workloads respectively.

6.2 Impacts to Graph Analytics

To verify the advantage of fine grained parallelism using synchronous parallel processing (with HSync) against asynchronous parallel and BSP processing for graph analytics, we tested PageRank, single source shortest path (SSSP), graph coloring, and alternative least squares (ALS) for matrix factorization. We implemented each algorithm in these different models and presented how fast they proceed over time. For ALS, we used the Netflix data [2] and the Yahoo! Music User Ratings [25], with 100,480,507 and 717,872,016 reviews respectively. For the rest, we used the social network data `twitter-mpi` and the web graph data `uk-2007-05`.

We adopt an "early termination" heuristics for PageRank: a vertex is consider stable after its last value change is less than 10^{-2}. We measured the residual, defined as the absolute difference between a vertex's PageRank value and the sum of its incoming vertices' PageRank values, averaged against all vertices. Although all three models guarantee to produce correct results eventually, as seen in Fig. 16(a) and 16(b), synchronous processing based on HSync has outperformed the BSP and asynchronous counterparts (converging to smaller errors faster).

For SSSP, the edge weights are randomly generated (and then fixed). A random source is selected, and we report the average results over multiple runs. We measured the number of exploited vertices over time (higher is better). An interesting discovery in Fig. 16(c) and 16(d) is that BSP has a "long tail" while the other two terminate quickly. This is due to the fact that BSP has to pay non-negligible overheads even when only a very small fraction of vertices are still "active" (unexplored), due to its barriers. HSync runs faster than asynchronous processing, thanks to its transaction-style synchronization: for asynchronous processing, two active vertices running concurrently may exploit a unvisited vertex u simultaneously, and thus add u into its work queue more than once. This phenomena could occur frequently in the dense "core" area of the graph. Synchronous processing like HSync avoids such overheads.

Graph coloring is to assign the minimum possible number of colors to all vertices such that the adjacent vertices are assigned different colors. Figures 16(e) and 16(f) show how the number of

	PR		SSSP		WCC		Color		ALS	
Dataset	T	U	T	U	T	U	T	U	N	Y
PowerGraph	1268	381	58.8	90.2	197	210	m	m	392	4956
PowerLyra	662	m	37.5	m	107	m	m	m	164	1784
GraphChi	3778	2424	701	2077	589	3090	848	820	>3000	>8000
HSync	181	42.7	48.8	66.7	30.1	31.9	174	59.8	74.6	901

Table 2: Efficiency of different systems. (End-to-end wall clock time in seconds. T: `twitter-mpi`, U: `uk-2007-05`, N: `netflix`, Y: `yahoo`. m: memory limit exceeded.)

	PR		SSSP		WCC		Color		ALS	
Dataset	T	U	T	U	T	U	T	U	N	Y
PowerGraph	7.0	8.9	1.2	1.4	6.5	6.6	-	-	5.3	5.5
PowerLyra	3.7	-	0.8	-	3.6	-	-	-	2.2	2.0
GraphChi	20.9	56.8	14.4	31.1	19.6	96.9	4.9	13.7	>40.2	>8.9

Table 3: Efficiency compared with HSync, running time as a ratio to HSync's running time. (T: `twitter-mpi`, U: `uk-2007-05`, N:`netflix`, Y: `yahoo`)

edges that have violated this rule (two neighbors still have the same color) decreases over time. Note the BSP in this case is too expensive to converge, and its results have been ignored in these figures. Clearly, the fine grained parallelism using HSync converges much faster than asynchronous processing; the latter has difficulty to converge on dataset `uk-2007-05`, possibly due to its smaller diameter and dense "core" (such that inconsistent readings and assignments in asynchronous processing are hard to converge).

ALS can be formalized as a bipartite graph. ALS works by fixing the values on the right side and updating the left side, then vice visa. Note that there is *no* asynchronous parallel processing algorithm that is able to guarantee correct results for ALS [33]. That said, one can still execute a synchronous parallel processing algorithm *in an asynchronous manner, without requiring the correctness of the final output, to understand its behavior*. As seen in Fig. 16(g) and 16(h), where they show how the root mean square error (RMSE) reduces over time, the asynchronous parallel processing approach could not converge at all, whereas both BSP and synchronous parallel processing have shown much better performance. And fine-grained parallelism using synchronous parallel processing with HSync has clearly outperformed BSP.

6.3 System Performance Comparison

We compared the performance of fine-grained parallelism using HSync against other graph analytics systems, including PowerGraph [15], PowerLyra [4], and GraphChi [24], using PageRank, SSSP, weakly connected component (WCC), graph coloring and ALS. We conducted the PowerGraph and PowerLyra experiments with a 16 node Amazon EC2 `m3.2xlarge` (8 cores, 30GB memory) cluster, and GraphChi on a `r3.8xlarge` instance with 32 cores, 244GB memory and 320GB SSD. The memory budget for GraphChi is set to 200GB which is much larger than the dataset. The (one-pass) data preparation time and I/O time are excluded.

We report the end-to-end wall clock running time of each approach in Table 2, and each system's running time as a ratio to HSync in Table 3. HSync outperforms other systems by 3x to 100x folds in most cases. Note that PowerGraph and PowerLyra are cluster-based with 128 cores in total (from the cluster), and Graphchi and HSync run on a single node with 32 cores.

7. RELATED WORK

Many existing graph systems including Neo4j [38], Trinity [55], FlockDB [41], InfiniteGraph [40], Allegrograph [37], NetflixGraph [39], Titan [36] and HyperGraph-DB [19] support transactional graph processing at different levels. Trinity only provides the primitive functions for developers to lock and unlock vertices. DEX allows at most one read-write transaction, plus unlimited number of concurrent read-only transactions. Neo4j and Titan use standard two-phase lock (2PL) to implement the vertex transaction scheduler. The details of other systems are unknown due to lack of publications and the fact that they are not open sourced.

There are also works in database systems where they assume static workloads (in particular, the types of transactions are known a priori) and they rely on static analysis for improving transaction scheduler's performance. For example, H-Store [56, 18, 20] proposes transaction processing systems based on the partition of data such that local transactions do not conflict and they can run concurrently without concurrency control. Calvin [57] is based on a similar approach. These approaches rely on high quality partitions of the data that lead to little or no cross-partition transactions. After that each worker is responsible for processing the transactions in one partition. Thus, they need strong knowledge about the transactions to execute a priori. These approaches work well on business or e-commerce workloads like TPC-C and YCSB since the data can be easily partitioned. However large scale graphs tend to form a "hyper-ball" [61] and are much hard to partition [29] while ensuring little or no cross-partition vertex transactions.

Mixing concurrency control schemes have been explored before in the context of transaction processing in RDBMS [28, 49, 26] where schedulers that combine two or more CC schemes were designed. For example in real-time systems, 2PL is used for the transactions that must be answered in a timely manner, otherwise the system uses OCC [26]. However all these approaches employ *serializable graph testing* to ensure the correct interaction between multiple (e.g., 2PL and OCC) schedulers. This hurts scalability and throughput since testing serializable graph is very expensive. Our approach does not require additional mechanism to maintain the correctness between two different transaction schedulers.

Lastly, note that we have already reviewed the most closely related work on different schedulers and parallel processing models for graph analytics in Sections 2 and 4.2.

8. CONCLUSION AND FUTURE WORK

We introduce a new design for fine grained parallelism using synchronous parallel processing for graph analytics. By exploring the particular properties in large scale free graphs, we designed and implemented the HSync scheduler that shows excellent throughput and scalability for processing vertex transactions. HSync integrates 2PL with OCC, and uses 2PL to schedule vertex transactions from high degree vertices to avoid aborting them, and uses OCC to schedule vertex transactions from low degree vertices to reduce the overall overheads they may introduce to the system. A careful analysis and design show that the interaction between the two types of schedulers in HSync lead to correct results. Experimental evaluation confirms the advantage of HSync over other approaches.

As for future work, it is interesting to explore how to utilize the new hardware, specially hardware transactional memory (HTM), non-volatile random-access memory (NVRAM) and remote direct memory access (RDMA) for even better parallelism. Our focus here is in-memory multi-core architecture on a single node, but it is possible to extend our hybrid scheduler to a distributed in-memory cluster [11, 60] with distributed transaction processing [12, 62, 5] on top of fast network infrastructures like InfiniBand and RoCE (RDMA). In principle, distributed schedulers, like distributed 2PL and distributed OCC can be combined together in a similar fashion to derive a distributed version of HSync. Nevertheless, there are still significant research challenges as how to combine two distributed schedulers safely to satisfy our aforementioned necessary and sufficient condition to achieve conflict serializability, i.e., satisfying commit order-preserving.

Acknowledgments

The authors thank the helpful comments from the anonymous reviewers. The work was supported by grant of Research Grants Council of the Hong Kong SAR, China No. 14209314, The Chinese University of Hong Kong Direct Grant No. 4055048. Feifei Li was supported in part by NSF grants 1251019 and 1302663. Feifei Li was also supported in part by NSFC grant 61428204. We also thank the generous gift from AWS Cloud Credits for Research from Amazon.

9. REFERENCES

[1] R. Angles and C. Gutierrez. Survey of graph database models. *ACM Comput. Surv.*, 40(1):1:1–1:39, Feb. 2008.

[2] J. Bennett, S. Lanning, and Netflix. The Netflix prize. KDD Cup and Workshop, 2007.

[3] P. A. Bernstein, V. Hadzilacos, and N. Goodman. *Concurrency Control and Recovery in Database Systems*. Addison-Wesley, 1987.

[4] R. Chen, J. Shi, Y. Chen, and H. Chen. Powerlyra: Differentiated graph computation and partitioning on skewed graphs. *EuroSys '15*, pp. 1:1–1:15, 2015.

[5] Y. Chen, X. Wei, J. Shi, R. Chen, and H. Chen. Fast and general distributed transactions using rdma and htm. *EuroSys '16*, page to appear, 2016.

[6] A. Clauset, C. R. Shalizi, and M. E. J. Newman. Power-law distributions in empirical data. *SIAM Rev.*, 51(4):661–703, Nov. 2009.

[7] T. David, R. Guerraoui, and V. Trigonakis. Everything you always wanted to know about synchronization but were afraid to ask. *SOSP '13*, pp. 33–48, 2013.

[8] J. Dean and S. Ghemawat. Mapreduce: Simplified data processing on large clusters. *Commun. ACM*, 51(1):107–113, Jan. 2008.

[9] C. Diaconu, C. Freedman, E. Ismert, P.-A. Larson, P. Mittal, R. Stonecipher, N. Verma, and M. Zwilling. Hekaton: Sql server's memory-optimized oltp engine. *SIGMOD '13*, pp. 1243–1254, 2013.

[10] S. N. Dorogovtsev, J. F. F. Mendes, and A. N. Samukhin. Structure of growing networks with preferential linking. *Phys. Rev. Lett.*, 85:4633–4636, Nov 2000.

[11] A. Dragojević, D. Narayanan, M. Castro, and O. Hodson. Farm: Fast remote memory. *NSDI '14*, pp. 401–414, Apr. 2014.

[12] A. Dragojević, D. Narayanan, E. B. Nightingale, M. Renzelmann, A. Shamis, A. Badam, and M. Castro. No compromises: Distributed transactions with consistency, availability, and performance. *SOSP '15*, pp. 54–70, 2015.

[13] J. M. Faleiro and D. J. Abadi. Rethinking serializable multiversion concurrency control. *Proc. VLDB Endow.*, 8(11):1190–1201, July 2015.

[14] A. Fekete, D. Liarokapis, E. O'Neil, P. O'Neil, and D. Shasha. Making snapshot isolation serializable. *ACM Trans. Database Syst.*, 30(2):492–528, June 2005.

[15] J. E. Gonzalez, Y. Low, H. Gu, D. Bickson, and C. Guestrin. Powergraph: Distributed graph-parallel computation on natural graphs. *OSDI '12*, pp. 17–30, 2012.

[16] J. Gray and A. Reuter. *Transaction Processing: Concepts and Techniques*. Morgan Kaufmann Publishers Inc., 1st edition, 1992.

[17] M. Grund, P. Cudré-Mauroux, J. Krueger, and H. Plattner. Hybrid graph and relational query processing in main memory. DESWEB '13, pp. 23–24, April 2013.

[18] S. Harizopoulos, D. J. Abadi, S. Madden, and M. Stonebraker. OLTP through the looking glass, and what we found there. *SIGMOD '08*, pp. 981–992, 2008.

[19] B. Iordanov. HyperGraphDB: a generalized graph database. WAIM '10, 2010.

[20] E. P. Jones, D. J. Abadi, and S. Madden. Low overhead concurrency control for partitioned main memory databases. *SIGMOD '10*, pp. 603–614, 2010.

[21] T. Kaler. Chromatic scheduling of dynamic data-graph computations. Master's thesis, Massachusetts Institute of Technology, 2013.

[22] T. Kaler, W. Hasenplaugh, T. B. Schardl, and C. E. Leiserson. Executing dynamic data-graph computations deterministically using chromatic scheduling. SPAA '14, 2014.

[23] Z. Khayyat, K. Awara, A. Alonazi, H. Jamjoom, D. Williams, and P. Kalnis. Mizan: A system for dynamic load balancing in large-scale graph processing. *EuroSys '13*, pp. 169–182, 2013.

[24] A. Kyrola, G. Blelloch, and C. Guestrin. Graphchi: Large-scale graph computation on just a pc. *OSDI '12*, pp. 31–46, 2012.

[25] Y. Labs. http://webscope.sandbox.yahoo.com/catalog.php?datatype=r. [Online; accessed 6-Mar-2016].

[26] K.-Y. Lam, T.-W. Kuo, B. Kao, T. S. Lee, and R. Cheng. Evaluation of concurrency control strategies for mixed soft real-time database systems. *Information Systems*, 27:149, 2002.

[27] P.-A. Larson, S. Blanas, C. Diaconu, C. Freedman, J. M. Patel, and M. Zwilling. High-performance concurrency control mechanisms for main-memory databases. *Proc. VLDB Endow.*, 5(4):298–309, Dec. 2011.

[28] G. Lausen. Concurrency control in database systems: A step towards the integration of optimistic methods and locking. *ACM '82*, pp. 64–68, 1982.

[29] J. Leskovec, K. J. Lang, A. Dasgupta, and M. W. Mahoney. Community structure in large networks: Natural cluster sizes and the absence of large well-defined clusters. *Internet Mathematics*, 6(1):29–123, 2009.

[30] J. Levandoski, D. Lomet, S. Sengupta, R. Stutsman, and R. Wang. High performance transactions in deuteronomy. CIDR '15, January 2015.

[31] J. Levandoski, D. Lomet, S. Sengupta, R. Stutsman, and R. Wang. Multi-version range concurrency control in deuteronomy. *Proc. VLDB Endow.*, 8(13):2146–2157, Sept. 2015.

[32] D. B. Lomet, A. Fekete, R. Wang, and P. Ward. Multi-version concurrency via timestamp range conflict management. ICDE '12, pp. 714–725, 2012.

[33] Y. Low, D. Bickson, J. Gonzalez, C. Guestrin, A. Kyrola, and J. M. Hellerstein. Distributed graphlab: A framework for machine learning and data mining in the cloud. *Proc. VLDB Endow.*, 5(8):716–727, Apr. 2012.

[34] T. Maehara, T. Akiba, Y. Iwata, and K. Kawarabayashi. Computing personalized pagerank quickly by exploiting graph structures. *PVLDB*, 7(12):1023–1034, 2014.

[35] G. Malewicz, M. H. Austern, A. J. Bik, J. C. Dehnert, I. Horn, N. Leiser, and G. Czajkowski. Pregel: A system for large-scale graph processing. *SIGMOD '10*, pp. 135–146, 2010.

[36] Aurelius Inc. http://thinkaurelius.github.io/titan/.

[37] Franz Inc. http://www.franz.com/agraph/allegrograph/.

[38] Neo Technology, Inc. . http://www.neo4j.org/.

[39] Netflix Inc. https://github.com/Netflix/netflix-graph.

[40] Objectivity Inc. http://www.objectivity.com/infinitegraph.

[41] Twitter Inc. https://github.com/twitter/flockdb.

[42] B. Mcmahan and M. Streeter. Delay-tolerant algorithms for asynchronous distributed online learning. *In Z. Ghahramani, M. Welling, C. Cortes, N. Lawrence, and K. Weinberger, editors,* NIPS '14, pp. 2915–2923, 2014.

[43] N. Narula, C. Cutler, E. Kohler, and R. Morris. Phase reconciliation for contended in-memory transactions. *OSDI '14*, pp. 511–524, 2014.

[44] T. Neumann, T. Mühlbauer, and A. Kemper. Fast serializable multi-version concurrency control for main-memory database systems. *SIGMOD '15*, pp. 677–689, 2015.

[45] D. Nguyen, A. Lenharth, and K. Pingali. A lightweight infrastructure for graph analytics. *SOSP '13*, pp. 456–471, 2013.

[46] J. Ousterhout, P. Agrawal, D. Erickson, C. Kozyrakis, J. Leverich, D. Mazières, S. Mitra, A. Narayanan, G. Parulkar, M. Rosenblum, S. M. Rumble, E. Stratmann, and R. Stutsman. The case for RAMClouds: Scalable high-performance storage entirely in dram. *SIGOPS Oper. Syst. Rev.*, 43(4):92–105, Jan. 2010.

[47] I. Pandis, R. Johnson, N. Hardavellas, and A. Ailamaki. Data-oriented transaction execution. *Proc. VLDB Endow.*, 3(1-2):928–939, Sept. 2010.

[48] C. Papadimitriou. *The Theory of Database Concurrency Control*. Computer Science Press, Inc., 1986.

[49] J.-F. Pons and J. F. Vilarem. Mixed concurrency control: Dealing with heterogeneity in distributed database systems. *VLDB '88*, pp. 445–456, 1988.
[50] V. Prabhakaran, M. Wu, X. Weng, F. McSherry, L. Zhou, and M. Haridasan. Managing large graphs on multi-cores with graph awareness. *USENIX ATC '12*, pp. 4–4, 2012.
[51] K. Ren, A. Thomson, and D. J. Abadi. Lightweight locking for main memory database systems. *Proc. VLDB Endow.*, 6(2):145–156, Dec. 2012.
[52] A. Rowstron, D. Narayanan, A. Donnelly, G. O'Shea, and A. Douglas. Nobody ever got fired for using hadoop on a cluster. *HotCDP '12*, pp. 2:1–2:5, 2012.
[53] M. Sadoghi, M. Canim, B. Bhattacharjee, F. Nagel, and K. A. Ross. Reducing database locking contention through multi-version concurrency. *Proc. VLDB Endow.*, 7(13):1331–1342, Aug. 2014.
[54] Z. Shang and J. X. Yu. Catch the wind: Graph workload balancing on cloud. *ICDE '13*, pp. 553–564, 2013.
[55] B. Shao, H. Wang, and Y. Li. Trinity: A distributed graph engine on a memory cloud. *SIGMOD '13*, pp. 505–516, 2013.
[56] M. Stonebraker, S. Madden, D. J. Abadi, S. Harizopoulos, N. Hachem, and P. Helland. The end of an architectural era: (it 's time for a complete rewrite). *VLDB '07*, pp. 1150–1160, 2007.
[57] A. Thomson, T. Diamond, S.-C. Weng, K. Ren, P. Shao, and D. J. Abadi. Calvin: Fast distributed transactions for partitioned database systems. *SIGMOD '12*, pp. 1–12, 2012.
[58] S. Tu, W. Zheng, E. Kohler, B. Liskov, and S. Madden. Speedy transactions in multicore in-memory databases. SOSP '13, pp. 18–32, 2013.
[59] G. Wang, W. Xie, A. Demers, and J. Gehrke. Asynchronous large-scale graph processing made easy. *CIDR '13*, 2013.
[60] Y. Wang, L. Zhang, J. Tan, M. Li, Y. Gao, X. Guerin, X. Meng, and S. Meng. Hydradb: A resilient rdma-driven key-value middleware for in-memory cluster computing. *SC '15*, pp. 22:1–22:11, 2015.
[61] D. J. Watts and S. H. Strogatz. Collective dynamics of 'small-world' networks. *Nature*, 393(6684):409–10, 1998.
[62] X. Wei, J. Shi, Y. Chen, R. Chen, and H. Chen. Fast in-memory transaction processing using rdma and htm. *SOSP '15*, pp. 87–104, 2015.
[63] G. Weikum and G. Vossen. *Transactional Information Systems: Theory, Algorithms, and the Practice of Concurrency Control and Recovery*. Morgan Kaufmann Publishers Inc., 2001.
[64] R. Xin, J. Gonzalez, M. Franklin, and I. Stoica. Graphx: A resilient distributed graph system on spark. *CIDR '13*, 2013.
[65] S. Yang, X. Yan, B. Zong, and A. Khan. Towards effective partition management for large graphs. *SIGMOD '12*, pp. 517–528, 2012.
[66] M. Zaharia, M. Chowdhury, T. Das, A. Dave, J. Ma, M. McCauly, M. J. Franklin, S. Shenker, and I. Stoica. Resilient distributed datasets: A fault-tolerant abstraction for in-memory cluster computing. NSDI '12, pp. 15–28, 2012.
[67] H. Zhang, G. Chen, B. C. Ooi, K. L. Tan, and M. Zhang. In-memory big data management and processing: A survey. *IEEE Transactions on Knowledge and Data Engineering*, 27(7):1920–1948, 2015.
[68] Y. Zhang, Q. Gao, L. Gao, and C. Wang. Priter: A distributed framework for prioritized iterative computations. *SOCC '11*, pp. 13:1–13:14, 2011.
[69] M. Zinkevich, J. Langford, and A. J. Smola. Slow learners are fast. NIPS '09, pp. 2331–2339, 2009.

APPENDIX

A. BACKGROUND ON TRANSACTION PROCESSING

In this section, we briefly introduce the basic concepts of transaction processing. We focus on the main intuitions without introducing too many technical details. For readers who are interested in an in-depth discussion on the theory of transaction processing, please refer to excellent discussion on this topic from the following books [3, 16, 48].

We denote the basic unit of a database as a data element. It could be a tuple in a relational database, a vertex in a graph database, and a key-value pair in a key-value database. Each transaction works by reading and writing data elements. It may read and write several data elements. After a number of reads and writes, the last operation of each transaction is either *abort* or *commit*. If a transaction aborts, the transaction must have no side effect on the database at all, like the transaction had never been submitted. On the other hand, if a transaction commits, all actions in the transaction must be executed and reflected by the database.

When transactions execute concurrently, their reads and writes may interleave and interfere. There are several standards to define whether a given execution is considered correct or not. A popular isolation level is serializability. Executing transactions serially (one after another) is considered correct because there is interleaving of actions from different transactions, hence, transactions do not interfere with each other at all. And all schedules that are equivalent to a serial ordering of transactions are considered correct too.

Formally, let T be a set of transactions, $T = \{t(1), t(2), \cdots\}$. A history for T is known when all transactions in T commit, and a serial history is a history in which $t(i) < t(j)$ or $t(j) < t(i)$ for $i \neq j$. By $t(i) < t(j)$ it means that all reads/writes for a transaction $t(i)$ are executed before all reads/writes of $t(j)$. A history is called serializable if it is equivalent to a serial history s' ($s \approx s'$). Several serializability variations are defined. Among them, conflict serializability is defined on the notion of conflict, where two operations p in $t(i)$ and q in $t(j)$ are *conflict*, for $i \neq j$, if both p and q access the same data element, and at least one of them is write. For any two conflict operations p and q and a history s, we say $p <_s q$ if p proceeds q in s, and q *depends on* p (for history s) in this case.

A history s is *conflict serializable* if there exits a serial history s' such that s and s' contain same set of operations and for any two conflict operations p and q, either $p <_s q$ and $p <_{s'} q$, or $q <_s p$ and $q <_{s'} p$. The class of conflict serializable schedules is denoted as *CSR*. For simplicity, we denote transaction $t(j)$ *depends on* $t(i)$ if one of $t(j)$'s operations depends on one of $t(i)$'s operations.

If each transaction is represented as a vertex in a graph, then the dependency relationships can be modeled as directed edges among these vertices. The graph is called *serializable graph*. A schedule of these transactions satisfies *(conflict) serializable* if and only if the corresponding serializable graph is *acyclic*.

Based on CSR, we introduce a subclass of CSR, denoted as *COCSR* for *commit order-preserving* conflict serializable. COCSR says, a history s is $\approx$ to a serial history s' with the additional restriction such that for any two different transactions $t(i)$ and $t(j)$, if $t(i) < t(j)$ in s' then $ct(i) < ct(j)$ in s (and s'), where $ct(i)$ denotes the time $t(i)$ commits, and $ct(i) < ct(j)$ means $t(i)$ commits before $t(j)$ commits. The commit time $ct(i)$ for transaction $t(i)$ is defined as the time when all parties reach a consensus that it shall commit. In other words, before commit time the transaction could commit or abort (depending on the system status, user inputs, and the states of other transactions), and after the commit time it will not be aborted (regardless other transactions' operations).

We note that *commit order preserving* is a sufficient (but not necessary) condition for CSR. If all transactions obey the *commit order preserving* rule, the conflict relationship is ordered by the $ct(\cdot)$s of all transactions, which is a total order, therefore the serializable graph is acyclic (so the schedule satisfies CSR).

B. PROOF OF THEOREM 1

We show that our hybrid approach in Algorithms 1, 2, 3 follows the COCSR, thus follows CSR. We begin with the following lemma.

Lemma 2.1: *Consider two committed transactions $t(i)$ and $t(j)$ in HSync, $ct(i) < ct(j)$ if $t(j)$ depends on $t(i)$.* □

PROOF. For simplicity, we assume $t(i)$ accesses vertex v before $t(j)$ (and at least one of them writes v). We denote the lock on v as L_v.

By the definition of *commit time*, a BIG transaction commits when it just enters *TX-COMMIT-B* and a SMALL transaction commits when it passes validation and is ready to write D[] (line 21 in Algorithm 3).

- Case-1: Both $t(i)$ and $t(j)$ are BIG transactions. They cannot acquire L_v simultaneously. Since $t(j)$ depends on $t(i)$, $t(j)$ acquires L_v after $t(i)$. Thus $t(j)$ must wait until $t(i)$ releases L_v. In other words, when $t(j)$ is still in its growing phase, $t(i)$ is already in its shrinking phase. Therefore $ct(i) < ct(j)$.
- Case-2: $t(i)$ is a BIG transaction whereas $t(j)$ is a SMALL transaction. In the validation phase of $t(j)$, if L_v can be acquired by $t(j)$, it means that $t(i)$ has released L_v so it is in its shrinking phase. Therefore $ct(i) < ct(j)$ since $t(j)$ has not started to commit yet. Otherwise, $t(j)$ cannot pass validation and commit. It violates our assumption that both of them had been committed.
- Case-3: $t(i)$ is a SMALL transaction. $t(j)$ could be BIG or SMALL. Note that at least one of $t(i)$ and $t(j)$ writes to v.
  - If $t(i)$ writes to v, at this time $t(i)$ shall already been committed which indicates $ct(i) < ct(j)$. Otherwise $t(j)$ is not able to observe this modification as $t(i)$ has not committed, which contradicts with the assumption that $t(j)$ depends on $t(i)$.
  - If $t(i)$ reads from v and $t(j)$ writes to v. Suppose $ct(i) > ct(j)$. Therefore $t(j)$ successfully acquires the lock and writes to v before $t(i)$ commits. $t(i)$ will never have a chance to pass validation and commit. This violates our assumption that both of them had successfully committed. Thus $ct(i) < ct(j)$.

Therefore we prove the Lemma 2.1. □

Since CO is a sufficient condition of CSR, this completes the proof of Theorem 1.

C. EFFICIENT HYBRID SCHEDULER

C.1 Performance Consideration

We consider a problem that the transactions are scheduled by two schedulers. We assume that scheduler S_h is responsible to process transactions when conflicts are common and scheduler S_l is responsible for transactions that are not likely to conflict. Besides the two schedulers, an additional machinery is used to make sure the combination of them produces serializable schedules.

We emphasize that the coordination cost must be taken into consideration. If not, the coordinator itself may simply implement a standalone 2PL so that it ensures serializability anyway regardless how S_h and S_l behave. We highlight three general necessary conditions for efficient main memory computing, which are listed below.

Rule 1: No memory hot-spot. Ensuring strong locality in modern CPU architecture often hinders the scalability and efficiency of implementing a centralized component. For example in the experiments of memory latency [7], process only needs 5 to 44 cycles to access memory address in CPU's cache line, but 355 cycles for any data that are not found in cache. The slowest case is to access data

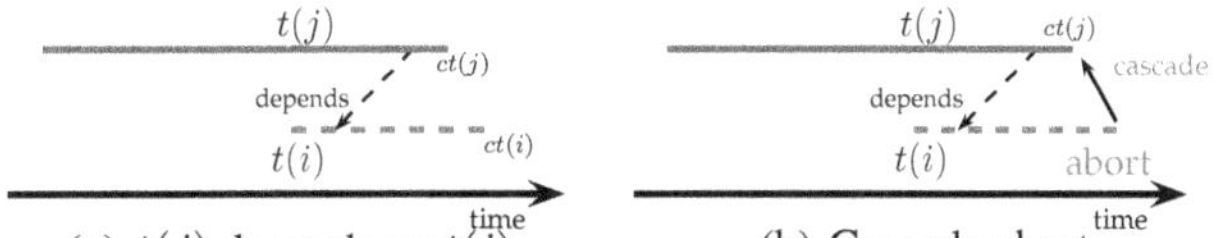

(a) $t(j)$ depends on $t(i)$ (b) Cascade abort

Figure 17: Violating commit order: S_h schedules t(j) and S_l schedules t(i).

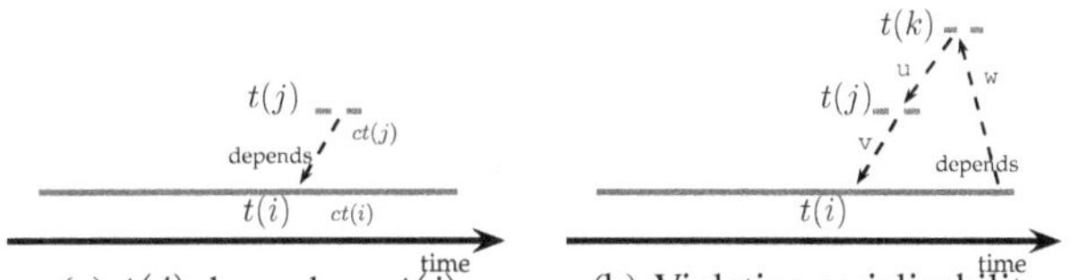

(a) $t(j)$ depends on $t(i)$ (b) Violating serializability

Figure 18: Violating commit order: S_h schedules t(i) and S_l schedules t(j).

that had just been modified by other CPUs (dirty access), which is as slow as 492 cycles.

Centralized memory access, or informally speaking, memory **hot-spot**, is a small area of memory that is frequently and repeatedly accessed by different CPUs. Having such hot-spot makes almost all access to it dirty. This phenomena is called cache thrashing. Memory hot-spot should be avoided if possible.

Rule 2: Linear overhead. In hard-disk based systems, disk access cost dominates the overall execution time. CPU and main memory operations are almost free. Hence, the amount of these main memory operations spent on transaction processing can be superliner to the size of data items involved in the transactions if needed. However in a main memory database, CPU and memory operations become dominating. It demands transaction processing schedulers to spend at most linear time, or even sub-linear time to the number of data items in a transaction.

Rule 3: No sacrifice for S_h. The hybrid scheduler should not abort S_h if possible. The reason is straightforward, transactions executed under scheduler S_h have a exponentially larger size like millions. Aborting these transactions are not worthwhile.

C.2 Key to Success: Commitment Order

We already showed CO is a sufficient condition for CSR and even COCSR in Section B. We will show, CO is also a necessary condition for an efficient hybrid scheduler. In other words, in order to keep the transactions CSR and do not break the aforementioned rules, *the coordination must obey commit order.*

We prove by contradiction. Assume there are two transactions $t(i)$ and $t(j)$, $t(j)$ depends on $t(i)$ and $ct(i) > ct(j)$, which means they do not satisfy CO.

- Suppose $t(j)$ is scheduled by S_h, whereas $t(i)$ is scheduled by S_l, as illustrated in Fig. 17(a). After $t(j)$ commits, if $t(i)$ aborts, then $t(j)$ may access some "dirty" values from $t(i)$, which violates the atomic property of transaction, and may cause cascade abort like shown Fig. 17(b).
- Next, suppose $t(i)$ is scheduled by S_h, whereas $t(j)$ is scheduled by S_l, as shown in Fig. 18(a). As illustrated in Fig. 18(b), after $t(j)$ commits, a transaction $t(k)$, that depends on $t(j)$ via accessing a value u, commits. However, $t(i)$ may depend on $t(k)$ via accessing a value w, which causes a cycle in the conflict graph. This violates CSR.

We show why such cycle is unavoidable. Firstly, when $t(k)$ tries to access the value u that $t(j)$ just committed, $t(k)$ is completely

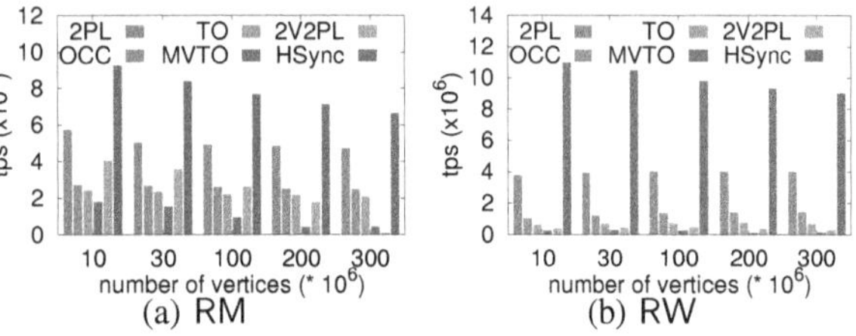

Figure 19: Synthetic graph: vary the number of vertices.

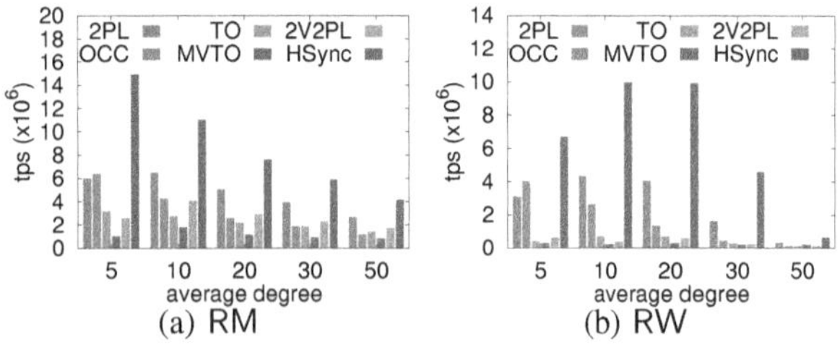

Figure 20: Synthetic graph: vary degree.

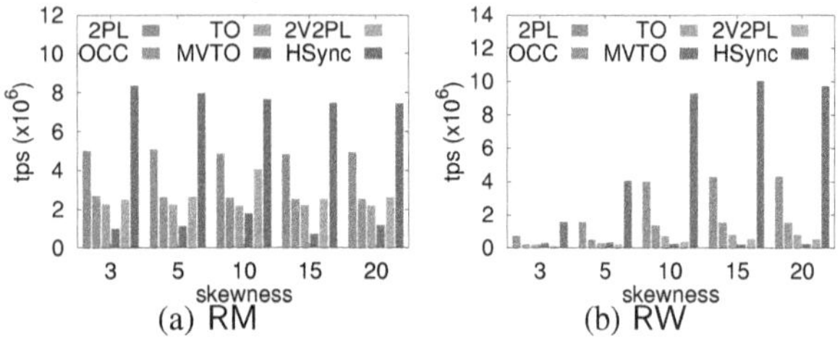

Figure 21: Synthetic graph: vary skewness.

unaware of $t(i)$. It cannot access the metadata of $t(i)$ directly, otherwise it violates the "no memory hot-spot" **Rule 1**. Neither can the liveness of $t(i)$ be stored in places associated with $t(j)$ or u, otherwise when $t(i)$ commits, it has to update its liveness flags there. Since the number of $t(i)$'s operations could be large, the number of such liveness flags could be even larger, this violates the "linear work" **Rule 2**. Thus $t(k)$ cannot infer whether the current value u's previous owner $t(j)$ has active dependencies or not, so with no information, it has to access u and causes conflict with $t(j)$. For the same reason, there is nothing that can prevent $t(k)$ to commit. After $t(k)$ has committed, it is entirely possible that $t(i)$ has to access a value w that $t(k)$ just committed. Allowing $t(i)$'s such access will violate the serializability. Denying it will force $t(i)$ to abort, or force both $t(j)$ and $t(k)$ to abort. For the later case, it is still possible that other transactions scheduled by S_h may have just accessed values updated by $t(j)$ or $t(k)$, hence had to abort. Therefore it violates **Rule 3**.

D. ADDITIONAL EXPERIMENTS

Synthetic Data. We also generate synthetic graph datasets to test different approaches. Given a vertex size V and an average degree D, we generate a graph G using the preference attachment method in [10]. Another parameter A (the "power-law-ness") is also used in the graph generation process. The smaller the value of $\frac{A}{D}$ is, the smaller the fraction of high-degree vertices is in the graph G. The range and default value of all parameters are shown in Table 4. For all experiments over synthetic graphs, we set $\tau = 10^3$.

Parameter	Range	Default
Size of V ($\times 10^6$)	10, 30, 100, 200, 300	100
Average degree D	5, 10, 20, 30, 50	20
Skew-ness A	3, 5, 10, 15, 20	10

Table 4: The parameters of synthetic data.

We measured the performance (tps, transactions per second) of different schedulers by varying the values of these parameters. In Fig. 19 we vary the number of vertices. HSync outperforms other schedulers regardless the size of the graphs for both RM and RW workloads. As the graph becomes bigger, the performance degenerates slightly due to the increasing density of the graph, which inherently limits the concurrency.

In Fig. 20 we vary the average degree of the graph. We note as the degree increases the amount of work in a transactions increases. When the average degree is small, OCC outperforms the 2PL since transactions conflicts are less likely to happen. Our scheduler HSync achieves the best performance among all cases.

In Fig. 21 we vary the skewness. Clearly, the performance gap between HSync and other schedulers increases as the graph degree distribution becomes skewer. It is contributed by the skewness-aware hybrid approach which schedules vertex transactions based on the degree of the vertex with different schedulers.

HSync in GraphLab. Lastly, we implemented HSync in GraphLab using GraphLab's communication primitives, to show that existing systems can also benefit from fine-grained parallelism using synchronous parallel processing with a scheduler like HSync. It is worth noting that the GraphLab is built on message passing, even in single computer mode, which limits the performance of good schedulers, since a scheduler needs to take a message round trip to verify before commitment.

In Fig. 22 we show how the training error reduces over time, while executing ALS on Netflix data. Clearly, the default fine-grained parallelism synchronous parallel processing in GraphLab has the worst performance: it converges much slower than both asynchronous and BSP approaches. This is due the ineffective scheduler it has used. It confirms the observations from GraphLab developers that fine-grained parallelism is not as fast as other engines. However, once using our hybrid scheduler HSync, fine-grained parallelism has outperformed all other engines in GraphLab including the asynchronous engine.

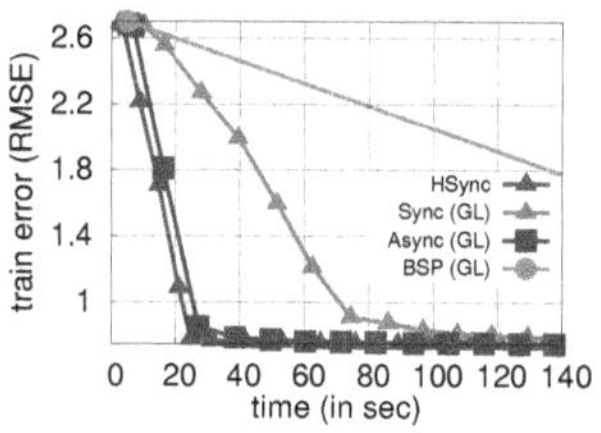

Figure 22: ALS in GraphLab

Hybrid Pulling/Pushing for I/O-Efficient Distributed and Iterative Graph Computing

Zhigang Wang†, Yu Gu†, Yubin Bao†, Ge Yu†, Jeffrey Xu Yu‡
†Northeastern University, China
‡The Chinese University of Hong Kong, China
wangzhiganglab@gmail.com, {guyu, baoyubin, yuge}@ise.neu.edu.cn, yu@se.cuhk.edu.hk

ABSTRACT

Billion-node graphs are rapidly growing in size in many applications such as online social networks. Most graph algorithms generate a large number of messages during iterative computations. Vertex-centric distributed systems usually store graph data and message data on disk to improve scalability. Currently, these distributed systems with disk-resident data take a push-based approach to handle messages. This works well if few messages reside on disk. Otherwise, it is I/O-inefficient due to expensive random writes. By contrast, the existing memory-resident pull-based approach individually pulls messages for each vertex on demand. Although it can be used to avoid disk operations regarding messages, expensive I/O costs are incurred by random and frequent access to vertices.

This paper proposes a hybrid solution to support switching between push and pull adaptively, to obtain optimal performance for distributed systems with disk-resident data in different scenarios. We first employ a new block-centric technique (b-pull) to improve the I/O-performance of pulling messages, although the iterative computation is vertex-centric. I/O costs of data accesses are shifted from the receiver side where messages are written/read by push to the sender side where graph data are read by b-pull. Graph data are organized by clustering vertices and edges to achieve high I/O-efficiency in b-pull. Second, we design a seamless switching mechanism and a prominent performance prediction method to guarantee efficiency when switching between push and b-pull. We conduct extensive performance studies to confirm the effectiveness of our proposals over existing up-to-date solutions using a broad spectrum of real-world graphs.

Keywords

I/O-Efficient; Distributed Graph Computing; Push; Pull

1. INTRODUCTION

The proliferation of popular online social networks such as Facebook and Twitter largely depends on graph analysis over billion-node graphs. In order to handle large graphs, many systems have been developed. *Pregel* [17] by Google as one of the early distributed systems takes a vertex-centric method based on the Bulk-Synchronous-Parallel [26] model (*BSP*) to process graph analysis jobs. *Pregel* is a Master-Slave framework (Fig. 1), where Master divides a job into several tasks assigned onto computational nodes, namely Slaves, in a cluster. Typically, tasks load graph data from a distributed file system and then partition data among themselves. Afterwards, they start computation in parallel through a set of iterations, called "supersteps". The workload in one superstep consists of local computation (i.e., invoking a user-defined function for each vertex) and exchanging intermediate results (i.e., messages). One computational node is referred to as a sender/receiver side when the task on it is sending/receiving messages. Without loss of generality, we assume that each node runs only one task. This paper thereby discusses communication among nodes, instead of tasks. Two consecutive supersteps are separated by a synchronization barrier to guarantee that the message exchange work is finished.

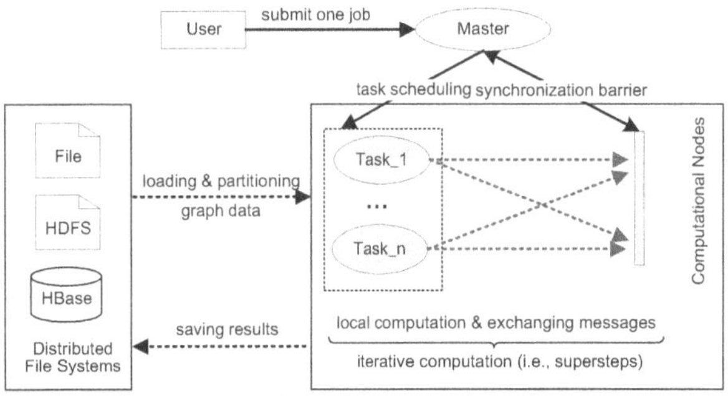

Figure 1: Illustration of iterative graph processing

The framework of *Pregel* has been driving much of the research on enhancing its performance, including graph partitioning [8, 23], communication [8, 20, 22], and convergence [25, 31]. This paper focuses on performing graph analysis on a cluster I/O-efficiently, as the memory resource of a given cluster can be easily exhausted due to two main factors. One is the drastically growing rate of real-world graph volumes, e.g., there are over 4.75 billion content items shared on Facebook daily. The other one is the increased message scale in proportion to the graph volume. Adding new physical nodes can alleviate memory pressure, but is not always feasible. The issue we investigate is to find an I/O-efficient way to handle a large number of messages received on every computational node.

Motivation: The fastest way to handle messages received is to keep them in memory. Take *Giraph* [2], an open-source *Pregel* implementation, as an example. In computing PageRank and the single source shortest path (SSSP) [17] over a web graph wiki with 5.7 million vertices and 130 million edges (disk storage size of 1GB) on a cluster of 5 computational nodes, it needs 10 times more memory than the original graph size to guarantee that the overall runtime will not increase rapidly due to disk I/O costs of messages and

SIGMOD'16, June 26-July 01, 2016, San Francisco, CA, USA
© 2016 ACM. ISBN 978-1-4503-3531-7/16/06...$15.00
DOI: http://dx.doi.org/10.1145/2882903.2882938

memory contention. Otherwise, the performance will drop significantly. As an indication of how *Giraph* scales when graph data and partial message data reside on disk, Fig. 2 shows the overall runtime and the percentage of messages on disk for PageRank (10 supersteps) and SSSP (converging after 284 supersteps). We vary the message buffer size from mem (all messages are kept in memory) down to 0.5 million on a computational node, while the percentage of messages that need to be stored on disk increases from 0% to 98%. As illustrated, the computing time increases from 130 to 510 seconds for PageRank, and from 490 to 780 seconds for SSSP, which confirms the expensive I/O cost incurred by messages. In particular the runtime of PageRank has largely increased from 130 to 160 seconds even though only 4% of messages reside on disk.

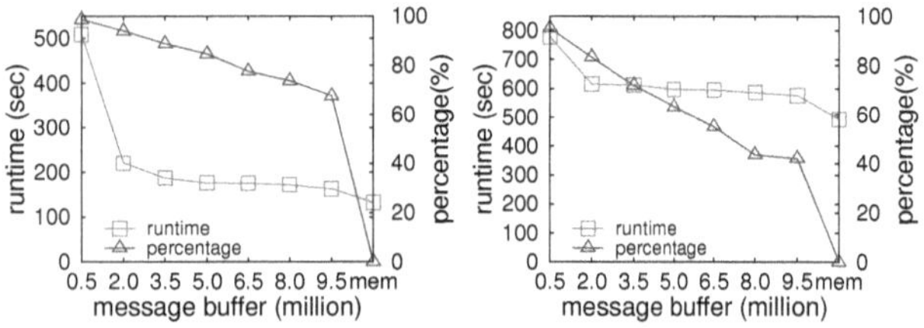

(a) PageRank (b) SSSP

Figure 2: The impact of messages (over wiki)

Problem Analysis: Almost all existing distributed graph systems [2, 20, 3], like *Giraph*, take a push-based approach to handle messages by pushing them from source vertices at the sender side to destination vertices at the receiver side. The push-based approach is efficient if most messages are kept in memory because every source vertex will be accessed only once in one superstep. However, it is most likely that the receivers need to store messages on disk, since the message volume can be large. That is I/O-inefficient as shown in Fig. 2, due to the poor temporal locality of messages among destination vertices, caused by writing data randomly. Another preferred approach is to pull messages from source vertices on demand when destination vertices are updating themselves. A receiver avoids writing/reading messages, as they can be consumed immediately after being generated. However, one source vertex may be read multiple times if it is the neighbor of several destination vertices. Since the graph volume is rapidly growing, graph data usually reside on disk. Thus, the I/O cost of reading vertices is still considerable, and may offset that of accessing messages in push, especially when the number of messages is decreasing during iterations. In fact, existing distributed pull-based systems such as *Seraph* [30] and *GraphLab PowerGraph* [8] are designed for memory-resident computation, and no special optimizations are considered for speeding up I/O access.

Obviously, push and pull are suitable for different scenarios, which is determined by the number of messages. However, neither of them works best in all cases. That motivates us to combine the two approaches and design a hybrid solution which supports switching between them adaptively. However, this is a non-trivial task due to the following two reasons. First, for current pull-based approaches, each destination vertex individually sends pull requests for desired messages. The frequent and random access to source vertices may cost more than writing/reading messages in push based on our test. Thus, directly combining them is not cost effective. Second, in order to gain optimal performance, some important issues such as the proper switching time and effective performance prediction model need to be explored, which are especially difficult in a complex distributed system.

Our Contributions: In order to solve the above two challenges, we propose a novel hybrid solution, called hybrid, to implement an I/O-efficient and adaptive message exchange mechanism for disk-resident graph computations.

First, we design a block-centric pull approach called b-pull to optimize the cost of accessing source vertices when pulling messages. Specifically, in b-pull, vertices in one block can send a block identifier to pull messages to be generated and sent for them, instead of sending requests for each one individually. b-pull shifts I/O costs of data accesses from messages to vertices. Recall that in a push-based system, messages received are from other computational nodes and are for different vertices. Their distribution might be random and not have patterns to follow. It is difficult to cluster messages received without high overhead. A similar problem also occurs for existing pull-based approaches, but data accessed are source vertices. However, in b-pull, graph data can be organized in an efficient way to reduce the I/O cost by clustering source vertices and edges based on the requested block.

Second, we propose a seamless switching mechanism by first decoupling push and b-pull, and then reorganizing the decoupled functions reasonably, to reduce extra switching costs. Additionally, a prominent performance metric is given through deeply analyzing the total communication and I/O costs for push and b-pull. We should stress that hybrid is not a replacement for our b-pull and existing push approaches. Instead, it always tries to choose a profitable one between them to run graph algorithms during iterations, although b-pull outperforms push in many cases. To this end, it employs b-pull and push as core components and builds a feasible switching scheme on top of them.

The major contributions of our work are summarized as below.

- We propose a new pull-based approach called b-pull which uses a block-centric mechanism to pull messages, in order to reduce the high I/O cost of dealing with messages received in iterations when the memory is not sufficient. A new data structure is designed to separate vertices and edges into different blocks. Furthermore, edges in one block can be clustered well to improve the locality when accessing vertices.

- We present a hybrid solution for handling iterative computations I/O-efficiently, by combining push and b-pull and switching between them adaptively. hybrid obtains optimal performance in different scenarios due to the seamless switching mechanism and the prominent performance prediction.

- We implement our proposals in a prototype system called *HybridGraph*, and then conduct experimental studies to confirm the efficiency of hybrid, in comparison with two typical push-based systems called *Giraph* and *MOCgraph*, and a well-known pull-based system *GraphLab PowerGraph*.

Paper Organization: The remainder of this paper is organized as follows. Section 2 discusses the related work. Section 3 introduces the overview of push, pull, and hybrid. Section 4 describes the b-pull technique and Section 5 presents the hybrid solution after analyzing the performance of push and b-pull. Section 6 reports our experimental studies. We conclude this work in Section 7.

2. RELATED WORK

A lot of representative distributed graph systems have been developed and we summarize them in Table 1.

Push-based Systems: As we all know, iterative graph algorithms generate a large number of messages [32], and it is a non-trivial task to efficiently manage them on external storage. Among existing distributed systems with disk-resident data, one policy employed by *PEGASUS* and *Gbase*, is to directly access messages using a distributed file system underneath, e.g., HDFS, for fault tolerance, leading to an expensive I/O-cost. Bu et al. design a Mapper Input Cache to keep data on local disks instead of HDFS for optimization, which reduces the runtime by nearly 20% based on their experiments [5]. Besides, *Giraph* manages messages on local disks if it cannot hold all of them in memory. Although the local disk has a superior performance, it is still far from ideal. As reported by Zhou et al. [32], for PageRank over their largest graph dataset, the runtime of *Giraph* with memory capacity of 1.5GB×46 is roughly 6 times more than that with memory capacity of 4GB×46, due to local I/O costs. In addition, *Pregelix* exploits "join" as used in the database community to model the matching operation between messages and vertices, and utilizes a B-tree to improve the disk performance, but the effect is limited for message-intensive algorithms, like PageRank.

Table 1: Distributed Graph Systems

Name	PUSH	PULL	DISK
Giraph++ [25]	✓		
Blogel [27]	✓		
GiraphX [24]	✓		
GPS [20]	✓		
GRE [29]	✓		
Mizan [15]	✓		
Naiad [18]	✓		
Pregel [17]	✓		
Trinity [22]	✓		
Faunus [1]	✓		✓
PEGASUS [14]	✓		✓
Gbase [13]	✓		✓
Giraph [2]	✓		✓
GraphX [9]	✓		✓
MOCgraph [32]	✓		✓
Hama [3]	✓		✓
Pregelix [4]	✓		✓
Surfer [6]	✓		✓
Chronos [10]	✓	✓	
Kineograph [7]	✓	✓	
Pregel+ [28]	✓	✓	
Kylin [11]		✓	
Seraph [30]		✓	
GraphLab PowerGraph [16, 8]		✓	
LFGraph [12]		✓	

Another preferred solution is to reduce the number of messages resident on disk. *Giraph* uses a Combiner to combine messages sent to the same vertex into a single one, which decreases the storage requirements at the receiver side. Furthermore, *MOCgraph* online processes messages received in a streaming manner, instead of keeping them until the next superstep. Combiner inherently requires messages involved in combining to be resident in memory. For online computing in *MOCgraph*, vertices also should be kept in memory. However, it is difficult to satisfy these requirements when processing extremely large graphs. In addition, neither of them works when messages are not commutative.

Many push-based systems also keep graph data on disk during iterations to improve the scalability. *Giraph* exchanges data between memory and disk using the LRU replacement strategy, but the poor locality of data accesses limits the effectiveness. *Hama* records the edge offset of each vertex to avoid loading unnecessary edges. It is suboptimal when all edges are required, such as PageRank. *GraphX* partitions vertices and edges into collections independently to process them in parallel, leading to many-to-many associations among collections. This data structure works well in memory, but is I/O-inefficient if collections reside on disk. The reason is that when performing "join" at an edge collection ("join site"), vertices from many vertex collections may be written/read on disk when the memory cannot hold them. *MOCgraph* organizes graph data by a hot-aware re-partitioning method, to keep more high in-degree vertices in memory for its online computing technique. Apparently, all of them ignore the cost of accessing vertex values, since vertex-centric push-based systems access each vertex once in a superstep. However, that is a problem in pull-based systems, and we design a new block-centric data structure to address it. Apart from the vertex-centric model, *Giraph++* and *Bolgel* propose a sub-graph centric model to accelerate graph analysis, as vertices in the same subgraph directly communicate with each other and can be updated by existing sequential algorithms. This is complement to our work and can be implemented when the partition structure on each computational node is opened up to users.

Pull-based Systems: As listed in Table 1, there exist several pull-based systems only designed for memory-resident computations. In these systems, destination vertices need to send pull requests to source vertices individually, which consumes much traffic even though some requests can be combined [7, 30, 28, 11]. *GraphLab PowerGraph* employs a vertex-cut mechanism to reduce the network cost of sending requests and transferring messages at the expense of incurring the space cost of vertex replications. Also, in these pull-based systems, reading a source vertex may be performed multiple times if it is the neighbor of different destination vertices, which is not free [10]. Since none of these systems considers the I/O cost, adapting their techniques for computations of disk-resident vertices may cause serious I/O-inefficiency. Finally, *Chronos*, *Kineograph*, and *Pregel+* support push and pull meanwhile, but either push or pull is used for a given algorithm. However, the hybrid solution presented in this paper can switch between push and our block-centric pull (b-pull) adaptively during iterations to obtain optimal performance. Our b-pull focuses on improving the I/O efficiency of reading vertices, and optimizing the communication cost of sending pull requests and exchanging messages. We stress that the push-based system *Blogel* supports block-level communication to save network resources, but only for specific algorithms like connected components. This is because a block is modeled as a sub-graph and vertices within it must share the same value, which makes it unsuitable for many algorithms, like PageRank and SSSP. *Blogel* and b-pull are technically orthogonal and have totally different implementation mechanisms.

3. OVERVIEW OF push, pull, AND hybrid

We model a graph as a directed graph $G = (V, E)$, where V is a set of vertices and E is a set of edges (pairs of vertices). For an edge (u, v), u is the source vertex denoted as svertex, and v is the destination vertex denoted as dvertex. The in-neighbors of u is a set of vertices that have an edge linking to u, and its out-neighbors is a set of vertices that u has an edge to link. The in-degree/out-degree of u is the number of its in-neighbors/out-neighbors. We state that the memory resource is limited if it cannot store messages entirely. In this case, the limited memory resource is supposed to be allocated for more I/O-inefficient messages in a high priority instead of graph data [32]. This paper thereby assumes graph data (vertices and edges) reside on disk. In the following, we introduce the logic of push-based and pull-based approaches, and then give an overview performance analysis for push, pull, and our hybrid.

Push: *Giraph* [2], an open-source implementation of *Pregel*, takes a vertex-centric mechanism for iterative graph analysis in a sequence of supersteps. In one superstep, every vertex u in G computes a user-defined function in parallel. We denote this function as compute(). For simplicity, let $M_I(u)$ and $M_O(u)$ denote the messages received and sent to/from u, then the compute is as follows and an implementation of PageRank is given in Fig. 3(a).

$$\text{compute}(u^i, M_I^i(u)) \rightarrow (u^{i+1}, M_O^{i+1}(u)) \tag{1}$$

Specifically, in the i-th superstep, first, u gets a message iterator msgs of $M_I^i(u)$ which keeps messages received from in-neighbors in the $(i$-$1)$-th superstep, and then initializes a sum to zero (Lines 2-3). Second, after computing the sum of message values (Lines 4-5), its value is updated from u^i to u^{i+1} (Lines 6-8). Third, u sends the new updated value divided by its out-degree as messages $M_O^{i+1}(u)$ to all its out-neighbors (Lines 9-11). M_O^{i+1} for all vertices are the basis to form M_I^{i+1} in superstep $(i$+$1)$. Finally, u will be inactive by *voting to halt* if the number of supersteps has reached to the maximal value maxNum. Note that an inactive vertex will become active again when it receives messages from its in-neighbors. We call this a push-based approach for the following two reasons. First, svertices send messages voluntarily. Second, messages are already available on local memory/disk when they are required by dvertices to execute compute().

```
1  Vertex.compute () {
2    Messages msgs = getRecMsg();
3    double sum = 0.0;
4    for (Message m: msgs.iterator())
5      sum = sum + m.getValue();
6    double newVal =
7      0.15/getNumVertices() + 0.85*sum;
8    setValue(newVal);

9    for (Edge e: getOutEdges().iterator())
10     sendMsgTo(e.Target(),
11           getValue() / getOutDegree());

12   if (getNumSupersteps() > maxNum)
13     voteToHalt();
14 }
```

(a) PageRank in push

```
1  Vertex.pullRes (dvertex v) {
2    if (getResFlag() is True)
3      get the edge e=(u, v); //u is svertex
4        sendMsgTo(e.Target(),
5              getValue() / getOutDegree());
6  }
7  Vertex.update () {
8    Messages msgs = getRecMsg();
9    double sum = 0.0;
10   for (Message m: msgs.iterator())
11     sum = sum + m.getValue();
12   double newVal =
13     0.15/getNumVertices() + 0.85*sum;
14   setValue(newVal);
15   if (getNumSupersteps() > maxNum)
16     voteToHalt();
17   else
18     setResFlag();
19 }
```

(b) PageRank in pull

Figure 3: push **and** pull

Fig. 4(a) gives a brief introduction to the data flow for a typical superstep i on one computational node. In *Giraph*, $M_I^i(u)$ and $M_O^{i+1}(u)$ may be possibly stored on disk when the memory is not enough to hold all of them.

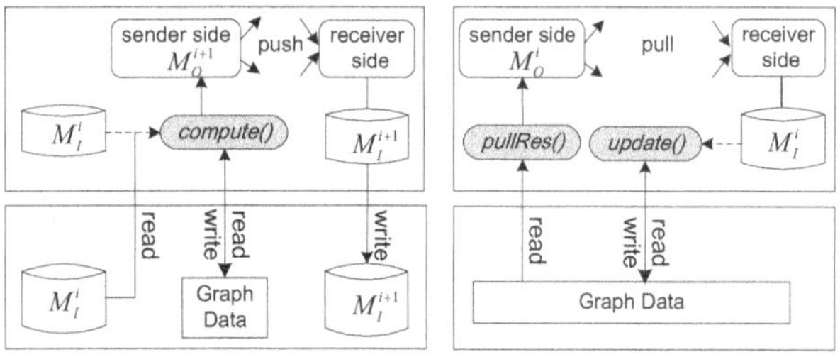

(a) push (b) pull

Figure 4: Data Flow: push **and** pull

Pull: The key idea of pull-based approaches is to decouple compute() into two functions, namely, pullRes() and update(), as shown in Eq. (2) and Eq. (3). We explain decoupled functions using PageRank in Fig. 3(b). The pullRes function is used by a svertex u to respond the pull request from a dvertex v for generating a desired message in $M_O^i(u)$/$M_I^i(v)$ (Lines 1-6). The update function is similar to the compute function in push-based systems without pushing messages. It updates v's value using the pulled messages $M_I^i(v)$. In particular, a vertex u indicates that it should send messages to its out-neighbors by calling a setResFlag function (Line 18). This signal is kept at u. On demand, in the next superstep, u will respond a pull request from any its out-neighbors dvertices if the signal is true (Line 2). We outline the implementation of pull in Fig. 4(b). Although existing pull-based systems assume that graph data reside in memory, it is most likely that we manage them on external storage when handling large graphs.

$$\text{pullRes}(u^i) \rightarrow M_O^i(u) \tag{2}$$

$$\text{update}(v^i, M_I^i(v)) \rightarrow v^{i+1} \tag{3}$$

Hybrid: In hybrid, we first decouple the computing logic for both push and pull, and then re-organize decoupled functions to support the switching operation. Thus, the performance of hybrid is determined by push and pull.

We analyze the total cost C in computing, for push and pull, as shown in Eq. (4). $\mathcal{N}$ represents the number of supersteps. In one superstep, we use C_{cpu}, C_{net}, and C_{io}, to represent the computation cost, communication cost, and I/O cost, respectively.

$$C = (C_{cpu} + C_{net} + C_{io}) \times \mathcal{N} \tag{4}$$

Note that the computing workload of pull is the same as push's but executed in two functions. Consequently, the difference between push and pull in terms of C_{cpu} can be considered to be negligible. Without loss of generality, suppose push and pull work using the synchronous computing model, even though both of them support the asynchronous iteration. push and pull thereby have the same $\mathcal{N}$ for a given algorithm. Obviously, we only need to discuss C_{net} and C_{io} below. For simplicity, we directly use network bytes and I/O bytes as the values of C_{net} and C_{io}.

First, compared with push, the extra cost of sending pull requests in pull, can be offset by the large communication gains due to concatenating/combining messages (described in Sec. 4.2), when the number of messages is large. Second, in push, messages in M_O^{i+1} are carried across two consecutive supersteps and may end up to be kept on disk if the message volume exceeds the allocated memory resource, which incurs high I/O costs. This problem is avoided in pull because messages produced in pullRes() are consumed in update() immediately in the same superstep. Nevertheless, when graph data reside on disk, pull will frequently and randomly access svertices to respond requests, which usually costs more than accessing messages on disk as reported in Sec 6.1.

In conclusion, first, when processing a large number of messages using limited memory resources, pull always outperforms push if the I/O cost of accessing svertices can be optimized. We make this condition satisfied by designing a new block-centric pull (b-pull) in Section 4. In addition, b-pull also optimizes C_{net} compared with pull. Second, the decreased number of messages inevitably narrows the gap between push and b-pull in terms of C_{net} and C_{io}, even making push beat b-pull. Thus, we design a hybrid solution to choose the profitable one to run iterative computations by switching between the two approaches adaptively (in Section 5).

4. BLOCK-CENTRIC PULLING METHOD

This section describes our block-centric pulling approach called b-pull by discussing three key issues. First, we present a data structure called VE-BLOCK for sending messages and storing a graph on disk. Second, we give the details on how to pull messages in block-centric using VE-BLOCK. Third, we discuss how to determine the proper number of blocks in VE-BLOCK to enhance the efficiency. Before that, we list important symbols in Table 2.

4.1 Efficient Graph Storage VE-BLOCK

The VE-BLOCK data structure consists of two components: Vblocks and Eblocks. The main purpose behind VE-BLOCK is to improve the efficiency when pulling messages while allowing fast access to update vertex values. Here, consider an adjacency list to represent a graph in which for every vertex it keeps a quadruple $(id, val, |V_o|, V_o)$, where we denote by id and val the id and value of one vertex, respectively. V_o is a list of out-neighbors, and $|V_o|$ is the out-degree. In VE-BLOCK, suppose that there are $\mathcal{V}$ fixed-sized Vblocks, b_1, b_2, ..., $b_{\mathcal{V}}$, in total. We simply range-partition all vertices into $\mathcal{V}$ blocks based on the vertex ids, since graph partitioning is an NP-hard problem.[1] A Vblock keeps a list of triples $(id, val, |V_o|)$. Given b_i, we have $\mathcal{V}$ variable-sized Eblocks, $g_{i1}, g_{i2}, \ldots, g_{i\mathcal{V}}$, to maintain outgoing edges from any svertex in b_i. In particular g_{ij} maintains any edge (u, v) for u in b_i and v in b_j, for $1 \leq j \leq \mathcal{V}$. Furthermore, in g_{ij}, edges from the same svertex u are clustered in a fragment. The svertex id id and an integer indicating the number of clustered edges, are the auxiliary data of a fragment.

Table 2: Definitions of symbols

Symbol	Definition
T_i	A computational node.
$\mathcal{T}$	Number of computational nodes.
$\mathcal{V}$	Number of vertex blocks (Vblocks) which store vertices.
b_i, X_i	The i-th vertex block b_i and its metadata X_i.
g_{ij}	An edge block (Eblock) which stores outgoing edges.
$E^t/\mathcal{E}^t$	Edges read from disk by push/b-pull at superstep t.
f	Number of fragments covering all outgoing edges in $\mathcal{E}^t$.
$\mathcal{M}$	Number of messages produced at one superstep.
M_{disk}	Messages resident on disk in push at one superstep.
C_{io}(push)/ C_{io}(b-pull)	Number of bytes of disk-resident data accessed by push/b-pull at one superstep.
BR$_i$/BS$_i$	Message receiving/sending buffer on T_i in b-pull.
B_i, B	Message receiving buffer on T_i in push, and $B=\sum B_i$.
B$_\perp$	Lower bound of B making C_{io}(push)<C_{io}(b-pull).
Q^t	Performance metric used in hybrid at superstep t.
s_{rr}/s_{rw}	Random read/write throughput of disk (MB/s).
s_{sr}	Sequential read throughput of disk (MB/s).
s_{net}	Network throughput (MB/s).

Accordingly, when a svertex needs to update its value, only a Vblock b_i it belongs to is accessed. On the other hand, messages are pulled based on b_i, which means that all vertices as dvertices in b_i will pull messages from svertices to update themselves. In this way, the cost of pull requests is minimized to a Vblock identifier. When a computational node receives the pull request, i.e., the Vblock id of b_i, it only needs to access Eblocks g_{ji} and Vblocks b_j, for $1 \leq j \leq \mathcal{V}$, to respond the request.

In order to further improve the efficiency, we also maintain the meta-information, X_j, for a Vblock b_j in the computational node where b_j is stored. Here, X_j keeps five items: the number of svertices in b_j (#), the total in-degree (ind) and out-degree ($outd$) of svertices, a bitmap x_j, and a Vblock responding indicator (res). X_j is used during pulling messages, as described in Section 4.2.

4.2 Pull Requesting and Pull Responding

Two components are used to pull messages. The pull requesting operation (Pull-Request) is performed at the computational node that requests messages to be consumed, and the pull responding operation (Pull-Respond) is performed at the computational node that sends messages on demand.

We discuss Pull-Request in Algorithm 1. In a superstep, each computational node T_x will invoke Pull-Request to request messages for every Vblock b_i held by it from any computational node T_y. Here, T_x works as the receiver. All messages received for vertices in b_i are kept in the message receiving buffer BR$_x$. At the same time, an active-flag vector is updated, to indicate whether a vertex value should be updated or not. After receiving all messages, each active vertex in b_i will perform the vertex-centric computation by calling update(). Like the active-flag vector, a responding-flag vector is used to indicate whether a svertex is supposed to send messages to its out-neighbors. Obviously, pulling messages is done in Vblocks, namely, the block-centric pulling mechanism.

In the same superstep, T_y needs to react to pull requests, as the sender. This is done by Pull-Respond (Algorithm 2). Assume T_y receives a pull request for Vblock b_i from T_x. It will check for every Vblock b_j that T_y holds, to see if there are any messages among vertices in b_j that need to be sent to vertices in b_i. To this end, T_y uses the meta-information X_j in three steps. 1) T_y checks the Vblock responding indicator res in X_j. If it is true, T_y needs to check further, i.e., checking the i-th bit in the bitmap x_j. 2) If the i-th bit is on, it indicates that there are edges directed from vertices in b_j to vertices in b_i. 3) When both are true, T_y calls pullRes() for any vertex u as svertex in b_j to generate messages, if u's responding-flag is true.

At the sender side, suppose that several svertices generate messages to a dvertex v. In Algorithm 2, these message values can be concatenated to share the same v's id. v's id is thereby transferred only once, which reduces communication costs. In addition, if the message value is commutative and associative [17], values are supposed to be combined into one, namely, the Combiner, to further improve the performance. Similarly, in Algorithm 1, messages received at the receiver side also can be concatenated or combined to save the memory space.

Algorithm 1: Pull-Request

foreach Vblock $b_i \in$ VE-BLOCK *on* T_x **do**
  foreach *each computational node* T_y **do**
    send a pull request for Vblock b_i to T_y;
    insert the messages received from T_y into a buffer BR$_x$;
    concatenate or combine messages in BR$_x$;
    update the active-flag vector;
  foreach *vertex* u *in* Vblock b_i **do**
    u.update() if u is active;
    update the responding-flag vector by invoking setResFlag();

Algorithm 2: Pull-Respond (Vblock b_i that T_x holds)

foreach *each* Vblock*'s metadata* X_j *on* T_y **do**
  if $X_j.res$ *is 1 and the i-th bit in* X_j*'s bitmap is 1* **then**
    foreach *each* fragment *in* Eblock g_{ji} **do**
      if u.getResFlag() *is true* **then**
        //u is the svertex of the fragment;
        insert u.pullRes() into a sending buffer BS$_y$;
        concatenate or combine messages in BS$_y$;
  send messages in BS$_y$ to T_x that requests messages for b_i;

4.3 The Number of Vblocks

In VE-BLOCK, all vertices of a graph are range-partitioned into $\mathcal{V}$ fix-sized Vblocks, and all edges are stored in $\mathcal{V} \times \mathcal{V}$ variable-sized Eblocks. The number of Vblocks, $\mathcal{V}$, becomes critical to determine the efficiency. We discuss it from two perspectives, the memory usage and the I/O cost.

Memory Usage: A computational node T_i holds two buffers for messages: BR$_i$ for receiving messages (in Pull-Request), and BS$_i$ for sending messages (in Pull-Respond). Note that the memory for metadata including X_i, and the active-flag and responding-flag vectors, is negligible. Suppose T_i keeps V_i vertices and outgoing edges from V_i. *Giraph* (push) uses B$_i$ as the maximum number

[1] VE-BLOCK can also be applied to any partitioning method by reordering vertices.

of messages in memory on T_i[2], i.e., available memory resources. We then analyze how to calculate a reasonable Vblock granularity $\mathcal{V}_i$ for T_i based on the size of BS_i and BR_i, for a given B_i, and the total number of Vblocks $\mathcal{V} = \sum \mathcal{V}_i$. For simplicity, we use n_i $(= |V_i|)$ to estimate $\mathcal{V}_i$.

Suppose there exist $\mathcal{T}$ computational nodes. BS_i is divided into $\mathcal{T}$ sub-buffers, as $\mathcal{T}$ computational nodes may send pull requests to T_i simultaneously. BS_i is inversely proportional to $\mathcal{V}$, because a large $\mathcal{V}$ can decrease the number of vertices in a Vblock, and then decrease the number of messages in the sub-buffer on T_i.

Messages are sent to T_i by $\mathcal{T}$ nodes in parallel, and may not be put into BR_i in time. To handle this case at the receiver side, we have two options which are separately setting a sub-buffer for each node, like BS_i, and controlling the data-flow during sending messages. The space complexity of the former is $O(\mathcal{T}\cdot\mathsf{BR}_i)$. The memory usage increases by ($\mathcal{T}$-1) times, compared with BR_i. Thus, we follow the latter idea in this paper. Once the sender starts the sending operation, messages will be sent to T_i in packages one by one. The new package will not be delivered until the old one has been handled by T_i (i.e., messages have been put into BR_i and concatenated/combined). Like BS_i, BR_i is inversely proportional to $\mathcal{V}_i$, as the decreased number of vertices in a Vblock can reduce the number of messages received.

For algorithms that support the Combiner, when a pull request is received by T_i, messages in a sub-buffer will not be sent until all messages from T_i are produced. The goal is to thoroughly combine messages to achieve high communication gains. Obviously, the maximum number of messages after being combined for one Vblock is equal to that of vertices as dvertices, $\frac{n_i}{\mathcal{V}_i}$. Thus, $\mathsf{BS}_i = \frac{n_i}{\mathcal{V}_i}\mathcal{T}$. $\mathsf{BR}_i = 2\frac{n_i}{\mathcal{V}_i}$, because we pre-pull messages for b_{i+1} when vertices in b_i are updating their values, to reduce the blocking time of pulling messages. Finally, we set $\mathcal{V}_i$ using Eq. (5).

For algorithms that only support concatenating, buffering all messages increases the memory usage since their values cannot be combined. Thus, at the sender side, we immediately flush out messages in each sub-buffer if the message scale exceeds a given sending threshold, like *Giraph*. BS_i is thereby negligible. At the receiver side, the number of message values received is determined by the sum of the in-degree per vertex in one Vblock. The pre-pulling optimization is disabled due to the increased memory usage. In this scenario, we set $\mathcal{V}_i$ using Eq. (6).

$$\mathcal{V}_i = \frac{2n_i + n_i\mathcal{T}}{\mathsf{B}_i} \quad (5)$$

$$\mathcal{V}_i = \frac{\sum_{u\in V_i} \textit{in-degree}(u)}{\mathsf{B}_i} \quad (6)$$

I/O Cost: It is worth noting that the main I/O cost is shifted from the receiver side in push to the sender side. Pull-Respond needs I/O costs to respond pull requests as shown in Algorithm 2. Recall that we can possibly arrange edges in each Eblock g_{ij} using fragments such that edges with the same svertex are clustered together, which significantly improves the locality. Nevertheless, for each fragment, we still need I/Os to access the fragment's auxiliary data and the corresponding svertex value in Vblock. Theorem 1 tells us that the totally expected number of fragments is proportional to $\mathcal{V}$. Because disk I/Os in Pull-Request are independent of $\mathcal{V}$, the total I/O costs of b-pull are proportional to $\mathcal{V}$.

THEOREM 1. *$\forall u \in V$, the expected number of its* fragments *is proportional to $\mathcal{V}$.*

[2] B_i indicates the message receiving buffer size. We ignore the space of the sending buffer because *Giraph* immediately flushes out messages at the sender side once a sending threshold is satisfied.

Following the analysis, we set $\mathcal{V}$ as small as possible on the prerequisite of providing sufficient memory for (BR_i+BS_i).

5. THE HYBRID SOLUTION

This section first gives a performance analysis of push, pull and b-pull, and then describes a hybrid solution to combine push and b-pull to obtain optimal performance for different scenarios.

5.1 Performance Analysis

Suppose that there exist four vertices, s_1, s_2, d_1, and d_2, which are distributed on two computational nodes T_1 (s_1 and s_2), and T_2 (d_1 and d_2), as shown in Fig. 5. As discussed in Section 3, we analyze C_{net} and C_{io}, the main factors affecting the performance.

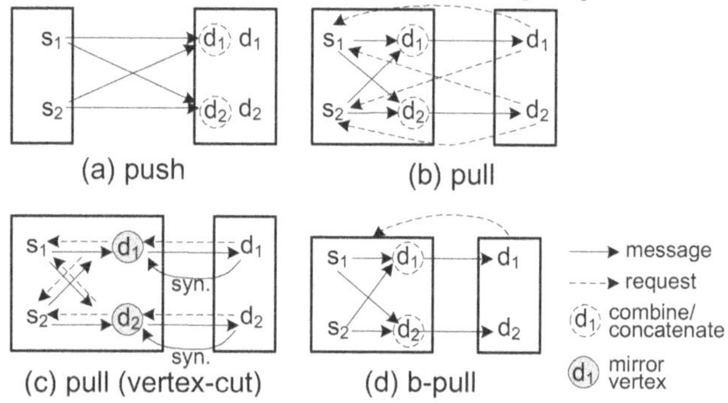

Figure 5: Comparisons of push, pull, pull (vertex-cut), and b-pull (block-centric)

Analyzing Communication Costs: Most push-based systems such as *Giraph* [2] and *GPS* [20] do not concatenate/combine messages at the sender side T_1, because the poor locality of messages among dvertices limits the communication gain. The gain usually cannot offset the cost of concatenating/combining. By contrast, in pull-based approaches, messages are generated for requested svertices on demand. For example, in Fig. 5 (b), all messages for d_1 are generated based on the requested d_1 and then can be concatencated/combined. This mechanism makes concatenating/combining cost effective, but incurs extra cost of sending pull requests. In the worst case, pull requests will be sent up to $(|V|\mathcal{T})$ times if we do not combine requests due to the poor locality among svertices. *GraphLab PowerGraph* employs a vertex-cut mechanism for efficiency and handles the computation by a Gather-Apply-Scatter model. As shown in Fig. 5(c), d_1 is cut into a master in T_2 and a mirror in T_1. Pull requests and messages are transferred between the master and mirrors in Scatter and Gather, respectively. Note that extra messages are used to synchronize mirror values in Apply. Obviously, the number of mirrors dominates the communication cost which is proportional to $|V|$ and increases with $\mathcal{T}$ sub-linearly [8]. Finally, for b-pull, the upper bound of the number of requests is $\mathcal{V}\mathcal{T} \ll |V|$. As shown in Fig. 5(d), suppose d_1 and d_2 are assigned into the same Vblock. The pull request will be sent only once. However, the number of messages is dominated by the data placement policy, and may be more than that for pull with vertex-cut because *GraphLab PowerGraph* designs many sophisticated yet special policies to optimize this problem. As a result, for C_{net}, b-pull beats push and pull, and can offer a comparable performance to pull with vertex-cut.

Analyzing I/O Costs: The cost of reading svertices in existing pull-based approaches is considerable, because sending pull requests for each dvertex individually leads to frequent and random disk accesses (as shown in Figs. 8 and 10). However, b-pull can decrease the upper bound of the number of I/O requests from $|E|$

in pull to the number of fragments in VE-BLOCK. Thus, in the following, we just analyze C_{io} for push and b-pull.

Let $G^t = (V^t, E^t)$ be the subgraph used in the t-th superstep, where $V^t \subseteq V$ and $E^t \subseteq E$. Also, $\mathcal{M}$ is the number of messages produced. $\mathcal{E}^t$ and E^t stand for the set of edges loaded from disk in b-pull and push, respectively. Now, we show the I/O cost of push in Eq. (7) and b-pull in Eq. (8), and then compare them in Theorem 2. Here, M_{disk} is the set of messages resident on disk in push, and F^t is the set of fragments covering all edges in $\mathcal{E}^t$. We denote by $IO(.)$ the number of bytes of the given data. Specifically, $2IO(M_{disk})$ is the total number of written and read bytes regarding messages. $IO(F^t)$/$IO(V^t_{rr})$ denotes the I/O cost of fragments' auxiliary data/values of svertices in Vblocks (i.e., V^t_{rr}) read by Pull-Respond. $IO(V^t)$ indicates the cost of updating vertex values, which is the same for both b-pull and push. Note that $IO(E^t)$ depends on the specific implementation of push [2, 32]. Without loss of generality, we only consider the implementation in *Giraph* [2], and others can also be used in our hybrid solution.

$$C_{io}(\text{push}) = IO(V^t) + IO(E^t) + 2IO(M_{disk}) \quad (7)$$
$$C_{io}(\text{b-pull}) = IO(V^t) + IO(\mathcal{E}^t) + IO(F^t) + IO(V^t_{rr}) \quad (8)$$

The size of M_{disk}, $|M_{disk}|$, is equal to $\mathcal{M} - B$, if $\mathcal{M} > B = \sum_{i=1}^{T} B_i$. Otherwise, it is 0 ($M_{disk}$=$\emptyset$). Let f be the size of F^t. Theorem 2 describes the sufficient condition of using b-pull. That is, $(\frac{|E|}{2} - f)$ is B's lower bound, namely $\mathsf{B}_\perp$, which makes push outperform b-pull in terms of I/O bytes. $|E|$ and f are available after building VE-BLOCK. Accordingly, we can decide whether using b-pull or not before starting to run iterative computations.

THEOREM 2. *Assume that each vertex in $V^t = V$ should broadcast messages to all of its neighbors at the t-th superstep. If $B \leq (\frac{|E|}{2} - f)$, then C_{io}(push) $\geq C_{io}$(b-pull).*

On the other hand, Theorem 2 only guarantees the effectiveness if each vertex should send messages to all its out-neighbors at every superstep, such as PageRank. For other algorithms, like SSSP, the number of vertices sending messages (called responding vertices) varies with iterations, i.e., $\mathcal{M}$ is not constant. In this scenario, the I/O cost comparison is non-deterministic, even though $B \leq \mathsf{B}_\perp$.

Favorite Scenarios: pull with vertex-cut is the up-to-date existing pull-based approach, but its performance is seriously degraded when graph data reside on disk, due to frequent svertex accesses. push also suffers from the performance degradation which is mainly caused by writing messages randomly and disabling combining/concatenating messages. By contrast, our b-pull avoids disk I/O costs incurred by messages and greatly reduces the cost of accessing svertices, while simultaneously offering a comparable communication efficiency to pull with vertex-cut. That makes b-pull outperform pull with vertex-cut in disk scenarios. b-pull also beats push in most cases, but the decrease of $\mathcal{M}$ narrows the gap, even making push beat b-pull. This is because b-pull will pay extra costs $IO(F^t)$ and $IO(V^t_{rr})$, compared with push. On the other hand, the I/O and communication cost of push is roughly proportional to $\mathcal{M}$. Not surprisingly, for SSSP-like algorithms, with the change of $\mathcal{M}$ during iterations, push and b-pull have different favorite scenarios, and using a single one can hardly achieve optimal performance.

5.2 Switching between push and b-pull

To support the switching operation between push and b-pull, hybrid should accommodate them from two perspectives: the computing functions for expressing processing logics, and the data storage for supporting consistent and efficient data accesses.

Computing Functions: Like pull, b-pull also decouples compute() in push into pullRes() and update(). For push, compute() is divided into three functions: load(), update(), and pushRes(). Here, load() loads messages received at the previous superstep into a local buffer (Eq. (9)), to prepare to be consumed in update(). $\Gamma^{in}(u)$ is the set of u's in-neighbors. Following update(), pushRes() is immediately invoked to broadcast new messages $M_O^{i+1}(u)$ to u's out-neighbors (Eq. (10)).

$$\text{load}(\sum_{x \in \Gamma^{in}(u)} M_O^{t-1}(x)) \rightarrow M_I^t(u) \quad (9)$$
$$\text{pushRes}(u^{t+1}) \rightarrow M_O^{t+1}(u) \quad (10)$$

Data Storage: The decoupling of compute() supports a seamless switching between push and b-pull. As shown in Fig. 6, when switching from b-pull to push, we first invoke b-pull's pullRes() and update() to update vertex values, and then immediately invoke push's pushRes() based on new values. Obviously, although b-pull and push are completed in a single superstep, update() is invoked only once for each vertex, which avoids reading/writing conflicts. Conversely, when switching from push to b-pull, load() and update() are invoked to update vertex values which will be used by pullRes() at the next superstep. In addition, the shared update() makes push and b-pull can share vertex values, i.e., Vblocks in VE-BLOCK. However, edges in Eblocks cannot be accessed efficiently in push, as pushRes() requires all outgoing edges of vertex u, but they are organized in fragments and distributed among different Eblocks. We thereby store edges twice. One is organized by Eblocks and used in b-pull. The other one is organized in an adjacency list, like *Giraph*, and used in push.

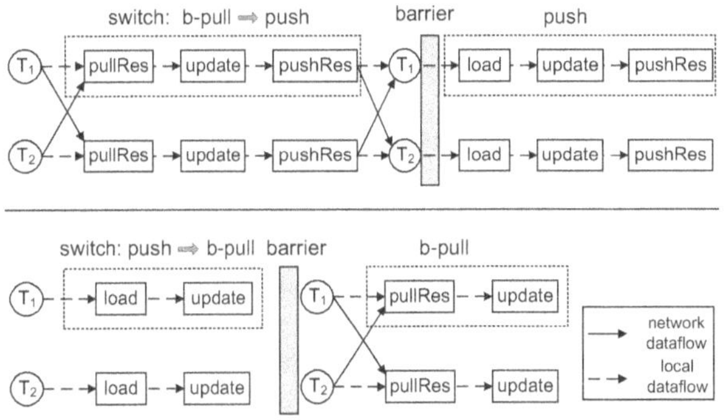

Figure 6: Switching between push and b-pull

5.3 Switching Time

The key to gain optimal performance in hybrid is deciding the right switching time, which is the focus of this section.

As we all know, many researchers have explored how to accurately predict metrics (e.g., the number of messages and active vertices) in iterations. Among them, Shang and Yu [21] present that metrics collected by the current superstep can be used to predict those of the remaining supersteps. They confirm the effectiveness for multiple algorithms over real graphs. This paper also adopts their method but the difference is that we should choose a metric which can characterize the performance of push and our b-pull.

Performance Metric and Switching Condition: The overall performance of push and b-pull is mainly dominated by the communication cost C_{net} and I/O cost C_{io}. Thus, at the t-th superstep, we use $\mathcal{M}_{co}$ (the number of concatenated or combined messages across network in b-pull) and C_{io} to estimate the performance. For

C_{net}, we assume that $Byte_m$ is the size of one destination vertex id if messages are concatenated, or a whole message if messages are combined. $\mathcal{M}_{co}Byte_m$ thereby denotes the extra communication volume of push, compared with b-pull. Recall that $IO(M_{disk})$ is the number of written/read bytes incurred by writing/reading messages in push. Thus, $\big(IO(E^t)+IO(M_{disk})-IO(\mathcal{E}^t)-IO(F^t)\big)$ is the difference of push and b-pull in terms of the number of sequential read bytes. On the other hand, $IO(V^t_{rr})$ stands for the number of random read bytes incurred by pulling messages. Finally, we give a metric Q^t to evaluate the performance difference between push and b-pull at superstep t in Eq. (11). Here, s_{rr}/s_{rw}/s_{sr} and s_{net} stand for the random-read/random-write/ sequential-read throughput (MB/s), and the network throughput (MB/s), respectively. Apparently, b-pull has superior performance if $Q^t \geq 0$.

$$Q^t = \frac{\mathcal{M}_{co}Byte_m}{s_{net}} + \frac{IO(M_{disk})}{s_{rw}} - \frac{IO(V^t_{rr})}{s_{rr}} + \frac{IO(E^t)+IO(M_{disk})-IO(\mathcal{E}^t)-IO(F^t)}{s_{sr}} \tag{11}$$

Switching Interval: If we use the dynamic information collected at the t-th superstep to predict the metric at the $(t+\Delta t)$-th superstep, the switching interval is Δt, $\Delta t \geq 1$. As reported by Shang et al. [21], the accuracy of prediction is proportional to $\frac{1}{\Delta t}$. The dynamic information required by $Q^{t+\Delta t}$ includes C_{io}(push), C_{io}(b-pull) and $\mathcal{M}_{co}$. When running push, we can figure out the set of required Eblocks if b-pull is run, based on the distribution of edges used in pushRes(). After that, C_{io}(b-pull) is estimated using the metadata of Eblocks. $\mathcal{M}_{co}$ is estimated by $\mathcal{M}R_{co}$, where R_{co} is the concatenating/combining ratio in the last superstep using b-pull. In contrast, we can easily calculate C_{io}(push) and other dynamic information when running b-pull. Note that $\mathcal{M}$ is not available if hybrid is switching from push to b-pull, because no new message is produced (as shown in Fig. 6). Besides, although no extra work is incurred during switching from b-pull to push, there still exists a slight performance loss caused by resource contention, since pullRes() and pushRes() are run in a single superstep. Obviously, frequent switching is not cost effective. We thereby set Δt as 2.

The Boundary of hybrid: Shang et al. [21] divide well-known graph algorithms into three categories based on the change of active vertices, namely, *Always-Active-Style*, *Traversal-Style*, and *Multi-Phase-Style*. We use the three categories to discuss the boundary of hybrid, as the number of active vertices dominates that of responding vertices and then decides $\mathcal{M}$. First, for *Always-Active-Style*, an accurate prediction of Q^{t+2} is always available and can be used by hybrid to make a smart choice between b-pull and push, as the behavior of vertices stays the same during iterations, like PageRank. Second, the number of active vertices for *Traversal-Style* algorithms, such as SSSP, usually varies with iterations. Thus, the prediction accuracy may be poor. However, hybrid still works well, because the variation usually keeps monotonic for a long time and then hybrid benefits from switching during several subsequent supersteps. Finally, the current hybrid is not suitable for *Multi-Phase-Style* algorithms. This is because they exhibit a periodical change in terms of the active vertex volume, which prevents hybrid from accumulating the switching gain.

5.4 Execution of hybrid

Now, we present the execution of hybrid in Algorithm 3. Here, maxNum is the maximum number of supersteps. The graph loading operation includes two tasks (Line 1): 1) storing graph data, including organizing vertices in Vblocks and storing edges twice, and 2) calculating $B_\perp$ used in Theorem 2. After that, we decide the initial execution mode based on Theorem 2, i.e., b-pull if $B \leq B_\perp$, and push, otherwise (Lines 2-3). During iterations, if $preMode$ is not equal to $curMode$, we start the switching operation as shown in Fig. 6 (Lines 13-14). Otherwise, runPull() or runPush() is invoked based on $curMode$ and returns the dynamic information which is used to estimate Q^{t+2} to determine $curMode$ of the next superstep (Lines 6-11).

Algorithm 3: Hybrid-Execution (B, G, $maxNum$)

1 loading G, and calculating $B_\perp$;
2 $preMode \leftarrow$ initMode(B,$B_\perp$);
3 $curMode \leftarrow preMode$;
4 **for** $t = 1$ to *maxNum* **do**
5   **if** *preMode* equals *curMode* **then**
6   **if** is_pull(*curMode*) **then**
7   [$\mathcal{M}_{co}$,C_{io}(push),C_{io}(b-pull)] $\leftarrow$ runPull();
8   **else**
9   [$\mathcal{M}_{co}$,C_{io}(push),C_{io}(b-pull)] $\leftarrow$ runPush();
10     $preMode \leftarrow curMode$;
11     $curMode \leftarrow$ evaluate($\mathcal{M}_{co}$,C_{io}(push),C_{io}(b-pull));
12   **else**
13   runSwitch($preMode$, $curMode$);
14     $preMode \leftarrow curMode$;

6. PERFORMANCE STUDIES

We have implemented our techniques in a prototype system called *HybridGraph*[3]. We compare it with the two push-based systems *Giraph* and *MOCgraph* and the well-known pull-based system *GraphLab PowerGraph*[4]. *MOCgraph* employs a message online computing technique to improve the performance of *Giraph* when messages are commutative. It is the up-to-date push-based system in terms of I/O-efficiency. *GraphLab PowerGraph* is memory-resident and we modify it to support access to vertices and edges on disk, to confirm the I/O-inefficiency of existing pull-based techniques. *GraphLab PowerGraph* is implemented using C++, while other systems tested are based on Java. We use b-pull to indicate our basic pull-based approach using the block-centric mechanism. Furthermore, we use hybrid to stand for our hybrid solution combining push and b-pull. *GraphLab PowerGraph*'s pull approach is represented by pull. In addition, we use push and pushM to indicate the push approach used in *Giraph* and *MOCgraph*, respectively.

We conduct testing using two clusters, a *local cluster* with HDDs (7,200 RPM) and an *amazon cluster* with SSDs. Each of them consists of 30 computational nodes with one additional master node connected by a Gigabit Ethernet switch, where one node is equipped with 4 CPUs. Other configurations are listed in Table 3.

We test four graph algorithms, namely, PageRank [17], SSSP [17], LPA [19], and SA [15], using 6 real graphs listed in Table 4. By default, we use 5 nodes for small graphs livej, wiki, and orkut, and 30 nodes for large graphs twi, fri and uk. A graph is partitioned by the range method [2] for *Giraph*, *MOCgraph*, and *HybridGraph*. Many intelligent partitioning methods are offered in *GraphLab PowerGraph*, but only Oblivious is used since others exhibit the similar I/O-performance. Fig. 3(b) gives the logic of PageRank, and other algorithms are described below.

- SSSP [17]: It finds the shortest distance between a given source vertex to any other vertex. Initially, the given source

[3]The source code is available at https://github.com/HybridGraph.

[4]We use the synchronous version of *MOCgraph* and *GraphLab PowerGraph* in the testing, and *HybridGraph* can be extended to support the asynchronous iteration.

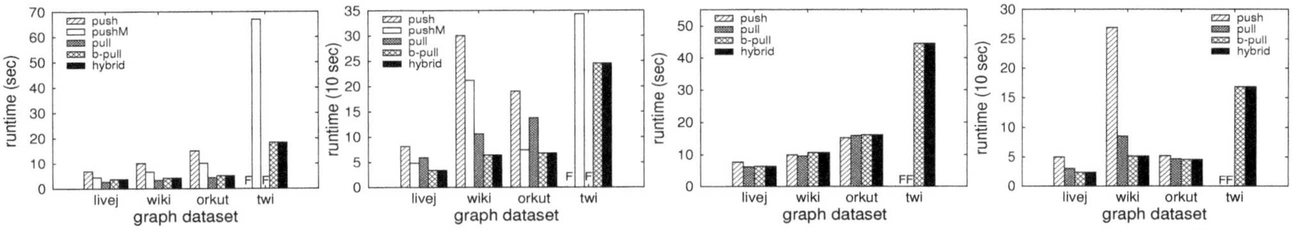

(a) Runtime of PageRank (b) Runtime of SSSP (c) Runtime of LPA (d) Runtime of SA

Figure 7: Testing runtime with *sufficient memory* on the *local cluster*

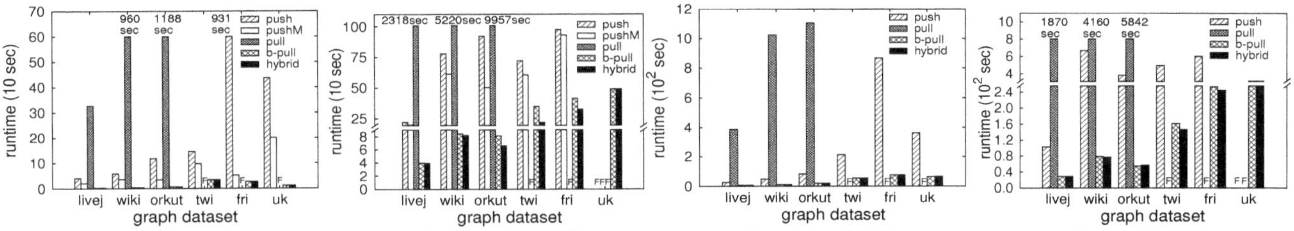

(a) Runtime of PageRank (b) Runtime of SSSP (c) Runtime of LPA (d) Runtime of SA

Figure 8: Testing runtime with *limited memory* on the *local cluster*

vertex is active and has the shortest distance 0 as its value. In every superstep, the value of a vertex is updated to be the minimum value received from its in-neighbors, if the minimum value is lower than the current one the vertex holds. The new minimum distance will be sent to its out-neighbors.

- LPA [19]: It is a near linear community detection algorithm based on label propagation. The label value of each vertex is initialized by its own unique vertex id. In the following supersteps, the value is updated by the label that a maximum number of its neighbors have. Messages, i.e., community labels, are thereby not commutative. All vertices must send messages to collect the whole information of all neighbors.
- SA [15]: It is to simulate advertisements on social networks. Each vertex represents a person with a list of favorite advertisements as its value. Selected vertices are identified as sources and send values to their out-neighbors. For one vertex, any received advertisement is either further forwarded to out-neighbors or ignored, which is decided by his/her interests. Advertisements as messages are not commutative if we update a value by the advertisement that a maximum number of its responding in-neighbors (i.e., sending messages) have.

Below, we first evaluate memory demands in particular when messages are far larger than the memory allowed to hold messages, to validate the effectiveness of b-pull and hybrid. Second, the detailed performance report of switching between push and b-pull is given. Third, we study scalability. Finally, we report the performance of loading raw graph data, and then analyze the blocking time and network traffic of push and b-pull. For PageRank and LPA, the average metrics (e.g., runtime and I/O bytes) of one superstep are reported, by totally running 5 supersteps, as the workload of each superstep is constant. SSSP and SA are run until they converge and we report the metrics of the whole iterations.

In particular, we state two testing scenarios: 1) *sufficient memory*. All systems tested manage data in memory. 2) *limited memory*. *Giraph* has multiple data management policies, and we take the same one given by Zhou et al. [32] for efficiency. That is, graph data reside on disk and message data may also reside on disk if the message buffer of one computational node B_i is full. We set the buffer as B_i=0.5 million for small graphs livej, wiki and orkut, B_i=1 million for the large graph twi, and B_i=2 million for larger graphs fri and uk. Correspondingly, *MOCgraph* and *GraphLab PowerGraph* use the buffer to cache vertices. Specially, we set a larger buffer for *GraphLab PowerGraph* (B_i=2.5 million) to guarantee that most vertices ($> 70\%$) reside in memory, because the runtime is unacceptable when B_i=0.5 million for small graphs. The LRU replacing strategy is used to manage vertices in *GraphLab PowerGraph*. For *MOCgraph*, other data (the remaining vertices, edges, and messages sent to disk-resident vertices) reside on disk. *GraphLab PowerGraph* manages edges and the remaining vertices on disk. Now, *HybridGraph* always stores data in VE-BLOCK on the external storage. However, B_i affects the number of Vblocks based on Eq. (5) and Eq. (6). In addition, missing bars labelled with 'F' in the figures reported indicate unsuccessful runs.

Table 3: Configurations of two clusters

Cluster	RAM	Disk	$s_{rr}/s_{rw}/s_{sr}$ †	s_{net} ‡
local	6.0GB	500GB	1.177/1.182/2.358MB/s	112MB/s
amazon	7.5GB	30GB	18.177/18.194/18.270MB/s	116MB/s

† Reported by the disk benchmarking tool *fio-2.0.13*, using the mixed I/O pattern "random/sequential mixed reads and writes, and 50% of the mix should be reads". This is because reads and writes are performed at the same time in a real system.
‡ Reported by the network benchmarking tool *iperf-2.0.5*.

Table 4: Real Graph Datasets (M: million)

Graph	Vertices	Edges	Degree	Type	Disk size
livej[5]	4.8M	68M	14.2	Social networks	0.50GB
wiki[6]	5.7M	130M	22.8	Web graphs	0.98GB
orkut[7]	3.1M	234M	75.5	Social networks	1.59GB
twi[8]	41.7M	1,470M	35.3	Social networks	12.90GB
fri[9]	65.6M	1,810M	27.5	Social networks	17.00GB
uk[10]	105.9M	3,740M	35.6	Web graphs	33.02GB

[5] http://snap.stanford.edu/data/soc-LiveJournal1.html
[6] http://haselgrove.id.au/wikipedia.htm
[7] http://socialnetworks.mpi-sws.org/data-imc2007.html
[8] http://an.kaist.ac.kr/traces/WWW2010.html
[9] http://snap.stanford.edu/data/com-Friendster.html
[10] http://law.di.unimi.it/webdata/uk-2007-05/

6.1 Overall Performance Evaluation

We test algorithms on all datasets in two scenarios: one is *sufficient memory* where push-based and pull-based approaches have different favorites (Fig. 7), and the other is *limited memory* where hybrid is supposed to be better (Fig. 8 and Fig. 9).

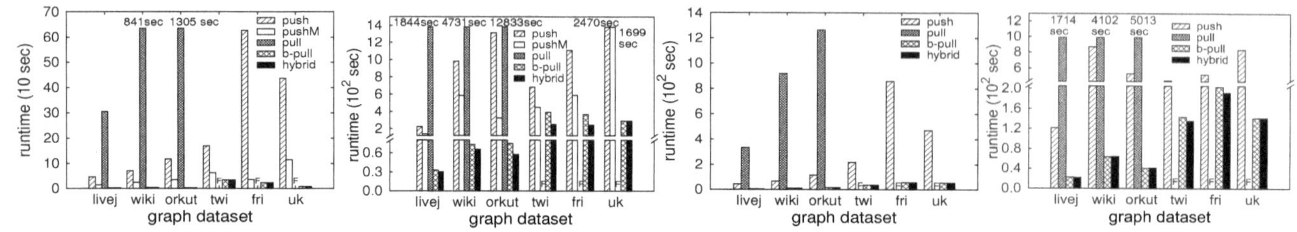

(a) Runtime of PageRank (b) Runtime of SSSP (c) Runtime of LPA (d) Runtime of SA

Figure 9: Testing runtime with *limited memory* on the *amazon cluster*

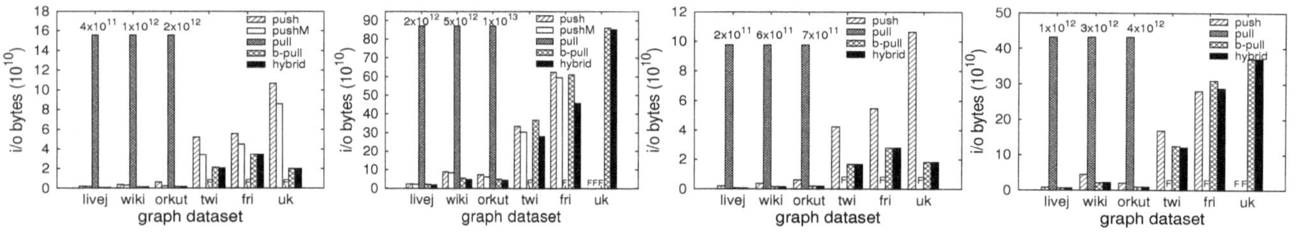

(a) PageRank (b) SSSP (c) LPA (d) SA

Figure 10: Testing I/O costs with *limited memory* on the *local cluster*

Runtime test using *sufficient memory* on the *local cluster*: In general, b-pull has superior performance to push, especially for SSSP and SA over the large diameter graph wiki, which has a long convergent stage where few vertices are updated. This is because b-pull reads edges based on the responding vertex set V_{res}, instead of the active vertex set V_{act} as push/pushM, where $V_{res} \subseteq V_{act}$. pushM beats push, because its message online computing can greatly alleviate the memory pressure to avoid starting Java garbage collection frequently. One observation we can make is that hybrid and b-pull even beat pull in some cases, as they send fewer pull requests than pull and can offer a comparable message transfer efficiency by combining messages. However, compared with pushM, the gains of hybrid and b-pull may be offset by extra costs of accessing svertices (e.g., SSSP over orkut). In *sufficient memory*, communication costs dominate the sign of Q^t. hybrid thereby runs b-pull since it can efficiently concatenate/combine messages, leading to the same performance as b-pull's.

Runtime test using *limited memory* on the *local cluster*: Since pull-based approaches can avoid the expensive message disk I/Os, the speedup of b-pull/hybrid compared with push is even up to a factor of 35 (PageRank over uk). Compared with pushM, b-pull/hybrid can still offer roughly 7x speedup for SSSP over wiki and 16x speedup for PageRank over uk. Note that for SSSP over twi, b-pull does not work well as expected (only 1.7x faster than pushM). The reason is that the highly skewed power-law degree distribution increases the number of fragments, and then the increasing costs of accessing svertices and auxiliary data of fragments are difficult to be offset, especially when the number of messages decreases. The optimal solution is to switch push and b-pull during iterations. For SSSP, hybrid contributes to decreasing the runtime of b-pull by up to 37.6% over twi. For SA, the gain achieved by hybrid is up to 9% over twi and fri.

Runtime test using *limited memory* on the *amazon cluster*: This suite of experiments is run on the *amazon cluster* to show the impact of SSDs (Fig. 9). As expected, pull, pushM, b-pull and hybrid benefit from SSDs since SSDs exhibit faster random reads/writes than HDDs. Generally, the speedup is between 1.74 and 3.6. In particular, for SSSP over twi, b-pull is only 1.1 times faster than pushM, instead of 1.7 times on the *local cluster*, as the fast random read/write performance of SSDs narrows the runtime gap. However, our hybrid is still 1.7 times faster than pushM. In conclusion, b-pull and hybrid still perform best. On the other hand, an interesting observation is that the performance of push is not improved, and even worse in some cases. This is because *Giraph* employs a sort-merge mechanism to handle disk-resident messages, where sorting is computation-intensive. However, each node in the *amazon cluster* is quipped with virtual CPUs. Its computing power is not so strong as the node's in the *local cluster* (physical CPUs).

Testing disk I/O costs using *limited memory* on the *local cluster*: In the same setting used in Fig. 8, Fig. 10 reports I/O costs, in terms of the total number of read and written bytes. Obviously, pull exhibits an extremely expensive I/O cost due to random and frequent access to svertices, even though we use LRU to manage vertices. pushM beats push, as its message online computing technique consumes messages sent for memory-resident dvertices immediately. Finally, when running SSSP over twi, the I/O cost of b-pull is usually more than that of push and pushM, since the gain achieved by avoiding message I/Os cannot offset the cost incurred by accessing svertices and auxiliary data of fragments. However, hybrid can optimize it by switching adaptively.

6.2 Analyzing hybrid during Iterations

We validate the effectiveness of hybrid using the same setting in Figs. 8 and 9. We first explore the features of the performance metric Q^t, including the prediction accuracy and the impact of hardware characteristics. After that, a detailed analysis is given to show the resource requirements of hybrid. Except for the impact of hardware characteristics, other experiments are run on the *local cluster*.

Testing the prediction accuracy of Q^t. The accuracy of predicting the performance metric is determined by C_{io}(push), C_{io}(b-pull) and $\mathcal{M}_{co}$. Figs. 11-13 report the prediction accuracy of them for SSSP and SA. The y-axis shows the ratio of the predicted value (collected at the t-th superstep) to the actual value (collected at the (t+2)-th superstep), since the switching interval is 2. The distance between the ratio and 1 is inversely proportional to the accuracy. We observe that the accuracy of SA is low, especially during supersteps 6-10. The reason is that the number of active vertices suddenly varies with iterations. For C_{io}(push), considering that edges are organized in blocks, even though one vertex is active, all edges in the corresponding edge block should be accessed. The I/O cost is thereby not sensitive to the variation of active vertices, which partially offsets the impact of the sudden change of message I/Os, based on Eq. (7). As a result, C_{io}(push) has an extremely high accuracy. The accuracy of C_{io}(b-pull) is further boosted, because C_{io}(b-pull) does not include message disk I/Os (Eq. (8)).

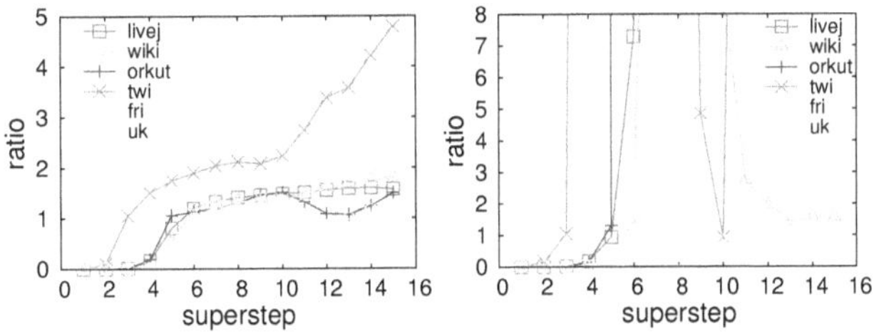

(a) SSSP (b) SA

Figure 11: The prediction accuracy of $\mathcal{M}_{co}$

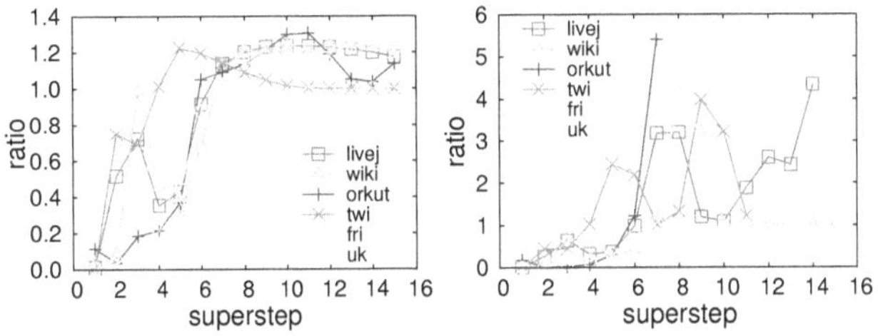

(a) SSSP (b) SA

Figure 12: The prediction accuracy of C_{io}(push)

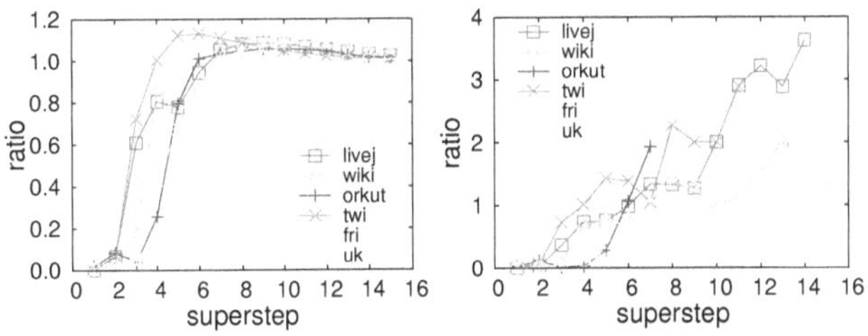

(a) SSSP (b) SA

Figure 13: The prediction accuracy of C_{io}(b-pull)

Evaluating the impact of hardware characteristics on Q^t. We explore the impact by running SSSP over twi, since hybrid achieves the most gain in this case, and other cases exhibit the similar phenomenon. Fig. 14 (a) shows values of Q^t on the *local cluster* (HDDs) and the *amazon cluster* (SSDs). There obviously exist two switching points: one happens at the 11th superstep, and the other happens at the 26th superstep. For the two clusters, we observe that the switching points do not change. A straightforward explanation is that both b-pull and push can benefit from the fast random read/write performance of SSDs. From the perspective of Q^t, when the sign of Q^t changes, the number of messages is usually small. As listed in Table 3, s_{net} is significantly more than $s_{sr}/s_{rd}/s_{rw}$. Thus, the impact of the communication volume can be ignored. Furthermore, s_{rr}, s_{rw}, and s_{sr}, are close in values. Based on Eq. (11), we can find that the final sign of Q^t is mainly dominated by $\big(C_{io}(\text{push}) - C_{io}(\text{b-pull})\big)$ which only relies on the graph topology and the special graph algorithm, and is orthogonal to the hardware characteristics. However, the absolute value of Q^t, $|Q^t|$, indicates the expected gain, which is affected by the hardware. For example, when $Q^t < 0$, $|Q^t_{HDD}| > |Q^t_{SSD}|$. That means, for the *local cluster*, switching from b-pull to push can achieve more gains, which is validated in Fig. 8 (b) and Fig. 9 (b). Taking SSSP over orkut and twi as examples, for HDDs, the gains of hybrid compared with b-pull are 19% and 38%, respectively. However, for SSDs, the gains are only 10% and 35%, respectively.

Analyzing resource requirements of hybrid. In this suite of experiments, we analyze resource requirements by running SSSP over twi. Here we ignore the report of SA since it has a similar performance with SSSP. We use push and b-pull as compared solutions, as hybrid always chooses one of them to execute iterative computations. Figs 14 (b)-(d) report the change of I/O-pressure, network communication costs, and memory usage. Generally, compared with push and b-pull, hybrid does not incur extra resource requirements if the switching operation does not happen, even though it maintains two replicas of edges. This is because when executing push/b-pull, hybrid only accesses edges in the adjacency list/Eblocks. However, in the case of switching from b-pull to push (at the 11th superstep), the resource requirements increase, because hybrid must pull messages from svertices, while simultaneously pushing new messages to dvertices. That means, at the 11th superstep, hybrid also processes messages which should have been handled at the 12th superstep in push. Although shifting the message processing does not incur extra work, the sudden increase of I/O-pressure, network costs, and memory usage, may slightly slow down the performance due to resource contention. Based on our test, hybrid takes 22.944s to accomplish the computation at superstep 11. Compared with the sum of 17.512s (b-pull at superstep 11) and 5.01s (push at superstep 12), the performance degradation does not exceed 2%. This can be easily offset by the switching gains (70%/38%, compared with push/b-pull). By contrast, when switching from push to b-pull at superstep 26, messages that should have been generated and pushed at this superstep will be pulled at superstep 27. The resource requirements will not increase. Note that the memory usage of hybrid is more than that of push, even though switching from b-pull to push has been done at superstep 11. The is because hybrid always needs to maintain the metadata information of VE-BLOCK (used by b-pull).

6.3 Scalability

We test the scalability of PageRank in Fig. 15 using the-state-of-the-art push-based and pull-based approaches: pushM and hybrid. All tests are run using *limited memory*. Obviously, decreasing the number of nodes increases the volume of data on each node, and then leads to more disk I/Os, i.e., writing/reading more messages for pushM, and reading more data in VE-BLOCK for b-pull integrated into hybrid. The former is much more expensive than the latter. Thus, we observe a super-linear performance degradation for pushM, when reducing the number of computational nodes. By contrast, the runtime increases sub-linearly for hybrid.

6.4 The performance of loading graph data

Fig. 16 reports the performance of loading graph data in *HybridGraph* using three data structures *adj* (i.e., adjacency list, used by push), VE-BLOCK (used by b-pull), and *adj*+VE-BLOCK (used by hybrid). We measure the performance in terms of runtime and I/O bytes written onto local disks. The y-axis indicates the performance ratio of *adj*/VE-BLOCK/*adj*+VE-BLOCK to *adj*. Building VE-BLOCK increases the runtime of loading data, as each adjacency list must be parsed into fragments (computation-intensive) and additional auxiliary data of fragments are written onto disk (I/O-intensive). Furthermore, compared with VE-BLOCK, although *adj*+VE-BLOCK keeps a replica of edges in an adjacency list, the overall loading runtime just slightly increases, due to the fast sequential write. Generally, for b-pull and hybrid, the extra cost in loading data can be easily offset by the performance gains during computation, as shown in Fig. 8 and Fig. 9.

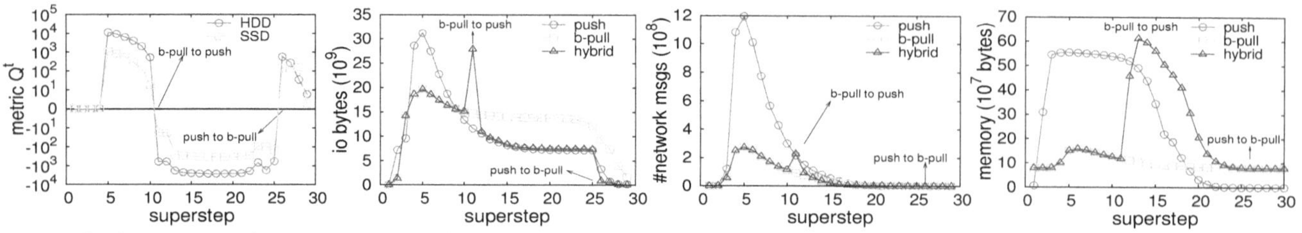

(a) Performance metric (b) Disk I/O costs (c) Network costs (d) Memory usage

Figure 14: Analyzing Q^t, I/O costs, network costs, and memory usage for hybrid (SSSP **over** twi, ***limited memory***)

6.5 Blocking time and network traffic

This section analyzes the efficiency of push and b-pull from the perspectives of blocking time and network traffic. Here, blocking time is the time of exchanging messages among computational nodes. We run PageRank in the same setting used in Fig. 7 (a). Fig. 17 shows the average value and fluctuant range (min-max) for blocking time over wiki and orkut datasets. Note that b-pull starts exchanging messages from the 2nd superstep.

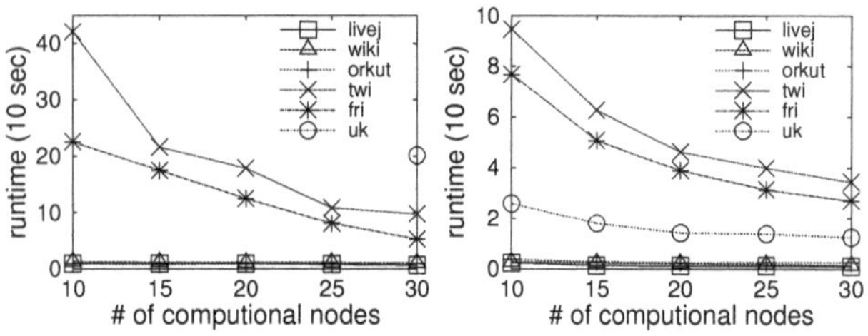

(a) pushM (PageRank) (b) hybrid (PageRank)

Figure 15: Scalability of computations (*local cluster*)

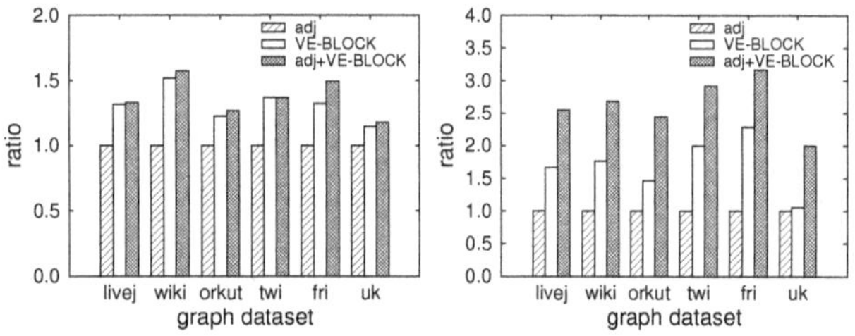

(a) Runtime (b) I/O costs

Figure 16: The performance of loading graph in *adj*, VE-BLOCK , and *adj*+VE-BLOCK , on the *local cluster*

Fig. 18 shows the network traffic for push and b-pull. The network traffic includes all input and output on bytes, and is extracted by GANGLIA [11], a cluster monitoring tool, where the monitoring interval is for every 2 seconds. In particular, we disable the combining function of b-pull, to reduce the impact on network traffic and then make a relatively fair comparison with push. Even so, the almost 50% reduction of network traffic is still achieved due to concatenating messages to the same destination vertices. In push, both concatenating and combining are disabled, as they are not cost-effective. The traffic of pushM is the same as push's, since it cannot optimize communication costs.

It is worth noting that in push and pushM, all distributed tasks will produce and send messages in parallel, whereas in b-pull, the message operation is triggered by pulling requests from destination vertex blocks. Our tests show b-pull offers a comparable parallelism and superior communication efficiency to push.

[11] Ganglia. http://ganglia.sourceforge.net/

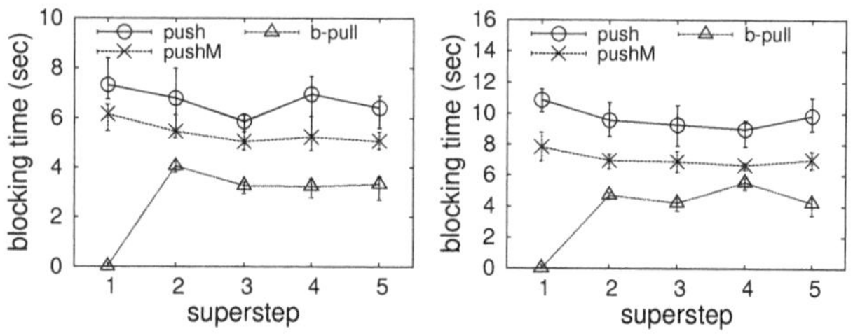

(a) Blocking time of wiki (b) Blocking time of orkut

Figure 17: Blocking time: push **vs.** b-pull

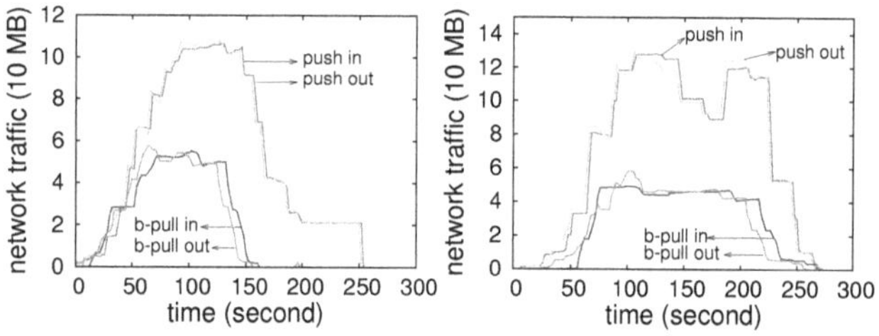

(a) Network traffic of wiki (b) Network traffic of orkut

Figure 18: Network traffic: push **vs.** b-pull

7. CONCLUSION

This paper proposes a new adaptive and I/O-efficient message processing mechanism based on the system *HybridGraph* we have developed for vertex-centric computing on Cloud. A large number of messages generated in iterations have to be stored on disk when memory is not sufficient, and it is most likely to happen when graphs become larger and larger. First, we show that the way of consuming messages received immediately will reduce the I/O cost at the receiver side to zero. The I/O cost reduction shifts to the sender side, and becomes the I/O cost of reading a graph. Therefore, by effectively organizing a graph beforehand, we design a new pulling approach b-pull to reduce I/O costs. Furthermore, to obtain optimal performance, push and b-pull are seamlessly combined in our hybrid framework and adaptively switched according to the variation in message scale. In experiments, we show that our proposed b-pull and hybrid methods can obviously outperform the up-to-date push-based and pull-based methods for computations of disk-resident graph data.

Acknowledgements. This work is supported by the National Basic Research Program of China (973 Program) under Grant No. 2012CB316201, the National Natural Science Foundation of China (61433008, 61472071, and 61272179), Research Grants Council of the Hong Kong SAR, China No. 14209314 and 418512, and China Scholarship Council. Authors are also grateful to anonymous reviewers for their constructive comments. Yu Gu is the corresponding author of this work.

8. REFERENCES

[1] Faunus. http://thinkaurelius.github.io/faunus/.

[2] Giraph. http://giraph.apache.org/.

[3] Hama. https://hama.apache.org/.

[4] Y. Bu, V. Borkar, J. Jia, M. J. Carey, and T. Condie. Pregelix: Big (ger) graph analytics on a dataflow engine. *Proc. of the VLDB Endowment*, 8(2):161–172, 2014.

[5] Y. Bu, B. Howe, M. Balazinska, and M. D. Ernst. Haloop: efficient iterative data processing on large clusters. *Proc. of the VLDB Endowment*, 3(1-2):285–296, 2010.

[6] R. Chen, X. Weng, B. He, and M. Yang. Large graph processing in the cloud. In *Proc. of SIGMOD*, pages 1123–1126. ACM, 2010.

[7] R. Cheng, J. Hong, A. Kyrola, Y. Miao, X. Weng, M. Wu, F. Yang, L. Zhou, F. Zhao, and E. Chen. Kineograph: taking the pulse of a fast-changing and connected world. In *Proc. of EuroSys*, pages 85–98. ACM, 2012.

[8] J. E. Gonzalez, Y. Low, H. Gu, D. Bickson, and C. Guestrin. Powergraph: Distributed graph-parallel computation on natural graphs. In *Proc. of OSDI*, volume 12, page 2, 2012.

[9] J. E. Gonzalez, R. S. Xin, A. Dave, D. Crankshaw, M. J. Franklin, and I. Stoica. Graphx: Graph processing in a distributed dataflow framework. In *Proc. of OSDI*, pages 599–613, 2014.

[10] W. Hant, Y. Miao, K. Li, M. Wu, F. Yang, L. Zhou, V. Prabhakaran, W. Chen, and E. Chen. Chronos: a graph engine for temporal graph analysis. In *Proc. of EuroSys*, page 1. ACM, 2014.

[11] L.-Y. Ho, T.-H. Li, J.-J. Wu, and P. Liu. Kylin: An efficient and scalable graph data processing system. In *Proc. of IEEE BigData*, pages 193–198. IEEE, 2013.

[12] I. Hoque and I. Gupta. Lfgraph: Simple and fast distributed graph analytics. In *Proc. of the First ACM SIGOPS Conference on Timely Results in Operating Systems*, page 9. ACM, 2013.

[13] U. Kang, H. Tong, J. Sun, C.-Y. Lin, and C. Faloutsos. Gbase: a scalable and general graph management system. In *Proc. of SIGKDD*, pages 1091–1099. ACM, 2011.

[14] U. Kang, C. E. Tsourakakis, and C. Faloutsos. Pegasus: A peta-scale graph mining system implementation and observations. In *ICDM*, pages 229–238. IEEE, 2009.

[15] Z. Khayyat, K. Awara, A. Alonazi, H. Jamjoom, D. Williams, and P. Kalnis. Mizan: a system for dynamic load balancing in large-scale graph processing. In *Proc. of Eurosys*, pages 169–182. ACM, 2013.

[16] Y. Low, D. Bickson, J. Gonzalez, C. Guestrin, A. Kyrola, and J. M. Hellerstein. Distributed graphlab: a framework for machine learning and data mining in the cloud. *Proc. of the VLDB Endowment*, 5(8):716–727, 2012.

[17] G. Malewicz, M. H. Austern, A. J. Bik, J. C. Dehnert, I. Horn, N. Leiser, and G. Czajkowski. Pregel: a system for large-scale graph processing. In *Proc. of SIGMOD*, pages 135–146. ACM, 2010.

[18] D. G. Murray, F. McSherry, R. Isaacs, M. Isard, P. Barham, and M. Abadi. Naiad: a timely dataflow system. In *Proc. of SOSP*, pages 439–455. ACM, 2013.

[19] U. N. Raghavan, R. Albert, and S. Kumara. Near linear time algorithm to detect community structures in large-scale networks. *Physical Review E*, 76(3):036106, 2007.

[20] S. Salihoglu and J. Widom. Gps: A graph processing system. In *Proc. of SSDBM*, page 22. ACM, 2013.

[21] Z. Shang and J. X. Yu. Catch the wind: Graph workload balancing on cloud. In *Proc. of ICDE*, pages 553–564. IEEE, 2013.

[22] B. Shao, H. Wang, and Y. Li. Trinity: A distributed graph engine on a memory cloud. In *Proc. of SIGMOD*, pages 505–516. ACM, 2013.

[23] I. Stanton and G. Kliot. Streaming graph partitioning for large distributed graphs. In *Proc. of SIGKDD*, pages 1222–1230. ACM, 2012.

[24] S. Tasci and M. Demirbas. Giraphx: parallel yet serializable large-scale graph processing. In *Euro-Par 2013 Parallel Processing*, pages 458–469. Springer, 2013.

[25] Y. Tian, A. Balmin, S. A. Corsten, S. Tatikonda, and J. McPherson. From" think like a vertex" to" think like a graph. *Proc. of the VLDB Endowment*, 7(3):193–204, 2013.

[26] L. G. Valiant. A bridging model for parallel computation. *Communications of the ACM*, 33(8):103–111, 1990.

[27] D. Yan, J. Cheng, Y. Lu, and W. Ng. Blogel: A block-centric framework for distributed computation on real-world graphs. *Proc. of the VLDB Endowment*, 7(14):1981–1992, 2014.

[28] D. Yan, J. Cheng, Y. Lu, and W. Ng. Effective techniques for message reduction and load balancing in distributed graph computation. In *Proc. of WWW*, pages 1307–1317, 2015.

[29] J. Yan, G. Tan, and N. Sun. Gre: A graph runtime engine for large-scale distributed graph-parallel applications. *arXiv preprint arXiv:1310.5603*, 2013.

[30] Z. Yang, J. Xue, Z. Qu, S. Hou, and Y. Dai. Seraph: An efficient system for parallel processing on a shared graph, 2013.

[31] J. Yin and L. Gao. Scalable distributed belief propagation with prioritized block updates. In *Proc. of CIKM*, pages 1209–1218, 2014.

[32] C. Zhou, J. Gao, B. Sun, and J. X. Yu. Mocgraph: Scalable distributed graph processing using message online computing. *Proc. of the VLDB Endowment*, 8(4):377–388, 2014.

APPENDIX

A. ARCHITECTURE OF *HybridGraph*

Fig. 19 gives the overview architecture of *HybridGraph* which is implemented on top of Apache Hama 0.2.0-incubating. Like *Giraph*, *HybridGraph* also employs a Master-Slave framework, consisting of a master node and multiple computational nodes. The master node is in charge of computational nodes through four components: 1) Task Scheduler, divides a graph job into several tasks and schedules them to computational nodes; 2) Synchronous Controller, coordinates the progress of tasks; 3) Fault Detector, detects failures during iterations; 4) Switcher, makes a smart decision on using push or b-pull for the next superstep. Currently, *HybridGraph* handles fault-tolerance by simply recomputing from scratch. Note that some algorithms always converge to the same results from any input. That motivates the need for a lightweight fault-tolerance solution which we plan to investigate as future work.

B. AN EXAMPLE USING b-pull

We discuss computing SSSP by our b-pull approach on two computational nodes, T_1 and T_2. Fig. 20 shows the VE-BLOCK for an example graph, where v_3 is the source vertex to compute. Given a vertex id v_i, val is the shortest distance, $|V_o|$ is the out-degree, and V_o is the out-neighbors of v_i. The vertices of the example graph G are partitioned into three Vblocks: $b_1 = \{v_1, v_2\}$, $b_2 = \{v_3, v_4\}$, and $b_3 = \{v_5\}$, and the edges of G are distributed into Eblocks accordingly. Here, b_i is with Eblocks, g_{i1}, g_{i2}, and g_{i3}. Suppose b_1 and b_2 with their Eblocks are assigned to the computational node T_1, and b_3 with its Eblocks is assigned to T_2. X_i is the meta-information of b_i, and only maintained by the computational node to which b_i belongs. In particular, for instance, the bitmap in X_1 (100) indicates that the vertices in b_1 only have out-neighbors in Eblock g_{11}. Here, the res of X_2 is set to be 1 since the value of source vertex v_3 is 0 and should be sent to its out-neighbors.

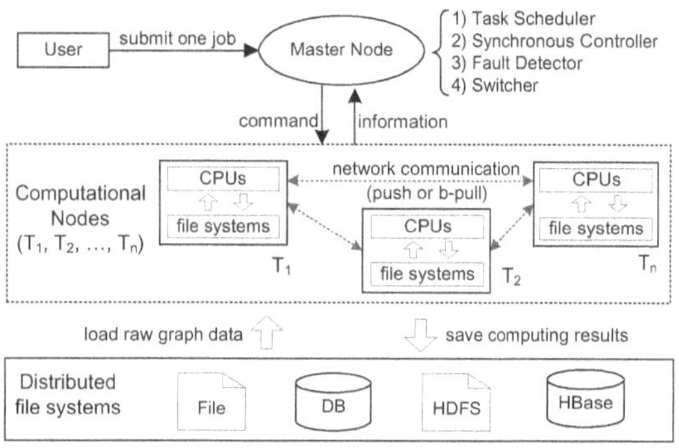

Figure 19: *HybridGraph* **Architecture**

We discuss the iterative process of push and our b-pull in Fig. 21. In the push-based approach, in the 1st superstep, the source-vertex v_3 updates its shortest distance to be zero and then pushes messages to its 3 out-neighbors v_2, v_4, and v_5. In the 2nd superstep, they update their shortest distances, and push messages to their out-neighbors. In every superstep, the messages will be stored at the receiver side to be used for the next superstep. The SSSP computation will terminate in 4 supersteps.

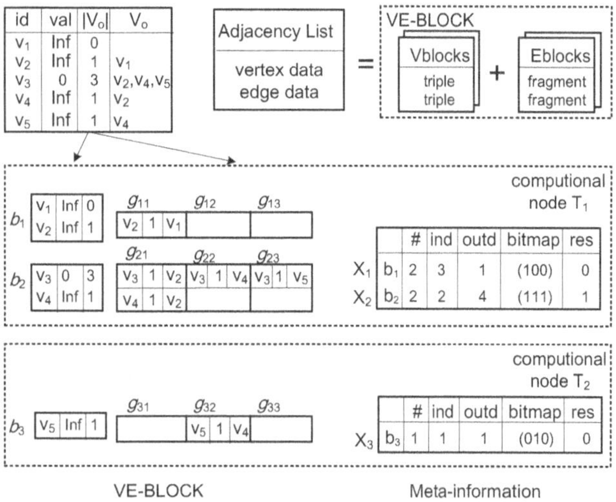

Figure 20: The VE-BLOCK **structure**

In our b-pull, in the 1st superstep, the source vertex v_3 only updates its value to be zero. There are no any messages sending. In the 2nd superstep, via pull requesting based on Vblock ids, v_2, v_4, and v_5 request messages to be sent from the vertex v_3, and then update their own values. Different from the push-based approach, the messages received in the same superstep will be consumed immediately. b-pull needs 5 supersteps, which is one more than push. But in the last one, no data are transferred except block-centric pull requests. The cost is negligible, and we thereby state that b-pull

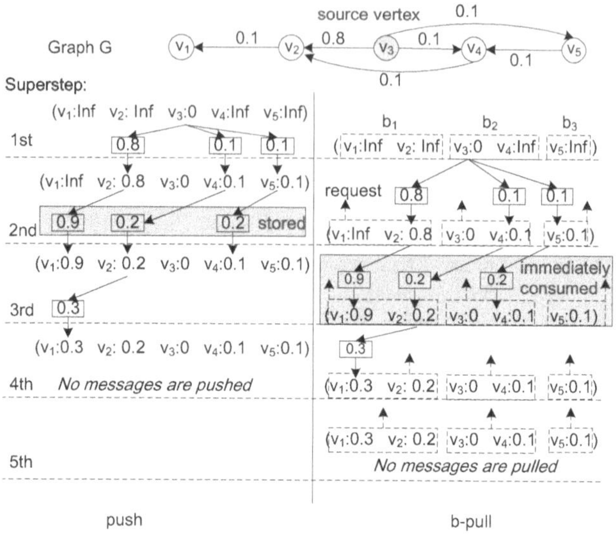

Figure 21: Illustration of SSSP **in** push **and** b-pull

and push have the same supersteps for a given algorithm in the synchronous computing model in Eq. (4).

Next, we further explain b-pull using Pull-Request (Algorithm 1) and Pull-Respond (Algorithm 2). Consider the 2nd superstep in our b-pull. The computational node T_1 sends pull requests for Vblocks b_1 and b_2, and the computational node T_2 sends pull requests for Vblock b_3 simultaneously. We discuss the process for requesting b_1 in Fig. 22. The other are the same. As shown in Fig. 22, ① T_1 sends the pull request for b_1 to T_1 and T_2. ② T_1 receives the request from itself, and then checks the meta-information for Vblocks T_1 holds. Vblock b_1 is skipped, as the res of X_1 is 0. However, the res of X_2 is 1 and the 1st bit in the bitmap in X_2 is 1, which indicates that some vertices in b_2 should broadcast the most recent values, and there exist edges from b_2 to b_1 in Eblock g_{21}. As a result, b_2 may produce messages to be sent to vertices in b_1. Then, v_3 and v_4 in b_2 are checked while scanning g_{21}. Since only v_3 is the responding vertex at the 1st superstep, we obtain the value of v_3 and the outgoing edge $(v_3, v_2, 0.8)$ with a weight 0.8. ③ T_1 invokes v_3.pullRes() to produce a message $(v_2, 0.8)$, and then puts it into the sub-buffer of BS_1. ④ Messages in sub-buffer are sent to T_1 and are kept in the receiving buffer BR_1. ⑤ When all messages have been pulled from T_1 and T_2, T_1 invokes update() for the active vertex v_2 in b_1 to update its value (v_2.update()). ⑥ The new value of v_2 is stored, and v_2 is marked as responding to respond pull requests at the next superstep.

C. TESTING THE IMPACT OF THE VEBLOCK GRANULARITY

We conduct testing to explore the impact of $\mathcal{V}$ using PageRank and SSSP over graphs livej and wiki, on 5 nodes of the *local cluster* (described in Section 6). Fig. 23 and Fig. 24 show the curve of the memory requirement measured by summing up the byte size of messages in buffer and metadata in VE-BLOCK, and I/O bytes, respectively, when varying the number of Vblocks. The x-axis is the number of Vblocks ($\mathcal{V}$) where x indicates that $\mathcal{V} = x \times 10$ Vblocks are used, and min is the minimum number 5 of Vblocks used, which means that each node has 1 Vblock. For PageRank, we set the number of supersteps as 10 and report the average. For SSSP, we run it until the algorithm converges, and report the maxi-

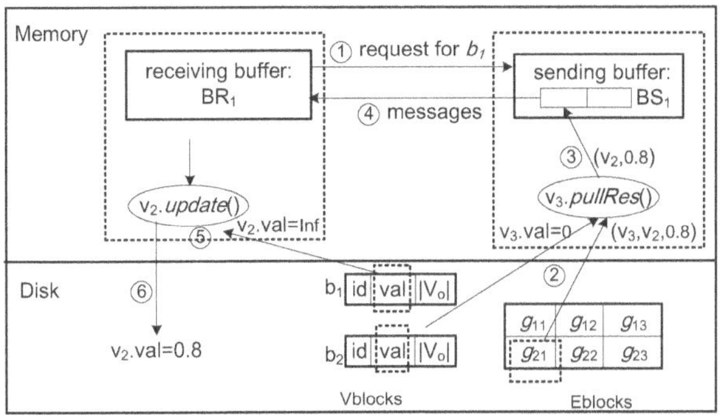

Figure 22: Message data-flow for b_1 on T_1 in the 2nd superstep

mum value among supersteps. With the increase of $\mathcal{V}$, the memory requirement rapidly drops, while the cost of I/O bytes significantly increases, as more fragments are generated (Theorem 1). We also show the overall runtime when varying $\mathcal{V}$ in Fig. 25. In particular, we find that for SSSP there exists a turning point between $\mathcal{V}$=5 (min) and $\mathcal{V}$=100 ($x = 10$). This is because the iterative computation of SSSP exhibits a gradual convergence stage where fewer edges are required. In this scenario, although a smaller $\mathcal{V}$, such as min, can decrease the number of fragments (Theorem 1), one Eblock stores more edges on average. Since data are scanned in Eblocks, many useless edges are accessed, which wastes I/O bandwith. This algorithm-specific characteristic does not violate Theorem 1. Besides, the prior knowledge about the number of required edges and the corresponding variation during iterations, is not easily achieved. Thus, we still calculate $\mathcal{V}$ using the rules described in Section 4.3 under the assumption that all edges are required.

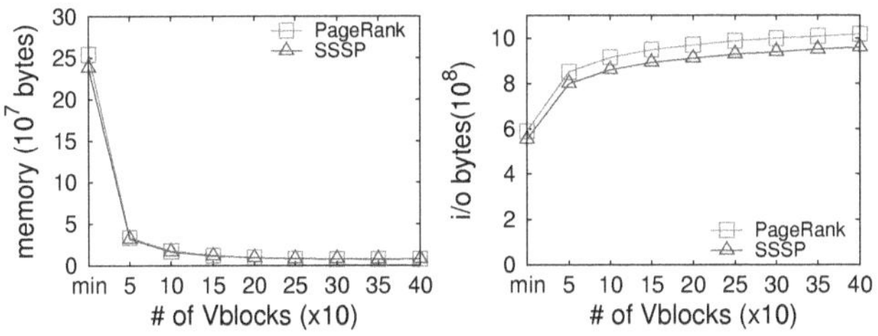

(a) Memory requirement (b) I/O bytes

Figure 23: Memory requirements and I/O bytes (over livej)

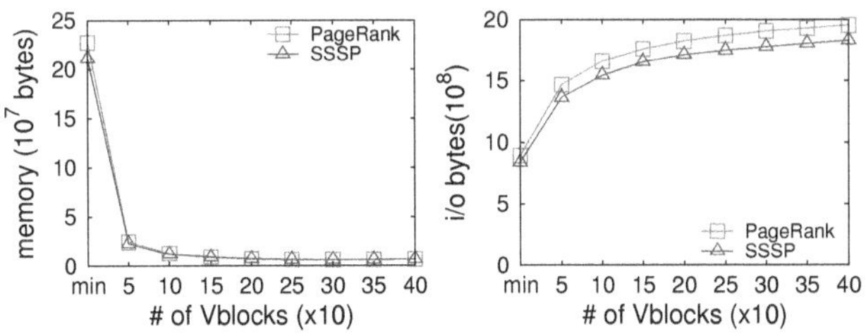

(a) Memory requirement (b) I/O bytes

Figure 24: Memory requirements and I/O bytes (over wiki)

D. PROOF

The proof of Theorem 1.

PROOF. Let $F[\mathcal{V}]$ denote the number of fragments associated with u as svertex in Vblock, and $\mathbb{E}(F[\mathcal{V}])$ is the expected $F[\mathcal{V}]$. Given a vertex u in Vblock b_i, let the indicator Z_j denote the event

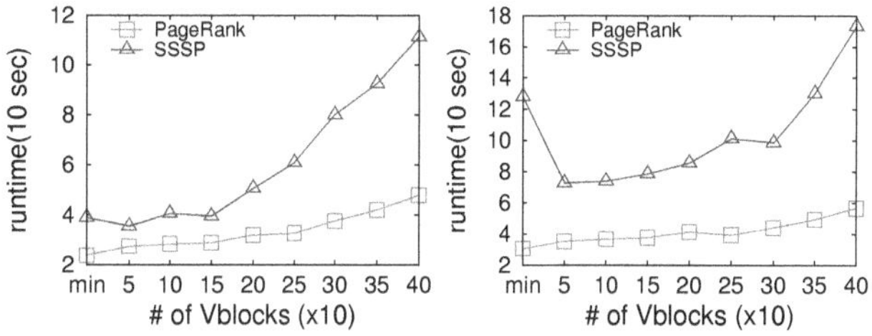

(a) livej (b) wiki

Figure 25: Overall runtime (PageRank and SSSP)

that there exists at least one of its outgoing edges in Eblock g_{ij}, i.e., one fragment exists in g_{ij}. The expectation Z_j is $\mathbb{E}(Z_j) = 1-(1-P[\mathcal{V}])^{d[u]}$, where $d[u]$ stands for the out-degree of u. Here, $P[\mathcal{V}]$ is the probability of putting an edge into Eblock g_{ij} among $\mathcal{V}$ Eblocks, and $P[\mathcal{V}] \propto \frac{1}{\mathcal{V}}$. The expected number of fragments is:

$$g(\mathcal{V}) = \mathbb{E}(F[\mathcal{V}]) = \sum_{j=1}^{\mathcal{V}} \mathbb{E}(Z_j) = \mathcal{V}\big(1-(1-P[\mathcal{V}])^{d[u]}\big).$$

As can be inferred, the first derivative is:

$$g^{'}(\mathcal{V}) = 1-(1+\frac{d[u]-1}{\mathcal{V}})(1-\frac{1}{\mathcal{V}})^{d[u]-1}.$$

Considering that $d[u] \geq 1$ for most graphs, the second derivative is:

$$g^{''}(\mathcal{V}) = -\frac{d[u](d[u]-1)}{\mathcal{V}}(1-\frac{1}{\mathcal{V}})^{d[u]-2} \leq 0.$$

Thus, we have: $g^{'}(\mathcal{V}) \geq g^{'}(\mathcal{V}\rightarrow+\infty) = 0$. Suppose $\mathcal{V}_1 \leq \mathcal{V}_2$. Obviously, $\mathbb{E}(F[\mathcal{V}_1]) \leq \mathbb{E}(F[\mathcal{V}_2])$, which means $\mathbb{E}(F[\mathcal{V}]) \propto \mathcal{V}$. □

The proof of Theorem 2.

PROOF. We use S_m, S_v, S_e, S_f represent the average size of per message, per vertex value, per edge, and auxiliary data of each fragment, respectively. We first analyze the features of accessing edges. For b-pull, at each superstep, edges may be involved in update() to update vertex values, besides being used in pullRes() to broadcast messages. By contrast, they are accessed only once in push because compute() covers the logics of update() and pullRes(). When all vertices broadcast messages to their neighbors along outgoing edges, $|E^t| = |E| = \mathcal{M}$. Accordingly, in the worst case, $IO(\mathcal{E}^t) = 2IO(E^t) = 2S_e|E| = 2S_e\mathcal{M}$. Second, the I/O bytes of accessing disk-resident messages in push is: $2(|E|-B)S_m$. For b-pull, considering that $S_m \geq S_v$ and $S_m \geq S_f$, we have:

$$IO(F^t) + IO(V^t_{rr}) \leq f(S_f + S_v) \leq 2fS_m.$$

Finally, suppose $B \leq (\frac{|E|}{2} - f)$, we can infer that:

$$C_{io}(\text{push}) - C_{io}(\text{b}-\text{pull}) \geq 2S_m(|E| - B - f) - S_e|E| \geq 0$$

, because $S_m \geq S_e$. □

E. THE EFFECTIVENESS OF COMBINING

Distributed systems usually set a sending threshold to control the communication behavior, in order to make full use of the network idle time and reduce the overhead of building connections. Assume that the threshold is 2. As shown in Fig. 5 (a), for push, s_1 generates two messages $m(s_1, d_1)$ and $m(s_1, d_2)$ for d_1 and d_2. Then the system starts the sending operation because a buffer overflow occurs. After that, s_2 also generates a message $m(s_2, d_1)$ for d_1. However, it cannot be combined with $m(s_1, d_1)$ since the latter is

Table 5: **Comparisons of runtime in five scenarios about** *GraphLab PowerGraph* **(seconds)**

scenarios	PageRank			SSSP			LPA			SA		
	livej	wiki	orkut	livej	wiki	orkut	livej	wiki	orkut	livej	wiki	orkut
original	3.0	3.6	5.0	58.8	105.7	120.8	7.4	11.1	18.6	30.4	80.5	47.5
ext-mem	3.1	4.1	5.9	60.2	108.8	129.6	7.6	11.7	19.2	31.6	85.5	49.0
ext-edge	3.9	4.8	7.1	93.5	207.4	220.6	8.6	12.5	21.6	41.6	163.7	64.6
ext-edge-v3	4.5	5.0	7.1	137.2	259.2	222.8	8.8	13.0	21.1	80.4	233.5	64.6
ext-edge-v2.5	654.7	960.4	1187.8	2318.4	5219.5	9956.5	387.0	1024.2	1103.4	1869.5	4160.3	5841.7

unavailable. Thus, the communication gain is limited and usually cannot offset the cost of executing combining. By contrast, for pull (including b-pull), messages are generated based on the demand of the destination vertex. For example, when d_1 sends a pull request, s_1 and s_2 will generate messages for it. This mechanism obviously guarantees that all messages for d_1 can be combined.

We modify *MOCgraph* to support combining messages at the sender side. The modified version is identified as pushM +com. We define the combining ratio as $\frac{\#\_of\_combined\_messages}{\#\_of\_total\_messages}$. Not surprisingly, as shown in Fig. 26 (a) (in the same setting used in Fig. 7 (a)), when varying the sending threshold from 1MB to 32MB, the runtime of pushM increases because a large threshold cannot make full use of the network idle time. By contrast, pushM +com works well, as many messages can be combined (i.e., a large combining ratio shown in Fig. 26 (b)), leading to a communication gain. However, the gain is easily offset by the cost of combining if the threshold is small. On the other hand, for b-pull, the communication gain is orthogonal to the threshold. Consequently, the only challenge for b-pull is to set a reasonable threshold to make full use of network resources. Fortunately, this constraint is relatively loose. As shown in Fig. 26, b-pull works well from 1MB to 4MB. This paper thereby uses 4MB as the default sending threshold.

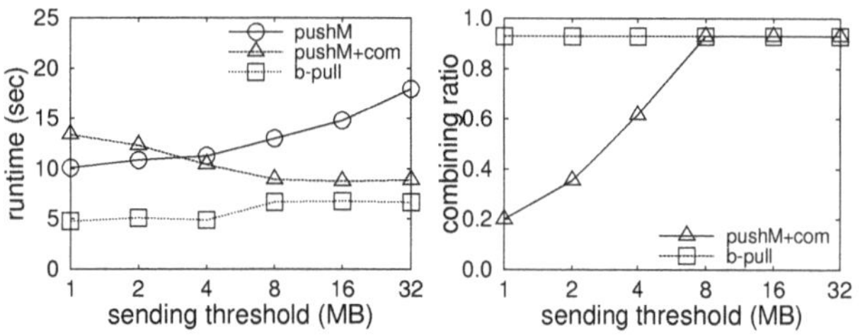

(a) Runtime (b) Combining ratio

Figure 26: Testing the effectiveness of combining for pushM **and** b-pull (PageRank **over** orkut)

F. EVALUATING THE PERFORMANCE OF MODIFIED *GraphLab PowerGraph*

In this suite of experiments, we use five testing scenarios to confirm that our extension does not incur extra costs compared with the original *GraphLab PowerGraph*. The first one is 1) *original*: using the original *GraphLab PowerGraph* to process data in memory. The other four scenarios use our disk extension: 2) *ext-mem*: all data are memory-resident, like *original*; 3) *ext-edge*: edges reside on disk and vertices are kept in memory; 4) *ext-edge-v3*: edges reside on disk and each task caches 3 million vertices at most in memory; 5) *ext-edge-v2.5*: edges reside on disk and each task caches 2.5 million vertices at most in memory.

Table 5 reports the performance in five scenarios using 5 computational nodes of the *local cluster*. Apparently, *ext-mem* achieves a comparable performance with the original *GraphLab PowerGraph*, which validates that our extension is reasonable. Furthermore, the runtime of *ext-edge* slightly increases, because edges are read only once per superstep. Finally, with the increase of the number of disk-resident vertices, the overall performance seriously degrades, due to frequently reading/writing disk-resident vertices, even though we have employed the LRU replacing strategy.

G. DETAILED DISCUSSION ON THE BOUNDARY OF hybrid

The switching mechanism of our hybrid relies on the sign of Q^t which is determined by sub-metrics C_{io}(push), C_{io}(b-pull) and $\mathcal{M}_{co}$. We predict them using the mechanism proposed by Shang et al. [21]. Shang et al. divide graph algorithms into three categories based on the change of active vertices, namely, *Always-Active-Style*, *Traversal-Style*, and *Multi-Phase-Style*. We discuss the boundary of hybrid accordingly.

Always-Active-Style: Every vertex in each superstep sends messages to all its neighbors. The typical algorithm is PageRank. We can always achieve the predicted Q^{t+2} accurately, since the behavior of vertices does not change. hybrid can choose an optimal mechanism based on Q^{t+2}.

Traversal-Style: Some vertices are treated as starting points, and the other ones are involved in computing based on the user-defined processing logic. SSSP follows this style. Not surprisingly, when the number of active vertices is drastically changing, the prediction mechanism proposed by Shang et al. [21] works poorly. Specifically, when the active vertex scale is decreasing, we have $Q^t > Q^{t+2}$, because Q^t is proportional to the number of messages. If we use Q^t as the predicted value of Q^{t+2}, the switching timing from b-pull to push (i.e., the sign changes from positive to negative) will be put off. Nevertheless, hybrid still achieves an impressive gain in runtime. This is because the sign of Q^t keeps unchanged in the subsequent n supersteps (due to a continuous decrease of the number of active vertices), and then hybrid can always benefit from the switching operation. Here, n depends on the specified algorithm and the graph topology. Take SSSP over twi as an example. n=15 after switching from b-pull to push (as shown in Fig. 14 (a)). Similarly, switching from push to b-pull will be put off when the number of active vertices is increasing. In conclusion, the total gain in runtime is up to 37.6%.

Multi-Phase-Style: The entire computation is divided into a number of phases, and each phase needs several supersteps. The behavior of vertices changes repeatedly among phases. That means the increase and decrease of the active vertex scale will occur periodically. Like *Traversal-Style*, the prediction accuracy is poor. But the difference is that the sum of gains after executing the delayed switching is negligible, because the sign of Q^t changes frequently. Taking the minimum spanning tree algorithm as an example [21], n=1 after switching from b-pull to push. A possible solution is to analyze the historical information of iterations to explore the change style, and then guide the switching operation. We will validate the effectiveness of this solution as future work.

Scalable Pattern Sharing on Event Streams*

Medhabi Ray
Worcester Polytechnic Institute
100 Institute Road
Worcester, MA 01609
medhabi@cs.wpi.edu

Chuan Lei
Worcester Polytechnic Institute
100 Institute Road
Worcester, MA 01609
chuanlei@cs.wpi.edu

Elke A. Rundensteiner
Worcester Polytechnic Institute
100 Institute Road
Worcester, MA 01609
rundenst@cs.wpi.edu

ABSTRACT

Complex Event Processing (CEP) has emerged as a technology of choice for high performance event analytics in time-critical decision-making applications. Yet it is becoming increasingly difficult to support high-performance event processing due to the rising number and complexity of event pattern queries and the increasingly high velocity of event streams. In this work we design the SPASS framework that successfully tackles these demanding CEP workloads. Our SPASS optimizer identifies opportunities for effective shared processing among CEP queries by leveraging time-based event correlations among queries. The problem of pattern sharing is shown to be NP-hard by reducing the Minimum Substring Cover problem to our CEP pattern sharing problem. The SPASS optimizer is designed that finds a shared pattern plan in polynomial-time covering all sequence patterns while still guaranteeing an optimality bound. To execute this shared pattern plan, the SPASS runtime employs stream transactions that assure concurrent shared maintenance and re-use of sub-patterns across queries. Our experimental study confirms that the SPASS framework achieves over 16 fold performance improvement for a wide range of experiments compared to the state-of-the-art solution.

Keywords

Complex Event Processing; Sharing; Sequence Pattern

1. INTRODUCTION

Motivation. Major businesses from fraud detection, online retail to health-care monitoring employ Complex Event Processing (CEP) technologies [6, 29, 42] to detect event patterns such as time-ordered or unordered sequence of events, along with the non-existence of events and other patterns, over high velocity event streams. Major advances have been made on the development of solutions for efficiently detecting event patterns in near real-time [6, 8, 27, 29, 42]. With the explosion in the number and type of such event analytics queries, these systems face workloads that often involve hundreds or even thousands of real-time event pattern queries [27]. Pattern queries in these workloads can have sub-patterns across numerous patterns that are *concurrently* executed in a *shared manner*. This points at a tremendous opportunity for scaling these compute intensive workloads.

However most existing CEP engines [6, 29, 42] process pattern matching queries *sequentially* without sharing nor maximizing concurrency among queries. With very high loads, such independent processing leads to *repeated and thus wasted computations*, exacerbating the problem of overload. This may cause a loss in the availability of service during peak hours, performance bottlenecks and potentially huge monetary loss for the organization due to not delivering results on time.

The running example shown in Figure 1 highlights the unique sharing opportunities available in a workload of pattern queries on a car location event stream similar to the Linear Road Benchmark data [2] for real-time traffic monitoring.

Motivating Example - Real-time Traffic Monitoring. The application monitors the motor vehicle expressways of a large metropolitan area. Monitoring movements of cars under various circumstances could be used for future route recommendations, toll adjustments and re-routing along with other intelligent traffic services. In this example, $Carloc$ represents a stream of car location reports. The application sends out warnings to cars about possible delays due to constructions or accidents in a certain route. The first pattern P_1 monitors cars that first pass $tollA$, then pass a construction site and finally take the next exit. P_2 searches for traffic patterns where cars take an exit after seeing an accident while P_3 monitors cars that pass by a parked emergency vehicle and then take an exit.

P_1: PATTERN SEQ (CL (CL.pos = tollA), CL1 (CL1.pos = WorkZone & CL1.id = CL.id), CL2 (CL2.pos = exitA & CL.id = CL2.id)) WITHIN 30 min on STREAM *Carloc*	P_2: PATTERN SEQ (CL (CL.pos = tollA), Accident (Accident.pos = tollA + 5 miles), CL1 (CL1.pos = exitA & CL.id = CL1.id)) WITHIN 30 min on STREAM *Carloc*

P_3: PATTERN SEQ (CL (CL.pos = tollA), CL1 (CL1.pos = CL.pos & CL1.type = EV & CL1.state = Parked), CL2 (CL2.pos = exitA & CL.id = CL2.id)) WITHIN 30 min on STREAM *Carloc*

Figure 1: Pattern Query Workload

The above queries are all monitoring the traffic around a particular toll booth ($tollA$) and contain similar sub-patterns SEQ (CL ($CL.pos$ $=$ $tollA$), $CL2$ ($CL2.pos$ $=$ $exitA$ & $CL.id$ $=$ $CL2.id$)). Hence intermediate results could potentially be shared when processing these pattern queries, thus saving computational resources and achieving speed-up. Numerous event analytics applications from online advertising, click-stream analysis, to social

*This work was done when Medhabi Ray and Chuan Lei were students at Worcester Polytechnic Institute. NSF grants IIS-1018443 and 0917017 support this project.

SIGMOD'16, June 26-July 01, 2016, San Francisco, CA, USA

© 2016 ACM. ISBN 978-1-4503-3531-7/16/06...$15.00

DOI: http://dx.doi.org/10.1145/2882903.2882947

networking services exhibit identical characteristics, namely, huge workloads composed of similar sequence pattern queries. The opportunity to share computations across such patterns is widespread.

Challenges. To design an effective infrastructure for scalable shared processing of a workload of sequence patterns, we must develop technologies to (1) first identify an effective pattern sharing plan, and (2) then to execute the shared pattern plan in an efficient concurrent manner.

• **Benefit Estimation for Pattern Sharing.** To identify sharable sub-patterns that minimize CPU costs, we need to establish an effective model to estimate the computational savings obtainable from sharing a given sub-pattern. One important observation here is that sharing a sequence pattern does not always result in true performance benefits. In our running example above, the events of witnessing a work zone in P_1 and witnessing an accident in P_2 are unlikely to co-occur. Thus the sharing of sub-patterns between P_1 and P_2 may even cause more harm than good by incurring unnecessary concurrency control overhead. Thus we propose to devise a lightweight yet effective method for estimating these *time-sensitive co-occurrence properties of event streams* to accurately capture the benefit of sharing sub-patterns of event pattern queries.

• **Intractable Search Space of Pattern Sharing Optimization.** Finding a set of sub-patterns to share among event patterns that minimizes the overall computation costs across the entire workload requires enumerating all possible combinations of sub-patterns. Similar to the view selection problem [30, 37], i.e., choosing a set of views to materialize over a database such that the cost of evaluating a given query workload is minimized, identifying an optimal set of sub-patterns to share is prohibitively expensive due to its exponential search space [35]. This necessitates the design of practical yet effective strategies for finding a logical pattern sharing plan.

• **Concurrent Shared Pattern Execution.** Once a promising solution for sharing sub-patterns has been identified, the workload must be transformed into a shared runtime plan that can be executed in a concurrent manner. This requires a run-time infrastructure that correctly handles shared sub-pattern matches leveraging concurrent execution on a modern architecture. Shared sub-pattern matches must be maintained correctly so as to enable concurrent accesses by other queries involved in the sharing process.

State-of-the-Art. Prior work in CEP has mainly focused on the design of execution strategies for efficient *event pattern processing* [6, 8, 26, 42]. These techniques adopt Nondeterministic Finite Automaton (NFA) execution strategy to process a *single pattern at a time*. Hence they do not concern themselves with exploiting sharing opportunities across the workload of pattern queries. While merging NFAs has been attempted in the context of XML-filtering [13, 14], it is limited to prefix-matching. On the other hand, SPASS supports sharing of any common sub-patterns not necessarily limited to prefix or suffix patterns. There have been some efforts to execute event pattern matching on a distributed architecture [5, 36]. However, these works fail to provide any guarantee to produce a globally optimal plan for multiple pattern sharing.

In **multiple query optimization** (MQO), much work has been accomplished for static relational databases [9, 11, 19]. Prior work focused on view materialization for shared results across multiple queries [11] and on sharing similar sub-expressions to avoid re-computation costs [9]. However, these prior techniques cannot be directly applied to our continuous pattern sharing problem because (1) our data is continuously under flux, and (2) the data-driven approach of CEP may trigger the pattern matching process to be spawned in various orders based on the arrival of events – in contrast to the traditional static processing frameworks where the execution is fully orchestrated.

There has also been some work on MQO for **continuous queries over data streams** [12, 28]. These works have focused on deciding at what level of data granularity (i.e., tuple, pane, or full window) to share a sub-expression across queries [28]. However without considering properties specific to pattern queries such as *inter-query event correlations*, optimization opportunities will be missed. This is now the focus of our work.

Proposed Solution. In this work we propose SPASS (Scalable PAttern Sharing on event Streams), a framework for the efficient detection of event sequences in data streams via shared concurrent pattern execution. The SPASS optimizer takes as input a set of pattern queries. It estimates the benefit of sharing the computation of sub-patterns based on the time-ordering across events and the *inter-query event correlation* hidden in the event streams. We prove that our problem of finding an optimal pattern sharing plan is equivalent to the NP-hard Minimum Substring Cover (MSC) problem [21]. The approximate solution to the MSC problem with practical bounds on optimality [21] can now be applied to solve our problem. The resulting near-optimal shared pattern plan is then executed in a concurrent manner. For effective concurrent execution paradigm, we extend the *continuous sliding views technology* [34], initially designed for a single pattern query, to synchronously cache and reuse intermediate results of shared sub-patterns across multiple patterns. Lastly we introduce a *stream transaction manager* that controls access to these shared sliding views to achieve efficient yet correct insertion, deletion, and reuse of the sub-pattern matches.

Contributions. The contributions of this work include:

1. We establish a cost model for estimating the benefit of sharing sub-patterns by exploiting both the overlapping *event ordering* among pattern queries and *inter-query event correlation* hidden in event streams (Sec. 3).
2. We show that our problem of optimizing a workload of sequence pattern queries to minimize computation costs is equivalent to the well-known NP-hard problem, called *Minimum Substring Cover* [21]. This leads us to a polynomial-time solution to the problem of sequence pattern sharing, yet with proven acceptable bounds on optimality [21] (Sec. 3).
3. We propose an effective runtime infrastructure that facilitates shared processing of common sub-patterns across multiple queries by using the *shared continuous sliding views* technology. A stream transaction manager is introduced to guarantee synchronous access to these shared views for concurrent pattern executions (Sec. 4).
4. Our extensive experiments on real world event streams illustrate that our proposed SPASS approach achieves over 16 fold performance improvement on average for a wide range of scenarios over the state-of-the-art non-sharing and sharing (i.e., prefix- and suffix-based) approaches [6, 14, 42] (Sec. 5).

2. PRELIMINARIES

2.1 Event Processing Basics

An *event instance* is defined as an occurrence of interest denoted by a lower-case letter (e.g., 'e'). The time of occurrence of an event instance e_i is given by a timestamp (referred to as $e_i.ts$). An *event type* E of an instance e_i denoted by $e_i.type$ describes the set of attributes associated with e_i. A specific attribute of the event instance e_i is referred to with $e_i.attr$. Predicates of the form $p_i(e_i.attr)$ can be specified on event instances. An event stream is an unbounded set of event instances e_i that arrive in order of their occurrence time. The timestamp of the last event instance that has arrived into the system is referred to as ts_{curr}.

Query Specification. We adopt a pattern query language commonly used in the literature [27, 42] to specify event pattern queries.

The example patterns in Figure 1 conform to the above query specification. We will explain each of these clauses below. The **PATTERN** clause denotes the event operator to be matched against the event stream specified in the **FROM** clause. In our SPASS framework, we support the common pattern operators, including SEQ, AND, OR and NOT [27, 42].

A **SEQ** operator outputs a event pattern match when a set of events conform to the order in timestamps and predicates specified in the operator within a given window.

$$SEQ(E_1 : p_1(E_1.attr), ..., E_n : p_n(E_n.attr)) \\ = \{\langle e_1, ..., e_n\rangle | ts_{curr} - Window < e_1.ts < ... < e_n.ts \\ < ts_{curr} \wedge (e_i.type = E_i) \wedge p_i(e_j.attr) = true\} \quad (1)$$

An **AND** operator outputs an event pattern match when a set of events occur within a certain time window in any order.

$$AND(E_1 : p_1(E_1.attr), ..., E_n : p_n(E_n.attr)) \\ = \{\langle e_1, ..., e_n\rangle \mid \forall e_i(i \in 1, \dots n)(ts_{curr} - Window < e_i.ts \\ \leq ts_{curr}) \wedge (e_i.type = E_i) \wedge p_i(e_i.attr) = true\} \quad (2)$$

An **OR** operator denotes a union of a set of alternate event types. It produces an output when it finds a match for any one of the specified event types.

$$OR(E_1 : p_1(E_1.attr), E_2 : p_2(E_2.attr), ..., E_n :: p_n(E_n.attr)) \\ = \{\langle e_1 : p_1(e_1.attr) = true \vee e_2 : p_2(e_2.attr) = true \\ \vee \dots \vee e_n : p_n(e_n.attr) = true\rangle\} \quad (3)$$

A **NOT (!)** operator, which can occur within a SEQ or AND operator, denotes the non-existence of an event. In $SEQ(E_1,\dots, E_i, !E_j, E_k,\dots, E_n)$ a pattern match $\langle e_1, \dots,e_i, e_k,\dots, e_n\rangle$ is the output when no event instance e_j exists in the stream such that $e_i.ts<e_j.ts<e_k.ts$. For $AND(E_1,\dots,E_i, !E_j, E_k,\dots, E_n)$ a pattern match $\langle e_1,\dots, e_i, e_k,\dots, e_n\rangle$ is the output if and only if no event instance e_j exists in the stream in the interval $[(ts_{curr}$ - $Window), ts_{curr}]$.

Furthermore these operators can be nested within one another. For instance the query $SEQ(E_{11},\dots,E_{1k}, AND(E_{21},\dots,E_{2n}), E_{1l},\dots,E_{1m})$ has an AND operator nested within a SEQ operator. Semantically it refers to event patterns where $\langle e_{11},\dots,e_{1k}, e_{1l},\dots,e_{1m}\rangle$ occur in order while events in the match $\langle e_{21},e_{22},\dots, e_{1n}\rangle$ occur in any order and $\forall$ e_{2i}, $e_{1k}.ts < e_{2i}.ts < e_{1l}.ts$.

Predicate qualifications can be specified on the attributes of each event in the SEQ, AND, OR and NOT patterns. For instance, in Figure 1, ($CL.pos$ = $tollA$) in $P1$ represents a predicate specification on an event CL that refers to a car passing a certain location on the highway.

The **WITHIN** clause defines the *sliding window constraint* common in continuous stream processing [27, 42]. The $window$ parameter stipulates that the time difference between the first to the last event instances matched by a pattern query falls within the $window$ constraint.

2.2 Problem Statement

Given a workload W of pattern queries {P_1, P_2, ..., P_k} specified in a stream S and the statistics of the event stream, the goal of ***Sequence Pattern Sharing*** *is to find a set of sub-patterns {SP_1, SP_2, ..., SP_m} with SP_i a sub-pattern of P_j and $P_j \in W$ to share that minimizes computational costs for the entire workload W and then to design a runtime infrastructure to concurrently execute the shared pattern plan achieving high processing performance.*

Finding the optimal solution for this problem is prohibitively expensive as all combinations of possible sub-patterns form an exponentially large search space. Moreover, orchestrating a concurrent shared sequence pattern execution requires a meticulous yet lightweight transaction management mechanism to guarantee the result correctness.

2.3 The SPASS Architecture

Figure 2 shows the main components of the SPASS architecture. The SPASS architecture is composed of 2 modules – **SPASS Optimizer** and **SPASS Runtime**. The SPASS Optimizer takes as input a sequence pattern workload and outputs a sequence pattern sharing plan. The SPASS Runtime first instantiates this sequence pattern sharing plan on a concurrent execution infrastructure. Thereafter, it receives the event stream from external sources and produces pattern matches for the sequence pattern workload.

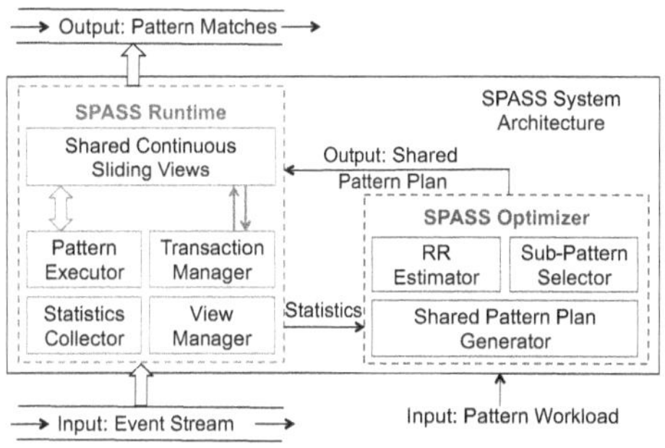

Figure 2: SPASS Architecture

2.3.1 SPASS Optimizer

The SPASS Optimizer adopts the principle of building an optimal sharing plan for the entire pattern workload [19] and then sharing similar components across these optimized queries when available [9]. To compute results for the workload of pattern queries with minimum CPU costs, the optimizer has to find a set of common sub-patterns that provides maximal sharing benefit.

RR Estimator. This module assigns a score referred to as *Redundancy Ratio* (RR) to candidate sub-patterns based on CPU cost savings reaped when sharing them. This score is computed periodically using a cost model and event statistics collected by the Statistics Collector in the SPASS Runtime infrastructure.

Sub-Pattern Selector. This module uses RR scores to identify the set of common sub-patterns to share across the pattern query workload. A polynomial-time algorithm produces a shared pattern plan covering the workload patterns with a bounded optimality.

Shared Pattern Plan Generator. The subset of sub-patterns chosen by the Sub-Pattern Selector is then transformed into a shared pattern plan by the Shared Pattern Plan Generator.

2.3.2 SPASS Runtime

The SPASS Runtime exploits stream transactions to support concurrent shared sequence pattern execution at runtime.

Pattern Executor. The Pattern Executor exploits the NFA-based pattern matching approach [6, 42] to compute pattern matches over event streams. It interacts with the View Manager to maintain and reuse sub-pattern matches in Shared Continuous Sliding Views.

Shared Continuous Sliding Views. The views are shared in-memory storage structures that store sub-pattern matches for reuse across multiple patterns. They are accessed by both the View Manager and Pattern Executor components.

View Manager. The View Manager adopts the continuous sliding view technology [34] to compute and re-use pattern matches across multiple patterns. It is responsible for making decisions regarding storing, retrieving and updating sub-pattern matches in a shared in-memory storage structure.

Transaction Manager. Concurrently accessing and updating shared sub-pattern matches across pattern queries could result in missing or duplicate pattern matches if view reads and writes are not carefully controlled. The Transaction Manager is responsible for access control of these shared views.

Statistics Collector. The runtime statistics used by the RR Estimator in the SPASS Optimizer are periodically collected by the Statistics Collector. Based on these periodic statistics, the SPASS Optimizer re-constructs a new sharing plan for the workload after these statistics are determined to have changed significantly [25].

3. SPASS OPTIMIZER

The goal of the SPASS Optimizer is to find a pattern sharing plan that minimizes the overall computational costs of the workload execution. To achieve this goal, we first establish a model to estimate the computational savings (*Redundancy Ratio*) achieved by sharing a specific sub-pattern. Second, we decide which subset of sub-patterns to share by reducing the well-known Minimum Substring Cover (MSC) [21] problem to our optimization problem. We exploit a polynomial-time algorithm for the MSC problem to efficiently find a near-optimal solution to our pattern sharing problem (Sec. 3.2). Lastly, we transform the selected sub-patterns into a hierarchical shared pattern plan covering all pattern queries in the workload (Sec. 3.3).

3.1 Redundancy Ratio of Sub-patterns

We now introduce the basis for the *Redundancy Ratio* (RR) scoring model used to reflect the candidate sub-patterns' re-usability across the pattern workload. The lower the score, the more benefit we achieve by sharing this sub-pattern. The redundancy in computational costs due to a common sub-pattern depends on the number of sub-pattern matches that are common across a given set of queries. The redundancy ratio also depends on the event ordering within an input stream. We refer to this factor as the *intra-query event correlation* as formally defined in Def. 1. We also define the *inter-query event correlation* across patterns that impacts the number of sub-pattern matches that can be shared across multiple queries.

Intra-query Event Correlation is essential for estimating the number of sub-pattern matches that can be formed in a given time interval. Intuitively it represents the percentage of events of type j (e_j) that follow an event of type i (e_i). This ratio can help us estimate the number of matches produced by a sequence pattern.

DEFINITION 1 (INTRA-QUERY EVENT CORRELATION). *For a time-ordered pattern $P = SEQ\ (E_1,\ldots E_i,\ldots E_j,\ldots,E_n)$, C_{Intra} is defined as:*

$$C_{Intra}(E_i, E_j) = \frac{|\langle e_i, e_j\rangle|_{window}}{|e_i| * |e_j|_{window}} \quad (1)$$

where $\langle\ e_i,e_j\ \rangle$ consists of e_i and e_j s.t $e_i.ts < e_j.ts$ and $|e_i|$ and $|e_j|$ denote the cardinality of event instances of type E_i and E_j respectively within one window.

Inter-query Event Correlation is used to estimate the sharing potential across multiple patterns. It is a ratio of the number of sub-pattern matches that are computed by two queries when they are shared to the total number of matches computed independently.

DEFINITION 2 (INTER-QUERY EVENT CORRELATION). *Given an input stream and a common sub-pattern SP of two patterns P_1 and P_2, the inter-query event correlation is defined as:*

$$C_{Inter}(P_i, P_j, SP) = \frac{|SP^{share}_{i,j}|_{window}}{|SP^{noshare}_{i,j}|_{window}} \quad (2)$$

where $|SP^{share}_{i,j}|$ denotes the cardinality of the sub-pattern matches found in the input stream that qualify to form complete pattern matches in P_i and P_j in a shared fashion, and $|SP|^{noshare}_{i,j}$ is the sum of the cardinalities of SP pattern matches produced by P_i and P_j separately.

Using the above defined notion of event correlation, our cost model estimates the costs for executing the sub-patterns in a shared versus an unshared manner. These cost functions are based on state-of-the-art physical implementations of operators as described in Appendix A.1. However, these functions could similarly be modeled for other operator implementations.

Time Period for Sampling. We propose to analyze the degree of sharing of sub-pattern matches over a certain time period, referred to as the *sample time period*. We then repeat this process on a periodic basis to accommodate event fluctuations. Within this time period, the optimizer constructs a stable sharing plan for the pattern workload. Choosing an appropriate sample time period has been well studied in the literature [16]. We leverage these techniques [16] to produce a stable execution plan designed to minimize CPU utilization. If the collected statistics significantly change, the SPASS Optimizer adapts to such change by migrating from the current shared pattern plan to the newly optimized one. For this we borrow plan adaptation techniques from the literature [31] to determine when plan migration becomes advantageous. Similarly, at the execution level we support caching for efficient plan migration [43] to avoid a full restart of the execution plan from scratch.

Analyzing the Cardinality of Sub-pattern Matches. Given a chosen sample time period, we compute the number of matches for a given sub-pattern within this time period. Figure 3 shows that the number of matches for a sub-pattern $SP = SEQ(A, B)$ produced by two parent patterns P_1 and P_2 may vary in a given time period. Consequently the number of pattern matches for SP that can be shared across P_1 and P_2 also varies with time.

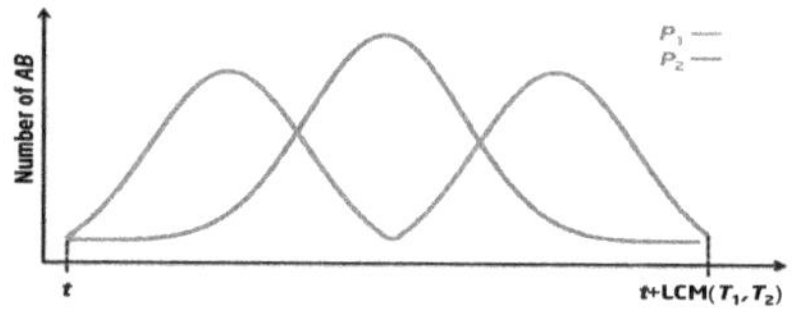

Figure 3: Non-Alignment of Cardinality of Pattern Matches

Observation 1. The cardinality of the sub-pattern matches varies over time. The crests and troughs of two such cardinalities plotted against time often may not align well. In fact, as depicted in Figure 3, the crests and troughs of P_1 and P_2 never align in this particular scenario even if their average cardinalities over time happen to be similar. Hence, the inter-query correlation between P_1 and P_2 with respect to AB would be quite low. Consequently, sharing this sub-pattern AB between P_1 and P_2 may even cause more harm than good by incurring unnecessary concurrency control overhead.

Observation 2. Even when the cardinalities of the sub-pattern matches happen to be the same for the two pattern queries along the time-axis, this still does not guarantee re-use. Consider two patterns $P_1 = SEQ(A, B, C, D)$ and $P_2 = SEQ(A, B, X, Y)$ both with a constant $window = 10s$. The matches for P_1 are $\{\langle a_2, b_3, c_5, d_{10}\rangle, \langle a_2, b_4, c_5, d_{10}\rangle\}$ while those for P_2 are $\{\langle a_5, b_7, x_9, y_{15}\rangle, \langle a_5, b_8, x_9, y_{15}\rangle\}$. In this case, the sub-pattern SEQ(A,B) is not common across P_1 and P_2 *at the event instance level*. This confirms that the benefit of sharing $SEQ(A, B)$ depends on the occurrences of the other sub-patterns in the parent pattern queries. We cannot solely rely on cardinality as decision criteria because the individual pattern matches may not actually overlap.

Redundancy Ratio Assignment. To accurately estimate the degree of the redundant computation of sub-pattern matches within each discrete time interval, we thus design a cost model $|C_S(SP_i, P_m, \ldots, P_n)|_j$ that denotes the cost to compute matches of the *shared* sub-pattern SP_i for all its parent patterns during the jth time interval. $|C(SP_i)|_j$ denotes the cost of producing all matches of SP_i for each parent pattern *separately*. Hence, the computation reuse is essentially the difference between $|C(SP_i)|_j$ and $|C_S(SP_i, P_m, \ldots, P_n)|_j$. The *Redundancy Ratio RR* of SP_i at the jth time interval, denoted by $RR(SP_i)_j$, can be defined as:

$$RR(SP_i)_j = \frac{|C_S(SP_i, P_m, \ldots, P_n)|_j}{|C(SP_i)|_j} \quad (3)$$

RR reflects the estimated cost benefit that can be achieved if sub-pattern SP_i is shared among its parent pattern queries for a given interval t_j in the event stream. The lower this RR is, the higher the benefit of sharing this sub-pattern. We compute these costs for these non-overlapping discrete intervals. We then take the average of these scores over the entire sampled time period. This average score assigned to each sub-pattern SP_i, denoted by $RR(SP_i)$ is:

$$RR(SP_i) = \frac{\sum_{j=0}^{t}\left[\frac{|C_S(SP_i, P_m, \ldots, P_n)|_j}{|C(SP_i)|_j}\right]}{t} \quad (4)$$

where t denotes the number of discrete intervals in the sampled time period. The number of discrete intervals is referred to as the level of granularity of discretization. Fine-grained analysis of sub-patterns highlights the actual re-usability of sub-pattern results across the parent queries.

		t_1	t_2	t_3	t_4	t_5	T	
AB	P_1	400	500	300	100	50	1350	No Sharing
	P_2	100	200	300	500	300	1400	
	$P_1 \cup P_2$	400	500	300	500	300	2000	Sharing
XY	P_1	400	500	300	400	50	1650	No Sharing
	P_2	100	100	100	500	300	1100	
	$P_1 \cup P_2$	400	500	300	500	300	2000	Sharing

Figure 4: Example of Discretized Granularity

EXAMPLE 1. *Consider the following two sub-patterns AB and XY. Assuming that the sampled period for both AB and XY is T, and T is discretized into 5 time intervals (i.e., t_1, t_2, t_3, t_4, and t_5). The number of matches computed with or without sharing in these intervals are shown in Figure 4.*

Now if we were to treat the entire period T as one time interval, then RR(AB) = 2000/(1350 + 1400) = RR(XY) = 2000/(1650 + 1100) = 0.727. In contrast, if the RR of both sub-patterns were to be calculated with finer granularity, the RR of AB and XY would be 0.741 and 0.759, respectively. Clearly sharing the sub-query AB would gain more computational savings compared to XY. Hence, the cost derived with a fine granularity of discrete time intervals more accurately reflects the degree of sharing.

Sharing Sub-patterns Across Multiple Window Sizes. Multiple window sizes for event patterns are easily accommodated in the Redundancy Ratio computation. When queries have different window sizes, we use the Lowest Common Multiple (LCM) of the window sizes as the smallest unit of time during which each query produces pattern matches for an integral number of window slides.

3.2 Sharing Sub-Patterns to Minimize Redundancy in Computation

Having the *RR* score assigned to each sub-pattern in the above step, the SPASS Optimizer needs to find the most suitable subset of sub-patterns to share. Given a set of pattern queries W, the ***sub-pattern sharing optimization problem*** is to find a subset of sub-patterns such that all pattern queries in the workload W can be answered, and the total redundancy ratio of this subset is minimal compared to all possible alternate solutions. We prove that this problem is equivalent to the well-known Minimum Substring Cover problem [21]. The SPASS Optimizer can thus employ a polynomial-time approximate solution to the Minimum Substring Cover problem to produce the set of sub-patterns to share. We now describe how the sequence sub-pattern sharing problem can be mapped to the Minimum Substring Cover Problem. In later subsections we extend this to consider other operators.

Minimum Substring Cover (MSC). For a given set of strings S, let $\Theta(S)$ denote the set of all *substrings* of strings in S. We define a *cover* of S to be a subset $C \in \Theta(S)$ such that any string $s \in S$ can be written as a concatenation of strings in C. The MSC problem is formally defined as follows.

DEFINITION 3 (MINIMUM SUBSTRING COVER). ***Instance:*** *A set of strings S, a weight function $F : \Theta(S) \rightarrow \mathbb{Q}_{0,1}$ where $\mathbb{Q}_{0,1}$ is the set of positive proper fractions.* ***Solution:*** *A cover C of S. That is, a set of strings $C \subseteq \Theta(S)$, where for each $s \in S$ a set $c_1, \ldots, c_p \subset C$ exists, with $s = c_1 \bullet \ldots \bullet c_p$ where $\bullet$ represents concatenation.* ***Measure:*** *The total weight of the cover, i.e., $F(C) = \Sigma_{c \in C} F(c)$ is minimal among all possible covers.*

Problem Mapping. We now show that having assigned weights to the sub-patterns which have the same properties as those of the weights of the substrings, the sub-pattern sharing problem is equivalent to the Minimum Substring Cover problem.

LEMMA 1 (REDUCTION). *If the Redundancy Ratio (RR) of the sub-patterns is in $\mathbb{Q}_{0,1}$, then every instance of the sub-pattern sharing problem can be reduced to a valid instance of the Minimum Substring Cover (MSC) problem (Def. 3).*

The proof can be found in Appendix A.4.

Approximate Algorithm to MSC. The well-known Local-Ratio (LR) algorithm [21] has been shown to find a cover of a set of strings C in polynomial time. Furthermore, it guarantees an approximation factor of m where m is the maximum length of the strings in the set of strings. We now leverage this algorithm to find the approximate set of sharing sub-patterns. The algorithm takes as input the pattern workload W and our RR scores of its sub-patterns. We output a list of pattern queries and their associated sub-patterns as a *query map* ($qMap\langle P_i$, list$\langle SP_i\rangle\rangle$). This data-structure subsequently facilitates easy construction of the *hierarchical execution plan*. We denote the set of all sub-patterns as $\Theta(W)$ and each individual sub-pattern in $\Theta(W)$ as SP_i. The solution $qMap$ is first set as empty (Line 1). The algorithm selects a pattern P_i not covered by $qMap$ (Line 3), and examines all sub-patterns in a temporary structure $qMap^c$ that are not already in $qMap$ (Lines 4). It then subtracts the minimum score $\epsilon =$

$\min\{RR\}$ from the cumulative RR (Lines 7), and recurs over the new weight function (Line 8).

Algorithm 1 LocalRatio(W, RR)

```
Input: A set of patterns W, RR : Θ(W) → Q_{0,1}
Output: A subset of sub-patterns C_W
 1: qMap = empty
 2: for every P_i ∈ W do
 3:   if P_i not covered by SP_i ∈ qMap of maximum length then
 4:     qMap^c ← SP_i ∈ Θ(W)\qMap
 5:     ε = min(sp) : SP_i ∈ qMap^c
 6:     RR1 = SP_i ∈ qMap^c ? ε : 0
 7:     RR2 = RR - RR1
 8:     qMap ← LR(W, RR2)
 9:     if qMap\P_i is a cover for W then
10:       qMap = (qMap\P_i)
11:       qMap.put(P_i, SP_i)
12:     end if
13:     return qMap
14:   end if
15: end for
```

3.2.1 Sharing Across Other Operators

The SPASS system supports a variety of event pattern operators including OR, AND and NOT with its optimization strategy described above with minor to no alteration. Both negation in SEQ or in AND patterns like $!E_i$ can be considered as a new symbol. Thus before using the solution to the MSC problem, each negated event type is mapped to a particular letter. The OR operator is simply a filter. Therefore it can be easily piggy-backed as part of the pattern detection process. We now describe how pattern matches can be shared across SEQ and AND operators.

While the previous derivation has been shown for sharing across multiple SEQ operators, the same can be extended to accommodate the AND operators. In essence an AND operator is a permutation of a set of events. Thus a SEQ and an AND operator with the same set of events would have some matches in common. For instance $AND(A,B)$ will produce matches for events A and B arriving in *any* order within the window, while $SEQ(A,B)$ will produce matches for events A and B arriving in order within the same window. Thus a subset of matches for AND operator will also qualify as matches for the SEQ operator. We can therefore share pattern matches between these different operators.

Our assumption here is that the most common type of CEP operator is the SEQ operator along with some AND operators. Hence given a workload composed of many SEQ and some AND operators, we slightly modify the above problem mapping to share pattern matches across both SEQ and AND. One important observations is that only those AND pattern matches can be shared with a SEQ operator that have events arriving in the same order specified in the SEQ operator. Thus as a first step to the MSC problem we rewrite the AND operator such that the events align with the SEQ operators. Given a set of m SEQ operators and k AND operators, we rewrite each AND operator in a maximum of m distinct ways such that each aligns with the operands in each SEQ operator. Using this rearrangement, it is now possible to see the overlap of event sub-patterns across SEQ and AND operators using the solution to the MSC problem. Thus the search space is only increased by a polynomial of mk rather than an exponential increase incurred by enumerating all permutations of AND.

The weights of sharing these sub-patterns across different operators correspond to the ratio of how many pattern matches are shared to the total number of pattern matches. Thus using the previous example of $SEQ(A,B)$ and $AND(A,B)$, if most pattern matches for AND are such that B arrives after A, then the *Redundancy Ratio* correctly reflects that with a lower score.

During execution, when SEQ and AND operators are shared, the implementation of the AND operator is deployed and the set of pattern matches arriving in the same order as the SEQ are pushed to the SEQ query. If multiple orderings of the same operands of the AND operator are chosen, they are identified in the step of building the shared pattern plan and are shared by multiple SEQ operators.

EXAMPLE 2. *Given $SEQ(X,B,A,Y,C,E)$, $SEQ(P,E,A,B,Q)$, $SEQ(D,E,B,A,C)$ and $AND(A,B,C,D,E)$. Here the AND query is rewritten as: $AND(D,B,A,C,E)$, $AND(C,D,E,A,B)$ and $AND(D,E,B,A,C)$. Thus there are now 6 patterns instead of 4 patterns as input to the MSC problem.*

3.3 Shared Pattern Plan

The solution to the minimum substring cover problem returns a map of pattern queries with their corresponding set of sub-patterns that cover this pattern query ($map\langle P_i$, list$\langle SP_i\rangle\rangle$). We now generate a shared pattern plan that compactly represents the multiple pattern workload. Algorithm 2 transforms the set of sub-patterns into a shared pattern plan. Such transformation-based approach is commonly used to generate shared query plans for traditional multi-query workloads [17, 24].

The shared pattern plan is represented as a graph *qGraph*. Each node in the graph represents a pattern or sub-pattern. Algorithm 2 iterates over the patterns in $qMap\langle P_i$, list$\langle SP_i\rangle\rangle$. For each pattern P_i, if a corresponding node is not found in *qGraph*, a root node is created. Its corresponding sub-patterns are scanned and the following action is taken: if a sub-pattern SP_j corresponds to an existing node in *qGraph*, no action is required. If a sub-pattern is seen for the first time, it is added to the *qGraph* as a child node of P_i. We illustrate Algorithm 2 using the following example.

Algorithm 2 Shared Pattern Plan Generation

```
Input: Map qMap
Output: Plan qGraph
subPatternList ← φ
while qMap != φ do
  P_i = qMap.remove()
  subPList ← qMap.get(P_i)
  while subPList != φ do
    subP ← subPList.remove()
    if subP ∉ qGraph then
      qGraph.addLeaf(newSubP)
    end if
    subP.addParent(P_i)
  end while
end while
return qGraph
```

EXAMPLE 3. *The following three pattern queries (i.e., P_1, P_2, and P_3 on the left) and the selected sub-patterns for sharing (on the right) are the inputs to our SPASS Optimizer.*
P_1: $(SEQ(A,B,C)) \rightarrow SEQ(A,B)$, $SEQ(B,C)$
P_2: $(SEQ(A,B,C,D)) \rightarrow SEQ(A,B,C)$, $SEQ(D)$
P_3: $(SEQ(A,B,X)) \rightarrow SEQ(A,B)$, $SEQ(X)$
Given the above selected sub-patterns to share, the algorithm loops through the patterns from P_1 to P_3. It scans the shortest sub-

patterns of P_1 which are $SEQ(A, B)$ and $SEQ(B, C)$. Therefore they are made leaves in the pattern DAG. $SEQ(A, B, C)$ is made the parent of these leaves. For P_2, the shortest sub-pattern $SEQ(D)$ is made a leaf. The next shortest pattern $SEQ(A, B, C)$ is then found to be already in the pattern DAG. Hence $SEQ(A, B, C, D)$ is made the parent of $SEQ(A, B, C)$ and $SEQ(D)$. For P_3, $SEQ(X)$ is added as a leaf node and $SEQ(A, B)$ already exists in the DAG. The final query DAG formed is depicted in Figure 5.

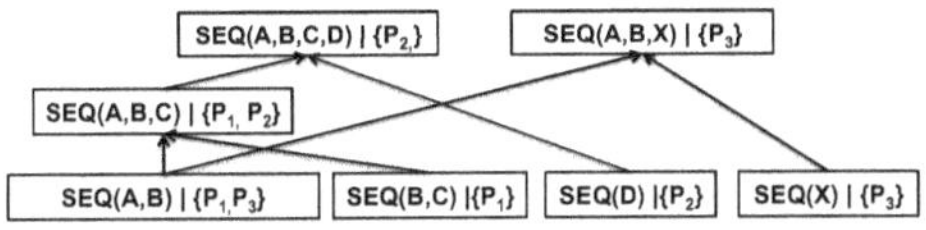

Figure 5: Shared Pattern Plan

type. All patterns composed of this event type access this shared buffer during the pattern matching process. On the other hand the *shared continuous sliding views* (S-CSV) cache intermediate results for sub-patterns. Each shared sub-pattern SP_i in the shared pattern plan has an associated S-CSV structure denoted by $view_{SP_i}$ that maintains matches for the sub-pattern SP_i.

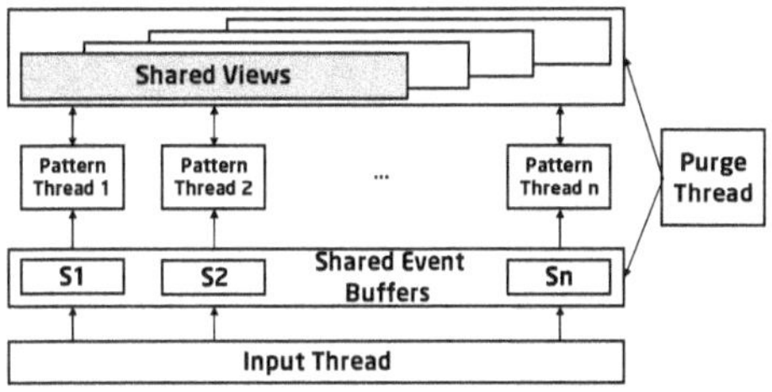

Figure 6: Shared Pattern Executor

4. SPASS RUNTIME

Given a shared pattern plan produced by the SPASS Optimizer, we now introduce the SPASS Runtime - our multi-threaded execution engine for concurrent shared pattern processing on event streams. We first describe the execution strategy for processing this plan assuming that only one pattern is processed upon the arrival of an event instance. Thereafter, we relax this restriction to handle (1) multiple events and (2) multiple patterns triggered simultaneously.

The key challenge of maintaining result matches for sub-patterns is tackled by plugging in *continuous sliding views* technology [34], which stores intermediate results of sub-patterns and incrementally updates and reuses them for answering a *single* sequence pattern query over sliding windows. We adopt and then extend this view technology from supporting a single pattern query to *shared continuous sliding views* to handle our multiple pattern scenario. We assume an identical window constraint of size $window$ which later is relaxed.

4.1 Shared Pattern Execution

SPASS Execution Model. The SPASS Runtime receives event tuples from their respective input event threads. The events are assumed to arrive in order. Each event type is associated with a shared event buffer. When an event arrives, it is inserted into its associated shared event buffers. Each pattern designates a *triggering event* that initiates the execution of this pattern. For the SEQ pattern $SEQ(A, B, C)$, the triggering event is C, which implies that the execution of $SEQ(A, B, C)$ begins only when an event of type 'C' arrives. When a sequence pattern execution is triggered by the arrival of its triggering event, all its sub-patterns are executed. Our execution adopts a *Non-deterministic Finite Automata (NFA)* approach to represent the structure of an event sequence. Namely, sequence patterns are computed using the NFA-based execution strategy by mapping successive event types to successive NFA states [6, 42]. Each sub-pattern execution is an independent thread that reads events from the shared event buffers. These partial sub-pattern matches are then stored in shared storage structures described next. These matches are not all computed from scratch. Instead sub-pattern matches that have once been computed are then stored in sequence views and subsequently reused by accessing the materialized views associated with that sub-pattern.

Shared Storage of Events and Intermediate Pattern Matches. Two types of shared storage units are used in the SPASS Runtime infrastructure (Figure 6). As is common in CEP systems [42], we utilize *shared event buffers* to store event instances for each event

Actions on Event Arrival. As events arrive into the SPASS Runtime, one of several actions is triggered. (1) **Append.** The arriving event is inserted into the respective event buffer via an *Append* operation on the shared event buffer. (2) **Read.** Pattern execution of a pattern P_i is triggered if the event is a *triggering event*. During pattern execution, events are read from shared event buffers and views as needed. These are modeled as *Read* operations. Sub-pattern matches are inserted into the corresponding shared views during pattern execution. This is modeled as an *Append* operation on the continuous sliding view structure. (3) **Purge.** Events from the buffers or sub-pattern matches in the shared views eventually expire out of the current window. They then should be purged. Assuming the new event e_i arrives at time i all events with timestamps less than (i - $window$) are deleted*. This is modeled as a $Purge$ operation. In summary, three types of operations, *Read*, *Append*, and $Purge$, are performed on the two types of shared memory structures, namely *shared event buffers* and *shared continuous sliding views*.

Pattern Execution via Shared Continuous Sliding Views. If a pattern P_i execution is triggered by the arrival of an event e_i, all its sub-patterns SP_i are executed one by one until completion. SEQ sub-patterns are computed using the NFA-based execution strategy [42, 6] while AND sub-patterns are executed using a traditional join operator. The sub-pattern matches are however not all computed from scratch. Instead sub-pattern matches that had previously been computed are stored in a $view$ associated with that sub-pattern. These sub-pattern matches stored in the views can then be shared across multiple patterns. Thus matches for sub-pattern SP_i produced and stored by one pattern P_j could be *reused* by another pattern P_k.

In order to facilitate collaborative re-use of *shared continuous sliding views*, we augment these view structures with timestamp-based indicators called the *View Validity Interval (VVI)*. These VVI indicate the interval of time for which the buffer contains the complete set of event matches. Further, when a pattern accesses these view structures, it looks for pattern matches within a certain time interval called the *View Lookup Interval (VLI)*. [34]. Based on whether this interval is currently valid for the shared view, pattern matches are read from the view ($Read_{View}$) or new matches are written to the view ($Append_{View}$). When new matches are appended to a view, the *VVI* is updated to reflect the latest state of the view. Example 4 demonstrates the above principles.

*We assume that events arrive in increasing order of timestamp.

EXAMPLE 4. *Consider the patterns P_1 and P_2 depicted in Figure 7. P_1 and P_2 both share the sub-pattern SP_c using its associated shared view $views_{SPc}$. For pattern P_1, SP_1 is executed followed by SP_c while for pattern P_2, SP_2 is executed followed by SP_c. Each pattern has a designated triggering event type (D for P_1 and Y for P_2). When event instance y_{13} arrives, P_2 is triggered and a match $\{\langle x_5 y_{13}\rangle\}$ is produced for sub-pattern SP_2 of P_2. Then sub-pattern SP_c is executed for the constrained View Lookup Interval (VLI) in this case is [13-10, 5] The view is thus updated to contain matches valid for the interval [3,5]. As the triggering event d_{17} for P_2 arrives, the match $\{\langle c_{16} d_{17}\rangle\}$ is produced for sub-pattern SP_1. SP_c is now updated for the interval [7, 16]. Four new sub-pattern matches are produced and stored in the $views_{SPc}$ for possible reuse. The view interval is now set to [7,16] to mark its completeness up to 16. Upon the arrival of event instance d_{18}, the view content is reused. Furthermore, when y_{20} arrives, P_2 triggers the update of SP_c for the interval [10, 18]. This process illustrates how we have step by step supported synchronous reuse and update of the views.*

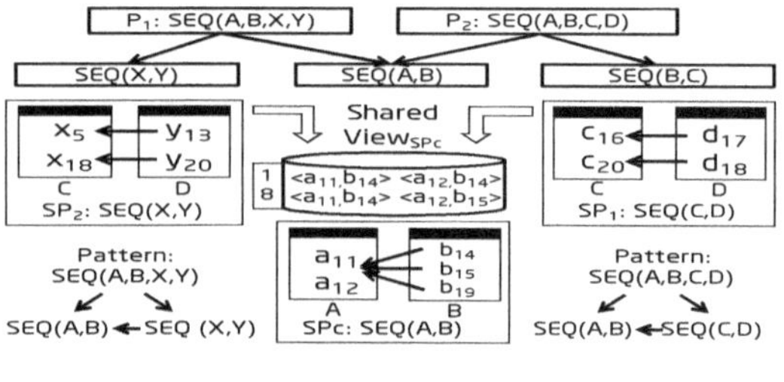

Figure 7: Shared SEQ Execution using Continuous Views

For simplicity we have described the execution when all patterns share the same window and no predicates exist. However multiple windows can be easily supported by keeping pattern matches for the largest window. Each pattern then filters out the matches relevant to its specific window.

The reuse, append, and purge of the shared continuous sliding view may require an additional step to ensure the result correctness based on the largest window among all windows associated to a view. Similarly, correlated predicates in the patterns can also be supported by an additional filtering phase. We adopt popular approaches for handling predicate sharing from the literature [20, 27]. For example, if a sub-pattern SP is shared across two patterns yet the two patterns specify different selection predicates C_1 and C_2 on this sub-pattern respectively, then the shared sub-pattern is rewritten as $(C_1 \vee C_2)$ to satisfy either selection predicate using well-known query rewriting techniques [27]and thus to be sharable. Predicate migration techniques such as push-down and pull-up [20] can be exploited in our SPASS Runtime as well. Further details are described in Appendix B.2.

4.2 Concurrent Shared Execution

We now relax the assumption that only one event is processed at a time until its completion. Instead we now consider the concurrent execution of two or more input events. As a consequence multiple pattern queries may be active at the same time. These concurrent execution threads could therefore attempt to access or update a *shared continuous sliding view* at the same time. This may lead to duplicate or missing results in the view.

EXAMPLE 5. *Figure 8 shows a time instance when the shared view contains all results valid during the time interval [5,10]. At*

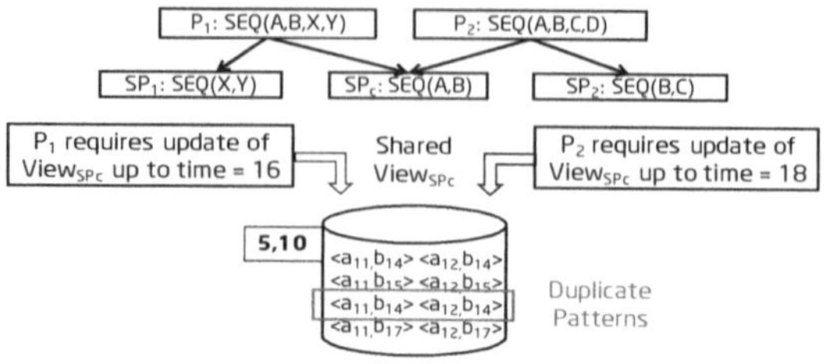

Figure 8: Duplicate Pattern Matches due to Concurrency

this instance, pattern P_1 requires to append the shared view up to time 16. At the same time P_2 is triggered and tries to also update the view up to timestamp 18. Without careful scheduling, P_2 might start updating while P_1 is still updating the view. This results in duplicate matches being produced namely $\{\langle a_{11} b_{14}\rangle, \langle a_{12}\ b_{14}\rangle\}$ as well as resources being wasted due to repeated computations.

The above example demonstrates how duplicate pattern matches may be produced during concurrent shared pattern execution. Thus our SPASS Runtime needs to deploy a concurrency control mechanism that avoids these erroneous results. As explained below, we use a transaction-based approach to guarantee correctness.

In the SPASS system, each event has a single point of entry. On arrival an event can trigger one or more of the following types of actions, namely, R_{View}, A_{View_t}, P_{View_t}, R_{Buffer_t}, A_{Buffer_t}, and P_{Buffer_t} ($R - Read$, $A - Append$, $P - Purge$). Given the indicators attached to shared views, namely the *View Validity Intervals*, we determine upon the entry of an event which data structures the event will need to read from and which it will need to update.

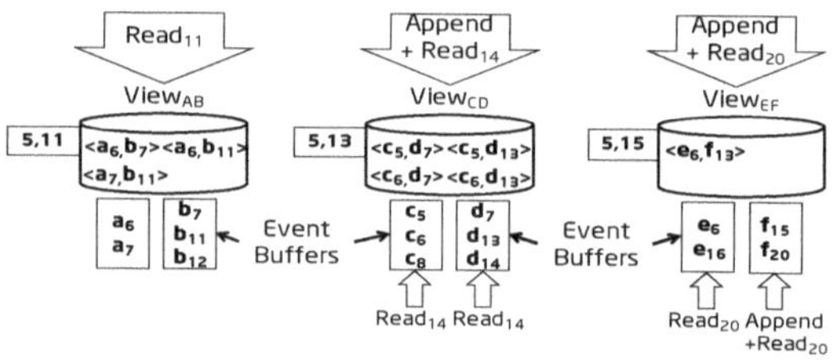

Figure 9: Actions on Event Buffers and Views

EXAMPLE 6. *Figure 9 depicts a pattern SEQ(A,B,C,D,E,F) that is partitioned into three parts namely SEQ(A,B), SEQ(C,D) and SEQ(E,F). When the event f_{20} arrives, the View Validity Intervals (VVIs) associated with the views $View_{EF}$, $View_{CD}$, and $View_{AB}$ are [5,15], [5,13], and [5,11], respectively. Judging from the shared event buffers it can be inferred that the $View_{EF}$ must be updated up to the time 20. In fact, the event buffer F must be updated as well as read from. The event buffer E must only be read from. Consequently, the event buffers of C and D must be read to update the $View_{CD}$ accordingly. The $View_{CD}$ will be updated to the time 14 as d_{14} is the last event in D that can join with the event instance e_{16} in E. For the $View_{AB}$, we can infer that it only needs to be read from as the last B event that can join with a C event to form valid matches is b_{11}. The $View_{AB}$ already contains matches up to this timestamp 11. Hence, the event buffers A and B do not need to be read from. Thus the actions triggered upon the arrival of event f_{20} are $A_{F_{20}}$, $R_{F_{20}}$, $R_{E_{20}}$, $A_{EF_{20}}$, $R_{EF_{20}}$, $R_{C_{14}}$, $R_{D_{14}}$, $A_{CD_{14}}$, $R_{CD_{14}}$, $R_{AB_{11}}$. Finally the last action is to purge events* *beyond the current window given by* $currentTime - window = 20 - 15 = 5$*, namely events with timestamp* < 5*.*

Notion of Correctness. As seen from the above example multiple actions are triggered upon the arrival of an event. Several of these actions can take place out of order, while for others a strict order must be enforced. These semantics include:
1. A_{View} must be preceded by $R_{Buffers}$. In order to append results to a given view, its associated event buffers must first be read.
2. If there are two append actions on different views A_{View1} and A_{View2}, any order of execution would be correct.
3. P_{View_t} or P_{Buffer_t} can be executed only when all operations before timestamp t have been completed.

The action A_{View} requires new pattern matches to be constructed and written to the view. Thus it needs to first read events from multiple event buffers ($R_{Buffer(s)}$). Hence $\{R_{Buffer(s)} + A_{View}\}$ must occur in order. On the other hand the actions A_{Buffer}, R_{View}, P_{Buffer}, P_{View} are independent of each other and thus can be executed in any order.

DEFINITION 4. *A SPASS Transaction is defined as the minimal set of SPASS actions that must be enforced to occur together as an atomic series of operations when an event arrives.*

Analysis of the SPASS Runtime reveals that there are the following set of atomic actions namely: $\{R_{View}\}$, $\{A_{View} + R_{Buffer(s)}\}$, $\{A_{Buffer}\}$, $\{P_{View/Buffer}\}$. Multiple transactions can be triggered upon the arrival of an event. They would each belong to one of the above four types of transactions. The above definition considers the notion that when a view is updated, it must be able to access the event buffers which form the raw events for the pattern matches. On the other hand, if an event triggers appends for two views, the two appends can take place completely independent of each other, thus allowing maximum parallelism. Further, the R_{View} transaction is separated from A_{View} to allow higher degree of parallelism as multiple R_{View} transactions can occur simultaneously while only one A_{View} is allowed on a view.

Lock Insertion and Compatibility: Locks are inserted upon the arrival of an event into the SPASS system. As shown in Example 6, the actions to be triggered in the SPASS system are determined as soon as an event arrives into the system. These actions are grouped into valid classes of transactions. Thus the locks required by these transactions can also be determined at this stage. These locks are then inserted into lock buffers associated with each shared storage i.e., event buffers and shared views. Thus a purge request P_{*_t} will be inserted only when requests for locks triggered by events arriving before t have all been inserted into lock buffers. This purge lock will not be granted until all other lock requests with an earlier timestamp have been processed.

Once locks have been inserted into respective lock buffers the atomic set of actions are ready to be triggered. Henceforth we adopt the well-known scheduling scheme of **Strict 2-Phase Locking (S2PL)** [38]. There is a pool of atomic actions that exist on a given shared buffer at any given time. Based on the lock compatibility protocol described below, some will be allowed to run. Figure 10 shows the compatibility of *Read*, *Append* and *Purge* locks. The read and append locks on *shared buffers* are completely independent of each other due to the sequential lock assignment. For *shared views*, append operations are not allowed to be executed concurrently. This avoids the creation of duplicate results. Lastly, the purge lock on shared buffers and views are most restrictive. In order to grant a purge request, the transaction manager must first make sure that the lock buffer for that resource does not contain any read requests on that resource that may try to read events or pattern matches purged by this purge transaction. This prevents any missing pattern matches to arise.

Acquired / Requested	Shared Buffer		Shared Views	
	Read	Append	Read	Append
Read	✓	✓	✓	✓
Append	✓	✓	✓	×
Requested				
Purge	×	✓	×	✓

Figure 10: Lock Compatibility in Transactions

5. PERFORMANCE EVALUATION

5.1 Experimental Setup

We have implemented our SPASS framework on top of the Chaos stream management system [40] using Java. Experiments were conducted on a PC with Intel Pentium IV 2.8 GHz CPU and 4GB RAM running Windows 7 system.

Methodology. We evaluate the efficiency and plan quality produced by our SPASS Optimizer. We compare our shared multiple sequence pattern execution strategy to the state-of-the-art approaches, including single sequence pattern query [42] evaluation without sharing sub-patterns, and shared sequence pattern query evaluation via prefix and suffix sharing [14]. Next we evaluate the efficiency and scalability of our SPASS Runtime by varying various parameters of the workload patterns. We show the performance benefits of the SPASS Runtime on a multi-core architecture by running it in single and multi-threaded mode.

Data sets and queries. We evaluate our techniques using two data sets, (1) real life stock trades data [1], which contains stock ticker and timestamp information, and (2) traffic data set using the data generator of the linear road [2]. In stock dataset, the portion of the trace holds 120,000 event instances. Each event has a stock ticker name and a timestamp information. To evaluate SPASS we create event patterns over these data sets, including SEQ, AND, and ! operators. We show experiments with the traffic dataset in the Appendix C.

Evaluation metrics. We compare the *average execution time* for computing multiple sequence pattern queries per window slide. After every window slide, the execution time is recorded for each pattern and averaged over the entire pattern workload run time. The average execution times for all patterns are then added to produce the average execution time per window for the entire workload.

5.2 Evaluating SPASS Optimizer

Here, we study the effectiveness and accuracy of our SPASS Optimizer for shared multiple plan generation. Specifically, we compare the *compile-time optimization performance* and the *quality* of the resulting plans for two alternative techniques, namely the approximate LR algorithm (LR) and exhaustive search (ES). The compile-time optimization performance is measured by the CPU time taken by either algorithm. We vary the key parameters that affect the performance of our SPASS Optimizer including the length and the number of the patterns. As baseline for the best quality shared pattern plan, we employ ES for finding the optimal plan for the given pattern workload. We generate pattern queries over the stock stream [1] data set to evaluate the SPASS Optimizer. Two types of workloads, only SEQ patterns as well as mixed patterns composed of SEQ and AND, are used to evaluate our optimizer.

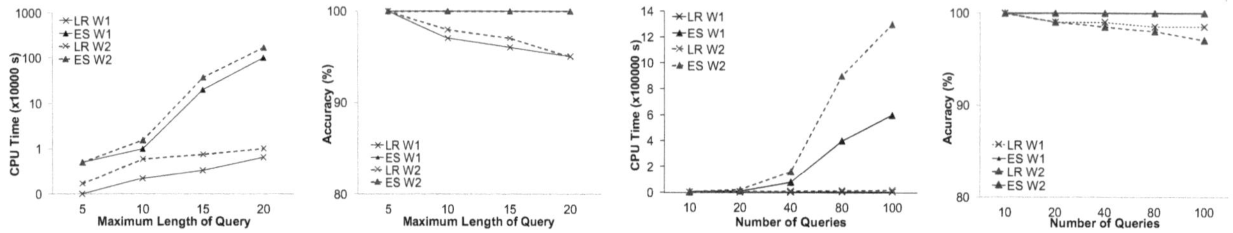

(a) Varying Pattern Length (l) (b) Varying Pattern Length (l) (c) Varying Pattern Number (k) (d) Varying Pattern Number (k)

Figure 11: Efficiency and Quality of SPASS Optimizer

5.2.1 *Effect of Varying the Pattern Length* l

Efficiency of SPASS Optimizer. We first evaluate the efficiency of the SPASS Optimizer with respect to plan generation time. We consider a workload of 10 patterns in which the length of the sequence pattern in each pattern is varied from $l = 5$ to 20. The continuous lines correspond to the workload with only SEQ queries while the dotted lines correspond to the mixed workload with SEQ and AND patterns. Our optimizer using the LR algorithm, as shown in Figure 11(a), is significantly more efficient than the alternative ES approach for both workloads. The total number of possible sub-patterns is proportional to the square of the length of the sequence pattern [21]. This drastically affects ES because this approach has to check all possible combinations in the search space. As depicted in Figure 11(a), the optimization time of ES increases exponentially (around 1,000,000 times) as the pattern length is increased from 10 to 20. In contrast, our proposed LR algorithm increases polynomially with the pattern length by a factor of around 6 times. The workload with mixed AND and SEQ patterns also maintains approximately the same ratio for ES and LR approaches.

Plan quality of SPASS Optimizer. Figure 11(b) shows the quality of the set of sub-patterns produced by our LR algorithm. The quality of the shared pattern plan is obtained by the total RR of the sub-patterns selected by the optimizer. The optimal solution should give the minimum total RR. As expected, the quality of the sub-pattern set from the LR algorithm slightly degrades as the length of the patterns increases. Compared to ES, the quality suffers from the degradation by 5% as the length of the sequence pattern increases from 10 to 20. In this case both workloads approximately has the same reduction in accuracy.

5.2.2 *Effect of Varying the Number of Patterns* k

Efficiency of SPASS Optimizer. We now examine the efficiency of the optimizer as the number of patterns varies from 10 to 100 while keeping the length of each pattern constant at 15 events. Our optimizer, as shown in Figure 11(c), is significantly more efficient than the ES approach. Again, the total number of possible sub-patterns is proportional to the number of patterns in the worst case. As depicted in Figure 11(c), ES is prohibitively expensive and thus is not practical. The optimization time of ES increases exponentially (around 400,000 times) as the number of patterns increases from 40 to 100. In contrast, our proposed LR optimizer increases linearly by wisely choosing the sub-patterns with lower redundancy RR (Section 3.1). Again, the mixed workload (depicted by the dotted lines) takes overall higher optimization time due to the extra search complexity incurred by AND patterns.

Plan quality of SPASS Optimizer. Figure 11(d) compares the quality of the set of sub-patterns produced by our LR algorithm with the optimal solution produced by ES for different numbers of patterns. As depicted in Figure 11(d), the quality degradation of our LR algorithm is almost negligible, i.e., 2.5% as the number of patterns increases from 10 to 100. The result again shows our LR algorithm is robust in the number of pattern variations.

5.3 Evaluating SPASS Runtime

We now evaluate the efficiency and scalability of the SPASS Runtime compared to the most prominent approach, i.e., SASE [42]. Using the SASE approach each pattern in the workload maintains its own event data-structures. The metric used in these experiments is the average execution time, i.e., the total pattern execution times (see Section 5.1) over all window slides divided by the number of window slides. It shows how quickly our SPASS Runtime produces the results for all pattern queries. That is the main concern from the application users' point of view. We vary three key parameters: (1) the length of shared sub-patterns, (2) the number of sequence patterns sharing the same sub-pattern, and (3) the window size. We work with three different workloads over the stock stream [1]. Workload $W1$ consists of only SEQ patterns, $W2$ has mixed SEQ and AND patterns, while $W3$ has SEQ patterns with ! sub-patterns.

In addition, we also evaluate the effectiveness of the SPASS weight assignment, concurrency mechanism, and overhead of statistics collection. In Sec. 5.4, we further compare our SPASS system against existing sub-pattern selection strategies such as prefix-sharing [14], suffix-sharing and random sub-pattern selection.

Effect of varying the window size w**.** As demonstrated in Figure 12(a), the window size w of the workloads is varied from $500ms$ to $2000ms$. The three workloads have 20 patterns each. The average execution time is computed for each window slide. As w increases, each window contains a larger number of events to process. This leads to more sharing opportunities and hence greater performance benefits. Figure 12(a) demonstrates that as the window size increases, the average execution time of both shared and unshared executions increases. The shared execution strategy avoids repeated computations. For both data sets, the execution time without sharing is approximately 16 times that of our SPASS execution when the window size is $500ms$. Moreover, as the window size increases from $500ms$ to $2000ms$ the performance of the unshared approach degrades significantly for all 3 workloads, while the SPASS shared execution exhibits a robust trend. At $w = 2000ms$, the unshared approach is approximately 26 times slower than our SPASS shared approach.

Effect of varying the number of shared patterns k**.** In this experiments, we vary the number of patterns in each workload k from 10 to 100. Here the length of the patterns (i.e., the number of event types in the patterns) is kept unchanged. As the number of shared patterns increases, we observe that our SPASS Runtime is 20 times faster compared to the unshared approach on average (Figure 12(b)). This difference in average execution time becomes

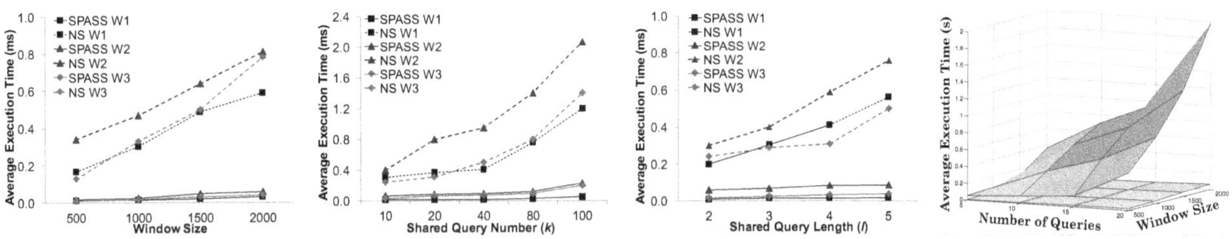

(a) Varying Window Size (w) (b) Varying Pattern Number (k) (c) Varying Pattern Length (l) (d) Varying All Together

Figure 12: SPASS Shared Execution with Varying Parameters

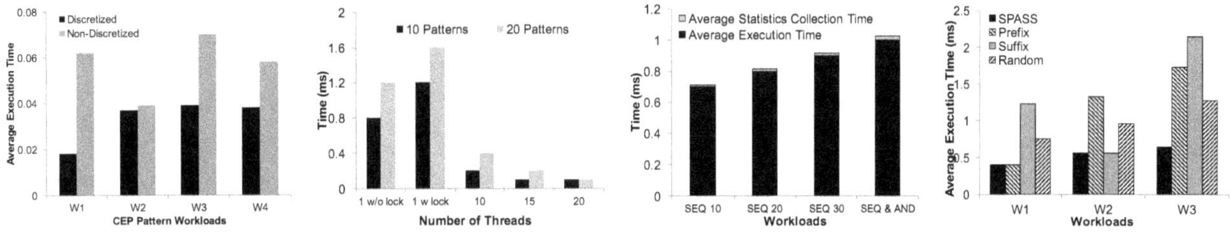

(a) Weight Accuracy (b) Concurrency (c) Statistics Overhead (d) Comparison with SOA

Figure 13: SPASS Runtime Performance

more significant when the number of patterns sharing common sub-patterns increases. This is because our shared execution avoids repeated computations by exploiting the shared views.

Effect of varying the shared sub-pattern length l. In this experiment we vary the length of the shared sub-patterns in each workload from 2 to 5. The window size is fixed at $1000ms$ for each workload. As the shared common sub-pattern length is increased, the repeated computations are saved to a greater extent. The average execution time shown in Figure 12(c) confirms the efficiency of the SPASS shared execution. As the length of the sequence patterns increases, the average execution times of both approaches increase. However, by sharing the computations of the shared sub-patterns, the average execution time is reduced by an average factor of 25 times from the unshared approach.

Effect of varying the window size w and the number of patterns k. Having seen the effects of one parameter at a time, we now vary two key parameters together to evaluate their interplay. We obtain a surface chart comparing the performance of shared and unshared execution strategies. Figure 12(d) shows the window sizes and number of pattern queries on the two planar (X and Y) axes. The vertical (Z) axis shows the average execution time. The surface for the shared approach is much closer to the XY plane while the unshared approach diverges from the shared plane as either window size or the pattern numbers or both are increased. As the window size and the number of patterns sharing a sub-pattern both increase, the shared execution achieves more performance gains. On average the shared approach performs 17 times faster average execution time compared to the unshared approach.

Evaluating the effectiveness of SPASS weight assignment. We now illustrate the effectiveness of our weight assignment approach to sub-patterns by analyzing redundancies in the sub-pattern match computation at a fine versus at a coarse granularity. We consider 4 different workloads of 10 pattern queries each. For each workload, the patterns are first run independently to obtain the exact counts of sub-pattern matches as described in Sec. 3.1. Then the time is discretized into fine $1sec$ intervals and the weights are computed. This results in a sharing plan SP_D. The alternate solution is to assign weight to the sub-patterns without discretizing time with the resulting sharing plan called SP_{ND}. The average execution time for each sharing plan is shown in Figure 13(a). On average, SP_D performs 2.5 times faster than SP_{ND} confirming the effectiveness of the discretized weight assignment approach.

Evaluating SPASS concurrency. In this experiment, we illustrate the efficiency of our proposed sequence transaction model with S2PL protocol. We use two workloads with 10 and 20 patterns each. Figure 13(b) shows that the average execution time with varying the number of threads. The first pair of bars represents the execution time of patterns run as a shared single threaded system without any locking mechanism. The second pair of bars corresponds to the execution time of the two workloads run with a single thread with the locking mechanism turned on. The difference between these two pairs of bars shows the overhead of adding the locking algorithm. Finally the following 3 pairs of bars show the execution time of running the two workloads with 10, 15 and 20 threads. As expected the performance improves with an increasing number of threads. However after adding a certain number of threads, 15 in this case, there is no further improvements in execution time.

Overhead of statistics collection in SPASS Optimizer. In this experiment, we have evaluated the runtime overhead of statistics collection for SPASS weight assignment relative to the overall query execution cost. As depicted in Figure 13(c), the overhead is negligible across all scenarios. On average 1.2% of the average execution time is spent on statistics collection for workloads composed of SEQ queries. The reason is threefold. First, the statistics are collected periodically as described in Sec 3.1. Second, we exploit the lightweight counting scheme of pattern matches [33] that is pushed into the sequence construction process. Third, our SPASS system only collects statistics for the common sub-patterns rather than all possible sub-patterns. For a mixed workload of SEQ and

AND queries, the overhead of the statistics collection is slightly higher, around 2% of the overall execution time. This is because the SPASS Runtime has to collect statistics for different permutations of the AND queries.

5.4 SPASS versus State-of-the-Art Sub-Pattern Selection Strategies

In this experiment (Figure 13(d)), we compare the SPASS Optimizer sub-pattern selection against existing sub-pattern selection strategies such as prefix-sharing [14], suffix-sharing and random sub-pattern selection. We use three different workloads with 20 queries each to compare the average execution time for the entire workload using each of these approaches. The workload $W1$ is characterized by 4 sets of 5 patterns sharing common prefixes across the queries. These patterns do not have any other sub-patterns in common. In this case both prefix-sharing and SPASS produce the same pattern sharing plan. They naturally outperform the other strategies in the order of random sub-pattern selection followed last by suffix-sharing. Similarly, the workload $W2$ consists of 4 sets of patterns with common suffixes. Again our SPASS Optimizer performs as good as suffix-sharing. In the third workload $W3$, the queries have common sub-patterns that not necessarily are a prefix or suffix sub-pattern. As expected, the SPASS system again outperforms all three state-of-the-art strategies at least 2 fold.

6. RELATED WORK

Complex Event Processing. Many CEP systems [6, 3, 42] have been proposed to process sequence pattern queries over event streams. SASE [3, 42] and Cayuga [6] follow an NFA-based approach for detecting sequence patterns where the arrival of events into the system are marked by state transitions. As opposed to NFA-based event processing, ZStream [29] uses tree-based query plans for both the logical and physical representation of query patterns. While these alternate operator implementations could also be used in the SPASS optimizer by adjusting the cost model, it is not the focus of this work. However, none of those systems treat the multiple pattern sharing problem as a first-class citizen.

There have also been some work on stream transaction model [39, 7]. While the model in [7] is general enough to support a broad range of stream queries, it does not take the append only characteristics of event streams into account. In [39], another transaction modelwas proposed for supporting concurrent updates in an active event processing system. Our transaction model in the context of sequence pattern sharing is significantly different from both of the above. Also our locking protocols are customized specifically for shared sequence execution exploiting multi-core architectures.

Multiple Query Optimization. Multiple query optimization (MQO) has been well studied [9, 11, 18] in static databases. However, optimizing multiple sequence pattern queries introduces new dimensions to the existing MQO problem due to time-ordered event correlations within and across patterns. Hence techniques for tackling the MQO problem in relational databases such as materialized views [11] and common sub-expression sharing [9, 18] are not sufficient for sharing sequence patterns over event streams.

MQO has received attention in the context of continuous query processing perspective too. The data stream processing system TelegraphCQ [10] has shared query processing as part of its native architecture. In [28], an adaptive tuple-level sharing technique was proposed to share multiple query processing over data streams with fluctuations. However, routing individual tuples between operators adds significant overheads. Our work instead produces a stable sharing plan [25] and re-optimizes only if there is significant change in statistics.

Preliminary efforts of merging the NFAs representing multiple event queries were made in RUMOR [23] based on the Cayuga [6] system. Their rule-based optimization follows a set of pre-defined steps that merge common sub-expressions across queries. A cost-based approach to decide which sub-expressions to share has not been provided. Further, they do not support the concurrent execution of multiple queries with shared sub-expressions. The XML-filtering work also adopts NFA-based processing [13, 14]. While merging NFAs has been explored in this context [13], it is limited to prefix-matching. In contrast, SPASS supports sharing of sub-patterns at any position within a sequence pattern, i.e., it is not necessarily limited to a prefix or a suffix only. In [22], the authors also incorporate materialization based optimization to improve the performance of processing a large number of XML stream queries. However, their approach takes neither window constraints nor event correlations into consideration, which are key factors in our SPASS optimization. Further they do not provide any techniques for maintaining views nor concurrently accessing them by multiple queries.

Materialized View Selection. The idea of using views to improve the query processing performance has been studied in static databases [4, 15, 30, 37]. The prior work primarily focussed on minimizing the overall query execution time by selecting a set of views to materialize, given limited memory space. Mistry et al. [30] proposed a greedy algorithm for selecting a set of views *without any guarantees of optimality*. Shukla et al. [37] targeted optimal view selection for *aggregation queries* but not for general sequence pattern queries. Our SPASS system tackles the more general sequence pattern sharing problem with time-ordered event correlations while still guaranteeing an optimality bound.

OctopusDB [15] addresses the problem of designing a good layout for different data access patterns without knowing the exact query patterns up front through adaptive view storage. However, its techniques are designed to optimize the access of different storage structures, rather than sharing common computations among different workloads. DBToaster [4] exploits viewlet transforms, a recursive finite differencing technique, to materialize a query and a set of deltas as views for incremental maintenance. They do not focus on windowed queries and hence fail to tackle the problem of time-ordered event correlations within and across patterns.

In the context of complex event processing, the continuous sliding views mechanism was proposed in [34] to address the problem of view maintenance over event streams for a single query. In our work, we now extend this mechanism with optimization techniques to support shared continuous sliding views for multiple windowed sequence pattern queries. Our proposed techniques provide on concurrent access to shared views for reading, for updating, and for view purging in a timely fashion for memory efficiency without missing or duplicating results.

7. CONCLUSION

This work addresses the sequence pattern sharing problem on event streams using the SPASS technology. The proposed SPASS Optimizer leverages event correlations within and across patterns to find an effective sharing plan. We proposed an approximate polynomial-time algorithm to find a shared pattern plan covering all sequence patterns with a guaranteed optimality bound. The SPASS Runtime then exploits the shared continuous sliding view technology to execute this shared pattern plan. A sequence transaction model on shared views is introduced to define the correctness of concurrent pattern executions. Our sequence-aware locking protocol guarantees correct execution while minimizing delays. SPASS achieves 16 folds performance improvement in CPU utilization compared to state-of-the-art techniques.

8. REFERENCES

[1] I. inetats. stock trade traces. http://davis.wpi.edu/dsrg/stockData/eventstream3.txt.

[2] Stanford Linear Road Benchmark. http://infolab.stanford.edu/stream/cql-benchmark.html.

[3] J. Agrawal, Y. Diao, D. Gyllstrom, and N. Immerman. Efficient pattern matching over event streams. In *SIGMOD*, pages 147–160, 2008.

[4] Y. Ahmad, O. Kennedy, et al. Dbtoaster: Higher-order delta processing for dynamic, frequently fresh views. *PVLDB*, 5(10):968–979, June 2012.

[5] M. Akdere, U. Çetintemel, and N. Tatbul. Plan-based complex event detection across distributed sources. *PVLDB*, 1(1):66–77, 2008.

[6] Alan J. Demers and Johannes Gehrke and Biswanath Panda and Mirek Riedewald and others. Cayuga: A general purpose event monitoring system. In *CIDR*, pages 412–422, 2007.

[7] I. Botan, P. M. Fischer, et al. Transactional stream processing. In *EDBT*, pages 204–215, 2012.

[8] B. Cadonna, J. Gamper, and M. H. Bohlen. Sequenced event set pattern matching. In *EDBT*, pages 33–44, 2011.

[9] U. S. Chakravarthy and J. Minker. Multiple query processing in deductive databases using query graphs. In *VLDB*, pages 384–391, 1986.

[10] S. Chandrasekaran, O. Cooper, A. Deshpande, et al. Telegraphcq: Continuous dataflow processing for an uncertain world. In *CIDR*, 2003.

[11] S. Chaudhuri, R. Krishnamurthy, S. Potamianos, and K. Shim. Optimizing queries with materialized views. In *ICDE*, pages 190 - 200, 1995.

[12] J. Chen, D. J. DeWitt, et al. Niagaracq: A scalable continuous query system for internet databases. In *ACM SIGMOD Record*, pages 379–390, 2000.

[13] Y. Diao, M. Altinel, M. J. Franklin, H. Zhang, and P. Fischer. Path sharing and predicate evaluation for high-performance xml filtering. *ACM TODS*, 28(4):467–516, 2003.

[14] Y. Diao, P. Fischer, M. J. Franklin, and R. To. Yfilter: Efficient and scalable filtering of xml documents. In *ICDE*, pages 341–342, 2002.

[15] J. Dittrich and A. Jindal. Towards a one size fits all database architecture. In *CIDR*, pages 195–198, 2011.

[16] M. G. Elfeky, W. G. Aref, et al. Stagger: Periodicity mining of data streams using expanding sliding windows. In *ICDM*, pages 188–199, 2006.

[17] G. Giannikis, G. Alonso, and D. Kossmann. Shareddb: killing one thousand queries with one stone. *PVLDB*, 5(6):526–537, 2012.

[18] G. Giannikis, P. Unterbrunner, et al. Crescando. In *SIGMOD*, pages 1227–1230, 2010.

[19] J. Grant and J. Minker. On optimizing the evaluation of a set of expressions. *International Journal of Computer & Information Sciences*, pages 179–191, 1982.

[20] J. M. Hellerstein and M. Stonebraker. Predicate migration: Optimizing queries with expensive predicates. In *SIGMOD*, pages 267–276, 1993.

[21] D. Hermelin, D. Rawitz, et al. The minimum substring cover problem. In *International Conference on Approximation and Online Algorithms*, pages 170–183, 2008.

[22] M. Hong, A. J. Demers, et al. Massively multi-query join processing in publish/subscribe systems. In *SIGMOD*, pages 761–772, 2007.

[23] M. Hong, M. Riedewald, C. Koch, J. Gehrke, and A. Demers. Rule-based multi-query optimization. In *EDBT*, pages 120–131, 2009.

[24] S. Krishnamurthy, M. J. Franklin, et al. The case for precision sharing. In *VLDB*, pages 972–984, 2004.

[25] C. Lei, E. Rundensteiner, and et al. Robust distributed stream processing. In *ICDE*, pages 817–828, 2013.

[26] M. Liu, E. Rundensteiner, and et al. High-performance nested cep query processing over event streams. In *ICDE*, pages 123 – 134, April, 2011.

[27] M. Liu, E. Rundensteiner, and et.al. E-cube: Multi-dimensional event sequence analysis using hierarchical pattern query sharing. In *SIGMOD*, pages 889–900, 2011.

[28] S. Madden and et al. Continuously adaptive continuous queries over streams. In *SIGMOD*, pages 49–60, 2002.

[29] Y. Mei and S. Madden. Zstream: a cost-based query processor for adaptively detecting composite events. In *SIGMOD*, pages 193–206, 2009.

[30] H. Mistry, P. Roy, S. Sudarshan, and K. Ramamritham. Materialized view selection and maintenance using multi-query optimization. In *ACM SIGMOD Record*, volume 30, pages 307–318, 2001.

[31] R. V. Nehme, K. Works, C. Lei, E. A. Rundensteiner, and E. Bertino. Multi-route query processing and optimization. *Journal of Computer and System Sciences*, 79(3):312–329, 2013.

[32] N. Onose, A. Deutsch, Y. Papakonstantinou, and E. Curtmola. Rewriting nested xml queries using nested views. In *SIGMOD*, pages 443–454, 2006.

[33] Y. Qi, L. Cao, et al. Complex event analytics: online aggregation of stream sequence patterns. In *SIGMOD*, pages 229–240, 2014.

[34] M. Ray, E. Rundensteiner, et al. High-performance complex event processing using continuous sliding views. In *EDBT*, pages 525–536, 2013.

[35] P. Roy and et al. Efficient and extensible algorithms for multi query optimization. In *SIGMOD*, pages 249–260, 2000.

[36] N. P. Schultz-Møller et al. Distributed complex event processing with query rewriting. In *DEBS*, pages 4:1–4:12, 2009.

[37] A. Shukla, P. Deshpande, J. F. Naughton, et al. Materialized view selection for multidimensional datasets. In *VLDB*, volume 98, pages 488–499, 1998.

[38] A. Thomasian. Two-phase locking performance and its thrashing behavior. *ACM TODS*, 18(4):579–625, 1993.

[39] D. Wang, E. A. Rundensteiner, and R. T. Ellison. Active complex event processing over event streams. *PVLDB*, 4(10):634–645, 2011.

[40] S. Wang, M. Hao, et al. Chaos: A data stream analysis architecture for enterprise applications. In *2009 IEEE conference on commerce and enterprise computing*, pages 33–40, 2009.

[41] S. Wang, E. Rundensteiner, et al. State-slice: New paradigm of multi-query optimization of window-based stream queries. In *VLDB*, pages 619–630, 2006.

[42] E. Wu, Y. Diao, et al. High-performance complex event processing over streams. In *SIGMOD*, pages 407–418, 2006.

[43] Y. Zhu, E. A. Rundensteiner, and G. T. Heineman. Dynamic plan migration for continuous queries over data streams. In *SIGMOD*, 2004.

APPENDIX

A. SPASS OPTIMIZER

A.1 Event Pattern Cost Model

Cost of Single SEQ Pattern Execution. For a sequence pattern operator P_i = $SEQ(E_1$,..., $E_n)$, the computation costs C_{Pi} of P_i using NFA-based pattern evaluation are formulated in Equation 5. Essentially it is the product of the cardinality of the event type E_i and E_j with the intra-event correlation that gives an estimate of the number of E_j events would follow E_i events in a given time window. The automata-based execution technique provides a special indexing technique [42] that can find sequence pattern matches without doing a cross-product of all events arriving in a given window. The total computation cost for k different query patterns would be $\sum_{i=1}^{k} C_{P_i}$.

$$C_{P_i} = \sum_{i=1}^{n} |E_i| * [\prod_{j=0}^{i} |E_j| * C_{Intra}(E_j, E_{j+1}) * P_{E_i}] \quad (5)$$

Cost of Single AND Pattern Execution. For an AND pattern operator P_i = $AND(E_1$,..., $E_n)$, the computation costs C_{Pi} of P_i using a evaluation are formulated in Equation 6. This cost is based on the execution model discussed in [8].

$$C_{P_i} = \prod_{i=1}^{n} |E_i| * P_{E_i} \quad (6)$$

Cost of Shared Pattern Execution. The shared execution of pattern queries chops the query into smaller sub-patterns $[SP_1 \ldots SP_k]$. Each sub-pattern SP_i is computed once and only once with the respective cost C_{SP_i} and shared across patterns. Several sub-patterns are then re-combined to form final results for pattern queries in the workload.

Assume two patterns P_1 and P_2 that share a common sub-pattern SP_{12}. P_1 is composed of sub-pattern SP_1 and SP_{12} while P_2 is composed of SP_2 and SP_{12}. The *inter-query correlation* factor gives reflects how many of these sub-pattern matches are common across the two parent patterns. Thus the shared cost of execution is obtained by subtracting the product of execution cost of the common sub-pattern with the the inter-query correlation from the sum cost of executing the parent patterns individually. This cost is shown in Equation 7. It is straightforward to generalize it for multiple sub-patterns shared across multiple queries.

$$C_S(P_1, P_2) = C_{P_1} + C_{P_2} - C_{Inter}(P_1, P_2, SP_{12}) * C_{SP12} \quad (7)$$

A.2 Multiple Windows and Predicates in SPASS Optimization

Sequence patterns in a workload might have different $windows$ as well as $predicates$ specified. The handling of queries with different predicates and window sizes has been already addressed by previous research using sliced time windows and shared data fragments [41]. In this paper, the SPASS optimizer's cost model takes such $window$ and $predicate$ specifications into account. However, its main focus is to identify shared sub-patterns based on event correlations within or across multiple pattern queries.

Our cost model captures redundant sub-pattern computations. Consider the two sub-patterns SP_1 = $SEQ(A$ ($A.color$=$orange$ & $A.color$=$blue$), B) and SP_2 = $SEQ(A$ ($A.color$=red & $A.color$ =$blue$), B). If most patterns satisfy the predicate ($A.color$=$blue$), then there could be a high degree of redundancy.

Similarly pattern queries with different sized $window$ parameters may still share sub-pattern matches across each other in our SPASS optimizer. Our redundancy ratio implicitly captures this information during the shared pattern plan generation. The reason is that the sample time period used to analyze sub-pattern matches is guaranteed to be larger than the largest window size among all pattern queries sharing this sub-pattern. For instance consider patterns P_1 = $SEQ(A,B,C)$ with $window$ = 10 and P_2 = $SEQ(A,B,D)$ with $window$ = 100. The events forming the pattern matches for P_1 can be directly reused by P_2.

A.3 Sharing Across Nested Patterns

In this work we focus primarily on optimizing flat CEP queries. However, SPASS system supports sharing operators across nested event patterns without considering optimization. Given a pattern *SEQ(X,AND(A,B,C),Y)* and another pattern *AND(A,B,C)*, it identifies the two AND operators with the same operands. It then shares the computation of this sub-pattern across two queries.

There has been prior work on rewriting nested patterns to exploit sharing opportunities [32, 26]. These techniques could be exploited to rewrite nested CEP patterns before applying our optimization principle. However using these principles [26] we often end up with an exponential number of flat queries which might result in exponential blow up of the input to the MSC problem. For instance the query *SEQ(X,AND(A,B,C,),Y)* when rewritten, would result in 6 different SEQ queries that each need to be run.

A.4 Proof of Lemma 1

PROOF. **Sub-pattern Sharing $\subseteq$ MSC Problem.** Given a set of pattern queries W, each pattern P_i is given as $SEQ(E_1$,E_2,..., E_n). For each event type we assign a specific letter. Thus each pattern is translated to a string of letters '$E_1E_2 \ldots E_n$'. Thus, the pattern query workload W is analogous to a set of strings S. The set of common sub-patterns across any two or more pattern queries is equivalent to substrings common across two or more strings. The weight function of RR (defined in Eq. 4) is $\Theta(W) \rightarrow \mathbb{Q}_{0,1}$ as RR is a ratio of two natural numbers where the denominator is guaranteed to be greater than the numerator. We define a cover C_W of W to be a set of sub-patterns in $\Theta(W)$, where for each $P_i \in W$ there exist $SP_1, \ldots, SP_k \in C_W$, with $P_i = (SP_1 \cdot \ldots \cdot SP_k)$. Thus finding the optimal solution for the MSC problem is equivalent to finding a cover C_W of the pattern workload W composed of a set of sub-patterns that has a minimum total RR, namely $Min(RR(C_W))$ for all possible covers C_W of W.

MSC $\subseteq$ Sub-pattern Sharing Problem. It is straightforward to reduce the MSC problem to the sub-pattern sharing problem as well. □

B. SPASS RUNTIME

B.1 Single Sequence Execution using Continuous Sliding Views

Continuous sliding views are effectively cached intermediate results for sequence sub-patterns. We briefly enumerate the steps in for a single sequence pattern execution using continuous views. We assume here that a sequence pattern S is composed of two sub-patterns SP_1 and SP_2 such that SP_1 is the right sub-pattern and SP_2 is the left sub-pattern. Sub-pattern matches for SP_2 are maintained in a view $view_{SP1}$.

1. When an event instance e_i arrives at time i, it is inserted into its respective storage unit called *event stack*.

2. Events in the event stacks that have timestamps $< i$ - $window$ are *purged* from the stacks.

3. If e_i is a *triggering event* then the right-most sub-pattern SP_1 is triggered execution. Sequence matches are computed from the events that are currently in the event stacks within the current $window$.

4. Once pattern matches for SP_1 have been computed, SP_2 is then executed following a right-to-left order processing. Matches for sub-pattern SP_2 are then re-used from $view_{SP1}$. *Continuous sliding views* are augmented with a view indicator that indicates the completeness status of the view. If the view is found to contain all required pattern matches, then they are re-used.

5. If the $view_{SP1}$ is found to be incomplete, new pattern matches for SP_2 are computed from the event stacks and *appended* to the view. The view indicator is also updated to indicate the updated state of the view. At the same time old pattern matches are *purged* from the view.

EXAMPLE 7. *Consider the pattern $SEQ(A, B, C, D)$ is executed as a combination of two sub-patterns SP_c = $SEQ(A, B)$ and SP_1 = $SEQ(C, D)$, the matches for sub-pattern SP_c are cached in the continuous view $view_{SPc}$ (Figure 14(a)). Pattern SP_1 is executed first followed by SP_c. When the triggering event d_{18} arrives, the sub-pattern SP_1 triggers pattern matching and the new match {$\langle c_{16}d_{18}\rangle$} is computed. The timestamp of the left most event in sub-pattern SP_1 constrains the pattern match for SP_c. Thus for the match {$\langle c_{16}d_{18}\rangle$}, the timestamp of the leftmost event C is 16. The matches for SP_c that can form complete matches for P_1 are those that occur within the time-interval of [$t_{current}$ - $window$, $t_{leftevent}$] = [18-10, 16]. Hence for this triggering event, SP_c is only computed for the range [8, 16]. Sliding views are augmented with special indicators called rightBound that indicates if the view contains all pattern matches up to a certain time. In this case the view has already contained sub-pattern matches for $SEQ(A, B)$ up to timestamp 16. Thus the sub-pattern matches are directly reused from the view. When event instance d_{21} arrives to the system (Figure 14(b)), the event a_{11} expires as the $window$ = 10. Consequently all sub-pattern matches containing a_{11} are also purged from the view. Further, d_{21} forms new sequence matches for the sub-pattern $SEQ(A,B)$ = {$\langle c_{16}d_{11}\rangle$, $\langle c_{20}d_{21}\rangle$}. Now the sub-pattern $SEQ(A,B)$ is looked up for the interval [11, 20]. However, the view currently contains sub-pattern matches up to a timestamp of 16. Thus the view requires an update thus adding the new sub-pattern match {$\langle a_{12}b_{19}\rangle$} to the view. Finally the indicator of the view is updated to 20.*

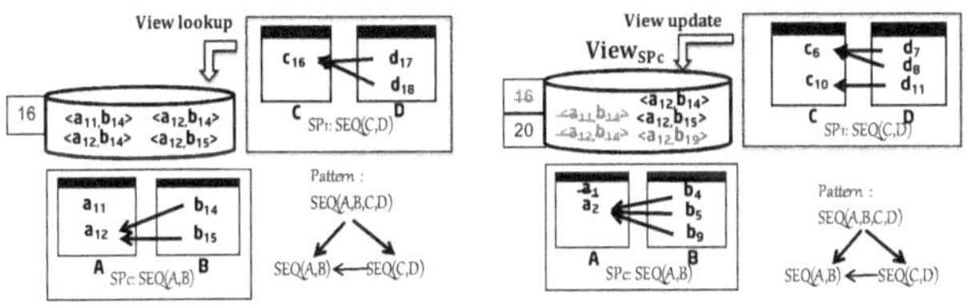

(a) Read (b) Update

Figure 14: Single Sequence Execution using Continuous Views

B.2 Multiple Windows and Predicates in SPASS Runtime

Support for Different Windows. Multiple sequence patterns could have different window sizes. The *shared continuous sliding view* technology could support multiple sequence patterns with different window sizes by maintaining pattern matches in the view for the larger window. The reuse, append, and purge operations can be easily modified to support this feature.

$window_{max}$. In order to support multiple windows, each shared view is associated with a $window_{max}$. For the set of patterns $\{P_1, \ldots P_k\}$ that access a view $View_{SPi}$ each pattern P_i has an associated window $window_i$. Then the largest window among all these $window_i$ is designated as $window_{max}$. $View_{SPi}$ contains all sub-pattern matches of SP_i that satisfy this largest window $window_{max}$.

Modified View Reuse, Append, and Purge. During the reuse phase, each pattern P_i thus filters out only those pattern matches that satisfy $window_i$ constraint. During the append phase pattern matches for the sub-pattern SP_i must be computed while satisfying the $window_{max}$ constraint. The purge operation on the view must be performed only when sub-pattern matches are to be expired out of the largest window, i.e., sub-pattern matches containing event instances e_i such that $i < t_{current}$ - $window_{max}$.

EXAMPLE 8. *For example, in Figure 7, if P_2 had a $window$ with size 20 and P_1 had a $window$ size 10, then the $view_{SP1}$ could contain pattern matches such as $\langle a_{11}, b_13\rangle$ where $b.ts$ - $a.ts$ > 10. Such matches would not qualify for pattern P_1. These matches must be filtered out by P_1 during the reuse phase. Further, if newly arrived events c_{25} and d_{30} formed a pattern match $\langle c_{25}, d_{30}\rangle$ for the sub-pattern SP_1 the view would be updated for the interval [$t_{current}$ - $window_{P1}$, 25] = [20, 25]. However if the $view_{SPc}$ is not complete, the view update must be done for an interval [$t_{current}$ - $window_{max}$, 25] = [10, 25].*

Support for Different Predicates. Next we extend our above treatment by considering how the presence of predicates in the pattern queries influence the shared execution process. Sequence patterns could have selection predicates specified on events or join predicates across events such as P_1 = SEQ(A:$A.color$ = $blue$, B:$B.id$ = $A.id$). In SPASS Runtime, we exploit the approaches on predicate sharing that have been extensively studied in the literature [20]. If a sub-pattern is shared across two patterns yet the two patterns specify different selection predicate on them, the sub-pattern is rewritten to satisfy both selection predicates using existing query rewriting techniques [27]. For instance, consider the above pattern P_1 and pattern P_2 = SEQ(A:$A.color$ = $black$, B:$B.id$ = $A.id$). In this case the selection predicates $A.color$ = $blue$ and $A.color$ = $black$ on P_1 and P_2 could be rewritten to ($A.color$ = $black$ or $A.color$ = $black$). For equijoin-like predicates across the entire sequence pattern (e.g., P_1), the views could be partitioned by the join attribute value [34]. Thus predicate migration techniques such as push-down and pull-up [20] which are effectively orthogonal to *shared continuous sliding views* can be adopted in our SPASS execution.

B.3 Lock Compatibility

Lock Compatibility on Event Buffers. The read and append locks on buffers are completely independent of each other. Similarly, two appends could take place at the same time on a buffer. This is due to the assumption that duplicate events do not arrive in the event stream. Thus the actions of appending two events to the same buffer are independent. Similarly, if a transaction is appending to the buffer, while another transaction has requested a read lock on the buffer, it means the buffer must already contain the events up to the timestamp requested by the read lock. This is guaranteed by the sequential lock assignment phase.

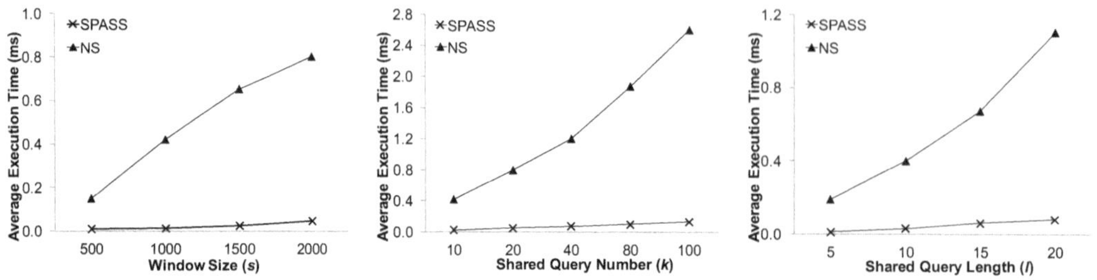

(a) Varying Window Size (w) (b) Varying Pattern Number (k) (c) Varying Pattern Length (l)

Figure 15: Shared Execution with Varying Parameters (Linear Road)

Lock Compatibility on Shared Views. In terms of transactions on views, if an A_{View} operation is in progress, another R_{View} transaction should be allowed to execute due to the sequential lock assignment phase. The sequential lock assignment must predetermine that a transaction only requests a read lock on a view if the validity interval of the view at the time of arrival of this event indicates that the view already contains the required pattern matches. Otherwise it must create two locks namely $R_{buffer(s)}$ and A_{View}. Two append operations are not allowed on a view at the same time. This avoids the creation of duplicate results.

Purge Lock. Finally the P_{Buffer} and P_{View} locks are considered most restrictive. Notice that purge locks could be denied even when there simply exists another request for a lock on that resource, even if it has not yet been granted. That is in order to grant a purge request, the transaction manager must make sure that the lock buffer for that resource does not contain any read requests on that resource that may try to read events or pattern matches purged by this purge transaction. This prevents any missing pattern matches.

C. EXPERIMENTAL EVALUATION

In this set of experiments, we evaluate the efficiency and scalability of our SPASS system with another dataset from the Linear Road Benchmark [2]. The dataset consists of car locations with timestamps. The pattern query workload comprises of finding sequences of locations that a car has traveled with a period of time. We vary the three parameters used in Sec. 5.3: (1) the length of shared sub-patterns, (2) the number of sequence patterns sharing the same sub-pattern, and (3) the window size. As depicted in Figure 15(a), as the window size is increased from $500s$ to $2000s$, the advantage of our SPASS system compared to the unshared solution in the average execution time increases from 10 folds to 20 folds. The reason is that the number of event tuples sharable in each window is substantially increased in the larger window. Similarly, when the number of the queries is increased from 10 to 100 as shown in Figure 15(b), the winning margin of our solution over unshared solution significantly increases, as more computational savings are obtained by exploiting more sharing opportunities in a larger query workload. Lastly, in Figure 15(b), when the length of queries is increased, the average execution time of our SPASS system is relatively stable compared to the unshared approach as expected. This is because the longer the common sub-patterns are, the more they contribute to the computational savings obtained by the queries sharing them.

How to Win a Hot Dog Eating Contest: Distributed Incremental View Maintenance with Batch Updates[*] [†]

Milos Nikolic Mohammad Dashti Christoph Koch
{milos.nikolic, mohammad.dashti, christoph.koch}@epfl.ch
École Polytechnique Fédérale de Lausanne

ABSTRACT

In the quest for valuable information, modern big data applications continuously monitor streams of data. These applications demand low latency stream processing even when faced with high volume and velocity of incoming changes and the user's desire to ask complex queries. In this paper, we study low-latency incremental computation of complex SQL queries in both local and distributed streaming environments. We develop a technique for the efficient incrementalization of queries with nested aggregates for batch updates. We identify the cases in which batch processing can boost the performance of incremental view maintenance but also demonstrate that tuple-at-a-time processing often can achieve better performance in local mode. Batch updates are essential for enabling distributed incremental view maintenance and amortizing the cost of network communication and synchronization. We show how to derive incremental programs optimized for running on large-scale processing platforms. Our implementation of distributed incremental view maintenance can process tens of million of tuples with few-second latency using hundreds of nodes.

1. INTRODUCTION

Many big data applications demand real-time analytics over high-velocity streaming data. In a growing number of domains – sensor network monitoring, clickstream analysis, high-frequency algorithmic trading, and fraud detection to name a few – applications continuously monitor rapidly-changing datasets in order to promptly detect certain patterns, anomalies, or future trends. Application users construct complex queries to reveal more information and expect to have fresh results available at all time. Such streaming applications usually have strict latency requirements, which frequently forces developers to build ad-hoc solutions in order to pull off utmost performance.

We identify three essential requirements for stream processing systems to serve these modern applications:

* *Support for complex continuous queries.* Modern streaming engines need to support continuous queries that can capture complex conditions, such as SQL queries with nested aggregates.
* *Low-latency (incremental) processing.* Online and responsive analytics enable data analysts to quickly react to changes in the underlying data. Streaming datasets evolve through frequent, small-sized updates, which makes refreshing query results using recomputation too expensive. Online systems rely on *incremental computation* to sustain high update rates and achieve low refresh latency.
* *Scalable processing.* Emerging big data applications demand scalable systems for querying and managing large datasets. Scalable processing aims to speed up query evaluation and accommodate growing memory requirements.

Modern data processing systems often fail to simultaneously address the above requirements. Traditional relational database systems support complex SQL queries but suffer from high query latencies despite their support for incremental computation of materialized views [18, 17, 14]. Conventional data stream SQL processing systems [26, 4] use incremental algorithms for evaluating continuous queries over finite windows of input data. Their usefulness is yet limited by their window semantics, inability to handle long-lived data, and lack of support for complex queries. Both classical databases and stream processing engines have limited scalability. Scalable stream processing platforms[1], like MillWheel [7], S4 [29], and Heron [25], offer low-level programming models that put the burden of expressing complex query plans on the application developer. Naiad [27] and Trill [11] focus mostly on flat LINQ-style continuous queries; encoding and efficiently incrementalizing complex queries with nested aggregates is a non-trivial task left to the user. Spark Streaming [39] supports running simple SQL queries but only over windowed data.

In this work, we study low-latency incremental processing of complex SQL queries in both local and distributed environments. Our approach derives, at compile time, delta programs that capture changes in the result for updates to the database. For efficient incremental computation, we build upon our previous work on recursive incremental view maintenance [20, 21], whose implementation inside the DBToaster system demonstrates $3-4$ orders of magnitude better performance than commercial database and stream processing engines in local settings [22].

DBToaster's recursive view maintenance can deliver μ-second latencies for single-tuple updates on standard database workloads.

[*]It is all about the bite size, and the best bite size is $1,000$ to $10,000$ tuples in local execution. We also address the distributed case.

[†]This work was supported by ERC Grant 279804.

[1]We will, throughout this paper, use stream processing and continuous queries interchangeably: We will not aim to ensure bounded state size by e.g. window semantics. This is vindicated by the common use of the term streaming in this relaxed way in recent times.

SIGMOD'16, June 26-July 01, 2016, San Francisco, CA, USA
© 2016 ACM. ISBN 978-1-4503-3531-7/16/06...$15.00
DOI: http://dx.doi.org/10.1145/2882903.2915246

In this work, we generalize this idea to batches of updates. We present a novel technique called *domain extraction* that enables efficient incremental maintenance of complex SQL queries with nested aggregates for batch updates. We study the trade-offs between single-tuple and batched incremental processing and identify the cases where batching can improve the performance of incremental view maintenance. Our experiments show that maintenance programs specialized for single-tuple processing can outperform generic batched implementations in many cases. These results refute the widespread belief that batching always wins over tuple-at-a-time processing [30].

Batched processing enables distributed incremental view maintenance and amortizes increased costs of communication and coordination in large-scale deployments. In this paper, we show how to transform local view maintenance code into programs capable of running on large-scale processing platforms. Our implementation of distributed incremental view maintenance inside DBToaster runs on top of Spark [38] and can process tens of million of updates with few-second latency on a scale of hundreds of workers.

Our system compiles SQL workloads into aggressively specialized query engines. We rely on a modern compiler framework, called LMS [35], to generate low-level native code that is free of overheads of classical query processing engines (e.g., template-based operators). We create custom data structures for storing materialized views that are optimized for the observed access patterns. We also specialize query engines for different batch sizes, for instance, to avoid materialization when processing single-tuple updates or to use columnar mode when serializing large batches.

In this work, we make the following contributions:

1. We present techniques for the efficient recursively incremental processing of queries with nested aggregates for batch updates. This part of the paper generalizes our previous work [20, 21, 22].
2. We study the trade-offs between single-tuple and batched incremental processing in local settings. We analyze the cases when batching can greatly reduce maintenance costs.
3. We describe a novel approach for compiling incremental view maintenance code into programs optimized for running in distributed environments.
4. We present techniques for code and data-structure specialization of incremental view maintenance programs.
5. Our single-node experiments show that single-tuple processing can often outperform batched processing. Our distributed view maintenance implementation can deliver few-second latencies of processing tens of million of tuples using hundreds workers.

This paper is organized as follows. We provide an overview of incremental view maintenance in Section 2. We discuss delta processing for batch updates in Section 3 and distributed incremental view maintenance in Section 4. We present our code and data-structure specialization techniques in Section 5, experimental evaluation in Section 6, and related work in Section 7.

2. VIEW MAINTENANCE

Database systems use materialized views to speed up execution of frequently asked queries. Materialized views require maintenance to keep their contents up to date for changes in the base tables. Refreshing materialized views using recomputation is expensive for frequent, small-sized updates. In such cases, applying only incremental changes (deltas) to materialized views is usually more efficient than recomputing views from large base tables.

2.1 Classical Incremental View Maintenance

Let $(Q, M(\mathbf{D}))$ denotes a materialized view, where Q is the view definition query and $M(\mathbf{D})$ is the materialized contents for a given database $\mathbf{D}$. When the database changes from $\mathbf{D}$ to $(\mathbf{D}+\Delta\mathbf{D})$, classical incremental view maintenance *evaluates* a delta query ΔQ in order to refresh $M(\mathbf{D})$.

$$M(\mathbf{D}+\Delta\mathbf{D}) = M(\mathbf{D}) + \Delta Q(\mathbf{D}, \Delta\mathbf{D})$$

The delta ΔQ often has a simpler structure than Q (e.g., has fewer joins) and involves smaller delta updates instead of large base tables. So, computing ΔQ and refreshing $M(\mathbf{D})$ becomes cheaper than re-evaluating Q from scratch. Incremental view maintenance derives one delta query for each referenced base table. The derivation process relies on a set of change propagation rules defined for each operator of the view definition language. The derived delta query takes its role in the associated view maintenance trigger.

EXAMPLE 2.1. *Let query Q counts the tuples of a natural join of $R(A,B)$, $S(B,C)$, and $T(C,D)$ grouped by column B. Intuitively, we write the delta query for updates to R as:*

$$\Delta_R Q := Sum_{[B]}(\Delta R(A,B) \bowtie S(B,C) \bowtie T(C,D))$$

Let M_R, M_S, and M_T denote the materialized base tables, then the maintenance trigger for updates to R looks as:

```
ON UPDATE R BY dR
  M_R(A,B) += dR(A,B)
  dQ(B)     := Sum_[B](dR(A,B) * M_S(B,C) * M_T(C,D))
  M_Q(B)    += dQ(B)
```

Here, `+=`, `:=`, *and* $*$ *denote bag union, assignment, and natural join. Under the standard assumption that $|\Delta R| \ll |R|$, incremental maintenance is cheaper than re-evaluation.* □

Incremental view maintenance is often cheaper than naïve re-evaluation but is not free. Computing deltas can be expensive, like in Example 2.1, where $\Delta_R Q$ is a non-trivial join of one (small) input update and two (potentially large) base tables.

2.2 Recursive Incremental View Maintenance

Delta queries can be expensive despite their simpler form. For instance, a delta of an n-way join still references $(n-1)$ base tables. Instead of computing such a delta query from scratch, we could re-apply the idea of incremental processing to speed up the delta evaluation: store previously computed delta results, just as any other query result, and compute the delta of a delta query (second-order delta) to maintain the materialized delta result. That way, the second-order delta query maintains the first-order delta view, which in turn maintains the top-level view. Assuming that with each derivation deltas become simpler, we could recursively apply the same procedure until we get deltas with no references to base tables. The described procedure is known as *recursive incremental view maintenance* [20, 21, 22].

Recursive incremental view maintenance materializes the top-level view along with a set of auxiliary views that support each other's incremental maintenance. The materialization procedure starts from the top-level view and derives its delta queries for updates to base relations. For each delta query, the procedure materializes its update-independent parts such that the delta evaluation requires as little work as possible. Formally, the procedure transforms $\Delta Q(\mathbf{D}, \Delta\mathbf{D})$ into an equivalent query $\Delta Q'$ that evaluates over a set of materialized views $M_1, \ldots, M_k$ and update $\Delta\mathbf{D}$:

$$\Delta Q(\mathbf{D}, \Delta\mathbf{D}) = \Delta Q'(M_1(\mathbf{D}), M_2(\mathbf{D}), ..., M_k(\mathbf{D}), \Delta\mathbf{D})$$

But note that $M_1, \ldots, M_k$ also require maintenance, which again relies on simpler materialized views. At first, it may appear counterintuitive that storing more data can reduce maintenance costs. However, the recursive incremental maintenance scheme makes the work required to keep all views fresh extremely simple. For flat queries, each individual aggregate value can be incrementally maintained using a constant amount of work [21], which is impossible to achieve with classical incremental maintenance or recomputation.

EXAMPLE 2.2. *Let us apply recursive incremental view maintenance on the query of Example 2.1 and updates to R. Considering $\Delta_R Q$, we materialize its update-independent part $S(B,C) \bowtie T(C,D)$ as an auxiliary view $M_{ST}(B)$. We projected away C and D as they are irrelevant for the computation of $\Delta_R Q$. Repeating the same procedure for updates to T, we materialize $R(A,B) \bowtie S(B,C)$ as $M_{RS}(B,C)$ to facilitate computing of $\Delta_T Q$. For updates to S, we materialize $R(A,B) \bowtie T(C,D)$ separately as $M_R(B)$ and $M_T(C)$*[2].

Next, we derive second-order deltas for M_{ST} and M_{RS}. Repeating the same delta derivation for updates to all three base relations, we materialize one additional view $M_S(B,C)$ representing the base relation S. Further derivation produces delta expressions with no base relations. Overall, recursive view maintenance materializes queries at three different levels: the top-level query M_Q, two auxiliary views M_{RS} and M_{ST}, and the base tables M_R, M_S, and M_T. The maintenance trigger for updates to R looks as:

```
ON UPDATE R BY dR
  M_Q(B)     += Sum_[B](dR(A,B) * M_ST(B))
  M_RS(B,C) += Sum_[B](dR(A,B) * M_S(B,C))
  M_R(B)     += Sum_[B](dR(A,B))
```

We similarly build triggers for updates to S and T. □

Recursive incremental view maintenance can produce triggers with lower complexity than classical maintenance triggers. In the previous example, each statement performs at most one join between the delta relation and one materialized view, which is clearly less expensive than the classical approach. In practice, DBToaster's recursive view maintenance can outperform classical view maintenance by several orders of magnitude for single-tuple updates [22].

2.3 Contributions

We summarize our contributions on our running example.

Domain extraction. Consider a modified query from Example 2.1 that reports only distinct B tuples. The delta of this query for updates to R is, unfortunately, more complex than the query itself as it reevaluates the whole query from scratch just to compute the incremental change. Clearly, that defeats the purpose of incremental computation.

In Section 3, we show how to incrementally maintain such delta queries. We observe that ΔR affects only the output tuples whose B value appears in ΔR. We present an algorithm that restricts the domain of delta evaluation to only those output tuples affected by the given input change. We also discuss the cases in which reevaluation is preferable over incremental computation.

Single-tuple vs. batch processing. We study the trade-offs between tuple-at-a-time and batched recursive incremental view maintenance in local settings. The former yields simpler maintenance code; in the trigger of Example 2.2, we can eliminate the loop around ΔR for single-tuple updates and achieve constant-time maintenance of M_Q and M_R. The latter can have positive or negative impacts on cache locality and can significantly reduce view maintenance cost; in the same example, we can pre-aggregate ΔR as $\text{Sum}_{[B]}(\Delta R(A,B))$ to keep only distinct B values along with their multiplicity. A small aggregated domain makes the maintenance code cheaper: our experiments show that batch pre-aggregation can bring up to 3 orders of magnitude performance improvements.

Distributed execution. In this work, we also study distributed execution of incremental programs. Distributed incremental view maintenance opens new problems compared to classical parallel and distributed query processing [24, 34]. First, we optimize multiple delta queries at once, where each query handles changes to one base relation. Second, during optimization we also need to consider the partitioning information of the target view being refreshed. Finally, recursive incremental view maintenance creates data-flow dependencies among statements maintaining auxiliary materialized views. These dependencies prevent arbitrary re-orderings of statements inside a trigger function. For instance, evaluating an n-th order delta relies on simpler, $(n+1)$-th order materialized views, whose contents is maintained (if necessary) in subsequent statements; in Example 2.2, we first maintain the query result, then the auxiliary view, and finally the base relation. That is, we maintain materialized views in decreasing order of their complexity. This property creates a DAG of dependencies among trigger statements, bringing more complexity to the problem.

Batch processing is essential for efficient implementation of distributed incremental view maintenance as it amortizes increased costs of network communication and synchronization. In Section 4, we show how to transform view maintenance code, like that from Example 2.2, into programs optimized for running in distributed settings. To achieve that goal, we redefine the query language with location-aware constructs, introduce new operators for exchanging data over the network, and develop a set of optimization rules that are specific to distributed environments.

Program specialization. Commercial database systems rely on embedded query evaluation mechanisms to compute deltas. In practice, they exhibit poor view maintenance performance due to overheads from components not directly related with view maintenance (e.g, logging, buffer management, concurrency control, etc.) and the use of general data structures and algorithms [22, 19, 28].

We argue that efficient view maintenance requires specialization of incremental programs. We observe that nowadays most applications have static query workloads with template-derived queries. Knowing the workload in advance allows us to tailor query processing based on the application requirements and avoid unnecessary features of database systems. Thus, we specialize incremental programs into low-level native or interpreted code and generate custom data structures to facilitate efficient maintenance operations.

EXAMPLE 2.3. *Let us show the idea of program specialization on the trigger from Example 2.2. At compile time, we analyze the access patterns inside triggers and create custom data structures with index support for storing the view contents. For instance, we optimize ΔR for scanning, while the other views may feature efficient lookup, update, and/or slice operations. Then, we transform trigger statements into function calls over these objects. For example, the R trigger may have the following functional representation:*

```
def onUpdateR(dR) {
  dR.foreach((k1,v1) =>        // key-value pairs
    mQ.update(k1.B, v1*mST.get(k1.B))
    mS.slice(k1.B, (k2,v2) =>
      mRS.update((k1.B,k2.C), v1*v2))
    mR.update(k1.B, v1)
  )
}
```

We cover the compilation process in more detail in Section 5. The take-away here is that, in the quest for maximum performance,

[2] Recursive incremental view maintenance avoids storing query results with disconnected join graphs for performance reasons [22].

we aspire to specialize high-level operators into optimized low-level implementations that enable efficient view maintenance at the speed of native code.

3. BATCHED DELTA PROCESSING

In this section, we focus on the problem of view maintenance for batch updates. First, we revisit the data model and query language from our previous work [22]; Appendix A provides more details.

3.1 Data Model and Query Language

Data Model. We materialize views as generalized multiset relations [22, 20, 21]. One relation contains a finite number of unique tuples with a non-zero, positive or negative, multiplicity. The data model generalizes tuple multiplicities from single count integers to multiple (potentially non-integer) values that correspond to different aggregate values (e.g., `SUM`, `AVG`). Traditional SQL represents these aggregates as separate columns in the query result, while this model keeps them in the multiplicities to facilitate incremental processing – updating aggregate values means changing tuple multiplicities rather than deleting and inserting tuples from the result. For simplicity, in this paper we associate each tuple with one count or aggregate multiplicity.

Query Language. The query language uses algebraic formulas to define queries (views) over generalized multiset relations. The language consists of relations $R(\vec{A})$, bag union $Q_1 + Q_2$, natural join $Q_1 \bowtie Q_2$, multiplicity-preserving projection $\text{Sum}_{\vec{A}}(Q)$, constants, values $f(var1, var2, \ldots)$, variable assignments $(var := value)$, and comparisons. To support queries with nested aggregates, the query language generalizes the assignment operator to take on arbitrary expressions instead of just values: $(var := Q)$ defines a finite-size relation containing tuples of expression Q with non-zero multiplicities extended by column var holding that multiplicity. Each output tuple has the multiplicity of 1. Expression Q may be correlated with the outside as usual in SQL.

EXAMPLE 3.1. *Consider a query over $R(A,B)$ and $S(B,C)$:*

```
SELECT COUNT(*) FROM R WHERE R.A <
  (SELECT COUNT(*) FROM S WHERE R.B = S.B)
```

The nested query is $Q_n := Sum_{[]}(S(B_2,C) \bowtie (B = B_2))$, where B comes from the outer query. The whole query is $Sum_{[]}(R(A,B) \bowtie (X := Q_n) \bowtie (A < X)))$. □

Variable assignment $(var := Q)$ can also express existential quantification. Assume the query of Example 3.1 had an `EXISTS` condition instead of the comparison. Then, we would write the condition part as $(X := Q_n) \bowtie (X \neq 0)$.

Delta Queries. Delta queries capture changes in query results for updates to base relations. For any query expression Q, we can construct a delta query ΔQ using a set of derivation rules defined for each operator of the query language. Our previous work studied these rules in detail [21, 22]; in short, the delta rules for updates ΔR to R are:

$$
\begin{aligned}
\Delta_R(R(A_1,A_2,\ldots)) &:= \Delta R(A_1,A_2,\ldots)\\
\Delta_R(Q_1 + Q_2) &:= (\Delta_R Q_1) + (\Delta_R Q_2)\\
\Delta_R(Q_1 \bowtie Q_2) &:= ((\Delta_R Q_1) \bowtie Q_2) + (Q_1 \bowtie (\Delta_R Q_2))\\
&\quad + ((\Delta_R Q_1) \bowtie (\Delta_R Q_2))\\
\Delta_R(\text{Sum}_{[A_1,A_2,\ldots]} Q) &:= \text{Sum}_{[A_1,A_2,\ldots]}(\Delta_R Q)\\
\Delta_R(var := Q) &:= (var := (Q + \Delta_R Q)) - (var := Q)
\end{aligned}
$$

where $-Q$ is syntactic sugar for $(-1) \bowtie Q$. For all other kinds of expressions, $\Delta_R(\cdot) := 0$.

3.2 Delta Evaluation for Batch Updates

In this section, we focus on the techniques for efficient evaluation of delta queries for batches of updates to base relations. For flat queries in which variable assignments involve only values, the delta rules always produce a simpler expression. Here, we define the complexity of a query in terms of its degree [21], which roughly corresponds to the number of referenced base relations. Replacing large base relations by much smaller delta relations reduces evaluation cost, favoring incremental maintenance over recomputation.

For queries with nested aggregates and existential quantification, the derivation rule for variable assignment prescribes recomputing both the old and new results to evaluate the delta, which clearly costs more than recomputing the whole query expression once. In general, these classes of queries might have no benefit from incremental maintenance. But, in many cases, we can specialize this delta rule to achieve efficient maintenance.

3.2.1 *Model of Computation*

We describe our model of computation to understand the advantages of alternative evaluation strategies. We represent an expression as a tree of operators, which are always evaluated from left to right, in a bottom-up fashion. Information about bound variables flows from left to right through the product operation. For instance, in expression $R(A) \bowtie S(A)$, the term $R(A)$ binds the A variable which is then used to lookup the multiplicity value inside $S(A)$. The evaluation cost for such an expression is $O(|R|)$, where $|R|$ is the number of tuples with a non-zero multiplicity in R.

Our model considers in-memory hash join as a reference join implementation. In this model, the ordering of terms has an impact on query evaluation performance. For example, when $S(A)$ is smaller than $R(A)$, commuting the two terms like $S(A) \bowtie R(A)$ results in fewer memory lookups in R. Note that commuting terms is not always possible – for instance, in expression $R(A) \bowtie A$, the two terms do not commute, unless A is already bound.

3.2.2 *Domain extraction*

We present a technique, called *domain extraction*, for efficient delta computation of queries with nested aggregates and existential quantification. We explain the idea on the problem of duplicate elimination in bag algebra. We formalize the technique afterwards.

For clarity of the presentation, we introduce $Exists(Q)$ as syntactic sugar for $\text{Sum}_{[\text{sch}(Q)]}((X := Q) \bowtie (X \neq 0))$, where $sch(Q)$ denotes the schema of Q. $Exists(Q)$ changes every non-zero multiplicity inside Q to 1. The delta rule for $Exists$ is $\Delta_R(Exists(Q)) = Exists(Q + \Delta_R Q) - Exists(Q)$.

First, we introduce the notion of domain expressions. A domain expression binds a set of variables with the sole purpose of speeding up the downstream query evaluation. All domain expression tuples have the multiplicity of one. For instance, we can write $R(A,B)$ as $Exists(R(A,B)) \bowtie R(A,B)$ without changing the original query semantics. Note that now $Exists(R(A,B))$ defines the iteration domain during query evaluation rather than $R(A,B)$.

EXAMPLE 3.2. *Consider an SQL query over $R(A,B)$*

```
SELECT DISTINCT A FROM R WHERE B > 3
```

or equivalently $Q := Exists(Sum_{[A]}(R(A,B) \bowtie (B > 3)))$. Let Q_n denotes the nested sum, then $\Delta Q_n := Sum_{[A]}(\Delta R(A,B) \bowtie (B > 3))$ and $\Delta Q := Exists(Q_n + \Delta Q_n) - Exists(Q_n)$. Note that ΔQ recomputes Q twice, once to insert new tuples and then to delete the old ones, which clearly defeats the purpose of incremental computation. Also, $(Q_n + \Delta Q_n)$ might leave unchanged many tuples in Q_n, so deleting those tuples and inserting them again is wasted work.

```
def extractDom(e: Expr): Expr = e match {
  case Plus(A, B) =>
    interDoms(extractDom(A), extractDom(B))
  case Prod(A, B) =>
    unionDoms(extractDom(A), extractDom(B))
  case Sum(gb, A) =>
    val domA  = extractDom(A)
    val domGb = inter(sch(domA), gb)
    if (domGb == gb) domA
    else if (domGb == Nil) 1
    else Exists(Sum(domGb, domA))
  case Assign(v, A) if A.hasRelations =>
    extractDom(A)
  case Rel(_)    =>
    if (e.hasLowCardinality) Exists(e) else 1
  case _         => e
}
```

Figure 1: The domain extraction algorithm. `interDoms` extracts common domains, `unionDoms` merges domains, `inter` is set intersection, and `sch(A)` denotes the schema of expression `A`.

Our goal is to transform ΔQ into an expression that changes only relevant tuples in the delta result. We want to iterate over only those tuples in Q_n whose A values appear in $\Delta R(A,B)$; other tuples are irrelevant for computing ΔQ. To achieve that goal, we capture the domain of A values in ΔR using $Exists(\Delta R(A,B))$[3]. To express only distinct values of A in ΔR, we write:

$$Q_{dom} := Exists(Sum_{[A]}(Exists(\Delta R(A,B)))).$$

The outer Exists keeps the multiplicity of 1. We prepend Q_{dom} to ΔQ in order to restrict the iteration domain.

$$\Delta Q' := Q_{dom} \bowtie (Exists(Q_n + \Delta Q_n) - Exists(Q_n))$$

We can make Q_{dom} more strict by including $(B > 3)$. □

Figure 1 shows the algorithm for domain extraction. The algorithm recursively pushes extracted domains up through the expression tree to bound variables in even larger parts of the expression. At leaf nodes, it identifies relations with low cardinalities that can restrict the iteration domain. We can either use cardinality estimates for each relation or rely on heuristics. We also include terms that can further restrict the domain size, like comparisons, values, and variable assignments over values.

For Sum aggregates, we recursively compute the domain of the subexpression and then, if necessary, reduce its schema to match that of the Sum aggregate. For instance, in Example 3.2, we project $Exists(\Delta R(A,B)) \bowtie (B > 3)$ on column A. If the domain schema is reduced, we enclose the expression with *Exists* to preserve the domain semantics; if the schema is empty, the extracted domain bounds no column and has little effect. When dealing with union, we intersect two subexpressions to find the maximum common domain that can be propagated further up in the tree; for the product operation, we union subexpressions into one common domain.

The domain extraction procedure allows us to revise the delta rule for variable assignments as:

$$\Delta(var{:=}Q) := Q_{dom} \bowtie ((var{:=}Q + \Delta Q) - (var{:=}Q))$$

where $Q_{dom} :=$ `extractDom`(ΔQ).

3.2.3 Re-evaluation vs. Incremental Computation

For non-nested queries, recursive incremental maintenance has lower parallel complexity than non-incremental evaluation [21], which often reflects in faster sequential execution in practice [22]. For queries with nested aggregates, there are cases when recomputing from scratch is better than computing the delta.

[3] ΔR can contain both insertions and deletions.

EXAMPLE 3.3. *Consider a query over $R(A,B)$ and $S(B,C)$.*

```
SELECT COUNT(*) FROM R
WHERE R.A < (SELECT COUNT(*) FROM S) AND R.B=10
```

The nested query computes an aggregate value and has no correlation with the outer query. The domain extraction procedure cannot restrict the domain of the delta query for updates to S, so re-evaluation is a better option. We can still speed up the computation by materializing the query piecewise, for instance, by precomputing and maintaining the expression $Sum_{[A]}(R(A,B) \bowtie (B = 10))$. Note that we can incrementally maintain the top-level query for updates to R by materializing the nested query result as a single variable.

Nested queries are often correlated with the outside query. When the correlation involves equality predicates, extracting the domain of the inner query might restrict some of the correlated variables. This range restriction can reduce the maintenance cost. In general, the decision on whether to incrementally maintain or recompute the query result requires a case-by-case cost analysis. In our experiments, we incrementally maintain a query whenever the extracted nested domain binds at least one equality-correlated variable.

3.3 Single-tuple vs. Batch Updates

Incremental programs for single-tuple updates are simpler and easier to optimize than batched incremental programs. The parameters of single-tuple triggers match the tuple's schema to avoid boxing and unboxing of the primitive data types in the input. We can inline these parameters into delta expressions and eliminate one-element loops. In local environments, we can process one batch of updates via repeated calls to single-tuple triggers. Aside from the increased invocation overhead, we identify three reasons why such an approach can be suboptimal.

Preprocessing batches. Preprocessing a batch of updates can merge or eliminate changes to the same input tuples. Static analysis of the query can identify subexpressions that involve solely batch updates (e.g., domain expressions). Then, we can precompute a batch aggregate by keeping only relevant batch columns of the tuples that match query's static conditions. Batch pre-aggregation can produce much fewer tuples, which can significantly decrease the cost of trigger evaluation; smaller batches also reduce communication costs in distributed environments. Batch pre-aggregation can have a limited effect when there is no filtering condition and there is a functional dependency between the aggregated columns and the primary key of the delta relation; then, we can eliminate only updates targeting the same key.

Skipping intermediate views states. When a maintenance trigger evaluates the whole query from scratch, batching can help us to avoid recomputation of intermediate query results. For instance, considering the query of Example 3.3 and updates to S, processing one batch of updates refreshes the inner query result once and triggers one recomputation of the outer query. In contrast, the tuple-at-a-time approach evaluates the outer query on every update.

Cache locality. Processing one update batch, in a tight loop, can improve cache locality and branch prediction for reasonably-sized batches; too large batches can have negative impacts on locality.

In our experiments, we evaluate these trade-offs between single-tuple and batch maintenance for different update sizes.

4. DISTRIBUTED VIEW MAINTENANCE

In this section, we present our compiler that transforms maintenance triggers generated for local execution into maintenance programs optimized for running on large-scale processing platforms with synchronous execution, like Spark or Hadoop. Our approach

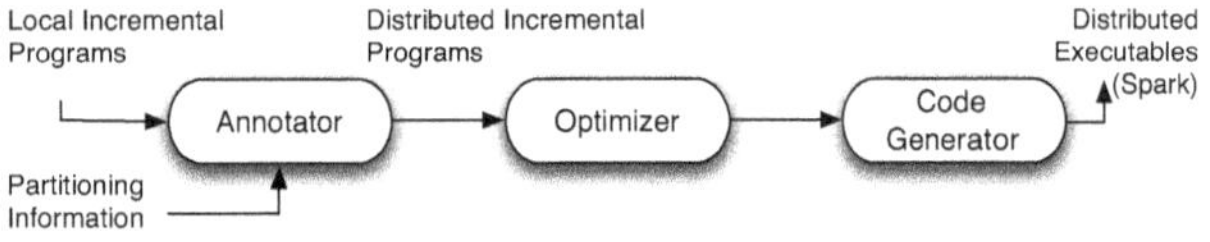

Figure 2: Compilation of incremental programs

is general and applies to any input program formed using our query language, not just recursive view maintenance programs.

Distributed Execution Model. We assume a synchronous execution model where one driver node orchestrates job execution among workers, like in Spark or Hadoop. Processing one batch of updates may require several computation stages, where each stage runs view maintenance code in parallel. All workers are stateful, preserve data between stages, and participate in every stage.

Our approach naturally leverages the fault tolerance mechanisms of the underlying execution platform, in our case, the Spark computing framework. Using data checkpointing, we can periodically save intermediate state to reliable storage (HDFS) in order to shorten recovery time. Checkpointing may have detrimental effects on the latency of processing, so the user needs to carefully tune the frequency of checkpointing based on application requirements.

Types of Materialized Views. We classify materialized views depending on the location of their contents. *Local views* are stored and maintained entirely on the driver node. They are suitable for materializing top-level aggregates with small output domains. *Distributed views* have their contents spread over all workers to balance CPU and memory pressure. Each distributed view has an associated partitioning function that maps a tuple to a non-empty set of nodes storing its replicas.

4.1 Compilation Overview

Figure 2 shows the process of transforming a local incremental program into a functionally equivalent, distributed program. The input consists of statements expressed using our query language. To distribute their execution, the compiler relies on partitioning information about each materialized view. Deciding on the optimal view partitioning scheme happens outside of the compilation process; we assume that such partitioning information is available (e.g., provided by the user).

The compilation process consists of three phases. First, we annotate a given input program with partitioning information and, if necessary, introduce operators for exchanging data among distributed nodes in order to preserve the correctness of query evaluation. Next, we optimize the annotated program using a set of simplification rules and heuristics that aim to minimize the number of jobs necessary for processing one update batch. Finally, we generate executable code for a specific processing platform. Only the code generation phase depends on the target platform.

4.2 Well-formed Distributed Programs

The semantics of the query operators, presented in Section 3.1 and Appendix A, cannot be directly translated to distributed environments. For instance, unioning one local and one distributed view has no clear meaning. Even among views of the same type, naïvely executing query operators at each distributed node might yield wrong results. For instance, a natural join between two distributed views produces a correct result only if the views are identically partitioned over the join (common) keys; otherwise, one or both operands need to be repartitioned.

We extend our query language with new location-aware primitives that allow us to construct *well-formed* query expressions. Such expressions preserve the correctness of distributed query evaluation for the given partitioning strategy.

Location Tags. To reason about the semantics and correctness of query evaluation, we annotate query expressions with location tags: 1) `Local` tag denotes the result is located on the driver node; 2) `Dist` ($\mathcal{P}$) tag marks the result is distributed among all workers according to partitioning function $\mathcal{P}$; and 3) `Random` tag denotes the result is randomly distributed among all workers.

A relation (materialized view) can take on a `Local`, `Dist`, or `Random` tag. Constants, values, comparisons, and variable assignments involving values are interpreted (virtual) relations whose contents is deterministic and never materialized. The location of such terms is irrelevant from the perspective of query evaluation, and they can freely participate in both local and distributed expressions; in distributed settings, one can view these terms as fully replicated.

Location Transformers. To support distributed execution, we extend the language with new operators for manipulating location tags and exchanging data over the network.

- $\texttt{Repart}_{\mathcal{P}_2}(Q^{\{\texttt{Dist}(\mathcal{P}_1),\texttt{Random}\}}) = Q^{\texttt{Dist}(\mathcal{P}_2)}$
  Partition the distributed result of Q using function $\mathcal{P}_2$.
- $\texttt{Scatter}_{\mathcal{P}}(Q^{\texttt{Local}}) = Q^{\texttt{Dist}(\mathcal{P})}$
  Partition the local result of Q using function $\mathcal{P}$.
- $\texttt{Gather}(Q^{\{\texttt{Dist}(\mathcal{P}),\texttt{Random}\}}) = Q^{\texttt{Local}}$
  Aggregate the distributed result of Q on the driver node.

The location transformers are the only mechanism for exchanging data among nodes. `Repart` and `Gather` operate over distributed expressions, while `Scatter` supports only local expressions.

Distributed Query Operators. We extend the semantics of our query operators with location tags.

- Relation $R(A_1, A_2, ...)^T$ stores the contents at location T.
- Bag union $Q_1^T + Q_2^T$ merges tuples either locally or in parallel on every node, and the result retains tag T. Requires the same location tag for both operands.
- Natural join $Q_1^T \bowtie Q_2^T$ has the usual semantics when $T = \texttt{Local}$. For distributed evaluation, both operands need to be partitioned on the join keys; the result is distributed and consists of locally evaluated joins on every node. Joins on `Random` are disallowed.
- $\text{Sum}_{[A_1,A_2,...]}Q^T$, when $T = \texttt{Dist}(\mathcal{P})$, computes partial aggregates on every node. The result has tag T only if Q is key partitioned on one of the group-by columns; otherwise, we annotate with a `Random` tag. In other cases, the result retains tag T.

All other language constructs – constants, values, comparisons, and variable assignments – are location independent and their semantics remain unchanged.

Next, we present an algorithm for transforming a local program into a well-formed distributed program based on the given partitioning information. The algorithm annotates and possibly extends the expression trees of the statements to preserve the semantics of each operator. For each statement, we start by assigning location tags to all relational terms in the expression tree. Then, in a bottom-up fashion, we annotate each node of the tree with a location tag. We introduce location transformers where necessary to preserve the semantics and correctness of each query operator, as discussed above. Upon reaching the root node, we ensure that the RHS query expression evaluates at the same location where the target LHS view is materialized, and, if necessary, introduce a `Gather` or `Scatter` transformer. To obtain a well-formed distributed program, we apply this procedure to every input statement.

EXAMPLE 4.1. *Let us construct a well-formed statement for*

$$M(A) \mathrel{+}= Sum_{[A]}(M_1(A,B) \bowtie M_2(A,B))$$

when $M(A)$ and $M_1(A,B)$ are partitioned by A, while $M_2(A,B)$ is partitioned by B. We associate location tags to the materialized views. We use $M(A)^{[A]}$ to denote that $M(A)$ is partitioned on column A. Since the join operands have incompatible location tags, we introduce Repart *around one of the operands (e.g., left):*

$$\texttt{Repart}_{[B]}(M_1(A,B)^{[A]})^{[B]} \bowtie M_2(A,B)^{[B]}$$

The join result remains partitioned on B. The Sum expression computes partial aggregates grouped by column A. Such an expression cannot have location tag [B] since B is not in the output schema; so, we assign a Random *tag to the expression. Now, we have reached the root of the expression tree. We need to ensure that the RHS expression has the same location tag as the target view. So, adding a* Repart *transformer produces a well-formed statement:*

$$M(A)^{[A]} \mathrel{+}= \texttt{Repart}_{[A]}(Sum_{[A]}(\texttt{Repart}_{[B]}(M_1(A,B)^{[A]})^{[B]} \bowtie M_2(A,B)^{[B]})^{Random})^{[A]}$$

□

The algorithm for constructing well-formed expressions has no associated cost metrics and might produce suboptimal solutions. In the above example, executing the final statement requires two communication rounds (Repart s) between the driver and workers. Such communication overhead is unnecessary – if we repartition the other join operand, we produce an equivalent, less expensive well-formed statement with only one communication round:

$$M(A)^{[A]} \mathrel{+}= \text{Sum}_{[A]}(M_1(A,B)^{[A]} \bowtie \texttt{Repart}_{[A]}(M_2(A,B)^{[B]})^{[A]})^{[A]}$$

To optimize well-formed programs we rely on a set of simplification and heuristic rules, which we present next.

4.3 Optimizing Distributed Programs

In this section, we describe how to optimize well-formed programs in order to minimize communication and processing costs. We divide this task into two stages. The first stage relies on a simple cost-based model to simplify each individual statement. The second stage exploits commonalities among statements to avoid redundant communication and minimize the number of jobs needed to execute the given program.

4.3.1 Intra-Statement Optimization

Intra-statement optimization aims to minimize the amount of network traffic required to execute one well-formed statement. Our cost model takes the number of communication rounds as the basic metric for cost comparison. Each location transformer (Repart, Scatter, and Gather) shuffles data over the network, so statements containing fewer of them require less communication. Our cost model also relies on few heuristics to resolve ties between statements with the same cost. We reshuffle expressions that involve batch updates rather than whole materialized views as the formers are usually smaller in size; we favor expressions with fewer Gather transformers to distribute computation as much as possible.

The optimizer uses a trial and error approach to recursively optimize a given statement. It tries to push each location transformer down the expression tree, following the rules from Figure 3. Note that these rules might produce more expensive expressions, in which case the algorithm backtracks. During each optimization step, the compiler tries to simplify the current expression using the rules from Figure 4. Each simplification rules always produces an equivalent expression with fewer location transformers.

$$\begin{aligned}
\texttt{Repart}_{\mathcal{P}}(Q_1 \bowtie Q_2) &\Leftrightarrow \texttt{Repart}_{\mathcal{P}}(Q_1) \bowtie \texttt{Repart}_{\mathcal{P}}(Q_2)\\
\texttt{Repart}_{\mathcal{P}}(Q_1 + Q_2) &\Leftrightarrow \texttt{Repart}_{\mathcal{P}}(Q_1) + \texttt{Repart}_{\mathcal{P}}(Q_2)\\
\texttt{Repart}_{\mathcal{P}}(\text{Sum}_{[A_1,A_2,\ldots]}(Q)) &\Leftrightarrow \text{Sum}_{[A_1,A_2,\ldots]}(\texttt{Repart}_{\mathcal{P}}(Q))\\
\texttt{Repart}_{\mathcal{P}}(var := Q) &\Leftrightarrow (var := \texttt{Repart}_{\mathcal{P}}(Q))
\end{aligned}$$

Figure 3: Bidirectional optimization rules for Repart. The same rules apply to Scatter and Gather.

$$\begin{aligned}
\texttt{Repart}_{\mathcal{P}}(Q^{\texttt{Dist}(\mathcal{P})}) &\Rightarrow Q^{\texttt{Dist}(\mathcal{P})}\\
\texttt{Gather}(Q^{\texttt{Local}}) &\Rightarrow Q^{\texttt{Local}}\\
\texttt{Repart}_{\mathcal{P}_1} \circ \texttt{Repart}_{\mathcal{P}_2} &\Rightarrow \texttt{Repart}_{\mathcal{P}_1}\\
\texttt{Repart}_{\mathcal{P}_1} \circ \texttt{Scatter}_{\mathcal{P}_2} &\Rightarrow \texttt{Scatter}_{\mathcal{P}_1}\\
\texttt{Gather} \circ \texttt{Repart}_{\mathcal{P}} &\Rightarrow \texttt{Gather}\\
\texttt{Gather} \circ \texttt{Scatter}_{\mathcal{P}} &\Rightarrow \texttt{Gather}\\
\texttt{Scatter}_{\mathcal{P}} \circ \texttt{Gather} &\Rightarrow \texttt{Repart}_{\mathcal{P}}
\end{aligned}$$

Figure 4: Simplification rules for location transformers. The ∘ sign denotes operator composition.

In Example 4.1, the optimizer pushes the outer $\texttt{Repart}_{[A]}$ through Sum and ⋈, and then simplifies $\texttt{Repart}_{[A]} \circ \texttt{Repart}_{[B]}$ to $\texttt{Repart}_{[A]}$. The optimized statement requires only one communication round.

4.3.2 Inter-Statement Optimization

Location transformers represent natural pipeline breakers in query evaluation since they need to materialize and shuffle their contents before continuing processing. In this section, we show how to analyze inter-statement dependencies to minimize the number of pipeline breakers and their communication overhead.

Single Transformer Form. To facilitate inter-statement analysis, we first convert a given program into single transformer form where each statement has at most one location transformer. The transformer, if present, always references one materialized view. In other words, we normalize the input program by: 1) materializing the contents being transformed (if not already materialized), 2) extracting the location transformers targeting the materialized contents into separate statements, and 3) updating the affected statements with new references. To achieve that, we recursively bottom-up traverse the expression tree of every statement.

Single transformer form sets clear boundaries around the contents that needs to be communicated, which eases the implementation of further optimizations. We apply common subexpression elimination and dead code elimination to detect expressions shared among statements and to eliminate redundant network transfers. In contrast to the classical compiler optimizations, our routines are aware of the location where each expression is executed.

Statement Execution Mode. The location tag associated with each statement determines where and how that statement is going to be executed. Statements targeting local materialized views are, as expected, executed at the driver node in *local mode*. Statements involving distributed views run in *distributed mode*, where the driver initiates the computation.

All location transformations run in local mode since the driver governs their execution. But, materializing the contents to be reshuffled can happen in both local and distributed mode. For instance, preparing contents for Scatter takes place on the driver node, while for Repart and Gather happens on every worker node.

Statement Blocks. Distributed statements are more expensive to execute than local statements. To run a distributed statement, the driver needs to serialize the task closure, ship it to all the work-

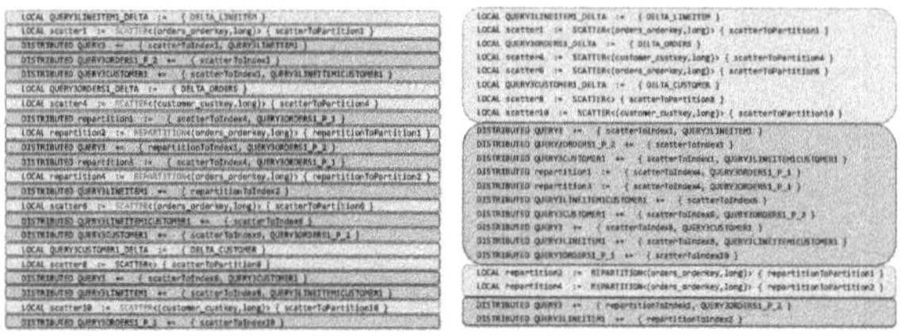

Figure 5: The block fusion effect in TPC-H Q3: before and after. Green blocks are local, blue blocks are distributed.

ers, and wait for the completion of each one of them. For short-running tasks, and recursive view maintenance is often such, non-processing overheads can easily dominate in the execution time.

To amortize the cost of executing distributed statements, we pack them together into processing units called *statement blocks*. A statement block consists of a sequence of distributed statements that can be executed at once on every node without comprising the program correctness. Apart from distributed blocks, we also introduce blocks of local statements whose purpose is to determine which network operations can be batched together (the driver initiates `Repart`, `Scatter`, and `Gather` in local mode).

Data-flow dependencies among statements prevent arbitrary re-orderings of statements and blocks. In Appendix C.3, we show methods for checking the commutativity of statements and blocks.

Block Fusion Algorithm. We prefer program execution plans with as few statement blocks as possible. Here, we describe an algorithm that reorders and merges together consecutive blocks to minimize their number. Appendix C.3 presents the algorithm.

First, we promote each statement into a separate block that keeps statement's execution mode (local or distributed). Then, the algorithm tries to fuse together the first block with the others that share the same execution mode and commute with all intermediate blocks. On success, the algorithm merges the new block sequence recursively; otherwise, it handles the remaining blocks recursively.

Figure 5 visualizes the effects of block fusion on the incremental program of TPC-H Q3. Before running the algorithm, the annotated input program contained 10 local and 12 distributed statement blocks. After reordering and merging these blocks, the algorithm outputs only 2 local and 2 distributed compound blocks.

4.4 Code Generation

Statement blocks considerably simplify code generation. Isolating distributed blocks enables workers to safely run code generated for single-node execution on their local data partitions. Pure local statements without transformers also correspond to unmodified single-node code. Distributed code generation, thus, relies to a great extent on single-node code generation.

Code generated for location transformers uses platform-specific communication primitives for exchanging data. To minimize network overhead, we encapsulate transformers of the same type into one compound request per block. For instance, we coalesce multiple `Scatter` transformers and their materialized data into just one `Scatter` request that uses a container data structure.

5. IMPLEMENTING VIEW MAINTENANCE

In this section, we describe how to compile queries of our language into low-level code that uses specialized data structures.

5.1 From Queries to Native Code

DBToaster compiles maintenance programs into imperative or functional code optimized for the execution in local mode (C++) or distributed mode (Scala for Spark). The compiler relies on the model of computation described in Section 3. As discussed, the query language exploits the notion of information flow, which is common in programming languages. The information about bound variables always flows from left to right during query evaluation, which eases compilation of the language construct. In generated code, we replace all high-level operators, like natural joins, unions, etc., with concrete operations over the underlying data structures.

When compiling a relational term, we distinguish several cases: (1) if all its variables are free, we transform it into a `foreach` loop that iterates over the whole collection; (2) if all its variables are bound, we replace it with a `get` (lookup) operation; (3) otherwise, we form a `slice` operation that iterates over only the elements matching the current values of the bound variables. Note that cases (2) and (3) may benefit from specialized index structures.

We use continuation passing style [8] to facilitate code generation and avoid intermediate materializations, such as redundant computations of bag unions and aggregates. The compilation process relies on an extensible compiler library, called LMS [36], to perform both classical optimizations, like common subexpression elimination, dead code elimination, loop unrolling and fusion, and also domain-specific optimizations, like data-structure specialization and automatic indexing.

Our compiler optimizes incremental programs for single-tuple processing. It specializes the parameters of single-tuple triggers to the concrete primitive types of the updated relation. Then, the native compiler can treat such parameters as constants and move them out of loops and closures when possible. Our compiler eliminates loops around one-element batches and uses primitive type variables rather than maps to store intermediate materializations.

5.2 Data Structure Specialization

The design of the data structure for storing materialized views depends on whether the view contents can change over time and the types of operations that need to be supported. Materialized views defined over static base relations are immutable collections of records stored in fixed-size arrays with fast lookup and scan operations. In typical streaming scenarios, however, updates to mutable base relations can be fast-moving and unpredictable, indicating that any array-based solution for storing tuples of dynamic materialized views might be expensive either in terms of the memory usage or maintenance overhead.

We materialize the contents of dynamic materialized views inside record pools, shown in Figure 6. One record pool stores records of the same format inside main memory and dynamically adapts its size to match the current working set. The pool keeps track of available free slots to facilitate future memory allocations and ease memory management. We specialize the format of pool records at compile time. Each record contains key fields corresponding to the schema of the materialized expression and value fields storing tuple multiplicities. The key fields uniquely identify each record.

5.2.1 Automatic Index Support

We can associate multiple index structures with one record pool, as shown in Figure 6. Each index structure provides a fast path to the records that match a given condition. We use unique hash indexes to provide fast lookups and non-unique hash indexes for slice operations[4]. Both indexes maintain an overflow linked list for each bucket. To shorten scanning in one bucket, non-unique hash indexes cluster records that share the same key. Pool records keep

[4]Studying other index types, like B++ trees (for range operations) or binary heaps (for min/max), we leave for future work.

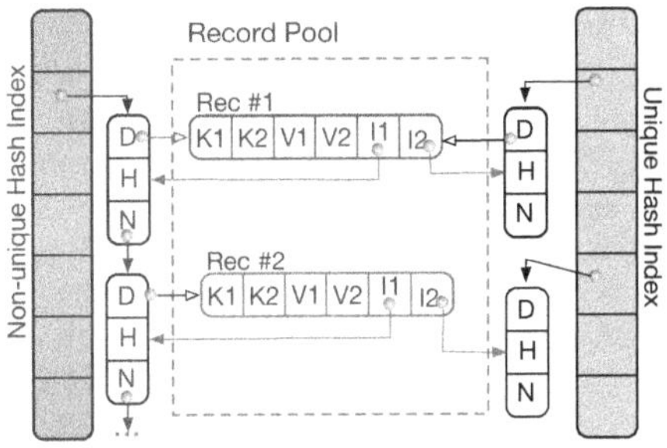

Figure 6: Multi-indexed data structure used for materialization. Each bucket (shaded cells) has a linked list of collisions. Legend: (D)ata, (H)ash, (N)ext, (K)ey, (V)alue, and (I)ndex.

back-references to their indexes to avoid hash re-computation and additional lookups during update and delete operations.

Our compiler analyzes the following access patterns: 1) scan over the entire collection (`foreach`), 2) lookup for a given unique key (`get`, `update`, `delete`), and 3) index scan for a given non-unique key (`slice`). We build a unique hash index for `get` operations, that is, when all lookup keys are bound at evaluation time. The same rule applies to `update`, `insert`, and `delete` operations. For `slice` operations, we create a non-unique index over the variables bound at evaluation time. When the access pattern analysis detects only `foreach` operations, we omit index creation.

DBToaster creates all relevant index structures. From our experience, most data structures produced during recursive compilation have only few indexes. For instance, the materialized views produced compiling the TPC-H queries usually have zero or one secondary indexes, with rare exceptions of up to three non-unique indexes. Our empirical results indicate that the benefit of creating these indexes greatly outperforms their maintenance overheads.

5.2.2 *Column-oriented layout*

Record pools keep tuples in a row-oriented format. Materialized views store aggregated results in which all unused attributes are projected away during query compilation. Thus, during query evaluation, each access to one record likely references all its fields.

The row-oriented layout is, however, unsuitable for efficient data serialization and deserialization, which are important considerations in distributed query evaluation. To speed up these operations, the compiler creates array-based data structures for storing serializable data in columnar mode. It also generates specialized transformers for switching between row- and column-oriented formats.

We also use columnar data structures for storing input batches. Batched delta processing often starts by filtering out tuples that do not match query's static conditions. As these conditions are often simple (e.g., $A > 2$), using a columnar representation can improve cache locality. After filtering, we typically aggregate input batches to remove unused columns and store the result in a record pool.

6. EXPERIMENTS

We evaluate the performance of recursive incremental view maintenance for batch updates of different sizes in local and distributed settings. In the single-node evaluation, we analyze the throughput and cache locality of C++ incremental programs generated using the DBToaster Release 2.2 [2]. In the distributed evaluation, we scale out incremental view maintenance to hundreds of Spark workers. Our experimental results show that:

- In local mode, view maintenance code specialized for tuple-at-a-time processing can outperform or be on par with batched programs for almost half of our queries.
- Preprocessing input batches can boost the performance of incremental computation by multiple orders of magnitude.
- Large batches can have negative impacts on cache locality. In local mode, the throughput of most of our queries peaks for batches with $1,000 - 10,000$ tuples.
- In distributed mode, we show that our approach can scale to hundreds of workers for queries of various complexities, while processing input batches with few second latencies.

Experimental Setup. We run single-node experiments on an Intel Xeon E5-2630L @ 2.40GHz server with 2×6 cores, each with 2 hardware threads, 15MB of cache, 256GB of DDR3 RAM, and Ubuntu 14.04.2 LTS. We compile generated C++ programs using GCC 4.8.4. For distributed experiments, we use 100 such server instances connected via a full-duplex 10GbE network and running Spark 1.6.1 and YARN 2.7.1. We generate Scala programs for running on Spark and compile using Scala 2.10.4.

Query and Data Workload. Our query workload consists of the TPC-H queries that are modified for streaming scenarios [22] and a subset of TPC-DS queries from [23] (excluding four queries with the OVER clause, which we currently do not support). We run these queries over data streams synthesized from TPC-H and TPC-DS databases by interleaving insertions to the base relations in a round-robin fashion. We process 10GB streams in local mode and 500GB streams in distributed mode. We run experiments with a one-hour timeout on query execution, not counting loading of streams into memory and forming input batches of a given size.

6.1 Single-node Evaluation

Our local experiments compare tuple-at-a-time and batched incremental programs. The former have triggers with tuple fields as function parameters, which can be inlined into delta computation; the latter consist of triggers accepting one arbitrary-sized columnar batch. In both cases, we generate single-threaded C++ code.

Batched incremental programs have extra loops inside triggers for processing input batches. To avoid redundant iterations over the whole batch, we materialize input tuples that match query's static conditions, retaining only the attributes (columns) used in incremental evaluation. These pre-aggregated batches are smaller in size due to having fewer attributes and, potentially, fewer matching tuples, which can significantly affect view maintenance costs. In contrast, single-tuple triggers avoid materialization of input batches.

6.1.1 *Batch Size vs. Throughput*

Figure 7 shows the normalized throughput of batched incremental processing of the TPC-H queries for different batch sizes using the tuple-at-a-time performance as the baseline. For ease of presentation, we use two graphs with different y-axis scales.

For almost half of our queries, batched incremental processing performs worse or just marginally better than specialized tuple-at-a-time processing. This result comes at no surprise once we start analyzing the pre-aggregated batches of these queries for updates to their largest (and usually most expensive) relation. For instance, Q5, Q9, and Q18 aggregate `LINEITEM` deltas by `orderkey` and, possibly, some other fields; Q16 aggregates `PARTSUPP` deltas by the primary key (`partkey`, `suppkey`). In these cases, batch pre-aggregation retains (almost) the same number of input tuples, bringing no performance improvements; on the contrary, it introduces extra materialization and looping overheads. For two-way join queries, Q4, Q12, and Q13, the simplicity of their view maintenance code makes these overheads particularly pronounced.

Batch pre-aggregation keeps only input tuples that match static query conditions. This step can speed up the rest of view maintenance code, bringing improvements that depend on the selectivity of query predicates. For instance, preprocessing in Q3, Q7, Q8, Q10, and Q14 filters out tuples of `LINEITEM` and `ORDERS` batches and yields improvements from 19% in Q7 to 306% in Q8.

Batch pre-aggregation can project input tuples onto a set of attributes with small active domains. For instance, Q1 projects a `LINEITEM` batch onto columns containing only few possible values, which enables cheap maintenance of the final 8 aggregates. So, the single-tuple implementation performs more maintenance work per input tuple. For Q2 and Q19, batch filtering and projection can give up to 1.3x and 5.1x better performance. This benefit can increase for queries with more complex trigger functions. For instance, Q22 filters and projects an `ORDERS` batch on `custkey`, while Q20 filters and projects `PARTSUPP` and `LINEITEM` batches on `suppkey`. In both cases, the projected columns have much smaller domains, bringing significant improvements, 2,243x in Q20 and 4,319x in Q22.

Incremental programs for single-tuples updates are easier to optimize than their batched counterparts due to having simpler input and fewer loops in trigger bodies. This virtue emerges in Q17 and Q21. For these queries, our compiler fails to factorize common subexpressions as efficiently as during the single-tuple compilation, which causes same expressions to be evaluated twice.

For Q11 and Q15, incremental view maintenance is more expensive than re-evaluation due to inequality-based nested aggregates. Increasing batch sizes results in fewer re-evaluations, which increases the overall throughput at the expense of higher latencies.

Bulk processing amortizes the overhead of invoking trigger functions. For instance, maintaining a single aggregate over `LINEITEM` in Q6 with batches of 10,000 tuples can bring up to 2x better performance than the single-tuple execution. However, these results hold only when function inlining is disabled. Since the single-tuple trigger body of Q6 consists of just one conditional statement, the C++ compiler usually decides to inline this computation, causing single-tuple execution to always outperform batched execution.

Comparison with PostgreSQL. Figure 8 compares the throughput of recursive incremental processing in C++ and re-evaluation and classical incremental view maintenance in PostgreSQL for TPC-H Q17. We implement incremental processing in PostgreSQL using the domain extraction procedure described in Section 3.2. The results show that the generated code outperforms PostgreSQL re-evaluation from 233x to 14,181x and classical incremental view maintenance from 120x to 10,659x, for different batch sizes.

Appendix B contains the performance numbers for the TPC-H and TPC-DS queries from our workload. The results show that, in all but four cases, recursive view maintenance outperforms classical view maintenance by orders of magnitude, even when processing large batches, for which the database system is optimized for.

Memory requirements. Recursive incremental view maintenance materializes auxiliary views in order to speed up the work required to keep all views fresh. The sizes of these auxiliary views created to maintain a given query, in general, depend on the query structure. Our query workloads, TPC-H and TPC-DS, are based on the star schema with one large fact table and several dimension tables. In such cases, auxiliary materialized views cannot have more tuples than the fact table due to integrity constraints. In practice, the sizes of materialized views are much smaller than the size of the fact table as their view definition queries often involve static filtering conditions. In addition, materialized views discard columns unused in a given query and aggregate over the remaining columns.

6.2 Distributed Evaluation

For distributed experiments, we use Spark [38] for parallelizing the execution of incremental view maintenance code. Spark offers a synchronous model of computation in which the driver governs job execution and coordination with workers.

We execute a subset of the TPC-H queries with different complexities on a 500GB stream of tuples. We chunk the input stream into batches of a given size, and, for each batch, we run one or more Spark jobs to refresh the materialized view. To avoid scalability bottlenecks caused by the driver handling all input data, we simulate a system in which every worker receives, independently of the driver and other workers, a fraction of the input stream. In our experiments, we ensure that each worker gets a roughly equal *random* partition of every batch. Each worker preloads its batch partitions before starting the experiment.

Materialized views are either stored locally on the driver or distributed among workers. The decision on how to partition materialized views in order to minimize their maintenance costs is a challenging problem, which might benefit from previous work on database partitioning [15, 31]. We leave this question for future work. For this paper, we rely on a simple heuristics rule: we partition materialized views on the primary key of a base table appearing in the view schema (e.g., `orderkey`); if there are multiple such primary keys of base tables (e.g., `orderkey`, `custkey`), we partition on the one with the highest cardinality (`orderkey`); otherwise, if there are no primary keys in the view schema, we assume the final aggregate has a small domain and can be stored on the driver.

Query Complexity in Spark. Generated Spark code runs a sequence of jobs in order to perform incremental view maintenance. Each job consists of multiple stages (e.g., map-reduce phases), and each stage corresponds to one block of distributed statements, defined in Section 4.3. The number of jobs and stages for a given query depends on the query structure and the provided partitioning information. Appendix C.1 shows the complexity of the TPC-H queries in terms of the number of jobs and stages necessary for processing one update batch, for the above partitioning strategy.

6.2.1 *Weak Scalability*

We evaluate the scalability of our approach when each worker receives batch partitions of size 100,000. Figure 9 shows the measured latency and throughput for a subset of the TPC-H queries.

Q6 computes a single aggregate over `LINEITEM`. Given the initial random distribution of batches and small query output size, we create one stage during which each worker computes a partial aggregate of its batch partition, and then, we sum these values up to update the final result at the driver. The purpose of running Q6 is to measure Spark synchronization overheads as a function of the number of workers. The query requires minimal network communication as each worker sends one 64-bit value per batch. Also each worker spends negligible time aggregating 100,000 tuples (6 ms on average), thus the results from Figure 9a are close to pure synchronization overheads of Spark. The median latency of processing a batch of size $(100{,}000 \times \#\text{workers})$ increases from 65 ms for 50 workers to 386 ms for 1,000 workers, while the throughput rises up to 267 million tuples per sec for 600 workers. Both metrics suffer from synchronization costs, which increase with more workers.

Q17 computes a two-way join with an equality-correlated nested aggregate. Incremental computation of Q17 relies on the domain extraction procedure described in Section 3.2. We partition both base relations on `partkey` and store the result at the driver. The execution graphs consists of two stages. The first stage pre-aggregates batch partitions and shuffles the result on `partkey`. The second

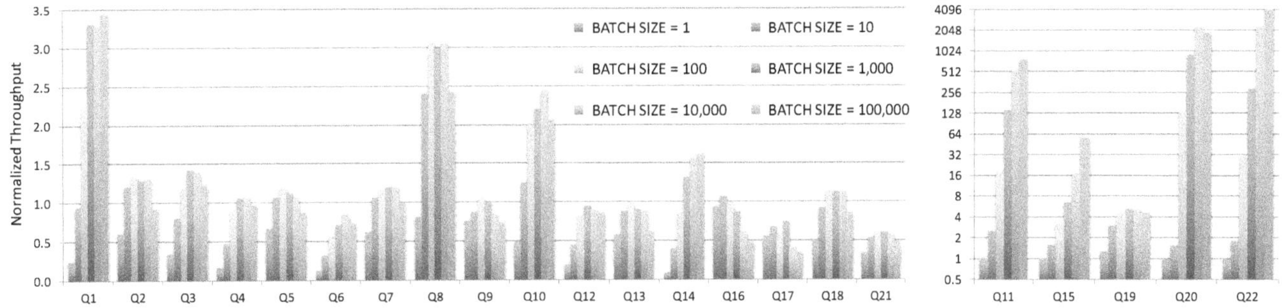

Figure 7: Normalized throughput of the TPC-H queries for different batch sizes with single-tuple execution as the baseline.

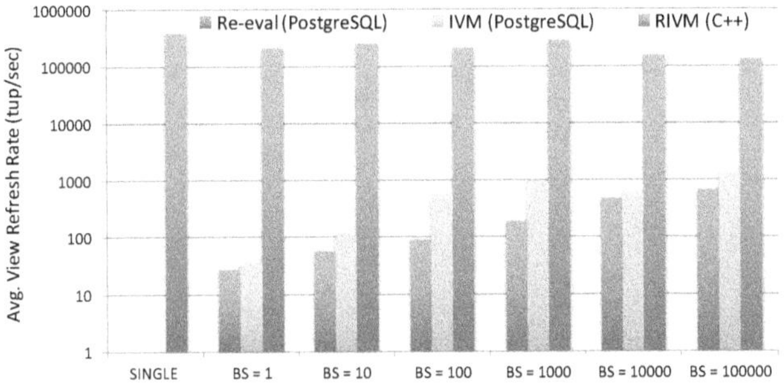

Figure 8: Throughput comparison for TPC-H Q17 of re-evaluation and incremental maintenance in PostgreSQL and recursive incremental maintenance in generated C++ code for different batch sizes. SINGLE denotes specialized single-tuple processing in C++.

stage refreshes the base relations and aggregates partial results at the driver to update the final result.

Figure 9b shows the performance of incremental maintenance of Q17. The throughput rises up to 600 nodes, while the median latency increases from 1.3s for 50 workers to 4s for 800 workers. Q17 achieves higher latency than Q6 due to several reasons: 1) workers perform more expensive view maintenance (526 ms on average), 2) the shuffling phase requires serialization and deserialization of data, writing to local disks, and reading from remote locations, and 3) more processing stages incur more synchronization overheads. Pre-aggregation of input batches reduces the amount of shuffled data from 7.6 MB to 1.8 MB per worker. This amount remains constant regardless of the number of workers.

Figure 9c shows that the average throughput of Q3 increases up to 400 workers. Compared with Q17, the median latency of Q3 is lower at smaller scales and almost identical when using more workers. Q3 uses one additional stage to replicate pre-aggregated `CUSTOMER` deltas and join them with materialized views partitioned over `orderkey`. The amount of shuffled data per worker grows with the batch size, from 439 KB for 50 workers to 2.4 MB for 1,000 workers. The trigger processing time per worker (excluding all other overheads) changes on average from 120 ms for 50 workers to 305 ms for 1,000 workers, with less than 10% deviation among workers in both cases. Thus, at larger scales, the increased shuffling cost dominates the processing time.

Q7 is one of the most complex queries in our workload from the perspective of incremental view maintenance. The driver stores the top-level result and runs three jobs to process one batch of updates. The median latency grows more rapidly compared to other queries, from 1.5s on 50 workers to 16.9s on 800 workers. The average running time of the update triggers per worker also increases but more steadily, from 0.6s to 3.7s, while the amount of shuffled data per worker grows from 2.1 MB to 8.4 MB. This increased network communication induces higher latencies and brings down the average throughput beyond 400 workers.

In all these cases, using more workers increases the variability of latency. From our experience with using Spark, stragglers can often prolong stage computation time by a factor of 1.5 – 3x despite almost perfect load balancing. We also observe that the straggler effect is more pronounced with queries shuffling relatively large amounts of data, such as Q3 and Q7. Examining logs and reported runtime metrics gives no reasonable explanation for such behavior.

6.2.2 *Strong Scalability*

We measure the scalability of our incremental technique for constant batch sizes and varying numbers of workers. Figure 10 shows the measured throughput for a subset of the TPC-H queries. We use batches with 50, 100, 200, and 400 million tuples to ensure enough parallelizable work inside update triggers. Figure 11 in Appendix C shows results for more TPC-H queries. We compare our approach against re-evaluation using Spark SQL for batches with 400 million tuples. Note that Spark SQL can handle only flat queries.

Figure 10a shows that the median latency of Q6 decreases with more workers until the cost of synchronization becomes comparable with the cost of batch processing. Processing 100 million tuples using 100 workers takes on average 14 ms per worker, leaving no opportunities for further parallelization. For the four batch sizes, the lowest median latencies are 98 ms, 130 ms, 153 ms, and 211 ms. Re-evaluating Q6 on each update using Spark SQL achieves the median latency of 32.8 seconds per batch on 100 nodes.

The incremental view maintenance of Q17 scales almost linearly, as shown in Figure 10b. The median latency of processing one batch of 400 million tuples declines by 10.7x (from 68.5s to 6.4s) when using 16x more resources (from 50 to 800 workers). Here, the amount of shuffled data per worker decreases from 77.4 MB to 4.2 MB, while the trigger processing time per worker drops from 27.3s to 2.3s. We observe similar effects when processing smaller batches. When using 800 workers, the median latency of processing different batch sizes varies from 3.6s to 6.4s.

Figure 10c shows that the median latency of processing Q3 decreases with more nodes, from 30s with 25 workers to 4.2s with 400 workers for input batches with 400 million tuples. Adding more workers decreases the amount of work performed inside each trigger and the amount of shuffled data per worker while at the same time increases synchronization overheads. Using larger batches creates more parallelizable work and enables scalable execution across more nodes, as shown in Figure 10c. Re-evaluating Q3 using Spark SQL performs slower than our incremental program for the corresponding batch size, from 8.5x using 25 workers to 20.9x using 400 workers.

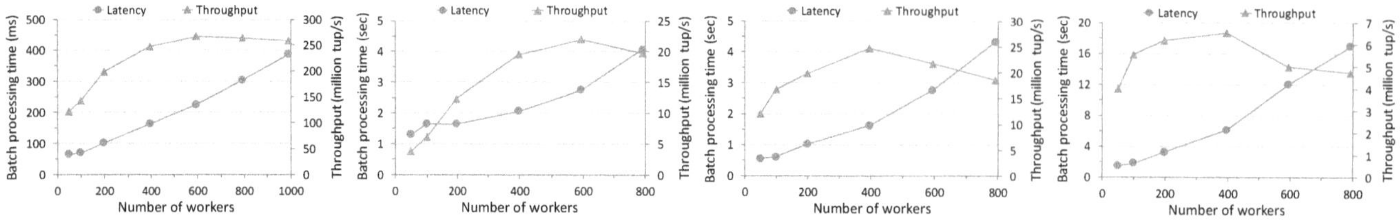

(a) Q6 (b) Q17 (c) Q3 (d) Q7

Figure 9: Weak scalability of the incremental view maintenance of TPC-H queries. Each worker processes batches of size 100,000.

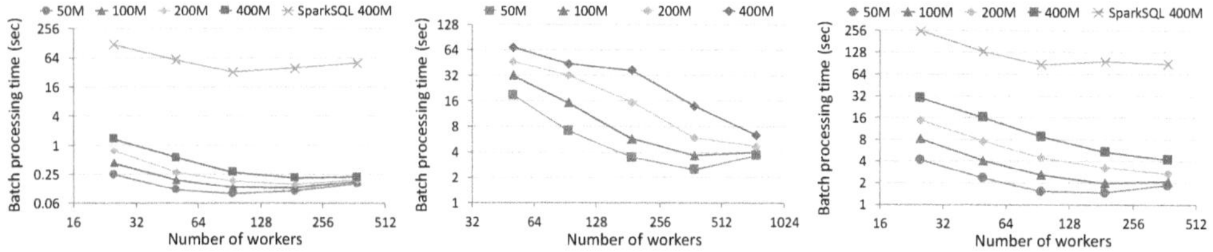

(a) Q6 (b) Q17 (c) Q3 (d) Q7

Figure 10: Strong scalability of the incremental view maintenance of TPC-H queries for different batch sizes (in million of tuples). Appendix C contains results for more TPC-H queries.

Q7 requires the most expensive maintenance work among the four TPC-H queries. The median latency of processing 100 million tuples drops from 44.8s with 25 workers to 10.4s with 200 workers. Beyond 200 workers, even though the size of shuffled data per worker decreases, managing large data creates stragglers that prolong execution time. Compared with Spark SQL re-evaluation, our approaches achieves 3.3x lower median latency with 200 workers.

Using fewer workers increases the variability of latency in almost all our queries due to larger amounts of shuffled data per worker. This observation confirms our previous conclusion that shuffling large data among many workers creates stragglers.

Optimization effects. We evaluate the effects of our optimization from Section 4 on TPC-H Q3. We present the numbers in Appendix C. We consider the naive implementation with all optimizations turned off; then, we include simplification rules for location transforms to minimize their number, followed by enabling the block fusion algorithm. Finally, we apply CSE and DCE optimizations to eliminate trigger statements doing redundant network communication during program execution. Our analysis indicates that merging together statements using the block fusion algorithm brings largest performance boosts and enables scalable execution.

7. RELATED WORK

Incremental view maintenance. Classical incremental view maintenance [17, 13, 14] is typically used for processing batch updates in data warehouse systems [6, 37, 33], where the focus is on achieving high throughput rather than low latency. Commercial database systems support incremental view maintenance but only for restricted classes of queries [3, 1]. Our approach is based on using recursive incremental view maintenance [20, 21]. The DBToaster system [22] implements recursive incremental processing for single-tuple updates in local mode. In contrast, we target batched execution in both local and distributed settings. To support efficient batched incremental maintenance of SQL queries, we develop a new technique, called domain extraction.

Scalable stream processing. Scalable stream processing platforms, such as MillWheel [7], Heron [25], and S4 [29], expose low-level primitives to the user for expressing complex query plans. S-Store [10] provides triggers for expressing data-driven processing with ACID guarantees in streaming scenarios. Naiad [27] and Trill [11] support flat LINQ-style continuous queries, while for complex queries with nested aggregates the user has to encode efficient execution plans. Spark Streaming [39] allows running simple SQL queries but only for windowed data. In contrast to these systems, our approach: 1) favors declaritivity as the user only needs to specify input SQL queries without execution plans; 2) can incrementally maintain queries with equality-correlated nested aggregates; 3) generates code tailored to the given workload; our compilation framework can target any scalable system with a synchronous execution model. Percolator [32] handles incremental updates to large datasets but targets latencies on the order of minutes. Scalable batch processing systems like Pig, Hive, and Spark SQL [9] aim for high throughput rather than low latency.

Distributed query processing. Our approach uses well-known techniques from distributed query processing [24, 16, 34], like the basic shuffling primitives and batch pre-processing for minimizing network communication. In contrast to classical distributed query optimization [5, 24, 12], the problem of optimizing recursive incremental programs is more complex since it has to keep track of data-flow dependencies among the program statements that maintain auxiliary views. These dependencies prevent arbitrary statement re-orderings inside trigger functions.

8. CONCLUSION

In this paper, we focus on the problem of low-latency incremental processing of SQL queries in local and distributed streaming environments. We present the domain extraction procedure for maintaining queries with equality-correlated nested aggregates. We study the effect of batch size on the latency of processing in local settings: we show that pre-processing input batches can boost the performance of incremental computation but also demonstrate that tuple-at-a-time processing can outperform batch processing using code specialization techniques (on roughly one half of the benchmarked queries). In local settings, our approach exhibit up to four orders of magnitude better performance than PostgreSQL in incremental batched processing. For distributed view maintenance, we show how to compile local maintenance programs into distributed code optimized for the execution on large-scale processing platforms. Our approach can process tens of million of tuples with few-second latency using hundreds of Spark workers.

9. REFERENCES

[1] Create Indexed Views. http://msdn.microsoft.com/en-us/library/ms191432.aspx.

[2] DBToaster Release 2.2 revision 3387, Nov. 27, 2015. http://www.dbtoaster.org/index.php?page=download.

[3] Materialized View Concepts and Architecture. http://docs.oracle.com/cd/B28359_01/server.111/b28326/repmview.htm.

[4] D. Abadi, Y. Ahmad, M. Balazinska, M. Cherniack, J. Hwang, W. Lindner, A. Maskey, E. Rasin, E. Ryvkina, N. Tatbul, Y. Xing, and S. Zdonik. The design of the Borealis stream processing engine. In *CIDR*, pages 277–289, 2005.

[5] S. Adali, K. S. Candan, Y. Papakonstantinou, and V. Subrahmanian. Query Caching and Optimization in Distributed Mediator Systems. In *ACM SIGMOD Record*, volume 25, pages 137–146. ACM, 1996.

[6] D. Agrawal, A. El Abbadi, A. Singh, and T. Yurek. Efficient View Maintenance at Data Warehouses. In *SIGMOD*, volume 26, pages 417–427, 1997.

[7] T. Akidau, A. Balikov, K. Bekiroğlu, S. Chernyak, J. Haberman, R. Lax, S. McVeety, D. Mills, P. Nordstrom, and S. Whittle. MillWheel: Fault-tolerant Stream Processing at Internet Scale. *PVLDB*, 6(11):1033–1044, 2013.

[8] A. W. Appel and T. Jim. Continuation-passing, closure-passing style. In *POPL*, pages 293–302, 1989.

[9] M. Armbrust, R. S. Xin, C. Lian, Y. Huai, D. Liu, J. K. Bradley, X. Meng, T. Kaftan, M. J. Franklin, A. Ghodsi, and M. Zaharia. Spark SQL: Relational Data Processing in Spark. In *SIGMOD*, pages 1383–1394, 2015.

[10] U. Cetintemel, J. Du, T. Kraska, S. Madden, D. Maier, J. Meehan, A. Pavlo, M. Stonebraker, E. Sutherland, N. Tatbul, K. Tufte, H. Wang, and S. Zdonik. S-Store: A Streaming NewSQL System for Big Velocity Applications. *Proc. VLDB Endow.*, 7(13):1633–1636, 2014.

[11] B. Chandramouli, J. Goldstein, M. Barnett, R. DeLine, D. Fisher, J. C. Platt, J. F. Terwilliger, and J. Wernsing. Trill: A High-performance Incremental Query Processor for Diverse Analytics. *PVLDB*, 8(4):401–412, 2014.

[12] S. Chaudhuri. An overview of query optimization in relational systems. In *PODS*, pages 34–43, 1998.

[13] S. Chaudhuri, R. Krishnamurthy, S. Potamianos, and K. Shim. Optimizing queries with materialized views. In *ICDE*, pages 190–200, 1995.

[14] R. Chirkova and J. Yang. Materialized Views. *Databases*, 4(4):295–405, 2011.

[15] C. Curino, E. Jones, Y. Zhang, and S. Madden. Schism: A Workload-driven Approach to Database Replication and Partitioning. *PVLDB*, 3(1-2):48–57, 2010.

[16] R. Epstein, M. Stonebraker, and E. Wong. Distributed Query Processing in a Relational Data Base System. In *SIGMOD*, pages 169–180, 1978.

[17] A. Gupta, I. S. Mumick, et al. Maintenance of materialized views: Problems, techniques, and applications. *IEEE Data Eng. Bull.*, 18(2):3–18, 1995.

[18] A. Gupta, I. S. Mumick, and V. S. Subrahmanian. Maintaining Views Incrementally. *SIGMOD Rec.*, 22(2):157–166, 1993.

[19] Y. Klonatos, C. Koch, T. Rompf, and H. Chafi. Building Efficient Query Engines in a High-level Language. *PVLDB*, 7(10):853–864, 2014.

[20] C. Koch. Incremental query evaluation in a ring of databases. In *PODS*, pages 87–98, 2010.

[21] C. Koch. Incremental query evaluation in a ring of databases, 2013. Technical Report EPFL-REPORT-183766, https://infoscience.epfl.ch/record/183766.

[22] C. Koch, Y. Ahmad, O. Kennedy, M. Nikolic, A. Nötzli, D. Lupei, and A. Shaikhha. DBToaster: Higher-order delta processing for dynamic, frequently fresh views. *VLDBJ*, 23(2):253–278, 2014.

[23] M. Kornacker, A. Behm, V. Bittorf, T. Bobrovytsky, C. Ching, A. Choi, J. Erickson, M. Grund, D. Hecht, M. Jacobs, et al. Impala: A Modern, Open-Source SQL Engine for Hadoop. In *CIDR*, 2015.

[24] D. Kossmann. The state of the art in distributed query processing. *CSUR*, 32(4):422–469, 2000.

[25] S. Kulkarni, N. Bhagat, M. Fu, V. Kedigehalli, C. Kellogg, S. Mittal, J. M. Patel, K. Ramasamy, and S. Taneja. Twitter Heron: Stream Processing at Scale. In *SIGMOD*, pages 239–250, 2015.

[26] R. Motwani, J. Widom, A. Arasu, B. Babcock, S. Babu, M. Datar, G. Manku, C. Olston, J. Rosenstein, and R. Varma. Query processing, approximation, and resource management in a data stream management system. In *CIDR*, 2003.

[27] D. G. Murray, F. McSherry, R. Isaacs, M. Isard, P. Barham, and M. Abadi. Naiad: A Timely Dataflow System. In *SOSP*, pages 439–455, 2013.

[28] T. Neumann. Efficiently Compiling Efficient Query Plans for Modern Hardware. *PVLDB*, 4(9):539–550, 2011.

[29] L. Neumeyer, B. Robbins, A. Nair, and A. Kesari. S4: Distributed Stream Computing Platform. In *ICDMW*, pages 170–177, 2010.

[30] S. Padmanabhan, T. Malkemus, A. Jhingran, and R. Agarwal. Block Oriented Processing of Relational Database Operations in Modern Computer Architectures. In *ICDE*, pages 567–574, 2001.

[31] A. Pavlo, C. Curino, and S. Zdonik. Skew-Aware Automatic Database Partitioning in Shared-Nothing, Parallel OLTP Systems. In *SIGMOD*, pages 61–72, 2012.

[32] D. Peng and F. Dabek. Large-scale Incremental Processing Using Distributed Transactions and Notifications. In *OSDI*, pages 1–15, 2010.

[33] D. Quass and J. Widom. On-line Warehouse View Maintenance. *SIGMOD Rec.*, 26(2):393–404, 1997.

[34] R. Ramakrishnan and J. Gehrke. *Database Management Systems*. McGraw-Hill, 2003.

[35] T. Rompf and M. Odersky. Lightweight modular staging: a pragmatic approach to runtime code generation and compiled DSLs. In *GPCE*, pages 127–136, 2010.

[36] T. Rompf and M. Odersky. Lightweight modular staging: a pragmatic approach to runtime code generation and compiled dsls. *Commun. ACM*, 55(6):121–130, 2012.

[37] J. Wiener, H. Gupta, W. Labio, Y. Zhuge, H. Garcia-Molina, and J. Widom. A System Prototype for Warehouse View Maintenance. 1995.

[38] M. Zaharia, M. Chowdhury, M. Franklin, S. Shenker, and I. Stoica. Spark: Cluster Computing with Working Sets. In *HotCloud*, 2010.

[39] M. Zaharia, T. Das, H. Li, T. Hunter, S. Shenker, and I. Stoica. Discretized Streams: Fault-tolerant Streaming Computation at Scale. In *SOSP*, pages 423–438, 2013.

	Re-evaluation (PostgreSQL)						IVM (PostgreSQL)						Recursive IVM (DBToaster, C++)						
Batch size	1	10	100	1000	10000	100000	1	10	100	1000	10000	100000	Single	1	10	100	1000	10000	100000
TPC-H 1	10	32	103	187	1003	2889	57	332	2478	9686	12250	12194	1267132	307715	1186926	2812549	4179921	4163385	4372480
TPC-H 2	11	146	427	493	5685	13420	28	125	193	4726	1995	12044	756611	456559	911141	1005175	971154	986810	691260
TPC-H 3	34	111	301	522	2120	5722	17	78	222	61	9100	5676	3736860	1251162	3004637	4401315	5323732	5182684	4580003
TPC-H 4	23	122	400	400	3713	7333	55	93	5857	10223	12550	12971	10076062	1603637	4652895	9012747	10687864	10790913	9752380
TPC-H 5	30	88	253	460	2304	5424	11	174	9	11	153	8665	584261	387568	625805	690475	658595	618632	509490
TPC-H 6	27	88	282	319	2500	6528	58	579	4065	11091	12742	12556	138216710	17017320	44270149	78310773	98176845	116931875	101327791
TPC-H 7	34	117	311	317	2985	7083	7	30	2	16	6908	5944	650650	397643	689015	753051	775288	770259	646018
TPC-H 8	35	114	338	335	2629	5886	28	8	21	19	222	5571	91221	73786	219613	279041	273387	277808	221020
TPC-H 9	30	151	335	513	1952	5999	14	25	22	21	197	1545	104370	78460	90949	109515	102940	86251	76296
TPC-H 10	32	88	322	207	2282	5701	33	165	372	123	7836	12306	2889537	1391237	3605282	5771226	6354245	7050705	5964290
TPC-H 11	22	61	191	366	1930	8734	23	71	220	367	2062	9414	768	776	1923	13500	109603	407547	591716
TPC-H 12	33	109	356	646	3279	4823	49	1050	6248	10837	630	5306	8675929	1678780	3905117	7131341	8236605	7706686	7469474
TPC-H 13	21	74	170	489	345	2578	33	94	283	267	2108	7334	779515	444588	685871	758725	701083	679684	474765
TPC-H 14	26	74	230	313	2322	6556	35	40	56	148	11686	11611	33041606	2769955	13146565	27984674	43468480	51827803	53436252
TPC-H 15	18	74	203	154	1613	4674	N/A	34	38	86	923	3944	17	17	27	52	109	285	964
TPC-H 16	19	58	203	330	1161	2822	18	35	302	1317	5304	10095	123936	115749	131902	121464	108208	75015	58721
TPC-H 17	27	57	88	194	481	666	36	111	564	948	589	1288	379303	210671	256882	208937	279930	155138	131964
TPC-H 18	20	66	207	223	1190	2114	20	18	17	77	676	5881	1133647	572132	1040612	1278945	1272541	1274853	971313
TPC-H 19	31	72	234	329	2218	6139	42	422	502	144	291	11944	1946309	2461229	5829592	8753856	9988084	9737049	8776165
TPC-H 20	6	9	15	18	36	56	11	7	5	21	25	43	977	950	1504	129092	874469	2191422	1871407
TPC-H 21	32	110	347	417	794	7333	31	54	24	10	10583	6797	836800	282532	449838	508128	501657	478923	407540
TPC-H 22	14	45	141	247	1551	5462	12	36	97	298	1252	741	189	183	336	5918	54459	434245	815903
TPC-DS 3	35	92	328	2045	3136	6694	164	1785	4457	5444	6866	8416	12309621	2072493	5945894	8116538	8718851	7740490	6442932
TPC-DS 7	1	14	109	219	1635	5000	98	1104	4262	4438	6721	6694	858649	361726	1024456	1227564	1076421	963048	392581
TPC-DS 19	1	106	132	264	2480	5056	0	78	232	82	7231	6139	30	29	29	29	29	25	7
TPC-DS 27	107	837	3706	5760	7307	8037	76	867	4326	6331	6846	8212	588394	196141	560333	669487	529235	497035	202849
TPC-DS 34	0	4	42	208	1821	4730	1	4	41	173	7510	6350	2803540	1019381	4742812	9219979	10612493	11445739	10689928
TPC-DS 42	9	79	405	196	4322	5594	153	1234	4607	5124	6766	7694	21127917	2589874	7953492	10242024	11325623	9460881	8530989
TPC-DS 43	0	4	42	201	1643	4411	91	710	3232	4702	7246	6972	3103901	589052	3488082	9893883	12851893	14494762	14605017
TPC-DS 46	0	4	43	204	2050	5040	0	1	14	56	6599	6611	185	149	149	149	149	147	90
TPC-DS 52	8	79	406	191	4289	6583	136	869	4266	5066	6808	8121	21005081	2456902	8102885	10552388	11401574	10311449	9074722
TPC-DS 55	31	97	294	875	2444	5444	52	1128	4639	5726	6528	6825	34822881	2343359	7680837	10282103	10993911	10028796	8951066
TPC-DS 68	0	4	42	202	2226	5238	0	1	14	57	6628	6361	182	149	149	149	149	147	88
TPC-DS 73	107	810	3866	5892	7308	8111	139	896	4352	6396	6919	8184	2104283	1028758	4739743	8906107	10620186	10460940	9176666
TPC-DS 79	0	4	39	197	1819	4066	1	4	41	170	5036	6111	838490	427822	1903781	3289301	3869664	3254954	2834858

Table 1: Throughput comparison of re-evaluation and incremental maintenance in PostgreSQL and recursive incremental maintenance in generated C++ code for different batch sizes (in tuples per second).

APPENDIX

A. QUERY LANGUAGE

Here, we revisit the query language from our previous work [22]. The language uses algebraic formulas to define queries (views) over generalized multiset relations. Valid queries result in relations with finite support, and because the tuples in a relation are unique, we can interpret query results as maps (dictionaries) with tuples being the keys and multiplicities being the values.

We first present a fragment of the language sufficient for expressing flat queries with aggregates.

- Relation $R(A_1, A_2, ...)$ represents the contents of a base table. It defines a mapping from every unique tuple of the relation to its multiplicity. The SQL equivalent is `SELECT A1, A2, ..., COUNT(*) FROM R GROUP BY A1, A2, ...`, modulo the aggregate value, which is now part of the multiplicity.
- Bag union $Q_1 + Q_2$ merges tuples of Q_1 and Q_2, summing up their multiplicities.
- Natural join $Q_1 \bowtie Q_2$ matches tuples of Q_1 with tuples of Q_2 on their common columns, multiplying the multiplicities.
- $\text{Sum}_{[A_1,A_2,...]}Q$ serves as multiplicity-preserving projection. The SQL equivalent is a group-by `SUM(1)` aggregate, except that the aggregate value is stored inside the multiplicity of the group-by tuples.
- Constant c can be interpreted as a singleton relation mapping the empty tuple to the multiplicity of c. The empty tuple joins with any other tuple.
- Value $f(var1, var2, \ldots)$ is an interpreted relation defining a mapping from tuple $\langle var1, var2, \ldots \rangle$ to its multiplicity determined by $f(var1, var2, \ldots)$. Constant c is a special case of a value term. Value terms are valid only if all variables are bound at evaluation time. For example, expression A has a free (unsafe) variable, thus it is invalid, while expression $R(A,B) \bowtie A$ has finite support. Note that the latter expression corresponds to the SQL query `SELECT A, B, SUM(A) FROM R GROUP BY A, B`.
- Variable assignment $(var := value)$ defines a singleton relation mapping a single-column tuple with the indicated value to a multiplicity of 1. Multiple assignments can be joined together to construct an arbitrary wide tuple.
- Comparison $(value_1 \, \theta \, value_2)$ is an interpreted relation where each tuple has a multiplicity of either 0 or 1 depending on the truthfulness of the boolean predicate. Joining an expression with a comparison filters out tuples that do not satisfy the predicate by setting their multiplicity to 0; the multiplicities of the matching tuples remain unchanged.

To support queries with nested aggregates, the query language generalizes the assignment operator to take on arbitrary expressions instead of just values. Then variable assignment $(var := Q)$ defines a finite-size relation containing tuples of expression Q with non-zero multiplicities extended by column var holding that multiplicity. Each output tuple has the multiplicity of 1. Expression Q may be correlated with the outside as usual in SQL.

B. SINGLE-NODE EXPERIMENTS

In this section, we provide more single-node experimental results, including a comparison of recursive incremental view maintenance in DBToaster and re-evaluation and classical incremental view maintenance in PostgreSQL.

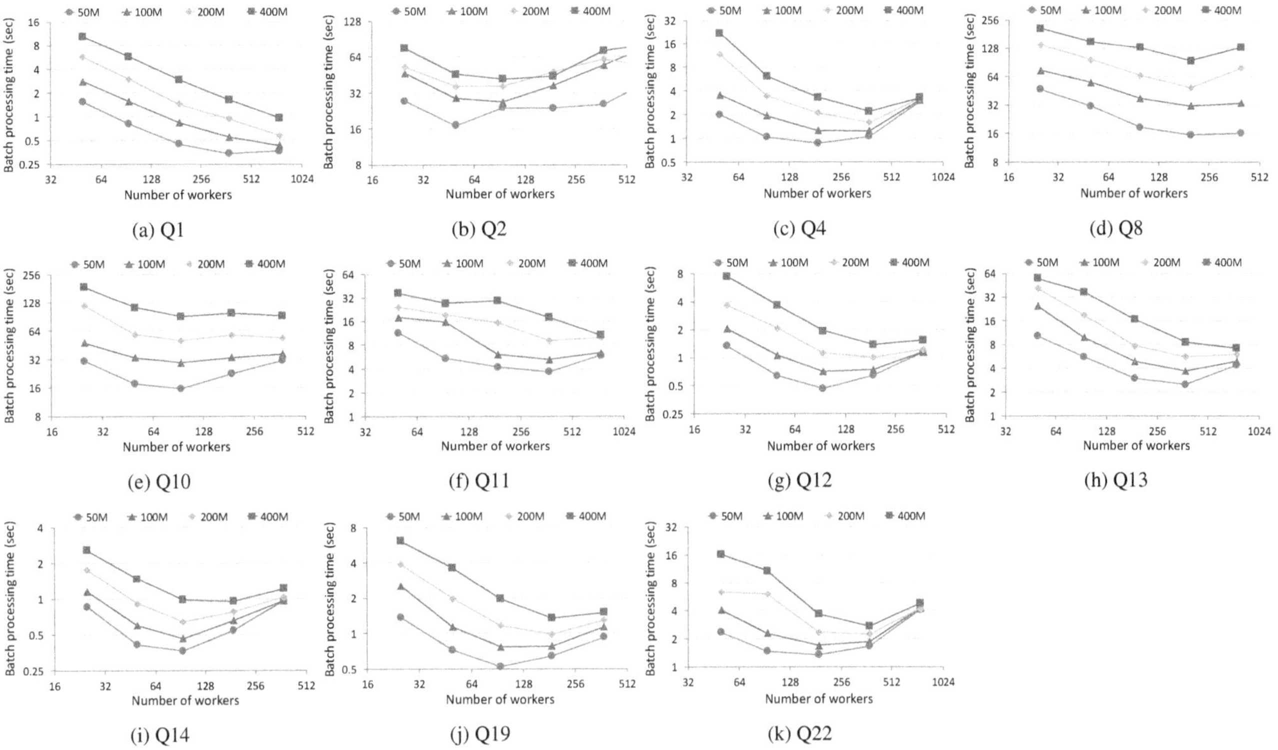

Figure 11: Strong scalability of the incremental view maintenance of TPC-H queries for different batch sizes (in million of tuples).

Batch size	Single	1	10	100	1000	10000	100000
instructs	19,633	145,670	33,407	17,199	15,750	15,425	15,868
I1 misses	2.0	6.8	3.5	2.0	1.8	1.8	1.4
LLC refs	485	683	533	424	402	578	668
LLC misses	369	562	416	302	258	302	316

Table 2: Cache locality of TPC-H Q3. All numbers are in millions.

B.1 Comparison with PostgreSQL

Table 1 compares the throughput of recursive incremental view maintenance using our generated C++ programs and re-evaluation and classical incremental view maintenance using PostgreSQL for TPC-H and TPC-DS queries. These numbers demonstrate that our view maintenance and code specialization techniques outperform, in all but few cases, the database system by orders of magnitude, even when processing large update batches.

B.2 Cache Locality

In this experiment, we measure the cache locality of generated programs for single-tuple and batched incremental processing on a 10GB input stream. We use perf 3.13.11 to monitor CPU performance counters during the view maintenance of TPC-H Q3. We start profiling after loading the streams and forming input batches. Table 2 presents the obtained results.

The numbers of retired instructions of the single-tuple and batched programs roughly correspond to the normalized throughput numbers from Figure 7. The batch processing with size 1 executes almost 10x more instructions than with size 1,000, which translates into a 4.3x slowdown in running time. The generated programs exhibit low numbers of L1 instruction cache misses compared to the total number of instructions. These results are indicators of good code locality of our view maintenance code.

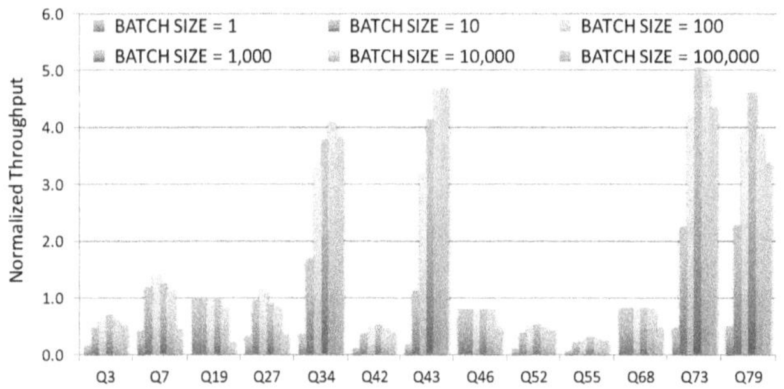

Figure 12: Normalized throughput of TPC-DS queries for different batch sizes with single-tuple execution as the baseline.

The second block shows the number of caches references and misses that reached the last level cache. Extremely large and small batch sizes have negative effects on cache locality. Relatively high numbers of cache misses are expected given that in this streaming scenario most input data passes through the query engine clearing out the cache and without being referenced again. Batched processing with size 1,000 exhibits the lowest number of cache references and cache misses, which corresponds to the result from Figure 7.

B.3 TPC-DS Benchmark

Figure 12 shows the normalized throughput of batched incremental processing of a subset of the TPC-DS queries for different batch sizes using the tuple-at-a-time performance as the baseline. These results show that single-tuple processing of TPC-DS queries often outperforms batched processing due to simpler maintenance code. Preprocessing input batches to filter out irrelevant tuples and remove unused columns can bring up to 5x better performance for four TPC-DS queries from our workload.

	Q1	Q2	Q3	Q4	Q5	Q6	Q7	Q8	Q9	Q10	Q11
Jobs	1	1	1	1	2	1	3	2	3	1	2
Stages	1	3	3	2	5	1	6	6	7	3	4

	Q12	Q13	Q14	Q15	Q16	Q17	Q18	Q19	Q20	Q21	Q22
Jobs	1	2	1	1	3	1	1	1	1	2	2
Stages	2	4	2	3	5	2	3	2	3	4	3

Table 3: View maintenance complexity of TPC-H queries in Spark.

C. DISTRIBUTED EXPERIMENTS

In this section, we present more scalability results of the TPC-H queries, shown in Figure 11, and provide additional information about our distributed incremental view maintenance approach.

C.1 Query Complexity in Spark

Generated Spark code runs a sequence of jobs in order to perform incremental view maintenance. Each job consists of multiple stages (e.g., map-reduce phases), and each stage corresponds to one block of distributed statements. In Table 3, we show the complexity of the TPC-H queries in Spark expressed as the number of jobs and stages necessary to process one batch of updates to base relations, assuming the partitioning strategy described in Section 6.2. The structure of each query determines the number of jobs and stages.

C.2 Optimization Effects

Figure 13 shows the effects of our optimizations from Section 4 on the distributed incremental view maintenance of TPC-H Q3 for input batches with 200 million tuples. We consider the naive implementation with all optimizations turned off; then, we include simplification rules for location transforms to minimize their number, followed by enabling the block fusion algorithm. Finally, we apply CSE and DCE optimizations to eliminate trigger statements doing redundant network communication during program execution.

Our results show that applying simplification rules can reduce the median latency of incremental processing of Q3 by 35% when using 400 workers. Grouping together trigger statements using the block fusion algorithm reduces the number of stages necessary to process one input batch, which enables scalable execution. Eliminating redundant network communication statements further decreases the latency by 11% for 400 workers. The final optimized program relies on the Spark framework to pipeline processing stages, bringing up to 22% performance improvements.

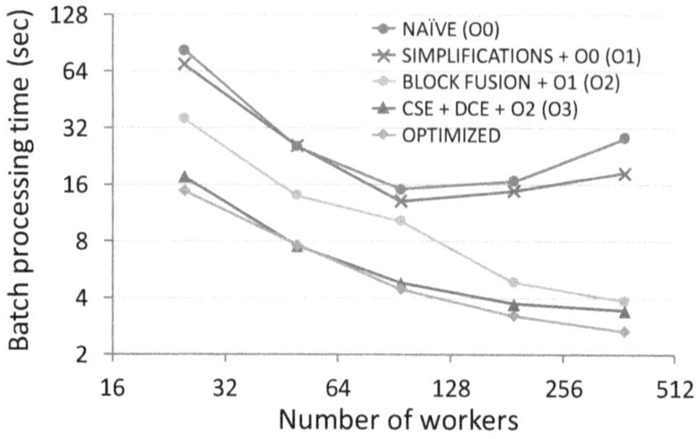

Figure 13: Optimization effects on the distributed incremental view maintenance of TPC-H Q3 for batches with 200 million tuples.

C.3 Block Fusion Algorithm

Here, we present the block fusion algorithm described in Section 4.3.2 for reordering and merging together consecutive statement blocks with the goal of minimizing their number.

```
def commute(s1: Stmt, s2: Stmt): bool =
  !s2.rhsMaps.contains(s1.lhsMap) &&
  !s1.rhsMaps.contains(s2.lhsMap)

def commute(b1: Block, b2: Block): bool =
  b1.stmts.forall(lhs =>
    b2.stmts.forall(rhs => commute(lhs, rhs)))

def mergeIntoHead(hd: Block, tl: List[Block]) =
  tl.foldLeft (hd,Nil) { case ((b1,rhs),b2) =>
    if (b1.mode == b2.mode &&
        rhs.forall(b => commute(b,b2)))
      (Block(b1.mode, b1.stmts++b2.stmts), rhs)
    else (b1, rhs :+ b2) }

def merge(blocks: List[Block]) = blocks match {
    case Nil => Nil
    case hd::tl =>
      val (hd2,tl2) = mergeIntoHead(hd,tl)
      if (hd == hd2) hd::merge(tl)
      else merge(hd2::tl2) }
```

Sharing-Aware Outlier Analytics over High-Volume Data Streams

Lei Cao[†], Jiayuan Wang[‡], Elke A. Rundensteiner[‡]
[†]IBM T.J. Watson Research Center Yorktown Heights, NY 10598, USA
[‡]Worcester Polytechnic Institute Worcester, MA 01609, USA
caolei@us.ibm.com, jwang1|rundenst@cs.wpi.edu

ABSTRACT

Real-time analytics of anomalous phenomena on streaming data typically relies on processing a large variety of continuous outlier detection requests, each configured with different parameter settings. The processing of such complex outlier analytics workloads is resource consuming due to the algorithmic complexity of the outlier mining process. In this work we propose a sharing-aware multi-query execution strategy for outlier detection on data streams called SOP. A key insight of SOP is to transform the problem of handling a *multi-query outlier* analytics workload into a *single-query skyline* computation problem. We prove that the output of the skyline computation process corresponds to the minimal information needed for determining the outlier status of any point in the stream. Based on this new formulation, we design a customized skyline algorithm called K-SKY that leverages the *domination relationships* among the streaming data points to minimize the number of data points that must be evaluated for supporting multi-query outlier detection. Based on this K-SKY algorithm, our SOP solution achieves minimal utilization of both computational and memory resources for the processing of these complex outlier analytics workload. Our experimental study demonstrates that SOP consistently outperforms the state-of-art solutions by three orders of magnitude in CPU time, while only consuming 5% of their memory footprint – a clear win-win. Furthermore, SOP is shown to scale to large workloads composed of thousands of parameterized queries.

Keywords

Outlier;Stream;Multi-query

1. INTRODUCTION

Motivation. Nowadays, high-speed data-intensive stream monitoring applications ranging from credit card fraud detection, network intrusion prevention, stock investment tactical planning to telephone fraud detection [16] necessitate the extraction of outliers from huge volumes of stream data in a near real-time fashion.

In recent years distance-based outlier methods [12, 18, 2, 5] have been widely adopted for the detection of outliers in high volume stream data due to their simplicity and insensitivity to concept drift.

SIGMOD'16, June 26-July 01, 2016, San Francisco, CA, USA

DOI: http://dx.doi.org/10.1145/2882903.2882920

The distance-based outlier model initially proposed in [12] originates from the basic notion of capturing abnormal phenomena in data which can be traced back to the seminal work by Hawkins [10]. In [10] Hawkins states that outliers can be identified based on assessing the similarity among points in a dataset. More specifically an outlier is an object O with fewer than k neighbors in the dataset D, where a neighbor is defined to be any other object in D that is within a distance range r from object O.

To discover abnormal phenomena from streaming data using this model of distance-based outliers, a set of input parameters have to be specified by the analyst. For example, when monitoring the potential credit fraud in bank transaction streams, analysts may look for unusual transactions whose values *in recent days* significantly differ from those of *the majority of* transactions made by peers at similar income levels. To detect such outliers utilizing the distance-based outlier technique, several parameter values have to be appropriately set. These include the r parameter that defines the notion of *significance* in transaction value dissimilarity and the k parameter that determines the *majority* of the peer transactions. In addition sliding window semantics [3] need to be applied to ensure that the outliers are continuously detected based on the *most recent* portion of the input stream only. Out-of-date information, such as the bank transactions made a long time ago, are typically no longer relevant for the interpretation of the recent outlier detection results. Thus they should be purged from the active stream window. Therefore the sliding window specific parameters, such as the *window size* and the *slide size*, also have to be specified by the analyst.

A stream outlier detection system may need to handle a large number of such parameterized queries for a variety of reasons. First, multiple analysts monitoring the same input stream may submit their outlier search requests with different parameter settings. In the credit fraud monitoring application, with a number of analysts monitoring the same bank transaction stream [16] – each may customize their outlier search requests by tuning their parameter settings using their personalized interpretation of abnormity. Even a single data analyst may submit multiple queries with distinct parameter settings, because determining apriori the most effective input parameters is difficult – if not impossible – especially when faced with an unknown or widely fluctuating input stream. In streaming environments, the continuous nature of streaming data emphasizes the necessity of supplying the most appropriate input parameters settings early on. Otherwise, the opportunity to accurately discover outliers in the segment of the stream gone by may be permanently lost. Furthermore, each analyst may provide their own personalized understanding of how large the "most recent" portion of the data to be considered is essential. Hence they may submit multiple outlier detection requests with different window related parameter settings ranging from a short-term minute long view to a long-term weekly or even monthly perspective.

For these plethora of reasons, a large number of outlier detection queries with different pattern and window related parameter settings may simultaneously need to be processed by the system. Thus, a stream processing system must be able to accommodate a large outlier analytics workload composed of hundreds or more of requests covering many, if not all, major parameter settings of an outlier query, and thus striving to capture the most valuable outliers in the stream.

Limitations of the State-of-the-Art. Although efforts have been made in developing efficient algorithms for distance-based outlier detection on data streams [7, 13, 1], these algorithms focus on handling *one single outlier request* with a fixed parameter setting. The simultaneous execution of multiple requests with varying *pattern* and *window* specific parameters remains largely unexplored.

Unfortunately LEAP [7], the state-of-the-art solution for handling a *single* outlier detection request over data streams, is not sufficient when applied to a large analytics workload composed of hundreds or more of such requests. This is caused by the high demand on both computational and memory resources to support each query in the workload *independently*. Our experiments confirm that LEAP indeed cannot meet the real time responsiveness requirements when handing a large workload (Sec. 6). It takes around 100 seconds to support a medium size workload (hundred queries) on a medium speed data stream (100KB per second).

While [13] also focuses on distance-based outlier detection for a single parameter setting, it also discusses an initial multiple outlier query solution. However this work is limited in that it only considers queries for a variation of pattern-specific parameters. The window-specific parameters are completely overlooked. Even for this pattern-specific parameter case, [13] continuous to rely on conducting routinely expensive range query searches that acquire all possible neighbors for all queries. Yet as already shown in [7], such range-query based solutions struggle to handle even one single outlier request when dealing with high volume streams [16].

Challenges. To handle a large workload composed of hundreds or even thousands of outlier requests over data streams in real time, effective processing strategies must be devised that cleverly shared the system resources.

This is complicated by the fact that requests with different parameter settings may cause totally different outliers to be identified. First, given a data point *p*, the evidence needed to prove its outlier status, i.e., whether it is an outlier or an inlier, with respect to distinct outlier interpretations (parameter settings) can differ. Clearly, variations in pattern-specific parameters lead to distinct criteria in defining the affinity among data points. Furthermore, due to variations in window-specific parameters even the data subpopulation of the data stream each query is posed against can differ dramatically.

Our Proposed SOP Approach. In this work we propose a innovative approach, called SOP, that efficiently handles an outlier analytics workload composed of a large number of outlier detection requests with arbitrary parameter settings, while still guaranteeing that each data point is processed *only once*.

As foundation of our solution we make the important observation that a workload composed of multiple outlier requests with arbitrary parameter settings can be correctly answered by directly utilizing *one single skyband query* [17] – a generalization of the well known *skyline* concept. Better yet we prove that given one data point, the *skyband* points discovered by the skyband query are the *minimal* yet *sufficient* evidence required to prove its outlier status with respect to *all* outlier queries in the workload.

Second, we design a customized skyband query algorithm called K-SKY that leverages the unique *domination relationships* among the streaming data points that presents their relative importance to the detection of outliers. We prove that K-SKY is guaranteed to discover all skyband points by examining only the *minimal number* of data points. Furthermore by prioritizing the processing order of the data points in the stream based on their arrival time, K-SKY naturally takes advantage of the common data populations among the data points covered by the active windows of queries with *distinct window-specific parameters*. This way redundant skyband point computations are eliminated. In short our K-SKY algorithm is optimal in minimizing the number of data points evaluated when processing an outlier analytics workload.

Based on the K-SKY algorithm our integrated strategy called SOP (Sharing-Aware Outlier Processing) achieves full sharing of both CPU computations and memory utilization for the processing of a workload of outlier queries. Computation-wise, in each active window, SOP only requires a single pass through the batch of new data points. That is, for each point we run *one single skyband query to answer all queries* in the workload. Memory-wise, SOP integrates all skyband points into a single compact data structure called LSKY. This assures that only *one single copy* of the neighbors shared across all queries is maintained.

Our experimental studies on real data streams demonstrate that SOP successfully drives down the CPU costs by over *three orders of magnitude* with significantly less memory utilization compared to [13, 7] for a rich diversity of scenarios. Furthermore, it is the only known method that scales to huge workloads composed of thousands of outlier requests.

Contributions. Our contributions include:

1) Our SOP framework is the first to tackle the problem of shared execution of multiple outlier requests with arbitrary pattern and window specific parameters in the stream context.

2) The key innovation of SOP is to transform the multi-query outlier problem into a single-query skyband problem. The output of the skyband query is proven to be minimal yet sufficient for determining the outlier status of each point for any parameter setting on the workload.

3) Our customized skyband algorithm is tuned to process outlier requests with diverse parameter settings. K-SKY is proven to be optimal in the number of points being evaluated.

4) Leveraging the commonality and dominance among the data populations, we are able to utilize one specific skyband query to support multiple queries with varying window specific parameters. By this full sharing is achieved across the query windows.

5) Our extensive experiments demonstrate that SOP routinely achieves three orders of magnitude or more speed up over the state-of-the-art methods [13, 7].

2. PROBLEM DEFINITION

Distance-Based Outliers in Sliding Windows. We first review the notion of distance-based outliers [12]. We use the term *data point* or *point* to refer to a multi-dimensional tuple in a data stream. The function $dist(p_i, p_j)$ denotes the distance between data points p_i and p_j. Distance-based outlier detection uses a range threshold *r* to define the *neighbor* relationship between any two points p_i and p_j.

Definition 1. *Two points p_i and p_j in a dataset D are said to be* ***neighbors*** *if $dist(p_i, p_j) \leq r$ with r a range threshold.*

The function $nn(p_i, r)$ represents the number of neighbors a data point p_i has within range *r*.

Definition 2. ***Distance-based Outlier.*** *Given a distance threshold r and a count threshold $k(k > 0)$, a data point p_i is regarded as an* ***outlier*** *in dataset D if $nn(p_i, r) < k$.*

Distance-based outlier detection only works for data sets for which an appropriate distance function can be defined. While this is straightforward for numerical attributes, textual or categorical attributes would typically have to be transformed into numerical attributes using existing methods in the literature [19].

We use $q_i(r_i, k_i)$ to denote the outlier detection query q_i with r_i and k_i the range and count thresholds respectively.

We focus on periodic sliding window semantics as proposed by CQL [3] and widely used in the literature [13, 7]. Such semantics can be either time or count-based. In both cases, each query q_i has a window size $q_i.win$ (either a time interval or a tuple count) and a slide size $q_i.slide$. For time-based windows each window W_c of q_i has a starting time $W_c.T_{start}$ and an ending time $W_c.T_{end}$ = $W_c.T_{start}$ + $Q.win$. Periodically the current window W_c slides, causing $W_c.T_{start}$ and $W_c.T_{end}$ to increase by $q_i.slide$. For count-based windows, a fixed number (count) of data points corresponds to the window size $q_i.win$. The window slides after the arrival of $q_i.slide$ new data points. The arrival time of point p is denoted as $p.time$. If $W_c.T_{start} \leq p.time < W_c.T_{end}$, p falls into W_c.

Outliers will be generated based on the points that fall into the current window W_c, also called the population of W_c. A point p in W_c might have a different outlier status (outlier or inlier) in the next window W_{c+1} if it is still alive in W_{c+1}, since each window has a different population.

Definition 3. ***Distance-Based Outlier Detection In Sliding Windows.*** *Given a stream S, a streaming distance-based outlier detection query $q_i(r_i, k_i, win_i, slide_i)$, q_i continuously detects and outputs the outliers in the current window W_c after the window slides from the previous to the current window W_c.*

Multiple Outlier Detection Optimization. Outlier detection requests on the same input stream can have arbitrary settings on all four parameters *r*, *k*, *win*, and *slide*. The set of outlier requests q_i that must be concurrently processed is denoted as query group $\mathbb{Q}$. Each query q_i in $\mathbb{Q}$ is called a member query of $\mathbb{Q}$. Our goal is to minimize both the processing time and the memory space needed to answer all queries in a large outlier analytics workload.

3. VARYING THE DISTANCE-BASED OUTLIER PARAMETERS

In this section we first introduce our transformation of processing a workload composed of queries with varying *r* but fixed *k* parameters into a skyband query. Then we present our K-SKY algorithm that supports such skyband query with optimality. Next we extend K-SKY to handle outlier detection queries with arbitrary *k* and *r* parameters. In this section we assume all queries share the same sliding window parameters *win* and *slide*.

3.1 K-SKY: Varying Parameter - r

Given a query group $\mathbb{Q}$ with *varying r* but *fixed k* parameters, the goal is to design an approach that supports all member queries in $\mathbb{Q}$ with each point *p* of data stream *S* processed only once in each current window W_c. The key insight here is that given such a query group $\mathbb{Q}$ and one data point *p* in current window W_c of stream *S*, the output of one single customized K-skyband query is sufficient yet necessary to determine the outlier status of *p* with respect to all queries in $\mathbb{Q}$.

3.1.1 *From Multi-Query Outlier Workloads to Single Query Skyband Processing*

K-skyband query is a generalization of the well known *skyline* concept. As defined in [17] a K-skyband query reports all points that are *dominated* by no more than K points. The case $K = 0$ corresponds to a conventional skyline. The key idea underlying this skyline concept is to define the *domination relationship* between any two data points. As a simple example consider a dataset *D* composed of *n* one dimensional data points, namely *n* distinct values $\{p_1, p_2, p_3, ..., p_n\}$. Assume the *domination relationship* between any pair of data points p_i and p_j ($1 \leq i, j \leq n$) is defined as p_i *dominates* p_j if $p_i > p_j$. Then the K-skyband (K=2) query on dataset *D* returns the top-3 largest points in *D*: $\{p_{max}, p_{max-1}, p_{max-2}\}$. p_{max-2} is dominated by the two data points p_{max} and p_{max-1}, while all other data points in *D* are dominated by at least these three top-3 points of *D*.

To map our problem of determining the *outlier status of a given point p* to the K-skyband problem, we have to similarly define the *domination relationship* between any pair of data points in the dataset D_{W_c}, i.e., the population of the current window W_c. The key observation here is that given any two points p_i and p_j, two key factors, namely their relative *arrival time* and the *distance* to the point *p* under evaluation, determine whether p_i is more important than p_j in terms of evaluating the outlier status of *p*.

Let us introduce a query group $\mathbb{Q}$ used in the remainder of this section. Assume we have a query group $\mathbb{Q}$: $\{q_1(r_1), q_2(r_2), ..., q_m(r_m), q_{m+1}(r_{m+1}), ..., q_n(r_n)\}$ [1], where r_m represents the r parameter of query q_m. The r parameter of q_1, q_2,...,q_n monotonically increases, that is, $r_1 < r_2 < ... < r_m < r_{m+1} < ... < r_n$.

Distance Dimension. In distance-based outlier definition (Def. 2), points in a dataset *D* are classified either as outliers or inliers. Thus, the process of identifying outliers in *D* is equivalent to the process of finding and eliminating inliers from it. By Def. 2, *p* is guaranteed to be an inlier once *k* neighbors are acquired in *D*. Given two points p_i and p_j, assume $dist(p_i, p) < r_m < dist(p_j, p) < r_{m+1}$. Then p_i is the neighbor of *p* with respect to query subset $\mathbb{Q}_i = \{q_m, ..., q_n\}$, while p_j is the neighbor of *p* only with respect to query subset $\mathbb{Q}_j = \{q_{m+1}, ..., q_n\}$. $\mathbb{Q}_i \supset \mathbb{Q}_j$. In other words p_i satisfies the neighbor requirement of more queries than p_j. For the evaluation of *p*, p_i is more important than p_j, because p_i makes the outlier status of *p* closer to be determined with respect to all queries in $\mathbb{Q}$ than p_j. In this perspective p_i *dominates* p_j.

On the other hand, assume $r_m < dist(p_i, p) < dist(p_j, p) < r_{m+1}$. Then p_i and p_j are both neighbors of *p* for the same set of queries $\{q_{m+1}, ..., q_n\}$. In this scenario p_i and p_j equally affect the outlier status of *p* although $dist(p_i, p) \neq dist(p_j, p)$. Based on this observation we now are ready to re-define the distance function $dist(p, p_i)$ so to normalize the distance between data points. The *original* distance function is denoted as $dist_o(p, p_i)$ instead.

Definition 4. *Given a query group $\mathbb{Q}$: $\{q_1(r_1), q_2(r_2), ..., q_m(r_m), q_{m+1}(r_{m+1}), ..., q_n(r_n)\}$ with $r_1 < r_2 < ... < r_m < r_{m+1} < ... < r_n$, $dist(p, p_i) = m + 1$ if $r_m < dist_o(p, p_i) \leq r_{m+1}$ for $0 \leq m \leq n$ with r_0 defined as $-\infty$ and r_{n+1} defined as ∞.*

By Def. 4, $dist(p_i, p) = dist(p_j, p)$ if $r_m < dist_o(p_i, p) < dist_o(p_j, p) < r_{m+1}$. This new *normalized distance* calculated using Def. 4 now accurately represents the importance of each data point to *p*.

[1] For the ease of readability, we only list those parameters in the query notation $q_i(r, k, win, slide)$ that vary. In this case $(k, win, slide)$ would be removed from q_i, since only parameter *r* is a variable.

Time Dimension. In the streaming context the presence of the time dimension further complicates matters. In particular we cannot simply claim that one data point p_i closer to p impacts the status of p more than the other points. Instead the arrival time of the data points also has to be taken into consideration. A point p_i that arrived later in the window may have a more *decisive* impact on the outlier examination process compared to an earlier arriving p_j even if p_i is not closer to p than p_j. This is so because the *younger* a data point p_i is, the longer its neighbor relationships (if any) with p will persist into the future.

Domination Relationship. We now define the *domination relationship* between the pair of points in dataset D_{W_c} that takes both the distance and time dimensions into consideration.

Definition 5. ***Domination Relationship.*** *Given a query group* $\mathbb{Q}$: $\{q_1(r_1),\ q_2(r_2), ..., q_m(r_m),\ q_{m+1}(r_{m+1}), ..., q_n(r_n)\}$ *with* $r_1 < r_2 < ... < r_m < r_{m+1} < ... < r_n$, *point* p_i ***dominates*** p_j *with respect to point p if: (1)* $p_i.time > p_j.time$; *(2)* $dist(p, p_i) \leq dist(p, p_j)$ $(p_i, p_j \in D_{W_c} - p)$ *and* $p \in D_{W_c}$; *(3)* $dist(p, p_i) \leq n$, *with* <u>*dist()*</u> *the normalized distance of* $\mathbb{Q}$ *defined in Def. 4.*

In other words, given a data point p_i, p_i dominates another point p_j only if p_i expires later than p_j from window W_c (Condition 1) and it is not further away from p than p_j (Condition 2). The third condition in the domination rule filters out any data point p_i that is not a neighbor of p for any query in $\mathbb{Q}$. As otherwise this p_i would never be influencing the outlier status of p.

Based on the domination relationship defined in Def. 5, the outlier status of p with respect to all queries in $\mathbb{Q}$ can now be correctly answered based on the skyband points delivered by one single $(k - 1)$-skyband query denoted as Q^s, namely the K-skyband query with K specified as *k-1* [2].

Lemma 1. *Given a query group* $\mathbb{Q}$*, for any data point p, the output of the skyband query* Q^s *corresponding to* $\mathbb{Q}$*, denoted as* $\mathbb{S}_p$*, is* ***sufficient*** *and* ***necessary*** *to continuously determine the outlier status of p with respect to all queries in* $\mathbb{Q}$*.*

While the formal proof of Lemma 1 can be found in Appendix A, below we sketch the key ideas of the proof.

Sufficiency. The sufficiency of this mapping is based on two observations, namely the *KNN* observation and the *K-distance* observation as explained below.

<u>KNN Observation.</u> First, Q^s always returns the *k nearest neighbors* of p as part of the skyband points. The k nearest neighbors of p denoted as $kNN(p)$ are k points in D_{W_c} that do not have larger distance to p than any other point in D_{W_c}. The proof of this observation is intuitive. Given any point $p_i \in kNN(p)$, at most $k - 1$ points in D_{W_c} are closer to p than p_i. By the domination relationship defined in Def. 5, at most $k - 1$ points in D_{W_c} dominate p_i. Therefore p_i is a skyband point of our skyband query Q^s.

K-distance Observation. Second, once $kNN(p)$ is discovered, the outlier status of p with respect to each query in $\mathbb{Q}$ can be determined by examining the distance between p and its kth-nearest neighbor called $k\text{-}distance(p)$. If $r_m <$ k-distance(p) $\leq r_{m+1}$, then p is guaranteed to be an **outlier** for queries $\{q_1,q_2,...,q_m\}$ and an **inlier** for queries $\{q_{m+1},...,q_n\}$.

Justifying this observation is straightforward. If k-distance(p) $\leq r_{m+1}$, then all points in $kNN(p)$ are neighbors of p for queries $\{q_{m+1},...,q_n\}$. Therefore p is an inlier for such queries. On the other hands, since k-distance(p) $> r_m$, p does not have k neighbors for queries $\{q_1,q_2,...,q_m\}$. Otherwise the points in $kNN(p)$ would not be the k nearest points to p in D_{W_c}. Thus p is an outlier to queries $\{q_1,q_2,...,q_m\}$.

[2]For simplicity this notation does not reflect p and $k - 1$.

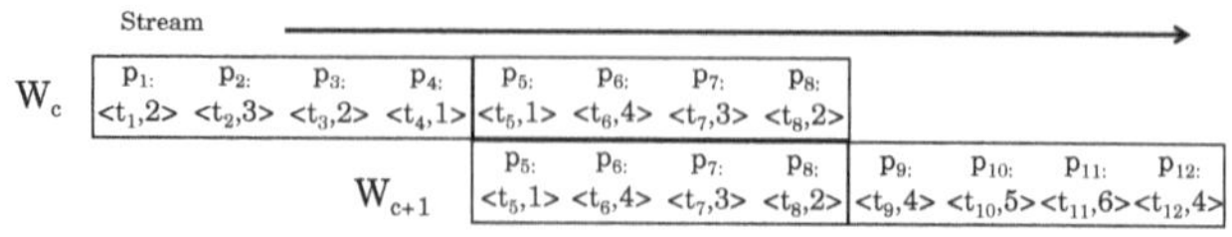

Figure 1: Sliding window stream

Next we illustrate these two observations with an example.

Example 1. *Given a query group* $\mathbb{Q}$: *{$q_1(1)$,$q_2(2)$,$q_3(3)$} with the k parameter set as 3 and the dataset* D_{W_c} *composed of points* p_i *represented in the arrival time and distance space* $(< t_i, d_i >)$: *{*$p_1 :< t_1, 2 >$, $p_2 :< t_2, 3 >$, $p_3 :< t_3, 2 >$, $p_4 :< t_4, 1 >$, $p_5 :< t_5, 1 >$, $p_6 :< t_6, 4 >$, $p_7 :< t_7, 3 >$, $p_8 :< t_8, 2 >$ *} as shown in Fig. 1. Here* t_i *indicates the arrival time of* p_i $(t_1 < t_2 <... <t_8)$ *and* d_i *indicates the distance of* p_i *to p. The* $(k - 1)$*-skyband query* $\mathbb{Q}^s$ *with* $k = 3$ *will return {*$p_4 :< t_4, 1 >$, $p_5 :< t_5, 1 >$, $< p_7 : t_7, 3 >$, $< p_8 : t_8, 2 >$*} as the skyband points in window* W_c*. A subset of this result, namely {*$p_4 :< t_4, 1 >$, $p_5 :< t_5, 1 >$, $p_8 :< t_8, 2 >$*} is the kNN of p. The k-distance of p thus is 2. By the k-distance observation we can correctly derive the outlier status of p. Namely p is an outlier for* q_1*, while being an inlier for* q_2 *and* q_3*.*

Necessity. Note in the above example since the skyband point $p_7 :< t_7, 3 >$ is not in the kNN(p) set of W_c, p_7 is not utilized to evaluate p in W_c. However p_7 arrived later than p_4 and p_5 in kNN(p). Potentially it might still benefit the evaluation of p in the future windows.

As shown in Fig. 1 when the window slides from W_c to W_{c+1}, $< t_4, 1 >$ will expire. Since all new arrivals p_i ($\{p_9, p_{10}, p_{11}, p_{12}\}$) in W_{c+1} are far from p, namely $dist(p, p_i) > 3$, now p_7 will be in kNN(p) = $\{< t_5, 1 >, < t_7, 3 >, < t_8, 2 >\}$ of W_{c+1}. As the third nearest neighbor of p, the distance between p_7 and p $dist(p_7, p) = 3$ will be utilized to determine the outlier status of p. Now p is an outlier for q_1 and q_2, while being an inlier only for q_3.

3.1.2 The K-SKY Algorithm

Although the traditional *K-skyband* algorithms could be applied to support our Q^s query [17, 21], we now design a customized algorithm called K-SKY that more efficiently supports the multiple outlier detection queries compared to existing algorithms [17, 21]. K-SKY encompasses two optimization principles, namely *time-aware prioritization* and *least examination*, that leverage the unique properties of the domination relationship among the streaming points shown in our outlier detection context. K-SKY is proven to be optimal in minimizing the number of data points to be evaluated in the skyband point discovery process.

Time-Aware Prioritization Principle. Given a data point p_i only two attributes are considered in the domination relationship of our skyband problem, namely the distance to a certain point p and the arrival time of p_i as defined in Def. 5. Furthermore, in sliding window streams the data points are naturally ordered by their arrival time. In other words, all data points can effectively been considered to be sorted on their arrival time attribute upon arrival. Therefore K-SKY effectively only needs to consider one attribute (distance to p) in the skyband point discovery process. By the definition of the domination relationship, later arrivals will never be dominated by the earlier arrivals. Leveraging this property we prioritize the order in which the K-SKY algorithm processes the data points. More specifically K-SKY always conducts the search with a later arriving data points first order. By this if one data point is not dominated by more than k points in the distance attribute and thus considered to be a skyband point, then it is not necessary to evaluate it again. This is so, because it will be guaranteed to never be dominated by other points evaluated later. Thus all skyband points can be discovered in one pass over the data set.

Better yet, given a data point p_i with $dist(p_i, p)$ no larger than the smallest r value r_1 in $\mathbb{Q}$, if p_i has already been dominated by k points when evaluated, K-SKY can be terminated immediately. This is so because all remaining (unevaluated) points would be dominated by at least these k points that dominate p_i. Therefore K-SKY can safely terminate without even examining all points.

Least Examination Principle. Second, in the sliding window context, the K-SKY search is applied in two situations. First, any *new* point p that just arrived in the current window W_c needs K-SKY to figure out its skyband points in the current window. Second, an existing point p needs K-SKY to update its skyband points when the stream slides to the current window W_c. In the first situation, for a newly arriving point p, K-SKY has to be conducted *from scratch* to search for the needed information of p. Instead in the second situation the key observation here is that given the skyband points of the window W_{c-1}, to acquire the skyband data points of a new window W_c, only a small fraction of data points in W_c need to be evaluated, namely the new arrivals and the unexpired skyband points of W_{c-1}.

This is so because any existing data point p_i in W_c could not possibly be a skyband point in window W_c if p_i is not also a skyband point in W_{c-1}. If p_i is not listed in the *skybandPoints* set of W_{c-1}, p_i must be dominated by at least k data points p_j in *skybandPoints*. By the domination rule defined in Def. 5, if p_j dominates p_i, $p_j.time > p_i.time$. This indicates p_j would not expire earlier than p_i. If p_i is still valid in window W_c, p_j would also remain valid. Therefore in W_c, p_i could not possibly be a skyband point, since it is still dominated by at least *k* data points.

Algorithm 1 K-SKY($p, W_c.plist, p.skyband, \mathbb{Q}$)

```
Output: skybandPoints //the k-1-skyband point set
1: if p.skyband == NULL then
2:     W_c.input = W_c.plist; // New point;search from scratch
3: else
4:     expireSkyband(p.skyband)
5:     W_c.input = p.skyband + W_c.pList.new; //Old point; search in new
       arrivals and unexpired skyband points
6: end if
7: for each p_i ∈ W_c.input from W_c.input.tail to W_c.plist.head do
8:     d = dist(p, p_i);
9:     if (TRUE == p_i.skyEvaluate(d,skybandPoints, Q)) then
10:        p.updateOutlierStatus(Q);
11:    else
12:        if d ≤ Q.r_min then
13:            break;
14:        end if
15:    end if
16: end for
```

K-SKY Algorithm. Next we show how K-SKY detects the (k-1)-skyband points in each window W_c. The skyband is computed every time when the window moves. In other words, the K-SKY algorithm is called after we receive a batch of new points based on the slide size. As shown in Alg. 1, the points of window W_c are stored in a list structure $W_c.plist$. When the streaming data arrives, the later arrivals are appended at the tail of $W_c.plist$. Therefore the points in $W_c.plist$ are naturally ordered by their arrival time. If p is a new point of W_c, then the search has to be conducted from scratch (Lines 1,2). Otherwise based on our *Least Examination* optimization principle K-SKY only search in the new arrivals and the unexpired skyband points of p (Lines 3-5).

Then guided by our *time-aware prioritization* optimization principle, K-SKY evaluates the data points of the input list $W_c.plist$ in the order from tail to head, i.e., via a "last come, first served" order (Line 7). After calculating the distance between p and some data point p_i, K-SKY evaluates whether p_i is dominated by at least k already discovered skyband candidate points. If not, p_i will be inserted into the candidate point set *skybandPoints* (Line 9). Otherwise if p_i is not a skyband point and $dist(p_i, p)$ is not larger than the smallest r parameter r_1 in $\mathbb{Q}$, K-SKY terminates (Lines 12,13). This is so because again by our *time-aware prioritization* principle, the remaining points does not have chance to be skyband points.

Leveraging the time-aware prioritization and least examination optimization principles, K-SKY is able to discover all skyband points by scanning the data set at most once. In other words, K-SKY is a *one pass* algorithm. Furthermore, it may terminate without even seeing all data points. We now show that it is *optimal* in minimizing the number of points being evaluated in the execution process.

Lemma 2. ***Optimality.*** *K-SKY correctly discovers the (k-1)-skyband points in window W_c by examining only the minimum number of data points.*

The proof of Lemma 2 can be found in Appendix B.

The skyEvaluate Algorithm. The complexity of K-SKY relies on the number of points being evaluated and on the cost of evaluating each point, that is, the cost to determine whether a given point p_i is a skyband point or not. This decision is computed by the subroutine $skyEvaluate$ of K-SKY. Since the number of points examined by K-SKY has already been proven to be minimal, the reduction of the second cost per point is now critical for high-performance of K-SKY. For this we must design an efficient $skyEvaluate$ algorithm.

Algorithm 2 skyEvaluate(d,skybandPoints, $\mathbb{Q}$)

```
Output: isSkyband; //Boolean: skyband point or not
1: layer = skybandPoints.getLayer(d);
2: count = 0;
3: for i =1; i++; i ≤ layer do
4:     count += skybandPoints.layerCount(i);
5: end for
6: if count ≤ k - 1 then
7:     skybandPoints.map(p_i);
8:     return true;
9: else
10:    return false;
11: end if
```

First we introduce the *core data structure* of the K-SKY algorithm called *LSky*. *LSky* is a layered data structure that stores the skyband points acquired in the execution process of K-SKY. It plays a critical role in assisting $skyEvaluate$ to effectively determine whether a point p_i is a skyband point.

In *LSky*, skyband points are organized into a layered two dimensional structure that preserves the order among the skyband points in both the distance and the time dimensions. As shown in Fig. 2, the points in each layer have the same distance to point p based on the normalized distance function in Def. 4. The points in the upper layer always have a smaller distance to p than the points in lower layers. Furthermore, in each layer the points are ordered based on their arrival time with the earliest arrival being at the head. By this, skyband points can be quickly expired when the window slides forward in time.

As shown in Fig. 2, given a data point p_i, skyEvaluate first calculates which layer it belongs to (Line 1). More specifically, given a query group $\mathbb{Q}$: $\{q_1(r_1), q_2(r_2), ..., q_m(r_m), q_{m+1}(r_{m+1}), ..., q_n(r_n)\}$ with $r_1 < r_2 < ... < r_m < r_{m+1} < ... < r_n$, a point p_i should be mapped to the layer corresponding to r_m (bucket B_m) if $r_{m-1} < dist(p, p_i) \le r_m$. This can be done in logarithmic time in the number of buckets using a binary search.

Next, $skyEvaluate$ evaluates whether a point p_i is a skyband point. Since K-SKY processes data points in the "last come, first served" order, a point p_i to be inserted into LSky is guaranteed to be dominated by the points falling in the same layer with p_i and the points within its upper layers. If in total there are fewer than k such points in LSky when p_i is processed, then p_i will be a skyband point (Lines 6 - 8). This can be easily determined by explicitly maintaining the cardinality of each layer (Lines 3 - 5).

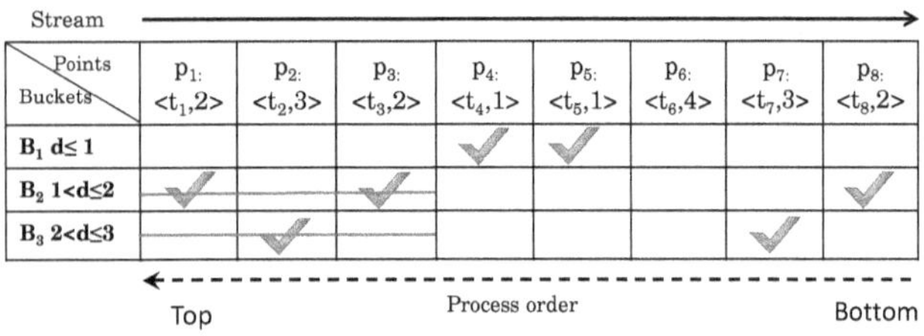

Figure 2: Skyband Point Search With LSky

Next we utilize an example to demonstrate how K-SKY detects the skyband points with the assistance of the LSky structure.

Example 2. *Given the stream and the queries in Example 1, point p_8 is processed first by K-SKY as shown in Fig. 2. Since 1 $< dist(p, p_8) = 2 \leq 2$, by Def. 4, p_8 is hashed into bucket B_2. The next point processed by K-SKY is p_7. Correspondingly p_7 is inserted into bucket B_3 because $2 < dist(p, p_7) = 3 \leq 3$. Point p_6 will be excluded from the skybandPoints set immediately since $dist(p, p_6) = 4$ is greater than the largest r parameter in query group $\mathbb{Q}$. Points p_5 and p_4 instead will be inserted into bucket B_1. By Def. 4, p_3, p_2, and p_1 should be hashed into buckets B_2, B_3, and B_2 correspondingly. However all of them are excluded from the LSky structure, since they are dominated by at least 3 data points. For example when we hash p_3 into bucket B_2, there are already 2 points in B_1 and 1 point in B_2. Therefore p_3 is dominated by 3 points and thus it is not a skyband point. In this example the skyband points are $\{< t_4, 1 >, < t_5, 1 >, < t_7, 3 >, < t_8, 2 >\}$.*

Complexity Analysis. With the assistance of the $LSky$ structure the overall complexity of K-SKY is $O(LB)$ with L the number of the points examined in K-SKY and B the number of the layers (buckets) visited when evaluating whether a point is a skyband point. We have already proven that K-SKY is optimal in L. Now let us assume that the points are uniformly distributed among all layers of $LSky$, then on average B equals to $\frac{|r|}{2}$, where $|r|$ represents the number of unique r parameter values in query group $\mathbb{Q}$. Given a window with $|W|$ data points, the complexity of processing the whole window therefore is $O(|W|L\frac{|r|}{2})$.

3.2 Handling Various K and R Parameters

We now relax our problem to consider varying not only k but also r parameters. One simple approach to handle a set of outlier detection queries with arbitrary pattern related parameters k and r would be to divide this workload into groups, each of which contains queries with the identical k parameter value. This then would simplify our problem into a *multi-skyband query problem* with only the k parameter varying. Intuitively our problem then could be handled by directly applying K-SKY on each group of queries. However this solution requires the independent identification and maintenance of the skyband points for each group of queries. Since a large number of skyband points are likely to be shared across these skyband queries, this naive solution inevitably leads to significant wastage of CPU and memory resources. We now tackle this shortcoming.

3.2.1 Sharing-Aware Multi-Skyband Solution

Next we propose a sharing-aware solution that efficiently solves this *multi-skyband query problem.* By maintaining the skyband points in one integrated LSky structure, given a point p_i, only one single skyband point evaluation operation is required to correctly answer all skyband queries. This way we assure that multiple skyband queries are supported by K-SKY, while still guaranteeing that each data point is evaluated exactly *only once*.

Given a query group $\mathbb{Q}$, $\mathbb{Q}$ is partitioned into sub-groups $\mathbb{Q}_j$: $\{(r_1, k_j), (r_2, k_j), ..., (r_n, k_j)\}$ $(1 \leq j \leq max, k_1 < k_2 ... < k_{max}$, $r_1 < r_2 ... < r_n)$. The member queries in each sub-group $\mathbb{Q}_j$ share the same k parameter value (k_j). Therefore each $\mathbb{Q}_j$ corresponds to one skyband query Q_j^s.

The key idea here is that our K-SKY algorithm can handle any number of skyband queries with distinct k parameter values with only some slight adjustment in the criteria used to determine whether a point p_i is a *skyband point* of at least one Q_j^s.

Definition 6. ***Skyband Point Rule.*** *p_i is a **skyband point** if:*
(1) p_i is hashed into some bucket B_m;
(2) $k' = \sum_{j=1}^{m} | B_j | < k_{max}$; and
(3) $dist(p,p_i) \leq max\{r_n of \mathbb{Q}_j \mid \forall k_j > k'\}$.

The first two conditions in Def. 6 correspond to the *examination rule* of the single query case except for replacing the k parameter of the single query with k_{max} (the largest k parameter value in $\mathbb{Q}$). However not all points satisfying these two conditions would be in the skyband point set. Now p_i is dominated by k' points. By the definition of k-skyband query, p_i would not be a skyband point of query Q_j^s unless k' is smaller than the k parameter k_j of queries in $\mathbb{Q}_j$ (the query sub-group corresponding to Q_j^s). Furthermore, any point p_i will be discarded by query Q_j^s if $dist(p, p_i)$ is larger than r_n of $\mathbb{Q}_j$ by the *domination relationship* defined in Def. 5. The above two conditions are captured by Condition 3 in Def. 6.

Optimality. Based on the discussion of our *time-aware prioritization optimization* principle it can be easily shown that K-SKY discovers all skyband points of multiple skyband queries in one pass over the data set. Here we provide the intuition. The processing order of K-SKY guarantees that the points added to *skybandPoints* during the execution of K-SKY would not be replaced later. Therefore similar to the case of processing a single skyband query, K-SKY correctly discovers the (k-1)-skyband points for *all* skyband queries with only the *minimum* number of points evaluated.

Complexity Analysis. Similar to handling a single skyband query, the complexity of K-SKY handling multiple skyband queries is determined by the number of the points being evaluated (L) and the number of the layers (B) that exist in $LSky$. Given a window with $|W|$ data points, the complexity of processing the whole window therefore is $O(|W|LB)$.

3.2.2 Outlier Detection With K-SKY

After acquiring the skyband points, these points then can be utilized to determine the outlier status of p with respect to each member query in $\mathbb{Q}$. For example, this can be done by first calculating the k-distance of p with respect to each query sub-group $\mathbb{Q}_j$ and then applying the *k-distance observation* (Sec. 3.1.1). However the key observation here is that to determine the status of p, this extra process is superfluous. In fact, we observe that the outlier status of p can be naturally derived as part of the *skyband point discovery* process as explained below.

Inlier Rule. Suppose we have a query sub-group $\mathbb{Q}_j$: $\{q_1(r_1, k_j), q_2(r_2, k_j), ..., q_m(r_m, k_j), q_{m+1}(r_{m+1}, k_j), ..., q_n(r_n, k_j)\}$. When evaluating whether p_i is a skyband point, if point p_i is found to be dominated by $k_j - 1$ points and mapped into bucket B_m of LSky, then p is guaranteed to be an inlier for a subset of queries in $\mathbb{Q}_j$: $\{q_m, q_{m+1}, ..., q_n\}$. This is so because all points dominating p_i are as close as p_i to p. Since p_i is mapped to bucket B_m, $dist(p_i, p) \le r_m$. Therefore p_i along with all points dominating p_i (in total k_j points) are neighbors of p for $\{q_m, q_{m+1}, ..., q_n\}$. By the outlier definition in Def. 2, p is thus an inlier for these queries.

As shown inliers are naturally recognized during the process of evaluating whether a point is a skyband point without introducing any extra overhead. This logic can be seamlessly applied in K-SKY (see Line 11 in Alg. 1) to mark p as inlier for the corresponding queries. Eventually p will be reported as outlier for those queries that do not mark p as inlier after K-SKY terminates.

Safe Inlier in Sliding Stream Windows. Furthermore, given a point p its outlier status might not always need to be evaluated in *each window* and against *every query* in $\mathbb{Q}$. Potentially skyband points discovered in the current window might provide sufficient evidence to prove that p is an inlier during its *entire remaining* life for a particular subset of queries in $\mathbb{Q}$, regardless of the characteristics of the future incoming stream. In this case, we would name p a guaranteed *safe inlier* with respect to a query subset $\mathbb{Q}_{safe}$ of query group $\mathbb{Q}$. This property arises due to the time order relationship among stream data points.

Safe Inlier Condition. We observe that p is guaranteed to be a *safe inlier* if the point p_i that triggers the above *inlier rule* arrives later than p. By the *domination relationship* definition in Def. 5, for each of the $k_j - 1$ points p_j that dominate p_i, $p_j.time > p_i.time > p.time$. In other words, all k_j neighbors of p would have arrived later than p and in turn would not expire before p. Therefore the neighbor relationship between p and p_i persists during the entire life of p. p is thus a safe inlier.

Evaluating the above *safe inlier condition* in K-SKY is straightforward. Namely when monitors the satisfaction of the *inlier rule* (Line 11 in Alg. 1), we also compare the arrival order of p_i and p.

Once p is determined to be a safe inlier, it is no longer necessary to evaluate p for $\mathbb{Q}_{safe}$: $\{q_m, q_{m+1}, ..., q_n\}$ in any future window. Thus the discovery of safe inliers can significantly improve the CPU and memory efficiency of K-SKY.

Next we demonstrate with an example how K-SKY determines whether a given point p is an outlier with respect to query group $\mathbb{Q}$.

Example 3. *Given two query groups QG_1 and QG_2 in Fig. 3, on stream in Fig. 4 we demonstrate how K-SKY supports outlier detection queries with varying k and r parameters. As shown in Fig. 4, p_8 is processed first and hashed to bucket B_2 of LSky. p_7 is processed next and inserted into bucket B_3. p_7 is dominated by one point in B_2. In other words, p_7 is dominated by $k_1 - 1$ points, where k_1 is the k parameter of QG_1. By the inlier rule this may cause p to be recognized as inlier for some queries in QG_1. By comparing $dist(p, p_7)$ against the r parameters in QG_1, p is confirmed to be inlier for queries $< k_1, r_3 >$ and $< k_1, r_4 >$, since $dist(p, p_7) \le r_3 < r_4$. Then K-SKY proceeds to hash p_6 into bucket B_4. p_6 is dominated by two points p_7 and p_8. This triggers the inlier status check for queries in QG_2 (k_2 = 3). Since $dist(p, p_6) \le r_4$, p is inlier for query $< k_2, r_4 >$. Next p_5 is processed and inserted into bucket B_1. When K-SKY processes p_4, p_4 is dominated by 2 (k_2-1) points. Furthermore, $dist(p, p_4) \le r_{min}$ of QG_2 (r_2 = 2). By the termination condition of K-SKY, QG_2 (k_2 = 3) is terminated now, since all queries in QG_2 classify p as inlier. Next p_3 will be excluded from LSky, since p_3 (in B_3) is dominated by four points and therefore is not a skyband point for any query group. After p_2 is evaluated, there are two points p_2 and p_5 in B_1 whose distance to p is not larger than r_{min} = r_1 = 1 of QG_1 (k_1 = 2). This satisfies the termination condition of QG_1. In turn p is classified as inlier by all queries in QG_1. This leads to the termination of the outlier status evaluation process for point p, because both query groups have been completed. The earliest arrival p_1 is not evaluated.*

	r \ k	r_1= 1	r_2 = 2	r_3=3	r_4=4
QG1	k_1 = 2	X		X	X
QG2	k_2 = 3		X	X	X

Figure 3: Queries with varying *k* and *r* parameters

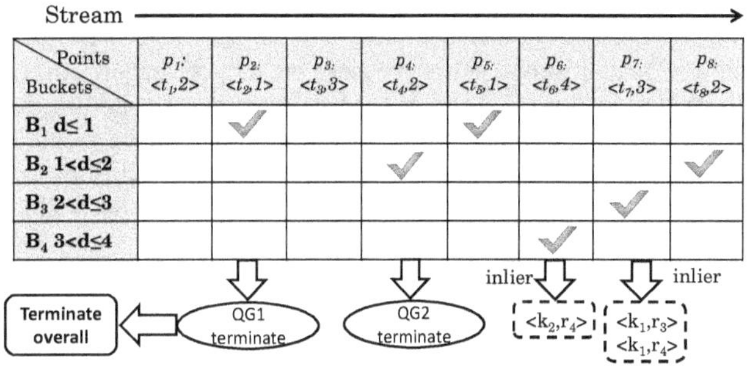

Figure 4: K-SKY for multiple queries

The Overall Outlier Detection Approach. The overall process of utilizing the K-SKY algorithm to continuously detect outliers from the sliding window stream is shown in Alg. 3.

Algorithm 3 detectOutlier($W_c.plist$,$\mathbb{Q}$)

```
Output: outliers; //the outlier sets
1: for each p ∈ Wc.plist do
2:    if (IsSafeInlier(p) == TRUE) then
3:       break;
4:    else
5:       K-SKY(p, Wc.plist,p.skyband,Q);
6:       Q_in = markInlierStatus(p, Q);
7:       markSafeInlier(p, Q);
8:       if Q - Q_in ≠ ∅ then
9:          insertOutlier(outliers,p,Q - Q_in);
10:      end if
11:   end if
12: end for
```

Given a point p in the current window W_c, Alg. 3 first checks whether p is a safe inlier (Line 2). The K-SKY algorithm will only execute on the points that are not marked as safe inliers (Lines 4, 5). Then based on the output of K-SKY, we mark p as inlier for the corresponding queries $\mathbb{Q}_{in}$ (Line 6). The safe inlier status of p will also be updated (Line 7). Finally p is inserted into the output set *outliers* if not all queries in $\mathbb{Q}$ classify p as inlier (Lines 8 - 10). Each element in the *outlier set* records one point p along with the member queries $q_i \in \mathbb{Q}$ - $\mathbb{Q}_{in}$ that classify p as outlier.

4. VARYING SLIDING WINDOW PARAMETERS

Next, we study the case that the window parameters can vary. The key observation here is that such multiple queries can be supported by utilizing one single customized skyband query. Therefore full sharing of both CPU and memory resources is achieved over sliding windows.

4.1 Varying the Window Parameter - Win

Here we first examine the scenario when the window sizes vary, while the slide size remains stable. Therefore all queries slide to a new window at the same time. In other words, they are *synchronized*. All queries require output at exactly the same moment, i.e., at time $W_c.end$ in Fig. 5. This observation leads to an important characteristic. Given a query group $\mathbb{Q}$ with member queries having the same slide size but arbitrary window sizes, $\mathbb{Q}$ can be supported with one skyband query with respect to q_{max} denoted as q^s_{max}, namely the member query with largest window in $\mathbb{Q}$ as in Fig. 5. Intuitively this is so because the largest window covers all smaller windows. Therefore skyband points discovered in the largest window can be utilized to answer all queries in the group.

Therefore by employing the K-SKY algorithm and collecting the skyband points for this special skyband query q^s_{max}, this outlier query group $\mathbb{Q}$ can be correctly answered with each point *p* in the data stream *S* evaluated only once in each window that contains *p*.

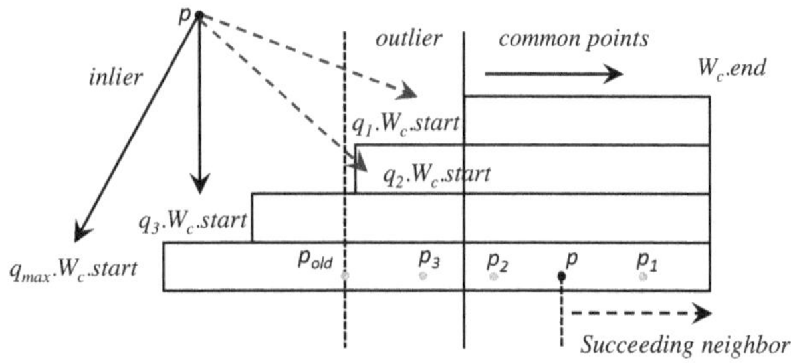

Figure 5: Queries with varying window sides

As shown in Sec. 3.1.2, K-SKY gives more preference to the points arriving later than the points arriving earlier. That is, K-SKY always processes the later arrivals first. On the other hand the later arrivals in the stream happen to be the common points among the data populations covered by the current windows of different queries (Fig. 5). Therefore K-SKY naturally leverages the data commonality among the windows of distinct queries. Redundant computations during the skyband point discovery process are eliminated.

Outlier Status Evaluation. After K-SKY terminates, as shown in Sec. 3.1.2, the outlier status of $p \in q_{max}.D_{W_c}$ with respect to q_{max} has already been determined. If q_{max} marks *p* as outlier, then *p* is guaranteed to be an outlier for any other query q_i in *Q*. Therefore it is not necessary to evaluate the outlier status of q_i anymore. However this is not the case if p instead is marked as an inlier for q_{max}. This is so because the neighbors of a particular q_i are only a subset of the neighbor set of q_{max}. Even if q_{max} has acquired enough neighbors to prove the inlier status of *p*, this does not guarantee that *p* has enough neighbors for other queries with smaller windows. Therefore an *extra outlier status evaluation step* is necessary for other member queries q_i in $\mathbb{Q}$ besides q_{max}. Fortunately, as we demonstrate below, to determine the outlier status of *p* with respect to the member queries in $\mathbb{Q}$, it is not necessary to examine all points in $q^s_{max}.skyband$.

Lemma 3. *Given a query group* $\mathbb{Q}$: $\{q_1, q_2, ..., q_m, q_{m+1}, ...,$ $q_{max}\}$ $(q_1.win < q_2.win < ... < q_{max}.win)$, *p is an outlier for queries* $\{q_1, q_2, ..., q_m\}$, *if* $q_{m+1}.W_c.start < p_{old}.time < q_m.W_c.start$, *where* p_{old} *is the oldest point in* $q^s_{max}.skyband$.

The formal proof of Lemma 3 can be found in Appendix C.

By Lemma 3 when *p* is an inlier of q_{max}, to determine the outlier status of *p* with respect to all other queries in $\mathbb{Q}$ we only need to evaluate one single skyband point p_{old}, namely the last skyband point acquired exactly when K-SKY terminates. This is achieved by locating the query q_m with largest window size whose current window W_c has not started yet at the time when p_{old} arrives. As shown in Fig. 5, queries q_1 and q_2 are outliers, because the oldest neighbor of *p*, namely p_{old} arrived earlier than the start time of the windows of q_1 and q_2.

Let us assume the queries in $\mathbb{Q}$ are ordered by their window sizes. In that case, the delimiter query q_m can be located in $O(\log | \mathbb{Q} |)$ time with a binary search style algorithm.

Safe Inlier. A point *p* declared as inlier by query q_{max} is not necessarily an inlier for all queries in $\mathbb{Q}$. However this is not the case when *p* is a *safe inlier.* Once *p* is confirmed as a safe inlier by q_{max}, *p* is guaranteed to be a safe inlier for all queries in $\mathbb{Q}$.

Since all queries in $\mathbb{Q}$ have the same slide size, their current window W_c ends at the same time point. Therefore all queries in $\mathbb{Q}$ share the same succeeding points of *p* in W_c, namely the points arriving later than *p*, but earlier than the end of the window as depicted in Fig. 5. This indicates that the *k* succeeding neighbors of *p* discovered by q_{max} are shared by all queries. Hence *p* is a safe inlier with respect to all queries in $\mathbb{Q}$.

Based on this **Safe-For-All** property, once *p* is determined by K-SKY to be a safe inlier of q_{max}, *p* can also be declared to be a safe inlier for all queries without requiring any further evaluation. It is then safe to exclude *p* from further evaluation in any future window. Therefore significant CPU and memory resources are saved.

In summary, we conclude that we only need to detect and maintain the skyband points for one single skyband query with respect to the outlier query with the largest window size. This then is sufficient to answer all outlier queries in the query group. Clearly, full sharing is achieved.

4.2 Varying the Slide Parameter

Next, we consider the case where all queries have the same window size, while their slide sizes vary. Unlike the previous varying window size case, these queries are not synchronized. That is, their windows move at a different pace. Therefore no stable relationship holds across the data populations covered by the active windows with respect to different queries. In other words there is no such query whose active window continuously contains the windows of other queries. Therefore the above strategy supporting queries with various window sizes does not handle this case. However independently generating output for this set of queries at different moments is not practical for large volume streams.

To solve this problem, given a query group $\mathbb{Q}$, we build a single *swift query* q_{sft} that correctly answers all member queries of $\mathbb{Q}$. Q_{sft} has the same window size as all member queries in *Q*, while its slide size is set as the greatest common divisor on the slide sizes of all the queries in $\mathbb{Q}$.

Intuitively by definition of the greatest common divisor, $\forall q_i \in \mathbb{Q}$, we have $q_i.slide \bmod q_{sft} = 0$. Therefore at any time t_j when $q_i \in \mathbb{Q}$ produces an outlier result $q_i.outlier$, q_{sft} would also be producing result $q_{sft}.outlier$. Furthermore, since $q_i.win = q_{sft}.win$, the points covered by the window of q_i and q_{sft} would be identical at t_j. Therefore at any t_j $q_i.outlier = q_{sft}.outlier$. Hence Q_{sft} is sufficient to represent all queries in $\mathbb{Q}$.

Therefore a query group $\mathbb{Q}$ with varying slide sides can be supported by one special skyband query with respect to this special outlier query q_{sft}. It is straightforward to determine at runtime when to output the outlier detection results and what query the output corresponds to by tracking for each query when the window slides.

Safe Inlier. Although potentially q_{sft} slides its window more frequently than any q_i in $\mathbb{Q}$, this swift query solution does wastes neither CPU nor memory resources. This is because q_{sft} is able to discover *safe inliers* and to terminate the outlier detection process at the earliest possible moment. This observation relies on the **Safe For All** property of q_{sft} similar to q_{max} in the varying window size case. Namely given a point p, if p is recognized as a safe inlier for the swift query q_{sft}, then p is a safe inlier for all $q_i \in \mathbb{Q}$. Next we briefly justify this observation.

We use $succ(p, q)$ to denotes the points arriving later than p in the current window W_c of query q. The **safe-for-all** property follows immediately from the fact that in any future window $succ(p, q_{sft})$ is a subset of $succ(p, q_i)$ for any query $q_i \in \mathbb{Q}$. This is so because in any future window when query q_i is scheduled to produce outlier status for p, all points succeeding to p in the current window of q_{sft} will not expire (since p has not expired). Furthermore, q_i will also get some additional new points into the future window.

Since q_{sft} is potentially scheduled more frequently than any query in $\mathbb{Q}$, the safe inliers will be discovered quicker.q_{sft} is able to discover and prune the safe inliers earlier than any query in $\mathbb{Q}$. Therefore CPU and memory resources are saved.

In conclusion, this swift query solution achieves full sharing by utilizing only one single skyband query to answer all member queries in $\mathbb{Q}$. Furthermore safe inliers are also discovered and discarded earlier than any actual member query, leading to additional saving in CPU and memory resources.

4.3 Varying Both Win and Slide Parameters

We now describe our solution for the case when both window parameters, namely win and slide, vary. This solution is a straightforward combination of the techniques introduced in the last two sections. In particular, we simply build one *single swift query* that has the largest window size among all member queries and its slide size as the greatest common divisor of the slide sizes of all member queries. A specific skyband query with respect to this single swift query will then be employed to collect skyband points, namely the evidence to prove the outlier status of a given point p. Similar to the varying slide size case the timing when each query is required to produce output is determined at runtime (see Sec. 4.2). Then Lemma 3 introduced in Sec. 4.1 is applied to decide the outlier status of each point for the queries requiring output based on the results of the swift skyband query. In short, this case of arbitrary window and slide sizes can be regarded as an arbitrary window size case with a fixed slide size whose value is the greatest common divisor of the slide sizes of all member queries.

5. VARYING ALL PARAMETER SETTINGS

Finally, we consider the most general case with arbitrary pattern and window-specific parameters. Although sharing among a group of totally arbitrary queries appears hard at first sight, we now demonstrate that this problem can be tackled utilizing the skyband query technique. This is possible, because as shown in Sec. 4.3, the skyband query technique designed for processing the outlier analytics workloads with varying *pattern-specific* parameters can be leveraged to answer multiple queries with arbitrary *window-specific* parameters.

SOP Outlier Detection Framework. As depicted in Fig. 6, SOP first employs a query parser to divide the queries in a query group $\mathbb{Q}$ into sub-groups $\mathbb{Q}_i$ based on their k parameters. Queries with the same k parameter are grouped into one sub-group $\mathbb{Q}_i$. The queries in each sub-group $\mathbb{Q}_i$ are then sorted based on their r parameters. The queries with same r parameters are further sorted based on their window sizes. Then the query parser will create one skyband query Q_i^s for each outlier query sub-group $\mathbb{Q}_i$. Its window size is set as the the largest window size among the member queries in $\mathbb{Q}_i$. Its slide size is then set as the greatest common divisor of the slide sizes of the member queries.

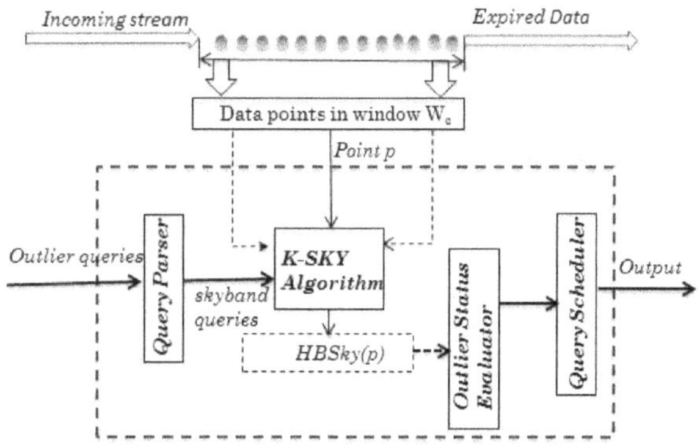

Figure 6: SOP Framework

After the query parser transforms the outlier detection queries into the skyband queries, the K-SKY algorithm for multiple skyband queries introduced in Sec. 3.2 will be applied to detect the skyband points. Then the outlier status evaluator determines the outlier status of each data point with respect to the outlier queries using the inlier rule introduced in Sec. 3.2.2.

Similar to the varying window sizes case if a data point p is classified as an outlier for the queries in some sub-group $\mathbb{Q}_i$, then p is guaranteed to be an outlier for all queries in $\mathbb{Q}_i$ no matter what their window sizes are. On the other hand if p is declared to be an inlier for some queries, Lemma 3 has to be applied to evaluate whether p is indeed an inlier for these queries by checking their window sizes as shown in Sec. 4.1.

Once the outlier status of p is determined for certain queries, the query scheduler determines whether it is time to output the outliers for these queries based on their slide sizes (per Sec. 4.2).

Conclusion. Computation-wise, SOP only requires a single pass through new data points, each collecting the minimum evidence to prove its outlier status with respect to all queries. Memory-wise, the evidence which proves the outlier status of each data point with respect to multiple queries is maintained only once. In short, SOP achieves full sharing for multiple distance-based outlier queries over sliding windows in terms of both CPU and memory resources.

6. PERFORMANCE EVALUATION

6.1 Experimental Methodology

We conducted experiments on a PC with 3.4G HZ Intel i7 processor and 6GB memory, running Windows 7 OS. All algorithms are implemented in JAVA on HP CHAOS stream engine [8].

Real Data Sources. We use the Stock Trading Traces Data (STT) [11]. It has one million transaction records throughout the trading hours of one day. All data has the same format of name, transId, time, volume, price, and type.

Synthetic Data. We also implement a data generator to create a dataset containing 100M points. This dataset is composed of Gaussian distributed data points as inlier candidates and uniform distributed ones as outliers. The outliers are randomly distributed in each time segment of the data stream.

Alternative Algorithms. We compare our proposed SOP algorithm with the two state-of-the-art solutions from the literature [13, 7]. Since MCOD [13] does not support variations in window-specific parameters, we have extended MCOD by inserting our

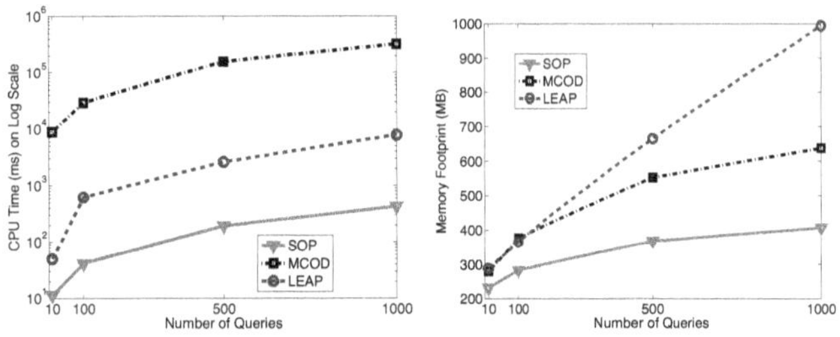

(a) CPU (log scale) (b) Memory (log scale)

Figure 7: Varying r values for queries on synthetic dataset

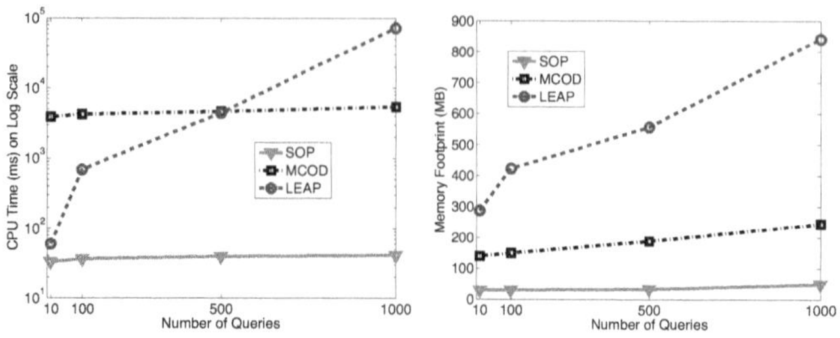

(a) CPU (log scale) (b) Memory (log scale)

Figure 8: Varying k values for queries on synthetic dataset

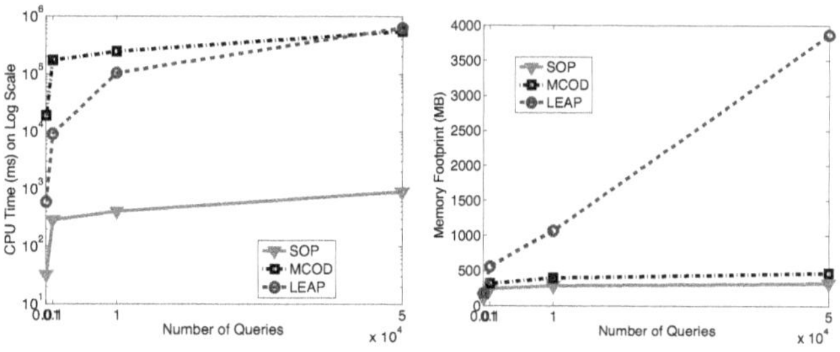

(a) CPU (log scale) (b) Memory (log scale)

Figure 13: Varying K, R, W and S values on synthetic dataset

window-specific techniques into MCOD. We now use this enhanced algorithm to compare against SOP. In addition, we also compare our sharing strategy against the state-of-the-art single query strategy LEAP [7]. Multiple queries are supported by applying LEAP independently to process each query in the query group.

Metrics. We measure two metrics common for stream systems, namely the average processing time (CPU time) per window and the peak memory consumption (MEM). The CPU time per window corresponds to the total amount of system time resources used to process the queries on the data in one window. The consumed memory metric corresponds to the memory required to store the information for each active object (i.e. the skyband points) and the outliers of all queries in the current window. All results are collected and calculated at the unit of one window at a time. Then they are averaged over all windows processed in the given experiments. All experiments are reported using the count-based window, with time-based window processing achieving similar results.

We also conduct scalability tests to validate the performance of the proposed algorithms with an increasing number of queries in the workload.

All in all our study covers important combinations of the four query parameters. They range from varying one specific parameter only at a time to the more general cases of varying all 4 of them among the queries populating the workload as shown in Table 1. The varying ranges of the parameters are listed in Table 2.

Workload	Pattern		Window	
	R	K	W	S
(A)	arbitrary	fixed	fixed	fixed
(B)	fixed	arbitrary	fixed	fixed
(C)	arbitrary	arbitrary	fixed	fixed
(D)	fixed	fixed	arbitrary	fixed
(E)	fixed	fixed	fixed	arbitrary
(F)	fixed	fixed	arbitrary	arbitrary
(G)	arbitrary	arbitrary	arbitrary	arbitrary

Table 1: Combinations of different workloads

Type	Name	Value
Pattern	K	[30,1500)
	R	[200,2000)
Window	W	[1Ks,500Ks)
	S	[50s,50Ks)

Table 2: The ranges of the parameters

6.2 Varying Pattern Specific Parameters

Our general methodology is to prepare four workloads with 10, 100, 500, 1000 queries respectively by randomly choosing the values of the pattern-specific parameters in a range for each query, while fixing the window-specific parameters. The synthetic dataset is utilized in this set of experiments to make sure the outlier rate is small ($< 5\%$) when varying the k and r parameters.

Arbitrary R Case. In the first experiment, we evaluate the performance of our SOP compared with the state-of-the-art MCOD [13] and LEAP [7] when only varying parameter r. We fix the window size to 10K, slide size to 0.5K and k parameter value to 30, while r is randomly selected in the range from 200 to 2000.

As shown in Fig. 7(a), SOP significantly outperforms MCOD and LEAP up to 3 orders of magnitude in CPU time. By mapping the multiple outlier query problem to the skyband query problem, SOP only needs to collect *minimum information* to prove the outlier status of each data point with respect to *all* queries. Instead, MCOD relies on routinely conducting a range query to detect outliers. That is, in each case it will compare each data point with all the other data points in each window and collect all the points satisfying the neighbor condition of any user query. On the other hand LEAP repeatedly detects outliers for each query from scratch. Its CPU performance thus degrades quickly as the number of queries increases. We thus confirm that the CPU efficiency of both MCOD and LEAP is significantly worse than that of SOP.

SOP is also superior in memory usage as shown in Fig. 7(b). This is because in each window given a data point p, MCOD keeps all data points satisfying the neighbor conditions of p with respect to any query. SOP instead determines that it is not necessary for the evaluation of the outlier status of p. On the other hand, LEAP, without leveraging the sharing opportunities across multiple queries, maintains the neighbors of each point independently for each query.

Arbitrary K Case. In this experiment, we analyze the performance of SOP by varying k parameter values of the queries. We use a fixed window size of 10K and a slide size of 0.5K. Parameter r is fixed at 700. A value for k is randomly selected in the range from 30 to 1500 for each query.

As shown in Fig. 8(a), similar to the case of varying r, the CPU performance of SOP outperforms the other two alternatives up to 4 orders of magnitude. Since the case of varying k can be treated as a special case of the case with arbitrary k and r values, this experiment demonstrates the effectiveness of our K-Sky algorithm when handling multiple skyband queries.

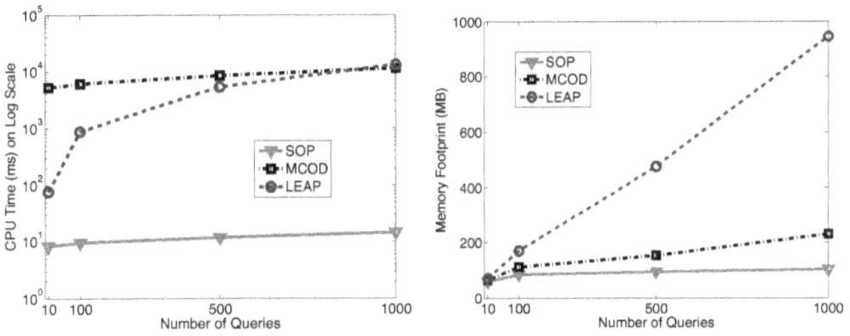

(a) CPU (log scale) (b) Memory (log scale)

Figure 9: Varying k and r values on synthetic dataset

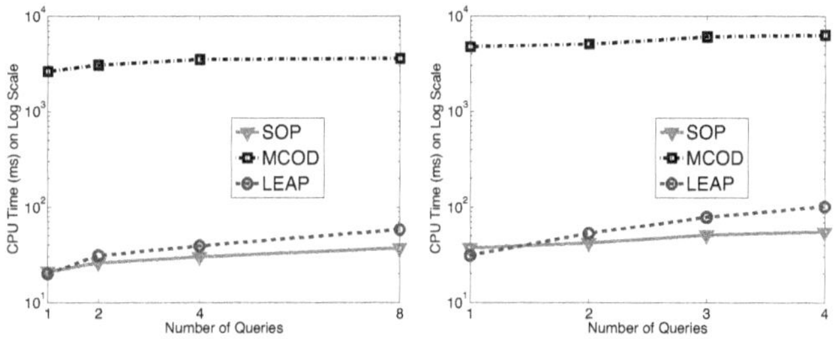

(a) Same attribute (b) Different attributes

Figure 10: CPU (log scale): small workload

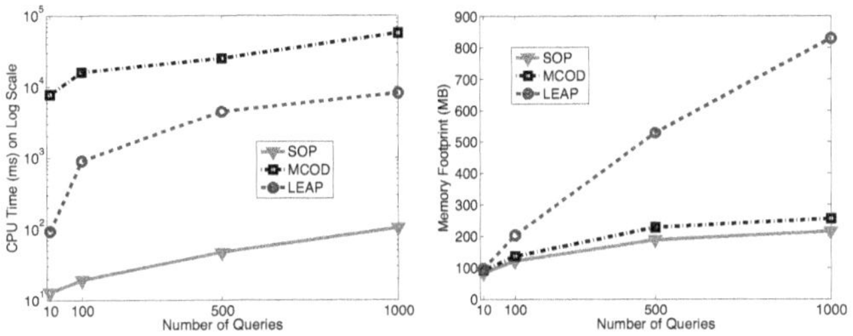

(a) CPU (log scale) (b) Memory (linear scale)

Figure 11: Varying Win for queries on STT dataset

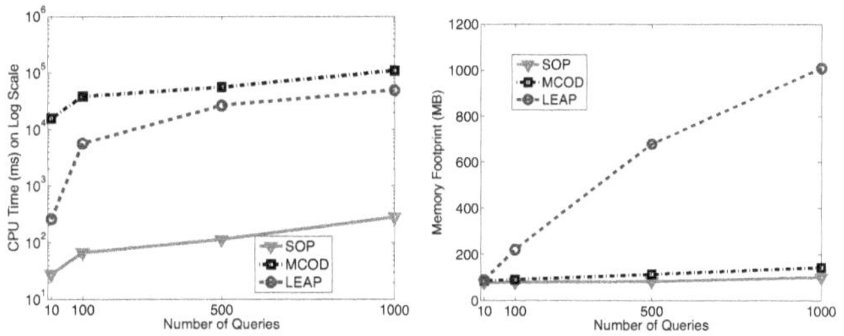

(a) CPU (log scale) (b) Memory (log scale)

Figure 12: Varying W and S values on STT dataset

The CPU resources utilized by SOP are very stable as the number of queries increases. This is because for each workload the k value is randomly selected in the same range. In each workload at least one of the randomly selected k is likely to get fairly close to the upper ceiling value in the range. In other words the maximum k in each workload is similar on average. Therefore this experiment demonstrates that the performance of SOP relies on the largest k value instead of on the number of queries in the workload. Therefore SOP scales to a potentially huge workload composed of a large number of queries. A similar trend can also be observed in memory utilization as shown in Fig. 8(b).

Arbitrary K and R Case. In this experiment, we assess the performance of the algorithms when varying both k and r. We fix the window size to 10K, slide size to 0.5K, while the values for both k and r are randomly generated in the range respectively from 30 to 1500 and from 200 to 2000 for each query.

Fig. 9 depicts the performance of the three algorithms in terms of CPU costs and memory consumption. We observe that SOP consistently outperforms MCOD and LEAP up to 3 orders of magnitude. This confirms that K-SKY not only effectively shares the computation among the queries with an identical k parameter, but it also achieves full sharing across multiple skyband queries with respect to different query groups with distinct k values. MCOD instead solves this case by *simulating* an outlier query using the largest k and smallest r values in the workload as its pattern parameters. Such a query can have much more restricted neighbor requirements and in turn more expensive range queries than any of the actual outlier queries. Huge CPU and memory resources may be wasted compared to SOP.

Small Workload. In this set of experiments, we test the performance of SOP when processing small workload. It is composed of two experiments. In the first experiment, all queries utilize the same set of attributes in the detection of outliers. We vary the size of the workload by containing 1, 2, 4, 8 queries. Again it confirms that SOP performs well even in this small workload case as shown in Fig. 10(a). In particular when the workload contains only one single query, SOP does not perform worse than the state-of-the-art single query approach LEAP. This shows that no much extra overhead is introduced by SOP.

Furthermore, we also evaluate the performance of SOP when handling queries utilizing different set of attributes. In this experiment, the queries are divided into 3 groups. The queries in the same group utilize the same set of attributes. We vary the number of queries in each group from 1 to 4. To support such workload SOP is slightly extended using a simple divide and conquer approach. As depicted in Fig. 10(b) our extended SOP approach continues to perform well. More specifically SOP is at least 150 times faster than MCOD and two times faster than LEAP even in this small number of queries case.

6.3 Varying Window Specific Parameters

Next, we focus on workloads composed of 10, 100, 500, 1000 queries respectively for the case when varying window-specific parameters, while using a fixed pattern-specific parameter setting. In this set of experiments the stock data [11] is utilized to evaluate how our SOP solution performs when handling real datasets.

Arbitrary Win Case. In this experiment, we study the performance of SOP for window sizes ranging from 1K to 500K. We fix the slide size as 0.5K, r as 200, and k as 30.

As shown in Fig. 11, SOP features significantly better performance on both CPU and memory consumption compared to MCOD and LEAP. Since MCOD leverages the sharing opportunities across the windows of multiple queries by adopting our swift query strategy, its CPU and memory usage is relatively stable compared to LEAP as the number of queries increases. However MCOD is still outperformed by SOP by at least 2 orders of magnitude in CPU time as shown in Fig. 11(a). This is because based on our *safe-for-all* observation in Sec. 4.1, SOP terminates and excludes p from any future evaluation process immediately once p is classified as safe inlier by the skyband query corresponding to the outlier query with the largest window size. As stated earlier, MCOD instead relies on a range query to detect these outliers. Even if a data point is recognized as safe inlier, this neighbor search continues completing the comparisons with all other untouched data points. Therefore a huge amount of CPU resources can be wasted.

Arbitrary Win and Slide Case. In this experiment, we investigate the performance of SOP when varying both window-specific parameters. We fix k as 30 and r as 200. The window and slide sizes are arbitrarily selected for each query from the range of 1K to 500K and from 50 to 50K respectively.

As illustrated in Fig. 12, the average CPU time consumed by SOP increases only from 28ms to 282ms (10 folds) as the number of queries increases from 10 to 1000 (100 folds). This continues to outperform the alternative algorithms by at least two orders of magnitudes. Clearly, results shown in Fig. 12 demonstrate the effectiveness of the swift query strategy for handling arbitrary win and arbitrary slide case.

6.4 Varying Pattern and Window Parameters

In this most general case, we prepare four workloads composed of 100, 1000, 10,000, 50,000 queries respectively by varying all window-specific and pattern-specific parameters.

We observe from Fig. 13(a) that similar to the cases of independently varying pattern-specific parameters and window-specific parameters SOP achieves tremendous gain in CPU utilization compared to (augmented) MCOD and (the non-shared) LEAP. Furthermore SOP shows excellent scalability in the cardinality of the workload. As the number of queries rises from 1000 to the extremely large cardinality of 50,000 queries, the CPU costs of SOP only increase from 32ms to 892ms. As the number of the queries increases, the sharing opportunities among the given set of queries also increase. Since SOP achieves full sharing across queries, it effectively reduces the CPU burden caused by the huge workload.

The memory usage of SOP also consistently outperforms the alternatives solutions as shown in Fig. 13(b). As previously stated, the reason is that LEAP detects outliers on the same streaming data for each query independently. Hence the memory consumed by the workload queries accumulates as the number of queries grows. On the other hand, MCOD always detects outliers by discovering and maintaining all neighbors for each point. However, SOP only requires minimal information to prove the outlier status of each point. As a result, SOP effectively avoids the usage of unnecessary space by purging redundant intermediate results. Therefore significant memory utilization is reduced by SOP.

7. RELATED WORK

Distance-based Outliers on Streaming Data. With the emergence of digital devices generating data streams, outliers on streaming data are one type of anomalies recently studied [7, 13, 1]. Existing work [7, 13, 1] focuses primarily on processing a single outlier detection request. In particular [1] leverages the observation that the neighbors p_i of a point p that arrived after p do not expire before p expires. They make a distinction between the preceding neighbors of p, P_p, i.e., those that will expire before p, and the succeeding neighbors of p, S_p, those that will persist during the entire lifetime of p. They first introduce the idea of a "safe inlier" as a point p with $\geq$ k succeeding neighbors.

[13] further improves on [1] by leveraging the *safe inlier* concept of [1]. That is, it organizes the data points into a queue based on the number of their succeeding neighbors, so that it can efficiently schedule the necessary checks that have to be made when the window slides. However it still relies on full range query searches to process the newly arriving points. Therefore it cannot provide real time responsiveness when applied to high velocity streaming data. Besides this single query technique, [13] also touches on supporting multiple outlier detection queries for the case of varying pattern-specific parameters. Given a data point p they first utilize a range query to find all points that satisfy the neighbor condition of all queries in the query group. Then a postprocessing step is applied to filter the unnecessary points from this large neighbor set to reduce the maintenance costs. In our work by directly transforming the multi-query outlier problem into the single query skyband problem, we only collect the necessary evidence that is sufficient to answer multiple outlier queries, therefore significantly outperforming this method as confirmed in our experiments.

Due to a deeper understanding the temporal relationships among stream data points, [7] overcomes the limitation of prior methods [1, 13] of undertaking full range query searches by discovering as early as possible safe inliers in the scan process. This allows it to better satisfy the performance requirements of modern streaming applications. However multiple outlier detection requests are not supported in [7].

Outliers on Sensor Streams. [20] proposes an online technique to detect outliers in sensor stream data. This work primarily focuses on how to reduce the message transmission and in turn reduce the power consumption of the sensors. First, it utilizes kernel density estimation to model the distribution of the sensor data. Then given a point p, [20] approximates whether p is an outlier by estimating the number of its neighbors using the density distribution function $f(p)$. However unlike our work focusing on detecting *exact* distance-based outliers, this *approximation* no longer assures complete results. Furthermore, they only support a single outlier detection query. No multi-query technique is discussed.

kNN Queries on Streams. Continuous kNN queries over sliding windows have indeed been studied in [15, 6]. Both works use a grid to index the stream data. To improve response time, they either postpone the processing of the new points which are not likely to be in kNN set [6] or eagerly pre-compute the possible kNN set for each future window as new data arrives [15].

However to determine the outlier status of p it is not necessary to always discover the full kNN of p. Rather one algorithm should stop evaluating p as long as any k neighbors of p have been discovered. Therefore the use of the streaming kNN algorithm to continuously detect outliers is not an efficient approach. Instead our customized skyband algorithm K-SKY always discovers the minimal information necessary to determine the outlier status of p.

General Multi-Query Optimization. Multiple query sharing has been widely studied as a general optimization problem in streaming environments. Previous research on sharing computations studied traditional SQL queries such as selection, join, and aggregation [4, 9, 22, 14]. Their methods include rewriting queries to expose common subexpressions, sharing indices, or segmenting input into partitions and sharing partial results over the partitions. However the key problem we address in this work, namely correctly answering multiple outlier detection queries by only collecting minimal information, is different from the more general purpose optimization effort required by the traditional SQL query sharing.

8. CONCLUSION

In this work, we present the first solution, called SOP, for efficient shared processing of a large number of distance-based outlier detection requests with diverse parameter instantiations over sliding window streams. SOP requires only one single pass over the data points to support a huge workload composed of a large number of outlier detection requests with arbitrary input settings for all pattern and window specific parameters. Our experimental study using both real and synthetic streaming datasets confirms that for the rich diversity of tested scenarios SOP outperforms the alternatives on average three orders of magnitude in CPU time, while using only 5 % memory space of its counterparts.

9. REFERENCES

[1] F. Angiulli and F. Fassetti. Distance-based outlier queries in data streams: the novel task and algorithms. *Data Min. Knowl. Discov.*, 20(2):290–324, 2010.

[2] F. Angiulli and C. Pizzuti. Fast outlier detection in high dimensional spaces. In *PKDD*, pages 15–26, 2002.

[3] A. Arasu, S. Babu, and J. Widom. The cql continuous query language. *VLDB J.*, 15(2):121–142, 2006.

[4] A. Arasu and J. Widom. Resource sharing in continuous sliding-window aggregates. In *VLDB*, pages 336–347, 2004.

[5] S. D. Bay and M. Schwabacher. Mining distance-based outliers in near linear time with randomization and a simple pruning rule. In *KDD*, pages 29–38, 2003.

[6] C. Böhm, B. C. Ooi, C. Plant, and Y. Yan. Efficiently processing continuous k-nn queries on data streams. In *ICDE*, pages 156–165, 2007.

[7] L. Cao, D. Yang, Q. Wang, Y. Yu, J. Wang, and E. A. Rundensteiner. Scalable distance-based outlier detection over high-volume data streams. In *ICDE*, pages 76–87, 2014.

[8] C. Gupta, S. Wang, I. Ari, M. C. Hao, U. Dayal, A. Mehta, M. Marwah, and R. K. Sharma. Chaos: A data stream analysis architecture for enterprise applications. In *CEC*, pages 33–40, 2009.

[9] M. A. Hammad, M. J. Franklin, W. G. Aref, and A. K. Elmagarmid. Scheduling for shared window joins over data streams. In *VLDB*, pages 297–308, 2003.

[10] D. M. Hawkins. *Identification of Outliers*. Springer, 1980.

[11] I. INETATS. Stock trade traces. *http://www.inetats.com/*.

[12] E. M. Knorr and R. T. Ng. Algorithms for mining distance-based outliers in large datasets. In *VLDB*, pages 392–403, 1998.

[13] M. Kontaki, A. Gounaris, A. N. Papadopoulos, K. Tsichlas, and Y. Manolopoulos. Continuous monitoring of distance-based outliers over data streams. In *ICDE*, pages 135–146, 2011.

[14] S. Krishnamurthy, C. Wu, and M. J. Franklin. On-the-fly sharing for streamed aggregation. In *SIGMOD Conference*, pages 623–634, 2006.

[15] K. Mouratidis and D. Papadias. Continuous nearest neighbor queries over sliding windows. *IEEE Trans. Knowl. Data Eng.*, 19(6):789–803, 2007.

[16] A. Nazaruk and M. Rauchman. Big data in capital markets. In *SIGMOD Conference*, pages 917–918, 2013.

[17] D. Papadias, Y. Tao, G. Fu, and B. Seeger. Progressive skyline computation in database systems. *ACM Trans. Database Syst.*, 30(1):41–82, 2005.

[18] S. Ramaswamy, R. Rastogi, and K. Shim. Efficient algorithms for mining outliers from large data sets. In *SIGMOD Conference*, pages 427–438, 2000.

[19] G. E. Rosario, E. A. Rundensteiner, D. C. Brown, and M. O. Ward. Mapping nominal values to numbers for effective visualization. In *InfoVis*, pages 113–120, 2003.

[20] S. Subramaniam, T. Palpanas, D. Papadopoulos, V. Kalogeraki, and D. Gunopulos. Online outlier detection in sensor data using non-parametric models. In *VLDB*, pages 187–198, 2006.

[21] Y. Tao and D. Papadias. Maintaining sliding window skylines on data streams. *IEEE Trans. Knowl. Data Eng.*, 18(2):377–391, 2006.

[22] S. Wang, E. A. Rundensteiner, S. Ganguly, and S. Bhatnagar. State-slice: New paradigm of multi-query optimization of window-based stream queries. In *VLDB*, pages 619–630, 2006.

APPENDIX

A. PROOF OF PROBLEM MAPPING

Lemma 1. *Given a query group $\mathbb{Q}$, for any data point p, the output of Q^s, denoted as $\mathbb{S}_p$, is* ***sufficient*** *and* ***necessary*** *to continuously determine the outlier status of p with respect to all queries in $\mathbb{Q}$, where Q^s represents the $(k-1)$-skyband query with respect to p with k as the neighbor threshold parameter defined in $\mathbb{Q}$.*

Proof. "$\Rightarrow$" we prove the sufficiency by showing that Q^s always returns the *k nearest neighbors* of *p* kNN(p) [3] as part of the skyband points. Assume the data points in D have been partitioned into t subsets S_1, S_2, ..., S_t. Each subset S_i contains all data points with the same distance to *p*. Assume here that the subsets $S_1, S_2, ..., S_t$ are sorted in an ascending order by their distance to *p*. Assume $\mid S_1 \mid + \mid S_2 \mid +, ..., + \mid S_x \mid < k$ and $\mid S_1 \mid + \mid S_2 \mid + ... + \mid S_x \mid + \mid S_{x+1} \mid \geq k$. All data points in $S_1 \cup S_2 \cup ... \cup S_x$ along with (k - ($\mid S_1 \mid + \mid S_2 \mid +, ..., + \mid S_x \mid$)) data points with largest timestamp in S_{x+1} will be returned by Q^s, since by the domination rule in Def. 5 they are dominated by at most k -1 data points. These k data points satisfy the $kNN(p)$ definition, since no other data point is closer towards *p* than they are. Then by the *k-distance* observation, kNN(p) is sufficient to prove the outlier status of *p* with respect to $\mathbb{Q}$. The sufficiency is proven.

"$\Leftarrow$" By contradiction. Given a point p_i ($p_i \in \mathbb{S}_p$ - *k*NN(p)), although by the *k-distance* observation, $\mathbb{S}_p - \{p_i\}$ is still sufficient to determine the status of *p* in the current window W_c, potentially *p* may be erroneously evaluated in the future window W_{c+x}. Assume that when the stream evolves to w_{c+x}, all points in $\mathbb{S}_r$ arriving earlier than p_i have expired. If all points p_j arriving after W_c are far from *p* ($dist(p, p_j) > r_i$), p_i should now be in kNN(p). Since the outlier status of *p* is determined by kNN(p), to correctly determine the outlier status of *p* in any future window, p_i has to be kept. The necessity is proven. ■

B. OPTIMALITY PROOF OF K-SKY

Lemma 2. *K-SKY correctly discovers the (k-1)-skyband points in window W_c by examining only the minimum number of data points.*

Proof. We prove Lemma 2 by showing that: (1) Any point inserted to skybandPoints during the execution of K-SKY is guaranteed to be a true *(k-1)-skyband* point; (2)No data point that could not be a *(k-1)-skyband* point is examined during the execution of K-SKY.

Proof of (1). In K-SKY the later arrivals are always evaluated earlier than the earlier arrivals. Therefore any point p_i already added into *skybandPoints* has a larger timestamp than any point p_j remaining to be evaluated. That is, $p_j.time < p_i.time$. By the domination rule defined in Def. 5, p_j cannot *dominate* p_i. Therefore p_i would not be replaced by any point evaluated later. Condition (1) holds.

Proof of (2). Proof in two steps. First, K-SKY stops immediately once the termination condition is satisfied. Namely K-SKY terminates immediately once one point p_i is dominated by k points if the distance between p_i and p is not larger than the smallest r parameter r_{min} in $\mathbb{Q}$. Therefore the remaining points that will not be in *skybandPoints* are not evaluated.

Second, we prove any data point evaluated during the execution of K-SKY is potentially a *(k-1)-skyband* point. Data point p_i is evaluated by K-SKY if and only if the termination condition has

[3]This kNN is based on the normalized distance function.

not yet been satisfied. In other words when p_i was evaluated, at most k - 1 data points p_j with dist(p,p_j) $\leq r_{min}$ existed at that time. Therefore p_i should be listed in $skybandPoints$ if dist(p,p_i) $\leq r_{min}$. That is, if we were not to consider p_i, then potentially an incorrect skyband point set may be reported. Furthermore, in K-SKY if p $\in W_c$ is an point that survived the stream data expiration, only the new arrivals in W_c and its unexpired unexpired skyband points in last window W_{c-1} will be examined. By our *least examination optimization* principle these points are the only points that will appear in the skyband point set of the new window W_c. This confirms that any point evaluated by K-SKY is indeed necessary to guarantee the correctness of the Q^s query. ■

C. PROOF OF LEMMA 3

Lemma 3. *Given a query group* $\mathbb{Q}$*:* $\{q_1, q_2, ..., q_m, q_{m+1}, ...,$ $q_{max}\}$ *(*$q_1.win < q_2.win, < ..., < q_{max}.win$*), p is an outlier for queries* $\{q_1, q_2, ..., q_m\}$*, if* $q_{m+1}.W_c.start < p_{old}.time < q_m.W_c.start$*, where* p_{old} *is the oldest point in* $q^s_{max}.skyband$*.*

Proof. q^s_{max} is a special skyband query with respect to the single outlier query $q_{max}(k, r)$. Since *p* is an inlier with respect to q_{max}, the skyband set $q^s_{max}.skyband$ contains *k* neighbors of *p*. p_{old} is dominated by k -1 points in $q^s_{max}.skyband$, because $p_{old}.time <$ $p_i.time$ ($\forall p_i \in q^s_{max}.skyband$). Since $q_{m+1}.W_c.start < p_{old}.time < q_m.W_c.start$, p_{old} falls in the current window W_c of $\{q_{m+1}, ..., q_{max}\}$, but is out of the W_c of $\{q_1, q_2, ..., q_m\}$. Therefore *p* has at most k - 1 neighbors in $q^s_{max}.skyband$ for $\{q_1, q_2, ..., q_m\}$. Furthermore, any point p_j out of $q^s_{max}.skyband$ cannot be a neighbor of *p* for $\{q_1, q_2, ..., q_m\}$ in their current window W_c. Otherwise p_{old} would also be dominated by p_j. Hence it would in total be dominated by *k* points. This contradicts the fact that p_{old} is a skyband point of q^s_{max}. ■

THEMIS: Fairness in Federated Stream Processing under Overload

Evangelia Kalyvianaki
City University London
sbbj913@city.ac.uk

Marco Fiscato
Imperial College London
mfiscato@doc.ic.ac.uk

Theodoros Salonidis
IBM TJ Watson Research Center
tsaloni@us.ibm.com

Peter Pietzuch
Imperial College London
prp@imperial.ac.uk

ABSTRACT

Federated stream processing systems, which utilise nodes from multiple independent domains, can be found increasingly in multi-provider cloud deployments, internet-of-things systems, collaborative sensing applications and large-scale grid systems. To pool resources from several sites and take advantage of local processing, submitted queries are split into *query fragments*, which are executed collaboratively by different sites. When supporting many concurrent users, however, queries may exhaust available processing resources, thus requiring constant load shedding. Given that individual sites have autonomy over how they allocate query fragments on their nodes, it is an open challenge how to ensure global fairness on processing quality experienced by queries in a federated scenario.

We describe THEMIS, a federated stream processing system for resource-starved, multi-site deployments. It executes queries in a globally fair fashion and provides users with constant feedback on the experienced processing quality for their queries. THEMIS associates stream data with its *source information content* (SIC), a metric that quantifies the contribution of that data towards the query result, based on the amount of source data used to generate it. We provide the BALANCE-SIC distributed load shedding algorithm that balances the SIC values of result data. Our evaluation shows that the BALANCE-SIC algorithm yields balanced SIC values across queries, as measured by Jain's Fairness Index. Our approach also incurs a low execution time overhead.

1. INTRODUCTION

Federated stream processing systems (FSPSs) [14, 13] continuously process data streams using computation and network resources from several autonomous sites [9]. Submitted queries are split into *query fragments*, which can be deployed across multiple sites. For example, a cloud-based stream processing system may span more than one cloud provider to benefit from lower costs, higher resilience or closer proximity to data sources. In collaborative e-science applications, FSPSs such as OGSA-DAI [3] and Astro-WISE [1] pool resources from multiple organisations to provide a shared processing service for high stream rates and computationally expensive queries. Participatory sensing and smart city infrastructures [5, 31] require deployments of systems that combine independent domains with distinct data or processing capabilities for a large user base.

SIGMOD'16, June 26-July 01, 2016, San Francisco, CA, USA
© 2016 ACM. ISBN 978-1-4503-3531-7/16/06...$15.00
DOI: http://dx.doi.org/10.1145/2882903.2882943

A challenge is that FSPSs are likely to suffer from long-term overload conditions. As a shared processing platform with many users, they can experience a "tragedy of the commons" [19] when users submit more queries than what can be sustained given the available resources. Instead of adopting a rigid admission policy, which rejects user queries when available resources are low, it is more desirable for an FSPS to use load-shedding techniques [33, 27]. Under load-shedding, the FSPS provides a best-effort service by reducing the resource requirements of queries through dropping a fraction of tuples from the input data streams.

Appropriate load shedding in an FSPS, however, is complicated by the fact that individual sites are autonomous and may implement their own resource allocation policies. For example, a site may prioritise queries belonging to local users at the expense of external query fragments. Without coordination of load-shedding decisions across sites, multi-site queries may experience significant variations in processing quality, depending on the load distribution across sites. *It is therefore an open challenge how to ensure that queries spanning multiple autonomous sites in an FSPS experience globally fair processing quality under overload conditions.*

Many stream processing systems support load shedding mechanisms to handle overload conditions. Load shedding mechanisms that operate at the granularity of individual nodes [33, 10, 35], however, cannot achieve fair shedding decisions for queries spanning multiple nodes. Proposals for distributed load shedding [34, 44] associate a utility function with query output rates and aim to maximise the sum of utilities, which is not a representative measure of fairness. In addition, they assume special structure and a-priori knowledge of utility functions. Load shedding decisions are controlled by a centralised entity or are based on pre-computed shedding plans—both of which are not practical in an FSPS in which domains retain control. Operator-specific semantic shedding approaches for, e.g. joins [21, 26, 17], aggregates [10, 35] or XML streams [38] cannot be applied in a federated context when users employ diverse sets of operators or customised, user-defined ones.

We describe a new approach for distributed load shedding in an FSPS that treats queries in a globally fair fashion. The key idea is to define a query-independent metric to measure the quality of processing that query fragments have experienced, and then to use this information for load shedding:

(1) We associate stream data with a metric called *source information content* (SIC), which represents the contribution of that data to the result in a query-independent way. The SIC metric quantifies the amount of source data that was used to generate a given query

result data item. Intuitively, data that was aggregated over many stream sources is considered to be more important to the final query result. The SIC metric thus decouples processing quality from the semantics of the operators and provides a query-independent way to capture the quality of query processing with respect to tuple shedding. This is particularly suited to accommodate a diverse set of user queries that executes operators of various semantics and even with user-defined operators.

(2) Overloaded nodes in the FSPS invoke a distributed semantic *fair load-shedding algorithm* that aims to balance the SIC values of query results across all queries, referred to as the BALANCE-SIC fairness policy. This policy balances the SIC values of query results (i.e. maximises the Jain's Fairness Index, a normalised scalar metric that quantifies balance). It effectively utilises the processing capacity of FSPS nodes, given the practical constraints of the placement of queries on sites and their autonomy.

When queries are assigned across FSPS sites, it becomes challenging to control per-node tuple shedding and yet provide global BALANCE-SIC fair processing. This stems from the fact that shedding tuples at a node affects its resource availability and also the processing quality of other queries. Since queries span across sites and share resources, such effects are spread across sites, affecting shedding decisions on the rest of the nodes. It is therefore nontrivial to control tuple shedding globally in a federated setting.

In our approach, each node takes independent yet informed shedding decisions about the overall processing quality of locally-hosted queries. Queries provide continuous feedback on their processing quality through the SIC metric. The shedding of tuples eventually converges to global fairness as each node continuously adjusts its shedding behaviour in response to that of other FSPS nodes.

To demonstrate the practicality of our fair load-shedding approach, we describe THEMIS, an FSPS for overloaded deployments.[1] Our evaluation of THEMIS shows that: (a) the SIC metric captures the result degradation across a variety of query types; (b) in contrast to the baseline of random shedding, THEMIS achieves 33% fairer query processing, according to Jain Fairness Index, even with skewed workload distributions; and (c) our approach has low overhead and scales well to the number of nodes and queries.

In summary, the contributions and the paper outline are:

1. a query-independent model and a metric called SIC for quantifying the quality of stream processing based on the amount of information contributed by data sources (§4) and a practical approximation for computing it (§6);
2. the definition of the BALANCE-SIC fairness in an overloaded FSPS based on the processing quality of queries; and a distributed algorithm for globally BALANCE-SIC-fair semantic load-shedding in an FSPS, which takes the loss of information suffered by queries into account (§5);
3. the design and implementation of THEMIS, an FSPS that implements efficiently the BALANCE-SIC fair load-shedding policy (§6); and
4. results from an experimental evaluation that demonstrate that the approach achieves fair query processing under various workloads in a federated setting (§7).

[1] According to the Greek mythology, THEMIS is the Titan goddess of law and order.

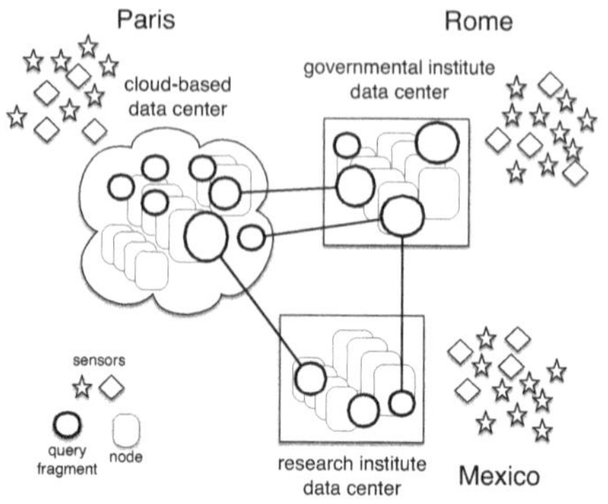

Figure 1: Example of a multi-site FSPS deployment for urban micro-climate monitoring

2. OVERLOAD IN FEDERATED STREAM PROCESSING

In this section, we describe the problem of fairness in query processing, which arises in an overloaded FSPS. We identify the key characteristics of an FSPS using an example application for query data processing over micro-climate sensor-generated data (§2.1). We then introduce the BALANCE-SIC fairness goal for an overloaded FSPS (§2.2) and discuss related work (§2.3).

2.1 Federated Stream Processing

Consider a use case of a globally-distributed FSPS for urban micro-climate monitoring. Figure 1 shows a deployment of such a system across three sites (i.e. Rome, Paris and Mexico), with environmental sensors as data sources. The FSPS collects data from a range of sensors, such as air temperature, humidity and carbon monoxide, and processes the data in real-time for analysis. Queries are issued, e.g. by government agencies for urban planning, transport authorities, citizens with respiratory problems and meteorological researchers. A sample high-level data streaming queries may continuously report: *"the 10 highest values of carbon monoxide concentration measurements on highways in Mexico every minute"* and *"the covariance matrix between measurements of (temperature, airflow) and (carbon dioxide, nitrogen) in Paris every 10 minutes"*.

Each site consists of a data centre with physical nodes running a local distributed stream processing system, and we assume seamless integration across all these systems at the federated sites [12]. Below, we provide a high-level overview of data stream processing in an FSPS. Sources generate *tuples* for processing by *queries*. Queries are subdivided into *query fragments* and deployed at one or more sites. A query fragment consists of one or more *operators*, and each fragment of the same query is deployed on a different FSPS node. Query fragments use resources, i.e. CPU, memory, disk space and network bandwidth, to process incoming tuples and generate output tuples. Output tuples may be further processed by fragments of the same query, until result tuples are sent to the user issuing the query. Nodes share their resources among fragments belonging to different queries.

Below, we identify three main characteristics regarding user behaviour and resource utilisation in such an FSPS:

C1. Skewed query workload distribution. Sites primarily host queries of local users so the overall load distribution across sites may be skewed, with some sites being more loaded than others. In general, query fragments cannot be allocated uniformly across sites due to local policy constraints or the reliance on local sources. For example, queries using forecasting algorithms may be restricted to running at a given site due to licensing constraints, which may limit the number of authorised users or remote sites using the system.

C2. Permanent resource overload. Due to the shared nature of an FSPS, we assume that the system is constantly overloaded, i.e. its resources are lower than required for perfect execution of all queries. In the above example, queries are issued by a large user population, leading to high demand. A common strategy for an FSPS to handle overload is to use *tuple shedding* [27, 33].

C3. Site autonomy. The collaborative nature of an FSPS means that a site should accept incoming queries, even under high load. However, sites belonging to different administrative domains are managed autonomously. It is therefore infeasible to assume centralised control over all tuple shedding decisions, enforced across all sites. Instead, sites elect to cooperate, having only a partial view of all resource allocation decisions across the whole FSPS.

2.2 Fairness in FSPS

The problem of how to implement *fair query processing* arises naturally in an overloaded FSPS. There exist many different approaches to address overload conditions. For example, admission control rejects incoming queries under overload [41, 40]. Such methods are not applicable in a federated context because the collaborative nature means that submitted queries must be accepted. Other approaches redistribute operators for load balancing [43, 40, 42, 11]. However, query placement in an FSPS is typically controlled by users, e.g. to leverage characteristics such as proximity.

We employ *distributed load shedding* to address overload conditions in an FSPS. By using load shedding, we assume that users agree to use the FSPS and receive *degraded query processing* for their queries. We assume that users submit queries whose results remain useful, even when their processing is degraded due to load shedding, such as aggregates [10], including averages, counts as well as top-k queries. Finally, we use *distributed* load shedding to comply with site autonomy (see C3 in §2.1).

There are two challenges to implement distributed load shedding. First, there is a need for a query-independent processing metric to capture the impact of shedding on the quality of query processing. Ideally, we require a measure for processing quality that quantifies the processing degradation under shedding but is *query-independent*, i.e. it does not have to be adapted manually to the semantics of specific queries. With such a measure, it becomes possible to compare the impact of tuple shedding across queries and hence guide shedding decisions according to a fairness policy. In §4, we introduce the SIC query-independent metric that captures the quality of processing by measuring the contribution of source tuples actually used for generating query results.

Second, depending on the deployment of query fragments to sites, some queries may get more penalised due to overload than others. We therefore want to achieve *global fairness* across all queries by enforcing load shedding at all sites so that all queries are equally penalised by the shedding. We achieve this by aiming to equalise a fairness measure of all queries after shedding. It is a challenge how to implement fairness across queries executing on overloaded, distributed and autonomous sites, regardless of their deployment. In §5, we present a new distributed load shedding algorithm that maintains BALANCE-SIC fairness of queries.

2.3 Related Work

The research community recognises the need for FSPSs, exploring relevant research challenges. Tatbul [32] argues for the integration of multiple stream processing engines for a variety of applications and pinpoints the challenges when dealing with heterogeneous query semantics. Botan et al. [12] present *MaxStream*, an FSPS for business intelligence applications. Our focus instead is on fairness in an overloaded FSPS using load shedding.

Centralised load shedding. Early proposals for load shedding focus on single-node systems [4, 33, 28]. A simple way to address overload is through *random shedding* [33] that discards arbitrary tuples. This baseline approach is easy to implement and has low overhead, however, it cannot be used to control the shed tuples.

In contrast, *semantic shedding* discards tuples using a function that correlates them with their contribution to the quality of the query output [33]. Tuples are discarded in a way that maximises result quality. Carney et al. [15] describe generic *drop-* and *value-based* functions to quantify the contribution of tuples on the result. A drop-based function specifies how the result quality of a query decreases with the number of discarded tuples. Many systems discard tuples as to maximise the output tuple rate [17, 34]. In some cases, a value-based function correlates the query output quality with the values of the output tuples [23]. In contrast, our goal is to maximise the contribution of the source tuples used for processing.

There exist semantic load shedding approaches for specific operator types, such as joins [21, 26, 17], aggregates [10, 35] and XML operators [38]. These approaches require domain knowledge of the operator semantics, while we treat operators as black-boxes.

Distributed load shedding. The problem of distributed load allocation has been studied for stream processing systems. Zhao et al. [44] consider the allocation problem for applications with tasks modelled as synchronous and asynchronous forks and joins, commenting that this approach can be applied to distributed stream processing. Their work emphasises a theoretical framework for convergence to an optimal solution and presents simulations over two queries and three output streams. In contrast, we provide a fair stream processing system based on the contributions of source tuples and evaluate a prototype implementation.

Tatbul et al. [34] employ distributed shedding to maximise the total weighted throughput of queries by computing the drop selectivity of random or window drop operators inserted at the input streams of a stream processing system. Shedding decisions are made sequentially by each node along a query, starting from the leaves and propagating through metadata up to the input nodes. They assume identical queries layouts to nodes (e.g. all root components are deployed on the same node), which is not applicable in a federated system. Finally, the scalability of the approach remains unclear, as the simulation-based evaluation only includes a handful of applications. In our prototype evaluation, we execute several hundreds of queries across tens of nodes.

Both approaches [34, 44] perform load shedding to maximise the sum of utility functions but sum maximisation does not achieve fairness. In addition, they require utility functions of special structure (either linear weighted functions [34] or concave functions [44] of rate), which does not capture query utility in practice. Finally, they require a-priori knowledge of the utility functions, which is challenging to estimate offline. In contrast, our approach targets fairness without assuming specific, a-priori utility functions. The only assumption is that the "utility" (as captured by the SIC metric) decreases with shedding and is implicitly modelled during system operation through the propagation and updating of the SIC metric in the data tuples.

An important issue for load shedding is the selection of drop locations in a query plan [33, 10]. The most efficient way is to discard tuples at upstream operators, close to sources [15, 20, 29]. This, however, is difficult to do in an FSPS because it requires global information about query plans that span multiple sites.

Metrics for query processing quality. The building block for a fairness mechanism is a metric that quantifies the processing degradation under shedding. A typical metric is the rate of query output tuples [17, 34, 44]. This metric intuitively increases when the rate of tuple shedding decreases. It remains unclear, however, how to compare performance degradation across queries with different semantics, which fundamentally may exhibit different output rates.

Our metric associates query performance with the contribution of source tuples required for perfect processing, which is related to the network imprecision metric (NI) [24] used in large-scale monitoring systems. The NI metric estimates the percentage of nodes available when calculating an aggregate value over a set of data sources. In contrast, our metric operates at the granularity of individual tuples and uses a time interval to reason about the impact of source tuples on the result.

Approximate query execution [22, 28, 15, 10, 7, 6] has the goal to reduce the resource footprint of queries by producing different, approximate answers compared to execution with abundant resources. Existing techniques in this area change operator semantics [28, 26, 17, 16, 30, 39]—instead, we approach queries as black-boxes and address overload by tuple shedding for fair processing.

Fairness. The notion of fairness in an FSPS remains largely unexplored. In early work, Babcock et al. [10] study the problem of load shedding across aggregation queries running over a single-node streaming engine. Although they do not discuss fairness directly, the goal of their work is to minimise, and hence equalise, the relative error caused by shedding for all queries. They employ a performance metric that is tailored for sliding window aggregation queries only. In a special case of their work, Zhao et al. [44] implement a weighted proportional fairness scheme on output stream rates. In contrast, we explore the concept of BALANCE-SIC fairness in the context of an overloaded FSPS.

3. FEDERATED PROCESSING MODEL

In this section, we describe our system model for an FSPS.

Data model. A tuple t is a set of three elements $(\tau, \text{SIC}, \mathcal{V})$ where τ is the tuple's logical timestamp; $\text{SIC} \in \mathbb{R}^+$ is the source information content meta-data, which we formally define in §4; and $\mathcal{V}$ is the set of payload values according to the tuple's schema. We use the notations t_τ, t_{SIC} and $t_\mathcal{V}$ to refer to the timestamp, meta-data and payload values, respectively, of a tuple t. A *stream* of tuples is an infinite, time-ordered sequence of tuples.

Query graph. A query q is a directed acyclic graph $q = (\mathcal{O}, \mathcal{M})$ where $\mathcal{O}$ is the set of operators and $\mathcal{M}$ is the set of streams. An operator takes one or more *input streams* and produces an *output stream* of *derived* tuples. Derived tuples are denoted by t^{out}. We assume that, for each operator $o \in \mathcal{O}$, there exists a time or count window that atomically emits tuples for processing by o.

In the query graph, the direction of edges indicates the direction of tuples flowing between operators. Certain operators in the query graph are connected to a finite set of *sources*, which are denoted by $\mathcal{S}$ and produce *source tuples* in time-variant rates. We assume sources of different rates per query. Every source is connected to a single operator in the query graph. We use t^s to denote that tuple t comes from source $s \in \mathcal{S}$. The domain of source tuples across sources $\mathcal{S}$ over time is given by $\mathbb{T}^S$. The timestamp t_τ indicates the time of tuple's t generation either by a source or by an operator in the case of a source or a derived tuple, respectively. There exists one *root operator* in the query graph to emit the *query result stream* containing result tuples for the user. Result tuples are denoted by t^r and the domain of result tuples is given by $\mathbb{T}^R$.

Query deployment. An FSPS consists of a set of nodes $\mathcal{D}$ with heterogeneous resources. Each node $d \in \mathcal{D}$ corresponds to a different autonomous site; without loss of generality, we focus on single-node sites as typically nodes within a site have similar capacities.

Upon deployment, the query graph is partitioned into *query fragments* that are disjoint sets of at least a single query operator. Each query fragment is deployed on a different FSPS node, and a query can span a subset or all of the FSPS nodes. We assume that query division to fragments and mapping of fragments to FSPS nodes are performed by the query user and remain the same throughout a query's execution. Finally, an FSPS node can host multiple fragments of different queries.

4. SOURCE INFORMATION CONTENT

We introduce the source information content (SIC) metric to quantify the quality of processing by accounting for the contributions of source tuples towards result tuples.

Query processing. We consider queries as black-boxes. For each query q, we use an abstract *query function* f_q to describe the collective processing by all operators in $\mathcal{O}$ over source tuples to produce result tuples, i.e. $f_q : \mathbb{T}^S \to \mathbb{T}^R$. A query function takes as input a set of source tuples T^S and outputs a set of result tuples $\mathcal{T}^R$ generated from operators processing $\mathcal{T}^S$, i.e. $f_q(\mathcal{T}^S) = \mathcal{T}^R$ where $\mathcal{T}^S \in \mathbb{T}^S$ and $\mathcal{T}^R \in \mathbb{T}^R$. Our goal is to enumerate the tuples of $\mathcal{T}^S$ and so to measure any loss of these tuples due to shedding.

Source information content. We now formally introduce the *source information content* (SIC) metric to quantify the information contribution from sources to query results.

The SIC value of a source tuple t^s_{SIC} measures its contribution to the result tuples in relation to the rest of tuples $\in \mathcal{T}^S$. We assign the SIC value of a source tuple as:

$$t^s_{SIC} = \frac{1}{|\mathcal{T}^S_s||\mathcal{S}|}. \tag{1}$$

Equation (1) captures our consideration that all source tuples from a given source s, denoted by $\mathcal{T}^S_s$, are equally important for the result. The more tuples a source generates, the less important each individual tuple becomes because it can be regarded as an *update*, e.g. multiple sensor readings at a higher sampling rate. Thus, the SIC value of an individual source tuple t^s is inversely proportional to $|\mathcal{T}^S_s|$ and is also normalised by the number of sources $|\mathcal{S}|$ in a query for a query-independent metric.

For a query q, the SIC value of its result tuples, q_{SIC}, is given by the sum of the SIC values of all source tuples used for the generation of the result tuples, i.e. tuples that are not dropped:

$$q_{\text{SIC}} := \sum_{t^s \in \widetilde{\mathcal{T}^S}} t^s_{SIC}, \tag{2}$$

where $\widetilde{\mathcal{T}^S} \subseteq \mathcal{T}^S$ is the set of source tuples *actually* processed for the result tuples. A source tuple is not used towards a result because it (or a tuple derived from it) was discarded due to load shedding.

The SIC value of the query result, q_{SIC}, lies in the range of $[0, 1]$. When $q_{\text{SIC}} = 1$, the result is *perfect*, and all source tuples are processed, $\widetilde{\mathcal{T}^S} = \mathcal{T}^S$. When $q_{\text{SIC}} \in (0, 1)$, the result is *degraded*, and a subset of source tuples are missing. The shed tuples are given by $\mathcal{T}^S / \widetilde{\mathcal{T}^S}$ and $f_q(\widetilde{\mathcal{T}^S}) = \widetilde{\mathcal{T}^R}$, where $\widetilde{\mathcal{T}^R} \subseteq \mathcal{T}^R$ is the set of result tuples derived from processing $\widetilde{\mathcal{T}^S}$. Finally, when $q_{\text{SIC}} = 0$, all source tuples were discarded, i.e. $\widetilde{\mathcal{T}^S} = \emptyset$.

However, it is challenging in practice to capture accurately the sets $\widetilde{\mathcal{T}^S}$, $\mathcal{T}^S$, $\widetilde{\mathcal{T}^R}$ and $\mathcal{T}^R$ because source tuples are successively transformed to derived tuples by operators and some are shed: de-

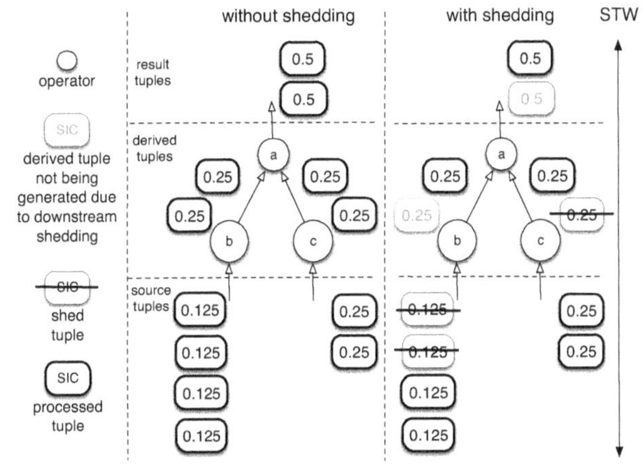

Figure 2: Example of SIC tuple values

rived tuples are "lost", e.g. due to filters and joins, which only select a subset of their input tuples. In other cases, tuples contribute to multiple derived tuples, e.g. sliding windows. Next, we introduce a practical way to (i) identify the source and result tuples in the corresponding sets of $\mathcal{T}^S$ and $\mathcal{T}^R$ such that $f_q(\mathcal{T}^S) = \mathcal{T}^R$ for perfect processing; and (ii) to measure the contribution of source tuples in $\widetilde{\mathcal{T}^S}$ for degraded processing.

Source time window. We introduce the concept of a *source time window* (STW), i.e. a period of time during which we account for all generated source tuples to contribute to certain result tuples. More formally, given a source tuple t^s and a result tuple t^r, $t^s \in \mathcal{T}^S$ and $t^r \in \mathcal{T}^R$ and $f_q(\mathcal{T}^S) = \mathcal{T}^R$ if and only if there exists a time index ρ such that $\rho \leq t^s_\tau, t^r_\tau \leq \rho + \text{STW}$. The duration of a STW should cover the *end-to-end processing latency* to allow enough time for source tuples to be processed by operators and produce result tuples. We always select a STW with significantly higher duration than the end-to-end latency, and it includes any network latencies for multi-fragmented queries.

SIC propagation from source to result tuples. Using the STW, we can calculate the query SIC value as in Equation (2). Rather than adding up the contributions of source tuples, we follow a bottom-up approach in which we propagate the SIC values of source tuples from $\mathcal{T}^S$ using derived tuples as they are processed by operators during the period of a STW. We then add the contributions of result tuples that contain the contributions of those source tuples *actually* processed towards the result tuples.

First, we calculate the SIC contribution of every derived tuple t^{out}:

$$t^{\text{out}}_{SIC} = \frac{\sum\limits_{t \in \mathcal{T}^o_{in}} t_{SIC}}{|\mathcal{T}^o_{out}|}, \tag{3}$$

where T^o_{in} is the set of all input tuples processed atomically by operator o, producing a set of output tuples given by T^o_{out} during a STW. Recall that in our model, we always consider a time or count window that atomically emits input tuples for an operator to process. In this way, the SIC values of source tuples are gradually passed from source tuples through derived tuples to result tuples. As derived tuples are discarded, their SIC values are not accounted for because they are not part of the set of input tuples $\mathcal{T}^o_{in}$ for operator processing. Finally, the query SIC value of result tuples is:

$$q_{\text{SIC}} := \sum_{t^r \in \widetilde{\mathcal{T}^R}} t^r_{\text{SIC}}, \tag{4}$$

where we only consider result tuples $t^r \in \widetilde{\mathcal{T}^R} \subseteq \mathcal{T}^R$ that are derived from source tuples $\in \widetilde{\mathcal{T}^S}$. The use of STW captures the relationship between source and result tuples, i.e. $f_q(\widetilde{\mathcal{T}^S}) = \widetilde{\mathcal{T}^R}$.

SIC example. Figure 2 provides a numerical example of the use of SIC values on source, derived and result tuples, the use of a STW and how result SIC values are calculated in the case of perfect processing and shedding. It shows a query with three operators, a, b and c. During a STW, operator b receives 4 source tuples and outputs 2 derived tuples; operator c receives 2 source tuples and outputs 2 derived tuples; and operator a receives 4 derived tuples and outputs 2 result tuples. All SIC values for source tuples are normalised to the 2 sources. Without shedding, $q_{\text{SIC}} = 1$, $\mathcal{T}^S$ contains 6 tuples in total and $\sum_{t^s \in \mathcal{T}^S} t^s_{SIC} = 4 * 0.125 + 2 * 0.25 = 1$; and, $\mathcal{T}^R$ has 2 tuples and $\sum_{t^r \in \mathcal{T}^R} t^r_{SIC} = 2 * 0.5 = 1$. Assuming that operator b sheds two of its input tuples and operator a sheds one of its input tuples (non-shed tuples are shown with bold), then: $q_{\text{SIC}} = \sum_{t^r \in \widetilde{\mathcal{T}^R}} t^r_{SIC} = 0.5$ and $\sum_{t^s \in \widetilde{\mathcal{T}^S}} t^s_{SIC} = 0.125 + 0.125 + 0.25 = 0.5$ because some of the source tuples do not contribute to the result tuples $\widetilde{\mathcal{T}^R}$. Although not discarded, one of the input source tuples of c does not contribute to the result tuple since a derived output tuple of c is shed.

The SIC metric enables direct comparisons among queries using only their source tuples and without considering their semantics. Such a query-independent metric is key to compare shedding amongst queries and to define BALANCE-SIC fairness.

5. BALANCE-SIC FAIRNESS

Given a deployment of streaming queries in an overloaded FSPS, the problem arises how to perform load shedding in a fair manner. Shedding the same amount of data from all queries is not desirable because different queries derive different utilities from the same amount of data. In practice, such utilities may not be known a-priori before actual system deployment. In addition, FSPS sites are distributed and autonomous, and they must achieve global fairness across queries in a fully decentralised manner.

We address the fairness problem by introducing the BALANCE-SIC fairness objective. This objective seeks to equalise the queries' SIC values while fully utilising all node resources. The SIC metric represents the contribution of *processed* source tuples of a query to produce its result. It also represents the degradation of query result as opposed to the "perfect" result achieved with no load shedding. Equalising SIC values of different queries leads to utility fairness—each of the queries will generate degraded results to the same degree with respect to no shedding of its data.

We introduce the BALANCE-SIC fairness distributed algorithm (Algorithm 1) to enforce this objective. The algorithm performs load shedding at each FSPS node to comply with site autonomy. Depending on the deployment of query fragments to nodes, some queries may be more penalised due to overload compared to others. Given a deployment plan of queries to nodes, our goal is to make all SIC values of query results to converge to the same values. Note that any converged SIC values would depend on several, often time-changing, factors such as queries' arrivals and departures, tuples rates and operators processing demands and heterogeneous nodes' capacities. To this end, our algorithm strives to *opportunistically* converge to equal SIC values while respecting these constraints. Our algorithm drops tuples from input streams to achieve BALANCE-SIC fairness and does so by selecting the tuples with the highest SIC values to increase node's utilisation with fewer processed tuples.

Algorithm 1: BALANCE-SIC Stream Processing Fairness

1 /* all variables refer to a single node */
2 c := number of tuples a node can process
3 $\mathcal{Q}$:= set of running queries
4 $\mathcal{T}$:= set of tuples for a STW
5 **foreach** STW **do**
6 $\quad\mathcal{X}$ = `selectTuplesToKeep`(c, $\mathcal{Q}$);
7 $\quad$`shedTuples`($\mathcal{T}/\mathcal{X}$);
8 **Procedure** `updateSIC`($\mathcal{Q}$)
9 $\quad\forall\, q \in \mathcal{Q}$ update q_{SIC}
10 **Procedure** `selectTuplesToKeep`(c, $\mathcal{Q}$)
11 $\quad$**while** $c > 0$ **do**
12 $\quad\quad q' = \arg\min_{q \in \mathcal{Q}}(q_{SIC})$
13 $\quad\quad \mathcal{Q}' = \mathcal{Q}/q'$
14 $\quad\quad q'' = \arg\min_{q \in \mathcal{Q}'}(q_{SIC}, q''_{SIC} \neq q'_{SIC})$
15 $\quad\quad$select set of tuples x from q' with aggregate SIC value $x_{SIC} := \sum_{t \in x} t_{sic}$, such that:
16 $\quad\quad \min\Big((q''_{SIC} - (q'_{SIC} + x_{SIC})), \max(x_{SIC})\Big)$
17 $\quad\quad\quad$subject to $(|x| < c)$
18 $\quad\quad c = c - |x|$
19 $\quad\quad X = X \cup x$
20 $\quad\quad$`updateSIC`($\mathcal{Q}$);
21 $\quad$**return** $\mathcal{X}$
22 **Procedure** `shedTuples`($\mathcal{T}/\mathcal{X}$)
23 $\quad$shed all tuples $\in \mathcal{T}/\mathcal{X}$

We first describe the algorithm operation on a single FSPS node. We then describe how it achieves BALANCE-SIC fairness across multi-fragment queries running on a multi-site FSPS.

5.1 Single node Balance-SIC fairness

Consider a node running a set of single-fragment queries, denoted by $\mathcal{Q}$. Assume that the node's capacity c is known and is defined by the number of tuples that the node can process before overloading during a STW (Assumption 1), i.e. a node is overloaded when the total number of input tuples of all queries combined exceeds the node's capacity as defined by the number of tuples to process. In §6, we describe a cost model that estimates c in an online fashion. Assume that, for each query $q \in \mathcal{Q}$, the set of its source tuples $\mathcal{T}^S$ is known at the start of its STW (Assumption 2), which means that the set of all $\mathcal{T}^S$ from all $q \in \mathcal{Q}$ can be defined as $\mathcal{T}$. Note that these assumptions are made primarily for the description of the Algorithm 1. In §6, we discuss practical ways to satisfy these assumptions. Extensive evaluation results in §7 show that the implementation of our algorithm efficiently enforces the BALANCE-SIC fairness policy in an overloaded FSPS despite these assumptions.

The BALANCE-SIC Algorithm 1 is executed each STW (lines 5–7) and defines the set of tuples to shed so that all running queries $q \in \mathcal{Q}$ converge to equal result SIC values for the current STW. For simplicity, we consider all queries to have the same STW. The algorithm first executes the procedure `selectTuplesToKeep()` (line 6) to select the set of source tuples $\mathcal{X}$ to retain for processing so that all q_{SIC} values for all queries $q \in \mathcal{Q}$ converge to the same value. Then, the algorithm sheds all remaining tuples i.e. $\mathcal{T}/\mathcal{X}$ (line 7) that cannot be processed due to limited capacity.

The procedure `selectTuplesToKeep`(c, $\mathcal{Q}$) (lines 10–21) iteratively selects tuples to process from each query until the total number of tuples to keep reaches the node's capacity c. In each iteration, the algorithm selects the two queries with the least q_{SIC} values, i.e. q' and q'' (lines 12–14). Given the lowest result SIC query q' (line 12), it selects as many tuples as required from q' so that q'_{SIC} reaches the result SIC value of the second lowest query q'' (lines 15–16). If there is more that one query with the same minimum SIC values, the algorithm selects one randomly. In case the aggregate number of tuples to accept is higher than the node's capacity, the algorithm only accepts as many as possible without exceeding the node's capacity (line 17).

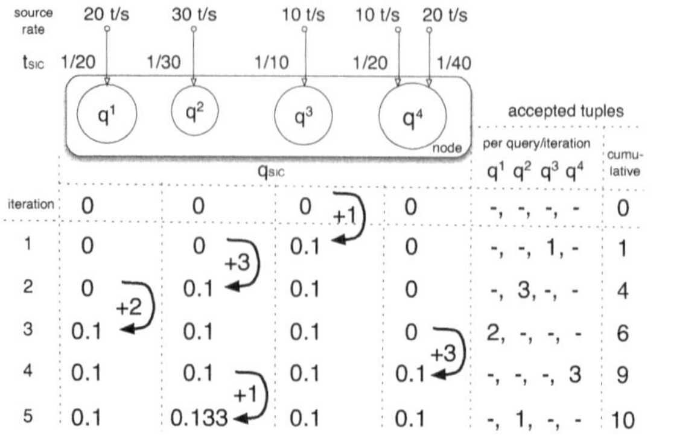

Figure 3: `selectTuplesToKeep()` on a single node with $c = 10$

For each query, the algorithm keeps the tuples with the highest SIC values, as shown in line 16 by $\max(x_{SIC})$. This maximises the aggregate SIC value of a query with the least possible number of tuples and so utilises nodes' resources efficiently. The accepted tuples are passed for processing and so q'_{SIC} is updated (line 20 and lines 8–9). We further explain in §5.2 the use of the $\mathcal{Q}$ argument in `updateSIC()` (line 20). The loop terminates when the number of accepted tuples reaches the node's capacity as measured by c. The remaining tuples $\mathcal{T}/\mathcal{X}$ are discarded (line 7) as shown by the function `shedTuples()` (lines 22–23).

The algorithm follows a gradient ascent approach to increase gradually the result SIC values of all queries while minimising the pairwise SIC differences of the two queries with the lowest SIC values. Iteratively, the algorithm minimises the pairwise SIC differences of the lowest two queries—eventually all queries' SIC values will converge as long as there are enough tuples from all queries to select (see Assumption 3).

Example of single node Balance-SIC fairness. Figure 3 shows an example of a single node with capacity c=10 with 4 single-fragment queries. Three of the queries have one source and query q^4 has two sources. Source rates and thus the normalised tuple t_{SIC} values are given. At the beginning, all queries have $q_{SIC} = 0$.

At iteration 1, the algorithm selects q^3 randomly to accept one tuple and so $q^3_{SIC} = 0.1$ At iteration 2, the lowest query is randomly selected to be q^2 and the next highest is q^3. The algorithm accepts 3 tuples from q^2 so that $q^2_{SIC} = q^3_{SIC} = 0.1$. At iteration 3, 2 tuples from q^1 are accepted to match $q^1_{SIC} = q^2_{SIC} = q^3_{SIC} = 0.1$. At iteration 4, the algorithm accepts 1 tuple from one of the q^4 sources and 2 tuples from the other source, i.e. $q^4_{SIC} = \frac{1}{20} + 2 * \frac{1}{40} = 0.1$.

After iteration 4, all queries' SIC values converge to the same value as they are all equal to 0.1. However, the node has remaining capacity ($9 < 10$) to process one more tuple, and so the algorithm accepts one more tuple (i.e. randomly from q^2) to fully utilise the node. The algorithm terminates after iteration 5 at which point the number of accepted tuples reaches 10 and equals the node's capacity. Eventually, three of the queries have exactly the same SIC values i.e. $q^1_{SIC} = q^2_{SIC} = q^3_{SIC} = 0.1$ and $q^4_{SIC} = 0.133$.

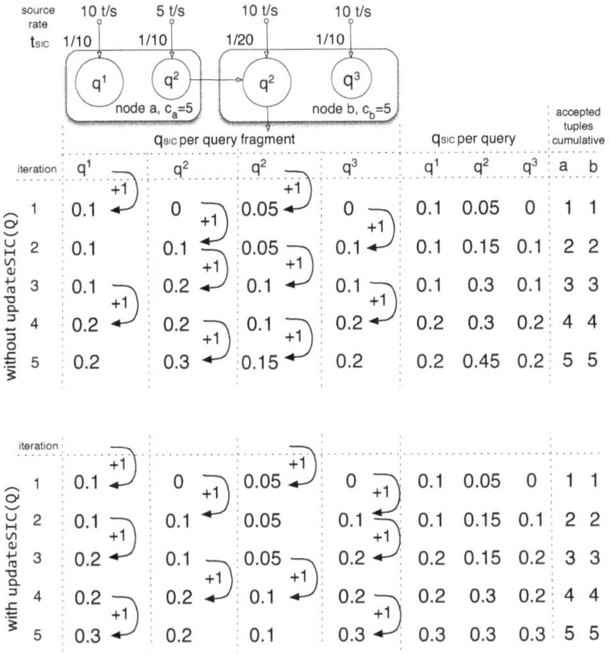

Figure 4: `selectTuplesToKeep()` on two nodes with c_a=5 and c_b=5 tuples

This example highlights that, in practice, the algorithm may not make all queries achieve exactly the same SIC values because of the involved node capacities and tuple rates, but it opportunistically tries to converge to equal SIC values.

5.2 FSPS Balance-SIC fairness

In the case of a multi-site FSPS, each node executes the same Algorithm 1 (lines 5–7). There are two main differences in the case of multi-fragment queries. First, the SIC value of a multi-fragment query is affected by the tuple shedding performed on other nodes. If such a query has the minimum SIC value among all co-located queries on the same node, the following problem emerges: all nodes running other fragments of these co-located queries attempt to maximise the SIC values of the same minimum SIC query, potentially overshooting and causing oscillations. To address this problem, the algorithm explicitly updates the result SIC value of the queries at each iteration so that all nodes eventually become aware of each other's shedding decisions (`updateSIC(`$\mathcal{Q}$`)` in line 20).

To better illustrate the use of `updateSIC(`$\mathcal{Q}$`)` for global convergence, we use the example in Figure 4 in which two nodes host three queries in total and query q^2 spans both nodes. The source rates of all queries and the nodes' capacities are shown in the figure. The top part of the figure illustrates the execution of the BALANCE-SIC without the use of the `updateSIC(`$\mathcal{Q}$`)` function. In each iteration, a node attempts to converge the SIC values of its running queries in isolation. In case of ties, the algorithm selects a query randomly. After iteration 5, the multi-fragment q^2 query has the highest result SIC value of all the single-fragment queries, and they all have different result SIC values ($q^2_{SIC} = 0.45 > q^1_{SIC} = 0.2 = q^3_{SIC} = 0.2$). This is because each node compares only the SIC values of the fragments of its hosted queries.[2]

[2]We consider that fragments of a query graph have the same structure. The SIC value of a fragment corresponds to the SIC value of the downstream operator, which outputs the tuples for the next downstream fragment in the case of multi-fragment queries, or the end-user in the case of a single-fragment query.

The bottom part of Figure 4 shows how the use of `updateSIC(`$\mathcal{Q}$`)` makes both nodes take informed shedding decisions for global convergence. At the end of each iteration, both nodes are updated with the result SIC values of their hosted queries and so become aware of each others' shedding decisions. In this case, the BALANCE-SIC algorithm converges and all result SIC values become equal ($q^1_{SIC} = q^2_{SIC} = q^3_{SIC} = 0.3$). The dissemination of the query SIC result values to the FSPS nodes hosting the query fragments for the use of `updateSIC(`$\mathcal{Q}$`)` is performed by the query coordinator described in §6.

In the description of the algorithm, we assumed no delays when updating the result SIC value of a query to the nodes hosting its query fragments: once a tuple is accepted by a query, its contribution to the result SIC value is assumed to be instantaneous (Assumption 3). This assumption is for the purposes of the explanation only—we provide a practical implementation in §6 to address delays, and our evaluation results that show that the algorithm works well with delayed updates in practice.

The second issue with multi-fragment queries is that an accepted tuple on a node from a multi-fragment query may be discarded by another node downstream, thus wasting processing resources at an upstream node. Rather than using back-pressure [44], our algorithm uses the actual SIC values of tuples to select the highest available value. Since, in our model, the SIC metric captures the importance of tuples, i.e. the higher the SIC value, the more important is the tuple, the algorithm thus always keeps the most valuable tuples ($\max(x_{SIC})$ in line 16).

The BALANCE-SIC algorithm aims to converge the SIC values of all queries by exploiting the overlap of queries fragments across nodes and by allowing each node to take informed shedding decisions based on the result SIC values of its hosted queries. In this way, nodes become aware of each others shedding decisions and converge to global fairness across the set of FSPS queries without centralised coordination. Our work considers FSPS in which all nodes are implicitly connected through the fragmentation of queries. This means that any accepted tuple on a node eventually affects the shedding on any other node transitively.

6. BALANCE-SIC FAIRNESS IMPLEMENTATION

Next we describe the integration of the BALANCE-SIC fairness approach with our FSPS system called THEMIS. THEMIS implements the performance model from §4 and associates stream tuples with meta-data about their SIC value. It uses this information for shedding decisions according to the BALANCE-SIC fairness. This section focusses on the practical aspects of the BALANCE-SIC fairness approach. In particular, we explain how to weaken our previous assumptions and, in §7, we will give experimental evidence on the convergence of the BALANCE-SIC algorithm. Figure 5 provides an overview of the architecture of a typical THEMIS node.

STW approximation. §4 introduced the STW concept as an interval, which captures the relationship between source and result tuples. The duration of the STW should exceed the end-to-end processing latency of the system in order to allow source tuples to be processed by all downstream operators. To model the continuous nature of stream processing and the generation of tuples from sources, THEMIS uses the concept of a *sliding window* to implement a STW, i.e. the STW logically slides continuously over time. This approximation allows us to handle the continuous generation of source tuples, relating them to result tuples.

There is a trade-off: the larger the STW size, the more unnecessary source tuples are part of it, i.e. ones that do not contribute to a

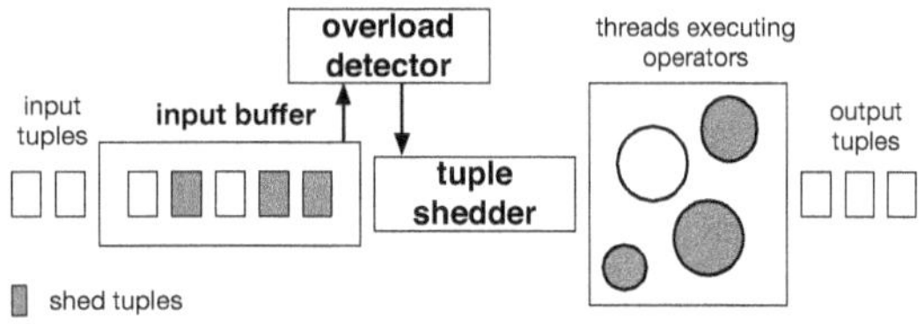

Figure 5: Architecture of a typical single THEMIS node

given result tuple. We find empirically that a STW that is an order-of-magnitude larger than the end-to-end processing delay and has a small slide, leads to an acceptable SIC precision. Furthermore, a large STW allows more tuples and therefore more queries to be selected by the BALANCE-SIC algorithm for global convergence.

SIC maintenance. In THEMIS, tuples are associated with SIC values. Based on a relational streaming model [8], each tuple has *fields* of a given schema. When an operator atomically outputs multiple tuples, they are grouped together into a *batch*. A batch contains a sequence of tuples preceded by a single header with the following fields: (a) the SIC value; (b) a unique identifier of the query that these tuples belong to; and (c) a timestamp of the tuple creation, in case of source tuples, or, of their generation, for derived tuples.

The assignment of SIC values to source tuples is performed as per Equation (1), which requires the number of source tuples per source per STW $\mathcal{T}_s^{\mathcal{S}}$ and the number of sources. Although the number of sources $\mathcal{S}$ per query is known a-priori—we consider queries with fixed sources—calculating the number of tuples in $\mathcal{T}_s^{\mathcal{S}}$ poses a challenge when source rates are unknown and time-varying. THEMIS uses the STW approximation of sliding windows to update the SIC values of all source tuples per slide online, before passing these for processing to downstream operators. By using a large STW and small slides, THEMIS can accurately capture time-changing source rates, thus providing a practical solution to relax Assumption 2 (see §5.1).

The assignment of SIC values to derived tuples is performed as per Equation (3), which requires the sets of input and output tuples. These groups are identified easily for tumbling windows before an operator emits tuples atomically for processing. In the case of sliding windows, we also provide a practical way to divide the SIC value of an input tuple across all its derived tuples per slide.

The dissemination of query result SIC values to nodes that host query fragments (i.e. `updateSIC()` in Algorithm 1) is performed by a logically-centralised *query coordinator* component. It is instantiated when a new query is deployed, and it is responsible for the query management during its lifecycle.

Overload detection. Each THEMIS node has an *input buffer* (IB) queue (Figure 5) in which all incoming tuples await processing. When the tuple arrival rate exceeds the node's capacity, the size of the IB grows, and the node overloads. To address overload, a node has an *overload detector* and a *tuple shedder* component.

The overload detector periodically checks the size of the IB. When its size exceeds a threshold c, the overload invokes the tuple shedder to discard excess tuples from the IB. The IB threshold represents the number of tuples that the node can process during a shedding interval. Its value changes and is estimated online based on a *cost model*. The tuple shedder discards batches until the size of the remaining tuples in the IB reaches c, as in Algorithm 1.

In case a node is momentarily not overloaded, THEMIS processes all tuples for all hosted queries. In this case, the BALANCE-SIC algorithm is independently invoked on all other overloaded nodes to balance SIC values across all FSPS nodes.

Cost model. The IB threshold depends on the properties of the operators. We adopt a cost model to calculate the average processing time spent on a tuple (see Assumption 1 in §5.1). This is calculated based on the number of processed tuples between successive invocations of the overload detector. We use a moving average over past estimations to calculate the average time required to process a tuple. Based on the time until the next invocation of the shedder, we estimate c. Our cost model works independently from the node's hardware capacity. It estimates online the processing capacity of any node as the average processing time per tuple. More complex cost models [37, 26] have been proposed, but they only apply to specific operator semantics.

Tuple shedder. The tuple shedder executes Algorithm 1 in each shedding interval. The interval is a fixed configuration parameter and sets a bound on the maximum waiting time of tuples in the IB. For low latency processing, it should be set to a short interval, e.g. a few hundred milliseconds. Setting a very low threshold, however, incurs a higher overhead. In §7.2, we evaluate the impact of the shedding interval on BALANCE-SIC fairness.

To reduce the impact of delays when disseminating the result SIC values by the query coordinator to nodes hosting query fragments, the load shedder estimates the result SIC values of queries based on its local shedding. The shedder assumes that all batches in the IB are discarded and then estimates the effect of discarding them on the result SIC values. It subtracts the sum of the SIC values of batches from the current updated query result SIC. In this way, it projects the effect that its shedding will have on the result SIC value. Furthermore, the periodic invocation of the shedder enables it to make informed decisions across a STW in a step-by-step fashion. In this way, THEMIS captures the real-time nature of tuple processing and any further downstream shedding that must consider the query result SIC value. The above heuristics enables us to address Assumption 3 (see §5.2) on zero delays between shedding and updating the result SIC values. Evaluation results show that FSPS queries converge to BALANCE-SIC fairness.

7. EVALUATION

We now evaluate the BALANCE-SIC fair processing under overload in an FSPS. The goals of the evaluation are to demonstrate:

1. the **correlation of the SIC metric with result correctness** when query processing is degraded due to load shedding (§7.1). The results show that the SIC metric captures result correctness across different types of queries and data distributions;
2. the **effectiveness of the BALANCE-SIC fairness algorithm** in reducing the spread of SIC values across queries (§7.2). The results show that our approach is fairer than random shedding: for a mixture of multi-fragment queries deployed across 18 nodes, it has a 33% higher Jain's Fairness Index metric. We also demonstrate convergence for different shedding intervals;
3. the **scalability of the fairness algorithm** (§7.3). We show that the algorithm maintains fair query shedding with an increasing number of nodes and queries;
4. the **impact on burstiness and wide-area networks** (§7.4) in applying BALANCE-SIC fairness is minimal;
5. the **comparison against related work** (§7.5). We show that our approach outperforms [34] and works agnostically in terms of the output utility function as opposed to [44], which leads to fairer allocations in complex deployments; and
6. the **overhead of our fair shedder implementation** (§7.6). We provide evidence that the load shedder increases the execution time of a base random shedder by only 11%.

Experimental set-up. We use queries from two workloads, an *aggregate* and a *complex* workload as described in Table 1. Aggre-

Aggregate workload
AVG: average value of tuples every sec: `Select Avg(t.v) from Src[Range 1 sec]`
MAX: maximum value of tuples every sec: `Select Max(t.v) from Src[Range 1 sec]`
COUNT: no of tuples with values $\geq$ 50 every sec. `Select Count(t.v) from Src[Range 1 sec] Having t.v` $\geq$ 50
Complex workload
AVG-all: average CPU usage of nodes every sec. `Select Avg(t.v) from AllSrc[Range 1 sec]`, (13 ops)
TOP-5: top 5 nodes with largest available CPU and free memory $\geq$ 100 MB every sec. `Select Top5(AllSrcCPU.id) From AllSrcCPU[Range 1 sec], AllSrcMem[Range 1 sec] Where AllSrcMem.free >= 100,000 and AllSrcCPU.id = AllSrcMem.id`, (29 ops)
COV: covariance of CPU usage of two nodes every sec. `Select Cov(SrcCPU1.value, SrcCPU2.value) SrcCPU1[Range 1 sec], SrcCPU2[Range 1 sec]`, (5 ops)

Table 1: Queries in CQL-like [8] syntax. `Src` represents a single source stream. `AllSrc` shows the union of multiple streams. For the *complex* queries, the number of operators/fragment is shown.

Local test-bed	
Server spec.	3 servers with 1.8 Ghz CPU, 4 GB mem, Linux 2.6.27-17-server, 1 Gbps LAN
THEMIS *deployment*	1 source node, 1 query submission node, 1 processing node
source rate	400 tuples/sec in 5 batches/sec of 80 tuples/batch per source
Emulab test-bed	
Server spec.	25 servers with 3 Ghz CPU, 2 GB mem, Linux RedHat 9, 1 Gbps LAN
THEMIS *deployment*	3 source nodes, 3 query submission nodes, up to 18 processing nodes
source rate	150 tuples/sec in 3 batches/sec of 50 tuples/batch per source

Table 2: Set-up of experimental test-beds

gate queries operate on a single source and perform basic aggregate functions; the complex workload implements a set of queries for monitoring the health of data center servers. It consists of monitoring queries over multiple sources, composed of various operators including average, max, top-k, group-by, filter, join and covariance.

The queries from the complex workload are split into fragments for multi-site deployment, as follows. Each fragment connects to sources and contains the same operators, performing equivalent processing as a single-fragment query in an incremental fashion. An AVG-all fragment connects to 10 sources; a TOP-5 fragment connects to 20 sources; and a COV fragment connects to 2 sources. The number of operators per fragment are shown in Table 1. For example, the most complex TOP-5 fragment consists of 29 operators, i.e. 10 CPU source data receivers, 10 memory receivers, 1 filter, 3 time windows, 2 averages, 1 join, 1 top-k and 1 output operator.

The query graphs, when running, are organised in two different ways: (1) in the case of the AVG-all query, a root fragment is connected to all other fragments and centrally aggregates partial results towards the final result forming a tree; and (2) for TOP-5 and COV queries, fragments form a chain, and the last fragment in the chain outputs the query result. Such graphs enable us to evaluate the effect of downstream shedding and the estimation of the result SIC values by the tuple shedder across two different query graphs.

Queries process either *synthetic* or *real-world* datasets. The data in the *synthetic* dataset follows either a *gaussian*, *uniform* or *exponential* distribution, with a mean of 50. We also use a *mixed* synthetic dataset, with values randomly chosen from any of the previous distributions. The *real-world* dataset are measurements of CPU and memory-related utilisation from PlanetLab nodes, as recorded by the CoTop project [36].

Table 2 describes our two *local* and *Emulab* [2] test-beds. We use the local test-bed for the SIC correlation to result correctness. We use the Emulab test-bed for the fairness and scalability experiments where all nodes are located within the same 100-Mbps LAN with a star topology and 5 ms of delay between nodes.

In all experiments, we set the STW duration to 10 secs and the shedding interval to 250 ms. The size of the STW should be set to an order of magnitude larger than the end-to-end processing delay across all queries, which emit new result tuples every 1 sec. We determined empirically that larger STW values do not effect the correct query SIC calculation. We deploy 10 TOP-5 queries with two fragments, and we measure their SIC values over STW set to 10 and 100 secs. In these underloaded cases, results show that the average SIC values across queries correctly measure perfect processing: 0.9700 ± 0.0064 and 1.0086 ± 0.0034, respectively. Therefore, we set the duration of the STW to 10 sec. In the rest of the paper, we report results over 5 minutes of execution after query deployment.

7.1 SIC Correlation

When using the SIC metric to provide feedback on processing quality, it is important that its value is correlated with the result error: a higher SIC value should indicate that the query result is *closer* to the perfect result.

We evaluate this correlation for different types of queries and source data. We use the local test-bed to deploy queries from the aggregate workload and the TOP-5 and COV queries from the complex workload. For each query type, we increase the number of queries on a single node to emulate different degrees of overload. For the aggregate workload and the COV queries, the source rate is 400 tuples/sec and, for the TOP-5 query, it is 20 tuples/sec. The node uses a shedder that discards tuples randomly every 250 ms.

Figure 6 shows the correlation between the result correctness and the SIC values for the aggregate workload. We quantify correctness by comparing to perfect processing. We report the *mean absolute error*, which quantifies the relative distance of the degraded result values, $\tilde{t}_{\mathcal{V}}^{r}$ from the perfect values, $t_{\mathcal{V}}^{r}$ for all result tuples n:

$$\left(\sum_{\forall t^r} \left| \frac{\tilde{t}_{\mathcal{V}}^{r} - t_{\mathcal{V}}^{r}}{t_{\mathcal{V}}^{r}} \right| \right) / n$$

The results show that, when the SIC values increase, the error decreases, which indicates that the degraded results approach the perfect results. Depending on the query type, this correlation is stronger (e.g. for COUNT) or weaker (e.g. for AVG).

For the AVG query in Figure 6(a), we observe small changes in the error after shedding because the average value of the underlying data distribution does not significantly change. For the COUNT query in Figure 6(b), however, the error is substantially higher because degraded processing discards tuples proportionally to the overload condition. For the MAX query, there is a small error for the synthetic dataset, which increases for the mixed and real-world datasets. As for the AVG query, the maximum value of the synthetic dataset does not change significantly when some data is discarded, which is not the case for the real-world dataset.

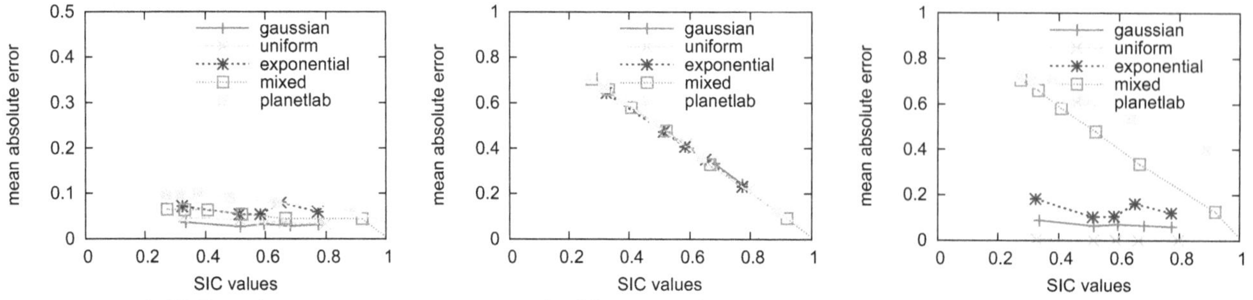

(a) AVG queries (b) COUNT queries (c) MAX queries

Figure 6: Correlation of SIC metric with result correctness for the aggregate query workload

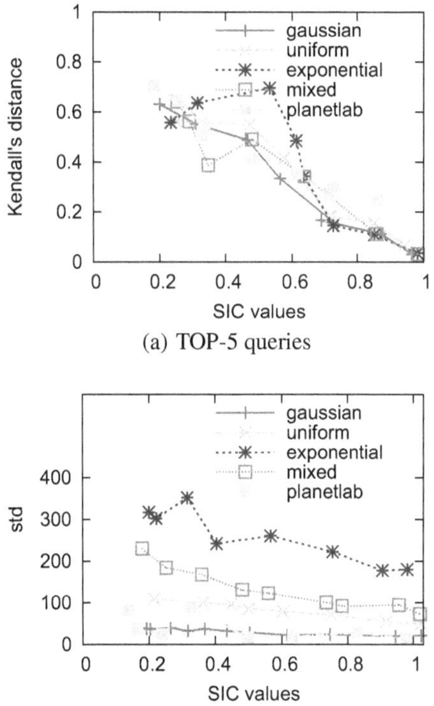

(a) TOP-5 queries

(b) COV queries

Figure 7: SIC correlation with results for the complex workload

Next, we consider the SIC correlation for the complex workload. For the TOP-5 query, we calculate the error between perfect and degraded results using the Kendall's distance metric [18]. It counts the differences—i.e. permutations and elements in only one list—of pairs of distinct elements between two lists. We plot the normalised Kendall's distance with a maximum error of 1.

For the COV query, we discard source data at random, which produces a series of sample covariance values. Since these values are random, their expected value should match the real covariance, obtained through perfect processing. We can estimate the deviation of the values from the perfect value through the standard deviation.

The results in Figure 7 show that there is a significant correlation. As the result SIC value increases, the distance/error to the perfect result decreases. For example, the TOP-5 query shows similar behaviour across synthetic and real-world datasets. For the COV query, the error is more prominent in the real-world than the synthetic dataset because discarding values from the synthetic distribution does not significantly change the covariance of the distribution.

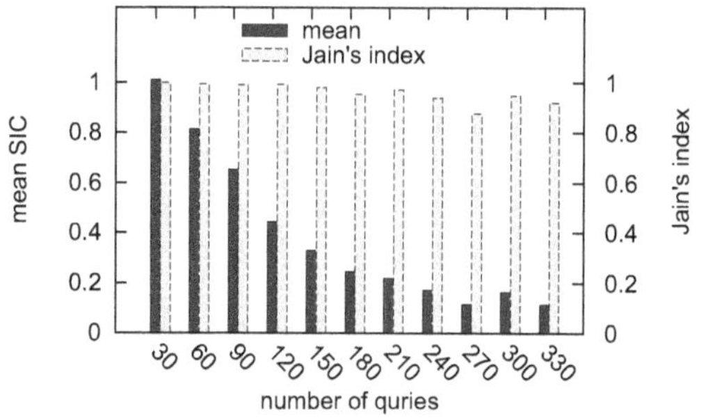

Figure 8: Single-node fairness

7.2 Balance-SIC Fairness

Next we evaluate the effectiveness of the BALANCE-SIC fairness approach to converge the result SIC values of queries. We start by validating that our approximation of the STW allows the algorithm to converge to BALANCE-SIC fairness on a single node. We also explore the behaviour of the algorithm for different shedding intervals. We continue to evaluate our approach in the case of a multi-node deployment, comparing to the baseline of random shedding. Finally, we study the effect of the ratio of multi-fragmented queries on the level of achieved fairness.

To measure the effectiveness of the BALANCE-SIC fairness approach, we use the *Jain's Fairness Index metric* [25]:

$$\text{Jain's index} := \frac{\left(\sum_{\forall q \in \mathcal{Q}} q_{\text{SIC}}\right)^2}{|\mathcal{Q}| * \sum_{\forall q \in \mathcal{Q}} (q_{\text{SIC}})^2},$$

where $\mathcal{Q}$ is the set of queries executed by the FSPS. Intuitively, the metric captures the proportion of queries whose differences in SIC values are small. The Jain's index values range from $1/|\mathcal{Q}|$ to 1; the higher the value, the fairer the system. When its value is 1, all queries have the same result SIC value.

Source time window approximation. We first explore the convergence of our algorithm to BALANCE-SIC fairness, validating the use of sliding window STW (see §6). We deploy queries of the complex workload on a local test-bed node. Over the course of this experiment, we did not observe any oscillation of SIC values and the standard deviation of values remained low.

Figure 8 shows that, with more queries, the load on the node increases, and the mean SIC values across queries decreases when more tuples are discarded. Our approach equalises the SIC values as shown by the Jain's index values close to 1. These results indicate that, even under extreme overload, i.e. when the total incoming input rate for all queries is 528,000 tuples/sec, the mean SIC value drops to values around 0.1 and the majority of the tuples are dropped, our approach can enforce fairness across queries.

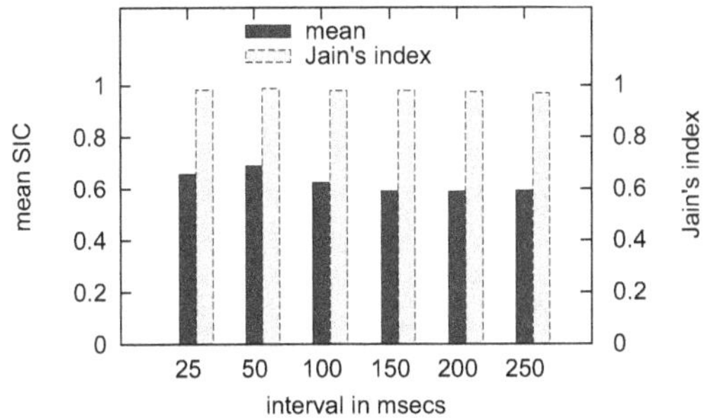

Figure 9: Shedding interval

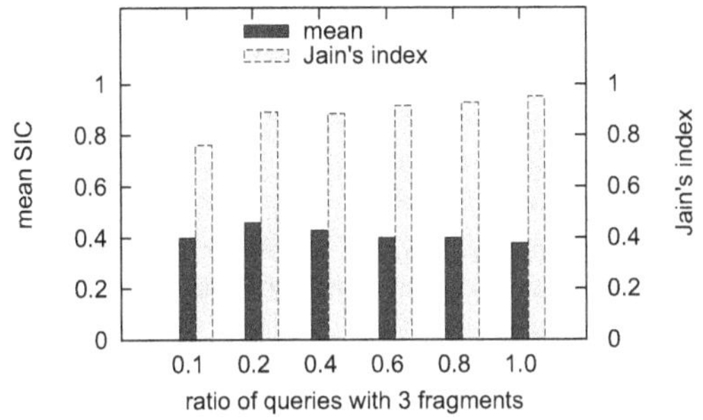

Figure 11: Fairness for multi-fragmented queries

Shedding interval. We study the effect of different shedding intervals, as shown in Figure 9. The shedding interval corresponds to the slide of the STW. In each case, we deploy 200 queries from the complex workload on 6 nodes, and each query has between 1 and 3 fragments. The results show that our algorithm achieves fair shedding regardless of the shedding interval, as shown by the close values for the mean and high values Jain's index metric.

BALANCE-SIC fairness across multiple nodes. Next, we deploy our fair shedding approach across 18 nodes. As we do not know the optimal fairness solution, we compare against random shedding as a practical baseline. We deploy multi-fragment, complex queries. We report results as we vary the number of fragments per query from 1 to 6 and when queries have a random number of fragments between 1 and 6 (mixed case). In all cases, the total number of fragments is the same, approximately 2,000.

Figure 10 shows that the BALANCE-SIC fair shedder provides a fairer solution in all cases compared to the random shedder. For the most realistic mixed workload, BALANCE-SIC is 33% better than the random approach, according to the Jain's index. In addition, BALANCE-SIC reduces the spread of SIC values across queries, as shown by the standard deviation (std) in Figure 10(b). The BALANCE-SIC shedder accepts tuples from the most degraded queries while it sheds tuples from the least degraded ones. In doing so, it better utilises resources towards processing more valuable source tuples, as supported by the increased mean SIC values in Figure 10(c). In contrast, the random shedder blindly sheds tuples regardless of their upstream processing.

Multi-fragmentation. We rely on query fragmentation to achieve our fairness. We study the effect that different ratios of multi-fragmented queries have. We vary the ratio of three-fragment over single-fragment queries from the complex workload across 10 nodes. The total number of fragments is about 2,000, and each node has roughly the same load. Figure 11 shows that, when more queries are multi-fragmented, the BALANCE-SIC fairness algorithm converges to a fairer system, as more queries span nodes.

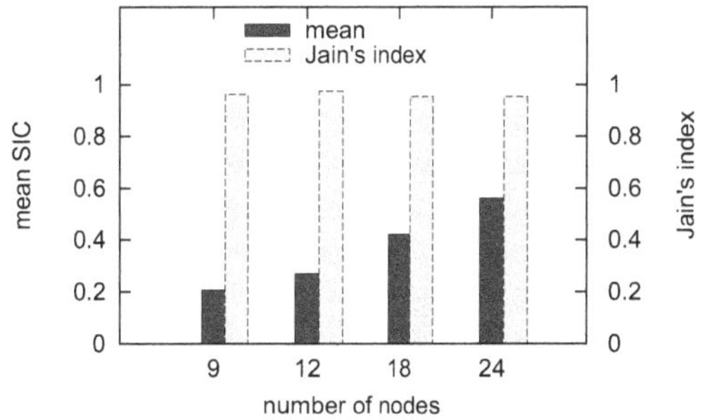

Figure 12: Fairness for increasing number of nodes

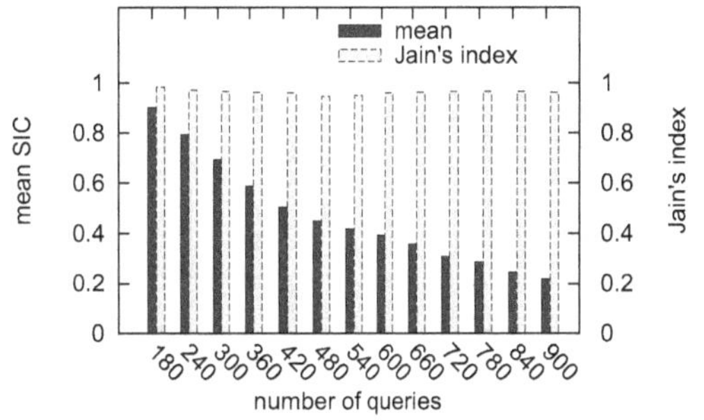

Figure 13: Fairness for increasing number of queries

7.3 Scalability

Next we evaluate the scalability of the BALANCE-SIC fairness algorithm. First we increase the number of nodes while hosting a constant number of 500 queries. We deploy queries from the complex workload and vary their fragments randomly from 1 to 6. Fragments are deployed according to a Zipf distribution.

As shown in Figure 12, BALANCE-SIC manages to utilise the increasing number of nodes as the mean SIC values increase. In all cases, our approach sheds tuples fairly, as the Jain's index metric approaches to 1. In Figure 13, we increase the number of queries for a fixed deployment on 18 nodes. The results show that, with more queries, tuples are discarded fairly. This is even the case when the large number of queries strain the resources of the system, decreasing the mean SIC value.

7.4 Burstiness and wide-area networks

We evaluate BALANCE-SIC fairness with bursty sources over a wide-area network, referred to as FSPS. We deploy THEMIS over a network with 4 nodes, and we emulate wide-area latencies between nodes of 50 ms. To introduce bursty source rates, we modify sources so that 10% of the time they generate tuples at 10× their normal rate. We also deploy queries on a LAN without burstiness as a baseline. We deploy queries from the complex workload with two query fragments, which are randomly assigned to nodes.

Figure 14 shows the average SIC values of queries after carrying out BALANCE-SIC shedding. The results show that, regardless of the deployment set-up, the average SIC values remain similar. This indicates that THEMIS can achieve BALANCE-SIC fairness in the presence of bursty sources and variation in nodes' latency.

7.5 Comparison against related work

We compare against the work on distributed data stream processing allocation from [34] and [44]. Both formulate a centralised optimisation problem: [34] maximises the sum of the outputs of weighted queries, and [44] maximises the sum of the utilities of query outputs. Both approaches rely on a-priori knowledge of query

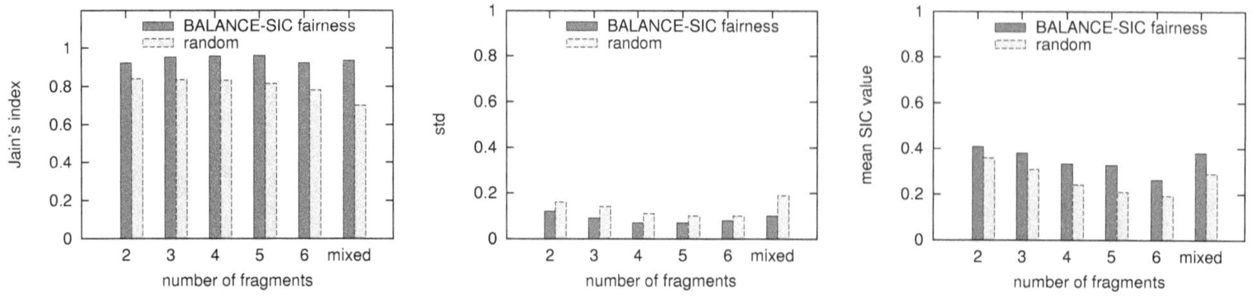

(a) Jain's index (b) std (c) mean

Figure 10: Comparison of BALANCE-SIC fairness against random tuple shedding

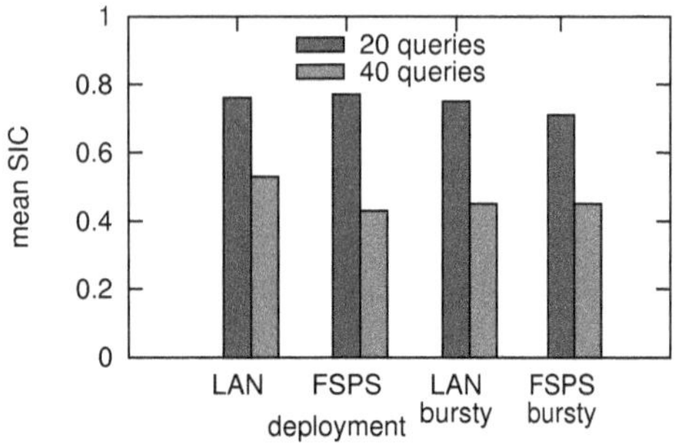

Figure 14: Fairness with source burstiness and wide-area latencies

parameter values. To address this limitation, we use the THEMIS cost model to calculate any unknown values.

We formulate the centralised problem of a fixed query deployment that closely matches the simple set-up used in the evaluation of [34]. It consists of two nodes and multiple two-operator queries in which all operators connecting to sources are collocated on the same node. We use 60 AVG-all queries of two fragments running on 2 nodes. As in [34], we use the GLPK tool to solve the optimisation problem. The optimal solution allows 3 out of the 60 queries to process all of their input tuples: one query discards a fraction of its input tuples; and all the other queries discard all of their tuples, which is clearly not a fair solution. This optimisation problem is not formulated to balance the throughput across queries (although all queries weights are set to 1).

To compare with [44], we first solve the problem for the same simple set-up of [34] as above, using the formulation of [44] and logarithmic output utility functions. For this simple set-up, [44] yields a fair solution as our approach. We further compare using a complex deployment of 20 AVG-all queries (3 fragments each), 20 COV and 20 TOP-5 queries (2 fragments each), and randomly deploying their fragments on 4 nodes. The solution of [44] is obtained using Matlab and the Jain's fairness index for the resulting utilities' distribution (normalised log-output rates) equals 0.87. This solution is less fair than our BALANCE-SIC solution where the Jain's fairness index for the resulting SIC values equals to 0.97, which is close to perfect fairness. Note that the solutions based on [34] are only applicable to concave utility functions.

Both approaches [34, 44] aim to solve the distributed shedding problem for specific deployments, and they rely on a-priori knowledge of values. Although [44] gives a fair allocation in simple deployments, with complex deployments and varying workloads, BALANCE-SIC provides a fairer allocation.

7.6 Overhead

We finally consider the overhead of BALANCE-SIC in terms of additional meta-data bytes and shedder execution time. In our prototype implementation, we use 10 bytes to store the SIC value per batch, which is a small amount compared to actual stream data.

In addition, our fair load shedder increases execution time only insignificantly compared to a random shedder. The average execution time per batch spent by the fair and the random shedders for the mixed workload (see Figure 10) are 0.088 ± 0.26 msec and 0.079 ± 0.32 ms, respectively. In summary, the BALANCE-SIC shedder incurs a 11% overhead.

Finally, each query coordinator submits the result SIC values to a query fragment as needed by `updateSIC()` in Algorithm 1. This creates a message of 30 bytes, which is sent at regular intervals to all query fragments. In the evaluation, we used intervals of 250 ms to match the shedding interval for update shedding. The additional data sent between nodes because of this operation is negligible when compared to high tuple rates in data stream processing.

8. CONCLUSIONS

It will be increasingly important to handle long-lasting overload in federated stream processing systems (FSPSs). This requires new decentralised designs to provide fairness in queries processing.

We describe a new fairness model for FSPSs under overload. We associate tuples with their *source information content* (SIC), i.e. the amount of information from data sources that they contain. This approach quantifies the perceived contribution of a tuple, without being dependent on processing semantics. We provide evidence that the contribution of source tuples is correlated with the quality of query results. We provide a new definition of BALANCE-SIC processing fairness in the context of FSPSs according to SIC values and describe a distributed algorithm that enables individual sites in an FSPS to perform BALANCE-SIC fair tuple shedding, reducing the skew in experienced processing quality.

Acknowledgments. This research work was partially supported by the EPSRC DISSP grant (EP/F035217/1), and the U.S. Army Research Laboratory and the U.K. Ministry of Defence under Agreement Number W911NF-06-3-0001.

9. REFERENCES

[1] Astronomical Wide-field Imaging System for Europe. http://www.astro-wise.org/.

[2] Network Emulation Testbed. http://www.emulab.net.

[3] OGSA-DAI: Open Grid Services Architecture. http://ogsadai.org.uk/.

[4] D. J. Abadi, D. Carney, et al. Aurora: A New Model and Architecture for Data Stream Management. *VLDB*, 12(2), 2003.

[5] K. Aberer, M. Hauswirth, and A. Salehi. A Middleware for Fast and Flexible Sensor Network Deployment. In *VLDB*, 2006.

[6] S. Agarwal, H. Milner, A. Kleiner, A. Talwalkar, M. Jordan, S. Madden, B. Mozafari, and I. Stoica. Knowing when You'Re Wrong: Building Fast and Reliable Approximate Query Processing Systems. In *SIGMOD*, 2014.

[7] S. Agarwal, B. Mozafari, A. Panda, H. Milner, S. Madden, and I. Stoica. BlinkDB: Queries with Bounded Errors and Bounded Response Times on Very Large Data. In *EuroSys*, 2013.

[8] A. Arasu, S. Babu, and J. Widom. The CQL Continuous Query Language: Semantic Foundations and Query Execution. *VLDB*, 15(2), 2006.

[9] A. Avetisyan, R. Campbell, et al. Open Cirrus: A Global Cloud Computing Testbed. *Computer*, 43(4), 2010.

[10] B. Babcock, M. Datar, and R. Motwani. Load Shedding for Aggregation Queries over Data Streams. In *ICDE*, 2004.

[11] M. Balazinska, H. Balakrishnan, and M. Stonebraker. Contract-based Load Management in Federated Distributed Systems. In *NSDI*, 2004.

[12] I. Botan, Y. Cho, R. Derakhshan, N. Dindar, L. Haas, K. Kim, and N. Tatbul. Federated Stream Processing Support for Real-Time Business Intelligence Applications. In *Enabling Real-Time Business Intelligence*, volume 41. 2010.

[13] I. Botan, R. Derakhshan, N. Dindar, L. Haas, R. J. Miller, and N. Tatbul. SECRET: A Model for Analysis of the Execution Semantics of Stream Processing Systems. *PVLDB*, 3(1-2), 2010.

[14] I. Botan and Y. C. et al. Design and Implementation of the MaxStream Federated Stream Processing Architecture. Technical Report 632, ETH, 2009.

[15] D. Carney, U. Çetintemel, et al. Monitoring Streams: A New Class of Data Management Applications. In *VLDB*, 2002.

[16] K. Chakrabarti, M. Garofalakis, R. Rastogi, and K. Shim. Approximate Query Processing using Wavelets. *VLDB*, 10(2), 2001.

[17] A. Das, J. Gehrke, and M. Riedewald. Approximate Join Processing over Data Streams. In *SIGMOD*, 2003.

[18] R. Fagin, R. Kumar, and D. Sivakumar. Comparing top k lists. In *SODA*, 2003.

[19] H. Garrett. The Tragedy of the Commons. *Science*, 162(3859), 1968.

[20] B. Gedik, K.-L. Wu, and P. Yu. Efficient Construction of Compact Shedding Filters for Data Stream Processing. In *ICDE*, 2008.

[21] B. Gedik, K.-L. Wu, P. Yu, and L. Liu. GrubJoin: An Adaptive, Multi-Way, Windowed Stream Join with Time Correlation-Aware CPU Load Shedding. *TKDE*, 19(10), 2007.

[22] L. Golab and M. T. Özsu. Issues in Data Stream Management. *SIGMOD Rec.*, 32(2), 2003.

[23] A. Jain, E. Y. Chang, and Y.-F. Wang. Adaptive Stream Resource Management using Kalman Filters. In *SIGMOD*, 2004.

[24] N. Jain, P. Mahajan, et al. Network Imprecision: A New Consistency Metric for Scalable Monitoring. In *OSDI*, 2008.

[25] R. Jain, D. Chiu, and W.Hawe. A Quantitative Measure of Fairness and Discrimination for Resource Allocation in Shared Computer System. Technical Report 301, DEC, 1984.

[26] J. K. Jeffrey, J. F. Naughton, and S. D. Viglas. Evaluating Window Joins over Unbounded Streams. In *ICDE*, 2003.

[27] B. B. Mayur, B. Babcock, M. Datar, and R. Motwani. Load Shedding Techniques for Data Stream Systems. In *MPDS*, 2003.

[28] R. Motwani, J. Widom, et al. Query Processing, Resource Management, and Approximation in a Data Stream Management System. In *CIDR*, 2003.

[29] C. Olston, J. Jiang, and J. Widom. Adaptive Filters for Continuous Queries over Distributed Data Streams. In *SIGMOD*, 2003.

[30] F. Reiss and J. M. Hellerstein. Data Triage: An Adaptive Architecture for Load Shedding in TelegraphCQ. In *ICDE*, 2005.

[31] I. Schweizer, C. Meurisch, et al. Noisemap - Multi-tier Incentive Mechanisms for Participative Urban Sensing. In *PhoneSense*, 2012.

[32] N. Tatbul. Streaming Data Integration: Challenges and Opportunities. In *ICDEW*, 2010.

[33] N. Tatbul, U. Çetintemel, et al. Load Shedding in a Data Stream Manager. In *VLDB*, 2003.

[34] N. Tatbul, U. Çetintemel, and S. Zdonik. Staying FIT: Efficient Load Shedding Techniques for Distributed Stream Processing. In *VLDB*, 2007.

[35] N. Tatbul and S. Zdonik. Window-Aware Load Shedding for Aggregation Queries over Data Streams. In *VLDB*, 2006.

[36] The PlanetLab Consortium. PlanetLab. http://www.planetlab.org, 2004.

[37] S. Wang and E. Rundensteiner. Scalable Stream Join Processing with Expensive Predicates: Workload Distribution and Adaptation by Time-slicing. In *EDBT*, 2009.

[38] M. Wei, E. A. Rundensteiner, and M. Mani. Utility-Driven Load Shedding for XML Stream Processing. In *WWW*, 2008.

[39] M. Wei, E. A. Rundensteiner, and M. Mani. Achieving High Output Quality Under Limited Resources Through Structure-based Spilling in XML Streams. *PVLDB*, 3(1-2), 2010.

[40] J. Wolf, N. Bansal, et al. SODA: An Optimizing Scheduler for Large-Scale Stream-Based Distributed Computer Systems. In *Middleware*, 2008.

[41] C. H. Xia, D. Towsley, and C. Zhang. Distributed Resource Management and Admission Control of Stream Processing Systems with Max Utility. In *ICDCS*, 2007.

[42] Y. Xing, J.-H. Hwang, U. Çetintemel, and S. Zdonik. Providing Resiliency to Load Variations in Distributed Stream Processing. In *VLDB*, 2006.

[43] Y. Xing, S. Zdonik, and J.-H. Hwang. Dynamic Load Distribution in the Borealis Stream Processor. In *ICDE*, 2005.

[44] H. C. Zhao, C. H. Xia, Z. Liu, and D. Towsley. A Unified Modeling Framework for Distributed Resource Allocation of General Fork and Join Processing Networks. In *SIGMETRICS*, 2010.

SABER: Window-Based Hybrid Stream Processing for Heterogeneous Architectures

Alexandros Koliousis[†], Matthias Weidlich[†‡], Raul Castro Fernandez[†], Alexander L. Wolf[†], Paolo Costa[♮], Peter Pietzuch[†]

[†]Imperial College London [‡]Humboldt-Universität zu Berlin [♮]Microsoft Research

{akolious, mweidlic, rc3011, alw, costa, prp}@imperial.ac.uk

ABSTRACT

Modern servers have become heterogeneous, often combining multi-core CPUs with many-core GPGPUs. Such heterogeneous architectures have the potential to improve the performance of data-intensive stream processing applications, but they are not supported by current relational stream processing engines. For an engine to exploit a heterogeneous architecture, it must execute streaming SQL queries with sufficient data-parallelism to fully utilise all available heterogeneous processors, and decide how to use each in the most effective way. It must do this while respecting the semantics of streaming SQL queries, in particular with regard to window handling.

We describe SABER, a *hybrid* high-performance relational stream processing engine for CPUs and GPGPUs. SABER executes window-based streaming SQL queries in a data-parallel fashion using all available CPU and GPGPU cores. Instead of statically assigning query operators to heterogeneous processors, SABER employs a new adaptive *heterogeneous lookahead scheduling* strategy, which increases the share of queries executing on the processor that yields the highest performance. To hide data movement costs, SABER pipelines the transfer of stream data between CPU and GPGPU memory. Our experimental comparison against state-of-the-art engines shows that SABER increases processing throughput while maintaining low latency for a wide range of streaming SQL queries with both small and large window sizes.

1. INTRODUCTION

The recent generation of stream processing engines, such as S4 [45], Storm [52], Samza [1], Infosphere Streams [13], Spark Streaming [56] and SEEP [17], executes data-intensive streaming queries for real-time analytics and event-pattern detection over high volumes of stream data. These engines achieve high processing throughput through *data parallelism*: streams are partitioned so that multiple instances of the same query operator can process *batches* of the stream data in parallel. To have access to sufficient parallelism during execution, these engines are deployed on shared-nothing clusters, scaling out processing across servers.

An increasingly viable alternative for improving the performance of stream processing is to exploit the parallel processing capability offered by *heterogeneous* servers: besides multi-core CPUs with dozens of processing cores, such servers also contain accelerators such as GPGPUs with thousands of cores. As heterogeneous servers have become commonplace in modern data centres and cloud offerings [24], researchers have proposed a range of parallel streaming algorithms for heterogeneous architectures, including for joins [36,51], sorting [28] and sequence alignment [42]. Yet, we lack the design of a *general-purpose* relational stream processing engine that can transparently take advantage of accelerators such as GPGPUs while executing arbitrary streaming SQL queries with windowing [7].

The design of such a streaming engine for heterogeneous architectures raises three challenges, addressed in this paper:

(1) When to use GPGPUs for streaming SQL queries? The speed-up that GPGPUs achieve depends on the type of computation: executing a streaming operator over a batch of data in parallel can greatly benefit from the higher degree of parallelism of a GPGPU, but this is only the case when the data accesses fit well with a GPGPU's memory model. As we show experimentally in §6, some streaming operators accelerate well on GPGPUs, while others exhibit lower performance than on a CPU. A streaming engine with GPGPU support must therefore make the right scheduling decisions as to which streaming SQL queries to execute on the GPGPU in order to achieve high throughput for arbitrary queries.

(2) How to use GPGPUs with streaming window semantics? While a GPGPU can naturally process a discrete amount of data in parallel, streaming SQL queries require efficient support for *sliding windows* [7]. Existing data-parallel engines such as Spark Streaming [56], however, tie the size of physical batches of stream data, used for parallel processing, to that of logical windows specified in the queries. This means that the window size and slide of a query impact processing throughput; current data-parallel engines, for example, struggle to support small window sizes and slides efficiently. A streaming engine with GPGPU support must instead support arbitrary windows in queries while exploiting the most effective level of parallelism without manual configuration by the user.

(3) How to reduce the cost of data movement with GPGPUs? In many cases, the speed-up achieved by GPGPUs is bounded by the data movement cost over the PCI express (PCIe) bus. Therefore, a challenge is to ensure that the data is moved to the GPGPU in a continuous fashion so that the GPGPU is never idle.

We describe the design and implementation of SABER, a **hybrid relational stream processing engine** in Java that executes streaming SQL queries on both a multi-core CPU and a many-core GPGPU to achieve high processing throughput. The main idea behind SABER is that, instead of offloading a fixed set of query operators to an accelerator, it adopts a *hybrid* execution model in which all query operators can utilise all *heterogeneous processors* in-

SIGMOD'16, June 26-July 01, 2016, San Francisco, CA, USA

DOI: http://dx.doi.org/10.1145/2882903.2882906

terchangeably. By "processor" we refer here to either an individual CPU core or an entire GPGPU. More specifically, SABER makes the following technical contributions:

Hybrid stream processing model. SABER takes a streaming SQL query and translates it to an operator graph. The operator graph is bundled with a batch of stream data to form a *query task* that can be scheduled on a heterogeneous processor. SABER's hybrid stream processing model then features two levels of data parallelism: (i) tasks run in parallel across the CPU's multiple cores and the GPGPU and (ii) a task running on the GPGPU is further parallelised across its many cores.

One approach for selecting the processor on which to run a given query operator is to build an offline performance model that predicts the performance of operators on each processor type. Accurate performance models, however, are hard to obtain, especially when the processing performance can change dynamically, e.g. due to skewed distributions of input data.

In contrast, SABER uses a new *heterogeneous lookahead scheduling (HLS)* algorithm: the scheduler tries to assign each task to the heterogeneous processor that, based on past behaviour, achieves the highest throughput for that task. If that processor is currently unavailable, the scheduler instead assigns a task to another processor with lower throughput that still yields an earlier completion time. HLS thus avoids the need for a complex offline model and accounts for changes in the runtime performance of tasks.

Window-aware task processing. When SABER executes query tasks on different heterogeneous processors, it supports sliding window semantics and maintains high throughput for small window sizes and slides. A *dispatcher* splits the stream into fixed-sized batches that include multiple fragments of windows processed jointly by a task. The computation of window boundaries is postponed until the task executes, thus shifting the cost from the sequential dispatching stage to the highly parallel task execution stage. For sliding windows, tasks perform incremental computation on the windows in a batch to avoid redundant computation.

SABER preserves the order of the result stream after the parallel, out-of-order processing of tasks by first storing the results in local buffers and then releasing them incrementally in the correct order as tasks finish execution.

Pipelined stream data movement. To avoid delays due to data movement, SABER introduces a *five-stage pipelining* mechanism that interleaves data movement and task execution on the GPGPU: the first three stages are used to maintain high utilisation of the PCIe bandwidth by pipelining the Direct Memory Access (DMA) transfers of batches to and from the GPGPU with the execution of associated tasks; the other two stages hide the memory latency associated with copying batches in and out of managed heap memory.

The remainder of the paper is organised as follows: §2 motivates the need for high-throughput stream processing and describes the features of heterogeneous architectures; §3 introduces our hybrid stream processing model; §4 describes the SABER architecture, focussing on its dispatching and scheduling mechanisms; and §5 explains how SABER executes query operators. The paper finishes with evaluation results (§6), related work (§7) and conclusions (§8).

2. BACKGROUND

2.1 High-throughput stream processing

Stream processing has witnessed an uptake in many application domains, including credit fraud detection [26], urban traffic management [9], click stream analytics [5], and data centre management [44]. In these domains, continuous streams of input data (e.g. transaction events or sensor readings) need to be processed in an online manner. The key challenge is to maximise processing *throughput* while staying within acceptable latency bounds.

For example, already in 2011, Facebook reported that a query for click stream analytics had to be evaluated over input streams of 9 GB/s, with a latency of a few seconds [49]. Credit card fraud detection systems must process up to 40,000 transactions per second and detect fraudulent activity within 25 ms to implement effective countermeasures such as blocking transactions [26]. In finance, the NovaSparks engine processes a stream of cash equity options at 150 million messages per second with sub-microsecond latency [46].

The queries for the above use cases can be expressed in a streaming relational model [7]. A stream is a potentially infinite sequence of relational *tuples*, and queries over a stream are window-based. A *window* identifies a finite subsequence of a stream, based on tuple count or time, which can be viewed as a relation. Windows may overlap—tuples of one window may also be part of subsequent windows in which case the window *slides* over the stream. Distinct subsequences of tuples that are logically related to the same set of windows are referred to as *panes* [41], i.e. a window is a concatenation of panes. Streaming relational query *operators*, such as projection, selection, aggregation and join, are executed per window.

To execute streaming relational queries with high throughput, existing stream processing engines exploit parallelism: they either execute different queries in parallel (*task parallelism*), or execute operators of a single query in parallel on different partitions of the input stream (*data parallelism*). The need to run expensive analytics queries over high-rate input streams has focused recent research efforts on data parallelism.

Current data-parallel stream processing engines such as Storm [52], Spark [56] and SEEP [17] process streams in a data-parallel fashion according to a *scale-out* model, distributing operator instances across nodes in a shared-nothing cluster. While this approach can achieve high processing throughput, it suffers from drawbacks: (i) it assumes the availability of compute clusters; (ii) it requires a high-bandwidth network that can transfer streams between nodes; (iii) it can only approximate time-based window semantics due to the lack of a global clock in a distributed environment; and (iv) the overlap between windows requires redundant data to be sent to multiple nodes or the complexity of a pane-based approach [11].

2.2 Heterogeneous architectures

In contrast to distributed cluster deployments, we explore a different source of parallelism for stream processing that is becoming increasingly available in data centres and cloud services: servers with *heterogeneous architectures* [10, 54]. These servers, featuring multi-core CPUs and accelerators such as GPGPUs, offer unprecedented degrees of parallelism within a single machine.

GPGPUs implement a *throughput-oriented architecture*. Unlike traditional CPUs, which focus on minimising the runtime of sequential programs using out-of-order execution, speculative execution and deep memory cache hierarchies, GPGPUs target embarrassingly parallel workloads, maximising total system throughput rather than individual core performance. This leads to fundamental architectural differences—while CPUs have dozens of sophisticated, powerful cores, GPGPUs feature thousands of simple cores, following the *single-instruction, multiple-data* (SIMD) model: in each cycle, a GPGPU core executes the same operation (referred to as a *kernel*) on different data. This simplifies the control logic and allows more functional units per chip: e.g. the NVIDIA Quadro K5200 has 2,304 cores and supports tens of thousands of threads [47].

GPGPU cores are grouped into streaming multi-processors (SM), with each SM supporting thousands of threads. Threads have their own dedicated sets of registers and access to high-bandwidth, shared on-chip memory. While modern CPUs hide latency by using a deep cache hierarchy, aggressive hardware multi-threading in GPGPUs allows latency to be hidden by interleaving threads at the instruction-level with near zero overhead. Therefore, GPGPU cores have only small cache sizes compared to CPUs: e.g. the NVDIA Quadro K5200 has a 64 KB L1 cache per SM and a 1,536 KB L2 cache shared by all SMs.

A dedicated accelerator typically is attached to a CPU via a PCIe bus, which has limited bandwidth.[1] For example, a PCIe 3.0 $\times 16$ bus has an effective bandwidth of approximately 8 GB/s. This introduces a fundamental throughput limit when moving data between CPU and GPGPU memory. Especially when data movements occur at a high frequency, as in streaming scenarios, care must be taken to ensure that these transfers happen in a pipelined fashion to avoid stalling the GPGPU.

The potential of GPGPUs for accelerating queries has been shown for traditional relational database engines. For example, Ocelot [32] is an in-memory columnar database engine that statically offloads queries to a GPGPU using a single "hardware-oblivious" representation. GDB [29] and HyPE [16] accelerate SQL queries by offloading data-parallel operations to GPGPUs. All these systems, however, target one-off queries instead of continuous streaming queries with window semantics.

2.3 Using GPGPUs for stream processing

The dataflow model of GPGPUs purportedly is a good match for stream processing. In particular, performing computation on a group of tuples that is laid out in memory linearly should greatly benefit from the SIMD parallelism of GPGPUs. At the same time, the scarcity of designs for relational stream processing engines on GPGPUs is evidence of a range of challenges:

Different acceleration potential. Not all stream processing queries experience a speed-up when executed on a GPGPU compared to a CPU. Any speed-up depends on a range of factors, including the amount of computation per stream tuple, the size of the tuples, any memory accesses to temporary state and the produced result size. For example, a simple projection operator that removes attributes from tuples typically is bottlenecked by memory accesses, whereas an aggregation operator with a complex aggregation function is likely to be compute-bound. This makes it challenging to predict if the performance of a given query can be improved by a GPGPU.

Existing proposals for accelerating traditional database queries (e.g. [37, 55]) assume that a comprehensive analytical model can establish the relation between a query workload and its performance on a heterogeneous processor. Based on such a performance model, they offload queries on a GPGPU either statically [32] or speculatively [29]. Fundamentally, performance models are vulnerable to inaccuracy, which means that they may not make the most effective use of the available accelerators, given an unknown query workload.

The challenge is to devise an approach that makes effective decisions as to which queries can benefit from GPGPU offloading.

Support for sliding windows. Any data-parallel stream processing must split streams into *batches* for concurrent processing, but each streaming SQL query also includes a window specification that affects its result. The batch size should thus be independent from the window specification—the batch size is a physical implementation parameter that determines the efficiency of parallel processing, whereas the window size and slide are part of the query semantics.

[1]Despite recent advances in integrated CPU/GPGPU designs [22, 30, 31], discrete GPGPUs have a substantial advantage in terms of performance and power efficiency.

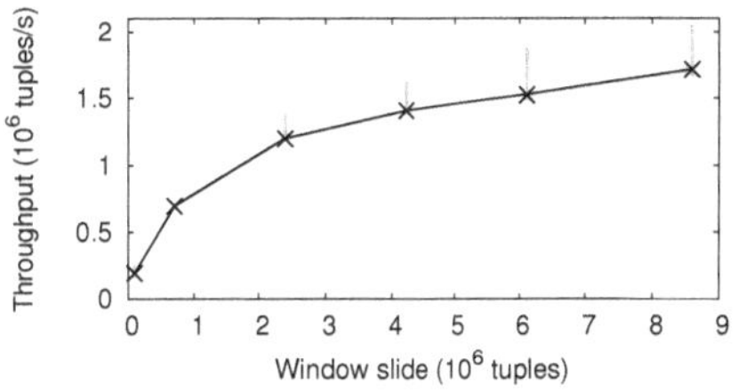

Figure 1: Performance of a streaming GROUP-BY query with a 5-second window and different window slides under Spark Streaming

Existing data-parallel engines, however, tie the definition of batches to that of windows because this simplifies window-based processing. For example, Spark Streaming [56] requires the window slide and the batch size to be a multiple of the window size, enabling parallel window computation to occur on different nodes in lockstep.

Such a coupling of batches and windows has a performance impact. In Fig. 1, we show the throughput of a streaming GROUP-BY query with a 5-second sliding window executing on Spark Streaming with a changing window slide. As the slide becomes smaller (i.e. there is more overlap between windows), the throughput decreases—when the batches are smaller, the parallel window processing becomes less efficient. This makes it infeasible to process queries with fewer than several million 64-byte tuples in each window slide while sustaining high throughput.

The challenge is how an engine can decouple batches and windows from each other and still ensure a consistently high throughput.

Cost of stream data movement. Since a stream processing engine processes continuous data, the bandwidth of the PCIe bus can limit the throughput of queries offloaded to the GPGPU. In particular, any data movement to and from the GPGPU causes a delay—a DMA-managed memory transfer from the CPU to the GPGPU takes around 10 microseconds [43], which is orders of magnitude slower than a CPU memory access.

The challenge is how an engine can amortise the delay of data movement to and from the GPGPU while processing data streams.

2.4 Stream data and query model

We assume a relational stream data model with window-based queries, similar to the *continuous query language* (CQL) [7].

Data streams. Let T be a universe of *tuples*, each being a sequence of values of primitive data types. A *stream* $S = \langle t_1, t_2, \ldots \rangle$ is an infinite sequence of such tuples, and T^* denotes the set of all streams. A tuple t has a timestamp, $\tau(t) \in \mathscr{T}$, and the order of tuples in a stream respects these timestamps, i.e. for two tuples t_i and t_j, $i < j$ implies that $\tau(t_i) \leq \tau(t_j)$. We assume a discrete, ordered time domain $\mathscr{T}$ for timestamps, given as the non-negative integers $\{0, 1, \ldots\}$. Timestamps refer to logical application time: they record when a given event occurred and not when it arrived in the system. There is only a finite number of tuples with equal timestamps.

Window-based queries. We consider queries that are based on *windows*, which are finite sequences of tuples. The set of all windows is $\hat{T}^* \subset T^*$, and the set of all, potentially infinite, sequences of windows is $(\hat{T}^*)^*$. A window-based query q is defined for n input streams by three components: (i) an n-tuple of *window functions* $\langle \omega_1^q, \ldots, \omega_n^q \rangle$, such that each function $\omega_i^q : T^* \to (\hat{T}^*)^*$, when evaluated over an input stream, yields a possibly infinite sequence of windows; (ii) a possibly compound n-ary *operator function* $f^q : (\hat{T}^*)^n \to \hat{T}^*$ that is applied to n windows, one per input stream, and produces a window result (a sequence of tuples); and (iii) a *stream function* $\phi^q : (\hat{T}^*)^* \to T^*$ that transforms a sequence of window results into a stream.

Common window functions define *count-* or *time-based* windows with a *window size* s and a *window slide* l: the window size determines the amount of enclosed data; the window slide controls the difference to subsequent windows. Let $S = \langle t_1, t_2, ...\rangle$ be a stream, and $\omega_{(s,l)}$ be a window function with size s and slide l that creates a sequence of windows $\omega_{(s,l)}(S) = \langle w_1, w_2, ...\rangle$. Given a window $w_i = \langle t_k, \dots, t_m\rangle, i \in \mathbb{N}$, if ω is count-based, then $m = k + s - 1$ and the next window is $w_{i+1} = \langle t_{k+l}, \dots, t_{m+l}\rangle$; if ω is time-based, then the next window is $w_{i+1} = \langle t_{k'}, \dots, t_{m'}\rangle$ such that $\tau(t_m) - \tau(t_k) \leq s$, $\tau(t_{m+1}) - \tau(t_k) > s$, $\tau(t_{k'}) - \tau(t_k) \leq l$, and $\tau(t_{k'+1}) - \tau(t_k) > l$. This model thus supports *sliding* ($l < s$) and *tumbling* windows ($l = s$). We do not consider predicate-based windows in this work.

Query operators. The above model allows for the flexible definition of an operator function that transforms a window into a window result, both being sequences of tuples. In this work, we support relational streaming operators [7], i.e. projection (π), selection (σ), aggregation (α) and θ-join ($\bowtie$). These operators interpret a window as a relation (i.e. the sequence is interpreted as a multi-set) over which they are evaluated. For the aggregation operator, we also consider the use of GROUP-BY clauses.

Operator functions may also be specified as *user-defined functions* (UDFs), which implement bespoke computation per window. An example of a UDF is an n-ary partition join, which takes as input an n-tuple of windows, one per input stream, and first partitions all windows based on tuple values before joining the corresponding partitions of the windows. Despite its similarity, a partition join cannot be realised with a standard θ-join operator.

Stream creation. Window results are turned into a stream by a stream function. We consider stream functions that are based on relation-to-stream operators [7]. The *RStream* function concatenates the results of windows under the assumption that this order respects the tuple timestamps: with $\langle w_1, w_2, ...\rangle$ as a sequence of window results, and $w_i = \langle t_{k_i}, \dots, t_{m_i}\rangle$ for $i \in \mathbb{N}$, the result stream is a sequence $S_R = \langle t_{k_1}, \dots, t_{m_1}, t_{k_2}, \dots, t_{m_2}, ...\rangle$. The *IStream* function considers only the tuples of a window result that were not part of the previous result: with $\langle \dots, t_{j_{i+1}}, \dots\rangle$ as the projection of w_{i+1} to all transitions $t_{j_{i+1}} \notin \{t_{k_i}, \dots, t_{m_i}\}$ that are not part of w_i, the result stream is $S_R = \langle t_{k_1}, \dots, t_{m_1}, \dots, t_{j_2}, \dots, t_{j_3}, \dots\rangle$.

Typically, specific operator functions are combined with particular stream functions [7]: using the IStream function with projection and selection operators gives intuitive semantics, whereas aggregation and θ-join operators are used with the RStream function. In the remainder, we assume these default combinations.

3. HYBRID STREAM PROCESSING MODEL

Our idea is to sidestep the problem of "when" and "what" operators to offload to a heterogeneous processor by introducing a *hybrid stream processing model*. In this hybrid model, the stream processing engine always tries to utilise *all* available heterogeneous processors for query execution opportunistically, thus achieving the aggregate throughput. In return, the engine does not have to make an early decision regarding which type of query to execute on a given heterogeneous processor, be it a CPU core or a GPGPU.

Query tasks. The hybrid stream processing model requires that each query can be scheduled on any heterogeneous processor, leaving the scheduling decision until runtime. To achieve this, queries are executed as a set of data-parallel *query tasks* that are runnable on either a CPU core or the GPGPU. For a query q with n input streams, a query task $v = (f^q, B)$ consists of (i) the n-ary operator function f^q specified in the query and (ii) a sequence of n *stream batches* $B = \langle b_1, \dots, b_n\rangle$, $b_i \in \hat{T}^*$, i.e. n finite sequences of tuples, one per input stream. We use $\iota(v) = q$ as a shorthand notation to refer to the query of task v (§4.2, Alg. 1).

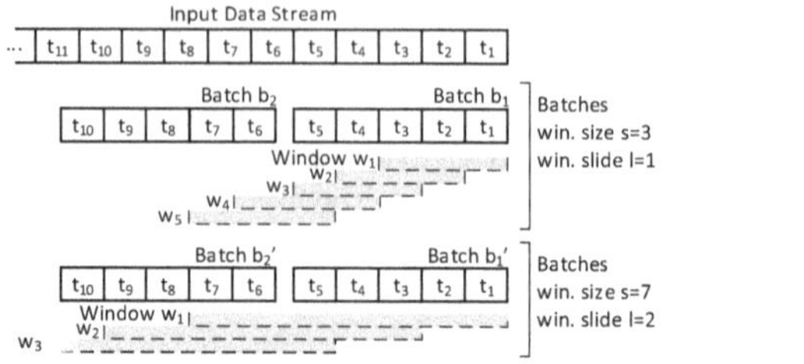

Figure 2: Stream batches under two different window definitions

The *query task size* φ is a system parameter that specifies how much stream data a query task must process, thus determining the computational cost of executing a task. Let $v = (f^q, B)$ with $B = \langle b_1, \dots, b_n\rangle$ be a query task, then the query task size is the sum $\Sigma_{i=1}^{n} |b_i|$ of the *stream batch sizes*. The size of a stream batch $b_i = \langle t_1, \dots, t_m\rangle$ is the data volume of its m tuples. The query task size equals the stream batch size in the case of single-input queries.

As we show experimentally in §6.4, a fixed query task size can in practice be chosen independently of the query workload, simply based on the properties of the stream processing engine implementation and its underlying hardware. There is a trade-off when selecting the query task size φ: a large size leads to higher throughput because it amortises scheduling overhead, exhibits more parallelism on the GPGPU and makes the transmission of query tasks to the GPGPU more efficient; on the other hand, a small size achieves lower processing latency because tasks complete more quickly.

Window handling. An important invariant under our hybrid model is that a stream batch, and thus a query task, are independent of the definition of windows over the input streams. Unlike pane-based processing [11,41], the size of a stream batch is therefore not determined by the window slide. This makes window handling in the hybrid model fundamentally different from that of existing approaches for data-parallel stream processing, such as Spark Streaming [56] or Storm [52]. By decoupling the parallelisation level (i.e. the query task) from the specifics of the query (i.e. the window definition), the hybrid model can support queries over fine-grained windows (i.e. ones with small slides) with full data-parallelism.

Fig. 2 shows the relationship between the stream batches of a query task and the respective window definitions from a query. In this example, stream batches contain 5 tuples. With a window definition of $\omega_{(3,1)}$, stream batch b_1 contains 3 complete windows, w_1, w_2, and w_3, and fragments of two windows, w_4 and w_5. The remaining tuples of the latter two windows are contained in stream batch b_2. For the larger window definition $\omega_{(7,2)}$, the first stream batch b'_1 contains only window fragments: none of w_1, w_2, and w_3 are complete windows. Instead, these windows also span across tuples in stream batch b'_2.

Operators. A stream batch can contain complete windows or only window fragments. Hence, the result of the stream query for a particular sequence of windows (one per input stream) is assembled from the results of multiple query tasks. That is, a window $w = \langle t_1, \dots, t_k\rangle$ of one of the input streams is partitioned into m *window fragments* $\{d_1, \dots, d_m\}$, $d_i \in \hat{T}^*$, such that the concatenation of the window fragments yields the window.

As shown in Fig. 3, this has consequences for the realisation of the n-ary operator function f^q: it must be decomposed into a *fragment operator* function f^q_f and an *assembly operator* function f^q_a. The fragment operator function $f^q_f : (\hat{T}^*)^n \to \hat{T}^*$ defines the processing for a sequence of n window fragments, one per stream, and yields a sequence of tuples, i.e. a window fragment result.

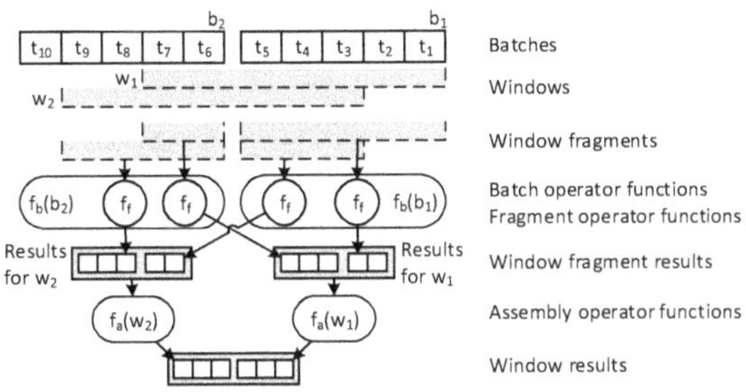

Figure 3: Example of computation based on window fragments

The assembly operator function $f_a^q : \hat{T}^* \rightarrow \hat{T}^*$ constructs the complete window result by combining the window fragment results from f_f^q. The composition of the fragment operator function f_f^q and the assembly operator function f_a^q yields the operator function f^q.

The decomposition of function f^q into functions f_f^q and f_a^q is operator-specific. For many associative and commutative functions (e.g. aggregation functions for count or max), both f_f^q and f_a^q are the original operator function f^q. For other functions, such as median, more elaborate decompositions must be defined [50].

The decomposition also introduces a synchronisation point in the data-parallel execution because the assembly function may refer to the results of multiple tasks. In §4.3, we describe how this synchronisation can be implemented efficiently by reusing threads executing query tasks to perform the assembly function.

Incremental computation. When processing a query task with a sliding window, it is more efficient to use *incremental computation*: the computation for a window fragment should exploit the results already obtained for preceding window fragments in the same batch.

The hybrid model captures this optimisation through a *batch operator* function $f_b^q : ((\hat{T}^*)^n)^m \rightarrow (\hat{T}^*)^m$ that is applied to a query task. The batch operator function takes as input m sequences of n window fragments, where n is the number of input streams and m is the maximum number of window fragments per stream batch in the task. It outputs a sequence of m window fragment results. The same result would be obtained by applying the fragment operator function f_f^q m-times to each of the m sequences of n window fragments.

Example. The effect of applying the hybrid stream processing model is shown in Fig. 3. Windows w_1 and w_2 span two stream batches, and they are processed by two query tasks. For each task, the batch operator function computes the results for the window fragments contained in that task. The assembly operator function constructs the window results from the window fragment results.

4. SABER ARCHITECTURE

We describe SABER, a relational stream processing engine for CPUs and GPGPUs that realises our hybrid stream processing model. We begin this section with an overview of the engine's architecture, and then explain how query tasks are dispatched (§4.1), scheduled (§4.2), and their results collected (§4.3).

Processing stages. The architecture of SABER consists of four stages controlling the lifecycle of query tasks, as illustrated in Fig. 4:

(i) A *dispatching* stage creates query tasks of a fixed size. These tasks can run on either type of processor and are placed into a single, system-wide queue.

(ii) A *scheduling* stage decides on the next task each processor should execute. SABER uses a new *heterogeneous lookahead scheduling* (HLS) algorithm that achieves full utilisation of all heterogeneous processors, while accounting for the different performance characteristics of query operators.

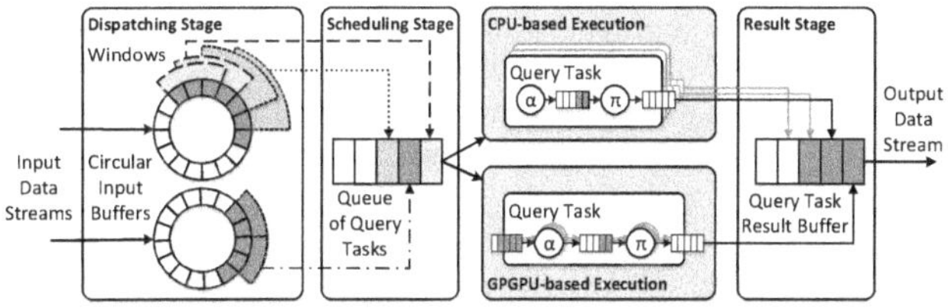

Figure 4: Overview of the Saber architecture

(iii) An *execution* stage runs the query tasks on a processor by evaluating the batch operator function on the input window fragments. A task executes either on one of the CPU cores or the GPGPU.

(iv) A *result stage* reorders the query task results that may arrive out-of-order due to the parallel execution of tasks. It also assembles window results from window fragment results by means of the assembly operator function.

Worker thread model. All four stages are executed by *worker threads*. Each worker is a CPU thread that is bound to a physical core, and one worker uses the GPGPU for the execution of query tasks. Worker threads handle the complete lifecycle of query tasks, which means that they are always fully utilised. This is in contrast to having separate threads for the dispatching or result stage, which could block due to out-of-order processing of query tasks.

Starting with the scheduling stage, the lifecycle of a worker thread is as follows: When a worker thread becomes idle, it invokes the scheduling algorithm to retrieve a task to execute from the system-wide task queue, indicating if it will execute the task on a CPU core or the GPGPU. The worker thread then executes the retrieved task on its associated heterogeneous processor. After task execution completes, the worker thread enters the result stage. In synchronisation with other worker threads, it orders window fragment results and, if possible, assembles complete window results from their fragments. Any assembled window results are then appended to the corresponding query's output data stream.

4.1 Dispatching of query tasks

Dispatching query tasks involves two steps: the storage of the incoming streaming data and the creation of query tasks. Query tasks are inserted into a system-wide queue to be scheduled for execution on the heterogeneous processors.

Buffering incoming data. To store incoming tuples, SABER uses a circular buffer per input stream and per query. By maintaining a buffer per query, processing does not need to be synchronised among the queries. Data can be removed from the buffer as soon as it is no longer required for query task execution.

The circular buffer is backed by an array, with pointers to the start and end of the buffer content. SABER uses byte arrays, so that tuples are inserted into the buffer without prior deserialisation. The implementation is lock-free, which is achieved by ensuring that only one worker thread inserts data into the buffer (worker threads are only synchronised in the result stage) and by explicitly controlling which data is no longer kept in the buffer. A query task contains a *start pointer* and an *end pointer* that define the respective stream batch. In addition, for each input buffer of a query, a query task contains a *free pointer* that indicates up to which position data can be released from the buffer.

A worker thread that executes a query task has only read-access to the buffer. Releasing data as part of the result stage, in turn, means moving the start pointer of the buffer to the position of the free pointer of a query task for which the results have been processed.

Query task creation. The worker thread that inserts data into a circular buffer also handles the creation of query tasks. Instead of first deserialising tuples and computing windows in the sequential dispatching stage, all window computation is handled by the highly parallel query execution stage.

In the dispatching stage, the data inserted into the buffer is added to the current stream batch and, as soon as the sum of stream batch sizes in all query input streams exceeds the query task size ϕ, a query task is created. A *query task identifier* is assigned to each task so that all tasks of a query are totally ordered. This permits the result stage to order the results of query tasks.

4.2 Scheduling of query tasks

The scheduling goal is to utilise all heterogeneous processors fully, yet to account for their different performance characteristics. The challenge is that the throughput of a given type of heterogeneous processor is query-dependent. Query tasks should therefore primarily execute on the processor that achieves the highest throughput for them. At the same time, overloading processors must be avoided because this would reduce the overall throughput. The scheduling decision must thus be query-specific and take the (planned) utilisation of the processors into account.

Instead of using a performance model, SABER observes the *query task throughput*, i.e. the number of query tasks executed per unit of time, defined per query and processor. Based on this, it estimates which processor type is preferred for executing a query task.

At runtime, the preferred processor may be busy executing other tasks. In such cases, SABER permits a task to execute on a non-preferred processor *as long as it is expected to complete before the preferred processor for that task would become available.*

Making scheduling decisions based on the observed task throughput has two advantages: (i) there is no need for hardware-specific performance models and (ii) the scheduling decisions are adaptive to changes in the query workload, e.g. when the selectivity of a query changes, the preferred processor for the tasks may also change. However, this approach assumes that the query behaviour is not too dynamic because, in the long term, the past execution of tasks must allow for the estimation of the performance of future tasks for a given query. Our experimental evaluation shows that this is indeed the case, even for workloads with dynamic changes.

Observing query task throughput. SABER maintains a matrix that records the relative performance differences when executing a query on a given type of processor. The *query task throughput*, denoted by $\rho(q,p)$, is defined as the number of query tasks of query q that can be executed per time unit on processor p. For the CPU, this value denotes the aggregated throughput of all CPU cores; for the GPGPU, it is the overall throughput including data movement overheads.

For a set of queries $Q = \{q_1, \ldots, q_n\}$ and two types of processors, $P = \{\text{CPU}, \text{GPGPU}\}$, we define the *query task throughput matrix* as

$$\mathscr{C} = \begin{pmatrix} \rho(q_1,\text{CPU}) & \rho(q_1,\text{GPGPU}) \\ \vdots & \vdots \\ \rho(q_n,\text{CPU}) & \rho(q_n,\text{GPGPU}) \end{pmatrix}.$$

Intuitively, in each row of this matrix, the column with the largest value indicates the preferred processor (highest throughput) for the query; the ratio $r = \rho(q,\text{CPU})/\rho(q,\text{GPGPU})$ is the speed-up ($r > 1$) or slow-down ($r < 1$) of the CPU compared to the GPGPU.

The matrix is initialised under a uniform assumption, with a fixed value for all entries. It is then continuously updated by measuring the number of tasks of a query that are executed in a certain time span on a particular processor. Based on the average time over a fixed set of task executions, the throughput is computed and updated.

Algorithm 1: Hybrid lookahead scheduling (HLS) algorithm

input : $\mathscr{C}$, a query task throughput matrix over $Q = \{q_1, \ldots, q_n\}$ and $P = \{\text{CPU},\text{GPGPU}\}$,
$p \in \{\text{CPU},\text{GPGPU}\}$, the processor for which a task shall be scheduled,
$w = \langle v_1, \ldots, v_k \rangle$, $k > 1$, a queue of query tasks, $\iota(v_i) \in Q$ for $1 \leq i \leq k$,
$count : Q \times P \rightarrow \mathbb{N}$, a function assigning a number of executions per query and processor,
st, a switch threshold.
output: $v \in \{v_1, \ldots, v_k\}$ - the query task selected for execution on processor p

```
1  pos ← 1 ;                                  // Initialise position in queue
2  delay ← 0 ;                                // Initialise delay
   // While end of queue is not reached
3  while pos <= k do
4      q ← ι(w[pos]) ;                        // Select query of task at current position
5      p_pref ← argmax_{p'∈P} C(q, p') ;      // Determine preferred processor
       // If p is preferred or preference ignored due to delay or switch threshold
6      if (p = p_pref ∧ count(q, p) < st) ∨
       (p ≠ p_pref ∧ (count(q, p_pref) ≥ st ∨ delay ≥ 1/C(q, p))) then
           // If preference was ignored, reset execution counter
7          if count(q, p_pref) ≥ st then count(q, p_pref) ← 0 ;
8          count(q, p) ← count(q, p) + 1 ;    // Increment execution counter
9          return w[pos] ;                    // Select task at current position
10     delay ← delay + 1/C(q, p_pref) ;       // Update delay
11     pos ← pos + 1 ;                        // Move current position in queue
12 return w[pos];
```

Hybrid lookahead scheduling (HLS). The HLS algorithm takes as input (i) a query task throughput matrix; (ii) the system-wide queue of query tasks; (iii) the processor type (CPU or GPGPU) on which a worker thread intends to execute a task; (iv) a function that counts how often query tasks have been executed on each processors; and (v) a switch threshold to ensure that tasks are not executed only on one processor. It iterates over the tasks in the queue and returns the task to be executed by the worker thread on the given processor.

At a high level, the decision as to whether a task v is selected by the HLS algorithm depends on the identified preferred processor and the outstanding work that needs to be done by the preferred processor for earlier tasks in the queue. Such tasks may have the same preferred processor and will be executed *before* task v, thereby delaying it. If this delay is large, it may be better to execute task v on a slower processor if task execution would complete before the preferred processor completes all of its other tasks.

To perform this *lookahead* and quantify the amount of outstanding work for the preferred processor, the HLS algorithm sums up the inverses of the throughput values (variable *delay*). If that delay is larger than the inverse of the throughput obtained for the current task with the slower processor, the slower processor leads to an earlier estimated completion time compared to the preferred processor.

Over time, the above approach may lead to the situation that tasks of a particular query are always executed on the same processor, rendering it impossible to observe the throughput of other processors. Therefore, the HLS algorithm includes a *switch threshold*, which imposes a limit on how often a given task can be executed on the same processor without change: a given task is not scheduled on the preferred processor if the number of tasks of the same query executed on the preferred processor exceeds this threshold.

The HLS algorithm is defined more formally in Alg. 1. It iterates over the tasks in the queue (lines 3–11). For each task, the query operator function of the task is selected (line 4). Then, the preferred processor for this query is determined by looking up the highest value in the row of the query task throughput matrix (line 5).

The current task is executed on the processor associated with the worker thread: (i) if the preferred processor matches the worker's processor, and the number of executions of tasks of this query on this processor is below the switch threshold or (ii) if the worker's

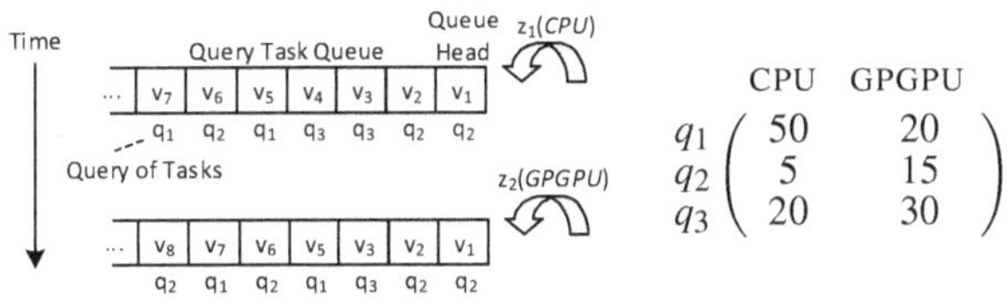

Figure 5: Example of hybrid lookahead scheduling

processor is not the preferred one but the accumulated delay of the preferred processor means that execution on the worker's processor is beneficial, or the number of tasks of this query on the preferred processor is higher than the switch threshold (line 6).

If a non-preferred processor is selected for the current task, the execution counter of the preferred processor is reset (line 7). The execution counter for the selected processor is incremented (line 8), and the current task is returned for execution (line 9). If the current task is not selected, the accumulated delay is updated (line 10), because the current task is planned to be executed on the other processor. Finally, the next query task in the queue is considered (line 11).

Example. Fig. 5 gives an example of the execution of the HLS algorithm. The query task queue contains tasks for three queries, q_1–q_3. Assuming that a worker thread z_1 for processor CPU becomes available, HLS proceeds as follows: the head of the queue, v_1, is a task of query q_2 that is preferably executed on GPGPU. Hence, it is not selected and the planned delay for GPGPU is set to $1/15$. The second and third tasks are handled similarly, resulting in an accumulated delay for GPGPU of $1/15 + 1/15 + 1/30 = 1/6$. The fourth task v_4 is also preferably executed on GPGPU. However, the estimation of the accumulated delay for GPGPU suggests that the execution of v_4 on CPU would lead to an earlier completion time, hence it is scheduled there. Next, if a worker thread z_2 that executes tasks on GPGPU becomes available, it takes the head of the queue because GPGPU is the preferred processor for tasks of query q_2.

4.3 Handling of task results

The result stage collects the results from all tasks that belong to a specific query and creates the output data stream. To maintain low processing latency, results of query tasks should be processed as soon as they are available, continuously creating the output data stream from the discretised input data streams. This is challenging for two reasons: first, the results of query tasks may arrive out-of-order due to their parallel execution, which requires reordering to ensure correct results; second, the window fragment results of a window may span multiple query tasks, which creates dependencies when executing the assembly operator function.

To address these challenges, the result stage reduces the synchronisation needed among the worker threads. To this end, processing of query task results is organised in three phases, each synchronised separately: (i) storing the task results, i.e. the window fragment results, in a buffer; (ii) executing the assembly operator function over window fragment results to construct the window results; and (iii) constructing the output data stream from the window results.

Result storage. When worker threads enter the result stage, they store the window fragment results in a circular *result buffer*, which is backed by a byte array. The order in which results are stored is determined by the query task identifiers assigned in the dispatch stage: a worker thread accesses a particular slot in the result buffer, which is the query task identifier modulo the buffer size.

To ensure that worker threads do not overwrite results of earlier query tasks stored in the result buffer, a *control buffer* records status flags for all slots in the result buffer. It is accessed by worker threads using an atomic compare-and-swap instruction. To avoid blocking a worker thread if a given slot is already populated, the result buffer has more slots than the number of worker threads. This guarantees that the results in a given slot will have been processed before this slot is accessed again by another worker thread.

Assembly of window results. After a worker thread has stored the results of a query task, it may proceed by assembling window results from window fragment results. In general, the results of multiple tasks may be needed to assemble the result of a single window, and assembly proceeds in a pairwise fashion. Given the results of two consecutive tasks, the windows are processed in their logical order, as defined by the query task identifier. The window result is calculated by applying the assembly operator function to all results of relevant fragments, which are contained in the two query task results. The obtained window results directly replace the window fragment results in the result buffer.

If additional fragment results are needed to complete the assembly for a window, i.e. the window spans more than two query task results, multiple assembly steps are performed. The assembly operator function is then applied to the result of the first assembly step and the fragment results that are part of the next query task result.

If a window spans more than two query tasks, and the assembly of window results is not just a concatenation of fragment results, the above procedure is not commutative—a window fragment result may be needed to construct the results of several windows, which are part of different evaluations of the assembly operator function. In that case, the pairwise assembly steps must be executed in the order defined by the query task identifiers. Such ordering dependencies can be identified by considering for each query task whether it contained windows that opened or closed in one of the stream batches. A query task result is ready for assembly either if it does not contain windows that are open or closed in one of the stream batches, or if the preceding query task result has already been assembled.

The information about task results that are ready for assembly and task results that have been assembled are kept as status flags in the control buffer. After a worker thread stores the result of a query task in the result buffer, it checks for slots in the result buffer that are ready for assembly. If there is no such slot, the worker thread does not block, but continues with the creation of the output stream.

Output stream construction. After window result assembly, the output data stream is constructed. A worker thread that finished assembly of window results (or skipped over it) checks if the slot of the result buffer that contains the next window result to be appended to the output stream is ready for result construction. If so, the worker thread locks the respective slot and appends the window results to the output stream. If there is no such slot, the worker thread leaves the result stage and returns to the scheduling stage.

5. QUERY EXECUTION

We now describe SABER's query execution stage in more detail. A challenge is that the performance of streaming operators may be restricted by their memory accesses. SABER thus explicitly manages memory to avoid unnecessary data deserialisation and dynamic object creation (§5.1). Whether the GPGPU can be utilised fully depends on how efficiently data is transferred to and from the GPGPU. SABER employs a novel approach to pipelined stream data movement that interleaves the execution of query tasks with data transfer operations (§5.2). Finally, we describe our implementation of streaming operators on the CPU (§5.3) and GPGPU (§5.4).

5.1 Memory management

Dynamic memory allocation is one of the main causes of performance issues in stream processing engines implemented in managed

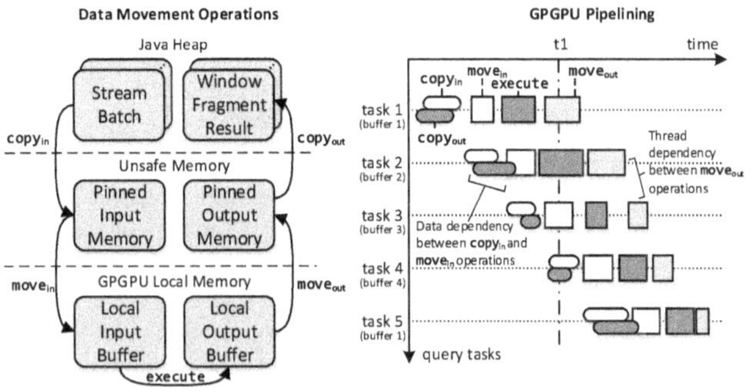

Figure 6: Data movement and pipelining for GPGPU-based execution of query tasks

languages with garbage collection, such as Java or C#. The SABER implementation therefore minimises the number of memory allocations by means of lazy deserialisation and object pooling.

Lazy deserialisation. To manage the data in input streams efficiently, SABER uses lazy deserialisation: tuples are stored in their byte representation and deserialised only if and when needed. Deserialisation is controlled per attribute, i.e. tuple values that are not accessed or needed to compute windows are not deserialised. Deserialisation only generates primitive types, which can be efficiently packed in byte arrays without the overhead of pointer dereferencing of object types. In addition, whenever possible, operators in SABER realise *direct byte forwarding*, i.e. they copy the byte representation of the input data to buffers that store intermediate results.

Object pooling. To avoid dynamic memory allocation on the critical processing path, SABER uses statically allocated pools of objects, for all query tasks, and of byte arrays, for storing intermediate window fragment results. To avoid contention for the byte arrays when many worker threads access it, each thread maintains a separate pool.

5.2 Pipelined stream data movement

Executing a query task on the GPGPU involves several data movement operations, as shown on the left side of Fig. 6: (i) the input data is copied from Java heap memory to pinned host memory ($\mathsf{copy}_{\mathsf{in}}$); (ii) using DMA, data is transferred from pinned host memory to GPGPU memory for processing ($\mathsf{move}_{\mathsf{in}}$); (iii) after the query task has executed (execute), the results are transferred back from the GPGPU memory to pinned host memory ($\mathsf{move}_{\mathsf{out}}$); and (iv) the results are copied back to Java heap memory ($\mathsf{copy}_{\mathsf{out}}$).

Performing these data movement operations sequentially would under-utilise the GPGPU. Given that stream processing handles small amounts of data in practice, the PCIe throughput becomes the bottleneck—executing the $\mathsf{copy}_{\mathsf{in}}$ and $\mathsf{copy}_{\mathsf{out}}$ operations sequentially would reduce the throughput to half of the PCIe bandwidth.

SABER therefore uses a *five-stage pipelining* mechanism, which interleaves I/O and compute operations to reduce idle periods and yield higher throughput. Pipelining is achieved by having dedicated threads execute each of the five data movement operations in parallel: two CPU threads copy data from and to Java heap memory ($\mathsf{copy}_{\mathsf{in}}$ and $\mathsf{copy}_{\mathsf{out}}$), and two GPGPU threads implement the data movement from and to GPGPU memory ($\mathsf{move}_{\mathsf{in}}$ and $\mathsf{move}_{\mathsf{out}}$). The remaining GPGPU threads execute query tasks (execute).

The right side of Fig. 6 shows the interleaving of data movement operations. Each row shows the five operations for a single query task. The interleaving of operations can be seen, for example, at time t1, when $\mathsf{move}_{\mathsf{out}}$ of task 1, execute of task 2, $\mathsf{move}_{\mathsf{in}}$ of task 3, and the copy operations of task 4 all execute concurrently.

The interleaving of operations respects data and thread dependencies. For a specific query task, all operations are executed sequentially because each operation relies on the data of the previous one. The CPU threads executing the copy operations, however, run in parallel so that the result data of the i-th task is copied by the $\mathsf{copy}_{\mathsf{out}}$ operation of the $(i{+}4)$-th task: as shown in Fig. 6, task 5's $\mathsf{copy}_{\mathsf{out}}$ operation returns the results of task 1. If task 1's $\mathsf{move}_{\mathsf{out}}$ operation has not completed, task 5 will be blocked until a notification from the dedicated GPGPU thread performing $\mathsf{move}_{\mathsf{out}}$.

The execution of each data movement operation by a thread also results in the sequential execution of the same operation of different tasks: in the example, task 2's $\mathsf{move}_{\mathsf{out}}$ operation must complete before the respective thread executes task 3's $\mathsf{move}_{\mathsf{out}}$ operation.

5.3 CPU operator implementations

To execute a query task on a CPU core, a worker thread applies the window batch function of a given query operator to the window fragments of the stream batches for this task. SABER implements the operator functions as follows.

Projection and selection operators are both stateless, and their batch operator function is thus a single scan over the stream batch of the corresponding query task, applying the projection or selection to each tuple. The assembly operator function then concatenates the fragment results needed to obtain a window result according to the stream creation function (see §2.4).

Aggregation operators, such as *sum*, *count* and *average*, over sliding windows exploit *incremental computation* [12, 50]. In a first step, the batch operator function computes window fragments by partitioning the stream batch of the query task into panes, i.e. distinct subsequences of tuples. To compute the aggregation value per window fragment, the batch operator function reuses the aggregated value—the result—of previous window fragments and incorporates tuples of the current fragment.

For an aggregation operator, a window result cannot be constructed by simply concatenating window fragment results, but the operator function must be evaluated for a set of fragment results. The assembly of window results from window fragment results is done stepwise, processing the window fragment results of two query tasks at a time. As described in §4.3, SABER keeps track for each fragment whether it is part of a window that opened, closed, is pending (i.e. neither opened nor closed), or fully contained in the stream batch of the query task. This is achieved by storing window fragment results in four different buffers (byte arrays) that contain only fragments that belong to windows in specific states.

SABER also supports the definition of `HAVING` and `GROUP-BY` clauses. The implementation of the `HAVING` clause reuses the selection operator. For the `GROUP-BY` clause, the batch operator function maintains a hash table with an aggregation value per group. To avoid dynamic memory allocation, SABER uses a statically allocated pool of hash table objects, which are backed by byte arrays.

Join operators implement a streaming θ-join, as defined by Kang et al. [35]. The execution of query tasks for the join is sequential because, unlike other task-parallel join implementations [27], SABER achieves parallelism by the data-parallel execution of query tasks.

5.4 GPGPU operator implementations

GPGPU operators are implemented in OpenCL [40]. Each operator has a generic code template that contains its core functionality. SABER populates these templates with tuple data structures, based on the input and output stream schemas of each operator, and query-specific functions over tuple attributes (e.g. selection predicates or aggregate functions). Tuple attributes are represented both as primitive types and vectors, which allows the implementation to use vectorised GPGPU instructions whenever possible.

Each GPGPU thread evaluates the fragment operator function. To exploit the cache memory shared by the synchronised threads on a single GPGPU core, tuples that are part of the same window are assigned to the same work group. The assembly operator function that derives the window results from window fragment results (see §4.3) is evaluated by one of the CPU worker threads.

Projection and selection. To perform a projection, the threads in a work group load the tuples into the group's cache memory, compute the projected values, and write the results to the global GPGPU memory. Moving the data to the cache memory is beneficial because the deserialisation and serialisation of tuples becomes faster. For the selection operator, the result from a fragment operator function is stored as a binary vector in the group's cache memory. Here, each vector entry indicates whether a tuple has been selected.

In a second step, SABER uses a prefix-sum (or scan) operation [14] to write the output data to a continuous global GPGPU memory region: it scans the binary vector and obtains continuous memory addresses to which selected tuples are written. These addresses are computed per window fragment and offset based on the start address of each fragment in order to compress the results for all fragments in a stream batch.

Aggregation first assigns a work group to each of the window fragments in the stream batch of the query task. For the implemented commutative and associative operator functions, each thread of the work group repeatedly reads two tuples from the global GPGPU memory and aggregates them. The threads thus form a reduction tree from which the window fragment result is derived. As in CPU-based execution (§5.3), the results are stored while keeping track for each fragment whether it is part of a window that opens, closes, is pending, or is fully contained in the stream batch.

To implement aggregations with `HAVING` clauses, SABER relies on the aforementioned approach for selection, which is applied to the aggregation results. For a `GROUP-BY` clause, every work group populates an open-addressing hash table. The table uses a linear probing approach combined with a memory-efficient representation. The size of the table and the hash function used on the CPU and GPGPU are the same to ensure that, given a tuple in the CPU table, it can be searched in the GPGPU table, and vice versa.

An additional challenge, compared to the CPU implementation, is to ensure that the hash table for a window fragment is thread-safe. We reserve an integer in the intermediate tuple representation to store the index of the first input tuple that has occupied a table slot. Threads try to atomically compare-and-set this index. When a collision occurs, a thread checks if the key stored is the same as the current key, in which case it atomically increments the aggregate value, or it moves to the next available slot.

If the window fragment is incomplete, the hash table is output as is—this is necessary because the result aggregation logic is the same for both CPU and GPGPU. Otherwise, all sparsely populated hash tables are compacted at the end of processing.

Join operators exploit task-parallelism, similar to the *cell join* [27]. To avoid quadratic memory usage, however, SABER adopts a technique used in join processing for in-memory column stores [32] and performs a join in two steps: (i) the number of tuples that match the join predicate is counted and (ii) the results are compressed in the global GPGPU memory, as for selection.

6. EVALUATION

We evaluate SABER to show the benefits of its hybrid stream processing model. First, we demonstrate that such a model achieves higher performance for both real-world and synthetic query benchmarks (§6.2). We then explore the trade-off between CPU and GPGPU execution for different queries (§6.3). After that, we investigate the impact of the query task size on performance (§6.4) and show that SABER's CPU operator implementations scale (§6.5). Finally, we evaluate the effectiveness of HLS scheduling (§6.6).

Datasets		Queries			
Name	# Attr.	Name	Windows	Operators	Values
Synthetic (Syn)	7	PROJ_m	*various*	$\pi_{a_1,\ldots,a_m}$	$1 \le m \le 10$
		SELECT_n	*various*	$\sigma_{p_1,\ldots,p_n}$	$1 \le n \le 64$
		AGG_f	*various*	α_f	$f \in \{\text{avg}, \text{sum}\}$
		$\mathsf{GROUP\text{-}BY}_o$	*various*	$\gamma_{g_1,\ldots,g_o}$	$1 \le o \le 64$
		JOIN_r	*various*	$\bowtie_{p_1,\ldots,p_r}$	$1 \le r \le 64$
Cluster Monitoring (CM)	12	CM_1	$\omega_{60,1}$	$\pi, \gamma, \alpha_{\text{sum}}$	
		CM_2	$\omega_{60,1}$	$\pi, \sigma, \gamma, \alpha_{\text{avg}}$	
Smart Grid (SG)	7	SG_1	$\omega_{3600,1}$	π, α_{avg}	
		SG_2	$\omega_{3600,1}$	$\pi, \gamma, \alpha_{\text{avg}}$	
		SG_3	$\omega_{1,1}, \omega_{1,1}$	$\pi, \sigma, \bowtie$	
Linear Road Benchmark (LRB)	7	LRB_1	ω_{∞}	π	
		LRB_2	$\omega_{30,1}, \omega_{\text{part}}$	$\pi_{\text{distinct}}, \bowtie$	
		LRB_3	$\omega_{300,1}$	$\pi, \sigma, \gamma, \alpha_{\text{avg}}$	
		LRB_4	$\omega_{30,1}$	$\pi, \gamma, \alpha_{\text{count}}$	

Table 1: Summary of evaluation datasets and workloads

6.1 Experimental set-up and workloads

All experiments are performed on a server with 2 Intel Xeon E5-2640 v3 2.60 GHz CPUs with a total of 16 physical CPU cores, a 20 MB LLC cache and 64 GB of memory. The server also hosts an NVIDIA Quadro K5200 GPGPU with 2,304 cores and 8 GB GDDR 5 memory, connected via a PCIe 3.0 (×16) bus. When streaming data to SABER from the network, we use a 10 Gbps Ethernet NIC. The server runs Ubuntu 14.04 with Linux kernel 3.16 and NVIDIA driver 346.47. SABER uses the Oracle JVM 7 with the *mark-and-sweep* garbage collector.

Table 1 summarises the query workloads and datasets in our evaluation. We use both synthetic queries, for exploring query parameters, and application queries from real-world use cases. The CQL representations of the application queries are listed in Appendix A.

Synthetically-generated workload (Syn). We generate synthetic data streams of 32-byte tuples, each consisting of a 64-bit timestamp and six 32-bit attribute values drawn from a uniform distribution—the default being integer values, but for aggregation and projection the first value being a float. We then generate a set of queries using the operators from §2.4, and vary key parameters: the number of attributes and arithmetic expressions in a projection; the number of predicates in a selection or a join; the function in an aggregation; and the number of groups in an aggregation with `GROUP-BY`.

Compute cluster monitoring (CM). Our second workload emulates a cluster management scenario. We use a trace of time-stamped tuples collected from an 11,000-machine compute cluster at Google [53]. Each tuple is a monitoring event related to the tasks of compute jobs that execute on the cluster, such as the successful completion of a task, the failure of a task, or the submission of a high-priority task for a production job.

We use two queries, CM_1 and CM_2, that express common cluster monitoring tasks [23,38]: CM_1 combines a projection and an aggregation with a `GROUP-BY` clause to compute the sum of the requested share of CPU utilisation per job category; and CM_2 combines a projection, a selection, and an aggregation with a `GROUP-BY` to report the average requested CPU utilisation of submitted tasks.

Anomaly detection in smart grids (SG). This workload focuses on anomaly detection in energy consumption data from a smart electricity grid. The trace is a stream of smart meter readings from different electrical devices in households [34].

We execute three queries, $\mathsf{SG}_{1\text{–}3}$, that analyse the stream to detect outliers. SG_1 is a projection and aggregation that computes the

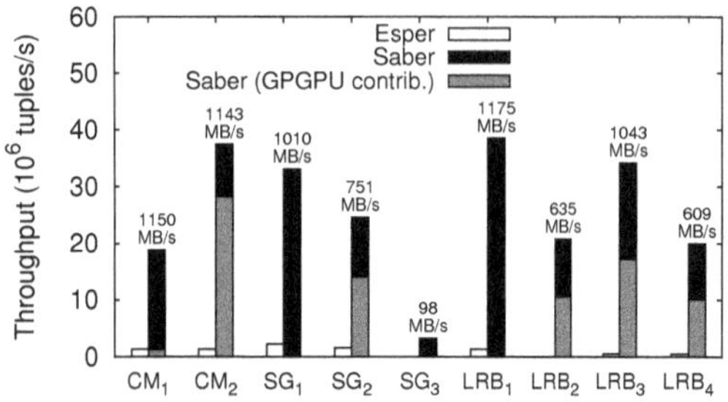

Figure 7: Performance for application benchmark queries

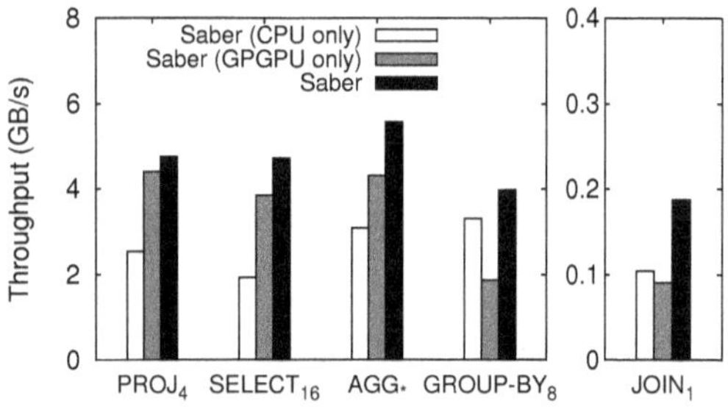

Figure 8: Performance for synthetic queries. AGG∗ evaluates all aggregate functions and GROUP-BY evaluates cnt and sum.

sliding global average of the meter load; SG_2 combines a projection and aggregation with a GROUP-BY to derive the sliding load average per plug in a household in a house; and SG_3 uses a join to compare the global load average with the plug load average by joining the results of SG_1 and SG_2, and then counts the houses for which the local average is higher than the global one.

Linear Road Benchmark (LRB). This workload is the Linear Road Benchmark [8] for evaluating stream processing performance. The benchmark models a network of toll roads, in which incurred tolls depend on the level of congestion and the time-of-day. Tuples in the input data stream denote position events of vehicles on a highway lane, driving with a specific speed in a particular direction.

6.2 Is hybrid stream processing effective?

We first explore the performance of SABER for our application benchmark queries. To put the achieved processing throughput into perspective, we also compare to an implementation of the queries in Esper [2], an open-source multi-threaded stream processing engine. The input streams for the queries are generated by a separate machine connected through a 10 Gbps network link.

Fig. 7 shows the processing throughput for SABER and Esper for the application queries. For SABER, we also report the split of the contribution of the CPU (upper black part) and the GPGPU (lower grey part) to the achieved throughput. SABER manages to saturate the 10 Gbps network link for many queries, including CM_1, CM_2 and LRB_1. In contrast, the performance of Esper remains two orders of magnitude lower due to the synchronisation overhead of its implementation and the lack of GPGPU acceleration.

Different queries exhibit different acceleration potential on the CPU versus the GPGPU, which SABER automatically selects according to its hybrid execution model. For CM_1, the aggregation executes efficiently on the CPU, whereas the selection in CM_2 on the GPGPU benefits from its high throughput, leaving aggregation over sliding windows to the CPU. SG_1 and LRB_1 do not benefit from the GPGPU because the CPU workers can keep up with the task generation rate. SG_2 and LRB_3 utilise both heterogeneous processors equally because they can split the load.

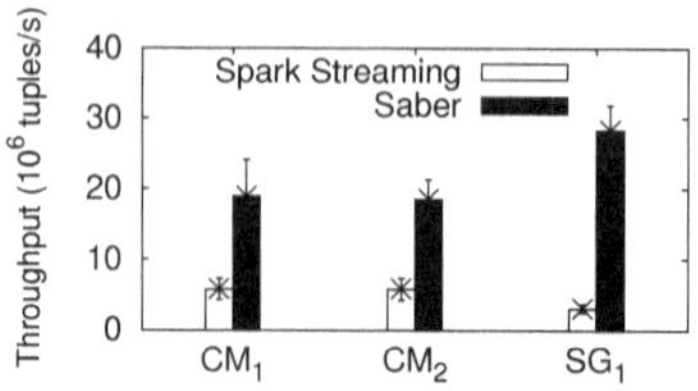

Figure 9: Performance compared to Spark Streaming

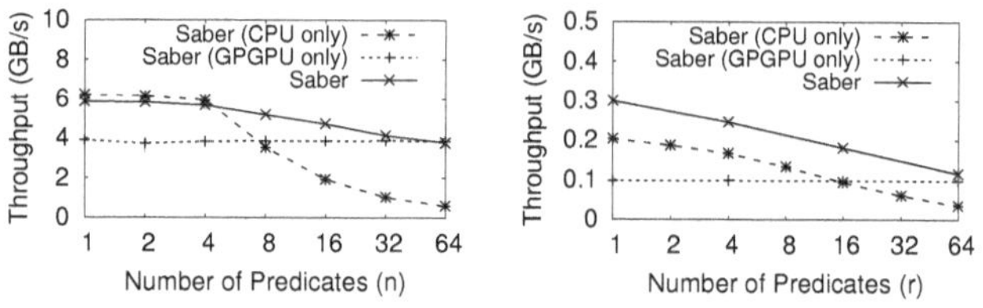

(a) SELECT_n with $\omega_{32KB,32KB}$ (b) JOIN_r with $\omega_{4KB,4KB}$

Figure 10: Performance impact of query parameters

Next, we use our synthetic operator queries to compare the performance achieved by SABER to CPU-only and GPGPU-only execution, respectively. Fig. 8 shows that the hybrid approach always achieves higher throughput than only using a single type of heterogeneous processor. The contention in the dispatching and result stages in SABER means that the combined throughput is less than the sum of the throughput achieved by the CPU and the GPGPU only.

Fig. 9 shows the performance of SABER and Spark Streaming with the CM_1, CM_2 and SG_1 queries. Since Spark does not support count-based windows, we change the queries to use 500 ms tumbling windows based on system time for comparable results. For CM_1 and CM_2, SABER's throughput is limited by the network bandwidth, while, for SG_1, SABER saturates 90% of the network bandwidth, showing a throughput that is 6× higher than Spark Streaming, which is limited due to scheduling overhead.

We put SABER's performance into perspective by comparing it against MonetDB [33], an efficient in-memory columnar database engine. We run a θ-join query over two 1 MB tables with 32-byte tuples. The tables are populated with synthetic data such that the selectivity of the query is 1%. In SABER, we emulate the join by treating the tables as streams and applying a tumbling window of 1 MB. In MonetDB, we partition the two tables and join the partitions pairwise so that the engine can execute each of the partial θ-joins in parallel. The output is the union of all partial join results.

When the query output has only two columns—those on which we perform the θ-join—MonetDB and SABER exhibit similar performance: with 15 threads, MonetDB runs the query in 980 ms and SABER in 1,088 ms.[2] When the query output includes all columns (`select *`), MonetDB is 2× slower than SABER because, as a columnar engine, it spends 40% of the time reconstructing the output table after the join evaluation. However, when we change the query to an equi-join with the same selectivity (rather than a θ-join), MonetDB is 2.7× faster because it is highly-optimised for such queries.

6.3 What is the CPU/GPGPU trade-off?

As we increase the complexity of some query operators, the CPU processing throughput degrades. Keeping the number of worker threads fixed to 15, Fig. 10 shows this effect for SELECT_n and JOIN_r when varying the number of predicates (the other operators yield similar results). For SELECT_n, we further observe that, for few predicates, the throughput is bound by the rate at which the dispatcher can generate tasks.

[2] We report the average of 5 runs. In all SABER runs, the GPGPU consumes approximately 1/3 of the dispatched tasks.

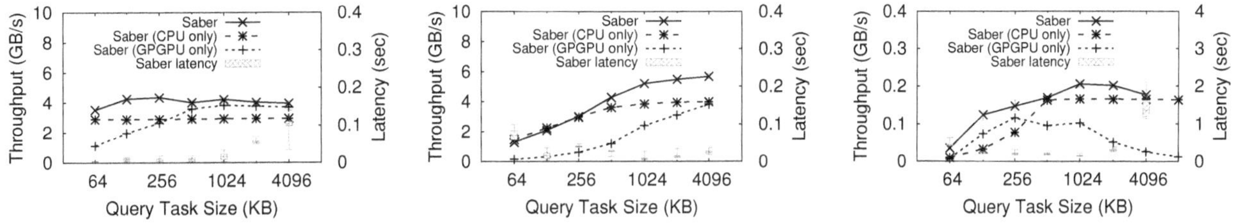

(a) $SELECT_{10}$ with $\omega_{32\,KB,32\,KB}$ (b) $AGG_{avg}GROUP\text{-}BY_{64}$ with $\omega_{32\,KB,32\,KB}$ (c) $JOIN_4$ with $\omega_{32\,KB,32\,KB}$

Figure 12: Performance impact of query task size ϕ for different query types

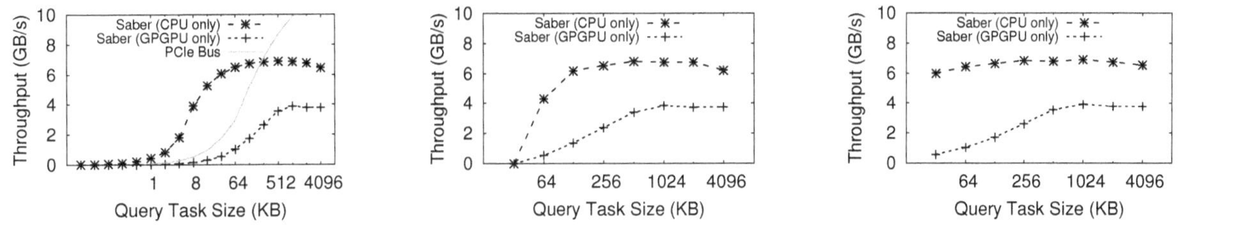

(a) $SELECT_1$ with $\omega_{32\,B,32\,B}$ (b) $SELECT_1$ with $\omega_{32\,KB,32\,B}$ (c) $SELECT_1$ with $\omega_{32\,KB,32\,KB}$

Figure 13: Performance impact of query task size ϕ for different window sizes and slides

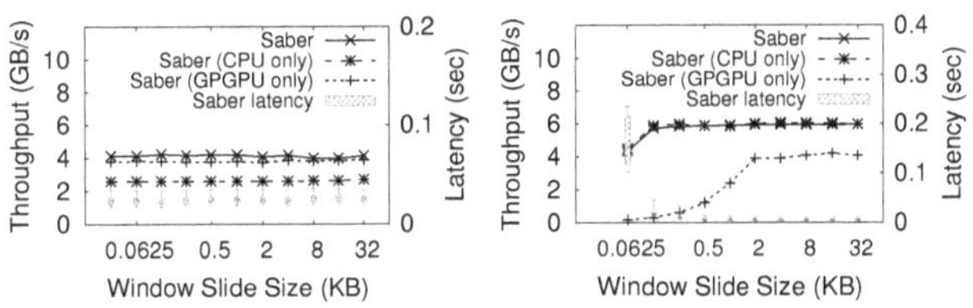

(a) $SELECT_{10}$ with $\omega_{32\,KB,x}$ (b) AGG_{avg} with $\omega_{32\,KB,x}$

Figure 11: Performance impact of window slide

We compare the CPU throughput with that obtained from using just the GPGPU. Fig. 10 shows that there are regions where the GPGPU is faster than the CPU, and vice versa. The GPGPU is bound by the data movement overhead, and any performance benefit diminishes when the query is not complex enough. Except for the case in which the dispatcher is the bottleneck because of a simple query structure ($SELECT_n$, $1 \leq n \leq 4$), hybrid execution is beneficial for both queries, achieving nearly additive throughput.

Fig. 11 shows the impact of the window slide on the CPU/GPGPU trade-off for two sliding window queries, $SELECT_{10}$ and AGG_{avg}, under a fixed task size of 1 MB. The window size is 32 KB, while the slide varies from 32 bytes (1 tuple) to 32 KB. As expected, the slide does not influence the throughput or latency on any processor for $SELECT_{10}$ because the selection operator does not maintain any state. For AGG_{avg}, the CPU uses incremental computation, which increases the throughput until it is bound by the dispatcher. On the GPGPU, an increase of the window slide reduces the number of windows processed, which increases throughput. At some point, however, the GPGPU throughput is limited by the PCIe bandwidth.

6.4 How does task size affect performance?

Next, we investigate the impact of the query task size on performance. Intuitively, larger tasks improve throughput but negatively affect latency. We first consider three queries, $SELECT_{10}$, $AGG_{avg}GROUP\text{-}BY_{64}$, and $JOIN_4$, with $\omega_{32\,KB,32\,KB}$. In each experiment, we measure the throughput and latency when varying query task sizes from 64 KB to 4 MB.

The results in Fig. 12 confirm our expectation. While the absolute throughput values vary across the different queries, they exhibit a similar trend: initially, the throughput grows linearly with the query task size and then plateaus at around 1 MB. The only exception is the GPGPU-only implementation of the JOIN query for which throughput collapses with query task sizes beyond 512 KB. This is due to a limitation of our current implementation: the computation of the window boundaries is always executed on the CPU.

To validate our claim that the batch size is independent from the window size and slide, we use a single type of query, $SELECT_1$, and vary the window size and slide: from a window size of just 1 tuple ($\omega_{32\,B,32\,B}$), to a slide of just 1 tuple ($\omega_{32\,KB,32\,B}$), and to a large tumbling window ($\omega_{32\,KB,32\,KB}$).

Fig. 13 shows that SABER achieves a comparable performance in all three cases, with the throughput growing approximately until 1 MB. This demonstrates that the batch size is independent from the executed query but only depends on the hardware.

6.5 Does Saber scale on the CPU?

We now turn our attention to the scalability of SABER's CPU operator implementations. We measure the throughput achieved by each operator in isolation when varying the number of worker threads. Fig. 14 shows the results for a $PROJ_6$ query with $\omega_{32\,KB,32\,KB}$ windows. We omit the results for the other operators because they exhibit similar trends. The results show that the CPU operator implementation scales linearly up to 16 worker threads. Beyond this number, the performance plateaus (or slightly deteriorates for some operators) due to the context-switching overhead when the number of threads exceeds the number of available physical CPU cores.

6.6 What is the effect of HLS scheduling?

We finish by investigating the benefit of hybrid lookahead scheduling (HLS). For this, we consider a workload W_1 with two queries, Q_1=$PROJ_6^*$ (i.e. $PROJ_6$ with 100 arithmetic expressions for each attribute) with $\omega_{32\,KB,32\,KB}$, and Q_2=$AGG_{cnt}GROUP\text{-}BY_1$ with $\omega_{32\,KB,16\,KB}$, executed in sequence. These queries exhibit opposite performance: when run in isolation, Q_1 has higher throughput on the GPGPU (1,475 MB/s vs. 292 MB/s), while Q_2 has higher throughput on the CPU (2,362 MB/s vs. 372 MB/s).

We compare the performance achieved by HLS against two baselines: a "first-come, first-served" (FCFS) scheduling policy and a static scheduling policy (Static), in which Q_1's tasks are scheduled

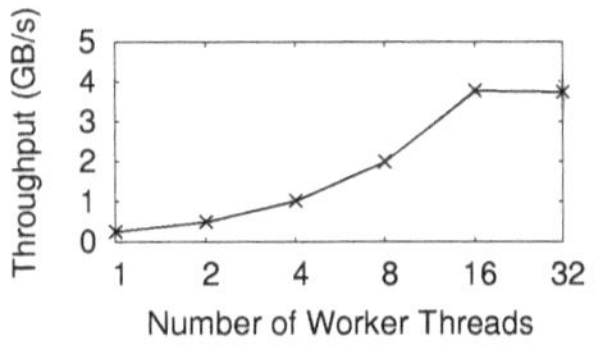

Figure 14: Scalability of CPU operator implementation

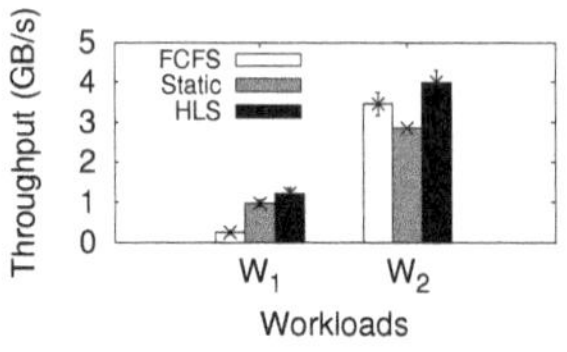

Figure 15: Performance impact of HLS scheduling

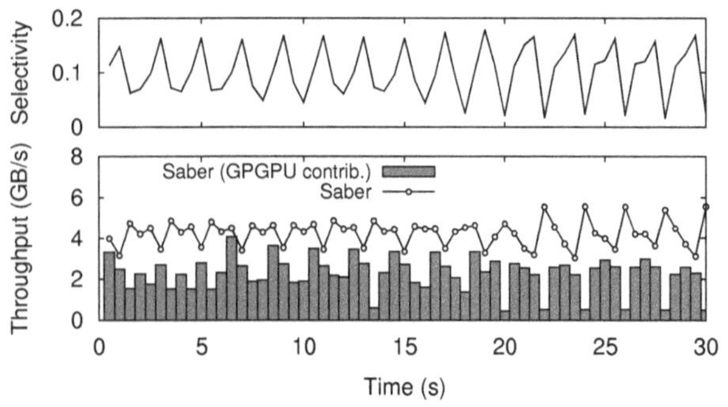

Figure 16: Adaptation of HLS scheduling

on the GPGPU and Q_2's task are scheduled on the CPU. Note that this policy is infeasible in practice with dynamic workloads.

Fig. 15 shows that, as expected, FCFS has the worst performance as tasks are not matched with the preferred processor. More interesting is the comparison between Static and HLS: although Static significantly improves over FCFS, HLS achieves higher throughput because it exploits all available resources.

Next, we consider a scenario in which Static would under-perform. Workload W_2 consists of two queries, Q_3=PROJ$_1$ with $\omega_{32\text{KB},32\text{KB}}$ and Q_4=AGG$_{\text{sum}}$ with $\omega_{32\text{KB},32\text{KB}}$, executed in sequence. Statically assigning Q_3 to the CPU and Q_4 to the GPGPU yields full utilisation of the GPGPU, but CPU cores are under-utilised. Reversing the assignment has the opposite effect. In Fig. 15, we show the latter assignment due to its higher throughput. Splitting the workload with FCFS, both CPU and GPGPU are fully utilised with a CPU/GPGPU split of approximately 1:1.5 for both Q_3 and Q_4. HLS saturates both processors too, but with peak throughput by converging to a better CPU/GPGPU split of 1:2.5 for Q_3 and 1:0.5 for Q_4. The results for W_1 and W_2 thus show the ability of HLS to support heterogeneous processors without *a priori* knowledge of the workload.

Fig. 16 shows how HLS adapts to workload changes. We run a SELECT$_{500}$ query over the cluster management trace, filtering task failure events. The selection predicate has the form $p_1 \wedge (p_2 \vee \cdots \vee p_{500})$ such that when a failure event is selected (p_1) all other predicates are evaluated too, making query tasks with high selectivity expensive to run. The trace contains a period with a surge of task failure events, which we repeat. The resulting selectivity is shown in the upper part of Fig. 16. To enable HLS to react to frequent changes, we update the query task throughput matrix every 100 ms.

Fig. 16 shows how HLS adapts: when selectivity is low, the CPU is faster than the GPGPU and monopolises the task queue—the GPGPU contribution is limited to tasks permitted to run by HLS's switch threshold rule. When the selectivity increases, the GPGPU is the faster processor. As the query task throughput for both processors changes, HLS adapts by scheduling more tasks on the GPGPU to sustain a high throughput.

7. RELATED WORK

Centralised stream processing engines have existed for decades, yet engines such as STREAM [6], TelegraphCQ [20], and NiagaraCQ [21] focus on single-core execution. Recent systems such as Esper [2], Oracle CEP [3], and Microsoft StreamInsight [39] support multi-core architectures at the expense of weakening stream ordering guarantees in the presence of windows. Research prototypes such as S-Store [18] and Trill [19] have strong window semantics with SQL-like queries. However, S-Store does not perform parallel window computation. Trill parallelises window processing through a map/reduce model, but it does not support hybrid query execution.

Distributed stream processing systems such as Storm [52], Samza [1] and SEEP [17] execute streaming queries with data-parallelism on a cluster of nodes. They do not respect window semantics by default. Millwheel [4] provides strong window semantics, but it does not perform parallel computation on windows and instead assumes partitioned input streams. Spark Streaming [56] has a batched-stream model, and permits window definitions over this model, thus creating dependencies between window semantics, throughput and latency. Recent work on adapting the batch size for Spark Streaming [25] automatically tunes the batch size to stay within a given latency bound. Unlike Streaming Spark, SABER decouples window semantics from system performance.

Window computation. Pane-based approaches for window processing [41] divide overlapping windows into panes. Aggregation occurs at the pane level, and multiple panes are combined to provide the final window result. In contrast to our hybrid stream processing model, the goal is to partition windows so as to avoid redundant computation, not to achieve data parallelism. Balkesen and Tatbul [11] propose pane processing for distribution, which incurs a different set of challenges compared to SABER due to its shared-nothing model.

Recent work [12, 50] has focused on the problem of avoiding redundant computation with sliding windows aggregation. This involves keeping efficient aggregation data structures, which can be maintained with minimum overhead [12], even for general aggregation functions that are neither invertible nor commutative [50]. Such approaches are compatible with the batch operator functions that SABER uses to process multiple overlapping window fragments.

Accelerated query processing. In-memory databases have explored co-processing with CPUs and GPGPUs for accelerating database queries for both in-cache and discrete systems. All such systems [15, 16, 22, 30, 48, 55], however, target one-off and not streaming queries, and they therefore do not require parallel window semantics or efficient fine-grained data movement to the accelerator.

GStream [57] executes streaming applications on GPGPU clusters, and provides a new API that abstracts away communication primitives. Unlike GStream, SABER supports SQL window semantics and deployments on single-node hybrid architectures.

8. CONCLUSIONS

We have presented SABER, a stream processing system that employs a new hybrid data parallel processing model to run continuous queries on servers equipped with heterogeneous processors, namely a CPU and a GPGPU. SABER does not make explicit decisions on which processor a query should run but rather gives preference to the fastest one, yet enabling other processors to contribute to the aggregate query throughput. We have shown that SABER achieves high processing throughput (over 6 GB/s) and sub-second latency for a wide range of streaming queries.

Acknowledgements. Research partially funded by the European Union Seventh Framework Programme (FP7/2007-2013) under grant agreement number 318521, the German Research Foundation (DFG) under grant agreement number WE 4891/1-1, and a PhD CASE Award by EPSRC/BAE Systems.

9. REFERENCES

[1] Apache Samza. http://samza.apache.org/. Last access: 09/02/16.

[2] Esper. http://www.espertech.com/esper/. Last access: 09/02/16.

[3] Oracle® Stream Explorer. http://bit.ly/1L6tKz3. Last access: 09/02/16.

[4] T. Akidau, A. Balikov, K. Bekiroğlu, S. Chernyak, J. Haberman, R. Lax, S. McVeety, D. Mills, P. Nordstrom, and S. Whittle. MillWheel: Fault-tolerant Stream Processing at Internet Scale. *Proc. VLDB Endow.*, 6(11):1033–1044, Aug. 2013.

[5] M. H. Ali, C. Gerea, B. S. Raman, B. Sezgin, T. Tarnavski, T. Verona, P. Wang, P. Zabback, A. Ananthanarayan, A. Kirilov, M. Lu, A. Raizman, R. Krishnan, R. Schindlauer, T. Grabs, S. Bjeletich, B. Chandramouli, J. Goldstein, S. Bhat, Y. Li, V. Di Nicola, X. Wang, D. Maier, S. Grell, O. Nano, and I. Santos. Microsoft CEP Server and Online Behavioral Targeting. *Proc. VLDB Endow.*, 2(2):1558–1561, Aug. 2009.

[6] A. Arasu, B. Babcock, S. Babu, M. Datar, K. Ito, R. Motwani, I. Nishizawa, U. Srivastava, D. Thomas, R. Varma, and J. Widom. STREAM: The Stanford Stream Data Manager. *IEEE Data Eng. Bull.*, 26(1):19–26, Mar. 2003.

[7] A. Arasu, S. Babu, and J. Widom. The CQL Continuous Query Language: Semantic Foundations and Query Execution. *The VLDB Journal*, 15(2):121–142, June 2006.

[8] A. Arasu, M. Cherniack, E. Galvez, D. Maier, A. S. Maskey, E. Ryvkina, M. Stonebraker, and R. Tibbetts. Linear Road: A Stream Data Management Benchmark. In *Proceedings of the 30th International Conference on Very Large Data Bases*, VLDB '04, pages 480–491. VLDB Endowment, 2004.

[9] A. Artikis, M. Weidlich, F. Schnitzler, I. Boutsis, T. Liebig, N. Piatkowski, C. Bockermann, K. Morik, V. Kalogeraki, J. Marecek, A. Gal, S. Mannor, D. Gunopulos, and D. Kinane. Heterogeneous Stream Processing and Crowdsourcing for Urban Traffic Management. In *Proceedings of the 17th International Conference on Extending Database Technology*, EDBT '14, pages 712–723. OpenProceedings.org, 2014.

[10] aws.amazon.com. Announcing Cluster GPU Instances for Amazon EC2. http://amzn.to/1RrDflL, Nov. 2010. Last access: 09/02/16.

[11] C. Balkesen and N. Tatbul. Scalable Data Partitioning Techniques for Parallel Sliding Window Processing over Data Streams. In *Proceedings of the 8th International Workshop on Data Management for Sensor Networks*, DMSN '11, 2011.

[12] P. Bhatotia, U. A. Acar, F. P. Junqueira, and R. Rodrigues. Slider: Incremental Sliding Window Analytics. In *Proceedings of the 15th International Middleware Conference*, Middleware '14, pages 61–72. ACM, 2014.

[13] A. Biem, E. Bouillet, H. Feng, A. Ranganathan, A. Riabov, O. Verscheure, H. Koutsopoulos, and C. Moran. IBM Infosphere Streams for Scalable, Real-time, Intelligent Transportation Services. In *Proceedings of the 2010 ACM SIGMOD International Conference on Management of Data*, SIGMOD '10, pages 1093–1104. ACM, 2010.

[14] G. E. Blelloch. *Vector Models for Data-parallel Computing*. MIT Press, 1990.

[15] S. Breß. The Design and Implementation of CoGaDB: A Column-oriented GPU-accelerated DBMS. *Datenbank-Spektrum*, 14(3):199–209, 2014.

[16] S. Breß and G. Saake. Why It is Time for a HyPE: A Hybrid Query Processing Engine for Efficient GPU Coprocessing in DBMS. *Proc. VLDB Endow.*, 6(12):1398–1403, Aug. 2013.

[17] R. Castro Fernandez, M. Migliavacca, E. Kalyvianaki, and P. Pietzuch. Integrating Scale out and Fault Tolerance in Stream Processing Using Operator State Management. In *Proceedings of the 2013 ACM SIGMOD International Conference on Management of Data*, SIGMOD '13, pages 725–736. ACM, 2013.

[18] U. Cetintemel, J. Du, T. Kraska, S. Madden, D. Maier, J. Meehan, A. Pavlo, M. Stonebraker, E. Sutherland, N. Tatbul, K. Tufte, H. Wang, and S. Zdonik. S-Store: A Streaming NewSQL System for Big Velocity Applications. *Proc. VLDB Endow.*, 7(13):1633–1636, Aug. 2014.

[19] B. Chandramouli, J. Goldstein, M. Barnett, R. DeLine, D. Fisher, J. C. Platt, J. F. Terwilliger, and J. Wernsing. Trill: A High-performance Incremental Query Processor for Diverse Analytics. *Proc. VLDB Endow.*, 8(4):401–412, Dec. 2014.

[20] S. Chandrasekaran, O. Cooper, A. Deshpande, M. J. Franklin, J. M. Hellerstein, W. Hong, S. Krishnamurthy, S. R. Madden, F. Reiss, and M. A. Shah. TelegraphCQ: Continuous Dataflow Processing. In *Proceedings of the 2003 ACM SIGMOD International Conference on Management of Data*, SIGMOD '03, pages 668–668. ACM, 2003.

[21] J. Chen, D. J. DeWitt, F. Tian, and Y. Wang. NiagaraCQ: A Scalable Continuous Query System for Internet Databases. *SIGMOD Rec.*, 29(2):379–390, May 2000.

[22] L. Chen, X. Huo, and G. Agrawal. Accelerating MapReduce on a Coupled CPU-GPU Architecture. In *Proceedings of the International Conference on High Performance Computing, Networking, Storage and Analysis*, SC '12, pages 25:1–25:11. IEEE Computer Society Press, 2012.

[23] X. Chen, C.-D. Lu, and K. Pattabiraman. Failure Analysis of Jobs in Compute Clouds: A Google Cluster Case Study. In *Proceedings of the 25th International Symposium on Software Reliability Engineering*, ISSRE '14, pages 167–177. IEEE Computer Society Press, 2014.

[24] S. Crago, K. Dunn, P. Eads, L. Hochstein, D.-I. Kang, M. Kang, D. Modium, K. Singh, J. Suh, and J. Walters. Heterogeneous Cloud Computing. In *Proceedings of the 2011 IEEE International Conference on Cluster Computing*, CLUSTER '11, pages 378–385. IEEE Press, 2011.

[25] T. Das, Y. Zhong, I. Stoica, and S. Shenker. Adaptive Stream Processing Using Dynamic Batch Sizing. In *Proceedings of the ACM Symposium on Cloud Computing*, SOCC '14, pages 16:1–16:13. ACM, 2014.

[26] feedzai.com. Modern Payment Fraud Prevention at Big Data Scale. http://bit.ly/1KCskD5, 2013. Last access: 09/02/16.

[27] B. Gedik, R. R. Bordawekar, and P. S. Yu. CellJoin: A Parallel Stream Join Operator for the Cell Processor. *The VLDB Journal*, 18(2):501–519, Apr. 2009.

[28] N. Govindaraju, J. Gray, R. Kumar, and D. Manocha. GPUTeraSort: High Performance Graphics Co-processor Sorting for Large Database Management. In *Proceedings of the 2006 ACM SIGMOD International Conference on Management of Data*, SIGMOD '06, pages 325–336. ACM, 2006.

[29] B. He, M. Lu, K. Yang, R. Fang, N. K. Govindaraju, Q. Luo, and P. V. Sander. Relational Query Coprocessing on Graphics Processors. *ACM Trans. Database Syst.*, 34(4):21:1–21:39, Dec. 2009.

[30] J. He, M. Lu, and B. He. Revisiting Co-processing for Hash

Joins on the Coupled CPU-GPU Architecture. *Proc. VLDB Endow.*, 6(10):889–900, Aug. 2013.

[31] J. He, S. Zhang, and B. He. In-cache Query Co-processing on Coupled CPU-GPU Architectures. *Proc. VLDB Endow.*, 8(4):329–340, Dec. 2014.

[32] M. Heimel, M. Saecker, H. Pirk, S. Manegold, and V. Markl. Hardware-oblivious Parallelism for In-memory Column-stores. *Proc. VLDB Endow.*, 6(9):709–720, July 2013.

[33] S. Idreos, F. Groffen, N. Nes, S. Manegold, K. S. Mullender, and M. L. Kersten. MonetDB: Two Decades of Research in Column-oriented Database Architectures. *IEEE Data Engineering Bulletin*, 35(1):40–45, 2012.

[34] Z. Jerzak and H. Ziekow. The DEBS 2014 Grand Challenge. In *Proceedings of the 8th ACM International Conference on Distributed Event-Based Systems*, DEBS '14, pages 266–269. ACM, 2014.

[35] J. Kang, J. Naughton, and S. Viglas. Evaluating window joins over unbounded streams. In *Proceedings of the 19th IEEE International Conference on Data Engineering*, ICDE '03, pages 341–352. IEEE Press, 2003.

[36] T. Karnagel, D. Habich, B. Schlegel, and W. Lehner. The HELLS-join: A Heterogeneous Stream Join for Extremely Large Windows. In *Proceedings of the 9th International Workshop on Data Management on New Hardware*, DaMoN '13, pages 2:1–2:7. ACM, 2013.

[37] T. Karnagel, M. Hille, M. Ludwig, D. Habich, W. Lehner, M. Heimel, and V. Markl. Demonstrating Efficient Query Processing in Heterogeneous Environments. In *Proceedings of the 2014 ACM SIGMOD International Conference on Management of Data*, SIGMOD '14, pages 693–696. ACM, 2014.

[38] S. Kavulya, J. Tan, R. Gandhi, and P. Narasimhan. An Analysis of Traces from a Production MapReduce Cluster. In *Proceedings of the 10th IEEE/ACM International Conference on Cluster, Cloud and Grid Computing*, CCGrid '10, pages 94–103. IEEE Computer Society, 2010.

[39] S. J. Kazemitabar, U. Demiryurek, M. Ali, A. Akdogan, and C. Shahabi. Geospatial Stream Query Processing Using Microsoft SQL Server StreamInsight. *Proc. VLDB Endow.*, 3(1-2):1537–1540, Sept. 2010.

[40] Khronos OpenCL Working Group. *The OpenCL Specification, version 1.2*, 2012.

[41] J. Li, D. Maier, K. Tufte, V. Papadimos, and P. A. Tucker. No Pane, No Gain: Efficient Evaluation of Sliding-window Aggregates over Data Streams. *SIGMOD Rec.*, 34(1):39–44, Mar. 2005.

[42] W. Liu, B. Schmidt, G. Voss, and W. Muller-Wittig. Streaming Algorithms for Biological Sequence Alignment on GPUs. *IEEE Trans. Parallel Distrib. Syst.*, 18(9):1270–1281, Sept. 2007.

[43] D. Lustig and M. Martonosi. Reducing GPU Offload Latency via Fine-grained CPU-GPU Synchronization. In *Proceedings of the 19th IEEE International Symposium on High Performance Computer Architecture*, HPCA '13, pages 354–365. IEEE Computer Society, 2013.

[44] M. L. Massie, B. N. Chun, and D. E. Culler. The ganglia distributed monitoring system: design, implementation, and experience. *Parallel Computing*, 30(7):817 – 840, July 2004.

[45] L. Neumeyer, B. Robbins, A. Nair, and A. Kesari. S4: Distributed Stream Computing Platform. In *Proceedings of the 2010 IEEE International Conference on Data Mining Workshops*, ICDMW '10, pages 170–177. IEEE Computer Society, 2010.

[46] Novasparks™. NovaSparks Releases FPGA-based Feed Handler for OPRA. `http://bit.ly/1kGbQ0D`, Aug. 2014. Last access: 09/02/16.

[47] NVIDIA®. Quadro K5200 Data Sheet. `http://bit.ly/1O3D0Yx`. Last access: 09/02/16.

[48] H. Pirk, S. Manegold, and M. Kersten. Waste not... Efficient co-processing of relational data. In *Proceedings of the 30th IEEE International Conference on Data Engineering*, ICDE '14, pages 508–519. IEEE Press, 2014.

[49] Z. Shao. Real-time Analytics at Facebook. Presented at the *Fifth Conference on Extremely Large Databases*, XLDB5, Oct. 2011. `http://stanford.io/1HqxPmw`. Last access: 09/02/16.

[50] K. Tangwongsan, M. Hirzel, S. Schneider, and K.-L. Wu. General Incremental Sliding-window Aggregation. *Proc. VLDB Endow.*, 8(7):702–713, Feb. 2015.

[51] J. Teubner and R. Mueller. How Soccer Players Would Do Stream Joins. In *Proceedings of the 2011 ACM SIGMOD International Conference on Management of Data*, SIGMOD '11, pages 625–636. ACM, 2011.

[52] A. Toshniwal, S. Taneja, A. Shukla, K. Ramasamy, J. M. Patel, S. Kulkarni, J. Jackson, K. Gade, M. Fu, J. Donham, N. Bhagat, S. Mittal, and D. Ryaboy. Storm@Twitter. In *Proceedings of the 2014 ACM SIGMOD International Conference on Management of Data*, SIGMOD '14, pages 147–156. ACM, 2014.

[53] J. Wilkes. More Google Cluster Data. Google Research Blog, `http://bit.ly/1A38mfR`, Nov. 2011. Last access: 09/02/16.

[54] wired.com. Google Erects Fake Brain With... Graphics Chips? `http://wrd.cm/1CyGIYQ`, May 2013. Last access: 09/02/16.

[55] Y. Yuan, R. Lee, and X. Zhang. The Yin and Yang of Processing Data Warehousing Queries on GPU Devices. *Proc. VLDB Endow.*, 6(10):817–828, Aug. 2013.

[56] M. Zaharia, T. Das, H. Li, T. Hunter, S. Shenker, and I. Stoica. Discretized Streams: Fault-tolerant Streaming Computation at Scale. In *Proceedings of the 24th ACM Symposium on Operating Systems Principles*, SOSP '13, pages 423–438. ACM, 2013.

[57] Y. Zhang and F. Mueller. GStream: A General-Purpose Data Streaming Framework on GPU Clusters. In *Proceedings of the International Conference on Parallel Processing*, ICPP '11, pages 245–254. IEEE Press, 2011.

APPENDIX

A. BENCHMARK QUERIES

A.1 Cluster monitoring

```
-- Query 1
--
-- Input:  TaskEvents
--         long   timestamp
--         long   jobId
--         long   taskId
--         long   machineId
--         int    eventType
--         int    userId
--         int    category
--         int    priority
--         float  cpu
--         float  ram
--         float  disk
--         int    constraints
-- Output: CPUusagePerCategory
```

```
--          long  timestamp
--          int   category
--          float totalCpu
--
select timestamp, category, sum(cpu) as totalCpu
from TaskEvents [range 60 slide 1]
group by category
--
-- Query 2
--
-- Input:  TaskEvents
-- Output: CPUusagePerJob
--          long  timestamp
--          long  jobId
--          float avgCpu
--
select timestamp, jobId, avg(cpu) as avgCpu
from TaskEvents [range 60 slide 1]
where eventType == 1
group by jobId
```

A.2 Smart grid

```
-- Query 1
--
-- Input:  SmartGridStr
--          long  timestamp
--          float value
--          int   property
--          int   plug
--          int   household
--          int   house
--         [int   padding]
-- Output: GlobalLoadStr
--          long  timestamp
--          float globalAvgLoad
--
select timestamp, AVG (value) as globalAvgLoad
from SmartGridStr [range 3600 slide 1]
--
-- Query 2
--
-- Input:  SmartGridStr
-- Output: LocalLoadStr
--          long  timestamp
--          int   plug,
--          int   household
--          int   house
--          float localAvgLoad
--
select timestamp, plug, household, house,
       AVG (value) as localAvgLoad
from SmartGridStr [range 3600 slide 1]
group by plug, household, house
--
-- Query 3
--
-- Input:  GlobalLoadStr, LocalLoadStr
-- Output: Outliers
--          long  timestamp
--          int   house
--          float count
--
(
select L.timestamp, L.plug, L.household,
       L.house
from LocalLoadStr  [range 1 slide 1] as L,
     GlobalLoadStr [range 1 slide 1] as G
 where L.house == G.house and
       L.localAvgLoad > G.globalAvgLoad
) as R
--
select timestamp, house, count(*)
from R
group by house
```

A.3 Linear Road Benchmark

```
-- Query 1
--
-- Input:  PosSpeedStr
--          long  timestamp
--          int   vehicle
--          float speed
--          int   highway
--          int   lane
--          int   direction
--          int   position
-- Output: SegSpeedStr
--          long  timestamp
--          int   vehicle
--          float speed
--          int   highway
--          int   lane
--          int   direction
--          int   segment
--
select timestamp, vehicle, speed,
       highway, lane, direction,
       (position/5280) as segment
from SegSpeedStr [range unbounded]
--
-- Query 2
--
-- Input:  SegSpeedStr
-- Output: VehicleSegEntryStr
--          long  timestamp
--          int   vehicle
--          float speed
--          int   highway
--          int   lane
--          int   direction
--          int   segment
--
select distinct
   L.timestamp, L.vehicle, L.speed, L.highway, L.lane,
   L.direction, L.segment
from SegSpeedStr [range 30 slide 1] as A,
     SegSpeedStr [partition by vehicle rows 1] as L
where A.vehicle == L.vehicle
--
-- Query 3
--
-- Input:  SegSpeedStr
-- Output: CongestedSegRel
--          long  timestamp
--          int   highway
--          int   direction
--          int   segment
--          float avgSpeed
--
select timestamp, highway, direction, segment,
       AVG(speed) as avgSpeed
from SegSpeedStr [range 300 slide 1]
group by highway, direction, segment
having avgSpeed < 40.0
--
-- Query 4
--
-- Input:  SegSpeedStr
-- Output: SegVolRel
--          long  timestamp
--          int   highway
--          int   direction
--          int   segment
--          float numVehicles
--
(
select timestamp, vehicle, highway, direction, segment,
       count(*)
from SegSpeedStr [range 30 slide 1]
group by highway, direction, segment, vehicle
) as R
--
select timestamp, highway, direction, segment,
       count(vehicle) as numVehicles
from R
group by highway, direction, segment
```

Range Thresholding on Streams

Miao Qiao
Massey University
New Zealand
m.qiao@massey.ac.nz

Junhao Gan
University of Queensland
Australia
j.gan@uq.edu.au

Yufei Tao
University of Queensland
Australia
taoyf@itee.uq.edu.au

ABSTRACT

This paper studies a type of continuous queries called *range thresholding on streams* (RTS). Imagine the stream as an unbounded sequence of elements each of which is a real value. A query registers an interval, and must be notified as soon as a certain number of incoming elements fall into the interval. The system needs to support multiple queries simultaneously, and aims to minimize the space consumption and computation time.

Currently, all the solutions to this problem entail quadratic time $O(nm)$ to process n stream elements and m queries, which severely limits their applicability to only a small number of queries. We propose the first algorithm that breaks the quadratic barrier, by reducing the computation cost dramatically to $O(n + m)$, subject only to a polylogarithmic factor. The algorithm is general enough to guarantee the same on weighted versions of the queries even in d-dimensional space of any constant d. Its vast advantage over the previous methods in practical environments has been confirmed through extensive experimentation.

CCS Concepts

•Information systems → Stream management;

Keywords

Range Thresholding; Streams; Algorithms

1. INTRODUCTION

Stream processing is an important topic, especially in today's big-data environments where applications with gigantic update volumes abound. *Continuous queries* [1, 2, 8, 17, 21] constitute a major analytical tool on stream data. Unlike queries in a traditional DBMS whose results are determined by the current state of the database, a continuous query is a long-running operation that monitors the incoming traffic in a non-stop manner, and triggers time-critical actions when certain conditions are fulfilled.

SIGMOD'16, June 26-July 01, 2016, San Francisco, CA, USA

DOI: http://dx.doi.org/10.1145/2882903.2915965

This paper studies a new type of continuous queries that we call *range thresholding on streams* (RTS). For a basic one-dimensional version, consider the stream as an unbounded sequence of elements $e_1, e_2, e_3, \ldots$, where each element e_i ($i \geq 1$) carries:

- a *value* $v(e_i)$, which is a real number
- a *weight* $w(e_i)$, which is a positive integer.

A query q specifies an interval $R_q = [x, y]$ and an integer $\tau_q \geq 1$. Let $S(q)$ be the set of stream elements e that

- are received after q is registered in the system, and
- have value $v(e)$ falling in R_q.

The query *matures* when the total weight of the elements in $S(q)$ exceeds τ_q for the first time. The system's job is to capture the maturity of q in real time. The challenge is to scale well to a huge number of simultaneous queries, in terms of both space and computation cost.

An RTS query, intuitively, detects when the interval R_q becomes a "hot spot", by having accumulated a total weight of τ_q. It is a crucial building brick in applications that demand rapid responses to such hot spots. As an example, in stock trading, a fund manager pays close attention to the trading volumes in sensitive price ranges. In particular, substantial selling may be an early sign of a significant price downfall. The manager must receive timely alerts about this, for which purpose a typical RTS query q has the form:

> *"Alert me when $\tau_q = 100,000$ shares of AAPL (Apple Inc.) have been sold in the price range $R_q = [100, 105]$ from now."*

Relevant to the query is the stream where each element e is an AAPL trading transaction with $v(e)$ equal to the selling price, and $w(e)$ equal to the number of shares sold. The maturity of such a query is a key factor in various financial models, whose outcome plays a vital role in trading decisions. The system must support a large number of queries of this sort, each with its own R_q and τ_q.

RTS may look deceptively easy at first glance: whenever a new element e arrives, check whether $v(e)$ is in R_q; if so, increase the weight of R_q by $w(e)$—clearly, a constant time operation overall. This method, unfortunately, scales poorly to the number m of queries running at the same time: now it costs $O(m)$ time to process e. The total cost of processing n stream elements thus becomes a prohibitive quadratic term $O(nm)$. This implies that the method is computationally intractable when m is large. Surprisingly, in spite of the fundamental nature of RTS and the obvious defects of "conventional solutions" like the above, currently no progress has been made to break the quadratic barrier.

Even less is understood when the dimensionality d departs from 1, in which case $v(e)$ and R_q become respectively a point and a rectangle in d-dimensional space, as in the following query q:

> *"Alert me when $\tau_q = 100,000$ shares of AAPL have been sold by transactions e satisfying*
>
> - *the selling price of e is in [100, 105], and*
> - *when e takes place, the NASDAQ index is at 4,600 or lower."*

Here, $v(e)$ is a point (price, NASDAQ), whereas R_q is the rectangle $[100, 105] \times (-\infty, 4600]$ in the same two-dimensional space. It is straightforward to design an $O(nm)$ time algorithm, but how to escape the quadratic trap is even more elusive.

Our Contributions. We present the first algorithm that circumvents the quadratic barrier for any constant dimensionality d. Our algorithms process m queries and n stream elements in a total of $\tilde{O}(n + m)$ time—where notation $\tilde{O}(.)$ hides a polylogarithmic factor—namely, $\tilde{O}(1)$ time per query and element amortized. Apparently, $\Omega(n+m)$ time is compulsory even just to see each query and element once. Therefore, our algorithm is asymptotically optimal up to only a polylogarithmic factor.

Perhaps even more interesting are the techniques we have devised to bring about the major improvement. The most crucial discovery is an observation on the connection between RTS and another surprisingly remote problem called *distributed tracking* [9] (a detailed account of which will appear in Section 3.1). The observation then leads to the development of a novel algorithmic paradigm which, we believe, serves as a powerful weapon for implementing real-time triggers such as RTS.

This paper also features an extensive experimental evaluation of the proposed techniques. The results are fully aligned with our theoretical analysis: our algorithm is faster than conventional approaches by a factor up to orders of magnitude.

Paper Organization. Section 2 formally defines the RTS problem. Section 3 reviews the previous work related to ours. Sections 4-7 describe our RTS algorithms, and prove their theoretical guarantees. Section 8 empirically compares the proposed solutions to alternative methods. Finally, Section 9 concludes the paper with a summary of our findings.

2. PROBLEM FORMULATION

We now encapsulate all the definitions in Section 1 into a coherent framework. Given a constant integer $d \geq 1$, we consider the *data space* $\mathbb{R}^d$, i.e., the d-dimensional Euclidean space where each dimension has a real-valued domain $\mathbb{R}$.

The *data stream* is an unbounded sequence of elements, where the i-th ($i \geq 1$) element is denoted as e_i, and is said to arrive at *time* i. Each element e carries two fields:

- A point $v(e)$—called the *value* of e—in the data space;
- A *weight* $w(e)$ which is a positive integer.

An RTS query q specifies a d-dimensional axis-parallel rectangle R_q and an integer *threshold* $\tau_q \geq 1$. If the query is issued after receiving e_j (for some $j \geq 1$) and t is an integer larger than j, we use $S(q, t)$ to represent the set of elements among $e_{j+1}, e_{j+2}, ..., e_t$ that are covered by R_q, i.e.,

$$S(q, t) = \{e_i \mid j < i \leq t \text{ and } e_i \in R_q\}.$$

Define:

$$W(q, t) \quad = \quad \sum_{e \in S(q,t)} w(e) \tag{1}$$

which sums up the weights of all the elements in $S(q, t)$. Since every $w(e)$ is positive, $W(q, t)$ monotonically increases with time. The *maturity time* of q is the smallest j' making the following hold

$$W(q, j') \geq \tau_q$$

at which moment the query *matures*.

Let n be total number of stream elements so far, i.e., the *length* of the stream at this point. For convenience, we abbreviate $S(q, n)$ as $S(q)$, and $W(q, n)$ as $W(q)$.

The system allows two operations:

- REGISTER(q): Accept a query at the current moment (after the arrival of e_n).
- TERMINATE(q): Stop and eliminate a query.

A query, which has been registered but not terminated, is *alive*. We denote by Q the set of alive queries. For every query $q \in Q$, the system *must* report the maturity of q at its maturity time. Such a query is then automatically removed from the system with a TERMINATE operation.

Denote by m the total number of queries ever registered in history. The system's efficiency goal is to *entail total computation cost of* $\tilde{O}(n+m)$. In addition, we require that it should consume $\tilde{O}(m_{alive})$ space at all times, where m_{alive} is the number of queries alive currently. This essentially implies that one cannot hope to store too many stream elements (if any at all).

This completes the definition of the RTS problem. A special instance—which we refer to as *counting RTS*—arises when $w(e) = 1$ for all the stream elements e. Later, we will discuss first the counting version, which allows us to elaborate on our central ideas, before including the extra details to solve the general RTS problem.

3. RELATED WORK

Section 3.1 discusses how RTS can be tackled using known techniques. Section 3.2 presents an introduction to the *distributed tracking* problem. Finally, Section 3.3 surveys other research that is relevant, but to a less extent.

3.1 Existing RTS Solutions

Section 1 has already mentioned a *baseline* approach for solving the RTS problem, which maintains the precise value of $W(q)$ for all alive queries q. Given an incoming stream element e, it simply checks whether $v(e) \in R_q$, and if so, increases $W(q)$ accordingly. This approach demands the minimum amount of space $O(m_{alive})$, but incurs $O(m_{alive})$ time processing e. It is easy to see that in the worst case its overall computation time can be as high as $O(nm)$.

Query indexing has become a standard method to tackle continuous queries. The rationale is to create an index structure on the *queries* (unlike a conventional database where indexes are on *data*). Each arriving stream element trickles down the index, and updates the relevant information therein. This motivates a better RTS approach that maintains a structure on the set Q of alive queries to support the *stabbing operation*:

> Given a point v in the data space $\mathbb{R}^d$, report the set of queries $q \in Q$ such that $v \in q$. These queries are said to be *stabbed* by v.

Such operations have been very well studied (see [20] for a full summary of the past results). In one-dimensional space, the *interval tree* [12] consumes $O(|Q|) = O(m_{alive})$ space, supports an insertion/deletion in $\tilde{O}(1)$ time, and performs a stabbing operation in $\tilde{O}(1+k)$ time, where k is the number of queries reported. Using standard layering techniques (see Chapter 5.3 of [12]), the interval tree can be extended to d-dimensional space, by paying a logarithmic factor in the space, update, and query overhead. For constant d, the resulting structure uses $\tilde{O}(m_{alive})$ space, supports an update in $\tilde{O}(1)$ time, and allows a stabbing operation in $\tilde{O}(1+k)$ time. For practical data, the *R-tree* [5, 16] is a dynamic structure that may exhibit satisfactory efficiency for the stabbing operation, although no attractive worst-case guarantees exist on updates and queries.

Given such an index, the *stabbing approach* launches, for each stream element e, a stabbing operation to find the queries stabbed by $v(e)$. Every such query q then has its $W(q)$ increased by $w(e)$. The stabbing approach is still captivated by the quadratic trap because the value of k—the number of queries stabbed by an incoming element—can be as large as m in the worst case, and thereby, necessitating $O(nm)$ time overall. However, better efficiency is expected in practice because, with a more careful analysis, one can easily show that the cost of the approach is bounded by $\tilde{O}(n) + O(m \cdot \tau_{max})$, where τ_{max} is the largest threshold of all queries. When viewed this way, the quadratic trap takes up a different form, i.e., with respect to m and τ_{max}.

3.2 Distributed Tracking

This problem is defined in a distributed environment with $h+1$ sites: one of them is the *coordinator* q, while the rest are *participants* $s_1, s_2, ..., s_h$. Communication exists between only the coordinator and the participants, whereas the participants do not talk to each other.

Each participant s_i $(1 \le i \le h)$ has an integer counter c_i. Initially, all the counters $c_1, c_2, ..., c_h$ are 0. At every timestamp, at most one of those counters gets increased by 1—in other words, it is possible that no counter is incremented, but never more than one. The coordinator's job is to report *maturity* when the following condition holds

$$\sum_{i=1}^{h} c_i = \tau$$

where $\tau > 0$ is an integer. To achieve the purpose, an algorithm instructs the sites to send messages strategically. The goal is to minimize the messaging cost, measured in the number of words transmitted.

A straightforward solution to this problem is to have a participant inform the coordinator whenever its counter increases. The total communication cost is apparently τ bits, which is expensive if τ is large. The problem admits another algorithm [9] that requires the communication of $O(h \log \tau)$ words. Note that this is far less than τ bits when τ is (realistically) much larger than h. Next, we describe the algorithm in full.

First, if $\tau \le 6h$, then solve the problem using the straightforward solution by sending $O(\tau) = O(h)$ words.

Consider now $\tau > 6h$. The coordinator q sends to every participant s_i $(1 \le i \le h)$ the value which we call the *slack*:

$$\lambda = \lfloor \tau/(2h) \rfloor. \qquad (2)$$

This requires h messages. Then, s_i intermittently sends a one-bit *signal* to q according to the following rule:

> Let $\bar{c}_i$ be the counter value at the time of the last signal to q (0, if no signal yet). Send a signal, as soon as $c_i - \bar{c}_i = \lambda$.

The coordinator keeps track of the number of signals received. When the number reaches h, it collects the precise counters from all the participants using h messages, and calculates:

$$\tau' = \tau - \sum_{i=1}^{h} c_i.$$

This finishes a *round*.

Notice that, at this moment, we are facing the same problem but with a reduced $\tau = \tau'$. The algorithm recursively solves it as above. Eventually, the value of τ drops to at most $6h$, in which case the problem is settled with a final round using the straightforward approach.

Each round clearly necessitates $O(h)$ messages. It is not hard to verify from $\tau > 6h$ that $\tau' \le 2\tau/3$, implying that the total number of rounds is $O(\log \tau)$. This explains why the total messaging cost is $O(h \log \tau)$ words.

3.3 Other Relevant Research

This subsection reviews several topics related to RTS, paying an effort to provide a chronological view on their development.

Triggers, a form of which RTS can be though of as, are one of the oldest concepts in database systems. As taught in standard textbooks, a conventional trigger typically serves a "passive" role, which is to ensure certain integrity constraints on the underlying relations. In the 1990's, the community started to introduce novel, more sophisticated, forms of triggers that allow a database to activate itself in response to a great variety of events. The functionalities of those "advanced" triggers eventually escalate to a level such that people decided to call them *event-condition-action* rules. Efficient implementation of such rules in DBMS has been extensively studied in the literature of *active databases*; see [11, 19] for a nice introduction.

Early research assumed datasets with low insertion/deletion frequency. Since the emergence of update-intensive applications at the beginning of the century, stream processing has been a major subfield in the database area. Continuous queries—a concept that, interestingly, had its first appearance in non-stream days [21]—are a main focus in the research of modern systems for managing stream data (e.g., [1, 2, 8, 17]). Our work also belongs to this line of research.

Triggers were revitalized on streams. This was reflected not only in the community's endeavor to *implement* triggers to meet the new efficiency requirements [7], but also in the creative *use* of triggers to build innovative application platforms, perhaps most notably, *publish/subscribe systems*; see some representative works [8, 14, 15, 18, 23] and the references therein. Such a system is built on a stream of elements (e.g., tweets, news articles, product orders, etc), only some of which may be interesting to a user. Instead of "publishing" everything, the system allows the user to "subscribe" to particular information. A subscription is essentially a trigger, specifying when the system should *push* information to the user, and if so, what information to push.

RTS, if not treated entirely as a continuous *query*, may also be counted as a stream trigger, or a form of content subscription. In the sense of the former, the user issuing an RTS query should get an alert at the query's maturity time. In the sense of the latter, on the other hand, the user implicitly subscribes to a form of information *aggregated* from the elements flowing through the system. Regardless of the perspective, however, RTS is unique in its own, especially given the fact that there does not exist an efficient algorithm—not counting the ones in Section 3.1 with the quadratic time complexity.

Finally, we note that active databases have also be rejuvenated on streams, yielding another line of research under the theme of *complex event processing*; see [10, 13, 22] for entry points of reading into this subfield. Our work complements that subfield by adding RTS as another "efficiently-supportable" atomic event type.

4. THE FIRST ALGORITHM

We will incrementally unfold our ultimate RTS algorithm. Let us start by constraining the problem in two ways:

- Counting RTS with $d = 1$, that is, the value of each stream element is one-dimensional, and its weight is 1.
- All the queries are registered at the beginning, namely, before receiving the first element. No query is accepted afterwards. Those queries remain alive until maturity. This is called the *one-time registration constraint.*

The goal of this section is to settle the above restricted problem using $\tilde{O}(m_{alive})$ space at any moment, and $\tilde{O}(n+m)$ time overall. The imposed constraints permit us to concentrate on explaining the most crucial ideas. Both constraints will be eventually removed in later sections; and our final algorithm still achieves the same space and query complexities.

To simplify our technical exposition, we will treat each query interval R_q as $[x, y)$, namely, open at the right end. This assumption does not lose generality because, as a standard technique, a closed interval $[x, y]$ can be regarded as $[x, y + \epsilon)$ for an infinitesimal $\epsilon > 0$.

The Endpoint Tree. Define Q^* as the set of registered queries. We create a binary search tree $\mathcal{T}$ on the endpoints of the queries' intervals; see Figure 1 for an example with 8 queries. The height of $\mathcal{T}$ is $O(\log m)$.

Every node u in $\mathcal{T}$ is naturally associated with a *jurisdiction interval* $I(u)$ as follows. Consider first that u is a leaf. Suppose that u stores an endpoint x, and u'—the leaf succeeding u—stores x' ($= \infty$ if u' does not exist); then, $I(u) = [x, x')$. Consider now u as an internal node with child nodes u_1, u_2; then $I(u) = I(u_1) \cup I(u_2)$. As an example, in Figure 1, the jurisdiction interval of leaf 8 is $[8, 9)$, that of leaf 16 is $[16, \infty)$, and that of u_1 is $[5, 9)$.

Let e be a stream element such that $v(e)$ is at least the leftmost endpoint in $\mathcal{T}$ (otherwise, e obviously can be safely ignored). At each level of $\mathcal{T}$, e is *covered* by precisely one node u: the one with $I(u)$ containing $v(e)$. These nodes can be easily found in $O(\log m)$ time by descending a single root-to-leaf path.

Every node u in $\mathcal{T}$ stores a counter $c(u)$, which equals the number of stream elements covered by u. The counters are initially set to 0, and maintained along with the arrival of each element e: if $I(u)$ covers $v(e)$, increase $c(u)$ by 1. We then discard e forever—our structure does not store any elements. It is thus clear that the maintenance takes $O(\log m)$ time per element.

We refer to $\mathcal{T}$ as the *endpoint tree*. It is rudimentary to construct it in $O(m \log m)$ time.

"Distributed" Tracking. We are ready to unveil how to leverage the distributed tracking (DT) algorithm in Section 3.2 for RTS.

Focus, for the time being, on an arbitrary query $q \in Q^*$. Its interval $R_q = [x, y)$ can be partitioned by the jurisdiction intervals of nodes that constitute the *canonical node set* U_q. This is the minimum set of nodes with *disjoint* jurisdiction intervals whose union equals R_q. U_q contains at most 2 nodes per level of $\mathcal{T}$, implying that $U_q = O(\log m)$. For instance, consider query q_5 in Figure 1: $U_{q_5} = \{u_1, u_2, u_3\}$. Given x, y, it is a standard exercise[1] to identify U_q in $O(\log m)$ time.

Next, we define a conceptual DT problem instance for q. Set $h_q = |U_q|$. There are h_q "participants", each of which is a node $u \in U_q$. The counter of "participant" u is simply $c(u)$. The query q itself is the "coordinator", whose mission is to capture maturity when the following condition holds:

$$\sum_{u \in U_q} c(u) = \tau_q.$$

Note that, by definition of U_q, the left hand side of the equation is precisely $W(q)$.

It must be emphasized that there is nothing "distributed" in this conversion. All the processing happens on a single machine in the context of RTS. The "distributed" viewpoint is sheerly to allow the reader to borrow the knowledge from Section 3.2 to see what is actually happening here.

We then "run" the algorithm in Section 3.2 to solve this DT instance, by *simulating* all of its steps. Whenever $c(u)$ increases by 1, we reflect so by thinking that the counter of the "participant" u has gone up by 1. Whenever the algorithm instructs a "participant" u to send a message (of no more than one word) to the "coordinator" q or the other way around, we spend $O(1)$ time to do so explicitly, so that both u and q can maintain the same information as demanded by the algorithm.

A piece of detail deserves a more careful look. In the DT algorithm, every node $u \in U_q$ keeps—as described in Section 3.2—the counter value $\bar{c}_q(u)$ at the time of the last

[1]Let z_1 and z_2 be the leaves storing x and y, respectively. Identify the lowest common ancestor u of z_1, z_2. Then, invoke the following procedure ADD(u). In general, the procedure first checks whether $I(u) \subseteq [x, y)$. If so, it adds u to U_q and finishes. Otherwise, it checks whether $I(u)$ is disjoint with $[x, y)$. If so, it adds nothing and finishes. If not, it recursively invokes ADD(u_1) and ADD(u_2), where u_1 and u_2 are the two child nodes of u.

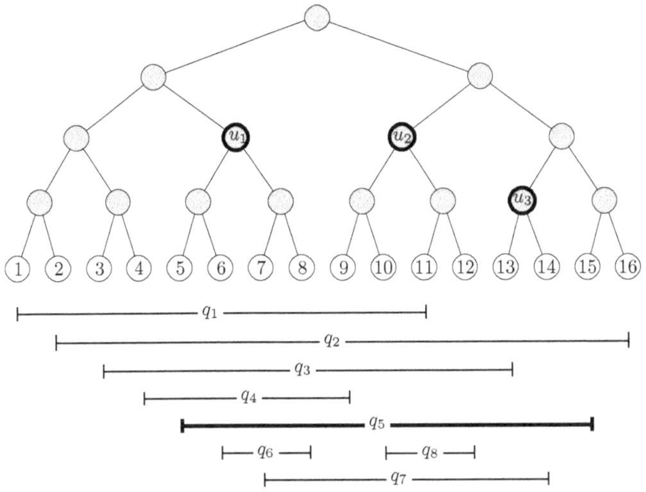

Figure 1: One-dimensional endpoint tree

signal to q. The next signal from u takes place when

$$c(u) - \bar{c}_q(u) = \lambda_q \tag{3}$$

where λ_q is the *slack* value given in (2). Node u needs to inspect the above condition *only* when its counter $c(u)$ changes. Hence, every incoming element triggers such slack inspection only at $O(\log m)$ nodes.

To analyze the computation cost, recall from earlier discussion that the time of maintaining the node counters is $O(n \log m)$. The same cost applies to inspecting the slack condition in (3). The rest of the DT algorithm is simulated with $O(1)$ time per "message". We already know from Section 3.2 that the algorithm needs $O(h_q \log \tau_q)$ messages to solve the DT instance of q. Therefore, in the RTS context, such *messaging cost* adds up to

$$O(h_q \log \tau_q) = O(\log m \cdot \log \tau_q) \tag{4}$$

in total.

Putting Together All Queries with Heaps. Every query $q \in Q^*$ defines a DT instance as above, which is solved by an instance of the algorithm of Section 2. In other words, conceptually, there are m algorithm instances in progress simultaneously. Our task is to implement such "concurrent" execution efficiently on our *sequential* CPU.

Two immediate observations are helpful. First, the maintenance of node counters (i.e., $c(u)$ of every node u in $\mathcal{T}$) is *common* to all instances. Therefore, such maintenance incurs only $O(n \log m)$ time in total for m queries.

Second, the messaging cost of each query q is specific to q itself, and is given by (4). Hence, the total messaging cost of all queries is:

$$\sum_{q \in Q^*} O(\log m \cdot \log \tau_q) = O(m \log m \cdot \log \tau_{max})$$

where τ_{max} the largest τ_q of all $q \in Q^*$.

It remains to discuss the cost of inspecting the slack condition (3). Concentrate on an arbitrary node u. Let $Q(u)$ be the set of queries that have u in their canonical node sets. For example, consider u_2 in Figure 1: $Q(u_2) = \{q_2, q_3, q_5, q_7\}$.

Carrying out the one-query strategy naively, when $c(u)$ changes, we would inspect the condition for all the queries in $Q(u)$. However, this, taking $O(|Q(u)|)$ time, is overly expensive, and will blow up the overall cost essentially to quadratic again. We overcome this issue by inspecting only *one* slack condition, instead of $|Q(u)|$, as explained next.

For each query $q \in Q(u)$, define

$$\sigma_q(u) = \lambda_q + \bar{c}_q(u). \tag{5}$$

Phrased differently, $\sigma_q(u)$ indicates the *future* value of $c_q(u)$ when the next signal from u to q should occur. For two queries $q_1, q_2 \in Q(u)$ such that $\sigma_{q_1}(u) < \sigma_{q_2}(u)$, $\sigma_{q_1}(u) > c(u)$ always implies $\sigma_{q_2}(u) > c(u)$. Namely, if a signal to q_1 is not necessary yet, neither is it to q_2.

Motivated by this, we maintain the $\sigma_q(u)$ of all the queries $q \in Q(u)$ in a min-heap $\mathcal{H}(u)$. Whenever $c(u)$ changes, we perform these steps:

1. Find the minimum $\sigma_q(u)$ in $\mathcal{H}(u)$ in $O(1)$ time.
2. If $c(u) < \sigma_q(u)$, then we are done.
3. Otherwise, remove $\sigma_q(u)$ from $\mathcal{H}(u)$, and instruct u to send a signal to q (as in the DT algorithm). This takes $O(\log |\mathcal{H}(u)|) = O(\log m)$ time. Then, repeat from Line 1.

It is evident that the above steps run in

$$O(1 + x \cdot \log m) \tag{6}$$

time, where x is the number of signals issued at Line 3.

We now bound the total cost of the 3 steps during the entire algorithm, including all nodes and queries. The $O(1)$ term in (6) occurs $O(n \log m)$ times, because each stream element can increase the counters of $O(\log m)$ nodes. To bound the sum of the term $x \log m$, we point out that the total number of signals throughout the algorithm is

$$\sum_{q \in Q^*} O(h_q \log \tau_q) = O(m \log m \cdot \log \tau_{max}). \tag{7}$$

Therefore, all the $x \log m$ terms add up to $O(m \log^2 m \cdot \log \tau_{max})$.

To complete the time analysis, we must note that $\mathcal{H}(u)$ demands additional cost for the insertions and deletions therein. Specifically, whenever the λ_q of a query q changes, so does $\sigma_q(u)$ for each $u \in U_q$; see (5). This incurs $O(\log m)$ time to remove the old $\sigma_q(u)$ from $\mathcal{H}(u)$ and to add back the new one. The number of λ_q changes equals the number of rounds in the DT algorithm for q, which as explained in Section 3.2 is $O(\log \tau_q)$. Hence, the total number of heap insertions and deletions (over all queries, all nodes) is also given by (7). Their cost is therefore $O(m \log^2 m \cdot \log \tau_{max})$.

Finally, as each query adds an entry in the heaps of $O(\log m)$ nodes, the total space consumption is bounded by $O(m \log m)$.

Handling Maturity. When a query q matures, we simply remove its entry from the $\mathcal{H}(u)$ of all nodes $u \in U_q$, in $O(h_q \log m) = O(\log^2 m)$ time. This adds $O(m \log^2 m)$ time to the overall computation cost.

Recall that we aim to use $\tilde{O}(m_{alive})$ space at all times. Our structure, as mentioned earlier, occupies $\tilde{O}(m)$ space, which can break the promise when $m_{alive} \ll m$, namely, after many queries have matured. Next, we explain how to deal with the issue with *global rebuilding*.

When m_{alive} has decreased to $m/2$, we destroy the whole structure, and re-start the entire algorithm from *scratch* with respect to the remaining set Q of alive queries which, importantly, have their thresholds adjusted. Specifically, for each query $q \in Q$, we obtain $W(q)$ (the actual number of elements that have already arrived and fallen into R_q, as defined in Section 2). The value of $W(q)$ equals the sum of the counters of all the nodes in U_q, and thus can be obtained in $O(\log m)$ time. From *now* on, q matures after another $\tau_q - W(q)$ subsequent elements get into R_q. We thus reset its threshold to $\tau_q - W(q)$. After all the threshold resetting is complete, we rebuild $\mathcal{T}$ in $O(m_{alive} \log m_{alive})$ time, after which the algorithm runs as if the stream had just started.

One global rebuilding takes $O(m \log m)$ time in total. This can be amortized on the $m/2$ queries that have matured, so that each of those query bears $O(\log m)$ time. As each query bears such cost only once, the total rebuilding cost is $O(m \log m)$ for the entire algorithm.

If Q^* is the set of queries alive at the moment of the most recent reconstruction, the above approach ensures that $m_{alive} \geq |Q^*|/2$. Therefore, our space consumption now becomes $O(|Q^*| \log |Q^*|) = O(m_{alive} \log m_{alive})$, as desired.

Remark. We now have solved the simplified RTS problem defined at the beginning of this section. Our algorithm guarantees $O(m_{alive} \log m_{alive}) = \tilde{O}(m_{alive})$ space at any moment, and performs $O(n \log m + m \log^2 m \cdot \log \tau_{max}) = \tilde{O}(n + m)$ time in total.

5. DYNAMIC QUERIES

This section will remove the "one-time registration" constraint, where queries are *static* in the sense that all of them need to be registered at the beginning of the stream. Next, we extend our algorithm of the previous section to the *dynamic* scenario, allowing the REGISTER and TERMINATE operations defined in Section 2 at any time.

Termination. The data structure behind our algorithm—namely the endpoint tree—easily supports a TERMINATE(q) operation, in the same manner as removing a matured query. Specifically, it suffices to delete the entry of q from the $\mathcal{H}(u)$ of all nodes $u \in U_q$. This takes $O(\log^2 m)$ time as explained before. Note that the underlying binary search tree $\mathcal{T}$ does not change after the termination (because $\mathcal{H}(u)$ is a secondary min-heap associated with u). After $m/2$ queries have disappeared (either matured or deleted), apply global rebuilding as described in Section 4 to maintain the space consumption $\tilde{O}(m_{alive})$.

Registration. Recall that $\mathcal{T}$ is built on the endpoints of the query intervals. To terminate a query, we can afford to retain the endpoints of the query's interval in $\mathcal{T}$, because this does not affect the algorithm's correctness (some redundancy is left in the structure, but the extra space is affordable, as proved earlier). To insert a new query with REGISTER(q), however, we must add the endpoints of R_q into $\mathcal{T}$; otherwise, the node counters in $\mathcal{T}$ do not allow us to derive $W(q)$ precisely, making it impossible to detect its maturity.

Inserting the endpoints of R_q may trigger *rebalancing operations* of $\mathcal{T}$ (i.e., splits or rotations, depending on the binary tree implementation). Accordingly, the secondary min-heaps will need to be reorganized, because rebalancing may disrupt the canonical node sets of many queries. For inquisitive readers, we mention that in theory this can be dealt with using *weight balancing techniques* (see, e.g., [4]), but the algorithm becomes too complicated to implement in practice.

We circumvent this problem by resorting to another, much more practical, algorithmic technique called the *logarithmic method* [3, 6]. It is a generic framework that allows one to convert a *semi*-dynamic structure supporting only deletions to a *fully*-dynamic structure that is able to support both deletions and insertions. In what follows, we explain how to instantiate the framework in our RTS context.

Our indexing scheme now consists of g endpoint trees $\mathcal{T}_1, \mathcal{T}_2, ..., \mathcal{T}_g$ satisfying all the properties below:

P1 $g = O(\log m)$.

P2 Every alive query is managed by one and exactly one tree.

P3 Let $m_{alive}(i)$ be the number of alive queries in $\mathcal{T}_i$ ($1 \leq i \leq g$). It must hold that $m_{alive}(i) \leq 2^{i-1}$. Note that $\mathcal{T}_i$ is allowed to be an empty tree (i.e., merely a placeholder) with $m_{alive}(i) = 0$.

At the very beginning, $g = 1$, and $\mathcal{T}_1$ is an empty tree. Consider, in general, that the system receives a REGISTER(q) operation. We handle it with these steps:

1. Identify the smallest $j \geq 1$ satisfying

$$\sum_{i=1}^{j} m_{alive}(i) \;<\; 2^{j-1}. \tag{8}$$

   If j does not exist, then set $j = g + 1$ (as we will see, in this case a new endpoint tree will be created).

2. Collect all the alive queries in $\mathcal{T}_1, \mathcal{T}_2, ..., \mathcal{T}_j$, together with the new query q, into a set Q^*. For each query $q' \in Q^*$, obtain $W(q')$ from the endpoint tree where it belongs. Reduce the threshold $\tau_{q'}$ of q' by $W(q')$.

3. Discard all of $\mathcal{T}_1, \mathcal{T}_2, ..., \mathcal{T}_j$. Construct $\mathcal{T}_j$ on Q^* from scratch. From now on, $\mathcal{T}_j$ is responsible for the queries of Q^* (with thresholds *modified*), treating them as if they were new with respect to the subsequent stream.

   Note that (8) ensures that $\mathcal{T}_j$ obeys Property ***P3***. Furthermore, $\mathcal{T}_1, \mathcal{T}_2, ..., \mathcal{T}_{j-1}$ are now all empty.

Given an incoming element e, we now use it to increase the node counters of all g trees. As the counter increasing for each tree takes $O(\log m)$ time, in total the processing time of e is bounded by $O(g \log m) = O(\log^2 m)$. The time is thus $O(n \log^2 m)$ for all the n stream elements.

Next, we analyze the cost of rebuilding the endpoint trees. Our algorithm ensures that if a query moves from $\mathcal{T}_i$ to $\mathcal{T}_{i'}$, it is always due to Line 3, which must have destroyed T_i and rebuilt $\mathcal{T}_{i'}$. This implies that $i' \geq i$ always holds, namely, a query *never* moves from a higher "ranked" endpoint tree to a lower one.

Line 3, whose cost dominates the other steps, builds $\mathcal{T}_j$ in $O(|Q^*| \cdot \log |Q^*|) = O(2^j \log m)$ time. On the other hand, the definition of j (c.f. (8)) implies

$$\sum_{i=1}^{j-1} m_{alive}(i) \;\geq\; 2^{j-2} \tag{9}$$

otherwise, j would have been smaller by at least 1. In other words, at least 2^{j-2} queries have moved from a lower ranked

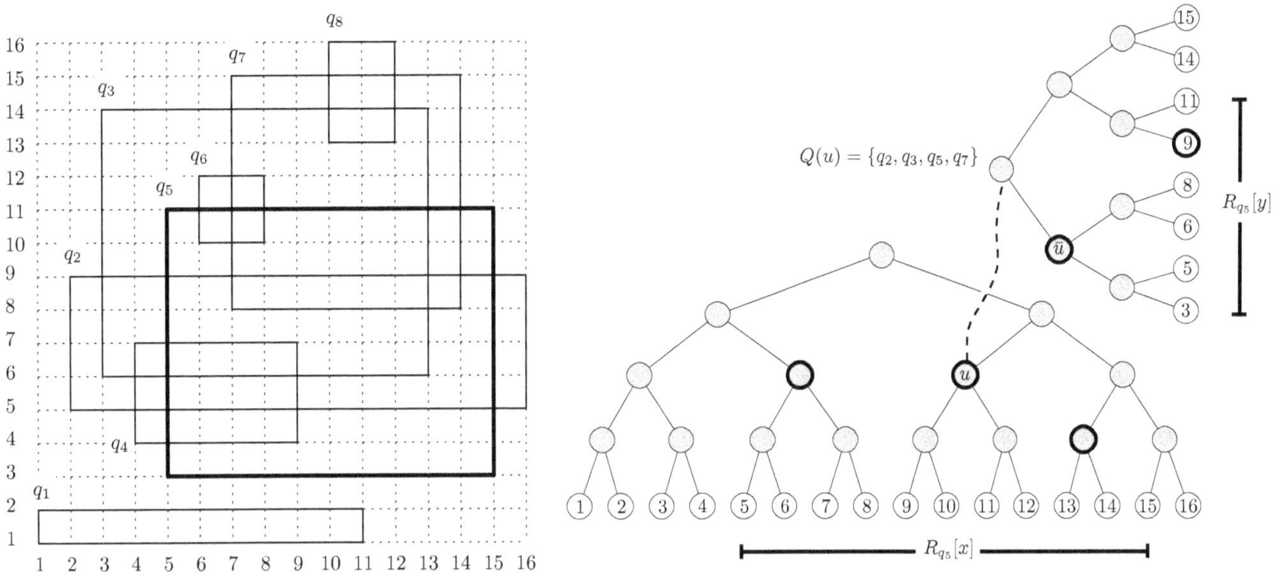

Figure 2: Two-dimensional endpoint tree

endpoint tree to $\mathcal{T}_j$. We can thus charge the $O(2^j \log m)$ construction time of $\mathcal{T}_j$ on those queries, each of which bears only $O(\log m)$. Property ***P1*** tells us that a query can be charged this way only $O(\log m)$ times, i.e., $O(\log^2 m)$ time in total. Therefore, the overall cost of rebuilding the endpoint trees is $O(m \log^2 m)$.

Why can our algorithm ensure ***P1***? Consider the moment when $\mathcal{T}_g$ has just been constructed at Line 3. (9) shows that $\mathcal{T}_g$ must contain more than 2^{g-2} queries. It thus follows that $m \geq 2^{g-2}$, and hence, $g = O(\log m)$.

None of the other parts of the time analysis in Section 5 is affected. In other words, our algorithm entails $O(n \log^2 m + m \log^2 m \cdot \log \tau_{max})$ time to process a stream of length n and m *dynamic* queries. As each endpoint tree uses space that is proportional to the number of alive queries therein (up to a logarithmic factor), Property ***P2*** ensures that the total space consumption is $\tilde{O}(m_{alive})$ at all times.

6. MULTIDIMENSIONAL QUERIES

We will describe how to solve, still, counting RTS, but in d-dimensional space $\mathbb{R}^d$ with a constant d. This, in fact, has become fairly easy under the algorithmic framework laid out in the previous sections. It should have become clear that there are two central ideas:

- Partition the search region R_q (i.e., an interval for $d = 1$) into $\tilde{O}(1)$ components, for each of which the number of elements within is kept precisely at a node.
- Many queries share the same components such that the total number of distinct components is $\tilde{O}(m_{alive})$.

Plugging almost any such partitioning scheme into our framework will yield an efficient algorithm. For $d = 1$, our scheme—based on canonical node sets—assumes a binary search tree. A natural extension to general d is to use ideas from the *range tree* (see Chapter 5.3 of [12]).

The subsequent discussion explains this for $d = 2$ because the generalization to higher d will then become straightforward. We will first work with the one-time registration constraint, namely, all the m queries are registered at the beginning of the stream. The constraint can be removed by the same technique in Section 5. Once again, for our technical exposition, we regard each R_q in the form of $[x_1, x_2) \times [y_1, y_2)$, with the "infinitesimal trick" explained in Section 4.

Two-Dimensional Endpoint Tree. Let Q^* be the set of all queries. Remember that, for each $q \in Q^*$, R_q is now a two-dimensional rectangle. Denote by $R_q[x]$ the projection of R_q onto the x-dimension, and by $R_q[y]$ the projection onto the y-dimension.

We create a binary search tree $\mathcal{T}$ on the endpoints of $R_q[x]$ of all $q \in Q^*$. As before, each query defines an *x-canonical node set*, which is the minimum set of nodes in $\mathcal{T}$ with disjoint jurisdiction intervals whose union is $R_q[x]$.

Focus now on a specific node u in $\mathcal{T}$. Denote by $Q(u)$ the set of queries that have u in their x-canonical node sets. We associate u with a secondary binary search tree $\mathfrak{T}(u)$, which indexes the endpoints of $R_q[y]$ of all $q \in Q(u)$.

Figure 2 illustrates this using an example with 8 queries—for the reader's convenience, the x-projections of the rectangles are exactly the intervals in our one-dimensional example of Figure 1. For the node u as indicated, $Q(u) = \{q_2, q_3, q_5, q_7\}$. Therefore, $\mathfrak{T}(u)$ is created on the endpoints of the y-projections of the four queries: $[5, 9)$, $[6, 14)$, $[3, 11)$, and $[8, 15)$.

$\mathcal{T}$ and all the the secondary trees $\mathfrak{T}(u)$ constitute our two-dimensional *endpoint tree*. It is rudimentary to construct the structure in $O(m \log m)$ time.

Query Decomposition. It is important to note the *geometric region* in $\mathbb{R}^2$ corresponding to every node u in $\mathcal{T}$, and to every node $\bar{u}$ in a secondary tree $\mathfrak{T}(u)$. Specifically, the jurisdiction interval $I(u)$—which is on the x-dimension—defines the vertical slab $I(u) \times (-\infty, \infty)$. The jurisdiction interval $I(\bar{u})$—which is on the y-dimension—defines the rectangle $I(u) \times I(\bar{u})$. For instance, consider node u and $\bar{u}$ in Figure 2: u corresponds to the slab $[9, 13) \times (-\infty, \infty)$, and $\bar{u}$ to $[9, 13) \times [3, 9)$.

We are ready to explain how the R_q of a query $q \in Q^*$

is partitioned by the above geometric regions. Let u be a node in the x-canonical node set of q. Then, q and u together define $U_q(u)$, which is the minimum set of nodes in $\mathcal{T}(u)$ with disjoint jurisdiction intervals whose union is $R_q[y]$. Consider, for instance, query q_5 and node u of $\mathcal{T}$ in Figure 2: $U_{q_5}(u) = \{\bar{u}, \text{leaf } 9\}$. The *y-canonical node set* of q—denoted as U_q—unions the $U_q(u)$ of all such nodes u.

The size of U_q is $O(\log^2 m)$, because $|U_q(u)| = O(\log m)$ while there are $O(\log m)$ such u. Every node $\bar{u} \in U_q$ is in some secondary tree; and the geometric regions of all the $\bar{u}$ form a disjoint partition of R_q.

Algorithm. Every node $\bar{u}$ in a secondary tree keeps a counter equal to the number of stream elements e such that $v(e)$ falls into the geometric region of $\bar{u}$. These counters can be easily maintained in $O(\log^2 m)$ time per element (descending one root-to-leaf path Π of $\mathcal{T}$, and then one root-to-leaf path of $\mathcal{T}(u)$ for each node $u \in \Pi$). The counter maintenance takes $O(n \log^2 m)$ time in total for n elements.

The rest of the algorithm directly follows that of Section 4. In particular, every query still defines a distributed tracking instance involving the h_q nodes in U_q, where $h_q = |U_q|$. The total number of heap insertions and deletions is still given by the left hand side of (7). As h_q here becomes $O(\log^2 m)$, the total cost of all the heap updates is bounded by $O(m \log^3 m \cdot \log \tau_{max})$.

Eliminating the one-time registration constraint with the logarithmic method (Section 5) increases the counter maintenance overhead by a logarithmic factor. Therefore, our two-dimensional algorithm entails the overall computation time of $O(n \log^3 m + m \log^3 m \cdot \log \tau_{max})$. The space consumption is $O(m_{alive} \log^2 m_{alive})$: essentially the total size of U_q of all the alive queries q.

Remark. Extending our algorithm to general d-dimensional space is at the standard expense of an extra logarithmic factor in both the running time and space per dimension: $O(n \log^{d+1} m + m \log^{d+1} m \cdot \log \tau_{max})$ and $O(m_{alive} \log^d m_{alive})$, respectively.

7. THE WEIGHTED VERSION

We are already very close to solving the most generic form of RTS. The only constraint left is that the element weights are still confined to 1. In this section, we will remove this last constraint.

Weighted Distributed Tracking. Before tackling elements with arbitrary weights, let us first consider a more general version of the DT problem in Section 3.2. As before, the setup involves a coordinator q, and h participants $s_1, s_2, ..., s_h$, such that s_i $(1 \le i \le h)$ keeps a counter c_i initially set to 0. At every timestamp, still at most one counter gets increased, but the increment can be any positive integer (instead of just 1). The coordinator aims to capture *maturity* subject to

$$\sum_{i=1}^{h} c_i \geq \tau. \tag{10}$$

The efficiency goal now is to achieve two purposes simultaneously:

- Communication cost $O(h \log \tau)$ messages (each one word in length).
- The coordinator and participants perform in total $O(n + h \log \tau)$ CPU time, where n is the total number of counter increases at all sites.

If communication *was* the only concern, the problem can be easily settled with $O(h \log \tau)$ messages as follows. Whenever c_i needs to increase by say w, s_i does so by increasing c_i w times, each time by 1. This conversion essentially transforms the current problem into the unweighted version, thus permitting the application of the same algorithm in Section 3.2.

The drawback of the simple reduction lies in the computation cost: as $O(1)$ time is spent on increasing a counter by 1, the total amount of work done becomes $O(\tau + h \log \tau)$. This can be substantially higher than our goal $O(n + h \log \tau)$ if $\tau \gg n$—this will lead to prohibitively high RTS processing cost when we plug the algorithm into our framework.

The astute reader may wonder why the issue did not arise in Section 3.2. In fact, for the old DT problem, there must be exactly $n = \tau$ counter increases at maturity; therefore, the trivially attainable CPU cost of $O(\tau + h \log \tau)$ is good, precisely the complexity $O(n + h \log \tau)$ that we want. This is no longer true for weighted DT.

Next, we explain how to modify the DT algorithm to suit our purposes. Again, if $\tau \le 6h$, we solve the problem by asking each participant to send all counter changes to q. This requires $O(\tau) = O(h)$ messages.

For $\tau > 6h$, q launches a *round* by informing every s_i $(1 \le i \le h)$ the slack $\lambda = \lfloor \tau/(2h) \rfloor$. The way s_i behaves is a bit different from Section 3.2:

> Let $\bar{c}_i$ be an integer that equals 0 at the round's beginning. When $c_i - \bar{c}_i \ge \lambda$:
>
> 1. Send a signal to q, and increase $\bar{c}_i$ by λ.
> 2. If $c_i - \bar{c}_i \ge \lambda$ still holds, repeat Line 1, *unless* q has announced the end of this round.

When the number of signals reaches h, q declares to all sites "the round has finished", and collects their precise counters. Maturity is reported if (10) is satisfied. Otherwise, q decreases τ by $\sum_{i=1}^{h} c_i$; and the next round starts.

The algorithm is correct because if a round still has not finished at the end of a timestamp, it must hold that

$$\begin{aligned}\sum_{i=1}^{h} c_i &\le \lambda \cdot (h-1) + \sum_{i=1}^{h} (c_i - \bar{c}_i) \\ &< \lambda \cdot h + \lambda \cdot h \le \tau.\end{aligned}$$

As in Section 3.2, $\tau > 6h$ ensures that a round decreases τ by at least $\tau/3$. Thus, the number of rounds is $O(\log \tau)$, making the total number of messages $O(h \log \tau)$. Furthermore, the computation time is $O(n + h \log \tau)$ because $O(1)$ time is spent (i) at a participant only if its counter is increased or it needs to send a message, and (ii) at the coordinator to send a message.

RTS. Our ultimate RTS algorithm—settling the problem defined in Section 2 entirely—requires only one more sentence to describe: replace the algorithm of Section 3.2 with the above one. All the analysis still holds directly. We thus have established the main result of this paper:

THEOREM 1. *For the RTS problem in constant dimensionality, there is an algorithm that processes n stream elements and m queries in $\tilde{O}(n + m)$ time.*

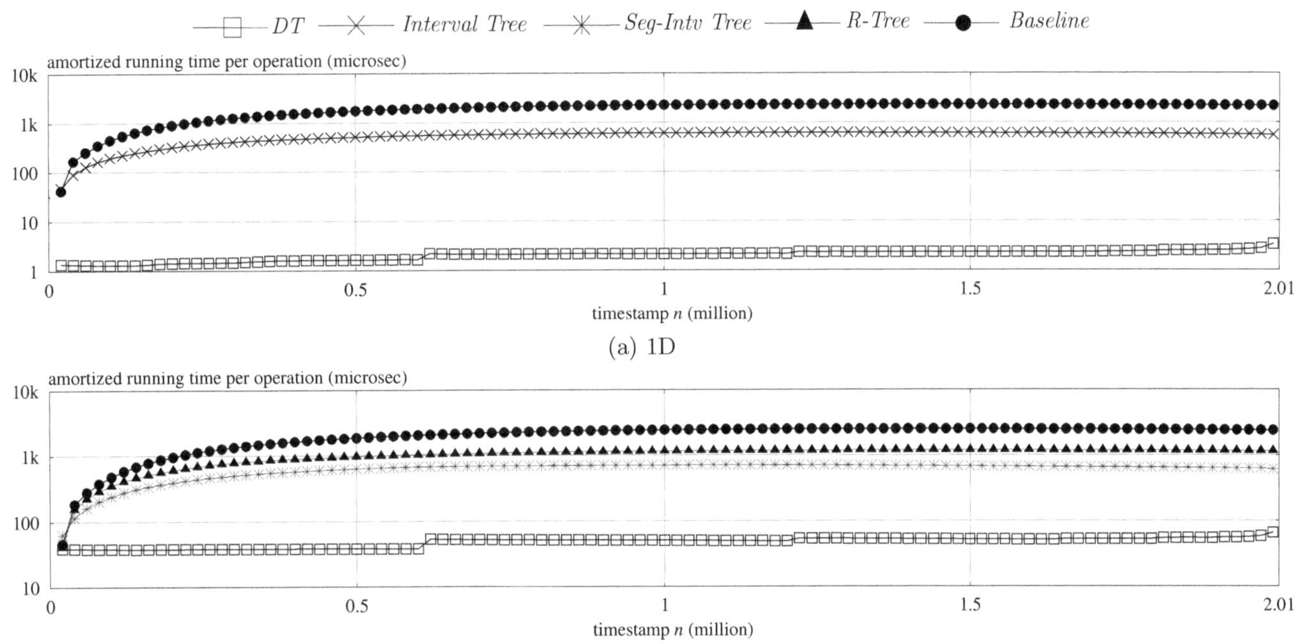

(a) 1D

(b) 2D

Figure 3: Efficiency as a function of time (m = 1 million, τ = 20 million, static queries)

8. EXPERIMENTS

This section presents an experimental evaluation of our techniques for the RTS problem in 1D and 2D spaces, using the existing solutions for comparison. Specifically, we examined the following methods:

- [1D, 2D] *Distributed tracking* (DT): The proposed algorithm in Theorem 1. The name reflects the new connection we established between RTS and the distributed tracking problem; see Section 4. As explained in Section 5, its time complexity for processing the whole stream is $O(n \log^{d+1} m + m \log^{d+1} m \cdot \log \tau_{max})$.
- [1D, 2D] *Baseline*: The approach described in Section 3.1 that probes all alive queries upon receiving a new element. Its time complexity is $O(nm)$.
- [1D] *Interval tree*: This is the stabbing approach described in Section 3.1 for 1D space, using the interval tree [12] as the stabbing structure. Its time complexity is $\tilde{O}(n) + O(m \cdot \tau_{max})$, as mentioned in Section 3.1.
- [2D] *Seg-Intv tree*: Again the stabbing approach in Section 3.1, but for 2D space, whose stabbing structure combines the segment tree and the interval tree [12]. Its time complexity is also $\tilde{O}(n) + O(m \cdot \tau_{max})$.
- [2D] *R-tree*: As the R-tree is commonly believed to offer competitive efficiency on multidimensional queries, we included another 2D stabbing approach that uses this access method as the stabbing structure. Its time complexity is $O(nm)$—the R-tree is a heuristic structure that does not have attractive efficiency guarantees.

Our machine was equipped with a 3.7GHz multi-core CPU and 16GB memory. The operating system was Linux (Ubuntu 14.04).

We separated the evaluation into two parts: inspecting first the scenario where all queries were registered at the beginning of the stream (Section 8.1), before moving to the second where queries were issued throughout the stream (Section 8.2). The former part studied how the intrinsic parameters m and τ of the RTS problem influence the behavior of alternative algorithms, without the complication caused by the dynamism of arbitrary query registration, the exploration of which was the aim of the latter part.

8.1 Scenario 1: Static Query Insertions

Setup. On each dimension, the data space had an integer domain of $[0, 10^5]$. For each stream element e, its value $v(e)$ was a d-dimensional point ($d = 1$ or 2) uniformly distributed in the data space, and its weight $w(e)$ followed the Gaussian distribution with mean 100 and standard deviation 15 (if this resulted in $w(e) < 1$, $w(e)$ was re-generated).

In each experiment, m queries were registered at the beginning of the stream, all given an identical threshold τ. The values of m and τ are the two primary varying parameters in this subsection. Each query q also specified a rectangle R_q, which was a square (for $d = 1$, an interval) with volume 10% that of the data space. The center of R_q was generated in such a way that each coordinate followed the Gaussian distribution with mean $5 \cdot 10^4$ and standard deviation set to 15% of the mean. The whole R_q was required to fall within the data space; otherwise, it was re-generated.

Notice that the generation simulated the situation where stream elements e are everywhere but queries tend to focus on "areas of common interest"—near the center of the data space. The uniformity of $v(e)$ had the importance of ensuring that *every* $v(e)$ should "stab" 10% of the queries currently alive in expectation, regardless of the locations of the query rectangles. This means that each query q had a 10% probability of having its $W(q)$ increased at every timestamp. Given that each increase had the expectation of 100, q was expected to mature after $\tau/(10\% \cdot 100) = \tau/10$ timestamps.

We allowed a query to be terminated before maturity. Specifically, at every timestamp, an alive query q was termi-

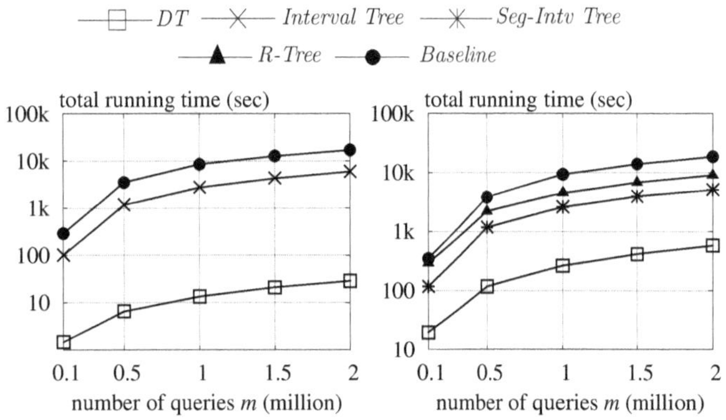

(a) 1D (b) 2D

Figure 4: Efficiency as a function of m (τ = 20 million, static queries)

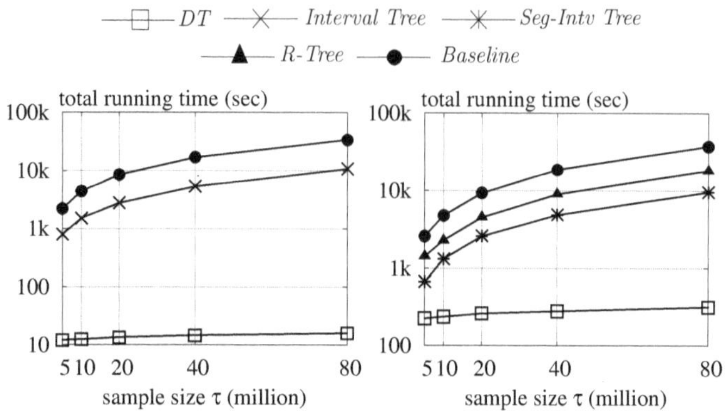

(a) 1D (b) 2D

Figure 5: Efficiency as a function of τ (m = 1 million, static queries)

nated with probability p_{del}, whose value was such that the probability for q to be terminated before reaching the $(\tau/10)$-th timestamp was 90%. In other words, 10% of the m queries were able to live till their expected maturity time, echoing the reality where a small fraction of the triggers would get activated eventually. This, intuitively, favored the algorithms falling prey to the quadratic trap because, once deleted, a query can no longer be stabbed by any subsequent elements. Nevertheless, we will see that our algorithm brought forward huge efficiency gains even in this case.

A stream kept evolving until all the queries had either matured or been terminated.

Results. Perhaps the most effective way to illustrate an algorithm's behavior is to *trace* its efficiency for the entire stream. The first set of experiments was designed for this purpose. We used each algorithm to process a 1D/2D stream with m set to 1 million and τ to 20 million, and kept track of the average per-operation cost (where each *operation* refers to the handling of an incoming element, or the insertion, deletion, or maturity of a query) as the stream evolved. Figures 3a and 3b present the 1D and 2D results, respectively.

The comparison reveals the significance of breaking the quadratic trap. The proposed algorithm *DT*—which took only *a fraction of a millisecond* per operation—outperformed all the competitors considerably: by a factor over two and one order of magnitude in 1D and 2D spaces, respectively (note that the y-axis is shown in log scale). Observe that all the other methods required nearly a *millisecond* to perform an operation. This is unacceptable, recalling that one millisecond is comparable to the time of a *disk* I/O, even thought everything was memory resident! The observation serves as strong manifestation of our original motivation that no existing technique can support large-scale RTS on a fast stream.

The figures also reveal several characteristics of the algorithms. At the beginning, each algorithm focused on constructing its underlying data structure, i.e., simply an array for *Baseline*, an endpoint tree for *DT*, and for every other method, the structure as indicated by its name. In any case, the construction cost—after amortization over m queries—was relatively low, compared to the cost of processing an incoming element. This explains the common pattern of all the curves: gradually increasing to a stable value. For *DT*, the occasional "bumps" on its curve indicate global rebuilding (see Section 4), caused by query maturity and deletions.

The next two sets of experiments were designed to examine scalability with respect to m and τ. To do so on m, we fixed τ to 20 million, and measured the total execution time of each algorithm in processing a stream, when the value of m changed from 100k to 2 million. Figures 4a and 4b present the 1D and 2D results, respectively. We investigated the scalability on τ in a similar fashion: fixing m to 1 million, and varying τ from 5 million to 80 million. The results are presented in Figure 5. As predicted by theory, *DT* scaled much better than the other approaches. Its performance advantage became increasingly significant with the growth of m and τ.

8.2 Scenario 2: Dynamic Query Insertions

We now proceed to the scenario where queries can be inserted any time during a stream.

Setup. Stream elements were generated in the same way as in Section 8.1. The total number of elements in a stream was fixed to 3 million. One million queries were registered in the system before the stream started; and then new queries were added according to a mode of dynamism from below:

- *Stochastic mode*: At every timestamp from 1 to 2 million, a new query was registered with probability p_{ins}, which is a parameter to vary in specific experiments.
- *Fixed-load mode*: A new query was registered as soon as an existing one matured or got terminated. In this mode, the number of alive queries remained unchanged during the whole stream.

In any case, a query (regardless of its registration time) was created in the same way as explained in Section 8.1, with its threshold τ set to 20 million. In particular, as before, at every timestamp each alive query had probability p_{del} to be terminated, where p_{del} was set to permit the query to live to its expected maturity time with 10% probability.

Results. Let us start with the stochastic mode. Focusing on $p_{ins} = 0.3$, Figure 6 shows the amortized per-operation cost as a function of the number of received elements. The overall trends, as well as the relative performance of all methods, are similar to those already demonstrated in Figure 3. It is worth pointing out that here the bumps on the curve of *DT*

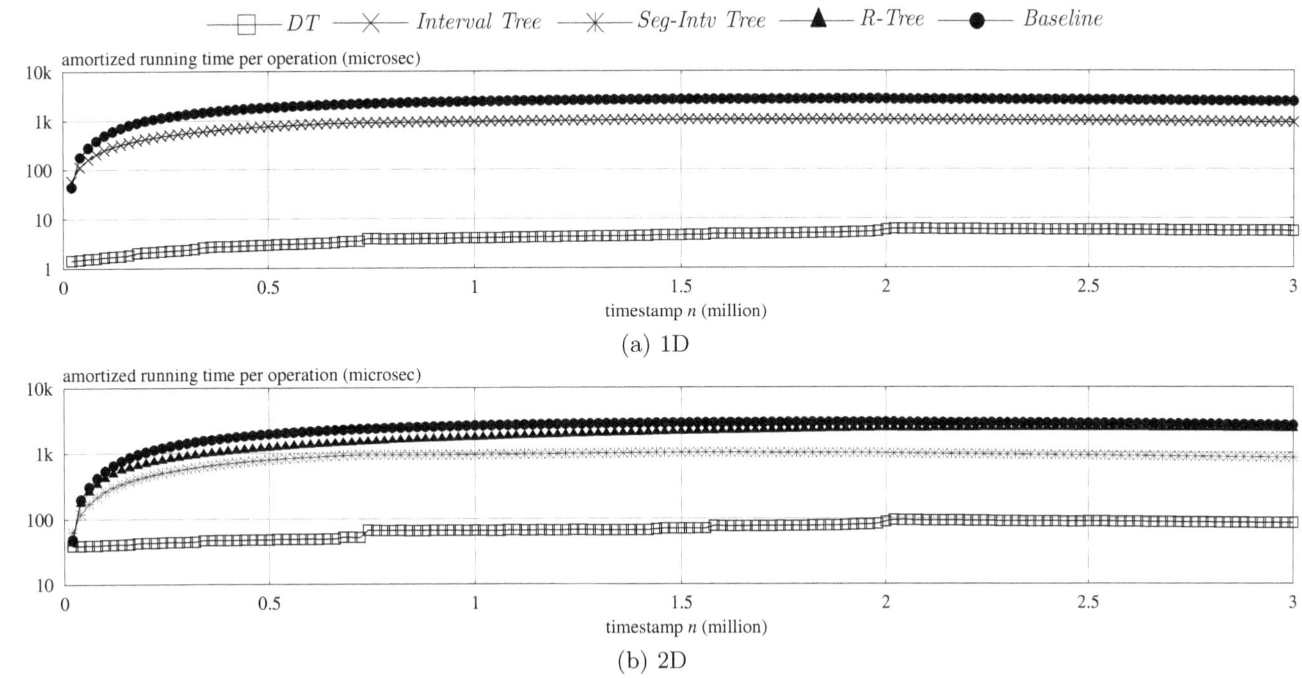

Figure 6: Efficiency as a function of time (dynamic queries, stochastic mode with $p_{ins} = 0.3$)

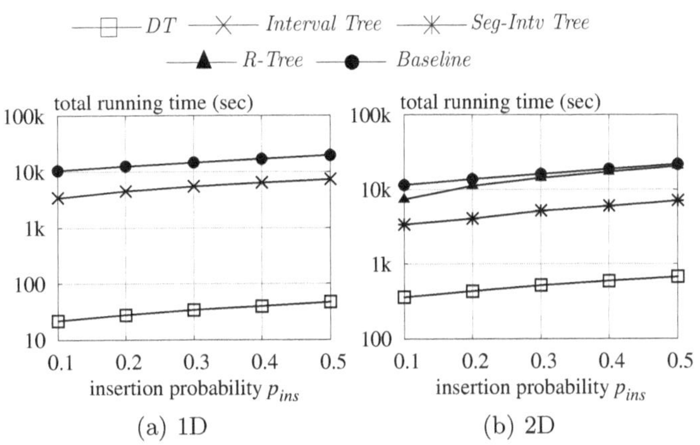

Figure 7: Efficiency as a function of p_{ins} (dynamic queries, stochastic mode)

were the effects of the reconstruction that took place either in global rebuilding or the logarithmic method (Section 5).

Next, we adjusted p_{ins} from 0.1 to 0.5, and measured for each method its total execution time for processing the whole stream. The results are presented in Figure 7. As expected, the running time increased as p_{ins} became larger (which implied more queries)—notice that $p_{ins} = 0.5$ corresponds to a very busy system: one query every two stream elements.

Finally, turning to the fixed-load mode, Figure 8 traces out the amortized per-operation cost of all the methods, confirming once again the significant speedup achieved by our algorithm over the other approaches. The results reflect what performance can be expected in an exceedingly busy system (where the number of alive queries never decreases). Note, interestingly, from Figure 8 that *R-tree* actually performed *worse* even than *Baseline*! This was caused by a well-known drawback of the R-tree's update algorithms: much less effective when the indexed objects have large and heavily overlapping extents. This was exactly the case for RTS (where queries tend to gather in "hot areas"). The problem was most exacerbated on fixed-load streams because they had the highest update volumes—although the astute reader may have also noticed the same phenomenon from Figure 7b.

9. CONCLUSIONS

Range thresholding on streams (RTS) supports user triggers of the form "*alert me when a specific number of stream elements have shown up in the region of my interest*". Such kind of triggers are extremely important in numerous system involving time-critical actions. Unfortunately, currently there does not exist an efficient algorithm for processing such triggers: all the known solutions incur prohibitive processing time—quadratic to the problem's input size.

In this paper, we have developed the first algorithm whose running time successfully escapes the quadratic trap—even better, the algorithm promises computation cost that is near-linear to the input size, up to only a polylogarithmic factor. Extensive experimentation has confirmed that the new algorithm, besides having rigorous theoretical guarantees, has excellent performance in practical scenarios, outperforming alternative methods by a factor up to orders of magnitude. It can therefore be immediately leveraged as a reliable fundamental tool for building sophisticated triggering mechanism in real systems.

10. REFERENCES

[1] D. J. Abadi, D. Carney, U. Çetintemel, M. Cherniack, C. Convey, S. Lee, M. Stonebraker, N. Tatbul, and S. B. Zdonik. Aurora: a new model and architecture for data stream management. *VLDB J.*, 12(2):120–139, 2003.

[2] A. Arasu and J. Widom. A denotational semantics for continuous queries over streams and relations. *SIGMOD Record*, 33(3):6–12, 2004.

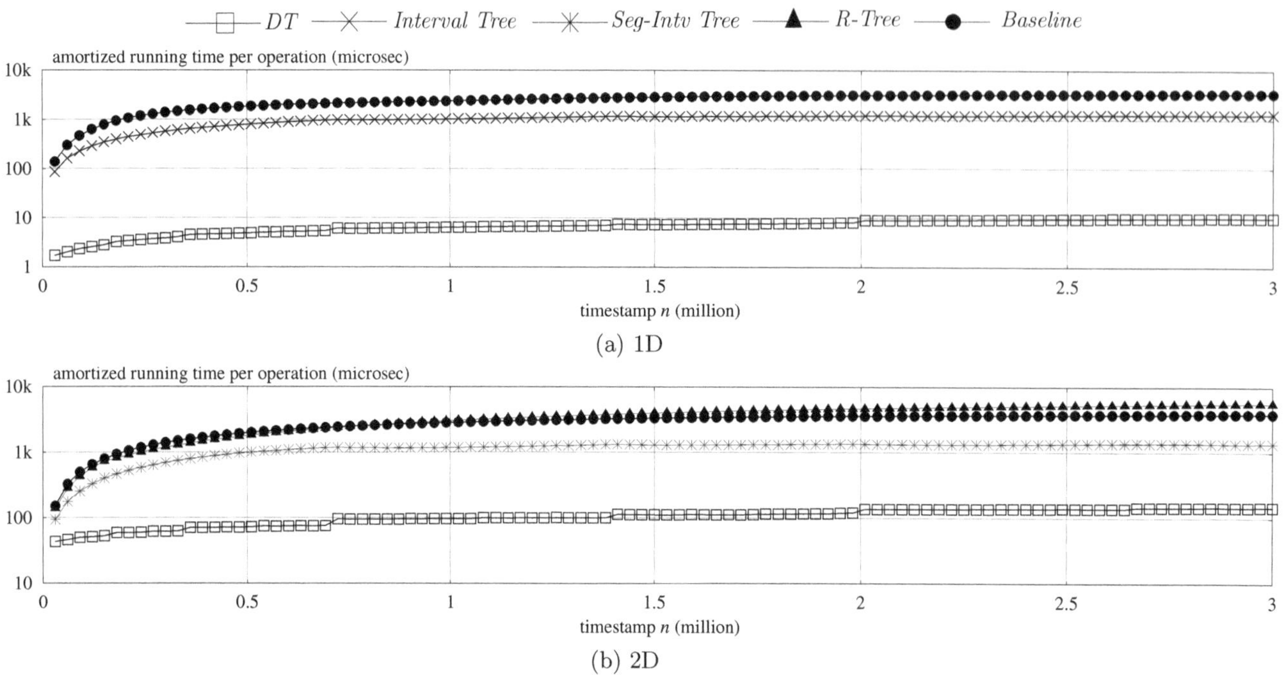

Figure 8: Efficiency as a function of time (dynamic queries, fixed-load mode)

[3] L. Arge and J. Vahrenhold. I/O-efficient dynamic planar point location. *Computational Geometry*, 29(2):147–162, 2004.

[4] L. Arge and J. S. Vitter. Optimal external memory interval management. *SIAM J. of Comp.*, 32(6):1488–1508, 2003.

[5] N. Beckmann, H. Kriegel, R. Schneider, and B. Seeger. The R*-tree: An efficient and robust access method for points and rectangles. In *SIGMOD*, pages 322–331, 1990.

[6] J. L. Bentley and J. B. Saxe. Decomposable searching problems I: Static-to-dynamic transformation. *Journal of Algorithms*, 1(4):301–358, 1980.

[7] D. Carney, U. Çetintemel, M. Cherniack, C. Convey, S. Lee, G. Seidman, M. Stonebraker, N. Tatbul, and S. B. Zdonik. Monitoring streams - A new class of data management applications. In *VLDB*, pages 215–226, 2002.

[8] J. Chen, D. J. DeWitt, F. Tian, and Y. Wang. Niagaracq: A scalable continuous query system for internet databases. In *SIGMOD*, pages 379–390, 2000.

[9] G. Cormode, S. Muthukrishnan, and K. Yi. Algorithms for distributed functional monitoring. *ACM Transactions on Algorithms*, 7(2):21, 2011.

[10] G. Cugola and A. Margara. Processing flows of information: From data stream to complex event processing. *ACM Comp. Surv.*, 44(3):15, 2012.

[11] U. Dayal, E. N. Hanson, and J. Widom. Active database systems. In *Modern Database Systems*, pages 434–456. 1995.

[12] M. de Berg, O. Cheong, M. van Kreveld, and M. Overmars. *Computational Geometry: Algorithms and Applications*. Springer-Verlag, 3rd edition, 2008.

[13] A. J. Demers, J. Gehrke, B. Panda, M. Riedewald, V. Sharma, and W. M. White. Cayuga: A general purpose event monitoring system. In *CIDR*, pages 412–422, 2007.

[14] Y. Diao, S. Rizvi, and M. J. Franklin. Towards an internet-scale XML dissemination service. In *VLDB*, pages 612–623, 2004.

[15] F. Fabret, H. Jacobsen, F. Llirbat, J. L. M. Pereira, K. A. Ross, and D. Shasha. Filtering algorithms and implementation for very fast publish/subscribe. In *SIGMOD*, pages 115–126, 2001.

[16] A. Guttman. R-trees: a dynamic index structure for spatial searching. In *SIGMOD*, pages 47–57, 1984.

[17] S. Madden, M. A. Shah, J. M. Hellerstein, and V. Raman. Continuously adaptive continuous queries over streams. In *SIGMOD*, pages 49–60, 2002.

[18] B. Nguyen, S. Abiteboul, G. Cobena, and M. Preda. Monitoring XML data on the web. In *SIGMOD*, pages 437–448, 2001.

[19] N. W. Paton and O. Díaz. Active database systems. *ACM Comp. Surv.*, 31(1):63–103, 1999.

[20] S. Rahul. Improved bounds for orthogonal point enclosure query and point location in orthogonal subdivisions in $\mathbb{R}^3$. In *SODA*, pages 200–211, 2015.

[21] D. B. Terry, D. Goldberg, D. A. Nichols, and B. M. Oki. Continuous queries over append-only databases. In *SIGMOD*, pages 321–330, 1992.

[22] E. Wu, Y. Diao, and S. Rizvi. High-performance complex event processing over streams. In *SIGMOD*, pages 407–418, 2006.

[23] A. Yu, P. K. Agarwal, and J. Yang. Processing a large number of continuous preference top-k queries. In *SIGMOD*, pages 397–408, 2012.

Bridging the Archipelago between Row-Stores and Column-Stores for Hybrid Workloads

Joy Arulraj
Carnegie Mellon University
jarulraj@cs.cmu.edu

Andrew Pavlo
Carnegie Mellon University
pavlo@cs.cmu.edu

Prashanth Menon
Carnegie Mellon University
pmenon@cs.cmu.edu

ABSTRACT

Data-intensive applications seek to obtain trill insights in real-time by analyzing a combination of historical data sets alongside recently collected data. This means that to support such hybrid workloads, database management systems (DBMSs) need to handle both fast ACID transactions and complex analytical queries on the same database. But the current trend is to use specialized systems that are optimized for only one of these workloads, and thus require an organization to maintain separate copies of the database. This adds additional cost to deploying a database application in terms of both storage and administration overhead.

To overcome this barrier, we present a hybrid DBMS architecture that efficiently supports varied workloads on the same database. Our approach differs from previous methods in that we use a single execution engine that is oblivious to the storage layout of data without sacrificing the performance benefits of the specialized systems. This obviates the need to maintain separate copies of the database in multiple independent systems. We also present a technique to continuously evolve the database's physical storage layout by analyzing the queries' access patterns and choosing the optimal layout for different segments of data within the same table. To evaluate this work, we implemented our architecture in an in-memory DBMS. Our results show that our approach delivers up to 3× higher throughput compared to static storage layouts across different workloads. We also demonstrate that our continuous adaptation mechanism allows the DBMS to achieve a near-optimal layout for an arbitrary workload without requiring any manual tuning.

1. INTRODUCTION

Organizations need to quickly transform freshly obtained data into critical insights. Such workloads, colloquially known as hybrid transaction-analytical processing (HTAP), seek to extrapolate insights and knowledge by analyzing a combination of historical data sets with real-time data [40, 48]. Data has immense value as soon as it is created, but that value diminishes over time. For many application domains, such as high-frequency trading and Internet advertising, it is imperative that this analysis uses the newest data for the results to have the most impact. Many organizations implement HTAP pipelines using separate DBMSs. The most common practice is to use one DBMS for transactions and another for analytical queries. With this model, the new information from transactions goes into an on-line transactional processing (OLTP) DBMS. Then in the background, the system uses an extract-transform-load utility to migrate data from the OLTP DBMS to a data warehouse for on-line analytical processing (OLAP).

There are several problems inherent in such a bifurcated environment. Foremost is that the time it takes to propagate changes between the separate systems is often measured in minutes or even hours. This data transfer inhibits an application's ability to act on data immediately when it is entered in the database. Second, the administrative overhead of deploying and maintaining two different DBMSs is non-trivial as personnel is estimated to be almost 50% of the total ownership cost of a large-scale database system [45]. It also requires the application developer to write a query for multiple systems if they want to combine data from different databases.

A better approach is to use a single HTAP DBMS that can support the high throughput and low latency demands of modern OLTP workloads, while also allowing for complex, longer running OLAP queries to operate on both hot (transactional) and cold (historical) data. What makes these newer HTAP systems different from legacy general-purpose DBMSs is that they incorporate many of the advancements over the last decade from the specialized OLTP and OLAP systems. The key challenge with HTAP DBMSs, however, is executing OLAP workloads that access old data along with new data in the database while simultaneously executing transactions that update the database. This is a difficult problem and existing HTAP DBMS resort to using separate query processing and storage engines for data that is stored in different layouts. That is, they employ a separate OLTP execution engine for row-oriented data that is better for transactions and a separate OLAP execution engine for column-oriented data that is better for analytical queries. They then have to use a synchronization method (e.g., two-phase commit) to combine the results from the two different parts of the system [5, 29, 47]. Cobbling systems together in this manner increases the complexity of the DBMS and degrades performance due to the additional overhead needed to maintain the state of the database across different runtimes. This in turn limits the types of questions that can be asked about data as soon as it enters the database, which is the main selling point of a HTAP DBMS.

To overcome this problem, we present a method to bridge the architectural gap between the OLTP and OLAP systems using a unified architecture. Our approach is to store tables using hybrid layouts based on how the DBMS expects tuples will be accessed in the future. This means that a table's "hot" tuples are stored in a format that is optimized for OLTP operations, while the other "cold" tuples in that same table are stored in a format that is more

SIGMOD'16, June 26-July 01, 2016, San Francisco, CA, USA

DOI: http://dx.doi.org/10.1145/2882903.2915231

amenable to OLAP queries. We then propose a logical abstraction over this data that allows the DBMS to execute query plans that span these different layouts without using separate engines and with minimal overhead. Our other contribution is a novel on-line reorganization technique that continuously enhances each table's physical design in response to an evolving query workload. This enables the DBMS to migrate the database to the near-optimal storage layout for an arbitrary application without requiring a human administrator to configure the DBMS for the particular application and in a transactionally safe manner.

To evaluate our approach, we implemented our storage and execution architecture in the Peloton HTAP DBMS [1]. We compare our methods with other state-of-the-art storage models and show that they enable the DBMS to achieve up to 3× higher throughput across different hybrid workloads. We also demonstrate that our reorganization method allows the DBMS to continuously modify the layout of tables without manual tuning and with minimal overhead.

The remainder of this paper is organized as follows. We first discuss the performance impact of a storage model, and the benefits of a flexible storage model for HTAP workloads in Section 2. Next, in Section 3, we describe the design of our system architecture based on this model. We then present the concurrency control mechanism that enables the DBMS to support hybrid workloads in Section 4, followed by our on-line layout reorganization technique in Section 5. We then present our experimental evaluation in Section 6. We conclude with a discussion of related work in Section 7.

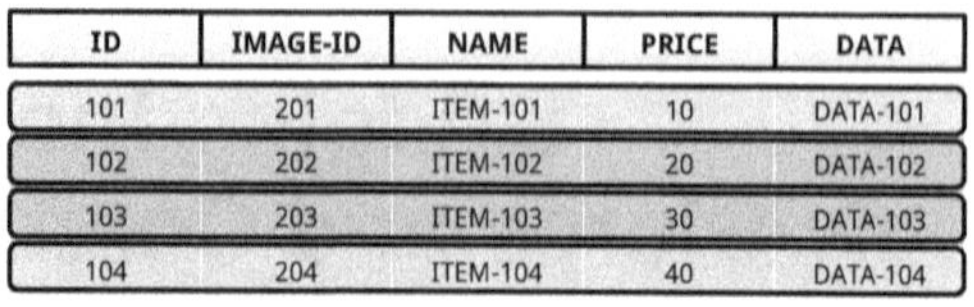

(a) OLTP-oriented N-ary Storage Model (NSM)

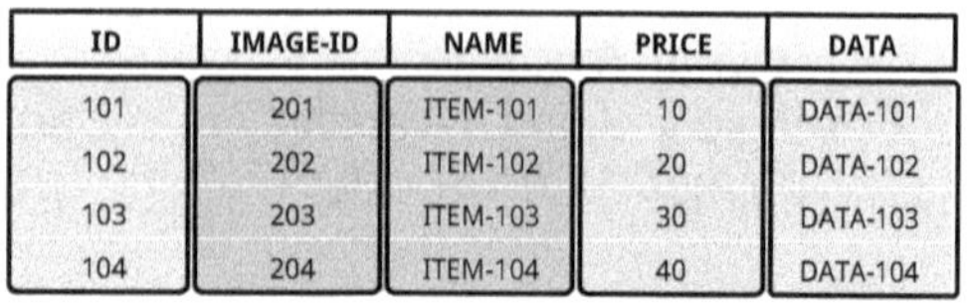

(b) OLAP-oriented Decomposition Storage Model (DSM)

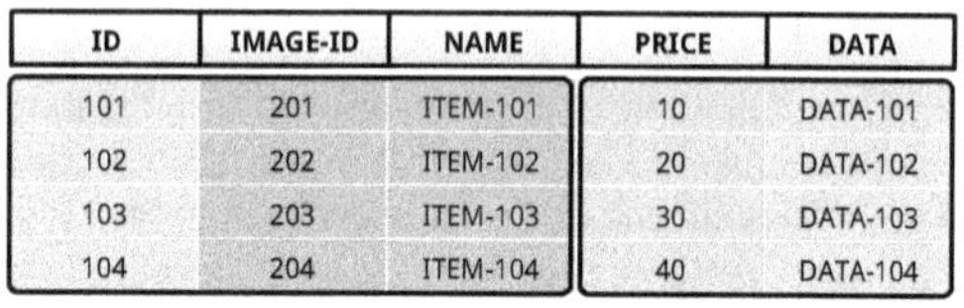

(c) HTAP-oriented Flexible Storage Model (FSM)

Figure 1: Storage Models – Different table storage layouts work well for OLTP, OLAP, and HTAP workloads. The different colored regions indicate the data that the DBMS stores contiguously.

2. MOTIVATION

We begin with an overview of the impact of the table's storage layout on the performance of the DBMS for different types of workloads. We then make the case for why a "flexible" storage model is the best choice for HTAP workloads.

2.1 Storage Models

There are essentially two ways that DBMSs store data: (1) the n-ary storage model and (2) decomposition storage model. These models prescribe whether the DBMS stores the data in a tuple-centric or in an attribute-centric manner. Note that the choice of the storage model is independent of whether the primary storage location of the database is on disk or in-memory.

All DBMSs that are based on the architecture of the original DBMSs from the 1970s (i.e., IBM System R, INGRES) employ the n-ary storage model (NSM). With this approach, the DBMS stores all of the attributes for a single tuple contiguously. In the example shown in Figure 1a, all the attributes belonging to the first tuple (`ID #101`) are stored one after another, followed by all the attributes of the second tuple (`ID #102`). NSM works well for OLTP workloads because the queries in transactions tend to operate only on an individual entity in the database at a time (e.g., a single customer record), and thus they need to access most (if not all) of the attributes for that entity. It is also ideal for insert-heavy workloads, because the DBMS can add tuples to the table using a single write.

NSM is not a good choice, however, for analytical queries in OLAP workloads. This is because these queries tend to access multiple entities in a table at the same time. These queries also typically only access a subset of the attributes for each entity. For example, a query might only analyze the location attribute for all of the customer records within a particular geographic region. But NSM-based DBMSs can only read tables tuple-at-a-time, and therefore they process the data in a tuple-centric manner within their query operators [21]. Prior research has shown that this execution strategy has lower CPU efficiency due to high interpretation overhead [15]. NSM-based DBMSs squander I/O and memory bandwidth when executing OLAP queries because they unnecessarily access and process attributes that are not even needed for the final result.

An alternate approach, known as the decomposition storage model (DSM), stores data attribute-at-a-time [7, 17]. That is, the DBMS stores the tuples' values for a single attribute in a table contiguously. This is the storage model employed in modern OLAP DBMSs, including Vertica [49] and MonetDB [15]. Figure 1b shows an example of the storage layout of a table using DSM: the DBMS allocates space for all the values belonging to the first attribute (`ID`), followed by those that belong to the second attribute (`IMAGE-ID`). DSM works well for OLAP workloads because the DBMS only retrieves the values belonging to those attributes that are needed by the query. They also process the data attribute-at-a-time, thereby improving the CPU efficiency due to lower interpretation overhead and skipping unnecessary attributes [6, 7].

But just like how NSM systems are inefficient for read-only OLAP workloads, DSM systems are not ideal for write-heavy OLTP workloads. This is because these workloads are comprised of queries that insert and update tuples into the table. Unlike in NSM, this is an expensive operation in DSM, as the storage manager needs to copy over the tuples' attributes to separate storage locations. Hence, the NSM and DSM architectures pose a problem for a DBMS supporting HTAP workloads that include transactions that update the state of the database while also executing complex analytical queries on this data. We contend that it is better for the DBMS to use a flexible storage model that provides the benefits of both the NSM and DSM for their respective workloads, while avoiding the problems that they encounter with the other workloads.

2.2 The Case for a Flexible Storage Model

We refer to a storage model that generalizes the NSM and DSM as the *flexible* storage model (FSM). It supports a wide variety of hybrid storage layouts where the DBMS co-locates the attributes that are frequently accessed together. We defer a detailed description of the FSM to Section 3. In the example shown in Figure 1c, all the values belonging to the first three attributes (`ID, IMAGE-ID, NAME`) are stored contiguously, followed by those belonging to the last two attributes (`PRICE, DATA`).

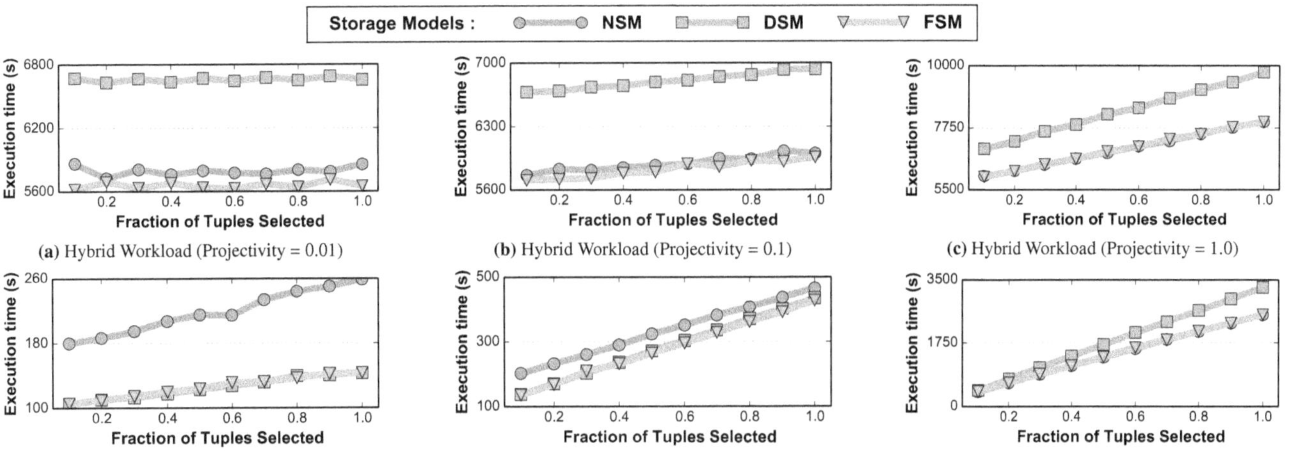

(a) Hybrid Workload (Projectivity = 0.01) (b) Hybrid Workload (Projectivity = 0.1) (c) Hybrid Workload (Projectivity = 1.0)

(d) Read-Only Workload (Projectivity = 0.01) (e) Read-Only Workload (Projectivity = 0.1) (f) Read-Only Workload (Projectivity = 1.0)

Figure 2: Performance Impact of the Storage Models – Time taken by the execution engine to run (1) a hybrid, and (2) a read-only workload on top of the NSM, DSM, and FSM storage managers.

FSM-based DBMSs can exploit a fundamental property of HTAP workloads in modern database applications. In these workloads, the access patterns of transactions are such that tuples are more likely to be updated in an OLTP transaction when they are first added to the database. Then, over time they become *colder* and thus are less likely to be updated again. For instance, more than half of the content that Facebook users access and interact with are shared by their friends in the past two days, and then there is a rapid decline in content popularity over the following days [13]. For these workloads, it is advantageous to store the hot data in a tuple-centric layout (NSM) since it is likely to be modified during this period. But then once a particular data item passes some threshold, the DBMS can reorganize the cold data to an attribute-centric layout (DSM) that works well for analytical queries [47]. A FSM-based DBMS can support these HTAP workloads efficiently by storing different parts of the same table under different hybrid storage layouts.

To better understand these issues, we now compare the performance impact of these different storage models in a motivating experiment. Consider a database with a single table $\mathcal{R}(a_0, a_1, \ldots, a_{500})$ that has 10m tuples. Each attribute a_k is a random integer value in the range $[-100, 100]$. The application for this database contains the following two queries:

Q_1: **INSERT INTO** R **VALUES** $(a_0, a_1, \ldots, a_{500})$
Q_2: **SELECT** $a_1, a_2, \ldots, a_k$ **FROM** R **WHERE** $a_0 < \delta$

The transactional query Q_1 inserts a tuple into the table R, while the analytical query Q_2 projects a subset of attributes $a_1, a_2, \ldots, a_k$ from all the tuples in the table R that satisfy the predicate $a_0 < \delta$. Note that different values for k and δ affect its projectivity and selectivity, respectively. We consider two workloads: (1) a *hybrid* workload of 1000 scan (Q_2) queries followed by 100m insert (Q_1) queries, and (2) a *read-only* workload of 1000 scan (Q_2) queries.

We measure the total time that an in-memory DBMS takes to execute these two workloads when its storage manager uses the NSM, DSM, and FSM storage layouts. For the FSM layout, the DBMS co-locates the attributes accessed in Q_2 together in the following layout: $\{\{a_0\}, \{a_1, \ldots, a_k\}, \{a_{k+1}, \ldots, a_{500}\}\}$. We consider three scenarios where we increase the projectivity of the scan query (Q_2) progressively from 1% to 100%. For each of these projectivity settings, we also vary the selectivity of the query from 10% to 100%. We note that the time taken to execute a scan query is higher than the time taken to execute an insert query. We defer the description of our experimental setup to Section 6.

Figures 2a to 2c present the results for the hybrid workload. We observe that NSM and FSM storage managers outperform the DSM storage manager by up to 1.3× across all scenarios. This is because DSM needs to split a tuple's attributes on every insert and store them in separate memory locations. FSM works well on this workload because it adopts wider vertical partitions similar to the NSM, and therefore executes insert queries faster than DSM. On the scan queries, FSM outperforms NSM because it stores the predicate attribute (a_0) and the projected attributes ($a_1, \ldots, a_k$) separate from the other attributes in the table. During both predicate evaluation and subsequent projection, the FSM storage manager retrieves only the attributes required for query processing.

The results for the read-only workload are shown in Figures 2d to 2f. We see that on this workload the DSM and FSM layouts outperform the NSM on low projectivity analytical queries. They execute the workload up to 1.8× faster than NSM due to better utilization of memory bandwidth. This experiment highlights the performance impact of the storage model on HTAP workloads. It is clear from this that neither a NSM nor a DSM storage layout is a good solution for HTAP workloads. A better approach is to use a FSM DBMS that can process data stored in a wide variety of hybrid layouts, including the canonical tuple-at-a-time and the attribute-at-a-time layouts. Given this, we now present our FSM-oriented DBMS architecture.

3. TILE-BASED ARCHITECTURE

We now describe a manifestation of the FSM approach that uses a storage abstraction based on *tiles*. A tile is akin to a vertical/horizontal segment of table. We begin with a description of a storage architecture based on *physical tiles*. We then describe how to hide the layout of these physical tiles from the DBMS's query processing components through *logical tiles*. We will present our concurrency control protocol for this architecture in Section 4 and the dynamic layout reorganization method in Section 5.

3.1 Physical Tile

The fundamental physical storage unit of the DBMS is a *tile tuple*. Informally, a tile tuple is a subset of attribute values that belong to a tuple. A set of tile tuples form a physical tile. We refer to a collection of physical tiles as a *tile group*. The storage manager physically stores a table as a set of tile groups. All the physical tiles belonging to a tile group contain the same number of tile tuples.

Consider the table layout shown in Figure 3. The table comprises

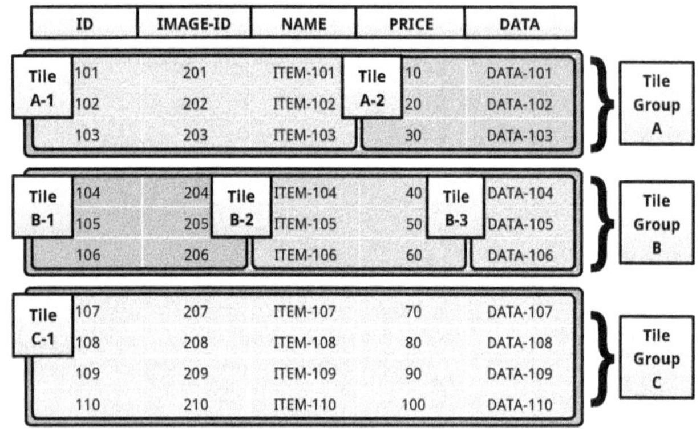

Figure 3: Physical Tile – An example storage layout of a table composed of physical tiles. This table comprises of three tile groups (A, B, C).

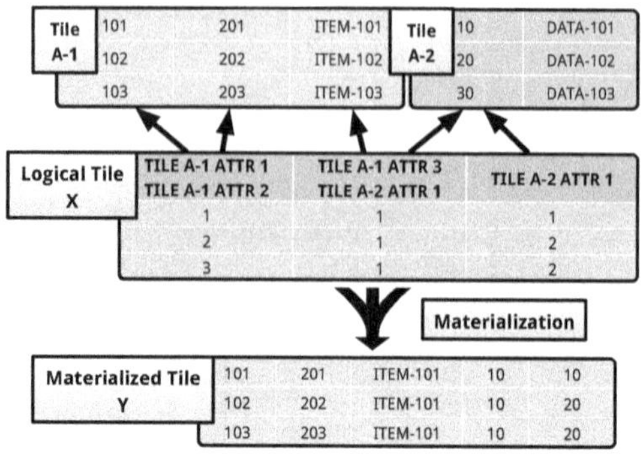

Figure 4: Logical Tile – An example of a logical tile representing data spread across a couple of physical tiles (A-1, A-2).

of three tile groups (A, B, C), that each contain a disparate number of physical tiles. The tile group A consists of two tiles (A-1, A-2). The tile A-1 contains the first three attributes (ID, IMAGE-ID, NAME) of the table, while the tile A-2 contains the remaining two attributes (PRICE, DATA). These two tiles form the tile group A.

A tuple can be stored in an FSM database using different layouts over time. For instance, the default approach is for the DBMS to store all the new tuples in a tuple-centric layout, and then as they become colder, it reorganizes them into a layout with narrower OLAP-friendly vertical partitions. This is done by copying over the tuples to a tile group with the new layout, and swapping the original tile group in the table with the newly constructed one. As we describe in Section 5, this reorganization occurs in the background and in a transactionally safe manner to avoid false negatives/positives.

We note that the NSM and DSM layouts are special cases of the FSM layout when using tiles. If each tile group consists of one tile that contains all the attributes of the table, then it is the same as the NSM's tuple-centric layout. On the other hand, if each tile consists of exactly one attribute, then it is equivalent to the DSM's attribute-centric layout. Besides supporting flexible vertical partitioning, this tile-based architecture also supports horizontal partitioning of a table. This design choice allows the DBMS to configure the number of tuples stored in a tile group, such that the tiles fit within the CPU cache. For two tables with different schemas, the DBMS can therefore choose to store different number of tuples per tile group.

3.2 Logical Tile

An architecture based on physical tiles enables the DBMS to organize data in any possible layout that works well for the HTAP workload. The problem with storing data in different layouts, however, is that it is difficult to efficiently execute queries over this data. This is because the design of the DBMS's query processing components is not optimized for a particular data layout. One solution is to transform each tuple into a standard format, independent of the layout of its tile group when a query reads the data. But this requires extra processing overhead for each query, and thus the DBMS loses the benefits of the OLTP- or OLAP-optimized storage layouts.

Another approach is for the DBMS to use multiple execution engines for query processing that are optimized for the different hybrid layouts. But this requires expensive merging of the results produced by the operators in the different execution engines [47]. In this case, the DBMS needs to employ an additional synchronization method (beyond its internal concurrency control protocol) to enforce ACID guarantees. Beyond these two issues, just having to maintain multiple execution paths in the DBMS's source code that are specialized for the different layouts is notoriously difficult [50].

To overcome this problem, we propose an abstraction layer in our architecture based on logical tiles. A *logical tile* succinctly represents values spread across a collection of physical tiles from one or more tables. The DBMS uses this abstraction to hide the specifics of the layout of the table from its execution engine, without sacrificing the performance benefits of a workload-optimized storage layout. We now illustrate the abstraction with an example.

For the example in Figure 4, the logical tile X points to data in the two physical tiles A-1 and A-2. Each *column* of a logical tile contains a list of offsets corresponding to the tuples in the underlying physical tiles. A column in a logical tile can represent the data stored in one or more attributes spread across a collection of physical tiles. The DBMS stores this mapping in the logical tile's metadata region. It records this information only once for a logical tile's column. For instance, the first column in X maps to the first and second attributes of A-1. When the DBMS materializes X, it uses the first column to construct the first two attributes of the materialized tile Y.

The value stored in the first column of the first row of X represents the values present in the first two attributes of the first tuple of A-1. During materialization, the DBMS transforms it into {101, 201}. Similarly, the value stored in the the second column of the first row of X maps to the third attribute of A-1 and the first attribute of A-2. On materialization, it becomes {ITEM-101, 10}.

For all the attributes that a column in a logical tile maps to, the DBMS uses the same list of tuple offsets during materialization. It is possible for two columns in a logical tile (with unique offset lists) to map to the same attribute in a physical tile. This is exemplified by the second and the third columns of X. To simplify the abstraction, we restrict logical tiles from referring to other logical tiles, meaning that every logical tile column maps to an attribute in a physical tile.

We contend that this logical tile abstraction provides expressive power even after this simplification. We next demonstrate how it enables a DBMS to process data organized in different layouts. During query execution, the DBMS can dynamically choose to materialize a logical tile, that is an intermediate query result, into a physical tile [6]. In this case, the operator constructs a *passthrough* logical tile with only one column that directly maps to the attributes in the materialized physical tile, and propagates that logical tile upwards to its parent in the plan tree.

3.3 Logical Tile Algebra

In order for the DBMS to benefit from storing data in physical tiles, it must be able to execute queries efficiently while still remaining agnostic to the underlying layouts of tuples. We refer to this property of abstracting away the physical layout of the data from the DBMS's query processing components as *layout transparency*. This reduces the coupling between the DBMS's storage manager and

```
SELECT R.c, SUM(S.z)
FROM R JOIN S ON R.b = S.y
WHERE R.a = 1 AND S.x = 2
GROUP BY R.c;
```

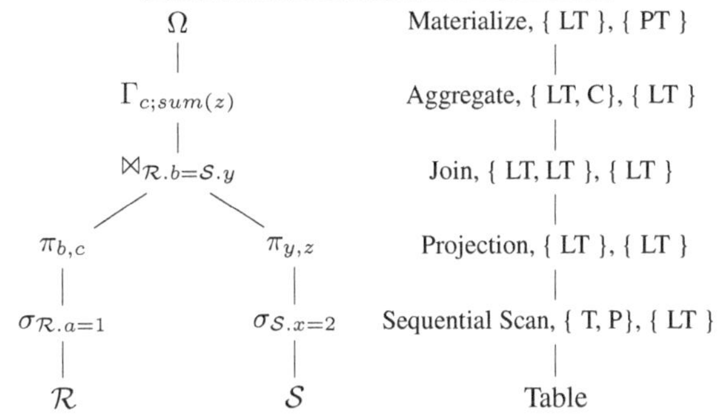

Figure 5: Sample SQL query and the associated plan tree for illustrating the operators of the logical tile algebra. We describe the name, inputs, and output of each operator in the tree. We denote the logical tile by LT, the physical tile by PT, the table by T, the attributes by C, and the predicate by P.

execution engine. We now present an algebra defined over logical tiles that allows the DBMS to achieve layout transparency.

Consider the SQL query that accesses the tables $\mathcal{R}(a, b, c)$ and $\mathcal{S}(x, y, z)$ and its corresponding plan tree shown in Figure 5. It selects some tuples from $\mathcal{R}$ based on a, and some tuples from $\mathcal{S}$ based on x. It then joins the resulting tuples based on b and y. Finally, it groups the resulting tuples by c, and for each group, it computes the sum over z. Using this query as an example, we now describe the operator semantics of our logical tile algebra.[1]

Bridge Operators: Most of the logical tile algebra operators produce and consume logical tiles, which means that they are oblivious to the storage layout of the underlying physical tiles. The only operators that interact with the storage manager are the ones at the bottom and the top of the tree. We refer to these operators as *bridge operators* because they connect logical tiles and physical tiles.

The bridge operators include the table access methods, such as the *sequential scan* and the *index scan* operators. The sequential scan operator generates a logical tile for every tile group in the table. Each logical tile only contains one column that is a list of offsets corresponding to all the tuples in the tile group satisfying the predicate. In Figure 5, the sequential scan (σ) operator associated with $\mathcal{R}$ emits logical tiles that represent the tuples that satisfy the predicate a=1. The *index scan* operator identifies the tuples matching the predicate using the index, and then constructs one or more logical tiles that contain the matching tuples.

The DBMS uses the *materialize* operator to transform a logical tile to a physical tile. It also uses this operator to perform early-materialization [6]. In Figure 5, the aggregate operator (Γ) constructs a physical tile with the aggregate tuples, and then wraps around it with a passthrough logical tile. In order to send the query result to the client, the DBMS runs the materialize operator (Ω) for transforming the passthrough logical tile returned by the aggregate operator to a physical tile. In this case, the materialize operator does not need to construct a new physical tile. Instead, it directly returns the physical tile underlying the passthrough logical tile.

Metadata Operators: The metadata of a logical tile includes information about the underlying physical tiles and a bitmap that represents the rows that must be examined by the operator processing the logical tile. This category of operators only modifies the metadata of the logical tile and not the data that it represents. The *projection* operator modifies the list of attributes in the schema of the input logical tile to remove the attributes that are not needed in the upper-levels of the query plan or in its final result. For the query in Figure 5, the projection operator (π) on top of the sequential scan operator (σ) associated with $\mathcal{R}$ outputs logical tiles that contains the attributes b and c. Another metadata operator is *selection*; this operator modifies the metadata of the input logical tile to mark any row corresponding to a tuple that does not satisfy the predicate as not being part of the logical tile.

Mutators: These operators modify the data stored in the table. The *insert* operator takes in a logical tile, and appends the associated tuples to the specified table. In this case, the operator first reconstructs the tuples represented by the logical tile, and then adds them into the table. It can also directly take tuples from the client and append them to the table.

The *delete* operator takes in a logical tile, and removes the tuples present in the underlying table. It uses the tuple offsets in the first column of the logical tile to identify the locations of the tuples that should be deleted, and then proceeds with their removal. It also supports a truncate mode to quickly erase all the tuples in the table. The *update* operator first removes the tuples present in the logical tile similar to the delete operator. It then constructs the newer version of the tuples by copying over their older version, and performing the requested modifications. Finally, it appends the newer version of the tuples into the table. As we discuss in Section 4, the mutators also control the visibility of tuples for transactions.

Pipeline Breakers: The last category of operators consume the logical tiles produced by their children in the plan tree. They block the execution of the upper-level operators while they wait for their children's output. This is necessary because these operators need to have all of the logical tiles from their children before they can produce their own output. This essentially breaks the streamlined flow of logical tiles between operators during the query execution [37].

The *join* operator takes in a pair of logical tiles, and then evaluates the join predicate over them. It first constructs an output logical tile, whose schema is obtained by concatenating the schemas of the two input logical tiles. When it iterates over each pair of tuples, if it finds a pair satisfying the predicate, then it concatenates them and appends them to the output logical tile. For the query shown in Figure 5, the join operator ($\bowtie$) examines every pair of logical tiles emitted by the projection (π) operators, and then produces a concatenated logical tile containing every pair of logical tile tuples that satisfy the join predicate $\mathcal{R}.b = \mathcal{S}.y$.

Set operators, such as *union* and *intersect*, are also pipeline-breakers. While going over the logical tiles produced by their children, they keep track of the tuples observed. Finally, they emit the logical tiles after marking the tuples that should be skipped by the set operation as not being part of the associated logical tiles.

Similarly, aggregation operators (e.g., *count*, *sum*), examine all the logical tiles from their child to construct the aggregate tuples. Unlike the set operators, these operators build new physical tiles to store the aggregate tuples. For instance, in Figure 5, the aggregate operator (Γ) constructs a physical tile that contain the sum over the attribute z for every group of tuples with a unique value for the attribute c. It then constructs a set of passthrough logical tiles, and propagates them upwards in the plan tree one logical tile at a time.

3.4 Discussion

We now discuss the benefits of the logical tile abstraction for an HTAP DBMS. These include the following:

Layout Transparency: The operators need not be specialized for

[1] A formal algebraic definition of all the operators in our logical tile algebra is presented in Appendix A.

all possible storage layouts because the logical tile algebra hides this information from them. This design obviates the need for expensive merge operations over results produced using different execution engines. It also reduces the DBMS's code complexity, thereby improving maintainability and testability.

Vectorized Processing: The iterator paradigm in many query-processing systems is implemented using executors that process data one tuple at a time [21]. This approach suffers from a high interpretation overhead and prevents key compiler optimizations such as loop pipelining [15]. In contrast, the operators in a tile-based DBMS process data logical tile at a time. As shown in prior research on columnar DBMSs, vectorized processing improves the CPU efficiency by reducing the interpretation overhead [7].

Flexible Materialization: Since neither early materialization nor late materialization is a universally good strategy [6], a tile-based DBMS can dynamically choose to materialize at any operator in the plan tree during the query execution. It can then propagate the passthrough logical tiles upwards in the plan tree. This flexible materialization strategy works well for HTAP workloads.

Caching Behavior: The DBMS can optimize several dimensions in how it creates tile groups, such as the number of tuples per tile group, to ensure that the tiles fit well within the cache hierarchy. Furthermore, the logical tiles' succinct representation enables the DBMS to more easily manage complex intermediate query execution results within the cache.

For the query shown in Figure 5, processing one logical tile at a time reduces the number of cache misses and function calls. The DBMS also copies less data and chases fewer pointers because it only materializes the logical tile in the aggregation operator. Lastly, our logical-tile algebra bridges the theoretical gap between row-stores and column-stores within a single DBMS architecture.

4. CONCURRENCY CONTROL

HTAP workloads are comprised of short-duration transactions that are executed alongside long-running analytical queries. The DBMS must ensure that these OLAP queries do not see the effects of transactions that start after they begin and the readers should not block on writers [41]. It is for this reason that most HTAP DBMSs employ multi-version concurrency control (MVCC) [34, 38, 46].

We now discuss how to use MVCC with our tile-based architecture. We adopt a similar approach taken in previous systems where the DBMS records the versioning information directly alongside the tuple data [30, 46]. When a new transaction is started, the DBMS assigns it a unique *transaction identifier* from a monotonically increasing global counter. When a transaction is ready to commit, the DBMS assigns it a unique *commit timestamp* that it obtains by incrementing the timestamp of the last committed transaction. Each transaction maintains a metadata context that includes: (1) the timestamp of last committed transaction that should be visible to this transaction, and (2) *references* to the set of tuple versions that the transaction either inserts or deletes during its lifetime. A reference contains only the location of the tuple and not its actual data. In our tile-based architecture, it includes the tile group identifier and the offset of the tuple within that tile group. Every tile group contains the following versioning metadata for each tuple:

- **TxnId:** A placeholder for the identifier of the transaction that currently holds a latch on the tuple.
- **BeginCTS:** The commit timestamp from which the tuple becomes visible.
- **EndCTS:** The commit timestamp after which the tuple ceases to be visible.

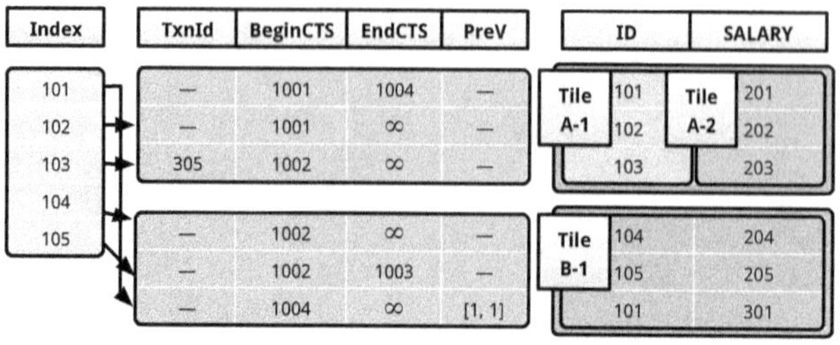

Figure 6: Concurrency Control – Versioning information that the DBMS records in the tile groups for MVCC.

- **PreV:** Reference to the previous version, if any, of the tuple.

Figure 6 shows an example of this versioning metadata. The DBMS stores this information separate from the physical tiles, so that it can handle all the physical tiles in a tile group in the same manner. The system uses the previous version field to traverse the version chain and access the earlier versions, if any, of that tuple. This version chain can span across multiple tile groups, and thus versions may be stored under different physical layouts in memory.

4.1 Protocol

We now discuss the operators in the execution engine that work with the storage manager to ensure transactional isolation. By default, the DBMS provides snapshot isolation.

Mutators: The *insert* operator starts by requesting an empty tuple slot from the DBMS. It then claims that slot by storing its transaction identifier in that tuple's `TxnId` field with an atomic compare-and-swap operation. The `BeginCTS` field is initially set to infinity so that the tuple is not visible to other concurrent transactions. When the transaction commits, the DBMS sets the tuple's `BeginCTS` field to the transaction's commit timestamp, and resets its `TxnId` field. In Figure 6, the first two tuples in the first tile group are inserted by the transaction with commit timestamp `1001`. The DBMS appends all the new tuples in a tile group with the default NSM layout.

The *delete* operator first acquires a latch on the target tuple by storing its transaction identifier in the tuple's `TxnId` field. This prevents another transaction from concurrently deleting the same tuple. At the time of committing the transaction, the DBMS sets the tuple's `EndCTS` to the transaction's commit timestamp, thereby ceasing its existence. In Figure 6, the tuple with `ID 105` is deleted by the transaction with commit timestamp `1003`.

The *update* operator begins with marking the older version of the tuple as invisible. It then constructs the newer tuple version by copying over the older one, and performing the requested modifications. Finally, it appends the newer tuple version into the table. In Figure 6, the transaction with commit timestamp `1004` updates the `SALARY` of the tuple with `ID 101`. Note that the `PrevV` field of the third tuple in the second tile group refers to the older version of tuple in the first tile group. At this point in time, the transaction with identifier `305` holds a latch on the tuple with `ID 103`.

Bridge Operators: The only other category of operators that are concerned about the visibility of tuples are the table access methods. The *sequential scan* and *index scan* operators emit one or more logical tiles for the matching tuples. Before predicate evaluation, they first determine if the tuple is visible to their transaction, by verifying whether the transaction's last visible commit timestamp falls within the the `BeginCTS` and `EndCTS` fields of the tuple. The tuple versions that are inserted by the transaction are also visible to these operators. Due to this design, all the other operators of the logical tile algebra are decoupled from the tuple visibility problem.

At any point in time, the DBMS can roll back an uncommitted

transaction by resetting the TxnId field of the tuples that it has latched, and releasing any unused tuple slots. Over time, the older versions of a tuple become invisible to any current or future transactions. The DBMS periodically garbage collects these invisible tuple versions in an asynchronous incremental manner. The garbage collection process not only helps in recovering the storage space, but also refreshes the statistics maintained by the query planner.

4.2 Indexes

A tile-based DBMS can use any order-preserving in-memory index (e.g., B+tree) for primary and secondary indexes. While the key stored in the index comprises of a set of tuple attributes, the value is a logical location of the latest version of a tuple. We do not store raw tuple pointers because then the DBMS would have to update them when it reorganizes the layout of the tile groups.

In Figure 6, the index entry for the tuple with ID 101 refers to the third tuple in the second tile group. An operator might encounter a version of the tuple that is not visible to its current transaction. When this occurs, it uses the PreV field to traverse the version chain to find the newest version of the tuple that is visible to the transaction. In this way, the DBMS does not need to redundantly maintain the versioning information in the table as well as in the indexes [30].

4.3 Recovery

Our DBMS architecture includes a recovery module that is responsible for the logging and recovery mechanisms. It employs a variant of the canonical ARIES recovery protocol that is adapted for in-memory DBMSs [12, 32, 35]. During regular transaction execution, the DBMS records the changes performed by the transaction in the write-ahead log, before committing the transaction. It periodically takes snapshots that are stored on the filesystem to bound the recovery time after a crash.

At the start of recovery, the DBMS first loads the latest snapshot. It then replays the log to ensure that the changes made by the transactions committed since the snapshot are present in the database. Changes made by uncommitted transactions at the time of failure are not propagated to the database. As we do not record the physical changes to the indexes in this log, the DBMS rebuilds all of the tables' indexes during recovery to ensure that they are consistent with the database [32]. We leave a detailed discussion of Peloton's recovery module as future work.

5. LAYOUT REORGANIZATION

All of the above optimizations in the design of our FSM-based DBMS are moot unless the system is able to efficiently and effectively reorganize the layout of the database to adapt with the changes in the HTAP workload. The crux of our approach is to track the recent query workload at runtime, and then periodically compute a workload-optimized storage layout for each table in the background. The DBMS then reorganizes the table to match the computed layout.

There are two approaches to perform data reorganization in a DBMS. The first is to combine query processing with data reorganization. In this case, the DBMS copies existing data to new tile groups with a query-optimized layout before processing the data [11]. This approach can be prohibitively expensive for some queries due to the additional I/O overhead.

An alternative is to decouple this reorganization from query execution and use a separate background process to reorganize the data in an incremental manner one tile group at a time. Over time, this process optimizes the storage layout for the workload and amortizes the cost across multiple queries. It is because this approach is incremental [25] that we adopt this second strategy. We now describe the information that the DBMS collects to guide this process.

Algorithm 1 Vertical Partitioning Algorithm

Require: recent queries Q, table T, number of representative queries k
  function UPDATE-LAYOUT(Q, T, k)
    # Stage I : Clustering algorithm
    for all queries q appearing in Q **do**
      for all representative queries r_j associated with T **do**
        if r_j is closest to q **then**
          $r_j \leftarrow r_j + w \times (q - r_j)$
        end if
      end for
    end for
    # Stage II : Greedy algorithm
    Generate layout for T using r
  end function

5.1 On-line Query Monitoring

The DBMS uses a lightweight monitor that tracks the attributes that are accessed by each query. The goal is to determine which attributes should be stored in the same physical tile in the new tile group layout. The monitor collects information about the attributes present in the query's SELECT clause, as well as those that are present in the WHERE clause [11, 36]. It distinguishes between these two sets of attributes because by co-locating only the attributes in the WHERE clause, rather than those in both clauses together, it needs to retrieve less data for predicate evaluation. It then stores this information as a time series graph for each individual table.

To reduce the monitoring overhead, the monitor only gathers statistics from a random subset of queries. In this case, it needs to ensure that the storage layout is not biased towards the more frequently observed transactions. To improve the overall throughput on HTAP workloads, it needs to optimize the layout for both the transactions and the data intensive analytical queries. The DBMS achieves this by recording the query plan cost computed by the optimizer [3]. It uses this plan cost information to derive a storage layout that also benefits the analytical queries. We next describe how the DBMS uses these query statistics to compute a workload-optimized vertical partitioning for each table.

5.2 Partitioning Algorithm

Computing the optimal storage layout for a workload based on its query statistics requires exponential space and time in the number of attributes. Consider a query workload Q with m queries, and a table with n attributes. For every query $q \in Q$, the naïve partitioning algorithm needs to examine 2^n groups of attributes. It then analyses all the possible attribute partitions of the table. The number of such partitions is referred to as a *Bell number*. Based on the asymptotic limit of the Bell number, the time complexity of this algorithm is $\mathcal{O}(e^{nln(n)} + mn2^n)$ and its space complexity is $\Theta(2^n)$ [19, 23].

As this is infeasible in practice, we adopt a more resource-efficient partitioning algorithm that converges towards the optimal storage layout over time. Our approach leverages the query statistics to compute the layout in two stages. As shown in Algorithm 1, it first employs a clustering algorithm to determine which set of attributes should be stored together in the same physical tile. It then uses a greedy algorithm that uses the output of the clustering algorithm to generate a workload-aware tile group storage layout.

For each table T in the database, the DBMS maintains statistics about the recent queries Q that accessed it. For each $q \in Q$, the DBMS extracts its metadata, such as the attributes it accessed. If the DBMS is able to identify the "important" queries, then it can optimize the storage layout of the table for these queries. It performs this identification using an on-line k-means clustering algorithm and dynamically updates the layout based on incoming queries [27].

For each query q, the clustering algorithm observes the referenced attributes, and assigns it to the jth cluster, whose mean representative query r_j is the most similar to q. The distance metric between two queries is defined as the number of attributes which are accessed by one and exactly one of the two queries divided by the number of attributes in T. Queries that access a lot of common attributes of T, therefore, tend to belong to the same cluster. After assigning the query to a cluster, it updates r_j to reflect the inclusion of the query q. The algorithm prioritizes each query based on its plan cost. If it treats all queries equally, the OLTP queries that tend to outnumber the long-running analytical queries will force the algorithm to quickly converge to a tuple-centric layout. The low projectivity analytical queries do not benefit from the tuple-centric layout. By prioritizing the queries based on their plan cost, the queries with higher I/O cost have a stronger influence on the layout of the table.

An attractive feature of the on-line clustering algorithm is that, over time, the means of the clusters drift towards the recent samples. To better understand this aspect, we now discuss the algorithm more formally. We define c_j to be the mean representative query of the jth cluster, and c_0 to represent that mean's initial value. Each cluster's mean is a vector of numbers whose length equals the number of the attributes in T. If the algorithm adds s query samples to the cluster over time, and prioritizes the older samples with a weight w at the time of addition, then the current mean of the cluster is given by:

$$c_j = (1-w)^s c_0 + w \sum_{i=1}^{s} (1-w)^{s-i} Q_i$$

The weight w determines the rate with which the older query samples are forgotten by the algorithm. The time complexity of each iteration of this algorithm is $\mathcal{O}(mnk)$ with a space complexity of $\mathcal{O}(n(m+k))$. Therefore, it is more efficient than a naïve partitioning algorithm. By using the clustering algorithm, the DBMS maintains the top k representative queries associated with each table in the database.

The next stage in Algorithm 1 is to use a greedy algorithm to derive a partitioning layout for the table using these representative queries. This algorithm iterates over the representative queries in the descending order based on the weight of their associated clusters. For each cluster, the algorithm groups the attributes accessed by that cluster's representative query together into a tile. It continues this process until it assigns each attribute in the table to some tile. In this manner, the DBMS periodically computes a layout for the table using the recent query statistics. We next describe how it reorganizes the table to the new layout.

5.3 Data Layout Reorganization

We use an incremental approach for data layout reorganization. For a given tile group, the DBMS first copies over the data to the new layout, and then atomically swaps in the newly constructed tile group into the table. Any concurrent delete or update operation only modifies the versioning metadata that is stored separate from the physical tiles. The newly constructed tile group refers to the versioning metadata of the older tile group. The storage space consumed by the physical tiles in the older tile group is reclaimed by the DBMS only when they are no longer referenced by any logical tiles. Due to its incremental nature, the overhead of data layout reorganization is amortized over multiple queries.

The reorganization process does not target hot tile groups that are still being heavily accessed by OLTP transactions. Rather, it transforms the cold data to new layouts. This approach works well with the MVCC protocol described in Section 4. The updated versions of the tuples start off in a tuple-centric layout, and then are gradually transformed to an OLAP-optimized layout. Hence, the reorganization process does not impact latency-sensitive transactions while benefiting the OLAP queries.

Some application could have periodic cycles in their workload that oscillate between different sets of queries. In this scenario, it would be better if the DBMS does not quickly reorganize tables to a new layout because then the workload would shift back after an expensive reorganization. This is particularly important in exploratory workloads with ad-hoc OLAP queries. To avoid this problem, the DBMS prioritizes the older query samples in the clustering algorithm with a larger weight, thereby dampening the adaption mechanism. On the other hand, if the workload shift is not ephemeral, then it proceeds with the reorganization. We examine strategies for controlling data reorganization in Section 6.5.

6. EXPERIMENTAL EVALUATION

We now present an analysis of the tile-based FSM architecture. We implemented our execution engine and FSM storage manager in the Peloton DBMS [1]. Peloton is a multi-threaded, in-memory DBMS that is designed for HTAP workloads. Its execution engine supports all the common relational operators, which are implemented using the logical tile abstraction. We also integrated the runtime components for on-line query monitoring and data reorganization described in Section 5.

We deployed Peloton for these experiments on a dual-socket Intel Xeon E5-4620 server running Ubuntu 14.04 (64-bit). Each socket contains eight 2.6 GHz cores. It has 128 GB of DRAM and its L3 cache size is 20 MB.

For each experiment, we execute the workload five times and report the average execution time. All transactions execute with the default snapshot isolation level. We disable the DBMS's garbage collection and logging components to ensure that our measurements are only for the storage and query processing components.

In this section, we begin with an analysis of the impact of query projectivity and selectivity settings on the performance of different storage models. We then demonstrate that a FSM DBMS can converge to an optimal layout for an arbitrary workload without any manual tuning. We then examine the impact of the table's horizontal fragmentation on the performance of the DBMS. We next perform a sensitivity analysis on the parameters of the data reorganization process. Lastly, we compare some of our design choices against another state-of-the-art adaptive storage manager [11].

6.1 ADAPT Benchmark

We first describe the benchmarks we use in our evaluation. Since there currently is a dearth of HTAP workloads for testing, we developed our own that we call the ADAPT benchmark that is composed of queries that are common in enterprise workloads [41]. This benchmark is inspired by the one that Alagiannis et al. developed for evaluating the H_2O adaptive storage manager [11].

The ADAPT database has two tables – a narrow table and a wide table. Each table contains tuples with a primary key (a_0) and p integer attributes ($a_1, \ldots, a_p$), each 4 bytes in size. The narrow table has $p = 50$ attributes, and the wide table has $p = 500$ attributes. The size of the tuples in these two tables is approximately 200 B and 2 KB, respectively. In all of our experiments, we first load 10m tuples into each table in the database.

The benchmark's workload consists of (Q_1) an *insert* query that adds a single tuple into the table, (Q_2) a *scan* query that projects a subset of attributes of the tuples that satisfy a predicate, (Q_3) an *aggregate* query that computes the maximum value for a set of attributes over the selected tuples, (Q_4) an *arithmetic* query that sums up a subset of attributes of the selected tuples, and (Q_5) a *join* query that combines the tuples from two tables based on a predicate defined over the attributes in the tables. The corresponding SQL for these queries is as follows:

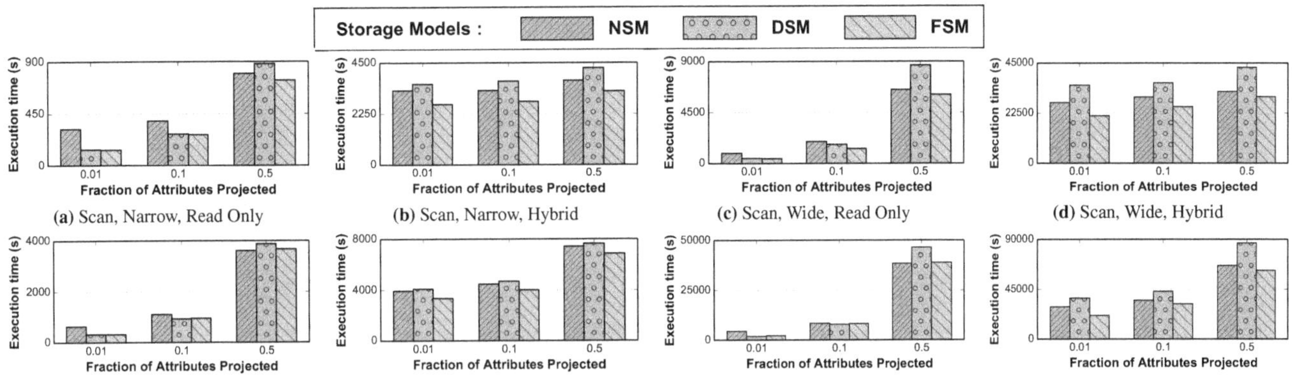

(a) Scan, Narrow, Read Only (b) Scan, Narrow, Hybrid (c) Scan, Wide, Read Only (d) Scan, Wide, Hybrid

(e) Aggregate, Narrow, Read Only (f) Aggregate, Narrow, Hybrid (g) Aggregate, Wide, Read Only (h) Aggregate, Wide, Hybrid

Figure 7: Projectivity Measurements – The impact of the storage layout on the query processing time under different projectivity settings. The execution engine runs the workload with different underlying storage managers on both the narrow and the wide table.

Q_1: **INSERT INTO** R **VALUES** $(a_0, a_1, \ldots, a_p)$
Q_2: **SELECT** $a_1, a_2, \ldots, a_k$ **FROM** R **WHERE** $a_0 < \delta$
Q_3: **SELECT** MAX(a_1),...,MAX(a_k) **FROM** R **WHERE** $a_0 < \delta$
Q_4: **SELECT** $a_1 + a_2 + \ldots + a_k$ **FROM** R **WHERE** $a_0 < \delta$
Q_5: **SELECT** X.a_1,...,X.a_k,Y.a_1,...,Y.a_k
FROM R **AS** X, R **AS** Y **WHERE** X.a_i < Y.a_j

Note that different values for k and δ alter the projectivity and the selectivity of the queries, respectively. We use different workloads comprised of these query types to evaluate the impact of the storage models on the performance of the DBMS.

6.2 Performance Impact of Storage Models

We begin with an analysis of the storage models when executing the scan (Q_1), aggregate (Q_2), and insert (Q_3) queries under different projectivity and selectivity settings. We consider two workloads in this experiment: (1) a *read-only* workload with one scan or aggregate query, and (2) a *hybrid* workload comprised of one scan or aggregate query followed by 1m insert queries. For each workload, we first load the database and execute the queries five times till the DBMS reorganizes the tables' layout. This is the ideal scenario for the FSM storage manager. We then execute the workload again using different storage managers and measure their completion time.

Figures 7a and 7b show the results for these two workloads with the scan query under different projectivity settings. For these experiments, we configure the scan query to select all the tuples. We observe that when the projectivity of the scan query is low, the DSM and FSM storage managers execute the read-only workload 2.3× faster than their NSM counterpart. This is because they make better use of memory bandwidth by only fetching the required attributes. As the query's projectivity increases, the performance gap decreases; when half of the attributes are included in the query's output, the DSM storage manager is 21% slower than the other storage managers. We attribute this to the increase in the tuple reconstruction cost. On the hybrid workload, under low projectivity settings, the FSM storage manager outperforms both NSM and DSM by 24% and 33%, respectively. This is because it processes the scan query faster than NSM and the insert queries faster than DSM.

The results in Figures 7c and 7d show that the differences between the storage managers are larger for the wide table. When half of the attributes are projected, DSM is 43% slower than FSM on the read-only workload in Figure 7c, but it is only 19% slower than FSM for the narrow table on the same workload and projectivity setting in Figure 7a. This is because the tuple reconstruction cost increases with wider tuples. This experiment shows that the benefits of FSM are more pronounced for the wide table.

These trends also occur for the aggregate query workloads shown in Figures 7e to 7h. We configure this query to compute the maximum value over all the tuples for the attributes of interest. The magnitude of the performance gaps between the different storage managers is smaller under the low projectivity settings. FSM executes the read-only workload upto 1.9× faster than NSM. This is because the execution engine needs to materialize the logical tiles consisting of the aggregate tuples for all the storage managers.

Figure 8 shows the results for the read-only and hybrid workloads under different selectivity settings. For these experiments, we fix the projectivity of the scan and aggregate queries to 0.1 (i.e., the query projects five attributes for the narrow table, and 50 attributes for the wide table). We vary the selectivity of these queries from 10–100%. Across all these settings, the execution time with FSM is either better or comparable to the other storage managers. This highlights the benefits of hybrid storage layouts for HTAP workloads.

We see that DSM outperforms NSM on the read-only workload, but then this order is flipped for the hybrid workload. This is because DSM executes the scan query faster than NSM on both the tables (Figures 8a and 8c). But NSM is faster than DSM on the insert queries (Figures 8d and 8h). FSM outperforms NSM on the read-only workload and DSM on the hybrid workload. This illustrates that the FSM storage manager can adapt to any HTAP workload unlike the DSM and NSM storage managers. In case of the workloads that contain the aggregate query, as shown in Figures 8e to 8h, the difference between the storage managers shrinks. We attribute this to the low projectivity setting of the aggregate query, which corroborates the findings in Figure 7.

6.3 Workload-Aware Adaptation

In the previous experiment, we examined a hybrid storage layout *after* the DBMS optimizes the layout for the workload. In the real world, this is not feasible due to the dynamic nature of workloads. Thus, we now examine the ability of FSM to adapt the storage layout at runtime, and compare it against static NSM and DSM layouts.

In this experiment, we execute a sequence of queries with changing properties. To mimic the temporal locality in HTAP workloads, and to clearly delineate the impact of the DBMS's storage layout on the different queries, the sequence is divided into *segments* of 25 queries that each correspond to a particular query type. This means that the DBMS executes the same type of query (with different input parameters) in one segment, and then switches to another query type in the next segment. We measure the execution time of each query in the sequence on the wide table for the NSM, DSM, and FSM storage managers. We configured the Peloton's reorganization process to speed up the adaptation process for the sake of demonstration.

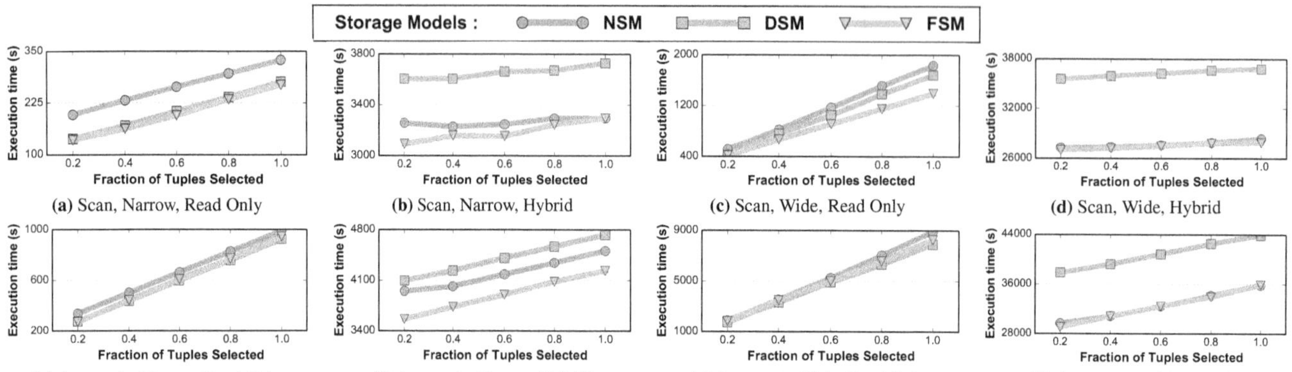

(a) Scan, Narrow, Read Only (b) Scan, Narrow, Hybrid (c) Scan, Wide, Read Only (d) Scan, Wide, Hybrid

(e) Aggregate, Narrow, Read Only (f) Aggregate, Narrow, Hybrid (g) Aggregate, Wide, Read Only (h) Aggregate, Wide, Hybrid

Figure 8: Selectivity Measurements – The impact of the storage layout on the query processing time under different selectivity settings. The execution engine runs the workload with different underlying storage managers on both the narrow and the wide table.

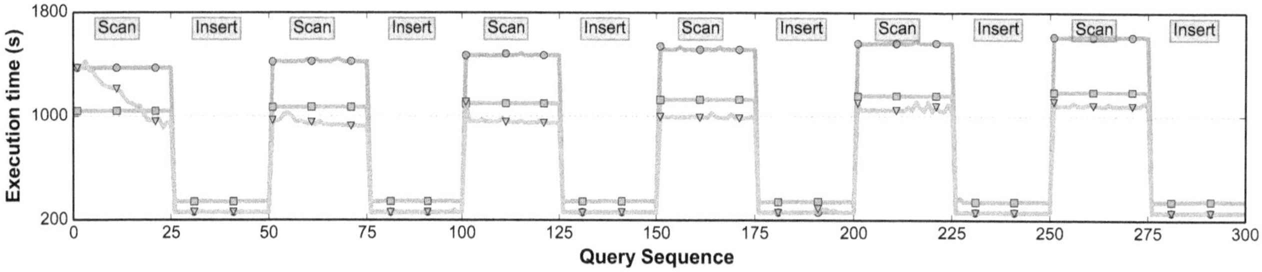

Figure 9: Workload-Aware Adaptation – The impact of tile group layout adaption on the query processing performance in an evolving workload mixture from the ADAPT benchmark. This experiment also examines the behavior of different storage managers while serving different query types in the workload.

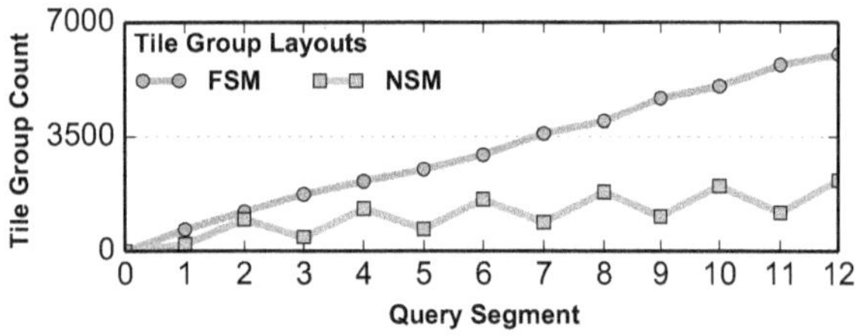

Figure 10: Layout Distribution – The variation in the distribution of tile group layouts of the table over time due to the data reorganization process.

The key observation from the time series graph in Figure 9 is that the FSM storage manager converges over time to a layout that works well for the particular segment. For instance, consider its behavior on the first query segment – a low-projectivity scan query (Q_2). When the tables are loaded into the database, FSM stores all the tuples in the default NSM layout because it has not yet seen any queries. The query execution time is, therefore, comparable to NSM. Over the next few queries, however, it starts reorganizing the data to the hybrid layout $\{\{a_0\}, \{a_1, \ldots, a_k\}, \{a_{k+1}, \ldots, a_{500}\}\}$, which is ideal for Q_2. After this happens, the query execution time drops and matches that of the DSM-based storage manager.

Next, when the workload shifts to the insert query segment (Q_1), we observe that both NSM and FSM fare better than DSM. This is because they perform fewer writes to different memory locations. After the insert queries, there is another shift in the workload back to the scan queries. FSM immediately outperforms NSM because it already reorganized most of the tile groups initially loaded into the table to an OLAP-optimized layout during the first scan query segment. The DBMS takes more time to process the scan queries in the third segment compared to those in the first segment because the table grows in size due to the interleaving insert query segment.

To better understand how the FSM is performing data reorganization, we analyze the distribution of the different tile group storage layouts over time. At the end of every query segment, we compute the number of tile groups per layout. The results shown in Figure 10 indicate that there are only two different layouts – the FSM layout mentioned above and the NSM layout. After every insert query segment, there is an increase in the number of tile groups with NSM layout. This is because the newly added tuples are stored in that layout. Over time, the number of tile groups with the FSM layout increases, as it works well for the scan query segment. This explains the better execution times on those segments in Figure 9.

6.4 Horizontal Fragmentation

We next measure the impact of horizontal fragmentation on the DBMS's performance. The goal is to compare query processing through logical tiles versus the canonical tuple-at-a-time iterator model [21]. We vary the number of tuples that the FSM storage manager stores in every tile group between 10–10000. We then measure the time it takes to execute the workloads comprising of scan queries (Q_2) from Section 6.2.

Figure 11a presents the results for the read-only workload on the narrow table. We observe that the execution time drops by 24% as we increase the number of tuples per tile group from 10 to 1000. We attribute this to the reduction in interpretation overhead. On the hybrid workload shown in Figure 11b, the performance gap reduces to 17%. We attribute this to the writes performed by the insert queries (Q_1) that are not affected by the horizontal fragmentation.

The results for the wide table are shown in Figures 11c and 11d. On the read-only workload, we see that the coarse-grained fragmentation setting outperforms the fine-grained one by 38%. This is because the logical tiles succinctly represent the data stored in these wide tables, and therefore the benefits of vectorized processing are more pronounced. We observe that the performance difference

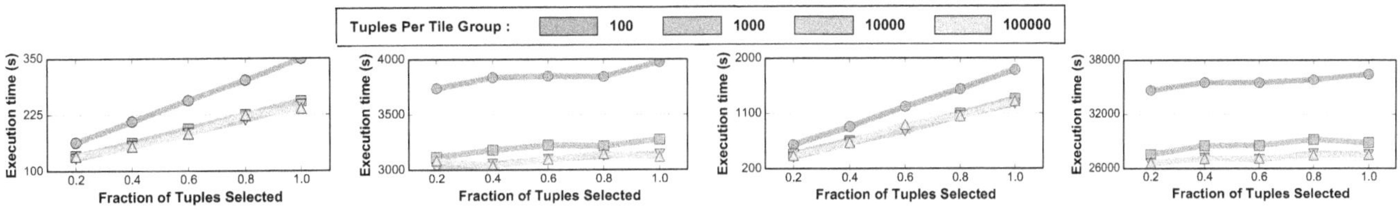

(a) Scan, Narrow, Read Only (b) Scan, Narrow, Hybrid (c) Scan, Wide, Read Only (d) Scan, Wide, Hybrid

Figure 11: Horizontal Fragmentation – The impact of horizontal fragmentation on the DBMS's performance. We execute the read-only and hybrid workloads comprising of scan queries on the tables in the ADAPT benchmark under different fragmentation settings.

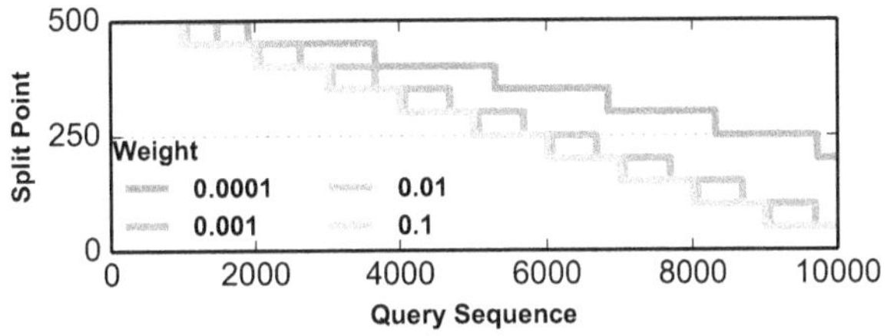

Figure 12: Weight Sensitivity Analysis – The impact of the weight w parameter on the rate at which the clustering algorithm of the data reorganization process adapts with the shifts in the HTAP workload.

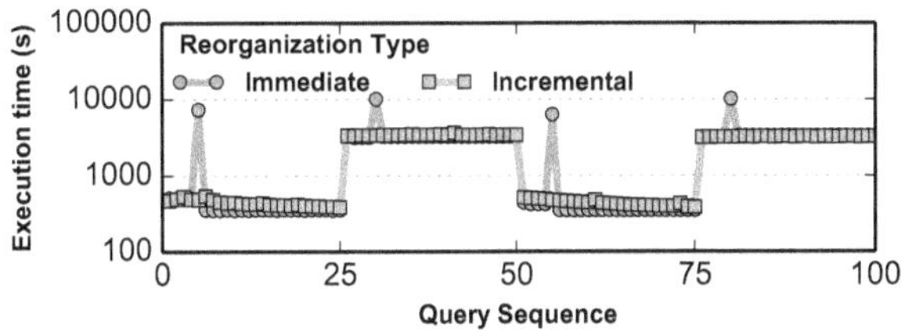

Figure 13: Data Reorganization Strategies – Comparison of the incremental and the immediate data reorganization strategies on a HTAP workload.

tapers off when we increase the number of tuples per tile group from 1000 to 10000. This is likely because the logical tiles no longer fit in the CPU caches beyond this saturation point.

6.5 Reorganization Sensitivity Analysis

We now perform a sensitivity analysis of the parameters of the reorganization process that optimizes the storage layout of the database for the workload. We are interested in how the weight w for older query samples affects the clustering algorithm's behavior. The workload contains a sequence of scan queries (Q_2) on the wide table. The sequence is divided into *segments* of 1000 queries. We gradually reduce the projectivity of the queries from 100% to 10% across the different segments.

As the DBMS executes the workload, it updates the table's layout to the form $\{\{a_0\}, \{a_1, \ldots, a_k\}, \{a_{k+1}, \ldots, a_{500}\}\}$, where k varies with the queries' projectivity in the current segment. We refer to this k as the *split point* in the layout, and we expect that k should decrease from 500 to 50. The rate at which k changes depends on the weight w for older query samples.

Figure 12 shows the fluctuation in the split point as the storage manager processes queries under different w settings ranging from 0.001 to 0.1. When w=0.0001, we observe that the rate at which the algorithm updates the split point is low. This is because the older query samples have a stronger impact on the partitioning layout. On the other hand, when w=0.1, the algorithm closely follows the shift in the workload. In this case, the storage manager reorganizes the data aggressively, and is therefore more susceptible to ephemeral workload shifts. We strike a balance at w=0.001. Under this setting, the storage manager adapts quickly enough for HTAP workloads, but is also not easily swayed over by ephemeral workload shifts.

6.6 Data Reorganization Strategies

Lastly, we compare the key design choices in our system with the H_2O adaptive storage manager [11]. As we described in Section 5, there are two approaches to on-line data reorganization. The first is to combine query processing with reorganization (H_2O), while the other is to reorganize data in an incremental manner (our approach in Peloton). We refer to these two approaches as *immediate* and *incremental* data reorganization strategies. We compare these two strategies using a workload comprising of scan (Q_2) and arithmetic (Q_4) queries on the wide table. We use a sequence of four segments each containing 25 queries. We alternate between these two queries in each query segment.

Figure 13 presents the time FSM takes to execute each query while adopting the different data reorganization strategies. We observe that when it adopts the former approach, there are spikes in the query latency. This is because when the partitioning algorithm derives a new layout after observing new queries, the storage manager transforms all the tile groups to the new layout within the critical path of query. Although this benefits the subsequent queries in the segment, that query incurs the entire data reorganization penalty. On the other hand, we do not observe such spikes when using the incremental strategy. This is because the reorganization cost is amortized across multiple queries. In this case, the query execution time gradually drops over time due to data reorganization. Thus, we contend that this approach is better for latency-sensitive applications.

Another important design choice is whether the storage manager can maintain multiple copies of the same piece of data with different layouts. H_2O chooses to create copies of the data with new layouts as part of the query execution. This improves the execution time of subsequent queries of the same type. But, it necessitates the construction of layout-specific access operators using code generation techniques. Our storage manager, however, only maintains one copy of the data with a particular layout at any given point in time. We adopt this approach to avoid the overhead of synchronizing the copies on write-intensive workloads.

7. RELATED WORK

We now discuss the previous research on optimizing DBMS storage and execution models for specific workloads, especially in the context of HTAP applications.

Storage Models: Several storage models have been proposed for optimizing the DBMS performance on different workloads. The ubiquitous NSM works well for OLTP workloads [17]. For OLAP workloads, the DBMS's I/O efficiency can be improved by adopting DSM, as it only fetches those columns that are required for query processing [24]. This approach also enhances the caching behavior by increasing the data locality across multiple tuples [14], but incurs high tuple reconstruction costs for OLTP queries. Hybrid NSM/DSM schemes address this trade-off by co-locating attributes accessed together in a query within the same partition [18], figuring out the optimal vertical and horizontal partitioning for a given workload [8], and employing different storage models in different replicas of a table [42].

Ailamaki et al. introduced the PAX model, where all of the data for a single tuple are stored together in a disk page similar to NSM, but it clusters the values of a particular column together for multiple tuples within that page [9, 10]. This helps improve the cache performance and bandwidth utilization by eliminating unnecessary memory references, and thereby reduce the overhead of OLAP queries with low projectivity.

Off-line Physical Design Tuning: Data Morphing generalizes the PAX storage model by decomposing the records into arbitrary groups of attributes [23]. It determines the optimal partitioning for a given workload using a hill-climbing algorithm evaluated over query workload statistics. Zukowski and Boncz show that for complex queries, different storage layouts work well for different parts of the same query plan [51]. MonetDB/X100 improves CPU efficiency by using vectorized primitives for query processing [15]. IBM's Blink horizontally partitions data to improve compression through fixed-length dictionary encoding, which enables efficient hash-based aggregation techniques and SIMD evaluation of predicates [43].

All of this work examines the performance impact of storage models on OLTP and OLAP workloads. They assume, however, that the workload is known a priori, and thus are unable to adapt to dynamic HTAP workloads. In contrast, our approach tunes the storage layout in tandem with the workload to support these applications.

On-line Physical Design Tuning: Database cracking performs index construction and maintenance as a part of regular query processing [25]. It dynamically sorts the tuples in a column-store based on the query workload, and minimizes the tuple reconstruction cost using auxiliary data structures [26]. This approach, however, does not handle co-located attributes. Bruno and Chaudhuri present an on-line algorithm for selecting indexes [16]. During query execution, DBMS estimates the improvement provided by a candidate index on the given workload and space constraints, and then automatically creates that index if it considers it to be beneficial. Autostore is an on-line self-tuning data store that uses a greedy algorithm for database partitioning [28].

Similar to our approach, this line of work addresses the problem of optimizing the physical design of the database during regular query processing. But all of them focus on auxiliary data structures (i.e., indexes), or they tightly couple the design of the DBMS's execution engine with that of its storage manager.

Hybrid DBMS Architectures: Since the beginning of the 21st century, there have been several DBMSs and add-ons developed for HTAP workloads. One of the first approaches, known as fractured mirrors, is where the DBMS maintains both separate NSM and DSM physical representations of the database simultaneously [42]. This approach has been recently implemented in Oracle's columnar add-on [39]. IBM's BLU is a similar columnar storage add-on for DB2 that uses dictionary compression [44]. Although these systems achieve better ad-hoc OLAP query performance than a pure row store DBMS, the cost of synchronizing the mirrors is high.

The HYRISE DBMS automatically partitions the tables into variable-length vertical segments based on how the attributes of each table are co-accessed by the queries [22]. HYRISE provides better cache utilization than PAX when scanning both narrow and wide projections. Based on the work from HYRISE, SAP developed the HANA in-memory DBMS that uses a split-storage model [31, 47]. Tuples start out in a NSM layout, and then migrate to a compressed DSM storage manager.

Another DBMS that supports dual NSM/DSM storage like HANA is MemSQL [4]. Like HANA, these storage layouts are managed by separate runtime components [5]. But MemSQL is different because the different layouts are not transparent to the application. That is, the administrator manually imports data into the DBMS as a disk-resident, read-only table stored in columnar format and then modifies their application to query those tables.

HyPer is an in-memory hybrid DBMS that stores the entire database in either a NSM or DSM layout (i.e., it cannot use hybrid layouts for tables) [29]. To prevent longer running OLAP queries from interfering with regular transactions, HyPer periodically creates copy-on-write snapshots by forking the DBMS's process and executes those queries on separate CPUs in the forked process. OLTP transactions are executed by the original process, and all OLAP queries are executed on the snapshots. All of the above DBMSs adopt static hybrid storage layouts. That is, they can only optimize the storage layout of the tables for a static workload.

Adaptive Stores: OctopusDB maintains multiple copies of a database stored in different layouts [20]. It uses a logical log as its primary storage structure and then creates secondary physical representations from the log entries. It does not address some problems with this architecture. Foremost is that the DBMS's query planner is unable to generate query plans that could span different representations. The system also incurs high synchronization costs.

H_2O is a hybrid system that dynamically adapts the storage layout with the evolving HTAP workload [11]. It maintains the same data in different storage layouts to improve the performance of read-only workloads through multiple execution engines. It combines data reorganization with query processing. Although Peloton shares many of the goals of the H_2O system, it uses a single execution engine to process data stored in different storage layouts. It performs data reorganization in the background to reduce the impact on query latency. Peloton stores a given tile group in only one storage layout, as it needs to support write-intensive workloads, where the overhead of synchronizing the copies of a tile group is high. It allows tile groups belonging to the same table to have different storage layouts.

8. CONCLUSION

This paper presented a DBMS architecture based on tiles to bridge the architectural gap between the OLTP and OLAP systems. The FSM storage manager stores tables using hybrid storage layouts based on how it expects the tuples to be accessed in the future. It organizes the hotter tile groups of a table in a format that is optimized for OLTP operations, while the colder ones are stored in a format that is more amenable to OLAP queries. We proposed a logical tile abstraction that allows the DBMS to execute query plans over data with these different layouts without using separate execution engines and with minimal overhead. Our on-line reorganization technique continuously enhances each table's physical design in response to an evolving query workload. This enables the DBMS to optimize the layout of a database for an arbitrary application without requiring any manual tuning. Our evaluation showed that the FSM-based DBMS delivers up to 3× higher throughput compared to static storage layouts across different HTAP workloads.

ACKNOWLEDGMENTS

This work was supported (in part) by the Intel Science and Technology Center for Big Data and the U.S. National Science Foundation (CCF-1438955). Thanks to Greg Thain for the paper title idea.

For questions or comments about this paper, please call the CMU Database Hotline at +1-844-88-CMUDB.

References

[1] Peloton Database Management System. http://pelotondb.org.

[2] Linux perf framework. https://perf.wiki.kernel.org/index.php/Main_Page.

[3] PostgreSQL Query Plan Cost. http://www.postgresql.org/docs/9.5/static/using-explain.html.

[4] MemSQL. http://www.memsql.com, 2015.

[5] MemSQL – Columnstore. http://docs.memsql.com/4.0/concepts/columnstore/, 2015.

[6] D. Abadi, D. Myers, D. DeWitt, and S. Madden. Materialization strategies in a column-oriented DBMS. In *ICDE*, 2007.

[7] D. J. Abadi, S. R. Madden, and N. Hachem. Column-stores vs. row-stores: How different are they really? In *SIGMOD*, 2008.

[8] S. Agrawal, V. Narasayya, and B. Yang. Integrating vertical and horizontal partitioning into automated physical database design. In *SIGMOD*, 2004.

[9] A. Ailamaki, D. J. DeWitt, M. D. Hill, and M. Skounakis. Weaving relations for cache performance. In *VLDB*, 2001.

[10] A. Ailamaki, D. J. DeWitt, and M. D. Hill. Data page layouts for relational databases on deep memory hierarchies. *The VLDB Journal*, 11(3):198–215, 2002.

[11] I. Alagiannis, S. Idreos, and A. Ailamaki. H2O: A hands-free adaptive store. In *SIGMOD*, 2014.

[12] J. Arulraj, A. Pavlo, and S. Dulloor. Let's talk about storage & recovery methods for non-volatile memory database systems. In *SIGMOD*, 2015.

[13] D. Beaver, S. Kumar, H. C. Li, J. Sobel, P. Vajgel, and F. Inc. Finding a needle in haystack: Facebook's photo storage. In *OSDI*, 2010.

[14] P. Boncz, S. Manegold, and M. L. Kersten. Database architecture optimized for the new bottleneck: Memory access. In *VLDB*, pages 54–65, 1999.

[15] P. Boncz, M. Zukowski, and N. Nes. Monetdb/x100: Hyper-pipelining query execution. In *CIDR*, 2005.

[16] N. Bruno and S. Chaudhuri. An online approach to physical design tuning. In *ICDE*, 2007.

[17] G. P. Copeland and S. N. Khoshafian. A decomposition storage model. In *SIGMOD*, 1985.

[18] D. Cornell and P. Yu. An effective approach to vertical partitioning for physical design of relational databases. In *IEEE TSE*, 1990.

[19] N. de Bruijn. *Asymptotic Methods in Analysis*. Dover, 1981.

[20] J. Dittrich and A. Jindal. Towards a one size fits all database architecture. In *CIDR*, pages 195–198, 2011.

[21] G. Graefe. Volcano – an extensible and parallel query evaluation system. In *IEEE TKDE*, volume 6, pages 120–135, Feb. 1994.

[22] M. Grund, J. Krüger, H. Plattner, A. Zeier, P. Cudre-Mauroux, and S. Madden. HYRISE: a main memory hybrid storage engine. In *VLDB*, pages 105–116, 2010.

[23] R. A. Hankins and J. M. Patel. Data morphing: An adaptive, cache-conscious storage technique. In *VLDB*, 2003.

[24] S. Harizopoulos, V. Liang, D. J. Abadi, and S. Madden. Performance tradeoffs in read-optimized databases. In *VLDB*, pages 487–498, 2006.

[25] S. Idreos, M. L. Kersten, and S. Manegold. Database cracking. In *CIDR*, 2007.

[26] S. Idreos, M. L. Kersten, and S. Manegold. Self-organizing tuple reconstruction in column-stores. In *SIGMOD*, 2009.

[27] A. K. Jain. Data clustering: 50 years beyond k-means. *Pattern Recognition Letters*, 2010.

[28] A. Jindal and J. Dittrich. Relax and let the database do the partitioning online. In *Enabling Real-Time Business Intelligence*, Lecture Notes in Business Information Processing, 2012.

[29] A. Kemper and T. Neumann. HyPer: A hybrid OLTP&OLAP main memory database system based on virtual memory snapshots. In *ICDE*, pages 195–206, 2011.

[30] P.-A. Larson, S. Blanas, C. Diaconu, C. Freedman, J. M. Patel, and M. Zwilling. High-performance concurrency control mechanisms for main-memory databases. In *VLDB*, 2011.

[31] J. Lee, M. Muehle, N. May, F. Faerber, V. Sikka, H. Plattner, J. Krüger, and M. Grund. High-performance transaction processing in SAP HANA. *IEEE Data Eng. Bull.*, 36(2):28–33, 2013.

[32] N. Malviya, A. Weisberg, S. Madden, and M. Stonebraker. Rethinking main memory OLTP recovery. In *ICDE*, 2014.

[33] S. Manegold, P. A. Boncz, and M. L. Kersten. Optimizing database architecture for the new bottleneck: Memory access. *VLDB Journal*, 2000.

[34] MemSQL. How MemSQL Works. http://docs.memsql.com/4.1/intro/.

[35] C. Mohan, D. Haderle, B. Lindsay, H. Pirahesh, and P. Schwarz. ARIES: a transaction recovery method supporting fine-granularity locking and partial rollbacks using write-ahead logging. *ACM TODS*, 17(1):94–162, 1992. ISSN 0362-5915.

[36] S. B. Navathe and M. Ra. Vertical partitioning for database design: A graphical algorithm. In *SIGMOD*, 1989.

[37] T. Neumann. Efficiently compiling efficient query plans for modern hardware. *Proc. VLDB Endow.*, 4(9):539–550, June 2011.

[38] T. Neumann, T. Mühlbauer, and A. Kemper. Fast Serializable Multi-Version Concurrency Control for Main-Memory Database Systems. In *SIGMOD*, 2015.

[39] Oracle. Oracle database in-memory option to accelerate analytics, data warehousing, reporting and OLTP. http://www.oracle.com/us/corporate/press/2020717, 2013.

[40] M. Pezzini, D. Feinberg, N. Rayner, and R. Edjlali. Hybrid Transaction/Analytical Processing Will Foster Opportunities for Dramatic Business Innovation. https://www.gartner.com/doc/2657815/, 2014.

[41] H. Plattner. A common database approach for OLTP and OLAP using an in-memory column database. In *SIGMOD*, 2009.

[42] R. Ramamurthy, D. J. DeWitt, and Q. Su. A case for fractured mirrors. In *Proceedings of the 28th International Conference on Very Large Data Bases*, VLDB '02, pages 430–441, 2002.

[43] V. Raman, G. Swart, L. Qiao, F. Reiss, V. Dialani, D. Kossmann, I. Narang, and R. Sidle. Constant-time query processing. In *ICDE*, 2008.

[44] V. Raman et al. DB2 with BLU acceleration: So much more than just a column store. In *VLDB*, volume 6, pages 1080–1091, 2013.

[45] A. Rosenberg. Improving query performance in data warehouses. *Business Intelligence Journal*, 11, Jan. 2006.

[46] D. Schwalb, M. Faust, J. Wust, M. Grund, and H. Plattner. Efficient transaction processing for Hyrise in mixed workload environments. In *IMDM*, 2014.

[47] V. Sikka, F. Färber, W. Lehner, S. K. Cha, T. Peh, and C. Bornhövd. Efficient transaction processing in SAP HANA database: The end of a column store myth. In *SIGMOD*, pages 731–742, 2012.

[48] V. Sikka, F. Farber, A. Goel, and W. Lehner. SAP HANA: The evolution from a modern main-memory data platform to an enterprise application platform. In *VLDB*, 2013.

[49] M. Stonebraker, D. J. Abadi, A. Batkin, X. Chen, M. Cherniack, M. Ferreira, E. Lau, A. Lin, S. Madden, E. O'Neil, P. O'Neil, A. Rasin, N. Tran, and S. Zdonik. C-store: A column-oriented dbms. VLDB, pages 553–564, 2005.

[50] A. H. Watson, T. J. Mccabe, and D. R. Wallace. Structured testing: A software testing methodology using the cyclomatic complexity metric. In *U.S. Department of Commerce/National Institute of Standards and Technology*, 1996.

[51] M. Zukowski and P. A. Boncz. Vectorwise: Beyond column stores. In *IEEE Data Engineering Bulletin*, 2012.

APPENDIX

A. LOGICAL TILE ALGEBRA

We formally define the semantics of the operators in logical tile algebra. For each operator, we describe the type of the input arguments and output, as well as an algebraic definition of the transformation from the input arguments to the output. We denote a multi-set of tuples that can contain duplicates by $\langle\ldots\rangle$, and a set of tuples where all the elements are unique by $\{\ldots\}$. $|S|$ represents the size of a multi-set or set S. Given this notation, we describe the operators based on the logical tile algebra shown in Table 1.

Category	Operator	Input Arguments	Output
Bridge Operators	SEQUENTIAL SCAN	T X, predicate P	$\{ \text{LT} \} \equiv \{ \text{LT w} \mid \text{w} \equiv \langle x \mid x \in X \wedge P(x) \rangle \}$
	INDEX SCAN	I X, predicate P	$\{ \text{LT} \} \equiv \{ \text{LT w} \mid \text{w} \equiv \langle x \mid x \in X \wedge P(x) \rangle \}$
	MATERIALIZE	LT X	PT Y
Metadata Operators	SELECTION	LT X, predicate P	$\text{LT} \equiv \langle x \mid x \in X \wedge P(x) \rangle$
	PROJECTION	LT X, attributes C	$\text{LT} \equiv X' \mid \text{schema}(X') = C$
Mutators	INSERT	T X, LT Y	$\text{T} \equiv \text{X} \Rightarrow X \vee Y_p$
	DELETE	T X, LT Y	$\text{T} \equiv \text{X} \Rightarrow X \setminus Y_p$
	UPDATE	T X, attributes C, expr E	$\text{T} \equiv \text{X} \Rightarrow (X \setminus Y_p) \vee Z_p$
Pipeline Breakers	JOIN	LT X, LT Y, predicate P	$\text{LT} \equiv \langle x \mid\mid y \mid x \in X \wedge y \in Y \wedge P(x, y) \rangle$
	UNION	LT X, LT Y	$\text{LT} \equiv \{ z \mid z \in X \vee z \in Y \}$
	INTERSECTION	LT X, LT Y	$\text{LT} \equiv \{ z \mid z \in X \wedge z \in Y \}$
	DIFFERENCE	LT X, LT Y	$\text{LT} \equiv \{ z \mid z \in X \wedge z \notin Y \}$
	UNIQUE	LT X	$\text{LT} \equiv \{ z \mid z \in X \}$
	COUNT	LT X	$\text{int} \equiv \mid X \mid$
	SUM	LT X, attributes C	$\text{LT} \equiv [\sum_{x \in X} x_c \; \forall \, c \in C]$
	MAX	LT X, attributes C	$\text{LT} \equiv [\; \max_{x \in X} x_c \; \forall c \in C]$

Table 1: Logical Tile Algebra – Algebraic definitions for the operators of the logical tile algebra. For each operator, we describe its category, input arguments, output, and the algebraic transformation. We denote the logical tile by **LT**, the physical tile by **PT**, the table by **T**, and the index by **I**.

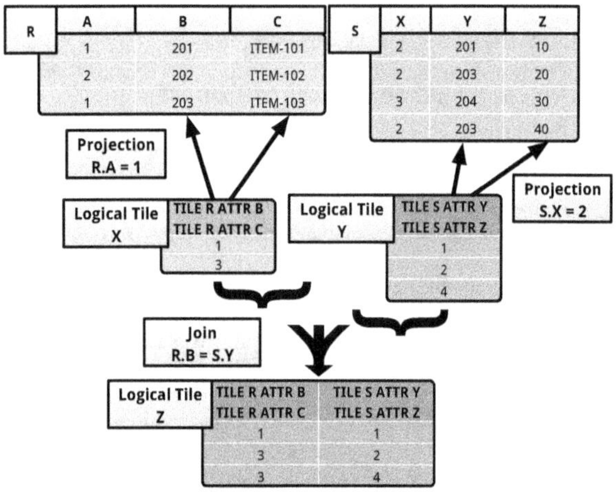

Figure 14: Logical Tile Operators – The runtime behavior of the sequential scan and join operators of the logical tile algebra for the sample query.

Bridge Operators: The bridge operators include the table access methods, such as the sequential scan and the index scan operators. The *sequential scan* operator generates a logical tile for every tile group in the table X that contains any tuple x satisfying the predicate $P(x)$. The output logical tile only contains one column, that is a list of offsets corresponding to the matching tuples in the tile group. Figure 14 shows the runtime behavior of the sequential scan operator in the plan tree presented in Figure 5. Here, the operator emits a logical tile X that represents the tuples in the physical tile R that satisfy the predicate a=1. The *index scan* operator identifies the tuples matching the predicate P using the index X, and then constructs one or more logical tiles representing those tuples. Each logical tile can only represent the matching tuples that are present within the same tile group.

The *materialize operator* transforms the logical tile X to a physical tile Y. The execution engine invokes this operator either before sending the result tuples to the client, or when it needs to perform early-materialization. In the latter case, it constructs a passthrough logical tile to wrap around the materialized tile Y, and passes it upwards in the plan tree.

Metadata Operators: The *projection* operator takes in a logical tile X, only modifies its metadata, and emits it as the output. It removes the attributes that need to be projected away from the metadata. The columns corresponding to these attributes are still present in the logical tile. The *selection* operator marks the tuples that do not satisfy the predicate P as invisible in the metadata of X. The rows corresponding to these tuples are still present in X. Due to these optimizations, these operators only need to alter the metadata of the logical tile.

Mutators: These operators directly modify the data stored in the table, and we therefore represent the transformation by $\Rightarrow$. The *insert* operator takes in a logical tile Y, and appends the associated tuples Y_p to the specified table X. The *delete* operator removes the tuples Y_p represented by Y from the table X. The *update* operator first marks the tuples Y_p represented by Y in the table X as dead. It then evaluates the expressions E associated with the attributes C over Y_p to construct newer versions of those tuples Z_p. Finally, it appends Z_p in the table. The mutators work with the transactional storage manager to control the lifetime of tuples.

Pipeline Breakers: These operators break the streamlined flow of logical tiles between them during query execution [37]. The *join* operator takes in logical tiles X and Y, and evaluates the join predicate $P(x, y)$ over them. It constructs an output logical tile by concatenating the schemas of X and Y. As iterates over every pair of tuples, if it finds a one that satisfies P, it concatenates them and appends them to the output logical tile. In Figure 14, we note that the output logical tile Z is obtained by concatenating the matching tuple pairs from the input logical tiles X and Y.

The *set* operators are also pipeline breakers. For instance, the *union* operator keeps track of the tuples that it observes, while going over all the input logical tiles from its children. Finally, it returns the logical tiles after marking the duplicate tuples as invisible.

The *aggregate* operators, such as the *count* and *sum* operators, examine all the logical tiles from the child operator to construct the aggregate tuples. Unlike the set operators, the aggregate operators build new physical tiles to store the aggregate tuples. Finally, they construct a set of passthrough logical tiles to wrap around these newly constructed physical tiles as depicted by [...], and propagate them upwards in the plan tree one logical-tile at a time.

We note that the logical tile abstraction has no limitations with respect to its expressiveness. Logical tiles are a "shorthand" notation for describing a set of tuples stored in one or more relations. Any relational operator can therefore be mapped to logical tile algebra.

B. JOIN QUERIES

In this section, we examine the performance impact of storage

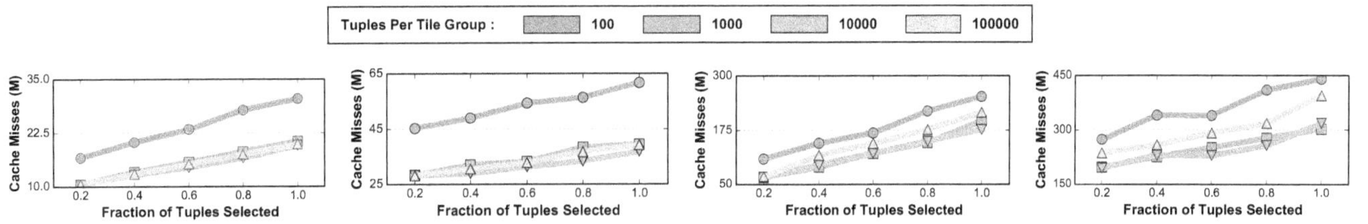

(a) Narrow, Read Only (b) Narrow, Hybrid (c) Wide, Read Only (d) Wide, Hybrid

Figure 15: Caching Behavior – Evaluation of the impact of horizontal fragmentation on caching behavior. We execute the read-only and hybrid workloads on the tables in the ADAPT benchmark under different horizontal fragmentation settings.

Number of Logical Tiles	Materialization Time(s)
1	17.7
10	18.3
100	25.7
1000	82.3
10000	640.4

Table 2: Indirection Overhead – Time taken to materialize 10000 tuples depending on the number of logical tiles representing them.

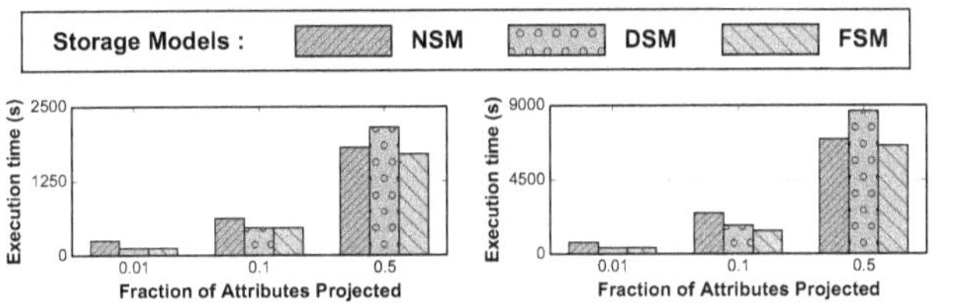

(a) Narrow Table (b) Wide Table

Figure 16: Join Measurements – The impact of the storage layout on the time taken to execute join queries under different projectivity settings. The execution engine runs the workload with different underlying storage managers on both the narrow and the wide table.

models on join queries. Our layout-agnostic join algorithms operate on logical tiles and compute the join using only the join keys. This approach is similar to cache-conscious join algorithms, like radix join [33], that evaluate the join by accessing only the attributes involved in the join. As such, the data layout does not significantly affect the join predicate evaluation [11]. However, the data layout does impact the post-join tuple reconstruction, wherein the storage manager needs to retrieve the projected attributes. The overall behavior of the join operator, while processing data stored under different layouts, is similar to that of the projection operator.

We demonstrate this using the self join query Q_5. We load the table R with 10m tuples. We then measure the time it takes to execute the join query Q_5 on the table. We vary the projectivity of the join query from 1% to 100%. We pick two random attributes a_i and a_j to construct the join predicate.

Figure 16a presents the results for the join query on the narrow table. We observe that when the projectivity of the join query is high, the NSM and FSM storage managers execute the join query 1.3× faster than their DSM counterpart. This is because these layouts reduce the cost of retrieving the projected attributes during tuple reconstruction. The results for the wide table are shown in Figure 16b. In this case, the NSM and FSM storage managers outperform the DSM storage manager by 1.5×. These results are similar to those observed in the projectivity experiment in Section 6.2.

C. CACHING BEHAVIOR

We next examine the impact of horizontal fragmentation on the DBMS's cache locality. In this experiment, we evaluate the reduction in the number of CPU cache misses due to the logical-tile-at-a-time processing model compared to the tuple-at-a-time iterator model [21]. We vary the number of tuples that the FSM storage manager stores in every tile group between 10–10000. We then count the number of cache misses incurred while executing the workloads from Section 6.2 under different horizontal fragmentation settings. We use event-based sampling in the *perf* framework [2] to track the caching behavior. We start this profiling after loading the database.

Figure 15a presents the results for the read-only workload on the narrow table. We observe that the number of cache misses drops by 1.5× when we increase the number of tuples stored in a tile group from 10 to 1000. We attribute this to the reduction in interpretation overhead. A similar drop in the number of cache misses is seen with the hybrid workload results shown in Figure 15b.

The results for the wide table are shown in Figures 15c and 15d. On the read-only workload, we see that the number of cache misses under the coarse-grained fragmentation setting is 1.7× smaller than that under the fine-grained setting. This shows that the benefits of the succinct representation of data by logical tiles are more pronounced for wide tables. We observe that the number of cache misses is higher when we increase the number of tuples per tile group from 1000 to 10000. This is because the logical tiles no longer fit in the CPU caches beyond this saturation point.

D. INDIRECTION OVERHEAD

We now focus on the performance overhead associated with the level of indirection in the logical tile abstraction to access the underlying physical tiles. To materialize a logical tile, the storage manager needs to look up the locations of the underlying physical tiles only once for all the tuples contained in the logical tile.

Table 2 presents the time taken to materialize 10000 tuples from the wide table that are represented by one or more logical tiles. We vary the number of tuples represented by each logical tile from 1 through 10000. When every logical tile represents only one tuple, the storage manager materializes 10000 such logical tiles. On the other hand, when the logical tile represents all the 10000 tuples, then the storage manager only materializes one such logical tile. We observe that the materialization time drops by 8× when the number of tuples represented by a logical tile increases from 1 to 10. As HTAP workloads frequently contain queries that produce longer logical tiles, we think that the indirection overhead will be tolerable.

An alternative approach to handle HTAP workloads is to use two separate OLTP and OLAP DBMSs [47]. However, the overhead of an atomic commitment protocol to coordinate transactions that span across data stored in these two different systems is higher than the overhead of indirection associated with the logical tile abstraction.

E. CONCURRENT HYBRID WORKLOADS

In this section, we examine the impact of storage layout on the performance of concurrent HTAP workloads. The workload consists of a random mixture of scan queries (Q_2) and insert queries (Q_1). The selectivity of the scan queries is set to 10% of all the tuples in the table. We configure the projectivity of the scan queries to 10%

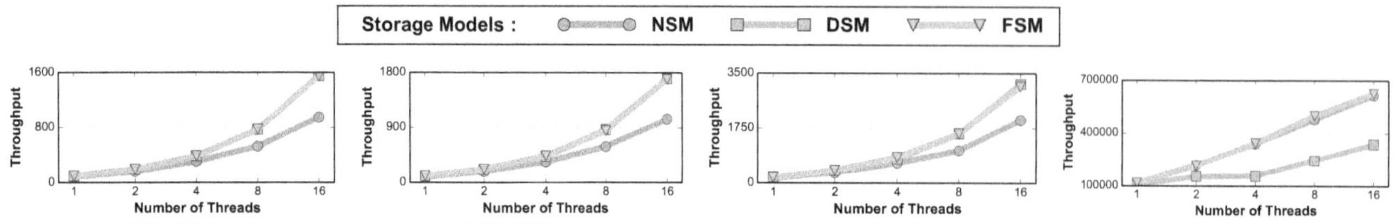

(a) Read Only (b) Read-heavy (c) Balanced (d) Write-only

Figure 17: Concurrent Hybrid Workloads – The impact of the storage layout on the query processing time under different concurrent hybrid workloads. The execution engine runs the workloads with different underlying storage managers on the narrow table.

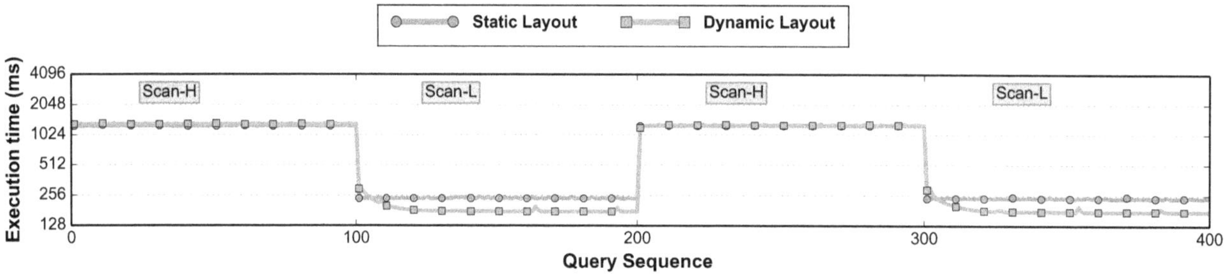

Figure 18: Dynamic Layout Adaptation – Benefits of dynamic layout adaptation on a HTAP workload.

of the attributes in the table. All the storage managers take more time to execute the scan query compared to the insert query. We examine four types of workload mixtures that allow us to vary the I/O operations that the DBMS executes. These mixtures represent different ratios of scan and insert queries:

- **Read-Only:** 100% *scans*
- **Read-Heavy:** 90% *scans*, 10% *inserts*
- **Balanced:** 50% *scans*, 50% *inserts*
- **Write-Heavy:** 10% *scans*, 90% *inserts*

We measure the throughput delivered by each storage manager on the different workload mixtures. On each workload mixture, we vary the number of concurrent clients from 1 through 16. We perform this experiment on a server with eight cores. Figure 17a presents the results on the read-only mixture. We observe that the throughputs delivered by the FSM and DSM storage managers are 1.7× higher than that of the NSM storage manager under higher concurrency settings. We attribute this to their better usage of memory bandwidth by only fetching the attributes required by the scan queries. We observe that the throughput scales linearly with the number of client connections. We notice similar trends on the read-heavy and balanced mixtures in Figures 17b and 17c.

The trend is reversed on the write-heavy mixture shown in Figure 17d. On this workload, FSM and NSM outperform DSM because they perform fewer writes to different memory locations while handling the insert queries. The absolute throughput is more than 400× higher than that observed on the read-only mixture. This is due to the lower overhead incurred by the storage manager while executing an insert query.

F. DYNAMIC LAYOUT ADAPTATION

We evaluate the benefits of dynamic layout adaptation on ad-hoc HTAP workloads in this section. Hyrise partitions the tables into vertical segments based on how the attributes of each table are co-accessed by the queries [22]. It assumes, however, that the access patterns are known a priori, and thus it generates a *static* storage layout for every table. Unlike Hyrise, Peloton dynamically adapts the storage layout based on the changes in the HTAP workload.

We consider an HTAP workload comprising of scan queries (Q_2) with high projectivity on the wide table in the ADAPT benchmark. We configure the projectivity to be 90% of the attributes. Hyrise computes an optimal storage layout for this workload where all the projected attributes are stored in a single physical tile.

In order to emulate a dynamic HTAP workload, we invoke *ad-hoc* query segments comprising of scan queries (Q_2) with low projectivity. These queries project only 5% of the attributes. Each query segment consists of 100 queries. This means that the DBMS executes the high projectivity scan queries in one segment, and then switches to the low projectivity scan queries in the next segment. We measure the execution time of each query in the sequence when we use the static layout computed by Hyrise and the dynamic layouts generated by the FSM storage manager.

The key observation from the time series graph in Figure 18 is that the FSM storage manager converges over time to a layout that works well for the particular segment. For instance, in the first query segment, it performs similar to Hyrise on the high projectivity scan queries. Next, when the workload shifts to the low projectivity query segment, we observe that it outperforms the static layout computed by Hyrise by 1.5×. This is because the layout reorganization process dynamically adapts the layout to work well for this segment.

G. FUTURE WORK

Peloton contains several knobs for controlling the layout reorganization process. Although we attempt to provide good default settings for these knobs, we believe that the DBMS should automatically adjust these knobs based on the HTAP workload. We plan to investigate the design of a self-driving module within the DBMS that dynamically adjusts these knobs to simplify the tuning process. We intend to explore code generation and data compression techniques for optimizing query execution as well as other facets of the DBMS's runtime operations.

An Effective Syntax for Bounded Relational Queries

Yang Cao[1,2] Wenfei Fan[1,2]

[1]School of Informatics, University of Edinburgh [2]RCBD and SLISDE, Beihang University

{Y.Cao-17@sms, wenfei@inf}.ed.ac.uk

ABSTRACT

A query Q is *boundedly evaluable* under a set $\mathcal{A}$ of access constraints if for all datasets D that satisfy $\mathcal{A}$, there exists a fraction D_Q of D such that $Q(D) = Q(D_Q)$, and the size of D_Q and time for identifying D_Q are both *independent of* the size of D. That is, we can compute $Q(D)$ by accessing a bounded amount of data no matter how big D grows. However, while desirable, it is undecidable to determine whether a query in relational algebra (RA) is bounded under $\mathcal{A}$.

In light of the undecidability, this paper develops an effective syntax for bounded RA queries. We identify a class of *covered* RA queries such that under $\mathcal{A}$, (a) every boundedly evaluable RA query is equivalent to a covered query, (b) every covered RA query is boundedly evaluable, and (c) it takes PTIME in $|Q|$ and $|\mathcal{A}|$ to check whether Q is covered by $\mathcal{A}$. We provide quadratic-time algorithms to check the coverage of Q, and to generate a bounded query plan for covered Q. We also study a new optimization problem for minimizing access constraints for covered queries. Using real-life data, we experimentally verify that a large number of RA queries in practice are covered, and that bounded query plans improve RA query evaluation by orders of magnitude.

Keywords

Bounded evaluability; query evaluation; big data

1. INTRODUCTION

Querying big data is cost prohibitive. Given a query Q and a dataset D, it is NP-complete to decide whether a tuple t is in the query answer $Q(D)$ when Q is an SPC query (selection, projection and Cartesian product), and PSPACE-complete if Q is in relational algebra (RA) [5]. When D is big, it is hard, if not impossible, to compute $Q(D)$ within constrained resources such as time and available processors.

To tackle this problem, a notion of boundedly evaluable queries has recently been studied [13, 14, 18, 19]. The idea is to compute $Q(D)$ by accessing only a fraction D_Q of D that suffices to answer Q in D, instead of the entire D. To identify D_Q, it makes use of a set $\mathcal{A}$ of access constraints, which are a combination of simple cardinality constraints and their indices. Under $\mathcal{A}$, Q is *boundedly evaluable* if for all datasets D that satisfy $\mathcal{A}$, there exists D_Q such that

- $Q(D_Q) = Q(D)$, and
- the time for identifying D_Q from D and hence the size $|D_Q|$ of D_Q are determined by Q and $\mathcal{A}$ only.

That is, $Q(D)$ can be computed by accessing (identifying and fetching) a small D_Q with the indices in $\mathcal{A}$, such that $|D_Q|$ is *independent of* $|D|$, no matter how big D grows.

The idea has proven effective: on some real-life datasets, 77% of SPC queries [14] and 60% of graph pattern queries [13] are found boundedly evaluable on average, under a few hundreds simple access constraints, outperforming conventional query evaluation approaches by orders of magnitude.

However, it is undecidable to determine whether an RA query Q is boundedly evaluable under a set $\mathcal{A}$ of access constraints [19]. Set difference (universal quantification) of RA makes the bounded evaluability analysis far more intriguing.

Example 1: Consider an example query Q_0 from Graph Search of Facebook [17]: *find me all restaurants in* NYC *which I have not been to, but in which my friends have dined in May, 2015.* The query is posed on dataset D_0, which consists of three relations: (a) friend(pid, fid), stating that fid is a friend of pid, (b) dine(pid, cid, month, year) indicating that a person pid dined in restaurant cid in month of year, and (c) cafe(cid, city), stating that cid is located in city.

Query Q_0 is given in RA, with constant p_0 denoting "me":

$$\begin{aligned} Q_0(\mathsf{cid}) &= Q_1(\mathsf{cid}) - Q_2(\mathsf{cid}), \text{ where} \\ Q_1(\mathsf{cid}) &= \pi_{\mathsf{cid}}\big(\mathsf{friend}(p_0, \mathsf{fid}) \bowtie_{\mathsf{fid}=\mathsf{pid}} \mathsf{dine}(\mathsf{pid}, \mathsf{cid}, \textsc{may}, 2015) \\ &\qquad \bowtie_{\mathsf{cid}=\mathsf{cid}'} \mathsf{cafe}(\mathsf{cid}', \textsc{nyc})\big), \text{ and} \\ Q_2(\mathsf{cid}) &= \pi_{\mathsf{cid}}\ \mathsf{dine}(p_0, \mathsf{cid}, \mathsf{month}, \mathsf{year}). \end{aligned}$$

Dataset D_0 may be big, with billions of users and trillions of friend links [21]. It is costly to compute $Q_0(D_0)$ directly.

Now consider a set $\mathcal{A}_0$ of real-life cardinality constraints:

- ψ_1: friend(pid $\to$ fid, 5000);
- ψ_2: dine((pid, year, month) $\to$ cid, 31);
- ψ_3: dine((pid, cid) $\to$ (pid, cid), 1);
- ψ_4; cafe(cid $\to$ city, 1).

Here ψ_1 specifies a constraint imposed by Facebook [16]: a limit of 5000 friends per user; ψ_2 states that each person dines in at most 31 restaurants each month; ψ_3 says that (pid, cid) is a "key" of the pair, and ψ_4 states that each restaurant id is associated with a single city. Indices can be built on D_0 based on ψ_1 such that given a person, it

SIGMOD'16, June 26-July 01, 2016, San Francisco, CA, USA

© 2016 ACM. ISBN 978-1-4503-3531-7/16/06...$15.00

DOI: http://dx.doi.org/10.1145/2882903.2882942

returns all the ids of her friends by accessing at most 5000 friend tuples; similarly for ψ_2, ψ_3 and ψ_4. These indices and constraints together are called *access constraints* [19].

Given the access constraints, we can compute $Q_1(D_0)$ by accessing at most 315000 tuples from D_0, instead of trillions. (1) We identify and fetch T_1 of at most 5000 fid's of friend tuples with pid $= p_0$, by using the index built for ψ_1. (2) For each fid value f in T_1, we fetch T_2 of at most 31 cid's of dine tuples with fid $= f$, year $= 2015$ and month $=$ MAY, leveraging the index for ψ_2. (3) For each cid in T_2, we fetch its cafe tuple by using the index for ψ_4, and return a set T_3 of cid's from these tuples with city $=$ NYC. The query plan fetches at most $5000 + 5000 \times 31 \times 2$ tuples only, all using indices, to compute $Q_1(D_0)$ no matter how big D_0 is. Therefore, Q_1 is boundedly evaluable under $\mathcal{A}_0$.

However, query Q_2 is not bounded under $\mathcal{A}_0$: we cannot make use of any indices above when accessing the (possibly huge) dine relation given pid $= p_0$ alone. Since the set difference operator in Q_0 forces us to check *all* tuples in $Q_2(D_0)$, one might think that Q_0 is not bounded either.

Nonetheless, observe that Q_0 is equivalent to $Q'_0(\mathsf{cid}) = Q_1(\mathsf{cid}) - Q_3(\mathsf{cid})$, where $Q_3(\mathsf{cid}) = Q_1(\mathsf{cid}) \ltimes_{\mathsf{cid}=\mathsf{cid}'} Q_2(\mathsf{cid}')$. Moreover, Q_3 is boundedly evaluable. Indeed, for each cid value returned by $Q_1(D_0)$ (*i.e.*, T_3 above), we can check whether (p_0, cid) is a pair occurring in relation dine, by accessing one tuple via the index for ψ_3. We return all those cid's that pass the check. Thus we can answer $Q_3(D_0)$ by accessing 5000×31 tuples. Therefore, Q_0 is equivalent to bounded Q'_0, with a query plan consisting of the plan for Q_1 above, followed by the plan for Q_3; it accesses at most 470000 tuples only, no matter how big D_0 grows. This shows that Q_0 is actually boundedly evaluable under $\mathcal{A}_0$. □

This example tells us that to decide whether an RA (SQL) query is bounded, it is often necessary to check query equivalence, which is undecidable for RA queries in the presence of set difference [5]. An *open question* [14, 18, 19] asks whether it is still possible to make practical use of bounded evaluability for answering RA queries, given the undecidability?

Contributions. This paper is to answer the open question. We approach the problem by identifying an *effective syntax* for boundedly evaluable RA queries. That is, a class $\mathcal{L}$ of RA queries such that under a set $\mathcal{A}$ of access constraints,

(a) every boundedly evaluable RA query is equivalent to a query in $\mathcal{L}$, *i.e.*, $\mathcal{L}$ expresses all bounded RA queries;

(b) every query Q in $\mathcal{L}$ is boundedly evaluable; and

(c) it takes PTIME (polynomial time) in $|Q|$ and $|\mathcal{A}|$ to syntactically check whether Q is in $\mathcal{L}$.

That is, $\mathcal{L}$ identifies the *core* subclass of boundedly evaluable RA queries, *without sacrificing their expressive power.*

The study of bounded evaluability is analogous, to an extent, to the study of safe relational calculus queries, which are also undecidable. Effective syntax was first studied 30 years ago [20, 32, 34], to express all safe queries up to equivalence. As observed in [20], "*several commercial database query systems give intuitively unexpected results on such queries*" (unsafe queries); this is evidenced by a real-life example tested with SQL and QUEL [35]. Effective syntax imposes syntactical restrictions on undecidable safe queries, such that the restricted class is efficiently decidable.

Along the same lines, effective syntax allows us to make practical use of bounded evaluability. (1) It provides us with a guideline for formulating bounded evaluable queries, just like its counterpart for safe queries. (2) As will be shown shortly, bounded evaluability analysis can be readily incorporated into commercial DBMS. Given an input RA query Q, it first checks whether Q is in $\mathcal{L}$, in PTIME by condition (c) above; if so, it generates a bounded query plan for Q by using indices in $\mathcal{A}$, which is warranted to exist by (b). (3) By (a), if Q is boundedly evaluable, it can be expressed in $\mathcal{L}$. Hence query rewriting rules can be implemented to transform Q to an equivalent query in $\mathcal{L}$, to an extent.

More specifically, we provide theoretical results and practical methods for the bounded evaluability of RA as follows.

(1) We develop an effective syntax $\mathcal{L}$ for boundedly evaluable RA queries (Section 3), referred to as *covered* queries. In a nutshell, an RA query Q is covered if for any relation in Q, its attributes *needed for answering* Q can be fetched via the indices in $\mathcal{A}$, in time bounded by the cardinality constraints of $\mathcal{A}$. We prove that every boundedly evaluable RA query under $\mathcal{A}$ is also covered by $\mathcal{A}$ (*i.e.*, property (a)).

(2) We develop an algorithm for checking covered queries (Section 4). Given an RA query Q and a set $\mathcal{A}$ of access constraints, the algorithm decides whether Q is covered by $\mathcal{A}$ in $O(|Q|^2 + |\mathcal{A}|)$-time, where $|Q|$ is the size of Q and $|\mathcal{A}|$ is the total length of access constraints in $\mathcal{A}$, independent of the size $|D|$ of dataset D. In practice, $|Q|$ and $|\mathcal{A}|$ are typically much smaller than $|D|$. This proves property (c).

(3) We provide an algorithm to generate query plans for covered queries (Section 5). Given an RA query Q covered by $\mathcal{A}$, the algorithm generates a query plan ξ of length $O(|Q||\mathcal{A}|)$ such that for any dataset D that satisfies $\mathcal{A}$, ξ computes $Q(D)$ by accessing a bounded amount of data determined by Q and $\mathcal{A}$. The algorithm is based on a nontrivial characterization of covered RA queries and takes $O(|Q|(|Q| + |\mathcal{A}|))$ time, again independent of $|D|$. This proves property (b).

(4) We also study a new optimization problem (Section 6). Given a query Q covered by $\mathcal{A}$, it is to find a subset $\mathcal{A}_m \subseteq \mathcal{A}$ such that Q remains covered by $\mathcal{A}_m$ and the estimated data access via $\mathcal{A}_m$ is minimized. We show that the problem is NP-complete and is not in APX, *i.e.*, it has no PTIME constant-factor approximation algorithm. Nonetheless, we develop efficient heuristic algorithms with performance guarantees, some with reasonable approximation bounds.

(5) We show how bounded evaluability analysis can be integrated into existing DBMS (Section 7). Given an RA query Q and a set $\mathcal{A}$ of access constraints, we check whether Q is covered by $\mathcal{A}$, and if so, we generate a bounded query plan for Q with minimal constraints in $\mathcal{A}$, and compute $Q(D)$ by accessing a small fraction D_Q of D, all by using the algorithms described above. We also show how access constraints can be discovered and incrementally maintained.

(6) We implement our approach on top of MySQL and PostgreSQL and experimentally evaluate its effectiveness using two real-life datasets and a commercial benchmark (query templates and datasets; Section 8). We find the following on the real-life data: under a set $\mathcal{A}$ of at most 266 access constraints, on average (a) 67.5% of randomly generated RA queries are boundedly evaluable, among which 83.5% are covered; (b) our query plans outperform MySQL and PostgreSQL that use the same indices by at least *3 orders of magnitude*, and the gap gets larger on bigger data; (c) our plans

access only 0.0019% of the data; that is, they "reduce" D from PB to GB; and (d) the indices account for 14.8% of the original data. We also find that (e) our algorithms for coverage checking, plan generation and minimizing access constraints are all efficient: they take at most 199ms in all cases.

These results settle the open question for the study of RA boundedly evaluability, from theory to practice. They suggest an approach to answering queries within bounded resources, by adding the functionality of bounded evaluation to existing DBMS. It is a common practice for decades in query evaluation to access as little data as possible, rather than the entire dataset, by making use of various indices. This work is an effort to formalize the idea, to decide when it is feasible to answer a query within bounded resources, and to provide a systematic method to achieve it.

Related work. We categorize previous work as follows.

Bounded evaluability and effective syntax. The study of bounded evaluability was motivated by the idea of scale independence [6, 7], which is to guarantee that a bounded amount of work is required to execute all queries in an application, regardless of the size of the underlying data. The notion was formalized in [19], focusing on query answering in a particular given dataset. Bounded evaluability was proposed in [18], which extends [19] by ranging over all datasets that satisfy a set $\mathcal{A}$ of access constraints. A query Q is called *boundedly evaluable* under $\mathcal{A}$ if it has a *bounded query plan*; such a plan allows data access only via indices embedded in $\mathcal{A}$, and interleaves data fetching and relational operations, to answer Q by accessing a bounded amount of data.

It is shown that for any SPCU query Q and any set $\mathcal{A}$ of access constraints, it is decidable but EXPSPACE-hard to decide whether Q is boundedly evaluable under $\mathcal{A}$ [18]; but it is undecidable when Q is in RA [19]. Effective syntax was explored for bounded SPC queries [18]. However, it was left open in [18] whether there exists an effective syntax for boundedly evaluable RA (*i.e.,* FO, first-order logic) queries.

This work answers the open question in positive by providing a PTIME effective syntax for boundedly evaluable RA queries. It is radically different from the one for SPC [18], which becomes Π_2^p-complete when extended to SPCU, and undecidable for RA. The result of this work allows existing DBMS to support boundedly evaluable RA queries.

Effective boundedness. A notion of effective boundedness was studied for SPC [14], based on a *restricted form* of query plans in which data fetching must be completed before any relational operations can start. It was also studied for graph pattern queries via simulation and subgraph isomorphism [13], which are quite different from relational queries.

This work differs from [14] in the following. (1) We study effective syntax for RA, while [14] focuses on checking and answering SPC queries of a special form. Our main result is an effective syntax for boundedly evaluable RA queries, which is nontrivial since *not* every query class has an effective syntax [32]. This issue is not considered in [14]. (2) Bounded evaluability is much harder to decide than effective boundedness. For SPC, bounded evaluability is EXPSPACE-hard [18], but effective boundedness is in PTIME [14]. (3) We study RA, in contrast to SPC [14]. RA is equivalent to FO on relations [5], while SPC is a conjunctive fragment of FO, and does not support disjunction (union) and universal quantification (set difference). (4) Our methods for checking covered RA queries and for generating query plans are different from those of [14]. While effective boundedness for SPC is characterized by five syntactic rules [14], it is impossible to extend the rules to RA. It is much harder to decide which attributes to retrieve and how their values propagate for RA queries. (5) Our results substantially extend [14] and allow existing DBMS to support bounded evaluable RA queries. Even when SPC is concerned, we provide a PTIME solution that allows generic query plans, as opposed to the restriction of [14]. (6) We also study a new optimization problem for minimizing estimated data access, which is nontrivial (NP-complete and not in APX) and is not studied by [14].

Access constraints. Related to query answering under access constraints is the notion of access patterns. They require a relation to be only accessed by providing certain combinations of attributes [10–12, 25, 28]. Unlike access patterns, access constraints impose both cardinality constraints and "restricted" data accesses via indices. Moreover, we study how to answer RA queries by accessing a bounded amount of data. Hence the results on bounded evaluability are quite different from those for access patterns. In addition, we develop effective syntax for bounded RA queries, an issue that has not been studied for access patterns.

2. BOUNDED EVALUABILITY

In this section we review the notions of access constraints and bounded evaluability, following [14, 18, 19].

Access schema. Over a relational schema $\mathcal{R}$, an *access schema* $\mathcal{A}$ is a set of *access constraints* of the form [14, 19]:

$$\psi = R(X \to Y, N),$$

where R is a relation schema in $\mathcal{R}$, X and Y are sets of attributes of R, and N is a natural number.

A relation instance D of R *satisfies* the constraint if

- for any X-value $\bar{a}$ in D, $|D_Y(X = \bar{a})| \leq N$, where $D_Y(X = \bar{a}) = \{t[Y] \mid t \in D, t[X] = \bar{a}\}$; and
- there exists an *index on* X *for* Y that given an X-value $\bar{a}$, retrieves $D_Y(X = \bar{a})$ by accessing at most N tuples.

That is, for any given X-value, there exist at most N distinct corresponding Y values in D, and these Y values can be retrieved by using the index for ψ. Intuitively, ψ is a combination of a cardinality constraint and its index.

We say D *satisfies* access schema $\mathcal{A}$, denoted by $D \models \mathcal{A}$, if D satisfies all the constraints in $\mathcal{A}$.

For instance, denote by $\mathcal{R}_0$ the collection of relation schemas friend, dine and cafe. Then the set $\mathcal{A}_0$ consisting of $\psi_1 - \psi_4$ given in Example 1 is an access schema over $\mathcal{R}_0$.

Remark. (1) Traditional functional dependencies (FDs) are a special case of access constraints ($N = 1$). (2) Access constraint discovery will be discussed in Section 7.

Query plans under access schema $\mathcal{A}$. We study relational algebra (RA) queries, defined over a relational schema $\mathcal{R}$ with selection σ, projection π, Cartesian product $\times$, union $\cup$, set-difference $-$ and renaming ρ operators [5]. Following [18], we define a *query plan* ξ *for* Q *under* $\mathcal{A}$ simply as a sequence of relational algebra operators and an additional fetch$(X \in T, R, Y)$ operator returning $\bigcup_{\bar{a} \in T} D_{XY}(X = \bar{a})$ from D, where T is returned by some operation in the sequence prior to it, such that the plan retrieves data with constants in Q and these fetch operations only (see formal definition in Appendix A). Intuitively, query plans under access schema restrict traditional query plans to access data in an *controlled and quantified* manner, via fetch operations.

Bounded evaluability [18]. A query plan ξ is *boundedly evaluable under an access schema $\mathcal{A}$* (or simply *bounded*) if

(1) for each operation $\mathsf{fetch}(X \in T, R, Y)$ in ξ, there exists an access constraint $R(X \to Y, N)$ in $\mathcal{A}$; and

(2) the length of ξ is determined by $|\mathcal{R}|$, $|\mathcal{A}|$ and $|Q|$ only, which are the sizes of $\mathcal{R}$, $\mathcal{A}$, and Q, respectively.

An RA query Q is *boundedly evaluable under $\mathcal{A}$* (or *bounded*) if it has a boundedly evaluable query plan under $\mathcal{A}$.

Intuitively, if Q is bounded, then there exists a bounded query plan ξ for Q such that for all instances D of $\mathcal{R}$ that satisfy $\mathcal{A}$, it fetches D_Q from D via the indices in $\mathcal{A}$ such that $Q(D) = Q(D_Q)$. Moreover, $|D_Q|$ is determined by Q and constants in $\mathcal{A}$ only, independent of $|D|$, where $|D|$ denotes the total number of tuples in D. The time for identifying D_Q (checking indices) and fetching D_Q is also independent of $|D|$ (assuming that given an X-value $\bar{a}$, it takes $O(N)$ time to fetch $D_{XY}(X = \bar{a})$ in D with the index in $R(X \to Y, N)$).

Example 2: Recall Q_0 and $\mathcal{A}_0$ from Example 1. A boundedly evaluable query plan for Q_0 under $\mathcal{A}_0$ is as follows.

$T_1 = \{p_0\}$, $T_2 = \mathsf{fetch}(T_1, \mathsf{friend}, \mathsf{fid})$, $T_3 = \pi_{\mathsf{fid}}(T_2)$,
$T_4 = \{2015\}$, $T_5 = \{\text{MAY}\}$, $T_6 = T_4 \times T_5$, $T_7 = T_3 \times T_6$,
$T_8 = \mathsf{fetch}(X \in T_7, \mathsf{dine}, \mathsf{cid})$, $T_9 = \pi_{\mathsf{cid}}(T_8)$,
$T_{10} = \mathsf{fetch}(X \in T_9, \mathsf{cafe}, \mathsf{city})$, $T_{11} = \sigma_{\mathsf{city}=\text{NYC}}(T_{10})$,
$T_{12} = \pi_{\mathsf{cid}}(T_{11})$,
$T_{13} = T_1 \times T_{12}$, $T_{14} = \mathsf{fetch}(X \in T_{13}, \mathsf{dine}, (\mathsf{pid}, \mathsf{cid}))$,
$T_{15} = \pi_{\mathsf{cid}}(T_{14})$, $T_{16} = T_{13} \setminus T_{15}$.

Note that the sequence $T_1, \ldots, T_{12}$ forms a boundedly evaluable query plan for sub-query Q_1 of Q_0 under $\mathcal{A}_0$. □

The analysis of bounded evaluability is more intriguing for RA queries than for SPC, as illustrated below.

Example 3: Consider an access schema $\mathcal{A}_1$ and RA query Q_4 defined on relation schemas $R(A, B, E)$ and $S(F, G, H)$:

∘ $\mathcal{A}_1 = \{R(AB \to E, N), S(F \to GH, 2), S(GH \to GH, 1)\}$.

∘ $Q_4 = Q_4^1 - Q_4^2$, where $Q_4^1 = \pi_x(R(1, x, y) \bowtie S(w, x, y) \bowtie S(w, 1, x) \bowtie S(w, x, x))$ and $Q_4^2 = \pi_x(R(1, x, x) \bowtie S(u, 1, x) \bowtie S(u, x, x))$, where $\bowtie$ denotes natural join.

At a first glance, Q_4 seems not boundedly evaluable, since we cannot retrieve x and w values using indices in $\mathcal{A}_1$ and thus cannot get y for Q_4^1. Similarly, we cannot get u and x values for Q_4^2. However, under $S(F \to GH, 2)$ in $\mathcal{A}_1$, observe that (x, y) must be equal to either $(1, x)$ or (x, x) in all tuples retrieved from instance of S by any query plan for Q_4^1. In other words, under $\mathcal{A}_1$, the SPC sub-query Q_4^1 reduces to SPCU $Q_4^{1'} \cup Q_4^{1''}$, where $Q_4^{1'} = \pi_x(R(1, 1, x) \bowtie S(w, 1, x) \bowtie S(w, x, x)$ and $Q_4^{1''} = Q_4^2$. Thus, under $\mathcal{A}_1$, Q_4 is equivalent to $Q_4^{1'}$, which is boundedly evaluable under $\mathcal{A}_1$. □

The presence of union ($\cup$) allows us to convert SPC to SPCU under $\mathcal{A}$ (*e.g.*, Q_4^1 to $Q_4^{1'} \cup Q_4^{1''}$), which may further interact with set difference ($-$) (*e.g.*, Q_4 and $Q_4^{1'}$).

Notations. We will use the following notations.

(1) Under an access schema $\mathcal{A}$, an RA query Q_1 is *$\mathcal{A}$-equivalent to* Q_2, denoted by $Q_1 \equiv_{\mathcal{A}} Q_2$, if for all instances D of $\mathcal{R}$ with $D \models \mathcal{A}$, $Q_1(D) = Q_2(D)$. That is, in all D satisfying $\mathcal{A}$, Q_1 and Q_2 return the same answer. This notion is stronger than the conventional equivalence $Q_1 \equiv Q_2$, which holds if for all instances D of $\mathcal{R}$, $Q_1(D) = Q_2(D)$ [5].

(2) To simplify the exposition, we consider RA queries Q in a *normal form* in which all occurrences of each relation name are made distinct via renaming. For an access constraint $\phi = R(X \to Y, N)$ and a renaming S of R in Q, we refer to $S(X \to Y, N)$ as the *actualized constraint* of ϕ on S, and to the set of all actualized constraints of $\mathcal{A}$ as the *actualized access schema* of $\mathcal{A}$ on Q. We consider *w.l.o.g.* normalized Q and actualized $\mathcal{A}$ only, based on the lemma below.

Lemma 1: *Given any* RA *query Q and access schema $\mathcal{A}$ over relational schema $\mathcal{R}$, one can compute the actualized access schema $\mathcal{A}'$ from Q and $\mathcal{A}$ in $O(|Q||\mathcal{A}|)$-time such that*

(1) for any instance D of $\mathcal{R}$, $D \models \mathcal{A}$ iff $D \models \mathcal{A}'$; and

(2) Q is boundedly evaluable under $\mathcal{A}$ iff Q' is boundedly evaluable under $\mathcal{A}'$ (iff for if and only if). □

3. AN EFFECTIVE SYNTAX

Essential to practical use of bounded evaluability is the following problem. Given a query Q and an access schema $\mathcal{A}$, it is to decide whether Q is boundedly evaluable under $\mathcal{A}$. The problem is undecidable for RA queries Q [19].

The undecidability motivates us to find an effective syntax $\mathcal{L}$ for boundedly evaluable RA queries (see Section 1). We identify such an $\mathcal{L}$, referred to as the class of *covered queries*.

Covered queries. We now define covered queries, starting with SPC. Intuitively, an SPC query Q is covered if for any relation S in Q, all the attributes of S needed to answer Q can be fetched via indices in $\mathcal{A}$ and moreover, their sizes are bounded by the cardinality constraints of $\mathcal{A}$.

Consider an SPC query $Q = \pi_Z \sigma_C(S_1 \times \ldots \times S_n)$ defined over a relational schema $\mathcal{R}$, where Z is a set of attributes of $\mathcal{R}$, C is the selection condition of Q, and S_i's are distinct relations after renaming (Lemma 1). We use Σ_Q to denote the set of all equality atoms $A = A'$ or $A = c$ derived from C by the transitivity of equality. For any sets X and X' of attributes of Q, we write $\Sigma_Q \vdash X = X'$ if $X = X'$ can be derived from Σ_Q, which can be checked in $O(\max(|X|, |X'|))$ time (after an $O(|Q|^2)$-time preprocessing of Q).

Coverage. The *set of covered attributes* of Q by an access schema $\mathcal{A}$, denoted by $\mathsf{cov}(Q, \mathcal{A})$, includes attributes that can be accessed via indices in $\mathcal{A}$. It is defined as follows:

∘ if $\Sigma_Q \vdash \sigma_{A=c}$, then $A \in \mathsf{cov}(Q, \mathcal{A})$;

∘ if $R(\emptyset \to X, N) \in \mathcal{A}$, then $R[X] \subseteq \mathsf{cov}(Q, \mathcal{A})$;

∘ if $R[X] \subseteq \mathsf{cov}(Q, \mathcal{A})$ and $\Sigma_Q \vdash R[X] = S[Y]$, then $S[Y] \subseteq \mathsf{cov}(Q, \mathcal{A})$; and

∘ if $R(X \to Y, N) \in \mathcal{A}$ and $R[X] \subseteq \mathsf{cov}(Q, \mathcal{A})$, then $R[Y] \subseteq \mathsf{cov}(Q, \mathcal{A})$.

Here $R(\emptyset \to X, N)$ is an access constraint stating that there are at most N distinct X values in an instance of R, *e.g.*, there exist at most 12 distinct months per year.

Covered SPC. Denote by X_Q the set of attributes in an SPC query Q that occur in either its selection condition C or the projection attributes Z of Q. We say that Q is

∘ *fetchable via $\mathcal{A}$* if $X_Q \subseteq \mathsf{cov}(Q, \mathcal{A})$; and

∘ *indexed by $\mathcal{A}$* if for each relation name S in Q, there is an actualized constraint $S(X \to Y, N)$ of $\mathcal{A}$ such that
  - $S[X] \subseteq \mathsf{cov}(Q, \mathcal{A})$, and
  - $S[XY]$ includes all attributes of S that are in X_Q, *i.e.*, attributes XY come from the same tuple.

An SPC query Q is *covered by $\mathcal{A}$* if Q is both fetchable via $\mathcal{A}$ and indexed by $\mathcal{A}$. That is, all attributes needed by Q can be fetched using indices of $\mathcal{A}$ and are bounded by $\mathcal{A}$.

Covered RA. We represent an RA query Q as its *query (syntax) tree* T^Q [5]. To simplify the discussion, we say that an RA query Q' is a *sub-query* of Q if $T^{Q'}$ is a sub-tree of T^Q.

A *max* SPC *sub-query* of Q is a sub-query Q_s such that

- Q_s is an SPC query, and
- there exists no sub-query Q'_s of Q such that it is also in SPC, $Q_s \neq Q'_s$, and Q_s is a sub-query of Q'_s.

An RA query Q is *covered by an access schema* $\mathcal{A}$ if for all max SPC sub-queries Q_s of Q, Q_s is covered by $\mathcal{A}$. Similarly, Q is *fetchable via* $\mathcal{A}$ (resp. *indexed by* $\mathcal{A}$) if each max sub-SPC sub-query is fetchable via $\mathcal{A}$ (resp. indexed by $\mathcal{A}$).

Intuitively, an RA query Q is "normalized" by pushing set difference to the top level, on (unions of) max SPC sub-queries. These max SPC sub-queries characterize all relation attributes that need to be accessed when answering Q.

Example 4: For the queries and $\mathcal{A}_0$ of Example 1, Q_1 and Q_3 are covered by $\mathcal{A}_0$, but Q_2 is not. Indeed, $X_{Q_1} = \{x_{p_0}, \mathsf{fid}, \mathsf{pid}, \mathsf{cid}, x_{\mathrm{MAY}}, x_{2015}, \mathsf{cid}', x_{\mathrm{NYC}}\} = \mathsf{cov}(Q_1, \mathcal{A}_0)$, where x_d denotes the attribute corresponding to a constant d in Q_1. Hence Q_1 is fetchable via $\mathcal{A}_0$; moreover, Q_1 is indexed by $\mathcal{A}_0$ since friend, dine and cafe are indexed by ψ_1, ψ_2 and ψ_4, respectively; similarly for Q_3. However, Q_2 is not fetchable via $\mathcal{A}_0$ since $\mathsf{cov}(Q_2, \mathcal{A}_0) = \{x_{p_0}\}$ but $X_{Q_2} = \{x_{p_0}, \mathsf{cid}\}$, and relation dine is not indexed by any constraint in $\mathcal{A}_0$ for Q_2. As a result, Q'_0 is covered by $\mathcal{A}_0$ since both of its max SPC sub-queries Q_1 and Q_3 are covered by $\mathcal{A}_0$. In contrast, Q_0 is not covered by $\mathcal{A}_0$ since Q_2 is not. □

The main result of the paper is as follows.

Theorem 2: *Under access schema $\mathcal{A}$, for any* RA *query Q,*

(1) if Q is boundedly evaluable under $\mathcal{A}$, then Q is $\mathcal{A}$-equivalent to an RA *query Q' that is covered by $\mathcal{A}$;*

(2) if Q is covered, then Q is boundedly evaluable; and

(3) it takes PTIME *to check whether Q is covered by $\mathcal{A}$.* □

That is, we reduce the problem of deciding RA bounded evaluability to syntactic checking of covered queries, *without losing the expressive power.* Indeed, all boundedly evaluable RA queries have an $\mathcal{A}$-equivalent covered version. For these RA queries, covered queries play the same role as range-safe RA queries for checking "the safety" SQL queries [5].

Proof sketch of Theorem 2(1). We will prove Theorem 2(3) and (2) in Sections 4 and 5, respectively. For (1), we show that for any RA query Q, if it has a bounded query plan ξ under $\mathcal{A}$, then ξ can be converted to a query Q_ξ covered by $\mathcal{A}$ such that $Q_\xi \equiv_{\mathcal{A}} Q$ (see Appendix B). □

4. CHECKING COVERED QUERIES

We next give a constructive proof of Theorem 2(3) by providing an algorithm for checking covered queries, denoted by CovChk. Given an access schema $\mathcal{A}$ and an RA query Q, CovChk returns "yes" if Q is covered by $\mathcal{A}$, and "no" otherwise. Below we show a result stronger than Theorem 2(3).

Proposition 3: *Given an access schema $\mathcal{A}$ and an* RA *query Q, algorithm* CovChk *determines whether Q is covered by $\mathcal{A}$ in $O(|Q|^2 + |\mathcal{A}|)$ time.* □

Note that checking is conducted at the meta level on Q and $\mathcal{A}$ only, independent of (possibly big) datasets D.

The algorithm is shown in Fig. 1, consisting of two parts. It first finds the set $\mathcal{S}_Q$ of all max SPC sub-queries of Q

Algorithm CovChk

Input: An RA query Q and an access schema $\mathcal{A}$.
Output: "yes" if Q is covered by $\mathcal{A}$ and "no" otherwise.

1. identify the set $\mathcal{S}_Q$ of all max SPC sub-queries of Q
2. **for each** max SPC sub-query Q_s in $\mathcal{S}_Q$ **do**
3.   **if** Q_s is not indexed under $\mathcal{A}$ **then return** "no";
4.   construct induced FDs $\Sigma_{Q_s,\mathcal{A}}$ for Q_s and $\mathcal{A}$;
5.   **if** $\Sigma_{Q_s} \not\models \hat{X}_C^{Q_s} \rightarrow \hat{X}_{Q_s}$ **then return** "no";
6. **return** "yes";

Figure 1: Algorithm CovChk

(line 1). It then checks whether all queries in $\mathcal{S}_Q$ are covered by $\mathcal{A}$ (lines 2–5). It returns "yes" if and only if so (line 6).

Identifying max SPC **sub-queries.** CovChk computes the set $\mathcal{S}_Q$ by a bottom-up scan of the query tree of Q. This is done in time linear in $|Q|$, since each relation of Q occurs in only one max SPC sub-query of Q, by the assumption that relation names in Q are distinct (see Section 2).

Checking coverage of SPC **sub-queries.** We next focus on how to check whether an SPC sub-query Q_s is covered by $\mathcal{A}$, *i.e.*, indexed by $\mathcal{A}$ and fetchable via $\mathcal{A}$ (Section 3). While index checking is straightforward, the fetching condition is more involved, and is based on its connection with the implication analysis of functional dependencies (FDs) [5]. To establish the connection, we need the following notions.

Unification. A *unification function* ρ_U is an *attribute* renaming function: for all attributes A and A' in $\mathcal{S}_Q$, $\rho_U(A) = \rho_U(A')$ (assigned the same name) if and only if $\Sigma_Q \vdash A = A'$. For a set X,we denote by $\rho_U(X)$ the set $\{\rho_U(A) \mid A \in X\}$.

Induced FDs. For $\phi = R(A \rightarrow B, N)$ in $\mathcal{A}$, we call $\rho_U(R[A]) \rightarrow \rho_U(R[B])$ an *induced* FD from Q and ϕ. We denote the set of all induced FDs from Q and constraints in $\mathcal{A}$ by $\Sigma_{Q,\mathcal{A}}$.

Example 5: For Q_1 and $\mathcal{A}_0$ of Example 1, define a unification function ρ_U such that $\rho_U(\mathsf{friend[pid]}) = \mathsf{pid}$, $\rho_U(\mathsf{friend[fid]}) = \mathsf{fid}$, $\rho_U(\mathsf{dine[pid]}) = \mathsf{fid}$, $\rho_U(\mathsf{dine[cid]}) = \mathsf{cid}$, $\rho_U(\mathsf{dine[year]}) = \mathsf{year}$, $\rho_U(\mathsf{dine[month]}) = \mathsf{month}$, $\rho_U(\mathsf{cafe[cid]}) = \mathsf{cid}$ and $\rho_U(\mathsf{cafe[city]}) = \mathsf{city}$. Then $\Sigma_{Q_1,\mathcal{A}_0}$ consists of the following induced FDs: pid $\rightarrow$ fid, (fid, year, month) $\rightarrow$ cid, (fid, cid) $\rightarrow$ (fid, cid), and cid $\rightarrow$ city. □

We now give the connection between induced FDs and fetchable SPC queries. For an SPC query Q_s, let X_{Q_s} be the set of all its attributes that occur in its selection condition or projection attributes, and $X_C^{Q_s} \subseteq X_{Q_s}$ be the set of attributes A in Q_s such that $\Sigma_{Q_s} \vdash A = c$ for some constant c. Let $\hat{X}_{Q_s} = \rho_U(X_{Q_s})$ and $\hat{X}_C^{Q_s} = \rho_U(X_C^{Q_s})$. Then we have:

Lemma 4: *An* SPC *query Q_s is fetchable under $\mathcal{A}$ if and only if $\Sigma_{Q_s,\mathcal{A}} \models \hat{X}_C^{Q_s} \rightarrow \hat{X}_{Q_s}$.* □

Here $\Sigma \models \varphi$ denotes the standard FD implication: for all databases D, if D satisfies Σ, then D also satisfies φ (see [5]).

Intuitively, $\hat{X}_C^{Q_s}$ is the set of attributes whose values are already provided by Q_s, and $\hat{X}_{Q_s}$ includes all the attributes whose values are needed for answering Q_s. The computation of $\mathsf{cov}(Q, \mathcal{A})$ (Section 3) is a chasing process with $\mathcal{A}$ to deduce $\hat{X}_{Q_s}$ from $\hat{X}_C^{Q_s}$. The process coincides with the implication analysis of $\Sigma_{Q_s,\mathcal{A}} \models \hat{X}_C^{Q_s} \rightarrow \hat{X}_{Q_s}$ (see Appendix B).

Lemma 4 reduces the problem of checking whether an SPC query Q_s is fetchable via $\mathcal{A}$ to the implication analysis of FDs. Based on the lemma, algorithm CovChk checks

Notation	Description
$\mathcal{A}$	(actualized) access schema
$\|\mathcal{A}\|$	the total length of access constraints in $\mathcal{A}$
$\\|\mathcal{A}\\|$	the number of constraints in $\mathcal{A}$
Q_s	a max SPC sub-query of Q
Σ_{Q_s}	equality $A = A'$ and $A = c$ derived from Q_s
X_Q	attributes in σ_C or π_Y of some max Q_s of Q
X_C^Q	attributes A such that $\Sigma_{Q_s} \vdash A = c$ for a Q_s of Q
X_Q^S	attributes in both S and X_{Q_s} for some Q_s of Q
$\rho_U(A)$	renaming of A with unification function ρ_U
$\rho_U(X)$	$\{\rho_U(A) \mid A \in X\}$
$\Sigma_{Q_s,\mathcal{A}}$	the set of induced FDs from Q_s and $\mathcal{A}$
ξ^c	canonical bounded query plan
$\xi_F^c(A)$	unit fetching plan for attribute A
$\mathcal{G}_{Q,\mathcal{A}}$	$\langle Q, \mathcal{A}\rangle$-hypergraph for Q and $\mathcal{A}$
Π_{V_S,u_A}	hyperpath from set V_S to node u_A

Table 1: Notations

whether Q_s is fetchable by firstly constructing the set $\Sigma_{Q_s,\mathcal{A}}$ of induced FDs from Q_s and $\mathcal{A}$, and then checking whether $\Sigma_{Q_s,\mathcal{A}} \models \hat{X}_C^{Q_s} \rightarrow \hat{X}_{Q_s}$ by invoking a linear-time FD implication algorithm [5] (lines 4–5). It checks whether Q_s is indexed under $\mathcal{A}$ simply by definition (line 3).

Example 6: Given Q_0, Q_0' and $\mathcal{A}_0$ of Example 1, by examining max SPC sub-queries, algorithm CovChk finds that Q_0' is covered by $\mathcal{A}_0$ but Q_0' is not (see Appendix C). □

Correctness & Complexity. The correctness of CovChk follows from the definition of covered queries and Lemma 4. Algorithm CovChk can be implemented in $O(|Q|^2 + |\mathcal{A}|)$ time (see Appendix D for more details). This completes the proof of Proposition 3 and Theorem 2(3).

The notations of the paper are summarized in Table 1.

5. GENERATING BOUNDED PLANS

We now verify Theorem 2(2) by proving a stronger result.

Theorem 5: *(1) For any* RA *query Q covered by an access schema $\mathcal{A}$, Q has a canonical bounded query plan under $\mathcal{A}$. (2) There exists an algorithm that given Q covered by $\mathcal{A}$, generates a canonical bounded query plan of length $O(|Q||\mathcal{A}|)$ in $O(|Q|(|Q| + |\mathcal{A}|))$ time.* □

Here canonical bounded query plans are boundedly evaluable query plans that characterize covered RA queries. That is, every covered query Q warrants a boundedly evaluable query plan ξ. Better still, ξ can be generated in a bounded amount of time and has a bounded length, both determined by Q and $\mathcal{A}$, independent of the underlying datasets.

The proof is nontrivial. Below we first introduce canonical bounded query plans (Section 5.1). We then provide an algorithm with the property of Theorem 5(2) (Section 5.2).

5.1 Capturing Covered Queries with Plans

We define canonical query plans and show that an RA query Q is covered by $\mathcal{A}$ *if and only if* Q has a canonical bounded plan under $\mathcal{A}$. From this Theorem 5(1) follows.

Canonical bounded query plans. For an RA query Q under an access schema $\mathcal{A}$, a *canonical bounded query plan* ξ^c is a boundedly evaluable query plan for Q that consists of a *fetching plan* ξ_F^c, followed by an *indexing plan* ξ_I^c and then an *evaluation plan* ξ_E^c, as follows (see Appendix A).

Fetching plan ξ_F^c: A fetching plan ξ_F^c is a sequence of *unit fetching plans* $\xi_F^c(A_1)$, ..., $\xi_F^c(A_m)$, for all attributes A_1, ..., A_m in X_Q of Q. Here unit plan $\xi_F^c(A_i)$ fetches all the necessary values for A_i; it may use fetch by employing an access constraint ϕ of $\mathcal{A}$, projections (π) and Cartesian-product ($\times$), but has no need for selection (σ).

Indexing plan ξ_I^c. An indexing plan ξ_I^c is a sequence of *unit indexing plans* $\xi_I^c(S_1)$, ..., $\xi_I^c(S_m)$ for all relations S_1, ..., S_m in Q. For each S_i, $\xi_I^c(S_i)$ ensures that the *combinations* of attributes fetched by $\xi_F^c(A_j)$ are from the same tuples in D. Let Q_s be the max SPC sub-query in which S_i occurs, $X_{Q_s}^{S_i} = \{A_1, \ldots, A_K\}$ be the set of attributes of S_i that are also in X_{Q_s}, and $S_i(X \rightarrow Y, N)$ be a constraint in $\mathcal{A}$ that indexes S_i. Then $\xi_I^c(S_i)$ works in three steps: (1) join $\xi_F^c(A_1)$, ..., $\xi_F(A_K)$ together; (2) apply fetch under $S_i(X \rightarrow Y, N)$; and (3) return the intersection of (1) and (2).

Evaluation plan ξ_E^c. Plan ξ_E^c is the RA expression of Q, in which each relation S_i in Q is replaced by T_k, where $T_k = \xi_I^c(S_i)$ is the output of the indexing plan $\xi_I^c(S_i)$ for S_i.

Intuitively, given a dataset D with $D \models \mathcal{A}$, a canonical bounded query plan ξ^c first executes ξ_F^c to fetch necessary data values from D via indices in $\mathcal{A}$. This is followed by ξ_I^c to combine and filter partial tuples for each relation that is needed for answering max SPC sub-queries of Q. Finally, ξ_E^c is executed against the fetched partial tuples instead of D directly. That is, ξ^c accesses data only via ξ_F^c and ξ_I^c.

By the definitions of bounded evaluability and canonical bounded query plans, one can verify the lemma below (see Appendix B for a proof), from which Theorem 5(1) follows.

Lemma 6: *For* RA *query Q and access schema $\mathcal{A}$, (1) Q is fetchable via $\mathcal{A}$ iff Q has a fetching plan under $\mathcal{A}$; and (2) Q is indexed by $\mathcal{A}$ iff Q has an indexing plan under $\mathcal{A}$.* □

5.2 Generating Canonical Bounded Plans

We next give a constructive proof of Theorem 5(2) by developing an algorithm that, given an access schema $\mathcal{A}$ and an RA Q covered by $\mathcal{A}$, returns a canonical bounded query plan ξ^c of bounded length in $O(|Q|(|Q| + |\mathcal{A}|))$ time. The idea of the algorithm is to encode Q and $\mathcal{A}$ in a hypergraph representation such that (i) there is a certain hyperpath in the hypergraph *iff* Q is fetchable under $\mathcal{A}$; and (ii) each such hyperpath encodes a canonical fetching plan for Q under $\mathcal{A}$.

Below we first introduce structures used by the algorithm. (see Table 1). We then present the algorithm.

$\langle Q, \mathcal{A}\rangle$-hypergraph $\mathcal{G}_{Q,\mathcal{A}}$. A *directed hypergraph* $\mathcal{H}$ (cf. [9]) is a pair (V, E), where V is a nonempty set of nodes and E is a set of hyperedges. A *hyperedge* e in E is an ordered pair (H, t), where $H \subseteq V$, $H \neq \emptyset$, and $t \in V \setminus H$. Here H and t are called the *head* and *tail* of e, and are denoted by head(e) and tail(e), respectively. The size $|\mathcal{H}|$ of $\mathcal{H}$ is the sum of the cardinality of its hyperedges, *i.e.*, $\sum_{e \in E} |\text{head}(e)|$. Hypergraphs have been used to model FDs with single attribute on their RHS (called RHS-FD) by its hyperedges [9].

Given an RA query Q and an access schema $\mathcal{A}$, we use a hypergraph to encode the induced FDs for all max SPC sub-queries of Q. For each induced FD $X \rightarrow Y$, there are $|Y \setminus X| + 1$ induced RHS-FDs $X \rightarrow \tilde{Y}$ and $\tilde{Y} \rightarrow Y_i$ for each $Y_i \in Y$, where $\tilde{Y}$ is a new attribute name denoting Y. A *$\langle Q, \mathcal{A}\rangle$-hypergraph* $\mathcal{G}_{Q,\mathcal{A}}$ for Q and $\mathcal{A}$ is a directed hypergraph (V, E) with a special node r, such that (1) E encodes all the induced RHS-FDs; (2) for all induced RHS-FDs of form $\emptyset \rightarrow \tilde{Y}$, $\emptyset$ is encoded by r; and (3) for each attribute A in $\{\rho_U(A) \mid A \in X_C^{Q_s}$, Q_s is a max SPC sub-query of $Q\}$, there is a hyperedge from r to the node encoding A (see Appendix A).

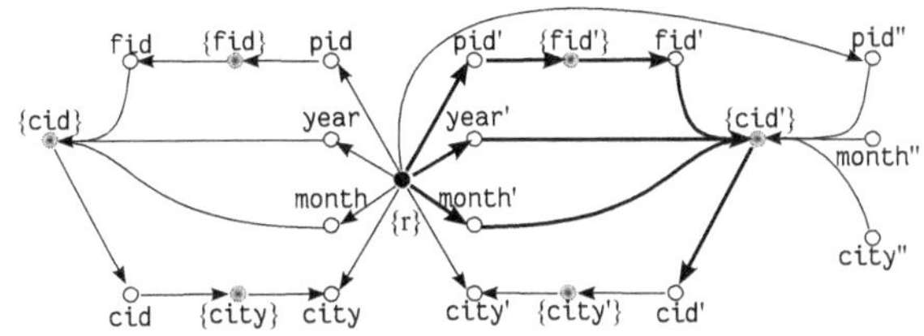

Figure 2: $\langle Q, \mathcal{A}\rangle$-hypergraph $\mathcal{G}_{Q'_0,\mathcal{A}_0}$ for Q'_0 and $\mathcal{A}_0$

Example 7: The $\langle Q, \mathcal{A}\rangle$-hypergraph $\mathcal{G}_{Q'_0,\mathcal{A}_0}$ for Q'_0 and $\mathcal{A}_0$ of Example 1 is depicted in Fig. 2 (see Appendix C). □

Hyperpath. A *sub-hypergraph* of $\mathcal{H} = (V, E)$ is a hypergraph $\mathcal{H}' = (V', E')$ such that $V' \subseteq V$, $E' \subseteq E$, and E' is restricted to V'. A *hyperpath* [9] in $\mathcal{H}$ from a set $S \subseteq V$ ($S \neq \emptyset$) to a target node $t \in V$ is a sub-hypergraph $\Pi_{S,t} = (V_{\Pi_{S,t}}, E_{\Pi_{S,t}})$ of $\mathcal{H}$ satisfying the following: if $t \in S$, then $E_{\Pi_{S,t}} = \emptyset$; otherwise its $k \geq 1$ hyperedges can be ordered in a sequence $\langle e_1, \ldots, e_k\rangle$ such that (a) for any $e_i \in E_{\Pi_{S,t}}$, $\mathsf{head}(e_i) \subseteq S \cup \{\mathsf{tail}(e_1), \ldots, \mathsf{tail}(e_{i-1})\}$; (b) $t = \mathsf{tail}(e_k)$; and (c) no sub-hypergraph of $\Pi_{S,t}$ other than itself is a hyperpath from S to t in $\mathcal{H}$. For example, a hyperpath $\Pi_{\{r\},u_{\mathsf{cid}'}}$ from r to $u_{\mathsf{cid}'}$ in $\mathcal{G}_{Q'_0,\mathcal{A}_0}$ of Example 7 is highlighted in bold in Fig. 2.

We now establish the connection between hyperpaths and canonical fetching plans as follows.

Lemma 7: *For any* RA *query Q, access schema $\mathcal{A}$ and attribute A in X_Q of Q, there exists a unit fetching plan $\xi^c(A)$ for Q under $\mathcal{A}$* if and only if *there exists a hyperpath from r to $u_{\rho_U(A)}$ in the hypergraph $\mathcal{G}_{Q,\mathcal{A}}$.* □

Lemma 7 tells us that to get a canonical fetching plan for Q under $\mathcal{A}$, it suffices to find hyperpaths from r to u_A in $\mathcal{G}_{Q,\mathcal{A}}$ for all attribute $A \in X_Q$. Based on this we develop our algorithm for canonical bounded plan generation.

Algorithm. The algorithm, denoted by QPlan and shown in Fig. 3, takes as input an access schema $\mathcal{A}$ and an RA query Q covered by $\mathcal{A}$; it returns a canonical bounded query plan $\mathcal{P}_{Q,\mathcal{A}}$ for Q under $\mathcal{A}$. It generates $\mathcal{P}_{Q,\mathcal{A}}$ in three steps: it first generates unit fetching plans for attributes in X_Q (lines 1-6). It then builds an indexing plan $\xi^c_I(S)$ for each relation name S that occurs in Q on top of the fetching plans (lines 7-9). Finally it adds the evaluation plan ξ^c_E (line 10).

More specifically, it first constructs the $\langle Q, \mathcal{A}\rangle$-hypergraph $\mathcal{G}_{Q,\mathcal{A}}$ for Q and $\mathcal{A}$ (line 1), and initializes data structures for storing unit fetching plans (L_F) and the final query plan ($\mathcal{P}_{Q,\mathcal{A}}$) (line 2). It then iteratively finds unit fetching plans for attributes in X_Q (lines 3-6). For each attribute A in X_Q, it finds a hyperpath $\Pi_{\{r\},u_A}$ from r to u_A that encodes A in $\mathcal{G}_{Q,\mathcal{A}}$, by invoking procedure findHP (line 4; not shown). Here findHP can be implemented in $O(|\mathcal{G}_{Q,\mathcal{A}}|) = O(|Q| + |\mathcal{A}|)$ time by traversing $\mathcal{G}_{Q,\mathcal{A}}$ [9]. It then converts the hyperpath into a unit fetching plan $\xi^c_F(A)$ via procedure transQP (line 5) (see Appendix D for details), and adds the plan to $\mathcal{P}_{Q,\mathcal{A}}$ (line 6). After these, algorithm QPlan generates indexing plans for all relations in Q, by manipulating the unit fetching plans stored in L_F, following the definition of indexing plan (lines 7-9). It finally adds the evaluation plan of Q to $\mathcal{P}_{Q,\mathcal{A}}$ (line 10), and returns $\mathcal{P}_{Q,\mathcal{A}}$ (line 11).

Example 8: Given Q'_0 and $\mathcal{A}_0$ of Example 1, QPlan first constructs the hypergraph $\mathcal{G}_{Q'_0,\mathcal{A}_0}$ shown in Fig 2 for Q'_0 and $\mathcal{A}_0$. It then iteratively finds unit fetching plans for attributes in $X_{Q'_0}$. Take cid$'$ in sub-query Q_1 of Q'_0 as an example

---

Algorithm QPlan

Input: An access schema $\mathcal{A}$ and an RA query Q covered by $\mathcal{A}$.
Output: A canonical bounded query plan ξ^c for Q under $\mathcal{A}$.

1. construct the $\langle Q, \mathcal{A}\rangle$-hypergraph $\mathcal{G}_{Q,\mathcal{A}}$ for Q and $\mathcal{A}$;
2. $L_F[\,] := nil$; $\mathcal{P}_{Q,\mathcal{A}} = nil$;
3. **for each** attribute $A \in X_Q$ of Q **do**
   /* find a hyperpath from r to $u_{\rho_U(A)}$ in $\mathcal{G}_{Q,\mathcal{A}}$ for $\rho_U(A)$ */
4. $\Pi_{\{r\},u_{\hat{A}}} :=$ findHP$(r, u_{\hat{A}}, \mathcal{G}_{Q,\mathcal{A}})$; /* $\hat{A} = \rho_U(A)$ */
   /* translate hyperpath to a unit fetching plan for A */
5. $L_F[A] :=$ transQP$(\Pi_{\{r\},u_{\hat{A}}})$;
6. append $L_F[A]$ to $\mathcal{P}_{Q,\mathcal{A}}$;
7. **for each** relation S in Q **do**
8. construct indexing plan $\xi^c_I(S)$ with $L_F[A]$ for all A in X^S_Q;
9. append $\xi^c_I(S)$ to $\mathcal{P}_{Q,\mathcal{A}}$;
10. append evaluation plan ξ^c_E for Q to $\mathcal{P}_{Q,\mathcal{A}}$;
11. **return** $\mathcal{P}_{Q,\mathcal{A}}$;

Figure 3: Algorithm QPlan

(recall the setting of Example 7 in Appendix C). It finds a hyperpath $\Pi_{\{r\},u_{\mathsf{cid}'}}$ in $\mathcal{G}_{Q'_0,\mathcal{A}_0}$, marked in bold in Fig. 2. It then translates $\Pi_{\{r\},u_{\mathsf{cid}'}}$ into a unit fetching plan consisting of T_1-T_9 given in Example 2. Similarly, it generates unit fetching plans for all the other attributes in $X_{Q'_0}$. It then finds indexing plans for relations in Q'_0. For instance, an indexing plan for dine$''$ is as follows: $T'_1 = T_9$ (since T_1, $\ldots$, T_9 form a unit fetching plan for cid$'$), $T'_2 = \{p_0\}$, $T'_3 = T'_1 \times T'_2$, $T'_4 = \mathsf{fetch}(X \in T'_3, \mathsf{dine}'', (\mathsf{pid}'', \mathsf{cid}'))$. Finally, it adds the evaluation plan. A complete canonical bounded query plan for Q'_0 under $\mathcal{A}_0$ is given in Appendix C, which is essentially the same as the one given in Example 2. □

Correctness & Complexity. The correctness of QPlan is ensured by Theorem 5(1) and Lemma 7. By Theorem 5(1), a covered Q has a canonical bounded query plan, including a unit canonical fetching plan $\xi^c_F(A)$ for each attribute A in X_Q of Q. By Lemma 7, there exists a hyperpath from r to u_A for each $A \in X_Q$, encoding $\xi^c_F(A)$. Hence QPlan is warranted to be able to find such a plan.

Algorithm QPlan can be implemented in $O(|Q|(|Q|+|\mathcal{A}|))$ time (See Appendix D for a detailed analysis).

The lemma below completes the proof of Theorem 5(2).

Lemma 8: *Given an* RA *query Q covered by $\mathcal{A}$,* QPlan *finds a canonical bounded query plan of length $O(|Q||\mathcal{A}|)$.* □

6. ACCESS MINIMIZATION

In this section, we study a new optimization problem for bounded evaluability, referred to as the *access minimization problem* and denoted by AMP$(Q, \mathcal{A})$. It is stated as follows.

- Input: Access schema $\mathcal{A}$, RA query Q covered by $\mathcal{A}$.
- Output: A subset $\mathcal{A}_m \subseteq \mathcal{A}$ such that Q is also covered by $\mathcal{A}_m$ and $\mathcal{A}_m$ is *minimum, i.e.,* for any other subset $\mathcal{A}' \subseteq \mathcal{A}$, if Q is also covered by $\mathcal{A}'$, then $\sum_{R(X\to Y,N)\in\mathcal{A}_m} N \leq \sum_{R(X\to Y,N)\in\mathcal{A}'} N$.

That is, it is to identify a small set $\mathcal{A}_m$ of access constraints in $\mathcal{A}$ that covers Q and moreover, $\mathcal{A}_m$ estimates a "minimum" amount of data to be accessed for answering Q. It also suggests how many access constraints we need to cover a query, and the size of indices built for the constraints.

While useful, the problem is hard. We show that the problem is intractable (Section 6.1). Nonetheless, we provide efficient algorithms with performance guarantees (Section 6.2).

6.1 Intractability & Approximation Hardness

The decision version of AMP, denoted $\mathsf{dAMP}(Q,\mathcal{A},K)$, is to decide, given access schema $\mathcal{A}$, RA query Q covered by $\mathcal{A}$ and a natural number K, whether there exists $\mathcal{A}_m \subseteq \mathcal{A}$ such that A_m covers Q and $\sum_{R(X\to Y,N)\in\mathcal{A}_m} N \le K$. Its corresponding optimization problem, denoted by $\mathsf{oAMP}(Q,\mathcal{A})$, is to find the minimum K for $\mathsf{dAMP}(Q,\mathcal{A},K)$ to answer "yes".

We also study two practical special cases. We say that a $\langle Q,\mathcal{A}\rangle$-hypergraph $\mathcal{G}_{Q,\mathcal{A}}$ is *acyclic* if $G_{Q,\mathcal{A}}$ is acyclic, where $G_{Q,\mathcal{A}}$ is a directed graph derived from $\mathcal{G}_{Q,\mathcal{A}}$ by replacing each hyperedge $e = (\{u_1,\ldots,u_p\},v)$ with p edges (u_1,v), $\ldots$, (u_p,v). Intuitively, $\mathcal{G}_{Q,\mathcal{A}}$ is acyclic when the dependency relation on attributes of Q imposed by $\mathcal{A}$ is not "recursive". We study the following two special cases:

- *acyclic*: when $\mathcal{G}_{Q,\mathcal{A}}$ is acyclic; and
- *elementary*: for each $\phi = R(X \to Y,N)$ in $\mathcal{A}$, either ϕ is an *indexing* constraint, *i.e.*, of the form $R(X \to X,1)$, or a *unit* constraint, *i.e.*, when $|X| = |Y| = 1$.

Both cases are quite common in practice: access constraints rarely incur recursive dependencies, and are often of the form of indexing or unit constraints. For example, (1) Q_0' and $\mathcal{A}_0$ in Example 1 are an acyclic case since $\mathcal{G}_{Q_0',\mathcal{A}_0}$ (Fig. 2) is acyclic; and (2) Q_0' and $\mathcal{A}_0 \setminus \{\psi_2\}$ are an elementary case.

These problems are nontrivial, even their special cases.

Theorem 9: *(1)* $\mathsf{dAMP}(Q,\mathcal{A},K)$ *is* NP*-complete.*
(2) $\mathsf{oAMP}(Q,\mathcal{A})$ *is not approximable within* $c{*}\log|X_Q \setminus X_C^Q|$ *for any constant* $c > 0$.
(3) When $(Q,\mathcal{A})$ *is acyclic or elementary,* $\mathsf{dAMP}(Q,\mathcal{A},K)$ *remains* NP*-hard, and* $\mathsf{oAMP}(Q,\mathcal{A})$ *is not in* APX. □

The class APX is the set of NP optimization problems that can be approximated by a constant-factor approximation algorithm, *i.e.*, a PTIME algorithm within *some* constant.

6.2 Approximation Algorithms

Theorem 9 tells us that for $\mathsf{AMP}(Q,\mathcal{A})$, any efficient algorithm is necessarily heuristic. Below we provide an efficient heuristic that *guarantees* to find a *minimal* $\mathcal{A}_m \subseteq \mathcal{A}$ that covers Q, *i.e.*, removing any constraint from $\mathcal{A}_m$ makes Q not covered by $\mathcal{A}_m$. Moreover, for the two special cases, there are approximation algorithms with accuracy bounds.

Theorem 10: *(1) There is an algorithm for* $\mathsf{AMP}(Q,\mathcal{A})$ *that finds minimal* $\mathcal{A}_m$ *in* $O(|Q|^2 + \|\mathcal{A}\|(|Q| + |\mathcal{A}|))$ *time.*
(2) For acyclic $(Q,\mathcal{A})$, $\mathsf{oAMP}(Q,\mathcal{A})$ *is approximable within* $O(1 + |X_Q \setminus X_C^Q|)$ *in* $O(|Q| + |\mathcal{A}|)$ *time.*
(3) For elementary $Q(Q,\mathcal{A})$, $\mathsf{oAMP}(Q,\mathcal{A})$ *is approximable within* $O(1+|X_Q\setminus X_C^Q|^{\epsilon})$ *in* $O((|Q|+|\mathcal{A}|)^{\frac{1}{\epsilon}}|X_Q\setminus X_C^Q|^{\frac{2}{\epsilon}}$ *time, for any constant* $\epsilon > 0$. □

As a proof, we outline the algorithms as follows.

General case. As a proof of Theorem 10(1), we give an algorithm for $\mathsf{AMP}(Q,\mathcal{A})$ for the general case, denoted by minA (not shown). It is based on the following heuristics: a constraint $\phi = R(X \to Y, N_\phi)$, if it is not used to index a relation (Section 3), then it is less likely in the optimum solution $\mathcal{A}_m$ if Q remains covered by $\mathcal{A}\setminus\{\phi\}$, and moreover, (a) $\mathsf{cov}(Q,\mathcal{A})\setminus\mathsf{cov}(Q,\mathcal{A}\setminus\{\phi\})$ is small; and (b) N_ϕ is large.

Based on the observation, algorithm minA works as follows. It first constructs the set $\Sigma_{Q,\mathcal{A}}$ of induced FDs of Q and $\mathcal{A}$. It then iteratively removes "redundant" FDs from $\Sigma_{Q,\mathcal{A}}$. In each iteration, it greedily selects an induced FD that corresponds to access constraint ϕ, such that (a) Q remains covered by $\mathcal{A}\setminus\{\phi\}$; and (b) $w(\phi) = \frac{c_1\cdot N_\phi}{c_2\cdot(|\mathsf{cov}(Q,\mathcal{A})\setminus\mathsf{cov}(Q,\mathcal{A}\setminus\{\phi\})|+1)}$ is maximum among all constraints $\mathcal{A}$, where c_1 and c_2 are user-tunable coefficients for normalizing the numbers. It returns all access constraints corresponding to the remaining FDs in $\Sigma_{Q,\mathcal{A}}$ when it cannot remove more FDs from $\Sigma_{Q,\mathcal{A}}$.

Example 9: Consider Q_1 and $\mathcal{A}_0$ given in Example 1. Let $\mathcal{A}_1$ consist of constraints in $\mathcal{A}_0$ and an additional ψ_5: $\mathsf{dine}((\mathsf{pid},\mathsf{year}) \to \mathsf{cid}, 366)$, *i.e.*, each person dines out at most 366 times per year. For $\mathsf{AMP}(Q_1,\mathcal{A}_1)$, algorithm minA returns $\mathcal{A}_m = \{\psi_1\ \psi_2, \psi_4\}$ (see details in Appendix C). □

Analysis. Algorithm minA always returns minimal $\mathcal{A}_m \subseteq \mathcal{A}$ for $\mathsf{AMP}(Q,\mathcal{A})$ since it keeps removing FDs until $\mathcal{A}_m$ is minimal, in $O(|Q|^2+\|\mathcal{A}\|^2(|Q|+|\mathcal{A}|))$ time (see Appendix D).

Acyclic case. We prove Theorem 10(2) by giving an approximation algorithm, denoted by $\mathsf{minA_{DAG}}$ (omitted). The algorithm capitalizes on the connection between hyperpaths and coverage (Lemma 7). It uses the following notion.

Weighted $\langle Q,\mathcal{A}\rangle$-hypergraph. For an RA query Q and an access schema $\mathcal{A}$, the *weighted $\langle Q,\mathcal{A}\rangle$-hypergraph* is a weighted hypergraph, where each hyperedge carries a weight defined as follows. Recall $\mathcal{G}_{Q,\mathcal{A}}$ from Section 5.2. For each induced FD $X \to Y$ in $\Sigma_{Q,\mathcal{A}}$ derived from an constraint $R(X \to Y,N)$ in $\mathcal{A}$, the hyperedge encoding the induced RHS-FD $X \to \tilde{Y}$ has weight N, and hyperedges encoding the remaining induced $\tilde{Y} \to Y_i$ (for $Y_i \in Y$) have weight 0. Moreover, all hyperedges emanating from the special node r have weight 0. For instance, for Q_1 and $\mathcal{A}_1$ of Example 9, its weighted $\langle Q,\mathcal{A}\rangle$-hypergraph $\mathcal{G}_{Q_1,\mathcal{A}_1}$ is depicted in Fig. 7 in Appendix C (see Appendix A for a formal definition).

Algorithm $\mathsf{minA_{DAG}}$. Based on this notion, $\mathsf{minA_{DAG}}$ simply computes the shortest hyperpaths from node r in $\mathcal{G}_{Q,\mathcal{A}}$ to nodes encoding attributes in $(\hat{X_Q} \setminus \hat{X_C^Q})$ (recall $\hat{X} = \rho_U(X)$ and Table 1) *w.r.t.* the sum of weights of hyperedges on it. It returns access constraints corresponding to the induced FDs encoded by edges of the hyperpaths, plus one constraint with the minimum N to index each relation S in Q (Section 3).

Example 10: For Q_1 and $\mathcal{A}_1$ of Example 9, its weighted $\langle Q,\mathcal{A}\rangle$-hypergraph $\mathcal{G}_{Q_1,\mathcal{A}_1}$ is acyclic (see Fig. 7 in Appendix B). Given Q_1 and $\mathcal{A}_1$, $\mathsf{minA_{DAG}}$ computes shortest hyperpaths from r to u_{pid}, u_{fid}, u_{cid}, u_{month}, u_{year} and u_{city}. For example, the shortest hyperpath from r to u_{cid} is the one containing edge $(\{\mathsf{fid},\mathsf{year},\mathsf{month}\},\mathsf{cid})$ with weight 31. Algorithm $\mathsf{minA_{DAG}}$ returns constraints ψ_1, ψ_2, ψ_4 in $\mathcal{A}_1$ that correspond to the edges in those hyperpaths. As Q_1 is already indexed by them, no more constraints are needed. □

Analysis. By Lemma 7, $\mathsf{minA_{DAG}}$ always returns $\mathcal{A}' \subseteq \mathcal{A}$ that covers Q. The approximation bound can then be proved based on the following (see details in Appendix B): the weight of the shortest hyperpaths from r to a node u_A denoting attribute A is the minimum "cost" to cover A with $\mathcal{A}$.

Observe that the search for shortest hyperpaths emanating from r can be conducted by BFS in $\mathcal{G}_{Q,\mathcal{A}}$ in $O(|\mathcal{G}_{Q,\mathcal{A}}|)$ time. Hence, algorithm $\mathsf{minA_{DAG}}$ is in $O(|Q| + |\mathcal{A}|)$ time.

Elementary case. As a proof of Theorem 10(3), we develop an algorithm, denoted by $\mathsf{minA_E}$ (omitted), for the elementary case $(Q,\mathcal{A})$ of $\mathsf{AMP}(Q,\mathcal{A})$. The idea is by reduction to the *directed minimum steiner arborescence* problem ($\mathsf{dminSAP}(G,u,V_T)$) (cf. [15]), which is to find the minimum

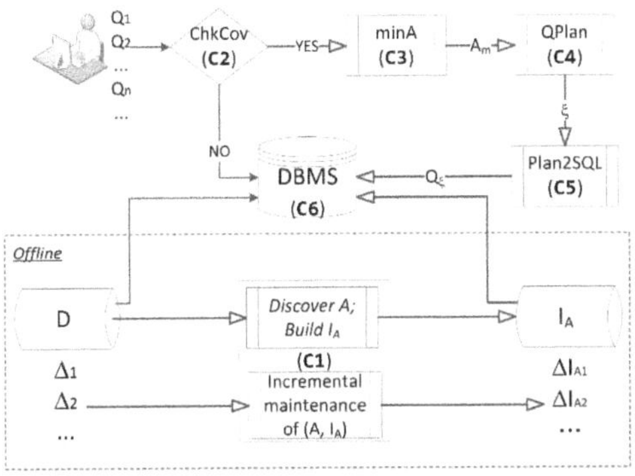

Figure 4: Bounded evaluability on DBMS

weighed arborescence rooted at node u spanning all nodes in a set V_T in a weighted directed graph G.

The reduction is as follows. Given an elementary case $(Q, \mathcal{A})$, we construct an instance (G, u, V_T) of dminSAP:

(a) G is the weighted $\langle Q, \mathcal{A}\rangle$-hypergraph $\mathcal{G}_{Q,\mathcal{A}_{ni}}$ for Q and $\mathcal{A}_{ni} \subset \mathcal{A}$, where $\mathcal{A}_{ni}$ contains all unit constraints in $\mathcal{A}$;

(b) u is the special node r in $\mathcal{G}_{Q,\mathcal{A}_{ni}}$; and

(c) V_T is the set of nodes in $\mathcal{G}_{Q,\mathcal{A}_{ni}}$ that correspond to attributes in $\hat{X}_Q \setminus \hat{X}_C^Q$ (see Table 1).

For elementary $(Q, \mathcal{A})$, $\mathcal{G}_{Q,\mathcal{A}_{ni}}$ is actually a weighted directed graph rooted at node r. Thus this is an instance of dminSAP(G, u). The reduction guarantees the following.

Lemma 11: *For elementary $(Q, \mathcal{A})$,* oAMP$(Q, \mathcal{A})$ *has a c-approximation algorithm that takes $O(f(Q, \mathcal{A}))$-time if* dminSAP$(\mathcal{G}_{Q,\mathcal{A}_{ni}}, r, V)$ *has a (c−1)-approximation algorithm in $O(f(|Q|, |\mathcal{A}_{ni}|) + |\mathcal{A}|)$-time.* □

Algorithm. Based on Lemma 11, algorithm minA$_E$ works as follows. (a) It first builds the reduction described above. (b) It then computes the minimum weighted arborescence DT_r rooted at r of $\mathcal{G}_{Q,\mathcal{A}_{ni}}$ that spans all nodes in V_T, for $(\mathcal{G}_{Q,\mathcal{A}_{ni}}, r, V_T)$ constructed in (a). (c) It returns the following constraints in $\mathcal{A}$: (i) constraints corresponding to edges in DT_r; and (ii) constraints that index relations in Q.

Analysis. It is known that for dminSAP$(\mathcal{G}_{Q,\mathcal{A}_{ni}}, r, V)$, there exists an $O(|V_T|^\epsilon)$-approximation algorithm that takes at most $O(|\mathcal{G}_{Q,\mathcal{A}_{ni}}|^{\frac{1}{\epsilon}} |V_T|^{\frac{2}{\epsilon}})$-time for any constant $\epsilon > 0$ [15]. Moreover, observe that $|V_T| = |\hat{X}_Q \setminus \hat{X}_C^Q| \leq |X_Q \setminus X_C^Q|$. Thus minA$_E$ is the algorithm promised by Theorem 10(3).

This completes the proof of Theorem 10.

7. SUPPORTING BOUNDED QUERIES

We next present a framework for incorporating bounded evaluation of RA queries into existing DBMS, based on covered queries. To simplify the discussion, we use $\mathcal{I}_\mathcal{A}$ to denote the indices for all constraints in an access schema $\mathcal{A}$.

A framework of bounded evaluation. The framework is shown in Fig. 4. Given an application for queries over instances of a relational schema $\mathcal{R}$, it works as follows. As *offline* preprocessing (**C1** in Fig. 4), it discovers an access schema $\mathcal{A}$ from (sample) instances of $\mathcal{R}$, builds indices $\mathcal{I}_\mathcal{A}$ for $\mathcal{A}$ on the instance D of $\mathcal{R}$ in use, and maintains $\mathcal{I}_\mathcal{A}$ in response to updates to D. Given a user RA query posed on D, it first checks whether Q is covered by $\mathcal{A}$ (**C2**). If so, it picks a minimum set $\mathcal{A}_m$ of $\mathcal{A}$ that covers Q (**C3**), generates a bounded query plan ξ for Q under $\mathcal{A}_m$ (**C4**), and translates it into an SQL query Q_ξ (**C5**). Query Q_ξ can then be evaluated directly by the underlying DBMS on a bounded dataset D_Q identified by the bounded plan ξ (**C6**). If Q is not covered, it is executed against D by the DBMS. As will be seen shortly, a large fraction of RA queries are covered and hence, can be evaluated by accessing a small D_Q.

We next present its components in more details.

(1) Building and maintaining $\langle \mathcal{A}, \mathcal{I}_\mathcal{A}\rangle$. It has three parts.

(a) Discovering $\mathcal{A}$. Like FDs, access constraints are defined on schema $\mathcal{R}$. They can be mined by extending dependency discovery tools [26], *e.g.,* TANE [23] for FDs. More specifically, on samples of a relation schema R, we search candidate attributes X and Y via revised FD mining, and use group_by on X and aggregates count on Y to form access constraint $R(X \to Y, N)$. These include those composed of attributes with a finite domain, *e.g.,* $R(X \to \text{month}, 12)$, stating that a year has 12 months. These constraints hold on *all instances* of $\mathcal{R}$, just like discovered FDs.

Discovered constraints also include those determined by policies and statistics, *e.g.,* ψ_1 of Example 1 imposing a limit of 5000 friends per person, and one stating that US airports host carriers of at most 28 airlines (see Section 8). Such constraints *may* change if Facebook changes their policy or some US airports expand, and are thus maintained (see below).

(b) Building indices $\mathcal{I}_\mathcal{A}$. For each discovered constraint $\phi = R(X \to Y, N)$ in $\mathcal{A}$, the index for ϕ is constructed by creating a partial table $T_{XY} = \pi_{XY}(D_R)$ and building a hash index on X over T_{XY}, where D_R is the instance of R in D. The index is no larger than $|D_R|$ and is constructed in $O(|D_R|)$ time. Thus, it takes $O(\|\mathcal{A}\||D|)$ time to build all indices in $\mathcal{A}$, and the total size $\mathcal{I}_\mathcal{A}$ is at most $O(\|\mathcal{A}\||D|)$.

(c) Incremental maintenance of $\langle \mathcal{A}, \mathcal{I}_\mathcal{A}\rangle$. Now consider updates ΔD to D, *i.e.,* sequences of tuple insertions and deletions (which can simulate value modifications). We show that in response to ΔD, both constraints in $\mathcal{A}$ and indices $\mathcal{I}_\mathcal{A}$ can be maintained by *bounded incremental* algorithms: their costs are determined by $\mathcal{A}$ and the size $|\Delta D|$ of updates ΔD only, and are independent of D and $\mathcal{I}_\mathcal{A}$. In practice, ΔD is typically small, and hence so are the costs.

Proposition 12: *In response to updates ΔD to D, both $\mathcal{A}$ and $\mathcal{I}_\mathcal{A}$ can be updated in $O(N_\mathcal{A}|\Delta D|)$ time, where $N_\mathcal{A} = \Sigma_{R(X\to Y,N)\in\mathcal{A}} N$.* □

(2) Checking whether Q is covered by $\mathcal{A}$. This can be carried out by algorithm CovChk of Section 4.

(3) Minimizing accessed data. This is conducted by the algorithms in Section 6 to minimize index access in $\mathcal{I}_\mathcal{A}$.

(4) Generating boundedly evaluable query plans $\xi_{(Q,\mathcal{A})}$. This is done by using algorithm QPlan of Section 5.

(5) Interpreting $\xi_{(Q,\mathcal{A})}$ as SQL query Q_ξ. We develop an algorithm, denoted by Plan2SQL (omitted), to translate a bounded plan ξ into an SQL query Q_ξ, such that Q_ξ can be directly executed by DBMS. Given ξ and $\mathcal{A}$, Plan2SQL returns Q_ξ such that for any dataset $D \models \mathcal{A}$, Q_ξ returns $Q(D)$ by accessing the same amount of data *in index $\mathcal{I}_\mathcal{A}$* as ξ does in D. For instance, recall Q_1 and $\mathcal{A}_0$ of Example 1, $\mathcal{A}_0'$ $= \mathcal{A}_0 \setminus \{\psi_3\}$, and the bounded query plan ξ for Q_1 under $\mathcal{A}_0'$ given in Example 2. Let the index relations in $\mathcal{I}_\mathcal{A}$ under ψ_1, ψ_2 and ψ_4 in $\mathcal{A}_0'$ be ind_friend, ind_dine and ind_cafe, respectively. Plan2SQL$(\xi, \mathcal{A}_0')$ returns the following SQL query:

```
select distinct cid
from   ind_cafe
```

```
where city = NYC and cid in
    (select distinct cid
     from   ind_dine /* no access to the underlying D */
     where  month = MAY and year = 2015 and pid in
            (select distinct fid from ind_friend where pid = p0))
```

Thus, bounded evaluation can be built on top of DBMS.

Added functionality. While indices and constraints are already employed by DBMS, their current mechanism stops short of taking advantage of bounded evaluation.

Indices and query plans. Query plans generated by conventional query engines fetch entire tuples first and then filter tuples based on the query (see, *e.g.*, [5]), by employing *tuple*-based indices, *e.g.*, hash index and tree-based index [31]. In contrast, a boundedly evaluable query plan makes use of *attribute*-based indices. It identifies what attributes are necessarily needed, fetches values of the attributes, infers their connection with other attributes, composes attribute values into tuples and validates the tuples (via the indexing condition of Section 3). However, existing DBMS stops short of exploring this, no matter what indices are provided.

This observation is verified by examining system logs of commercial DBMS, which shows excessive duplicated and unnecessary attributes in tuples fetched by DBMS, and the redundancies get inflated rapidly when joins are involved.

We also check whether a query Q is boundedly evaluable before Q is executed, as opposed to conventional DBMS.

(2) Constraints. Query optimization has been studied for reformulating a query Q as another query by "chasing" Q with constraints [5, 24, 30]. However, to the best of our knowledge, conventional query engines have made little use of it, partly because the chasing process is costly and may not even terminate. Moreover, cardinality constraints have not been explored for this purpose. In contrast, we use cardinality constraints to generate boundedly evaluable query plans, instead of query reformulation. These constraints are easy to reason about and can be readily supported by DBMS.

(3) Join ordering. Query engines may reorder joins in a query plan to minimize estimated data access [22, 27]. It is an effective optimization strategy complementary to this work. However, to comply with bounded data access via access constraints, some joins in a boundedly evaluable query plan cannot be reordered. It is an interesting topic to study what joins can be reordered in boundedly evaluable plans.

8. EXPERIMENTAL STUDY

Using real-life data, we conducted two sets of experiments to evaluate (1) the effectiveness of the RA-query evaluation approach based on the bounded evaluability analysis, and (2) the efficiency of algorithms ChkCov, QPlan and minA.

Experimental setting. We used three datasets: two real-life (AIRCA and TFACC) and one benchmark (MCBM).

(1) US Air carriers (AIRCA) records flight and statistic data of US air carriers from year 1987 to 2014. It consists of Flight On-Time Performance data [4] for departure and arrival data, and Carrier Statistic data [3] for airline market and segment data of the air carriers. It has 7 tables, 358 attributes, and over 162 million tuples, about 60GB of data.

(2) UK traffic accident (TFACC) integrates the Road Safety Data [2] of road accidents that happened in the UK from 1979 to 2005, and National Public Transport Access Nodes (NaPTAN) [1]. It has 19 tables with 113 attributes, and over 89.7 million tuples in total, about 21.4GB of data.

(3) Mobile communication benchmark (MCBM) was generated by using a commercial benchmark from Huawei Technologies Co. Ltd. The dataset consists of 12 relations with 285 attributes, simulating mobile communication scenarios. We varied the number of tuples from $2^{-5} \times 360$ to 360 million, and used 360 million by default, about 90GB of data.

All of the three datasets were stored in MySQL.

Access schema. We extracted 266, 84 and 366 access constraints for AIRCA, TFACC and MCBM, respectively, by using the discovery method in Section 7. For example, a constraint on AIRCA is OnTimePerformance(Origin $\rightarrow$ AirlineID, 28), *i.e.*, each airport hosted carriers of at most 28 airlines. On TFACC, we had Accident((data, police_force) $\rightarrow$ accident_ID, 304), *i.e.*, each police force in the UK had handled no more than 304 accidents within a single day from 1979 to 2005. In fact there are many more access constraints in the datasets, which were not used in our tests. We built indices for the constraints by using DBMS (see Section 7).

RA queries generator. We generated queries by using attributes that occurred in the access constraints and constants randomly extracted for those attributes. For MCBM, the query generation also complied with the provided query templates. We generated 300 RA queries Q on these datasets, 100 for each. The queries vary in the number #-sel of equality atoms in the selection conditions in the range of [4, 9], #-join of joins in the range of [0,5] and #-unidiff of set difference and union operators in the range of [0, 5].

Algorithms. We implemented the following algorithms in Python: (1) ChkCov (Section 4) to check whether an RA query is covered; (2) QPlan (Section 5) to generate canonical query plans for covered queries; (3) minA, minA_{DAG} and minA_{E} (Section 6) to find minimum access constraints for covered queries; (4) Plan2SQL to interpret canonical query plans generated by QPlan as SQL queries (Section 7); (5) evalQP^- and evalQP to evaluate the translated queries Q_ξ with and without minimized $\mathcal{A}_m$ (via minA; by Plan2SQL) using DBMS, respectively; and (6) evalDBMS that directly uses DBMS engine for query evaluation, with a configuration in favor of DBMS, which is described as follows.

Configuration. For DBMS, we used MySQL 5.5.44 (MyISAM engine) and PostgreSQL 9.3.9, both with optimization enabled. Both original queries and query plans generated by our algorithms are executed on the same database server. In favor of MySQL and PostgreSQL, besides indices for access constraints, we also built extra indices when testing original queries on the DBMS, *e.g.*, primary and foreign key indices and B-tree on numerical attributes, while these were all disabled when testing our query plans. The experiments were conducted on an Amazon EC2 d2.xlarge instance with 14 EC2 compute units and 30.5GB memory. All the experiments were run 3 times. The average is reported here.

Experimental Results. We next report findings. As results for PostgreSQL are even worse than MySQL when compared with ours, we mainly report MySQL to save space.

Exp-1: Effectiveness of bounded evaluability.
(I) Percentage of bounded evaluable and covered RA queries. Varying the number of access constraints, we tested the percentage of covered queries (via ChkCov) and boundedly evaluable queries (by manual examination). The results

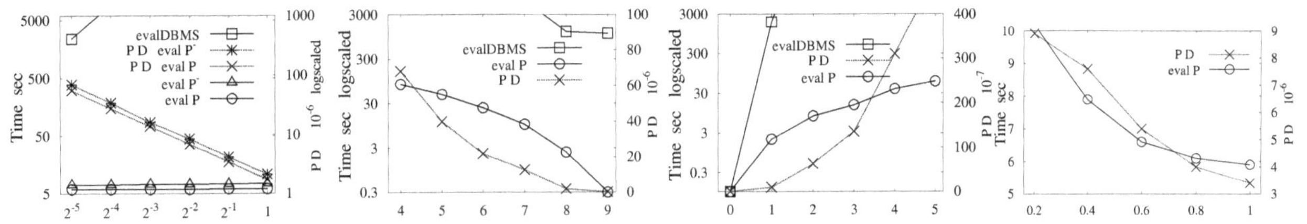

(a) AIRCA: varying $|D|(\times 60\text{GB})$ (b) AIRCA: varying #-sel (c) AIRCA: varying #-join (d) AIRCA: varying $\|\mathcal{A}\|(\times\|A\|)$

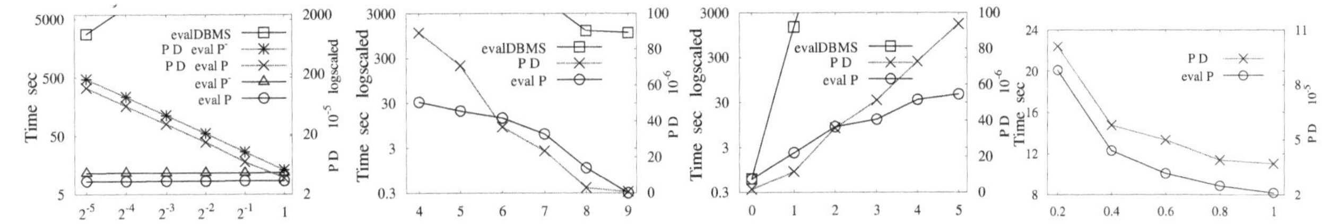

(e) TFACC: varying $|D|(\times 21.4\text{GB})$ (f) TFACC: varying #-sel (g) TFACC: varying #-join (h) TFACC: varying $\|\mathcal{A}\|(\times\|A\|)$

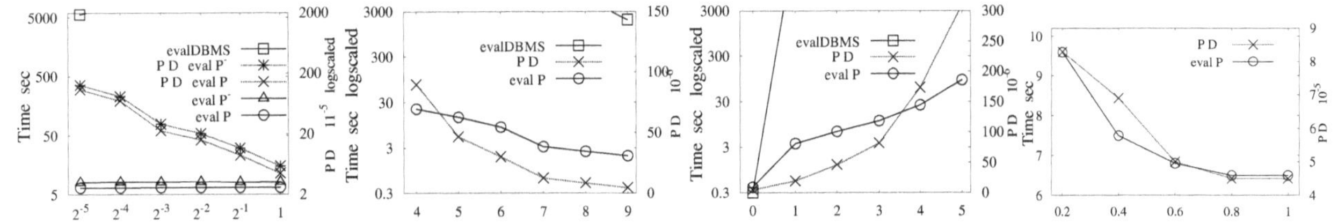

(i) MCBM: varying $|D|$ $(\times 90\text{GB})$ (j) MCBM: varying #-sel (k) MCBM: varying #-join (l) MCBM: varying $\|\mathcal{A}\|(\times\|A\|)$

Figure 5: Effectiveness of bounded evaluability

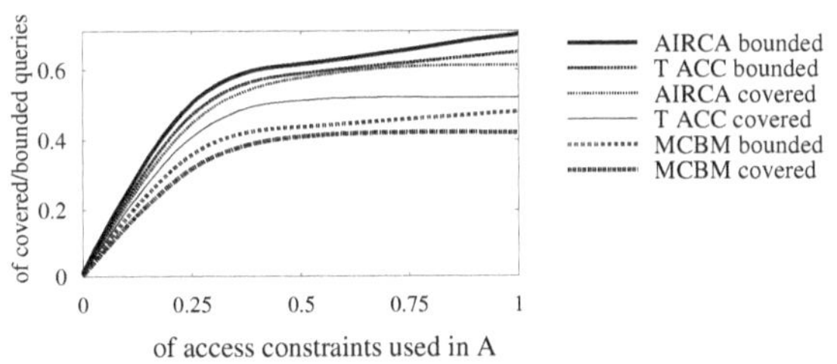

Figure 6: Percentage of covered (bounded) queries

are shown in Figure 6, and tell us the following. (a) When all the discovered constraints are used, (i) at least 70, 65 and 48 out of 100 queries are boundedly evaluable, and (ii) 61, 52 and 42 are covered, on AIRCA, TFACC and MCBM, respectively. That is, at least 70%, 65% and 51% of the queries are boundedly evaluable, and among them 87%, 80% and 87.5% are covered. Hence, covered queries are indeed effective for determining the bounded evaluability of RA queries. (b) The more access constraints are used, the more queries are covered and boundedly evaluable, as expected. Nonetheless, among all the covered queries, 78.7%, 84.6% and 80.9% are already covered by only 25% of the discovered access constraints on AIRCA, TFACC and MCBM, respectively. That is, a large number of queries can be covered by a small number of constraints.

(II) Effectiveness of covered queries. We next evaluated the effectiveness of query plans generated by QPlan, by comparing the run time of evalQP and evalDBMS, both executed by MySQL. The results are reported in Figure 5, on datasets AIRCA, TFACC and MCBM, by varying $|D|$, Q and $\|\mathcal{A}\|$. We report (i) the average evaluation time (the left y-axis), and (ii) ratio $P(D_Q) = |D_Q|/|D|$, measuring the total amount of data D_Q accessed by our query plans (the right y-axis), which is assessed by using MySQL's EXPLAIN statement. Unless stated otherwise, we used the full-size datasets, all access constraints, and 5 covered queries randomly chosen.

(1) Impact of $|D|$. To evaluate the impact of $|D|$, we varied the datasets by using scale factors from 2^{-5} to 1. As shown in Figures 5(a), 5(e) and 5(i), the results tell us the following.

(a) The evaluation time of evalQP is indifferent to the size of D, as expected for covered queries.

(b) Bounded query plans work well with large D. Indeed, evalQP took less than 5.9s, 8.3s, 6.5s with MySQL, and 5.5s, 9.0s, 7.0s with PostgreSQL, on AIRCA, TFACC and MCBM, respectively, no matter how large the datasets were. In contrast, even on the smallest subsets with scale factor 2^{-5}, evalDBMS took 2398s, 2759s, 5675s by MySQL, and 3598s, 3851s, 7301s by PostgreSQL; it could not terminate within 2 hours for all larger subsets. This is why few points are reported for evalDBMS in the figures. In fact, evalDBMS could not finish within 14 hours on all three full-size datasets (both MySQL and PostgreSQL). That is, evalDBMS is at least 8.5×10^3, 6.1×10^3 and 7.8×10^3 times slower on AIRCA, TFACC and MCBM, respectively. The larger the dataset is, the bigger the gap between evalDBMS and evalQP is.

(c) Query plans generated by QPlan accessed a very small fraction of the data: $P(D_Q)$ is 1.7×10^{-6}, 3.7×10^{-5}, 2.2×10^{-6} on full-size AIRCA, TFACC and MCBM. *i.e.*, 0.00017%, 0.0037% and 0.00022% of these datasets, respectively.

Remark. As shown above, evalQP outperforms evalDBMS by at least 3 orders of magnitude, for reasons explained in Section 7. We also find that when queries Q use key attributes only, evalDBMS is as fast as evalQP if extra key/foreign key indices are built for MySQL and PostgreSQL, *e.g.,* less than 3s with one join on full AIRCA. However, as long as Q involves non-key attributes, evalDBMS performs poorly on big tables, even provided with all indices. It gets worse when the number of non-key attributes increases. By looking into MySQL's log and its EXPLAIN output, we verified that this is partially due to the following. Given an access constraint $R(X \rightarrow Y, N)$, evalQP fetches only distinct values of the relevant XY attributes, but evalDBMS fetches entire tuples with irrelevant attributes of R, although those attributes are not needed for answering Q at all, no matter what indices are provided. This led to duplicated (X, Y) values when X is not a key, and the duplication got rapidly inflated by joins, *e.g.,* EXPLAIN output shows that MySQL consistently accesses entire tables when there are non-key attributes.

(2) Impact of Q. To evaluate the impact of queries, we varied #-sel of Q from 4 to 9, #-join from 0 to 5 and #-unidiff of set operators (union and set-difference) from 0 to 5, while keeping the other factors unchanged.

The results are reported in Figures 5(b), 5(f), 5(j) for varying #-sel and Figures 5(c), 5(g), 5(k) for varying #-join. We find the following. (a) The complexity of Q has impacts on the query plans generated by QPlan. The larger #-sel or the smaller #-join is, the faster the query plans are, and the smaller data D_Q is accessed. This is because with more selections or fewer joins, our plans generated by QPlan took less steps to fetch all attribute values needed. (b) Algorithm evalQP scales well with #-sel and #-join. It found answers for largest Q within 89.5s, on the three full-size datasets. (c) Algorithm evalDBMS is almost indifferent to #-sel; in fact it only terminated within 3000s on extremely restricted (constant) selection queries, with at most one join on non-key attribute. But it is very sensitive to #-join: it did the best when #-join = 0, *i.e.,* if there is no join (or Cartesian product) at all; but it cannot finish the job within 3000s for queries with 2 joins on all three datasets.

Our query plans are indifferent to #-unidiff (hence the results are not shown). This is because our query plans fetch data via max SPC sub-queries, independent of the number of union and set-difference operations in the queries. We do not report the results of evalDBMS since it did not complete its computation within 3000s on all three datasets.

(3) Impact of $\|\mathcal{A}\|$. To evaluate the impact of access constraints, we varied $\|\mathcal{A}\|$ with scale factors from 0.2 to 1 in 0.2 increments, and tested the queries that are covered. Accordingly we varied the indices used by evalDBMS. We report $P(D_Q)$ and run time of evalQP. As shown in Figures 5(d), 5(h) and 5(l), (a) more constraints help QPlan generate better query plans, as expected. For example, when all access constraints were used, evalQP took 5.8s, 8.5s and 6.3s for queries on AIRCA, TFACC and MCBM, respectively, while they took 10.2s, 20.1s and 9.6s given 20% of the constraints. (b) The more access constraints are used, the smaller $|D_Q|$ is, as QPlan can find better plans given more options. (c) Algorithm evalDBMS did not produce results in any test within 3000s, even given the indices in full-size $\mathcal{A}$ of constraints.

(III) Effectiveness of minA. We also evaluated the effectiveness of minA for minimizing access schemas by comparing evalQP and evalQP$^-$. As reported in Figures 5(a), 5(e) and 5(i), (1) minA helps QPlan generate query plans that access less data; indeed, evalQP accessed much smaller D_Q than evalQP$^-$ in most cases; for example, $P(D_Q)$ is 0.0037% for evalQP on full-size TFACC, while it is 0.0051% for evalQP$^-$; and (2) minA also enables query plans to use indices of smaller size (*i.e.,* index relations; not shown). For example, on full-size TFACC, evalQP used index no larger than 2.1% of the size of D while it was 3.3% for evalQP$^-$.

(IV) Size and creation time of indices. The total indices for all access constraints are of 7.7GB, 3.6GB and 9.5GB, accounting for 12.8%, 16.8% and 10.6% of $|D|$. They are smaller than the bound estimated in Section 7, since many constraints use attributes with small domains. They took 3.1, 2.2 and 4.2 hours to build offline for AIRCA, TFACC and MCBM, respectively, and were used to answer all queries.

Exp-2: Efficiency. The second set of experiments evaluated the efficiency of our algorithms ChkCov, QPlan, minA, minA$_{\mathsf{DAG}}$ and minA$_{\mathsf{E}}$ on queries and access schemas for each of AIRCA, TFACC and MCBM. We found that ChkCov, QPlan, minA, minA$_{\mathsf{DAG}}$ and minA$_{\mathsf{E}}$ took at most 65ms, 199ms, 86ms, 84 ms and 74 ms, respectively, for all queries on three datasets, with all the access constraints.

Summary. From the experiments we find the following. (1) Covered queries give us a practical effective syntax for boundedly evaluable RA queries. Over 80% of boundedly evaluable queries are covered. (2) Bounded evaluability is promising for querying large datasets. Indeed, (a) it is easy to find access constraints from real-life data, and many queries are covered under a small number of such constraints; and (b) for covered queries, the evaluation time and the amount of data accessed are *independent of* the size of the underlying dataset. As a result, on a real-life dataset of 60GB, evalQP answers queries in 5.9 seconds by accessing at most 0.00017% of the data on average, while evalDBMS is unable to find answers within 3000 seconds even on a dataset of 3.75 GB, with even more indices than evalQP can use. The performance gap between evalQP and evalDBMS gets bigger on larger datasets. (3) The size of the indices needed is 13.4% of $|D|$ on average. (4) Our algorithms are efficient: they take at most 0.2 second in all cases tested.

9. CONCLUSION

We have answered an open question about the bounded evaluability of RA. Our solution consists of both fundamental results and practical algorithms. Our experimental results have shown that it is promising to make practical use of bounded evaluability. Indeed, a large number of RA queries are covered, and covered queries can be efficiently evaluated without worrying about the size of the underlying datasets.

One topic for future work is to develop algorithms for discovering a (minimum) set of access constraints to cover a workload. While an approach is outlined in Section 7, the topic needs a full treatment. Another topic is to develop algorithms that, when a query is not boundedly evaluable, compute its approximate answers with provable accuracy bound, by accessing only a small fraction of data.

Acknowledgments. Fan and Cao are supported in part by 973 Program 2014CB340302 and 2012CB316200, NSFC 61421003 and 61133002, ERC 652976, EPSRC EP/J015377/1 and EP/M025268/1, NSF III 1302212, Shenzhen Peacock Program 1105100030834361, Guangdong Innovative Research Team Program 2011D005. Shenzhen Science and Technology Fund JCYJ20150529164656096 and Guangdong Applied R&D Program 2015B010131006.

10. REFERENCES

[1] *http://data.gov.uk/dataset/naptan.*

[2] *http://data.gov.uk/dataset/road-accidents-safety-data.*

[3] *www.transtats.bts.gov/DatabaseInfo.asp?DB_ID=110.*

[4] *www.transtats.bts.gov/DatabaseInfo.asp?DB_ID=120.*

[5] S. Abiteboul, R. Hull, and V. Vianu. *Foundations of Databases.* Addison-Wesley, 1995.

[6] M. Armbrust, K. Curtis, T. Kraska, A. Fox, M. J. Franklin, and D. A. Patterson. PIQL: Success-tolerant query processing in the cloud. *PVLDB*, 5(3), 2011.

[7] M. Armbrust, A. Fox, D. A. Patterson, N. Lanham, B. Trushkowsky, J. Trutna, and H. Oh. SCADS: Scale-independent storage for social computing applications. In *CIDR*, 2009.

[8] G. Ausiello, P. Crescenzi, G. Gambosi, V. Kann, A. Marchetti-Spaccamela, and M. Protasi. *Complexity and Approximation,Combinatorial optimization problems and their approximability properties.* Springer, 1999.

[9] G. Ausiello, P. G. Franciosa, and D. Frigioni. Directed hypergraphs: Problems, algorithmic results, and a novel decremental approach. In *ICTCS*, 2001.

[10] M. Benedikt, P. Bourhis, and C. Ley. Analysis of schemas with access restrictions. *TODS*, 40(1):5, 2015.

[11] M. Benedikt, J. Leblay, and E. Tsamoura. Querying with access patterns and integrity constraints. *PVLDB*, 8(6), 2015.

[12] A. Calì and D. Martinenghi. Querying data under access limitations. In *ICDE*, 2008.

[13] Y. Cao, W. Fan, J. Huai, and R. Huang. Making pattern queries bounded in big graphs. In *ICDE*, 2015.

[14] Y. Cao, W. Fan, and W. Yu. Bounded conjunctive queries. *PVLDB*, 2014.

[15] M. Charikar, C. Chekuri, T. Cheung, Z. Dai, A. Goel, S. Guha, and M. Li. Approximation algorithms for directed steiner problems. In *SODA*, 1998.

[16] Facebook, 2013. *http://newsroom.fb.com.*

[17] Facebook. Introducing graph search. *https://en-gb.facebook.com/about/graphsearch*, 2013.

[18] W. Fan, F. Geerts, Y. Cao, T. Deng, and P. Lu. Querying big data by accessing small data. In *PODS*, 2015.

[19] W. Fan, F. Geerts, and L. Libkin. On scale independence for querying big data. In *PODS*, 2014.

[20] A. V. Gelder and R. W. Topor. Safety and translation of relational calculus queries. *TODS*, 16(2), 1991.

[21] I. Grujic, S. Bogdanovic-Dinic, and L. Stoimenov. Collecting and analyzing data from e-government facebook pages. In *ICT Innovations*, 2014.

[22] A. Gubichev and T. Neumann. Exploiting the query structure for efficient join ordering in SPARQL queries. In *EDBT*, 2014.

[23] Y. Huhtala, J. Kärkk ainen, P. Porkka, and H. Toivonen. TANE: An efficient algorithm for discovering functional and approximate dependencies. *Comput. J.*, 42(2):100–111, 1999.

[24] I. Ileana, B. Cautis, A. Deutsch, and Y. Katsis. Complete yet practical search for minimal query reformulations under constraints. In *SIGMOD*, pages 1015–1026, 2014.

[25] C. Li. Computing complete answers to queries in the presence of limited access patterns. *VLDB J.*, 12(3), 2003.

[26] J. Liu, J. Li, C. Liu, and Y. Chen. Discover dependencies from data - A review. *TKDE*, 24(2), 2012.

[27] G. Moerkotte, P. Fender, and M. Eich. On the correct and complete enumeration of the core search space. In *SIGMOD*, 2013.

[28] A. Nash and B. Ludäscher. Processing first-order queries under limited access patterns. In *PODS*, 2004.

[29] C. H. Papadimitriou. *Computational Complexity.* Addison-Wesley, 1994.

[30] L. Popa. Object/relational query optimization with chase and backchase. *IRCS Technical Reports Series*, 2001.

[31] R. Ramakrishnan and J. Gehrke. *Database management systems.* McGraw Hill, 2000.

[32] A. P. Stolboushkin and M. A. Taitslin. Finite queries do not have effective syntax. In *PODS*, 1995.

[33] R. R. Stoll. Set theory and logic. *W. H. Freeman and Co., San Francisco, Calif.-London*, 1961.

[34] J. D. Ullman. *Principles of Database Systems, 2nd Edition.* Computer Science Press, 1982.

[35] J. D. Ullman. *Principles of Database and Knowledge-Base Systems, Volume I.* Computer Science Press, 1988.

APPENDIX A: Formal Definitions

Query plans (Section 2)

We define a *query plan ξ for Q under $\mathcal{A}$* as a sequence:

$$\xi(Q, \mathcal{R}) : T_1 = \delta_1, \ldots, T_n = \delta_n,$$

such that (1) for all instances D of $\mathcal{R}$, $T_n = Q(D)$; and (2) for all $i \in [1, n]$, δ_i is one of the following:

- $\{a\}$, where a is a constant in Q; or
- $\mathsf{fetch}(X \in T_j, R, Y)$, where $j < i$, and T_j has attributes X; for each $\bar{a} \in T_j(D)$, it retrieves $D_{XY}(X = \bar{a})$ from D, and returns $\bigcup_{\bar{a} \in T_j(D)} D_{XY}(X = \bar{a})$; or
- $\pi_Y(T_j)$ or $\sigma_C(T_j)$, for $j < i$, a set Y of attributes in T_j, and Boolean condition C defined on T_j; or
- $T_i \times T_k$, $T_j \cup T_k$ or $T_j \setminus T_k$, for $j < i$ and $k < i$.

We denote T_n by $\xi(D)$, as *the result of applying ξ to D*.

Canonical bounded query plans (Section 5.1).

Fetching plan ξ^{c}_F: A fetching plan ξ^{c}_F is a sequence of *unit fetching plans* $\xi^{\mathsf{c}}_F(A_1)$, ..., $\xi^{\mathsf{c}}_F(A_m)$, for all attributes A_1, ..., A_m in X_Q of Q, where $\xi^{\mathsf{c}}_F(A_i)$ is inductively defined as follows (assuming A_i is in a max SPC sub-query Q_s of Q):

(i) if $A_i \in X^{Q_s}_C$, then $\xi^{\mathsf{c}}_F(A_i)$ is $\{c\}$, where $\sigma_{A_i = c}$ is in Q_s;

(ii) if $\sigma_{A_i = A'}$ is in Q_s and there exists a unit fetching plan $\xi^{\mathsf{c}}_F(A')$ for A', then $\xi^{\mathsf{c}}_F(A_i) = \xi^{\mathsf{c}}_F(A')$; and

(iii) if there exists a constraint $R(W \to U, N)$ in $\mathcal{A}$ such that $A_i \in R[U]$, and moreover, if for each $w_i \in R[W] = \{w_1, \ldots, w_m\}$, there exists a unit fetching plan $\xi^{\mathsf{c}}_F(w_i)$ for w_i, then $\xi^{\mathsf{c}}_F(A_i)$ is:

- $T_1 = \xi_F^c(w_1)$, ..., $T_m = \xi_F^c(w_m)$,
- $T_{m+1} = T_1 \times \cdots \times T_m$,
- $T_{m+2} = \mathsf{fetch}(X \in T_{m+1}, R, U)$,
- $T_{m+3} = \pi_{A_i}(T_{m+2})$.

Indexing plan ξ_I^c. An indexing plan ξ_I^c is a sequence of *unit indexing plans* $\xi_I^c(S_1)$, ..., $\xi_I^c(S_m)$ for all relations S_1, ..., S_m in Q. For each S_i, let Q_s be the max SPC sub-query in which S_i occurs, $X_{Q_s}^{S_i} = \{A_1, \ldots, A_K\}$ be the set of attributes of S_i that also occur in X_{Q_s}, and $S_i(X \to Y, N)$ be a constraint in $\mathcal{A}$ that indexes S_i. Then $\xi_I^c(S_i)$ is as follows:

- $T_1 = \xi_F^c(A_1)$, ..., $T_K = \xi_F^c(A_K)$,
- $T_{K+1} = T_1 \times \cdots \times T_K$,
- $T_{K+2} = \pi_{S_i[X]}(T_{K+1})$,
- $T_{K+3} = \mathsf{fetch}(X \in T_{K+2}, S_i, Y)$, and
- $T_{K+4} = T_{K+1} \cap T_{K+3}$ (expressed in terms of $\times$, σ, π).

That is, ξ_I^c ensures that each S_i in Q is indexed.

$\langle Q, \mathcal{A}\rangle$-hypergraph $\mathcal{G}_{Q,\mathcal{A}}$ (Section 5.2)

Given an RA query Q and an access schema $\mathcal{A}$, we use a hypergraph to encode the induced FDs for all max SPC sub-queries of Q. Let $\Sigma_{Q,\mathcal{A}}$ be the union of $\Sigma_{Q_s,\mathcal{A}}$ (the set of induced FDs for Q_s and $\mathcal{A}$) for all max SPC sub-queries Q_s in Q. We assume *w.l.o.g.* that for any two max SPC sub-queries Q_s and $Q_{s'}$ of Q, $\Sigma_{Q_s,\mathcal{A}} \cap \Sigma_{Q_{s'},\mathcal{A}} = \emptyset$. A $\langle Q, \mathcal{A}\rangle$-*hypergraph* (or simply hypergraph) $\mathcal{G}_{Q,\mathcal{A}}$ for Q and $\mathcal{A}$ is a directed hypergraph (V, E) derived from $\Sigma_{Q,\mathcal{A}}$ as follows.

(1) For each induced FD $X \to Y$ in $\Sigma_{Q,\mathcal{A}}$, with $X = \{x_1, \ldots, x_p\} (p \geq 1)$ and $Y \setminus X = \{y_1, \ldots, y_q\} (q \geq 1)$, there are $p + q + 1$ nodes u_{x_1}, ..., u_{x_p}, u_{y_1}, ..., u_{y_q} and u_Y in V to encode x_1, ..., x_p, y_1, ... y_q and the set Y, respectively, and there exist $q + 1$ hyperedges $e_1 = (\{u_{x_1}, \ldots, u_{x_p}\}, u_Y)$, $e_2 = (\{u_Y\}, u_{y_1})$, ..., $e_{q+1} = (\{u_Y\}, u_{y_q})$ in E.

(2) There is a dummy node r such that for each induced FD $\emptyset \to Y$ in $\Sigma_{Q,\mathcal{A}}$ with $Y = \{y_1, \ldots, y_q\}$ $(q \geq 1)$, there exist $q + 1$ nodes u_Y, u_{y_1}, ..., u_{y_q} in V and $q + 1$ hyperedges $(\{r\}, u_Y)$, $(\{u_Y\}, u_{y_1})$, ..., $(\{u_Y\}, u_{y_q})$ in E.

(3) For each attribute A in $\hat{X}_C^Q = \{\rho_U(A) \mid A \in X_C^{Q_s}$, Q_s is a max SPC sub-query of $Q\}$, there exist a node u_A in V and a hyperedge $(\{r\}, u_A)$ in E.

Weighted $\langle Q, \mathcal{A}\rangle$-hypergraph (Section 6.2).

For an RA query Q and an access schema $\mathcal{A}$, the *weighted $\langle Q, \mathcal{A}\rangle$-hypergraph* is a pair $(\mathcal{G}_{Q,\mathcal{A}}, w(\cdot))$, where $\mathcal{G}_{Q,\mathcal{A}} = (V, E)$ is the $\langle Q, \mathcal{A}\rangle$-hypergraph for Q and $\mathcal{A}$, and $w(\cdot) : E \to \mathbb{N}^+$ assigns an natural number $w(e)$ to each hyperedge e in E. More specifically, $w(\cdot)$ is defined as follows. Recall the definition of $\mathcal{G}_{Q,\mathcal{A}}$ given above. For each induced FD $X \to Y$ in $\Sigma_{Q,\mathcal{A}}$ with $X = \{x_1, \ldots, x_p\}$ and $Y \setminus X = \{y_1, \ldots, y_q\}$, suppose that $X \to Y$ is derived from $R(X \to Y, N)$ in $\mathcal{A}$. Then

(i) $w(e_1) = N$, where e_1 is the hyperedge $(\{u_{x_1}, \ldots, u_{x_p}\}, u_Y)$ in $\mathcal{G}_{Q,\mathcal{A}}$ *w.r.t.* $X \to Y$;

(ii) $w(e_2) = \ldots = w(e_{q+1}) = 0$, for $e_2 = (\{u_Y\}, u_{y_1})$, ..., $e_{q+1} = (\{u_Y\}, u_{y_q})$; and

(iii) $w(\{r\}, u_A) = 0$ for all hyperedges emanating from the dummy node r of $\mathcal{G}_{Q,\mathcal{A}}$.

APPENDIX B: Proofs

Proof sketch of Theorem 2(1)

It suffices to show that for any boundedly evaluable query plan ξ under $\mathcal{A}$, there exists a covered RA query Q_ξ such that $Q_\xi \equiv_{\mathcal{A}} \xi$, *i.e.*, $Q_\xi(D) = \xi(D)$ for any $D \models \mathcal{A}$. We show this in two steps. We first rewrite ξ into an equivalent RA query Q' by replacing every $\mathsf{fetch}(X \in T_j, R, Y)$ with $\pi_{S[XY]}\sigma_{Y_{Q_j}=S[X]}(Q_j \times R(X, Y, Z))$, where Q_j is the rewriting of the first j operations $T_1 = \delta_1$, ..., $T_j = \delta_j$ of ξ, and Y_{Q_j} is the set of attributes of the output relation of Q_j. We then show by induction on the length of Q_ξ that Q_ξ can be transformed into an equivalent Q'_ξ that is covered by $\mathcal{A}$, by equivalence-preserving rewriting laws of set algebra [33]. □

Proof of Lemma 4

Since $\Sigma_{Q_s,\mathcal{A}} \models \hat{X}_C^{Q_s} \to \hat{X}_{Q_s}$ iff $\hat{X}_{Q_s} \subseteq (\hat{X}_C^{Q_s})^*$ (cf. [5]), to show that Q_s is fetchable via $\mathcal{A}$ iff $\Sigma_{Q_s,\mathcal{A}} \models \hat{X}_C^{Q_s} \to \hat{X}_{Q_s}$, we just need to show that $X_{Q_s} \subseteq \mathsf{cov}(Q_s, \mathcal{A})$ iff $\hat{X}_{Q_s} \subseteq (\hat{X}_C^{Q_s})^*$, where $(\hat{X}_C^{Q_s})^*$ is the FD closure of $\hat{X}_C^{Q_s}$ under $\Sigma_{Q_s,\mathcal{A}}$. We prove this by showing the following:

(1) $X_{Q_s} \subseteq \mathsf{cov}(Q_s, \mathcal{A})$ iff $\rho_U(X_{Q_s}) \subseteq \rho_U(\mathsf{cov}(Q_s, \mathcal{A}))$; and

(2) $\rho_U(\mathsf{cov}(Q_s, \mathcal{A})) = (\rho_U(X_C^{Q_s}))^*$ (recall $\rho_U(X) = \hat{X}$).

Here (1) can be prove by contradiction based on the definitions. We prove (2) below. We first define a chasing procedure that computes $\mathsf{cov}(Q_s, \mathcal{A})$ for any SPC query Q_s under $\mathcal{A}$. Based on it we then show $\rho_U(\mathsf{cov}(Q_s, \mathcal{A})) = (\rho_U(X_C^{Q_s}))^*$.

A chasing sequence of $\mathsf{cov}(Q_s, \mathcal{A})$ for Q_s is defined as

$$\mathsf{cov}(Q_s, \mathcal{A}) = \mathsf{cov}_0(Q_s, \mathcal{A}), \ldots, \mathsf{cov}_n(Q_s, \mathcal{A}),$$

such that (1) $\mathsf{cov}_0(Q_s, \mathcal{A}) = X_C^{Q_s}$, and (2) for each $i \geq 0$, $\mathsf{cov}_{i+1}(Q_s, \mathcal{A})$ is obtained by applying some rules given in the definition of coverage $\mathsf{cov}(Q, \mathcal{A})$ so that $\mathsf{cov}_i(Q_s, \mathcal{A}) \neq \mathsf{cov}_{i+1}(Q_s, \mathcal{A})$. Obviously such a chasing sequence is terminal; moreover, by the definition of $\mathsf{cov}(Q_s, \mathcal{A})$, the result $\mathsf{cov}_n(Q_s, \mathcal{A})$ of the chasing sequence (the last element) is exactly $\mathsf{cov}(Q_s, \mathcal{A})$ for Q_s and $\mathcal{A}$. One can show $\rho_U(\mathsf{cov}(Q_s, \mathcal{A})) = (\rho_U(\mathsf{cov}_0(Q_s, \mathcal{A})))^*$ (thus $= (\rho_U(X_C^{Q_s}))^*$) by induction on the length n of the chase. □

Proof of Lemma 6

By the definition of indexed queries, Q is indexed by $\mathcal{A}$ iff Q has an indexing plan. Below we show that Q is fetchable via $\mathcal{A}$ iff Q has a fetching plan under $\mathcal{A}$.

[$\Rightarrow$] Assume that Q is fetchable via $\mathcal{A}$. Then each max SPC sub-query Q_s is fetchable via $\mathcal{A}$, *i.e.*, $X_{Q_s} \subseteq \mathsf{cov}(Q_s, \mathcal{A})$. Thus for each attribute $A \in X_{Q_s}$, $A \in \mathsf{cov}(Q_s, \mathcal{A})$. Consider the chasing sequence $\mathsf{cov}(Q_s, \mathcal{A}) = \mathsf{cov}_0(Q_s, \mathcal{A})$, ..., $\mathsf{cov}_n(Q_s, \mathcal{A})$ described in the proof of Lemma 4, where $\mathsf{cov}_0(Q_s, \mathcal{A}) = X_C^{Q_s}$ and $\mathsf{cov}_n(Q_s, \mathcal{A}) = \mathsf{cov}(Q_s, \mathcal{A})$. There must exist $i \in [0, n]$ such that $A \in \mathsf{cov}_i(Q_s, \mathcal{A})$ but $A \notin \mathsf{cov}_{i-1}(Q_s, \mathcal{A})$ (if exists). We refer to $\mathsf{cov}_0(Q_s, \mathcal{A})$, ..., $\mathsf{cov}_i(Q_s, \mathcal{A})$ as the *deduced chasing* for attribute A. One can verify that there exists a unit fetching plan for A under $\mathcal{A}$ by induction on the length of the deduced chasing for A.

[$\Leftarrow$] This direction can be readily verified by induction on the length of $\xi_F^c(A)$, by the definitions of unit fetching plans and fetchable queries, similar to above. □

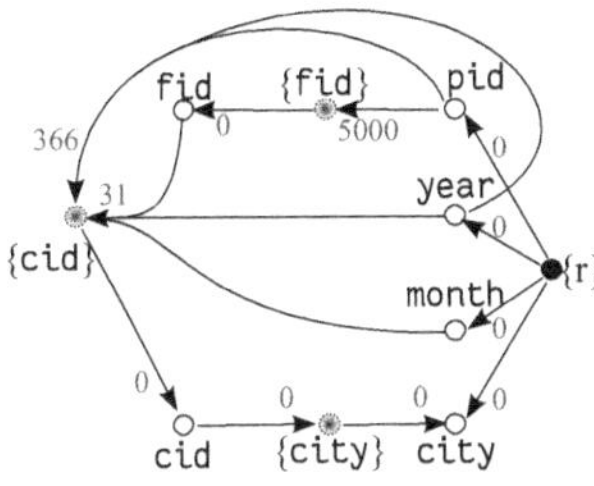

Figure 7: Weighted $\mathcal{G}_{Q_1,\mathcal{A}_1}$ for Q_1 and $\mathcal{A}_1$

Proof of Lemma 7

This is verified by giving translation algorithms Γ_ξ from $\xi^c(A)$ to $(\{r\}, u_{\rho_U(A)})$, and Γ_r from $(\{r\}, u_{\rho_U(A)})$ to $\xi^c(A)$. Below we outline Γ_r, which will be used later in our algorithm. Given a hyperpath $\Pi_{\{r\},u_A}$ from $\{r\}$ to u_A, Γ_r inductively generates fetching plans as follows: (a) if $\Pi_{\{r\},u_A}$ is a hyperedge $(\{r\}, u_A)$ constructed in case (3) of $\langle Q, \mathcal{A}\rangle$-hypergraph above, then return $T_1 = \{\mathsf{c}\}$; (b) if $\Pi_{\{r\},u_A}$ is a hyperedge $(\{r\}, u_Y)$ constructed in case (2) for induced FD $\emptyset \to Y$, then return $T_1 = \xi^c_F(A')$; and (c) if the last hyperedge of $\Pi_{\{r\},u_A}$ is a hyperedge (V_Y, u_A) constructed in case (1) of $\langle Q, \mathcal{A}\rangle$-hypergraph, and if for each u_{B_i} in $V_S = \{u_{Y_1}, \ldots, u_{Y_p}\}$, the unit fetching plan translated from hyperpath $\Pi_{\{r\},u_Y}$ is $\xi^c_F(Y_i)$, then return $T_1 = \xi^c_F(Y_1), \ldots, T_p = \xi^c_F(Y_p)$, $T_{p+1} = T_1 \times \cdots \times T_p$, $T_{p+2} = \mathsf{fetch}(X \in T_{p+1}, R, Y)$, and $T_{p+3} = \pi_A(T_{p+3})$. □

Proof of Theorem 9

(1) For $\mathsf{dAMP}(Q, \mathcal{A}, K)$, we give an NP algorithm that guess $\mathcal{A}_m$ and checks whether Q is covered by $\mathcal{A}_m$ in PTIME. The lower bound follows from (3) below.

(2) We show the approximation-hardness of $\mathsf{oAMP}(Q, \mathcal{A})$ by L-reduction from the MINIMUM SET COVER problem [29].

(3) We show that $\mathsf{dAMP}(Q, \mathcal{A}, K)$ is NP-hard for both special cases by reduction from the VERTEX COVER problem, which is NP-complete (cf. [29]). We show the approximation-hardness of the special cases by AP-reduction from the MINIMUM SET COVER problem, which is not in APX [8]. □

Proof of Lemma 11

We prove Lemma 11 by showing step (c) of algorithm $\mathsf{minA_E}$ maps feasible solutions to dminSAP with approximation ratio c to feasible solutions to oAMP with approximation ratio $c+1$ in the elementary case. This can be verified along the same lines as the performance bound analysis of $\mathsf{minA_{DAG}}$ outlined in Section 6.2, and the analysis of approximation bound of algorithm $\mathsf{minA_{DAG}}$ in Appendix D below. □

APPENDIX C: Examples

Example 6 (Section 4). Given Q_0 and $\mathcal{A}_0$ of Example 1, algorithm CovChk examines the max SPC sub-queries Q_1 and Q_2 of Q_0, and finds that Q_1 is covered by $\mathcal{A}_0$ while Q_2 is not. It first computes the set $\Sigma_{Q_1,\mathcal{A}_0}$ of induced FDs from Q_1 and $\mathcal{A}_0$ (see Example 5), with $\hat{X}_{Q_1} = \{\mathsf{pid}, \mathsf{fid}, \mathsf{cid}, \mathsf{year}, \mathsf{month}, \mathsf{city}\}$ and $\hat{X}^{Q_1}_C = \{\mathsf{pid}, \mathsf{year}, \mathsf{month}, \mathsf{city}\}$. It verifies that Q_1 is covered by $\mathcal{A}_0$ since $\Sigma_{Q_1,\mathcal{A}_0} \models \hat{X}^{Q_1}_C \to \hat{X}_{Q_1}$, and Q_1 is indexed by $\mathcal{A}$ (see Example 4). Along the same lines, it finds that Q_2 is not covered, and concludes that Q_0 is not covered. In contrast, it finds that max SPC sub-queries Q_1 and Q_3 of Q_0' are both covered by $\mathcal{A}_0$, and thus so is Q_0'. □

Example 7 (Section 5). For Q_0' and $\mathcal{A}_0$ of Example 1, its $\langle Q, \mathcal{A}\rangle$-hypergraph $\mathcal{G}_{Q_0',\mathcal{A}_0}$ is depicted in Fig. 2, after the following conversions. We write $Q_0' = Q_1 - Q_3$ ($Q_3 = Q_1(\mathsf{cid}) \bowtie_{\mathsf{cid}=\mathsf{cid}'} Q_2(\mathsf{cid}')$) in the normal form of Section 2 such that it keeps relation names of Q_1 unchanged, and renames (a) each relation S in sub-query $Q_1(\mathsf{cid})$ of Q_3 to S' (*e.g.*, dine of $Q_1(\mathsf{cid})$ in Q_3 is renamed to dine$'$), and (b) each relation S in sub-query $Q_2(\mathsf{cid}')$ of Q_3 to S'' (*e.g.*, dine of $Q_2(\mathsf{cid})$ in Q_3 to dine$''$). In Fig. 2, we extend the unification function ρ_U given in Example 5. (a) For each attribute $S'[A]$ that occurs in sub-query $Q_1(\mathsf{cid}')$ of Q_3, if $\rho_U(S[A]) = A$ in Q_1, then $\rho_U(S'[A]) = A'$ for $Q_1(\mathsf{cid}')$ in Q_3. (b) For sub-query $Q_2(\mathsf{cid})$ of Q_3, $\rho_U(\mathsf{dine}''[\mathsf{pid}]) = \mathsf{pid}''$, $\rho_U(\mathsf{dine}''[\mathsf{cid}]) = \mathsf{cid}'$, $\rho_U(\mathsf{dine}''[\mathsf{month}]) = \mathsf{month}''$ and $\rho_U(\mathsf{dine}''[\mathsf{year}]) = \mathsf{year}''$. □

Example 8 (Section 5). A complete fetching plan for Q_0' under $\mathcal{A}_0$ is as follows.

$T_1 = \{p_0\}$ $(\xi^c_F(\mathsf{pid}))$,
$T_2 = \mathsf{fetch}(X \in T_1, \mathsf{friend}, \mathsf{fid})$;
$T_3 = \pi_{\mathsf{fid}}(T_2)$ $(\xi^c_F(\mathsf{fid})$;
$T_4 = \{2015\}$ $(\xi^c_F(\mathsf{year}))$;
$T_5 = \{\text{MAY}\}$ $(\xi^c_F(\mathsf{month})$;
$T_6 = T_3 \times T_4$;
$T_7 = T_6 \times T_5$;
$T_8 = \mathsf{fetch}(X \in T_7, \mathsf{dine}, \mathsf{cid})$;
$T_9 = \pi_{\mathsf{cid}}(T_8)$ $(\xi^c_F(\mathsf{cid}))$;
$T_{10} = \{\text{NYC}\}$ $(\xi^c_F(\mathsf{city}))$;
$T_{11}, \ldots, T_{20}$; $T_{21} = \{p_0\}$ $(\xi^c_F(\mathsf{pid}''))$.

Here T_{11} - T_{20} are unit fetching plans for attributes in Q_3, and are the same as T_1 - T_{10} *w.r.t.* attribute renaming.

An indexing plan $\xi^c_I(\mathsf{dine}'')$ for relation dine$''$ is:

$T^I_1 = T_{19}$;
$T^I_2 = T_{20}$;
$T^I_3 = T_{19} \times T_{20}$;
$T^I_4 = \mathsf{fetch}(X \in T^I_3, \mathsf{dine}, (\mathsf{pid}, \mathsf{cid}))$;

similar for other relations. Finally, an evaluation plan for Q_0' under $\mathcal{A}_0$ is exactly Q_0' with each relation name S replaced by the T_S with $T_S = \xi^c_I(S)$. □

Example 9 (Section 6). For $\mathsf{AMP}(Q_1, \mathcal{A}_1)$, algorithm minA works as follows. It first finds that either ψ_2 and ψ_3, or ψ_3 and ψ_5 can be removed from $\mathcal{A}_1$ while keeping Q_1 covered. It then calculates $w(\psi_2) = \frac{c_1 \cdot 31}{c_2 \cdot 1}$ and $w(\psi_5) = \frac{c_1 \cdot 366}{c_2 \cdot 1}$. Suppose that $c_1 = c_2 = 1$. Then minA greedily picks ψ_5 instead of ψ_2. It finds that no more constraints can be removed while keeping Q_1 covered. Thus minA returns $\mathcal{A}_m = \{\psi_1\ \psi_2,\ \psi_4\}$. □

Example 10 (Section 6). The complete weighted $\langle Q, \mathcal{A}\rangle$-hypergraph $\mathcal{G}_{Q_1,\mathcal{A}_1}$ for Q_1 and $\mathcal{A}_1$ is shown in Fig. 7. □

APPENDIX D: Algorithm Analysis

Complexity of algorithm CovChk (Section 4)

We next show that CovChk can be implemented in $O(|Q|^2 + |\mathcal{A}|)$ time. (1) It takes $O(|Q|)$ time to compute the set $\mathcal{S}_Q$

of all max SPC sub-queries of Q. (2) Checking whether all Q_s's in $\mathcal{S}_Q$ are indexed by $\mathcal{A}$ can be implemented in $O(|Q| + |\mathcal{A}|)$ time, by building an index from relations in Q to constraints of $\mathcal{A}$ in $O(|Q|+|\mathcal{A}|)$ time before the iteration. (3) It takes $O(|Q_s|^2)$ time to construct induced FDs $\Sigma_{Q_s,\mathcal{A}}$, and the size of $\Sigma_{Q_s,\mathcal{A}}$ is bounded by $|\mathcal{A}_{Q_s}|$ for each Q_s. (4) FD implication checking can be done in linear time (cf. [5]), *i.e.*, $O(|\Sigma_{Q_s,\mathcal{A}}|+|X_C^{Q_s}|+|X_{Q_s}|) = O(|\mathcal{A}_{Q_s}|+|Q_s|)$ for each Q_s. Putting these together, CovChk is in $O(|Q|^2+|\mathcal{A}|)$ time.

Complexity of Algorithm QPlan (Section 5)

Algorithm QPlan can be implemented in $O(|Q|(|Q| + |\mathcal{A}|))$ time. Indeed, (1) constructing the $\langle Q, \mathcal{A}\rangle$-hypergraph $G_{Q,\mathcal{A}}$ takes $O(|Q| + |\mathcal{A}|)$ time. (2) In each iteration (lines 3-6), findHP takes $O(|Q| + |\mathcal{A}|)$ time to find hyperpath $\Pi_{\{r\},u_{\hat{A}}}$ (cf. [9]), and transQP takes $O(|\Pi_{\{r\},u_{\hat{A}}}|) = O(\|\mathcal{A}\|)$ time to translate P into a unit fetching plan, where $\|\mathcal{A}\|$ denotes the cardinality of $\mathcal{A}$. There are no more than $|Q|$ iterations. (3) Indexing plan generation takes $O(|Q|)$ time in total. (4) The size of the evaluation plan is bounded by $|Q|$. Putting these together, QPlan takes $O(|Q|+|\mathcal{A}|) + O(|Q|(|Q|+|\mathcal{A}|+\|\mathcal{A}\|))$ $+ O(|Q|) + O(|Q|) = O(|Q|(|Q| + |\mathcal{A}|))$ time in total.

Algorithm transQP (Section 5.2)

It is the translation algorithm Γ_r given in the proof of Lemma 7 in Appendix B.

Complexity of Algorithm minA (Section 6.2)

Algorithm minA can be implemented in $O(|Q|^2+\|\mathcal{A}\|^2(|Q|+|\mathcal{A}|))$ time. Indeed, (1) it takes $O(|Q|^2 + |\mathcal{A}|)$ time to construct $\Sigma_{Q,\mathcal{A}}$; (2) it iterates at most $\|\mathcal{A}\|$ times; and (3) in each iteration, it takes $O(\|\mathcal{A}\| \cdot |\Sigma_{Q,\mathcal{A}}|) = O(\|\mathcal{A}\|(|Q| + |\mathcal{A}|))$ time to update the scores of all constraints in $\mathcal{A}$ and check whether removing each of them will make Q not covered.

Approximation bound of Algorithm minA$_{\text{DAG}}$ (Section 6.2).

Let $c(\mathcal{A})$ denote the sum of the N's in all the constraints in $\mathcal{A}$. Let $\mathcal{A}'_I$ be the set of constraints in $\mathcal{A}'$ indexing a relation, and $\mathcal{A}'_{ni}$ be all the other constraints. Let $\mathcal{A}^{OPT}$ be the optimal solution to AMS$(Q, \mathcal{A})$. We define $\mathcal{A}_I^{OPT}$ and $\mathcal{A}_{ni}^{OPT}$ analogous to $\mathcal{A}'_I$ and $\mathcal{A}'_{ni}$, respectively. One can verify that $\frac{c(\mathcal{A}')}{c(\mathcal{A}^{OPT})} = \frac{c(\mathcal{A}'_{ni})+c(\mathcal{A}'_I)}{c(\mathcal{A}_{ni}^{OPT})+c(\mathcal{A}_I^{OPT})} \leq \frac{k*c(\mathcal{A}_{ni}^{OPT})+c(\mathcal{A}'_I)}{c(\mathcal{A}_{ni}^{OPT})+c(\mathcal{A}_I^{OPT})} \leq$ $k + 1$, where $k = |\rho_U(X_Q) \setminus \rho_U(X)| \leq |X_Q \setminus X_C^Q|$.

Wander Join: Online Aggregation via Random Walks

Feifei Li [1], Bin Wu [2], Ke Yi [2], Zhuoyue Zhao [3]
[1]University of Utah, Salt Lake City, USA
[2]Hong Kong University of Science and Technology, Hong Kong, China
[3] Shanghai Jiao Tong University, Shanghai, China
lifeifei@cs.utah.edu {bwuac, yike}@cse.ust.hk zzy7896321@sjtu.edu.cn

ABSTRACT

Joins are expensive, and online aggregation over joins was proposed to mitigate the cost, which offers users a nice and flexible tradeoff between query efficiency and accuracy in a continuous, online fashion. However, the state-of-the-art approach, in both internal and external memory, is based on ripple join, which is still very expensive and even needs unrealistic assumptions (e.g., tuples in a table are stored in random order). This paper proposes a new approach, the *wander join* algorithm, to the online aggregation problem by performing random walks over the underlying join graph. We also design an optimizer that chooses the optimal plan for conducting the random walks without having to collect any statistics *a priori*. Compared with ripple join, wander join is particularly efficient for equality joins involving multiple tables, but also supports θ-joins. Selection predicates and group-by clauses can be handled as well. Extensive experiments using the TPC-H benchmark have demonstrated the superior performance of wander join over ripple join. In particular, we have integrated and tested wander join in the latest version of PostgreSQL, demonstrating its practicality in a full-fledged database system.

1. INTRODUCTION

Joins are often considered as the most central operation in relational databases, as well as the most costly one. For many of today's data-driven analytical tasks, users often need to pose ad hoc complex join queries involving multiple relational tables over gigabytes or even terabytes of data. The TPC-H benchmark, which is the industrial standard for decision-support data analytics, specifies 22 queries, 17 of which are joins, the most complex one involving 8 tables. For such complex join queries, even a leading commercial database system could take hours to process. This, unfortunately, is at odds with the low-latency requirement that users demand for interactive data analytics.

The research community has long realized the need for interactive data analysis and exploration, and in 1997, initialized a line of work known as "online aggregation" [19]. The observation is that such analytical queries do not really need a 100% accurate answer. It would be more desirable if the database could first quickly return an approximate answer with some form of quality guarantee (usually in the form of confidence intervals), while improving the accuracy as more time is spent. Then the user can stop the query processing as soon as the quality is acceptable. This will significantly improve the responsiveness of the system, and at the same time saves a lot of computing resources.

SIGMOD'16, June 26-July 01, 2016, San Francisco, CA, USA

DOI: http://dx.doi.org/10.1145/2882903.2915235

Unfortunately, despite of many nice research results and well cited papers on this topic, online aggregation has had limited practical impact—we are not aware of any full-fledged, publicly available database system that supports it. The "CONTROL" project at Informix [18] in year 2000 reportedly had implemented ripple join as an internal project, prior to its acquisition by IBM. But no open source or commercial implementation of the "CONTROL" project exists today. Central to this line of work is the ripple join algorithm [15]. Its basic idea is to repeatedly take samples from each table, and only perform the join on the sampled tuples. The result is then scaled up to serve as an estimation of the whole join. However, the ripple join algorithm (including its many variants) has two critical weaknesses: (1) Its performance crucially depends on the fraction of the randomly selected tuples that could actually join. However, we observe that this fraction is often exceedingly low, especially for equality joins (a.k.a. natural joins) involving multiple tables, while *all* queries in the TPC-H benchmark (thus arguably most joins used in practice) are natural joins. (2) It demands that the tuples in each table be stored in a random order.

This paper proposes a different approach, which we call *wander join*, to the online aggregation problem. Our basic idea is to not blindly take samples from each table and just hope that they could join, but make the process much more focused. Specifically, wander join takes a randomly sampled tuple only from one of the tables. After that, it conducts a random walk starting from that tuple. In every step of the random walk, only the "neighbors" of the already sampled tuples are considered, i.e., tuples in the unexplored tables that can actually join with them. Compared with the "blind search" of ripple join, this is more like a guided exploration, where we only look at portions of the data that can potentially lead to an actual join result. To summarize, we have made the following contributions:.

- We introduce a new approach called *wander join* to online aggregation for joins. The key idea is to model a join over k tables as a join graph, and then perform random walks in this graph. We show how the random

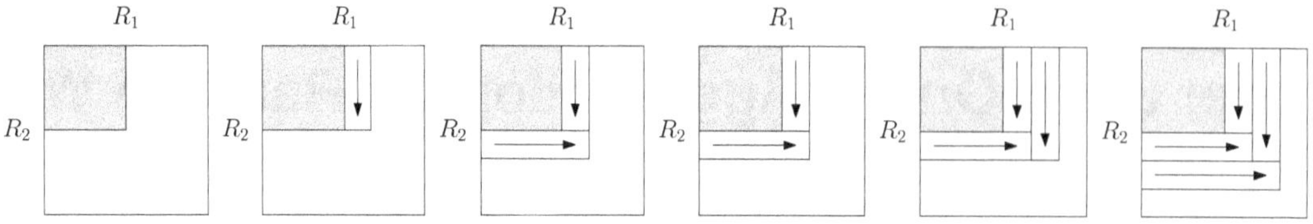

Figure 1: Illustration of the ripple join algorithm [15] on two tables R_1 and R_2.

walks lead to unbiased estimators for various aggregation functions, and give corresponding confidence interval formulas. We also show how this approach can handle selection and group-by clauses. These are presented in Section 3.

- It turns out that for the same join, there can be different ways to perform the random walks, which we call *walk plans*. We design an optimizer that chooses the optimal walk plan, without the need to collect any statistics of the data *a priori*. This is described in Section 4.
- We have conducted extensive experiments to compare wander join with ripple join [15] and its system implementation DBO [9,26]. The experimental setup and results are described in Section 5. The results show that wander join has outperformed ripple join and DBO by orders of magnitude in speed for achieving the same accuracy for in-memory data. When data exceeds main memory size, wander join and DBO initially have similar performance, but wander join eventually outperforms DBO on very large data sets.
- We have implemented wander join in PostgreSQL. On the TPC-H benchmark with tens of GBs of data, wander join is able to achieve 1% error with 95% confidence for most queries in a few seconds, whereas PostgreSQL may take minutes to return the exact results for the same queries.

Furthermore, we review the background of online aggregation, formulate the problem of online aggregation over joins, and summarize the ripple join algorithm in Section 2. Additional related work is surveyed in Section 6. The paper is concluded in Section 7 with remarks on a few directions for future work.

2. BACKGROUND, PROBLEM FORMULATION, AND RIPPLE JOIN

Online aggregation. The concept of online aggregation was first proposed in the classic work by Hellerstein et al. in the late 90's [19]. The idea is to provide approximate answers with error guarantees (in the form of confidence intervals) continuously during the query execution process, where the approximation quality improves gradually over time. Rather than having a user wait for the exact answer, which may take an unknown amount of time, this allows the user to explore the efficiency-accuracy tradeoff, and terminate the query execution whenever s/he is satisfied with the approximation quality.

For queries over one table, e.g., `SELECT SUM(quantity) FROM` R `WHERE discount` $>$ `0.1`, online aggregation is quite easy. The idea is to simply take samples from table R repeatedly, and compute the average of the sampled tuples (more precisely, on the value of the attribute on which the aggregation function is applied), which is then appropriately scaled up to get an unbiased estimator for the `SUM`. Standard statistical formulas can be used to estimate the confidence interval, which shrinks as more samples are taken [14].

Online aggregation for joins. For join queries, the problem becomes much harder. When we sample tuples from each table and join the sampled tuples, we get a sample of the join results. The sample mean can still serve as an unbiased estimator of the full join (after appropriate scaling), but these samples are *not* independently chosen from the full join results, even though the joining tuples are sampled from each table independently. Haas et al. [14,16] studied this problem in depth, and derived new formulas for computing the confidence intervals for such estimators, and later proposed the *ripple join* algorithm [15]. Ripple join repeatedly takes random samples from each table in a round-robin fashion, and keep all the sampled tuples in memory. Every time a new tuple is taken from one table, it is joined with all the tuples taken from other tables so far. Figure 1 illustrates how the algorithm works on two tables, which intuitively explains why it is called "ripple" join.

There have been many variants and extensions to the basic ripple join algorithm. First, if an index is available on one of the tables, say R_2, then for a randomly sampled tuple from R_1, we can find all the tuples in R_2 that join with it. Note that no random sampling is done on R_2. This variant is also known as *index ripple join*, which was actually noted before ripple join itself was invented [32,33]. In general, for a multi-table join $R_1 \bowtie \cdots \bowtie R_k$, the index ripple join algorithm only does random sampling on one of the tables, say R_1. Then for each tuple t sampled from R_1, it computes $t \bowtie R_2 \bowtie \cdots \bowtie R_k$, and all the joined results are returned as samples from the full join.

Problem formulation. The type of queries we aim to support is the same as in prior work on ripple join, i.e., a SQL query of the form

> `SELECT g, AGG(expression)`
> `FROM` $R_1, R_2, \ldots, R_k$
> `WHERE join conditions AND selection predicates`
> `GROUP BY g`

where `AGG` can be any of the standard aggregation functions such as `SUM, AVE, COUNT, VARIANCE`, and `expression` can involve any attributes of the tables. The `join conditions` consist of equality or inequality conditions between pairs of the tables, and `selection predicates` can also be applied to any number of the tables.

At any point in time during query processing, the algorithm should output an estimator $\tilde{Y}$ for `AGG(expression)` together with a confidence interval, i.e.,

$$\Pr[|\tilde{Y} - \texttt{AGG(expression)}| \leq \varepsilon] \geq \alpha.$$

Here, ε is called the *half-width* of the confidence interval and α the *confidence level*. The user should specify one of them and the algorithm will continuously update the other as time goes on. The user can terminate the query when it reaches the desired level. Alternatively, the user may also specify a time limit on the query processing, and the algorithm should return the best estimate obtainable within the limit, together with a confidence interval.

3. WANDER JOIN

3.1 Wander join on a simple example

For concreteness, we first illustrate how wander join works on the natural join between 3 tables R_1, R_2, R_3:

$$R_1(A, B) \bowtie R_2(B, C) \bowtie R_3(C, D), \tag{1}$$

where $R_1(A, B)$ means that R_1 has two attributes A and B, etc. The natural join returns all combinations of tuples from the 3 tables that have matching values on their common attributes. We assume that R_2 has an index on attribute B, R_3 has an index on attribute C, and the aggregation function is SUM(D).

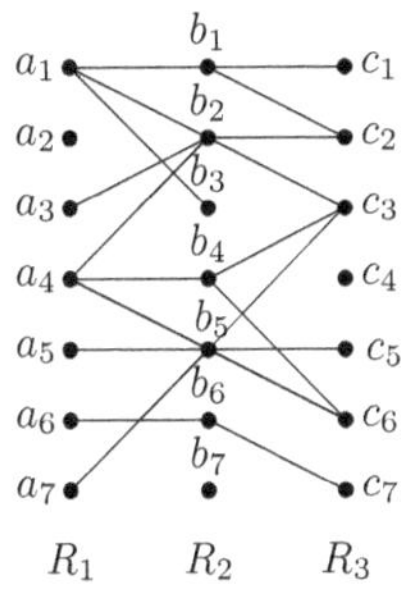

Figure 2: The 3-table join data graph: there is an edge between two tuples if they can join.

We model the join relationships among the tuples as a graph. More precisely, each tuple is modeled as a vertex and there is an edge between two tuples if they can join. For this natural join, it means that the two tuples have the same value on their common attribute. We call the resulting graph the *join data graph* (this is to be contrasted with the *join query graph* introduced later). For example, the join data graph for the 3-table natural join (1) may look like the one in Figure 2. This way, each join result becomes a path from some vertex in R_1 to some vertex in R_3, and sampling from the join boils down to sampling a path. Note that this graph is completely *conceptual*: we do not need to actually construct the graph to do path sampling.

A path can be randomly sampled by first picking a vertex in R_1 uniformly at random, and then "randomly walking" towards R_3. Specifically, in every step of the random walk, if the current vertex has d neighbors in the next table (which can be found efficiently by the index), we pick one uniformly at random to walk to.

One problem an acute reader would immediately notice is that, different paths may have different probabilities to be sampled. In the example above, the path $a_1 \to b_1 \to c_1$ has probability $\frac{1}{7} \cdot \frac{1}{3} \cdot \frac{1}{2}$ to be sampled, while $a_6 \to b_6 \to c_7$ has probability $\frac{1}{7} \cdot 1 \cdot 1$ to be sampled. If the value of the D attribute on c_7 is very large, then obviously this would tilt the balance, leading to an overestimate. Ideally, each path should be sampled with equal probability so as to ensure unbiasedness. However, it is well known that random walks in general do not yield a uniform distribution.

Fortunately, a technique known in the statistics literature as the *Horvitz-Thompson estimator* [20] can be used to remove the bias easily. Suppose path γ is sampled with probability $p(\gamma)$, and the expression on γ to be aggregated is $v(\gamma)$, then $v(\gamma)/p(\gamma)$ is an unbiased estimator of $\sum_\gamma v(\gamma)$, which is exactly the SUM aggregate we aim to estimate. This can be easily proved by the definition of expectation, and is also very intuitive: We just penalize the paths that are sampled with higher probability proportionally. Also note that $p(\gamma)$ can be computed easily on-the-fly as the path is sampled. Suppose $\gamma = (t_1, t_2, t_3)$, where t_i is the tuple sampled from R_i, then we have

$$p(\gamma) = \frac{1}{|R_1|} \cdot \frac{1}{d_2(t_1)} \cdot \frac{1}{d_3(t_2)}, \tag{2}$$

where $d_{i+1}(t_i)$ is the number of tuples in R_{i+1} that join with t_i.

Finally, we independently perform multiple random walks, and take the average of the estimators $v(\gamma_i)/p_i$. Since each $v(\gamma_i)/p_i$ is an unbiased estimator of the SUM, their average is still unbiased, and the variance of the estimator reduces as more paths are collected. Other aggregation functions and how to compute confidence intervals will be discussed in Section 3.4.

A subtle question is what to do when the random walk gets stuck, for example, when we reach vertex b_3 in Figure 2. In this case, we should not reject the sample, but return 0 as the estimate, which will be averaged together with all the successful random walks. This is because even though this is a failed random walk, it is still in the probability space. It should be treated as a value of 0 for the Horvitz-Thompson estimator to remain unbiased. Too many failed random walks will slow down the convergence of estimation, and we will deal with the issue in Section 4.

3.2 Wander join for acyclic queries

Although the algorithm above is described on a simple 3-table *chain join*, it can be extended to arbitrary joins easily. In general, we consider the *join query graph* (or *query graph* in short), where each table is modeled as a vertex, and there is an edge between two tables if there is a join condition between the two. Figure 3 shows some possible join query graphs.

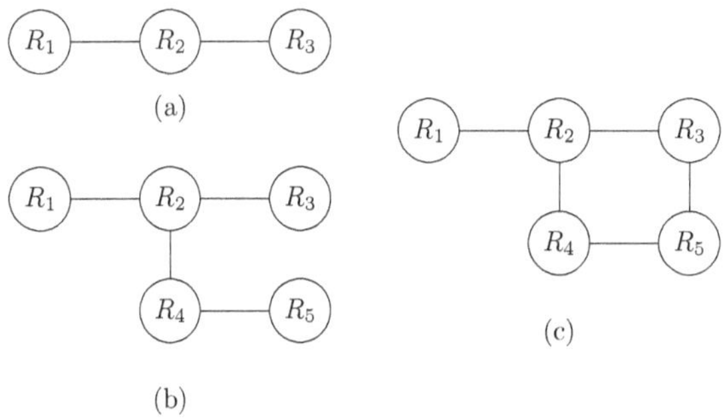

Figure 3: The join query graph for a (a) chain join; (b) acyclic join; (c) cyclic join.

When the join query graph is acyclic, wander join can be extended in a straightforward way. First, we need to fix a *walk order* such that each table in the walk order must be adjacent (in the query graph) to another one earlier in the order. For example, for the query graph in Figure 3(b), R_1, R_2, R_3, R_4, R_5 and R_2, R_3, R_4, R_5, R_1 are both valid walk orders, but R_1, R_3, R_4, R_5, R_2 is not since R_3 (resp. R_4) is not adjacent to R_1 (resp. R_1 or R_3) in the query graph. (Different walk orders may lead to very different performances, and we will discuss how to choose the best one in Section 4.)

Next, we simply perform the random walks as before, following the given order. The only difference is that a random walk may now consist of both "walks" and "jumps". For example, using the order R_1, R_2, R_3, R_4, R_5 on Figure 3(b), after we have reached a tuple in R_3, the next table to walk to is R_4, which is connected to the part already walked via R_2. So we need to jump back to the tuple we picked in R_2, and continue the random walk from there.

Finally, we need to generalize Equation (2). Let $d_j(t)$ be the number of tuples in R_j that can join with t, where t is a tuple from another table that has a join condition with R_j. Suppose the walk order is $R_{\lambda(1)}, R_{\lambda(2)}, \ldots, R_{\lambda(k)}$, and let $R_{\eta(i)}$ be the table adjacent to $R_{\lambda(i)}$ in the query graph but appearing earlier in the order. Note that for an acyclic query graph and a valid walk order, $R_{\eta(i)}$ is uniquely defined. Then for the path $\gamma = (t_{\lambda(1)}, \ldots, t_{\lambda(k)})$, where $t_{\lambda(i)} \in R_{\lambda(i)}$, the sampling probability of the path γ is

$$p(\gamma) = \frac{1}{|R_{\lambda(1)}|} \prod_{i=2}^{k} \frac{1}{d_{\lambda(i)}(t_{\eta(i)})}. \tag{3}$$

3.3 Wander join for cyclic queries

The algorithm for acyclic queries can also be extended to handle query graph with cycles. Given a cyclic query graph, e.g., the one in Figure 3(c), we first find any spanning tree of it, such as the one in Figure 3(b). Then we just perform the random walks on this spanning tree as before. After we have sampled a path γ on the spanning tree, we need to put back the non-spanning tree edges, e.g., (R_3, R_5), and check that γ should satisfy the join conditions on these edges. For example, after we have sampled a path $\gamma = (t_1, t_2, t_3, t_4, t_5)$ on Figure 3(b) (assuming the walk order R_1, R_2, R_3, R_4, R_5), then we need to verify that γ should satisfy the non-spanning tree edge (R_3, R_5), i.e., t_3 should join with t_5. If they do not join, we consider γ as a failed random walk and return an estimator with value 0.

3.4 Estimators and confidence intervals

To derive estimators and confidence interval formulas for various aggregation functions, we establish an equivalence between wander join and sampling from a single table with selection predicates, which has been studied by Haas [14]. Imagine that we have a single table that stores all the paths in the join data graph, including both full paths, as well as partial paths (like $a_1 \to b_3$). Wander join essentially samples from this imaginary table, though non-uniformly.

Suppose we have performed a total of n random walks $\gamma_1, \ldots, \gamma_n$. For each γ_i, let $v(i)$ be the value of the expression on γ_i to be aggregated, and set $u(i) = 1/p(\gamma_i)$ if γ_i is a successful walk, and 0 otherwise. With this definition of u and v, we can rewrite the estimator for `SUM` as $\frac{1}{n}\sum_{i=1}^{n} u(i)v(i)$. We observe that this has exactly the same form as the one in [14] for estimating the `SUM` for a single table with a selection predicate, except for two differences: (1) in [14], $u(i)$ is set to 1 if γ_i satisfies the selection predicate and 0 otherwise; and (2) [14] does uniform sampling over the table, while our sampling is non-uniform. However, by going through the analysis in [14], we realize that it holds for any definition of u and v, and for any sampling distribution. Thus, all the results in [14] carry over to our case, but with u and v defined in our way. We give the estimators and confidence intervals for various estimators in Appendix A; here we just point out that any of them can be computed easily in $O(n)$ time.

3.5 Selection predicates and group-by

Wander join can deal with arbitrary selection predicates in the query easily: in the random walk process, whenever we reach a tuple t for which there is a selection predicate, we check if it satisfies the predicate, and fail the random walk immediately if not.

If the starting table of the random walk has an index on the attribute with a selection predicate, and the predicate is an equality or range condition, then we can directly sample a tuple that satisfies the condition from the index, using Olken's method [38]. Correspondingly, we replace $|R_{\lambda(1)}|$ in (3) by the number of tuples in $R_{\lambda(1)}$ that satisfy the condition, which can also be computed from the index. This removes the impact of the predicate on the performance of the random walk, thus it is preferable to start from such a table. More discussion will be devoted on this topic under walk plan optimization in Section 4.

If there is a `GROUP BY` clause in the query, the algorithm remains the same, except that each random walk path will end up in one of the groups and an estimator (and its confidence interval) is maintained for each group separately. However, this simple strategy will not work well when different groups have very different selectivities: popular groups tend to get hit by more random walks, while small groups may have few hits, leading to estimates with large confidence intervals. For queries on a single table (i.e., non-joins), there is a powerful technique to address this issue, known as *stratified sampling* [2, 28]. But how to extend this technique to handling joins remains an open problem.

3.6 Justification for using indexes

Our random walk based approach crucially depends on the availability of indexes. For example, for the 3-table chain join in (1), R_2 needs to have an index on its B attribute, and R_3 needs to have an index on its C attribute. In general, a valid walk order depends on which indexes over join attributes are available. Insufficient indexing will limit the freedom of choices of random walk orders, which will be discussed in detail in Section 4.

However, we would argue that having plenty of indexes is actually a reasonable assumption: (1) Indexes can speed up general query processing tremendously. Without indexes, any query will require at least one full scan of the entire table, so indexes should have been built for any table that is queried often. (2) The main concern of not having an index is the maintenance cost, i.e., the cost and overhead (such as locking) to update the index when new data records are inserted or deleted from the base table. But note that complex analytical (OLAP) queries, for which online aggregation is most useful, usually work in a data warehousing environment, which only sees batch updates that take place in offline time (e.g., at night). Even for online updates, new indexes are now available, such as the *fractal tree index* [5] (already implemented in MySQL and MongoDB), and recent work on adaptive and holistic indexing [12, 13, 17, 22, 41] with transaction and concurrency control support, that support such updates much more efficiently than traditional database indexes. (3) The ripple join algorithm also requires an index if tuples are to be maintained in a random order [15]. (4) When an index is not available, we could first build an index over the join attribute on the fly; building a secondary, unclustered index is usually cheaper than evaluating the join in full, say, with sort-merge joins.

3.7 Comparison with ripple join

It is interesting to note that ripple join and wander join take two "dual" approaches. Ripple join takes uniform but non-independent samples from the join, while random walks return independent but non-uniform samples. It is difficult to make a rigorous analytical comparison between the two approaches: Both sampling methods yield slower convergence compared with ideal (i.e., independent and uniform) sampling. The impact of the former depends the amount of correlation, while the latter on the degree of non-uniformity, both of which depend on actual data characteristics and the query. Thus, an empirical comparison is necessary, which will be conducted in Section 5. Here we give a simple analytical comparison in terms of *sampling efficiency*, i.e., how many samples from the join can be returned after n sampling steps, while assuming that non-independence and non-uniformity have the same impact on converting the samples to the final estimate. This comparison, although crude with many simplifying assumptions, still gives us an intuition why wander join can be much better than ripple join.

Consider a chain join between k tables, each having N tuples. Assume that, for each table $R_i, i = 1, \ldots, k-1$, every tuple $t \in R_i$ joins with d tuples in R_{i+1}. Suppose that ripple join has taken n tuples randomly from each table, and correspondingly wander join has performed n random walks (successful or not).

Consider ripple join first. The probability for k randomly sampled tuples, one from each table, to join is $(\frac{d}{N})^{k-1}$. If n tuples are sampled from each table, then we would expect $n^k(\frac{d}{N})^{k-1}$ join results. Note that if the join attribute is the primary key in table R_{i+1}, we have $d_i = 1$. As a matter of fact, *all* join queries in the TPC-H benchmark, thus arguably most joins used in practice, are primary key-foreign key joins. Suppose $N = 10^6, k = 3, d = 1$, then we would need to take $n = (\frac{N}{d})^{\frac{k-1}{k}} = 10,000$ samples from each table until we get the first join result. Making things worse, this number grows with N and k.

Now let us consider wander join. In fact, under the assumption that each tuple joins with d tuples in the next table, the random walk will always be successful. In general, the efficiency of the random walks depends on the fraction of tuples in a table that have at least one joining tuple in the next table. We argue that this should not be too small. Indeed, for primary key-foreign key joins, each foreign key should have a match in the primary key table, so this fraction is 1. But if we walk from the primary key to the foreign key, this may be less than one. In general, this fraction is not too small, since if it is small, computing the join in full will be very efficient anyway, so users would not need online aggregation at all. Now we assume that this fraction is at least 1/2 for each table. Then the success rate of a random walk is $\geq 1/2^{k-1}$, i.e., we expect to get at least $n/2^{k-1}$ samples from the join after n random walks have been performed. This leads to the most important property of our random walk based approach, that its efficiency does not depend on N, which means that it works on data of *any* scale, at least theoretically. Meanwhile, it does become worse exponentially in k. However, k is usually small; the join queries in the TPC-H benchmark on average involve 3 to 4 tables, with the largest one having 8 tables. But regardless of the value of k, wander join is better than ripple join as long as $n/2^{k-1} \geq n^k/N^{k-1}$ (assuming $d = 1$), i.e., $n/N \leq 1/2$. Note that $n/N > 1/2$ means we are sampling more than half of the database. When this happens and the confidence interval still has not reached the user's requirement, online aggregation essentially has already failed.

Computational costs. There is also a major difference in terms of computational costs. Computing the confidence intervals in ripple join requires a fairly complex algorithm with worst-case running time $O(kn^k)$ [14], due to the non-independent nature of the sampling. On the other hand, wander join returns independent samples, so computing confidence intervals is very easy, as described in Section 3.4. In fact, it should be clear that the whole algorithm, including performing random walks, computing estimators and confidence intervals, takes only $O(kn)$ time, assuming hash tables are used as indexes. If B-trees are used, there will be an extra log factor.

Run to completion. Another minor thing is that ripple join, when it completes, computes the full join exactly. Wander join can also be made to have this feature, by doing the random walks "without replacement". This will introduce additional overhead for the algorithm. A more practical solution is to simply run wander join and a traditional full join algorithm in parallel, and terminate wander join when the full join completes. Since wander join operates in the "read-only" mode on the data and indexes, it has little interference with the full join algorithm.

Worst case. Note that the fundamental lower bounds shown by Chaudhuri et al. [8] for sampling over joins apply to wander join as well. In particular, both ripple join and wander join perform badly on the hard cases constructed by Chaudhuri et al. [8] for sampling over joins. But in practice, under certain reasonable assumptions on the data (as described above and as evident from our experiments), wander join outperforms ripple join significantly.

4. WALK PLAN OPTIMIZER

Different orders to perform the random walk may lead to very different performances. This is akin to choosing the best physical plan for executing a query. So we term different ways to perform the random walks as *walk plans*. A relational database optimizer usually needs statistics to be collected from the tables *a priori*, so as to estimate various intermediate result sizes for multi-table join optimization. In this section we present a walk plan optimizer that chooses the best walk plan without the need to collect statistics.

4.1 Walk plan generation

We first generate all possible walk plans. Recall that the constraint we have for a valid walk order is that for each table R_i (except the first one in the order), there must exist a table R_j earlier in the order such that there is a join condition between R_i and R_j. In addition, R_i should have an index on the attribute that appears in the join condition. Note that the join condition does not have to be equality. It can be for instance an inequality or even a range condition,

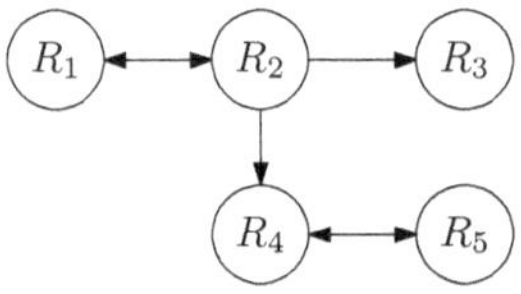

R_1, R_2, R_3, R_4, R_5
R_1, R_2, R_4, R_3, R_5
R_1, R_2, R_4, R_5, R_3
R_2, R_1, R_3, R_4, R_5
R_2, R_1, R_4, R_3, R_5
R_2, R_1, R_4, R_5, R_3
R_2, R_3, R_1, R_4, R_5
R_2, R_3, R_4, R_1, R_5
R_2, R_3, R_4, R_5, R_1
R_2, R_4, R_1, R_3, R_5
R_2, R_4, R_1, R_5, R_3
R_2, R_4, R_3, R_1, R_5
R_2, R_4, R_3, R_5, R_1
R_2, R_4, R_5, R_1, R_3
R_2, R_4, R_5, R_3, R_1

Figure 4: A directed join query graph and all its walk plans.

such as $R_j.A \leq R_i.B \leq R_j.A + 100$, as long as R_i has an index on B that supports range queries (e.g., a B-tree).

When there is at least one valid walk order. Under the constraint above, there may or may not be a valid walk order. We first consider the case when at least one walk order exists. In this case, each walk order corresponds to a walk plan.

To generate all possible walk orders, we first add directions to each edge in the join query graph. Specifically, for an edge between R_i and R_j, if R_i has an index on its attribute in the join condition, we have a directed edge from R_j to R_i; similarly if R_j has an index on its attribute in the join condition, we have a directed edge from R_i to R_j. For example, after adding directions, the query graph in Figure 3(b) might look like the one in Figure 4, and all possible walk plans are listed on the side. These plans can be enumerated by a simple backtracking algorithm. Note that there can be exponentially (in the number of tables) many walk plans. However, this is not a real concern because (1) there cannot be too many tables, and (2) more importantly, having many walk plans does not have a major impact on the plan optimizer, which we shall see later.

We can similarly generate all possible walk plans for cyclic queries, just that some edges will not be walked, and they will have to be checked after the random walk, as described in Section 3.3. We call them *non-tree* edges, since the part of the graph that is covered by the random walk form a tree. An example is given in Figure 5.

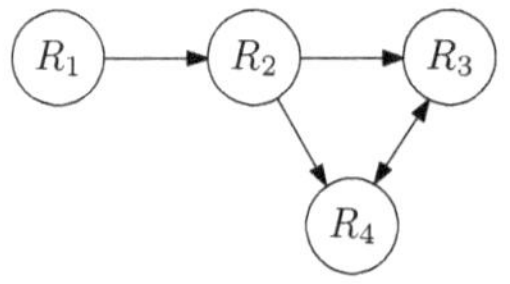

R_1, R_2, R_3, R_4. non-tree edge: (R_2, R_4)
R_1, R_2, R_4, R_3. non-tree edge: (R_2, R_3)

Figure 5: Walk plan generation for a cyclic query graph.

When there is no valid walk order. The situation gets more complex when there is no valid walk order, like for the two query graphs in Figure 6 (dashed edges are also part of the query graph). First, one can easily verify that the sufficient and necessary condition for a query graph to admit at least one valid walk order is that it has a directed spanning tree[1]. When there are not enough indexes, this condition may not hold, in which case we will have to decompose the query graph into multiple components such that each component has a directed spanning tree. Figure 6 shows how the two query graphs can be decomposed, where each component is connected by solid edges.

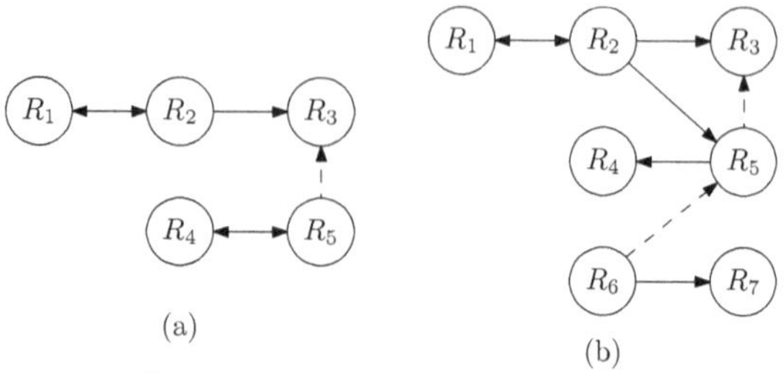

Figure 6: Decomposition of the join query graph into directed spanning trees. Dashed edges are non-tree edges.

After we have found directed spanning tree decomposition, we generate walk orders for each component, as described above. A walk plan now is any combination of the walk orders, one for each component. Then, we will run ripple join on the component level and wander join within each component. More precisely, we perform random walks for the components in a round-robin fashion, and keep all successful paths in memory. For each newly sampled path, it is joined with all the paths from other tables, i.e., checking that the join conditions on the edges between these components are met. For example, we check (R_3, R_5) in Figure 6(a) and (R_5, R_6) in 6(b). Note that (R_3, R_5) in 6(a) is checked by wander join for the component $\{R_1, R_2, R_3, R_4, R_5\}$. For every combination of the paths, one from each table, we use the HT estimator as in Section 3, except that $p(\gamma)$ is replaced by the product of the $p(\gamma_i)$'s for all that paths γ_i's involved.

Directed spanning tree decomposition. It remains to describe how to find a directed spanning tree decomposition. We would like to minimize the number of components, because each additional component pushes one more join condition from wander join to ripple join, which reduces the sampling efficiency. In the worst scenario, each vertex is in a component by itself, then the whole algorithm degrades to ripple join.

Finding the smallest directed spanning tree decomposition, unfortunately, is NP-hard (by a simple reduction from set cover). However, since the graph is usually very small (8 in the largest TPC-H benchmark query), we simply use exhaustive search to find the optimal decomposition.

For a given query graph $G = (V, E)$, the algorithm proceeds in 3 steps. In step 1, for each vertex v, we find the set of all vertices reachable from v, denoted as $T(v)$. Then, we remove $T(v)$ if it is dominated (i.e., completely contained) in another $T(v')$. For example, for the query graph in Figure 6(b), only $T(R_1) = \{R_1, R_2, R_3, R_4, R_5\}$ and $T(R_6) = \{R_3, R_4, R_5, R_6, R_7\}$ remain, since other $T(v)$'s are dominated by either $T(R_1)$ or $T(R_6)$. Denote the remaining set of vertices as U.

In step 2, we find the smallest subset of vertices C such that $\bigcup_{v \in C} T(v)$ covers all vertices, by exhaustively checking all subsets C of U. This gives the smallest cover, not a decomposition, since some vertices may be covered by more than one $T(v)$. For example, $T(R_1)$ and $T(R_6)$ are the optimal cover for the query graph in Figure 6(b), and they both cover R_3, R_4, R_5.

In step 3, we convert the cover into a decomposition.

[1]A *directed tree* is a tree in which every edge points away from the root. A *directed spanning tree* of a graph G is a subgraph of G with all vertices of G, and is a directed tree.

Denote the set of multiply covered vertices as M, and let $G_M = (M, E_V)$ be the induced subgraph of G on M. We will assign each $u \in M$ to one of its covering $T(v)$'s. However, the assignment cannot be arbitrary. It has to be *consistent*, i.e., after the assignment, all vertices assigned to $T(v)$ must form a single connected component. To do so, we first find the strongly-connected components of G_M, contract each to a "super vertex" (containing all vertices in this strongly-connected component). Then we do a topological sort of the super vertices; inside each super vertex, the vertices are ordered arbitrarily. Finally, we assign each $u \in M$ to one of its covering $T(v)$'s by this order: if u has one or more predecessors in G_M that have already been assigned, we assign u to the same $T(v)$ as one of its predecessors; otherwise u can be assigned to any of its covering $T(v)$'s. For the query graph in Figure 6(b), the topological order for M is R_5, R_3, R_4 or R_5, R_4, R_3, and in this example, we have assigned all of them to $T(R_1)$. In Appendix B, we give a proof that this algorithm produces a consistent assignment.

4.2 Walk plan optimization

We pick the best walk plan by choosing the best walk order for each component in the directed spanning tree decomposition. Below, we simply assume that the entire query graph is one component.

The performance of a walk order depends on many factors. First, it depends on the structure of the join data graph. Considering the data graph in Figure 7, if we perform the random walk by the order R_1, R_2, R_3, then the success probability is only 2/7, but if we follow the order R_3, R_2, R_1, it is 100%.

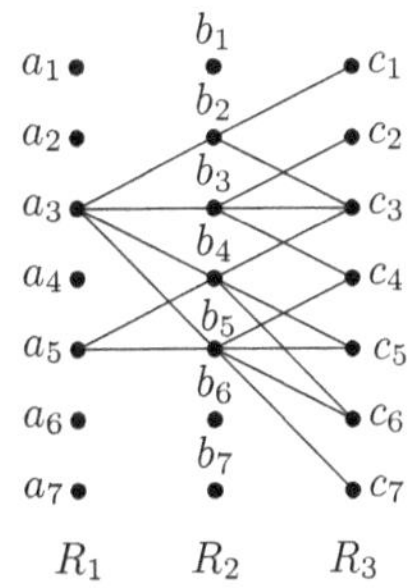

Figure 7: Structure of the join data graph has a significant impact on the performance of different walk plans.

Second, as mentioned, if there is a selection predicate on an attribute and there is a table with an index on that attribute, it is preferable to start from that table. Thirdly, for a cyclic query graph, which edges serve as the non-tree edges also affects the success probability. And finally, even if the success probability of the random walks is the same, different walk orders may result in different non-uniformity, which in turn affects how fast the variance of the estimator shrinks.

Instead of dealing with all these issues, we observe that ultimately, the performance of the random walk is measured by the variance of the final estimator after a given amount of time, say t. Let X_i be the estimator from the i-th random walk (e.g., $u(i)v(i)$ for SUM if the walk is successful and 0 otherwise), and let T be the running time of one random walk, successful or not. Suppose a total of W random walks have been performed within time t. Then the final estimator is $\frac{1}{W}\sum_{i=1}^{W} X_i$, and we would like to minimize its variance.

Note that W is also a random variable, we cannot just break it up as in standard variance analysis. Instead, we should do a conditioning on W, and use the *law of total variance* [36]:

$$\begin{aligned}
&\mathsf{Var}\left[\frac{1}{W}\sum_{i=1}^{W} X_i\right]\\
=&\mathsf{E}\left[\mathsf{Var}\left[\frac{1}{W}\sum_{i=1}^{W} X_i \,\middle|\, W\right]\right] + \mathsf{Var}\left[\mathsf{E}\left[\frac{1}{W}\sum_{i=1}^{W} X_i \,\middle|\, W\right]\right]\\
=&\mathsf{E}[\mathsf{Var}[X_1]/W] + \mathsf{Var}[\mathsf{E}[X_1]] \quad //\mathsf{Var}[X_i] = \mathsf{Var}[X_j] \text{ and}\\
&\qquad\qquad //\mathsf{E}[X_i] = \mathsf{E}[X_j] \text{ for any } i, j\\
=&\mathsf{Var}[X_1]\mathsf{E}[1/W] + 0\\
=&\mathsf{Var}[X_1]\mathsf{E}[T/t]\\
=&\mathsf{Var}[X_1]\mathsf{E}[T]/t.
\end{aligned}$$

Thus, for a given amount of time t, the variance of the final estimator is proportional to $\mathsf{Var}[X_1]\mathsf{E}[T]$.

The next observation is that both $\mathsf{Var}[X_1]$ and $\mathsf{E}[T]$ can also be estimated by the random walks themselves! In particular, $\mathsf{Var}[X_1]$ is just estimated as in Section 3.4 and Appendix A; for $\mathsf{E}[T]$, we simply count the number of index entries looked up, or the number of I/Os in external memory, in each random walk and take the average.

Now, for each walk order, we perform a certain number of "trial" random walks and estimate $\mathsf{Var}[X_1]$ and $\mathsf{E}[T]$. Then we compute the product $\mathsf{Var}[X_1]\mathsf{E}[T]$ and pick the order with the minimum $\mathsf{Var}[X_1]\mathsf{E}[T]$. How to choose the number of trials is the classical sample size determination problem [6], which again depends on many factors such as the actual data distribution, the level of precision required, etc. However, in our case, we do not have to pick the very best plan: If two plans have similar values of $\mathsf{Var}[X_1]\mathsf{E}[T]$, their performances are close, so it does not matter which one is picked anyway. Nevertheless, we do have to make sure that, at least for the plan that is picked, its estimate for $\mathsf{Var}[X_1]\mathsf{E}[T]$ is reliable; for plans that are not picked, there is no need to determine exactly how bad they are. Thus, we adopt the following strategy: We conduct random walks following each plan in a round-robin fashion, and stop until at least one plan has accumulated at least τ successful walks. Then we pick the plan with the minimum $\mathsf{Var}[X_1]\mathsf{E}[T]$ that has at least $\tau/2$ successful walks. This is actually motivated by association rule mining, where a rule must both be good and have a minimum support level. In our implementation, we use a default threshold of $\tau = 100$.

Finally, we observe that all the trial runs are not wasted. Since each random walk, no matter which plan it follows, returns an unbiased estimator. So we can include all the random walks, before and after the optimal one has been picked, in computing the final estimator. The confidence interval is also computed with all these random walks. This is unlike traditional query optimization, where the cost incurred by the optimizer itself is pure "overhead".

5. EXPERIMENTS

5.1 Experimental setup

We have evaluated the performance of wander join in comparison with ripple join and its variants, the DBO engine, under two settings, which are described in detail below.

Standalone implementation. We first implemented both wander join and ripple join in C++. For wander join, data in each table is stored in primary key order in an array (using `std::vector`); for each join key, a hash table index is built (using `std::unordered_map`); for each key having a selection predicate, a binary search tree (BST) is built as the index (using `std::ordered_map`). Note that using these index structures, each step of the random walk takes $O(1)$ time and sampling from a table with a selection predicate takes $O(\log N)$ time. We ensure that all the index structures fit in memory; in fact, all the indexes combined together take space that is a very small fraction of the total amount of data, because they are all secondary indexes, storing only pointers to the actual data records, which have many other attributes that are not indexed. Furthermore, building these indexes is very efficient; in fact, they can be built with very minimum overhead while loading data from the file system to the memory (which one has to do anyway).

Similarly, for ripple join, we give it enough memory so that all samples taken can be kept in memory. For all samples taken from each table, we keep them in a hash table (also using `std::unordered_map`). Ripple join can take random samples in two ways. If the table is stored in a random order (in an array), we can simply retrieve the tuples in order. Alternatively, if an index is available, we can use the index to take a sample. The first one takes $O(1)$ time to sample a tuple and is also very cache-efficient. However, when there is a selection predicate, then the algorithm still has to read all tuples, but only keep those that satisfy the predicate. In this case, the second implementation is better (when the index is built on the selection predicate), though it takes $O(\log N)$ time to take a sample. We have implemented both versions; for the index-assisted version, indexes (BSTs) are built on all the selection predicates.

The idea for the standalone implementation is to give an ideal environment to both algorithms without any system overhead, so as to have a "barebone" comparison between the two algorithms.

System implementation. To see how the algorithms actually perform in a real database system, we have implemented wander join in the latest version of PostgreSQL (version 9.4; in particular, 9.4.2). Our implementation covers the entire pipeline from SQL parsing to plan optimization to physical execution. We build secondary B-tree indexes on all the join attributes and selection predicates.

The only system implementation available for ripple join is the DBO system [9, 25, 26]. In fact, the algorithm implemented in DBO is much more complex than the basic ripple join in order to deal with limited memory, as described in these papers. We compared wander join in our PostgreSQL implementation with Turbo DBO, using the code at http://faculty.ucmerced.edu/frusu/Projects/DBO/dbo.html, as a system-to-system comparison. Note that due to the random order storage requirement, DBO was built from ground up. Currently it is still a prototype that supports online aggregation only (i.e., no support for other major features in a RDBMS engine, such as transaction, locking, etc.). On the other hand, our integration of wander join into PostgreSQL retains the full functionality of a RDBMS, with online aggregation just as an added feature. Thus, this comparison can only be to our disadvantage due to the system overhead inside a full-fledged DBMS for supporting many other features and functionality.

Note that the original DBO papers [25] compared the DBO engine against the PostgreSQL database by running the same queries in both systems. We did exactly the same in our experiments, but simply using the PostgreSQL version with wander join implemented inside its kernel.

Data and queries. We used the TPC-H benchmark data and queries for the experiments, which were also used by the DBO work [9, 25, 26]. We used 5 tables, `nation`, `supplier`, `customer`, `orders`, and `lineitem`. We used the TPC-H data generator with the appropriate scaling factor to generate data sets of various sizes. We picked queries Q3 (3 tables), Q7 (6 tables; the `nation` table appears twice in the query) and Q10 (5 tables) in the TPC-H specification as our test queries.

5.2 Results on standalone implementation

We first run wander join and ripple join on a 2GB data set, i.e., the entire TPC-H database is 2GB, using the "barebone" joins of Q3, Q7, and Q10, where we drop all the selection predicates and group-by clauses. In Figure 8 we plot how the *confidence interval* (CI) shrinks over time, with the confidence level set at 95%, as well as the *estimates* returned by the algorithms. They are shown as a percentage error compared with the true answer (which were obtained offline by running the exact joins to full completion). We can see that wander join (WJ) converges much faster than ripple join (RJ), due to the much more focused search strategy. Meanwhile, the estimates returned are indeed within the confidence interval almost all the time. For example, wander join converges to 1% confidence interval in less than 0.1 second whereas ripple join takes more than 4 seconds to reach 1% confidence interval. The full exact join on Q3, Q7, and Q10 in this case is 18 seconds, 28 seconds, and 19 seconds, respectively, using hash join.

Next, we ran the same queries on data sets of varying sizes. Now we include both the random order ripple join (RRJ) and the index-assisted ripple join (IRJ). For wander join, we also consider two other versions to see how the plan optimizer has worked. WJ(B) is the version where the optimal plan is used (i.e., we run the algorithm with every plan and report the best result); WJ(M) is the version where we use the median plan (i.e., we run all plans and report the median result). WJ(O) is the version where we use the optimizer to automatically choose the plan, and the time spent by the optimizer is included. In Figure 9 we report the time spent by each algorithm to reach $\pm 1\%$ confidence interval with 95% confidence level on data sets of sizes 1GB, 2GB, and 3GB. We also report the time costs of the optimizer in Table 1. From the results, we can draw the following observations:

(1) Wander join is in general faster than ripple join by two orders of magnitude to reach the same confidence interval.

(2) The running time of ripple join increases with N, the data size, though mildly. Recall from Section 3.7 that ripple join expects to get $n^k(\frac{d}{N})^{k-1}$ sampled join results after n tuples have been retrieved from each of the k tables. Thus, to obtain a given sample size s from the join, it needs $n = s^{1/k}(\frac{N}{d})^{(k-1)/k}$ samples from each table. This partially explains the slightly-less-than-linear growth of its running time as a function of N.

(3) The running time of wander join is not affected by N. This also agrees with our analysis: When hash tables are used, its efficiency is independent of N altogether.

(4) The optimizer has very low overhead, and is very ef-

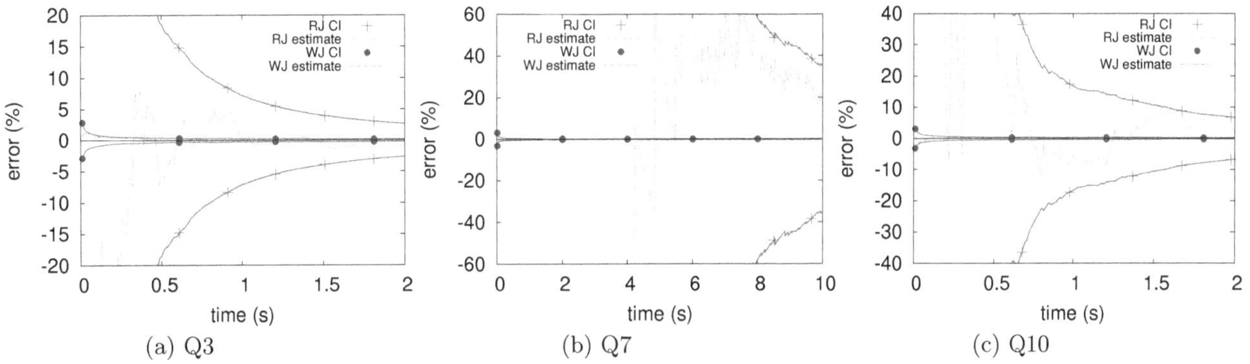

Figure 8: Standalone implementation: Confidence intervals and estimates on barebone queries on 2GB TPC-H data set; confidence level is 95%.

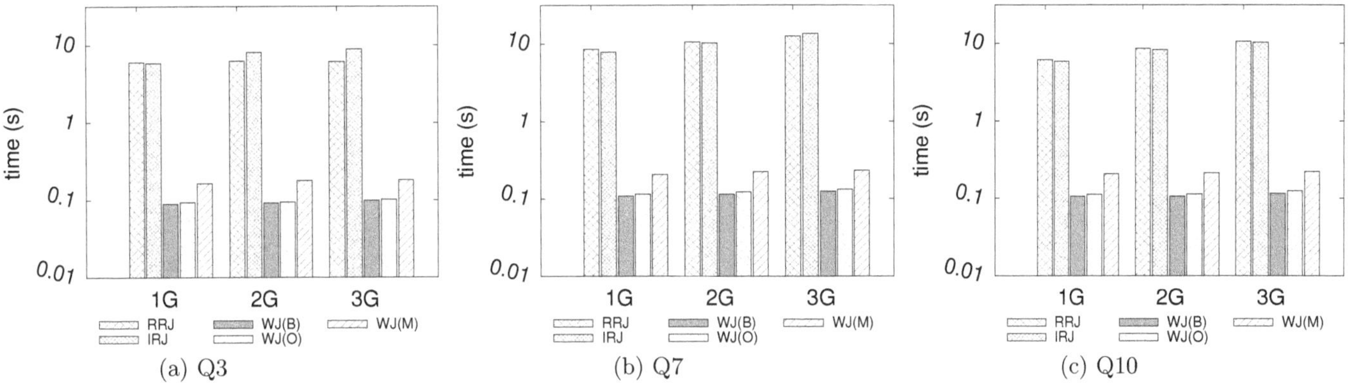

Figure 9: Standalone implementation: Time to reach ±1% confidence interval and 95% confidence level on TPC-H data sets of different sizes.

	size (GB)	optimization (ms)	execution (ms)
Q3	1	2.8	88.7
	2	2.8	91.3
	3	2.9	101.9
Q7	1	6.4	106.1
	2	6.4	112.1
	3	6.6	123.7
Q10	1	7.0	105
	2	7.3	105.6
	3	8.8	116

Table 1: Standalone implementation: Time cost of walk plan optimization (execution time to reach ±1% confidence interval and 95% confidence level on TPC-H data sets of different sizes).

fective. In fact, from the figures, we see that WJ(B) and WJ(O) have almost the same running time, meaning that the optimizer spends almost no time and indeed has found either the best plan or a very good plan that is almost as good as the best plan. Recall that all the trial runs used in the optimizer for selecting a good plan are not wasted; they also contribute to building the estimators. For barebone queries, many plans actually have similar performance, as seen by the running time of WJ(M), so even the trial runs are of good quality.

Finally, we put back the selection predicates to the queries. Figure 10 shows the time to reach ±1% confidence interval with 95% confidence level for the algorithms on the 2GB data set, with one selection predicate of varying selectivity, while Figure 11 shows the results when all the predicates are put back. Here, we measure the overall selectivity of all the predicates as:

$$1 - (\text{join size with predicates})/(\text{barebone join size}), \quad (4)$$

so higher means more selective.

From the results, we see that one selection predicate has little impact on the performance of wander join, because most likely its optimizer will elect to start the walk from that table. Multiple highly selective predicates do affect the performance of wander join, but even in the worst case, wander join maintains a gap with ripple join of more than an order of magnitude.

These experiments also demonstrate the importance of the plan optimizer: With multiple highly selective predicates, a mediocre plan can be much worse than the optimal one, and the plan optimizer almost always picks the optimal or a close-to-optimal plan with nearly no overhead. Note that in this case we do have poor plans, so some trial random walks may contribute little to the estimation. However, the good plans can accumulate $\tau = 100$ successful random walks very quickly, so we do not waste too much time anyway.

5.3 Results on system implementation

For the experimental evaluation on our PostgreSQL implementation of wander join, we first tested how it performs when there is sufficient memory, and then tested the case when memory is severely limited. We compared against Turbo DBO in the latter case. Turbo DBO [9] is an improvement to the original DBO engine, that extends ripple join to data on external memory with many optimizations.

When there is sufficient memory. Due to the low-

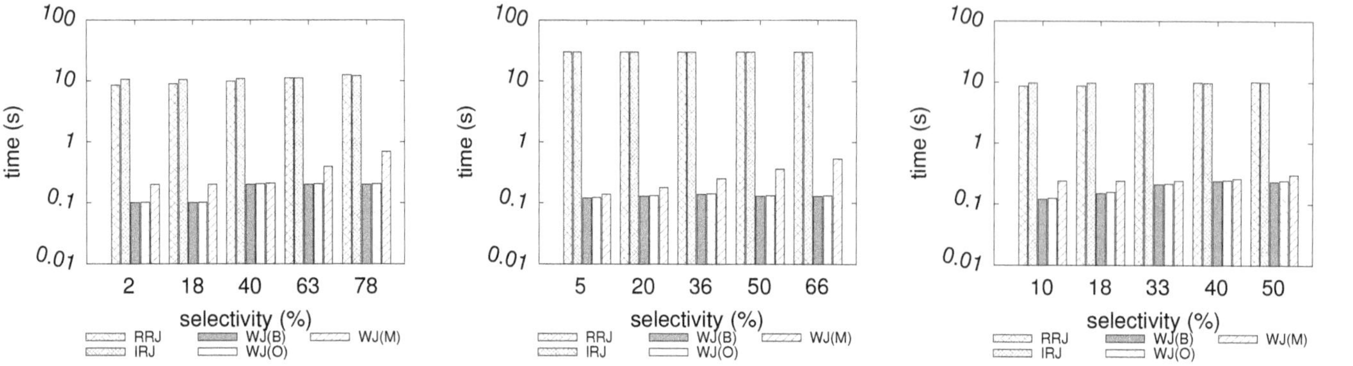

(a) Q3 (b) Q7 (c) Q10

Figure 10: Standalone implementation: Time to reach ±1% confidence interval and 95% confidence level on the 2GB TPC-H data set with one selection predicate of varying selectivity.

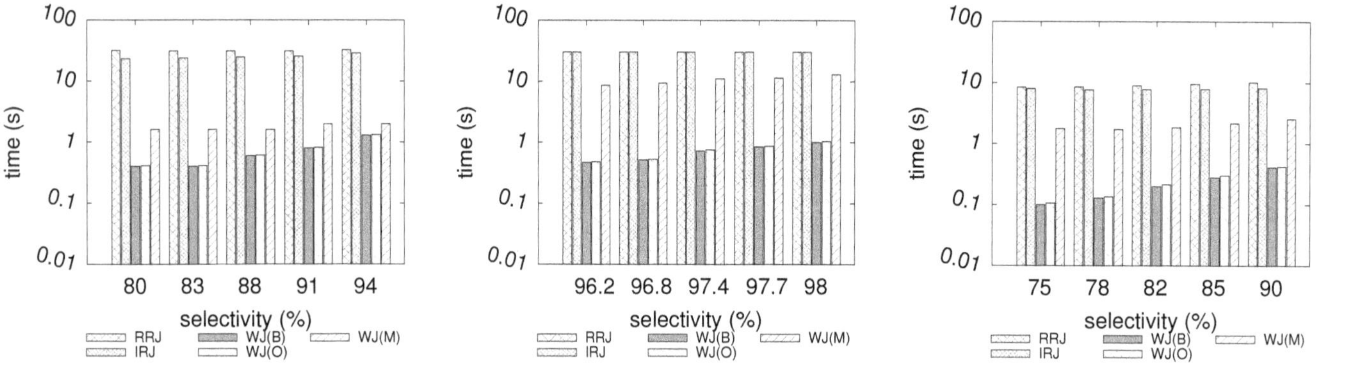

(a) Q3 (b) Q7 (c) Q10

Figure 11: Standalone implementation: Time to reach ±1% confidence interval and 95% confidence level on the 2GB TPC-H data set with multiple selection predicate of varying selectivity.

latency requirement for data analytical tasks and thanks to growing memory sizes, database systems are moving towards the "in-memory" computing paradigm. So we first would like to see how our system performs when there is sufficient memory. For this purpose, we used a machine with 32GB memory and data sets of sizes up to 20GB. We ran both wander join (implemented inside PostgreSQL) and the built-in PostgreSQL full join on the same queries, both through the standard PostgreSQL SQL query interface. We extended PostgreSQL's parser, plan generator, and query executor to support keywords like `CONFIDENCE`, `WITHINTIME`, `REPORTINTERVAL`, and `ONLINE`. We also integrated the plan optimizer of wander join into the query optimizer of PostgreSQL. For example, an example based on Q3 of TPC-H benchmark is:

```
SELECT ONLINE
SUM(l_extendedprice * (1 - l_discount)), COUNT(*)
FROM customer, orders, lineitem
WHERE c_mktsegment='BUILDING' AND c_custkey=o_custkey
AND l_orderkey=o_orderkey
WITHINTIME 20 CONFIDENCE 95 REPORTINTERVAL 1
```

This tells the engine that it is an online aggregation query, such that the engine should report the estimations and their associated confidence intervals, calculated with respect to 95% confidence level, for both `SUM` and `COUNT` every 1 second for up to 20 seconds.

Note that since we have built indexes on all the join attributes and there is sufficient memory, the PostgreSQL optimizer had chosen index join for all the join operators to take advantage of the indexes. We used Q3, Q7, and Q10 with all the selection predicates, but without the group-by clause.

The results in Figure 12 clearly indicate a linear growth of the full join, which is as expected because the index join algorithm has running time linear in the table size. Also because all joins are primary key-foreign key joins, the intermediate results have roughly linear size. On the other hand, the data size has a mild impact on the performance of wander join. For example, the time to reach ±1% confidence interval for Q7 merely increases from 3 seconds to 4 seconds, when the data size increases from 5GB to 20GB in Figure 12(b). By our analysis and the internal memory experimental results, the total number of random walk steps should be independent of the data size. However, because we use B-tree indexes, whose access cost grows logarithmically as data gets larger, so the cost per random walk step might grow slightly. In addition, on larger data sets, the CPU cache may not be as effective as on smaller data sets. These system reasons might have explained the small performance drop of wander join on larger data sets. Nevertheless, PostgreSQL with wander join reaching 1% CI has outperformed the PostgreSQL with full join by more than one order of magnitude when data size grows.

We have also run Turbo DBO in this case. However, it turned out that Turbo DBO spends even more time than PostgreSQL's full join, so we do not show its results. This seems to contradict with the results in [26]. In fact, this is because DBO is intentionally designed for large data and

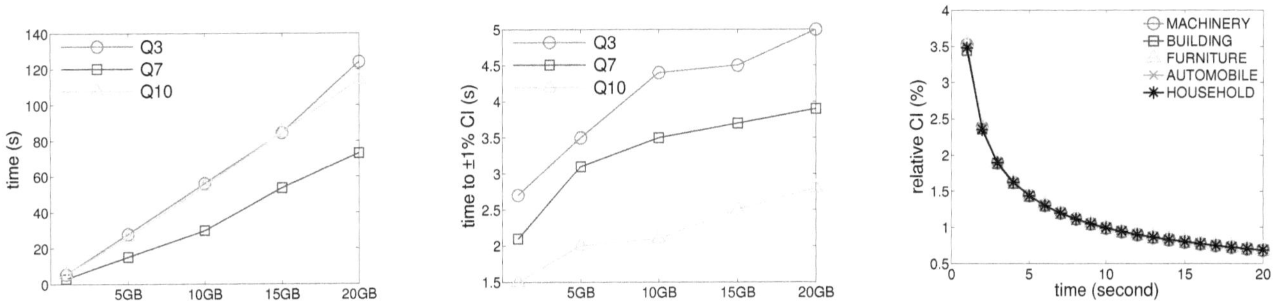

(a) PostgreSQL full join (b) Wander join in PostgreSQL (c) Wander join in PostgreSQL: Q10 with "GROUP BY c_mktsegment" on 10GB data

Figure 12: System implementation experimental results with sufficient memory: 32GB memory.

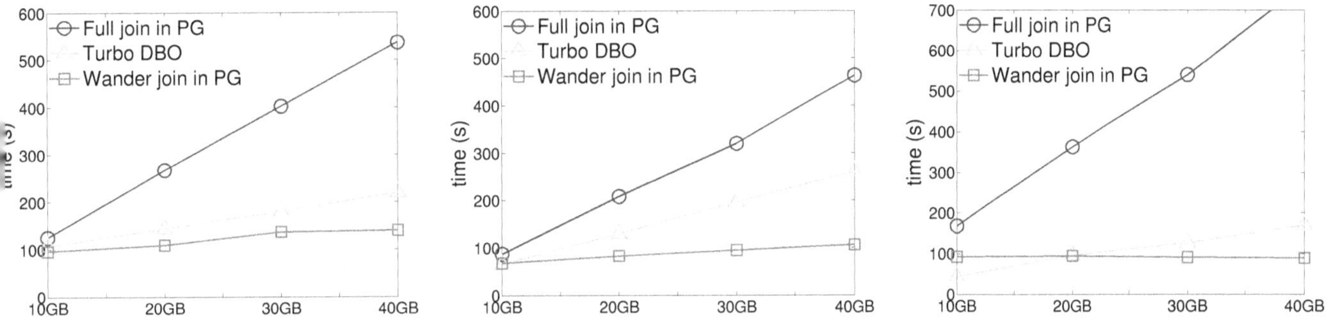

(a) Q3 (b) Q7 (c) Q10

Figure 13: System implementation experimental results with limited memory, 4GB memory.

small memory. In the experiments of [26], the machine used had only 2GB of memory. With such a small memory, PostgreSQL had to resort to sort-merge join or nested-loop join for each join operator, which is much less efficient than index join (for in-memory data). Meanwhile, DBO follows the framework of sort-merge join, so it is actually not surprising that it is not as good as index joins for in-memory data. In our next set of experiments where we limit the memory size, we do see that DBO performs better than the full join.

We also tested wander join with Q10 with a "`GROUP BY c_mktsegment`" clause. The confidence intervals as time goes on for each group are plotted in Figure 12(c). In the data set, data is evenly distributed among the groups defined by `c_mktsegment`, so the confidence intervals of all the groups reduce at the rate.

When memory is limited. In our last set of experiments, we used a machine with only 4GB memory, and ran the same set of experiments as above on data sets of sizes starting from 10GB and increasing to 40GB. The time for wander join inside PostgreSQL and Turbo DBO to reach ±5% confidence interval with 95% confidence level, as well as the time of the full join in PostgreSQL, are shown in Figure 13.

From the results, we see that a small memory has a significant impact on the performance of wander join. The running time increases from a few seconds in Figure 12 to more than 100 seconds in Figure 13, and that's after we have relaxed the target confidence interval from ±1% to ±5%. The reason is obviously due to the random access nature of the random walks, which now has a high cost due to excessive page swapping. Nevertheless, this is a "one-time" cost, in the sense that each random walk step is now much more expensive, but the number of steps is still not affected. After the one-time, sudden increase when data size exceeds main memory, the total cost remains almost flat afterward. In other words, the cost of wander join in this case is still independent of the data size, albeit to a small increase in the index accessing cost (which grows logarithmically with the data size if B-tree is used). Hence, wander join still enjoys excellent scalability as data size continues to grow.

On the other hand, both the full join and DBO clearly have a linear dependency on the data size, though at different rates. On the 10GB and 20GB data sets, wander join and DBO have similar performance, but eventually wander join would stand out on very large data sets.

Anyway, spending 100 seconds just to get a ±5% estimate does not really meet the requirement of interactive data analytics, so strictly speaking both wander join and DBO have failed in this case (when data has significantly exceeded the memory size). Fundamentally, online aggregation requires some form of randomness so as to have a statistically meaningful estimation, which is at odds with the sequential access nature of hard disks. This appears to be an inherent barrier for this line of work. However, as memory sizes grow larger and memory clouds get more popular (for example, using systems like RAMCloud [39] and FaRM [10]), with the SSDs as an additional storage layer, in the end we may not have to deal with this barrier at all. What's more, as shown in Figure 13, wander join (and DBO) still shows much better latency (for an acceptable confidence interval like 5%) than the full join, and the gap only becomes larger as data size continues to grow. So it is still very useful to have online aggregation over joins as a valuable tool available for data analysts.

Effectiveness of walk plan optimization. In the standalone implementation, we have observed that the walk plan optimizer has low overhead and can generate walk plans much better than the median plan. Similarly, we conducted experiments with our PostgreSQL implementation of wander join to see the effectiveness and the overhead of the walk plan optimizer, with either sufficient memory or limited memory. The results are shown in Table 2 (in Appendix C). In Table 2, instead of reporting the time of a median plan, we used the plan as constructed from the input query and used by PostgreSQL. From the results, we see that with sufficient memory, the results are similar to those on the standalone implementation, namely, there is very little overhead in the walk plan optimization. With limited memory, the optimizer tends to spend more time, due to system overhead and the page faults incurred by the round-robin exploration. But the total time (walk plan optimization + plan execution) is not much more expensive than the best plan execution itself, and is still much better than the plan used by PostgreSQL.

In summary, we see that in all cases, the optimizer can pick a plan that is much better than the plan generated from the input query and used by PostgreSQL. And generally speaking, query optimizer in a database engine tries to optimize the full join, not online aggregation. That's the value of having our own walk plan optimizer for wander join, and our walk plan optimization is both very effective and very efficient.

Comparing with a commercial-level database system. Finally, to gauge how our PostgreSQL (PG) implementation of wander join performs in comparison to a commercial-level database system, we ran the queries (in full) on System X[2], and then see how much accuracy our PG (with wander join) and DBO can achieve with 1/10 of the System X's full query time for the same query. System X uses the same machine and builds the same indexes as PG with wander join does.

We ran these experiments on both sufficient memory and limited memory for TPC-H data of different size (from 10GB to 40GB), using Q3, Q7, and Q10. The results are reported in Table 3 (in Appendix C). These results clearly demonstrate the benefits of wander join in getting high-quality approximate results in just a fraction of the time needed to get the accurate result, even when compared to state-of-the-art commercial-level database systems. Note that in many cases, DBO did not return any results in the time given, which is consistent with previously reported results, that DBO usually starts to return results after a few minutes [9,26].

6. RELATED WORK

The concept of online aggregation was first proposed in [19], and since then has generated much follow-up work, including the efforts in extending it to distributed and parallel environments [40,42,43,47,50] and multiple queries [48]; a complete survey of these work is out of the scope of this paper. In particular, related to our problem, online aggregation over joins was first studied in [15], where the ripple join algorithm was designed. Extensions to ripple join were done over the years [9,25,26,35], in particular, to support ripple join in DBO for large data on external memory. Note that we have already reviewed the core ideas in online aggregation and ripple join in Section 2.

Online aggregation is closely related to another line of work known as *query sampling* [8,21,38,45]. In online aggregation, the user is only interested in obtaining an aggregate, such as `SUM` or `AVE`, on a particular attribute of all the query results. However, a single aggregate may not be expressive enough to represent sufficient properties of the data, so the user may require a random sample, taken uniformly and independently, from the complete set of query results that satisfy the input query conditions. Note that query sampling immediately solves the online aggregation problem, as the aggregate can be easily computed from the samples. But this may be an overkill. In fact, both wander join and ripple join have demonstrated that a non-uniform or a non-independent sample can be used to estimate the aggregate with quality guarantees. Nevertheless, query sampling has received separate attention, as a uniform and independent sample can serve more purposes than just computing an aggregate, including many advanced data mining tasks; in some cases, the user may just want the sample itself.

In addition to these efforts, there are also extensive work on using sampling for approximate query processing, selectivity estimation, and query optimization [1,2,7,11,27–30, 37,44,46,49,51,52]. In partiluar, there is an increasing interest in building sampling-based approximate query processing systems, e.g., represented by systems like BlinkDB, Monte-Carlo DB, Analytical Bootstrap, DICE and others [1–3,23,24,31,37,51,52], but these systems do not support online aggregations over joins.

7. FUTURE DIRECTIONS

This work has presented some promising results on wander join, a new approach to online aggregation for joins. Yet, it has a lot of potential to be further exploited. Here we list a few directions for future work:

- Wander join is an "embarrassingly parallel" algorithm, and it should be very easy to implement it on a multi-core machine or a cluster. In particular, we are working on integrating wander join with SparkSQL [4]. Because wander join works much better for in-memory data than data from external memory on hard disks, Spark's massively parallel, in-memory computing framework provides an ideal platform for wander join. Recent efforts on extending traditional online aggregation techniques to Spark SQL in systems like G-OLA have already shown promising results [50].
- Because wander join can estimate `COUNT` very quickly, we can run wander join on any sub-join and estimate the intermediate join size. This in turn provides important statistics to a traditional cost-based query optimizer. It would be interesting to see if this can lead to improved query plan selection for full join computation.
- When the query has a group-by clause and the groups are highly unbalanced, some groups might be under-sampled. This problem can be in general solved by *stratified sampling* [1,2,34,50,52]. If the group-by attributes are from a single table, wander join can easily handle by simply starting the random walks from that table, but the problem is more complicated when the group-by involves attributes from different tables, which deserves further investigation.

[2]Legal restrictions prevent us from revealing the actual vendor name.

8. ACKNOWLEDGMENTS

Feifei Li was supported in part by NSF grants 1251019, 1302663, and 1443046. Feifei Li was also supported in part by NSFC grant 61428204. Bin Wu and Ke Yi are supported by HKRGC under grants GRF-621413, GRF-16211614, and GRF-16200415.

9. REFERENCES

[1] S. Agarwal, H. Milner, A. Kleiner, A. Talwalkar, M. I. Jordan, S. Madden, B. Mozafari, and I. Stoica. Knowing when you're wrong: building fast and reliable approximate query processing systems. In *SIGMOD*, pages 481–492, 2014.

[2] S. Agarwal, B. Mozafari, A. Panda, H. Milner, S. Madden, and I. Stoica. Blinkdb: queries with bounded errors and bounded response times on very large data. In *EuroSys*, pages 29–42, 2013.

[3] S. Agarwal, A. Panda, B. Mozafari, A. P. Iyer, S. Madden, and I. Stoica. Blink and it's done: Interactive queries on very large data. In *Proceedings of the VLDB Endowment*, volume 5, 2012.

[4] M. Armbrust, R. S. Xin, C. Lian, Y. Huai, D. Liu, J. K. Bradley, X. Meng, T. Kaftan, M. J. Franklin, A. Ghodsi, and M. Zaharia. Spark sql: Relational data processing in spark. In *Proc. ACM SIGMOD International Conference on Management of Data*, 2015.

[5] M. A. Bender, M. Farach-Colton, J. T. Fineman, Y. Fogel, B. C. Kuszmaul, and J. Nelson. Cache-oblivious streaming B-trees. In *Proc. ACM Symposium on Parallelism in Algorithms and Architectures*, 2007.

[6] G. Casella and R. L. Berger. *Statistical Inference*. Duxbury Press, 2001.

[7] S. Chaudhuri, R. Motwani, and V. Narasayya. Random sampling for histogram construction: how much is enough? In *Proc. ACM SIGMOD International Conference on Management of Data*, 1998.

[8] S. Chaudhuri, R. Motwani, and V. Narasayya. On random sampling over joins. In *Proc. ACM SIGMOD International Conference on Management of Data*, 1999.

[9] A. Dobra, C. Jermaine, F. Rusu, and F. Xu. Turbo charging estimate convergence in dbo. In *Proc. International Conference on Very Large Data Bases*, 2009.

[10] A. Dragojevic, D. Narayanan, M. Castro, and O. Hodson. FaRM: Fast remote memory. In *NSDI*, pages 401–414, 2014.

[11] P. B. Gibbons and Y. Matias. New sampling-based summary statistics for improving approximate query answers. In *Proc. ACM SIGMOD International Conference on Management of Data*, 1998.

[12] G. Graefe, F. Halim, S. Idreos, H. A. Kuno, and S. Manegold. Concurrency control for adaptive indexing. *PVLDB*, 5(7):656–667, 2012.

[13] G. Graefe, F. Halim, S. Idreos, H. A. Kuno, S. Manegold, and B. Seeger. Transactional support for adaptive indexing. *VLDB J.*, 23(2):303–328, 2014.

[14] P. J. Haas. Large-sample and deterministic confidence intervals for online aggregation. In *Proc. Ninth Intl. Conf. Scientific and Statistical Database Management*, 1997.

[15] P. J. Haas and J. M. Hellerstein. Ripple joins for online aggregation. In *Proc. ACM SIGMOD International Conference on Management of Data*, pages 287–298, 1999.

[16] P. J. Haas, J. F. Naughton, S. Seshadri, and A. N. Swami. Selectivity and cost estimation for joins based on random sampling. *Journal of Computer and System Sciences*, 52:550–569, 1996.

[17] F. Halim, S. Idreos, P. Karras, and R. H. C. Yap. Stochastic database cracking: Towards robust adaptive indexing in main-memory column-stores. *PVLDB*, 5(6):502–513, 2012.

[18] J. M. Hellerstein, R. Avnur, and V. Raman. Informix under control: Online query processing. *Data Min. Knowl. Discov.*, 4(4):281–314, 2000.

[19] J. M. Hellerstein, P. J. Haas, and H. J. Wang. Online aggregation. In *Proc. ACM SIGMOD International Conference on Management of Data*, 1997.

[20] D. G. Horvitz and D. J. Thompson. A generalization of sampling without replacement from a finite universe. *Journal of the American Statistical Association*, 47:663–685, 1952.

[21] X. Hu, M. Qiao, and Y. Tao. Independent range sampling. In *Proc. ACM Symposium on Principles of Database Systems*, 2014.

[22] S. Idreos, S. Manegold, and G. Graefe. Adaptive indexing in modern database kernels. In *EDBT*, pages 566–569, 2012.

[23] R. Jampani, F. Xu, M. Wu, L. L. Perez, C. Jermaine, and P. J. Haas. The monte carlo database system: Stochastic analysis close to the data. *ACM Trans. Database Syst.*, 36(3):18, 2011.

[24] P. Jayachandran, K. Tunga, N. Kamat, and A. Nandi. Combining user interaction, speculative query execution and sampling in the DICE system. *PVLDB*, 7(13):1697–1700, 2014.

[25] C. Jermaine, S. Arumugam, A. Pol, and A. Dobra. Scalable approximate query processing with the DBO engine. In *Proc. ACM SIGMOD International Conference on Management of Data*, 2007.

[26] C. Jermaine, S. Arumugam, A. Pol, and A. Dobra. Scalable approximate query processing with the DBO engine. *ACM Transactions on Database Systems*, 33(4), Article 23, 2008.

[27] R. Jin, L. Glimcher, C. Jermaine, and G. Agrawal. New sampling-based estimators for OLAP queries. In *ICDE*, page 18, 2006.

[28] S. Joshi and C. M. Jermaine. Robust stratified sampling plans for low selectivity queries. In *ICDE*, pages 199–208, 2008.

[29] S. Joshi and C. M. Jermaine. Sampling-based estimators for subset-based queries. *VLDB J.*, 18(1):181–202, 2009.

[30] A. Kim, E. Blais, A. G. Parameswaran, P. Indyk, S. Madden, and R. Rubinfeld. Rapid sampling for visualizations with ordering guarantees. *PVLDB*, 8(5):521–532, 2015.

[31] A. Klein, R. Gemulla, P. Rösch, and W. Lehner. Derby/s: a DBMS for sample-based query answering. In *SIGMOD*, 2006.

[32] R. J. Lipton and J. F. Naughton. Query size estimation by adaptive sampling. In *Proc. ACM Symposium on Principles of Database Systems*, 1990.

[33] R. J. Lipton, J. F. Naughton, and D. A. Schneider. Practical selectivity estimation through adaptive sampling. In *Proc. ACM SIGMOD International Conference on Management of Data*, 1990.

[34] S. Lohr. *Sampling: Design and analysis*. Thomson, 2009.

[35] G. Luo, C. J. Ellmann, P. J. Haas, and J. F. Naughton. A scalable hash ripple join algorithm. In *Proc. ACM SIGMOD International Conference on Management of Data*, 2002.

[36] R. Motwani and P. Raghavan. *Randomized Algorithms*. Cambridge University Press, 1995.

[37] S. Nirkhiwale, A. Dobra, and C. M. Jermaine. A sampling algebra for aggregate estimation. *PVLDB*, 6(14):1798–1809, 2013.

[38] F. Olken. *Random Sampling from Databases*. PhD thesis, University of California at Berkeley, 1993.

[39] J. K. Ousterhout, P. Agrawal, D. Erickson, C. Kozyrakis, J. Leverich, D. Mazières, S. Mitra, A. Narayanan, D. Ongaro, G. M. Parulkar, M. Rosenblum, S. M. Rumble, E. Stratmann, and R. Stutsman. The case for ramcloud. *Commun. ACM*, 54(7):121–130, 2011.

[40] N. Pansare, V. R. Borkar, C. Jermaine, and T. Condie. Online aggregation for large mapreduce jobs. In *Proceedings of the VLDB Endowment*, volume 4, 2011.

[41] E. Petraki, S. Idreos, and S. Manegold. Holistic indexing in main-memory column-stores. In *SIGMOD*, pages 1153–1166, 2015.

[42] C. Qin and F. Rusu. Parallel online aggregation in action. In *SSDBM*, pages 46:1–46:4, 2013.
[43] C. Qin and F. Rusu. PF-OLA: a high-performance framework for parallel online aggregation. *Distributed and Parallel Databases*, 32(3):337–375, 2014.
[44] D. Vengerov, A. C. Menck, and M. Zait. Join size estimation subject to filter conditions. In *Proc. International Conference on Very Large Data Bases*, 2015.
[45] L. Wang, R. Christensen, F. Li, and K. Yi. Spatial online sampling and aggregation. In *Proc. International Conference on Very Large Data Bases*, 2016.
[46] M. Wu and C. Jermaine. Outlier detection by sampling with accuracy guarantees. In *SIGKDD*, pages 767–772, 2006.
[47] S. Wu, S. Jiang, B. C. Ooi, and K. Tan. Distributed online aggregation. *PVLDB*, 2(1):443–454, 2009.
[48] S. Wu, B. C. Ooi, and K. Tan. Continuous sampling for online aggregation over multiple queries. In *SIGMOD*, pages 651–662, 2010.
[49] F. Xu, C. M. Jermaine, and A. Dobra. Confidence bounds for sampling-based group by estimates. *ACM Trans. Database Syst.*, 33(3), 2008.
[50] K. Zeng, S. Agarwal, A. Dave, M. Armbrust, and I. Stoica. G-OLA: generalized on-line aggregation for interactive analysis on big data. In *SIGMOD*, pages 913–918, 2015.
[51] K. Zeng, S. Gao, J. Gu, B. Mozafari, and C. Zaniolo. ABS: a system for scalable approximate queries with accuracy guarantees. In *SIGMOD*, pages 1067–1070, 2014.
[52] K. Zeng, S. Gao, B. Mozafari, and C. Zaniolo. The analytical bootstrap: a new method for fast error estimation in approximate query processing. In *SIGMOD*, pages 277–288, 2014.

APPENDIX

A. ESTIMATORS AND CONFIDENCE INTERVALS

For any function $f, h : \mathbb{N} \to \mathbb{R}$, we introduce the following notation:

$$T_n(f) = \frac{1}{n}\sum_{i=1}^{n} f(i),$$

$$T_{n,q}(f) = \frac{1}{n-1}\sum_{i=1}^{n}(f(i) - T_n(f))^q,$$

$$T_{n,q,r}(f,h) = \frac{1}{n-1}\sum_{i=1}^{n}(f(i) - T_n(f))^q(h(i) - T_n(h))^r.$$

The estimators for a few common aggregation functions, as well as estimators for their variances, are given by:

$$\texttt{SUM} : \tilde{Y}_n = T_n(uv), \tilde{\sigma}_n^2 = T_{n,2}(uv);$$

$$\texttt{COUNT} : \tilde{Y}_n = T_n(u), \tilde{\sigma}_n^2 = T_{n,2}(u);$$

$$\texttt{AVE} : \tilde{Y}_n = T_n(uv)/T_n(u), \tilde{\sigma}_n^2 =$$

$$\frac{1}{T_n^2(u)}\left(T_{n,2}(uv) - 2R_{n,2}T_{n,1,1}(uv,u) + R_{n,2}^2 T_{n,2}(u)\right),$$

where $R_{n,2} = T_n(uv)/T_n(u)$.

Please see [14] for formulas for `VARIANCE` and `STDEV`.

Finally, after we have obtained an estimate $\tilde{\sigma}_{n(t)}^2$ for the variance of an estimator $\tilde{Y}$, the half-width of the confidence interval is computed as (for a confidence level threshold α)

$$\varepsilon_n = \frac{z_\alpha \tilde{\sigma}_n}{\sqrt{n}}, \tag{5}$$

where z_α is the $\frac{\alpha+1}{2}$-quantile of the normal distribution with mean 0 and variance 1.

B. ADDITIONAL PROOFS

Lemma 1 *The algorithm produces a consistent assignment.*

PROOF. Suppose that after the assignment, some $T(v)$ is disconnected. Then there must be a $u \in T(v) \cap M$ such that all its predecessors in $T(v)$ have been assigned to other $T(v')$'s, but u remains in $T(v)$. If any of u's predecessors is assigned before u, then the algorithm cannot have assigned u to $T(v)$. If all of u's predecessors are assigned after u, then they must be in the same strongly-connected component as u, and u does not have other predecessors in M. This means that u is directed connected to $T(v) \setminus M$. □

C. ADDITIONAL TABLES

Table 2 (see next page) presents the results on the effectiveness and overhead of walk plan optimization for wander join in PostgreSQL. Table 3 (see next page) presents our PostgreSQL implementation of wander join against both DBO and a commercial database system (denoted as System X). For results in both Tables 2 and 3, we investigated both sufficient memory and limit memory scenarios. The results of which have been discussed in the end of Section 5.

	SF[1]	sufficient memory					limited memory				
		total time[2]	optimized plan[3]		PG plan[4]		total time	optimized plan		PG plan	
			time	AE[5]	time	AE		time	AE	time	AE
Q3	10	9.24	9.03	0.26	20.2	0.09	330	323	0.95	556	2.91
	20	11.27	11.05	0.39	21.4	0.34	390	382	0.43	673	0.05
	30	11.28	11.03	0.23	21.5	0.37	429	422	1.22	702	0.49
	40	11.38	11.04	0.30	21.5	0.27	455	447	3.63	706	0.56
Q7	10	9.18	9.02	0.19	51.6	0.03	126	90	1.23	937	0.45
	20	9.32	9.22	0.42	56.4	0.07	188	131	3.90	1359	1.72
	30	8.47	8.17	0.28	60.5	0.11	215	145	1.67	1613	0.53
	40	8.56	8.27	1.16	60.6	0.30	230	157	1.00	1742	0.71
Q10	10	3.23	3.05	1.19	3.12	0.11	71	61	0.31	95	0.43
	20	3.33	3.17	0.39	4.34	0.02	96	79	0.51	118	1.03
	30	3.35	3.06	0.45	5.54	0.84	107	90	2.22	125	1.17
	40	4.22	4.07	0.06	7.87	0.76	111	93	2.48	134	0.97

Table 2: PostgreSQL with wander join: time cost of walk plan optimization and total execution time (and the actual error achieved).

[1] SF: scale factor (GB).
[2] total time: the total wall clock time for walk plan optimization and plan execution to reach the target confidence interval (CI) with 95% confidence level. The target CI is 1% for sufficient memory and 5% for limited memory.
[3] optimized plan: time taken and actual error achieved to reach the target CI by directly using the best plan selected by wander join's query optimizer (i.e., the plan execution time from the total time).
[4] PG plan: time taken and actual error achieved to reach the target CI by using the plan constructed from the input query and used by PostgreSQL.
[5] AE: actual error (%).

	SF[1]	sufficient memory					limited memory				
		System X[2]	DBO		PG+WJ[5]		System X	DBO		PG+WJ	
			CI[3]	AE[4]	CI	AE		CI	AE	CI	AE
Q3	10	32.24	–	–	1.18	0.09	107.27	–	–	15.9	7.8
	20	74.29	–	–	0.78	0.43	249.94	–	–	11.1	4.3
	30	65.17	–	–	0.84	0.40	428.39	–	–	9.6	4.5
	40	90.23	–	–	0.76	0.26	707.04	48.50	30.60	8.1	4.7
Q7	10	33.62	–	–	1.15	0.24	103.3	–	–	15.1	4.1
	20	73.03	–	–	0.70	0.35	205.7	–	–	11.2	3.4
	30	57.82	–	–	0.79	0.35	326.35	–	–	9.6	1.7
	40	77.92	–	–	0.69	0.05	445.86	–	–	8	0.3
Q10	10	40.43	–	–	0.75	0.01	146.57	47.71	23.24	13.7	1.2
	20	98.96	82.06	21.93	0.47	0.02	326.67	35.62	14.60	8.7	2.1
	30	109.19	138.29	66.50	0.46	0.05	697.06	26.43	6.69	6.9	1.3
	40	138.87	97.68	11.99	0.42	0.06	829.97	11.31	1.32	5.2	0.5

Table 3: Accuracy achieved in 1/10 of System X's running time for computing the full join.

[1] SF: scale factor (GB).
[2] System X: full join time on System X (seconds).
[3] CI: half width of the confidence interval (%).
[4] AE: actual error (%).
[5] PG+WJ: Our version of PostgreSQL with Wander Join implemented inside the PostgreSQL engine.
–: no result reported in the time given.

Quickr: Lazily Approximating Complex AdHoc Queries in BigData Clusters

Srikanth Kandula, Anil Shanbhag, Aleksandar Vitorovic, Matthaios Olma, Robert Grandl, Surajit Chaudhuri, Bolin Ding
Microsoft
msr-quickr@microsoft.com

ABSTRACT

We present a system that approximates the answer to complex ad-hoc queries in big-data clusters by injecting samplers on-the-fly and without requiring pre-existing samples. Improvements can be substantial when big-data queries take multiple passes over data and when samplers execute early in the query plan. We present a new *universe* sampler which is able to sample multiple join inputs. By incorporating samplers natively into a cost-based query optimizer, we automatically generate plans with appropriate samplers at appropriate locations. We devise an accuracy analysis method using which we ensure that query plans with samplers will not miss groups and that aggregate values are within a small ratio of their true value. An implementation on a cluster with tens of thousands of machines shows that queries in the TPC-DS benchmark use a median of 2× fewer resources. In contrast, approaches that construct input samples even when given 10× the size of the input to store samples improve only 22% of the queries, i.e., a median speed up of 0×.

1. INTRODUCTION

This paper considers the problem of approximating jobs in big-data clusters. Jobs specified as a mash-up of relational expressions and user-defined code increasingly dominate the big-data ecosystem, due in large part to the growth of frameworks such as Hive [40], Pig [37], SCOPE [18], Spark-SQL [12] and Dremel [33].

Queries in big-data clusters are approximatable but are complex and use many datasets. As an example, consider a production cluster at Microsoft with tens of thousands of machines that supports millions of queries per day for Bing and other services. (1) The distribution of queries over inputs is heavy-tailed. We find that the smallest subset of inputs which supports half of the queries is 20PB in size. The next 30% of queries touch another 40PB of inputs. (2) Further, queries are complex. They have many joins; median value is 3 and 90th percentile is 11. The execution graphs are deep, with the median graph having 192 operators and a depth of 28. Further, queries touch many columns from each dataset; the median query uses 8 columns per dataset and 49 at the 90th percentile. However, queries also have aggregations and their output is much smaller than the input indicating the potential for speed-up from approximation.

SIGMOD'16, June 26-July 01, 2016, San Francisco, CA, USA

ISBN 978-1-4503-3531-7/16/06. . . $15.00

DOI: http://dx.doi.org/10.1145/2882903.2882940

Approximating big-data queries, i.e., trading off degradation in answer quality to improve performance, has many use cases. We use performance colloquially here to refer to both query response time and cluster throughput. Since queries process large volumes of data on expensive clusters, even a modest decrease in resource usage, say 2×, would reduce the bill from Azure by 2× and production clusters which are capacity limited can run 2× more queries. Data scientists can tolerate imprecise answers for exploratory analysis and faster responses increase productivity [17, 25]. Two use cases are especially important: (a) queries that generate aggregated dashboard reports by analyzing logs if sped up would increase the refresh rate of the dashboards at no extra cost and (b) machine learning queries that build models by iterating over datasets (e.g., k-means) can tolerate approximations in their early iterations.

Unfortunately, state-of-art techniques cannot approximate complex queries. Most SQL databases and big-data systems offer the uniform sample operator. The user can sample as desired. But the systems do not reason about the accuracy of the resulting answer. A rich vein of prior research [6, 7, 9, 14, 20, 39] builds samples over input datasets. They deliver immense benefit to *predictable* queries that touch only one large dataset, i.e., any joins have to be with small dimension tables on foreign keys. However, they cannot support joins over more than one large table, queries that touch less frequently used datasets or query sets that use a diverse set of columns. As explained above, such queries and datasets dominate in big-data clusters. For example, on the TPC-DS [4] benchmark, our experiments show that when given 1×(4×) the size of the input to store samples, a state-of-the-art input sampling system BlinkDB [9] offers a benefit for 11% (17%) of the queries.

Our system, QUICKR, has three goals. First, offer turn-key support for approximations: that is, given a query, decide whether or not it can be sampled and output an appropriate query plan with samplers. In particular, input samples, views or indices may not be available. Next, support complex queries, i.e., support the large portion of SQL shown in Table 1. Finally, ensure that answers will be accurate; that is, with high probability (whp), none of the groups will be missed in the answer and that the computed value of aggregations is within a bounded ratio of their true value (say ±10%). We are unaware of any system that achieves these goals.

A key observation in QUICKR is that big-data queries perform multiple passes over data. This is partly due to the queries being complex and partly due to parallel plans. For example, a hash join requires two passes over data and one shuffle across the network. If data were sampled in the first pass, all subsequent computation could be sped up. The novel advantage of such *inline sampling* is that the gains from sampling have negligible apriori overhead. The disadvantage is that the *best case gains* are potentially smaller relative to apriori sampling which can execute the query on a very small sample of input. In our cluster, the median query has 2.4 *effective*[1] passes over data and 6.5 passes at the 90th percentile. Furthermore, the first pass over data is often embarrassingly parallel. Hence, inline sampling offers sizable performance gains without apriori overhead.

We note that QUICKR is complementary to building apriori samples. The latter is suited for simple predictable queries on popular datasets whereas QUICKR can approximate the more complex queries over infrequently used datasets with zero overhead.

A novel aspect that lets QUICKR cover many more queries than prior methods is a *universe sampler* that samples multiple join inputs. It is well known that joining a p probability sample of inputs is akin to a p^2 probability sample of the join output [21, 24]. Hence, sampling the join inputs improves performance at the cost of substantial degradation in answer quality. On the other hand, when queries join large inputs, sampling the join output offers limited speed-up. With the universe sampler, joining a p probability sample of inputs is statistically equivalent to a p probability universe sample of the join output. The key idea is to *consistently* sample the join inputs without any coordination (such as exchanging histograms of join keys [6, 22]). We will show that the universe sampler is applicable broadly, i.e., it supports multiple equi-joins and only requires the group-by columns and the value of aggregates to be uncorrelated with the sampled column set.

QUICKR offers turn-key support for approximations by picking for every newly arriving query an execution plan with samplers. In this paper, we pick the best performing plan among those that have no worse than the specified amount of error. Since queries can be unapproximable (more on this later), a legitimate outcome is to output a plan without samplers. QUICKR solves several challenges along the way. Which sampler to pick and where to place the samplers in the plan is a complex decision, in part, because QUICKR uses three different samplers each of which is most appropriate under some conditions. The *universe* sampler is described above. The *uniform* sampler mimics a Bernoulli process. The *distinct* sampler ensures that no groups will be missed by *stratifying*, i.e., picking some rows for every distinct value of the group-by columns. To place these samplers at arbitrary locations in the plan, QUICKR requires that samplers run in one pass over data, with bounded memory and in parallel; that is, different sampler instances independently process partitions of data.

There are two broad ways to find a good plan with samplers: add samplers on top of the plan output by a query optimizer or treat samplers as first-class operators within the query optimizer. QUICKR adopts the latter approach because the former is computationally expensive and leads to poor quality plans. Since any operator can be followed by a sampler, there are exponentially many sampled plans. Reasoning about the performance and accuracy of each of these possible plans is complex and requires statistics that are harder to acquire outside the QO. Most importantly, adding samplers can lead to dramatically different query plans. For example, because a sampler reduces cardinality, joins may become implementable more cheaply or parallel portions of the plan can be replaced with the much simpler sequential plans. By treating samplers as first-class operators in a Cascades-style [27] cost-based query optimizer, QUICKR effectively navigates a large space of possible sampled plans.

We call the resulting algorithm **ASALQA**, short for place **a**ppropriate **s**amplers at **a**ppropriate **l**ocations in the **q**uery plan **a**utomatically. **ASALQA** begins by placing a sampler optimistically before every aggregation. Then, several new transformation rules generate alternative plans by moving samplers closer to the input, i.e., to before database operators such as join, select, and project. **ASALQA** picks

[1]computed as $\left(\sum_{\text{task } t} \text{input}_t + \text{output}_t\right)$ / (job input + job output)

Selection	Arbitrary (user-defined) expressions specified as f(*col*1, *col*2, ...) <=> *Constant*. Also, composing several such literals with ∨ or ∧.
Aggregates	DISTINCT, COUNT, SUM, AVG and their *IF equivalents. User-defined aggregates need annotations.
Join	All but full-outer join. Includes joins over multiple tables, outer joins and star queries with foreign key joins.
Others	Projects, Order By, Windowed aggregates, ...

Table 1: Types of parallel SQL queries that are handled by QUICKR. In particular QUICKR can deal with arbitrary depth queries.

the best plan by costing both performance and accuracy. To do so, ASALQA uses statistics such as cardinality and distinct value counts which are computed in one effective pass by the first query that touches an input and are derived by ASALQA for sub-expressions. The plans output by ASALQA often have multiple samplers. Many plans have samplers deep in the query plan. ASALQA declares roughly 25% of the TPC-DS queries to be unapproximable for various reasons. An illustrative example is in §2.

ASALQA can reason about the accuracy of a sampled expression. Our method transforms a query expression with arbitrarily many samplers to an equivalent expression with one sampler at the root. In particular, we generalize prior work that only considered SUM-like aggregates [35] to the case where answers can have groups. We also generalize the method to a broader class of samplers that are not generalized-uniform-samplers; our universe and distinct samplers are not uniformly random. Furthermore, we compute the error metrics for ASALQA plans in one effective pass over data whereas in general error bounds require a self-join [35] or bootstrap [10, 44].

We have implemented QUICKR in a production query optimizer. Experiments over queries in the TPC-DS benchmark show a median reduction of 2× in resources used; a few queries improve by over 5×. For over 90% of queries, QUICKR does not miss groups. Most of the misses are due to `LIMIT 100` on the aggregation column. When considering the *full* answer, QUICKR does not miss groups for 99% of queries. Aggregations are within ±10% of their true value in 80% of the queries; 92% of queries are within ±20%. We carefully explain the causes of high error. In contrast, BlinkDB [9] has a median gain of 0% even when given 10× the input size to store samples. That is, at least half the queries receive no benefit. In a parameter sweep, we find that the best coverage is 22% of queries and the best median speed-up *among the covered queries* is 35%.

To sum up, our key contributions are:

- QUICKR offers a new way to lazily approximate complex adhoc queries with zero apriori overhead.
- Through careful analysis over queries in a big-data cluster, we find apriori samples are untenable because query sets make diverse use of columns and queries are spread across many datasets. The large number of passes over data per query makes the case for lazy approximations.
- We introduce a new sampler operator – universe – that effectively samples multiple join inputs.
- We consider query optimization over samples much more extensively. Our ASALQA algorithm automatically outputs sampled query plans only when appropriate.
- We present implementation results from a production big-data system.

We believe that this is just the first step towards practical lazy approximations. Queries can be sped up further by reusing sampled views [28] and by progressive execution [29]. In the rest of this paper, we describe our analysis of queries from our production cluster in §3. We describe our samplers in §4.1, the ASALQA algorithm in §4.2 and our accuracy analysis is in §4.3. Experimental results and a summary of related work are in §5 and §6.

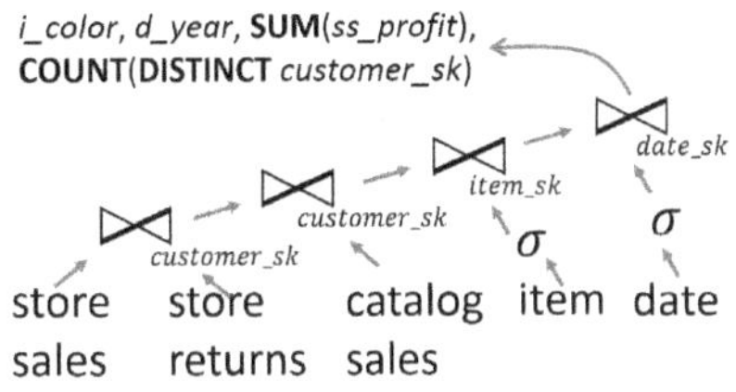

Technique	How sampled
Input sampling	Stratify store_sales on {item_sk, date_sk, customer_sk}
QUICKR	Universe sample all three fact tables on customer_sk

Figure 1: A simple example that mimics many TPC-DS queries.

2. MOTIVATING EXAMPLE

Consider the query in Figure 1. Per item color and year, the query computes the total profit from store sales and the number of unique customers who have purchased and returned from stores and purchased from catalog. Item and date are dimension tables joined on a foreign key. The other three are large fact tables joined on shared keys. Since joining a pair of fact tables requires two reads and one shuffle, this query incurs many passes over its input data.

Stratification on a column set C guarantees that the sampler will pick some rows for every distinct value of C. The most useful input sample stratifies `store_sales` on {`item_sk`, `date_sk`, `customer_sk`} because `store_sales` is the largest table and not stratifying can miss groups in the answer. However, such a sample is as large as the input since the three columns have many distinct combinations leading to zero performance gains.

The universe sample on a column set C picks all rows whose hash of the value of columns in C falls in a randomly chosen subspace. QUICKR yields a very different sampled query plan: at extraction on all fact tables, universe sample on `customer_sk`. This works because QUICKR reasons that (a) universe sampling all fact tables on the join key `customer_sk` and then joining them is identical to a universe sample of the join output, (b) the group columns {`i_color`, `d_year`} are independent with `customer_sk` since different random subsets of customers have similar likelihood of purchasing different colored items over years and (c) the group has only a few distinct values and since the fact tables have over 10^9 rows, there are many rows per group. Interestingly, the universe sample can also estimate the number of unique customers, which is the same column whose value it sub-samples on. The reason is that the number of unique customers in the chosen subspace can be projected up by the fraction of subspace that is chosen. QUICKR speeds up this query substantially. The data in-flight after the first pass reduces by the sampled probability and there are up to 4 subsequent passes over this dataset.

Note that small changes in the query can lead to very different sampled plans. If some user-defined operator applies on `store_sales`, QUICKR *could* place the universe sampler *after* that UDO. Indeed, we find in our evaluation that many queries have samplers in the middle of the query plan. Consider a more substantial change: if the query only had `store_sales`, i.e., no joins with the other fact tables, QUICKR would prefer a uniform sample of `store_sales`. As we show later, the uniform sampler has smaller variance than the universe sampler. If the answer were also grouped on `i_category` and `i_name` from `item`, the group could then contain so many distinct values that QUICKR would distinct sample the `store_sales` table on `ss_item_sk`. That is, QUICKR stratifies on join keys to mimic stratification on columns from `item`. Finally, if the answer has one group per day, that is group on `d_date` instead of `d_year`, then QUICKR may declare the query unapproximable since stratifying `store_sales` on {`ss_item_sk`, `ss_date_sk`} will not reduce rowcount. In our evaluation, we see that all three samplers are used often. Many plans use multiple samplers. QUICKR finds that 25% of the examined TPC-DS queries are unapproximable.

A ninja data scientist can probably reason about this large space of sampled plans quickly and correctly. Early in the project, it took us about an hour to manually analyze each query. QUICKR offers a turn-key solution. In practice, QUICKR also generates slightly better plans since we found that human experts fail to fully explore the space of possible plans. Also, experts did not have access to automatic derivations of cardinality and the number of distinct values.

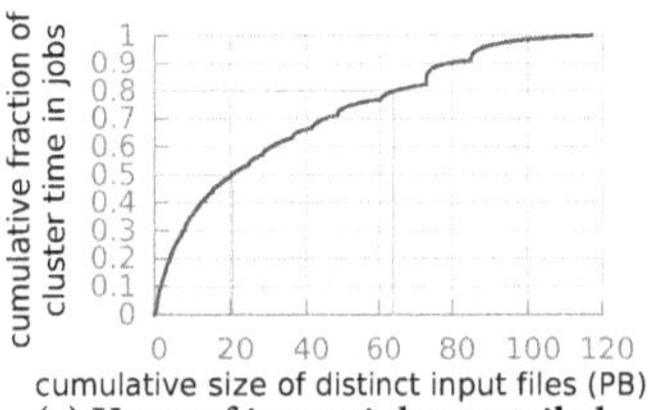

(a) Usage of inputs is heavy tailed.

Metric	Percentile value				
	25th	50th	75th	90th	95th
# of Passes over Data	1.83	2.45	3.63	6.49	9.78
1/firstpass duration fract.	1.37	1.61	2.09	6.38	17.34
# operators	143	192	581	1103	1283
depth of operators	21	28	40	51	75
# Aggregation Ops.	2	3	9	37	112
# Joins	2	3	5	11	27
# user-defined aggs.	0	0	1	3	5
# user-defined functions	7	27	45	127	260
size of QCS+QVS	4	8	24	49	104

(b) Characterizing some $O(10^8)$ queries that ran in a production big-data cluster over a two month span.

Figure 2: Analysis of the queries and datasets used in a large cluster. Equivalent estimates for publicly available benchmarks are in Table 9.

3. PRIMER: APPROXIMABILITY OF BIG-DATA QUERIES

A key departure in QUICKR is to inject sampling operators into the query plan. Suppose query Q over input I has answer $Q(I)$. Apriori sampling techniques search for the *best* sample of input I' such that $Q(I') \approx Q(I)$. Instead, QUICKR searches over the space of sampled query plans for the *best* plan Q' such that $Q'(I) \approx Q(I)$. In both cases, *best* can imply best performance subject to the accuracy needs or vice-versa. Clearly the approaches are complementary. Here, we document aspects of queries observed in a large production cluster that lead us to believe that QUICKR is necessary.

We analyzed the production queries in Microsoft's Cosmos clusters over a two month period. The clusters have tens of thousands of servers. Overall, $O(10^8)$ queries were submitted by $O(10^4)$ unique developers. The query language is a mash-up of relational and user-defined operations [18]. The query set includes: ad-hoc queries written by developers and production jobs which cook new data (e.g., ETL), or mine logs to construct dashboard reports. Figure 2 summarizes our findings.

Heavy Tail over Inputs: If most queries touch a small number of inputs, then it may be worthwhile to store apriori samples for those inputs. Per Figure 2a however, we find that queries access many different inputs. The figure is generated as follows for a two week period: (1) Per input, compute the total cluster hours used by queries that read the input. (2) When a query has multiple inputs, apportion its cluster hours among the inputs proportional to input size. (3) Sort inputs in decreasing order of their cluster hours. (4) Traversing in that order, compute the cumulative size of the input and the cumulative cluster hours. We see that jobs that account for half the cluster-hours touch 20PBs of distinct files. The last 25% of queries, the *tail*, access another 60PBs of files.

To store differently stratified samples, apriori storage techniques typically use sample storage of 1× to 10× the size of the input (eg. BlinkDB [9]). We see from Figure 2a that the smallest input set used by 20% of queries is 3PB. Hence, assuming input popularity can be predicted perfectly, covering 20% of queries will require between 3PB and 30PB of apriori samples. Such a large sample set is already a substantial fraction of the total input size (120PB). QUICKR targets the vast majority of other queries and needs no apriori samples.

Recall that no stored samples implies that QUICKR has to read all input data once. Per Figure 2b, the median query in the cluster takes 2.25 effective passes over data.[2] By sampling on the first pass, we can estimate that QUICKR may speed-up the median job by 2.25×. 10% of queries can speed up by over 6×. The practical gains can be less because not all queries are approximable (for reasons below) or much more because the samplers can also speed up the computation on the first pass (e.g., fewer data to partition and write out).

Query Approximability: Query answers can be aggregates such as a `SUM`, `COUNT`, `AVG` or aggregations over groups such as `SELECT X, SUM(Y)`. The goal of approximation is to avoid processing all the data, yet still obtain (a) an unbiased estimate of the answer per group[3] that is within a small ratio of the true answer with high probability (or whp.), (b) ensure that no groups are missed whp., and (c) offer an estimate of the expected error per aggregation. Queries for which this is possible, we say, are *approximable*.

A key intuition behind the approximability of a query is the *support* per group of the answer. By *support* we refer to the number of data rows in the input that contribute to each group. Simple aggregations have support equal to the number of rows in the input. The support may vary across groups. In general, queries with large support receive high performance gains from approximation since even a small probability sample can produce an answer that is close to the true answer. If the underlying data value has high variance, more support is needed (more on this later). We observe that typical big data queries have large support due in part to their large inputs.

Per Figure 2b, typical queries also have joins, selects, projects and user-defined code, all of which further complicate approximability. We distinguish between row-local operations that take one or more columns and yield a column such as `DayOf(X : date)` and aggregations that take a collection of rows having a common value of the group-by columns and yield zero or more rows such as `X, MODE(Y)`. We call the former user-defined functions (UDFs) and the latter user-defined aggregates (UDAs). The median query has tens of UDFs and a few UDAs. The median query also has a handful of joins, several of which are not foreign-key joins.

To quantify the complexity of these operations, we co-opt the phrase Query Column Set (QCS) from BlinkDB [9] to refer to the subset of the input columns that appear in the answer or impact which rows belong in the answer. For example, the QCS of `SELECT X, SUM(Y) WHERE Z > 30` is $\{X, Z\}$. The corresponding query value set (QVS) is $\{Y\}$, i.e., the columns that appear in aggregates. We recursively replace newly generated columns that appear in the QCS or QVS with the columns that were used to generate that column. We see that the size of QCS ∪ QVS is over 8 for 50% of queries. Further, the size of the median QCS is also 8. Comparing with equivalent estimates for benchmarks in Tables 3 and 9, we see that queries in the production cluster tend to be more complex. BlinkDB [9] constructs stratified samples on the QCS sets. Observing that the value of columns in the QVS can have high skew, StratifiedSampling [20] stratifies on QCS ∪ QVS.

Armed with the above background, we posit that apriori sampling has poor query coverage even when given storage space that is many times the size of that dataset. First, the QCSets have many columns. Since the goal of stratification is to store some rows for every distinct value of the columns in QCS, the more columns in the QCS, the more the distinct values and larger the stratified sample for that QCS. Second, queries have very diverse QCSets. Queries with different QCS will not benefit from the same stratified sample. Roughly, the smaller the intersection between the two QCSets, the less useful the sample will be. In the extreme case, when the QCSets have no overlap, sharing the sample can have the same error profile as a random sample[4] or worse if the QCSets have correlated values. As a result, given a storage budget, apriori sampling techniques must choose very carefully which QCSets to stratify on to help the largest set of queries [9, 20]. By injecting samplers into the query graph, QUICKR completely avoids this problem.

Further, many queries that appear unapproximable for input samples can be sped up by QUICKR. Consider a query with a large QCS. A stratified sample on that QCS may be as large as the input. However, QUICKR can place a sampler *after* selections or joins whose (complex) predicates contributed many of the columns in the QCS. If the selects are pushed down to the first parallel pass on data, the gains from QUICKR will be substantial.

Handling Joins: None of the known approximation systems handle joins well. Note that join between a fact and a dimension table is effectively a select since the foreign key relationship ensures that exactly one row will match out of the dimension table. Most prior work samples only one of the join inputs; doing so does not speed up queries where both input relations require a lot of work. To understand the issue with sampling both inputs, consider a two table join where `T1` has 80 rows with `X = 1` and `T2` has 1 row with `X = 1`. The join is on column X. To ensure that each tuple appears in the output with the same probability, a 25% sample on the join output requires 50% samples of both inputs.[5] That is, the join inputs have to be sampled with a quadratically higher probability. Even so, sample-and-join has a higher variance. For example, the probability that rows with `X = 1` disappear after sample-and-join is 0.5 whereas with join-and-sample, it is 10^{-10}.[6] The problem arises because the join output depends on the *joint distribution* over the two inputs but such joint distribution does not exist apriori. Further, it is expensive to compute when these relations are intermediate content generated in the midst of executing a deep query. A better sampler would have over-sampled the rows with `X = 1` in T_2 since that value occurs more often in T_1. Such correlation-aware samplers exist [6, 7, 21] but they are cumbersome to implement in parallel (since they build statistics and indices on one join input and use that to sample the other input) and are somewhat ineffective because the sampler cannot be pushed down further on the inputs. QUICKR's universe sampler uniquely samples both join inputs without any data exchange between the inputs at runtime, thereby allowing QUICKR to speed-up many more queries than prior work.

In summary, our analysis reveals the following:

- Distribution of queries over input datasets is heavy-tailed. Individual queries use many columns and a diverse set of

[2] computed as $\left(\sum_{\text{task } t} \text{input}_t + \text{output}_t\right) / (\text{job input} + \text{job output})$
[3] true sum ≈ 20 * `sum` for a 5% sample. Also see Table 8.

[4] uniform sample = strat sampler with empty QCS.
[5] since a tuple will appear in output only if both its constituent tuples in the inputs are sampled and $0.25 = 0.5 * 0.5$
[6] T_1, T_2 and $T_1 \bowtie T_2$ have 80, 1, 80 rows with `X = 1` respectively. Hence, the probability of missing `X = 1` in join-and-sample is $(1 - 0.25)^{80} = 10^{-10}$ and in sample-and-join is $(1 - 0.5)^{80} + 0.5 = 0.5$.

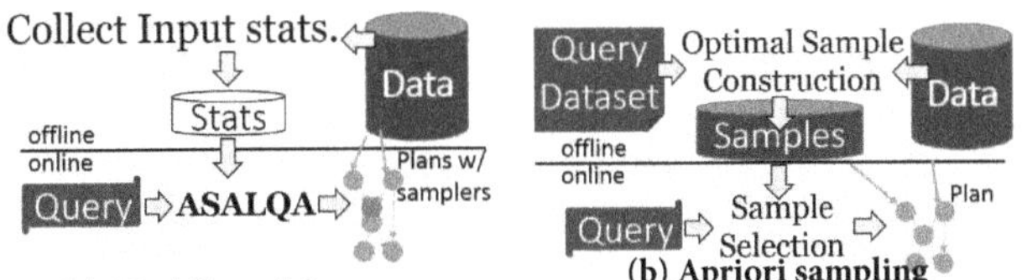

(a) Workflow of QUICKR (b) Apriori sampling

Figure 3: Overview of QUICKR and how it differs from prior methods.

columns such that the additional storage space required to store samples can be prohibitively large.

- Queries typically have aggregation operators, large support, and output $\ll$ input, so they are approximable.
- Several factors hinder approximability: queries use a diverse set of columns requiring extensive stratification. Many queries join large input relations.
- Queries are deep, involving multiple effective passes over data including network shuffles.

4. JUST-IN-TIME SAMPLING

Figure 3a shows an overview of QUICKR. QUICKR uses statistics of the input datasets to generate at query optimization time an execution plan with samplers placed at appropriate locations. The samplers are described in §4.1. The algorithm that determines how best to place the samplers is in §4.2. Analysis of the error and properties of the transformation rules is in §4.3. We briefly recount our goals:

- Minimal overhead to the administrator: That is, assume no apriori samples, indices or views and support ad-hoc queries.
- Support a large fraction of the queries in SQL and big-data scenarios; including general joins and UDFs.
- Performance gains should be sizable; either reducing the resource needs of a query or a faster completion time or both.
- Offer accurate answers: That is, with high probability miss no groups, offer confidence intervals, and estimate aggregate values to within a small ratio of their true values.

4.1 Samplers

QUICKR uses three types of samplers. Each sampler passes a subset of the input rows. The subset is chosen based on the policies that we describe next. In addition, each sampler appends a metadata column representing the *weight* associated with the row. The weight is used to estimate the true value of aggregates and the confidence intervals. Our samplers are required to run in a *streaming* and *partitionable* mode. They have to execute in one pass over data with a memory footprint well below the size of the input or output. Furthermore, when many instances of a sampler run in parallel on different partitions of the input, the union of their output should mimic the output of one sampler instance examining all of the input. These minimal assumptions enable placing the samplers at arbitrary locations in a parallel query plan.

4.1.1 Uniform sampler

Given probability p, the uniform sampler Γ_p^{U} lets a row pass through with probability p uniformly-at-random. The weight column is set to $1/p$. In contrast, alternatives that pick a desired *number* of input rows uniformly-at-random with or without replacement [24] are neither streaming nor partitionable. If implemented with reservoir sampling so as to finish in one pass over data, their memory usage grows up to the desired output size and the parallel instances have to be synchronized and coordinated. The number of rows output by Γ_p^{U} is governed by a binomial distribution and each row can be picked at most once.

4.1.2 Distinct sampler

The uniform sampler is simple but it has some issues that limit it from being used widely. Queries with group-by such as `SELECT X, SUM(Y) GROUP BY X` can miss groups in the answer, especially those corresponding to values of `X` that have low support. For such queries, QUICKR uses a distinct sampler which intuitively guarantees that at least a certain number of rows pass per distinct combination of values of a given column set. The distinct sampler also helps when aggregates have high skew. To see this problem, consider a three row input with the values 1, 1, 100 for column `Y`. The true answer for `SUM(Y)` is 102 but the projected answer changes dramatically based on whether the value of 100 is sampled or not; even at 50% sampling, the most likely answers are 2 and 202, each of which happen with likelihood 1/4.

Given a column set C, a number δ, and probability p, the distinct sampler $\Gamma_{p,C,\delta}^{\mathsf{D}}$ passes at least δ rows for every distinct combination of values of the columns in C.[7] Subsequent rows with the same value are let through with probability p uniformly-at-random. The weight of each passed row is set correspondingly; i.e., 1 if the row passes because of the frequency check and $1/p$ if it passes due to the probability check. QUICKR picks the parameters $\{C, \delta, p\}$ as a by-product of query optimization+sampling (§4.2)

To see how the distinct sampler improves over the uniform sampler, consider the following examples. Columns that form the group and those used in predicates can be added to the column set C. Since the distinct sampler will pass some rows for every distinct value of the columns in C, none of the groups will be missed and some rows will pass the predicate. QUICKR also allows stratifying on functions over columns. For the skewed aggregates example (input has $\mathtt{Y} = \{1, 1, 100\}$) stratifying on $\lceil Y/100 \rceil$ ensures that $Y = 100$ will appear in the sample.

Since QUICKR may employ the distinct sampler on any intermediate relation, the sampler must execute in a single pass, have a bounded resource footprint, and be partitionable. A naive implementation would maintain the observed frequency count per distinct value of column set C. Then, it would pass a row while the frequency seen thus far is below δ with weight 1 and pick subsequent rows with probability p and hence a weight of $1/p$. This naive approach has three problems. The first problem is bias. The first few rows *always* pass through and are more likely to impact the answer. Worse, the first few rows *picked in the probabilistic mode* have a relatively disproportionate impact on the answer since their weight $1/p$ is much larger than the previous rows whose weight is 1. Only the more frequently occurring values of C are free from bias since enough rows will be picked for those values in the probabilistic mode. Second, the memory footprint can be as large as the number of distinct values in C. Finally, when running in a partitioned mode, it is not possible to track how many rows with a particular value of C have been selected by the other (parallel) instances of the sampler. Hence, it is hard to ensure that all instances cumulatively pass *at least* δ rows and p *probability henceforth.*

QUICKR solves the problems of the naive approach. To be **partitionable**, we carefully adjust δ based on the degree-of-parallelism of the sampler D. That is, each instance of the distinct sampler takes a modified parameter set $\{C, \lceil \frac{\delta}{D} \rceil + \varepsilon, p\}$ wherein ε is carefully chosen to tradeoff between passing too many rows and passing too few rows by considering these two extreme cases–(1) all rows with the same value of C are seen by one sampler instance or (2) rows are uniformly spread across instances. The total number of rows passed by all instances is $(\delta/D) + \varepsilon$ for case (1) and $\delta + D\varepsilon$ for case (2). Case (1) is less frequent, but can happen if the input is ordered by the col-

[7]Precisely, at least min(δ, number of rows with that distinct value of C)

umn set C. QUICKR uses $\varepsilon = \delta/D$ since, in practice, the distribution of rows across instances more closely resembles case (2).

For **small memory footprint**, QUICKR adapts a sketch that identifies heavy hitters in one pass over data [32]. Crucially, using this sketch QUICKR maintains *approximate* frequency estimates for only the *heavy hitters* in memory that is *logarithmic* in the number of rows. Our key insight is that the distinct sampler's gains arise from probabilistically dropping rows that correspond to values of C that occur very frequently; tracking only the heavy-hitters achieves most of these gains. In particular, for an input of size N and constants s, τ, our sketch identifies values with frequency above $sN \pm \tau N$ and estimates their frequency to within $\pm\tau N$ off their true frequency. The memory usage is $\log(\tau N)/\tau$. QUICKR uses $\tau = 10^{-4}$ and $s = 10^{-2}$ for a memory footprint of 20MB with $N = 10^{10}$ input rows.

To reduce **bias**, QUICKR holds in a reservoir rows that are *early* in the probabilistic mode and passes them with the correct weight. In more detail: per distinct value, pass the first δ rows with weight 1. Subsequently, maintain a reservoir of size S. When more than $\delta + S/p$ rows are seen, flush the rows held in the reservoir with weight $1/p$. From then on, pick rows with probability p, i.e., without a reservoir. When the sampler has seen all rows, flush the rows in all non-empty reservoirs with weight $(\text{freq} - \delta)/S$ where freq is the number of observed rows. To see this method in action, suppose $\delta = 10, p = 0.1, S = 10$. It is easy to see that distinct values of C with freq in $[1, 10]$ will not use a reservoir. All their rows pass with weight 1. Those with freq in $(\delta, \delta + S/p] = [11, 110]$ are more interesting. For a value with freq of 30, its first ten rows pass right away, the next twenty go into the reservoir and a random subset of ten rows will be flushed *at the end* with a weight of $(\text{freq} - \delta)/S = 2$. Notice that the probability of a row numbered in $[11, 30]$ to be emitted is $1/2$. Finally, values with freq above 110 *lose* their reservoir once the 111'st row is seen. At that point, ten rows from the reservoir are passed with weight of 10. This method reduces bias because samples passed by the reservoir receive a weight that exactly corresponds to the probability with which the row was chosen. Further, only a small reservoir is kept (no more than S) and only for distinct values that have observed frequency between δ and $\delta + S/p$. Hence, the memory footprint is much smaller than straightforward reservoir sampling.

In summary, we are not aware of any other stratified sampler that functions in a streaming and partitionable manner. Furthermore, we believe that supporting stratification over functions of columns is novel. Though we use a column set C in the above description, this sampler can support a vector of functions whose domain is a subset of C. This allows for *just enough* stratification.

4.1.3 Universe sampler

Universe sampler is a new operator that uniquely allows QUICKR to sample the inputs of joins. Consider this example:

```
SELECT COUNT(DISTINCT order), SUM(ws.profit)
FROM ws JOIN wr ON ws.order = wr.order
```

Web-sales (ws) and web-returns (wr) are large fact tables being joined on a shared key. As discussed in §3, uniform sampling both the join inputs is not useful. Distinct sampling both the inputs has limited gains if the join keys have many columns and hence, many distinct values. *Correlation-aware* samplers [6, 21, 22, 24] are inefficient (since they construct histograms or indices on join inputs) and ineffective (since they require samplers to immediately precede the join). More details are in §6. Generalizing this example, similar cases happen with self-joins and *set operations* such as counting the number of orders that occur in one table, both tables, or exactly one table. All such cases are approximable (have aggregations and output $\ll$ input) but existing samplers do not help.

We now explain the insight behind universe sampler. Much of the trouble in sampling join inputs arises because the inputs have to *sampled independently* and their *joint behavior* has to be statistically meaningful. Suppose the value of the join keys is projected into some high dimensional *space* (e.g., using a hash function) and samplers on both inputs pick the ***same*** *random* portion of this space. That is, on both join inputs pick all rows whose value of join keys falls in some chosen subspace. For example, pick from the tables `ws` and `wr` rows that have `Hash(order)%4 = 2`. This yields a 25% sample. A join over these samples is statistically equivalent to sampling after the join (i.e., picking rows in join output that belong to the chosen subspace). Our implementation uses a cryptographically strong hash function. Hashing lets us pick a subspace without apriori knowledge of the *range* of values and we can vary the desired sample size by choosing a corresponding portion of the hash range.

More formally, the universe sampler takes as input a column set C and a fraction p. It chooses a p fraction of the value space of the columns in C. And, passes all rows whose value of columns in C belong to the chosen subspace. Related pairs of samplers will pick the same subspace. Note that the universe sampler is partitionable and needs only one pass: whether or not a row passes depends only on the values of the columns in C, so the sampler keeps no state across rows. As a corollary, different instances that process different subsets of the input would make the same decisions.

4.1.4 Limitations and interactions between samplers

We summarize the applicability of each sampler (e.g., guard conditions) and how the samplers complement each other and together expand the applicability of samplers as a family. All three samplers are broadly applicable in the sense that we can ensure commutativity with other database operations; although analyzing the accuracy of answers generated by universe and distinct samplers requires new methods because these samplers are not uniformly random (§4.3). Among the samplers, the uniform sampler is the most general. QUICKR uses the uniform and universe samplers only when the stratification requirements, if any, can be met. That is, either there is high support per group or the columns that need stratification (e.g., group by columns) are independent with the universe columns. For some aggregations, such as `COUNT` and `COUNT DISTINCT`, we note that column independence is not needed for the answer to be unbiased (e.g., `COUNT DISTINCT order` in §4.1.3). The universe sampler is applicable for equi-joins over arbitrarily many columns. Further, the universe sampler can be used for multiple joins in a query as we saw in Figure 1. More precisely, universe sampling can be used for *exactly one set of columns* in any query sub-tree that has an aggregate at the root. The three samplers together expand the range of applicability of samplers. That is, by integrating with the query optimizer (§4.2), QUICKR considers various join orders, choices of stratification and/ or universe columns, and choices of sampler locations to pick an appropriate plan. Consequently, our results will show that many otherwise unapproximable queries benefit from QUICKR.

4.2 Samplers + QO (or ASALQA)

Since every operator in the plan can potentially be followed by a sampler, the search space of possible sampled plans is very large. Further, for each possible choice of samplers and locations in the plan, one has to reason about the *performance and accuracy* of the corresponding plan. Given an input query, `ASALQA` outputs an execution plan with appropriate samplers inserted at appropriate locations. Our current target is the plan that achieves the best performance with accuracy as the constraint.

There are at least two choices as to how we can obtain a good plan that contains samplers: (a) Insert samplers a posteriori into a

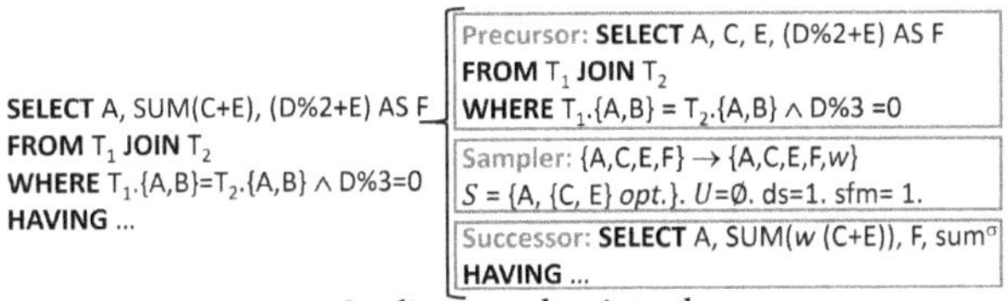

Figure 4: Seeding samplers into the query.

plan that is output by a traditional relational query optimizer or (b) Incorporate samplers as first-class operators along with the other database operators and explore the larger combined space of possible plans within a query optimizer. Notice that option (b) can yield plans that cannot be obtained from using option (a). For example, when a sampler reduces cardinality downstream join operations can be implemented differently and more efficiently as a cross join instead of a hash-join [8]. As another example, for queries with many joins and selects, option (a) may offer a plan on which all simple edits to insert samplers appear infeasible (inaccurate). Yet, a different ordering of the joins or selects may allow samplers to be inserted. Hence, we chose option (b); we offer a new **ASALQA** algorithm that incorporates samplers as native operators into a Cascades-style cost-based optimizer [18, 27].

Query optimization in Cascades consists of two main phases. In the *logical plan exploration* phase, a set of transformation rules generate alternative plans. The *physical plan creation* phase converts each logical operation to a physical implementation. **ASALQA** modifies both these phases and proceeds as follows. Samplers are injected into the query execution tree before every aggregation (§4.2.2). Intuitively, this represents the *potential to approximate* at that location. Next, QUICKR has a set of new transformation rules that push samplers closer to the raw input (§4.2.3–§4.2.5). The alternatives generated by a rule have no worse accuracy but can have better performance. Furthermore, a new rule changes the degree-of-parallelism (§A) of sampled query sub-expressions which can in turn trigger other changes to the overall plan. Finally, plan costing uses data statistics to identify the best plan, both in terms of performance and accuracy (§4.2.6, §4.3).

4.2.1 Sampler: logical and physical state

During the logical exploration phase, the requirements on a sampler are encoded in what we call the *logical state.* The requirements of the sampler change when the samplers are moved by the transformation rules. Furthermore, they may be implementable by one or more physical samplers. After logical exploration, **ASALQA** picks the best sampler that meets the requirements (§4.2.6). We denote the logical state by $\{S, U, \mathsf{ds}, \mathsf{sfm}\}$. S and U are the columns that the sampler needs to stratify or universe sample upon respectively. We also refer to them as *strat cols* and *univ cols* respectively. ds and sfm are short for downstream selectivity (i.e., the cumulative selectivity of operators between the sampler and the answer) and stratification frequency multiplier; their use will be described shortly.

4.2.2 Seeding samplers

We seed samplers by replacing each statement that has aggregations with three statements–a precursor, a sampler and a successor–as shown in Figure 4. This is optimistic; that is, **ASALQA** replaces the sampler with a pass-through operation if the error goal cannot be met. The *precursor* mimics the original statement but for aggregations. In particular, the precursor receives all of the JOIN clauses, WHERE clauses, UDOs and AS projections from the original statement. Aggregations in the precursor are replaced with their corresponding input columns. The *successor* performs these aggregations by replacing each with (a) an unbiased estimator of the true value computed over the sampled rows and (b) appends an optional column that offers a confidence interval. Table 8 shows how QUICKR rewrites some example aggregations. The successor also receives the HAVING clause from the original statement. A *sampler* statement is introduced between the precursor and successor. Columns that appear in the answer, e.g., A in Figure 4, are added to the stratification column requirement (S) in the sampler. Further, columns in the `*IF` clauses, in `SUM` and in `COUNT(DISTINCT)` (e.g., `C`, `E` in Figure 4) are optionally added to the set S (details in §4.2.3). Recall from §4.1 that stratification on these columns ensures that no groups are missed and corrects for value skew. Figure 4 also shows the initial values for the rest of the logical state ($U = \emptyset$; $\mathsf{ds} = 1$; $\mathsf{sfm} = 1$).

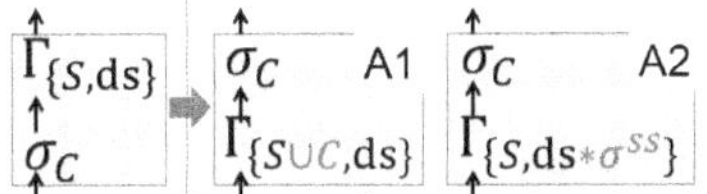

Figure 5: Pushing sampler past select: See §4.2.3.

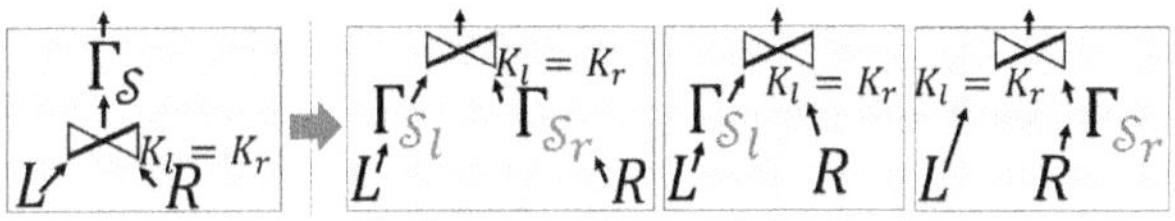

Figure 6: Pushing sampler past join: See §4.2.4.

4.2.3 Pushing sampler past Select

We start with a simple yet non-trivial transformation rule that pushes samplers past select operators. For the expression on the left in Figure 5, **ASALQA** generates the two alternatives on the right. Here σ_C denotes a select that uses columns C in its predicate. Let σ^{ss} be its selectivity.[8] We only show the relevant fields in the logical sampler state. To understand why this rule helps, note the following logic.

Alternative `A1` (Figure 5 middle) stratifies additionally on the predicate columns C. Doing so guarantees that the error will be no worse than the expression on the left since at least some rows pass the sampler for every distinct value of C. Unfortunately, the performance can be worse by a lot. This is because the more columns in C, the greater the number of distinct values in the stratified column set $S \cup C$, forcing the sampler to pass many more rows. The second alternative `A2` (Figure 5 right) retains perf gain potential at the cost of additional error. If the sampler were to not stratify on the columns in C, its performance is no worse than before. But, there will be fewer rows in the answer by a factor of σ^{ss}. Therefore, this plan is more likely to miss groups or have a higher variance for aggregates. It is easy to see when each alternative is preferable: (a) if the select has many predicate columns but is not very selective, `A2` is better; (b) if the select is highly selective, `A1` may be better; (c) otherwise, neither alternative is better.

Observe also that in both alternatives the sampler reduces the work for the select since it now operates on fewer rows. If the select is a conjunctive predicate ("and"), the logic above is applied per conjunction. When some predicate columns C are already in the strat cols S, observe that `A1` needs no correction. For `A2`, **ASALQA** uses a heuristic to reduce ds by a smaller amount than σ^{ss}.

4.2.4 Pushing sampler past Join

We highlight the transformation rules to push sampler past an equi-join because it has deep implications on performance and illustrates novel aspects of our technical contributions. As shown in Figure 6, the sampler can be pushed down to one or both inputs. Let L, R be the input relations and K_l, K_r be the corresponding join keys. When pushing a sampler past join, two key considerations arise: (i) continue to meet the stratification and universe requirements in the

[8] σ^{ss} = rows in output of σ/rows in input.

Inputs:
$\mathcal{S}$: Sampler state = $\{S, U, \text{sfm}, \text{ds}\}$
L, R: relational inputs of join with columns L^c, R^c respectively
K_l, K_r: Columns used as join keys // assume equi-join
Output: Vector of alternate samplers on one or both inputs of join.

1 **Func:** NumDV(R, C) : // distinct value count of columns C in R

2 **Func:** ProjectColSet$(S, \pi_{C_1 \to C_2})$: // S, C_1, C_2 are column sets. $|C_1| = |C_2|$. Replace columns in $S \cap C_1$ with corresponding ones in C_2.

3 **Func:** OneSideHelper$(\mathcal{S}, L, R, K_l, K_r, U_l)$:
4 $\vec{\mathcal{A}} \leftarrow \{\}$ // vector of state of alternative samplers on left relation
5 $S_f \leftarrow$ ProjectColSet$(\mathcal{S}.S, \pi_{K_r \to K_l})$//Normalize; these are "full" strat cols
6 $S_l \leftarrow S_f \cap L^c$// strat cols defined on left
7 sfm $\leftarrow \mathcal{S}$.sfm
8 **if** $|S_f - S_l| > 0$ **and** $|K_l - S_l| > 0$// *missing some strat cols* **then**
9 sfm $\leftarrow$ sfm $* \dfrac{\min(\text{NumDV}(L, K_l - S_l),\ \text{NumDV}(R, S_f - S_l))}{\text{NumDV}(R, \text{ProjectColSet}(K_l - S_l, \pi_{K_l \to K_r}))}$
10 $S_l \leftarrow S_l \cup K_l$ // append join keys to strat cols
11 $K\text{rem} \leftarrow K_l - S_l$
12 **foreach** *subset S of Krem* **do**
13 $S_{\text{skip}} \leftarrow K\text{rem} - S$// will strat on S, these join keys remain.
14 ds $\leftarrow \mathcal{S}.ds$ / NumDV(L, S_{skip}) $*$ // penalize by increasing ds $\min\left(\text{NumDV}(L, S_{\text{skip}}),\ \text{NumDV}(R, \text{ProjectColSet}(S_{\text{skip}}, \pi_{K_l \to K_r}))\right)$
15 // **omitted detail:** check for dissonance
16 $\vec{\mathcal{A}} \leftarrow \{S_l \cup S,\ U_l,\ \text{sfm},\ \text{ds}\}$
17 **return** $\vec{\mathcal{A}}$

18 **Func:** PrepareUnivCol(U, K):
19 **if** $U = \emptyset$ **or** $U = K$ **then return** K // Else, cannot do universe ;

20 **Func: PushSamplerOnOneSide**$(\mathcal{S}, L, R, K_l, K_r)$:
21 $U_l \leftarrow$ ProjectColSet$(\mathcal{S}.U, \pi_{K_r \to K_l})$
22 **if** $U_l - L^c = \emptyset$// *can push to one side iff other side has no univ col.* **then**
23 **return** OneSideHelper$(\mathcal{S}, L, R, K_l, K_r, U_l)$
24 **return** $\{\}$ // no alternatives

25 **Func: PushSamplerOntoBothSides**$(\mathcal{S}, L, R, K_l, K_r)$:
26 $U_l \leftarrow$ PrepareUnivCol(ProjectColSet$(\mathcal{S}.U, \pi_{K_r \to K_l}), K_l)$
27 $U_r \leftarrow$ PrepareUnivCol(ProjectColSet$(\mathcal{S}.U, \pi_{K_l \to K_r}), K_r)$
28 **if** $U_l = \emptyset$ **or** $U_r = \emptyset$ **then return** $\{\}$// cannot use univ ;
29 $\vec{\mathcal{A}}_l \leftarrow$ OneSideHelper$(\mathcal{S}, L, R, K_l, K_r, U_l)$
30 $\vec{\mathcal{A}}_r \leftarrow$ OneSideHelper$(\mathcal{S}, R, L, K_r, K_l, U_r)$
31 **return** $\vec{\mathcal{A}}_l \times \vec{\mathcal{A}}_r$ // cross product, output is vector of state-pairs

Figure 7: Pseudocode for pushing samplers past join.

sampler's logical state $\mathcal{S}$ and (ii) account for the additional changes to the answer due to the join following the sampler.

The PushSamplerOnOneSide function in Figure 7 shows how ASALQA considers pushing the sampler to the left input. Its goal is to find sampler $\mathcal{S}_l$ such that $\Gamma_{\mathcal{S}_l}(L) \bowtie R$ is an alternate for $\Gamma_{\mathcal{S}}(L \bowtie R)$. We first try to satisfy the universe and stratification requirements in $\mathcal{S}$. If any of the universe columns $\mathcal{S}.U$ appear only on the right relation, then pushing to the left is not possible; since some univ cols are unavailable on the left, picking rows in the desired value subspace of $\mathcal{S}.U$ is not possible. (See the check for $U_l - L^c = \emptyset$ in PushSamplerOnOneSide.) If some of the strat cols $\mathcal{S}.S$ are missing on the left, however, ASALQA stratifies on the left join keys. (See lines 8–10 in OneSideHelper.) In the example in Figure 1, stratifying `store_sales` ⋈ `date` on `d_year` can be approximated by stratifying `store_sales` on the left join key `sold_date_sk`. Intuitively, stratifying on join key ensures that some rows will appear on the sampled left to match every row from the right. However, the join keys may have more or fewer distinct values than the columns that they replace. In the above example, the join key has 365× more

row count	
Average*, Variance*	per *interesting*† column
Number of Distinct Values	
Heavy-Hitter Values and Freq.	

* : for columns with numerical values; † : columns that appear in select filters, join clauses or contained in the eventual answer.

Table 2: Statistics used by Quickr to facilitate sampler selection

distinct values than `d_year`; hence the support per group *appears* much smaller than it is. ASALQA uses sfm (stratification frequency multiplier) to correct for this difference. Intuitively, when replacing a stratified column with a join key having more (or fewer) distinct values, the value of sfm goes up (or down) and sfm is used as a multiplier when computing the group support (§4.2.6). We note that this has been a crucial enabler in pushing samplers onto large relations while properly accounting for stratification needs. Finally, accounting for the additional changes to the answer due to the join is similar to the case of select (see §4.2.3). Either the new sampler stratifies on the join keys or gets a smaller downstream selectivity. Lines 12–16 of OneSideHelper show how ASALQA considers different subsets of Krem to add to strat cols and adjusts ds accordingly.

The PushSamplerOntoBothSides function in Figure 7 shows how ASALQA considers pushing a sampler to both join inputs. Its goal is to find samplers $\mathcal{S}_l, \mathcal{S}_r$ such that $\Gamma_{\mathcal{S}_l}(L) \bowtie \Gamma_{\mathcal{S}_r}(R)$ is an alternate for $\Gamma_{\mathcal{S}}(L \bowtie R)$. Note the calls to OneSideHelper to push on to each side of the input. The only substantial change is adding join keys to the corresponding univ cols. As shown in PrepareUnivCol (line#19), ASALQA adds new universe requirements if univ cols do not exist already ($U = \emptyset$) or if they are identical to the join keys ($U = K$) as in the example query in Figure 1. As before, ASALQA picks the best option from among these alternatives.

ASALQA checks for dissonance between the stratification and universe requirements (line#15 in Figure 6). Columns that appear in both the S and U sets are troublesome because the universe sampler will only pick a subset of the values of such columns whereas stratification requires all values. ASALQA allows overlap in the requirements only when $|S \cap U| \ll |S|$; i.e., if only a few columns overlap, the column sets can be considered effectively independent. Further, overlap is allowed for columns that appear in S only because of `COUNT` or `COUNT DISTINCT` since such aggregates can be estimated correctly (see Table 8).

4.2.5 *Other transformation rules, Parallel plans and Global constraints*

We conclude the discussion of transformation rules by noting that ASALQA pushes samplers past many other operators including projections, union-alls and outer joins. In some cases, it is strictly better to push down the sampler. In other cases, ASALQA uses the costing that will be described in §4.2.6 to decide whether pushing down a sampler is better and to pick among the various choices. We mention two important issues here, the details of which are in §A. First, for the universe sampling property to hold, both input relations of a join should have an identical universe sampler (same column sets and probability). We ensure that this and other such *global requirements* are satisfied on the bottom-up pass of the query optimization. Next, parallel plan performance can improve further if samplers are followed by exchanges since the cardinality reduction due to the sampler can translate into a degree-of-parallelism reduction leading to more efficient serial sub-plans or better implementation choices. More details are in §A.

4.2.6 *Costing Sampled Expressions*

In this section, we describe how to cost sampled expressions. Costing helps pick between alternatives and determines how best to implement a sampler while meeting all of its requirements.

A key input to costing is the cardinality estimates per relational expression (how many rows) and the number of distinct values in each column subset. Table 2 shows the statistics that QUICKR collects for each input table. If not already available, the statistics are computed by the *first* query that reads the table [8]. Using these input statistics, ASALQA *derives* the corresponding statistics for each query sub-expression. The derivation improves upon prior work [16] by using heavy hitter identity and frequency.

Armed with the above stats, we reason about how best to implement a sampler so as to meet the requirements encoded in its logical state $\mathcal{S} = \{S, U, \text{sfm}, \text{ds}\}$. We use two high level simplifications. To ensure that the performance gains are high, we disallow sampling with probability above 0.1. Next, we use a fixed error goal: with high probability, do not miss groups in answer and keep aggregate value within ±10% of the true value. We defer a more graceful trade-off between speed-up and accuracy to future work.

Meeting these goals translates to the following sequence of checks: (C1) Is stratified column requirement S empty or can some sample probability $p \in [0, 0.1]$ ensure that, with high probability, each distinct value of the columns in S receives at least k rows? (C2) Is univ col requirement U empty? Answering C1 requires the cardinality and distinct value derivations described above for the input relation. Further, these numbers are multiplied by ds $*$ sfm. Recall that downstream selectivity ds is the probability that a row passed by this sampler will make its way to the answer (after downstream selections or joins). And, sfm is a multiplier to correct the effect of replacing strat cols with join keys (§4.2.4). If the answer to both C1 and C2 is true, the sampler is implemented using the uniform sampler (§4.1.1). If only C1 is true, a universe sampler is chosen. If only C2 is true, a distinct sampler may be chosen; we check whether there will be any data reduction, i.e., at least k_l rows exist per distinct value of columns in S. We choose $k_l = 3$. The default option is to not-sample i.e., implement sampler as a pass-through operator.

Intuitively, the reasoning is that if S and U are empty or if there is substantial support, a uniform sampler suffices. Universe sampler has higher variance and is chosen only when needed ($U \neq \emptyset$) and stratification needs are met ($S = \emptyset$, or enough support, or $|S \cap U| \ll |S|$). Finally, a query plan without samplers is chosen and is the desired option when (a) the per-group support is small or (b) downstream selectivity ds is so small or stratification requirements are so restrictive that the number of rows per distinct value of S is below k_l. Physical sampler parameters (e.g., sample probability p, δ for distinct) are chosen as the smallest values that satisfy (C1). We use $k = 30$ because anecdotally 30 samples are needed by central-limit-theorem which we use to estimate confidence intervals. In our evaluation, a parameter sweep shows that the plans output by ASALQA are similar for $k \in [5, 100]$.

4.3 Accuracy analysis

Given a query plan $\mathcal{E}$, with many samplers at arbitrary locations, QUICKR offers unbiased estimators of aggregate values as well as the probability of missing groups and the confidence intervals for aggregates. We briefly describe how to do this. First, suppose that a sampler immediately precedes the aggregation and group by operator. We use the well-known *Horvitz-Thompson (HT) estimator* [24] to calculate unbiased estimators of the true aggregate values and the variance of these estimators. The details are in §B.1. Then, we can use central-limit-theorem to compute confidence intervals. This does not suffice, however, because the samplers in $\mathcal{E}$ can be arbitrarily far away from the aggregates. In fact, QUICKR pushes samplers further away to improve performance.

Next, to analyze the case when samplers are at arbitrary locations we introduce a novel notion of *dominance* between query expressions whose output is identical when samplers are removed from both: $\mathcal{E}_2$ is said to dominate $\mathcal{E}_1$ denoted as $\mathcal{E}_1 \stackrel{*}{\Rightarrow} \mathcal{E}_2$, iff the *accuracy* of $\mathcal{E}_2$ is no worse than that of $\mathcal{E}_1$. This definition mathematically distills the necessary and sufficient conditions to ensure that $\mathcal{E}_2$ has no worse variance of estimators and no higher probability of missing groups than $\mathcal{E}_1$. The details are in §B.2, Proof of Proposition 5.

We then show that dominance transitively holds across database operators. Suppose that $\pi, \sigma, \bowtie$ denote a project, select and join.

Proposition 1 (Dominance Transitivity). *For pairs of expressions $\mathcal{E}_1$, $\mathcal{E}_2$ and $\mathcal{F}_1$, $\mathcal{F}_2$ that are equivalent if all samplers were removed:*

i) $\mathcal{E}_1 \stackrel{*}{\Rightarrow} \mathcal{E}_2$ *implies* $\pi(\mathcal{E}_1) \stackrel{*}{\Rightarrow} \pi(\mathcal{E}_2)$;

ii) $\mathcal{E}_1 \stackrel{*}{\Rightarrow} \mathcal{E}_2$ *implies* $\sigma(\mathcal{E}_1) \stackrel{*}{\Rightarrow} \sigma(\mathcal{E}_2)$;

iii) $\mathcal{E}_1 \stackrel{*}{\Rightarrow} \mathcal{E}_2$ *and* $\mathcal{F}_1 \stackrel{*}{\Rightarrow} \mathcal{F}_2$ *implies* $\mathcal{E}_1 \bowtie \mathcal{F}_1 \stackrel{*}{\Rightarrow} \mathcal{E}_2 \bowtie \mathcal{F}_2$, *if samplers in $\mathcal{E}_i$ are independent on samplers in $\mathcal{F}_i$ or $\mathcal{E}_i$ and $\mathcal{F}_i$ share the same universe sampler.*

The proof is in §B.2 Proposition 1.

To analyze the accuracy of a plan, we use the dominance rules to inductively *unroll* ASALQA. That is, just for the sake of analysis, we find an equivalent query expression $\mathcal{E}'$ which has only one sampler just below the aggregation such that $\mathcal{E}' \stackrel{*}{\Rightarrow} \mathcal{E}$. We use the above HT estimators on $\mathcal{E}'$. By dominance, the accuracy of $\mathcal{E}$ is no worse. An illustration of this process for the query in Figure 1 is in Figure 9.

Finally, we can prove that the analysis above requires only one effective pass over the sample; the details are in §B.1 Proposition 2.

Proposition 2 (Complexity). *For each group G in the query output, QUICKR needs $O(|\mathcal{E}(G)|)$ time to compute the unbiased estimator of all aggregations and their estimated variance where $|\mathcal{E}(G)|$ is the number of sample rows from G output by expression $\mathcal{E}$.*

In summary, we colloquially mention three novel aspects of our accuracy analysis; the details are in the Appendix. Note that prior work [35] applies for SUM-like aggregates, uniformly-random samplers and uses self-joins to compute variance. In contrast, ASALQA handles different aggregate types including the case when the answer has multiple aggregates. Next, we compute all relevant error measures in one effective pass over data. Finally, to analyze a more general class of samplers, we use two ideas. Any sampler that is strictly more likely to pass a row relative to some uniformly random sampler is analyzable. Further, any sampler that has equivalent error when convolved with all database operators is also analyzable. Our distinct and universe samplers fall into each category respectively. We believe that other samplers exist in each category. These intuitions lead to our definition of sampler dominance.

5. EVALUATION

We have implemented QUICKR's samplers and query optimization and deployed it in our production clusters. Here, we present results to answer the following questions:

- How much do queries speed-up? Our evaluation is relative to a version of the QO that is identical in all respects to QUICKR except for samplers. We also compare with a state-of-the-art input sampling technique–BlinkDB [9].
- How often are the output plans correct? Every query that receives a sampled plan should meet its error guarantee (with high probability, no groups are missed in the answer and all aggregates are within a small ratio of true value). Further, unapproximable queries should receive a plan with no samplers.
- Where do the gains come from? And, how may these results translate to other queries?

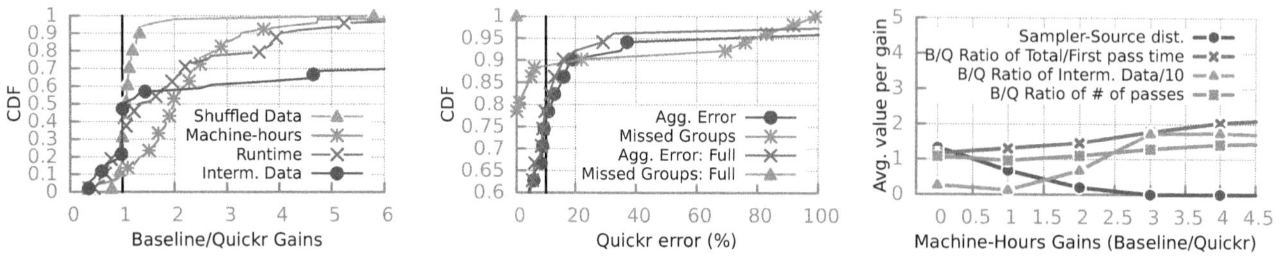

(a) Comparing runtime and resources used (b) Quantifying error (c) Correlating perf. gains to aspects of queries

Figure 8: Comparing QUICKR with Baseline– the production QO in our cluster that is identical to QUICKR except for samplers

5.1 Methodology

Comparables: Both of the systems that we compare QUICKR against are state-of-the-art. We refer to the production QO without samplers as **Baseline**. Thousands of man-years have gone into developing Baseline, and it is hardened from several years of production use. Baseline supports almost the entirety of T-SQL, has extensive support for UDOs, generates parallel plans and has carefully tuned parallel implementations of many operators. The authors of BlinkDB shared their MILP algorithm to choose which samples to construct. BlinkDB's logic to match a query to available input samples requires queries to recur in order to build the error-latency-profile. We give BlinkDB the benefit of perfect matching by running each query on all of the input samples and use the "best" sample.

Query sets: To share results publicly, we use the queries and datasets from the TPC-DS benchmark [4]. The results here are from a 500GB dataset (scale factor: 500). Results for the 2TB dataset were similar. Table 3 shows some query characteristics. Comparing with Figure 2b we see that TPC-DS queries are simpler than the queries in our cluster– they have fewer passes over data, fewer joins, and smaller QCS. Table 9 reports similar measures for queries from a variety of benchmarks (these queries were run on a Hive cluster) and shows that queries in other benchmarks are even simpler. We chose TPC-DS because it is closest to the workload on our cluster.

Performance Metrics: To compare performance, we measure query runtime as well as the usages of various resources. **Machine-hours** is the sum of the runtime of all tasks. This translates to cluster occupancy and is a measure of throughput. **Intermediate Data** is the sum of the output of all tasks less the job output, i.e., corresponds to the intermediate data written. **Shuffled Data** is the sum of data that moves along the network across racks. Together, the last two measure the excess IO footprint of the query.

Error Metrics: By **Missed Groups**, we refer to the fraction of groups in the answer that are missed. **Aggregation Error** denotes the average error between the estimated and true value of all aggregations in a query. We compute these metrics by analyzing the query output.

Cluster: We evaluate QUICKR on the same cluster that ran the production queries that were analyzed in Figure 2b. The servers in this cluster are *datacenter-standard*. That is, each has about ten cores, roughly 100GB of memory, a couple of high RPM disks, some SSDs and a couple of 10Gbps NICs.

5.2 Performance gains

Figure 8a plots a CDF of the various performance metrics. The x axis is a ratio between the values of Baseline and QUICKR. An x-value of 2 represents 2× improvement whereas those below 1 represent a regression. We see from the line with star points ("machine-hours") that QUICKR lowers resource usage of the median query by over 2×. The improvements in runtime, the line with x points, can be more or less than that of the resource usage due to two factors.

Metric	Percentile value					
	10th	25th	50th	75th	90th	95th
# of passes	1.12	1.18	1.3	1.53	1.92	2.61
Total/First pass time	1.26	1.44	1.67	2	2.63	3.42
# Aggregation Ops.	1	1	3	4	8	16
# Joins	2	3	4	7	9	10
depth of operators	17	18	20	23	26	27
# operators	20	23	32	44	52	86
size of QCS + QVS	2	4	5	7	12	17
size of QCS	0	1	3	5	9	11
# user-defined func.	1	2	4	9	14	24

Table 3: Characteristics of the TPC-DS queries used in evaluation.

(1) Queries that process a small amount of data such as TPC-DS q22 are critical-path limited. That is, since our cluster offers much more degree-of-parallelism than needed by some queries, their runtime equals the sum of duration of tasks on the critical path. (2) Other queries gain in runtime by more than expected. When the work to be done reduces, as it does with sampled plans, schedulers can marshall their tasks better. Overall, we find that query runtime improves by a median 1.6×. Roughly 20% of the queries speed up by over 3×. A handful speed up by over 6×. Please note however that roughly 20% of the queries have slightly longer runtimes. This is primarily because (a) query runtime is influenced by task failures and outliers [11, 41] and (b) our cluster scheduler uses fair-sharing and hence the resources offered to queries vary substantially from one execution to another [8, 26]. Regression in machine-hours happens less often and to a smaller degree; this is mostly because our samplers are in C#, but the rest of the query executes in C++ which leads to needless overhead in converting rows from one language format to another. In general, we find runtime to be a noisy metric on our cluster and believe machine-hours which is akin to job makespan to be a more stable metric to compare plan efficiency.

We now focus on some reasons behind these gains. The line with circular points ("interm. data") shows that the total amount of intermediate data written by sampled plans is much smaller. Almost 40% of the queries have reductions larger than 4×. For about 50% of the queries, the intermediate data written is about the same and some plans write even more data. The line with triangle points ("shuffled data") shows that the shuffled volume does not decrease as much as intermediate data. Two facts explain these findings. (1) QUICKR triggers parallel plan improvements that build upon the reduced cardinality due to samplers (§A). That is, when the data in flight becomes small, QUICKR decreases degree-of-parallelism (DOP) so that hash joins are replaced with cheaper broadcast joins etc. The benefit is faster completion time. The cost, however, is that more data has to be shuffled and written to adjust the DOP (§A). (2) QUICKR outputs plans *without samplers* for roughly 25% of the queries. These queries still receive a limited benefit (an average of 25%) because QUICKR triggers parallel plan improvements when cardinality reduces due to other aspects such as filters. Such queries will shuffle more data.

To summarize, QUICKR offers substantial performance gains to a large fraction of the complex queries in the TPC-DS benchmark.

Metric	Percentile value					
	10th	25th	50th	75th	90th	95th
Baseline QO time	0.38	0.49	0.51	0.54	0.56	0.57
Quickr QO time	0.48	0.5	0.52	0.55	0.57	0.58

Table 4: Query Optimization (QO) times (sec.)

Metric	Value					
	0	1	2	3	4	9
Samplers per query	25%	51%	9%	11%	2%	2%
Sampler-Source dist.	60%	12%	10%	17%	0%	0%

Table 5: Number of samplers per query and their locations

Since production queries have many more passes over data, we observe larger gains overall but defer those results for future work.

5.3 Quantifying error

Figure 8b plots a CDF of the error metrics over all the examined TPC-DS queries. The line with star points ("Missed Groups") shows that up to 20% of queries have missing groups. Upon careful examination, we find that every one of these cases is due to applying `LIMIT 100` on the answer after sorting over the aggregation column. Errors in aggregates change the rank of groups and hence the approximate answer picks a different top 100. We acknowledge that Quickr should more carefully consider this case. To the best of our knowledge, none of the prior AQP schemes handle this scenario either. We make one change to the queries: output the answer before `LIMIT 100` and call that the *full* answer. The line with triangle points ("Missed Groups: Full") shows that Quickr misses no groups in full answers (line is a point on the top left). This is indeed the desired behavior.

In Figure 8b, the lines with circle and x points ("Agg. Error" and "Agg. Error: Full") depict the error for aggregates. We see that 80% of the queries have error within ±10% and over 90% are within ±20%. This is quite good. Careful examination of the outliers reveals two prevalent causes. (a) Support is skewed across groups. Since Quickr assumes an even distribution except for heavy hitters, some groups receive fewer rows than desired and have high error. (b) SUMs that are computed over values with high skew have high error. As discussed in §4.1.1, the fix is to stratify on such columns. However, a complication is that value skew changes when passing through predicates. For example, WHERE $X > 10^6 \vee X < 10^{-3}$ increases skew and WHERE $X \in [10, 11]$ decreases it. We are working towards *deriving* the value skew statistic. If both of these causes are fixed, and we believe they can be, over 95% of the TPC-DS queries will have aggregates within ±10% of true answer.

5.4 Characterizing what Quickr does

Figure 8c correlates the performance gains with query characteristics. It shows the average metric value for a range in the machine-hours gains. The line with circle points ("Sampler-Source dist.") shows that the gains increase when the samplers are closer to the sources. We next compare some query aspects between the baseline plans and Quickr. The line with x points ("Total/First pass time") and the one with star points ("# of passes") show that the gains due to Quickr are larger for deeper queries. Finally, the line with triangle points ("Interm. Data/10") shows that queries that gain most by Quickr have substantial reductions in intermediate data (up to 19×, since the graph shows values divided by 10).

Table 4 shows the query optimization time for Quickr and Baseline. We expect longer QO times for Quickr since it considers samplers natively and hence explores more alternatives. We ran each query three times and pick the median QO time. The table shows that the increase in QO latency is below 0.1 seconds.

Table 5 shows that 51% of the queries have exactly one sampler. Many have multiple samplers. Further, 25% of the queries are unapproximable. The table also shows where the samplers are in the query plan. "Sampler-Source distance" is the number of IO passes between the extraction stage and the sampler. We see that 60% of the samplers are on the first pass on data. Recall that sampling on the first pass is likely to improve performance the most. We also see that Quickr places samplers in the middle of the plan in many queries; moving such samplers past the next database operator does not yield a better performance vs error tradeoff.

Table 7 shows how often various samplers are used. Overall, uniform sampler is used roughly twice as frequently as the distinct and universe samplers. The distinct sampler is often replaced by the uniform because when there is enough support for groups, the latter is accurate enough but has better performance. Analogously, the universe sampler is often optimized away because it is dominated by both the uniform and the distinct samplers (see Proposition 6 in §B.3). Quickr uses the universe sampler only for queries that join two large relations. This happens more often in our production queries. We note that even complex queries with multiple joins receive plans with only a few samplers. A key reason is that Quickr converts stratification requirements on columns from the smaller relations to stratification over join keys in the larger relations (see discussion on sfm in §4.2.4). Without our sampling+QO logic (§4.2), *evaluating* the accuracy and performance of the many possible sampled plans requires complex reasoning and is time-consuming even for an experienced data scientist.

Storage Budget	Coverage	Median Perf. gain: All	Median Perf. gain: Covered	Median Error
Default parameters (specifically, K=M=10^5).				
0.5×	0/64	0%	–	–
1×	0/64	0%	–	–
4×	9/64	0%	27%	6%
10×	14/64	0%	24%	5%
Tuned for small group size (K=M=10^1).				
0.5×	8/64	0%	35%	6%
1×	7/64	0%	35%	6%
4×	11/64	0%	32%	6%
10×	12/64	0%	24%	6%

Table 6: BlinkDB's performance on TPC-DS.

5.5 Quickr vs. Apriori samples

The fundamental problem with apriori samples is the poor coverage for any feasible storage budget. That is, when queries are rich, tables have many columns and a dataset has many tables, any choice of differently stratified samples of the inputs has poor coverage for feasible storage budgets. To illustrate this aspect, we evaluate BlinkDB [9], the best exemplar system of this approach, on the TPC-DS benchmark. BlinkDB's MILP to decide which samples to obtain works only for one table and extending to multiple tables is non-trivial due to reasons described below. We use the MILP to generate samples for the `store_sales` table because (a) it is the largest table in the TPC-DS benchmark and (b) it has the highest potential to improve query performance; out of the 64 queries that we consider, 40 use the `store_sales` table. Next, we run each query on *all* of the samples chosen by the MILP and pick the sample with the best possible performance that meets the error constraint (no groups missed and less than ±10% error for aggregates). We vetted our methodology and the results with the authors of BlinkDB.

Table 6 shows our findings when using the same parameter values as in the BlinkDB paper. We ran the queries in Hive [40] atop Tez [2]. The samples are not explicitly stored in memory but the file-system cache does help since no other queries ran on the cluster during our experiment. We see that very few queries benefit. For most queries, none of the constructed input samples yield an answer with zero missed rows and within ±10% error on aggregates.

For sample-set sizes equal to or smaller than the input, the best coverage was 13%. A parameter sweep on BlinkDB's internal parameters reveals that the best coverage overall was 22%, obtained at 10× the size of the input. Of the 14 queries that benefited, the median speed-up was 24%. It is more feasible to store the entire input in memory than such large sample-sets.

Digging a bit further, we find that BlinkDB's MILP generates over 20 differently stratified samples on `store_sales`. Most are on one column but several are on column pairs. Many TPC-DS queries have a large QCS (see Table 3); large QCSets have a large sample size and hence samples on column-pairs were picked by the MILP only at high storage budgets.

We take care to point out that apriori samples can be useful. Predictable aggregation queries that touch only one large dataset will greatly benefit. Especially if the data distribution is sparse, i.e. the number of distinct values per group is much smaller than the row count. Then, each stratified sample will be small and many different stratified samples can be feasibly stored per popular dataset. However, this does not happen in TPC-DS or in our production clusters. Further complications include: keeping samples consistent when datasets churn continuously and choosing which among the available samples (if any) would help an ad-hoc query that differs from the queries used when constructing samples. Storing apriori samples for queries that join more than one large table is problematic because the same tables can be joined on multiple columns and the samples constructed for a particular join-of-tables do not help queries that join in a different manner (for example, nine queries join `store_sales` and `store_returns` in TPC-DS with four different options for join columns).

6. RELATED WORK

Many big data systems support relational queries [12, 18, 33, 37, 40]. Several offer a (uniform) sampler operator. But none automatically decide which queries can be sampled, place appropriate samplers at appropriate locations or offer guarantees on answer quality.

A rich vein of literature samples input datasets. See [24] for an excellent overview. Some update the samples as datasets evolve [6]. Most assume knowledge of the queries and the datasets. Congressional sampling [7] keeps both uniform and stratified samples on the group-by columns used by queries. STRAT [20] computes the optimal sample-set to store given a budget. Chaudhuri et.al. [19] maintains an *outlier index* to better support skew. Babcock et. al. [14] stores the more uncommon values explicitly. SciBORQ [39] stores multiple layers of *impressions* where each layer can have a different focus and level of detail. Similar to STRAT, BlinkDB [9] also optimally chooses stratified samples. Uniquely, it stores samples in memory and computes an error-latency-profile for repetitive queries to meet error or performance targets. For complex ad-hoc queries with a heavy-tailed distribution on inputs, apriori sampling has substantial shortcomings (see §5.5).

Online aggregation (OLA) [29, 30, 43] progressively processes more of the input and keeps updating the answer. The use-case is exciting since the user can run the query until the answer is satisfactory. QUICKR looks at all tuples once (early in the plan) and retains a small subset for the remainder of the query. Hence, QUICKR can offer good error bounds without any assumptions on physical layout (e.g., input being randomly ordered) and with less computational overhead (e.g., does not need bootstrap). Further, OLA requires specialized join operators and in-memory data-structures to efficiently update the answers of a complex query [23, 38].

When sampling, QUICKR does not use existing indices on tables as well as some others do [24, 36]. While this choice makes QUICKR more widely applicable, for example on unstructured data or when no index exists, leveraging such metadata can make QUICKR more effective. For example, by sampling blocks or sub-trees of a B-tree instead of examining every tuple. This is key future work.

Our accuracy analysis technique (§4.3) improves in three ways over the closest related technique [35]. First, the previous technique [35] only applies for generalized uniform samplers (GUS). Neither our universe nor our distinct sampler belong to the class of GUS. We offer a new notion of sampler dominance that is a significant generalization. Second, we also analyze the likelihood of missing groups and consider aggregates beyond SUM (see §B, §C). Finally, while [35] requires self-joins to compute the variance, QUICKR computes variance and other error metrics in effectively one pass (§4.3).

Recently, there has been some work in using bootstrap to determine which apriori sample is suited for a query [10]. Since bootstrap can need thousands of trials, each of which resample from a sample [44], recent work shows how to symbolically execute bootstrap (by using probability annotations and new relational operators that convolve random variables) [44]. However, neither offset the shortcomings of apriori samples. Since QUICKR samples in-line, our accuracy analysis is simpler, faster and has good guarantees.

Our uniform sampler (§4.1.1) is the standard Poisson sampler [24] used by several prior works. The novelty in our distinct sampler (§4.1.2) derives largely from its execution in a streaming and partitioned manner: specifically in the way we lower bias and reduce memory footprint. To the best of our knowledge, the universe sampler (§4.1.3) is novel. Prior efforts on sampling both inputs of a join are much more complex [6, 21, 22, 24]. They use detailed statistics or indices on one or more of the input relations of the join (e.g., Strategy Stream Sample [21]). Since the join inputs in big data queries are intermediate data that is generated on the fly, obtaining such statistics has substantial overhead. It requires an additional pass over data and affects parallelism since the sampler on one input has to wait for the stat collector on the other. Worse, prior work requires samplers to *immediately precede* the join. That is, they cannot be pushed down past other database operations since maintaining the required statistics becomes even more complex. Our universe sampler requires no data exchange between the join inputs at execution time (the hash function and the portion of hash space to be picked are parameters from the query plan). Finally, we are aware of no prior work that reasons about samplers natively in the context of a query optimizer.

7. FINAL THOUGHTS

We offer a new way to approximate complex ad-hoc queries. Our insight is to leverage the many passes over data that such queries perform to sample lazily on the first pass. The ability to sample multiple join inputs precisely and reasoning about samplers natively in a query optimizer allowed us to offer a turn-key solution where the user only needs to submit a query and the system would automatically determine if and how best that query can be approximated. Initial results are very promising. In regimes where previously known techniques deliver no gains, QUICKR offers substantial speedup. The speed-up often translates to lower cost (e.g., when using public clouds), faster results or the ability to support many more queries without increasing cluster size by up to 2×. We also extend the state-of-art in analyzing the error of sampled expressions.

8. ACKNOWLEDGMENTS

We thank Chris Douglas, Alekh Jindal, Konstantinos Karanasos, Suman Nath, Raghu Ramakrishnan, Jingren Zhou and the Cosmos team at Microsoft for their feedback, advice and support. This draft also benefited from feedback from the SIGMOD reviewers.

9. REFERENCES

[1] AMPLab BigData Benchmark. http://bit.ly/1uyuBE8.
[2] Apache Tez. http://tez.apache.org/.
[3] Intel Big-Data-Benchmark. http://bit.ly/1HlFRHo.
[4] TPC-DS Benchmark. http://bit.ly/1J6uDap.
[5] TPC-H Benchmark. http://bit.ly/1KRK5gl.
[6] S. Acharya et al. The aqua approximate query answering system. In *SIGMOD*, 1999.
[7] S. Acharya et al. Congressional samples for approximate answering of group-by queries. In *SIGMOD*, 2000.
[8] S. Agarwal et al. Re-optimizing data parallel computing. In *NSDI*, 2012.
[9] S. Agarwal et al. Blinkdb: Queries with bounded errors and bounded response times on very large data. In *EuroSys*, 2013.
[10] S. Agarwal et al. Knowing when you're wrong: Building fast and reliable approximate query processing systems. In *SIGMOD*, 2014.
[11] G. Ananthanarayanan et al. Reining in the Outliers in MapReduce Clusters Using Mantri. In *OSDI*, 2010.
[12] M. Armbrust et al. Spark sql: Relational data processing in spark. In *SIGMOD*, 2015.
[13] B. Babcock et al. Models and issues in data stream systems. *PODS*, 2002.
[14] B. Babcock et al. Dynamic sample selection for approximate query processing. In *SIGMOD*, 2003.
[15] Z. Bar-Yossef et al. Counting distinct elements in a data stream. In *RANDOM*, 2002.
[16] K. Beyer, P. J. Haas, B. Reinwald, Y. Sismanis, and R. Gemulla. On synopses for distinctvalue estimation under multiset operations. In *SIGMOD*, 2007.
[17] J. Brutlag. Speed matters for Google web search. http://bit.ly/1b4RKoZ, 2009.
[18] R. Chaiken et al. SCOPE: Easy and Efficient Parallel Processing of Massive Datasets. In *VLDB*, 2008.
[19] S. Chaudhuri et al. Overcoming limitations of sampling for aggregation queries. In *ICDE*, 2001.
[20] S. Chaudhuri et al. A robust optimization-based approach for approximate answering of aggregate queries. *SIGMOD*, 2001.
[21] S. Chaudhuri, R. Motwani, and V. Narasayya. On random sampling over joins. In *SIGMOD*, 1999.
[22] S. Chaudhuri, R. Motwani, and V. R. Narasayya. Random sampling for histogram construction: How much is enough? In *SIGMOD 1998*, 1998.
[23] T. Condie et al. Mapreduce online. In *NSDI*, 2010.
[24] G. Cormode et al. Synopses for massive data: Samples, histograms, wavelets, sketches. *Found. Trends databases*, 2012.
[25] J. R. Dabrowski and E. V. Munson. Is 100 Milliseconds Too Fast? In *CHI*, 2001.
[26] A. Ferguson et al. Jockey: Guaranteed Job Latency in Data Parallel Clusters. In *EuroSys*, 2012.
[27] G. Graefe. The cascades framework for query optimization. *IEEE Data Eng. Bull.*, 1995.
[28] A. Halevy. Answering queries using views: A survey. 2001.
[29] J. M. Hellerstein, P. J. Haas, and H. J. Wang. Online aggregation. In *SIGMOD*, 1997.
[30] C. M. Jermaine et al. Scalable approximate query processing with the DBO engine. In *SIGMOD*, 2007.
[31] T. Johnson et al. Sampling algorithms in a stream operator. In *SIGMOD*, 2005.
[32] G. S. Manku and R. Motwani. Approximate frequency counts over data streams. In *VLDB*, 2002.
[33] S. Melnik et al. Dremel: Interactive analysis of web-scale datasets. In *VLDB*, 2010.
[34] R. Motwani et al. Query processing, resource management, and approximation in a data stream management system. *CIDR*, 2003.
[35] S. Nirkhiwale, A. Dobra, and C. Jermaine. A sampling algebra for aggregate estimation. In *PVLDB*, 2013.
[36] F. Olken. *Random Sampling from Databases*. PhD thesis, UCBerkeley, 1993.
[37] C. Olston et al. Pig Latin: A Not-So-Foreign Language for Data Processing. In *SIGMOD*, 2008.
[38] N. Pansare et al. Online aggregation for large mapreduce jobs. In *VLDB*, 2011.
[39] L. Sidirourgos et al. Sciborq: Scientific data management with bounds on runtime and quality. In *CIDR*, 2011.
[40] A. Thusoo et al. Hive- a warehousing solution over a map-reduce framework. In *VLDB*, 2009.
[41] Y. Kwon, M. Balazinska, B. Howe, J. Rolia. Skew-Resistant Parallel Processing of Feature-Extracting Scientific User-Defined Functions. In *SOCC*, 2010.
[42] Y. Yan et al. Error-bounded sampling for analytics on big sparse data. In *VLDB*, 2014.
[43] K. Zeng, S. Agarwal, A. Dave, M. Armbrust, and I. Stoica. G-ola: Generalized on-line aggregation for interactive analysis on big data. In *SIGMOD Demo*, 2015.
[44] K. Zeng et al. The analytical bootstrap: a new method for fast error estimation in approximate query processing. In *SIGMOD*, 2014.

APPENDIX

A. FURTHER DETAILS OF ASALQA

In §4.2.6, we see how QUICKR translates each logical sampler to a physical implementation. Next, the QO costs sampled sub-expressions. To enable this, we make the following changes: (1) Assign the correct cardinality for the samplers based on their sample probability p except for the distinct sampler which will leak more rows due to the requirement to pass at least δ rows for each distinct value of strat cols. (2) Assign the correct processing costs to the samplers per input and output row. The uniform sampler is the most efficient since it only tosses a coin per row. The universe sampler comes next since it uses a cryptographic hash. The distinct sampler has the highest processing cost because it invokes the heavy-hitter sketch and uses more memory for both the sketch and the reservoirs.

Sampler→{Sampler, Exchange}: Reducing the degree-of-parallelism (DOP) is necessary to get more gains from samplers. To see why, say a sampler reduces the number of rows in a relation by 10×, the work does become $\frac{1}{10}$'th now but start-up costs and other overheads remain the same. Reducing the DOP amortizes this overhead and triggers further improvements later in the plan. For example, hash joins can be replaced with cross joins, re-partitions can be avoided and parallel plans can be replaced with a serial plan when data in flight is small [8]. QUICKR introduces exchange operators to reduce the DOP. However, since an exchange shuffles data it increases the cost (in terms of latency and resources to shuffle) and hence `ASALQA` places an exchange only when the cost is smaller than the gains in subsequent portions of the execution plan.

Global requirements and Caveats: To ensure that both sides of a join are implemented with the same universe sampler parameters (if

Metric	Sampler Type		
	Uniform	Distinct	Universe
Distribution across samplers	54%	26%	20%
Queries that use at least 1 sampler of a certain type	49%	24%	9%

Table 7: Frequency of use of various samplers.

True value		Estimate rewritten by QUICKR
SUM(X)	COUNT(*)	SUM(w· X) | SUM(w)
AVG(X)		SUM(w · X)/SUM(w)
SUM(IF(F(X)? Y: Z))		SUM(IF(F(X)? w· Y: w· Z))[‡]
COUNT(DISTINCT X)		COUNT(DISTINCT X)·(univ(X)? w:1)

‡ : COUNTIF and COUNT(X) are rewritten analogous to SUMIF.

Table 8: How QUICKR rewrites aggregation operations.

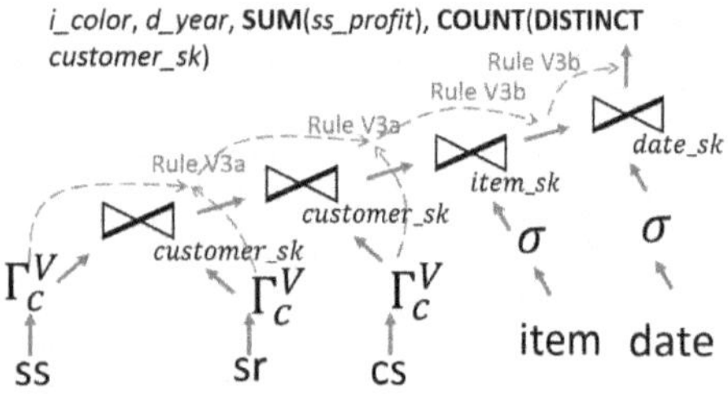

Figure 9: For the example in Figure 1, the query plan computed by ASALQA. The dashed arrows show how our error analysis unrolls ASALQA and the dominance rules (§B.3) used at each step. The result is an expression with a single sampler just below the aggregation.

Metric	Percentile values					
	50th			90th		
Total/First pass time	1.2	1.4	1.3	2.8	4.3	2
# of Passes over Data	3.1	1.1	1.0	4.0	1.2	1.3
# Aggregation Ops.	3	1	2	8	3	5
# Joins	4	2	2	9	5	7
depth of operators	20	18	16	26	24	27
size of QCS+QVS	5	5	5	12	9	4
size of QCS	3	3	4	9	8	3

Table 9: Analyzing query attributes from different workloads: TPC-DS [4], TPC-H [5] and Other (BigBench [3] ∪ BigData [1] ∪ ...). Queries are written in Hive and executed with Tez as the AM in Yarn.

at all), on the bottom-up pass of the query optimization, ASALQA rejects plans that do not satisfy such *global* requirements. It then falls back to the next best choice. Further, QUICKR does not allow nested samplers. Because the performance gains from sampling a relation that has been sampled already is not worth the added potential for error. This too is implemented during the bottom-up pass. Finally, we admit that a few aspects of QUICKR are as yet unimplemented. QUICKR does not push samplers past spools and full outer joins. Heavy hitter information is not used as well as it should be. And, though we obtain column value variance at the inputs, we do not yet derive the value variance past other operations. In our evaluation, we point out the effect of these caveats. The first two lower QUICKR's coverage and performance gains- fewer queries benefit and by less than they should- and the last adds to error when computing SUM over skewed columns. Our results are already quite good, however.

B. ANALYZING SAMPLED PLANS

We formally analyze our samplers and push-down rules. We focus here on queries that perform SUM-like aggregations over groups; other aggregates are covered in §C. Let group G denote all the tuples that have the same value in group-by columns of the output. The answer contains for each group G the aggregate $w(G) = \sum_{t \in G} w(t)$, where $w(t)$ is the value associated with tuple t. Given a query E, QUICKR's ASALQA algorithm outputs a query plan $\mathcal{E}$ with samplers at various locations. Our goal is to compare the answer of E (unsampled query) with that of $\mathcal{E}$ on two aspects: the *expected squared error* of group values (i.e., variance of $w(G)$) and the *group coverage probability* (i.e., likelihood of not missing a group).

For all three samplers used by QUICKR, we first offer closed-form expressions upon immediate use. That is, when the samplers are placed near at the root of the query plan just before group-by and aggregation (see §B.1). To compute similar expressions when samplers are at arbitrary locations in the query tree, intuitively, we address the following issue: when pushing a sampler past another database operator, how do the error expressions change? (See §B.2.) We introduce the concept of *sampling dominance* between query expressions which ensures that the error is no worse. Using this, we establish in §B.3 a collection of sampler transformation rules. which guide our exploration of alternatives as well as our accuracy analysis.

B.1 Estimating Sampler Accuracy

QUICKR uses the *Horvitz-Thompson (HT) estimator* [24] to relate the answers on sampled query plans to their true values and to estimate the expected squared error. For each group G in the answer of an unsampled query E, the sampled plan $\mathcal{E}$ outputs a subset of the rows in G, $\mathcal{E}(G) \subseteq G$. We estimate $w(G)$ as:

$$\hat{w}_{\mathcal{E}}(G) = \sum_{t \in \mathcal{E}(G)} \frac{w(t)}{\mathbf{Pr}[t \in \mathcal{E}(G)]}. \quad (1)$$

It is easy to see that the above (HT) estimator is unbiased, i.e., $\mathbf{E}[\hat{w}_{\mathcal{E}}(G)] = w(G)$. Hence, its variance is *expected squared error*:

$$\mathbf{Var}[\hat{w}_{\mathcal{E}}(G)] = \sum_{i,j \in G} \left(\frac{\mathbf{Pr}[i,j \in \mathcal{E}(G)]}{\mathbf{Pr}[i \in \mathcal{E}(G)]\,\mathbf{Pr}[j \in \mathcal{E}(G)]} - 1 \right) \cdot w(i) w(j).$$

From the sample $\mathcal{E}(G)$, $\mathbf{Var}[\hat{w}_{\mathcal{E}}(G)]$ can be estimated as:

$$\hat{\mathbf{Var}}[\hat{w}_{\mathcal{E}}(G)] = \quad (2)$$

$$\sum_{i,j \in \mathcal{E}(G)} \left(\frac{\mathbf{Pr}[i,j \in \mathcal{E}(G)]}{\mathbf{Pr}[i \in \mathcal{E}(G)]\,\mathbf{Pr}[j \in \mathcal{E}(G)]} - 1 \right) \cdot \frac{w(i) w(j)}{\mathbf{Pr}[i,j \in \mathcal{E}(G)]}.$$

Recall our three samplers: *uniform sampler* Γ_p^{U} (uniform sampling probability p), *distinct sampler* $\Gamma_{p,C,\delta}^{\mathsf{D}}$ (each value of column set C has support at least δ in the sample), and *universe sampler* $\Gamma_{p,C}^{\mathsf{V}}$ (sampling values of column set C with probability p). It could help to think of the universe sampler as a predicate that passes only the rows whose values of C belong to the chosen subspace.

We apply the HT estimator to compute variance for all the samplers. To do so, we compute the terms $\mathbf{Pr}[i \in \mathcal{E}(G)]$ and $\mathbf{Pr}[i,j \in \mathcal{E}(G)]$ for each sampler as follows:

Proposition 3 (To Compute HT Estimator and the Variance).

- *For Γ_p^{U}, for any tuples $i,j \in G$, we have $\mathbf{Pr}[i \in \mathcal{E}(G)] = p$, and, if $i \neq j$, $\mathbf{Pr}[i,j \in \mathcal{E}(G)] = p^2$.*
- *For $\Gamma_{p,C,\delta}^{\mathsf{D}}$, let $g(i)$ be the set of tuples with the same values on C as tuple i in the input relation. We have*

$$\mathbf{Pr}[i \in \mathcal{E}(G)] = \begin{cases} 1 & |g(i)| \le \delta \\ \max(\delta/|g(i)|, p) & |g(i)| > \delta \end{cases};$$

  if $i \neq j$, $\mathbf{Pr}[i,j \in \mathcal{E}(G)] = \mathbf{Pr}[i \in \mathcal{E}(G)]\,\mathbf{Pr}[j \in \mathcal{E}(G)]$.
- *For $\Gamma_{p,C}^{\mathsf{V}}$, let $g(i)$ be the set of tuples with the same values on C as i in the input relation. We have $\mathbf{Pr}[i \in \mathcal{E}(G)] = p$, and*

$$\mathbf{Pr}[i,j \in \mathcal{E}(G)] = \begin{cases} p & g(i) = g(j) \\ p^2 & g(i) \neq g(j) \end{cases}, \ \text{if } i \neq j.$$

A few imprecisions are worth mentioning. The universe sampler does choose its subspace at random. So while the formula above is technically accurate, tuples that belong to the subspace will be in the sample and those outside the subspace would not. Our implementation of the distinct sampler, because of its requirements to finish in one pass and with a small memory footprint, introduces some correlation between tuples and a slight bias as noted already.

Complexity of Computing Estimate and Error.
Proposition 2 posits that the computation requires only one effective pass over the sample. The proof follows from Proposition 3 and Equations(1)-(2). Since each tuple i in the sample $\mathcal{E}(G)$ also contains the probability $\mathbf{Pr}[i \in \mathcal{E}(G)]$ in its weight column, $\hat{w}_{\mathcal{E}}(G)$ can be computed in one scan using Equation(1). A naive way to compute $\hat{\mathbf{Var}}[\hat{w}_{\mathcal{E}}(G)]$ using (2) requires a self-join and can take quadratic time since it checks all pairs of tuples in the sample. We do better by observing that only the pairs having $\mathbf{Pr}[i, j \in \mathcal{E}(G)] \neq \mathbf{Pr}[i \in \mathcal{E}(G)]\,\mathbf{Pr}[j \in \mathcal{E}(G)]$ need to be considered. For the uniform and distinct samplers, the summation in (2) goes to zero for $i \neq j$ and so their variance can be computed in one pass. For the universe sampler, there are two types of pairs: i) (i, j) with $g(i) = g(j)$, and ii) (i, j) with $g(i) \neq g(j)$. Per Proposition 3, the summation term is zero for pairs of the latter type. For the former type, we maintain per-group values in parallel and use a shuffle to put them back into (2). Since the number of groups can be no larger than the number of tuples, the computation is linear. Further the shuffle often has much less work to do (per group) than the first pass (per sampled tuple) leading to our one-effective-pass claim.

Group Coverage Probability.
A group G will miss from the answer if all the tuples in G are missed in the sample $\mathcal{E}(G)$. We show how QUICKR makes this unlikely.

Proposition 4 (Group Coverage Probability). *When samplers immediately precede the aggregate, the probability that a group G appears in the answer is:*

- *For* Γ^{U}_{p}, $\mathbf{Pr}[G] = 1 - (1-p)^{|G|}$.
- *For* $\Gamma^{\mathsf{D}}_{p,C,\delta}$,
$$\mathbf{Pr}[G] \begin{cases} = 1, & \textit{if } C \textit{ contains the group-by dimensions} \\ \geq 1-(1-p)^{|G|}, & \textit{otherwise} \end{cases}.$$
- *For* $\Gamma^{\mathsf{V}}_{p,C}$, $\mathbf{Pr}[G] = 1-(1-p)^{|G(C)|}$, *where* $G(C)$ *is the set of distinct values of tuples in G on dimensions C.*

Using Proposition 4, we see that both uniform and distinct samplers rarely miss groups. Recall that QUICKR checks before introducing samplers that there is enough support, i.e., $p * |G| \geq k$ (§4.2.6). For example, when $k = 30$ and $p = 0.1$, the likelihood of missing G is below 10^{-14}. For the universe sampler, note that $|G(C)| \in [1, |G|]$. However, recall that QUICKR uses the universe sampler only when the stratification requirements can be met. That is, the overlap between universe columns and those defining the group is small. Hence, $|G(C)| \sim |G|$ and groups are missed rarely.

Sampling from Join.
The advantage of universe sampler $\Gamma^{\mathsf{V}}_{p,C}$ lies in sampling from join. To draw a p fraction of tuples from the join of two relations, the universe sampler only needs a p fraction from input relations. But, both the uniform and distinct samplers need to draw a $\sqrt{p}$ fraction of tuples. Not only is the $\sqrt{p}$ sample more expensive to compute but both the variance and the group coverage probability become worse (when p is replaced with $\sqrt{p}$ in Propositions 3 and 4).

B.2 Sampling Dominance

We now formalize our notion of sampling dominance between query expressions. Suppose $\mathcal{E}$ is an expression on database relations possibly with samplers. The *core* $\Lambda(\mathcal{E})$ denotes the expression generated by removing all samplers from $\mathcal{E}$. We say an expression $\mathcal{E}_1$ is dominated by another expression $\mathcal{E}_2$ if and only if the expressions have the same core and $\mathcal{E}_2$ has no higher variance and no higher probability of missing groups than $\mathcal{E}_1$. More formally, we have:

Definition 1 (Sampling Dominance). *Given two expressions* $\mathcal{E}_1$ *and* $\mathcal{E}_2$ *with* $\Lambda(\mathcal{E}_1) = \Lambda(\mathcal{E}_2)$ *and having* $\mathcal{R}_1$ *and* $\mathcal{R}_2$ *as the respective output relations, we say* $\mathcal{E}_2$ dominates $\mathcal{E}_1$, *or* $\mathcal{E}_1 \overset{*}{\Rightarrow} \mathcal{E}_2$, *iff*

$$(\textit{v-dominance } \mathcal{E}_1 \overset{\mathsf{V}}{\Rightarrow} \mathcal{E}_2) \quad \forall i, j: \tag{3}$$
$$\frac{\mathbf{Pr}[i \in \mathcal{R}_1, j \in \mathcal{R}_1]}{\mathbf{Pr}[i \in \mathcal{R}_1]\,\mathbf{Pr}[j \in \mathcal{R}_1]} \geq \frac{\mathbf{Pr}[i \in \mathcal{R}_2, j \in \mathcal{R}_2]}{\mathbf{Pr}[i \in \mathcal{R}_2]\,\mathbf{Pr}[j \in \mathcal{R}_2]}, \textit{ and}$$
$$(\textit{c-dominance } \mathcal{E}_1 \overset{\mathsf{C}}{\Rightarrow} \mathcal{E}_2) \quad \forall t: \mathbf{Pr}[t \in \mathcal{R}_1] \leq \mathbf{Pr}[t \in \mathcal{R}_2]. \tag{4}$$

Note that *sampler dominance* subsumes the *SOA-equivalence* definition from [35]. Two expressions $\mathcal{E}_1, \mathcal{E}_2$ are SOA equivalent iff $\mathcal{E}_1 \overset{*}{\Rightarrow} \mathcal{E}_2$ and $\mathcal{E}_2 \overset{*}{\Rightarrow} \mathcal{E}_1$. Intuitively c-dominance says that all tuples are strictly more likely to appear in the output and v-dominance helps relate the variance. By using (3) and (4) in (1) and the above propositions, it is not hard to see that if $\mathcal{E}_2$ dominates $\mathcal{E}_1$, $\hat{w}_{\mathcal{E}_2}(G)$ is better than $\hat{w}_{\mathcal{E}_1}(G)$ in terms of variance and group coverage probability. We formally state this result below.

Proposition 5 (Dominance and Accuracy). *For any group G in the output of a SUM-like aggregate query, consider two execution plans* $\mathcal{E}_1$ *and* $\mathcal{E}_2$ *with independent (uniform, distinct, universe) samplers, with the same core plan* $\Lambda(\mathcal{E}_1) = \Lambda(\mathcal{E}_2)$. *If* $\mathcal{E}_1 \overset{\mathsf{V}}{\Rightarrow} \mathcal{E}_2$, *we have*
$$\mathbf{Var}[\hat{w}_{\mathcal{E}_1}(G)] \geq \mathbf{Var}[\hat{w}_{\mathcal{E}_2}(G)].$$
And if $\mathcal{E}_1 \overset{\mathsf{C}}{\Rightarrow} \mathcal{E}_2$ *and the values on the join dimension and the grouping dimension (if any) are sampled independently, we have*
$$\mathbf{Pr}[G \textit{ is missed in } \mathcal{E}_1] \geq \mathbf{Pr}[G \textit{ is missed in } \mathcal{E}_2].$$

Hence, $\mathcal{E}_1 \overset{*}{\Rightarrow} \mathcal{E}_2$, implies that the latter has a strictly better answer.

Dominance Transitivity across Database Operators.
Eventually, we want the dominance relationship to hold at the root of a plan so that we can bound the variance and the group-missing probability in the answer according to Proposition 5. We show that dominance is transitive across database operators, from the root to leaves in the plan. We focus on three operators: π_C (projection on a subset of columns C), σ_C (selection on C), and $\bowtie_C$ (join on C).

This leads us to Proposition 1 which states the conditions under which the dominance relationship is transitive. The proof follows.

Proof. Note that projection holds by definition. We focus on select (ii) and join (iii) below.

Let $\mathcal{R}_i$ be the set of rows output by $\mathcal{E}_i$, and R be the set of rows output by $\Lambda(\mathcal{E}_i)$. For a row $i \in \sigma_C(R)$, we have
$$\mathbf{Pr}[i \in \sigma_C(\mathcal{R}_i)] = \begin{cases} \mathbf{Pr}[i \in \mathcal{R}_i] & i \in \sigma_C(R) \\ 0 & i \notin \sigma_C(R) \end{cases}. \tag{5}$$

ii) can be proved by putting (5) into (3) and (4).

To prove $\mathcal{E}_1 \bowtie_C \mathcal{F}_1 \overset{*}{\Rightarrow} \mathcal{E}_2 \bowtie_C \mathcal{F}_2$, it suffices to prove $\mathcal{E}_1 \times \mathcal{F}_1 \overset{*}{\Rightarrow} \mathcal{E}_2 \times \mathcal{F}_2$ (i.e., cross product) since $\bowtie_C$ is equivalent to composing $\times$ with selection σ_C and we can apply ii) for the latter. Suppose $\mathcal{S}_i$ is the set of rows output by $\mathcal{F}_i$, and S is the set of rows output by $\Lambda(\mathcal{F}_i)$. For $\mathcal{E}_1 \times \mathcal{F}_1 \overset{\mathsf{V}}{\Rightarrow} \mathcal{E}_2 \times \mathcal{F}_2$ to hold, we need to show that
$$\frac{\mathbf{Pr}[(r,s) \in \mathcal{R}_1 \times \mathcal{S}_1, (r',s') \in \mathcal{R}_1 \times \mathcal{S}_1]}{\mathbf{Pr}[(r,s) \in \mathcal{R}_1 \times \mathcal{S}_1]\,\mathbf{Pr}[(r',s') \in \mathcal{R}_1 \times \mathcal{S}_1]}$$
$$\geq \frac{\mathbf{Pr}[(r,s) \in \mathcal{R}_2 \times \mathcal{S}_2, (r',s') \in \mathcal{R}_2 \times \mathcal{S}_2]}{\mathbf{Pr}[(r,s) \in \mathcal{R}_2 \times \mathcal{S}_2]\,\mathbf{Pr}[(r',s') \in \mathcal{R}_2 \times \mathcal{S}_2]}. \tag{6}$$

To this end, we consider the following two cases.

Case a) $\mathcal{E}_i$ and $\mathcal{F}_i$ share a universe sampler $\Gamma^{\mathsf{V}}_{p,\mathcal{D}}$. Let $r_{\mathcal{D}}$ be the value of a row r on dimensions $\mathcal{D}$. In this case, the event "$(r,s) \in \mathcal{R}_i \times \mathcal{S}_i$" is equivalent to that r and s have the same values on dimensions $\mathcal{D}$, i.e., $r_{\mathcal{D}} = s_{\mathcal{D}}$, and the value $r_{\mathcal{D}}$ is picked by the universe sampler. Because, when $r_{\mathcal{D}} \neq s_{\mathcal{D}}$ or $r'_{\mathcal{D}} \neq s'_{\mathcal{D}}$, we have both sides of (6) equal to 0; when $r_{\mathcal{D}} = s_{\mathcal{D}}$ and $r'_{\mathcal{D}} = s'_{\mathcal{D}}$, we have

$$\mathbf{Pr}\left[(r,s) \in \mathcal{R}_i \times \mathcal{S}_i, (r',s') \in \mathcal{R}_i \times \mathcal{S}_i\right] = \mathbf{Pr}\left[r \in \mathcal{R}_i, r' \in \mathcal{R}_i\right]$$
$$\text{and } \mathbf{Pr}\left[(r,s) \in \mathcal{R}_i \times \mathcal{S}_i\right] = \mathbf{Pr}\left[r \in \mathcal{R}_i\right]. \qquad (7)$$

From (7) and $\mathcal{E}_1 \stackrel{*}{\Rightarrow} \mathcal{E}_2$, $\mathcal{F}_1 \stackrel{*}{\Rightarrow} \mathcal{F}_2$ we have $\mathcal{E}_1 \times \mathcal{F}_1 \stackrel{*}{\Rightarrow} \mathcal{E}_2 \times \mathcal{F}_2$.

Case b) $\mathcal{E}_i$ and $\mathcal{F}_i$ do not share a universe sampler. In this case, we know that samplers on the two sides of the join operator (or $\times$) are independent, i.e., rows from $\mathcal{R}_i$ and the ones from $\mathcal{S}_i$ are drawn independently. So based on this independence condition, we have

$$\mathbf{Pr}\left[(r,s) \in \mathcal{R}_i \times \mathcal{S}_i, (r',s') \in \mathcal{R}_i \times \mathcal{S}_i\right]$$
$$= \mathbf{Pr}\left[r \in \mathcal{R}_i, r' \in \mathcal{R}_i\right] \cdot \mathbf{Pr}\left[s \in \mathcal{S}_i, s' \in \mathcal{S}_i\right], \text{and} \qquad (8)$$
$$\mathbf{Pr}\left[(r,s) \in \mathcal{R}_i \times \mathcal{S}_i\right] = \mathbf{Pr}\left[r \in \mathcal{R}_i\right] \cdot \mathbf{Pr}\left[s \in \mathcal{S}_i\right]. \qquad (9)$$

Putting (8) and (9) into (6), we can see that $\mathcal{E}_1 \stackrel{*}{\Rightarrow} \mathcal{E}_2$ and $\mathcal{F}_1 \stackrel{*}{\Rightarrow} \mathcal{F}_2$ suffice for $\mathcal{E}_1 \times \mathcal{F}_1 \stackrel{*}{\Rightarrow} \mathcal{E}_2 \times \mathcal{F}_2$. □

B.3 Sampler Switching and Pushing Rules

For the same sampling rate p, we have the following ranking among samplers in the order of accuracy from lower to higher.

Proposition 6 (Switching Rule). *For any relation R, we have* $\Gamma^{\mathsf{V}}_{p,C}(R) \stackrel{*}{\Rightarrow} \Gamma^{\mathsf{U}}_{p}(R) \stackrel{*}{\Rightarrow} \Gamma^{\mathsf{D}}_{p,C,\delta}(R)$.

The proof follows from observing the terms for variance and group coverage of each sampler. Since the distinct sampler has lower performance gain, it is used only when needed for accuracy.

We now list a few useful *transformation* rules based on our dominance definition and transitivity proofs.

Proposition 7 (Pushing past Projection). *For any relation R and a projection π_C where C is a subset of columns of R, we have*
Rule-U1: $\Gamma^{\mathsf{U}}_{p}(\pi_C(R)) \stackrel{*}{\Rightarrow} \pi_C(\Gamma^{\mathsf{U}}_{p}(R))$;
Rule-D1: $\Gamma^{\mathsf{D}}_{p,\mathcal{D},\delta}(\pi_C(R)) \stackrel{*}{\Rightarrow} \pi_C(\Gamma^{\mathsf{D}}_{p,\mathcal{D},\delta}(R))$, *if* $\mathcal{D} \subseteq C$;
Rule-V1: $\Gamma^{\mathsf{V}}_{p,\mathcal{D}}(\pi_C(R)) \stackrel{*}{\Rightarrow} \pi_C(\Gamma^{\mathsf{V}}_{p,\mathcal{D}}(R))$, *if* $\mathcal{D} \subseteq C$.

The rules show that it is strictly better to push samplers below projects. Indeed, the sampler column set $\mathcal{D}$ is always a subset of the columns returned by the project C.

Pushing samplers past selections is complicated by one aspect. If the columns used in the select are not explicitly stratified, the group sizes vary before and after pushing. Hence, we introduce the *weak dominance relationship*, denoted as $\stackrel{\sim}{\Rightarrow}$. With weak dominance, v- and c- dominance only hold for large groups in a probabilistic way.

Proposition 8 (Pushing past Selection). *For any relation R and a selection σ_C with selection formula on a subset C of columns of R,*
Rule-U2: $\Gamma^{\mathsf{U}}_{p}(\sigma_C(R)) \stackrel{*}{\Rightarrow} \sigma_C(\Gamma^{\mathsf{U}}_{p}(R))$;
Rule-D2a: $\Gamma^{\mathsf{D}}_{p,\mathcal{D},\delta}(\sigma_C(R)) \stackrel{*}{\Rightarrow} \sigma_C(\Gamma^{\mathsf{D}}_{p,\mathcal{D}\cup C,\delta}(R))$;
Rule-D2b: $\Gamma^{\mathsf{D}}_{p,\mathcal{D},\delta}(\sigma_C(R)) \stackrel{\sim}{\Rightarrow} \sigma_C(\Gamma^{\mathsf{D}}_{p,\mathcal{D},\delta/\sigma^{\mathsf{SS}}}(R))$;
Rule-D2c: $\Gamma^{\mathsf{D}}_{p,\mathcal{D},\delta}(\sigma_C(R)) \stackrel{\sim}{\Rightarrow} \sigma_C(\Gamma^{\mathsf{D}}_{p,\mathcal{D},\delta}(R))$;
Rule-V2: $\Gamma^{\mathsf{V}}_{p,\mathcal{D}}(\sigma_C(R)) \stackrel{\sim}{\Rightarrow} \sigma_C(\Gamma^{\mathsf{V}}_{p,\mathcal{D}}(R))$, *if* $|\mathcal{D} \cap C| \ll |\mathcal{D} \cup C|$.
The selectivity of σ_C on R, denoted as σ^{SS}, is $|\sigma_C(R)|/|R|$.

Finally, we list the rules for pushing samplers past joins.

Proposition 9 (Pushing past Join). *For relations R_1 and R_2, with columns C_i respectively and an equi-join $\bowtie_C$ on columns C, we have*
Rule-U3: $\Gamma^{\mathsf{U}}_{p}(R_1 \bowtie_C R_2) \stackrel{c}{\Rightarrow} \Gamma^{\mathsf{U}}_{p_1}(R_1) \bowtie_C \Gamma^{\mathsf{U}}_{p_2}(R_2)$, *if* $p = p_1 \cdot p_2$;
Rule-D3a: $\Gamma^{\mathsf{D}}_{p,\mathcal{D},\delta}(R_1 \bowtie_C R_2) \stackrel{*}{\Rightarrow} \Gamma^{\mathsf{D}}_{p,\mathcal{D}\cup C,\delta}(R_1) \bowtie_C R_2$;
Rule-D3b: $\Gamma^{\mathsf{D}}_{p,\mathcal{D},\delta}(R_1 \bowtie_C R_2) \stackrel{\sim}{\Rightarrow} \Gamma^{\mathsf{D}}_{p,\mathcal{D},\delta}(R_1) \bowtie_C R_2$, *if* $\mathcal{D} \subseteq C_1$;
Rule-V3a: $\Gamma^{\mathsf{V}}_{p,\mathcal{D}}(R_1 \bowtie_C R_2) \stackrel{*}{\Rightarrow} \Gamma^{\mathsf{V}}_{p,\mathcal{D}}(R_1) \bowtie_C \Gamma^{\mathsf{V}}_{p,\mathcal{D}}(R_2)$, *if* $C = \mathcal{D}$ *or* $\mathcal{D} \subseteq C_1, C_2$;
Rule-V3b: $\Gamma^{\mathsf{V}}_{p,\mathcal{D}}(R_1 \bowtie_C R_2) \stackrel{\sim}{\Rightarrow} \Gamma^{\mathsf{V}}_{p,\mathcal{D}}(R_1) \bowtie_C R_2$, *if* $\mathcal{D} \subseteq C_1$.

Note that Rule-U3 includes the cases when uniform sampler is pushed to only one side, i.e., set $p_1 = 1$ or $p_2 = 1$. Observe that for rules D3a, D3b and V3b, wherein the sampler is only pushed to R_1, there are analogous rules that push the sampler only to R_2.

C. GENERAL AGGREGATIONS

So far, we have considered groups with SUM-like aggregates. Here, we extend our analysis to other aggregations such as `COUNT` and to the case where a result has multiple aggregations such as `SELECT x, SUM(y), COUNT(z)`. QUICKR allows users to annotate user-defined aggregates with functional expressions which it uses to obtain various accuracy measures; details are left for future work.
Other aggregations: Analyzing `COUNT` directly follows from `SUM` by setting $w(t) = 1\ \forall t$. `AVG` translates to $\frac{\texttt{SUM}}{\texttt{COUNT}}$ but its variance is harder to analyze due to the division [24]. In implementation, QUICKR substitutes `AVG` by `SUM/COUNT` and divides the corresponding estimators. QUICKR also supports `DISTINCT`, which translates to a group with no aggregations and `COUNT(DISTINCT)`. Error for the former is akin to missing groups analysis. For `COUNT(DISTINCT)`, the value estimator varies with the sampler– by default it is the value computed over samples. Only when universe sampling is on the same columns, the value over samples is weighted up by the probability. Further, distinct sampler offers unbiased error and zero variance. With uniform sampler, the variance is small but there is some negative bias since though unlikely due to QUICKR's requirement for sufficient support, some rare values may not appear. We defer analyzing the error for other aggregations to future work.
Multiple aggregation ops: QUICKR naturally extends to the case when multiple aggregations are computed over the same sampled input relation. The key observation is that the estimators of true values for each aggregation only require the value in the sampled tuple, the corresponding *weight* which describes the probability with which the tuple was passed and in rare cases the type of the sample (e.g., for `COUNT DISTINCT`). The first two are available as columns in the sampled relation. The third we implement as a corrective rewriting after `ASALQA` chooses the samplers.

D. ADDITIONAL RELATED WORK

We mention a few relevant threads of substantial research: synopses and sketches [15, 20, 42], view matching [28] and data streams [13, 31, 34]. Sketches and synopses on input datasets can offer more speed-up than samples. However, they are generally harder to reason with for ad-hoc queries and hence QUICKR prefers sampling. However, we do use the heavy-hitter sketch to reduce memory needs of our distinct sampler. Sampling in data streams has some similar constraints to what we pose on our samplers such as bounded memory footprint and streaming execution. However, while QUICKR samples partitioned data in parallel for ad-hoc queries, stream management systems focus on (known) queries that effectively execute forever. Reusing sampled sub-expressions generated by previous queries can improve QUICKR and hence view matching is an area of future work for us.

A Study of Sorting Algorithms on Approximate Memory

Shuang Chen[1,2*] Shunning Jiang[1,2*] Bingsheng He[2] Xueyan Tang[2]

[1]Shanghai Jiao Tong University, Shanghai, China
[2]Nanyang Technological University, Singapore

ABSTRACT

Hardware evolution has been one of the driving factors for the redesign of database systems. Recently, approximate storage emerges in the area of computer architecture. It trades off precision for better performance and/or energy consumption. Previous studies have demonstrated the benefits of approximate storage for applications that are tolerant to imprecision such as image processing. However, it is still an open question whether and how approximate storage can be used for applications that do not expose such intrinsic tolerance. In this paper, we study one of the most basic operations in database–sorting on a hybrid storage system with both precise storage and approximate storage. Particularly, we start with a study of three common sorting algorithms on approximate storage. Experimental results show that a 95% sorted sequence can be obtained with up to 40% reduction in total write latencies. Thus, we propose an *approx-refine* execution mechanism to improve the performance of sorting algorithms on the hybrid storage system to produce precise results. Our optimization gains the performance benefits by offloading the sorting operation to approximate storage, followed by an efficient refinement to resolve the unsortedness on the output of the approximate storage. Our experiments show that our *approx-refine* can reduce the total memory access time by up to 11%. These studies shed light on the potential of approximate hardware for improving the performance of applications that require precise results.

1. INTRODUCTION

Approximate computing [15, 41, 42, 52, 54, 60] is a hot research area that trades the accuracy/precision of application results for performance and/or energy efficiency. In all the previous studies [15, 41, 42, 52, 54, 60], approximate computing targets at the applications with intrinsic tolerance to inaccuracies in computation, such as computer vision and image processing. Meanwhile, the idea of approximate computing has been expanded to storage (i.e., *approximate storage* [36, 54, 48]). Nowadays, the scaling of common memory technologies like DRAM and flash is approaching its limit. New memory technologies, such as non-volatile memory (NVRAM), are emerging. For example, multi-level cell phase change memory (MLC PCM), the leading contender among NVRAMs, is shown to be a competitive choice for databases [47, 12, 27], and other applications [54].

In recent years, several kinds of approximate storage have been proposed to improve the energy efficiency and performance of memory systems [36, 48, 51, 35, 54]. They trade the precision of results for increased write performance or reduced energy consumption. A previous study shows 1.7× improvement on write latencies with quality loss under 10% for MLC PCM [54]. This is significant in PCM performance, because write latency issues almost drag the adoption of PCM reported by previous studies [30, 34]. Approximate storage also imposes little burden on manufacturers in the sense that it requires only reasonable modification to the existing hardware [54].

Despite the performance and power advantage of approximate hardware, its application scope is limited to the applications with inherent error tolerances, as in all the previous studies [15, 41, 42, 52, 54, 60]. Yet, many real applications are without intrinsic tolerance, which we define to be *precise computing*. The results of these applications are often required to be precise. For example, an imprecision in bank account storage can lead to millions of dollars in loss. A natural and challenging question is whether approximate storage can still be used for improving the performance and/or energy efficiency of precise computing.

In this paper, we study sorting, an important operation in (database) systems impacting the performance of various operators and algorithms [32], in the context of approximate memory. With heavier sorting workloads arising in high performance computing, engines of web indexing, and database systems, memory performance becomes an increasingly serious problem in conventional sorting algorithms [23]. The sorting algorithm requires a precisely sorted output, based on the input data. We conduct our study in two steps.

Step 1. We study the trade-off between sortedness and write performance if sorting is performed in the approximate memory *only*. The results and findings in this step are considered as the best performance/energy gains that we can achieve by leveraging approximate memory.

Step 2. To expand traditional approximate computing to a broader scope, how can we leverage the approximate

*Shuang Chen and Shunning Jiang contribute equally to this work and are listed alphabetically.

SIGMOD'16, June 26-July 01, 2016, San Francisco, CA, USA

DOI: http://dx.doi.org/10.1145/2882903.2882908

memory to improve the performance of sorting algorithms, but still produce *precise results*?

Particularly, we revisit three classic and popular sorting algorithms: *quicksort*, *mergesort*, and *radixsort* (the first two are comparison-based, while the last is not) using approximate main memory. Simulation results show that without the requirement of precise outputs, *quicksort* and *radixsort* can get a nearly sorted sequence while reducing 30% – 40% write latencies on the approximate memory.

Unlike previous studies that focus on approximate computing with approximate hardware, we design a sorting mechanism on the hybrid memory system with both precise and approximate memory for guaranteeing precise results. We use a novel algorithmic level execution mechanism on hybrid approximate/precise memory to produce precise results. Specifically, we propose an *approx-refine* mechanism in which the approximate memory acts as an accelerator. We first copy the input data from the precise memory to the approximate memory, and then perform an existing sorting algorithm on the approximate memory. Finally, the approximate results are refined to become precise in the precise memory. If the sorting algorithm can deliver a nearly sorted output on approximate memory, only a lightweight refinement is needed afterwards. As a result, the cost of refinement and data copies between precise memory and approximate memory can be compensated by the gain of offloading the sorting algorithm to the approximate hardware. Our *approx-refine* scheme is generally applicable to different sorting algorithms with little modification. Simulation results show that, up to 11% write latencies can be saved using the *approx-refine* mechanism in hybrid precise/approximate memory. However, *mergesort* does not show any benefit under the hybrid execution. Therefore, approximate storage is not favored by every sorting algorithm.

This paper has made the following major contributions. First, we showcase that approximate hardware can also be used for improving the performance of *precise* computing, which broadens the application scope of approximate hardware. Previously, approximate hardware is only used for approximate computing. Second, we develop and evaluate common sorting algorithms on the hybrid storage systems with both precise and approximate storage, and demonstrate the system and architectural insights of achieving precise computation on approximate hardware. To the best of our knowledge, this is the first systematic study of sorting algorithms on approximate storage.

The rest of the paper is organized as follows. Section 2 introduces the approximate memory model. In Section 3, we study sorting using approximate memory only, without the requirement of precise results. In Section 4, to produce precise results, we propose the *approx-refine* mechanism and introduce the detailed design of the refinement. Section 5 presents the experimental results using the *approx-refine* mechanism. Section 6 reviews the related work. Finally, Section 7 concludes the paper.

2. BACKGROUND

In this paper, we focus on phase change memory (PCM), as PCM is a kind of promising NVRAM and is shown to be a competitive choice for databases [47, 12, 27]. This section briefly introduces the basics and modeling of precise memory, and the approximate memory model from Sampson et al. [54]. The model from Sampson et al. captures the performance and precision tradeoff on PCM. For more details on the modeling of PCM, we refer readers to the following papers: approximate memory modeling [54], unidirectional shift [67], PCM programming feedback control loop [44], and successive approximation analog-to-digital-converter (ADC) for PCM systems [46].

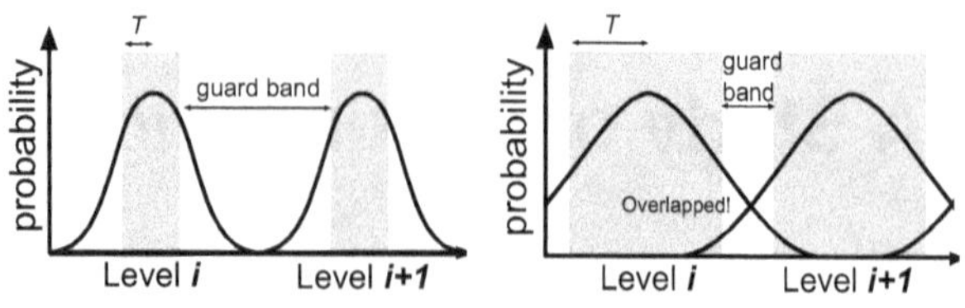

(a) Precise MLC (b) Approximate MLC

Figure 1: Differences between a precise (a) and approximate (b) multi-level cell (adapted from [54]).

2.1 Modeling Multi-Level Cell

NVRAM stores data as an analog value. For density scaling purpose, multi-level cell (MLC) stores multiple bits in one cell by dividing the range of the underlying analog value into more levels than single-level cell (SLC). SLC exposes only two states (logic "1" and "0"). The target analog range of each digital level in MLC is narrower than SLC. The multiple levels are separated by *guard bands*, which is controlled by the width of target analog range T as illustrated in Figure 1(a). The curves in Figure 1(a) show the probability of the analog value read from a cell after writing to it. In the precise MLC, the guard band is wide enough to distinguish two consecutive levels safely.

We adopt the MLC model from Sampson et al. [54], which abstracts the read/write model of MLC as follows. Let v be the internal analog value of a cell. In a cell write operation, a digital value d is first converted to the corresponding analog value v_d, Due to the non-determinism of analog writes, v would then be set to $WRITE(v_d)$ instead of v_d, where $WRITE$ is a function to produce an acceptable analog value by an iterative *program-and-verify* (P&V) process within a PCM write. A cell read operation retrieves an analog value $READ(v)$ and quantizes it to a digital value, where $READ$ is a function involving the perturbation. In the following, we present more details on $WRITE$ and $READ$.

2.1.1 MLC Write

Cell write operations are inherently non-deterministic on account of the analog nature. Due to process variation and material fluctuations, a single *cell write* pulse is usually insufficient to program the target analog value precisely. Hence, in both industry and academia, most MLC designs, including PCM [5, 7, 16, 43, 44, 46] and Flash [57], adopt an iterative *program-and-verify* (P&V) process to guarantee that the analog value is programmed within the exact value range.

Each write operation first resets the analog value to zero, and then iteratively performs P&V until the actual analog value reaches the target range (i.e., the grey area in Figure 1). Pseudo code of a cell write operation is shown in **Function** WRITE. The non-determinism of each programming iteration can be modeled as a normal distribution $N(\mu, \sigma^2)$ [54]. Positive constant β reflects the disturbance of a single programming step. T is an important parameter for the P&V process, and represents the width of target analog range. Both T and β determine the average number of programming iterations to finish a cell write.

Function WRITE(v_d) (adopted from [54])

Input: v_d - the analog value to be programmed
Output: v - the actual analog value after P&V

begin
    $v \leftarrow 0$; $\#P \leftarrow 0$;
    /* This while loop represents P&V process. The number of iterations $\#P$ is inversely proportional to cell write performance. */
    while v *has not reached* $[v_d - T, V_d + T]$ **do**
        $v \leftarrow v + N(v_d - v, |\beta(v_d - v)|)$;
        $++\#P$;
    end
    return v ;
end

2.1.2 MLC Read

Reading from MLC involves retrieving an analog value and quantizing it. The latency of a quantization is linear in the number of bits, as suggested by Qureshi et al. [46]. In practice, cells suffer from variation and unidirectional shift. The read model of Sampson et al. [54] is given as below.

$$READ(v) = v + N(\mu, \sigma^2) \cdot log_{10} t_w$$

where $N(\mu, \sigma^2)$ represents the variation modeled as a normal distribution [67], and t_w is the time elapsed after the cell write operation. $log_{10} t_w$ is the multiplier on account to drift. The drift is modeled as the logarithm of time elapsed since the cell was written.

2.2 Approximate MLC

An approximate MLC configuration reduces the guard band to provide better write performance and energy efficiency. The basic idea is to reduce the number of P&V iterations by increasing the parameter T; intuitively, larger target range leads to less latency. Figure 1(b) shows the differences of an approximate MLC from the precise one.

To study the average number of P&V iterations ($\#P$) of MLC with different precisions, we take 4-level MLC as an example and vary T from 0.025 (almost precise) to 0.125 (no guard band), and for each value of T, we conduct a Monte-Carlo simulation: writing a random value to a 4-level MLC cell/a random 32-bit number to sixteen concatenated 2-bit cells, for 100,000,000 times respectively. Fig. 2 shows the write performance and error rate of 4-level MLC cell.

Overall, the approximate cell model used in this paper can be simply considered as a probabilistic error model with parameter T. Varying T implies different trade-offs between error rate and write performance. When T is small ($T \leq 0.025$), the memory is precise because of the large guard band. With the increase of T, the guard band shrinks and errors occur with higher probability, which results in a smaller $\#P$ and hence better write performance. Take $T = 0.1$ as an example. The average number of iterations in a P&V process ($\#P$) is halved in comparison with

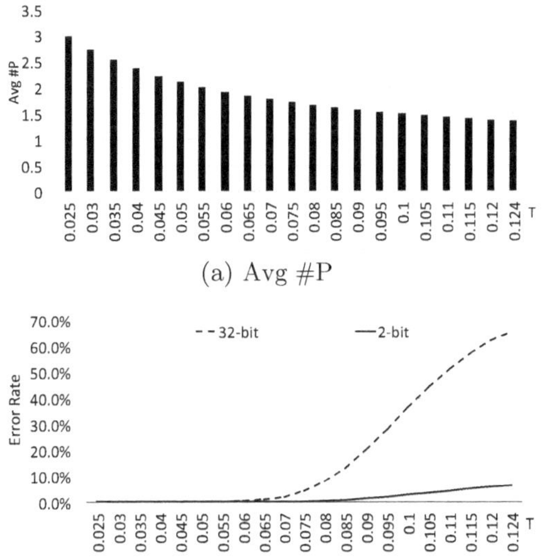

(a) Avg #P

(b) Error Rate

Figure 2: The impact of T on write performance and accuracy for 2-bit MLC cell (from Monte-Carlo simulation).

$T = 0.025$, showing around 50% reduction in cell write latency.

For the analysis in Section 4.3, we define

$$p(t) = \frac{avg.\ \#P\ when\ T = t}{avg.\ \#P\ when\ T = 0.025} \approx \frac{avg\ \#P\ when\ T = t}{3}$$

as the ratio of the numbers of P&V iterations required on approximate memory that on precise memory. The lower $p(t)$ is, the more the write latency is reduced, and the higher the degree of imprecision in the approximate memory is.

2.3 Interfaces for Approximate Memory

The approximate MLC used in this paper can be produced by the same manufacturing process as precise MLC, except for a different analog range width, which piles little pressure on memory chip manufacturers. Hence, an approximate memory module can be integrated with other precise modules on the same memory channel.

The programming interfaces and assembly language support used in this paper are similar to previous literature [54]. Specifically, method *approx_alloc(size)* allocates an array on approximate memory and returns a pointer. All memory access statements to an approximate array are compiled to *ld.approx* and *st.approx*. The OS kernel is modified to allow *approx_alloc* to allocate space only on approximate DIMMs, and to translate *ld/st.approx* back to normal *ld/st* with approximate array addresses.

We study sorting algorithms on a hybrid memory system with both precise and approximate memory support. Figure 3 shows how the approximate memory is integrated into the system. The juxtaposition of precise memory and approximate memory lies upon the storage system; OS kernel and assembly language are enhanced to support memory page allocation and translation of hybrid memory system. CPU and cache architecture in the case of hybrid memory system is the same as original system.

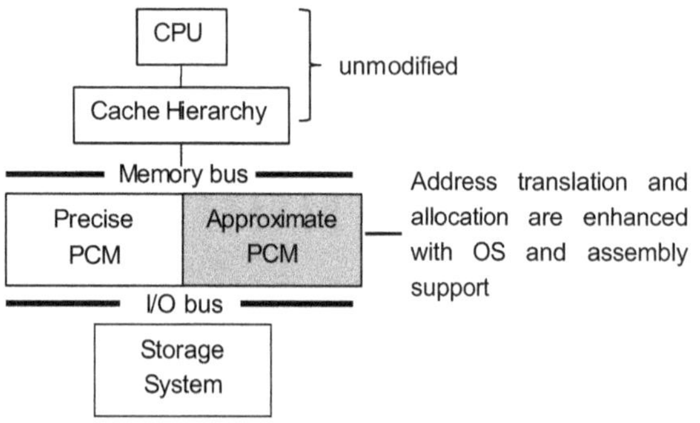

Figure 3: Memory System with Approximate Memory

L1 cache	32KB, LRU, write through
L2 cache	2MB, 4-way, LRU, write through
L3 cache	32MB, 8-way, LRU, 10ns access latency, write through
Main Memory	8GB PCM, 4KB page, 4 ranks of 8-bank each, 32 entries write queue/bank, 8 entries read queue/bank, read priority scheduling
Precise PCM Latency	T=0.025 data read: 50ns, data write: $1\mu s$

Table 1: Memory simulator parameters

Category	Parameter	Note
Level	$L = 4$	each cell stores 2 bits
Read model	$\mu = 0.067$ $\sigma = 0.027$	read fluctuation
	$t = 10^5 s$	elapsed time for *drift*
Write model	$\beta = 0.035$	write fluctuation
	$T = 0.025$	precise case: #P=2.98
	$T \in (0.025 \ldots 0.125)$	approximate cases

Table 2: Parameters for precise and approximate MLC. We reuse the parameter of Sampson et al. [54].

3. SORTING IN APPROXIMATE MEMORY

We start with a study of common sorting algorithms on approximate memory. The entire main memory used in this section's experiments is approximate memory; the imprecision of approximate memory causes unsortedness in the output of sorting executions. In this section, we focus on two issues: 1) how the approximate memory would impair different sorting algorithms, and 2) the trade-off between sortedness and write performance.

3.1 Sorting Algorithms

The following three classic sorting algorithms are studied: *mergesort*, *quicksort* and *radixsort*. Our implementation has inherited various implementation techniques from the previous studies (e.g., [6, 4]). To reduce writes, some of the write-optimized techniques including write combining by software managed buffers [4] are adopted whenever appropriate. More details are given below. The input data are assumed to be an array X of n elements (or *records*).

Mergesort Mergesort is a comparison-based divide-and-conquer sorting algorithm, and is commonly used in databases. A mergesort execution on array X requires $nlog_2n$ data write operations. At the first level of mergesort, the input chunk size is designed to fit into the L2 cache.

Quicksort Quicksort is also a commonly used comparison-based sorting algorithm. On average, it takes $nlog_2n$ data comparisons and $\frac{nlog_2n}{2}$ data writes to sort n items. The average time complexity of quicksort is $O(nlog_2n)$, but its worst case is $O(n^2)$. We implement a randomized quicksort algorithm. The pivot is chosen randomly to reduce the probability of worst cases.

Radix sort Radixsort is a non-comparative sorting algorithm which sorts elements by grouping those who share the same value in some significant position. Two variants are studied here: *Least Significant Digit Radix Sort* (LSD) and *Most Significant Digit Radix Sort* (MSD). LSD starts from the least significant digit and moves towards the most significant digit, while MSD works the other way around. We implement a simple version of LSD and MSD using queues as buckets. We have adopted and tuned multi-pass partitioning in radixsort like the previous study [4]. The number of bins in each pass for LSD and MSD is an important tuning parameter, and we evaluate 3-bit, 4-bit, 5-bit and 6-bit for the study, i.e., with 8, 16, 32 and 64 buckets, respectively. Unless stated otherwise, LSD and MSD represent 6-bit LSD and 6-bit MSD, respectively, since they usually achieve the best total write latency among different numbers of bins.

3.2 Methodology

As no approximate memory product is available in market and no simulator with PCM support is open-source, we ran experiments using an in-house memory simulator which models PCM reads and writes in detail. Because of large data sets, the simulator is trace-driven, where traces are obtained from the actual execution on a real machine. The machine is configured with Intel Xeon Processor E5-1650 and 8GB DDR3 SDRAM. For simplicity, only one core is used while collecting memory traces.

Table 1 gives the detailed parameters of our memory simulator. The settings of those parameters are consistent with previous literatures [30, 12]. For simplicity, we assume a write-through cache, which ensures that every data write must go to the main memory. As write performance is a dominated factor for sorting algorithms on PCM, we mainly look at the total latencies spent on memory writes. Table 2 gives the detailed parameters of our MLC PCM modeling which are inherited from [54]. We use 4-level (2-bit) PCM cell for our simulation, as 2-bit MLC is the most popular choice in NAND Flash reported by Micron Inc. [37]. As suggested in previous studies [8, 38, 54], the raw bit error rate (RBER) of precise MLC is typically 10^{-8}.

A 32-bit integer is stored in sixteen concatenated 2-bit cells [54]. Input data contain an array of keys and an array of payload in the form of integers (i.e., record IDs). The key values are uniformly distributed 32-bit integers. The payload (record IDs) is essential in database workloads to complete the entire query processing according to the sorted results [49]. In the next section, the record IDs are stored in the precise memory, and are used to refine and "recover" the totally sorted data.

3.3 Measure of Sortedness

Suppose an array of n elements, X, is to be sorted in increasing order. During the execution in the approximate memory, the elements of X may become imprecise, and thus the final X may not be fully sorted. To describe the sortedness of a sequence X after sorting in the approximate memory, we choose the measure *Rem* [9], which is defined as

$$Rem(X) = n - max\{k | X \textit{ has an ascending subseq. of length } k\}.$$

Intuitively, *Rem* indicates the number of elements that should be removed to produce a sorted sequence. *Rem* ratio (i.e., $\frac{Rem(X)}{n}$) should be small if the array X is nearly sorted.

There are other measures of sortedness, as surveyed in the previous study [20]. Still, we choose the definition of *Rem*, because it is more intuitive than other measures like *Inv* (the number of inversion pairs in a sequence [20]). It motivates us to design a lightweight refine algorithm introduced in Section 4.2. More details on how to leverage the sortedness are given in Section 4.

3.4 Experimental Results

To study the correlation between the proportion of imprecise elements and the sortedness (i.e. *Rem* ratio), we vary the size of guard band by tuning T to sort 16,000,000 (16M) random integers in the approximate memory. Since our target is to study the imprecision rather than to recover the sorted data, the payload array is not accessed in the study of this section. We define *write reduction* as the percentage of total memory write latency saved from using approximate memory compared with using precise memory only. More formally, total memory write latency is abbreviated to *TMWL*, then

$$Write\ Reduction = 1 - \frac{TMWL \textit{ using approximate memory}}{TMWL \textit{ using precise memory}} \quad (1)$$

When $T = 0.025$, the guard band is large and the memory can be considered precise [54]. As mentioned in Section 2.1.1, T should be less than $\frac{1}{8}$ to provide guard bands, i.e., $T < 0.125$. We vary T from 0.025 to 0.1. The cases where $T > 0.1$ are omitted because the imprecision behavior dominates the execution. Results are shown in Figure 4. The error rate denotes the proportion of elements in X whose values deviate from their original values after sorting in the approximate memory. For all the sorting algorithms, both error rate and *Rem* ratio grow rapidly when $T > 0.06$.

However, as shown in Figure 2(a), the average number of P&V iterations drops slowly when $T > 0.06$. Also, write reduction is increasing slower with larger T as shown in Figure 4(c). As a result, T should not be tuned to be arbitrarily large. These results of error and acceleration are consistent with those in the previous study [54].

To give more intuition, we take $n = 160,000$ as an example and visualize the shape of X after sorting. The results for larger input sizes (e.g., 16 million) are similar. The initial X contains 160,000 random integers, which are uniformly distributed between 0 and $2^{32} - 1$. The goal is to sort the 160,000 integers in increasing order. We show how X looks like after the sorting execution in the approximate memory with different precisions in Figures 5, 6, and 7, when $T =$ 0.03, 0.055, and 0.01, respectively. The X-axis of each figure represents n indexes, which ranges from 1 to n. The Y-axis is the value of each index after sorting in the approximate memory. A strictly increasing line represents a fully sorted sequence.

T	Quicksort	LSD	MSD	Mergesort
0.03	0.0019%	0.0009%	0.0007%	0.0025%
0.055	1.92%	1.02%	1.00%	55.80%
0.1	96.89%	95.68%	83.82%	99.95%

Table 3: *Rem* ratio of X after quicksort, LSD, MSD and mergesort in the approximate memory

Table 3 gives the detailed *Rem* ratio of X after quicksort, LSD, MSD and mergesort in the approximate memory. When T is small, errors hardly occur and X is almost sorted as shown in Figure 5. As T increases, more errors occur. When $T = 0.055$ in Figure 6, write latency is reduced by 33% (shown in Figure 2(a)) while X is still nearly sorted after quicksort and radixsort with the *Rem* ratio lower than 2%. The remaining elements are just like noises, and the amount is relatively small. However, if T keeps increasing, errors can burst almost exponentially (as observed in Figure 4(a)). When $T = 0.1$ in Figure 7, though write latency is reduced by 50%, X is still in chaos after sorting in the approximate memory, with the high *Rem* ratio over 90% for most sorting algorithms.

3.5 Discussions on Different Algorithms

Our study clearly shows that sorting algorithms have very different behaviors on approximate memory. As shown in Figure 4(b), Figure 6(d) and Figure 7(d), mergesort exposes different behavior from quicksort and radixsort, rendering itself vulnerable to imprecision. The execution of mergesort starts with divide-and-conquer, and the number of elements involved in a merge execution increases in later merge runs, so does the number of imprecise elements. Erroneous behaviors caught in the merge execution exacerbate in the last run, which involves the most imprecise elements, resulting in a sequence not being able to be labeled as "nearly sorted". LSD also has similar behaviors with mergesort, but not all errors in LSD matter. Unlike mergesort, errors in lower bits does not cause disorders in later runs because it only looks at specific bits in each pass. Therefore, LSD is much more tolerant to imprecision than mergesort.

In contrast, quicksort and MSD have rather smooth tradeoff between imprecision and performance. In each run of quicksort, if the picked pivot divides the sequence nearly equally, the first half should be strictly smaller than the second half. This fact makes fewer elements involved in later dividing processes, by which the detrimental effect of an imprecise element is minimized. The same reason applies to MSD.

4. SORTING UNDER APPROX-REFINE

Approximate storage is designed for those applications that do not require accurate results or are tolerant of imprecision. However, in many scenarios of sorting, especially in database applications, the results are required to be precise. Therefore, unlike existing work in the area of approximate computing [15, 41, 42, 52, 54, 60], this paper intends to take advantage of approximate storage while producing pre-

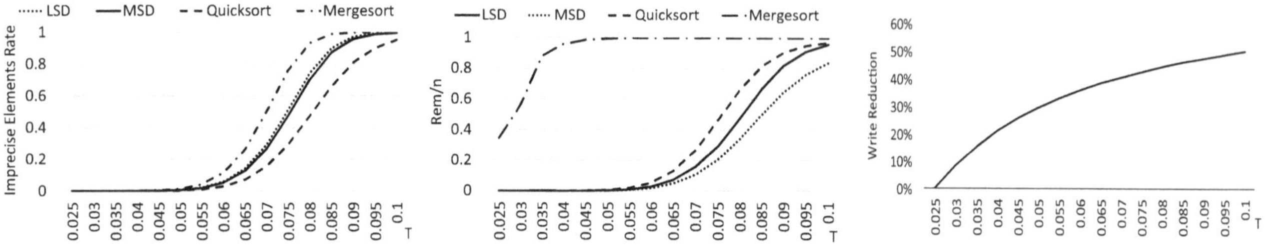

(a) Error rate (b) *Rem* ratio (c) Write reduction

Figure 4: Sorting 16M random integers in the approximate memory.

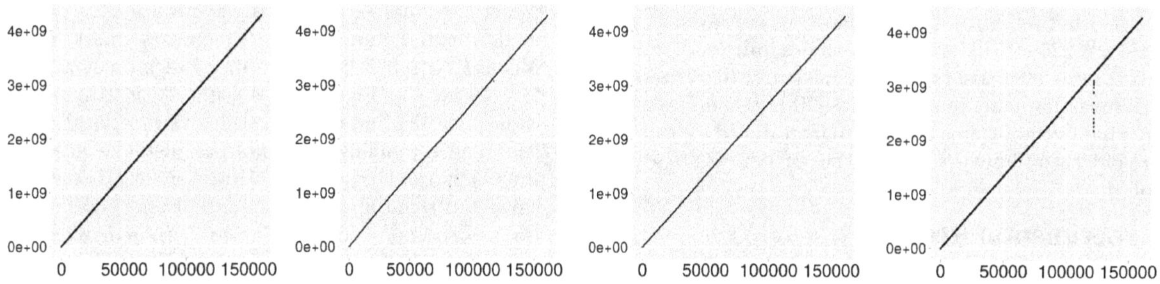

(a) Quicksort (b) LSD (c) MSD (d) Mergesort

Figure 5: Sequence X after sorting in the approximate memory when $T = 0.03$.

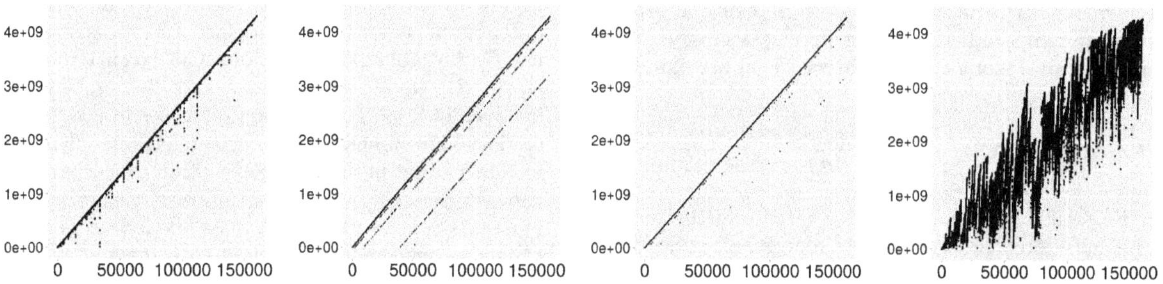

(a) Quicksort (b) LSD (c) MSD (d) Mergesort

Figure 6: Sequence X after sorting in the approximate memory when $T = 0.055$.

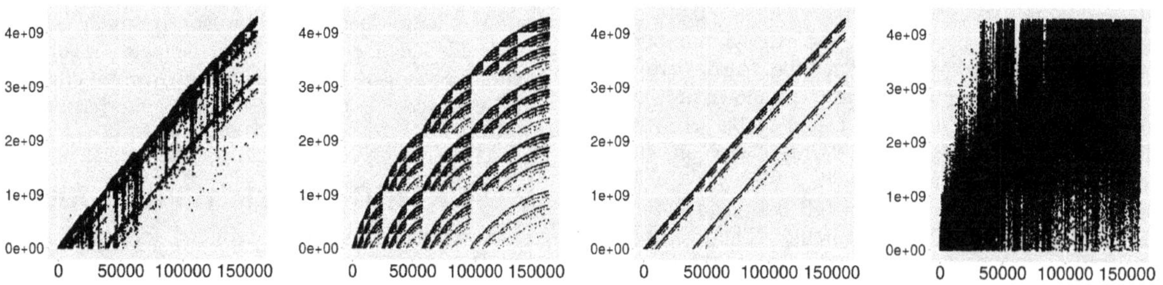

(a) Quicksort (b) LSD (c) MSD (d) Mergesort

Figure 7: Sequence X after sorting in the approximate memory when $T = 0.1$.

cise results. We propose a mechanism called *approx-refine* to refine the approximate outputs to precise results. The *approx-refine* mechanism makes use of both approximate memory and precise memory. Particularly, the previous section clearly shows the performance benefits of sorting algorithms on approximate memory, which can generate nearly sorted output in the approximate memory. We propose a lightweight refinement stage to transform the nearly sorted output to a totally sorted output. Also, the total cost of sorting on the approximate memory and the overhead caused by refinement should be smaller than that of sorting on the precise memory only. By dividing the sorting algorithm into multiple stages, we offload the main sorting algorithm to approximate memory, which is also similar to the concept of accelerator. In fact, a number of previous studies have similar designs [25, 28].

During the design and implementation, we take two special considerations into account. First, the *approx-refine* mechanism should be applicable to an arbitrary sorting algorithm on the precise memory. To the end of our design, an arbitrary sorting algorithm (e.g., three common sorting algorithms in our study) can be used as a component in our approx-refine mechanism. Second, the refinement should be lightweight and adaptive to the degree of unsortedness. Intuitively, the higher the sortedness of the output from the sorting on approximate memory, the smaller overhead the refinement stage should incur. In our design, the refinement scheme of *approx-refine* is adaptive to *Rem* (defined in Section 3).

4.1 Overview

As precise sorting is often required in applications for data management purposes where each tuple has a key along with a record ID. We assume that the input data to be sorted contains n <Key, ID> pairs, which are stored in two arrays $Key0$ and ID. The final precise output should contain a fully sorted sequence of n <Key, ID> pairs in increasing order of key values. All the inputs and outputs are stored in the precise memory. Approximate memory is only used during the sorting process.

The *approx-refine* process contains five stages, including *warm-up, approx preparation, approx stage, refine preparation,* and *refine stage*. We introduce the five stages as follows. A running example is given in Figure 8.

Warm-up Both $Key0$ and ID are in the precise memory initially. This study assumes that the input data is in the main memory. If the data is initially in the hard disk, we need to adopt more advanced external memory sorting algorithms [49], for which the proposed *approx-refine* scheme can be used in their in-memory sorting steps.

Approx Preparation Array $Key0$ is copied from precise memory to approximate memory (denoted as $\widetilde{Key}$). During this process, some of the keys may become imprecise (e.g. the sixth element changes from 35 to 32 in Figure 8). That means, $\widetilde{Key}$ is an imprecise version of $Key0$, and the degree of imprecision depends on the approximate memory configuration. Array ID remains in the precise memory.

Approx Stage We perform a sorting algorithm on $\widetilde{Key}$ together with the corresponding array ID. We study the three sorting algorithms described in Section 3.1: mergesort, quicksort and radix sort. The sorting algorithm we deploy in this stage is almost the same as the one in the

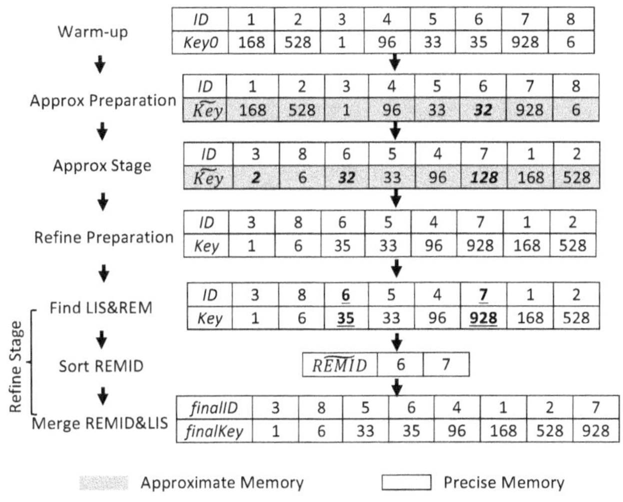

Figure 8: Overview of approx-refine for sorting. Imprecise elements are marked in bold and italic. Disorders after the approx stage are marked in bold and underlined.

precise memory, except for memory operations. During the sorting process, all reads and writes of keys are performed in the approximate memory, and operations on ID are in the precise memory. More keys become imprecise with more writes performed during the process. As a result, disorders are generated due to the occasional imprecision. For example, in Figure 8, $Key0_5 < Key0_6$ but $\widetilde{Key}_5 > \widetilde{Key}_6$ in the approximate memory, which results in the disorder of their corresponding IDs (ID_5 and ID_6).

Refine Preparation After the *approx* stage, we are only able to obtain a nearly sorted sequence of keys $\{Key_i\} = \{Key0_{ID_i}\}$. For example, ID_3 and ID_4 form an inversion pair because $Key_3 > Key_4$. In fact, to save more memory writes, we do not generate array Key in the *refine preparation* stage. We always make use of array $Key0$ and $\{Key_i\} = \{Key0_{ID_i}\}$ to get Key with memory reads. The notation of Key is only defined for convenience.

Refine Stage The goal of this stage is to adjust Key and ID to achieve fully sorted results in the precise memory. The increasing array of key values is denoted as $finalKey$, and the corresponding array of record IDs is denoted as $finalID$. We give the detailed design of the *refine stage* in Section 4.2. This is essentially an off-loading computing model, where the majority of the sorting algorithm is off-loaded to be performed on approximate memory in **Approx Stage**.

4.2 Refine Stage

The sequence Key is almost sorted after the *approx stage*. Our goal in the *refine stage* is to design a lightweight algorithm to refine the results with partial disorders and produce strictly sorted sequences. The algorithm should be efficient enough with as few memory write operations as possible, as writes are the dominated cost on NVRAM.

An intuitive solution is to use some adaptive sorting algorithms that benefit from the presortedness in the input sequence. Many existing adaptive sorting algorithms [20] benefiting from presortedness target at the asymptotic time complexity but not the number of memory writes. Thus, they typically introduce $3n$ or even more memory writes (n is the number of input records). In contrast, our refine algorithm, with a lightweight and efficient heuristics, introduces fewer than $3n$ memory writes and has a low time complexity as well. Note that, intuitively, the lower bound of the number of memory writes should be $2n$, n for keys and another n for record IDs. The refine algorithm introduced below has fewer than $3n$ memory write operations, which is very close to the lower bound.

The *refine stage* is further decomposed into 3 steps.

Step 1. Find an ascending subsequence of the maximum length (also known as *Longest Increasing Subsequence (LIS)* [55]) in array Key. This step is motivated by Figure 6 and the measure of sortedness *Rem* introduced in Section 3.3. LIS is already sorted, while the remaining elements in Key are not.

Step 2. Sort the remaining elements in Key in increasing order. Together with LIS, we would get two sorted subsequences afterwards.

Step 3. Merge the two sorted subsequences to get the final sorted sequence.

We now present the implementation details of each step.

Step 1: Find LIS&REM. For simplicity, we denote LIS as the *Longest Increasing Subsequence* in Key, and REM as the remaining elements in Key (the size of REM is *Rem*). $LISID$ and $REMID$ are the corresponding record IDs of LIS and REM. To find LIS and REM, classical algorithms [55] have time complexity of at least $O(nlogn)$ and introduce at least $2n$ intermediate outputs to record states for the optimal solution (costly memory writes). To reduce the overhead of refinement to the maximum extent, we develop some heuristics to get an approximate LIS (denoted as $\widetilde{LIS}$) with time complexity of $O(n)$ and almost no intermediate memory writes. The corresponding approximate $LISID$, *Rem*, REM and $REMID$ under the heuristics are denoted as $\widetilde{LISID}$, $\widetilde{Rem}$, $\widetilde{REM}$ and $\widetilde{REMID}$. The heuristics make best use of the near-sortedness of Key after the *approx stage* and are relatively easy to implement.

```
/*
Input:
  Array ID: all the record IDs after the
       approx stage
  Array Key0: all the original key values
       in the precise memory
Output:
  Array REMID to record pairs that are not
       in LIS
*/
std::vector<keyType> REMID;
LIStail=Key0[ID[1]]; //assume the first key
     is in LIS(X)
for (i=2; i<n; ++i) {
  if (Key0[ID[i]]>=LIStail && Key0[ID[i]]<=
       Key0[ID[i+1]]) {
  //Key[i]/Key0[ID[i]] is in approximate
       LIS as it forms a non-decreasing
       order with its two neighbors,
    LIStail=Key0[ID[i]];
  }
  else {
    REMID.push_back(ID[i]);
  }
}
if (LIStail>Key0[ID[n]]) {
  REMID.push_back(ID[n]);
}
```

Listing 1: Find LIS&REM

Listing 1 shows the pseudo code of the first step in the *refine stage*. It finds <Key, ID> pairs whose key values are not in $\widetilde{LIS}$, e.g., bold and underlined pairs in Figure 8. The heuristics to get $\widetilde{LIS}$ scan ID only once and append a record ID to $\widetilde{REMID}$ if the corresponding key value does not form an ascending order with its left and right keys. In Figure 8, the third key value 35 and the sixth key value 928 are greater than their right key values, therefore, the third and the sixth record IDs are in $\widetilde{REMID}$.

In total, it only introduces *Rem* intermediate data write operations in this step. Note that we only record $\widetilde{REMID}$ here to save more intermediate memory writes during the *refine stage*. Also, recording $\widetilde{REMID}$ is sufficient to get all information that we need, including $\widetilde{REM}$, $\widetilde{LIS}$, $\widetilde{LISID}$. $\widetilde{REM}$ can be easily obtained by $\{\widetilde{REM_i}\} = \{Key0_{\widetilde{REMID}_i}\}$ though it introduces an additional data read. However, as a PCM write is very much slower than a PCM read, it deserves replacing a PCM write with a PCM read. $\widetilde{LISID}$ consists of all elements in ID except for those in $\widetilde{REMID}$. $\widetilde{LIS}$ can then be obtained by $\{\widetilde{LIS_i}\} = \{Key0_{\widetilde{LISID}_i}\}$

Step 2: Sort $\widetilde{REMID}$. Since Key is almost sorted, REM is small ($|REM| << n$) and thus we do not need to further extract any sorted subsequence from REM. In this step, we directly sort $\widetilde{REMID}$ in increasing order of their key values. Since $|REM| << n$, we can choose any reasonable algorithm to sort $\widetilde{REMID}$, because it does not make any significant difference. For simplicity, we just use the sorting algorithm in the *approx stage* to sort $\widetilde{REMID}$. For example, if we apply quicksort in the *approx stage* to sort n <Key, ID> pairs, we still use quicksort to sort $\widetilde{REMID}$ with $\widetilde{Rem}$ items. If Key is nearly sorted as expected and our heuristics work well, *Rem* should be very small and $\widetilde{Rem} \approx Rem$. Thus, the intermediate memory writes during sorting is negligible comparing to the total write latency in the *approx stage*. However, if Key is not nearly sorted, significant overhead will be introduced to sort $\widetilde{REMID}$, and the approximate memory will not act as an accelerator.

```
/*
Input:
  Array Key0: all the original keys in the
       precise memory
  Array ID: all the record IDs after the
       approx stage
  Array REMID after being sorted
Output:
  Array finalKey & finalID: n <Key, ID>
       pairs in increasing order of key
       values
*/

std::set<int> REMIDset;
//REMIDset is used to identify LISID later
for (i=0; i<REMID.size(); ++i) {
  REMIDset.insert(REMID[i]);
}

```

```
LISptr=1;
REMptr=0;
finalptr=1;
while (LISptr<=n) {
//find the next element in LISID
  while (LISptr<=n && REMIDset.count(ID[
      LISptr])>0) ++LISptr;
  if (LISptr>n) break;
//merge two sorted subsequences
  if (REMptr<REMID.size() && Key0[REMID[
      REMptr]]<Key0[ID[LISptr]]) {
    finalID[finalptr]=REMID[REMptr];
    finalKey[finalptr++]=Key0[REMID[REMptr
        ++]];
  }
  else {
    finalID[finalptr]=ID[LISptr++];
    finalKey[finalptr]=Key0[finalID[
        finalptr]];
    finalptr++;
  }
}
while (REMptr<REMID.size()) {
  finalID[finalptr]=REMID[REMptr];
  finalKey[finalptr++]=Key0[REMID[REMptr
      ++]];
}
```

Listing 2: Merge

Step 3: Merge $\widetilde{REMID}$&$\widetilde{LISID}$. Listing 2 gives the pseudo code of the final merge step in the *refine stage*. As we only have $\widetilde{REMID}$, we need to rescan array ID and find elements in $\widetilde{LISID}$. This strategy introduces more data reads but reduces data write operations. This write-limiting ideology also appears in previous study [63]. The merge step introduces $2n + \widetilde{Rem}$ data writes, among which $2n$ (n for array $finalID$ and n for array $finalKey$) are unavoidable.

4.3 Cost Analysis

Though approximate memory trades off precision for performance, the overhead of the *refine stage* offsets some of the benefits. We make a mathematical analysis to quantify the benefit that approximate memory brings under the *approx-refine* mechanism. Because memory write operations dominate the total execution time of a sorting algorithm on NVRAM [12], we analyze the total memory write latency under the *approx-refine* mechanism. We compare the results with sorting entirely in the precise memory to show the role of approximate memory.

Formally, let

$$\alpha_{alg}(n) = \#memory\ writes\ of\ keys\ using\ alg\ to\ sort\ n\ elements$$

For instance, suppose sorting is performed entirely in main memory, $\alpha_{quicksort}(n) \approx \frac{nlog_2 n}{2}$, $\alpha_{mergesort}(n) \approx nlog_2 n$. Obviously, $\alpha_{alg}(n)$ is a monotone increasing function of n.

Unlike the *write reduction* defined by Equation 1 in Section 3.4, in the case of the *approx-refine* mechanism, *write reduction* is defined as

$$Write\ Reduction = 1 - \frac{TMWL\ under\ approx\&refine}{TMWL\ using\ precise\ memory} \quad (2)$$

For simplicity, we assume that the memory write latency is a constant. Therefore, memory write latency is proportional to the number of memory write operations. Therefore, if total equivalent number of precise memory writes is abbreviated to $TEPMW$, then we define the following function to represent the write latency reduction of our proposed approx-refine scheme in comparison with the one running in the precise memory only.

$$WR_{alg}(n,t) = 1 - \frac{TEPMW\ under\ approx\&refine}{TEPMW\ under\ traditional\ sorting} \quad (3)$$

where one approximate memory operation is equivalent to $p(t)$ (defined in Section 2.2) precise memory operation, and traditional sorting is performed using precise memory only.

The total number of writes for traditional sorting in the precise memory is $2\alpha_{alg}(n)$: $\alpha_{alg}(n)$ times for key values and $\alpha_{alg}(n)$ times for record IDs.

As for the *approx-refine* mechanism, we calculate the effective number of precise memory write operations in different stages respectively.

1. In the *approx preparation* stage, n key write operations are needed to copy all the keys from precise memory to approximate memory. The equivalent number of write operations in the precise memory is $p(t)n$.
2. In the *approx* stage, $\alpha_{alg}(n)$ data write operations of keys in the approximate memory and $\alpha_{alg}(n)$ data write operations of record IDs in the precise memory are needed. In total, the equivalent number of write operations in the precise memory is $(p(t)+1)\alpha_{alg}(n)$.
3. In the *refine* stage, all the write operations are performed in the precise memory. The first step of the *refine* stage needs $\widetilde{Rem}$ data writes to record $\widetilde{REMID}$.
4. In the second step of the *refine* stage, $\alpha_{alg}(\widetilde{Rem})$ data writes are needed to sort $\widetilde{REMID}$.
5. Finally, $\widetilde{Rem} + 2n$ write operations are needed for the final merge.

In total, during the hybrid execution, $(p(t)+1)\alpha_{alg}(n) + 2\widetilde{Rem} + (2+p(t))n + \alpha_{alg}(\widetilde{Rem})$ effective precise memory writes are performed.

Finally,

$$WR_{alg}(n,t) = \frac{1-p(t)}{2} - \frac{\widetilde{Rem} + (1+0.5p(t))n}{\alpha_{alg}(n)} - \frac{\alpha_{alg}(\widetilde{Rem})}{2\alpha_{alg}(n)} \quad (4)$$

Therefore, the effect of our *approx-refine* mechanism is related to the guard band of the approximate memory, the size of dataset, the sorting algorithm, and the effects of our heuristics. To maximize WR, we definitely hope to minimize $p(t)$ and $\widetilde{Rem}$. However, given the sorting algorithm and n, $p(t)$ decreases but $\widetilde{Rem}$ increases with the increase of t. We will show the trade-off between $p(t)$ and $\widetilde{Rem}$ in the experiments of Section 5. With obtaining WR in the cost analysis, we can decide whether the approx-refine approach on the hybrid memory is better than the sorting algorithm on precise memory only, and switch between the two approaches accordingly.

5. EVALUATION OF APPROX-REFINE

In this section, we evaluate the *approx-refine* mechanism in hybrid approximate/precise memory, and compare the results with traditional sorting in the precise memory only.

We use the same methodology as the simulation studies in Section 3.2.

We focus on the impact of using approximate memory in sorting algorithms. We evaluate *write reduction* (defined by Equation 2 in Section 4.3) that quantifies the benefit of hybrid execution. As analyzed in Section 4.3, write reduction is determined by the algorithm, the input size and the precision of approximate memory. Therefore, we evaluate the influence of T and n under quicksort, mergesort, and radix sort (LSD, MSD).

Impact of T We vary T from 0.025 to 0.1 at intervals of 0.005, and show the write reduction of all sorting algorithms with 16M (16,000,000) records in Figure 9. We have the following observations:

1. Except for mergesort, all the algorithms achieve the maximum write reduction when $T = 0.055$. Radix sort can achieve a maximal write reduction of about 10%, while quicksort achieves write reduction up to 4%. Mergesort does not show any gain using approximate memory, and we have discussed the underlying reasons in Section 3.5.

2. When $T \leq 0.03$, write reduction may be negative because as shown in Equation 4, $p(t) \approx 1$, therefore $\frac{1-p(t)}{2} \approx 0$. Since the remaining two items are always positive, it is highly possible that write reduction is negative.

3. When $T \geq 0.07$, write reduction may also become negative because the overhead of refinement is significant. Since $p(t) \approx 0$ and $\widetilde{Rem} \approx n$, we have $\frac{1-p(t)}{2} - \frac{\alpha(\widetilde{Rem})}{2\alpha(n)} \approx 0$. As the second item is always positive, the final write reduction is negative.

4. Both LSD and MSD have slightly decreasing write reduction with more bins mainly because the total write latency decreases and the fixed overhead of copying keys in *approx preparation* takes a larger fraction in the total write latency.

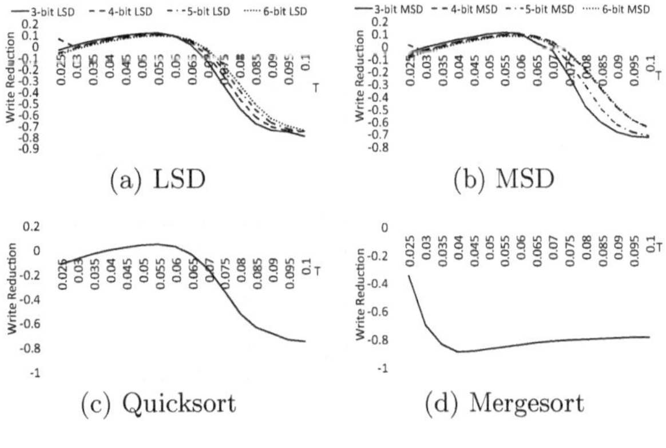

(a) LSD (b) MSD

(c) Quicksort (d) Mergesort

Figure 9: Relationship between write reduction and T.

Impact of n In this experiment, we set $T = 0.055$ because it produces the largest write reduction for most sorting algorithms. We change the size of input elements n from 1.6K (16000) to 16M (16,000,000). 3-bit LSD, 3-bit MSD and quicksort achieve the maximal write reduction of $11\%, 10.3\%$ and 4% respectively. From Figure 10, we see larger write reduction with large n except for LSD, which partially demonstrates the scalability of the *approx-refine* mechanism for most sorting algorithms. Equation 4 in Section 4.3 has indicated the scalability.

1. Since $\alpha_{quicksort}(n) \approx \frac{nlog_2 n}{2}$ and $\widetilde{Rem}$ is $O(n)$ (observed from experiments), given t, $WR_{quicksort}(n,t)$ is a monotone increasing function with respect to n. Thus, the performance gain of approx-refine increases for larger inputs in quicksort.

2. Since $\frac{\alpha_{MSD}(n)}{n}$ is a constant and $\widetilde{Rem}$ is also $O(n)$, given t, $WR_{MSD}(n,t)$ is a monotone increasing function with respect to n. Thus, the performance gain of approx-refine increases for larger inputs in MSD.

3. Like MSD, $\frac{\alpha_{LSD}(n)}{n}$ is also a constant. However, $\widetilde{Rem}$ is not $O(n)$ under LSD, which introduces more overhead in the *refine* stage. It shows some similar behavior of mergesort as discussed in Section 3.5. Therefore, given t, $WR_{LSD}(n,t)$ is not a monotone increasing function with respect to n.

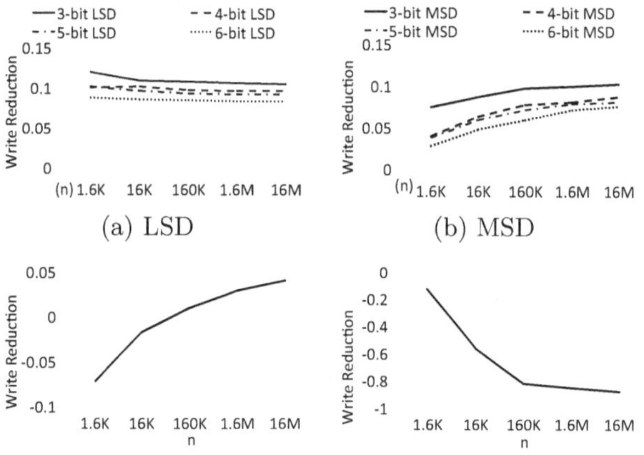

(a) LSD (b) MSD

(c) Quicksort (d) Mergesort

Figure 10: Relationship between write reduction and n.

We set $T = 0.055$ and $n = 16M$, and show the *normalized* total write latency under the approx-refine mechanism for each algorithm in Figure 11 (normalized to the write latency of 3-bit-LSD in the *approx* stage). Write latencies are further decomposed into *approx* and *refine*. Both LSD and MSD have smaller total write latencies with more bins (6-bit achieves the best performance). 6-bit MSD radixsort and Quicksort are the most efficient sorting algorithms with the least memory write latencies. The overhead of *refine* is negligible except for merge sort.

Summary. We have the following key findings. First, approximate memory is beneficial for sorting algorithms that require precise output, with up to 11% of write reduction in our experiments. The improvement is achieved through the proposed approx-refine scheme, i.e., taking advantage of approximate memory as well as a carefully designed and lightweight refinement stage. Second, sorting algorithms can

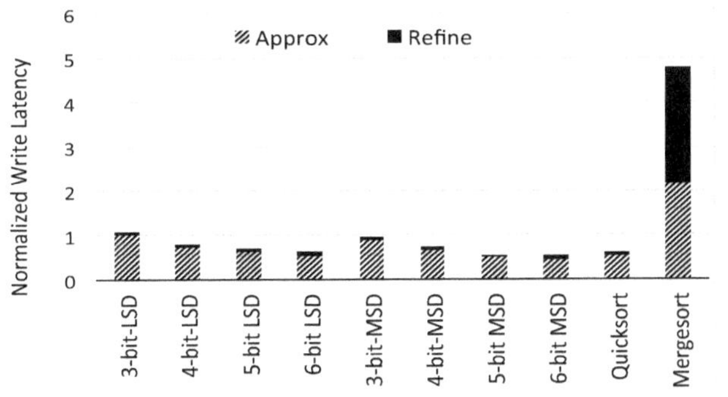

Figure 11: Breakdown of write latencies in *approx* and *refine* stages.

have very different performance behaviours. Radix sort and quick sort generally acquire reasonable performance gain whereas using approximate hardware has negative impact on merge sort.

The performance study can be extended in a couple of ways. First, we have tested the impact of some of the more advanced techniques including multithreading, memory prefetching and non-temporal streaming instructions in our implementations. We observed insignificant impacts of these factors. Second, we have extended and evaluated our approx-refine proposal in another approximate memory model [51] for energy saving. The preliminary results demonstrate the energy saving by 13.4%. More details can be found in Appendix A. Third, since approx-refine has the flexibility of allowing us to explore other sorting implementations, we have evaluated an open-source implementation of radixsort [45] which has used SIMD instructions extensively and histogram-based implementation. The preliminary results demonstrate the write latency reduction of around 10%. More details can be found in Appendix B. Finally, we are further extending a more complete memory model for approximate memory. Currently, we assume that the performance of random writes is the same as that of sequential writes. A more detailed model of PCM should capture the performance difference between random and sequential writes. In the *approx* stage, most write operations of the studied algorithms are random writes on PCM. However, in the *refine* stage, most writes are instead sequential writes. With a more detailed model of PCM, the approx-refine scheme should receive a higher gain of write reduction.

6. RELATED WORK

We review the related work in the following categories: approximate computing, sorting, and hybrid storage systems.

6.1 Approximate Computing

Approximate computing has attracted a lot of research attention. A large body of previous work has tackled approximate computing from various aspects: from architecture and hardware design, software and programming language support, model and tolerance analysis to approximate processing in databases. We refer the readers to a recent survey on approximate computing [26].

Architecture and Hardware Design. Approximate hardware design has been a hot research topic, due to the limited scaling of hardware. Mohapatra et al. [40] presented an algorithm/architecture co-design of voltage-scalable, process variation aware motion estimator. It leverages a fact in a video system that, not all computations are equally significant. Esmaeilzadeh et al. [18] proposed efficient mapping of disciplined approximate programming onto hardware. Venkataramani et al. [62] proposed a design of approximate circuits, an embodiment of quality programmable processor architecture [60], and a programmable and quality-configurable neuromorphic processing engine to execute approximate neural networks [61]. Sampson et al. [54] proposed approximate storage for non-volatile memory. Rahimi et al. [48], Lucas et al. [36], Song et al. [35] and Ranjan et al. [51] explored the energy efficient approximate storage in the context of different memory architectures (such as associative memristive memory, DRAM, and spintronic memory). We conjecture that our approx-refine scheme can be applicable to those approximate memory designs. This study adopts the approximate memory design from PCM [54]. Also, we focus on how to leverage the approximate memory to improve the performance of sorting algorithms to produce precise results.

Software and Programming Language Support. A number of software and programming systems have been proposed to exploit the tradeoff on precision and performance/energy consumption of approximate hardware. Green [3] is a simple and flexible framework to trade off QoS and energy consumption with controlled approximation. Esmaeilzadeh et al. [19] defined a programming model which helps offload approximable code regions to *neural processing unit* to trade precision for improved performance. Enerj [53] is proposed to isolate the approximate part from precise executions using type qualifiers. ApproxIt [68] is a lightweight quality estimator which dynamically scales the approximation quality over successive iterations. Still, most of those studies focus on applications with intrinsic tolerance to inaccuracy in computation.

Model and tolerance analysis. Models and tools have been developed to analyze the resilience of an application to imprecision. Nair et al.[41, 42] outlined the model and technique of approximate computing. Chippa et al. [15] proposed a framework to characterize the resilience of applications. ASAC [52] automatically generates annotations by sensitivity analysis to allow approximation.

Approximate processing in databases. Approximate query processing in databases [1, 11, 24, 56, 2] and sensor networks [58, 59] mainly leverage pre-computed synopses, sampling engines, or temporal and spatial localities to produce approximate answers within a certain error bar. Those studies do not leverage approximate hardware.

6.2 Sorting

The design and implementation of sorting algorithms are heavily impacted by architectures. They have been revisited in parallel architectures such as GPUs [25] and FPGAs [33], and emerging memories such as PCM [63] and Flash [65]. On PCM, write performance is a key problem for sorting, which involves a lot of memory writes [63]. The refinement stage in this study is write-optimized, which reduces writes with reasonably more reads in the design.

Another category of related work to our refinement stage is adaptive sorting algorithms [9, 39]. Many adaptive algorithms have been developed for nearsortedness [20, 9, 39]. However, they are mostly algorithms with theoretically good asymptotic time complexity. They are far more complicated to implement in practice, and are not optimized with writes. Thus, we use simple and lightweight heuristics to leverage the nearsortedness.

6.3 NVRAM and Hybrid Memory Systems

Previous papers have explored PCM as main memory [29, 34]. Recently, researchers have been revisiting database algorithms to better utilize PCM. Chen et al. [12] calibrated B^+-tree and join algorithms to favor PCM. Viglas et al. [63] proposed a write-limited notion to reduce write operations of sorts and joins. Chi et al. [14] also proposed to reduce write operations of $B+$-tree implementation. Data consistency problems have been addressed for index structures [66, 13]. New on-line transaction processing engines have been redesigned on NVRAM (e.g., [64, 22]). This paper extends the scope of PCM to approximate PCM, and proposes an efficient and general mechanism to provide precise sorting executions. Our approach is orthogonal to those previous studies, because approximate memory improves the performance by reducing programming iterations of each write operation.

Previously proposed hybrid storage often integrates two different memories such as PCM/DRAM [31, 50, 21], on/off-package DRAM [17], and LPDRAM/RLDRAM [10]. Our hybrid mechanism integrates the same material with different precision configuration, only by varying the guard band range. Memory modules needed by our mechanism are exactly the same in terms of material.

7. CONCLUSIONS

Approximate hardware has become an emerging research dimension in computer architecture for performance and energy consumption. Yet, most existing studies on approximate computing concentrate on applications with intrinsic tolerance to inaccuracy in computation. This paper argues that approximate hardware can also be used for improving the performance of applications with precise output requirement. Specifically, we exploit approximate memory to reduce write latencies for sorting algorithms on PCMs. We study how the precision of PCM affects the sortedness of the final output and propose a novel *approx-refine* mechanism to produce precise results. This mechanism first sorts in approximate storage to get nearly sorted sequences, and then reorders the sequence in precise storage with a lightweight recovery heuristics. We have studied three common algorithms including quicksort, merge sort and radix sort. Simulation results show that the total write latency is reduced by up to 11%. Sorting algorithms can have very different performance behaviors on approximate hardware. Radix sort and quick sort generally acquire reasonable performance gain whereas using approximate hardware has negative impact on merge sort. Therefore, we conclude that approximate memory is able to unleash the memory bound of sorting algorithms, and has the potential to be a special accelerator for sorting algorithms. Though system interfaces should be carefully redesigned to support hybrid approximate/precise main memory, the modification in hardware is lightweight and easy to implement.

As for future work, the *approx-refine* scheme has raised an interesting design strategy for leveraging approximate hardware for database systems. This paper makes the first and important step of utilizing approximate hardware for database operations. More research efforts have to be made in the future, e.g., other database operations (such as aggregations) on approximate hardware and reducing the overhead of refinement stage.

8. ACKNOWLEDGMENTS

The work of Shunning Jiang and Shuang Chen was done when they were visiting students at Nanyang Technological University, Singapore. This work is supported by Singapore Ministry of Education Academic Research Fund Tier 2 under Grant MOE2012-T2-2-067, and Academic Research Fund Tier 1 under Grant 2013-T1-002-123.

9. REFERENCES

[1] S. Agarwal, H. Milner, A. Kleiner, A. Talwalkar, M. Jordan, S. Madden, B. Mozafari, and I. Stoica. Knowing when you're wrong: Building fast and reliable approximate query processing systems. In *Proceedings of the 2014 ACM SIGMOD International Conference on Management of Data*, SIGMOD '14, pages 481–492. ACM, 2014.

[2] S. Agarwal, B. Mozafari, A. Panda, H. Milner, S. Madden, and I. Stoica. Blinkdb: queries with bounded errors and bounded response times on very large data. In *Proceedings of the 8th ACM European Conference on Computer Systems*, pages 29–42. ACM, 2013.

[3] W. Baek and T. M. Chilimbi. Green: a framework for supporting energy-conscious programming using controlled approximation. In *ACM Sigplan Notices*, volume 45, pages 198–209. ACM, 2010.

[4] C. Balkesen, G. Alonso, J. Teubner, and M. T. Özsu. Multi-core, main-memory joins: Sort vs. hash revisited. *Proceedings of the VLDB Endowment*, 7(1):85–96, 2013.

[5] F. Bedeschi, R. Fackenthal, C. Resta, E. M. Donze, M. Jagasivamani, E. C. Buda, F. Pellizzer, D. W. Chow, A. Cabrini, G. Calvi, et al. A bipolar-selected phase change memory featuring multi-level cell storage. *Solid-State Circuits, IEEE Journal of*, 44(1):217–227, 2009.

[6] G. S. Brodal, R. Fagerberg, and K. Vinther. Engineering a cache-oblivious sorting algorithm. *J. Exp. Algorithmics*, 12:2.2:1–2.2:23, June 2008.

[7] A. Cabrini, S. Braga, A. Manetto, and G. Torelli. Voltage-driven multilevel programming in phase change memories. In *Memory Technology, Design, and Testing, 2009. MTDT'09. IEEE International Workshop on*, pages 3–6. IEEE, 2009.

[8] Y. Cai, E. F. Haratsch, O. Mutlu, and K. Mai. Error patterns in mlc nand flash memory: Measurement, characterization, and analysis. In *Design, Automation & Test in Europe Conference & Exhibition (DATE), 2012*, pages 521–526. IEEE, 2012.

[9] S. Carlsson, C. Levcopoulos, and O. Petersson. Sublinear merging and natural mergesort. *Algorithmica*, 9(6):629–648, 1993.

[10] N. Chatterjee, M. Shevgoor, R. Balasubramonian, A. Davis, Z. Fang, R. Illikkal, and R. Iyer. Leveraging heterogeneity in dram main memories to accelerate critical word access. In *Microarchitecture (MICRO),*

2012 45th Annual IEEE/ACM International Symposium on, pages 13–24. IEEE, 2012.

[11] S. Chaudhuri, G. Das, and V. Narasayya. A robust, optimization-based approach for approximate answering of aggregate queries. In *ACM SIGMOD Record*, volume 30, pages 295–306. ACM, 2001.

[12] S. Chen, P. B. Gibbons, and S. Nath. Rethinking database algorithms for phase change memory. In *CIDR*, pages 21–31, 2011.

[13] S. Chen and Q. Jin. Persistent b+-trees in non-volatile main memory. *Proc. VLDB Endow.*, 8(7):786–797, Feb. 2015.

[14] P. Chi, W.-C. Lee, and Y. Xie. Making b+-tree efficient in pcm-based main memory. In *Proceedings of the 2014 international symposium on Low power electronics and design*, pages 69–74. ACM, 2014.

[15] V. K. Chippa, S. T. Chakradhar, K. Roy, and A. Raghunathan. Analysis and characterization of inherent application resilience for approximate computing. In *Proceedings of the 50th Annual Design Automation Conference*, page 113. ACM, 2013.

[16] X. Dong and Y. Xie. Adams: Adaptive mlc/slc phase-change memory design for file storage. In *Design Automation Conference (ASP-DAC), 2011 16th Asia and South Pacific*, pages 31–36. IEEE, 2011.

[17] X. Dong, Y. Xie, N. Muralimanohar, and N. P. Jouppi. Simple but effective heterogeneous main memory with on-chip memory controller support. In *Proceedings of the 2010 ACM/IEEE International Conference for High Performance Computing, Networking, Storage and Analysis*, pages 1–11. IEEE Computer Society, 2010.

[18] H. Esmaeilzadeh, A. Sampson, L. Ceze, and D. Burger. Architecture support for disciplined approximate programming. In *ACM SIGPLAN Notices*, volume 47, pages 301–312. ACM, 2012.

[19] H. Esmaeilzadeh, A. Sampson, L. Ceze, and D. Burger. Neural acceleration for general-purpose approximate programs. In *Proceedings of the 2012 45th Annual IEEE/ACM International Symposium on Microarchitecture*, pages 449–460. IEEE Computer Society, 2012.

[20] V. Estivill-Castro and D. Wood. A survey of adaptive sorting algorithms. *ACM Comput. Surv.*, 24(4):441–476, Dec. 1992.

[21] S. Gao, B. He, and J. Xu. Real-time in-memory checkpointing for future hybrid memory systems. In *Proceedings of the 29th ACM on International Conference on Supercomputing*, ICS '15, pages 263–272, New York, NY, USA, 2015. ACM.

[22] S. Gao, J. Xu, B. He, B. Choi, and H. Hu. Pcmlogging: Reducing transaction logging overhead with pcm. In *Proceedings of the 20th ACM International Conference on Information and Knowledge Management*, CIKM '11, pages 2401–2404, New York, NY, USA, 2011. ACM.

[23] P. Garcia. Multithreaded architectures and the sort benchmark. In *Proceedings of the 1st international workshop on Data management on new hardware*, page 1. ACM, 2005.

[24] M. N. Garofalakis and P. B. Gibbons. Approximate query processing: Taming the terabytes. In *VLDB*, 2001.

[25] N. Govindaraju, J. Gray, R. Kumar, and D. Manocha. Gputerasort: high performance graphics co-processor sorting for large database management. In *Proceedings of the 2006 ACM SIGMOD international conference on Management of data*, pages 325–336. ACM, 2006.

[26] J. Han and M. Orshansky. Approximate computing: An emerging paradigm for energy-efficient design. In *Test Symposium (ETS), 2013 18th IEEE European*, pages 1–6, May 2013.

[27] B. He. When data management systems meet approximate hardware: Challenges and opportunities. *Proceedings of the VLDB Endowment*, 7(10), 2014.

[28] B. He, M. Lu, K. Yang, R. Fang, N. K. Govindaraju, Q. Luo, and P. V. Sander. Relational query coprocessing on graphics processors. *ACM Transactions on Database Systems (TODS)*, 34(4):21, 2009.

[29] E. Ipek, J. Condit, E. B. Nightingale, D. Burger, and T. Moscibroda. Dynamically replicated memory: building reliable systems from nanoscale resistive memories. In *ACM SIGARCH Computer Architecture News*, volume 38, pages 3–14. ACM, 2010.

[30] L. Jiang, B. Zhao, Y. Zhang, J. Yang, and B. R. Childers. Improving write operations in mlc phase change memory. In *High Performance Computer Architecture (HPCA), 2012 IEEE 18th International Symposium on*, pages 1–10. IEEE, 2012.

[31] D. Kim, S. Lee, J. Chung, D. H. Kim, D. H. Woo, S. Yoo, and S. Lee. Hybrid dram/pram-based main memory for single-chip cpu/gpu. In *Proceedings of the 49th Annual Design Automation Conference*, pages 888–896. ACM, 2012.

[32] D. E. Knuth. *The art of computer programming: sorting and searching*, volume 3. Pearson Education, 1998.

[33] D. Koch and J. Torresen. Fpgasort: A high performance sorting architecture exploiting run-time reconfiguration on fpgas for large problem sorting. In *Proceedings of the 19th ACM/SIGDA International Symposium on Field Programmable Gate Arrays*, FPGA '11, pages 45–54, New York, NY, USA, 2011. ACM.

[34] B. C. Lee, E. Ipek, O. Mutlu, and D. Burger. Architecting phase change memory as a scalable dram alternative. *ACM SIGARCH Computer Architecture News*, 37(3):2–13, 2009.

[35] S. Liu, K. Pattabiraman, T. Moscibroda, and B. G. Zorn. Flikker: saving dram refresh-power through critical data partitioning. *ACM SIGPLAN Notices*, 47(4):213–224, 2012.

[36] J. Lucas, M. Alvarez-Mesa, M. Andersch, and B. Juurlink. Sparkk: Quality-scalable approximate storage in dram. 2014.

[37] Micron. MLC NAND Flash. http://www.micron.com/products/nand-flash/mlc-nand, 2015.

[38] N. Mielke, T. Marquart, N. Wu, J. Kessenich, H. Belgal, E. Schares, F. Trivedi, E. Goodness, and L. R. Nevill. Bit error rate in nand flash memories. In

Reliability Physics Symposium, 2008. IRPS 2008. IEEE International, pages 9–19. IEEE, 2008.

[39] A. Moffat, G. Eddy, and O. Petersson. Splaysort: Fast, versatile, practical. *Software: Practice and Experience*, 26(7):781–797, 1996.

[40] D. Mohapatra, G. Karakonstantis, and K. Roy. Significance driven computation: a voltage-scalable, variation-aware, quality-tuning motion estimator. In *Proceedings of the 2009 ACM/IEEE international symposium on Low power electronics and design*, pages 195–200. ACM, 2009.

[41] R. Nair. Models for energy-efficient approximate computing. In *Proceedings of the 16th ACM/IEEE international symposium on Low power electronics and design*, pages 359–360. ACM, 2010.

[42] R. Nair. Big data needs approximate computing: Technical perspective. *Commun. ACM*, 58(1), Dec. 2014.

[43] T. Nirschl, J. Philipp, T. Happ, G. Burr, B. Rajendran, M. Lee, A. Schrott, M. Yang, M. Breitwisch, C. Chen, et al. Write strategies for 2 and 4-bit multi-level phase-change memory. In *Electron Devices Meeting, 2007. IEDM 2007. IEEE International*, pages 461–464. IEEE, 2007.

[44] A. Pantazi, A. Sebastian, N. Papandreou, M. Breitwisch, C. Lam, H. Pozidis, and E. Eleftheriou. Multilevel phase change memory modeling and experimental characterization. *Proceedings of EPCOS*, 2009.

[45] O. Polychroniou and K. A. Ross. A comprehensive study of main-memory partitioning and its application to large-scale comparison-and radix-sort. In *Proceedings of the 2014 ACM SIGMOD international conference on Management of data*, pages 755–766. ACM, 2014.

[46] M. K. Qureshi, M. M. Franceschini, L. A. Lastras-Montaño, and J. P. Karidis. Morphable memory system: a robust architecture for exploiting multi-level phase change memories. In *ACM SIGARCH Computer Architecture News*, volume 38, pages 153–162. ACM, 2010.

[47] M. K. Qureshi, V. Srinivasan, and J. A. Rivers. Scalable high performance main memory system using phase-change memory technology. *ACM SIGARCH Computer Architecture News*, 37(3):24–33, 2009.

[48] A. Rahimi, A. Ghofrani, K.-T. Cheng, L. Benini, and R. K. Gupta. Approximate associative memristive memory for energy-efficient gpus. In *Proceedings of the 2015 Design, Automation & Test in Europe Conference & Exhibition*, pages 1497–1502. EDA Consortium, 2015.

[49] R. Ramakrishnan and J. Gehrke. *Database Management Systems*. Osborne/McGraw-Hill, Berkeley, CA, USA, 2nd edition, 2000.

[50] L. E. Ramos, E. Gorbatov, and R. Bianchini. Page placement in hybrid memory systems. In *Proceedings of the international conference on Supercomputing*, pages 85–95. ACM, 2011.

[51] A. Ranjan, S. Venkataramani, X. Fong, K. Roy, and A. Raghunathan. Approximate storage for energy efficient spintronic memories. In *Design Automation Conference (DAC), 2015 52nd ACM/EDAC/IEEE*, pages 1–6. IEEE, 2015.

[52] P. Roy, R. Ray, C. Wang, and W. F. Wong. Asac: automatic sensitivity analysis for approximate computing. In *Proceedings of the 2014 SIGPLAN/SIGBED conference on Languages, compilers and tools for embedded systems*, pages 95–104. ACM, 2014.

[53] A. Sampson, W. Dietl, E. Fortuna, D. Gnanapragasam, L. Ceze, and D. Grossman. Enerj: Approximate data types for safe and general low-power computation. In *ACM SIGPLAN Notices*, volume 46, pages 164–174. ACM, 2011.

[54] A. Sampson, J. Nelson, K. Strauss, and L. Ceze. Approximate storage in solid-state memories. In *Proceedings of the 46th Annual IEEE/ACM International Symposium on Microarchitecture*, pages 25–36. ACM, 2013.

[55] C. Schensted. Longest increasing and decreasing subsequences. In *Classic Papers in Combinatorics*, pages 299–311. Springer, 1987.

[56] J. Spiegel and N. Polyzotis. Tug synopses for approximate query answering. *ACM Transactions on Database Systems (TODS)*, 34(1):3, 2009.

[57] K. Takeuchi, T. Tanaka, and T. Tanzawa. A multipage cell architecture for high-speed programming multilevel nand flash memories. *Solid-State Circuits, IEEE Journal of*, 33(8):1228–1238, 1998.

[58] X. Tang and J. Xu. Adaptive data collection strategies for lifetime-constrained wireless sensor networks. *Parallel and Distributed Systems, IEEE Transactions on*, 19(6):721–734, 2008.

[59] X. Tang and J. Xu. Optimizing lifetime for continuous data aggregation with precision guarantees in wireless sensor networks. *IEEE/ACM Transactions on Networking (TON)*, 16(4):904–917, 2008.

[60] S. Venkataramani, V. K. Chippa, S. T. Chakradhar, K. Roy, and A. Raghunathan. Quality programmable vector processors for approximate computing. In *Proceedings of the 46th Annual IEEE/ACM International Symposium on Microarchitecture*, pages 1–12. ACM, 2013.

[61] S. Venkataramani, A. Ranjan, K. Roy, and A. Raghunathan. Axnn: energy-efficient neuromorphic systems using approximate computing. In *Proceedings of the 2014 international symposium on Low power electronics and design*, pages 27–32. ACM, 2014.

[62] S. Venkataramani, K. Roy, and A. Raghunathan. Substitute-and-simplify: A unified design paradigm for approximate and quality configurable circuits. In *Proceedings of the Conference on Design, Automation and Test in Europe*, pages 1367–1372. EDA Consortium, 2013.

[63] S. D. Viglas. Write-limited sorts and joins for persistent memory. *Proc. VLDB Endow*, 2014.

[64] T. Wang and R. Johnson. Scalable logging through emerging non-volatile memory. *Proc. VLDB Endow.*, 7(10):865–876, June 2014.

[65] C.-H. Wu. Data sorting in flash memory. In *Proceedings of the 27th Annual ACM Symposium on Applied Computing*, SAC '12, pages 1847–1849, New York, NY, USA, 2012. ACM.

[66] J. Yang, Q. Wei, C. Chen, C. Wang, K. L. Yong, and B. He. Nv-tree: Reducing consistency cost for nvm-based single level systems. In *Proceedings of the 13th USENIX Conference on File and Storage Technologies*, FAST'15, pages 167–181, Berkeley, CA, USA, 2015. USENIX Association.

[67] S. Yeo, N. H. Seong, and H.-H. S. Lee. Can multi-level cell pcm be reliable and usable? analyzing the impact of resistance drift. In *the 10th Ann. Workshop on Duplicating, Deconstructing and Debunking (WDDD)*, 2012.

[68] Q. Zhang, F. Yuan, R. Ye, and Q. Xu. Approxit: An approximate computing framework for iterative methods. In *Design Automation Conference (DAC), 2014 51st ACM/EDAC/IEEE*, pages 1–6. IEEE, 2014.

APPENDIX

A. EVALUATION WITH ANOTHER APPROXIMATE STORAGE

To demonstrate that our *approx-refine* mechanism can be applied to other approximate memory models, we make a preliminary study by using the model from Ranjan et al [51]. In the following, we briefly introduce the memory model, followed by the preliminary experimental results.

Approximate Spintronic Memory Model: Spintronic memory has great potential as future on-chip memories, which is a kind of NVRAM. Ranjan et al. [51] proposed an approximate model of spintronic memory to improve its energy efficiency. By adjusting the voltage and/or current of the magnetic tunnel junction (MTJ), they can achieve reduced read and write energy, resulting in an increased probability of read and write errors. As the energy consumption of a write operation can be over an order of magnitude higher than that of a read operation in spintronic memories, we mainly focus on the energy saving on writes by adopting the approximate memory model, and assume that reads are always precise for simplicity. Particularly, we revisit the three sorting algorithms on the approximate design of spintronic memories [51], and study the energy saving of our proposed approx-refine scheme.

Experimental Results: We explore four different configurations on the tradeoff between energy saving and precision in the approximate spintronic memory model. For each memory write operation, the energy consumption saving per write on the approximate memory is 5%, 20%, 33% and 50% of the original write energy in precise spintronic memory, with about 10^{-7}, 10^{-6}, 10^{-5} and 10^{-4} write error probability per bit respectively. The higher energy consumption saving per write, the higher error probability on the approximate memory.

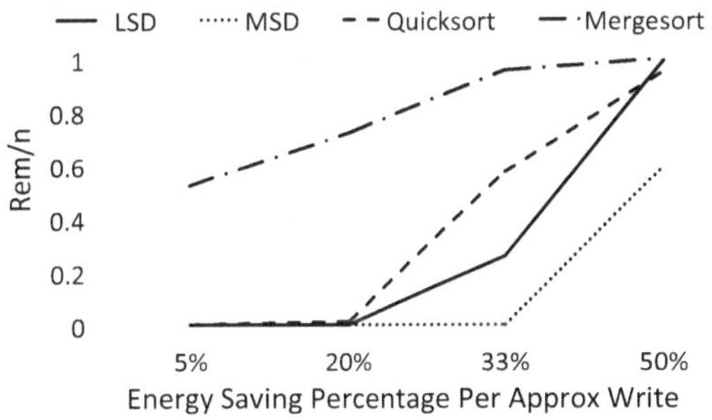

Figure 12: *Rem* ratio under the approximate memory model [51].

With 16M random 32-bit integers as an input, Figure 12 shows the change of *Rem* ratio with the percentage of write energy saving after quicksort, 6-bit LSD, 6-bit MSD and mergesort. When saving only 5% energy per write, errors are rare and the input sequence is nearly sorted. However, when saving 50% energy per write (error rate per bit is about 10^{-4}), the input sequence is still almost random after sorting in approximate memory. This observation is similar to that in Section 3.

Figure 13 shows the total write energy saving under different write error probabilities after applying our *approx-refine* mechanism in the approximate spintronic memory. We set

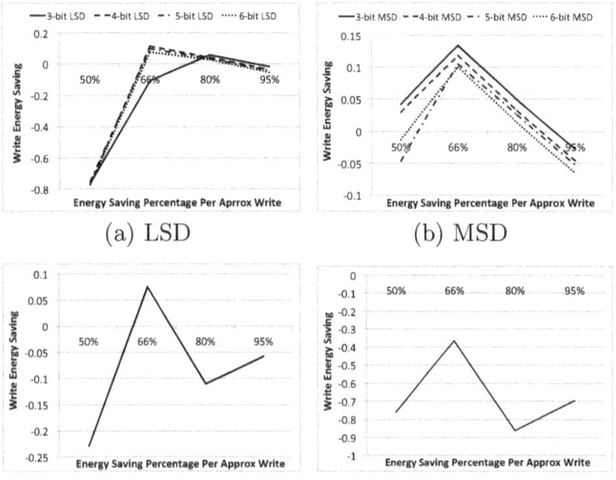

(a) LSD (b) MSD

(c) Quicksort (d) Mergesort

Figure 13: Write energy reduction in comparison with the precise memory model.

$n = 16M$. Except for mergesort, all the other three algorithms achieve better write energy consumption when the energy consumption saving of a write operation on the approximate model is 20% or 33% of the energy consumption per write on the precise model. Radix sort can achieve a maximal write energy saving of about 13.4%, while quicksort achieves write energy reduction up to 7.5%.

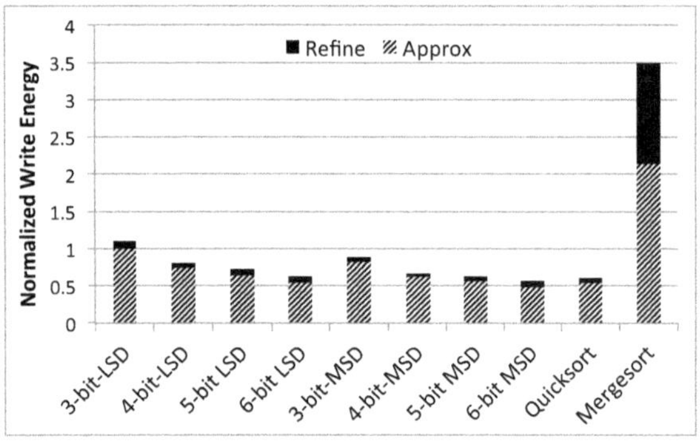

Figure 14: Breakdown of write energy in *approx* and *refine* stages.

We set the write energy saving per write in approximate spintronic memory as 33% of the precise write energy and $n = 16M$. We show the normalized total write energy consumption under the approx-refine mechanism for each algorithm in Figure 14 (normalized to the write energy of 3-bit-LSD in the *approx* stage).

Write energy is further decomposed into *approx* and *refine*. We can see that the energy consumption of the *refine* stage is mostly negligible except for merge sort.

Summary: This study shows that our approx-refine scheme can achieve up to 13.4% energy saving on the approximate spintronic memory model [51]. Through this study, we demonstrate that our *approx-refine* mechanism is not restricted to any specific model, but can be generally applied to many other approximate memory model.

B. EVALUATION WITH ANOTHER SORT IMPLEMENTATION

To demonstrate that our *approx-refine* mechanism is applicable to other sorting implementation, we make a preliminary study by using an open-source implementation of radix sort by Polychronious et al. [45]. The implementation includes both LSD and MSD, which uses SIMD instruction heavily and also includes a histogram-based scheme for better memory locality. We use the same methodology as presented in Section 3.2.

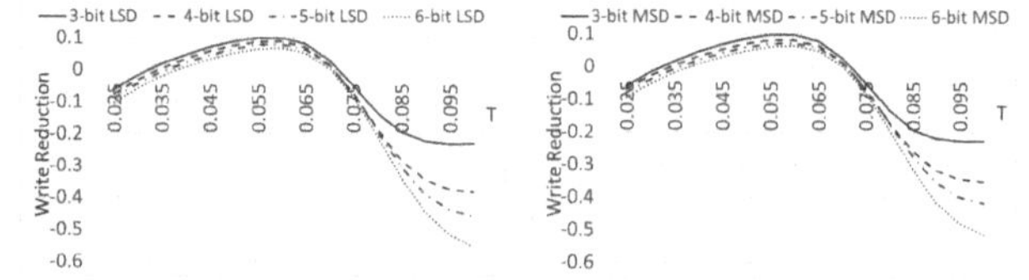

(a) LSD (b) MSD

Figure 15: Write Reduction of LSD and MSD of Polychronious's implementation [45] with approximate memory model from Sampson et al [53].

We change T from 0.025 to 0.1 and plot the write reduction of 3-bit to 6-bit LSD and MSD with $n = 16M$ in Figure 15. We have the following observations:

1. All of these algorithms achieve the most write reduction when $T = 0.055$ or $T = 0.06$. This is consistent with the results of our LSD and MSD implementations.
2. 3-bit LSD and MSD can achieve around 10% write reduction. 6-bit LSD and MSD can achieve around 5% write reduction. The gain is slightly smaller than the study of LSD and MSD using our own implementations. We further investigate this performance difference. This is due to different implementations of radix-sorts during each pass. The histogram-based scheme in this implementation further reduces the number of writes. Therefore, with the same overhead of the *refine* stage, there is smaller write reduction in this implementation. Note that, we have also tested the implementation by enabling/disabling the SIMD and NUMA options and get almost the same write reductions.

Distributed Wavelet Thresholding for Maximum Error Metrics

Ioannis Mytilinis
Computing Systems Laboratory
National Technical University of Athens
gmytil@cslab.ece.ntua.gr

Dimitrios Tsoumakos
Department of Informatics
Ionian University
dtsouma@ionio.gr

Nectarios Koziris
Computing Systems Laboratory
National Technical University of Athens
nkoziris@cslab.ece.ntua.gr

ABSTRACT

Modern data analytics involve simple and complex computations over enormous numbers of data records. The volume of data and the increasingly stringent response-time requirements place increasing emphasis on the efficiency of approximate query processing. A major challenge over the past years has been the efficient construction of fixed-space synopses that provide a deterministic quality guarantee, often expressed in terms of a maximum error metric. For data reduction, wavelet decomposition has proved to be a very effective tool, as it can successfully approximate sharp discontinuities and provide accurate answers to queries. However, existing polynomial time wavelet thresholding schemes that minimize maximum error metrics are constrained with impractical time and space complexities for large datasets. In order to provide a practical solution to the problem, we develop parallel algorithms that take advantage of key-properties of the wavelet decomposition and allocate tasks to multiple workers. To that end, we present i) a general framework for the parallelization of existing dynamic programming algorithms, ii) a parallel version of one such DP-based algorithm and iii) a new parallel greedy algorithm for the problem. To the best of our knowledge, this is the first attempt to scale algorithms for wavelet thresholding for maximum error metrics via a state-of-the-art distributed runtime. Our extensive experiments on both real and synthetic datasets over Hadoop show that the proposed algorithms achieve linear scalability and superior running-time performance compared to their centralized counterparts. Furthermore, our distributed greedy algorithm outperforms the distributed version of the current state-of-the-art dynamic programming algorithm by 2 to 4 times, without compromising the quality of results.

1. INTRODUCTION

The technological and societal developments of our era have resulted in an unprecedented production and processing of enormous data volumes, referred to with the term "Big Data". Applications, businesses, government organizations and digital infrastructures alike contribute to this Big Data reality. Processing over huge, heterogeneous and often imprecise data (the Internet of Things [3] is such an example) is considered common practice nowadays.

SIGMOD'16, June 26-July 01, 2016, San Francisco, CA, USA
© 2016 ACM. ISBN 978-1-4503-3531-7/16/06...$15.00
DOI: http://dx.doi.org/10.1145/2882903.2915230

Approximate query processing has emerged as a viable alternative for dealing with the huge amount of data and the increasingly stringent response-time requirements [5]. Due to the *exploratory nature* of many data analytics applications, there exists a number of scenarios in which an exact answer is not required. Users are often willing to forgo accuracy in favor of achieving better response times. In one such example, visualizing available tradeoffs between accuracy and execution-time helps users to fine-tune the execution of queries [30]. Moreover, approximate answers obtained from appropriate *synopses* of the data may be the only option when the base data is remote and unavailable[7].

To that end, several approximation techniques have been developed, including: sampling [5, 14, 4], histograms [19, 15, 20], wavelets [9, 13, 22, 24, 23] and sketches [16, 6]. Wavelet decomposition [29] provides a very effective data reduction tool, with applications in data mining [25], selectivity estimation [26], and approximate and aggregate query processing of massive relational tables [9, 31] and data streams [17, 11]. In simple terms, a wavelet synopsis is extracted by applying the wavelet decomposition on an input collection (considered as a sequence of values) and then summarizing it by retaining only a select subset of the produced *wavelet coefficients*. The original data can be approximately reconstructed based on this compact synopsis. Previous research has established that reliable and efficient approximate query processing can then be performed solely over such concise wavelet synopses [9].

Wavelet thresholding is the problem of determining the coefficients to be retained in the synopsis given an available space budget B. A conventional approach to this problem features a linear-time deterministic thresholding scheme that minimizes the overall mean squared error [29]. Still, the synopses produced by this method exhibit significant drawbacks [13], such as the high variance in the quality of data approximation, the tendency for severe bias in favor of certain regions of the data and the lack of comprehensible error guarantees for individual approximate answers. On the other hand, synopses that minimize maximum error metrics on individual data values prove more robust in accurate data reconstruction [12, 13].

However, the existing algorithms that minimize maximum error metrics are strictly centralized and are usually based on dynamic programming (DP) approaches, that demand a lot of communication, memory and processing power. As such, they cannot be executed over modern analytics platforms and fail to scale to big datasets. In [22], *GreedyAbs*, a heuristic-based solution is proposed, that is linear in practice. GreedyAbs is more efficient in terms of running-time than the DP-based algorithms but at the cost of loosened quality guarantees. Yet, this algorithm cannot scale to big data either, as it follows a sequential path of execution that prevents a data-parallel approach.

In this work, we present a general framework for adapting the existing DP algorithms to run over scalable, high-throughput modern platforms. We also present *DGreedyAbs*, a new distributed greedy algorithm for the problem. In this way, we offer scalable solutions to the wavelet thresholding for maximum error metrics problem and thus, we enhance the usability of wavelets in modern applications. To our knowledge, this is the first effort to adapt such algorithms towards big data scenarios. In summary, we make the following contributions:

- We present a general and scalable framework for the parallelization of all the existing DP algorithms for the problem and calculate its communication overhead. Our framework is based on a novel error tree decomposition that allows parallel processing of DP table rows. We demonstrate that our proposed partitioning scheme has general applicability, proving to be very efficient for other wavelet-based algorithms. In order to demonstrate the benefits of our approach, we create the *DIndirectHaar* algorithm, by applying the proposed framework on *IndirectHaar* [24], that is the current state-of-the-art. For datasets demanding intensive computations, we show that DIndirectHaar outperforms IndirectHaar by a factor of 2.7.
- We propose *DGreedyAbs*, a new distributed, heuristic-based algorithm and study its computational complexity. Our algorithm is based on three key ideas: 1) locality-preserving partitioning similar to the one applied for the DP algorithms, 2) speculative execution of the centralized greedy algorithm and 3) merging and filtering of intermediate results. DGreedyAbs is 2×–4× faster than DIndirectHaar and over 7 times faster than the centralized greedy algorithm. Moreover, our experiments show that, compared to GreedyAbs, the achieved performance exhibits no quality degradation.
- We implement[1] DGreedyAbs and DIndirectHaar on top of the Hadoop processing framework and perform an extensive experimental evaluation using both synthetic and real datasets. Previous approaches on the problem used datasets of up to 262K datapoints. To put emphasis on the merits of our approach, we experiment with datasets of up to 537M datapoints, demonstrating the applicability of our algorithms over big data scenarios.

The remainder of this paper is organized as follows: Section 2 presents the basic theoretical background for the wavelet decomposition. In Section 3, we give an overview of the related work. Section 4 proposes a novel framework for the parallelization of the DP algorithms and Section 5 presents DGreedyAbs. Finally in Section 6, we experimentally evaluate our algorithms and in Section 7, we present the conclusions.

[1]https://github.com/giagulei/dwmaxerr.git

Table 1: Wavelet decomposition example

Resolution	Averages	Detail Coef.
3	$[5, 5, 0, 26, 1, 3, 14, 2]$	–
2	$[5, 13, 2, 8]$	$[0, -13, -1, 6]$
1	$[9, 5]$	$[-4, -3]$
0	$[7]$	$[2]$

2. WAVELET PRELIMINARIES

Wavelet analysis is a major mathematical technique for hierarchically decomposing functions in an efficient way. The wavelet decomposition of a function consists of a coarse overall approximation together with detail coefficients that influence the function at various scales [29]. Thus, wavelets can successfully approximate sharp discontinuities. In this Section, we provide the basic background to the Haar wavelet transform and its properties.

2.1 Haar Wavelets

Haar wavelets constitute the simplest possible orthogonal wavelet system. Assume a one-dimensional data vector A containing $N = 8$ data values $A = [5, 5, 0, 26, 1, 3, 14, 2]$. The Haar wavelet transform of A can be computed as follows: We first average the values in a pairwise fashion to get a new "lower-resolution" representation of the data with the following average values: $[5, 13, 2, 8]$. The average of the first two values (i.e., 5 and 5) is 5, the average of the next two values (i.e., 0 and 26) is 13, etc. It is obvious that, during this averaging process, some information has been lost and thus the original data values cannot be restored. To be able to restore the original data array, we need to store some *detail coefficients* that capture the missing information. In Haar wavelets, the detail coefficients are the differences of the (second of the) averaged values from the computed pairwise average. In our example, for the first pair of averaged values, the detail coefficient is 0 (since $5 - 5 = 0$) and for the second is -13 ($13 - 26 = -13$). After applying the same process recursively, we generate the full wavelet decomposition that comprises a single overall average followed by three hierarchical levels of 1, 2, and 4 detail coefficients respectively, in order of increasing resolution (see Table 1). In our example, the wavelet transform (also known as the wavelet decomposition) of A is $W_A = [7, 2, -4, -3, 0, -13, -1, 6]$. Each entry in W_A is called a *wavelet coefficient*. The main advantage of using W_A instead of A is that, for vectors containing similar values, most of the detail coefficients tend to have very small values. Therefore, eliminating such small coefficients from the wavelet transform (i.e., treating them as zeros) introduces only small errors when reconstructing the original array and thus results to a very effective form of lossy data compression.

2.2 Error Trees

The *error tree*, introduced in [26], is a hierarchical structure that illustrates the key properties of the Haar wavelet decomposition. Figure 1 depicts the error tree for our simple example data vector A. Each internal node c_i $(i = 0, ..., 7)$ is associated with a wavelet coefficient value, and each leaf d_i $(i = 0, ..., 7)$ is associated with a value in the original data array. Given an error tree T and an internal node c_k of T, we let $leaves_k$ denote the set of data nodes in the subtree rooted at c_k. This notation is extended to $leftleaves_k$ ($rightleaves_k$) for the left (right) sub-tree of c_k. We denote

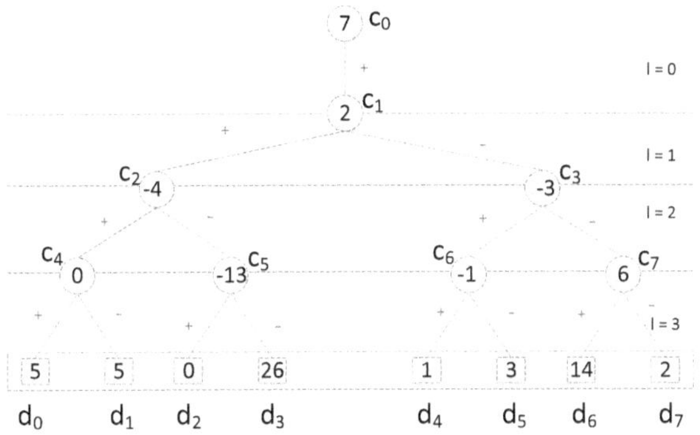

Figure 1: An error tree that illustrates the hierarchical structure of the Haar wavelet decomposition

$path_k$ as the set of all nodes with nonzero coefficients in T which lie on the path from a node c_k (d_k) to the root of the tree T. Moreover, for any two data nodes d_l and d_h, we use $d\,(l:h)$ to denote the range sum $\Sigma_{i=l}^{h} d_i$.

Given the error tree representation T of a one-dimensional Haar wavelet transform, we can reconstruct any data value d_i using only the nodes that lie on the path from d_i to the root of T. That is $d_i = \Sigma_{c_j \in path_i} \delta_{ij} \cdot c_j$, where the factor $\delta_{ij} = 1$ if $d_i \in leftleaves_j$ or $j = 0$ and $\delta_{ij} = -1$ otherwise. For example, in Figure 1, value $d_5 = 7 - 2 - 3 - (-1) = 3$. A range sum $d(l:h)$ can be computed using only nodes $c_j \in path_l \cup path_h$, by $d(l:h) = \Sigma_{c_j \in path_l \cup path_h} x_j$, where $x_j = (h - l + 1) \cdot c_j$, if $j = 0$ and $x_j = (|leftleaves_{j,l:h}| - |rightleaves_{j,l:h}|) \cdot c_j$, otherwise. Here, $leftleaves_{j,l:h} = leftleaves_j \cap \{d_l, d_{l+1}, .., d_h\}$ and $rightleaves_{j,l:h} = rightleaves_j \cap \{d_l, d_{l+1}, .., d_h\}$. That means that node c_j contributes to the range sum $d\,(h:l)$ positively as many times as there are leaf nodes of the left sub-tree of c_j in the summation range, and negatively as many times as there are leaf nodes of the right sub-tree of c_j, while the value of c_0 contributes positively for each leaf node in the summation range. In our example, $d\,(3:6) = (-1)\cdot(-13) + (-1)\cdot(-4) + (-2)\cdot 2 + 4 \cdot 7 + 1 \cdot (-3) + 6 = 44$.

Thus, reconstructing a single data value involves summing at most $logN + 1$ coefficients and reconstructing a range sum involves summing at most $2logN + 1$ coefficients, regardless of the width of the range.

2.3 Wavelet Thresholding

The complete Haar wavelet decomposition W_A of a data vector A is a representation of equal size as the original array. Given a budget constraint $B < N$, the problem of *wavelet thresholding* is to select a subset of at most B coefficients that minimize an aggregate error measure in the reconstruction of data values. The non-selected coefficients are implicitly set to zero. The resulting wavelet synopsis $\hat{W_A}$ can be used as a compressed approximate representation of the original data.

We consider the decomposition of Figure 1 and assume that only coefficients $\{c_0, c_5, c_3\}$ are retained in the synopsis, whereas all the rest are implicitly set to zero. In this case, the reconstructed value for d_5 is $\hat{d_5} = 7 - 3 = 4$ instead of the actual value $d_5 = 3$. For assessing the quality of a wavelet synopsis, many aggregate error-measures have been proposed [10]. Among the most popular metrics are the *mean squared error* (L_2), the *maximum absolute error* (max_abs) and the *maximum relative error* (max_rel):

$$L_2\left(W_A, \hat{W_A}\right) = \sqrt{\frac{1}{N}\sum_{i=1}^{N}\left(\hat{d_i} - d_i\right)^2} \quad (1)$$

$$max\_abs\left(W_A, \hat{W_A}\right) = max_{i=1}^{N}\left\{|\hat{d_i} - d_i|\right\} \quad (2)$$

$$max\_rel\left(W_A, \hat{W_A}\right) = max_{i=1}^{N}\left\{\frac{|\hat{d_i} - d_i|}{max\{|d_i|, S\}}\right\} \quad (3)$$

In the above equations, $\hat{d_i}$ denotes the reconstructed (approximate) value for d_i and S is a *sanity bound* used to prevent the influence of very small values in the aggregate error [31, 12, 13].

A preliminary approach to the thresholding problem is based on two basic observations about a coefficient's contribution in the reconstruction of the original data values (and range-sums). The first observation is that coefficients of larger values are more important, since their absence causes a larger absolute error in the reconstructed values. Second, a coefficient's significance is larger if its level in the error tree is higher, as it participates in more reconstruction paths of the error tree. Putting both together, the significance c_i^* of a coefficient is defined by $c_i^* = |c_i|/\sqrt{2^{level(c_i)}}$, where $level\,(c_i)$ denotes the level of resolution at which the coefficient resides (0 corresponds to the "coarsest" resolution level).

Accordingly, the conventional thresholding scheme is to retain the B wavelet coefficients with the greatest significance. It has been shown [29] that this approach minimizes the L_2 error. Nevertheless, the L_2 error minimization does not provide maximum error guarantees for individual approximate answers. As a result, the approximation error of individual values can be arbitrarily large, resulting into high variance in the quality of data approximation and severe bias in favor of certain regions of the data. This problem is particularly striking whenever a series of omitted coefficients lies along the same path of the error tree. Metrics max_abs and max_rel prove more robust error measures [12, 13], since they set a maximum error guarantee on individual values. The problem of minimizing these error metrics can be formulated as follows:

PROBLEM 1. *Given a data vector A of size N and a budget B, construct a representation $\hat{W_A}$ of A that minimizes a maximum error metric, while it retains at most B non-zero coefficients.*

For ease of readability, we also define the dual of Problem 1:

PROBLEM 2. *Given a data vector A of size N and an error bound ϵ, construct a representation $\hat{W_A}$ of A such that $max\_abs \leq \epsilon$ and the number of non-zero entries s^* in $\hat{W_A}$ is minimized.*

In this work, we focus on designing algorithms for Problem 1 that can specifically scale in big data scenarios. The existing algorithms for the problem either need to load the whole data set in memory or work on a small working set and make very often disk accesses to update it. The increasing sizes of data to be processed render centralized approaches (with excessive disk accesses) unusable in terms of performance and scalability. In this work, we instead propose a novel problem decomposition to smaller local sub-problems that can be more easily handled. Following that, we utilize partial and parallel computed solutions to derive the final one.

Table 2: Notation

Symbol i∈0..N-1	Semantics
A	Input data array
W_A	Wavelet transform array
N	Number of data points
B	Target size of synopsis
T_i	Error tree rooted at node i
$T_L(c_i)$ $(T_R(c_i))$	Sub-tree rooted at left (right) child of node i
d_i	Data value at cell i of the data array
$\hat{d_i}$	Reconstructed data value at cell i
$leaves_i$	Set of data nodes in T_i
c_i	Wavelet coefficient at cell i
M	Matrix used by DP algorithm
err_i	Signed accumulated error for d_i
R	Size of the root sub-tree
S	Size of a base sub-tree

3. RELATED WORK

In this Section, we present an overview of the existing approaches to Problem 1 and discuss the relation of our work to past research. In [12], a probabilistic DP algorithm that minimizes the maximum error metrics was proposed for the wavelet thresholding. The running-time of the algorithm is $O\left(N\delta^2 Blog\left(\delta B\right)\right)$, where δ is a quantization factor. However, as there is always a possibility of a "bad" sequence of coin flips, this approach can lead to a poor quality synopsis.

For this reason, a deterministic DP-based approach is proposed in [13]. Unfortunately, the optimal solution provided has a high time complexity of $O\left(N^2 BlogB\right)$, where N is the total number of coefficients and B the synopsis size.

In [23], the Haar+ tree is presented. This is a modified error tree that allows the design of a DP algorithm with running-time complexity of $O\left(\left(\frac{\Delta}{\delta}^2\right) NB\right)$, where Δ is the range of dataset values.

These solutions are very expensive in terms of time and space complexity. Such requirements render the solution impracticable for the purpose it is meant to be for, namely the quick and space-efficient summarization of data into manageable general-purpose synopses [9].

In order to decrease space complexity, Guha introduces a generally applicable, space efficient technique [18] for all these DP-based approaches. This technique only needs to keep a small subset of the data in memory while all the rest reside on disk. Nevertheless, such an approach considerably increases the I/O cost.

Furthermore, all the approaches mentioned so far contain, in their complexity formula, a term for budget B which can be $O(N)$ and can thus lead to quadratic or cubic complexity. Such running-times are prohibitive for big datasets, which may be in the order of gigabytes or terabytes. In order to eliminate term B from the complexity, a different DP-based approach is proposed in [24], where Problem 2 [24, 27, 28] is exploited and the resulting complexity is $O\left(\left(\frac{\mathcal{E}}{\delta}\right)^2 N\left(log\epsilon^* + logN\right)\right)$, where $\mathcal{E}$ is the minimum maximum error that can be achieved with $B-1$ coefficients and ϵ^* is the real maximum error. This algorithm is considered to be the current state-of-the-art for the problem, as it provides the optimal data reconstruction for the given budget and has the best running-time complexity among the corresponding DP algorithms.

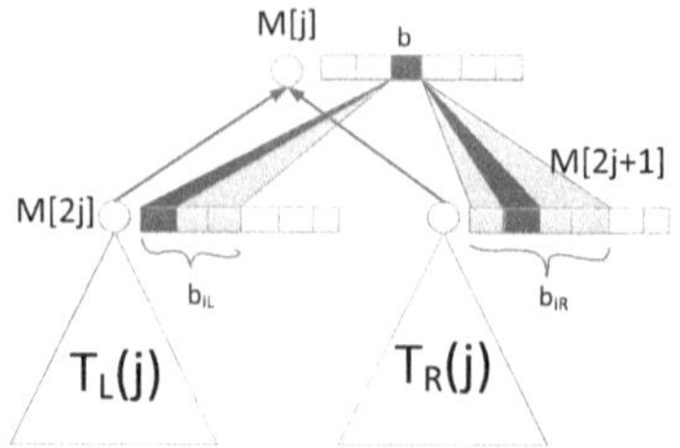

Figure 2: DP recursion on the error tree. Node c_j combines the M-rows of its children in order to produce $M[j]$

However, all of these algorithms run in a centralized fashion and, to the best of our knowledge, there is no proposed solution that adapts them to a distributed environment. Thus, problems like excessive demand for main memory capacity and disk I/O have not yet been resolved.

In order to decrease running-time, greedy algorithms have been proposed [22] for the minimization of the maximum absolute and relative error with worst-case running-time complexities of $O\left(Nlog^2N\right)$ and $O\left(Nlog^3N\right)$ respectively. These algorithms present almost linear behavior in practice and require less memory capacity than most of the DP-based ones. Nevertheless, as data scales close to the memory constraints of the machine, their performance significantly deteriorates. Moreover, these algorithms have inherent difficulties in their parallelization and thus, the decomposition to local sub-problems is not an easy task to accomplish.

Finally, the work in [21] considers a distributed setting for the wavelet decomposition, implemented on top of Hadoop, but it only targets the conventional thresholding scheme, which is a considerably easier task.

4. SCALING DP ALGORITHMS

Since the majority of the proposed algorithms for Problem 1 are based on dynamic programming, in this Section we present a general framework that can be used for their parallelization and efficient execution over modern distributed platforms. To achieve that, we exploit the structure of the error tree as well as the local properties of these algorithms and propose a locality-preserving partitioning scheme.

In all these algorithms, each row of the DP-matrix M is assigned to a node of the error tree. The contents of such a row differ between algorithms. Despite the different structure of the rows of M, all these algorithms follow a bottom-up fashion, where the rows corresponding to the leaves of the error tree are computed first. The row for each internal node is computed by combining the already computed rows of its children according to an optimality criterion. To compute the values for a single cell of a row j, many cells of the children-rows are examined and, eventually the one that optimizes a defined metric is selected, according to each algorithm. Thus, computing the row for any node of the error tree, demands two more rows to be in memory.

For example, in the MinRelVar algorithm presented in [12], each row $M[j]$ stores three values for every possible space allotment b to the sub-tree rooted at c_j. Thus, each cell $M[j,b]$ of a row is 3-dimensional and contains the following three values: $M[j,b].v, M[j,b].y, M[j,b].l$, which represent: i) the minimum error, ii) the probability to retain

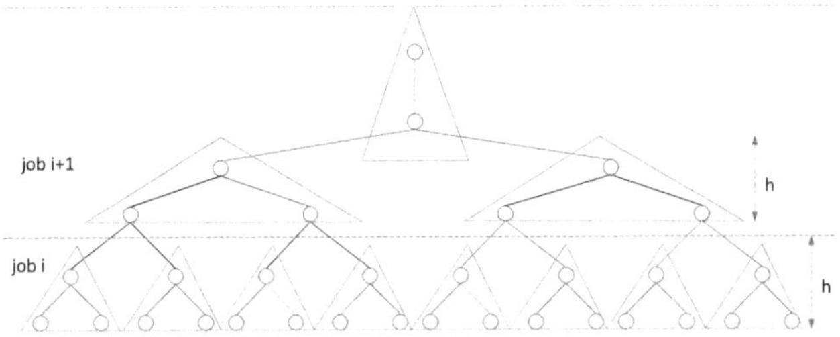

Figure 3: Partitioning used for parallelizing DP-based algorithms for Problem 1

coefficient c_j, and iii) the space allotment for the left subtree respectively. In order to compute $M[j,b]$, the algorithm needs to examine all $M[2j, b_{i_L}], b_{i_L} \in [0, b - M[j,b].y]$ and all $M[2j+1, b_{i_R}], b_{i_R} \in [0, b - M[j,b].y - b_{i_L}]$ and finally select the cells from $M[2j]$ and $M[2j+1]$ that incur the minimum error $M[j,b].v$. This procedure is illustrated in Figure 2. The shadowed cells represent the examined values and the bold colored ones the finally selected values.

In Figure 2, we observe that the left and right sub-tree of node c_j ($T_L(j)$ and $T_R(j)$ respectively) can be computed independently of each other. Based on this observation, the idea is to apply a partitioning scheme that hierarchically decomposes the error tree to sub-trees of a fixed height $h, h < logN$. Such a partitioning is presented in Figure 3 and results to $\lceil \frac{logN}{h} \rceil$ layers of sub-trees. We denote $Layer_i$ to be all the sub-trees located in layer i and it holds that:

$$|Layer_i| = \begin{cases} \frac{N}{2^{h \cdot i + i - 1}} & i = 1, .., \lfloor \frac{logN+1}{h+1} \rfloor \\ 1 & i = \lceil \frac{logN+1}{h+1} \rceil \end{cases} \quad (4)$$

For the parallelization of the existing DP algorithms for both Problems 1 and 2, we use Algorithm 1. The idea is to first run the DP algorithm in parallel over the sub-trees of the bottommost layer. When the processing is over, the computed rows for the roots of these sub-trees are sent over to the next layer in order to repeat the same process towards the root. More specifically, if the local root is the node c_j, the emitted key-value is $(j, M[j])$. The workers of the next stage collect the emitted key-values and repeat the same process. Naturally, a proper partitioning should be applied between different stages, in order to preserve the sub-tree locality in the next layer.

Algorithm 1 Parallel execution of a DP algorithm for Problem1

```
Require: Data size N, sub-tree height h
Partition the error tree to sub-trees of fixed height h.
i = 1
while i ≤ ⌊(logN+1)/(h+1)⌋ do
    if i > 1 then Combine M-rows from layer i − 1
    for all T_j ∈ Layer_i in parallel do
        Run DP on T_j
        Send the computed row of node j to the next layer
    end for
    i = i + 1
end while
Run DP on topmost sub-tree.
```

As a distributed approach, it is clear that this idea incurs a communication overhead. For every sub-tree of the error tree, the row of M that corresponds to the local root is transferred over to the workers of the next stage. Let $|M[j]|$ denote the size of the row corresponding to node c_j. Then, according to Equation 4, the communication overhead for the i-th stage is:

$$O(|Layer_i| \cdot max_{j \in Layer_i}\{|M[j]|\}) = O\left(\frac{1}{2^{h \cdot i + i - 1}} N \cdot max_{j \in Layer_i}\{|M[j]|\}\right) \quad (5)$$

and thus, the overall communication overhead:

$$O\left(\sum_{i=1}^{\lfloor \frac{logN+1}{h+1} \rfloor} \frac{1}{2^{h \cdot i + i - 1}} N \cdot max_{j \in Layer_i}\{|M[j]|\}\right) = O\left(\frac{N \cdot max\{|M[j]|\}}{2^h}\right) \quad (6)$$

Equation 6 represents the generic communication complexity of all DP algorithms when our partitioning scheme is applied. The maximum M-row size $max\{|M[j]|\}$, which determines the complexity, depends on the used algorithm.

After the completion of Algorithm 1, it is only the optimal approximation error for Problem 1 (synopsis size for Problem 2) that is computed and not the synopsis itself. To compute the synopsis, all DP algorithms require one additional step: a top-down recursive procedure on the error tree in order to select the appropriate coefficients. Starting from the root this time, we re-enter the sub-problem of the topmost sub-tree and select the coefficients to retain. When the processing of the topmost sub-tree is over, we know which coefficients are retained from this sub-tree and also the leaves of the sub-tree know which cells of the M-rows of their children are the best choice in order to obtain the optimal synopsis. Thus, each leaf-node of the topmost sub-tree sends a message to its children to inform them about the optimal choice they can make. With this message, the children recursively re-enter the sub-problems of the next layer of sub-trees.

Unfortunately, the space complexity of most DP algorithms for Problem 1 relies on budget B. Thus, for a bad case scenario where B is large enough ($O(N)$), matrix M may not fit in memory even for a moderate or small-sized sub-tree. Furthermore, in such a case, the communication overhead may be also too high to sustain. For example, for the algorithm in [12] it holds that $max\{|M[j]|\} = O(B \cdot \delta)$. If we substitute this quantity in Equation 6, the communication complexity is $O\left(\frac{NB\delta}{2^h}\right)$, which can become $O(N^2)$.

In order to avoid the impact of budget B, we focus on Problem 2 instead. The DP algorithm that solves the dual problem and on which we are going to apply the proposed framework is MinHaarSpace [24]. At each visited node c_j, MinHaarSpace computes the corresponding M-row, $M[j]$. $M[j]$ holds an entry $M[j,v]$ for each possible *incoming* value v at node c_j. An *incoming* value v at node c_j is a value reconstructed in the path of ancestor coefficients from the root node up to c_j. For example, in Figure 1, the incoming value of c_2 is $7 + 2 = 9$. For a specified incoming value v, $M[j,v]$ is a 3-dimensional cell that contains: (i) the minimum number of non-zero coefficients that need to be retained in the sub-tree T_j, (ii) the optimal value[2] to assign at c_j, and (iii) the actual minimum error in the scope of c_j.

[2]We use MinHaarSpace for unrestricted wavelets

By applying the proposed framework, we create algorithm *DMHaarSpace*, the new distributed version of MinHaarSpace. The workers of DMHaarSpace execute MinHaarspace over local data and emit the M-row of the local-root node, in a manner similar as described before. The running-time complexity of DMHaarSpace is the same as that of MinHaarspace, i.e., $O\left(\left(\frac{\epsilon}{\delta}\right)^2 NlogN\right)$ and the communication complexity is $O\left(\frac{N\epsilon}{\delta 2^h}\right)$, as derived from Equation 6 and the size of the M-row that is $O\left(\frac{\epsilon}{\delta}\right)$ [24], where δ is a user-defined parameter that quantizes the solution space.

Since DMHaarSpace targets Problem 2, we need to run the algorithm multiple times to derive the final solution. For this reason in [24], there is the IndirectHaar that solves Problem 1 by running MinHaarSpace multiple times. Algorithm 2 presents DIndirectHaar, a modified version of IndirectHaar that uses DMHaarSpace instead of MinHaarSpace.

As Algorithm 2 describes, the DIndirectHaar algorithm performs binary search in the space of possible errors. Obviously, this results in multiple distributed jobs of input size N. Furthermore, in order to compute the lower and upper error bounds (lines 1-2), an overhead of two extra jobs is required. For the lower bound, we compute the (B+1)-largest coefficient. Each worker emits its local wavelet coefficients in reverse order, i.e., largest first, and in a next step these coefficients are merged and the first $B+1$ are retained. For the upper bound, assuming that a B-term synopsis fits in memory, we load the B-largest-terms synopsis in the main memory of each worker and we bottom-up compute the max_abs.

Algorithm 2 DIndirectHaar

1: e_u =maximum absolute error for B-largest-terms synopsis
2: $e_l = (B+1)$-largest coefficient
3: $e_{low} = e_l; e_{high} = e_u$
4: **while** not finished **do**
5: $\quad e_{mid} = \frac{e_{high}+e_{low}}{2}$
6: $\quad \hat{W}_A$ =DMHaarSpace(e_{mid});$\bar{B}$ =size of $\hat{W}_A$
7: $\quad \bar{e}$ =actual maximum absolute error of $\hat{W}_A$
8: $\quad$**if** $\bar{B} < B$ **then**
9: $\quad\quad \tilde{W}_A$ =DMHaarSpace($< \bar{e}$);$\tilde{B}$ =size of $\tilde{W}_A$
10: $\quad\quad$**if** $\tilde{B} > B$ **then** finished=1
11: $\quad\quad$**else** $e_{high} = \bar{e}$
12: $\quad$**else**
13: $\quad\quad$**if** $\bar{B} > B$ **then** $e_{low} = e_{mid}$
14: $\quad\quad$**else** finished=1
15: $\quad$**end if**
16: **end while**

5. A DISTRIBUTED GREEDY APPROACH

As the DP-based solutions incur high computational overhead, there is often a need for a faster approach at the cost of approximation quality. This is exactly what the GreedyAbs [22] algorithm achieves. However, as explained in Section 3, this algorithm is not easily parallelizable and cannot scale for big datasets. In this Section, we present a fully parallelizable version of the greedy algorithm based on: (i) a partitioning scheme similar to the one presented in Section 4, (ii) speculative execution of the centralized algorithm, (iii) merging and filtering of results. We present our idea in detail for the maximum absolute error metric and discuss the modifications needed to support the maximum relative error metric problem.

5.1 GreedyAbs

For the ease of understanding of our algorithm, we first give a description of the GreedyAbs algorithm presented in [22]. Let $err_j = \hat{d_j} - d_j$ be the signed accumulated error for a data node d_j in a synopsis $\hat{W_A}$, yielded by the deletions of some coefficients. To assist the iterative step of the greedy algorithm, for each coefficient c_k not yet discarded, we introduce the *maximum potential absolute error* MA_k that c_k will contribute on the running synopsis, if discarded:

$$MA_k = max_{d_j \in leaves_k}\{|err_j - \delta_{jk} \cdot c_k|\} \quad (7)$$

Computing MA_k normally requires information about all err_j values in $leaves_k$. A naive method to compute MA_k is to access all $leaves_k$, where err_j are explicitly maintained. The disadvantages of this approach are the explicit maintenance of all err_j values at each step and the cost required to update MA_k values after the removal of a coefficient.

A more efficient solution for updating MA_k is reached by exploiting the fact that the removal of a coefficient equally affects the signed costs of all data values in its left or right sub-tree. For example, in Figure 1, the removal of coefficient $c_2 = -4$ increases the signed errors of data nodes d_0, d_1, and decreases the signed errors of d_2, d_3 by 4. Accordingly, the maximum and minimum signed errors in the left (right) sub-tree of a removed coefficient c_i are decreased (increased) by c_i. The maximum absolute error incurred by the removal necessarily occurs at one of these four positions of existing error extremum. Hence, the computation of MA_k requires that only four quantities be maintained at each internal node of the tree. These are the maximum and minimum signed errors for the $leftleaves_k$ and $rightleaves_k$, and are denoted by max_k^l, min_k^l, max_k^r, and min_k^r, respectively. It follows that Equation 7 is equivalent to:

$$MA_k = max\{|max_k^l - c_k|, |min_k^l - c_k|, \\ |max_k^r + c_k|, |min_k^r + c_k|\} \quad (8)$$

In the complete wavelet decomposition, these four quantities are all 0, since $err_j = 0, \forall d_j$. Thus, $MA_k = |c_k|, \forall k$ and the greedy algorithm removes the smallest $|c_k|$ first. In order to efficiently decide which coefficient to choose next, all coefficients are organized in a min-heap structure based on their MA_k. After the removal of a coefficient c_k, err_j for all $leaves_k$ changes, so the information of all descendants and ancestors of c_k must be updated. All the error quantities of the descendants in the left (right) sub-tree of c_k are decreased (increased) by c_k. During this process, a new MA_i is computed for each descendant c_i of c_k. In accordance, the changes in error quantities are propagated upwards to ancestors c_i of c_k and MA_i values are updated as necessary. While updating error quantities and MA values, the position of c_k's descendants and affected ancestors are dynamically updated in the heap. These procedure of removing nodes is repeated until only B nodes are left on the tree.

Another important thing to note is that the maximum absolute error does not change monotonically when a coefficient is removed. In other words, after deleting a coefficient c_k the maximum absolute error of its affected data values may decrease. As a result, choosing exactly B coefficients may not be the best solution given a space budget B. For this

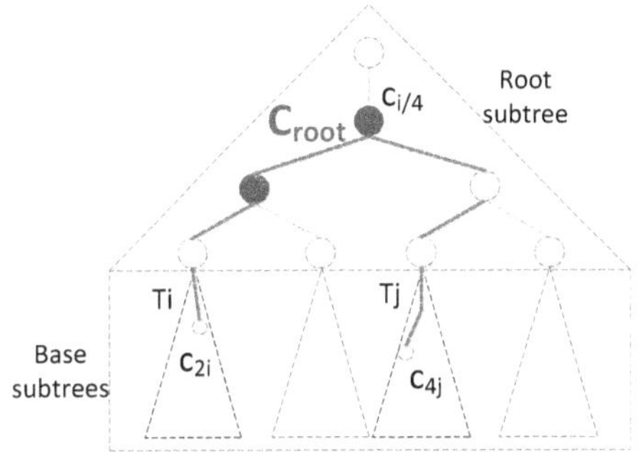

Figure 4: Partitioning used for parallelizing GreedyAbs. The red line illustrates an example of communication of two base sub-trees through the root sub-tree. The blue-filled nodes show a possible C_{root} set.

reason, we keep removing coefficients also after the limit of B has been reached, until no coefficient remains in the tree. From all B + 1 coefficient sets (B coefficients left, B-1 coefficients left, etc) produced at the last B steps of the algorithm, the one with the minimum *max_abs* is kept.

5.2 Scaling the Greedy Algorithm

GreedyAbs presents an inherent drawback for its parallelization. At each step, the algorithm needs global knowledge of the whole error tree. To solve the problem in parallel, we need to consider a partitioning similar to the one we used for the parallelization of the DP algorithms. In the proposed scheme, the error tree is partitioned into one *root sub-tree* and many *base sub-trees*, as shown in Figure 4.

At each iteration of GreedyAbs, the node c_k with the smallest MA is selected to be discarded. After its deletion, all the other nodes that lie either in $path_k$ or T_k may update their MA values. Ideally, we would like to take decisions at each base sub-tree independently of each other. For the parallelization of the algorithm, the main difficulty is that the base sub-trees communicate with each other through the root sub-tree. For example, consider a scenario, like the one depicted in Figure 4, where node c_{2i} is selected to be removed from the base sub-tree T_i and node c_{4j} is selected from T_j. The removal of c_{2i} updates the MA value of node $c_{i/4} \in path_{2i}$ to $MA'_{i/4}$. Suppose also that for node c_{4j} holds $c_{i/4} \in path_{4j} \wedge (MA_{4j} < MA_{i/4})$ and also $MA'_{i/4} < MA_{4j}$. This means that the removal of c_{2i} in T_i changed the preference of GreedyAbs in T_j. This example shows that the communication of base sub-trees through the root sub-tree can change the order in which nodes are discarded and interferes with a straight-forward parallel implementation.

In order to proceed towards a parallel and correct computation, we need to offer more isolation to the partitions base sub-trees. The idea behind our solution is the following. Let us assume that we somehow know which nodes of the root sub-tree are retained in the final synopsis. Let us call this set of nodes C_{root}. Having selected the retained nodes from the root sub-tree, we can remove the remaining root sub-tree and there are $B - |C_{root}|$ nodes that remain to be selected.

Consider now a base sub-tree T_j. The deletion of the nodes $c_i \in$ root sub-tree$\setminus C_{root}$ incurs an incoming error to T_j. For example, in the error tree of Figure 1, if we delete nodes $\{c_0, c_2\}$, there is an incoming error $-7 - 4 = -11$ to sub-tree T_5. Thus, if the incoming error to sub-tree T_j is e_{in}, we set then the signed accumulated errors to: $err_i = \delta_j e_{in}, \forall d_i \in T_j$ ($\delta_j = -1$ if T_j is a left sub-tree and 1, otherwise) and we run GreedyAbs on T_j. The output of $GreedyAbs\,(T_j)$ is an ordered list L_j of $|T_j|$ coefficients. The list is ordered according to the order that GreedyAbs discards the coefficients $c_i \in T_j$. More specifically, each element of the list is a tuple $(error, index)$ that indicates the maximum incurred absolute error when this node is discarded and the index of the discarded node in the error tree. This procedure of locally executing GreedyAbs on a sub-tree, is carried out in parallel for all base sub-trees.

When this stage of parallel GreedyAbs runs is over, we collect, sort error-wise and merge all the outputs from all the base sub-trees (i.e., $\forall T_j \in$ base sub-trees, sort and merge L_j), thus obtaining a globally ordered list. By keeping the $B - |C_{root}|$ elements of the list with the highest error, let us call them C_{base}, we form the final synopsis: $C_{root} \cup C_{base}$.

We have already mentioned that, in GreedyAbs, the error does not change monotonically when a coefficient is removed. For example, consider the key-values $KV_1 = (50, 8)$, $KV_2 = (42, 10)$ discarded in respective order. At the final global order, we expect KV_1 prior to KV_2, since node 8 was discarded first. However, as the error of KV_2 is smaller than the one of KV_1, the sorting will place KV_1 after KV_2. In order to avoid this unwanted behavior, we modify the logic according to which L_j lists are emitted to the sorting and merging mechanism. Instead of emitting a single node per key-value, we emit a list of nodes. While the error incurred by the deletion of a node is smaller or equal to the maximum so far error, we append the node to be discarded to a list. Otherwise, we emit the key-value and create a new one with an empty list. Consider the key-values KV_1, KV_2 of the previous example. Instead of emitting both of them, we emit $(50, [8, 10])$. Apart from correctness, in this way we also achieve better I/O efficiency, since the $|T_j|$ coefficients are emitted in batches and not one at a time.

This scheme, where lists are emitted as values, can be further improved. Assume the error from discarding a node is 132.44 and the error for the next node is 132.45. As the absolute difference is very small, we may decide that we can tolerate this error and, for I/O efficiency, we do not emit two different key-values. In general, we consider a user-specific parameter e_b and partition the domain of errors to buckets of width e_b. The algorithm is then modified as to emit a new key-value only when an error from the next bucket appears. In Algorithm 3 we present the modified *discardNode* function that we use for GreedyAbs. So far, we have ignored the procedure that finds the appropriate nodes to be retained from the root sub-tree, assuming it is "magically" available. As we cannot compute a-priori which these nodes are, we need to *speculatively* create the synopses for different C_{root} sets and finally retain the one that produces the best approximation. Let R denote the size of the root sub-tree. Since we do not know the number of nodes that

Algorithm 3 *discardNode*

Require: node index k, error e_k incurred by the deletion of node k, width e_b of the error bucket, list L of discarded nodes, the current max error *max_error*

$\hat{e} = \lfloor \frac{e_k}{e_b} \rfloor \cdot e_b$
if $\hat{e} \leq max\_error$ **then**
  L.append(c_k)
else
  emit $(\hat{e}, L)$;$max\_error = \hat{e}$;$L = []$
end if

should be retained from the root sub-tree, we should compute the synopsis for at least $min\{R, B\}+1$ different C_{root} sets, with each candidate C_{root} having different size: The empty set, as we may keep none of these nodes, keep only 1 node, keep 2 nodes, etc, until we examine the case where $min\{R, B\}$ nodes are kept. In order to find $min\{R, B\}+1$ candidate C_{root} sets, we run GreedyAbs on the root sub-tree. The intuition behind this choice is that, since only the root sub-tree is considered known at this stage, we should try to optimize the local problem and each time discard the node that incurs the minimum error. The candidate C_{root} sets are generated by the *genRootSets* function presented in Algorithm 4.

For example, we consider as root sub-tree the nodes $\{c_0, c_1, c_2, c_3\}$ of the error tree depicted in Figure 1. The run of GreedyAbs selects to discard the nodes according to the following order: $[c_1, c_3, c_2, c_0]$. Thus, the candidate C_{root} sets are the following 5: $\{c_1, c_3, c_2, c_0\}$,$\{c_3, c_2, c_0\}$,$\{c_2, c_0\}$,$\{c_0\}$,$\{\}$

Algorithm 4 *genRootSets*

Require: root sub-tree,B
$L_{root} = GreedyAbs$(root sub-tree)
$C = \{\{\}\}$
$lastIndex = L_{root}.size$
for $(i = lastIndex; i > lastIndex - B; i = i - 1)$ **do**
  $C_{root,i} = \{L_{root}[i], .., L_{root}[lastIndex]\}$
  $C = C \cup \{C_{root,i}\}$
end for
return C

In order to execute our algorithm in a distributed environment, we use the following scheme. Initially, we run GreedyAbs, in a centralized fashion, on the root sub-tree and we get as output a set C with all the candidate C_{root} sets. Since the root sub-tree can be exponentially smaller than the original dataset, its processing on a single machine can be done without compromising performance. For the distributed processing of the remaining dataset, we consider an architecture of two *levels* of workers. Each base sub-tree T_j is assigned to a different level-1 worker. Level-1 worker j runs GreedyAbs over its local data for every $C_{root} \in C$ that affects the incoming error to T_j. For every list of nodes that the GreedyAbs discards, the worker emits a key-value, in the form $([C_{root}, error], List)$ to the next level of workers. Therefore, apart from the maximum incurred error, the key contains information on which nodes are retained from the root sub-tree, for this run of GreedyAbs.

From the description of the algorithm above, it is derived that each worker runs GreedyAbs for all $C_{root} \in C$ that affect the incoming error. As we emit every node for each run of GreedyAbs, we observe that each initial coefficient is emitted $O(min\{R, B\}+1)$ times. This quantity can be multiple times the size of the initial dataset and leads to significant I/O overhead.

In order to avoid the excessive I/O, instead of emitting the list of the actual coefficients, we emit a histogram. For each emitted key-value, we keep the key as is and as value we emit the number of nodes that are discarded producing a maximum error that falls in a specific error bucket. For example, instead of emitting the key-value $(50, [8, 10])$ as in the previous example, we now emit $(50, 2)$, where 2 is the length of the list $[8, 10]$. This way, we emit sizeOf(int) bytes instead of the actual size of the list. We call *ErrHistGreedyAbs* the modified version of GreedyAbs that emits error histograms.

With the use of an appropriate partitioning scheme, all the emitted key-values that refer to the same C_{root} end up at the same level-2 worker. Key-values are sorted and merged according to the error information that is stored in the key, with the node yielding the highest error expected to appear first. When sorting and merging are over, there is a global ordering of all the nodes of the dataset for a particular C_{root}. By examining the first $B+1$ key-values, the B most important nodes are identified and the worker extracts the best achieved maximum absolute error. When the processing is over, each level-2 worker has computed the best error for the C_{root} sets it was assigned. We call *combineResults* the described procedure and we formally describe it in Algorithm 5. In a final step, all the level-2 workers send their results to a single process that decides the most accurate synopsis.

Algorithm 5 combineResults

Require: space budget B
Require: the set C' of C_{root} sets the worker is responsible for
Require: a list $L_{C_{root}} = [L_{1,C_{root}}, L_{2,C_{root}}, ..], \forall C_{root} \in C'$, where $L_{j,C_{root}}$ is the emitted key-values for C_{root} from sub-tree T_j.
$minError = infinity, bestCroot = \{\}$
for all $C_{root} \in C'$ **do**
  $L = merge(L_{C_{root}})$
  if $L[B - |C_{root}|].error < minError$ **then**
    $minError = L[B - |C_{root}|].error$
    $bestCroot = C_{root}$
  end if
end for
return $(minError, bestCroot)$

With the level-1 workers emitting histograms, when the job is over, we do not know which coefficients to choose for the synopsis but only which C_{root} we should use and what is the best error that can be achieved. By knowing the nodes that should be retained from the root sub-tree, we initiate a second job that computes and constructs the synopsis. In this second job, each level-1 worker runs exactly once GreedyAbs over its local data, only for the C_{root} that yields the best quality synopsis. This time, the workers do not emit histograms but the actually removed nodes. Furthermore, as at this time the final error ϵ^* is known, the workers do not have to emit all the nodes of their local sub-tree but only the ones that their removal incurs an error higher than ϵ^*. We call our algorithm DGreedyAbs and we formally describe it in Algorithm 6.

5.3 Complexity Analysis

The worst-case cost of GreedyAbs is $O(Nlog^2N)$ [22]. However, as we will see in the experimental Section, the algorithm's complexity is linear in practice and also leads to linear behavior of our algorithm. Assume $R = min\{R, B\}$. The run of GreedyAbs on the root sub-tree produces a powerset C, such that:
$|C| = R+1 \wedge \forall C_{root,i} \in C, 0 \leq |C_{root,i}| \leq R$
$\wedge |C_{root,i}| \neq |C_{root,j}| \forall i, j \in [0, R-1], i \neq j$
That means that every two different C_{root} sets differ from each other by at least one coefficient and since $|C| = R+1$, eventually all the coefficients of the root sub-tree will be selected, one at a time. In this way, we have a different incoming error to T_k for every node in $path_k$. Since the length of the path of each base sub-tree to the root is

Algorithm 6 DGreedyAbs

```
Require: error tree, space budget B
C = genRootSets(root sub-tree,B)
Assign base sub-trees to level-1 workers
for all T_j ∈ base sub-trees in parallel do
    for all C_root ∈ C that affect incoming error in T_j do
        e_in = incoming error in T_j from C_root
        err_i = err_i + δ_j e_in, ∀err_i ∈ T_j
        ErrHistGreedyAbs (T_j)
    end for
end for
minError = infinity, bestCroot = {}
for all w ∈ level-2 workers in parallel do
    Let C_w ⊆ C, the C_root sets that w is responsible for.
    (error, Croot) = combineResults (B, C_w, L_{C_w})
    if error < minError then
        minError = error
        bestCroot = Croot
    end if
end for
for all T_j ∈ base sub-trees in parallel do
    e_in = incoming error in T_j from bestCroot
    err_i = err_i + δ_j e_in, ∀err_i ∈ T_j
    L_j = GreedyAbs (T_j) {emit only nodes yielding error
        higher than minError}
end for
L = merge(L_j lists)
return {L[0], .., L[B − |bestCroot|]}
```

$logR + 1$, each mapper runs GreedyAbs exactly $logR + 2$ times; one for every node in $path_k$ and one for the empty set. Thus, the running-time complexity for the level-1 workers is $O\left((logR + 2)\, Nlog^2N\right) = O\left(logRNlog^2N\right)$. For a fixed size of base sub-trees, it holds that $R \sim N$, that is for a new $N' = 2^kN$ the new size of the root sub-tree will be $R' = 2^kR$ and so our solution is linearly scalable, as there is only a constant overhead in the running-time complexity of a level-1 worker. The running-time complexity of a level-2 worker is $O(N)$, as it only merges the already sorted outputs from the previous stage of execution.

An interesting question relates the size of the base and root sub-trees. Does the size of the sub-trees affect performance? Which is a "good" size for them? We study again the running-time complexity for a level-1 worker. Let us denote with S the size of a base sub-tree. It holds that $N = R + R \cdot S$. Consider now the same dataset N, but differently partitioned, so as $R' = 2^kR$. Since the dataset is the same, we have:

$$R + R \cdot S = R' + R' \cdot S' \Rightarrow S' = \frac{S+1}{2^k} - 1$$

So, the complexity becomes:

$$O\left(logR'S'log^2S'\right) = O\left((logR + k)\left(\frac{S+1}{2^k} - 1\right) log^2\left(\frac{S+1}{2^k} - 1\right)\right) = O\left(logRSlog^2S\right) \quad (9)$$

Next, we examine the communication complexity between level-1 and level-2 workers. In the worst case, where each node is discarded with a different error, S key-values are emitted for each $C_{root} \in C$. As $|C| = R+1$, there are $O(RS)$ emitted key-values. In practice, the communication is much lower, as with the described algorithm many discarded nodes are compacted to a single emitted key-value.

Finally, we compute the impact that the size of the sub-trees has on communication. As before, we consider a different partitioning with R', S'. It holds that:

$$O\left(R'S'\right) = O\left(2^kR\left(\frac{S+1}{2^k} - 1\right)\right) = O(RS)$$

We see that the size of the base sub-trees does not asymptotically affect neither running-time nor communication.

5.4 Maximum Relative Error

Minimizing the maximum relative error is arguably more essential compared to absolute error minimization in approximate query processing, as the same absolute error in two different data values may express huge differences in relative error. At the same time, relative error measures tend to be inordinately dominated by small data values. For instance, returning 2 as the approximate answer for 1 amounts to an 100% relative error, while in fact it is insignificant in a data context dominated by much larger values. In order to overcome such problems, several techniques have been developed for combining absolute and relative error metrics [31]. As in earlier approaches ([12], [13]), we have opted for the relative error metric with a sanity-bound S > 0. Our aim is to produce wavelet synopses in near-linear time and space such that, for each approximation $\hat{d}_i$ of a data value d_i, the ratio is kept lower than a feasible bound.

For this problem, in [22] the GreedyRel algorithm is presented. GreedyRel follows the greedy paradigm introduced in Section 5.1, wherein, instead of using MA_k, it chooses to discard the coefficient with the minimum *maximum potential relative* error, defined as follows:

$$MR_k = max_{d_j \in leaves_k}\left\{\frac{|err_j - \delta_{jk} \cdot c_k|}{max\left(|d_j|, S\right)}\right\} \quad (10)$$

Nevertheless, the four error quantities of Equation 8 cannot be used for the calculation or update of the MR_k. The reason is the denominator in Equation 10, which implies that the effect a coefficient c_k is different in the signed relative error of different data values.

In order to provide a scalable solution to this problem, we use a similar approach with that of DGreedyAbs, but instead of using GreedyAbs at the workers, we use GreedyRel.

6. EXPERIMENTAL EVALUATION

In the experimental Section we focus on evaluating the utility of the proposed distributed algorithms with respect to their efficiency (measuring creation time and approximation accuracy), data- and resource-based scalability and discuss parameters that affect their performance. All algorithms are implemented in Java. The distributed algorithms were developed using the MapReduce programming model.

Datasets. The experiments were conducted using both synthetic and real datasets. Synthetic data (SYN) allows easy testing over different data distributions and value ranges. Distributions utilized are uniform and zipfian (with exponents 0.7 and 1.5). Data values lie between $[0, M]$, with $M \in \{1K, 100K, 1000K\}$. For the real-life datasets we utilize NYCT [2] and WD [1]. NYCT describes taxi trips in the New York City in 2013 containing records for the trip time in seconds. WD consists of observations on wind direction that were captured by sensors in the U.S.A. during the hurricanes Ike, Bill, Bertha and Katrina. Wind direction is reported in azimuth degrees. Both datasets were partitioned

Table 3: Characteristics of NYCT and WD datasets

Name	#Records	Avg	Stdv	Max
NYCT2M	2M	672	483	10800
NYCT4M	4M	511	519.5	10800
NYCT8M	8M	255	646.6	10800
NYCT16M	16M	127	745	10800
NYCT32M	32M	63	3566.3	4293410
NYCT64M	64M	31	25410.3	4294966
WD2M	2M	121	119.7	655
WD4M	4M	122	119.9	655
WD8M	8M	138	119.4	655
WD16M	16M	127	118.8	655

in order to test scalability over different sizes. The smallest partition comprised the first $2M$ records, while each subsequent partition was twice as big as the previous one. Table 3 gives an overview of all real datasets used.

Platform setup. For our deployment platform, we used a Hadoop 2.6.0 cluster of 9 machines, each featuring eight Intel(R) Xeon(R) CPU E5405 @ 2.00GHz cores and 8 GB of main memory. One machine was used as the master node with the remaining ones setup as slaves. Each slave was allowed to run simultaneously up to 5 map tasks and 2 reduce tasks. Each of these tasks was assigned 1 physical core and 1 GB of main memory. For all the remaining properties, we kept the default Hadoop configuration.

DGreedyAbs and DIndirectHaar were deployed on the described platform. For the centralized algorithms, i.e., GreedyAbs and IndirectHaar, we used one machine with the same configuration as the ones of our Hadoop cluster.

6.1 Scalability

In this subsection, we assess the scalability of the algorithms with respect to the sub-tree size, the budget space for the synopsis B, the number of datapoints N and the number of tasks running in parallel. For the scalability experiments of this Section, we use a synthetic dataset of uniformly distributed data values in the range of $[0, 1K]$.

Varying sub-tree size. In the described distributed algorithms and according to the proposed partitioning schemes, each worker is assigned to process a sub-tree of the error tree. A first question we need to answer is how the size of the local sub-problems affects the overall performance of the algorithm. Figure 5a presents the running-time of the DIndirectHaar and DGreedyAbs algorithms when different sub-tree sizes are used. We examine values from $131K$ (2^{17}) to $1M$ (2^{20}) nodes per sub-tree. Values smaller than $131K$ are not appropriate as the resulting partitions are too small and incur a very high overhead to Hadoop. Similarly, values bigger than $1M$ do not fit in our mapper's main memory, degrading performance. For this experiment we use a dataset of $N = 17M$ and a budget space $B = N/8$. Figure 5a shows that the size of the sub-trees does not significantly affect the running-time of the job. This observation verifies the theoretical complexity for both algorithms. For the remainder of the experiments we consider a sub-tree size of $1M$ nodes for both algorithms.

Varying budget space. In the next experiment we examine the scalability to the budget space B. We run both DGreedyAbs and DIndirectHaar for a data size $N = 17M$ and we vary B from $N/64$ to $N/8$. Results are shown in Figure 5b. The running-time of DGreedyAbs is not considerably affected by the size of the synopsis. This is not always true for the DIndirectHaar algorithm. As we can see for $B = 0.5M$ for DIndirectHaar, the running-time may decrease as B is increased. This is because higher B-values lead to tighter errors and thus higher convergence rate for the algorithm. As the running-time of our algorithms is not significantly affected by B, for all subsequent experiments, we consider $B = N/8$.

Varying data size and number of parallel tasks. Figures 5c, 5d show the scalability with respect to N and the number of tasks running in parallel for DGreedyAbs and DIndirectHaar respectively. We vary the datasize from 2M to 537M datapoints for all the algorithms and the number of parallel map tasks from 10 to 40. For DGreedyAbs, we fix the number of reducers to four, as they do not have a high impact on performance and for DIndirectHaar we use only one reducer. We also compare both algorithms with the corresponding centralized implementations in order to assess the difference in performance. For DIndirectHaar, we set the parameter δ to 50, as for this value it achieves the best running-time results. We also note that the y-axis follows a logarithmic scale in these Figures.

Both algorithms scale linearly with the dataset size. The running-time is almost constant at first, when all data can be processed fully in parallel, and is linearly growing as the cluster is fully utilized and more tasks need to be serialized for execution. Linear scalability is also observed with the number of parallel running tasks. By halving the capacity of the cluster, running-time is doubled for DGreedyAbs and is increased by a factor of 1.7 on average for DIndirectHaar.

Compared to the centralized GreedyAbs, DGreedyAbs is 7.4× faster for a dataset of 17M datapoints. For sizes greater than $17M$ points, neither GreedyAbs nor IndirectHaar could run, as their execution demanded more main memory than the available 8GB. In Figure 5d, we see that IndirectHaar is faster than DIndirectHaar when the dataset size is small or there are few parallel running tasks. That is because the centralized implementation loads the whole dataset in memory and the multiple jobs required by IndirectHaar do not need to perform I/O operations. Therefore, in order to get benefit from DIndirectHaar, we need large datasets and compute-intensive jobs, where parallelization can be exploited. The degree of compute-intensity of a job is dependent on the dataset. We remind that the complexity of IndirectHaar (DIndirectHaar) is $O\left(\left(\frac{\mathcal{E}}{\delta}\right)^2 N\left(log\epsilon^* + logN\right)\right)$. For two same-sized datasets, running-time is determined by the term $\left(\frac{\mathcal{E}}{\delta}\right)^2$, which is dataset-specific.

6.2 Dataset impact

In this subsection, we use synthetic datasets to evaluate the impact of different data distributions and value ranges on both running-time and approximation quality. For all the experiments in this subsection, we use datasets of size $N = 17M$ and synopsis size $B = N/8$.

Varying distribution and δ. As the parameter δ of DIndirectHaar provides a "knob" for tuning the tradeoff between resource requirements and solution quality, in Figure 6 we show the impact of data distribution on DIndirectHaar when different δ-values are used. The main observation is that biased distributions favor both the synopsis construction time and the approximation quality [28]. In Figure 6a, we see that for the Zipf-0.7 distribution and for all δ-values, the algorithm is about 25% faster compared to the Uniform

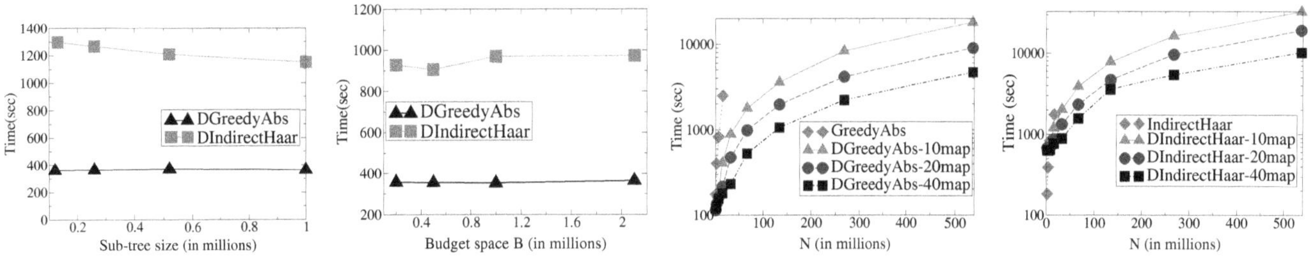

(a) Scalability with the sub-tree size.

(b) Scalability with the budget space

(c) Scalability of DGreedyAbs with N and cluster size.

(d) Scalability of DIndirectHaar with N and cluster size.

Figure 5: Scalability with the sub-tree size, budget space, dataset size and number of parallel tasks

distribution. Furthermore, the run for the Zipf-1.5 distribution outperforms the one for Zipf-0.7 by 45% when $\delta = 10$ and 20% when $\delta = 20$. Accordingly, in Figure 6b we see that when the Zipf-1.5 distribution is the case, the maximum absolute error is 8.4 times smaller than the one achieved for the Uniform data.

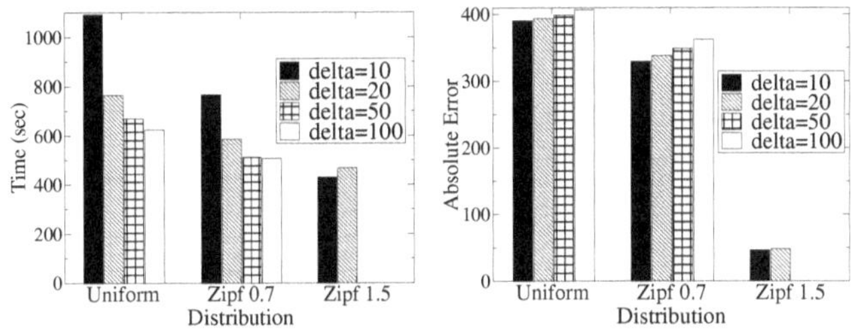

(a) Running-time

(b) Approximation quality

Figure 6: Impact of data distribution and δ on the performance and approximation quality of DIndirectHaar.

We also see that usually the smaller δ is, the higher is the running-time of the algorithm and the better the approximation quality, since more candidate values are examined for the incoming values and the wavelet coefficients. For values of δ equal to 50 or 100 we see that the algorithm reaches its lower bound of execution time on this data and thus, higher values for δ do not affect performance. For the Zipf-1.5, we see that the run for $\delta = 10$ outperforms the one for $\delta = 20$. As we get more approximate results for higher values of δ, DIndirectHaar requires more jobs to converge and provide the final answer. Moreover, the algorithm could not run for Zipf-1.5 and $\delta = 50, 100$ as these values were higher than the space they need to quantize.

Varying distribution and value ranges. Figure 7 shows how both DIndirectHaar and DGreedyAbs are affected by the range of dataset values. For the DIndirectHaar, we use $\delta = 20$, as it could not run for the Zipf-1.5 distribution when higher values for δ were used. For both algorithms and for all data distributions, we observe that datasets with wide ranges to select values from, lead to higher running-time and maximum absolute error. Intuitively, the larger the range of data values, the more likely are discontinuities present and thus, more coefficients are needed for an accurate synopsis. Since we keep the budget space fixed to $N/8$, we expect the maximum error to increase with the value range. In Figures 7b and 7d we observe that for the Uniform and the Zipf-0.7 distributions, an increase of an order of magnitude in the range of values is reflected to a corresponding increase to the maximum absolute error.

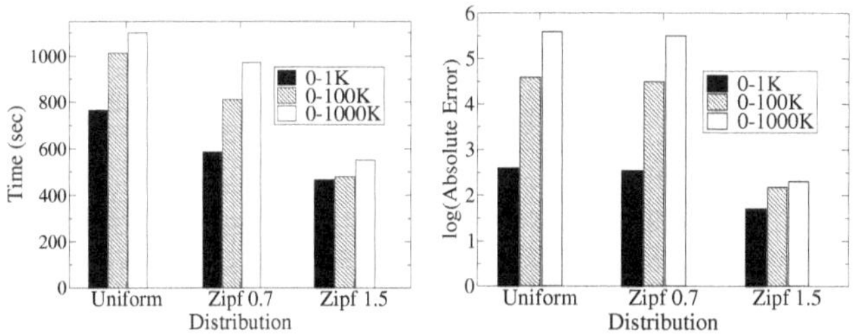

(a) DIndirectHaar Running-time

(b) DIndirectHaar Approximation quality

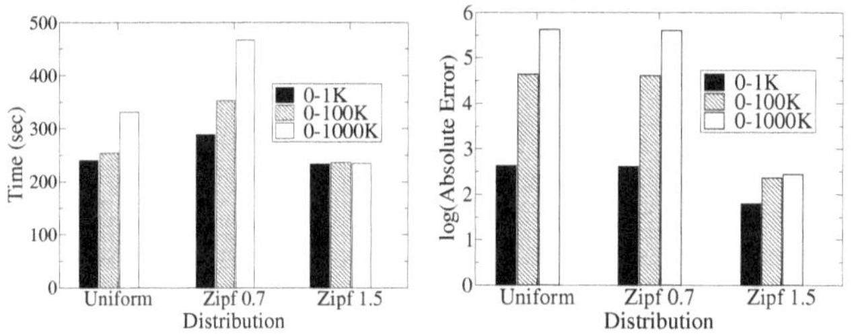

(c) DGreedyAbs running-time

(d) DGreedyAbs Approximation quality

Figure 7: Impact of different data value ranges and distributions on the performance and approximation quality.

However, as we can see from the example of the Zipf-1.5 distribution for both algorithms, both the achieved running-time and error for very biased datasets are very robust to changes in the range of data values. Moreover, in Figures 7a and 7c we observe that, for all distributions, running-time is more affected by the range of data values for DIndirectHaar than for DGreedyAbs. For example, the running-time of DIndirectHaar for the range $[0, 100K]$ is 25% higher than for $[0, 1K]$ for both Uniform and Zipf-0.7 distributions. The corresponding numbers for DGreedyAbs are 5% for the Uniform and 15% for the Zipf-0.7.

In Figure 7c, we notice a counter-intuitive result: The best running-time is achieved for the Uniform distribution. This is due to the I/O cost between the map and the reduce phase. In the case of the Uniform distribution, when the root of the error tree is not retained in the C_{root}, the first deletion of a node causes a large absolute error X. This first deleted node c_k happens to be located in the last level of the error tree and thus it affects only the nodes in $path_k$, i.e., $logS$ nodes. The algorithm continues by discarding other nodes. As the deletion of the majority of the nodes causes an error $e < X$, in this case, almost the whole sub-tree is emitted as a single key-value achieving high I/O-efficiency.

6.3 Direct Comparison

In this subsection we compare DGreedyAbs and DIndirectHaar with each other, as well as with their centralized counterparts using real-life datasets. Furthermore, we compare them against algorithms that construct a conventional synopsis (i.e., L_2-optimal). As these algorithms are less compute-intensive, we want to investigate the tradeoffs in running-time and produced maximum error. For constructing the conventional synopsis we implement CON, a parallel algorithm that uses the partitioning scheme described in Section 4 and retains the B largest coefficients in absolute normalized value. We also use Send-Coef [21], which computes in parallel the conventional synopsis by using a different partitioning. Both CON and Send-Coef are described in detail in Appendix A. For the approximation quality experiments, we do not include IndirectHaar and Send-Coef, as they theoretically achieve exactly the same results with DIndirectHaar and CON respectively.

NYCT dataset. In Figure 8, we present the results for the NYCT dataset. For the IndirectHaar and the DIndirectHaar we set $\delta = 50$, as for this value they achieve the best execution times. The construction of an accurate synopsis for this dataset is a difficult task to accomplish as it contains values of high magnitude and variance. In Table 3, we see that the NYCT64M dataset for example, has a maximum value 4294966 and standard deviation 25410.3. The difficulty in approximating NYCT is illustrated in Figure 8b, where the maximum absolute error for $B = N/8$ is more than 550 for all data sizes and algorithms. However, the most important deduced result from Figure 8b is that DGreedyAbs does not compromise approximation quality for the performance gain it offers and achieves the same maximum absolute error with its centralized counterpart. The synopsis produced by DGreedyAbs is 3 to 4.5 times more accurate, with respect to max_abs, than the conventional one.

Figure 8a presents the running-time results for the same dataset. With the maximum absolute error over 570 for all data sizes, the multiplicative factor $\left(\frac{\varepsilon}{\delta}\right)^2$ of the complexity formula of IndirectHaar and DIndirectHaarand is equal to 121. As such, for this dataset, the execution of the DP algorithms is very compute-intensive. Nevertheless, as we have already mentioned, datasets that demand intensive computations favor DIndirectHaar over IndirectHaar which is 2.7 times slower for a 17M dataset. As seen in Section 6.2, the execution of DGreedyAbs is more robust to different datasets and thus, its running-time is not significantly affected by the data distribution. DGreedyAbs is the most time-efficient algorithm, targeting maximum absolute error, being 5× faster than GreedyAbs for a 17M dataset and 1.8×–2.9× faster than DIndirectHaar for all data sizes. As the conventional synopsis is easier to be computed, we observe CON to be 4.2× and Send-Coef 2.8× faster on average than DGreedyAbs. CON outperforms Send-Coef, due to its partitioning scheme that preserves sub-tree locality.

WD dataset. Figure 9 shows the results for the WD dataset. In this experiment, we run IndirectHaar and DIndirectHaar with $\delta = 20$, as they could not run for larger values of δ. The values of this data set do not present large discontinuities and can thus be more easily approximated. This is verified in Figure 9b, where the maximum absolute errors are about 5 times smaller than the corresponding ones for the NYCT dataset. Regarding approximation quality, DGreedyAbs achieves again the same maximum absolute error

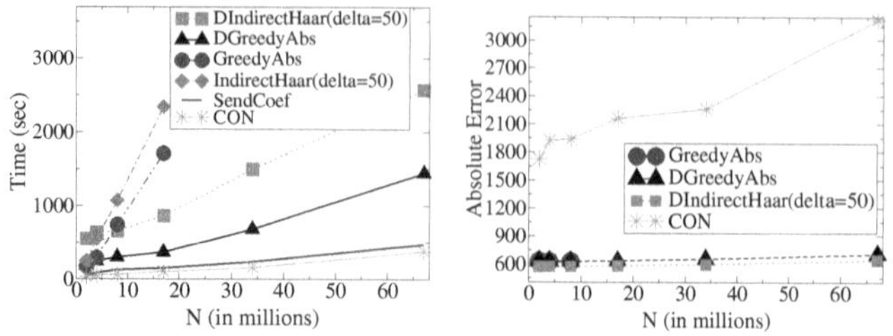

(a) Running-time (b) Approximation quality

Figure 8: Comparison for the NYCT dataset, $B = N/8$.

with GreedyAbs and on average 2.6× smaller than CON.

With a maximum absolute error about 125, the factor $\left(\frac{\varepsilon}{\delta}\right)^2$ is only 36 and thus, the execution of the DP algorithms demands fewer computations than for the NYCT dataset. Similarly to Section 6.1, in Figure 9a we see that IndirectHaar outperforms DIndirectHaar for data sizes up to 8M datapoints. We also observe that for this dataset and for all data sizes, IndirectHaar outperforms GreedyAbs and CON outperforms Send-Coef. Still, the most efficient algorithm, that targets the minimization of maximum error metrics, is DGreedyAbs as it outperforms GreedyAbs by a factor of 4.4 for a $17M$ dataset and achieves half the running-time of DIndirectHaar for all data sizes.

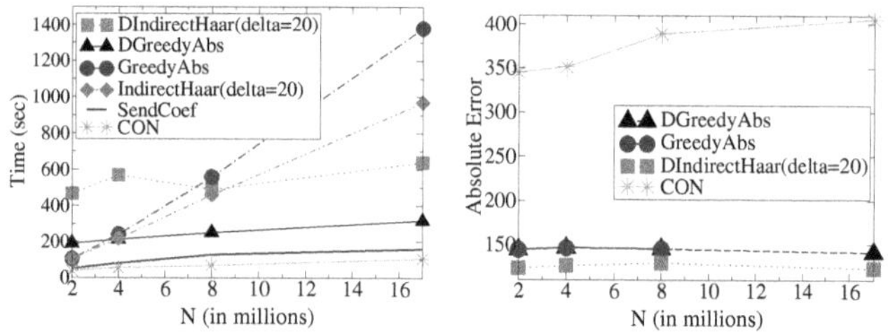

(a) Running-time (b) Approximation quality

Figure 9: Comparison for the WD dataset, $B = N/8$.

7. CONCLUSIONS

In this paper, we have examined the problem of wavelet thresholding aiming at the minimization of maximum error metrics. Having established that the existing approaches do not scale for big datasets, we focused on designing algorithms with linear scalability over scale-out infrastructures. We first presented a novel technique that allows the parallel decomposition of an error tree and can be used to support all the existing DP algorithms for the problem. In order to demonstrate the power of the proposed technique, we applied it on IndirectHaar thus implementing the DIndirectHaar algorithm. Our results show that DIndirectHaar scales linearly to data sizes that IndirectHaar is incapable of processing. Moreover, in order to further improve the running-time for the synopsis construction, we proposed DGreedyAbs, a new heuristic-based algorithm based on GreedyAbs. DGreedyAbs is over 7 times faster than GreedyAbs for a 17M dataset and 2–4 times faster than DIndirectHaar for all data sizes. Despite its efficient execution time, DGreedyAbs does not compromise quality, as in all experiments it achieves the same approximation results with its centralized counterpart.

8. ACKNOWLEDGEMENTS

The research leading to these results has been partially supported by the European Commission, in terms of the ASAP FP7 ICT Project under grant agreement no 619706.

9. REFERENCES

[1] Linked sensor data. https://wiki.knoesis.org/index.php/SSW_Datasets.

[2] Nyc taxi trip data 2013. https://archive.org/details/nycTaxiTripData2013.

[3] The Internet of Things, Hadoop, and the Big Data Approach. http://data-informed.com/internet-things-hadoop-big-data-approach/.

[4] S. Acharya, P. B. Gibbons, V. Poosala, and S. Ramaswamy. Join synopses for approximate query answering. In *ACM SIGMOD Record*, volume 28, pages 275–286. ACM, 1999.

[5] S. Agarwal, B. Mozafari, A. Panda, H. Milner, S. Madden, and I. Stoica. Blinkdb: queries with bounded errors and bounded response times on very large data. In *Proceedings of the 8th ACM European Conference on Computer Systems*, pages 29–42. ACM, 2013.

[6] N. Alon, Y. Matias, and M. Szegedy. The space complexity of approximating the frequency moments. In *Proceedings of the twenty-eighth annual ACM symposium on Theory of computing*, pages 20–29. ACM, 1996.

[7] L. Amsaleg, M. J. Franklin, A. Tomasic, and T. Urhan. Improving responsiveness for wide-area data access. In *IEEE Data Engineering Bulletin*. Citeseer, 1997.

[8] P. Cao and Z. Wang. Efficient top-k query calculation in distributed networks. In *Proceedings of the twenty-third annual ACM symposium on Principles of distributed computing*, pages 206–215. ACM, 2004.

[9] K. Chakrabarti, M. Garofalakis, R. Rastogi, and K. Shim. Approximate query processing using wavelets. *The VLDB Journal–The International Journal on Very Large Data Bases*, 10(2-3):199–223, 2001.

[10] G. Cormode, M. Garofalakis, P. J. Haas, and C. Jermaine. Synopses for massive data: Samples, histograms, wavelets, sketches. *Foundations and Trends in Databases*, 4(1–3):1–294, 2012.

[11] G. Cormode, M. Garofalakis, and D. Sacharidis. Fast approximate wavelet tracking on streams. In *Advances in Database Technology-EDBT 2006*, pages 4–22. Springer, 2006.

[12] M. Garofalakis and P. B. Gibbons. Wavelet synopses with error guarantees. In *Proceedings of the 2002 ACM SIGMOD international conference on Management of data*, pages 476–487. ACM, 2002.

[13] M. Garofalakis and A. Kumar. Deterministic wavelet thresholding for maximum-error metrics. In *Proceedings of the twenty-third ACM SIGMOD-SIGACT-SIGART symposium on Principles of database systems*, pages 166–176. ACM, 2004.

[14] P. B. Gibbons and Y. Matias. New sampling-based summary statistics for improving approximate query answers. In *ACM SIGMOD Record*, volume 27, pages 331–342. ACM, 1998.

[15] P. B. Gibbons, Y. Matias, and V. Poosala. Fast incremental maintenance of approximate histograms. In *VLDB*, volume 97, pages 466–475, 1997.

[16] A. C. Gilbert, Y. Kotidis, S. Muthukrishnan, and M. Strauss. Surfing wavelets on streams: One-pass summaries for approximate aggregate queries. In *VLDB*, volume 1, pages 79–88, 2001.

[17] A. C. Gilbert, Y. Kotidis, S. Muthukrishnan, and M. J. Strauss. One-pass wavelet decompositions of data streams. *Knowledge and Data Engineering, IEEE Transactions on*, 15(3):541–554, 2003.

[18] S. Guha. Space efficiency in synopsis construction algorithms. In *Proceedings of the 31st international conference on Very large data bases*, pages 409–420. VLDB Endowment, 2005.

[19] Y. E. Ioannidis and V. Poosala. Histogram-based approximation of set-valued query-answers. In *VLDB*, volume 99, pages 174–185, 1999.

[20] H. V. Jagadish, N. Koudas, S. Muthukrishnan, V. Poosala, K. C. Sevcik, and T. Suel. Optimal histograms with quality guarantees. In *VLDB*, volume 98, pages 275–286, 1998.

[21] J. Jestes, K. Yi, and F. Li. Building wavelet histograms on large data in mapreduce. *Proceedings of the VLDB Endowment*, 5(2):109–120, 2011.

[22] P. Karras and N. Mamoulis. One-pass wavelet synopses for maximum-error metrics. In *Proceedings of the 31st international conference on Very large data bases*, pages 421–432. VLDB Endowment, 2005.

[23] P. Karras and N. Mamoulis. The haar+ tree: a refined synopsis data structure. In *Data Engineering, 2007. ICDE 2007. IEEE 23rd International Conference on*, pages 436–445. IEEE, 2007.

[24] P. Karras, D. Sacharidis, and N. Mamoulis. Exploiting duality in summarization with deterministic guarantees. In *Proceedings of the 13th ACM SIGKDD international conference on Knowledge discovery and data mining*, pages 380–389. ACM, 2007.

[25] T. Li, Q. Li, S. Zhu, and M. Ogihara. A survey on wavelet applications in data mining. *ACM SIGKDD Explorations Newsletter*, 4(2):49–68, 2002.

[26] Y. Matias, J. S. Vitter, and M. Wang. Wavelet-based histograms for selectivity estimation. In *ACM SIGMOD Record*, volume 27, pages 448–459. ACM, 1998.

[27] S. Muthukrishnan. Subquadratic algorithms for workload-aware haar wavelet synopses. In *FSTTCS 2005: Foundations of Software Technology and Theoretical Computer Science*, pages 285–296. Springer, 2005.

[28] C. Pang, Q. Zhang, D. Hansen, and A. Maeder. Unrestricted wavelet synopses under maximum error bound. In *Proceedings of the 12th International Conference on Extending Database Technology: Advances in Database Technology*, pages 732–743. ACM, 2009.

[29] E. J. Stollnitz, T. D. DeRose, and D. H. Salesin. *Wavelets for computer graphics: theory and applications*. Morgan Kaufmann, 1996.

[30] I. Trummer and C. Koch. An incremental anytime algorithm for multi-objective query optimization. In *Proceedings of the 2015 ACM SIGMOD International Conference on Management of Data*, pages 1941–1953. ACM, 2015.

[31] J. S. Vitter and M. Wang. Approximate computation of multidimensional aggregates of sparse data using wavelets. In *ACM SIGMOD Record*, volume 28, 1999.

APPENDIX

A. CONSTRUCTING THE CONVENTIONAL SYNOPSIS IN PARALLEL

In this Appendix, we describe in detail the CON and Send-Coef [21] algorithms used in Section 6.3 for computing the conventional wavelet synopsis. Moreover, we describe the Send-V and H-WTopk algorithms that also compute the conventional synopsis in parallel and are presented in [21]. All the algorithms in [21] compute wavelet synopses over histograms. Thus, in order to compare them against our algorithms, we first modify them not to compute histograms and perform the wavelet transform directly on the input data. For all the descriptions that follow, we denote N as the dataset size, m the number of map tasks, S the input size of a map task and R the size of the root sub-tree in datapoints.

A.1 The CON Algorithm

In order to compute the conventional synopsis in parallel, we partition the data as described in Section 4 (see Figure 3). Each mapper reads a portion of the input in the size of a power of two and locally constructs the corresponding sub-tree by pairwise averaging and differencing coefficients, as explained in Section 2. As the wavelet transform is of linear complexity and the mapper computes the coefficients only for its local data, the computational complexity of each map task is $O(S)$. After the construction of the sub-trees is over, each mapper emits all the computed coefficients to the reduce stage. Thus, the communication between the map and reduce phase is $O(N)$. The reducer reads all the coefficients that are computed in the map phase and inserts them in a priority queue, where only the B largest ones in absolute normalized value are retained. It also computes the wavelet coefficients of the root sub-tree and inserts them in the queue as well. When this process is over, there are B coefficients in the queue which comprise the conventional synopsis.

A.2 Send-V

The simplest algorithm presented in [21] for the computation of a conventional synopsis is Send-V. The Send-V algorithm computes a histogram in the map phase of the job. The reducer centrally computes the wavelet coefficients and retains the B largest ones. As the histogram computation is not required in our case, Send-V is, in effect, a sequential algorithm, where the reducer reads and centrally computes the wavelet transform for all the input data.

A.3 Send-Coef

Send-Coef is based on another method to compute wavelet coefficients, that is used especially in streaming settings. This method uses the wavelet basis vectors. The first wavelet basis vector is $\psi_0 = [1,..,1]/\sqrt{N}$, where $[1,..,1]$ is a vector of ones. To define the other $N-1$ basis vectors, we first introduce, for $j = 1,..,logN$ and $k = 0,..,2^j - 1$, the vector:

$$\phi_{j,k}(l) = \begin{cases} 1 & k\frac{N}{2^j} + 1 \leq l \leq k\frac{N}{2^j} + \frac{N}{2^j} \\ 0 & elsewhere \end{cases} \tag{11}$$

For $j = 1,..,logN - 1$ and $k = 0,..,2^j - 1$, we define the i-th wavelet basis vector for $i = 2^j + k + 1$ as $\psi_i = (-\phi_{j+1,2k} + \phi_{j+1,2k+1}) / \sqrt{\frac{N}{2^j}}$, where $\sqrt{\frac{N}{2^j}}$ is a scaling factor. If A is the data vector, the wavelet coefficients are the dot product of A with these wavelet basis vectors, i.e., $w_i = \langle A, \psi_i \rangle$, for $i = 1,..,N$.

The distributed computation of Send-Coef is based on the following observation:

$$w_i = \langle A, \psi_i \rangle = \sum_{j=1}^{m} \langle A_j, \psi_i \rangle,$$

where A_j is the j-th partition of the initial input data. Thus, every wavelet coefficient is a linear combination of the data values that belong to its sub-tree in the error tree.

Send-Coef partitions the data in a different way than the one proposed in Section 4. Each mapper takes up as many datapoints that fit as possible in a HDFS block size. The block size does not need to be aligned to a power of two. For every datapoint d_i, the mapper computes its contribution to the final value of every wavelet coefficient in $path_{d_i}$. Thus, a mapper partially computes all the coefficients along the path from its datapoints to the root of the error tree and thus sub-tree locality is not preserved. The reducer computes the final coefficients by aggregating the partially computed values and then retains the B largest ones in absolute normalized value. Algorithm 7 gives the pseudocode for the mappers of the Send-Coef algorithm.

As data locality is not preserved and for every data value we need to compute its contribution to $logN + 1$ nodes (the path to the root), the computational complexity of a mapper is $O(SlogN)$. Furthermore, every mapper emits $O(S(logN - logS))$ key-values to the reducer. By having m mappers, the whole communication cost is $O(mS(logN - logS)) = O(N(logN - logS))$. Compared to Send-Coef, our approach in Section A.1 achieves better computational complexity by a factor of $logN$ and communication cost by $logN - logS$.

Algorithm 7 *Send-CoefMapper*

Require: S: mapper input data
for all datapoints $d_i \in S$ **do**
  for all error tree nodes $j \in path_{d_i}$ **do**
    compute contribution $c_{i,j}$ of d_i to coefficient c_j
    if c_j is fully computed **then** emit (j, c_j)
  end for
end for
for all datapoints $d_i \in S$ **do**
  for all error tree nodes $j \in path_{d_i}$ **do**
    if c_j is partially computed **then** emit $(j, c_{i,j})$
  end for
end for

A.4 H-WTopk

In order to reduce the communication cost between the map and the reduce phase, the H-WTopk algorithm is proposed in [21]. H-WTopk is based on the TPUT [8] algorithm for the distributed top-k problem. In contrast to TPUT, H-WTopk can handle both positive and negative values, as both are possible for a wavelet coefficient. The intuition behind the algorithm is to use a partial sum to prune items that cannot be in the top-k. Thus, a mapper does not need to send all of its data to the reducer but only a set of candidate nodes, according to the local partial sums. The algorithm requires three communication rounds between the mappers and the reducer. For a coefficient x, $c(x)$ denotes its value and $c_j(x)$ its partially computed value at mapper j.

Round 1: Each mapper first emits the coefficients with the k highest and k lowest (i.e., most negative) values. For each coefficient x seen at the reducer, a lower bound $\tau(x)$ is computed on its total value's magnitude $|c(x)|$ (i.e., $|c(x)| \geq \tau(x)$), as follows. First, an upper bound $\tau^+(x)$ and a lower bound $\tau^-(x)$ are computed on its total value $c(x)$ (i.e., $\tau^-(x) \leq c(x) \leq \tau^+(x)$): If a mapper sends out the value of x, its exact value is added. Otherwise, for $\tau^+(x)$, the k-th highest value this mapper sends out is added and for $\tau^-(x)$ the k-th lowest value is added. Then we set $\tau(x) = 0$ if $\tau^+(x)$ and $\tau^-(x)$ have different signs and $\tau(x) = min\{|\tau^+(x)|, |\tau^-(x)|\}$ otherwise. Doing so ensures $\tau^-(x) \leq c(x) \leq \tau^+(x)$ and $|c(x)| \geq \tau(x)$. Now, the k-th largest $\tau(x)$, denoted as T_1, is used as a threshold for the magnitude of the top-k coefficients.

Round 2: A mapper j next emits all local coefficients x having $|c_j(x)| > T_1/m$. This ensures a coefficient in the true top-k in magnitude must be sent by at least one mapper after this round, because if a coefficient is not sent, its aggregated value's magnitude can be no higher than T_1.

Now, with more values available from each mapper, upper and lower bounds $\tau^+(x), \tau^-(x)$ are refined for each coefficient $x \in L$, where L is the set of coefficients ever received. If a mapper did not send the value for some x, T_1/m $(-T_1/m)$ is now used for computing $\tau^+(x)$ $(\tau^-(x))$. This produces a new better threshold, T_2 (calculated in the same way as computing T_1 with improved $\tau(x)$'s), on the top-k coefficients' magnitude.

Next, coefficients are further pruned from L. For any $x \in L$ a new threshold $\tau'(x) = max\{|\tau^+(x)|, |\tau^-(x)|\}$ is computed based on refined upper and lower bounds $\tau^+(x), \tau^-(x)$. If $\tau'(x) < T_2$, coefficient x is deleted from L. The final top-k coefficients must be in the set L.

Round 3: Finally, the values of all coefficients in L are requested from each mapper. Then the aggregated values of exactly these coefficients are computed, and the k of largest magnitude among them are selected as the synopsis.

A.5 Experimental Evaluation of Algorithms for the Conventional Synopsis

For any given dataset, all four described algorithms produce exactly the same synopses. Thus, we do not need to compare them in terms of approximation quality. In this Section, we evaluate their performance with respect to running time. For the evaluation we use the NYCT and WD datasets over the same platform presented in Section 6. For all the experiments, we have configured a cluster for 20 available map and 1 reduce slots.

Figure 10 shows the running time results for both datasets when a synopsis of size $B = N/8$ is requested. Since Send-V ends up to be a sequential algorithm, it presents much worse running time performance than CON and Send-Coef for both examined datasets.

In Figure 10, we also observe that our algorithm (CON) is the most time-efficient for computing the conventional synopsis. The performance gain of CON stems from its locality-preserving partitioning, which results in less computational and communication complexity. CON is 1.5× faster on average than Send-Coef, that is the second most efficient algorithm, both for the NYCT and the WD datasets.

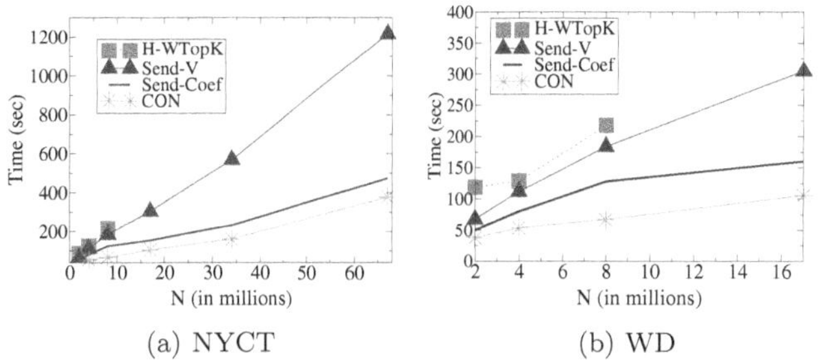

Figure 10: Running time comparison for constructing a conventional synopsis with $B = N/8$.

For both datasets, we observe that despite the communication optimizations, H-WTopk presents the worst performance. Furthermore, for datasizes larger than 8 millions of datapoints, it runs out of memory. This is because of the selected synopsis size. H-WTopk can be very efficient if B is much smaller than the input size of the mapper. Otherwise, since it needs to emit the B largest and B smallest coefficients, it ends up emitting twice the input size. Furthermore, it also has the extra overhead of three MapReduce jobs. In [21], the wavelet transform was applied to a histogram and thus, data had been already compacted and smaller budget space was needed to achieve accurate results. The impact of B in the communication cost is discussed in [21], where the corresponding values were only chosen in the range [10, 50].

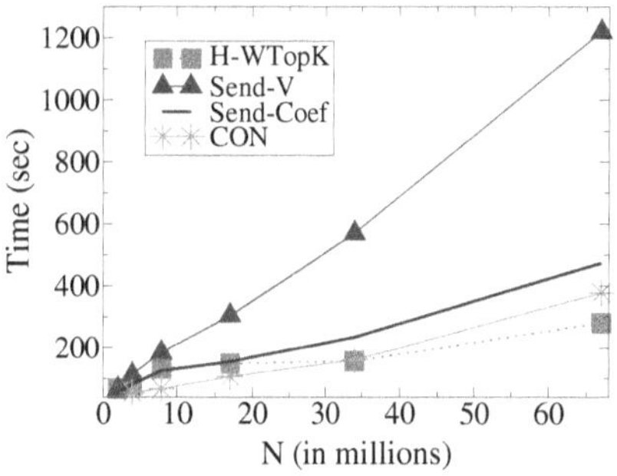

Figure 11: Running time results for the NYCT dataset and B=50.

Figure 11 shows the corresponding results for the NYCT dataset when a synopsis of stable size $B = 50$ is used. This figure verifies the results of [21]: H-WTopk dominates the other approaches only when B is very small and the dataset size large enough to not be affected by the overhead of the three MapReduce jobs. Thus, in our case, where the transform is applied directly on the data and not on a histogram, this algorithm is not of practical use as it is very difficult to construct a good quality synopsis with so few coefficients.

Sample + Seek: Approximating Aggregates with Distribution Precision Guarantee

Bolin Ding[1] Silu Huang[2]* Surajit Chaudhuri[1] Kaushik Chakrabarti[1] Chi Wang[1]
[1]Microsoft Research, Redmond, WA
[2]University of Illinois, Urbana-Champaign, IL
{bolind, surajitc, kaushik, chiw}@microsoft.com, shuang86@illinois.edu

ABSTRACT

Data volumes are growing exponentially for our decision-support systems making it challenging to ensure interactive response time for ad-hoc queries without increasing cost of hardware. Aggregation queries with Group By that produce an aggregate value for every combination of values in the grouping columns are the most important class of ad-hoc queries. As small errors are usually tolerable for such queries, approximate query processing (AQP) has the potential to answer them over very large datasets much faster. In many cases analysts require the distribution of (group, aggvalue) pairs in the estimated answer to be guaranteed within a certain error threshold of the exact distribution. Existing AQP techniques are inadequate for two main reasons. First, users cannot express such guarantees. Second, sampling techniques used in traditional AQP can produce arbitrarily large errors even for SUM queries. To address those limitations, we first introduce a new precision metric, called *distribution precision*, to express such error guarantees. We then study how to provide fast approximate answers to aggregation queries with distribution precision guaranteed within a user-specified error bound. The main challenges are to provide rigorous error guarantees and to handle arbitrary highly selective predicates without maintaining large-sized samples. We propose a novel sampling scheme called *measure-biased sampling* to address the former challenge. For the latter, we propose two new indexes to augment in-memory samples. Like other sampling-based AQP techniques, our solution supports any aggregate that can be estimated from random samples. In addition to deriving theoretical guarantees, we conduct experimental study to compare our system with state-of-the-art AQP techniques and a commercial column-store database system on both synthetic and real enterprise datasets. Our system provides a median speed-up of more than 100x with around 5% distribution error compared with the commercial database.

1. INTRODUCTION

Enterprises are collecting large volumes of data and are increasingly relying on analysis of the data to drive their businesses. For example, data analysts in a retail enterprise slice and dice their sales data to understand the sales performance along different dimensions like product and geographic location with a varying set of filtering conditions. Interactive query response time is critical in such data exploration; studies in human-computer interaction show that the analyst typically loses the analysis context if the response time is above one second [26]. Unfortunately, as data volume (*i.e.*, number of rows) and complexity of filtering conditions increase (*e.g.*, arbitrary user-given logical expression on multiple dimensions), the response time to answer such queries becomes longer unless additional hardware resources are leveraged. Is it possible to fend off the need for additional resources by leveraging the fact that "small" errors are acceptable for such exploratory queries?

For arbitrary SQL queries, it is hard to take advantage of the flexibility of answering queries with "small" errors, because of the difficulty of defining "error" in an easy-to-understand manner. Fortunately, there is a very important class of queries for which we can both crisply formalize the notion of "small" errors and take advantage of this flexibility in bringing down response time using *approximate query processing* (AQP) techniques. A query in this class is a SQL query with aggregation on a few *measure* attributes (*e.g.*, sales and population) along with a filter predicate and a group-by operator (see Section 2.1). Such *aggregation queries* are very common in OLAP and many business intelligence (BI) applications.

Limitations of existing AQP systems. For many tasks, analysts require the returned distribution of (group, aggvalue) pairs to be within a certain error threshold of the exact distribution. Suppose the analyst wants to visualize the (group, aggvalue) pairs using a pie-chart. She would require the error between the two distributions to be small such that the pie-chart based on the returned answer is similar to that based on the exact answer in terms of relative areas for the different groups. Existing sampling-based AQP systems, *e.g.*, in [3, 12, 7, 5], fall short in such tasks for two main reasons:

• *Inadequate semantics of precision metrics*: *Confidence interval (CI)* [3, 5] used by existing AQP systems are inadequate to express the above guarantees. A 90% confidence interval CI $=$ $[\text{est} - w, \text{est} + w]$ means that, informally, with 90% probability (pre-sampling), the resulting CI covers the true value, where est is the estimated value for a group [22]. CI-based techniques measure the error for each group independently, but *not* for the entire distribution: a 90% CI for every group does not mean they are correct for all groups at the same time with 90% probability. What we seek is a precision metric that captures errors across groups. While *mean squared (relative) error (MSE)* [12, 7] provides another alternative to measure precision, MSE can be estimated after the query has been evaluated but cannot be guaranteed in advance.

• *Unbounded (data-dependent) errors*: Consider a SUM query. For a sample S_m of m rows drawn from n rows (in one group) on the

*Work done while visiting Microsoft Research

SIGMOD'16, June 26-July 01, 2016, San Francisco, CA, USA

ISBN 978-1-4503-3531-7/16/06...$15.00

DOI: http://dx.doi.org/10.1145/2882903.2915249

ID	C_1	C_2	C_3	M
1	0	0	0	1
...	0	0	0	1
90	0	0	0	1
91	0	1	0	10
...	0	1	0	10
100	0	1	0	10
101	1	0	0	1
...	1	0	0	1
198	1	0	0	1
199	1	0	0	100
200	1	0	1	100

(a) Example table T: rows 1-90 / 91-100 / 101-198 have the same dimension values

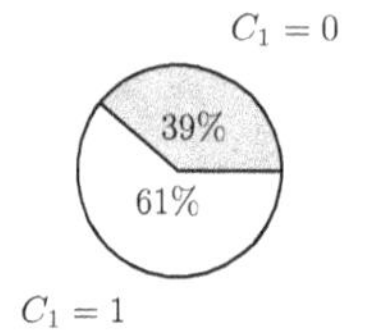

(b) Distribution answer

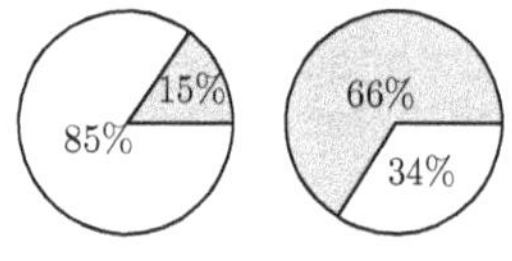

(c) Case I (d) Case II

Figure 1: Table and Answer to aggregation query

measure attribute, the CI width is proportional to $\mathrm{std}(S_m)/\sqrt{m}$ [16, 5] for uniform sampling and stratified sampling – $\mathrm{std}(S_m)$ is the *sample standard deviation* on the measure attribute. In particular, for SUM, the 90% CI width is $w \approx 1.65n \cdot \mathrm{std}(S_m)/\sqrt{m}$ (the constant 1.65 is determined by the confidence level 90% and central limit theorem). This result has a profound implication. Since $\mathrm{std}(S_m)$ depends on data and can be arbitrarily large, the CI width can be arbitrarily large. As a consequence, it is not possible to support AQP with a user-specified error bound in many situations.

We illustrate the above drawbacks using an example.

EXAMPLE 1.1. *Consider a table T with C_1 (state), C_2 (product), C_3 (customer group), a measure M (sales), and 200 rows, in Figure 1(a). An analyst wants to find sales number per state with*

Q: SELECT C_1, SUM(M) FROM T GROUP BY C_1.

The answer is a set of (group, aggvalue)-pairs: {(C_1 = 0, 190), (C_1 = 1, 298)}. We can normalize the answer as a distribution $\mathbf{x}$ $= \langle 190/488, 298/488\rangle = \langle 0.39, 0.61\rangle$ *(pie-chart in Figure 1(b)).*

Suppose a sample of 20 rows are drawn uniformly from T to answer Q. With high chance, 9 rows from rows 1-90 with $M = 1$ and 1 row from rows 91-100 with $M = 10$ are picked for the first group ($C_1 = 0$). For the second group ($C_1 = 1$), there are two cases with high probability. Case I: when exactly one of rows 199 and 200 is in the sample, the answer is estimated as {(C_1 = 0, 19/0.1), (C_1 = 1, 109/0.1)}, which can be normalized as $\langle 19/128, 109/128\rangle = \langle 0.15, 0.85\rangle$ *(pie-chart in Figure 1(c)). Case II: when neither of rows 199 and 200 is taken, the answer is estimated as {(0, 19/0.1), (1, 10/0.1)} and normalized as* $\langle 19/29, 10/29\rangle = \langle 0.66, 0.34\rangle$ *(pie-chart in Figure 1(d)). This shows that uniform sampling can produce large errors. Stratified sampling in [5, 3] and small group sampling in [7] cannot help here. They use different sampling rates for groups of different sizes. But the two groups in the answer to Q have the same size. These techniques end up with drawing uniform samples from each group, and suffer from the same issue.*

As mentioned above, for SUM, *we have the CI width* $w = 1.65n \cdot \mathrm{std}(S_m)/\sqrt{m}$. *For the second group in the above (C_1 = 1), the true value is 298. In Case I, we have* est $= 1090$, *and* $w \approx 1470$ *– CI correctly covers the true value but is too wide as* $\mathrm{std}(S_m)$ *is large. In Case II, we have* est $= 100$, *and* $w = 0$ *(as* $\mathrm{std}(S_m) = 0$*), which does not cover the true value. In both cases, it is difficult to guarantee the error to be within a user-given threshold.*

Contributions. In this paper, we build an AQP system to answer aggregation queries with interactive speed that addresses the above two limitations. It *processes aggregation queries with precision of answers guaranteed within a user-given error bound.* We first focus on queries on single table with predicates and COUNT/SUM aggregates, which are central to many BI tasks. We also describe how our techniques are extended for queries with foreign-key joins on multiple tables, and a large class of predicates and aggregates.

Our approach, referred to as *sample+seek* is driven by several key insights. First, we want to find a way to capture precision of the entire distribution across groups. To address this issue, we introduce the notion of *distribution precision*. Second, we assert that AQP is not effective with unbounded data-dependent errors, as illustrated in Example 1.1. Therefore, we must look beyond traditional uniform/stratified sampling-based techniques to find an effective sampling schema aided by indexes if necessary, which is not subject to unbounded errors and able to deal with a large class of queries, including those with highly selective predicates. To address the second issue, we introduce a combination of novel sampling strategy (*measure-biased sampling*) and indexes (*measure-augmented inverted index* and *low-frequency group index*). We describe these three key aspects of our framework below.

- *Precision metric.* We propose to use, *distribution precision*, to measure the precision of the entire distribution over all groups (as opposed to the precision of individual groups) and to allow the analyst to express the desired guarantees. Distribution precision is defined to be the L^2 distance between normalized distributions of the approximate answer and the exact one. In Example 1.1, the distribution answer $\mathbf{x} = \langle 0.39, 0.61\rangle$. And if we give an approximation $\hat{\mathbf{x}} = \langle 0.40, 0.60\rangle$, their L^2 distance is $\|\mathbf{x}-\hat{\mathbf{x}}\|_2 = \sqrt{0.01^2 + 0.01^2}$ $= 0.014$. The analyst specifies the value of a *single parameter*, error upper bound ϵ, and our system *guarantees* to produce an approximation $\hat{\mathbf{x}}$ s.t. with high probability (*e.g.*, 0.9), $\|\mathbf{x} - \hat{\mathbf{x}}\|_2 \leq \epsilon$.
- *Measure-biased sampling.* We address the challenge of avoiding data-dependent error bound by developing a novel sampling scheme called *measure-biased sampling*. The insight is to pick a row with probability proportional to its value on the measure attribute. For SUM-queries without predicates, we show that a *measure-biased sample* of $\mathrm{O}(1/\epsilon^2)$ rows suffices to give answers under our distribution precision guarantee with errors independent of the (sample) standard deviation of measure values.
- *Indexes for selective predicates.* Large samples have to be maintained to handle queries with highly selective predicates. We address this challenge by building two auxiliary indexes, *measure-augmented inverted index* and *low-frequency group index*, to aid in-memory samples. For selective predicates, we identify rows that satisfy the predicate by looking up these two indexes instead of maintaining prohibitively large samples in memory. The insight is that since we need to lookup rows only for highly selective predicates, we need very few data accesses to guarantee the distribution precision. In particular, we need at most $\mathrm{O}(1/\epsilon^2)$ random I/O's to answer selective queries under our precision guarantee.

Extensibility. Our solution enjoys *the same degree of extensibility* as other sampling-based AQP techniques (*e.g.* [7, 5]) do and thus supports a range of aggregate functions like AVG, STDEV, and COUNT(DISTINCT ·). Specialized summaries like views [6], data cube [18], and histograms [17] do not have such extensibility. Our solution can be easily extended for foreign key joins in a star/snowflake schema. The predicates we can handle range from (dis)conjunctions of constraints on categorical dimensions to range constraints and arbitrary AND-OR logical expressions of them.

Our experiments show that compared to the state of the art AQP systems, our sample+seek solution provides answers with equal or less error in orders of magnitude faster response time.

Organization. Section 2 introduces the class of aggregation queries our system can handle and formalizes our distribution precision guarantee. Section 3 overviews our sample+seek approach and system architecture. Details about the "sample" part, *i.e.*, how to construct and utilize uniform and measure-biased samples, is introduced in Section 4, and the "seek" part, *i.e.*, auxiliary indexes, is in Section 5. Section 6 discusses extensions of our approach. Experimental study is reported in Section 7, followed by related work in Section 8 and conclusion in Section 9. Proofs of most non-trivial theorems and additional experiments are in the appendix.

2. PRELIMINARIES

We first define the class of queries that we focus on, and formalize the precision guarantee our system offers for query answers.

2.1 Single-Block Aggregation Queries

$T(D_1, \ldots, D_{d_C}, M_1, \ldots, M_{d_M})$ is a table with $d_C + d_M$ dimensions. $D_1, \ldots, D_{d_C}$ are group-by and predicate dimensions and $M_1, \ldots, M_{d_M}$ are measure attributes. Types of dimensions are defined by data owner. A column can be both a group-by/predicate dimension and a measure at the same time in different queries.

For a row $t \in T$, let t_D and t_M be the values of dimension D and measure M on this row, respectively, and t_{ID} denote the ID of a row. Let $|T| = n$ be the number of rows in T.

Table aggregation queries. For the ease of explanation, we first focus on queries in the form of $Q(\mathcal{G}, F(M), \mathcal{P})$, called *table aggregation queries*, on a single table T to introduce our techniques:

$$\text{SELECT } \mathcal{G},\ F(M) \text{ FROM } T \text{ WHERE } \mathcal{P} \text{ GROUP BY } \mathcal{G}. \quad (1)$$

- *Group-by dimensions* $\mathcal{G} \subseteq \{D_1, \ldots, D_{d_C}\}$ are a subset of dimensions of T on which rows are aggregated on.
- *Aggregate measure* $F(M)$ is COUNT(*) or SUM(M) where $M \in \{M_1, \ldots, M_m\}$ is a measure attribute.
- *Predicate* $\mathcal{P}$ consists of equality constraints on categorical dimensions $\{D_1, \ldots, D_{d_C}\}$, in the form of "$D_i = v_i$". $\mathcal{P}$ is an AND-OR expression of multiple such constraints.

For simplicity of discussion, we assume that values of a measure M are non-negative when presenting our techniques. How to handle measures with negative values will be introduced in Section 6.1 .

Single-block aggregation queries. Our techniques can be extended for a more general class, *single-block aggregation queries*, which generalizes the class of table aggregation queries in three aspects: i) **(schema)** to support foreign key joins on a star/snowflake schema; ii) **(predicates)** to support range constraints on numeric dimensions and arbitrary AND-OR logical expressions $\mathcal{P}$ of equality constraints and range constraints; iii) **(aggregates)** support more aggregates, *e.g.*, AVG(M), STDEV(M), and COUNT(Distinct M). We introduce how our system handles the above extensions in Section 6.2. The class of aggregates supported by us is the same as the class supported by state of the art AQP systems like BlinkDB [5].

Answers and distributions. An output to an aggregation query Q is a set of (group, value)-pairs, $\{(g_1, z_1), (g_2, z_2), \ldots, (g_r, z_r)\}$, where r is the number of distinct values on the product of group-by dimensions $\mathcal{G} = \{G_1, \ldots, G_l\}$. Each $g_i \in G_1 \times G_2 \times \ldots G_l$ is said to be a *group*, and z_i is the corresponding aggregate value. We can present the output to be an r-dim vector $\mathbf{z} = \langle z_1, \ldots, z_r \rangle$.

The query output $\mathbf{z}$ can be *normalized as a distribution* on all groups $G_1 \times \ldots \times G_l$: let $x_i \leftarrow z_i / \sum_{j=1}^{r} z_j$, for $i = 1, 2, \ldots, r$. The vector $\mathbf{x} = \langle x_1, \ldots, x_r \rangle$ is said to be a *distribution answer* (or *answer* for short) to the query Q. Our guarantee about precision introduced next is w.r.t. the distribution answer with the goal of preserving the relative ratio/order of groups in the query output.

2.2 Distribution Precision Guarantee

Computing the exact output or distribution answer $\mathbf{x}$ to a query Q can be expensive on large tables. Our system produces an estimated distribution answer $\hat{\mathbf{x}} = \langle \hat{x}_1, \ldots, \hat{x}_r \rangle$. We propose to measure the *error* in $\hat{\mathbf{x}}$ using the L^2*(Euclidean)-distance* between $\mathbf{x}$ and $\hat{\mathbf{x}}$, *i.e.*, $\|\mathbf{x} - \hat{\mathbf{x}}\|_2 = \sqrt{\sum_{i=1}^{r} (x_i - \hat{x}_i)^2}$. For the ease of understanding, we can rephrase $\|\mathbf{x} - \hat{\mathbf{x}}\|_2$ in words as follows:

$$\sqrt{\sum_{\text{group } i} \left(\frac{\text{group } i\text{'s value}}{\text{total group value}} - \frac{\text{estimated group } i\text{'s value}}{\text{total est. group value}} \right)^2}. \quad (2)$$

Our system allows users to specify an error bound ϵ which is *independent* on both the query Q and the data distribution in table T. The estimated answer $\hat{\mathbf{x}}$ is called an ϵ*-approximate answer* or ϵ*-approximation* of the true distribution answer $\mathbf{x}$ if $\|\mathbf{x} - \hat{\mathbf{x}}\|_2 \le \epsilon$.

System task and precision guarantee. Our AQP system processes single-block aggregation queries and promises ϵ*-distribution precision guarantee*: that is, for a user-specified error bound ϵ, our system can produce an estimated answer $\hat{\mathbf{x}}$ for any given single-block aggregation query Q, s.t. $\hat{\mathbf{x}}$ must be an ϵ-approximation of the exact answer $\mathbf{x}$ to Q, *i.e.*, $\|\mathbf{x} - \hat{\mathbf{x}}\|_2 \le \epsilon$, with high probability.

As discussed in Section 1, compared to CI, our distribution precision guarantee based on L^2-distance is more rigorous, easier to be interpreted, and has only one parameter ϵ that consistently measures how two answers differentiate globally.

Another good property of our guarantee is: $\max_i |x_i - \hat{x}_i| \le \|\mathbf{x} - \hat{\mathbf{x}}\|_2 \le \epsilon$. It says that, when ϵ-distribution precision guarantee holds, the max of errors $|x_i - \hat{x}_i|$ for all groups is also bounded by ϵ, with high probability. It implies that the order of groups or the top-k groups derived from $\hat{\mathbf{x}}$ can be wrong by at most ϵ.

3. SYSTEM OVERVIEW

We give an overview of our solution in Section 3.1, including sample/index building and aggregation query processing, and summarize the main theoretical results we obtain. In Section 3.2, we introduce the architecture of our system.

3.1 Overview of Our Approach

To tackle the inherent deficiency of sampling-based approach when handling queries with very selective predicates, we propose a novel *sample+seek* framework. We classify queries into *large queries* and *small queries* based on how many rows satisfy the predicates. For large queries, with many rows satisfying their predicates, we are able to collect enough number of rows satisfying their predicates from a *uniform sample* or a new sample designed for SUM aggregates, called *measure-biased sample*, to obtain ϵ-approximate answers. For small queries, random samples are not sufficient, so we propose two new index structures, called *measure-augmented inverted index* and *low-frequency group index*, to evaluate them for ϵ-approximations using index *seeks*.

3.1.1 Classification of Queries

We classify queries using *(measure) selectivity* into *large queries* and *small queries*, based on the hardness of being answered.

DEFINITION 1. (Selectivity and Measure selectivity) *The* selectivity *of predicate $\mathcal{P}$ in a query Q against a table T is $s(\mathcal{P}) = |T_{\mathcal{P}}|/|T|$ where $|T|$ is the number of rows in T and $T_{\mathcal{P}} \subseteq T$ is the set of rows that satisfy the predicates $\mathcal{P}$ in T.*

The measure selectivity *of predicate $\mathcal{P}$ in a query Q against a table T on measure M is $s_M(\mathcal{P}) = M(T_{\mathcal{P}})/M(T)$, where $M(T_{\mathcal{P}}) = \sum_{t \in T_{\mathcal{P}}} t_M$ and $M(T) = \sum_{t \in T} t_M$.*

DEFINITION 2. (Large queries and small queries) *For a selectivity threshold s_0, a query Q with* COUNT *aggregate is a s_0-*large *query iff $s(\mathcal{P}) \ge s_0$ and otherwise a s_0-*small *query.*

Similarly, a query Q with SUM(M) *is a s_0-*large query *iff we have $s_M(\mathcal{P}) \ge s_0$, and otherwise a s_0-*small query.

Input: aggregation query $Q(\mathcal{G}, F(M), \mathcal{P})$
Output: ϵ-approximate answer distribution
1: If F = COUNT then
2: $(\hat{\mathbf{x}}, \sup_{\hat{\mathbf{x}}}) \leftarrow$ ProcessWithDataBubble(Q, T^0);
3: Else If F = SUM then
4: $(\hat{\mathbf{x}}, \sup_{\hat{\mathbf{x}}}) \leftarrow$ ProcessWithDataBubble(Q, T^M).
5: If $\sup_{\hat{\mathbf{x}}} \geq 1/\epsilon^2$ then
6: Output $\hat{\mathbf{x}}$;
7: Else
8: If the *low-frequency group index* is usable
9: $\hat{\mathbf{x}} \leftarrow$ ProcessWithLFIndex(Q);
10: Else
11: $\hat{\mathbf{x}} \leftarrow$ ProcessWithMAIndex(Q);
12: Output $\hat{\mathbf{x}}$.

Algorithm 1: Processing Aggregation Queries

We set s_0 to be $1/\sqrt{n}$, where n is the number of rows in T, in most of discussion and analysis later on. We simply call the two classes large queries and small queries when $s_0 = 1/\sqrt{n}$.

3.1.2 Offline Sampling and Index Building

For a table T with d_C group-by and predicate dimensions, d_M measures, and n rows, we build three types of samples/indexes.

The first one is called *data bubble*. Each data bubble is a *random sample* of rows drawn from T. We draw a *uniform sample* $T^0 \subseteq T$ containing $O(\sqrt{n}/\epsilon^2)$ rows to answer COUNT-queries, and a *measure-biased sample* containing $O(\sqrt{n}/\epsilon^2)$ rows T^M used to answer SUM(M)-queries for each measure dimension M. So there are a total of $d_M + 1$ data bubbles. The basic idea of measure-biased sampling is to pick a row t in T with replacement with probability proportional to t_M, to get ϵ-approximate answers to SUM(M)-queries using a minimum number of sample rows. As their sizes are sublinear in n, we load them into memory in pre-processing.

The second one is called *measure-augmented inverted index*. For each value of a categorical dimension, we keep a *postings list* of row IDs where this value appears in the corresponding dimension. Up until now, it is similar to an inverted index in IR systems. We then augment each postings list with rough values of measures. For example, if $t_M = 2^8 + 10$, we store 8 (*i.e.*, $\mathsf{apx}(t_M) = 2^8$) for t_M in the index to save space. Similar to measure-biased sampling, these rough values $\mathsf{apx}(t_M)$'s will be used to guide our online sampling when processing SUM-aggregation queries. We keep this index on disk if we do not have enough memory, but each postings list is stored sequentially s.t. it can be efficiently read when needed.

The third one is called *low-frequency group index*. In this index, for each value that is *infrequent* in a categorical dimension, *i.e.*, the number of rows containing it is no more than $\sqrt{n}$, we materialize these rows sequentially on disk. The motivation of this index is that, if an infrequent value appears in the predicate of a query as part of a conjunction, we can simply scan these rows sequentially on disk to calculate the answer. For example, consider the table T in Figure 1(a) and a predicate "$C_2 = 1$ AND $C_3 = 0$". Only 10 rows satisfy $C_2 = 1$, so we can simply scan them for the answer.

3.1.3 Sample+Seek Processing of Queries

Our system does *not* estimate queries' selectivities. For every incoming query, we first proceed with our uniform sample or measure-biased samples. If enough number $(1/\epsilon^2)$ of rows satisfying its predicate are collected from the samples, an ϵ-approximation can be produced. For large queries, the processing can be terminated at this point with high probability. Only when our system does not collect enough number of rows satisfying the predicate from the samples, it continues to use the other two deterministic auxiliary indexes to evaluate the query for ϵ-approximation.

Our query processing algorithm is outlined in Algorithm 1. We process a query with the data bubble samples first (lines 1-4). Let $\hat{\mathbf{x}}$ be the estimated distribution answer, and $\sup_{\hat{\mathbf{x}}}$ be the number of sample rows satisfying the predicate $\mathcal{P}$ (those used to calculate $\hat{\mathbf{x}}$). If $\sup_{\hat{\mathbf{x}}} \geq 1/\epsilon^2$, we can terminate with an ϵ-approximate answer $\hat{\mathbf{x}}$ (lines 5-6); otherwise, $\hat{\mathbf{x}}$ is not accurate enough, so we will continue to check whether the low-frequency group index is usable (lines 8-9), or refer to the measure-augmented inverted index (lines 10-11).

Section 4 introduces how to create and utilize data bubble samples. Section 5 presents how to build and process queries with measure-augmented inverted index and low-frequency group index.

3.1.4 A Summary of Theoretical Guarantees

We now present the performance guarantees of our system for producing ϵ-approximations, in an informal way.

Main results. For a table T with d_C group-by/predicate dimensions, d_M measures, and n rows. We need to keep $O(\sqrt{n}/\epsilon^2)$ rows in each of the $d_M + 1$ data bubbles. For any aggregation query $Q(\mathcal{G}, F(M), \mathcal{P})$, we need to scan *one* of the data bubbles to compute ϵ-approximate answer in linear time $O(|\mathcal{G}| \cdot \sqrt{n}/\epsilon^2)$. If Q is a large query, we can terminate with an ϵ-approximation with high probability. If Q is a small query and the low-frequency group index can be used to answer it, we scan at most $\sqrt{n}$ rows in the index to get its answer. If the low-frequency group index cannot be used, we can always use the measure-augmented inverted index to perform $O(1/\epsilon^2)$ random I/O's for an ϵ-approximation.

Parameters. Both the error bound ϵ and the selectivity threshold s_0 are tunable. Our theoretical results and system can be extended for general parameter settings. The precision parameter ϵ can be specified by users or administrators to trade-off between precision and indexing/processing cost. The selectivity threshold s_0 is set as $1/\sqrt{n}$ by default. Generally, the size of each sample needs to be $O((1/s_0) \cdot (1/\epsilon^2))$ to get ϵ-approximations for s_0-large queries.

Error bound and accuracy probability in big O notations. All the theoretical results about obtaining ϵ-approximation in this paper hold *with high probability* ("*w.h.p.*" for short) – we mean that, with probability at least $1 - \delta$ (*e.g.*, 0.95) for some constant δ (*e.g.*, 0.05), our estimation is an ϵ-approximation. For a fixed error bound ϵ, there is a tradeoff between the sample sizes/processing costs (those in "main results" above) and the accuracy probability $1-\delta$: theoretically, for an accuracy probability $1-\delta$, there is an additional factor $\log(1/\delta)$ behind the $O(\cdot)$ notations about the sample sizes/processing costs. However, since δ does not have to be arbitrarily small, we can treat $\log(1/\delta)$ as a constant for simplicity of presentation. So in all $O(\cdot)$ or $\Omega(\cdot)$ notations in the main body of this paper, we omit all the small logarithmic terms like $\log(1/\delta)$ and $\log(1/\epsilon)$ when presenting theoretical results. These terms will be found in the proofs of our theorems in the appendix.

3.2 System Architecture

The architecture of our system is in Figure 2. Our system can be attached to a database with its independent storage and query processing engine. It connects to a data source in the *column-based format* using a component called *data connector*, which can be customized for different database systems. In the index building stage, the three of indexes, *data bubbles*, *measure-augmented inverted index*, and *low-frequency group index*, are created from the column-based storage. After index building is finished, our *query processor* needs to access the data bubbles (in memory) and the other two indexes (on disk) to process aggregation queries.

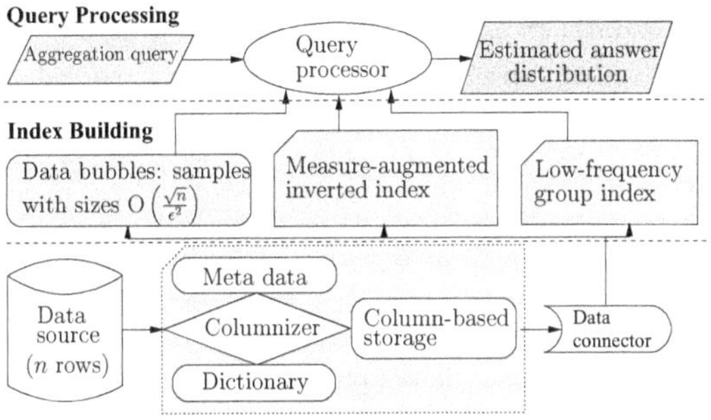

Figure 2: System Architecture

Input: aggregation query $Q(\mathcal{G}, F(M), \mathcal{P})$ and sample T'
Output: ϵ-approximate answer $\hat{\mathbf{x}}$ and support $\text{sup}_{\hat{\mathbf{x}}}$
1: $\hat{\mathbf{x}} \leftarrow \mathbf{0}$; $\text{sup}_{\hat{\mathbf{x}}} \leftarrow 0$;
2: For each sample row $t \in T'$:
3: If t satisfies $\mathcal{P}$ then
4: Let i be the group t belonging to on $\mathcal{G}$;
5: $\hat{x}_i \leftarrow \hat{x}_i + 1$; $\text{sup}_{\hat{\mathbf{x}}} \leftarrow \text{sup}_{\hat{\mathbf{x}}} + 1$;
6: Normalize $\hat{\mathbf{x}}$ to be a distribution on all groups on $\mathcal{G}$;
7: Output $(\hat{\mathbf{x}}, \text{sup}_{\hat{\mathbf{x}}})$.

Algorithm 2: ProcessWithDataBubble(Q, T'): processing aggregation queries with a data bubble (sample)

4. SAMPLE: UNIFORM OR BIASED

We now introduce the two sampling schemes, *uniform sampling* and *measure-biased sampling*, and how to use them to answer large COUNT and SUM-queries with ϵ-approximation, respectively.

4.1 Uniform Sampling

Uniform sampling is a very natural idea to approximate the answer distribution $\mathbf{x}$ for an aggregation query Q. The sampling process can be formally described as follows. For a given sample size m, we repeat drawing a row with replacement from a table T for m times – each row $t \in T$ is chosen into T^0 with equal probability

$$\mathbf{Pr}\left[t \text{ is picked}\right] = 1/n. \tag{3}$$

The resulting m sample rows in T^0 are stored in memory for processing queries. We show that a pre-drawn uniform sample with size $O(\sqrt{n}/\epsilon^2)$ suffices for all large COUNT-queries against T.

Algorithm 2 shows how the uniform sample T^0 can be used to estimate answers to aggregation queries. When $Q(\mathcal{G}, \text{COUNT}(*), \mathcal{P})$ comes, we process it with T^0 using one scan. For each row $t \in T^0$, we check whether t satisfies $\mathcal{P}$ (line 3); if yes and t belongs to the ith group on group-by columns $\mathcal{G}$, we increase $\hat{x}_i$ by 1 (lines 4-5). Finally, we normalize $\hat{\mathbf{x}} = \langle \hat{x}_1, \ldots, \hat{x}_r \rangle$ as a distribution and also report the number of rows satisfying $\mathcal{P}$ as $\text{sup}_{\hat{\mathbf{x}}}$ (lines 6-7).

The follow theorem formally shows that why T^0 with sample size $O(\sqrt{n}/\epsilon^2)$ suffices for all large COUNT-queries.

THEOREM 3. (Precision of Uniform Sampling) *We use uniform sampling to draw $O((1/s_0) \cdot (1/\epsilon^2))$ rows to form a sample T^0 from a table T of n rows. For any COUNT-aggregation query on T, $Q(\mathcal{G}, \text{COUNT}(*), \mathcal{P})$, let $\mathbf{x}$ be the exact answer to Q. If the selectivity of predicates $\mathcal{P}$ is no less than s_0, $s(\mathcal{P}) \geq s_0$, Algorithm 2 uses T^0 to calculate an estimated answer $\hat{\mathbf{x}}$ s.t. with high probability, $\|\mathbf{x} - \hat{\mathbf{x}}\|_2 \leq \epsilon$. In particular, if the selectivity threshold $s_0 = 1/\sqrt{n}$, a uniform sample of $O(\sqrt{n}/\epsilon^2)$ rows suffices.*

A special case of Theorem 3 with selectivity threshold $s_0 = 1$ has been studied in [1], as stated in Corollary 4 below. Our proof of Theorem 3 generalizes it extensively from two aspects: i) to show $\mathbf{E}\left[\|\mathbf{x} - \hat{\mathbf{x}}\|_2^2\right] \leq O(\epsilon^2)$, we need to utilize the fact that the number of sample rows satisfying $\mathcal{P}$, denoted as $m_{\mathcal{P}}$, concentrates on $\Omega(1/\epsilon^2)$ (w.h.p.); and ii) we need to generalize McDiarmid's inequality to complete the proof for $\|\mathbf{x} - \hat{\mathbf{x}}\|_2 \leq \epsilon$ (w.h.p.).

COROLLARY 4. (Without Predicate [1]) *We use uniform sampling to draw $O(1/\epsilon^2)$ rows T^0 from a table T of n rows. For any aggregation query Q with COUNT aggregate on T and no predicate, let $\mathbf{x}$ be the exact answer to Q. We can use T^0 to calculate an estimated answer $\hat{\mathbf{x}}$ s.t. with high probability, $\|\mathbf{x} - \hat{\mathbf{x}}\|_2 \leq \epsilon$.*

Optimality. The information-theoretic lower bound in [1] also implies the optimal sampling size for COUNT, *i.e.*, at least $\Omega(1/\epsilon^2)$ sample rows are needed to obtain an ϵ-approximate answer (with probability at least $1 - \delta$) for a COUNT-query with no predicate.

Early termination. We can derive an early termination condition for Algorithm 2 from Corollary 4. In order to be an ϵ-approximate distribution answer to a query Q, $\hat{\mathbf{x}}$ needs a sample of $O(1/\epsilon^2)$ rows among all rows that satisfy Q's predicate. So we can track the size of this sample using $\text{sup}_{\hat{\mathbf{x}}}$ in Algorithm 2. When $\text{sup}_{\hat{\mathbf{x}}} \geq 2/\epsilon^2$, we can exit the loop of lines 2-5 and output the normalized $\hat{\mathbf{x}}$. We have integrated this early termination condition in our implementation. It offers significant performance gain for large queries whose selectivities $s(\mathcal{P})$'s are much larger than $1/\sqrt{n}$, as for those queries, only a small portion of rows in the $O(\sqrt{n}/\epsilon^2)$-sample need to be scanned to get a sample of $2/\epsilon^2$ rows satisfying $\mathcal{P}$.

4.2 Measure-biased Sampling

To extend the uniform sampling schema for queries with SUM aggregates on any measure dimension M, a naive way is to change "$\hat{x}_i \leftarrow \hat{x}_i + 1$" to "$\hat{x}_i \leftarrow \hat{x}_i + t_M$" on line 5 of Algorithm 2 (recall that t_M is the value of measure M on a row t). This simple extension, however, is not accurate enough. We can show that using a uniform sample with size $m = O(\sqrt{n}/\epsilon^2)$, the expected squared error $\mathbf{E}\left[\|\mathbf{x} - \hat{\mathbf{x}}\|_2^2\right]$ for large queries is *no less* than $\mathbf{Var}\left[M\right] \cdot \epsilon^2$, where $\mathbf{Var}\left[M\right] = \frac{1}{n}\sum_{t \in T}(t_M/\bar{M} - 1)^2$ and $\bar{M}$ is the average value of measure M. Later in Proposition 7, we will also prove that $\mathbf{E}\left[\|\mathbf{x} - \hat{\mathbf{x}}\|_2^2\right]$ is upper bounded by $O(\Delta^3 \cdot \epsilon^2)$ with the same sample size, if measure M takes value in $[1, \Delta]$. Both $\mathbf{Var}\left[M\right]$ and Δ could be very large for a general data distribution on M.

Recall cases I and II in Example 1.1. If we use the above naive adaption of uniform sampling to process query Q, we will get an estimated answer either in Figure 1(c) or in 1(d) with high probability. Both are far away from the true answer.

We now introduce a new sampling schema called *measure-biased sampling*. For each measure M, we first need to construct (randomly) a *measure-biased sample* T^M in preprocessing, which will be used to estimate answers for SUM-queries with high accuracy.

Constructing measure-biased samples. To construct T^M with a given sample size m, we repeat drawing a row with replacement from T for m times – each row t is picked into T^M with probability proportional to its value t_M on measure M, *i.e.*,

$$\mathbf{Pr}\left[t \text{ is picked}\right] = \frac{t_M}{\sum_{t' \in T} t'_M} \sim t_M; \tag{4}$$

All the rows drawn are kept in T^M. Note that each row may appear multiple times in T^M, *i.e.*, T^M could be a multi-set. We will show that for a table T with n rows, a measure-biased sample T^M with size $O(\sqrt{n}/\epsilon^2)$ suffices for all large SUM(M)-queries.

If there are d measure attributes, we need to maintain d measure-biased samples, each for one measure. We can construct all the measure-biased samples together with the uniform sample in two scans of the table T. Please refer to Appendix B for details.

Estimating using measure-biased samples. When using T^M to estimate the answer for a $\mathsf{SUM}(M)$-query Q, it is a bit surprising that we can reuse Algorithm 2 – we only need to call the procedure $\mathsf{ProcessWithDataBubble}(Q, T^M)$. Readers may wonder why in line 5, $\hat{x}_i$ is increased by 1 instead of the measure value t_M for a sample row t. The reason is, informally, that since the sampling probability of t is proportional to t_M (as in (4)), we need to calibrate row t's contribution to the estimation $\hat{\mathbf{x}}$ with t_M^{-1}. This idea is similar to Horvitz-Thompson estimator (which is for single-point estimation), but here we are estimating a distribution $\mathbf{x}$. Refer to the following example for more intuition.

EXAMPLE 4.1. (Continue Example 1.1) *Let's look at the query Q in Example 1.1, for which uniform sample fails. We draw a measure-biased sample T^M with rows 1, 26, 51, 76, 92, 94, 96, 98, 111, 136, 161, and 186 each appearing once, and 199 and 200 each appearing four times (considering their values on M – refer to Example B.1 and Figure 9 in Appendix B on how they were drawn). Reusing Algorithm 2, call* $\mathsf{ProcessWithDataBubble}(Q, T^M)$ *– the estimation it gives is $\hat{\mathbf{x}} = \langle 8/20, 12/20\rangle = \langle 0.40, 0.60\rangle$, which is very close to the exact answer $\mathbf{x} = \langle 0.39, 0.61\rangle$.*

The following theorem formally shows that, for each measure M, a measure-biased sample T^M with size $O(\sqrt{n}/\epsilon^2)$ suffices for all large $\mathsf{SUM}(M)$-queries to give ϵ-approximation.

THEOREM 5. (Precision of Measure-Biased Sampling) *We apply measure-biased sampling on measure attribute M and draw $O((1/s_0)\cdot(1/\epsilon^2))$ rows T^M from a table T of n rows. For any aggregation query, $Q(\mathcal{G}, \mathsf{SUM}(M), \mathcal{P})$, with aggregate $\mathsf{SUM}(M)$ on T, let $\mathbf{x}$ be the exact answer to Q. If the measure selectivity of predicates $\mathcal{P}$, $s_M(\mathcal{P})$, is no less than s_0, Algorithm 2 uses T^M to calculate an estimated answer $\hat{\mathbf{x}}$ s.t. with high probability, $\|\mathbf{x}-\hat{\mathbf{x}}\|_2 \le \epsilon$. In particular, if the selectivity threshold $s_0 = 1/\sqrt{n}$, a measure-biased sample of $O(\sqrt{n}/\epsilon^2)$ rows suffices.*

Optimality of measure-biased sampling. Our measure-biased sampling for SUM-queries draws the same number of sample rows as the uniform sampling does for COUNT-queries. Since COUNT is a special case of SUM (when the measure attribute is a constant 1), the low-bound result in [1] also implies that for SUM-queries with no predicate ($s_0 = 1$), we need at least $\Omega(1/\epsilon^2)$ sample rows to obtain an ϵ-approximate answer with high probability.

Early termination. The same early termination condition introduced in Section 4.1 for the uniform samples can be applied here for measure-biased samples. When we collect $\sup_{\hat{\mathbf{x}}} \ge 2/\epsilon^2$ samples rows that satisfy the predicate in Q, we can exit the loop of lines 2-5 of Algorithm 2 and output the normalized $\hat{\mathbf{x}}$. This condition is also integrated in our implementation and offers significant performance gain for queries with high measure selectivities.

5. SEEK: RANDOM OR SEQUENTIAL

Large queries with (measure) selectivity no smaller than s_0 ($= 1/\sqrt{n}$ by default) have been handled by uniform and measure-biased samples. So what left here are small queries with (measure) selectivity smaller than s_0. For example, for such a small COUNT aggregation query, we know that the number of rows satisfying its predicate is no more than $\sqrt{n}$. We will keep this property in mind when designing the two indexes to handle small queries.

5.1 Measure-Augmented Inverted Index

As we first focus on aggregation queries with categorical dimensions in their predicates, it is a natural idea to apply *inverted indexes* from IR systems in our problem. For each value v of each dimension D_i, we can keep a *postings list* of rows that have value v on dimension D_i. Then for a query $Q(\mathcal{G}, F(M), \mathcal{P})$, there have been extensive studies on how to efficiently retrieve all rows satisfying $\mathcal{P}$ using those postings lists, such as [8]. For a predicate that is a conjunction (with only ANDs) of equi-constraints, it is equivalent to computing the intersection of postings lists. After that, we only need to scan the retrieved rows once for aggregation.

There are, however, at least two optimizations we can do in the scenario of aggregation queries processing. First, we cannot keep full rows in the postings list, as each row could be wide (in terms of the number of bits), especially if the number of dimensions is non-trivial (*e.g.*, 30). We can keep only the IDs of those rows, and later seek their dimension/measure values in the original table.

Secondly, of course, random seek based on row ID is expensive. Our basic idea is that, after we get the IDs of rows that satisfy the predicate $\mathcal{P}$, we draw a random sample from these IDs, and perform random seeks only for the sample IDs. The two sampling schemes introduced in Section 4 can be applied here online to draw proper samples to achieve our ϵ-approximation precision guarantee. To this end, besides row IDs, we need approximate measure values to guide our online measure-biased sampling.

We introduce how to construct and utilize *measure-augmented inverted index* in this subsection.

5.1.1 Construction

Our measure-augmented inverted index is described in Figure 3. For each value v of a categorical dimension D, we maintain a *measure-augmented postings list* $\mathsf{inv}(D, v)$. Each of our measure-augmented postings lists consists of two parts.

First, $\mathsf{inv}(D, v)$ maintains IDs of rows that have value v on D just as in an IR-style postings list. This part is depicted in the left of Figure 3. From the ID of a row t, denoted as t_{ID}, we can access the value of each the dimension or measure of t from our column-based storage, using one random seek (I/O).

Second, let's use $\mathsf{inv}(D, v)$ also to denote the set of rows that have value v on D. For each row $t \in \mathsf{inv}(D, v)$, we maintain the values of measures $M_1, \ldots, M_{d_\mathsf{M}}$ on this row. Note that keeping all the exact measure values is still too expensive (*e.g.*, for ten 64-bit integers). So we only keep an approximation $\mathsf{apx}(t_{M_i})$ of measure t_{M_i} in order to save the space as well as to speedup the access of $\mathsf{inv}(D, v)$. $\mathsf{apx}(t_{M_i})$ only needs to be an *2-approximation* of t_{M_i}:

$$\mathsf{apx}(t_{M_i}) \le t_{M_i} < 2\cdot\mathsf{apx}(t_{M_i}). \tag{5}$$

So the number of bits we need is at most $\log\log\Delta(M_i)+1$, where $\Delta(M_i)$ is the range of values in measure M_i.

The construction of measure-augmented inverted index is similar to constructing traditional IR inverted index, which can be done within one scan of all the rows in linear time.

EXAMPLE 5.1. (Continue Example 1.1) *For the example table T with* 200 *rows in Figure 1(a), Figure 4(a)-4(b) shows the measure-augmented postings lists* $\mathsf{inv}(C_2, 0)$ *and* $\mathsf{inv}(C_3, 0)$*, respectively. Values on measure M,* i.e., *t_M, are rounded to $\mathsf{apx}(t_M)$ as $2^0, 2^1, 2^2, \ldots$, so that (5) is satisfied. For example, t_M for row 100 is rounded to 8 from 10 in* $\mathsf{inv}(C_3, 0)$ *and t_M for row 200 is rounded to 64 from 100 in* $\mathsf{inv}(C_2, 0)$*. The number of bits needed for each $\mathsf{apx}(t_M)$ is $\log_2\log_2\Delta(M) + 1$. In this example, the range of M is $\Delta(M) = 100$, so we need only $\log_2\log_2 100 + 1 = \log_2 6 + 1 = 3$ bits, as $\mathsf{apx}(t_M)$ can only be $2^0, 2^1, \ldots, 2^6$.*

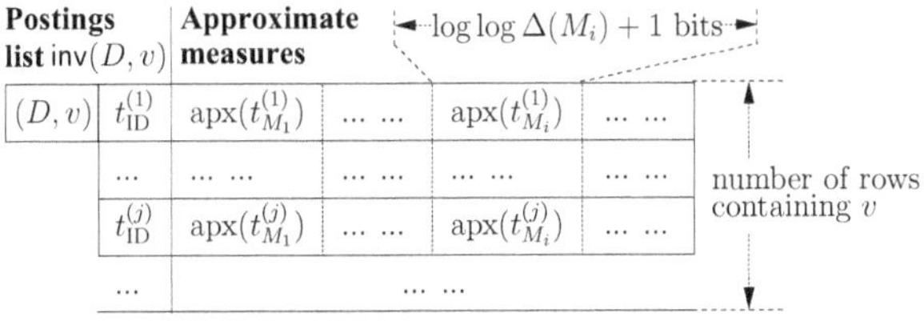

Figure 3: Measure-Augmented Inverted Index

ID	apx(M)
1	1
...	1
90	1
101	1
...	1
198	1
199	64
200	64

(a) inv$(C_2, 0)$

ID	apx(M)
1	1
...	1
90	1
91	8
...	8
100	8
101	1
...	1
198	1
199	64

(b) inv$(C_3, 0)$

ID	apx(M)
1	1
...	1
90	1
101	1
...	1
198	1
199	64

(c) inv$(C_2, 0) \cap$ inv$(C_3, 0)$

Figure 4: Two Measure-Augmented Postings Lists

Size of index. Our measure-augmented inverted index is composed of row IDs and approximate measures. Suppose a table has n rows and d_{C} dimensions. Each row ID needs $\mathrm{O}(\log n)$ bits and is stored d_{C} times in the index, one time for each dimension. For each row ID and each measure M_i, we need $\mathrm{O}(\log\log \Delta(M_i))$ bits to store the approximate measure $\mathsf{apx}(t_{M_i})$. So the index size is:

THEOREM 6. *For a table with n rows, d_{C} dimensions, and d_{M} measures, the measure-augmented inverted index needs a total of* $\mathrm{O}\Big(n \cdot d_{\mathsf{C}} \cdot (\log n + \Sigma_{i=1}^{d_{\mathsf{M}}} \log\log \Delta(M_i))\Big)$ *bits.*

Each postings list inv(D, v) can be compressed using standard techniques as it will only be accessed sequentially. We will report the actual size of such indexes in our experiments.

5.1.2 Processing Queries

To process a query $Q(\mathcal{G}, F(M), \mathcal{P})$ using measure-augmented inverted index, we first retrieve IDs of all rows that satisfy $\mathcal{P}$. Let $T_{\mathcal{P}}$ be the set of all such rows, and $T_{\mathcal{P}}^{\mathsf{ID}}$ be the set of their IDs. For a predicate expression with AND, OR, and NOT operators on equi-constraints in the form of "$D_i = v_i$", this is equivalent to computing set intersection, union, and minus of postings lists inv(D_i, v_i), and we only need one scan of those lists.

After we get IDs of rows in $T_{\mathcal{P}}^{\mathsf{ID}}$, we can seek the original table T for their dimension and measure values to finish the aggregation. But $|T_{\mathcal{P}}^{\mathsf{ID}}|$ random seeks are expensive.

A very natural idea is to draw a random sample from $T_{\mathcal{P}}^{\mathsf{ID}}$, and perform random seeks only for the sample rows.

For COUNT aggregates, from Corollary 4, a uniform sample of $\mathrm{O}(1/\epsilon^2)$ rows suffice for an ϵ-approximate answer $\hat{\mathbf{x}}$.

For SUM aggregates, we propose *approximate measure-biased sampling* to estimate an ϵ-approximate answer.

Online approximate measure-biased sampling. We start with a proposition about the sample size needed for an ϵ-approximation if *uniform sampling* is used. We prove that, with uniform sampling, it suffices to seek $\mathrm{O}(\Delta^3/\epsilon^2)$ sample rows, where Δ is the range of measure values. This result itself is discouraging as Δ^3 is large. Our *approximate measure-biased sampling* scheme will improve the sample size to $\mathrm{O}(1/\epsilon^2)$ using approximate measures $\mathsf{apx}(\cdot_M)$.

PROPOSITION 7. (Uniform Sample for SUM) *We draw a uniform sample of $\mathrm{O}(\Delta^3/\epsilon^2)$ rows $T'_{\mathcal{P}}$ from $T_{\mathcal{P}}$, assuming values of measure M are within range $[1, \Delta]$. For a SUM aggregation query Q with predicate $\mathcal{P}$, let $\mathbf{x}$ be the exact answer to Q. We can use $T'_{\mathcal{P}}$ to get an estimation $\hat{\mathbf{x}}$ s.t. $\mathbf{E}\,[\|\mathbf{x} - \hat{\mathbf{x}}\|_2] \le \epsilon$.*

```
Input:   aggregation query Q(G, F(M), P) and table T
Index:   measure-augmented inverted index inv
Output:  ε-approximate answer distribution x̂
1: x̂ ← 0;
2: Compute T_P^ID ← {t_ID | rows t that satisfy P} using inv;
3: Repeat min{1/ε², |T_P^ID|} times:
4:     Randomly pick t_ID ∈ T_P^ID: for each t_ID ∈ T_P^ID,
           Pr[t_ID is picked] = apx(t_M) / Σ_{t'∈T} apx(t'_M) ~ apx(t_M);   (6)
5:     t ← seeking T using t_ID for other dimensions;
6:     Let i be the group t belonging to on G;
7:     x̂_i ← x̂_i + t_M/apx(t_M);
8: Normalize x̂ to be a distribution and output x̂.
```

Algorithm 3: ProcessWithMAIndex(Q): online approximate measure-biased sampling and processing

How to process a query using the approximate measure-biased sampling technique is described in Algorithm 3. Inspired by the idea of measure-biased sampling (recall (4)), the sample size can be reduced tremendously to $\mathrm{O}(1/\epsilon^2)$ if rows in $T_{\mathcal{P}}$ can be sampled with probability proportional to t_M. In measure-augmented inverted index, t_M is not available, but an approximation to t_M, $\mathsf{apx}(t_M)$, is available. A row t in $T_{\mathcal{P}}$ is drawn into sample $T'_{\mathcal{P}}$ with probability proportional to $\mathsf{apx}(t_M)$ (line 4). If t is picked, we retrieve its dimension and measure values by seeking our column-based storage (line 5), and let i be the group it belongs to (lines 6). Let $t_{M'} = t_M/\mathsf{apx}(t_M)$ be the weight of t in the estimation $\hat{x}_i$ (line 7). Finally, $\hat{\mathbf{x}}$ is normalized and output (line 8). We know that, for any t, $1 \le t_{M'} < 2$, from how $\mathsf{apx}(\cdot_M)$ is chosen as in (5). The reduction in sampling complexity is achieved by shrinking Δ in Proposition 7. Intuitively, from Proposition 7, if $\Delta = 2$, which is true for $t_{M'}$, a sample of size $\mathrm{O}(1/\epsilon^2)$ should suffice. Before proving the formal result in Theorem 8, we use an example to demonstrate the online approximate measure-biased sampling.

EXAMPLE 5.2. (Continue Example 5.1) *For the table T with 200 rows in Figure 1(a), consider such a query Q:*

SELECT C_1, SUM(M) FROM T
WHERE $C_2 = 0$ AND $C_3 = 0$ GROUP BY C_1.

The answer $\mathbf{x} = \langle 90/288, 198/288\rangle = \langle 0.31, 0.69\rangle$. Using our measure-augmented postings lists in Figures 4(a)-4(b), we can first compute the IDs of rows that satisfy "$C_2 = 0$ AND $C_3 = 0$". We get $T_{\mathcal{P}}^{\mathsf{ID}} = \{1, \ldots, 90, 101, \ldots, 198, 199\}$ as in Figure 4(c). There are 188 rows in $T_{\mathcal{P}}^{\mathsf{ID}}$ with $\mathsf{apx}(t_M) = 1$, and 1 row (199) with $\mathsf{apx}(t_M) = 64$. So if we draw 20 rows with probability proportional to $\mathsf{apx}(t_M)$ from $T_{\mathcal{P}}^{\mathsf{ID}}$, with high likelihood, we will get 7 rows from $\{1, \ldots, 90\}$, 8 rows from $\{101, \ldots, 198\}$, 5 copies of row 199. From line 7 in Algorithm 3, we can estimate $\hat{\mathbf{x}} =$

$$\langle \frac{7 \times 1}{7 + 8 + 5 \times 100/64}, \frac{8 \times 1 + 5 \times 100/64}{7 + 8 + 5 \times 100/64} \rangle = \langle 0.30, 0.70\rangle.$$

THEOREM 8. (Sample using Approximate Measures) *We can draw $\mathrm{O}(1/\epsilon^2)$ rows $T'_{\mathcal{P}}$ from $T_{\mathcal{P}}$ biased on approximate measure $\mathsf{apx}(\cdot_M)$ of M (in (6)). For an aggregation query $Q(\mathcal{G}, \mathsf{SUM}(M), \mathcal{P})$, let $\mathbf{x}$ be the exact answer to Q. We can use the measure-biased sample $T'_{\mathcal{P}}$ to calculate an approximate answer $\hat{\mathbf{x}}$ (as in Algorithm 3) s.t. with high probability, we have $\|\mathbf{x} - \hat{\mathbf{x}}\|_2 \le \epsilon$.*

Query processing cost. We observe the bottleneck in cost lies on the second step, because the first step only involves sequential scans of postings lists, but the second step needs random seeks. The number of random seeks, however, is bounded by $\min\{1/\epsilon^2, |T^{\mathsf{ID}}_{\mathcal{P}}|\}$ for each dimension in the query to get an ϵ-approximation.

THEOREM 9. *A query Q with predicate $\mathcal{P}$ can be processed using our measure-augmented inverted index (with Algorithm 3) to get an ϵ-approximation. Let $T_{\mathcal{P}}$ be the set of rows satisfying $\mathcal{P}$. The total number of random seeks to our index and the column-based storage is $O(\min\{1/\epsilon^2, |T_{\mathcal{P}}|\} \cdot d_Q)$, where d_Q is the number of dimensions and measures in the query Q.*

5.2 Low-Frequency Group Index

Low-frequency group index is designed to benefit a special class of predicates in the form of

$$\mathcal{P} : D_1 = v_1 \text{ AND } \ldots \text{ AND } D_l = v_l \text{ AND } (\ldots), \tag{7}$$

i.e., a conjunction of one or more equi-constraints and some other constraints. For example, for table T in Figure 1(a), "$C_2 = 1$ AND ($C_3 = 0$ OR $C_3 = 1$)" is such a predicate.

The construction and processing using low-frequency group index is quite straightforward. If there is less than $\sqrt{n}$ rows (out of all the n rows in the table T) with value v on a dimension D, we simply store these rows sequentially in the index. Any query in the form (7) with "$D = v$" in its predicate is a small query and cannot be handled by our samples. Processing such queries using the low-frequency group index is easy: we only need to scan the $\sqrt{n}$ rows sequentially in the index. More details are in Appendix C.

Not all small queries can be processed using this index. For example, when $T_{D_1=v_1}$ and $T_{D_2=v_2}$ are both large (with $> \sqrt{n}$ rows and thus not in the index), their intersection $T_{D_1=v_1} \cap T_{D_2=v_2}$ could be small. We still rely on our measure-augmented inverted index to answer the query with predicate "$D_1 = v_1$ AND $D_2 = v_2$".

6. EXTENSIONS

6.1 From Distributions to Absolute Answers

We now introduce how to convert a distribution answer $\hat{\mathbf{x}}$ to an absolute answer $\hat{\mathbf{z}}$. For the distribution answer obtained from low-frequency group index, since it is exact, the conversion is trivial. So let's focus on SUM-queries with estimated distribution obtained from measure-biased sampling. Measure-augmented inverted index also relies on (approximate) measure-biased sampling, so it is similar. And COUNT is a special case of SUM.

Consider a SUM(M)-query Q with predicate $\mathcal{P}$ against a table T. Suppose its output is $\mathbf{z} = \langle z_1, \ldots, z_r \rangle$, where z_i is the aggregate value of the ith group. $\mathbf{z}$ can be normalized to a distribution $\mathbf{x} = \langle x_1, \ldots, x_r \rangle$ as in Section 2.1. Let $T_{\mathcal{P}} \subseteq T$ be the set of rows satisfying $\mathcal{P}$ and $T_i \subseteq T_{\mathcal{P}}$ be the set of rows in the ith group of the output to Q. For a set of rows S, let $M(S) = \sum_{t \in S} t_M$. So we can easily derive that $x_i = M(T_i)/M(T_{\mathcal{P}}) = z_i/M(T_{\mathcal{P}})$.

In the measure-biased sample T^M, let m be the number of sample rows in T^M, $m_{\mathcal{P}}$ be the number of sample rows satisfying $\mathcal{P}$ in T^M, and m_i be the be the number of rows belonging to the ith group in T^M. So from Algorithm 2, we have $\hat{x}_i = m_i/m_{\mathcal{P}}$.

Since $|\hat{x}_i - x_i| \le \epsilon$ (implied by our distribution precision guarantee $\|\mathbf{x} - \hat{\mathbf{x}}\|_2 \le \epsilon$), informally, we have

$$x_i = z_i/M(T_{\mathcal{P}}) \approx m_i/m_{\mathcal{P}} = \hat{x}_i.$$

So it is intuitive to estimate $\hat{z}_i = M(T_{\mathcal{P}}) \cdot m_i/m_{\mathcal{P}}$. Both m_i and $m_{\mathcal{P}}$ are known from Algorithm 2, but $M(T_{\mathcal{P}})$ is unknown. Alternatively, we can estimate $M(T_{\mathcal{P}})$ as $M(T) \cdot m_{\mathcal{P}}/m$, and therefore,

$$\hat{z}_i = M(T) \cdot m_i/m = \hat{x}_i \cdot M(T) \cdot m_{\mathcal{P}}/m.$$

Negative values on measures. For a measure attribute M with both positive values and negative values, we can create two versions of M: M^+ takes only positive values and is set to 0 if the row has a negative value on M; and similarly, M^- takes only negative values and is set to 0 if the row has a positive value on M. Using the above tricks, we can get estimated answers for both M^+ and M^-. The estimation for M can be obtained from the difference between the estimated M^+ and M^- on each group. In this way, we can at least handle negative values for both SUM and AVG.

Input: aggregation query $Q(\mathcal{G}, F(M), \mathcal{P})$ and sample T'
$\hat{S}_i \leftarrow \varnothing$ for all groups i's; sup $\leftarrow 0$;
For each sample row $t \in T'$:
  If t satisfies $\mathcal{P}$ then
    Let i be the group t belonging to on $\mathcal{G}$;
    $\hat{S}_i \leftarrow \hat{S}_i \cup \{t\}$; $\mathsf{w}(t) \leftarrow \mathbf{Pr}[t \in T']$; sup $\leftarrow$ sup $+1$;
For each group i: $\hat{\mathbf{x}}_i \leftarrow \mathsf{Estimator}(\hat{S}_i, \mathsf{w}(\cdot), F)$;
Output $(\hat{\mathbf{x}}, \text{sup})$.

Algorithm 4: ProcessWithDataBubble(Q, T'): extended for general measure F on uniform/measure-based sample

Input: aggregation query $Q(\mathcal{G}, F(M), \mathcal{P})$ and table T
Index: measure-augmented index MAInd
$\hat{S}_i \leftarrow \varnothing$ for all groups i's;
Compute $T^{\mathsf{ID}}_{\mathcal{P}} \leftarrow \{t_{\mathsf{ID}} \mid \text{rows } t \text{ that satisfy } \mathcal{P}\}$ using MAInd;
Repeat $\min\{1/\epsilon^2, |T^{\mathsf{ID}}_{\mathcal{P}}|\}$ times:
  Randomly pick $t_{\mathsf{ID}} \in T^{\mathsf{ID}}_{\mathcal{P}}$: for each $t_{\mathsf{ID}} \in T^{\mathsf{ID}}_{\mathcal{P}}$,
    If MeasureBiased = true: $\mathbf{Pr}[t_{\mathsf{ID}}] \sim \mathsf{apx}(t_M)$;
    Else (uniform sampling): $\mathbf{Pr}[t_{\mathsf{ID}}] = 1/|T^{\mathsf{ID}}_{\mathcal{P}}|$;
  $t \leftarrow$ seeking T using t_{ID} for other dimensions;
  Let i be the group t belonging to on $\mathcal{G}$;
  $\hat{S}_i \leftarrow \hat{S}_i \cup \{t\}$; $\mathsf{w}(t) \leftarrow \mathbf{Pr}[t_{\mathsf{ID}}]$;
For each group i: $\hat{\mathbf{x}}_i \leftarrow \mathsf{Estimator}(\hat{S}_i, \mathsf{w}(\cdot), F)$;
Output $\hat{\mathbf{x}}$.

Algorithm 5: ProcessWithMAIndex(Q, MeasureBiased): extended for general measure F on uniform/measure-based sample

6.2 Extensibility of Our Techniques

Foreign key joins and star schema. In order for our system to support aggregate queries with foreign key joins in a star schema, our samples and indexes can be extended as follows.

Uniform/measure-biased samples are drawn from the fact table in the same way as introduced in Section 4. But for each dimension table, we have two options. i) We can join it with the samples from the fact table in the offline sampling stage and attach the additional dimensions to the samples; or ii) we can perform the join when processing aggregation queries using samples, if one or more of its dimensions appear in the query. Option ii) is feasible when the dimension table is small enough to be fit into the memory. In our implementation, we choose option i). For the complex schema in TPC-H, Table 1 shows the space overhead of all uniform and measure-biased samples, which is affordable in memory even though samples are attached with dimensions from all tables.

For the measure-augmented inverted index and the low-frequency group index, we construct them in the view that joins the fact table with all the dimensions. For TPC-H, Table 1 shows their total sizes.

In a snowflake schema with multiple fact tables and multi-level dimensions, the above extensions can still be applied.

Range predicates. Our samples can already be used to handle any predicate that is based on existing dimensions. To handle range predicates like "$D \geq s$ AND $D \leq t$" for small queries, we introduce the following *measure-augmented B+ tree index*.

• *Measure-augmented B+ tree.* In a B+ tree built on a numerical dimension D, each leaf node is associated with a list of D's values within certain range. In our measure-augmented B+ tree, for each D's value at each leaf, we associate it with IDs (pointers) of the rows with this value on D and also approximate measure $\mathsf{apx}(t_M)$ for each measure (as in (5)) of these rows – recall that these approximate measures need much less bits than the exact measure values.

When a range constraint $s \leq D \leq t$ is in the predicate, we can use this measure-augmented B+ tree to retrieve IDs of rows with $s \leq t_D \leq t$ as well as their approximate measures. Our approximate measure-biased sampling introduced in Section 5.1.2 can then be used to pick $O(1/\epsilon^2)$ row IDs and seek their dimension values in the original table to answer a query with ϵ-approximation.

Extension for other aggregates. We now focus on how to extend our sample+seek solution to a wide range of aggregates.

• *Simple extensions.* We can convert both estimated distributions for SUM and COUNT to absolute answers using the way introduced in Section 6.1. Then some measure like AVG can be easily supported as it is nothing but the ratio of SUM to COUNT.

• *Generic aggregates.* To support a generic range of aggregates in Algorithm 1, we extend processing with uniform/measure-biased samples (Algorithm 2) and processing with measure-augmented index (Algorithm 3) to Algorithm 4 and Algorithm 5, respectively. Processing with low-frequency group index is trivial: one can get the exact value of any aggregate by scanning rows in the index.

The main idea behind Algorithms 4-5 is that, no matter with i) uniform/measure-biased samples or ii) with measure-augmented indexes, our estimations are made based on a set of sample rows with different sampling probabilities. For each group in the answer, with i), sample rows have been pre-drawn and kept in memory, so Algorithm 2 can directly use them. With ii), Algorithm 3 does online sampling/seeking in lines 4-5, and make use of the sample rows for estimation in lines 6-7. So it is intuitive to replace the specific estimation methods in Algorithm 2 (lines 4-5) and Algorithm 3 (lines 6-7) with generic estimators to handle other aggregates.

In Algorithm 4, when scanning rows in a (uniform or measure-biased) sample T', we keep rows from each group i in $\hat{S}_i$ as well as the probability of seeing each row t in $\mathsf{w}(t)$ (line 5). After the scan, for each group i, a point estimation of its aggregate F can be made based on the set of sample rows $\hat{S}_i$ from group i and their weights $\mathsf{w}(\cdot)$, using a generic estimator $\mathsf{Estimator}(\hat{S}_i, \mathsf{w}(\cdot), F)$ (line 6).

The extension in Algorithm 5 is similar, but the sampling is conducted online, either uniformly (line 6) or biased on measure (line 5). Again, rows collected from sampling are kept in $\hat{S}_i$ for group i together with sampling probabilities in $\mathsf{w}(\cdot)$ (line 9). After enough number of rows are collected, estimation of aggregate value F for each group can be made using $\mathsf{Estimator}(\hat{S}_i, \mathsf{w}(\cdot), F)$.

Estimator is a customizable component and *any sample-based point estimator* for the aggregate F can be applied. It takes a set of sample rows $\hat{S}$, their sampling weights $w(\cdot)$, and F as the input, but does not rely on other components of our system. So our solution enjoys the same extensibility as other sampling-based AQP techniques (*e.g.* [7, 5]) do to support a generic range of aggregates. For example, if F is STDEV(M), the sample standard deviation estimator can be used as Estimator; if F is COUNT(DISTINCT M), the estimator GEE proposed in [10] can be used as Estimator.

We will evaluate such extensions in experiments.

7. EVALUATION

We compare our system with a commercial RDB and two state of the art AQP solutions with stratified sampling: Babcock *et al.* [7] (workload-independent) and BlinkDB [5] (workload-aware).

• SPS: Our *sample+seek* solution introduced in this paper.
• DBX: A standard commercial database system with column-store indexes built for all tables on all columns.[1]
• SMG: Small group sampling introduced in [7].
• BLK: BlinkDB with multi-dim stratified sampling [5].

More implementation details of SPS.

• *Parameters.* Our SPS has two parameters. The selectivity threshold s_0 is set to $1/\sqrt{n}$, where n is the total number of rows in a table. The requested error bound ϵ varies from 0.025 to 0.1, and is set as 0.05 if not specified. We use constants 1 behind all $O(\cdot)$'s in our theoretical results. For uniform/measure-biased sampling, our analysis shows that $O(\sqrt{n}/\epsilon^2)$ rows in each sample suffice – we pick exactly $\sqrt{n}/\epsilon^2$ rows for each sample. Similarly, from Theorem 8, we pick exactly $1/\epsilon^2$ rows to perform random seeks.

• *Independent storage.* We implement our storage/index and query execution engine in SPS using C# from sketch. Our custom implementation (of all the components in Figure 2 except "data source") does not reply on other database systems. In our system architecture in Figure 2, we have the original data kept in a column-based storage with dictionary compression on disk. Our samples/indexes are constructed from it, with samples loaded into memory and the other two types of indexes maintained on disk. DBX has a better optimized column-based storage engine – we do not utilize it for SPS, as we want to highlight the speedups brought by our samples/indexes and processing algorithms with early termination.

• *Column-store v.s. row-store.* Our sample+seek framework is independent on the actual data storage of tables, but we choose column-store for uniform/measure-biased samples, and row-store for low-frequency group indexes based on the ways they are accessed. For in-memory samples, a query may touch only a few dimensions of sample rows and only data on these dimensions need to be read. So to take the best advantage of data locality and cache, it is more efficient to store the data column by column. For on-disk low-frequency group indexes, since at most $\sqrt{n}$ rows need to be scanned to answer a query, it is more efficient to store the data row by row so that only one random access is required per query. Dictionary compression is applied on both types of storages.

SMG and BLK are implemented on the same storage engine (to store data and samples) as SPS, and all the samples from SMG and BLK are pre-loaded into memory for fair comparison.

7.1 Experiment Settings and Summary

All of our experiments are conducted on a Windows server with 8 core 2.27GHz CPUs and 64 GB memory. DBX is given 4 cores for better performance, and each of the rest uses one core.

Datasets. We use two datasets (a real one and a benchmark):

• LOG: This is a real dataset about service logs in a Fortune 500 company. It is a single table with 29 columns – 19 of them are categorical dimensions (for group-by), and the rest 10 are numerical dimensions/measures. The numbers of distinct values in the categorical dimensions range from 2 to 3000. The whole table has 1.12 billion rows. To test the scalability of different systems, we extract two sub-tables from LOG, LOG-S with 310 million rows and LOG-M with 620 million rows.

• TPC-H: With a scaling factor 100, we produce a 100 GB star-

[1]We tried different types of indexes. Column-store indexes turn out to be the best option for our aggregation query workloads.

Datasets	# of rows (n)	Size on disk	On-disk indexes				In-memory uniform and measure-biased samples (only needed for one ϵ)								
			MA index		LF index		$\epsilon = 0.025$		$\epsilon = 0.050$		$\epsilon = 0.075$		$\epsilon = 0.010$		time
			size	time	size	time	budget	size	budget	size	budget	size	budget	size	
LOG-S	310M	60GB	26GB	0.2h	36GB	0.3h	0.0909	11GB	**0.0227**	2.8GB	0.0101	1.2GB	0.0056	0.68GB	0.2h
LOG-M	620M	120GB	41GB	0.5h	6GB	0.4h	0.0643	16GB	**0.0161**	4.1GB	0.0071	1.8Gb	0.0040	1.1GB	0.4h
LOG	1120M	202GB	70GB	1.0h	8GB	0.7h	0.0478	22GB	**0.0120**	5.5GB	0.0053	2.4GB	0.0030	1.4GB	0.7h
TPC-H	600M	100GB	62GB	0.6h	6GB	0.4h	0.0653	15GB	**0.0163**	3.8GB	0.0073	1.7GB	0.0041	0.94GB	0.5h

Table 1: Data size and error bound v.s. sampling budget, sample sizes, and index sizes

schema database using TPC-H benchmark, in which the fact table LINEITEM has a total of 600 million rows.

Workloads. For both datasets, we randomly generate workloads of aggregation queries with predicates, group-bys, and aggregates, and foreign key joins (in TPC-H). We vary the number of group-by columns from 1 to 4 and the number of dimensions in predicates from 0 to 4. COUNT/SUM aggregates are used for experiments in Sections 7.3-7.4. SUM and COUNT(DISTINCT $\cdot$) are tested in Section 7.5. In each aggregation query, the measure M involved is chosen randomly from all the measures. Group-by dimensions and predicate dimensions are chosen uniformly at random from all the categorical dimensions in all tables, with key/id columns excluded (as they are not likely to appear in aggregation queries). In Sections 7.3-7.4, a predicate consists of 0 to 4 (dimension, value) pairs, which represent conjunction (ANDs) of constraints "$D = v$" – v is picked randomly from all values of dimension D. More complex predicate types are tested in Section 7.5.

There are 20 such workloads: each one W.X.Y ($X = 1, 2, 3, 4$ and $Y = 0, 1, 2, 3, 4$) is the set of queries with X group-by dimensions and Y predicate dimensions generated in the above way. We randomly generate 50 queries for each workload W.X.Y. Note that for TPC-H, our workloads are different from the standard TPC-H queries, in order to mimic real-world analytical workloads and to cover more column combinations for each workload. Each standard TPC-H benchmark query (if it is an aggregation query) only covers one particular combination of dimensions and values.[2]

Performance metrics. We report both *Response Time* (ms) and *Speedup* of aggregation query processing in different system. Response time is the time to processing a query. Speedup is the relative ratio of response time in two systems.

Error metrics. We use the L^2 distance between the normalized estimated answer and the true one, $\|\mathbf{x} - \hat{\mathbf{x}}\|_2$, to measure the *Error* in answers produced by different systems. For the ease of understanding, please refer to (2) in Section 2.2 for a more concrete form.

Parameter ϵ in our system specifies *Requested Error*, but the *Actual Error* of answers produced by AQP systems could be different.

Summary of results. We report the cost of constructing and storing samples and indexes in Section 7.2. We compare our SPS with DBX in Section 7.3. The actual error in answers produced by SPS is almost always lower than the requested error bound (specified by ϵ). When ϵ is 5%, SPS achieve a speedup of 100x for 90% of the queries in our workloads. For very selective queries, the speedup is less significant but still around 10x. When compared with other AQP systems SMG and BLK in Section 7.4, our SPS solution produces much less error when the response time is similar; and to produce answers with the same quality, SPS is much faster. The errors in the estimated answers given by SPS have much smaller standard deviations, which implies that the error is more likely to be bounded consistently in SPS. When applied on general aggregates with complex predicates in Section 7.5, our SPS still has the best performance gain compared to SMG and BLK.

[2]Although we use TPC-H in our experiments, the queries used in our experiments are quite different from standard TPC-H benchmarks. So our results do not reflect TPC-H benchmark numbers.

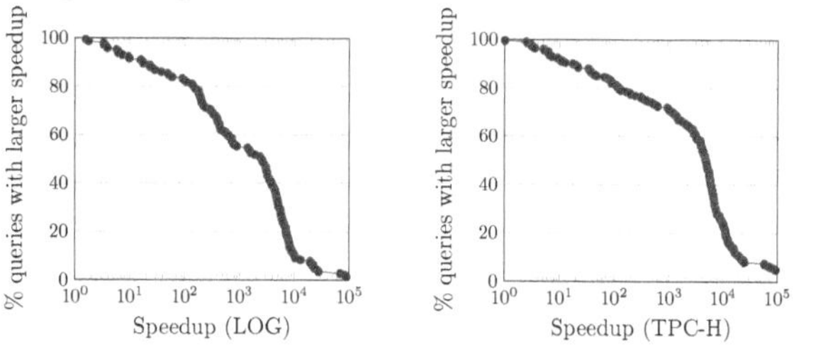

Figure 5: Speedup for the whole workload (twenty together)

7.2 Sampling Budget and Index Size

We first report the overhead of our samples/indexes in terms of both their sizes and construction time in Table 1.

Sampling budget and in-memory samples. Recall that the size of each sample is function of both the required error bound ϵ and the number of rows n, *i.e.*, $\sqrt{n}/\epsilon^2$. The *sampling rate* or *sampling budget* is $(\sqrt{n}/\epsilon^2)/n = (1/\sqrt{n}) \cdot (1/\epsilon^2)$. So one property of our system is that *the sampling rate/budget decreases when the data size increases*, which is a significant advantage for "big data."

The right part of Table 1 gives the sampling budgets (column "budget") and the total sizes of uniform and measure-biased samples (column "size") for different values of error bound ϵ in datasets of different sizes. Dictionary compression is applied on these samples. Because of the above property about sampling budget, the sample sizes increase very slowly for larger datasets for fixed ϵ.

On-disk indexes. Table 1 also gives the size of our measure-augmented indexes, denoted as "MA index" there. Its size is independent on the error bound ϵ, but roughly linear to the data size. The size of the low-frequency group indexes ("LF index" in Table 1) is also independent on ϵ, but is stable for larger datasets. This is because the selectivity threshold $s_0 = 1/\sqrt{n}$ decreases in larger datasets, so fewer values have "low-frequency."

The total proportion of samples and indexes to the original data size decreases for larger datasets (from 1.08 in LOG-S to 0.41 in LOG for $\epsilon = 0.05$) – so our solution is more suitable for "big data."

Construction time. The time needed to build samples and indexes is independent on the error bound but linear to the data size (# rows and # columns), as samples and indexes are constructed during scans of tables. The building time is reported in Table 1 for each portion. The total building time (pre-processing) ranges from 0.7 hour for the smallest LOG-S to 2.4 hours for the largest LOG. Considering that one query in LOG may take several minutes to be completed in DBX and the performance gain of SPS, the cost of this one-time building process is reasonable and profitable.

7.3 Performance Gain over DBMS

We compare our SPS solution with a commercial database product DBX. For our workloads of aggregation queries, column-store indexes give the best performance in DBX, and the memory in our machine is large enough to allow DBX to cache column-store indexes in memory. For TPC-H, we run DBX on a view table that materializes all the foreign-key joins for DBX's best performance.

We compare SPS with DBX on all the twenty workloads W.X.Y (X = 1 ... 4 and Y = 0 ... 4) for both COUNT and SUM.

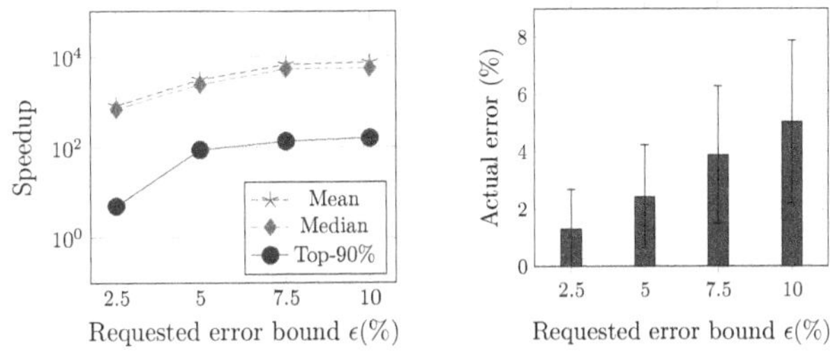

(a) Speedup over DBX (b) Actual error

Figure 6: Varying requested error bound ϵ (LOG)

Exp-I: Overall speedup. Figure 5 reports the overall speedup gained in our SPS system over DBX on all the twenty workloads for SUM aggregates in LOG and TPC-H. The x-axis in Figure 5 is the speedup ratio obtained by each query in our system, and the y-axis is the percentage of queries that obtain higher speedup. For example, a point $(10^2, 90)$ means 90% of all queries are sped up more than 100 times. We can find that, in both LOG and TPC-H, 90% queries in the workload get around 100x speedup or more, and the median speedup is over 10^3x and close to 10^4x.

The requested error bound ϵ is set to 0.05 here. As shown in Exp-II, the actual error is lower than ϵ most of the time.

Exp-II: Vary requested error bound ϵ. Such tremendous speedup is, of course, at the cost of error in the approximate answers produced by SPS. However, the error can be easily controlled by users using the parameter ϵ. We vary the request error bound ϵ, and report the speedups in Figure 6(a) and actual errors in Figure 6(b), where we use all the twenty LOG workloads with SUM aggregates. The error bounds ϵ requested by users are varied from 0.025 to 0.1.

Figure 6(a) plots 90-percentile / median / mean speedups. With larger ϵ, *i.e.*, if users can tolerate a bit larger error, they can gain more significant speedups. But even when they request the error to be no more than $\epsilon = 0.025$, the median / mean speedup is from 10^2 to 10^3. Figures 6(b) plots the average errors together with error bars representing one standard deviation, which are roughly the ranges of min/max error, for each ϵ. The average actual error (even plus standard deviation) is much lower than the requested error bound.

The speedups and errors for TPC-H have very similar trend to LOG. And SPS gets even lower actual errors for COUNT workloads. So those figures are omitted due to the space constraint.

Additional experiments. Exp-III (vary database size), Exp-IV (vary selectivity of queries), and Exp-V (vary number of dimensions in queries) are reported in Appendix D.

7.4 Comparing with Stratified Sampling

We compare our AQP system SPS with BLK and SMG. We use the real dataset LOG-S for this comparison.

Parameters and settings. For both BLK and SMG, we try different values of their parameters and choose the best ones in our experiments. In SMG, there is a threshold for the size of "small groups", and the best value we find in the testing dataset is 2000. In BLK, the similar parameter K (refer to Section 8 for a brief introduction) is set to be 10000 for the best performance. The space budget for samples in BLK is set to be 50% of the dataset size (the same as in [5]) so that we are able to load all the samples of BLK into memory for the fastest possible processing with these samples.

We give the distribution of the 20 SUM-workloads W.X.Y (X = 1-4 and Y = 0-4) (refer to the definitions Section 7.1) to BLK's optimization module which chooses the best set of stratified samples to cover them. Then we use the same workloads for comparison.

Comparison results and analysis. BLK can guarantee response time. For each query, we continuously enlarge the requested response time, so that the actual error in its answer can be reduced. SPS makes such tradeoff between time and error by varying ϵ and early termination. Similar tradeoff can be enabled in SMG by randomly permuting rows in the samples of SMG (in the preprocessing), so errors in SMG keep reducing as a query is being evaluated.

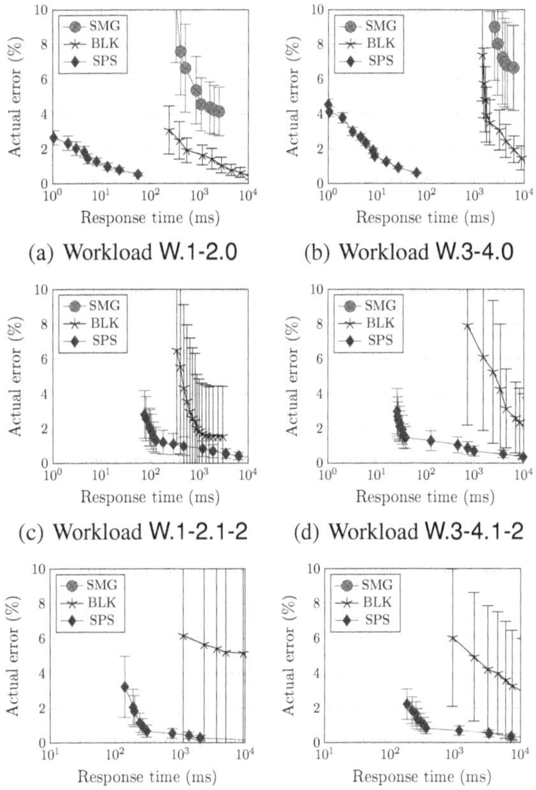

(a) Workload W.1-2.0 (b) Workload W.3-4.0

(c) Workload W.1-2.1-2 (d) Workload W.3-4.1-2

(e) Workload W.1-2.3-4 (f) Workload W.3-4.3-4

Figure 7: Time-error tradeoff in different systems

The 20 workloads are partitioned into six sets as in Figure 7. W.X_1-X_2.Y_1-Y_2 means all queries in W.X.Y with X = X_1 or X_2, and Y = Y_1 or Y_2. The comparison results for the three are reported in Figures 7(a)-7(f) for in-depth analysis. In each figure, one point (x, y) in a chart corresponds to "(the average response time, the average actual error)" of queries. The actual error is associated with an error bar with a width of one standard deviation to show how stable the actual error is for certain requested response time.

- **Queries with no predicates.** W.1-2.0 and W.3-4.0 (in Figures 7(a)-7(b)) are queries without predicates. All the three systems perform reasonably well for them, producing answers with error less than 0.1 within seconds. It is also obvious that our SPS has the narrowest error bar and the lowest average error for the same response time. This is because of our fundamentally different sampling scheme, measure-biased sampling, which produces precision guarantee independent on the underlying data distribution.
- **Queries with predicates.** For queries with predicates (the rest four sub-workloads in Figures 7(c)-7(f)), results about SMG are not plotted, because either its error is much higher than SPS and BLK, or its response time is too long. The reason is that SMG's small group sampling is a stratified sampling on only one dimension, so for selective predicates, its stratified samples can only capture a small number of rows satisfying the predicate, which makes its estimation inaccurate. We also observe that, SPS outperforms BLK a lot on error when the response time is similar. This is due to both our new sampling technique and the novel index structures. With the help of the indexes, our online sampling only needs $1/\epsilon^2$

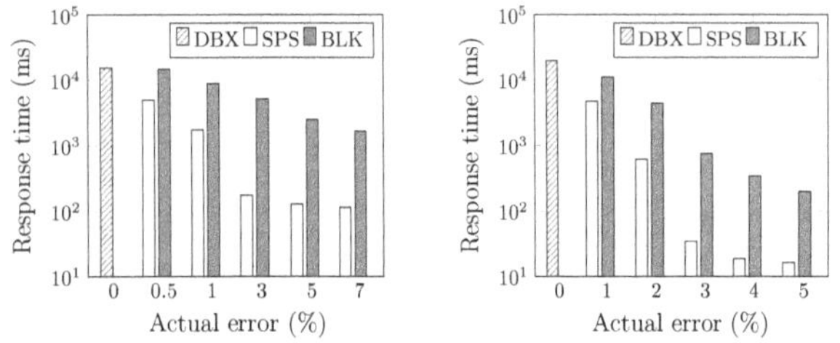

(a) SUM(M) (b) COUNT(DISTINCT M)

Figure 8: With complex predicates and general aggregates

random seeks to produce an ϵ-approximation for any small query. On the other hand, when only very few rows satisfy a small query's predicate, if the predicate's column set is not covered exactly by the columns of any stratified sample selected by BLK's optimization module, BLK will suffer from the same problem as SMG (although it happens less frequently than in SMG).

7.5 Extensibility

We conduct experiments on more general workloads (generic aggregates with range constraints and complex logical expressions as predicates) to evaluate the extensibility of SPS as introduced in Section 6.2. SPS still outperforms the others on such workloads.

The workloads are generated on LOG-S with 1-4 group-by dimensions, and complex logical expressions on 4 dimensions as predicates, such as "$(C_1 = v_1 \text{ OR } v_2' \leq C_2 \leq v_2'') \text{ AND } (C_3 = v_3 \text{ OR } v_4' \leq C_4 \leq v_4'')$". We generate two such workloads with aggregates SUM(M) and COUNT(DISTINCT M), respectively. We always include 2 equality constraints on categorical dimensions and 2 range constraints on numerical dimensions in a predicate. For each of such workloads, dimensions, values, and logical expressions are randomly picked to form 200 queries.

Results for the two workloads are reported in Figure 8. We plot the average response time of SPS and BLK when achieving certain actual error, and compare them with DBX (we ignore SMG as it is dominated by the other two). Overall, our SPS provides much better tradeoff between time and error than BLK does, and is always faster than BLK when with the same error.

The performance gain of SPS over BLK and DBX on SUM is significant (Figure 8(a)) because of the strong theoretical guarantee. SPS can benefit from measure-biased samples on other aggregates AVG and STDEV as well even though the theoretical guarantees are weaker for them. It benefits from our samples and indexes also on COUNT(DISTINCT M) (Figure 8(b)). So when the error is above 2% or 1%, SPS is still the best option with significant performance gain and smooth tradeoff between time and accuracy. In particular, SPS still gets 100x speedup when the error is 5%.

8. RELATED WORK

AQP has been studied extensively during last few decades. There are three related lines, including i) online sampling – drawing samples after each query comes, ii) offline sampling – drawing samples before queries come; and iii) non-sampling based approaches.

Online sampling/aggregation. Online aggregation [19, 14, 24] streams data in a random order or assumes that sample rows can be randomly drawn from the underlying database, and uses them to estimated query answers. The disadvantage is that drawing rows randomly from the table for each query means many random I/O accesses, which are costly at query time, resulting in high latency. Such techniques are orthogonal to our ideas of sampling and building indexes before queries come, and can be integrated into our system to provide estimations before index building is finished.

Offline sampling. This line of work is especially relevant to ours. The idea is to create random samples before queries come, and calibrate their sampling rates carefully using stratified (or importance) sampling [22] to reduce variance when using them to answer queries. There are two types of offline sampling techniques: one calibrates sampling rates without the knowledge of workload; and the other utilizes historical workload distribution.

• **Workload-independent sampling.** Aqua [3, 2] proposes congressional sampling. For all possible queries, consider combinations of group-by dimensions. For each combination, the sampling rate is set based on a weighting function that considers the group sizes for all subsets of the group-by dimensions in this combination. For d possible group-by dimensions, there are 2^d combinations, which renders it impractical for datasets with dozens or hundreds of possible group-by columns. In addition, Aqua operates on a single sample which has to be very general-purpose in nature but only loosely appropriate for any particular query [7].

To overcome such shortcomings, Babcock *et al.* [7] proposes small group sampling, a stratified sampling technique that builds a biased sample on each single column. Uniform sampling does a satisfactory job at providing good estimates for the large groups in a group-by query. A group here is the set of all rows with certain (the same) value on a group-by dimension. For small groups, uniform sampling fails to draw enough number of rows for each. So all the rows from the small groups are included in the biased sample on their dimension. A query is executed on the union of the uniform sample and all biased samples whose dimensions appear in the query for an estimated answer. Using similar heuristics, outlier indexing [11] is proposed to include rows with outlier values in additional samples to improve estimation accuracy.

• **Workload-aware sampling.** Workload information can be used to optimize samples' constitution. For example, Aqua [2] can be adapted to workloads. Workloads are also used in [15] to construct "self-tuning" biased samples. STRAT [12, 13] aims to minimize the expected relative error of workloads. [23] requires building a new sample for each query template. SciBORQ [27] targets scientific analysis and creates samples based on past query results with no guarantees on error margin. However, the assumption of these works that workloads are stable can easily be wrong in practice.

BlinkDB [5] abstracts workload to query column set (QCS), *i.e.*, the set of columns that appear in a query, allowing it to tolerate moderate workload change. A group is the set of all rows with the same values on a QCS. A stratified sample can be created for each QCS by sampling K rows for each group on this QCS – if a group has less than K rows, all of its rows are put in the sample. BlinkDB formulates an optimization problem to decides how to allocate space budget across QCSs based on previous workloads. It provides either time guarantee or CI-based error guarantee.

Related work on requested error v.s. actual error, non-sampling approaches, and other AQP systems is discussed in Appendix E.

9. CONCLUSIONS

We propose an AQP system based on a novel sample+seek framework. Distribution precision is guaranteed in answers to aggregation queries. A new measure-biased sampling technique is introduced to approximately process SUM aggregation queries with less selective predicates and achieve this precision guarantee. For queries with more selective predicates, sampling is not enough, and we propose two novel indexes to aid in-memory samples. The number of random seeks using our indexes can be bounded to achieve the same precision guarantee. Thus, our system is efficient for queries with various selectivities. Our system can extend to support a generic range of aggregates with complex predicates.

10. REFERENCES

[1] J. Acharya, I. Diakonikolas, C. Hegde, J. Z. Li, and L. Schmidt. Fast and near-optimal algorithms for approximating distributions by histograms. In *PODS*, 2015.

[2] S. Acharya, P. B. Gibbons, and V. Poosala. Congressional samples for approximate answering of group-by queries. In *SIGMOD*, 2000.

[3] S. Acharya, P. B. Gibbons, V. Poosala, and S. Ramaswamy. The aqua approximate query answering system. In *SIGMOD*, 1999.

[4] S. Agarwal, H. Milner, A. Kleiner, A. Talwalkar, M. Jordan, S. Madden, B. Mozafari, and I. Stoica. Knowing when you're wrong: building fast and reliable approximate query processing systems. In *SIGMOD*, 2014.

[5] S. Agarwal, B. Mozafari, A. Panda, H. Milner, S. Madden, and I. Stoica. Blinkdb: queries with bounded errors and bounded response times on very large data. In *Eurosys*, 2013.

[6] S. Agrawal, S. Chaudhuri, and V. R. Narasayya. Automated selection of materialized views and indexes in sql databases. In *VLDB*, 2000.

[7] B. Babcock, S. Chaudhuri, and G. Das. Dynamic sample selection for approximate query processing. In *SIGMOD*, 2003.

[8] P. Bille, A. Pagh, and R. Pagh. Fast evaluation of union-intersection expressions. In *ISAAC*, 2007.

[9] K. Chakrabarti, M. Garofalakis, R. Rastogi, and K. Shim. Approximate query processing using wavelets. *VLDBJ*, 10(2-3), 2001.

[10] M. Charikar, S. Chaudhuri, R. Motwani, and V. R. Narasayya. Towards estimation error guarantees for distinct values. In *PODS*, 2000.

[11] S. Chaudhuri, G. Das, M. Datar, R. Motwani, and V. Narasayya. Overcoming limitations of sampling for aggregation queries. In *ICDE*, 2001.

[12] S. Chaudhuri, G. Das, and V. Narasayya. A robust, optimization-based approach for approximate answering of aggregate queries. In *SIGMOD*, 2001.

[13] S. Chaudhuri, G. Das, and V. Narasayya. Optimized stratified sampling for approximate query processing. *TODS*, 32(2), 2007.

[14] T. Condie, N. Conway, P. Alvaro, J. M. Hellerstein, K. Elmeleegy, and R. Sears. Mapreduce online. In *NSDI*, 2010.

[15] V. Ganti, M.-L. Lee, and R. Ramakrishnan. Icicles: Self-tuning samples for approximate query answering. In *VLDB*, 2000.

[16] M. N. Garofalakis and P. B. Gibbons. Approximate query processing: Taming the terabytes. In *VLDB*, 2001.

[17] A. C. Gilbert, Y. Kotidis, S. Muthukrishnan, and M. J. Strauss. Optimal and approximate computation of summary statistics for range aggregates. In *PODS*, 2001.

[18] J. Gray, S. Chaudhuri, A. Bosworth, A. Layman, D. Reichart, M. Venkatrao, F. Pellow, and H. Pirahesh. Data cube: A relational aggregation operator generalizing group-by, cross-tab, and sub-totals. *Data Min. Knowl. Discov.*, 1(1), 1997.

[19] J. M. Hellerstein, P. J. Haas, and H. J. Wang. Online aggregation. *SIGMOD*, 1997.

[20] A. Kim, E. Blais, A. G. Parameswaran, P. Indyk, S. Madden, and R. Rubinfeld. Rapid sampling for visualizations with ordering guarantees. *PVLDB*, 8(5), 2015.

[21] A. Kleiner, A. Talwalkar, S. Agarwal, I. Stoica, and M. I. Jordan. A general bootstrap performance diagnostic. In *KDD*, 2013.

[22] S. L. Lohr. *Sampling: Design and Analysis*. Thomson, 2009.

[23] C. Olston, E. Bortnikov, K. Elmeleegy, F. Junqueira, and B. Reed. Interactive analysis of web-scale data. In *CIDR*, 2009.

[24] N. Pansare, V. R. Borkar, C. Jermaine, and T. Condie. Online aggregation for large mapreduce jobs. *PVLDB*, 4(11), 2011.

[25] N. Potti and J. M. Patel. Daq: a new paradigm for approximate query processing. *PVLDB*, 8(9), 2015.

[26] B. Shneiderman. Response time and display rate in human performance with computers. *ACM Computing Surveys*, 1984.

[27] L. Sidirourgos, M. L. Kersten, and P. A. Boncz. Sciborq: Scientific data management with bounds on runtime and quality. In *CIDR*, 2011.

[28] J. S. Vitter and M. Wang. Approximate computation of multidimensional aggregates of sparse data using wavelets. In *SIGMOD*, 1999.

[29] K. Zeng, S. Gao, B. Mozafari, and C. Zaniolo. The analytical bootstrap: a new method for fast error estimation in approximate query processing. In *SIGMOD*, 2014.

APPENDIX

A. PROOFS

Proof of Theorem 3. Suppose there are r groups in the answer $\mathbf{x}$ to Q. For each group $i \in \{1, \ldots, r\}$, let n_i be the number of rows belonging to the ith group and satisfying the predicate $\mathcal{P}$, and $n_{\mathcal{P}}$ be the total number of rows satisfying $\mathcal{P}$. So of course, $\sum_{i=1}^{r} n_i = n_{\mathcal{P}}$ and $s(\mathcal{P}) = n_{\mathcal{P}}/n$.

We draw a uniform sample of m rows T^0 from T. Similarly, in the sample T^0, let m_i be the number of rows belonging to the ith group and satisfying the predicate $\mathcal{P}$, and $m_{\mathcal{P}}$ be the number of rows satisfying $\mathcal{P}$.

Consider the answer $\mathbf{x}$ to Q and the estimated answer $\hat{\mathbf{x}}$, we have $x_i = n_i/n_{\mathcal{P}}$ and $\hat{x}_i = m_i/m_{\mathcal{P}}$. So,

$$\mathbf{E}\left[\|\mathbf{x} - \hat{\mathbf{x}}\|_2^2\right] = \mathbf{E}\left[\sum_{i=1}^{r}\left(\frac{n_i}{n_{\mathcal{P}}} - \frac{m_i}{m_{\mathcal{P}}}\right)^2\right] \tag{8}$$

$$= \mathbf{E}\left[\frac{n^2}{m^2 n_{\mathcal{P}}^2}\sum_{i=1}^{r}\left(m \cdot \frac{n_i}{n} - m \cdot \frac{n_{\mathcal{P}}}{n} \cdot \frac{m_i}{m_{\mathcal{P}}}\right)^2\right]. \tag{9}$$

$m_{\mathcal{P}}$ can be interpreted as the number of successes in m independent Bernoulli trials with success probability $n_{\mathcal{P}}/n$. So $\mathbf{E}[m_{\mathcal{P}}] = m \cdot n_{\mathcal{P}}/n \triangleq \bar{m}_{\mathcal{P}}$. Similarly, m_i can be interpreted as the number of successes in m independent Bernoulli trials with success probability n_i/n. So $\mathbf{E}[m_i] = m \cdot n_i/n \triangleq \bar{m}_i$. From Chernoff bound, for $0 < \epsilon < 1$, we have

$$\mathbf{Pr}\left[m_{\mathcal{P}} \geq (1+\epsilon)\bar{m}_{\mathcal{P}}\right] \leq e^{-\epsilon^2 \bar{m}_{\mathcal{P}}/3}, \tag{10}$$

$$\text{and } \mathbf{Pr}\left[m_{\mathcal{P}} \leq (1-\epsilon)\bar{m}_{\mathcal{P}}\right] \leq e^{-\epsilon^2 \bar{m}_{\mathcal{P}}/2}. \tag{11}$$

Consider two events: $\mathsf{E}_{\text{in}} = [(1-\epsilon)\bar{m}_{\mathcal{P}} < m_{\mathcal{P}} < (1+\epsilon)\bar{m}_{\mathcal{P}}]$ and $\mathsf{E}_{\text{out}} = [m_{\mathcal{P}} \geq (1+\epsilon)\bar{m}_{\mathcal{P}} \vee m_{\mathcal{P}} \leq (1-\epsilon)\bar{m}_{\mathcal{P}}]$. We can then rewrite (9) using conditional probability:

$$\mathbf{E}\left[\|\mathbf{x} - \hat{\mathbf{x}}\|_2^2\right] = \mathbf{E}\left[\frac{1}{\bar{m}_{\mathcal{P}}^2}\sum_{i=1}^{r}\left(\bar{m}_i - \bar{m}_{\mathcal{P}} \cdot \frac{m_i}{m_{\mathcal{P}}}\right)^2\right] = \tag{12}$$

$$\mathbf{E}\left[\frac{1}{\bar{m}_{\mathcal{P}}^2}\sum_{i=1}^{r}\left(\bar{m}_i - \bar{m}_{\mathcal{P}} \cdot \frac{m_i}{m_{\mathcal{P}}}\right)^2 \middle| \mathsf{E}_{\text{in}}\right] \cdot \mathbf{Pr}\left[\mathsf{E}_{\text{in}}\right] \tag{13}$$

$$+ \mathbf{E}\left[\frac{1}{\bar{m}_{\mathcal{P}}^2}\sum_{i=1}^{r}\left(\bar{m}_i - \bar{m}_{\mathcal{P}} \cdot \frac{m_i}{m_{\mathcal{P}}}\right)^2 \middle| \mathsf{E}_{\text{out}}\right] \cdot \mathbf{Pr}\left[\mathsf{E}_{\text{out}}\right]. \tag{14}$$

Let $m_{\mathcal{P}}/\bar{m}_{\mathcal{P}} = \alpha$. (13) can be upper bounded as:

$$(13) \leq \mathbf{E}\left[\frac{1}{\bar{m}_{\mathcal{P}}^2}\sum_{i=1}^{r}\left(\bar{m}_i - \frac{m_i}{\alpha}\right)^2 \middle| 1-\epsilon < \alpha < 1+\epsilon\right] \tag{15}$$

$$\leq \max_{1-\epsilon<\alpha<1+\epsilon} \frac{1}{\bar{m}_{\mathcal{P}}^2}\sum_{i=1}^{r}\mathbf{E}\left[\left(\bar{m}_i - \frac{m_i}{\alpha}\right)^2\right] \tag{16}$$

$$= \max_{1-\epsilon<\alpha<1+\epsilon} \frac{1}{\bar{m}_{\mathcal{P}}^2}\sum_{i=1}^{r}\left(\frac{1}{\alpha^2}\mathbf{Var}\left[m_i\right] + \frac{(\alpha-1)^2}{\alpha^2}\bar{m}_i^2\right) \tag{17}$$

$$\leq \frac{2}{\bar{m}_{\mathcal{P}}^2}\left(\sum_{i=1}^{r}\mathbf{Var}\left[m_i\right] + \sum_{i=1}^{r}\epsilon^2\bar{m}_i^2\right) \quad (\epsilon \leq 0.5 \text{ is small}). \tag{18}$$

Since m_i is the number of successes in m Bernoulli trials,

$$\sum_{i=1}^{r}\mathbf{Var}\left[m_i\right] = \sum_{i=1}^{r} m \cdot \frac{n_i}{n} \cdot \left(1 - \frac{n_i}{n}\right) \leq \frac{m \cdot n_{\mathcal{P}}}{n} = \bar{m}_{\mathcal{P}}. \tag{19}$$

From Cauchy-Schwarz inequality, we have

$$\sum_{i=1}^{r} \epsilon^2 \bar{m}_i^2 \leq \epsilon^2 \left(\sum_{i=1}^{r} \bar{m}_i \right)^2 = \epsilon^2 \cdot \bar{m}_{\mathcal{P}}^2 \tag{20}$$

Putting (19) and (20) back to (18), we have

$$(13) \leq \frac{2}{\bar{m}_{\mathcal{P}}} + 2\epsilon^2. \tag{21}$$

Now we upper bound (14). From (10) and (11),

$$\mathbf{Pr}\left[\mathsf{E}_{\mathsf{out}}\right] \leq e^{-\epsilon^2 \bar{m}_{\mathcal{P}}/3} + e^{-\epsilon^2 \bar{m}_{\mathcal{P}}/2} \leq 2e^{-\epsilon^2 \bar{m}_{\mathcal{P}}/3}. \tag{22}$$

For the values of $m_{\mathcal{P}}/\bar{m}_{\mathcal{P}} = \alpha$ in event $\mathsf{E}_{\mathsf{out}}$, we have

$$\mathbf{E}\left[\frac{1}{\bar{m}_{\mathcal{P}}^2} \sum_{i=1}^{r} \left(\bar{m}_i - \bar{m}_{\mathcal{P}} \cdot \frac{m_i}{m_{\mathcal{P}}} \right)^2 \middle| \mathsf{E}_{\mathsf{out}} \right] \tag{23}$$

$$\leq \frac{1}{\bar{m}_{\mathcal{P}}^2} \mathbf{E}\left[\sum_{i=1}^{r} \bar{m}_i^2 + \sum_{i=1}^{r} \left(\bar{m}_{\mathcal{P}} \cdot \frac{m_i}{m_{\mathcal{P}}} \right)^2 \right] \leq 2. \tag{24}$$

where the second inequality of (24) is from Cauchy-Schwarz inequality and linearity of expectation. Putting (22) and (24) back to (14), together with (13) and (21), we have

$$\mathbf{E}\left[\|\mathbf{x} - \hat{\mathbf{x}}\|_2^2\right] \leq \frac{2}{\bar{m}_{\mathcal{P}}} + 2\epsilon^2 + 4e^{-\epsilon^2 \bar{m}_{\mathcal{P}}/3} \leq 6\epsilon^2, \tag{25}$$

if $\bar{m}_{\mathcal{P}} = \Omega\left(\frac{1}{\epsilon^2} \log \frac{1}{\epsilon^2}\right)$, and from Jensen's inequality,

$$\mathbf{E}\left[\|\mathbf{x} - \hat{\mathbf{x}}\|_2\right] \leq \sqrt{\mathbf{E}\left[\|\mathbf{x} - \hat{\mathbf{x}}\|_2^2\right]} \leq 3\epsilon. \tag{26}$$

We can conclude the proof using a generalized McDiarmid's inequality. Rewrite $\phi(t_1, \ldots, t_m) \triangleq \|\mathbf{x} - \hat{\mathbf{x}}\|_2$, where t_i is a sample row from the table T and $\{t_i \mid i = 1, \ldots, m\}$ are mutually independent. Consider a different estimation $\hat{\mathbf{x}}' = \langle \hat{x}_1', \ldots, \hat{x}_r' \rangle$, where $\hat{x}_i' = m_i/\bar{m}_{\mathcal{P}}$ (and truncate $\hat{x}_i'$ at 1). Note that $\bar{m}_{\mathcal{P}}$ is unknown so $\hat{\mathbf{x}}'$ is only conceptually feasible. Similarly, let $\phi'(t_1, \ldots, t_m) \triangleq \|\mathbf{x} - \hat{\mathbf{x}}'\|_2$. Using Chernoff bound as (10), if $\bar{m}_{\mathcal{P}} = \Omega\left(\frac{1}{\epsilon^2} \log \frac{1}{\delta}\right)$,

$$\mathbf{Pr}\left[1 - \epsilon \leq \frac{\|\mathbf{x} - \hat{\mathbf{x}}\|_2}{\|\mathbf{x} - \hat{\mathbf{x}}'\|_2} \leq 1 + \epsilon\right] \geq 1 - \delta. \tag{27}$$

For any two random samples $\{t_1, \ldots, t_i, \ldots, t_m\}$ and $\{t_1, \ldots, t_i', \ldots, t_m\}$ differing at only one pair of tuples t_i and t_i', the function ϕ' satisfies the Lipschitz property that

$$|\phi'(t_1, \ldots, t_i, \ldots, t_m) - \phi'(t_1, \ldots, t_i', \ldots, t_m)| = c_i \leq 2/\bar{m}_{\mathcal{P}}.$$

and $\sum_{i=1}^{m} c_i^2 \leq 4/\bar{m}_{\mathcal{P}}$. So using McDiarmid's inequality,

$$\mathbf{Pr}\left[\|\mathbf{x} - \hat{\mathbf{x}}'\|_2 > \mathbf{E}\left[\|\mathbf{x} - \hat{\mathbf{x}}'\|_2\right] + \epsilon\right] \leq e^{-8\epsilon^2 \bar{m}_{\mathcal{P}}} = \delta. \tag{28}$$

Thus, from (26), (27), and (28), we have

$$\mathbf{Pr}\left[\|\mathbf{x} - \hat{\mathbf{x}}\|_2 \leq \epsilon\right] \geq 1 - \delta, \tag{29}$$

if $m = \Omega\left(\frac{1}{s_0} \cdot \frac{1}{\epsilon^2} \cdot \left(\log \frac{1}{\epsilon^2} + \log \frac{1}{\delta}\right)\right)$ (note $\bar{m}_{\mathcal{P}} = m \cdot s_0$). □

Proof of Theorem 5. Let's first focus on a special case where $s_0 = 1$ and the query $Q(\mathcal{G}, \mathsf{SUM}(M), \varnothing)$ has no predicate.

Suppose there are r groups in the answer $\mathbf{x} = \langle x_1, \ldots, x_r \rangle$ to Q. Let $T_i \subseteq T$ be the set of rows belonging to the ith group for $i = 1, \ldots, r$. Recall that, for a set T of rows, $M(T) = \sum_{t \in T} t_M$ is the sum of values of measure M over all rows in T. So we have $x_i = M(T_i)/M(T)$.

Let m be the number of rows in the measure-biased sample T^M, and let m_i be the number of rows belonging to the ith group in T^M. Recall that, in our estimated answer $\hat{\mathbf{x}} = \langle \hat{x}_1, \ldots, \hat{x}_r \rangle$, we have $\hat{x}_i = m_i/m$. So we can rewrite

$$\mathbf{E}\left[\|\mathbf{x} - \hat{\mathbf{x}}\|_2^2\right] = \frac{1}{m^2} \sum_{i=1}^{r} \mathbf{E}\left[\left(\frac{M(T_i)}{M(T)} \cdot m - m_i\right)^2\right]. \tag{30}$$

In our measure-biased sampling, a row in the ith group T_i is drawn into T^M with probability $p_i^M = M(T_i)/M(T)$. So m_i is the number of successes of in m independent Bernoulli trials with success probability p_i^M. We have $\mathbf{E}[m_i] = mp_i^M$ and $\mathbf{Var}[m_i] = mp_i^M(1 - p_i^M)$. (30) can be rewritten as

$$\mathbf{E}\left[\|\mathbf{x} - \hat{\mathbf{x}}\|_2^2\right] = \frac{1}{m^2} \sum_{i=1}^{r} \mathbf{Var}[m_i] = \frac{1}{m} \sum_{i=1}^{r} p_i^M(1 - p_i^M) \leq \frac{1}{m}.$$

The rest part is similar to the proof of Theorem 3. Let $m = \Omega\left((1/\epsilon^2) \cdot \log(1/\delta)\right)$. Using Jensen's inequality, we could have $\mathbf{E}\left[\|\mathbf{x} - \hat{\mathbf{x}}\|_2\right] \leq 1/\sqrt{m} \leq \epsilon$. As replacing one row in T^M changes $\|\mathbf{x} - \hat{\mathbf{x}}\|_2$ at most by $1/m$, using McDiarmid's inequality, $\|\mathbf{x} - \hat{\mathbf{x}}\|_2 \leq 2\epsilon$ with probability at most $1 - \delta$.

Now consider the general case with $0 < s_0 \leq 1$ and a query $Q(\mathcal{G}, \mathsf{SUM}(M), \mathcal{P})$ with measure selectivity $s_M(\mathcal{P}) \geq s_0$. The idea is identical to the proof of Theorem 3 so we only sketch it in the following part.

Let $T_{\mathcal{P}} \subseteq T$ be the set of rows satisfying $\mathcal{P}$ in T, and $T_i \subseteq T_{\mathcal{P}}$ be the set of rows satisfying $\mathcal{P}$ and belonging to the ith group in T. Also, let $m_{\mathcal{P}}$ be the number of rows satisfying $\mathcal{P}$ in the sample T^M, and m_i be the number of rows satisfying $\mathcal{P}$ and belonging to the $i$the group in T^M.

In our measure-biased sampling, it is not hard to see $\mathbf{E}[m_{\mathcal{P}}] = m \cdot M(T_{\mathcal{P}})/M(T) \triangleq \bar{m}_{\mathcal{P}}$. Similar to the proof of Theorem 3, consider two events: $\mathsf{E}_{\mathsf{in}} = [(1 - \epsilon)\bar{m}_{\mathcal{P}} < m_{\mathcal{P}} < (1 + \epsilon)\bar{m}_{\mathcal{P}}]$ and $\mathsf{E}_{\mathsf{out}} = [m_{\mathcal{P}} \geq (1 + \epsilon)\bar{m}_{\mathcal{P}} \vee m_{\mathcal{P}} \leq (1 - \epsilon)\bar{m}_{\mathcal{P}}]$. Decompose $\mathbf{E}\left[\|\mathbf{x} - \hat{\mathbf{x}}\|_2^2\right]$ as in (13)-(14) into

$$\mathbf{E}\left[\|\mathbf{x} - \hat{\mathbf{x}}\|_2^2\right] = \mathbf{E}\left[\|\mathbf{x} - \hat{\mathbf{x}}\|_2^2 \mid \mathsf{E}_{\mathsf{in}}\right] \cdot \mathbf{Pr}\left[\mathsf{E}_{\mathsf{in}}\right] \tag{31}$$

$$+ \mathbf{E}\left[\|\mathbf{x} - \hat{\mathbf{x}}\|_2^2 \mid \mathsf{E}_{\mathsf{out}}\right] \cdot \mathbf{Pr}\left[\mathsf{E}_{\mathsf{out}}\right]. \tag{32}$$

We can show that $\mathbf{Pr}\left[\mathsf{E}_{\mathsf{out}}\right]$ is small enough so that (32) only adds a term ϵ. On the other hand, in the event E_{in}, $\mathbf{E}\left[\|\mathbf{x} - \hat{\mathbf{x}}\|_2^2 \mid \mathsf{E}_{\mathsf{in}}\right]$ can be upper bounded similarly as in the above special case by $1/\bar{m}_{\mathcal{P}}$ with high probability. Putting them together with a generalized argument using McDiarmid's inequality completes the proof. □

Proof of Proposition 7. In the answer $\mathbf{x} = \langle x_1, \ldots, x_r \rangle$ to Q, there are r groups. Let $T_i \subseteq T_{\mathcal{P}}$ be the set of rows belonging to the ith group for $i = 1, \ldots, r$. For a set T of rows, recall $M(T) = \sum_{t \in T} t_M$. So we have $x_i = M(T_i)/M(T_{\mathcal{P}})$. Let m be the number of rows in $T_{\mathcal{P}}'$ and T_i' be the set of rows belonging to the ith group in $T_{\mathcal{P}}'$. We estmate $\hat{x}_i = M(T_i')/M(T_{\mathcal{P}}')$.

We rewrite $\mathbf{E}\left[\|\mathbf{x} - \hat{\mathbf{x}}\|_2^2\right] =$

$$= \frac{1}{M(T_{\mathcal{P}}')^2} \sum_{i=1}^{r} \mathbf{E}\left[\left(x_i \cdot M(T_{\mathcal{P}}') - M(T_i')\right)^2\right] \tag{33}$$

$$\leq \frac{1}{m^2} \sum_{i=1}^{r} \mathbf{E}\left[\left(x_i \cdot M(T_{\mathcal{P}}') - M(T_i')\right)^2\right]. \tag{34}$$

Now focus on the ith group. Consider one random draw of a row t in $T_{\mathcal{P}}'$. Let $\mathrm{I}_{t,i}$ be indicator variable of the event that $t \in T_i$ (*i.e.*, $\mathrm{I}_{t,i} = 1$ if $t \in T_i$ and $\mathrm{I}_{t,i} = 0$ otherwise). Define random variable $Z_{t,i} = x_i \cdot t_M - t_M \cdot \mathrm{I}_{t,i}$. We can rewrite the term in (34) as $x_i \cdot M(T_{\mathcal{P}}') - M(T_i') = \sum_{t \in T_{\mathcal{P}}'} Z_{t,i}$. It is not hard to see that $\mathbf{E}_t[Z_{t,i}] = 0$. And because the m rows in $T_{\mathcal{P}}'$ are drawn independently, we have

$$\mathbf{E}\left[\left(\Sigma_{t\in T'_{\mathcal{P}}} Z_{t,i}\right)^2\right] = m\mathbf{E}_t\left[Z_{t,i}^2\right].$$

Putting it back to (34), we have

$$\mathbf{E}\left[\|\mathbf{x}-\hat{\mathbf{x}}\|_2^2\right] \le \frac{1}{m}\sum_{i=1}^{r}\mathbf{E}_t\left[Z_{t,i}^2\right]. \quad (35)$$

We upper bound $\mathbf{E}_t\left[Z_{t,i}^2\right]$ in the rest part.

$$\mathbf{E}_t\left[Z_{t,i}^2\right] = \mathbf{E}_t\left[x_i^2 \cdot t_M^2 - 2x_i \cdot t_M^2 \cdot \mathrm{I}_{t,i} + t_M^2 \cdot \mathrm{I}_{t,i}^2\right]. \quad (36)$$

Let $n = |T_{\mathcal{P}}|$ and $n_i = |T_i|$. Using the fact that $t_M \in [1, \Delta]$ for any row t, we have

$$\mathbf{E}_t\left[x_i^2 \cdot t_M^2\right] = x_i^2 \cdot \sum_{t\in T_{\mathcal{P}}}\frac{t_M^2}{n} \le x_i^2 \cdot \frac{n\Delta^2}{n} = x_i^2\Delta^2.$$

And similarly, from $n_i/n \le x_i\Delta$, we have

$$\mathbf{E}_t\left[t_M^2 \cdot \mathrm{I}_{t,i}^2\right] = \sum_{t\in T_i}\frac{t_M^2}{n} \le \frac{n_i\Delta^2}{n} \le x_i\Delta^3,$$

Putting them back to (36), we have

$$\mathbf{E}_t\left[Z_{t,i}^2\right] \le x_i^2\Delta^2 + x_i\Delta^3 \le (\Delta^3+\Delta^2)\cdot x_i. \quad (37)$$

And putting (37) back to (35), we have

$$\mathbf{E}\left[\|\mathbf{x}-\hat{\mathbf{x}}\|_2^2\right] \le \frac{1}{m}\sum_{i=1}^{r}(\Delta^3+\Delta^2)\cdot x_i = \frac{\Delta^3+\Delta^2}{m}.$$

Let $m = \Omega(\Delta^3/\epsilon^2)$ and then we have $\mathbf{E}\left[\|\mathbf{x}-\hat{\mathbf{x}}\|_2^2\right] \le \epsilon^2$, and from Jessen's inequality, we complete the proof. □

Proof of Theorem 8. In the answer $\mathbf{x} = \langle x_1, \ldots, x_r\rangle$ to Q, there are r groups. Let $T_i \subseteq T_{\mathcal{P}}$ be the set of rows belonging to the ith group. Let $n = |T_{\mathcal{P}}|$ and $n_i = |T_i|$. For a set T of rows, recall $M(T) = \sum_{t\in T} t_M$. So we have $x_i = M(T_i)/M(T_{\mathcal{P}})$.

Let m be the number of rows in the approximate measure-biased sample $T'_{\mathcal{P}}$, and let T'_i be the set of rows belonging to the ith group in $T'_{\mathcal{P}}$. Recall that we estimate x_i as $\hat{x}_i = M'(T'_i)/M'(T'_{\mathcal{P}})$. We can rewrite $\mathbf{E}\left[\|\mathbf{x}-\hat{\mathbf{x}}\|_2^2\right] =$

$$= \frac{1}{M'(T'_{\mathcal{P}})^2}\sum_{i=1}^{r}\mathbf{E}\left[\left(x_i \cdot M'(T'_{\mathcal{P}}) - M'(T'_i)\right)^2\right]. \quad (38)$$

(38) is analogous to (33). The probability of drawing a row from T_i is $p_i = \sum_{t\in T_i}\mathsf{apx}(t_M)/\sum_{t\in T_{\mathcal{P}}}\mathsf{apx}(t_M)$. It is not hard to show $p_i \le 2x_i$. Similar to (33)-(37), we can show

$$\mathbf{E}\left[\|\mathbf{x}-\hat{\mathbf{x}}\|_2^2\right] \le \frac{12}{m},$$

with $\Delta = 2$. So with $m = \Omega(1/\epsilon^2)$, we have $\mathbf{E}\left[\|\mathbf{x}-\hat{\mathbf{x}}\|_2^2\right] \le \epsilon^2$, and from Jessen's inequality, we have $\mathbf{E}\left[\|\mathbf{x}-\hat{\mathbf{x}}\|_2\right] \le \epsilon$.

Finally, replace one row in $T_{\mathcal{P}}$ changes $\|\mathbf{x}-\hat{\mathbf{x}}\|_2$ at most by $2/m$ (because $1 \le t_{M'} < 2$). So, using McDiarmid's inequality, we have that $\|\mathbf{x}-\hat{\mathbf{x}}\|_2 \le 2\epsilon$, with probability at most $1-\delta$, if $m = \Omega\left((1/\epsilon^2)\cdot\log(1/\delta)\right)$. □

B. DRAWING SAMPLES EFFICIENTLY

In the first scan, for each measure M, we compute $M(T) = \sum_{t\in T} t_M$, *i.e.*, the sum of values on M over all rows in T. We generate m random real numbers $S^M(m)$ uniformly from the range $[0, M(T))$. Then in the second scan, we maintain a partial sum of measure values when scanning rows; more specifically, for each row t, we maintain the sum of t'_M for all rows t' that were scanned before arriving at t, denoted as $\sigma_M(t)$. We add one copy of t into T^M if there exists $s \in S^M(m)$ s.t. $\sigma_M(t) \le s < \sigma_M(t) + t_M$, and k copies of t if there are k such samples s in $S^M(m)$.

The intuition behind the above implementation is that a row t occupies an interval $[\sigma_M(t), \sigma_M(t)+t_M)$ with width t_M on the whole range $[0, M(T))$, so a uniformly picked number from the range falls into the interval of t with probability exactly proportional to t_M (as required in (4) by measure-biased sampling). A simplified version can be used for generating uniform samples.

We illustrate this sampling procedure using an example.

EXAMPLE B.1. (Continue Example 1.1) *Let's use the table T with 200 rows in Figure 1(a) and measure M to demonstrate how to implement measure-biased sampling in two scans. To draw a measure-biased sample T^M with 20 rows, in the first scan, we calculate $M(T) = \sum_t t_M = 488$. We draw 20 random numbers $S^M(20)$ uniformly from the range $[0, 488]$. For example, we could have $S^M(20) = \{0, 25, 50, \ldots, 450, 475\}$.*

We maintain partial sums on M during the second scan of rows from 1 to 200. For row 26, the partial sum is 25 and we have 25 in $S^M(20)$, so row 26 is put into T^M. For row 199, the partial sum is 288 and $\{300, 325, 350, 375\} \subseteq S^M(20)$ falling into the range $[288, 388)$, so 4 copies of row 199 are put into T^M. Figure 9 shows how the measure-biased sample T^M is constructed from random numbers in $S^M(20)$. When there are multiple measures, the second scans for all of them can be easily merged (by maintaining partial sums on all the measures simultaneously).

C. LOW-FREQUENCY GROUP INDEX

Construction. For a dimension D and a value v, let $T_{D=v}$ be the set of rows with value v on dimension D. In a table of n rows, it is obvious that if there is an equi-constraint $D_i = v_i$ in the predicate of Q with $|T_{D_i=v_i}| \le \sqrt{n}$ (or $n \cdot s_0$), then Q must be a (s_0-)small query. For each (dimension,value)-pair (D, v), iff $|T_{D=v}| \le \sqrt{n}$, the low-frequency group index *materializes* $T_{D=v}$, *i.e.*, explicitly stores rows in $T_{D=v}$ sequentially. Note that in our measure-augmented inverted index, $\mathsf{inv}(D, v)$ points to the same set of rows as $T_{D=v}$ does. But $\mathsf{inv}(D, v)$ keeps only row IDs and approximate measures, while in our low-frequency group index, $T_{D=v}$, if presents, keeps these rows with all dimensions and measure attributes in a row-oriented format.

We cannot get a tight theoretical bound of the size of this index as the set of pairs (D, v) with $|T_{D=v}| \le \sqrt{n}$ is dependent on the frequency distribution of dimension D. But since $\sqrt{n}$ is small, in both benchmark and real datasets, we observe that its size is usually very small (see "LF index" in Table 1). We store it on disk. When the disk space budget is a problem, we can choose to not build it, as measure-augmented inverted index suffices for all small queries.

Processing queries. For a query Q, we check two conditions: whether i) its predicate $\mathcal{P}$ is in the form of (7) and ii) $\mathcal{P}$ contains an equi-constraint "$D_i = v_i$" with $T_{D_i=v_i}$ stored in the index. If yes, we simply need to scan up to $\sqrt{n}$ rows in $T_{D_i=v_i}$ sequentially to get the exact answer. It corresponds to ProcessWithLFIndex(Q) in lines 8-9 of Algorithm 1. For example, the following query

SELECT C_1, SUM(M) FROM T GROUP BY C_1
WHERE $C_2 = 1$ AND ($C_3 = 0$ OR $C_3 = 1$)

can be answered by scanning rows $T_{C_2=1}$.

THEOREM 10. *If a query Q satisfies the above conditions i) and ii), the low-frequency group index can be used to answer Q. On*

t_{ID}	1	26	51	76	92	94	96	98	111	136	161	186	199	200
Partial sum $\sigma_M(t)$	0	25	50	75	100	120	150	170	200	225	250	275	288	388
Numbers in $S^M(20)$	0	25	50	75	100	125	150	175	200	225	250	275	$300, 325, 350, 375$	$400, 425, 450, 475$
$\sigma_M(t) + t_M$	1	26	51	76	110	130	160	180	201	226	251	276	388	488
# copies of t in T^M	1	1	1	1	1	1	1	1	1	1	1	1	4	4

Figure 9: Drawing a Measure-biased Sample T^M

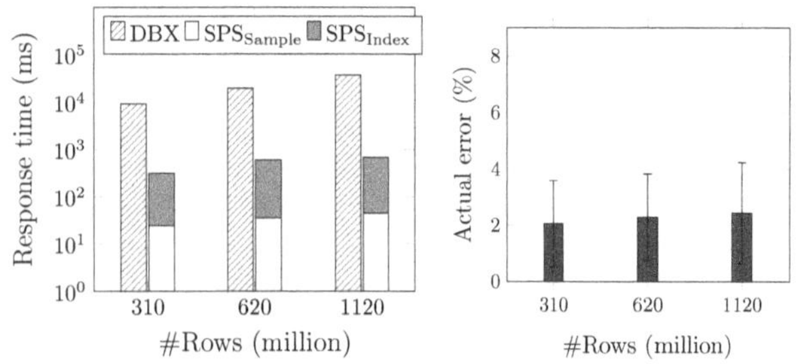

Figure 10: Varying number of rows (LOG)

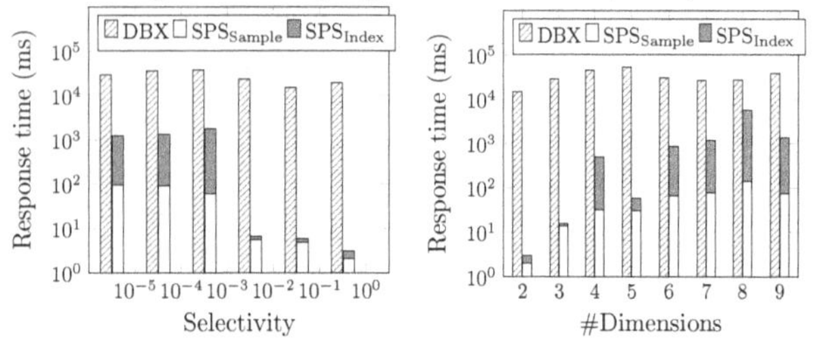

(a) Varying selectivity (b) Varying # dimensions

Figure 11: Selectivity and # dimensions of queries (LOG)

a table of n rows, we need to retrieve at most $\sqrt{n}$ rows sequentially from the disk to compute its answer.

D. ADDITIONAL EXPERIMENTS

Exp-III: Vary database size. We test the scalability of our system and compare it with DBX for datasets with different sizes. We use datasets LOG-S, LOG-M, and LOG (refer to Table 1) and set $\epsilon = 0.05$. Average response time (in DBX and SPS) and average actual error with one standard deviation (in SPS) for queries in all the twenty workloads are plotted in Figure 10. First of all, we find that the actual error is quite stable for different databases, which is not surprising because of our rigorous theoretical guarantees.

For response time of SPS, we decompose it into $\text{SPS}_{\text{Sample}}$ and $\text{SPS}_{\text{Index}}$, which represent the time SPS spends on in-memory samples and on-disk indexes, respectively. It can be seen that response time in SPS increases slightly for larger datasets, but the $\text{SPS}_{\text{Index}}$ part is quite stable. That is because the number of random accesses needed in our algorithm is independent on the database size (Theorem 8). On the other hand, DBX's response time increases linearly to the number of rows, because column-store indexes are used.

Exp-IV: Vary selectivity of queries. Selectivity (ratio of # rows satisfying the predicate to total # rows) may affect the response time of our system SPS. It is because large queries (with selectivity higher than $1/\sqrt{n}$) only need to scan in-memory samples, but small queries may also need to use on-disk indexes. So we partition queries in all the twenty workloads into six buckets with selectivities in $(10^{-1}, 1]$, $(10^{-2}, 10^{-1}]$, ..., $(0, 10^{-5}]$. Average response time in each bucket is plotted in Figures 11(a) for LOG with $\epsilon = 0.05$. The one for TPC-H looks quite similar.

We find that $\text{SPS}_{\text{Sample}}$ increases as selectivity becomes smaller. It is because of the early termination condition when scanning samples: an ϵ-approximation $\hat{\mathbf{x}}$ needs to collect $1/\epsilon^2$ rows that satisfies the query predicate from the sample – if the predicate has large selectivity, this condition can be satisfied earlier in the scan. $\text{SPS}_{\text{Index}}$ tends to be stable for small selectivity as the number of random accesses is upper bounded by both $1/\epsilon^2$ (Theorem 9).

Average actual error is steadily below the requested bound 0.05 because of our rigorous theoretical guarantee.

Exp-V: Vary number of dimensions in queries. We partition queries into buckets based on the numbers of dimensions (in group-bys, predicates, and measure of each query). In our workloads, the number of dimensions varies from 2 to 9. Average response time in each bucket is plotted in Figure 11(b) for LOG with $\epsilon = 0.05$. The one for TPC-H is similar and thus omitted here. With more dimensions, the response time of SPS increases because of two reasons: i) smaller selectivity (so $\text{SPS}_{\text{Index}}$ increases); and ii) more columns to be scanned (so $\text{SPS}_{\text{Sample}}$ increases). SPS always has significant speedup over DBX and tends to be stable after six dimensions.

E. ADDITIONAL RELATED WORK

Requested error v.s. actual error. Most of sampling-based systems estimate error bars using central limit theorem (CLT), Hoeffding inequality [6], or bootstrap [29]. In particular, BlinkDB [5] estimates error bar using standard closed-form formulas during online query. It is then claimed in [4] that the estimated error bar fails a lot in real query workload (also refer to our Example 1.1). A recent diagnostic algorithm (Kleiner *et al.* [21]) is extended by [4] to diagnose the failure of error bar estimation.

So requested (or estimated) error is not always below the actual error. That is also one motivation why we introduce a more rigorous notion, distribution predication guarantee, in this work. As far as we are concerned, our work is the first to provide such theoretical guarantees in AQP. One of our theoretical result on uniform sampling is inspired by the result in Acharya *et al.* [1]. It proves that uniform sampling achieves a tight bound in histogram approximation, which can be applied in our problem when the query has no predicate and the aggregate function is COUNT.

Non-sampling based approaches. Another orthogonal line of work are view materialization [6] and datacube [18] which precompute answers to some queries and create summaries to accelerate OLAP query processing. Histograms [17] and wavelets [28, 9, 17] create compressed synopses of relational tables to support some aggregates. These techniques either have too large space overhead (super-linear) to be applicable for enterprise-scale workloads and datasets, or are applicable for only a subclass of aggregates supported by ours (*e.g.*, without joins and complex predicates).

Other AQP systems. Deterministic approximate querying (DAQ) schemes are recently proposed in [25]. It proposes novel bit-sliced indexes to store columns separately so that a query can be evaluated on the first few bits while ignoring the remaining bits for each row. However, the bitwise DAQ still needs to exhaust all bits when doing equality check on categorical dimensions, and in general it needs to scan all rows for the most significant bits, so the speedup is limited for the query class we support. However, it would be a very interesting line of future work to incorporate such bit-sliced indexes into sampling-based systems, as these two lines of works are orthogonal and can mutually enhance each other.

Ordering guarantee in AQP is studied by Kim *et al.* [20]. It proposes an optimal online sampling algorithm to guarantee the right order of groups with the help of efficient indexes.

Stop-and-Stare: Optimal Sampling Algorithms for Viral Marketing in Billion-scale Networks

Hung T. Nguyen
CS Department
Virginia Commonwealth Univ.
Richmond, VA, USA
hungnt@vcu.edu

My T. Thai
CISE Department
University of Florida
Gainesville, Florida, USA
mythai@cise.ufl.edu

Thang N. Dinh
CS Department
Virginia Commonwealth Univ.
Richmond, VA, USA
tndinh@vcu.edu

ABSTRACT

Influence Maximization (IM), that seeks a small set of key users who spread the influence widely into the network, is a core problem in multiple domains. It finds applications in viral marketing, epidemic control, and assessing cascading failures within complex systems. Despite the huge amount of effort, IM in billion-scale networks such as Facebook, Twitter, and World Wide Web has not been satisfactorily solved. Even the state-of-the-art methods such as TIM+ and IMM may take days on those networks.

In this paper, we propose SSA and D-SSA, two novel sampling frameworks for IM-based viral marketing problems. SSA and D-SSA are up to 1200 times faster than the SIGMOD'15 best method, IMM, while providing the same $(1 - 1/e - \epsilon)$ approximation guarantee. Underlying our frameworks is an innovative *Stop-and-Stare* strategy in which they *stop at exponential check points* to verify (*stare*) if there is adequate statistical evidence on the solution quality. Theoretically, we prove that SSA and D-SSA are the first approximation algorithms that use (asymptotically) minimum numbers of samples, meeting strict theoretical thresholds characterized for IM. The absolute superiority of SSA and D-SSA are confirmed through extensive experiments on real network data for IM and another topic-aware viral marketing problem, named TVM.

Keywords

Influence Maximization; Stop-and-Stare; Sampling

1. INTRODUCTION

Viral Marketing, in which brand-awareness information is widely spread via the word-of-mouth effect, has emerged as one of the most effective marketing channels. It is becoming even more attractive with the explosion of social networking services such as Facebook[1] with 1.5 billion monthly active users or Instagram[2] with more than 3.5 billion daily like connections. To create a successful viral marketing campaign, one needs to seed the content with a set of individuals with high social networking influence. Finding such a set of users is known as the *Influence Maximization* problem.

Given a network and a budget k, Influence Maximization (IM) asks for k influential users who can spread the influence widely into the network. Kempe et al. [1] were the first to formulate IM as a combinatorial optimization problem on the two pioneering diffusion models, namely, *Independent Cascade* (IC) and *Linear Threshold* (LT). They prove IM to be NP-hard and provide a natural greedy algorithm that yields $(1 - 1/e - \epsilon)$-approximate solutions for any $\epsilon > 0$. This celebrated work has motivated a vast amount of work on IM in the past decade [2, 3, 4, 5, 6, 7, 8, 9, 10, 11, 12]. However, most of the existing methods either too slow for billion-scale networks [1, 2, 4, 5, 6, 7] or ad-hoc heuristics without performance guarantees [13, 3, 14, 15].

The most scalable methods with performance guarantee for IM are TIM/TIM+[8] and latter IMM[16]. They utilize a novel RIS sampling technique introduced by Borgs et al. in [17]. All these methods attempt to generate a $(1 - 1/e - \epsilon)$ approximate solution with minimal numbers of RIS samples. They use highly sophisticated estimating methods to make the number of RIS samples close to some theoretical thresholds θ [8, 16]. However, they all share two shortcomings: 1) the number of generated samples can be arbitrarily larger than θ, and 2) the thresholds θ are not shown to be the minimum among their kinds.

In this paper, we 1) unify the approaches in [17, 8, 16] to characterize the necessary number of RIS samples to achieve $(1 - 1/e - \epsilon)$-approximation guarantee; 2) design two novel sampling algorithms SSA and D-SSA aiming towards achieving minimum number of RIS samples. In the first part, we begin with defining RIS framework which consists of two necessary conditions to achieve the $(1 - 1/e - \epsilon)$ factor and classes of *RIS thresholds* on the sufficient numbers of RIS samples, generalizing θ thresholds in [8, 16]. The minimum threshold in each class is then termed *type-1 minimum threshold*, and the minimum among all type-1 minimum thresholds is termed *type-2 minimum threshold.*

In the second part, we develop the *Stop-and-Stare Algorithm* (SSA) and its dynamic version D-SSA that guarantee to achieve, within constant factors, the two minimum thresholds, respectively. Both SSA and D-SSA follow the *stop-and-stare* strategy which can be efficiently applied to many optimization problems over the samples and guaran-

[1] http://newsroom.fb.com/company-info/

[2] https://instagram.com/press/

SIGMOD'16, June 26-July 01, 2016, San Francisco, CA, USA

DOI: http://dx.doi.org/10.1145/2882903.2915207

tee some constant times the minimum number of samples required. In short, the algorithms keep generating samples and *stop* at *exponential check points* to verify (*stare*) if there is adequate statistical evidence on the solution quality for termination. This strategy will be shown to address both of the shortcomings in [8, 16]: 1) guarantee to be close to the theoretical thresholds and 2) the thresholds are minimal by definitions. The dynamic algorithm, D-SSA, improves over SSA by automatically and dynamically selecting the best parameters for the RIS framework. We note that the Stop-and-Stare strategy combined with RIS framework enables SSA and D-SSA to meet the minimum thresholds without explicitly computing/looking for these thresholds. That is in contrast to previous approaches [17, 8, 16] which all find some explicit unreachable thresholds and then probe for them with unbounded or huge gaps.

Our experiments show that both SSA and D-SSA outperform the best existing methods up to several orders of magnitudes w.r.t running time while returning comparable seed set quality. More specifically, on Friendster network with roughly 65.6 million nodes and 1.8 billion edges, SSA and D-SSA, taking 3.5 seconds when $k = 500$, are up to 1200 times faster than IMM. We also run CELF++ (the fastest greedy algorithm for IM with guarantees) on Twitter network with $k = 1000$ and observe that D-SSA is $2 \cdot 10^9$ times faster. Our contributions are summarized as follows.

- We generalize the RIS sampling methods in [17, 8, 16] into a general framework which characterizes the necessary conditions to guarantee the $(1 - 1/e - \epsilon)$-approximation factor. Based on the framework, we define classes of RIS thresholds and two types of minimum thresholds, namely, type-1 and type-2.
- We propose the Stop-and-Stare Algorithm (SSA) and its dynamic version, D-SSA, which both guarantee a $(1-1/e-\epsilon)$-approximate solution and are the first algorithms to achieve, within constant factors, the type-1 and type-2 minimum thresholds, respectively. Our proposed methods are not limited to solve influence maximization problem but also can be generalized for an important class of hard optimization problems over samples/sketches.
- Our framework and approaches are generic and can be applied in principle to sample-based optimization problems to design high-confidence approximation algorithm using (asymptotically) *minimum number of samples*.
- We carry extensive experiments on various real networks with up to several billion edges to show the superiority in performance and comparable solution quality. To test the applicability of the proposed algorithms, we apply our methods on an IM-application, namely, Targeted Viral Marketing (TVM). The results show that our algorithms are up to 1200 times faster than the current best method on IM problem and, for TVM, the speedup is up to 500 times.

Note that this paper does not focus on distributed/parallel computation, however our algorithms are amenable to a distributed implementation which is one of our future works.

Related works. Kempe et al. [1] formulated the influence maximization problem as an optimization problem. They show the problem to be NP-complete and devise an $(1 - 1/e - \epsilon)$ greedy algorithm. Later, computing the exact influence is shown to be #P-hard [3]. Leskovec et al. [2] study the influence propagation in a different perspective in which they aim to find a set of nodes in networks to detect the spread of virus as soon as possible. They improve the simple greedy method with the lazy-forward heuristic (CELF), which is originally proposed to optimize submodular functions in [18], obtaining an (up to) 700-fold speedup.

Several heuristics are developed to find solutions in large networks. While those heuristics are often faster in practice, they fail to retain the $(1-1/e-\epsilon)$-approximation guarantee and produce lower quality seed sets. Chen et al. [19] obtain a speedup by using an influence estimation for the IC model. For the LT model, Chen et al. [3] propose to use local directed acyclic graphs (LDAG) to approximate the influence regions of nodes. In a complement direction, there are recent works on learning the parameters of influence propagation models [20, 21]. The influence maximization is also studied in other diffusion models including the majority threshold model [22] or when both positive and negative influences are considered [23] and when the propagation terminates after a predefined time [22, 24]. Recently, IM across multiple OSNs have been studied in [11] and [25] studies the IM problem on continuous-time diffusion models.

Recently, Borgs et al. [17] make a theoretical breakthrough and present an $O(kl^2(m+n)\log^2 n/\epsilon^3)$ time algorithm for IM under IC model. Their algorithm (RIS) returns a $(1-1/e-\epsilon)$-approximate solution with probability at least $1 - n^{-l}$. In practice, the proposed algorithm is, however, less than satisfactory due to the rather large hidden constants. In sequential works, Tang et al. [8, 16] reduce the running time to $O((k + l)(m + n)\log n/\epsilon^2)$ and show that their algorithm is also very efficient in large networks with billions of edges. Nevertheless, Tang's algorithms have two weaknesses: 1) intractable estimation of maximum influence and 2) taking union bounds over all possible seed sets in order to guarantee a single returned set.

Organization. The rest of the paper is organized as follows: In Section 2, we introduce two fundamental models, i.e., LT and IC, and the IM problem definition. We, subsequently, devise the unified RIS framework, RIS threshold and two types of RIS minimum thresholds in Section 3. Section 4 and 5 will present the SSA algorithm and prove the approximation factor as well as the achievement of type-1 minimum threshold. In Section 6, we propose the dynamic algorithm, D-SSA and prove the approximation together with type-2 minimum threshold property. Finally, we show experimental results in Section 7 and draw some conclusion in Section 8.

2. MODELS AND PROBLEM DEFINITION

This section will formally define two most essential propagation models, e.i., *Linear Threshold* (LT) and *Independent Cascade* (IC), that we consider in this work and followed by the problem statement of the Influence Maximization (IM).

We abstract a network using a weighted graph $G = (V, E, w)$ with $|V| = n$ nodes and $|E| = m$ directed edges. Each edge $(u, v) \in E$ is associated with a weight $w(u, v) \in [0, 1]$ which indicates the probability that u influences v.

2.1 Propagation Models

In this paper, we study two fundamental diffusion models, namely, Linear Threshold (LT) and Independent Cascade

(IC). Assume that we have a set of seed nodes S, the propagation processes under these two models happen in rounds. At round 0, all nodes in S are activated and the others are not activated. In the subsequent rounds, the newly activated nodes will try to activate their neighbors. Once a node v becomes active, it will remain active till the end. The process stops when no more nodes get activated. The distinctions of the two models are described as follows:

Linear Threshold (LT) model. The edge weights in LT model must satisfy the condition $\sum_{u \in V} w(u, v) \leq 1$. At the beginning of the propagation process, each node v selects a random threshold λ_v uniformly at random in range $[0, 1]$. In round $t \geq 1$, an inactivated node v becomes activated if $\sum_{\textbf{activated neighbors } u} w(u, v) \geq \lambda_v$. Let $\mathbb{I}(S)$ denote the expected number of activated nodes given the seed set S, where the expectation is taken over all λ_v values from their uniform distribution. We call $\mathbb{I}(S)$ the *influence spread* of S under the LT model.

Independent Cascade (IC) model. In IC, when a node u gets activated, initially or by another node, it has a single chance to activate each inactive neighbor v with the probability proportional to the edge weight $w(u, v)$. After that moment, the activated nodes remain its active state but they have no contribution in later activations.

Table 1: Table of Symbols

Notation	Description
n, m	#nodes, #edges of graph $\mathcal{G} = (V, E, w)$.
$\mathbb{I}(S)$	Influence Spread of seed set $S \subseteq V$.
OPT_k	The maximum $\mathbb{I}(S)$ for any size-k seed set S.
$\hat{S}_k$	The returned size-k seed set of SSA/D-SSA.
S_k^*	An optimal size-k seed set, i.e., $\mathbb{I}(S_k^*) = OPT_k$.
R_j	A random RR set.
$\mathcal{R}$	A set of random RR sets.
$\mathrm{Cov}_{\mathcal{R}}(S)$, $S \subseteq V$	#RR sets in $\mathcal{R}$ incident at some node in S.
c	$c = 2(e-2) \approx \sqrt{2}$.
$\Upsilon(\epsilon, \delta)$	$\Upsilon(\epsilon, \delta) = 2c \ln \frac{1}{\delta} \frac{1}{\epsilon^2}$.
Λ_1	$\Lambda_1 = (1 + \epsilon_1)(1 + \epsilon_2)\Upsilon(\epsilon_3, \delta/3)$.
Λ_2	$\Lambda_2 = (1 + \epsilon_2)\Upsilon(\epsilon_2, \delta_2)$.

2.2 Problem Definition

Given the propagation models defined previously, we formally state the Influence Maximization (IM) problem as in the following definition.

DEFINITION 1 (INFLUENCE MAXIMIZATION (IM)). *Given a graph $G = (V, E, w)$, $k \in Z^+$ and a propagation model, the Influence Maximization problem asks for a seed set $\hat{S}_k \subset V$ of k nodes that maximizes its influence spread, $\mathbb{I}(\hat{S}_k)$.*

3. UNIFIED RIS FRAMEWORK

This section will present the unified RIS framework which generalizes the methods of using RIS sampling for IM problem. The unified framework characterizes the sufficient conditions to guarantee an $(1 - 1/e - \epsilon)$-approximation in the framework. Subsequently, we will introduce the concept of RIS threshold in terms of the number of necessary samples to guarantee the solution quality and two types of minimum RIS thresholds, i.e., type-1 and type-2.

3.1 Preliminaries

3.1.1 RIS sampling

The major bottle-neck in the traditional methods for IM [1, 2, 4, 26] is the inefficiency in estimating the influence spread. To address that, Borgs et al. [17] introduced a novel sampling approach for IM, called Reverse Influence Sampling (in short, RIS), which is the foundation for TIM/TIM+[8] and IMM[16], the state-of-the-art methods.

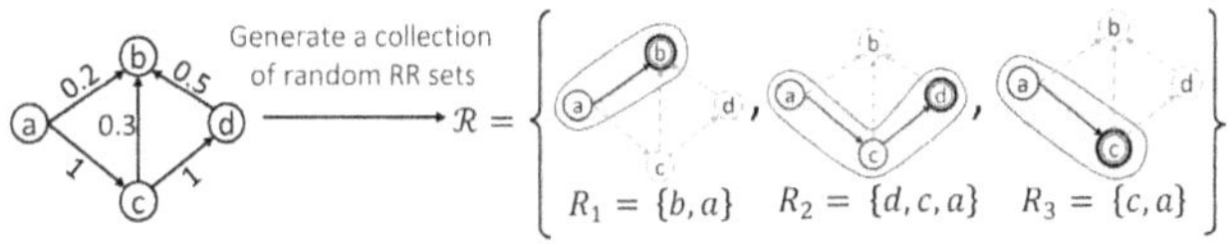

Figure 1: An example of generating random RR sets under the LT model. Three random RR sets R_1, R_2 and R_3 are generated. Node a has the highest influence and is also the most frequent element across the RR sets.

Given a graph $G = (V, E, w)$, RIS captures the influence landscape of G through generating a set $\mathcal{R}$ of random *Reverse Reachable (RR) sets*. The term 'RR set' is also used in TIM/TIM+ [8, 16] and referred to as 'hyperedge' in [17]. Each RR set R_j is a subset of V and constructed as follows,

DEFINITION 2 (REVERSE REACHABLE (RR) SET). *Given $G = (V, E, w)$, a random RR set R_j is generated from G by 1) selecting a random node $v \in V$ 2) generating a sample graph g from G and 3) returning R_j as the set of nodes that can reach v in g.*

Node v in the above definition is called the *source* of R_j. Observe that R_j contains the nodes that can influence its source v. If we generate multiple random RR sets, influential nodes will likely appear frequently in the RR sets. Thus a seed set S that *covers* most of the RR sets will likely maximize the influence spread $\mathbb{I}(S)$. Here a seed set S covers an RR set R_j, if $S \cap R_j \neq \emptyset$. For convenience, we denote the coverage of set S as $\mathrm{Cov}_{\mathcal{R}}(S) = \sum_{R_j \in \mathcal{R}} \min\{|S \cap R_j|, 1\}$. An illustration of this intuition and how to generate RR sets is given in Fig. 1. In the figure, three random RR sets are generated following the LT model with sources b, d and c, respectively. The influence of node a is the highest among all the nodes in the original graph and also is the most frequent node across the RR sets. This observation is rigorously captured in the following lemma in [17].

LEMMA 1. *Given $G = (V, E, w)$ and a random RR set R_j generated from G. For each seed set $S \subset V$,*

$$\mathbb{I}(S) = n \Pr[S \text{ covers } R_j]. \quad (1)$$

Lemma 1 says that the influence of a node set S is proportional to the probability that S intersects with a random RR set. Thus, to find S that optimizes $\mathbb{I}(S)$, we can alternatively optimize over the proportional probability which can be approximated by sampling many R_j. This relation is the soul of the RIS-based approaches on IM problem.

3.1.2 (ϵ, δ)-approximation

We recall the (ϵ, δ)-approximation and two criteria of achieving such approximation in [27] that will be used in our framework and later proofs.

DEFINITION 3 ((ϵ, δ)-APPROXIMATION). *Let $Z_1, Z_2, \ldots$ be independently and identically distributed samples according* *to Z in the interval [0, 1] with mean μ_Z and variance σ_Z^2. A Monte Carlo estimator of μ_Z,*

$$\hat{\mu}_Z = \frac{1}{T}\sum_{i=1}^{T} Z_i \tag{2}$$

is said to be an (ϵ, δ)-approximation of μ_Z if

$$\Pr[(1-\epsilon)\mu_Z \leq \hat{\mu}_Z \leq (1+\epsilon)\mu_Z] \geq 1-\delta \tag{3}$$

Having defined the (ϵ, δ)-approximation, the first inherent question is how (when) we can achieve that approximation. We investigate two criteria in Lems. 2 and 3.

Define $\Upsilon(\epsilon, \delta/2) = 2c\ln(2/\delta)/\epsilon^2$ with $c = 2(e-2)$ and $\mathrm{Cov}(Z) = \sum_{i=1}^{T} Z_i$. The following lemma is called *Zero-One Estimator Theorem* [27] stating the first criterion.

LEMMA 2 ([27]). *Let θ^* be the optimal number samples that guarantee an (ϵ, δ)-approximation of μ_Z, if $T = \frac{\Upsilon(\epsilon,\delta/2)}{\mu_Z}$, then $\hat{\mu}_Z = \frac{\mathrm{Cov}(Z)}{T}$ is an (ϵ, δ)-approximate of μ_Z and*

$$T \leq c_1 \cdot \theta^* \tag{4}$$

where c_1 is a constant.

Based also on [27], we have the second criterion to guarantee (ϵ, δ)-approximation as stated below.

LEMMA 3 ([27]). *Let θ^*, μ_Z be defined as in Lem. 2 and T be the number of samples at which $\mathrm{Cov}(Z) \geq 1 + (1+\epsilon)\Upsilon(\epsilon, \delta/2)$, then $\hat{\mu}_Z$ is an (ϵ, δ)-approximation of μ_Z and $T \leq (1+\epsilon)c_1 \cdot \theta^*$ where c_1 is the constant in Lem. 2.*

Note that if only one side of the event in Eq. 3 is required, then $\Upsilon(\epsilon, \delta/2)$ becomes

$$\Upsilon(\epsilon, \delta) = 2c\ln\frac{1}{\delta}\frac{1}{\epsilon^2} \tag{5}$$

3.2 RIS Framework and Thresholds

Based on Lem. 1, the IM problem can be solved by the following two step algorithm.

- Generate a collection of RR sets, $\mathcal{R}$, from G.
- Use the greedy algorithm for the Max-coverage problem [28] to find a seed set $\hat{S}_k$ that covers the maximum number of RR sets and return $\hat{S}_k$ as the solution.

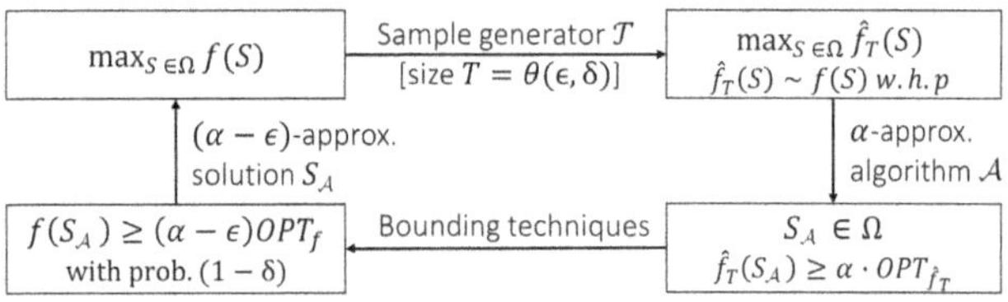

Figure 2: Overview of algorithms based on optimization over samples (ϵ is the error from approximating $f(S)$ by $\hat{f}_T(S)$, OPT_f and $OPT_{\hat{f}_T}$ are optimal solutions of $f(.)$ and $\hat{f}_T(.)$).

This two-step algorithm is actually an instance of a general class of methods illustrated in Fig. 2. The original problem is an maximization problem of $f(.)$ over Ω_S which is usually very hard to solve/approximate directly. Instead, we find an estimate $\hat{f}_T(.)$ of $f(.)$. The estimation function $\hat{f}_T(.)$ is constructed by generating $T = \theta(\epsilon, \delta)$ samples where $\theta(\epsilon, \delta)$ is an **explicit** threshold. The threshold $\theta(\epsilon, \delta)$ decides the estimation quality of $\hat{f}_T(.)$ compared to $f(.)$ and usually is the most critical point in the methods. After having the function $\hat{f}_T(.)$, an $\alpha-$approximation algorithm $\mathcal{A}$ which is easier and efficient to find the final solution $S_\mathcal{A}$ of $\hat{f}_T(.)$ as well as $f(.)$. The function $f(.)$ that characterizes our maximization objective covers a wide range of important problems, e.g., targeted viral marketing [29], densest subgraph [30], which have very high complexity to approximate and hence, need to rely on sampling algorithms. Thus, our proposed *stop-and-stare* methods can be modified to address many other optimization problems under this category. We illustrate this ability by extending SSA and D-SSA to solve the targeted viral marketing in our experiments section.

Similar to determining θ, the core question in applying the above algorithm for influence maximization problem is that: *How many RR sets are sufficient to provide a good approximate solution?* In this case, the function $f(S)$ is the influence function $\mathbb{I}(S)$ and the samples are generated by RIS sampling. [8, 16] propose two such theoretical thresholds and two probing techniques to realistically estimate those thresholds. However, their thresholds are not known to be any kind of minimum and the probing method is *ad hoc* in [8] or far from the proposed threshold in [16]. Thus, they cannot provide any guarantee on the optimality of the number of samples generated.

Since the probing for an explicit threshold is seen to admit certain limitations, we propose a new approach. Instead of explicitly expressing a theoretical threshold and trying to probe for it, we characterize the conditions that all the RIS-based algorithms need to attain and state the sufficient number of samples to satisfy those conditions. Thus, we can define the minimum samples according to the necessary conditions and further, propose SSA and D-SSA to achieve the minimum. We will first define our RIS framework as enforcing the necessary conditions to guarantee the best known solution quality and then propose two minimum thresholds based on the precision parameters in our framework.

Suppose that there is an optimal seed set, S_k^*, which has the maximum influence in the network. If there are multiple optimal sets with influence, OPT_k, we choose the first one alphabetically to be S_k^*. Given $0 \leq \epsilon, \delta \leq 1$, our unified RIS framework enforces two conditions:

$$\Pr[\hat{\mathbb{I}}(\hat{S}_k) \leq (1+\epsilon_a)\mathbb{I}(\hat{S}_k)] \geq 1-\delta_a \tag{6}$$

and

$$\Pr[\hat{\mathbb{I}}(S_k^*) \geq (1-\epsilon_b)OPT_k] \geq 1-\delta_b \tag{7}$$

where $\delta_a + \delta_b \leq \delta$ and $\epsilon_a + (1-1/e)\epsilon_b \leq \epsilon$.

Based on the above conditions, we define the RIS threshold as the following.

DEFINITION 4 (RIS THRESHOLD). *Given a graph G, $0 \leq \epsilon_a, \epsilon_b, \delta_a, \delta_b \leq 1$, $N(\epsilon_a, \epsilon_b, \delta_a, \delta_b)$ is called an RIS Threshold in G w.r.t $\epsilon_a, \epsilon_b, \delta_a, \delta_b$ if any number $|\mathcal{R}| \geq N(\epsilon_a, \epsilon_b, \delta_a, \delta_b)$ of random RR sets generated from G is sufficient to guarantee both Eqs. 6 and 7.*

With the two above conditions, we now prove that any $N \geq N(\epsilon_a, \epsilon_b, \delta_a, \delta_b)$ RR sets are sufficient to guarantee $(1-1/e-\epsilon)$-approximation ratio.

THEOREM 1. *Given a graph G, $0 \leq \epsilon_a, \epsilon_b, \delta_a, \delta_b \leq 1$, let $\epsilon \geq \epsilon_a + (1-1/e)\epsilon_b$ and $\delta \geq \delta_a + \delta_b$, if the number of RR sets $|\mathcal{R}| \geq N(\epsilon_a, \epsilon_b, \delta_a, \delta_b)$, then the two-step algorithm in our RIS framework returns $\hat{S}_k$ satisfying*

$$\Pr[\mathbb{I}(\hat{S}_k) \geq (1 - 1/e - \epsilon)OPT_k] \geq 1 - \delta \tag{8}$$

which means $\hat{S}_k$ is an $(1 - 1/e - \epsilon)$-approximate solution.

For brevity, the proof is presented in the appendix.

Existing RIS thresholds. For any $\epsilon, \delta \in (0, 1)$, Tang et al. established in [8] an RIS threshold,

$$N(\frac{\epsilon}{2}, \frac{\epsilon}{2}, \frac{\delta}{2\binom{n}{k}}, \frac{\delta}{2\binom{n}{k}}) = (8 + 2\epsilon)n\frac{\ln 2/\delta + \ln\binom{n}{k}}{\epsilon^2 OPT_k}$$

In a later study [16], they reduced this number to another RIS threshold,

$$N(\epsilon_1, \epsilon - \epsilon_1, \frac{\delta}{2\binom{n}{k}}, \frac{\delta}{2\binom{n}{k}}) = 2n\frac{((1 - 1/e)\alpha + \beta)^2}{\epsilon^2 OPT_k},$$

where $\alpha = (\frac{\ln 2}{\delta})^{\frac{1}{2}}$, $\beta = (1 - 1/e)^{\frac{1}{2}}(\frac{\ln 2}{\delta} + \ln\binom{n}{k})^{\frac{1}{2}}$ and $\epsilon_1 = \frac{\epsilon \cdot \alpha}{(1-1/e)\alpha+\beta}$.

Unfortunately, computing OPT_k is intractable, thus, the proposed algorithms have to generate $\theta\frac{OPT_k}{KPT^+}$ RR sets, where KPT^+ is the expected influence of a node set obtained by sampling k nodes with replacement from G and the ratio $\frac{OPT_k}{KPT^+} \geq 1$ is not upper-bounded. That is they may generate many times more RR sets than needed.

3.3 Two Types of Minimum Thresholds

Based on the definition of RIS threshold, we now define two strong theoretical limits, i.e. type-1 minimum and type-2 minimum thresholds. In Section 5, we will prove that our first proposed algorithm, SSA, achieves, within a constant factor, a type-1 minimum threshold and later, in Section 6, our dynamic algorithm, D-SSA, is shown to obtain, within a constant factor, the strongest type-2 minimum threshold.

DEFINITION 5 (TYPE-1 MINIMUM THRESHOLD). *Given $0 \leq \epsilon, \delta \leq 1$ and $0 \leq \epsilon_a, \epsilon_b, \delta_a, \delta_b \leq 1$ satisfying $\delta_a + \delta_b \leq \delta$ and $\epsilon_a + (1 - 1/e)\epsilon_b \leq \epsilon$, $N^1_{min}(\epsilon_a, \epsilon_b, \delta_a, \delta_b)$ is called a type-1 minimum threshold w.r.t $\epsilon_a, \epsilon_b, \delta_a, \delta_b$ if $N^1_{min}(\epsilon_a, \epsilon_b, \delta_a, \delta_b)$ is the smallest number of RR sets that satisfies both Eq. 6 and Eq. 7.*

If $N(\epsilon_a, \epsilon_b, \delta_a, \delta_b)$ is an RIS threshold, then any N such that $N \geq N(\epsilon_a, \epsilon_b, \delta_a, \delta_b)$ is also an RIS threshold. We choose the smallest number over all the RIS thresholds to be type-1 minimum as defined in Def. 5. All the previous methods [17, 8, 16] try to approximate $N^1_{min}(\epsilon_a, \epsilon_b, \delta_a, \delta_b)$ for some setting of $\epsilon_a, \epsilon_b, \delta_a, \delta_b$, however, they fail to provide any guarantee on how close their numbers are to that threshold. In contrast, we show that SSA achieves, within a constant factor, an type-1 minimum threshold in Sec. 5. Next, we give the definition of the strongest type-2 minimum threshold which is achieved by D-SSA as shown in Sec. 6.

DEFINITION 6 (TYPE-2 MINIMUM THRESHOLD). *Given $0 \leq \epsilon, \delta \leq 1$, $N^2_{min}(\epsilon, \delta)$ is called the type-2 minimum threshold if*

$$N^2_{min}(\epsilon, \delta) = \min_{\epsilon_a, \epsilon_b, \delta_a, \delta_b} N^1_{min}(\epsilon_a, \epsilon_b, \delta_a, \delta_b) \tag{9}$$

where $\epsilon_a + (1 - 1/e)\epsilon_b = \epsilon$ and $\delta_a + \delta_b = \delta$.

From Def. 6, it follows that type-2 minimum is the strongest possible threshold that we can achieve in the RIS-framework.

3.4 Achieving the Minimum Thresholds

In the following sections, we propose two approximation algorithms, namely, *Stop-and-Stare* (SSA) and the dynamic version D-SSA, which respectively achieve the two theoretical minimum thresholds as well as the best known worst-case approximation ratio. In more details, both SSA and D-SSA employ the stop-and-stare strategy that doubles the number of RIS samples and checks the quality of current solution by an independent influence estimation step. This strategy guarantees that we do not oversample, i.e., doubling the necessary number in the worst case. On a specific setting of the tuple $\{\epsilon_a, \epsilon_b, \delta_a, \delta_b\}$, SSA guarantees a type-1 minimum threshold corresponding to that configuration.

By specifically setting the parameters, SSA algorithm is simpler than the dynamic D-SSA. D-SSA achieves the type-2 minimum threshold through dynamically finding the best set of parameter values at each exponential checking points. Thus, $\{\epsilon_a, \epsilon_b, \delta_a, \delta_b\}$ are not specified in advance but automatically detected by D-SSA. Further, D-SSA can reuse the RR sets generated in the independent influence estimation without changing the independence property of RR sets in subsequent iterations.

4. STOP-AND-STARE ALGORITHM (SSA)

In this section, we describe our first Stop-and-Stare Algorithm (SSA) in details. SSA keeps generating RR sets until doubling the current number and *stops* to check the solution obtained from the total RR sets generated. It uses Max-Coverage (Alg. 2) to find the solution, $\hat{S}_k$. Since the influence of $\hat{S}_k$ calculated from those RR sets is biased, SSA independently generates another collection of RR sets in Estimate-Inf procedure (Alg. 3) to obtain an unbiased estimation of $\hat{S}_k$ influence. Then it *stares* at the two influences and if they are close enough (satisfying SSA's stopping conditions), it halts and returns the found solution.

Algorithm 1 SSA Algorithm

Input: Graph G, $0 \leq \epsilon, \delta \leq 1$, and a budget k.
Output: An $(1 - 1/e - \epsilon)$-optimal solution, $\hat{S}_k$ with at least $(1 - \delta)$-probability.

Compute $\epsilon_1, \epsilon_2, \epsilon_3$ according to Eq. 18
$\Lambda_1 \leftarrow (1 + \epsilon_1)(1 + \epsilon_2)2c\ln\frac{3}{\delta}\frac{1}{\epsilon_3^2}$
$\mathcal{R} \leftarrow$ Generate Λ_1 random RR sets by RIS
repeat
    $<\hat{S}_k, \hat{\mathbb{I}}(\hat{S}_k)> \leftarrow$ Max-Coverage($\mathcal{R}$, k, n)
    if $\mathrm{Cov}_{\mathcal{R}}(\hat{S}_k) \geq \Lambda_1$ **then**
        $\mathbb{I}_c(\hat{S}_k) \leftarrow$ Estimate-Inf($G, \hat{S}_k, \epsilon_2, \frac{\delta}{3}, |\mathcal{R}|\frac{1+\epsilon_2}{1-\epsilon_2}\frac{\epsilon_3^2}{\epsilon_2^2}$)
        if $\hat{\mathbb{I}}(\hat{S}_k) \leq (1 + \epsilon_1)\mathbb{I}_c(\hat{S}_k)$ **then**
            return $\hat{S}_k$
        end if
    end if
    $\mathcal{R} \leftarrow$ Generate $|\mathcal{R}|$ random RR sets by RIS
until $|\mathcal{R}| \geq (8 + 2\epsilon)n\frac{\ln\frac{2}{\delta} + \ln\binom{n}{k}}{\epsilon^2}$
return $\hat{S}_k$

4.1 SSA Algorithm

This subsection will detail the main procedure of SSA where Max-Coverage (described in Alg. 2) and Estimate-Inf (described in Alg. 3) are incorporated. The precision parameters $\epsilon_1, \epsilon_2, \epsilon_3, \delta_1, \delta_2$ are specified in Eq. 18 and discussed in

Subsection 5.2.1. An illustration of those precision parameters in SSA (and also later for D-SSA) is provided in Fig. 3. This figure also demonstrate our bounding technique in our framework (Fig. 2): The overall error is accumulated from the sampling errors to estimate of $\mathbb{I}(S_k^*)$ and $\mathbb{I}(\hat{S}_k)$ and the approximation error of Max-Coverage to find the set $\hat{S}_k$.

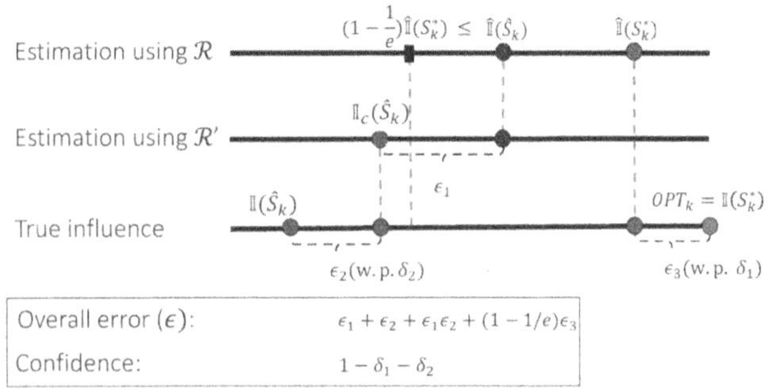

Figure 3: Illustration of precision parameters $\epsilon_1, \epsilon_2, \epsilon_3, \delta_1, \delta_2$ ($\mathbb{I}(.)$ denotes the true influence function, $\hat{\mathbb{I}}(.), \mathbb{I}_c(.)$ are the estimates of $\mathbb{I}(.)$ by the collection $\mathcal{R}$ of RR sets in the main algorithm and by another independent collection $\mathcal{R}'$ of the Estimate-Inf, S_k^* is an optimal solution).

The SSA algorithm is presented in Alg. 1. SSA starts with initializing the values of three variables ϵ_1, ϵ_2 and ϵ_3 which are critical in deciding the stopping conditions and will be specified in our analysis (Eq. 18) where we prove the type-1 minimum threshold of SSA. Having obtained those values, the algorithm, then, computes Λ_1 (Line 2) which determines the lower bound for the degree of the selected seed set, $\hat{S}_k$. The central part of our algorithm iterates round by round: at round 0, SSA generates Λ_1 random RR sets (Line 3) simply because that is the lowest number we can expect to meet the first condition at Line 6; at round $i \geq 1$, it doubles the number of random RR sets by introducing $|\mathcal{R}|$ more sets (Line 12). In each round, a candidate seed set $\hat{S}_k$ is selected by Max-Coverage together with its estimated influence. SSA obtains another estimated influence which is returned by the Estimate-Inf (Line 7) and denoted by $\mathbb{I}_c(\hat{S}_k)$. The two influences are used in the second condition (Line 8). Thus, SSA contains two *stopping conditions*:

(C1) The first condition $\text{Cov}_{\mathcal{R}}(\hat{S}_k) \geq \Lambda_1$ (Line 6) ensures that the coverage of the returned solution is at least Λ_1 which is important to guarantee the approximability of $\hat{S}_k$ and S_k^* as shown in Lem.5 and 6. This condition remains true after the first time it is established.

(C2) The second condition $\hat{\mathbb{I}}(\hat{S}_k) \leq (1+\epsilon_1)\mathbb{I}_c(\hat{S}_k)$ (Line 8) compares estimates of $\mathbb{I}(\hat{S}_k)$ obtained by Max-Coverage and by the Estimate-Inf procedure. This comparison is only active after the first stopping condition is met and the number of RR sets is large enough to trigger the Estimate-Inf. If these two estimates are close enough (within a multiplicative factor of $1+\epsilon_1$), we confirm the approximability of $\hat{S}_k$ (Lem. 5).

As we will prove in Sec. 5, the two stopping conditions are sufficient to guarantee the $(1-1/e-\epsilon)$-approximation of $\hat{S}_k$. Note that we use a threshold $(8+2\epsilon)n\frac{\ln\frac{2}{\delta}+\ln\binom{n}{k}}{\epsilon^2}$ which is taken from TIM+ [8] when considering $OPT_k = 1$ to stop SSA in cases of bad events.

Algorithm 2 Max-Coverage procedure

Input: RR sets ($\mathcal{R}$), k and number of nodes (n).
Output: An $(1-1/e)$-optimal solution, $\hat{S}_k$ and its estimated influence $\mathbb{I}_c(\hat{S}_k)$.
$\hat{S}_k = \emptyset$
for i=1 **to** k **do**
  $\hat{v} \leftarrow \arg\max_{\{v \in V\}}(\text{Cov}_{\mathcal{R}}(\hat{S}_k \cup \{v\}) - \text{Cov}_{\mathcal{R}}(\hat{S}_k))$
  Add $\hat{v}$ to $\hat{S}_k$
end for
return $<\hat{S}_k, \text{Cov}_{\mathcal{R}}(\hat{S}_k) \cdot n/|\mathcal{R}|>$

4.2 Finding Max-Coverage

We describe the Max-Coverage procedure to find a $(1-1/e)$-coverage set. This algorithm plays the role of the α-approximation algorithm in Fig. 2 where $\alpha = 1-1/e$. Alg. 2 illustrates the greedy Max-Coverage algorithm to select a size-k seed set. The whole procedure goes through k iterations in which, at each step, a node with maximum relative coverage, with respect to the previously chosen ones, is selected into the seed set $\hat{S}_k$. As a well-known result [31], we have the following lemma.

LEMMA 4. *The greedy Max-Coverage returns an $(1-1/e)$-approximate seed set $\hat{S}_k$.*

This algorithm can be implemented in linear time in terms of the total size of all the RR sets as in [17, 8, 16] and, as a result, the complexity is upper-bounded by the generating RR sets. Thus, the complexity of the whole algorithm actually depends only on that for generating RR sets.

4.3 Influence Estimation

Estimating influence of a given seed set S is a key component in our method and is used in the places where we have a candidate seed set and need to check whether the estimate of that set in the main algorithm is good enough. Our goal is to obtain a good approximation (within a certain multiplicative-error) of the given seed set influence.

Algorithm 3 Estimate-Inf procedure

Input: Graph G, a seed set S, $0 \leq \epsilon_2, \delta_2 \leq 1$ and maximum number of samples, T_{max}.
Output: $\mathbb{I}_c(S)$ such that $\mathbb{I}_c(S) \leq (1+\epsilon_2)\mathbb{I}(S)$ with at least $(1-\delta_2)$-probability or exceeding T_{max}.
1: $\Lambda_2 = 1 + 2c(1+\epsilon_2)\ln\frac{1}{\delta_2}\frac{1}{\epsilon_2^2}$
2: Cov = 0
3: **for** T **from** 1 **to** T_{max}
4:   Generate $R_j \leftarrow$RIS(G)
5:   Cov = Cov + $\min\{|R_j \cap S|, 1\}$
6:   **if** Cov $\geq \Lambda_2$ **then**
7:     **return** $n \times \text{Cov}/T$ {n: number of nodes}
8:   **end if**
9: **end for**
10: **return** -1 {Exceeding T_{max} RR sets}

The estimating procedure is called Estimate-Inf and detailed in Alg. 3. Given a node set S and two parameters, ϵ_2, δ_2, Estimate-Inf returns an estimate $\mathbb{I}_c(S)$ of $\mathbb{I}(S)$ such that $\mathbb{I}_c(S) \leq (1+\epsilon_2)\mathbb{I}(S)$ with at least $(1-\epsilon_2)$-probability. The most crucial point in the procedure is determining Λ_2 (Line 1) and the related condition (Line 6) which compares the coverage of S with Λ_2. In our analysis, we show that the condition is sufficient to guarantee $\mathbb{I}_c(S) \leq (1+\epsilon_2)\mathbb{I}(S)$ with at least $(1-\epsilon_2)$-probability. The main step in this procedure is the **for** loop in which random RR sets are drawn one at a time until satisfying the condition. The loop iterates through the maximum of T_{max} iterations where, as described in Alg. 1, T_{max} is a constant multiply of the total number of RR sets generated in the main algorithm at that point. Choosing T_{max} is a crucial point of this algorithm since we run this at every iteration in SSA. At the beginning when the solution $\hat{S}$ is not

We define a random variable $X = \min\{|R_j \cap S|, 1\}$, where R_j is a random RR set and $\mu_X = \mathbb{I}(S)/n$ (Lem. 1). From Lem. 3 of the (ϵ, δ)-approximation criteria, we obtain a direct corollary as stated below,

COROLLARY 1. *The Estimate-Inf procedure of SSA returns an estimate, $\mathbb{I}_c(S)$, of $\mathbb{I}(S)$ such that*

$$\Pr[\mathbb{I}_c(S) \leq (1+\epsilon_2)\mathbb{I}(S)] \geq 1-\delta_2 = 1-\delta/3 \quad (10)$$

5. SSA GUARANTEE AND PERFORMANCE ANALYSIS

In this section, we will prove that SSA returns a $(1-1/e-\epsilon)$-approximate solution with at least $(1-\delta)$-probability in Subsec. 5.1. Subsequently, SSA is shown to require no more than a constant factor of a type-1 minimum threshold of RR sets with the same probability in Subsec. 5.2.

5.1 Approximation Guarantee

In this subsection, we will prove that SSA achieves the approximation factor of $(1-1/e-\epsilon)$ with at least $(1-\delta)$-probability. The proof essentially contains two core components which are two conditions in our RIS framework (Subsection 3.2): 1) prove that at termination SSA achieves a good approximation of the selected solution, $\hat{S}_k$, (Lem. 5) and 2) the hidden optimal solution, S_k^*, is also well-estimated (Lem. 6). Thus, combining these with Theo. 1 (Subsection 3.2) gives us the approximation factor $(1-1/e-\epsilon)$ stated in Theo. 2.

The first component states the quality of the estimated influence of the returned solution, $\hat{\mathbb{I}}(\hat{S}_k)$, that SSA has at termination is shown in Lem. 5.

LEMMA 5. *SSA returns a seed set, $\hat{S}_k$, with*

$$\Pr[\hat{\mathbb{I}}(\hat{S}_k) \leq (1+\epsilon_{12})\mathbb{I}(\hat{S}_k)] \geq 1-\delta/3 \quad (11)$$

where $\epsilon_{12} = \epsilon_1 + \epsilon_2 + \epsilon_1\epsilon_2$.

The proof is presented in the appendix. Based on Lem. 5, we prove the second component which also contains the influence estimation of the optimal solution, S_k^*.

LEMMA 6. *SSA terminates with*

$$\Pr[\hat{\mathbb{I}}(S_k^*) \leq (1-\epsilon_3)OPT_k \text{ or } \hat{\mathbb{I}}(\hat{S}_k) \geq (1+\epsilon_{12})\mathbb{I}(\hat{S}_k)] \leq 2\delta/3$$

Thus,

$$\Pr[\hat{\mathbb{I}}(S_k^*) \geq (1-\epsilon_3)OPT_k] \geq 1-2\delta/3 \quad (12)$$

Lem. 5 and 6 are sufficient to prove the approximation quality of SSA as stated by the following theorem.

THEOREM 2. *Given $0 \leq \epsilon, \delta \leq 1$ and $\epsilon_1, \epsilon_2, \epsilon_3$ satisfying $\epsilon_1+\epsilon_2+\epsilon_1\epsilon_2+(1-1/e)\epsilon_3 \leq \epsilon$, SSA returns a seed set, $\hat{S}_k$, such that*

$$\Pr[\mathbb{I}(\hat{S}_k) \geq (1-1/e-\epsilon)OPT_k] \geq 1-\delta \quad (13)$$

PROOF. To prove the theorem, we will show that $|\mathcal{R}|$ is an RIS threshold and then apply Theo. 1 to obtain the $(1-1/e-\epsilon)$-approximation property of SSA. Actually, we will later prove in Sec. 5 that $|\mathcal{R}|$ is not just RIS threshold but, to within a constant factor, a type-1 minimum threshold.

The first condition to become an RIS threshold is taken from Lem. 5,

$$\Pr[\hat{\mathbb{I}}(\hat{S}_k) \leq (1+\epsilon_1)(1+\epsilon_2)\mathbb{I}(\hat{S}_k)] \geq 1-\delta/3 \quad (14)$$

The second condition is obtained from Lem. 6,

$$\Pr[\hat{\mathbb{I}}(S_k^*) \geq (1-\epsilon_3)OPT_k] \geq 1-2\delta/3 \quad (15)$$

From Eq. 14 and Eq. 15, we conclude that $|\mathcal{R}|$ is an RIS threshold with $\epsilon_a = (1+\epsilon_1)(1+\epsilon_2)-1$, $\epsilon_b = \epsilon_3$, $\delta_a = \delta/3$ and $\delta_b = 2\delta/3$. Notice that $\epsilon_a + (1-1/e)\epsilon_b = \epsilon$ and $\delta_a + \delta_b = \delta$. By Theo. 1, we have

$$\Pr[\mathbb{I}(\hat{S}_k) \geq (1-1/e-\epsilon)OPT_k] \geq 1-\delta \quad (16)$$

which completes the proof of Theo. 2. □

5.2 Achieving Type-1 Minimum Threshold

We will analyze the number of RR sets generated in both the main and Estimate-Inf procedures and show that SSA requires no more than a constant times a type-1 minimum RR sets. That makes SSA the first method to achieve a type-1 minimum threshold.

5.2.1 Parameter Settings

In Theo. 2, we rely on the assumptions that $\epsilon_1, \epsilon_2, \epsilon_3$ are given such that

$$\epsilon_1+\epsilon_2+\epsilon_1\epsilon_2+(1-1/e)\epsilon_3 \leq \epsilon. \quad (17)$$

Determining their values plays an important role in the algorithm. Ideally, we want to generate just enough RR sets in the main algorithm to have a good estimate of $\hat{S}_k$ and then check the influence by Estimate-Inf procedure. That is because we will discard all the RR sets in the Estimate-Inf after running and, thus, if we start checking too early, we will waste a wealth of RR sets. On the other hand, because of the doubling scheme in the main algorithm, if starting checking way latter, we will generate a lot of unnecessary RR sets in the main procedure. In SSA, we determine the values of $\epsilon_1, \epsilon_2, \epsilon_3$ based on experiments and prove in next subsection that SSA generates only a constant times the type-1 threshold w.r.t these settings. In Sect. 6, we propose a dynamic algorithm, D-SSA, to tune and find the best values during the execution and it requires, within a constant factor, the strongest type-2 minimum threshold RR sets.

We carried experiments on various values of ϵ_1, ϵ_2 and ϵ_3 which satisfy Eq. 17 and found the following values robustly giving low number of RR sets,

$$\begin{aligned}\epsilon_1 &= \epsilon/6\\ \epsilon_2 &= \epsilon/2\\ \epsilon_3 &= \epsilon/4(1-1/e)\end{aligned} \quad (18)$$

5.2.2 Number of RR sets in the main algorithm

Here, we will analyze the number of RR sets generated in the main algorithm and show that this number is at most constant times $N_{min}^1(\epsilon_a, \epsilon_b, \delta_a, \delta_b)$ where $\epsilon_a = \epsilon_{12} = \epsilon_1+\epsilon_2+\epsilon_1\epsilon_2$, $\epsilon_b = \epsilon_3$ and $\delta_a = \delta/3, \delta_b = 2\delta/3$. From Subsec. 5.1,

$$\Pr[\hat{\mathbb{I}}(\hat{S}_k) \leq (1+\epsilon_a)\mathbb{I}(\hat{S}_k)] \geq 1-\delta_a \quad (19)$$

and

$$\Pr[\hat{\mathbb{I}}(S_k^*) \geq (1-\epsilon_b)OPT_k] \geq 1-\delta_b \quad (20)$$

are obtained by enforcing two stopping conditions:

$$\mathrm{Cov}_{\mathcal{R}}(\hat{S}_k) \geq \Lambda_1 \quad \text{(C1)}$$

and

$$\hat{\mathbb{I}}(\hat{S}_k) \leq (1+\epsilon_1)\mathbb{I}_c(\hat{S}_k) \quad \text{(C2)}$$

Now, to determine the number of RR sets generated in SSA, we will start from $N^1_{min}(\epsilon_a, \epsilon_b, \delta_a, \delta_b)$ RR sets where Eq. 19 and Eq. 20 are satisfied and determine how many more RR sets needed to meet (C1) and (C2). More specifically, we prove that in the cases that the inequalities in Eq. 19 and Eq. 20 hold with $N^1_{min}(\epsilon_a, \epsilon_b, \delta_a, \delta_b)$ RR sets, SSA needs at most $\frac{c_1}{1-1/e-\epsilon} N^1_{min}(\epsilon_a, \epsilon_b, \delta_a, \delta_b)$ RR sets, where c_1 is a constant defined in Lem. 2. Thus, SSA will need no more than $\frac{c_1}{1-1/e-\epsilon} N^1_{min}(\epsilon_a, \epsilon_b, \delta_a, \delta_b)$ RR sets with the same probability that two inequalities in Eq. 19 and Eq. 20 hold which is at least $1-\delta$. The satisfaction of (C1) is stated as follows.

LEMMA 7. *Suppose that with $N^1_{min}(\epsilon_a, \epsilon_b, \delta_a, \delta_b)$ RR sets, we have*

$$\hat{\mathbb{I}}(\hat{S}_k) \leq (1+\epsilon_a)\mathbb{I}(\hat{S}_k) \quad (21)$$

and

$$\hat{\mathbb{I}}(S_k^*) \geq (1-\epsilon_b)OPT_k \quad (22)$$

Then SSA needs at most $\frac{c_1}{1-1/e-\epsilon} N^1_{min}(\epsilon_a, \epsilon_b, \delta_a, \delta_b)$ RR sets to satisfy condition (C1).

The proof is presented in the appendix. The following lemma states that condition (C2) is also satisfied with the same number of RR sets.

LEMMA 8. *Given all the assumptions as in Lem. 7, SSA needs at most $\frac{c_1}{1-1/e-\epsilon} N^1_{min}(\epsilon_a, \epsilon_b, \delta_a, \delta_b)$ RR sets to satisfy condition (C2) with at least $(1-\delta/3)$-probability.*

From Lem. 7 and Lem. 8 and the fact that SSA stops when two stopping conditions, i.e., (C1) and (C2), are satisfied, we have the following lemma.

LEMMA 9. *The main algorithm of SSA generates, within a constant factor, $N^1_{min}(\epsilon_a, \epsilon_b, \delta_a, \delta_b)$ RR sets with at least $(1-\delta)$-probability.*

PROOF. From Lems. 7 and 8, we obtain that the number of RR sets $|\mathcal{R}| \geq \frac{c_1}{1-1/e-\epsilon} N^1_{min}(\epsilon_a, \epsilon_b, \delta_a, \delta_b)$ is the necessary condition to satisfy both (C1) and (C2) with the probability accumulated from Eq. 19, Eq. 20 and Lem. 8 that is $1 - \delta_b - \delta/3 = 1-\delta$ (follows from Lem. 6 that the inequalities in Eq. 19 and 20 are both satisfied with probability $1-\delta_b$). Therefore, due to the doubling scheme, SSA will generate at most $\frac{2c_1}{1-1/e-\epsilon} N^1_{min}(\epsilon_a, \epsilon_b, \delta_a, \delta_b)$ which remains to be a constant times $N^1_{min}(\epsilon_a, \epsilon_b, \delta_a, \delta_b)$. □

5.2.3 *Number of RR sets in* Estimate-Inf *procedure*

As presented in Alg. 3, the number of RR sets generated in Estimate-Inf procedure is always smaller than $\frac{1+\epsilon_2}{1-\epsilon_2}\frac{\epsilon_3^2}{\epsilon_2^2}$ times the number of RR sets currently in the main algorithm. Therefore, the total number of RR sets generated during the running of SSA is smaller than $\frac{1+\epsilon_2}{1-\epsilon_2}\frac{\epsilon_3^2}{\epsilon_2^2}$ times the sum of RR sets present at each iteration in the main algorithm. In turn, due to the doubling behavior, the sum of RR sets is smaller than twice that number at the last iteration. Thus, based on Lem. 9, we have the following lemma.

LEMMA 10. *Estimate-Inf procedure of SSA generates, to within a constant factor, $N^1_{min}(\epsilon_a, \epsilon_b, \delta_a, \delta_b)$ RR sets with at least $(1-\delta)$-probability.*

The constant in the lemma is $2\frac{1+\epsilon_2}{1-\epsilon_2}\frac{\epsilon_3^2}{\epsilon_2^2}$ times that in Lem. 9 that makes it

$$2\frac{1+\epsilon_2}{1-\epsilon_2}\frac{\epsilon_3^2}{\epsilon_2^2}\frac{2c_1}{1-1/e-\epsilon}N^1_{min}(\epsilon_a, \epsilon_b, \delta_a, \delta_b) \quad (23)$$

Combining Lems. 9 and 10, we conclude the overall number of RR sets by the following theorem.

THEOREM 3. *SSA generates, to within a constant factor, $N^1_{min}(\epsilon_a, \epsilon_b, \delta_a, \delta_b)$ RR sets with at least $(1-\delta)$-probability.*

The total number in this theorem is the sum of those in Lems. 9 and 10,

$$(1+2\frac{1+\epsilon_2}{1-\epsilon_2}\frac{\epsilon_3^2}{\epsilon_2^2})\frac{2c_1}{1-1/e-\epsilon}N^1_{min}(\epsilon_a, \epsilon_b, \delta_a, \delta_b) \quad (24)$$

6. DYNAMIC ALGORITHM

In this section, we propose the dynamic algorithm, named D-SSA, that automatically selects $\epsilon_1, \epsilon_2, \epsilon_3, \delta_1, \delta_2$ during its execution. While maintaining the $(1-1/e-\epsilon)$-approximate solution as in SSA, D-SSA requires, to within a constant factor, the type-2 minimum threshold. This is the strongest result over all IM methods following the RIS framework.

6.1 D-SSA Algorithm

In Section 4, SSA can be seen as generating two independent collections of RR sets: one is in the main algorithm to find the maximum seed set and the another is for estimating the influence of the seed set found in the main procedure. Recall from Section 5 that we want to start checking the influence of $\hat{S}_k$ at the moment of having generated just enough RR sets so that the RR sets for checking are not wasted. However, detecting that moment is challenging since it depends not only on the networks but also the particular execution of generating RR sets.

The dynamic algorithm D-SSA, described in Alg. 4, addresses thoroughly these issue by dynamically computing the values of $\epsilon_1, \epsilon_2, \epsilon_3, \delta_1, \delta_2$ along its execution and stops whenever the success probability meets the requirement (Line 12). D-SSA also reuses the checking RR sets for finding seed set without affecting the independence of RR sets in subsequent iterations (Line 16). More specifically, D-SSA uses the newly generated RR sets to estimates the influence of the seed set found in the previous iteration and obtain the current value of ϵ_1 (Line 7). From the value of ϵ_1, ϵ_2 and ϵ_3 can be computed accordingly (Line 8). The formula for computing ϵ_2 and ϵ_3 are based on the condition that

$$\epsilon_1 + \epsilon_2 + \epsilon_1\epsilon_2 + \epsilon_3(1-1/e) \leq \epsilon \quad (25)$$

and considering $\epsilon_2 + \epsilon_1\epsilon_2$ and $\epsilon_3(1-1/e)$ having similar roles. After that it relies on the two stopping conditions mentioned in SSA to calculate δ_1 and δ_2. D-SSA stops when sum of δ_1 and δ_2 is less than or equal to θ which signifies that the success probability meets the requirement.

6.2 D-SSA Analysis

We will sequentially show that D-SSA achieves $(1-1/e-\epsilon)$-approximation factor in Subsec. 6.2.1 and requires only, to within a constant factor, the strongest type-2 minimum threshold of the RR sets in Subsec. 6.2.2.

Algorithm 4 D-SSA Algorithm

Input: Graph G, $0 \leq \epsilon, \delta \leq 1$, and k.
Output: An $(1-1/e-\epsilon)$-optimal solution, $\hat{S}_k$.
1: $\Lambda \leftarrow 2c(1+\epsilon)^2 \ln \frac{2}{\delta} \frac{1}{\epsilon^2}$
2: $\mathcal{R} \leftarrow$ Generate Λ random RR sets by RIS
3: $<\hat{S}_k, \hat{\mathbb{I}}(\hat{S}_k)> \leftarrow$ Max-Coverage$(\mathcal{R}, k)$
4: **repeat**
5: $\quad \mathcal{R}' \leftarrow$ Generate $|\mathcal{R}|$ random RR sets by RIS
6: $\quad \mathbb{I}_c(\hat{S}_k) \leftarrow \mathrm{Cov}_{\mathcal{R}'}(\hat{S}_k) \cdot n/|\mathcal{R}'|$
7: $\quad \epsilon_1 \leftarrow \hat{\mathbb{I}}(\hat{S}_k)/\mathbb{I}_c(\hat{S}_k) - 1$
8: $\quad$ **if** $(\epsilon_1 \leq \epsilon)$ **then**
9: $\quad\quad \epsilon_2 \leftarrow \frac{\epsilon-\epsilon_1}{2(1+\epsilon_1)}$, $\epsilon_3 \leftarrow \frac{\epsilon-\epsilon_1}{2(1-1/e)}$
10: $\quad\quad \delta_1 \leftarrow e^{-\frac{\mathrm{Cov}_{\mathcal{R}}(\hat{S}_k) \cdot \epsilon_3^2}{2c(1+\epsilon_1)(1+\epsilon_2)}}$
11: $\quad\quad \delta_2 \leftarrow e^{-\frac{(\mathrm{Cov}_{\mathcal{R}'}-1)(\hat{S}_k) \cdot \epsilon_2^2}{2c(1+\epsilon_2)}}$
12: $\quad\quad$ **if** $\delta_1 + \delta_2 \leq \delta$ **then**
13: $\quad\quad\quad$ **return** $\hat{S}_k$
14: $\quad\quad$ **end if**
15: $\quad$ **end if**
16: $\quad \mathcal{R} \leftarrow \mathcal{R} \cup \mathcal{R}'$
17: $\quad <\hat{S}_k, \hat{\mathbb{I}}(\hat{S}_k)> \leftarrow$ Max-Coverage$(\mathcal{R}, k)$
18: **until** $|\mathcal{R}| \geq (8+2\epsilon)n \cdot \frac{\ln \frac{2}{\delta} + \ln \binom{n}{k}}{\epsilon^2}$
19: **return** $\hat{S}_k$

6.2.1 Approximation Guarantee

We show that D-SSA preserve the $(1-1/e-\epsilon)$-approximation factor of SSA by the following theorem.

THEOREM 4. *Given a graph G, $0 \leq \epsilon \leq 1-2/e$ and $0 \leq \delta \leq 1$ as the inputs, D-SSA returns a $(1-1/e-\epsilon)$-approximate solution.*

PROOF. we prove that the two stopping conditions in SSA are still hold in D-SSA and thus D-SSA has the same approximation factor as SSA does.

Directly from the Alg. 4, when D-SSA terminates, the following conditions are satisfied,

$$\mathrm{Cov}_{\mathcal{R}}(\hat{S}_k) = 2c(1+\epsilon_1)(1+\epsilon_2) \ln \frac{1}{\delta_1} \frac{1}{\epsilon_3^2} \tag{26}$$

and

$$\mathrm{Cov}_{\mathcal{R}'}(\hat{S}_k) = 1 + 2c(1+\epsilon_2) \ln \frac{1}{\delta_2} \frac{1}{\epsilon_2^2} \tag{27}$$

with $\epsilon_1 + \epsilon_2 + \epsilon_1\epsilon_2 + (1-1/e)\epsilon_3 = \epsilon$ and $\delta_1 + \delta_2 = \delta$.

Eq. 26 is the first stopping conditions in SSA. Eq. 27 is the checking condition in the Estimate-Inf procedure in SSA and, together with the setting of ϵ_1, we obtain the second stopping condition in SSA.

$$\hat{\mathbb{I}}(\hat{S}_k) \geq (1+\epsilon_1)(1+\epsilon_2)\mathbb{I}(\hat{S}_k) \tag{28}$$

Thus, the $(1-1/e-\epsilon)$-approximation factor is followed from SSA which completes the proof. □

6.2.2 Achieving the Type-2 Minimum Threshold

Here, we will prove a much stronger result than that of SSA that D-SSA requires only, to within a constant factor, the type-2 minimum of RR sets $N^2_{min}(\epsilon, \delta)$. Since $\epsilon^*_a \leq \epsilon$ and $\delta^*_b \leq \delta$, let denote the constant

$$M = \frac{\ln \frac{2}{\delta^*_b}}{\ln \frac{1}{\delta^*_b}} \frac{4 \cdot (1+\epsilon^*_a)^2}{(\frac{1}{2} - \frac{1}{e} - \frac{\epsilon}{2})^3} \leq \frac{\ln \frac{2}{\delta}}{\ln \frac{1}{\delta}} \frac{4 \cdot (1+\epsilon)^2}{(\frac{1}{2} - \frac{1}{e} - \frac{\epsilon}{2})^3} \tag{29}$$

Alternatively speaking, for a given graph G, we will show that D-SSA terminates when the number of RR sets in $\mathcal{R}$ is larger than or equal to $M\mathsf{c}_1 N^2_{min}(\epsilon, \delta)$, where c_1 is a constant defined in Lem. 2, with at least $(1-\delta)$-probability. Due to the doubling scheme, D-SSA will generate no more than twice that number. More specifically, we will prove that the stopping condition (Line 11) is satisfied. Recall $N^2_{min}(\epsilon, \delta)$ RR sets implies

$$\Pr[\hat{\mathbb{I}}(\hat{S}_k) \leq (1+\epsilon^*_a)\mathbb{I}(\hat{S}_k)] \geq 1 - \delta^*_a \tag{30}$$

and

$$\Pr[\hat{\mathbb{I}}(S^*_k) \geq (1-\epsilon^*_b)OPT_k] \geq 1 - \delta^*_b \tag{31}$$

where

$$N^1_{min}(\epsilon^*_a, \epsilon^*_b, \delta^*_a, \delta^*_b) = \min_{\epsilon_a, \epsilon_b, \delta_a, \delta_b} N^1_{min}(\epsilon_a, \epsilon_b, \delta_a, \delta_b)$$

Apply Theo. 1, we have

$$\Pr[\mathbb{I}(\hat{S}_k) \geq (1-1/e-\epsilon)OPT_k] \geq 1 - \delta \tag{32}$$

First, we show that the value of ϵ_1 is upper bounded by the following lemma.

LEMMA 11. *Given $0 \leq \epsilon \leq 1-2/e$ and $0 \leq \delta \leq 1$, if $|\mathcal{R}| \geq M\mathsf{c}_1 N^2_{min}(\epsilon, \delta)$, then,*

$$\Pr[\epsilon_1 \leq \frac{\epsilon^*_a + \epsilon^*_b/2}{1 - \epsilon^*_b/2}] \geq 1 - \delta \tag{33}$$

where c_1 is a constant defined in Lem. 2.

The proof is presented in the appendix. Based on the result of Lem. 11, we next prove that D-SSA will terminate when $|\mathcal{R}| \geq M\mathsf{c}_1 N^2_{min}(\epsilon, \delta)$ with at least $(1-\delta)$-probability.

LEMMA 12. *If $|\mathcal{R}| \geq M\mathsf{c}_1 N^2_{min}(\epsilon, \delta)$ and $\epsilon_1 \leq \frac{\epsilon^*_a + \epsilon^*_b/2}{1-\epsilon^*_b/2}$, then,*

$$\delta_1 + \delta_2 \leq \delta \tag{34}$$

Therefore, D-SSA needs at most a constant times the type-2 minimum with the probability of $\Pr[\epsilon_1 \leq \frac{\epsilon^*_a + \epsilon^*_b/2}{1-\epsilon^*_b/2}]$ which is at least $1-\delta$. Since we double the RR sets every round, the actual number of RR sets is at most twice the necessary one. Thus, we conclude that D-SSA generates at most a constant times the type-2 minimum with probability of at least $1-\delta$.

THEOREM 5. *Given a graph G, $0 \leq \epsilon \leq 1-2/e$ and $0 \leq \delta \leq 1$, let $N^2_{min}(\epsilon, \delta)$ be the type-2 minimum threshold of RR sets. D-SSA generates no more than, to within a constant factor, $N^2_{min}(\epsilon, \delta)$ RR sets with the probability of at least $(1-\delta)$.*

The Theo. 5 follows directly from Lems. 11 and 12.

7. EXPERIMENTS

Backing by the strong theoretical results, we will experimentally show that SSA and D-SSA outperform the existing state-of-the-art IM methods by a large margin. Specifically, SSA and D-SSA are several orders of magnitudes faster than IMM and TIM+, the best existing IM methods with approximation guarantee, while having the same level of solution quality. SSA and D-SSA also require several times less memory than the other algorithms. To demonstrate the applicability of the proposed algorithms, we apply our methods on a critical application of IM, i.e., Targeted Viral Marketing (TVM) introduced in [29] and show the significant improvements in terms of performance over the existing methods.

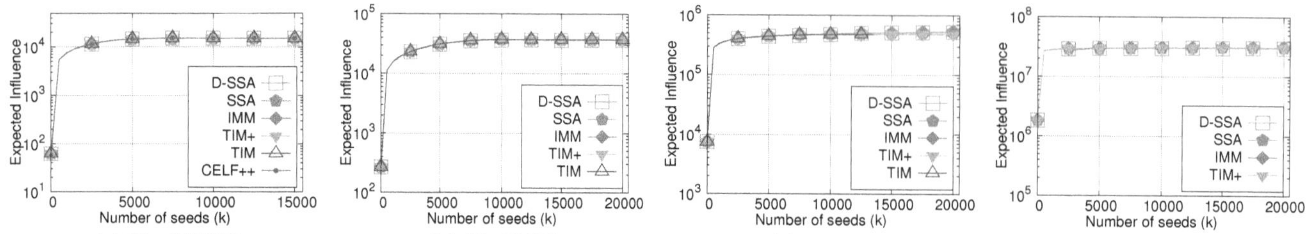

(a) NetHEPT (b) NetPHY (c) DBLP (d) Twitter

Figure 4: Expected Influence under LT model.

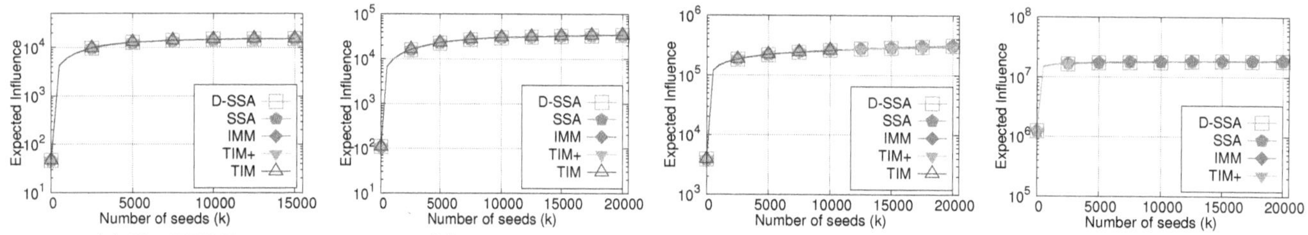

(a) NetHEPT (b) NetPHY (c) DBLP (d) Twitter

Figure 5: Expected Influence under IC model.

Table 2: Datasets' Statistics

Dataset	#Nodes	#Edges	Avg. degree
NetHELP[3]	15K	59K	4.1
NetPHY[3]	37K	181K	13.4
Enron[3]	37K	184K	5.0
Epinions[3]	132K	841K	13.4
DBLP[3]	655K	2M	6.1
Orkut[3]	3M	117M	78
Twitter [32]	41.7M	1.5G	70.5
Friendster[3]	65.6M	1.8G	54.8

7.1 Experimental Settings

All the experiments are run on a Linux machine with 2.2Ghz Xeon 8 core processor and 100GB of RAM. We carry experiments under both LT and IC models on the following algorithms and datasets.

Algorithms compared. On IM experiments, we compare SSA and D-SSA with the group of top algorithms that provide the same $(1 - 1/e - \epsilon)$-approximation guarantee. More specifically, CELF++ [33], one of the fastest greedy algorithms, and IMM [16], TIM/TIM+ [8], the best current RIS-based algorithms, are selected. For experimenting with TVM problem, we apply our Stop-and-Stare algorithms on this context and compare with the most efficient method for the problem, termed KB-TIM, in [29].

Datasets. For experimental purposes, we choose a set of 8 datasets from various disciplines: NetHEPT, NetPHY, DBLP are citation networks, Email-Enron is communication network, Epinions, Orkut, Twitter and Friendster are online social networks. The description summary of those datasets is in Table 2. On Twitter network, we also have the actual tweet/retweet dataset and we use these data to extract the target users whose tweets/retweets are relevant to a certain set of keywords. The experiments on TVM are run on the Twitter network with the extracted targeted groups of users.

Parameter Settings. For computing the edge weights, we follow the conventional computation as in [8, 13, 4, 26], the weight of the edge (u, v) is calculated as $w(u, v) = \frac{1}{d_{in}(v)}$ where $d_{in}(v)$ denotes the in-degree of node v.

In all the experiments, we keep $\epsilon = 0.1$ and $\delta = 1/n$ as a general setting or explicitly stated otherwise. For the other parameters defined for particular algorithms, we take the recommended values in the corresponding papers if available. We also limit the running time of each algorithm in a run to be within 24 hours.

7.2 Experiments with IM problem

To show the superior performance of the proposed algorithms on IM task, we ran the first set of experiments on four real-world networks, i.e., NetHEPT, NetPHY, DBLP, Twitter. We also test on a wide spectrum of the value of k, typically, from 1 to 20000, except on NetHEPT network since it has only 15233 nodes. The solution quality, running time, memory usage are reported sequentially in the following. We also present the actual number of RR sets generated by SSA, D-SSA and IMM when testing on four other datasets, i.e., Enron, Epinions, Orkut and Friendster.

7.2.1 *Solution Quality*

We first compare the quality of the solution returned by all the algorithms on LT and IC models. The results are presented in Fig. 4 and Fig. 5, respectively. The CELF++ algorithm is only able to run on NetHEPT due to time limit. From those figures, all the methods return comparable seed set quality with no significant difference. The results directly give us a better viewpoint on the basic network property that a small fraction of nodes can influence a very large portion of the networks. Most of the previous researches only find up to 50 seed nodes and provide a limited view of this phenomenon. Here, we see that after around 2000 nodes have been selected, the influence gains of selecting more seeds become very slim.

7.2.2 *Running time*

We next examine the performance in terms of running time of the tested algorithms. The results are shown in Fig. 6 and Fig. 7. Both SSA and D-SSA significantly outper-

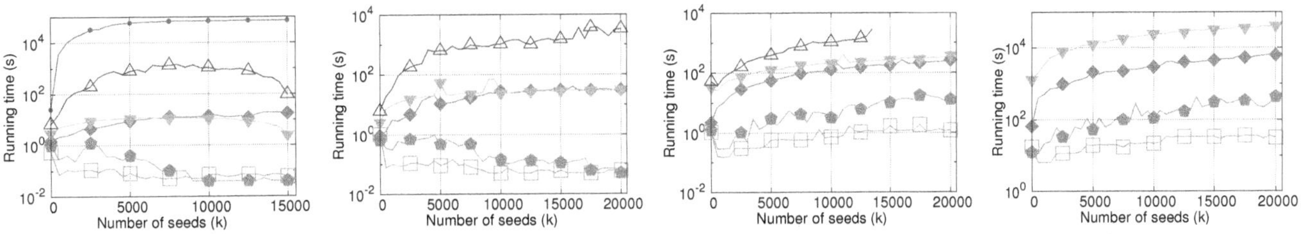

(a) NetHEPT (b) NetPHY (c) DBLP (d) Twitter

Figure 6: Running time under LT model

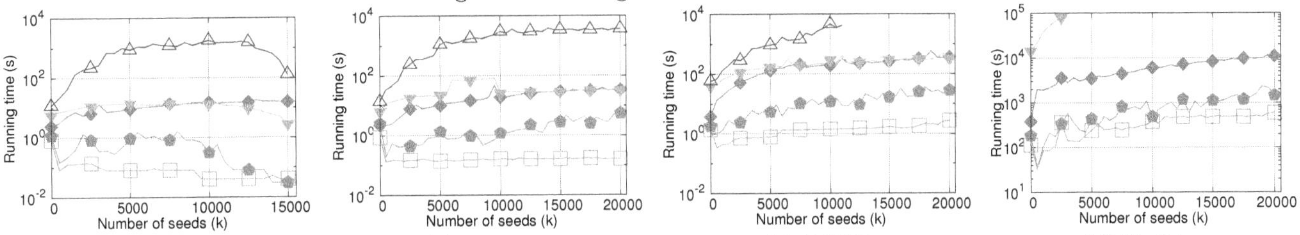

(a) NetHEPT (b) NetPHY (c) DBLP (d) Twitter

Figure 7: Running time under IC model

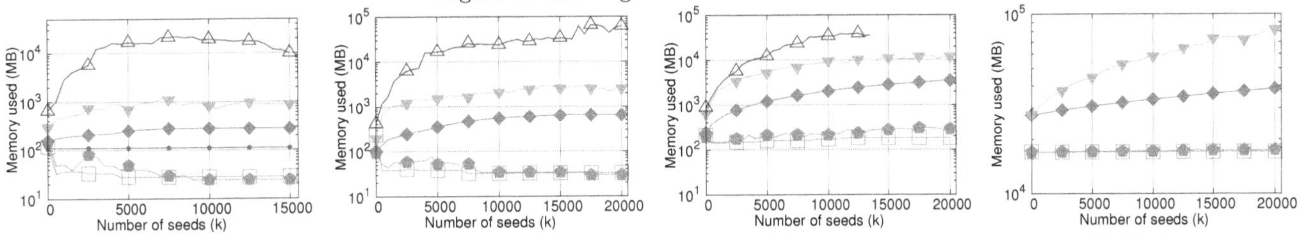

(a) NetHEPT (b) NetPHY (c) DBLP (d) Twitter

Figure 8: Memory usage under LT model

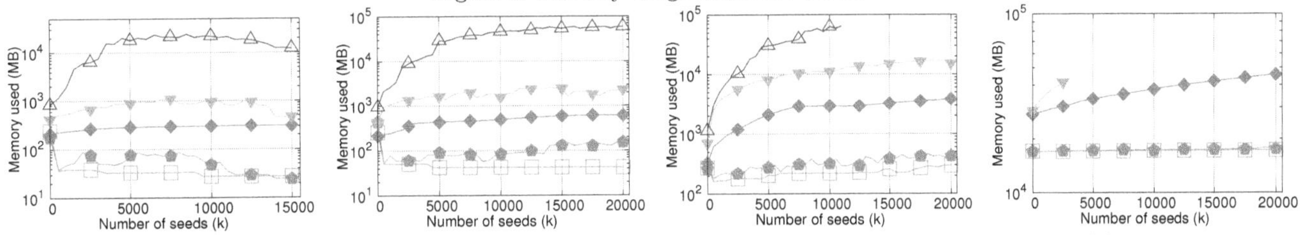

(a) NetHEPT (b) NetPHY (c) DBLP (d) Twitter

Figure 9: Memory usage under IC model

Data	**running time**(s)									**number of RR sets**(thousands)								
	$k = 1$			$k = 500$			$k = 1000$			$k = 1$			$k = 500$			$k = 1000$		
	D-SSA	SSA	IMM	D-SSA	SSA	IMM	D-SSA	SSA	IMM	D-SSA	SSA	IMM	D-SSA	SSA	IMM	D-SSA	SSA	IMM
Enron	**0.2**	0.6	0.7	**0.1**	0.2	3.1	**0.2**	0.6	6.9	**120**	180	2.8	**30**	60	580	**120**	180	910
Epin.	**0.4**	0.8	0.8	**0.1**	**0.1**	4.4	**0.3**	0.7	12.1	**160**	300	400	**40**	60	1214	**160**	240	1852
Orkut	**0.5**	1.1	2.1	**0.6**	3.4	17.4	**0.6**	4.3	45.5	**30**	60	124	**60**	240	760	**60**	240	1392
Frien.	**6.7**	10.3	270	**3.5**	5.9	4321.8	**12.4**	27.7	8028	**60**	120	262	**30**	60	1322	**120**	240	2250

Table 3: Across dataset view of performance of SSA, D-SSA and IMM on various datasets under LT model.

form the other competitors by a huge margin. Comparing to IMM, the best known algorithm, SSA and D-SSA run up to several orders of magnitudes faster. TIM+ and IMM show similar running time since they operate on the same philosophy of estimating optimal influence first and then calculating the necessary samples to guarantee the approximation for all possible seed sets. However, each of the two steps displays its own weakness. In contrast, SSA and D-SSA follows the Stop-and-Stare mechanism to thoroughly address those weaknesses and thus exhibit remarkable improvements.

Comparing between SSA and D-SSA, since D-SSApossesses the type-2 minimum threshold compared to the weaker type-1 threshold of SSA with the same precision settings ϵ, δ, D-SSA achieves considerably better performance and commits up to an order of magnitudes speedup.

7.2.3 Memory Usage and Number of RR sets

This experiment is divided into two parts: 1) we report the memory usage in the previous experiments and 2) since the gain in influence peaks at the selection of 1 to 1000 nodes, we carry new experiments on four other datasets, i.e., Enron, Epinion, Orkut and Friendster, with $k \in \{1, 500, 1000\}$ to show the view across datasets of SSA, D-SSA and IMM.

Memory Usage. The results on memory usage of all the algorithms are shown in Fig. 8 and Fig. 9. We can see that there is a strong correlation between running time and memory usage. It is not a surprise that SSA and D-SSA require much less memory, up to orders of magnitude, than the other methods since the complexity is represented by the number of RR sets and these methods achieve type-1 and type-2 minimum thresholds of RR sets.

Across datasets view. We ran SSA, D-SSA and IMM on four other datasets, i.e., Enron, Epinions, Orkut and Friendster, with $k \in \{1, 500, 1000\}$ under LT model. The results are presented in Table 3. In terms of running time, the table reflects our previous results that SSA and D-SSA largely outperform IMM, up to several orders of magnitudes. In particular, for Friendster - the largest network in our testbed with more than 65 million nodes, D-SSA is 1200-fold faster than IMM in case of $k = 500$. The same pattern happens in terms of the number of RR sets generated. As shown, even in the most extreme cases of selecting a single node, SSA and D-SSA require several times fewer RR sets than IMM.

7.3 Experiments with TVM problem

In this experiments, we will modify our Stop-and-Stare algorithms to work on Targeted Viral Marketing (TVM) problem and compare with the best existing method, i.e., KB-TIM in [29] to show the drastic improvements when applying our methods. In short, we will describe how we select the targeted groups from actual tweet/retweet datasets of Twitter and how to modify D-SSA and SSA for TVM problem. Then, we will report the experimental results.

7.3.1 TVM problem and methods

Targeted Viral Marketing (TVM) is a central problem in economics in which, instead of maximizing the influence over all the nodes in a network as in IM, it targets a specific group whose users are relevant to a certain topic and aims at optimizing the influence to that group only. Each node in the targeted group is associated with a weight which indicates the relevance of that user to the topic. The best current method for solving TVM is proposed in [29] in which the authors introduce weighted RIS sampling (called WRIS) and integrate it into TIM+ method [8] to derive an approximation algorithm, termed KB-TIM. WRIS only differs from the original RIS at the point of selecting the sampling root. More specifically, WRIS selects the root node proportional to the node weights instead of uniform selection as in RIS.

In the same way, we incorporate WRIS into D-SSA and SSA for solving TVM problem. By combining the analysis of WRIS in [29] and our previous proofs, it follows that the modified D-SSA and SSA preserve the $(1 - 1/e - \epsilon)$-approximation property as in IM problem.

7.3.2 Extracting the targeted groups

We use tweet/retweet dataset to extract the users' interests on two political topics as described in [32]. We choose two groups of most popular keywords as listed in Table 4,

Table 4: Topics, related keywords

Topic	*Keywords*	#Users
1	**bill clinton, iran, north korea, president obama, obama**	997,034
2	**senator ted kenedy, oprah, kayne west, marvel, jackass**	507,465

and mine from the tweet data who posted tweets/reweets containing at least one of those keywords in each group and how many times. We consider those users to be the targeted groups in TVM experiments with the relevance/interest of each user on the topic proportional to the frequency of having those keywords in their tweets.

7.3.3 Experimental results

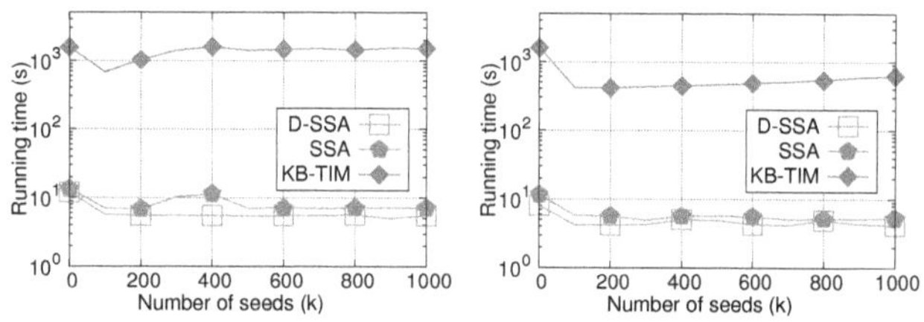

(a) Topic 1 (b) Topic 2

Figure 10: Running time on Twitter network

We run SSA, D-SSA and KB-TIM on Twitter network under LT model with the targeted groups extracted from tweet dataset as described previously. Since all the algorithms have the same guarantee on the returned solution, we only measure the performance of these methods in terms of running time and the results are depicted in Fig. 10. In both cases, D-SSA and SSA consistently witness at least two order of magnitude improvements (up to 500 times) in running time compared to KB-TIM. D-SSA is also consistently faster than SSA due to the more optimal type-2 threshold.

8. CONCLUSION

In this paper, we make several significant contributions in solving the fundamental influence maximization (IM) problem. We provide the unified RIS framework which generalizes the best existing technique of using RIS sampling to find an $(1 - 1/e - \epsilon)$-approximate solution in billion-scale networks. We introduce the RIS threshold that all the algorithms following the framework need to satisfy and two minimum thresholds, i.e., type-1 and type-2. Interestingly, we are able to develop two novel algorithms, SSA and D-SSA, which are the first methods meeting the two minimum thresholds. Since IM plays a central roles in a wide range of practical applications, e.g., viral marketing, controlling diseases, virus/worms, detecting contamination and so on, the developments of SSA and D-SSA will immediately result in a burst in performance and allow their applications to work in billion-scale domains.

9. ACKNOWLEDGMENTS

The work of My T. Thai is partially supported by NSF CCF 1422116.

10. REFERENCES

[1] D. Kempe, J. Kleinberg, and É. Tardos, "Maximizing the spread of influence through a social network," in *KDD'03*, pp. 137–146, ACM New York, NY, USA, 2003.

[2] J. Leskovec, A. Krause, C. Guestrin, C. Faloutsos, J. VanBriesen, and N. Glance, "Cost-effective outbreak detection in networks," in *ACM KDD '07*, (New York, NY, USA), pp. 420–429, ACM, 2007.

[3] W. Chen, C. Wang, and Y. Wang, "Scalable influence maximization for prevalent viral marketing in large-scale social networks," in *ACM KDD '10*, (New York, NY, USA), pp. 1029–1038, ACM, 2010.

[4] A. Goyal, W. Lu, and L. Lakshmanan, "Simpath: An efficient algorithm for influence maximization under the linear threshold model," in *Data Mining (ICDM), 2011 IEEE 11th International Conference on*, pp. 211–220, IEEE, 2011.

[5] A. Goyal, W. Lu, and L. Lakshmanan, "Celf++: optimizing the greedy algorithm for influence maximization in social networks," in *Proceedings of the 20th international conference companion on World wide web*, pp. 47–48, ACM, 2011.

[6] E. Cohen, D. Delling, T. Pajor, and R. F. Werneck, "Sketch-based influence maximization and computation: Scaling up with guarantees," in *Proceedings of the 23rd ACM International Conference on Conference on Information and Knowledge Management*, pp. 629–638, ACM, 2014.

[7] N. Ohsaka, T. Akiba, Y. Yoshida, and K.-i. Kawarabayashi, "Fast and accurate influence maximization on large networks with pruned monte-carlo simulations," in *Twenty-Eighth AAAI Conference on Artificial Intelligence*, 2014.

[8] Y. Tang, X. Xiao, and Y. Shi, "Influence maximization: Near-optimal time complexity meets practical efficiency," in *Proceedings of SIGMOD international conference on Management of data*, pp. 75–86, ACM, 2014.

[9] D. T. Nguyen, H. Zhang, S. Das, M. T. Thai, and T. N. Dinh, "Least cost influence in multiplex social networks: Model representation and analysis," in *Data Mining (ICDM), 2013 IEEE 13th International Conference on*, pp. 567–576, IEEE, 2013.

[10] T. N. Dinh, Y. Shen, D. T. Nguyen, and M. T. Thai, "On the approximability of positive influence dominating set in social networks," *Journal of Combinatorial Optimization*, vol. 27, no. 3, pp. 487–503, 2014.

[11] Y. Shen, T. N. Dinh, H. Zhang, and M. T. Thai, "Interest-matching information propagation in multiple online social networks," in *Proceedings of the 21st ACM International Conference on Information and Knowledge Management*, CIKM '12, (New York, NY, USA), pp. 1824–1828, ACM, 2012.

[12] H. T. Nguyen, M. T. Thai, and T. N. Dinh, "Cost-aware targeted viral marketing in billion-scale networks," in *INFOCOM, 2016 Proceedings IEEE*, pp. 55–59, IEEE, 2013.

[13] W. Chen, Y. Wang, and S. Yang, "Efficient influence maximization in social networks," in *KDD '09*, (New York, NY, USA), pp. 199–208, ACM, 2009.

[14] K. Jung, W. Heo, and W. Chen, "Irie: Scalable and robust influence maximization in social networks," in *Data Mining (ICDM), 2012 IEEE 12th International Conference on*, pp. 918–923, IEEE, 2012.

[15] Y. Wang, G. Cong, G. Song, and K. Xie, "Community-based greedy algorithm for mining top-k influential nodes in mobile social networks," in *Proceedings of the 16th ACM SIGKDD international conference on Knowledge discovery and data mining*, pp. 1039–1048, ACM, 2010.

[16] Y. Tang, Y. Shi, and X. Xiao, "Influence maximization in near-linear time: A martingale approach," in *Proceedings of SIGMOD International Conference on Management of Data*, pp. 1539–1554, ACM, 2015.

[17] C. Borgs, M. Brautbar, J. Chayes, and B. Lucier, "Maximizing social influence in nearly optimal time," in *Proceedings of the Twenty-Fifth Annual ACM-SIAM Symposium on Discrete Algorithms*, SODA '14, pp. 946–957, SIAM, 2014.

[18] M. Minoux, "Accelerated greedy algorithms for maximizing submodular set functions," in *Optimization Techniques* (J. Stoer, ed.), vol. 7 of *Lecture Notes in Control and Information Sciences*, pp. 234–243, Springer, 1978.

[19] N. Chen, "On the approximability of influence in social networks," *SIAM Journal of Discrete Mathematics*, vol. 23, no. 3, pp. 1400–1415, 2009.

[20] A. Goyal, F. Bonchi, and L. Lakshmanan, "Learning influence probabilities in social networks," in *Proceedings of the third ACM international conference on Web search and data mining*, pp. 241–250, ACM, 2010.

[21] K. Kutzkov, A. Bifet, F. Bonchi, and A. Gionis, "Strip: stream learning of influence probabilities," in *Proceedings of the 19th ACM SIGKDD international conference on Knowledge discovery and data mining*, pp. 275–283, ACM, 2013.

[22] T. Dinh, H. Zhang, D. Nguyen, and M. Thai, "Cost-effective viral marketing for time-critical campaigns in large-scale social networks," *Networking, IEEE/ACM Transactions on*, 2014.

[23] H. Zhang, T. Dinh, and M. Thai, "Maximizing the spread of positive influence in online social networks," in *Distributed Computing Systems (ICDCS), 2013 IEEE 33rd International Conference on*, pp. 317–326, July 2013.

[24] W. Chen, W. Lu, and N. Zhang, "Time-critical influence maximization in social networks with time-delayed diffusion process," in *Twenty-Sixth AAAI Conference on Artificial Intelligence*, 2012.

[25] N. Du, L. Song, M. Gomez-Rodriguez, and H. Zha, "Scalable influence estimation in continuous-time diffusion networks," in *Advances in neural information processing systems*, pp. 3147–3155, 2013.

[26] H. Nguyen and R. Zheng, "On budgeted influence maximization in social networks," *Selected Areas in Communications, IEEE Journal on*, vol. 31, no. 6, pp. 1084–1094, 2013.

[27] P. Dagum, R. Karp, M. Luby, and S. Ross, "An optimal algorithm for monte carlo estimation," *SIAM J. Comput.*, vol. 29, pp. 1484–1496, Mar. 2000.

[28] S. Khuller, A. Moss, and J. S. Naor, "The budgeted

maximum coverage problem," *Information Processing Letters*, vol. 70, no. 1, pp. 39–45, 1999.
[29] Y. Li, D. Zhang, and K.-L. Tan, "Real-time targeted influence maximization for online advertisements," *Proceedings of the VLDB Endowment*, vol. 8, no. 10, 2015.
[30] S. Bhattacharya, M. Henzinger, D. Nanongkai, and C. Tsourakakis, "Space-and time-efficient algorithm for maintaining dense subgraphs on one-pass dynamic streams," in *Proceedings of the Forty-Seventh Annual ACM on Symposium on Theory of Computing*, pp. 173–182, ACM, 2015.
[31] G. L. Nemhauser and L. A. Wolsey, "Maximizing submodular set functions: formulations and analysis of algorithms," *North-Holland Mathematics Studies*, vol. 59, pp. 279–301, 1981.
[32] H. Kwak, C. Lee, H. Park, and S. Moon, "What is twitter, a social network or a news media?," in *Proceedings of the 19th international conference on World wide web*, pp. 591–600, ACM, 2010.
[33] A. Goyal, W. Lu, and L. V. Lakshmanan, "Celf++: optimizing the greedy algorithm for influence maximization in social networks," in *Proceedings of the 20th international conference companion on World wide web*, pp. 47–48, ACM, 2011.

APPENDIX

In our proof, we utilize the following version of Chernoff-Hoeffding's inequality,

LEMMA 13 ([27]). *Let $Z_1, Z_2, ...$ be independently and identically distributed samples according to Z in the interval [0, 1] with mean μ_Z and variance σ_Z^2. Let $\hat{\mu}_Z = \frac{1}{T}\sum_{i=1}^{T} Z_i$ be an estimate of μ_Z. For any fixed $T > 0, 0 \geq \epsilon \geq 1$,*

$$\Pr[\hat{\mu} \geq (1+\epsilon)\mu] \leq e^{\frac{-T\mu\epsilon^2}{2c}} \tag{35}$$

and

$$\Pr[\hat{\mu} \leq (1-\epsilon)\mu] \leq e^{\frac{-T\mu\epsilon^2}{2c}}. \tag{36}$$

Proof of Theorem 1

According to Def. 4, if the number of RR sets generated $|\mathcal{R}| \geq N(\epsilon_a, \epsilon_b, \delta_a, \delta_b)$ then Eqs. 6 and 7 hold. From Eq. 6, we have

$$\Pr[\hat{\mathbb{I}}(\hat{S}_k) \leq (1+\epsilon_a)\mathbb{I}(\hat{S}_k)] \geq 1-\delta_a \tag{37}$$

which is equivalent to

$$\Pr[\mathbb{I}(\hat{S}_k) \geq \hat{\mathbb{I}}(\hat{S}_k) - \epsilon_a \mathbb{I}(\hat{S}_k)] \geq 1-\delta_a \tag{38}$$

Let $S_{kmax} \in V$ be the size-k set with maximum coverage in $\mathcal{R}$. The greedy strategy in finding max-coverage returns the set, $\hat{S}_k$, with $\hat{\mathbb{I}}(\hat{S}_k) \geq (1-1/e)\hat{\mathbb{I}}(S_{kmax})$ [31]. Since $\hat{\mathbb{I}}(S_{kmax}) \geq \hat{\mathbb{I}}(S_k^*)$, $\hat{\mathbb{I}}(\hat{S}_k) \geq (1-1/e)\hat{\mathbb{I}}(S_k^*)$. Thus,

$$\Pr[\mathbb{I}(\hat{S}_k) \geq (1-1/e)\hat{\mathbb{I}}(S_k^*) - \epsilon_a \mathbb{I}(\hat{S}_k)] \geq 1-\delta_a$$

Now by substituting $\hat{\mathbb{I}}(S_k^*)$ in this probability with that from Eq. 7 and noting that the right hand side is updated to $1-\delta_a-\delta_b \geq 1-\delta$ to account for the probability in Eq. 7. Hence,

$$\Pr[\mathbb{I}(\hat{S}_k) \geq (1-1/e)(1-\epsilon_b)OPT_k - \epsilon_a \mathbb{I}(\hat{S}_k)] \geq 1-\delta$$

Since $\mathbb{I}(\hat{S}_k) \leq OPT_k$,

$$\Pr[\mathbb{I}(\hat{S}_k) \geq (1-1/e)(1-\epsilon_b)OPT_k - \epsilon_a OPT_k] \geq 1-\delta$$

or,

$$\Pr[\mathbb{I}(\hat{S}_k) \geq (1-1/e-(1-1/e)\epsilon_b - \epsilon_a)OPT_k] \geq 1-\delta$$

and, finally, due to $\epsilon \geq \epsilon_a + (1-1/e)\epsilon_b$,

$$\Pr[\mathbb{I}(\hat{S}_k) \geq (1-1/e-\epsilon)OPT_k] \geq 1-\delta$$

That completes the proof of Theo. 1.

Remark: As shown in [8], the number of RR sets represent the complexity of an RIS based method. Let KPT be the expected time to generate an RR set, then $|\mathcal{R}|KPT$ is the complexity of generating all the RR sets. Moreover, the finding Max-coverage step can be done in linear time w.r.t the total size of RR sets which is upper-bounded by the generating RR sets.

Proof of Lemma 5

Recall that SSA terminates when the selected seed set, $\hat{S}_k$, satisfies two conditions,

$$\mathrm{Cov}_{\mathcal{R}}(\hat{S}_k) \geq \Lambda_1 \tag{39}$$

and

$$\hat{\mathbb{I}}(\hat{S}_k) \leq (1+\epsilon_1)\mathbb{I}_c(\hat{S}_k) \tag{40}$$

From Corollary 1, we have

$$\Pr[\mathbb{I}_c(S) \leq (1+\epsilon_2)\mathbb{I}(S)] \geq 1-\delta/3 \tag{41}$$

Substitute $\mathbb{I}_c(\hat{S}_k)$ in Eq. 41 with that of Eq. 40,

$$\Pr[\hat{\mathbb{I}}(\hat{S}_k) \leq (1+\epsilon_1)(1+\epsilon_2)\mathbb{I}(\hat{S}_k)] \geq 1-\delta/3 \tag{42}$$

This completes the proof of Lem. 5.

Proof of Lemma 6

To prove the lemma, we first find a lower-bound of the number of RR sets, $|\mathcal{R}|$, generated and, thus, show that $|\mathcal{R}| \geq \frac{\Upsilon(\epsilon_3,\delta/3)n}{OPT_k}$ with high probability and, then, apply Chernoff-Hoeffding's inequality. Recall that

$$\hat{\mathbb{I}}(\hat{S}_k) = \frac{\mathrm{Cov}_{\mathcal{R}}(\hat{S}_k)n}{|\mathcal{R}|} \tag{43}$$

Apply the first stopping condition, $\mathrm{Cov}_{\mathcal{R}}(\hat{S}_k) \geq \Lambda_1$,

$$\hat{\mathbb{I}}(\hat{S}_k) \geq \frac{\Lambda_1 n}{|\mathcal{R}|} = \frac{(1+\epsilon_1)(1+\epsilon_2)\Upsilon(\epsilon_3,\delta/3)n}{|\mathcal{R}|}$$

where $\Upsilon(\epsilon_3, \delta/3) = 2c\ln(3/\delta)1/\epsilon_3^2$.
Now, combine the result of Lem. 5 with the above inequality, we have

$$\Pr[\frac{\Upsilon(\epsilon_3,\delta/3)n}{|\mathcal{R}|} \leq \mathbb{I}(\hat{S}_k)] \geq 1-\delta/3$$

Thus,

$$\Pr[|\mathcal{R}| \geq \frac{\Upsilon(\epsilon_3,\delta/3)n}{\mathbb{I}(\hat{S}_k)}] \geq 1-\delta/3 \tag{44}$$

and due to $\mathbb{I}(\hat{S}_k) \leq OPT_k$,

$$\Pr[|\mathcal{R}| \geq \frac{\Upsilon(\epsilon_3,\delta/3)n}{OPT_k}] \geq 1-\delta/3 \tag{45}$$

Eq. 45 says that $|\mathcal{R}| \geq \frac{\Upsilon(\epsilon_3,\delta/3)n}{OPT_k}$ with at least $(1-\delta/3)$-probability. In cases that $|\mathcal{R}| \geq \frac{\Upsilon(\epsilon_3,\delta/3)n}{OPT_k}$ happens, we use Chernoff-Hoeffding's inequality (Lem. 13) on the optimal solution, S_k^*, with random variable $Z = \min\{1, |R_j \cap S_k^*|\}$ and $\mu_Z = OPT_k/n$ to obtain

$$\Pr[\hat{\mathbb{I}}(S_k^*) \leq (1-\epsilon_3)OPT_k] \leq e^{-\frac{|\mathcal{R}|OPT_k\epsilon_3^2}{n2c}} \quad (46)$$

Then, due to $|\mathcal{R}| \geq \frac{\Upsilon(\epsilon_3,\delta/3)n}{OPT_k}$,

$$\Pr[\hat{\mathbb{I}}(S_k^*) \leq (1-\epsilon_3)OPT_k] \leq e^{-\frac{\Upsilon(\epsilon_3,\delta/3)\epsilon_3^2}{2c}} = \delta/3 \quad (47)$$

Thus, combining Eq. 45 and Eq. 47 gives

$$\Pr[\hat{\mathbb{I}}(S_k^*) \leq (1-\epsilon_3)OPT_k \text{ or } \hat{\mathbb{I}}(\hat{S}_k) \geq (1+\epsilon_{12})\mathbb{I}(\hat{S}_k)] \leq 2\delta/3$$

which completes the proof of Lem. 6.

Proof of Lemma 7

From Lem. 2, to achieve the approximation described in Eq. 20, we need at least $\frac{\Upsilon(\epsilon_b,\delta_b)n}{OPT_k}$ and

$$\frac{\Upsilon(\epsilon_b,\delta_b)n}{OPT_k} \leq \mathsf{c}_1 \cdot \theta^* \quad (48)$$

Since θ^* is the sufficient number of RR sets to achieve Eq. 19 only and $N^1_{min}(\epsilon_a,\epsilon_b,\delta_a,\delta_b)$ is enough to obtain both Eq. 19 and Eq 20, we get $\theta^* \leq N^1_{min}(\epsilon_a,\epsilon_b,\delta_a,\delta_b)$ and, thus,

$$\frac{\Upsilon(\epsilon_b,\delta_b)n}{OPT_k} \leq \mathsf{c}_1 \cdot N^1_{min}(\epsilon_a,\epsilon_b,\delta_a,\delta_b) \quad (49)$$

Multiply both sides by $\frac{1}{1-1/e-\epsilon}$,

$$\frac{\Upsilon(\epsilon_b,\delta_b)n}{(1-1/e-\epsilon)OPT_k} \leq \frac{\mathsf{c}_1 \cdot N^1_{min}(\epsilon_a,\epsilon_b,\delta_a,\delta_b)}{1-1/e-\epsilon} \quad (50)$$

Since $\mathbb{I}(\hat{S}_k) \geq (1-1/e-\epsilon)OPT_k$ as a consequence of Eq, we have

$$\frac{\Upsilon(\epsilon_b,\delta_b)n}{\mathbb{I}(\hat{S}_k)} \leq \frac{\mathsf{c}_1 \cdot N^1_{min}(\epsilon_a,\epsilon_b,\delta_a,\delta_b)}{1-1/e-\epsilon} \quad (51)$$

Recall that $\hat{\mathbb{I}}(\hat{S}_k) = \frac{\mathrm{Cov}_{\mathcal{R}}(\hat{S}_k)n}{|\mathcal{R}|}$ or $|\mathcal{R}| = \frac{\mathrm{Cov}_{\mathcal{R}}(\hat{S}_k)n}{\hat{\mathbb{I}}(\hat{S}_k)}$. Thus, the condition $\mathrm{Cov}_{\mathcal{R}}(\hat{S}_k) \geq \Lambda_1$ is equivalent to

$$|\mathcal{R}| \geq \frac{\Lambda_1 n}{\hat{\mathbb{I}}(\hat{S}_k)} = \frac{(1+\epsilon_b)\Upsilon(\epsilon_b,\delta_b)n}{\hat{\mathbb{I}}(\hat{S}_k)} \quad (52)$$

Since $\hat{\mathbb{I}}(\hat{S}_k) \leq (1+\epsilon_a)\mathbb{I}(\hat{S}_k)$, we also have

$$\frac{\Upsilon(\epsilon_b,\delta_b)n}{\mathbb{I}(\hat{S}_k)} \geq \frac{(1+\epsilon_b)\Upsilon(\epsilon_b,\delta_b)n}{\hat{\mathbb{I}}(\hat{S}_k)} \quad (53)$$

From Eq. 52 and Eq. 53, observe that if we set $|\mathcal{R}| = \frac{\Upsilon(\epsilon_b,\delta_b)n}{\mathbb{I}(\hat{S}_k)}$ then Eq. 52 will hold and, in turn, we achieve $\mathrm{Cov}_{\mathcal{R}}(\hat{S}_k) \geq \Lambda_1$. Based on that and Eq. 51, we conclude that $\frac{\mathsf{c}_1 \cdot N^1_{min}(\epsilon_a,\epsilon_b,\delta_a,\delta_b)}{1-1/e-\epsilon}$ RR sets are sufficient to satisfy the condition (C1).

Proof of Lemma 8

In this case, the necessary number of RR sets is the same as that to satisfy Eq. 19 where $\epsilon_a = \epsilon_1 + \epsilon_2 + \epsilon_1\epsilon_2$. The only question here is whether the Estimate-Inf succeeds and returns $\mathbb{I}(\hat{S}_k)$ when the main algorithm has $|\mathcal{R}|$ random RR sets. Recall that it fails in the case that the number of RR sets required in Estimate-Inf exceeds $|\mathcal{R}|\frac{1+\epsilon_2}{1-\epsilon_2}\frac{\epsilon_3^2}{\epsilon_2^2}$, however, from Eq. 51,

$$|\mathcal{R}| \geq \frac{\Upsilon(\epsilon_b,\delta_b)n}{\mathbb{I}(\hat{S}_k)} = 2c\ln\frac{3}{\delta}\frac{1}{\epsilon_3^2}\frac{n}{\mathbb{I}(\hat{S}_k)} \quad (54)$$

Multiply both side with $\frac{1+\epsilon_2}{1-\epsilon_2}\frac{\epsilon_3^2}{\epsilon_2^2}$,

$$|\mathcal{R}|\frac{1+\epsilon_2}{1-\epsilon_2}\frac{\epsilon_3^2}{\epsilon_2^2} \geq \frac{1+\epsilon_2}{1-\epsilon_2}2c\ln\frac{3}{\delta}\frac{1}{\epsilon_2^2}\frac{n}{\mathbb{I}(\hat{S}_k)} \quad (55)$$

Based on Lem. 2, $2c\ln\frac{3}{\delta}\frac{1}{\epsilon_2^2}\frac{n}{\mathbb{I}(\hat{S}_k)}$ random RR sets are sufficient to obtain

$$\Pr[\mathbb{I}_c(\hat{S}_k) \geq (1-\epsilon_2)\mathbb{I}(\hat{S}_k)] \leq 1-\delta/3 \quad (56)$$

Thus, combine Eq. 55 and Eq. 56,

$$\Pr[|\mathcal{R}|\frac{1+\epsilon_2}{1-\epsilon_2}\frac{\epsilon_3^2}{\epsilon_2^2} \geq (1+\epsilon_2)2c\ln\frac{3}{\delta}\frac{1}{\epsilon_2^2}\frac{n}{\mathbb{I}_c(\hat{S}_k)}] \leq 1-\delta/3$$

or,

$$\Pr[\frac{\mathbb{I}_c(\hat{S}_k)}{n}|\mathcal{R}|\frac{1+\epsilon_2}{1-\epsilon_2}\frac{\epsilon_3^2}{\epsilon_2^2} \geq (1+\epsilon_2)2c\ln\frac{3}{\delta}\frac{1}{\epsilon_2^2}] \geq 1-\delta/3$$

The left hand side, $\frac{\mathbb{I}_c(\hat{S}_k)}{n}|\mathcal{R}|\frac{1+\epsilon_2}{1-\epsilon_2}\frac{\epsilon_3^2}{\epsilon_2^2}$, is the coverage, Cov, in Estimate-Inf procedure when $|\mathcal{R}|\frac{1+\epsilon_2}{1-\epsilon_2}\frac{\epsilon_3^2}{\epsilon_2^2}$ RR sets are generated and the whole inequality is the condition to succeed. That means with $|\mathcal{R}|$ RR sets in the main algorithm, the Estimate-Inf returns a good estimation of $\mathbb{I}(\hat{S}_k)$ with at least $(1-\delta/3)$-probability.

Proof of Lemma 11

To prove the lemma, we begin by showing that $\mathbb{I}(S_k^*)$ has an better approximation when $|\mathcal{R}| \geq M\mathsf{c}_1 N^2_{min}(\epsilon,\delta)$. Let $X^* = \min\{1, |R_j \cap S_k^*|\}$ (R_j is a random RR set) be a random variable with $\mu_{X^*} = OPT_k/n$. Apply Lem. 2 on the approximation of μ_{X^*} to achieve Eq. 31, we have

$$\frac{\Upsilon(\epsilon_b^*,\delta_b^*)}{\mu_{X^*}} \leq \mathsf{c}_1 N^2_{min}(\epsilon,\delta) \quad (57)$$

Multiply both sides by M, we have

$$\frac{M\Upsilon(\epsilon_b^*,\delta_b^*)}{\mu_{X^*}} \leq M\mathsf{c}_1 N^2_{min}(\epsilon,\delta) \quad (58)$$

In other words,

$$|\mathcal{R}| \geq \frac{M\Upsilon(\epsilon_b^*,\delta_b^*)}{\mu_{X^*}} \quad (59)$$

Then, since

$$M\Upsilon(\epsilon_b^*,\delta_b^*) = \frac{\ln\frac{2}{\delta_b^*}}{\ln\frac{1}{\delta_b^*}}\frac{4(1+\epsilon_a^*)^2}{(\frac{1}{2}-\frac{1}{e}-\frac{\epsilon}{2})^3}\Upsilon(\epsilon_b^*,\delta_b^*) \geq \Upsilon(\frac{\epsilon_b^*}{2},\frac{\delta_b^*}{2}),$$

thus,

$$|\mathcal{R}| \geq \frac{\Upsilon(\frac{\epsilon_b^*}{2},\frac{\delta_b^*}{2})}{\mu_{X^*}} \quad (60)$$

Apply Lem. 2 with the number of RR sets specified in Eq. 60, we have

$$\Pr[\hat{\mathbb{I}}(S_k^*) \geq (1-\epsilon_b^*/2)OPT_k] \geq 1-\delta_b^*/2 \quad (61)$$

Combine Eq. 30 and Eq. 61 and apply Theo. 1,

$$\Pr[\mathbb{I}(\hat{S}_k) \geq (1 - \frac{1}{e} - \epsilon)OPT_k] \geq 1 - \delta_a^* - \frac{\delta_b^*}{2} \quad (62)$$

In Eq. 59, $|\mathcal{R}|$ depends on $\mu_{X^*} = OPT_k/n$ and in Eq. 62, we obtained the relation between $\mathbb{I}(\hat{S}_k)$ and OPT_k and, thus, we can represent $|\mathcal{R}|$ in terms of $\mathbb{I}(\hat{S}_k)$,

$$\Pr[|\mathcal{R}| \geq \frac{M\Upsilon(\epsilon_b^*, \delta_b^*)(1 - 1/e - \epsilon)}{\mathbb{I}(\hat{S}_k)/n}] \geq 1 - \delta_a^* - \frac{\delta_b^*}{2}$$

and since $M\Upsilon(\epsilon_b^*, \delta_b^*)(1 - 1/e - \epsilon) \geq \Upsilon(\frac{\epsilon_b^*}{2}, \frac{\delta_b^*}{2})$,

$$\Pr[|\mathcal{R}| \geq \frac{\Upsilon(\frac{\epsilon_b^*}{2}, \frac{\delta_b^*}{2})}{\mathbb{I}(\hat{S}_k)/n}] \geq 1 - \delta_a^* - \frac{\delta_b^*}{2} \quad (63)$$

Notice that in each iteration D-SSA generates $|\mathcal{R}|$ new random RR sets and put them in $\mathcal{R}'$ to compute $\mathbb{I}_c(\hat{S}_k)$. Thus,

$$\Pr[|\mathcal{R}'| \geq \frac{\Upsilon(\frac{\epsilon_b^*}{2}, \frac{\delta_b^*}{2})}{\mathbb{I}(\hat{S}_k)/n}] \geq 1 - \delta_a^* - \frac{\delta_b^*}{2} \quad (64)$$

In the cases that $|\mathcal{R}'| \geq \frac{\Upsilon(\frac{\epsilon_b^*}{2}, \frac{\delta_b^*}{2})}{\mathbb{I}(\hat{S}_k)/n}$, apply Lem. 2,

$$\Pr[\mathbb{I}_c(\hat{S}_k) \geq (1 - \epsilon_b^*/2)\mathbb{I}(\hat{S}_k)] \geq 1 - \delta_b^*/2 \quad (65)$$

Combine with the probability in Eq. 64, we have

$$\Pr[\mathbb{I}_c(\hat{S}_k) \geq (1 - \epsilon_b^*/2)\mathbb{I}(\hat{S}_k)] \geq 1 - \delta_a^* - \delta_b^* \quad (66)$$

or, equivalently,

$$\Pr[\mathbb{I}(\hat{S}_k) \leq \frac{1}{1 - \epsilon_b^*/2}\mathbb{I}_c(\hat{S}_k)] \geq 1 - \delta_a^* - \delta_b^* \quad (67)$$

Thus, from Eq. 30 and Eq. 67 with a note that Eq. 30 was used to derive Eq. 67 and, thus, the probability that both happen is actually the probability in Eq. 67, we achieve

$$\Pr[\hat{\mathbb{I}}(\hat{S}_k) \leq \frac{1 + \epsilon_a^*}{1 - \epsilon_b^*/2}\mathbb{I}_c(\hat{S}_k)] \geq 1 - \delta_a^* - \delta_b^* \quad (68)$$

Then, since $\epsilon_1 = \frac{\hat{\mathbb{I}}(\hat{S}_k)}{\mathbb{I}_c(\hat{S}_k)} - 1$ and from Eq. 68,

$$\Pr[\epsilon_1 \leq \frac{1 + \epsilon_a^*}{1 - \epsilon_b^*/2} - 1] \geq 1 - \delta_a^* - \delta_b^* \quad (69)$$

and due to $\delta_a^* + \delta_b^* \leq \delta$,

$$\Pr[\epsilon_1 \leq \frac{\epsilon_a^* + \epsilon_b^*/2}{1 - \epsilon_b^*/2}] \geq 1 - \delta \quad (70)$$

which completes the proof.

Proof of Lemma 12

Notice that since $\epsilon \leq 1 - 2/e$, we have $\frac{\epsilon_a^* + \epsilon_b^*/2}{1 - \epsilon_b^*/2} \leq \epsilon$ and the condition in Line 9 is satisfied. Given $\epsilon_1 \leq \frac{\epsilon_a^* + \epsilon_b^*/2}{1 - \epsilon_b^*/2}$, we compute ϵ_2, ϵ_3 as,

$$\epsilon_2 = \frac{\epsilon - \epsilon_1}{2(1 + \epsilon_1)} \geq \frac{1/2 - 1/e - \epsilon/2}{1 + \epsilon_a^*}\frac{\epsilon_b^*}{2} \quad (71)$$

and

$$\epsilon_3 = \frac{\epsilon - \epsilon_1}{2(1 - 1/e)} \geq (1/2 - 1/e - \epsilon/2)\frac{\epsilon_b^*}{2} \quad (72)$$

Since $\epsilon_1 \leq \frac{\epsilon_a^* + \epsilon_b^*/2}{1 - \epsilon_b^*/2}$ also implies that all the inequality used in the proof of Lem. 11 hold, then

$$\hat{\mathbb{I}}(S_k^*) \geq (1 - \epsilon_b^*/2)OPT_k \quad (73)$$

Combine with $\hat{\mathbb{I}}(\hat{S}_k) \geq (1 - 1/e)\hat{\mathbb{I}}(S_k^*)$, we have

$$\hat{\mathbb{I}}(\hat{S}_k) \geq (1 - 1/e)(1 - \epsilon_b^*/2)OPT_k \quad (74)$$

Replace OPT_k in $\mu_{X^*} = OPT_k/n$ by that in the above inequality, we get $\mu_{X^*} \leq \frac{\hat{\mathbb{I}}(\hat{S}_k)}{n(1-1/e)(1-\epsilon_b^*/2)} \leq \frac{\hat{\mathbb{I}}(\hat{S}_k)}{n(\frac{1}{2} - \frac{1}{e} - \frac{\epsilon}{2})}$ and then the number of RR sets in Eq. 59 is rewritten as,

$$|\mathcal{R}| \geq \frac{\ln \frac{2}{\delta_b^*}}{\ln \frac{1}{\delta_b^*}} \frac{4(1 + \epsilon_a^*)^2}{(\frac{1}{2} - \frac{1}{e} - \frac{\epsilon}{2})^2} \frac{\Upsilon(\epsilon_b^*, \delta_b^*)}{\hat{\mathbb{I}}(\hat{S}_k)/n} \quad (75)$$

or, equivalently,

$$|\mathcal{R}|\frac{\hat{\mathbb{I}}(\hat{S}_k)}{n} \geq 2c \ln \frac{2}{\delta_b^*} \frac{4(1 + \epsilon_a^*)^2}{(\frac{1}{2} - \frac{1}{e} - \frac{\epsilon}{2})^2 \epsilon_b^{*2}} \geq 2c \ln \frac{2}{\delta_b^*} \frac{1}{\epsilon_b^{*2}}$$

The left hand side is the coverage of $\hat{S}_k$ in $\mathcal{R}$, $\mathrm{Cov}_{\mathcal{R}}(\hat{S}_k)$. Combining that and the calculated $\epsilon_1, \epsilon_2, \epsilon_3$ to find δ_1,

$$\delta_1 = e^{-\frac{\mathrm{Cov}_{\mathcal{R}}(\hat{S}_k) \cdot \epsilon_3^2}{2c(1+\epsilon_1)(1+\epsilon_2)}} \leq e^{-\frac{2c \ln \frac{2}{\delta_b^*} \frac{1}{\epsilon_3^2} \cdot \epsilon_3^2}{2c(1+\epsilon_1)(1+\epsilon_2)}} \leq \delta_b^*/2 \quad (76)$$

To compute the value of δ_2, we base on the fact that $|\mathcal{R}'| = |\mathcal{R}|$ and Eq. 64,

$$\delta_2 = e^{-\frac{\mathrm{Cov}_{\mathcal{R}'}(\hat{S}_k) \cdot \epsilon_2^2}{2c(1+\epsilon_2)}} \leq e^{-\frac{2c \ln \frac{2}{\delta_b^*} \frac{1}{\epsilon_2^2} \cdot \epsilon_2^2}{2c(1+\epsilon_2)}} \leq \delta_b^*/2 \quad (77)$$

From Eq. 76 and Eq. 77, we conclude

$$\delta_1 + \delta_2 \leq \delta_b^*/2 + \delta_b^*/2 = \delta_b^* \leq \delta \quad (78)$$

which proves Lem. 12.

Spheres of Influence for More Effective Viral Marketing

Yasir Mehmood
Pompeu Fabra University
Barcelona, Spain
yasir.mehmood@gmail.com

Francesco Bonchi
ISI Foundation
Turin, Italy
francesco.bonchi@isi.it

David García-Soriano
Eurecat
Barcelona, Spain
david.garcia@eurecat.org

ABSTRACT

What is the set of nodes of a social network that, under a probabilistic contagion model, would get infected if a given node s gets infected? We call this set the *sphere of influence* of s. Due to the stochastic nature of the contagion model we need to define a notion of "expected" or "typical" cascade: this is a set of nodes which is the closest to all the possible cascades starting from s.

We thus formalize the *Typical Cascade* problem which requires, for a given source node s, to find the set of nodes minimizing the expected Jaccard distance to all the possible cascades from s. The expected cost of a typical cascade also provides us a measure of the *stability* of cascade propagation, i.e., how much random cascades from a source node s deviate from the "typical" cascade. In this sense source nodes with lower expected costs are more reliable.

We show that, while computing the quality of a candidate solution is #**P**-hard, a method based on (1) sampling random cascades and (2) computing their Jaccard Median, can obtain a multiplicative approximation with just $O(1)$ samples. We then devise an index that allows to efficiently compute the sphere of influence for any node in the network.

Finally, we propose to approach the influence maximization problem as an instance of set cover on the spheres of influence. Through exhaustive evaluation using real-world networks and different methods of assigning the influence probability to each edge, we show that our approach *outperforms in quality* the theoretically optimal greedy algorithm.

Categories and Subject Descriptors

H.2.8 [**Database Management**]: [Database Applications-Data Mining]; G.2.2 [**Discrete Mathematics**]: [Graph Theory-Graph Algorithms]

Keywords

uncertain graphs; typical cascade; sphere of influence; influence maximization

SIGMOD'16, June 26-July 01, 2016, San Francisco, CA, USA

ISBN 978-1-4503-3531-7/16/06...$15.00

DOI: http://dx.doi.org/10.1145/2882903.2915250

1. INTRODUCTION

The phenomenon of influence-driven cascades in social networks has received tremendous attention in the last years thanks to its applications, among which the most appealing is *viral marketing*. The idea of viral marketing is to exploit a pre-existing social network in order to increase brand awareness or to achieve other marketing objectives (such as product sales) through self-replicating viral processes, analogous to the spread of viruses. More concretely, the idea is to target a few "influentials", in the hope that, through word-of-mouth mechanism, they will be able to spread the marketing message to a large portion of the network, as it was a viral contagion.

This notion was formalized by Kempe et al. [24] in the *Influence Maximization* problem, i.e., the problem of finding the set of k influential nodes (usually named "seed set") such that activating them maximizes the expected number of nodes that eventually get activated in a social network where the contagion is governed by a stochastic propagation model. This problem has received a great deal of attention by the research community in the last decade.

However, Watts [39, 40, 41] challenges what he calls *"The Influentials Hypothesis"*, i.e., the assumption that a small set of super-star users can act as sparks to start a large forest fire. Watts states that influence processes are highly unpredictable and unreliable, and relying on a small seed set simply aggravates the unpredictability. Therefore, in order to implement viral marketing in the real world, Watts suggests we should target a large seed set of ordinary individuals who might trigger their small, but more reliable, *sphere of influence*. Even if each seed manages to activate a handful of other users, the large size of the seed set makes possible to reach a critical mass that can make the campaign go viral.

Inspired by this vision, in this paper we study how to compute the sphere of influence of each node s in the network, together with a measure of stability of such sphere of influence, representing how predictable the cascades generated from s are. We then devise an approach to influence maximization based on the spheres of influence and maximum coverage, which is shown to outperform in quality the theoretically optimal method for influence maximization when the number of seeds grows.

In order to better explain our contributions, we first need to provide some preliminary background on the influence maximization problem.

Influence maximization. Kempe et al. [24] modeled viral marketing as a discrete optimization problem, named *influence maximization*, and based on the concept of propagation model: i.e., a stochastic model that governs how users influence each other and thus how contagion happens. Given a propagation model and a set of nodes $S \subseteq V$, the expected number of nodes "infected" in the viral cascade started with S is called the *expected spread* of S, denoted by $\sigma(S)$. For a given $k \in \mathbb{N}$ the influence maximization problem asks for a set $S \subseteq V$, $|S| = k$, such that $\sigma(S)$ is maximum.

The most studied propagation model is the so called *Independent Cascade* (IC) model. We are given a directed probabilistic graph $\mathcal{G} = (V, E, p)$ where each arc $(u, v) \in E$ is labeled with a contagion (or influence) probability $p_{u,v} \in (0, 1]$, representing the strength of the influence of u over v. At a given time step, each node is either active (an adopter of product) or inactive. At time 0, a set S of seeds are activated. Time unfolds deterministically in discrete steps. When a node u first becomes active, say at time t, it has one chance to influence each inactive neighbor v with probability $p_{u,v}$, independently of the history thus far. If the attempt succeeds, v becomes active at time $t + 1$.

Influence maximization is generally **NP**-hard [24]. Kempe et al., however, show that the objective function $\sigma(S)$ is *monotone*[1] and *submodular*[2]. When equipped with such properties, the simple greedy algorithm that at each iteration greedily extends the current set of seeds S with the node w providing the largest marginal gain $\sigma(S \cup \{w\}) - \sigma(S)$, gives a $(1 - 1/e)$-approximation to the optimum [30, 24].

Another source of complexity is the fact that the computation of the expected spread which is itself #**P**-hard. Therefore in the work of Kempe et al. Monte Carlo simulations are run sufficiently many times to obtain an accurate estimate of the expected spread. In particular they show that for any $\phi > 0$, there is a $k = \text{poly}(n/\phi)$ such that by using k samples, we can obtain a $(1 - 1/e - \phi)$-approximate solution for influence maximization.

Finally, it is important to note that the $(1 - 1/e)$ approximation ratio for influence maximization cannot be further improved, at least under the IC propagation model. This is due to the fact that influence maximization under the IC model encodes max-k-cover as a special case, which has been shown to be not approximable within ratio $(1 - 1/e + \epsilon)$ unless **P**= **NP** [15]. For this reason, while a very literature has been produced on the efficiency and scalability of influence maximization, understandably very little attention has been devoted to improving the quality (at least in practice, given that in theory it is not possible).

Problem studied. The problem studied in this paper is, abstractly, to compute the set of nodes that, under a probabilistic contagion model, would get infected if a given node s get infected. This can be seen as a novel type of reachability query in *uncertain* or *probabilistic* graphs [31, 23]. More in details, our data is a probabilistic directed graph $\mathcal{G} = (V, E, p)$, where $p : E \to (0, 1]$ is the contagion probability, i.e., the probability that the arc will exist, or participate, in a contagion cascade. Our query is a source node $s \in V$, and the result is a set of nodes $C \subseteq V$, which we call the *sphere of influence* of s, i.e., the set of nodes that would get infected if the node s get infected.

This type of query can find application in many contexts besides viral marketing: from epidemics (*given an ebola case, which other individuals should we quarantine?*), to corporate workflows, computer and financial networks (*given a node failure, which is the typical cascade we can expect?*).

[1] $\sigma(S) \leq \sigma(T)$ whenever $S \subseteq T$.
[2] $\sigma(S \cup \{w\}) - \sigma(S) \geq \sigma(T \cup \{w\}) - \sigma(T)$ whenever $S \subseteq T$.

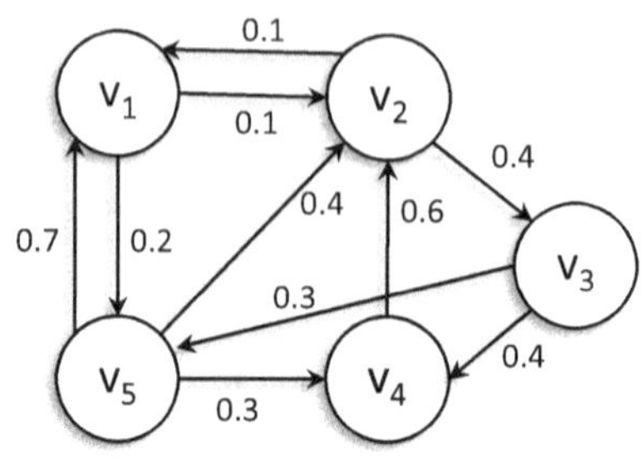

Figure 1: An example probabilistic graph.

As the contagion is a stochastic process, we need to define a way to identify a unique set of nodes C. In fact, each possible subset of V can be a possible cascade from s, each one with its own probability of materializing.

EXAMPLE 1. *Consider the probabilistic graph in Figure 1 and suppose v_5 is our query node. The probabilities associated to the arcs define a probability distribution over the possible subsets of $\{v_1, v_2, v_3, v_4\}$. For instance the set $\{v_1\}$ is the cascade of v_5 with probability* $0.7 \cdot (1 - 0.4) \cdot (1 - 0.3) \cdot (1 - 0.1) = 0.2646$ *(i.e., the arc (v_5, v_1) succeeds transmitting the contagion, while (v_5, v_2), (v_5, v_4), and (v_1, v_2) all fail). Similarly the set $\{v_2, v_4\}$ is the cascade of v_5 with probability* $(1 - 0.7) \cdot 0.3 \cdot (1 - ((1 - 0.4) \cdot (1 - 0.6)) \cdot (1 - 0.1) \cdot (1 - 0.4) = 0.036936$ *(i.e., the arc (v_5, v_1) fails transmitting the contagion, (v_5, v_4) succeeds and at least one among (v_5, v_2) and (v_4, v_2) succeeds, finally (v_2, v_1) and (v_2, v_3) both fail).*

As a final example, the set $\{v_1, v_3, v_4\}$ has null probability of being the cascade of v_5 as v_3 can only be infected by v_2.

Thus, how to identify a unique set of nodes C from this probability distribution? One could think to select the most probable cascade, but this would not be a good choice as explained next. If we have $|V| = n$ nodes there are 2^n possible cascades and n is usually large. This means that we have a probability distribution over a very large discrete domain, with all the probabilities that are very small. As a consequence the most probable cascade still has a tiny probability, not much larger than many other cascades. Finally, the most probable cascade might be very different from many other equally probable cascades.

Instead in this paper we study the problem of computing set of nodes which is the closest (in expectation) to all the possible cascades of s. For our purpose we need a set-similarity measure: the Jaccard similarity is the most natural choice and it has the benefit of being a metric.

Paper contributions. The main contributions of this paper are summarized as follows:

- We formalize the *Typical Cascade* problem which requires, for a given source node s, to find the sets of nodes minimizing the expected Jaccard distance to all the possible cascades from s. Such expected cost also represents, for a given node s, a measure of the *stability* of its sphere of influence, i.e., how much a random cascades from a source node s deviate from the "typical" cascade. In this sense source nodes with lower expected cost are preferable: e.g., in the context of viral marketing they can be considered more reliable influencers.
- We show that for a given source node s, computing the expected cost for a candidate set of nodes is #**P**-hard.

- We then devise a solution based on sampling possible worlds and then computing the *Jaccard median* [11] of the obtained cascades.
- The next question we face is how many samples are needed in order to get a "good" approximation. We answer this question by providing theoretical bounds showing that, quite surprisingly, we can obtain a multiplicative approximation with a constant number samples, i.e., not dependent on the size of the network.
- Backed by our theoretical results, we turn our attention to the practical deployment of our algorithm and we devise an index that allows to efficiently compute the sphere of influence for any node in the network.
- Finally, we apply our framework to the influence maximization problem and propose a max-cover based solution over the spheres of influence. Trough exhaustive evaluation using real-world networks and different methods of assigning the influence probability to each arc, we show that our approach *outperforms in quality* the theoretically optimal greedy algorithm.

Our method based on spheres of influence has several interesting features that can explain its quality.

The first observation is that with our method we intuitively steer the attention of the greedy algorithm from the average size of cascades (i.e., the expected spread), to the size of the "average cascade". This gives us a more reliable approach to the influence maximization problem. In fact, as suggested by intuition, the typical cascade of a node gets larger when all the possible cascades from that node have a large common portion, or in other terms, are similar. Therefore, by picking nodes with large typical cascades, not only do we pick nodes that are influential, but we also implicitly favor influentials that are reliable. The connection between the size of the typical cascade and its cost is confirmed empirically in Section 6.3.

We also show empirically that, as the seed set size grows, at a certain point the standard influence maximization approach reaches a saturation point where it is no longer able to distinguish well among nodes to be added to the solution. Essentially, by focusing on the marginal gain w.r.t. the expected spread, the standard method finds itself choosing among many practically equivalent nodes. Instead our method, by focusing on the sets themselves, is still able to distinguish the next good candidate when the standard influence maximization has reached its saturation point. From this moment on (that is to say, for large seed sets) our method starts outperforming the theoretically optimal algorithm w.r.t. the expected spread objective function.

Our empirical findings are consistently confirmed by a thorough experimentation over several influence networks which are the typical benchmarks used in the influence maximization literature, and by using different ways of learning/assigning the influence probability to each link.

To the best of our knowledge our work is the first to show consistent improvement in terms of quality over the standard greedy algorithm for influence maximization.

For repeatability sake our software and datasets are publicly available at http://tinyurl.com/pxl9h89.

Roadmap. In Section 2 we first provide preliminary notions and notations, then we introduce the Typical Cascade problem, and study its hardness. In Section 3 we develop the theory behind our method based on sampling and Jaccard median, and we derive the bounds on the number of samples needed to have a good multiplicative approximation. In Section 4 we present the practical algorithm, while in Section 5 we show the application to influence maximization. Section 6 contains our experiments, Section 7 covers the related work, and Section 8 concludes the paper by summarizing the results and discussing future lines of investigation.

2. THE TYPICAL CASCADE PROBLEM

2.1 Preliminaries

Let $\mathcal{G} = (V, E, p)$ be a probabilistic directed graph, where $p : E \rightarrow (0, 1]$ is a function that assigns a probability of existence to each edge. Following the literature, we consider the edge probabilities independent [31, 22, 23, 6]. In this setting, the *possible-world* semantics [1, 13] is a principled way of defining the meaning of a query over uncertain data. Specifically, the possible-world semantics interprets $\mathcal{G}$ as a probability distribution over subgraphs of (V, E) defined by choosing every edge $e \in E$ independently at random with probability $p(e)$. That is, the probability of observing any possible world $G = (V, E_G) \sqsubseteq \mathcal{G}$ is:

$$\Pr(G) = \prod_{e \in E_G} p(e) \prod_{e \in E \setminus E_G} (1 - p(e)). \tag{1}$$

Let $q(G)$ be a function that when applied to a deterministic graph G returns a value in $\mathbb{R}$. Following the possible-world semantics querying q over the probabilistic graph $\mathcal{G}$ is typically done by asking for its expected value:

$$q(\mathcal{G}) = \mathop{\mathbb{E}}_{G \sim \mathcal{G}} q(G) = \sum_{G \sqsubseteq \mathcal{G}} q(G) \Pr(G).$$

When $q(G)$ is a binary predicate then the expectation corresponds to the probability that the predicate is satisfied. For example, this is the case for instance of *reachability* query $r(u, v)$, which returns true if v is reachable trough a directed path from u. In the context of probabilistic graphs, the corresponding *reliability* query would ask for the probability of v being reachable from u.

In this paper we are interested in a type of query which returns neither a scalar nor a binary, but a set of nodes. Given a directed probabilistic graph $\mathcal{G} = (V, E, p)$ and a node $s \in V$ we are interested in the *cascade* originated from s, i.e., the set of nodes that would get infected if s get infected. In the case of a deterministic, graph that would be the set of nodes reachable from s trough directed paths. But how to determine the typical cascade in a probabilistic graph?

2.2 Problem statement

In a sense we want to define a notion of "expected" or "typical" cascade: this is a cascade which is *the closest to the set of possible cascades of* s. Towards formalizing this intuition, we need a metric to compute the distance among two possible cascades. As previously stated, a cascade simply corresponds to a set of nodes, we therefore use *Jaccard distance*. Given two sets of nodes $A, B \subseteq V$, their Jaccard distance is defined as

$$d_J(A, B) = 1 - \frac{|A \cap B|}{|A \cup B|} = \frac{|A \oplus B|}{|A \cup B|},$$

which is known to be a metric (see, e.g., [10]).

Given a deterministic graph $G \sqsubseteq \mathcal{G}$ and a node $s \in V$, we denote by $R_s(G)$ the set of nodes reachable from s in G. Given $\mathcal{G}$, $s \in V$ and a set of nodes $C \subseteq V$, we define the *expected cost*, $\rho_{\mathcal{G},s}(C)$, of C as the expected Jaccard distance between C and a random cascade generated from s:

$$\rho_{\mathcal{G},s}(C) = \mathbb{E}[d_J(R_s(G), C)] = \sum_{G \sqsubseteq \mathcal{G}} d_J(R_s(G), C) \Pr(G).$$

(We omit the dependence on $\mathcal{G}$ or s when appropriate.)

This represents a measure of the *stability*, i.e., how much random cascades from s deviate from C. It is therefore desirable to find the set $C^* \subseteq V$ that minimizes the expected cost $\rho_s(C^*)$. This set represents the *typical cascade* of the node s, or what we abstractly call its sphere of influence.

PROBLEM 1 (TYPICAL CASCADE). *Given a probabilistic graph $\mathcal{G} = (V, E, p)$ and a source node $s \in V$ find the set $C^* \subseteq V$ that minimizes the expected cost:*

$$C^* = \arg\min_{C \subseteq V} \rho_{\mathcal{G},s}(C).$$

We next study the complexity of our problem.

2.3 Complexity of Problem 1

The first source of complexity for the Typical Cascade problem is that for a given source, computing the expected cost of a set of nodes is #**P**-hard.

THEOREM 1. *Given a probabilistic graph $\mathcal{G} = (V, E, p)$, a source node $s \in V$, and a set of nodes $C \subseteq V$, computing $\rho_{\mathcal{G},s}(C)$ is #**P**-hard.*

PROOF. We employ a reduction from s-t reliability on graphs: given a directed probabilistic graph G and two nodes $s, t \in V(G)$, compute the probability that there is a path from s to t, denoted $rel(G, s, t)$. This problem was shown #**P**-hard by Valiant [38].

Consider an instance $\langle G, s, t \rangle$ of s-t reliability, where $G = (V, E)$. Let $n = |V|$ and consider the graph G' which is equal to G except that we add an arc from t to every node in the graph with existence probability 1. We calculate the cost of the two candidate medians $H_1 = V$ and $H_2 = V \setminus \{t\}$ and show that determining the reliability $rel(G, s, t)$ can be reduced in polynomial time to the computation of $\rho_{G',s}(H_1)$ and $\rho_{G',s}(H_2)$, proving the theorem.

Denote by $R(C)$ the event that a random cascade C from s in G reaches t, and let $U(C) = 1 - R(C)$ denote the complementary event. Note that there is a natural measure-preserving mapping ϕ between cascades in G and cascades in G': $\phi(C) = V$ if $R(C)$ holds, and $\phi(C) = C$ otherwise. In particular, for very $X \subseteq V$ it holds that

$$\rho_{G',s}(X) = \mathbb{E}_C[d_J(\phi(C), X)].$$

For any cascade C in G two cases may occur:

(a) $R(C) = 1$ (i.e., $t \in C$). Then $\phi(C) = V$ so $d_J(\phi(C), H_1) = 0$ and $d_J(\phi(C), H_2) = \frac{1}{n}$.

(b) $R(C) = 0$ (i.e., $t \notin C$). Then $\phi(C) = C$ so $d_J(\phi(C), H_1) = \frac{n-|C|}{n}$ and $d_J(\phi(C), H_2) = \frac{n-1-|C|}{n-1}$.

Therefore

$$\begin{aligned}\rho_{G',s}(H_1) &= \mathbb{E}_C\left[R(C) \cdot 0 + U(C) \cdot \frac{n-|C|}{n}\right] \\ &= \mathbb{E}_C\left[U(C) \cdot \frac{n-|C|}{n}\right] \\ \rho_{G',s}(H_2) &= \mathbb{E}_C\left[R(C) \cdot \frac{1}{n} + U(C) \cdot \frac{n-|C|-1}{n-1}\right] \\ &= \mathbb{E}_C\left[(1 - U(C)) \cdot \frac{1}{n} + U(C) \cdot \frac{n-|C|-1}{n-1}\right].\end{aligned}$$

Manipulating these expressions yields

$$\begin{aligned}&n \cdot \rho_{G',s}(H_1) - (n-1) \cdot \rho_{G',s}(H_2) = \\ &\mathbb{E}_C[U(C) \cdot (n - |C|)] - \\ &- \mathbb{E}_C\left[(1 - U(C)) \cdot \frac{n-1}{n} + U(C) \cdot (n - |C| - 1)\right] = \\ &\mathbb{E}_C\left[U(C) \cdot \left(2 - \frac{1}{n}\right) - 1 + \frac{1}{n}\right] = q \cdot \left(2 - \frac{1}{n}\right) - 1 + \frac{1}{n},\end{aligned}$$

where $q = \mathbb{E}_C[U(C)] = \Pr_C[t \notin C]$ is the unreliability probability of t from s. Therefore the reliability is

$$rel(G, s, t) = 1 - q = \frac{1 - \frac{1}{n} - n\rho_{G',s}(H_1) + (n-1)\rho_{G',s}(H_2)}{2 - \frac{1}{n}},$$

which shows that evaluating $\rho_{G',s}$ is #**P**-hard. □

A natural approach to deal with some #**P**-hard problems is by means of Monte-Carlo sampling: this means to sample a large enough number ℓ of independent cascades $\mathcal{S} = \{S_1, \ldots, S_\ell\}$ from s, and use them to compute an estimate $\bar{\rho}_s(C)$ as the empirical mean of $d_J(C, s_i)$ over the cascades sampled:

$$\bar{\rho}_s(C) = \frac{1}{\ell} \sum_{i \in [\ell]} d_J(C, \tau_i).$$

This is an unbiased estimator of the actual cost $\rho_s(C)$ as defined above, so one may hope to use $\bar{\rho}_s(C)$ as a proxy for the actual cost $\rho_s(C)$ and attempt to solve the following related optimization problem:

PROBLEM 2 (JACCARD MEDIAN). *Given a finite set V and a collection $\mathcal{S}$ of ℓ sets $S_1, \ldots, S_\ell \subseteq V$, find a set $\bar{C}^* \subseteq V$ that minimizes the average Jaccard distance of $\bar{C}^*$ from the elements of $\mathcal{S}$.*

$$\bar{C}^* = \arg\min_{C \subseteq V} \bar{\rho}_s(C).$$

Chierichetti et al. [11] show that Problem 2 is **NP**-hard, and present a polynomial-time approximation scheme.

The difference between Problems 1 and 2 is that in the latter we are given a list of sets, while the first one defines implicitly a distribution over exponentially many sets. Neither one seems easily reducible to the other, though: on the one hand, enumerating all subgraphs to apply Jaccard median to our problem would require exponential time; on the other hand, a solution to the typical cascade problem may not extend to a general solution to Jaccard median, since the set of possible cascades from a vertex in a graph has certain special properties (for example, closure under unions).

3. SAMPLING AND JACCARD MEDIAN

In the previous section we hinted at a possible approach to tackle the Typical Cascade problem:

1. sample ℓ random cascades from source nodes s;
2. compute their Jaccard median as the typical cascade.

An important question is how many deterministic graphs we need to sample in order to obtain a good estimate of the median quality, and to avoid overfitting in the scheme above. To fix notation, let $\mathcal{C}$ denote a distribution over non-empty subsets of $[n]$ (for example, $\mathcal{C}$ could be the reachability sets from a given vertex in an n-vertex uncertain graph). Let

$$\rho(X) = \mathop{\mathbb{E}}_{C \sim \mathcal{C}}[d_J(C, X)]$$

denote the cost of a candidate solution X, and

$$M^* = \arg\min_{M \subseteq [n]} \rho(M)$$

denote an optimal median with cost $\epsilon^* = \rho(M^*)$.

Recall that we cannot evaluate $\rho(X)$ efficiently, so we resort to sampling ℓ independent elements of $\mathcal{C}$ and using the empirical mean $\widetilde{\rho}(X)$ as an estimator for $\rho(X)$. Then we derive a median M that approximately minimizes $\widetilde{\rho}_s$ on the sample, with the hope that its actual cost $\rho(M)$ will be close to optimal.

While one can easily show that the cost of any particular set X is approximately preserved (with additive error) in the sample, this may not hold simultaneously for all sets. The situation is analogous with the problem of overfitting in learning theory: while the error of any given classifier can be accurately estimated from the training set, if the learner's hypothesis class is large enough it may happen that we find a hypothesis that does exceptionally well on the training set, but performs badly on the test set. (In our setting, the set $2^{[n]}$ of all "candidate medians" play the role of the hypothesis class.) In fact, as there are 2^n candidate medians, a naive estimate via the union bound would suggest that $\Theta(n)$ samples are needed, which is too large a sampling size to be practical (recall that n is the number of nodes of the graph in our application). Fortunately this is far from tight: our next result shows that these bounds can be substantially improved, as long as the cost of the optimal median is small: a *constant* number of samples suffice to get good *multiplicative* approximations.

THEOREM 2. *Let* $\widetilde{M^*} = \arg\min_{X \subseteq [n]} \widetilde{\rho}(X)$. *For* $\delta \geq \exp(-\ell/10)$, *the following holds with probability at least* $1-\delta$*:*

$$\rho(\widetilde{M^*}) \leq \left(1 + O\left(\epsilon^* + \sqrt{\frac{\log(\ell/\delta)}{\ell}}\right)\right)\epsilon^*,$$

More generally, whenever $\widetilde{\rho}(\widetilde{Y}) \leq (1+\beta)\widetilde{\rho}(\widetilde{M^*})$, *we have*

$$\rho(\widetilde{Y}) \leq \left(1 + O\left(\beta + \epsilon^* + \sqrt{\frac{\log(\ell/\delta)}{\ell}}\right)\right)\epsilon^*,$$

In particular, for any $\alpha > \epsilon^*$, a sample of size $\ell = \log(1/\alpha)/\alpha^2$ suffices to obtain an $(1 + O(\alpha))$-approximate median. This is remarkable, because the number of samples is independent of n and moreover, it does not suffice in general to estimate the cost of a candidate solution with small multiplicative error (this would require $\ell = \Omega(1/\epsilon^*)$). This means that the empirical and true costs may differ significantly, yet the cost of the *solution* found by solving the empirical problem is very close to the true optimal. The result also yields a sublinear-time randomized approximation algorithm for *standard* Jaccard median (Problem 2) when the number of input sets is large: sample $O(\log(1/\alpha)/\alpha^2)$ of the input sets and work on the smaller instance.

Roughly speaking, the proof of Theorem 2 proceeds as follows. We show that a) any nearly optimal median X gives rise to an easily manageable approximate cost function f_X with certain properties implying that no median can do much better than X (Lemma 1); and b) these properties of f_X are approximately preserved after sampling (Lemma 2). This trick allows us to convert the statement "for all candidate medians, their sample cost is not much smaller than $\rho(M^*)$" into a statement regarding the *single* function f_X (see Lemma 2), which can be proved directly. The proof of these intermediate lemmas may be found in Appendix A.

LEMMA 1. *Let* $X \subseteq [n]$ *and define*

$$f_X(Y) = \mathop{\mathbb{E}}_{C \sim \mathcal{C}}\left[\frac{|Y \oplus C|}{|X \cup C|}\right].$$

The following hold for all $Y, Y' \subseteq [n]$*:*

(a) $d_J(Y, Y') \leq \min\left(\rho(Y) + \rho(Y'), 6(\rho(X) + f_X(Y) + f_X(Y')\right)$.

(b) If $X \cap Y \neq \emptyset$, *then* $1 - d_J(X, Y) \leq \frac{\rho(Y)}{f_X(Y)} \leq \frac{1}{1-d_J(X,Y)}$.

(c) If $\rho(Y) \leq \rho(X)$, *then* $f_X(Y) \leq \frac{f_X(X)}{1-2f_X(X)}$.

Intuitively, in order to prove that X is a nearly optimal median, it suffices to show that X is an approximate minimizer of $f_X(Y)$.

Denote by $\mathcal{D}$ the uniform distribution over the sample $S_1, \ldots, S_\ell$, and observe that $\widetilde{\rho}(X) = \mathbb{E}_{D \sim \mathcal{D}}[d_J(X, D)]$.

LEMMA 2. *Let* $X \subseteq [n]$. *Define* $Z = \arg\min_{Y \subseteq [n]} f_X(Y)$ *and* $\widetilde{Z} = \arg\min_{Y \subseteq [n]} \widetilde{f}_X(Y)$, *where* $\widetilde{f}_X(Y) = \mathbb{E}_{D \sim \mathcal{D}}\left[\frac{|Y \oplus D|}{|X \cup D|}\right]$. *With probability at least* $1 - \delta$,

$$f_X(\widetilde{Z}) \leq \left(1 + O\left(\sqrt{\frac{\log(\ell/\delta)}{\ell}}\right)\right) f_X(Z),$$

provided $\rho(X)$ *is below some constant and* $\delta \geq \exp(-\ell/10)$.

Moreover, whenever $\widetilde{f_X}(Y) \leq (1+\beta)\widetilde{f}_X(\widetilde{Z})$, *we have*

$$f_X(\widetilde{Y}) \leq \left(1 + O\left(\beta + \sqrt{\frac{\log(\ell/\delta)}{\ell}}\right)\right) f_X(Z).$$

We are now equipped with the tools needed to prove Theorem 2.

PROOF. Consider the optimal median M^* with cost $\rho(M^*) = \epsilon^*$, and the optimal solution to the empirical median $\widetilde{M^*} = \arg\min_X \widetilde{\rho}(X)$. Since $f_X \leq 1$, we may assume ϵ^* is bounded above by a suitable constant. By Lemma 2, with probability at least $1 - \delta$ it holds that $\widetilde{\rho}(M^*) \leq \rho(M^*)(1 + O(\sqrt{\log(\ell/\delta)/\ell})) \triangleq \lambda$. By definition, $\rho(M^*) \leq \rho(\widetilde{M^*})$ and $\widetilde{\rho}(\widetilde{M^*}) \leq \widetilde{\rho}(M^*)$, so by applying Lemma 1 to $\mathcal{C}$ and $\mathcal{D}$,

$$2d_J(M^*, \widetilde{M^*}) \leq (\rho(M^*) + \rho(\widetilde{M^*})) + (\widetilde{\rho}(M^*) + \widetilde{\rho}(\widetilde{M^*})),$$

i.e., $d_J(M^*, \widetilde{M^*}) \leq \epsilon^* + \lambda$.

We introduce the following shorthand notation for comparing costs: $x \preceq y$ if $x \leq y/(1 - O(\epsilon^* + \lambda))^{O(1)}$, $x \succeq y$ if $y \preceq x$, and $x \approx y$ if both $x \succeq y$ and $x \preceq y$ hold. Let Z minimize $f_{M^*}(Y)$ and $\widetilde{Z}$ minimize $\widetilde{f}_{M^*}(Y)$. Then we have $d_J(M^*, Z) \leq \rho(M^*) + f_{M^*}(M^*) + f_{M^*}(Z) = 2f_{M^*}(M^*) + f_{M^*}(Z) \leq 3\epsilon^*$, and $\rho(Z) \leq \epsilon^*/(1 - 3\epsilon^*) = O(\epsilon^*)$ for small enough ϵ^*. Likewise, $d_J(\widetilde{M}^*, Z) \leq \rho(\widetilde{M}^*) + \rho(Z) \leq O(\lambda + \epsilon^*)$ and $d_J(\widetilde{M}^*, \widetilde{Z}) \leq \widetilde{\rho}(\widetilde{M}) + f_{\widetilde{M}}(\widetilde{Z}) \leq \lambda + 2\widetilde{f}_M(\widetilde{M}) \leq O(\lambda + \epsilon^*)$.

By definition, $f_{M^*}(Z) \leq f_{M^*}(M^*)$ and $\widetilde{f}_{M^*}(\widetilde{Z}) \leq \widetilde{f}_{M^*}(Z)$. By Lemma 1, $f_{M^*}(M^*) \preceq f_{M^*}(Z)$, so $f_{M^*}(Z) \approx f_{M^*}(M^*) = \rho(M^*)$. The same lemma applied to $\widetilde{f}_{M^*}$ yields $\widetilde{f}_{M^*}(\widetilde{M}^*) \approx \widetilde{f}_{M^*}(\widetilde{Z}) \leq \widetilde{f}_{M^*}(Z)$, thus $f_{M^*}(\widetilde{Z}) \preceq f_{M^*}(Z)$ and so $f_{M^*}(\widetilde{Z}) \approx f_{M^*}(Z)$. Hence, by Lemma 2, with probability at least $1 - O(\delta)$,

$$f_{M^*}(\widetilde{M}^*) \approx f_{M^*}(\widetilde{Z}) \approx f_{M^*}(Z).$$

If we divide δ by a constant factor and repeat the argument, we obtain the first part Theorem 2. The second part is proved similarly by using the "moreover" part of Lemma 2. □

4. PRACTICAL ALGORITHMS

Next we put together the pieces from the theoretical insights introduced in the previous section, and discuss practical efficiency considerations. First, we describe an indexing scheme enabling efficient simulations of the cascades needed. Then we present the main algorithm to compute a typical cascade for every node of $\mathcal{G}$.

In order to obtain the typical cascade for a given vertex v, we first need to produce a certain number ℓ of cascades from v. As we saw before, taking $\ell = O(\log(1/\alpha))$ samples is enough to obtain a $(1 + \alpha)$-approximation provided that the cost is $\Omega(\alpha)$; if we wish this guarantee to hold simultaneously for all vertices, we may take $\ell = O(\log(n/\alpha)/\alpha^2)$. Rather than sampling separately for each vertex, we sample ℓ possible worlds $G_1, \ldots, G_\ell$ from $\mathcal{G}$, each of which implicitly defines a sample cascade from each vertex $v \in V(G)$, which may be obtained by performing a DFS traversal of G rooted at v.

A key observation that we exploit to speed up this process is that all the vertices in the same *strongly connected component* (SCC) have the same reachability set: since any two vertices u, v in the same SCC are reachable from each other, any vertex reachable by u is also reachable by v, and viceversa. Therefore we can represent each sampled possible world G_i by its SCC structure. Representing G_i in terms of its SCCs yields savings in both space usage and computational runtime, because of the compactness of representation and because a single DFS is sufficient to identify the reachability set of all vertices in the same component.

Based on these observations we build an index that contains for all the sample possible worlds $G_1, \ldots, G_\ell$:

1. the *condensation* C_i of G_i, that is, the directed acyclic graph of links between SCCs, obtained by contracting [42] each component of G_i to a single vertex;

2. for each vertex v and index i, the identifier of the connected component of v in G_i (see Figure 2);

Computing the SCCs and performing their contraction can be performed in time linear in the total number of vertices and edges of the graphs sampled [36].

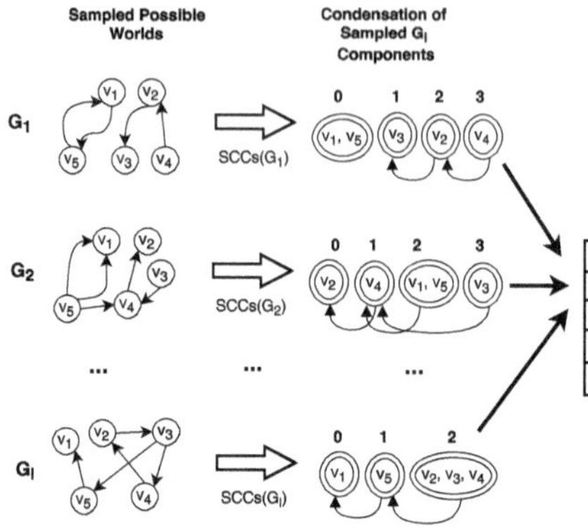

	G_1	G_2	...	G_l
v_1	0	2	...	0
v_2	2	0	...	2
v_3	1	3	...	2
v_4	3	1	...	2
v_5	0	2	...	1

Figure 2: Cascade index: for each sampled possible world G_i it is stored the structure made of the condensation of the SCCs and a matrix indicating for each vertex v and each possible world G_i, the index of the component to which v belongs in G_i.

Algorithm 1: Index construction

Input : Input graph $\mathcal{G}$ and number of samples ℓ.
Output: Index $\mathcal{I}$, Component Pointers $\mathcal{P}$

$\mathcal{I} \leftarrow [|V| \times \ell]$
$\mathcal{P} \leftarrow [1 \times \ell]$
for $i \leftarrow 1$ *to* k **do**
  Sample G_i from $\mathcal{G}$
  $SCCs \leftarrow StronglyConnectedComponents(G_i)$
  $\mathcal{P}[i] \leftarrow transitiveReduction(SCCs)$
  foreach $v \in V$ **do**
    $\mathcal{I}[v, i] \leftarrow nodeComponentIndex(v,\ SCCs)$
  end
end
return $(\mathcal{I}, \mathcal{P})$

To further reduce the space consumption, we perform the transitive reduction [3] of the condensation of C_i, i.e., find the unique graph T_i (not necessarily a subgraph of C_i) with vertex set $V(C_i)$ that preserves the reachability/non-reachability between every pairs of vertices of C_i and has the smallest number of edges. While the worst-case computational complexity of this task is theoretically equivalent to that of Boolean matrix multiplication [3], for which the best algorithms known run in time $O(n^{2.373})$, in the practical instances arising in our experiments the algorithm from [3] proved adequate.

The procedure to construct the index is summarized in Algorithm 1.

Given a node v and $i \in [\ell]$, the cascade of v in G_i can be obtained as follows: look at the identifier of the SCC of v in G_i; recursively follow the links from the associated condensed vertex in C_i to find all the reachable components; and output the union of the elements in the reachable components. The time to perform this computation is linear in the number of nodes of the output and the number of edges of the condensation C_i, which is typically much smaller than the number of edges of G_i.

For the computation of the typical cascade C_v of a node v, we need to compute an approximate Jaccard median of the collection of ℓ cascades $S_1, \ldots, S_\ell$ from v. To this end, we use the work of Chierichetti et al. [11]. Their PTAS to achieve arbitrarily good approximations is mostly of theoretical interest, so we use the algorithm described in Section 3.2 of [11], which achieves an $1+O(\epsilon)$ factor approximation (where ϵ is the cost of the optimal median of the instance) and runs in time $\widetilde{O}(k+\sum_i |S_i|)$.

Algorithm 2: All Typical Cascades

```
Input  : Input graph 𝒢, number of samples ℓ.
Output: The typical cascades for each v ∈ G.
(ℐ, 𝒫) ← Index(𝒢, ℓ)
for vinG do
    S ← [1 × ℓ] (list of cascade sets)
    for i ← 1 to ℓ do
        c ← ℐ[v, i]
        cG ← reachable_components(𝒫[i], c)
        S[i] ← ⋃{nodes(c) | c ∈ cG}
        C_v ← JaccardMedian(S) (by Chierichetti et al. [11])
    end
end
return {(v, C_v) | v ∈ V(𝒢)}
```

---

5. INFLUENCE MAXIMIZATION

In this section we present, as an application of the typical cascade computation, a novel approach to influence maximization. While our approach is heuristic in nature, it is motivated by the observations below.

1. Given a seed set $\mathbb{S}$, we can define its stability as the expected cost of its typical cascade C^* exactly as we have done for singleton nodes in Section 2. If this cost is small we say that the seed set is reliable.

2. If $\mathbb{S}$ is a highly reliable seed set, the size of its typical cascade C^* is very close to the mean size of cascades from $\mathbb{S}$ (see [11]). In other words, by optimizing for size of the typical cascade we are also indirectly optimizing for expected spread, unless the optimal solution is unreliable (which is ruled out by the next item).

3. It is an empirically observable phenomenon (see the stability analysis in Sec. 6) that the expected cost of the typical cascade of $\mathbb{S}$ tends to decrease as $\mathbb{S}$ grows. Intuitively, this means that the cascading process becomes more and more deterministic (or predictable) as the size of the seed set increases. We want to leverage this fact by acting as if the cascade from $\mathbb{S}$ were effectively C^*. However, for sake of efficiency, in our method we will not use the typical cascade of $\mathbb{S}$, but instead we will use the union of the typical cascades of all the seed nodes in $\mathbb{S}$. This is justified by the next point.

4. It can be shown that some nearly optimal typical cascade from seed set $\mathbb{S}$ is a superset of the typical cascades for the cascades induced by the individual elements of $\mathbb{S}$. This is because if the typical cascade has cost ϵ, then simply selecting all elements that are present with probability at least $1/2$ can be proved to be a solution with cost at most $\epsilon + O(\epsilon^{3/2})$ [11]. But note that the probability that a given vertex is reachable from $\mathbb{S}$ is monotonically increasing with $\mathbb{S}$, so the set of elements reachable with probability at least $1/2$ is monotonically increasing as well. Consequently the nearly optimal typical cascade for $\mathbb{S}$ can be assumed to contain the typical cascades for all its elements. (It may contain further elements, which would increase the solution size and decrease its cost, so we are being conservative by ignoring them.)

These observations motivate us to approach the influence maximization problem as max-cover problem over the typical cascades of the singleton nodes. Let $\mathbb{S} \subseteq V$ denote a set of nodes and let C_v be the median cascade of each $v \in V$. Write $\Phi(\mathbb{S}) = \bigcup_{v\in\mathbb{S}} C_v$ for the elements covered by the typical cascades of all the nodes in $\mathbb{S}$, Now, given an finite integer $k \leq |V|$, our goal is to find a set $\mathbb{S}^*$ such that the coverage $\Phi(\mathbb{S}^*)$ is maximized for $|\mathbb{S}^*| = k$.

Formally,

$$\mathbb{S}^* = \underset{\substack{\mathbb{S}\subseteq V:\\ |\mathbb{S}|=k}}{\arg\max}\, \Phi(\mathbb{S})$$

This is an instance of the maximum coverage problem, which can be approximated by the standard greedy algorithm that runs for k iterations and at each iteration it selects a node v whose addition increases the value of Φ the most. This approach, whose pseudocode is shown in Algorithm3, is named InfMax_TC: *Influence Maximization using Typical Cascades.*

Algorithm 3: InfMax_TC

```
Input  : Typical cascades for all v ∈ V: {C_1, C_2, ··· , C_|V|}
Output: Seed set of k nodes: S*
S* ← ∅
for i ← 1 to k do
    u = arg max_{u∈V\S*} Φ(S* ∪ u)
    S* ← S* ∪ u
end
return S*
```

In the next section we compare this method for influence maximization with the standard method, w.r.t. the objective function of the influence maximization problem: the expected spread.

6. EXPERIMENTS

In our experiments we first report basic statistics about the spheres of influence (or typical cascades) and their computation, such as their size, cost and the running time of our procedure. We then focus on the main goal of our experimental assessment which is to show the performance, in terms of quality, of our method for influence maximization.

The majority of the literature on influence maximization uses a set of benchmark social graphs, where the influence probability for each edge is artificially assigned according to some certain standard methods. Perhaps more appropriately, some authors [16, 33] have started to use influence probabilities learnt from a log of past user activity. In our experiments, for sake of exhaustiveness, we follow both approaches. We use six datasets which are often used as benchmarks in the literature for influence maximization: in three of these the edge probabilities are *learnt*, whereas for the other three the probabilities are *assigned* artificially as described later. Moreover, we use two different methods for learning the contagion probabilities and two different methods for assigning them. This gives us a total of 12 datasets to work with.

Datasets	$\|V\|$	$\|E\|$	Type	Probabilities
Digg	$68K$	$875K$	directed	learnt
Flixster	$137K$	$1.2M$	undirected	learnt
Twitter	$23K$	$650K$	undirected	learnt
NetHEPT	$15K$	$31K$	undirected	assigned
Epinions	$76K$	$509K$	directed	assigned
Slashdot	$77K$	905	directed	assigned

Table 1: Dataset characteristics.

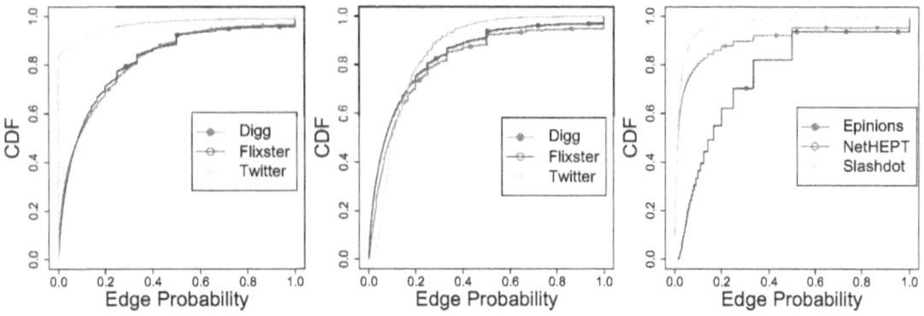

Figure 3: CDF of edge probabilities learnt from Saito (left), Goyal (center), and WC model (right). We do not report the distribution for the fixed probability method as this is not meaningful.

6.1 Dataset description

The three datasets that come with a log of users activity and can thus be used for learning the influence probabilities are Digg, Flixster and Twitter.

Digg is a news portal that allows users to submit news stories, as well as rate the posted stories by means of *voting*. The ratings are then used to promote stories on the front page of Digg portal. The data snapshot we use is related to the the voting history of all the stories *promoted* during June, 2009 [20]. It has $3M$ votes for $3.5K$ stories. The data also provides a *fan network* from which a directed social graph is induced.

Flixster is an online social networking service (https://flixster.com/) enabling its users to rate and review movies. Here, we have user ratings from November 2005 to November 2009 [21]. This amounts to $8.2M$ ratings for $49K$ items/movies.

Twitter. The final dataset in this category is a snapshot of Twitter, obtained by crawling its public timeline[3]. The items in Twitter represent the URLs propagating across the network. Unlike the previous two datasets, in Twitter the user activity corresponds to sharing/resharing of the URLs instead of rating items. The data contains $6K$ items and $383K$ user activities.

The other three datasets are from the SNAP dataset collection [28]. These include NetHEPT, Epinions, and Slashdot. The first is a network of citations, whereas the other two are social networks. These datasets are widely used in the study of social networks and influence maximization [35, 9]. Table 1 reports basic statistics on the datasets used. When a graph is undirected, we just consider the edges existing in both directions.

[3]https://dev.twitter.com/rest/reference/get/statuses/user_timeline

Datasets	$avg(\|\widetilde{C^*}\|)$	$sd(\|\widetilde{C^*}\|)$	$max(\|\widetilde{C^*}\|)$
Digg-S	9.0	22.2	263
Flixster-S	4.3	12.0	439
Twitter-S	17.0	86.4	1459
Digg-G	7.3	17.0	130
Flixster-G	999.5	822.7	2589
Twitter-G	24.9	58.4	1727
NetHEPT-W	3.0	1.2	13
Epinions-W	3.6	8.6	684
Slashdot-W	4.8	19.4	420
NetHEPT-F	1067.5	915.5	4138
Epinions-F	4774.5	1574.4	6345
Slashdot-F	1337.0	841.5	5574

Table 2: In the table $|\widetilde{C^*}|$ denotes the size of the approximated typical cascade computed and we report its average, standard deviation, and maximum over all nodes in the graph.

6.2 Edge probabilities

Below we describe the two different ways of learning the influence probabilities, and the two different ways of artificially assigning the influence probabilities, that we use in our experiments.

Learning from real-world cascades. The datasets in the first category (Digg, Flixster, and Twitter) provide us two key elements: (i) a social network (ii) log of user activities (for different items) with the corresponding timestamps. Both methods we use exploit these two pieces of input to learn the edge probabilities. The first method is by Saito et al. [33], which model the learning of the influence probabilities as a likelihood maximization problem and devise an EM algorithm to solve it.

The second method by Goyal et al. [16] follows a frequentist approach. Among the various models they propose we use the simplest one: the probability assigned to an edge (u, v) is simply the number of times in the propagation log in which v performs an action after u, divided by the number of actions performed by u [16].

In the following we will use a suffix -S and a suffix -G to denote the datasets with the probabilities learnt by following Saito et al. [33] and Goyal et al. [16] respectively.

Artificial assignments. For the second group of datasets (NetHEPT, Epinions, and Slashdot), we use two different methods for artificially assigning probability to each edge. The first the methods is the weighted cascade (WC) model [9], which sets the probability $p_{u,v}$ over an edge (u, v) as: $p_{u,v} = \frac{1}{inDeg(v)}$. Here, $inDeg(v)$ is the in-degree of node v. In the second method, we assign a fixed probability $p_{u,v} = 0.1$ to each edge (u, v).

In the following we will use a suffix -W and a suffix -F to denote the datasets with the probabilities assigned by weighted cascade method and fixed respectively.

Using the methods of learning/assigning edge probabilities explained above, we have 12 datasets in total for our experiments detailed in this section. Figure 3 reports the CDFs of the edge probabilities in all datasets.

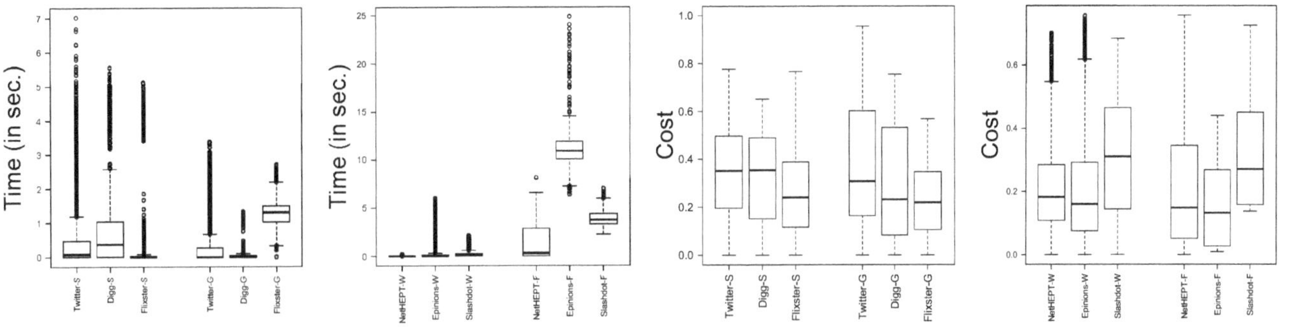

Figure 4: Time taken to compute the typical cascade $\widetilde{C^*}$ (two left-most plots) and its expected cost $\rho_{\mathcal{G},s}(\widetilde{C^*})$ (two right-most plots).

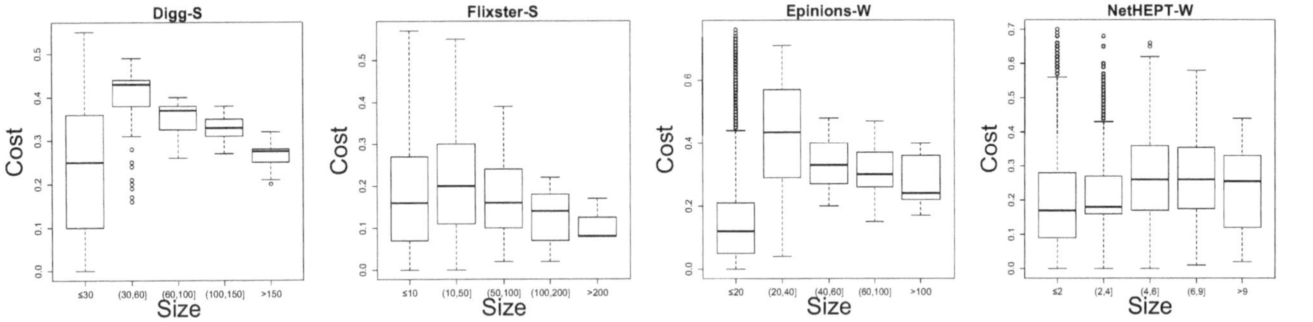

Figure 5: Distribution of the expected cost $\rho_{\mathcal{G},s}(\widetilde{C^*})$ of the typical cascade w.r.t. its size.

6.3 Computing the typical cascades

Table 2 reports basics statistics on the size of the sampled cascades (S_i) and the typical cascade computed from the samples ($\widetilde{C^*}$). Given that the edge probabilities learnt using the method of Goyal et al. [16] are larger than the probabilities learnt by means of Saito et al. [33] method (See Figure 3), not surprisingly also the average size of typical cascades is larger for the former than for the latter.

The pattern is even more evident in Flixster, which showcases the fact that different strategies used to assign probabilities may greatly impact the size of the samples, and thereby, the size of the corresponding typical cascade. We also note that when artificially assigned, the probabilities set fixed to 0.1 also result in larger sampled cascades, and thus larger typical cascade, than produced when assigning probabilities by means of the WC model.

In Figure 4 we report the time taken to compute the typical cascade $\widetilde{C^*}$ and its expected cost $\rho_{\mathcal{G},s}(\widetilde{C^*})$, excluding the index construction. That is, this is the time to extract the cascades from the index and run the Jaccard median approximation on this instance. (Recall that we are using 1000 samples so the number of elements to process per vertex is often in the hundreds of thousands.) The times reported use a Python implementation, on a Intel Xeon 2.2 Ghz with 6 cores and 16 GB memory. As depicted, the time remains almost always well under 1 second except for a small number of nodes. As regards the expected costs they rarely exceed 0.4, and in most of the dataset the average is around 0.2.

Figure 5 reports the distributions of the expected cost w.r.t. the size of the typical cascade, in order to assess whether the quality (or reliability) of the solution also depends on its size. In every plot, if we disregard the bucket of very small cascades, which is in any case not very interesting for applications, we can observe that the larger is the typical cascade, the more reliable it is (smaller cost). This becomes even more evident when observing the maximum cost observed: it is practically impossible to find a large typical cascade with large cost. This matches the intuition discussed in Section 1.

6.4 Influence maximization

We next present our main practical result: the fact that our method for influence maximization based on spheres of influence (presented in Section 5) outperforms the standard influence maximization method for what concerns quality, i.e., the expected spread achieved.

Quality of influence maximization. In the following, the standard greedy (theoretically optimal) algorithm for influence maximization [24] is denoted InfMax_std, and our greedy algorithm for maximum coverage using the sphere of influence (typical cascade) of each node is denoted InfMax_TC. In all the experiments we use $k = 200$ for the seed set size and we use the same number of sampled cascades (1000) for both methods: to estimate the expected spread for InfMax_std, and for computing the typical cascades for InfMax_TC. The expected spread $\sigma(S)$ is reported in each iteration of the two greedy algorithms from $|S| = 1$ to 200. For the standard greedy algorithm for influence maximization InfMax_std we use the implementation provided by [18].

The results for all 12 combinations of datasets and ways of assigning edge probabilities are reported in Figure 6: on the X-axis we report the size of the seed set $|S|$, on the Y-axis we report the expected spread $\sigma(S)$. We can observe the same pattern emerging in all settings: InfMax_std outperforms InfMax_TC in the selection of the first several seeds, but at a certain point, as the seed set size grows, the two curves cross and InfMax_TC starts outperforming the standard method.

Point of saturation analysis. In order to gain more insight into why this happens we study the "point of saturation": i.e., when the greedy algorithm starts seeing all the nodes as indistinguishable w.r.t. the marginal gain. Recall that the general strategy of greedy algorithms is to select the next seed that provides the maximum gain w.r.t. the objective function (expected spread InfMax_std and maximum coverage for InfMax_TC).

More in detail, at an arbitrary iteration j, let MG_i^j denote the node that is ranked i^{th} position for what concerns the marginal gain it will add to the current solution. Any greedy algorithm, so both InfMax_std and InfMax_TC would select MG_1^j. In this test we check the ratio MG_{10}^j/MG_1^j, i.e., we compare how much the marginal gain of the selected node is larger than that of the node which is ranked 10th. This ratio is by definition in $[0,1]$: a ratio closer to 0 means that the selected node is much better than the 10th node in the ranking, while a ratio closer to 1, means that the improvement provided by the selected node is no different than other potential candidates. A ratio close to 1 means that the greedy algorithm can no longer distinguish well among candidates and thus its choice becomes essentially random. At this point we say that the saturation has likely arrived.

Before presenting the results, it is worth noting that running this test is costly. In fact we need to run the standard greedy algorithm with no optimization at all (for instance we cannot use the optimizations in [18]). For this reason we cannot scale. Therefore we report experiments only on the smaller datasets, Twitter-S and NetHEPT-F. Moreover, we start from the 50th iteration of the greedy algorithm and compute the marginal gain ratio for a little more than 30 iterations.

The results of this experiment are shown in Figure 7, where we can observe that, as expected the ratios grow with the iterations, but also that InfMax_std has a ratio already much larger than InfMax_TC at the 50th iteration, and very close to 1 already at the 65th iteration. At this point InfMax_std is already unable to distinguish between the top-10 nodes with the largest marginal gain.

From this perspective, our method has more power to discriminate among interesting nodes, as it reaches its saturation point much later.

Stability analysis. As we already discussed in Section 5, we can define the stability of a seed set $\mathbb{S}$, as the expected cost of its typical cascade C^* exactly as we have done for singleton nodes: the smaller this expected cost the more stable (or reliable) is the seed set. In this last experiment we compare the expected cost of the seed sets selected by InfMax_std and InfMax_TC. These costs are reported in Figure 8 for six datasets.

We can observe that the seed sets selected by InfMax_TC are consistently more stable than the seed sets selected by InfMax_std. In some of the cases the two methods have similar stability at the beginning of the greedy process (small seed sets), but then they start diverging quite early. In other cases (e.g., NetHEPT-W and Slashdot-W) InfMax_std starts by selecting very unstable influential nodes. This confirms one of the motivations behind our work (previously described in Example 2 in Section 1): nodes that have a very high expected spread are not necessarily reliable.

In conclusion, our method not only constantly outperforms the classic (and theoretically optimal) greedy algorithm in terms of expected spread, but the seed sets it produces are also more reliable than those produced by the standard greedy. This could be an important feature, when it comes to real-world deployment.

7. RELATED WORK

To the best of our knowledge, no prior formulation of the problem finding the *sphere of influence* of a node in terms of its typical cascade exists in the literature.

A related line of research studies *reliability* in uncertain graphs [44, 23, 2]. This, for instance, includes finding the probability of connection between two nodes, also known as 2-terminal reliability [8]. Other variants of this problem ask to compute the probability that all nodes are pairwise connected or all nodes in a subset are pairwise connected [19, 34]. However, it has been shown that even the basic problem of computing 2-terminal reliability is #**P**-complete [38]. For this reason, several approximation schemes have been proposed mainly exploiting Monte Carlo sampling methods to estimate connection probabilities. Quite recently, these ideas have been developed to formulate *reliability search* problem in order to efficiently find all nodes reachable from a set of source nodes greater than a probability threshold [25].

Another related line of research is the data-driven vaccination problem: Given a set of already infected people in a population, what are the healthy people who should be immediately given vaccines to best control the epidemic? [43]

For what concerns influence maximization we have already covered the main main background information in the Introduction. The first algorithmic treatment of the problem was provided by Domingos and Richardson [14, 32], who modeled the diffusion process in terms of Markov random fields, and proposed heuristic solutions to the problem. Later, Kempe *et al.* [24] introduced influence maximization as a discrete optimization problem: this is the definition that has been followed in the subsequent literature. As explained previously most of the effort in this area has been devoted to improve the efficiency and scalability of influence maximization [27, 9, 17, 18].

Recently, Borgs et al. [7] proposed a near-linear time randomized algorithm based on the idea of sampling *"reverse-reachable"* (RR) sets in the graph. These ideas were extended to obtain a more practical algorithm – *Two-phase Influence Maximization (TIM)* – by Tang et al. [35]. Cohen et al. [12] proposed a sketch-based design for fast computation of influence spread, achieving efficiency and effectiveness comparable to TIM.

Most of this literature on efficient algorithms for influence maximization assumes the weighted social graph given, and do not address how the link influence probabilities $p_{u,v}$ can be obtained. Saito et al. [33] were the first to study the problem of learning the probabilities for the independent cascade model from a set of past observations, formalizing it as likelihood maximization and applying Expectation Maximization (EM) to solve it. Later Goyal et al. [16] provided a simpler and more scalable frequentist definition.

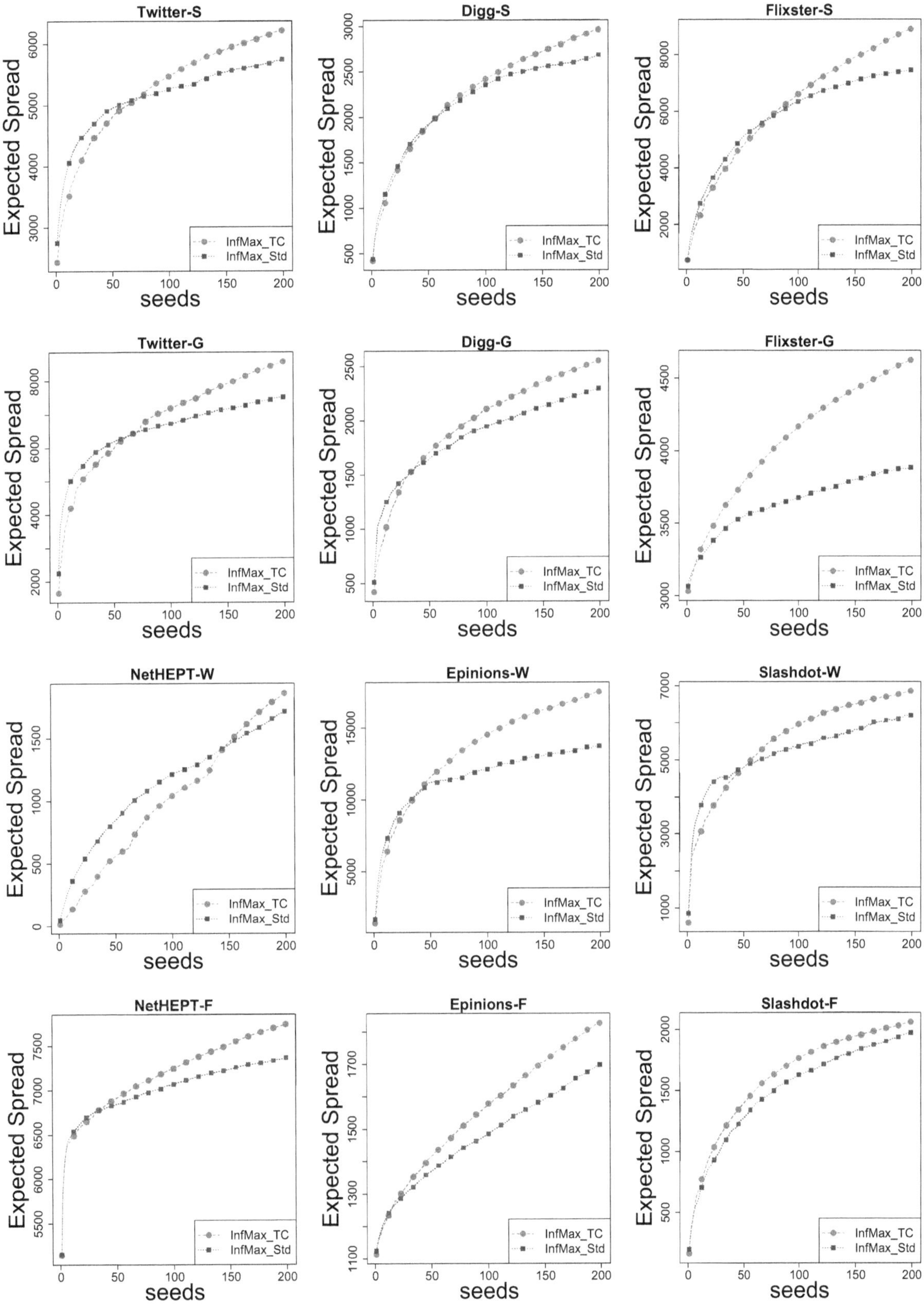

Figure 6: Influence maximization experiments in all 12 settings: on the X-axis we report the size of the seed set $|S|$, on the Y-axis we report the expected spread $\sigma(S)$.

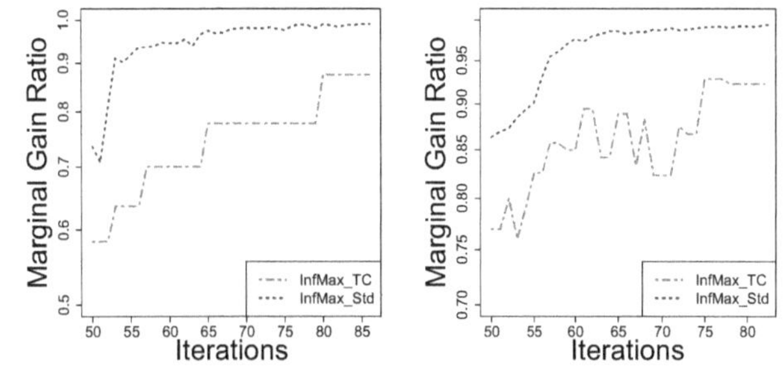

Figure 7: Marginal gain ration provided by seeds in NetHEPT-F (left) and Twitter-S (right).

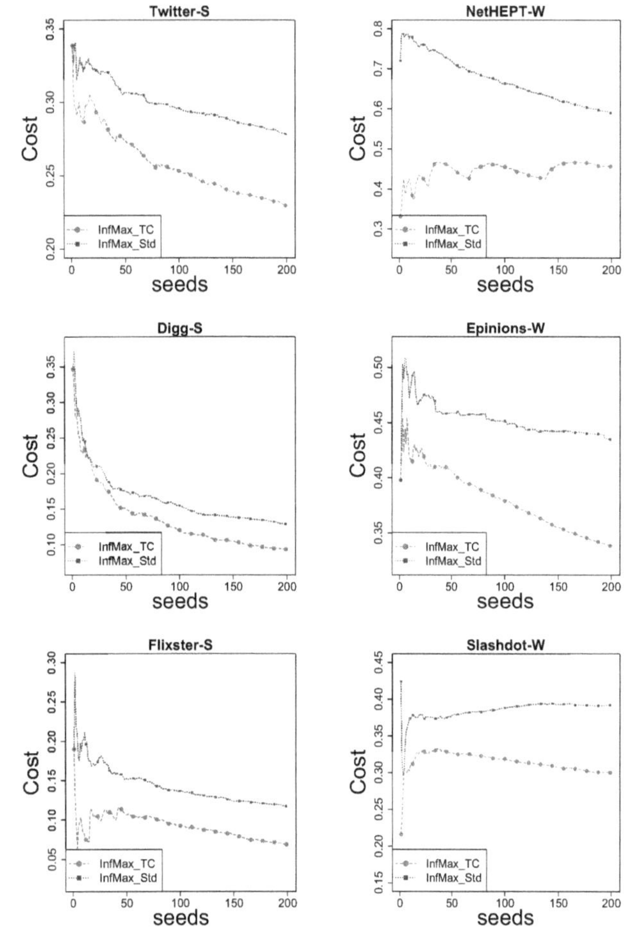

Figure 8: Stability analysis: expected cost of the seed sets extracted by InfMax_std and InfMax_TC over six datasets. By expected cost we mean the expected Jaccard distance between the typical cascade generated by the seed set and 1000 random cascades generated by the same seed set. The smaller this value, the more reliable the behaviour of the seed set.

Following the likelihood maximization of [33], Mathioudakis et al. [29] studied the problem of sparsifying the influence network to a prefixed extent while maximizing the likelihood of generating the propagation traces in the given log. Barbieri et al. [5] use a similar EM approach of [33] to learn *topic-aware* influence probabilities.

Following the frequentist definition of [16] Kutzkov et al. [26] studied the problem of learning influence probabilities in a big data scenario, where the network topology might not fit in memory and there is a continuous stream of actions (e.g., a stream of tweets in Twitter). Following the same definition of Goyal et al. [16], Tassa and Bonchi [37] studied the privacy and security implications of learning influence strength in a social network, and devised secure multiparty protocols.

8. CONCLUSIONS AND FUTURE WORK

In this paper we study the problem of computing the sphere of influence for each node in a social influence network. We formalize this as the Typical Cascade problem over a probabilistic directed graph where each directed edge (u, v) has associated a probability representing the contagion probability, or the strength of influence of u over v. We devise a method based on sampling and computing the Jaccard median of the samples. Then we propose a novel approach to influence maximization based on max-cover applied to the sphere of influence of all nodes in the network.

Our main theoretical result is a bound showing that we can obtain a multiplicative approximation to our problem with a constant number samples, i.e., not dependent on the size of the network (Theorem 2).

Our main practical contribution is the first method for influence maximization outperforming the theoretically optimal greedy algorithm for influence maximization, for large seed sets (Figure 6).

To the best of our knowledge *our work is the first to show consistent improvement in terms of quality over the standard greedy algorithm for influence maximization*, as confirmed by our thorough experimentation using several different benchmark networks and different ways of assigning the influence probabilities to the edges.

Given that the classic greedy algorithm is essentially optimal in terms of quality under standard complexity assumptions, a very interesting line of research for future investigation is to characterize which graph properties of real-world datasets allow the greedy algorithm, either the classic one or our variant based on spheres of influence, to provide better approximations. One may also exploit the gadget for the max-cover greedy algorithm developed in [4] to obtain tight bounds on the optimality gap of the solutions found.

The computations of the sphere of influence might find applications in other contexts, that we plan to investigate in our future research. First of all, remaining in the viral marketing context, having the spheres of influence precomputed and stored in an index might provide a direct solution to several variants of influence maximization. Consider for instance the case where different segments of market (set of users) have different values for a viral marketing campaign. In our setting this is directly achieved by means of a weighted max-cover using the available spheres of influence. Then when the next campaign is run, and the users have different values, we can again reuse the same spheres of influence. Other examples might include viral marketing campaigns under different types of constraints, such as, e.g., when different nodes have different costs to become a seed.

Outside of viral marketing, we can consider application of spheres of influence in contagion problems, or in the vaccination problem [43].

9. REFERENCES

[1] S. Abiteboul, P. Kanellakis, and G. Grahne. On the representation and querying of sets of possible worlds. In *SIGMOD*, 1987.

[2] K. Aggarwal, K. Misra, and J. Gupta. Reliability evaluation a comparative study of different techniques. *Microelectronics Reliability*, 14(1):49–56, 1975.

[3] A. V. Aho, M. R. Garey, and J. D. Ullman. The transitive reduction of a directed graph. *SIAM J. Comput.*, 1(2):131–137, 1972.

[4] R. A. Baeza-Yates, P. Boldi, and F. Chierichetti. Essential web pages are easy to find. In *WWW*, 2015.

[5] N. Barbieri, F. Bonchi, and G. Manco. Topic-aware social influence propagation models. In *ICDM*, 2012.

[6] F. Bonchi, F. Gullo, A. Kaltenbrunner, and Y. Volkovich. Core decomposition of uncertain graphs. In *KDD*, 2014.

[7] C. Borgs, M. Brautbar, J. Chayes, and B. Lucier. Maximizing social influence in nearly optimal time. In *SODA*, 2014.

[8] T. B. Brecht and C. J. Colbourn. Lower bounds on two-terminal network reliability. *Discrete Applied Mathematics*, 21(3):185–198, 1988.

[9] W. Chen, Y. Yuan, and L. Zhang. Scalable influence maximization in social networks under the linear threshold model. In *ICDM*, 2010.

[10] F. Chierichetti and R. Kumar. LSH-preserving functions and their applications. *Journal of the ACM*, 62(5):33, 2015.

[11] F. Chierichetti, R. Kumar, S. Pandey, and S. Vassilvitskii. Finding the jaccard median. In *SODA*, 2010.

[12] E. Cohen, D. Delling, T. Pajor, , and R. F. Werneck. Sketch-based influence maximization and computation: Scaling up with guarantees. In *CIKM*, 2014.

[13] N. Dalvi and D. Suciu. Efficient query evaluation on probabilistic databases. In *VLDB*, 2004.

[14] P. Domingos and M. Richardson. Mining the network value of customers. In *KDD*, 2001.

[15] U. Feige. A threshold of $\ln n$ for approximating set cover. *Journal of the ACM*, 45(4):634–652, 1998.

[16] A. Goyal, F. Bonchi, and L. V. Lakshmanan. Learning influence probabilities in social networks. In *WSDM*, 2010.

[17] A. Goyal, F. Bonchi, and L. V. Lakshmanan. A data-based approach to social influence maximization. *PVLDB*, 5(1):73–84, 2011.

[18] A. Goyal, W. Lu, and L. V. Lakshmanan. CELF++: optimizing the greedy algorithm for influence maximization in social networks. In *WWW*, 2011.

[19] G. Hardy, C. Lucet, and N. Limnios. K-terminal network reliability measures with binary decision diagrams. *IEEE Transactions on Reliability*, 56(3):506–515, 2007.

[20] T. Hogg and K. Lerman. Social dynamics of digg. *EPJ Data Science*, 1(1):1–26, 2012.

[21] M. Jamali. Flixster data set. http://www.cs.ubc.ca/~jamalim/datasets/.

[22] R. Jin, L. Liu, and C. C. Aggarwal. Discovering Highly Reliable Subgraphs in Uncertain Graphs. In *KDD*, 2011.

[23] R. Jin, L. Liu, B. Ding, and H. Wang. Distance-Constraint Reachability Computation in Uncertain Graphs. *PVLDB*, 4(9):551–562, 2011.

[24] D. Kempe, J. M. Kleinberg, and É. Tardos. Maximizing the Spread of Influence through a Social Network. In *KDD*, 2003.

[25] A. Khan, F. Bonchi, A. Gionis, and F. Gullo. Fast reliability search in uncertain graphs. In *EDBT*, 2014.

[26] K. Kutzkov, A. Bifet, F. Bonchi, and A. Gionis. STRIP: stream learning of influence probabilities. In *KDD*, 2013.

[27] J. Leskovec, A. Krause, C. Guestrin, C. Faloutsos, J. M. VanBriesen, and N. S. Glance. Cost-effective outbreak detection in networks. In *KDD*, 2007.

[28] J. Leskovec and A. Krevl. SNAP Datasets: Stanford large network dataset collection. http://snap.stanford.edu/data.

[29] M. Mathioudakis, F. Bonchi, C. Castillo, A. Gionis, and A. Ukkonen. Sparsification of influence networks. In *KDD*, 2011.

[30] G. L. Nemhauser, L. A. Wolsey, and M. L. Fisher. An analysis of approximations for maximizing submodular set functions - I. *Mathematical Programming*, 14(1):265–294, 1978.

[31] M. Potamias, F. Bonchi, A. Gionis, and G. Kollios. k-Nearest Neighbors in Uncertain Graphs. *PVLDB*, 3(1):997–1008, 2010.

[32] M. Richardson and P. Domingos. Mining knowledge-sharing sites for viral marketing. In *KDD*, 2002.

[33] K. Saito, R. Nakano, and M. Kimura. Prediction of information diffusion probabilities for independent cascade model. In *KES*, 2008.

[34] A. R. Sharafat and O. R. Ma'rouzi. All-terminal network reliability using recursive truncation algorithm. *IEEE Transactions on Reliability*, 58(2):338–347, 2009.

[35] Y. Tang, X. Xiao, and Y. Shi. Influence maximization: Near-optimal time complexity meets practical efficiency. In *SIGMOD*, 2014.

[36] R. E. Tarjan. Depth-first search and linear graph algorithms. *SIAM J. Comput.*, 1(2):146–160, 1972.

[37] T. Tassa and F. Bonchi. Privacy preserving estimation of social influence. In *EDBT*, 2014.

[38] L. G. Valiant. The complexity of enumeration and reliability problems. *SIAM J. Comput.*, 8(3):410–421, 1979.

[39] D. Watts. Challenging the influentials hypothesis. *WOMMA Measuring Word of Mouth, Volume 3*, pages 201–211, 2007.

[40] D. Watts and P. Dodds. Influential, networks, and public opinion formation. *Journal of Consumer Research*, 34(4):441–458, 2007.

[41] D. Watts and J. Peretti. Viral marketing for the real world. *Harvard Business Review*, pages 22–23, May 2007.

[42] D. B. West. *Introduction to Graph Theory (2nd Edition)*. Prentice Hall, Aug. 2000.

[43] Y. Zhang and B. A. Prakash. Dava: Distributing vaccines over networks under prior information. In *SDM*, 2014.

[44] K. Zhu, W. Zhang, G. Zhu, Y. Zhang, and X. Lin. Bmc: an efficient method to evaluate probabilistic reachability queries. In *Database Systems for Advanced Applications*, pages 434–449. Springer, 2011.

APPENDIX

A. MISSING PROOFS FROM SECTION 3

Before showing the required proofs, we need to establish a couple of technical lemmas. The first gives a relationship between Jaccard distance and size of the union of two sets; the second gives a tight bound on the expectation of the inverse denominators of $d_J(X, C)$.

LEMMA 3. *If $A \cap B \neq \emptyset$, then $|A \cup B| \leq \frac{\min(|A|,|B|)}{1-d_J(A,B)}$.*

PROOF. Compute the Jaccard similarity of A and B:

$$J(A,B) = \frac{|A \cap B|}{|A \cup B|} \leq \frac{\min(|A|,|B|)}{|A \cup B|} \leq \frac{|A|}{|A \cup B|} \leq \frac{1}{1+\alpha},$$

so their Jaccard distance satisfies

$$d_J(A,B) = 1 - J(A,B) \geq \frac{\alpha}{1+\alpha}.$$

□

LEMMA 4. *For all X,*

$$\frac{1}{|X|} \geq \mathop{\mathbb{E}}_{C \sim \mathcal{C}}\left[\frac{1}{|X \cup C|}\right] \geq \frac{1-2\sqrt{\rho(X)}}{|X|}.$$

PROOF. The first inequality is obvious.
To show the second, we first prove that, for all $\alpha \in (0,1)$,

$$\Pr\left[\frac{|C|}{|X|} \notin [1-\alpha, 1+\alpha]\right] \leq \frac{1+\alpha}{\alpha}\rho(X).$$

To see this, $B(C)$ denote the "bad event" $\frac{|C|}{|X|} \notin [1-\alpha, 1+\alpha]$. Note that $1/(1-\alpha) > 1+\alpha$, so by Lemma 3, $B(C)$ implies $d_J(C,X) \geq \frac{\alpha}{1+\alpha}$. Then

$$\mathbb{E}[d_J(C,X)] \geq \Pr[B(C)] \cdot d_J(C,X),$$

so

$$\Pr[B(C)] \leq \frac{\mathbb{E}[d_J(C,X)]}{\alpha/(1+\alpha)} = \frac{1+\alpha}{\alpha}\rho(X).$$

Setting $\epsilon \triangleq \rho(X)$ and $\alpha \triangleq \sqrt{\epsilon}$, we obtain

$$\begin{aligned}
\mathbb{E}\left[\frac{1}{|X \cup C|}\right] &\geq \frac{\Pr[|X \cup C| \leq (1+\alpha)|X|]}{(1+\alpha)|X|} \\
&\geq \frac{1 - \frac{1+\alpha}{\alpha}\epsilon}{(1+\alpha)|X|} \\
&= \frac{1}{|X|}\left(\frac{1}{1+\alpha} - \frac{\epsilon}{\alpha}\right) \\
&\geq \frac{1}{|X|}\left(1 - \alpha - \frac{\epsilon}{\alpha}\right) \\
&= \frac{1}{|X|}(1 - 2\sqrt{\epsilon}).
\end{aligned}$$

□

A.1 Proof of Lemma 1

PROOF. (a) Since d_J is a metric and the support of $\mathcal{C}$ is nonempty,

$$\begin{aligned}
d_J(Y,Y') &= \mathop{\mathbb{E}}_{C \in \mathcal{C}}[d_J(Y,Y')] \\
&\leq \mathop{\mathbb{E}}_{C \in \mathcal{C}}[d_J(Y,C) + d_J(C,Y')] \\
&= \rho(Y) + \rho(Y').
\end{aligned}$$

On the other hand, observe that $|Y \oplus C| + |X \oplus C| \geq |X \oplus Y|$ (the triangle inequality for the Hamming metric), so by Lemma 4,

$$\begin{aligned}
f_X(Y) + \rho(X) &= f_X(Y) + f_X(X) \\
&= \mathbb{E}\left[\frac{|Y \oplus C| + |X \oplus C|}{|X \cup C|}\right] \\
&\geq \mathbb{E}\left[\frac{|X \oplus Y|}{|X \cup C|}\right] \\
&\geq \frac{|X \oplus Y|}{|X|}\left(1 - 2\sqrt{\rho(X)}\right) \\
&\geq \frac{|X \oplus Y|}{|X \cup Y|}\left(1 - 2\sqrt{\rho(X)}\right) \\
&= d_J(X,Y)\left(1 - 2\sqrt{\rho(X)}\right).
\end{aligned}$$

Thus

$$\begin{aligned}
d_J(X,Y) &\leq \min\left(1, \frac{f_X(Y) + \rho(X)}{1 - 2\sqrt{\rho(X)}}\right) \\
&\leq (f_X(Y) + \rho(X)) \cdot \min\left(\frac{1}{\rho(X)}, \frac{1}{1 - 2\sqrt{\rho(X)}}\right) \\
&\leq 6\,(f_X(Y) + \rho(X)),
\end{aligned}$$

by an easy case distinction ($\rho(X) \leq 1/6$ vs $\rho(X) > 1/6$).
Likewise, $d_J(X,Y') \leq 6\,(f_X(Y') + \rho(X))$, so by the triangle inequality,

$$\begin{aligned}
d_J(Y,Y') &\leq d_J(Y',X) + d_J(X,Y') \\
&= O(\rho(X) + f_X(Y) + f_X(Y')).
\end{aligned}$$

(b) Let $\tau = d_J(X,Y)$. Using Lemma 3,

$$\begin{aligned}
|X \cup Y \cup C| &\leq |X \cup C| + |Y \setminus X| \\
&= |X \cup C| + (|X \cup Y| - |X|) \\
&\leq |X \cup C| + \left(\frac{1}{1-\tau}|X| - |X|\right) \\
&= |X \cup C| + \frac{\tau}{1-\tau}|X| \\
&\leq |X \cup C|\left(1 + \frac{\tau}{1-\tau}\right) \\
&= \frac{|X \cup C|}{1-\tau}.
\end{aligned}$$

Likewise, we have $|X \cup Y \cup C| \leq \frac{|Y \cup C|}{1-\tau}$. Thus,

$$|X \cup C|, |Y \cup C| \leq \frac{|X \cup C|}{1-\tau}, \frac{|Y \cup C|}{1-\tau}.$$

and

$$(1-\tau)\frac{|Y \oplus C|}{|X \cup C|} \leq \frac{|Y \oplus C|}{|Y \cup C|} \leq \frac{1}{1-\tau}\frac{|Y \oplus C|}{|X \cup C|}.$$

Taking expectations over C, we obtain

$$(1-\tau)f_X(Y) \le \rho(Y) \le \frac{1}{1-\tau} f_X(Y).$$

(c) By parts a) and b), $\rho(Y) \le \rho(X)$ implies $d_J(X,Y) \le \rho(Y) + \rho(X) \le 2\rho(X)$ and $(1 - d_J(X,Y))f_X(Y) \le \rho(Y) \le \rho(X) = f_X(X)$.

□

A.2 Proof of Lemma 2

We need an auxiliary lemma.

LEMMA 5. *Let $\widetilde{z}$ be the average of $t \ge 3$ independent random variables in $[0,1]$ each with expectation $z > 0$. Then*

(a) If $z \le \frac{1}{30}$,

$$\Pr\left[\widetilde{z} > \frac{1}{3}\right] \le \frac{30z}{e^{t/3}}.$$

(b) For all $C > 0$,

$$\Pr\left[\widetilde{z} > z + \sqrt{\frac{C}{t}}\right] \le e^{-2C}.$$

PROOF. (a) Let $\delta = \frac{1}{3z} - 1$. By the multiplicative Chernoff bound,

$$\begin{aligned}\Pr\left[\widetilde{z} > \frac{1}{3}\right] &\le \left(\frac{e^\delta}{(1+\delta)^{1+\delta}}\right)^{zt} \\ &= (e^{1-3z} \cdot 3z)^{t/3} \\ &\le (3ez) \cdot (3ez)^{t/3-1} \\ &\le (3ez) \cdot e^{1-t/3} \\ &= (3e^2 z) \cdot e^{-t/3} \\ &\le 30ze^{-t/3}.\end{aligned}$$

(b) Let $\tau = \sqrt{C/t}$. By the additive Chernoff bound,

$$\Pr[\widetilde{z} > z + \tau] \le e^{-2t\tau^2} = e^{-2C}.$$

□

We proceed to prove Lemma 2.

PROOF. For all $i \in [n]$, define

$$a_i = \mathop{\mathbb{E}}_{C\sim\mathcal{C}} \frac{[i \in Z \oplus C]}{|X \cup C|}, \qquad b_i = \mathop{\mathbb{E}}_{C\sim\mathcal{C}} \frac{[i \notin Z \oplus C]}{|X \cup C|}.$$

By linearity of expectation,

$$\begin{aligned}f_X(Y) &= \mathop{\mathbb{E}}_{C\sim\mathcal{C}}\left[\frac{\sum_{i\in[n]}[i \in Y \oplus C]}{|X \cup C|}\right] \\ &= \sum_{i\in[n]} \mathop{\mathbb{E}}_{C\sim\mathcal{C}} \frac{[i \in Y \oplus C]}{|X \cup C|} \\ &= \sum_{i\in Z\oplus C} a_i + \sum_{i\in Y\oplus Z} b_i \\ &= \sum_{i\notin Y\oplus Z} a_i + \sum_{i\in Y\oplus Z} b_i,\end{aligned}$$

where we used $Y \oplus C = (Z \oplus C) \oplus (Y \oplus Z)$. In particular,

$$f_X(Z) = \sum_{i\in[n]} a_i,$$

and the optimality of Z implies $f_X(Z \oplus \{i\}) \ge f_X(Z)$, i.e., $a_i \le b_i$ for all $i \in [n]$.

Now define the empirical counterparts of a_i, b_i:

$$\widetilde{a}_i = \mathop{\mathbb{E}}_{D\sim\mathcal{D}} \frac{[i \in Z \oplus D]}{|X \cup D|}, \qquad \widetilde{b}_i = \mathop{\mathbb{E}}_{D\sim\mathcal{D}} \frac{[i \notin Z \oplus D]}{|X \cup D|}.$$

Likewise, we have

$$\widetilde{f}_X(Y) = \sum_{i\notin Y\oplus Z} \widetilde{a}_i + \sum_{i\in Y\oplus Z} \widetilde{b}_i.$$

Let $\widetilde{Z}$ minimize $\widetilde{f}_X(Y)$. Then

$$Z \oplus \widetilde{Z} = \{i \in [n] \mid \widetilde{a}_i > \widetilde{b}_i\},$$

so

$$\begin{aligned}f_X(\widetilde{Z}) &= \sum_{i\notin\widetilde{Z}\oplus Z} a_i + \sum_{i\in\widetilde{Z}\oplus Z} b_i \\ &= \sum_{\widetilde{a}_i\le\widetilde{b}_i} a_i + \sum_{\widetilde{a}_i>\widetilde{b}_i} b_i\end{aligned}$$

and

$$f_X(\widetilde{Z}) - f_X(Z) = \sum_{\widetilde{a}_i>\widetilde{b}_i} (b_i - a_i).$$

Note that

$$\mathop{\mathbb{E}}_{C\sim\mathcal{C}}\left[\frac{1}{|X \cup D|}\right] = a_i + b_i \triangleq \alpha$$

and, by Lemma 4,

$$\frac{1 - 2\sqrt{\rho(X)}}{|X|} \le \mathop{\mathbb{E}}_{D\sim\mathcal{D}}\left[\frac{1}{|X \cup D|}\right] = a_i + b_i \triangleq \widetilde{\alpha}.$$

We set the following parameters for convenience:

$$\lambda \triangleq \sqrt{\frac{3 + 3\ln(2\ell/\delta)}{\ell}}, \quad \gamma \triangleq |\alpha - \widetilde{\alpha}|, \quad C = 10\log(\ell/\delta).$$

Since $\widetilde{\alpha}$ is the expectation of independent random variables in $[0, 1/|X|]$, we can apply the additive Chernoff bound:

$$\Pr\left[|X| \cdot \gamma > \sqrt{\frac{\ln(4/\delta)}{2\ell}}\right] \le 2\exp\left(-2\ell\frac{\ln(4/\delta)}{2\ell}\right) = \frac{\delta}{2}.$$

In particular, with probability at least $1 - \delta/2$, $\gamma \le \frac{\lambda}{|X|}$ and $\alpha - \gamma \le \widetilde{\alpha} \le \alpha + \gamma$.

Observe that $\widetilde{a}_i$ is the average of ℓ independent random variables in $[0, 1/|X|]$. Since $a_i = 0$ implies $\widetilde{a}_i = 0$ and hence $\widetilde{a}_i \le \widetilde{b}_i$ almost surely, we may assume $a_i > 0$ for all i. Letting $z_i = |X| \cdot a_i$ and using Lemma 5, we conclude that

(a) If $z_i \le \frac{1}{30}$,

$$\Pr\left[|X| \cdot \widetilde{a}_i > \frac{1}{3}\right] \le \frac{30|X|a_i}{e^{\ell/3}}.$$

(b) For all $C > 0$,

$$\Pr\left[|X| \cdot \widetilde{a}_i > \sqrt{\frac{C}{\ell}}\right] \le e^{-2C}.$$

Write

$$B_1 = \left\{ i \in [n] \mid z_i \le \frac{1}{30} \wedge \widetilde{b}_i \ge \widetilde{a}_i \right\},$$

$$B_2 = \left\{ i \in [n] \mid z_i > \frac{1}{30} \wedge b_i \ge a_i + \sqrt{\frac{C}{\ell}} \right\},$$

$$A = [n] \setminus (B_1 \cup B_2).$$

Note that for small enough λ, the conditions $\widetilde{b}_i \ge \widetilde{a}_i$ and $|\alpha - \widetilde{\alpha}| \le \lambda$ imply $z_i > 1/30$. By the above,

$$\begin{aligned}
\mathbb{E}\left[\sum_{i \in B_1} (b_i - a_i)\right] &\le \frac{1}{|X|} \mathbb{E}[|B_1|] \\
&= \frac{1}{|X|} \sum_{i \mid z_i \le 1/30} \Pr[i \in B_1] \\
&\le \frac{30|X|}{|X| e^{\ell/3}} \sum_{z_i \le 1/30} a_i \\
&= \frac{30}{e^{\ell/3}} f_X(Z) \\
&\le O(\delta \cdot \lambda f_X(Z))
\end{aligned}$$

by our choice of λ, so Markov's inequality implies that with probability at least $1 - \delta/4$ we have

$$\sum_{i \in B_1} (b_i - a_i) \le O(\lambda f_X(Z)).$$

Likewise,

$$\begin{aligned}
\mathbb{E}\left[\sum_{i \in B_2} (b_i - a_i)\right] &\le \frac{1}{|X|} \mathbb{E}[|B_2|] \\
&= \frac{1}{|X|} \sum_{z_i > 1/30} \Pr[i \in B_2] \\
&\le \frac{e^{-2C}}{|X|} \left| \left\{ i \in [n] \mid a_i > \frac{1}{30|X|} \right\} \right|
\end{aligned}$$

The size of the set $B_3 = \{i \in [n] \mid a_i > \frac{1}{30|X|}\}$ is at most $30|X| \sum_{i \in B_3} a_i \le 30|X| f_X(Z)$, therefore with probability at least $1 - \delta/4$ we have

$$\sum_{i \in B_2} (b_i - a_i) \le \frac{120 e^{-2C} f_X(Z)}{\delta} = O(\lambda f_X(Z)).$$

Finally, notice that

$$\begin{aligned}
\sum_{i \in A \wedge \widetilde{a}_i < \widetilde{b}_i} (b_i - a_i) &\le \sum_{a_i \ge 1/30} \sqrt{\frac{C}{\ell}} \\
&\le 30 \sqrt{\frac{C}{\ell}} \sum_i a_i \\
&= 30 \sqrt{\frac{C}{\ell}} f_X(Z) \\
&\le O(\lambda f_X(Z)).
\end{aligned}$$

Therefore with probability at least $1 - \delta$,

$$f_X(\widetilde{Z}) \le (1 + O(\lambda)) f_X(Z).$$

This establishes the first part of the theorem. To prove the second, suppose that $\widetilde{f}_X(Y) \le (1 + \beta) \widetilde{f}_X(\widetilde{Z})$. Observe that

$$f_X(\widetilde{Y}) - f_X(Z) = \sum_{i \in \widetilde{Y} \oplus Z} b_i - a_i.$$

and

$$\widetilde{f}_X(\widetilde{Y}) - \widetilde{f}_X(\widetilde{Z}) = \sum_{i \in \widetilde{Y} \oplus \widetilde{Z}} \widetilde{b}_i - \widetilde{a}_i \le \beta \widetilde{f}_X(\widetilde{Z}).$$

If we split the set $T = \widetilde{Y} \oplus \widetilde{Z}$ into $T \cap B_1, T \cap B_2$ and $T \cap A$ and apply our bounds for the size of B_1 and B_2, we conclude that with probability $1 - \delta$,

$$\sum_{i \in \widetilde{Y} \oplus \widetilde{Z}} (b_i - a_i) \le O(\lambda) \cdot \widetilde{f}_X(\widetilde{Z}) + \sum_{i \in T \cap A, z_i \le 1/30, \widetilde{b}_i \le \widetilde{a}_i} (b_i - a_i)$$

and

$$\begin{aligned}
\sum_{i \in T \cap A, z_i \le 1/30, \widetilde{b}_i \le \widetilde{a}_i} (b_i - a_i) &= \sum_{i \in T \cap A, z_i \le 1/30, \widetilde{b}_i \le \widetilde{a}_i} O(\widetilde{b}_i - \widetilde{a}_i) \\
&= O(\beta f_X(\widetilde{Z})).
\end{aligned}$$

Thus

$$\begin{aligned}
f_X(\widetilde{Y}) - f_X(Z) &\le |f_X(\widetilde{Z}) - f_X(Z)| + \sum_{i \in \widetilde{Y} \oplus \widetilde{Z}} (b_i - a_i) \\
&= O(\beta + \lambda) f_X(Z).
\end{aligned}$$

□

Continuous Influence Maximization: What Discounts Should We Offer to Social Network Users?*

Yu Yang[1], Xiangbo Mao[1,2], Jian Pei[1] and Xiaofei He[2]
[1]Simon Fraser University, Burnaby, BC, Canada
[2]Zhejiang University, Hangzhou, China
{yya119, xiangbom, jpei}@sfu.ca, xiaofeihe@gmail.com

ABSTRACT

Imagine we are introducing a new product through a social network, where we know for each user in the network the purchase probability curve with respect to discount. Then, what discount should we offer to those social network users so that the adoption of the product is maximized in expectation under a predefined budget? Although influence maximization has been extensively explored, surprisingly, this appealing practical problem still cannot be answered by the existing influence maximization methods. In this paper, we tackle the problem systematically. We formulate the general continuous influence maximization problem, investigate the essential properties, and develop a general coordinate descent algorithm as well as the engineering techniques for practical implementation. Our investigation does not assume any specific influence model and thus is general and principled. At the same time, using the most popularly adopted independent influence model as a concrete example, we demonstrate that more efficient methods are feasible under specific influence models. Our extensive empirical study on four benchmark real world networks with synthesized purchase probability curves clearly illustrates that continuous influence maximization can improve influence spread significantly with very moderate extra running time comparing to the classical influence maximization methods.

Categories and Subject Descriptors

H.2.8 [**Database Applications**]: Data Mining

Keywords

Influence Maximization; Coordinate Descent

*Yang, Mao and Pei's research is supported in part by an NSERC Discovery grant, the Canada Research Chair program, and a Yahoo! Faculty Research and Engagement Program (FREP) award. Mao and He's research is supported in part by National Natural Science Foundation of China (Grant No: 61233011) and National Program for Special Support of Top-Notch Young Professionals. All opinions, findings, conclusions and recommendations in this paper are those of the authors and do not necessarily reflect the views of the funding agencies.

SIGMOD'16, June 26-July 01, 2016, San Francisco, CA, USA
© 2016 ACM. ISBN 978-1-4503-3531-7/16/06...$15.00
DOI: http://dx.doi.org/10.1145/2882903.2882961

1. INTRODUCTION

Influence maximization [8, 13] is a critical technique in many social network applications, such as viral marketing. The intuition is that, by targeting on only a small number of nodes (called seed nodes), it is possible to trigger a large cascade of information spreading in a social network. Technically, in a social network, influence maximization tries to identify a set of nodes such that if the selected nodes are committed to spread a piece of information to their neighbors, such as adopting a product, the expected spread in the social network is maximized. There have been abundant studies on various models and computational methods for influence maximization. We will review some representative milestone studies in Section 2.

All existing works on influence maximization, except for [10], assume a node is either a seed or not. Eftekhar *et al.* [10] generalized the assumption one step further by assuming that nodes are divided into groups and each group takes a predefined probability to be part of the seeds. However, many demands in practice are still not addressed.

Imagine a company is introducing a new product through a social network by providing discounts to users in the network in the hope of maximizing the influence spread. The total discount is constrained by a budget defined by the company. It is well known that different users in a social network may have a different capability in spreading influence. Consequently, the company naturally wants to offer different users different discounts. It is reasonable to assume that the more discount a user is offered, the more likely the user may adopt the product and spread the influence to her neighbors, which is also known in marketing research as the *purchase probability curve* being monotonic with respect to discount. At the same time, different users may have different purchase probability curves. Given a budget and the users' purchase probability curves, what discounts should the company offer to the users so that the expected influence spread is maximized? Apparently, this is an interesting question that is asked again and again in various applications where influence maximization is used. At the same time, unfortunately the existing influence maximization techniques cannot answer the question.

Motivated by the practical demands, in this paper, we investigate the questions about what discounts we should offer to social network users. In general, given a social network, a budget, and, for each user in the network, the seed probability function on discount (corresponding to the purchase probability curve with respect to discount in the above motivation example), the continuous influence maximization problem is to find the optimal configuration, which consists of a discount rate for each user, that maximizes the influence spread in expectation. We make several contributions.

First, to the best of our knowledge, we are the first to identify and systematically study the problem of continuous influence maximization, which has significant applications in practice. We show that the continuous influence maximization problem is a generalization of the existing influence maximization problem, which focuses on discrete configurations. Consequently, we investigate the hardness of the problem, and analyze several essential properties of the problem. We do not assume any specific influence model, and thus all properties explored are general.

Second, we develop a general coordinate descent framework for the general continuous influence maximization problem. Again, this algorithm does not assume any specific influence model. We analyze the practical challenges in implementation, and suggest the corresponding engineering techniques.

Third, we demonstrate that more efficient methods are feasible for specific influence models. As a concrete example, we consider the independent cascade model [13], which is the most popularly used influence model in literature. We develop two simple yet effective algorithms based on the latest, state-of-the-art polling-based framework [1].

Last, we report an extensive empirical evaluation using four benchmark real social network data sets with synthesized purchase probability curves. The largest data set has almost 4 million nodes and 70 million edges. The experiment results clearly show that continuous influence maximization can significantly improve influence spread. At the same time, the extra running time remains moderate.

The rest of the paper is organized as follows. We review the related work in Section 2 and formulate the problem of continuous influence maximization in Section 3. In Section 4, we investigate the properties of the expectation of influence spread. We present the general coordinate descent framework in Section 5. We study in Section 6 the relationship between continuous influence maximization developed in this paper and the existing influence maximization problem. In Section 7, we examine the challenges of implementing the coordinate descent algorithm in practice, and provide the corresponding engineering techniques. In Section 8, we develop two algorithms under the independent cascade model. We report an extensive empirical evaluation in Section 9, and conclude the paper in Section 10.

For the interest of space, all mathematical proofs are given in Appendix.

2. RELATED WORK

Domingos *et al.* [8] proposed to take advantage of peer influence between users in social networks for marketing. The essential idea is that, by targeting on only a small number of users (called seed users), it is possible to trigger a large cascade of users purchasing a specific product through a social network. Consequently, the technical challenge is to find a small set of users who can trigger the largest cascade in the network. Kempe *et al.* [13] formulated the problem as a discrete optimization problem, which is well known as the influence maximization problem. Since then, influence maximization has drawn much attention from both academia and industry [4, 5, 6, 12, 9, 23, 22].

Most influence maximization algorithms are designed for triggering models [13]. Among these algorithms, a polling-based method [1] has the lowest worst-case time complexity, $O((k+l)(n+m)\log^2 n/\varepsilon^3)$. Tang *et al.* [23, 22] further improved the method to make it run in $O((k+l)(n+m)\log n/\varepsilon^2)$ expected time. The empirical studies showed that their improved algorithms are orders of magnitude faster than the other influence maximization algorithms. Lei *et al.* [14] proposed a method that learns the propagation probabilities while running the viral marketing campaigns.

Another line of algorithmic viral marketing research is budgeted influence maximization [25, 19]. Under such problem settings, every user in a social network is assigned with a threshold value that indicates the amount of money a company needs to spend to persuade her/him to be an initial adopter. One key problem of this setting is how to obtain users' threshold values. Singer [20] proposed a mechanism that can elicit users' true threshold values if they are rational agents. Chen *et al.* [3] provided a comprehensive survey on influence maximization algorithms.

Farajtabar *et al.* [11] modeled social events using multivariate Hawkes processes, and developed a convex optimization framework to determine the incentives on users for stimulating a social event of a desired activity level. Although the objective function in [11] is flexible since it only requires that the objective is a concave utility function, both the properties explored in [11] and the algorithm proposed are only suitable for multivariate Hawkes processes rather than a general influence model. Descriptive influence models, such as the independent cascade model and the linear threshold model [13], the two most widely used models, cannot fit in the framework in [11].

Eftekhar *et al.* [10] discovered that sometimes instead of targeting on very few individual users, persuasion attempts on groups of users, for example, displaying advertisements to them, may lead to wider range cascades in social networks. The motivation of persuasion on groups is that by spending less money on a targeted individual a company can target on much more users and, as a result, in expectation such a strategy may bring more initial adopters [24]. Eftekhar *et al.* [10] assumed that the probability that a user is persuaded to be a seed user is given and fixed, if she/he is targeted. A more realistic strategy is that we can adjust the resource spent on a specific individual to manipulate the probability she/he becomes a seed user, which is the subject studied in this paper.

3. PROBLEM DEFINITION

A social network is a graph $G = \langle V, E \rangle$, where V is a set of users and E is a set of relationships between users. Denote by $n = |V|$ the number of users and $m = |E|$ the number of relationships, that is, edges.

An influence cascading model (influence model for short) describes the process of how influence is cascaded in a social network. Two most widely used influence models are the independent cascade model and the linear threshold model [13]. In an influence cascade process, a cascade is started by a small number of users, whom we call *seed users* (or *seeds* for short). We call the set of seed users the *seed set*, denoted by S. Every influence model has an *influence function* $I : 2^V \to R$, where $I(S)$ is the expected size of the cascade triggered by the seed set S and is also called the *influence spread* of S. Usually, $I(S)$ is assumed monotonic and submodular [13, 18], which capture the intuition about influence spreading.

In this paper, we are interested in customizing a discount for every user in a social network to maximize influence cascading. With a discount of 0%, a user has to pay the full price. With a discount of 100%, the product is free for the user. Please note that the notion of discount here can also be used to model in general the cost that we would like to pay to a user to turn the user into a seed.

Technically, a user $u \in V$ is associated with a *seed probability function* $p_u : [0,1] \to [0,1]$, which models the probabilistic distribution that u is attracted to become a seed user given a discount between 0% to 100%. Denote by c_u the discount we offer to u. Then, $p_u(c_u)$ is the probability that u becomes a seed user given such a discount. In this paper, we assume that a seed probability function $p_u(\cdot)$ has the following properties: (1) $p_u(0) = 0$; (2) $p_u(1) = 1$; (3) $p_u(c_u)$ is monotonic with respect to c_u; and (4) $p_u(c_u)$ is continuously differentiable. Conditions (1) and (2) are also assumed in the classical influence maximization problem.

The existing marketing research [2, 21] estimates user purchase probability. Most of the existing work focuses on the adoption rate of the whole population rather than each individual, and estimations are on specific goods. In reality, a user's purchasing behavior may change over time and on different types of goods [7]. Thus, the best way to decide a user's seed probability function (purchase probability curve) is to learn from data. Since seed probability functions can take many different forms, it is important to design a general marketing method that can handle all kinds of such functions.

We assume that different users become seed users independently. Denote by an n-dimensional vector $C = (c_1, c_2, ..., c_n)$ a *configuration* of discounts assigned to all users in G. It is clear that, unlike the situation in the influence maximization problem, the seed set S in our problem setting is probabilistic. Given a social network $G = \langle V, E\rangle$ and a configuration C, the probability that a subset $S \subseteq V$ of users is the seed set is

$$Pr(S;V,C) = \prod_{u\in S} p_u(c_u) \prod_{v\in V-S} (1-p_v(c_v)) \tag{1}$$

For a specific influence model with an influence function $I(S)$, the *expected influence spread* is

$$UI(C) = \sum_{S\in 2^V} Pr(S;V,C)I(S) \tag{2}$$

Now we define the *continuous influence maximization* problem (*CIM* for short) studied in this paper as follows. Given a social network $G = \langle V, E\rangle$, a budget B, a seed probability function $p_u(c_u)$ for every user u, and an influence model with an influence function $I(S)$, find the configuration C that is the optimal solution to the following continuous optimization problem.

$$\begin{aligned} \text{maximize} \quad & UI(C) \\ \text{s.t.} \quad & 0 \le c_u \le 1, \forall u \in V \\ & \sum_{u\in V} c_u \le B \end{aligned} \tag{3}$$

We call a configuration satisfying the constraints in Eq. 3 a *feasible* configuration. Please note that the budget B here is a safe budget in general. When discounts here are used to model the costs committed to each user, it models the total cost. When discounts here are explained as discount rates, the budget is the worst-case budget. We leave the exploration of other forms of the budget constraint to future work, such as the expected budget under the discount rate explanation.

The classical influence maximization problem is a special case of the continuous influence maximization problem, since it can be written in a similar way as follows.

$$\begin{aligned} \text{maximize} \quad & UI(C) \\ \text{s.t.} \quad & c_u = 0 \text{ or } c_u = 1, \forall u \in V \\ & \sum_{u\in V} c_u \le B \end{aligned} \tag{4}$$

We call a configuration satisfying the constraints in Eq. 4 an *integer* configuration. Apparently, an integer configuration is also a feasible configuration.

In the rest of the paper, for the sake of clarity, we also call the classical influence maximization problem *discrete influence maximization* (*DIM* for short). Table 1 summarizes the frequently used notations.

Notation	Description
$G = \langle V, E\rangle$	Social network G, where V is the set of users and E is the set of relationships
$n = \|V\|$	The number of nodes in G
$m = \|E\|$	The number of edges in G
$p_u(c_u)$	The probability that u becomes a seed user if u is offered a discount c_u
$C = (c_1, c_2, ..., c_n)$	A configuration, where c_u $(0 \le c_u \le 1)$ is the discount offered to user u
$Pr(S;V,C)$	The probability of a subset of users $S \subseteq V$ is the seed set S (Eq. 1)
$UI(C)$	The expected influence spread caused by configuration C (Eq. 2)

Table 1: Frequently used notations.

4. EXPECTED INFLUENCE SPREAD

The CIM problem is to optimize the expected influence spread $UI(C)$. In this section, we discuss the computation of $UI(C)$ and the monotonicity of $UI(C)$, which prepare us for the solution development in the next sections.

4.1 Computing $UI(C)$

Given $G = \langle V, E\rangle$, an influence function $I(S)$, and a seed probability function $p_u(c_u)$ for every $u \in V$, how can we obtain $UI(C)$? It is known that, for many popular influence models, computing $I(S)$ is #P-hard [4, 6]. What is the hardness of computing $UI(C)$?

THEOREM 1 (COMPLEXITY). *Given a configuration C, computing $UI(C) = \sum_{S\in 2^V} Pr(S;V,C)I(S)$ is #P-hard if computing $I(S)$ is #P-hard.*

Since $UI(C)$ is the expectation of $I(S)$ over the random variable S, we can use Monte Carlo simulations to estimate $UI(C)$. Because every user becomes a seed user independently, randomly generating a seed set S according to $Pr(S;V,C)$ is equivalent to simply adding each user u to S independently with probability $p_u(c_u)$. We have the following result.

THEOREM 2 ((ε,δ) ESTIMATION). *Suppose we have an influence spread oracle that can return the influence spread $I(S)$ of a given seed set S. By calling the influence spread oracle $\frac{n^2 \ln\frac{2}{\delta}}{2\varepsilon^2(\sum_{u\in V} p_c(c_u))^2}$ times, we can have an (ε,δ) estimation [17] of $UI(C)$.*

As mentioned before, computing $I(S)$ is #P-hard for some influence functions. The good news is that there exists a FPRAS[1] (Fully Polynomial Randomized Approximation Scheme) [17, 16] for estimating $I(S)$. We prove that if $I(S)$ can be estimated efficiently, so is $UI(C)$. Similar to influence maximization where the number of seeds B is assumed to be $\Omega(1)$, we assume that the expected number of seeds $\sum_{u\in V} p_u(c_u)$ is also $\Omega(1)$.

THEOREM 3 (FPRAS ESTIMATION). *For an influence function $I(\cdot)$, if there is a FPRAS for estimating $I(\cdot)$, there is a FPRAS for estimating $UI(\cdot)$.*

For the two most widely used influence models, namely the independent cascade model and the linear threshold model [13], we have the following upper bound on the time complexity of Monte Carlo simulations needed for obtaining an (ε,δ) approximation of $UI(C)$.

[1] An FPRAS is an algorithm which returns an (ε,δ) estimation of the desired value in time polynomial to n (size of input), $\frac{1}{\varepsilon}$ and $\ln\frac{1}{\delta}$.

THEOREM 4 (APPROXIMATION RUNTIME). *Under the independent cascade model and the linear threshold model, we can use* $O(\frac{mn^2 \ln \frac{1}{\delta}}{2\varepsilon^2(\sum_{u \in V} p_u(c_u))^2})$ *time to obtain an* (ε, δ) *approximation of* $UI(C)$.

In summary, the results in this subsection establish that, as long as $I(S)$ can be computed efficiently (that is, in polynomial time), $UI(C)$ can also be computed efficiently. This strong relation makes comparing two different configurations C_1 and C_2 computationally feasible, since we can efficiently estimate $UI(C_1)$ and $UI(C_2)$ accurately.

4.2 Monotonicity of $UI(C)$

Eq. 3 contains an inequality constraint $\sum_{u \in V} c_u \leq B$. According to the assumption that $p_u(c_u)$ is monotonic with respect to c_u, we can prove that the inequality constraint $\sum_{u \in V} c_u \leq B$ can be substituted by an equation constraint $\sum_{u \in V} c_u = B$.

LEMMA 1. *Given configurations* $C_1 = (c_1^1, c_2^1, ..., c_n^1)$ *and* $C_2 = (c_1^2, c_2^2, ..., c_n^2)$*, if there exists* u $(1 \leq u \leq n)$ *such that* $c_u^1 \geq c_u^2$*, and* $\forall v \in V - \{u\}$*,* $c_v^1 = c_v^2$*, then* $UI(C_1) \geq UI(C_2)$.

For two configurations $C_1 = (c_1^1, c_2^1, ..., c_n^1)$ and $C_2 = (c_1^2, c_2^2, ..., c_n^2)$, we write $C_1 \succeq C_2$ if $\forall u$, $c_u^1 \geq c_u^2$. By the transitivity of $\geq$ and Lemma 1, we have the following immediately.

THEOREM 5 (MONOTONICITY). *If* $C_1 \succeq C_2$*, then* $UI(C_1) \geq UI(C_2)$.

According to Theorem 5, it is obvious that the optimal C for the continuous influence maximization problem must use up the budget B. Thus, the continuous influence maximization problem can be rewritten as follows.

$$\begin{aligned} \text{maximize} \quad & UI(C) \\ \text{s.t.} \quad & 0 \leq c_u \leq 1, \forall u \in V \\ & \sum_{u \in V} c_u = B \end{aligned} \tag{5}$$

5. A GENERAL COORDINATE DESCENT FRAMEWORK

In this section, we develop a coordinate descent algorithm to solve the continuous influence maximization problem. Our algorithm is a general framework, since we do not compose any constraints on the specific form of the influence function $I(S)$ and the seed probability function $p_u(c_u)$. We only assume that $p_u(c_u)$ is monotonic and continuously differentiable.

5.1 Gradient

For a node $u \in V$, we can rewrite $UI(C)$ as follows.

$$\begin{aligned} & UI(C) \\ = & \sum_{S \in 2^V \wedge u \in S} Pr(S; V, C) I(S) + \sum_{S \in 2^V \wedge u \notin S} Pr(S; V, C) I(S) \\ = & \sum_{S \in 2^{V-\{u\}}} Pr(S; V - \{u\}, C) I(S)[1 - p_u(c_u)] \\ & + \sum_{S \in 2^{V-\{u\}}} Pr(S; V - \{u\}, C) I(S \cup \{u\}) p_u(c_u) \\ = & p_u(c_u) \cdot \sum_{S \in 2^{V-\{u\}}} Pr(S; V - \{u\}, C)[I(S \cup \{u\}) - I(S)] + const \end{aligned}$$

where *const* is a constant with respect to c_u. Given a graph $G = \langle V, E \rangle$ and influence function $I(S)$, for a node $u \in V$, $Pr(S; V - \{u\}, C)$, $I(S)$ and $I(S \cup \{u\})$ are constants with respect to c_u. Therefore, using a node $u \in V$ we can rewrite the objective function $UI(C)$ into a linear function of $p_u(c_u)$, where c_u is the only variable.

Assuming $p_u(c_u)$ is continuously differentiable, we can take the partial derivative of $UI(C)$ with respect to c_u, that is,

$$\frac{\partial UI(C)}{\partial c_u} = p_u'(c_u) \sum_{S \in 2^{V-\{u\}}} Pr(S; V - \{u\}, C)[I(S \cup \{u\}) - I(S)] \tag{6}$$

In this way, we can compute the gradient of $UI(C)$ with respect to a specific configuration C. The gradient information will be used in the coordinate descent algorithm to be developed next.

5.2 A Coordinate Descent Algorithm

The coordinate descent algorithm is an iterative algorithm. In each iteration, we pick only two variables c_i and c_j, and fix the rest $n-2$ variables. We try to increase the value of the objective function $UI(C)$ by changing only the values of c_i and c_j.

As stated in Eq. 5, $\sum_{u \in V} c_u = B$. Thus, when we fix c_u for all $u \in V - \{i, j\}$, $\sum_{u \in V - \{i,j\}} c_u$ is a constant. Let $B' = B - \sum_{u \in V - \{i,j\}} c_u = c_i + c_j$. In other words, $c_j = B' - c_i$. Combining the other constraints $0 \leq c_i \leq 1$ and $0 \leq c_j \leq 1$ in Eq. 5, we have an equivalent constraint $max(0, B' - 1) \leq c_i \leq min(1, B')$.

Thus, in each iteration, increasing $UI(C)$ can be achieved by solving the following optimization problem.

$$\begin{aligned} \text{maximize} \quad & UI(C) \text{ w.r.t. } c_i \text{ and } c_j = B' - c_i \\ \text{s.t.} \quad & max(0, B' - 1) \leq c_i \leq min(1, B') \end{aligned} \tag{7}$$

To solve the above optimization problem, we further rewrite $UI(C)$ by fixing c_u for all $u \in V - \{i, j\}$ and setting $c_j = B' - c_i$. That is,

$$\begin{aligned} UI(C) = & \sum_{S \in 2^{V-\{i,j\}}} Pr(S; V - \{i, j\}, C) \Big\{ \\ & [1 - p_i(c_i)][1 - p_j(B' - c_i)] I(S) \\ & + [1 - p_i(c_i)] p_j(B' - c_i) I(S \cup \{j\}) \\ & + [1 - p_j(B' - c_i)] p_i(c_i) I(S \cup \{i\}) \\ & + p_i(c_i) p_j(B' - c_i) I(S \cup \{i, j\}) \Big\} \end{aligned} \tag{8}$$

In Eq. 8, except for $p_i(c_i)$ and $p_j(B' - c_i)$, all terms can be regarded as constants. Therefore, we have a new form of $UI(C)$ with respect to c_i and $c_j = B' - c_i$ as follows.

$$\begin{aligned} UI(C) = & (A_1 + A_2 - A_3 - A_4) p_i(c_i) p_j(B' - c_i) \\ & + (A_3 - A_1) p_i(c_i) + (A_4 - A_1) p_j(B' - c_i) + const, \end{aligned} \tag{9}$$

where

$$\begin{aligned} A_1 &= \sum_{S \in 2^{V-\{i,j\}}} Pr(S; V - \{i, j\}, C) I(S) \\ A_2 &= \sum_{S \in 2^{V-\{i,j\}}} Pr(S; V - \{i, j\}, C) I(S \cup \{i, j\}) \\ A_3 &= \sum_{S \in 2^{V-\{i,j\}}} Pr(S; V - \{i, j\}, C) I(S \cup \{i\}) \\ A_4 &= \sum_{S \in 2^{V-\{i,j\}}} Pr(S; V - \{i, j\}, C) I(S \cup \{j\}) \end{aligned} \tag{10}$$

```
Input: Budget B, social network G, seed probability function
       p_u(c_u), ∀u ∈ V, and influence function (influence
       model) I(S)
Output: Configuration C
1: Initialize C such that C satisfies constraints in Eq. 5
2: while not converge do
3:     Pick two variables c_i and c_j
4:     B' ← c_i + c_j
5:     Find all x ∈ (max(0, B' − 1), min(B', 1)) that
       dUI(C)/dc_i |_{c_i = x} = 0
6:     c_i ← argmax_{c_i ∈ {x, max(0, B'−1), min(1, B')}} UI(C)
7:     c_j ← B' − c_i
8: end while
9: return C
```

Algorithm 1: The Coordinate Descent Algorithm

In Eq. 9, $UI(C)$ only has one variable c_i. We take the derivative of $UI(C)$, that is,

$$\begin{aligned}\frac{\mathrm{d}UI(C)}{\mathrm{d}c_i} =&(A_1+A_2-A_3-A_4)[p_i^{'}(c_i)p_j(B'-c_i)\\ &-p_i(c_i)p_j^{'}(B'-c_i)]+(A_3-A_1)p_i^{'}(c_i)\\ &-(A_4-A_1)p_j^{'}(B'-c_i)\end{aligned} \tag{11}$$

Since $p_i(c_i)$ and $p_j(B'-c_i)$ are both continuously differentiable on $(max(0,B'-1), min(B',1))$, the value $c_i \in [max(0,B'-1), min(B',1)]$ that maximizes the objective function in Eq. 7 must be in one of the following three situations: (1) $c_i = max(0,B'-1)$; (2) $c_i = min(B',1)$; or (3) $c_i = x$, where $x \in (max(0,B'-1), min(B',1))$ and $\frac{\mathrm{d}UI(C)}{\mathrm{d}c_i}|_{c_i=x} = 0$. Thus, we only need to check these three types of points and set c_i to the one that results in the maximum value of $UI(C)$ with respect to c_i and $c_j = B'-c_i$.

Based on the above discussion, the pseudo-code of the coordinate descent algorithm for solving the continuous influence maximization problem is given in Algorithm 1.

We do not assume any specific seed probability function $p_u(c_u)$ and influence function $I(S)$. Thus, Algorithm 1 is a general framework for solving the continuous influence maximization problem.

In Line 3 of Algorithm 1, we do not specify which c_i and c_j should be picked. One heuristic that may help here is to use the partial derivative $\frac{\partial UI(C)}{\partial c_u}$ as a heuristic. For example, we can pick a variable with a large partial derivative and another variable that has a small partial derivative. Limited by space, we leave the exploration of effective heuristics to future work.

The convergence of Algorithm 1 is guaranteed by the following observations. First, $UI(C) \leq n$, where n is the number of nodes in the social network. Second, after each iteration in Algorithm 1, the updated configuration C ensures that the value of $UI(C)$ is at least as good as the previous one, that is, the value of $UI(C)$ is non-decreasing.

Algorithm 1 approaches a stationary configuration as the limit, which is a necessary condition for finding local optima. Since the objective function $UI(C)$ is not necessarily convex or concave, even when the stationary point is a local optima, it may not be the global optima. At the same time, because in each iteration the value of our objective cannot be decreased, when taking a configuration C and applying Algorithm 1, we can always find a configuration C' no worse than C.

6. CIM AND DIM

In this section, we examine the relation between the continuous influence maximization problem (CIM) studied in this paper and the classical and well studied (discrete) influence maximization problem (DIM).

Our first result is that, when the influence function $I(S)$ and the seed probability function $p_u(c_u)$ satisfy certain conditions, the continuous influence maximization problem and the discrete influence maximization problem share the same optimal solution.

THEOREM 6 (CIM AND DIM). *Given an influence function $I(S)$ that is monotonic and submodular, a budget B that is a positive integer, and a seed probability function $p_u(\cdot)$ for every node such that $\forall u \in V, \forall c_u \in [0,1]$, $p_u(c_u) \leq c_u$, the optimal objectives of CIM and DIM are equivalent.*

COROLLARY 1. *Given an influence function $I(S)$ that is monotonic and submodular, an integer budget B, if $\forall u \in V, \forall c_u \in [0,1]$, $p_u(c_u) \leq c_u$, then there exists an integer configuration C that is optimal to CIM.*

Theorem 6 also immediately indicates the complexity of the continuous influence maximization problem.

COROLLARY 2. *If maximizing $I(S)$ is NP-hard, and $I(S)$ is monotonic and submodular, then given a social network $G = \langle V,E \rangle$, a budget B and the seed probability function $p_u(c_u)$ for each $u \in V$, maximizing $UI(C)$ over C is also NP-hard.*

To further understand the significance of Theorem 6, we notice that the seed probability function $p_u(c_u)$ represents how user u is sensitive to discount c_u. If $p_u(c_u) \leq c_u$, user u is insensitive to discount. Theorem 6 indicates that, if all users in the network are insensitive to discount, then we would better give free products to some seed users, that is, setting $c_u = 1$, to trigger a sizeable cascade propagation.

Although under some conditions, CIM and DIM share the same optimal objectives, it can be shown that in some situations it is not the case, particularly when some users are sensitive to discount.

EXAMPLE 1. *Consider a social network $G = \langle V,E \rangle$ where $E = \emptyset$. In other words, G is a graph of n isolated nodes. In the independent influence model or the linear cascade model, if the budget $B = 1$, and for each node u, the seed probability function $p_u(c_u) = \sqrt{c_u}$, then the optimal solution for discrete influence maximization is to pick an arbitrary node u and the optimal influence spread is 1. However, the optimal solution to continuous influence maximization is to assign $\frac{1}{n}$ discount to each node, and the optimal influence spread is $\sqrt{n}$. Thus, not only the optimal solution to discrete influence maximization is not optimal to continuous influence maximization in some cases, but also such solutions to DIM can be arbitrarily bad for CIM as the size of the network becomes very large.*

It can be easily shown that CIM can always achieve influence spread no smaller than DIM. Given a budget B, one can first run a DIM algorithm to find a seed set of $\lfloor B \rfloor$ seeds. Then, by taking the corresponding integer configuration C of the seed set as the initial configuration, after applying the coordinate descent algorithm, a configuration C' that $UI(C') \geq UI(C)$ can be found.

7. PRACTICAL CIM SOLUTIONS

In this section we first discuss some challenges that the coordinate descent algorithm faces in practical implementation. Then, we introduce a practical strategy. Although the strategy cannot guarantee a global or local optimal solution to the continuous influence maximization problem, it can always find a solution no worse than a solution to the discrete influence maximization problem that a known method can produce.

7.1 Practical Challenges for the Coordinate Descent Algorithm

In the coordinate descent algorithm, we need to compute 3 coefficients, $(A_1+A_2-A_3-A_4)$, A_3-A_1, and A_4-A_1. Similar to $UI(C)$, these three coefficients can only be estimated by sampling techniques if computing $I(S)$ is #P-hard. All the three coefficients can be very close to 0. Consequently, estimating them may be very challenging.

To tackle the challenge, a practical trick is not to solve $\frac{dUI(C)}{dc_i}|_{c_i=x}=0$. Instead, we can estimate $UI(C)$ directly by trying all possible values of $c_i \in [max(0,B'-1), min(B',1)]$. This makes good sense in practice since a budget typically carries a minimum unit. For example, if we want the absolute error of C to be up to 0.01, at most we only need to try 101 different values of c_i because $min(B',1)-max(0,B'-1)\leq 1$.

However, even the above trick may face serious challenges in some situations. A key observation is that the gain obtained in an iteration of the coordinate descent algorithm is limited.

THEOREM 7 (GAIN IN AN ITERATION). *In the coordinate descent algorithm, let the configuration before an iteration and that after the iteration be C and C_1, respectively. Then, after the iteration, we have*

$$\begin{aligned}&UI(C_1)-UI(C)\\ \leq&\operatorname*{argmax}_{u\in V}\sum_{S\in 2^{V-\{u\}}} Pr(S;V-\{u\},C)\big(I(S\cup\{u\})-I(S)\big)\end{aligned}$$

Theorem 7 indicates that sometimes the gain after one iteration in the coordinate descent algorithm can be very small, because $I(S\cup\{u\})-I(S)$ can be close to 0. While very often we can only calculate $UI(C)$ by Monte Carlo simulations, such sampling techniques may fail to detect a very small difference between two highly similar configurations.

7.2 Unified Discount Configuration

A practical engineering strategy to design discounts is to offer a unified discount to some users in a social network. That means, for each node u in G, c_u is either a predefined value c or 0. Thus, for finding a good configuration C, we can optimize over the unified discount c. Although c is continuous, because we have to use up all budget due to the monotonicity of $UI(C)$, to optimize over c, we only need to consider situations when $c=\frac{B}{\lceil B\rceil},\frac{B}{\lceil B\rceil+1},\ldots,\frac{B}{n}$. Now, the problem becomes how we can find the optimal configuration when c is fixed.

When c is fixed, finding the optimal configuration C is to find the optimal set of users to offer each of them discount c. Suppose we choose the set S of users to offer discounts, denote by $Pr(S';S,c)$ the probability of generating a seed set S' when the unified discount is c, that is,

$$Pr(S';S,c)=\prod_{u\in S'}p_u(c)\prod_{v\in S-S'}(1-p_v(c)) \tag{12}$$

We define $UI(S;c)$ as the expected influence spread when we offer each user in S with a unified discount c. That is,

$$UI(S;c)=\sum_{S'\in 2^S}Pr(S';S,c)I(S') \tag{13}$$

We observe the following nice property of $UI(S;c)$ when c is fixed.

THEOREM 8 (MONOTONICITY AND SUBMODULARITY). *If $I(S)$ is monotonic and submodular with respect to S, then $UI(S;c)$ is also monotonic and submodular with respect to S.*

The monotonicity and submodularity of $UI(S;c)$ with respect to S imply that, when c is fixed, we can apply a greedy algorithm to find a set of users S to offer discounts which can cause influence spread at least $(1-\frac{1}{e})$ times of the influence spread caused by the optimal set of users S^*. In such a case, when the influence model and seed probability function for each user are given, some efficient influence maximization algorithms [15, 23, 22] can be applied here.

8. CIM ALGORITHMS UNDER THE INDEPENDENT CASCADE MODEL

In this paper, we demonstrate how we can develop specific algorithms for continuous influence maximization under some specific influence model. Since the independent cascade model is the most popularly used influence model [5, 4, 13, 23], we design two simple yet effective algorithms to solve the continuous influence maximization problem under the independent cascade model. Note that our main contribution in this paper is the general framework, the discussion in this subsection is for providing an example that how a specific influence model is plugged into our framework.

Recently, a polling-based algorithmic framework [1, 23, 22] was proposed for triggering models [13] like the IC model and was shown the most efficient influence maximization algorithm so far. Our algorithms are also polling-based algorithms.

Let us first briefly review how a polling method works for influence maximization.

Given a graph $G=\langle V,E\rangle$, a poll is conducted as follows: a node $v\in V$ is picked in random and then we try to find out which nodes are likely to influence v. We run a Monte Carlo simulation of IC propagation from v on the transpose graph [2] G^T. Note that the propagation probability of an edge (v,u) in G^T is pp_{uv}, the propagation probability of edge (u,v) in G. Such "reverse" propagation process from v is used for finding v's potential "influencers". Suppose the set of nodes reached in this poll is h. We call h a random hyper-edge. The intuition of the poll process is that if a node u has high influence, then the probability that u appears in a random hyper-edge h is high.

Then the polling method consists of two major steps.

1. Random Hyper-graph Construction. Generate a random hyper-graph H by generating a certain number of random hyper-edges. Note that nodes in H are still nodes in G. A node u and a hyper-edge $h\in H$ are incident if $u\in h$. Denote by $deg_H(S)$ the degree of the set of nodes S, which is the number of hyper-edges in H incident to at least one node of S. The greater $deg_H(S)$ is, the more likely the influence spread of S is high.

2. Maximum Coverage on Radom Hyper-graph. Greedily choose B nodes to add to the seed set S such that the selected node can increase $deg_H(S)$ the most.

One key property that makes the polling method work well is that when the number of random hyper-edges mH is fixed, $\frac{deg_H(S)*n}{mH}$ is an unbiased estimation of $I(S)$, the influence spread of S in G [1].

[2] $G^T=\langle V,E^T\rangle$ is the transpose graph of $G=\langle V,E\rangle$ if $\forall(u,v)\in E$, $(v,u)\in E^T$

Thus, as long as mH is sufficiently large, the seed set returned by the polling method has good quality guarantees. Tang *et al.* [23, 22] illustrated how to estimate the lower bound of mH that makes the result of the polling method a $(1-1/e-\varepsilon)$-approximation with probability at least $1-\frac{1}{n}$ given ε.

To solve the continuous influence maximization problem, we can employ a similar method that also constructs a random hyper-graph.

THEOREM 9. *Given a graph $G=\langle V,E\rangle$ and seed probability functions of all nodes, a random hyper-graph H with mH hyper-edges generated according to G and a configuration C, $\frac{n*\sum_{h\in H}[1-\prod_{u\in h}(1-p_u(c_u))]}{mH}$ is an unbiased estimation of $UI(C)$.*

According to Theorem 9, we build a random hyper-graph H by simply setting mH to a predefined number, usually in $O(n\log n)$. Two continuous influence maximization algorithms are devised based on H.

The first algorithm is called *Unified Discount* (UD). In Section 7.2, we discussed that in reality, instead of offering different users different discounts, a company can select a set of users and offer each of them the same discount c. We prove that, under such a situation, $UI(S;c)$ is monotonic and submodular if $I(S)$ is monotonic and submodular, which is true under the IC model. One can also easily prove that $\sum_{h\in H}[1-\prod_{u\in h}(1-p_u(c_u))]$ is also monotonic and submodular when $c_u=c$ or 0. Thus, when c is fixed, a simple greedy algorithm with the CELF pruning technique [15] can be applied to find a set S that is at least $(1-1/e)$ optimal with respect to maximizing $\sum_{h\in H}[1-\prod_{u\in h}(1-p_u(c_u))]$. Obviously the configuration C returned satisfies that $c_u=c$ if $u\in S$, otherwise $c_u=0$. For finding the best discount c, we adopt a simple heuristic that is based on the fact that normally discount offered by companies is a multiple of 5%. Therefore, we simply run an exhaustive search of c by setting $c=5\%,10\%,...,95\%,100\%$. One can choose some other step interval as needed.

The second algorithm, called Coordinate Descent (CD), takes the configuration returned by the Unified Discount algorithm as the initial values and a coordinate descent procedure is conducted to further improve $UI(C)$. Like Unified Discount, this algorithm is also run on the random hyper-graph H. Thus, the formulation that the optimization Coordinate Descent tries to solve is

$$\begin{aligned} \text{maximize} \quad & \sum_{h\in H}[1-\prod_{u\in h}(1-p_u(c_u))] \\ \text{s.t.} \quad & 0\le c_u\le 1, \forall u\in V \\ & \sum_{u\in V} c_u\le B \end{aligned} \tag{14}$$

In our implementation, in each iteration, instead of picking a pair of coordinates c_i and c_j from $O(n^2)$ potential pairs in Algorithm 1, we only pick c_i and c_j from coordinates that have non-zero values in the initial configuration C. Note that the initial configuration C has at most $\frac{B}{5\%}=O(B)$ non-zero entries, and $B\ll n$. Efficiency is the major reason to do this. In the experiments, we run iterations in total 100 rounds. In each round, every pair of non-zero c_i and c_j are picked and optimized over.

EXAMPLE 2. *Fig. 1 is a toy example illustrating the differences between integer configuration, unified discount configuration, and continuous configuration. In Figure 1, the propagation model is the IC model and the propagation probabilities along edges are all 0.1. Suppose the seed probability functions for the nodes in this graph are all $p_u(c_u)=2c_u-c_u^2$, that is, the users are sensitive to discount. When $B=1$, the optimal seeding strategy for DIM is to choose node v1 as the single seed, which leads to the best integer configuration is $C_1=(1,0,0,0,0)$ and $UI(C_1)=1.4$. If we apply the unified discount strategy, the best unified discount value is 0.2. Correspondingly the best unified discount configuration is $C_2=(0.2,0.2,0.2,0.2,0.2)$ and $UI(C_2)=1.89216$. If we apply the coordinate descent algorithm and set $C_2=(0.2,0.2,0.2,0.2,0.2)$ as the initial value of configuration, we get a better continuous configuration $C_3=(0.38312,0.15422,0.15422,0.15422,0.15422)$ and $UI(C_3)=1.93533$.*

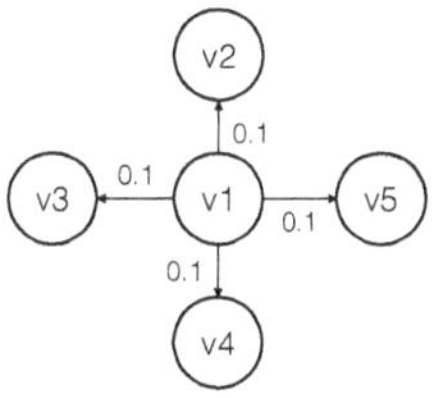

Figure 1: An example illustrating the differences among integer configuration, unified discount configuration and continuous configuration.

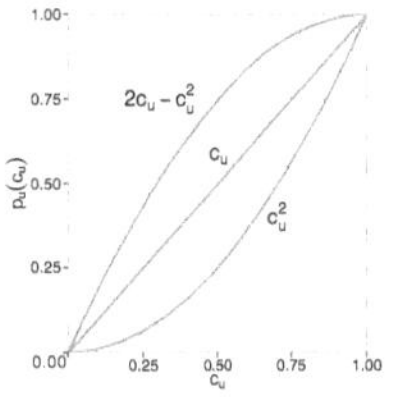

Figure 2: The seed probability functions used in the experiments.

9. EMPIRICAL EVALUATION

To examine the effectiveness and efficiency of our methods, in this section, we report experiments on four real networks with synthesized seed probability functions to test our proposed methods. The experiment results show that the continuous influence maximization strategy can significantly improve influence spread without incurring dramatic extra overheads compared to discrete influence maximization.

Network	n	m	Average Degree	mH
wiki-Vote	7,115	103,689	14.6	0.25M
ca-AstroPh	18,772	396,220	21.1	1M
com-dblp	317,080	2,099,732	6.6	20M
com-LiveJornal	3,997,962	69,362,378	17.3	40M

Table 2: Datasets

9.1 Expertmental Settings

We ran our experiments on four real network data sets that are publicly available in SNAP (http://snap.stanford.edu/data/index.html). Table 2 shows the details of the four data sets. All networks are treated as directed graphs, which means if a network is undirected, every undirected edge (u,v) is processed as two directed edges (u,v) and (v,u).

In our experiments, we adopted the Independent Cascade (IC) model as the influence model, which is the most widely used in literature [5, 4, 13, 23]. Following the most popular settings of the IC model [5, 4, 13, 23], we set the propagation probability of a directed edge (u,v) to $\frac{\alpha}{in-degree(v)}$, where $\alpha \in \{0.7, 0.85, 1\}$.

For seed probability functions, unfortunately we do not have access to any such real data sets for the purpose of experiments. Thus, we used synthesized seed probability functions. Given a network $G = \langle V, E \rangle$, we randomly picked 5% nodes to assign $p_u(c_u) = c_u^2$, and 10% nodes to assign $p_u(c_u) = c_u$ as their seed probability functions. These users (nodes) were insensitive to discount. The rest 85% nodes were assigned with $p_u(c_u) = 2c_u - c_u^2$, which means that those users are sensitive to discount. When c_u is close to 0, the probability that u becomes a seed is roughly twice of c_u. As c_u increases, the ratio $\frac{2c_u - c_u^2}{c_u}$ decreases gradually. Figure 2 shows the curves of the two seed probability functions as well as the function $p_u(c_u) = c_u$ as the reference.

To compare the continuous influence maximization strategy and the existing discrete one, we compare the results of our algorithms to the result of discrete influence maximization. Since the IC model was used in our experiments, all algorithms implemented are based on the IC model. Therefore, in our experiments, all algorithms were implemented based on the polling framework. All algorithms were implemented in C# and ran on an Apple Mac Pro (Late 2013) computer with Intel Xeon 3.70GHz CPU, 64GB main memory. In the algorithms developed in Section 8, we need to set a parameter mH. The value for each dataset is also listed in Table 2.

9.2 Experimental Results

9.2.1 *Effectiveness*

Fig. 3 shows the influence spread of each algorithm under different settings of parameters. Since our methods introduce extra uncertainty in the seed set, we also report one standard deviation interval of influence spread in Fig. 3. All influence spreads and standard deviations are obtained by 20,000 Monte Carlo simulations. From the results we find that both the Unified Discount (UD) algorithm and the Coordinate Descent (CD) algorithm can significantly increase the expected influence spread compared to discrete influence maximization (IM). Although the standard deviations of UD and CD algorithms are larger than that of IM, the gap is not large. In most cases the ratio of the first two to the last one is no more than 1.5. The CD algorithm can always achieve a higher influence spread and a lower standard deviation than the UD algorithm. Worth noting that 100 rounds of iterations for the CD algorithm are enough on datasets used in experiments. The CD algorithm converges within 100 rounds in all cases in our experiments.

Tang *et al.* [22] pointed out that, for the IM algorithm, to achieve a $(1 - \frac{1}{e} - \varepsilon)$-approximation of the optimal solution with at least $1 - \frac{1}{n}$ probability, the number of hyper edges mH should be set to at least $\frac{2n(1-\frac{1}{e})(\log\binom{n}{k} + \log n + \log 2)}{OPT\varepsilon^2}$. Therefore, when mH is fixed and the influence spread of the solution of the IM algorithm is known, we can figure out ε accordingly, and know how good the solution is. Thus, we also report the approximation lower bound of the influence maximization algorithm. Here we use the influence spread of the seed set returned by the IM algorithm as a lower bound of OPT. Fig. 4 shows that the approximation lower bound of the IM algorithm under our experimental settings is greater than 55% usually. Note that $(1 - \frac{1}{e}) \approx 63\%$ is the approximation upper bound of any polynomial time algorithm if $P \neq NP$. This means our implementation of the baseline algorithm (IM) in the experiments is fairly good.

Fig. 5 shows how the influence spread varies with respect to the unified discount c in the Unified Discount algorithm. Limited by space, we only report the influence values when $\alpha = 1$ and $B = 50$ on each dataset. From Fig. 5 we can see that finding a best unified discount is necessary because different values of c can result in very different influence spreads.

Dataset	B	1% Search Step	5% Search Step	Reduction Percentage
Wiki-Vote	10	311	311	0%
	20	463	460	0.7%
	30	562	562	0%
	40	650	642	1.2%
	50	719	710	1.3%
Ca-Astro	10	1241	1241	0%
	20	1760	1760	0%
	30	2120	2120	0%
	40	2422	2422	0%
	50	2680	2680	0%
Com-Dblp	10	1896	1896	0%
	20	3290	3290	0%
	30	4489	4489	0%
	40	5578	5563	0.3%
	50	6557	6530	0.4%
Com-LiveJournal	10	46906	46845	0.1%
	20	69185	69126	0.1%
	30	86469	86469	0%
	40	100027	99948	0.1%
	50	111086	110967	0.1%

Table 3: Effect of the parameter search step in calculating the best unified discount c.

We also tested the effectiveness of the search step 5% we chose in the Unified Discount algorithm. Table 3 shows the difference of using 1% and 5% as the search step when finding the best unified discount c. Here α was set to 1. The column "Reduction Percentage" means how much influence the best spread is decreased if we change the search step from 1% to 5%. From Table 3 we find that the reduction is tiny. In other words, the Unified Discount algorithm is insensitive to this parameter.

9.2.2 *Sensitivity to User Purchase Probability Curves*

We also tested the sensitivity of our methods with respect to user purchase probability curves. We still used the three purchase probability curves mentioned in Section 9.1, since they are representative and stand for users being sensitive to discounts, benchmark sensitivity to discounts and user being insensitive to discounts, respectively. To test the effect of purchase probability curves on the results, we reduced the portion of sensitive users and correspondingly increased the number of insensitive users. Specifically, for each social network, we randomly generated another two instances of it where different populations were assigned to those purchase probability curves. In the first instance, the portions of the three purchase probability curves were changed to 75%, 15% and 10%, respectively. In the second instance, 65%, 20% and 15%, respectively. We ran our methods on those new instances by setting $\alpha = 1$. Then we compared the new results with the original result where there are 85% sensitive users.

Table 4 shows the changes. Please note that different assignments of purchase probability curves to users may lead to different results. Moreover, it is possible that influence spread is higher when the portion of sensitive users is smaller. This is because the purchase probability curves were randomly assigned to users. Thus, even when the portion of sensitive users is smaller, it is possible that more influential users are assigned with sensitive purchase probability curves. We ran a good number of random assignments on the four data sets. The results are consistent in trend. From Table 4 we can see that the influence spread only decreases slightly after we reduced the number of sensitive users.

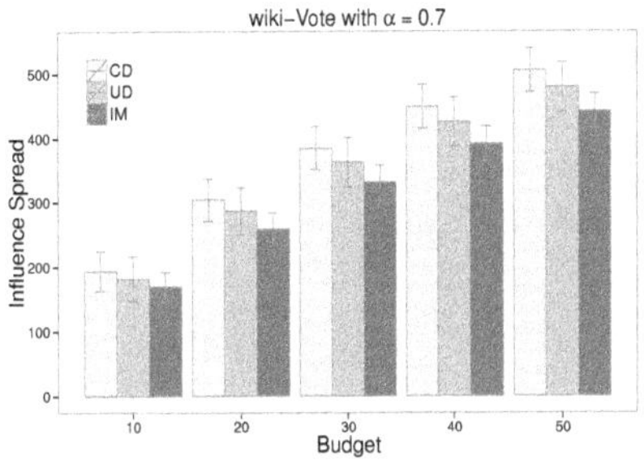

(a) on wiki-Vote with $\alpha = 0.7$

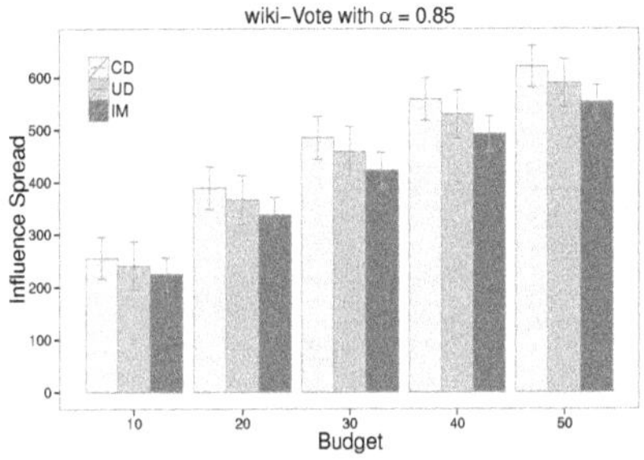

(b) on wiki-Vote with $\alpha = 0.85$

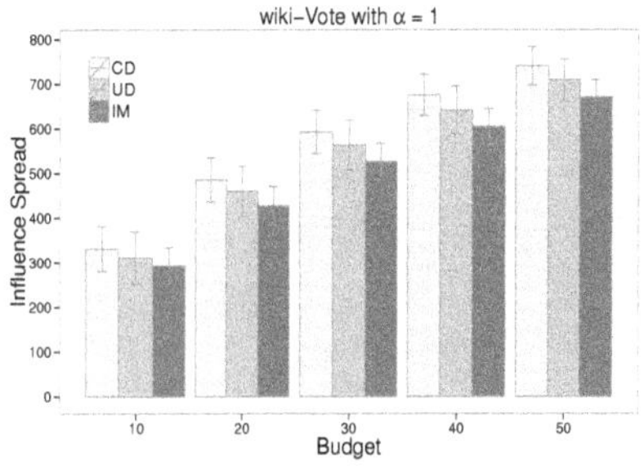

(c) on wiki-Vote with $\alpha = 1$

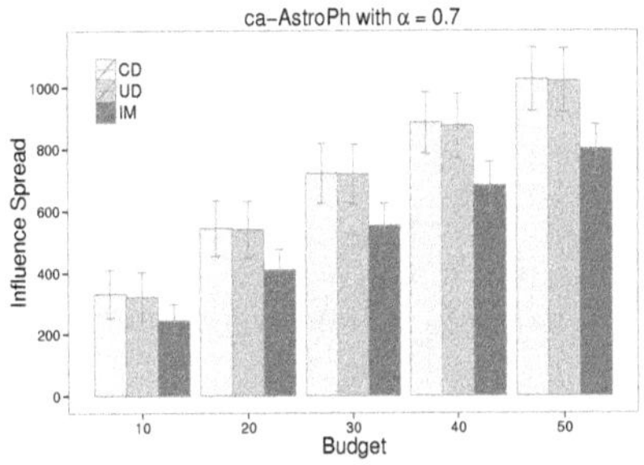

(d) on ca-AstroPh with $\alpha = 0.7$

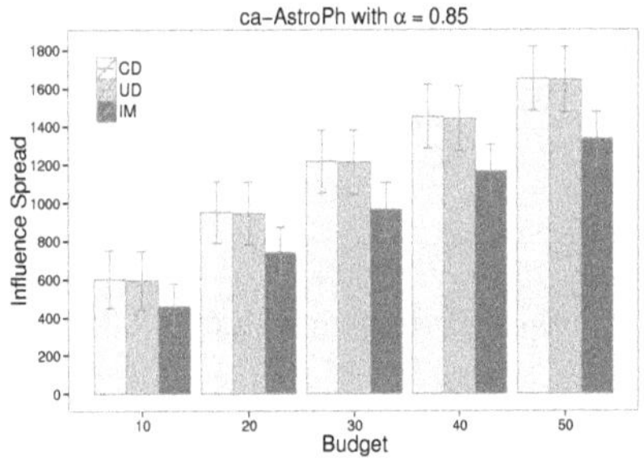

(e) on ca-AstroPh with $\alpha = 0.85$

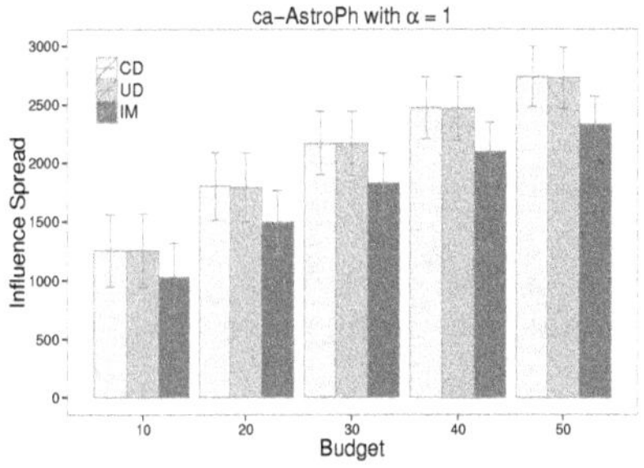

(f) on ca-AstroPh with $\alpha = 1$

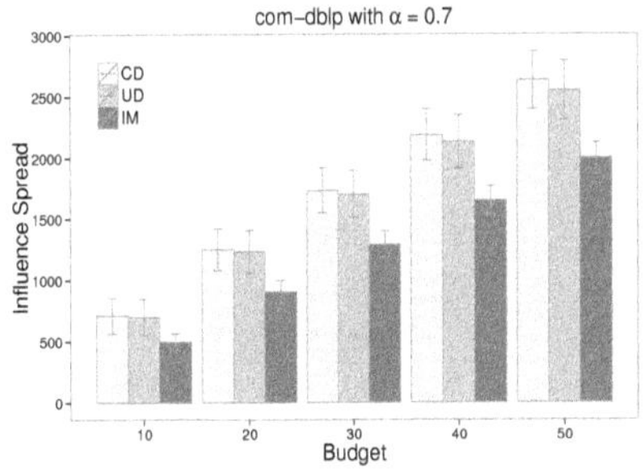

(g) on com-dblp with $\alpha = 0.7$

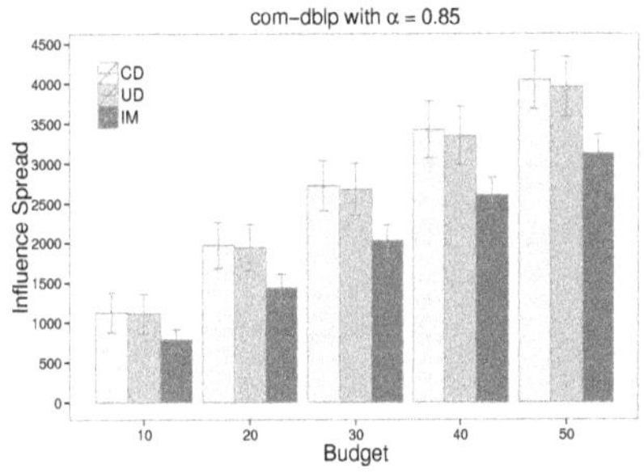

(h) on com-dblp with $\alpha = 0.85$

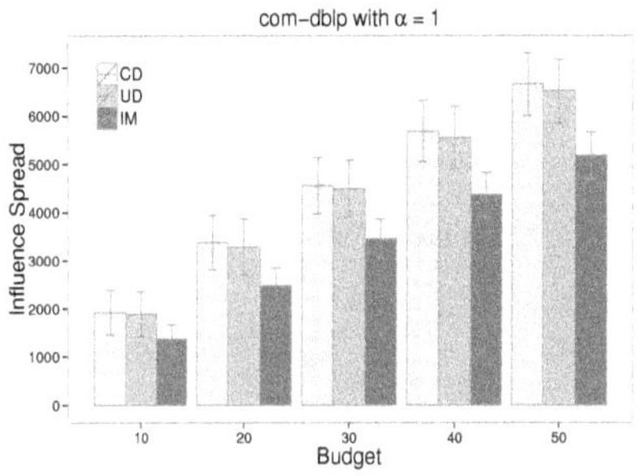

(i) on com-dblp with $\alpha = 1$

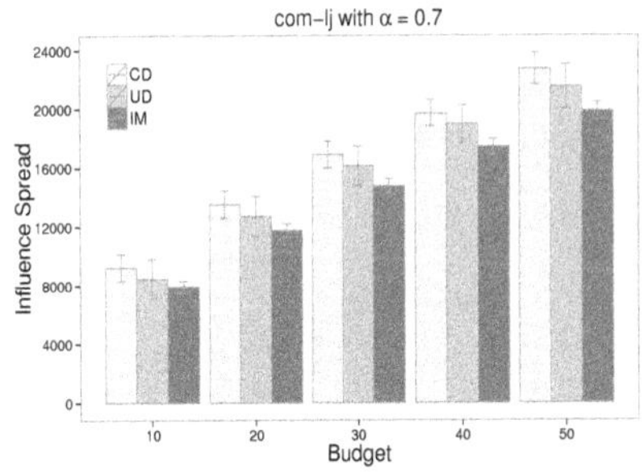

(j) on com-LiveJournal with $\alpha = 0.7$

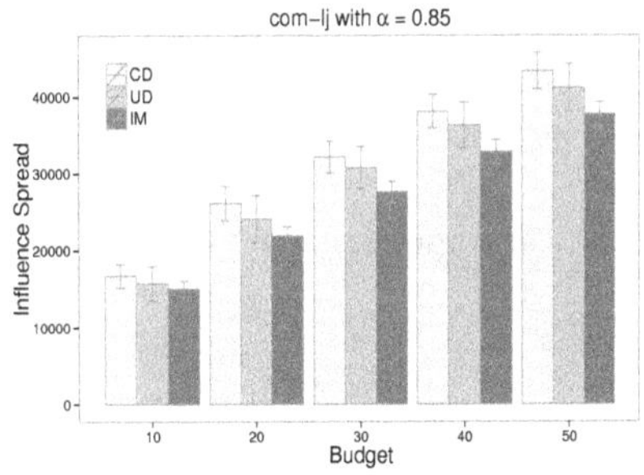

(k) on com-LiveJournal with $\alpha = 0.85$

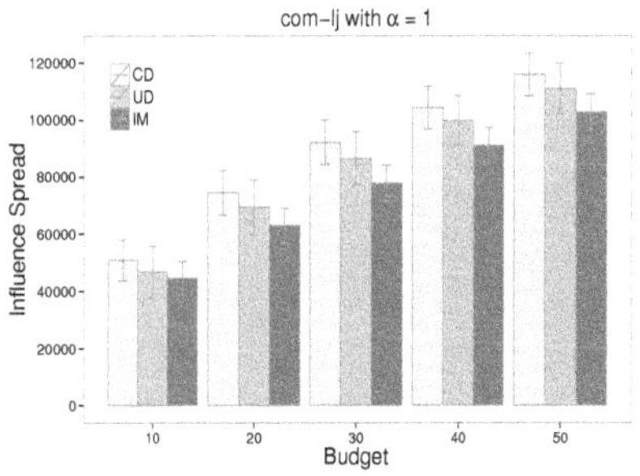

(l) on com-LiveJournal with $\alpha = 1$

Figure 3: Influence spread

9.2.3 Scalability

We also tested the scalability of the algorithm and report the results in Fig. 6. GBT is the time of building the hypergraph. According to Fig 6, as the scale of network increases, the gap on the running time between our algorithm and the of the IM algorithm decreases. On the smallest dataset wiki-Vote, the running time of the Coordinate Descent algorithm is about 10 times of that of IM. The gap is reduced to no more than 4 times on the ca-AstroPh dataset and less than twice on the com-dblp dataset. On the largest dataset com-LiveJournal, the running time of the CD algorithm is only 1.5 times of that of IM. The reason is that the computational cost of building the hypergraph is high, while the configuration computation phase is relatively efficient. In addition, we only ran at most 100 rounds of iterations in CD in all experiments, and in each round we only need to optimize over $O(k^2)$ pairs of c_i and c_j, if the initial value of CD has k non-zero entries. Thus, in smaller networks, the portion of iterations in total running time is higher because the cost of CD iterations is relatively stable while the cost of building hyper graph is proportional to the scale of the network.

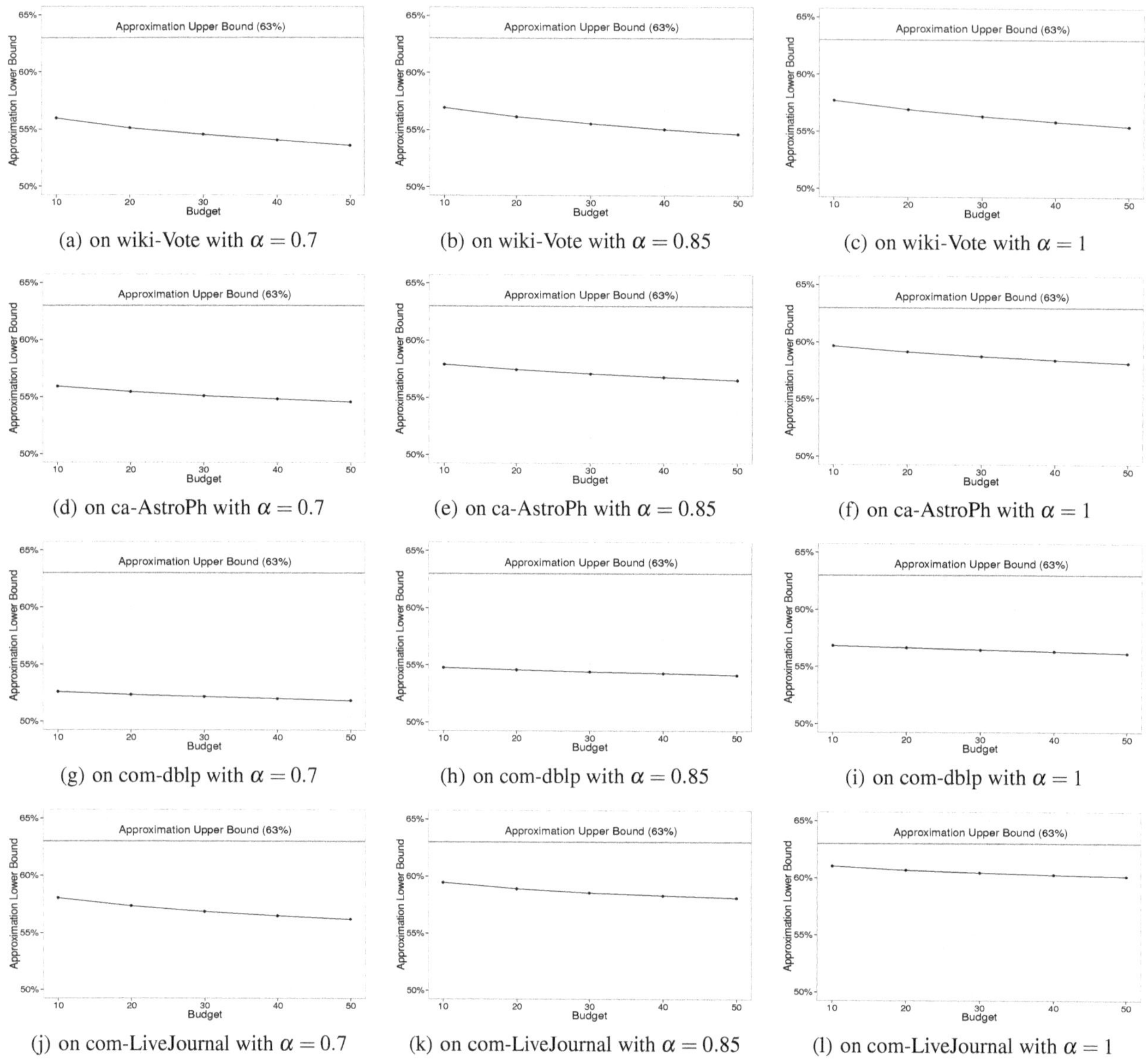

(a) on wiki-Vote with $\alpha = 0.7$ (b) on wiki-Vote with $\alpha = 0.85$ (c) on wiki-Vote with $\alpha = 1$

(d) on ca-AstroPh with $\alpha = 0.7$ (e) on ca-AstroPh with $\alpha = 0.85$ (f) on ca-AstroPh with $\alpha = 1$

(g) on com-dblp with $\alpha = 0.7$ (h) on com-dblp with $\alpha = 0.85$ (i) on com-dblp with $\alpha = 1$

(j) on com-LiveJournal with $\alpha = 0.7$ (k) on com-LiveJournal with $\alpha = 0.85$ (l) on com-LiveJournal with $\alpha = 1$

Figure 4: Approximation Lower Bound

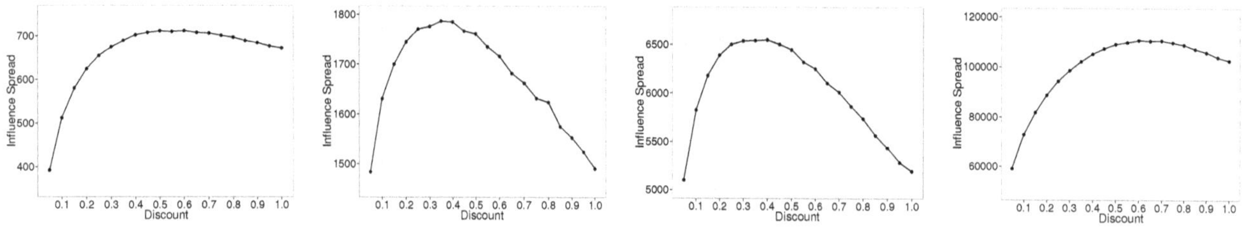

(a) on wiki-Vote with $\alpha = 1$ and $B = 50$ (b) on ca-AstroPh with $\alpha = 1$ and $B = 50$ (c) on com-dblp with $\alpha = 1$ and $B = 50$ (d) on com-LiveJournal with $\alpha = 1$ and $B = 50$

Figure 5: Influence Spread w.r.t. unified discount c

10. CONCLUSIONS

In this paper, we proposed to offer users in social networks discounts rather than free products to trigger social cascades. We model the continuous influence maximization problem. Some key properties of the continuous influence maximization problem were studied and a coordinate descent framework was devised. Based on this framework, we proved that under certain conditions the continuous influence maximization problem and the original influence maximization problem share the same optimal solutions. We

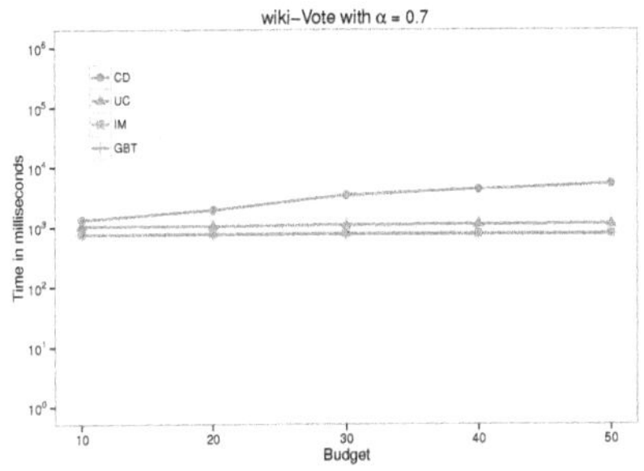

(a) on wiki-Vote with $\alpha = 0.7$

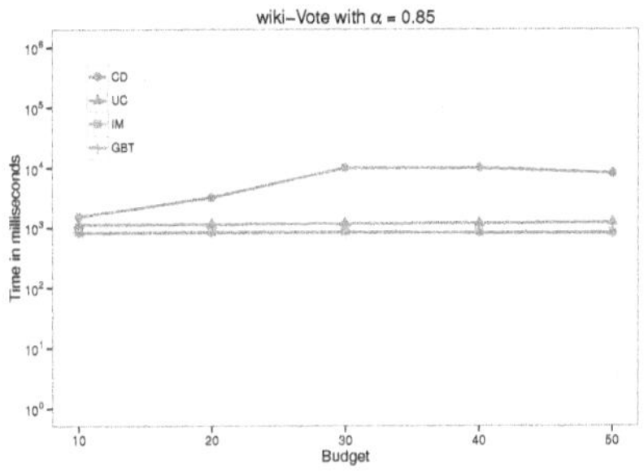

(b) on wiki-Vote with $\alpha = 0.85$

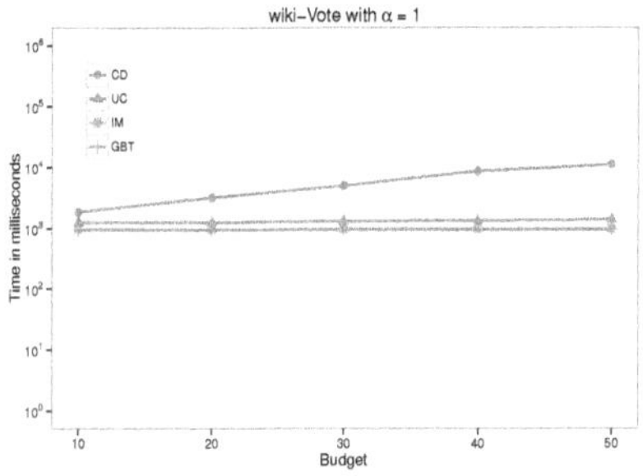

(c) on wiki-Vote with $\alpha = 1$

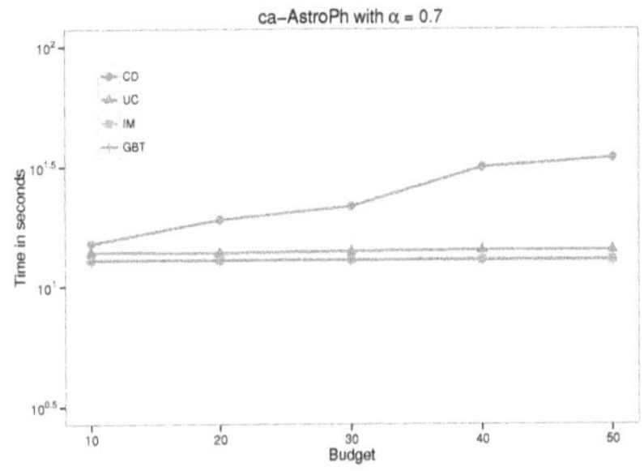

(d) on ca-AstroPh with $\alpha = 0.7$

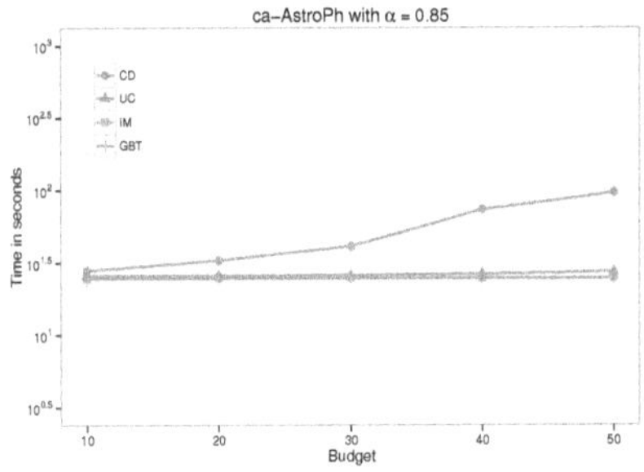

(e) on ca-AstroPh with $\alpha = 0.85$

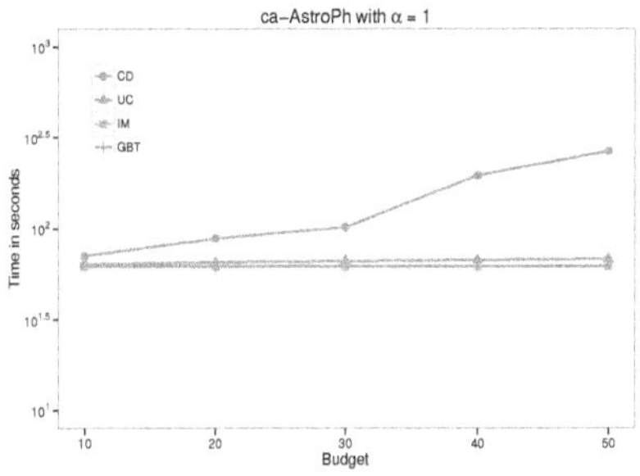

(f) on ca-AstroPh with $\alpha = 1$

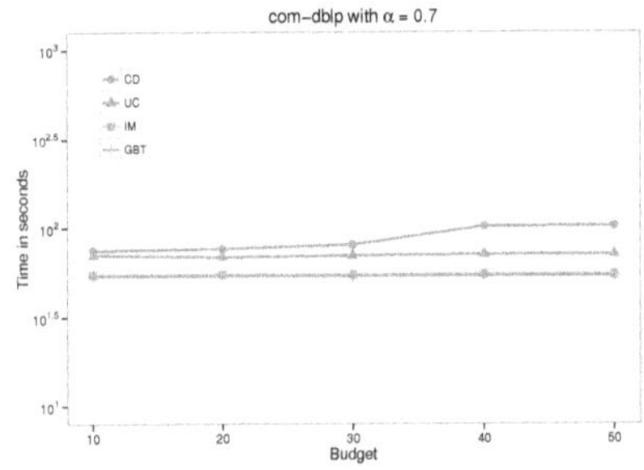

(g) on com-dblp with $\alpha = 0.7$

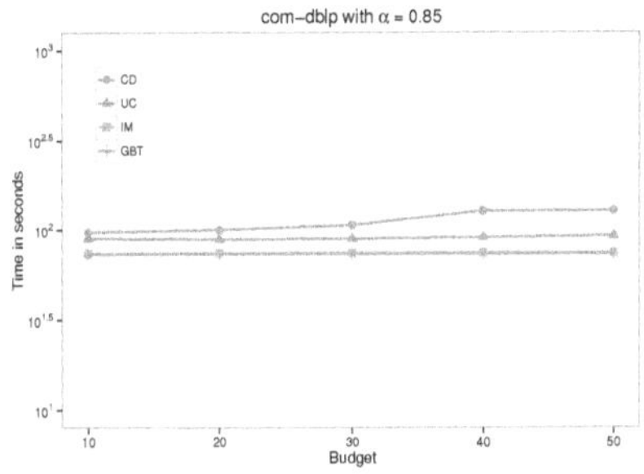

(h) on com-dblp with $\alpha = 0.85$

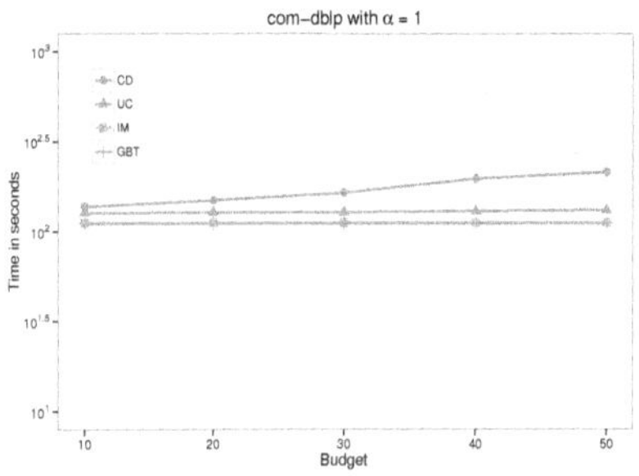

(i) on com-dblp with $\alpha = 1$

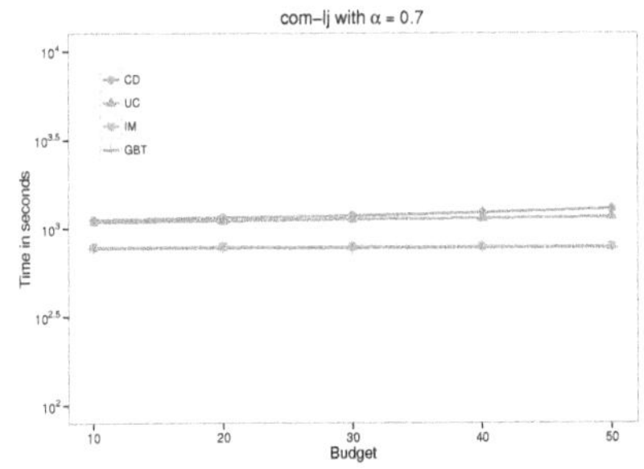

(j) on com-LiveJournal with $\alpha = 0.7$

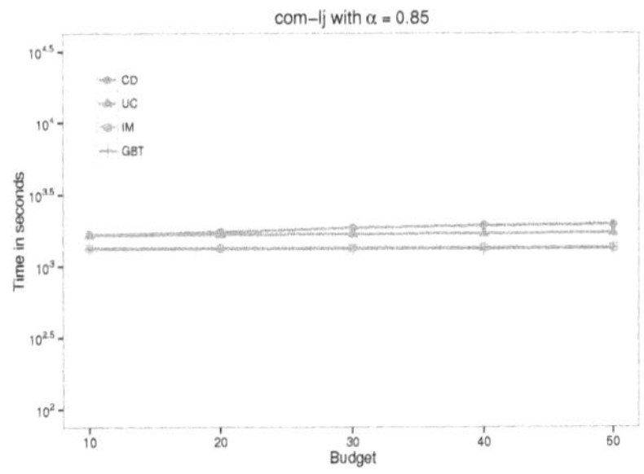

(k) on com-LiveJournal with $\alpha = 0.85$

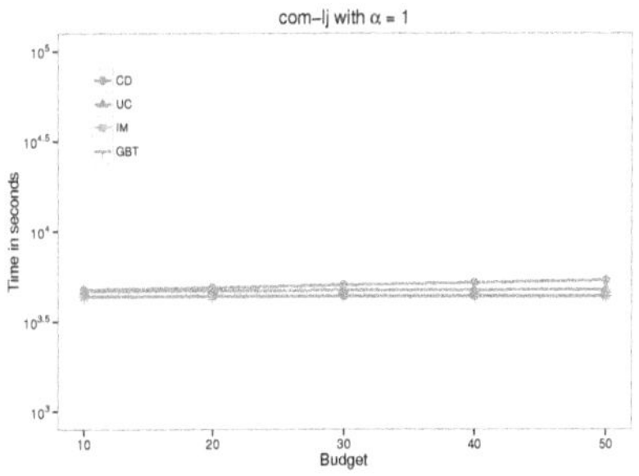

(l) on com-LiveJournal with $\alpha = 1$

Figure 6: Running time

then pointed out the key challenges in practically implementing the coordinate descent framework and proposed feasible engineering techniques that work in practice. The experiment results demonstrated that our methods can improve influence spread significantly, while the extra running time over the classical discrete influence maximization algorithm remains moderate.

We believe that this work opens a new direction for future work. For example, it is imperative to investigate whether our objective function $UI(C)$ is convex or concave, and how the form of $p_u(c_u)$ may affect the convexity/concavity of $UI(C)$? Moreover, the coordinate descent algorithm is only guaranteed to converge to a stationary point. Under what conditions can it converge to a local optima? Efficient continuous influence maximization algorithms for specific influence models are essential for real life applications. For example, in the experiments, we designed two simple algorithms Unified Discount (UD) and Coordinate Descent (CD) that work well in practice. In UD, we conduct a brute force search for finding the optimal discount c. Is there a better algorithm for searching c? For

Dataset	B	Unified Discount					Coordinate Descent				
		85% Sensitive	75% Sensitive	Reduction Percentage	65% Sensitive	Reduction Percentage	85% Sensitive	75% Sensitive	Reduction Percentage	65% Sensitive	Reduction Percentage
Wiki-Vote	10	311	319	-2.6%	319	-2.6%	332	332	0%	337	-1.5%
	20	460	463	-0.7%	455	1.1%	487	480	1.4%	473	2.9%
	30	562	564	-0.4%	551	2.0%	593	586	1.2%	575	3.0%
	40	642	648	-1.0%	631	1.7%	675	671	0.6%	656	2.8%
	50	710	715	-0.7%	696	2.0%	745	742	0.4%	725	2.7%
Ca-Astro	10	1241	1251	-0.8%	1173	5.5%	1252	1269	-1.4%	1184	5.4%
	20	1760	1754	0.3%	1663	5.5%	1785	1785	0%	1698	4.9%
	30	2120	2111	0.4%	2027	4.4%	2159	2147	0.6%	2065	4.4%
	40	2422	2405	0.7%	2328	3.9%	2461	2445	0.7%	2370	3.7%
	50	2680	2656	0.9%	2577	3.8%	2720	2702	0.9%	2626	3.5%
Com-Dblp	10	1896	1861	1.9%	1827	3.8%	1925	1917	0.4%	1882	2.2%
	20	3290	3210	2.4%	3158	4.0%	3338	3271	2.0%	3220	3.5%
	30	4489	4356	3.0%	4284	4.6%	4650	4449	4.3%	4379	5.8%
	40	5563	5409	2.8%	5331	4.2%	5694	5564	2.3%	5471	4.0%
	50	6530	6371	2.4%	6273	4.0%	6675	6522	2.3%	6429	3.7%
Com-LiveJournal	10	46845	46973	-0.3%	46722	0.3%	51500	48423	6.0%	49630	3.6%
	20	69126	68605	0.8%	67763	2.0%	74309	72675	2.2%	71909	3.2%
	30	86469	85536	1.1%	83237	3.7%	92201	90524	1.8%	85653	7.1%
	40	99948	98766	1.2%	95897	4.1%	104267	102080	2.1%	100541	3.6%
	50	110967	109660	1.2%	106268	4.2%	115870	113364	2.2%	111568	3.7%

Table 4: Sensitivity to user purchase probability curves.

both UD and CD, how does the number of hyper-edges mH affect the quality of the solutions?

Another interesting direction to investigate is minimizing the budget of our continuous seeding strategy for covering a given portion of users in a social network. While minimizing budget under integer seeding strategy can be easily obtained by slightly modifying the greedy algorithm for influence maximization, it is far from trivial to design a new algorithm for our continuous seeding strategy.

11. REFERENCES

[1] C. Borgs, M. Brautbar, J. Chayes, and B. Lucier. Maximizing social influence in nearly optimal time. In *Proceedings of the Twenty-Fifth Annual ACM-SIAM Symposium on Discrete Algorithms*, pages 946–957. SIAM, 2014.

[2] M. Brennan. Constructing demand curves from purchase probability data: an application of the juster scale. *Marketing Bulletin*, 6(May):51–58, 1995.

[3] W. Chen, L. V. Lakshmanan, and C. Castillo. Information and influence propagation in social networks. *Synthesis Lectures on Data Management*, 5(4):1–177, 2013.

[4] W. Chen, C. Wang, and Y. Wang. Scalable influence maximization for prevalent viral marketing in large-scale social networks. In *Proceedings of the 16th ACM SIGKDD international conference on Knowledge discovery and data mining*, pages 1029–1038. ACM, 2010.

[5] W. Chen, Y. Wang, and S. Yang. Efficient influence maximization in social networks. In *Proceedings of the 15th ACM SIGKDD international conference on Knowledge discovery and data mining*, pages 199–208. ACM, 2009.

[6] W. Chen, Y. Yuan, and L. Zhang. Scalable influence maximization in social networks under the linear threshold model. In *Data Mining (ICDM), 2010 IEEE 10th International Conference on*, pages 88–97. IEEE, 2010.

[7] Y. B. Cho, Y. H. Cho, and S. H. Kim. Mining changes in customer buying behavior for collaborative recommendations. *Expert Systems with Applications*, 28(2):359–369, 2005.

[8] P. Domingos and M. Richardson. Mining the network value of customers. In *Proceedings of the seventh ACM SIGKDD international conference on Knowledge discovery and data mining*, pages 57–66. ACM, 2001.

[9] N. Du, L. Song, M. Gomez-Rodriguez, and H. Zha. Scalable influence estimation in continuous-time diffusion networks. In *Advances in Neural Information Processing Systems*, pages 3147–3155, 2013.

[10] M. Eftekhar, Y. Ganjali, and N. Koudas. Information cascade at group scale. In *Proceedings of the 19th ACM SIGKDD international conference on Knowledge discovery and data mining*, pages 401–409. ACM, 2013.

[11] M. Farajtabar, N. Du, M. Gomez-Rodriguez, I. Valera, H. Zha, and L. Song. Shaping social activity by incentivizing users. In *NIPS*, 2014.

[12] A. Goyal, W. Lu, and L. V. Lakshmanan. Simpath: An efficient algorithm for influence maximization under the linear threshold model. In *Data Mining (ICDM), 2011 IEEE 11th International Conference on*, pages 211–220. IEEE, 2011.

[13] D. Kempe, J. Kleinberg, and É. Tardos. Maximizing the spread of influence through a social network. In *Proceedings of the ninth ACM SIGKDD international conference on Knowledge discovery and data mining*, pages 137–146. ACM, 2003.

[14] S. Lei, S. Maniu, L. Mo, R. Cheng, and P. Senellart. Online influence maximization. In *Proceedings of the 21st ACM SIGKDD international conference on Knowledge discovery and data mining*, pages 645–654. ACM, 2015.

[15] J. Leskovec, A. Krause, C. Guestrin, C. Faloutsos, J. VanBriesen, and N. Glance. Cost-effective outbreak detection in networks. In *Proceedings of the 13th ACM SIGKDD international conference on Knowledge discovery and data mining*, pages 420–429. ACM, 2007.

[16] C. Long and R.-W. Wong. Minimizing seed set for viral marketing. In *Data Mining (ICDM), 2011 IEEE 11th International Conference on*, pages 427–436. IEEE, 2011.

[17] M. Mitzenmacher and E. Upfal. *Probability and computing: Randomized algorithms and probabilistic analysis.* Cambridge University Press, 2005.

[18] E. Mossel and S. Roch. On the submodularity of influence in social networks. In *Proceedings of the 39th annual ACM*

symposium on Theory of computing, pages 128–134. ACM, 2007.

[19] H. Nguyen and R. Zheng. On budgeted influence maximization in social networks. *Selected Areas in Communications, IEEE Journal on*, 31(6):1084–1094, 2013.

[20] Y. Singer. How to win friends and influence people, truthfully: influence maximization mechanisms for social networks. In *Proceedings of the fifth ACM international conference on Web search and data mining*, pages 733–742. ACM, 2012.

[21] E. Suh, S. Lim, H. Hwang, and S. Kim. A prediction model for the purchase probability of anonymous customers to support real time web marketing: a case study. *Expert Systems with Applications*, 27(2):245–255, 2004.

[22] Y. Tang, Y. Shi, and X. Xiao. Influence maximization in near-linear time: A martingale approach. In *Proceedings of the 2015 ACM SIGMOD international conference on Management of data*. ACM, 2015.

[23] Y. Tang, X. Xiao, and Y. Shi. Influence maximization: Near-optimal time complexity meets practical efficiency. In *Proceedings of the 2014 ACM SIGMOD international conference on Management of data*, pages 75–86. ACM, 2014.

[24] G. Ventures. Business advertising. http://www.gaebler.com/Business-Advertising.htm.

[25] Y. Wang, W. Huang, L. Zong, T. Wang, and D. Yang. Influence maximization with limit cost in social network. *Science China Information Sciences*, 56(7):1–14, 2013.

Appendix

Proof of Theorem 1 We prove by a simple reduction from computing $I(S)$. For any S, we can make a configuration C such that $c_u = 1$ if $u \in S$ and $c_u = 0$ otherwise. Clearly we have $UI(C) = I(S)$. Thus, if computing $I(S)$ is #P-hard, so is computing $UI(C)$. ∎

Proof of Theorem 2 Recall that $UI(C) = \sum_{S \in 2^V} Pr(S;V,C)I(S)$. $\forall S \in 2^V$, we have $0 \le I(S) \le n$. We can estimate $UI(C)$ by a Monte Carlo method. By applying the Hoeffding bound, we have

$$Pr(|\widehat{UI}(C) - UI(C)| \ge \varepsilon UI(C)) \le 2e^{-\frac{2R^2\varepsilon^2 UI^2(C)}{Rn^2}},$$

where R is the number of MC simulations. Since $UI(C) \ge \sum_{u \in V} p_u(c_u)$, to achieve the goal that $Pr(|\widehat{UI}(C) - UI(C)| \ge \varepsilon UI(C)) \le \delta$, we can set $R \ge \frac{n^2 \ln \frac{2}{\delta}}{2\varepsilon^2(\sum_{u\in V} p_u(c_u))^2}$. ∎

Proof of Theorem 3 If there is a FPRAS for estimating $I(S)$, in $O(\mathrm{POLY}(\frac{n}{\varepsilon'}\ln\frac{1}{\delta'}))$ time we can obtain an (ε', δ') approximation of $I(S)$. If we set $\delta' = \frac{\delta_1}{O(\mathrm{POLY}(\frac{n}{\varepsilon'}\ln\frac{1}{\delta_1}))}$, the time we need is $O(\mathrm{POLY}(\frac{n}{\varepsilon'}\ln\frac{O(\mathrm{POLY}(\frac{n}{\varepsilon'}\ln\frac{1}{\delta_1}))}{\delta_1})) = O(\mathrm{POLY}(\frac{n}{\varepsilon'}\ln\frac{1}{\delta_1}))$.

According to Theorem 2, if we can access the value of $I(S)$, we can have an (ε', δ_1) approximation of $UI(C)$ by calling the oracle $O(\mathrm{POLY}(\frac{n}{\varepsilon'}\ln\frac{1}{\delta_1}))$ times. Suppose $R = O(\mathrm{POLY}(\frac{n}{\varepsilon'}\ln\frac{1}{\delta_1}))$, and we have R randomly generated seed sets $\{S_1, S_2, ..., S_R\}$. Let $\widehat{UI}(C) = \sum_{i=1}^{R} I(S_i)$, $\widehat{I}(S_i)$ be the estimated influence spread of S_i using the FPRAS in $O(\mathrm{POLY}(\frac{n}{\varepsilon'}\ln\frac{1}{\delta_1}))$ time, and $\widehat{\widehat{UI}}(C) = \sum_{i=1}^{R}\widehat{I}(S_i)$. Clearly, $Pr\{|\widehat{UI}(C) - UI(C)| > \varepsilon' UI(C)\} < \delta_1$, and $Pr\{|\widehat{\widehat{UI}}(C) - \widehat{UI}(C)| > \varepsilon'\widehat{UI}(C)\} < \delta_1$ (by Union Bound). Applying union bound, we have $Pr\{|\widehat{\widehat{UI}}(C) - UI(C)| < \varepsilon'(2+\varepsilon')UI(C)\} > 1 - 2\delta_1$.

Setting $\varepsilon'(2+\varepsilon') = \varepsilon$ and $2\delta_1 = \delta$, which means $\varepsilon' = \sqrt{1+\varepsilon} - 1$ and $\delta_1 = \frac{\delta}{2}$, we can obtain an (ε, δ) approximation of $UI(C)$ in $O(\mathrm{POLY}(\frac{n}{\varepsilon'}\ln\frac{1}{\delta_1})) \times O(\mathrm{POLY}(\frac{n}{\varepsilon'}\ln\frac{1}{\delta_1})) = O(\mathrm{POLY}(\frac{n}{\varepsilon'}\ln\frac{1}{\delta_1}))$ time. Note that $\frac{1}{\varepsilon'} = \frac{1}{\sqrt{1+\varepsilon}-1} = \frac{\sqrt{\varepsilon+1}+1}{\varepsilon} \le \frac{3}{\varepsilon} = O(\frac{1}{\varepsilon})$, and $\ln\frac{1}{\delta_1} = O(\ln\frac{1}{\delta})$. So in $O(\mathrm{POLY}(\frac{n}{\varepsilon}\ln\frac{1}{\delta}))$ time we can have an (ε, δ) approximation of $UI(C)$. ∎

Proof of Theorem 4 We firstly prove $UI(C)$ equals the influence spread of a fixed seed sets on a gadget graph. Given a graph $G = \langle V, E\rangle$ and a configuration C, we create a gadget graph $G' = \langle V', E'\rangle$ by adding a gadget node u' for each node u in G, and adding a direct edge (u', u) with propagation probability $p_u(c_u)$. Using the equivalent live edges random process of independent cascade model or linear threshold model [13], it can be easily proved that $UI(C) = I(V' - V) - n$. So we can use the same Monte Carlo simulation for computing influence spread of a given seed set to estimate $I(V' - V)$ and then obtain $UI(C)$. Applying a simple Hoeffding bound to obtain an (ε, δ) approximation of $UI(C)$, we obtain the number of Monte Carlo simulations needed as $O(\frac{n^2\ln\frac{1}{\delta}}{2\varepsilon^2(\sum_{u\in V} p_u(c_u))^2})$. Since each Monte Carlo simulation takes $O(m)$ time. in total we can have an (ε, δ) approximation of $UI(C)$ in $O(\frac{mn^2\ln\frac{1}{\delta}}{2\varepsilon^2(\sum_{u\in V} p_u(c_u))^2})$ time. ∎

Proof of Lemma 1 Because $p_u(c_u)$ is monotonic with respect to c_u, we have $p_u(c_u^1) \ge p_u(c_u^2)$. Thus, $p_u(c_u^1) - p_u(c_u^2) = \alpha \ge 0$. We have

$$\begin{aligned} UI(C) = &\sum_{S\in 2^{V-\{u\}}} Pr(S; V - \{u\}, C)I(S)[1 - p_u(c_u)] + \\ &\sum_{S\in 2^{V-\{u\}}} Pr(S; V - \{u\}, C)I(S \cup \{u\})p_u(c_u) \end{aligned}$$

Therefore,

$$\begin{aligned} &UI(C_1) - UI(C_2) \\ &= \sum_{S\in 2^{V-\{u\}}} Pr(S; V - \{u\}, C_1)I(S \cup \{u\})\alpha \\ &- \sum_{S\in 2^{V-\{u\}}} Pr(S; V - \{u\}, C_2)I(S)\alpha \\ &= \sum_{S\in 2^{V-\{u\}}} \alpha Pr(S; V - \{u\}, C_2)[I(S \cup \{u\}) - I(S)] \end{aligned}$$

Due to the monotonicity of $I(S)$, $I(S \cup \{u\}) - I(S) \ge 0$ and $UI(C_1) - UI(C_2) \ge 0$. Thus, we have $UI(C_1) \ge UI(C_2)$. ∎

Proof of Theorem 6 The major idea of our proof is to show that, for an arbitrary feasible configuration C, there is an integer configuration C' such that $UI(C') \ge UI(C)$. As $p_u(c_u) \le c_u$ stated in the theorem, we consider two cases.

First, we consider the situation where $\forall u \in V, p_u(c_u) = c_u$. For any feasible configuration C, in Line 3 of Algorithm 1, if C contains a component c_i that is not an integer, since B is an integer, C must contains another component c_j $(i \ne j)$ such that c_j is not an integer, either. Therefore, we can always pick non-integers c_i and c_j. Then, we optimize over c_i and c_j by solving the optimization problem in Eq. 7. Due to Eq. 9, we have

$$\begin{aligned} UI(C) = &(A_1 + A_2 - A_3 - A_4)c_i(B' - c_i) + \\ &(A_3 - A_1)c_i + (A_4 - A_1)(B' - c_i) \end{aligned}$$

which is a quadratic form of c_i and the coefficient of the quadratic term is $-(A_1+A_2-A_3-A_4)$. Since $I(S)$ is submodular, we have $I(S\cup\{i,j\})-I(S\cup\{j\})\leq I(S\cup\{i\})-I(S)$. Thus, $(A_1+A_2-A_3-A_4)\leq 0$, which means $UI(C)$ is a convex function with respect to c_i. Therefore, the value of x that makes $\frac{dUI(C)}{dc_i}|_{c_i=x}=0$ is the global minimum. Since we are interested in only the maximum, we can ignore the root of $\frac{dUI(C)}{dc_i}=0$ completely. This means that, after optimization, c_i must be either $max(0,B'-1)$ or $min(B',1)$.

Let us examine the value of c_i and c_j after optimization under different situations of B'. There are two possible cases.

- If $B'\geq 1$, then $B'-1\leq c_i\leq 1$. After optimization over c_i and c_j, if $c_i=B'-1$, then $c_j=1$. If $c_i=1$, then $c_j=B'-1$.
- If $B'<1$, then $0\leq c_i\leq B'$. After optimization over c_i and c_j, if $c_i=0$, then $c_j=B'$. If $c_i=B'$, then $c_j=0$.

Thus, after optimization over c_i and c_j, at least one variable of c_i and c_j takes an integer value. In other words, after one iteration we eliminate at least one non-integer c_u. Apparently, after at most n iterations we can make all c_u's integers. Since in every iteration the objective function does not decrease, the final integer configuration C' can achieve an influence spread no smaller than the initial configuration. Therefore, we only need to consider integer configurations, which means CIM degenerates into DIM.

Second, we consider the situation when there exists at least one node u such that $p_u(c_u)<c_u$. In other words, we consider for each u, $p_u(c_u)\leq c_u$. Let $\bar{p}_u(c_u)$ be the seed probability function such that for each u, $\bar{p}_u(c_u)=c_u$. Denote by $\overline{UI}(C)$ be the influence spread using $\bar{p}_u(c_u)$ with respect to configuration C. For each u, due to the assumption that $\bar{p}_u(\cdot)$ is continuous, we have $\bar{c}_u$ such that $p_u(c_u)=\bar{p}_u(\bar{c}_u)\leq c_u=\bar{p}_u(c_u)$. Consider two configurations $C=(c_1,\ldots,c_n)$ and $\overline{C}=(\bar{c}_1,\ldots,\bar{c}_n)$. Clearly, $\overline{C}\preceq C$. Due to the monotonicity of $UI(C)$, we have $UI(C)=\overline{UI}(\overline{C})\leq\overline{UI}(C)$. As the first case, we already prove that $\overline{UI}(C)$ has the same objectives in CIM and DIM when C is an integer configuration. Note that for any integer configuration C, $UI(C)=\overline{UI}(C)$. Thus, the theorem holds in this general case. ∎

Proof of Theorem 7 Suppose in this iteration c_i and c_j are picked for optimization. Clearly after optimization over c_i and c_j, if c_i and c_j change, then one of them increases and the other decreases, because the sum of c_i and c_j remains a constant. Without loss of generality, assume c_i increases by α and $p_i(c_i+\alpha)-p_i(c_i)=\beta$. Apparently, since $0\leq p_i(c_i)\leq 1$ and $p_i(c_i)$ is monotonic, $\beta\leq 1$.

Let C_2 be a new configuration such that $C_2(j)=C_1(j)+\alpha$ and all other entries of C_2 are identical to those in C_1. Due to the monotonicity of $UI(C)$, since $C_2\succeq C_1$, we have $UI(C_2)\geq UI(C_1)$. Moreover,

$$UI(C_2)-UI(C)=\beta\sum_{S\in 2^{V-\{i\}}}Pr(S;V-\{i\},C)\big(I(S\cup\{u\})-I(S)\big).$$

Therefore,

$$\begin{aligned}&UI(C_1)-UI(C)\leq UI(C_2)-UI(C)\\&\leq\sum_{S\in 2^{V-\{i\}}}Pr(S;V-\{i\},C)\big(I(S\cup\{u\})-I(S)\big)\\&\leq\operatorname*{argmax}_{u\in V}\sum_{S\in 2^{V-\{u\}}}Pr(S;V-\{u\},C)\big(I(S\cup\{u\})-I(S)\big)\end{aligned}$$

∎

Proof of Theorem 8 The monotonicity can be immediately proved using Theorem 5. Next, we show the submodularity of $UI(S;c)$.

Suppose we have two sets S_1 and S_2 such that $S_1\cup\{v\}=S_2$. Let u be a node such that $u\notin S_2$. Then,

$$\begin{aligned}&UI(S_1\cup\{u\};c)-UI(S_1;c)\\&=\sum_{S\in 2^{S_1}}Pr(S;S_1,c)\Big(p_u(c)I(S\cup\{u\})+(1-p_u(c))I(S)\Big)-\\&\quad\sum_{S\in 2^{S_1}}Pr(S;S_1,c)I(S)\\&=p_u(c)\sum_{S\in 2^{S_1}}Pr(S;S_1,c)\Big(I(S\cup\{u\})-I(S)\Big)\end{aligned}$$

We also have

$$\begin{aligned}&UI(S_2\cup\{u\};c)-UI(S_2;c)\\&=\sum_{S\in 2^{S_1}}Pr(S;S_1,c)\Big(p_v(c)p_u(c)I(S\cup\{u,v\})+\\&\qquad p_v(c)(1-p_u(c))I(S\cup\{v\})+\\&\qquad p_u(c)(1-p_v(c))I(S\cup\{u\})+\\&\qquad (1-p_u(c))(1-p_v(c))I(S)\Big)-\\&\quad\sum_{S\in 2^{S_1}}Pr(S;S_1,c)\Big(p_v(c)I(S\cup\{v\})+(1-p_v(c))I(S)\Big)\\&=\sum_{S\in 2^{S_1}}Pr(S;S_1,c)\Bigg(p_u(c)p_v(c)\Big(I(S\cup\{u,v\})-I(S\cup\{v\})\Big)+\\&\qquad p_u(c)(1-p_v(c))\Big(I(S\cup\{u\})-I(S)\Big)\Bigg)\\&\leq\sum_{S\in 2^{S_1}}Pr(S;S_1,c)\Bigg(p_u(c)p_v(c)\Big(I(S\cup\{u\})-I(S)\Big)+\\&\qquad p_u(c)(1-p_v(c))\Big(I(S\cup\{u\})-I(S)\Big)\Bigg)\\&=p_u(c)\sum_{S\in 2^{S_1}}Pr(S;S_1,c)\Big(I(S\cup\{u\})-I(S)\Big)\\&=UI(S_1\cup\{u\};c)-UI(S_1;c)\end{aligned}$$

That is, we prove

$$UI(S_1\cup\{u\};c)-UI(S_1;c)\geq UI(S_2\cup\{u\};c)-UI(S_2;c).$$

By a simple induction, we can show that, if $S\subseteq T$ and $u\notin T$, $UI(S\cup\{u\};c)-UI(S;c)\geq UI(T\cup\{u\};c)-UI(T;c)$, which means $UI(S;c)$ is submodular with respect to S. ∎

Proof of Theorem 9 Recall that in the proof of Theorem 4 we illustrated that $UI(C)=I(V'-V)-n$ on the gadget graph $G'=\langle V',E'\rangle$. Consider a poll process on G' similar to it on G: we firstly randomly pick a node $v\in V$, then starting from v we run the random reverse propagation to generate a random hyper-edge h' on G'. According to the equivalent living edges process of IC model, this random reverse propagation process can be divided into two steps. (1) We randomly reversely "propagate" to nodes in V; and (2) we reversely "propagate" to nodes in $V'-V$. Clearly ,the first step is equivalent to generating a random hyper edge on G. Denoted by $h'^G=h'\cap V$ the set polled in the first step.

Denote by $Pr(h'^G=h)$ the probability that in the first step the set of nodes h is polled and $Pr(h'\cap(V-V')\neq\varnothing)$ the probability that at least one node in $V'-V$ is reversely propagated to. Similar to [1], $Pr\{h'\cap(V-V')\neq\varnothing\}=\frac{I(V'-V)-n}{n}$. According to the equivalent living edges process of the IC model, given $h'^G=h$, the conditional probability $Pr\{h' \cap (V - V') \neq \varnothing \mid h'^G = h\} = 1 - \prod_{u \in h}(1 - p_u(c_u))$.

Now we consider for a random hyper-edge h the expectation of $1 - \prod_{u \in h}(1 - p_u(c_u))$,

$$
\begin{aligned}
& E[1 - \prod_{u \in h}(1 - p_u(c_u))] \\
&= \sum_{S \in 2^V} Pr(h = S)[1 - \prod_{u \in S}(1 - p_u(c_u))] \\
&= \sum_{S \in 2^V} Pr(h'^G = S) Pr\{h' \cap (V - V') \neq \varnothing \mid h'^G = S\} \\
&= Pr\{h' \cap (V - V') \neq \varnothing\} \\
&= \frac{I(V' - V) - n}{n}
\end{aligned}
$$

Apparently,

$$E[\sum_{h \in H}[1 - \prod_{u \in h}(1 - p_u(c_u))]] = mH * E[1 - \prod_{u \in h}(1 - p_u(c_u))]$$

Since $UI(C) = I(V' - V) - n$, $\frac{n * \sum_{h \in H}[1 - \prod_{u \in h}(1 - p_u(c_u))]}{mH}$ is an unbiased estimation of $UI(C)$. ■

Holistic Influence Maximization: Combining Scalability and Efficiency with Opinion-Aware Models

Sainyam Galhotra* Akhil Arora* Shourya Roy
Text and Graph Analytics (TGA), Xerox Research Centre India (XRCI), Bangalore, India
sainyam@cs.umass.edu {akhil.arora, shourya.roy}@xerox.com

ABSTRACT

The steady growth of graph data from social networks has resulted in wide-spread research in finding solutions to the influence maximization problem. In this paper, we propose a *holistic* solution to the influence maximization (*IM*) problem. (1) We introduce an *opinion-cum-interaction* (OI) model that closely mirrors the real-world scenarios. Under the OI model, we introduce a novel problem of *Maximizing the Effective Opinion (MEO)* of influenced users. We prove that the *MEO* problem is NP-hard and cannot be approximated within a constant ratio unless P=NP. (2) We propose a heuristic algorithm *OSIM* to efficiently solve the MEO problem. To better explain the *OSIM* heuristic, we first introduce *EaSyIM* – the opinion-oblivious version of *OSIM*, a scalable algorithm capable of running within practical compute times on commodity hardware. In addition to serving as a fundamental building block for *OSIM*, *EaSyIM* is capable of addressing the scalability aspect – *memory consumption* and *running time*, of the IM problem as well.

Empirically, our algorithms are capable of maintaining the deviation in the spread always within 5% of the best known methods in the literature. In addition, our experiments show that both *OSIM* and *EaSyIM* are effective, efficient, scalable and significantly enhance the ability to analyze real datasets.

1. MOTIVATION

Growth and pervasiveness of online social networks is no longer a new phenomenon. They have become an integral part of the day-to-day life of almost every Internet user. Their wide-spread reach paves the way for a host of applications – (1) *Viral marketing/ad-targeting* [9,24,44], (2) *Outbreak detection* [25,35], (3) *Community formation, evolution and detection* [10, 12, 40], (4) *Recommendations* using social-media [14, 49] and many more. The *influence maximization* (IM) problem [32] with its applicability in solving the above mentioned problems and beyond, has thus, been one of the most widely studied problems over the past decade. This problem is to identify a set of *seed nodes* so that the overall *spread* of information in a network, which is the potential collective impact of imparting that piece of information to these nodes, is maximized.

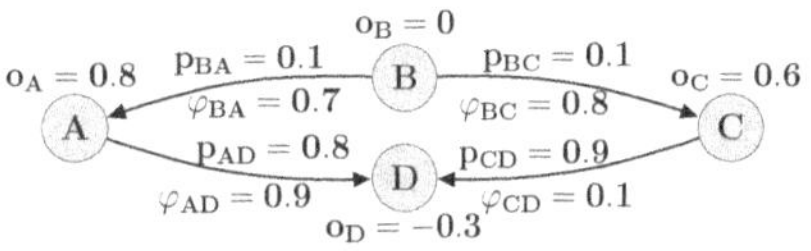

Figure 1: **A sample representation of the Twitter network.**

Given that the objective of IM is to maximize the *spread* of information about a content, which can be a product, person, event and many more, an important aspect of this problem is the underlying *information diffusion* model. A diffusion model defines the dynamics of information propagation and also controls the way this information is perceived by the nodes in a network. Nevertheless, a substantially large fraction of the literature in this field has focussed on devising efficient and scalable algorithms [13, 17–19, 21–23, 28, 29, 31–33, 35, 42, 46] for IM using the classical information diffusion models [32, 44]. The two fundamental diffusion models proposed by Kempe et al. [32] – *Independent Cascade* (IC) and *Linear Threshold* (LT) have been almost exclusively followed in majority while extended in a small fraction of all the subsequent work.

Having said that, the most obvious limitation of these models is that the notion of *spread*, of a set of seed-nodes S, is defined as a function of the number of nodes that get activated using these seeds. The problem with this definition is two fold – (1) Each node is considered to be contributing fully and positively towards the *spread* of information about a content without considering the personal *opinion* of the nodes which could be even negative, (2) A newly active node is always considered to perceive the information with the same intent as that of the node that activated it, while the former may tend to disagree with the latter owing to the *interactions* between them in the past. These scenarios are not scarce in real-world settings, where a node can possess an *opinion* (Def. 4) towards a content which is the subject of IM. Moreover, usually past *interactions* (Def. 5) between a pair of nodes govern the way in which any new information originating from one of the two would be perceived by the other and vice-versa. To better understand these aspects, let us consider a (sample) real-world scenario in Example 1.

EXAMPLE 1. *Suppose Apple wants to market, utilizing the notion of viral-marketing, the iPhone 6 Plus using the Twitter network given a marketing budget of* 1 *seed-node. Figure 1 portrays a snapshot of such a network consisting of* 4 *nodes. Nodes A and C follow B, while D follows A and C. The opinion (o) of a node towards the new iPhone can be calculated using its opinion towards similar products in the past – previous iPhone models or phones belonging to the same market segment. For example, the node A has* $o_A = 0.8$, *which means that she held highly positive opinions towards previous iPhone models or similar products. The opinion for other nodes can be computed in a similar way. Moreover, each*

*The first two authors have contributed equally to this work.

SIGMOD'16, June 26-July 01, 2016, San Francisco, CA, USA
 ISBN 978-1-4503-3531-7/16/06... $15.00
DOI: http://dx.doi.org/10.1145/2882903.2882929

edge possesses an additional parameter, called the interaction (φ) *probability. In our example, the directed edge BC has $\varphi_{BC} = 0.8$ which means that the node C perceives the information originating from the node B with the same intent 4 out of 5 times. In other words, C agrees with B 4 out of 5 times while disagrees otherwise.*

In the light of above discussions, it is intuitive that despite of being widely adopted, the fundamental (opinion-oblivious) diffusion models lack the power to leverage the expressibility of the social networks of today, namely – *Facebook*, *Twitter* etc. Thus, there is a need to explore potential extensions, over and above these models, with the ability to better model information diffusion under real-world scenarios. To further this cause, we incorporate the concepts of *opinion* and *interaction* [27,38,43] from the social media domain and propose a new *Opinion-cum-Interaction* (OI) model of information diffusion capable of addressing the limitations discussed above. Using the OI model, we define a more realistic notion of *opinion-spread* (Defs. 6 and 7).

Let us try to analyze the importance of *opinion-spread* using the example in Figure 1. As discussed earlier, opinion-oblivious diffusion models, viz. IC, rely on the influence probability (p) alone without paying heed to the personal opinion of the activated nodes, which may even be negative. Thus, the likelihood of C being chosen as a seed under the IC model is fairly high, owing to the high value of p_{CD} which in turn results in high (opinion-oblivious) *spread*. However, owing to o_D being negative it will always decrease the overall *opinion-spread* if activated. Thus, C might not be the best choice for a seed-node. Moreover, a model capable of capturing the effect of *opinions*, viz. OI, will penalize C and thus decrease its likelihood of being chosen as a seed node.

We strengthen the above mentioned observation further, by plotting the *opinion-spread* against the number of seeds for different real datasets (details in Sec. 4). Figure 2 shows that the opinion-spread obtained by the seeds selected using the OI model is much better when compared to that using the IC model, and thus, establishes the importance of *OI* over the IC/LT models of information-diffusion with better conformance to the real-world scenarios.

As mentioned above, there has not been much research in devising *opinion-aware* information-diffusion models, with *IC-N* [16] and *OC* [48] being the only two models capable of incorporating *negative opinion* in the diffusion process. Despite of their capability to model opinions, they possess the following limitations.

(1) Constrained and Specific: The IC-N model is rather simplistic, where a negatively activated node retains its opinion throughout its lifetime, while a *quality-factor* qf (same for each node) defines the probability of transitioning to a negative opinion for the positively activated nodes. Although, a uniform qf allows retention of submodularity, which further facilitates extension of existing algorithms for IM to this setting, it renders the model too *specific*.

(2) Simplistic diffusion dynamics: The IC-N model possesses a strict constraint that a negatively activated node will always activate other nodes as negative. This assumption ignores the personal opinion of a node completely, and will be violated when the target node possesses a highly positive opinion about a content.

The OC model, where the change in opinion of a node is dependent upon its own opinion and the opinion of the nodes that activate it, does not possess the above two limitations. The OC model thus, facilitates a more involved process of modelling opinions at an added cost of losing submodularity.

(3) Lack capability to capture Interaction: Both IC-N and OC lack the capability to capture the way in which information is perceived between a pair of nodes (*interaction*) in the network.

(4) Lack of backward-compatibility with fundamental diffusion models: The IC-N model is tuned to work with IC at the first layer, while the OC model is designed to work with LT alone.

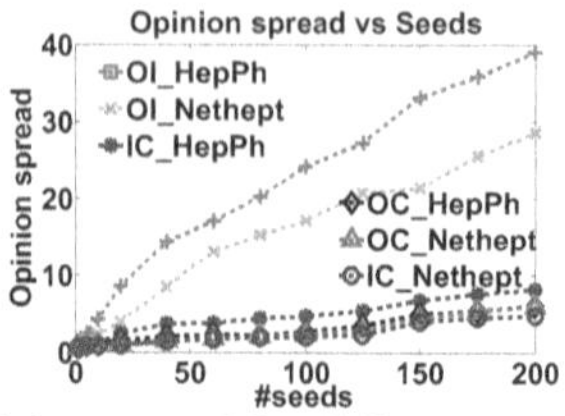

Figure 2: **Opinion spread for different diffusion models.**

The OI model attempts to address these limitations by allowing – (1) Nodes to possess different opinions, (2) Edges to possess an *interaction* probability for modelling the perception of information between a node-pair, and (3) Capability of working with both IC and LT at the first layer. In addition to the analytical explanations, Figure 2 also shows that the opinion-spread with seeds selected using OI is better when compared to those selected using OC. In summary, the OI model is a more generic, natural and realistic model when compared to IC-N and OC.

Having successfully motivated (both qualitatively and empirically) and differentiated (from current state-of-the-art) the OI model, we propose a novel problem (MEO) of maximizing the *spread* of information under opinion-aware settings. Since *MEO* is NP-hard and difficult to approximate within a constant ratio, we incorporate ideas from the *opinion-oblivious* scenarios to design *scalable* algorithms for the *opinion-aware* case. We propose *OSIM*, capable of maximizing the *opinion-spread* while accommodating for the change of *opinion* as the information propagates. To this end, we first analyze a representative set of algorithms for IM under the fundamental diffusion models.

Although, the Kempe's GREEDY algorithm [32] provides the best possible approximation guarantees for the IM problem, it is inefficient. The CELF++ [28] algorithm with optimizations over GREEDY renders it as the most efficient technique within this class of algorithms. However, these techniques never improved the asymptotic time-complexity of IM and thus, cannot be employed for large graphs. To further this, recent works employed the use of *sampling* with *memoization* [13,23,45,46], with TIM$^+$ and its improvement IMM being the most efficient, to achieve superior efficiency while retaining approximation guarantees. However, these algorithms cannot be termed *scalable* owing to their *exorbitantly high* memory footprint. For example, the memory footprint of TIM$^+$ can be as high as 100 GB for a graph with $1M$ nodes and $3M$ edges which is not uncommmon these days. Owing to these limitations, neither CELF++ nor TIM$^+$ serve as potential candidates for extensions to *opinion-aware* scenarios. Our proposition, *EaSyIM*, tackles these problems by incorporating the idea that influence of a node can be estimated using a function of the number of simple paths starting at that node. Note that paths of length l from a node u can be calculated as the sum of all paths of length $l-1$ from its neighbors. We exploit this idea to devise data-structures and algorithms capable of running in *linear space* and *time*. This renders our algorithm *scalable* yet *efficient*. Therefore, *EaSyIM* is chosen for extensions to the *opinion-aware* case to produce *OSIM*, which being fundamentally similar possesses the same analysis as *EaSyIM*.

Contributions. In summary, we make the following contributions. We propose a *holistic* solution to the IM problem. Towards that,

- We introduce the OI model (Sec. 2.2) which, to the best of our knowledge, is the most generic information diffusion model with the ability to address most of the limitations in the existing models and closely mirror real-world scenarios. In addition to this, we are the first to motivate the need of *opinion-aware* models by citing a novel application analyzing churn, using real-world data (Sec. 4.1.2).

- Under OI, we propose a novel problem of maximizing the effective opinion of influenced users, called *MEO* (Sec. 2.3).
- We propose effective, efficient and scalable algorithms (Sec. 3), namely – *OSIM* and *EaSyIM*, that run in linear time $O(k\mathcal{D}(m+n))$ and space $O(n)$.
- We provide thorough theoretical analyses (Sec. 3.4) to prove the effectiveness of our algorithms. We believe that such an in-depth analysis for the algorithms that estimate influence as a function of simple paths is not present in the literature.
- Through an in-depth empirical analysis (Sec. 4), we show that our algorithms are the first to possess the capability of handling *huge* graphs on *commodity-hardware* and provide the best trade-off between *running-time* and *memory consumption*, while retaining the quality of *spread*.

The rest of the paper is organized as follows. In Section 2, we introduce a generic opinion-aware information diffusion model and present the problem statement. Section 3 describes our algorithm and its analysis. In Section 4, experimental results are presented. Section 5 highlights the related work before Section 6 concludes. For details and elaborate version of the proofs, the reader is referred to a full version of this paper in *arXiv 1602.03110*.

2. OPINION AWARE IM

In this section, we first introduce the basic concepts of the IM problem and build upon them to describe the Opinion-cum-Interaction (OI) model for information diffusion in detail. The notations used in the rest of the paper are summarized in Table 1.

2.1 Preliminaries

The objective of the IM problem is to capture the dynamics of information diffusion for maximizing the spread of information in a network. To this end, we first define the notions of *seed* and *active* nodes in the context of fundamental (opinion-oblivious) information diffusion models, namely – IC and LT. Next, we use these concepts to define the notion of *spread* of information in a network.

DEFINITION 1 (SEED NODE). *A node $v \in V$ that acts as the source of information diffusion in the graph $G(V, E)$ is called a seed node. The set of seed nodes is denoted by S.*

DEFINITION 2 (ACTIVE NODE). *A node $v \in V$ is deemed active if either (1) It is a seed node ($v \in S$) or (2) It receives information, under the dynamics of information diffusion models, from a previously active node $u \in V_{(a)}$. Once activated, the node v is added to the set of active nodes $V_{(a)}$.*

Given a seed node $s \in S$ and a graph $G(V, E)$, an information diffusion model $\mathcal{I}$ defines a step-by-step process for information propagation. Having defined the notions of seed and active nodes, we now introduce the dynamics of the IC and LT models. For both the IC and LT models, the first step requires a seed node $s \in S$ to be activated and added to the set of active nodes $V_{(a)}$. Under the IC model, at any step i each newly activated node $u \in V_{(a)}$ gets one independent attempt to activate each of its outgoing neighbours $v \in \textbf{Out}(u)$ with a probability $p_{(u,v)}$. However, under the LT model, a node v gets activated if the sum of weights $w_{(u,v)}$ of all the incoming edges (u, v) originating from active nodes $\forall u \in \textbf{In}(v)_{(a)}$ [1] exceeds the activation threshold θ_v of v, i.e., $\sum_{u \in \textbf{In}(v)_{(a)}} w(u, v) \geq \theta_v$. Once a node becomes active, it remains active in all the subsequent steps. This diffusion process runs for each seed-node $s \in S$ until no more activations are possible. Eventually, the cardinality of the set of active nodes $|V_{(a)}|$, barring the number of seeds $k = |S|$, constitute the spread of a given set of seed nodes. Formally,

[1] $X_{(a)}$, for any set X, denotes the set of active nodes in that set.

Item	Definition
$\textbf{Out}(u)$	Set of outgoing neighbours of u.
$\textbf{In}(v)$	Set of incoming neighbours of v.
o_v	Personal opinion of v; $o_v \in [-1, 1]$.
$\varphi_{(u,v)}$	Interaction probability from u to v.
$\Gamma(S)$	Spread obtained by set of seed nodes (S).
$\sigma(S)$	Expected value of spread by seeds in S; $\mathbb{E}(\Gamma(S))$.
$V_{(a)}$	The set of active nodes; $V_{(a)} \subseteq V$.
λ	Penalty parameter on negative opinion spread.
$\gamma_v(u)$	Contribution of v to $\sigma(u)$, using approximate scores (Sec. 3.2).
$\gamma^*_v(u)$	Contribution of v to $\sigma(u)$, using GREEDY [32].
$\mathbb{P}_{uv}$	The set of all u-v paths; $\{u \rightsquigarrow v\}$
$\Delta^l(u)$	Score assigned to u, using all $u \rightsquigarrow v$ paths of length $\leq l$.

Table 1: **Summary of the notations used.**

DEFINITION 3 (SPREAD). *Given an information diffusion model $\mathcal{I}$ (opinion-oblivious), the spread $\Gamma(S)$ of a set of seed nodes S is defined as the number of nodes, barring the nodes in S, that get activated using these seed nodes. Mathematically, $\Gamma(S) = |V_{(a)}| - |S|$.*

Given the above defined concepts, the IM problem aims at identifying a set of seed nodes capable of maximizing the *expected spread* of information in a network under a fixed budget on the number of seed nodes. More formally, Given a graph $G = (V, E)$, a fundamental (opinion-oblivious) information diffusion model $\mathcal{I}$ (IC/LT) with specifics defined as above and a budget k, find a set of seed nodes, $S \subseteq V \mid k = |S|$, that maximizes the expected value of information spread $\sigma(S) = \mathbb{E}[\Gamma(S)]$ in this graph.

2.2 Opinion-cum-Interaction (OI) Model

The OI model for information diffusion serves as an extension over the IC and LT models to facilitate opinion-aware IM. The fundamental models are modified to include a second layer attributed to modelling the diffusion and change of *opinion*(Def. 4) in the network. As opposed to the IC/LT models, where a newly activated node (oblivious to its *opinion*) is always considered to be contributing positively towards the information spread (Def. 3), the OI model considers the *spread* (opinion-spread, Defs. 6 and 7) of information under an *opinion-aware* scenario – where the contribution of a newly activated node could as well be negative.

The OI model can be easily tuned, with minor modifications, to work with both IC and the LT models. The specifics of OI, thus, change depending on the underlying fundamental information diffusion model. Before moving to the model specifics, it is useful to introduce the notions of *opinion* (o) of a node and *interaction* (φ) between two nodes. Usually, the objective of IM is to maximize the spread of information about a specific content viz. product, topic, person, event etc. Having said that, the opinion of a node is always defined in the context of a particular content to denote the personal preference of this node towards that content. Formally,

DEFINITION 4 (OPINION). *The opinion of a node $v \in V$ consists of two sub-components – (1) an orientation ({negative, neutral, positive}) towards a content and (2) strength ([0, 1]) that quantifies its preference towards that content. The opinion of a node is, thus, denoted as $o_v \in [-1, 1]$.*

As opposed to *opinion* which is associated with properties of a node alone, *interaction* aims at capturing the effect of the dyadic relationship between any two nodes to better model the process of information diffusion. Formally,

DEFINITION 5 (INTERACTION). *The interaction probability (directed) between two nodes $u, v \in V$, denoted as $\varphi_{(u,v)} \in [0, 1]$, is defined as a fraction of the times an information content shared by u gets accepted by v with the same orientation as that of u.*

For example, if two nodes u and v agree with each other 1 out of 5 times in the past, then $\varphi_{(u,v)} = \varphi_{(v,u)} = 1/5 = 0.2$. As discussed in Sec. 1, the opinion of a node towards a new content can be estimated from the previously held opinions by this node towards similar contents in the past. As opposed to this, the interaction probabilities (directed, $\varphi_{(u,v)}$ might not be equal to $\varphi_{(v,u)}$) between two nodes is rather generic and can be estimated[2] by accounting for all possible interactions between these nodes in the past. Next, we describe the specifics of the OI model.

We model the underlying network as a directed graph $G = (V, E)$ with parameters p, w, θ, o, φ, where $|V| = n$ and $|E| = m$ denote the set of vertices and edges respectively. The parameters have similar meanings as discussed earlier in this section. Oblivious to the underlying information diffusion model (IC or LT), each node $v \in V$ possesses an opinion towards a new content denoted by $o_v \in [-1, 1]$. Specifically the sign of o_v indicates the *orientation* and the value denotes the *strength*. More formally, $o_v > 0$, $o_v = 0$, and $o_v < 0$ indicate positive, neutral and negative orientation respectively. In addition, $o_v = -1$ denotes a strong negative opinion while $o_v = +1$ denotes a strong positive opinion. Moreover, each edge $(u, v) \in E$ possess $\varphi_{(u,v)} \in [0, 1]$, that refers to the probability of a node v acquiring the same opinion as that of u, considering only the contribution from node u. $\varphi_{(u,v)} = 0$ indicates that v never agrees with u, while $\varphi_{(v,u)} = 0.5$ indicates that u agrees with v half of the time. The dynamics of the model are as follows.

Under the IC model, the first step involves activation of each seed node s, in the selected seed set S ($|S| = k$), with its opinion[3] $o_s, \forall s \in S$, while all other nodes remain inactive. At any step i, if a node u (which was activated at step $i - 1$) activates another node v then the final opinion (o'_v) of v is dependent upon both, its initial opinion o_v and the final opinion (o'_u) of the node u. More formally, each node u, contributes o'_u with a probability $\varphi_{(u,v)}$ and $-o'_u$ with a probability $1 - \varphi_{(u,v)}$. The final opinion of the node v is $o'_v = \frac{o_v + (-1)^{\alpha} o'_u}{2}$, where $\alpha = 0$ with a probability of $\varphi_{(u,v)}$ and $\alpha = 1$ with a probability of $1 - \varphi_{(u,v)}$.

Under the LT model, the first step witnesses the same set of initializations as done for OI under the IC model. At any step i, if a node v gets activated (by the set of nodes $\mathbf{In}(v)_{(a)}$, activated at previous steps) then the final opinion o'_v of v is dependent upon both, its initial opinion o_v and the final opinion o'_u for all the nodes $u \in \mathbf{In}(v)_{(a)}$. The contributions made by each node to the opinion of the node v is the same as discussed above for OI under the IC model. The final opinion of the node v is $o'_v = (o_v + \frac{1}{|\mathbf{In}(v)_{(a)}|} \sum_{u \in \mathbf{In}(v)_{(a)}} (-1)^{\alpha_{(u,v)}} o'_u)/2$, where $\alpha_{(u,v)} = 0$ with a probability of $\varphi_{(u,v)}$ and $\alpha_{(u,v)} = 1$ with a probability of $1 - \varphi_{(u,v)}$.

Once a node becomes active, it remains active with the same effective opinion in all the subsequent steps. The information propagation process runs until no more activations are possible. With these extensions, we aim to solve the IM problem under settings that closely mirror real-world scenarios. Before moving ahead, we revisit Example 1 and analyze the difference between *spread* and *opinion-spread* with stating the importance of the latter in real-world scenarios using Example 2.

EXAMPLE 2. *Let us consider the construction described in Example 1 with all the model-specific parameters present in Figure 1. For the sake of brevity, the analysis of spread in this scenario assumes (1) the IC model and (2) the OI model using IC at the first-layer. The influence probability (p, of an edge) possesses the same meaning as for the fundamental models. Since* $p_{AD} = 0.8$, *the expected spread of A under the IC model* ($\sigma(A)$) *is* 0.8. *Similarly for other nodes:* $\sigma(B) = 0.3628$, $\sigma(C) = 0.9$ *and* $\sigma(D) = 0$. *Thus, C is selected as the seed node. Since D agrees with A with a probability of* φ_{AD} *and disagrees otherwise, the expected opinion-spread of A under the OI model is expressed as* $\sigma^o(A) = p_{AD}\big(\varphi_{AD}(o_D + o_A)/2 + (1 - \varphi_{AD})(o_D - o_A)/2\big) = 0.8\big(0.9(-0.3 + 0.8)/2 + 0.1(-0.3 - 0.8)/2\big) = 0.136$. *Similarly for other nodes:* $\sigma^o(B) = -0.022564$, $\sigma^o(C) = -0.351$ *and* $\sigma^o(D) = 0$. *Thus, A is selected as the seed node. An interesting observation is that, the seed identified using the IC model, i.e. C, would have resulted in the worst-possible opinion-spread. This clearly shows the importance of the notion of opinion-spread under the OI model, over opinion-oblivious spread using the IC model, in real-world scenarios where opinion of nodes and interaction between nodes play an important part in governing the process of information propagation.*

Next, we formally state the *MEO* problem followed by its tractability analysis.

2.3 Problem Formulation

Using the concepts described in the previous sections, we formally define the notion of spread under the opinion-aware (OI) model, called *Opinion Spread*. While, under the opinion oblivious models spread can simply be stated as the total number of nodes that get activated with a given set of seed nodes, a more involved notion of spread is required under the *opinion-aware* settings.

DEFINITION 6 (OPINION SPREAD). *Opinion spread of a seed set S, denoted by* $\Gamma^o(S)$, *is defined as the sum of final opinions of the nodes in the activated set* $V_{(a)} \setminus S$, *when S is the chosen seed set, i.e.,* $\Gamma^o(S) = \sum_{v \in V_{(a)} \setminus S} o'_v$.

DEFINITION 7 (EFFECTIVE OPINION SPREAD). *Effective opinion spread of a seed set S, denoted by* $\Gamma^o_\lambda(S)$, *is defined as the weighted difference between the opinion spread of nodes with positive orientation and the opinion spread of nodes with negative orientation, i.e.,* $\Gamma^o_\lambda(S) = \big(\sum_{o'_v > 0} o'_v - \lambda \sum_{o'_v < 0} |o'_v|\big); \forall v \in V_{(a)} \setminus S$, *in the set of activated nodes* $V_{(a)} \setminus S$, *where* λ *is the penalty on negative opinion spread.*

The problem of maximizing the effective opinion spread under the OI model is called: *Maximizing the Effective Opinion of the Influenced Users (MEO)* problem, and is defined formally as follows.

PROBLEM 1. *Given a graph* $G = (V, E)$, *the opinion-aware (OI) model with specifics defined as in Sec. 2.2 and a budget k, find a set of seed nodes,* $S \subseteq V \mid k = |S|$, *that maximizes the expected value of the effective opinion spread* $\sigma^o_\lambda(S) = \mathbb{E}[\Gamma^o_\lambda(S)]$.

2.4 Properties of MEO under the OI model

2.4.1 NP-hardness

LEMMA 1. *The MEO problem is NP-hard.*

PROOF. The IM problem is reducible to an instance of the MEO problem under the OI model, when $o_v = 1, \forall v \in V$ and $\varphi_{(u,v)} = 1, \forall (u, v) \in E$. It is known that any generalization of a NP-hard problem is also NP-hard. Since, the IM problem is NP-hard [32], the MEO problem is NP-hard as well. □

[2]We have discussed one possible way to estimate opinion and interaction. These notions are rather generic and other approaches can be employed for their estimation as well.

[3]The final opinion of the seeds is same as their initial personal opinion, $o'_s = o_s$.

2.4.2 *Submodularity*

A function $f(\cdot)$ is submodular if the marginal gain from adding an element to a set S is at least as high as the marginal gain from adding it to a superset of S. Mathematically,

$$f(S \cup \{x\}) - f(S) \geq f(T \cup \{x\}) - f(T)$$

for all elements x and all pairs of sets (S, T), where $S \subseteq T$. For submodular and monotone functions, the greedy algorithm of iteratively adding the element with the maximum marginal gain approximates the optimal solution within a factor of $(1 - 1/e)$ [41].

LEMMA 2. *The opinion spread as a function $\Gamma(\cdot)$ in a graph G, is neither monotone nor submodular.*

PROOF. Please see Appendix A. □

Using Lemma 2, it is evident that a greedy algorithm cannot produce a $1 - 1/e$ approximate solution to the *MEO* problem. Next, we further prove that $\nexists$ any algorithm capable of approximating *MEO* within a constant ratio.

THEOREM 1. *Approximating MEO within a constant ratio is not possible unless $P = NP$.*

PROOF. Please see Appendix B. □

3. ALGORITHM

3.1 Outline of our Algorithm

To solve the *MEO* problem efficiently, we propose a technique as outlined in Algorithm 1. We first assign a score (line 4), to each node $u \in V$ of the graph $G(V, E)$, by aggregating the contributions of all paths starting at u. We prove that if the score assignment is correct (we will specify exactly what is meant by "correct" later), then the expected value of the influence spread achieved using our algorithm is the same as that achieved using the GREEDY gold standard [32]. The correctness of our score assignment algorithms, both for the opinion-oblivious (EaSyIM) and the opinion-aware (OSIM) case, holds perfectly for trees. Moreover, in a conclusive discussion, we show that the error introduced in case of graphs is small as well. Through detailed analyses and experiments we show that our results do not deviate much from that of the GREEDY algorithm.

On completion of the score assignment step, the node possessing the maximum score is selected as the seed node (lines 5–9). In order to ensure the sets of nodes activated by each selected seed node to be disjoint; the last step of the seed-selection algorithm (line 11) keeps track of all the previously activated nodes as a set ($V_{(a)}$). This enables the score assignment step to discount the contributions of all the previously activated nodes in subsequent iterations. The above process continues until k seeds are selected.

Next, we describe the score-assignment algorithms – (1) *EaSyIM* and its extension (2) *OSIM* in detail. The algorithms are fundamentally similar for both, *opinion-oblivious* and *opinion-aware*, cases.

3.2 Score Assignment

The score assignment step, similar to ASIM [26], leverages the idea that the probability of a node v to get activated by a seed node u is dependent upon the number of simple paths from u to v in G. Thus, a simple function of the number of paths from a node u to all other nodes $v \in V \setminus \{u\}$ can be used to assign a score to u. This score-assignment is further used to rank all the nodes $v \in V$ in an order determining their expected spread $\sigma(v)$. To this end, the scores assigned to a node u ($\Delta^l(u)$), is computed by aggregating

Algorithm 1 ScoreGREEDY

```
Input: Graph G = (V, E),#seeds k = |S|, l
Output: Seed set S
 1: S, V_(a) ← ∅
 2: for i = 1 to k do
 3:     max, maxId ← 0
 4:     Δ^l ← AssignScore(G(V \ V_(a), E), o, p, φ, l)
 5:     for each u ∈ V do
 6:         if Δ^l(u) > max then
 7:             max ← Δ^l(u), maxId ← u
 8:         end if
 9:     end for
10:     S ← S ∪ {maxId}
11:     Update V_(a) with nodes activated by the newly selected seed-node (maxId)
12: end for
```

Algorithm 2 AssignScore

```
Input: Graph G = (V, E), o, p, φ, l
Output: Δ^l
if ¬ Opinion then
    Δ^l ← EaSyIM(G(V, E), p, l) //Opinion-Oblivious
else
    Δ^l ← OSIM(G(V, E), o, p, φ, l) //Opinion-Aware
end if
```

the contributions of all $u \rightsquigarrow v$ paths of length at most l[4] ($\mathcal{L}(u \rightsquigarrow v) \leq l$). We start with a description of the score assignment step for the opinion-oblivious (EaSyIM) case and then follow it up with the opinion-aware (OSIM) case. The following explanations of the score assignment algorithms assume the IC model of information diffusion. Their extensions to the *linear threshold* (LT) and the *weighted cascade* (WC) models are discussed in Sec. 3.3.

3.2.1 *EaSyIM*

As mentioned in Sec. 3.2, a function of the number of directed simple paths from a node u to another node v can be used to estimate the influence of the former on the latter. However, direct application of this notion to design solutions for the influence maximization problem poses two inherent challenges of maintaining – 1) Scalability and Efficiency, 2) Correctness guarantees. Since, counting the number of s-t paths is shown to be in $\#P$-Complete [47], computing the expected influence of a node is $\#P$-hard for both the IC [17] and the LT [19] models. This further shows that it is impossible to come up with a score-assignment algorithm capable of correctly selecting a seed-node with maximum influence.

Although counting s-t paths is $\#P$-Complete, there exists a polynomial time algorithm to count all possible walks of length at most l between all node-pairs ($\forall (u, v) \in V$) in G that takes $O(n^3 \log l)$ time and consumes $O(n^2)$ memory. The $Path\text{-}Union$ (PU) algorithm (Algorithm 3) extends this algorithm by initializing the adjacency matrix of the graph M with the pair-wise influence probabilities (line 2). Since the contributions of these paths cannot be simply aggregated, we define a new operator $\otimes$ for matrix multiplication (line 4). Under this operator, the multiplication of ith row ($M[i][:]$) with j^{th} column ($M[:][j]$) is defined using Eq. 1. This algorithm has an inherent problem that it counts cyclic paths as well, which eventually serves as a source of error while computing the influence of a node. We try to reduce the impact of this error for each node, by removing the contributions of the walks that pass through the node itself (lines 5–7). Finally, the score of each node u is computed as indicated in line 10.

$$M[i][j] = M[i][:] \otimes M[:][j] = \bigcup_{k=1}^{n} M[i][k] \times M[k][j]. \quad (1)$$

[4] l is the maximum path length considered for score assignment, where $l \leq \mathcal{D}$. $\mathcal{D}$ is the diameter of the graph.

Algorithm 3 *Path-Union(PU)*

```
Input: Graph G = (V, E), n = |V|, p, l
Output: Δ^l
1: Matrix M^{n×n} ← 0, PU ← I^{n×n}
2: Δ^0(u) ← 0 (∀u ∈ V), M[u][v] ← p_(u,v) (∀u, v ∈ V)
3: for each i ∈ {1, ..., l} do
4:     PU ← PU ⊗ M
5:     for each v ∈ V do
6:         PU[v][v] ← 0
7:     end for
8:     for each u ∈ V do
9:         for each v ∈ V do
10:            Δ^i(u) ← Δ^{i−1}(u) + PU[u][v]
11:        end for
12:    end for
13: end for
14: return Δ^l
```

Owing to its huge time and space complexity, the *PU* algorithm cannot be used in practice. The *EaSyIM* algorithm (Algorithm 4) describes a score-assignment method, with efforts to tackle this scalability bottleneck. Paths of length l from a node u can be calculated as the sum of all paths of length $l-1$ from its neighbors. $\Delta^l(u)$ ($\forall u \in V$) is defined as the weighted sum of the number of paths of length at most l starting from u and is computed as indicated in line 5 of Algorithm 4. The weight for each path is defined as the product of probabilities $p_{(u,v)}$ of the edges composing that path. EaSyIM score of a node u tries to mimic closely the expected value of the spread when u is chosen as a seed node.

For every iteration of *EaSyIM*, the outgoing neighbours $\mathbf{Out}(u)$ of each node $u \in V$ are visited to accumulate the contribution of paths of different lengths (l). The parameter l can be as large as the diameter ($\mathcal{D}$) of the graph. Thus, the total time taken by the score-assignment step using the *EaSyIM* algorithm is $O(\mathcal{D}(m+n))$, in the worst-case. Moreover, the total time taken for selecting k seeds using our modified greedy algorithm (ScoreGREEDY) is $O(k\mathcal{D}(m+n))$. The space complexity of this algorithm is $O(n)$, as the only additional overhead is the storage of a score ($O(1)$) at each node. A detailed analysis on the correctness of *PU* and *EaSyIM* algorithms is present in Sec. 3.4.1.

3.2.2 OSIM

We now describe the *OSIM* algorithm (Algorithm 5), to assign a score to each node of a graph for the opinion-aware case. This algorithm extends *EaSyIM* by accommodating for the change in opinion (Sec. 2.2) during the information propagation process. Since, the change in opinion is captured using a second layer over and above the activation step of a node, we incorporate the use of the following intermediate terms α_i, or_i and sc_i for each node. At each iteration, these intermediate terms contain only the contributions for a given path length $i \leq l$. For a given node u, the term $or_i(u)$ contains the weighted sum of the initial 2opinions of all nodes, reachable via paths of length i starting at u (line 6). In other words, $or_i(u)$ constitutes the contribution of nodes reachable by u via paths of length i to its score ($\Delta^i(u)$), without considering the change in opinion during information propagation. Similarly, the term $\alpha_i(u)$ computes the weighted sum of the interaction probabilities (φ) associated with all the paths of length i, starting at u (line 7). For a given path of length i ($\mathcal{L}(u \rightsquigarrow v) = i$), $sc_i^v(u)$ contains the contributions of all nodes in this path to the change in opinion of node v (line 8). The term $sc_i(u)$ further contains the aggregation of $sc_i^v(u)$ for all i length paths starting at u (line 10).

Similar to *EaSyIM*, the weight for each path is defined as the product of probabilities $p_{(u,v)}$ of the edges composing that path. Moreover, the weight, for term α_i, additionally incorporates the interaction probabilities ($\varphi_{(u,v)}$) as well. In line 11, the score for a node u ($\Delta^i(u)$) is iteratively updated with the aggregation of all the intermediate terms ($or_i(u)$, $\alpha_i(u)$, and $sc_i(u)$). Finally, $\Delta^l(u)$ contains the score of a node u with the contributions of all paths of length at most l, starting at u. Note that, since the loop invariants in lines 2, 3 and 5 of *OSIM* is exactly the same as that of *EaSyIM* (lines 2, 3 and 4), its time and space complexity analysis is exactly the same as *EaSyIM*.

Algorithm 4 EaSyIM

```
Input: Graph G = (V, E), p, l
Output: Δ^l
1: Δ^i(v) ← 0 (∀i ≤ l, ∀v ∈ V)
2: for each i ∈ {1, ..., l} do
3:     for each u ∈ V do
4:         for each v ∈ Out(u) do
5:             Δ^i(u) ← Δ^i(u) + p_(u,v)(1 + Δ^{i−1}(v))
6:         end for
7:     end for
8: end for
9: return Δ^l
```

Algorithm 5 OSIM

```
Input: Graph G = (V, E), o, p, φ, l
Output: Δ^l
1: α_0(u) ← 1, or_0(u) ← o_u, sc_0(u), Δ^0(u) ← 0 (∀u ∈ V)
2: for each i ∈ {1, ..., l} do
3:     for each u ∈ V do
4:         α_i(v), or_i(v), sc_i(v) ← 0
5:         for each v ∈ Out(u) do
6:             or_i(u) ← or_i(u) + p_(u,v) or_{i−1}(v)
7:             α_i(u) ← α_i(u) + p_(u,v) α_{i−1}(v)(2φ_(u,v) − 1)/2
8:             sc_i(u) ← sc_i(u) + p_(u,v) sc_{i−1}(v)
9:         end for
10:        sc_i(u) ← sc_i(u) + o_u α_i(u)
11:        Δ^i(u) ← Δ^{i−1}(u) + (or_i(u) + sc_i(u) + o_u α_i(u)) / 2
12:    end for
13: end for
14: return Δ^l
```

3.3 Extensions

Please see Appendix C.

3.4 Analysis of Score Assignment

As a first step towards analyzing our algorithms, we prove that the ScoreGREEDY algorithm produces a $1 - 1/e$ approximate solution to the IM problem, under the condition that the score assigned to each node captures the expected value of spread using that node.

LEMMA 3. *Given a graph $G(V, E)$, if score-assignment is correct, i.e., the score assigned to each node $\Delta^l(u)$ captures the expected value of its spread $\Delta^l(u) = \sigma_{\sigma(S)}(\{u\})$ where S is the set of seed nodes, then $\sigma(S_k) = \sigma(S_k^*)$ where S_k is the set of seed nodes selected using the ScoreGREEDY algorithm while S_k^* is the set selected using GREEDY algorithm.*

PROOF. Please see Appendix E. □

CONCLUSION 1. *Given a correct score assignment algorithm, the ScoreGREEDY algorithm produces a $1 - 1/e$ approximate solution to the IM problem.*

As discussed in Sec. 3.2, it is impossible to devise a scoring algorithm that captures the expected value of spread for each node, for graphs. Thus, the ScoreGREEDY algorithm cannot produce a $1-1/e$ approximate solution to the IM problem. Next, we show a detailed analysis of both EaSyIM and OSIM score assignment strategies.

3.4.1 EaSyIM

In this section, we first state the causes for the introduction of errors in *PU* & *EaSyIM*, and follow it up by a concrete analysis on the exact quantification of these errors.

We first show the amount of error introduced by *PU* for DAGs[5]. Although, the *PU* algorithm can enumerate the exact number of paths for DAGs, errors might still creep in while assigning scores, owing to the presence of non-disjoint paths between any pair of nodes as shown in Figure 3a. More specifically errors are introduced in the score-assignment of a node when none of the paths starting from that node to any other node in the graph are disjoint.

LEMMA 4. *Given a DAG, $G(V, E)$ and a set of paths, $\mathbb{P}_{uw}$, s.t. $(w, v) \in E$, if the contribution of w in the score of u is correct then the maximum possible relative error introduced by v in the score of u using the PU algorithm is $\epsilon_1^{DAG} = \sum_{w \in In(v)} \left((p_{(w,v)} - 1)A_1\right)$, where $A_1 = \sum_{\rho \in \mathbb{P}_{uw}} \prod_{e \in \rho} p_e$.*

PROOF. Please see Appendix F. □

LEMMA 5. *Given a DAG, $G(V, E)$ and a set of paths, $\mathbb{P}_{uv}$, the maximum possible relative error (w.r.t PU) introduced by v in the score of u using the* EaSyIM *algorithm is $\epsilon_2^{DAG} \leq B_1 = \sum_{\rho \in \mathbb{P}_{uv}} \prod_{e \in \rho} p_e$.*

PROOF. Please see Appendix G. □

Using Lemma 4 and 5 the total error (worst-case) introduced by *EaSyIM* for DAGs is $\epsilon_1^{DAG} + \epsilon_2^{DAG} \leq \sum_{w \in \mathbf{In}(v)} (2p_{(w,v)} - 1)A_1$.

Moving ahead, we analyze the errors introduced by *PU* and *EaSyIM* on graphs. The error due to cycles that end up at a node u itself are discounted using the *PU* algorithm (lines 5–7). The largest amount of error would be introduced by cycles of length 3, owing to the exponential decrease of the influence probabilities with length of a path. Next, we analyze the errors introduced by other cyclic paths as shown in Figure 3b.

LEMMA 6. *Given a graph $G(V, E)$ and a set of cyclic paths $\mathbb{P}_{ww}$, s.t. $(u, w) \in E$, the maximum possible relative error, assuming just the effect of cycles, introduced by w in the score of u using approximate score-assignment algorithms (PU and* EaSyIM*) is $\epsilon^{cycle} = \sum_{\rho \in \mathbb{P}_{ww}} (\prod_{e \in \rho} p_e)/|\rho|$, where $|\rho| \leq \mathcal{D}$.*

PROOF. Please see Appendix H. □

THEOREM 2. *Given the expected spread of u is greater when compared to the spread of v using the* GREEDY *algorithm i.e., $\sigma^*(u) > \sigma^*(v)$, the corresponding expected spreads achieved using seeds selected by any approximate score-assignment algorithm preserve this relationship i.e., $\sigma(u) > \sigma(v)$, if $\frac{\epsilon_v}{\sigma^*(v)} - \frac{\epsilon_u}{\sigma^*(u)} \leq \frac{\sigma^*(u) - \sigma^*(v)}{\sigma^*(v)}$, where $\epsilon_u = \sigma(u) - \sigma^*(u)$ and $\epsilon_v = \sigma(v) - \sigma^*(v)$.*

PROOF. Let ϵ_u and ϵ_v be the errors introduced in u and v respectively using any approximate score-assignment algorithm. Given $\sigma^*(u) > \sigma^*(v)$, for $\sigma(u)$ and $\sigma(v)$ to violate this relationship the relative error introduced in v ($\frac{\epsilon_v}{\sigma^*(v)}$) should exceed the relative error introduced in u ($\frac{\epsilon_u}{\sigma^*(u)}$) by the amount of gap between u and v relative to v. Figure 3c portrays this observation. Mathematically,

$$\frac{\epsilon_v}{\sigma^*(v)} - \frac{\epsilon_u}{\sigma^*(u)} \leq \frac{\sigma^*(u) - \sigma^*(v)}{\sigma^*(v)}. \ Since,\ \sigma^*(u) > \sigma^*(v)$$

$$\Rightarrow \epsilon_v - \epsilon_u \leq \sigma^*(u) - \sigma^*(v) \Rightarrow \sigma(v) \leq \sigma(u). \tag{2}$$

Thus, if the above condition holds then the errors introduced by any approximate score-assignment algorithm preserves the relative ordering between σ^* and σ. □

[5]Directed acyclic graphs would be abbreviated as DAGs.

3.4.2 Discussion

Eq. 2 (theorem 2) presents the condition for any approximate score-assignment algorithm to maintain the same relative ordering of nodes as produced by the greedy-gold standard[6]. This condition evaluates to $\epsilon_1 - \epsilon_2 \leq \frac{\sigma^*(u)}{\sigma^*(v)} - 1$, where $\epsilon_1 = \frac{\epsilon_v}{\sigma^*(v)}$ and $\epsilon_2 = \frac{\epsilon_u}{\sigma^*(u)}$ are the relative errors incurred in the scores of v and u respectively. This condition could further be simplified, by putting $\epsilon_1 - \epsilon_2 = \epsilon$, to $\sigma^*(v) \leq \frac{\sigma^*(u)}{1+\epsilon}$. Let us now analyze the above mentioned condition and identify the cases where it gets violated. Firstly, when $\epsilon << 1$, i.e., $1 + \epsilon \approx 1$, the condition always holds as it is given that $\sigma^*(u) > \sigma^*(v)$. Now, when ϵ is large, we can rewrite the condition as $\epsilon \leq \frac{\sigma^*(u)}{\sigma^*(v)} - 1$. A large ϵ means that the difference of relative errors in the two chosen nodes is high. Given this, if $\sigma^*(v)$ and $\sigma^*(u)$ are close then choosing any one of u and v as a seed-node would not impact the expected spread much, thus, producing a correct ordering is no longer important. On the other hand, when $\sigma^*(v)$ and $\sigma^*(u)$ are far apart, we can safely assume $\sigma^*(v)$ to be equal to $\sigma^*(u)$ in the worst case[7]. Finally, the only case for which the condition in Eq. 2 gets violated is when $\epsilon > 0$. To better explain the previous result, we provide an in-depth analysis of lemma's 4, 5, and 6 to get an expression for the relative error. Please note that, unlike above, all the analyses in the following discussion are based on the score of a node v w.r.t contribution of another node w.

Using lemma 4 and 5, it is evident that the relative error, for DAGs, introduced by v in the score of u using the *EaSyIM* algorithm is $\leq \sum_{w \in \mathbf{In}(v)} (2p(w, v) - 1)A_1$. To quantify this error, we evaluate A_1 under different information-diffusion models. Considering the average degree of the underlying graph to be η, the expected value of the total number of u-v paths of a given length (l) can be upper-bounded by η^{l-1}. Under the IC model, the contribution of a path of length l is $\prod p_e = p^l$ where $p = 0.1$ which simplifies A_1 to $\sum_{i=2}^{l-1} \eta^{i-1} p^i$. It can be seen that this error is not as large as it looks, since the number of paths usually do not increase exponentially (w.r.t η) with the increase in length. Let us consider a graph with small value of η, i.e., $\eta p < 1$ and analyze the growth of A_1 with the addition of paths of increasing length. With the addition of paths of a given length i, A_1 increases by $(\eta p)^{i-1} p$, which in turn decreases exponentially since $\eta p < 1$. Thus, we can observe that A_1 grows sub-logarithmically. On the contrary, when η is large it dominates the growth of A_1 and thus, the error increases with the increase in path-length. However, the path-length is upper-bounded by the diameter $\mathcal{D}$ of the graph, which is usually small for large η [34]. Hence, the overall error introduced by the *EasyIM* algorithm is upper-bounded by $\eta(2p - 1)A_1$, which is small in case of DAGs. Similarly, lemma 6 computes the error introduced by v in the score of u due to cycles by the *PU* algorithm. Eq. 11 can be re-written as $\sum_{i=2}^{l} (\eta^{i-1} p^i)/i$, which is similar to the error term evaluated for DAGs. Using similar analysis as above, this term is also small. Moreover, *EaSyIM* incurs an additional error owing to the cycles of varying lengths that contain u. It is evident that the error due to these cycles is similar to that of the *PU* algorithm. Thus, the total error introduced by *EaSyIM* is not large for graphs as well.

Under the WC model, we can safely assume that $\eta p = 1$ as the probability associated with each edge $e = (u, v)$ is $1/\text{in-degree}(v) \approx 1/\eta$. The analysis for the IC model holds for this case as well and thus, the error is small. Our results are even stronger for the LT model, as *EaSyIM* always maintains the same ordering of nodes

[6]GREEDY ranks the nodes in the order of their expected influence.

[7]The chance of any score-assignment algorithm to distort the relative ordering by introducing errors would be the highest when $\sigma^*(u)$=$\sigma^*(v)$.

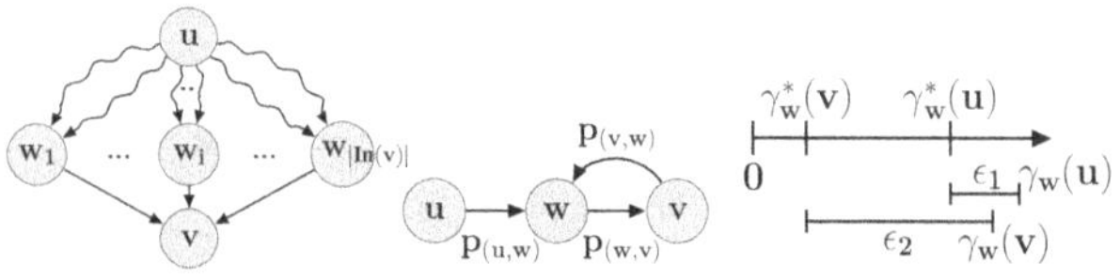

(a) Non-Disjoint Paths (b) Cycles (c) Relative Error

Figure 3: **Error analysis for the score-assignment step.**

as produced by the GREEDY algorithm for DAGs. This clearly follows from the live-edge model, where each node possesses at most one incoming edge and thus, in our analysis all the $\cup$'s can be replaced by $\sum$'s which in turn eradicates all the sources of errors for DAGs (and other simpler structures as well). One can also observe that using a similar analysis, the error introduced by *EaSyIM* for tree-like structures is 0 for the IC and WC models as well. Moreover, the errors introduced for graphs are due to the cycles alone, and following the similar analysis as above (edge probabilities are $1/\text{in-degree}$), the overall error remains small.

Now we revisit the expression $\epsilon > 0$. Since ϵ_1 is not close to ϵ_2, we can conclude, owing to the above analysis that the error increases significantly with length only if the number of paths increase exponentially, that there exist a large number of longer paths contributing to ϵ_1. Let there be t_1 paths of length l_1 which contribute towards ϵ_1 and t_2 paths of length l_2 which contribute towards ϵ_2. Assuming that the other set of paths introduce an equal amount of error in both u and v, the expression $\epsilon > 0$ reduces to $t_1 p^{l_1} - t_2 p^{l_2} > 0$ for the IC model. Thus, the condition in Eq. 2 gets violated if the length of the paths contributing to v, i.e., $l_2 < l_1 < l_2 - \log_p(\frac{t_1}{t_2})$. Considering an alternate analysis, we can see that if there are t paths of length l, with an individual contribution of p^l, ending at a node v, then the correct score would be $\cup p^l = 1 - (1 - p^l)^t$. Since $p^l << 1$ this expression reduces to $\approx 1 - (1 - tp^l) = tp^l$. This is the same as the score assigned using the *EaSyIM* algorithm.

In summary, we identify the conditions where the error introduced by *EaSyIM* does not distort the relative ordering of nodes, as produced by the greedy gold standard. For the cases, where this relative ordering cannot be maintained we show that the error introduced is small, and thus the overall impact to the spread of a given set of seed-nodes is also small. Before analyzing *OSIM*, we state the conclusions drawn on the results presented in this section.

CONCLUSION 2. *Score-assignment using the* EaSyIM *algorithm captures the expected spread of a node for tree-like structures, under the IC, WC and LT models of information diffusion. Thus, the ScoreGREEDY algorithm produces a* $1 - 1/e$ *approximate solution to the IM problem for tree-like structures.*

CONCLUSION 3. *Score-assignment using the* EaSyIM *algorithm captures the expected spread of a node for DAGs under the LT model. Thus, the ScoreGREEDY algorithm produces a* $1 - 1/e$ *approximate solution to the IM problem for DAGs under the LT model.*

3.4.3 OSIM

Please see Appendix I.

4. EXPERIMENTS

All the simulations were done using the Boost graph library [7] in C++ on an Intel(R) Xeon(R) 20-core machine with 2.4 GHz CPU and 100 GB RAM running Linux Ubuntu 12.04. We present results on real (large) graphs, taken from the arXiv [3] and SNAP [6] repositories, as described in Table 2. In addition to these, a snapshot of the *Twitter* network crawled from Twitter.com in July 2009 was downloaded from a publicly available source [1]. We consider a mix of both directed and undirected graphs, however to ensure uniformity the undirected graphs were made directed by considering, for each edge, the arcs in both the directions. As a conventional practice, the *spread*, and hence the *opinion-spread* as well, is calculated as an average over $10K$ Monte Carlo (MC) simulations[8]. Next, we state the *information-diffusion* models and the *algorithms* used for obtaining the results described in the rest of this section.

Dataset	n	m	Type	Avg. Degree	90-%ile Diameter
NetHEPT	15K	62K	Undirected	4.1	8.8
HepPh	12K	237K	Undirected	19.75	5.8
DBLP	317K	2.1M	Undirected	6.63	8
YouTube	1.13M	5.98M	Undirected	5.29	6.5
SocLiveJournal	4.85M	69M	Directed	14.23	6.5
Orkut	3.07M	234.2M	Undirected	76.29	4.8
Twitter	41.6M	1.5B	Directed	36.06	5.1
Friendster	65.6M	3.6B	Undirected	54.88	5.8

Table 2: **Datasets.**

Information-Diffusion Models: We incorporate the use of three fundamental diffusion models, namely – IC, WC and LT [32], for the *opinion-oblivious* case. The IC model is used with a uniform probability $p_{(u,v)} = 0.1$, assigned to all the edges $(\forall(u,v) \in E)$ of the graph G. On the other hand, the WC model associates a probability of $p_{(u,v)} = \frac{1}{|\mathbf{In}(v)|}$ with all the edges, where $|\mathbf{In}(v)|$ denotes the in-degree of v. As opposed to the IC and WC models, the LT model requires an additional parameter, apart from the weights $w_{(u,v)} = \frac{1}{|\mathbf{In}(v)|}$ associated with all the edges, on all the nodes of the graph specifying the node threshold $\theta_v = rand(0,1)$, $\forall v \in V$. Note that the $rand(0,1)$ function generates numbers randomly and uniformly between 0 and 1. Moreover, all these parameter assignments follow the conventional practice in the literature [28, 32, 35, 46]. For the *opinion-aware* case, we employ the use of two diffusion models, namely – OC [48] and OI (Sec. 2.2). This choice is driven by our thorough analytical comparisons in Sec. 1 and later in Sec. 5 with other related models. The details about dataset preparation using the opinion-aware model parameters – *opinion* (o) and *interaction* (φ) are present in Sec. 4.1.

Algorithms: We portray the effectiveness of *OSIM* by comparing with the Modified-GREEDY (Appendix K) algorithm which, being tuned to maximize the *effective opinion spread* (Def. 7), serves as a baseline to evaluate the *quality of spread* for the *opinion-aware* scenario. We compare *EaSyIM* for effectiveness, efficiency and scalability with a representative set of state-of-the-art algorithms and heuristics, as established by us in Secs. 1 and 5, namely – CELF++, TIM$^+$, IRIE and SIMPATH. For all these algorithms, we adopt the C++ implementations made available by their authors.

Parameters: The value of spread reported by the Modified-GREEDY, CELF++ [28], *OSIM* and *EaSyIM* algorithms is an average over $10K$ MC simulations. Thus, we report the total time taken to complete all the MC simulations for these algorithms. Unless otherwise stated, we set $l = 3$ and $\lambda = 1$ for the score-assignment step of *OSIM* and *EaSyIM*. For the TIM$^+$ [46] algorithm we use $\epsilon = 0.1$. We set the IRIE parameters α and θ to 0.7 and $1/320$, respectively, and SIMPATH's parameters η and l to 10^{-3} and 4, respectively. All the parameters have been set according to the recommendations by the authors of [29, 31, 46].

Comments: Note that we do not perform scalability comparisons of *OSIM* with the OVM algorithm [48] as (1) Asymptotically, the time complexity of *OSIM* $\big(O(k\mathcal{D}(m+n))$, where $\mathcal{D}$ is a small constant$\big)$ is better when compared to OVM $\big(O(k^2(m+n))\big)$, (2) It is rather difficult to extend OVM to work with the OI model and (3) OVM is designed to work with just the LT model at the first-layer while OSIM works with both IC and LT models. Moreover, since the time and space complexity analysis of *OSIM* is exactly

[8]These instances were run in parallel on 20-cores for *OSIM*, *EaSyIM* and Modified-GREEDY. However, for a fair comparison with other techniques we report the total time taken.

the same as that of *EaSyIM*, the scalability comparisons performed for the latter serve for the former as well.

4.1 Opinion-Aware

4.1.1 Real Data: Twitter

To motivate the importance of the OI model in real-world scenarios, we employed the use of data extracted from the *Twitter* social network. This data has two aspects, namely – (1) the underlying (directed) social network, and (2) the tweets by users of this network. A snapshot of the *Twitter* network, crawled in June 2009 containing $41.6M$ users (nodes) and $1.5B$ connections (edges), available publicly from [1] is used as the underlying graph. A collection of $476M$ tweets gathered from a subset ($17M$ users) of the users ($41.6M$) in the underlying graph, crawled during the period of June 2009 to December 2009, available publicly from [6] constitutes the second part of our dataset. This dataset contains the following information for each tweet, namely – (1) user-id, (2) time-stamp, and (3) the original text message or the tweet.

As discussed in previous sections, the motive of IM, and hence MEO, is to maximize the spread of information about a content, which can be a product, person, event and many more. For instance, in Twitter, the diffusion of information about a topic corresponds to the retweeting of or replying to a tweet or even tweeting about the topic. In fact, the temporal sequence of tweets by users, about a topic, guided by their connections in the network, defines the spread of information about that topic. Thus, as a first step towards analyzing information diffusion in real-world settings, there is a need to extract *topic-focussed subgraphs*.

To this end, we pre-processed our dataset to retain all the tweets that possess at least one *hashtag* (#), where *hashtags* constitute our *topics*. Thus, we were left with $48.5M$ tweets corresponding to $1.6M$ users. Moreover, we projected the underlying twitter network on this identified subset of $1.6M$ users. This gave us a graph of $1.6M$ users with $75M$ edges among them. We denote this graph with the term *background graph* in the rest of this section. Moving ahead, we describe the procedure for construction of topic-focussed subgraphs. A *topic-focused subgraph* evolves by including nodes and edges when users tweet (or retweet) on the same topic, thus (re)activating the edges between them. Following this procedure, we scan the tweets in the increasing order of their time-stamps, and the users associated with the tweets are added as nodes incrementally. Moreover, a directed edge is constructed from a node A to another node B if this edge (directed) exists in the *background graph* and vice versa. All the nodes with an in-degree of 0 are considered to be originators or seeds of information. We stop growing a topic-graph if no new seed-nodes were added for a significant amount of elapsed time and start growing a new topic graph. The threshold on the elapsed time was learnt from the data. We look at the average frequency of tweets and identify a time difference as threshold that deviates significantly from the expected. This procedure resulted in $\approx$ 10–12 topic-focussed subgraphs per *hashtag*. Note that the construction of topic-focused subgraphs requires just a single scan of the *background graph*.

With all the data preparation steps in place, next, we use popular sentiment analysis APIs [4, 5] to extract *opinions* from the tweets. These sources learn a hierarchical classifier, which first determines whether a tweet is neutral or not. Neutral tweets are assigned an *opinion* score of 0. If the tweet was not neutral, then another classifier determines the probability of this tweet towards the positive class. Finally, we map this probability value ($[0, 1]$) to our *opinion* scores ($[-1, 1]$). Note that the error introduced by the sentiment classifier would equally effect all the following results and thus, it can be safely ignored for all the analsyes.

Next, we show our analyses using topic-focussed subgraphs extracted from high frequency *hashtags* (top-100), each of which possesses at least $50K$ tweets. Unless otherwise stated, the following portrayed results are averaged over all the topic-subgraphs and the *normalized root-mean-square* error is used as the quality metric. We first show the results of opinion estimation for nodes on unseen topics. The opinions extracted from the tweets of a user, may include the effects of (1) her personal opinion, (2) the influence of her social contacts and (3) external factors. Modelling of external factors is relatively hard from the data, and thus, we consider just the first two factors. As discussed in Sec. 1, we estimate the opinion of a node for a given topic, by considering the opinions of this node for similar topics. Since our topics possess a temporal aspect as well, we estimate the opinion of a node for a topic A, by performing a weighted average of the opinion of this node on all the related topics in the past. In addition, since we also possess the *true* value of the opinion of nodes for the topic A, as output by our classifier, we portray the quality of this estimation procedure from our data. We were able to estimate the opinions of the *seed-nodes* with an error[9] of 3.43% and the opinions of all other nodes with an error of 8.57%. Note that the error on non-seed nodes is higher when compared to that on the seed nodes. This is indicative of the fact that the tweets of the seed-nodes indeed express their personal opinion, however the tweets of other nodes additionally include the effect of the opinions of their network. Moreover, this also proves that there is a need for models that: (1) consider the *change of opinion* during information diffusion, and (2) consider the effect of *interaction* between two nodes.

Having computed the *opinion* of each node, the *interaction* associated with an edge between two nodes (directed) is calculated as the fraction of the times they agree with each other across the subgraphs corresponding to all the topics in the past and not just those corresponding to the related topics. Note that both the parameters for the OI model, namely – *opinion* and *interaction*, can be easily computed during the topic-subgraph construction step and do not incur any additional cost for their estimation. As mentioned earlier in this section that topic-subgraph construction is a required step for analyzing information diffusion, thus, the parameter estimation cost for the OI model is amortized constant.

Next, we show that the *opinion-spread* in real-world follows the OI model. For this experiment, we consider the top-100 extracted topic-subgraphs and use the identified seeds or originators of information from the real-world, as the seed nodes for the information diffusion process to measure the *opinion spread*. For each topic subgraph we calculate the opinion-spread using the opinions extracted from their tweets, which serves as our *ground truth*. Similarly, we use the estimated parameters on these topic subgraphs and obtain the *opinion spread* under the OI, OC and the IC models. Although, depending upon the distribution of opinions and interactions, the opinion-spread achieved using all the three models can fall on the either side of the ground-truth, our results in Figure 4a show that the opinion-spread obtained under the OI model is always closest to the ground-truth opinion-spread and thus, possesses the least error. Moreover, Figure 4b shows a similar analysis on the average opinion-spread using the OI, OC and IC models with varying seeds, and it is evident that the *opinion-spread* under the OI model possesses the least error.

Having empirically proved that the OI model closely mirrors the *opinion-spread* in real world scenarios, finally, we show our results on opinion-aware IM. As mentioned earlier in this section, we show the average opinion-spread achieved for different topics by performing the information diffusion process on the entire *back-*

[9] The error in estimation can be on the either side of the true value.

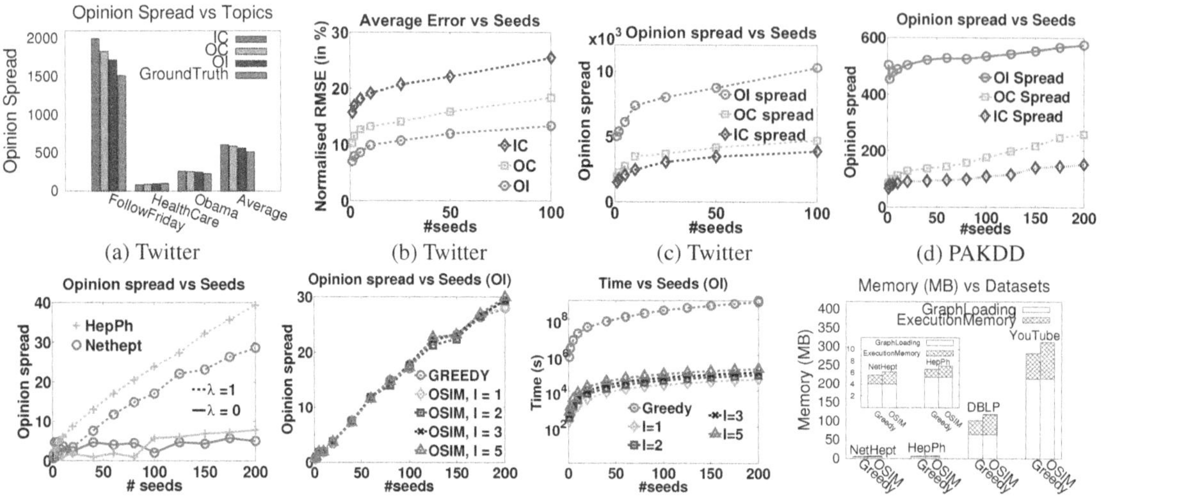

(a) Twitter (b) Twitter (c) Twitter (d) PAKDD

(e) NetHEPT and HepPh (f) NetHEPT (g) NetHEPT (h) Medium Datasets

Figure 4: **Comparison of average opinion-spread under OI, OC and IC with ground-truth for different topic-graphs on Twitter data with (a) k=50 seeds and (b) varying seeds. Opinion-spread ($\lambda = 1$) comparison of OI with OC and IC on (c) Twitter data and (d) PAKDD data (churn analysis). (e) Opinion-spread comparison of $\lambda = 1$ with $\lambda = 0$ on NetHept and HepPh. (f) Growth of opinion-spread ($\lambda = 1$) with l and k on NetHEPT (OI). (g) Growth-rate of running time with l and k on NetHEPT (OI). (h) Memory consumed for $k = 100$ on Medium Datasets.**

ground graph. Figure 4c shows that the opinion-spread achieved using the seeds selected by the OI model is much better when compared to that of the OC and the IC model. Apart from the results on quality, *OSIM* with $l = 1$, took 497 minutes and $1.72GB$ of RAM to identify 100 seeds on the *background graph*.

4.1.2 Real Data: Analyzing Customer Churn

We used the PAKDD 2012 data mining competition dataset, available publicly from [2], to motivate the applicability of *MEO* and the OI model in solving real-world problems. The dataset contains profiles of $\approx 100K$ customers, including billing information, usage data, service requests and complaints, of a large telecommunications company for a period of 1 year from January 1, 2011 to December 31, 2011. The data also contains information about the *churn* (termination of services) date for each customer, where $17K$ customers are churners and the rest are non-churners. Using this data, the objective of the challenge was to predict which customers are liable to churn. We extend this problem of modelling *customer-churn* further to perform a novel analysis using *opinion-aware* IM. Since the main objective of this paper is not churn-prediction, to make the data preparation step for our analysis simpler we work on a balanced subset of the original data containing $34K$ customers with equal number of churners and non-churners.

Owing to the increasing popularity of *label propagation* [50] and similarity based learning [20], we build upon the hypothesis that customers with *similar* attributes possess similar *churn* behavior. Under this hypothesis, we induce a graph, of *customers*, using *attribute-value* similarity and a similarity *threshold* to construct edges between two customers. The graph obtained thus, consists of $34K$ nodes (customers) and $1.5M$ edges (relationships), with churners assigned a label of -1 and non-churners that of 1. Using this data, we build a model using label-propagation to predict the susceptibility of a customer towards churn. After convergence, the value ($[-1, 1]$) at each node represents the *affinity*, or in other words the *opinion*, of a customer to churn with -1 and 1 denoting strong affinity towards churn and non-churn respectively. In this way, we estimate the *opinion* (o) parameter of the OI model. The attribute-value similarity defines the influence-proability (p) associated with each edge, while the *interaction* probability (φ) for each edge is generated using the $rand(0, 1)$ function described above.

Acquainted with the likelihood of customers to churn combined with the availability of a churn-prediction model, a service provider would like to identify potential targets, under a marketing buget, capable of maintaining its reputation, thus, indirectly preventing the *cascades* of churn. This task boils down to identifying seeds that maximize the difference of positive and negative opinions, or in other words maximize the effective opinion (MEO). Figure 4d shows that the opinion-spread achieved using the seeds selected by the OI model is much better when compared to that of the OC and the IC model. This proves the importance of the OI model and the notions of *opinion* and *interaction* in solving real-world problems.

4.1.3 Other Real Datasets

Having highlighted the importance of *opinion*, *interaction*, the OI model and the MEO problem using two real-world datasets in the previous sections, here we present an in-depth analysis of *opinion-aware* IM on the benchmark datasets (Table 2) used for the evaluation of classical IM. Since these datasets do not inherently possess the properties of *opinion* and *interaction* with nodes and edges of the graph respectively, we annotate them as follows. The *opinions* are generated by two methods, namely – (a) $o \sim rand(-1, 1)$, where the opinion of each node is generated uniformly at random in the range $[-1, 1]$ and, (b) $o \sim \mathcal{N}(0, 1)$, where the generated opinions follow the standard normal distribution, while the *interaction* probability for each edge is only generated uniformly and randomly using the function $\varphi \sim rand(0, 1)$. The reported results are averaged over 3 different instances of the generated data. For additional results please see Appendix J.

Quality: The first set of results show the importance of the choice of optimization-objective. We compare the *effective opinion-spread* ($\lambda = 1$) with the *opinion-spread* ($\lambda = 0$) for the NetHEPT dataset using *OSIM* under the OI model. It is evident from Figure 4e that $\lambda = 1$ outperforms $\lambda = 0$ and hence, maximizing the effective opinion-spread is better. With this, we fix $\lambda = 1$ for a comparison of the effective opinion-spread obtained using *OSIM* (with varying l) with Modified-Greedy for different datasets. Fig-

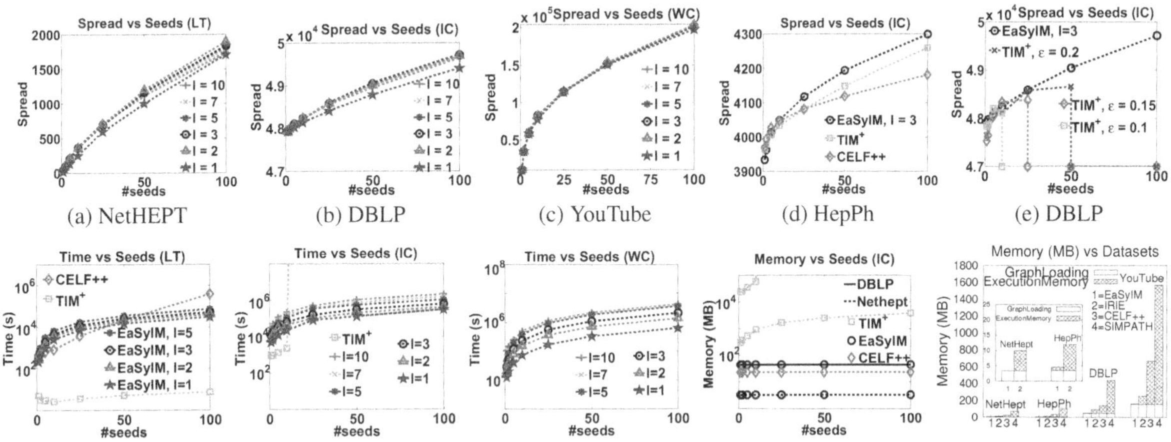

(a) NetHEPT (b) DBLP (c) YouTube (d) HepPh (e) DBLP

(f) NetHEPT (g) DBLP (h) YouTube (i) NetHEPT and DBLP (j) Medium Datasets

Figure 5: **Growth of spread with l and k on (a) NetHEPT (LT), (b) DBLP (IC) and (c) YouTube (WC). Spread comparison of *EaSyIM* with TIM$^+$ and CELF++ on (e) HepPh (IC), (f) DBLP (IC). Running time comparison of *EaSyIM* with CELF++ and TIM$^+$ on (h) NetHEPT (LT), (i) DBLP (IC) and (j) YouTube (WC). Memory consumption comparison of *EaSyIM* with CELF++ and TIM$^+$ on (m) NetHEPT and DBLP (IC), and with all algorithms for $k = 100$ on (n) Medium Datasets (IC).**

ure 4f presents the results with varying seeds for NetHEPT under the OI model ($o \sim \mathcal{N}(0,1)$). It can be seen that the reported opinion spread improves with increase in l, however, it starts to dip when $l \to \mathcal{D}$ owing to a significant increase in the number of cyclic paths, which in turn causes the error in the assigned scores to increase as discussed in Sec. 3.4.2. Using these results, we conclude that $l = 3$ serves as the best choice for *OSIM*. Moreover, *OSIM* closely mirrors Modified-GREEDY with respect to the quality of obtained *opinion-spread*.

Efficiency: In continuation to the comparison on quality, here we compare *OSIM* with Modified-GREEDY on its running-time for the NetHEPT dataset. Figure 4g shows that *OSIM* is at least 10^3 times more efficient when compared to Modified-GREEDY with the gain going as high as 10^5 for some cases. Moreover, this figure (with y-axis in log-scale) also shows that the running-time of *OSIM* grows linearly with increase in l.

Scalability: Figure 4h shows a comparison of the memory-consumed by *OSIM* with Modified-GREEDY for all the 4 datasets discussed above. It is important to note that the memory consumption of these algorithms is independent of the parameters, namely – path-length (l), number of seeds (k) and the number of MC simulations. Both the algorithms scale linearly in the size of the graph and require constant-factor overheads to solve the MEO problem. This is indicated by the stacked bars, which show that these algorithms require only a small amount (constant-factor) of memory over and above the memory required to load the graph.

As stated earlier, in addition to the scalability and efficiency analysis for *OSIM*, next, we present a more involved analysis for *EaSyIM* which serves the purpose for the former as well.

4.2 Opinion-Oblivious

Quality: The first set of results portray the effect of the parameter l on the *spread* obtained using *EaSyIM*. Figures 5a, 5b and 5c present the results with varying seeds on the NetHEPT, DBLP and the YouTube datasets under the LT, IC and WC models respectively. It can be seen that the reported spread follows a similar pattern as that of *OSIM*, i.e., it improves with increase in l, however, it starts to dip when $l \to \mathcal{D}$. Using these results, we conclude that $l = 5$ serves as the best choice for *EaSyIM*, with $l = 3$ being marginally worse when compared to $l = 5$. Moreover, owing to $l = 3$ being ≈ 2 times more efficient when compared to $l = 5$ (detailed analysis on efficiency in the following paragraph), we fix $l = 3$ for a comparison of the spread obtained using *EaSyIM* with other algorithms. Figures 5d and 5e present the spreads obtained for the HepPh and DBLP datasets under the IC model. Note that the sudden drop in the spread of TIM$^+$ in Figure 5e indicates that it crashed on our machine after that point. These results show that *EaSyIM* mirrors the state-of-the-art techniques closely for majority of the datasets, while being *even better* at certain instances, with respect to the quality of the obtained *spread*.

Efficiency: Figures 5f, 5g and 5h show a comparison of the running-times of *EaSyIM* with CELF++ and TIM$^+$ for varying seeds on the NetHEPT, DBLP and the YouTube datasets under the LT, IC and WC models respectively. These figures show that *EaSyIM* grows linearly (y-axis in log-scale) with the parameters l and k, therefore *EaSyIM* is ≈ 2 times faster for $l = 3$ when compared to $l = 5$. Owing to the marginal improvement in the spread from $l = 3$ to $l = 5$ (quality analysis in the previous paragraph), we choose $l = 3$ for *EaSyIM* as it provides the best tradeoff between efficiency and quality. Moreover, it can be seen that neither CELF++ nor TIM$^+$ scale well with the increase in graph size. CELF++ was not able to complete on the DBLP and the YouTube datasets even after running for 7 days, while TIM$^+$ crashed on the DBLP dataset for $k > 10, 25, 50$ with $\epsilon = 0.1, 0.15, 0.2$ respectively owing to its huge memory requirement. In addition, it is evident from Tables 3 and 4 that *EaSyIM* is 10–15 times more efficient while consuming 3-4 times less memory when compared to CELF++, and requires 8–10 times more time to run while its memory-footprint is ≈ 500 times smaller when compared to TIM$^+$. We argue that since *EaSyIM* can be efficiently parallelized owing to the independence of the MC simulations, its lack of efficiency when compared to TIM$^+$ can be easily mitigated by running it in parallel on 8 cores[10] while ensuring the memory gain to be the same.

Scalability: Figure 5i portrays the growth of the memory-footprint of *EaSyIM*, CELF++, and TIM$^+$ with varying seeds for the NetHEPT and the DBLP datasets. It is evident that the memory-consumption of all other techniques, barring TIM$^+$ (which grows at a much faster rate), grows linearly with the number of seeds. It is also clear that *EaSyIM* possesses the smallest memory-footprint, being ≈ 4 and ≈ 500 times smaller when compared to CELF++ and TIM$^+$

[10]Considering the ease of availability of multiple cores in a single machine when compared to large amount of RAM.

Dataset	Running Time (min)			Memory (MB)		
	TIM^+	EaSyIM (l=1)	Gain	TIM^+	EaSyIM (l=1)	Gain
DBLP	783.1	2183	0.36x	35234.75	46.5	**758x**
YouTube	NA	5089.5	∞	NA	158.3	∞
socLive	NA	15433.33	**∞**	NA	974.94	∞

Table 3: **Comparing *EaSyIM* with TIM$^+$**, $k = 50$, $\epsilon = 0.1$.

Dataset	Running Time (min)			Memory (MB)		
	CELF++	EaSyIM (l=1)	Gain	CELF++	EaSyIM (l=1)	Gain
NetHEPT	5352.25	118	**45.35x**	23.26	3.39	6.86x
HepPh	9746.74	230	**41x**	24.60	3.47	7.08x
DBLP	NA	5071.67	**∞**	NA	44.73	**∞**

Table 4: **Comparing *EaSyIM* with CELF++**, $k = 100$.

respectively. Moreover, TIM$^+$ ($\epsilon = 0.1$) crashed for $k > 10$ on the DBLP dataset due to going out of memory on our machine. To further this, our experiments revealed that even after relaxing ϵ to 0.15 and 0.2 it crashed for $k > 25$ and $k > 50$ respectively. This analysis unravels the obvious problem with TIM$^+$, i.e., though being efficient it requires an exorbitantly high amount of main-memory and thus, cannot be termed *scalable*. Figure 5j shows the additional amount of memory required, over and above the memory required to load the graph, by each of our benchmarking algorithms for 4 different datasets. It is clear that *EaSyIM* possesses the least overhead while SIMPATH possesses the highest. Note that we omit the bar corresponding to TIM$^+$, as it hinders the comparison with other techniques owing to its memory consumption being too high. This shows that *EaSyIM* possesses the capability of scaling to very large graphs. For additional results please see Appendix J.

In summary, both *OSIM* and *EaSyIM* provide the best trade-off between *memory-consumption* and *running-time*, and possess the capability to perform IM on large graphs using moderately sized machines or even a laptop.

5. RELATED WORK

The IM problem has been studied extensively over the past decade, thus, it is rather difficult to write a complete literature review in one section. A detailed comparison of the OI model with both IC-N [16] and OC [48], the only other models for *opinion-aware* IM, has been done qualitatively (Sec. 1) and empirically (Sec. 4). Here, we overview the existing works that overlap with our problem.

(1) *Topic-Aware and Competitive IM*: The motive of topic-aware IM [8, 11, 15] is to design strategies for maximizing the collective *spread* of information under a given topic-distribution. It allows different influence probabilities for each topic (assuming a joint distribution of topics), without considering the opinions (of a node) towards these topics. On the other hand, the objective of competitive IM [30, 36, 39] is to maximize the *spread* of information, about a specific content, in the presence of competitors. It is rather intuitive that competitive IM is similar to topic-aware IM, thus, both of them suffer with same set of deficiencies, i.e., (a) the absence of opinions and negatively activated nodes, and (b) the incapability of capturing their change as information propagates. In addition, another limitation for competitive IM lies with the information-diffusion process, where each node (strictly) propagates information about a particular content and any newly activated node (by the former) also (strictly) follows the same content. In summary, both of them consider maximization of the number of active nodes (opinion-oblivious notion of *spread*), rendering the spread function to be submodular and thus, are closer to the *classical* IM problem.

(2) *IM in signed networks*: IM in signed networks [37] considers the presence of an opinion, from a binary valued set containing exactly opposite opinions, at each node with the notion of *friends* – capable of activating a node with their own opinion and *foes* – capable of doing the opposite. The major limitation in this model is the stringent constraint on the parameters to attain values from a *discrete binary* valued set. On the contrary, OI allows *opinions* and *interactions* to come from a real-valued domain. Moreover, the *interaction* between two nodes is given a *probabilistic* aspect which is missing in the signed network voter model. In fact, the signed network voter model is rather a *special-case* of the OI model.

(3) *Classical IM*: Kempe et al. [32] proved that finding an optimal solution for the IM problem is NP-Hard, and that a simple greedy (GREEDY) algorithm provides the best approximation guarantees in polynomial time. It required $O(kmnr)$ time to produce a solution, where r is the number of MC simulations (usually $r \approx 10K$). This high time complexity renders the GREEDY algorithm inapplicable to the networks of today. Since then, a host of works have introduced optimizations in GREEDY with CELF++ [28] being the most efficient of all within this class of algorithms. Note that these optimizations never improved the asymptotic time complexity of the algorithm. In pursuit of better time complexity, researchers have recently resorted to techniques that use *sampling* with *memoization* [13, 23, 45, 46], to portray superior efficiency while retaining approximation guarantees. Among them, TIM$^+$ [46], that runs in $O((k+l)(m+n)\log n/\epsilon^2)$ expected time and produces a $(1 - \frac{1}{e} - \epsilon)$-approximate solution, where ϵ is a constant, with probability as high as $1 - n^{-l}$, and its improvement IMM [45] are the most efficient. Despite their superior efficiency these algorithms lacked *scalability*, owing to their exorbitantly high memory footprint. The worst case space complexity of TIM$^+$ is $O(n^2 \log \binom{n}{k}/\epsilon^2)$, which can be very high for small values of ϵ. In addition to the above mentioned techniques, literature has witnessed many heuristic algorithms [17–19, 29, 31]. Among them, IRIE and SIMPATH [29, 31] are considered state-of-the-art heuristics for the IC and LT models respectively. Although, these techniques build upon a similar idea as that of *EaSyIM*, its algorithm design and analysis is very different from them with an additional advantage of running in linear space and time. Moreover, as shown in Sec. 4, both of these techniques are not capable of scaling to larger datasets.

6. CONCLUSIONS AND FUTURE WORK

In this paper, we addressed the problem of influence maximization in social networks under a very generic opinion-aware setting, where the nodes can possess any one of the – positive, neutral and negative opinions. To this end, we introduced the novel *MEO* problem and devised a *holistic* solution to the influence maximization problem; by coming up with an opinion-cum-interaction (*OI*) model, and scalable algorithms – *OSIM* and *EaSyIM*. Since majority of the works in the literature operate oblivious to the existence of opinions and are not scalable, there are efficiency concerns in real-world scenarios with huge graphs. Consequently, we designed efficient algorithms that run in time linear to the size of the graph. Moreover, the space complexity of our algorithms is also linear; which is orders of magnitude better when compared to the state-of-the-art techniques. Our empirical studies on real-world social network datasets showed that our algorithms are effective, efficient, scale well – providing the best trade-off between running time and memory consumption, and are practical for large real graphs. In future, we would like to come up with a distributed version of our algorithms, thus enabling it scale to even larger graphs.

Acknowledgements

We would like to thank Sayan Ranu, Arnab Bhattacharya, Srikanta Bedathur and Jeff Ullman for providing valuable suggestions and insights throughout the course of this work. We also thank Manish Gupta (Director – XRCI) for providing such a great platform to work on cutting-edge research problems.

7. REFERENCES

[1] http://an.kaist.ac.kr/traces/WWW2010.html.

[2] http://lamda.nju.edu.cn/zhangt/dm2012/Project4.html.

[3] arXiv. http://www.arxiv.org.

[4] Empath: Sentiment, Topic, and Demographic Analysis. https://www.parc.com/services/focus-area/bigdata/.

[5] Natural Language Sentiment Analysis API. http://text-processing.com/demo/sentiment/.

[6] SNAP Datasets. https://snap.stanford.edu/data/.

[7] The Boost Graph Library. http://www.boost.org.

[8] Ç. Aslay, N. Barbieri, F. Bonchi, and R. A. Baeza-Yates. Online topic-aware influence maximization queries. In *EDBT*, pages 295–306, 2014.

[9] C. Aslay, W. Lu, F. Bonchi, A. Goyal, and L. V. S. Lakshmanan. Viral marketing meets social advertising: Ad allocation with minimum regret. *PVLDB*, 8:814–825, 2015.

[10] L. Backstrom, D. Huttenlocher, J. Kleinberg, and X. Lan. Group formation in large social networks: Membership, growth, and evolution. In *KDD*, pages 44–54, 2006.

[11] N. Barbieri, F. Bonchi, and G. Manco. Topic-aware social influence propagation models. In *ICDM*, pages 81–90, 2012.

[12] N. Barbieri, F. Bonchi, and G. Manco. Cascade-based community detection. In *WSDM*, pages 33–42, 2013.

[13] C. Borgs, M. Brautbar, J. Chayes, and B. Lucier. Maximizing social influence in nearly optimal time. In *SODA*, pages 946–957, 2014.

[14] V. Chaoji, S. Ranu, R. Rastogi, and R. Bhatt. Recommendations to boost content spread in social networks. In *WWW*, pages 529–538, 2012.

[15] S. Chen, J. Fan, G. Li, J. Feng, K.-l. Tan, and J. Tang. Online topic-aware influence maximization. *PVLDB*, 8:666–677, 2015.

[16] W. Chen, A. Collins, R. Cummings, T. Ke, Z. Liu, D. Rincon, X. Sun, Y. Wang, W. Wei, and Y. Yuan. Influence Maximization in Social Networks When Negative Opinions May Emerge and Propagate. In *SDM*, 2011.

[17] W. Chen, C. Wang, and Y. Wang. Scalable influence maximization for prevalent viral marketing in large-scale social networks. In *KDD*, pages 1029–1038, 2010.

[18] W. Chen, Y. Wang, and S. Yang. Efficient influence maximization in social networks. In *KDD*, pages 199–208, 2009.

[19] W. Chen, Y. Yuan, and L. Zhang. Scalable influence maximization in social networks under the linear threshold model. In *ICDM*, pages 88–97, 2010.

[20] Y. Chen, E. K. Garcia, M. R. Gupta, A. Rahimi, and L. Cazzanti. Similarity-based classification: Concepts and algorithms. *Journal of Machine Learning Res*, 10:747–776, 2009.

[21] S. Cheng, H. Shen, J. Huang, W. Chen, and X. Cheng. Imrank: influence maximization via finding self-consistent ranking. In *SIGIR*, pages 475–484, 2014.

[22] S. Cheng, H. Shen, J. Huang, G. Zhang, and X. Cheng. Staticgreedy: solving the scalability-accuracy dilemma in influence maximization. In *CIKM*, pages 509–518, 2013.

[23] E. Cohen, D. Delling, T. Pajor, and R. F. Werneck. Sketch-based influence maximization and computation: Scaling up with guarantees. In *CIKM*, pages 629–638, 2014.

[24] T. N. Dinh, H. Zhang, D. T. Nguyen, and M. T. Thai. Cost-effective viral marketing for time-critical campaigns in large-scale social networks. *IEEE/ACM Trans. Netw.*, 22:2001–2011, 2014.

[25] S. Eubank, H. Guclu, V. S. Anil Kumar, M. V. Marathe, A. Srinivasan, Z. Toroczkai, and N. Wang. Modelling disease outbreaks in realistic urban social networks. *Nature*, 429(6988):180–184, 2004.

[26] S. Galhotra, A. Arora, S. Virinchi, and S. Roy. Asim: A scalable algorithm for influence maximization under the independent cascade model. In *WWW (Companion Volume)*, 2015.

[27] H. Gao, J. Mahmud, J. Chen, J. Nichols, and M. X. Zhou. Modeling user attitude toward controversial topics in online social media. In *ICWSM*, 2014.

[28] A. Goyal, W. Lu, and L. V. Lakshmanan. Celf++: Optimizing the greedy algorithm for influence maximization in social networks. In *WWW (Companion Volume)*, pages 47–48, 2011.

[29] A. Goyal, W. Lu, and L. V. Lakshmanan. Simpath: An efficient algorithm for influence maximization under the linear threshold model. In *ICDM*, pages 211–220, 2011.

[30] X. He, G. Song, W. Chen, and Q. Jiang. Influence blocking maximization in social networks under the competitive linear threshold model. In *SDM*, pages 463–474, 2012.

[31] K. Jung, W. Heo, and W. Chen. Irie: Scalable and robust influence maximization in social networks. In *ICDM*, pages 918–923, 2012.

[32] D. Kempe, J. Kleinberg, and E. Tardos. Maximizing the spread of influence through a social network. In *KDD*, pages 137–146, 2003.

[33] J. Kim, S.-K. Kim, and H. Yu. Scalable and parallelizable processing of influence maximization for large-scale social networks? In *ICDE*, pages 266–277, 2013.

[34] J. Leskovec, J. Kleinberg, and C. Faloutsos. Graphs over time: Densification laws, shrinking diameters and possible explanations. In *KDD*, pages 177–187, 2005.

[35] J. Leskovec, A. Krause, C. Guestrin, C. Faloutsos, J. VanBriesen, and N. Glance. Cost-effective outbreak detection in networks. In *KDD*, pages 420–429, 2007.

[36] H. Li, S. S. Bhowmick, J. Cui, Y. Gao, and J. Ma. Getreal: Towards realistic selection of influence maximization strategies in competitive networks. In *SIGMOD*, pages 1525–1537, 2015.

[37] Y. Li, W. Chen, Y. Wang, and Z.-L. Zhang. Influence diffusion dynamics and influence maximization in social networks with friend and foe relationships. In *WSDM*, pages 657–666, 2013.

[38] K. W. Lim and W. Buntine. Twitter opinion topic model: Extracting product opinions from tweets by leveraging hashtags and sentiment lexicon. In *CIKM*, pages 1319–1328, 2014.

[39] W. Lu, F. Bonchi, A. Goyal, and L. V. S. Lakshmanan. The bang for the buck: fair competitive viral marketing from the host perspective. In *KDD*, pages 928–936, 2013.

[40] Y. Mehmood, N. Barbieri, F. Bonchi, and A. Ukkonen. CSI: community-level social influence analysis. In *ECML/PKDD*, pages 48–63, 2013.

[41] G. Nemhauser, L. Wolsey, and M. Fisher. An analysis of approximations for maximizing submodular set functionsi. *Mathematical Programming*, 14(1):265–294, 1978.

[42] N. Ohsaka, T. Akiba, Y. Yoshida, and K. Kawarabayashi. Fast and accurate influence maximization on large networks with pruned monte-carlo simulations. In *AAAI*, pages 138–144, 2014.

[43] A. Pak and P. Paroubek. Twitter as a corpus for sentiment analysis and opinion mining. In *LREC*, 2010.

[44] M. Richardson and P. Domingos. Mining knowledge-sharing sites for viral marketing. In *KDD*, pages 61–70, 2002.

[45] Y. Tang, Y. Shi, and X. Xiao. Influence maximization in near-linear time: A martingale approach. In *SIGMOD*, pages 1539–1554, 2015.

[46] Y. Tang, X. Xiao, and Y. Shi. Influence maximization: Near-optimal time complexity meets practical efficiency. In *SIGMOD*, pages 75–86, 2014.

[47] L. G. Valiant. The complexity of enumeration and reliability problems. *SIAM Journal on Computing*, 8:410–421, 1979.

[48] H. Zhang, T. N. Dinh, and M. T. Thai. Maximizing the spread of positive influence in online social networks. In *ICDCS*, pages 317–326, 2013.

[49] X. W. Zhao, Y. Guo, Y. He, H. Jiang, Y. Wu, and X. Li. We know what you want to buy: A demographic-based system for product recommendation on microblogs. In *KDD*, pages 1935–1944, 2014.

[50] X. Zhu and Z. Ghahramani. Learning from labeled and unlabeled data with label propagation.

APPENDIX

A. PROOF OF LEMMA 2

PROOF. Let us consider a bipartite graph $G(V, E)$ (Figure 6a) containing two sets of nodes X and $Y = V \setminus X$. The set X contains $n_x = |X|$ nodes while the set Y contains $n_y = |Y|, n_y \geq 2n_x$ nodes. Moreover, let us assume that the opinions of the nodes $\forall x_i \in X$ to be $o_{x_i} = +1$, while that of nodes $\forall y_j \in Y$ to be $o_{y_j} = 0$. There exist directed edges from each node $x_i \in X$ to two consecutive nodes $y_{2i-1}, y_{2i} \in Y$. Further, the influence probabilities are initialized as $p_{(u,v)} = 1, \forall(u,v) \in E$ and the interaction probabilities φ associated with all but the last two edges is 1, which attain a value of 0. Mathematically, $\varphi_{x_i,y_j} = 1 \mid 1 \leq i \leq n_x - 1, j = 2i - 1$ or $j = 2i$ while $\varphi_{x_i,y_j} = 0 \mid i = n_x, j = 2i - 1$ or $j = 2i$. An analysis of the properties of the spread function $\Gamma(\cdot)$, assuming the above construction, is presented next.

Consider a scenario where the set of seeds S is initialized with a single node $x_i \mid 1 \leq i \leq n_x - 1$. With this seed, both of the nodes y_{2i-1} and y_{2i} will get activated with final opinion $+1/2$. Hence, the effective spread $\Gamma^o(S) = 2 \times (1/2) = +1$. Now if the node $x_{|X|}$ is added to the set S, the nodes $y_{2|X|-1}$ and $y_{2|X|}$ will also get activated. The final opinion of these newly activated nodes will be $-1/2$ each. The effective spread of the updated seed set is $\Gamma^o(S) = 1 - 1 = 0$. On adding another node $x_j \mid j \neq i$ and $1 \leq j \leq n_x - 1$ to the set S, the nodes y_{2j-1} and y_{2j} will become active with a final opinion of $1/2$ each. Thus, the effective spread is now $\Gamma^o(S) = 0 + 1 = 1$. In the above case it can be seen that the effective spread varied from $1 \rightarrow 0 \rightarrow 1$ on subsequent additions of nodes to the seed set. This clearly shows that the opinion spread function $\Gamma^o(S)$ is neither monotone nor submodular. □

B. PROOF OF THEOREM 1

PROOF. We show that the classical set cover problem can be decided in polynomial time if an approximation, with a constant ratio, for MEO exists in polynomial time. To this end, we reduce the set cover problem to an instance of MEO. Given a set of elements $Q = \{q_1, \ldots, q_n\}$ and a collection of subsets $R = \{R_1, \ldots, R_m\}$ where $R_i \subseteq Q, \forall i \in \{1, \ldots, m\}$,

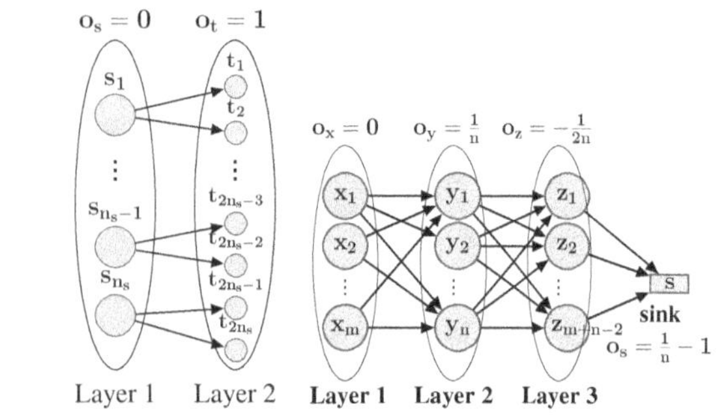

(a) Submodularity (b) Tractability

Figure 6: Reductions for the submodularity and tractability analysis of MEO.

the set-cover decision problem returns true if $\exists C \subseteq R; |C| = k$ and $\cup C_j = Q, \forall C_j \in C$.

Now given the set-cover problem, we construct a graph as shown in Figure 6b to obtain an instance of MEO by adding three layers of nodes in addition to a sink node. For each subset $R_i \in R$, a node x_i is added in the first layer of the graph with opinion $o_{x_i} = 0$. In the second layer, for each element $q_i \in Q$, we add a node y_i with opinion $o_{y_i} = \frac{1}{n}$. We add a third layer containing $m+n-2$ nodes denoted by z_i with opinion $o_{z_i} = -\frac{1}{2n}$. Moreover, we add a sink node s with opinion $o_s = -1+\frac{1}{n}$. Now, a directed edge (x_i, y_j) is added iff $q_i \in R_j$. For each node y_i in the second layer, edges $(y_i, z_j), \forall j \in \{1, 2, \ldots, m+n-2\}$ are added in the graph. To finalize this construction, we add the edge $(z_i, s), \forall i \in \{1, 2, \ldots, m+n-2\}$.

For the IC model, all the edges $(u, v) \in E$ are assigned $p_{(u,v)} = 1$ and $\varphi_{(u,v)} = 1$. Moreover, the LT model uses the same activation threshold for each node $\theta_u = 1$. It can be seen that for both these models, the seeds should be chosen from the first layer (any of the x_i's), because they will activate y_j's which in turn will activate any of the z_i's and thus, s would always be activated.

We instantiate MEO with $\lambda = 1$. Without loss of generality, assuming $\exists$ a set-cover of size k, $C = \{x_1, x_2, \ldots, x_k\}$, then choosing these nodes as seeds ensures the maximum spread. The final opinion of y_i, $o'_{y_i} = (0 + \frac{1}{n})/2 = \frac{1}{2n}$. Similarly, the final opinion of z_i, $o'_{z_i} = \frac{1}{2n} - \frac{1}{2n} = 0$ and the final opinion of s, $o'_s = (0 - 1 + \frac{1}{n})/2 = -\frac{1}{2} + \frac{1}{2n}$. Hence, the spread $= n\frac{1}{2n} + 0 - \frac{1}{2} + \frac{1}{2n} = \frac{1}{2n} > 0$. When a set cover of size k does not exist, the maximum spread achieved is $|Q'|\frac{1}{2n} + 0 - \frac{1}{2} + \frac{1}{2n} \leq (n-1)\frac{1}{2n} - \frac{1}{2} + \frac{1}{2n} = 0$, where Q', $|Q'| \leq n-1$ is the maximum number of elements covered by the k chosen sets. Hence, the maximum spread achieved when the set-cover does not exist is 0.

If there is a polynomial time algorithm which approximates MEO within a constant ratio, then we can decide the set-cover problem in polynomial time using the above mentioned reduction. In other words, if an approximate algorithm gives a spread ≤ 0 on the reduced graph, then a set-cover does not exist while a set-cover exists if the spread > 0. This renders the set-cover problem decidable in polynomial time, which means P=NP. Therefore, approximating MEO within a constant ratio is NP-hard. □

C. EXTENSIONS

The extension to the WC model is rather trivial, as instead of assuming a fixed value of p (usually $p = 0.1$ for IC), we assign $\forall(u, v) \in E, p_{(u,v)} = 1/|\textbf{In}(v)|$. All the previously presented algorithms can readily accommodate this change. However, the changes required for the LT model are much more involved.

Extension to the LT model is difficult when considering its classical definition where each node possesses a threshold, while it is quite intuitive using the *live-edge* model. Kempe et al. proved the equivalence between the LT and the live-edge model in [32]. Similar to the IC and WC models, under the live-edge model each edge $(u, v) \in E$ possesses a probability with which u activates its neigbour v. Moreover given an instance of the graph, it has an additional constraint of each node possessing one (live) incoming edge. The expected value of spread is then calculated using the spreads achieved for each of these graph instances. Thus, by associating influence probabilites with each edge and generating various graph instances satisfying the above constraint, our algorithms get extended to the *live-edge* model and hence, the LT model without undergoing any change. Since each node can possess only a single incoming edge, the error introduced in score-assignment owing to the non-disjoint nature of the paths gets completely removed (a unique u–v path $\forall u, v \in V$), which in turn facilitates stronger theoretical analysis for the LT model when compared to the IC and WC models.

Next, we present a detailed analysis for the *EaSyIM* and the *OSIM* algorithms for score-assignment, assuming the IC model of information diffusion. Sec. 3.4.2 provides discussions on methods to extend these analyses to the WC and LT models as well.

D. LEMMA 7

As a first step towards analyzing our algorithms, we derive a relation between the expected value of spread achieved using a set of seed-nodes and any possible partition of this set.

LEMMA 7. $\sigma(A \cup B) = \sigma(A) + \sigma_{\sigma(A)}(B)$

PROOF. Using Kempe's [32] analysis of the IC model it can be seen that,

$$\begin{aligned}\sigma(A \cup B) &= \sum_X P(X)\sigma_X(A \cup B) \\ &= \sum_X P(X)\sigma_X(A) + \sum_X P(X)\big(\sigma_X(B) - \sigma_X(A \cap B)\big) \\ &= \sigma(A) + \sigma_{\sigma(A)}(B). \end{aligned} \tag{3}$$

A similar analysis can be done for the LT model using the reduction to the *live-edge* model [32]. Under the live-edge model each node possesses a single (live) incoming edge, thus, a node v is activated via a path either from a node in A or in B.

$$\begin{aligned}\sigma(A \cup B) &= \sum_X P(X)\sigma_X(A \cup B) \\ &= \sum_X P(X)\sigma_X(A) + \sum_X P(X)\sigma_X(B)\end{aligned}$$

Since, $\sigma(A)$ and $\sigma(B)$ are disjoint,

$$\sigma(A \cup B) = \sigma(A) + \sigma_{\sigma(A)}(B). \tag{4}$$

□

E. PROOF OF LEMMA 3

PROOF. If $k = 1$, $\sigma(S_k) = \sigma(S^*_k)$ because ScoreGREEDY(G, k, l) chooses the node with the maximum score. Since the score assigned to each node captures the expected value of its spread, the seed-node selected by the former is the same as that selected by the GREEDY algorithm. Let us assume that $\sigma(S_k) = \sigma(S^*_k)$ holds for $k = i$. Now for $k = i + 1$,

$$\sigma(S^*_{i+1}) = \sigma(S^*_{i+1}) - \sigma(S^*_i) + \sigma(S^*_i)$$

Paritioning S_{i+1} as $S_i \cup \{u_{i+1}\}$, Lemma 7 yields the following,

$$\begin{aligned}&= \sigma_{\sigma(S^*_i)}(\{u_{i+1}\}) + \sigma(S^*_i) \\ &= \sigma_{\sigma(S_i)}(\{u_{i+1}\}) + \sigma(S_i) \\ &= \Delta^l(\{u_{i+1}\}) + \sigma(S_i) \\ &= \sigma(S_{i+1}).\end{aligned}$$

Since $\sigma(S_{i+1}) = \sigma(S^*_{i+1})$, by the principle of mathematical induction $\sigma(S_k) = \sigma(S^*_k)$ holds $\forall k$. □

F. PROOF OF LEMMA 4

PROOF. The exact contribution of a node v to the score of another node u is

$$\gamma^*_v(u) = \sum_{w \in \textbf{In}(u)} \Big(p_{(w,v)} \bigcup_{\rho \in \mathbb{P}_{uw}} \prod_{e \in \rho} p_e\Big). \tag{5}$$

Similarly, the contribution of v to the score of u using the PU algorithm is

$$\gamma_v(u) = \bigcup_{\rho \in \mathbb{P}_{uv}} \prod_{e \in \rho} p_e. \tag{6}$$

Using the standard inclusion-exclusion principle,

$$\bigcup_{\rho \in \mathbb{P}_{uv}} \prod_{e \in \rho} p_e = \Big(\sum_{\rho \in \mathbb{P}_{uv}} \prod_{e \in \rho} p_e - \sum_{\rho' \in \mathbb{P}_{uv}} \sum_{\rho \in \mathbb{P}_{uv} \setminus \{\rho'\}} \prod_{e \in \rho} p_e \prod_{e' \in \rho'} p_{e'} + \ldots + (-1)^{|\mathbb{P}_{uv}|-1} \prod_{\rho \in \mathbb{P}_{uv}} \prod_{e \in \rho} p_e \Big).$$

Thus, Eq. 5 and 6 can be written as follows.

$$\gamma_v^*(u) = \sum_{w \in \mathbf{In}(u)} \Big(p_{(w,v)} \big(A_1 - A_2 + \ldots + (-1)^{t-1} A_{t^*} \big) \Big).$$

$$\gamma_v(u) = B_1 - B_2 + \ldots + (-1)^{t-1} B_t.$$

where $t^* = |\mathbb{P}_{uw}|$, $t = |\mathbb{P}_{uv}|$ and $A_i, i \leq t^*$, $B_j, j \leq t$ stand for the larger terms in the expansion of $\bigcup_{\rho \in \mathbb{P}_{uw}} \prod_{e \in \rho} p_e$ and $\bigcup_{\rho \in \mathbb{P}_{uv}} \prod_{e \in \rho} p_e$ respectively.

Assuming $A_2 << A_1$ and henceforth $B_2 << B_1$, all the higher order terms can be neglected (significance of this assumption is described in Sec. 3.4.2). Moreover, the relationship between A_1 and B_1 is defined as follows.

$$\sum_{w \in \mathbf{In}(v)} p_{(w,v)} A_1 = \sum_{w \in \mathbf{In}(v)} p_{(w,v)} \Big(\sum_{\rho \in \mathbb{P}uw} \prod_{e \in \rho} p_e \Big) = \sum_{\rho \in \mathbb{P}uv} \prod_{e \in \rho} p_e = B_1.$$

Neglecting the summation over the pair-wise product of the paths between different intermediary nodes $w_i, w_j, \forall (i,j) \mid w_i, w_j \in \mathbf{In}(v)$, we devise a relationship between B_2 and A_2.

$$\begin{aligned} B_2 &= \sum_{\rho \in \mathbb{P}_{uv}} \sum_{\rho' \in (\mathbb{P}_{uv} \setminus \{\rho\})} \prod_{e \in \rho} p_e \prod_{e' \in \rho'} p'_e \\ &\geq \sum_{w \in \mathbf{In}(v)} p^2_{(w,v)} \sum_{\rho \in \mathbb{P}_{uw}} \sum_{\rho' \in (\mathbb{P}_{uw} \setminus \{\rho\})} \prod_{e \in \rho} p_e \prod_{e' \in \rho'} p'_e \\ &= \sum_{w \in \mathbf{In}(v)} p^2_{(w,v)} A_2. \end{aligned}$$

The relative error ϵ_1^{DAG}, is now defined as,

$$\epsilon_1^{DAG} = \frac{|\gamma_v^*(u) - \gamma_v(u)|}{\gamma_v^*(u)} \approx \frac{B_2 - \sum_{w \in \mathbf{In}(v)} p_{(w,v)} A_2}{\sum_{w \in \mathbf{In}(v)} p_{(w,v)} (A_1 - A_2)}$$

$$\begin{aligned} &Since,\ A_2 << A_1,\ A_2 < A_1^2 \\ &\approx \frac{\sum_{w \in \mathbf{In}(v)} p_{(w,v)} (p_{(w,v)} - 1) A_2}{\sum_{w \in \mathbf{In}(v)} p_{(w,v)} A_1} \\ &\leq \sum_{w \in \mathbf{In}(v)} \big((p_{(w,v)} - 1) A_1 \big). \end{aligned} \tag{7}$$

□

G. PROOF OF LEMMA 5

PROOF. Using the same nomenclature as Lemma 4, the contribution of v in the score of u using the PU and the *EaSyIM* algorithm is stated as follows

$$\gamma_v^{PU}(u) = \sum_{i=1}^{t} (-1)^{i-1} B_i \approx B_1 - B_2. \tag{8}$$

$$\gamma_v^{EaSyIM}(u) = B_1. \tag{9}$$

The relative error (w.r.t PU) ϵ_2^{DAG}, can now be stated as follows

$$\epsilon_2^{DAG} = \frac{B_2}{B_1 - B_2} \approx \frac{B_2}{B_1} \leq B_1. \tag{10}$$

□

H. PROOF OF LEMMA 6

PROOF. The contribution of a node w in the score of another node u, considering the effect of cycles exclusively, is dependent upon all possible cyclic paths that contain w. Moreover, since the combined contribution of the participating nodes in each cycle ρ should only be considered once to the score of u, we scale $\gamma_w(u)$ by $1/|\rho|$. Mathematically,

$$\gamma_w(u) = \sum_{\rho \in \mathbb{P}_{ww}} p_{(u,w)} (1 + 1/|\rho|) \prod_{e \in \rho} p_e.$$

However, the contribution using the GREEDY algorithm is

$$\gamma_w^*(u) = p_{(u,w)}.$$

Now, the relative error ϵ^{cycle}, is

$$\epsilon^{cycle} = \frac{|\gamma_w^*(u) - \gamma_w(u)|}{\gamma_w^*(u)} = \frac{\sum_{\rho \in \mathbb{P}_{ww}} p_{(u,w)} (1/|\rho|) \prod_{e \in \rho} p_e}{p_{(u,w)}} = \sum_{\rho \in \mathbb{P}_{ww}} \Big(\prod_{e \in \rho} p_e \Big) / |\rho|. \tag{11}$$

□

I. ANALYSIS OF OSIM

Since the analysis over generic graphs is quite complex, we analyze *OSIM* on DAGs with fixed value of $\varphi_{(u,v)}$. Moreover, since *OSIM* is fundamentally similar to EaSyIM and the analysis involving opinions is complex, thus, we reduce (without introducing any limitation in the algorithm) the analysis effort with results on a single path and not for all possible paths from a node. These results can further be easily extended.

Both the below mentioned results talk about the expected spread of a single node. Since the overall function is neither submodular nor monotone, we cannot employ the use of a greedy algorithm to achieve a constant approximation. (Proof in Sec. 2).

The following notation would assume these definitions for the rest of this section. $\delta_j(\{A\})$ is the *Dirac*[11] measure, $\psi_i = \frac{2\varphi_{(u_{i,i+1})} - 1}{2}$ and $\mathrm{P}_j = p_{(u_j, u_{j+1})}$.

LEMMA 8. *Given a path of length l, consisting of nodes $u_0, u_1, \ldots, u_l$, with the penalty parameter on opinion spread, $\lambda = 1$, the effective opinion spread under the OI model of information-diffusion, considering this path, on choosing u_0 as the seed node is* $\sigma^o(\{u_0\}) = \sum_{i=1}^{l} \Big(\Big(\prod_{j=1}^{i} \mathrm{P}_{j-1} \Big) \sum_{j=0}^{i} \Big(\frac{o_{u_j}}{2} \big(1 + \delta_j(\{0\})\big) \prod_{k=1}^{i-j} \psi_{i-k} \Big) \Big)$.

PROOF. It is evident that the contribution of a path of length l in the expected opinion spread of a seed node u_0, is the sum of expected effective opinions of nodes in that path. Now we try to solve the following recursive

[11]The Dirac measure $\delta_j(\{A\})$ is defined for any set A, where $\delta_j(\{A\}) = 1$ if $j \in A$ and 0 otherwise.

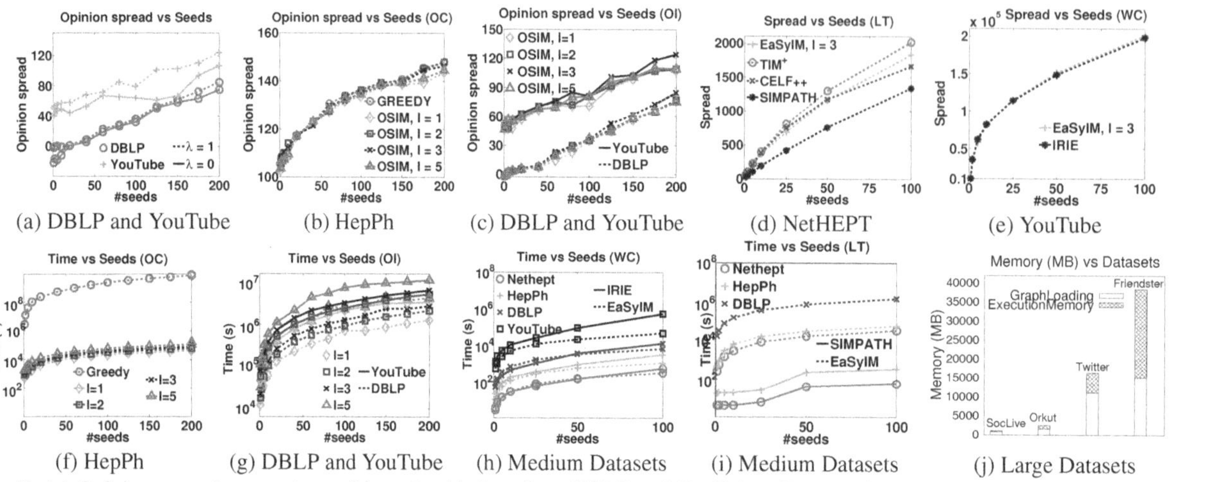

(a) DBLP and YouTube (b) HepPh (c) DBLP and YouTube (d) NetHEPT (e) YouTube
(f) HepPh (g) DBLP and YouTube (h) Medium Datasets (i) Medium Datasets (j) Large Datasets

Figure 7: (a) Opinion-spread comparison of $\lambda = 1$ with $\lambda = 0$ on DBLP and YouTube. Growth of opinion-spread ($\lambda = 1$) with l and k on (b) HepPh (OC), and (c) DBLP and YouTube (OI). Spread comparison of *EaSyIM* with SIMPATH and IRIE on (d) NetHEPT (LT) and (e) YouTube (WC). Growth-rate of running time of *OSIM* with l and k on (f) HepPh (OC) and (g) DBLP and YouTube (OI). Running time comparison of *EaSyIM* with IRIE on (h) Medium Datasets (WC), and SIMPATH on (i) Medium Datasets (LT). (j) Memory consumption of *EaSyIM* for $k = 100$ on Large Datasets.

relation to get a closed expression for the expected opinion of the nodes.

$$o'_{u_i} = \frac{o_{u_i}}{2} + \psi_{i-1} o'_{u_{i-1}}$$

$$o'_{u_{i-1}} = \frac{o_{u_{i-1}}}{2} + \psi_{i-2} o'_{u_{i-2}}$$

$$\vdots$$

$$o'_{u_1} = \frac{o_{u_1}}{2} + \psi_0 o'_{u_0}$$

On solving the telescopic sum and substituting $o'_{u_0} = o_{u_0}$

$$o'_{u_i} = \sum_{j=1}^{i} \Big(\frac{o_{u_j}}{2} \prod_{k=1}^{i-j} \psi_{i-k} \Big) + o_{u_0} \prod_{k=1}^{i} \psi_{i-k}$$

$$= \sum_{j=0}^{i} \Big(\frac{(1 + \delta_j(\{0\})) o_{u_j}}{2} \prod_{k=1}^{i-j} \psi_{i-k} \Big).$$

$$\sigma^o(\{u_0\}) = \sum_{i=1}^{l} \Big(o'_{u_i} \prod_{j=1}^{i} \mathrm{p}_{j-1} \Big)$$

$$= \sum_{i=1}^{l} \Big(\Big(\prod_{j=1}^{i} \mathrm{p}_{j-1} \Big) \sum_{j=0}^{i} \Big(\frac{o_{u_j}}{2} (1 + \delta_j(\{0\})) \prod_{k=1}^{i-j} \psi_{i-k} \Big) \Big).$$

□

LEMMA 9. *Given a path of length l and $\lambda = 1$, the score assigned to a node u using the* OSIM *algorithm captures the effective opinion spread, considering the contribution of this path, on choosing u as the seed node. Mathematically, $\Delta^l(u) = \sigma^o(\{u\})$.*

PROOF. Please see the full version in *arXiv 1602.03110*. □

J. ADDITIONAL EXPERIMENTAL RESULTS

Quality: It is evident from Figure 7a that $\lambda = 1$ outperforms $\lambda = 0$ and hence, maximizing the effective opinion-spread is better. Figures 7b and 7c present the results with varying seeds for HepPh under the OC model ($o \sim \mathcal{N}(0, 1)$), and DBLP & YouTube under the OI model ($o \sim rand(-1, 1)$) respectively. We omit the results for the Modified-GREEDY algorithm in Figure 7c owing to its lack of scalability. Figures 7d and 7e present the spreads obtained for the NetHEPT and YouTube datasets under the LT and WC models respectively.

Efficiency: Figures 7f show that *OSIM* is at least 10^3 times more efficient when compared to Modified-GREEDY with the gain going as high as 10^5 for some cases. Figure 7g portrays the running time of *OSIM* for the DBLP and the YouTube datasets. Note that the solid line overlapping with the y-axis and the horizontal top part of the plot shows the time for Modified-GREEDY, which is indicative of the fact that it did not complete even after a month's time. Figures 7h and 7i show a comparison of the running times of *EaSyIM* with the state-of-the-art heuristics – IRIE (WC) and SIMPATH (LT). It is evident that both of these techniques do not scale well. *EaSyIM* is $2 - 3$ and $4 - 6$ times faster when compared to IRIE for small and medium sized datasets respectively. It is slower when compared to SIMPATH on smaller datasets, however, highly efficient for the medium sized datasets as SIMPATH did not complete even after 5 days on the DBLP dataset.

Scalability: Eventually as a part of our scalability experiments, we present the memory required by *EaSyIM* for the 4 large graph datasets (Table 2) in Figure 7j. This shows that *EaSyIM* possesses the capability of scaling to graphs with billion-scale edges.

K. MODIFIED-GREEDY ALGORITHM

Algorithm 6 Modified-GREEDY

Input: Graph $G = (V, E)$,#seeds $k = |S|$
Output: Seed set S

```
S ← ∅
for i = 1 to k do
    maxId = arg max_{w ∈ V \ S} (Γ^o_λ(S ∪ {w}) − Γ^o_λ(S))
    S ← S ∪ {maxId}
end for
```

L. ADDITIONAL NOTE ON CELF++

This algorithm exploits the sub modularity of the problem by using a "lazy-forward" optimization while selecting seeds. This technique calculates marginal gain of nodes in decreasing order of their probability of being a seed node, which in turn is calculated form its marginal gain in previous iterations. Another optimization which helped engineer the running time of this algorithm was to ignore the nodes which do not hold a chance to become a seed node in consequent iterations.

Potential and Pitfalls of Domain-Specific Information Extraction at Web Scale

Astrid Rheinländer*, Mario Lehmann, Anja Kunkel, Jörg Meier, and Ulf Leser*
Humboldt-Universität zu Berlin, Department of Computer Science, Berlin, Germany
*{rheinlae,leser}@informatik.hu-berlin.de

ABSTRACT

In many domains, a plethora of textual information is available on the web as news reports, blog posts, community portals, etc. Information extraction (IE) is the default technique to turn unstructured text into structured fact databases, but systematically applying IE techniques to web input requires highly complex systems, starting from focused crawlers over quality assurance methods to cope with the HTML input to long pipelines of natural language processing and IE algorithms. Although a number of tools for each of these steps exists, their seamless, flexible, and scalable combination into a web scale end-to-end text analytics system still is a true challenge.

In this paper, we report our experiences from building such a system for comparing the "web view" on health related topics with that derived from a controlled scientific corpus, i.e., Medline. The system combines a focused crawler, applying shallow text analysis and classification to maintain focus, with a sophisticated text analytic engine inside the Big Data processing system Stratosphere. We describe a practical approach to seed generation which led us crawl a corpus of ~1 TB web pages highly enriched for the biomedical domain. Pages were run through a complex pipeline of best-of-breed tools for a multitude of necessary tasks, such as HTML repair, boilerplate detection, sentence detection, linguistic annotation, parsing, and eventually named entity recognition for several types of entities. Results are compared with those from running the same pipeline (without the web-related tasks) on a corpus of 24 million scientific abstracts and a third corpus made of ~250K scientific full texts. We evaluate scalability, quality, and robustness of the employed methods and tools. The focus of this paper is to provide a large, real-life use case to inspire future research into robust, easy-to-use, and scalable methods for domain-specific IE at web scale.

SIGMOD'16, June 26-July 01, 2016, San Francisco, CA, USA

ISBN 978-1-4503-3531-7/16/06...$15.00

DOI: http://dx.doi.org/10.1145/2882903.2903736

Keywords

Focused crawling; Information extraction; Massively parallel data analysis

1. INTRODUCTION

The analysis of information published on the web is valuable for a plethora of applications, e.g., to analyze customer product reviews [21], to investigate relationships between politicians and their sponsors [12], or to predict flu waves and assess their treatments [7], to name just a few. Analyzing web data is not trivial due to its scale, distribution, heterogeneity, redundancy, and questionable quality. Compared to traditional text analytics, already obtaining the data to be analyzed is difficult, requiring either access to an existing (open) large web crawl or the set-up and running of a proper crawler. For applications requiring domain-specific texts, like the one we focus on here, special care must be taken to restrict the crawl to this domain, typically by applying text classification on the crawl or during the crawling [8]. Another severe issue arises from the extreme heterogeneity of web documents and their cluttering with navigational elements, advertisements, script code, formatting instructions etc. [29]. Many projects circumvent this problem by focusing on a single or a few data sources, typically the big social media platforms such as Twitter, Facebook or Flickr; however, this excludes literally billions of additional knowledge sources. Finally, the filtered and cleansed web texts must be analyzed by information extraction (IE) algorithms to obtain the desired facts, which in itself is a challenging task when the text collection is large and the requirements regarding data quality are high.

In this paper, we report on our experiences from building a comprehensive system for domain-specific text analytics on the open web. Building such systems for long was only possible for large web companies; however, advances in cloud computing, IE, and crawler techniques together with falling prices for storage, computing power, and network bandwidth put such systems – in principle – also into the realm of mid-size organizations. But putting this theoretical possibility into practise still is a highly challenging task. Therefore, the goal of this experience paper not only is to describe such a system, with a focus on design issues regarding robustness, data quality, and scalability, but also to pinpoint the most critical issues that need to be solved when building such systems, with the ultimate intention to foster more research into this important and challenging area.

As a concrete use case, we applied the system to crawl a 1 TB collection of web text from the biomedical domain

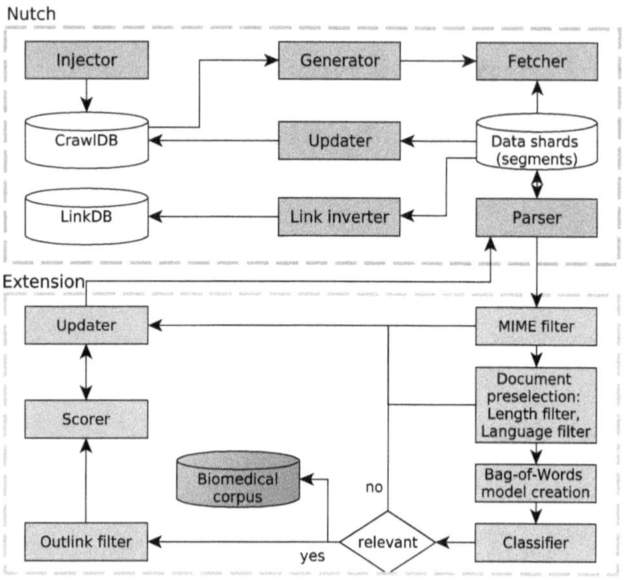

Figure 1: Architecture of a topical crawler based on Apache Nutch.

with the goal to retrieve a high quality corpus in terms of precision with respect to our target domain. This corpus was cleansed and filtered by specific modules for web texts, linguistically preprocessed using methods from statistical natural language processing (NLP), and eventually analyzed by a series of domain-specific IE programs to find mentions of important entities in this field, such as genes, drugs, or diseases. We then ran the same pipeline on two much more controlled sets, i.e., all abstracts in the Medline collection of scientific articles, and a set of approximately 250.000 biomedical full texts. A fourth corpus was built from all web pages deemed out-of-domain by the focused crawler. Next, we compared results from a linguistic analysis and from the domain-specific IE on the four corpora to each other, finding notable differences in many aspects, including simple metrics such as average sentence and document length, more linguistically motivated properties such as the use of negation or abbreviations, and, eventually, the sets and frequencies of occurring domain-specific entities. The system applies advanced machine learning (ML) in every phase of its collection and analysis pipeline, i.e, text classification during the focused crawling, snipped classification for the extraction of net text from HTML pages, sequential classification with Hidden Markov Models for the NLP, and classification, pattern matching and Conditional Random Fields for the IE tasks. Most notably, the entire process for web text analysis (excluding the crawling) was specified, optimized, and executed using a small set of data flows in a single, homogeneous, and declarative framework for specifying UDF-heavy data flows, i.e., the Stratosphere system [2, 23]. Using this framework allowed us to systematically evaluate the entire extraction process with respect to scalability, efficiency, and quality of the involved tools. We believe our approach implements a notable advancement compared to the current state-of-the-art for building such systems, which boils down to manually created scripts implementing an ad-hoc assembly of existing tools. This practice clearly interferes with today's needs in Big Data analytics; instead, we envision complex information acquisition and extraction from the web as an almost effortless end-to-end task.

The remainder of this paper is structured as follows: Section 2 explains the retrieval of biomedical web pages by means of focused web crawling at large scale. Section 3 reviews the data analytics platform, discusses data flows we used for analyzing the crawl. Section 4 evaluates efficiency and scalability of crawling and presents results of our analysis with respect to language structure and contents of the crawled documents. Section 5 summarizes lessons learned in this study and highlights open engineering and research challenges for efficient text analytics at large scale. We conclude this paper in Section 6.

2. FOCUSED CRAWLING: THE BASIS FOR DOMAIN-SPECIFIC TEXT ANALYTICS

The goal of our research is to perform advanced IE on domain-specific collections of web documents. A proper way to obtain such a collection are focused crawlers [8]. A focused web crawler traverses parts of the web to find documents relevant for a certain topic. To speed-up the crawling and to obtain good harvest rates (i.e. a large density of relevant pages among all crawled pages), a major objective during focused crawling is to visit only those outgoing links of a website that appear to be particularly relevant for a given topic. To decide whether a link is relevant or not, the assumption is made that relevant pages are most likely linked to other relevant pages whereas irrelevant pages point more often to other irrelevant pages and thus constitute an endpoint during the crawl. To assess the relevance of page, a focused crawler is equipped with a text classifier trained on a set of pre-classified documents. We built a focused crawler which follows this approach: It downloads web pages, classifies them as relevant or not, and only further considers links outgoing from relevant pages. We did not follow the alternative approach of classifying links based on its surroundings because this would require the laborious creation of a training corpus of links; in contrast, obtaining a training corpus of relevant documents is comparably simple. For our study, we trained on a set of randomly selected abstracts from Medline[1]), considered as relevant, and an equal-sized set of randomly selected English documents taken from the common crawl corpus[2]), considered as irrelevant. This approach is cheap and simple; note, however, that it introduces some bias as a typical Medline abstract is quite different from a typical web page (see Section 4.3.1).

2.1 Crawler architecture

To obtain a large corpus of reasonable quality, the setup of the focused crawler is crucial. Web crawlers should be insusceptible to so-called spider traps, i.e., websites containing programming errors or dynamically generated links that cause the crawler to be trapped in an infinite loop. A crawler also needs to respect the implicit and explicit rules of a domain (e.g., maximum number of simultaneous requests, rules contained in the "robots.txt" file). Finally, it must be implemented in a distributed manner to allow for using multiple machines in parallel. There exist a number of frameworks which implement such functionality; we built our system on

[1]http://www.ncbi.nlm.nih.gov/pubmed
[2]http://www.commoncrawl.org

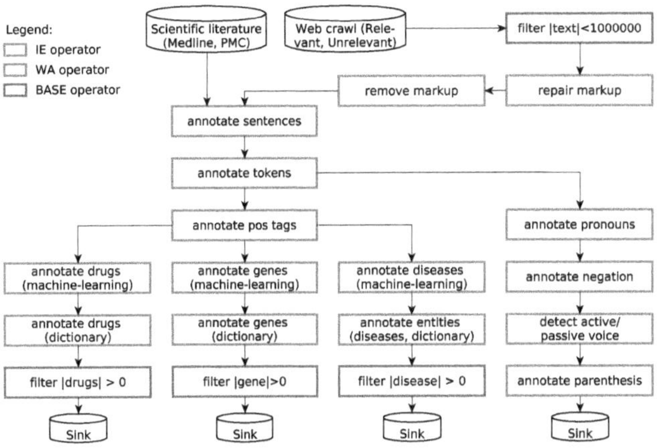

Figure 2: Consolidated high-level data flow for analyzing biomedical documents from scientific publications and the internet. Isochromatic frames indicate Sopremo operator package.

top of the open-source framework Apache Nutch[3]. Nutch is based on Apache Hadoop[4] to enable scalable and distributed crawling. It lacks a component for focusing a crawl, but has a clean extension interface which we used to plug-in a classifier and the necessary logic. Figure 1 shows the architecture of Nutch together with our custom extensions. The part implemented in Nutch (upper part of Fig. 1) is fairly conventional; an injector reads seed URLs from a text file and adds these to the crawl database (CrawlDB) acting as the crawl frontier. A set of fetcher threads reads lists of not yet visited URLs from this database, downloads the respective web pages and forwards them to a parser for link and content extraction; unseen links are added to the CrawlDB. Besides, a link database (LinkDB) stores the graph structure of the crawled pages.

To add focus to the crawling process, we extended Nutch with the following components (lower part of Fig. 1): After parsing a web page, we first check whether it is of textual content using a MIME type filter. We also remove pages that are too short and pages that are written in languages other than English by using an n-gram based language filter, because subsequent IE tools used in this analysis are sensitive to language. Afterwards, the main text of a page is extracted using the tool Boilerpipe [15]. To classify a document, its extracted net text is converted to a Bag-of-Words model and classified for its biomedical relevance. We use a Naïve Bayes algorithm due to its robustness with respect to class imbalance (we have no rational guess on the expected percentage of biomedical pages during a focused crawl) and its ability to update its model incrementally, although we currently don't use this feature. If a page is classified as relevant, it is added to the corpus and all its outlinks are added to CrawlDB; otherwise, it is discarded. The crawling and classification process is repeated iteratively until either CrawlDB is empty, the desired corpus size is reached, or it is stopped manually by the user.

2.2 Seed generation

A very important issue in crawling, and especially in focused crawling, is the determination of the set of seed URLs used to initiate the crawl. The typical way of obtaining a large set of seeds is to issue keyword queries to one or more search engines. For focused crawling, keywords are chosen such that they retrieve domain-specific seeds with high probability. Since all search engine APIs restrict the number of allowed queries and limit the number of returned results, one often uses (a) multiple search engines in parallel and (b) large sets of queries - which creates the necessity to generate thousands of high quality queries. For our case study, we utilized five different search engines, namely Bing, Google, Arxiv, Nature, and Nature blogs. For each search engine, we generated queries with (a) general biomedical terms, obtained from National Cancer Institute[5] and the Genetic Alliance glossary[6] and (b) highly specific molecular terms extracted from the Gene Ontology[7], Drugbank[8], and the UMLS/MeSH sub-tree for diseases [9]. Exemplary keywords are shown in Table 1 together with the total number of search terms for each category. Clearly, the chosen queries give the resulting corpus a certain direction; in our case, we intended to focus on genetic facts about diseases.

In a first experiment, we used only a subset of keywords from our data sources (see Table 1, numbers in bracket). All search results from the different search engines obtained with these keywords were merged to a single list of 45,227 seed URLs. However, the resulting crawl terminated quickly due to an emptied CrawlDB, i.e., all pages in the frontier of pages reachable from these seeds were classified as irrelevant. Debugging this crawl, we found several reasons for this situation. First, the search terms chosen were too general. For these, the search engines return rather general pages, which they considered as authoritative for the respective topic, such as front pages of portals. These pages very often immediately were classified as irrelevant, i.e., this branch of the crawl stopped after just one step. Second, we found that biomedical sites generally are only weakly linked; most often, all outgoing links from a page were navigational leading to pages on the same host (see Sect. 4.1 for details).

Note that not stopping the crawl of such irrelevant pages immediately but after n steps (e.g., $n = 2$, $n = 3$) is a viable alternative to increase the size of the crawl, since many front pages of portals deemed irrelevant link to relevant content for our domain. Yet, crawling time will significantly increase since many irrelevant pages will be explored as well. Since the entire crawling process already stretched to more than two months while stopping immediately when visiting an irrelevant page (see Section 4.1 for details), we decided to increase the set of seed URLs to obtain a larger crawl instead. Consequently, we performed a second seed generation run, this time using 15,000 queries resulting in a total number of 485,462 seed URLs. These seeds were used for crawl described previously.

3. DATA FLOWS FOR WEB-SCALE INFORMATION EXTRACTION

Information extraction (IE) and statistical natural language processing (NLP) tasks on large text collections are

[3]http://nutch.apache.org

[4]http://hadoop.apache.org

[5]http://www.cancer.gov

[6]http://www.geneticalliance.org.uk/glossary.htm

[7]http://geneontology.org

[8]http://www.drugbank.ca

[9]http://www.nlm.nih.gov/mesh/

Category	No. of terms	Example search terms
general terms	500 (166)	cancer, chronic pain
disease-specific	5000 (468)	thymoma, nausea, cough
drug-specific	4000 (325)	GAD-67, Aspirin
gene-specific	6500 (246)	BRCA, Cactin

Table 1: Total number and exemplary search terms by category used for seed URL retrieval. Numbers in brackets denote the number of search terms for the first crawl (see text).

time- and resource-consuming because of the complexity of the involved tasks [5]. Our aim was to apply state-of-the-art techniques in biomedical information extraction. This requires the use of several heavy-weight tools and algorithms, some of which have a runtime complexity that is quadratic in the text length (see below). Due to the embarrassingly parallel nature of information extraction at the entity level, a natural choice to alleviate runtime problems is to parallelize all analysis on a cluster. To this end, we implemented and wrapped a variety of IE and NLP tools for use with Stratosphere[10], a parallel data processing platform for large-scale, UDF-heavy data analytics. A detailed description of Stratosphere can be found in [2], in the following, we very briefly summarize key concepts of Stratosphere and then discuss in detail the data flow we implemented to perform text analytics on the crawled corpus and other texts.

3.1 Stratosphere

Stratosphere is a system for parallel execution of UDF-heavy data flows. These data flows are specified in a declarative scripting language called Meteor (note that there also exist other APIs) [13]. Meteor scripts are composed of primitive operators, which are defined in domain-specific packages, i.e., self-contained libraries of the operator implementations, their syntax, and semantic annotations. A Meteor script is parsed into an algebraic representation, logically optimized [23], and compiled into a parallel data flow program of parallelization primitives (e.g., map, reduce, cross) embracing the operators implementations. Subsequently, the parallel data flow program is physically optimized, translated into an execution graph and deployed on the given hardware [2].

Currently, the system ships more than 60 different operators organized in four packages, i.e., general purpose (BASE), information extraction (IE), web analytics (WA), and data cleansing (DC). The BASE package comprises relational operators, such as filter, projection, transformation, or join. The IE package includes operators for annotating texts with syntactic annotations (e.g., sentence boundaries, part-of-speech tags) and semantic annotations (e.g., mentions of different entity types, relationships between entities), and for merging annotations using different schemes. The WA package contains operators specific to the analysis of web documents, such as link extraction, markup removal, or markup repair. Eventually, the DC package brings operators for data cleansing and data integration, addressing common challenges in processing dirty or heterogeneous data sources.

[10]Stratosphere was recently renamed into Flink and is now an Apache Top-Level project; our code builds on release 0.4.2.

3.2 Data flow for Crawl Analysis

The ultimate goal of our study was to compare the domain-specific "information content" of biomedical web pages with that of a corpus of scientific publications, either as full texts or as abstracts. Furthermore, we wanted to compute general linguistic characteristics of the different corpora we studied, such as average sentence length or frequency of negated sentences. The latter has two purposes: First, we find it of general interest to differentiate properties of different types of texts in a given domain. Second, these properties have consequences on the tools which are used to analyze the texts. Eventually, we were also interested in the link topology of the biomedical pages to test some common assumptions on these structures.

Processing a large set of documents to compute a number of measures and to extract a variety of different information requires a complex set of tasks. Specifically, our scenario encompasses three different sub-problems, namely document preprocessing and HTML cleansing, linguistic document analysis, and biomedical entity extraction. Each of these sub-problems requires the use of a bunch of different tools; for instance, high-quality entity extraction is only possible using separate and highly optimized tools for each entity class. Furthermore, the different processing steps have various dependencies. Ideally, all tasks and their dependencies are expressed using a single data flow program to enable a holistic optimization and seamless analysis. Stratosphere allows such a concise specification; Fig. 2 displays the high-level data flow we developed for this case study. The complete data flow comprising all required analysis for this study consists of 38 elementary operators. Web pages are first filtered to exclude extremely long documents. Next, HTML markup is detected, errors are repaired, and all markup is removed from each page. All documents are annotated with sentence and token boundaries. For linguistic analysis, each sentence is analyzed for occurrences of pronouns, negation, and parenthesis using different sets of regular expressions, and each found mention of any of these categories is added to the result set together with information on document ID, sentence ID, and start/end positions. For the biomedical content analysis, we then annotate three types of biomedical entities, namely genes, drugs, and diseases.

Note that biomedical IE is considered particularly challenging because of ambiguous naming conventions, multi-word names, acronyms, etc., and specialized methods, dictionaries, and models are needed to achieve satisfactory results with respect to extraction accuracy [18]. The accuracy of all tools applied to web documents is difficult to predict, since all current tools were trained and evaluated only on scientific articles, and mostly only on abstracts. Therefore, we chose to apply two different extraction methods for each entity type on the entire data set: A classical fuzzy dictionary-matching tool, and ML-based entity taggers using Conditional Random Fields (CRF). In this field, dictionary-based entity extraction typically achieves good precision yet low recall because dictionaries are necessarily incomplete in a field developing as fast as biomedical research. On the other hand, ML-based extraction methods often show much improved recall and they also show superior precision. Besides, they usually exhibit a significantly slower processing speed.

Note that none of the tools we applied was developed for this study; instead, they were chosen from available open

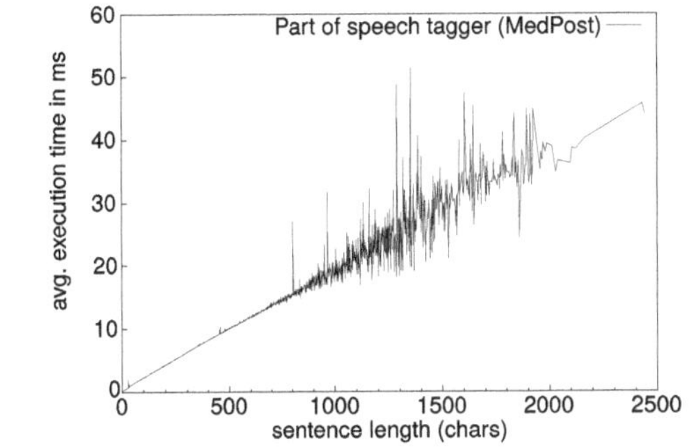

(a) Part-of-speech tagging.

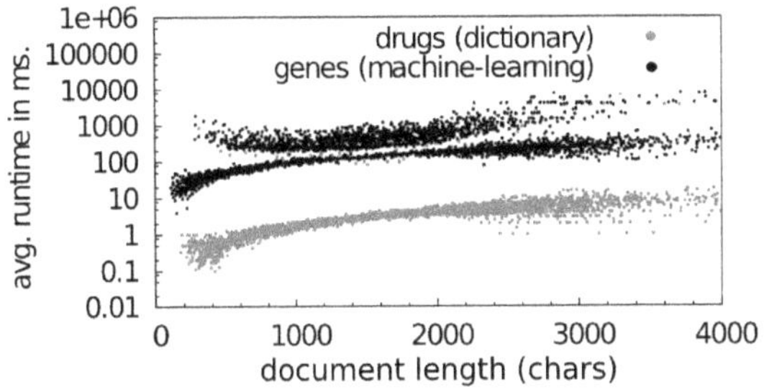

(b) Named entity recognition. Black: ML, red: dictionary.

Figure 3: Runtimes information extraction tools with respect to the length of the input texts.

source software following a best-of-breed strategy. For dictionary matching, we used an automaton-based matching algorithm that quickly retrieves mentions of entities even for large dictionaries [11]. To account for some variations, we transformed each dictionary term into a regular expression. The largest dictionary employed here, that for gene names, contains more than 700,000 entries; dictionaries for disease and drug names were significantly smaller with 61,438 and 51,188 entries, respectively. As ML-based tool for drug names we used ChemSpot [24], for gene names we applied BANNER [17], and for diseases we integrated a previously developed tool in our group directly building on the CRF library Mallet[11]. Note that also ChemSpot and BANNER use Mallet.

4. EVALUATION

In this section, we perform a detailed evaluation of the many facets of our case study in domain-specific web-scale information extraction. Specifically, we first give a technical evaluation of the focused crawl itself, which implies assessing the harvest rate of the crawler, the quality of the text classifier used to keep focus and the quality of the boilerplate detection algorithm we applied. Next, we focus on the performance and scalability of the information extraction pipeline, which includes identifying the most time-consuming steps, contrasting dictionary-based entity recognition with ML-based approaches in terms of recognition speed, and experiments for showing the scale-out our pipeline achieves thanks to the underlying processing system Stratosphere. Eventually, we provide a detailed analysis of our biomedical web corpus in contrast to three other corpora, i.e., the set of pages classified as irrelevant during the crawl, the complete set of approximately 21 million abstracts from Medline (until year 2013), and a set of approximately 250,000 full texts from the PLoS open data mining collection (PMC).

4.1 Quality of the Focused Crawler

The premise of our study is to enable seamless information extraction on large sets of crawled, domain-specific documents on a mid-size cluster. We run our crawler on a cluster of 5 servers, each equipped with at least 32 CPU cores and connected with a 1 GB line to a 10 GB switch connected to the Internet backbone. Politeness rules of web servers were respected and the sizes of host-specific fetch lists was limited to 500 to prevent threads from blocking each other. Each downloaded page passing the initial filtering was subjected to boilerplate removal and to text classification. With this set-up, our crawler achieved a download rate of 3-4 documents per second, which is notably slower compared to other systems (e.g., [20] considers download rates between 10 and 100 pages per second as representative) due to the complex filtering and classification steps employed in our setup. This sums up to more than 80 days of pure crawling and classification for downloading and analyzing approx. 21 million web pages. The crawl yielded 373 GB presumably relevant and 607 GB presumably irrelevant pages, which corresponds to a harvest rate of 38%. This seems to be a typical value for such systems (e.g., [3, 22] report harvest rates between 25% and 45%). Document pre-selection was very effective: MIME-type filtering decreased the number of documents to be analyzed by 9.5%, language filtering by 14%, and document length filtering by 17%.

Evaluating a focused crawler is notoriously difficult for multiple reasons. First, experiments cannot be repeated due to the highly dynamic nature of the web. Starting a crawl with exactly the same set of seeds will result in a largely different result even if the repetition is performed shortly after the first run, as many pages will have changed leading to different link chains. Due to this fact, one cannot easily compare the performance of, for instance, two crawls using different classifiers, different relevance thresholds, or just different prioritization rules for the fetch queue. Second, the recall of a crawler cannot be determined; even estimating it is impossible as this would require a certain set of pages one expects to be found; but whether or not a crawler finds them largely depends on the seeds which cannot be set in an "unbiased" fashion. Third, yield and harvest rate depend largely on the seed lists, which usually are not published.

Classifier and Boilerplate Detection. The quality of the crawled corpus for our purposes, i.e., its specificity for the biomedical domain, depends on mostly two factors: The quality of the classifier, and the quality of the boilerplate detection. We assessed the quality of both components on a gold standard data set during development and on a small, randomly drawn sample of the crawl.

Our classifier achieved a precision of 98% at a recall of 83% in 10-fold cross validation on its training corpus. We then manually checked a randomly drawn set of 100 pages from the relevant corpus and 100 pages from the irrelevant corpus. On these 200 pages, precision was estimated at 94% at a recall of 90%, which roughly confirms the results on the training data (note that these are quality measures of the classifier, not of the the entire crawler; see discussion

[11]http://mallet.cs.umass.edu

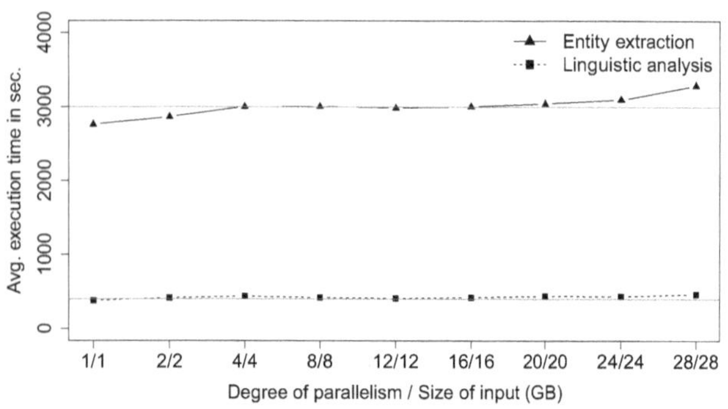

Figure 4: Scale up of linguistic and entity extraction partial data flows. Ideal scale up is displayed in red.

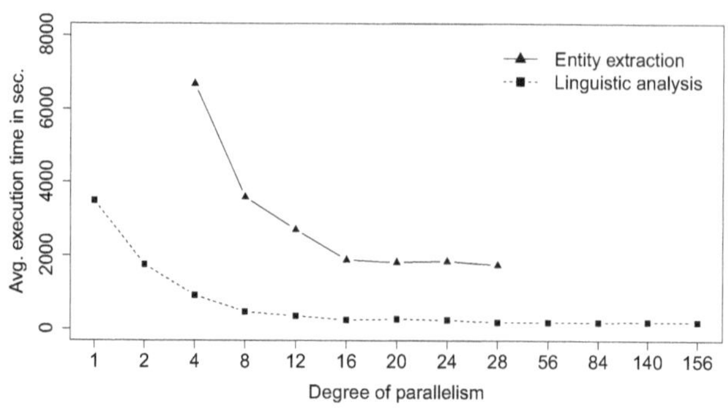

Figure 5: Scale out of linguistic and entity extraction data flows.

above). Differences are notable, but in expectable ranges gives the different characteristics of the texts and the small sample size. An analysis of the false positives showed that these are often web pages at the fringe of what we consider biomedical; for instance, pages describing chemical support for body builders or technical devices used for medical purposes such as wheel chairs. Note that the classifier model we used is geared towards high precision as classifier recall plays a minor role in focused crawling; assuming that the web is essentially infinite, one can simply let the crawler run for longer to obtain more relevant documents. Whether this assumption was reasonable will be discussed in Sect. 5.

In an initial evaluation on a gold standard data set, the boilerplate detection tool we used achieved a precision of 90% at a recall of 82% on average, evaluated on a set of 1906 web pages. These quality measures are computed based on the amount of net text being correctly identified by the algorithm. We assessed the quality of the method on the same 200 web pages used for judging the text classifier. Results indicate a precision of 98% at a recall of 72%. Manual inspection revealed that tables and lists, which often contain valuable facts, are not recognized properly in many cases.

Table 2 lists the top 30 ranked domains according to page rank. Manual inspection revealed that many of them clearly relate to biomedical content, which suggests that the crawling process points to our target domain. Sub-classes of seemingly irrelevant sites, such as slideshare.net or blogger.com often also contain some biomedical material (e.g., blogs, personal journals, reports). It is also not surprising that domains such as arxiv.org and nature.com are ranked within the top 30, because seeds were generated by the search APIs of these domains, which return results only for content hosted there.

4.2 Scalability of Information Extraction

We evaluated the performance of the extraction and analysis data flow in terms of scalability and performance of the individual IE components. These experiments were carried out on a 28 node cluster, where each node was equipped with 24 GB RAM, 1 TB HDD, and a Intel Xeon E5-2620 CPU with 6 cores. Accordingly, the maximum degree of parallelism (DoP) was 168. In the following, we always report as runtimes the average of 3 runs of the analysis flows on each corpus. Input and output of all tasks was stored in HDFS with one data node per compute node and a data replication factor of 3.

Runtime characteristics of the different IE tools. All NLP and IE tools available for Stratosphere were originally designed and implemented by third parties. Many of them are complex applications encompassing several thousand lines of code with multiple dependencies to external libraries. This implies that we usually have no influence on the speed or memory consumption of these tools; there are very rare cases where command-line parameters can be used that impact these properties. Of course, we do heavily influence the speed of each tool on the entire data set by parallelizing its execution on different partitions of the data set.

Prior to analyzing the entire data set of crawled documents, we first evaluated the individual runtimes of each involved component using a random sample of 10,000 documents, which were analyzed using a single thread on a single server. The two dominant steps with respect to runtime are entity extraction, consuming 70% of the total execution time, and part-of-speech tagging, requiring 12% of the runtime. The distribution of the runtimes of part-of-speech tagging (a) and entity annotation (b) by sentences are shown in Fig. 3. Two observations are particularly interesting. First, our part-of-speech tagger, MedPost, uses a Hidden Markov Model of order three, whose runtime is, in principle, linear in the length of the text being analyzed. There are, however, large runtime fluctuations in practice (see Fig. 3(a)) and even occasional crashes, especially when the tagger is applied to very long sentences. Clearly, it is highly questionable whether the very long sentences we observe in our data (with more than 2000 characters) are really reasonable sentences or just errors of the sentence detection method; however, such errors are inevitable in a web environment, considering that the input to the splitter are parts, possibly wrongly extracted by the boilerplate detection, of arbitrary web pages possibly without any sentence structures (see also Sect. 5). One work-around would be to introduce an upper limit on sentence length, but finding a good threshold, trading runtime robustness for information yield, will be non-trivial. Second, Fig. 3(b) shows that the execution time needed for annotating entities varies greatly between annotation methods. Dictionary- and ML-based methods differ in runtime by up to three orders of magnitude. This is a consequence of the differing computational complexity of the underlying algorithms; essentially linear for dictionary matches (the regular expression transformations almost only affect very short word suffixes), yet quadratic for the Conditional Random Fields underlying our ML-based tools [28].

Scalability. We tested the scalability or our IE data flow using a random sample of 20 GB from our crawl. Experiments were carried out separately for the linguistic analysis and the biomedical entity annotation to gain insights into their specific behavior. To this end, we created two separate data flows. Both first filter long texts, repair and remove HTML markup, and annotate sentence and token boundaries (cf. Fig. 2). Subsequently, the linguistic data flow detects pronouns, negation, and parenthesis, while the entity extraction flow first annotates part-of-speech tags and then drug, gene, and disease names using either dictionary or ML-based tools.

We first evaluated both flows on the 20 GB sample with varying DoPs, which led to a number of interesting observations. First, we could not execute the entity extraction data flow with a DoP smaller than 4 due to the excessive runtimes of the ML-based taggers (see above). Furthermore, we could not run this flow with DoPs larger than 28 due to the very high memory requirements of the dictionary-based taggers which each require between 6 and 20 GB of main memory per worker thread. Very likely, this is due to the fact that they transform each dictionary entry (i.e., a regular expression) into a the corresponding non-deterministic finite automaton, which usually greatly increases space requirements. However, the nodes we used have only 24 GB main memory; thus, we could not run more than one instance of these tools per node in the cluster. In contrast, the much less demanding linguistic data flow could be scaled out over the entire range of DoPs without any problems.

As shown in Fig. 5, scale out for both tested flows was satisfactory until DoP=16 for entity extraction, with a decrease in execution time of up to 72%, and until DoP=12 for the linguistic analysis, with a decrease in execution time of up to 95%. Using more nodes brought only marginal further improvements in execution times. This behavior can be explained by the relatively high start-up times of certain tools. For instance, the dictionary-based gene name recognition algorithm needs approximately 20 minutes (!) to load the dictionary and to create the internal data structures used for text matching. These 20 minutes are a hard lower bound for the runtime of this task, regardless of the number of nodes being used. It is not possible to work around this bound in a non-intrusive manner; one either has to use another tool or perform substantial changes to the tool itself. Scale-out of the linguistic flow was considerably better because in this data flow, startup costs of all involved tasks are negligible.

Clearly, the concrete DoP beyond which no more performance gains are obtained depends on the size of the input data, which was rather small in our scale-out experiments. Therefore, we also performed scale-up experiments, where we increased the number of available compute nodes synchronously to the amount of input data. As can be seen from Fig. 4, the linguistic data flow exhibits an almost ideal scale-up, whereas the entity extraction flow scales sub-linear for large DoPs and input sizes, which is consistent to the result of the scale-out experiments.

Processing the entire crawl - a war story. Although Stratosphere offers an elegant and powerful way of specifying complex IE data flows and is also capable of optimizing

about.com	arxiv.org
bettermedicine.com	biomedcentral.com
blogs.nature.com	blogger.com
cancer.net	cancer.org
cdc.gov	definition-of.com
disqus.com	farlex.com
g2conline.org	healthline.com
hhs.gov	lexiophiles.com
mpg.org	mypacs.net
nih.gov	omniture.com
ourhealth.com	reuters.com
rightdiagnosis.com	sideeffects.embl.de
slideshare.net	statcounter.com
thefreedictionary.com	wikimedia.org
wikipedia.org	wordpress.org

Table 2: Domains of 30 top-ranked sites according to page rank.

and parallelizing them on the given cluster, we could not execute the complete flow on the available hardware. This had mostly three reasons:

First, as described above, the dictionary-based entity taggers come along with very high main memory requirements. The complete data flow as shown in Fig. 2 needs roughly 60 GB main memory per worker thread, which clearly exceeds the amount of RAM available on each node. Unfortunately, the scheduling component of Stratosphere does not consider memory consumption per worker node as optimization goal, for that reason we could not run an entire flow on any of the nodes.

Second, another issue occurred with the ML-based disease recognition tool. This tool brings its own linguistic preprocessing, which is imported from the OpenNLP library, version 1.4[12]. However, all other OpenNLP operators we integrated into Stratosphere (such as tokenization and sentence splitting) are based on version 1.5, which is not downward compatible to 1.4. Unfortunately, the Java class loader employed in the system's runtime engine is not capable of using two different versions of the same library.

Third, in most popular Big Data analysis scenarios, a very large input is scanned and subsequently aggregated into smaller and smaller intermediate results. Accordingly, the bulk of the network traffic for accessing and inputs and writing outputs of tasks is usually spent by those tasks that are at the beginning of the analysis flows, whereas latter tasks often process only small data sets. However, the situation is quite different in a text analytics scenario like ours, where texts are piped through a series of tasks, each adding specific annotations (POS tags, entity annotation, token boundaries etc.) and thus actually increasing the size of the data throughput the analysis pipeline. In our case, the total amount of data produced is 1,6 TB, consisting of 400 GB entity annotations and 1,2 TB linguistic annotations, on top of the 1 TB raw text. Storing and accessing these large intermediate data sets through HDFS over-stressed the cluster network (nodes are connected by a 1 GB switch), leading to unpredictable network delays which in turn led to time-out induced crashes in some of the annotation tools.

To cope with these problems, we had to take several dras-

[12]http://opennlp.apache.org/

	Size in GB	No. of docs.	Mean no. of chars.
Relevant crawl	373	4,233,523	88,384
Irrelevant crawl	607	17,704,365	37,625
Medline	21	21,686,397	865
PMC	19	250,440	55,704

Table 3: Summary of data sets.

tic measures. First, we split up the flow into different parts such that each part only required memory within the given limits; essentially, we created one flow for all linguistic analysis and one flow per entity class of the biomedical analysis. Still, the memory requirements (see above) put severe constraints on the number of threads executable per node, which grossly hampered the overall DoP and thus greatly increased the overall runtime. Eventually, we spinned of gene recognition, being the most space-consuming task, and executed it on a single server with 1 TB RAM using 40 threads. In the same manner, we had to perform disease name extraction in a separate run to overcome versioning problems. To cope with the network problems, we furthermore splitted the crawled data into chunks of 50 GB and executed the different flows separately on these chunks.

Alternatively to splitting the data flow into separate parts and analyzing the crawled data chunk-wise, we considered renting cloud systems for our experiments but quickly disregarded this option due to high rental costs. Since memory requirements of IE operators is the most limiting factor in our study, only cloud instances with more than 35 GB RAM come into question, which are still rather costly. For example, renting a 28 node cluster of instance type "m4.4xlarge" with 64GB of RAM available per node from AWS costs approximately 650 USD per day as of March 2016[13].

4.3 Content analysis

A main interest in this project is to compare extraction results from the web to the scientific literature to identify commonalities and differences between biomedical texts from the web and from peer reviewed journals. Thus, we also analyzed abstracts and full-texts from Medline and PMC using the same IE flow (downstream from the HTML treatment) as for the crawled data. As a forth text collection, we used all pages crawled but classified as irrelevant. Table 3 summarizes the data sets enclosed in this analysis.

We performed an in-depth analysis and comparison of the results obtained on these four corpora. Our analysis is split into a linguistic part, concerning properties such as article lengths, sentence structure, and usage of grammatical structures, and a domain-specific part, comparing the occurrence frequencies and distributions of three biomedical entities, i.e., drugs, genes, and diseases.

4.3.1 Linguistic analysis

Analyzing the linguistic structure of texts is important for assessing the complexity of texts and to judge whether existing IE tools, which were trained and developed for different corpora, might perform well in web documents. Particularly, we examine document lengths, sentence lengths, incidence of negation, and incidence of pronouns and parenthesis. Differences in obtained measures were statistically assessed using the Mann-Whitney-Wilcoxon signed rank test. This test produces a P-value, which estimates the probability that the observed differences are due to random effects in the data.

Document and sentence lengths. Sentence lengths impact IE and NLP in different ways. First, the execution time of IE and NLP tools usually directly depends on the lengths of the sentences to be analyzed. Second, the difficulty of constituent and dependency sentence parsing and the difficulty of modern relation extraction methods rises with sentence lengths [27]. Likewise, if crawled web documents contain shorter sentences than Medline or PMC, we expect the former to be easier to analyze. Other important measures are the document lengths in the different corpora, as these must be considered when comparing the frequency of entity mentions.

Figure 6(a) displays the distribution of document lengths and Fig. 6(b) displays mean sentence lengths across the different data sets. Mean document lengths in relevant documents were significantly shorter than in PMC ($P < 0.01$), but significantly longer compared to irrelevant documents ($P < 0.01$) and to Medline abstracts ($P < 0.01$). Document lengths for the relevant corpus show the largest variance, which increases the need for appropriate load balancing in a distributed setting. Differences in sentence lengths between the four corpora are also significant, confirming previous findings from [6] regarding Medline abstracts and PMC full texts. These differences have to be kept in mind when selecting tools for IE that are based on gold standard data. Most tools we are aware of were trained and evaluated on Medline abstracts and thus on rather short sentences; accordingly, we expected a lower performance of these tools on longer sentences than reported in the literature.

Incidence of negation. Detecting negation is important in many areas of natural language processing (e.g., sentiment analysis, relation extraction) and is particularly important for analyzing biomedical texts [1]. Here, we used a rather simple method for determining negations in sentences, using a set of regular expressions to find mentions of the words *not*, *nor*, and *neither*. As shown in Fig. 6(c), the incidence of negation in the four corpora is significantly different ($P < 0.01$) regarding the overall incidence of negation and the relative frequency of negation with respect to document length. Specifically, texts in the set of relevant documents have a lower incidence of negation than in PMC and the irrelevant pages and a higher incidence of negation than in Medline. Accordingly, appropriate treatment of negation will be more important for web data than for scientific articles.

Incidence of pronouns and parenthesized text. Pronominal anaphora are important in biomedical IE to perform co-reference resolution [10]. To measure the amount of such co-references in our corpora, we counted six different classes of pronouns in each data set. Interestingly, the incidence of demonstrative, relative, and object pronouns, which are the most important pronoun classes for co-reference resolution, was significantly lower both in relevant and irrelevant texts compared to texts from PMC (data not shown). We expected this observation concerning irrelevant texts since these texts are significantly shorter than texts from PMC. Our observation is surprising for relevant texts as these are significantly longer than documents from PMC. This finding

[13]http://aws.amazon.com/ec2/pricing/

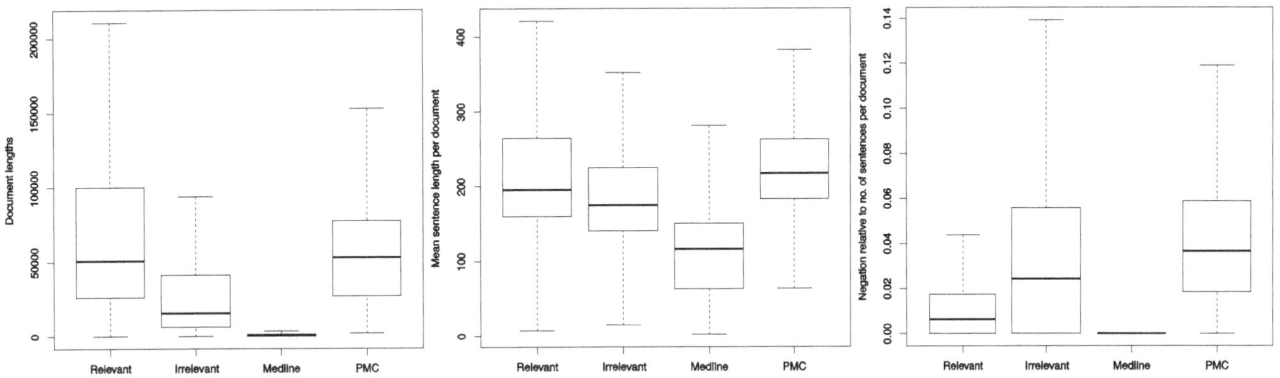

(a) Distribution of document length (b) Distribution of mean sentence length (c) Incidence of negation

Figure 6: Distribution and incidence of linguistic properties per document in different data sets.

might indicate that co-reference resolution on crawled texts is not as vital as in analyzing biomedical full-text literature.

Parentheses can hint to abbreviations, paper references, synonyms of named entities, etc., which are very important during NLP processing. Properly treating parenthesis is also highly important for syntactic parsing, as text in parentheses does typically not conform to the sentence grammar. We extracted parenthesized text using a set of regular expressions and found that that their incidences differ significantly ($P < 0.01$) between all data sets (data not shown). We observed the highest incidence in texts from PMC, followed by relevant web documents and Medline, and the lowest in irrelevant documents.

Data set	Method	Disease	Drug	Gene
Relevant	Dict.	26,344	17,974	73,435
	ML	629,384	28,660	5,506,579
Irrelevant	Dict.	5,318	8,456	22,131
	ML	119,638	15,875	991,010
Medline	Dict.	11,194	12,164	29,928
	ML	343,184	20,282	4,715,194
PMC	Dict.	12,291	15,013	92,319
	ML	277,211	25,462	1,858,709

Table 4: Number of distinct entity names by corpus.

4.3.2 *Biomedical entities*

The result we were most interested in this study from an application point-of-view was the degree of differences in the biomedical entities that are mentioned on the web versus the scientific literature. Table 4 lists the number of distinct names that were found in the two crawled corpora, in Medline, and in PMC for the entity classes disease, drug, and gene. As expected, ML-based annotation produces substantially more annotations for each entity type than dictionary-based annotation. We also notice that the total number of distinct annotations is significantly different between relevant and irrelevant pages both for dictionary- and ML-based approaches, with much larger numbers of annotations in relevant documents for each entity class, which is reassuring of the crawl quality. In the following, we compare named entity annotations in the different corpora more deeply for each entity type.

Disease names. As shown in Fig. 7(a), the incidence of disease names per document is higher in PMC articles and relevant web documents compared to Medline abstracts and irrelevant crawled documents, which rarely mention more than one disease (presumably mostly false positives with abbreviations). Differences of the mean number of disease annotations per 1000 sentences between relevant ($avg_{rel} =$ 128.49) and irrelevant ($avg_{irrel} = 4.57$), relevant and Medline ($avg_{medl} = 204.92$), and Medline and PMC ($avg_{pmc} =$ 117.51) are all highly significant ($P < 0.01$). One explanation for the smaller incidence of disease names in Medline abstracts compared to web and PMC full-text documents even when normalized to per-sentence measures is the shorter average sentence length in the abstracts. Furthermore, the large number of disease names in the relevant web document is certainly a result of the way we generated seeds, often using disease names as keywords. Accordingly, our crawl should be enriched for disease-related websites, such as information websites for patients or disease-specific support groups.

Drug names. Figure 7(b) displays the incidence of drug names per document in the different data sets. In relevant documents, more drug mentions were recognized on average compared to irrelevant documents and abstracts taken from Medline. The means of drug name annotations for both annotation methods combined per 1000 sentences differ significantly ($P < 0.01$) between relevant ($avg_{rel} = 97.83$) and irrelevant ($avg_{irrel} = 6.85$) documents, and between relevant documents and Medline ($avg_{medl} = 293.95$) abstracts and PMC documents ($avg_{pmc} = 275.95$). Possible reasons for the differences between crawled relevant documents and Medline abstracts are the same as for disease names, as disease-related web sites often are also full of drug names.

Gene names. Similar to results for disease and drug names, differences in the number of gene mentions per document are significant between relevant and irrelevant documents, and between relevant and Medline ($P < 0.01$) and the means of gene name annotations per 1000 sentences for dictionary-based annotation differ significantly between all sets ($avg_{rel} = 128.23$, $avg_{irrel} = 4.39$, $avg_{medl} = 415.58$, $avg_{pmc} = 74.12$). However, the most striking observation regarding the incidences of gene names are the extremely large differences between the dictionary-based extraction method

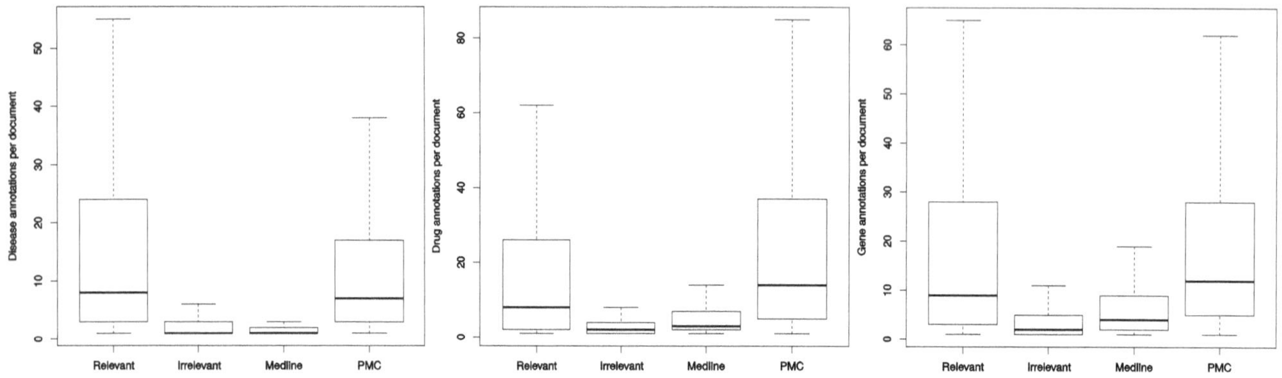

(a) Diseases (b) Drugs (c) Genes

Figure 7: Incidence of named entity annotations per document in the different corpora.

and the ML-based algorithm. Using ML, we recognized more than 5.5 million distinct gene names in relevant documents, whereas dictionary-based annotation only finds 73,435 different gene names (cf. Table 4). It is immediately clear that the vast majority of annotations produced by BANNER must be false positives, because there exist only roughly 900,000 distinct gene names (including synonyms) in the public gene-related databases. The reason for this presumably excessive amount of wrong annotations is the fact that BANNER was trained on a small set of selected Medline abstracts, which exhibit different language characteristics than web documents (see Sect. 4.3.1). Upon manual inspection, we noticed that a very large number of false positives are three letter acronyms (TLA), which are almost always tagged as genes by our tool; this strategy is correct for the gold standard abstracts used for developing and evaluating the tool, but leads to catastrophic performance on any other documents. Therefore, we filtered all TLAs from the list of ML-tagged gene names prior to further analysis, reducing, for instance, the number of distinct gene names in the relevant web corpus from 5.5 million to 2.3 million. Figure 7(c) displays the incidence of gene names in the different data sets after filtering.

Annotation overlap and difference. Finally, we determined the differences in the sets of extracted entities between the different data sets to assess whether focused crawling has the potential to open up new sources of biomedical knowledge and to exclude the potential danger of simply having many scientific abstracts in the relevant crawl. Figure 8 shows the overlap and non-overlaps of dictionary-based entity annotations. For all evaluated entity types, we found that the overlap of extracted names between relevant and irrelevant documents is notable but rather small, i.e., approximately 15% for disease names, approximately 30% for drug names (86% out of which were also found in Medline and PMC), and 17% for gene names. The overlap between relevant and Medline and relevant and PMC is considerably larger and ranges from 6% (ML-based gene extraction) to 60% (dictionary-based gene extraction).

We also assessed the statistical significance of these differences using the Jensen-Shannon divergence (JSD), an information-theoretic measure for assessing the difference between two probability distributions based on the Kullback-Leibler divergence. JSD is a symmetric measure and results in values bounded for two distributions A, B with $0 \leq JSD_{A,B} \leq 1$, where similar distributions approach a JSD close to 0, and dissimilar distributions approach 1. For each data set and entity type, we determined the probability distribution of entity names and computed for each combination of data sets the JSD (data not shown). Relevant and irrelevant documents exhibit larger JSDs, i.e., significantly different distributions ($0.4463 \leq JSD_{rel,irrel} \leq 0.6548$), for any entity type compared to documents from Medline and relevant ($0.2864 \leq JSD_{rel,medl} \leq 0.3596$), and PMC and relevant ($0.1673 \leq JSD_{rel,pmc} \leq 0.3354$). This indicates that documents classified as relevant during crawling actually are more similar to the biomedical literature and thus relevant for the target domain. Similarly, JSD between irrelevant and Medline ($0.4528 \leq JSD_{irrel,medl} \leq 0.6850$) and irrelevant and PMC ($0.3941 \leq JSD_{irrel,pmc} \leq 0.6633$).

Together, these findings give clear evidence that there is a significant amount of information on the web which is not contained in the scientific literature, indicated by several thousand distinct entity names for each entity type which appear only in relevant web documents. Studying these sets in more detail will be the next step in our research.

5. LESSONS LEARNED AND CHALLENGES FOR FUTURE RESEARCH

In this paper, we reported our experiences with a study in crawling and deeply analyzing a large domain-specific corpus from the web, exemplified for the field of biomedical research. From a domain-knowledge point-of-view, our results are highly interesting as they indicate that there is indeed a large body of biomedical knowledge on the web that is not present in the scientific literature. Clearly, much more research is necessary to substantiate this hypothesis and to assess the usefulness of this knowledge, which could be, for instance, reports of high quality that were not (yet) published or important text book knowledge that is so established that one cannot find scientific publications discussing it; however, a large fraction presumably are also false positive matches of the taggers or information of dubious quality and reliability. Our study also brought up a number of technical pitfalls of focused crawling and large-scale, high quality text processing using a best-of-breed strategy for choosing text analytics tools. In the following, we highlight some of these challenges.

Reliable MIME-type detection. Large files down-

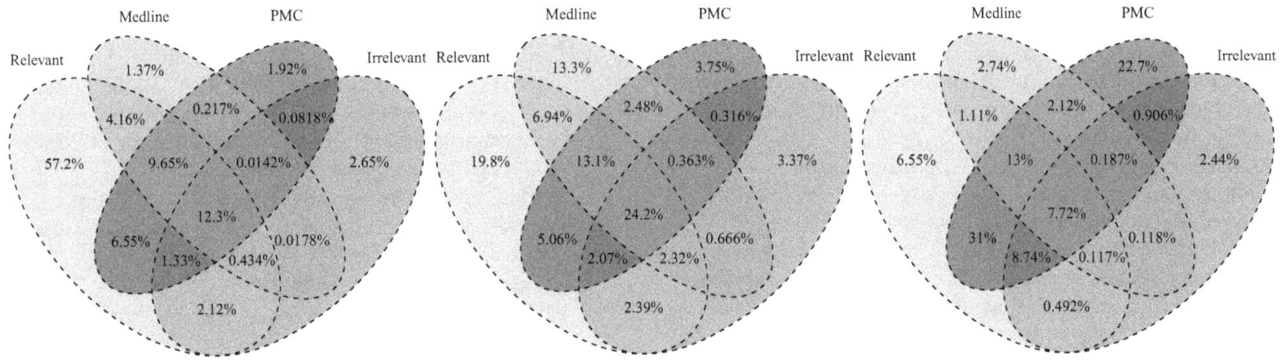

(a) Disease (b) Drug (c) Gene

Figure 8: Annotation overlap of distinct entity names in % for different entity types and dictionary-based annotation.

loaded during crawl are often not textual but embedded presentation slides or formatted documents, which were wrongly classified as plain textual. Filtering by document size only, as we did, is unsatisfactory as it easily misses relevant (and extensive) content. However, we are not aware of any robust tools or ongoing research for reliable MIME-type detection; instead, detecting MIME-types usually is carried out by regular expression matching on the file name extension or by analyzing the first n bytes of a document. We used the Apache Tika[14] library during crawling, which ships only with a list of a handful common MIME-types.

Robust HTML markup removal. According to [19], 95% of HTML documents on the web do not adhere to W3C HTML standards. 13% of the analyzed websites had so sever issues that they could not be transcoded. However, correctly formatted HTML pages seem to be a prerequisite for most boilerplate detection algorithms. In the course of this study, we evaluated different markup removal algorithms and found them to perform reasonably well on a gold-standard set of 1,906 pages (details omitted). Applying these tools to our crawled documents, however, revealed that they are highly sensitive to markup errors, often resulting in crashes or empty results. Developing boilerplate detection algorithms that are more robust against errors in real life web pages is essential for seamless and comprehensive text analytics from web documents.

Resource consumption of extraction tools. Even though the NLP and IE tools we used require only a moderate amount of memory for each running instance, these numbers sum-up notably when running multiple instances on a multi-threaded machine. In our study, this grossly hampered the DoP we could achieve, leading to sub-optimal resource usage and long analysis times. Furthermore, several tools produced Java out-of-memory errors when applied to long texts; as we could not find a workaround for this behavior, we eventually had to define a hard upper limit on the texts to be analyzed. These findings indicate that the current tools, at least in the biomedical domain, are not well prepared to be applied on large text collections. This is consistent with the observation that research in this field is obsessed with small improvements in extraction quality on small gold standard data sets, and rarely considers runtime or space consumption when used in true applications. The situation might be different in other fields, but research in more robust NER tools, with configurable memory consumption, seems highly desirable.

NLP and IE models for web documents. It is well known that ML tools work best on data sets that exhibit similar language characteristics as those used for training. Most research into NER tools in biomedicine is performed on Medline abstracts, both with respect to training data and evaluation data. On such data, ML-based NER is clearly superior to other approaches, as shown in many recent studies and international competitions [25]. Accordingly, all ML-based methods used in this project employ models trained on Medline abstracts since no other training data is available. However, our study reveals that web documents and documents from Medline and PMC are significantly different in several aspects. This leads to an enormous amount of false positive matches by these tools, which are often short abbreviations. We believe that there is a great need for more sophisticated models for domain-specific entity recognition from web documents. Note that the current research into this direction typically targets rather simple entity types, such as persons, places, or products [9]. To our knowledge, the performance of such methods on the more difficult biomedical entity types has not yet been evaluated.

Trade-off between precision and yield in focused crawling. When setting-up our system, we focused on a high-precision text classifier as we believed that the number of true positives can be improved more easily with longer crawls than with a high-recall classifier, which might also bring many false positive pages. However, we actually observed that this strategy was not as effective as we thought. Actually, the size of the crawl we obtained was bound by the fact that our crawl frontier eventually emptied. As described in Sect. 2.2, we already had to significantly extend our seed list to obtain a crawl of at least the size we have now. Several strategies could be followed to create larger focused crawl. For instance, one could produce even larger seed lists, but this requires substantial preparation time given the current limits of the search engine APIs. Another approach would be to also follow links from pages classified as irrelevant, but only with a small margin. Finally, one could tune the classifier towards more recall during crawling, and classify each crawled text later a second time with a model geared

[14]http://tika.apache.org

towards high precision. Which of these ways is the most promising one, remains an open question.

Crawling and text analytics as a consolidated process. This project pursued a two-staged approach, where crawling and text analytics was performed in two separate phases using very different infrastructures. However, the result of the IE pipeline could actually be a valuable input for the classifier during a crawl, as the occurrence of gene names or disease names are strong indicators for biomedical content. We believe it would be a worthwhile undertaking to research systems that would allow specifying crawling strategies, classification, and domain-specific IE in a single framework. Such a framework would greatly reduce the time it takes to build web-scale domain-specific text analysis systems.

6. CONCLUSION

In recent years, web-scale information extraction by means of Big Data processing tools has gained much attention. However, most works focus on comparable simple IE techniques [26, 16] or consider only singular extraction tasks [4, 14]. Moreover, we are not aware of any research has in the interplay of web crawling and state-of-the-art information extraction, especially when applied in a domain-specific setting. Accurate acquisition of web documents by means of focused web crawls was in the focus of research in the late 1990s and early 2000s, but this topic seems to have lost momentum in recent years, despite the often reiterated importance of the web for Big Data scenarios. We can only speculate about the reasons for this apparent contradiction. One reason could be the difficulty to compare and assess the quality of focused web crawling; another reason probably is the fact that such research requires considerable investments both in terms of hardware (large clusters, high bandwidth, etc.) and in terms of software (complex analysis pipelines, best-of-breed tool selection, parallelization).

We described methods to simplify the creation of such systems using and extending open source systems. The experiences we report partly seem devastating, uncovering a series of issues in essentially all components that prevent their seamless and scalable application, at least on a mid-size cluster as was available to us. Of course, our experiences are specific to the frameworks we used and might have been different with other base systems; yet, we are not aware of any other system offering such a rich set of NLP and (biomedical) IE tools ready-to-use (with all caveats described in this work) than Stratosphere. Nevertheless, it is our frank intention to create more attention to the interesting and challenging topic of sophisticated, domain-specific web-scale information extraction in the data management research community.

Acknowledgments

This research is funded by the German Research Foundation under grant FOR 1306. We thank Philippe Thomas and Tim Rocktäschel for providing models and software we used during entity recognition.

7. REFERENCES

[1] S. Agarwal and H. Yu. Biomedical negation scope detection with conditional random fields. *J. Am. Med. Inform. Assn.*, 17(6):696–701, 2010.

[2] A. Alexandrov, R. Bergmann, S. Ewen, J.-C. Freytag, F. Hueske, A. Heise, O. Kao, M. Leich, U. Leser, V. Markl, F. Naumann, M. Peters, A. Rheinländer, M. J. Sax, S. Schelter, M. Höger, K. Tzoumas, and D. Warneke. The stratosphere platform for big data analytics. *VLDB J.*, 23(6):939–964, 2014.

[3] S. Chakrabarti, M. van den Berg, and B. Dom. Focused crawling: A new approach to topic-specific web resource discovery. *Comput. Netw.*, 31(11-16):1623–1640, 1999.

[4] B. Chandramouli, J. Goldstein, and S. Duan. Temporal analytics on big data for web advertising. In *Proc. 28th IEEE Int. Conf. on Data Engineering*, pages 90–101, 2012.

[5] L. Chiticariu, R. Krishnamurthy, Y. Li, S. Raghavan, F. R. Reiss, and S. Vaithyanathan. Systemt: An algebraic approach to declarative information extraction. In *Proc. 48th Annual Meeting of the Association for Computational Linguistics*, 2010.

[6] K. B. Cohen, H. L. Johnson, K. Verspoor, C. Roeder, and L. Hunter. The structural and content aspects of abstracts versus bodies of full text journal articles are different. *BMC Bioinformatics*, 11:492, 2010.

[7] L. Covolo, S. Mascaretti, A. Caruana, G. Orizio, L. Caimi, and U. Gelatti. How has the flu virus infected the web? 2010 influenza and vaccine information available on the internet. *BMC Public Health*, 13(1):83, 2013.

[8] B. D. Davison. Topical locality in the web. In *Proc. 23rd Annual Int. ACM SIGIR Conf. on Research and Development in Information Retrieval*, pages 272–279, 2000.

[9] O. Etzioni, M. Cafarella, D. Downey, A.-M. Popescu, T. Shaked, S. Soderland, D. S. Weld, and A. Yates. Unsupervised named-entity extraction from the web: An experimental study. *Artif. Intell.*, 165(1):91–134, 2005.

[10] C. Gasperin and T. Briscoe. Statistical anaphora resolution in biomedical texts. In *Proc. 22nd Int. Conf. on Computational Linguistics - Volume 1*, pages 257–264, 2008.

[11] M. Gerner, G. Nenadic, and C. M. Bergman. Linnaeus: A species name identification system for biomedical literature. *BMC Bioinformatics*, 11:85, 2010.

[12] A. Heise and F. Naumann. Integrating open government data with stratosphere for more transparency. *J. Web Semant.*, 14:45–56, 2012.

[13] A. Heise, A. Rheinländer, M. Leich, U. Leser, and F. Naumann. Meteor/Sopremo: An Extensible Query Language and Operator Model. In *Proc. Int. Ws. on End-to-End Management of Big Data*, 2012.

[14] V. N. Khuc, C. Shivade, R. Ramnath, and J. Ramanathan. Towards building large-scale distributed systems for twitter sentiment analysis. In *Proc. 27th Annual ACM Symposium on Applied Computing*, pages 459–464, 2012.

[15] C. Kohlschütter, P. Fankhauser, and W. Nejdl. Boilerplate detection using shallow text features. In *Proc. 3rd ACM Int. Conf. on Web Search and Data Mining*, pages 441–450, 2010.

[16] R. Krishnamurthy, Y. Li, S. Raghavan, F. Reiss, S. Vaithyanathan, and H. Zhu. Systemt: A system for

declarative information extraction. *SIGMOD Rec.*, 37(4), 2009.

[17] R. Leaman and G. Gonzalez. Banner: An executable survey of advances in biomedical named entity recognition. In *Pacific Symposium on Biocomputing*, pages 652–663, 2008.

[18] U. Leser and J. Hakenberg. What makes a gene name? named entity recognition in the biomedical literature. *Brief. Bioinform.*, 6(4):357–369, 2005.

[19] E. Ofuonye, P. Beatty, S. Dick, and J. Miller. Prevalence and classification of web page defects. *Online Inform. Rev.*, 34(1):160–174, 2010.

[20] C. Olston and M. Najork. Web crawling. *Found. Trends Inf. Retr.*, 4(3):175–246, 2010.

[21] B. Pang and L. Lee. Opinion mining and sentiment analysis. *Found. Trends Inf. Ret.*, 2(1-2):1–135, 2008.

[22] G. Pant and P. Srinivasan. Learning to crawl: Comparing classification schemes. *ACM T. Inform. Syst.*, 23(4):430–462, 2005.

[23] A. Rheinländer, A. Heise, F. Hueske, U. Leser, and F. Naumann. Sofa: An extensible logical optimizer for udf-heavy data flows. *Inform. Syst.*, 52(C):96–125, 2015.

[24] T. Rocktäschel, M. Weidlich, and U. Leser. Chemspot: a hybrid system for chemical named entity recognition. *Bioinformatics*, 28(12):1633–1640, 2012.

[25] I. Segura-Bedmar, P. Martínez, and M. Herrero-Zazo. Lessons learnt from the ddiextraction-2013 shared task. *J. Biomed. Inform.*, 51:152–164, 2014.

[26] W. Shen, A. Doan, J. F. Naughton, and R. Ramakrishnan. Declarative information extraction using datalog with embedded extraction predicates. In *Proc. 33rd Int. Conf. on Very Large Data Bases*, pages 1033–1044, 2007.

[27] D. Tikk, I. Solt, P. E. Thomas, and U. Leser. A detailed error analysis of 13 kernel methods for protein-protein interaction extraction. *BMC Bioinformatics*, 14:12, 2013.

[28] A. Viterbi. Error bounds for convolutional codes and an asymptotically optimum decoding algorithm. *IEEE T. Inform. Theory*, 13(2):260–269, 2006.

[29] L. Yi, B. Liu, and X. Li. Eliminating noisy information in web pages for data mining. In *Proc. 9th ACM SIGKDD Int. Conf. on Knowledge Discovery and Data Mining*, pages 296–305, 2003.

Robust and Noise Resistant Wrapper Induction*

Tim Furche[1] and Jinsong Guo[1] and Sebastian Maneth[2] and Christian Schallhart[1]

[1]University of Oxford firstname.lastname@cs.ox.ac.uk

[2]University of Edinburgh smaneth@inf.ed.ac.uk

ABSTRACT

Wrapper induction is the problem of automatically inferring a query from annotated web pages of the same template. This query should not only select the annotated content accurately but also other content following the same template. Beyond *accurately* matching the template, we consider two additional requirements: **(1)** wrappers should be *robust* against a large class of changes to the web pages, and **(2)** the induction process should be *noise resistant*, i.e., tolerate slightly erroneous (e.g., machine generated) samples. Key to our approach is a query language that is powerful enough to permit accurate selection, but limited enough to force noisy samples to be generalized into wrappers that select the likely intended items. We introduce such a language as subset of XPATH and show that even for such a restricted language, inducing optimal queries according to a suitable scoring is infeasible. Nevertheless, our wrapper induction framework infers highly robust and noise resistant queries. We evaluate the queries on snapshots from web pages that change over time as provided by the Internet Archive, and show that the induced queries are as robust as the human-made queries. The queries often survive hundreds sometimes thousands of days, with many changes to the relative position of the selected nodes (including changes on template level). This is due to the few and discriminative anchor (intermediately selected) nodes of the generated queries. The queries are highly resistant against positive noise (up to 50%) and negative noise (up to 20%).

1. INTRODUCTION

Web wrappers are programs that extract information from web pages. For instance a wrapper may extract the names of movie directors from movie listings such as IMDB. Wrappers have always played a significant role in accessing the web as data—whether to extract competitors' prices for competitive intelligence (see [10] for a recent survey) or as bridge between traditional web pages and linked data [19]. Wrapper induction is then the process of inferring a wrapper from a given sample of annotated data which follows a certain template. A good wrapper is expected to select the same intended information also from other pages of the same template. For instance, given a sample with "Martin Scorsese" (more specifically, its enclosing span-node) annotated, a wrapper that searches for this particular string would be far too specific in most cases: it works only for movies of this single director. A wrapper is **(1)** *accurate* if it infers the full set of intended information from the given examples. This is a notion common to most wrapper induction approaches. Our wrappers should additionally be **(2)** *robust* against structural changes of the web page over time, and—different from previous approaches—**(3)** the induction process should be *resistant to noise* in the annotations. E.g. if all but one of several movie directors are annotated on a page, then the induced wrapper should select all directors, i.e., treating the missing director as noise.

Previous wrapper induction approaches [18, 1, 16] have focused on the *supervised* setting where a human annotator provides a perfect set of annotations. We consider a very different setting for wrapper induction, motivated by a recent rise in automated data extraction [15, 5, 13] and wrapper maintenance approaches [22]. Samples are no longer provided by humans but automatically by entity recognizers [5, 13] or by finding known instances in new [15] or modified [22] web pages. For both cases, only as much annotations may be provided for any single page or site as there is overlap between the page's items and the recognized entities or known instances. Different from the supervised setting, automatically generated samples can be *noisy*—some annotations might be missing and others might be incorrectly placed.

Thus, our wrapper induction method considers samples that may be both noisy and minimal, allowing wrappers to be induced from annotations for a single page and from as little as a single sample. It achieves this primarily through the careful choice of an *expressive subset* of XPATH, that is sufficient to express most wrappers, but limited enough to force noisy annotations to be generalized into wrappers that select the likely intended items. The proposed method achieves remarkable robustness. It does so in a very different fashion than previous approaches—by optimizing for *short, selective wrappers* that use HTML's *semantic markup* for selection where possible: our approach favors **(1)** *short* expressions with a small number of steps over multi-step expressions. It also prefers **(2)** *selective* expressions that drill down quickly into a small portion of the HTML page over expressions that are unselective (though possibly shorter). Selective expressions are less likely to be affected by changes in unrelated parts of the document. It is also heavily biased towards exploiting hints about the **(3)** *se-*

*Corresponding author: Jinsong Guo. The research leading to these results has received funding from the European Research Council under the ERC grant DIADEM, no. 246858 and ExtraLytics, no. 641222, as well as from the EPSRC programme grant VADA, no. EP/M025268/1. The current affiliation of Christian Schallhart is Google London (email address: christian.schallhart@gmail.com).

SIGMOD'16, June 26-July 01, 2016, San Francisco, CA, USA

ISBN 978-1-4503-3531-7/16/06...$15.00

DOI: http://dx.doi.org/10.1145/2882903.2915214

mantic role of elements in the template. In HTML, these are typically expressed in `id` or `class` attributes and often used for styling and scripting. HTML5's Microdata adds further semantic attributes such as `itemprop`. Many templates also provide static labels, either visible or in form of `title` tooltips. These criteria are designed to mimic human-created robust XPATH expressions.

As an example, consider the following wrapper, extracting (`span`-elements of) directors from IMDB movie pages:

```
descendant::div[starts-with(.,"Director:")][1]/
    descendant::span
```

This XPATH query selects the first `div`-element with text-value of the form "Director: ...". Starting from this `div`-element, the query selects all descendant `span`-elements. There is only one such span-element, and this element contains precisely the director names of the movie. Thus, the above is an accurate wrapper for extracting director names. However, this query is *not* robust against changes to the web page: **(1)** Imagine more `span` elements (containing non-director information) are inserted under the correct div-element. The wrapper would wrongly select all of them. **(2)** Imagine that more `div`-elements (without director information) are inserted *before* the `div`-element containing the director information. The wrapper would select the wrong `div`-element and return its contained `span` elements, if any. Our approach does *not* attempt to build an accurate model of changes done to a specific web site or class of web sites. Instead, we aim to model heuristics for building robust wrappers on any type of web site.

What then, is a robust wrapper for this example?

```
descendant::div[starts-with(.,"Director:")]/
    descendant::span[@itemprop="name"]
```

This wrapper q_{director} is the most robust one in our setting. It follows the heuristic outlined above for short, selective wrappers that prefer semantic features in their predicates. It increases the selectiveness of the `span` step by using a predicate on a semantic attribute (`itemprop`) and shortens the `div` step by removing the positional predicate that is no longer needed (because of the `itemprop`-attribute). We often refer to the intermediate nodes selected by an XPATH expression as "anchors". Figure 1 shows a fragment of the tree structure of an IMDB movie page with "Martin Scorsese" as director; the red shaded nodes are anchors of q_{director}.

Contributions. We present a novel approach for inducing wrappers under the combined requirements of robustness and noise resistance.

(1) We define *directed XPath with sideways checks* (for short, dsXPath). dsXPath is powerful enough to capture a large class of wrappers and is weak enough to support the generalization to correct queries from noisy samples.

(2) We define a natural framework for computing the *robustness* of a query. The essential feature of this framework is its composability: the robustness score of a composed query can be computed from the scores of its constituents.

(3) We show that computing the top-k most robust queries is intractable, hence there is no hope for an exact solution.

(4) We devise a recursive bottom-up scheme for estimating the top-k most robust dsXPath queries for a given set of samples.

(5) We experimentally evaluate our approach using old versions of popular pages from the Internet Achieve.

Noise Resistance. To deal with noisy samples, we restrict to a particularly small XPATH fragment. This fragment is *not* selection complete, i.e., there are annotated documents for which no query in the fragment selects the annotated positions accurately. For instance, our fragment cannot select all but some particular elements of a list. Most notably, the fragment misses important features such as negation and union. Interestingly, while trying to keep the XPATH fragment as restricted and small as possible, we found that certain axes are crucially required in order to achieve full accuracy for all our samples. Besides the four base axis of XPATH (`child`, `parent`, `descendant`, and `ancestor`), we found that the two "sideways" axes `following-sibling` and `preceding-sibling` are essential for our wrappers. For instance, often we want to select all elements of a list appearing *after* a specific determining element.

Experiments. Our evaluation validates three claims: **(1)** The approach generates robust wrappers, that remain effective as long as the relevant data is present, often for hundreds of days. **(2)** The generated wrappers have comparable or higher robustness than human-created ones. **(3)** The approach is able to generate such wrappers even in presence of significant amount of noise in the annotations. We selected over 100 popular web pages from more than 50 different sites. We track the evolution of the pages over *six years* in the Internet Archive in 20 day intervals. For each of these over $> 10k$ "page versions", we evaluate the human crafted wrapper, the wrapper produced by our system, and a simple baseline wrapper.

Related Work

This paper introduces a novel wrapper induction approach tailored to the emerging setting of automatic, rather than human provided annotations. Wrapper induction is the process of inducing an extraction program, often one or more XPATH or similar expressions over the HTML tag tree, from a set of examples.

Supervised Induction. Initially, wrapper induction approaches [18, 1] have been **supervised** where annotations are provided by humans (see [12]). The supervised setting has seen a flurry of industrial tools such as Lixto [1] or Mozenda, http://mozenda.com/. In fact, a simple incarnation of these inducers has become an essential tool for web developers, to inspect web sites and find relevant nodes. Firebug, as well as the developer tools provided with Chrome, Firefox, and Safari, allow to induce XPATH expressions from single samples. For neither of these approaches has robustness of the expressions been a primary concern. For the latter, e.g., the induced expressions are often one-off means for debugging and thus optimized for simplicity. In fact, most of these tools provide expressions close to the canonical path (see Section 2), at most exploiting unique `id` attributes if present. These expressions are typically not *robust* per se, as noted in [8, 9]. Furthermore, all of these tools assume a perfect input and *only* return expressions that cover all and only the given examples with no *noise*. Some of the more advanced systems, such as [1], can infer a wrapper for a list of template items from only a few examples of that list and thus deal with a limited form of negative noise, but even in these cases positive noise is not considered.

That lack of robustness of earlier supervised approaches has been noted in [8, 9, 6] and let to two methods that partially address that issue: **(1)** The first [8, 9] aims to find a more robust wrapper the selects the exact same data items as the given one. However, the approach is limited by the choice of wrapper language, a fairly narrow subset of XPATH. Most importantly, it does not address attributes and attribute values at all, yet the choice of attributes and values is among the most crucial choices for robust wrappers (see Section 6). **(2)** The second is focused on learning probabilistic models of the evolution of web pages over time to rank XPATH expressions by their robustness [6]. This allows to tailor robustness to the specific change behavior of a web site. However, the used XPATH fragment is strictly weaker than the one used here (only `child` and `descendant` axis, at most one predicate per step, only equality predicates). Furthermore, our results demonstrate that expensive, site-specific training of change models is not required to achieve long term robustness. This work is extended to the notion of an optimal wrapper [21] with respect to a probabilistic and a adversarial (worst-case) change model.

Automatic Induction. Supervised wrapper induction requires significant supervision and human effort. Thus lately a number of automated approaches to wrapper induction have been suggested. Generally, these approaches are focused on inducing wrappers for a list of search results or single-entity (e.g., product) pages following the same template structure. They fall into three categories depending on the primary means to identify the elements of such a list: **(1)** *Pure template discovery:* The earliest approaches attempt to discover the template structure purely from the visual and structural similarity of the items of the template. As for wrapper induction, there is a notion of robustness for template discovery (see, e.g., [20]). However, robustness here measures how well a certain method is able to deal with a wide variety of sites and application domains. **(2)** *Entity extraction-based:* These approaches [23, 5, 7, 13] use domain-specific entity extractors to annotate the relevant items on the page. They employ fairly standard XPATH wrapper induction approaches that can not deal with positive noise and only with limited negative noise if any. Thus, their main contribution and difference lies in how they are reconciling the annotations in a pre-processing step before the XPATH induction: ODE [23] uses annotations only for post-processing to filter and label the item lists identified through template discovery, [5] considers multiple subsets of the annotations, [13] combines the annotation with, among others, a novel template discovery component that filters the given annotations to maximize regularity of the detected template items. In both cases, annotation noise is eliminated in elaborate and costly post-processing steps, which may be not be necessary at all or could be simplified if combined with the induction method suggested here. **(3)** *Redundancy-based:* Finally, methods such as [4, 3, 15, 2] exploit overlapping sources in the same domain. They consider many candidate item lists and select ones that maximize cross-domain instance-level redundancy. In many ways, the techniques for inducing a robust wrapper discussed in this paper are orthogonal to these approaches, as also pointed out in [5]. Most of these approaches [5, 7, 13] use XPATH induction once the relevant list items are identified, a few use regular expression-like patterns [23], or queries against some form of visual representation of a page [20]. For none of the automatic induction approaches robustness of the induced wrapper is a primary concern, though [5] employs, among others, the induction method from [6]. In most cases, our induction method could be integrated with these systems, thus yielding more robust wrappers, as shown in Section 6.

2. PRELIMINARIES

We assume the reader to be familiar with the basics of XPATH 1.0 and use HTML and XML syntax freely. An (HTML or XML) *document D* is a text containing markup and attribute definitions. The latter two give rise to a tree structure, containing element nodes, attribute nodes, and text nodes. An example of a document's tree structure is shown in Figure 1. Element nodes are depicted as ellipses. The attributes of an element give rise to attribute nodes. These attribute nodes are depicted as boxes, which are connected by dotted lines to their element nodes. The dotted line is labeled by the name of the attribute (prepended by the @-symbol), while the box contains the attribute's value. For instance, the document fragment `<h4 @class="inline">Director:</h4>` gives rise to the circled `h4`-node in the lower left of the figure, and to the `inline`-labeled attribute box connected to it.

Wrappers. Let D be a document. XPATH queries are evaluated relative to a given node u of D. We denote by $q_D(u)$ the set of target nodes of q when evaluated relative to u in D, and simply write $q(u)$ if D is clear from the context. A *wrapper* is an XPATH expression q. These expression will be evaluated relative to the root of D, thus, $q_D(r)$ is the result set of the wrapper expression on D, where r is the root node of D. We denote $q_D(r)$ also by $q(D)$. *Wrapper induction* is an algorithm I that given a document D and a set of nodes V of D, returns a wrapper $q = I(D,V)$. We say a wrapper q "matches" a target node n from a context u if $n \in q_D(u)$, omitting u if $u = r$.

Canonical Path. Let D be a document and let u be an element or text node of D. The *canonical path of u*, denoted $\mathsf{canon}(u)$, is an XPATH query defined recursively as follows. If u is the root node then $\mathsf{canon}(u) = /$. Otherwise, let $p = \mathsf{canon}(v)$ where v is the (element) parent node of u, $k \geq 1$ such that u is the k-th child of v, and t is a node test for u (i.e., `text()` if u is a text node, or *name* if u is a *name*-labeled element node). Then, $\mathsf{canon}(u) = p/t[k]$.

For Figure 1, the canonical path of the director node on an IMDB director page (the red `span` element) is:

```
/html[1]/body[1]/ ... /div[4]/a[1]/span[1]
```

The dashed line in Figure 1 and the dots in the expression above refer to a part of the path that is not shown (consisting of eleven XPATH steps, seven of which are `divs`).

Let $\mathcal{D} = \langle D_1, \ldots, D_n \rangle$ be a sequence of documents all containing a given node v (typically a sequence of versions of a single page, e.g., snapshots of an IMDB director page). Then, we say that there are k *c-changes* in $\mathcal{D}$ w.r.t. v, if $k = |\{D_{i+1} : \{v\} \neq \mathsf{canon}(v)(D_i)\}|$. The number of c-changes is a measure for changes in $\mathcal{D}$ that affect the path from v to the document root. Such changes are far more likely to affect any query selecting v than changes in regions of the document far from v.

Robustness. Let q be a wrapper and let D and D' be documents. The query q is *robust* (*for D and D'*), if there exists a bijection π between $q(D)$ and $q(D')$ so that for all nodes v in $q(D)$: $D/v = D'/\pi(v)$. Here, D/v denotes the (abstract, nodeId-free) subtree of D rooted at node v. Note that since $q(D)$ is a set (and not a sequence), our robustness definition is order independent.

Noise Resistance. Let D be a document and V, V' be sets of nodes of D such that V' is obtained from V by adding and deleting nodes. A wrapper induction is *noise resistant* (*for V, V' and D*), if given D and V' it returns the same query q as for input D and V. A wrapper induction I is *k%-robust*, if for k% of all pairs (D, D') and sets of nodes V from D, the wrapper $I(D,V)$ is robust. A wrapper induction I is *k%-noise resistant*, if for k% of all documents D and sets of nodes V, V' of D, the wrapper $I(D,V)$ is noise resistant.

Precision, Recall, and F-Score. Imagine a set B approximating another set A. The elements in $B \cap A$ are called *true positives* and t^+ denotes their number $|B \cap A|$. The elements in $B - A$ are called *false positives* and we define $f^+ = |B - A|$. The elements in $A - B$ are called *false negatives* and we define $f^- = |A - B|$. The *precision* of B with respect to A is calculated as $\mathsf{prec}(A,B) = t^+/(t^+ + f^+)$. The *recall* of B with respect to A is $\mathsf{rec}(A,B) = t^+/(t^+ + f^-)$. The *F-score* $\mathsf{F}_\beta(A,B)$ measures the accuracy biased toward precision ($\beta < 1$) or recall ($\beta > 1$): $\mathsf{F}_\beta(A,B) = \frac{(1+\beta^2)\mathsf{prec}(A,B)\mathsf{rec}(A,B)}{\beta^2\mathsf{prec}(A,B)+\mathsf{rec}(A,B)}$.

3. XPATH FRAGMENT DSXPATH

In this section we define our XPath fragment, called *directed XPath with sideways checks* (for short, dsXPath). The idea of

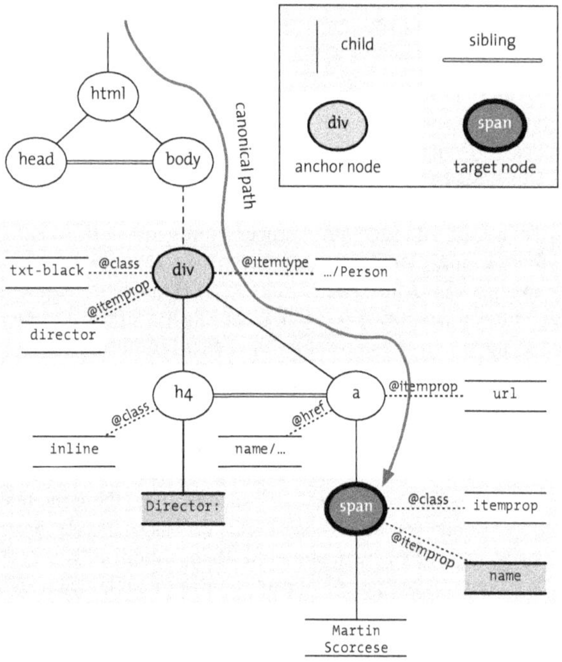

Figure 1: Tree structure of an IMDB movie page

dsXPath is to be **(1)** *general enough* to cover all samples with 100% precision and recall and **(2)** *restricted enough* as to enforce noise resistant queries. In Section 4, we show how the careful choice of the language fragment together with a straightforward, but flexible scoring of expressions yields a noise resistant, yet accurate and robust wrapper induction.

Query Syntax. The syntax of dsXPath queries is presented in Figure 2. A query consists of one or more steps. Each step con-

⟨*Query*⟩	::=	⟨*Step*⟩ ('/' ⟨*Step*⟩)*
⟨*Step*⟩	::=	⟨*Axis*⟩ '::' ⟨*Nodetest*⟩ ('[' ⟨*Predicate*⟩ ']')*
⟨*Axis*⟩	::=	**child** | **attribute** | **descendant** | **following-sibling**
	|	**parent** | **ancestor** | **preceding-sibling**
⟨*Nodetest*⟩	::=	'*' | 'node()' | 'text()' | ⟨*TagName*⟩
⟨*Predicate*⟩	::=	⟨*Int*⟩ | 'last()' '-' ⟨*Int*⟩
	|	**attribute** '::' ⟨*AttrName*⟩
	|	⟨*Function*⟩ '(' ⟨*Content*⟩ ',' ⟨*String*⟩ ')'
⟨*Function*⟩	::=	equals | contains | starts-with | ends-with
⟨*Content*⟩	::=	**attribute** '::' ⟨*AttrName*⟩ | normalize-space(.)

Figure 2: Syntax of our XPATH Fragment

sists of an axis, a nodetest, and an arbitrary number of predicates. The axis is any of XPATH's navigational axes (including the attribute axis), except the following and preceding axes. The nodetest is any of XPATH's nodetests. The nonterminals ⟨*TagName*⟩ and ⟨*AttrName*⟩ in Figure 2 refer to the strings allowed as element and attribute names. A predicate is either positional (i.e., consisting of a number or of last() minus a number), the test for the existence of an attribute, or one of four possible Boolean functions on strings. The second argument to a Boolean string-function is an arbitrary string of characters (indicated by the nonterminal ⟨*String*⟩). The first argument to a Boolean string-function is either an attribute selection (given by the attribute axis followed by a name) or a text access. The only text access that we consider is the fixed expression normalize-space(.). This expression selects and normalizes (i.e., removes extra whitespace) the text-value of the current node. E.g., applied to the div-node in Figure 1 we obtain "Director: Martin Scorsese". For brevity, we write only . instead of normalize-space(.) and abbreviate **attribute** with @ as in XPATH.

We explain the semantics of XPATH using examples, see [14] for details. We implicitly assume a given document D. A query q is evaluated starting at a given node u of D. The result $q(u)$ is a set of nodes of D. Consider the following query q.

```
descendant::div[starts-with(.,"Director:")]/
    descendant::span[(@class="itemprop")]
```

The evaluation of q on the root of a document D goes step-wise through the XPath query: first all div-labeled descendants of the root node are selected, and of those, the ones with text-value starting with "Director:". Finally, we select from these nodes the span-labeled descendants with class-attribute equal to "itemprop" and return them as result.

The above query uses two anchor nodes to characterize the target span. An *anchor node of q* is a node of D that is selected during the evaluation of $q(r)$ on D. We do not give a formal definition but note that red-marked nodes in Figure 1 are the anchors of this query.

dsXPath Queries. We now define *directed* XPATH *queries with sideways checks* (dsXPath Queries) as a restriction of the syntactical fragment given in Figure 2. We choose this fragment for two reasons, namely, to obtain a feasible search space and to foster generalization during induction to avoid overfitting of noisy query samples. Such queries are either *one-* or *two-directional.* Intuitively, a one-directional query does not change its up/down direction, i.e., it strictly traverses the tree either top-down or bottom-up (but not mixtures thereof). However, in a one-directional query we do additionally allow "sideways checks". A sideways check is a subquery consisting of the following- and preceding-sibling axes. A two-directional query is the concatenation of two one-directional queries. Given a query $q = a_1 :: t_1P_1/a_2 :: t_2P_2/\ldots/a_n :: t_nP_n$ with axes a_i, node tests t_i, and predicates P_i, we define $\mathsf{axes}(p) = a_1 \ldots a_{n-1}$ if $a_n =$ attribute and $\mathsf{axes}(p) = a_1 \ldots a_n$ otherwise. The query q is *one-directional,* if $\mathsf{axes}(q)$ matches one of the following regular expressions with **following-sibling*** | **preceding-sibling*** $= \langle sideways \rangle$:
(1) ((**parent** | **ancestor**) ⟨*sideways*⟩)* or
(2) ((**child** | **descendant**) ⟨*sideways*⟩)*.

Finally, for a given sequence of documents $\mathcal{D} = (D_1, \ldots, D_n)$, and a given dsXPath query q, we say that q is *plausible*, if all constants appearing in the predicates of q also appear in the considered document. Recall that the text-value of a document is the concatenation of all texts in the document. The query q is plausible, if it is generated by the EBNF in Figure 2 in such a way that **(1)** each string is either a substring of the text-value of a document in $\mathcal{D}$, or is a substring of an attribute value of a document in $\mathcal{D}$, and **(2)** each integer produced by the nonterminal ⟨*Int*⟩ is not larger than the number of nodes of any document in $\mathcal{D}$. From now on, we only consider plausible dsXPath queries.

4. WRAPPER INDUCTION

We first introduce the query model and types of induced queries. Then our ranking is defined and the query induction problem is shown to be infeasible (**NP**-hard).

Query Model. Given a document D, a *query sample* is a pair $\langle u, V\rangle$, where u is a node of D and V is a non-empty set of nodes of D. Our query induction induce takes a sequence of query samples $S = (\langle u_1, V_1\rangle, \ldots, \langle u_n, V_n\rangle)$ over the documents $\mathcal{D} = (D_1, \ldots, D_n)$ (possibly containing duplicates) as input and returns a ranked set of *query instances* $Q = \mathsf{induce}(S)$. A query instance $q = \langle p, t^+, f^+, f^-\rangle$ consists of an XPATH expression $p = \mathsf{query}(q)$ and the corresponding numbers of true positives, false positives, and false negatives, i.e., the numbers $t^+ = \Sigma_{i=1}^{n} |p(u_i) \cap V_i|$, $f^+ = \Sigma_{i=1}^{n} |p(u_i) - V_i|$, and $f^- = \Sigma_{i=1}^{n} |V_i - p(u_i)|$. Given q, we write $t^+(q)$, $f^+(q)$, and $f^-(q)$ for the individual values of q. We also write $q(u)$ in lieu of $p(u)$ with $p = \mathsf{query}(q)$. Ideally, each XPATH expression $p = \mathsf{query}(q)$ for $q \in \mathsf{induce}(S)$ should lead from u_i to V_i, i.e., $p(u_i) = V_i$ (evaluated in D_i) for all $1 \le i \le n$. Note however that a fully accurate expression p is not always possible or – in case of noisy input – not even desired.

Ranking. In order to deal with noisy additional annotations, we choose $\beta = 0.5$ for the F-score. We rank the query instances q by maximizing the F-score $\mathsf{F}_{0.5}(q)$ and minimizing the robustness score $\mathsf{score}(q)$. More precisely, we define the order $<$ with $q < q'$ iff (1) $\mathsf{F}_{0.5}(q) > \mathsf{F}_{0.5}(q')$ or (2) $\mathsf{F}_{0.5}(q) = \mathsf{F}_{0.5}(q')$ and $\mathsf{score}(q) < \mathsf{score}(q')$. The *robustness score* $\mathsf{score}(q)$ is a positive number computed recursively from the structure of the query expression $\mathsf{query}(q)$. The *smaller* the score, the more favorable the query. The robustness score of an XPATH expression is computed as the sum of the scores of its steps, because we favor shorter queries over longer ones; we call this *plus-composability*. The scores of steps are multiplied by a power of a *decay-factor* δ. This allows to favor cheaper steps towards the end (beginning), i.e., closer to (further from) the target node, by choosing $\delta \le 1$ ($\delta \ge 1$). We define $\mathsf{score}(a_1 :: t_1P_1/\cdots/a_n :: t_nP_n) = \Sigma_{i=1}^{n} \mathsf{score}(a_i :: t_iP_i) \cdot \delta^{i-1}$. where for $i \in \{1, \ldots, n\}$, a_i is an axis, t_i is a node test, and P_i is a sequence of predicates.

For each axis a (such as **descendant** of **child**) we fix a constant score s_a. Similarly, for each node test t we fix a constant s_t. Note, that different tags can thus be scored differently, e.g., `div`'s differently from `script` tags, though in most cases a default value $c_{default}$ is used. The score for a single step $a :: tP$ is now computed as the sum of the scores for axis, node test, and predicates $P = p_1 \ldots p_m$: $\mathsf{score}(a :: t p_1 \cdots p_m) = s_a + s_t + \Sigma_{j=1}^{m} \mathsf{score}(p_j)$.

The score for a predicate p is computed as follows. If p is a positional predicate, i.e., of the form $p = [n]$ or $p = [\texttt{last()} - n]$ where n is a positive integer, then the score for p is $\mathsf{score}(p) = c_{\text{pos}} \cdot n$, where c_{pos} is a fixed constant.

If p is of the form `[f(attribute::a, w)]` or `[attribute::a]` (in the latter case we set $\mathsf{length}(w)$ and s_f to zero) where a is an attribute name, f is a function (such as "equals" or "contains"), and w is a string, then the score for p is the sum of a fixed score s_f, a *no-function-penalty* constant y, a fixed score s_a, and the product of the fixed length factor c_f and the length of the string w: $\mathsf{score}(p) = s_f + y + s_a + c_f \cdot \mathsf{length}(w)$, where y has a non-zero value only if $p=$`[attribute::a]`. For a predicate with text access of the form $p=$`[f(.,w)]` where f is a function (such as "equals" or "contains") and w is a string, we define $\mathsf{score}(p) = s_f + s_{\text{text}} + c_f \cdot \mathsf{length}(w)$, where s_{text} is a fixed score. If q contains no predicate, we add to $\mathsf{score}(q)$ a *no-predicate-penalty*. The two penalty scores *no-function-penalty* and *no-predicate-penalty* bias the scoring towards queries with predicates that are likely more selective.

Query Induction Problem. We define the query induction problem and prove that it is infeasible. The query induction problem is the optimization problem of finding a selection of the best ranked query instances among the plausible directed expressions in dsXPath, where optimality is in terms of the ranking given in the previous section. For a natural number K, a top-K set is a set of ranked query instances with the highest achievable scores; there might be several such top-K sets achieving the same scores.

DEFINITION 1 (QUERY INDUCTION PROBLEM). *Given a sequence $S = (\langle u_1, V_1\rangle, \ldots, \langle u_n, V_n\rangle)$ of query samples over implicit documents $\mathcal{D} = (D_i, \ldots, D_n)$ and a constant K, the* query induction problem *is to find a top-K set of plausible query instances.*

THEOREM 1. *The query induction problem is* **NP***-hard, even with query samples of the form $\langle u, \{v\}\rangle$, requiring an optimal query instance leading from u to v.*

The theorem can be reduced to Minimum Set Cover.

5. DSXPATH INDUCTION ALGORITHM

In this section our query induction algorithms are explained, first for single-target query samples, and then for multiple-target query samples. We always work in the context of a given number K, and compute sequences of "K-best" query instances (ordered according to our ranking). The resulting algorithm has polynomial runtime since it executes a polynomial number of XPATH queries of polynomial size over the analyzed document. We define the *set B of base axes* as $B := \{$**child**, **parent**, **following-sibling**, **preceding-sibling** $\}$, and define **child**.transitive = **descendant** and **parent**.transitive = **ancestor**. Further, we set α.transitive $= \alpha$ for $\alpha \in \{$**following-sibling**, **preceding-sibling**$\}$. For an axis β, we say that node v is *β-reachable* from u if and only if $v \in q(u)$ for the query $q = \beta :: *$.

Single-Target Query Samples. Let D be a document and u a node of D. Here we consider the restricted case of one target node, i.e., $V = \{v\}$ where v is in D. Our algorithms are constructed in such a way that v is guaranteed to be reachable from u via the transitive axis of one of our base axes. The most interesting case of our induction algorithm, is for the case that v is a descendant of u, i.e., for the **child** base axis. The cases for the other base axes follow from this case in a straightforward way. Let us thus discuss now the case that v is a descendant of u. We denote the sequence of nodes on the path from u to v by $\mathsf{spine}(u, v)$, and refer to the nodes in $\mathsf{spine}(u, v)$ as *possible anchors*. To compute the best-K query instances leading from u to v, we incrementally compute the best-K instances $best(n)$ for each node n in $\mathsf{spine}(u, v)$. Initially, we set $best(v)[1] = \langle \varepsilon, 1, 0, 0\rangle$ and $best(v)[k] = \langle \bot, 0, 0, 0\rangle$ for $2 \le k \le K$, The "empty query" ε occurs only as intermediate result; When applied to $best(v)$, it selects only the node v itself. By $\bot$ we denote the "fail query" which always returns $\emptyset$. We now recursively compute for each node $n \in \mathsf{spine}(v, u) - \{v\}$, the superset $cand(n) \supseteq best(n)$ of *candidate instances*, by using the already computed best-K sets $best(t)$ for nodes t preceding n in the sequence $\mathsf{spine}(v, u)$. From this superset, we assign the best-K instances to $best(n)$ and proceed along the spine until we have computed $best(u)$, which is returned as result. The superset $cand(n)$ is computed as $cand(n) = \bigcup_{t \in \mathsf{spine}(v,n) \setminus \{n\}} \mathsf{stepPattern}(n, t, \mathsf{axis}, K) \times best(t)$ as shown in Algorithm 2. Here, axis is the unique base axis in B such that t is axis.transitive reachable from n, i.e., axis =**child** for the case discussed here. The function $\mathsf{stepPattern}(n, t, \mathsf{axis}, K)$ computes the best-K query instances that match t from n along axis (possibly involving "sideways detours" but no intermediate anchors), and $\times$ yields the concatenated instances of the cross-product of the two instance sets. We next explain function $\mathsf{stepPattern}(n, t, \mathsf{axis}, K)$ performing induction along the spine.

Spine Step Induction. The function stepPattern(n,t,axis,K) shown in Algorithm 1 generates the available spine patterns to match spine node t while moving along axis (or its transitive closure) starting at context node u; only the case of the child-axis is shown. Note that in the return specification of the algorithm, axis.reverse refers to the reverse of an axis, i.e., **child**.reverse = **parent** (and vice versa), **descendant**.reverse = **ancestor** (and vice versa), and **following-sibling**.reverse = **preceding-sibling** (and vice versa). This algorithm works as follows. We first compute for axis = child recursively through inducePath (Lines 2–5). Note, child is the *unique* axis for which we ever produce sideways checks in our algorithms! This explains that in the recursive case (for the child axis), we iterate over all siblings s of t (Line 2), compute the node patterns for s (Line 3) and the best-K paths from s to t recursively (Line 4). Note that each such path consists of exactly one XPATH step that uses either the **following-sibling** or **preceding-sibling** axis (depending on the position of s with respect to t). Then we add all possible concatenations between node patterns and paths (Line 5). Thus, each query in P starts with a node test. As all recursive calls to inducePath generate a path along the sibling axes, the subsequent calls to stepPattern will be handled non-recursively (because of Line 1).

Algorithm 1: Step Induction stepPattern(n,t,axis,K)

```
input   : node t is axis.transitive-reachable from node n
returns : path set P such that ∀p ∈ P and all nodes x
          if x is axis.reverse.transitive-reachable from t,
          then {t} ⊆ p(x)
1 if axis = child then
2     for s ∈ siblings(t) do
3         P' := nodePattern(s);
4         P'' := inducePath(s, {t}, K);
5         P := P ∪ {p'/p'' | p' ∈ P' and p'' ∈ P''};
6 else P := nodePattern(t);
7 R := {axis.transitive :: p | p ∈ P};
8 if t ∈ axis(n) then R := R ∪ {axis :: p | p ∈ P};
9 return rescore(n, {t}, R);
```

Let us discuss the function nodePattern. Given a node u, this function iteratively computes a set of possible node tests followed by at most two predicates. In a first step, a node test for the node u is generated. This starts with the most general such test `node()` followed by the test of the tag name of node u. Then one predicate with an attribute (or text-value) equality-comparison is produced. The resulting queries, with axis prepended are tested on node n. If u is *not* uniquely matched, then an additional positional predicate is concatenated. Thus, each pattern returned by nodePattern contains at most two predicates: one attribute (or text) comparison (possibly) followed by a positional predicate. The selection of attribute names and text functions follows our definition of scoring for such query constructs (see Section 4). As an example if the node u is labeled `div`, then the first few node patterns that are returned by the call nodePattern(u) are of the form:

```
node()                          div
div[@id='x']                    div[@class='y']
div[contains(.,'z')]
```

Note that x, y, z are constrained to be single strings that appear in the input document as follows: either as single words (space-separated and/or bordered) or as the full text-value of a node.

The node tests P at hand, we complete these patterns by prepending axis.transitive to all patterns in P (Line 7). If t is reachable with a single step along axis, we prepend axis to all patterns in P (Line 8). At last, the algorithm returns the resulting patterns R, scored as expressions matching only t from context node u (Line 9).

As an example, consider the sample $\langle u, \{v\}\rangle$ where u is the body-node and v the em-node in this document:

```
<body>
  <div class="content">
    <div id="main">
      <em class="highlight">The Target</em>
</div></div></body>
```

This means that we have four nodes on the spine from u to v: the body-node, the two div-nodes, and the em-node. We now generate stepPatterns, starting at the lower div-node (with id-attribute), and matching the em-node. E.g. these expressions are generated:

```
descendant::em
child::em
child::node()[class="highlight"]
```

Next, similar patterns are generated for expressions matching the em-node, starting at the upper div-node, and then starting at the body-node. In the next step we generate stepPatterns for the lower div-node; first, starting from the div-node above it, e.g., the expressions `descendant::div` and `descendant::div[@id="main"]`. Next, patterns are generated that match the lower div-node, starting at the body-node, e.g., the expression `descendant::div[@id="main"]`. Note however that the expression `descendant::div` it *not* generated at this step, because it matches both div-nodes, and hence is not accurate (strictly speaking, the expression may be generated, but receives a very low score). To update the best patterns (from u to v), we now also generate combined patterns such as patterns such as

```
descendant::div[@id="main"]/child::em
```

Finally, stepPatterns for the upper div-node are generated, starting from the body-node, and are combined with the previous expressions, so that for instance the expression

```
descendant::div[@class="content"]/child::div[@id="main"]
                                                  /child::em
```

is generated. The precise ranking of these expressions depends on the parameter; see Section 6.3 for typical parameter choices.

Algorithm 2: Axis Path Induction inducePath$(u, V, K, \text{axis}, best, tar)$

```
input   : node u and node set V ≠ ∅,
          ∀v ∈ V : v is axis.transitive-reachable from u,
          K > 0 best-K bound,
          best initial table with best-K paths (wrt. score),
          tar table of reachable target nodes
returns : query instances q with q(u) ≈ V, ranked by score
for v ∈ V do
    for t ∈ spine(v, u) − {u} do
        for n ∈ spine(u, t) − {t} do
            V' := tar(n);
            for 1 ≤ k ≤ K and p ∈ stepPattern(n, t, axis) do
                p' := p/best(t)[k];    M := p'(n);
                q := ⟨p', |M ∩ V'|, |M − V'|, |V' − M|⟩;
                if q < best(n)[K] then
                    insert q into best(n);
return best(u);
```

Multiple-Target Query Samples. We now generalize to multipe-target query samples, i.e., samples $\langle u, V\rangle$ with $|V| > 1$. Thus, $\mathsf{inducePath}$ takes u, V, and K as arguments, along with pre-initialized tables *best* and *tar*, respectively for the best-K instances and the relevant targets to be matched (explained below). The *best* table is initialized as before to $\langle\bot, 0, 0, 0\rangle$ for all relevant entries, except for the first entry in every target node $v \in V$ which is set to $\langle\varepsilon, 1, 0, 0\rangle$. The table *tar* contains for each relevant node n the axis-reachable targets in V, where axis is the direction of the one-directional $\mathsf{dsXPath}$ reaching from u to V Both tables are handed in as arguments to enable the reuse of this algorithm in more general settings beyond the base case. For dealing with $|V| > 1$, the algorithm iterates over all targets $v \in V$ (Line 1) while maintaining a single best-K table *best* throughout all iterations. In each iteration v, $\mathsf{inducePath}$ induces the best-K instances which match v from u, possibly along with other targets from V. However, to produce accurate results, $\mathsf{inducePath}$ evaluates the accuracy of the induced instances against V (or subsets of V in for intermediate instances). Hence, $best(u)$ contains upon loop termination the so-far best expressions matching V and is returned as result (Line 10). The sign $\approx$ in the specification of the algorithm means that the query instances select *some* nodes of the sample. Note that $q < best(n)[K]$ in Line 8 of means that the ranking of q is strictly smaller than the ranking of the K-th query instance in the table $best(n)$.

For each v, $\mathsf{inducePath}$ computes for all nodes $n \in \mathsf{spine}(u, v) - \{v\}$ the best instances to match v and evaluates them against all reachable targets $tar(n) = V \cap \mathsf{axis.transitive}(n)$, given *tar* is initialized accordingly. To enable a dynamic programming approach, we need to ensure that the entries in *best* are already computed when the algorithm reads these entries. Thus, we first iterate (Line 2) over all possible anchors $t \in \mathsf{spine}(v, u) - \{u\}$ and in an inner loop (Line 3) over all nodes n for which t could serve as anchor, i.e., $n \in \mathsf{spine}(u, t) - \{t\}$. In each inner iteration, we enumerate all instances in $\mathsf{stepPattern}(n, t, \mathsf{axis}, K) \times best(t)$ (Line 5) but only add those to $best(n)$ which beat the K-best know instance (Lines 8–9). This way, $best(t)$ is not altered anymore, once the algorithm reads $best(t)$ to generate candidates for $best(n)$. The remaining lines in Algorithm 2 deal with the accuracy evaluation of the generated instances: we obtain the relevant targets V' and wrap each generated XPATH expression p' into an instance q with the true positives, false positives and negatives evaluated against V'.

Two-Directional Paths and Multiple Samples. Our general induction algorithm is shown in Algorithm 3. It uses $\mathsf{inducePath}$ from Algorithm 2 as subprocedure, and generalizes our previous considerations to two-directional paths and multiple samples. Two-directional paths are needed if a match node $v \in V$ is not a descendant (and not an ancestor) of the context node u.

(1) *Samples requiring two-directional paths* (Lines 5–15). A two-directional path from u_i to V_i is required, if not all nodes in V are reachable via the same base axis. Then induce searches for the closest node l_i such that u_i and V_i are both reachable via one-directional paths from l_i. This node l_i is the least common ancestor of either V_i or $V_i \cup \{u_i\}$ (Lines 5–7). Once l_i is fixed, induce first computes the best-K tail instances from l_i to V_i. For computing the final result, the algorithm induces instances leading from u_i to l_i, but with an deviating initialization: First, we take standard initialization for *best* (Line 8) but *initialize* $best(l_i)$ *with the tail instances* from l_i to V_i (Line 11). Then, the overall induced expressions lead from u_i to l_i and continue with one of the expressions in $best(l_i)$ to match the nodes in V_i. Second, we set the *targets for computing the accuracy* of the obtained instances to V_i, i.e., we set $tar(n) = V_i$ for all $n \in \mathsf{spine}(u_i, l_i) - \{l_i\}$, since we want to match V_i from each node between u_i and l_i.

Algorithm 3: Path Induction $Q = \mathsf{induce}(S, K)$

input : samples $S = \{\langle u_1, V_1\rangle, \ldots, \langle u_n, V_n\rangle\}$ such that $V_i \neq \emptyset$ for all $1 \leq i \leq n$, $K > 0$ as best-K bound
returns : query instances Q with $q(u_i) \approx V_i$ for all $q \in Q$ and $1 \leq i \leq n$

1 **for** $\langle u_i, V_i\rangle \in S$ **do**
2   **if** $\exists a \in B\ \forall v \in V_i$: v *is* $\mathsf{axis.transitive}$*-reachable from* u_i **then**
3     $Q_i := \mathsf{inducePath}(u_i, V_i, K, a, \mathsf{init}(u_i, V_i, K))$;
4   **else**
5     $l_i := \mathsf{lca}(V_i)$;
6   **if** $\nexists a \in B$: l_i *is* $a.\mathsf{transitive}$*-reachable from* u_i **then**
7       $l_i := \mathsf{lca}(V_i \cup \{u_i\})$;
8     $\langle best, \_\rangle := \mathsf{init}(u_i, \{l_i\}, K)$;
9     $a :=$ unique axis in B so that $\forall v \in V_i$:
10   v is $a.\mathsf{transitive}$-reachable from l_i
11     $best(l_i) := \mathsf{inducePath}(l_i, V_i, K, a, \mathsf{init}(l_i, V_i, K))$;
12   **for** $n \in \mathsf{spine}(u, l_i) - \{l_i\}$ **do** $tar(n) := V_i$;
13     $a :=$ unique axis in B so that l_i
14   is $a.\mathsf{transitive}$-reachable from u_i
15     $Q_i := \mathsf{inducePath}(u_i, \{l_i\}, K, a, best, tar)$;
16 **return** $\mathsf{aggregate}(\bigcup_{i=1}^{n} Q_i)$;

(2) *Multiple Samples.* We deal with multiple samples by first computing a best-K set Q_i for each sample $\langle u_i, V_i\rangle$ individually, and second choosing from these instances the ones which perform best on all samples (Line 16).

6. EVALUATION

Our experiments show that our wrapper induction produces accurate and robust XPATH expressions even from noisy query samples. We first compare our system with two state-of-the-art XPath wrapper induction system [6, 2]. We first evaluate the robustness of our induction system and look at change frequencies occurring on the involved pages (Section 6.2). Finally, we point out some characteristics of the induced expressions (Section 6.3) and analyze the noise resistance of the wrapper induction (Section 6.4).

Running time of the wrapper induction is generally in the same order of magnitude as page retrieval and loading. For a single node expression, it ranges from a few milliseconds to several seconds, with a median of 1.4 seconds and more than 60% of the cases running faster than page retrieval and loading.

6.1 State-of-the-Art Comparison

For robust wrapper induction, [6] presents one of the seminal approaches and includes experiments on IMDB pages. As the system is not available, we rather replicate their experiments as faithfully as possible: as in [6], we take 15 snapshots of director names on IMDB movie pages taken at 2 months intervals. If within such a 2 month interval, no new snapshot is available, we extend the interval until one becomes available, in order to ensure that we use 15 distinct snapshots. We use their success ratio measure as the percentage of snapshots at time t where the induced wrapper still works on the immediately following snapshot at time $t + 1$. We tried to approximate the likely time period used in their paper by considering the following three snapshot periods: 2004–2006, 2005–2007, and 2006–2008. Our approach achieves a success ratio of 100%, 86%, 86%, respectively. This compares to 86% reported in their paper [6], where the precise time period is not mentioned.

Site	Induced / Human XPATH queries	valid days	c-changes
S1	`descendant::div[@id="console"]/descendant::p`	400	4
	`descendant::div[starts-with(.,"Top")]/descendant::p`	400	4
S2	`descendant::h3[@class="f-quote"]`	382	16
	`descendant::div[@id="channel0"]/child::h3`	382	16
S3	`descendant::img[@class="adv"][1]` (rank=1)	300	2
	`descendant::div[@class="contentSmLeft"]/descendant::img[@class="adv"]` (rank=3)	456	2
	`descendant::div[@class="contentSmLeft"]/descendant::img[contains(@class,"adv")]` (rank=5)	1999	34
	`descendant::img[ancestor::div[1][@class="contentSmLeft"]]`	1999	34

S1 = www.foxnews.com, **S2** = espn.go.com, **S3** = www.wellsfargo.com

Table 1: Matching single nodes, two typical queries and one difficult case

We also compare with a more recent, automatic wrapper induction system [2] (WEIR). WEIR is based on the observation that different sources for a certain type of data often have some overlapping and is able to induce wrappers automatically in many cases. The trade-off is that WEIR requires multiple pages that follow the same template as input for each source, and each induced XPath expression matches at most one node per page. The induced expressions are generally of two types: absolute expressions that are similar to canonical paths, but starting from the closest anchestor of the target node with a unique ID. The second type of expressions are relative to a close-by "template" node, i.e., a node with a text content that is likely fixed (such as "Director"). To tailor to the limitations of WEIR, we select hotel pages from Tripadvisor with the same template. We let WEIR induce expressions from 10 such pages from 2012, and average over 5 such sets with differing pages and/or target nodes. WEIR exploits the availability of 10 pages to guess which nodes contain static content (such as "Country") and which contain variable values. WEIR's induction returns an unranked set of on average 30 expressions. We compare the robustness of these expressions over the time period from 2012 to 2016 against our system. For our system, we provide only a *single* page with the same target node as for WEIR. The top-10 expressions returned by our system survive on average 67% of the time period, compared with 32% on average for the 10 expressions returned by WEIR. If we compare the most robust expression returned by each system, ours survive for 93% of the period compared to 56% for WEIR. If we only consider the top ranked expression for our case, we survive 92%—our ranking very closely models robustness—of the period. Also note, that our top-ranked and best expressions are robust for the entire period in well over 80% of the cases, compared with around 15% for WEIR.

6.2 Robustness

We evaluate the robustness of the generated expressions in Figures 3 and 4 respectively for single and multiple target nodes. For both cases, we assembled a data set of 50 test tasks respectively, each specifying a URL u together with a manually crafted XPATH expression q leading to a single node in the first set or multiple nodes in the second set (between 3 and 59 nodes with an average of 10). The sites in the dataset come from over 20 different verticals, such as "Movies", "News", and "Travel", and include some of the most visited websites on the web. The data sets select nodes from a range of different node types arising in the construction of site wrappers: Such wrappers do not only select a single type of data on a page but navigate to the data via forms and links to extract multiple objects which are dispersed over multiple pages. To build such a wrapper, one needs to induce expressions matching form elements, menu entries, next links, and data attributes. Our data sets are assembled to reflect this variety of use cases.

To check the robustness of induced expressions, we obtain from the Internet Archive a sequence of snapshots taken from u. On the first snapshot we induce an expression q' to match the same nodes as q does. The induction is restricted to expressions which do not refer to textual data contents, i.e., texts that are not part of the template but belong to changing data, such as article titles. Such textual content would be too volatile and would cause the induced expression to break quickly.

Once induced, we evaluate each such expression q' on subsequent snapshots of u taken at 20 day intervals until **(1)** q' does not match the same nodes as q, **(2)** q breaks itself, or **(3)** we reach a given end date. We check whether q is still correctly working by evaluating a pre-specified predicate on the nodes matched of q. For example, such a predicate might check that the matched nodes belong to a certain class or start with certain string. When these predicates did not match anymore, we manually verified that q did break; if q was still valid, we improved the corresponding predicates. If the Internet Archive does not contain a required snapshot, we search for the closest existing snapshot as replacement. Our evaluations start 01-01-2008 and end 12-31-2013.

We compare the robustness of induced wrappers with canonical wrappers that consist of absolute XPATH from root node to target nodes, and human wrappers carefully designed by experienced experts. Note that many human wrappers are *not* in dsXPath using axes such as `following`, see query **S3** in Table 2. When designing human wrappers, we aimed at making them as robust as possible, in some cases even rewriting a wrapper that broke by manually inspecting the snapshot.

Results for matching a single node. Figure 3 shows a density distribution comparing the robustness of induced, canonical, and human wrappers. Intuitively, the higher the curve is towards the right, the more robust wrappers it contains. From the generated 53 expressions, 6 break within 100 days, however, most of these expressions are not robustly wrappable, since in 5 of these cases the corresponding manually crafted expressions fail as well. 27 expressions remain valid between 100 and 400 days, and 20 expressions remain valid for more than 400 days. Thus, discounting the 5 expressions which have no robust wrapper, we only fail in a single case, i.e., our wrapper induction is over 98%-robust.

Table 1 shows the induced expressions for three cases taken from our dataset (following the same format as Table 2). For sites **S1** and **S2**, we show the top-ranked induced expression in the first line and the manually written expression in the second line; for **S3** we show three induced expression and the manual one. In addition to the number of days the expression remained valid, we also show the number of changes in the canonical path leading to the target node during this period, as a very rough indicator for the amount of changes occurring on the page. **S1** achieves maximal robustness, since the top video is replaced by list of videos and thus it

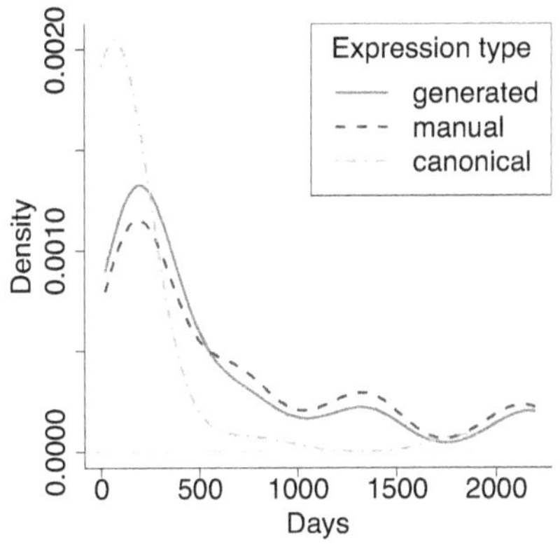

Figure 3: Robustness of expressions for matching a single node

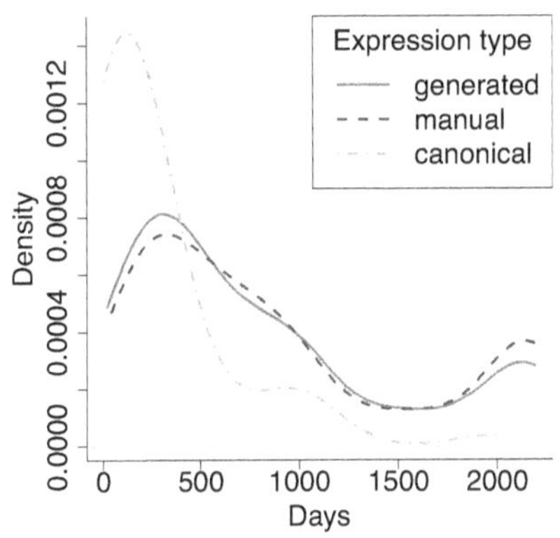

Figure 4: Robustness of expressions for matching multiple nodes

is unclear what the intended selection should be. **S2** also achieves maximal robustness, as the targeted quotation disappears from the site. **S3** is a hard case; our ranking does not work perfectly, since in the top-ranked expression the positional predicate just outruns the expressions involving a second step which is necessary for more robustness. On the other hand, the 5th induced expression would already deliver a very good result – after 1999 days, the involved attributes obtain new names which cannot be anticipated at all.

The **break reasons** for the wrappers fall into five groups:

(a) The first group contains wrapper pairs (induced/human) where both wrappers work over the *full test period* (2008–13), i.e., these are the most robust wrappers. From the 51 wrappers, four fall into this group. For instance, the IMDB search field is selected by this induced wrapper `descendant::input[@name="q"]` and, as the reader may verify, this wrapper still works today.

(b) For 7 wrappers, both human and induced wrapper fail at the *same* time, yet the target information is still present after the break date. This is typically the case when the markup has changed considerably, causing the wrappers to break. In fact, these changes typically coincide with a site-wide visual redesign. Preeminent for these 7 queries are changes in the values of important attributes: e.g., class attributes change from `"hp-content-block"` to `"homepage-content-block"`, or from `"headline20"` to `"headline16"`, or the id-attribute changes from `"searchInputArea"` to `"searchArea"`. We believe that these cases could be dealt with by incorporating more sophisticated text queries. We leave this issue for future work.

(c) For another 7 wrappers the induced wrapper works *longer*. This may seem surprising, but coincidentally our heuristics chose here an expression that proofed more robust. For example, the induced wrapper (on salesforce.com) q = `descendant::input[@type="text"][last()]` works during the entire period, while the human query `descendant::*[@id="search_box_hm"]/`q breaks after 1.5 years.

(d) Conversely, there are 2 cases where the induced query *breaks before*han the human one: first, the induced query `descendant::div[(@id="cnnT1Col")]/descendant::h1` breaks after 241 days, while the human query `descendant::*[@class="cnnT1Txt"]/descendant::h1` breaks only after 681 days. Coincidentally, in this case the `class` attribute proves to be more robust than the `id` attribute. In the last case, the human query `/descendant::img[@id="jobs"]/ancestor::a[1]` lasts for 1201 days, while the induced query `descendant::a[@href="http://www.jobs.nih.gov/"]` breaks after 1170 days, when a second node with the same `href` value is added to the page.

(e) 7 wrappers break because of *erroneous archive snapshots* which are either empty or structurally broken.

(f) 24 wrappers break when the *relevant targets were removed* from their respective pages; thus, no wrapper could survive such a change. Strictly speaking, these wrappers belong to Group **(a)**, as they did not break in the maximally possible (but not full) time range. Here we categorize them as an independent group to illustrate the fact that *no wrappers* could still work.

Results for matching multiple nodes. The results in Figure 4 for the expressions matching multiple nodes show similar but slightly better results. For example, only 2 out of 50 expressions are less than 100 days valid, with an average of 815 days and a median of 568 days. It is interesting to observe that in both datasets, after the initial density peaks at 250 (single node) and 350 days (multiple nodes), the density falls until reaching a minimum at 1500 days. Apparently, the cases before 1500 belong to sites which do change significantly eventually, while the cases beyond belong to sites which are never updated significantly at all.

Table 2 shows four of our multi-target wrappers. For sites **S1–S3** the top-ranked induced expression is shown in the first line, and the manually written expression in a line below; for **S3** we additionally first show the 49th-ranked induced expression. We show the number of target nodes, the number of days the expression remained valid, and the number of c-changes. The latter is a rough indicator of the amount of changes to the document that directly affect the path from the document root to the target nodes (see Section 2).

S1 matches a list of "channels" which are moved to another page after 219 days. Both the human and generated expression achieves perfect robustness. Note that the induced expression does not rely on textual content but on attributes only. **S2** does not break during the full observation period. The induced expression prefers the shorter string but is otherwise identical to the manual one. **S3** shows a good but suboptimal result: the `class`-attribute of our top-ranked expression is removed at day 339; in contrast, the manual expression (relying on textual contents) only breaks at day 622. Interestingly, our rank-49 induced expression (using no attributes or text) holds even for 700 days.

We checked by hand the **break reasons** of the wrappers. This time, no induced wrapper ever worked longer than the human made, so we have only four groups: **(a)** 6 wrapper pairs work over the full period, selecting general lists such as "latest news" items. **(b)** 10 wrapper pairs break at the same time. **(c)** There are no cases where the induced wrapper works

Site	Inferred / Human XPATH queries	#res	valid days	c-changes
S1	`descendant::a[contains(@class,"hpCH2")]/preceding-sibling::a[contains(@class,"hpCH")]`	22	219	1
	`descendant::div[contains(.,"Channels")]/descendant::a[@class="hpCH"]`		219	1
S2	`descendant::tr[contains(.,"News")]/following-sibling::tr`	7	2056	2
	`descendant::tr[contains(.,"News and Latest Reviews")]/following-sibling::tr`		2056	2
S3	`descendant::div[(@class="tvgrid")]/following-sibling::node()/descendant::li` (rank=1)	8	339	12
	`descendant::p/following-sibling::node()/descendant::li` (rank=49)		622	13
	`descendant::p[contains(., "Hit")]/following::ul[1]/descendant::li`		700	13

S1 = www.about.com, **S2** = www.mobiletechreview.com, **S3** = imdb.com

Table 2: Matching multiple nodes, queries with sibling axes (top-ranked / human)

longer than the human one. **(d)** 3 induced wrappers break before the human one. For example, the induced top-ranked wrapper `descendant::div[@class="widePanel"]/descendant::a` breaks after 817 days, while the human wrapper is robust for the entire 5 year period. However, the 30th ranked induced expression is fully robust too: it first selects the text `"offers:"` from a header and then continues with `/following-sibling::node()/descendant::a`. Another example is **S3** from Table 2, where the human selects a node containing the text `"Hit"`, while the induced query uses a `class` attribute. **(e)** 10 wrapper pairs break due to issues with the internet archive. **(f)** 21 wrapper paris break due to diminishing targets. Often, the removal of the list information co-occurs with a complete visual redesign of the respective site.

Both examples of induced wrappers that fail before the human ones suggest that selection through the text-value of nodes gives more robust wrapper than through attributes. This is confirmed by analyzing the 10 cases where induced and human wrappers break simultaneously: often the only possible robust approach is based on selecting keywords within the target list. We believe that our approach can induce robust queries for these cases; however, as we mostly target volatile data entries, our configuration is biased to deal with (relatively) dynamic item lists.

Change Rate. Here our discussions will be for both, single- and multiple-target wrappers. We use a very rough change measure: only if the *canonical path* to the target nodes change, do we count this as one change. Thus, if such a "c-change" occurs, then we increase the change counter, induce a new path, and continue in the same way. Recall that the canonical path consists only of element names and position numbers. In this way, we obtain *very low* change frequencies, the largest being 25 (obviously, many more things change on the pages, even considering attribute values on the canonical path gives completely different numbers). Since the canonical path is our yardstick for a simple wrapper, we find c-changes an appropriate measure. For single-target wrappers, 11 wrappers survive more than 5 c-changes; 16 wrappers survive exactly 1 c-change (that being the largest group). The average is at 4.1 c-changes. For multiple-target wrapper, 13 wrappers survive more than 5 c-changes, but the highest number is only 19 (versus 25 for single). Interestingly, the average is again 4.1 c-changes. We only checked two sites (IMDB and espn) by hand to see what kind of canonical path changes occur. The most frequent here, were positional changes on div nodes. For instance, in a typical path (from IMDB) `html[1]/.../layer[1]/div[1]/div[3]/div[4]/form[1]/input[1]` the `div[4]` becomes a `div[3]` in a new version. Next frequent changes are inserted or removed div nodes on the canonical path (i.e., changing the length of the path).

6.3 Expression Characteristics

Parameter Choices. As explained in Section 4, the typical expression characteristics are chosen as suggested by our experience, as well as previous literature on wrapper induction, e.g., that `descendant` is preferred over `child`. These are further discussed below. The most important other parameter of our approach is the *decay factor*, which favors anchors further away from the targets. Our decay factor is $\delta = 2.5$, as was determined as optimal through a sequence of experience varying delta between 0.5 and 5.

For single- and for multiple-target wrapper induction we use the *same* ranking parameters. We use *no* specific scores for different tags, but merely $c_{\text{node()}} = c_* = 1$ and $c_{default} = 10$. Our positional factor is 20, *no-function-penalty* is 15, and *no-predicate-penalty* is 1000. All other parameters are as follows:

Axes		Attributes		Functions	
descendant	1	id	1	equals	1
attribute	1	type	1	position	1
foll.-sibling	1	title	1	contains	5
child	10	class	5	starts-with	5
parent	10	for	10	norm.-space	5
ancestor	20	name	50	last	20
prec.-sibling	25	*default*	1000	string	100

As an example, for `descendant::img[@class="adv"][1]` we compute as score $c_{\text{descendant}} + c_{default} = 1 + 10 + 1 = 11$ plus the two predicates. The first one gives $s_{\text{class}} = 5$ plus $1 \cdot 3$, and `[1]` gives 21. The final score equals 40.

Analysis. Starting with the 53 expressions generated to match a single node, we see that 34 of these expressions have 1 step, 19 expressions have 2 steps, amounting to 72 total XPATH steps. All of these steps follow the `descendant` axis. Figure 5 gives some details on the characteristics of these expressions: On the left the figures shows that 26 of the 72 steps check for `div` elements, followed by `input`, and `a` elements. Of these 72 nodetests, 62 are refined by at least one predicate, and 10 are refined by two predicates, yielding again coincidentally 72 predicates. As shown in the right of Figure 5, these predicates check in 26 cases for an `id` attribute, in 18 cases for an `class` attribute, and in 17 cases for a position. In contrast, textual contents are only checked in 2 cases. This data suggest the following pattern: If the expression contains two steps, the first step identifies the region containing the targets by typically matching a `div`, `input`, or `a` node, predicated with an `id` or `class` attribute or position. The second step matches the target node, referring to a wide range of different tag names and often checking for its position within the context.

The expressions to match multiple nodes have quite different characteristics than the ones for single nodes. Fist of all, only 9 out of 50 examples use a single step, 34 employ 2 steps, and 7 need

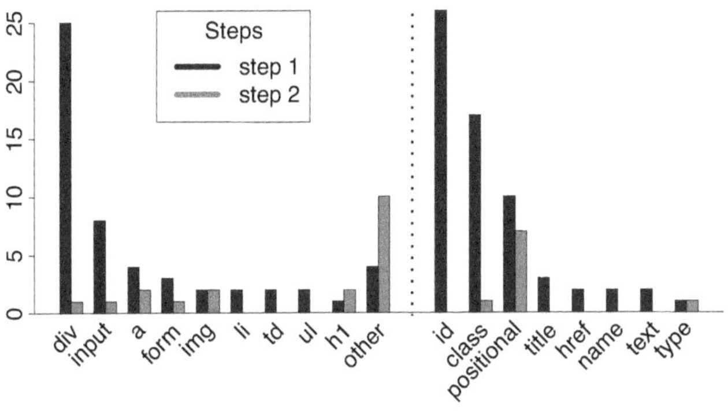

Figure 5: Nodetests/predicates of single-target queries

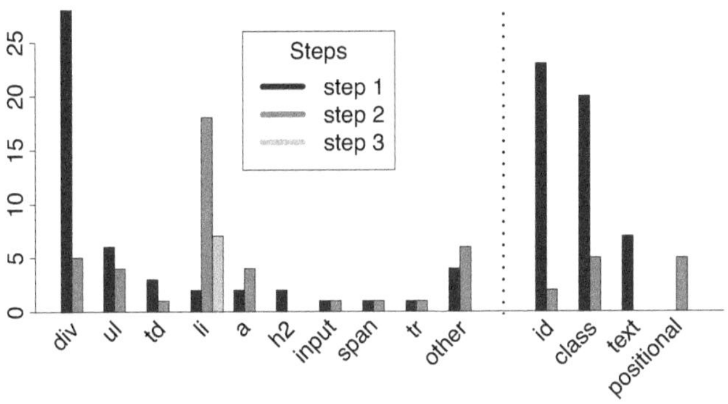

Figure 6: Nodetests/predicates of multiple-target queries

3 steps, yielding a total of 98 steps. These steps employ a bigger variety of axes, although 88 still rely the `descendant` axis; 7 steps use `following-sibling`, 2 step use `preceding-sibling`, and 1 step `child`. The use of the sibling axes is at first surprising, as most useful node lists are grouped below a common ancestor. However, to identify the correct subset of siblings belonging to our target list to avoid, e.g., adverts at the beginning or end, robustly matching lists require sibling anchors. For instance, query **S3** in Table 2 selects the first ul-sibling that follows the h3-node, and similarly, query **S4** (at rank 49) select all list items under following siblings of a p-node. The nodetests, shown on the left of Figure 6, also check in 33 cases for the `div` tag. However, the next nodetests check for unordered lists and table entries with `ul` and `td` as tags containing or neighboring the target nodes. Finally, the 27 steps checking for list items with the `li` occur mostly in the second and third step to match the sequence of target nodes. The right of Figure 6 shows the the distribution of the 62 predicates occurring in the induced expressions. These predicates mostly check for `id` and `class` attributes. However in contrast to the single-target cases, the expressions for multiple targets do not check for any other attribute; aside these, only 7 expressions check in the first step for textual contents, and only 5 expressions check in their second step for positions.

6.4 Accuracy and Noise Resistance

Real-Life Noise. In this experiment, we verify that indeed our approach is able to deal with realistic noise as produced by a real-life entity recognizer. We use the Stanford NER [11] to annotate 10 pages randomly sampled from a set of product listing websites (cf. [13]). We only select pages that contain at least one list of entities supported by the Stanford NER, here one of date, person, location, organisation, money. The size of the lists vary between 8 and 77 elements. For each of these pages, we run the Stanford NER and map its annotations to DOM nodes that serve as target nodes for our approach. The resulting input contains on average 32% negative and 28% positive noise, though both vary widely: $0-67\%$ for negative and $0-145\%$ for positive noise, with each page having at least some noise.

Our approach deals surprisingly well with these noisy samples: in 80% of the cases, our top-ranked expression identifies the correct intended set of nodes, ranging from dates, book authors, artists, and event locations to prices. There are two cases where it fails. **(1)** For "organisations" on newyorknewyork.com, the NER returns 145% positive noise, yet misses 55% of the sought-for target nodes. The returned expression is overgeneralized to a significantly larger set of nodes. **(2)** For "persons" on waterstones.com, the NER returns 50% positive, and 28% negative noise. The target nodes are authors of books returned by a search. Unfortunately, most of the positive noise is structural, annotating a list of author names in a sidebar list used to refine the query. The generated expression selects that list rather than the intended one. Both of these cases could be addressed by limiting the induction to the main content area, obtained by removing boilerplate content [17]. However, this is out of the scope of this paper. It is worth pointing out, that even if we eliminate the two cases where the system fails, noise remains significant (30% negative and 11% positive on average), yet in all of these cases our method compensate flawlessly for that noise.

Synthetic noise. Here we evaluate noise resistance by adding or removing a precentage of the target nodes of a sample. We evaluate different four types of noise: **(N1)** *negative random noise* **(N2)** *negative mid-random noise* where the first and last nodes (in document order) of a target set are not removed, **(N3)** *positive structured noise* where we add random nodes chosen from a node set which is structurally related (via an XPATH expression) to the target nodes. Finally, we consider **(N4)** *positive random noise* where we add random leaf nodes to the target set. We use two datasets: The first one for negative noise has 100 query samples matching between 3 and 59 nodes, with a median of 6 and an average 9.43 nodes. The second one for positive noise features 50 query samples matching between 2 and 100 nodes, with a median of 20 and an average of 34.92.

Figure 7 summarizes our results for all noise types. We show for the noise intensities of 10, 30, 50, and 70% the percentage of cases where the induction with and without noise delivered identical results. Thus, we evaluate the noise resistance in the most aggressive way. Typically, with negative noise, around 10% of the cases deliver with noise a result which is at least within the top 50 results induced without noise. With positive noise, the fraction of such expressions is negligible. Our system deals well with **(N1)** negative random noise at 10 and 30% intensity in achieving *identical* results in respectively 88% and 74% of the cases, thus showing that our approach is 88%- and 74%-noise resistant. However, at 50 and 70% intensity, 38 and 70% of the cases deliver non-identical results. Seemingly unsatisfying, this relatively low noise resistance is caused by removed head and tail nodes – which are critical to determine the start and end of a sequence of list entries. Therefore, we consider **(N2)** negative mid-random noise where we keep the very first and last node (in pre-order) and choose the noisily removed nodes only from the remaining nodes in between. In this case, our system returns identical results in 93, 83, 72, and 66% of the cases for the analyzed intensities. Our system deals exceptionally well with positive noise. For **(N3)** structural positive noise until 50% intensity, our system achieves in at least 90% of the cases an iden-

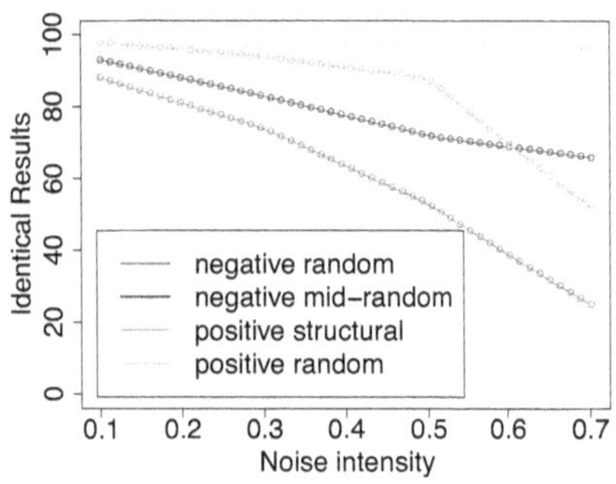

Figure 7: Result degradation with increased presence of noise

tical expression with and without noise. At 70% intensity however, this percentage drops to 54%. For **(N4)** we see almost no effect on the results, e.g., at 70% noise intensity, our system delivers the same result as without noise in 96% of the cases. Even at a noise intensity of 300%, we obtain identical results in 84% of the cases.

7. CONCLUSION

We present a wrapper induction algorithm that combines the ability to deal with noisy samples with a robustness that allows generated wrappers to often survive until the selected data is no longer present in the page. The experiments point to a number of further directions to improve our methods: **(1)** Extending the method to deal with *multi-node wrappers* where not only a single item or list of items, but multiple related items are to be extracted, is a natural step forward. Our method is already designed to allow the induction not only of absolute, but also of relative expressions and thus should be a great fit for a multi-node wrapper as in [13]. **(2)** *Learning an effective scoring* for different types of node types, textual values, and axes from a given corpus of websites. This is particularly relevant to distinguish different text fragments used to identify the same node and to best reflect specifics of a scenario. **(3)** Entity extractors, as used in information extraction or to generate automatic annotations in, e.g., [5], can provide information about the type of entity (e.g., "director") of a piece of text. Using such types in a wrapper to identify the containing node may yield more robust wrappers. **(4)** No matter how sophisticated the wrapper language or scoring, without constraints on the shape of future versions of a page, the robustness of a single wrapper will always be limited. Therefore, we are now *inducing multiple wrappers* that use a variety of independent means for selecting a target node.

Acknowledgements

We thank the anonymous referees for many insightful comments which greatly helped to improve the quality of this paper.

8. REFERENCES

[1] R. Baumgartner, S. Flesca, and G. Gottlob. Visual Web Information Extraction with Lixto. In *VLDB*, pages 119–128, 2001.

[2] M. Bronzi, V. Crescenzi, P. Merialdo, and P. Papotti. Extraction and integration of partially overlapping web sources. *Proc. VLDB Endow.*, 6(10):805–816, Aug. 2013.

[3] S. L. Chuang, K. C. C. Chang, and C. Zhai. Collaborative wrapping: A turbo framework for web data extraction. In *Data Engineering, 2007. ICDE 2007. IEEE 23rd International Conference on*, pages 1261–1262, April 2007.

[4] S.-L. Chuang, K. C.-C. Chang, and C. Zhai. Context-aware wrapping: Synchronized data extraction. In *Proceedings of the 33rd International Conference on Very Large Data Bases*, VLDB '07, pages 699–710. VLDB Endowment, 2007.

[5] N. Dalvi, R. Kumar, and M. Soliman. Automatic wrappers for large scale web extraction. *PVLDB*, 4(4):219–230, 2011.

[6] N. N. Dalvi, P. Bohannon, and F. Sha. Robust web extraction: an approach based on a probabilistic tree-edit model. In *SIGMOD*, pages 335–348, 2009.

[7] N. Derouiche, B. Cautis, and T. Abdessalem. Automatic extraction of structured web data with domain knowledge. In *ICDE*, pages 726–737, 2012.

[8] B. Fazzinga, S. Flesca, and A. Tagarelli. Learning robust web wrappers. In *DEXA*, pages 736–745, 2005.

[9] B. Fazzinga, S. Flesca, and A. Tagarelli. Schema-based web wrapping. *Knowl. Inf. Syst.*, 26(1):127–173, 2011.

[10] E. Ferrara, P. D. Meo, G. Fiumara, and R. Baumgartner. Web data extraction, applications and techniques: A survey. *Knowledge-Based Systems*, 70(0):301 - 323, 2014.

[11] J. R. Finkel, T. Grenager, and C. Manning. Incorporating non-local information into information extraction systems by gibbs sampling. In *ACL*, pages 363–370, New York, NY, USA, 2005. ACM.

[12] S. Flesca, G. Manco, E. Masciari, E. Rende, and A. Tagarelli. Web wrapper induction: A brief survey. *AI Commun.*, 17(2):57–61, 2004.

[13] T. Furche, G. Gottlob, G. Grasso, X. Guo, G. Orsi, C. Schallhart, and C. Wang. DIADEM: Thousands of websites to a single database. *PVLDB*, 7(14):1845–1856, 2014.

[14] G. Gottlob, C. Koch, R. Pichler, and L. Segoufin. The complexity of XPath query evaluation and XML typing. *J. ACM*, 52(2):284–335, 2005.

[15] P. Gulhane, R. Rastogi, S. H. Sengamedu, and A. Tengli. Exploiting content redundancy for web information extraction. In *WWW*, pages 1105–1106, 2010.

[16] W.-S. Han, W. Kwak, H. Yu, J.-H. Lee, and M.-S. Kim. Leveraging spatial join for robust tuple extraction from web pages. *Inf. Sci.*, 261:132–148, 2014.

[17] C. Kohlschütter, P. Fankhauser, and W. Nejdl. Boilerplate detection using shallow text features. In *WSDM*, pages 441–450, New York, NY, USA, 2010. ACM.

[18] N. Kushmerick, D. S. Weld, and R. Doorenbos. Wrapper Induction for Information Extraction. In *IJCAI*, pages 729–737, 1997.

[19] J. Lehmann, T. Furche, G. Grasso, A.-C. N. Ngomo, C. Schallhart, A. Sellers, C. Unger, L. Bühmann, D. Gerber, D. L. Konrad Höffner and, and S. Auer. DEQA: Deep Web Extraction for Question Answering. In *ISWC*, pages 131–147, 2012.

[20] W. Liu, X. Meng, and W. Meng. Vide: A vision-based approach for deep web data extraction. *IEEE Transactions on Knowledge and Data Engineering*, 22(3):447–460, 2010.

[21] A. G. Parameswaran, N. N. Dalvi, H. Garcia-Molina, and R. Rastogi. Optimal schemes for robust web extraction. *PVLDB*, 4(11):980–991, 2011.

[22] J. Raposo, A. Pan, M. Álvarez, and J. Hidalgo. Automatically maintaining wrappers for semi-structured web sources. *Data Knowl. Eng.*, 61(2):331–358, 2007.

[23] W. Su, J. Wang, and F. H. Lochovsky. ODE: Ontology-Assisted Data Extraction. *TODS*, 34(2), 2009.

Author Index

www.ingramcontent.com/pod-product-compliance
Lightning Source LLC
LaVergne TN
LVHW080103011026
849160LV00013B/1021